The ENCYCLOPEDIA
of CHRISTIANITY

Volume 5
Si–Z

The
of

Volume 5

editors

translator and English-language editor

statistical editor

WILLIAM B. EERDMANS PUBLISHING COMPANY

BRILL

ENCYCLOPEDIA CHRISTIANITY

Si–Z

Erwin Fahlbusch†
Jan Milič Lochman†
John Mbiti
Jaroslav Pelikan†
Lukas Vischer

Geoffrey W. Bromiley

David B. Barrett

GRAND RAPIDS, MICHIGAN / CAMBRIDGE, U.K.
LEIDEN / BOSTON

Originally published in German as
Evangelisches Kirchenlexikon, Dritte Auflage (Neufassung)
© 1986, 1989, 1992, 1996, 1997
Vandenhoeck & Ruprecht, Göttingen, Germany

English translation © 2008 by
Wm. B. Eerdmans Publishing Company

Published jointly 2008 by
Wm. B. Eerdmans Publishing Company
2140 Oak Industrial Drive N.E., Grand Rapids, Michigan 49505
www.eerdmans.com
and by
Koninklijke Brill NV
Leiden, the Netherlands
www.brill.nl

Printed in the United States of America

14 13 12 11 10 09 08   10 9 8 7 6 5 4 3 2 1

Library of Congress Cataloging-in-Publication Data

Evangelisches Kirchenlexikon. English.
   The encyclopedia of Christianity / editors, Erwin Fahlbusch . . . [et al.];
translator and English-language editor, Geoffrey W. Bromiley;
statistical editor, David B. Barrett; foreword, Jaroslav Pelikan.
      p.   cm.
   Contents: v. 5. Si–Z.
   ISBN 978-0-8028-2417-2 (cloth: v. 5: alk. paper)
   1. Christianity — Encyclopedias.   I. Fahlbusch, Erwin.
II. Bromiley, Geoffrey William.   III. Title.
BR95.E8913   2008
230'.003 — dc21   98-45953
                                                        CIP

Brill ISBN 978 90 04 14596 2

Contents

List of Entries

This list does not include headings that simply refer the reader to a cross-reference.

Introduction

This introduction provides a brief guide to the editorial conventions followed throughout the *Encyclopedia of Christianity,* as well as to the statistical information specially prepared for the *EC* by David Barrett.

ALPHABETIZATION

Articles are arranged alphabetically word by word (not letter by letter), with hyphens and apostrophes counted as continuing the single word; all commas are ignored. For example:

> Antiochian Theology
> Anti-Semitism, Anti-Judaism
> . . .
> Augsburg Confession
> Augsburg, Peace of
> . . .
> Calvin, John
> Calvinism
> Calvin's Theology
> . . .
> Church Year
> Churches of Christ

STATISTICS

The *EC* includes separate articles for each of the six major areas (formerly "continents") currently recognized by the United Nations (i.e., Africa, Asia, Europe, Latin America and the Caribbean, Northern America, and Oceania). It also presents separate articles for all independent countries of the world, omitting only those whose population, according to U.N. estimates for 1995, is less than 200,000 (e.g., Andorra, Nauru).

Accompanying each country article is a standard statistical box with the following format:

Argentina

	1960	1980	2000
Population (1,000s):	20,616	28,094	37,032
Annual growth rate (%):	1.55	1.51	1.19

Area: 2,780,400 sq. km. (1,073,518 sq. mi.)

A.D. 2000

Population density: 13/sq. km. (34/sq. mi.)
Births / deaths: 1.90 / 0.78 per 100 population
Fertility rate: 2.44 per woman
Infant mortality rate: 20 per 1,000 live births
Life expectancy: 74.2 years (m: 70.6, f: 77.7)
Religious affiliation (%): Christians 92.9 (Roman Catholics 90.2, Protestants 5.9, indigenous 5.4, marginal 1.4, unaffiliated 1.1, other Christians 0.6), nonreligious 2.2, Muslims 2.0, Jews 1.5, other 1.4.

The demographic information in these boxes is taken from the *World Population Prospects: The 1996 Revision* (New York [United Nations], 1998). Depending on the presentation in U.N. tables, figures for 1960, 1980, and 2000 are either for that year alone or for a five-year period beginning with that year. In each case where the United Nations provides three estimates, the medium variant estimates are cited. Information on country area is taken from the *1996 Britannica Book of the Year* (Chicago, 1996). For countries like Argentina, where the birth rate minus the death rate (1.12 per 100 population) does not equal the annual growth rate (1.19), the difference is due to migration — in this case, *into* the country.

David Barrett, editor of the *World Christian Encyclopedia* (2d ed.; 2 vols.; New York, 2001) and senior researcher at the Center for the Study of Global Christianity, Gordon-Conwell Theological Seminary, South Hamilton, Massachusetts, has provided all the information on religious affiliation in the statistical boxes. In the first place, the boxes present the breakdown of overall religious affiliation for each country, using the following sixteen categories:

atheists — persons professing atheism, skepticism, or disbelief, including antireligious (opposed to all religion)

Baha'is — followers of the Baha'i World Faith, founded in the 19th century by Bahā' Allāh

Buddhists — followers of any of the branches of Buddhism; worldwide, 56 percent are Mahayana (northern), 38 percent Theravada (Hinayana, or southern), 6 percent Tantrayana (Lamaism)

Chinese folk religionists — followers of the traditional Chinese religion, which includes local deities, ancestor veneration, Confucian ethics, Taoism, divination, and some Buddhist elements

Christians — followers of Jesus Christ, either affiliated with churches or simply identifying themselves as such in censuses or polls

Confucianists — non-Chinese followers of Confucius and Confucianism, mostly Koreans in Korea

Hindus — followers of the main Hindu traditions; worldwide, 70 percent are Vaishnavas, 25 percent Saivas, 3 percent Saktas, 2 percent neo-Hindus and reform Hindus

Jews — adherents of Judaism

Muslims — followers of Islam; worldwide, 83 percent are Sunnites, 16 percent Shiites, 1 percent other schools

new religionists — followers of Asian 20th-century new religions, new religious movements, radical new crisis religions, and non-Christian syncretistic mass religions, all founded since 1800 and most since 1945

nonreligious — persons professing no religion, nonbelievers, agnostics, freethinkers, dereligionized secularists indifferent to all religion

Shintoists — Japanese who profess Shinto as their first or major religion

Sikhs — followers of the Sikh reform movement arising out of Hinduism

spiritists — non-Christian spiritists, spiritualists, thaumaturgists, medium-religionists

Taoists — followers of the religion developed from the Taoist philosophy and from folk religion and Buddhism

tribal religionists — primal or primitive religionists, animists, spirit-worshipers, shamanists, ancestor-venerators, polytheists, pantheists, traditionalists, local or tribal folk-religionists

The country boxes list each religious group that numbers at least 1.0 percent of the population of that county; any groups that number 0.9 percent or less of the population are grouped together under "other." Because of rounding, the totals of all the religious groups in a country may not equal 100.0 percent.

Second, for the category "Christians," the information in the boxes shows in parentheses the break-down by ecclesiastical bloc, using the following seven categories:

Anglicans — persons in a church that is in fellowship with the archbishop of Canterbury, especially through its participation in the Lambeth Conference; Episcopalians

indigenous — Christians in denominations, churches, or movements who regard themselves as outside of mainline Anglican/Orthodox/Protestant/Roman Catholic Christianity; autonomous bodies independent of foreign origin or control (e.g., Independent Charismatic Churches [Braz.], house church movement [China], isolated radio believers [Saudi Arabia], Zion Christian Church [S.Af.], Vineyard Christian Fellowship [U.S.])

marginal — followers of para-Christian or quasi-Christian Western movements or deviations out of mainline Protestantism, not professing Christian doctrine according to the classic Trinitarian creeds (i.e., Apostles', Nicene) but often claiming a second or supplementary or ongoing source of divine revelation in addition to the Bible (e.g., Christian Scientists, Jehovah's Witnesses, Mormons, Unitarians)

Orthodox — Eastern (Chalcedonian), Oriental (Pre-Chalcedonian, Non-Chalcedonian, Monophysite), Nestorian (Assyrian), and nonhistorical Orthodox

Protestants — persons in churches that trace their origin or formulation to the 16th-century Reformation and thus typically emphasize justification by faith alone and the Bible as the supreme authority, including (1) churches in the Lutheran, Calvinistic, and Zwinglian traditions; and (2) other groups arising before, during, or after the Reformation (e.g., Waldenses, Bohemian Brethren, Baptists, Friends, Congregationalists, Methodists, Adventists, Pentecostals, Assemblies of God)

Roman Catholics — persons in a church that recognizes the pope, the bishop of Rome (with the associated hierarchy), as its spiritual head

unaffiliated — professing Christians not associated with any church

As with the different religions, so for the different types of Christians, any group that numbers at least 1.0 percent of the population of the country is listed. Any groups of Christians that number 0.9 percent or less of the population are included together under "other Christians." Because of rounding, the totals of all the individual Christian groups may not equal the total percentage of

Christians. Furthermore, where persons affiliate themselves with, or are claimed by, two Christian groups at once, the total of the percentages of the individual Christian groups in a country may exceed the countrywide percentage of Christians. This problem of double counting (evident, for example, in the Argentina box on p. x) is left unresolved in the *EC*.

Accompanying each major area article are three tables that list most of the information appearing in the individual country statistical boxes. The first table displays demographic information; the second, data on overall religious affiliation; the third, data on church affiliation. The religion tables list separately the 12 most popular religions worldwide (i.e., the above list of 16 minus Baha'is, Confucianists, Shintoists, and Taoists), with all the others accounted for under "Other." In the tables showing ecclesiastical breakdown, all Christians are counted in one of the seven categories (or, in cases of double counting, in more than one category). The tables of religion and of Christianity report country by country all adherents of a religious position or Christian grouping that total at least 0.1 percent of the population. In addition, all tables present totals for the major area as a whole, as well as for each region that U.N. statistics distinguish within the major area. (The tables accompanying "Africa," for example, show totals for the whole continent; for the regions of eastern, middle, northern, southern, and western Africa; and also for each country that has a separate article in the *EC*.) Finally, for purposes of comparison, relevant figures for the whole world appear as the top row of each major area table.

CROSS-REFERENCES

A variety of cross-references aid the reader in locating articles or specific sections of articles. One type appears as a main title, either (1) making clear where a subject is treated or (2) indicating the exact article title. For example:

(1) **Aid** → Christian Development Services; Development 1.4

    Anathema → Confessions and Creeds

(2) **Ancient Church** → Early Church

    Ancient Oriental Churches → Oriental Orthodox Churches

Other cross-references appear within the text of articles. Those referring to other sections of the present article have the form "(see 1)," "(see 3.2)."

Cross-references to other articles cited as such appear (3) within parentheses in the text, following a cross-reference arrow and using the exact spelling and capitalization of the article title, and (4) on a separate line after the text proper and before the bibliography. In both cases, multiple cross-references are separated by semicolons, and only a single, initial arrow is used. Items cross-referenced within the text of an article normally do not also appear following the text of the article.

(3) In the latter part of the 20th century some churches in the United States and Europe have tried to revive the right of church asylum for some refugees whom the government refused to recognize as political refugees (→ Sanctuary 3; Resistance, Right of, 2).

As such, dance rejects an antibiblical dualism (→ Anthropology 2.3 and 3.2; Soul).

The Roman Catholic Church reacted negatively, placing Beccaria's book on the Index (→ Censorship; Inquisition 2). Then in the 19th century F. D. E. Schleiermacher (1768-1834; → Schleiermacher's Theology) criticized theologically the theory of retribution.

(4) → Anglican Communion 4; Clergy and Laity; Consensus 4; Councils of the Church

→ Catholicism (Roman); Church 3.2; Lay Movements

→ Communities, Spiritual; Ethics 2; Monasticism 3.2.2; Property, esp. 3.2-3

Finally (5), cross-references also appear within the flow of the text, with an arrow appearing before a word or phrase that points clearly (but not necessarily exactly) to the title of another article. Specific sections referred to are indicated by section marks and numbers in parentheses. Normally (6), the exact name of an article is used if a specific section is cited.

(5) The extension of the problem to political matters makes it necessary to define the relations between the obedience of → faith (§3), → freedom (§2), and → reason.

In the controversy with the → Pelagians Augustine's main concern was to show that grace is not limited to external aids like the →

law (§§3.1-2) or the teaching and example of Christ.

Jewish → proselyte baptism incorporates the baptized not only into the religious fellowship but also into God's → covenant → people. This matter is relevant in the dialogue between Israel and the → church (§§1.4.1.3, 2.1, 5.5.3).

(6) . . . the 19th-century → apocalyptic movement in the United States.

vs. . . . the 19th-century apocalyptic movement (→ Apocalypticism 3) in the United States.

BIBLIOGRAPHIES

Within a bibliography (or separate section of a bibliography), entries are ordered first by author, then by title (disregarding an initial article in any language). Successive articles by the same author(s) are separated by semicolons.

In individual bibliographic entries, the names of series are included only if the title is omitted (typically only for biblical commentaries). For works appearing both in a non-English language and in English translation, normally only the English title is cited.

Consulting Editors

ULRICH BECKER *Education*
EUGENE L. BRAND *Liturgy; Worship*
FAITH E. BURGESS *Women's Studies/Issues*
CARSTEN COLPE *Religious Studies*
HANS-WERNER GENSICHEN† *Asia; Mission Studies*
MARTIN GRESCHAT *Biographies; Church History*
HEIMO HOFMEISTER *Philosophy*
HUBERTUS G. HUBBELING† *Philosophy*
ANASTASIOS KALLIS *Orthodoxy*
LEO LAEYENDECKER *Sociology*

EKKEHARD MÜHLENBERG *Church History*
HANS-JÜRGEN PRIEN *Latin America*
DIETRICH RITSCHL *Systematic Theology; Ethics*
JÜRGEN ROLOFF† *New Testament*
JOACHIM SCHARFENBERG† *Practical Theology; Psychology*
TRAUGOTT SCHÖFTHALER *Sociology*
RUDOLF SMEND *Old Testament*
ALBERT STEIN† *Law; Church Law*

Contributors

JÚLIO CÉZAR ADAM, *Novo Hamburgo, Braz.*
Worship 7
NADIA AL-BAGDADI, *Budapest*
Syria
BROOKS ALEXANDER, *Berkeley, Calif.*
Witchcraft
FRANCES M. ALGUIRE, *Chapel Hill, N.C.*
World Methodist Council
CARMELO E. ÁLVAREZ, *Chicago*
Spirituality 3
S. WESLEY ARIARAJAH, *Madison, N.J.*
Sri Lanka
J. KWABENA ASAMOAH-GYADU, *Accra, Ghana*
Spirituality 2; Worship 5
HANS-MARTIN BARTH, *Marburg, Ger.*
Temptation
WOLFGANG BARTUSCHAT, *Hamburg*
Spinozism

ĽUBOMÍR BATKA, *Bratislava, Slovakia*
Slovakia
RICHARD BÄUMLIN, *Oberwiel, Switz.*
State
DANIEL H. BAYS, *Grand Rapids*
Three-Self Patriotic Movement
D. W. BEBBINGTON, *Stirling, Scot.*
Spurgeon, Charles Haddon
HANS-JÜRGEN BECKEN, *Stuttgart, Ger.*
South Africa
ULRICH BECKER, *Hannover, Ger.*
Sunday School 4
HEINRICH BEDFORD-STROHM, *Bamberg, Ger.*
Social Ethics 1
BIRGIT BENDER-JUNKER, *Darmstadt, Ger.*
Utopia
GUSTAV ADOLF BENRATH, *Mainz, Ger.*
Socinianism

BRUCE R. BERGLUND, *Grand Rapids*
Totalitarianism

REINHOLD BERNHARDT, *Basel, Switz.*
Theologia crucis

THOMAS F. BEST, *Geneva*
United and Uniting Churches

JAMES A. BEVERLEY, *Pickering, Ont.*
Unification Church

WERNER BÖCKENFÖRDE†, *Freiburg, Ger.*
Vicar-General

RICHARD BOECKLER, *Stuttgart, Ger.*
Stewardship

ARNO BÖHLER, *Vienna*
Theism

GIORGIO BOUCHARD, *Turin, It.*
Waldenses 4

HANNE BRAUN, *Stuttgart, Ger.*
Young Women's Christian Association

GEOFFREY W. BROMILEY, *Santa Barbara, Calif.*
Sinai; Visitation 1

JOHANNES BROSSEDER, *Cologne*
Teaching Office 1

CANDY GUNTHER BROWN, *Bloomington, Ind.*
Vineyard Christian Fellowships

ROBERT F. BROWN, *Newark, Del.*
Sign 1-2; Subjectivism and Objectivism;
Symbol 1-2; Theodicy; Universalism and
Particularism; Utilitarianism; Voluntarism

STEPHEN F. BROWN, *Boston*
William of Ockham

MICHAEL VON BRÜCK, *Munich*
Upanishads

ANTON A. BUCHER, *Salzberg, Aus.*
Symbol 1-2

WALTER BÜHL, *Munich*
Subculture

BRUNO BÜRKI, *Neuchâtel, Switz.*
Symbol 4

A. B. T. BYARUHANGA-AKIIKI, *Kampala, Uganda*
Uganda

JOHN D. CARLSON, *Tempe, Ariz.*
War

PAUL A. CATHEY, *Grand Junction, Colo.*
Zealots

KIM-KWONG CHAN, *Hong Kong*
Tibet

MARK D. CHAPMAN, *Oxford*
Theology in the Nineteenth and Twentieth
Centuries 4

JEAN-MARIE CHARPENTIER, *Arles, Fr.*
Trust 2; Worker-Priests

SATHIANATHAN CLARKE, *Washington, D.C.*
Third World Theology

GIANCARLO COLLET, *Münster, Ger.*
Theology of Revolution

KENNETH J. COLLINS, *Wilmore, Ky.*
Wesley, John

CARSTEN COLPE, *Berlin*
Soul 1; Theogony; Transcendental Meditation;
Visions; Xenophobia; Yezidis; Yoga

JAMES H. CONE, *New York*
Slavery 3

LAWRENCE CUNNINGHAM, *Notre Dame, Ind.*
Xavier, Francis

CHARLES E. CURRAN, *Dallas, Tex.*
Social Ethics 2

NÉSTOR DA COSTA, *Montevideo, Uruguay*
Uruguay

LISA E. DAHILL, *Columbus, Ohio*
Spirituality 0

HEIDI DAHLES, *Amsterdam*
Tourism

KARL-FRITZ DAIBER, *Hannover, Ger.*
Social Science; Sociology of Churches

ALLAN K. DAVIDSON, *Auckland, N.Z.*
Solomon Islands

MIGUEL A. DE LA TORRE, *Denver, Colo.*
Social Ethics 3

REBECCA KONYNDYK DEYOUNG, *Grand Rapids*
Sin 5

BALWANT SINGH DHILLON, *Amritsar, India*
Sikhs

JÖRG DIERKEN, *Hamburg*
Spiritualism

FRANCE M. DOLINAR, *Ljubljana, Slovenia*
Yugoslavia / Montenegro; Serbia

HANS-DIETER DÖPMANN, *Berlin*
Slavic Mission

ANGELIKA DÖRFLER-DIERKEN, *Grosshansdorf, Ger.*
Teresa of Ávila

ULRICH ERNST, *Wuppertal, Ger.*
Word Square

LARRY ESKRIDGE, *Wheaton, Ill.*
Student Christian Movements

GEORG EVERS, *Raeren, Belg.*
Social Ethics 5

HEIJE FABER†, *Maarn, Neth.*
Superstition

ERWIN FAHLBUSCH†, *Montouliers, Fr.*
Slavery 0, 2

WOLF-ECKART FAILING, *Darmstadt, Ger.*
Social Education

JENNIFER S. FEENSTRA, *Orange City, Iowa*
Social Psychology

PAVEL FILIPI, *Prague*
Slovakia

CONTRIBUTORS

Július Filo, *Svätý Jur, Slovakia*
Youth Work 1-3

Rainer Flasche, *Marburg, Ger.*
Umbanda

David B. Fletcher, *Wheaton, Ill.*
Substance Abuse

Robert Fortner, *Grand Rapids*
Technology

Karl Suso Frank†, *Freiburg, Ger.*
Subintroductae

Gerhild Frasch, *Frankfurt*
Young Women's Christian Association

Helmut Frenz, *Hamburg*
Torture

Jakob Frey†, *Aarau, Switz.*
Taizé Community

Volkmar Fritz, *Bad Schwartau, Ger.*
Tabernacle 1; Temple 2

Herbert Frost†, *Cologne*
Usury

Peter Galadza, *Ottawa, Ont.*
Worship 3

Thomas Gandow, *Berlin*
Youth Religions

Günther Gassmann, *Tutzing, Ger.*
Tradition; Unity

Erwin Gatz, *Vatican City*
Vatican

Wolfgang Gern, *Frankfurt*
Third World

Wilhelm Goerdt, *Münster, Ger.*
Sophiology

Dietrich Goldschmidt†, *Berlin*
University

Adolfo González Montes, *Almería, Sp.*
Spain

T. David Gordon, *Grove City, Pa.*
Theocracy 1-4

Friedrich Wilhelm Graf, *Munich*
Troeltsch, Ernst

Helga Grebing, *Göttingen, Ger.*
Social Movements

Gene L. Green, *Wheaton, Ill.*
Thessalonians, Epistles to the

Paulos Gregorios†, *New Delhi*
Syrian Orthodox Churches in India

Hans-Jürgen Greschat, *Marburg, Ger.*
Taboo

Lee Griffith, *Beaver Dams, N.Y.*
Terrorism

Bernhard Grom, *Munich*
Stigmatization

Joachim Guhrt, *Bad Bentheim, Ger.*
World Alliance of Reformed Churches

Steven R. Guthrie, *Nashville, Tenn.*
Theology and Music

Peter Haenger, *Basel, Switz.*
Sierra Leone

Wolfgang Hage, *Marburg, Ger.*
Stylites

Martin Hailer, *Bayreuth, Ger.*
Soul 2

Daniel C. Harlow, *Grand Rapids*
Synoptics

Peter Hauptmann, *Überlingen, Ger.*
Slavophiles; Starets; Stundism

Robert D. Hawkins, *Columbia, S.C.*
Spirituals; Stabat Mater Dolorosa

Günther Hegele, *Landau, Ger.*
Youth Work 4

Göran Hellberg, *Karjaa, Fin.*
Sports and Faith 1

Reinhard Hempelmann, *Berlin*
Temple Society

Reinhard Henkel, *Zagreb, Croatia*
Zambia

Wolfram Herrmann, *Leipzig*
Ugarit

Timothy Hessel-Robinson, *Fort Worth, Tex.*
Spirituality 4

Joachim Heubach†, *Eutin-Fissan, Ger.*
Vestments

Andrew M. Hill, *York, Eng.*
Unitarians

Teresia Hinga, *Santa Clara, Calif.*
Social Ethics 4

Paul R. Hinlicky, *Salem, Va., and Bratislava, Slovakia*
Status confessionis

Norman A. Hjelm, *Wynnewood, Pa.*
Söderblom, Nathan; Transdenominational Movements; Visser 't Hooft, W. A.

John F. Hoffmeyer, *Philadelphia*
Trinity 2

Heimo Hofmeister, *Heidelberg, Ger.*
Transcendentals

J. W. Hofmeyr, *Pretoria, S.Af.*
South Africa

Karl Hoheisel, *Bonn*
Spiritism; Theosophy 1-3

William J. Hoye, *Münster, Ger.*
Summa; Transcendental Theology

Britta Hübener, *Stuttgart, Ger.*
Terre des Femmes

Hans Hübner, *Göttingen, Ger.*
Sin 2; Wrath of God 2

Jürgen Hübner, *Heidelberg, Ger.*
Worldview 2

WILHELM HÜFFMEIER, *Berlin*
Teaching Office 2

PETER HUGHES, *Toronto*
Universalism, Universalists

PAUL JUNGGAP HUH, *Seoul, South Korea*
Worship 6

KRISTIAN HUNGAR, *Heidelberg, Ger.*
Solidarity

HAROLD JAP-A-JOE, *Paramaribo, Suriname*
Suriname

PAUL JENKINS, *Basel, Switz.*
Sierra Leone

OTTFRIED JORDAHN, *Hamburg*
Wedding Ceremony 1

KLAUS-PETER JÖRNS, *Berlin*
Suicide

OTTO KAISER, *Marburg, Ger.*
Wisdom Literature

AHMET T. KARAMUSTAFA, *St. Louis, Mo.*
Sufism

VELI-MATTI KÄRKKÄINEN, *Pasadena, Calif.*
Theosis 2

THOMAS KAUFMANN, *Göttingen, Ger.*
Zwingli, Ulrich

ARTHUR L. KENNEDY, *Brighton, Mass.*
Theology in the Nineteenth and Twentieth
Centuries 2; Vatican I and II

THOMAS D. KENNEDY, *Valparaiso, Ind.*
Teleology

SEBASTIAN KIM, *York, Eng.*
South Korea

OTTO KIMMINICH†, *Regensburg, Ger.*
UNESCO

NOEL Q. KING, *Corralitos, Calif.*
Sikhs

HUBERT KIRCHNER, *Berlin*
Syllabus of Errors; Trent, Council of;
Ultramontanism; Union

WOLFRAM KISTNER, *Johannesburg, S.Af.*
South Africa

MICHAEL KLESSMANN, *Wuppertal, Ger.*
Supervision

ERNST AXEL KNAUF, *Bern, Switz.*
Tribes of Israel

LIVIA KOHN, *Magdalena, N.M.*
Taoism and Chinese Popular Religion

ROBERT KOLB, *St. Louis, Mo.*
Two-Kingdoms Doctrine

PAUL KORTENHOVEN, *Grand Rapids*
Sierra Leone

WOLFGANG KROHN, *Bielefeld, Ger.*
Technology 1

LEO LAEYENDECKER, *Bunnik, Neth.*
Sociology; Sociology of Religion; Weber, Max;
Worldview 1

RISTO LEHTONEN, *Helsinki, Fin.*
World Student Christian Federation

ANZA A. LEMA†, *Dar es Salaam, Tanz.*
Tanzania

WILLIAM E. LESHER, *Berkeley, Calif.*
World's Religions, Parliament of the

ULRIKE LINK-WIECZOREK, *Oldenburg, Ger.*
Suffering; Time and Eternity 2

PETER LODBERG, *Århus, Den.*
State Church

JOSEPH LOWRY, *Philadelphia*
Theocracy 5

SCOTT C. LUCAS, *Tucson, Ariz.*
Sunna; Sunnism, Sunnis

ROGER LUNDIN, *Wheaton, Ill.*
Transcendentalism

WILHELM LÜTTERFELDS, *Passau, Ger.*
Solipsism

PERTTI LUUMI, *Helsinki, Fin.*
Sunday School

MICHAEL J. MCCLYMOND, *St. Louis, Mo.*
Theology of Revival

FOSTER R. MCCURLEY, *Mohnton, Pa.*
Sin 1, 4

INGE MAGER, *Hamburg*
Syncretistic Controversy

LOIS MALCOLM, *St. Paul, Minn.*
Word of God 3

ROMAN MALEK, *St. Augustin, Ger.*
Taiwan

KLAUS MALETTKE, *Marburg, Ger.*
Thirty Years' War 1

CHRISTOPH MARKSCHIES, *Berlin*
Tertullian

BRUCE D. MARSHALL, *Dallas, Tex.*
Thomism

MICHAEL MARTEN, *Edinburgh*
Turkey

BERNICE MARTIN, *Egham, Surrey, Eng.*
Youth

MARTIN E. MARTY, *Chicago*
United States of America

HANS-PETER MATHYS, *Basel, Switz.*
Typology

MELANIE A. MAY, *Rochester, N.Y.*
Theological Education

JOACHIM MEHLHAUSEN†, *Tübingen, Ger.*
Synod

VOLKER MEJA, *St. John's, Nfld.*
Sociology of Knowledge

CONTRIBUTORS

John P. Meno, *Teaneck, N.J.*
Syrian Orthodox Church

Harding Meyer, *Kehl-Marlen, Ger.*
Transdenominational Movements

Joel Mitchell, *Boston*
Western Sahara

Nathan D. Mitchell, *Notre Dame, Ind.*
Worship 2.1-2

George Monsma, *Grand Rapids*
Unemployment

Viggo Mortensen, *Århus, Den.*
Theology of Religions

Ambrose M. Moyo, *Harare, Zim.*
Zimbabwe

Lewis S. Mudge, *Berkeley, Calif.*
SODEPAX

Isabel Mukonyora, *Bowling Green, Ky.*
Zimbabwe

Constantine M. Mwikamba, *Nairobi*
Somalia

Allen C. Myers, *Grand Rapids*
Solomon; Wisdom Literature; Zechariah, Book of; Zephaniah, Book of

Hubertus Mynarek, *Odernheim, Ger.*
Theosophy 4

Ludwig Nagl, *Vienna*
Structuralism

Wolf-Dieter Narr, *Berlin*
Social Systems

Helga Neumann, *Wernigerode, Ger.*
Symbolism of Animals

Peter Neuner, *Munich*
Synergism

Klaus Nientiedt, *Freiburg, Ger.*
Traditionalist Movement

Sibongile C. Nxumalo, *Mbabane, Swaziland*
Swaziland

Bernd Oberdorfer, *Augsburg, Ger.*
Zinzendorf, Nikolaus

Klaus Otte, *Frankfurt*
Speculative Theology

Elisabeth Ottmüller, *Nürnberg, Ger.*
Women's Missions

John Michael Owen, *Nedlands, Austral.*
Theology

Alan G. Padgett, *St. Paul, Minn.*
Truth 2-3

Johannes Panagopoulos†, *Athens*
Theosis 1; Transfiguration of the World

Aristotle Papanikolaou, *New York*
Theology in the Nineteenth and Twentieth Centuries 3

Joseph Parsalaw, *Usa River, Tanz.*
Tanzania

Georg Pfeffer, *Berlin*
Totemism

Peter C. Phan, *Washington, D.C.*
Viet Nam

Richard V. Pierard, *Hendersonville, N.C.*
Soviet Union; United Nations; World Evangelical Alliance; Worldwide Church of God

Peter Plank, *Würzburg, Ger.*
Synaxarion

Thomas Poiss, *Berlin*
Stoicism

Günther Pöltner, *Vienna*
Time and Eternity 1

Bernard J. Power, *Victoria, Austral.*
Tunisia; United Arab Emirates; Yemen

Reiner Preul, *Kiel, Ger.*
Socialization

Horst Dietrich Preuss†, *Neuendettelsau, Ger.*
Yahweh

Joseph L. Price, *Whittier, Calif.*
Sports and Faith 2

Hans-Jürgen Prien, *Lübeck, Ger.*
Sublimis Deus; Uruguay; Venezuela

Ondrej Prostrednik, *Bratislava, Slovakia*
Youth Work 1-3

Michael Pye, *Marburg, Ger.*
Zen

Gottfried Reeg, *Berlin*
Synagogue

A. James Reimer, *Waterloo, Ont.*
Tillich, Paul

Hans-Diether Reimer†, *Stuttgart, Ger.*
Swedenborgianism

Paolo Ricca, *Rome*
Waldenses 1-3

Joachim Ringleben, *Göttingen, Ger.*
Theology of History

Dietrich Ritschl, *Reigoldswil, Switz.*
Soul 2-3; Systematic Theology

Ronald G. Roberson, *Washington, D.C.*
Syrian Orthodox Churches in India

Robert Owen Roberts, *Maryville, Tenn.*
Whitefield, George

Gabriel C. Rochelle, *Allentown, Pa.*
Spiritual Direction

Wolfgang Röd, *Innsbruck, Aus.*
Transcendental Philosophy

Carole Rogel, *Columbus, Ohio*
Slovenia

Wolfgang G. Röhl, *Stuttgart, Ger.*
Wandering Jew

Dieter Roll, *Bad Emstal, Ger.*
Young Men's Christian Association

PHILIP A. ROLNICK, *St. Paul, Minn.*
Trinity 1

JÜRGEN ROLOFF†, *Erlangen, Ger.*
Sociohistorical Exegesis 3; Wine

MICHAEL ROOT, *Columbia, S.C.*
Simul iustus et peccator

JOHN ROXBOROGH, *Dunedin, N.Z.*
Singapore; Social Ethics 5

MURRAY A. RUBINSTEIN, *New York*
Taiwan

A. JAMES RUDIN, *New York*
Zionism

ENNO RUDOLPH, *Heidelberg, Ger.*
Sign 1-2; Skepticism; Symbol 3

ALENA AMATO RUGGERIO, *Ashland, Oreg.*
Women's Movement

WILLIAM G. RUSCH, *New York*
World Council of Churches

HORACE O. RUSSELL, *Rosemont, Pa.*
Voodoo

BJÖRN RYMAN, *Uppsala, Swed.*
Sweden

DOROTHEA SATTLER, *Münster, Ger.*
Systematic Theology

GERHARD SAUTER, *Bonn*
Theology in the Nineteenth and Twentieth
Centuries 1; Tolerance

WALTER SAWATSKY, *Elkhart, Ind.*
Tajikistan; Turkmenistan; Ukraine; Uzbekistan

JOHANNES SCHILLING, *Kiel, Ger.*
Stations of the Cross

MARGARETE SCHLÜTER, *Frankfurt*
Talmud; Torah

HANS-CHRISTOPH SCHMIDT-LAUBER, *Vienna*
Worship 1, 2.3-4

PETER SCHMIECHEN, *Lancaster, Pa.*
Sin 3

THADDEUS A. SCHNITKER, *Zurich*
Sunday; Tonsure; Water, Holy

WALTER SCHÖPSDAU, *Bensheim, Ger.*
Social Encyclicals; Subsidiarity

HERMANN SCHULZ, *Bremen, Ger.*
Sociohistorical Exegesis 1-2

DOUGLAS J. SCHUURMAN, *Northfield, Minn.*
Vocation; Work

KARL SCHWARZ, *Vienna*
Vow

WILLIAM SCHWEIKER, *Chicago*
Social Gospel

ALBRECHT SCRIBA, *Mainz, Ger.*
Theophany

KURT-VICTOR SELGE, *Berlin*
Tertiaries

ALAN P. F. SELL, *Milton Keynes, Eng.*
Westminster Assembly and Confession of Faith

VOLKER SELLIN, *Heidelberg, Ger.*
Social History

FRANK C. SENN, *Evanston, Ill.*
Sign of the Cross; Worship 2.3-4

JON F. SENSBACH, *Gainesville, Fla.*
Trinidad and Tobago

MARK H. SENTER III, *Deerfield, Ill.*
Youth Work 5

NOTGER SLENCZKA, *Mainz, Ger.*
Sign 3; Ubiquity; Wrath of God 3

RUDOLF SMEND, *Göttingen, Ger.*
Wrath of God 1

MARK SMITH, *Oxford*
United Kingdom

HERMANN SPIECKERMANN, *Göttingen, Ger.*
Word of God 1

CHRISTA SPRINGE, *Mainz, Ger.*
Urban Rural Mission

MAX L. STACKHOUSE, *Princeton*
Troeltsch, Ernst

PAUL STADLER, *St. Gallen, Switz.*
Zaire / Congo-Kinshasa

WERNER STEGMAIER, *Greifswald, Ger.*
Vitalism

ALBERT STEIN†, *Brühl, Ger.*
Superintendent

JÜRGEN STEIN, *Bremen, Ger.*
Simony; Technology 2; Tithe

ERNST STEINKELLNER, *Vienna*
Tibetan Religions

W. P. STEPHENS, *Penzance, Cornwall, Eng.*
Zwingli's Theology

BRIAN STILTNER, *Fairfield, Conn.*
Weapons of Mass Destruction

MICHAEL STOLLEIS, *Frankfurt*
State Ethics

PETER STRACK, *Osnabrück, Ger.*
Terre des Hommes

JOCHEN STREITER, *Wuppertal, Ger.*
Venezuela

GERLINDE STROHMAIER-WIEDERANDERS, *Berlin*
Tabernacle 2

ROBERT SUMSER†, *Dayton, Ohio*
Socialism

THEO SUNDERMEIER, *Heidelberg, Ger.*
Syncretism; Tribal Religions

ERNST C. SUTTNER, *Vienna*
Uniate Churches

HERBERT R. SWANSON, *Lansing, Mich.*
Thailand

ESZTER SZABÓ, *Budapest*
Slavery 2

CONTRIBUTORS

HANS JOACHIM THILO†, *Lübeck, Ger.*
Wedding Ceremony 2

OWEN C. THOMAS, *Berkeley, Calif.*
Temple, William

PRADIP THOMAS, *Brisbane, Austral.*
World Association for Christian
Communication

MICHAEL TRESCHOW, *Kelowna, B.C.*
Wycliffe, John

PEDRO TRIGO, *Caracas, Venezuela*
Venezuela

THEO TSCHUY†, *Tannay, Switz.*
SODEPAX

JAKOB M. M. DE VALK, *Rotterdam, Neth.*
Society

MARY NOLL VENABLES, *Cork, Ire.*
Visitation 2

ERICH VIERING, *Bremen, Ger.*
Togo

WOLFGANG VORTKAMP, *Berlin*
University

GERHARD VOSS, *Niederaltaich, Ger.*
Una Sancta Movement

RUDOLF G. WAGNER, *Heidelberg, Ger.*
Taiping Rebellion

HERIBERT WAHL, *Trier, Ger.*
Trauma

GEOFFREY WAINWRIGHT, *Durham, N.C.*
Spirituality 1

JOHANNES WALLMANN, *Bochum, Ger.*
Thirty Years' War 2

KEVIN WARD, *Leeds, Eng.*
Third World

REGINA WEGEMUND, *Hamburg*
Sudan

ROLF WEIBEL, *Stans, Switz.*
Switzerland

MARTIN WEIMER, *Kiel, Ger.*
Trust 1

SAMUEL WELLS, *Durham, N.C.*
Virtue

KAREN WESTERFIELD TUCKER, *Boston*
Worship 8

JAMES F. WHITE†, *Notre Dame, Ind.*
Worship 4

ULRIKE WIETHAUS, *Winston-Salem, N.C.*
Spirituality 5

ROWAN D. WILLIAMS, *London*
Soteriology; Virgin Birth

DAVID WILLIS-WATKINS, *Princeton*
Theologia crucis

JÖRG WINTER, *Karlsruhe, Ger.*
Visitation 2

ALBERT WIRZ†, *Berlin*
Slavery 1

JOHN WOLFFE, *Milton Keynes, Eng.*
Wilberforce, William

MICHAEL WOLTER, *Bonn*
Twelve, The; Word of God 2

J. ROBERT WRIGHT, *New York*
Thirty-nine Articles

ERNST WÜRTHWEIN†, *Marburg, Ger.*
Song of Solomon

CHOO-LAK YEOW, *Singapore, Republic of Singapore*
Singapore

CARLOS ZUBILLAGA, *Montevideo, Uruguay*
Uruguay

Abbreviations

Abbreviations generally follow those given in the *Journal of Biblical Literature* "Instructions for Contributors." For those not listed there, the abbreviations in the second edition of S. M. Schwertner's *Internationales Abkürzungsverzeichnis für Theologie und Grenzgebiete* (Berlin, 1992) are used; for works of theology or related fields not listed in either source, new abbreviations have been formed.

Writings listed below under the section "Early Church Writings" include those of writers through Augustine.

BIBLICAL BOOKS, WITH THE APOCRYPHA

Gen.	Genesis	Zeph.	Zephaniah
Exod.	Exodus	Hag.	Haggai
Lev.	Leviticus	Zech.	Zechariah
Num.	Numbers	Mal.	Malachi
Deut.	Deuteronomy	Add. Est.	Additions to Esther
Josh.	Joshua	Bar.	Baruch
Judg.	Judges	Bel	Bel and the Dragon
Ruth	Ruth	1-2 Esdr.	1-2 Esdras
1-2 Sam.	1-2 Samuel	4 Ezra	4 Ezra
1-2 Kgs.	1-2 Kings	Jdt.	Judith
1-2-3-4 Kgdms.	1-2-3-4 Kingdoms	Ep. Jer.	Epistle of Jeremiah
1-2 Chr.	1-2 Chronicles	1-2-3-4 Macc.	1-2-3-4 Maccabees
Ezra	Ezra	Pr. Azar.	Prayer of Azariah
Neh.	Nehemiah	Pr. Man.	Prayer of Manasseh
Esth.	Esther	Sir.	Sirach / Ecclesiasticus / Wisdom of Jesus, Son of Sirach
Job	Job		
Ps(s).	Psalm(s)	Sus.	Susanna
Prov.	Proverbs	Tob.	Tobit
Eccl.	Ecclesiastes	Wis.	Wisdom of Solomon
Cant.	Canticles / Song of Solomon / Song of Songs	Matt.	Matthew
		Mark	Mark
Isa.	Isaiah	Luke	Luke
Jer.	Jeremiah	John	John
Lam.	Lamentations	Acts	Acts of the Apostles
Ezek.	Ezekiel	Rom.	Romans
Dan.	Daniel	1-2 Cor.	1-2 Corinthians
Hos.	Hosea	Gal.	Galatians
Joel	Joel	Eph.	Ephesians
Amos	Amos	Phil.	Philippians
Obad.	Obadiah	Col.	Colossians
Jonah	Jonah	1-2 Thess.	1-2 Thessalonians
Mic.	Micah	1-2 Tim.	1-2 Timothy
Nah.	Nahum	Titus	Titus
Hab.	Habakkuk	Phlm.	Philemon

ABBREVIATIONS

Heb.	Hebrews	1-2-3 John	1-2-3 John
Jas.	James	Jude	Jude
1-2 Pet.	1-2 Peter	Rev.	Revelation

OLD TESTAMENT PSEUDEPIGRAPHA

2 Apoc. Bar.	Syriac *Apocalypse of Baruch*	*Jub.*	*Jubilees*
Asc. Isa.	*Ascension of Isaiah*	*Odes Sol.*	*Odes of Solomon*
1 Enoch	Ethiopic *Enoch*		

EARLY CHURCH WRITINGS, WITH NAG HAMMADI TRACTATES

Ambrose
    In Ps.   *In Psalmum*
Athanasius
    Contra Arian.   *Apologia contra Arianas*
    De incar.   *De incarnatione Dei Verbi*
    Ep. Mar.   *Epistula ad Marcellinum de interpretatione Psalmorum*
    Vita Ant.   *Vita Antonii*
Augustine
    Conf.   *Confessions*
    De cat. rud.   *De catechizandis rudibus*
    De civ. Dei   *De civitate Dei*
    De doc. Christ.   *De doctrina Christiana*
    De mor. eccl.   *De moribus ecclesiae catholicae et de moribus Manichaeorum*
    De Trin.   *De Trinitatae libri quindecim*
    Enarr. in Ps.   *Enarrationes in Psalmos*
    In Evang. Iohan.   *In Evangelium Iohannis Tractatus*
    Sol.   *Soliloquia*
Basil the Great
    Hex.   *Homiliae in hexaemeron*
Chrys. [Chrysostom]
    In Ps.   *In Psalmum*
1-2 Clem.   *1-2 Clement*
Clement of Alexandria
    Paed.   *Paedagogus*
    Protr.   *Protrepticus*
Cyprian of Carthage
    Ad Quir.   *Ad Quirinum*
    De pat.   *De bono patientiae*
Cyril of Jerusalem
    Cat.   *Catecheses*
Did.   *Didache*

Eusebius
    Hist. eccl.   *Historia ecclesiastica*
Gregory of Nazianzus
    Or. theol.   *Orationes theologicae*
    Herm. Sim.   *Hermas, Similitude(s)*
Hippolytus
    Haer.   *Refutatio omnium haeresium*
    Trad. apos.   *Traditio apostolica*
Ign. [Ignatius]
    Eph.   *Letter to the Ephesians*
    Pol.   *Letter to Polycarp*
Irenaeus
    Adv. haer.   *Adversus omnes haereses*
    Demon.   *Demonstration of the Apostolic Preaching*
Justin Martyr
    1 Apol.   *1 Apologia*
    Dial.   *Dialogue with Trypho*
    Mart. Pol.   *Martyrdom of Polycarp*
    Odes Sol.   *Odes of Solomon*
Origen
    Comm. in Ioan.   *Commentarii in Ioannem*
    De princ.   *De principiis*
    Prot. Jas.   *Protevangelium of James*
Tertullian
    Ad uxor.   *Ad uxorem*
    Adv. Marc.   *Adversus Marcionem*
    Adv. Prax.   *Adversus Praxeam*
    Apol.   *Apologeticus pro Christianis*
    De bapt.   *De baptismo*
    De cor.   *De corona*
Theodore of Mopsuestia
    Cat. serm.   *Catechetical Sermons*

DEAD SEA SCROLLS

1QS	*Serek hayyaḥad (Rule of the Community, Manual of Discipline)*	11QTemple	*Temple Scroll*

CLASSICAL TARGUMS AND RABBINIC WRITINGS

b.	Babylonian Talmud	*Giṭ.*	*Giṭṭin*
y.	*Jerusalem Talmud*	*Pesaḥ.*	*Pesaḥim*
m.	Mishnah	*Qoh. Rab.*	*Qohelet Rabbah*
'Abot	*'Abot*	*Sanh.*	*Sanhedrin*
'Abot R. Nat.	*'Abot de Rabbi Nathan*	*Ta'an.*	*Ta'anit*
Gen. Rab.	*Genesis Rabbah*	*Tamid*	*Tamid*

OTHER ANCIENT, MEDIEVAL, AND EARLY MODERN WRITINGS

Aristotle
Eth. Nic.	*Ethica Nicomachea*
Meta.	*Metaphysica*
Ph.	*Physica*
Pol.	*Politica*

Boethius
Consol.	*De consolatione philosophiae*
De Trin.	*De Trinitate*
Opus. sac.	*Opuscula sacra*

CA	Confessio Augustana (Augsburg Confession)
CA Apol.	Apology of the Confessio Augustana

Calvin, J.
Comm. Jer.	*Commentary on Jeremiah*
Inst.	*Institutes of the Christian Religion*

Cassian
Conf.	*Conferences*

Cicero
De fin.	*De finibus*

Dionysius the Pseudo-Areopagite
De cael. hier.	*De caelesti hierarchia*

Formula of Concord
Ep.	Epitome
SD	Solid Declaration

Herodotus
Hist.	*History*

John of Damascus
De fide orth.	*De fide orthodoxa*

Josephus
Ag. Ap.	*Against Apionem*

Ant.	*Jewish Antiquities*
J.W.	*Jewish War*

Kant, I.
Prol.	*Prolegomena zu einer jeden zukünftigen Metaphysik*

Locke, J.
Essay	*An Essay concerning Human Understanding*

Marcus Aurelius
Med.	*Meditations*

Peter Lombard
Sent.	*Sentences*

Plato
Leg.	*Leges*
Phd.	*Phaedo*
Phdr.	*Phaedrus*
Prot.	*Protagoras*
Rep.	*Republic*
Ti.	*Timaeus*

Richard of St.-Victor
De Trin.	*De Trinitate*

Thomas Aquinas
Contra. impug.	*Contra impugnantes Dei cultum et religionem*
Quod.	*Quaestiones de quodlibet I-XII*
Sent.	*Scriptum super libros Sententiarum*
Summa c. Gent.	*Summa contra Gentiles*
Summa theol.	*Summa theologiae*
Super 1 Cor.	*Super Primam Epistolam ad Corinthios lectura*

MODERN PUBLICATIONS AND EDITIONS

AB	Anchor Bible	AggBeh	*Aggressive Behavior*
ABD	*Anchor Bible Dictionary*	*AHDE*	*Anuario de historia del derecho español*
AbNTC	Abingdon NT Commentaries	*AJPs*	*American Journal of Psychology*
AcadLP	*Academy: Lutherans in Profession*	*AmA*	*American Anthropologist*
AEL	*Ancient Egyptian Literature*	*AmPs*	*American Psychologist*

ABBREVIATIONS

AnBoll	Analecta Bollandiana	CTM	Concordia Theological Monthly
ANEP	Ancient Near East in Pictures	CTQ	Concordia Theological Quarterly
AnPont	Annuario pontificio	Daed.	Daedalus: Journal of the American Academy of Arts and Sciences
AnthQ	Anthropological Quarterly		
Antiph.	Antiphon: A Journal for Liturgical Renewal	DCS	A Dictionary of Christian Spirituality (ed. Gordon S. Wakefield)
AOB	Altorientalische Bilder zum Alten Testament	DEM	Dictionary of the Ecumenical Movement (2d ed., 2002)
ARG	Archiv für Reformationsgeschichte	DFTh	Dictionary of Fundamental Theology (René Latourelle and Rino Fisichella, 1994)
ARSoc	Annual Review of Sociology		
ASR	American Sociological Review		
ASV	American Standard Version	DH	Denzinger-Hünermann, Enchiridion symbolorum (37th ed., 1991)
ATD	Das Alte Testament Deutsch		
ATJ	Africa Theological Journal	Diak.(US)	Diakonia. A Quarterly Devoted to Advancing Orthodox-Catholic Dialogue
BAW.AO	Bibliothek der alten Welt. Reihe: Der Alte Orient		
		DSp	Dictionnaire de spiritualité, ascétique et mystique
BC	Biblical Commentary (Edinburgh)		
BerOl	Berit Olam: Studies in Hebrew Narrative and Poetry	DTC	Dictionnaire de théologie catholique
		dü	Der Überblick. Zeitschrift für ökumenische Zusammenarbeit und weltweite Begegnung
BICMR	Bulletin on Islam and Christian-Muslim Relations in Africa		
BiDi	Bibliotheca dissidentium	DV	Douay-Rheims Version
BKAT	Biblischer Kommentar: Altes Testament	EC	Enciclopedia cattolica
BNTC	Black's New Testament Commentaries	EDCC	Economic Development and Cultural Change
BRTh	Baptist Review of Theology (Gormley, Ont.)		
		EDNT	Exegetical Dictionary of the New Testament
BSOAS	Bulletin of the School of Oriental and African Studies		
		EK	Evangelische Kommentare
BW	Biblical World	EKKNT	Evangelisch-katholischer Kommentar zum Neuen Testament
CAsJ	Central Asiatic Journal		
CChr.SL	Corpus Christianorum, Series Latina	EKL	Evangelisches Kirchenlexikon (1st ed., 1956-59; 2d ed., 1962; 3d ed., 1986-97)
CD	K. Barth, Church Dogmatics		
CDWC	Corpus Dictionary of Western Churches (Washington, D.C., 1970)	ELC	Encyclopedia of the Lutheran Church
		EMZ	Evangelische Missionszeitschrift
CEurH	Central European History	EncJud	Encyclopaedia Judaica (1971)
CGG	Christlicher Glaube in moderner Gesellschaft	EncPh	Encyclopedia of Philosophy
		EncRel(E)	The Encyclopedia of Religion (ed. M. Eliade)
CGRev	Conrad Grebel Review		
CH	Church History	EncWRNA	Encyclopedia of Women and Religion in North America
ChiSt	Chicago Studies: An Archdiocesan Review		
ChM	Churchman: A Journal of Anglican Theology	EpiJ	Epiphany Journal
		ER	Ecumenical Review
ChrTo	Christianity Today	ERE	Encyclopaedia of Religion and Ethics
CIC	Codex Iuris Canonici	ESL	Evangelisches Soziallexikon
ConJ	Concordia Journal	EStL	Evangelisches Staatslexikon (3d ed.)
CP	Classical Philology	EtB	Études bibliques
CPUB	Centro Pro Unione Bulletin	EvQ	Evangelical Quarterly
CRef	Corpus Reformatorum	EvT	Evangelische Theologie
CRJ	Christian Research Journal	Exchange	Exchange: Journal of Missiological and Ecumenical Research
CSBull	Christian Spirituality Bulletin		
CSEL	Corpus scriptorum ecclesiasticorum latinorum	GGB	Geschichtliche Grundbegriffe
		GOTR	Greek Orthodox Theological Review
CT	Concilium Tridentinum (13 vols.; Friburg, 1963-76)	Greg.	Gregorianum
		HAT	Handbuch zum Alten Testament

HBT	*Horizons in Biblical Theology*
HDThG	*Handbuch der Dogmen- und Theologiegeschichte*
HFTh	*Handbuch der Fundamentaltheologie*
HibJ	*Hibbert Journal: A Quarterly Review of Religion, Theology, and Philosophy*
HJ	*Historisches Jahrbuch der Görres-Gesellschaft*
HKG(J)	*Handbuch der Kirchengeschichte* (ed. H. Jedin)
HKKR	*Handbuch des katholischen Kirchenrechts*
HLit	*Handbuch der Liturgik* (3d ed., 2003)
HNT	Handbuch zum Neuen Testament
HO	*Handbuch der Orientalistik*
HÖ	*Handbuch der Ökumenik*
HR	*History of Religions*
HThG	*Handbuch theologischer Grundbegriffe*
HTR	*Harvard Theological Review*
HWP	*Historisches Wörterbuch der Philosophie*
HZ	*Historische Zeitschrift*
ICC	International Critical Commentary
IDB	*Interpreter's Dictionary of the Bible*
IGI	*In God's Image*
IJPsa	*International Journal of Psychoanalysis*
IJST	*International Journal of Systematic Theology*
Interp.	Interpretation: A Commentary for Teaching and Preaching
ISBE	*International Standard Bible Encyclopedia* (rev. ed.)
JAC	*Jahrbuch für Antike und Christentum*
JACT	*Journal of African Christian Thought*
JAF	*Journal of American Folklore*
JASPs	*Journal of Abnormal and Social Psychology*
JBTh	*Jahrbuch für biblische Theologie*
JCTR	*Journal for Christian Theological Research*
JEH	*Journal of Ecclesiastical History*
JETS	*Journal of the Evangelical Theological Society*
JFPs	*Journal of Family Psychology*
JHBS	*Journal of the History of the Behavioral Sciences*
JHI	*Journal of the History of Ideas*
JLH	*Jahrbuch für Liturgik und Hymnologie*
JPCCo	*Journal of Pastoral Care and Counseling*
JPS	Jewish Publication Society Holy Scriptures (1917)
JPs	*Journal of Psychology*
JPSP	*Journal of Personality and Social Psychology*
JR	*Journal of Religion*
JRA	*Journal of Religion in Africa*

JRAI	*Journal of the Royal Anthropological Institute of Great Britain and Ireland*
JSOT	*Journal for the Study of the Old Testament*
JSSR	*Journal for the Scientific Study of Religion*
JSSt	*Journal of Semitic Studies*
JThWS	*Journal of Third World Studies*
JTS	*Journal of Theological Studies*
JTSA	*Journal of Theology for Southern Africa*
JUHS	*Journal of the Universalist Historical Society*
JusEcc	*Jus ecclesiasticum*
JUUH	*Journal of Unitarian Universalist History*
JWCI	*Journal of the Warburg and Courtauld Institutes*
KAI	H. Donner and W. Rollig, *Kanaanäische und aramäische Inschriften*
KEK	Kritisch-exegetischer Kommentar über das Neue Testament
KJ	*Kirchliches Jahrbuch für die EKD*
KJV	King James Version
KuD	*Kerygma und Dogma*
LJ	*Liturgisches Jahrbuch*
LPs	*Lexikon der Psychologie*
LQ	*Lutheran Quarterly*
LS	*Louvain Studies*
LTK	*Lexicon für Theologie und Kirche*
LuJ	*Luther-Jahrbuch*
LuthFor	*Lutheran Forum*
LW	*Luther's Works*, "American Edition" (55 vols.; St. Louis and Philadelphia, 1955-76)
MdEZW	*Materialdienst der Evangelische Zentralstelle für Weltanschauungsfragen*
MdKI	*Materialdienst des Konfessionskundlichen Instituts*
MDOG	*Mitteilungen der Deutschen Orient-Gesellschaft zu Berlin*
MECW	Karl Marx and Friedrich Engels, *Collected Works*
MeE	*Maria et ecclesia*
MHRC	*Mental Health, Religion, and Culture*
Miss.	*Missiology*
MoTh	*Modern Theology*
NBL	*Neues Bibel-Lexikon*
NBl	*New Blackfriars*
NCBC	New Century Bible Commentary
NCE	*New Catholic Encyclopedia* (1967-79)
NCE (2d ed.)	*New Catholic Encyclopedia* (2003)
NEQ	*New England Quarterly*
NGDMM	*New Grove Dictionary of Music and Musicians*
NHThG	*Neues Handbuch theologischer Grundbegriffe*

ABBREVIATIONS

NICNT	New International Commentary on the New Testament	SacPa	Sacra pagina
NICOT	New International Commentary on the Old Testament	Saec.	Saeculum. Jahrbuch für Universalgeschichte
NIDNTT	New International Dictionary of New Testament Theology	SC	Sources chrétiennes
NIDOTTE	New International Dictionary of Old Testament Theology and Exegesis	SCJ	Sixteenth Century Journal: A Journal for Renaissance and Reformation Students and Scholars
NIGTC	New International Greek Testament Commentary	SE	Sacris eruditi. Jaarboek voor godsdienstwetenschappen
NJBC	New Jerome Bible Commentary	SJOT	Scandinavian Journal of the Old Testament
NRSV	New Revised Standard Version	SJT	Scottish Journal of Theology
NTR	New Testament Readings	SM	Sacramentum mundi. Theologisches Lexikon für die Praxis
NTS	New Testament Studies		
NZSTh	Neue Zeitschrift für systematische Theologie	SocAn	Sociological Analysis
		SocComp	Social Compass
OCA	Orientalia Christiana analecta	SocFor	Social Forces
ODCC	Oxford Dictionary of the Christian Church (3d ed.)	SocRes	Social Research
		Spec.	Speculum: A Journal of Mediaeval Studies
ÖR	Ökumenische Rundschau	SThKAB	Schriften des Theologischen Konvents Augsburgischen Bekenntnisses
ÖR.B	Ökumenische Rundschau. Beiheft		
OR(E)	L'osservatore romano (English ed.)	StPatr	Studia patristica: Papers Presented to the International Conference on Patristic Studies
OS	Ostkirchliche Studien		
OTGu	Old Testament Guides		
OTL	Old Testament Library	StPM	Stromata patristica et mediaevalia
PastOrS	Pastoral Orientation Service	SVTQ	St. Vladimir's Theological Quarterly
PG	Patrologia Graeca	TDNT	Theological Dictionary of the New Testament
PhQ	Philosophical Quarterly		
PhTop	Philosophical Topics	TDOT	Theological Dictionary of the Old Testament
PL	Patrologia Latina		
PNTC	Pillar New Testament Commentary	THAT	Theologisches Handwörterbuch zum Alten Testament
PsBull	Psychological Bulletin		
PsInq	Psychological Inquiry	ThPr	Theologia practica
PsRev	Psychological Review	TLOT	Theological Lexicon of the Old Testament
PsT	Psychology Today	TLZ	Theologische Literaturzeitung
PTh	Pastoraltheologie	TMPR	Totalitarian Movements and Political Religions
PuN	Pietismus und Neuzeit		
PWSup	Supplement to Pauly-Wissowa, Real-Encyclopädie der classischen Altertumswissenschaft	TRE	Theologische Realenzyklopädie
		TRu	Theologische Rundschau
		TS	Theological Studies
QGPRK	Quelle zur Geschichte des Papsttums und des römischen Katholizismus	TToday	Theology Today
		TTZ	Trierer theologische Zeitschrift
RAmCul	Religion and American Culture	TUAT	Texte aus der Umwelt des Alten Testaments
RelEE	Religion in Eastern Europe		
RelSRev	Religious Studies Review	TUHS	Transactions of the Unitarian Historical Society
RelStSo	Religion, State, and Society		
RelW	Religions of the World (5 vols.; Santa Barbara, Calif., 2002)	VCSup	Vigilae Christianae Supplements
		VJTR	Vidyajyoti Journal of Theological Reflection
RGG	Religion in Geschichte und Gegenwart		
RHR	Revue de l'histoire des religions	VT	Vetus Testamentum
RP	Review of Politics	WA	M. Luther, Werke. Kritische Gesamtausgabe (Weimarer Ausgabe)
RRelRes	Review of Religious Research		
RSV	Revised Standard Version	WA.B	— Briefwechsel
RW	Reformed World	WBC	Word Biblical Commentary

WCE	*World Christian Encyclopedia* (2d ed., 2 vols., 2001)	ZDPV	*Zeitschrift des deutschen Palästina-Vereins*
		ZEE	*Zeitschrift für evangelische Ethik*
WM	*Wörterbuch der Mythologie*	ZKT	*Zeitschrift für katholische Theologie*
WTJ	*Wesleyan Theological Journal*	ZNW	*Zeitschrift für die neutestamentliche Wissenschaft*
WüJA	Würzburger Jahrbucher für Altertumswissenschaft		
WzM	*Wege zum Menschen*	ZTK	*Zeitschrift für Theologie und Kirche*
ZAW	*Zeitschrift für die alttestamentliche Wissenschaft*	ZZ	*Zwischen den Zeiten*

STATES AND PROVINCES

Ala.	Alabama	N.C.	North Carolina
Ariz.	Arizona	Nebr.	Nebraska
B.C.	British Columbia	Nfld.	Newfoundland
Calif.	California	N.H.	New Hampshire
Colo.	Colorado	N.J.	New Jersey
Conn.	Connecticut	N.M.	New Mexico
D.C.	District of Columbia	N.Y.	New York
Del.	Delaware	Okla.	Oklahoma
Fla.	Florida	Ont.	Ontario
Ga.	Georgia	Oreg.	Oregon
Ill.	Illinois	Pa.	Pennsylvania
Ind.	Indiana	R.I.	Rhode Island
Ky.	Kentucky	S.C.	South Carolina
Mass.	Massachusetts	Tenn.	Tennessee
Md.	Maryland	Tex.	Texas
Mich.	Michigan	Va.	Virginia
Minn.	Minnesota	Vt.	Vermont
Mo.	Missouri	Wash.	Washington
Mont.	Montana	Wis.	Wisconsin

GENERAL

A.D.	*anno Domini,* in the year of the Lord	c.	*corpus articuli,* the body of the article (Thomas Aquinas)
Akkad.	Akkadian		
anniv.	anniversary	ca. (c.)	circa
app.	appendix	can(s).	canon(s)
Arab.	Arabic	cent(s).	century, centuries
Aram.	Aramaic	cf.	*confer,* compare
Arg.	Argentina	chap(s).	chapter(s)
art(s).	article(s)	Chin.	Chinese
aug.	augmented	CIA	Central Intelligence Agency (U.S.)
Aus.	Austria	comm.	commentary
Austral.	Australia	comp(s).	compiler(s)
b.	born	C.R.	Costa Rica
B.C.	before Christ	d.	died
Belg.	Belgium	Den.	Denmark
bk.	book	diss.	dissertation
Braz.	Brazil	dist.	distinction
c.	chapter (in citing U.K. statutes)	doc.	document

ABBREVIATIONS

DtrH	Deuteronomistic redaction, historically oriented	MDut.	Middle Dutch
DtrP	Deuteronomistic redaction, prophetically oriented	MEng.	Middle English
		mi.	mile(s)
E	Elohistic source	MS(S)	manuscript(s)
ed(s).	edited (by), edition(s), editor(s)	MT	Masoretic Text
e.g.	*exempli gratia,* for example	NATO	North Atlantic Treaty Organization
Egypt.	Egyptian	n.d.	no date
EKD	Evangelische Kirche in Deutschland	Neth.	Netherlands
Eng.	England, English	NGO(s)	nongovernmental organization(s)
ep.	*epistula(e),* letter(s)	no(s).	number(s)
esp.	especially	Norw.	Norway
est.	estimated, estimate	n.p.	no place
ET	English translation	n.s.	new series
et al.	*et alii,* and others	NT	New Testament
etc.	*et cetera,* and so forth	N.Z.	New Zealand
exp.	expanded	OECD	Organization for Economic Cooperation and Development
f	females	OEng.	Old English
ff.	and following	orig.	original(ly)
fig(s).	figure(s)	OT	Old Testament
Fin.	Finland	p(p).	page(s)
fl.	*floruit,* flourished	par.	parallel(s), parallel to
Fr.	France, French	par(s).	paragraph(s)
FS	Festschrift	Pers.	Persian
ft.	foot, feet	pl.	plural
fut.	future	Pol.	Polish
Ger.	Germany, German	pop.	population
Gk.	Greek	posth.	posthumously
Heb.	Hebrew	P.R.	Puerto Rico
Hiph.	Hiphil	pres.	president
Hung.	Hungarian	prooem.	*prooemium,* preface
ibid.	*ibidem,* in the same place	pseud.	pseudonym
i.e.	*id est,* that is	pt.	part
IRA	Irish Republican Army	pub.	published
Ire.	Ireland	Q	hypothetical source of material common to Matthew and Luke but not found in Mark
It.	Italy, Italian		
Jam.	Jamaica		
Jpn.	Japanese	q(q).	question(s)
KGB	(acronym in Russian for "Committee for State Security")	repr.	reprint(ed)
		resp.	*respondeo dicendum quod,* I answer that . . . (Thomas Aquinas)
km.	kilometer(s)		
Kor.	Korean	rev.	revised (by, in)
κτλ.	κατὰ τὰ λοιπά, and so forth	Russ.	Russian
L	material in Luke not found in Matthew or Mark	S.Af.	South Africa
		Scot.	Scotland
Lat.	Latin	sess.	session
lect(s).	lecture(s)	sing.	singular
lit.	literal(ly)	Skt.	Sanskrit
LXX	Septuagint	sol.	solution
M	material in Matthew not found in Mark or Luke	Sp.	Spain, Spanish
		sq.	square
m	males	SSR	Soviet Socialist Republic
m.	meter(s)	St.	Saint
marg.	marginal reading	Sumer.	Sumerian

s.v.	*sub verbo, under the word*		USSR	Union of Soviet Socialist Republics
Swed.	Sweden, Swedish		v(v).	verse(s)
Switz.	Switzerland		Vg	(Latin) Vulgate
Syr.	Syriac		vol(s).	volume(s)
Tanz.	Tanzania		vs.	versus
trans.	translated by, translator(s), translation		Yid.	Yiddish
Turk.	Turkish		YMCA	Young Men's Christian Association
U.K.	United Kingdom		YWCA	Young Women's Christian Association
U.N.	United Nations		Zim.	Zimbabwe
UNESCO	United Nations Educational, Scientific, and Cultural Organization		→	cross-reference to another article
			*	passim (with Bible references)
U.S.	United States		§	section

Si

Sierra Leone

	1960	*1980*	*2000*
Population (1,000s):	2,241	3,236	4,866
Annual growth rate (%):	1.60	2.05	2.20

Area: 71,740 sq. km. (27,699 sq. mi.)

A.D. 2000

Population density: 68/sq. km. (176/sq. mi.)
Births / deaths: 4.41 / 2.21 per 100 population
Fertility rate: 5.62 per woman
Infant mortality rate: 146 per 1,000 live births
Life expectancy: 41.1 years (m: 39.6, f: 42.6)
Religious affiliation (%): Muslims 46.3, tribal religionists 40.0, Christians 11.4 (Protestants 3.8, indigenous 3.6, Roman Catholics 3.5, other Christians 1.6), nonreligious 2.1, other 0.2.

1. General Situation
2. Religious Situation

1. General Situation

1.1. The Republic of Sierra Leone is an extremely poor West African nation with tremendous inequality in income distribution. While it possesses substantial mineral, agricultural, and fishery resources, its economic and social infrastructure is not well developed, and serious social disorders continue to hamper economic development. Over 60 percent of the working-age population engages in subsistence agriculture. Manufacturing is minimal, consisting mainly of processing raw material and some light manufacturing in the urban centers. Alluvial diamond mining, which remains the major source of hard-currency earnings, accounts for nearly half of Sierra Leone's exports. The fate of the economy depends on the maintenance of domestic peace and the continued receipt of aid from abroad, both of which are essential to offset the country's severe trade imbalance.

Recent improvement in political stability has led to a revival of some economic activity such as the rehabilitation of bauxite mining. A presidential election was scheduled for mid-2007, bringing with it the potential for increased social unrest, which would have a negative influence on the whole economic and social structure.

1.2. Portuguese reports from the 16th century (e.g., by Valentim Fernandes and Andre Alvares d'Almada) indicate that most of the 18 ethnic groups currently in Sierra Leone were already present prior to European arrival. The Krio people illustrate a special case. They were freed slaves of multiethnic background who, toward the end of the 18th century, returned and settled on the Sierra Leone Peninsula, where they developed an autonomous culture and language. They were aided in this endeavor by the British antislavery movement, which included police action by the British fleet after 1807 (→ Slavery).

In precolonial Sierra Leone the difficult ecological conditions (woodlands) and the comparatively small volume of trade prevented the development of centralized forms of government. Several of the ethnic groups such as the Yalunka, the Kono, and the Kuranko became warrior societies, which lived for the most part in densely populated and strongly defended settlements. Secret societies for men and for women became established in most ethnic groups and were called by various names: Poro, Sande, Gbangbani, and Sogo. These secret societies served as regulating powers and had considerable political influence.

1.3. With the expansion of the areas under British rule, the Krio played a central role as traders and → missionaries. Tension between the crown colony dominated by the Krio and the Protectorate culminated in 1898 in the so-called Hut Tax War, led by the Temne warrior-chief Bai Bureh, in which a large percentage of the Protectorate population rose up against the British colonial powers. Later, the shared interests of the non-Krio educated elite and the traditional rulers led to the formation of organized national movements, one of which, the Sierra Leone People's Party (SLPP), rose to become the first indigenous government party of the country (1955). Ethnic rivalries and general economic dissatisfaction led to a violent turnover of power in 1967, resulting in a one-party rule by the All Peoples' Congress (APC). The APC was led by Siaka Stevens until 1986, when he turned over power to his handpicked successor, Major General Joseph Saidu Momoh.

1.4. The Revolutionary United Front (RUF) started a civil war in 1991 from its base in Liberia. Initial rebel attacks, led by RUF commander Foday Sankoh, began in southeastern Sierra Leone near the Liberian border. In 1992 President Momoh was ousted by a military coup. By 1994 the → war had reached the Northern Province, and by 1997 it had spread throughout the country. A second rebel force, the Armed Forces Revolutionary Council (AFRC), joined the RUF in 1996 and began a reign of terror that lasted for over four years.

Horrible atrocities were committed by the RUF/AFRC, which eventually led to involvement of the international community in peacemaking operations led by the → United Nations. From 1997 to 2000 more than 15,000 U.N. military troops were sent to Sierra Leone, which was the largest U.N. peacemaking operation in the world at that time. In addition, a West African peacekeeping force, ECOMOG, consisting of 3,000 troops (mainly from Nigeria), was present from 1996 to 2001. Also, 800 British troops arrived in 2001 and helped facilitate the present peace accord.

2. Religious Situation

2.1. Although → Islam claims over 40 percent of the population and Christianity 10 percent, *traditional African religion* permeates all religious groups in Sierra Leone. Religious life is to a large degree determined by secret societies, whose designation differs from one ethnic group to another but whose organization and function are virtually identical across all groups. The secret societies are closely connected to veneration of → ancestors, for supernatural ancestral authority legitimates the earthly power of the association. The rites of initiation for young boys and girls are directed by the secret society. In the initiation schools, ethnic handicrafts and music are taught, along with traditional law.

2.2. *Islam* (→ Sunni, Sunnis) is concentrated mostly in the northern and western areas of the republic. The Susu, Vai, Bullom, Kuranko, Yalunka, and Fula people are predominantly Muslim, and even in the Temne group Muslims are strongly represented. The Ahmadiya Mission arrived in the country in 1957 and continues to be active, mainly in educational institutions.

2.3. By African standards, → *Protestantism* has had a comparatively long tradition in Sierra Leone. The first generation of freed slaves who settled in Sierra Leone founded their own Methodist-oriented denomination. Protestant missions before 1800 (mostly Methodists and Anglicans; → Methodism; Anglican Communion) concentrated on the growing Krio population, who received a continuous influx of freed slaves from almost all parts of Africa. The Krio minority (2 percent) constitutes the only completely Christianized ethnic group in Sierra Leone. With the British display of power, the mission work of the various Protestant churches and denominations expanded to all the other ethnicities of the land (with the exception of the northern Susu and the southeastern Vai; → Colonialism; Mission 3.4). In the 19th century the middle-class, Western-educated, Victorian Krio population was the exemplary instance of the effect of missionary work in Africa.

In addition to → evangelism, the efforts of mission also brought about pioneering scientific work of lasting significance. Notable are the comparative ethnolinguistic studies of Sigismund Wilhelm Koelle (1820-1902; *Polyglotta Africana* [1854]) and the systematic exploration of the Temne language and literature by the missionary C. F. Schlenker. The racist arrogance of European missionaries (→ Racism) and the striving for cultural independence led early (1844) to a division of the local Methodist community and to the founding of an indigenous Creole church. For the Anglicans, Sierra Leone is the cradle of the so-called Native Pastorates. Bishop Samuel Crowther (ca. 1807-91) began his career in that church. On the whole, however, the results of Protestant evangelization were strikingly modest. Besides the Krio, only about 8 percent of the population belong to one of the non–Roman Catholic denominations.

2.4. Since the late 19th century the *Roman Catholic* mission has been active in nearly all areas of Sierra Leone and has had considerable success in primary, secondary, and postsecondary education (→ Catholic Missions). Indigenous clergy, lay leaders trained and supported by the Xaverian order, and the Holy Ghost Fathers are now emerging as the leaders in Catholic evangelization. Exact church membership figures are difficult to obtain, but their numbers in the rural areas certainly are equal to or exceed those of the Protestant missions.

2.5. As of 2006, the overall Christian population in Sierra Leone was growing at a rate greater than that of the early European mission era. In large part this growth is the result of an educated and committed indigenous clergy and lay leadership.

Bibliography: D. B. Barrett, G. T. Kurian, and T. M. Johnson, *WCE* (2d ed.) 1.658-61 • J. R. Cartwright, *Politics in Sierra Leone, 1947-67* (Toronto, 1970) • C. M. Fyle, *Historical Dictionary of Sierra Leone* (Lanham, Md., 2005) • G. O. Roberts, *The Anguish of Third World Independence: The Sierra Leone Experience* (Washington, D.C., 1982) • H. A. Sawyer, *God: Ancestor or Creator?* (London, 1970) • R. G. Saylor, *The Economic System of Sierra Leone* (Durham, N.C., 1967) • G. T. Stride and C. Ifeka, *Peoples and Empires of West Africa* (New York, 1971) • A. Wyse, *The Krio of Sierra Leone: An Interpretive History* (London, 1989).

Paul Jenkins, Peter Haenger, and Paul Kortenhoven

Sign

1. Term

A *sign* in the most general sense is something understood to stand for something else, for something other than the sign itself. To serve as a sign, it must be recognized as signifying what it stands for. People and computer programs recognize and employ signs. To determine whether other animals do too depends on what counts as a sign, and on the assessment of their cognitive and instinctual functions. There is no unanimity as to what counts as a sign or how to classify different sorts of signs.

Some signs have a direct or natural connection between their characteristics or occurrence, and what they signify. For instance, thunder is a common but not infallible sign of imminent rainfall. Although our experience strongly connects the two, thunder is neither a necessary nor a sufficient condition for rain. Sometimes there is rain without thunder, sometimes thunder without rain.

Other signs rely on convention to make them signifiers. For instance, a red octagonal sign tells a motorist to come to a stop before proceeding. Society picked this sign to indicate stopping, although there is no natural connection of this color and shape with the consequent action.

There is disagreement as to whether → language originated as a set of conventional signs, of sounds selected to point to various objects. Some words function in this way, but others (such as "if" and "now") do not.

Another issue concerns whether a → symbol is just a kind of sign, or belongs to a field partially overlapping with that of signs, or is a distinctive communicator in its own right. Some treat sign and symbol synonymously, or nearly so; others do not.

2. Philosophical Aspects

2.1. *Aristotle and Plato*

The *De interpretatione* of Aristotle (384-322 b.c.; → Aristotelianism) presents a theory of signs that is foundational for → hermeneutics, or interpretive method, and for modern semiotics, or theory of signs. Aristotle treats the sign *(symbolon)* as an inadequate means of indicating something other than itself, as representing it insufficiently. Words are typical examples. Words by themselves are neither true nor false; they are just "mere signs." Truth content belongs only to sentences, to specific combinations of words. Until corrected in the 20th century, the subsequent history of the concept of signs perpetuated this primarily negative sense of sign.

Aristotle's account is a critical reaction to the *Cratylus* dialogue of Plato (427-347 B.C.; → Platonism). Plato views words as instruments crafted by the mind in order to name things (388B). We must first know the thing if we are to locate the appropriate instrument for naming it. Word formation is secondary and conventional; knowledge of the thing named is prior and what is important. With respect to the status of words as such, there is no essential difference between Plato and Aristotle.

But Plato goes further, in saying that root words must be utilized if one is to know which other words are suitable names (438A-C). Knowledge of language makes word formation possible. Plato derives an entire etymology of names and concepts from this "idealism of root words." So Plato points from word-signs themselves to a prior eidetic knowing. Aristotle, in contrast, says that knowledge is possible only from the connected use of signs in sentences, not from the signs as such.

2.2. *Leibniz*

G. W. Leibniz (1646-1716) synthesized features of those two theories. Mathematical → logic expresses the ontological or conceptual content of the signs that Aristotle devalued. It furnishes the paradigm for expressing the sign's independent, ontological integrity. For Leibniz, a mathematical function is a typical example of a sign. He sees its conventional symbols and their relations as the summation of all the possible predicates of the geometric magnitudes that it designates. It both indicates something other than itself and embodies in itself the perfect principle of what it signifies. Leibniz understands the monad, or simple substance, to be a sign too, one inclusive of all the features of that to which it points, because a monad reflects within itself the whole universe.

In uniting Plato's eidetic, or idea-based, approach with Aristotle's conventionalist interpretation, Leibniz stands in continuity with the teaching of Nicholas of Cusa (1401-64) that the world is a symbol of God. On that view a symbol is the kind of sign that functions not only as a proxy for → meaning but also as itself the bearer of meaning.

2.3. *Modern Period*

The culmination of the concept of signs came with C. S. Peirce (1839-1914), who interpreted signs as "human forms." For Peirce, thoughts are sign-processes, so that the things the linguistic signs, or words, point to are understood in turn to be signs themselves. The indicating sign is interpreted as something produced by the sign-object (what it sig-

nifies) and as a suitable representative of it. So we have Peirce's "triangle," formed by the lines connecting the sign as symbol, the sign-object, and the interpretation, or signification. The nexus of indication is endless, linking each sign to further signs. The meaning of one sign is always discovered from another sign. Consequently, Peirce views reality as what is signified by all the signs, which are convertible into one another. There is no absolute point of interpretation within this triangle; each interpretation is subject to further interpretation if elucidation of its meaning is to be understood and made understandable. The model of discourse it involves is one of "shifting symbols," not one of the subject as absolute authority regarding the meaning of signs. This model opens the door to a modern "ethics of discourse" and the final abandonment of Aristotelian conventionalism. The sign forms a unity with the meaning it represents, a unity constitutive of the concept of symbol. After Peirce, the concept of symbol became increasingly detached from the concept of sign.

Peirce's model was basic to the semantic theory of Gottlob Frege (1848-1925) in modern logic. Frege introduced a semantic triad of sense, sign, and reference, or meaning. The sense is the interpretation or elucidation, the sign is the linguistic symbol, and the reference is what the sign designates. It is crucial that there can be substantial differences between different signs that have the same reference. Frege's famous example is "the evening star" and "the morning star," which refer differently to the planet Venus when it appears in different positions in the sky. The contrast in signs depends upon the mode of the referent's presentation. Frege's triangle involves more separation of sign from sense than does Peirce's distinction of symbol from signification.

According to Ludwig Wittgenstein (1889-1951) in his later thought, there are no ultimate objects or ultimate interpretations. There are just referential signs and the processes of interpretation. Without expressly saying so, this modern philosophy of signs has adopted some basic theses of the hermeneutic tradition deriving from Friedrich → Schleiermacher (1768-1834; → Schleiermacher's Theology). That tradition understands the hermeneutic process to be an open dialogue among interpretations, signs, and further interpretations. It sets out from the nature of the dialogue of interpreter and interpretation, rather than from symbolic representations of interpretations in the symbols themselves.

The theory of symbolic forms advanced by Ernst Cassirer (1874-1945) fully develops this sense of representation, in a manner also with roots in Peirce. Cassirer views the entire history of human culture through his historical phenomenology of the forms by which people in various eras symbolized their worldviews, and also their practical relationships. He identifies five primal cultural phenomena or symbolic forms: → myth, → religion, language, scientific knowledge, and art. Cassirer reinterprets the signification of the world by representative signs as a constitution of the world by symbols. This process is foundational for → culture. The first stage, mythic consciousness, discloses the sign-character of signs in a normative way for all subsequent forms of symbolism. Mythic consciousness grasps the natural phenomenon both as the real presence of the supernatural and as a representative sign for it, as indicating it. The advance of culture resolves this ambivalence in the sign by means of the symbol, by annulling the difference between the sign and its hidden signification. The two coalesce by interpretation and the creation of new symbols. Cassirer understands the world to be a macrocosm of symbolisms. More like Peirce than Leibniz, however, he does not depict the world as a completed symbol system, as divine, but instead as developing itself in a symbolizing process.

The linguist Ferdinand de Saussure (1857-1913) sought a new definition of the relationship between signifier and thing signified. He linked them in the sign, yet stressed, more than Peirce or Cassirer, the conventional nature of language signs. Their meaning is to be explained from the social circumstances of their origins. His sociolinguistic starting point influenced the later movement of → *structuralism,* although with very different effect (→ Linguistics).

Roland Barthes (1915-80) carried over into the literary sphere Saussure's anti-idealistic thesis of the autonomy of linguistic systems. He calls for recognition of the ambiguity of literary communication. For Barthes the language of literature is symbolic; it is structurally plural. Signs are symbol-elements, and symbols are macro-signs. The function of symbolic language is to rearrange the certitudes of everyday speech into a second language. It can do so because of the sign-character of symbols, which are complexes of possible meanings.

Poststructuralism radicalized the tendency of structuralism to be critical of → metaphysics. The *deconstructionism* program of Jacques Derrida (1930-2004) declares any quest for a nonrepresentative sense linked to signs to be meaningless. There is no reality to be accessed apart from the signs themselves. Thus it completes the dismissal of the traditional theory of meaning.

Bibliography: W. ALSTON, "Sign and Symbol," *EncPh* 7.437-41 • R. BARTHES, *A Barthes Reader* (New York, 1982) • E. CASSIRER, *The Philosophy of Symbolic Forms* (3 vols.; New Haven, 1953) • J. DERRIDA, *Of Grammatology* (Baltimore, 1976); idem, *Writing and Difference* (Chicago, 1978) • U. ECO, *Semiotics and the Philosophy of Language* (Bloomington, Ind., 1984) • G. FREGE, *The Frege Reader* (ed. M. Beaney; Oxford, 1997) • J. HOPKINS, *A Concise Introduction to the Philosophy of Nicholas of Cusa* (Minneapolis, 1980) • G. LEIBNIZ, *Philosophical Papers and Letters* (Dordrecht, 1970) • C. PEIRCE, *The Collected Papers of C. S. Peirce* (8 vols.; Cambridge, Mass., 1931-58) • E. RUDOLPH and H. WISMANN, eds., *Sagen, was der Zeit ist. Analysen zur Zeitlichkeit der Sprache* (Stuttgart, 1992) • F. DE SAUSSURE, *Course in General Linguistics* (New York, 1959) • F. SCHLEIERMACHER, *Hermeneutics: The Handwritten Manuscripts* (Missoula, Mont., 1977) • D. SEDLEY, *Plato's Cratylus* (Cambridge, 2003) • L. WITTGENSTEIN, *Philosophical Investigations* (Oxford, 1953).

ENNO RUDOLPH and ROBERT F. BROWN

3. Theological Aspects
3.1. *Biblical*
Signs in the Bible are seldom just conventional indicators. They function to reassure those who receive them and to serve as reminders to them. Signs do not just point to something that is not present; they manifest what they signify. They confirm that a past institution of → salvation remains in force. Examples include the rainbow, the practice of → circumcision, and the → Sabbath, which are all signs of God's → covenant (Gen. 9:12; 17:9-14; Exod. 31:13; Ezek. 20:12). Signs and wonders confirm God's power (Judg. 6:17; Mark 8:11-12; John 20:30). Some signs mark the onset of coming events. These include prophetic signs (Jer. 13:1-11; 19:1-13; 27; 32; Ezek. 4–5) and signs of the times (Matt. 11:1-6; 16:1-4; 24:3-34; Mark 13; Luke 21:7-36).

3.2. *Augustine*
→ Augustine (354-430; → Augustine's Theology) decisively influenced the concept of signs in the Western Christian tradition. In the model of symbolic actions in the Eastern church, the thing signified is present in → images, pictorial screens, → icons, and the → liturgy experienced as a participation in the heavenly liturgy. In contrast, Augustine paralleled the distance *(diastasis)* of the sign from what it signifies (the *res*), with the universal categorial antithesis of use *(uti),* as differentiated from enjoyment *(frui),* as the source of blessedness. For him, this antithesis ultimately expresses the dis-

tinction of the world from God (*De doc. Christ.* 1-2). As the *res* that is not signifying anything other than itself, God is distinct from the → creation, which is itself *res,* but one that bears the distinct impress of what points to the Creator (ibid. 1.4.4). From this domain of created things that also signify, we must distinguish the domain of realities that do nothing but signify, namely, that of → language.

Augustine's definition of sign (*De doc. Christ.* 2.1.1), as something that represents in the mind what is other than itself, is important because it portrays the connection between sign and thing signified for both the originator of the sign and those to whom it is addressed. So the sign does not actually manifest what it signifies. Instead, based on convention or on an outward similarity, it initiates a movement of the recipient's mind toward something not identical with the sign, and perhaps not even present.

Augustine's distinction between thing *(res)* and sign *(signum)* is taken up in a threefold distinction: the *res* to be enjoyed (which is God), the *res* to be used, and the *res* to be both used and enjoyed. The *Sentences* of Peter Lombard (ca. 1100-1160) puts the relation of sign to thing signified into the framework of → dogmatics. God as *res* (in bk. 1) is distinguished from sacramental signs (bk. 4). The doctrine of creation (bk. 2) serves as the route used to the Creator. → Christology and moral teachings (bk. 3) concern what is to be both used and enjoyed. All created realities have the character of signs, a conviction expressed in the medieval concept of the *analogia entis* (analogy of being).

3.3. *Aquinas*

The → sacraments in particular fall under the heading of signs in all medieval dogmatics. Thomas Aquinas (ca. 1225-74) states explicitly, "The sacrament belongs to the species of the sign" (*Summa theol.* III, q. 60, art. 1, resp.); sacraments exhibit an outward likeness to what they signify. The sacraments of the new covenant, unlike those of the old covenant, not only signify something but also effectively mediate the signified reality. Peter Lombard's *Sentences* states: "In the means [of the sacrament] there is a sign of God's → grace and the formal cause of invisible grace, so that it bears the image of grace and is its cause" (4.1.4.2). This sacramental concept, already found in Augustine, juxtaposes the signifying and causative functions (the latter emphatically arising from the sign-concept) and portrays the fundamental mediatorial function in the discussion of sacraments in the Western church.

Aquinas advocates in exemplary fashion an in-

nate efficacy of the sacramental elements, via the grace present in them. In contrast, the → Franciscans (Bonaventure and Duns Scotus) and the → nominalists (→ William of Ockham, Pierre d'Ailly, and Gabriel Biel) usually grasp the sacrament in the strict sense as a mere sign, to be fulfilled by an immediate operation of God's grace on the soul.

3.4. *Reformation*

Reformation-era controversies about the meaning of the eucharistic sign focus on the association but separation of *res* and *signum.* Ulrich → Zwingli (1484-1531) understood the sacramental sign as the occasion pointing us to the → passion of Christ. By virtue of the sign's likeness to it, the sign makes one spiritually contemporary with the passion and seizes one in → faith *(manducatio spiritualis).* Partaking in the common meal is evidence of belonging to the Christian community. The antitheses of spirit and corporeality, of God and world, with reference to faith and the physical means, place their imprint on the relationship of *signum* and *res.* The physical elements are relegated to being just a setting for a spiritual contemporaneity, as outward indication of spiritual realities, but not themselves as mediating spirit or as the bedrock of faith.

Martin → Luther (1483-1546; → Luther's Theology) carried on the understanding of sign in the theological tradition when he designated both Word and sacrament as "effective signs." They are effective not as instruments of grace working on the soul but instead as realities that mediate the "for me" of salvation. For Luther, the eucharistic sign is not the bread but is the real presence of Christ's body (therefore, the scholastic *res et sacramentum*). Here the *res* is the forgiveness of sins that becomes one's own in faith. The sign has the character of encouragement. It does not point to something external but instead mediates a verbal meaning that counts as one's own ("your sins are forgiven you"). So the sacramental sign has its setting as the moment of → promise within the context of word and faith. The word is the fundamental sign, as it is for Augustine. *Res* and *signum* are no longer related as spirit is to body. The sign itself is the manifestation and guarantee of a promise of God, on which faith relies in adhering to this "visible word."

3.5. *Modern Period*

Since the end of the 19th century, both Roman Catholic theology and High Church circles within Protestantism have endeavored to get beyond a purely conventional concept of sign in the interest of reorienting liturgical practice and, as a result, of advancing ecumenical discussion (→ Ecumenical Dialogue). Leading the way is research into "nondualistic" understandings of reality in which a sign is representative of transcendent power. These include worldviews that are mythical and magical, as well as those from the biblical, Hellenistic, and early medieval eras. There are also phenomenological descriptions of the immediate experience of corporeality at a level where soul-body dualism is completely suspended, with body graspable as the soul's manifestation and medium of realization. As a result, Roman Catholic theologians of the liturgical movement (Odo Casel, Romano Guardini, and Josef Jungmann) describe the church's liturgical and sacramental actions as symbolic actions in which the reality they signify makes itself present and manifest. The research of Max Thurian (1921-96), a Reformed member of the → Taizé community who became a Roman Catholic, yielded comparable results with the concept of recollection *(anamnesis)* in liturgical actions. This liturgical model overcame the antithesis of sign to signified reality, of the signifying and effective function of the sacrament to the liturgical sign. It established the concept of a sign that is efficacious and contemporaneous in its very signifying character.

This concept of sign was important in discussions of the *transsignification* teaching within Roman Catholic circles, but as a result also in ecumenical dialogue between Roman Catholic and Protestant churches. This dialogue took place after World War II, first at the Benedictine monastery in Chevetogne, Belgium (1958), and then also at a global level. The final report of this dialogue between Protestants and the Roman Catholic Secretariat (now Pontifical Council) for Promoting Christian Unity, entitled "The Presence of Christ in the Church and the World" (1977, doc. 2, esp. 503-10), points to a consideration of nondualistic categories as the requisite path to unity. It is debatable whether such a concept of sign is a settled matter and is suited to overcoming denominational differences.

Bibliography: F. DILLISTONE, *Traditional Symbol and the Contemporary World* (New York, 1973) • R. GUARDINI, *The Spirit of the Liturgy* (New York, 1998; orig. ed., Paris, 1930) • G. LOCHER, *Zwingli's Thought: New Perspectives* (Leiden, 1981) • H. DE LUBAC, *The Mystery of the Supernatural* (New York, 1967) • W. NICOL, *The Sēmeia in the Fourth Gospel* (Leiden, 1972) • N. SLENCZKA, *Realpräsenz und Ontologie* (Göttingen, 1993) • W. STÄHLIN, *Vom Sinn des Leibes* (Stuttgart, 1951) • P. TILLICH, *Systematic Theology* (3 vols.; Chicago, 1951-63).

NOTGER SLENCZKA

Sign of the Cross

The sign of the cross may be used to trace the shape of the → cross on oneself or over an assembly or over things that are being set aside for sacramental use.

1. The earliest form of crossing oneself was to trace a cross on one's forehead with one thumb. Later, during the Arian controversy (→ Arianism), the sign of the cross was made during Trinitarian invocations or benedictions. It is typically made by drawing the right hand from forehead to breast, then from shoulder to shoulder, and back to the center of the breast. In the Eastern church the cross is made from right to left; in the Western church, from left to right.

→ Tertullian is the earliest witness to Christians crossing themselves "in every act of coming and going . . . in all the ordinary actions of everyday life" (*De cor.* 3). The custom of Christians crossing themselves at some or every point in domestic life is reflected in Martin → Luther's Small → Catechism, in which he recommends that Christians cross themselves upon arising in the morning and retiring at night as a part of morning and evening → devotions (*Book of Concord*, 363).

Worshipers have crossed themselves at several places in the → liturgy, especially at invocations in the name of the Father and of the Son and of the Holy Spirit, in remembrance of → baptism; at the words in the creeds "(I believe) in the resurrection of the body"; and at the announcement of gospel reading (→ Readings, Scripture), when small thumb-crossings are made on the forehead, on the lips, and over the heart.

Hippolytus is a witness to the use of the sign of the cross "as a shield" against the → devil (*Trad. apos.* 37). It came to be used in → exorcisms and conjurations as a weapon against the demonic. The sign of the cross has also been traced on persons using oil in the acts of baptismal anointing and → healing. → Augustine of Hippo held that the sign of the cross was needed for the "due performance" of sacramental acts (*In Evang. Iohan.* 118). Under his influence the sign of the cross came to be regarded as essential to the valid consecration of the sacrament elements and therefore seemed to be an integral part of the *opus operatum* view in medieval sacramental theology. The use of the sign of the cross in blessings was therefore rejected by some → Reformers, although it continued to be used by Lutherans generally and by Anglicans only in connection with baptism. The → Book of Common Prayer rejected the idea that the sign of the cross is part of "the substance of the sacrament" but retained it as "a lawful outward ceremony and honorable badge, whereby the person who has been baptized is dedicated to the service of him that died upon the Cross."

2. The sign of the cross has been made by → bishops and → priests or → pastors over the congregation in → blessing. The priest or pastor may make one large graceful sign of the cross over the assembly to accompany words of absolution or blessing. Bishops may make three small signs of the cross over the congregation, first toward the center and then toward the bishop's left and right.

The continuing personal use of the sign of the cross hinges on its connection with baptism. The most explicit demonstration of this link is seen in the custom of Christians dipping their hands in water and tracing the cross on themselves on entering or leaving the church.

Bibliography: Book of Concord (ed. R. Kolb and T. J. Wengert; Minneapolis, 2000) • R. D. H. Bursell, *Liturgy, Order, and the Law* (Oxford, 1996) • P. J. Elliott, *Ceremonies of the Modern Roman Rite* (rev. ed.; San Francisco, 2005) • B. Fischer, *Signs, Words, and Gestures* (New York, 1981) • J. A. Jungmann, *The Mass of the Roman Rite* (vol. 1; New York, 1951) • L. L. Mitchell, *Baptismal Anointing* (London 1966).

Frank C. Senn

Sikhs

1. Origin
2. Scripture
3. Teachings
4. The Khalsa
5. Military and Political Significance

1. Origin

The name "Sikh" (Skt. *shishya*, "disciple") signifies a person who follows the teachings of the ten Sikh gurus and of Guru Granth Sahib, the holy book. The first guru, Nanak (1469-1539), founded a new fellowship that was open to all, irrespective of → caste, creed, or gender. He considered himself a divine minstrel whose chief avocation was to sing the glories of God. Never claiming that he himself was an incarnation of God, he conveyed the will of God through his *bani* (utterances).

Guru Nanak forthrightly criticized the contemporary evil order, whether social, religious, or politi-

cal. He preached a message of the unity of God and the brotherhood of humankind, and he composed a number of → hymns, using them for devotional singing. He went on long journeys throughout Asia and interacted with a wide variety of religious people, many of whom became attracted to his teachings. In the various places he would organize his disciples (Sikhs) into a *sangat*, or congregation. Finally, he settled at Kartarpur (now in Pakistan), a small town he established on the right bank of the river Ravi. There he founded a religious center known as Dharamsala (lit. "rest house," also a place in which to practice religion), where a group of dedicated disciples gathered around him. He taught them the basic principles of his faith and instructed them in the Sikh way of life. Besides worshiping together in the Dharamsala, they ate together from a *langar*, or common kitchen.

Before his death in 1539, Guru Nanak chose Guru Angad, one of his disciples, to succeed him on his mission. The line of successors established by Guru Nanak continued till 1708, when the tenth guru, Gobind Singh, was assassinated. The Sikhs believe that though the Sikh gurus were different in person, yet they all were carriers of one Jyoti (spirit), the "spirit of Nanak."

2. Scripture

The Sri Guru Granth Sahib (lit. "the honorable teacher, the book"), the Sikh holy book, comprises the sacred writings of Guru Nanak, his five successors, medieval Hindu Bhaktas (→ Bhakti), Muslim → Sufis, and other God-oriented persons associated with the Sikh gurus. Its history dates back to the time of Guru Nanak, whose hymns provided a powerful stimulus to his successors to add new hymns to the received texts. It is in the vernacular of Punjab, written in characters called Gurmukhi (from the mouth of the guru), especially developed for it by Guru Angad.

Ever since its canonization by the fifth guru, Arjan, and its subsequent installation in 1604 in Darbar Sahib (honorable court), Amritsar, it has been considered the most authentic repository of the divine Word (→ India 2.3). Some 36 authors have contributed, yet the whole text is essentially unified. It encompasses the spiritual experiences of the prominent religious persons of the Indian subcontinent during the period of its compilation. Except for the liturgical sections and the epilogue, almost the whole text is set to music, arranged in 31 musical modes *(ragas)*, some of which are composite. It presents a unique blend of music and poetry that is most suitable for devotional and public singing. The variety of languages, musical modes, and vocabulary transcends the boundaries of region and religion. All these features of the Sikh scripture make it unique among the world's holy books.

The Guru Granth Sahib enjoys an unparalleled reverence and significance in the Sikh way of life. Throughout its history the Sikh community has turned to it for guidance whenever confronted by contentious issues, either secular or religious. In this sense the holy book is not merely an ancient scripture but has been a perpetual guru for Sikhs. The Dasam Granth includes works by the tenth guru, Gobind Singh (1675-1708), and his companions but does not have the same supreme rank.

The Gurdwara ("doorway of the guru" or "doorway to God"), the Sikh religious place of worship, is the setting for devotion, fellowship, edification, and service. The focus of → worship is simply the holy book, Sri Guru Granth Sahib, which is installed in each Gurdwara. The Gurdwara functions as a counseling center where visitors receive practical training in the Sikh way of life. It is the fountainhead or sanctuary of Sikh → spirituality, of which the essential parts are meditation on the Word, truthful living, honest work, love, service, and sharing. Ablutions take place there. A key feature is the Guru ka Langar, or "guru's kitchen," where meals are provided after the services. All participants sit in rows without distinction and eat in fellowship together, without any payment. The Gurdwara may have a *serai* (rest house) attached to it, which provides lodging to pilgrims and travelers — again, with no discrimination. The Gurdwara is the axis of community life, the focus of congregational devotion and other social activities of the Sikhs.

3. Teachings

Guru Granth Sahib is the principal source from which Sikh teachings derive their authority and meaning. It begins with an invocation affirming that ultimate reality in all its detail is → God, who is one, beyond form, birth, and death. The emphasis is on the all-sovereign, self-illuminating, transcendent, and omnipresent God, on whom the whole universe depends for its existence. He not only listens but responds to a sincere supplication. He can be encountered directly and personally but is beyond any rational and empirical verification and is likewise beyond any human form or shape. One way of knowing him is the way of → love, a constant awareness of his sacred presence everywhere and at all times. Briefly speaking, the unity of the Godhead, his character as sui generis and eternal, puts Sikhism in the category of → monotheistic religions. The unity of God is not merely a metaphysical idea but a supreme value to be practiced here in this world. For example, since God is the Creator, the sole cause of → creation, humankind thus has a common origin. This belief establishes the idea of brotherhood/sisterhood and personal equality. When Sikhs assemble in a Gurdwara for worship and afterward partake of food from the Langar, no distinctions are made among participants (because of caste, creed, financial status, etc.).

The traditional Indian → worldview had been one of negation. Although the Sikh teachings do not dispute the perishable nature of the world, yet they do not despise the world as simply an illusion. The world is a reality, though it is not as real as its Creator. The Sikh worldview takes into account all the spheres of life, including "mother nature." The whole of this world is a Dharamsala, a sacred place in which to live and practice religion. The world has not been divided into two distinct and opposite realms: → sacred and profane. Sikhism teaches neither withdrawal from the world nor acceptance of the decadent social order as it is. It calls for struggle not only to eradicate → evil but to establish a renewed world order where higher values such as truth, justice, honesty, goodness, love, brotherhood, equality, and compassion are in full flower. Sikh teachings do not preach pessimism but emphasize an active and purposeful life. Normal family life is not an impediment in the way to communion with God. The believer is exhorted to live a detached life amid worldly temptations. The teachings, which take into account the whole gamut of human relationship, discourage an otherworldly attitude and encourage Sikhs to become useful citizens of the world.

A human being is not a physical body alone; he or she also possesses a spiritual element that belongs to the creative genius of God. It is an interior place where the person can realize God in a mystical manner. Human beings are supreme among all living beings. They are distinguished from the animal world, which in turn confers upon them special status and dignity in the cosmic plane (→ Human Dignity). Human life is a gift of God, a mission and an opportunity to achieve the summum bonum of life. Although a person enjoys → freedom of will, he or she carries responsibility to understand the meaning of being a human; failure to do so means regressing to the level of animals. Ego is the root cause of alienation from God and of evil in this world. The antidote is meditation on the name of God, which finds expression in truthful living. In God's court, the status of a person is measured only in terms of that person's good deeds.

Sikh teachings endeavor to develop an integrated personality, one that is perfect, free from eternal and external constraints of life. An enlightened person participates in worldly affairs in a positive manner to improve the whole environment of → society. He or she does not shun social responsibilities but maintains equilibrium even in adverse circumstances and remains ever ready to serve society. There is no legitimacy in dividing human beings along the lines of caste, creed, race, ethnicity, or region. All distinctions between one person and another have been rendered invalid. The stress is on equality and brotherhood, which are rooted in the principle of the common origin of humankind. Sikh teachings stand for a casteless and classless society that guarantees equal → rights to all citizens.

Sikh teachings are frequently summed up in three terse phrases:

Kirat Karo: earn your livelihood by the sweat of
    your labor;
Naam Japo: meditate on the name of God; and
Vand Chako: share your earnings with others.

The Sikh institutions such as guruship, Sangat, Gurdwara, Langar, Guru Granth, and Guru Panth (the mystic body of the Khalsa) that emerged were in direct response to the ideals propounded by Guru Nanak. All these institutions expressed the values cherished by Sikhs and provided practical manifestations of them. The Sikh concept of God, world, and humankind, along with the resultant attitudes and institutional organizations, were largely instrumental in establishing Sikhism as a separate and independent religion.

4. The Khalsa

Under the third and fourth gurus, the Sikhs were settled in and around the Punjab. During the fifth guru the number of Sikhs increased, spreading to most of the important cities of Mughal India. In 1577 Guru Ram Das founded the city of Ramdaspur, where he excavated Amrit Sarovar, or "pool of nectar." In 1589 Guru Arjan laid the foundation of the central Sikh shrine in the middle of Amrit Sarovar, and subsequently the city of Ramdaspur came to be known as Amritsar. Here the Sri Guru Granth Sahib is installed in the central Sikh shrine, known as Harmandir Sahib (the exalted sanctuary of God). It is often called the Golden Temple because of the golden work inlaid on its roof, walls, and domes. In the same precinct the Akal Takht (throne of the Timeless One), built by the sixth guru, stands witness to the Sikh idea of sovereignty. It symbolizes the interlocking of the temporal with

the spiritual in Sikhism. As the highest temporal seat, it is where the Sikhs hold discussion on matters concerning the community.

Up to the death of Emperor Akbar in 1605, relations between the Sikhs and the Mughals were friendly. Thereafter Emperor Jahangir (1605-27) followed a policy of religious intolerance, doing all he could to stop the spread of Sikhism. Consequently, in 1606 the fifth guru, Arjan, died as a martyr in the cause of Sikh faith at the hands of Mughals. It was the turning point in the history of Sikhs. Thereafter Sikhs organized themselves militarily under the sixth guru, Hargobind (1606-44). It ushered in an era of armed conflict between the Sikhs and Mughals. In 1675 the ninth guru, Tegh Bahadur, was arrested and thrown into prison by the Mughal state. He had championed the cause of Kashmiri pandits against the Mughal policy of converting them forcibly to the fold of → Islam. In November 1675 Guru Tegh Bahadur was publicly beheaded in the Chandani Chowk (bazaar) of Delhi on the orders of Emperor Aurangzeb (1658-1707).

On the day of Vaisakhi (March 29) in 1699, the tenth guru, Gobind Singh, instituted the Khalsa (Arab. *khālisah,* "pure, free"), a core of dedicated Sikhs directly under the control of the guru and also wedded to military and religious discipline. It was to defend the Sikh community against the attacks of Mughals and their allies. Women as well as men were admitted to this order by baptism with Amrit (ambrosia), made up of sugar water stirred in a steel cauldron with a double-edged sword by five Sikhs one by one while they recited certain hymns of the Sikh gurus. After the baptism women took the name "Kaur" (princess), and men the name "Singh" (lion). Besides adhering to a specific code of conduct, they were to keep five symbols, known as the five Ks: Kesh (uncut hair), Kirpan (sword), Kachh (short trousers), Kangha (comb), and Kara (steel bracelet).

In the struggle that ensued between the Sikhs and the Mughals, four sons of Guru Gobind Singh fell as martyrs, two youths fighting in the battle and two infants bricked alive in a wall by the Mughal officials of Punjab. Guru Gobind Singh wrote a long letter (the *Zafarnama,* "notification of victory") to Aurangzeb, reminding him of injustice that the guru suffered and of the guru's resolve to fight the tyrannical Mughal state. On the invitation of new emperor, Bahadur Shah (1707-12), Guru Gobind Singh traveled to Deccan, where in 1708 he fell to a fatal blow struck by two Pathan soldiers of the Mughal army. Before his death Guru Gobind Singh abolished the line of succession and invested the authority of guruship for all time in the Guru Granth. In addition, the Guru Panth was elevated permanently to the status of guru.

5. Military and Political Significance

After the death of Guru Gobind Singh, political leadership came into the hands of Banda Singh Bahadur, whom the guru had commissioned to continue the struggle against the Mughals in Punjab. He led the Sikhs in liberating a large tract of Punjab territory, replacing the Mughal authority with a new administration. The first Sikh rule, which lasted only a short while (1710-15), could not long survive against the military might of the Mughal empire. Banda Singh Bahadur and his fellow Sikhs were besieged, and ultimately 740 Sikhs were taken as prisoners to Delhi, where in June 1716 they were tortured and executed publicly. It signaled the beginning of a reign of terror for the Sikhs. The Mughal emperors and their governors at Lahore followed a relentless policy of exterminating the Sikhs as a religious community. Prices were fixed on their heads, and they were hunted down like wild beasts. Their execution in public in the most barbaric manner in the chowks of Lahore was a common practice.

Despite the odds against them, the Sikhs eventually managed to overthrow the Mughal rule. In 1765 they occupied Lahore and became the sovereign rulers of Punjab. They had complete sway over the country from the Indus River in the northwest to the Jamuna River in the east. Under Maharaja Ranjit Singh (1780-1839) the Sikhs set up their own kingdom at Lahore. It ranked among the world powers of its time. The Sikhs successfully defended it against the Mughals, as well as the neighboring Afghan chiefs and Hindu princes. In the early 19th century they resisted the colonial British, keeping them at bay until 1849.

After annexation, the Sikh kingdom of Lahore became a province of British India. Because of their skills the Sikhs were welcomed into British rule, especially the military service. The socioreligious reform movements of the 1860s led in the 1870s to the emergence of Singh Sabha, a movement attempting to define and defend Sikhism. It ushered in an era of Sikh renaissance that is best known for reorganization and Sikh self-distinction vis-à-vis → Hinduism, Islam, and Christianity. The Sikh struggle for Gurdwara reforms resulted in the Gurdwara Act of 1925, whereby Sikhs gained the right to manage their shrines. The Sikh holy places were reclaimed from corrupt priests, and yeoman service was also rendered to the cause of independence.

Between the partition of India in 1947 (when 40 percent of the 6.5 million Sikhs were uprooted) and the establishment of a Punjabi-speaking state in 1966, the Sikhs created a miracle of economic, industrial, and agricultural development, as well as taking a leading part in two wars against Pakistan. In June 1975, however, Indira Gandhi (1917-84) declared an internal emergency in India and had all opposition leaders put into prison. The Sikhs in Punjab launched the Save Democracy Campaign, and about 40,000 Sikhs courted arrest. It was the beginning of distrust between the Sikhs and the central government of India, led by the Congress Party.

When in 1981 the central government failed to respond to Sikh demands for greater self-determination, transfer of Chandigarh and Punjabi-speaking areas to Sikh control, and Punjab's rights over its river waters, resentment began to mount. In May 1984 a small group of armed Sikhs led by Sant Jarnail Singh Bhindrawale entrenched themselves in the Golden Temple. In June 1984 the central government imposed a curfew all over the Punjab, totally cut it off from the rest of the country, and ordered the Indian army to storm the Golden Temple. This action resulted in the killing of hundreds of pilgrims and innocent Sikhs, besides destroying the Akal Takht and much else. Sikhs all over the world were outraged at the attack on the Golden Temple and the destruction of Akal Takht. Four months later the Sikh reaction to the army attack became clear, as two Sikh members of the bodyguard of Prime Minister Indira Gandhi assassinated her on October 31. Gruesome riots in Delhi and other Indian cities broke out in which thousands of Sikhs were massacred and their properties looted, set on fire, and destroyed.

In 2001 there were more than 19 million Sikhs in India, of whom 14.5 million were concentrated in Punjab. In addition, between 1 and 2 million Sikhs are scattered around the world in the Sikh diaspora, with the largest numbers in England, Canada, and the United States. In May 2004 Manmohan Singh, a renowned economist, became prime minister of India, the first Sikh to hold this office. His appointment has deepened relations between the Sikhs and the central government of India.

Bibliography: *Sikh texts:* G. S. Talib, trans., *Sri Guru Granth Sahib* (4 vols.; Patiala, 1984-90) • M. Thiel-Horstmann, trans., *Leben aus der Wahrheit. Texte aus der heiligen Schrift der Sikhs* (Zurich, 1988) • Trilochan Singh et al., trans., *Selections from the Sacred Writings of the Sikhs* (London, 1960) • C. Vaudeville, trans., *Kabīr* (Oxford, 1984).

Secondary works: W. O. Cole and P. S. Sambhi, *The Sikhs: Their Religious Beliefs and Practices* (London, 1978; 2d ed., Brighton, Eng., 1995) • Daljeet Singh, *Essentials of Sikhism* (Amritsar, 1994) • G. S. Dhillon, *India Commits Suicide* (Chandigarh, 1995) • Ganda Singh and Teja Singh, *A Short History of the Sikhs (1469-1765)* (Bombay, 1950; repr., Patiala, 1989) • J. S. Grewal, *The Sikhs of the Punjab* (rev. ed.; Cambridge, 1998) • H. R. Gupta, *History of the Sikhs* (6 vols.; New Delhi, 1978-91) • Harbans Singh, ed., *The Encyclopedia of Sikhism* (4 vols.; Patiala, 1992) • Jagjit Singh, *The Sikh Revolution* (New Delhi, 1981) • M. Juergensmeyer and N. G. Barrier, eds., *Sikh Studies: Comparative Perspectives on a Changing Tradition* (Berkeley, Calif., 1979) • Kapur Singh, *Parasharprasna; or, The Baisakhi of Guru Gobind Singh* (Jullundur, 1959; rev. ed., Amritsar, 1989) • Khushwant Singh, *A History of the Sikhs* (2 vols.; Princeton, 1963; rev. ed., Delhi, 2004) • M. A. Macauliffe, *The Sikh Religion: Its Gurus, Sacred Writings, and Authors* (6 vols.; Oxford, 1909; repr., Delhi, 1985) • W. H. McLeod, *Guru Nanak and the Sikh Religion* (New Delhi, 1969) • G. S. Mansukhani, *Introduction to Sikhism* (New Delhi, 1967) • Sher Singh, *Philosophy of Sikhism* (Amritsar, 1979) • M. Thiel-Horstmann, "Guru Nanak und der Sikhismus," *Große Religionsstifter* (ed. P. Antes; Munich, 1992) 115-32.

Balwant Singh Dhillon and Noel Q. King

Simony

1. The term "simony" took its origin from Simon Magus in Acts 8:18-24. It involves making, or trying to make, spiritual office or gifts a commercial matter. In 451 the Council of → Chalcedon began systematizing this offense, and we still find signs of it in the Roman Catholic 1983 → CIC (cans. 149.3, 188, and 1380) and in Anglican → church law (can. 1969.16). The CIC has come under criticism for leaving many questions open (E. Eichmann).

Simony is not just a disciplinary offense but a sacrilege or → heresy. Gehazi in 2 Kgs. 5:20-27 has given his name to the special offense of selling spiritual blessings. The fee paid → priests from endowments for special → masses is not regarded by the → Roman Catholic Church as simony, since the priest is here performing his duty by command of the church.

2. The rulings and writings against simony show how temptations and threats to the integrity of the → church grew with its → power and responsibili-

ties. Penalties such as loss of office, → excommunication, and the invalidating of ministries were meant to ward off simony. Criticism of simony was historically important in the question of the secular holdings of bishops in the → Investiture Controversy. → Bishops had to prove that simony had played no part in their appointment. Eventually the church policy of the emperor and kings came under the general charge of simony, which the papacy was successful in opposing (→ Empire and Papacy).

3. To avoid simony, the Protestant churches have passed disciplinary measures and taken steps to control appointments. The cooperation of → congregations and → elders in supervising the right administration of the → sacraments and the proper discharge of the pastoral office is a further safeguard.

Bibliography: H. E. J. Cowdrey, *Pope Gregory VII, 1073-1085* (Oxford, 1998) esp. 242-48 • J. Gilchrist, "Simony," *NCE* (2d ed.) 13.135-36 • J. H. Lynch, *Simoniacal Entry into Religious Life from 1000 to 1260: A Social, Economic, and Legal Study* (Columbus, Ohio, 1976) • T. Reuter, "Gifts and Simony," *Medieval Transformations: Texts, Power, and Gifts in Context* (ed. E. Cohen and M. B. de Jong; Leiden, 2001) 157-68 • R. A. Ryder, *Simony: An Historical Synopsis and Commentary* (Washington, D.C., 1931) • J. Wycliffe, *On Simony* (trans. T. A. McVeigh; New York, 1992).

Jürgen Stein

Simul iustus et peccator

1. Bible
2. Augustine and Medieval Theology
3. Luther and the Reformation Debate
4. Modern and Ecumenical Discussions

The formula *simul iustus et peccator* (*siep*, "simultaneously justified and a sinner") was used by Martin → Luther (1483-1546; → Luther's Theology) and adopted as a central term of Lutheran theology in the 20th century. It refers to the continuing sinfulness of the justified person. Earlier a focus of doctrinal disagreement between Protestant (esp. Lutheran) and Roman Catholic theology, it recently has been the subject of official ecumenical agreement.

1. Bible

While the formula *siep* dates only from the → Reformation, it has roots in the NT. On the one hand, various strands of the NT, including both Pauline (Rom. 6:18, 22) and Johannine (1 John 3:9) texts, affirm that the justified person is freed from → sin. On the other hand, various NT texts recognize the justified person's ongoing struggle with sin. In Galatians, Paul recognizes that the Christian must still resist the "desires of the flesh" that remain in the justified (Gal. 5:16-17). First John goes further in stating, "If we say that we have no sin, we deceive ourselves" (1:8).

Much premodern exegesis understood Paul to be speaking of himself as a Christian when he referred to "the sin that dwells within me" (Rom. 7:17), which drives him to do "the evil I do not want" (v. 19). The interpretation of Romans 7, which became central to later disputes, has recently shifted, with most commentators today understanding this passage to refer to Paul in his preconversion life. (The significance of the referent of Romans 7 should not be exaggerated; → Augustine in his later writings, Thomas Aquinas, Luther, and the Council of → Trent all agreed that this text referred to the Christian Paul, and thus the debate did not turn on this question.) The NT contains no doctrine of *siep*, but it does pose the problem of understanding how the justified person is freed from sin and yet struggles with an internal drive to sin.

2. Augustine and Medieval Theology

Augustine (354-430; → Augustine's Theology) formulates the categories in which the debate is later carried out in his discussion of three central concepts: → baptism, sin, and concupiscence (i.e., the disordered desires of the self, which remain following baptism). Augustine often equated original sin with the disordering of the self in which reason, will, and desire are no longer rightly subordinated to one another and to God. Baptism removes the guilt of concupiscence, but an "infirmity" remains in the self that must be resisted. While Augustine generally does not refer to concupiscence as itself sin, he is not always consistent, and he does equate concupiscence with the "law of sin" that Paul says dwells in his members (Rom. 7:23). He was thus appealed to by both sides in the later debate.

Theologians of the 12th and 13th centuries came to understand the grace given in baptism as a form or quality that inheres in the justified (e.g., Aquinas, *Summa theol.* I of II, q. 110, art. 2). This analysis was thoroughly Augustinian, for it implied that what justifies in no sense comes from the person but must be infused from without. If that which justifies is a quality of the self and this quality is understood as incompatible with the presence of sin, then sin

cannot be present in the justified. All sin, strictly understood, is mortal sin, which damns. Sins that do not damn (i.e., venial sins), which the justified often commit, can thus be called sin only analogously (see, e.g., ibid., q. 88, art. 1, ad 1). This anthropology of sin and grace framed the later Catholic response to *siep*.

3. Luther and the Reformation Debate

Martin Luther's assertion of *simul iustus et peccator* was rooted in the conjunction of his understanding of → justification as participation in the righteousness of Christ (and thus not primarily a quality inhering in the self) and the reading of specific biblical texts. Signs of his new thinking can be seen in his early interpretations of Pss. 32 and 51 (*LW* 10.145-47, 235-41) and, more clearly, of Romans, where Luther uses the formula *siep* (ibid. 25.260). While the formula did not become common in Luther's writings, the underlying convictions became a permanent aspect of his teaching

Luther's most comprehensive explanation and defense of *siep* is his Against Latomus (1521, *LW* 32.133-260), in which he defends the statement that the good works of the saints are also sins. In agreement with Augustine, Luther stresses the presence of disordered desires in the self after baptism and justification. Justification does mean that these desires no longer rule the self but are ruled (p. 203). Nevertheless, he insists that these disordered desires can rightly be called sin, appealing to Paul's language in Romans 7 (p. 219), although he clearly differentiates such sin from mortal sin, which is incompatible with faith (p. 218). In addition, the self that struggles successfully with such desires is still not obeying the central commandment to love God with all one's heart and mind. The justified truly do good works, yet as the works of a divided self, they do not in themselves fulfill the law and are thus rightly called sin (p. 212). The formula *siep* affirms the continuing dependence of the justified on the righteousness of Christ.

Interpreters of Luther have noted that *siep* has two aspects: partial and total. On the one hand, the justified is partially sinner (the disorders of the self are still present) and partially justified (a new self is born of faith). On the other hand, the total → self is just (as clothed in faith by the perfect righteousness of Christ), and yet if God were to judge by the commandment of undivided love, the total self would be judged a sinner. In neither case, however, does *siep* represent a static coexistence of justification and sin. In its partial aspect, the new self rules the sin that remains and is called increasingly to control and suppress that sin. In its total aspect, justification in Christ is the decisive truth about the self, whose sinfulness is passing away.

Other Reformers, such as Philipp → Melanchthon (1497-1560) and John → Calvin (1509-64; → Calvin's Theology), affirm the sinfulness of remaining concupiscence, appealing to Romans 7, without explicit use of the formula *siep,* which did not become a slogan during the Reformation period.

The Council of Trent (1545-63) saw the affirmation of the continuing sinfulness of the justified as an aspect of a more comprehensive Reformation denial of both the authentic renewal of the justified and the power of baptism. While granting that Paul does sometimes call concupiscence sin, even in the justified, the council denied that such concupiscence is "truly and properly" called sin and condemned those who say otherwise (DH 1515).

4. Modern and Ecumenical Discussions

While the sinfulness of remaining concupiscence became a standard Protestant assertion, the formula *siep* did not enter the theological vocabulary until the rediscovery of Luther's *Lectures on Romans* (*LW* 25) at the beginning of the 20th century. Initially reclaimed in Roman Catholic critiques of Luther, *siep* was adopted by many Lutheran theologians, especially after Rudolf Hermann's (1887-1962) study of the phrase (1930), as a focal point of a Reformation doctrine of justification. While some theologians emphasized the formula's contradiction of Roman Catholic teaching (E. Jüngel), other theologians, both Protestant (K. → Barth) and Catholic (K. → Rahner and H. U. von Balthasar), defused the formula's controversial character by a detailed attention to what it affirmed.

Roman Catholic–Lutheran → ecumenical dialogues in both the United States and Germany found that while Lutheran and Catholic theology reflected different concerns, realized in different definitions of "sin," the resulting disagreements need not be church-dividing. This agreement was ratified in 1999 by the Roman Catholic Church and the churches of the Lutheran World Federation in the → *Joint Declaration on the Doctrine of Justification* (*JDDJ,* esp. pars. 28-30). While the initial Roman Catholic response to the *JDDJ* was critical of its handling of *siep,* the subsequent Annex not only clarified matters sufficiently for the Catholic Church to affirm the *JDDJ* but also included a limited affirmation of *siep* by the church.

Following the ratification of the *JDDJ,* the ecumenical study group Ökumenischer Arbeitskreis in Germany produced the most thorough study of the topic to date, with extensive historical essays, providing further support for the ecumenical agreement (T. Schneider and G. Wenz).

Bibliography: H. G. Anderson, T. A. Murphy, and J. A. Burgess, eds., *Justification by Faith* (Minneapolis, 1985) • H. U. von Balthasar, *The Theology of Karl Barth: Exposition and Interpretation* (San Francisco, 1992) • K. Barth, *CD* IV/1 • R. Hermann, *Luthers These "Gerecht und Sünder zugleich"* (Gütersloh, 1930; 2d ed., 1960) • E. Jüngel, *Justification: The Heart of the Christian Faith; A Theological Study with an Ecumenical Purpose* (Edinburgh, 2001) • K. Lehmann and W. Pannenberg, eds., *The Condemnations of the Reformation Era: Do They Still Divide?* (Minneapolis, 1990) • The Lutheran World Federation and The Roman Catholic Church, *Joint Declaration on the Doctrine of Justification* (Grand Rapids, 2000) • K. Rahner, "Justified and Sinner at the Same Time," *Theological Investigations* (vol. 6; Baltimore, 1969) 218-30 • T. Schneider and G. Wenz, *Gerecht und Sünder zugleich? Ökumenische Klärungen* (Freiburg, 2001) • D. S. Yeago, "Martin Luther on Renewal and Sanctification: Simul Iustus et Peccator Revisited," *Sapere teologico e unità della fede* (ed. C. A. Valls, C. Dotolo, and G. Pasquale; Rome, 2004) 655-74.

Michael Root

Sin

1. OT

To understand the meaning of "sin," a powerful theological concept in the OT, the interpreter first needs to study the terms in the Hebrew Bible that translators have rendered into English as "sin." The meaning of these terms can often be approximated by studying the nontheological passages in which they appear. How the words describe interactions among humans provides clues about the interaction between humans and God. (G. von Rad, K. Koch, and K. D. Sakenfeld have demonstrated in some detail the use of this method.) Second, the depiction of sin is not limited to the use of the obvious words but extends to a variety of actions that tear at the relationship between God and his people. Third, consideration of words and actions that are presented as the opposites of sin can heighten our understanding of the term. Fourth, the interconnectedness of sin and its subsequent → guilt and → punishment throws further light on the subject.

1.1. Terms

The Hebrew words usually discussed in a study of sin are various forms of the roots *ḥṭ'*, *pš'*, *'wn*, and *'šm*. Those words frequently appear together, even in synonymous parallelism in poetic passages, and for the most part they should be understood similarly. Unfortunately, in rendering the Hebrew Bible into Greek (the → Septuagint), the translators had at their disposal primarily the Greek term *hamartia*, meaning a mistake or missing the goal of an ethical code. This factor has served to obscure the implication of rebellion in the Hebrew words.

The nontheological uses of *ḥṭ'*, the most common term, indicate a more personal affront, even the dishonoring of a person with whom a relationship exists. Saul admits to David that he had "done wrong" *(ḥṭ')* to him and promises he will not again do him harm (1 Sam. 26:21). Elsewhere, David protests his innocence and asks Jonathan about the nature of his sin against Saul, using both *ḥṭ'* and *'wn* (1 Sam. 20:1). Later, Shimei confesses, "I have sinned [*ḥṭ'*]," and the description of his action in the following verse indicates he has "cursed the LORD's anointed," David (2 Sam. 19:20-21). Reuben tells his brothers that their betrayal of their brother Joseph and their selling him into slavery was a "wrong [*ḥṭ'*]" against Joseph (Gen. 42:22). These passages and many others indicate that *ḥṭ'* represents not merely the erring from a code of behavior but a personal dishonoring of, even harm against, another person.

With that nontheological background in mind, the theological use of *ḥṭ'* to express that same personal affront is highlighted by other "sin" words that accompany it. In Ps. 78:17 the psalmist, in describing Israel's sinning *(ḥṭ')* against the Lord in the wilderness, uses the parallel verb *mrh,* "rebel." The exilic prophet reports God's speech to the exiles in Babylon that they have sinned *(ḥṭ')* against the Lord from the beginning and have rebelled *(pš')* ever since (Isa. 43:27; see also Job 13:23). In Ezek. 16:51-52, the Lord accuses Israel of sins *(ḥṭ')* that exceeded those of Samaria by committing a host of "abominations" (idolatrous acts associated with Canaanite religion and practice). Likewise, Hosea describes Israel's sin *(ḥṭ')* as making and worshiping idols (Hos. 13:2), and Jeremiah defines *ḥṭ'* and *'wn* as forsaking the Lord through idolatry and breaking the → Torah (Jer. 16:10-11).

1.2. Broken Relationship with God

Apart from these specific words, Israel's affront against the honor of God is variously portrayed as the breaking of the → covenant relationship that God established with the people through Moses. While we consider the → Decalogue to be Israel's ethical code, the Ten Commandments in Exod. 20:3-17 are set within the context of the Lord's claim to be Israel's God on the basis of redeeming them from the bondage in Egypt. Sin is therefore not simply the breaking of the code but a dishonoring of the Lord's authority established in the act of redemption. Not surprisingly, then, the prophets Hosea and Jeremiah focus on the pathos of God, the Lord's heart-broken pain (A. Heschel), as Israel acts, on the one hand, as the Lord's adulterous wife (Jer. 3:1, 20; Hos. 1:2; 3:1) and, on the other, as the Lord's rebellious son or faithless child (Jer. 3:14, 19; Hos. 11:1-2). Isaiah speaks of this forsaking of the Lord in terms of empty worship and vain sacrifices, along with injustice to the poor in courts of law (Isa. 1:4-17), and Ezekiel reports that the Lord accused Israel of the sin of Sodom, namely, failing to care for the poor and the needy (Ezek. 16:49). Even when specific reference is made to some of the Ten Commandments (e.g., Hos. 4:1b-2), the context is the affront to God's exclusive claim to be "the LORD your God" (Exod. 20:2).

Likewise, without using any of the terms for sin, the story of eating the forbidden fruit in the Garden of Eden vividly portrays the first couple's rejection of the authority of God. After the serpent's enticement that "you will be like God, knowing good and evil" (Gen. 3:5), they asserted their own independence and ran for the forbidden fruit. While the story does not bear all the weight of "the fall" that → Augustine and later theology imposed on Genesis 3, it nevertheless remains a potent narrative about the nature of sin as → autonomy (i.e., self-rule) over against the honoring of God's authority. It is significant that such rebellion begins with the first human couple and becomes the prototype of human sinfulness (Hos. 6:7). Indeed, that first act of human sinfulness describes the experience of all people (1 Kgs. 8:46; Eccl. 7:20).

1.3. The Opposites of Sin

The opposites of sin support the understanding of sin's personal nature. The rebellion against God's authority by breaking commandments results in a divine lawsuit against the people of Israel (Hos. 4:1-3); what God desires of the people are sin's opposites: "steadfast → love [ḥsd]" and "knowledge [dᶜt] of God" (Hos. 6:6). N. Glueck and K. D. Sakenfeld (1978) have demonstrated that the word ḥsd (often translated, as here, "steadfast love") is a highly relational term indicating "loyalty within a covenant relationship." As is well known, dᶜt in biblical Hebrew is not merely an intellectual awareness but an intimate relationship (e.g., Gen. 4:1; Amos 3:2). Even the term ṣdqh/ṣdq (righteousness) is likewise not so much a legal or moral matter but a fulfilling of expected roles within particular relationships (G. von Rad, *OT Theology*, 370-83). What God desires, in other words, is not simply meeting the goals of an ethical or ritual standard but proving oneself to be faithful within the covenant relationship. Sin must be understood as the opposite of such fidelity.

1.4. Sin, Guilt, and Punishment

The study of sin in the OT becomes quite complex when several of the terms for sin bear the extended meanings "guilt," "punishment," and even "sin offering" (i.e., the means for removing the consequences of the sins). K. Koch shows that the Hebrew understanding of ᶜwn, for example, permits no distinction between sin and its resulting punishment. The word ʾšm describes the potential "guilt" of Isaac's deception against Abimelech at Gen. 26:10, but it is used also for "penalty" (i.e., the offering of a sheep or goat, Lev. 5:6) or "guilt offering" (Lev. 5:15). D. Kellermann shows that in that dual role ʾšm functions much like ḥṭʾ in its nominal form ḥṭʾt.

The terms seem to indicate that the OT reflects the common ancient Near Eastern pattern of a specific evil a person commits coming back to roost on one's head. Yet God's response to the personal nature of sin points in a different direction. The story of rebellion in the Garden of Eden results not in punishment that corresponds directly to eating forbidden fruit but in a series of broken relationships between humans, between humans and snakes, between humans and the soil, and so forth (C. Westermann). Since sin in the OT is an affront against the person of God and God's honor, God's judgment against Israel involves removing the signs that had demonstrated the covenant relationship, namely, the land God gave to Israel (Jer. 29:4), the land and the people (Isa. 6:10-13), and the divine → Word that created and enlivened the community (Amos 8:11-12). The dishonoring of God throws the individuals who constitute the community into a milieu of disaster, even death for a person (Exod. 10:16-17) and for one's entire family (1 Kgs. 13:34). Surely ḥṭʾ and ᶜwn result in "barriers between you and your God" (Isa. 59:2).

God, however, never allows sin to have the last word. Even while expelling Adam and Eve from the garden, "the LORD God made garments of skins for the man and for his wife, and clothed them" (Gen. 3:21). Against the history of human rebellion through Genesis 3–11, God called Abraham to serve as the means by which all the families of the earth would be blessed (Gen. 12:3). In spite of Israel's constant dishonoring of their Lord, God established the entire sacrificial system in order to renew repeatedly the relationship with Israel, including the use of a scapegoat to bear away the sins of the people. Specifically, God commissioned the Servant to suffer "for our transgressions [pš]" and "for our iniquities [ᶜwn]," and the Lord "laid on him the iniquity [ᶜwn] of us all" (Isa. 53:5-6). God provides the means of → forgiveness and thus gives → hope to Israel and to all humankind, even within the milieu of sin and death.

Bibliography: D. I. BLOCK, *The Book of Ezekiel: Chapters 1–24* (Grand Rapids, 1997) 509-10 • T. L. BRODIE, *Genesis as Dialogue* (Oxford, 2001) 142-56 • W. BRUEGGEMANN, *Genesis* (Atlanta, 1982) 40-54 • B. CHILDS, *The Book of Exodus* (Philadelphia, 1974) 385-439 • N. GLUECK, *Hesed in the Bible* (Cincinnati, 1967) • A. HESCHEL, *The Prophets* (2 vols.; New York, 1962) • D. KELLERMANN, "אָשָׁם *ʾāshām*" etc., *TDOT* 1.429-37 • K. KOCH, "חָטָא *chāṭāʾ*" etc., *TDOT* 4.309-19; idem, "עָוֹן *ʿāwōn*" etc., *TDOT* 10.546-62; idem, *The Prophets,* vol. 1, *The Assyrian Period;* vol. 2, *The Babylonian and Persian Periods* (Philadelphia, 1983-84) • G. QUELL, "Ἁμαρτάνω κτλ. A: Sin in the OT," *TDNT* 1.267-86 • G. VON RAD, *Genesis: A Commentary* (rev. ed.; Philadelphia, 1972) 86-102; idem, *OT Theology* (vol. 1; New York, 1962) • K. D. SAKENFELD, *Faithfulness in Action* (Philadelphia, 1985); eadem, *The Mean-

ing of Hesed in the Hebrew Bible (Missoula, Mont., 1978) • C. WESTERMANN, *Genesis 1–11: A Commentary* (Minneapolis, 1984).

FOSTER R. McCURLEY

2. NT

The OT view of sin as sin against God is also found in the NT. But a more radical concept of sin occurs, namely, as a power. The NT writers either ignore the cultic dimension of → forgiveness or contest it theologically. → Paul offers the most profound theological discussion, which provides the fullest picture of the NT doctrine of sin.

2.1. *Paul*

Paul depicted sin within the context of his theology of → justification. Only thus could he show the depths of the fearsome reality of sin. Especially in the Epistle to the Romans he put sin and the sinner theologically together in a way that no other NT author could achieve, but always in the context of the → salvation that God grants in Christ. If we fail to speak of sin in its connection with soteriology, we can know only its secondary reality. Paul distinguishes between sin *(hamartia)* and the act of sin *(parabasis, paraptōma)*. Outside or prior to Christ, we are all subject to sin as to a power in which, as in a person, Paul finds demonic features. Sin defines the essence of sinners, so that they *are* their sin (→ Anthropology 2). Sin is an annihilating power that is at work within us. Paradoxically, it is both nonidentical with us and yet also identical. In this sense the word "flesh" *(sarx)*, which is so often misunderstood, denotes the individual locus of the power that cannot be defined individually (→ Anthropology 2.3). Sinners are flesh insofar as sin finds concrete form in them. But sin exists long before acts of sin. Sinners commit acts of sin because they are essentially and totally defined by sin. The acts do not constitute the power of sin, not even the first act of → Adam (Rom. 5:12). The introduction to the list of vices in Gal. 5:19-21 is important, for all of them — including *porneia* (fornication) — are works of the flesh. In a sense it is easy to misunderstand the much-quoted formula of Rudolf Bultmann (1884-1976) that a sin came into the world through sinning (*Theology*, 1.251). We can observe the power of sin in the acts described in Rom. 1:18–3:9. The worst act of all is perverting the worship of God into idolatry (Rom. 1:18-23). Rom. 5:12-21 shows us the cosmic and prehistorical dimension of sin and salvation.

A noetic perspective is needed, as well as an ontological one. In Rom. 7:15 sinners who are under the power of sin and its indwelling (vv. 14-23) do not recognize how disastrous their situation is.

Romans 7 depicts the depth of a sinful existence from the standpoint of those who are freed from sin. Only the redeemed in Christ can see how sin has entered our innermost core and destroyed us. As flesh under sin's power, we are sold to sin as slaves (v. 14). We are under the illusion that our sinful being is harmless. We do not even see that sin has perverted the law (vv. 8-13). The fact that sin is known by the law can only mean (since Rom. 3.20 is the conclusion of 1:18–3:20 and since, given the flow of the argument in Romans, the act of redemption has not yet been taken into account) that through the → law sinners recognize that acts of sin that have their origin in sin but do not yet know sin itself as their generating force.

Paul thinks of sin as a sphere of power (Rom. 3:9). But he did not see human existence only in history, as Bultmann supposed. Paul also saw it spatially. God's redeeming act that frees us from sin gives us a new space, a being in Christ, a being under the righteousness of God. As sin gave birth to acts of sin, the new being (→ New Self) gives birth to acts of righteousness: action follows being *(agere sequitur esse)*. Paul refers to sins *(hamartiai)* only in formulas (Gal. 1:4; 1 Cor. 15:3; see also Matt. 26:28). This view of sin receives classic formulation in the Deutero-Paulines: God "has rescued us from the power of darkness and transferred us into the kingdom of his beloved Son, in whom we have redemption, the forgiveness of sins" (Col. 1:13-14; see also Eph. 2:1-10).

2.2. *Jesus*

While Paul's view of sin must seen in the context of his theology of justification, that of → Jesus must be seen in the context of his proclamation of the → kingdom of God. Like Paul, Jesus could harshly accuse those who on the basis of their own devotion to the law wanted to be righteous before God. But his attack on legalism belongs to a different theological context. We see it in relation to the merciful nearness of God that is extended to sinners. God receives sinners (Luke 15). When Jesus says in Mark 2:17 that he has not come to call the righteous but sinners, he was dealing ironically with the Pharisaic judgment of who sinners are, and he was rejecting their definitions, which were based on purity laws (see also Mark 7:15; Rom. 14:14, 20; → Cultic Purity). Sin for Jesus involves the despising of others, but also a lack of faith in God, who in his → grace and with his claims draws as close to us as possible.

In interpreting the proclamation and conduct of Jesus, we need to highlight the inner connection between his battle against sin and the satanic world, his sharpening of the law in some of the antitheses of the → Sermon on the Mount, and his acceptance of sinners in the name of God. We may debate whether he himself forgave sinners (Mark 2:1-12) or simply pronounced God's forgiveness. It is hard, also, to find a satisfactory explanation of the unforgivable sin of blaspheming the → Holy Spirit (Mark 3:29 and par.). But these questions do not basically affect Jesus' view of sin.

2.3. The Johannine Literature

Except in the account of → John the Baptist in John 1:29, the word *hamartia* occurs in the Gospel of John only in chaps. 8 and 9, once or twice in the Farewell Discourses (chaps. 14–17), and in 19:11 and 20:23. Using "sin" in the singular brings out its cosmic extent (1:29) and its power to enslave those who commit it (cf. Paul). For John, sin is both a power and an act. Jesus speaks of the sins of unbelieving Jews (8:24). As in Paul, sin leads to death (8:21 and 24). Another resemblance to Paul is that the unbelieving → Pharisees do not see their sin (sing.); they are blind (9:41).

In the Farewell Discourses of the Fourth Gospel, Jesus refers to the Paraclete, who will convict the world of its sin (→ Holy Spirit 1.2.4). Here, as in chaps. 8 and 9, sin is unbelief (16:8-9). The risen Lord gives the disciples the power to forgive sins (20:23).

In 1 John the word for sin occurs more frequently. There seems to be a → dualism here that we do not find in the Gospel of John. Those who commit sin are of the → devil, whereas those who are born of God do not sin (3:8-9). Verses 1:7, 2:2, and 3:5 are to be seen in light of John 1:29. More stress than in the Gospel of John falls on the atoning character of the death of Jesus (in 2:2 note *hilasmos*, "means by which sins are forgiven"; → Atonement).

2.4. Hebrews

Hebrews, a letter-sermon, is an admonition dealing with a specific situation. The theological terms thus have a function of encouragement (→ Parenesis), even though they rest on a theological basis found in the so-called dogmatic sections. The recipients seem not to have reckoned with the bitter experiences of postbaptismal sin, and we must interpret sin *(hamartia)* theologically with reference to the aim of the letter (B. Lindars and others). The result is a certain breach between the rhetorical and the theological forms of argument.

Hebrews was under Pauline influence, as we see from the term "sin." Its frequent use in the singular brings out, as in Romans, its character as a power. It deceives us (3:13; see also Rom. 7:11) and "clings so closely" to us (12:1). The recipients must fight more intensively against it (12:4). They need to listen to God's Word and, as hearers, should not harden their hearts (3:7-15; Ps. 95:7b-11). The doctrine of sin thus stands in the context of the central thought of the Word of God. As in Paul, a distinction is made between sin and an act of sin (*parabasis*, 2:2). In a Word-of-God theology, sin is disobedience to the Word. But sin may also be the act of sin. Though its character as a power is seen in 3:13, it can also be an act, such as unbelief (3:12, 19). It thus follows that most of the occurrences of "sin" in Hebrews are in the plural, and indeed they take place in criticisms of the cult. The OT sacrifices cannot put away sins. Forgiveness comes only through the once-for-all sacrifice of Jesus Christ, the high priest (chap. 9). The cultic way of thinking is overcome by the atoning death of Christ, which is itself paradoxically put in cultic terms, which means also an end to cultic ideas of sin.

It is hard to say what is meant by statements that a second repentance is not possible (6:4-8; 10:36-39; 12:16-17). Did this rigorist view simply stress the earnestness of the decision we must make in favor of God's grace, so that we are not to press them too literally (I. Goldhahn-Müller)? The debate continues. Similar discussion rages around the relation between sinlessness in 1 John 3:4-10 and inclination to sin in 1 John 1:6–2:2.

Bibliography: H. W. ATTRIDGE, *The Epistle to the Hebrews* (Philadelphia, 1989) • E. BRANDENBURGER, *Adam und Christus. Exegetisch-religionsgeschichtliche Untersuchung zu Röm. 5:12-21 (1. Kor. 15)* (Neukirchen, 1962); idem, *Fleisch und Geist. Paulus und die dualistische Weisheit* (Neukirchen, 1968) • R. E. BROWN, *The Gospel according to John*, vol. 2, *Chapters 13–21* (Garden City, N.Y., 1970) 1039-45 • R. BULTMANN, *Theology of the NT* (2 vols.; New York, 1951-55) 1.239-53, 2.231-36 • G. GELARDINI, ed., *Hebrews: Contemporary Methods, New Insights* (Leiden, 2005) • I. GOLDHAHN-MÜLLER, *Die Grenze der Gemeinde. Studien zum Problem der Zweiten Buße im Neuen Testament* (Göttingen, 1989) • W. GRUNDMANN, "Ἁμαρτάνω κτλ. F: Sin in the NT," *TDNT* 1.302-16 • H. HÜBNER, *Biblische Theologie des Neuen Testaments,* vol. 2, *Die Theologie des Paulus und ihre neutestamentliche Wirkungsgeschichte* (Göttingen, 1993) 258-306 • R. JEWETT, *Romans: A Commentary* (Minneapolis, 2007) • L. T. JOHNSON, *Hebrews: A Commentary* (Louisville, Ky., 2006) • E. KÄSEMANN, *Commentary on Romans* (Grand Rapids, 1980) 33-90, 171-212 • B. LINDARS, *The Theology of the Letter to the Hebrews* (Cambridge, 1991) • W. MICHAELIS, "Παραπίπτω, παράπτωμα," *TDNT* 6.170-73 • H. RIDDERBOS, *The Gospel of John: A Theological Commentary* (Grand Rapids, 1997) • J. SCHNEI-

DER, "Παράβασις," *TDNT* 5.739-40 • E. SCHWEIZER, "Σάρξ E: The NT," *TDNT* 7.124-51 • G. STRECK, *Theology of the NT* (Louisville, Ky., 2000).

HANS HÜBNER

3. Doctrine

3.1. *Term and Distinctions*

The Christian doctrine of sin holds the key for understanding both the doctrine of → creation and the doctrine of → salvation. On the one hand, it defends → monotheism by affirming the goodness of the creation and denying that the material world is evil; on the other hand, it points to salvation as the redemption of life in this world, without demonizing or forsaking earthly existence. In general, any view of sin takes many forms. In the → church fathers of the first four centuries, sin is joined with death and demonic powers, which are overcome by the → resurrection and new life in Christ. While this perspective remains central in the churches of the East, the Western churches tend to be dominated by the views of → Augustine (354-430; → Augustine's Theology), which have been appropriated but modified in various ways by both Roman Catholics and Protestants.

3.1.1. Sin can refer to *a break in relations* of humans with God or with other persons, *an act* that violates commandments and rules, or *a power* that tempts and dominates (see 1 and 2). Because of this range in usage, the nature and consequences of sin are described in different ways. In relation to God, sin is described as rebellion, idolatry, or mistrust, leading to alienation. As an act, it is violation of divine and community law, leading to division, anger, and fear. As a → power, sin tempts, controls, and dominates (see Romans 1–8). In our time, destructive social forces such as → racism, → war, and economic oppression have been described as powers of sin. Two images are repeatedly used to describe this domination — illness and bondage, both of which imply loss of freedom and assert that humans are unable to save themselves.

3.1.2. Several distinctions should be noted. One is between *being* and *act*. If sin is a turning away from God, then it must be located in whatever is deemed to be the center of selfhood and considered a continuing state of being rather than merely a momentary act unrelated to our minds and hearts. As a state of being, sin affects the entire person from whom specific acts arise. Thus it is appropriate to → confess our *sin,* which endures as a state of mind and heart, as well as to confess specific acts or *sins.*

A second distinction is between acts of *commission* and acts of *omission* — that is, what we have actually done and not done. Since humans are commanded to → love God with their whole life, the sin of omission is quite relevant.

The third distinction is between *active* and *passive* sin. As we shall see, the tradition has tended to emphasize strong, active rebellion, self-love, and the misuse of all things for ourselves. Liberationists remind us that sin also takes the form of accepting servitude or of not becoming what God intends us to be (→ Liberation Theology). This perspective implies that in some cases (e.g., repressive family and social systems) → grace must take the form of liberation instead of forgiveness. At issue here is the difficult task of sorting out what we have actually initiated and what has been inflicted upon us.

3.2. *The Fall*

The doctrine of creation — that all things are created by one God and that all things are good — leads to the question of the origin and nature of moral → evil. Christians find the answer in the narratives of Genesis 3–11, the story of the fall (→ Primeval History [Genesis 1–11]). In chaps. 2 and 3 humans created in the image of God are free to enjoy paradise, but they may not pretend to be God. This limit is symbolized by the prohibition against eating the fruit of the tree of the knowledge of good and evil, itself the representation of divine knowledge. When humans choose to be like gods, such pretension denies their humanity and changes their relation to God and to one another; they become afraid of each other and must hide from God. That Adam blames God for giving him Eve (3:12) only shows the depth of the alienation. In Genesis 4–11 the situation only gets worse, as the alienation between the original pair is played out in murder (Cain), universal selfishness (the contemporaries of Noah), and the arrogance of nations (at Babel).

Despite their naive and anthropomorphic style, the early stories of Genesis focus on the central idea that sin enters the world through the misuse of human freedom, wherein human beings seek to become gods and rule over one another apart from the true God. There is no point in blaming the serpent (or the devil as a fallen angel), since such an approach requires that we then explain how an angel could fall, thereby repeating the same story at a different level. Sin is neither natural nor necessary but enters the world by personal rebellion against God, born of some combination of → anxiety, → fear, and selfishness. For reasons we cannot fully explain, we love ourselves and the world in ways we should not. That the stories are filled with mistrust and self-deception only reveals the participation of our hearts and minds (reason) in our turning from God. The human condition has been drastically altered, the responsibility for which must be placed on humans rather than on God or a devil. What we have here is a level of "moral realism," so central to Christian thought, that declares that the problem is with us.

3.3. Original Sin

3.3.1. Augustine

The most definitive expression of moral realism is found in Augustine. In his early life, he resisted baptism, living instead a libertine lifestyle as he taught philosophy and rhetoric. Even as he was attracted to → Manichaeanism and its preoccupation with the dualistic struggle of good and evil (→ Dualism), he continually struggled with the origin and nature of moral evil. Augustine overcame that impasse by combining two ideas. The first was the Platonic notion that all things are essentially good but become evil as the good is subject to privation or corruption. In this way he broke out of the dualistic framework, which assumed two ultimate sources, and thus moved toward affirmation of the one God, who created everything. The second was the biblical idea of creation and fall, an idea that gave primacy not to cosmic evil outside humans but to evil as the creation of the human will.

Given his personal journey, it should not be surprising that Augustine defines sin in terms of the pride and self-love that so dominate a person that they create habits that over time become compulsive behavior. As life turns more and more in upon itself, humans lose their original freedom to will and achieve the very good that they desire and that God commands. Augustine thus readily uses the images of illness and bondage to describe the consequence of sin: we can neither heal ourselves nor free ourselves. The cause and blame for this plight is not to be placed on God or on external forces but only upon ourselves. Furthermore, what began with the individual now characterizes all of our common life and institutions. Augustine designates the loss of our freedom and capacity to do the good as *original sin*. This bondage to selfishness becomes the new state of human life. In a fateful and debatable move, Augustine connects self-love with sexual desire and then argues that original sin was passed from generation to generation by the natural process of procreation.

3.3.2. Pelagius

Augustine was opposed by a contemporary, the Celtic monk Pelagius (ca. 354-after 418; → Pelagianism), who maintained confidence in human → freedom and the capacity to do the good. For Pelagius, God would not require humans to do things that they are unable to do. Although Augustine's view has repeatedly been endorsed by both Roman Catholics and Protestants, the → optimism of Pelagius reappears in every generation, either as confidence in → reason and the complete goodness of humans or as an assault on Augustine as being morbidly negative. The influence of Pelagius thus continues to this day through views that are often called semi-Augustinian or semi-Pelagian. Such views share some degree of confidence in the human ability to do the good.

By contrast, the Augustinian view insists on what has here been called moral realism: the full recognition of the depth of moral evil and the consequent necessity of reliance solely on grace rather than human effort. For those claiming Augustine, there is little room for utopianism or theories of historical progress based on human capability. Nor may we divide the world between good and evil, since such a division claims absolute purity on our side while demonizing our enemies. Sin is real, and it has changed the human condition in such a way that salvation can be only by the grace of God in Jesus Christ.

3.3.3. The Augustinian Legacy

Augustine's legacy includes some fateful consequences that have promoted continuing debate. First, if sin is transmitted biologically, then this doctrine becomes a rationale for defending the → virgin birth of Jesus. But eliminating Joseph in the process of Jesus' conception solves only half the problem; centuries later, in 1854, the → Roman Catholic Church therefore promulgated the doctrine of the immaculate conception, namely, that Mary herself was conceived without sin (→ Mariology 1.3.3).

Second, Augustine affirmed that the burden of original sin was removed by → baptism, whereas the burden of actual sins is removed by penance (→ Penitence) and forgiveness. In addition to fostering a mechanistic view of baptism, this view lends support for such questionable practices as the → emergency baptism of dying infants.

Third, Augustine connected sin with selfishness, self-love, and sexual desire, a connection that drove him toward → celibacy — a move adopted by the Roman tradition.

Fourth, the connection of sin with sexual desire has led to negative views of human → sexuality.

Finally, by defining sin as a privation of the good or an incapacity of the will, Augustine opened the way for discussions of grace as a corrective power that enables the will to do the good. How nature (i.e., our impaired will) and grace (i.e., God's saving action) relate to each other prompted a variety of views, some of them having a Pelagian twist. One arose in the 14th century, when → William of Ockham (ca. 1285-1347) affirmed that grace is given only to those who first seek to do the good.

3.4. *The Reformation*

The continuing debate between the Augustinian and semi-Pelagian views became a major issue for the Protestant → Reformers. Their reliance on Paul led them to revive Augustine, only to find his realism compromised by the reliance of some on Pelagian optimism. Moreover, the force of Augustine's view was often muted by complex discussions involving the difference between unforgivable ("mortal") sins and forgivable ("venial") sins; the distinction between attrition, the fear of punishment, and contrition, or genuine repentance; the comparison of humans' love for God and God's love for humans; and the system of penance, which codified how sinners may receive the grace of God. When Martin → Luther (1483-1546; → Luther's Theology) confessed his terror regarding his unworthiness before God, he was comforted with counsel that had a decidedly Pelagian ring: do the best you can, and God will not deny grace. Not surprisingly, Luther's rediscovery of the gospel involved reading both Paul and Augustine, two writers who affirm both our bondage to sin and the necessity of total reliance on grace.

The vehemence of the Reformers' attack on the views of the Middle Ages reflects their zeal to revive the biblical view of sin, with Augustine as their guide. For them, sin is pride and rebellion against God, as well as the loss of our capacity to know or love God. Attempts to categorize and subdivide sin and repentance, our action and God's grace, and even to fit it all neatly into a system of penance appeared to them to miss the point: sin is a state of mind and heart as well as particular acts; it is rebellion against and mistrust of God and the consequent attempt to use all things for ourselves; it has infected the entire world as well as the heart, mind, and will of all individual persons. Thus, when Luther denied the freedom of the will in his literary debate with → Erasmus (1469?-1536), what was at stake was not human ability to analyze or reason about worldly things in order to make sound judgments but whether human beings have within themselves the capacity to achieve the will of God.

Finally, it should be noted that Luther adopted Paul's realism regarding the continuation of sin in the Christian's life, even after our justification by grace. This position resulted in his declaration that the Christian is simultaneously righteous and a sinner *(→ simul iustus et peccator)*. Others moved beyond this paradox of sin and grace. John → Calvin (1509-64; → Calvin's Theology) gave greater attention than Luther to → sanctification, affirming the so-called third use of the law, namely, the law as teacher or moral guide; and John → Wesley (1703-91) preached growth in grace, while other → free church leaders went further in asserting that one could "cross over" from sin to a redeemed life of holiness.

3.5. *The Modern Period: Protest and Revival*

In the modern age the doctrine of sin has been severely criticized in the name of freedom and → innocence. The idea of original sin, it has been claimed, denies human freedom and condemns humans for sins they have not committed. Augustine's willingness to connect sin to sexual desire clearly makes the doctrine negative and repressive. The fact that some Christians exemplify these traits only reinforces the idea that the doctrine of original sin denigrates all pleasure, especially the sexual. In the → Enlightenment this protest appeared by positing the individual, rational → self, who acts on the basis of his or her own freedom and self-interest, as the basic unit of society. Immanuel Kant (1724-1804; → Kantianism) gave forceful expression to this view, proclaiming that "enlightenment" is emancipation from self-imposed bondage. By affirming the ability of the self to reform itself, the individual is freed from the external demands of church, state, and tradition. In the modern age this drive for → autonomy is often joined with the rejection of God, who is regarded as a threat to the freedom of the individual. From this perspective, Genesis 3 is repudiated on the grounds that the prohibition against seeking knowledge is a blameworthy attempt by God to keep humans in a state of childish dependence.

The result of this protest is a rejection of moral realism in favor of innocence and optimism. This choice is seen in every area of modern life — for example, the affirmation of the innocence of children, the rejection of checks and balances in political life, and the need for regulation regarding economics and the environment. The innocence of the individual is protected by attempts to explain moral failures as resulting from traumatic events in one's past or other psychological disorders, thus eliminating moral responsibility. The innocence of the nation is upheld by claims of "purity" (e.g., in international relations) or by relegating horrors such as the → Holocaust or American → slavery to being merely isolated events of the past. In short, moral optimism sees evil as external to the self, residing primarily in social forces that restrict and repress. In the last 40 years, both liberal and conservative groups have tended to embrace forms of optimism and innocence, although they tend to focus on different aspects of life, such as the purity of the individual or the purity of institutions like nations, corporations, or churches.

In 20th-century American thought, Reinhold → Niebuhr (1892-1971) led the revival of moral realism. He saw that races, nations, and classes reveal only greater degrees of a selfishness that is forever justified by an appeal to "universal values." For Niebuhr, it was naive to assume that individual and social conflicts are the result merely of lack of knowledge, poor communication, or other misunderstandings. He held that at the heart of all social conflict lies a conflict of wills, struggles for power, and interests at odds with one another. Niebuhr, who began with strong liberal and pacifistic views, reversed his own course by embracing the theology of Paul and Augustine. However, he formulated the classic orthodox view of sin in modern language. For him, the fall points to the fact that humans, anxious because of their finitude, overreach in their quest for power, knowledge, and goodness. Thus out of anxiety regarding finitude arises the denial of finitude and the pretense that humans are gods. There appears to be no limit to our desire to use all things, including God, for our own glorification, or to conceal such self-interest by hypocrisy and the presumption of good intentions.

Significantly, moreover, by using historical and social categories, Niebuhr found no need to adopt Augustine's idea of the sexual transmission of original sin. Instead, "original sin" describes the historical and social environment of self-interest and warfare into which all individuals are born. Niebuhr regarded Adam's sin as inevitable but not necessary, and the same can be said of every member of the race. The basic idea that all humans participate in a corporate structure of sin and are tempted to turn from God set Niebuhr against the naive claims of innocence advanced by liberal and conservative groups alike. Similarly, this insight prompted him to oppose the great tyrannies of the 20th century.

Two other developments have shaped contemporary discussions of sin. One is the extension in → liberation theology of the doctrine of sin to include social, economic, political, and patriarchal structures that oppress the poor and powerless. The other is the feminist concern that sin be defined not only in terms of active, strong rebellion against God but also in terms of passive acceptance of suffering (→ Feminism; Feminist Theology).

3.6. Sin and Salvation

The basic elements of the doctrine of sin — the fall, original sin, and human subjugation to demonic powers — are affirmed in both Eastern and Western Christianity. In the West, though, the Augustinian view has dominated and contributed to the emphasis on moral realism, the tension of sin and grace, and the → sacraments as the forgiveness of sins. Notable exceptions to this dominance are the → Anabaptist and pietistic traditions, as well as modern liberal Protestantism (→ Liberal Theology). The Augustinian view has always required careful interpretation, given its ambiguous relation to two traditions that have cast negative shadows over much of Christianity: one is legalism, which transforms concern for holiness into rigid moralistic practices, with rewards and punishments allocated on the basis of human actions; the other is an otherworldly → piety that derives from pessimism regarding this world of sin and sorrow.

The great alternative to Augustinianism in the West continues to be Pelagian optimism. Perhaps such optimism is irrepressible as a reaction to legalism and otherworldly piety. Pelagianism denies that sin totally controls human reason, freedom, or the capacity to do the good; instead, it emphasizes human goodness, reason, and the power to achieve self-actualization.

This summary highlights the direct correlation between the doctrine of sin and salvation. Moral realism leads directly to the idea of salvation as redemption from sin through the grace of God in Jesus Christ. Because sin represents the corruption of the good, salvation requires, not the destruction of sinners, but their release from the power of sin. For moral realism, there can be no salvation without the intervention of God. The Pelagian view, with all of its variations in popular religion, opens the door to theories of salvation based on education, therapy, self-discipline, and self-help. Jesus, in this view, is more of a teacher than the Savior, an example rather than the Lord.

Bibliography: J. CALVIN, *Institutes of the Christian Religion* (2 vols.; Philadelphia, 1960) • G. GUTIÉRREZ, *A Theology of Liberation* (rev. ed.; Maryknoll, N.Y., 1988) • S. KIERKEGAARD, *The Concept of Dread* (Princeton, 1944); idem, *Fear and Trembling; and, The Sickness unto Death* (Garden City, N.Y., 1955) • M. LUTHER, *The Bondage of the Will* (LW 33; Philadelphia, 1972); idem, *Lectures on Romans* (LW 25; St. Louis, 1972) • R. NIEBUHR, *Moral Man and Immoral Society: A Study in Ethics and Politics* (New York, 1932); idem, *The Nature and Destiny of Man: A Christian Interpretation*

(New York, 1941) • C. Plantinga Jr., *Not the Way It's Supposed to Be: A Breviary of Sin* (Grand Rapids, 1995) • W. Rauschenbusch, *A Theology for the Social Gospel* (Louisville, Ky., 1997; orig. pub., 1917) • V. Saiving, "The Human Situation: A Feminine View," *JR* 40 (April 1960) 100-112 • P. Schmiechen, *Saving Power: Theories of Atonement and Forms of the Church* (Grand Rapids, 2005) • J. Segundo, *Evolution and Guilt* (Maryknoll, N.Y., 1974).

                                          Peter Schmiechen

4. Practical Theology

People seldom attend worship services or Christian education classes with the word "sin" uppermost in their minds. Neither do they normally seek pastoral → counseling with the intention of dealing with their sin. What people bring with them — with or without realizing or articulating it — are their concerns about various consequences of sin. The insights of Karl Menninger (1893-1990) about the overwhelming sense of → guilt without an understanding of sin as its root cause are as valid today as the day he wrote his book *Whatever Became of Sin?*

4.1. *Sin as Rebellion*

A biblical, theological, and pastoral approach to sin compels us to acknowledge that sin is a rebellious power against God that affects the ways we treat one another. Just as the commands to "love the Lord your God" and "love your neighbor" (Matt. 22:34-39; Mark 12:28-31; Luke 10:25-27) are so intertwined that speaking of loving God but hating our → neighbor condemns us as liars (1 John 4:20), so sin against God is barely distinguishable from dishonoring and neglecting our neighbors, and vice versa. Sin is a terminal illness that affects all our relationships in our thoughts and actions. We see this illness clearly in our personal and corporate failure to provide care for, and to honor, the vulnerable — the poor, the hungry, the homeless. We experience sin's power when adults abuse children and when children abuse parents and one another. Pastoral counselors all too often hear about sin revealing itself in physical and verbal abuse between husbands and wives and their acts of dishonoring one another through infidelity, deception, and neglect. The pains and fears we experience daily, along with their resulting guilt, resentments, frustrations, anger, humiliation, and grief, are consequences of sin. Sin is so deceptive that its power lurks even in our apparently good actions.

Discerning sin as a universal rebellion out of which myriad consequences flow is basic to an understanding of the Bible. The author of Genesis 3 describes the sin of the first human couple as their rebellious assertion of → autonomy against God, and then "because you have done this" (v. 14), the painful symptoms of sin in daily life — as present today as they were in the garden — follow immediately (vv. 14-24). The apostle Paul defines sin as idolatry (Rom. 1:18-23) and then begins his lists of the consequences of that sin with the words "therefore" (v. 24), "for this reason" (v. 26), and "since they did not see fit to acknowledge God" (v. 28). When we focus on the consequences of sin — the daily signs of brokenness and the individual sins — rather than on sin itself, we fall into the deadly trap of thinking that we can take control of the action in life's drama.

4.2. *The Deceits of Sin*

The desire for control lies at the deceptive heart of sin itself. First, if sin is merely the breaking of an ethical code (religious or societal), then each individual has the power to change inappropriate behavior into acceptable actions that would reestablish the person in the religious or social community and in the eyes of God. This assumed power enables one to demonstrate moral discipline and thereby to maintain the sense of controlling one's life.

Second, a focus on isolated actions can lead people to develop a hierarchy of sins that is evident in the way we harangue about certain moral concerns, often holding the worst sins to be of a sexual nature and the least worrisome to be irresponsibility for the poor and other vulnerable persons. Such a hierarchy of offenses enables us to control the determination of whose sins are greater or lesser than our own.

Third, when sin is considered merely an inappropriate act against God or another person or community, then the offender can consider the matter resolved by performing an appropriate act, like offering an apology. An apology has the effect of leading the offender to think that he or she has done all that can be expected and that, now having controlled or managed the issue, accepting or rejecting the apology is the problem of the offended party.

Fourth, when a person is pained by having committed a particular offense, a well-meaning adviser can suggest the need to "forgive yourself." The advice is appealing, because it implies that resolution to the problem lies within one's own control. However, it is not biblical, not theological, not pastoral, and ultimately not effective.

4.3. *Pastoral Care*

While "sin" is not the first word on people's minds, it does not have the last word either. → Pastoral care, whether in the congregational opportunities of → preaching and teaching or in the private mo-

ments of counseling, begins and ends with the →
Word of God.

4.3.1. *Comfort and Affliction*

The prophetic Word of God comforts the afflicted
and afflicts the comfortable. In the theology of Martin → Luther (1483-1546; → Luther's Theology),
these two ways in which God confronts us are called
gospel and law (→ Law and Gospel). God's word of
good news is sufficient and does not require help,
but God speaks to us in a dialogic context. The effect
of the Word comes not simply from what is said but
also in the context in which it is heard. "I am the
Lord your God" can be comforting to someone lost
and forsaken, already knowing affliction. Likewise,
the same divine claim can be afflicting to those who
are comfortable with their own mastery of life; the
Word convicts them of sin (see Luther's Large Catechism on the Ten Commandments). Pastoral care of
persons requires the loving proclamation of this
two-edged word, because the listening individuals
know from day to day varying degrees of affliction,
as well as varying forms of comfort. The preaching
and teaching of the Word about Jesus Christ both
exposes our sin and accuses us; that same Word forgives our sin, enabling us to live even within the
conflict of comfort and affliction (G. O. Forde).

4.3.2. *Sin and the Crucified Christ*

Humanity's sin is most revealed as we see its opposite: the life and faith that Jesus himself demonstrated. The temptation stories in Matthew (4:1-11)
and Luke (4:1-13) announce that immediately following his baptism as the Son of God, Jesus was
tempted by the devil. The three temptations challenged Jesus to use his divinely endowed identity as
the Son of God for personal gain and immunity
from → suffering. Jesus showed how the person of
faith responds to the temptations of magical wonder, worldly power, and guarantee of safety. Jesus refused to dishonor God and his own God-given mission, thus demonstrating how faith reveals its
opposite, namely sin. Later in Luke's gospel Jesus
faces another threefold temptation that he exert his
power and control to demonstrate that he is who he
claims to be: the messianic Son of God. The leaders
of the crowd, the soldiers, and one of the thieves delivered the temptations, but instead of giving in to
sin's call for infidelity, Jesus forgave them, promised
paradise to the thief, and sacrificially commended
his spirit to God (Luke 23:32-43). Jesus showed that
the opposite of self-seeking sin is the sacrifice of self
to the will of God and the loving forgiveness of others, even of enemies. The execution of the sinless
Son of God at the hand of God (Matt. 26:31: "I will
strike the shepherd") reveals the extent to which sin

has disabled us. God's sacrificial love to become one
of us convicts all humanity in our quest to "be like
God."

Pastoral care can provide comfort, first of all, in
the astonishing announcement that the Word of
God took on our flesh (→ Incarnation). The Jesus
who did not sin bore the consequences of our sin.
He knew rejection by religious and political persons.
He knew betrayal by those nearest to him. He knew
the physical pain we experience, the death that is
common to us all as the wages of our sin. As he endured all this agony on the cross, Jesus even knew
the forsakenness of God we feel in our grief and suffering. Paradoxically, then, as we experience even
God's absence in our lives, we come closer to the
crucified Christ. Furthermore, the risen and victorious Lord we worship is none other than the Servant
who knows intimately all our pains and sorrows.

Second, pastoral care is founded upon the
equally astonishing message that the cross of Christ
defeats sin and effects the → salvation of humanity.
If sin is a power in which all humankind has been
complicit and results in a separation from God and
from one another, then God must take control and
offer the divine forgiveness that alone will restore us
to God and to one another (2 Cor. 5:21; Gal. 3:13-
14). The word of the cross, as foolish as it sounds to
the world, is the power and wisdom of God with
which we are graciously endowed (1 Cor. 1:18-25;
→ Theologia crucis).

4.3.3. *Goal*

The goal of pastoral care, then, is to proclaim in various settings the love of God in Jesus Christ, which
alone exposes the depth of our sin and simultaneously brings us again and again into dynamic relationships with God and with one another. This
restoration from sin's disintegrating power is accomplished neither by the monologue of an apology
nor by forgiving oneself. What opens sinners to restoration is our humbling ourselves before God and
before persons we have dishonored by asking, "Will
you forgive me?" (see Matt. 6:12; Luke 11:4). Faithful preaching and teaching enable the petitioner to
hear the answer to that question again and again
and to continue the dialogue within a life of hope.

Bibliography: A. Dueck and C. Lee, *Why Psychology
Needs Theology* (Grand Rapids, 2005) • G. O. Forde,
Justification by Faith: A Matter of Death and Life (Phila-
delphia, 1982) • D. J. Hall, *God and Human Suffering:
An Exercise in the Theology of the Cross* (Minneapolis,
1986); idem, *Lighten Our Darkness: Toward an Indige-
nous Theology of the Cross* (rev. ed.; Lima, Ohio, 2001) •
E. Käsemann, *Commentary on Romans* (Grand Rapids,

1980) 33-52 • A. E. McGrath, *Luther's Theology of the Cross* (Grand Rapids, 1990) • K. Menninger, *Whatever Became of Sin?* (New York, 1973) • R. R. Reno, *Redemptive Change: Atonement and the Christian Cure of the Soul* (Harrisburg, Pa., 2002) • F. N. Watts, *Theology and Psychology* (Burlington, Vt., 2002).

Foster R. McCurley

5. The Seven Deadly Sins

The seven deadly sins — known for most of their early history as the seven capital vices — constituted an important schema of sins that was used by Christians for self-examination, → confession, → preaching, and spiritual formation for nearly a millennium. Popular treatments of the seven use "sin" and "vice" as synonymous terms. Technically, however, "vice" is a more specific term than "sin," since it refers only to a character trait, rather than applying to a general human condition ("original sin," "sinful nature"), a specific action ("sins of thought, word, or deed"), or social structures ("institutional racism, a structural sin").

The seven vices can be traced back as far as Evagrius Ponticus (346-99), in his practical guides to the → ascetic life of the desert anchorite. John Cassian (ca. 360-after 430) transmitted it to the Latin monastic tradition, → Gregory the Great (ca. 540-604) gave it authoritative status, scholastic theologians systematized it in the 13th century, and it appeared extensively in penitential and preaching manuals after the Fourth Lateran Council (1215), the most famous of which was the *Summa de vitiis et virtutibus* by the 13th-century Dominican William Peraldus. The heptad was widely used in Western Christianity on account of its diagnostic power, memorability, and comprehensiveness.

The seven vices were called principal or capital (from Lat. *caput*, "head") on account of their being the head — meaning principle or source — of many other sins. The term "principal vices" originates in Cassian's writings (*Conf.* 5) and was further explained by Gregory in his widely disseminated *Moralia in Iob*. Authors and illustrators commonly depicted the seven as a tree, with pride as the common root, the seven vices as the main branches, and other sins as their offshoots and poisonous fruit. The organic metaphor emphasized identifying the ultimate source of sin in one's heart and excising it at that level.

Thomas Aquinas (ca. 1225-74) argued that these seven vices were "source sins" because their objects are goods closely affiliated with → happiness, which are then pursued in an excessive or idolatrous way.

The vices thus manifest a structure identified by → Augustine (354-430): They are disordered loves — that is, desires for created goods in place or, or in excess of, love for God the Creator (*Conf.* 1.20, 2.5). Furthermore, they are motivated by pride, in which we seek to define the good on our own terms and procure happiness for ourselves (2.6). For example, avaricious people seek in money (a temporal, finite good) the sufficiency and contentment that can be found only in God (an eternal, infinite good), and they depend on themselves to provide that good rather than trusting God to do so. The intensely desirable ends of the seven vices spawn other sins that serve those ends or are the effects of one's excessive pursuit of them. For example, the offspring of avarice typically includes "fraud" and "insensibility to mercy."

The list of vices in its most typical form includes pride. Alternately, on the basis of Sir. 10:15 ("Pride is the beginning of all sin," DV), Gregory named seven other vices, including vainglory, offshoots of pride. However, pride occasionally competed for status as the chief vice with avarice, given the apostle Paul's statement that love of money is the root of all evil (1 Tim. 6:10). The seven are often divided into spiritual vices and carnal vices. Pride, envy, and sloth directly regard spiritual goods like our love for others and God, while avarice, vainglory, and anger concern goods like power, honor, and justice; gluttony and lust, in contrast, have bodily pleasures in view.

There was some variation in the list throughout much of its history. Evagrius included sloth and sadness, vainglory and pride, as well as avarice, anger, lust, and gluttony, for a total of "eight evil thoughts [*logismoi*]." In addition to making pride the root, Gregory added envy and subsumed Evagrian and Cassianic sloth under sadness. Gregory's list was authoritative for hundreds of years but gradually shifted to include pride again, replace sadness with sloth, and drop vainglory because of its similarity to pride. The list in its current form has *pride, envy, sloth, avarice, anger, lust, and gluttony.*

The list is also known as the seven deadly sins, after the 13th-century distinction between mortal (deadly) and venial sin, a distinction denied in Protestant theology. But even theologians whom Catholic theology takes as authoritative, like Aquinas, denied that all these vices always or only have a deadly form and preferred the term "capital vices."

The Christian tradition used the vices to guide self-examination and confession, and a parallel set of virtues to guide spiritual formation and the practice of holiness. The process of casting off vice and cultivating virtue was framed in terms of Paul's distinction between taking off the old → self, or sinful nature, and putting on the new self, redeemed and sanctified by → grace (Eph. 4:22-24; Col. 3:5-14).

The list of virtues paralleling the vices usually included the seven principal virtues — → faith, → hope, and → love (1 Cor. 13:13), along with prudence, justice, courage, and temperance (Wis. 8:7). The cardinal virtues were a Greek philosophical inheritance, although Augustine reframed them as kinds of love (*De mor. eccl.* 25.15; → Greek Philosophy). The vices were not directly opposed to the seven virtues, however. Instead, for example, pride was to be countered by the Christian virtue of → humility (as in → Benedict's Rule), and anger overcome by patience or long-suffering (Prudentius, *Psychomachia*). While the virtues had an explicit scriptural basis, the heptad of vices did not, although Cassian tried to assign it a metaphoric one (i.e., the seven tribes driven out of Canaan in Deut. 7:1). Despite its origin in distinctly Christian practices, then, the inability of academic theologians to find a satisfying theoretical or scriptural basis for the list and the shift from a virtue- to a law-based ethics may have been factors in its gradual decline after the Middle Ages. Nevertheless, the seven deadly sins continue to capture the popular imagination, as is attested by regular treatments of the topic in both scholarly literature and entertainment culture, up to the present day (e.g., the MTV special *Seven Deadly Sins*, which aired in August 1993).

Bibliography: Selected primary sources (in English): J. CASSIAN, *The Conferences* (trans. B. Ramsey; New York, 1997); idem, *The Institutes* (trans. B. Ramsey; New York, 2000) • EVAGRIUS OF PONTUS, *The Greek Ascetic Corpus* (trans. R. E. Sinkewicz; Oxford, 2003) • THOMAS AQUINAS, *On Evil* (trans. R. Regan; Oxford, 2003).

Secondary (scholarly): M. BLOOMFIELD, *The Seven Deadly Sins* (Lansing, Mich., 1952; repr., 1967) • R. G. NEWHAUSER, *The Treatise on Vices and Virtues in Latin and the Vernacular* (Turnhout, 1993); idem, ed., *In the Garden of Evil: The Vices and Culture in the Middle Ages* (Toronto, 2005) • S. WENZEL, "The Seven Deadly Sins: Some Problems of Research," *Spec.* 43 (1968) 1-22.

Secondary (general or pastoral): H. FAIRLIE, *The Seven Deadly Sins Today* (Washington, D.C., 1978; repr., Notre Dame, Ind., 1995) • S. SCHIMMEL, *The Seven Deadly Sins: Jewish, Christian, and Classical Reflections on Human Psychology* (Oxford, 1997).

REBECCA KONYNDYK DeYOUNG

Sinai

In the story of the exodus → Moses leads the people to Sinai and receives the → law there (Exodus 20–Numbers 10). In the earliest Hebrew poetry it represents God's dwelling place (Deut. 33:2); God comes forth from Sinai to help his people (Judg. 5:5; Ps. 68:8), and he returns there (Hos. 5:15). "Horeb" is an alternative name in the Pentateuch (also in 1 Kgs. 8:9; 19:8; 2 Chr. 5:10; Ps. 106:19; Mal. 4:4).

It is not clear whether "Sinai" refers to a single mountain or to a range, nor is the meaning of the name or the location clear. Various sites in the Sinai Peninsula and northwestern Arabia have been suggested, dependent largely on proposals for the route of the exodus, consideration of the association with Seir and Edom (Judg. 5:4-5) and Midian (Hab. 3:7), and interpretations of the conquest and settlement accounts (→ Tribes of Israel). The suggestion that Sinai is a volcano (based on Exod. 19:18) does not tally with Exod. 19:16, 19.

For Christians, as for Jews, fixing the geographic location of Sinai is secondary to its theological significance. Here Moses meets God in the burning bush (Exodus 3), receives the law (Exodus 20–23), and mediates the → covenant (§1) with God that undergirds Israel as a nation and people (see the application to Christians in 1 Pet. 2:9; Rev. 1:6). The parallels between Jesus' transfiguration (Matt. 17:1-8 and par.) and Moses' mountaintop encounter with God point to Jesus as fulfillment of the law and reveal him as the Messiah and successor to Moses. In Gal. 4:24-25 Paul presents Sinai as a symbol for the law, which, although it is divinely revealed and given, subjects us to bondage because we fail to keep it. In contrast is the → gospel, the culmination of divine revelation in Christ and the covenant of promise, which brings freedom by expiation and forgiveness.

Hebrews 12:18-24 presents a similar picture, contrasting Sinai (the place of terror) with Mount Zion (the place of joy). At Sinai Christians come under conviction of sin as they learn the divine requirements and see their inability to meet them. But the God of law and judgment is also the God of grace, who through Christ gives them a place among the redeemed on the heavenly Zion.

Yet Sinai still has significance in the living of the Christian life, for if the ceremonial and civil ordinances have ceased to be valid with Christ's coming, the moral demands represent God's eternal will for his people and constitute a permanent guide to a life that is pleasing to God and in conformity with his purpose.

Bibliography: B. BERNSTEIN, *Sinai: The Great and Terrible Wilderness* (New York, 1979) • B. S. CHILDS, *The Book of Exodus* (Philadelphia, 1974) • E. W. NICHOLSON, *Exodus and Sinai in History and Tradition* (Richmond, Va., 1973).

GEOFFREY W. BROMILEY

Singapore

	1960	1980	2000
Population (1,000s):	1,634	2,415	3,587
Annual growth rate (%):	2.81	2.30	1.03

Area: 641 sq. km. (247 sq. mi.)

A.D. 2000

Population density: 5,596/sq. km. (14,523/sq. mi.)
Births / deaths: 1.30 / 0.53 per 100 population
Fertility rate: 1.79 per woman
Infant mortality rate: 5 per 1,000 live births
Life expectancy: 78.1 years (m: 75.9, f: 80.5)
Religious affiliation (%): Chinese folk religionists 41.4, Muslims 18.3, Buddhists 14.5, Christians 13.0 (Roman Catholics 4.9, Protestants 4.2, indigenous 2.4, other Christians 1.5), Hindus 5.4, nonreligious 4.7, new religionists 1.8, other 0.9.

1. General Situation
2. Religious Situation

1. General Situation

The island of Singapore was obtained from Malay rulers in Johor in 1819 by Stamford Raffles (1781-1826). Established as a free trading port, it became part of the British Straits Settlements along with Malacca and Penang. The British surrendered to the Japanese in February 1942, and in 1946 Singapore became a crown colony. After independence in 1963 it was part of the Federation of Malaysia until 1965.

Under the leadership of Lee Kwan Yee (prime minister 1959-90), Singapore became a prosperous modern state, acutely conscious of the importance of identity, social cohesion, religious and political stability, and economic strength for its political survival. It continues to value technical and business skills, guards its reputation for freedom from economic corruption, and successfully brokers its rich cultural and linguistic links with China and other parts of Asia and the West. These traits are reflected in the energy, faith, pragmatism, and missionary expansion of Singaporean churches today.

2. Religious Situation

2.1. The pre-European inhabitants of Singapore were Malay Muslims and animist seafaring *orang laut* (sea people). From its beginnings under British administration, Singapore attracted traders from the region and further afield, including Portuguese descendants, Chinese, Indians, and Malays. A diverse multireligious society was rapidly created whose primary common concern was business.

It was over a decade before churches were built, and education facilities were also slow to develop. Many Portuguese were from Melaka and Penang, and the first Roman Catholic chapel was built in 1831. The Armenian Church, opened in 1835, is the oldest remaining church building in Singapore. Scots and English administrators and traders set up Presbyterian and Anglican congregations in the late 1830s, including St. Andrews Cathedral. → Missionaries included the London Missionary Society (LMS) Ultra Ganges Mission based in Melaka, American Congregationalists, and independent itinerants. Most left for China in the 1840s after the First Opium War (1839-42) provided access to Canton. The LMS commitment to printing and education was significant in the long term, rather than immediately fruitful.

After the British extended their control in the Malay Peninsula following the Treaty of Pangkor in 1874 (→ Colonialism), Christians among immigrants from India, Sri Lanka, and China were fundamental to the growth of the church. American Methodist missionaries arrived in 1895, and their schools, energy, and commitment quickly extended their network to the Malay States, Borneo, Sumatra, and the Philippines. Converts were almost entirely Chinese and Indian. Christianity remained part of the cultural identity of Eurasian Portuguese Catholics, Mar Thoma Christians from Kerala and Sri Lanka, and a small community of Armenian traders.

2.2. As it expanded, Singapore faced many social problems. Today it may be difficult to imagine the once-filthy streets and gutters that contributed to unhealthy living, with beggars scavenging for decaying vegetables and fish. Opium addiction, secret societies, and the abuse of women were common. The British colonizers brought in thousands of convicts from Hong Kong and India as cheap labor. Church growth, like civic administration, was hampered by the diversity of languages. Malay, several Chinese dialects, and numerous Indian and Indonesian languages were all heard. Many expatriates sought to return home rather than settle down; only after World War II did the majority of Singapore's population begin to sink its roots in Singapore soil.

2.3. During the "Japanese time" most expatriate church leaders either left after the invasion or were interned in Changi Prison, though a few Catholic clergy, and for a time the Anglican bishop, were able to remain relatively active. Conviction of the need to work more closely together and to provide for locally trained leadership was translated in 1948 into the formation of the Malayan Christian Council ($\rightarrow$ National Councils of Churches) and the opening of Trinity Theological College by the Anglican, Methodist, and Presbyterian churches to educate pastors "in an ecumenical setting." In 1952 a faith and order commission was set up to initiate church union conversations, but by 1962 it had become obvious that the participants were unable to resolve doctrinal differences attached to external traditions, and local leadership did not see the relevance of the expatriate ecumenical vision.

After Singapore had to leave the Federation of Malaya in 1965, many churches and ecumenical institutions developed separate Singaporean identities. The National Council of Churches, Singapore (NCCS) was formed by older mainline Protestant churches in 1974 and for a time supported an industrial mission in Jurong. Other Protestant churches set up the Evangelical Fellowship of Singapore (EFOS) in 1980, but both groups have struggled to sustain their relevance in the Singapore context. The $\rightarrow$ Christian Conference of Asia was headquartered in Singapore from 1974 until the end of 1988, when it was asked to leave. The Association for Theological Education in Southeast Asia (ATESEA) is the only remaining ecumenical body with links to other ecumenical bodies in the region, but a number of international evangelical organizations have regional bases and training centers in Singapore.

2.4. Between 1950 and 1964 the Anglicans ($\rightarrow$ Anglican Communion), Brethren, Methodists ($\rightarrow$ Methodism; Methodist Churches), and Presbyterians initiated 20 new congregations. The $\rightarrow$ Roman Catholic Church also grew numerically. The $\rightarrow$ Baptists, Bible-Presbyterians, Christian Nationals Evangelism Commission, and Lutherans ($\rightarrow$ Lutheran Churches) set up 22 new congregations. During this period, many churches doubled their membership. In addition to holding the weekly services, many of these churches conduct weekday programs, including counseling, social welfare services, student chaplaincy work, evangelistic programs, missionary work, and youth fellowship activities. From the 1970s the $\rightarrow$ charismatic movement and the growth of independent $\rightarrow$ Pentecostal churches became strong features of Singaporean Christianity. From the 1990s many Singaporean churches became directly involved in Christian mission in Southeast Asia and beyond. Christians are well represented in the professions. Parachurch organizations are a sig-

nificant part of mission and an important avenue for lay leadership development.

The Inter Religious Organization, formed in 1950, brings together religious leaders of all faiths. It has, however, very few programs. In 1990 the government passed the Religious Harmony Act, which authorized it to take any necessary actions to preserve peace among the religions. Churches in Singapore may copartner with the government to bring about racial and religious harmony. What has become a Singapore model of church-state understanding, in which church leaders avoid confrontation, demonstrate loyalty, and exercise discretion in constructive relationships with the government, has significance for a number of other political contexts in Asia.

Bibliography: R. P. Balhetchet, *Metamorphosis of a Church: A Study on the People of God in the Republic of Singapore; Analysis and Projection* (Rome, 1976) • E. Chew and E. Lee, eds., *A History of Singapore* (Singapore, 1991) • T. R. Doraisamy, *Forever Beginning: One Hundred Years of Methodism in Singapore* (2 vols.; Singapore, 1985-86) • R. B. H. Goh, *Christianity in Southeast Asia* (Singapore, 2005) • R. M. Greer, *A History of the Presbyterian Church in Singapore* (Singapore, 1959) • F. G. Lee, *The Catholic Church in Malaya* (Singapore, 1963) • Malayan Christian Council, *The Churches Working Together* (Singapore, 1959) • B. E. K. Sng, *In His Good Time: The Story of the Church in Singapore, 1819-1978* (2d ed.; Singapore, 1993).

John Roxborogh, with Choo-Lak Yeow

Sinti $\rightarrow$ **Roma**

Sisterhoods $\rightarrow$ **Communities, Spiritual**

Skepticism

1. Antiquity
2. Christian Approaches
3. Modern Period
4. Hegel and Positivism

1. Antiquity

Skepticism (from Gk. *skeptomai,* "examine") is a principle of thought, constantly modified in the history of $\rightarrow$ philosophy, whereby $\rightarrow$ doubt is cast on everything. It originated with the founder of the third post-Aristotelian school, Pyrrho of Elis (ca. 360-ca. 272 b.c.). Pyrrho's teachings were handed down by Sextus Empiricus (fl. early 3d cent. a.d.), which gave rise to the traditional equating of Pyrrhonism and skepticism. Pyrrho established the possibility of a radical skepticism with his argument that there are no convincing reasons for distinguishing between, for example, just and unjust, or beautiful and ugly, or ultimately true and false. Everything is in the last resort indifferent *(adiaphoron)* and thus exposed in principle to doubt. Distinctions are simply posited arbitrarily by us. Withholding judgment *(epochē)* is thus the best attitude for those who have this insight and who demonstrate their wisdom in general by a state of unshakability of heart *(ataraxia)* such as → Stoicism advocated.

This position contains features of the ethical → relativism that was developed later by the "new skepticism" of Aenesidemus (1st cent. B.C.) and worked systematically by means of ten basic principles of a skeptical approach. Pyrrho and Aenesidemus expressly linked up with the Sophist tradition, whose influence the Platonic academy (→ Platonism) had weakened but not destroyed. One might speak of a skeptical reaction to the crisis of → metaphysics in antiquity (→ Greek Philosophy).

2. Christian Approaches
→ Augustine (354-430; → Augustine's Theology) set the course for the Christian handling of skepticism in his work *Contra academicos* (Against the skeptics). Here the skeptical tradition is the natural opponent of the certainty of Christian → faith. Later, however, Duns Scotus (ca. 1265-1308; → Scotism) and → William of Ockham (ca. 1285-1347; → Nominalism) viewed transition through doubt as a way to assurance of faith and to convincing arguments on its behalf. Along with this methodological coalition between faith and doubt was an existential coalition that came to a head in → mysticism. Here a skeptical attitude to the world served as a basis for the only abiding certainty, → mystical union. B. → Pascal (1623-62) pioneered this approach for the postmedieval tradition.

3. Modern Period
In the → modern period skeptics like M. Montaigne (1533-92) and antidogmatists like P. Bayle (1647-1706) appealed to the Pyrrhonian tradition and made it influential in the modern world (→ Modernity). D. Hume (1711-76) based his programmatic skepticism chiefly on a theory of human knowledge, though by way of Montaigne he also saw confirmation in Pyrrho and made Pyrrhonian skepticism a vital force in the → Enlightenment. Hume doubted whether apart from → experience there can be any concepts that might guide or establish our knowledge of → nature. He thus taught that the concept of → causality, a fundamental category of modern science, does not originate a priori in thought but is simply a term for a belief resting on experience of the regularity of certain phenomena. The feature that is skeptical here in the classical sense is that Hume cut from under natural science the sure ground of the regularity of natural phenomena, since we can base regularity only on physical effects and not on unquestionable concepts.

I. Kant (1724-1804; → Kantianism) found critical provocation in this position (see his *Critique of Pure Reason,* B786-97). On the one hand, he wanted to guarantee for knowledge and → ethics a sure foundation in rational thought, but on the other, he wished to preserve a place for a skepticism that is critical of → dogmatism and → ideology. Between skepticism on the one side and dogmatism on the other, he thus took a third path, which he definitively adopted into the canon of philosophical methods, namely, that of skeptical method. He claimed, "Only to → transcendental philosophy . . . does this skeptical method belong essentially" (B452). Kant, though, plainly differentiated it from the methodical skepticism of R. Descartes (1596-1650; → Cartesianism).

Unlike Pyrrhonian skepticism, Kant's skeptical method does not entangle human reason in neutralizing self-contradictions (→ Antinomy) but shows that reason has a sure knowledge that is beyond the confines of human understanding as its premise. In this way Kant enlightens Pyrrhonism itself regarding its own presuppositions. A self-certainty of the human understanding replaces Pyrrhonian *epochē*/skepticism. This result does not, as in Descartes, take the form of evidence that overcomes all doubt. In each act of → cognition it must be achieved afresh, with balanced reciprocal control between empirical observation and conceptual thinking.

4. Hegel and Positivism
G. W. F. Hegel (1770-1831; → Hegelianism) further radicalized this form of constructive skepticism in his *Phenomenology of Mind* (chap. B.4.B), and at the same time tried to overcome it in a way typical of German → idealism. He saw in skepticism a negative form of omniscience that with its knowledge disputes all knowledge. This negative position feeds on its own negation, so that we can properly portray it only dialectically (→ Dialectic). Hegel offers this account in the form of the dialectical path of self-conceptualizing knowledge that, by double negation, achieves a position of certain knowledge and thus overcomes skepticism.

In the 20th century Kant's skeptical method, modified as methodological skepticism, became an incontestable element in → epistemology (→ Philosophy of Science). The progress of the school of → positivism rests on its triumph over Hegel's enormous effort to overcome skepticism.

Bibliography: D. C. ALLEN, *Doubt's Boundless Sea: Skepticism and Faith in the Renaissance* (Baltimore, 1964) • M. BURNYEAT, ed., *The Skeptical Tradition* (Berkeley, Calif., 1983) • M. J. FERREIRA, *Scepticism and Reasonable Doubt: The British Naturalist Tradition in Wilkins, Hume, Reid, and Newman* (New York, 1986) • M. N. FORSTER, *Hegel and Skepticism* (Cambridge, Mass., 1989) • D. HUME, *Enquiries concerning the Human Understanding and Concerning the Principles of Morals* (ed. L. B. Selby-Bigge; Westport, Conn., 1980; repr. from 1777 ed.) • P. D. KLEIN, *Certainty, a Refutation of Scepticism* (Minneapolis, 1981) • G. E. MOORE, "Four Forms of Skepticism," *Philosophical Papers* (London, 1959) 193-222 • T. PENELHUM, *God and Skepticism: A Study in Skepticism and Fideism* (Boston, 1983) • R. H. POPKIN, *The History of Skepticism from Erasmus to Descartes* (New York, 1964) • E. RUDOLPH, *Skepsis bei Kant* (Munich, 1978) • SEXTUS EMPIRICUS, *Scepticism, Man, and God: Selections from the Major Writings of Sextus Empiricus* (ed. P. P. Hallie; Middletown, Conn., 1964) • C. L. STOUGH, *Greek Skepticism: A Study in Epistemology* (Berkeley, Calif., 1969) • B. STROUD, *The Significance of Philosophical Scepticism* (Oxford, 1984).

ENNO RUDOLPH

Slavery

Overview
1. Sociological Aspects
2. History
3. Theological and Ethical Aspects

Overview

The "Slavs," an ancient people of east-central Europe, were conquered and sold into bondage so frequently during the Middle Ages that their name eventually became synonymous with the state of servitude. "Sclavus," their original title, came into MEng. as *sclave,* with the meaning "one bound to servility" attached as early as the ninth century. Evidently, by that time it already made no difference to which race these "slaves" belonged.

By means of slavery, whether the ownership and dependence be physical or otherwise, certain people become the property of others and are obliged to offer service, being given the degrading status of no more than useful objects. Slavery was a social institution in antiquity. The Christian West at times found it offensive but did not totally end it, and with European expansion from the 15th century onward (→ Colonialism 2), it took on a mercantile form (the African-American slave trade). This form of slavery persisted into the 20th century and is seen today in the discriminatory treatment of people of different skin color (→ Racism) or different gender (→ Sexism), as well as in the inhumane exploitation of workers (forced labor camps of → totalitarian regimes), social and economic need (→ Poverty), and commercial sex (→ Prostitution). Thus far the universal condemnation of slavery by the U.N.'s Universal Declaration of Human → Rights (1948) has not been able to check new and concealed forms of slavery.

The investigation of slavery by the → social sciences examines the subject and describes and evaluates the data and the consequences. The OT and NT writings regarding slavery, theological reflection on the subject, church practice throughout church history, and the controversy over the slavery question in the 19th century (see 2) demonstrate by example the following: insight into revelation of the will of God (→ Law), decisions of → conscience, and concrete ethical action (→ Social Ethics 1) together merge faith and understanding, objective situation and subjective interest, and they differ according to the corresponding contextual circumstances (→ Contextual Theology). The theological and ethical arguments for and against slavery, abolitionist postulates, the condemnation of slavery on humanitarian and human-rights grounds, and the corresponding calls for action result from perspectives that tell us more about the position of the observer than about what is observed. A change of perspective to the victims of slavery leads to criticism and correction of the observer's position and focuses on the practical (sometimes militant) implementation of liberation, justice, → equality, and → freedom among all people (→ Liberation Theology; Black Theology; Third World Theology).

In the following sections various aspects of the topic are discussed, from which we see that slavery poses a problem and task for the theology, ethics, and practice of the church and demands a process of mediation that will demonstrate and verify what is specifically Christian.

ERWIN FAHLBUSCH†

1. Sociological Aspects

1.1. Various forms of slavery may be found in societies almost everywhere in the world and throughout history, from the time of the invention of agricultural implements. In a few places such as classical Greece (except Sparta) and ancient → Rome, slavery was so important for the ruling classes that we are forced to speak of slave societies. The same applies in the → modern period to European plantation colonies in the Caribbean countries, the United States, and Latin America (→ Colonialism 2) before the gradual abolition of slavery in the course of the 19th century. Today → international law condemns slavery (the League of Nations in 1926 and art. 4 of the U.N. Declaration of Human Rights in 1948). Despite the prohibition, however, the practice of slavery goes on in poor countries. Conditions in totalitarian labor camps were as bad as any under slavery (→ Totalitarianism; Torture).

1.2. In slave societies, both ancient and modern, as many as 30 percent and more of the people could be slaves, mainly prisoners of war and aliens from often distant lands. The American plantations gave rise to the biggest forced human migration in history. From the 16th century to the end of the 19th, some 11 million Africans were forcibly shipped across the Atlantic to America. By 1542 the Spanish → Dominican Bartolomé de Las Casas (1484-1566), a critic of colonialism, had already forbidden the enslaving of Indians. By way of comparison, from the 7th century to the 20th, about 17 million slaves were traded to North Africa and the Middle East.

In America slaves worked mostly on the land or in mines. So long as their prices were relatively low, they were exploited without regard for loss. The situation changed when Great Britain outlawed the slave trade in 1807. Slaveholders now had to see to it that their slaves bore and reared children (→ Sexism). The result was improvement in the material lot of slaves. On the eve of the American Civil War (1861-65), slaves in the U.S. Southern states were better off economically than many European peasants and workers. But they were still without any → rights. In particular, their owners would not grant any rights of paternity. In 1685, in an effort to humanize the → institution, the French *Code noir* had recognized slave marriages (→ Humanity), but the provision had little influence on practice. Whenever possible, slaves set up their own families, just as they cultivated their own → culture, in spite of the harshest of living conditions. Religious → rites, → dance, a rich folk literature, and music (→ Spirituals) bear witness to this fact. In the United States, in distinction from other slave societies, only comparatively few slaves were set free by their masters (→ Freedom).

Slavery in antiquity and in non-Western societies differs from that on the plantations by reason of the fact that slaves not only engaged in heavy agricultural, industrial, and domestic work but might also be soldiers or high-ranking officials. Slaves could also own property and in unusual cases have their own slaves. Another feature in many African societies is that slaves are sought not so much to provide cheap labor as to increase the numbers of the groups, which is true in matrilinear societies. House slaves who have grown up in the owner's home may not be sold again. Across the generations a process of incorporation takes place. Slavery is thus less an economic matter than a way of producing dependents. The difference between slaves and their descendants and free people is that the former have no personal rights and no legal relatives apart from their owners. But in traditional African societies the "free" are not free in the sense of civil rights; they are tied to the group and part of its → property and potential. We also find the institution of slavery for debts whereby individuals are pledged to creditors.

In → Islam, the liberation of slaves counts as a pious deed. Yet slavery persists in Islam, as it did in → Judaism and Christianity.

1.3. As a whole, the history of slavery is also a history of resistance to it (→ Emancipation 2; Resistance, Right of). One of the most important slave revolts was that of the gladiator trainee Spartacus (d. 71 B.C.), the third Roman slave war (73-71). In Brazil in 1605 runaway slaves set up the kingdom of Palmares, which survived until 1694. The revolt of slaves in French St. Domingue in 1791 resulted in the founding of independent Haiti. Nor should we forget the day-by-day resistance in the form of feigned submission, indolence, flight, and the forming of religious societies (→ African-American Cults; Black Churches 1; Voodoo). The abolition of slavery was a victory for → Enlightenment thinking, with its stress on human equality and on the value of the individual (→ Adulthood; Anthropology), though the lead in the campaign came from men and women of strong Christian convictions (esp. William → Wilberforce), support being provided by philanthropists and merchants.

In southern Europe slavery increased once again in the late → Middle Ages. Elsewhere it was replaced by serfdom. In other continents it was followed by other forms of compulsory labor, such as contract work and leasehold. The spreading → racism that also followed slavery limited the scope of emancipation. Europeans, however, justified the colonial subjection of Africa as a part of the fight against slavery. The transatlantic slave trade and the abolition of slavery in America had led to its spread in Africa.

Scholars are divided on the contribution of slavery to the industrial development of Europe (→ Industrial Society).

Bibliography: C. van der Anker, ed., *The Political Economy of New Slavery* (New York, 2004) • M. L. Bush, *Servitude in Modern Times* (Malden, Mass., 2000) • D. B. Davis, *Slavery and Human Progress* (New York, 1984) • M. I. Finley, *Ancient Slavery and Modern Ideology* (ed. B. D. Shaw; rev. ed.; Princeton, 1998) • E. D. Genovese, *Roll, Jordan, Roll: The World the Slaves Made* (New York, 1974) • B. Lewis, *Race and Slavery in the Middle East* (New York, 1990) • P. E. Lovejoy, *Transformations in Slavery: A History of Slavery in Africa* (Cambridge, Mass., 1983) • C. Meillassoux, *The Anthropology of Slavery: The Womb of Iron and Gold* (Chicago, 1991) • O. Patterson, *Slavery and Social Death: A Comparative Study* (Cambridge, Mass., 1982) • A. Wirz, *Sklaverei und kapitalistisches Weltsystem* (Frankfurt, 1984).

ALBERT WIRZ†

2. History

2.1. In antiquity slavery was considered a natural institution; a full middle-class lifestyle called for the possession of slaves. Aristotle (384-322 b.c.; → Aristotelianism) thought that a slave, being uneducated, was destined by nature to serve as a "living tool" (*Eth. Nic.* 8.11.6; *Pol.* 1.2.1). Plato (427-347; → Platonism) described slaves as inferior beings equipped only with physical force who were deficient in reason (*Leg.* 6.776-77E). Their employment and treatment might vary with circumstances, but they never enjoyed legal recognition as persons. The → Stoic doctrine of natural human → equality ascribed an inner → freedom to slaves, but it did not affect their outward status, though offering public opinion a more humane assessment and helping to improve the lot of slaves. A similar attitude was the concern of the → early church to make slaves children of God (Irenaeus; → Alexandrian Theology) and to assist them to "inner freedom" (→ Origen; Origenism), though with no challenging of the institution in principle. → Utopian philosophy was the first to point out the contradiction of being at the same time a person and a thing, for the → "golden age" (→ Paradise 3 and 5) would not need slaves.

2.2. In Israel the owning of menservants and maidservants was part of the patriarchal constitution and lifestyle (Gen. 14:14; 24:35; 26:14), but clear regulations were laid down regarding their legal relation and the participation of servants in the cult (Exod. 21:1-11; Deut. 12:18; Gen. 17:12). Purchased slaves differed from those born in the house-

hold (Gen. 17:12-13). Foreign prisoners of war, including women (Judg. 5:30; 1 Sam. 30:3), might be bought and sold as slaves (Exod. 21:32; Num. 31:7-9, 18, 32-47; Deut. 20:13-14; Ezek. 27:13; Amos 1:9; 1 Macc. 3:41; 2 Macc. 8:11) and employed in labor projects (2 Sam. 12:31; 1 Kgs. 9:15-21).

A concern for slaves may be seen in the laws protecting them (Exod. 21:20, 26-27; Lev. 19:20-22), which make provision for manumission (Deut. 15:12-18; the year of jubilee) and allow the purchase of freedom (Lev. 25:49). Job 31:13-15 speaks of the natural rights of slaves as creatures of God. In a transferred sense vassals, subjects, courtiers, and others might be called slaves (1 Sam. 8:14-15; 17:32; 2 Sam. 12:18; 2 Kgs. 18:24). Dependence on God and commitment to him might also be called a slave relation (Judg. 2:8; 1 Sam. 7:3-4; also Judg. 10:6, 10, 13, 16 RSV). It is an honor to be called the servant or slave of God (2 Kgs. 18:12; Judg. 2:8; Ps. 105:42; → Servant of the Lord).

2.3. The NT presupposes and uncritically accepts slavery as an institution. The → parables of Jesus mention it (Matt. 18:23-35; 25:14-30; Luke 12:42-48; 17:7-10), but faith in Christ makes slaves and freemen equal before God (Gal. 3:26-28). Because believers have the eschatological → kingdom of God in view, social distinctions fade, and the community of faith is to assemble in → love for Christ. → Paul, then, can direct slaves to obey their masters, and masters to deal with their servants in a way that is pleasing to God (Eph. 6:5-8; Col. 3:22–4:1, → Household Rules; see also 1 Pet. 2:18-25). Paul emphatically calls himself a "slave of (Jesus) Christ" (Rom. 1:1; Gal. 1:10 NRSV marg.) and points to the new being "in Christ Jesus" (Gal. 3:26, 28; see also 2:20), which makes all believers brothers and sisters (Phlm. 16).

As regards → salvation, stress falls on the relation to God and on the freedom from bondage to → sin that Christ has won for us, so that the → gospel tends to lose its impact when it comes to social revolution. Liturgical praise, the sacramental ratification of salvation, personal and collective appropriation of salvation, and the objective working out of salvation by the → church determine the secular dimensions of the gospel. Slaves have a place in the Christian community, but slavery is still part of the social and economic order. It is highly questionable whether the early church as a tiny and alien minority could have brought about any effective change.

2.4. → Tertullian (ca. 160-ca. 225) thought little of earthly manumission: "Though it seems to [provide] liberty, yet it will come to be found bondage" (*De cor.* 13). → Augustine (354-430; → Augustine's

Theology) believed that "the prime cause . . . of slavery is sin" (*De civ. Dei* 19.15). Thomas Aquinas (ca. 1225-74; → Thomism) declared that we must distinguish between our natural equality as "spiritual beings" and the law that is naturally set up and regulated by → reason. This law allows slavery on the basis of its "utility" (*Summa theol.* II of II, q. 57, art. 3), but it "regards the body, not the soul" (q. 104, art. 6), thus establishing a limit in natural law. → Grace delivers from bondage to sin but not from physical bondage that is regulated by human laws. Theologians and popes could thus accept slavery as a necessary and legitimate evil, although penalties were sometimes imposed for the unjust and cruel treatment of slaves, and laws were passed to prevent it.

Gregory XVI (1831-46) was the first to press for abolition of slavery on the grounds of justice and humanity, in his constitution *In supremo apostolatus fastigio* (1839). Leo XIII (1878-1903) was finally ready to resolutely condemn slavery, doing so in his encyclicals *In plurimis* (1888) and *Catholicae Ecclesiae* (1890).

2.5. With the view that Christian freedom is not dependent on social institutions, M. → Luther (1483-1546; → Luther's Theology) accepted the traditional evaluation of slavery. But the → Hussites (Taborites), the → Bohemian Brethren, and the left wing of the → Reformation saw the social-revolutionary side of the gospel. From the 18th century onward, actual contact with slavery and the slave trade on the mission field changed the outlook on slavery. The interest of → Pietism in giving Christianity practical expression inspired the change and led to humanitarian enterprises. The assessment and conduct of missionary churches, however, was not uniform. They sometimes argued that inhumanity to slaves and their demoralizing degradation besmirched Christianity (G. Warneck). At the same time, the antislavery agitation of the founder of the White Fathers (→ Catholic Missions 5), Cardinal Charles M. A. Lavigerie (1825-92), helped to foster colonial imperialism (H. Gründer).

The incompatibility of faith and → force, and the Christian commandment of love, motivated the → Mennonites, Methodists (→ Methodism 2.4), and Quakers (→ Friends, Society of) to advocate the freeing of slaves and the abolition of slavery. In 1780 itinerant Methodist preachers were forbidden to own slaves. In Great Britain W. → Wilberforce (1759-1833), an Anglican Evangelical member of Parliament, with support from converted slave-trader John Newton, associates in the so-called Clapham Sect, and a campaign to change public opinion, succeeded after a difficult struggle in seeing the slave trade outlawed in 1807, with the abolition of slavery in all British territories finally to follow in 1834. In the following decades similar laws were enacted in other countries, although these steps did not at first mean the total ending of slavery or the slave trade. At the 1890 Brussels Conference the great powers at last made themselves responsible for putting an end to the slave trade in Africa.

In the United States the question of slavery split the states and the Protestant churches. The Southern states, with their large slave population, defended slavery on economic and theological grounds, but from 1828 onward several abolitionist societies in the North called for a total end to the institution. The issue caused the Methodists to divide in 1844 into the Methodist Episcopal Church and the Methodist Episcopal Church, South (→ Black Churches 1; Methodist Churches 2.3). In 1845 the → Baptists (§1) split into Southern and Northern Conventions, and in 1857 and 1861 we find similar division in the Presbyterian Church (→ Reformed and Presbyterian Churches 4.2). The General Convention in the Southern states split off from the → Christian Churches in 1854, and in 1863 Lutherans formed the separate Evangelical Lutheran Church in the South (→ Lutheran Churches 6.1). Different views of the slave question within the American Board of Commissioners for Foreign Missions (→ North American Missions 2.1) led in 1846 to the founding of the antislavery American Missionary Association.

In time, most of these divisions were healed, and the prohibiting of slavery prevailed as a matter of human → rights. Nevertheless, the favored position of whites is still a problem for the churches, one that occupies the ecumenical movement (→ Racism; Program to Combat Racism; Ecumenism, Ecumenical Movement).

Bibliography: On 2.1: P. Hunt, *Slaves, Warfare, and Ideology in the Greek Historians* (New York, 1998) • W. L. Westermann, *The Slave System of Greek and Roman Antiquity* (Philadelphia, 1955; repr., 1984) • R. Zelnick-Abramovitz, *Not Wholly Free: The Concept of Manumission and the Status of Manumitted Slaves in the Ancient Greek World* (Boston, 2005).

On 2.2 and 2.3: P. Garnsey, *Ideas of Slavery from Aristotle to Augustine* (New York, 1996) • J. A. Glancy, *Slavery in Early Christianity* (New York, 2002) • D. Goldenberg, *The Curse of Ham: Race and Slavery in Early Judaism, Christianity, and Islam* (Princeton, 2003) • J. A. Hill, *Slaves in the NT: Literary, Social, and Moral Dimensions* (Minneapolis, 2006).

On 2.4 and 2.5: R. Blackburn, *The Making of New*

World Slavery: From the Baroque to the Modern, 1492-1800 (New York, 1997) • W. G. Clarence-Smith, *Islam and the Abolition of Slavery* (London, 2006) • S. Deyle, *Carry Me Back: The Domestic Slave Trade in American Life* (New York, 2005) • H. Gründer, *Welteroberung und Christentum. Ein Handbuch zur Geschichte der Neuzeit* (Gütersloh, 1992) • J. O. Horton and L. E. Horton, *Slavery and the Making of America* (New York, 2004) • M. Lengellé, *L'esclavage* (6th ed.; Paris, 1992; orig. pub., 1955) • D. P. Mannix and M. Cowley, *Black Cargoes: History of the Atlantic Slave Trade, 1518-1865* (London, 2002; orig. pub., 1962) • M. A. Noll, *The Civil War as a Theological Crisis* (Chapel Hill, N.C., 2006) • J. S. Panzer, *The Popes and Slavery* (New York, 1996) • UNESCO, *The African Slave Trade from the Fifteenth to the Nineteenth Century* (Paris, 1979) • G. Warneck, *Die Stellung der evangelischen Mission zur Sklavenfrage* (Leipzig, 1889).

Erwin Fahlbusch† and Eszter Szabó

3. Theological and Ethical Aspects

3.1. Slavery is a form of human bondage in which persons are defined as the property of others. Throughout most of their history, Christian churches and their theologians have unfortunately accepted slavery as God's will for some persons, especially when those persons have not been Europeans. Most have used the Bible as the chief reason for their acceptance and promotion of slavery. As a human book, the Bible does not make an unequivocal condemnation of slavery. However, Jesus did proclaim a gospel that emphasized "release to the captives" and taught us to "let the oppressed go free" (Luke 4:18). Since Christians claimed Jesus Christ to be the heart of Christianity, it seems that they, instead of accepting slavery as God's will, would have been its most ardent opponents.

3.2. Although early Christians and their descendants did not condemn slavery, many historians and theologians of the churches claim that their gospel of "brotherhood" ameliorated the condition of the slaves. In other words, Christian masters often treated their slaves "better." Paul's return of Onesimus to Philemon, emphasizing that he be received "no longer as a slave" but as "a beloved brother" (v. 16), and his accent on the oneness of all humanity in Christ (Gal. 3:28) — these and other similar incidents and passages have been cited as evidence for this claim. However, if one looks at slavery, not from the perspective of the masters or of the churches that accepted it, but rather from the vantage point of the slaves — the people who suffered under it — it is not likely that *amelioration*

will be a major theme in one's analysis of the churches' relationship to this institution. Rather, the question will be: How could the churches claim to preach and to live the gospel of → freedom, as defined by Jesus Christ, and still at the same time not only tolerate human servitude but actually participate in holding others in bondage? As long as theologians and churches avoided that question, the more they tolerated slavery and other forms of injustice in their midst. There is nothing that one can say to make the churches' failure to condemn slavery acceptable to people with a modicum of moral decency.

Living between the patristic period and the beginning of the Middle Ages, → Augustine (354-430), bishop of Hippo, attributed slavery to the sins of the slaves. His theology of slavery defined the churches' doctrinal and ethical teachings for centuries. It is noteworthy that the Protestant → Reformation happened during the same time as the European slave trade. As millions of Africans were stolen from their homeland, Catholic and Protestant theologians hardly referred to it in their theological and ethical reflections; and of the few who did, most did not oppose the importation of Africans as the property of Europeans. From the perspectives of European theologians, it was God's will that whites rule over blacks, because the former were racially superior to the latter.

In North America, white churches and their theologians are well known for their advocacy of slavery as the will of God. Initially, slave masters objected to the evangelization of slaves by missionaries and preachers because they feared that biblical references to freedom might lead their slaves to claim a similar status for themselves. But white theologians and preachers convinced slave masters that Christianity actually made blacks better slaves, that is, obedient and docile. They taught slaves that they should obey their masters because it was God's will. To disobey the master, therefore, was to disobey God. With the exception of the Quakers (→ Friends, Society of), no denominational churches took a stand against slavery. In fact, most churches owned slaves themselves.

3.3. It is important to note that the black victims of slavery did not accept the white preachers' views of the gospel. On the contrary, they contended that God willed their freedom and not their slavery. As evidence, they pointed to the exodus of the Israelite slaves from Egypt, the → prophets' stand for justice, and Jesus' identification with the poor, dying on the cross like them. Most of the more than 250 slave revolts were religiously inspired and were led by black preachers. Approximately 2,000 slaves ran away to freedom annually. Those who could not escape from bondage expressed their desire for freedom in songs, prayers, and other sayings — usually in secret meetings that were held in the woods at night, often called the invisible institution.

Free blacks in the North founded their own churches to demonstrate their refusal to accept segregation in white churches and also to prove that they were human beings, and thus quite capable of running their own institutions just like whites. The African Methodist Episcopal Church (A.M.E.) was founded in 1816, and the African Methodist Episcopal Zion Church (A.M.E.Z.) and many Baptist churches followed soon afterward. These churches served as the heart of the black resistance against slavery.

Although legal slavery ended in the United States in 1865, segregation took its place. Many blacks concluded that segregation, in the words of Martin Luther → King Jr. (1929-68), was "just another form of slavery dressed up in certain niceties of complexity." White churches were even more firmly committed to segregation than they had been to slavery. With social Darwinism dominating the intellectual life of America and Europe, whites thought of themselves as superior to blacks and other people of color. Slavery, colonization, and segregation were not regarded as cruel but a blessing for its victims. White churches therefore promoted "white over black" in their congregational life, as well as in the society. No American theologian made the liberation of black people from slavery or segregation the starting point of his or her understanding of the gospel of Jesus. This is the great difference between black and white reflections on the gospel. Being the victims, blacks have always recognized that the Christian gospel began and ended with the liberation of the poor from bondage.

The appearance of Martin Luther King Jr. in the 1950s and the rise of → black theology in the 1960s are largely responsible for slavery and segregation becoming an issue of Christian doctrine and ethics in the United States. While Reinhold → Niebuhr (1892-1971), usually regarded as America's most prominent 20th-century theologian, could say, "We must not consider the Founding Fathers immoral just because they were slaveholders," King, in contrast, defined slavery and segregation as the greatest moral issue in American history. He contended that unless churches took an unequivocal stand against → racism in all its expressions, they could not claim an identity with Jesus Christ.

Black theology extended King's claim even fur-

ther. Its proponents claimed that the real bearers of the Christian tradition in America were not whites who ignored the theological and ethical demands of the gospel; rather, the true meaning of the gospel of Jesus is found in the history and culture of the black slaves and their descendants. With liberation as the main theme of the gospel, black theologians contended that a church's or a person's stand regarding slavery and segregation must serve as the litmus test in defining the meaning of Christian identity.

One's definition of slavery and one's attitude toward it are, to a great extent, defined by whether one is a descendant of the victims or of the victimizers. If the latter, one is more likely to analyze the church in terms of the ameliorating role it played, making life a little better for the slaves until slavery was legally abolished. If the former, one is more likely to analyze the church in terms of its support of slavery, even to the point of owning slaves, and its slowness in regarding human servitude as a contradiction of the gospel it preached. This writer is a descendant of slaves and thus cannot find any theological justification for the church's failure to take an uncompromising stand against such obvious forms of injustice as slavery and its cousin, segregation.

Bibliography: D. B. Davis, *The Problem of Slavery in Western Culture* (Ithaca, N.Y., 1966) • J. A. Harrill, *Slaves in the NT: Literary, Social, and Moral Dimensions* (Minneapolis, 2006) • O. Patterson, *Slavery and Social Death: A Comparative Study* (Cambridge, Mass., 1982) • A. J. Raboteau, *Slave Religion: The "Invisible Institution" in the Antebellum South* (New York, 1978) • L. B. Scherer, *Slavery and the Churches in Early America, 1619-1819* (Grand Rapids, 1975) • H. S. Smith, *In His Image, but . . . : Racism in Southern Religion, 1780-1910* (Durham, N.C., 1972) • E. Troeltsch, *The Social Teaching of the Christian Churches* (2 vols.; Louisville, Ky., 1992; orig. pub., 1912) • G. S. Wilmore, *Black Religion and Black Radicalism: An Interpretation of the Religious History of African Americans* (3d ed.; Maryknoll, N.Y., 1998).

James H. Cone

Slavic Mission

Whereas Latin and Byzantine missions went hand in hand with expansion, the adoption of Christianity by Slavic tribes helped to stabilize independent states (→ Mission 3.3).

1. After a mainly Frankish mission to Slavs who had settled in Illyria in the sixth and seventh centuries, and to southern Slavs in Slovenia and Croatia, mis-

sionary work increased with the destruction of the Avars' kingdom in Pannonia (ca. 500-803) by Charlemagne (768-814) and the Bulgars in 811. The Drava River became the boundary of the influence of Aquileia, in northern Italy, and of the more recent missionary metropolis of Salzburg. Magyars (Hungary) who had settled in Pannonia founded the Diocese of Zagreb in Croatia in 1091. Soon, however, there came a move in the direction of Byzantine Slavic mission.

2. Having achieved political independence, Prince Rastislav of Moravia (846-70) sought to break free from the connection with the Salzburg archdiocese. When Pope Nicholas I (858-67) turned down his request for missionaries, Rastislav asked Constantinople to send missionaries who could teach the Slavs church doctrine in their own language. Sent by the Eastern church in 862, the brothers Cyril (ca. 827-69) and Methodius (ca. 815-85) created an alphabet for the purpose (Glagolitic) and, by means of translations of the Bible (→ Bible Versions), liturgical texts, and books of → church law, pioneered an ecclesiastical Slavic literature.

The papal elevation of Methodius to the archbishopric of Sirmium (near modern Sremska Mitrovica, Serbia) shows that Rome's aim was to win other Slavic peoples with the help of these writings. Thus John VIII (872-82) wrote a letter in May 873, our earliest evidence for the existence of Serbian Christianity, to the Serbian prince Mutimir (ca. 860-91), asking him to come under this archdiocese, of which Methodius was archbishop. But the Serbian church refused to abandon Eastern Orthodoxy (→ Orthodox Church 2.2).

3. The work of Cyril and Methodius stood under the banner of church unity. But a clash came between Roman and Byzantine universalism in the simultaneous attempt to Christianize the first Bulgarian kingdom (681-1018), which Slavs and Turkish Proto-Bulgars had founded. After first agreeing to accept Latin Christianity from the Franks, Bulgarian prince Boris (czar 852-89) felt compelled in 864/65 to adopt Christianity from the hereditary political foe, → Byzantium. Seeking ecclesiastical autonomy, Boris played off Rome against Byzantium, subjecting his young church to the papacy in 866 but then returning to Constantinople in 870. The actions of the Latin → missionaries — for example, demanding → celibacy of the clergy, imposing Latin-style → fasting, repeating the → sacrament of chrismation (→ Church Membership 2), and bringing the addition of the →

filioque into the creed, which Rome itself had not yet done, along with the reaction to the papal claim to primacy on the part of Constantinople, which viewed the five → patriarchs as of equal status (→ Pope, Papacy; Pentarchy) — point us to the differences that resulted in the great East-West schism of 1054 (→ Heresies and Schisms 3).

On the death of Methodius in 885, the use of the Slavic liturgy was forbidden in Moravia and Pannonia. Driven out, the disciples of Methodius found a new home in Bulgaria. Bishop Clement of Ochrid (ca. 840-916) did more translating and composed model sermons for the Slavic clergy whom he ordained. The Cyrillic alphabet, which originated in Bulgaria, became the basis of the literature of both the Orthodox Serbs and the East Slavs. Sava (1169-1236), patron of Serbia, established the → autocephaly of the Serbian church in 1219.

4. Kiev princess Olga received → baptism in Constantinople in 957. Then, together with the German king Otto I (936-73), she had Adalbert of Trier (d. 981) consecrated bishop of Kiev. The famous Kiev baptism followed in 988, when Prince Vladimir (980-1015), who was honored as a saint, accepted Christianity from Byzantium after examining, according to the oldest Russian chronicles, the religions of neighboring peoples, though the political development of his marriage to the emperor's sister Anna was probably the decisive factor (→ Russian Orthodox Church 1.1). The Kiev church was organized as a metropolitan church under Constantinople. The taking over of church Slavic writings gave rise to a specific culture and helped to bring the different peoples together. It was important that the developing of this church took place after the 1054 schism, to which early Kiev writings bear witness.

After 1240 we see the identity of church and nation in two ways. In 1240 the fall of the Kiev state and the beginning of almost 250 years of Tatar rule resulted in Moscow (founded in the 12th cent.) becoming the ecclesiastical center. Then, northwestern Russia had to be defended against Swedish armies and the Teutonic Knights from the Latin West. In 1439 the Council of Florence tried to force Byzantium into union with Rome (→ Councils of the Church), but Byzantium broke free again in 1448.

5. Among the West Slavs, Czech nobles had received baptism in 845 at Regensburg, the court of Louis the German (817-76). In Bohemia, however, Christianity spread only at the end of the ninth century through the work of → Moravian priests.

Poland had had contacts with the Orthodox Church in the ninth century, but it was Latin Christianity that came to it from Bohemia when Mieszko I (ca. 963-92) married a Czech princess and in 966 accepted baptism. With the establishing of an archbishopric in 1000, the Poles put their land under papal protection and reduced German influence.

For some 200 years Poland and Lithuania ruled over what are now the Ukraine and Belarus. The resultant union with Rome that was arranged for the Orthodox in these areas — the Union of Brest-Litovsk, in 1595/96 — became the source of permanent tension (→ Union 2.1; Uniate Churches).

Bibliography: H.-D. Döpmann, "Die Annahme des Christentums bei den Slawen-Völkern Südosteuropas. Anmerkungen in vergleichend historischer Sicht," *Études balkaniques* (Sofia) 26 (1990) 46-53; idem, *Die orthodoxe Kirchen* (Berlin, 1991); idem, *Die Ostkirchen von Bilderstreit bis zur Kirchenspaltung von 1054* (Leipzig, 1991) • E. G. Farrugia, ed., *Christianity among the Slavs: The Heritage of Saints Cyril and Methodius* (Rome, 1988) • C. Hannick, "Die byzantinischen Missionen," *Kirchengeschichte als Missionsgeschichte* (vol. II/1; Munich, 1978); idem, "Les nouvelles chrétientés du monde byzantin. Russes, Bulgares et Serbes," *Évêques, moines et empereurs (610-1054),* vol. 4 of *Histoire du christianisme des origenes à nos jours* (ed. J.-M. Mayeur; Paris, 1993) 909-39 • L. Müller, *Die Taufe Rußlands. Die Frühgeschichte des russischen Christentums bis zum Jahre 988* (Munich, 1987) • T. Piffl-Perčević and A. Stirnemann, eds., *Der heilige Method, Salzburg und die Slawenmission* (Innsbruck, 1987) • A.-E. M. Tachiaos, *Cyril and Methodius of Thessalonica: The Acculturation of the Slavs* (Crestwood, N.Y., 2001) • A. P. Vlasto, *The Entry of the Slavs into Christendom: An Introduction to the Medieval History of the Slavs* (Cambridge, 1970).

Hans-Dieter Döpmann

Slavophiles

When Russian philosophy became independent in the early 19th century, a prominent question was that of the relation of Russia to Europe, which J. P. Chaadayev (1794-1856) raised in his *Lettres philosophiques* (1827-31; ET *Philosophical Letters* [Knoxville, Tenn., 1969]). A "Western" group of thinkers wanted a full and swift adoption of the achievements of the West, but another group, the Slavophiles, argued for Russia's independence and even superiority and hence advocated separate enterprises. It is hard to draw a distinction between stricter and less strict Slavophiles, or between older Slavophiles, with their religious concerns, and younger Slavophiles, who linked together Pan-Slavism and Russian Orthodox → spirituality (→ Orthodoxy Christianity; Russia 1.1).

The most important spokesmen of the Slavophiles were the author S. T. Aksakov (1791-1859), the lay theologian A. S. Khomyakov (1804-60), the philosopher I. V. Kireevsky (1806-56), the historian K. S. Aksakov (1817-60), the champion for the emancipation of the serfs Y. F. Samarin (1819-76), the scientist N. Y. Danilevsky (1822-85), and the publicist I. S. Aksakov (1823-86). Though not of this group, F. M. Dostoyevsky (1821-81) represented a similar view with his Russian → messianism.

The influence of the Slavophiles on the → Russian Orthodox Church (→ Orthodox Church) may be seen in the way that Archbishop Filaret (Gumilevsky, 1805-66) from Chernigov argued in his history of the church that the pagan Slavs were by no means hostile to Christianity. The great writer on the → philosophy of religion V. S. Solovyov (1853-1900) was at first fascinated by the Slavophiles but later abandoned them, though he remained faithful to their basic concerns. In one way or another, modern religious thought in Russia still bears the imprint of the legacy of the Slavophiles.

Bibliography: P. K. Christoff, *An Introduction to Nineteenth-Century Russian Slavophilism* (4 vols.; The Hague, 1961-91) • W. Goerdt, *Russische Philosophie. Zugänge und Durchblicke* (Freiburg, 1984) • A. S. Khomiakov and I. Kireevsky, *On Spiritual Unity: A Slavophile Reader* (ed. B. Jakim and R. Bird; Hudson, N.Y., 1998) • A. Osipov, "The Theological Conceptions of Slavophiles," *Holy Russian Church and Western Christianity* (ed. G. Alberigo and O. Beozzo; Maryknoll, N.Y., 1996) 33-48 • D. Pospielovsky, "The Neo-Slavophile Trend and Its Relation to the Contemporary Religious Revival in the USSR," *Religion and Nationalism in Soviet and East European Politics* (ed. P. Ramet; Durham, N.C., 1984) 41-58 • S. Rabow-Edling, *The Intellectuals and the Idea of the Nation in Slavophile Thought* (Stockholm, 2001); eadem, "The Role of 'Europe' in Russian Nationalism: Reinterpreting the Relationship between Russia and the West in Slavophile Thought," *Russia in the European Context, 1789-1914: A Member of the Family* (ed. S. P. McCaffray and M. Melancon; New York, 2005) 97-112 • B. Schultze, *Russische Denker. Ihre Stellung zu Christus, Kirche und Papsttum* (Vienna, 1950) • A. Walicki, *The Slavophile Controversy: History of a Conservative Utopia in Nineteenth-Century Russian Thought* (Oxford, 1975).

Peter Hauptmann

Slovakia

	1960	*1980*	*2000*
Population (1,000s):	4,145	4,976	5,372
Annual growth rate (%):	1.02	0.65	0.13

Area: 49,035 sq. km. (18,933 sq. mi.)

A.D. 2000

Population density: 110/sq. km. (284/sq. mi.)
Births / deaths: 1.20 / 1.07 per 100 population
Fertility rate: 1.50 per woman
Infant mortality rate: 11 per 1,000 live births
Life expectancy: 72.3 years (m: 68.0, f: 76.6)
Religious affiliation (%): Christians 85.6 (Roman Catholics 72.0, Protestants 11.2, unaffiliated 1.0, other Christians 1.4), nonreligious 11.0, atheists 3.4.

1. History
2. Churches
3. Jewish Community
4. Ecumenical Relations
5. Theological Training
6. Church and State

1. History

After the breakup of the Austro-Hungarian Empire in 1918, and during the years 1918-38 and 1945-92, Slovakia was part of Czechoslovakia. Its population of 5.4 million (2006) includes a substantial Hungarian minority of about 10 percent. The capital is Bratislava (Ger. Pressburg, Hung. Pozsony).

The Christianization of Slovakia began in the ninth century (a Christian church was dedicated in Nitra in 828) and was marked by a contest between the Eastern and Western churches. A brief but significant episode was the Slavo-Byzantine mission of Cyril (ca. 827-69) and of Methodius (ca. 815-85). Methodius was later appointed by Hadrian II (867-72) as archbishop of Moravia and Sirmium (near modern Sremska Mitrovica, Serbia) in Pannonia, with its seat in Nitra. Soon, however, Slovakia came under the cultural sphere of influence of the Western church, partly because of the political influence of the Hungarian dynasty of the house of Árpád, which incorporated Slovakia into its kingdom in about the year 1000.

Attempts at reform in the medieval church (esp. through the → Waldensian movement) met with some response among the German population, who colonized some regions of Slovakia from the 12th century. Aided by "gracious rides," or the military campaigns of 1428-35 in Hungary, the Hussite movement penetrated deep in the land of Slovakia,

leaving its mark on Slovak popular and intellectual circles, with the idea of church services in the vernacular and Communion *sub utraque specie,* or "under each kind" (→ Hussites 1). Through Martin → Luther, the influence of the → Reformation spread rapidly in Slovakia and led to the creation of special → confessions of faith based on the → Augsburg Confession (1530): the Confessio Pentapolitana, issued by five eastern Slovak towns in 1549; the Confessio Heptapolitana (or Montana), established by seven central Slovak mining towns in 1559; and the Confessio Scepusiana, issued by the priest brotherhood of Spiš in northern Slovakia in 1569. Synods in Žilina (1610) and in Spišské Podhradie (1614) organized the Lutheran church as independent of Rome.

While the Slovak and German populations embraced the ideas of the Lutheran Reformation, the Hungarians were influenced more by → Calvinism. The Reformed Christian Church was constituted in 1567 at the Synod of Debrecen, in the former Hungarian kingdom, where it accepted the → Heidelberg Catechism (1563) and Second → Helvetic Confession of Faith (1566) as its confessional writings. In addition, → Anabaptists from Switzerland and Germany settled in western parts of Slovakia but never gained official recognition.

Counter-Reformation activity was supported by the Hapsburgs after 1526 but met with resistance from the Protestant nobility (Štefan Bočkaj, Gabriel Bethlen, Juraj I Rákoci, Imrich Tököli, František II Rákoci) and thus was not completely successful (→ Catholic Reform and Counterreformation). It came to an end with the enlightened absolutism of Austrian emperor Joseph II (1780-90; → Josephinism) and his Toleration Edict of 1781.

In the 19th century Lutheran pastors and teachers in particular contributed to the national revival and growth of Slovak culture (by codifying the Slovak language in 1843, and by contributing to literature and education), supporting the Slovak nation in its struggle against Hungarian influence (esp. after 1867). This influence lasted until World War I and the breakup of the Austro-Hungarian monarchy.

2. Churches

2.1. The result of Counter-Reformation activity in Slovakia was that the → *Roman Catholic Church* regained its majority position. Today it is the largest Christian church in the country, with 3.7 million believers in four dioceses and two archdioceses. The tendency toward secularization and the atheist propaganda of the former socialist regime, however, have left their mark, especially in industrial areas, on what was once a church of the people. Its political influence, too, has clearly declined in comparison with the period before the Second World War, despite the prestige it gained from consistent opposition to the socialist regime.

2.2. The *Greek Catholic (→ Unitate) Church* came into existence when a large number of Orthodox believers joined the Catholic Church of the Eastern Rite in the 17th and 18th centuries. The Prešov eparchy was canonically founded by a bull of Pope Pius VII in 1818. In 1950 this church was forced to join the → Orthodox Church, from which it separated again in 1989 and formed the Greek Catholic Church. In 2001 it numbered 220,000 believers.

2.3. Eastern Christianity is represented in the Slovak Republic by the *Orthodox Church of the Czech Lands and Slovakia* (in 2001: 50,000 believers, two eparchies). The church gained → autocephalous status from the Moscow Patriarchate in 1951 as the Orthodox Church in Czechoslovakia. Today it is very active in Slovakia. The Orthodox Academy in Slovakia, in Michalovce, serves as a center for information, education, and culture.

2.4. The *Slovak Evangelical Church of the Augsburg Confession* did not free itself from Hungarian structures until 1918, when it established itself as an independent church with two church districts. In 1939-45 a group of German-speaking congregations (42 parishes, with 30,000 members) seceded from it. In 2001 it had 372,000 members in 327 congregations. It is a synodical-presbyterial church body divided into East and West districts and led by a general bishop and a general director. The church is a member of the → Lutheran World Federation and maintains close links with Slovak Lutheran minorities in the United States, the former Yugoslavia, Romania, and the Czech Republic.

2.5. The *Reformed Church of Slovakia* was formed as an independent church after the breakup of the Austro-Hungarian monarchy in 1918. In 1938 the southern part of Slovakia, with a majority of Reformed parishes, became a part of Hungary. After World War II many Hungarians were displaced to Hungary. The unclear situation after 1945 prevented the consolidation of the church. The government recognized the Reformed Church in 1948, and its constitution was accepted in 1952. As with other churches, its work and life were hindered by the atheistic regime.

In 2001 the church had 300 congregations, with 110,000 believers; it is divided into seven Hungarian and two Slovak districts. The majority of its members and congregations, primarily on the southern borders of Slovakia, are Hungarian-speaking; only about 10 percent are Slovak. The church is a member of the → World Alliance of Reformed Churches.

2.6. The remaining Protestant churches in the Slovak Republic were established in modern times, mostly with help from outside the country. The largest is the Evangelical Methodist Church (7,500 adherents, 5 congregations, in Slovakia from 1924) and → Pentecostalism, represented by the Apostolic Church (4,000 members in 2001, in 25 congregations) and smaller bodies, and the Seventh-day → Adventists (3,400 members, in 43 congregations). Representing the heritage of revivalism and the → free churches are the Baptist Union (3,600 adherents, in 17 congregations) and the Church of the Brethren (3,200 members, 35 congregations).

3. Jewish Community

The lively Jewish religious community, which numbered 135,000 in 1930, was virtually destroyed during World War II, when the Slovak government supported the deportation of Jews to concentration camps. Nowadays the community numbers only 2,300.

4. Ecumenical Relations

The level of ecumenical cooperation on the local level varies from region to region. The annual Week of Prayer for Christian Unity attracts considerable interest. On the official level, the churches are represented on the Ecumenical Council of Churches in Slovakia (ECCS), established in 1993 (after the division of the Ecumenical Council of the Czechoslovak Republic). It aims to coordinate church activity in relations with public institutions (education, social work, prisons, the military, etc.) and with foreign ecumenical bodies, and also to develop mutual relationships in the spiritual and theological spheres. In 2002 the ECCS had eight full members and four observers (Roman Catholic Church, Greek Catholic Church, Apostolic Church, and the Seventh-day Adventist Church).

The churches in the Slovak Republic are members of international ecumenical organizations that correspond to their denominational affiliation. In addition, some belong to the → World Council of Churches, the → Conference of European Churches, and the → Leuenberg Agreement. Since 1993 the Slovak → Bible Society has been involved in the printing and distribution of Bibles. In 1997 it completed the ecumenical translation of the NT and Psalms into Slovak. Catholic and Protestant scholars are currently working on a new ecumenical translation of the OT (→ Bible Versions).

5. Theological Training

Theological training at the university level can be acquired at the theological faculties of four state universities: Bratislava (Roman Catholic, Lutheran), Komárno (Reformed), Banská Bystrica (evangelical churches), and Prešov (Orthodox and Greek Catholic). In addition, the churches are establishing their own teaching institutions.

6. Church and State

→ Church and state have never been separated in Slovakia, although there have been a number of determined supporters of such a move, including the first Czechoslovak president, T. G. Masaryk (1850-1937). Even the socialist state supported the churches financially and assumed responsibility for paying the salaries of church workers as compensation for the nationalization of church property (state law 218, 1949). In this way, it gained control over the life of the churches and influenced the selection of church personnel. This authority of the state over the life of the churches was removed with the fall of the socialist regime (1989), when discrimination against Christians ceased and the churches gained access to public (state) services and institutions. Currently, religion classes are taught in the public schools.

In November 2000 the Roman Catholic Church signed an accord with Slovakia, establishing the church's legal status. On behalf of the churches of the ECCS, a similar treaty was signed by the government and by representatives of 11 churches and religious communities.

Bibliography: M. Čeplíková, *Štát, cirkvi a právo na Slovensku* (State, churches, and law in Slovakia) (Košice, 2005) • D. P. Daniel, "The Reformation and the Creation of National Intelligentsias in the Kingdom of Hungary," *The First Millennium of Hungary in Europe* (ed. K. Papp and J. Barta; Debrecen, 2002) 365-76 • G. Eyal, *The Origins of Postcommunist Elites: From Prague Spring to the Breakup of Czechoslovakia* (Minneapolis, 2003) • S. Fisher, *Political Change in Post-Communist Slovakia and Croatia: From Nationalist to Europeanist* (New York, 2006) • E. Harris, *Nationalism and Democratisation: Politics of Slovakia and Slovenia* (Aldershot, 2002) chaps. 1-4 • K. Henderson, *Slovakia: The Escape from Invisibility* (London, 2002) • S. J. Kirschbaum, *A History of Slovakia: The Struggle for Survival* (2d ed.; New York, 2005) • J. Kvačala, *Dejiny reformácie na Slovensku* (The history of the Reformation in Slovakia) (Liptovský Mikuláš, 1935) • P. Mulík, *Prehľad registrovaných cirkví a osobností náboženského života v Slovenskey republike* (An overview of the registered churches and figures of religious life in the Slovak Republic) (Bratislava, 1998).

Pavel Filipi and Ľubomír Batka

Slovenia

	1960	1980	2000
Population (1,000s):	1,580	1,832	1,914
Annual growth rate (%):	0.63	0.52	−0.20
Area: 20,256 sq. km. (7,821 sq. mi.)			

A.D. 2000

Population density: 94/sq. km. (245/sq. mi.)
Births / deaths: 0.95 / 1.15 per 100 population
Fertility rate: 1.30 per woman
Infant mortality rate: 7 per 1,000 live births
Life expectancy: 74.3 years (m: 70.3, f: 78.3)
Religious affiliation (%): Christians 92.1 (Roman Catholics 87.7, indigenous 1.8, Protestants 1.5, other Christians 1.0), nonreligious 5.2, atheists 2.6, other 0.1.

1. General Situation
2. Religious Situation
   2.1. Roman Catholic Church
   2.2. Other Religious Communities

1. General Situation

1.1. The independent state of Slovenia, established in 1991, is bordered by Italy, Austria, Hungary, and Croatia. Slovenes have lived in this part of Europe since the mid-sixth century, where they settled an area nearly twice the country's current size. In the mid-700s Bavarians and Franks established political rule over them. At this time Slovenes were also Christianized by Irish → missionaries, agents of the Franks, who brought them religion and the Latin alphabet. Thus the Slovenes' political and religious future was locked into a western European mode. When Charlemagne (768-814) established the Holy Roman Empire, Slovene lands were included, and they remained a part of various feudal domains for nearly a millennium thereafter.

Of the feudal rulers, Hapsburgs made the greatest impact on Slovene development. The family established a foothold in central Europe in 1282, expanding its realm over the centuries into a major political force that would last until 1918. Areas where Slovenes lived were considered part of the original accessions, or "hereditary lands," of the Hapsburgs. After 1477 the Hapsburg ruler was continually the Holy Roman emperor and therefore the most important Catholic ruler in Europe.

1.2. In the 16th century the Hapsburgs and the Slovenes, mostly peasant serfs, became embroiled in the political and religious struggles of the → Reformation. → Humanism, which was strong among the clergy in the Slovene lands, by 1525 introduced → Protestantism — essentially → Lutheranism — among religious reformers. Protestantism, except in some eastern Slovene lands, was eradicated in the following century by the Hapsburg Catholic ruler and counterreform religious institutions (→ Catholic Reform and Counterreformation). Slovene humanist reformers, however, made a lasting impact on their culture. They produced the first printed books in Slovene (until then the written language existed only in the Freising Fragments, religious MSS of the 10th cent.). In 1550 the religious reformer Primož Trubar (1508-86) published the first Slovene primer and a → catechism, followed by other religious books, 31 in all. By 1584 Jurij Dalmatin (ca. 1547-89), another reformer, had completed and published his Slovene translation of the Bible. Today's independent Slovenia, a largely Catholic country, pays tribute to these men who established the basis for a Slovene literary language, honoring them on Reformation Day, October 31, a national holiday.

The Hapsburg lands were named the Austrian Empire in the early 19th century, at a time when all national groups in that state were experiencing cultural awakening — Slovenes included. Intellectuals, many of them Catholic clergy, played key roles in furthering Slovene national goals. One was Bishop Anton Slomšek (1800-1862), who promoted the use of Slovene-language readers in elementary schools and also helped found a publishing house that survives to this day. By midcentury, cultural awareness led to political activity, and in 1848 Slovene leaders offered their first political program: union of Austria's Slovene lands and use of the national language in schools and administration. These goals were not met in that revolutionary time, but Austria in the later 1860s began to evolve politically toward representative rule. A parliament was established, and by 1906 all men had the vote. Slovene political parties were organized in the 1890s. There were three groups: Clericals, Liberals, and Social Democrats. The Clericals tended to be very pro-monarchy and Rome-oriented, the Liberals and Social Democrats much less so or not at all. This difference led to a clerical-anticlerical cleavage that was common to many European Catholic countries.

1.3. After World War I and Austria's dismemberment, Slovenes became part of a Yugoslav state, where they remained for 70 years. Between 1918 and 1941 the Kingdom of Serbs, Croats, and Slovenes (renamed Yugoslavia in 1929) included two-thirds of Europe's Slovenes. A few had been left in the postwar Austrian republic, some remained in Hungary, but nearly a third fell to Italy. For those who lived in Yugoslavia in the interwar years, there was the benefit of living among other southern Slavs, a goal some Slovenes had worked for, but there were the drawbacks of Serbian dominance. The state had a Serbian dynasty, a constitution that centralized power in the Serbian capital, Belgrade, a regime that favored Eastern Orthodoxy (→ Orthodox Christianity) and Serbian culture, and one incapable of organizing postwar economic recovery, much less economic advances. The worldwide depression of the 1930s and European fascists finished off royal Yugoslavia. The country was invaded in 1941 by the Germans, after which the state was divided among its neighbors, most of them allies of Germany or Italy.

1.4. The second Yugoslavia was established in 1945 by Communists headed by Tito (Josip Broz, 1892-1980), who had led the resistance to foreign occupiers. The Communists' Liberation Front defeated the invaders, but it also battled a Slovene Home Guard movement that emerged in the fall of 1943. The latter was supported by the Slovene Catholic Church leadership, which opposed Communism, railed against its own Christian Socialists who had joined Tito's movement, and ultimately collaborated with the enemy. (Slovenes, unlike many peoples in interwar Europe, did not have a native fascist movement.) The ideological war between clericals and anticlericals bitterly divided the Slovenes; the clerical losers went abroad. (Thousands of them, who were repatriated by the British forces from occupied southern Austria in 1945, were summarily executed upon their return.) Over the decades the clerical voice of opposition was sustained by the diaspora in Italy, Austria, the United States, South America, and Australia. Since 1991 it has established renewed political clout in independent Slovenia.

From 1945 to 1991 Yugoslavia remained under Communist rule. Initially, this relationship meant adhering to the Stalinist model of development: rapid industrialization, collectivization of agriculture, Communist Party rule, ideological conformity, and purging of class enemies. Churches came under attack, religious education was discontinued, and the university's theology faculty was abolished. But already in the mid-1950s Yugoslavia broke from the Soviet bloc and pursued its own road to → socialism, known as Titoism.

41

The Slovenes eventually experienced benefits from living in the Socialist Federal Republic of Yugoslavia. For the first time ever, they had their own republic, one of six in Yugoslavia. It was called Slovenia, and most Italian Slovene territory lost after 1918 was joined to it in peace settlements after 1945. As a separate entity with a separate language (Serbo-Croatian was used in most of the rest of Yugoslavia), Slovenes slowly found their way toward making the system work for them. In the 1960s a thaw allowed market economic innovations and opened the country to Western influences. The Slovenes, having a border with Italy and Austria, took advantage of liberalized border regulations. Slovenes worked and shopped regularly abroad, improved their living standard, and prospered economically, at least relative to the rest of Yugoslavia. Ideology, too, was modified, with the arts and the church benefiting. In 1966 an agreement was reached between Yugoslavia and the Vatican that allowed more religious activities; formal diplomatic relations between the two were reestablished in 1970. Briefly in the late 1960s Slovenes even had a reform government. It was followed by a return to Communist hard-liners in the 1970s, some of whom continued into the 1980s, well after the death of Tito in 1980, the war leader who had forged together the disparate Yugoslav state.

1.5. Slovenia's independence was achieved against a backdrop of momentous developments across Europe. In the late 1980s Communism collapsed in Eastern Europe, and the USSR let its satellites go. In the west 12 European states announced firm plans to create a European Union in 1992. In Yugoslavia new leaders emerged to fill the vacuum left by Tito's death; alas, the strongest were republican presidents who generated damaging interethnic tensions in their grab for power. This development pitted Slovenia, which favored greater autonomy, political pluralism, a capitalist economy, and strong ties with the West, against Serbia, where Great Serbism stood behind strong central-party rule and firm central (i.e., Serbian) control of the economy. On June 25, 1991, after five years of growing confrontations, Slovenia — together with Croatia, a neighboring Yugoslav republic — declared independence. This bold step precipitated a tragic war that did not end until late 1995.

The war, which began in Slovenia, lasted only ten days there before moving southward to Croatia. The European community brokered a truce in early July, and the Serb-led Yugoslav army pulled out of Slovenia by October. The new state thus turned to its reform agenda of enacting a democratic constitution (December 1991), holding new multiparty elections (1992), privatizing the economy (still in progress), and reinvigorating economic life in general. Internationally, Slovenia's independence was recognized by the European Union in January 1992; the Vatican offered recognition already in late 1991. Slovenes were soon members of the → United Nations and the Organization for Security and Cooperation in Europe (OSCE). They coveted membership in NATO and the European Union (EU), but it was not forthcoming until 2004. (None of the other former republics of Yugoslavia are yet members of either.) Since 1991 Slovenia has held four elections and has experienced six peaceful changes of government (four center-left and two center-right). Its economy, compared with that of other former Communist states, has excelled. In 2005 Slovenia held the presidency of the OSCE, and in 2008 Slovenia is scheduled to preside over the EU.

2. Religious Situation
2.1. *Roman Catholic Church*
The constitution of 1991 set forth the principle of separation of → church and state. Also, religious affiliation and practice were recognized as the equal right of all citizens. About 30 religious communities have registered in Slovenia, but by far the largest is the → Roman Catholic, with approximately 70 percent of the population, according to the 1991 census. The Catholic Church has become a powerful institution in independent Slovenia. Even in the 1980s, it had been gaining position under the leadership of liberal archbishop and metropolitan Alojzij Šuštar (1980-97). In 1987 Catholic → Mass was again celebrated publicly at Christmas, a sign that times were changing. The archbishop supported Slovenia's reformers who brought about independence in 1991.

Two major issues that have occupied Šuštar and his successors, France Rode (1997-2004) and Alojzij Uran (2004-), have been denationalization of church property and religious education. On the issue of returning church properties, the most obvious cases have been resolved, with church buildings and adjacent properties being awarded to the church. The disposition of vast estates, however — mostly forest land, some confiscated in the 18th century by the Hapsburgs — is still pending. The result will probably be a partial restitution of real estate, together with an award of income-bearing bonds.

As to religious education, the church has reestablished a Faculty of Theology at the University of Ljubljana, which on doctrinal matters defers to

Rome. Some private elementary and secondary Catholic schools have also been opened. The church's push, particularly under Archbishop Rode, to introduce religious instruction in all schools, has been rejected. Religion may be taught only as an elective subject and never as a matter of doctrinal teaching in public schools.

An agreement with the Vatican has set the parameters of church-state relations for Slovenia. Negotiations began in 1999, and although an accord was signed at the end of 2001, the government referred it to the constitutional court for review. After nearly two years and much popular debate, the court ruled that the accord was acceptable as long as the church observed Slovenia's sovereignty and the separation of church and state. The accord went into effect in January 2004.

2.2. *Other Religious Communities*

Of the remaining religious communities, the two largest are the Orthodox (about 46,000), and the Muslim (47,500; → Islam). The Orthodox are primarily Serbs; the Muslims, largely Bosnians and Kosovo Albanians — both from the former Yugoslavia. The Muslim community recently proposed building a → mosque in Ljubljana, Slovenia's capital. A referendum rejected the proposal; the constitutional court, however, ruled the vote unconstitutional for violating freedom of religious expression.

Slovenia also has about 16,000 Protestants of several denominations. The largest is the Evangelical Christian Church in Slovenia (14,700), whose strength is in eastern Slovenia; its antecedents go back to the 16th-century Reformation. Independent Slovenia's first president, Milan Kučan, was from an evangelical family.

Slovenia has never had many Jews. There were Jewish communities in medieval towns, but Hapsburg rulers expelled them during the Counter-Reformation. Currently, the Jewish population of Slovenia is only about 100.

Bibliography: J. BENDERLEY and E. KRAFT, *Independent Slovenia: Origins, Movements, Prospects* (New York, 1994) • J. Gow and C. CARMICHAEL, *Slovenia and the Slovenes: A Small State and the New Europe* (Bloomington, Ind., 2000) • L. PLUT-PREGELJ and C. ROGEL, *Historical Dictionary of Slovenia* (2d ed.; Lanham, Md., 2007) • S. P. RAMET, *Balkan Babel: The Disintegration of Yugoslavia from the Death of Tito to the Fall of Milosevic* (4th ed.; Boulder, Colo., 2002) esp. 81-99, "The Catholic Church" • C. ROGEL, *The Breakup of Yugoslavia and Its Aftermath* (Westport, Conn., 2004); eadem, *The Slovenes and Yugoslavism, 1890-1914* (New York, 1977).

CAROLE ROGEL

Social Education

1. Term and Theme
2. Historical Development
3. Fields of Work
4. As a Science

1. Term and Theme

The term "social education" is of German origin (*Sozialpädagogik,* used by K. Mager in 1844, and by F. Diesterweg in 1850). Similar words in other languages did not arise at the same time, but in almost all European countries there are similar fields of work using the same procedures. There are of course great differences in the various national conditions of work, in the contents of the education, in the means of delivery, and in the social and professional status of the educators. Thus we find the "resident social worker" in Great Britain; the *Erzieher* (educator) or *Sozialpädagoge* (social pedagogue) in Germany, Austria, and Switzerland; the *inrichtingswerker* (worker in a [social] institution) in Holland; the *éducateur spécialisé* in France and *éducateur social* in Belgium — all with differently emphasized functions. The similarities are great enough, however, to justify treating them together.

The difference in Germany and some other European countries between (educationally oriented) social education and (help-centered) "social work" is foreign to Anglo-Saxon countries, especially the United States. Insofar as the term "social work" has an integral function, there are convergences between the two fields. But in Germany, "social education" denotes a nuanced sphere of action (1) that in the social sector has the task, by means of material help and personally delivered services, of contributing to the security and control of one's life; (2) that in theory belongs to the sphere of → education (→ Pedagogy); and (3) that is a profession requiring a degree in the social sciences, in the area of social education.

2. Historical Development

The historical presuppositions for the work of social education were the same in all industrialized lands (→ Industrial Society). The industrial process and the related social changes had produced mass poverty and the very real threat of wider crises among the population. The problems diagnosed as neglect and as endangerment were answered by both a liberal socioeconomic system (→ Liberalism) and an authoritarian state system that exercised an element of punishment and control over divergent social and political groups. In tackling the comprehensive character of this social upheaval, conservative, re-formed, and revolutionary views were all in agreement in the 19th century.

There arose, not only a bewildering variety of social-educational practices, but also a double front (1) against the inhumane features of the industrial-capitalist system (→ Capitalism) and (2) against a one-sided and unrealistic tendency toward an individualistic education that would ignore social and political matters. Significant changes in the liberal view of economics, the state, and society brought an increasing development of social politics as a result of the union of a social-hygienic principle of prevention with a sociopolitical concept of protection.

As rules were set up concerning the care of young people and the protection of workers, decisive conditions were established between 1878 and 1928 for work in social education. The field took on its special quality in concrete relationship with social politics. This development fostered a change of function in social-educational practices that was favorable in principle but hard to realize in practice. The focus ceased to be a matter of punishment and control; instead, the issue was one of including a social sphere in public education. At first, social education was defined only in terms of what it was not (i.e., not the education provided by family, church, school, or job), or only as an education for those in need or in poverty; such understandings gave it a secondary status. Gradually, however, it became a primary system of education recognized by the → state and by → society. It thus assumed an infrastructural quality and ceased to apply only to adolescents.

With its recognition by the state and society, the state linked public education, apart from the → family and the → school, with a design for sociopolitical care in an all-embracing social sector. This change meant that social-educational action became increasingly a special vocation with its own training.

3. Fields of Work

The double function of social education in a social → democracy covers (1) prevention and the resolving of educational defects and other social handicaps and (2) the acceptance of the qualitatively new needs of society in social education. The work of social education is thus part of social politics and, increasingly, an element in a politics of culture and education that has no clear guidelines scholastically. It is a rightful possession of all citizens so far as material, social, and cultural resources are concerned and broadly aims to increase each person's security

and success in life. The changes and influences in the → environment (§1) and in real-life situations that it brings apply to all individuals and groups that are affected by (or are causing) the problems. A varied concept of need, risk, and education decides the modes of action, which are not primarily the giving of interventionist help point by point but the working toward social-critical → development (§2). The specific work of social education will be determined by the problem and the social and economic situation, using the multiple forms of education, development, and the giving of material aid, support, and counseling either in acute crises or in problems of transition at the personal level.

The fields of activity differ accordingly, and so does the field of social-educational theory as a whole. The specific work might consist of preschool education or education at home, training for a job, counseling for parents and teachers, the teaching of health, preparation for adulthood, work among children and young people, help for the elderly, social planning, help for adult groups, and so forth. Because it is decided more by conflicts than by individual defects, social education must know the attitudes of those it deals with. It reconstructs the life context of socially restricted people and therefore the institutionalized forms of its intervention. Its competence in both theory and practice does not focus on vicarious handling of the problem but on vicariously interpreting it. Interpretative work, other-centered understanding, and typological generalizing not only deepen knowledge of the problem but open up critical perspectives. In active concern to deal openly with social conflicts and to help against negative institutional forces, social education seeks to minimize its own work structurally to moments of suitable intervention, using a minimum of control.

The concern to introduce a support that is alien to the life of others and to make it effective in action is hardly a comprehensive description of the work of social education. The task of ethical reflection is also involved (→ Ethics). For one thing, it must be determined how far social-educational reflection has its basis in a practice founded on justice. A foundation also in social philosophy and ethics is needed (→ Social Ethics), which is more than specific vocational ethics. Furthermore, social-educational action needs critical interaction with subjective structures of meaning. Successful forms of accepting and dealing with reality should be developed in the context of a person's own biographical history. Any action that promotes the ability of individuals to lead their own lives has an ethical dimension.

4. As a Science

Social education sees itself as an integral component of the science of education. It thus must face two central pedagogical issues that arise: (1) the socially defined relations between generations, or the conditions that make individual development possible, and (2) the openness to, or ability for, fitting into present-day society. Fundamental pedagogical criteria are involved. Social education aims at processes of individual and collective → emancipation, at the promoting of competence for action, and at an individual's personal → autonomy and self-determination.

The connection of social education with general pedagogy does not mean that it ceases to be what has been called a pedagogy of the social state, for it primarily relates to the gaining or losing of economic, social, and cultural opportunities. It is a genuine form of pedagogy. Pedagogy loses its connection to social politics if it does not incorporate the focus peculiar to social education.

Social education is not a global concept but relates to specific social threats, to educational intervention, to social counseling, and to the offering of aid. It nevertheless can achieve a greater methodical self-limitation and greater relative independence of ordinary educational development, of therapy, and, in a different sense, of social work.

→ Socialization

Bibliography: G. Albrecht and H.-U. Otto, eds., *Social Prevention and the Social Sciences* (Berlin, 1991) • C. Cannan and C. Warren, eds., *Social Action with Children and Families: A Community Development Approach to Child and Family Welfare* (London, 1997) • C. B. Germain and A. Gitterman, *The Life Model of Social Work Practice* (2d ed.; New York, 1996) • W. Lorenz, *Social Work in a Changing Europe* (London, 1994) • L. Lowy, *Sozialarbeit/Sozialpädagogik als Wissenschaft im angloamerikanischen und deutschsprachigen Raum* (Freiburg, 1983) • K. Mollenhauer, *Einführung in die Sozialpädagogik. Probleme und Begriffe der Jugendhilfe* (Weinheim, 2001) • *The Social Work Reference Library* (electronic resource; Washington, D.C., 1997) • H. Sunker and H.-U. Otto, eds., *Education and Fascism: Political Identity and Social Education in Nazi Germany* (London, 1997) • K. Woodroofe, *From Charity to Social Work in England and the United States* (London, 1974) • C. Woyshner, J. Watras, and M. S. Crocco, eds., *Social Education in the Twentieth Century: Curriculum and Context for Citizenship* (New York, 2004).

Wolf-Eckart Failing

Social Encyclicals

1. The Roman Catholic social movement developed with the industrialization of Europe. Leo XIII (1878-1903) gave the movement a dogmatic basis in 1891 in the first of the social encyclicals, *Rerum novarum (RN)*. Henceforth, social teaching presented itself as a continuous developing and updating of *RN*, especially on the occasion of its decennial anniversaries (→ Encyclicals; Social Ethics). Leo sharply criticized revolutionary → socialism (→ Marxism) but also supported a reforming policy over against romantic and conservative Christian socialism, supported a reforming policy that would curb the abuses of → capitalism by fair wages, representation in (Catholic) worker associations, and state intervention.

RN had only the labor question in view, but Pius XI (1922-39) in *Quadragesimo anno* (*QA*, 1931) dealt with "the reconstruction of the social order" (title). He advocated a vertical organization of associations or cooperatives of the workers in a given field (including employers and employees; *QA* 87) as a third way between capitalism and the class conflict (→ Class and Social Stratum) and decreed that socialism, which "affirms that human association has been instituted for the sake of material advantage alone" (118), absolutely "cannot be reconciled with the teachings of the Catholic Church" (117; → Marxism and Christianity)

In his radio messages → Pius XII (1939-58) followed an abstract deduction by → natural law. John XXIII (1958-63), though, had a more open sociological analysis that made discussion of things rather than texts possible. In *Mater et magistra* (1961) he shifted the accent from the more liberal → subsidiarity of *QA* to a more social and worldwide → solidarity. Judgment on socialism is deferred, and in *Pacem in terris* (1963) he addressed "all men of good will," told Roman Catholics cautiously to work together with other political and social movements, and accepted the tradition of human and civil → rights.

In his encyclical *Populorum progressio* (1967), Paul VI (1963-78) challenged the market ideology of industrial countries (→ Economy). He acknowledged unjust worldwide development, attacked capitalism, rejected the inviolability of private → property, and failed to condemn in principle revolutionary violence (→ Force, Violence, Nonviolence; Industrial Society; Revolution; Third World).

In *Laborem exercens* (1981) John Paul II (1978-2005), on the basis of a religious → anthropology of human → work, urged more generally, "We must emphasize and give prominence to the primacy of man in the production process, *the primacy of man over things*" (12). In *Sollicitudo rei socialis* (1987) he distinguished between true, personal development and mechanistic → progress. *Centesimus annus* (*CA*, 1991), on the occasion of the 100th anniversary of *RN*, warns against a capitalism that shares a materialistic view of humanity with the socialism that broke apart in 1989 (→ Materialism) and that does not ethically integrate economic freedom. Instead, *CA* affirms a capitalist economic system that relies upon creative responsibility on the part of enterprises, the market, and private property within the boundaries of the common good.

2. By a right understanding of true humanity and its destiny, achieved by social philosophy and theology, the social teaching of the → Roman Catholic Church tries to show us the true way to the structuring of human life together in a new social order that will conform to objective and generally acceptable criteria (*Guidelines,* 6). Under Paul VI, in the apostolic letter *Octogesima adveniens* (1971), social doctrine ceases to be a deductive doctrine that applies abstract principles to situations and teaches models to → society, becoming instead social reflection that accepts the situation itself as the "theological place" of knowledge.

John Paul II expresses again the universal character of this doctrine as the nexus of "leading principles," "criteria of judgment," and "laws of right conduct" in place of the idea, common in → liberation theology, of theory as deriving from praxis. In the face of the postmodern declaration of the death of man (→ Modernity; Postmodernity), he sets the principle of → revelation: "The Church's *social teaching* is itself a valid *instrument of evangelization.* As such, it proclaims God and his mystery of salvation in Christ to every human being, and for that very reason reveals man to himself" (*CA* 54). With the claim to possess both "the Christian view of the human person" and "a correct picture of society" (13), there goes hand in hand an organic view of social life that is free of conflict (*Guidelines,* 39) and an antimodernistic insistence on "the essential bond between human freedom and truth" (*CA* 4).

→ Dependence; Economics Ethics

Bibliography: C. E. CURRAN, *Catholic Social Teaching, 1891-Present: A Historical, Theological, and Ethical Analysis* (Washington, D.C., 2002) • *Guidelines for the Study and Teaching of the Church's Social Doctrine in the Formation of Priests* (Rome, Congregation for Catholic Education, 1988) • J. HOLLAND, *Modern Cath-*

olic Social Teaching: The Popes Confront the Industrial Age, 1740-1958 (New York, 2003) • R. W. ROUSSEAU, *Human Dignity and the Common Good: The Great Papal Social Encyclicals from Leo XIII to John Paul II* (Westport, Conn., 2002).

WALTER SCHÖPSDAU

Social Ethics

1. General

1.1. *Term*

Though the term "social ethics" occurred in the 19th century, development of this field as a theological discipline took place only in the 20th century. In ethics a distinction is usually made between individual and social ethics (→ Ethics 7.1.2). But the distinction should not become separation, for individual ethics, having to do with the conduct of individuals in their own fields of activity and the pertinent attitudes, → virtues, and → duties involved, cannot be divorced from the related social, institutional, and structural conditions (→ Society 4). Individual actions cannot be separated from their effect on political and social conditions, and social patterns of life deeply shape individual morality, so that all ethics is social ethics (E. Wolf). Similarly, we cannot divorce reflection on social and political actions from the individual subjects of action (→ Action Theory 3).

"Social ethics" as the place of scholarly discourse on moral action must be distinguished from "social doctrine." The latter describes a → consensus reached on moral actions that can be seen as binding to a certain degree. From a Roman Catholic perspective the guarantee of this binding quality lies in the → teaching office of the → hierarchy, but from a Protestant perspective it can rest only on a process of communication, as comprehensive as possible, by the → church on a biblical basis. While the emphases differ, in both cases tradition and Scripture play a key role. Because of the difficulty in formulating the content of the consensus, the term "social doctrine" is seldom used in Protestantism.

1.2. *Task*

The task of social ethics may be described in terms of four central functions. The *hermeneutic function* consists in helping to understand the problems of modern → society (→ Individualism; Pluralism 1; Secularism; Science and Theology; Technology). In view of the increasingly complex problems, social ethics points out the various dimensions of the problems with the help of the available empirical data provided by the social sciences. Considering the short-term and long-term consequences and the ultimate ends toward which it aims, this function describes the conflicts in goals and the possible alternative decisions.

The *directing function* of social ethics is to aim at decision between different alternatives. On the basis of → reason, → experience, and → tradition, including the biblical data, it develops formal rules and principles that can shape just, loving, and re-

sponsible action (→ Responsibility) in the given circumstances.

In reflecting on this action, social ethics also has a *public function.* The findings of social ethics are not an end in themselves but serve to further public discourse in the church and society on the conditions of a meaningful and fulfilling social life (→ Church and State; Politics). Social ethics lives in a mutual exchange between political and social experience in → everyday life on one hand and academic reflection on the other.

Within academic reflection it has an *interdisciplinary function,* taking up empirical → social sciences into the construction of philosophical or theological theories. Similarly, on the basis of philosophical or theological standards, it reminds the sciences of their responsibility for the consequences of their research.

1.3. *Basis*

Roman Catholic and Protestant churches have found different bases for social ethics. Roman Catholic → natural law (§5), which goes back to Thomas Aquinas (ca. 1225-74; → Thomism), begins with certain transcendental ethical principles that apply to all people. Its ethics, then, is strongly influenced by moral philosophical considerations (→ Moral Theology).

The Protestant *sola Scriptura* (→ Reformation Principles) has traditionally given the biblical and theological element a greater role in the ethical tradition. Yet on the Protestant side the role of biblical contents for material ethical statements has always been contested. Reasons from natural law or a theology of creation (W. Elert, P. Althaus, H. Thielicke), with a common appeal to the → two-kingdoms theology of Martin → Luther, stand over against a Christological basis that lays claim to the kingship of Christ (→ Kingdom of God 3.2) and that stresses the fundamental significance of biblical contents, even for the political and social sphere (K. → Barth and E. Wolf, as do A. Kuyper and E. Brunner, who also stress a creational theology).

In the latter part of the 20th century, both within Protestant ethics and among the denominations, there has been a certain convergence on the basis that the links between a grounding of ethics in reason and in the Bible need not be too far apart. Independently of whether we stress the importance of biblical impulses for rational reflection (W. Huber, C. Frey, R. → Niebuhr, P. Ramsey) or an expansion of social-ethical knowledge by biblical contents (M. Honecker, P. Lehmann), in Protestant social ethics there is a broad consensus on the need to communicate ethical concerns as far as possible outside the limits of the Christian faith (J. L. Adams, M. Stackhouse, W. Schweiker). This position leads to a convergence with many portions of Roman Catholic social ethics, which, in critical rejection of the assumed privilege of the teaching office, offers an "autonomous morality" (A. Auer) or a universalistic "theonomous" morality that is intelligible to all people.

1.4. Development

The economic and social upheavals in Europe in the 18th and 19th centuries (→ Modern Period) raised the basic question that led to the development of a theory of social ethics: How can social and governmental → institutions be so shaped that they can stand up to scrutiny by ethical standards?

1.4.1. Roman Catholic

In the 20th century, on the basis of the papal → social encyclicals, Roman Catholic social doctrine has attempted to describe a responsible order of → state and society in terms of Christian ethics, and in particular has taken into view the increasing significance of the → economy. The encyclicals *Rerum novarum* (1891) of Leo XIII (1878-1903) and *Quadragesimo anno* (1931) of Pius XI (1922-39) linked their criticism of → socialism and liberal → capitalism primarily with antimodernistic motifs (→ Modernism), but new impulses came with John XXIII (1958-63) that plainly influenced Roman Catholic social doctrine. His *Mater et Magistra* (1961) and *Pacem in terris* (1963), influenced by French social Catholicism (P. Bigo, P. Pavan, M. D. Chenu, L. J. Lebret; → Marxism and Christianity 2.1), opened the door to the challenges of modern society (→ Catholicism [Roman] 1.2.3). This opening may be seen in the clearer perception of the worldwide scope of the social problem, in the adoption of the idea of political and social human → rights, and in the linking of justice and → peace as related problems. The style of argument runs from neoscholastic thinking about natural rights (→ Neoscholasticism) to the adoption of the findings of the social sciences.

On this basis two pairs of concepts developed that in different ways constituted the system of coordinates of Roman Catholic social ethics. The *principle of human dignity* and the *principle of common good* both form the anthropological foundation. The human character as in the image of God (→ Anthropology 3.4) constitutes the unchangeable and inviolable dignity of the human person (→ Human Dignity), which excludes all forms of collectivism and → totalitarianism. Personal human existence, however, is reliant on community. Our social character (→ Society 3-4) is bound up with consid-

erations that are both philosophical (the human being as *zōon politikon*) and theological (as member of the → people of God). It cannot be reconciled with → individualism, liberal capitalism, or modern forms of → hedonism.

The principles of → subsidiarity and → solidarity are the theoretical cornerstones in moving from the principles of both person and community to social-structural questions. An essential principle in interpreting them is their complementarity (F. Furger). The *subsidiarity principle* appeared first in *Quadragesimo anno,* deriving from G. Gundlach, although its roots were in ecclesiological debates. It limits the action of institutional governing bodies to what is necessary for the well-being of the whole. Where possible, corresponding tasks should be left to smaller and relatively independent forms of social organization. The *solidarity principle* was first set forth in *Mater et Magistra.* It gives basic responsibility to society, and especially to its weakest members, that all political and social decisions should be measured by this standard. It forbids the interpretation of the subsidiarity principle that would disadvantage the weak. This approach parallels the Protestant adoption of certain themes from J. Rawls in American Protestant ethics (R. W. Lovin, P. Williams).

Roman Catholic social ethics worked out the consequences of these four basic principles for the economy (→ Economic Ethics). Approaches that especially stress the precedence of labor over capital postulated in *Laborem exercens* (1981) and that gain an important stimulus from conversations with labor unions (O. von Nell-Breuning, F. Hengsbach) go along with the guaranteeing of private property (L. Roos, A. Rauscher, D. Hollenbach; → Property 4.1). Common everywhere is a stress on the need to link the efficiency of the marketplace with social responsibility.

Newer approaches of Catholic social ethics increasingly move beyond what is felt to be a static Catholic social doctrine (see F. Hengsbach, B. Emunds, and M. Möhring-Hesse). There is interdisciplinary dialogue with the social sciences (W. Dreier; → Practical Theology 3.3.2) that stresses the adoption of concepts in discourse theory (H.-J. Höhn; → Ethics 1.4), a politically liberating dimension of theology (J. B. Metz), narrative orientation to ethical models (D. Mieth), reflection on the practice of → social movements (F. Hengsbach, H. Büchele), and the acknowledgment of the gender perspective (M. Heimbach-Steins).

1.4.2. Eastern Orthodox

In the Eastern → Orthodox Church there has been

little development of social ethics. The reasons lie in the theological and ecclesiastical tradition and also in the historical and social fields. The subjection of → Christology to pneumatology (→ Holy Spirit), the related mystical tradition in Orthodox theology (→ Orthodox Christianity 3), and the strong influence of → monasticism all limited the grounds on which, in both the church and theology, reflection on Christian responsibility for the world could be worked out in social ethics. Most of the Orthodox churches, too, have lacked the possibility of working in a democratic framework. They have thus had little chance of developing ethical theory in a critical balance of state and society.

Impulses from the ecumenical movement, especially in the conciliar process for justice, peace, and the integrity of creation (→ Conciliarity 3; Modern Church History 1.4.4), along with the collapse of states in eastern Europe, have brought about promising signs. The new work shows what a rich potentiality the Orthodox tradition has for theorizing in this area. In a Trinitarian framework Christology is made fruitful for ethical reflection on institutions and structures (S. Harakas).

1.4.3. *Protestant*

In the Protestant sphere social ethics developed as a theological discipline in the middle of the 20th century. A forerunner was E. → Troeltsch (1865-1923), who in debate with M. → Weber (1864-1920) opened up for theology a scholarly access to the secularized modern world (→ Modernity 4.3). Similar predecessors were the religious socialists (C. Blumhardt, L. Ragaz, P. → Tillich; → Religious Socialism) and those in the American → Social Gospel tradition (W. → Rauschenbusch, W. Gladden, W. Mueller, P. Wogaman), who, unlike the champions of the Lutheran doctrine of orders (see 1.3), used the Christian faith as the basis both of the need to change and of the changeability of structures in state and society.

A fully developed social ethics in Europe, unlike in the United States, came only with the new approaches of the ecumenical movement after World War II. On the basis of the discussion by J. H. Oldham (1874-1969) of the → middle axioms, the → World Council of Churches at its First Assembly, at Amsterdam in 1948, developed the concept of the responsible society, which has a goal of social justice and a comprehensive democratization of society (→ Democracy 3). Driven by the ecumenical theorizing, E. Wolf (1902-71) applied theological reflection to the problem of institutions and specially emphasized their changeability. H.-D. Wendland (1900-1992) then developed a Christian → humanism that

had in view real humanity in the modern world, interpreted by social-scientific methods and understood in the light of the coming → kingdom of God; on this basis he described the tasks of the "social → diakonia" of the church.

At the World Conference on Church and Society, in Geneva in 1966 (→ Ethics 7.4), modern social and technological revolutions were discussed, with a great public echo in the churches. The question of the right way of dealing with modern challenges is basic for social theory. With different accents, two approaches are prominent. The first lays special stress on modern life, using as a starting point the → freedom of the individual person (→ Self) in its theological roots. The emphasis thus falls on the chances and opportunities of modernity (T. Rendtorff). The other stresses the ambivalence of modern life and pleads for a critical approach to the crises of the modern world in terms of creative discipleship (H. E. Tödt). The theological axis is an understanding of "communicative freedom" that assumes an equal dignity of sociality and individuality (W. Huber).

1.4.4. *European Churches and Social Responsibility*

The memoranda *(Denkschriften)* of the Evangelical Church in Germany serve as a means to communicate social-ethical theory in the public realm. Using both technical competence and theological reflection on central social themes, they deal, for example, with the ethics of peace (1981, 1994, 2001), the social aspects of the European process of unity (1991), the social and ecological reform of market economies (1991), social justice and solidarity in German society (1997), the ethical problems of modern biotechnologies (2002), or poverty (2006).

Across Europe the conciliar process for justice, peace, and the integrity of creation in the 1980s has produced important impulses for ethical discussion in both church and nonchurch circles (e.g., in 1989 at the European assembly at Basel). An interesting note has been the high degree of unity on these issues among Roman Catholic, Protestant, and Orthodox ethical thinkers.

In the new millennium questions of bioethics and a just reorientation of globalization have been among the most intensively discussed themes in the European churches. The issue of social justice has gained a special relevance, since numerous eastern European countries with low wage levels have been included in the common European market, putting the high social standards of western European countries under increasing pressure. Recent social ethics tries to find answers to these issues in a dialogue between Catholic, Protestant, and Orthodox traditions (I. Gabriel, A. Papaderos, and U. Körtner).

In the search for a tenable basis within Christian traditions in dialogue with other traditions, human and civil → rights are of central significance. There may be controversies on the way of describing political and social rights and debate about the plausibility of cultural rights, but the rights issue is the starting point of basic ethical and legal consensus beyond natural and cultural frontiers.

1.5. Themes

1.5.1. Justice

Economic ethics is concerned with the socioethical implications of economic justice. In contrast to continuous Roman Catholic discussions in social ethics (see 1.4.1), Protestant ethics, apart from G. Wünsch's *Evangelische Wirtschaftsethik* (Protestant economic ethics, 1927), long neglected this field. But new efforts began in the 1980s, thanks to A. Rich's basic work (1984-90). With the globalization of the economy and increasingly global competition, the question of social justice and a fair distribution of the increasing material wealth is posed all the more urgently.

On the basis of biblical perspectives and philosophical theory (J. Rawls), new concepts of justice must be developed on the basis of the option for the poor (→ Poverty). In both national and international economic politics (→ Development 1; Third World), measures must be taken to balance the distribution of resources but also to promote a stronger participation of the weak in the economic process. Enterprises themselves are true subjects of ethical responsibility. An ethics of enterprises has therefore been developed as a distinct field in ethics (C. McCoy, P. Ulrich, K. Homann; for recent German literature, see E. Stübinger).

1.5.2. Globalization

The debate on justice in social ethics must be made fruitful for the concrete issues connected with globalization. The common ground of the biblical option for the poor has not yet led to a common view of globalization. While many churches of the North see both opportunities and risks in the process of economic globalization and argue for shaping globalization responsibly (Evangelical Church in Germany, 2001), many churches of the South are fundamentally critical of globalization. The so-called AGAPE Document ("*A*lternative *G*lobalization *A*ddressing *P*eoples and *E*arth"), which was the basis of the discussion of globalization at the Ninth Assembly of the World Council of Churches, in Porto Alegre, Brazil, in 2006, sees in "neoliberal globalization" the reason for increasing poverty in the world.

Other Christian voices see globalization under certain circumstances as a possible instrument for overcoming poverty (M. Stackhouse and P. Paris, 2000). Whatever one's position, the dispute in social ethics on globalization must be grounded in an appropriate linkage between the option for the poor and a sober look at economic data and theory.

1.5.3. Peace

Until the late 1980s discussions of peace (→ Peace 1.3, 2.3; Peace Movements) were based on the East-West confrontation and the arms race. The churches had come to an increasing consensus on the need to do away with → weapons of mass destruction and on the impossibility of using war as a means of resolving → conflicts (§2). The conditions of modern war with its mass destructive consequences resulted in a wide agreement between the different social-ethical positions, ranging from a pacifist position of not using → force in principle to the position that advocates the traditional doctrine of a just war (→ War 4.3). Under the conditions of nuclear deterrence both positions opted for the nonuse of military force (→ Pacifism).

The failure of diplomacy in resolving new regional conflicts after the end of the East-West system of nuclear deterrence has again raised the question whether, in a last resort, the use of force not only might be tenable in situations of extreme injustice from a Christian standpoint, but might even be demanded. In any case, political mechanisms for avoiding conflict and nonmilitary methods of sanctions should be strengthened and further developed. In this field the → United Nations has a vital role. In ecumenical agreement on the ethics of peace there is an indissoluble connection between justice and peace. It is thus part of the peace task of the church to constantly stress the injustice of the global economic system as a threat to peace.

1.5.4. Integrity of Creation

Increasing destruction of the basis of life has given increased significance to ecological questions in social ethics (→ Ecology; Environment). While dealing with the role of Christianity in shaping cultural values that favored the destruction of nature, Christian ethics has also begun to reflect on the limits of legitimate intrusion into → nature by civilization. A key position in this regard is the question of our relation to the nonhuman world (→ Creation 4). We may adopt a clearly anthropocentric view, according to which nature is solely for our human use. Or we may ascribe to nature a value of its own, on the basis of which it is not under our control and serves its own purpose. In terms of the environmental consequences there is wide-ranging agreement in both views. Both demand an ecological reorientation of the economy. A fundamental aspect of this reorientation is an ecological restructuring of the internal cost system of the economy, for example, by increasing the cost of → energy consumption.

In global measures to protect the environment, we cannot ignore the difference between North and South or the related need of the poor countries to catch up. In emphasizing the connection between justice and the integrity of creation, the churches have a special role. Along with global pleas for the alteration of economic and political strategies, they must argue for a reorientation of civilization in the direction of a more conscious approach to material → consumption and of the restoration of a basic respect for life.

1.5.5. Medical Ethics

More recently, → medical ethics has developed as a social-ethical field of its own. Technical progress in human medicine has raised problems in ethics that go far beyond the realm of individual decision. Especially, new possibilities in connecting genetic engineering and modern → reproduction technologies have led to increased international ethical discussion. Should it be allowed to genetically screen in-vitro-fertilized embryos in order to select them according to their genetic quality (preimplantation genetic diagnosis)? Should embryos be used to gain embryonic stem cells for research in order to develop new medical therapies? Should embryos be cloned to gain such stem cells with a matching genetic code (therapeutic, or research, cloning; → Genetic Counseling)? Answers to these questions depend to a large degree on whether embryos in their first weeks of existence are seen as developing human beings with full human dignity or whether they are seen only as potential human life, only gradually developing into human beings with dignity.

Bioethical problems at the end of life include the use of life-prolonging modern intensive medicine, the question of indirect, passive, or active → euthanasia, and the question of the determination of death in organ givers. The social-ethical relevance is increased by the mix of economic and research interest and humanitarian motives, sometimes hard to distinguish. In interdisciplinary conversation the ethical dimensions of research and the use of newer medical technologies must be made conscious. Along with legal matters, a new definition of the ethos of medicine is needed, along the lines of a culture of self-limitation. No matter where one sees the exact beginning of human life and its status as a human person, social ethics must attempt to sharpen the sense of the dignity of human life that, for

Christian faith, is grounded in the divine likeness but, at the same time, is plausible for all people of goodwill.

Bibliography: On 1.3 (Basis): W. H. LAZARETH, *Christians in Society: Luther, the Bible, and Social Ethics* (Minneapolis, 2001) • R. NIEBUHR, *Moral Man and Immoral Society: A Study in Ethics and Politics* (New York, 1949) • W. SCHWEIKER, *Theological Ethics and Global Dynamics: In the Time of Many Worlds* (Malden, Mass., 2004) • W. SCHWEIKER and C. T. MATHEWES, eds., *Having: Property and Possession in Religious and Social Life* (Grand Rapids, 2004) • M. L. STACKHOUSE, *Christian Social Ethics in a Global Era* (Nashville, 1995).

On 1.4 (Development): A. J. VAN DER BENT, *Commitment to God's World: A Concise Critical Survey of Ecumenical Social Thought* (Geneva, 1995) • EVANGELICAL CHURCH IN GERMANY, *For a Future Founded on Solidarity and Justice: A Statement of the Evangelical Church in Germany and the German Bishops' Conference on the Economic and Social Situation in Germany* (Hannover, 1997) • I. GABRIEL, A. PAPADEROS, and U. KÖRTNER, *Perspektiven ökumenischer Sozialethik. Der Auftrag der Kirchen im größeren Europa* (Mainz, 2005) • D. HOLLENBACH, , *Justice, Peace, and Human Rights: American Catholic Social Ethics in a Pluralistic World* (New York, 1988) • W. HUBER, *Violence: The Unrelenting Assault on Human Dignity* (Minneapolis, 1996) • D. P. NILES, ed., *Between the Flood and the Rainbow: Interpreting the Conciliar Process of Mutual Commitment (Covenant) to Justice, Peace, and the Integrity of Creation* (Geneva, 1992) • W. RAUSCHENBUSCH, *A Theology for the Social Gospel* (Louisville, Ky., 1997; orig. pub., 1918) • T. RENDTORFF, *Ethics* (vol. 1, Philadelphia, 1986; vol. 2, Minneapolis, 1989) • U. SCHMITTHENNER, *Contributions of Churches and Civil Society to Justice, Peace, and the Integrity of Creation* (Frankfurt, 1999).

On 1.5 (Themes): U. DUCHROW and F. J. HINKELAMMERT, *Property for People, Not for Profit: Alternatives to the Global Tyranny of Capital* (London, 2004) • D. FORRESTER, *Christian Justice and Public Policy* (Cambridge, 1997) • D. HALLMAN, *Ecotheology: Voices from South and North* (Geneva, 1994) • S. HAUERWAS, *A Better Hope: Resources for a Church Confronting Capitalism, Democracy, and Postmodernity* (Grand Rapids, 2000) • L. L. RASMUSSEN, *Earth Community, Earth Ethics* (Geneva, 1996) • A. RICH, *Wirtschaftsethik* (2 vols.; Gütersloh, 1984-90) • M. L. STACKHOUSE, with P. J. PARIS, eds., *God and Globalization,* vol. 1, *Religion and the Powers of the Common Life* (Harrisburg, Pa., 2000) • M. L. STACKHOUSE, with D. S. BROWNING, eds., *God and Globalization,* vol. 2, *The Spirit and the Modern Authorities* (Harrisburg, Pa., 2001) • M. L. STACKHOUSE, with D. B. OBENCHAIN, eds., *God and Globalization*, vol. 3, *Christ and the Dominions of Civilization* (Harrisburg, Pa., 2002) • W. STORRAR and A. MORTON, eds., *Public Theology for the Twenty-first Century* (London, 2004) • E. STÜBINGER, "Zu neueren Publikationen aus dem Bereich der Wirtschaftsethik," *ZEE* 49 (2005) 284-313 • WORLD COUNCIL OF CHURCHES, *Science, Faith, and New Technologies: Transforming Life*, vol. 2, *Genetics, Agriculture, and Human Life* (Geneva, 2005).

HEINRICH BEDFORD-STROHM

2. North America

2.1. *Development and Methodology*

Christian social ethics in the United States developed at the beginning of the 20th century with the rise of the → Social Gospel movement, which criticized the individualistic → piety of the mainstream Protestant churches. In light of the growing urban poverty associated with the industrial revolution, Walter → Rauschenbusch (1861-1918) and others called for the churches to recognize that the → kingdom of God calls for social change and justice in our world. Although the Social Gospel has been criticized for being naive, too utopian, and not conscious enough of human sinfulness, the movement has had important and lasting ramifications for the discipline of Christian social ethics and for the life of the churches in the United States and Canada.

The two world wars and the intervening economic depression occasioned the development of Christian realism, especially the work of Reinhold → Niebuhr (1892-1971). Reacting to the optimism of secular and religious → liberalism, Niebuhr insisted that we must recognize the presence of → sin and → conflict in the world, the inability to apply → love directly to the social situation, and the need for → power to counterbalance existing power structures.

Although European theologians had a great influence on American theology in general, American Protestant social ethics tended to be more homegrown. On the Roman Catholic scene, the influence of papal teaching had a very significant influence on the development of a natural-law tradition of social justice (see 1.4), as illustrated before 1950 in the writings of John A. Ryan (1869-1945). Ryan advocated a living wage, the need for labor unions, and the role of the government as intervening for the sake of social justice. Before 1960, however, there was little or no ecumenical dialogue and exchange.

The Niebuhrian influence was seen throughout the cold war and continues today in different forms, including a small number of neoconservatives (e.g., M. Novak; → Conservatism 2.1; Modern Church History 2.6.3; North American Theology 7.1). The majority of Christian ethicists in the United States have in general adopted a method employing Scripture, → tradition, → reason, and → experience and have often criticized aspects of American life, especially in the areas of → race, → poverty, and → war (→ Pacifism; Peace). Significant methodological developments have recently occurred. Discussions continue about the sources of Christian → ethics (§§3-4, 6-7) and the proper use of the Scriptures, the sciences, and social analysis (→ Sociology). In the 1960s P. Lehmann's koinonia ethics rated context (→ Contextual Theology) more highly than ethical principles (see Joseph Fletcher's situation ethics), but P. Ramsey (1913-88) employed a deontological method insisting on some absolute norms. Black power (J. Cone; → Black Theology) and feminist, womanist, and mujerista ethics (B. W. Harrison; → Feminist Theology) not only dealt with the social evils of racism and patriarchy but have introduced a praxis-oriented and liberationist methodology for dealing with all of Christian social ethics (→ Liberation Theology). Ecofeminism, for example, sees domination and hierarchical ordering as the reason for our exploitation of the earth and its resources (→ Ecology; Organization).

Contemporary Christian social ethics is very much in dialogue with philosophical developments (→ Analytic Ethics; Analytic Philosophy; Process Philosophy). Many are conscious today of the role of historicity and the greater relativity (→ Relativism) involved in Christian ethics. Debates rage about foundationalism — the position that involves a commitment to certain basic beliefs or principles, from which all other justification derives. Some philosophers go further to maintain that moral → identity is tradition-constituted, and some Christian theologians in this perspective emphasize the distinctiveness of the Christian story and its unique application to the Christian community but not directly to those outside the community (S. Hauerwas). Many of these philosophical developments and the liberationist approaches mentioned above challenge the liberal acceptance of human → reason that can develop universally agreed-upon → norms and structures. Most Christian social ethicists, however, cannot accept the postmodern denial of any universal values or norms such as human → rights. Likewise today communitarians, both philosophical and theological, strongly disagree with individualistic → liberalism (e.g., R. Bellah).

The ecumenical aspect of Christian ethics has been growing. Especially since the 1960s, Protestant and Roman Catholic ethicists have been in regular dialogue with one another and have learned from each other, for example, in the discussion of → natural law (J. C. Murray). A broader ecumenism is occurring in the discussion about comparative religious ethics (→ Religion 2; Theology of Religions). In this connection, an influx of new evangelical voices from Christian colleges and seminaries has reintroduced basic concerns for biblically and theologically based ethics, including concerns for → public theology.

2.2. *Society of Christian Ethics*
The growth of the discipline of Christian social ethics is best illustrated in the life of the Society of Christian Ethics (founded 1959), the professional organization of the discipline that in 2005 had 950 members, primarily from the United States, Canada, and Europe. The original members taught in theology schools, but by 1983 more members taught in colleges and universities — a trend that has continued to grow. The discipline is thus related to both the church and the academy, but the academic aspects of the discipline (e.g., publication) have become more prominent with the shift to the college and university setting. The original founding members were white, male Protestants. Roman Catholics started joining the society in 1963 and now form a strong contingent within the group. Blacks also became prominent in the life of the society in the 1960s and have continued to play a significant role. The growing presence of women began in the 1970s and is continuing at a rapid pace. Also, the Society of Jewish Ethics has been formed, which now meets jointly with the Society of Christian Ethics.

2.3. *Issues*
The agenda or particular issues discussed in Christian social ethics have been set by the important events of the times. In the 1950s and early 1960s racial discrimination against blacks was a most significant issue that was generally strongly condemned by ethicists and the mainstream churches. The later approach of black theology and of black power proved to be more controversial.

The most controversial issue in the late 1960s and early 1970s concerned the United States' involvement in Viet Nam. Most Christian ethicists appealed to just-war principles (→ War 4.3), many condemning the U.S. involvement (J. C. Bennett). A strong pacifist position also came to the fore (J. H. Yoder). Many Christian social ethicists raised critical questions about the cold war and U.S. involvement in other countries, but many defended the need for humanitarian intervention. In addition to the pacifist and just-war approaches, G. Stassen and others have proposed just-peacemaking — an ethic that articulates specific alternatives to war.

In the 1970s great interest developed in bioethics because of the medical advances of the time (→ Ethics 1.5; Medical Ethics). Debate about health care and its proper distribution, → abortion, dying, and → euthanasia continue to dominate and divide both ethicists and individual churches. The growing feminist movement, both in general and in Christian social ethics in particular, has challenged the patriarchal and dominating structures present both in the church and in the world (→ Sexism). Furthermore, debates about → homosexuality not only have divided church bodies but have prompted vigorous debate among ethicists.

Christian ethicists have responded in various ways to the charge first raised in the late 1960s that the divine command to subdue the earth has contributed to many of our ecological problems (→ Ecology). Others have seen it as a call to develop a more responsible → technology. International ethics has discussed the world political scene, with emphasis on the cold war, deterrence, democratic structures, the breakup of the Soviet Union, the growing gap between the rich and the poor nations of the world (→ Development 1.2; Third World), human rights, and problems in eastern Europe and the former Soviet Union. More recently, the debates about the Middle East, → "terrorism," the Iraq War, and Iranian nuclear capabilities have captured much attention.

Domestic issues have included the important role of the family in society, the role and function of law, the involvement of the churches in public-policy debates (→ Church and State), the growing problem of → cities, the role of → minorities, and economic systems and concerns. Some have challenged → capitalism in the name of a humanistic socialism (→ Christians for Socialism 2), at least until the collapse of the Soviet Union and the liberation movement in Central America. Some neoconservatives have defended the existing system, and many have contributed to the growing field of business ethics.

2.4. *Role of the Churches*
The last decades of the 20th century witnessed a growing social role of the churches. This role included not only involvement of church people in trying to change social structures but also statements made in the name of the churches. Mainstream Protestant churches and the → National Council of the Churches of Christ have traditionally been prominent in this area. The 1980s saw two significant → pastoral letters by the U.S. Roman Catholic bishops on peace and the economy. The 1980s also witnessed the growing social involvement of

the evangelical churches (→ Evangelical Movement 3), which tended to favor a more conservative social policy. Evangelical churches, however, are also home to liberal and even radical social ethicists. In Canada the Anglican, Roman Catholic, and United Churches have been working together to protect and enhance the rights of native peoples (→ Canada 4). And on all sides there is a growing engagement with issues of globalization.

Bibliography: H. BECKLEY, Passion for Justice (Louisville, Ky., 1992) • D. S. BROWNING et al., From Culture Wars to Common Ground: Religion and the American Family (Louisville, Ky., 2000) • L. S. CAHILL, Theological Bioethics: Participation, Justice, and Change (Washington, D.C., 2005) • K. G. CANNON, Black Womanist Ethics (Atlanta, 1988) • J. H. CONE, Risks of Faith: The Emergence of a Black Theology of Liberation, 1968-1998 (Boston, 1999) • C. E. CURRAN, Catholic Social Teaching, 1891-Present: A Historical, Theological, and Ethical Analysis (Washington, D.C., 2002) • G. J. DORRIEN, Soul in Society: The Making and Renewal of Social Christianity (Minneapolis, 1995) • S. HAUERWAS and S. WELLS, eds., The Blackwell Companion to Christian Ethics (Malden, Mass., 2004) • K. LEBACQZ, Justice in an Unjust World: Foundations for a Christian Approach to Justice (Minneapolis, 1987) • E. L. LONG, Academic Bonding and Social Concern: The Society of Christian Ethics, 1959-1983 (Boston, 1984) • S. F. PARSONS, Feminism and Christian Ethics (New York, 1996) • M. L. STACKHOUSE et al., eds., God and Globalization (3 vols.; Harrisburg, Pa., 2000-2002) • G. H. STASSEN and D. P. GUSHEE, Kingdom Ethics: Following Jesus in Contemporary Context (Downers Grove, Ill., 2003) • J. WALLIS, God's Politics: Why the Right Gets It Wrong and the Left Doesn't Get It (San Francisco, 2005) • J. WITTE JR. and J. D. VAN DER VYVER, eds., Religious Human Rights in Global Perspective, vol. 1, Religious Perspectives; vol. 2, Legal Perspectives (The Hague, 1996) • J. P. WOGAMAN, Christian Perspectives on Politics (Louisville, Ky., 2000).

CHARLES E. CURRAN

3. Latin America
3.1. History
On January 13, 1493, Native Americans' blood was first spilled by Christopher Columbus's men, a prelude to one the greatest → genocides of human history. The → Roman Catholic Church played a prominent role in this colonial venture (→ Colonialism). By 1494 Pope Alexander VI (1492-1503) had assigned all ecclesiastical powers operating in what was called New Spain to the Crown. Through *patronato real* (the king's patronage), the king was given the right to appoint the high ecclesiastical of-

fices and administer the tithes. In effect, the king of Spain became a vice-pope, appointing → bishops whose first allegiance was to the Crown.

While the official church complied with Spain's power structures, → priests of various → religious orders became defenders of the dispossessed Indians. Their vows of poverty led them to live and struggle with the marginalized. A two-tiered, informal ecclesiastical structure evolved, consisting first of those who represented Christendom, agents for the colonialists, and those who represented the church, followed by the body of believers (mostly outcasts). Clerics like Bartolomé de Las Casas (1484-1566), Antonio Montesinos (ca. 1486-1540), Diego de Medellín (1496-1593), and Juan del Valle (d. 1561) preached against the inhumanity faced by the natives and promoted resistance to oppressive policies. For many, these first voices of protest became the forerunners of what would become a Latin American liberationist movement.

With the Latin American wars for independence during the 1800s, the emerging nations sought to maintain the same control over the church that Spain previously held and continued the two-tiered perspective. At the forefront was Christendom, the space carved out by the ruling power, which in turn provided religious legitimacy to the existing social structures. On the underside of Christendom was the church of the poor, the peasants, and the marginalized. Although independence was declared, Latin America found itself dependent on the economic power of first the British Empire, and then the United States.

Five major events contributed to the modern development of the liberationist perspective. The first was John XXIII's (1958-63) Second → Vatican Council (1962-65), which produced the pastoral constitution *Gaudium et spes* (1965), emphasizing the church's responsibility for "those who are poor or afflicted in any way" (§1). Second, the 1968 Medellín conference attempted to implement Vatican II within the Latin American context (→ Latin American Councils 2.4). Third, Gustavo Gutiérrez published *Teología de la liberación,* (1971), a reflection on how theology can be formed by learning from the daily struggle of the poor. Fourth, Christian → base communities (CBCs) began to develop, in which the dispossessed gathered to discover how to turn their Christian conviction into the reality of their marginalized lives. Fifth, the earlier 1959 Cuban revolution also served to demonstrate that nations in Latin American could break free from U.S. hegemony. While Cuba was never accepted as a model to emulate, it did prove that society need not be organized along a pro-U.S. capitalist paradigm.

3.2. *Thought of Liberation*

Moral theologian Francisco Morena Rejón observes that a salient note in → liberation theology and ethics is rooted in the effort to reconcile the requirements of a theoretical, academic order with a pastoral concern. Thus → moral theology, far from repeating timeless ahistorical principles, presents itself as a reflection vigorously involved with the people's daily experience. The framework established for doing social ethics is based on the model of seeing–judging–acting, a model influenced by the Catholic Church's constitution *Gaudium et spes* and the apostolic letter *Octogesima adveniens* (1971). The "acting" part of the model serves as a "first act," with reflections and contemplation on the praxis taken then becoming what is called theology. Praxis is informed by considerations of social analysis, philosophy, and biblical hermeneutics.

Additionally, all social-ethical praxis chosen is derived from the perspective of the oppressed — specifically, the social location of the poor. From the underside of power and privilege, a worldview is developed from which to address the existing structural injustices. The key goal of social ethics becomes (1) liberation from all forms of social, political, economic, and institutional exploitation; (2) the establishment of a more human and dignified life by providing humans control over determining each person's own destiny; (3) the creation of a new being in Christ delivered from the consequences of sin as oppression; (4) the abolition of injustice; and (5) the formation of a new social order based on sociopolitical freedom and redistribution of economic resources.

3.3. *Debate and Dialogue*

Several critiques have arisen concerning the social ethics derived from liberation theology.

The continued necessity for liberation. During the 1980s, military dictatorships gave way to elected civilian governments. With the collapse of Communism and the election of leftists and a few former guerrillas to public office, some began to question the relevance of liberation theology. This critique led Gustavo Gutiérrez, during the 1996 conference of the American Academy of Religion, held in New Orleans, to declare that he did not believe in liberation theology; rather, he believed in Jesus Christ. For theologians like Gutiérrez, all theologies are contextual to a specific place and time and thus should be abandoned when they no longer address the needs of the faithful (→ Contextual Theology). Still, the poor and oppressed will continue to exist, to whom liberation theologians look in describing the theological and ethical perspectives of the marginalized faith community.

The triumph of neoliberalism. Another consequence of the collapse of Communism is the globalization of "free markets." The rise of neoliberalism has contributed to a series of economic and political changes, both in Latin America and in the international arena. Faced with a new world order, many of the original statements and discussions of liberation theologians in the 1960s and 1970s are no longer relevant to today's economic challenges.

The primacy of Eurocentric thought. One of the main claims of liberation theologians has been their insistence that they are articulating the theological reflections emerging from the grassroots faith community. Yet these reflections actually appear to be very Eurocentric and Catholic. When we consider that most of the poor are a mixture of races and cultures, we are left to wonder where the indigenous elements of the faith of the people are incorporated. Some would argue that a very Catholic and European liberation theology is destructive to indigenous cultures, participating in "colonizing" a discourse that is hostile to Native people. Missing from liberation theology is the reflection of the religious faith of the poor whose beliefs are shaped by their Indian or African cultures.

The accusation of being Marxist. A major critique of liberation theology has been its supposed link with → socialism or → Marxism. It is true that most (if not all) liberation theologians express opposition to → capitalism and multinational corporations. It is also true that a few liberation theologians have considered themselves to be Marxist (although several have moved away from this self-identification); nevertheless, liberation theologians have consistently argued that their commitment has always been for liberation, not → Marx. They insist on employing whatever social-scientific methodologies can best elucidate the cause of oppression. Several found Marxist economic theories helpful in explaining the plight of the poor. While such theories have been employed from time to time, other aspects of Marxism are disapproved, for example, Marx's rejection of God and sin.

The lack of feminist perspectives. During the height of political repression, many liberation theologians avoided controversial issues like women's ordination, birth control, abortion, sexual orientation, or clerical celibacy (for Catholics). Missing from liberation theology was a feminist social critique. Theologians like Marcella Althaus-Reed critique liberation theologians for relegating and limiting women's contributions to issues related to Mariology, and for failing to incorporate a sexual praxis.

3.4. New Challenges

With the end of the East-West confrontation in 1989 and the entrenchment of neoliberalism, new challenges arose for social ethics, social doctrine, and liberation theology in Latin America. For one, grassroots liberationist movements were forced to deal with the full might of the United States, which trained over 60,000 Latin American soldiers in commando operations, psychological warfare, and counterinsurgency techniques committed to eliminating all parties the United States deemed hostile to its interests. The training manuals produced by the Pentagon advocated executions, torture, false arrest, blackmail, censorship, payment of bounty for murders, and other forms of physical abuse against enemies. According to former CIA officer John Stockwell, "Encouraging techniques of raping women and executing men and children is a coordinated policy of the destabilization program" (quoted in W. I. Robinson and K. Norsworthy, 56-57). The long list of U.S.-trained operatives includes two of the three officers cited for the assassination of Archbishop Romero (March 1980); three of the four officers cited in the rape and murder of four churchwomen, three of whom were Maryknoll nuns (December 1980); Roberto D'Aubuisson, the founder of El Salvador's death squads; 10 of the 12 officers responsible in the massacre of 900 civilians in El Mozote (December 1981); 19 of the 26 officers cited in the murder of six Jesuit priests, their housekeeper, and her teenage daughter (November 1989); and the brutal military dictators that ruled Argentina (Roberto Viola and Leopoldo Galtieri), Bolivia (Hugo Banzer), Ecuador (Guillermo Rodríguez), Guatemala (Efraín Ríos Montt and Fernando Romeo Lucas García), Honduras (Juan Melgar Castro and Policarpo Paz García), Panama (Manuel Noriega), and Peru (Juan Velasco Alvarado).

José Comblin was among the first to question how theology must change to meet the challenge of the new century, which is transforming the ethos of those oppressed in Latin America. He realized that the Brazilian poor left the → poverty of rural life and moved into urban areas in search of employment. This migration further weakened the CBCs, already decimated by decades of bloody rural repression. Until now, the CBCs had been successful in outlying *barrios*, but not among middle-class traditional churchgoers within the parish center, nor among the very poor of the city and surrounding countryside. Economic changes as well as migration

have since brought the CBCs to a standstill. Even people who continue to struggle for land now live in the city. And should they obtain land, they may work on it for a while but inevitably return to the city.

Meanwhile, the rich elite have isolated themselves from their poorer compatriots, moving to exclusive gated suburbs and hiring security guards for protection. While exclusion is not a new phenomenon, what is new is their abandonment of the lower middle classes, who remain trapped in the city together with the incoming poor. The newly rich are no longer the old bourgeoisie *patrones* who may have felt paternalistic pity toward those under them. The new elite are the "executives" who have accumulated wealth through profitable sales instead of production and who feel little obligation to the poor. For their part, the poor are unable to take advantage of their client relations.

According to a Latin American saying, "While liberation theologians made a preferential option for the poor, the poor made a preferential option for evangelicalism." Scholars such as Philip Berryman do not see the future as belonging to the CBCs, which are in decline. Instead, the future belongs to evangelical Protestantism, particularly in its Pentecostal form (→ Evangelical Movement; Pentecostalism). The explosive growth of these non-Catholic groups is contributing to a new face of religious reality in urban Latin America. The emphasis that some evangelical Protestant groups place on prosperity theology makes this new religious movement more compatible with the tenets of capitalism. This new religious focus on personal piety and prosperity is unlikely to challenge neoliberalism.

Bibliography: M. ALTHAUS-REID, *Indecent Theology: Theological Perversions in Sex, Gender, and Politics* (London, 2000) • P. BERRYMAN, *Religion in the Megacity: Catholic and Protestant Portraits from Latin America* (Maryknoll, N.Y., 1996) • J. COMBLIN, *Called for Freedom: The Changing Context of Liberation Theology* (trans. P. Berryman; Maryknoll, N.Y., 1998) • M. DE LA TORRE, *Doing Christian Ethics from the Margins* (Maryknoll, N.Y., 2005) • I. ELLACURÍA and J. SOBRINO, *Mysterium Liberationis: Fundamental Concepts of Liberation Theology* (Maryknoll, N.Y., 1993) • G. GUTIÉRREZ, *A Theology of Liberation* (15th anniv. ed.; trans. C. Inda and J. Eagleson; Maryknoll, N.Y., 1988) • P. RICHARD, *Death of Christendoms, Birth of the Church* (trans. P. Berryman; Maryknoll, N.Y., 1987) • W. I. ROBINSON and K. NORSWORTHY, *David and Goliath: The U.S. War against Nicaragua* (New York, 1987) • C. SMITH, *The Emergence of Liberation Theology: Radi-*

cal Religion and Social Movement Theory (Chicago, 1991).

MIGUEL A. DE LA TORRE

4. Africa

4.1. *Three Traditions: African Indigenous Religions, Islam, and Christianity*

Africa is heir to three religiocultural traditions: African Indigenous Religions (AIRs), → Islam, and Christianity. Each of these traditions embodies a distinct → worldview, with distinctive notions of God, human nature, and human destiny, as well as of the relationship between human beings, God, and the nonhuman world.

These three traditions, each of which claims millions of adherents, have coexisted on the continent for centuries, although sometimes the various social ethics linked with these traditions are in contrast or in tension with each other. Simultaneously, however, there is often remarkable continuity or overlap between them. Some of these continuities derive from the encounter and interaction between these traditions and the inevitable mutual borrowings.

These continuities may not be recognized by all involved. Many prefer to claim a radical difference and even superiority over other traditions sharing the same religiocultural landscape. Such presumptions have led to numerous conflicts regarding various socioethical issues, with some insisting that the normative traditions to which they adhere constitute the best possible answers in matters of social ethics. In the African context the normative traditions arising out of Islam and Christianity have, more often than not, been assumed to be superior and prior to those arising out of the AIRs. African social ethics, understood as social ethics flowing specifically from the indigenous religions of Africa, has often been assumed to be nonexistent, since AIRs themselves have only recently begun to be recognized as such. The continent has long been interpreted in social Darwinist terms and has been considered to be too close to the bottom of the evolutionary ladder for Africans to have evolved a coherent belief system (→ Evolution 2), let alone a coherent ethical system, a perspective captured metaphorically in the depiction of Africa as the Dark Continent. In analyzing and navigating the multiple controversies regarding one or another aspect of social ethics in Africa, this tendency to ignore or belittle African perspectives on the basis that they really do not matter becomes a contentious issue.

While some of the tensions in African social ethics may arise out of the rather chauvinistic tendencies in the traditions prevailing in Africa, some of the tensions arise out of conflicting interpretation of the respective social ethics and the process of discerning the normative response to specific situations. We consider here issues arising in the areas of → marriage, the view of human nature, and the locus of moral authority.

4.1.1. *Marriage*

In issues of marriage, controversies have long surrounded plural marriage (polygamy). From the perspective of AIRs, polygamy, though not obligatory, is morally permissible. The same is the case for Islam. Christianity, in contrast, considers monogamy as the normative ideal.

It is noteworthy that the religious or theological legitimation for plural marriages in AIRs is different from that of Islam. For the former, plural marriages are permitted as part of the religioethical imperative to nurture, protect, and grow family and community. In this framework, a widowed woman and her children are entitled to the continued protection of the family of her deceased husband. This protection is legitimated and guaranteed through the practice of levirate marriage (L. Magesa 1997, 115-59). Ideally, such marriage functions as a kind of economic and social protection for the bereaved family. A similar logic is implicit in the permissibility of polygamy in Islam, though in this case no man is allowed more than four wives. Islamic teaching insists that, given the need to provide for the material and social welfare of the women concerned, a man must be able to care adequately for every wife he marries.

In contrast to AIRs and Islam, Christian ethical systems proscribe polygamy, primarily because it violates the principle of the accountability of the man and the woman to each other as a couple and before God. Moreover, the goals and purposes of marriage in Christianity center more on the couple's mutual companionship and exclusive exchange of conjugal rights. Though children are important in the Christian understanding of marriage and its purposes, childlessness does not invalidate marriage. Incapacity for sexual activity, however, could invalidate a marriage and become grounds for annulment of a marriage, while a breach of the moral duty of exclusive conjugal rights between the husband and wife jeopardizes the marriage, perhaps leading to divorce.

In the African indigenous context, children are more central to the definition of marriage, and childlessness looms larger as a threat to a marriage. Consequently, in the interest of "consummating the marriage" by having children, AIRs recognize the moral permissibility of involving a third party to help a couple have children (through taking a second wife if the wife is infertile, or through engaging the help of a brother or even a friend if the man is infertile).

Moreover, it is also important to note that whereas marriage in the Christian context is an agreement between two individuals who through marriage become one, marriage in the African indigenous context is in addition a means of growing and enriching the larger community. John Mbiti thus characterizes African marriage as a religious and social duty. Marriage is a focal point in an African community involving the couple, the living, the dead, and the yet to be born (p. 148). Moreover, the centrality of children in African notions of marriage is also intertwined closely with questions of personal → immortality, since it is believed that the more children one has, the greater one's chances for personal immortality, since a person is believed to live in and through the children and in being remembered by them. A childless marriage, then, is considered incomplete, a negative condition for both the couple and the community.

In their turn, perspectives that prioritize the community in the rationale for marriage have also occasioned controversy and criticism spearheaded by feminist ethicists and analysts of → culture and → religion who are concerned that prioritizing the community may well undermine the individual human → rights of women (→ Women's Movement). Continuing controversy thus surrounds the moral permissibility of levirate marriage, at times referred to rather misleadingly as widow inheritance.

Such different understandings of marriage, rooted as these are in differences in worldviews, often lead to heated debates regarding what is morally permissible and what is not in regard to marriage and related issues in the African context. Furthermore, the centrality of children in marriage and their importance both for the couple and for the extended community may well lie behind some of the resistance to the use of contraceptives and to the practice of celibacy and abstinence, even when these may be indicated as prophylactics for disease. Similarly, some of the controversies regarding same-sex unions may also stem from this notion of the centrality of children as a legitimating purpose for sexual relationships.

4.1.2. Human Nature

The three main religious traditions in Africa also embody competing and often contradictory → anthropologies, or views of human nature and human destiny. The AIRs typically define the person as an integral whole, constituting the outer person (the body) and the inner self (moyo), with neither considered superior to the other. This perspective contrasts with some versions of Christian anthropology derived largely from Christianity's encounter with Greek/Platonic thought, which features a rigid dualism between body (sōma) and soul (psychē)/spirit (pneuma). In addition, Christianity in some respects prioritizes the soul/spirit over the body. In Euro-Christian anthropology, it is desirable that one learns to "subdue the body" in order to ensure the salvation of the soul, whereas in AIRs there is a clear emphasis on the celebration of the whole person, body and all.

In AIR anthropology the human person is defined in terms of one's interrelationship and interconnection with others. This notion is well captured by Mbiti, who maintains that whereas the prevailing Euro-anthropology embraces the Cartesian idea "I think, therefore I am," thus prioritizing the place of the mind and reason in the definition of personhood, in the African context individuals can only say, "We are, therefore I am" (p. 106). One's ubuntu (personhood) is defined and shaped by what Magesa calls the "relationship imperative" (1997, 64). The prevailing notion in AIRs is that of corporate identity, in which to be, is to be in relationship with others. While this notion of personhood is reminiscent of notions of corporate identity, particularly in the biblical world before its encounter with → Hellenism, it does differ from the Christian anthropology based on Hellenistic worldviews.

These different anthropologies yield different responses to specific issues of social ethics. The notion of personhood based on the relationship imperative thrives on interdependence and therefore favors solidarity and community, while the notion of personhood that prioritizes the individual and reason favors individual → autonomy and choice and the assertion of individual rights in determining what is morally admissible or reprehensible in matters of social ethics. In the African context, the principle "we are, therefore I am" has been applied relatively successfully in political and public spheres throughout Africa.

In Kenya, for example, in the years immediately after independence in 1963, citizens were encouraged to participate collectively in the urgent project of nation building by adopting the spirit of Harambee — an ideology of solidarity based on African notions of interconnectedness and interdependence. It entails working synergistically and pooling efforts and resources to accomplish a common goal. In the spirit of Harambee, many low-cost schools and health clinics were built in Kenya in the 1970s by communities working collaboratively.

Similarly, Tanzania's first president, Julius Nyerere, experimented with what he called African socialism, appealing to the African notion of Jamaa, or family, to mobilize African notions of corporate identity, interdependence, and interconnectedness. Describing the nation as one big family, he reminded citizens that families thrive best when people work together *bega kwa bega* (shoulder to shoulder). Through the ideology of Ujamaa (familyhood), Nyerere encouraged citizens to think of each other as brothers and sisters. This notion of corporate identity has fueled many liberation movements among indigenous peoples (e.g., the Ogoni of Nigeria, the Maasai of Kenya, and the San people of the Kalahari Desert).

The related concept of *ubuntu*, with its emphasis on the interconnectedness of all human beings and their destiny, has been popularized in South Africa and exemplified in the theological and socioethical thought and practice of Bishop Desmond Tutu. It has been mobilized successfully to dismantle apartheid and to forge a new identity for postapartheid South Africa as a multiracial nation marked by radical → pluralism, → tolerance, and respect for → human dignity across racial lines, despite the trauma and vandalization particularly of Africans and their *ubuntu* under the apartheid regime. (See D. Tutu 1994.)

Simultaneously, greater emphasis on individual rights and individual freedoms is also evident in contemporary African social ethics and is commensurate with the global emphasis in this regard, particularly since the Universal Declaration of Human Rights in 1948. Many African countries are signatories to international compacts like the Convention on the Elimination of All Forms of Discrimination against Women (CEDAW), adopted in 1979 by the U.N. General Assembly, as well as the Convention on the Rights of the Child (1989; → United Nations). Drawing on such global compacts, many NGOs in Africa push in their respective countries for implementation of the protocols to which the states have signed and also document ways in which the countries may contradict in practice what they have agreed to in principle.

4.1.3. *Moral Authority*

Other areas of debate in the African religiocultural moral landscape are occasioned by the differences regarding sources of authority in determining what is morally appropriate. Within the Christian tradition, for example, although the Bible is considered authoritative in determining what ought to be done in social ethics, there are controversies regarding who has authority to read, interpret, and apply the Bible in contemporary issues. For many, particularly in the Protestant traditions, the individual's reading, interpretation, and application of the Bible is necessary and sufficient in ethical decision making. In → Roman Catholic Christian circles, however, though the Bible is a resource in making ethical decisions, its interpretation is mediated within the framework of the institutional church, which identifies itself as "Mother and Teacher of all nations" (the encyclical *Mater et Magistra* [1961], §1, of John XXIII [1958-63]). In fulfilling its role as teacher, the church over the years has developed a body of literature cumulatively and collectively referred to as Catholic social teaching (→ Social Encyclicals), which is intended to be a road map for Catholic faithful worldwide. Such social thought is also initiated, mediated, and disseminated by regional bishops' councils. The Association of Member Episcopal Conferences in Eastern Africa (AMECEA), for example, has frequently issued → pastoral letters designed to offer guidance involving contemporary socioethical issues, including issues of human rights in Africa, → peace and justice, as well as the HIV/AIDS crisis. Since the local Catholic Church is also part of the universal church, controversies can occur in the course of trying to apply the rather general principles in these teachings in specific local situations. To address just such issues, the Synod on Africa was convened in Rome in 1996.

This picture is further complicated by the fact that → Shari'a, Islamic law, is also applied in places where Islam has a substantive presence (e.g., Nigeria). As for the AIRs, the authority derived from their custodians of moral traditions, such as elders, seers, and healers, is hardly ever consulted in contemporary African social ethics, though customary law based on ethnic sensibilities is recognized. This reality is controversial and morally problematic in itself.

4.2. *The Impact and Legacy of Colonialism*

A nuanced understanding of social ethics in Africa demands recognition of the impact and legacy of → colonialism, as well as of neocolonialism. At the 1884 Berlin Conference, Africa was divided up into colonies and distributed among the various European colonial powers. This unilateral usurpation of African territory and consequent exploitation of the land and its peoples became a major factor in African social ethics at various levels. At one level this colonization was prefaced and indeed justified through ethnocentric, racist, and social-Darwinist depictions of Africa prevailing in the 19th century. In a provocative essay subtitled "The Genealogy of the Myth of the Dark Continent," Patrick Brantlinger identifies 19th-century literature that conjured up in Europeans' minds the image of Africa as the Dark Continent, a metaphor used to signify the alleged primitiveness, mystery, and radical moral inadequacy of the African peoples.

Having imbibed the myth of the Dark Continent as reality, Europeans proceeded to encroach on the continent, ostensibly to save it from the impact of such moral inadequacy and to accelerate Africans' development up the evolutionary ladder from primitiveness to civilization. According to the diagnosis of David Livingstone (1813-73), Africa was in need of what came to be referred to as the three Cs: Christianity, (European) civilization, and commerce. Here "commerce" was meant to replace the slave trade, for which Africans were increasingly and exclusively blamed. These prescriptions for transforming and "enlightening" the Dark Continent involved an all-encompassing and damaging fourth C: colonialism. Such colonialism and the supporting → racism and ethnocentrism (engines that continue to drive neocolonialism) are at the core of the sustained injustice that Africa continues to suffer and are keys, if not defining issues, in African social ethics.

European versions of Christianity were considered integral to European civilization, and so the mission of Christianizing Africa became part and parcel of the so-called civilizing mission — that is, the Europeanization of Africa. Since Europe and its ways were considered the model and pinnacle of development and civilization, Europeans with a rather misplaced notion of moral legitimacy set about reconstructing Africa in European terms. According to V.-Y. Mudimbe, this reconstruction was a three-pronged process that involved the usurpation and domination of physical space, the domestication of the minds of the natives, and the integration of local economic and political histories into a Western framework. These three distinct but complementary projects yielded what Mudimbe has called "the invention of Africa" (pp. 1-2). The missionary Christianity of the 19th century was therefore wittingly or unwittingly implicated in the colonization of Africa (→ Mission 3.4; Colonialism and Mission), a situation that Jean-Marc Ela labels the "moral ambiguity of mission" (chap. 2). To the extent that Euro-Christianization of Africa was part of the project of domesticating the natives' minds in preparation for physical colonization, missionary Christianity itself emerges as a pressing ethical issue.

In response to the moral ambiguity of missionary Christianity, thousands of so-called African → Independent Churches arose on the continent, both in protest to the ethnocentric practices of the colo-

nial churches and in an effort to reclaim their sovereignty in view of the religiocultural imperialism implicit in colonial Christianity. The informal theology of decolonization embedded in the practices of Independent Churches was a precursor of the more formal efforts to theologically decolonize the African mind. These theologies of decolonization later concretized in the 1960s in the emergence of African and → black theologies of liberation in South Africa and elsewhere on the continent and its diasporas. Such theologies of liberation have been defined as theologies "of the oppressed, by the oppressed, for the liberation of the oppressed" (→ Liberation Theology). By definition they are "in search of new symbols by which to affirm black humanity" (B. Moore, ix), where this humanity has been denied, erased, and often brutally vandalized under colonialism and more recently under neocolonialism and global → capitalism.

Theologies of inculturation promulgated by theo-ethicists like Jean-Marc Ela and Laurenti Magesa (2004) have also appeared on the continent in an effort to formally redeem and reclaim the theological and moral efficacy of African indigenous worlds. The goal is to reclaim and apply in real life what Magesa (1997) refers to as Africa's "moral traditions of abundant life," which are embedded in AIRs. Such inculturation is considered a necessary, though possibly not sufficient, dimension that is integral to the liberation and decolonization of Africa.

4.3. *The Emerging African Feminism*

An additional complexity in Africa is that most of the interpretation of the sacred writings of the three major traditions, as well as the exposition of these in commentaries, pastoral letters, and religious teachings, is androcentric. The voice of women as moral agents and therefore as legitimate interpreters of religion, culture, and ethics has been marked until recently by its conspicuous absence. However, the androcentric and patriarchal nature of social practices in Africa has increasingly been named as a major dimension of injustice on the continent. This is particularly true since the resurgence worldwide of second-wave → feminism in the 1960s and 1970s. In her book *Daughters of Anowa*, Mercy Oduyoye describes what she calls the eruption of African women into the arena of theological and social ethics and cites a number of social movements, including the 1960s → civil rights movement, the 1960s → peace movement against the Viet Nam War, and, most important, the ferment stimulated by a series of U.N.-sponsored global conferences on women.

The 1985 U.N. Nairobi Conference and the 1995 Beijing Conference (the U.N.'s Fourth World Conference on Women) were perhaps the most instrumental in drawing African women from the margins to the center of social ethics, not just as victims of androcentric and patriarchal policies, but also as key players and actors in the African socioethical scene. The Beijing Platform for Action has become a universal tool for women determined to name, shame, and transform patriarchal society both locally and globally. Energized by the momentum generated by these global movements and conferences, and in many cases reconstructing and reclaiming their agency undermined by colonialism, African women have worked to transform both their personal lives and the African public sphere, in which policies that affect their lives are designed and implemented. "Mainstreaming gender" in all aspects of society has thus been a key goal of feminist social ethics. At the same time, however, feminist ethicists in Africa and beyond have embraced what they refer to as a hermeneutics of suspicion and have also been critical of "mainstream" ethics and policies when such policies have sabotaged women's human dignity and welfare.

While such feminist ethics is not exclusively "faith-based" or coterminous with the contours of religious boundaries in Africa, it is noteworthy that such feminist social ethics has crystallized in a palpable way though several faith-based forums, including the women's programs of the → All Africa Conference of Churches and the → World Council of Churches (WCC) and its member national Christian councils, which focus on women's issues in church and society.

A major forum for feminist social ethics is the Circle of Concerned African Women Theologians (hereafter, the Circle). Founded in 1989 under the leadership of Mercy Amba Oduyoye, who was then a deputy secretary of the WCC, the Circle deliberately draws its membership from AIRs, Islam, and Christianity. Since its founding, the Circle has embarked on a sustained program of collaborative research, writing, and publishing on matters pertaining to the role of religion and culture in shaping the lives of women on the continent. They aim to identify and encourage that which is life-serving and conducive to the human dignity of all, particularly women, and to identify in order to jettison that which is subversive to life and inimical to human dignity in all the religiocultural traditions in Africa. Having adopted a proactive but critical "cultural hermeneutics," they have done research and published substantively on issues of socioethical concerns in Africa, including HIV/AIDS, poverty and its feminization, violence against women, and women's

rights. Also, from a feminist postcolonial perspective, they have been rereading the scriptures and "oratures" (such as myths, proverbs, and other forms of folktalk) of the AIRs, Islam, and Christianity in order to unmask that which facilitates → sexism, patriarchy, and other systems of domination, while at the same time reconstructing and reclaiming from these same sources that which facilitates life and human dignity. Circle books based on this research and analysis include works by E. Amoah, R. A. M. Kanyoro, J. N. Njoroge, and Oduyoye.

African feminist social ethics as exemplified by the Circle is also studied in solidarity with similarly concerned others within and beyond the continent. In particular, the Circle has collaborated with feminist theo-ethicists in the United States such as Margaret Farley, Rosemary Ruether, Letty Russell, and Elisabeth Schüssler Fiorenza, as well as with womanist ethicists like Katie Canon, Shawn Copeland, and Jacqueline Grant in black feminist circles in the United States. Elsewhere, the Circle is in close touch with the theo-ethicists in the global South, particularly through the Women's Commission of the → Ecumenical Association of Third World Theologians (EATWOT). This forum allows mutual enrichment and empowerment among women as social ethicists in the global South, including Asia and Latin America. Moreover, recognizing that dialogue and solidarity are crucial for a sustainable resolution of some of the glaring issues of social justice that plague Africa and the world today, African women are reaching out to other circles of solidarity, including solidarity with men who have the same passion to humanize the continent and indeed the world so that all, particularly women, can call the world home.

4.4. *Three Crises*

While decolonizing all aspects of African social and public spheres continues to preoccupy African social ethicists today, the liberative project of social ethics has gained an accelerated urgency in the last several decades because of three staggering crises in Africa and indeed the global village: the scandal of massive extreme → poverty, the challenge of HIV/AIDS, and the escalated ecological crisis (→ Ecology; Environmental Ethics). The fallout from all these three crises has cumulatively and disproportionately affected Africa and its peoples.

4.4.1. *Poverty*

There is an emerging recognition that the massive poverty in Africa is the foremost urgent bioethical issue in the continent; poverty frequently and routinely kills. On average, 15,000 people die daily from the so-called diseases of poverty — treatable diseases that thrive on lack of basics of life (esp. clean water, food, and shelter) and that haunt millions on the continent.

Social ethicists have increasingly recognized the inadequacy of charity, the traditional ethical response to poverty. Charity is necessary but not sufficient to deal adequately with the crisis of extreme poverty in Africa and elsewhere. Recognizing that this poverty is the cumulative result of intersecting forces in Africa's history, particularly colonialism, neocolonialism, and racism, new strategies to respond ethically to poverty focus on these root causes.

Elsewhere, a similar approach is recommended by Jeffrey Sachs in his book *The End of Poverty* (2005). He urges analysts and ethicists to adopt what he calls "clinical economics" and to address root causes if we are to make poverty history, as he is convinced we can and should by the year 2020 ($\rightarrow$ Economic Ethics). Furthermore, it is also increasingly recognized that in the context of Africa, as elsewhere in the global South, eliminating poverty demands, as Vandana Shiva insists, getting the history of poverty right by recognizing its roots in the colonial and neocolonial history of the continent. Feminist ethicists have also highlighted the fact that most of the impoverished and even enslaved are women and children, particularly girls. They have identified sexism as a compounding feature in what they call the feminization of poverty in Africa.

It is noteworthy that the need to address root causes of poverty, as well as the global nature of the scope and etiology of the problem, is gaining momentum. The Jubilee 2000 campaign, for example, appealed to the biblical idea of Jubilee to call for the cancellation of the crippling debt that Africa and other global South regions had accumulated under the notorious "structural adjustment programs" prescribed by the International Monetary Fund in the 1990s. Having identified this overwhelming debt as a major causative factor in the impoverishment of Africa masses, activists from around the world waged a campaign to cancel the debt in the spirit of Jubilee described in Leviticus 25.

Similarly, it has been recognized that the root causes of the massive poverty in the world today include global capitalism, which insists on making a profit, apparently by "any means necessary." Multinational corporations and their role in the de facto neocolonization of the continent have also been identified as part of the root causes of massive indigence in Africa. The concerted efforts globally to address these root causes and to pave the way for an alternative future world have recently crystallized in the World Social Forum, designed to identify and address the problematic dimensions of globalization as they relate to the impoverishment of Africa and others, mostly in the global South. It is interesting to note in this context that, before the recently concluded Seventh World Social Forum, held in Nairobi in January 2007, a preconference of liberation theologians from Africa, Asia, and Latin America was held to flesh out the theo-ethical ramifications of the negative side of globalization and its relationship to issues of freedom and justice in Africa. There seems to be an increasing sense of joint purpose and conviction that a better, alternative world in which extreme poverty is history is indeed possible, and many are determined to work together toward this end.

4.4.2. *HIV/AIDS*

The global nature of HIV/AIDS and its intimate link with the other "viruses" of poverty — sexism, racism, and social stigma — are increasingly recognized in African social ethics. Rejecting the earlier rather simplistic and at times ethnocentric and sexist responses to AIDS as it pertains to Africa, analysts increasingly urge ethical responses that address the intersection of HIV/AIDS with these other forces, which work cumulatively to make HIV particularly lethal in Africa. There is an urgency, therefore, to rethink received ethics regarding marriage, sexuality, and even theology itself, to the extent, for example, that a sexist theology of marriage that subordinates the female to the male makes women more vulnerable to HIV/AIDS. Such a gendered rethinking of Africans social ethics in the face of HIV has, for example, preoccupied the Circle in the last decade; they have held several consultations, as well as produced several publications (e.g., by I. A. Phiri), on this urgent issue.

4.4.3. *The Ecological Crisis*

Africa has clearly suffered disproportionately from the global ecological crisis and its fallout. It is increasingly clear that the effect of ecological degradation in Africa (esp. desertification and deforestation) has provoked many of the numerous situations of violent conflicts. So-called ethnic or tribal clashes have often in reality been conflicts over diminishing and nonrenewable natural resources, particularly land, water, and forests. The global nature of this crisis is also increasingly recognized in the role of multinational companies like BP and Shell in the oil-based armed conflicts in the Niger Delta, as well as the many multinational agribusiness corporations in Africa who profit from the so-called cash crops, notably coffee, tea, tobacco, cotton, and, recently, horticultural products like fresh-cut flowers. Some of the chronic shortage of land to grow food crops is due to using land for these cash crops. The result is the chronic and ubiquitous famine in Africa.

Against this background, social ethicists have urged a multipronged response that involves not only teaching peasants about their misuse and abuse of nature (by overgrazing, cutting too many trees for fuel, etc.), as has been the rather simplistic response in the past, but also calling for greater responsibility at the global level and calling other players in the global village to account. In particular, it is increasingly recognized that certain religiocultural approaches to the relationship between the human and nonhuman worlds have played a role in the crisis. The individualistic moral anthropocentrism with regard to nature that prevails in the Western ethical tradition and that is based on anthropocentric readings of the Genesis accounts of creation, in which man is created in God's image and is to exercise dominion over the rest of the created world, has been named as a facilitator of the exploitative approaches to the nonhuman world of animals and plants.

This approach contrasts sharply with attitudes toward → nature embedded in AIRs, which view the human and nonhuman worlds as interconnected. This perspective results in greater reverence for nature, a reverence that was too quickly dismissed by 19th-century missionaries as symptomatic of aberrant spirituality, with Africans being accused of being nature worshipers. Increasingly, these alternative worldviews that are more conducive to "earth keeping" and "earth healing" are being recognized worldwide (see the Earth Charter, www.earthcharter.org/). It is interesting to note that the worldview of the AIRs seems to provide a more direct resource for healing the earth, although rereading the Christian Bible in a way that awakens stewardship rather than confirming the prevailing ruthless exploitation of nature is also an ongoing strategy to respond ethically to the escalating ecological crisis in Africa. African ethicists are thus revisiting and reconstructing the nature-friendly insights to be found in Africa's rich threefold heritage of the AIRs, Islam, and Christianity.

4.5. Contributions to a Global Ethic

Faced with the multiple and intersecting socioethical issues that plague Africa and indeed the world today, and in recognition of the global nature, scope, and etiology of many of these issues, and recognizing that sustainable solutions demand the collaborative efforts of all around the globe, African social ethics is increasingly becoming collaborative and trans-African in its approach. It is also geared toward nurturing practical responses in concrete, socially transformative action. There is evidence, therefore, that African social ethics is increasingly becoming applied ethics.

Some socioethical projects are collaborative, involving Christian and Muslims in solidarity and in dialogue. Such was the case, for example, in South Africa, where in the 1980s Moslems and Christians worked together to dismantle apartheid. Moslems had declared apartheid *haramu* (forbidden), while concerned Christians declared it a heresy (→ Status confessionis 3.1). In addition, a joint conference between various socially engaged theological organizations operational in Africa — including the Circle of Concerned Women, the All Africa Conference of Churches, and the Organization of Africa Independent Churches (OIC) — engaged in a collaborative consultation in which they hammered out a joint communiqué that identified 20 areas of specific socioethical concern, including escalating poverty, landlessness, and HIV/AIDS, and vowed to work individually and collaboratively to deal with these issues.

This collaborative spirit, which is largely in response to the imperative of solidarity, also reaches outward beyond Africa. For example, a number of African social ethicists participated in the conference "Catholic Ethics World Wide," held in Padua, Italy, in July 2006. Although African ethicists have in the past participated in few such events, their engagement in this effort is a hopeful sign that Africa has a perspective to offer to the rest of the world in the quest for a global ethic.

The recognition of Africa's potential to make such a contribution is long overdue, considering that Africa has given the world some of the most outstanding examples of leadership in the humanization of the global public square. This list includes South African *Desmond Tutu,* who led the Truth and Reconciliation Commission to jump-start the healing of wounds inflicted by apartheid. *Nelson Mandela,* whose unequivocal stance against apartheid cost him 27 years of imprisonment, has become a major role model and example of servant-leadership at work. Ghanaian *Kofi Annan,* U.N. secretary-general from 1997 to 2007, proposed the Global Compact in 1999 to nurture corporate social responsibility among those doing business in the contemporary world. They are urged to conduct their business with greater commitment to ten universal ethical principles that better protect human rights, as well as ecology, in the process of doing business. More recently, and in recognition of her many years of activism focusing on the rehabilitation of a vandalized ecology, both locally and globally, Kenyan professor *Wangari Maathai* received the 2004 Nobel Peace Prize for her efforts in reforestation. As a whole, leaders such as these have built their exemplary careers on insights embedded in African thought (including the ideas of *ubuntu* and of interconnectedness, which nurtures a more reverent approach to nature).

Many have built on the efforts of ordinary people who have also embraced the project to humanize Africa as their own. For example, Maathai worked hard to "re-green" Africa, not alone, but in solidarity with hundreds of women who are members of the Greenbelt Movement. In Rwanda, scene of horrific → genocide in 1994, Rwandese people have reached deep into their indigenous belief and ethical system to rediscover and apply the notion of Gacaca (community courts) to promote healing of their traumatized nation. All these are signs that Africa can and will contribute to the global ethic and the quest for global healing.

Bibliography: *On 4.1:* AFRICA FAITH AND JUSTICE NETWORK, *The African Synod: Documents, Reflections, Perspectives* (Maryknoll, N.Y., 1996) • C. CURRAN, *Catholic Social Teaching: A Historical and Ethical Analysis, 1891-Present* (Washington, D.C., 2002) • B. KISEMBO, L. MAGESA, and A. SHORTER, *African Christian Marriage* (2d ed.; Nairobi, 1998) • L. MAGESA, *African Traditional Religions: The Moral Traditions of Abundant Life* (Maryknoll, N.Y., 1997) • J. MBITI, *African Religions and Philosophy* (2d ed.; London, 1990) • R. S. MOSHA, *The Heartbeat of Indigenous Africa: A Study of the Chagga Educational System* (New York, 1999) • P. J. PARIS, *The Spirituality of African Peoples: The Search for a Common Moral Discourse* (Minneapolis, 1995) • J. PLATVOET, J. COX, and J. OLUPONA, eds., *The Study of Religions in Africa: Past, Present, and Prospects* (Cambridge, 1996) • M. P. SOMÉ, *The Healing Wisdom of Africa: Finding Life Purpose through Nature, Ritual, and Community* (New York, 1999) • D. TUTU, *The Rainbow People of God: The Making of a Peaceful Revolution* (New York, 1994).

On 4.2: P. BRANTLINGER, "Victorians and Africans: The Genealogy of the Myth of the Dark Continent," *"Race," Writing, and Difference* (ed. H. L. Gates Jr.; Chicago, 1986) 185-222 • J.-M. ELA, *African Cry* (Maryknoll, N.Y., 1986) • P. KANYANDAGO, *Marginalized Africa: An International Perspective* (Nairobi, 2002) • J. KUNNIE, *Is Apartheid Really Dead? Pan-Africanist Working-Class Cultural Critical Perspectives* (Boulder, Colo., 2000) • L. MAGESA, *Anatomy of Inculturation: Transforming the Church in Africa* (Maryknoll, N.Y., 2004) • B. MOORE, ed., *The Challenge of Black Theology in South Africa* (Atlanta, 1974) • V.-Y. MUDIMBE, *The Invention of Africa: Gnosis, Philosophy, and the Order of Knowledge* (Bloomington, Ind., 1988) • P. I. ODOZOR, ed., *Africa: Towards Priorities of Mission* (Enugu, Nigeria, 2000).

On 4.3: D. AKINTUNDE, *African Culture and the Quest for Human Rights* (Ibadan, Nigeria, 2001) • E. AMOAH, *Where God Reigns: Reflection of Women in God's World* (Accra, 1997) • W. M. DUBE, *Other Ways of Reading: African Women and the Bible* (Atlanta, 2001); idem, *Postcolonial Feminist Interpretation of the Bible* (St. Louis, 2000) • R. A. M. KANYORO and J. N. NJOROGE, eds., *Groaning in Faith: African Women in the Household of God* (Nairobi, 1996) • M. A. ODUYOYE, *Daughters of Anowa: African Women and Patriarchy* (Maryknoll, N.Y., 1995) • M. A. ODUYOYE and R. A. M. KANYORO, *The Will to Arise: Women, Tradition, and the Church in Africa* (Maryknoll, N.Y., 1992) • C. PEMBERTON, *Circle Thinking: African Women Theologians in Dialogue with the West* (Leiden, 2003).

On 4.4: L. S. CAHILL, *Theological Bioethics: Participation, Justice, Change* (Washington, D.C., 2005) • R. CHIRIMUTA and R. CHIRIMUTA, *AIDS, Africa, and Racism* (London, 1989) • S. K. GITAU, *The Environmental Crisis: A Challenge to African Christianity* (Nairobi, 1999) • J. KEENAN, ed., *Catholic Ethicists on HIV Prevention* (New York, 2002) • I. A. PHIRI, ed., *African Women, HIV/AIDS, and Faith Communities* (Pietermaritzburg, 2003) • R. RUETHER, ed., *Women Healing the Earth: Third World Women on Ecology, Feminism, and Religion* (Maryknoll, N.Y., 1996) • J. SACHS, *End of Poverty: How We Can Make It Happen in Our Lifetime* (London, 2005) • V. SHIVA, "How to End Poverty: Making Poverty History and the History of Poverty," *ZNET Daily Commentaries,* May 11, 2005, www.zmag.org/sustainers/content/2005-05/11shiva.cfm.

On 4.5: M. BATTLE, *Reconciliation: The Ubuntu Theology of Desmond Tutu* (Cleveland, 1997) • O. F. IKE, ed., *Globalization and African Self-Determination: What Is Our Future?* (Enugu, Nigeria, 2004) • H. KÜNG, *Global Responsibility: In Search of a New World Ethic* (New York, 1991) • W. MAATHAI, *Unbowed: A Memoir* (New York, 2006) • V. SHIVA, *Stolen Harvest: The Hijacking of the Global Food Supply* (Cambridge, Mass., 2000); eadem, "The Suicide Economy of Corporate Globalisation," *ZNET Daily Commentaries,* February 19, 2004, www.zmag.org/sustainers/content/2004-02/19shiva.cfm.

TERESIA HINGA

5. Asia

5.1. *Situation*

Asia embodies the promise of economic development and increasing global influence, along with the social tensions and problems of rapid social change, systemic poverty, overpopulation, environmental abuse, economic exploitation (→ Economy; Economic Ethics), lack of full political and religious freedom, and violations of human → rights. Issues of medical ethics, personal and community values, corruption, the role and status of women, the protection of children, the sex trade and → tourism, and the ability of minority cultures to survive the challenges of modernization, globalization, and nationalism also concern churches and Christians.

On the whole, Christians are more confident about publicly addressing moral issues about which there is a degree of consensus than they are about addressing questions about which Christian communities are themselves divided. Churches found it easier to criticize colonial governments than confront the leaders of postcolonial independent nations, but the broad Christian support for actions leading to the overthrow of President Ferdinand Marcos in the Philippines in 1986 is one exception at least. Taiwan and South Korea are other societies where public protest is not unknown. Some issues are deeply ambiguous. In the 1830s British Christians in India opposed the opium trade but prayed for the access to China that the Opium Wars facilitated. As Malaya approached independence in 1957 and the question of religious freedom in a majority Muslim country was debated, Christian leaders advocated a secular constitution like that of India but struggled to rise above the appearance of self-interest.

Questions surrounding abortion, organ donation, and child labor, or even → ancestor veneration, may appear relatively straightforward in theory. Some issues may be possible to address by law and regulation, but difficult in terms of culture and practice. When responses require biblical reflections that go beyond the obvious, as in the case of homosexuality, or in the contextualization of a Christian theology of affluence, it is more difficult again. The pressing needs of poverty, interfaith relations, and political survival can combine with the popularization and politicization of issues within the global Christian marketplace of ideas to inhibit biblical and theological reflection.

By reason of their minority status — 8.3 percent (2000) in Asia as a whole, and a good deal lower in most Asian nations — Christians can do justice to their mission only in dialogue and cooperation with other traditions. This is also true in the Philippines, with its significant Muslim minority and a dominant Christianity. Interfaith ethical dialogue can help extend lines of communication in societies where Christians may be in danger of being ghettoized by either their majority or their minority status. Personal and social ethics, and emerging ecological concerns, are fruitful areas of common interest for Christians, Muslims, and Buddhists (→ Theology of Religions). Theological reflection on large-scale tragedies, such as the 2004 tsunami devastation, can highlight both shared humanitarian values and differences in spiritual understanding. Of significant impact is the unconscious influence of Christians in general, many of whom are in independent indigenous churches, living out their faith in the terms in which they understand it. Some emerging churches also deliberately seek to impact society through a theology that values the workplace, business, and home as places requiring integrity and witness.

In the history of China, India, the Philippines, Indonesia, and other countries, schools (→ Mission Schools), colleges, universities, and hospitals have been a significant dimension of Christian mission. Education was seen as a contribution to the needs of society, and medicine an expression of Christian love and an extension of the healing ministry of Christ (→ Medical Missions). The relationship of education to → evangelism was debated, but practical engagement with society was acknowledged as important. The Baptist missionary Timothy Richard (1845-1919), secretary of the Society for the Diffusion of Christian and General Knowledge in Shanghai, was moved by his experience of floods and famines to address China's needs for technology and development. In postindependence Indonesia the Christian churches took an active part in national development, although local relationships have at times been problematic as intercommunal violence spread in several areas in the late 1990s. The church's reception of the Pancasila ("five pillars") ideology was determined by an attitude of critical cooperation.

5.2. Regional Organizations

In addition to groups concerned with supporting education, such as the United Board for Christian Higher Education in Asia, numbers of institutes have been founded dealing with social doctrine and problems. In the Philippines the Association of Christian Institutes for Social Concern in Asia (ACISCA) was founded at Manila as a subgroup of the → World Council of Churches to coordinate the churches' efforts to coordinate the social sector. In India the Christian Institute for the Study of Religion and Society of the → Church of South India (→ India 3.3) at Bangalore (founded 1957 and directed by P. D. Devanandan and M. M. Thomas), and the Indian Social Institute of the → Jesuits in New Delhi have been important sources of studies. There are similar groups elsewhere, including the Institute for the Church and Society in Colombo, Sri Lanka. These institutes advise church leaders and prepare material for national and international statements or addresses to congregations (→ Pastoral Letters).

The → Christian Conference of Asia has long had an organization to deal with urban and rural mission (→ Urban Rural Mission), now located in Hong Kong. The Federation of Asian Bishops' Conferences (FABC; → Asian Theology 5) maintains the Central Office for Human Development, in Manila, with national branches that coordinate the work in the social sector and provide training for personnel.

5.3. Theological Influences and Directions

In terms of theology, social ethics is seen as a necessary reflection on the basis of faith in a God concerned for the whole world and of Jesus' example of meeting people's needs. Asian churches have commonly understood themselves as a voice of conscience in their societies. Although the Jesuit missions to the Chinese and Mogul courts had a wide view of the relationship of Christian faith to Asian societies, the beginnings of theoretical dealing with questions of social ethics in Asia are European and North American. Asian Catholics have been influenced by papal encyclicals demanding contextual responses to social issues, including *Rerum novarum* (1891) and *Gaudium et spes* from Vatican II. During a visit in 1997 Pope John Paul II reminded Singapore Catholics that the church needed the poor in order to be the body of Christ.

The → Social Gospel strongly influenced discussion in China and other Asian nations during the 1930s and 1940s. Later, Latin American → liberation theology extended this influence. In the history of the reception of this theology, which found acceptance mainly in the Philippines, a part was played by independent Asian developments (→ Asian Theology 1-4). In Korea, minjung theology used memories of experiences of oppression and exploitation to create dances, songs, and other forms of expression as ways to reflect on the causes of social injustice and possible means to overcome it. In India, controversy about the class structure (→ Caste), along with the fact that most Christians belong to the lower castes or are tribal, helped produce Dalit theology, *dalit* meaning "beaten down, enslaved." A related focus is a concern for aboriginal minority peoples in various Asian countries whose languages, customs, and worldviews are threatened.

5.4. Themes

In the regional Asian conferences of the → Ecumenical Association of Third World Theologians (EATWOT) and their international commissions, the themes of Christian social ethics appear strongly. In contrast to a social doctrine operating on the basis of → natural law with abstract general principles, as in the papal → social encyclicals, the stress of Asian theologians is on an empirical analysis of society that seeks to take into account cultural, economic, political, historical, and religious factors. Asian contributions to Christian social ethics reckon with, and seek to make use of, the various religious and philosophical approaches of Asian traditions. Over against the West, which begins with individually understood human and civil rights, Asian theologians emphasize the paradigm of human liberation within social connections.

Asian feminist theologians, including Filipino, Chinese, and Indonesian, have an increasing influence on social ethics (→ Feminist Theology). They have their own contribution to make to the issue of the integrity of creation (→ Ecology), to the position of women in society, and to the tasks of the Christian community in education and hygiene (→ Public Health). Many female action groups deal with such questions, among them the Chipko movements in the Himalayas to protect primeval forests and the group Gabriela in the → Philippines (§2.4).

Asian churches remain sensitive to their responsibilities as citizens, which include careful attention to their relationships with governments, other faith communities, and the global and local social issues of their time. Social concern and ethical engagement as such are no longer distinctive markers of one Christian tradition over against another, but their actual responses may reflect different sensitivities. Successive generations of Asian Christians continue to face the need for a wide range of responses in different social contexts and in facing new critical issues.

Bibliography: P. Casperz, "Asia's Third World Response to Catholic Social Thought," *VJTR* 55 (1991) 561-68, 631-38, 698-705 • P. D. Devanandan and M. M. Thomas, *Christian Participation in Nation-Building* (Bangalore, 1960) • G. Dietrich, "Feminist and Ecological Concerns in Asia," *IGI* 12 (1993) 31-42 • P. Digan, *Churches in Contestation: Asian Christian Social Protest* (New York, 1984) • J. C. England et al., eds., *Asian Christian Theologies: A Research Guide to Authors, Movements, Sources* (3 vols.; Maryknoll, N.Y., 2002-4) • V. Fabella, *Asia's Struggle for Full Humanity: Towards a Relevant Theology* (New York, 1980) • T. C.

Fox, *Pentecost in Asia: A New Way of Being Church* (Maryknoll, N.Y., 2002) • P. FRESTON, *Evangelicals and Politics in Africa, Asia, and Latin America* (Cambridge, 2001) • F. GOMEZ, *Social Ethics, Doctrine, and Life* (Manila, 1991) • D. T. NILES, *Christian Action in the Asian Struggle* (Singapore, 1973) • L. F. PFISTER, "Rethinking Mission in China: James Hudson Taylor and Timothy Richard," *The Imperial Horizons of British Protestant Missions, 1880-1914* (ed. A. Porter; Grand Rapids, 2003) 183-212 • M. N.-C. POON, ed., *Pilgrims and Citizens: Christian Social Engagement in East Asia Today*, vol. 1, *Christianity in Asia* (Adelaide, 2006) • V. SHIVA, *Staying Alive: Women, Ecology, and Survival in India* (New Delhi, 1988).

JOHN ROXBOROGH, with GEORG EVERS

Social Gospel

1. History
2. Theology
    2.1. Key Persons
    2.2. Content
    2.3. Practice
3. Assessment

1. History

1.1. The Social Gospel was a movement within Protestant churches in the United States during the late 19th and early 20th centuries (→ Modern Church History 2.6.3). This movement was a response to what American and European thinkers called the "social question." The social question centered on conflicts between labor and capital, the rapid growth of industrialized cities and towns, as well as problems in determining a just wage and in addressing economic depression (→ Capitalism; Industrial Society; Social Movements). Many Christian thinkers began to believe that "industrial capitalism" was manifestly unjust insofar as its specific institutional mechanisms seemingly bred widespread poverty and the many other social ills that follow poverty. Salvation would require a transformation of the social order to enable individuals to escape cycles of poverty and oppression. Social Gospel thinkers and other progressivists often endorsed some socialist ideas as well as workers' rights, while advocating an important role for government in national society.

1.2. During the late 19th century various socialist movements (→ Socialism) challenged the reigning → ideology of laissez-faire capitalism and the religious and moral → individualism found in the United States and Europe (→ Modern Period). During the Victorian period there had been an emphasis in Christian thought on individual sin and salvation, coupled with a call to personal holiness that too often was removed from the demands for social justice. Within the Christian community there then arose increasing awareness of the intrinsically social character of Christian faith and therefore a criticism of the privatization of religion. Christian leaders and theologians sought to demonstrate the import of Christian faith for the social order in an age of increasing → secularization (→ North American Theology 5, 8).

The Social Gospel was the Protestant expression of these developments. It sought to demonstrate the social relevance of Christian faith in an age of dramatic change, with sustained attention to the problems of industrialization, urban growth, and labor. From roughly 1890 to the 1930s the Social Gospel won a following in Congregational, Baptist, Methodist, Episcopal, and Presbyterian churches. The theology of the Social Gospel sought to articulate the meaning of this movement for the sake of widening its social and religious influence.

Concern for the social question and for the social implications of faith, however, was not limited to Protestant theologians. American Roman Catholic thinkers such as John A. Ryan (1869-1945) and the development of the papal social → encyclicals from Leo XIII (1878-1903) onward represent an attempt to address the social question from within a theological and ethical framework.

1.3. The Social Christian movement within Protestant churches was expressed in conservative, progressive, and radical forms. The progressive form of this movement, especially among the middle → class, was, in the strict sense, called the Social Gospel. The theology of the Social Gospel was a → liberal theology that accepted biblical criticism, → evolution, and social → progress centered on the → kingdom of God. Theologians of the Social Gospel sought to draw on the insights of the historical and social sciences in conjunction with the message of Jesus and the Hebrew prophets in order to address basic social questions and articulate the social meaning of Christian faith.

1.4. The themes of the wider social movement also found literary expression among authors whose work is now engrained in American literature, ranging from Charles Sheldon's (1857-1946) famous *In His Steps* (1896) and also *The Reformer* (1902), to the works of Josiah Strong (1847-1916), Harold Bell Wright (1872-1944), and Josiah Holland (1819-81). Especially important works were Edward Bellamy's

(1850-98) *Looking Backward* (1888) and Upton Sinclair's (1878-1968) seminal book about the plight of immigrant workers in Chicago, *The Jungle* (1906). These authors explored the plight of industrialization in the United States and also expressed some of the insights of progressive thought and the Social Gospel. In some cases, like Sinclair's *The Jungle,* literary expression provoked social reform. The intensity of social concern manifest in these and other literary works indicates that the Social Gospel was just one expression, albeit an extremely important one, of a widespread desire among many progressive thinkers and groups to confront the social question.

2. Theology

2.1. *Key Persons*

Washington Gladden (1836-1918), a liberal Congregational pastor in Columbus, Ohio, and author of many books on social issues, has been called the father of the Social Gospel. Gladden, a champion of liberal social views, challenged the notion that economic life is beyond the scope of Christian ethics (→ Economic Ethics). As a social principle, he advocated rational self-love and the → Golden Rule. The Social Gospel did not so much attack capitalistic society as it sought to reform it from the inside.

Walter → Rauschenbusch (1861-1918) was the main theologian of the movement. Rauschenbusch, the son of a German-born Baptist minister, confronted the reality of the social question while pastor of the German Baptist Church in the "Hell's Kitchen" area of New York City. He had studied the theologies of Albrecht Ritschl (1822-89) and Adolf von Harnack (1851-1930; → Theology in the Nineteenth and Twentieth Centuries), and he drew on those resources in articulating a theology for the Social Gospel. He described himself as a practical socialist. He developed his theology in several important books, including *Christianity and the Social Crisis* (1907), *Christianizing the Social Order* (1912), and *A Theology for the Social Gospel* (1917).

2.2. *Content*

Rauschenbusch and other Social Gospelers looked to the teachings of the historical Jesus, discovered through scholarly means, to provide principles for individual and social life. The central message of Jesus was the kingdom of God, which was seen as a historical possibility of social harmony and justice. God was understood to be working through the processes of nature and history to fulfill the divine purposes of love and cooperation. "The Kingdom of God is humanity organized according to the will of God" (*A Theology for the Social Gospel,* 142). It is

this-worldly and ethical, with transforming and redemptive power. The Social Gospel affirmed human potentialities for contributing, with historical progress, to the coming of the kingdom by → education and social changes.

The ethics of the kingdom of God stressed the law of → love and concern for the common good. → Sin was understood as individual selfishness, "a private kingdom of self-service" that is opposed to the divine reign of love and cooperation. Social salvation requires the transformation of the individual to care for the social good and also the "Christianizing" of the social order. Systemic and superpersonal forces are saved when they come under the law of Christ. The reality of this salvation entails the demand for economic and legal reform concerning taxes, child labor, and the minimum wage; for the formation of educational institutions; for international cooperation; and for the humane treatment of children, women, and the poor. The underlying idea was that individuals could escape sinful habits and ways of life only by being empowered to leave the unjust economic and social conditions that fostered sinful patterns of existence. The work of the church, accordingly, was to enable conversion and life within the Christian community while also addressing the conditions that drove people to despair.

In sum, the theology of the Social Gospel insisted that true religion could no longer be conceived as a matter of personal → conversion and salvation. Every Christian doctrine had to be recast in terms of the social meaning of Christian faith. The church is to be the social factor in salvation, which requires that it embody Christ.

2.3. *Practice*

The practical concern of the Social Gospel movement centered on economic issues and general social reform. The intent was to replace competition and strife with cooperation. Many Social Gospelers were pacifists, especially in the period between the two world wars (→ Pacifism). The range of influence of the Social Gospel on the churches was seen first in the "Social Creed of the Churches," adopted by the Federal Council of Churches in 1912. Similarly, many denominations have subsequently adopted social statements or creeds aimed at reducing social conflict and redressing economic and political injustice.

3. Assessment

3.1. By the 1930s several criticisms of the Social Gospel appeared in the United States. Reinhold → Niebuhr (1892-1971) and others criticized the overly optimistic assessment of human existence found in the theology of the Social Gospel. Niebuhr also criticized liberal theology in general for too easily identifying Christian love with prudential mutuality.

Niebuhr's brother, H. Richard Niebuhr (1894-1962), insisted that Jesus does not command love for its own sake. What filled Jesus' soul was not love as such but God. The Social Gospel is theologically mistaken, which manifests itself in its ethics. As H. R. Niebuhr put it in his book *The Kingdom of God in America* (1937), liberalism meant that "a God without wrath brought men without sin into a kingdom without judgment through the ministration of a Christ without a cross" (p. 193).

Similarly, developments in economics, law, politics, and social reform challenged the method of social analysis used by the Social Gospel. Theologians also have questioned the use of the Bible in the theology of the Social Gospel, arguing that the teachings of Jesus cannot simply be translated into contemporary life.

3.2. Recently, other criticisms, as well as adaptations of the themes of the Social Gospel, have appeared on the American scene. For many Christian theologians the idea of Christianizing the social order is nothing less than simple accommodation of the Christian message to American political and economic power. The drive to accommodation is the basic weakness of every form of liberal theology, including the Social Gospel. Accordingly, the task of the church is not to transform society but, rather, to foster a community of peace empowered to witness to a sinful world. The social message of the church, in other words, is its own distinctive order of life.

Other theologians worry less about the possible accommodation of the Social Gospel to the wider society and its values, since, manifestly, the church always has engaged and always must engage social realities. These thinkers, however, insist that a vision of Christian faith delimited to the political and economic situation in one nation fails to grasp the complexity of the emerging global social reality. In the age of globalization and worldwide ecological endangerment, forms of economic, political, social, and ethical analysis must be widened in order to address these new realities. Like the Social Gospelers, these thinkers argue that one must show the relevance of Christianity to the present age. The fact is that present global realities exceed the framework of thought found in the original Social Gospel movement.

Finally, it has been argued that the feminist and womanist movements among the various Christian churches represent and yet also revise many of the impulses of the Social Gospel. From the early femi-nist movement until today, it is clear that the plight of women within any society is linked to economic and political forms of oppression and exclusion. In order to further women's equality, power, and flourishing, it is necessary, thereby, to transform the social order. This transformation also requires a revising of Christian faith in order to address systemic forms of → sexism and oppression. In this way some of the themes of the Social Gospel have been adapted to a new situation.

3.3. Granting these criticisms and adaptations, the theology of the Social Gospel has left a lasting mark on progressive Protestant thought in the United States. The churches owe to it their deep awareness of social realities, their concern for social justice, and their hope of possible social change. Moreover, as theologians increasingly explore the centrality of praxis for theological reflection and assert the need to examine, criticize, and transform the social order (→ Liberation Theology), the Social Gospel provides resources for articulating the relation between Christian faith and social justice.

Bibliography: A. ABELL, *American Catholicism and Social Action: A Search for Social Justice* (Garden City, N.Y., 1960) • H. BECKLEY, *Passion for Justice: Retrieving the Legacies of Walter Rauschenbusch, John Ryan, and Reinhold Niebuhr* (Louisville, Ky., 1992) • W. J. D. EDWARDS et al., eds., *Gender and the Social Gospel* (Carbondale, Ill., 2003) • C. H. EVANS, *The Social Gospel Today* (Louisville, Ky., 2001) • W. C. GRAHAM, *Half-Finished Heaven: The Social Gospel in American Literature* (Lanham, Md., 1995) • R. HANDY, ed., *The Social Gospel in America, 1870-1920* (New York, 1966) • H. HOPKINS, *The Rise of the Social Gospel in American Protestantism, 1865-1915* (New Haven, 1942) • H. R. NIEBUHR, *The Kingdom of God in America* (New York, 1937) • D. OTTATI, "Social Gospel," *New and Enlarged Handbook of Christian Theology* (ed. D. W. Musser and J. Price; Nashville, 2003) 468-70 • W. SCHWEIKER, *Theological Ethics and Global Dynamics: In the Time of Many Worlds* (Oxford, 2004).

WILLIAM SCHWEIKER

Social History

1. Theme, Questions, and Methods
2. Development of Research
3. Social and Economic History
4. Religion and Religious Societies as Themes
5. Cultural History
   5.1. Ways of Thinking
   5.2. Everyday History
6. History of Society

1. Theme, Questions, and Methods

In its subject matter, social history is a branch of historical science; in its formulations and methods, it brings a specific approach to historical research. If we define it by its subject as a part of history, then its field of research is → society rather than the → state, in the sense of G. W. F. Hegel's (1770-1831; → Hegelianism; Idealism 6) "system of needs." Its interest is in the internal differentiation of society according to strata and classes and groups, as well as in the forces and movements at work in them in history (→ Class and Social Stratum). As a specific approach to historical research, social history becomes determinative when social phenomena are the deciding factors in developments in other spheres of reality. From this angle it becomes the social history of → politics, → law, literature, medicine, the churches, and so forth.

The questions of social history typically lead to the research of collective phenomena, processes, and structures. It uses both hermeneutical/philosophical and analytic methods, as we find them also in the social sciences (→ Social Psychology; Sociology).

2. Development of Research

Up to the 20th century "history" predominantly meant political history or history of the state. This approach was well to the fore in Germany and was partially replaced only after World War II. This one-sided political orientation covered especially the history of the last two centuries, as well as medieval and early modern history, so that in these centuries the social and political spheres were intermingled in the sense of the *societas civilis sive politica*.

Against the dominance of political history, Werner Conze (1910-86) in the 1950s called for a social history that would appeal to the dichotomy of the → state and → society and would treat the history of society as a separate issue. He showed the need for this approach by arguing that we cannot understand social history as a phenomenon if we see it only in the light of political history.

In a first phase the new social history aimed to discuss particularly the interactions between the society and the state since the double political and economic → revolution at the end of the 18th century. Its interest was in → social movements and organizations that sought to bring social needs and concerns into the processes of the state and in the social results of state legislation. Characteristic fields of research were social movements, parties, and associations on the one side, and agrarian and industrial reforms and state social politics on the other. The history of the labor movement became a favorite field of research at this time. Political history itself increasingly took sociohistorical formulations and determinants into its calculation, so that the borders between social and political history became fluid.

3. Social and Economic History

The field of social and economic history takes into account the reality that the economy and society are closely connected. Certain forms of society go hand in hand with certain forms of economics. For example, we distinguish agrarian and industrial societies. Economic changes cause social changes, just as social factors hinder or help economic developments (→ Economic Ethics; Economy). In large part the social history of the → modern period is the history of social changes that were brought about by the industrial revolution (→ Industrial Society; Technology).

Consideration of economic background is all the more essential in social history, the more strongly it devotes its attention to the material aspects of social reality (e.g., standard of living, social status, diet). Yet social history differs from economic history in that it deals also with cultural phenomena and anthropological questions (→ Anthropology; Education; Everyday Life; Family; Popular Religion).

4. Religion and Religious Societies as Themes

In Europe → religion is present primarily in the form of the Christian → churches and → sects, and we find a form of religion (→ Religion, Personal Sense of) among both the elite and the people. But religion in the sense of the modern → sociology of religion can be analyzed independently of any one church or religious group. Popular piety may be seen as an independent phenomenon quite outside of any orientation to church doctrine or religious fellowship, as a sign of religion that may also be seen in substitute religions of all kinds (→ Civil Religion).

In comparison with the situation in France and the English-speaking countries, modern social historical research in Germany has shown stronger interest in religion and the church. During the 1950s a strong interest developed in social movements and parties and the church associations of the 19th century, in Protestant and Catholic → lay movements, in the churches' social initiatives to the various social questions, and later in the Christian labor unions and party structures (→ Modern Church History).

Sociohistorical research on those whom the churches employ (priests, pastors, and church workers of various kinds) in terms of their social origins, social class, and pattern of advancement is only in its infant stages. For the 19th century new works on the religious changes in popular ways of thought and on what W. Schieder has called directed popular religion began to appear. Church festivals ($\rightarrow$ Church Year), the worship of $\rightarrow$ saints, and $\rightarrow$ pilgrimages have become an important theme in social history ($\rightarrow$ Popular Catholicism).

5. Cultural History

Social history long focused particularly on the material conditions of life. The "social question" of the industrial age was a key point in sociohistorical research. The traditional linking of social and economic history promoted this perspective, as did its overlapping with political history, which treated the state as the creator of a social balance of interests. Later than in France and the Anglo-Saxon countries, social history in Germany drew out the ramifications of the insight that concentration on material existence means a constriction and an abstraction. Social behavior relating to material need takes place according to cultural $\rightarrow$ norms. It involves collective dimensions of constructions of meaning relevant to actions (F. Neidhardt). Researching and discovering these collective constructions is the task of a new kind of cultural history whose interest remains in the meaning of social behavior. The underlying concept of culture corresponds to $\rightarrow$ ethnology (or cultural anthropology; $\rightarrow$ Culture 4), rather than to the history of art and literature.

As cultural history, social history is still in its early stages. Research is being done in the culture of workers, the culture of the people *(Volk)*, family history ($\rightarrow$ Family 1), and social protest. Social history is gradually turning into a basic cultural history (U. Daniel).

5.1. *Ways of Thinking*

One kind of cultural history is a history of a people's way of thinking. This topic involves cultural models and mental certainties that influence behavior. The French Annales school developed this line of study from the 1920s under the leadership of Marc Bloch (1886-1944) and Lucien Febvre (1878-1956). It studies the cultural influences at the interface between mental orientation and behavior and thus points to the forces that constitute a given culture. An example of this approach may be seen in the research of Michel Vovelle (b. 1933) on the process of dechristianization in 18th-century France.

5.2. *Everyday History*

A history of culture in a broader sense covers everyday history. As "history from below" (E. P. Thompson), everyday history demands regard for the behavior, perceptions, and experiences of nameless people apart from the tribunes of great politics, but also regard for a sociohistorical analysis of structures and processes. Advocates of everyday history in this sense emphasize its closeness to life, its range of possible subjects, and the help received thereby in attempting to understand past behavior. Critics point to the lack of criteria for identifying what is significantly historic and thus to arbitrary favoritism in the choice of subject matter.

In reality, the outstanding publications that use this method (e.g., the monumental work of Martin Broszat, *Bayern in der NS-Zeit*) give evidence of what is typical and of more lasting value, of which structures transcend the individuals studied. We can see this focus from the title of a work on everyday history by the French historian Fernard Braudel: *Les structures du quotidien* (ET *The Structures of Everyday Life*).

6. History of Society

As a history of a sector of society, social history does not cover all the sectors dealt with by a history of economics, politics, or culture. Showing the interdependence of the sectors and the total force of their various factors is the goal of a history of society as an integrated study. A "history of society," in contrast to a mere "social history" (E. Hobsbawm), has long been discussed in Anglo-Saxon research. It corresponds to the *histoire totale* in the French Annales school. Hans-Ulrich Wehler (b. 1931) has developed the same concept in Germany. In this conception, history is a process with three dimensions in control: government, economics, and culture. The three mutually affect and condition one another, but no one of them seems to be the primary factor.

Bibliography: On 1-3: P. Burke, ed., *New Perspectives on Historical Writing* (2d ed.; University Park, Pa., 2001) • W. Conze, *The Shaping of the German Nation* (London, 1979) • D. Cressy, *Society and Culture in Early Modern England* (Aldershot, 2003) • N. Z. Davis, *Society and Culture in Early Modern France* (Stanford, Calif., 1975) • J. Kocka, *Sozialgeschichte. Begriff—Entwicklung—Probleme* (2d ed.; Göttingen, 1986); idem, ed., *Sozialgeschichte im internationalen Überblick. Ergebnisse und Tendenzen der Forschung* (Darmstadt, 1989) • C. Tilly et al., *The Rebellious Century, 1830-1930* (Cambridge, 1975).

On 4: J. Baumgartner, ed., *Wiederentdeckung der Volksreligiosität* (Regensburg, 1979) • B. Plongeron, *Religion et sociétés en Occident, XVIe-XXe siècles* (new ed.; Paris, 1982); idem, ed., *La religion populaire dans l'occident chrétien. Approches historiques* (Paris, 1976) • W. Schieder, ed., *Religion und Gesellschaft im 19. Jahrhundert* (Stuttgart, 1993) • F. Senn, *The People's Word: A Social History of the Liturgy* (Minneapolis,

2006) • J. Sperber, *Popular Catholicism in Nineteenth-Century Germany* (Princeton, 1984).

On 5: M. L. B. Bloch, *The Historian's Craft* (New York, 1961) • F. Braudel, *Les structures du quotidien. Le possible et l'impossible* (Paris, 1979; ET *The Structures of Everyday Life: The Limits of the Possible* [New York, 1981] = vol. 1 of *Civilization and Capitalism, 15th-18th Century* [3 vols.; Berkeley, Calif., 1992]) • M. Broszat, *The Hitler State* (New York, 1981) • M. Broszat et al., eds., *Bayern in der NS-Zeit* (6 vols.; Munich and Vienna, 1977-83) • P. Buhle, ed., *Popular Culture in America* (Minneapolis, 1987) • P. Burke, *Popular Culture in Early Modern Europe* (London, 1978; repr., 1994) • U. Daniel, *Kompendium Kulturgeschichte* (Frankfurt, 2001); idem, *The War from Within: German Working-Class Women in the First World War* (New York, 1997) • R. van Dülmen, *Kultur und Alltag in der Frühen Neuzeit* (3 vols.; Munich, 1990-94) • L. P. V. Febvre, *Life in Renaissance France* (Cambridge, Mass., 1997); idem, *A New Kind of History: From the Writings of Febvre* (ed. P. Burke; London, 1973) • S. L. Kaplan, ed., *Understanding Popular Culture: Europe from the Middle Ages to the Nineteenth Century* (Berlin, 1984) • D. Sabean, *Power in the Blood: Popular Culture and Village Discourse in Early Modern Germany* (Cambridge, 1984) • W. Schieder and V. Sellin, eds., *Sozialgeschichte in Deutschland* (4 vols.; Göttingen, 1986-87) • V. Sellin, "Mentalität und Mentalitätsgeschichte," *HZ* 241 (1985) 555-98 • L. Stone, *The Family, Sex, and Marriage in England, 1500-1800* (London, 1977) • E. P. Thompson, *The Making of the English Working Class* (new ed.; Harmondsworth, 1968) • M. Vovelle, *The Revolution against the Church: From Reason to the Supreme Being* (Columbus, Ohio, 1991).

On 6: E. J. Hobsbawm, *The Age of Extremes: A History of the World, 1914-1991* (New York, 1996); idem, *Behind the Times: The Decline and Fall of the Twentieth-Century Avant-gardes* (New York, 1999); idem, *On History* (New York, 1997) • H. U. Wehler, *Deutsche Gesellschaftsgeschichte* (4 vols.; Munich, 1987-2003); idem, *Nationalismus. Geschichte–Formen–Folgen* (3d ed.; Munich, 2007).

VOLKER SELLIN

Social Justice → Righteousness, Justice, 1, 3.2

Social Movements

1. Term
2. History
3. Motives, Goals, Agents
4. Movements after 1945

1. Term

From the middle of the 18th century, radical liberals used the term "social movements" to refer to the labor movement. But a historical outlook could not support such a limited definition, especially when there was a minimum consensus regarding its general features. In pre- and postrevolutionary crises (→ Revolution), then, it became the form of a mostly radical protest against prevailing social structures and relations, along with a claim for their radical reconstruction, often with an appeal to a vision of the future. Only historically, however, can we really see what social movements are.

2. History

In antiquity there were early forms of social movements with slave revolts (→ Slavery). The → Middle Ages featured movements of the poor, → heresies, → sects, and peasant revolts (→ Peasants' War), which continued up to the early → modern period. Even before the → Enlightenment, middle-class social movements arose out of the formation of sects in connection with the beginnings of middle-class society in the Netherlands (16th cent.) and in England (17th cent.; → Bourgeois, Bourgeoisie 2). Such movements could lead in fact to a claim to equal rights (e.g., the social protests of the English Levelers and Diggers).

In the early stages of industrialist-capitalist production there were pre- and early-socialist and communist protest movements that show the beginnings of a real social movement (esp. labor unions, Luddites, and utopian socialists; → Capitalism; Religious Socialism 1; Socialism). But the first comprehensive modern social movement was the labor movement, as Friedrich Engels (1820-95) called it in 1845, for, as a movement of emancipation aimed at the whole of → society, it had in view a radical reconstruction of relations by organized self-help (→ Emancipation 2).

In consolidated middle-class societies in the second half of the 19th century, a differentiation of interests or pluralism of social forces occurred that for the most part was directly interested in reform (e.g., movements for women, peace, youth, and Bible and tract distribution; → Bible Societies 4; Fellowship Movement 2; Liturgical Movement 1; Lux Mundi; Mission 3; Modern Church History 1.3.3-5; Oxford Movement; Women's Movement). The 20th century also saw more violent movements of social bandits, peasant communists, and city mobs, usually only of regional interest and not going beyond protests, hunger revolts, or strikes.

With the successful shaping of social relations by

social movements organized for emancipation, conservative counterforces arose (→ Conservatism 1). In the case of fascist movements, they managed to integrate large portions of society and may thus be called social movements of their own (→ Revolution 4.1-2).

After World War II movements of national independence in the former colonial lands called for notice (e.g., in India and Algeria; → Colonialism 2.6), though they were only in part social movements, for most of the leaders did not come from the lower classes but were intellectuals. The same is true of ethnic and ethnic-religious movements of liberation in, for example, the United States (→ Modern Church History 2.7) and the → Third World, though → liberation theology is part of the movement of modern social protest.

In the late 1970s and 1980s the Western world saw new social movements (→ Counterculture) that, attaching themselves to older countercultural lifestyles, were pursued more in networks than in social counteraction (e.g., the peace movement and the women's movement). In such movements emancipatory-progressive and value-conservative motives have combined in political and social action.

3. Motives, Goals, Agents

3.1. In the Middle Ages (particularly in the 10th and 11th cents.), internal church reform and social → lay movements were directed equally against the church and the world. Both were to be made subject to transcendence in a world shaped by → salvation history, as is put forward in → millenarianism, the doctrine of the 1,000-year rule of Christ on earth. At the beginning of the 15th century the followers of Jan → Hus (ca. 1372-1415; → Hussites), following doctrines of John → Wycliffe (ca. 1330-84), tried to organize a social-revolutionary movement in Bohemia with strongly chiliastic features in the congregations (→ Bohemian Brethren). In the mid-15th century the Taborites split off from the Hussites, settling in communities and cities in southern Bohemia.

3.2. The → Reformation at first bypassed the stream of chiliastic revolutionary ideas, as illustrated by Thomas → Müntzer (ca. 1489-1525; → Reformers 3.3) and the → Anabaptists. Between the medieval tradition and the beginning of the modern world, we have the peasants' movement of social revolution that culminated in the Peasants' War of 1524/25. The phrase "common man" best describes those who led the revolt. The rapid growth of the antithesis between the rich and the poor, rapidly increasing taxes, and the restrictions on the independence of village communities were the main causes

of the revolt of the common man, which sought to replace the old law by a new divine law. This law saw the gospel as having direct implications for the secular order. Such an interpretation called forth the protest in principle of Martin → Luther (1483-1546; → Luther's Theology, 4.2; Two Kingdoms Doctrine), which cost the Reformation much of its support as a popular movement.

3.3. Under the influence of → Calvinism, the Puritan movement in 17th-century England had a great effect on the carrying through of capitalist forms of production. The → Puritans stood for a free biblical Christianity and an ascetic lifestyle (→ Asceticism). But radical elements in the Puritan movement became independent. The Levelers (→ Equality 2.6) represented the interests of small landowners, and the Diggers the interests of the poor, calling for the abolition of all private → property. Behind all their ideas was the concept of the equality of all Christians before God.

3.4. The ideas of chiliastic social movements lived on in Christian social teachings (→ Social Ethics) and partly took a secular turn (→ Secularization) in favor of → emancipation. The workers' social movement of the early 1830s grew out of it. Utopian (early) socialism and communism (→ Utopia) was held by intellectuals, tradesmen, and factory wage-laborers in this period, especially in France and Germany. They fought for what was at times a religiously inspired communism of equality, with a revolutionary dictatorship and a reform of society by joining together in collectives. The early social-democratic labor movement, carried mainly by manual laborers, which reached its first high point in the revolution of 1848/49, remained, however, strictly a social reforming movement and was inclined to favor trade unions and cooperative associations.

The anarchist version of the labor movement that arose at the same time (→ Anarchy 3-4) adopted as natural a rational order of society that would rest on the free consent of individuals. Without the aid of government and social control (→ State), it would establish itself by means of libertarian resistance or syndicalist revolutionary actions. Into the 20th century, in Russia, Spain, and France, anarchism found considerable support from peasants, farm workers, workers in small businesses, and even intellectuals.

The social-democratic and revolutionary labor movement began mobilizing the masses from the 1860s throughout Europe. The mass of modern industrial workers in the great cities and industrial conurbations embraced it; intellectuals and socially discriminated groups (Jews; → Anti-Semitism, Anti-Judaism) favored it, though not farm workers or the members of old and new middle classes. In its ideology the labor movement was mainly dominated by the theorems of Karl → Marx (1818-83; → Marxism 1.2.1), who thought that with the necessary collapse of capitalism, a revolutionary overthrow of society by the power of the organized proletariat was inevitable. After the initial dictatorship of the proletariat a new form of social relations, free of all government, would become possible (→ Marxism 1.3).

3.5. Christian social movements took a middle road between conservative insistence on the status quo and socially reforming change. The Roman Catholic variant (→ Catholicism [Roman] 1.2.3) had its roots in the 1830s and later found its main support among the miners in the Saar, the Ruhr, and Upper Silesia (→ Religious Socialism 1). Roman Catholic social teaching (see the encyclical *Rerum novarum* [1891]; → Social Encyclicals) stressed the social duty of property and championed a reforming social policy that would see to the rights of workers under priestly supervision.

The Protestant version first limited itself to philanthropic efforts but then recognized the collective rights of workers and pleaded for their integration into the church and the state (A. Stoecker, F. Naumann; → Religious Socialism 2). Early criticism of capitalism and ideas of a Christian socialism (R. Todt) did not really take hold (→ Conservatism 1.2.3; Marxism and Christianity 3).

Religious socialism in the 20th century, primarily a Protestant effort, was not itself a social movement but a marginal phenomenon of the socialist movement. It had started with F. D. Maurice (1805-72) and C. Kingsley (1819-75) in the 19th century, then appeared in the → Social Gospel in the latter part of the 19th and on into the 20th century, and finally found its way into Switzerland and Germany (P. → Tillich; → Theology in the Nineteenth and Twentieth Centuries; Religious Socialism 5), where in criticism of a capitalist economy it offered a theologically exacting attempt at a counterpoise to the existing social reality.

3.6. The disillusionment caused by the failure of the labor movement in Europe between 1914 and 1918 resulted in the totalitarian variant that led after the war in many countries to the formation of Communist parties (→ Political Parties). Originally we can speak, especially in Russia and Germany, of the rise of Communist parties as a movement, in light of the mass mobilization, the ideological radicalization (→ Ideology), and the setting aside of traditional organizational structures in the labor movement. In the mid-1920s the process began of changing Communist parties into instruments of bureaucratic and terrorist dictatorship (→ Bureaucracy; Russia 3).

3.7. The character of → fascism (understood as a generic concept) diverged from conservative and conservative revolutionary circles, clubs, groups, and parties and gained popular support as a paramilitary voluntary corps (→ Populism). Fascist movements that went far beyond minority positions were marked by the mass mobilization of members from all social classes, including the working classes. They won over adherents with a racist (→ Racism), nationalistic (→ Nation, Nationalism), and antiemancipatory ideology, a cult of the Führer, and an exaltation of → power potential. The mass outlook expressed a radical protest against the crisis of capitalism and liberal democracy, and it turned the social movements into a legitimation of total rule in the so-called Third Reich (→ Totalitarianism).

4. Movements after 1945

4.1. In the Weimar Republic one could see the contours of a total rejection of middle-class life in all branches and directions of the labor movement. After 1945, then, we find a differentiation into institutional and organizational segments that are distinguished only by their tasks and possibilities of working together in the democratic-parliamentarian welfare state and in a democratic-pluralist society (→ Democracy; Pluralism; State Ethics). This development is evident in Sweden and Britain and goes hand in hand with the deproletarianizing of society and general acceptance of the welfare state and of the tasks of the labor movement as a social movement.

4.2. The students' movement of the 1960s and 1970s, inspired by a radical, emancipatory, revolutionary Marxism, showed intelligence for the first time as the agent of a social movement and tried to break through social taboos. Through its demonstrations and provocations, as well as its practice of alternative forms of collective life, it failed to win general acceptance in society and lost itself in dogmatic sects or terrorist activities (→ Terrorism), although it did realize some success in dealing with institutions.

The same is true of the → women's movement, which claimed to be only a single social movement but split off in many directions. Its successes have been mainly in integrated work relating to existing institutions and organizations.

The → peace movement, however, which has many different supporters and foundations (Christian, Enlightenment, socialist, philosophical) and means, has won general acceptance in society, sustains ongoing momentum with its deep roots (e.g., back to I. Kant's treatise *Eternal Peace* [1795]; → Idealism 3; Kantianism), and shows itself capable of achieving class-transcending political and cultural goals and worldwide → communication. Its ideas about the way to achieve an enhanced quality of life in a peaceful world give it its mobilizing activity (→ Peace).

→ Achievement and Competition; Christians for Socialism; Class and Social Stratum; Economic Ethics; Economy; Humanity; Industrial Society; Politics

Bibliography: G. CHESTERS and I. WELSH, *Complexity and Social Movements: Multitudes at the Edge of Chaos* (New York, 2006) • J. M. CONWAY, *Praxis and Politics: Knowledge Production in Social Movements* (New York, 2006) • D. DELLA PORTA and M. DIANI, *Social Movements: An Introduction* (2d ed.; Malden, Mass., 2006) • M. GIUGNI, *Social Protest and Policy Change: Ecology, Antinuclear, and Peace Movements in Comparative Perspective* (Lanham, Md., 2004) • H. GREBING, *Die deutsche Arbeiterbewegung. Zwischen Revolution, Reform und Etatismus* (Mannheim, 1993); idem, *The History of the German Labour Movement* (London, 1969) • D. S. GUTTERMAN, *Prophetic Politics: Christian Social Movements and American Democracy* (Ithaca, N.Y., 2005) • I. NESS, ed., *Encyclopedia of American Social Movements* (4 vols.; Armonk, N.Y., 2004) • W. WIPPERMANN, *Europäischer Faschismus im Vergleich (1922-1982)* (Frankfurt, 1983) • B. M. YARNOLD, ed., *The Role of Religious Organizations in Social Movements* (New York, 1991).

HELGA GREBING

Social Psychology

1. Background
2. Topics
   2.1. Social Influence and Obedience
   2.2. Attitudes
   2.3. Attribution Theory
   2.4. The Self and Relationships
   2.5. Social Problems
3. Critique

Social psychologists study a wide range of social phenomena, from attitudes to group influences to attraction. Largely differentiated from other fields studying social phenomena by a focus on the individual and the use of the scientific method, social psychology can be defined as the scientific study of individuals' cognitions, actions, and feelings as they relate to and are influenced by others. Although social psychology is often considered a branch of psychology, a largely nonexperimental part of the field is sociologically oriented (G. Collier, H. L. Minton, and G. Reynolds). Some have argued that social psychology should be defined as a field separate from both → psychology and → sociology (T. M. Newcomb).

1. Background
With a focus on the individual in relation to others, the topics studied by social psychologists are many and varied. Social psychologists generally attribute the first studies conducted in the field to American Norman Triplett (1898) or to French professor of agricultural engineering Max Ringelmann (1913, as cited in D. A. Kravitz and B. Martin). The work of these two was on group influences that would later be known as social facilitation (Triplett) and social loafing (Ringelmann). H. Haines and G. M. Vaughn suggest that this early research did not launch the field but were simply two of many studies that became relevant to social psychology once its methods became clearly defined.

Interest in → groups and their effect on the individual has long been important to social psychologists, with the most famous research on group influence occurring in the 1950s and 1960s. Group influences were studied by M. Sherif, with research showing the development of a group → norm in situations involving an ambiguous judgment. One of Sherif's most often cited studies involved two groups of boys at a summer camp (Sherif and C. W. Sherif). After allowing the groups to create strong identities, the researchers brought the boys together in a number of competitive situations and, after a week of conflict between the groups, attempted to reduce tension and hostility. The greatest success in this endeavor came with goals the boys could not reach without working together (so-called superordinate goals).

Kurt Lewin also worked in this area of the field and proposed a holistic approach involving observations of the field, or total situation, in which specific elements were embedded. According to K. Danziger, "Lewinian grand theory really never got off the ground" (p. 341) but was an inspiration for the next generation of social psychologists and important to the development of social psychology as a scientific discipline.

2. Topics
2.1. *Social Influence and Obedience*
Social influence was addressed in a notable study by

Solomon Asch (1956). In his research, participants were faced with the task of making a public declaration concerning a perceptual judgment comparing line lengths. Others in the situation who appeared to be participants but were actually working with the experimenter were making clearly wrong judgments. A surprising number of the participants in Asch's study went along with the obviously incorrect judgments of the group and against their own perceptions.

Stanley Milgram conducted what has become one of the most famous experiments in the field (1963). Milgram was interested in understanding obedience because of the events of Nazi Germany. The participants in his initial study (all men) were asked to give electrical shocks to another participant, the learner, any time he got an answer to a learning task wrong. The majority of the participants continued giving shocks when the experimenter asked them to continue, all the way to shocks marked "XXX," or beyond the "Danger: Severe Shock" marking on the apparatus. The learner was actually working with the experimenter and received no shocks. Besides showing how obedient to authority the average person can be, the study ignited a debate in the field about the use of deception and the risks of psychological harm to participants in research studies.

2.2. Attitudes

Another long-standing research interest for social psychologists has been attitudes. The topic of attitude change became particularly important with the propaganda of World War II. Carl I. Hovland was involved in research assessing the effectiveness of U.S. army propaganda, and he later wrote about his work (with A. A. Lumsdaine and F. D. Sheffield). With the work of L. Festinger (1957), J. W. Brehm and A. R. Cohen (1962), and others, attitude change became one of the largest areas in social psychology until the late 1960s, when a more cognitive focus became popular. One research program that included a more cognitive focus involving person perception and attitudes is that of Fritz Heider. Heider's balance theory proposed that cognitive consistency was of vital importance to individuals such that, put simply, one must love what one's friends love and hate what one's enemies love.

An area related to attitudes that has received continued focus is that of → prejudice and discrimination, as these issues have been a persistent problem around the world (G. W. Allport, R. T. LaPiere, and C. M. Steele and J. Aronson). One line of work focuses on nonconscious, automatic attitudes toward groups, known as implicit attitudes (P. G. Devine;

also work by A. G. Greenwald, D. E. McGhee, and J. K. L. Schwartz). Implicit attitudes may influence an individual's treatment of members of particular social groups, even when the individual is not consciously aware of these attitudes (J. F. Dovidio, K. Kawakami, and S. L. Gaertner). Stereotypes may also influence how an individual, as a member of a stereotyped group, may act in a situation relevant to that stereotype ("stereotype threat"; Steele and Aronson).

2.3. Attribution Theory

Attribution theory arose in the 1960s, as psychology as a whole became more focused on cognitive processes (→ Cognition). Researchers in this area tried to understand how and why individuals made the attributions they made about themselves and others (E. E. Jones and K. E. Davis). One of the most important developments in this area was the idea of the fundamental attribution error. Such an error is the tendency of people to make dispositional inferences about other's behavior, ignoring situational factors that may have contributed to that behavior (L. Ross).

2.4. The Self and Relationships

Another major area that has long been of interest is the → self. Social psychologists have investigated what individuals know about the self and how they think about the self (self-knowledge and self-concept), as well as how individuals present themselves to others (self-presentation). Among the major findings from this area is that how one views oneself, one's self-schema, influences how information is processed (H. Markus 1977). Cultural differences in views of self have been found to have a large impact on how people think and feel and on what motivates them (Markus and S. Kitayama).

Attraction and close relationships is one current area of interest to social psychologists. Some researchers argue that belongingness is a basic need (R. F. Baumeister and M. R. Leary). Unmet belongingness needs can create problems in mental and physical health and contribute to social problems such as school shootings (M. R. Leary et al.). Social psychologists have developed theories of love (E. Hatfield and R. L. Rapson; R. J. Sternberg) and of the continuation of relationships. J. M. Gottman, for example, identified factors predictive of marital dissolution.

2.5. Social Problems

Social psychologists focus on particular social issues or problems, often sparked by local, national, or world events and challenges. B. Latane and J. M. Darley embarked on a line of research on helping behaviors after the report of a murder of a young woman that involved over 30 neighbors being aware of the attack but failing to provide help. The effect of exposure to media violence has been a subject of research for a number of years (A. Bandura; B. J. Bushman and C. A. Anderson). Social psychology has also made contributions to the areas of health (S. E. Taylor et al.), education (R. Rosenthal), and law (G. Wells, R. Malpass, and R. C. L. Lindsay).

3. Critique

In 1973 Kenneth Gergen attacked the field, arguing that social psychology is not the scientific study of behavior but rather simply a current history of human behavior. Social psychology, he claimed, ignored the historical and cultural influences on individuals, rendering any findings applicable only to the particular population studied. Social psychologists responded to the attack both by clarifying their objectives and approaches and by increasing their focus on cross-cultural work and making greater use of a variety of research methods.

As is evident in this overview of social psychology, although many interesting topics are studied, the field suffers from a lack of unifying theory or organizing framework (Markus 2005). The varied research findings of social psychologists provide an ever greater understanding of humans in relation to one another, but this variety may also result in fragmentation of the discipline and lack of any coherent message.

Bibliography: Background and critique: G. COLLIER, H. L. MINTON, and G. REYNOLDS, *Current Thought on American Social Psychology* (New York, 1991) • K. DANZIGER, "Making Social Psychology Experimental: A Conceptual History, 1920-1970," *JHBS* 36 (2000) 329-47 • K. GERGEN, "Social Psychology as History," *JPSP* 26 (1973) 309-20 • H. HAINES and G. M. VAUGHAN, "Was 1898 a 'Great Date' in the History of Social Psychology?" *JHBS* 15 (1979) 323-32 • D. A. KRAVITZ and B. MARTIN, "Ringelmann Rediscovered: The Original Article," *JPSP* 50 (1986) 936-41 • K. LEWIN, *Field Theory in Social Science* (ed. D. Cartwright; New York, 1951); idem, "Group Decisions and Social Change," *Reading in Social Psychology* (ed. T. M. Newcomb and E. L. Hartley; New York, 1947) 330-41 • T. M. NEWCOMB, "Social Psychological Theory: Integrating Individual and Social Problems," *Social Psychology at the Crossroads* (ed. J. H. Rohrer and M. Sherif; New York, 1951) 31-49 • M. SHERIF, *The Psychology of Social Norms* (New York, 1936) • M. SHERIF and C. W. SHERIF, *Groups in Harmony and Tension: An Integration of Studies of Intergroup Relations* (New York, 1953) • N. TRIPLETT, "The Dynamogenic Factors in Pacemaking and Competition," *AJPs* 9 (1898) 507-33.

Topics: Social influence and obedience: S. E. ASCH, *Studies of Independence and Conformity: A Minority of One against a Unanimous Majority* (Washington, D.C., 1956) • S. MILGRAM, "Behavioral Study of Obedience," *JASPs* 67 (1963) 371-78.

Topics: Attitudes: G. W. ALLPORT, *The Nature of Prejudice* (Reading, Mass., 1954) • J. W. BREHM and A. R. COHEN, *Explorations in Cognitive Dissonance* (New York, 1962) • P. G. DEVINE, "Stereotypes and Prejudice: Their Automatic and Controlled Components," *JPSP* 56 (1989) 181-89 • J. F. DOVIDIO, K. KAWAKAMI, and S. L. GAERTNER, "Implicit and Explicit Prejudice and Interracial Interaction," *JPSP* 81 (2002) 62-68 • L. FESTINGER, *A Theory of Cognitive Dissonance* (Evanston, Ill., 1957) • A. G. GREENWALD, D. E. MCGHEE, and J. K. L. SCHWARTZ, "Measuring Individual Differences in Implicit Cognition: The Implicit Associations Test," *JPSP* 74 (1998) 1464-80 • F. HEIDER, "Attitudes and Cognitive Organization," *JPs* 21 (1946) 107-12; idem, "Social Perception and Phenomenal Causality," *PsRev* 51 (1944) 358-74 • C. I. HOVLAND, A. A. LUMSDAINE, and F. D. SHEFFIELD, *Experiments on Mass Communications* (Princeton, 1949) • R. T. LAPIERE, "Attitudes versus Actions," *SocFor* 13 (1934) 230-37 • C. M. STEELE and J. ARONSON, "Stereotype Threat and the Intellectual Test Performance of African Americans," *JPSP* 69 (1995) 797-811.

Topics: Attribution theory; the self and relationships: R. F. BAUMEISTER and M. R. LEARY, "The Need to Belong: Desire for Interpersonal Attachments as a Fundamental Human Motivation," *PsBull* 117 (1995) 497-512 • J. M. GOTTMAN, "A Theory of Marital Dissolution and Stability," *JFPs* 7 (1993) 57-75 • E. HATFIELD and R. L. RAPSON, "Passionate Love: New Directions in Research," *Advances in Personal Relationships* (vol. 1; ed. W. H. Jones and D. Perlman; Greenwich, Conn., 1987) 109-39 • E. E. JONES and K. E. DAVIS, "From Acts to Disposition: The Attributional Process in Person Perception," *Advances in Experimental Social Psychology* (vol. 2; ed. L. Berkowitz; New York, 1965) 219-66 • M. R. LEARY, R. M. KOWALSKI, L. SMITH, and S. PHILLIPS, "Teasing, Rejection, and Violence: Case Studies of the School Shootings," *AggBeh* 29 (2003) 202-14 • H. MARKUS, "On Telling Less Than We Can Know: The Too Tacit Wisdom of Social Psychology," *PsInq* 16 (2005) 180-84; idem, "Self-Schemata and Processing Information about the Self," *JPSP* 35 (1977) 63-78 • H. R. MARKUS and S. KITAYAMA, "Culture and the Self: Implications for Cognition, Emotion, and Motivation," *PsRev* 98 (1991) 224-53 • L. ROSS, "The Intuitive Psychologist and His Shortcomings: Distortions in the Attribution Process," *Advances in Experimental Social*

Psychology (vol. 10; ed. L. Berkowitz; New York, 1977) 173-220 • R. J. Sternberg, "The Triangular Theory of Love," *PsRev* 93 (1986) 119-35.

　　Topics: Social problems: A. Bandura, *Aggression: A Social Learning Analysis* (Englewood Cliffs, N.J., 1973) • B. J. Bushman and C. A. Anderson, "Media Violence and the American Public: Scientific Facts versus Media Misinformation," *AmPs* 56 (2001) 477-89 • B. Latane and J. M. Darley, "Social Determinants of Bystander Intervention in Emergencies," *Altruism and Helping Behavior* (ed. J. Macaulay and L. Berkowitz; New York, 1970) 13-27; idem, *The Unresponsive Bystander: Why Doesn't He Help?* (New York, 1970) • R. Rosenthal, "Covert Communication in Classrooms, Clinics, Courtrooms, and Cubicles," *AmPs* 57 (2002) 839-49 • S. E. Taylor, M. E. Kemeny, G. M. Reed, J. E. Bower, and T. L. Gruenwald, "Psychological Resources, Positive Illusions, and Health," *AmPs* 55 (2000) 99-109 • G. Wells, R. Malpass, and R. C. L. Lindsay, "From the Lab to the Police Station: A Successful Application of Eyewitness Research," *AmPs* 55 (2000) 581-98.

Jennifer S. Feenstra

Social Science

1. Historical Development
2. Data Collection and Research Methods
3. Academic Controversy
4. Empirical Social Science and Theology

1. Historical Development

The beginnings of empirical social science lie in the field of statistics of the 17th and 18th centuries. Under the influence of the Belgian Adolphe Quetelet (1796-1874), "moral statistics," already common in Germany, was developed as an attempt to show the causal dependency of the individual on general social factors. In addition, under Quetelet among others, official governmental statistics began to be gathered in the second half of the 19th century. The first scientific collections of data were then commissioned in connection with the social questions of the Verein für Soziolpolitik (Association for social policy). In the 1920s research institutions in the area of empirical social research began to be formed, such as those in Cologne, Frankfurt, and Vienna. Varied theoretical conceptions began to emerge that are still influential today.

　　After 1945, German empirical social research was greatly influenced by developments in North America, where differentiated procedures of social research were developed much earlier. The methods of qualitative analysis, as well as standardized surveys,

were further developed. The present situation, especially in Germany but also in other countries such as the United States, is characterized by the fact that quantifiable empirical social research has lost its predominance. Qualitative data collection techniques (e.g., group discussions and narrative interviews), which were preferred from the outset in critical sociology (the Frankfurt school; → Critical Theory), are again stirring interest. Processes of interpretive anthropology in the sense of the "thick description" of Clifford Geertz are used. Additionally, to some extent the active participation of the researcher is encouraged in the processes of social change (action research) that the research itself triggers.

2. Data Collection and Research Methods

The most widely used technique of data collection is still that of the interview, with its standardized form of questionnaire. In addition, group discussion is used to collect data. Observation can also provide sociologically relevant information. Written materials are unpacked by means of methodologically safeguarded analysis of content.

　　Three important criteria must be observed in the development and use of techniques:

> Validity: A collection must measure what it is meant to measure.
>
> Reliability: The instrument must be dependable, yielding the same results after multiple attempts under the same conditions.
>
> Representivity: The group investigated, if not interviewed in its entirety, must be constituted so that it is possible to obtain results characteristic of the larger social group.

Today the processing of data is done with computers, using statistical techniques, which makes it possible to test the mutual dependencies of individually researched factors and demonstrate multifactor correlations.

　　Empirical research oriented to social science is — contrary to research by survey, with some exceptions — guided by theory in both its descriptive and its explanatory investigations. Under the theory, a cross-section of social reality is interpreted, or explained. Hypotheses grow out of the theory, and empirical research is designed so that these formulated hypotheses are tested by the material. The process of testing involves interpretation of the data under the guidance of theory.

3. Academic Controversy

The usual theoretical concept in empirical social science plainly echoes a positivist view of → science

(→ Positivism). As in the phenomena that natural science investigates, it finds the principle of → causality in social relations. The main interest in exposition is to distinguish and interpret the factors that are causes and those that are effects. It is thus suspected, not unjustly, that a *stimulus-response model of behaviorism* is the basic theory in empirical social science. Hence the projects of empirical social science are of limited scope as experiments or as field research. The hypotheses are also limited, as are the theories that are built on them or that underlie them. Empirical social science does not work with a theory of → society that is a "developed existential judgment" (M. Horkheimer). It can understand reality descriptively but not criticize it.

An opposing theoretical position that engages in criticism of empirical social science, and especially of its standardized techniques, is *hermeneutical sociology* (→ Hermeneutics), which sees complexity of meaning. Closely related is the sociological version of → *action theory,* which tries to understand the subject not merely as reacting but as, at the same time, giving meaning and shaping society. Not least in this connection we must also refer to *critical theory,* which in the interest of liberation seeks to bring to light the inhumane structures of existing society by critically presenting from a theoretical standpoint the nature of a prevailing social form. The fact that empirical social science is possible only within a positivist understanding of social science may be seen, on the one side, from the efforts of action-theory sociologists to redevelop qualitative procedures and, on the other, from the research of critical theory, especially the study of authoritarianism by T. W. Adorno and the Berkeley group.

4. Empirical Social Science and Theology

The adoption of empirical social science by → theology is mainly praxis oriented, which was true especially in the 19th and early 20th centuries. F. D. E. → Schleiermacher regarded church statistics as a theological task (*Brief Outline,* §§232-50). For him, along the lines of an earlier concept, church statistics meant "knowledge of the existing social situation in all the different parts of the Christian church" (§195). Later the Lutheran theologian Alexander von Oettingen (1827-1906) adopted the procedure of "moral statistics" (see 1). His aim was to develop a → social ethics on an empirical basis. In the 1920s theologians did empirical studies of workers and young working people.

After 1945 theologians were hesitant to adopt the methods of social science. Sociologists, not theologians, did the first sociological studies of the churches (→ Sociology of Churches). The new orientation in → practical theology from the mid-1960s was an essential factor in the adoption of empirical social science by theology. It was then hoped that empirical social science would help to solve the crisis in the European churches of dwindling attendance and the growing exodus of members.

The main significance of the various forms of empirical social science for theology is that they make possible an intersubjective extension of the → everyday experience of individuals. This extension enables them to control their own primary experience and, not least, to be sensitive to social conditions. The results of empirical social science can also be significant for the church by bringing observable social reality and normative claims to bear on each other. In the development of new church concepts, empirical social science has the function of testing to see how close the concepts are to reality. The importance of empirical social science for the practice of the church usually grows when the approach is discussed with practical theologians and the research team and when those interested in the research work out the results in a process of joint discussion.

In → systematic theology empirical social science and → sociology in general can make possible the viewing of theologically relevant facts from a nontheological standpoint. In ecclesiology, for example, it is necessary to deal with the character of the → church as an → institution or → organization. The question of → faith and → piety necessitates a study of the social conditions that might lead to faith or unbelief. The view made possible by empirical research demands comprehensive theological reflection and enhances its possibility. But the use of the procedures of empirical social science in theological discussion, or assessment of the results of empirical research, cannot avoid asking about the theoretical presuppositions. The possible danger of a duplicating of reality by empirical research needs to be considered. The objection that empirical research treats people as things must also be weighed and might lead those taking part either to plunge more strongly into the process of research or to develop techniques that will bring out clearly the significance of individuals as acting subjects.

→ Philosophy of Science; Sociology of Religion

Bibliography: T. W. ADORNO et al., *The Positivist Dispute in German Sociology* (New York, 1976; orig. pub., 1969) • H. ALBERT, *Between Social Science, Religion, and Politics: Essays in Critical Rationalism* (Amsterdam, 1999) • H. M. BLALOCK and A. B. BLALOCK, eds., *Meth-*

odology in Social Research (New York, 1968) • K.-F. DAIBER, *Grundriß der praktischen Theologie als Handlungswissenschaft. Kritik und Erneuerung der Kirche als Aufgabe* (Munich, 1977) • A. DIEKMANN, *Empirische Sozialforschung* (14th ed.; Hamburg, 2005) • C. GEERTZ, *The Interpretation of Cultures* (New York, 2001; orig. pub., 1973) • H. HARTMANN, *Empirische Sozialforschung. Probleme und Entwicklungen* (Munich, 1970) • S. N. HESSE-BIBER and P. LEAVY, eds., *Emergent Methods in Social Research* (Thousand Oaks, Calif., 2006) • F. N. KERLINGER and H. B. LEE, *Foundations of Behavioral Research* (4th ed.; Fort Worth, Tex., 2000) • H. KROMREY, *Empirische Sozialforschung. Modelle und Methoden der standardisierten Datenerhebung und Datenauswertung* (11th ed.; Stuttgart, 2006) • G. LENSKI, *The Religious Factor: A Sociological Study of Religion's Impact on Politics, Economics, and Family Life* (Westport, Conn., 1977; orig. pub., 1961) • R. MAYNTZ, K. HOLM, and P. HÜBNER, *Introduction to Empirical Sociology* (Harmondsworth, 1976) • A. VON OETTINGEN, *Die Moralstatistik und die christliche Sittenlehre* (2 vols.; Erlangen, 1868-73) • K. R. POPPER, *The Logic of Scientific Discovery* (London, 1992; orig. pub., 1935) • F. SCHLEIERMACHER, *Brief Outline on the Study of Theology* (Richmond, Va., 1966; orig. pub., 1811) • P. ZEDLER and H. MOSER, eds., *Aspekte qualitativer Sozialforschung* (Opladen, 1983).

KARL-FRITZ DAIBER

Social Stratum → Class and Social Stratum

Social Systems

1. Term and History
2. Problem
3. Religion and Church

1. Term and History

1.1. In antiquity, "system" (Gk. *systēma*) referred to a whole formed of several parts. In the → modern period, "social system" has become a central term. Jurisprudence (→ Law and Legal Theory), → theology, and, above all, theologically inspired → philosophy (→ Philosophy and Theology) reached their peak in social systems theory. According to Heinrich Rombach, with Spinoza and since Spinoza, philosophy becomes a system; the philosophy of the system is philosophy as system (→ Spinozism). The concept of system means principally a necessary connection between the individual and the whole; the individual experiences its truth in and through the whole. Idealistically (→ Idealism), and also apodictically, G. W. F. Hegel (1770-1831) stated, "The true is actual only as system" (preface to *Phenomenology of Spirit*). Although system proposals are still being made (see most recently Gerold Prauss), radical critics of the conditions of the possibility of systems have increased. The line reaches from S. → Kierkegaard (1813-55) through F. → Nietzsche (1844-1900) and up to representatives of so-called → postmodernism.

The more recent usage of "system" stands in no direct continuity with the early modern philosophical tradition. The concept of system is applied to problems of mathematics, nonlinear physics, machines, and organisms, as well as to social and psychological systems. No area of reality is excepted. Behind this practice is the assumption of the fundamental continuity of reality, in which the differences in the sense of a differentiation of systems are integrated. This assumption becomes fruitful in the possibility of the → analogy between the systems. In particular, the assumption of living systems propounded by Ludwig von Bertalanffy (1901-72) became widely accepted, according to which the same basic unity exists in all systems, with their functional status varying according to the context and the degree of the differentiation of the systems.

Corresponding to general system theory, strict analogies to information systems emerge. Basic unity (cell or information/bit), variance according to size and degree of differentiation, feedback, self-direction, and much more recur. In biotechnology and the still-developing biochip, as well as in cybernetics, the assumption of system is applied practically.

1.2. In the social sciences, systems theory derives from one of its founding fathers, August Comte (1798-1857). The leading patterns of system-theoretical argumentation were influenced first in the 1930s by Talcott Parsons (1902-79), in the form of structural-functional systems theory, and since the 1960s by Niklas Luhmann (1927-98), in the form of functional-structural systems theory (→ Structuralism). The difference between the two consists in the degree of generality. Functional-structural systems theory is considerably more abstract and connects more directly to general systems theory, comprehending all conceivable systems. Structure-functional systems theory is used more for ordering taxonomically, while the latter is used more analytically and heuristically.

In the systems theory of Luhmann, three relations are decisive for the analysis of functions and their diverse structural consequences: (1) from a system to its → environment (§1); (2) from one system to other systems; and (3) from a system to itself. The environmental connection, which constitutes the system, is simultaneously its existential presupposition and its challenge. The system illustrates a specific reduction of the overcomplex environment in that it attains through its special selectivity a measure of intrinsic complexity that marks it as special. Systems differ in the measure of this intrinsic complexity and the related system and subsystem formation. On this feature depends the degree of their self-reference and capability for autopoiesis (i.e., for self-managed preservation and renewal). An evolutionary process is assumed (→ Evolution). The differentiation of systems grows and, with it, its self-reference ("reflexivity") and autopoiesis.

1.3. The term "system" is used in everyday speech (→ Everyday Life) and in part also analytically to designate economically and politically differing societies. The most familiar and effective became the difference between the Soviet, or "real socialist," system (→ Socialism) and the Western, or free market/capitalistic, system (→ Capitalism). This difference, though, lost meaning with the end of the → Soviet Union in 1991.

2. Problem

The theory of social systems possesses considerable advantages. It permits the elaboration of functional requirements from structures, and structural requirements from functions. It allows the ordering of a variety in phenomena in terms of assumed structural-functional requirements. It makes it possible to discover to what degree → institutions have formed themselves and correspond to their functions. In so-called modernization theory, which has been used especially in assessing the deficits and requirements of country development, systems theory remains influential to this day. In the functional variants of systems theory, there are many heuristic, even investigative, powers, for the question is constantly asked whether and to what degree functionally specific systems can persist, given the risk represented by their intrinsic complexity in the face of the permanent challenges of an unharmonious, uncontrollable environment.

The dangers of systems theory in its differing variants are also considerable. It suffers from its overabstraction and a resulting arbitrariness; it easily becomes a falsely systematic terminological game. It is crypto-normative (→ Norms) and continues the tradition of the subjectivization of institutions and instruments of knowledge that charac-

terizes → modernity. It has rather antihistorical, even historical-philosophical, implications.

3. Religion and Church

For their part, → religion and → church are understood as differentiated systems. Religion's own "medium" of → faith, in terms of system theory, can be assessed in its distinctive capacity and limits, as can the distinctiveness of organized religion as a subsystem of modern systems. The functional characteristics of → organizations, which can be highlighted by means of systems theory, fall into conflict with the specifically functional meaning of religion. The dispute between science and its function, on the one hand, and religion, on the other, cannot be settled by the use of systems theory.

Bibliography: K. C. Bausch, *The Emerging Consensus in Social Systems Theory* (New York, 2001) • L. von Bertalanffy, *General System Theory: Foundations, Development, Applications* (rev. ed.; New York, 1973) • E. Cassirer, *Substance and Function: And Einstein's Theory of Relativity* (New York, 1953; orig. pub., 1910) • J. Habermas, *The Theory of Communicative Action* (2 vols.; Oxford, 2004) • N. Luhmann, *Funktion der Religion* (5th ed.; Frankfurt, 1999; orig. pub., 1977); idem, *Social Systems* (trans. J. Bednarz Jr.; Stanford, Calif., 1995; orig. pub., 1984) • W.-D. Narr, *Theoriebegriffe und Systemtheorie* (4th ed.; Stuttgart, 1976) • T. Parsons, *The Social System* (new ed.; London, 1991; orig. pub., 1951) • G. Prauss, *Die Welt und wir* (2 vols. in 4 pts.; Stuttgart, 1990-2006) • H. Rombach, *Substanz, System, Struktur* (Freiburg, 1966) • I. M. Wallerstein, *World-Systems Analysis* (Durham, N.C., 2004).

Wolf-Dieter Narr

Socialism

1. Background
2. European Socialist Parties
3. Communist Movements
4. Resurgence of Socialist Parties
5. U.S. Socialists

From the 1840s to the 1950s, "socialism" referred to those authors and organizations whose ideas and activities were intended to further the interests of the working class (→ Class and Social Stratum). By 1960, socialists expanded their constituency to include the middle classes. Until the 1950s, socialist parties tended to be Marxist insofar as their ultimate goal — whether through gradual reform (E. Bernstein), spontaneous insurrection (R. Luxemburg), or planned → revolution (V. Lenin) — was the conquest of the state and the abolition of → capitalism. By 1960, however, most socialist parties in the West had become committed to capitalism, albeit one managed in a way to support broad social programs. The exceptions were the socialist regimes primarily in eastern Europe and Asia that effectively abolished capitalism.

1. Background

There were important antecedents to the emergence of comprehensive socialist theories and formal organizations in the second half of the 19th century, especially Thomas More's (1478-1535) and Jean-Jacques Rousseau's (1712-78) radical critique of private → property, Gracchus Babeuf's (1760-97) radical communalism and the Jacobin Clubs in revolutionary France, the "Utopian" reformers of the Restoration (Saint-Simon, Charles Fourier, Robert Owen), the Chartist movement in Great Britain, and the French proletarian agitators (Louis-Auguste Blanqui) in the 1830s. The various utopian and communitarian experiments in the United States in the 19th century are also important in understanding the development of socialism (→ Perfection 5).

The writings of Karl → Marx (1818-83) and Friedrich Engels (1820-95) went beyond the concern for → human dignity and social justice of previous humanistic texts by providing a theoretical basis for socialist organizations at the end of the 19th century and beyond. Synthesizing French insurrectionism, Hegelian philosophy, and English economic theory, historical, or dialectical, → materialism constituted the general framework within which socialists analyzed history. As Marx and Engels wrote in *The Communist Manifesto* (1848), "The history of all hitherto existing society is the history of class struggle." Of more immediate importance was Marx and Engels's analysis of capitalism. Three ideas were particularly important: that capitalism would experience increasingly volatile economic crises, eventually imploding under the force of its own contradictions (catastrophe thesis); that the capitalist class would become increasingly small (proletarianization thesis); and that the growing proletariat would become increasing poor (pauperization thesis).

2. European Socialist Parties

Founded in 1890, the Sozialdemokratische Partei Deutschlands (SPD, German Social Democratic Party) was the earliest, largest, and best-organized socialist party in the world, serving as the model for most Continental working-class parties. Its organi-

zational antecedents include Ferdinand Lassalle's (1825-64) General German Workers' Association (1863), August Bebel's (1840-1913) and Wilhelm Liebknecht's (1826-1900) Social Democratic Workers' Party (1869), and the Socialist Workers' Party (1875). In its combination of revolutionary rhetoric and reformist practices, the SPD became typical of socialist parties throughout Europe. At Erfurt in 1891 the orthodox Marxist Karl Kautsky (1854-1938) made Marxism the official theory of the SPD; German workers, ever growing in number, had but to wait for the inevitable final economic crisis, which would provide them the requisite context to launch the revolution and abolish capitalism. In contrast, the revisionist Eduard Bernstein (1850-1932) focused on the practical, daily demands of the workers, paying scant attention to the ultimate goal of socialism.

Bernstein's *Evolutionary Socialism* (1899) legitimized the fundamentally reformist orientation of all socialist parties in Europe and presaged trends in the 20th century, as he argued that workers should, as indeed Marx did, support activities designed to democratize the state, develop welfare programs, and regulate the market. Bernstein's revisionism was based in part on the fact that Marx's theory did not correspond to reality: the capitalist class was not shrinking, and poverty among the workers was not growing. Neither did capitalism seem on the verge of collapse. Another source of reformist socialism was the union leaders who, as their organizations developed, grew weary, and later frightened, by functionaries who threatened armed struggle and mass strikes. This pattern was particularly evident in the United States. Union leaders were concerned with wages, working conditions, benefits, and, above all, institutional solvency.

Consequently, socialist conferences were hardly forums to analyze the intricacies of dialectics or the theory of surplus value. The French socialists, under the direction of Jean Jaurès (1859-1914), paid little attention to Marxist theory. Debates within the Italian Socialist Party and the Finnish Socialist Party centered on practical issues, especially the value of cooperation with nonsocialist forces; that their electoral constituencies were strongest among agricultural laborers, rather than industrial workers, does not appear to have caused much concern. In Britain labor leaders generally disassociated their organizations from anything remotely connected to Marxism, until 1918, when the Labour Party formally committed itself to the public ownership of the means of production; the reforms of Liberals and the practical orientation of unions clearly moderated British socialism. Throughout Europe theory was conspicuously irrelevant to policies; note the remarkable convergence of demands by highly Marxist parties (Germany, Russia, Spain), untheoretical socialist parties (France), nonsocialist labor parties (Britain), and unpolitical trade unions (almost everywhere).

As a result, when monarchs declared war in 1914, all socialist parties, except for the British Socialist Party, the Bolsheviks, and the Mensheviks, voted in favor of the war. The outbreak of war exposed socialist parties throughout Europe to a range of problems. For example, socialists had to abandon their ideologically mandated emphasis on industrial workers in order to defend the → "nation" and cultivate patriotic credentials. German socialists opted to support their government to protect the organizational and electoral achievements from the retrogressive effects of a possible Russian victory; socialists in eastern Europe supported a war that would deliver them from oppressive multinational empires.

3. Communist Movements

The most lasting consequence of World War I in Europe and the United States was the collapse of the Second International (1899-1916). At its height, this loose federation of socialist parties and trade unions included 21 countries and some 4 million members; its goals included an eight-hour workday, the prevention of → war, and the end of → colonialism. With its demise, communist parties emerged, which challenged socialists as the sole representatives of the Left. The greatest success was in Russia, where the Bolsheviks, led by Vladimir Lenin (1870-1924), came to power in October 1917. Lenin made three contributions to Marxist theory. First, he argued that, given the unparliamentary character of czarist Russia, Russian socialists could not imitate the democratic structures of socialist movements elsewhere in Europe; instead, Russian socialism must be organized by a small, highly trained group of professional revolutionaries. Second, given the weakness of the Russian → bourgeoisie, a dictatorship of the proletariat was needed to facilitate Russia's transition from → feudalism to capitalism. Third, Lenin argued that European imperialism functioned to stabilize capitalism by ameliorating the problem of overproduction. Other contributions from Russia include Leon Trotsky's (1879-1940) notion of "permanent revolution" to counter the reactionary tendencies of bureaucracies, and Joseph Stalin's (1878-1953) "socialism in one country," which effectively detached the development of Soviet communism from the support of socialist parties elsewhere in

Europe. Under Stalin, the Soviet Union became a formidable economic and military power.

The impact of the Soviet Union on Europe and the United States was profound. In 1919 Lenin founded the Third International (1919-43), which expanded membership to 41 countries, largely by mobilizing parties outside of Europe. Most notably, the Moscow-controlled Third International sought to end European colonialism. Most infamous, however, were its erratic and often catastrophic directives to communist parties outside the Soviet Union. For example, Moscow's sectarianism forbade German communists from joining forces with other antifascist forces until 1934, when it was too late. Stalin's 1939 pact with Hitler undermined antifascism as a unifying force. After World War II Moscow imposed and maintained Stalinist regimes in the countries that had been liberated by the Red Army (in Poland, East Germany, Hungary, Romania, Bulgaria, Czechoslovakia, Estonia, Latvia, Lithuania, and, to a lesser extent, Albania and Yugoslavia). These regimes, which lasted until 1991, nationalized industry and collectivized agriculture. While the economic performance of these command economies did not measure up to those in the capitalist West, they did make dramatic industrial, technological, and scientific advancements (esp. in the Soviet Union and East Germany). The governments of Eastern European communist regimes were highly centralized, authoritarian regimes, which paid little heed to civil and individual → rights. Notwithstanding their provision of universal health care and education, rent control and utility subsidies, and extensive state-financed cultural programs, Eastern European governments suffered from chronic legitimacy problems. State-directed economies were simply not able to satisfy consumer expectations.

Communist movements appeared throughout the undeveloped world after 1945. These movements sought to displace colonial regimes, advance economic autonomy, and restore national sovereignty. They typically promised the nationalization of key industries and the redistribution of land. The most important success in Asia was the establishment of the People's Republic of China in 1949 by Mao Zedong (1893-1976). While heavily influenced by Stalinist Russia, Mao contributed to Marxist theory by his emphasis on the peasants as the revolutionary force. Mao also developed a strategy of protracted war (or three-stage guerrilla war: strategic defensive, strategic stalemate, strategic offensive), which proved effective against the Japanese and American-backed Nationalist forces in the 1930s and 1940s; his strategy was applied successfully against colonial powers and proxy regimes in places as different as Cuba and Viet Nam. Mao's legacy is contradictory. On the one hand, he is credited with reestablishing China's sovereignty, modernizing industry and agriculture, and increasing literacy and life-expectancy rates; on the other hand, he is associated with devastating famines, a cult of personality, dictatorship, and the corruption of cultural-intellectual life in China.

4. Resurgence of Socialist Parties

In central and western Europe in the 1920s, communist parties, with the exception of those in Germany and France, were marginal political forces, never posing a revolutionary, or even parliamentary, threat. They created widespread fear and were plagued by ill-conceived directives from Moscow. In contrast, socialist parties did well in the 1920s and beyond: in Britain, Spain, France, Germany, Denmark, and Sweden socialists formed governments (alone or in coalition) or represented strong parliamentary opposition. Fascist regimes in Italy, Germany, and Spain destroyed local socialist and communist organizations; a similar fate awaited those parties in countries that the Germans conquered after 1939.

Just as socialist parties dominated the Left in the 1920s, communist parties prevailed between 1945 and 1948. Communist insurrections in Albania and Yugoslavia abolished capitalism and established a one-party state, independent of the USSR; Greek communists likewise revolted but were crushed by U.S.-backed forces; and the communists were represented in ruling coalitions in France, Italy, Norway, Belgium, Austria, and Finland. By 1948, however, the electoral strength of communist parties, except in France and Italy, fell well behind their socialist counterparts; everywhere the communists were expelled from government. The communists' success was due primarily to their resistance to Nazism, which provided them with much-needed patriotic credentials. Their sudden demise was due primarily to the cold war; it was very difficult for populations occupied by, or in the shadow of, the United States to embrace or even tolerate communism.

Socialists in the West recovered control of the Left (except in France and Italy, where the communists remained very strong), which they were generally capable of translating into electoral success. In the 1950s socialists in Norway, Sweden, and Denmark controlled the governments; in Austria, Holland, Belgium, and Finland they served in coalition governments; in France, Germany, Britain, and Italy,

however, they were in opposition. In the 1960s the socialists were generally more successful. Throughout Europe, governments established social welfare programs (national health insurance, old-age pension, full employment, family allowances, public housing, maternity and disability leave), and governments in Britain and France nationalized specific industries (transportation, communication, coal, and steel).

These programs certainly represent the legacy, but not necessarily the work, of European socialists, for social welfare programs had multiple agencies (confessional, Liberal, and Right parties) and functions (social justice, wage control, political legitimacy). There are no uniform correlations between socialist governments and social welfare programs, taxation rates, or public expenditure. Even nationalization received the support of Conservatives in Britain and Gaullists in France, and for reasons that had nothing to do with abolishing capitalism. The catastrophes of the first half of the 20th century had presumably made Europeans recognize the imperative of stabilizing capitalism, even if this effort entailed a commitment to welfare programs, market regulations, and state intervention.

The electoral success of socialists after World War II (40 percent on average by the 1960s) was the result of, first, their historical associations with welfare programs and, second, their increasing capacity to form coalitions. The latter was achieved by formally abandoning revolutionary jargon, by soliciting middle-class voters, and, above all, by accepting capitalism as the means to finance social welfare programs. At Bad Godesberg in 1959, the SPD program did not mention Marxism or identify socialism as an end goal; in Britain, Anthony Crosland (1918-77) endorsed Keynesian economic policies; at their 1961 Blackpool Conference, Labour did not even use the term "socialism." In Austria, Belgium, and Italy socialists renounced their traditional hostility toward religion. When in government, socialists never pursued fundamental political or economic changes; they aligned easily with center-right parties.

After 1968 socialist parties experienced strong challenges from two directions. First, high energy costs and unemployment, inflation, low growth, and the decline of manufacturing threatened the ability of the European state to finance social programs; also, decline in union membership and dramatic increases in female, part-time workers challenged socialism's traditional base and conventional view of the working class. Second, new social movements (e.g., → feminism, → ecology, → pacifism) challenged the hierarchical and compromising (i.e., coalition-building) character of socialist parties, forcing leaders to expand the traditional parameters of party agendas. The so-called New Left of the 1960s in Europe and the United States rejected Soviet-style socialism and also organized opposition to the Viet Nam War and racial discrimination. It also produced a refreshingly vibrant academic culture, as represented by such figures as Herbert Marcuse (1898-1979), Noam Chomsky (b. 1928), and Angela Davis (b. 1944), to name only a few.

By the 1980s socialist parties, initially conceived to liberate the (male) industrial working class, had become instruments to emancipate women, protect the environment, and prevent nuclear war. Socialists, early champions of women's suffrage, supported abortion and divorce rights, equal pay, child-care, parental leave, and female quotas. Socialists were also responsive to ecological issues and either co-opted Green platforms or formed coalitions with Green parties. Finally, socialists sought to improve East-West relations and reverse the arms race (→ Weapons of Mass Destruction).

The immediate postwar period saw a left-center consensus, which facilitated the success of socialist parties, but the 1980s and 1990s revealed a right-center, neoliberal consensus, which obliged socialist parties to alter almost all of their historic principles. The market, regulated by legislation, not public property, was accepted as the best means of maintaining welfare programs; capitalism, not socialism, was the preferred mode to modernize the economy, especially in southern Europe and Great Britain; the abolition of capitalism as an end goal was deleted from most socialist programs; emphasis shifted from full-employment programs (to benefit workers) to consumer-oriented anti-inflationary programs (to benefit the middle class); relations between unions and socialist parties became increasingly tenuous; aversion to European-wide economic integration weakened; and communist parties abandoned traditional symbols (flowers replaced hammers and sickles). Even in the Soviet Union, Mikhail Gorbachev (b. 1931) initiated reforms to decentralize the economy.

5. U.S. Socialists

In the United States, socialists were generally unable to build an enduring political movement that had a dominant base in the labor movement and that extended over generations. Capitalism, though, was not without its detractors, as witnessed by the numerous social critics and communitarian experiments of the 19th century. Moreover, in the first de-

cades of the 20th century socialism was a formidable political and social force. Between 1901 and 1912 membership in the Socialist Party of America (SPA, founded in 1901) grew from 10,000 to 118,000. The SPA fielded 1,200 public officials, among whom many were workers. There was also a rich working-class culture, as indicated by some 300 periodicals and numerous educational and leisure activities. The SPA represented the convergence of progressive and, in some cases, anticapitalist forces of the 19th century, such as the Socialist Labor Party, People's Party, Social Democratic Party, and some constituent elements in the American Federation of Labor (AFL). The rapid and geographically widespread growth of the SPA between 1901 and 1920 was both cause and effect of its ideological flexibility and democratic structure. Orthodox and revisionist Marxists, agrarian utopians, populists, urban trade unionists, farmers of the Southwest, foreign and native-born Americans, Protestant ministers, and middle-class intellectuals all found a place in the party. There was no party line to uphold: positions on revolution and evolution, race and immigration, unions and party, strikes and sabotage, and worker-farmer alliances differed wildly.

The most important American socialist was Eugene Debs (1855-1926), who founded the American Railroad Union in 1893 and cofounded the Industrial Workers of the World (IWW) in 1905. He was SPA candidate for president five times. In 1912, in his best showing, Debs received 6 percent of the vote; in 1920 he ran from prison (having been sentenced for opposing America's entry into World War I). Despite his electoral efforts, as a member of the SPA, Debs emphasized organizing workers rather than winning elections. While he was wary of the IWW's readiness to strike and sabotage, he was also critical of the limited vision of nonsocialist craft unions that dominated the AFL. Debs further distinguished himself by denouncing → racism. (As an organization, the SPA did very little to organize black workers or to oppose racism.)

Contrary to Marxist theory, socialism did not advance significantly in the United States, the most economically developed country in the world. By 1920 the American Left had declined considerably, as socialist, communist, and labor parties together could count only some 36,000 members, and socialist mayors declined from 74 in 1911 to 18 in 1917. Two factors were most important to the decline of the SPA specifically, and the American Left generally. First, the SPA's antiwar position was met with vigilante terror and government policies of obstruction, prosecution, and deportation, especially in the West and South.

Second, the Bolshevik Revolution brought about the formation of rival communist and labor parties in 1919; the intractable disputes over the applicability of Bolshevism in the United States and the authority of the Moscow-controlled Third International paralyzed the Left. Increasingly marginalized in the 1920s, American socialists and communists, like their European counterparts, were unable to benefit politically from the presumably propitious "objective conditions" of the Great Depression of the 1930s. Despite their significant influence in labor, social welfare, cultural expression, and elsewhere, neither group was able to advance electorally. The post–World War II Red Scare spelled the end of a socially or politically relevant American Left.

Bibliography: P. J. BAILEY, China in the Twentieth Century (2d ed.; Oxford, 2001) • I. T. BEREND, Central and Eastern Europe, 1944-1993 (Cambridge, 1996) • M. J. BUHLE, P. BUHLE, and D. GEORGAKAS, eds., Encyclopedia of the American Left (Urbana, Ill., 1990) • R. V. DANIELS, ed., A Documentary History of Communism (rev. ed.; 2 vols.; Hanover, N.H., 1984) • A. FRIED and R. SANDERS, eds., Socialist Thought: A Documentary History (New York, 1992) • R. S. GOTTLIEB, Marxism, 1844-1990: Origins, Betrayal, Rebirth (New York, 1992) • S. M. LIPSET and G. MARKS, It Didn't Happen Here: Why Socialism Failed in the United States (New York, 2000) • K. MARX and F. ENGELS, The Communist Manifesto (ed. J. E. Towns; Boston, 1999; orig. pub., 1848) • M. MEISNER, Mao's China and After (3d ed.; New York, 1999) • D. SASSOON, One Hundred Years of Socialism (New York, 1996) • G. SWAIN and N. SWAIN, Eastern Europe since 1945 (New York, 2003) • J. WEINSTEIN, The Decline of Socialism in America, 1912-1925 (New Brunswick, N.J., 1984).

ROBERT SUMSER†

Socialization

1. General
2. Religious

1. General

1.1. The term "socialization" became a basic concept in American sociology in the 1930s and 1940s. It describes all the planned and unplanned influences that a → society exerts upon its growing members and the learning processes or mechanisms by which individuals adopt and appropriate these influences. It is the process by which a society reproduces itself as a sociocultural system and by which, since the socialized individual is also a productive subject, it continually evolves. Individuals receive from society certain elements that are held in common and without which society could have neither stability nor flexibility: → language, models or roles of conduct, techniques of self-control, cultural values, → norms and moral principles (→ Ethics), philosophical and religious conceptions, → myths, and paradigms. Perhaps the most important academic root of the sociological theory of socialization is the social philosophy of G. H. Mead (1863-1931), for whom the basic anthropological phenomenon was not the individual linguistic or rational process but the social process, which is worked out in so-called interactionism (esp. by T. Parsons).

In view of the many processes involved, the concept of socialization was adopted by nearly all disciplines in the humanities and the social sciences — besides sociology, by cultural anthropology (→ Culture 4), → psychology, → communication theory, sociolinguistics, → ethnology, and → education. Along with the "empirical turn" in the German philosophy of education, the expression has found a home in Germany since the 1960s, for education made socialization its experiential basis.

1.2. The pedagogical reception of the concept of socialization sets the task of conceptual precision before academic educational policy.

What is the relation of socialization to traditional views of education, but also to new terms that are used for the process of human development such as "maturity," "influence," "personalization," "individuation," "inculturation," or "development" itself? Various relations are possible here, and they all make sense, whether socialization involves only one aspect (influence by social relations and groups), or whether it is used for the total process. In the latter case it is congruent with the term "education," when this takes into account what may be called functional or unplanned education by means of the relationships and circumstances of life. In such a case, we may lose the concept of education in the narrower sense.

Since education influences socialization, the question of the goals of socialization arises. The answer depends on what the relation is thought to be between the individual and society, or the person (→ Self) and the → institution. If individuals are seen as the agents of social roles, and if they are to maintain their independence and individuality (→ Individualism) over against social expectations, how can their → autonomy find expression? In view of this tension a theorem of "balancing identity" (E. Goffman, J. Habermas) has been worked out, and forces that make for identity such as role distance, → empathy, and tolerance of ambiguity have all been given a place in the repertoire of educational goals. But the ethical questions raised by these goals have not yet been answered.

As regards the structure of the socialization process, a distinction is made between "primary" (i.e., preschool) and "secondary" forms. Further distinction is made among the sources of socialization, which include → family, → kindergarten, school, job, and peer groups, with particular significance attaching to the → mass media and to the "scene" in youth cultures (→ Subculture; Youth Work). The structures relating to these sources can also be linked up with "phase models" in → psychoanalysis or developmental psychology. The return of younger generations to the thinking and behavior of older generations is now seen as "retroactive socialization."

1.3. The various methods of research, some interdisciplinary, show various interests. Important research impulses derive from organizing curricular reform and concrete courses of instruction. But → social education and social politics (esp. the family), along with legislation and the administration of justice, all rely on the results of socialization research, especially concerning the influence of the milieu, one's social → class, and the social status of values, behavior, language, and lifestyle.

2. Religious

2.1. The term "religious socialization" makes us aware that the appropriating of religious ideas, norms, and models of conduct takes place in a social context — that is, by means of → group communication and interaction, within the framework of institutions. A question arises, however, whether we should simply call it a special case of general socialization.

The idea that the Christian → faith is communicated and appropriated in exactly the same way as, for example, language, ways of dealing with people, customs, or clichés is to be resisted on theological grounds, for it ignores the fact that the Christian understanding of reality achieves subjective allegiance only by means of an act of existential decision. The semantically clear and credible presentation of Christian witness by persons, groups, or institutions that are the means of religious socialization are a necessary, but not the only prerequisite, in making a decision of this kind.

Sociology and social theory can also give us reason not to regard religious socialization as a special instance of general socialization. If we do make this equation, as, for example, T. Luckmann does on the basis of his definition of → religion as the existing basic and integrative system of values or complex of → meaning in a society, then at its core all socializa-

tion is religious socialization. In view of the actual effects of traditional religion on human action, we must agree that religious socialization is important, even though the influence of religion may be in decline, or at any rate less obvious than in earlier epochs. For where the Christian understanding of reality is regarded and accepted as true, it *eo ipso* governs human thinking, feeling, and willing.

2.2. If too broad an understanding of religious socialization is inappropriate, so too is too narrow a view. Its concern is not merely with questions of what elements of traditional religion, in what ways, and with what results enter the consciousness of modern adults or young people and influence their religious development. Such an approach would leave out of consideration the dependence of religious development on other lines of personal → development such as the cognitive, the psychosexual (→ Sexuality), and the moral, along with the impact of religious factors on these other forms of human development. The true theme of a theory of religious socialization, then, is the total process of socialization in a given sociocultural setting, the main issue being that of the relation between this total process and the elements of religious development within it.

2.3. Empirical research in religious socialization orients itself, on the one hand, to questions arising in the → sociology of religion and of the churches. They include all the measures of religious education that are taken in the family, kindergarten, school, and church. The form, intensity, and efficacy of religious education are investigated in relation to structural social changes, specific factors of environment and → class and stratum, specific profiles of → piety, strategies of church work, and changes in the educational system.

On the other hand, the orientation, along with psychological and psychoanalytic theories of development, is to particular situations of decision in personal development, with a view to establishing the interaction between religion and general developmental problems and formulating criteria for an experience-oriented educational practice. For example, what form will the idea of God and one's relationship with him take in relation to typical crises in personal development as psychoanalysis brings these to light? What positive or pathogenic influence (→ Neurosis) will religious → symbols and practices (→ Devotion; Prayer; Worship) have on the development of self-worth (narcissus crisis), on the formation of → conscience (Oedipus crisis), or on the finding of self-identity (puberty crisis; → Identity)?

The dominant functional approach in all such investigations should not be discredited by theology.

We do not have here a relativizing of the truth claims of the Christian faith but an attempt to clarify their practical significance in relation to experience.

→ Biography, Biographical Research; Christian Education; Development 2-3; Ego Psychology; Environment; Identity; Psychology of Religion; School and Church; Sociology of Churches; Sociology of Religion

Bibliography: On 1: S. BERMAN, *Children's Social Consciousness and the Development of Social Responsibility* (Albany, N.Y., 1997) • H. BLUMER, *George Herbert Mead and Human Conduct* (Walnut Creek, Calif., 2004) • C. FLANAGAN, *Early Socialisation: Sociability and Attachment* (New York, 1999) • D. A. GOSLIN, ed., *Handbook of Socialization Theory and Research* (Chicago, 1971) • B. KRZYWOSZ-RYNKIEWICZ and A. ROSS, eds., *Social Learning, Inclusiveness, and Exclusiveness in Europe* (Stoke on Trent, Eng., 2004) • T. PARSONS and R. F. BALES, *Family, Socialization and Interaction Process* (Glencoe, Ill., 1955) • A.-N. PERRET-CLERMONT et al., eds., *Joining Society: Social Interaction and Learning in Adolescence and Youth* (New York, 2004) • B. ROGOFF, *The Cultural Nature of Human Development* (New York, 2003) • K.-J. TILLMANN, *Sozialisationstheorien* (13th ed.; Reinbek, 2004).

On 2: J. A. BECKFORD, *Social Theory and Religion* (Cambridge, 2003) • J. W. FOWLER, K. E. NIPKOW, and F. SCHWEITZER, eds., *Stages of Faith and Religious Development: Implications for Church, Education, and Society* (New York, 1991) • H.-J. FRAAS, *Religiöse Erziehung und Sozialisation im Kindesalter* (3d ed.; Göttingen, 1978); idem, *Die Religiosität des Menschen. Ein Grundriß der Religionspsychologie* (2d ed.; Göttingen, 1993) • K. E. HYDE, *Religion in Childhood and Adolescence: A Comprehensive Review of the Research* (Birmingham, Ala., 1990) • F. K. OSER and W. G. SCARLETT, eds., *Religious Development in Childhood and Adolescence* (San Francisco, 1991) • R. PREUL, *Religion, Bildung, Sozialisation* (Gütersloh, 1980) • F. SCHWEITZER, *Lebensgeschichte und Religion* (4th ed.; Gütersloh, 1999); idem, *The Postmodern Life Cycle: Challenges for Church and Theology* (St. Louis, 2004) • K. TAMMINEN, *Religious Development in Childhood and Youth* (Helsinki, 1991).

REINER PREUL

Society

1. Term

The term "society" means (1) people living together; (2) a more or less independent association of people with institutionalized relations (→ Institution) that are regulated by sanctions, and also with certain common values, aims, and interests (e.g., → Nation, Nationalism); and (3) an → organization set up for a specific purpose (distinguished by F. Tönnies from the society that grows up of itself and has its purpose within itself). For the most part the term has sense (2) in modern → sociology. The derived term "association" may sometimes be used for the movement whereby a → group or institution merges into a larger society, giving up its own → autonomy in order to perform a specific function within the larger unit.

The concept of society is relatively late. Besides the → family, the Greeks knew only the polis, which embraced the → state, the society, and → religion (→ Greek Religion). The distinction between → church and state played a major role in the Middle Ages. When the middle classes developed, with their striving for → democracy and a modern economy not regulated by the state (→ Modern Period), the English and French thinkers of the → Enlightenment began to use the phrase "civil society" (first in A. Ferguson's *Essay on the History of Civil Society* [1767]). I. Kant (1724-1804; → Kantianism) distinguished between political and natural (civil) society. G. W. F. Hegel (1770-1831; → Hegelianism) related the two dialectically. Burgeoning sociology (which began with A. Comte) viewed society as its proper theme, and from now on the state came to be regarded as only one of various social institutions.

2. History

When people lived as → nomads or seminomads, society was identical with the extended clan. Only as agriculture developed and the population became more settled could larger social units come on the scene. An important development was the rise of cities as centers of government, trade, and culture. For centuries the land (where most people lived) and the → city were in stable balance. This society of agrarians and craftsmen characterized Europe from the Middle Ages up to the 18th century.

In the 19th century new techniques of production and communication, along with the triumph of middle-class groups (→ Bourgeois, Bourgeoisie) over the older feudal order, led to the development of the new type of → industrial society. Modern industrial society is essentially urban. The division of labor, constantly improving technology, and the rationalization of all life are outstanding features. The transition from an agrarian to an industrial society was so radical that all 19th-century sociologists examined it theoretically. C. H. Saint-Simon (1760-1825), Comte (1798-1857), and later É. Durkheim (1858-1917) drew attention to increasing interdependence as a result of the division of labor. They regarded this development as good because it promoted human → solidarity. K. → Marx (1818-83) allowed that people are more interdependent, but he also argued that they have conflicting interests. In particular, the distinction between those who have capital and those who have only their labor to offer leads to inequality (→ Equality) and thus gives rise to social classes (→ Class and Social Stratum; Marxism; Socialism).

Others pointed out that with the increasing size and complexity of society, and with the expansion of rationalizing and bureaucracy, we face the loss of traditional values and human relations (Tönnies) or the destruction of human → freedom in an ever more individualistic society (A. de Tocqueville). The modern term "mass society" (→ Masses, The) describes a society of large, centralized, bureaucratic institutions in which there are many human contacts, but which are superficial, fleeting, and impersonal. In the late 20th century, when relatively more people found themselves in administrative, cultural, and service sectors than in the industrial sector, the new term "postindustrial society" came into use. → Science and → technology hold a predominant place in this new form (→ Service Society).

3. Sociology

Sociologically, the most important problem of society is that of the relation between structure and → culture. Historical → materialism (Marx) regards the nexus of social relations (primarily economic relations) as decisive for ideas and values. This nexus shapes the cultural superstructure, which is determined by the infrastructure (relations of production, esp. class distinctions). In contrast, other sociologists (M. → Weber) point out that although economic factors are important, we cannot deduce ideas and religious conceptions from them alone. These, too, exert an influence, among other things, on economic life.

A second basic problem concerns the formation of society. Society is less a natural entity than a human institution (as most societies bear witness), but to what degree has it been consciously established? It is probably to be seen as the end result of innumerable human decisions that originally were taken with some immediate aim in view but that in com-

bination produced institutions and relations that were not at first envisioned and yet that showed a great capacity for survival once they were established. Furthermore, these institutions are constructs that are made more complex by conflicting revitalizations, so that it is hard to grasp their mutual relations and development.

A third sociological problem is that of the cohesion of a society. Are inner contradictions suppressed by compulsion and → manipulation, or can there be some high degree of integration whereby the parts contribute to the survival of the whole? A related question is what changes a society. Do we look at changes in the relations of production, at demographic developments, or at changes in ideas?

4. Philosophical and Social Ethics

The fundamental philosophical question of society is whether to give priority to the individual or to groups and institutions. Is society a consequence of our social nature (Aristotle, Thomas Aquinas), or is it an artificial construct by way of contracts between individuals (Protagoras, J.-J. Rousseau, and other representatives of the social-contract theory)? There are also intermediate solutions. Thus Kant viewed human beings as unsociably social.

In the same connection the question arises how far one can make individuals or groups responsible for the society in which they live. Although a society is probably not the intended result of human actions, the problem of → responsibility is all the harder because society, consisting of a complex web of institutions, defies easy comprehension. This means that no one can say for certain what the results of human intervention will be, and it is thus best to exercise great caution in attempts at social direction.

A related question is whether one can regard society as a good environment for people. Is it a benevolent mother (Aristotle, Durkheim), or does it alienate us from our true being — in principle (Rousseau), in its present form as class society (Marx), or as one-dimensional society (H. Marcuse)? Much modern criticism of society arises at this point, from revolutionary to reforming and nonconformist (→ Counterculture; Subculture).

An interesting question in social ethics is the following: When we strive for social ideals, how far must we reckon with existing economic, technological, and political relations, especially the power structures, which we can neither fundamentally ignore nor merely accept?

5. Problems

The most important present-day problems of society are threefold. The first is the process of → secularization, in which society loses a comprehensive value system (→ Norms) and, in its place, is left only with → pluralism or a relativizing of values. Since a society needs a minimum of common values to validate its institutions and orient the actions of its members, many efforts have been made to develop a rational, nontranscendental value system to fulfill the function formerly fulfilled by religion (Comte). This theme underlies the debate about → civil religion.

The second problem is the process of individualizing, which sets individual freedom and personal self-fulfillment above subordination to a common goal. This can be a danger for society but paradoxically also for human freedom itself. The breaking or weakening of many social ties (to → family, → church, village, or profession) means that the state alone is left as an organizing force. Extreme → individualism can thus result in a totalitarian society (Tocqueville).

The final problem is that of the growing autonomy of science and technology and their breaking loose from a comprehensive system of values and meaning. Because and to the extent that science and technology follow only their own → logic, they acquire an increasingly threatening character.

→ Anthropology 5; Capitalism; Critical Theory; Development 1; Emancipation; Politics; Progress; Social Systems

Bibliography: R. Aron, *Eighteen Lectures on Industrial Society* (trans. M. K. Bottomore; London, 1967) • D. Bell, *The Coming of Post-industrial Society* (New York, 1999; orig. pub., 1973) • D. Frisby and D. Sayer, *Society* (New York, 1986) • A. Giddens, *The Constitution of Society* (Cambridge, 1986); idem, *The Third Way: The Renewal of Social Democracy* (Cambridge, 1999) • W. Kornauser, *The Politics of Mass Society* (New York, 1965) • K. Mannheim, *Man and Society in an Age of Reconstruction* (rev. ed.; London, 1980; orig. pub., 1940); idem, *Systematic Sociology: An Introduction to the Study of Society* (Westport, Conn., 1984) • F. Tönnies, *Community and Civil Society* (trans. J. Harris; Cambridge, 2001; orig. pub., 1887) • A. Touraine, *The Post-industrial Society: Tomorrow's Social History, Classes, Conflicts, and Culture in the Programmed Society* (trans. L. F. X. Mayhew; London, 1974).

JAKOB M. M. DE VALK

Society of Jesus → Jesuits

Socinianism

1. Fausto Sozzini
2. Doctrines
3. Evaluation and Development

1. Fausto Sozzini

Socinianism takes its name from the Italian Protestant Fausto Sozzini (Lat. Socinus, 1539-1604). It is a collective term for the anti-Trinitarians of Poland in the 17th century (→ Anti-Trinitarianism), describing both their doctrine and their church structure.

Influenced by the dogmatic statements of his uncle Lelio Sozini (last name with one *z*, 1525-62), which challenged Protestant → orthodoxy (§§1-2; → Calvinism 3), Fausto left Florence, where he had served the Medicis until 1574, and after periods in Basel (1574-78) and Klausenburg in Transylvania (now Cluj-Napoca in Romania, 1578-79), he arrived in Kraków in 1580. After a lengthy period of doctrinal controversies about infant → baptism, military service, and the 1,000-year reign of Christ (→ Millenarianism), which were then afflicting the Reformed Church *(Ecclesia maior)*, Sozzini succeeded in gathering together a → Unitarian minority *(Ecclesia minor;* → Reformation 4.9, 11) and giving its congregations a common doctrinal foundation. He was the organizer and theological authority of the Polish Brethren (the Fratres Poloni), which, with the protection of the nobility and in spite of the violent opposition of Roman Catholics, Reformed, and Lutherans, became almost a fourth church and denomination in Poland in the first half of the 17th century. At its main center in Raków (formed only in 1579, some 50 km. / 80 mi. northeast of Kraków), it established after 1600 both a college and a printing press, which attracted many students and teachers from abroad.

2. Doctrines

The unifying confessional statement of Socinianism was the Racovian → Catechism, which was published in Polish in 1605, later also in German (1608) and Latin (1609). It was drawn up by Valentin Schmalz (1572-1622) of Gotha and Johann Völkel (d. 1618) of Grimma, two students of Fausto. An enlarged Latin edition was prepared in 1684 by H. Johann Crellius, Jonas Schlichting, and Martin Ruarus.

The statement asserts that the way to eternal life begins with a proper knowledge of the one, all-powerful God and of Jesus Christ. Jesus Christ is one in will with the Father but should not be called

God because he has only the one, human nature. The orthodox doctrine of the → Trinity and the two-nature doctrines of Christ (→ Christology 2) are thus rejected. Of the three offices of Christ the prophetic is the most important. The → Eucharist is just a ceremony, not a → sacrament. It is not a sacrifice for the remission of sins, nor does it strengthen faith; it merely recalls and proclaims the loving sacrifice of Jesus Christ on the cross. Baptism is simply an → initiation rite for adults, although infant baptism, not attested in the Bible, is a tolerable error.

Christ guarantees believers eternal life by his exemplary earthly life, which they are to follow (→ Discipleship), and also by his death and → resurrection. The orthodox doctrine of satisfaction (→ Christology 2.3.2; Salvation 4.2) is rejected on the ground that it contradicts the gracious character of the Christian religion (→ Grace). Faith is a trusting → obedience before the commands, which believers accept by free will (a rejection of the doctrine of the fall and original sin). The outward sign of the church is simply a salutary doctrine of the → promises and commands, and the congregations will see to its observance with the help of → church discipline.

3. Evaluation and Development

The underlying philological and biblicist dogmatic criticism (→ Biblicism), which avoids all → allegory and which A. Ritschl (1822-89) and A. Harnack (1851-1930) characterized as a union of humanism with the nominalist and Pelagian tradition (→ Nominalism; Pelagianism), might be seen as an early "supernatural → rationalism" (§3) that accepts the truth and certainty of an exclusively preferred NT, but without the divine → authority of Christ, his supernatural → miracles, or his resurrection.

The next generation of Socinians, until they were driven out of Poland (1658), tried to set forth the exegetical foundation of their critical theology in numerous scholarly works, but the rational arguments and the strict → moralism came rapidly to the fore, and the supernatural elements began to fade. Along these lines Andreas Wissowatius (Wiszowaty, 1608-78), a nephew of Fausto, demanded in his *Religio rationalis* (1685) that in principle we must use the judgment of sound reason also in theology. Around 1700 both the exegetical findings and this methodological principle called for increasing attention among Protestant theologians in both the Netherlands and England (→ Deism). They were then taken up by the broader historical-critical → exegesis (§2.1.5) of the → Enlightenment and became the common legacy of theological rationalism.

The Christological motifs of Socinianism are still maintained by the Transylvanian Unitarian Church (→ Romania 2.3.2). Among the Unitarians of the United States, however, which have crossed 19th-century Romantic and idealistic elements with universalist and, more recently, humanistic and humanitarian elements (→ Universalism, Universalists), they are hardly recognizable at all.

Bibliography: C. ANDRESEN, *HDThG* 3.2.1, 3-5 • *BiDi* 8, 12-15, 18, 23 (1987, 1990-93, 1997, 2004) • A. M. HILL, "Unitarier," *TRE* 34.332-39 • P. KNIJFF and S. J. VISSER, comps., *Bibliographia Sociniana: A Bibliographical Reference Tool for the Study of Dutch Socinianism and Antitrinitarianism* (Hilversum, 2004) • M. MULSOW and J. ROHLS, eds., *Socinianism and Arminianism: Antitrinitarians, Calvinists, and Cultural Exchange in Seventeenth-Century Europe* (Leiden, 2005) • J. P. OSIER, *Faust Socin; ou, Le christianisme sans sacrifice* (Paris, 1996) • F. P. SOZZINI, *De Jesu Christo Servatore* (On Jesus Christ the Savior, 1578) (Basel, 1594) • W. URBAN, *Der Antitrinitarismus in den böhmischen Ländern und in der Slowakei im 16. und 17. Jahrhundert* (Baden-Baden, 1986); idem, "Sozzini, Sozinianer," *TRE* 31.598-604 • E. M. WILBUR, *A History of Unitarianism*, vol. 1, *Socinianism and Its Antecedents*; vol. 2, *In Transylvania, England, and America* (Cambridge, Mass., 1945-52) • A. WISSOWATIUS, *Religio rationalis* (1685) (Wolfenbüttel, 1982).

GUSTAV ADOLF BENRATH

Sociohistorical Exegesis

1. General
   1.1. Term
   1.2. History
   1.3. Method
2. OT
3. NT

1. General

1.1. *Term*

The term "sociohistorical exegesis" covers various sociologically oriented analyses of the literary sources of the OT and NT. Biblical categories of sources and text types can usually be put in different religious-social, sociopolitical, and cultural groups and movements that may differ locally, regionally, and also in time.

1.2. *History*

This type of exegesis involves several types of research. → Social history plays a large part in recent international study. Economic history is a central theme in the study of the ancient Near East, of classical antiquity, and of → Hellenism. Since the 19th century the various disciplines have paid more and more attention methodologically to social, economic, and cultural history, for example, in biblical archaeology or in the study of the country and period (→ Exegesis, Biblical; Archaeology 1; History, Auxiliary Sciences to). Much information had been gathered on Hebrew archaeology by the 19th century, with information on the country, the culture, and religious history (J. Benzinger).

The first comprehensive sociohistorical surveys appeared in 1920 (M. → Weber) and 1937 (Antonin Causse). → Liberation theology is one of the more recent theological streams influencing sociohistorical exegesis. We are indebted especially to F. Belo and N. K. Gottwald for information on historical and cultural material influences.

1.3. Method

Sociohistorical exegesis uses literary and sociological methods that specify source category, types of texts, and normative cultural assumptions. One must differentiate the historical, economic, social, political, and legal problems. The sources also provide ancient Oriental or classical sociocultural meanings that can be correctly interpreted only through the perspective of normative exegetical methods. Analyses of individual literary documents (→ Literature, Biblical and Early Christian) take into account nonliterary sources (archaeological and iconographic findings; → Iconography), as well as historical and socioreligious reconstructions (→ Sociology of Religion). Contributions by the biblical sciences to the analysis of text types (genres, history of forms), criticism of trends, and determination of the historical source have developed socioliterary approaches that are at least implicit. Sociohistorical exegesis calls for differentiated comparative methods — economic, religious, and cultural — whose horizon cannot be limited to the ancient Oriental and classical cultures.

2. OT

Basic to the sociohistorical exegesis of the OT are the results of Palestinian archaeology, which help to clarify hypotheses regarding especially disputed sociohistorical problems of the Israelite occupation and settlement (→ Israel 1.2). They are an irrefutable test when rightly applied. Excavations uncover, as far as possible, the individual ancient sites and disclose the material culture of various epochs.

Problems of the social structure and dynamics of ancient Israel arise at several levels. Sources and texts are often influenced by tribal forms and ways

of life. We can try to understand OT tribalism with the help of → ethnology. In this context we must allow that forms of social change cannot be pressed into a single epoch or process that led by way of the wanderings (→ Tribes of Israel), conquest, and formation of the state to the religiously and legally regulated and authorized → theocracy of the Persian period. From Judges 9 we have reliable sociopolitical information regarding the city government (→ City) of Canaanite Israel that lasted until the period of the monarchy, and from Nehemiah 5 (middle of the 5th cent. B.C.) we gain information regarding preexilic indebtedness and personal responsibility (→ Guilt 2). The relation between (corporate) priestly, levitical, political-military, administrative, economic, and tribal groups and relations, groups of relatives and households, and ritual and ethnic subsidiary groups (→ Slavery 2) can no longer be reconstructed from the OT with any detail. Violent clashes (Exod. 32:25-29; Deuteronomy 13; 2 Kings 10; 23:4-20, etc.) resulted from religious and sociopolitical conflicts, among which the forcible setting up of the monotheism of → Yahweh by Josiah (639-609) was of particular social and historical importance (→ Monotheism).

Monarchical institutions and city government gave emphasis to conflicts of division. From the middle of the eighth century Amos, Hosea, Isaiah, and Micah criticized the socially devastating practice of loans and illegitimate enrichment by means of trade that was increasingly regulated by a money economy (Amos 2:6-8; 4:1-3; 5:7-15; 6:1-3; 8:4-6; Mic. 2:1-10; 3:1-3; Hos. 4:1-3; 12:7-8; Isa. 5:8-10; 10:1-2). The remission of debts in an (un)regulated way (Leviticus 25; Deuteronomy 15) could not compensate for the typical dynamic of inequality that beset agrarian relations in the ancient Near East and antiquity. With obvious gaps, social development also shows epochal continuity.

Bibliography: On 1: F. BELO, *A Materialist Reading of the Gospel of Mark* (Maryknoll, N.Y., 1981) • J. BENZINGER, *Hebräische Archäologie* (3d ed.; Leipzig, 1927) • C. E. CARTER and C. L. MEYERS, eds., *Community, Identity, and Ideology: Social Science Approaches to the Hebrew Bible* (Winona Lake, Ind., 1996) • A. CAUSSE, *Du groupe ethnique à la communauté religieuse. Le problème sociologique de la religion d'Israël* (Paris, 1937) • A. R. CERESKO, *Introduction to the OT: A Liberation Perspective* (rev. ed.; Maryknoll, N.Y., 2001) • N. K. GOTTWALD, *The Tribes of Yahweh: A Sociology of the Religion of Liberated Israel, 1250-1050 B.C.E.* (Sheffield, 1999) • N. K. GOTTWALD and R. A. HORSLEY, eds., *The Bible and Liberation: Political and Social Hermeneutics* (rev. ed.;

Maryknoll, N.Y., 1993) • R. WORTHAM, *Social-Scientific Approaches in Biblical Literature* (Lewiston, N.Y., 1999).

On 2: M. AVI-YONAH and E. STERN, eds., *Encyclopedia of Archaeological Excavations in the Holy Land* (4 vols.; Oxford, 1975-78) • M. D. CARROLL R., ed., *Rethinking Contexts, Rereading Texts: Contributions from the Social Sciences to Biblical Interpretation* (Sheffield, 2000) • D. J. CHALCRAFT, ed., *Social-Scientific OT Criticism* (Sheffield, 1997) • F. CRÜSEMANN, *The Torah: Theology and Social History of OT Law* (Minneapolis, 1996) • H. EILBERG-SCHWARTZ, *The Savage in Judaism: An Anthropology of Israelite Religion and Ancient Judaism* (Bloomington, Ind., 1990) • P. F. ESLER, ed., *Ancient Israel: The OT in Its Social Context* (Minneapolis, 2006) • I. FINKELSTEIN, *The Archaeology of the Israelite Settlement* (Jerusalem, 1988) • B. LANG, ed., *Anthropological Approaches to the OT* (Philadelphia, 1985) • N. P. LEMCHE, *Early Israel: Anthropological and Historical Studies on the Israelite Society before the Monarchy* (Leiden, 1985) • S. NAKANOSE, *Josiah's Passover: Sociology and the Liberating Bible* (Maryknoll, N.Y., 1993) • R. NEU, *Von der Anarchie zum Staat* (Neukirchen, 1992) • M. NOTH, *Aufsätze zur biblischen Landes- und Altertumskunde* (ed. H. W. Wolff; Neukirchen, 1971) • H. SCHULZ, *Leviten im vorstaatlichen Israel und im Mittleren Osten* (Munich, 1987) • R. N. WHYBRAY, *The Good Life in the OT* (New York, 2002) • R. R. WILSON, *Sociological Approaches to the OT* (Philadelphia, 1984).

HERMANN SCHULZ

3. NT

3.1. Historical-critical → exegesis (§2.2) recognizes that to expound a text it is not enough to understand the intentions and ideas of its author. We must also see the concrete conditions of life in which he or she was raised. This fact raises the problems of sociohistorical exegesis (→ Social History). In the first third of the 20th century important steps were made in this direction. The question of primitive Christian forms of society (→ Primitive Christian Community) was raised, as were its relation to the Hellenistic form (E. Hatch) and the social aspects of the primitive Christian mission (A. von Harnack; → Mission 3.2). Papyrus findings brought to light the world of lower social classes as the social background of the NT (A. Deissmann). Exegesis made good use of the economic and social situation of → Palestine at the time of → Jesus (J. Jeremias) and of the insights won by historians of the society and economy of late antiquity (M. Rostovtzeff). In particular, *Formgeschichte* (→ Exegesis, Biblical, 2.2.3), with its question of the *Sitz im Leben*, or life-setting, of the various texts gave evidence of the un-

derlying social milieu. From roughly 1900 to 1930, the Chicago school of theology went even further with its demand that we should show the history of primitive Christianity as the developing social experience of a group with religious interests (S. J. Case).

3.2. Sociohistorical exegesis was marginalized between 1930 and 1970 by → dialectical theology and existential interpretation (→ Existential Theology 2), but it came back with a vengeance, holding itself together with a methodological consolidation. For modern sociohistorical exegesis it was not enough to consider the social and cultural relations in which the NT texts arose and to which they related. The texts had to be seen as manifestations of the social processes and processes of development behind them. To this extent we have here a renewal and development of the program of *Formgeschichte* (G. Theissen) insofar as the question of the life setting derives from restriction to the religious interests of the community.

Recourse is needed here to sociological theories (→ Sociology). Especially Max → Weber's (1864-1920) "interpretive sociology," with its conception of "charismatic authority" and "routinizations of charisma" (→ Charisma 2), is often used to describe the forms and developments of everyday primitive Christian community life (Theissen; B. Holmberg). The theory of a → sociology of knowledge as developed by Max Scheler (1874-1928) and Karl Mannheim (1893-1947) also plays a certain role (J. H. Elliott).

3.3. Sociohistorical exegesis has given rise to many new perspectives. It might be that the setting for important parts of the → Synoptic tradition, especially for → Q, do not lie in settled communities but in groups of wandering and ascetic charismatics ("wandering radicalism," G. Theissen). The explanation of the rise of Pauline theology warrants research into the economic and social relations of the congregations (e.g., in Corinth and Thessalonica) and into the complex relations of the primitive Christians to authority (B. Holmberg). The important role of city culture (→ City 1) in late antiquity, both as the soil of primitive Christianity and as an influential force in the development of forms of church life, also calls for notice (W. A. Meeks).

→ New Testament Era, History of

Bibliography: On Paul and specific places and groups: D. L. BALCH, ed., *Social History of the Matthean Community: Cross-disciplinary Approaches* (Minneapolis, 1991) • J. H. ELLIOTT, *A Home for the Homeless: A Sociological Exegesis of 1 Peter, Its Situation and Strategy* (Philadelphia, 1981) • K. C. HANSON and D. E.

Oakman, *Palestine in the Time of Jesus: Social Structures and Social Conflicts* (Minneapolis, 1998) • M. Hengel, *Judaism and Hellenism: Studies in Their Encounter in Palestine during the Early Hellenistic Period* (Philadelphia, 1981) • B. Holmberg, *Paul and Power* (Philadelphia, 1980) • J. Jeremias, *Jerusalem in the Time of Jesus: An Investigation into Economic and Social Conditions during the NT* (Philadelphia, 1969) • P. Lampe, *From Paul to Valentinus: Christians at Rome in the First Two Centuries* (Minneapolis, 2003) • W. A. Meeks, *The First Urban Christians: The Social World of the Apostle Paul* (2d ed.; New Haven, 2003) • J. H. Neyrey, ed., *The Social World of Luke-Acts* (Peabody, Mass., 1991) • G. Theissen, *The Social Setting of Pauline Christianity: Essays on Corinth* (Philadelphia, 1982) • D. C. Verner, *The Household of God: The Social World of the Pastoral Epistles* (Chico, Calif., 1983) • F. Watson, *Paul, Judaism, and the Gentiles: A Sociological Approach* (Cambridge, 1986).

More general works: S. J. Case, *The Social Origins of Christianity* (Chicago, 1923) • J. H. Elliott, *What Is Social-Scientific Criticism?* (Minneapolis, 1993) • P. F. Esler, *The First Christians in Their Social Worlds: Social-Scientific Approaches to NT Interpretation* (London, 1994) • J. G. Gager, *Kingdom and Community* (Englewood Cliffs, N.J., 1975) • M. Hengel, *Property and Riches in the Early Church: Aspects of a Social History of Early Christianity* (Philadelphia, 1974) • B. Holmberg, *Sociology and the NT* (Minneapolis, 1990) • H. C. Kee, *Christian Origins in Sociological Perspective* (Philadelphia, 1980); idem, *Knowing the Truth: A Sociological Approach to NT Interpretation* (Minneapolis, 1989) • H. G. Kippenberg, *Religion und Klassenbildung im antiken Judäa. Eine Religionssoziologische Studie zum Verhältnis von Tradition und gesellschaftlicher Entwicklung* (2d ed.; Göttingen, 1982); idem, *Die vorderasiatischen Erlösungsreligionen in ihrem Zusammenhang mit der antiken Stadtherrschaft* (Frankfurt, 1991) • A. Malherbe, *Social Aspects of Early Christianity* (2d ed.; Philadelphia, 1983) • B. J. Malina, *The NT World: Insights from Cultural Anthropology* (3d ed.; Louisville, Ky., 2001) • *NDIEC* • C. Osiek and D. L. Balch, *Families in the NT World: Households and House Churches* (Louisville, Ky., 1997) • R. L. Rohrbaugh, ed., *The Social Sciences and NT Interpretation* (Peabody, Mass., 1996) • M. I. Rostovtzeff, *The Social and Economic History of the Hellenistic World* (3 vols.; Oxford, 1941) • T. Schmeller, *Urchristliche Wandercharismatiker im Prisma soziologisch orientierter Exegese* (Stuttgart, 1989) • L. Schottroff, *Lydia's Impatient Sisters: A Feminist Social History of Early Christianity* (Louisville, Ky., 1995) • W. Schottroff and W. Stegemann, eds., *God of the Lowly: Socio-historical Interpretations of the Bible* (Maryknoll, N.Y., 1984) •

J. E. Stambaugh and D. L. Balch, ed., *The NT in Its Social Environment* (Philadelphia, 1986) • G. Theissen, *The First Followers of Jesus: A Sociological Analysis of the Earliest Christianity* (London, 1978) • M. White and O. L. Yarbrough, eds., *The Social World of the First Christians* (Minneapolis, 1995).

Jürgen Roloff†

Sociology

1. Concept and Criteria
2. Historical Overview
   2.1. The Genesis of Sociology and Its Problems
   2.2. Eighteenth and Nineteenth Centuries
      2.2.1. England
      2.2.2. France
      2.2.3. Germany
      2.2.4. Evolutionism
   2.3. Classic Period
      2.3.1. Marx
      2.3.2. Durkheim
      2.3.3. Tönnies, Simmel, Weber
      2.3.4. Sociology in the United States
3. Contemporary Directions

1. Concept and Criteria

1.1. There is no generally acknowledged definition of sociology. In the broadest sense the word refers to *the science of → society,* that is, the science of people living together, especially of the constantly changing structures that spring from the common activities of people and that, in themselves, determine people's activities (→ Action Theory).

This general definition allows varying emphases. Sociology can, for example, be defined either *analytically,* as the researching of systems and/or structure and → culture of a society, with its resulting processes, or *concretely,* as the research of → institutions or → groups or the configurations of people's life together (N. Elias).

1.2. Sociology is tied to the knowledge that people acquire in the process of living together. Sociological knowledge itself (→ Epistemology), however, differs from this "social knowing" in that it must prove itself in terms of the criteria of scientific rigor, namely, systematic coherence, verifiability, and relevance. That is, social reality must be described with concepts that are clear and are connected in an orderly manner. The connections between social phenomena must be presented and explained with the help of a comprehensible ordering of judgments (i.e., a theory). The judgments must be able to be tested empirically; in addition, the insights gained must be relevant for the development of a theory, its practical use, or both.

These criteria stand in an irresolvable tension. It is difficult to test a comprehensive theory and also to develop a general theory on the basis of empirically derived judgments. And in both cases the practical usefulness leaves something to be desired. An acceptable equilibrium between the named criteria thus remains a difficult task. A de facto concentration on one or another of these criteria is one reason for the different approaches in sociology. Other reasons emerge from the peculiarities of the object and its problems, and from the related choice of method.

2. Historical Overview

2.1. *The Genesis of Sociology and Its Problems*

Sociology arose in the 17th and 18th centuries, when the concept "society" received a new meaning. It came to be used for citizens' → organizations such as commercial firms or learned societies. Such groups developed first and, for the most part, in contrast to older organizational forms of → state, → church, and guild, so that "society" received also a polemical connotation; it stood for an area (the "civil society") on which state and church were to have no influence (→ Bourgeois, Bourgeoisie, 2; Society 1). According to J. Locke (1632-1704), it possesses a preferential place ahead of the state, which accordingly has a serving function.

In the ebb and flow of social changes, fundamental questions arise that have since been a constant challenge for sociological thinking, namely, the problems of social order, social change, and social inequality.

2.1.1. The problem of *social order* arose with the increasing → individualism and a growing consciousness of individual → freedom. Statistical results demonstrated order and regularity in society, yet it remained unclear how this order could emerge from the actions of innumerable free individuals. The philosophical question of the relationship between order and freedom became here the sociological question of how society is possible. It contains as the basic problem the relationship between the individual and the overarching whole (→ Society 3-4).

This problem is solved either by viewing the society as a specific whole (i.e., holism; → Organism) or by understanding the social construction as the result of the interplay of individual decisions, actions, and goals (i.e., atomism). Or one may conceive of the individual and the whole as mutually presupposing and conditioning each other.

The problem can be addressed by the following specific questions: Does order arise out of the role behavior of individuals (the atomistic market model)? Does it arise from the domination of the few over the many (holistic or atomistic conflict model)? Or does it rest on a → consensus about the building of society (holistic harmony model)? The answers are connected to the political ideologies of → liberalism, right- and left-wing radicalism, and → conservatism.

2.1.2. In addition, *social change* was a new phenomenon, at least in regard to its speed, extent, and intensity. In view of this problem, three positions are possible: a society can be seen as basically *static*, so that change requires an explanation; or as *dynamic*, in which case stability must be explained; or with change and stability viewed as two sides of a coin. These positions correspond, each in turn, to holism, atomism, or the joining of the two. Specific problems are the question of the causes of change and the question of the direction and assessment of the change as → progress. The theme of change forms the common boundary between sociology and the historical sciences (→ Development 1; Evolution).

2.1.3. Because freedom and → equality become ideals, the existing *social inequality* becomes not only an allocation problem but also a theoretical problem: is it rooted in the differing capabilities of individuals, is it an unavoidable aspect of society, or can both viewpoints be combined? Inequality is a starting point for the question of whether the social sciences must be normative or value-neutral.

2.1.4. Because of the concentration on one or two of the three fundamental problems and because this choice is always characterized by one's → worldview, sociology has from its very onset been pluralistic. The basic positions have broadened into a multifaceted panorama of "paradigms," each of which has methodological implications. The most important methodological question remains whether sociological methods should be those of the sciences or those of the humanities.

2.2. *Eighteenth and Nineteenth Centuries*

2.2.1. *England*

The above-mentioned variations correspond roughly to cultural differences in Europe in the 18th and 19th centuries. In England, liberalism influenced the despotic-society model of T. Hobbes (1588-1679), as well as the market model of Locke and A. Smith (1723-90). A. Ferguson (1723-1816) spoke of the mutual dependence of individual and society ("both associating and speaking . . . are coaeval with the species of man"). He also reflected on the unintended consequences of human action, namely, institutions; as the basic elements of human society, institutions are for him "the result of human action, but not the execution of any human design." In the 19th century J. Bentham (1748-1832) and J. Stuart Mill (1806-73) founded an atomistic social science according to utilitarian principles (→ Utilitarianism).

2.2.2. France
In Roman Catholic France the organic-consensus model was favored (→ Organism 3.9). J.-J. Rousseau (1712-78) made culture responsible for inequality and argued for a reorganization of society on the basis of a general will *(volonté générale)*, in the formation of which → civil religion (§2) would play a role.

A. Comte (1798-1857) coined the term "sociology" and is called the father of sociology. The overcoming of the intellectual crisis after the French → Revolution (§2.4) called for a new kind of thinking, a dependable, positive method that would lead to surer, more precise, and more useful knowledge of the facts (→ Positivism). Comte formulated the law of the three stages, which said that thinking, after having passed a theological stage and a metaphysical stage, enters finally into a third stage — the positive. The transition to this third stage was accomplished first by astronomy, then physics and chemistry, all of which proceed atomistically, and finally by biology and sociology, which operate holistically. Comte applied the biological differentiation between anatomy and physiology to sociology as statics (order) and dynamics (progress). Statics rests on a consensus; dynamics applies the three-stages law to societal development.

2.2.3. Germany
In contrast to the science-oriented sociology of England and France, Germany had other emphases, which slowed the development of sociology there. I. Kant (1724-1804; → Kantianism) and G. W. F. Hegel (1770-1831; → Hegelianism) brought important elements to social science. M. → Weber's (1864-1920) thesis on value-neutrality was based on Kant's differentiation of being and ought, while Hegel influenced Marxist theory (see 2.3.1). The thesis of J. G. → Herder (1744-1803) was significant — that a people is a historically determined, organic whole that is accessible to an individualizing, understanding, hermeneutical procedure rather than a positivistic one (→ Hermeneutics 3.1.2; Historicism; Romanticism 3).

2.2.4. Evolutionism
In the 19th century the strong influence of evolutionism on the historical and social sciences was seen especially in H. Spencer (1820-1903). He formulated the following cosmic law of development:

on all levels of reality, a transition from incoherent homogeneity to coherent heterogeneity takes place through processes of differentiation and functional specialization, which go together with an integration of the differentiated units. This triad of differentiation, specialization, and integration is highly significant in all modernization theories and gave great weight to the question of the driving forces of this development (climate, race, environment, economic relationships, etc.). The social Darwinism initiated by Spencer described societal development as a struggle for survival (→ Evolution 2.2). Its conceptualization (conflict and conquest) was used by L. Gumplowicz (1838-1909), G. Ratzenhofer (1842-1904), and F. Oppenheimer (1864-1943) for the processes of formation of the → state.

In the United States W. G. Sumner (1840-1910) represented a conservative variation that rejected any intervention into society. L. Ward (1841-1913) held to a reformist variety that acknowledged and advocated a social evolution through human intervention, along with natural evolution.

2.3. Classic Period
The foundation for modern sociology was laid in the classic period. The most important authors lived in the time of the transition to the → industrial society and reflected the problems that accompanied it. Besides discussion of the basic problems mentioned above (see 2.1), they attempted to make sociology an independent science through a definition of the object and the method that was as precise as possible.

2.3.1. Marx
K. → Marx (1818-83; → Marxism) was not interested in drawing boundaries between scientific disciplines. Sociologically, his thinking was normative and evolutionary. He regarded society as a whole defined by opposites and thus as the condition that makes classes possible; these classes drive forward a process of change that takes place in phases and ultimately produces social equality. In this way he sought to connect the conditioning societal whole and human action. Later, however, he fell back into a holistic determinism.

2.3.2. Durkheim
In contrast to the psychologizing approach of G. Tarde (1843-1904), who understood society simply as a gathering of people who, through processes of imitation, gain a certain unity and develop themselves by innovation, opposition, and similarity, É. Durkheim (1858-1917) held social facts to be realities sui generis. They are "ways of thinking, acting, and feeling" that come to the individual from the outside and exert a compelling power; they can-

not be traced back to organic or psychological facts but spring from the common actions of people. The society is the most important social fact; it possesses a religious character (→ Sociology of Religion 2.2) and is the source of the forms of viewing and understanding time, space, cause, result, and so forth (an approach that intends to sociologize the Kantian → categories). The social realities are to be handled as though they were things; thus, positive methods (involving observation, measurement, and statistics) are appropriate. Durkheim sees the society in transition from a mechanical → solidarity based on equality to an organic solidarity based upon a division of labor. In this transition the basis for a new social order arises. If this process proceeds too quickly, then every order can break apart, leading to anomie. He sees inequality as the necessary element of a differentiated society; it must, however, have giftedness as its standard.

2.3.3. *Tönnies, Simmel, Weber*

In Germany the position of sociology became problematic because of the differently defined opposition of the natural sciences and the humanities (→ Philosophy of History; Historiography 3.7). Although its object is historical-social reality, it cannot proceed solely by looking for social laws (i.e., nomothetically). But as soon as it proceeds by describing specific historical phenomena (i.e., idiographically), such as → Calvinism or → capitalism, and/or hermeneutically, the historical sciences become its strong competitor. It thus, on the one hand, must develop general concepts; on the other, it must conduct empirical (social) research. For F. Tönnies (1855-1936) this division of tasks led to the differentiation between pure, applied, and empirical sociology. His conceptual dichotomy between *Gemeinschaft* (community) and *Gesellschaft* (society), which should characterize societal change, is well known. Within the same division of tasks, G. Simmel (1858-1918) developed a sociology of the "forms of socialization," which in the end gave sociology an ahistorical character.

M. Weber sought to overcome the contradiction. For him, human social action was the object of sociology, and with this view he chose an atomistic starting point. Sociology must "understand clearly and thus explain causally" this object and thereby avoid value judgments (i.e., proceed in a manner that is *Wertfrei,* "value-neutral"; → Culture 4). For the purpose of bringing order to social phenomena, Weber developed generalizable "ideal types," which at the same time should allow "understanding." He used them also in the analysis of historical phenomena (→ Calvinism 4; Capitalism 2.2; Achievement

and Competition 3) and processes (rationalization; → Industrial Society 1; Rationalism 2).

In his analysis of society Weber emphasized that action is driven by material and ideal interests, but in a way that is determined by cultural values and models. Between the various spheres of value (→ Politics; Economy; Science and Theology; Religion), but also between groups and organizations within each of these spheres, → conflicts are unavoidable. His particular interest focused on the specifically Western process of rationalization, whose religious roots he sought (→ Sociology of Religion 2.2).

2.3.4. *Sociology in the United States*

In the United States sociology was institutionalized earlier than in other countries. As a reaction to theories of evolution, there was a turning to the empirical research of urban social problems, stimulated especially through R. E. Park (1864-1944). He belonged to the famous Chicago school, along with W. I. Thomas (1863-1947), E. W. Burgess (1886-1966), and W. F. Ogburn (1886-1959), among others. Their empirical definitions were generally deficient in theoretical content. Ogburn was especially well known because of his empirical research of social change and his theory of "cultural lag," which was received as the description of a cultural delay after technological development.

A second focus of American sociology was the "social behaviorism" of G. H. Mead (1863-1931), later called "symbolic interactionism" (→ Everyday Life 2.7 and 3.5). The behavioristic stimulus-and-response model was supplemented by the assumption that the "stimulus" is interpreted before a "response" follows, because people communicate with each other through the medium of interpretable → symbols and not on the basis of instincts (→ Communication 1). People develop a "self" in the process of communication; "mind" arises as a reflection upon the person's communication with his or her self. In this view, social behaviorism is related to → pragmatism. The "looking-glass self" first came into play with C. H. Cooley (1864-1929), while W. I. Thomas had already pointed to the element of interpretation in activity with his "definition of the situation."

3. Contemporary Directions

3.1. Sociology is well established today in universities. The numerous directions of research and a large number of scientific journals show a wide spectrum of fields of work and of tasks. Scientific conferences, both national and international (e.g., the International Sociological Association), make possible the exchange of themes and results of research.

3.2. The continuing differentiation of society is reflected in the specialization of sociology, while the fundamental problems to which sociology owes its existence constantly demand new expression in a changing society.

3.2.1. As far as the *level of analysis* is concerned, one can distinguish macrosociology, which deals with large societal connections and with → culture (§5); organizational sociology, which works on the middle level of → organizations; and microsociology, which researches smaller groups. As regards *content,* there is a growing number of specializations, for example, political sociology (→ Politics 2), economic sociology, sociology of families (→ Family 1), sociology of scientific knowledge, → sociology of churches, → sociology of knowledge, and → sociology of religion.

Cutting across all these specializations are the two categories of theoretic and empirical sociology, which are not mutually exclusive but have different emphases. In addition, there is an application-oriented sociology of management (or administration).

The *methods* of sociology, although refined for some time, still show the differences between the approach of science and the approach of the humanities. Classic evolutionism, with its monocausal thinking, was replaced with a neo-evolutionism in several paradigms (e.g., in systems theory).

3.2.2. The legacy of Marx appears in a less significant neo-Marxist sociology, but it forms an important source of inspiration for the Frankfurt school and its heritage (→ Critical Theory; Social Science 3). Some viewpoints of Durkheim and Weber were taken up by → functionalism and system theory (R. K. Merton, T. Parsons, R. Münch, N. Luhmann). Conflict sociology (→ Conflict) builds on Weber (R. Dahrendorf) and Simmel (L. Coser). Symbolic interactionism has not gone much beyond the stage developed by Mead and summarized by H. Blumer.

Newer, sometimes more radical variations are phenomenological sociology and ethnomethodology (→ Everyday Life 2.7.2; Phenomenology). Behavioristic tendencies are seen again in learning and utility theories (G. C. Homans, S. Lindenberg, K. D. Opp) and in the related rational-choice theory (J. Coleman). Noteworthy are the figuration and civilization theory of N. Elias (1897-1990) and historical sociology, following on his and Weber's work.

In addition, the structuration theory of A. Giddens and the strictly empirical sociology of P. Bourdieu, working with the concepts of habitus and field, should be mentioned. They embody three contrasting attempts to transcend the tension between social form and individual action (i.e., between holism and atomism; see 2.1.1).

3.3. Sociology continues to offer an extremely complex picture. Although the specific national directions have lost ground in favor of an internationalization of sociology, they have, admittedly, not completely disappeared.

Bibliography: Works mainly before 1900: A. COMTE, *Cours de philosophie positive* (6 vols.; Paris, 1830-42; 3d ed., 1869); idem, *The Essential Comte: Selected from "Course de philosophie positive"* (ed. S. Andreski; London, 1974) • A. FERGUSON, *An Essay on the History of Civil Society* (Edinburgh, 1767; repr., ed. F. Oz-Salzberger; Cambridge, 1995) • L. GUMPLOWICZ, *Grundriß der Soziologie* (Vienna, 1885) • J. G. VON HERDER, *Werke* (3 vols.; Munich, 1984-2002) • T. HOBBES, *Leviathan; or, The Matter, Form, and Power of a Commonwealth Ecclesiastical and Civil* (London, 1651; repr., ed. J. C. A. Gaskin; Oxford, 1996) • J. LOCKE, *Two Treatises on Government* (1690; repr., New York, 1960) • K. MARX, "The German Ideology" (1845-46), *MECW* 5.19-539 • J.-J. ROUSSEAU, *Discours sur l'origine et les fondements de l'inégalité parmi les hommes* (Amsterdam, 1755; ET *A Discourse on Inequality* [Harmondsworth, 1984]); idem, *The Social Contract* [1762]; and, *The First and Second Discourses* (ed. S. Dunn; New Haven, 2002) • A. SMITH, *The Wealth of Nations* (1776) (Harmondsworth, 1970) • H. SPENCER, *The Study of Sociology* (London, 1873; repr., Ann Arbor, Mich., 1961) • G. TARDE, *On Communication and Influence: Selected Writings* (Chicago, 1976) • *The Utilitarians: "An Introduction to the Principles of Morals and Legislation"* [by] *Jeremy Bentham. "Utilitarianism" and "On Liberty"* [by] *John Stuart Mill* (Garden City, N.Y., 1961).

Works mainly after 1900: L. M. BARKER, *Learning and Behavior: Biological, Psychological, and Sociocultural Perspectives* (Upper Saddle River, N.J., 1997) • T. BOTTOMORE and R. NISBET, eds., *A History of Sociological Analysis* (London, 1979) • P. BOURDIEU and L. J. D. WACQUANT, *An Initiation to Reflexive Sociology* (Chicago, 1992) • J. COLEMAN, *Foundations of Social Theory* (Cambridge, Mass., 1990) • C. H. COOLEY, *The Two Major Works of Charles H. Cooley: Social Organization* [1909]; *Human Nature and the Social Order* [1902] (Glencoe, Ill., 1956) • É. DURKHEIM, *Les règles de la méthode sociologique* (Paris, 1895; ET *The Rules of Sociological Method* [New York, 1982]) • S. N. EISENSTADT, with M. CURELARU, *The Form of Sociology: Paradigms and Crises* (New York, 1976) • N. ELIAS, *Über den Prozeß der Zivilisation. Soziogenetische und psychogenetische Untersuchungen* (2 vols.; Basel, 1939; new ed., Frankfurt, 1993; ET *The Civilizing Process:*

Sociogenetic and Psychogenetic Investigations, vol. 1, *The History of Manners;* vol. 2, *State Formation and Civilization* [rev. ed.; Oxford, 2000]) • A. GIDDENS, *The Constitution of Society: Outline of the Theory of Structuration* (Cambridge, Mass., 1984) • W. LEPENIES, *Geschichte der Soziologie* (4 vols.; Frankfurt, 1981) • G. H. MEAD, *Mind, Self, and Society* (Chicago, 1934) • W. F. OGBURN, *Social Change with Respect to Culture and Original Nature* (New York, 1922; repr., 1950) • R. E. PARK and E. W. BURGESS, *Introduction to the Science of Sociology* (Chicago, 1921; 3d ed., 1969) • G. SIMMEL, *On Individuality and Social Forms: Selected Writings* (ed. D. N. Levine; Chicago, 1971); idem, *Soziologie* (Berlin, 1908) • P. A. SOROKIN, *Contemporary Sociological Theories* (New York, 1928) • W. G. SUMNER, *Folkways: A Study of the Sociological Importance of Usages, Manners, Customs, Mores, and Morals* (New York, 1906; repr., 1959) • W. I. THOMAS, *On Social Organization and Social Personality: Selected Writings* (Chicago, 1966) • F. TÖNNIES, *Gemeinschaft und Gesellschaft* (Leipzig, 1887; 8th ed., 1935; ET *Community and Society* [New York, 1957]) • M. WEBER, *Wirtschaft und Gesellschaft* (1922; ET *Economy and Society: An Outline of Interpretive Sociology* [2 vols.; Berkeley, Calif., 1978]).

LEO LAEYENDECKER

Sociology of Churches

1. Definition
2. History
3. Theory
4. Research Fields
5. Institutes

1. Definition

The sociology of churches is part of the → sociology of religion. It deals with the social forms of Christianity, its influence on → society in general, and the way in which it is affected by social factors. Compared with the sociology of religion, it has its own essentially narrower themes. It differs from pastoral sociology inasmuch as, like the sociology of religion, it is value-free. But the distinction is fluid. In general, pastoral sociology is the scholarly social analysis of the phenomena of religion and the church in the interests of the church's action. In this sense it is a discipline of → practical theology.

2. History

The sociology of churches has been a special discipline only from the 1950s and 1960s, and particularly in Germany. In the Anglo-Saxon world, the sociology of religion is more dominant. Pastoral sociology has been known in Holland since the 1950s (W. Banning).

Even earlier, however, corresponding studies were of great importance for the development of the discipline, such as the empirical investigation of Protestantism by A. von Oettingen (1827-1906) or the analysis of the German territorial churches by P. Drews (1858-1912) and his associates (from 1902). We might also refer to detailed studies of individual problems, such as that of the relation of workers to the church by P. Piechowski and others. Finally, there were the works devoted to religion and geography (→ Geography of Religion) by G. LeBras and F. Boulard in France and by J. P. Kruijt in Holland.

A specific sociology of churches arose in Germany after World War II. In the 1960s this focus resulted in critical and even unhelpful questions, but then a theoretically based and empirically sensitive sociology of churches developed that was more aware of its limits vis-à-vis the broader field of → religion. It was important in this regard that the Roman Catholics and Lutherans in West Germany initiated inquiries entrusted to G. Schmidtchen and also to church-related planning groups. Since that time there has been fairly intensive research into problems of church work.

In the United States the sociology of churches, as a study of institutionalized Christianity, is a branch of the sociology or science of religion. It is in the hands of many scholarly societies that are supported by the → denominations and their colleges, so that many research projects are possible, over which there have been lively exchanges.

3. Theory

For a long time the sociology of churches lacked a theoretical basis. It was often in the hands of theologians and church workers who knew little of sociology, which perhaps explains the difficulty of its finding a true place among sociological disciplines. A basic change came only after the 1960s. The functionalist approach of O. Schreuder and others linked the sociology of churches to general theoretical development. Influential, too, was N. Luhmann's approach to religious sociology in terms of system theory (→ Social Systems). Luhmann's studies on the problem of the organization of religion were basic to inquiry in this area.

Technically, the sociology of churches now uses all the instruments of empirical → social science at its disposal, dominated by standardized procedures using the complex techniques of measurement and evaluation. Since the publication of results is often meant for a broader church public, however, the complexity of the procedures employed is not always apparent.

4. Research Fields

In general, the obvious forms of institutionalized religion are a main theme in research into the sociology of churches. This is especially true when we consider that the great polling institutes (Allensbach and EMNID in Germany, Gallup in the United States) include questions on church positions and related conduct. Often basic assumptions about the situation of religion and the churches in modern society play a part in interpretation of the results. The function, range, and extent of so-called → secularization are a matter for discussion. Studies by Schmidtchen, H. Hild, and J. Hanselmann deal with the situation of the mainline churches in the Federal Republic. There are comparable studies in Holland, Sweden, Finland, Austria, Switzerland, and the United States. Increasingly, attention focuses on those who are not attached to the church or who have left it (→ Church Membership 5).

Individual studies in Germany since the 1950s deal with the congregation (D. Goldschmidt, F. Greiner, and H. Schlesky; → Congregation 3), with offices (pastor, deacon and deaconess, teacher; → Ministry, Ministerial Offices), and with religious → socialization (§2), including that of theologians. Another important theme is that of → youth and religion, or youth and the church (→ Youth Religions). We also have studies of church rituals and forms of communication in the broadest sense (→ Communication; Preaching), of leadership bodies (→ Church Government), and of churches as social systems. In this connection we might refer to the studies of Roman Catholicism by F.-X. Kaufmann and his students (→ Catholicism [Roman] 2.3).

In Germany most of the work focuses on the mainline churches. Research into the → free churches or the Christian → sects is rare.

5. Institutes

Much of the work is done by special church or church-related institutes. The Roman Catholics have the Katholiek Sociaal Kerkelijk Instituut in Holland and similar institutes in Essen, Vienna, and Saint Gall. The German Evangelical Church has an institute in Hannover; the Evangelical Lutheran Church of Finland has the Church Research Institute in Tampere. Work is also conducted by the planning divisions of the church bureaucracies and by the theological faculties or individual sociologists on the sociology faculties (e.g., at the Roman Catholic universities in Belgium, Holland, Poland, and the United States). In the United States there are many societies or sections of societies, and in Europe we find the International Society for the Sociology of Religion, which resulted from work in the field in Holland, Belgium, and France.

→ Church 4; Civil Religion; Class and Social Stratum; Organization; Subculture

Bibliography: Older works: W. Banning, ed., *Handboek pastorale sociologie* (7 vols.; The Hague, 1953-62) • P. L. Berger, *The Noise of Solemn Assemblies: Christian Commitment and the Religious Establishment in America* (Garden City, N.Y., 1961) • P. Drews et al., eds., *Evangelische Kirchenkunde* (7 vols.; Leipzig, 1902-19) • D. Goldschmidt, F. Greiner, and H. Schelsky, *Soziologie der Kirchengemeinde* (Stuttgart, 1960) • G. LeBras, *Études de sociologie religieuse* (2 vols.; Paris, 1955-56) • A. von Oettingen, *Die Moralstatistik und die christliche Sittenlehre* (2 vols.; Erlangen, 1868-73) • P. Piechowski, *Proletarischer Glaube* (Berlin, 1927) • O. Schreuder, *Kirche im Vorort. Soziologische Erkundung einer Pfarrei* (Freiburg, 1962) • E. Troeltsch, *The Social Teaching of the Christian Churches* (Louisville, Ky., 1992; orig. pub., 1912) • M. Weber, *The Protestant Ethic and the Spirit of Capitalism* (Los Angeles, 1998; orig. pub., 1904-5) • J. M. Yinger, *Religion, Society, and the Individual* (New York, 1957).

More recent works: K.-F. Daiber, ed., *Religion und Konfession* (Hannover, 1989) • K. Gabriel and F.-X. Kaufmann, eds., *Zur Soziologie des Katholizismus* (Mainz, 1980) • G. Gallup Jr., *The Spiritual Life of Young Americans* (Princeton, 1999) • G. Gallup Jr. and J. Castelli, *The People's Religion: American Faith in the 90's* (New York, 1989) • G. Gallup Jr. and D. M. Lindsay, *Surveying the Religious Landscape: Trends in U.S. Beliefs* (Harrisburg, Pa., 1999) • C. Y. Glock, ed., *Religion in Sociological Perspective* (Belmont, Calif., 1973) • J. Hanselmann, H. Hild, and E. Lohse, eds., *Was wird aus der Kirche?* (Gütersloh, 1984) • H. Hild, ed., *Wie stabil ist die Kirche?* (Berlin, 1974) • W. Huber, ed., *Kirche in der Vielfalt der Lebensbezüge. Die vierte EKD-Erhebung über Kirchenmitgliedschaft* (Gütersloh, 2006) • P. Jenkins, *The Next Christendom: The Coming of Global Christianity* (Oxford, 2002) • F.-X. Kaufmann, *Kirche begreifen. Analysen und Thesen zur gesellschaftlichen Verfassung des Christentums* (Freiburg, 1979) • N. Luhmann, *Funktion der Religion* (5th ed.; Frankfurt, 1999; orig. pub., 1977) • D. A. Roozen and C. K. Hadaway, *Church and Denominational Growth* (Nashville, 1993) • G. Schmidtchen, *Zwischen Kirche und Gesellschaft* (Freiburg, 1972) • M. A. Thung, *The Precarious Organisation: Sociological Ex-

plorations of the Church's Mission and Structure (The Hague, 1976) • J.-P. WILLAIME, *Sociologie du protestantisme* (Paris, 2005) • R. WUTHNOW, *The Restructuring of American Religion: Society and Faith since World War II* (Princeton University Press, 1988).

Journals: Archives des sciences sociales des religions (1973- [1956-72, *Archives de sociologie des religions*]) • *Journal for the Scientific Study of Religion* (1961-) • *Social Compass* (1953-) • *Sociological Analysis* (1964-).

KARL-FRITZ DAIBER

Sociology of Knowledge

1. Term and Tasks
2. History of Knowledge
3. Scheler and Mannheim
4. Recent Trends

1. Term and Tasks

The sociology of knowledge investigates the relation between knowledge and being, as well as the connection between categories of thought, the claims of knowledge, and its social reality. It is a basic, theoretical, and specialized type of → sociology. From the outset, it lays claim to providing a total analysis.

2. History of Knowledge

2.1. French and Scottish → Enlightenment philosophy (→ Modern Church History 1.2) recognized that all social differences have social causes and are thus potentially subject to human control. Social, economic, and political factors determine the genesis, structure, and content of the human consciousness. Hence the philosophers of the Enlightenment anticipated what became a major thrust of the proponents of the sociology of knowledge.

In the main, however, philosophers have tried to show that such a sociology is neither possible nor desirable. I. Kant (1724-1804) allowed that perception always involves → categories of understanding and concepts, but he viewed the understanding itself as a priori (→ Kantianism 1). Empiricists of the most widely varied persuasions have argued that (scientific) knowledge is warranted by direct → experience not dependent on social conditions (→ Empiricism). At best, nontheoretical factors might influence the genesis of ideas, but not the structure and content of thought itself (→ Epistemology 1).

2.2. K. → Marx (1818-83) paved the way for a sociological analysis of knowledge by arguing that social and economic factors determine the ideological superstructure (→ Marxism). His theory of →

ideology (§1.2) became the central thesis of the sociology of knowledge and produced in the writings of, for example, G. Lukács (1885-1971) exemplary analyses of intellectual works.

É. Durkheim (1858-1917) was also a forerunner of sociology of knowledge, although he was not so successful in offering a comprehensive model of the processes of classification he sought to present. In *De quelque formes primitives de classification* (1903; ET *Primitive Classification* [Chicago, 1963]) and *Les formes élémentaires de la vie religieuse* (1912; ET *The Elementary Forms of the Religious Life* [London, 1915]), which he wrote in collaboration with M. Mauss, Durkheim argued that the central categories of perception and experience (space, time, causality, etc.) had their origin in the social structure. Durkheim and Mauss (1873-1950), by research into the classification processes of primitive → societies, reached the conviction that all the important categories of human thought are socially conditioned. Their thesis that the classification of things reproduces the classification of people (e.g., into clans) is often still a starting point for sociological research.

2.3. In the 1920s the decisive development of the sociology of knowledge came from M. Scheler (1874-1928) and K. Mannheim (1893-1947). Their contribution was a symptomatic product of a deep-rooted crisis in the historical and social consciousness of the day. → Historicism, → relativism, and → skepticism were under lively debate. What was often a naive belief in progress came under attack by distrust and skepticism.

3. Scheler and Mannheim

In this situation the sociology of knowledge became the doctrine of the rise and fall of social processes, relations, and depictions proper to the cultural sphere of knowledge (Scheler), and especially it became the doctrine of the link between knowledge and society (Mannheim). In contrast to the Marxist criticism of ideology, the sociology of knowledge lays less emphasis on the concealing intention of statements and more on the varied structures of consciousness possessed by the different subject types in history and society.

3.1. Scheler coined the term "sociology of knowledge." In his own investigations he was concerned to demonstrate its independent worth. He recognized, however, that there are factors of reality that condition thinking in various historical periods and in the most varied social and cultural systems of thought. He spoke of the impotence of the intellect face-to-face with such factors.

3.2. Mannheim's ambitious program was to lay a foundation for a sociological analysis of knowledge. Like Scheler, he took a broader view of the Marxist concept of superstructure and argued that psychological, biological, intellectual, and religious factors, as well as the purely economic, lay behind it. He investigated the social conditions of various forms of knowledge but excluded the sociological analysis of scientific and technological knowledge. Along with his *Ideologie und Utopie* (1929), his studies in the sociology of knowledge dealing with academic rivalry, conservative thought (→ Conservatism), and generational problems are still good examples of what the sociology of knowledge can achieve. He thought that the sociology of knowledge can play a part in intellectual and political life by showing that social conditions help to give rise to political philosophies, ideologies, cultural achievements, and competing systems of thought. He held the important view that the sociology of knowledge plays a key role in strategies that attempt to relate → reason to → politics.

4. Recent Trends

Recent trends in the sociology of knowledge include a stress on everyday awareness (→ Everyday Life 2), which classic sociology of knowledge had usually neglected. Specific attention was also paid to the scientific and technological forms of knowledge. P. Berger and T. Luckmann in their *Social Construction of Reality* (1966), with its reference to the social phenomenology of A. Schütz (→ Everyday Life 2.7) and the philosophical → anthropology (§4.2) of A. Gehlen (1904-76), deliberately set aside the classic approach and its epistemological and methodological questions. They take as their theme everything that counts as knowledge in the society.

Inspired by developments in the history of knowledge, the sociology of knowledge has recently attempted an empirical analysis of the "manufacture" of natural-scientific knowledge. The most important research tools have been ethnographies of laboratory life (B. Latour and S. Woolgar, K. Knorr-Cetina). These studies have led to a reassessment of the limitations of various types of knowledge, of the conditions of their origin, and of their structural qualities. Traditional theoretical assumptions about the specific rationality of scientific knowledge have also been revised.

→ Philosophy of Science; Science and Theology

Bibliography: P. L. Berger and T. Luckmann, *The Social Construction of Reality* (Garden City, N.Y., 1966) • D. Kettler and V. Meja, *Karl Mannheim and the Crisis of Liberalism* (New Brunswick, N.J., 1995) • K. Knorr-Cetina, *Epistemic Cultures: How the Sciences Make Knowledge* (Cambridge, Mass., 1999); eadem, *The Manufacture of Knowledge: An Essay on the Constructivist and Contextual Nature of Science* (New York, 1980) • B. Latour and S. Woolgar, *Laboratory Life: The Social Construction of Scientific Facts* (Beverly Hills, Calif., 1979) • K. Mannheim, *From Karl Mannheim* (2d ed.; ed. K. H. Wolff; New Brunswick, N.J., 1993); idem, *Ideologie und Utopie* (Bonn, 1929; 8th ed., Frankfurt, 1995; ET *Ideology and Utopia: An Introduction to the Sociology of Knowledge* [London, 1936]) • V. Meja and N. Stehr, eds., *Der Streit um die Wissenssoziologie* (2 vols.; Frankfurt, 1982; ET *Knowledge and Politics: The Sociology of Knowledge Dispute* [London, 1990]); idem, eds., *The Sociology of Knowledge* (2 vols.; Chichester, 2000) • M. Scheler, *Die Wissensformen und die Gesellschaft* (1926), vol. 8 of *Gesammelte Werke* (Bern, 1980; ET *Problems of a Sociology of Knowledge* [trans. M. S. Frings; London, 1980]) • N. Stehr, *Knowledge Societies* (London, 1994) • N. Stehr and V. Meja, eds., *Society and Knowledge: Contemporary Perspectives in the Sociology of Knowledge and Science* (New Brunswick, N.J., 2005) • S. Woolgar, ed., *Knowledge and Reflexivity: New Frontiers in the Sociology of Knowledge* (London, 1988).

Volker Meja

Sociology of Religion

1. Theme and Methods
2. History
3. Fields of Research

1. Theme and Methods

1.1. The theme of the sociology of religion is *religion as a social phenomenon.* General agreement obtains regarding the universal and directly perceptible features of religious social phenomena. Phenomena of this kind are the result of a process of institutionalizing, in the course of which the original religious experience of an individual or group has gradually taken fixed forms in the shape of a → myth or a doctrine (→ Dogma). This doctrine finds ritual expression in the cult (→ Rite). Regulations also emerge for the faithful, who together form a more or less organized fellowship. The sociology of religion investigates the development of these phenomena of creed, cult, code, and communion, how they have changed, and what their interaction is with other social phenomena.

Basic differences exist regarding the specifically religious character of these forms, for it is no longer taken for granted that religion (in the West) is the same thing as *church* religion. As a result the term "religion" is now less clear-cut. The most important conflict is between positions that describe anything that gives → meaning or stability as religion and those that regard the idea of a transcendent reality as essential. The first position changes the sociology of a religion into a sociology of meaning (see 2.3).

1.2. Religion as a social phenomenon is studied with all the methods and the aids of all the theoretical perspectives (or paradigms) that modern → sociology places at its disposal. Since the sociology of religion is an empirical science (→ Empiricism) and, as such, value-free, it takes no position on the question of whether religion may be reduced to social (and/or psychological) factors or has a transcendent origin. Most sociologists of religion subscribe to a methodological → agnosticism and limit themselves to establishing observable data.

In this way the sociology of religion differs from the criticism of religion (→ Religion, Criticism of), which preceded it historically, and also from → theology. Criticism of religion had and has the aim of unmasking religious phenomena as individual or social → illusions, while theology embraces the task of giving a rational account of → faith. Tension may arise between the sociology of religion and theology, especially when it comes to the sociology of the churches. Along with the → psychology of religion, the → phenomenology of religion, and the → history of religion, the sociology of religion is part of → religious studies, a field embracing many disciplines (→ Philosophy of Religion).

2. History

2.1. Older social interpretations of religion came under the heading of the criticism of religion *(Religionskritik)*. According to A. Comte (1798-1857; → Positivism), people in the *theological phase* of history were seeking an explanation of reality on the presupposition of some supernatural being (→ Transcendentalism). At the second, *metaphysical, stage* (→ Metaphysics), such a being or beings became abstractions (e.g., → soul, being, → natural law). At the third, *positivist, stage,* positive scientific explanations are dominant that regard religion as scientifically outmoded. Yet Comte could later outline a positive religion with its own festivals, for he was convinced that some system of insights and rituals was necessary for communal life (→ Social Systems). This integration thesis is still important in the sociology of religion.

According to K. → Marx (1818-83; → Marxism; Marxism and Christianity), religion is an ideological cover (→ Ideology) for alienating relations of force and exploitation. It will wither away when these factors are removed and → classes fade from the scene. Until then it can give comfort to sufferers in their distress. It is thus both "the sigh of the afflicted" and "the opium of the people" — the compensation thesis. At the same time, religion is also a protest against suffering and has played a limited revolutionary role (→ Revolution). The sociology of religion has clung to this thought of religion as both offering comfort and demanding resistance, though without the critical accent.

2.2. In the classic sociology of religion of É. Durkheim (1858-1917) and M. → Weber (1864-1920), the element critical of religion largely vanished, and the foundations for the later sociology of religion were laid. Durkheim offered for the first time a definition of religion on a logical deductive basis. He viewed it as an interconnected whole of convictions and cultic practices with reference to the sacred that makes its adherents a fellowship or → church (§4). He sought its origin along evolutionary lines in the → totemism of the least-developed societies. In totemism the emblems that are depicted (i.e., → animals or plants) and the members of the clan that are thus symbolized (→ Symbol) have a sacral character. They derive from this system a social force that is not supernatural but that itself originates in their common life. This force is a superior entity that has moral power and on which people depend. The power of the common life finds supreme manifestation in collective rites that individuals may not shirk, since the rites intensify and strengthen feelings. At these rites they experience a collective force, and this force is related to the totem, which represents the collective. Feelings that unite people can be experienced in the rites of modern social life.

Durkheim analyzed various types of rites and worked out their most important functions, namely, the upholding of society and the strengthening of faith. In this way he was an advocate of the integration thesis. As he saw it, the integrative function can be performed in our modern differentiated → society only by a religion that in fact concerns something that is common to all, namely, humanity. The result is the cult of the individual, in which the human being is God and the believer at the same time.

We may distinguish two different lines in Weber's work. First, in the chapters on the sociology of religion in his *Wirtschaft und Gesellschaft* (Economy and society), he discusses historically and globally various aspects of the world religions. His themes here are magicians, → priests, the concept of

→ God, religious → ethics, → prophets, community, → sects, → theodicy, redemption (→ Soteriology), → regeneration, ways of redemption, and the relation between religious ethics and the world. Many of these themes are an integral part of the sociology of religion today.

The insights gained were important for the second line, which Weber followed in his *Gesammelte Aufsätze zur Religionssoziologie* (Collected essays in the sociology of religion), in which he examines the significance of religion in the development of modern Western societies (→ Modern Period). Basic here is the general historical question as to the roots of Western rationality. By this term Weber means in particular the rationality of ends, the effective and efficient relating of means to end, and the systematic deduction of the right lines from universal rules. This type of rationality arose in the West and has penetrated almost all areas of life, as we see in modern → capitalism and → bureaucracy. Essential to the development of modern capitalism were certain conditions that might be present even in areas where it did not develop because there was lacking the fundamental rational attitude that derives from a certain type of religion.

Weber saw two types of religion. The one rests on the idea of an impersonal and immanent supreme power, to which we may attain by → contemplation. Typical here is the *exemplary prophet,* who by his way of living shows others the road to → salvation and who represents a world-rejecting, mystical openness to the divine (→ Mysticism 1).

The other type of religion is governed by ideas of a personal, transcendent, creative God (→ Creation). Typical here is the *ethical prophet,* who proclaims the will of this creating God and calls for an active ascetic life in the world (→ Asceticism). The religions of India and China offer examples of the first type; those of Iran, the Near East, and then, arising from these, the religiousness of the West offer examples of the second, with early → Calvinism serving as a particularly good expression.

In his famous thesis, which is still a matter of debate, Weber claimed that Calvinism strongly favored the development of capitalism, since it summoned one to hard work and an ascetic life in the world (this-worldly asceticism). In this way it sanctioned the lifestyle of the commercial middle class (→ Bourgeois, Bourgeoisie). Their related success later came to be seen as a mark of election (→ Predestination). An "elective affinity" thus arose between Calvinistic thinking and the ideas and material interests of the middle class. Unintentionally, this influence made the capitalist ethos independent, which slowly forced religion to the margins of society.

Unlike Marx, Weber gave religion a dynamic function. He thus represented the transformation, or → secularization, thesis. With Marx, however, he perceived a relation between religious attitude and social position and interests. For Weber, the religions bear the imprint of their carriers.

2.3. The analyses of religion by Marx, Weber, and Durkheim all stand within the framework of macrosociological analyses of society. They are heavily theory-laden and closely linked to sociology in general. Provisionally, however, this route was then abandoned for some time to come. The sociology of religion became the sociology of the churches, which had fewer contacts with sociology in general and was poor in theory, having a more practical interest. The themes of this sociology thus became less extensive. Church religion was reduced to a smaller area, and as a result the sociology of the churches dealt with narrower fields and smaller segments of society — specifically, older people (→ Old Age), women, and children (→ Childhood). This shift of focus meant also a decrease of church-oriented religiosity. And finally it appeared more and more difficult for people today to think of reality dualistically in such terms as → nature and supernature, or the world and God (→ Dualism).

These features of → secularization (§2) made necessary a reorientation of the concept of religion in detachment from traditional institutional forms and with a new secular content. A key role in this process was played by T. Luckmann's *Das Problem der Religion in der modernen Gesellschaft* (1963; ET *The Invisible Religion* [New York, 1967]). In this work Luckmann defined religion as the transcending of biological nature in the process of becoming human (→ Anthropology). Primarily, then, we must seek religion in the concrete world of each individual. It consists of what is most important in life for the individual. Religion does not need a relation to the supernatural or the transcendent in the classic sense. This development greatly widened the scope of the sociology of religion. It now became the sociology of (the establishing of) meaning. In this way it can again find a link to sociological theory and to analyses of modern society.

3. Fields of Research

3.1. No consensus exists regarding this new definition of religion. Many scholars still want a substantial definition that will carry a reference to the transcendent or to some supernatural or different reality. Others want a functional definition that will describe as religion anything that does what church religion was earlier said to do (integration, compensation, transformation, giving of meaning). We often find here an appeal to the description offered by P. → Tillich (1886-1965; → Existential Theology), namely, that religion is that which is of ultimate concern to us. This ultimate concern may be a supernatural reality, ultimate values that give → meaning to life, or ultimate problems such as → suffering and → death, which must have a place in the construction of meaning (R. N. Bellah).

3.2. In investigating the new forms of religion, Luckmann looks for ultimate values. His themes include individual → autonomy, self-development, self-depiction, and → sexuality. Death has no place, for the autonomous individual is supposedly always young and never dies.

Other scholars are tracing ultimate problems and the related coping strategies. These problems may be such classic ones as that of life after death, or they may take a modern form such as building relations or dealing with environmental questions. The coping strategies may be individual or collective, such as seeking help from a → pastor or psychotherapist (R. Machalek and M. Martin, J. M. Yinger; → Psychotherapy) or taking part in social activities. Some try to look at both aspects of religion and also examine modern definitions of a possible supreme reality that Luckmann ignored (M. A. Thung).

In all these areas of "invisible religion," there is reference to a more or less autonomous selection of sacral themes that may be found in a society's culture. We see here both the fragmentary character and the strong individualism of modern → culture. The claim often made in modern research is that the meaning of life is the meaning that people give to it. We hear of a marketplace of worldviews from which we may choose at will. Since there are no institutional forms, however, the individual packages have no stability. These structural features appear even in the religion of the churches, for people relate selectively to what the churches offer and may also add their own "alien" elements.

3.3. → New religions may also take the form of new religious movements or, more commonly, "cults." Numbers and size are less than often assumed. The groups are the result of renewal or of imports (e.g., from Asia) and are normally viewed as religiously or culturally aberrant (R. Stark and W. S. Bainbridge).

The "audience cult" is poorly organized, if at all. People gather for lectures or courses or learn from journals, books, the radio, or television (→ Mass Media). The "client cult" involves a relation between a therapist or counselor and clients. This movement can be well organized, but in the case of the clients it usually is not. "Cult movements" offer a comprehensive orientation of life, though it may not be religious. The degree of organization is generally low, though at times we find strict authoritarian forms of organization (→ Church of Scientology). Except in the (few) strongly organized cults, individuals may be autonomously selective. As a result, most cults have little stability. They depend on the popularity of what they offer and on the changing tastes of individual consumers, whom we may describe as seekers.

The many offerings reveal only a limited number of themes. The cosmos and the world may be seen as a harmonious whole (holism). This whole is the theater of autonomous individual self-fulfillment. For this self-fulfillment the term "wholeness" might again be used, for both the psychological and the physical aspects of life are concerned. For this reason therapeutic relations are so important. High value attaches to → experience, which gives intuitive certainty and has the power to change life. In contrast, knowledge has less value, for analytic discourse does not yield the same results. These groups have a strong anti-institutional thrust. What is sought is fellowship and in some cases support from (charismatic) leaders.

In individual forms of the new religions, we often find the compensation function of religion. We may well ask, however, whether these movements have the power to transform lives. It seems far from certain that they do. Nor are the prospects good for integration, though some have argued that → civil religion can achieve it (Bellah, T. Parsons, N. Luhmann).

3.4. The sociology of religion has long considered the topic of secularization, understood as the disappearance of religion from public (and private) life (K. Dobbelaere). There has recently been a revaluation, however, since it has become clear that religion has not disappeared as easily as had been expected by a number of sociologists (P. Berger). In this context the new definition of religion is useful for the understanding of secularization, for by reason of a functional definition secularization becomes religious change; religion does not disappear but changes its form. Many scholars speak now of a "return of the sacred" (D. Bell). The long-term development of religion is described along evolutionary lines (Bellah, R. Döbert, G. Dux; → Evolution).

3.5. Interest in traditional religions remains alive in the sociology of churches and has also received encouragement from the historical sociology of religion, which in particular goes back to Weber (W. Schluchter). Historians and other scholars still test the tenability of Weber's thesis.

The dynamic role of religion also has a place in investigations and theorizing relative to the vertical structuring of society (i.e., pillarization; → Secularization 2), in which the → worldview is a decisive criterion in the formation of → groups and → organizations. Many western European societies in the early 20th century (e.g., in the Netherlands and Switzerland) manifested this feature, which had a liberating effect on the religious groups concerned. Intensive research into it began after 1950.

3.6. Sociological theorizing plays an important role in research into these themes. Functionalism and system theory, and especially differentiation theory along the lines of Durkheim (Parsons, Luhmann), appear in discussions about civil religion and about applying a sociological concept of evolution to the long-term development of religion (Bellah, Döbert). The action approach in sociology relates to new reflections on Weber, to the study of new forms of religion (Luckmann), and to a sociology-of-knowledge approach to religion (Berger, Luckmann). More recently, the rational-choice theory of religion has become an interesting and important approach (L. A. Young, S. Bruce) Theorizing about social movements also plays a part in the analysis of religious movements (J. A. Hannigan).

Bibliography: D. BELL, "The Return of the Sacred," *The Winding Passage: Essays and Sociological Journeys, 1960-1980* (Cambridge, Mass., 1980) 324-54 • R. N. BELLAH, *Beyond Belief: Essays on Religion in a Post-traditional World* (New York, 1970) • P. L. BERGER, *The Sacred Canopy: Elements of a Sociological Theory of Religion* (Garden City, N.Y., 1967); idem, ed., *The Desecularization of the World: Resurgent Religion and World Politics* (Washington, D.C., 1999) • S. BRUCE, *Choice and Religion: A Critique of Rational Choice Theory* (Oxford, 1999) • A. COMTE, *Cours de philosophie positive* (6 vols.; Paris, 1830-42; ET *The Positive Philosophy* [New York, 1974]) • K. DOBBELAERE, *Secularization: An Analysis at Three Levels* (Brussels, 2002) • R. DÖBERT, *Systemtheorie und die Entwicklung religiöser Deutungssysteme* (Frankfurt, 1973) • É. DURKHEIM, *The Elementary Forms of Religious Life* (New York, 1995; orig. pub., 1912) • G. DUX, *Die Logik der Weltbilder* (Frankfurt, 1982) • J. A. HANNIGAN, "Social Movement Theory and the Sociology of Religion: Toward a New Synthesis," *SocAn* 52 (1991) 311-31 • T. LUCKMANN, *The Invisible Religion* (New York, 1967) • N. LUHMANN, *Die Religion der Gesellschaft* (Frankfurt,

2000) • R. MACHALEK and M. MARTIN, "Invisible Religions: Some Preliminary Evidence," *JSSR* 15 (1976) 311-21 • K. MARX and F. ENGELS, *On Religion* (New York, 1964) • T. PARSONS, *Action Theory and the Human Condition* (New York, 1978) • W. SCHLUCHTER, ed., *Max Webers Sicht des okzidentalen Christentums* (Frankfurt, 1988) • R. STARK and W. S. BAINBRIDGE, *The Future of Religion: Secularization, Revival, and Cult Formation* (Berkeley, Calif., 1985) • M. A. THUNG et al., *Exploring the New Religious Consciousness* (Amsterdam, 1985) • M. WEBER, *Economy and Society* (Berkeley, Calif., 1978; orig. pub., 1922); idem, *The Protestant Ethic and the Spirit of Capitalism* (Mineola, N.Y., 2003; orig. pub., 1904-5) • J. M. YINGER, "A Comparative Study of the Substructures of Religion," *JSSR* 16 (1977) 67-86 • L. A. YOUNG, *Rational Choice Theory and Religion* (New York, 1997).

LEO LAEYENDECKER

SODEPAX

1. Inception
2. Development
3. Achievements and Demise

1. Inception

The Joint Committee on Society, Development, and Peace, known by the acronym SODEPAX, arose in 1968 as a product of the energy and creativity generated by the → social encyclicals of Popes John XXIII (1958-63) and Paul VI (1963-78), by the Vatican II Pastoral Constitution on the Church in the Modern World (*Gaudium et spes,* 1965), and by the → World Council of Churches' Conference on Church and Society (Geneva, 1966). In operation until 1980, this body was for a time the only agency responsible both to the WCC and the Holy See, and hence well positioned to bring WCC social thought into encounter with Roman Catholic reflection and practice, and vice versa. With its secretariat in Geneva, SODEPAX was intended to promote the emergence of a common ecumenical → social ethic.

2. Development

At first the small and dynamic staff of SODEPAX organized several international conferences on volatile issues such as worldwide → development (Beirut, 1968), support for development (Montreal, 1969), and → peace as an imperative for our time (Baden, Austria, 1970). The results of these meetings were published and became the basis for discussions that sprang up across the globe.

In a second stage of work, from 1971 to 1974,

SODEPAX concentrated on problems arising in particular contexts, such as ecumenical work in India and Japan and interconfessional conversations in the context of the civil war in Northern Ireland.

A third phase of work, from 1974 to 1980, saw a series of national and regional conferences devoted to discussion of a new world economic order, parallel to discussions going on in the → United Nations and elsewhere. The results were published in the periodical *Church Alert* (English and French) and were widely discussed. In all, SODEPAX made significant contributions in the fields of economic development research, → education, → communication, and → peace.

3. Achievements and Demise

The work of SODEPAX came to an end in 1980. Its theological work had dramatized the differences in social thought between the Protestant and Roman Catholic traditions. While one might observe remarkable areas of agreement on issues such as human → rights, → religious liberty, economic development, → racism, and the like, rarely was SODEPAX able to generate joint official actions or statements arising from such regions of accord. There were also Vatican-WCC tensions in matters of procedure. The Vatican, after long and careful study, would speak cautiously and in generalities. The WCC would convene short-term meetings that spoke specifically and prophetically. Behind these differences of style and practice were more profound theological and ecclesiological tensions, for example, the difference between inquiries under the conviction of Christ's lordship over history, which sought "divine revelation in the uniqueness and freshness of each event" (T. S. Derr, 9), and those derived from → "natural law" accounts that lead more readily to general principles expressed in abstract terms.

Diminishing financial support made matters still more difficult. After the initial three years of funding from international financial institutions, which made possible a somewhat opulent lifestyle, SODEPAX had to depend largely on what the WCC and the Vatican could make available. In time, both sponsoring bodies began to see the needed support as an unnecessary burden.

In the end, the actions and positions of SODEPAX likely exceeded the ecumenical and administrative readiness of both the Holy See and the WCC. The SODEPAX experiment made clear the structural and institutional difficulties of WCC–Roman Catholic cooperation, not least in the enterprise's independent style of operation, which sometimes duplicated other work being pursued in both camps and disturbed those on both sides who desired more programmatic control.

Bibliography: A. VAN DER BENT, *Commitment to God's World: A Concise Critical Survey of Ecumenical Social Thought* (Geneva, 1995) • T. S. DERR, *Barriers to Ecumenism: The Holy See and the World Council of Churches on Social Questions* (Maryknoll, N.Y., 1983) • M. ELLINGSEN, *The Cutting Edge: How Churches Speak on Social Issues* (Grand Rapids, 1993) • L. S. MUDGE, "Ecumenical Social Thought," *A History of the Ecumenical Movement,* vol. 3, *1968-2000* (ed. J. Briggs, M. A. Oduyoye, and G. Tsetsis; Geneva, 2004) 279-321 • T. STRANSKY, "SODEPAX," *DEM* 1055-56.

THEO TSCHUY† and LEWIS S. MUDGE

Söderblom, Nathan

1. Early Life
2. Theological Publication
3. Archbishop
4. Life and Work Movement
5. Other Ecumenical Initiatives

1. Early Life

Lars Olof Jonathan Söderblom (called Nathan; 1866-1931), born in Trönö in the central Swedish province of Hälsingland, was the son of Jonas Söderblom, a pietistic pastor of the Church of Sweden. In 1883 he enrolled in Uppsala University, and in 1886 he received his first degree, Filosofie kandidat (equivalent to a B.A), in Latin, Greek, Semitic and Nordic languages, philosophy, and geology. As he pursued further studies in → theology at Uppsala, he was active in student affairs, being elected to "O.D.," the still-renowned male chorus Orphei Dränger, and also to the presidency of the Uppsala student body.

In 1890 he traveled to the United States in order to participate in the then-famous Northfield, Massachusetts, student Christian conference. The leaders of that conference — John R. → Mott (1865-1955), Dwight L. → Moody (1837-99), and Ira D. Sankey (1840-1908) — made a deep impression on Söderblom. At this conference the young Swedish student formulated a prayer, recorded in his diary, that was to guide his life and career: "Lord, give me humility and wisdom to serve the great cause of the free → unity of thy church."

In 1893 Nathan Söderblom was ordained a → priest in the Church of Sweden by Gottfried Billing (1841-1925), then → bishop of Västerås. The next year he was married to Anna Forsell (1870-1955); the couple was to have 12 children. That same year, 1894, the couple traveled to France, where he became → pastor to Swedish churches in Calais and Paris.

While in France, Söderblom pursued doctoral studies at the Sorbonne, and in 1901, with Auguste Sabatier (1839-1901) having been his principal teacher, he defended his dissertation, "La vie future d'après le Mazdéisme," a study in the eschatology of Ahura Mazda, the supreme Zoroastrian deity (→ Iranian Religions 6-7). The same year he became professor of theological prenotions and theological encyclopedia at Uppsala University, a chair he held until 1914. (His title was the result of lengthy developments in the study of theology as an academic discipline. Today, Söderblom's chair would probably be simply "professor of the history of religion.") During this time at Uppsala, he was also an honorary canon (prebendary) of the historic Holy Trinity Church, located in the heart of the university area. This was a period of considerable academic accomplishment and publication for Söderblom and also a time when he made important trips to such places as Rome, Athens, and Constantinople. Moreover, in 1912 he was named professor of the → history of religion at the University of Leipzig in Germany, a position he held simultaneously with his professorship at Uppsala.

2. Theological Publication

The breadth of Nathan Söderblom's theological interests is amazing. He was a student of the history of religions, and his most fruitful theological work perhaps had to do with "the problem of religion" as such, and with the problem of → revelation in particular. One of his two most important works, *The Nature of Revelation,* was first published in 1903 at the beginning of Söderblom's career as just one essay, "The Religion of Revelation." It was reissued in 1932 with two additional chapters, "Portals of Revelation" and "Continued Revelation." An English translation appeared in 1933 and was reprinted in 1966 with a most helpful introduction to the work and its author.

The Nature of Revelation should be studied in connection with the second of his most important works, the publication of the internationally important Gifford Lectures, which he was invited to deliver in Edinburgh in 1931 and 1932. The first set of lectures was published in English as *The Living God;* the second set was never delivered.

But Söderblom had other interests and made other contributions. He published several works on Martin → Luther, beginning as early as 1893 with two untranslated works, *The Origin of the Lutheran Reformation* and *Luther's Religion.* Perhaps most important, he also published a collection of studies, also untranslated, *Humor and Melancholy and Other Luther Studies* (1919).

Some of his reflections on ecclesial and ecumenical concerns appear in a work that appeared in English under the title *Christian Fellowship.* He also made heavy use of the notion → "evangelical catholicity" (he preferred "evangelic catholicity").

3. Archbishop

In 1914 the Archbishopric of Uppsala became vacant, and in the Swedish system, Söderblom's name was the third of the three candidates presented to the king of Sweden for his government's decision. The other two candidates, Bishops Hjalmar Danell (1860-1938) of the Diocese of Skara and J. Eklund (1863-1945) of Karlstad, together had more than 80 percent of the votes cast in the complicated Swedish system of the time, involving → clergy, laity, and members of the theological faculty. It was a major surprise, then, that the government named Nathan Söderblom archbishop of Uppsala, primate of the Church of Sweden. With this position, he also became, ex officio, pro-chancellor of Uppsala University.

While he was archbishop, a great many matters affecting the life of the Church of Sweden occupied Söderblom's attention: lengthy formal → visitations to all parishes in the archdiocese; negotiations over crucial issues between the state and the church (→ Church and State), not least the role of the rising labor movement in Swedish society; coordination of relief work in Germany and Austria after World War I; participation with all Swedish bishops in a protest in 1923 over the crisis between the French and Germans in the Ruhr Valley; and leadership of a special → evangelism effort in the archdiocese in 1926.

4. Life and Work Movement

Nathan Söderblom, as primate of the Church of Sweden, is chiefly remembered, however, for his remarkable international and ecumenical accomplishments. His early visit to the United States and his period of residency in France indelibly imprinted international concerns on his consciousness. These concerns resulted in his tireless efforts for peace before, during, and after World War I, not least through his involvement in the leadership of the World Alliance for Promoting International Friendship through the Churches. This involvement with the → peace movement dovetailed with his commitment to the → Life and Work movement, one of the major streams in the early modern ecumenical movement.

His identification with Life and Work reached its climax in 1925 at the Universal Christian Conference on Life and Work, held in Stockholm (and Uppsala). Regarded as one of the events most formative of the modern ecumenical movement, the Stockholm conference owed much to the genius and commitment of the Swedish archbishop, whose vision was that this meeting on social issues should support the idea of an ecumenical council of churches. To be sure, the → Roman Catholic Church did not accept Söderblom's invitation to participate in this meeting, but virtually every other strain in Christendom did — Orthodox, Anglican, and Protestant. In material prepared for the event, it was stated that the words "life and work" were an expression of the determination to set forth "the Christian way of life" as "the world's greatest need." It was the aim of the conference "to formulate programmes and devise means . . . whereby the *fatherhood of God and the brotherhood of all peoples* will become more completely realized through the church of Christ." And famously, the conference deliberately avoided theological issues with the slogan "Doctrine divides, while service unites" (quoted in P. Abrecht, 691).

It can be argued that the Stockholm Conference was the victim of its own idealism. The complexities of the world after World War I were perhaps not fully grasped. Its statements were soon recognized as vague and far too general. Nevertheless, this gathering was a milestone in the creation both of ecumenical and of sociopolitical awareness. Christians who previously had had little or no contact encountered each other in worship, discourse, and decision making, and the results shaped much of the ecumenical development that was to come in the 20th century.

5. Other Ecumenical Initiatives

The ecumenical insights and commitments of Nathan Söderblom were not limited to the Life and Work movement. Indeed, he saw the crucial importance of → Faith and Order as well and gave much to that movement, largely in support of the work of another ecumenical pioneer, the American Episcopal bishop Charles H. Brent (1862-1929). At the First Conference on Faith and Order, held in 1927 in Lausanne, Switzerland, a kind of parallel to the earlier Stockholm Conference of Life and Work, Söderblom chaired the key section "The Unity of Christendom and the Relation Thereto of Existing Churches."

It was also largely as a result of the initiative of Archbishop Söderblom, and after a period of bold steps forward, that the 1920 Lambeth Conference of Anglican bishops officially acknowledged that the Church of Sweden had maintained the historic episcopate (→ Episcopacy) throughout its existence and that there was really nothing to inhibit intercommunion between it and the → Anglican Communion. Since then, for example, it has been the rule that bishops from each church participate in the → consecration of new bishops in the partner body.

Söderblom also worked to strengthen relations between the Church of Sweden and other → Lutheran churches. For instance, he had a special love for the Augustana Lutheran Church in America, a body that traced its roots to Swedish immigration in the 19th century and that the archbishop referred to as the daughter church of his own.

At various times in its history, which began in 1860, the immigrant church had, in point of fact, felt deserted by the mother church, and there was even some hostility toward Söderblom himself, who was perceived by some as far too liberal a theologian. For four months in 1923 the archbishop and his wife visited the Augustana Church in order to demonstrate not simply friendship but solidarity within the wider Lutheran tradition.

In 1930 Archbishop Nathan Söderblom was awarded the Nobel Peace Prize. In his comments at the presentation ceremony in Oslo, Söderblom used a favorite metaphor of body and soul: "The peoples are members of an organism, but a body must have a soul, else it becomes at best a dead mechanism. This soul will be the love and righteousness of the Gospel and not the devil of selfishness. Thus the work of peace must begin in one's own heart."

After years of battling heart disease, Söderblom died on July 12, 1931.

→ Ecumenism, Ecumenical Movement

Bibliography: Primary sources: Christian Fellowship; or, The United Life and Work of Christendom (Chicago, 1923) • *The Living God: Basal Forms of Personal Religion* (London, 1933; repr., Boston, 1962) • *The Mystery of the Cross* (Milwaukee, 1933) • *The Nature of Revelation* (Philadelphia, 1966).

Secondary works: P. Abrecht, "Life and Work," *DEM* 691-92 • C. R. Bråkenhielm and G. W. Hollman, eds., *The Relevance of Theology: Nathan Söderblom and the Development of an Academic Discipline* (Uppsala, 2002) • C. J. Curtis, *Söderblom: Ecumenical Pioneer* (Minneapolis, 1967); idem, *Söderblom: Theologian of Revelation* (Chicago, 1966) • S. Dahlgren, ed., *Nathan Söderblom as a European* (Uppsala, 1992) • C. F.

HALLENCREUTZ and Ö. SJÖHOLM, eds., *Nathan Söderblom. Präst, Professor, Ärkebiskop* (Uppsala, 2000) • S. RUNESTAM, *Söderblomsstudier* (Uppsala, 2004) • E. J. SHARPE, *Nathan Söderblom and the Study of Religion* (London, 1990) • B. SUNDKLER, *Nathan Söderblom: His Life and Work* (Lund, 1968); idem, *Nathan Söderblom och hans möten* (Stockholm, 1975).

NORMAN A. HJELM

Solidarity

1. Term
2. Social Movements
3. Social Policy
4. Social Law
5. Theology
6. Churches

1. Term

The expression "to show solidarity" describes the activity of mutual support and the acceptance of responsibility (in the sense of "one for all and all for one"). It derives from the experience of mutual dependence and responsibility. Remembered experience is combined here with the hope for a renewal, the surpassing or correction of such experience (→ Kingdom of God), a connection from which moral and legal expectations of behavior from self or others are easily derived (→ Moral Theology; Law and Legal Theory; Action Theory). Admittedly they mean something only if the freedom *not* to fulfill such expectations also is included. Frequent use or misuse of the word "solidarity" offers barely concealed hints of the misery of the experienced world.

In terms of the current conditions of globalization, the following definition of "solidarity" is clear: "the awareness of a common humanity and global citizenship and the voluntary acceptance of the responsibilities which go with it. It is the conscious commitment to redress inequalities both within and between countries. It is based on a recognition that in an interdependent world, poverty or oppression anywhere is a threat to prosperity and stability everywhere" (International Labor Organisation, 41).

2. Social Movements

The word "solidarity" became a concept of commercial law in the course of the medieval reception of Roman jurisprudence (H. J. Berman), in particular, for the joint liability of businesspeople who were not related to each other. Accordingly, the Code Civile (1804) stipulates that, aside from the free will of the sovereign ruler (→ State), mutual liability can be established only through the free choice of legally competent private citizens (→ Property). As early as 1791 in France, traditional social organizations were considered dissolved, and the formation of new associations or coalitions was prohibited.

In a countermove C. Fourier (1772-1837) and his students (see H. Renaud and A. E. Bestor 1948) built on the idea that "solidarity" designates a durable agreement between strangers. They set aside the restrictive legal definition of solidarity in favor of the praxis of solidarity. In the course of countless labor struggles, solidarity became a basic value of workers' parties and unions, which was true outside of France as well, especially as international solidarity (G. Reisz).

There is a particular irony in the fact that this term, narrowly defined in the Marxist Internationale as a battle concept and appropriated by the party to legitimate its doctrine after the Russian revolution, served as the dominant concept to delegitimize the ruling system with the formation of the trade union Solidarność (Solidarity) in Poland in 1980. There, intellectuals and church representatives allied themselves with the workers (L. Kolakowski, A. Michnik, J. Tischner).

3. Social Policy

Since 1895 solidarity has characterized the social policy of the radical socialists of France under the leadership of L. Bourgeois (1851-1925; see Bourgeois 1896). Sociologically, É. Durkheim (1858-1917; → Sociology) developed the distinction between organic solidarity (linkage on the basis of complementary difference; → Achievement and Competition) and mechanical solidarity (linkage on the basis of similarity; Durkheim 1893).

No doubt influenced by the Dreyfus Affair in 1894, Durkheim expanded this concept in accordance with the practical and political acceptance of responsibility and sought integration in a collective moral consciousness (→ Sociology of Religion) that is formed by public intervention on behalf of individuals in crisis situations whose dignity and rights have been violated (→ Democracy). This consciousness is mediated through → education (Durkheim 1898). Durkheim initiated the reflection about social cohesion, that is, about the relationship between factual and normative interdependence in individualized and differentiating → industrial societies (H. Brunkhorst; → Individualism).

H. Pesch (1854-1926), taking up French impulses, developed the basic concepts of Roman Catholic social doctrine (→ Subsidiarity). At this time in the churches the term "social" (→ Social Gospel) suffices to designate the initiatives and movements engaging the social questions (→ Religious Socialism).

4. Social Law

A sociological understanding of the social state is achieved by T. H. Marshall (1893-1982): through the institutionalization of social → rights, along with civil freedoms and political rights of participation, citizenship achieves an integrative status. The → United Nations pursues this political approach as "human development" (United Nations Development Program). The individualistic world society is confronted by two problems of inclusion: individualization on the basis of further discrimination, and exclusion of large portions of the population. Both can be met with weak as well as strong solidarity (M. Walzer, Brunkhorst).

The → counterculture and self-help movements practice weak solidarity, making use of the media (S. Serra) against the background of an emerging worldwide legal system made up of human-rights pacts and conventions. Human rights are specified concretely as women's rights, children's rights, and minority rights (K. Heidel). Their enforcement is subject to review. Strong solidarity develops where institutions effectively guarantee social rights. Between weak and strong solidarity lies the guarantee of social rights through the Charter of Basic Rights of the European Union (E. Riedel, M. Telò).

It can be shown sociologically that solidarity, or, in other words, "communitarian commitment," has a specific opportunity in modern, individualized circumstances. Where support is lacking — from relatives and from social security — actions of solidarity can be a bridge when, on the basis of voluntarism and worldview neutrality, those in need participate as those who can give, and accessible, well-organized, professionally staffed agencies assume the task of mediation (K. O. Hondrich and C. Koch-Arzberger, W. Sullivan, R. Rorty).

5. Theology

Since the 1960s theological thought has taken up the term "solidarity," with an expanding temporal horizon. That is, the term embraces both memorializing, anamnetic solidarity with the dead (H. Peukert, J. B. Metz, J. Sobrino and J. H. Pico) and anticipatory solidarity with future generations (→ Political Theology; Liberation Theology).

Building on Nelson Glueck's work, H. Gollwitzer (1908-93) probably moves the theological discussion along furthest with the suggestion that "solidarity" translates Heb. *ḥesed* and Gk. *charis* (→ Grace). In so doing, he conveys to this term a distinctive contour by probing the biblical references. In a way similar to the more routine combination of "justice and righteousness," which is to be distinguished from it, *ḥesed* occurs primarily in two characteristic phrases: *ḥesed wĕraḥămîm* (solidarity and mercy) and *ḥesed we'ĕmet* (solidarity and faithfulness, or reliability). Both designate extraordinary historical interhuman experiences and are used to testify to the experience of God.

Gollwitzer draws the anthropological and ethical consequences in defining the hearer of the → Word of God as one liberated for solidarity: "The more our communal life in society approximates to a real togetherness, and the more through solidarity — so far as laws can compel it and educate men toward it — they show *chesed,* solidarity, to each other, by that much more there comes into being an earthly horizon of grace for the earthly life of men, in a measure that is possible for them, and by that much more such a communal life will become a 'parable' of the Kingdom of God, similar to it for all its dissimilarity" (pp. 204-5).

6. Churches

The churches have reacted to the sobering challenges created by the transformative crises of world society both in ways that are not specifically designated as solidarity (e.g., → worker-priests, the → Program to Combat Racism, the conciliar process, "God's preferential option for the poor"; → Poverty) and in ways that refer explicitly to solidarity ("a church in solidarity with the poor," J. de Santa Ana; Ecumenical Decade of the Churches in Solidarity with Women, M. A. Oduyoye).

Bibliography: On 1-2: H. J. BERMAN, *Law and Revolution: The Formation of the Western Legal Tradition* (Cambridge, Mass., 1983) • A. E. BESTOR, *Backwood Utopias: The Sectarian Origins and Owenite Phases of Communitarian Socialism in America, 1663-1829* (Philadelphia, 1950; 2d ed., 1970); idem, "The Evolution of the Socialist Vocabulary," *JHI* 9 (1948) 259-303 • C. GIDE, "Solidarity," *The New Palgrave: A Dictionary of Economics* (London, 1987) 4.421 • INTERNATIONAL LABOR ORGANISATION, *A Fair Globalization: Creating Opportunities for All* (Geneva, 2004) • L. KOLAKOWSKI, "Ist der bürokratische Sozialismus reformierbar? Thesen über Hoffnung und Hoffnungslosigkeit" (1971), *Marxismus–Utopie und Anti-Utopie* (Stuttgart, 1974) 117-42 • A. MICHNIK, *The Church and the Left* (Chicago, 1993; orig. pub., 1977) • G. REISZ, *Solidarität in Deutschland und Frankreich. Eine politische Deutungs-*

analyse (Opladen, 2006) • H. Renaud, *Solidarité. Vue synthétique de la doctrine de Charles Fourier* (Paris, 1842) • J. Tischner, *The Spirit of Solidarity* (San Francisco, 1984).

On 3-4: L. Bourgeois, *Solidarité* (Paris, 1896) • H. Brunkhorst, *Solidarity: From Civic Friendship to a Global Legal Community* (Cambridge, 2005) • É. Durkheim, *The Division of Labor in Society* (New York, 1984; orig. pub., 1893); idem, "Individualism and the Intellectuals" (1898), *On Morality and Society: Selected Writings* (ed. R. N. Bellah; Chicago, 1973) 43-57 • K. Heidel, *Poverty Reduction Strategy Papers: Children First! A Case Study on PRSP Processes in Ethiopia, Kenya, and Zambia from a Child Rights Perspective* (Heidelberg, 2005) http://www.sarpn.org.za/documents/d0002048/index.php • K. O. Hondrich and C. Koch-Arzberger, *Solidarität in der modernen Gesellschaft* (Frankfurt, 1992) • T. H. Marshall, *Citizenship and Social Class* (Cambridge, 1950) • E. Riedel, "Solidarität," *Kommentar zur Charta der Grundrechte der Europäischen Union* (ed. J. Meyer; 2d ed.; Baden-Baden, 2005) 323-432 • R. Rorty, *Contingency, Irony, and Solidarity* (Cambridge, 1989); idem, "Solidarity or Objectivity?" *Post-Analytic Philosophy* (ed. J. Rajchman and C. West; New York, 1986) 3-19 • S. Serra, "Multinationals of Solidarity: International Civil Society and the Killing of Street Children in Brazil," *Globalization, Communication, and Transnational Civil Society* (ed. S. Bramann; Cresskill, N.J., 1996) 219-41 • W. Sullivan, "American Social Reform and a New Kind of Modernity," *Toward a Global Civil Society* (ed. M. Walzer; Providence, R.I., 1995) 201-7 • M. Telò, *Europe, a Civilian Power? European Union, Global Governance, World Order* (Basingstoke, 2006) • United Nations Development Program, *Human Development Report* (New York, yearly since 1990) • M. Walzer, *Thick and Thin: Moral Argument at Home and Abroad* (Notre Dame, Ind., 1994).

On 5-6: N. Glueck, *Hesed in the Bible* (Cincinnati, 1967; orig. pub., 1927) • H. Gollwitzer, *An Introduction to Protestant Theology* (Philadelphia, 1982) • J. B. Metz, *Faith in History and Society: Toward a Practical Fundamental Theology* (New York, 1980) • M. A. Oduyoye, *Who Will Roll the Stone Away? The Ecumenical Decade of the Churches in Solidarity with Women* (Geneva, 1990) • H. Peukert, *Science, Action, and Fundamental Theology: Toward a Theology of Communicative Action* (Cambridge, Mass., 1984) • R. Rosenzweig, *Solidarität mit den Leidenden im Judentum* (Berlin, 1978) • J. de Santa Ana, ed., *Towards a Church of the Poor* (Geneva, 1979) • J. Sobrino and J. H. Pico, *Theology of Christian Solidarity* (Maryknoll, N.Y., 1985).

Kristian Hungar

Solipsism

1. "Solipsism" (Lat. *solus*, "alone," and *ipse*, "self") is a term whose history goes back to the 17th century. For I. Kant (1724-1804; → Kantianism) it meant the practical idea of self-obsession, which M. Stirner (1806-56) later radicalized as egoism. In the 19th century it found a use in → epistemology and → metaphysics. In general, "solipsism" denotes a philosophical conviction according to which the → self or ego is granted a radical special position both in theory and in practice.

While the *epistemological solipsism* of R. Descartes (1596-1650; → Cartesianism) holds the contents of the ego's awareness to be the basis of the fundamental certainty of human knowledge of the world (→ Worldview), J. Locke (1632-1704), G. Berkeley (1685-1753), and D. Hume (1711-76) held that all external reality was cognitively or ontologically dependent on ideas and perception (→ Cognition; Ontology).

Metaphysical solipsism, which, as in J. G. Fichte's (1762-1814) early thought, is the consequence of a subjective → idealism, declares by contrast that the self is the only existing reality and that all other reality is the content of its consciousness. For A. Schopenhauer (1788-1860) this variation was possible "only in a madhouse."

An epistemological form of solipsism, according to which only one's own sensory data can be the basis for the knowledge of experience, was favored by B. Russell (1872-1970), who, like H. Driesch (1867-1941), took solipsism only hypothetically or methodologically, not metaphysically. This is true for the solipsism thesis of present-day constructivism (e.g., of E. von Glasersfeld), according to which the whole world of experience is a construction of the human → organism. Above all, metaphysical solipsism necessarily ends up in practical aporia. Furthermore, it rests on an inconsistent view of the *solus ipse* (H. Rickert), contradicts itself performatively in the linguistic formulation of its own thesis, and somehow does not do justice to the process of being seen by the other (J.-P. Sartre).

The modern theory of interpersonality ends up in the same way, for example, in the → phenomenology of E. Husserl (1859-1938), with its egological constitution of the other. Similarly, R. Carnap (1891-1970; → Positivism) considered one's own psyche as a methodological basis of the physical world, as well as of the alien psychic realm, and thus rejected metaphysical solipsism as a meaningless, illusory problem. Existential variations on solipsism are found in the fundamental ontology of M. Heidegger (1889-1976), according to which → fear reveals existence as the *solus ipse* in the world, as well as in the → existentialism of K. Jaspers (1883-1969), wherein the solipsism of existence permanently endangers existential → communication.

2. The modern problem of solipsism is above all influenced by L. Wittgenstein (1889-1951), who removed solipsism from the context of consciousness and discussed it in the framework of linguistic philosophy (→ Language 5; Linguistics 3.7). Whereas in his early work he advocated the thesis of the → truth of solipsism, which allows itself only to be thought and not to be said, he later decisively rejected this view. Here the solipsism problem appears as that of a radical private language that, as a language of one's own conscious experiences, on logical grounds could not be understood by other persons (→ Logic). This semantic modification of Cartesianism, including its solipsistic core, was criticized by Wittgenstein on the ground that a private person with a subjective internal language for his or her own objects of experience does not know the rules of a correct language game that apply only for linguistic → signs with public semantics.

In the center of the current discussion about private language (P. F. Strawson, S. Kripke, J. Hintikka) is the question of what kind of language can be used to correctly express verbally our condition of consciousness without ending up in the aporia of the private-language models and still do justice to the truth of solipsism.

→ Analytic Philosophy; Autonomy; Ego Psychology; Subjectivism and Objectivism

Bibliography: C. Dore, *God, Suffering, and Solipsism* (New York, 1989) • M. Frank, ed., *Selbstbewußtseinstheorien von Fichte bis Sartre* (2d ed.; Frankfurt, 1993) • A. A. Johnstone, *Rationalized Epistemology: Taking Solipsism Seriously* (Albany, N.Y., 1991) • S. A. Kripke, *Wittgenstein on Rules and Private Language* (Cambridge, Mass., 1982) • H. O. Mounce, "Philosophy, Solipsism, and Thought," *PhQ* 47 (1997) 1-17 • G. Ryle, *The Concept of Mind* (London, 1949) esp. chap. 1 • M. Theunissen, *The Others: Studies in the Social Ontology of Husserl, Heidegger, Sartre, and Buber* (Cambridge, Mass., 1996).

WILHELM LÜTTERFELDS

Solomon

The second son of → David and Bathsheba, Solomon was Israel's third king and ruled over its golden age (ca. 970-930 B.C.; → Israel 1.4).

Solomon consolidated his father's kingdom, dividing all except Judah into districts that cut across the old tribal boundaries, thus consolidating the government at Jerusalem. He built the → temple (§2; 1 Kings 5–7; 2 Chronicles 2–4), accomplishing what his father had only envisioned, as well as his own magnificent palace (1 Kgs. 7:1-8). He levied heavy taxation and employed forced labor, largely of foreign captives, in an extensive building program (5:13-18), fortifying Jerusalem and other important cities, including Megiddo, Hazor, and Gezer (9:15-22).

Under Solomon the empire reached its greatest extent (1 Kgs. 4:20-21). It was especially important in commerce, with ships sailing to the end of the known world (9:26-28; 10:22). He made numerous commercial and military treaties with neighboring states, often sealed by marriage alliances (5:12; 11:1-3). Unfortunately, his foreign wives diverted Solomon from the pure worship of the God of Israel (Neh. 13:26), for which is blamed the division of the united monarchy after his death (1 Kgs. 11:8-13).

Both Solomon's wisdom (1 Kgs. 4:32-34; 10:23-24; Sir. 47:13-17; Matt. 12:41-42; Luke 11:31) and his great wealth (Matt. 6:29; Luke 12:27) were proverbial. He humbly asked of God "an understanding mind to govern your people, able to discern between good and evil" (1 Kgs. 3:9), a capacity displayed in his juridical skills (3:16-28) and encyclopedic knowledge (4:29-34; 10:1-9, 23-24; Wis. 7:17-22). He is characterized as a true Renaissance man (1 Kgs. 4:32-33) and so came to be associated with the books of Proverbs (1:1; 10:1; 25:1), Ecclesiastes (1:1, 12ff.), Wisdom (9:7-8), and the Song of Songs (1:1; 3:11), as well as the pseudepigraphal Psalms of Solomon, Odes of Solomon, and Testament of Solomon.

The summary of Solomon's accomplishments in 1 Kgs. 10:23-24 portrays him as an incomparable ruler. His own priestly activities expanded the role of the king (8:14-64; 9:25). The temple, perhaps his crowning glory, was an inducement to → piety and → obedience to God's → Torah (1 Kgs. 8:22-53, 56-61), a symbol of God's presence in the midst of his people and testimony to his sovereignty.

Jesus contrasts Solomon's splendor as minimal in comparison to God's creation (Matt. 6:29; Luke 12:27). Testifying that the wisdom of Solomon was sufficient to prove his divine appointment as king, → Jesus points to himself as "something greater than Solomon" (Matt. 12:42; Luke 11:31). Matthew includes Solomon among Jesus' ancestors (Matt. 1:6-7).

In both Judaism and Christianity the association of Solomon with demonology and magic flourished in late antiquity, and the "Solomonic" wisdom books influenced early Christian → mysticism. Later Christian thought portrayed him as a great moral teacher and leader, the model of kingly prudence (Dante, *Paradiso* 13.94-108) and a type of Christ (M. → Luther, *LW* 14.327). Nevertheless, Solomon's reign is testimony to both the uses and abuses of God's gifts and to the consequences of those actions (1 Kgs. 4:20-21, 24-25; 11–12).

Bibliography: L. K. HANDY, ed., *The Age of Solomon* (Leiden, 1997) • T. ISHIDA, *Studies in the Period of David and Solomon* (Winona Lake, Ind., 1982) • K. W. WHITELAM, *The Just King: Monarchical Judicial Authority in Ancient Israel* (Sheffield, 1979).

ALLEN C. MYERS

Solomon Islands

	1960	1980	2000
Population (1,000s):	118	227	444
Annual growth rate (%):	2.99	3.50	3.05
Area: 28,370 sq. km. (10,954 sq. mi.)			

A.D. 2000

Population density: 16/sq. km. (41/sq. mi.)
Births / deaths: 3.42 / 0.38 per 100 population
Fertility rate: 4.57 per woman
Infant mortality rate: 19 per 1,000 live births
Life expectancy: 72.8 years (m: 70.7, f: 75.1)
Religious affiliation (%): Christians 95.8 (Protestants 38.5, Anglicans 35.1, Roman Catholics 13.5, indigenous 5.6, unaffiliated 1.9, marginal 1.1), tribal religionists 3.0, other 1.2.

1. Pre-Christian Society
2. Early Missionary Contact
3. Colonization and Christianization
4. The Second World War and After
5. Independence and After

1. Pre-Christian Society

The name "Solomon Islands" originated from the first European contact made by a Spanish expedition led by Alvaro de Mendana in 1568. The archipelago consists of a chain of large parallel islands running northwest to southeast, with numerous outlying and smaller groups of islands. The people had no overall natural, political, or linguistic unity in the precontact period, speaking over 70 languages. The first settlers, largely in the west, spoke languages connected to the early inhabitants of Papua New Guinea. Austronesian-speaking settlers,

comprising the majority of the population, spread throughout Solomon Islands from the west and are linked to the speakers of Oceanic languages. Despite this linguistic complexity, there was a history of trade, warfare, and intermarriage between different tribal groups.

The pre-Christian religion reflected common beliefs in ghosts of → ancestors and spirits but manifested local differentiation in terms of → myths and religious practices. The spiritual world was a source of fear and power, with → magic and sorcery being used to try to control these forces. Payback was endemic, leading to recurring fighting, with feasting and compensation payments used to facilitate reconciliation. While there were some chiefly groupings, many areas were marked by local fragmentation and the acquisition of *mana* by "big-men" who were noted for their prowess in a particular field such as sorcery or the accumulation of material wealth. Community solidarity was expressed among closely knit kin groups. The roles of men and women were clearly separated. Both patrilineal and matrilineal groupings are found in Solomon Islands.

2. Early Missionary Contact

→ Conversion of the islanders was one of the Spanish explorers' objectives. Mendana was accompanied by four Franciscans and conferred the names of popular saints on some islands (→ Catholic Missions). The earliest Solomon Islanders to receive → baptism were three people abducted by the Spanish. Mendana's attempt to establish a colony on the island of Santa Cruz (Ndende) in 1595 was abandoned.

The first sustained missionary attempt was made in 1845 by French Catholic Marist → priests and brothers. They were led by Bishop Jean-Baptiste Epalle, who was attacked on Santa Isabel and died within three weeks of his arrival. The death of four → missionaries from sickness and three by violence, as well as the failure to achieve any converts, led Jean-George Collomb, Epalle's successor, to withdraw the mission in 1847. Malaria and sickness, tribal jealousies, cultural ignorance, conflicting worldviews, and an insular Marist spirituality conspired to defeat the missionaries. A French naval punitive expedition in 1848 brought retaliation to the missionaries' murderers.

The first Anglican → bishop in New Zealand, George Augustus Selwyn, inaugurated the Melanesian Mission in 1849. Initially young men and later young women were recruited and taken back to New Zealand and (from 1867) Norfolk Island for training before returning to their own people as teachers of Christianity. Mota, the language of a small island in northern Vanuatu, was adopted as the mission's lingua franca. European missionaries later took up residence in the islands for longer periods with the establishment of permanent mission stations in Gela, San Cristobal, Santa Isabel, and Guadalcanal. John Coleridge Patteson was consecrated as missionary bishop in 1861. He was killed at Nukapu in the Santa Cruz group in 1871, possibly as a payback for the unscrupulous activities of labor recruiters. Stephen Taroaniara from San Cristobal and Joseph Atkin died from injuries sustained at this time. The mission was noted for its encouragement of indigenous → evangelism and positive respect for local cultures. In R. H. Codrington, W. G. Ivens, and C. E. Fox, the mission produced outstanding missionary anthropologists and linguists.

3. Colonization and Christianization
Following the proclamation in 1893 of a British protectorate over eastern and central Solomon Islands, a British resident commissioner was appointed in 1896. British governance, the growth of the copra trade, improved medical practice, regular shipping links with Sydney, and exposure to European influences made Solomon Islands a more favorable environment for missionary work. Missions became significant agents of pacification, preaching peace and bringing basic health care, → education, and → literacy.

French Marist missionaries returned in 1898 to both the northern (Bougainville) and southern Solomon Islands, setting up mission stations under priests who trained local catechists. Catholics competed with the increasing Protestant and Anglican influences. Jean Ephrem Bertreux, prefect apostolic of South Solomons from 1903, became bishop in 1912.

A Methodist mission, supported from Australia and New Zealand, commenced in the western Solomons in 1902 under the dominating leadership of John Francis Goldie, who was chairman of the mission until 1951 (→ Methodist Churches). Methodists adopted Roviana as their common language. Significant use was made of Pacific Islander missionaries from Samoa, Fiji, and Tonga, who undertook pioneering work in remote areas, with Europeans residing at district mission stations. Local people were trained as teachers, but the mission gave no encouragement for them to be ordained.

The recruitment of laborers from Solomon Islands for Australian sugar plantations led Florence Young to establish in 1886 an interdenominational → "faith mission," the Queensland Kanaka Mission.

After the ending of labor trade in 1901 the mission began work among returned laborers in Malaita. Led by Dr. Northcote Deck, Young's nephew, the renamed South Sea Evangelical Mission (SSEM) competed with Catholic and Anglican missions and adopted a largely negative attitude toward local culture. The arrival of Seventh-day → Adventist missionaries in the western Solomons from 1914 triggered further missionary rivalry.

Anglican expansion in the 19th century was slow. Cecil Wilson, bishop 1894-1911, stimulated the establishment of mission stations and schools in the islands. After the First World War the training of local leaders was shifted from Norfolk Island to Solomon Islands, and English was adopted for church boarding schools. The creation of the Melanesian Brotherhood in 1925 by Ini Kopuria and Bishop John Steward encouraged the growth of an indigenous religious order, grounded in traditional culture, which proved to be a significant evangelistic force in the church in Solomon Islands and beyond.

4. The Second World War and After
The Japanese invasion in 1942 brought destruction, as well as disruption to mission work. Most European missionaries withdrew from the western Solomons, with local people showing considerable initiative in sustaining church life. Anglican and Catholic missionaries in the central and southern islands stayed at their posts. Advancing allied soldiers and airmen were surprised by the vigorous Christianity they encountered. J. F. Kennedy, a future American president, was rescued by Solomon Islands Christians. Marching Rule, an indigenous political-religious movement, grew from the war. Solomon Islanders in Malaita and Guadalcanal demanded a voice in the government and greater control of their affairs, but the movement was suppressed.

Methodist slowness in ordaining Solomon Islanders in part gave rise in 1960 to the Christian Fellowship Church, a breakaway independent church led by Silas Eto. Rapid localization of ordained ministry followed this split (→ Ordination). In 1968 Methodists joined the United Church of Papua New Guinea and Solomon Islands. Leslie Boseto from Choiseul was the church's first indigenous bishop in the Solomon Islands, moderator of the whole church, an international ecumenical leader, and later a politician. In 1996 the United Church in Solomon Islands became an autonomous church.

The South Sea Evangelical Church replaced the SSEM in 1964, becoming an autonomous church in 1975. The visit of Muri Thompson in 1970, a Maori evangelist, stimulated a vigorous Pentecostal revival. The church has a strict attitude to cultural and moral behavior, as well as links with international charismatic and fundamentalist organizations.

Dudley Tuti and Leonard Alufurai were ordained assistant Anglican bishops in 1963. The Anglican Church of Melanesia became an autonomous province of the → Anglican Communion in 1975, with Norman Palmer as its first indigenous archbishop. Since then, a number of new dioceses have been created. The Mothers' Union provides significant avenues for women's leadership in villages and dioceses and nationally. Theological training at Bishop Patteson Theological College from 1966 continues the long-standing emphasis on local ordination training (→ Theological Education). Anglicans and Catholics both support contextualization in worship, architecture, and theology. Catholics still largely depend on expatriate priests and bishops.

5. Independence and After

In 1978 Solomon Islands became an independent state within the British Commonwealth. Conflict between peoples from Malaita and Guadalcanal, from 1999 to 2003, created political instability. This crisis led to a government invitation to Australia, New Zealand, and Pacific nations to send peacekeeping help, which arrived in the form of the Regional Assistance Mission to Solomon Islands (RAMSI). The conflict resulted in the death of a Catholic priest in 2002 and seven Melanesian brothers in 2003. Church leaders and notably the Melanesian Brotherhood played significant roles as mediators and peacemakers during the conflict.

Over 95 percent of Solomon Islanders are classified as Christians. While the majority of people identify with the original mission churches, breakaway and parachurch groups present some threats to this dominance. New religious movements such as → Baha'i, → Jehovah Witnesses, and → Assemblies of God have small followings. Churches still play important roles in secondary education and health care, in partnership with the government, with Seventh-day Adventists maintaining their own education system. The Solomon Islands Christian Association, founded in 1967, provides ecumenical coordination. Churches face considerable demands in a country where a high birth rate and young population, a weak economic base, and potentially divisive political and ethnic forces challenge national unity.

Bibliography: J. A. BENNETT, *Wealth of the Solomons: A History of a Pacific Archipelago, 1800-1978* (Honolulu, 1987) • G. G. CARTER, *Ti.è Varanè: Stories about People of Courage from Solomon Islands* (Rabaul, 1981) • M. ERNST, ed., *Globalization and the Re-shaping of Christianity in the Pacific Islands* (Suva, 1994) • D. HILLIARD, *God's Gentlemen: A History of the Melanesian Mission, 1849-1942* (Brisbane, 1978) • H. LARACY, *Marists and Melanesians: A History of Catholic Missions in the Solomon Islands* (Canberra, 1976); idem, ed., *Pacific Protest: The Maasina Rule Movement, Solomon Islands, 1944-1952* (Suva, 1983) • B. MACDONALD-MILNE, *The True Way of Service: The Pacific Story of the Melanesian Brotherhood, 1925-2000* (Leicester, 2003) • A. R. TIPPETT, *Solomon Islands Christianity: A Study in Growth and Obstruction* (London, 1967) • D. L. WHITEMAN, *Melanesians and Missionaries: An Ethnohistorical Study of Religious Change in the Southwest Pacific* (Pasadena, 1983).

ALLAN K. DAVIDSON

Somalia

	1960	1980	2000
Population (1,000s):	2,711	4,961	8,697
Annual growth rate (%):	2.27	3.20	3.17
Area: 637,000 sq. km. (246,000 sq. mi.)			

A.D. 2000

Population density: 14/sq. km. (35/sq. mi.)
Births / deaths: 4.67 / 1.51 per 100 population
Fertility rate: 6.46 per woman
Infant mortality rate: 103 per 1,000 live births
Life expectancy: 51.0 years (m: 49.4, f: 52.6)
Religious affiliation (%): Muslims 97.9, Christians 1.8 (Orthodox 1.5, other Christians 0.4), other 0.3.

Note: Figures do not include former British Somaliland.

1. Population and History
  1.1. Before Independence
  1.2. From Independence (1960) to Collapse of the Central Government (1991)
  1.3. Somaliland and Puntland
  1.4. From 1991 to the Present
2. Religion and Somali Society
  2.1. Islam
  2.2. Christianity
  2.3. Cultural and Religious Critique

1. Population and History

Somalia is situated on the Horn of Africa, with the Indian Ocean and the Gulf of Aden on its coast and Ethiopia, Kenya, and Djibouti along its borders. It is a product of the colonial scramble for Africa, originally being divided into five colonies: in the north-

northwest, Djibouti (French Somaliland); in the north, along the Gulf of Aden, Punt (British Somaliland); in the west, Ogaden (Ethiopian Somaliland); in the central region and south, Juba (Italian Somaliland); and in the southwest, Kenya's Northern Frontier District (Kenya Somaliland), administered by the British from Kenya (→ Colonialism). The national flag has a white star on a blue background. The five points of the star represent the five areas or countries in which Somalis live. It further symbolizes the goal of a Greater Somalia that would unify Somalis from all five regions.

In 2006 the population of Somalia was estimated at between 9 and 12 million people, with an estimated 2-3 million of this number in the north in Somaliland. Worldwide, the Somali diaspora numbered approximately 2-3 million.

Somalia is not a nation of unified people who speak one language, have a homogeneous religion, or share a single culture. Throughout the land, six major clans (all with many variations in spelling) vie for control: in the north, Dir, Daarood, and Isaaq; in the south, Hawiye, Rahanwayn, and Digil, along with several segments of the Daarood. Traditionally, all these clans and ethnic minorities occupied specific regions, and each clan had its own way of managing its territorial resources, as well as its own judicial, cultural, religious, and social life.

1.1. *Before Independence*

From time immemorial, Somalia maintained cultural and commercial contacts with the ancient world, particularly Egypt, Arabia, and Persia. In the seventh century Abdulmalik ibn Marwan (685-705) from Arabia sent his troops to conquer Mogadishu and to collect tribute from neighboring states in East Africa. Mogadishu eventually rebelled, and the Arabs occupied Juba.

Islamic sultanates ruled Somalia and were hostile to Christian Abyssinia in the north (→ Ethiopian Orthodox Church) and the Bantu and expanding Oromo to the west. The rulers of Somalia found help from the Yemenite king and soon founded, in the region of Harer (in eastern Ethiopia), the Adal Sultanate. In the 14th and early 15th centuries, Ethiopian emperor Dawit I (1382-1411) waged war against Adal. After long fighting, the Muslim king Sa'ad ad-Din II (ruled ca. 1400) was captured in Zeila (modern Seylac) and executed. After his defeat a victory song was composed around 1415 that contains the first written record of the word "Somalia." Ethiopia controlled Somalia from the 1420s until 1527.

In 1527, under the leadership of Imam Ahmad Guray (ca. 1506-43, orig. name Ahmad ibn Ibrahim al-Ghazi), Adal recovered and reached its peak. The northern clans Daarood, Isaaq, and Dir supported Ahmad and his followers, who in 30 years of war (1529-59) conquered the heartland of Abyssinia, slaughtering any Ethiopian who refused to convert from Orthodox Christianity to → Islam. The Portuguese, however, came onto the scene, and a joint Portuguese-Ethiopian Christian force defeated the Muslim army in 1543. Ahmad Guray was killed in the decisive battle of Wayna Daga.

From 1698 to 1774 the sultan of Muscat and Oman controlled the northeastern coast, which later fell to the rule of Egypt. The sultan of Zanzibar (→ Tanzania) controlled the southeastern coast from 1866 to 1892.

In the 19th century the occupation by outsiders met with resistance. One notable antiforeigner leader was Muhammad Abdille Hasan (1864-1920). Born in Ogaden, Mad Mullah, as the British called him, began agitating for expulsion of the British infidels from Somaliland. He challenged his coreligionists on the dangers of accepting the introduction of Christianity. His oratorical skills helped him gather an initial army of 3,000. In 1899 he declared war on infidels, killing those who resisted rule by Islamic law and any fellow Somalis who tried to convert to Christianity. For 20 years he and his followers unleashed terror, killing thousands of Somalis. He built his headquarters in Taleh, with materials coming from Yemen. In 1920 British warplanes bombed his headquarters and killed thousands of people, including Hasan, thus ending his dream of creating a supertribal, superclan political structure governed by Islamic law. Some consider him to be the forerunner of modern Somali nationalism.

After World War II pressure increased for independence. The first registered political party agitating for freedom was the Somali Youth League (SYL), formed in 1945, followed by many others based on clan and ethnic group. In 1948 the foreign powers in Somalia made efforts to solve the "Somali question," and the → United Nations debated the issue in 1949. Eventually, Italy was given nominal trusteeship of Somalia for ten years. The SYL, though, opposed the idea and argued for immediate independence. In 1959 the Italian administration phased out and prepared to hand over power to Somalis.

1.2. *From Independence (1960) to Collapse of the Central Government (1991)*

On June 26, 1960, British Somaliland gained its independence. Then by prearrangement a few days later, on July 1, it merged with the U.N. Trust Territory of Somalia to become the independent Somali Republic. The capital of Somaliland, in the north, was Hargeysa; the capital of the new republic was Mogadishu, on the southern coast.

The first president was Aden Abdulle Osman, with Abdirashid Ali Shermarke as prime minister. Even from the outset, however, the rifts and divisions within Somalia were apparent. The differences between the north and the south, the official languages used (respectively, English and Italian), and the different currencies and cultural priorities were only some of the obstacles to achieving a solid national unity.

The early postindependence era in Somalia was marked by a political ideology of Pan-Somalism. The driving force of Pan-Somalism was the idea of uniting all Somalis, even those living in neighboring countries. Between 1967 and 1969 this position led to border tensions with neighboring Kenya and Ethiopia. Somalia was forced to reconsider its stand, and Prime Minister Ibrahim Egal (Igaal) sought peace and reconciliation with the neighboring countries, renouncing territorial claims. Shermarke, president since 1967, was assassinated in 1969. This was one of the factors that led to a coup on October 21, 1969, which catapulted Mohamed Siad Barre into power as the president. He detained Prime Minister Egal, releasing him only in 1982 after mounting internal and external pressure.

From 1971 to 1973 the Supreme Revolutionary Council (SRC), chaired by Barre, pursued "scientific → socialism," though without supporting → atheism, and gained support from the Soviet Union and China. The Somali language acquired a written form as a national language, giving Somalis a sense of linguistic identity. The newly named Democratic Socialist Republic of Somalia tried to unite all ethnic Somalis into a single state, making overt claims on Ethiopia, Djibouti, and Kenya.

In 1973 Mengistu Haile Mariam came to power in Ethiopia, and from 1974 he was supported by the USSR. In 1977 Somalia invaded Ethiopia, launching the Ogaden War (1977-78), during which Ethiopia received support from both the Soviet Union and Cuba. Somali troops were driven out of Ethiopia in March 1978, but border conflicts continued. After the war, Somalia abandoned its "scientific socialism" and turned to the West for support. Between 1977 and 1991 it received a great deal of assistance, with hundreds of Western aid workers caring for 100,000 → refugees from the Oromo territory. From 1982 to 1988 the United States viewed Somalia as a partner in defense in the context of the cold war.

In the 1980s, frustrated with losing the Ogaden War, Barre's government began to violently suppress opposition groups, particularly from the Isaaq clan.

The army and various factions of society became dissatisfied with Barre. The Somali National Movement (SNM), composed of mainly the Isaaq clan, was founded in Hargeysa in 1981 with the single objective of overthrowing the regime. Other opposition movements, with support from other clans, included the United Somali Congress (USC, Hawiye), the Somali Salvation Democratic Front (Majeerteen), and the Somali Democratic Movement (Digil/Rahanwayn).

In 1988 Barre had the Somali air force bomb Hargeysa, an attack that killed 10,000 civilians and insurgents. This act strengthened the resolve of the various militias to overthrown Barre, now seen as a dictator. Barre declared a state of emergency in 1990 as he faced serious military operations from all sides and could no longer govern the whole country. In January 1991 he was ousted and fled the country.

Before Somalia's government collapsed in 1991 and fighting escalated among clans seeking control of the country, → education was free and compulsory for children between the ages of 6 and 14. The → literacy rate increased from 5 percent of the adult population in the early 1970s to 24 percent in 1990, following an intensive government-sponsored literacy campaign. As a result of Somalia's civil war, however, the educational system collapsed and most schools closed, including the Somali National University (1954-91) in Mogadishu, which had an enrollment of about 4,600 before the war. In 1996 primary schools enrolled only 8 percent of school-aged children, and general secondary schools enrolled a mere 5 percent.

1.3. *Somaliland and Puntland*

On the departure of Barre, the former colony of British Somaliland declared its withdrawal from the 1960 union with Somalia and in May 1991 reasserted its own independence as a sovereign state, the Republic of Somaliland. By 2006, however, it had received recognition from no other state. It has a bicameral legislature, an independent judiciary, and several political parties. In 2003 and 2005 it had national elections that independent observers described as free and fair.

In 1998 the leaders of Puntland, the region to the northeast of Mogadishu around the point of the "horn," declared it to be an autonomous state, the Puntland State of Somalia. It does not seek outright independence from Somalia but desires recognition as a federal division within a united Somalia. As in Somaliland, the support the Puntland leaders receive is based primarily on tribal and clan loyalty. Furthermore, both areas obtain economic and political support from Ethiopia.

1.4. *From 1991 to the Present*

With Barre out of the picture, fighting between rival factions erupted in the south, leading to 40,000 casualties in 1991 and 1992. During the same period, drought and banditry produced a famine in which as many as 300,000 Somalis perished. These tragedies led the international community, including the United States, to launch a U.N. mission to the area, at first only to provide humanitarian relief, and later to attempt to restore law and order. When 24 Pakistan U.N. personnel were killed in June 1993, and then in October when 18 Americans were killed and their bodies were dragged through the streets of Mogadishu, the United States, and later the United Nations, abandoned the mission.

Somalia has been fortunate in receiving a significant amount of international humanitarian support. While this aid has no doubt saved many lives, it also has created the problem of international dependency. The Somali Aid Coordination Body, comprising U.N. agencies, individual donors, NGOs, the U.S. Agency for International Development, and the European Union, coordinates all foreign aid. In 2002 international aid for Somalia totaled $174.4 million, with remittances from Somalis living abroad estimated at $250 million. By 2006 the level of remittances from abroad was estimated at between $800 million and $1 billion.

The migration of Somalis to different parts of the world has a global effect. Their presence in different areas influences regional dynamics at all levels — intercultural, interreligious, economic, and political. In 2006 an estimated 80,000 Somalis were living in Toronto, with as many as 50,000 in Minneapolis and St. Paul, Minnesota. It is hoped that the experience of Somali emigrants all over the world may in the long term have some positive, trickle-down effect on life in Somalia.

Since 1991 there have been several transitional governments in Somalia. Altogether 14 peace attempts have been made, involving the efforts of many other countries, including Ethiopia, Italy, Yemen, and Kenya. An important recent peace initiative was by the Organization of African Unity (OAU), through the East African Inter-Governmental Authority on Development, which sponsored four years of peace talks in Kenya. These efforts led to a peace agreement among various factions of Somalia. In October 2004 the delegates who had gathered in Kenya elected Abdullahi Yusuf Ahmed as interim Somalian president, who took the oath of office in Nairobi. (Ahmed had been president of Puntland, an office he then resigned.) The cabinet, formed in 2005, operates from Baydhabo (Baidoa), not Mogadishu, for reasons of security. Some have dismissed this effort as a puppet government not mandated directly by the Somalia people. Others see it as a step forward toward peace.

In June 2006 the militia of the Islamic Courts Union (ICU) seized Mogadishu, ousting the warlords who had controlled the city since 1991 and restoring a measure of order to the city. The ICU sought to restore peace and order by enforcing Islamic law (→ Shari'a). Many, especially women, viewed the situation with great suspicion, given the history of repressive tendencies by Islamic → fundamentalists. If Islamic law was applied, would there be any future for non-Muslim groups in Somalia? Would the → rights of individuals continue to be trampled? Furthermore, serious questions were raised regarding the amount of arms being smuggled into Somalia or sold to the ICU, which posed a significant threat to the whole Horn of Africa, if not globally. Such developments would seem to jeopardize the worldwide efforts against → terrorism.

One thing is clear: the regional and international community is getting tired of the chaos in Somalia. Primarily, it is up to the people of Somalia to restore peace and order in their country. To do so, however, the spirit of nationhood or → state must be encouraged. Are Somalis willing to go beyond clanism, family ties, and ethnicity? Can Somalis somehow gain a true vision of a → nation that transcends tribe, clan, and family, even if divided into two or three states? Or, since Somaliland has declared its independence, is it time to let other Somalias be created?

2. Religion and Somali Society
2.1. *Islam*

Somalis are predominantly Muslims, of whom 90 percent are → Sunni of the Shafi'ite rites. Islam is part of most Somalis' national identity, with some Somalis claiming to be able to trace their forefathers to the Prophet Muhammad. Somalis were the first African people to convert to Islam.

Somalis for centuries related relatively well with neighboring Christian Ethiopia. This tolerance is attributed to a hadith of the Prophet instructing Muslims not to attack Ethiopia unless attacked. The reason for this allowance is that, in the very early days of Islam, Ethiopians in Arabia protected the first followers of the Prophet.

Three Sufi orders exist in Somalia: Qadiriyah, Ahmadiyah-Idrisiyah, and Salihiyah (the later two interwoven). All these orders seek closer personal relationship with Allah through spiritual disciplines. The members are expected to practice self-renunciation, in some cases including poverty and seclusion. Members of these orders are known as dervishes (Pers. *darvīsh,* "beggar"). The dervishes founded *jamaat* (sing. *jamaa*), or religious agricultural communities. Besides giving spiritual nourishment and development, these *jamaat* functioned as buffer zones between hostile groups or clans, for the *jamaa* centers were considered holy. In 1950 these orders had perhaps 35,000 members. Current statistics are unavailable, but some observers estimate that they may have at least doubled in size.

These orders could be instrumental in the peace process in Somalia. It needs to be noted, however, that fundamentalists are gaining ground faster than the Sufi mystical orders. Fundamentalists have established NGOs supported by groups and individuals from Sudan, South Africa, North America, Europe, Kuwait, Pakistan, Saudi Arabia, Iran, and other countries.

2.2. Christianity

The few Christians in Somalia are mostly Roman Catholics. The → Roman Catholic Church began → missionary work in 1881, facing a hostile reception from Muhammad Abdille Hasan. In the 1970s the church established 20 schools. In 1971 three Franciscan missionaries were driven out of Somalia; in 1972 missionary activity was banned and church properties were nationalized.

An unknown assassin gunned down Italian-born bishop Salvatore Colombo at the cathedral of Mogadishu in 1989. He had served as the bishop of Mogadishu since 1976 and was an outspoken critic of the government. In 2006 Bishop Giorgio Bertin of Djibouti had oversight of the church in Somalia, which Vatican circles refer to as an invisible church.

Swedish Lutherans began the first Protestant mission efforts in 1898 (→ Scandinavian Missions; Lutheran Churches). Their work was in the south, mostly among Bantus, who were former → slaves. In 1935 they gave up their work at the request of the Italian colonial authorities.

The → Mennonites arrived in Somalia in 1953, and the Sudan Interior Mission (SIM) in 1954, both having worked previously in Ethiopia. Like the Lutherans, the Mennonites concentrated on medical and educational work, as well as agricultural development (→ Medical Missions). SIM workers completed a translation of the Bible into Somali, a task that had been started earlier by Roman Catholics in British Somaliland and by English and Swedish missionaries. In 1975 Mennonites ordained the first Somali pastor. Until 1976 the Mennonites served with state consent in the medical sphere.

In 1963 instruction in the → Qur'an became mandatory for all schools, and church and religious instruction was prohibited. In conjunction with na-

tional Islamization, all missions had to leave Somalia in 1976. The churches were allowed to continue but had to receive permission for any mission activity (→ Church and State).

Throughout the history of Somalia, Christians have consistently faced → persecution and denial of their rights. In 2003 at the Somali National Reconciliation Conference, held in Nairobi, Peter Ahmed Abdi, leader of the tiny Mogadishu Pentecostal Church, stated that Somalia Christians live in constant fear. They have no rights and were participating in the conference as a Christian group to demand their rights of expression and freedom of worship. The conference endorsed Islam as the official religion, with the Christian delegation expressing fears that this step could lead to official persecution.

2.3. Cultural and Religious Critique

In two prominent cases, Somali women have recently broken ranks with tradition and have let their voices be heard. Hawa Aden Mohamed has become the "voice of the voiceless" in Somalia. In Mogadishu she founded the Women Adult Education Development Center; in Juba, the Women's Development Centre; but especially she is known for the Galkayo Education Center for Peace and Development, in Puntland. The center agitates in particular against female genital mutilation, which is a traditional rite of passage for most Somali women. She spreads the message that this mutilation is not a religious ordinance from the Qur'an but rather is a form of cultural control. The mission of the center is to strengthen and empower women to advocate for their rights in all spheres of life, with education seen as a tool for liberation for both women and men.

Ayaan Hirsi Ali (Hirsi Magan) is a Somali-born critic of Islam who served in the Dutch Parliament (2003-6) before moving to the United States. Her stand against so-called honor killings and on behalf of the position of women in Islam generally brought her to public attention in the 1990s, especially through the script she wrote for the film *Submission,* whose director, Theo van Gogh, was murdered by a radical Muslim in Amsterdam in broad daylight in 2004.

Bibliography: A. J. AHMED, ed., *The Invention of Somalia* (Lawrenceville, N.J., 1995) • D. B. BARRETT, G. T. KURIAN, and T. M. JOHNSON, *WCE* (2d ed.) 1.671-75 • M. BRONS, *Society, Security, Sovereignty, and the State in Somalia: From Statelessness to Statelessness?* (Utrecht, 2001) • M. DIRIYE ABDULLAHI, *Culture and Customs of Somalia* (Westport, Conn., 2001) • J. GARDNER and J. EL BUSHRA, eds., *Somalia–the Untold Story: The War through the Eyes of Somali Women* (London, 2004) •

A. Kusow, ed., *Putting the Cart before the Horse: Contested Nationalism and the Crisis of the Nation-State in Somalia* (Trenton, N.J., 2004) • I. M. Lewis, "Conformity and Contrast in Somali Islam," *Islam in Tropical Africa* (ed. I. M. Lewis; London, 1966) 253-67; idem, *A Modern History of Somalia* (rev. ed.; London, 1980) • P. D. Little, *Somalia: Economy without State* (Oxford, 2003) • T. Lyons, *Somalia: State Collapse, Multilateral Intervention, and Strategies for Political Reconstruction* (Washington, D.C., 1995) • A. A. Mazrui and C. Wondji, eds., *Africa since 1935* (Oxford, 1999) • N. Mburu, *Bandits on the Border: The Last Frontier in the Search for Somali Unity* (Trenton, N.J., 2005) • S. Ragusa, "Somalia: Rights Denied," *New People* (Nairobi) 102 (March–April 2006) on Hawa Aden Mohamed • S. Shai, "Somalia–Background and Historical Review," *The Red Sea Terror Triangle: Sudan, Somalia, Yemen, and Islamic Terror* (New Brunswick, N.J., 2005) 63-102.

Constantine M. Mwikamba

Son of David → Christological Titles 3.5

Son of God → Christological Titles 3.3

Son of Man → Christological Titles 2

Song of Solomon

1. Contents and Form
2. Origin
3. Time and Place
4. History of Exposition

1. Contents and Form

The Song of Solomon (also Canticles, also Songs of Songs — i.e., the finest song) is ascribed to → Solomon (1:1). It is a collection of some 30 love lyrics. In 12 of these a woman is speaking; she expresses her longing for her lover, describes her dreams of love, and speaks of her union with her lover and of his handsome form. In 8 songs a man speaks, recounting the beauty of his beloved, of the good fortune and riches that she means for him, and of his union with her. In 6 songs both speak, admiring one another and expressing the joy of their love even to the point of physical union. In the "Wedding Dance of the Bride" (6:13–7:5), onlookers describe her charm as she dances.

Typical genres are songs of admiration, descrip-

tion, longing, and praise. The language, with its vivid images (topoi), is artistic and poetic. We should call the Song of Solomon literary poetry rather than popular poetry. The influence of the Near East, especially Egypt, may be seen in many of the motifs.

2. Origin

The artistic form and alien influences suggest an origin in educated circles (the "wise"). The many wedding references point to a setting of the many days of a wedding feast (still common in the Near East) as the pair begins their joint life together. It is hard to think that there would be in → Judaism a lyricizing of free love as G. Gerleman proposed.

3. Time and Place

The usage (one Persian loanword, one Greek, various Aramaisms) favors a later origin (3d-2d cent. b.c.), but it is possible that much older songs have been adapted. Jerusalem is the probable place of origin ("daughters of Jerusalem," 1:5; 2:7, etc.).

4. History of Exposition

Offense was early taken at the erotic and sensual character of this canonical work. For this reason it has mostly been taken allegorically or typologically during the last two millennia. Judaism understood it as referring to the relation between → Yahweh and → Israel (to be read at → Passover); Christianity, to the relation between Christ and the church or between God and his people or members of his people, especially → Mary. This interpretation still holds good today.

Since the 18th century (G. von Herder), however, a more natural view of the Song of Solomon as love songs has also come to the fore in Protestantism. The idea that the Song of Solomon is a drama, common in the 19th century, has now been rejected. An understanding in terms of the cultic myth of a divine wedding (Ishtar and Tammuz) is unprovable and improbable.

The Song of Solomon certainly has a place in the canon as a joyous affirmation of married → love in all its aspects.

Bibliography: Commentaries: D. Bergant and D. W. Cotter (BerOl; Collegeville, Minn., 2001) • G. Gerleman (BKAT; 2d ed.; Neukirchen, 1981) • T. Longman III (NICOT; Grand Rapids, 2001) • M. H. Pope (AB; New York, 1977) • H. Ringgren (ATD; 3d ed.; Göttingen, 1981) • E. Würthwein (HAT; 2d ed.; Tübingen, 1969).

Other works: A. C. Hagedorn, ed., *Perspectives on*

the Song of Songs (Berlin, 2005) • O. Loretz, *Das althebräische Liebeslied* (Neukirchen, 1971) • E. A. Matter, *The Voice of My Beloved: The Song of Songs in Western Medieval Christianity* (Philadelphia, 1990) • H. Schmökel, *Heilige Hochzeit und Hoheslied* (Wiesbaden, 1956) • E. Würthwein, "Zum Verständnis des Hohen Liedes," *TRu* 32 (1967) 177-212.

Ernst Würthwein†

Sophiology

The concept of Sophiology embraces the intentionally related but different and antinomic/paradoxical theorems of Russian religious thinkers, especially V. S. Solovyov (1853-1900), P. Florensky (1882-1937), and S. Bulgakov (1871-1944), in relation to God, humanity, and the world. On the basis of particular mystical experiences (→ Mysticism), the Bible (Proverbs, Song of Solomon, Sirach, John, etc.), and → patristic texts, along with → iconography (→ Icons), they point to Sophia, the Wisdom of God, as the personal being in the decisive interrelating and union of ourselves with God.

The starting point is the view into innerworldly chaos, the division between all that is and humanity, and the desire of nature and ourselves for resolution, for the union of all with all, for cosmic union. → Sin, the falling away of the world soul from God, explains worldly chaos. The striving for unity is explicable as the longing of the world soul for its origin, seen here as Sophia. The world is thus "Sophianic"; as such, it pursues the supercosmic process of the union of nature and humanity as a "becoming absolute," with God, the true Absolute, behind the process. Sophia brings about the union in a historical → theodicy in which God works in and with us as the God-man, preshadowed in Christ (= Sophia). Sophia speculation leads to paradoxical definitions (→ Paradox): Sophia is created and uncreated, an essence of God, a fourth hypostasis, the innermost life of the → Trinity, Christ Logos, eternal feminine, creative beginning of the world, divine mother, → church, and more.

When Sophiologists advance their spiritual theses, controversy in the church and theology is unavoidable, as in the case of Bulgakov, whose doctrines were condemned in 1935 by Metropolitan (later Patriarch) Sergius of Moscow. Sophiology as a → theology that is open to the world continues to be disputed, but it lives on in Russian philosophy as a high metaphysical and religious speculation (→ Metaphysics; Speculative Theology).

→ Gnosis, Gnosticism; Orthodox Christianity; Orthodox Church; Philosophy of Religion; Theosophy

Bibliography: A. Arjakovsky, "The Sophiology of Father Sergius Bulgakov and Contemporary Western Theology," *SVTQ* 49/1-2 (2005) 219-35 • S. N. Bulgakov, *Sophia, the Wisdom of God: An Outline of Sophiology* (rev. ed.; Hudson, N.Y., 1993; orig. pub., 1937) • A. Louth, "Wisdom and the Russians: The Sophiology of Fr Sergei Bulgakov," *Where Shall Wisdom Be Found?* (ed. S. C. Barton; Edinburgh, 1999) 169-81 • B. Schultze, "Maria und Kirche in der russischen Sophia-Theologie," *MeE* 10 (1960) 51-141 • Archbishop Seraphim Sobolev, *The Defense of the Sophianic Heresy by Archpriest S. Bulgakov* (in Russian) (Sofia, 1937); idem, *The New Teaching concerning Sophia, the Wisdom of God* (in Russian) (Sofia, 1935) • P. Valliere, "Sophiology as the Dialogue of Orthodoxy with Modern Civilization," *Russian Religious Thought* (ed. J. D. Kornblatt and R. F. Gustafson; Madison, Wis., 1996) 176-98 • A. Walker, "Sophiology," *Diak.(US)* 16/1 (1981) 40-54 • V. V. Zenkovsky, *A History of Russian Philosophy* (2 vols.; London, 1953; repr., 2003).

Wilhelm Goerdt

Soteriology

1. Biblical Aspects
   1.1. Place within Theology
   1.2. Central Theme
   1.3. NT Images
2. Systematic Aspects
   2.1. Early Attempts at Synthesis
   2.2. Anselm, Aquinas, Abelard
   2.3. Reformation
   2.4. Legacy of the Reformation
   2.5. Liberal Protestantism

1. Biblical Aspects
1.1. *Place within Theology*
Soteriology is the systematic consideration of the Christian doctrine of salvation. It deals with the difference that Christ makes to human subjectivity and human history and, above all, to the relationship between human beings and God. In this connection, it raises fundamental questions about Christian → anthropology, the person of Christ (→ Christology), and the nature and will of → God. The working out of a soteriology also involves issues of → ethics, → politics, and → spirituality.

Sometimes in the history of Christian theology a concern with soteriology has been used as a means of bracketing "speculative" questions (e.g., about Christology), as if the effects of the work of Christ could be treated in abstraction from these broader matters. This attitude is often associated with Philipp → Melanchthon's (1497-1560; → Reformers 3.1.1) dictum that "to know Christ is to know his benefits," and it can be traced in both → Pietism and → liberal theology. The consensus has been, though, that the doctrine of salvation enables us to consider the whole shape of Christian doctrine. The way in which diverse theologies and theologians use the classic images of salvation tells us much about their whole conception of God, humanity, and history.

1.2. Central Theme

It is significant that imagery has played so great a part in the development of soteriology. All theories of salvation are heavily marked by particular → metaphors, and — as in the NT itself — Christian → worship has always employed a wide range of such metaphors. A classic discussion of the effects of Christ's → death and → resurrection is Thomas Aquinas's (ca. 1225-74; → Thomism) treatment in *Summa theol.* III, qq. 49 and 53, which deliberately weaves together a number of metaphors and refuses to limit itself to a single authoritative theory.

The goal of the passion and resurrection is clearly defined as the raising of human beings to perfect communion with the → glory of God. It is a highly biblical perspective: for Paul, John, and the writer of Hebrews, it is clear that all the varied images focus upon a single theme, namely, that because of Christ's death and exaltation, it is possible for human beings to enjoy the same intimacy with the Father as the Son has, in → time and eternity (§2).

1.3. NT Images

This positive message of soteriology is elucidated in the NT in five main clusters of imagery:

- victory over diabolical powers enslaving human beings, or decisive judgment and sentence of banishment against them (the Synoptic → exorcism stories; also, for example, John 12:31; 16:7-11 and 33; Romans 6 and 8; 1 Corinthians 15; Colossians 1)
- a price paid or ransom handed over (Mark 10:45 and par.)
- a law court in which God acquits us of the charges against us, so "justifying" us, declaring us righteous (above all, Romans 3–8)
- a perfect atoning sacrifice (Hebrews above all, but also the metaphor of Christ as Lamb in John 1 and in 1 Peter and Revelation), or a → sacrifice sealing the → covenant of God with his people

(the eucharistic words in Mark 14:24 and par. and 1 Cor. 11:25)
- the bearing by an innocent person of the → punishment of the guilty (1 Pet. 3:18, perhaps 2 Cor. 5:15-21).

In several of these metaphors there is implicit or explicit appeal to the perfect → obedience of Jesus to the will of God in life and death. This element makes it plain that the human freedom, the subjectivity, of Jesus has an indispensable role in the process of salvation, and that his nonviolent response to the threat of suffering and death can be presented as a model to us (Philippians 2; 1 Peter 2).

Although the focus is normally on the cross (→ Theologia crucis), it must also be remembered that the resurrection concretely sets in motion the forming of a new and reconciled humanity (taught throughout Romans, 1 and 2 Corinthians, Colossians, and Ephesians; → Reconciliation), the new → creation; otherwise, salvation would be a primarily negative transaction. This theme also reinforces the significance of the role of the → Holy Spirit in salvation, as the power guaranteeing cohesion and mutual nurture in community.

2. Systematic Aspects

2.1. Early Attempts at Synthesis

In the history of Christian doctrine many attempts have been made to synthesize the images of the NT. In the earliest period there was still more concentration on the goal than on the means of salvation; what Christ and the Spirit bestow is → *theōsis*, a share in the divine nature (2 Pet. 1:4), the restoring of the divine image lost by Adam's fall (→ Sin). "God became human so that human beings might become divine" (→ Athanasius [d. 373] *De incar.* 54.3; see also → Irenaeus [d. ca. 200]). The incarnate Word reveals the beauty of God's image in us by perfect love and obedience to the Father (Irenaeus) and, after the resurrection, exalts human nature to the heavenly places. The glorified humanity of Christ is given to us in the Eucharist (→ Eucharistic Ecclesiology), thus conveying → immortality to our flesh (so Ignatius [d. ca. 107], Gregory of Nyssa [d. ca. 395], and → Cyril of Alexandria [d. 444]).

The cross is an atoning sacrifice and ransom, but there is little theoretical discussion of how it operates. Very occasionally we find the idea, frequent in later medieval piety, that the incarnate form of Christ is a kind of disguise to deceive the devil (→ Origen; Augustine), so that he is persuaded to admit Jesus to the realm of the dead, whence he will lead out the souls of the redeemed. Early and medieval → liturgy, as well as the poetry and religious drama of the → Middle Ages, make much of the language of Christ as victor in the battle with Satan, assaulting Hades to rescue the trapped souls; the motif is common in → iconography, Eastern and Western.

2.2. *Anselm, Aquinas, Abelard*

Eastern Christianity (→ Orthodox Christianity) in general remains within this frame of reference. Western Christianity, from the early Middle Ages, also developed a variety of theoretical accounts, the first being → Anselm's (1033-1109) treatment in *Cur Deus homo?* (1098): Adam's disobedience to God is an offense to an unlimited honor and majesty, and no finite agent can repair this infinite damage or insult. Yet it must be a human agent who repairs the breach if humans are to be reconciled. Thus God must act *as* a human agent. Because God's acts are of infinite worth or merit, they will atone for the infinite offense. The terms of this theory are obviously shaped by feudal notions of public honor and repute (→ Feudalism) and their role in cementing the social bond.

Anselm's theory was significantly modified later by Aquinas (*Summa theol.* III, q. 48, art. 2), who asserts that the Son must offer the Father something the Father loves more than he hates sin, namely, himself. Such a view links soteriology more firmly with the Trinitarian nature of God (→ Trinity).

Peter Abelard (1079-1142) employs a completely different strategy, insisting that Christ's cross is a demonstration of God's unreserved → love; there is nothing God will not do or endure to show us his love, and the change made by the cross is a change in our hearts. It is we, not the Father, who must be persuaded by Christ's death. Again, Aquinas (*Summa theol.* III, q. 49, art. 1) adopts and modifies: Our love for God is the formal cause of our → forgiveness, even though the act of God is the efficient cause; the cross must create in us a state of "friendship" with God. Aquinas, it should be noted, gives a more central place to the resurrection in the work of salvation than does either Anselm or Abelard.

2.3. *Reformation*

The → Reformation reacted strongly against what was seen as an overemphasis on the causal role of our human love for God. Martin → Luther's (1483-1546; → Luther's Theology) insistence on justification by faith alone (→ Reformation Principles) gives central place to Paul's legal imagery. We are declared guiltless by the free act of God, and that declaration empowers us to live differently, in → freedom and fellowship (→ Justification 2). Luther can use in addition the whole repertoire of biblical and patristic metaphor, notably the language of triumph in battle over the demons, but justification remains the focus.

John → Calvin (1509-64; → Calvin's Theology) gives a far more significant role to the human obedience of Christ (reflecting the difference between his and Luther's Christology). Christ re-forms humanity in every stage of its growth (so also Irenaeus), serving, loving, and obeying the Father in all circumstances, even on the cross, where he suffers the pains of a damned soul, the sense of utter separation from God. By union with his risen life, in the trust formed in us by the Spirit, we share the benefit of his obedience. We are treated as if we were obedient, and so adopted into the sonship of Jesus. This model is paralleled in the theology of John → Knox (ca. 1513-72), who lays special stress on adoption and union with the glorified humanity of Jesus.

2.4. *Legacy of the Reformation*

Both Protestant traditions, in the centuries following, lost something of the strongly biblical and patristic flavor of the best of Luther and Calvin. Lutheran → orthodoxy (§1) increasingly isolated justification from → sanctification, so damaging the unity of what is achieved in the cross and resurrection. Calvin's insistence on Christ bearing the → punishment of the damned, the punishment we deserve, became more and more central to some strands of → Calvinism, at the expense of other factors. Protestant revivalism (→ Revivals) and → fundamentalism in the last two centuries have regularly insisted on "penal substitution" as the only legitimate theology of the → atonement.

The strengths of the Reformed tradition were, however, richly developed by Karl → Barth (1886-1968; → Dialectical Theology), above all in *CD* IV/1 and 2, where Barth argues that "the Judge judged in our place" (IV/1, §59.2) absorbs in himself all possibilities of condemnation and loss. None but he can judge, and he has chosen to bear and so to cancel all judgment. His obedience in this work is the same thing as the Word's eternal response to the Father, and through this sovereignly free obedience, the dignity of the "royal man" is shared with all humanity.

2.5. *Liberal Protestantism*

Liberal Protestantism (esp. Albrecht Ritschl in Germany and Hastings Rashdall in England) tended to favor a rather weakened version of Abelard's approach. Jesus' role is to inspire us to greater love for God and each other. Friedrich → Schleiermacher (1768-1834; → Schleiermacher's Theology) gave complicated expression to this view. Christ's work consists of the living influence of his perfect God-consciousness on human freedom, summoning us to a new level of conscious life and making us capable of it, thus freeing us for life in society.

Such an approach found few defenders among 20th-century theologians. Even those, such as the Roman Catholic Karl → Rahner (1904-84; → Transcendental Theology) and the Protestant Wolfhart Pannenberg (b. 1928), who give a central place in their thought to the model of Jesus fulfilling the human vocation to self-transcendence in fellowship with God, have stressed the concreteness of divine action in this process, not merely the contingency of a great man's virtue.

The emptiness of regarding Christ as primarily an example has also been underlined, from quite different perspectives, by → liberation and → feminist theologies, which have insisted that our relation with God is distorted not only by individual sin but also by sinful structures, distorted patterns of → power (as in patriarchy and → colonialism). The saving work of Jesus must be seen as the construction of a community of just and reconciled relations (as both Schleiermacher and G. W. F. Hegel, in their radically different idioms, had argued in the 19th century). Here, too, there can be a risk of overstressing the role of human initiative and undervaluing the resourcefulness of God's grace in meeting our failure (i.e., God does more than simply inspire our effort).

All serious theologies of salvation must eventually draw us back to the conviction that God acts to re-create human possibility through the life, death, and resurrection of Jesus. Otherwise, salvation becomes no more than an attractive *ideal* of liberation and → healing, instead of the historical and concrete *reality* of renewed humanity (→ New Self).

Bibliography: G. AULÉN, *Christus Victor: An Historical Study of the Three Main Types of the Idea of the Atonement* (London, 1970; first ET, 1931) • K. BARTH, *CD* IV/1-2 • M. HENGEL, *The Atonement: The Origins of the Doctrine in the NT* (London, 1986) • J. MCINTYRE, *The Shape of Soteriology: Studies in the Doctrine of the Death of Christ* (Edinburgh, 1992) • W. PANNENBERG, *Jesus, God and Man* (2d ed.; Philadelphia, 1977) pt. 2 • K. RAHNER, *Foundations of Christian Faith* (New York, 1982) 116-37 • H. RASHDALL, *The Idea of Atonement in Christian Theology* (London, 1919) • A. RITSCHL, *Die Christliche Lehre von der Rechtfertigung und Versöhnung* (3 vols.; 3d ed.; Bonn, 1888-89; ET *The Christian Doctrine of Justification and Reconciliation,* vol. 1, *A Critical History* [Edinburgh, 1872]; vol. 3, *The Positive Development of the Doctrine* [Clifton, N.J., 1966]) • P. K. STEVENSON and S. I. WRIGHT, *Preaching the Atonement* (London, 2005) • M. VOLF, *Free of Charge: Giving and Forgiving in a Culture Stripped of Grace* (Grand Rapids, 2005) • J. G. VAN DER WATT, ed., *Salvation in the NT: Perspectives on Soteriology* (Leiden, 2005).

ROWAN D. WILLIAMS

Soul

1. Religious History
   1.1. Variety of Terms and Views
   1.2. Soul-Body Problem
2. Theology and Philosophy
   2.1. Concept
   2.2. Greek and Biblical Views
   2.3. Church Tradition, Arab Philosophy, and Thomas Aquinas
   2.4. Descartes and Subsequent Positions
   2.5. God and the Soul in Church Usage
3. Practical Theology
   3.1. Not an Express Theme
   3.2. The Empirical Sciences
   3.3. Transmigration and Esotericism

1. Religious History

1.1. *Variety of Terms and Views*

The word "soul" (cf. Ger. *Seele*) embraces the meanings of many other words with a history of their own. These meanings differ not only in ancient cultures but also among themselves. They stand for various human experiences, of which we no longer know whether they were as numerous as the terms used — but do know that historically they represent basic realities of existence. A common feature of these realities is that they are regarded as essentially different from the materials of which we and nature and our world are composed.

We may divide these basic realities as follows: First we have → *ecstasy,* in which we view ourselves substantially as outside ourselves. Then we have complementary *yearnings for* → *immortality,* which in substance involves something other than that which perishes in the grave and which carries with it a desire for a continuation of living contact with the deceased who are close to us. Third is the gift of *clairvoyance* (→ Visions), which demands an organ enabling the eye to function in times and places beyond those to which the physical eye is restricted. Next is the belief in a substantialized *vital force,* even in smaller spheres of existence than that represented by either a human being or an → animal as a whole (→ Vitalism). Finally, we have the recognition that certain kinds of feeling give us a different reality, or a different kind of reality, from that supplied by thought, a reality that demands a special agent to feel it that is beyond mind, understanding, or reason.

It has always been found right, then, to describe these basic immaterial realities in terms of "soul," even though this is a collective word that demands nuanced usage. Our own word "soul" covers a great variety of notions that ancient peoples expressed by such terms as

> *ba* or *ka* (Egyptians; → Egyptian Religion),
>
> *napištu* (Babylonians; → Babylonian and Assyrian Religion),
>
> *rûaḥ, nepeš* or *rûḥ, nafs* (Hebrews, Arabs, and Muslims; → Judaism; Islam),
>
> *armaiti, baodah, daēna, daēva, fravaši, grīva, gyān, hoš, mainyu, urva, uštāna* (Iranians; → Iranian Religions),
>
> *brahman, ātman,* (Hindus; → Hinduism),
>
> *daimōn, pneuma, thymos, idea, psychē, nous, logos* (Greeks, the three last of these terms being used also by Christians; → Greek Religion), and
>
> *animus, anima, mens* (Romans; → Roman Religion).

An even greater number of words exists among illiterate peoples, such as those that find a place for → shamanism. Among other peoples like the Chinese we find natural and cosmic forces similar to souls, which might be interpreted in various ways as deities, as among the Indians.

None of the basic experiences has to be the primary one in human history, nor can any one term be regarded as original. Certain features of the basic realities of the soul hereby posited have produced universal theories of origin and development such as → animism, animatism, or dynamism, which, in view of their monism of phenomenon or causality, have become → ideologies and are thus responsible for one-sided views that can be considered from other standpoints than that of the history of religion. But this standpoint, when properly adopted, can contribute to intercultural enlightenment and objective anthropological programs. It is probable, however, that our word "soul" has gained something from the Christian singling out of the personal relation to God, from the Gnostic idea of the soul as *salvator salvandus* (saved savior; → Gnosis, Gnosticism), and from the Neoplatonic concept, still echoed up to early modern times, of the unity of all souls in their plurality (→ Platonism).

1.2. *Soul-Body Problem*

The majority of incorporeal realities, that is, the historical, can be summarized as substances; their minority, those in the present, as functions. The so-called body-soul problem connects the present and historical findings, insofar as we find the same kind of variety in both. Each function of the soul today differs from all others to the same degree in which, earlier, the "soul" differed from all other essences. If one has reclaimed for the soul the function of a remaining substratum of psychological processes, then, both in this regard and in respect of its function as a concept of differentiation from the body, it has lost all concreteness. According to L. J. Pongratz, the phrase "psychology without soul," coined by F. A. Lange (1828-75), applies to modern scientific → psychology as a whole.

Bibliography: J. BEMPORAD et al., "Soul," *EncRel(E)* 13.426-65 • J. N. BREMMER, *The Early Greek Concept of the Soul* (Princeton, 1983) • C. COLPE, "Seele," *WM* 4.430-32 • K. JASPERS, *General Psychopathology* (Baltimore, 1997; orig. pub., 1913) • F. A. LANGE, *History of Materialism* (3 vols.; 2d ed.; London, 1879-81; orig. pub., 1866) • L. LÉVY-BRUHL, *How Natives Think* (Princeton, N.J., 1985; orig. pub., 1922); idem, *The "Soul" of the Primitive* (New York, 1966; orig. pub., 1927) • S. MORENZ, *Egyptian Religion* (Ithaca, N.Y., 1973) • I. PAULSON, *Die primitiven Seelenvorstellungen der nordeurasischen Völker* (Stockholm, 1958) • L. J. PONGRATZ, "Leib-Seele-Problem" and "Seele," *LPs* 2.415-18 and 3.290-91 • E. ROHDE, *Psyche: The Cult of Souls and Belief in Immortality among the Ancient Greeks* (Chicago, 1987; orig. pub., 1894) • A. SCHIMMEL, *Mystical Dimensions of Islam* (Chapel Hill, N.C., 1975) • B. SNELL, *The Discovery of the Mind: The Greek Origins of European Thought* (Cambridge, Mass., 1953) • T. STCHERBATSKY, *The Soul Theory of the Buddhists* (2d ed.; Varanasi, 1970).

CARSTEN COLPE

2. Theology and Philosophy

2.1. *Concept*

Since the term "soul," at any rate in the older and the newer European languages, denotes many things and is largely interchangeable with other terms like "life," "heart," "breath," and "person," investigating its etymological origins helps us little, nor need we attempt a definition. In ordinary speech (→ Analytic Philosophy), its imprecision causes little difficulty because the context is usually clear. Academically, the term defies reduction to a concept.

It is best, then, not to treat the OT *nepeš* or the NT *psychē* as concepts but to accept them in the imprecision of their normal usage. As a rule, the context will show what is meant, at least in the OT. The situation differs in the NT. For example, it is quite clear what "soul" means in 1 Pet. 3:20 (the eight "souls" saved through water in the days of → Noah), but less precise interpretations are possible in the very same epistle at 1:9 ("the outcome of your faith, the salvation of your souls"). The same problems arise today in the academic use of "soul" or *psyche,* for example, when we read of "psychological factors" in psychosomatics. We look for definitions, but they are not forthcoming.

2.2. Greek and Biblical Views

Behind and alongside both Greek and biblical usage stand many traditions and shamanistic practices (→ Shamanism) in which ideas of the soul occur, expressed in mythical or cultic speech, of which we can achieve some understanding today only by means of contextual analysis of the implied → anthropologies of these cultures or traditions.

From the many ideas of the soul — for example, as vital force, good or evil spirit, individual self, rarefied substance of the power of individual organs, "free" soul that can leave the body during sleep, or transmigrating soul — Greek philosophy (→ Psychology 2) first created, in the language of → myth, a dualistic understanding of soul and body. The many souls became one soul, though divided in dimensions or components. The soul controls the body as the horseman does unruly steeds (Plato *Phdr.* 246A, an image adopted also by M. → Luther). Deepened in Neoplatonism, though along with the momentous thought of a world soul, which the church could not accept (→ Platonism 3), this thought had a strong influence on the Christian tradition and is still taken seriously with respect to the relation between the soul and the brain (J. Eccles; see 3.2). The Platonic soul is immortal and does not have to be of a fine substance, as in many Stoic views (→ Stoicism). The much-discussed Greek trichotomy of soul, spirit, and body is a product of this dualistic understanding but is also an expression of human unity.

Another view entered harmoniously along with the Platonic tradition, namely, the monistic concept of the soul as the formal principle of the body. This was the view of Aristotle (384-322 B.C.; → Aristotelianism). Aristotle adopted Plato's (427-347) → dualism of ideas and reality into his concept of the entelechy in things and living creatures, and the horseman-soul analogy into his threefold concept of souls: the vegetative soul of plants; the animal soul of animals, which has the gift of perception; and the free rational soul of humans, which has its roots in the first two.

In contrast, the OT writings show an almost completely uniform understanding of *nepeš* in direct relation to → life. The soul is the power and principle of life, an expression, certainly, of appetites and emotions, yet not conceivable without the body. Gen. 35:18 ("as her soul was departing [for she died] . . .") and 1 Kgs. 17:21 ("let this child's life [*nepeš*] come into him again") are to be understood along these lines. OT passages become more ambiguous only in light of the church's interpretations, for example, when the concept of the *imago Dei,* as in Thomas Aquinas (ca. 1225-74; → Thomism), is linked to Aristotle's doctrine of the soul.

In general the NT presupposes the OT view, although Greek concepts also intrude. Thus Matt. 10:28, which says that we are not to fear those who can kill only the body and not the soul, raises this question, along with similar passages in the Judaic-Hellenistic martyrdom records. In the NT, however, the soul is not our rational part but the self that cannot function without the body. When the body perishes at death, the soul does not take its place. The self persists, but it acquires a new body (2 Cor. 5:1-10). Alongside the soul is the *pneuma,* which is ours by nature but then also a gift of God as the Spirit of Christ (→ Holy Spirit). As the self, the *psychē* is thus the lower power, the *pneuma* the higher (K. Berger). The *sōma* (body) is the sum of our outward relations insofar as such distinctions can be conceptualized.

2.3. Church Tradition, Arab Philosophy, and Thomas Aquinas

In the → early church a combination of NT and Platonic-Neoplatonic dualistic conceptions held sway from the first acts of the martyrs (→ Martyrs, Acts of the) to → Augustine (354-430; Augustine's Theology). The Aristotelian doctrine of the soul had little influence on the view of the soul in the early church. The soul would survive the → death of the individual, and OT and NT passages were interpreted accordingly. This position — strictly speaking, not in accordance with 1 Corinthians 15 — is still, with modifications, Roman Catholic teaching, and we find it also in John → Calvin (1509-64; → Calvin's Theology) and the Reformed, Lutheran, and Anglican traditions. (If *psychē* in the NT does denote the human self, then we might perhaps still use "immortality of the soul" as a way of speaking of the → resurrection.)

A truly new and deeper version of the doctrine of the soul came with Thomas Aquinas, thanks to the Arab philosophers and physicians who had reintroduced Aristotle to the West (→ Islamic Philosophy). Avicenna (980-1037) had taught the eternity of the world, as had Averroës (1126-98), who with the concept of a single soul common to all (as distinct from the mortal individual soul) had a great intellectual attraction for Aquinas and later theologians. These thinkers could not unite such concepts, however, with the Christian tradition. The basic structure of hylemorphism (i.e., the form gives reality to the possibility of matter) was accepted for both the soul and body, but not the eternity of a common soul or the mortality of the individual soul (→ Time and Eternity).

Aquinas linked the doctrine of → creation (§3), and especially the biblical concept of the *imago Dei,* to both the traditional Christian and the Aristotelian teachings about the soul. Souls are created individually. The soul is the final cause of creation. The human soul is the sum of all forms in the world and thus the culmination of the creaturely. There is here no disparagement of the body, such as is often attributed to the church. The body has its own dignity and function. After death the soul exists improperly, for it can be only the form of the body. It awaits reunion with the resurrected body. In quasi-philosophical terms Aquinas uses biblical materials to remedy certain defects in the traditional Neoplatonic doctrine of the soul.

2.4. *Descartes and Subsequent Positions*
This full and comprehensive explanation of God's creation and the human soul, however, did not solve every problem. The unity of → truth broke up, and with it the theological explanatory power of the Thomistic theological synthesis of → nature and the supernatural. The idea of two truths came to be accepted — that of revelation and that of reason. Only with R. Descartes (1596-1650; → Cartesianism), though, did a dualism that divides explanation of the world find expression. This dualism put the soul in the one sphere and the body in the other. With some truth, there has been found here the beginning of the philosophical justification of purely somatic medicine, which began its victorious march in the 19th century and shut out the soul. (Only 20th-century psychosomatic medicine sought to bring about reunion, though unfortunately the term speaks of two different entities.)

G. W. Leibniz (1646-1716; → Philosophy of Nature 2.2) made the dualism of Descartes into a harmoniously synchronizing parallelism that finds reflection today in wholly new concepts in neuropsychology (D. B. Linke). In the English-speaking world, however, → empiricism gained the upper hand, not → rationalism. According to J. Locke (1632-1704; → Self), the soul of the newborn is like a blank slate, though Locke did allow for some innate abilities to coordinate sense impressions. By way of G. Berkeley (1685-1753) and D. Hume (1711-76), empiricism led basically to behaviorism and to B. F. Skinner (1904-90).

The Continental tradition, following Cartesian dualism, did make possible the branch known as empirical → psychology (§2), which found a distinctive offshoot in the Pietist doctrine of self-scrutiny (→ Pietism). In the main, however, teaching about the soul was integrated into → metaphysics, as in C. Wolff (1679-1754).

I. Kant (1724-1804; → Kantianism) decisively modified this dualism. He recognized the validity of empirical psychology but contested the ability of philosophy to prove the existence of the soul, whether as a substance or as a guarantee of immortality. One cannot prove the soul as self-identity but only posit it as a postulate or regulative idea.

An opposing view found support in F. W. J. Schelling (1775-1854; → Idealism 5), who stressed the indissoluble unity of body and soul as against dualism, and in G. W. F. Hegel (1770-1831; → Hegelianism), who argued that the soul is the seat of powers we can describe empirically, that as such it knows itself, but that it knows itself as an element of the subjective consciousness and therewith as a necessary part of self-objectification of the spirit. We can overcome Kant's rejection of proof of the existence of the soul by uniting it to the objective spirit. Hegel's *Encyclopedia of the Philosophical Sciences* is the last effort to speak of the soul within the framework of a total philosophical or theological system, which the emancipation of psychology as a discipline negated. In modern discussion (see 3.2) there is constant reflection of the alternatives of rationalism and empiricism.

2.5. *God and the Soul in Church Usage*
The original dualism derived from Greek philosophy concerned the soul and the body. The OT with its unitary view is no witness in this regard, as parts of the NT are. There is no doubt at all, however, that the full biblical tradition, even in early, medieval, and Reformation exposition, views the soul as the point of contact between God and us. Augustine's desire to "know fully only God and the soul" (*Sol.* 1.2.7) may be an untenable compression of the gospel of God's turning to the world, but it unquestionably points us in this direction. Many approaches in → pastoral psychology, in the → psychology of religion, and in the teaching of → pastoral care devote themselves to these two themes (see 3.1). We find a variation based on the psychology of C. G. Jung (1875-1961) in E. Drewermann.

If one views the soul chiefly as the human self, theology can deal with the soul and God without restriction and in spite of the criticism of Kant and the "end of metaphysics." We receive the Word of God, and the soul, the human self, is preserved in

God after death. But this kind of usage is popular and imprecise, even though it is common in the church. The free use of such terms on a biblical basis has been influenced by culture-specific ideas of the soul and thus may not carry the same traditional significance in the churches of Africa and Asia as in Europe.

In all parts of the church, however, the soul has to do with the inner being, with the site of meeting with God, with the place of insight into → sin and → forgiveness, and with the seat of → love and → hope, including hope of eternal life. Souls may be touched, guided, won, saved, or lost. Even in a critical and thoughtful setting believers are familiar with such terms, although they themselves may not use them. The same applies to the Roman Catholic idea of masses for the souls of the dead, which those of other denominations who do not practice them can understand, or to the "soul brothers" of African Christians. When some conservative believers limit the church's task mainly to the "saving of souls," the difference does not lie in the concept of the soul as such but in the fear on the part of others that this narrow focus will separate soul and body, the salvation of the soul and social justice. In popular speech "soul" usually denotes our inner core, and it is related to continued existence after death.

Bibliography: Early Greek and biblical themes: K. BERGER, Historische Psychologie des Neuen Testaments (Stuttgart, 1991) • A. P. BOS, The Soul and Its Instrumental Body: A Reinterpretation of Aristotle's Philosophy of Living Nature (Boston, 2003) • E. ROHDE, Psyche: The Cult of Souls and Belief in Immortality among the Ancient Greeks (Chicago, 1987; orig. pub., 1894) • H. SONNEMANS, Seele, Unsterblichkeit, Auferstehung. Zur griechischen und christlichen Anthropologie und Eschatologie (Freiburg, 1984) • R. J. TESKE, "Soul," Augustine through the Ages: An Encyclopedia (ed. A. D. Fitzgerald; Grand Rapids, 1999) 807-12 • H. W. WOLFF, Anthropology of the OT (Philadelphia, 1974).

Other themes: J. ASSMANN, ed., Die Erfindung des inneren Menschen. Studien zur religiösen Anthropologie (Gütersloh, 1993) • I. C. BRADY, "Soul, Human," NCE (2d ed.) 13.336-45 • W. S. BROWN et al., eds., Whatever Happened to the Soul? Scientific and Theological Portraits of Human Nature (Minneapolis, 1998) • E. DREWERMANN, Tiefenpsychologie und Exegese (2 vols.; Olten, 1984-85) • J. C. ECCLES, How the Self Controls Its Brain (Berlin, 1994) • J. W. FOWLER, Stages of Faith: The Psychology of Human Development and the Quest for Meaning (San Francisco, 1981) • A. GEHLEN, Man, His Nature and Place in the World (New York,

1988; orig. pub., 1940) • J. B. GREEN and S. L. PALMER, eds., In Search of the Soul: Four Views of the Mind-Body Problem (Downers Grove, Ill., 2005) • B. GROM, Religionspsychologie (Munich, 1992) • D. B. LINKE and M. KURTHEN, eds., Parallelität von Gehirn und Seele (Stuttgart, 1988) • N. C. MURPHY, Bodies and Souls, or Spirited Bodies? (Cambridge, 2006) • C. A. VON PEURSEN, Body, Soul, Spirit (London, 1966) • G. RYLE, The Concept of Mind (New York, 1949) • J. SEIFERT, Das Leib-Seele-Problem in der gegenwärtigen philosophischen Diskussion (Darmstadt, 1979) • E. TUGENDHAT, Self-Consciousness and Self-Determination (Cambridge, 1986).

DIETRICH RITSCHL and MARTIN HAILER

3. Practical Theology

3.1. Not an Express Theme

Practical theology uses the term "soul" sparingly. It does so partly because it is imprecise (see 2.1) and partly because it cannot be a true theme in this discipline, any more than music itself can be in musicology. Especially as the teaching of → pastoral care, → practical theology does deal with dimensions relating to the soul — for example, the → development (§2) of the child (→ Childhood) and its → conscience, the emotions, also the relation of the soul to the body, to → grief, and to sickness (→ Health and Illness) — but not with the soul as a separate theme. Pastoral care, → religious education, the → psychology of religion, → psychotherapy, and → psychiatry all take up matters relating to the soul and its functions, dimensions, and relations.

3.2. The Empirical Sciences

The question arises whether indirectly in the empirical sciences of our day classical ideas of the soul have not reemerged under such terms as "the ego" (→ Ego Psychology) or "the self," and relative to the steering functions investigated in neurophysiology (see research into the two hemispheres of the brain). With its turning in the 1960s to concepts and constructs used by the empirical sciences, practical theology has begun to touch upon at least some aspects of the classical theological question about the soul. The older psychoanalytic concepts of the self in C. G. Jung (1875-1961), S. Freud's (1856-1939) structural theory of the personality, and ego psychology (A. Freud, H. Hartmann, R. White, E. Erikson, et al.) can be understood along such lines (→ Development 2; Psychoanalysis). In these interpretations "personality" and "the ego," with some degree of truth, stand in for that which traditionally has been called the soul. In this context → pastoral psychology, particularly in the United

States (→ Clinical Pastoral Education), again speaks quite freely about the soul, and congruence is seen at many points between Jung's theory and Christian belief.

A similar affinity to the classical Christian understanding of the soul is often seen in the dualistic interactionistic theory of J. C. Eccles (1903-97), which he developed along with K. Popper's concept of the world of physics, conscious perception, and the *I* in its → identity and continuity (1977), all in opposition to the monistic and materialistic theory of D. M. Armstrong and others that would ultimately explain all functions of the soul physiologically (→ Monism; Materialism). Eccles argues for the soul's relative independence of the body, for wholly new layers of reality that we cannot derive from the deep layers of the function of the brain. His position has stirred up debate in neuropsychology and run into strong criticism on account of its methodological dualism. Here, as in other apparently purely scientific central problems, we see reflected the classical philosophical and theological alternatives that in Eccles's own case we may relate to his early training in Thomistic thinking. Theology must consider carefully whether confirmation of a dualistic view is theologically useful.

3.3. *Transmigration and Esotericism*

Today churches in Europe and North America, along with practical theology, are challenged by modern interests in → meditation (→ Transcendental Meditation), → mysticism (§1), transmigration of souls (→ Karma; Reincarnation), and → esotericism (→ New Age; New Religions; Youth Religions). They partly encounter in these fields → Gnostic and newly received Eastern religious traditions, in which the soul has a central role (→ Buddhism; Hinduism; Jainism; Zen). In addition to thorough historical and systematic analyses of these movements, the Protestant churches especially will need ecumenical stimulation (→ Ecumenism, Ecumenical Movement; Ecumenical Theology) to learn from the riches of the churches of Africa and Asia and from the mysticism of the → Roman Catholic Church and the → Orthodox Church, in whose insights into the mysteries of the human soul they might find as yet unexcavated treasures (→ Spirituality). At the same time, they must avoid any naive idealizing of holism or false hopes of a scientific rehabilitating of their classic ideas of the soul (→ Science and Theology). They will do well to see in the word "soul" an irreplaceable metaphor for the mystery of human individuality and to safeguard and use it as such.

→ Pastoral Theology

Bibliography: M. von Brück, *The Unity of Reality: God, God-Experience, and Meditation in the Hindu-Christian Dialogue* (New York, 1990) • O. D. Creutzfeldt, J. C. Eccles, and J. Szentágothai, *The Brain-Mind Problem* (Louvain, 1987) • É. Durkheim, *The Elementary Forms of Religious Life* (New York, 2001; orig. pub., 1912) • J. C. Eccles, *Facing Reality: Philosophical Adventures by a Brain Scientist* (New York, 1970) • H. M. Enomiya-Lassalle, *Living in the New Consciousness* (Boston, 1988); idem, *Zen und christliche Spiritualität* (Munich, 1987) • E. Fromm, *The Heart of Man: Its Genius for Good and Evil* (New York, 1968) • D. B. Linke and M. Kurthen, eds., *Parallelität von Gehirn und Seele* (Stuttgart, 1988) • A. Pieris, *Love Meets Wisdom: A Christian Experience of Buddhism* (Maryknoll, N.Y., 1988) • K. R. Popper and J. C. Eccles, *The Self and Its Brain* (New York, 1977) • J. Sudbrack, *Mystik. Selbsterfahrung, kosmische Erfahrung, Gotteserfahrung* (Mainz, 1988) • T. Sundermeier, *The Individual and Community in African Traditional Religions* (Piscataway, N.J., 1998).

Dietrich Ritschl

South Africa

	1960	1980	2000
Population (1,000s):	17,396	29,170	46,257
Annual growth rate (%):	2.62	2.49	2.09
Area: 1,223,201 sq. km. (472,281 sq. mi.)			

A.D. 2000

Population density: 38/sq. km. (98/sq. mi.)
Births / deaths: 2.80 / 0.70 per 100 population
Fertility rate: 3.52 per woman
Infant mortality rate: 43 per 1,000 live births
Life expectancy: 67.4 years (m: 64.6, f: 70.3)
Religious affiliation (%): Christians 81.5 (indigenous 44.6, Protestants 27.0, Roman Catholics 8.1, Anglicans 5.3, unaffiliated 4.5, other Christians 1.0), tribal religionists 9.9, Hindus 2.5, Muslims 2.4, nonreligious 2.3, other 1.4.

1. General Situation
2. Christian Churches
3. Church and State
4. Non-Christian Religions

1. General Situation

In 2007 the Republic of South Africa had an estimated 45 million inhabitants of various races, creeds, languages, and cultures. The executive government is in Pretoria, but the National Assembly meets in Cape Town. The Court of Appeal resides in

Bloemfontein, and the overarching Constitutional Court of South Africa has its basis in Johannesburg. South Africa is subdivided into nine provinces with regional governments, but there is currently a debate about whether to return to an earlier arrangement with fewer provinces.

After 1652 European settlers started arriving in South Africa, coming primarily from the Netherlands, France, and Germany. They began to restrict the subsistence farming of the African population and started to make the indigenous people economically dependent. The settlers also quickly practiced and implemented various forms of racial segregation.

In the 19th century the conflict between British imperialism and Afrikaner nationalism in the South African context became a harsh reality. It had very major social, political, economic, and ideological effects in the further historical and political development of South Africa. The discovery of diamonds in 1867 and gold in 1886 led to mining, which favored the urbanization of the African peoples. The conflict of the first and second Anglo-Boer wars (1880-81, 1899-1902), between the British Empire and the Boer Republics, proved to be a very sad and painful experience in the development of South African society in the decades to come.

Swift industrialization after World War II accelerated the trend of urbanization. Facing African competition, white South Africans, especially Afrikaners, supported the policy of apartheid pursued by the National Party after 1948 (→ Racism). The result was economic sanctions against South Africa and its international isolation. The rural population fell into increasing poverty, made worse by droughts. In the search for work, people took to living in shack dwellings outside the cities. Unemployment was rife, and even where work was available, it meant uprooting from the original homes. In 1986, because of tension and conflict, the government undertook a gradual dismantling of discriminatory laws. But it also sought to quench the opposition by declaring a state of emergency. Finally in 1990 the apartheid policy was overthrown by F. W. de Klerk, and the way was opened up for a new constitution that would give the vote to all citizens. In the ensuing election (April 27, 1994) the African National Congress (ANC) gained 60 percent of the seats in Parliament and thus concluded an 80-year fight for equal treatment of the black population. On May 9, 1994, Nelson Mandela was elected president, thus ending 342 years of white minority rule.

A new constitution was formulated through extended negotiations between all the relevant parties present in South Africa, with eventually some of the best values and principles of a modern nonracial democratic tradition guaranteed in it. It entered into effect in February 1997. Freedom of individual speech and opinion is basic. The rule of law is also essential to the new South African society. South Africa no longer defines itself as a Christian state; all citizens enjoy religious liberty. English and Afrikaans had formerly been the official languages, but these 2 were replaced by 11 official languages. South Africa at that stage stood on the verge of tremendous social as well as political change.

2. Christian Churches

Approximately 80 percent of the population of South Africa are Christians. The percentages are as follows, with double-counting not accounted for here: African → Independent Churches 33.5 percent, Dutch Reformed Church (Nederduitse Gereformeerde Kerk) 13.4 percent, → Roman Catholic Church 11.4 percent, Methodist Church of South Africa (→ Methodist Churches) 8.8 percent, Anglican Church (→ Anglican Communion) 5.7 percent, Apostolic Faith Mission (→ Apostolic Churches) 4.8 percent, → Pentecostal and charismatic churches 3.9 percent, → Lutheran Church 3.8 percent, Presbyterian Church (→ Reformed and Presbyterian Churches) 2.2 percent, United Congregational Church 1.9 percent, Dutch Reformed Church (Nederduitsch Hervormde Kerk) 1.3 percent, → Baptist churches 1.2. percent, Reformed Church (Gereformeerde Kerk) 0.8 percent, and others (Rhema, → Salvation Army, → Mormons, etc.) 6.9 percent. Comparison with earlier statistics shows a rapid growth of Independent Churches, a dip in established churches that have been strongly influenced by European structures and traditions, and growth of Pentecostal and charismatic churches and similar evangelical groups (→ Evangelical Movement).

2.1. The Dutch East Indies Company established itself on the southern tip of Africa in 1652. It did not form a settlement but simply a point at which to take care of its ships (→ Colonialism). Under the aegis of the company a Christian congregation was set up in what is now South Africa. The only church recognized was the Dutch Reformed Church (Nederduitse Gereformeerde Kerk), under the supervision of the Dutch authorities at Amsterdam. Muslims (→ Islam) in other Dutch colonies in Africa and Asia who resisted Dutch colonial rule were deported as slaves to the Cape Colony (→ Slavery). Christians in turn gave the slaves Christian instruction (→ Mission). The Synod of Dordt (1618/19; → Councils of the Church 8) had determined that slaves should be freed, but in practice little was done to implement this resolution. As a result of the Napoleonic Wars, Britain took over the Cape Colony, and in 1804 it established → religious liberty. Anglicans, Presbyterians, and Methodists began work at the Cape, and in 1838 work was also initiated by a Roman Catholic bishop.

As a result of the forming of missionary societies arising from revivalism in Europe and America (→ Revivals; Theology of Revival), several mission groups came to South Africa, including the → Moravians in 1737 and 1792, the London Missionary Society in 1799 (→ British Missions), the Wesleyan Methodist Missionary Society in 1816, the Scottish Missionary Society in 1824, the Rhenish Mission in 1842 (→ German Missions), the Norwegian Lutheran Mission (→ Scandinavian Missions) and the Hermannsburg Mission in 1854, the Swedish Church Mission in 1876, and the American Lutheran Mission in 1928 (→ North American missions).

The discovery of diamonds and gold brought many immigrants from Europe and North America and drew African laborers from their native villages. The various missions moved their locations to the new cities, where Pentecostal and evangelical societies found a favorable setting for their work.

2.2. Along with → evangelism, the missions and churches have also engaged in education. The Lutherans and Dutch Reformed have aimed at broad cultural work on a popular level, but churches in the British tradition have shown more interest in higher education. They founded seminaries and universities such as we find in Western countries. Roman Catholics tried to do both. The educational work done by Anglicans, Congregationalists, and Roman Catholics helped to develop African leaders, who in time challenged the government of Europeans in both state and church. Even among less educated people a movement of protest and resistance also took hold that objected to the leadership of European missionaries in the churches and led to the establishing of many African Independent Churches, which had no European or American roots (→ African Theology; European Theology [Modern Period]). The newly developing African churches were seeking a worship style that would conform to African thinking and correspond to African needs. Special importance was attached to healing by prayer. In the 20th century → contextual theology of this type became the most powerful movement among Africans.

The theological training of pastors took place for the most part in church seminaries. Later, in line with a tradition in British missions, a common Federal Theological Seminary was set up at Alice and also Pietermaritzburg, which later closed down. The

Lutherans had their own Lutheran Theological College at Umphumulo in Natal but have since moved to the University of Kwazulu/Natal. Churches can now also make use of the theological faculties at the various universities for residential study, and extracurricular courses exist at the University of South Africa. Lutheran and Reformed missions have feared that the flight to the cities and adjustment to a civilization that levels down distinctions between various traditions might be unsettling for Africans. But this concern did not coincide with the political interests of the Boers. The missionary reports of the Dutch Reformed Church in 1936 established separation by races and languages, and politicians soon found a way to exploit this racial distinction.

3. Church and State

In 1948 racial separation and discrimination were established by law, and what had long been the practice of European settlers now became an all-embracing system. The violation of basic human → rights and attempts to justify apartheid on biblical grounds led to controversies, not only between church and state, but also between churches and even within individual churches. Tensions arose, for example, within and among the Dutch Reformed churches that supported the policies of the government and found biblical arguments in their favor. Among those who suffered under apartheid political movements and labor unions began to emerge. These aimed to bring about change, first by negotiation, then by demonstrations and campaigns of civil disobedience, and finally by armed resistance. Christians took part in these actions.

The Sharpeville Massacre of March 1960, in which South African police opened fire on an unarmed crowd of black protesters, killing 69 persons, compelled some of the churches to resolutely and radically oppose apartheid. But other churches rejected their stand. At the Cottesloe Consultation in December 1960, the World Council of Churches (WCC) tried to resolve the tensions among its South African members. Most of the delegates were in favor of reconciliation, but the effort failed because of the resistance of white Reformed synods. The Dutch Reformed member churches withdrew from the WCC after Cottesloe. Measures against apartheid began to be taken only after the setting up of the South African Council of Churches (SACC; → National Councils of Churches) in 1968 to replace the Christian Council, founded in 1936. An uproar was caused in 1968 when the council and the Christian Institute issued *A Message to the People of South Africa,* which condemned apartheid as a worship of idols. In 1974 the council raised the question of the legitimacy of the South African government, but it was ten years before the matter was taken up again. Through a parliamentary commission of inquiry (the Eloff Commission), the government tried to prove that the SACC was provoking revolt. The aim was to discredit the SACC and to hamper its activity, but this attempt failed. The insight gained ground in the SACC that all Christians had the duty of opposing apartheid.

In the struggle for justice, → reconciliation, and human rights, the SACC and the South African Catholic Bishops' Conference worked closely together. Yet the path from liberal opposition to an illegitimate regime to measures of civil disobedience against it would hardly have been thinkable without the support of independent Christian societies of witness and service, the denominational world federations, and the WCC. Under the leadership of C. F. Beyers Naudé (1915-2004), the Christian Institute questioned the validity of apartheid in the Reformed churches, described it as intrinsically evil, called for resistance to it, and cited the experiences of the Confessing Church in Nazi Germany and the insights of black theology. A ban was placed on the institute in 1977.

The movement of black theology tied in closely with the black consciousness movement that arose after 1969. The starting point was the divine likeness, and on this basis a call went out for resistance to a system of political injustice. Under the influence of the Institute for Contextual Theology, a theology expressly directed to the South African situation developed. This theology made an impact with the help of the Kairos Document of 1985/86, which aroused widespread interest in the ecumenical world. Distinguishing theologies of the state, church, and prophecy, it attacked the feeble understanding of reconciliation in the traditional churches, which would not allow Christians to protest against injustice. The movement Concerned Evangelicals put out a similar document. At regional and local levels smaller organizations took part in helping Christians to see that they were responsible for all South Africans receiving equal treatment and that they must make a stand against injustice.

Opposition to apartheid united Christians and adherents of other religions. The South African branch of the World Conference on Religion and Peace made important contributions to questions of peace and justice in South Africa and put forward proposals to protect religious liberty in the new South Africa and to secularize the state in a way that would still leave it open to religious influence.

The Lutherans and Dutch Reformed were still separating their congregations by race. In the face of this separation and of the churches' toleration of and support for apartheid, the → Lutheran World Federation and the → World Alliance of Reformed Churches made the duty of opposing racial discrimination a → *status confessionis* and suspended the membership of white member churches. The Lutheran Federation readmitted the white member churches in 1992, but they remained under the exclusion of the Reformed Alliance. The Reformed Church (Gereformeerde Kerk) would not legitimize apartheid in a 1986 statement, but it also would not say whether it objected to apartheid as such or only to its unjust application.

In the South African crisis the witness of the SACC, of the various churches, and of individual Christians would hardly have been possible without the accompanying help of the WCC. The WCC called upon Christians all over the world to do their duty by opposing racism, by initiating programs to fight it, and by supporting an economic and trade boycott of South Africa. When in 1990 the dismantling of apartheid and an opening up of the democratic process began (→ Democracy), the churches at once called for mediation in political conflicts. At a very representative and inclusive conference of church leaders at Rustenburg in November 1990, also including the Dutch Reformed churches, they issued a common declaration of guilt and a summons both to remedy past injustices and to make a new beginning in human relationships. It was not clear, however, how far the churches were bound by this declaration.

As far as other developments in the churches are concerned, the following points are of great importance: the introduction of African experiences and perceptions into church life, new beginnings in Bible interpretation, pastoral care that links the public responsibility of the churches to concern for individual needs and problems, the church's position in a secular state, participation of all church members in decision making in the churches, concern to end the rapidly rising number of shack dwellings, and the contribution the churches can make to economic justice.

In general, the transition to the new South Africa was very peaceful. The role of political leaders like Nelson Mandela (pres. 1994-99) and Thabo Mbeki (pres. 1999-) in reconciling many differences in South African society has been quite positive. The role of the largely successful Truth and Reconciliation Commission (TRC), under the leadership of Archbishop Desmond Tutu (b. 1931), also cannot be underestimated. While South Africa has largely managed to work through its political and cultural revolution peacefully, the economic transformation and issues like crime and AIDS remain high on the agenda. In this process of transition, the various religions and the Christian churches still have a substantial role to play.

4. Non-Christian Religions

Many other religions exist in South Africa. Some 5 million Africans belong to → tribal religions. The Bushmen (Khoisan) of the Cape and the Bantus that came down from the north held to an unwritten monotheistic religion (→ Monotheism). They worship a Creator God either with or without ancestor worship. Transition to Christianity is not too difficult in these cases. Medicine men (→ Shamanism) have a ministry to both soul and body. They have a part in the tribal hierarchy but are not organized, even though their religion has undergone revitalization. Many Africans belong to a tribal religion and also consider themselves Christians.

→ Hinduism arrived with Indian settlers who worked in the sugar industry in Natal. The first Hindu temple was built in Durban in 1869. Most Hindus are of the Vedanta tradition. We find groups like Hindu Mahasabba, Divine Life Society, as well as Krishna Consciousness International and Ramakrishna Mission.

In the 17th century the Dutch brought in Islamic deportees from Indonesia, and Sheikh Yusuf set up their first organization in 1694. When slavery was abolished in 1838, about two-thirds of the mixed population at the Cape were Muslims. The Sunnites are the most common (→ Sunna). They play an important part in economic and political life and are well organized. The Call of Islam, the Muslim Youth Movement, and Qibla are active religious groups.

Most of the Jews now in South Africa are Orthodox (→ Judaism). They opened their first → synagogue in Cape Town in 1841. They are all organized in the Union of Orthodox Synagogues. About 20 percent belong to Reformed synagogues, and their synagogues all belong to the South African Union for Progressive Judaism.

We might also mention → Buddhism and → Confucianism, but these are → minorities without regional or national structures. They have little impact on social or political life.

In the final analysis, the current situation in South Africa is relatively stable. Factors like a large religious population, the rule of law, a highly respected constitution, and a parliamentary democracy give substantial hope for the future.

Bibliography: L. ALBERTS and F. CHIKANE, eds., *The Road to Rustenburg: The Church Looking Forward to a New South Africa* (Cape Town, 1991) • COTTESLOE CONSULTATION, *The Report of the Consultation among South African Member Churches of the World Council of Churches: 7-14 December 1960 at Cottesloe* (Johannesburg, 1961) • D. CRAFFORD and G. GOUS, eds., *Een liggaam–baie lede. Die kerk se ekumeniese roeping wêreldwyd en in Suid-Afrika* (Pretoria, 1993) • J. W. DE GRUCHY and S. DE GRUCHY, *The Church Struggle in South Africa* (25th anniv. ed.; Minneapolis, 2005) • J. DU PLESSIS, *A History of Christian Missions in South Africa* (London, 1911; repr., Cape Town, 1965) • R. ELPHICK and R. DAVENPORT, *Christianity in South Africa: A Political, Social, and Cultural History* (Cape Town, 1997) • J. W. HOFMEYR and G. J. PILLAY, eds., *A History of Christianity in South Africa* (Pretoria, 1994) • *The Kairos Document: Challenge to the Church* (2d ed.; Johannesburg, 1986) • A. PRIOR, ed., *Catholics in Apartheid Society* (Cape Town, 1982) • M. PROZESKY, ed., *Christianity in South Africa* (Cape Town, 1990) • E. STRASSBERGER, *Ecumenism in South Africa, 1936-1960, with Special Reference to the Mission of the Church* (Johannesburg, 1974) • D. G. THOMAS, *Councils in the Ecumenical Movement of South Africa, 1904-1975* (Johannesburg, 1979) • C. VILLA-VICENCIO, *Trapped in Apartheid: A Socio-theological History of the English-Speaking Churches* (Maryknoll, N.Y., 1988).

WOLFRAM KISTNER, HANS-JÜRGEN BECKEN, and J. W. HOFMEYR

South Korea

	1960	1980	2000
Population (1,000s):	25,003	38,124	46,883
Annual growth rate (%):	2.64	1.36	0.72

Area: 99,274 sq. km. (38,330 sq. mi.)

A.D. 2000

Population density: 472/sq. km. (1,223/sq. mi.)
Births / deaths: 1.39 / 0.67 per 100 population
Fertility rate: 1.65 per woman
Infant mortality rate: 8 per 1,000 live births
Life expectancy: 73.5 years (m: 70.0, f: 77.0)
Religious affiliation (%): Christians 40.9 (Protestants 19.8, indigenous 17.3, Roman Catholics 7.9, marginal 1.9, other Christians 1.1), tribal religionists 16.2, new religionists 15.3, Buddhists 14.9, Confucianists 10.7, nonreligious 1.6, other 0.4.

1. General Situation
2. Religion and State
3. Development of Christianity
4. Characteristics of South Korean Christianity

1. General Situation

According to legend, Korea was founded by Dangun (Tangun) in 2333 B.C. as Gojoseon (Chosŏn). This was followed in the first century B.C. by the establishment of the three kingdoms of Goguryeo (Koguryŏ), Baekje (Paekche), and Silla, each of which had sophisticated systems of state organization and military force. The battle for supremacy between the three kingdoms in the peninsula intensified, and eventually Silla, with the aid of T'ang China, unified them in A.D. 668. Unified Silla was at the peak of its power and prosperity during the eighth century. It was succeeded by the Goryeo (Koryŏ) Dynasty (918-1392), which introduced the Confucian state model and Buddhist social conduct. It later suffered from Mongol invasion in the 12th century and internal conflict between military and civilian officers. It was followed by the Joseon (Yi) Dynasty (1392-1910), which established the *yangban* (noble) class as rulers of the kingdom. Under them, the land enjoyed peace and stability, especially during the region of King Sejong (1418-50), who invented the Korean alphabet — Hangeol (Han'gŭl) — among many other contributions.

In the latter part of the 19th century, the dynasty was under great threat from the imperial powers of Japan, Russia, and the Western nations. Despite people's resistance movements such as Donghak (Tonghak), Korea was eventually annexed by Japan for 36 years (1910-45). After liberation, Korea was divided in two by the Soviet and American forces. In 1950 the Korean War broke out, which resulted in the deaths of over 2.5 million people. In addition, the war led to the separation of over 10 million family members between the South and the North.

The land remains divided as North Korea, a Communist state, and South Korea; tension and occasional conflict continue, although peace talks are taking place. Since the war South Korea has gone through a series of military-backed governments but since 1988 has had a democratically elected government (→ Democracy). South Korea has become the world's 11th largest economy, with strengths in information technology, manufacturing, and construction.

2. Religion and State

In its history Korea has known a succession of → religions, which have often been closely associated with rulers or the dominant class as state religions. Accordingly, the religions that are out of favor have suffered unfavorable treatment and even persecution by the state. Contemporary South Korea guarantees freedom of religion (→ Religious Liberty); the state does not favor any particular religion.

The dominant belief system in ancient Korea was shamanistic; shamans were intermediaries who contacted the ancestors, who, with the spirits and demons, were regarded as present in every object in the world, seen and unseen. With the introduction of Buddhism and Confucianism, → shamanism faded away from the public domain, but the beliefs were assimilated into the organized religions and became deeply rooted in the religiosity of Koreans.

→ Buddhism was introduced in A.D. 327. It soon became the state religion of the three kingdoms and was regarded as giving spiritual endorsement to the authorities. During the Goryeo Dynasty in particular, Buddhism received strong support from the monarchy and the aristocrats and produced rich art, literature, and architecture. Though Buddhism suffered at the hands of the policies of the Confucian leaders of Joseon and was forced to the periphery of the political and urban life of the people, it has remained the dominant religion for Koreans. In more recent years, Buddhism has been experiencing a revival among the younger generation.

Although → Confucianism was introduced to Korea as early as the Three Kingdoms period, it became the official ideology only in the Joseon Dynasty, which developed a Confucian system of education, ceremony, and civil administration. Toward the end of the dynasty there was criticism of the close integration of government officials and Confucian scholars, which was contributing to corruption, and of the internal rivalry between different schools, which hampered the smooth operation of government. Confucianism, with its philosophical and cultural vigor, has recently been reintroduced into the modern and diverse society of South Korea.

There is also an indigenous religion, Cheondogyo (Ch'ŏndogyo), which was related to the Donghak movement and which upholds one supreme God, Haneullim. This religion has given expression to resistance to foreign influence in Korean society.

3. Development of Christianity

Christianity arrived in Korea in an unusual way. In the 18th century a Korean scholar by the name of Seng-Hoon Lee went to China to study, where he met a Jesuit missionary. Lee eventually became a Christian and was baptized in Peking in 1784. He returned to Korea and started to share his Christian faith, which led to many conversions. In 1789, when Jesuit missionaries first came to Korea, they discovered that there were already about 4,000 Catholic Christians on the Korean Peninsula. The → Roman

Catholic Church grew rapidly, but between 1801 and 1867 it faced great → persecution because of the refusal of Christians to practice → ancestor veneration or worship, which was regarded as essential for national stability, and because of accusations that the Christians were in contact with European imperial powers. The persecution of 1866 was especially severe; about 8,000 Christians were → martyred, and almost the same number later starved to death when they fled to the mountains. The country remained closed to the outside world until the Japanese imposed a trade agreement in 1876.

While the Korean Peninsula was still closed, several Protestant → missionaries who were working in China became interested in Korea. In 1832 K. A. Gützlaff briefly visited Korea, as did Robert Thomas in 1865 and 1866 (suffering martyrdom on his latter visit). The reports of their encounters drew the attention of other missionaries, who ventured to this hidden kingdom. John Ross and John MacIntyre, through the help of some Korean converts, completed the translation of the first Korean NT, which was published in China in 1887. The first ordained Protestant missionaries came to Korea in 1885 from North America and were soon followed by other missionaries. As they started work in many different parts of Korea, together with Korean evangelists, the church began to grow through a series of revivals, the most significant of which was the great revival in Pyeungyang (P'yŏngyang) in 1907 (→ Theology of Revival 7.3).

Persecution of Christians, however, continued. During the latter part of the colonial period, the Japanese authorities imposed worship at the → Shinto shrines upon the Korean Christians, persecuted Christians who refused, and burned down many churches. After independence in 1945, the Korean church had to face yet another persecution, this time by the Communists. During the Korean War, Christians in Communist-held areas were accused of being pro-American or capitalist, and many were killed by the Communist army and local militias.

After the war the churches in South Korea, both Catholic and Protestant, grew rapidly. Christianity has become a major religion, not only in numbers, but also in its influence on society in terms of education, medical work, and social reform. At the same time, churches have grown numerically through their engagement in → evangelism and church planting. According to the 2005 census, 29.2 percent of the population are Christians (Protestants, 18.3 percent; Roman Catholics, 10.9 percent). The majority of Protestants are Presbyterians, but there is also a strong presence of Methodist, Baptist, and Holiness churches; altogether there are 230 different denominations and groups.

The National Christian Council was formed in 1924; in 1946 it changed its name to the Korea → National Council of Churches (KNCC). It represents the liberal section of Protestant Christianity in South Korea. In 1989 the conservative Christian Council of Korea (CCK) was founded, consisting of 20 South Korean Protestant denominations. Since then the KNCC and CCK have often expressed sharply differing views, especially on the issue of Korean reunification.

In recent years Protestant churches have been engaged in sending missionaries overseas through over 160 Korean and international mission agencies. There are cooperative associations such as Korean World Missions Association and Mission Korea. In the area of media, the Christian Broadcasting System (1954) and Far East Broadcasting Company (1956) are two major Christian radio and TV stations, and there are increasing numbers of cable TV stations and one mass-circulation daily newspaper, *Kukminilbo* (1988), run by churches. Most churches utilize media technology and Internet Web sites for broadcasting church worship and for interacting with their members (→ Christian Communication).

4. Characteristics of South Korean Christianity

Christianity in South Korea has developed with a strong emphasis on the Scriptures. This emphasis stems from the heavy influence of the Confucian-oriented Korean education system, with its unquestioning approach to authoritative texts. Once Korean Christians accepted Christian sacred texts, they revered them as the supreme authority. Believers have employed the Confucian method of repeated reading and memorization as they studied the Christian Scriptures. There has also been a great eagerness to follow literally what the text teaches. Besides an emphasis on the Bible, South Korean Protestant churches show a charismatic tendency in → worship, which dates from the early revivals.

Korean Christianity has a tendency to stress pietistic living and separation from politics, but we also must note the contribution to society of minjung theology, or Korean liberation theology. Korea in the 1970s experienced a need for a new understanding of Christian faith that would meet the needs of the urban poor, who were victims of highly competitive, capitalist market practices. The minjung movement was sparked when Jun Tae-il died by self-immolation in November 1970 in a protest against the exploitation of fellow factory workers. Christian leaders took up this problem as a major issue and began standing for, and with, the poor and exploited. Minjung theologians, both Catholic and Protestant, captured people's imagination and brought the issue of → poverty and exploitation to public attention (→ Asian Theology 4.2). Minjung theology has made a significant contribution to Korean church and society through its understanding of liberation and justice, which showed the poor and oppressed that they should not be the objects of exploitation and that their protest was legitimate. Minjung theology was a major instrument of the minjung, or civil rights, movement, which challenged both church and society to deal with the problems of socioeconomic and political injustice; it also contributed to the democratization of Korean politics in the late 1980s.

The conflict between the two Koreas is certainly the dominant concern for Koreans and has affected the lives of Koreans ever since the division of Korea. Though the desire for reunification has been the most important agenda item for political leaders, opinions about how to achieve this goal have differed widely, as the two Koreas have been at the forefront of the cold war ideological conflict. Until the early 1980s, most churches in South Korea either took a conservative, anti-Communist position or maintained a policy of separation from politics. The most significant contribution of the churches to reconciliation occurred in 1988, when the KNCC issued the "Declaration of the Churches of Korea on National Reunification and Peace," a document that made a significant impact both within the church and on the whole nation. The declaration made practical suggestions to both governments, including the withdrawal of the U.S. army and the dismantling of the U.N. head office in South Korea. The declaration also proclaimed the year 1995 as a "jubilee year for peace and reunification," when Koreans could celebrate the 50th anniversary of the liberation from Japan. More recently, the churches have been involved in various ecumenical humanitarian projects such as the South-North Sharing Campaign, founded in 1993.

Although the churches in Korea endured severe persecutions during the 19th century, during the Japanese occupation, and throughout the Korean War, they not merely survived but have grown in significant numbers. The challenge to the church in South Korea remains not only to meet the needs of its own members but also to engage more deeply in meeting the needs of the wider public, thus genuinely becoming "salt and light" in the midst of the dynamic and yet diverse contemporary societies of North and South Korea.

Bibliography: G. Baek, *The History of Protestant Mission in Korea, 1832-1910* (1927; repr., Seoul, 1987) • R. E. Buswell Jr., ed., *Religions of Korea in Practice* (Princeton, 2007) • J. H. Grayson, *Korea: A Religious History* (rev. ed.; London, 2002) • C.-S. Yu, ed., *The Founding of Catholic Tradition in Korea* (Mississauga, Ont., 1996); idem, ed., *Korea and Christianity* (Fremont, Calif., 2004).

Sebastian Kim

Soviet Union

1. Background
2. The Bolshevik, or Communist, Revolution
3. The Soviet State
4. The Stalin Era
5. The Soviet Union after Stalin

1. Background

The 74-year Soviet period was a significant interlude in the vast sweep of Russian history. Its origins lay in the deepening unrest during the reign of the last czar, Nicholas II (1894-1917), and the crisis of World War I. A variety of political movements existed, some of which operated underground and were supported by exiles. They ranged from moderate conservatives and liberals to radical agrarian socialists who wanted to remake Russia along the lines of the rural peasant land communes and Western-style Marxists who stressed industrialization and building → socialism on the basis of the working class. In 1905 violent → revolution shook the imperial regime, and through the October Manifesto the czar granted a limited constitution establishing a popularly elected legislature (Duma). Other reforms followed, including religious toleration for adherents to non-Orthodox faiths, easing of residence requirements for Jews, and assistance to peasants who wished to leave their village communes and become freehold farmers.

The Marxist Social Democrats, meeting in exile in Brussels in 1903, divided over the issue of party organization. The leader of the Bolshevik (Russ. *bol'she*, "bigger, more"; i.e., majority) faction, Vladimir Ilyich Lenin (1870-1924), held that, in contrast to traditional Marxist dogma (→ Marxism), the workers (proletariat) could come to power in Russia when they had a strong, centralized party organization. Then in backward Russia the proletariat, allied with the oppressed peasantry, would industrialize the country and usher in socialism. During his years in exile Lenin developed his theories and kept the revolutionary vision alive, even as the Russian economy prospered and industrial growth was rapid. The promised → religious liberty was somewhat illusory, but evangelicals and Baptists grew in numbers.

World War I sealed the fate of the czarist regime. Inept leadership and inadequate armaments resulted in enormous losses on the fronts. Food shortages at home and scandals within the royal family eroded public confidence, and the radical political groups demanded change. The regime finally collapsed in the face of strikes and mass demonstrations, and Nicholas II abdicated on March 15, 1917. A Duma-appointed "Provisional Government" dominated by liberals and moderate socialists took charge of the administration, granted civil liberties, and set elections for a constitutional assembly.

2. The Bolshevik, or Communist, Revolution

Because the Provisional Government unwisely kept Russia in the war, the socialist groups went into opposition. Their strength lay in the *soviets,* popularly elected councils of workers and soldiers that sprang up around the country and demanded immediate peace, food for the starving populace, and land redistribution for the peasants. Lenin returned to Russia and immediately demanded that all power be given to the soviets. Turmoil racked the republic as the war effort floundered and both right- and left-wing groups attempted coups. Then, on November 6-7, 1917, on the eve of a national meeting of delegates from the soviets, Lenin and his Bolsheviks overthrew the Provisional Government in the name of the soviets, set up a new "Council of People's Commissars" with Lenin as chair for the Russian Soviet Federated Socialist Republic (RSFSR), and embarked on remaking the country. Its actions included negotiations to end the war, repudiation of the czarist debt, dispossession of property owners, elimination of all other political parties, secularization of education, complete separation of → church and state, and the requisitioning of foodstuffs from the peasants. The RSFSR constitution, introduced in July 1918, defined the state as "a dictatorship of the urban and rural proletariat and the poorest peasantry" (art. 2.9) and as a "republic of soviets of workers', soldiers', and peasants' deputies" that would effect a "transition" to socialist society (1.1, 2.9).

Elections took place for a constituent assembly, but pro-Bolshevik troops broke up the meeting when it convened in January 1918. Most Europeans assumed that the government of the ragtag, inexperienced Bolsheviks would soon collapse, but Lenin and his associates quickly established a one-party dictatorship and brutally suppressed all dissent

through a new secret police, the Cheka. Lenin insisted that the humiliating peace settlement that Russia concluded with the Central Powers in March was a tactical move to secure the Bolshevik regime and prepare the way for world revolution. Meanwhile, he moved the capital from the exposed St. Petersburg to Moscow in the Russian heartland and, harking back to Karl → Marx (1818-83) in 1848, adopted the name "Communist" for the ruling party, thus linking revolution and dictatorship in the service of extreme socialism. The party rapidly evolved into the centralized, bureaucratic institution that would dominate all the institutions of Soviet life for the next seven decades.

Then followed a brutal civil war, as the "Whites" endeavored to regain control of Russia. They were assisted for a time by Western powers who desired the elimination of Communist rule, because in early 1919 Lenin had created the Comintern (i.e., *Com*munist *Inter*national, or Third International) to promote Bolshevism and overthrow → capitalism everywhere. To meet the challenge, the Soviet government charged Leon Trotsky (1879-1940), a hardline revolutionary, Lenin's right-hand man and source of some of his ideas, with creating a "Workers' and Peasants' Red Army." Organized along lines of strict military discipline, commanded by former czarist officers (supervised by loyal Communists as "military commissars"), and using conscripted soldiers, it became an effective fighting force. The Reds won after three years of bitter struggle because they had the advantages of a unified command, control over the center of Russia (thus having internal lines of communication), an ethnically homogeneous population that responded to a nationalist appeal, access to large supplies of war matériel left over from the old regime, and a common revolutionary vision, whereas the Whites were deeply divided politically and were fighting on the periphery. The civil war, intervention, and the alignment of Western Communist parties with Moscow left a bitter legacy of hostility between Soviet Russia and the Western "capitalist" nations. It was a time of great suffering, and millions perished in the fighting and accompanying famines.

3. The Soviet State

As the period of "War Communism" ended in 1921, Lenin faced the daunting task of building socialism in the context of a national economy that had almost totally collapsed. He drew up the New Economic Policy (NEP), a bold program that allowed a modest return of capitalism. Food seizures ceased, and peasants (now disparagingly labeled *kulaks*) became small businesspeople. Smaller firms were returned to private hands, while the state retained control of the largest enterprises. To resolve the issue of the restive ethnic groups or nationalities of the old czarist empire, the Union of Soviet Socialist Republics was formed on December 29, 1922. It included Ukraine, White Russia (Byelorussia or Belarus), and eight other Caucasian and central Asian "Soviet Socialist Republics," while the RSFSR now would have its own boundaries within this larger state.

→ Persecution of the Russian Orthodox Church continued unabated. Religious holidays were abolished, church properties and art objects expropriated, clerics subjected to show trials, and → atheism officially propagated through the League of the Godless and antireligious magazines. The pro-regime "Living Church" was formed in 1922 to undermine the patriarchal church, but it faded from the scene when it was no longer useful. Jewish religious practices were sharply curtailed. Only small groups like the → Baptists and the → Mennonites were allowed a measure of freedom, the assumption being that, since they had been oppressed by czarism and the Orthodox establishment, they would be sympathetic to the regime.

4. The Stalin Era

To help keep discipline in the Communist Party, the post of general secretary was created in 1922. Its occupant was Joseph V. Stalin (1879-1953), an ambitious Georgian, who used his position to outmaneuver Trotsky as successor to Lenin (who died in January 1924). By 1928 Stalin was master of the Soviet state. He rejected Leninist internationalism in favor of "socialism in one country," and the Comintern compelled Communist parties worldwide to align their policies with that of the Soviet Union. He replaced the NEP with a series of five-year plans that fostered advance in heavy industry, using capital squeezed out of the agricultural sector by the collectivization of farms. When the kulaks resisted, millions were exiled or killed, and food production dropped dramatically. The old empire was restored through a process of Russification in the Soviet republics. The paranoid Stalin eliminated potential opposition through Moscow show trials that condemned former associates of Lenin, military leaders, and intellectuals, while on the slightest of pretexts the secret police dispatched millions more to the labor camps of the gulag, where the death rates approached 90 percent. Stalin's brutality showed him to be the modern-day heir of the 16th-century Ivan the Terrible.

The Religious Associations Law of 1929 restricted churches to worship alone and banned their educational, missionary, and philanthropic activities. Clergy and simple believers alike were liquidated or languished in the prison camps. The Soviet constitution of 1936 mandated separation of church and state while permitting both freedom of worship and antireligious propaganda. By 1939 the institutional structures of the churches were in shambles. Only → Islam in the distant republics was more or less left alone.

When Germany invaded the Soviet Union in June 1941, the country was woefully unprepared. Stalin had tried to maintain peaceful relations with Hitler, while the purges had decapitated the leadership of the Red Army. The Soviet dictator had to summon all available forces, including the churches, for the "Great Patriotic War." Church leaders immediately pledged their unconditional support, while atheistic propaganda and active persecution of believers ceased. In 1943 the Orthodox Church was allowed to call a synod, elect a patriarch, publish a church paper, and reopen schools, churches, and monasteries. In 1944 the regime permitted the two Baptist bodies to unite as the Evangelical Christians–Baptists and to resume their work. After 1945, however, pressure on the churches returned and intensified, especially as the cold war set in. It was exacerbated by the tendency of the churches in the West to promote anticommunism. For their part, the Orthodox and other churches in the USSR had to follow the Soviet line in all their pronouncements.

World War II enabled the nationalistic Stalin to regain all the lost territories of the czarist era, and they were incorporated into the USSR as republics (Estonia, Latvia, Lithuania, and Moldova [Moldavia]). At the same time, fearful of Western opposition to Soviet Communism, he formed a satellite empire of friendly socialist states kept in line by the Red Army. The Western "containment" policy reinforced his belief that capitalist powers had encircled the Soviet Union with hostile intent and that it could survive only through its own resources and persistence. Marxist-Leninist ideology was used to legitimize the Soviet → bureaucracy and define the foreign threat, which justified the sacrifices of the system.

5. The Soviet Union after Stalin

Bitter infighting among Stalin's potential successors followed his death in 1953, but an era of reform followed the emergence of Nikita Khrushchev (1894-1971) in 1955. To justify his program he launched a process of de-Stalinization that blamed the evils of Soviet society on Stalin's tyranny. Most of the labor camps were closed, housing conditions improved, food supplies increased, censorship on writers was eased, and impressive achievements in space travel occurred. The relaxation led to unrest at home and in the satellite states, which resulted in crackdowns. With the Soviet Union closing the gap with the West in nuclear → weapons, Khrushchev continued cold-war posturing, especially over Berlin, U.S. spy plane surveillance, and Cuba. After the Cuban missile crisis (1962), which brought the superpowers closer to nuclear conflict than at any time during the cold war, a modest easing of tensions took place. As for the churches, the Russian Orthodox joined the → World Council of Churches; the Evangelical Christians–Baptists attended the first → Baptist World Alliance meeting since the 1920s, where one of their number was elected a vice-president; and Bibles were printed for the first time in Soviet history. In the early 1960s, however, Khrushchev tightened the screws on religious bodies, and the Council on Religious Affairs kept a close eye on the churches.

Khrushchev was forced into retirement in 1964, and his successor, Leonid Brezhnev (1906-82), endeavored to hold the Soviet Union and its slowly disintegrating bloc together through the military Warsaw Pact and the Council for Mutual Economic Assistance (COMECON), which mirrored NATO and the European Common Market. In the cultural realm artists and writers were censored, pressure on the churches increased, and → anti-Semitism grew in intensity. The human → rights movement and a religious renaissance, reflected in the underground literature (samizdat) that circulated in the country and was smuggled out to the West, grew ever more significant. Détente was in the air as arms agreements relaxed some cold war tensions and the Soviets participated in the Helsinki accords of 1975, but economic growth was at a standstill, and Brezhnev's aged successors, Yuri Andropov (1914-84) and Konstantin Chernenko (1911-85), were unable to halt the decline.

The youthful Mikhail Gorbachev (b. 1931), who was elected general secretary in March 1985, brought the vision of reform through openness (glasnost'), restructuring (perestroika), and limited democratization, and he halted the uncompromising conflict against all forms of religion. The celebration of the millennium of Christianity in Russia in 1988 accelerated the thaw in religious tolerance, and the Orthodox and other churches grew exponentially as new Soviet religious laws, as well as new laws in the Russian and Ukrainian republics, laid a fresh foundation for religious societies and brought improved conditions. He also negotiated an end to the cold war and agreed to the dismantlement of the satellite empire. As various member states of the Soviet Union declared their independence, it was transformed into the → Commonwealth of Independent States. On December 25, 1991, Gorbachev resigned as president of the USSR, and the red hammer-and-sickle flag was lowered from the Kremlin for the last time. The Soviet period had come to an end.

→ Russia; Russian Orthodox Church

Bibliography: H. J. Coleman, *Russian Baptists and Spiritual Revolution, 1905-1929* (Bloomington, Ind., 2005) • D. J. Dunn, *The Catholic Church and Russia: Popes, Patriarchs, Tsars, and Commissars* (London, 2004) • M. K. Dziewanowski, *Russia in the Twentieth Century* (6th ed.; Upper Saddle River, N.J., 2003) • S. Fitzpatrick, *The Cultural Front: Power and Culture in Revolutionary Russia* (Ithaca, N.Y., 1992) • W. C. Fletcher, *A Study in Survival: The Church in Russia, 1927-1943* (New York, 1965) • B. Fowkes, *The Disintegration of the Soviet Union: A Study in the Rise and Triumph of Nationalism* (New York, 1996) • I. Halfin, *From Darkness to Light: Class Consciousness and Salvation in Revolutionary Russia* (Pittsburgh, 2000) • P. Kenez, *A History of the Soviet Union from the Beginning to the End* (2d ed.; New York, 2006) • D. R. Marples, *The Collapse of the Soviet Union, 1985-1991* (Harlow, Eng., 2004) • D. Peris, *Storming the Heavens: The Soviet League of the Militant Godless* (Ithaca, N.Y., 1998) • R. Pipes, *Russia under the Bolshevik Regime* (New York, 1994) • D. Priestland, *Stalinism and the Politics of Mobilization* (New York, 2007) • R. Sakwa, *The Rise and Fall of the Soviet Union: 1927-1991* (London, 2001) • W. Sawatsky, *Soviet Evangelicals since World War II* (Scottdale, Pa., 2007) • R. Service, *A History of Twentieth-Century Russia* (Cambridge, Mass., 1997) • L. H. Siegelbaum, *Soviet State and Society between Revolutions, 1918-1929* (New York, 2004) • P. D. Steeves, *Keeping the Faith: Religion and Ideology in the Soviet Union* (New York, 1989) • J. M. Thompson, *Russia and the Soviet Union* (5th ed.; Boulder, Colo., 2004).

Richard V. Pierard

Spain

1. The Roman Catholic Church and Other Churches
   1.1. Historical Development
   1.2. Freedom of Worship
   1.3. Roman Catholics
       1.3.1. Administrative and Educational Units and Church Personnel
       1.3.2. Church Life

	1960	*1980*	*2000*

Population (1,000s): 30,455 37,542 39,801
Annual growth rate (%): 1.02 0.49 −0.03
Area: 504,783 sq. km. (194,898 sq. mi.)

A.D. 2000

Population density: 79/sq. km. (204/sq. mi.)
Births / deaths: 0.94 / 1.00 per 100 population
Fertility rate: 1.22 per woman
Infant mortality rate: 7 per 1,000 live births
Life expectancy: 78.6 years (m: 75.3, f: 82.0)
Religious affiliation (%): Christians 93.8 (Roman Catholics 97.2, other Christians 1.8), nonreligious 4.4, atheists 1.2, other 0.6.

  1.4. Protestants
    1.4.1. Anglicans
    1.4.2. Reformed
    1.4.3. Baptists
    1.4.4. Others
  1.5. Orthodox
2. Ecumenical Relations
3. Church and State
  3.1. Roman Catholics
  3.2. Protestants
4. Non-Christian Religions
  4.1. Judaism
  4.2. Islam
  4.3. Other Groups

1. The Roman Catholic Church and Other Churches

Spain is an example of a Roman Catholic country. For some Spaniards Roman Catholicism is the country's vital nerve. For others it is the ancient faith that disrupted → toleration between Christians, Moors, and Jews. (Toleration, though, has been an achievement only of → modernity.) Spain was a Christian → nation before the Islamic invasion in the eighth century, which could not Islamicize it but long delayed the development of a Spanish-Gothic population. The Reconquista (lasting from the early 8th cent. to 1492) brought into being a Christian and European Spain.

1.1. Historical Development

The historical origins of Christianity in Spain are obscure. Did → Paul reach Tarragona, as he planned (Rom. 15:24, 28; *1 Clem.* 5.7)? By the third century, congregations were meeting under the leadership of → bishops, and presbyters and were fighting apostasy and → heresy (Cyprian *Ep.* 67) and also were dealing with → persecution (e.g., under Decian, in 250/51; → Martyrs, Acts of the). The canons of the Council of Elvira (ca. 306; → Councils of the

Church) are the first church document from Spain. Hosius of Córdoba (ca. 256-357/58) went to live at Alexandria and soon afterward at Nicaea. Toward the end of the fourth century Priscillianism was a threat (→ Asceticism), and in the fifth century Germanic tribes brought → Arianism to Iberia.

Religious peace came with the conversion of Visigoth king Recared (586-601) at the Third Council of Toledo (589). Spanish-Gothic Catholicism was now in control, with a goal of making further progress throughout the peninsula. Without being a → theocracy, the Spanish monarchy found support in it and also protected the church, giving it a certain independence from Rome. One example is the use of the Spanish West Gothic, or Mozarabic, → liturgy, which in 1078 replaced the Roman liturgy and has now been renewed and is reintroduced on occasion. Christianity in Spain was always aware of its apostolicity, finding a sign for it in the grave of the apostle → James (→ Santiago Cult).

During the → Renaissance and in the 16th century, some groups turned aside from the Catholic spirit of Spain. In the 15th century the "Catholic monarchs" Ferdinand (1479-1516) and Isabella (1474-1504) made a decisive contribution to political and religious → unity, though at the cost of persecuting the Jews (→ Anti-Semitism, Anti-Judaism). In the 16th century the spirit of the → Reformation breathed through the enlightened, such as the Erasmians (→ Humanism), the quietists (→ Quietism), and the mystical movement of the *recogidos* (the "withdrawn"; → Mysticism). Not least, it strengthened the Lutheran circles at Seville and Valladolid. The 18th century saw the crisis of the → Enlightenment.

The → Inquisition suppressed and hampered these movements. Historical research today shows, however, that the success of Roman Catholicism in Spain depended not only on the Inquisition but on Spain's sense of history (→ Theology of History) and on the wide-ranging → Catholic reforms of the 15th century (esp. under Cardinal Ximénez de Cisneros). This sense of history extended to America, with the discovery and colonizing of the New World, which Spanish and Portuguese → missionaries evangelized (→ Mission 3.4). "By God's grace" the church influenced the acts of the monarchy in favor of → evangelism and fought against the abuses of the conquest (Hadrian VI in the bull *Omnimoda* [1522] and the School of Salamanca, inaugurated by Francisco de Vitoria). The church engaged in a critical defense of the Indians and inspired Rome as well, notably in the Laws of Burgos of 1512/13 (the first laws written by Europeans to govern the behavior of settlers in the New World) and in Paul III's bull → *Sublimis Deus* (1537).

1.2. *Freedom of Worship*

The Cádiz constitution of 1812 did not allow freedom of worship or religion, although it was the first in Spain to do away with public recognition of the Inquisition. In 1869 the new constitution granted → religious liberty (art. 21). Anglicans (→ Anglican Communion), Methodists (→ Methodism), → Baptists, and other Protestant → denominations sent foreign missionaries from England, Scotland, Ireland, Holland, Switzerland, and North America in support of their work of bringing a so-called second reformation to Spain. The work of → Bible societies and organizations with goals similar to those of the Spanish Evangelization Society also contributed. A central council of the Reformed churches was set up in Gibraltar (Consistorio Central de la Iglesia Reformada Española).

Religious liberty was retained in 1876 with the return of the Bourbons, but the position of Roman Catholicism was strengthened. At the end of the 19th century there were some 10,000 Spanish Protestants. The constitution of 1931 (Second Republic) provided for full → religious liberty, though with an anticlerical, anti-Catholic bias. In 1936 there were 15,000 non–Roman Catholics. Given the relative tolerance of the regime of Generalissimo Franco (1936-75), there were 30,000 non-Catholics by 1955, even though the Leyes Fundamentales (basic laws) of Francoism favored Roman Catholicism until 1967.

1.3. *Roman Catholics*

According to the church's Office of Statistics and Sociology, 88.13 percent of Spaniards declared themselves Catholic in 1990, rising to 90.34 percent in 1996. That same year 1.8 percent declared that they practiced another religious confession, 3.0 percent said they were atheists, and 4.5 percent identified themselves as agnostics.

According to a survey conducted in 2005 by the autonomous state agency Centro de Investigaciones Sociales (CIS), only 79.3 percent of the population declared themselves Catholics. Of this group, 47 percent almost never attended mass, and 52 percent went to church with varying frequency. This relatively high percentage of church attendance is offset by the general disinterest of Spanish young people in the church.

1.3.1. *Administrative and Educational Units and Church Personnel*

1.3.1.1. According to the *Guía de la Iglesia Católica en España 2006,* the → Roman Catholic Church comprised 69 dioceses, 14 ecclesiastical provinces, and a military archbishopric. The primary see is in Toledo. According to the 2002 edition of *Statistics* of the Catholic Church in Spain, in the year 2000 there were 24,648 priests (775 in → Opus Dei), 8,710 religious, 205 permanent deacons (priests and nonpriests), and 58,406 nuns. There were 918 communities of contemplative nuns, and 43 of contemplative monks.

1.3.1.2. *Evangelization and → mission* play a large part among Roman Catholics (→ Evangelism). They include both → proclamation and instruction, with emphasis on education and → health. Spanish missions not only have evangelized America and the Philippines but are presently at work throughout the world. According to the 2006 report of the Pontifical Mission Societies, 17,260 Spaniards work as missionaries in the areas of evangelization, education, and health care, 11,304 of whom serve in the Americas. The Spanish missionary force includes 9,677 religious women, 5,489 religious (priests and nonpriests), 910 secular priests, and 770 laypeople. In all, 92 Spanish bishops oversee Spanish dioceses and prelatures, as well as apostolic administrations outside of Spain. To these must be added the pastoral labor of priests and laypeople in Spanish Catholic communities abroad on five continents.

1.3.1.3. In → *education* four historic Roman Catholic → universities call for notice: the Pontifical University "Comillas" (Madrid), the Pontifical University of Salamanca, the Catholic University of Deusto (Bilbao), and the University of Navarra (Pamplona). The Pontifical University of Salamanca is under the Conferencia Episcopal Española (CEE, Spanish Bishops' Conference). It was founded in 1940 with the reopening of the faculties of theology and canon law from the earlier university, which had been closed in the 19th century (→ Theological Education). Today the university has nine faculties and many schools, as well as other educational centers throughout the country.

The → Jesuits operate the University of Deusto in Bilbao, as well as the university "Comillas"; Opus Dei operates the University of Navarra. More recently, three new Catholic universities have been founded (at Ávila, Murcia, and Valencia), to which we must add two more of Catholic inspiration in Barcelona (Ramon Llull University) and Madrid (San Pablo-CEU University).

The Catholic Church also maintains faculties of theology in Barcelona, Burgos-Vitoria, Granada, Madrid, and Valencia, as well as 138 university schools and centers of higher education sponsored by the university schools. In 2000 there were 125,386 students matriculated in universities and higher centers of the church, 1,681 of whom were studying in faculties of theology and university institutes belonging to the seminaries. The church has 4,820 school centers: 2,265 for early and primary-school education, 2,058 for secondary school, and 497 for postsecondary education. In 1999/2000 there was a total of 1.3 million students. There also are 173 centers for professional, special, and adult education.

1.3.1.4. In the area of *health and social welfare,* the Catholic Church supports 305 family medical centers, 107 hospitals, 128 public clinics and dispensaries, 876 homes for the elderly and those chronically sick or disabled, 937 orphanages and centers for the protection of children, 321 nursery schools and day-care centers, 365 educational and rehab centers, and 2,502 social centers. In the year 2000 about 2 million people, both short-term and longer-term residents, were helped by these church centers. Overall, however, the state increasingly cares for such health and social needs.

1.3.2. *Church Life*

Church life has been in decline since the last decades of the 20th century, but the great riches of popular piety in Spanish Catholicism constitute a permanent source of its own renewal (→ Popular Catholicism). Catholicism has inspired Spanish culture, with literature and religious art in the Renaissance and baroque periods marking Spanish history and creating a mentality or worldview that is difficult to separate from Catholic faith itself. The secular elites who direct and promote the → secularization process of modern Spanish society advocate a nonreligious interpretation of the cultural heritage. For its part, the church attempts to prevent secular politics from appropriating the church's literary creations and historical artistic heritage as mere cultural elements, which tends to neutralize the catechetical and evangelizing reach of Catholicism.

Franco's regime, arising from the Civil War, granted the Catholic Church the status of state church, restoring and protecting its historic rights after the cruel religious persecution suffered from 1934 to the end of the war. Although the political Left tried to justify religious persecution by appealing to an alleged agreement between the church and the bourgeoisie, historical studies are making it clear that the church, even though stripped of its property under the 19th-century secularization of religious orders, was still capable of inspiring a Catholic social movement of deep significance, nourished by the modern social doctrine of the church from the time of Leo XIII (1878-1903). The agrarian Catholic labor unions arose from such

teaching, and they created the first savings and loan banks, which were called Círculos Católicos (Catholic Circles) and Montes de Piedad (Mountains of Piety), which would support the economic needs and social initiatives of the working classes. Social Catholicism continued to inspire the activities of → Catholic Action by means of the so-called apostolate of the working class.

The recent canonizations carried out by John Paul II (1978-2005) of some hundreds of the more than 7,000 priests, religious, and laity killed for their faith during the Second Republic are not a political declaration against the regime but simply a recognition by the church of martyrdom. Their deaths make tangible the reality of religious repression by the Republican regime, which was marked by an → ideology of anticlericalism and by the revolutionary elements of → Marxism and → anarchism. This period was one of deep division in Spanish society.

Since the end of the Civil War, Catholic Action has declined both internally and in society, but strong new spiritual movements, including → base communities, have offset this decline. Here we may mention Cursillos de Cristianidad, a movement started in Majorca in 1944 that trains laypeople; Comunidades Neocatecumenales, a growing ministry of adult faith formation, founded in 1964 by Kiko Argüello; the Catholic → Charismatic Renewal, which started in 1966 at Duquesne University (Pittsburgh, Pa.) and which has a large following in Spanish-speaking America and, to a lesser extent, in Spain; and Comunidades Populares, a movement inspired by Catholic Action that began in the late 1960s in the working-class suburbs in Madrid and that was part of the dialogue between Catholicism and Marxism. The last two efforts have become somewhat weakened in recent years. Opus Dei is still at work, along with several missionary societies.

Vatican II gave rise to a movement of deep reform of the church in Spain. The initial postconciliar period, however, was marked by disputes among various groups, associations, and movements within the church, including base communities, associations of theologians in favor of → liberation theology, the "We Are Church" movement, and others (*Teología y secularización en España a los cuarenta años de la clausura del Conc. Vaticano II* [Theology and secularization in Spain 40 years after the end of Vatican II], CEE, 86th Assembly, March 2006).

After a notable religious decline in the 1970s and 1980s, which even threatened to close down the processions of Semana Santa (Holy Week, esp. in Seville), the brotherhoods have again begun to enroll new members, the majority of whom are young people with a definite zeal for the church. Popular piety can ultimately become the means for a new evangelization of a dechristianized society, leading to Christian education and social commitment to the needy and to the missions; to eucharistic devotion, which had a profound influence on the spirituality and art of the baroque; and to Marian devotion, so characteristic of Hispanic religiosity, with numerous shrines of the Virgin Mary (including Our Lady of Covadonga, of Pilar [i.e., "the pillar"], of Guadalupe, of Montserrat, of Almudena, and of Rocío [i.e., "the dew"]).

After the postwar return to a confessionally Catholic state (or "national Catholicism"), the Roman Catholic Church fully embraced Vatican II in the 1960s, distancing itself from the political regime. Since the restoration of the parliamentary monarchy with the constitution of 1978, the church has been affected by secularization and the ideology of progressivism, which has led to diminishing religious practice. In doctrine and in morals, the church is facing the risk of slowly assimilating to agnostic European culture, which is far removed from observing Christian guidelines for life.

Because of this risk, the evangelizing effort of Catholics, especially under the impulse of John Paul II, has focused since 1980 on pastoral plans elaborated by the CEE for evangelizing society. One emphasis is on calling laypeople to be active in all areas of public life, which goes against the tendency of ideological laicism to privatize the faith. (See *"Testigos del Dios vivo": Sobre la misión e identidad de la Iglesia en nuestra sociedad* ["Witnesses of the living God": On the mission and identity of the church in our society], 1985; *Los católicos en la vida pública* [Catholics in public life], 1986; and a national congress on evangelization, held in Madrid in 1985.)

A second emphasis is on transmission of the faith to the younger generation (*La iniciación cristiana* [Christian initiation], 1998), including a defense of religion classes and of the teaching of Catholic morality in the schools. Since the 1980s, however, Parliament has passed six laws that have increasingly destabilized the educational system. Laws passed by the Spanish Socialist Workers' Party in 1985 and 1990, as well as one in April 2006, have restricted the teaching of religion in the schools. In 1988 the Bishops' Commission of Education and Catechizing prepared a critical report about the law that was passed in 1990, outlining the church's serious reservations with the bill. Neither then nor with the final law, however, was attention given to the

comments of the bishops or of the Federación de Religiosos de la Enseñanza (Federation of Religious in Education).

1.4. *Protestants*
The Iglesia Cristiana Española (ICE, Spanish Christian Church) was formed in 1871. In 1880 a group of Anglican congregations separated from this body, forming the Iglesia Española Reformada Episcopal (IERE, Spanish Reformed Episcopal Church), with J. B. Cabrera (1837-1916) as its first bishop. They accepted basic articles and a church order in 1899. The remaining Protestant churches took the name "Iglesia Evangélica Española" (IEE, Spanish Evangelical Church).

The Federación de Entidades Religiosas Evangélicas (FEREDE, Federation of Evangelical Religious Entities) estimates that it represents evangelical churches totaling 400,000 members. Of this number, it estimates that 30 percent are Latin American and African immigrants who came to Spain between 1990 and 2000.

The secretariat of the Commission for Interconfessional Relations of the CEE, however, estimates that there are only 130,000 evangelical Christians, divided among the Pentecostals (50,000), Baptist churches (40,000), Brethren Assemblies (20,000), the IEE (10,000), and other evangelical communities (10,000). Overall, Protestantism in Spain is not growing, and its story must be told with impartial objectivity.

The Ministry of Justice, in its Register of Religious Entities, has enrolled 1,064 evangelical entities. They include local church congregations, plus centers for education, health, publishing, and social activities administered by the Protestant churches.

1.4.1. *Anglicans*
The family of Anglican churches includes some 16,000 faithful, divided among the IERE (with 6,000 members and 15 centers for worship) and the Anglican Communion (10,000 faithful and 16 chaplaincies, largely for tourists and British residents temporarily in the country). The latter is officially assigned to the Spanish section of the Church of England's Diocese in Europe, which has its seat in Madrid. This European Anglican diocese is structured as a federation of churches and chaplaincies established in Spain; since 1842 it has constituted a jurisdiction of the Anglican Communion.

Although Anglican in spirit, the IERE turned to the Spanish-Gothic church for part of its liturgy. It is in full fellowship with other national independent churches (e.g., the Lusitanian Church in Portugal) and with → Old Catholic Churches. Its main church is in Madrid, with a bishop at its head. The IERE has been in full communion with the Anglican Communion since 1980, and its canonical ordination is Anglican (→ Church Law). It is a full member of the → World Council of Churches (WCC).

1.4.2. *Reformed*

The Iglesia Evangélica Española is strongly presbyterian and congregational in form and Calvinistic in doctrine (→ Calvinism). The *Guide to Organizations* (2004) of the Ministry of Justice lists 25 places of worship for the IEE. It also mentions 14 different evangelical churches of the Reformed tradition, as well as some Methodist churches (→ Methodism).

The IEE is a founding member of the → World Alliance of Reformed Churches (1870) and belongs to the WCC, the → World Methodist Council, the → Conference of European Churches (CEC), and the Conferencia de Iglesias Protestantes de los Países Latinos de Europa (CEPPLE, Conference of Protestant Churches of the Latin Countries of Europe). It regards itself as an heir of the → Reformation and appeals to Holy Scripture as its sole norm. It has seven presbyteries (corresponding to the old regions), which serve between the synod and the local congregations. Notwithstanding the historical limitation of religious freedom, the IEE has pursued social and educational goals and rendered basic service to its members. The IEE, together with the IERE, maintains the United Theological Seminary in Madrid and a Bible school that has programs of distance learning. It also has a modest program of publication.

1.4.3. *Baptists*

The → Baptist churches, which inherit the Anabaptist legacy of the 16th century, are closely linked to U.S. Southern Baptists. In the 19th century foreign missionaries to Spain began work first in Madrid and subsequently in Barcelona, Valencia, and a few other places, opening a Baptist seminary in Barcelona. Some of the Baptists are part of the Unión Evangélica Bautista Española (UEBE, Spanish Evangelical Baptist Union), which has 91 congregations (according to the 2004 *Guide to Organizations*); others belong to the Federación de Iglesias Evangélicas Bautistas Libres de España (FIEBLE, Federation of Free Evangelical Baptist Churches of Spain), which has 40 registered congregations. According to CIS, there were 125 local Baptist entities in 2005. The UEBE has a seminary in Madrid and does much social, educational, and publishing work. A national convention chooses its leaders.

1.4.4. *Others*

There are many other Protestant churches, some of them fundamentalistic (→ Fundamentalism) and some coming together in the Asambleas de Dios.

The Iglesia Evangélica Filadelfia, which consists primarily of → Roma, has 50,000 members (2000). There are 228 groups of Plymouth Brethren, with 20,000 total members. The Unión de Iglesias Cristianas Adventistas del Séptimo Día de España (UICASDE, Union of Seventh-day → Adventist Christian Churches of Spain), which dates from 1958, though Adventist missionaries were present in Spain since 1903, has 78 congregations, with 15,000 members. Other Protestant groups in Spain include the Salvation Army and the Mennonites.

1.5. *Orthodox*

Until the 1990s the Orthodox Church was represented in Spain by small communities of Greek and Romanian Orthodox in Madrid and Barcelona. Recent immigration, however, has increased the Orthodox presence significantly. Currently there are about 255,000 Orthodox faithful with legal status in the country: 150,000 Romanians, 50,000 Bulgarians, 40,000 Ukrainians, 5,000 Greeks, and 10,000 others. The Romanian Orthodox Church in Spain has 20 parishes.

As of December 2005, immigrants from eastern European countries numbered 192,134 Romanians (one-third of them Greek Catholics), 56,329 Bulgarians, 49,812 Ukrainians (half of them Eastern Rite Catholics, or Greek Catholics; → Uniate Churches), and 22,223 Russians. There is also much illegal immigration, which equals about a third of all the registered immigration from eastern Europe. In January 2003 the Greek Orthodox Church in Spain, which recognizes the Ecumenical Patriarchate of Constantinople, erected the new Diocese of Spain and Portugal, independent of the Archbishopric of Paris, to which it had belonged since 1949.

2. Ecumenical Relations

Ecumenical relations were developed in the 1950s in the setting of the Week of Prayer for Christian Unity (a circle around P. Couturier), although the Obra del Oriente Cristiano (Work of the Christian East) had an influence from the 1940s. Non–Roman Catholics founded the Comité Cristiano Interconfesional de España, and the Roman Catholic Bishops' Conference set up a committee for relations between the denominations that established conferences for → theology, → pastoral care, and → ecumenism. During the 1980s and 1990s these meetings were organized interconfessionally, thanks to the collaboration of the IERE, IEE, UEBE, and Madrid's Romanian and Greek Orthodox communities. Since 2000 this collaboration has led to an organization of seminaries or conferences on theological or pastoral studies, with invitations to other groups. The CEE Commission for Interconfessional Relations annually holds ecumenical conferences on theology and pastoral issues. Professors and pastors of other churches are also invited to these conferences, even as speakers.

Pastoral collaboration is fraternal. The Roman Catholic Church has offered the use of its churches to other Christian confessions for their worship celebrations and has offered various forms of aid to the organization of the communities of Christian non-Catholic immigrants. Centers for ecumenical worship and gathering have also been opened in Almería, Las Palmas, Málaga, Tenerife, and Valencia, in part because of the need to care for tourists. A new Catholic institute for women in orders was founded in Segovia in 1962 with a dedication to unity, the Instituto Misioneras de la Unidad (Missionaries for Unity Institute).

In the academic field, we might mention an ecumenical translation of the NT (1978), which was produced thanks to the collaboration of the United Bible Societies and, on behalf of the Catholic Church in Spain, the Biblioteca de Autores Cristianos and the publisher EDICABI (for *Edi*ciones de la *Ca*sa de la *Bí*blia). The same groups have been involved in a new translation of the OT, which is completed but awaiting final revision. There also is the Centro de Estudios Orientales y Ecuménicos Juan XXIII, which develops meetings and programs for study and research, even internationally, and offers a master's degree in theology and the history of ecumenism. The center, which is part of the papal university at Salamanca, began publishing *Diálogo Ecuménico* in 1966. The IERE and IEE, which are members of the → Conference of European Churches, promote ecumenical conferences, such as the Iberian Conference for Spanish and Portuguese Protestants, which meets periodically.

3. Church and State
Relations between → church and state have historically been determined by the Catholic character of Spain.

3.1. *Roman Catholics*
During the 19th century, tension between clericalism and anticlericalism marked the relations between the state and the Roman Catholic Church until radicalization came during the Second Republic (1931-39) and the Civil War (1936-39). The → concordat of 1953 fixed relations after the war, though with difficulty. The problems stemmed from the state's historic role as the patron of the church, from the 15th century onward (→ Patronage, Ecclesiasti-

cal), which allowed it to intervene in the election of bishops.

With the Law of Religious Liberty of 1967, the regime conformed to the doctrine of Vatican II in its declaration *Dignitatis humanae* (1965), which calls for "social and civil liberty in religious matters" (title). Spain accepted new principles, agreed upon between the Spanish state and the Holy See, for church-state relations, on the pattern of separation and collaboration, which found expression in five international agreements between the two states. King Juan Carlos I freely renounced the privilege of involvement in the election of bishops, and by the agreement of July 1976, the state renounced this same privilege, which had been exercised during the Second Republic; also the church renounced the legal privileges of priests. Four agreements in January 1979 followed, dealing with legal matters, educational and cultural affairs, economic matters, and religious support for the armed forces and the military service of priests and religious. The agreements were ratified by the Spanish Parliament in 1979.

The following decades made clear the sociopolitics of Catholic Spain. The Partido Socialista Obrero Español (PSOE, Spanish Socialist Workers' Party) came to power in 1982, even as John Paul II was being warmly received by the multitudes on his first trip to Spain. The PSOE retained power for 12 years, faithful to the three pillars of political and social consensus reflected in the Constitution of 1978: Spain as (1) a parliamentary monarchy; (2) a nonconfessional state, but with "appropriate cooperation relations with the Catholic Church and other confessions" (art. 16); and (3) a state of "self-governing communities" (part 8), on the basis of equal civic → rights for all. In 1994 the Partido Popular (PP, Popular Party) gained control of the government from the PSOE, with the socialists reclaiming power a decade later in the elections held a few days after the attack of March 11, 2004, the most serious terrorist attack in the history of Spain. This terrorist act left 192 dead at the Atocha train station in Madrid and other nearby stations. The attack was attributed to Islamic extremists, who gave no motive for their actions.

As a member of the Commissio Episcopatuum Communitatis Europensis (COMECE, Commission of the Bishops' Conferences of the European Community), with its headquarters in Brussels, the CEE cooperates with the Catholic bishops of the European Union for the passage of a European constitutional statement that acknowledges Europe's Christian roots, while at the same time concerning itself with social peace in a Europe that is experiencing immigration and growing religious pluralism, above all because of the presence there of 20 million followers of Islam. The CEE is also a member of the Consilium Conferentiarum Episcoporum Europae (CCEE, Council of European Bishops' Conferences), an instrument of collaboration for Catholic bishops, who deal with common problems facing the churches in Europe, collaborating ecumenically with the non-Catholic CEC.

The church has guided the moral conscience of those citizens who condemn the nationalistic terrorism of ETA (an acronym in Basque for "Basque fatherland and liberty"), operative since 1959 and a serious threat to democracy. Basque nationalism is promoted by the Partido Nacionalista Vasco (PNV, Nationalist Basque Party), which argues for the ethnic identity of the Basques, their historic territories, and their right of political self-determination. The 19th-century program of its founder, Sabino Arana (1865-1903), is summed up in the phrase *Dios y leyes viejas* (God and [the] old laws). The bishops have condemned the terrorism of ETA, which is motivated by extreme nationalism and elements of Marxist ideology (CEE, 79th Assembly, 2002). The stand of the CEE against ETA terrorism can be understood in the framework of the bishops' teaching about the decisive contribution of the church to the Spanish transition toward democracy and to social peace (statements issued in January 1973 and February 1986). Their teachings recognize the international détente needed, as well as Spain's new position in Europe.

More moderate in its strategy, Catalan nationalism claims a historical cultural identity based on the Catalan language and seeks to establish a politically autonomous region. Within this region, a minority seeks independence, while a majority is satisfied to remain as a Spanish region with political and administrative autonomy. To some extent the Montserrat Shrine of the Black Virgin has served as a catalyst of the nationalistic Catholicism of Catalonia, moderated by the teaching of the bishops of the ecclesiastical province of Tarraconensis (see *Las raíces cristianas de Cataluña* [The Christian roots of Catalonia, 1985]).

The teaching of the bishops has guided the role of Catholics in society, dealing with the relationship between the civil-democratic and the moral aspects of society (see statement from the 65th Assembly, 1966). The bishops have also addressed critically the secular mentality of the laws of the 1980s that legalized abortion and liberalized divorce, that introduced the idea of homosexual union as comparable

with marriage, and that permitted assisted reproduction and the manipulation of embryos (CEE, 81st Assembly, November 2003).

3.2. *Protestants*

Protestants, too, have long enjoyed recognition by, and collaboration with, the state. They united in the Comisión de Defensa Evangélica Española, which prepared the way for the FEREDE. In 1992 this group reached an agreement with the Spanish government regarding the diaconal, educational, and catechetical work of Protestants and the related financial issues.

4. Non-Christian Religions

→ Judaism and → Islam have each played a significant role in Spanish history.

4.1. *Judaism*

Though Sephardic Jews were expelled from Spain in 1492, the Jewish presence never ceased. Today Spanish Jews see themselves as heirs of those expelled in the 15th century (→ Judaism 3.3). According to CIS, in 2005 there were between 40,000 and 50,000 Jews in Spain, with 16 registered organizations, whose relationship with the Spanish population is one of friendship and full integration. This positive relationship was manifested in the joint celebration held on October 28, 2005, by the CEE and the Federación de Comunidades Israelitas de España for the 40th anniversary of Vatican II's *Nostra aetate*, the Declaration on the Relation of the Church to Non-Christian Religions.

Friendly bilateral conversations were started in 1947. The Asociación Hispano-Judía holds international conferences, and the Centro de la Comunidad Israelita and the Centro de Estudios Judeo-Cristianos are both at work in Madrid.

4.2. *Islam*

With the conquest of Granada in 1492, most Muslims were driven out of Spain, and the rest lost their citizenship in 1609 (the "expulsion of the Moriscos"). Muslims in Spain today are either immigrants (usually from Morocco or elsewhere in the Maghreb) or students. The 50,000 Muslims in the autonomous enclave cities of Ceuta and Melilla on the north coast of Morocco are an exception. They either have accepted Spanish citizenship or are the children of citizens.

As of 2005 about one million out of the 3.7 million immigrants to Spain were Muslims, with more than a half million of the Muslims coming from Morocco. Islam has 254 registered organizations, most of them belonging to the Comisión Islámica de España (CIE, Islamic Commission of Spain). These groups, which reflect the various tendencies within Islam, receive economic and political aid from various sources.

The construction of mosques in Spain illustrates the variety of Islamic sponsors. The largest mosque is the 'Umar ibn al-Khattāb Mosque, in Madrid's Centro Cultural Islámico. Opening in 1992, it was financed by King Fahd (1962-2005) of Saudi Arabia. A second mosque in Madrid is the Abū Bakr Mosque (1988), financed by the Asociación Musulmana en España, which has Syrian, Jordanian, and Palestinian support. Saudi financing helped erect the mosque in Marbella (1981, the first Spanish mosque since the reconquest). In Córdoba "El Morabito," a mosque built during the Spanish Civil War for the Moorish troops that helped Franco, now belongs to the city government but since 1992 has been leased to the Muslim community. The Sohail Mosque in Fuengirola, near Málaga, was built in 1993 by an Arab consulate. Finally, the mosque of Valencia receives Kuwaiti financing. It belongs to the Federación Española de Entidades Religiosas Islámicas (FEERI, Spanish Federation of Islamic Religious Bodies).

The CIE includes two federations: FEERI and the Unión de Comunidades Islámicas de España (UCIDE, Union of Islamic Communities of Spain), which promotes sociocultural activities to help immigrants. UCIDE, which defines itself as an Islamic religious federation, is a founding member of the Conseil Islamique de Coopération en Europe.

Many Islamic or Islamic-Christian societies seek to promote mutual understanding and cooperation. In 1968 the Asociación para la Amistad Islamo-Christiana (Association for Islamic-Christian Friendship) came into being. In 1992 Jews and Muslims reached an agreement with the Spanish government, approved by Parliament, regulating their religious work in the country.

In contrast, some Islamic associations propose, as an alternative to Christian Spain, a return to Al-Andalus, the Spain of Muslim domination of the Caliphate of Córdoba. These groups have their origins in the Islamic al-Murabitún movement of the London Da'wah Center of Abdelkader as-Sufi al-Murabit. Clusters from this movement went first to Morocco, then Spain, where they embraced various Islamic tendencies. In 1983 this community moved to Seville, where it suffered from various splits, out of which the Junta Islámica arose, as well as the Comunidad Islámica en España, developer of the mosque in Granada's Albaicín.

4.3. Other Groups

Other religious groups and sects in Spain include → Jehovah's Witnesses, which has about 800 officially registered places of worship (2005 Guide to Organi-zations). On the average, persons remain as members of this group for no more than ten years.

Also worthy of notice are the → Mormons, who report about 35,000 members. They settled in Spain toward the end of the 1970s, and their temple in Madrid serves Spain, Portugal, and southern France. Their official administrative headquarters are in San Fernando de Henares, in Madrid.

Religions and sects from the Far East, especially the so-called → youth religions, continue to attract the attention of Christian churches and their educators. Even though their impact has lessened in recent years, small religious groups continue to multiply, which constitutes a source of concern for the churches.

Bibliography: Early Spain: E. P. Colbert, *The Martyrs of Córdoba, 850-859* (Washington, D.C., 1962) • E. James, ed., *Visigothic Spain: New Approaches* (Oxford, 1980) • J. Orlandis, *La Iglesia en la España visigótica y medieval* (Pamplona, 1976) • M. Sotomayor y Muro, *La Iglesia en la España romana y visigoda (siglos I–VIII)*, vol. 1 of *Historia de la Iglesia en España* (ed. R. García Villoslada; Madrid, 1979) 7-400 • A. K. Ziegler, *Church and State in Visigothic Spain* (Washington D.C., 1930).

Islamic domination, Christian kingdoms (English works): R. I. Burns, *Moors and Crusaders in Mediterranean Spain* (London, 1978) • A. Castro, *The Spaniards: An Introduction to Their History* (Berkeley, Calif., 1971) • T. F. Glick, *Islamic and Christian Spain in the Early Middle Ages* (2d ed.; Leiden, 2005) • D. W. Lomax, *The Reconquest of Spain* (London, 1978).

Islamic domination, Christian kingdoms (Spanish works): T. de Azcona, *Isabel la Católica. Estudio crítico de su vida y reinado* (Madrid, 1964) • I. de las Cagigas, *Los mozárabes* (2 vols.; Madrid, 1947-48) • L. Fernández Suárez, *Los Reyes Católicos* (5 vols.; Madrid, 1989-90) • J. García Oro, *Cisneros y la reforma del clero español en tiempos de los Reyes Católicos* (Madrid, 1971) • N. López Martínez, *Los judaizantes castellanos y la Inquisición en los tiempos de Isabel la Católica* (Burgos, 1954) • E. Mitre Fernández, *Judaísmo y cristianismo. Raíces de un gran conflicto histórico* (Madrid, 1980) • C. Sanchez-Albornoz, *España, un enigma histórico* (Barcelona, 1956) • L. Vázquez de Parga and J. Uría Ríu, *Las peregrinaciones a Santiago de Compostela* (3 vols.; Madrid, 1948-49).

16th century to the present (English works): A. Brassloff, *Religion and Politics in Spain: The Spanish Church in Transition, 1962-96* (Basingstoke, 1998) • W. J. Callahan, *The Catholic Church in Spain, 1875-1998* (Washington, D.C., 2000); idem, *Church, Politics, and Society in Spain, 1750-1874* (Cambridge, Mass., 1984) • L. Hanke, *The Spanish Struggle for Justice in the*

Conquest of America (Philadelphia, 1949) • G. Jackson, *The Spanish Republic and the Civil War, 1931-1939* (Princeton, 1965) • H. Kamen, *The Spanish Inquisition: A Historical Revision* (New Haven, 1998) • F. Lannon, *Privilege, Persecution, and Prophecy: The Catholic Church in Spain, 1875-1975* (Oxford, 1987) • J. C. Nieto, *Juan de Valdés and the Origins of the Spanish and Italian Reformation* (Geneva, 1970) • S. G. Payne, *The Franco Regime, 1936-1975* (Madison, Wis., 1987); idem, *Spanish Catholicism: An Historical Overview* (Madison, Wis., 1984) • E. A. Peers, *Spain, the Church, and the Orders* (London, 1945) • P. Rodríguez, F. Ocáriz, and J. L. Illanes, *Opus Dei in the Church* (Dublin, 1994) • J. M. Sánchez, *Reform and Reaction: The Politico-Religious Background of the Spanish Civil War* (Chapel Hill, N.C., 1964) • J. B. Scott, *The Spanish Origin of International Law: Francisco de Vitoria and His Law of Nations* (Union, N.J., 2000; orig. pub., 1934) • W. E. Shiels, *King and Church: The Rise and Fall of Patronato Real* (Chicago, 1961).

16th century to the present (Spanish works): J. Alvárez Gómez et al., eds., *El postconcilio en España* (Madrid, 1988) • Biblioteca de Autores Cristianos, *Historia de las diócesis españolas* (10 vols.; 10 more vols. projected; Madrid, 2002ff.) • P. Borges Morán, *El envío de misioneros a América durante la época española* (Salamanca, 1977) • V. Cárcel Ortí, *La persecución religiosa en España durante la Segunda República, 1931-1939* (Madrid, 1990) • J. M. Cuenca Toribio, *Catolicismo social y político en la España contemporánea (1870-2000)* (Madrid, 2003) • A. Domínguez Ortiz and B. Vincent, *Historia de los moriscos* (Madrid, 1978) • J. P. Fusi and F. García de Cortázar, *Política, nacionalidad e Iglesia en el País Vasco* (San Sebastián, 1988) • E. La Parra López and M. Suárez Cortina, eds., *El anticlericalismo español contemporáneo* (Madrid, 1998) • M. López Rodríguez, *La España protestante. Crónica de una minoría marginada, 1937-1975* (Madrid, 1976) • F. Meer Lecha-Marzo, *La cuestión religiosa en las Cortes Constituyentes de la II República* (Pamplona, 1975) • Ministerio de Justicia, *Confesiones minoritarias en España. Guía de entidades y Vademécum normativo* (ed. J. Mantecón; Madrid, 2004) • P. Moa Rodríguez, *Los orígenes de la guerra civil* (Madrid, 1999) • A. Montero Moreno, *Historia de la persecución religiosa en España, 1936-1939* (2d ed.; Madrid, 2004) • L. Palacios Bañuelos, *Círculos de obreros y sindicatos agrarios en Córdoba, 1877-1923* (2d ed.; Córdoba, 1980) • V. Pérez-Díaz, B. Álvarez-Miranda, and E. Chuliá, *La inmigración musulmana en Europa* (Barcelona, 2004) • J. L. Sánchez Nogales, *El islam entre nosotros. Cristianismo e islam en España* (Madrid, 2004) • C. Seco Serrano, *La cuestión social en la Iglesia española contemporánea* (Madrid, 1981) • J. F. Serrano Oceja, ed., *La Iglesia frente al terrorismo de ETA* (Madrid, 2001) • L. Usoz y Río, ed., *Reformistas antiguos españoles* (24 vols.; Madrid, 1847-80; repr., 1980).

Adolfo González Montes

Speculative Theology

1. Speculative theology, often connected with German → idealism, has a much earlier origin. K. → Rahner (1904-84), distinguishing it from positive → theology in the Roman Catholic sphere, points back beyond the historical framework to a universal religious and theological foundation. Part of speculation as a scientific method is that, on the basis of a supposed → dialectic of being, a counterpart, as in a mirror *(speculum),* is always thought of not just in a historically comparative way but in a dynamic and cognitive way that sheds light on being itself (→ Cognition). Speculation was made a philosophical instrument especially by G. W. F. Hegel (1770-1831; → Hegelianism), who found in speculative theology not just a fashionable place for speculation but a rediscovery and, at the same time, a further development of a way of thought originally Christian, such as he found in Pauline dialectic (see 1 Cor. 13:12; Rom. 4:17, etc.).

2. With specific modifications, speculative theologians, taking up Christian → dogma and showing the real basis of the community, accepted the view that everything has an opposite, working both really and spiritually, both practically and ideally, simultaneously and without division. Hegel's dialectical method, which reproduces the process of world reason in the dialectic immanent to the subject, determines the course of things in the history of the faith. Dogma is critically enlightened and is exalted to the source of faith. Identification of God and man in Jesus Christ (→ Christology 2.5.3) creates neither interchange nor mixing in a supernaturalistic sense (→ Hegelianism 2) but a dialectical process immanent to being, or a dynamic identity of the nonidentical.

3. The great themes of speculative theology may be listed, but without a calculation of the dialectical, dynamic → ontology, which goes back to Paul. Thus although the speculative dialectical interpretation of the → Trinity is seen as opposed to one that is nondialectical, suspicion falls on the doctrine of

God and Christology because God reveals himself more strongly as absolute spirit *(actus purus)* to reason than as the personal God and takes up all antitheses pantheistically into himself (→ Pantheism). Christ is seen not as the personal Savior but as the principle of salvation for all humanity, or as the first to be redeemed. → Sin, as the antithesis of the finite to the infinite, counts as little (Hegel's "blessing of the fall"), as does history, with the result that everything comes to be seen as a mere "shifting of clouds."

4. In Roman Catholic theology, though not in contrast to positively defined theology, speculative theology, based on all the results of preceding historical exposition and a critical analysis of empirical materials (A. E. Biedermann, *Dogmatik* [1884/85] §3.9), is seen as the coherence of all that is positively understood. Speculation goes back to the working of the Logos in both rediscovery and expression, as found in Philo (15-10 B.C.–A.D. 45-50), John, and Paul. As a basis of knowledge it forms the constitutive religious principle of the church (§2), in the same way as D. → Bonhoeffer's (1906-45) "Christ existing as the community." Inductively, it draws near to the speculation of the empirical, works down to ultimate bases, achieves both positive and negative criticism, and, in the eminent sense of the word, arrives at a summary in thought of all that is most inward (§4.8). This does not take place in a way that is formally didactic. Ontological speculation sets ideal and material being in an original relationship and relates the subject of consciousness to its object (§20).

5. The centers of speculative theology were Heidelberg, with C. Daub (1765-1836), and Berlin, with W. Vatke (1806-82). In Zurich A. E. Biedermann (1819-85) gathered together the thinking of D. F. Strauss (1808-74), Hegel, and F. D. E. → Schleiermacher (1768-1834; → Schleiermacher's Theology) and wrote a strongly speculative Christian dogmatics in 1869 and 1884/85. He claimed that the real principle that lies behind the church leads by way of rational criticism of the doctrinal tradition, with the help of speculation, to a purified → dogmatics. A comparable work is that of the Berlin teacher I. A. Dorner (1809-84), who through the faith of the church, with a belief that is rational and penitentially rests on the church, the Scriptures, and the sacraments, attained to a consciousness of both the self and of God.

From the criticism of A. Ritschl (1822-89) and his pupils, speculative theology underwent further development right up to M. Werner (1887-1964) and F. Buri (1907-95). It also influenced so-called → dialectical theology in its dealings with → paradox, though here it never plumbed the depths of liberal speculative theology. Unlike the *Church Dogmatics* of → Barth, the Anglo-Saxon speculative theology of the "Beloved Community" developed the interesting proof of God of J. Royce (1855-1916; → God, Arguments for the Existence of), openness to the speculative question of being in his student E. Hocking (1873-1966), and preparation for interreligious → dialogue with W. M. Urban (1873-1952).

6. Speculative theology takes up a central Christian concern against a rationalistically flattened theology, on the one side, and, on the other, a higher order of Herrnhut theology in Schleiermacher. It is scientifically exact, both empirical and theoretical, and seeks to set forth a true biblical faith in a Reformation sense. Its achievement is to subject theology to methodological criticism, not merely analyzing the ontology of this method, but deriving it from the Christological center. The dialectical ontology that is sought makes possible both an operation of thinking that moves across boundaries and analyses of existence. It must be asked, however, whether it achieves an understanding of being in the light of which Paul (see Gal. 3:28) found a dynamic, universal community to be possible (i.e., existence that has a genuinely Christological basis) or whether the idealistic schematism is not too demanding.

Similarly, speculative theology has done little for symbols in the worship of God, and after two world wars, with the pressure of dialectical theology, it tended to lose its force. Yet its turning to methodological criticism, universal ontology, and the Christological center provided fresh hermeneutical activity (→ Hermeneutics) and → dialogue (§2) between the religions. Its real principle of community must be universally understood, and its thinking can give rise to a global → theology of religion. Approaches to a speculative theology of religion may be seen in Buddhist philosophy (→ Buddhism) and in the Japanese Kyoto school (Nishitani Keiji).

→ Theology in the Nineteenth and Twentieth Centuries

Bibliography: K. Barth, *Protestant Theology in the Nineteenth Century* (new ed.; Grand Rapids, 2002) • F. Buri, *Theology of Existence* (Greenwood, S.C., 1965) • I. A. Dorner, *A System of Christine Doctrine* (4 vols.; Edinburgh, 1880-81) • F. W. Graf, *Kritik und Pseudo-Spekulation. David Friedrich Strauss als Dogmatiker im*

Kontext der positionellen Theologie seiner Zeit (Munich, 1982) • E. HIRSCH, *Geschichte der neuern evangelischen Theologie* (5 vols.; 3d ed.; Münster, 1984) • K. KRÜGER, *Der Gottesbegriff der spekulativen Theologie* (Berlin, 1970) • R. ŌKŌCHI and K. OTTE, *Tan-ni-sho: Die Gunst des reinen Landes. Begegnung zwischen Buddhismus und Christentum* (Bern, 1979) • K. OTTE, *Durch Gemeinde zur Predigt. Zur Verhältnisbestimmung von Theologie und Predigt bei Alexander Schweitzer und Alois Emanuel Biedermann* (Frankfurt, 1979); idem, *Das Sprachverständnis bei Philo von Alexandrien* (Tübingen, 1968) • J. E. SMITH, *Royce's Social Infinite: The Community of Interpretation* (New York, 1950) • H. STEPHAN and M. SCHMIDT, *Geschichte der evangelischen Theologie in Deutschland seit dem Idealismus* (3d ed.; New York, 1973) • F. WAGNER, *Die vergessene spekulative Theologie* (Zurich, 1987) • C. WELCH, ed. and trans., *God and Incarnation in Mid-nineteenth Century German Theology: G. Thomasius, I. A. Dorner, A. E. Biedermann* (New York, 1965) • R. WELLEK, "The Minor Transcendentalists and German Philosophy," *NEQ* 15 (1942) 652-80 • M. WERNER, *The Formation of Christian Dogma* (New York, 1957).

KLAUS OTTE

Speech → Language

Spinozism

1. Term
2. Key Features
3. Development

1. Term

Spinozism is a special type of → metaphysics deriving from Baruch de Spinoza (1632-77). Spinoza, a Dutch philosopher of Jewish background who had grown up in the spirit of → Cartesianism, developed this type of metaphysics in his main work, *Ethica* (1677). A previous work, the *Tractatus theologico-politicus* (1670), which Spinoza published anonymously, ultimately brought about a broader reception of his philosophy.

2. Key Features

The characteristic feature of Spinoza's metaphysics is a → monism of substance that carries with it a denial of transcendence (→ Transcendental Philosophy). This theory offers a rational explanation of the world and an → ethics that relies exclusively on theoretical insights into the necessary structures of the world. In the one substance of → God all the ele-

ments of the personal and creative (understanding and will) are obliterated. The essence of God is nothing but productive power, which achieves fulfillment in the things produced, the *modi* (immanent → causality). This view of the nature of God leads to a strict determination of the world. Consequently, there is as little room in the world for the possible or for chance as there is for freedom of the will, belief in which expresses only a defective knowledge (→ Epistemology). What we can do does not show the ability of a subject with its own powers and standing apart from the → nature that encompasses it.

Mind and body are of the same origin but are not related causally. They find their unity in the nature of God, which consists of essentially different productive attributes. Mental and bodily events run parallel to one another. By reflection on ideas of the corporal, we can find the true origin of our ideas in the divine attribute of thought. We see here that which is eternal (*sub specie aeternitatis;* → Time and Eternity), and in this knowledge we know ourselves to be eternal. This form of knowledge is our blessedness, and it gives us a possible → freedom in which our adequate knowledge corresponds with our own nature. Knowledge is an act of the individual (→ Individualism; Self), and its essential feature is a striving for self-preservation, from which Spinoza derives a theory of the emotions and a rational orientation to the world (→ Worldview). Knowledge has the power of action only if we are emotionally involved by it. It reaches its purest form in intellectual → love for God, in which we love the God who is the cause of all things, the God to whom we owe all that we can do or think, and whom we can thank only by adequately recognizing him.

People who do not achieve this recognition are referred for their own → happiness to forms of organization that are congruent with → reason but that do not rely on the individual practice of reason. This is where → politics and → religion find their place. Religion is a doctrine of the good life that is adapted to the power of those addressed but that has no claim to → truth. It is no rival to → philosophy, for it differs from it only by its form of presentation.

3. Development

In its development Spinozism did not follow all the teachings of Spinoza but only specific aspects. The first phase had to do with the polemics against the *Tractatus* and the doctrine of God in the *Ethica*. One of the figures in J. G. → Herder's (1744-1803) essay "God" sums up these polemics: Spinoza was an atheist and a pantheist (→ Atheism; Pantheism) who taught blind necessity and was a foe of → revelation, a scoffer at religion, a devourer of states (→ State) and all civil society — in short, an enemy of the human race. Only marginally were the elements of Spinozism adopted (by A. J. Cuffeler in Holland; F. W. Stosch, T. L. Lau, and J. G. Wachter in Germany; and H. deBoulainviller in France).

G. W. Leibniz (1646-1716), with a theory of possible worlds and with the distinction between the logical and the factual, tried to overcome Spinozism by a different concept of God. The criticism of P. Bayle (1647-1706) was effective; he described Spinozism as a monstrous and meaningless system (→ Social Systems). G. E. Lessing's (1729-81) confession of Spinozism as published by F. H. Jacobi (1743-1819) opened up a new phase in Germany. M. Mendelssohn (1729-86), based upon Wolffian → rationalism, defended a purified Spinozism that would allow for religion and morality. Jacobi, however, derived atheism on the rationalistic premises of Spinozism itself. Whereas prior to this debate it had aroused little interest, Spinozism now was considered a type of metaphysics of the first order. Herder went on to work out the dynamic element in the power of God in a way that gave him a theory of self-organizing → life.

J. W. Goethe (1749-1832) found an affinity to his own worldview in a pantheistic Spinozism that allows specific being for each individual. F. D. E. → Schleiermacher (1768-1834; → Schleiermacher's Theology) found a theistic element in the intellectual love of God (→ Theism). In the philosophy of German → idealism Spinozism could offer help in giving a deeper foundation and eminent meaning to the subjective philosophy of I. Kant (1724-1804; → Kantianism). It offered a valid model for a theory of the absolute. J. G. Fichte (1762-1814) believed it would best enlighten his own system. F. W. J. Schelling (1775-1854) regarded himself as a Spinozist in his youth, and even in old age he believed that no one could advance what was true and complete in philosophy who had not plunged into the depths of Spinozism. G. W. F. Hegel (1770-1831; → Hegelianism) thought the standpoint of Spinozism was the essential beginning of philosophy because the → soul needed to bathe in the "ether" of a substance in which everything that one had held to be true was destroyed.

With decreasing interest in speculative philosophy in the later 19th century, Spinozism became a mere subject in the history of philosophy. M. Hess (1812-75), who took up its political theory, and L. Feuerbach (1804-72), who viewed the system materialistically (→ Materialism) and thus opened up the door to → Marxism, were the only exceptions.

In the 20th century the study of → Judaism revived interest in the philosophy of Spinoza, and since the 1960s French → structuralism has given it relevance in criticism of the concept of the subject. It has also found reception among theories of science and systems, within a philosophy of the mind, and in connection with an understanding of nature that is no longer seen from an anthropological angle.

Bibliography: W. BARTUSCHAT, *Spinozas Theorie des Menschen* (Hamburg, 1992) • E. CURLEY, *Spinoza's Metaphysics* (Cambridge, Mass., 1969) • A. R. DAMASIO, *Looking for Spinoza: Joy, Sorrow, and the Feeling Brain* (Orlando, Fla., 2003) • G. DELEUZE, *Expression in Philosophy* (New York, 1992; orig. pub., 1968) • S. HAMPSHIRE, *Spinoza and Spinozism* (Oxford, 2005) • E. E. HARRIS, *Salvation from Despair: A Reappraisal of Spinoza's Philosophy* (The Hague, 1973) • J. I. ISRAEL, *Radical Enlightenment: Philosophy and the Making of Modernity, 1650-1750* (Oxford, 2001) • R. MASON, *The God of Spinoza* (Cambridge, 1997) • A. MATHERON, *Individu et communauté chez Spinoza* (2d ed.; Paris, 1988) • P.-F. MOREAU, *Spinoza. L'expérience et l'éternité* (Paris, 1994) • S. NADLER, *Spinoza: A Life* (Cambridge, 1999) • R. H. POPKIN, *Spinoza* (Oxford, 2004) • D. B. STEINBERG, *On Spinoza* (Belmont, Calif., 2000) • L. STRAUSS, *Spinoza's Critique of Religion* (Chicago, 1997; orig. pub., 1930) • J. WETLESEN, *The Sage and the Way: Spinoza's Ethics of Freedom* (Assen, 1979) • Y. YOVEL, *Spinoza and Other Heretics* (2 vols.; Princeton, 1989) • S. ZAC, *Spinoza et l'interprétation de l'Écriture* (Paris, 1965).

WOLFGANG BARTUSCHAT

Spiritism

Contrasting with → animism, spiritism (or spiritualism) believes that all things have spirits, or → souls, that the dead and other spiritual beings have fellowship with each other, and that humans can make contact with the souls of the dead and with spiritual beings. Spiritists believe that the spirits of the dead can cause noises or make things disappear, give answers to questions about the hereafter, explore the other world, and offer information as to the → future.

1. We can distinguish the various kinds of spiritism according to the media by which these messages are transmitted. If they are derived from rappings or movements chiefly of round tables, they are spoken

of as table movings. Since the end of the 1950s tape recorders have been used in an effort to rule out ambiguities that result from the interpretation of these rappings and movements. Thus the answer to a question spoken on the tape is derived from the recorded "tone" of noise-free spaces or even from a radio program that might be picked up, with music or a language that no one understands.

The messages are clearer and longer if gifted mediums, usually in a trance (→ Ecstasy) under the influence of certain spirits, speak or write automatically in known languages, interpret their own systems of signs, or announce something inwardly seen or heard. In theosophical circles (→ Theosophy), astral travel (or projection) is especially valued for the investigation of the spirit world. To be sure, since such messages transmitted by individual mediums cannot be controlled in any way, the door is open to fraud and pranks.

Between physical and personal communication, there are vibrations or rappings on glass, among other phenomena, in which the movements are tied to letters and thus can produce linguistic messages.

2. Modern spiritism had forerunners in phenomenologically comparable forms of invoking the dead or oracles (→ Dead, Cult of the) among more primitive and also highly civilized peoples. In ancient Israel, trying to find the future with the help of the dead was an abomination to → Yahweh (Deut. 18:10-12; Lev. 19:31; 20:6, 27). In spite of the conviction that the dead know nothing about this world (Job 14:21; 21:21; Eccl. 9:5-6), necromancy was still practiced (1 Sam. 28:3, 9; 2 Kgs. 21:6; 23:24), probably under Canaanite or Egyptian influence.

More recently, spiritism has taken the form of mesmerism, which began around the middle of the 1800s under the Fox family in Hydesville, New York. In the Romance-language countries, the linking prevailed between spiritism and belief in → reincarnation, as promoted by French scholar Hippolyte Rivail (1804-69), who published spiritist works under the pseudonym "Allan Kardec."

3. In spiritism paranormal phenomena do take place that cannot be explained by ordinary means. It is hard to verify or falsify whether they are caused by spirits or other spiritual powers. Psychokinesis and telepathy suffice to explain them, but spiritism itself is a hypothesis or an object of faith. The same applies to experimental proofs of the survival of the dead.

4. Biblically, confessional Christians have no ground for thinking that evil spirits or Satan (→ Devil) are necessarily at work in spiritism. There can be reason for such beliefs only when all other attempts at explanation have failed (→ Occultism). By countering an enlightened and abbreviated Christianity that left no room for → heaven, the hereafter, spirits, or demons, spiritism, by questioning famous personalities such as Buddha, Lao-tzu, → Jesus, or → Peter, has attained the position of an independent and loosely organized religion of → revelation with much more than Christian features. Indeed, the conditions after death, according to mediums, are almost completely contrary to what Christian → dogmatics teaches. The most that can be said is that spiritism deserves the same respect that all other non-Christian religions can claim.

Bibliography: C. B. BECKER, *Paranormal Experience and Survival of Death* (Albany, N.Y., 1993) • G. W. BUTTERWORTH, *Spiritualism and Religion* (London, 1944) • A. GAULD, *The Founders of Psychical Research* (London, 1968); idem, *Mediumship and Survival: A Century of Investigations* (London, 1982) • F.-W. HAACK, *Rendezvous mit dem Jenseits. Der moderne Spiritismus* (Hamburg, 1973) • L. B. PATON, *Spiritism and the Cult of the Dead in Antiquity* (New York, 1921) • F. PODMORE, *Modern Spiritualism: A History and a Criticism* (2 vols.; London, 1902).

KARL HOHEISEL

Spiritual Direction

1. Setting
2. History
3. The Ministry of Direction

1. Setting

Spiritual direction is a historic, practical, and classic ministry of the Christian church. It is tied to the church's sacramental life, especially to practices of → confession and absolution, but practitioners (known variously as, e.g., → *starets* in the Slavic tradition, *gerōn* among Greeks, "counselor" or "director" in the West) are not identical to confessors. The practice originated in the monastic movement.

Spiritual direction relates both to the cultural milieu and to the tenor in which the church is located, but it acts independently from, or at times even at cross-purposes to, that milieu. Since the popularization of the term → "spirituality," spiritual direction has become detached, in some quarters, from its traditional roots in the life and faith of a given church. Training to become a spiritual director in a college or seminary program is a novelty of the late 20th century, as is the growth of Spiritual Directors International, an association that crosses religious boundaries in its constituency.

Spiritual direction as a discipline practiced across and even apart from ecclesiastical boundaries occurred only recently. This is both gain and loss: gain because current practice uses a variety of models for growth (including, e.g., Jungian psychology, a popular grounding for many spiritual directors), which is inviting to people who see themselves as spiritual explorers. It is loss because the practice has traditionally been tied to the community and cannot function apart from the signs, symbols, rituals, and rites of the church in which it grew.

Spiritual direction has its own history within churches and has been in the process of revival since the late 20th century. It began in the East, though in recent years renewal has come mostly from and within Western churches, particularly the → Anglican, Lutheran (→ Lutheranism), and → Roman Catholic traditions.

2. History

The roots of spiritual direction include the prophetic tradition of Hebrew religion, wherein the → prophet addressed people with the need to return to the faith of the → covenant. The prophet served as a mediator between the will of God and the life of the people. This prophetic ministry was transformed in the early Christian community as people sought ways to live in the light of the resurrection promise. This search to live in the light would naturally involve discerning how to live in the → Holy Spirit, who gathers the community and leads it into all truth.

The Christian approach was forged in the deserts of Sinai and Egypt. People would go to seek a "word" from one of the elders, male and female, who lived in prayer and solitude in order to receive others on a deep, self-emptied level. Indeed, they created solitude as a virtue rather than an absence, and the paucity of their words was more than compensated by the extravagance of their charity. Thousands of people consulted these enigmatic figures of the desert for a word that would guide their souls (→ Stylites).

A person under direction was obedient to an elder, not in rigid conformity to the elder's whim, but out of free choice in the belief that he or she was taking the path to full → freedom. The paradox of freedom-in-obedience is at the heart of the mystery of direction. The directee trusts that the Holy Spirit guides the director, especially to know his or her own limits and boundaries.

The *Conferences* of John Cassian (ca. 360-after

430) took the desert tradition and regularized it in a way that also provided models of pastoral ministry that embraced the ascetic traditions. Cassian exerted a powerful influence on both → Benedict of Nursia (ca. 480-ca. 547) and → Gregory the Great (590-604).

The early high point in the Western development of spiritual direction was the powerful papal reign of Gregory the Great, whose *Pastoral Rule* (ca. 591) was hugely influential for hundreds of years in establishing pastoral praxis, including that of spiritual direction, across the church. Gregory's work, however, shows the tension regarding spiritual direction between parish practice and monastic practice. Different figures adjusted the developing models to accommodate both sides of the tension. → Athanasius (ca. 297-373), for example, loved Anthony of Egypt (251?-356) as a charismatic spiritual director; in contrast to Anthony, however, Athanasius insisted on the centrality of the episcopacy in matters of faith and interpretation. This tension had practical ramifications insofar as decisions had to be made about candidates for → ordination: some leaders preferred to stress the ascetic side of a person's development, others the clerical side.

Another stream that fed into spiritual direction was the Irish penitential practices. In Gaelic lands, especially in Ireland, where travel was difficult and priests were few, people consulted with spiritual elders male and female (called *anmchara,* "soul friends"), who would counsel them apart from the sacramental practice of confession and absolution.

The spiritual center of Eastern practices and tradition was the monastic center of Mount → Athos, on the Chalcidice peninsula in northeast Greece. The tradition reached a high point in eastern Europe, the Ukraine, and Russia, especially in the 19th century at such monasteries as Optino in Russia, Valamo in Karelia, and the Kievan Caves in the Ukraine. Paissy Velichkovsky's (1722-94) masterful translation into Russian of the → *Philokalia,* an extensive collection of spiritual writings, was a key impetus for the flowering of spiritual direction. Seraphim of Sarov (1759-1833), beloved Russian monk and counselor to many, said, "I give others only what God has given me," showing the role of → prayer and self-denial in working with others.

Among Protestants a form of spiritual direction developed based on seeking the meaning of faith for individual lives. Called *Seelsorge* (spiritual care) in German, this practice was related to and grew out of the faith of the church in worship and Scripture. This approach may be defined as a personal application of the proclaimed faith to the individual. Martin → Luther (1483-1546; → Luther's Theology) and John → Calvin (1509-64; → Calvin's Theology), in particular, wrote incisive letters of spiritual direction that sought to bring their addressees into a deeper relationship with Jesus Christ. Later Reformed and Lutheran scholastics outlined a full process of → sanctification in stages, which they called the *ordo salutis* (→ Order of Salvation). The Pietist tradition sought to overcome a rigid systematization of the faith in favor of a return to emphasis upon love of God and the faith of the heart.

In the middle of the 20th century, under pressure from the growing dominance of → psychotherapy and → psychoanalysis in the general culture, a blurring of lines between psychological pastoral counseling models and older forms of spiritual direction occurred, to the detriment of the latter. Today we see a trend to separate these once again into distinct but mutually useful disciplines, each one enriching the other with its insights.

3. The Ministry of Direction

The aim of spiritual direction is union with or participation in God, or → *theōsis.* A director aids a person to discover ways in which he or she is separated from God and thus inwardly broken. Healing takes place through *metanoia,* repentance, by which one is turned around to face God once more, after walking in the wrong direction, away from God. Part of *metanoia* is confession of past sins and receiving absolution, but *metanoia* encompasses the orientation of one's entire life.

Christian faith is not abstract belief. Faith is based in experience. Spiritual direction enables persons to reflect on this experience.

Traditional understandings of direction follow a threefold model of purgation, illumination, and union, which is a way to distinguish aspects of relationships to God, self, and others. One does not progress in an orderly fashion through these stages so much as experience them as constantly interweaving and overlapping.

Spiritual direction is a ministry of → healing. Bad faith is not solely a matter of wrong thinking but leads to moral and spiritual decay in need of repair. Thus early spiritual directors were called "physicians of the soul." Anthony of Egypt, founder of → monasticism, said that the fathers and mothers went to the desert to find healing in accord with Christ's injunction "Physician, heal thyself" and then began to heal others. Roman Catholic teacher Henri Nouwen (1932-96) wrote of the "wounded healer," whose wounds become signs to aid in healing others, which he modeled in his own life.

The ground for healing and union is the person of Jesus Christ. Through his humanity persons are drawn back to God. This process of reunion with God is often related to both justification and sanctification in the West, to *theōsis,* or divinization, in the East. As Christ's human nature was united to the divine nature in one person, so human nature can be united, by grace but not by nature, to God. Persons do not become God, which is impossible, but may become "participants of the divine nature" (2 Pet. 1:4). Such participation is not static but a process of constant growth. We grow by rooting out the urges that drive us toward sin and away from God. Spiritual directors bring insight to challenge this dark part of the soul in order to assist the directee to move away from these urges into the Light of God. Gregory of Nyssa (ca. 330-ca. 395), in his *Life of Moses,* reasoned that since God is the fullness of beauty, humans constantly reach out beyond themselves toward union with God, for beauty is an endless unveiling of God.

The agent for healing and union is the Holy Spirit, who leads the church into all the truth of God (John 16:13) and who inspires the faithful through → baptism and chrismation. Church leaders from John Climacus (ca. 570-ca. 649), abbot of Sinai, to Martin Luther and beyond stressed repentance as "return to baptismal grace"; hence, the movement of the human spirit to return to God is always inspired and guided by the Holy Spirit. The vocation of a spiritual director is to assist a person to track the movement of the Holy Spirit in his or her life.

Bibliography: J. Allen, *Inner Way: Eastern Christian Spiritual Direction* (Grand Rapids, 1994) • D. Bonhoeffer, *Spiritual Care* (Philadelphia, 1985) • I. Chariton, comp., *The Art of Prayer: An Orthodox Anthology* (ed. T. Ware; London, 1966) • J. Chryssavgis, *Soul Mending: The Art of Spiritual Direction* (Brookline, Mass., 2000) • G. Demacopoulos, *Five Models of Spiritual Direction in the Early Church* (Notre Dame, Ind., 2006) • M. Guenther, *Holy Listening: The Art of Spiritual Direction* (Boston, 1992) • I. Hausherr, *Spiritual Direction in the Early Christian East* (Kalamazoo, Mich., 1990) • V.-M. Kärkkäinen, *One with God: Salvation as Deification and Justification* (Collegeville, Minn., 2004) • K. Leech, *Soul Friend: Spiritual Direction in the Modern World* (rev. ed.; Harrisburg, Pa., 2001) • J. T. McNeill, *History of the Cure of Souls* (New York, 1951) • T. Merton, *Spiritual Direction and Meditation* (Collegeville, Minn., 1986) • H. Nouwen, *The Wounded Healer* (New York, 1979).

Gabriel C. Rochelle

Spiritualism

1. Term
2. In Antiquity
3. Middle Ages, Reformation, and Pietism
4. Early Modern Period
5. Classic German Philosophy
6. Nineteenth and Twentieth Centuries

1. Term

Developed in the 17th century, "spiritualism" (from Lat. *spiritus,* and representing Gk. *nous* or *pneuma*) became in the 18th and 19th centuries a master term for philosophical systems that made mind or spirit their supreme principle. Mind or spirit, however, is a complex phenomenon and covers a broad spectrum, and we cannot give any comprehensive or precise and positive meaning to the term "spiritualism." Counterpositions are → materialism and → positivism.

If one uses the term in philosophy, it must be differentiated from an understanding of spiritualism stemming especially from Eng. "spiritualism," which among other things also includes irrational, spiritistic practices such as the conjuring of dead spirits (→ Irrationalism; Spiritism). In contrast, the spectrum of meanings of the strongly context-dependent term "spiritualism" must be deduced from the problems that lead to the development of rational forms of the philosophy of the spirit. Related to the concepts of → God, being, → soul or → reason, thought, and consciousness, and set in relation to conceptual oppositions like → nature and history, body and society, a philosophy of spirit has to do with the basic dynamic relations of particularity and universality, or of the → self and others, in which the spirit or mind achieves its self-determination by contact with those around it.

Although spiritualism in its many meanings has largely disappeared from philosophical terminology, it is used in a very particular way in the history of theology, in which from the 19th century onward it denotes a strain in Reformation theology that sees the direct working of the Holy Spirit in the religious consciousness as a key to the knowledge of God and finds little value in institutional mediations of → salvation such as Scripture, the → church, the Word (→ Word of God 3), or the → sacraments.

2. In Antiquity

The mind, which Anaxagoras (ca. 500-ca. 428 B.C.) placed among the principles of → philosophy, became with Parmenides (ca. 540-after 480) the mode of thinking that is most congruent with the one true being (→ Greek Philosophy). For him, as for Plato (427-347; → Platonism), knowledge does not derive from the changeable world of the senses but rests on unchangeable primal ideas (→ Epistemology). They are perceived by the mind as an "eye" of the → soul (§2) and are constantly recalled on the basis of an original acquaintance. Aristotle (384-322; → Aristotelianism), in contrast, stressed the sensory perceptions of the mind, which — given all the possibilities — is itself what it actually thinks. In the process of thought the mind focuses on what it thinks, and in these things it thinks itself. As mind or spirit, God, the origin of all movement, is thus determined.

Against this background a spiritualism developed in late antiquity in which, as in Stoicism (Seneca, Cicero), a substantialized *pneuma* (spirit) organically permeates the world, or, as in Neoplatonism (Plotinus, Porphyry), the *nous* (mind), especially in human beings, forms a connection between the supremely simple divine being and the emergent plurality of the cosmos. In distinction from the various → Gnostic systems, which assumed a → dualism of spirit and matter, Neoplatonic → monism understood the nonspiritual as nonexistent and conceived the one being as the goal for the ecstatic return of that which had derived by → emanation from it.

For → Augustine (354-430; → Augustine's Theology), who was under Neoplatonic influence, a substantialized concept of spirit helped to form both his concept of God and his religious pneumatology. Also under the influence of Neoplatonism was the older Christian → mysticism (§2; Dionysius the Pseudo-Areopagite, John Scotus Erigena), which focuses on the ascent of the soul to God that its spiritual nature makes possible.

3. Middle Ages, Reformation, and Pietism

Medieval German mysticism was an important influence, with its motif of union with God on the basis of the divine nature of the soul. Other influences were *devotio moderna* (new devotion), with its commendation of suffering as a way to God; Christian → humanism, with its ethic of development; and the Reformation concentration on salvation by subjective appropriation of → justification.

Against this background a radical Protestant theology developed in the 16th century that made either a mystic-ecstatic or a rational understanding of the work of spirit the principle of all religious life and thought. The very differently oriented groups, described polemically as *Schwärmer* (enthusiasts) by M. → Luther (1483-1546; → Luther's Theology), regarded dogma as the epitome of the objective facts of salvation, despised the visible church as a salvific institution and the Word and → sacraments as means of salvation, and upheld the subjective awareness of salvation, the invisible communion of the regenerate, and the working of God in the spirit.

Individualistic spiritualism differs from → Anabaptism by its scorning of all definite social forms of religion, though there were contacts in Upper Germany and Switzerland. We find here apocalyptic and revolutionary motifs (T. → Müntzer; → Apocalypticism 4; Millenarianism 5), but spiritualism stresses in fact the inwardness of the kingdom of God in a faith kindled in the spirit (A. Karlstadt, H. Denck, S. Franck). Ethically, it insists on → tolerance, and in an antinomian way (→ Antinomian Controversies) favors a → sanctification of the flesh in the spirit (K. Schwenckfeld). In the immediacy to God of this belief, which is both speculative and existential, spiritualism formed a bridge between the cosmological phenomenon of → nature and the nature of God, in which all life, even that of → evil, has its comprehensive place (Paracelsus, V. Weigel, J. Böhme).

Spiritualism was important in the relatively tolerant Netherlands (D. Coornheert), in which, as later also in England, regular spiritualistic societies flourished (Jorists, Familists [Family of Love], Labadists, and the Quakers). Influence was also exerted on → Pietism (J. Arndt, G. Arnold, J. K. Dippel) and on Protestant mysticism (D. Czepko, J. Scheffler). The basic motifs of the speculative direction, more than Reformation theology itself, anticipated the course of modern → Protestantism, with its emphasis on the subjectivity of faith in God.

4. Early Modern Period

Early modern philosophy increasingly dematerialized the mind or spirit and linked it to a self-embracing subjectivity of processes of consciousness (→ Subjectivism and Objectivism). Thus R. Descartes (1596-1650; → Cartesianism) viewed the mind as thought, which was contrasted with outward extension. B. Spinoza (1632-77; → Spinozism) turned this → dualism of spirit and body into speculative monism by seeing in thought and extension independent attributes of the intellectual divine substance, so that any difference between them lies always in a living, internal relation. G. W. Leibniz (1646-1716), however, viewed spirit as a perspectively individualized way of looking by monads at the processes of the universe, which God by "preestablished harmony" has joined together and also joined them to the lower world of the physical.

A development of English Platonism, with its stress on spirit as the supreme principle in world architecture (R. Cudworth, H. More), was the idealistic spiritualism of G. Berkeley (1685-1753), who went beyond the subject of perception to the thesis of *esse est percipi* (existence = perception). For him the body is not substantial but is a complex of ideas that God imparts to our self-contained spirit.

5. Classic German Philosophy

In contrast to this "dogmatic spiritualism," but also to an abstruse but influential spiritism (E. Swedenborg), I. Kant (1724-1804; → Kantianism) consequently carried the desubstantializing of the spirit to its goal by binding the unity of the consciousness functionally to the processes of its thinking, which is related to the manifold things in time and space that are given for our perception. If this position rules out any subjective spirit that makes it something objective, the question arises how it is to properly view itself.

Chronologically close to an aestheticization of the concept of spirit already seen in Kant, through which it symbolizes the conceptually unachievable view of the self as the enlivening principle of the mind (Kant) or even as "the life of life" (J. W. Goethe), the "intellectual intuition" advances in J. G. Fichte (1762-1814) to a central philosophical concept. Its use constitutes a nonconceptual self-relationship of the ego, which leads the ego to construct a world different from itself, which is necessary for its concrete determination. Thus the subjectivity of the spirit takes the place of the → absolute. This point finds expression in the early philosophy of F. W. J. Schelling (1775-1854), who, under Fichte's influence, argued that in light of intellectual intuition and for the sake of the relationship of the spirit to itself, the spirit unfolds its natural and historical genesis.

The systematic philosophy of G. W. F. Hegel (1770-1831; → Hegelianism) forms the high point of rational spiritualism. Here the absolute is the spirit insofar as it reveals the reflexiveness of subjectivity at the place of objectivity and contains in both an embedded, free, and symmetrical relationship of the self and others in full correspondence. The spirit does not simply comprehend nature but also is present in historical and cultural objectivations. This is the source of → religion as the best imaginative presentation of the absolute spirit that embodies a perfect correspondence of its concept and its reality. In it God is Spirit because it is part of his true determination to be truly realized in free → faith.

The rather different thinking of F. D. E. → Schleiermacher (1768-1834; → Schleiermacher's Theology) also has a spiritualist feature insofar as it conceives of religion as the culture of the self-dealings of human subjectivity and finds God in the common spirit of the total life that is instituted by Christ.

6. Nineteenth and Twentieth Centuries

In the 19th century the progress of science and history brought with it criticism of speculative spiritualism. Spirit, understood psychologically, and its cultural objectifications became the theme of empirical research (→ Empiricism). Against the materialist, positivist, or historicist drive to objectivity came the spiritualist protest related to the motifs of → Romanticism, which sought to anchor the rationality of reality in a spiritual divine being who gives himself to us in what is mainly intuitive faith (I. H. Fichte, C. H. Weisse, G. T. Fechner, R. H. Lotze; → Intuition). A spiritualist → metaphysics that resubstantializes spirit occurred also in French thinking during the 19th century (F. Maine de Biran, V. Cousin). It continues on in → vitalism (H. Bergson).

The legacy of German spiritualism made its mark in the irrational emphasizing of the higher independence of the spirit (R. Eucken), its ontological objectivity (N. Hartmann; → Ontology), and its vitalistic integration into the power of life (K. Joël; → Life 2). Life and spirit could also form the opposing principles of a universal → anthropology (M. Scheler). Since later idealistic spiritualism avoids rational investigation and, especially in the late 19th century, began to deal with supersensory phenomena, the concept of spiritualism largely disappeared from rational philosophy in the 20th century.

When explicit references are not made to older traditions, the 20th century, with the exception of the strictly monadological and subjective theory of the spirit in W. Cramer (1901-74), focused on the philosophical problems of the spirit under such terms as "existence," "the self," "history," → "society," or → "meaning." In the wake of the latest developments in the life sciences and the bioethical discussion of these developments, old controversies between spiritualism and materialism are breaking out in new paradoxes. While biotechnical and computer-technical visionaries see human life centered in the information content of the genome and want to preserve it in optimized mechanical storage media, the biological process of the merging of the sperm and the egg is valued in the conservative Christian view as the empirical conception of the image of God.

Philosophy and theology can evade the issues of a theory of the spirit only at the cost of leaving the level that has been reached because the point of interest is the contextualizing self-perception of human subjectivity as a whole. In the common legacy of thought in concepts of spirit and mind that links theology and → philosophy, and under an ascetic use of the term "spiritualism," the theme of a theory of the spirit offers a fruitful field for modern discussion between philosophy and theology.

Bibliography: H. Bornkamm, *Luther's World of Thought* (St. Louis, 1958); idem, *Mystik, Spiritualismus und die Anfänge des Pietismus in Luthertum* (Giessen, 1926) • H.-P. Dürr and C. Zimmerli, eds., *Geist und Natur. Über den Widerspruch zwischen naturwissenschaftlicher Erkenntnis und philosophischen Welterfahrung* (Bern, 1989) • H. Fast, ed., *Der linke Flügel der Reformation. Glaubenszeugnisse der Täufer, Spiritualisten, Schwärmer und Antitrinitarier* (Bremen, 1962) • B. R. Hoffman, *Luther and the Mystics* (Minneapolis, 1976) • A. Jacob, *De naturae natura: A Study of Idealistic Conceptions of Nature and the Unconscious* (Stuttgart, 1992) • C. W. Marsh, *The Family of Love in English Society, 1550-1630* (Cambridge, 1993) • T. J. Saxby, *The Quest for the New Jerusalem: Jean de Labadie and the Labadists, 1610-1744* (Dordrecht, 1987) • A. Séguenny, *Spiritualistische Philosophie als Antwort auf die religiöse Frage des XVI. Jahrhunderts* (Wiesbaden, 1978) • E. Troeltsch, *The Social Teaching of the Christian Churches* (2 vols.; Louisville, Ky., 1992) 2.729-807, "Mysticism and Spiritual Idealism" • F.-W. Wentzlaff-Eggebert, *Deutsche Mystik zwischen Mittelalter und Neuzeit* (3d ed.; Berlin, 1969) • G. H. Williams, *The Radical Reformation* (3d ed.; Kirksville, Mo., 1992; orig. pub., 1962).

Jörg Dierken

Spirituality

Overview

Overview

Since the latter decades of the 20th century, the term "spirituality" has taken on increasing prominence within North American Christianity and popular culture. While a large majority of adults in the United States professes belief in God, how such belief is expressed and lived has shifted dramatically in these decades, and "spirituality" is a catchword for such change; being "spiritual but not religious" defines large numbers of Americans, particularly in younger generations. And people construct their spirituality in ways that can seem amorphous, idiosyncratic, or resistant to definition.

To define the term, a look at its etymology may help. "Spirituality" translates Lat. *spiritualitas,* a noun derived in the fifth century from *spiritualiter,* the Lat. equivalent of the NT Gk. *pneumatikos,* "spiritual" (from Gk. *pneuma,* "spirit"). Within Paul's → anthropology, flesh and spirit *(sarx* and *pneuma)* refer not to a body/soul dualism but, respectively, to life apart from or life rooted in the living Spirit of Jesus Christ. To the extent that the whole being — body and soul — of persons participates in the reality of God opened in Jesus Christ through the Holy Spirit, such persons are *pneumatikoi* (1 Cor. 3:1; Gal. 6:1). Thus the NT language from which the term "spirituality" arose had a holistic orientation encompassing physical, emotional/psychic, and ethical/social dimensions of persons' lives, as well as their relationship with God.

Over the centuries, however, the term took on a strongly dualistic flavor (B. McGinn). Moving into English via French Roman Catholic thinkers, the term often carried connotations of body-denying or otherworldly private interiority. In English-language contexts, however, two movements bearing on the meaning of the term took place in the 20th century. As non-Catholic writers adopted the language of spirituality, and as Roman Catholics after → Vatican II rethought categories of sanctity and the Chris-

tian life, "spirituality" in contemporary Christian understanding has generally come to reflect a world- and body-embracing reality: in effect, a turn toward the original Pauline inflection of the term. Yet at the same time the term has also moved far beyond the Christian context, resulting in a bewildering diversity of meanings. What, then, *is* spirituality?

Scholars have distinguished three levels of meaning for the term (W. Principe). First, one may speak of spirituality at the most basic level as a person's primal, conscious (even if unarticulated) experience of participation in ultimate reality as he or she understands it — for Christians, in the reality of the triune God disclosed in Jesus Christ. Sandra Schneiders has developed a definition that encompasses both religiously framed and nonreligious spiritualities: "spirituality" refers to "the experience of conscious involvement in the project of life integration through self-transcendence toward the ultimate value one perceives" (1998, 1 and 3). This first level of experiential participation in or toward one's ultimate reality is that to which people typically refer when they speak of the mystery of another person's spirituality or of wanting to develop their own spirituality.

At a second level, we speak of spirituality as such experience of ultimate reality takes articulated or expressive form in some way, as people give words or some other tangible expression to their first-level experience. Here "spirituality" refers to what is mediated in the writings, → liturgies, → hymns, poetry, visual art, journals, sermons, actions, and so forth of a person or group of people, making their experience in some way accessible to others. Thus one might speak of being interested in Dietrich → Bonhoeffer's spirituality or in Anabaptist or Russian Orthodox spirituality. As at the first level, we are still speaking of an experience of God or ultimate reality, but here we have in mind such experience as expressed or discerned in historical or present-day artifacts — written, verbal, or enacted forms — that give some expression to experience of God.

Finally, one may speak of spirituality on a third level as the scholarly investigation of these historical or contemporary glimpses of human God-experience: the academic discipline of, for example, Christian spirituality. The remainder of this entry explores primarily this third meaning of spirituality, with reference specifically to the scholarly study of the *Christian* experience of God.

Within this discipline, a variety of types of study has emerged. Some scholars examine the history of Christian spirituality, tracing particular figures or movements or texts/artifacts, including biblical texts, with an eye to the ways people interpreted and negotiated their experience of the Christian God within their social, cultural, gendered context and personal circumstances (see, e.g., the scriptural and historical essays in the *Blackwell Companion to Christian Spirituality* [A. Holder] and the *New Westminster Dictionary of Christian Spirituality* [P. Sheldrake]; see 1, 5). Other scholars look at contemporary Christian experience in various cultures or social or gendered locations (see 2-4); essays in the dictionaries cited in the bibliography provide many more. Some works in Christian spirituality trace topical questions such as the shape of → mysticism or images of God and the embodied human person in a given spiritual context, or the role of nonviolence or particular art forms for a given person or tradition; still others treat methodological questions such as the role of the Bible or theology in norming and reflecting Christian spiritual expression.

As may be obvious from even this brief sketch, investigation into phenomena as complex and diverse as Christian experiences of God requires both exquisite care in negotiating the relative locations of scholar and person(s) under study and a rigorous, interdisciplinary methodology able to trace the interwoven questions of, for example, history, → sociology, → psychology, literary analysis, gender dynamics, or → culture — or some other fields altogether — that the experience of the figure(s) under study may call for. This breadth of consideration gives rise to two implications for the study of Christian spirituality.

First, such study *requires attention to hermeneutical questions* (Schneiders 1998 and 2005; → Hermeneutics). Whether the text in question is an actual writing or, for example, an art form, a political legacy, a sermon, or an institutionalized practice, such a text can be encountered as potentially mediating human God-experience only by means of interpretation.

Second, given how conceptually slippery is "experience," the term at the center of this discipline, a further implication of the complexity of its study is that the discipline *focuses paradigmatically on the particular*. If → systematic theology attempts to articulate categories for communicating Christian truth about God, Jesus Christ, or human persons in general, Christian spirituality traces how, within that larger theological story, *particular* persons or movements actually seem to have constructed their identity or lived their life or articulated their faith in encounter with God. Because experience includes resonances of meaning determined by circumstances of language, culture/social location, and personal narrative — resonances never the same for others, no matter how intuitively similar they may appear — work in Christian spirituality becomes more powerful not at ever higher levels of abstraction but at ever more fine-grained levels of particularity, for only there is the degree of attention this complexity requires feasible. To speak meaningfully of *Christian* spirituality is possible; to speak of *Anglican* spirituality, more precise; and to speak of the spirituality of *Desmond Tutu*, as a particular Anglican Christian, allows for a nuanced study attuned to the complexity of human experience of God.

If the subject matter of Christian spirituality is profoundly personal, its study becoming more vivid and fine-grained as its particularity of focus increases, this emphasis could seem to suggest a diffusing of what is distinctively Christian as particularity devolves into idiosyncrasy. What, after all, could an analysis of the eucharistic devotions of a convent of Benedictine nuns in 14th-century Germany share with a study of conversion narratives among African-American Baptists in mid-20th-century Alabama? Or with ways NT accounts of Jesus' temptation functioned among early desert monastics? Yet for all its staggering complexity and diversity across time and space, reflective of the unrepeatable distinctiveness of each human being in his or her actual embodied/gendered/cultured experience of God, Christian spiritual life shares in common experience of *this God:* encounter with the triune mystery revealed in Jesus Christ. Each study in this discipline opens some glimpse into particular human refractions of that primal, life-transforming encounter at the heart of every authentic Christian spirituality. From his Nazi prison cell in 1945, Dietrich Bonhoeffer (1906-45) wrestled with the question of "who Christ really is, for us today" (p. 279); and to the extent it is truly Jesus Christ being encountered — the one known in Scripture, attested in creeds and doctrines, tasted and heard and touched in Word and sacrament, liturgy and music, art and icon, and the compounding plethora of practices and devotions, desires, actions, and lives flowing forth from this Word made flesh — then all Christian experience does have some recognizable familial relationship. Precisely in probing the particular one discerns the Incarnate. And some degree of attention to the Incarnate One characterizes and connects the most disparate-seeming Christian experiences, even as the forms of experience, modes of its articulation, or scholarly tools used to trace these are indeed diverse.

Questions of discernment thus prove to be central not only to the Christian spiritual life but to the scholarship devoted to studying such life. The scholar brings explicit and implicit conceptions of how encounter with the triune Christian God "looks," and such conceptions not only shape what in the subject's experience the scholar chooses to pursue but will themselves be challenged precisely by the otherness of the subject's experience. The study of Christian spirituality can itself become a mediation of the life-transforming encounter with God under study. For this reason scholars in the discipline speak of the "self-implicating" nature of this scholarship, itself a complex question (see E. A. Dreyer and M. S. Burrows, pt. 2). And emerging with the discipline in a postmodern world, debate continues as to the place of the scholar's own Christian spiritual practice within the overall process of research, study, teaching, and contribution to the field. That is, are practicing Christians the best ones to study Christian spirituality?

Bibliography: D. BONHOEFFER, *Letters and Papers from Prison* (ed. E. Bethge; enlarged ed.; New York, 1972) • S. CHASE, *The Tree of Life: Models of Christian Prayer* (Grand Rapids, 2005) • K. J. COLLINS, ed., *Exploring Christian Spirituality: An Ecumenical Reader* (Grand Rapids, 2000) • M. DOWNEY, *Understanding Christian Spirituality* (New York, 1997) • E. A. DREYER and M. S. BURROWS, eds., *Minding the Spirit: The Study of Christian Spirituality* (Baltimore, 2005) • A. HOLDER, ed., *The Blackwell Companion to Christian Spirituality* (Oxford, 2005) • B. P. HOLT, *Thirsty for God: A Brief History of Christian Spirituality* (2d ed.; Minneapolis, 2005) • B. H. LESCHER and E. LIEBERT, eds., *Exploring Christian Spirituality* (New York, 2006) • R. MAAS and G. O'DONNELL, eds., *Spiritual Traditions for the Contemporary Church* (Nashville, 1990) • B. McGINN, "The Letter and the Spirit: Spirituality as an Academic Discipline," *CSBull* 1/2 (Fall 1993) 1-10 • M. A. McINTOSH, *Discernment and Truth: The Spirituality and Theology of Knowledge* (New York, 2004) • P. H. PFATTEICHER, *Liturgical Spirituality* (Valley Forge, Pa., 1997) • W. PRINCIPE, "Toward Defining Spirituality," *Exploring Christian Spirituality,* ed. Collins, 43-60 • S. M. SCHNEIDERS, "Approaches to the Study of Christian Spirituality," *The Blackwell Companion to Christian Spirituality* (ed. A. Holder; Oxford, 2005) 15-33; eadem, "A Hermeneutical Approach to the Study of Christian Spirituality," *CSBull* 2/1 (Spring 1994) 9-14; eadem, "The Study of Christian Spirituality: Contours and Dynamics of a Discipline," *CSBull* 6/1 (Spring 1998) 1-12 • P. SHELDRAKE, *Spirituality and History: Questions of Interpretation and Method* (2d ed.; London, 1998); idem, *Spirituality and Theology: Christian Living and the Doctrine of God* (London, 1999); idem, ed., *The New Westminster Dictionary of Christian Spirituality* (Louisville, Ky., 2005) • *Spiritus: A Journal of Christian Spirituality* (Baltimore) www.press.jhu.edu/journals/spiritus • R. J. WOODS, *Christian Spirituality: God's Presence through the Ages* (exp. ed.; Maryknoll, N.Y., 2006).

LISA E. DAHILL

1. Old Christendom

1.1. *Content and Theological Location*

As faithful existence in the → Holy Spirit, Christian spirituality is characterized at all levels and in all realms by *dying to sin* and *living for God* (Romans 6). Ritually, this process is initially expressed by the solemn renunciation of → evil and the profession of the creed (in the Orthodox liturgy of initiation, an "about-face" is enacted whereby the candidate leaves [*apotaxis*] the ranks of Satan and enlists [*syntaxis*] with Christ and the Holy Trinity). Sacramentally, one is given a share in the death and resurrection of Christ (in → baptism) and in his sacrifice and his communion with the Father in the divine kingdom (in the → Eucharist). Ethically, the Christian aims to root out the works of the flesh and to cultivate the fruits of the Spirit (Galatians 5). The history of spiritual theology speaks of ascesis (discipline) and mysticism (communion). The acme of Christian spirituality is a martyr's death, which ensures immediate access to the → kingdom of heaven.

Spirituality is a meeting point for Christian dogma and local culture. The focus of this encounter resides chiefly in → soteriology, that is, the saving work of Christ and its appropriation. Here the following questions are of central importance: How is the human condition after the fall understood? What has the Redeemer done to repair the deficit? How is salvation conceived and experienced? The various answers given to these questions are culturally conditioned, while in turn the gospel of Jesus Christ has played its own part in the development of particular cultures. Christian spirituality is in principle universal at the same time as it is culturally particular; thus there are "saints" whose fame is spread throughout the whole church, while the recognition of others is regionally limited.

1.2. *Geographic-Cultural Typology*

The spirituality of old Christendom can be sketched according to a geographic and cultural typology that is in part historical. In many regions (see 1.2.1-5) a symbiosis between → faith and → culture predominates; in others (see 1.2.6-8) the contrast between the two is more apparent.

1.2.1. *Greek*

According to → Athanasius of Alexandria (ca. 297-373), whose treatise *On the Incarnation* is a principal source of Eastern Orthodox soteriology, human fallenness consists in a loss of being, which springs from culpable ignorance toward God. This condition can be described as blindness and darkness. To reverse this mortal decay, the creative Logos became incarnate as Jesus Christ, whose teaching and entire life served the renewal of the knowledge of God among humankind. By his resurrection he brought → life and → immortality to light (2 Tim. 1:10). His saving work may be designated enlightenment or illumination.

Here Christian soteriology is conceived on the backdrop of a Platonic ontology and epistemology. The Hellenistic concept of *theōria* is matched by a spirituality of vision and light. The contemplation of sacred → icons gives insight into the divine figures, who thereby make themselves present and open to veneration. Looking at the Lord radiant with the light of heaven (the transfiguration and resurrection of Jesus are favorite themes in iconography) has a transformative effect on believers, who are changed by the Spirit from glory unto glory according to the likeness of the Lord (2 Cor. 3:18).

The inward efficacy of → contemplation depends on God's own → incarnation and leads to the "divinization" (→ Theosis) of human beings. By the Holy Spirit, who rested and remains on the Son of God, believers are made partakers of the divine nature (2 Pet. 1:4). The most intimate instance of communion between God and human beings is the sharing that the Spirit accords us in Christ's flesh and blood in the Eucharist. By its concretely corporeal character, Christianity is clearly distinguished from Platonic philosophy but also is brought close to the Hellenistic → mystery religions.

As the Jesus Prayer demonstrates (→ Prayer 3.4), Greek spirituality is marked by a Christological concentration: "Lord Jesus Christ, Son of God, have mercy upon me" is prayed with the rhythm of breathing. But the context and range of this prayer is Trinitarian. Christian existence finds its beginning and end in the Holy Trinity. The unity of each individual human being and the unity of human beings together is achieved in personal communion with the one God, who is himself a tri-unity. Thus the problem of the one and the many — a theme of Greek as of other philosophies — is resolved in a salutary manner.

The eternal God, however, remains transcendent over his creatures, so that human knowledge of God is always qualified by an initial and final reserve — *apophasis,* or negation (Gregory of Nyssa, *The Life of Moses*; → Apophatic Theology). Patristic spirituality finds its continuation or renewal in Simeon the New Theologian (949-1022), Gregory Palamas (ca. 1296-1359; → Palamism), the → *Philocalia* of Nicodemus of the Holy Mountain (ca. 1749-1809), and the Hesychastic revival of the 20th century (→ Hesychasm).

1.2.2. *Roman*

The chief legacy of Roman civilization lies in the area of → law. Latin soteriology reckons with the justice of God, which is both strict and generous. The feudal version of it is the satisfaction theory of → Anselm of Canterbury (1033-1109). The moral life is governed by the *lex Christi* (Gal. 6:2), which supplies precepts and counsels.

The character of Roman Christianity was displayed also in the → liturgy. In contrast to the picturesque, emotional, and prolix style of the Frankish and Visigothic rites of Gaul and Spain, the ideas of the Roman liturgy are "simple and elementary," its expressions "pregnant and precise," its actions "plain and practical," and its ceremonies "solemn and imposing": "Mystery never flourished in the clear Roman atmosphere, and symbolism was no product of the Roman religious mind" (E. Bishop, 10).

The *lex romana* was accompanied by military energy. Characteristic of Roman (Catholic) spirituality is the multiplicity of → "religious orders," whether the → Benedictines, oriented to a central rule of common life in the monastery and to the daily office as *opus Dei;* or the → Dominicans, as an "order of preachers" directed to the spreading of "the true faith"; or the → Jesuits, devoted to the special service of the → pope. Over the centuries the saints canonized by Rome have come predominantly from the ranks of the religious orders and congregations. These saints are held up to laypeople and "secular priests" for their inspiration and as models of the Christian life.

1.2.3. *Celtic*

Much remains obscure about the pre-Christian Celts. From their use of animal and plant forms in ornamentation it is possible to deduce a sense of closeness to nature. The harmonious control of the cosmic powers was probably important to them. In this context, the Christ who stilled the storm (Matt. 8:23-27) and is now enthroned at God's right hand (Phil. 2:9-11; Col. 3:1; Heb. 1:3) could be received as "high king of heaven."

An Irish "breastplate-prayer" *(lorica)* of the eighth or ninth century, traditionally attributed to St. Patrick (mid or late 5th cent.), has a Trinitarian framework ("I bind unto myself today the strong name of the Trinity") and a Christological center ("Christ be with me"). Redemption is brought into the context of → creation and continued in God's providential care of the believer: the believer first binds to himself (in C. F. Alexander's translation) "Christ's incarnation, his baptism in the Jordan river, his death on [the] cross for my salvation, his bursting from the spicèd tomb, his riding up the heavenly way, his coming at the day of doom"; then "the virtues of the starlit heaven, the glorious sun's life-giving ray, the whiteness of the moon at even, the flashing of the lightning free, the whirling wind's tempestuous shocks, the stable earth, the deep salt sea around the old eternal rocks"; and finally "the power of God to hold and lead, his eye to watch, his might to stay, his ear to hearken to my need, the wisdom of my God to teach, his hand to guide, his shield to ward, the word of God to give me speech, his heavenly host to be my guide."

That Celtic Christian spirituality is no mere matter of sentiment is shown by the fact that Irish piety often expressed itself in harsh ordeals of faith "in the desert" (lengthy immersion of the body in cold streams etc.), difficult → pilgrimages, and even voluntary exile. From Ireland stems also the practice of private penance that was taken by missionaries to the European continent.

1.2.4. *Germanic*

How Christ could be received by a warrior society may be read from the ninth-century Saxon gospel, *The → Heliand.* According to this diatessaron the runes of the "godspell" were written and sung by four heroes in the following way (borrowing G. R. Murphy's translation): The chieftain of mankind *(manno drohtin)* was born in David's fort; three lords from the East bring gifts to the all-ruler's child; the people's protector is immersed in the Jordan by his loyal thane John; the country's guardian fights off the loathsome enemy in the desert; the mighty rescuer chooses 12 from his retinue to be his companions; Christ enters Fort Jerusalem; he eats his last mead-hall feast with his men; before the final battle even the mightiest of kings kneels to the ground in prayer; his precious sweat drips down like blood welling out of wounds; Peter the swordsman defends him boldly; God's own son is hanged from the criminal tree; God's peace-child rises up, as the noble ladies report from the grave; the risen Christ joins the two heroes on their way to the castle at Emmaus. In short: "The many bolts on the doors of hell were unlocked; the road from this world up to heaven was built."

According to Gustav Aulén's study *Christus Victor* (1930), the conquering Christ constituted the "classic" description of redemption in the writings of → Irenaeus (ca. 130-ca. 200) and other → church fathers. Son of God and son of man, Jesus Christ by his cross and resurrection has defeated the hostile powers of sin, death, and the devil. Martin → Luther (1483-1546) rediscovered this powerful image for Christ's work of salvation (notably in "A Mighty Fortress"). In J. S. Bach's *St. John Passion,* John 19:30 is rendered: "Judah's hero gains a mighty victory and ends the strife: It is finished." Believers are indeed "under attack" *(angefochten),* for they fight not against human enemies but against the evil spirits of this dark world; but they have the complete armor of God, the breastplate of righteousness, the shield of faith, the helmet of salvation, and the sword of the Spirit, which is the word of God (Eph. 6:10-20); and through Christ they are "more than conquerors" (Rom. 8:37).

1.2.5. *Modern Western*

Since the → Renaissance, Western culture has been marked by a new → humanism, whose soteriology was already prepared in the writings of Peter Abelard (1079-1142). The love of God revealed in Christ is to be received, answered, imitated, and spread among humankind. The humanity of Christ is underlined, and his religious life and moral conduct are taken as exemplary.

The Song of Songs becomes the source of a bridal → mysticism between Christ and the human soul (already in → Bernard of Clairvaux [1090-1153] and → Catherine of Siena [1347-80]). → Francis of Assisi (1181/82-1226) concentrates on the birth of Christ (Francis is credited with having made the first model of the crib), Christ's poverty (Francis was devoted to "Lady Poverty," "la Povertà"), and Christ's passion (Francis received the stigmata). Thomas à Kempis recommends the "imitation of Christ" by the *via purgativa* and the *via illuminativa.* French-speaking Christianity knows the "pious humanism" of Francis de Sales (1567-1622) and Jane Frances de Chantal (1572-1641), as well as the eucharistic piety of Pierre de Bérulle (1575-1629), known as the Apostolus Verbi Incarnati (based on his major work *Grandeurs de Jésus* [1623]; → Eucharistic Spirituality). Spain has both the Christ mysticism of → Teresa of Ávila (1515-82) and John of the Cross (1542-91) and — in the land of St. James, *caballero de Cristo* (→ Santiago Cult 4) — the quasi-military Company of Jesus of → Ignatius Loyola (1491-1556).

In England, → Julian of Norwich (ca. 1342-after 1416) depicts Christ as our mother. The *Scale of Perfection* of Walter Hilton (ca. 1343-96) announces the theme of moral earnestness that will characterize English spirituality in various forms, whether Calvinistic Puritanism (John Bunyan, *The Pilgrim's Progress*), classic Anglicanism (Jeremy Taylor, *Holy*

Living and *Holy Dying;* William Law, *A Serious Call to a Devout and Holy Life*), or Methodism (John → Wesley's perfectionism).

In Switzerland and the Low Countries, the Calvinistic reform met cultures ripe for the rise of the → bourgeoisie and mercantilism. The elect exercise their divine calling in human professions; worldly success is to be sought as a confirmation of election.

In the 18th century, western and central Europe experienced a so-called → Enlightenment, which set the older humanism on the road to a rationalistic anthropocentrism that was in large part critical of religion (→ Religion, Criticism of). → Rationalism was countered in Germany by → Pietism and in England by → Methodism. Yet here also there was a danger that such spiritualities as these latter would emphasize the "experience" of believers in a one-sidedly subjective way. Thus in the 19th and 20th centuries many contemporaries achieved at best a reverence for the purely human Jesus as teacher and example (e.g., A. → Schweitzer).

1.2.6. *Coptic-Syrian*
Already in the → early church, some Christians desired to distance themselves not only spiritually but also physically from the world of heathen civilization. This movement of withdrawal or retirement (i.e., → anchoritism) gained in attraction after the Christianization of the Roman Empire had turned the church in a worldly direction. → Monasticism, which took forms both solitary (eremetical) and communal (coenobitic), entailed criticism not only of society but also of the church. Biblically, the desert was the place of Jesus' → temptations — and his faithfulness (Matt. 4:1-11). His later disciples followed him into the wildernesses of Egypt and Syria. (Syria witnessed the strange sight of pillar-saints [→ stylites] and tree-saints [dendrites].) Monasticism remains for the Eastern Orthodox churches a prophetic testimony to the kingdom of God; in the Western Catholic tradition the religious life is known as "white martyrdom."

1.2.7. *Russian*
The conversion of Russia had both its political and its aesthetic dimensions (one need only remember the report of the ambassadors from Prince Vladimir of Kiev concerning the worship in the Church of the Holy Wisdom at Constantinople), and a certain symbiosis between faith and culture has maintained itself in the liturgical and iconographic splendor found at both imperial and popular levels (→ Russian Orthodox Church 1). But a "Syrian" line, too, is found in the cave communities of Kiev.

Specially characteristic of the critical spirituality of Russia are the *yurodivye*, the so-called holy idiots,

or "fools for the sake of Christ" (1 Cor. 4:10; see also 3:18), whose crazy behavior bears witness to the foolishness of God, which in the cross of Christ showed itself wiser than human wisdom (1 Cor. 1:18–2:16). A well-known example is Basil of Moscow (1468-1552); in literature, the "Idiot" of Dostoyevsky (1821-81) belongs to the *yurodivye*.

1.2.8. *Anabaptist*
Unlike the revolutionary Thomas → Müntzer (ca. 1489-1525), the majority of → Anabaptists took the way of → pacifism, and indeed often in the face of severe → persecution. (According to Conrad Grebel, true Christians are like sheep among wolves.) Their stories are told in *The Bloody Theater; or, Martyrs' Mirror* of Thieleman Janszoon van Braght (1625-64). They understood themselves as faithful followers of Jesus, instructed by the → Sermon on the Mount. (No one can truly know Christ without following him in life, said Hans Denk.) As the "little flock" (Luke 12:32), they established their own communities distinguished by their plain lifestyles in contrast to social luxury, as well as by the distance they took from civil authorities. Many fled from Switzerland and the Netherlands and found refuge in North America, where they have contributed to the variegated pattern of religious freedom.

1.3. *Twentieth Century*
Through the modern means of communication the earth became in the 20th century a "global village" in which the exchange of information and goods was unhappily accompanied also by the intensification of conflicts. At the level of spirituality, the ecumenical movement among Christians did not lead to uniformity but rather developed toward an eclectic communion of traditions (→ Ecumenism, Ecumenical Movement). In Africa, memory returned to the pre-Christian cultural heritage insofar as it represents a "preparation for the gospel." In Asia, there was much interest in dialogue with non-Christian religions, and many spoke — whether in approval or rejection — of → syncretism. At stake soteriologically was the unique status and universal role of Jesus Christ (Acts 4:12; see the declaration *Dominus Iesus* issued by the Roman Congregation for the Doctrine of the Faith in 2000).

In the 1960s many Western liberal theologians (under the influence of the methodological atheism of the natural sciences, the psychological atheism of Sigmund Freud, the philosophical and moral atheism of Friedrich → Nietzsche, and the political atheism of Karl → Marx, as well as the sociologically observed privatization of religion in North Atlantic societies) spoke of a process of → "secularization," which should lead to a → "religionless Christianity."

Appeal was made to a paradoxical saying in the later writings of Dietrich → Bonhoeffer (1906-45): In a world come of age, one should live before God as though there were no God (*etsi Deus non daretur*).

By the 1980s, reports of the "death of God" turned out to have been exaggerated (→ God Is Dead Theology). Among evangelicals and Pentecostals, many began seeking to understand their place in the larger Christian tradition. Within the mainstream churches were to be found not only a recovery of some classical interests but also liberationist (see 3) and feminist (see 4) approaches to spirituality. Attention and energies were devoted to the healing of fissures in human society and to the preservation of the natural environment.

At the turn of the century, two figures emerged as the leading paradigms of saints in the making: Mother Teresa (1910-97), Albanian Catholic nun and caretaker of the dirt-poor in the slums of Calcutta; and Pope John Paul II (1920-2005), pastor, poet, philosopher, politician, an active man whose final years of suffering demonstrated strength perfected in weakness (see 2 Cor. 12:9).

1.4. *Today and Tomorrow*

The last two decades of the 20th century saw a flurry of publications at various levels containing the phrase "Christian spirituality" in their titles. By the first decade of the 21st century, however, the word "spirituality" — this time with no qualifying adjective — had also become the favored term in the sophisticated West for a vague, subjectivist, gnostically inclined religiosity that wished to have no connection with "organized religion," and certainly not with "institutional Christianity."

Apart from any "reevangelization" of old Christendom, two factors at the global level may help to preserve or restore the association of the word "spirituality" with the Holy Spirit, third person of the Trinity as confessed by the Christian faith: first, the "southward shift" in the demographics and energy of Christendom seems to be producing a form of ecclesial life with a marked "pentecostal," or at least "pneumatic," flavor; second, the apparently growing likelihood of martyrdom for the sake of Christ in some parts of the world will be a reminder that the ultimate witness cannot be made, as → Tertullian recognized, "unless the Spirit of God is in us" (*Adv. Prax.* 39; → Martyrs).

Bibliography: General: L. Bouyer et al., *History of Christian Spirituality,* vol. 1, *The Spirituality of the NT and the Fathers;* vol. 2, *The Spirituality of the Middle Ages;* vol. 3, *Orthodox Spirituality and Protestant and Anglican Spirituality* (New York, 1982) • L. S. Cunningham and K. J. Egan, *Christian Spirituality: Themes from the Tradition* (Mahwah, N.J., 1996) • C. Jones, G. Wainwright, and E. Yarnold, eds., *The Study of Spirituality* (London, 1986) • J. A. Jungmann, *Christian Prayer through the Centuries* (New York, 1978) • B. McGinn et al., *Christian Spirituality,* vol. 1, *Origins to the Twelfth Century;* vol. 2, *High Middle Ages and Reformation;* vol. 3, *Post-Reformation and Modern* (New York, 1985-89) • J. Pelikan, *Jesus through the Centuries: His Place in the History of Culture* (New Haven, 1985) • P. Sheldrake, ed., *The New Westminster Dictionary of Christian Spirituality* (Louisville, Ky., 2005) • J. R. Tyson, ed., *Invitation to Christian Spirituality: An Ecumenical Anthology* (New York, 1999) • M. Viller et al., eds., *Dictionnaire de spiritualité ascétique et mystique. Doctrine et histoire* (16 vols.; Paris, 1932-94) • G. Wainwright, "Christian Spirituality," *EncRel(E)* 3.452-60 • R. Williams, *Christian Spirituality: A Theological History from the NT to Luther and St. John of the Cross* (Atlanta, 1979) • R. J. Woods, *Christian Spirituality: God's Presence through the Ages* (exp. ed.; Maryknoll, N.Y., 2006).

Special topics: J. Aumann, *Christian Spirituality in the Catholic Tradition* (San Francisco, 1985) • E. Bishop, *Liturgica Historica* (Oxford, 1918) 1-19 ("The Genius of the Roman Rite") • D. Burton-Christie, *The Word in the Desert: Scripture and the Quest for Holiness in Early Christian Monasticism* (New York, 1993) • C. W. Bynum, *Jesus as Mother: Studies in the Spirituality of the High Middle Ages* (Berkeley, Calif., 1982); eadem, *Wonderful Blood: Theology and Practice in Late Medieval Northern Germany and Beyond* (Philadelphia, 2007) • N. K. Chadwick, *The Age of the Saints in the Early Celtic Church* (London, 1961) • C. Davis, ed., *English Spiritual Writers: From Aelfric of Eynsham to Ronald Knox* (London, 1961) • D. Freydank and G. Sturm, eds., *Das Väterbuch des Kiewer Höhlenklosters* (Leipzig, 1988) • L. Gillet, *The Jesus Prayer* (Crestwood, N.Y., 1987) • D. B. Hart, *The Beauty of the Infinite: The Aesthetics of Christian Truth* (Grand Rapids, 2003) • A. Louth, *The Origins of the Christian Mystical Tradition: From Plato to Denys* (Oxford, 1981) • G. L. Mantzaridis, *The Deification of Man: St. Gregory Palamas and the Orthodox Tradition* (Crestwood, N.Y., 1984) • G. R. Murphy, *The Heliand: The Saxon Gospel* (New York, 1992) • J. Saward, *Perfect Fools: Folly for Christ's Sake in Catholic and Orthodox Spirituality* (Oxford, 1980) • F. Senn, ed., *Protestant Spiritual Traditions* (New York, 1986) • P. Sheldrake, *Spirituality and History: Questions of Interpretation and Method* (New York, 1992); idem, *Spirituality and Theology: Christian Living and the Doctrine of God* (Maryknoll, N.Y., 1998) • W. M. Thompson, *Christology and Spirituality* (New York, 1991) • G. Wainwright, "The Holy

Spirit," *The Cambridge Companion to Christian Doctrine* (ed. G. Gunton; Cambridge, 1997) 273-96; idem, *The Holy Spirit, Witness, and Martyrdom: The Duquesne University Annual Holy Spirit Lecture* (Pittsburgh, 2006) • D. WEINSTEIN and R. M. BELL, *Saints and Society: The Two Worlds of Western Christendom* (Chicago, 1982) • F. M. YOUNG, *Brokenness and Blessing: Towards a Biblical Spirituality* (Grand Rapids, 2007). Many primary sources appear in the series "The Classics of Western Spirituality," published by Paulist Press and SPCK.

GEOFFREY WAINWRIGHT

2. African

Spirituality belongs firmly to the interconnected realms of religious belief, → faith, practice, and → experience. The word itself relates directly to Lat. *spiritus,* "breath" or "spirit," which renders Heb. *rûaḥ* and Gk. *pneuma,* each of which the Bible uses to refer to the → Holy Spirit. The Spirit of God is always God at work in his → creation. Thus in the creation stories of the Book of Genesis, the Spirit, or "breath/wind" of God, breathes life into a lifeless human form and restores order to a chaotic expanse of previously unconnected elements, just as the Holy Spirit invigorates the disciples for Christian mission at → Pentecost.

"God is spirit," and this sense of "spirit" as invisible presence is found in most religious traditions. In the context of religion, therefore, the existence of spirit beings implies a powerful world of the "wholly other," the *numen,* "sacred" or "holy," to which humans beings look for life and animation. This thought of a primordial spirit as the source of life and the ground of being is familiar to African → mythology. In Africa the relationship between humans and the spirit world is defined by a set of religious or numinous experiences, ritual observances, and practices that are meant to shore up life in a powerless and uncertain human world in anticipation of filling it with meaning and purpose. This is the end to which spirituality is generally directed.

2.1. *Cosmology*

The nature and sources of African traditional spirituality are thus located in the ontological realities of the peoples of Africa. In the African context certain routine and formal activities and behavior, whether overtly religious or not, are deemed to possess religious dimensions requiring the performance of ritual and the observance of religious protocol. Celebrations of festivals, installations of chiefs, the clearing of farms, the felling of particular trees, rites of passage, prayers, meditations, pilgrimages, sacrifices, offerings, and private and public morality may

all be accompanied by religious observances meant to sustain the relationships between human beings and their objects of worship. Spirituality therefore becomes an ongoing human quest for deeper relationships with transcendence through the observance of religious exercises, rites, and rituals, including paying attention to personal and communal obligations. Within the traditional African worldviews or African religiocultural realities, these elements define spirituality in indigenous contexts.

The African worldview assumes the presence of two asymmetrical realms of existence in the universe: the physical and the spiritual, or the world of humans and the world of spirits. Unlike in contemporary Western philosophical thought, however, the two worlds are not neatly compartmentalized. In African cosmology there are usually no fine distinctions made between the sacred and secular realms of life (→ Sacred and Profane). The natural and supernatural, the seen and unseen, the physical and spiritual worlds encroach upon each other, leading to general descriptions of Africans as being "deeply," "notoriously," or even "incurably" religious.

African cosmology includes many features, but five are particularly important for defining the parameters of African spirituality.

2.1.1. There is a basic and strong belief in *transcendent realities*. This transcendent world features the existence of a Supreme Being conceived of in the various traditions as Almighty God, who is also creator of the universe. Among the Mende of Sierra Leone, God is Leve (Supreme Creator); the Akan of Ghana call him Onyame (Creator and All-Sufficient One); the Ibo of Nigeria call him Chineke (Creator) or Chuku (Great Spirit), and in the same Nigerian context, the Yoruba call him Olodumare (Almighty or Supreme God). The ontological meaning of the Gye Nyame (lit. "except God"), symbol of the Akan, is "without God nothing has meaning" or "without God nothing holds together."

In African religious thought the Supreme Being is universal; he cannot be owned by particular peoples or cultures and mediated to others. He has revealed himself everywhere. Generally, he has no priests and no shrines because he cannot be domesticated in a particular geographic location. God in African religious thought is therefore sustainer of all things and the provider of sustenance for all his creation.

2.1.2. God is not alone in the transcendent world. There are also *lesser deities,* ancestors of clans and lineages, and other benevolent and malevolent powers, all of which can influence lives either for good or for ill. The African environment is enchanted. Lesser deities may be located in mountains, rocks, rivers, or stones. Unlike the Supreme Being, for whom they may serve as mediators, lesser deities have shrines and are served by religious mediators. They can be domesticated, even personally or communally owned. The Supreme Being is permanent, but the gods can be temporal, and they are retained or disposed of according to whether or not they fulfill human aspirations. The → ancestors who also belong to the realm of transcendence are clan and lineage elders. The living-dead, as they are sometimes called, are the custodians of morality; together with the deities, they reward and punish people according to their deeds.

2.1.3. Because of *human finiteness, impurity, and weakness,* each person must rely on the Supreme Being and the benevolent ancestors and spirit powers for protection against the inimical ways of evil spirits, demons, and earthborn powers such as witches and those with evil eyes (→ Evil).

2.1.4. There is belief in *the divine source and sanctity of human → life.* The human person may be finite, but everyone possesses a divine destiny that, for instance, makes the shedding of innocent blood abhorrent in African societies. This value appears in the Akan (Ghana) proverb "All humans without exception are children of Almighty God; none originates from the earth." This proverb, as does Hebrew mythology, acknowledges the transcendent source of all human life and has implications for the African conception of life as being sacred.

2.1.5. To be human in Africa is to belong to *the whole community* and to participate in its life. Thus the traditional ontology of Africa is expressed, not as *cogito ergo sum* (I think, therefore I am), but as *cognatus ergo sum* (I am related, therefore I am). This sense of community has implications both for caring for the gifts of nature and for upholding the sanctity of human life and thus has profound implications for spirituality.

2.2. *Mother Earth*

Mother Earth is also greatly revered in African philosophical thought. The biblical thought that "the earth is the LORD's and all that is in it" (Ps. 24:1) is not alien to African spirituality, in which the earth is God's and much more. It is animated with its own divine principle. Thus in Chinua Achebe's novel *Things Fall Apart,* Okonkwo pays a heavy fine for physically assaulting his wife during a sacred week observed in honor of the earth, during which there was to be no violence. "The evil you have done can ruin the whole clan," Okonkwo was reminded; "the earth goddess whom you have insulted may refuse to give us her increase, and we shall all perish" (p. 30).

In African spirituality, the earth has a broader reference than land. All the gifts of → nature and the → environment, through which communities eke out a living, possess a divine principle. African traditional festivals therefore usually revolve around rivers, forests, and even the sea because they are the sources of life and sustenance. Against the backdrop of such a → worldview, not only is the earth to be revered as the source of life and abundance, but such reverence also has implications for the destiny of the whole community. This interconnection affirms the view that African spirituality is more than an individual affair, for it involves seeking the well-being of the community; it is a corporate enterprise in which everyone has a stake.

2.3. *Human Weakness and Religious Ritual*

Human beings are vulnerable, which is related to the belief in spiritual causality that is present in African cultures. Since events have causes, African shrines create the necessary sacred spaces that serve as ritual locations in which evil can be dealt with. This human sense of vulnerability is further balanced by the belief that human beings and communities can enter into relationships with the world of benevolent transcendent beings and so share in its rewards, that is, the powers, blessings, abundance, and protection of that realm.

African spirituality is driven strongly by this firm belief in invisible spiritual forces, especially → witchcraft (§3) and other forms of supernatural evil. People therefore resort to shrines and diviners and, in the context of indigenous Christianity, to pastors and prophets to offer rituals, prayers, and offerings that are deemed effective against the powers of evil. → Prayer, → fasting, and ritual are therefore integral to African spirituality as means of communication with the supernatural realm, where power, strength, protection, and healing are located. Rituals possess efficacious effects by attracting benevolent powers and keeping at bay the malevolent ones.

In other words, Africans perform religious ritual — prayers, offerings, sacrifices, and observance of sacred weeks — in the search for cures for their ills, answers to the complexities of life, and guidance for an unknown future.

2.4. *Characteristics*

2.4.1. These features of traditional religion have several implications for spirituality in the African context. First, African spirituality exists in dependence on a transcendent realm of spirit beings for life and vitality. One's humanity, in African understanding, makes sense only within the context of relationship with God.

2.4.2. African spirituality is both vertical and

horizontal in that the relationship with God must be manifested in relationship with other human beings and the created order or the cosmos as a whole. → Individualism is an abomination and may be said to provoke mysterious diseases, epidemics, and disrupted purposes in life at the instigation of gods, ancestors, and spirits, who are immediate guardians and custodians of public and private morality.

2.4.3. African spirituality is guided by the conviction that indigenous African religion is often a means to an end. The ends include health, fertility, rain, power of procreation, and protection and power against evil. They are impossible without relational harmony with all the parties in the African cosmic order.

Libation prayer, for instance, always includes segments that petition for personal and communal enemies to be defeated so that nothing — physical or spiritual — will stand in the way of personal and communal well-being and security for all. This interdependence is powerfully seen in the religious ontology of the traditional African world. In the African universe, the constant engagement with the realm of "unseen" powers is what the Akan of Ghana call *nkwa,* or fullness of life. "Life" here is very similar to Heb. *shalom,* with its implications of peace, health, vitality, abundance, and general personal and communal well-being.

2.4.4. Spirituality in African traditions has a moral dimension. As noted, African religion encapsulates all the activities that drive and motivate lives of faith, so that the relationship between human beings and their gods or God can be sustained for the enjoyment of the good things sought for in prayer. These graces are usually communal in nature (→ Group and Group Dynamics).

2.5. *Christianity and African Spirituality*
A biblical book such as Ezekiel has become popular in African Christianity because it offers a poignant image of the Spirit of God as the source of life and animation. Here, like the breath of God in the Book of Genesis, "winds" of the Spirit restore life and vitality to lifeless bones in a valley (chap. 37). Western → secularization, it is often said in African Christianity, has drained the former heartlands of Christianity of its sense of the presence of the Spirit. Thus certain fundamental teachings of the Bible, largely neglected in sections of Western Christianity, have been embraced in Africa because, in the biblical context, the auspicious presence of the Spirit of God is a sign of meaning, restoration, power, and hope. These are the precise ends to which African spiritualities, both traditional and Christian, are also generally directed.

Christianity in Africa is indeed spreading, partly because in its indigenous, independent forms it has well synthesized traditional African and Christian spiritualities. African indigenous Christianity largely rejects traditional beliefs and practices as belonging to the realm of the devil. Nevertheless, traditional beliefs in a world of benevolent and malevolent transcendent powers, mystical causality, and the efficacy of such ritual actions as prayer and the worldviews underlying them still inform the types of Christianity that may be described as truly African.

Bibliography: C. Achebe, *Things Fall Apart* (London, 1959) • K. A. Appiah, *In My Father's House: Africa in the Philosophy of Culture* (Oxford, 1992) • K. Bediako, *African Christianity: The Renewal of a Non-Western Religion* (Edinburgh, 1985) • K. A. Dickson, *Theology in Africa* (London, 1984) • P. Jenkins, *The New Faces of Christianity: Believing the Bible in the Global South* (Oxford, 2006) • E. Y. Lartey, *In Living Color: An Intercultural Approach to Pastoral Care and Counseling* (2d ed.; London, 2003) • A. E. McGrath, *Christian Spirituality* (Oxford, 1999) • J. S. Mbiti, *African Religions and Philosophy* (2d ed.; London, 1989) • J. K. Olupona, ed., *African Spirituality: Forms, Meanings, and Expressions* (New York, 2000) • J. S. Pobee, *African Theology* (Nashville, 1979).

J. Kwabena Asamoah-Gyadu

3. Latin American and Caribbean

Latin American and Caribbean spirituality expresses a journey in faith of Latin American and Caribbean people and their search for → freedom. For more than 500 years of crisis these people have struggled to overcome colonial structures of domination and exploitation (→ Colonialism). The roots of oppression in Latin America and the Caribbean are linked to the conquest and colonization of these lands by the Portuguese and Spanish empires (→ Colonialism and Mission). These empires brought a messianism and providentialism based on the ideological and theological principles of a dominant culture, promoted by an aggressive → mission and → evangelism. It was a conquering Christendom. When Christopher Columbus (1451-1506) arrived in these lands, he was convinced that his enterprise, true to his own name, consisted in being a "Christbearer." The indigenous people soon discovered, however, that the "scourged Christ" was the real Christ. The conflict between these two Christs is part of the history of oppression and the hope for liberation so pervasive in the daily life and devotion of the poor in this region.

3.1. During the 19th century the Protestant missionary movement brought along two new dimensions of Christology: the liberal, civilizing Christ and the pious-docile evangelical Christ. A charismatic-Pentecostal Christ irrupted at the beginning of the 20th century with an emphasis on a sanctifying spirituality.

In the second half of the 20th century, repressive regimes in South America, the war in Central America, and the emancipatory movements in the Caribbean gave way to a spirituality of resistance in times of → persecution, → torture, → martyrdom, and exile. The struggle for liberation involved indigenous people, the Afro-Latin American and Afro-Caribbean sectors, marginalized and abused women, alienated young people, and abandoned children in the streets — that is, the majority of the population in the region.

The real value of a spirituality of liberation lies in the fact that, in the midst of all these obstacles and problems, people find in their praxis of faith the main source for their hope (→ Liberation Theology). Why do people still imagine and dream of a better future when so many negative forces surround them? They are victims of an oppressed system, but in faith they envision new and viable structures in a more just → society.

3.2. The socioeconomic situation of the late 1980s and the 1990s saw the implementation of a neoliberal → economy, with structural adjustments and market economy as part of the globalization process. The contradictions of this global economy produced not only poverty but misery; people are considered outcasts of the economic system and are excluded. These conditions create the conditions for an ecumenical → solidarity, a global solidarity in networks of service, education, housing, cultural life, recreation, and health. These areas of life and well-being become spiritual values.

The spiritual journey of the people of Latin America and the Caribbean continues. The people are facing structural violence, depletion of natural resources, environmental pollution, injustice, and corruption — in short, the lack of moral and spiritual values in society. A new millennium is here, and pressing issues confront and challenge these societies. The Latin American and Caribbean people need to affirm once more their determination in discerning the signs of the times and in reclaiming an authentic faith that calls them to a conversion process in prayer, reflection, celebration, and renewed praxis in transforming existing conditions of oppression.

Bibliography: C. ALVAREZ, *People of Hope: The Protestant Movement in Central America* (New York, 1991) • L. BOFF, *The Path to Hope: Fragments from a Theologian's Journey* (trans. P. Berryman; Maryknoll, N.Y., 1993) • I. GEBARA, *Out of the Depths: Women's Experience of Evil and Salvation* (trans. A. P. Ware; Minneapolis, 2002) • J. SOBRINO, *The Principle of Mercy: Taking the Crucified People from the Cross* (Maryknoll, N.Y., 1994).

CARMELO E. ÁLVAREZ

4. North American

4.1. *Framework*

Christian spirituality refers to the dynamic engagement between the Spirit of God and human experience in its religious, social, political, psychological, and moral dimensions. Interest in spirituality rose dramatically among North American Christians in the last part of the 20th century. Yet, while popular fascination with things labeled spiritual is evident in everything from book sales to crowded retreat centers, this same phenomenon produces consternation among scholars, primarily because religious experience does not easily submit to established methods of intellectual inquiry. Many theologians worry that what passes for spirituality in the popular sense is often unreflective and unmoored from the texts, traditions, practices, and communities that have historically shaped Christian piety. Some observers fear that the North American culture of individual → autonomy (→ Individualism) and consumer choice often drives what passes for spirituality; the phrase "spiritual but not religious" has become a cliché.

These phenomena raise questions about the character of North American spirituality. It has recently been demonstrated that this eclecticism and experimentation has characterized North American spirituality from the beginning. Since the time of its colonization, North America has been a continent filled with "restless souls" (L. E. Schmidt). In 1782 J. Hector St. John de Crèvecoeur observed that, as Europeans settled in North America, "the strict modes of Christianity, as practised in Europe, are lost." He noted that wherever a group of believers established their religious practice, they "worship the Divinity agreeably to their own peculiar ideas. Nobody disturbs them" (p. 48). While scholars have long debated whether North America possesses a unique character or religious identity (the question of American exceptionalism), it has generally been agreed that this laissez-faire approach to religious practice and the resulting diversity are primary characteristics of North American religiosity. Although many zealots have not been content to "live and let live" with regard to religious practice, the eclecticism and consumerist ideals of North American culture in general have shaped the character of its spirituality (→ Religion, Personal Sense of).

In fact, it is neither accurate nor useful to speak of a single North American spirituality. Rather, there are and have always been multiple forms of religious practice and many Christian spiritualities in North America. Rather than viewing such variety as evidence of a shallow piety ready to succumb to every fashionable trend, perhaps the spirit of experimentation just described can be regarded as a strength of North American religiosity that has resulted in the flourishing of Christian spiritual practice.

North America is a vast region, and it is impossible to generalize about the nature of North American Christian spirituality. This article highlights only some of the elements and traditions that have shaped North American spirituality, primarily within the United States. It ignores vast wells of spiritual experience and wisdom that have been prominent in North America and are found in, for example, Roman Catholicism, varieties of Eastern Orthodoxy, and many Protestant traditions.

There is no sign of diminishing interest in spirituality in North America. Within the American Academy of Religion, an academic field has arisen to study and interpret the phenomenon of Christian spirituality. Seminaries and churches increasingly demand that students preparing for ministry have adequate formation in spiritual practices and disciplines. And the culture of restless longing and relentless experimentation continues to ensure that the experiential and affective dimensions of religious life will not be ignored.

4.2. Puritanism

Puritan spirituality is often viewed as the characteristic form of religious life in colonial North America. This understanding ignores the practices of the indigenous peoples who had populated the continent for centuries before European arrival by adopting the view of the "New World" as unspoiled wilderness free of human habitation posited by the early English pilgrims. It also neglects the presence of Roman Catholic and other Christian communities in the colonial period. In at least one sense, however, → Puritans represent something characteristic about North American spirituality; harassed in their native land, they sought a location where they could practice their preferred form of religious life free from outside interference.

The Puritan movement emerged within the religious and political ferment of 16th- and 17th-century England. Described as "a hotter sort of Protestant," Puritans rejected the Elizabethan Settlement and longed for more radical reforms in the Church of England that would emphasize devout and intense → piety. Puritanism — many of whose adherents were known as "the godly," since "Puritan" was often a derisive term — was a diverse movement, encompassing a range of temperaments, from radicals who advocated complete separation from the Church of England to more irenic figures who worked for further reform within the institution. Among current traditions that trace some part of their lineage through the English Puritans are Presbyterians, Congregationalists, and Baptists.

Puritan piety was marked by a zealous devotion to Scripture as the sole authority and guide in matters of → liturgy, → devotion, and ecclesiastical organization. Whether working within the existing church or advocating separation, Puritans held forth the ideal of a visible church purified of moral and spiritual laxity. The early Puritan settlers in North America viewed the continent as a gift of God's providence that presented the opportunity to establish a holy commonwealth that would serve as a model of godly society on earth. Puritan spirituality reflected the theological influence of John → Calvin (1509-64; → Calvin's Theology) and the Reformed tradition, which emphasized God's sovereignty, human sinfulness, the gift of grace in Jesus Christ, and progressive → sanctification through a disciplined life.

The sterner sides of Puritan devotion have often been emphasized to the point of caricature. More recent scholarship, however, has illuminated a rich affective, experiential, and imaginative strain of Puritan piety that emphasized delight in the created order and sensuous, intimate engagement with the Creator. Such devotion is reflected in numerous commentaries and sermons on the Song of Songs by figures as prominent as John Cotton (1585-1652).

Undergirding this strand of piety is an emphasis on mystical union with Christ prominent in Calvin's writings. Puritans also borrowed devotional practices from Roman Catholics, such as the contemplative reading of Scripture, introspective examination of their interior lives, journal keeping, and poetry writing to nurture their sense of God's presence. The poetry of Anne Bradstreet (ca. 1612-72) and Edward Taylor (1645?-1729), both anthologized in every major collection of American literature, reflects this introspective and mystical piety. It also reflects the importance that Puritans placed upon detecting the movements of God's Spirit in ordinary earthly affairs. Puritan spirituality emphasized sanctification in the course of human living, a piety practiced in domestic life, economic affairs, and political events.

4.3. *Pietism and Evangelicalism*

Evangelicalism has developed into one of the most prominent forms of Christian practice in North America. Like North American spirituality itself, however, the → evangelical movement is quite varied, encompassing a variety of communities and personalities, from the Willow Creek Community Church, with its many and various ministries, to the Sojourners movement, which practices intentional community and radical action for social justice. Traits held in common by evangelicals include devotion to Jesus as Savior in a very personal, heartfelt relationship, commitment to the Bible as the Word of God and as sole authority for faith and practice, reliance upon God's → grace as that which saves and sustains believers, and dedication to a life of personal evangelistic witness.

Contemporary North American evangelicalism has roots in Reformed, Wesleyan, and Pietist traditions as they evolved in the 18th and 19th centuries. The Great Awakening of the mid-18th century arose out of stagnation within the Puritan movement. Jonathan → Edwards (1703-58) and George → Whitefield (1714-70), among others, emphasized dramatic → conversion, heartfelt piety, and continuing progress in holiness. Edwards, a Congregationalist, developed systematic categories for evaluating religious experience that integrated the intellectual and affective dimensions of spirituality. Whitefield, an Anglican who had contributed to the development of the Wesleyan movement in England, organized and preached several series of mass revival meetings in North America, emphasizing conversion and the intense experience of salvation. Whitefield's emphasis, however, fell more upon the emotional dimensions of spirituality than did that of Edwards. Whitefield, who was widely celebrated for his dramatic and compelling preaching style, is also regarded as a pioneer in evangelistic outreach. His mass meetings are sometimes regarded as early experiments with public media that proved effective in communicating a new form of spirituality in a market-oriented society.

The Second Great Awakening, in the early decades of the 19th century, was perhaps even more influential than the first in shaping North American evangelical spirituality. Groups like the Disciples of Christ, Methodists, and Baptists appealed to the restless egalitarian spirit of the North American frontier, establishing forms of congregational life that were not dependent upon the more hierarchical and established European denominations (→ Christian Church [Disciples of Christ]; Methodist Churches; Baptists). Characteristic of "frontier spirituality" was an emphasis on lay leadership, pragmatism in congregational organization, devotion to Scripture, the importance of individual salvation and holiness, and a continued emphasis on affective piety. Charles G. → Finney (1792-1875) was the most prominent revivalist of the day, experimenting with new forms of → evangelism in protracted "tent meetings" that could last for weeks and employing techniques like the "mourner's bench" to stimulate conversions. Whitefield's and Finney's influence has been regarded as reaching all the way to the present, manifesting itself in the rise of televangelism and in the seeker-church movement of the late 20th century.

During the last decades of the 20th century, evangelicals and other theologically conservative Christians became active in the political arena. Leaders like Jerry Falwell and James Dobson advocated evangelical involvement in political activities in order to restore what they defined as "traditional values" in the public arena and to reemphasize the ostensibly Christian national character of the United States. The Southern Baptist Church, the largest Protestant denomination in the United States, came under the control of its most theologically and politically conservative leaders, who also became involved in conservative political causes. Dobson's Focus on the Family Ministries perfected the use of media technology (long embraced by evangelicals) to exercise enormous influence over evangelical church life. Dobson's radio show boasts millions of listeners, he has written many bestselling books, and he organized the Family Research Council as a think tank and political lobbying organization. Dobson's primary emphasis is on providing resources for marriage and family life from a Christian perspective. This is a contemporary outworking of the early Protestant and Reformed stress upon God's grace as it works in domestic affairs and upon the life of → discipleship as it is lived out within the home. Out of the emphasis on family and marriage, Dobson and other evangelicals insist on Christian involvement in the public square in addressing such issues as legalized abortion, same-sex marriage, and prayer in the public schools.

Evangelicals with other political leanings share with their more conservative associates the conviction that spirituality is authenticated in public action. Jim Wallis, Ronald Sider, and others have promoted a discipleship embodied in social action that addresses issues such as → poverty, → racism, consumerism, and environmental stewardship.

4.4. *Hispanics*

The term "Hispanic" is imprecise, used in the United States to refer to persons whose ancestry derives from Spain or one of the diverse countries and cultures of Spanish-speaking Latin America. "Latino/a" is often used interchangeably with "Hispanic." Either term, however, tends to homogenize communities and individuals whose ancestry is diverse, and thus there is no typical Hispanic spirituality to describe. "Mestizaje" refers to the mixed racial and cultural heritage of Hispanic North Americans that emerged from the contact between Native Americans, Spanish and other Europeans, and Africans. Theologians have reflected on the term as a way to describe the theological and spiritual reality of Hispanic North Americans.

Spanish and Portuguese explorers accompanied by priests had traversed much of the Americas by the time English, French, and Dutch colonists arrived in the early 17th century. Spanish conquistadores forcibly converted native inhabitants of the New World to Roman Catholic Christianity, while Dominican, Franciscan, and Jesuit missionaries subsequently set up missions throughout the western portion of North America (→ Colonialism and Mission; Reductions).

The early history of colonization established Roman Catholicism as the dominant religion among the Indians of southern and western North America, supplanting the sacred symbols and rituals of the Aztecs, Mayas, and other native peoples. Today, there are many Pentecostal, evangelical, and mainline Protestant Latinos/as as well. Over time, contact between the native cultures and Catholic Christianity resulted in particular inculturated forms of Christian spirituality and practice, some of which endure in Protestant contexts.

Often referred to as popular religion, one form of spirituality shaped by the lived experiences of Latinos/as is the Virgin of Guadalupe. The Guadalupe tradition emerged from a time after the Spanish conquest of Mexico. Juan Diego (1474-1548), a poor Indian, encountered Mary in the form of a mestizo virgin who sent him to the Spanish bishop with instructions to build a shrine to her. The bishop ignored Juan Diego until Mary imprinted her image on an apron Juan Diego used to carry roses to the bishop. The bishop then repented and followed Juan Diego's instructions. The Virgin of Guadalupe functions for Hispanic Christians, especially for Mexican and Mexican American Roman Catholic Christians, as an affirmation of their mestizo identity. Because she vindicated the poor, powerless Juan Diego against the powerful colonial bishop, she is regarded as a symbol of affirmation and empowerment for the downtrodden and marginalized (→ Mariology; Mary, Devotion to).

Las Posadas, another form of popular religiosity, ritualizes Jesus' identification with the sense of dislocation characteristic of mestizo identity. Beginning each year on the night of December 16 and continuing for nine days, people ritually journey with Mary and Joseph to seek lodging. With songs and chants the procession goes from place to place, only to be told, "No room!" When "lodging" is finally found, a festive celebration ensues.

Each of these traditions exemplifies elements of the mestizo spirituality described by pioneering theologian Virgilio Elizondo, whose work has focused on Jesus as a "marginalized Galilean Jew, a borderland reject" (p. 54), a mestizo Messiah who shares and dignifies the marginal status of a mestizo people. Yet this mestizo Christ also illuminates the hopeful possibilities of new creation, exemplified in the new people who emerge from the coming together of many cultures, ethnicities, and races in Hispanic communities. The mestizo Christ exemplifies a spirituality of → reconciliation.

The party that concludes Las Posadas embodies another characteristic of North American Hispanic spirituality: enduring and festive → hope. Despite a history of marginalization and suffering, Hispanic worship and spirituality is marked by the spirit of fiesta — spontaneous and celebratory ritual affirming God's presence as liberator and provider.

4.5. *African Americans*

African American Christian spirituality is rooted in the historical experience of → slavery, with its radical dislocation and brutal oppression. Yet it is also characterized by resilience, hope, and joy. This Christianity has been shaped by the meeting of African traditional religious worldviews, European interpretations of Christianity, and the experience of seeking liberation from slavery and equality after emancipation. Traditional African cosmologies, which make no sharp distinction between the sacred and the secular, affirmed the goodness of creation and the dignity of humanity within that creation (see 2). The value of kinship and community has been central to African American spirituality, as African cosmologies also affirmed the relatedness of all things within creation. Identity and dignity have thus been defined by one's relatedness to family, as well as to the larger community. Africans forcibly transported to North America and enslaved maintained these worldviews with their ritual expressions, even as they received their oppressors' religion (often shared in order to encourage docility and acceptance of their enslavement), subverting it in order to affirm their own human worth and to hold forth the hope of freedom and justice.

Music and worship have been prominent and distinctive means of nurturing and expressing African American Christian spirituality. African rhythms, Christian theology, and allegorical biblical language blended during slavery to create a distinctive genre of Christian song — the → spirituals. The exodus is a prominent theme in the spirituals, expressing identification with Israel's experience of slavery in Egypt and nurturing the hope of freedom. Contemporary African American worship styles, found throughout African American congregations, regardless of denominational heritage, exemplify ecstatic, embodied, holistic forms of contemplative expression that remember the historical experience of oppression but allow the community to express its sense of gratitude and joy before God. In worship, African American Christians overcome the social structures imposed by the dominant culture to affirm their creation as people of worth to God, and God's ever-present sustaining work in their lives. "Come Sunday," by Duke Ellington (1899-1974), part of *Black, Brown and Beige*, his masterly musical interpretation of the African American experience, expresses this ideal well: "Often we grow weary / but [God] knows our every care / go to him in secret / he will hear your every prayer . . . but Sunday, Oh come Sunday, that's the day."

African American Christian spirituality has contributed significantly to social transformation in North America. Martin Luther → King Jr. (1929-68) and other → civil rights leaders of the mid-20th century drew upon their African American and Christian heritages to call North Americans of European ancestry to fulfill their ideals of human equality and Christian discipleship by rejecting racism and granting equal status to African Americans. King and others prepared those who joined the work for equality by instructing them in nonviolent tactics inspired by Jesus' teachings and the life of Mohandas Gandhi (1869-1948). Singing and preaching, however, were also prominent in preparing and sustaining civil rights marchers throughout the 1950s and 1960s. King's writings often reveal a profound, almost mystical practice of private prayer that sustained him throughout his public ministry.

One of King's mentors was Howard Thurman (1900-1981), whose written work and experiments in developing racially reconciled congregations distinguish him as one of the great figures of 20th-century North American spirituality. In his work Thurman developed a portrait of a "disinherited"

Jesus in which he was most closely identified with the marginalized existence of African Americans. As thus identified, said Thurman, African Americans in their sociological and religious realities uniquely reveal something about the nature of God.

4.6. *Pentecostals and Charismatics*

Pentecostal spirituality is a remarkable phenomenon that represents one of the most distinctive contributions of North American Christianity to the rest of the world. Several theological streams have contributed to the development of → Pentecostalism, the most significant one being Wesleyan. Early Methodist revival meetings included exuberant and emotional manifestations of the Spirit. John → Wesley's (1703-91) doctrine of the "second blessing" (i.e., the gift of sanctification received after conversion) was equated with the baptism of the Holy Spirit as narrated in the Book of Acts. Early Pentecostalism developed as a primitivist movement attempting to recapture the NT experience of receiving the Holy Spirit, the evidence of which included the personal experience of salvation and sanctification, → glossolalia, miraculous → healings, and an expectation of Christ's imminent return (→ Parousia).

Charles Fox Parham (1873-1929), a disaffected Methodist minister, began preaching the gospel of healing, premillennialism, and the "third blessing" in Topeka, Kansas, near the turn of the 20th century. Parham's teaching touched an African American evangelist named William Seymour (1870-1922) during a series of meetings held in Houston, Texas. When Seymour accepted a pastorate in Los Angeles, he took with him the gospel of Spirit baptism and speaking in tongues. The Azusa Street Revival that Seymour instigated in 1906 remains a historical watershed for identifying the beginnings of Pentecostalism as a worldwide movement. Meetings lasted all day and well into the night and were characterized by spontaneous and emotional displays, exuberant singing, and praying in tongues. Seymour's African American heritage shaped the public worship of early Pentecostalism as spirituals and free expressions of emotional release figured prominently in public gatherings. The Azusa Street meetings were also notable for attracting multiracial crowds. The character of early Pentecostalism was remarkably egalitarian; women, racial minorities, and those from the lower rungs of the socioeconomic ladder had their voices and dignity affirmed by the direct experience of the Holy Spirit's power.

In addition to its emphasis on ecstatic worship experiences, faith in divine healing, and exuberant prayer, Pentecostal spirituality is also thoroughly evangelistic. Spreading quickly around the world from its beginnings in Topeka and Los Angeles, Pentecostalism is often identified as the fastest growing religious movement of the 20th and early 21st centuries. The early revival spread quickly to Canada, Central America, and South America. The "Korean Pentecost" took place in 1907-8, and aspects of it have continued to shape Protestant Christian spirituality in Korea (→ Theology of Revival 7-9). Many denominational groups claim a Pentecostal and charismatic heritage, the largest being the Church of God in Christ and the → Assemblies of God, with each reporting membership of several millions. Charismatic movements have also appeared in several traditional, established churches. While charismatic movements in the Roman Catholic and Anglican/Episcopal churches have provoked controversy, they have provided sources of renewal as well.

4.7. Quakers

The Religious Society of → Friends emerged amid the political and religious ferment within 17th-century England. An early Quaker leader was George Fox (1624-91), a leatherworker who underwent a series of mystical experiences convincing him that each human person possesses the capacity for direct, unmediated communion with the Holy Spirit. After the restoration of the English monarchy in 1660, Quakers and other → dissenters from the Church of England were frequently persecuted, leading many to migrate to North America. The experimental and experiential character of Quakerism easily found its place within the pluralistic and seeker-oriented culture of North American spirituality, conducive as it has been to dissenters, radicals, and democratic forms of religious organization. The primary characteristics of Quaker spirituality include radical egalitarianism among believers, voluntary simplicity, quiet contemplative worship in which the assembly awaits a word from the Spirit, the practice of discernment, and a commitment to nonviolence and social justice.

John Woolman (1720-72) was a leading exemplar of Quaker spirituality in the 18th century. Woolman's journal is a spiritual classic, demonstrating his opposition to slavery, his advocacy on behalf of Native Americans, his commitment to simplicity, and his prescient connection of conspicuous → consumption with economic and social injustices. Rufus Jones (1863-1948) was a 20th-century Quaker mystic who deeply influenced Howard Thurman. Thurman's moral philosophy and the pastoral wisdom he offered to African American civil rights leaders were grounded in the conviction that racial reconciliation and social transformation

are rooted in the ecstatic religious experience of oneness with God and God's creation.

Today, Quaker spirituality is influential beyond the numerical strength of the Society of Friends. Richard Foster's books on spiritual disciplines have been enormously influential in renewing appreciation for disciplined devotional practice, especially among evangelicals. The American Friends Service Committee organizes people to respond to various justice and peace-oriented causes. Pendle Hill, a Quaker retreat center in Wallingford, Pennsylvania, offers a variety of programs and retreats focused on prayer, nonviolence, multiculturalism, and interfaith dialogue.

Bibliography: M. BATTLE, *The Black Church in America: African American Christian Spirituality* (Malden, Mass., 2006) • V. ELIZONDO, *Galilean Journey: The Mexican American Promise* (Maryknoll, N.Y., 2000) • J. FARINA, ed., *Sources of American Spirituality* (25 vols.; New York, 1978) • R. FOSTER, *Celebration of Discipline: The Path to Spiritual Growth* (25th anniv. ed.; San Francisco, 1998) • C. HAMBRICK-STOWE, *Charles G. Finney and the Spirit of American Evangelicalism* (Grand Rapids, 1996); idem, *The Practice of Piety: Puritan Devotional Disciplines in Seventeenth-Century New England* (Chapel Hill, N.C., 1982) • B. A. HOLMES, *Joy Unspeakable: Contemplative Practices of the Black Church* (Minneapolis, 2004) • L. G. JONES, "A Thirst for God or Consumer Spirituality? Cultivating Disciplined Practices of Being Engaged by God," *MoTh* 13 (1997) 3-28 • B. LANE, *Landscapes of the Sacred: Geography and Narrative in American Spirituality* (Baltimore, 2001) • G. MURSELL, ed., *The Story of Christian Spirituality: Two Thousand Years from East to West* (Minneapolis, 2001) • W. C. ROOF et al., "Forum: American Spirituality," *RAmCul* 9 (Summer 1999) 131-57 • H. ST. JOHN DE CRÈVECOEUR, *Letters from an American Farmer* (ed. S. Manning; Oxford, 1997; orig. pub., 1782) • L. E. SCHMIDT, *Restless Souls: The Making of Spirituality in America from Emerson to Oprah* (San Francisco, 2005) • A. TAVES, *Fits, Trances, and Visions: Experiencing Religion and Explaining Experience from Wesley to James* (Princeton, 1999); eadem, *The Household of Faith: Roman Catholic Devotions in Mid-Nineteenth-Century America* (Notre Dame, Ind., 1986) • G. WACKER, *Heaven Below: Early Pentecostals and American Culture* (Cambridge, Mass., 2001) • R. WUTHNOW, *After Heaven: Spirituality in America since the 1950s* (Berkeley, Calif., 1998).

TIMOTHY HESSEL-ROBINSON

5. Feminine

5.1. Historically, Christian spirituality has evolved around three thematic centers: (1) the →

Trinity, with God as Creator, Jesus Christ as Redeemer, and the Holy Spirit as Sustainer; (2) the community of believers (→ Church); and (3) both individual and collective → sanctification of life. → Contemplation and → meditation have generated theological, ecclesiological, and eschatological insight. Social action, prophetic utterance, and a spectrum of ecstatic states have served to translate abstract ideas into spiritual practice. In all these contexts Christian spirituality has vacillated between apophatic, cataphatic (i.e., positive, normative), and metaphoric approaches to the Divine (→ God 3) and its relationship to → creation.

Any understanding of feminine spirituality must be created in dialogue with masculine spirituality and feminist studies and cannot be assumed to be stable across place and time. Changing economic and historical contexts dramatically impact masculine and feminine roles; any assumptions about gender thus must be analyzed through the lens of ethnicity, sexual orientation, and class. Except for the biological ability to menstruate and, to varying degrees, the choice to become pregnant, to give birth, and to lactate, men and women may choose behaviors and roles associated with either gender. In the strictest sense, feminine spirituality thus concerns itself with the sacred dimensions of fertility and childbirth, which constitute an important, but not necessarily central, phase in the life span of a female human being. An extension of this biologically determined gendered aspect of human life is constituted by a focus on the → family, children, and → sexuality, including threats to women's and children's safety. A less narrow definition of feminine spirituality would claim that women and men are essentially rather than biologically different, and that this difference operates independently from the biological ability to give birth, thus permitting women and men to access different psychological, spiritual, and emotional worlds.

Feminist scholarship asserts that all social, theological, and historical aspects of Christianity are shaped by dualistic and asymmetrical definitions of gender (→ Dualism) that do not allow women to reach their full human potential and to participate as equal members in church and society (→ Feminism 4; Feminist Theology 3). It seeks to uncover the → sexist interpretation of the three central Christian themes of the Trinity, the church, and sanctification and to develop a new paradigm that will promote the full humanity of women, men, and children in right relation to creation and the Creator. This development includes economic, environmental, and gender justice on the personal and pub-

lic levels. Given the profound impact of feminist scholarship, it is appropriate to say that contemporary feminine spirituality is inherently feminist, even if its adherents disagree about the precise meaning of feminism and related movements such as mujerista theology, womanism, and indigenous and queer spiritualities.

In order to reach this goal, feminist spirituality aims to be ecumenical and dialogic and is committed to a critical reception of past spiritual traditions. This approach implies that the relationship between → sexism and other oppressive structures such as heterosexism, → classism, → racism, → anti-Semitism, and the exploitation of → nature must be acknowledged, and that liberating alternatives must be created.

5.2. In terms of the new understanding of the Divine, contemporary feminine spirituality draws from a number of resources. These include a creative rereading of biblical and historical writings, non-Christian goddess traditions as found in various world religions, and the work of feminist theology in Christian and other world traditions. To explore and fully experience the sacredness of femininity, it seeks inspiration in → liturgy (§4), rituals (→ Rite 2), spiritual texts, scholarly work, and → dreams; based on these resources, it seeks to describe the Divine metaphorically. Crucial here is the retrieval of ancient female symbols of the Divine such as earth, water, caves, rocks, darkness, and the moon (→ God 2). Divine creation (God) as feminine is often associated with the womb and organic processes of gestation and maturing. Divine redemption (Christ), reinterpreted as liberation from dominion and deceit, focuses on archetypal symbols of wisdom and insight (e.g., in the figure of Sophia; → Proverbs, Book of, 2.1) and on metaphors of change and transformation that move beyond patriarchal models of → sacrifice (→ Suffering 3.2) and victimization. Finally, an understanding of divine sustenance (Holy Spirit) is expanded by focusing on specifically female processes of protective growth and nurturing, as in gardening, weaving, or preparing food. Unlike traditional spirituality, with its oftentimes drastic split between → good and → evil, feminist spirituality often honors the "dark side" of the Divine as part of creation, as cosmic mystery, as divine "aliveness," and as necessary vulnerability (→ Process Theology).

In its rebuilding of community/church, feminist spirituality is anchored in the tradition of radical egalitarian movements founded throughout Christian history, but it adds a gender-conscious dimension that includes issues of → class, ethnicity, sexual identity, and other factors. An appreciation for embodied and often nature-based vocabularies for the Divine is reflected in attempts to create an earth-based model of community/church that includes all of nature and that stresses the creation of local ecofeminist communities of "celebration and resistance" (R. Ruether 1992). Constructive tension with outdated patriarchal church structures has elicited three distinct responses among feminist spiritual practitioners: to create a "church in exile," the so-called woman church; to work from within the church to transform it; or to leave it altogether in order to found post-Christian alternative communities.

The fact that values such as being-in-relation, process, intimacy, and healing are so crucial to feminine spirituality is also mirrored in a feminist appropriation of transcendence (→ Immanence and Transcendence) and the cosmic, mystical dimension of → life and → death. Experientially, interactive rituals and liturgies are designed to minimize centralized leadership, to encourage the creative participation of all members, and to honor the embodied dimensions of human life. Contemplation, meditation, and ecstatic celebration (→ Ecstasy) are highly valued, as are grassroots justice movements. Many aspects of life are affirmed as paths to the sacred, but special emphasis is often given to sexuality and the female life cycle. Rather than perpetuating a dualism between transcendence and immanence, feminist spirituality attempts to fuse the two and bring into → dialogue the diverse traditions that have formed Christianity globally, including culturally indigenous, pre-Christian religions.

Bibliography: P. Cha, S. S. Kang, and H. Lee, Growing Healthy Asian American Churches: Ministry Insights from Groundbreaking Congregations (Downers Grove, Ill., 2006) • J. W. Conn, Women's Spirituality: Resources for Christian Development (New York, 1996) • C. Eller, Living in the Lap of the Goddess: The Feminist Spirituality Movement in America (New York, 1993) • J. Grant, White Women's Christ and Black Women's Jesus: Feminist Christology and Womanist Response (Atlanta, 1989) • L. H. Hollies, Sister to Sister: Devotions for and from African-American Women (Valley Forge, Pa., 1999) • U. King, Women and Spirituality: Voices of Protest and Promise (New York, 1989) • B. J. Lanzetta, Radical Wisdom: A Feminist Mystical Theology (Minneapolis, 2005) • D. O'Murchu, Consecrated Religious Life: The Changing Paradigms (Maryknoll, N.Y., 2005) • J. Plaskow and C. P. Christ, eds., Weaving the Visions: New Patterns in Feminist Spirituality (San Francisco, 1992) • M. Procter-Smith and J. R. Walton, eds., Women at Worship: Interpretations of North American Diversity (Louisville, Ky., 1993) • J. Rodriguez, Stories We Live: Hispanic Women's Spirituality = Cuentos que vivimos (New York, 1996) • R. Ruether, Gaia and God: An Ecofeminist Theology of Earth Healing (San Francisco, 1992); eadem, Goddesses and the Divine Feminine: A Western Religious History (Berkeley, Calif., 2005) • M. E. Schumacher, ed., Women in Christ: Toward a New Feminism (Grand Rapids, 2004) • W. G. Storey, A Book of Prayer: For Gay and Lesbian Christians (New York, 2002) • G. Wade-Gayles, ed., My Soul Is a Witness: African-American Women's Spirituality (Boston, 2002) • S. Young, ed., An Anthology of Sacred Texts by and about Women (New York, 1993).

Ulrike Wiethaus

Spirituals

1. Negro spirituals were anonymous songs of enslaved blacks in North America (17th-19th cents.; → Slavery) that commented on and gave meaning to their plight. The spirituals allowed slaves to voice weariness, patience, optimism, eventually the → hope of liberation, and the role of Christian → faith in a society that otherwise excluded them. As they reflected on their oppression, individual slaves raised their experience to universal application in largely improvised song.

2. The origins of spirituals are complex. Based on African vocal and instrumental music, they were also influenced by English and Scottish → hymns (I. Watts, the Wesley brothers) that slaves encountered in their evangelization (→ Evangelism) in Southern plantation schools and slave churches. The 19th-century socioeconomic and political upheavals (agrarian to industrial economy, the Civil War) also profoundly affected the slaves' lives and were reflected as well in spirituals. Abraham Lincoln's (1809-65) Emancipation Proclamation (1863) officially freed slaves, technically ending that which gave the spirituals their birth. The Jubilee Singers of Fisk University, founded in 1866 in Nashville, Tennessee, both legitimized and popularized spirituals as a musical form in their concerts in North America and Europe. The first collection of spirituals, Slave Songs of the United States, was published in 1867. Although spirituals were romanticized for a time and dismissed as derivatives of white spirituals, recent scholarship has established their integrity and authentic African heritage.

3. Forms include the shout, a simple call-response pattern of soloist and group traced to the African ring → dance. The soloist improvises a story in one-line segments, with a mantralike response sung by others. While the images and characters might well be drawn from the Bible, they often serve as coded messages of liberation (Israel = slaves to be led to the "Promised Land"). Group responses include "Glory hallelujah!" or "O Jerusalem! Early in the morning!" indicating joyful anticipation of → freedom or even the time of escape (early morning). Other forms include slow ballads focused on endurance and release ("Swing Low, Sweet Chariot" or "Go Down, Moses"). Typical is the four-line stanza with repeating refrain. Popular "wandering verses" appear in a number of spirituals, borrowed as needed.

Unique musical characteristics include the insistent, duple rhythms of the African shout. Shouts often were danced as well as sung when slaves were allowed to gather after church. Syncopated rhythms marked the livelier spirituals, later influencing ragtime, Dixieland, and jazz. Altered scales ("bent" and "blues" notes), pentatonic scales, and the frequent use of microtones, almost impossible to write in manuscript, shape melodic and harmonic structure. The blues, emerging in the early 20th century, draws its inspiration from spirituals as well.

→ Black Churches; Church Music; Gospel Song; Theology and Music

Bibliography: J. H. Cone, *The Spirituals and the Blues* (Maryknoll, N.Y., 1971) • D. J. Epstein, *Sinful Tunes and Spirituals* (Champaign, Ill., 1977) • M. M. Fisher, *Negro Slave Songs in the United States* (New York, 1953) • W. B. McClain, *Come Sunday: The Liturgy of Zion* (Nashville, 1990) • A. J. Raboteau, *Slave Religion* (New York, 1978) • C. J. Rivers, *Soulfull Worship* (Washington, D.C., 1974) • H. Roach, *Black American Music: Past and Present* (2d ed.; Malabar, Fla., 1992) • J. S. Roberts, *Black Music of Two Worlds* (Tivoli, N.Y., 1974) • E. Southern, *The Music of Black Americans: A History* (3d ed.; New York, 1997) • J. M. Spencer, *Protest and Praise: Sacred Music of Black Religion* (Minneapolis, 1990) • W. T. Walker, *"Somebody's Calling My Name": Black Sacred Music and Social Change* (Valley Forge, Pa., 1979).

Robert D. Hawkins

Sports and Faith

1. Europe
2. United States
   2.1. Biblical Metaphors
   2.2. Colonial Conflicts
   2.3. Victorian Convergences
   2.4. Contemporary Collaboration
   2.5. Theological Significance

1. Europe

1.1. Sport as an exercise, a contest, or simply → play (swimming, fencing, boxing, shooting, ball games, and much more) is well known in all cultures and, in many cases, is related to worship and religious → rites. The Greeks instituted the Olympic Games in 776 B.C. (continuing until A.D. 393) in honor of the gods and as part of divine worship (→ Greek Religion 2). In Roman religion → dance formed part of the cult. In ancient → Rome sporting events were, in part, a training for soldiers.

1.2. The Bible seldom refers to any physical activity resembling sports. We learn of playing and dancing in the OT cult (2 Sam. 6:14; Exod. 15:20; Jer. 31:13; Ps. 30:11), and the NT refers to games metaphorically in the spiritual lives of Christians (1 Cor. 9:24-27; Phil. 3:13-14; 1 Tim. 4:8; 2 Tim. 2:5). The early church opposed the games for several reasons: waiting for the return of Christ (→ Parousia), a negative attitude to nakedness, the decline of the Olympic ideal in later antiquity, and the Neoplatonic view that the physical counts less than the spiritual (→ Platonism 3; Anthropology 3).

Later, the cloister schools (→ Monastery 4) found a place for exercise, and the → Reformers (e.g., U. → Zwingli) and → humanists gave it a place in the curriculum. Daily gymnastics had a role in the religious → pedagogy (§2.4) of J. A. Comenius (1592-1670).

In the 19th century sports and play became essential elements in the education of young people. The → Young Men's Christian Association (founded 1844) chose the motto *mens sana in corpore sano* (a healthy mind in a healthy body) and took up basketball and volleyball as Christian sports.

1.3. Sporting theory sees humans as developing and active beings who can be educated and who grow through both physical and spiritual exercise and practice. Theological → anthropology then considers them in their relationship to God and as God's creatures. The two lines of thought complement one another except when a theory of social Darwinism dominates sports and gives precedence to the strong at the expense of the weak (→ Evolution). On a Christian view, we are psychosomatic wholes, and a concern for physical well-being is part of what God made us for (→ Creation 2) and part of our human personality (→ Self). If we detach sports from the totality and see in them an end in themselves, we destroy them and miss their true goal. On a theological view, along with the struggle, emphasis falls on cooperation and mutual participation, so that the effort will be self-rewarding, bring real joy, and have a wholesome effect.

The healthy aspects of sports are important (→ Health and Illness), though we should not overestimate them, for sports are really play. Today sports are a source of recreation (→ Leisure), but they are also very expensive, for the market follows where the interests of people lie. At the highest level of a sport, participants are dependent on sponsoring, but athletes should not allow themselves to be bought, thus becoming means and objects. The value of a person is based on his or her creation by God, not on physical achievements.

1.4. Since the 1960s in some countries of Europe, the church has been working with sports on three levels. First, church → youth work has brought congregations into deeper cooperation with sporting clubs. Churches take part in training programs as part of their curriculum. An important part of this cooperation developed with meetings of the European church academies.

Second, pastors focusing on sports have made a significant contribution. As a rule, they play the role of interested but critical partners who show solidarity but are not part of the hierarchy of sports. They view participants not only from an angle of achievement but pastorally, being concerned with these people of normal human limitations as they are confronted with often unlimited expectations (→ Pastoral Care), faithfully accompanying them in the atmosphere of an important contest, which can be both attractive and depressing. (For example, several of the Finnish Olympic teams, as well as the Nordic skiing team, have their own pastor, who is on site during training sessions and at competitions.)

Finally, since the 1970s the churches have played an active part in the planning of international games and have offered their services both to the contestants and to the residents. At all main events the organizers provide, in cooperation with the churches and the spiritual leaders of other religions, a fully staffed religious center in the athletes' village.

Bibliography: G. BAUM and J. COLEMAN, eds., Sport (Edinburgh, 1989) • M. MALKAMÄKI, ed., Kyrkan och idrotten (Helsingfors, 1987) • E. F. MORITZ, ed., Sports, Culture, and Technology (Sottrum, 2003) • S. J. OVERMAN, The Influence of the Protestant Ethic on Sport and Recreation (Aldershot, 1997) • H.-G. ULRICHS, T. ENGELHARDT, and G. TREUTLEIN, eds., Körper, Sport und Religion. Interdisziplinäre Beiträge (Idstein, 2003).

GÖRAN HELLBERG

2. United States
2.1. *Biblical Metaphors*
Throughout its history, Christianity has intersected with sports in both conflicting and congruous ways. In the earliest Christian literature, the apostle → Paul used metaphors from the world of sports to align faith with the demands of discipline and the quest for victory that orient athletic activities. Although the earliest Christian writings do not address issues related to the acceptability of sports within the faith, they create a positive attitude toward dedication and competition, which are constitutive aspects of athletic activities.

The most expansive of Paul's sports metaphors appears in 1 Corinthians: "Do you not know that in a race the runners all compete, but only one receives the prize? Run in such a way that you may win it. Athletes exercise self-control in all things; they do it to receive a perishable wreath, but we an imperishable one. So I do not run aimlessly, nor do I box as though beating the air; but I punish my body and enslave it, so that after proclaiming to others I myself should not be disqualified" (9:24-27; see also Heb. 12:1). Similarly, in 1 Timothy an appreciation of pugilism appears in the urging to "fight the good fight of the faith" (6:12), and images of athletic training direct the reader to a sympathetic understanding of the value of discipline and preparation (4:7b-8). In Philippians Paul also invokes the image of the finish line in a race as a way of focusing attention on the singular goal of → faith: "This one thing I do: forgetting what lies behind and straining forward to what lies ahead, I press on toward the goal for the prize of the heavenly call of God in Christ Jesus" (3:13b-14).

Throughout Christian history theologians and church leaders have continued to use popular sports imagery to express the challenges, processes, and goals of faith. During the late 20th century, for instance, two gospel songs drew upon baseball and football for their inspiration, albeit with what many would consider a lack of propriety: "Jesus at the Home Plate" and "Drop Kick Me, Jesus, through the Goal Posts of Life." Although neither of these songs manifests the insight of Paul's epistles, both rely on sports images to convey a basic Christian message.

2.2. *Colonial Conflicts*
Despite both the early and recent appreciation of sports, much of American history has seen a conflict between sports and Christianity. In Puritan communities in the colonial period, sports and games were forbidden on Sundays, since such → play was seen as conflicting with the divine command to honor the → Sabbath. Sports and play were gener-

ally discouraged by → Puritans, since playful, athletic contests were thought to deflect interest and energy away from → work and moral actions.

Throughout the 19th century sports posed moral challenges to many Christian leaders. Ministers and pious commentators were troubled, not merely because of the time and energy that sports consumed, but also because it was felt that many sports (like horse racing or card playing) promoted gambling, while others (like rugby, baseball, and football) too often led to rowdy or violent behavior.

2.3. *Victorian Convergences*

By the mid-19th century, however, sports and Christianity had begun to converge in movements and ideals that spanned the Atlantic. Foremost among these movements was the founding of the → Young Men's Christian Association (YMCA) in England in 1844 and its quick transplantation to North America. This organization sought to infuse Christian values into exercise and health, especially for an increasingly industrialized society. Shortly after the establishment of the YMCA, an ideal known as muscular Christianity emerged in England and, in similar fashion, migrated quickly to the United States. Originally used pejoratively to describe an adolescent male believer who had developed his Christian character in playing rugby, the phrase "muscular Christian" quickly became accepted as an adequate way to identify the "manly" possibilities of faith, which were enumerated as strength, courage, and patriotism.

The recognition of sports as distinct activities apart from religious, cultural, or social rituals emerged with the rise of → leisure — the separation of a growing middle class from members of the laboring class (→ Class and Social Stratum). The development of sport as we now know it is a modern phenomenon that has coincided with the emergence of privileged classes, which are able to enjoy leisure and play. In the 19th and 20th centuries, however, an ironic twist occurred in the way the culture of leisure produced the professionalization of sports, shifting sports from expressions of play to exercises of work and thus, paradoxically, separating sports from the playful stimulus that had led to their rise to professional stature.

While the professionalization of sports developed in conjunction with the emergence of a leisure-oriented society, the muscular-Christian model similarly flourished in an increasingly industrialized society. To a certain extent American football and American liberal arts colleges, which were almost always founded as an extension of the mission of a Christian denomination, grew up together.

In addition, coaches at major research and state universities infused their athletic programs with Christian practices and values. At the University of Chicago Amos Alonzo Stagg (1862-1965), one of the most successful football coaches in collegiate history, introduced the practice of pregame prayer for his teams. And at the University of Michigan, Coach Fielding H. "Hurry-Up" Yost (1871-1946), whose teams in one four-year period amassed a total of almost 2,300 points while allowing their opponents fewer than 50, directed his teams to put the → Golden Rule into action by practicing clean living and good sportsmanship. These two coaches placed an indelible mark on the complex culture of collegiate athletics, combining football instruction, Christian values, and academic study.

During the Victorian period the perspective of muscular Christianity began to influence the opinions of ministers who had previously expressed reservations about sports and athletics. Recognizing the benefits of parishioners' participation in sports, ministers as a whole started to accept a regulated role for sports in connection with church life.

By the end of the 19th century the YMCA and the ideal of muscular Christianity had changed the course of American and international sports. James Naismith (1861-1939), a Canadian who had graduated from the YMCA College at Springfield, Massachusetts, invented the games of basketball and volleyball. In creating these sports, he sought to develop games that would require little equipment and few rules and that would encourage participation by involving all players simultaneously, interactively, and somewhat equally. Such games could be easily exported to foreign fields by → missionaries, who used the sports to attract persons to participate and then to hear the gospel (→ Evangelism).

2.4. *Contemporary Collaboration*

During the 20th century, sports increasingly provided a means for Christians to celebrate fellowship among the faithful and to reach out or minister to unbelievers and unaffiliated Christians. In that regard, throughout the United States churches of all sizes and most denominations participated in basketball and softball leagues, while many of the larger churches offered extensive recreational programs that included golf, karate, cycling, and tennis. By the end of the century, Christian colleges and seminaries were offering undergraduate majors and graduate programs in "sports ministry," and universities had created centers and institutes to focus on "sports ethics" and "spirituality and sports."

While church programs in sports and recreation grew, so also nondenominational Christian organizations arose to meet the spiritual needs of players in various sports. During midcentury the Fellowship of Christian Athletes (1954) developed as a special-interest focus out of the evangelical initiatives of Campus Crusade for Christ, and Athletes in Action (1966) was formed to field semiprofessional basketball and baseball teams that could use their competition as a platform for the players offering testimonies about their spiritual experiences. Within professional ranks, Baseball Chapel was established in 1973 to address the spiritual needs of ballplayers, whose travel and game schedules prevent their ongoing participation in a congregation during the season. Similarly, recognizing the spiritual needs of itinerant drivers, crews, and their families, Motor Racing Outreach worked with the National Association for Stock Car Auto Racing (NASCAR) to establish formal chaplaincy positions in 1988.

At the turn of the new century, sports are increasingly being accepted by U.S. Christian denominations and interfaith organizations. Many churches (esp. larger ones) have fully embraced sports programs, with churches in major cities often accommodating their programs to support professional teams and their schedules. At some churches in Dallas, for instance, worship times are shifted during the football season to minimize scheduling conflicts between worship services and the football games of the Dallas Cowboys. Other churches in the area feature postworship gatherings to view the games on large-screen televisions, a practice that became fairly common for churches throughout the country on Super Bowl Sunday, the day of the annual championship game of the National Football League. (It is uncertain whether this latter practice will continue, for in 2007 the NFL threatened legal action against churches in the Indianapolis area who advertised on-site parties for watching the Super Bowl.)

2.5. Theological Significance

The theological roots that nurtured ideas of muscular faith were an incarnational theology that celebrated the fullness of God's disclosure in the person of Jesus and that featured the recognition that each believer's body is a temple of God (2 Cor. 6:16). And the theological expansion of that idea has been grounded in an understanding of the sacramental potential of sports, which can be experienced as "flow," as the psychologist and prolific author Mihaly Csikszentmihalyi holds, or a "peak experience," as the psychologist Abraham Maslow (1908-70) suggested.

The spiritual experience of athletes in their performance of sport involves the introspective pursuit of personal, foundational truths that constitute the core of their identity, and it includes their appreciation of simplicity and harmony in team play. In a different manner, fans also reflect religious values in their engagement with sports. They manifest the religious power of sports in their expressions of allegiance and depth of devotion to teams, or as communities of like-minded, passionate, faithful fans. They often express their fervor in rituals of identification with a team, wearing its clothing, displaying its paraphernalia, and cheering for its success. Sports help players and fans alike confront the uncertainties of "fate" by playing out contingencies in games and by recognizing the role that chance plays in the outcome of contests. Similarly, sports help persons confront their anxieties and dreads about failure, aging, betrayal, and guilt, while competitive sports engage participants in situations that embody these challenges in every contest and season.

Sports generate rituals, institutions, and communities that for many make life meaningful and provide a source for temporal hope. They appeal to passions of heart and soul as they require courageous athletic performance and a quest for perfection, while also dramatizing conflicts between self and other, forces of good and threats of evil — cosmic struggles that potentially underlie each play and each contest. Through their symbols and rituals, sports provide occasions for experiencing a sense of ultimacy and for prompting personal transformation. The sacramental possibility of sports derives from their basic spiritual dimensions, namely, their capacity to evoke a sense of wonder, awe, wholeness, harmony, ecstasy, transcendence, or solitude. Sports often enable participants and spectators to transcend self, to experience the Other in a radical way, and to express deep passion. In this regard the intensity and perseverance of sports activity and sports watching can transfix and transform participants. While sports exercise this incredible lure and power, they also present a demonic possibility: unchecked, they can supplant Christian devotion with an idolatrous faith in sports themselves.

In building upon the incarnational and sacramental dimensions in muscular Christianity, sports can enable players and fans to experience and explore levels of selfhood, identity, and self-transcendence that otherwise remain inaccessible; sports can establish a means for bonding in communal relations with other devotees; sports can model ways to deal with contingencies and fate while playing by the rules; and sports can provide the prospect for experiencing a taste of victory — in all these ways providing, at least in an anticipatory and rudimentary way, the taste of abundant life.

Bibliography: W. J. Baker, *Playing with God: Religion and Modern Sport* (Cambridge, Mass., 2007) • J. Byrne, *O God of Players: The Story of the Immaculata Mighty Macs* (New York, 2003) • R. J. Higgs, *God in the Stadium: Sports and Religion in America* (Lexington, Ky., 1995) • S. J. Hoffman, ed., *Sport and Religion* (Champaign, Ill., 1992) • S. A. Jackson and M. Csikszentmihalyi, *Flow in Sports: The Keys to Optimal Experiences and Performances* (Champaign, Ill., 1999) • T. Ladd and J. A. Mathisen, *Muscular Christianity: Evangelical Protestants and the Development of American Sport* (Grand Rapids, 1999) • R. E. Neale, *In Praise of Play: Toward a Psychology of Religion* (New York, 1969) • J. L. Price, *Rounding the Bases: Baseball and Religion in America* (Macon, Ga., 2006); idem, ed., *From Season to Season: Sports as American Religion* (Macon, Ga., 2001) • C. Putney, *Muscular Christianity: Manhood and Sports in Protestant America, 1880-1920* (Cambridge, Mass., 2001).

Joseph L. Price

Spurgeon, Charles Haddon

Charles Haddon Spurgeon (1834-92), a Baptist preacher, was the son and grandson of ministers of the Independent denomination living in Essex, England. At the age of 15 he was converted under the ministry of a Primitive Methodist local preacher. Four months later, while serving as a schoolteacher, he was baptized as a believer and became a village preacher, acting as → pastor of the small church in the village of Waterbeach, near Cambridge. In 1854, while still under 20, Spurgeon was called to the prestigious pulpit of New Park Street Baptist Church in South London, where his rare combination of resolute evangelical theology and vividly phrased → preaching gathered a large congregation. The chapel was extended, Spurgeon had to move to the Surrey Gardens Music Hall to accommodate his hearers, and eventually, in 1861, a huge new auditorium, the Metropolitan Tabernacle, was opened for his use. The church grew from 232 members on Spurgeon's arrival to 5,311 at the end of 1891. Assisted by his brother James, Spurgeon organized a vast enterprise that issued a monthly church magazine, *The Sword and the Trowel*, maintained an orphanage from 1867, and from the following year included some almshouses. Spurgeon himself was one of the sights of London, a burly figure who was known for his pungent wit. His sermons were published weekly as *The Metropolitan Tabernacle Pulpit*, a series that continued down to 1917.

Spurgeon's theology remained Reformed at a time when most of his contemporaries were moving to broader beliefs. "I cannot sever Evangelicalism," he declared in 1884, "from → Calvinism." In 1868 he republished Thomas Watson's *Body of Divinity* (1692) as a declaration of faith. Yet he was prepared to have Methodists professing an Arminian theology preach from his pulpit and to commend authors of much wider views in his immensely popular six-volume commentary on the Psalms, *The Treasury of David* (1870-85). He also modified his theological stance. During 1858 he embraced the idea that Christian mission was best conducted on the faith principle (→ Faith Missions), and by 1861 he had accepted premillennial teaching (→ Millenarianism). He was a doughty champion of the Baptist position he had adopted, in 1864 charging the Evangelical clergy of the Church of England with bad faith for remaining in an institution that upheld baptismal regeneration. Gradually, however, Spurgeon began to fear that his colleagues in the Baptist ministry were following the Congregationalists in tolerating unbiblical opinions. In 1887 he left the Baptist Union because, he believed, it was on a theological downgrade toward inadequate views of the → atonement, the → inspiration of Scripture, and → justification by faith. Refusing to name those whom he suspected of error, Spurgeon was subjected to severe criticism by many of his fellow ministers. Nevertheless, this "downgrade controversy" helped stiffen the resolution of conservative groupings in the evangelical world and so contributed to the early stirrings of opinion that would crystallize as → fundamentalism.

In the wake of the controversy Spurgeon was a solitary figure, isolated in politics as well as religion. In 1886 he left the Liberal Party, which had championed the cause of Nonconformity, because its leader, W. E. Gladstone, proposed home rule for Ireland, a policy that Spurgeon feared would lead to Roman Catholic ascendancy there. He also suffered in his later years from rheumatic gout and Bright's disease, causing acute discomfort and the need to rest. It was while recuperating at Menton in the south of France that he died in 1892. Yet his legacy was immense. His short books, *John Ploughman's Talk* (1868) and *Sermons in Candles* (1890), proved to be best-sellers. Modeled on the Book of Proverbs, they supplied a draft of homely wisdom that sparkled with the common sense of the author.

Spurgeon's enduring appeal rested on his invocation of the manly and patriotic → virtues, holding cultured pretensions in contempt. These were the values that Spurgeon taught the students whom he trained for ministry at the college he ran from 1856 onward. He insisted that men should be admitted without regard to their ability to pay and should lodge with ordinary folk so as not to lose the common touch. By the end of the preacher's life 863 men had been trained at the institution, which continues to this day as Spurgeon's College. They constituted over one-fifth of the Baptist ministers of England and Wales and played a large part in the development of Baptist life in lands such as South Africa and Australia (→ Baptists). Through his men as well as through his publications, Spurgeon's influence continued to bolster evangelical convictions long into the 20th century.

Bibliography: Primary sources: Autobiography (4 vols.; London, 1897-1900; rev. ed., 2 vols., London, 1962-73) • *Lectures to My Students* (3 vols.; London, 1875-94; new ed., London, 1954) • *The Metropolitan Tabernacle Pulpit* (56 vols.; London, 1863-1917) • *The New Park Street Pulpit* (7 vols.; London, 1856-62).

Secondary works: D. W. Bebbington, "Spurgeon and British Evangelical Theological Education," *Theological Education in the Evangelical Tradition* (ed. D. G. Hart and R. A. Mohler; Grand Rapids, 1996) 217-34; idem, "Spurgeon and the Common Man," *BRTh* 5 (1995) 63-75 • M. Hopkins, *Nonconformity's Romantic Generation: Evangelical and Liberal Theologies in Victorian England* (Carlisle, 2004) • P. S. Kruppa, *Charles Haddon Spurgeon: A Preacher's Progress* (New York, 1982).

D. W. Bebbington

Sri Lanka

	1960	1980	2000
Population (1,000s):	9,889	14,819	18,821
Annual growth rate (%):	2.43	1.61	1.07
Area: 65,610 sq. km. (25,332 sq. mi.)			

A.D. 2000

Population density: 287/sq. km. (743/sq. mi.)
Births / deaths: 1.78 / 0.60 per 100 population
Fertility rate: 2.10 per woman
Infant mortality rate: 13 per 1,000 live births
Life expectancy: 74.1 years (m: 71.9, f: 76.4)
Religious affiliation (%): Buddhists 68.4, Hindus 11.7, Muslims 9.0, Christians 7.9 (Roman Catholics 6.8, other Christians 1.5), nonreligious 2.1, other 0.9.

1. General Situation
2. Ethnic Conflict
3. Religious Situation

1. General Situation

The island of Sri Lanka, just south of the Indian subcontinent, was called Ceylon until it recovered its original name in 1972. It is an independent nation — the Democratic Socialist Republic of Sri Lanka. Two-thirds of the population are Buddhists (→ Buddhism), with a sizable population of Hindus, Christians, and Muslims. The majority Buddhists speak Sinhalese, a language spoken only in the island. The minority Hindus speak Tamil, which is also the language of the state of Tamil Nadu in India (→ Hinduism). The Christian community is drawn in almost equal numbers from the two linguistic groups and is therefore placed in a significant position in the prolonged conflict between the two linguistic-ethnic groups.

2. Ethnic Conflict

2.1. The Sinhalese and the Tamil communities, which are part of the prehistoric migrations from the Indian mainland, absorbed and integrated much of the aboriginal peoples of the island. Today the Veddas, a small remnant of the original peoples, live in the north-central part of the country. In the early periods there was much interaction and intermarriage between the Sinhalese and the Tamils who had migrated from the mainland. Their linguistic identities, however, kept them apart as distinct communities, and the Tamils of Sri Lanka settled and controlled mostly the north and the east of the island.

Historical enmities between the two communities stem from wars between the Sinhala kings, who controlled the southern and central regions of the country, and Tamil kings from South India, who sought to exercise their influence over the neighboring island. Another Tamil group, referred to as Indian Tamils, was brought into the island during the British period as indentured laborers to develop and work in the tea and rubber estates in the central regions.

2.2. When the first colonizers arrived in Sri Lanka, the Tamils and the Sinhalese had their separate kingdoms (→ Colonialism). The Portuguese and the Dutch administered them as separate territories. The British, however, integrated the country and made English the official language of the island. Under British rule, the minority Tamils and those who had converted to Christianity had many advantages over the Sinhala-Buddhist majority. Therefore when the island became independent of British rule in 1948, there was an outbreak of Sinhala-Buddhist nationalism. In the enthusiasm to reestablish the place of the Sinhala language and Buddhism, the successive Sinhala majority governments undermined Tamil nationalism, a development that lies at root of the current conflict. The problems magnified when Sinhalese was made the only official language of the country and Buddhism the favored religion to be fostered and protected by the state. Furthermore, many steps were taken to correct what was perceived as undue advantages that the minority Tamils had enjoyed in education and employment opportunities. The problems exaggerated when successive governments attempted to change the demography of the country through state-sponsored colonization of Sinhalese in what Tamils considered their traditional homelands.

These offenses resulted in Tamils mounting a nonviolent campaign to gain their rights, led by the Federal Party, which demanded a federal constitution. The nonviolent campaign met with a military response, eventually leading to all-island ethnic riots in 1958 in which many Tamils were attacked and killed. Others fled to the Tamil areas of the island. The lack of any progress in resolving the issue politically eventually resulted in an armed youth movement within the Tamil community demanding a separate state, Eelam, for the Tamil people in the north and east of the country. Even though many armed Tamil militant groups came to the forefront, the Liberation Tigers of Tamil Eelam (LTTE) has emerged as the strongest and most formidable militant group.

Because of the linguistic affinity, in its early stages the Tamil struggle in Sri Lanka was embraced by many groups in Tamil Nadu in India. Successive Indian administrations, at both the state and central levels, became involved in attempts to resolve the Sri Lankan crisis. In 1987 the late Indian prime minister Rajiv Gandhi attempted to force a settlement, which included sending an Indian peacekeeping force to the troubled island. But the attempt failed, and India began to withdraw from its engagement after the assassination of Rajiv Gandhi in 1991 by a suicide bomber, alleged to be from the LTTE.

The strife has continued over the decades, with its periodic escalation into island-wide riots. A major ethnic riot in 1983 resulted in tens of thousands of Tamils either fleeing the country or becoming internally displaced persons living in → refugee camps. Several attempts to come to negotiated settlement failed, and in recent years the Norwegian government has taken an interest in mediating a peace accord. It succeeded in bringing the parties together for new negotiations and even brokered a cease-fire agreement. Because of the lack of progress in achieving a political agreement, however, the cease-fire is often broken, and the island is under the constant threat of being engulfed in even deeper conflict.

3. Religious Situation

3.1. Buddhism is believed to have been introduced into Sri Lanka during the reign of Emperor Aśoka (d. 238? B.C.) in India, who is said to have sent his sister, Sangamitra, with the Buddhist message. Hinduism came to Sri Lanka with the prehistoric Tamil migrants from South India and became the primary religion of the Tamil people. → Islam was established as traders from the Arabian Peninsula made regular visits to the island and eventually settled down in small pockets.

The presence of a small Christian community in Sri Lanka already in A.D. 537 is reported by a Nestorian Christian visitor (→ Nestorians). But significant Christian presence began with the coming of the colonial powers. The Portuguese arrived in 1505 and brought Roman Catholicism with them. But in 1656 Sri Lanka fell into the hands of Dutch colonial powers, who introduced Reformed Christianity. The Dutch Reformed Church, now called the Presbytery of Lanka, dates back to 1642, but is now reduced to a small church by the emigration of the Dutch and Portuguese descendants to Australia.

The British took over the island 150 years later, bringing with them the other major Protestant → denominations. The Anglicans (Church of Ceylon; → Anglican Communion), who form the largest of Protestant church today, held their first worship service in Sri Lanka in 1796. The Church Missionary Society (→ British Missions) sent British clergy in 1818. Methodist → missionaries arrived on the southern coast in 1814 (→ Methodist Churches; Methodism). The smaller Baptist church (→ Baptists) had its origins in 1812 as a result of the work of the Baptist Missionary Society under the influence of William Carey (1761-1834). → Pentecostal churches and smaller sects are also widely prevalent.

The Jaffna Diocese of the → Church of South India (from 1947), predominant in the north among the Tamils, was originally the work of American Congregationalists (→ Congregationalism; North American Missions), who opened their mission in 1816 as an extension of the work in India. An attempt to bring the Protestant churches into → union failed in 1975.

3.2. All Christian missions and churches in Sri Lanka concentrated from the very beginning on education and health work among the people. The churches established and managed most of the major educational and health institutions, with government aid. They also organized work among orphans and the destitute. Jaffna College, founded in 1823, was the first in Asia to offer modern higher education in English.

Churches also engaged in a number of development projects in villages and slums, offering employment opportunities to the rural and urban poor (→ Poverty). During the ethnic conflict over the past decades the churches have moved significantly into the area of refugee relief and rehabilitation, bringing the assistance of the world Christian community to the tens of thousands of displaced persons.

Active → mission and evangelization goes on in Sri Lanka, especially under the auspices of many new denominations and sects that entered the country in the 20th century. Nevertheless, there has not been any significant Christian growth in recent times. The continuing missionary work among the Buddhist population, especially by sectarian groups supported by funds from outside, however, has become a major issue between the Christians and the Buddhist movements within the country. Many attempts have been made to curb Christian missions and to outlaw → conversions, which has contributed to tensions between the Christians and Buddhists in the island.

3.3. Lay Christian organizations like the → YMCA and → YWCA, as well as movements among the youth like the Student Christian Movement, Evangelical Fellowship, Youth for Christ, and Campus Crusade (→ Student Christian Movements), also have a history in Sri Lanka. The National Christian Council of Sri Lanka (→ National Councils of Churches) was founded in 1923 and is the main forum for the interdenominational activities of the churches. The church has also been active in social and renewal movements. The ashram movement, the Christian Worker's Fellowship, Movement for Justice, Equality and Human Rights, and movements that work toward peace building have been essential parts of the church's ministry in Sri Lanka (→ Peace Movements).

Other interdenominational activities concentrate on issues of study and → dialogue. The Ecumenical Institute for Study and Dialogue, in Colombo, and the Christian Institute for the Study of Religion and Society, based at the Christa Seva Ashram in Jaffna, are closely linked with Protestant churches. Roman Catholic study centers, like the Center for Society and Religion, in Colombo, and the Center for Research and Encounter, in Tulana, also work on an ecumenical basis. The Protestant churches prepare their ministers in a common Protestant seminary, the Theological College of Lanka, situated near Kandy. The → Roman Catholic

Church has a number of regional seminaries and a national seminary in Ampitiya, also near Kandy. There is considerable ecumenical cooperation between the mainline Protestant churches and the Roman Catholic Church. The Sri Lankan church has also produced outstanding theologians like D. T. Niles (1908-70), Lynn A. De Silva (1919-82), Tissa Balasuriya (b. 1924), and Aloysius Pieris (b. 1934), recognized for their contributions in the global Christian community.

3.4. The Sri Lanka constitution guarantees freedom of religion to all its citizens (→ Church and State; Religious Liberty [Modern Period]). The churches are free to believe and practice their faith and to engage in educational, social, and evangelistic activities. The constitution, however, gives a special status to Buddhism, stipulating that it is the duty of the state to promote, protect, and foster the Buddhist religion and culture.

Most Buddhists feel that the churches had unjust advantages during the colonial period and that the churches have used their schools, colleges, and hospitals as the main tools of missionary activity. In 1961, therefore, the government nationalized, without compensation, church-run schools that were subsidized by government grants. Churches were still entitled to run schools, but they were no longer entitled to assistance from public funds. The teaching of the religion of the parents to the pupils was also made compulsory in all schools. In the same year the government also discontinued all the religious orders from other countries (mainly Roman Catholic nuns) that worked as nursing sisters and nurses in government hospitals. A limit was placed on missionary recruitment from abroad.

In another attempt to promote Buddhism, the government abolished → Sunday as the day of rest and introduced holidays on Poya days (i.e., special days in the monthly lunar cycle), which were significant for Buddhism. In 1972 this change was withdrawn, and Sunday was restored for reasons of commerce and international communications. In general, apart from the Buddhist grievances related to conversions, Christian relations with Buddhists, Hindus, and Muslims have been cordial. The race riots that plague the nation, for instance, have never taken on an explicitly religious tone.

→ Asian Theology; Social Ethics 5

Bibliography: S. Bose, States, Nations, Sovereignty: Sri Lanka, India, and the Tamil Eelam Movement (New Delhi, 1994) • J. Cartman, Hinduism in Ceylon (Colombo, 1957) • K. M. De Silva, Reaping the Whirlwind: Ethnic Conflict, Ethnic Politics in Sri Lanka (New Delhi,

1998) • W. L. A. D. PETER, *Studies in Ceylon Church History* (Colombo, 1964) • N. WICKRAMASINGHE, *Sri Lanka in the Modern Age: A History of Contested Identities* (London, 2006) • A. J. WILSON, *Sri Lankan Tamil Nationalism* (London, 2000) • D. WINSLOW and M. D. WOOST, *Economy, Culture, and Civil War in Sri Lanka* (Bloomington, Ind., 2004).

S. WESLEY ARIARAJAH

Stabat Mater Dolorosa

The Stabat Mater Dolorosa (lit. "the sorrowful mother was standing," from the first line) is a sequence → hymn focusing on Jesus' passion from the Virgin Mary's perspective. This hymn, composed in the 13th century by Jacopone da Todi (d. 1306) for the Feast of Our Lady of Sorrows (September 15), expands upon the verse ". . . and a sword will pierce through your own soul" (Luke 2:35a RSV) in 20 strophes. → Mary's anguish yet steadfastness at the crucifixion serves as a model for the Christian (→ Mariology).

The sequence was first developed in the 9th century to be sung after mass readings on festivals. Over 5,000 sequences had been composed by the 16th century, prompting the Council of → Trent (1545-63) to curtail the use of all but four. The Stabat Mater Dolorosa was expanded in 1727, quickly popularized by oratorio-influenced settings (e.g., by Pergolesi, Rossini, and Verdi). The Lutheran tradition accepted vernacular versions of several, primarily for → Christmas and → Pentecost. The U.S. *Lutheran Book of Worship* (1978) includes the Stabat Mater Dolorosa as a hymn for Holy Week (#110; → Lutheran Churches).

Bibliography: G. ABOS, *Stabat Mater* (ed. J. V. Bondin; Middleton, Wis., 2003) musical score with facsimiles • F. BLUME, *Protestant Church Music: A History* (New York, 1974) • G. FELLERER, *Geschichte der katholischen Kirchenmusik* (vol. 2; Kassel, 1976) • *Musikalische Gattungen in Einzeldarstellungen,* vol. 2, *Die Messe* (Munich, 1985) • S. SADIE, "Stabat Mater Dolorosa," *NGDMM* 18.36-37.

ROBERT D. HAWKINS

Starets

A *starets* (Russ., lit. "old man, elder"; pl. *startsy*) is a spiritual adviser in the → Orthodox Church, not necessarily a priest, recognized for his → piety and spiritual insight. The choice of an experienced ascetic (→ Asceticism) who deserved special honor as an older Christian (Gk. *gerōn* = Russ. *starets*) to act as a confessor was an early feature of Eastern → monasticism (→ Orthodoxy Christianity). In view of the Russian term for *gerōn,* such men came to be known as startsy toward the end of the 18th century, when they became most influential in Russia. With the development of monasteries the → abbot in rare cases might take on also the role of starets. Usually the startsy had a kind of charismatic character (→ Charisma) in institutionalized monasticism and were regarded in various ways as a lower order. The most important of the startsy were selected by pilgrims for many different reasons, but especially as confessors and counselors (→ Pilgrimage; Penitence).

In 1746 the Ukrainian Paisi Velichkovsky (1722-94) became a monk on Mount → Athos, where his austerity attracted a large community of Romanians and Slavs. In 1763 he left Athos with 60 pupils, going to the Dragomirna Monastery in Moldavia, where he became the abbot and the leading figure in the revival of both → Hesychasm and the startsy in Russia.

The greatest starets of the 19th century, and one of the greatest of all Russian saints, was Seraphim of Sarov (1759-1833), who from 1815 until his death received a steady stream of pilgrims from all over Russia. In his role as → spiritual director, he acted as confessor, teacher, healer, and spiritual adviser.

After Seraphim's death the Optina Hermitage (in the Kaluga region of Russia, southwest of Moscow) took up the work of the startsy. The main representatives were Fathers Leonid (1768-1841), Macarius (1788-1860), and Ambrose (1812-91). Their most famous pilgrims were Ivan Kireevsky (1806-56), Fyodor Dostoyevsky (1821-81), Leo Tolstoy (1828-1910), and Vladimir Solovyov (1853-1900).

In 1923 the Soviets closed Optina, with its startsy. Then in the fall of 1987 the → Russian Orthodox Church (§6) was allowed to reopen the hermitage, resuming the role of starets. The last great Russian starets, Archimandrite Pafnutij (Rossocha), known as Feofil and most recently bearer of the Great Schema in the Kiev Monastery of the Caves, which was reopened in 1988, died on March 22, 1996, at the age of 65. Today no fewer than 75 great Russian startsy are venerated by the Moscow Patriarchate. (This group includes two archpriests who were not monks.)

Bibliography: J. J. ALLEN, *Inner Way: Toward a Rebirth of Eastern Christian Spiritual Direction* (Grand Rapids, 1994) • ARISTARCH (Lochanov), *Velikie russkie starcy. Zhitiia, chudesa, duchovnye nastavleniia* (Great Russian startsy: Lives, miracles, spiritual direction) (Moscow, 2001) • S. CHETVERIKOV, *Starets Paisii Velichkovskii: His*

Life, Teachings, and Influence on Orthodox Monasticism (Belmont, Mass., 1980) • I. M. KONTEVITCH, "Eldership," *EpiJ* 9/4 (1989) 35-44 • I. SMOLITSCH, *Leben und Lehre der Starzen* (2d ed.; Cologne, 1952).

PETER HAUPTMANN

State

1. Definition
2. Historical Development
3. Modern States
4. Liberal Representative States
5. Constitutional States
6. States and Economies
7. States and Society
8. National States and the World Market
9. State Problems in the Third World
10. The Future of the State

1. Definition

In a provisional definition that reflects the influence of Max → Weber (1864-1920), a state is a political community whose government holds a monopoly on the use of force within a given territory (→ Force, Violence, Nonviolence 1). A government's officeholders are typically held accountable to function according to given rules articulated in a basic law or → constitution (§2). A state ruled by arbitrary or unaccountable dictatorial decree is generally judged to be illegitimate.

We might take this definition as an ideal type that is realized historically in widely diverse ways. The state is not a fixed, unchanging entity but a complex network of → institutions, laws, and processes that have developed and continue to develop historically. A purely instrumental view of the state, which is predominant in Weber and also found in → Marxism (§1) and in some liberal ideologies, presumes that the state's governing apparatus is nothing more than a means used by a more fundamental actor (e.g., the monarchy, the propertied class, the middle class, or the proletariat) to achieve its preferred ends.

A historical and concrete analysis of states will examine their particular institutional divisions and tasks. Next to the enforcement functions (i.e., securing the peace both internally and externally; → Peace 1), attention must be given to the state's importance as an agent of society's → development and its significance for legitimating diverse social practices (→ Legitimation). No political system can long endure on the basis of naked power alone (→

Social Systems). It also needs the means of → consensus building, adjudication, accountability, and representation.

2. Historical Development

States have not always existed. They are an outcome of human historical development, linked to specific religious, social, and economic circumstances. Earlier types of political order characterized by different patterns of governance included empires, feudal estates, and extended clans.

The first political entities that might be called states developed offices of governance that continued independently from those who held them. Such states existed perhaps as early as 5,000 years ago, for example, the city-states of Mesopotamia, where a ruling class took over agriculture and could recruit the labor needed to build canals and monuments. An analogous development also took place in Egypt, India, China, central America, and Peru. Some historians think that internal conflicts aided the development of states, while others point to external conflicts as the primary catalyst.

3. Modern States

The state as we know it today emerged gradually in Europe with the collapse of both the feudal system and diverse forms of government held together loosely under the → Roman Catholic Church's legal and moral authority. → Feudalism was a complex system of obligations based on a personal, ascending, hierarchical loyalty. No dualism of public and private spheres existed. → Power was based on possessions, with the chief owner commanding the loyalty of his vassals. Feudalism depended on an order of religious and → natural law. All persons had their own place, → duties, and limited rights (→ Law and Legal Theory).

The modern state manifests a concentration of political power within and over a specified territory. Yet it is distinguished in its relation to the simultaneous development of wide-ranging social differentiation, entailing the distinction of political government from economic, academic, religious, and other institutions. We can see this understanding of the state emerge in the writings of Marsilius of Padua (ca. 1280-ca. 1343), N. Machiavelli (1469-1527), John → Calvin (1509-64), and Johannes Althusius (1557-1638), to mention only a few.

The first modern states were absolute monarchies that claimed a divine right to rule. They were defended in France by Jean Bodin (1530-96) and in England by Thomas Hobbes (1588-1679). The monarch was both the sovereign legislator who made the law and the supreme judge in applying the law. The foundations of monarchical power were the army and the → bureaucracy, which acted as agents to discipline the population and exact tax revenues from landowners and merchants. Dynastic → wars and religious civil wars helped give rise to absolutism. We thus sometimes hear the one-sided thesis that war is the father of the modern state.

Even under absolute monarchies a relationship existed between the state and the development of capitalist economies (→ Capitalism). Maintaining a bureaucracy and an army depends on a money economy. The modern state is a taxing state. It must tap into the fruits of entrepreneurial production and commerce. The economic policy of early mercantilism that arose under absolute monarchies was not inspired by "the spirit of capitalism," but monarchical power politics did serve as a force behind industry. At the same time, enlightened despotism made use of agrarian and capitalist interests as a necessary agency of development. In this way the state acted in different ways to modernize and unify public law, to protect external trade and economic development, and to allow the differentiation of certain nonstate spheres of life.

4. Liberal Representative States

First in Britain, Holland, and Switzerland, and then in North America and France, limited and representative government took hold on the basis of the constitutional delimitation of state authority relative to economic and other spheres of life. While Hobbes saw in an absolute monarch a guarantee of peace in the face of "the war of all against all," John Locke (1632-1704) counted on a sufficiently integrated ruling class, made up of both the nobility and the middle class, to look after its interests in parliamentary institutions. The relatively weak and short-lived British form of absolutism gave way to the cooperation of the king and the upper and lower houses of Parliament, with power gradually shifting to the lower house. This arrangement by no means led to the emergence of a weak state.

From their beginnings, mercantilist and capitalist economic interests sought a state structure that would have sufficient power and legitimacy (1) to protect property (a central aim of the state, according to Locke and Adam Smith), (2) to develop an adequate form of order for the economy by guaranteeing contract and property rights and freedom of trade, and (3) to organize the necessary public infrastructure — the monetary, legal, and other conditions necessary to establish and maintain capitalist production.

5. Constitutional States

In constitutional states the constitution serves as the basic law that both establishes government and limits its authority by protecting certain civil rights. Montesquieu (1689-1755) argued that a division of powers should be included in a constitution as the best method of ensuring a balance between the king, the nobility, and the citizens. In the United States the separation of governmental powers acts as a guard against rapid change, as well as an assurance of diverse kinds of accountability.

6. States and Economies

During the last third of the 19th century, a change began to take place in the tasks of the state relative to the rapidly developing industrial economies. Better organized and regulated economic systems became necessary because of the rise of cartels, monopolies, and trade and labor associations, as well as the growing interdependence of states and their economies. This was true whether the primary pressure came from economic interests, as in the United States, the United Kingdom, and Switzerland, or from the state, as in Germany and Italy. The state no longer simply made room for entrepreneurial activity but began to promote economic and social development. The outcome was the modern welfare state, which is engaged in nearly every aspect of education, job training, health care, and economic development. Today the extension of these changes is evident at the international level in organizations such as the World Trade Organization, the World Bank, the International Monetary Fund, the European Union, and free-trade organizations among groups of states.

7. States and Society

The modern state, therefore, is no longer merely a dispenser of a few social and economic services (a process that began with Bismarck [1815-98] in Germany) but must now try to guarantee harmonious social growth (→ Industrial Society 1-2). State intervention aims, for example, to regulate social conflicts, to ensure full employment and price stability, to promote technological modernization, to provide social security for seniors and access to health care for the general population, and to deal with destructive environmental effects (→ Ecology) of economic growth. Contemporary states also face rapidly increasing migration of peoples both within their territories and across borders.

8. National States and the World Market

Among the additional problems affecting the ability of individual states to solve their own problems is the growth of international economic interdependence. Market economies, even when looking outward, used to function almost entirely within a national framework. Since World War II, however, states have been drawn more and more into a world market. This development undermines the economic and financial policies of some individual states. In extreme cases, especially in the Third World, it sometimes forces states to seek credit or investment on conditions that do not necessarily enhance the long-term development and eventual independence of the receiving state.

Given the pace of globalization, population growth, and competition for scarce resources, many commentators now say that so much is demanded of the state today that it may be reaching its limits. The question is whether international and transnational modes of governance, such as the one emerging with the European Union, are possible on an even larger scale. Or will the competition among major states such as China, India, Japan, Russia, the United States, and those in the European Union lead to new catastrophes, including new world wars?

In addition to economic globalization, there is also the growth in numbers and kinds of nonstate actors that ignore national borders. Among the most threatening of these actors are terrorist organizations, mafia-type crime syndicates, and arms merchants.

9. State Problems in the Third World

The special problems of the most underdeveloped, ill-governed, and poverty-stricken countries in the world result not only from economic → dependence but also from endogenous causes, including unjust governments, many of which manifest the negative consequences of → colonialism. Also to be noted is the failure of many weak or failing states to promote the education of their citizens, to encourage the differentiated development of state, economy, and society, and to control wanton violence.

10. The Future of the State

The state is not likely to disappear soon, and in some parts of the world the greatest need is for the formation of a just state with sound government institutions. But the growing interdependence of peoples and states in the world is rapidly challenging the ability of states to achieve internationally what each has been able to do, or struggled to do, within its own borders.

→ Church and State; Equality; Fascism; International Law; State Ethics

Bibliography: Y. BARZEL, *A Theory of the State: Economic Rights, Legal Rights, and the Scope of the State* (New York, 2002) • R. BÄUMLIN, "Rechtsstaat," *EStL* 2.2806-28 • H. J. BERMAN, *Law and Revolution* (2 vols.; Cambridge, Mass., 1983-2003) • P. B. EVANS, D. RUESCHEMEYER, and T. SKOCPOL, eds., *Bringing the State Back In* (Cambridge, 1985) • S. E. FINER, *The History of Government* (3 vols.; Oxford, 1997-98) • O. O'DONOVAN and J. L. O'DONOVAN, eds., *From Irenaeus to Grotius: A Sourcebook in Christian Political Thought* (Grand Rapids, 1999) • D. PHILPOTT, *Revolutions in Sovereignty* (Princeton, 2001) • G. POGGI, *The Development of the Modern State* (Stanford, Calif., 1978) • M. VAN CREVELD, *The Rise and Decline of the State* (Cambridge, 1999).

RICHARD BÄUMLIN

State Church

Overview
1. The Early Church and the Roman Empire
2. Developments in Orthodoxy
3. The West through the Middle Ages
4. The Reformation
5. Religious Freedom and the Separation of Church and State

Overview

The relationship between state and church can be organized in various ways as determined by history, politics, and theology (→ Church and State). State and church often include the same people, but they represent different organizational forms, with different aims and styles of work. There are basically two ways of relating state and church: the *state church,* with the church financed and regulated by the state, and the → *free church,* with the church financially and administratively independent of the state. Between these two poles a number of different systems organizing the two entities have developed.

State-church relationships are regulated through systems of civil and ecclesiastical law (→ Law and Legal Theory). The diversity of these systems mirrors the diversity of national cultures and identities. In Europe differences between these systems come from a variety of historical influences: the → early church, the → Middle Ages, the → Reformation, the Wars of Religion of the 16th and 17th centuries, the 18th-century → Enlightenment, and the development of liberal democratic states after World War II. States like Portugal and Spain were almost untouched by events before 1945, while political and theological events during the Reformation resulted in dramatic developments in northern Europe, where state church systems were established. These systems, moreover, were different in different countries. In Germany and the Netherlands, for example, the state church system allowed different → denominations of approximately equal strength to coexist. In the 17th and 18th centuries most European states were marked by some form of absolutist state control of the church. Separation of state and church became an issue in Europe in the 19th and 20th centuries as a consequence of ideologies like → Marxism, → socialism, and secular → liberalism, all under the influence of the Enlightenment.

1. The Early Church and the Roman Empire

The early church was a free church — at times accepted by the Roman state, and at other times persecuted by the empire on the grounds that Christians refused to participate in the official state cult. Christians typically were loyal Roman citizens as long as their faith was not compromised by the empire. During the reign of Emperor Constantine (306-37) Christianity was granted full freedom by the Edict of Milan (313), which held the state to be neutral with regard to religion. The process of the recognition of the Christian religion in the Roman Empire was crowned by an edict on February 28, 380, by the three emperors who between them ruled East and West: Gratian (375-83), Valentinian II (375-92), and Theodosius I (379-95). The ruling proscribed heresy and established Christianity as the state religion.

The edict from 380 confirmed the Constantinian alliance established at Milan in 313 and the practice both of state control over orthodoxy of doctrine and state involvement in the internal affairs of the church. In the East the relationship between state and church developed into caesaropapism, the idea of a harmonious "symphony" between the two entities. According to this view, the state and the church have one and the same head, Jesus Christ; the emperor governs the state and defends the orthodox faith in the name of Christ, and the church is loyal to the emperor and makes decisions solely in the ecclesiastical domain. This system came close to being theocratic. But after the reign of Emperor Julian ("the Apostate," 360-63), who tried to restore → paganism as the imperial religion and abolished the privileges that Constantine had granted to the Christian religion, → persecutions, backed by the power of the empire, of non-Christian citizens and persons labeled heretics became endemic.

2. Developments in Orthodoxy

In Armenia in about the year 301, King Tiridates III (259-314), who had been converted by Gregory the Illuminator (ca. 240-332), made Christianity the state religion, the first nation in the world to take this step. The process of indigenization and institutionalization of Christianity in Armenia followed in the fourth and fifth centuries. In 365 the Armenian church declared its complete independence from Constantinople.

The system of caesaropapism was by and large the fundamental principle and system in the Orthodox churches until the 20th century. In Russia the system collapsed with the Bolshevik Revolution in 1917-18, and in countries like Romania, Bulgaria, and Serbia the same collapse took place after World War II. The persecution of Christians was rampant in the Communist countries because of the Marxist atheistic ideology, with very many being imprisoned and killed, and churches were closed and church property confiscated. After World War II a certain degree of cooperation was established between the → Russian Orthodox Church and the Communist regime in the USSR because the church had been able to serve as a national symbol of unity and resistance during the war. In Albania all religions were prohibited in 1967, when the dictator Enver Hoxha (1944-85) declared Albania the first atheistic state in the world. Since the collapse of Communism in 1989 (→ Marxism), churches in eastern Europe have tried to establish new relationships with the states that respect the principle of the religious neutrality of the state and the independence of the churches.

3. The West through the Middle Ages

In the West the → Roman Catholic Church was able to retain a certain amount of independence because of the weakness and ultimate collapse of the → Roman Empire when the Goths under Alaric (ca. 370-410) captured and sacked Rome in 410. → Augustine of Hippo (354-430; → Augustine's Theology) was challenged to explain why the Roman Empire ended. Was it because of the neglect of the gods, or because of some fault of Christianity? His answer is formulated in *The City of God,* where he distinguishes two symbolic cities: *civitas terrena* (the earthly city) and *civitas Dei* (the City of God). People live their lives together until they are separated at the → last judgment and united with either the good or the bad angels. The church is not to be identified with the city of God; it is a "mixed body" of good and evil people. According to Augustine, the city of God must be seen in an eschatological perspective and is not to be identified with the institutional church. Augustine held that → wars against evil forces can be justified in order to guarantee peace, justice, and order in society. Thus, according to Augustine, it was not the fault of the Christian church that the Roman Empire had collapsed.

In the course of history, Augustine's eschatological perspective was forgotten, and the church came to be seen as an institution that represented the heavenly city in matters of → politics. The authority of the church was that of a higher spiritual power, and the → pope was superior to all earthly authority. This pseudo-Augustinian interpretation gave rise to theocratic concepts such as the medieval notions of the Holy Roman Empire and of the *corpus Christianum* (the body of all Christians).

After his election to the papacy in 590, → Gregory the Great (590-604) proved to be a figure of considerable strength and importance. He organized the resistance to the oppression of the Lombards by making his own troops available for the struggle; the city of Rome was now defended by pontifical soldiers. After making peace with the Lombards, Gregory laid the foundations for the pontifical state, administering large estates in Italy, Sicily, France, and North Africa (→ Papal States). As a major territorial ruler with considerable political strength, Gregory set the scene in the West for the lengthy struggle, marked by both competition and cooperation, between church and state that has done much to shape European history. Eventually, this struggle led to the idea of "criticism of power" *(Machtkritik),* which has become a basic component in European politics.

A high point of imperial power over the church was reached on Christmas Day 800, when Pope Leo III (795-816) crowned Charlemagne (768-814) during a mass in St. Peter's in Rome. This relationship between church and state continued when Pope John XII (955-64) anointed and crowned King Otto (936-73) as emperor in 962. The coronation ceremony marked the beginning of the Holy Roman Empire, which lasted, at least nominally, until 1806. Otto understood himself as the defender and ruler of the church *(defensor et rector ecclesiae)* — Christendom was one, a unique body, and the royal reign and the holy priesthood *(regnum et sacerdotium)* converged at the top in the person of the king.

Encouraged by the Cluniac reform movement, → Gregory VII (1073-85) initiated a process designed to liberate the church from lay power by attaining independence from lay → investiture, the right claimed by royalty to invest bishops and abbots with the symbols of their office. An important step in this process was the reform of papal elections at the Lateran Synod of 1059, which empowered a few members of the Roman clergy to elect the pope instead of the Roman aristocracy. This step was the origin of the college of → cardinals and the institution of the conclave as known today. The Investiture Controversy reached its climax in the bitter struggle between Gregory VII and Emperor Henry IV of Saxony (1056-1106). A solution was reached by their successors Henry V (1106-25) and Callixtus II (1119-24) when in 1122 they signed the Concordat of Worms. This agreement guaranteed the canonical elections of bishops and abbots, while the emperor was allowed to attend elections and to intervene when there were disputes. The power limits on both sides had become clear.

In the many years that followed, the papacy worked consistently and successfully to become the feudal overlord of the world. A significant part of this goal was the → Crusades, which began in 1096 and were regarded by kings and other rulers as a sacred task. The Crusades were an expression of the combined spiritual and secular leadership claimed by the papacy. During the reign of → Innocent III (1198-1216) the papacy reached the climax of its spiritual and political power. In 1302 Boniface VIII (1294-1303) faced unexpected consequences when he issued his bull *Unam sanctam,* which was directed against French king Philip IV (1285-1314), who had imposed taxes on the French clergy. Philip made no concession and in fact imprisoned Boniface. The king subsequently forced the election of Clement V (1305-14), a Frenchman, who in 1309 moved the papal see from Rome to Avignon, France, where it remained until 1377 (the so-called Babylonian captivity of the church).

4. The Reformation

This "Babylonian captivity" had a great impact on Christianity in the West. Rome lost its authority to local kings and rulers. In the latter centuries of the Middle Ages in countries like England and Denmark, the state's (i.e., the king's) influence over the national church grew considerably. This development was furthered in Germany, England, Scotland, and the Nordic countries during the → Reformation with the establishment of state churches.

The German Augustinian friar Martin → Luther (1483-1546; → Luther's Theology) set off what became the Reformation by challenging → indulgences, both the theology behind them and their actual sale by the Roman Church. To him, the human person is fundamentally a forgiven sinner because of the grace of God manifested in the suffering, death, and resurrection of Jesus Christ. It is the task of the church to proclaim the gospel and administer → baptism and the Lord's Supper (→ Eucharist), sacraments that are visible words *(verbum visibilis).* The → Word of God, baptism, and the Lord's Supper are thus the visible signs of the church and its only authority. Luther encouraged the state (i.e., the prince) to use its temporal power to ensure peace and stability in the country so that people could work without fear at home, in the fields, and in the marketplace. If the princes failed to live up to their responsibility, Luther often corrected their misbehavior in his writings and public statements. Christians should serve both the spiritual and the temporal kingdoms or regimens through which persons are enabled to serve both God and neighbor.

Luther's division of roles between church and state, the spiritual and the temporal regimens, was severely challenged in 1524-25 by the upheaval caused by the → Peasants' War. The peasants were under heavy financial pressure because of inflation, and they demanded an economic reform directed especially against the clerical landowners. Luther polemicized against the leader of the revolt, Thomas → Müntzer (ca. 1489-1525), and asked the territorial rulers to crush the movement and to reorganize society and the congregations. The 1526 Reichstag in Speier and successive meetings increased the authority of the territorial princes over the evangelical congregations. The princes became the guardians of orthodox Lutheran doctrine and morals. The idea of the one unique Christian society composed of spiritual and temporal elements remained intact in the Reformation, and the old Constantinian alliance was maintained at the territorial level. The Lutheran Reformation settled the competition between state and church to the advantage of the state.

Another Reformer, John → Calvin (1509-64; → Calvin's Theology), shared Luther's understanding of the visible marks of the church. The Ecclesiastical Ordinances of 1541, the constitution drawn up at Calvin's insistence for the Reformed Church of Geneva, describe a new ecclesiastical body, the consistory, designed to represent the church and defend it against the interference of the civil authorities. This body made it easier in the Reformed tradition to maintain the independence of the church from the state as compared with the Lutheran tradition, where there was a closer link between the church and the territorial regimes. Calvin also favored the idea of the *corpus Christianum* but, unlike Luther, did not want to restore the Constantinian alliance. Officials in public life are, according to Calvin, accountable to God and not to the church.

The principle of the territorial prince as the leader of a territorial church was consolidated in the 1555 Peace of Augsburg, when it was agreed by the parties to the first wars of religion in Germany that all subjects should subscribe to the religion of their prince (i.e., the principle of *cuius regio eius religio;* → Augsburg, Peace of). This principle was followed in most of Europe, including Roman Catholic areas, until the beginning of the 19th century. It was already in place in England, where in 1534 Henry VIII (1509-47) announced that he was the only supreme head on earth of the Church of England. In 1560 a Calvinistic confession of faith, largely formulated by John → Knox (ca. 1513-72), was approved by the Scottish Parliament, which saw the Reformation as a means to get rid of occupying French Catholic troops.

In Denmark the Reformation was introduced in 1536 by King Christian III (1534-59) as part of an internal civil war. He achieved → secularization by the confiscation of church property. During the period of absolute monarchy in Denmark (1660-1849), various laws stipulated the king's supreme authority to appoint → bishops and → pastors. The Danish Church Ordinance of 1537/39 was ratified in Norway (then a Danish province) by diets at Oslo and Bergen.

The Reformation in Sweden was introduced by the first Swedish king, Gustav Vasa (1496?-1560), who broke the union with Denmark in 1523. He also wanted to break the economic power of the Roman Catholic Church and confiscate its property. In 1544 the Diet of Västerås proclaimed Sweden an evangelical Lutheran state, and Roman practices such as the veneration of saints and pilgrimages were abolished. After several attempts to reintroduce the Roman Catholic form of Christianity, the Diet of Uppsala in 1593 definitively proclaimed the establishment of the Reformation in Sweden and Finland.

5. Religious Freedom and the Separation of Church and State

In the post-Reformation period the state, understood as a Christian authority, was obligated to protect the territorial church, even by force if necessary. The civil life of people was closely related to and regulated by the church.

Not until the last half of the 18th century did the issue of the separation of church and state become important. The Constitution of the United States of America, adopted in 1787 and soon thereafter amended, held that the country should have no established state church, and leaders of the young na-

191

tion soon called for "a wall of separation" between church and state. The American churches became free churches and were accepted as such by the state. The French Revolution in 1789 introduced freedom of religion, although in 1801 Napoleon signed a concordat with the pope whereby the religiously neutral French state recognized the Roman Catholic Church as a state church, since most French citizens belonged to that church. Reformed, Lutheran, and Jewish communities were also supported financially by the state. After the collapse of the Holy Roman Empire in 1806, the German states, in a new territorial situation, organized a state-church relationship after the French pattern.

The issue of → religious liberty became extremely important in the 19th century, and inspired by the American system, a number of free churches were established in, for example, Scotland and Switzerland. In England and the Nordic countries the use of force in religious matters was abandoned. In those countries degrees of religious freedom were granted, although the basic relationship between the state and the national church was maintained, the head of state being required to belong to the church that previously had been the established state church. In Denmark the state committed itself in its constitution of 1849 to support the Evangelical Lutheran Church as a national folk church as long as a majority of the Danish population belonged to the church.

The idea of the folk (or people's) church was introduced by the German theologian Friedrich → Schleiermacher (1768-1834; → Schleiermacher's Theology) as an element in his efforts to democratize the state church. The idea also became important in those countries where the Parliament, as the representative assembly of the nation's people, held the right to legislate in matters relating to the church.

The idea of freedom in religious matters was strongly supported by N. F. S → Grundtvig (1783-1872), a Danish theologian, hymn writer, pedagogue, and member of Parliament. It was his basic conviction that faith can thrive only in freedom and that the church is the local worshiping congregation where people — the "folk" — freely pray, confess, and sing together. He regarded the state as the best defender of the freedom of the church as long as it respected the church as a civil institution that possessed no political power or aspirations. In Sweden theologian and bishop Einar Billing (1871-1939) played an important role in understanding the Church of Sweden as an offer and a gift from God to the Swedish people, the community formed to preach the forgiveness of sins. The local parish church is an expression of this work of the grace of God through history. Grundtvig and Billing stand out in the Nordic countries as theologians who formulated an ecclesiological understanding of the Lutheran church as the national people's church. After the collapse of the absolutistic state church system, they were instrumental in helping the Lutheran churches to adapt to the new realities of liberal democracy and the welfare states.

During the 20th century efforts were made to move the power in church legislation and administration from the parliaments to local church councils, national synods, and bishops' councils in the Nordic countries and the United Kingdom. In Denmark local church councils were established in 1903, but they have no legislative power, which remains with the Parliament. Sweden established a new system of state-church relationships in 2000 — now frequently referred to as disestablishment — that affirms equality among the different churches and denominations as one of its main principles. Several links remain between the Swedish state and the (Lutheran) Church of Sweden, but these changes have also in unexpected ways led to closer relations between the state and the other churches and denominations (e.g., in relation to the church tax system and the maintenance of religious buildings of historic importance).

In Germany the state church system was abolished by the Weimar Constitution of 1919, thus separating (although this word is not used) the church from the state. However, cooperation between the two in matters such as religious instruction in the public school system, the church tax, and military chaplaincy has remained. The Federal Republic of Germany and its constitutent states have established a number of concordats and treaties with the German churches. The Reichskonkordat of 1933 between the German government of Adolf Hitler and the Roman Catholic Church was not revoked after World War II, although its relation to the present German Basic Law is unclear. Church-state treaties with the Evangelical Church in Germany (EKD), whether by the federal government or the states, are treated as being in a category similar to that of international treaties. These treaties provide for cooperation between the state and the bishops, arrangements for religious education in public schools, the role of theological faculties in German universities, military chaplains, and the position of the church in the public sphere in matters such as the financing of local parishes.

The separation of state and church was established in France in 1905 after many years of discussion. The 1905 law is based on the religious neutrality of the state. Under the doctrine of *laïcité,* the state must ensure that everyone has the possibility of attending worship and of being instructed in the beliefs proper to his or her chosen religion. This equality among the different religions implies that there is no state religion; the legislation of 1905 was designed to make religion a private matter and, as such, subject only to individual control. The religious denominations in France in principle do not have any direct or officially approved relations with the political system, although religious representatives are regularly consulted in ethical debates of national importance.

A new dimension of the state-church relationship was added by the signing of the Treaty on European Union (EU) in February 1992, a treaty that extended the scope of European unification through cultural and social components. Its scope now extends to areas that directly concern the churches in the areas of education, culture, and labor and tax laws. The EU respects the ways the member states have decided to organize relationships with churches and denominations, and today three basic types of civil ecclesiastical law systems exist within the EU. The first is characterized by the existence of a state church or predominant religion (Greece, Malta, the United Kingdom, the Nordic countries). The second type is based on the idea of a strict separation of church and state (France, Ireland, the Netherlands). The third type features the basic separation of state and church while simultaneously recognizing a multitude of common tasks (Austria, the Baltic States, Belgium, Hungary, Italy, Poland, Portugal, Spain). The tendency in most countries is toward the disestablishment of established churches and the acknowledgment of the right of self-determination for religious communities.

Churches in Asia, Africa, Latin America, and the Middle East established by Christian missions in recent times are free churches. As minority churches, some of them have experienced persecution and harassment by hostile governments, especially when the churches have advocated justice, democracy, and the rule of law. In 1992, for example, the Protestant Christian Batak Church in North Sumatra was attacked by Indonesia's internal security agency, which appointed its own choice for ephorus (archbishop). Church members were arbitrarily detained, houses were searched without warrants, and press coverage was banned. The incident illustrates the ongoing tension that exists in the relationship between state and church in many parts of the world.

Bibliography: B. J. BAILEY and J. M. BAILEY, *Who Are the Christians in the Middle East?* (Grand Rapids, 2003) • J. BRIGGS, M. A. ODUYOYE, and G. TSETSIS, eds., *A History of the Ecumenical Movement,* vol. 3, *1968-2000* (Geneva, 2004) • A. CUNNINGHAM, ed., *The Early Church and the State* (Philadelphia, 1982) • E. DUSSEL, ed., *The Church in Latin America: 1492-1992* (London, 1992) • W. H. C. FREND, *The Rise of Christianity* (Philadelphia, 1984) • P. HAMBURGER, *Separation of Church and State* (Cambridge, Mass., 2002) • C. LONGLEY, *Chosen People: The Big Idea That Shapes England and America* (London, 2002) • J. N. K. MUGAMBI, ed., *Democracy and Development in Africa: The Role of the Churches* (Nairobi, 1997) • M. REUVER, *Requiem for Constantine: A Vision of the Future of Church and State in the West* (Kampen, 1996) • G. ROBBES, ed., *State and Church in the European Union* (Baden-Baden, 2005) • B. RYMAN, ed., *Nordic Folk Churches: A Contemporary Church History* (Grand Rapids, 2005) • C. SMITH, *American Evangelicalism* (Chicago, 1998) • B. SUNDKLER and C. STEED, *A History of the Church in Africa* (Cambridge, 2000) • K. D. WALD, *Religion and Politics in the United States* (Oxford, 2003) • J. F. WILSON and D. L. DRAKEMAN, eds., *Church and State in American History: Key Documents, Decisions, and Commentary from the Past Three Centuries* (3d ed.; Boulder, Colo., 2003) • J. WITTE, *Law and Protestantism: The Legal Teachings of the Lutheran Reformation* (Cambridge, 2002) • P. WORSLEY, *The Three Worlds: Culture and World Development* (Chicago, 1984).

PETER LODBERG

State Ethics

1. Terminology
2. Relation between the State and Ethics
3. Ethics of Rulers
4. The State and Morals
5. Contrary Tendencies
6. Twentieth-Century Problems
7. The State and Its Citizens

1. Terminology

"State ethics" is an unusual term for English-speaking readers and must be explained in view of its continental European presuppositions. The term "state ethics" in the sense of governmental ethics would mean, if it were used at all, rules of "good administration" — thus, dependability and punctuality, as well as lack of corruption or discrimination. The heart of the problem of different semantics lies in the image of → "state." In Anglo-American legal circles it is difficult to imagine that the government, understood as a superindividual entity, should be subject to an ethics of its own. According to the English constitution one could speak only of the ethics of the "king in parliament," because he is the bearer of sovereignty. In the United States, administration and government have not become the abstract "state," as they have on the European continent.

In contrast, especially in France and Germany, one can speak of the ethics of the state (see 2-6), that is, the rules that shape the personified state internally and are self-imposed. They can also be understood as the ethical rules by which it is measured externally (see 7). Finally, the "state" that is formed and legitimated by the society makes decisions on ethical questions in its parliament — questions concerning issues such as the → death penalty, → abortion, atomic energy, humanitarian intervention, generally in → war and concerning the question of "just war," and, not least, → "torture for reasons of state" and all illegal activities of secret services.

2. Relation between the State and Ethics

If one concentrates on the continental European perspective, one must see that the European "state" was formed around monarchs in a long historical process from the High Middle Ages to the end of the ancien régime (1789) and became continually more abstract. This abstraction tended to objectify government and administration and make it independent of the unpredictable character of individuals. In the 18th century the ruler symbolically bowed to the state and called himself its "first servant." The nation and the people no longer were the private property of the prince but were the legal entity (persona moralis) of the state.

Since the 16th century, state and law, morality and politics have been separating. → Religion lost its central place as a comprehensive normative system. In the confessional conflicts, the old unity broke apart. From this division emerged the ethics of the individual, as well as politics without ethics and positive law without religion. That politics must operate free from individual ethics and religious commandments was the message of Niccolò Machiavelli (1469-1527), particularly in chap. 18 of his *Il principe* (1513). In the mid-16th century, "reason of state" (*ragione di stato*) replaced → ethics.

3. Ethics of Rulers

In order to avoid a total lack of protection from thinking and decisions based upon reason of state, there was a turning to the ethics of the rulers. The *Fürstenspiegel* (lit. "mirror for princes," i.e., a moral handbook) of modern times was not only to serve the education of the young princes but also to guarantee the nation and its inhabitants that the prince, whose religious ties could no longer be fully depended upon, was at least personally bound by a basic level of moral → norms.

The weal and woe of the nation were dependent upon the prince; he needed to be influenced by the fundamental propositions of ethics. In a continuation of the medieval catalog of virtues, the prince's highest goal was the common good (*bonum commune*), particularly seen in the Aristotelian tradition transmitted by Thomas Aquinas (ca. 1225-74; → Thomism). The ruler was to be righteous and strict but also mild; he should reward the "good" and punish the "evil"; he should live a virtuous and Christian life, install and oversee good civil servants, attend to swift justice, and strive to be respected by all. On this ethical foundation, relevant misbehavior could be criticized, such as corruption in administration and the courts, immorality among the nobility, the use of mistresses, squandering of money belonging to the subjects, and even the undignified behavior of the ruler himself.

These ethical requirements were supported by the doctrine of national law of the 16th to 18th centuries. The *ius publicum universale,* the general state theory based on natural law, restricted the sovereignty of the prince through a threefold set of limits. The ruler could not contravene divine law (*ius divinum*), → natural law (*ius naturale*), or the basic laws (*leges fundamentales*), understood as contracts. Thus he was legally bound, although without sanctions, to *ius divinum* as a Christian subject, to *ius naturale* as a rational being, and as a legal entity to the solemn contracts, which, in spite of their often fictitious character, were indissoluble.

At the end of the 18th century, the state ethics contained in this tradition were laid down in → constitutions and furnished with a new legitimacy. The constitutions differed from the older *leges fundamentales* in that they not only limited the ruler but also supplied normative legitimization for him, which until then had been dependent on religiously bound natural law. The constitutions now served the twofold goal of the justification of rule and, at the same time, its limits; they became the only authoritative text. In the American variation, the free people are the source of rule ("we the people"). The constitution is at the same time limited by an enumeration of rights to freedom that are exempt from the ruler's powers. On the European continent, the early constitutions stood as a protective wall against the continuing absolutistic machinery steered by a monarch with direct divine legitimization. They did not constitute a free society but first had to create a space for it by forcing back absolutism. This factor explains their strong defensive character and the political traces of compromise between the people and monarchs.

Because the European constitutions turned against absolutism, the ethics contained in them also turned against the 18th century. No longer is there any mention of the old formula of the common good, which in the late 18th century had been replaced by the formula of "happiness." It was discredited, first through Immanuel Kant's (1724-1804; → Kantianism) criticism of traditional eudaemonism, then through the fact that "happiness" was identified with absolutism. Since 1789 the revolutionary postulates of equality, freedom, and fraternity, of a nation of laws and citizens' political rights, together have worked to destroy the old ethical postulate of "happiness" or "welfare."

The English tradition is different. The traditionally stronger empirical and pragmatic basis of political thought regarding the "pursuit of happiness" did not experience this sharp break with the Aristotelian tradition. Between the old formula of the goal of → happiness and the utilitarianism of Jeremy Bentham (1748-1832), there are only differences in accent but no turning away from the former line of thought. Continuity of theory corresponds also to political continuity. To form a "nation" sharply divided from the society was not necessary under these circumstances. Therefore, there is no state ethics related to it. Also lacking is the spiritualization of the state, typical for Germany, raising it to the level of a "moral being" (G. W. F. Hegel, F. J. Stahl), which is understood not only as a romantic reaction to the utilitarian doctrine of the → Enlightenment but also as an attempt to reconcile the political tensions between a monarchical state and a liberal society.

4. The State and Morals

The idealistic state philosophy of the early 19th century thus began again with energetic appeals to understand the state as an instrument of the "moral education of humanity." The philosophical systems of subjective and objective → idealism understood the state partly as an instrument of → moral education, partly as the realization of morality that is the result of life in a well-ordered state, and partly itself as the "reality of the moral idea" (Hegel) or as the "moral kingdom" (Stahl). There was now wide agreement that the state image of the Enlightenment must be rejected and, with it, its construction through a contract, its goal as "shelter" against → power, and in the

end its function as a rationally constructed machine. The state was considered now to be an → organism of higher dignity. In it human morality is perfected; it is the highest form of human existence.

These doctrines may have been more or less conscious strategies to overcome the tensions between the monarchical institutional state and middle-class society, perhaps also attempts to take the sting from the emerging class struggle (→ Class and Social Stratum) through a promotion of morality. Its *impetus* comes first from a reaction to the Enlightenment and the French → Revolution; its *content* comes from the connection of cosmopolitan ideals of the end of the 18th century with the postulates of the movement toward nationhood and freedom. At the same time, on the opposing conservative side (→ Conservatism 1), the spiritualization observable in the Christian confessions brings about a re-Christianization of the state. Throne and altar come together once again and assign duties to each other somewhat symbiotically.

5. Contrary Tendencies

Admittedly, the 19th century contains opposing tendencies, which grow increasingly stronger. With → agnosticism and → atheism, first declared openly in the 18th century, the idea of God as the end point of responsibility for the state was called into question. The reduction of the state to a strictly worldly and transcendence-free view was now possible — its background in intellectual history is formed by the paradoxically parallel development of, first, the secularized understanding of politics of the Italian → Renaissance and, second, Martin → Luther's (1483-1546) → two-kingdoms doctrine. The latter had a different intention, but in the fading of the spiritual background, it left the state as a "worldly thing."

In the mid-19th century → "realism" and → "positivism" became widespread in all intellectual disciplines. One spoke of the "collapse" of idealistic philosophy. The triumphal march of the natural sciences began and required a reaction from political doctrine and the political sciences in general. State ethics was increasingly ignored. Accordingly, between 1860 and 1900 the discipline of the theory of the state almost completely disappeared. It was now expected of the state that it comprehend the rationally defined society as a permanent form and guarantee society's development, and that it administer the power granted to it by law and forcefully represent it externally.

The resulting ethical vacuum was increasingly filled with "realistic" ideas in the last third of the 19th century. The doctrines of state power understood in terms of constitutional positivism, the biologically inspired ideas of social Darwinism and → racism, the historical → materialism and the dogma of class struggle were, for all the heterogeneity of their positions, united in their antimetaphysical stance. State ethics was for them simply → metaphysics, or disguised ideology.

To the extent that they were historically realized in the → fascist dictatorships, in Stalinism (→ Marxism), and in all typologically comparable systems of repression, they showed what degree of barbarism these kinds of apparatus could reach. In addition, these systems used moral arguments with a great deal of propaganda and demanded of their peoples the highest kind of idealism (→ Totalitarianism).

6. Twentieth-Century Problems

6.1. In the 20th century, the attempts to formulate state ethics with a general consensus from all sides was no longer successful. The renaissances of a renewed moral education or a re-Christianization of political activity following state catastrophes made no headway. Society, which had simultaneously become egalitarian and pluralized (→ Pluralism 1), apparently found no agreement about a coherent material ethics. In that it more strongly emphasizes process and seeks to avoid any attempt at formulating a state ethics, seeing it as a retreat to a "closed society," society appears to acknowledge only a de-ethicized state and individual ethics (→ Social Ethics 1).

The program of constitutional positivism worked out since the middle of the 19th century divided law and ethics. In the radical version of Hans Kelsen (1881-1973), the state was identical with the self-legitimizing system of national legal norms. State ethics could therefore no longer be meaningfully spoken of from a judicial viewpoint. It lay "outside" of law and thereby outside of the state. This methodical purism was bearable as long as the legislature possessed a supply of legitimacy and its content appeared rational. In any case, even then it could not be overlooked that even the democratic model converging with legal positivism does not function without minimal ethical basic propositions: the consensus arrived at before every vote, majority decisions not revisable with force, the protection of structurally permanent weak → minorities, ethically based care for the unborn and for those not capable or entitled to vote, and perhaps also concern for future generations.

Democratic models are consistently based upon optimistic anthropological premises (→ Anthropology 4-5), namely, the assumption of the participants' capacity to learn and their ability to structure

action rationally and to move beyond their own → prejudices. Even the concept of the open society, which forgoes a minimally binding state ethics precisely for the sake of the individual's freedom to develop, cannot function without recourse to ethical ideas. These ideas, however, cannot be "marketed" actively by the state but must constantly be generated and renewed by the society. There are ethical constitutional presuppositions and expectations, which come to expression in a word like "constitutionality"; the constitution "lives" from them.

6.2. Since the constant renewal and activation of state ethics would, however, overwhelm the energies of → institutions (→ families, schools [→ School and Church], → church, associations, → political parties, and clubs), there is a need to relieve the load. In the Western type of modern state, this relief is found in the constitutions, along with their preambles, guarantees of basic rights, rules of procedure, and statements regarding the purposes of the state. Not only do they contain at a very high level of abstraction the normative focus of law, but they form the codex of state ethics accepted by the society.

The *bridging of the distance between general postulate and concrete individual situations* is the task of the constitutional jurisdiction established especially for that purpose. Its duty is not limited to the judicial process of decision making. It also contains, to a high degree, political and ethical components relating to the state. It is also known and declared to all participants that the procedures of electing members to the constitutional courts are regarded as strategically key processes. It is no different in the American model, with its balance between administration, legislature, and the pronouncements of the Supreme Court. The judges not only decide questions of law but implicitly define the basic ethical propositions of the society — notably, regarding abortion, torture, capital punishment, ethical boundaries in medicine and research, and the validity of universal human rights.

6.3. In this way, state ethics unexpectedly appeared again in judicial garb. The less closed the canon of values of a "multicultural" society (→ Virtue), the stronger the constitutional superstructure needs to be — and the more ethical elements it appears to contain. Thus at the end of the 20th century we did not witness a constantly accelerating decline of state ethics; rather, we saw complex processes of exchange between state and society, law and ethics. The need for ethical management appears, on the whole, to be relatively constant, while the satisfaction of this need can arise from different sources.

Particularly in immigration societies, the more

strongly ethical subsystems of the various ethnic, language, and cultural communities are differentiated, the more national institutional pressure grows to guarantee the basic ethical propositions of life together and to practice them in the educational system. It is precisely in liberal societies that limits to integration of groups with differing ethics are increasingly visible. This limitation has to do with differing understandings of gender roles, ethical values with regard to age groups, attitudes toward violence, consumer behavior, and much more.

7. The State and Its Citizens

7.1. To this point, state ethics has been discussed in the sense of ethics belonging to the state. One can, however, change perspective and inquire about ethics seen critically from outside the state, that is, ethics carried over to the state by its subjects or citizens. This "state ethics" is an abbreviation for all those postulates that were formulated in the course of history as expectations, hopes, and criticisms. It is basically — in mirror image — the same thing. That the king should be just and mild, reward the good and punish the bad, protect widows and orphans, avoid war, create useful institutions, prevent corruption, and have a listening ear for the complaints of the people — these correspond to the traditional demands. But there is a difference in tone between state ethics seen from the view of the state and those seen from the view of its citizens. To the extent that the citizens express themselves, their perspective is determined by how strongly they are affected. War and → peace, justice and civil service, taxation, and steering of the economy and social institutions all directly affect their lives. Their ethical impetus is directed to the improvement of → everyday life, to the relieving of the daily burdens and difficulties and less to an abstract formula that comprehends the common good as a whole. The contents of ethics therefore change in the wake of historical development, while the simple wish for a "good prince," a "good regime," or a "government oriented to the common good" continues to be heard.

Within an academic context, one might therefore doubt whether this summation of ethical postulates can even be called state ethics. In point of fact, there is no doubt that there are in modern societies relatively widespread and constantly normative propositions that form a "state ethics" *from below*. The dissatisfaction that has been observed in recent years with politics and politicians refers to moral expectations. It has to do with a rejection of corruption and mismanagement of tax revenues, with a disapproval of the holding of important and remunerative positions by unqualified party politicians, with the criticism of the → manipulation of important decisions without public participation, as well as with the feeling that the "true needs" and concerns of the population would be disregarded by a political class that had become all too secure in its possession of power. The propositions of this ethics are formulated negatively, but the existence of its implicitly positive counterpart constantly contributes to the thought process, even if it is seldom verbally expressed.

7.2. Unhappy citizens who criticize the officials they themselves have elected would in effect rather be subjects than citizens. Only by taking on the duties and burdens of a "civil society" do they become full members of it. "Citizen virtues" are thus the real basis of state ethics. Only an active citizen behaves responsibly. The model of the "responsible citizen" has become a cliché, to be sure, and it cannot be expected, in the circumstances of an → industrialized society based on division of labor that divides → responsibility and thus renders it invisible, that the modern citizen can take part and have a say in the fate of the whole society, in the way of ancient Athens. But the ethical model of responsibility is the only resistance that can be marshaled against the many powers that are interested in reducing the influence of the individual — for instance, within the fields of advertising and consumerism (→ Consumption), media and politics.

Concerning *duties,* however, the traditional elements are there: obedience to the law, payment of taxes, military and local service obligations, acceptance of voluntary positions in local administration and law courts, and the periodic exercise of a morally understood duty to vote. The question of whether membership in a political party should be a national ethical requirement is debated, in view of the enormous and unavoidable significance of these organizations in the formation of the public will. In the aim of hindering corrupt and power-hungry oligarchies, however, it surely must be advocated.

Concerning *activity,* the model of the responsible citizen can support an ethics of involvement and inconvenience, as well as the disturbance of intellectual and spiritual cartels of conformity — in short, the kind of criticism that has the courage to stand solidly on one's own judgment. Only through these critical and constantly self-activating state ethics can a community be kept robust. The legal and institutional superstructure is not the deciding factor — the citizen virtues are.

Bibliography: B. A. Ackerman, *We the People* (2 vols.; Cambridge, Mass., 1991-98) • A. M. Bickel, *The Least*

Dangerous Branch: The Supreme Court at the Bar of Politics (2d ed.; New Haven, 1986) • E.-W. Böckenförde, *Der Staat als sittlicher Staat* (Berlin, 1978) • R. M. Dworkin, *Law's Empire* (Cambridge, Mass., 1986); idem, *Taking Rights Seriously* (Cambridge, Mass., 1978) • J. H. Ely, *Democracy and Distrust: A Theory of Judicial Review* (Cambridge, Mass., 1980) • E. Forsthoff, *Der Staat der Industriegesellschaft* (2d ed.; Munich, 1977) • G. Jellinek, *Allgemeine Staatslehre* (Berlin, 1900; 3d ed., 1914) • H. Krüger, "Verfassungsvoraussetzungen und Verfassungserwartungen," *Festschrift für Ulrich Scheuner* (Berlin, 1973) 285-306 • W. Kymlicka, *Multicultural Citizenship: A Liberal Theory of Minority Rights* (Oxford, 1995) • J. Rawls, *A Theory of Justice* (Cambridge, Mass., 1971; rev. ed., 1999) • C. Schmitt, "Staatsethik und pluralistischer Staat," *Kant-Studien* 35 (1930) 28-42 • C. Taylor, *Multiculturalism and "The Politics of Recognition"* (Princeton, 1992).

Michael Stolleis

States of the Church → Papal States

Stations of the Cross

The stations of the cross (a term coined by William Wey in 1472) are an ancient form of → devotion involving the treading and contemplating of Christ's way of suffering. Usually today there are 14 stations. They are based on the gospels (→ Gospel), with only the Veronica station being legendary. The progress is from Pilate's house (the condemnation of → Jesus) to the entombment. In more recent discussion a 15th station is the goal (the → resurrection).

The starting point is the Good Friday → liturgy and → procession in → Jerusalem, which goes back to the fourth century. The development in the West and the fixing on 14 stations of the cross were the work of the priest Bethlem in his book on the subject (1518), Christiaan Cruys (1533-85, called Adrichomius) in his books *Jerusalem sicut Christi tempore floruit* (1584) and *Theatrum terrae sanctae* (1590, published posthumously), and Leonhard von Porto Maurizio (1676-1751) in his sermons on the theme. In 1731 and 1742 the Congregation of Indulgences adopted its teaching on → prayers for the stations of the cross as a norm. Related to these devotions were → indulgences, which might also be secured for the dead.

Pictorial representations of the stations of the cross have been common from the 15th century. In Spain plein-air paintings date from 1423. Lübeck

had a depiction in 1468. Around 1505 Adam Kraft (d. 1508/9) set up seven stations of the cross on the way to the Johannis burial ground in Nürnberg. Many stations of the cross lead to Calvaries, which were common from the 15th century onward, especially under the sign of the → Catholic Reformation (e.g., in northern Germany, Lombardy, and esp. Brittany), often on hillsides. From the early 18th century plein-air paintings found a continuation in stations of the cross in Roman Catholic churches. Depictions were common in the mid-18th century and among the German Nazarener (Lucas Brotherhood). Today there are many pictures in books of → meditation and devotion, and most Roman Catholic churches have stations of the cross arranged around the walls of the building.

→ Christian Art; Iconography; Passion, Accounts of the; Piety

Bibliography: B. Brown, "Stations of the Cross," *NCE* (2d ed.) 13.499-501 • J. Murphy-O'Connor, "The Geography of Faith: Tracing the Via Dolorosa," *BibRev* 12 (1996) 32-41 • M.-J. Picard, "Croix (Chemin de)," *DSp* 2.2576-606 • H. Thurston, *The Stations of the Cross: An Account of Their History and Devotional Purpose* (London, 1906) • A. Walker, *Journey into Joy: Stations of the Resurrection* (London, 2001).

Johannes Schilling

Status confessionis

1. Term
2. Reformation Concerns
3. Contemporary Discussion

1. Term

The Latin term *status confessionis* means the stance of a witness summoned to testify. In the 20th century the term acquired the technical sense among Protestants of a binding doctrinal stance on sociopolitical questions.

The roots of this theological motif lie in the intertestamental theology of the holy remnant of Israel during the time of Hellenization and later of the early Christian → martyrs and confessors. Important biblical sources include the statement of → Jesus on the necessity of confessing him before others (Matt. 10:32 par. Luke 12:8), as cited in the Solid Declaration of the → Formula of Concord (SD 10.17), and the stance taken against → Peter by → Paul in Antioch for the truth of the gospel manifest in the table fellowship of Jewish and Gentile believers (Gal. 2:11-21; SD 10.10-15).

The modern usage evolved from the Old Lutheran "confessional stance" against the Prussian Church → Union early in the 19th century. The technical term *status confessionis* found its way from there into scholarly discussion of the Lutheran confessional writings. Dietrich → Bonhoeffer (1906-45), among others, took it up and gave it new provenance in the church debate about "the Jewish question." Bonhoeffer analyzed the crisis brought on by the Nazi Aryan Clause in terms of a dynamic understanding of the → two-kingdoms doctrine: the state's failure within its own jurisdiction to protect certain citizens, the Jews, is linked with its interference in the church's jurisdiction, which is founded upon baptism, not race. Bonhoeffer thus correlated the ecclesial and the civil problems. This interpretation of the confessional stance as public protest working to resituate and redefine authority was taken up and developed by Robert Bertram (1921-2003) years later in his interpretation of a declaration of the → Lutheran World Federation (LWF) at Dar es Salaam in 1977 (see 3).

2. Reformation Concerns

The special concern of the 16th-century → Reformers, however, was not *status* but *casus* — not the stance of witness, but the special situation *(casus)* of being called to the stand. How is this extraordinary situation to be discerned in distinction from the ongoing witness of the church *(confessio continua)*?

Controversy occurred over the degree of permissible collaboration with the victorious papal party among defeated Lutherans during the Leipzig Interim (1548-52). Philipp → Melanchthon (1497-1560) took the view that collaboration on indifferent things (e.g., ceremonies) is permitted, so long as the doctrinally correct preaching of → grace is not compromised. Matthius Flacius (1520-75) took the opposite view: even trifling compromise with persecutors scandalized the suffering church. In this grave situation, the uncompromising witness of Galatians 2 is needed for the sake of the confused and frightened church; likewise the public confession of Matthew 10 is required by God as testimony against the persecutors.

SD 10 sided with Flacius's contention that *nihil est adiaphoron in casu confessionis et scandali* (there are no indifferent matters when it comes to confessing the faith or giving offense; → Adiaphora). The formulators defined the "case" of confession as the attempt to "use violence or chicanery in such a way that undermines true worship of God" (10.10). The SD affirms that in normal times the church is free to change ceremonial practices. But in the extraordinary case of → persecution, all are "obligated according to God's Word to confess true teaching and everything that pertains to the whole of religion freely and publicly . . . not only with words but also in actions and deeds. In such a time they shall not yield to the opponents even in indifferent matters" (ibid.).

3. Contemporary Discussion

3.1. The contemporary usage of *status confessionis* since the time of the → church struggle in Germany has been fraught with controversy, with traditional tensions between Lutheran and Reformed sensibilities never far from the surface. Is the *status confessionis* a matter of the martyr's witness in the precise case of persecution of gospel proclamation? Or may it be ethically generalized to include active, political work for change against whatever contradicts the will and way of Jesus Christ?

Thinking along the latter lines, the Reformierter Bund (RB) of the Evangelische Kirche in Deutschland (EKD), following the lead of the Nederlandse Hervormde Kerk in the Netherlands, declared in 1982 that a *status confessionis* had arisen in regard not merely to the possible use, but to the very possession, of nuclear → weapons (§5.2). This stance summoned the Western churches in the name of the faith to embrace unilateral nuclear disarmament, explicitly repudiating the "calculation, the equilibrium, ambiguity, and indecision" of the (predominantly Lutheran) EKD (D. J. Smit, 25). In 1977, however, *status confessionis* had been similarly invoked at Dar es Salaam by the LWF, declaring that, "on the basis of faith and in order to manifest the unity of the church, churches would publicly and unequivocally reject the existing apartheid system" and "work for change" (A. Sovik, 180; → Social Ethics 4.5).

Difficult questions arose immediately. The 1982 RB statement did not demand church discipline against the erring Christians of the EKD who accepted nuclear deterrence, as though the contradictory stances could exist in ongoing dialogue and debate. The LWF declaration, in contrast, eventuated in church discipline when two small Lutheran churches in South Africa were expelled at the Budapest assembly of the LWF in 1984 for insufficient opposition to apartheid. But one also had to ask: if peaceful "work for change" were to fail, does the *status confessionis* against apartheid sanction revolutionary violence to bring change about? For some, this question exposed an underlying political theology closer to Thomas → Müntzer (ca. 1489-1525) than to Martin → Luther (1483-1546).

3.2. The incompatibility of Christian faith with

weapons of mass destruction, apartheid, or many other contemporary evils is not seriously in dispute in the argument about *status confessionis*. Rather, the direct linkage of the church's proclamation of the gospel with political ultimatums, fallible analysis, and utopian calls to action has been hotly contested. The objections are as follows. First, when there is still time for active political work for change, the church is not yet in the "case" of confession. Second, the content of the "case" of confession is the integrity of the church as the communion of Christ — the Galatians' correlation of the gospel of free grace with the table fellowship of Jew and Gentile. Third, the danger of holy crusade arises when struggles for social justice are directly sanctioned as the cause of Christ in the present hour. Fourth, the church's ministry of → reconciliation as mediator of political conflict in society is forfeited when ultimatums are issued. Fifth, the continuing confession of the church suffices to muster the people of God to "work for change," which is the political vocation of all the baptized. Sixth, "work for change" must in any case remain open to challenge, dialogue, debate, and political compromise.

3.3. Thinking along these lines, an LWF consultation in 1982 developed criteria for discerning the *casus,* that is, determining how social and political problems might become an occasion for "special confessing of the faith" (a new formulation offered in place of the easily misunderstood "status confessionis"). Since the being of the church in society as the creature of the Word depends on the preaching of the gospel, such occasions may arise when (1) more than the gospel is regarded as necessary for salvation, (2) the life-giving good news is distorted into a demand that kills, (3) the whole gospel with all its implications for life no longer finds expression, (4) the church by its adherence to alien principles becomes a scandal and obstacle to faith, or (5) the church's proclamation of the gospel is made impossible. Not only, as traditionally, is violent persecution from the outside in view. Now a spotlight falls on the intrusion of alien ideologies into the church itself. If in this connection the church relies directly on the coercive power of the state, or even indirectly through conformity to social discrimination, the occasion for special confessing may be discerned.

3.4. Dutch Reformed South African theologian Dirk J. Smit came to similar conclusions in his interpretation of the resolution of the 1982 Ottawa meeting of the → World Alliance of Reformed Churches (WARC). On account of "the inflationistic use which eventually made the expression [*sta-*

tus confessionis] so commonplace that it actually became meaningless — many theologians and church leaders today are inclined to abandon the term" (p. 29). Acknowledging Lutheran-Reformed tensions over "the direct route from confession to politics," Smit urged that "one can only talk of 'ethical heresy' when that false doctrine is presented or defended in the name of the Gospel or the Bible" (pp. 43, 42). Smit thus called attention to the case made in Ottawa by Allan Boesak, who had argued that apartheid is not merely an evil → ideology but "a pseudo-religious ideology which was born in and is still being justified out of the bosom of Reformed Christianity" (p. 27). The Ottawa Resolution on Racism and South Africa accordingly found that apartheid "is a sin, and that the moral and theological justification of it is a travesty of the gospel, and in its persistent disobedience to the word of God, a theological heresy" (§1). This approach comports well with the fourth criterion of the LWF consultation listed above.

Yet Smit's deeper point was that there is, or should be, nothing special or extraordinary about forming the mind of the church in such a theological judgment. Such judgment is the normal work of dogmatic theology. Smit's description of the invocation of *status confessionis* as "inflationistic" — what Bertram had called "ethical protest with the volume turned up" (p. 104) — is telling. The striking thing about the apocalyptic resort to *status confessionis* in the 20th century is the absence it reflects of normal processes of doctrinal theology and → church discipline (what we could call the *processus confessionis*). The widespread failure to engage in → dogmatics — but in a lurch to call down fire on others — is what gave rise to M. Schloemann's caustic judgment on "making an easily revocable ecclesiological-ethical signal with a church-Latin code word" (p. 84). No doubt such misunderstanding, if not abuse, occurs. Yet the WARC and LWF were not wrong to pronounce the judgment of faith against apartheid. "Unless one takes a position that everything is God, the question of what is not God and not of God remains unavoidable" (C. Morse, 33).

The confused struggle over *status confessionis* reflects a basic need in Protestantism to rediscover theology as the church discipline that critically tests the church's confession of the Word of God before the world, not only in the extraordinary circumstance of persecution and scandal.

Bibliography: R. BERTRAM, "Confessing as Re-defining Authority: Ethical Implications of Augsburg's 'Time for Confessing,'" *The Debate on Status Confessionis:*

Studies in Christian Political Theology (ed. E. Lorenz; Geneva, 1983) 95-104 • D. Bonhoeffer, "The Church and the Jewish Question," *No Rusty Swords* (ed. E. H. Robinson; New York, 1965) 217-25 • G. Bornkamm, "Das Wort Jesu vom Bekennen," *Gesammelte Aufsätse,* vol. 3, *Geschichte und Glaube,* pt. 1 (Munich, 1968) 30-35 • Formula of Concord, Solid Declaration, art. 10, *The Book of Concord: The Confessions of the Evangelical Lutheran Church* (ed. R. Kolb and T. Wengert; Minneapolis, 2000) 635-40 • W. H. C. Frend, *Martyrdom and Persecution in the Early Church: A Study of a Conflict from the Maccabees to Donatus* (Grand Rapids, 1965) • H. P. Hamann, "Apartheid and (the) Status Confessionis," *A Lively Legacy: Essays in Honor of Robert Preus* (ed. K. E. Marquart, J. R. Stephenson, and B. W. Teigen; Fort Wayne, Ind., 1985) 40-51 • R. Hanhart, "Der status confessionis Israels in Hellenistischer Zeit," *ZTK* 92 (1995) 315-28 • P. R. Hinlicky, "Confession: A New Look at Some Old Theology," *AcadLP* 39 (1983) 57-80; idem, "The Debate over Status Confessionis," *LuthFor* 18/4 (1984) 24-29 • E. Lorenz, "The Criteria of Status Confessionis," *LuthFor* 17/4 (1983) 20-22 • U. Moeller, "Status Confessionis? Confessing our Faith in the Context of Economic Injustice," *RW* 46 (1996) 138-44 • C. Morse, "Testing the Spirits Today," *Not Every Spirit: A Dogmatics of Christian Disbelief* (Valley Forge, Pa., 1994) chap. 3 • O. K. Olson, *Matthias Flacius and the Survival of Luther's Reform* (Wiesbaden, 2002) • S. G. Ray, *Do No Harm: Social Sin and Christian Responsibility* (Minneapolis, 2003) • M. Schloemann, "The Special Case for Confessing: Reflections on the Casus Confessionis (Dar es Salaam, 1977) in the Light of History and Systematic Theology," *The Debate on Status Confessionis,* ed. Lorenz, 47-94 • D. J. Smit, "A Status Confessionis in South Africa?" *JTSA* 47 (1984) 21-46 • A. Sovik, ed., *In Christ–a New Community: The Proceedings of the Sixth Assembly of the Lutheran World Federation; Dar-es-Salaam, Tanzania, June 13-25, 1977* (Geneva, 1977) • E. TeSelle, "How Do We Recognize a Status Confessionis?" *TToday* 45 (1988) 71-78.

PAUL R. HINLICKY

Stewardship

The biblical parables and motif of the steward, or manager (Luke 12:42; 16:1, 8; 1 Cor. 4:1-2; 1 Pet. 4:10) — symbolizing Christian calling — might not be the basis of stewardship, but it certainly gave force to the concept as it developed in the North American churches, especially those of → free church persuasion. The idea is that Christians are trustees of the gifts and goods that God has en-

trusted to them and that they should be ready to support the work of the Christian → congregation with time, money, and involvement. Financial support might come first, but stewardship demands also time and involvement in evangelistic and diaconal initiatives (→ Evangelism; Diakonia).

Whether this form of lay responsibility can be transported to national churches in Europe is a moot question. American Lutherans warmly commended it to the German churches at the 1952 assembly of the → Lutheran World Federation, at Hannover, and the idea of being God's stewards appealed to the postwar Christians of Germany in their longing for a new life (Hanns Lilje). A movement of stewardship began with visiting and preparation for service and spilled over into the Scandinavian churches in the 1960s. Wherever it went, stewardship proved to be a biblically deepening perspective in the theological motivating of lay responsibility. It can include not merely the proper handling of money but also → visitation, diaconal ministry, singing in the church choir, action in economic matters, and working for world → peace and justice (H.-H. Ulrich).

Bibliography: T. A. Kantonen, *A Theology for Christian Stewardship* (Philadelphia, 1956) • R. S. Rodin, *Stewards in the Kingdom: A Theology of Life in All Its Fullness* (Downers Grove, Ill., 2000) • G. A. E. Salstrand, *The Story of Stewardship in the United States of America* (Grand Rapids, 1956) • T. Schober, ed., *Haushalterschaft als Bewährung christlichen Glaubens* (Stuttgart, 1981).

RICHARD BOECKLER

Stigmatization

In the history of → piety, the spontaneous occurrence of wound marks that resemble the flogged, thorn-crowned, and crucified → Jesus is called stigmatization. Stigmata, which were first exhibited by → Francis of Assisi (1181/82-1226), have been ascribed to numerous others who as a rule possessed a strong piety regarding the passion of Christ, the majority of whom were Roman Catholic women. The most famous examples are Anna Katharina Emmerick (1774-1824) and Therese Neumann of Konnersreuth in Bavaria (1898-1962).

Many people have inflicted wounds upon themselves out of a need for validation. Among the few stigmatized who were medically examined ("Madeleine," a patient of P. Janet, or the Capuchin monk Pio of Pietrelcina [1887-1968]), only shallow wounds were found, yet they bled profusely. A supernatural cause cannot be excluded, yet stigmatization can possibly be more simply explained as psychogenic bleeding and reddened swelling of the skin. Extremely sensitive people can produce these skin changes by autosuggestion as a result of compassion with the suffering Jesus. Although a strictly scientific explanation remains lacking, the hypothesis is supported by the fact that stigmata can be produced through external suggestion (A. Lechler) and through hypnosis in people who are disposed to produce the random bleeding of purpura (D. P. Agle, O. D. Ratnoff, and M. Wasman). Whether motivated by thankful and deeply affected emotions, tendencies to self-punishment, or hysterical needs for validation or experience, stigmatization needs to be researched case by case.

→ Lives of the Saints; Mystical Union; Mysticism; Parapsychology; Popular Religion; Saints, Veneration of; Visions

Bibliography: P. Adnès, "Stigmates," *DSp* 14.1211-43 • D. P. Agle, O. D. Ratnoff, and M. Wasman, "Conversion Reactions in Autoerythrocyte Sensitization: Their Relationship to the Production of Ecchymoses," *Archives of General Psychiatry* 20 (1969) 438-47 • T. Harrison, *Stigmata: A Medieval Mystery in a Modern Age* (London, 1994) • A. Lechler, *Das Rätsel von Konnersreuth im Lichte eines neuen Falles von Stigmatisation* (Elberfeld, 1933) • O. Schmucki, *The Stigmata of St. Francis of Assisi: A Critical Investigation in the Light of Thirteenth-century Sources* (St. Bonaventure, N.Y., 1991) • H. Thurston, *The Physical Phenomena of Mysticism* (London, 1952) • F. A. Whitlock and J. V. Hynes, "Religious Stigmatization: An Historical and Psychophysiological Enquiry," *Psychological Medicine* 8 (1978) 185-202 • I. Wilson, *Stigmata: An Investigation into the Mysterious Appearance of Christ's Wounds in Hundreds of People from Medieval Italy to Modern America* (San Francisco, 1989).

BERNHARD GROM

Stoicism

1. Survey
2. Teaching
   2.1. Physics
   2.2. Ethics
   2.3. Logic and Grammar
3. Methods and Problems
4. Influence

1. Survey

The formula *homologoumenōs zēn,* "living in harmony," makes clear the goal of the Stoics, a movement initiated by Zeno of Citium (ca. 335-ca. 263 B.C.). A *stoa* (colonnade) in Athens gave it its roof and its name. Cleanthes of Assos (331/30-232/31) added to the ambiguous goal of living in harmony the words *tē physei,* "with nature." His hymn to Zeus combines philosophical speculation with the religious tradition.

Chrysippus of Soli (ca. 280-ca. 206 B.C.) systematized Stoicism. It then took further shape in controversy with academic skepticism, the Peripatetics, and the Epicureans (→ Greek Philosophy). Panaetius of Rhodes (ca. 180-109) could accept with Aristotle (384-322; → Aristotelianism) the eternity of the world, and in encounter with Rome he differentiated the forms of ethical action (Ethics 1.3). Poseidonius of Apamea (ca. 135-ca. 51) united → philosophy of nature, geography, and history on an anthropological model and thought of the cosmos as a living entity. Cicero (106-43) discussed Stoic theorems in the context of competing schools.

Under the → Roman Empire the ethical and practical aspect came strongly to the fore. Seneca (ca. 4 B.C.–A.D. 65), Epictetus (ca. 55-ca. 135), and Marcus Aurelius (121-180) stressed the motif of self-persuasion, but they too showed an increasing turn to religion. Epictetus linked personal religion to the *logos.* Stoicism made its main impact as intellectual practice (→ Asceticism), as the true fulfillment of the *logos* (*Stoicorum veterum fragmenta* [*SVF*] 3.293), as a *forma vivendi* (form of life; Cicero *De fin.* 3.23).

2. Teaching

As a system (→ Social Systems), Stoicism tried to combine Heraclitus's conception of the *logos* and fire (see 2.1) with the Socratic postulate of the autonomy of virtue. Only → virtue is needed for success. But virtue derives from a firm insight into the *logos* structure of the cosmos and humanity (→ Anthropology 4; Reason).

2.1. *Physics*

Stoicism viewed itself as monistic (→ Monism) → materialism. The *logos,* as God, as the active material principle *(to poioun),* works on inert matter, a passive element *(to paschon);* nature *(physis)* achieves being as "creative fire" (*SVF* 1.171). The *logos,* as pneuma, coherently permeates the cosmos and gives it its inner tension *(tonos)* analogous to the → soul, which is the directing seed of the *logos* (*hēgemonikon, logos spermatikos*) in individual beings. The *logos,* as providence *(pronoia)* and destiny *(heimarmenē),* foreordains the process of the world, so that we can foresee it in detail (*SVF* 2.1187ff.); it takes a cyclic form, for after a cosmic conflagration *(ek-*

pyrōsis), a new but identical phase emerges (*SVF* 2.623ff.; → Apocatastasis).

2.2. *Ethics*

The resultant → fatalism gave Stoicism room for an adaptation of the individual (*SVF* 2.998). The primary motif in → life is self-preservation (*oikeiōsis, SVF* 3.661) by keeping one's rational nature against false views and affections *(pathē).* Freedom from emotion *(apatheia)* is a condition of autonomous virtue. By making impulses *(hormē)* and goals dependent on agreement with *logos,* it is possible to achieve the primary end. In relation to this primary end, one may distinguish relative advantages *(proēgmena)* such as → health and well-being, but these do not add to virtue, and hence all such values are ultimately → adiaphora.

Since there is such a thing as → natural law, the Stoics could be politically active (*SVF* 3.661). Rational action (*kathēkon, officium;* → Duty) in accordance with nature achieves what is right *(katorthōma)* in accordance with good insight. "The wages of a good deed is to have done it" (Seneca *Ep.* 81.19); the → happiness that results is characterized as the flowing of life (*SVF* 1.184). Over against the deforming of virtue, → suicide is accepted (e.g., Marcus Aurelius *Med.* 9.2). After death the souls of the wise live on in a sublunar heaven, but not beyond the cosmic conflagration.

2.3. *Logic and Grammar*

The criterion of Stoic → epistemology is perception *(katalēpsis),* a kind of combination model by which the *logos* lays hold of ideas *(phantasia)* implanted in the soul and tests them (*SVF* 1.66). Only when confirmed *(synkatathesis)* by the *logos* is there valid evidence for a thing. On this basis the Stoics could build up principles that they linked together in a complex modal logic of statements. By the use of analysis and norms they could ensure the freedom of their statements from ambivalence, and many of our grammatical → categories show a Stoic origin. Stoic semiotics (→ Sign 1) can point to an independent meaning *(sēmainomenon, lekton),* as well as to the subject *(tynchanon)* and sign *(sēmainon, SVF* 2.166). Its immaterial character may be a threat to monism, but the rigorous physical and ethical dogmas can be logically analyzed and applied.

3. Methods and Problems

Extreme caution is needed in relation to the fragmentary account of Stoicism in Cicero. Modern research gives evidence of its rapid development. Even in antiquity Stoic paradoxes came under debate (e.g., that there is no gradation of actions). As the logic that has been brought to light only in the 20th century suggests, we are not to understand a broad outline of Stoic teaching naively. A closer analysis of the Stoic use of words is needed.

Stoicism is, despite its dogmas, a continuation of Platonic and Aristotelian reflection on principles. Its premise of a rational materiality radically circumvents the problems of matter/form and body/soul, but it creates problems in explaining the manifold nature of the world. Why should not the cosmos be eternal in accordance with providence? Is strict perception *(katalēpsis)* possible (→ Skepticism)? How can we safeguard a sensory doctrine of knowledge against the emotions? Can the ideals of the wise ever be reached? Stoicism turned more and more to a reaching forward *(prokoptōn, proficiens)* that finds support in daily action.

4. Influence

Cicero was decisively important for the Latin West. His Stoic-oriented work *De officiis* influenced Christian → ethics by way of Ambrose (ca. 339-97), and it also made a significant impact on the development of → humanism by way of Petrarch (1304-74). Stoic → allegory (*SVF* 2.1088ff.), which scientifically interpreted the → polytheism of the myths of antiquity, also played a part in shaping exegesis (esp. in → Origen; → Alexandrian Theology; Exegesis, Biblical).

In the second century Stoicism integrated the models of union and ascent of → Platonism; from the third century onward, it merged into the stream of Neoplatonism. In the fourth century affinities between Stoicism and Christianity led to the appearance of a fictional exchange of letters between Paul and Seneca. → Augustine (354-430; → Augustine's Theology) passed on implicitly Stoic concepts to the → Middle Ages. Even in the → modern period we hold self-preservation to be one of our fundamental theorems, a value that comes from a Stoic or neo-Stoic basis.

Bibliography: Primary sources: M. T. Cicero, *De natura deorum* (trans. H. Rackham; New York, 1933) • *Die Fragmente zur Dialektik der Stoiker* (4 vols.; ed. K. Hülser; Stuttgart, 1987) • *Panaetii Rhodii fragmenta* (ed. M. van Straaten; Leiden, 1962) • Poseidonius, *Die Fragmente* (2 vols.; ed. W. von Theiler; Berlin, 1982) • Sextus Empiricus, *Against the Logicians* (trans. R. Bett; Cambridge, 2005); idem, *The Skeptic Way: Sextus Empiricus's Outlines of Pyrrhonism* (trans. B. Mates; New York, 1996) • *Stoicorum veterum fragmenta* (4 vols.; ed. H. von Arnim; Leipzig 1903-24).

Secondary works: T. Brennan, *The Stoic Life: Emotions, Duties, and Fate* (Oxford, 2005) • M. L. Colish,

The Stoic Tradition from Antiquity to the Early Middle Ages (2 vols.; Leiden, 1985) • A. GRAESER, *Plotinus and the Stoics* (Leiden, 1972) • B. INWOOD, *Ethics and Human Action in Early Stoicism* (Oxford, 1985); idem, *Reading Seneca: Stoic Philosophy at Rome* (New York, 2005); idem, ed., *The Cambridge Companion to the Stoics* (New York, 2003) • M. V. LEE, *Paul, the Stoics, and the Body of Christ* (New York, 2006) • A. A. LONG, ed., *Problems in Stoicism* (London, 1971) • B. MATES, *Stoic Logic* (Berkeley, Calif., 1953) • M. MORFORD, *Stoics and Neostoics: Rubens and the Circle of Lipsius* (Princeton, 1991) • M. POHLENZ, *Die Stoa* (2 vols.; 7th ed.; Göttingen, 1992) • J. M. RIST, ed., *The Stoics* (Berkeley, Calif., 1978) • J. SELLARS, *The Art of Living: The Stoics on the Nature and Function of Philosophy* (Aldershot, 2003); idem, *Stoicism* (Berkeley, Calif., 2006) • G. VERBEKE, *The Presence of Stoic Thought in Medieval Thought* (Washington, D.C., 1983).

THOMAS POISS

Structuralism

1. Term
2. Linguistic Structuralism
3. Structuralism and Ethnology
4. Theological Impact of Structuralism

In the various forms of structuralism, the aim, generally speaking, is to derive the elements of an orderly whole from its total structure (Lat. *struo*, "erect, put together, put in order").

1. Term
The term "structuralism" is used in many disciplines, such as in modern structuralist mathematics (D. Hilbert, the research group of N. Bourbaki), in which theories are explained by the differences from, and relations to, axiomatically given basic structures (→ Axiom). We also find it in the natural sciences, for example, in atomic theory, in the chemical theory of molecules, and in the doctrine of crystal lattices. Structural attempts at explanation are found also in modern biology, such as in the interpretations of the modes of functioning of cells and organs (L. Bertalanffy).

2. Linguistic Structuralism
From the beginning of the 20th century, influenced by the innovations of the Genevan linguist Ferdinand de Saussure (1857-1913) in → linguistics, the widespread use of structuralism began its career, which would take it into French → ethnology (C. Lévi-Strauss) and, in latter decades of the century, into French literature (R. Barthes), history (M. Foucault), and → philosophy (L. Althusser). Saussure initiated the synchronic (or "simultaneous") view of language, which, in place of the earlier dominant diachronic method, which had primarily researched the historical origin of language, sought to relativize it along structural lines. For Saussure, *langue* (i.e., → language) is a supraindividual → social system whose structure cannot be known from an analysis of *parole* (i.e., concrete speech) but can be explained only by the formal characteristics of the system of linguistic → signs, that is, by investigation of the differences that distinguish one from another and their mutual limitations. Every sign stands in relative opposition to other signs. It has a double function: on the one hand, it signifies (the *signifiant*, e.g., the sound sequence "it snows"); on the other, it is something signified (the *signifié*, here, snow falling). The connection between the two functions is not natural but arbitrary, joined by social convention and necessary for the functioning of the language.

Languages are thus viewed as systems of (partly unconscious) structural rules, which modern linguistics investigates. The Prague School (N. S. Trubetzkoy, R. Jacobson, J. Mukarovský), the Copenhagen Circle (L. Hjelmslev), and the American school of linguists (L. Bloomfield) have all followed this synchronic approach.

3. Structuralism and Ethnology
Structural interpretations can be used not only for the interpretation of language but also for an explanation of institutionally ordered forms of interaction (→ Institution), which was something Saussure realized when he said that "language is a system of signs that express ideas, and is therefore comparable to a system of writing, the alphabet of deaf-mutes, symbolic rites, polite formulas, military signals, etc." (p. 16).

The French ethnologist Claude Lévi-Strauss (b. 1908), often called the father of French structuralism, helped to give the new approach to *langue* a worldwide influence by applying the method of structural linguistics analytically to institutions, using it, with the help of motifs of S. Freud and K. → Marx (→ Marxism; Psychoanalysis), to explain structurally the relationships of primitive peoples. Lévi-Strauss analyzed the marriage rules that determined the structure of archaic societies, in which an exogamous exchange of women that met the → taboo against incest, played a central role. Along the lines of structural linguistics he also investigated the code of → totemism, with its concepts of opposites (heaven and earth, up above and down below). He also explained the content of → myths with a similar set of opposing pairs (the raw and the cooked, honey and tobacco).

The "classic structuralism" of Saussure and Lévi-Strauss was reinterpreted in French "poststructuralism," or "neostructuralism" (G. Deleuze, J. Derrida). This position focuses, among other things, on the critique of "centered," "closed" structures (M. Frank).

4. Theological Impact of Structuralism

The example of Lévi-Strauss in the interpretation of myths, as well as the structural narrative analyses of the Russian formalists T. Todorov (b. 1939) and V. Propp (1895-1970), made an impact on biblical → exegesis and opened up a discussion of methods. As exegesis that operated exclusively in terms of historical criticism ran into a crisis, new models of → hermeneutics and interpretative exposition came on the scene. The attempt of R. Barthes (1915-80) and J. Courtès (b. 1936) to explain the text of Acts 10–11 by structural narrative analysis, reading it as a system of mythical ideas, might serve to show how structuralism was influencing theology.

P. Ricoeur (1913-2005), who advocated a hermeneutical theory of interpretation in philosophy and psychoanalysis, as well as in biblical exegesis, pointed out that, although theological discourse would be enhanced by a structural reading of biblical texts that dealt with the system of narrative antitheses, this method, used in isolation, would be void of meaning. Only if hermeneutics is able to return from the abstractness of a structural-systemic analysis of *langue* to the dimension of *parole* (speech) can we grasp the meaning of texts. Ricoeur thus raises the question whether any absolutized structuralism in exegesis would not lead into error.

→ Anthropology; Culture; Epistemology; Meaning; Phenomenology

Bibliography: On 1-3: W. Balzer and C. U. Moulines, eds., *Structuralist Theory of Science: Focal Issues, New Results* (Berlin, 1996) • P. Caws, *Structuralism: A Philosophy for the Human Sciences* (Atlantic Highlands, N.J., 1997) • J. D. Culler, *Structuralist Poetics: Structuralism, Linguistics, and the Study of Literature* (London, 2002) • M. Frank, *What Is Neostructuralism?* (trans. S. Wilke and R. Gray; Minneapolis, 1989) • E. Kurzweil, *The Age of Structuralism: From Lévi-Strauss to Foucault* (New Brunswick, N.J, 1996) • C. Lévi-Strauss, *Introduction to the Science of Mythology* (trans. J. Weightman and D. Weightman; New York, 1969) • R. Macksey and E. Donato, eds., *The Structuralist Controversy* (Balti-more, 1972) • F. de Saussure, *Course in General Linguistics* (ed. C. Bally and A. Sechehaye; trans. W. Baskin; New York, 1959).

On 4: J. Dunnill, "Structuralism and Biblical Study" and "Structuralism and Hermeneutics," *Covenant and Sacrifice in the Letter to the Hebrews* (Cambridge, 1992) 48-57 and 58-63 • D. Greenwood, *Structuralism and the Biblical Text* (Berlin, 1985) • W. Harnisch, *Die Neutestamentliche Gleichnisforschung im Horizont von Hermeneutik und Literaturwissenschaft* (Darmstadt, 1982) • X. Léon-Dufour, ed., *Exegese im Methodenkonflikt. Zwischen Geschichte und Struktur* (Munich, 1973) with contributions by Barthes, Courtès, and Ricoeur • W. Schenk, *Die Sprache des Matthäus. Die Text-Konstituenten in ihren makro- und mikrostrukturellen Relationen* (Göttingen, 1987) • G. Schiwy, *Structuralism and Christianity* (trans. H. J. Koren; Pittsburgh, 1971) • D. R. Stiver, "Structuralism and Poststructuralism," *The Philosophy of Religious Language: Sign, Symbol, and Story* (Cambridge, Mass., 1996) 163-92.

Ludwig Nagl

Student Christian Movements

1. Early History
2. Late Nineteenth and Early Twentieth Centuries
3. Rise of American Evangelical Groups
4. Current Scope and Prospects

Student Christian Movements represent an important dimension of Protestant missionary and evangelistic work during the 19th and 20th centuries, particularly within the English-speaking evangelical world, and especially in the United States. While originating among, and targeting, university and college students, the movements and organizations that have arisen as part of this impulse have had a much wider impact within the wider Protestant community as a source of pride and inspiration, a practical training ground for future workers and leaders, and a laboratory for new strategies and techniques. Traditionally marked by an emphasis on → evangelism and a broad, grassroots → ecumenism, the movement split in the 1920s with the rise of liberal Protestantism and the fundamentalist-modernist controversy (→ Liberal Theology; Fundamentalism). Gradually since the 1930s, the growth sector of such organizations has tilted overwhelmingly toward conservative, North American–based, evangelical parachurch organizations. Moving into the 21st century, these well-funded evangelical ministries have become the predominant

Protestant presence on most secular college and university campuses worldwide.

1. Early History

Student-led renewal and evangelistic movements can trace their origins back to the very beginnings of the evangelical → revivals of the early 18th century in models like the so-called Holy Club at Oxford in the early 1730s, centered on John and Charles Wesley. Similar groups sprang up at Harvard, Yale, Brown, and other universities in the newly independent United States as part of the revivals associated with the Second Great Awakening at the turn of the 19th century. One of these groups, the Rising Sun at Williams College in western Massachusetts, provided the participants at the famous "Haystack Prayer Meeting," in which several missions-minded students discussed missionary service while seeking shelter from a thunderstorm in the summer of 1806. One of the students, Samuel Mills, subsequently played an influential role in the efforts that led in 1810 to the formation of the American Board of Commissioners for Foreign Missions (→ Mission; Missionary).

Throughout the early and mid 19th centuries the ranks of pious evangelical college students proved fertile recruiting grounds for various evangelical Protestant causes in Britain and the United States. A major impetus to Christian student movements came with the creation in 1844 of the → Young Men's Christian Association (YMCA) in London and the spread of the YMCA movement to North America in the early 1850s. By the end of that decade there were more than 200 associations scattered across the United States, with the "Y" having moved on to college campuses such as the Universities of Virginia and Michigan in conjunction with the "prayer meeting revival" of 1857/58.

2. Late Nineteenth and Early Twentieth Centuries

The latter decades of the 19th century marked a major upsurge in student-centered Protestant movements. In Britain, students at Cambridge formed the Cambridge Inter-Collegiate Christian Union in 1877, followed in 1879 by its equivalent at Oxford. The size and work of these groups were greatly enhanced by a series of successful revivals on British campuses led by the American evangelist D. L. → Moody (1837-99) in the early 1880s. Back in the United States, Moody repeated his British collegiate success in revival meetings held at Princeton, Harvard, Yale, and Dartmouth.

In the summer of 1886 Moody invited nearly 600 missions-minded college students to the Mount Hermon conference grounds on his farm in Northfield, Massachusetts, for a monthlong meeting. By the time it was over, 100 young people — the "Mount Hermon Hundred" — had come forward to pledge their lives to missionary service. The meetings expanded the next year, and one of the Hundred, Cornell graduate and newly appointed YMCA secretary John R. → Mott (1865-1955), helped organize the Student Volunteer Movement (SVM) in 1888. Guided by its motto "The evangelization of the world in this generation," the SVM became a phenomenon within American Protestantism. By the time of its first convention in 1891, more than 6,000 American college and Bible institute students had volunteered for overseas service.

The success of the SVM in America inspired similar efforts in Britain, Germany, and Scandinavia during the 1890s. In an attempt to network these movements, representatives from ten countries in Europe and North America met at Vadstena Castle in Sweden in 1895 to form the → World Student Christian Federation (WSCF). Committed to world evangelization, the WSCF quickly became an integral part of the growing ecumenical movement and in 1911 moved beyond its Protestant origins, inviting the participation of Orthodox Christians.

The prominence of student-centered and student-led groups continued into the first two decades of the 20th century. By 1913 the American YMCA was reporting meteoric growth, adding to the size and number of its facilities at such a rate that the value of its national physical plant doubled in a mere six-year period. Meanwhile in that same year, Mott reported at the annual WSCF convention that there were over 2,300 local, student-led Christian associations scattered across the globe. And on a personal level, heroic figures like the young American dairy millionaire William Borden (1887-1913) — "Borden of Yale," who renounced his fortune in favor of missionary service and died in Cairo, Egypt, en route to China — inspired young and old Protestants alike to greater piety and support for the missionary endeavor.

The coming of the First World War in 1914 and the growing impact of new intellectual trends and theological strife in the churches marked a dividing line that would by the 1920s, particularly in America, divide the great Pan-Protestant student Christian movements along liberal and conservative lines. Traumatized by the war, the WSCF shifted its postwar focus to ecumenism, social welfare, and the achievement of world → peace. Meanwhile, the American YMCA, under pressure from an increasingly secularized culture and liberal Protestant connections and leadership, gradually dropped its support for revivalism during the 1920s, replacing its former emphasis on personal evangelism and Bible study with a broad educational and recreational mission.

3. Rise of American Evangelical Groups

The liberal drift of these organizations was not well received within conservative Protestant circles in the United States. The grumblings of one Philadelphia youth pastor in the mid-1920s that one could "take the 'C' out of the YMCA and no one would ever know the difference" fairly reflected conservatives' growing dissatisfaction with the established Protestant youth organizations. The first major fundamentalist attempt to promote work with North American university students began in 1925 with the establishment of the League of Evangelical Students (LES) by a group of conservative theologians headed up by the Presbyterian J. Gresham Machen. Based at Princeton, and then from Machen's secessionist Westminster Theological Seminary, the LES was characterized by a fortress mentality and a focus on theology; by 1937 it had small chapters on over 60 campuses, primarily in the eastern half of the country.

The major breakthrough in conservative student movements came with the establishment of the British Inter-Varsity Christian Fellowship (IVCF) in 1928. Inter-Varsity, a split with Britain's WSCF-related Student Christian Movement, began work in Canada the next year at a conference in Kingston, Ontario (→ Evangelical Movement 3). IVCF began work in the United States in 1940 with 4 full-time staff and chapters on 22 American campuses. By the end of the decade the organization had expanded to over 40 staff and chapters at 229 colleges and universities. The success of IVCF spurred an effort to create a worldwide umbrella organization for evangelical students that would counterbalance the presence of the WSCF. In August 1947 representatives from evangelical student groups in seven North American and European countries, plus Australia, New Zealand, and China, met in Boston to create the International Fellowship of Evangelical Students (IFES). By the early 1960s, chapters of the IFES had been established in 14 additional countries.

Fed by the massive expansion of U.S. college enrollment in the postwar era, IVCF and other groups targeting American college students continued their growth apace through the 1950s. The Navigators (1933), originally targeting Southern California high school students and then American servicemen during World War II, followed its membership onto several college campuses in the postwar era as American war veterans pursued educational opportunities under the G.I. Bill. By the late 1950s the group was established on nearly 60 campuses across the country. A similar organization, Campus Crusade for Christ (CCC), was created in Southern California in 1951 by Bill Bright (1921-2003), a recent graduate of the evangelical Fuller Theological Seminary. By 1960 CCC had groups on over 40 U.S. campuses and had established work with students in Pakistan and South Korea. InterVarsity, for its part, had nearly 750 chapters (including about 300 chapters of the Nurses' Christian Fellowship), 100 full-time staff, and an annual budget of almost $750,000.

The 1960s and 1970s marked the true "boom" period in American evangelical college ministries as a result of a combination of factors, including (1) the arrival of the postwar "Baby Boom" generation on college and university campuses; (2) the growing strength and prosperity of the American evangelical movement; (3) a solid foundation of expanding evangelical youth work among American young people by such high school–oriented organizations as Youth for Christ, Young Life, and the Fellowship of Christian Athletes; and (4) the onset of the → "Jesus People" movement among → countercultural youth in the late 1960s and early 1970s. IVCF continued its prominent role with its triennial "Urbana" conferences at the University of Illinois. This event became an important source of potential missionaries and Christian workers, attracting upward of 15,000 students by the mid-1970s. By 1980 the American branch of IVCF could claim nearly 29,000 official members in 629 chapters and an operation that cost over $15 million per year.

But easily the biggest success story in perhaps the entire evangelical movement during this period was the stunning growth and diversification of Campus Crusade. By the end of the 1960s the group boasted nearly 2,000 full-time staff and had ventured into working with military personnel and athletes, as well as pioneering lay evangelistic training and mass evangelism. The decade of the 1970s saw even more spectacular results as CCC nearly quintupled in size. Although the revamped Campus Crusade of the 1980s and beyond sponsored dozens of evangelistic enterprises, its work among American students remained its core purpose, as well as the fount of many of its workers (→ Northern America 4).

4. Current Scope and Prospects

From relatively humble beginnings in the mid-third of the 20th century, American evangelical groups had by the early 21st century come to dominate collegiate ministry in North America and had become important cogs in the larger domestic and international evangelical movement beyond their original student constituency and missions focus. Once centered almost exclusively upon evangelism, they have increasingly reflected a more holistic concern for relief and education-oriented projects as part of their mission, in keeping with the widening view of the Christian mandate on the part of the larger evangelical subculture. By 2005 the American IVCF had a budget of $68 million, over 1,000 full-time staff, and annually sent hundreds of students overseas for evangelistic and humanitarian projects. The Navigators, which had begun evangelistic and discipleship programs that targeted adolescents and various minorities in the United States, in 2005 had a budget of $92 million, which supported nearly 2,000 workers in the United States and another 2,000 in over 100 other countries. Meanwhile, Campus Crusade counted over 26,000 full-time staff in 191 countries, boasted 550,000 "trained volunteers," and wielded an annual budget in excess of $400 million.

The vast resources of these groups and other youth-oriented organizations promised that evangelical student movements would maintain a strong conservative Protestant presence on American college and university campuses well into the future. Perhaps more important, however, they represented an influential resource and model for work overseas, both through their own organizations and through connections with groups like the IFES (representing national evangelical student groups in 150 countries by 2005). With the burgeoning of Christianity — particularly → Pentecostalism — in the global South in the late 20th and early 21st centuries, these student-oriented evangelical groups were in a strategic position to influence the spiritual, cultural, and political formation of the expanding elite in many Third World societies for years to come.

→ Youth Work 5.4-5

Bibliography: J. A. CARPENTER, *Revive Us Again: The Reawakening of American Fundamentalism* (New York, 1997) • C. H. HOPKINS, *History of the YMCA in North America* (New York, 1951) • K. HUNT and G. HUNT, *For Christ and the University: The Story of InterVarsity Christian Fellowship of the U.S.A., 1940-1990* (Downers Grove, 1991) • D. JOHNSON, *A Brief History of the International Fellowship of Evangelical Students* (Lausanne, 1964); idem, *Contending for the Faith: A History of the Evangelical Movement in the Universities and Colleges* (Leicester, 1979) • J. R. MOTT, *Five Decades and a Forward View* (New York, 1939) • P. POTTER and T. WIESER, *Seeking and Serving the Truth: The First Hundred Years of the World Student Christian Federation* (Geneva, 1997) • R. QUEBEDEAUX, *I Found It! The Story of Bill Bright and Campus Crusade* (San Francisco, 1979) • M. RICHARDSON, *Amazing Faith: The Authorized Biography of Bill Bright* (Colorado Springs, Colo., 2000) • B. L. SKINNER, *Daws: A Man Who Trusted God; The Inspiring Life and Compelling Faith of Dawson Troutman, Founder of the Navigators* (Colorado Springs, 1994).

LARRY ESKRIDGE

Stundism

Stundism refers to a → free church movement that arose in 1861 in southern Russia. It called itself the Brethren of the Friends of God, but it came to be known as Stundism (Ger. *Stunde,* "hour") because of its link with the German Reformed "observing of the hours" at Rohrbach, near Odessa. For the Stundists, reading and discussing the Bible came to be viewed as more important than maintaining the external Orthodox rites of worship (→ Bible Study). The movement arose in the context of other indigenous → sects going back to the middle of the 18th century, including those of so-called spiritual Christianity (e.g., the Doukhobors and their offshoot the Molokans). As in these earlier movements, so among the Stundists we find a rejection of → liturgy, the → sacraments, ordained → ministry, and church → organization. The removal of household → icons sealed its separation from the → Orthodox Church. Sociologically, the movement was made up of middle- and lower-class farmers, artisans, and discharged soldiers. It had a group of steadfast leaders (e.g., M. Ratushny, G. Balaban, and I. Ryaboshapka) but no single teacher.

Although it divided Stundism, the incursion of the → Baptists beginning in 1869 led to a deeper piety centered on Christ, as well as the development of an ordered congregational life even outside of Stundo-Baptism. Together with the Baptists and the circles gathered by Colonel V. A. Pashkov (1831-1902) and Count M. M. Korff (1842-1933), which belonged to the neo-Methodist revival movement (→ Methodism) sparked by the preaching of Lord Radstock in St. Petersburg in 1874, the congregations arising out of Stundism have been united since 1944 in the Union of Evangelical Christians–Baptists.

A split away from this group in 1961 was the Church of Evangelical Christians–Baptists (the "Initiativniki" Baptists), which took a firmer line against state religion. With the change of policy under M. Gorbachev the church's congregations rose from 281 to 704 between 1988 and 1991, and during the same period the number of churches in the Union fell from 2,325 to 2,249. The two groups together have about half a million baptized members, though a much higher number attend worship.

In 1988 the church had only one seminary for training pastors, with 125 students. By 1991 there were six seminaries with 332 students. The collapse of the → Soviet Union led to the formation of separate churches for the new republics, but they came together at the end of 1992 as the Euro-Asiatic Federation of the Union of Evangelical Christians–Baptists.

Bibliography: S. BOLSHAKOFF, *Russian Nonconformity: The Story of "Unofficial" Religion in Russia* (Philadelphia, 1950) • H. BRANDENBURG, *The Meek and the Mighty: The Emergence of the Evangelical Movement in Russia* (New York, 1977) • H.-C. DIEDRICH, *Siedler, Sektierer und Stundisten. Die Entstehung des russischen Freikirchentums* (2d ed.; Neuhausen-Stuttgart, 1997) • L. N. MITROKHIN, *Baptizm. Istoriya i sovremennost'* (Baptists: Past and present) (St. Petersburg, 1997) • S. I. ZHUK, "The Stundists," *Russia's Lost Reformation: Peasants, Millennialism, and Radical Sects in Southern Russia and Ukraine, 1830-1917* (Baltimore, 2004) 153-99.

PETER HAUPTMANN

Stuttgart Declaration of Guilt → Church Struggle 6; Visser 't Hooft, W. A., 3

Stylites

In the spirit of strict → asceticism, Syrian monks (→ Monasticism 4.2), for whom it was part of their lifestyle to live in confined spaces under the open sky, began to live, whether for a span of time or for the rest of their lives, on a platform atop a pillar, there either in a little hut or fully exposed to the elements. They thus became known as Stylites (Gk. *stylos,* "pillar").

The first to live in this manner was Simeon Stylites the Elder (ca. 390-459), who spent some 40 years on a pillar, eventually some 15 m. (50 ft.) high, on a mountain spur northwest of Aleppo (the pilgrimage center Qal'at Sim'ān). For the many pilgrims who flocked to him, Simeon acted as preacher and counselor, and he thus became the model for many male and female Stylites on into the Middle Ages in Syria, Palestine, Asia Minor, Constantinople, and Egypt, and even into the 19th century in Russia and Georgia (→ Pilgrimage).

The only known Stylite in the West — a St. Wulflaicus living near the Ardennes in the sixth century — was driven off by the bishop, and his pillar demolished.

→ Monastery 2

Bibliography: E. A. S. DAWES, *Three Byzantine Saints* (Oxford, 1948) • R. DORAN, trans., *The Lives of Simeon Stylites* (Kalamazoo, Mich., 1992) • H. DELEHAYE, *Les saints stylites* (Brussels, 1923; repr., 1989) • H. LIETZMANN, *Das Leben des heiligen Simeon Stylites* (Leipzig, 1908) • A. VÖÖBUS, *History of Asceticism in the Syrian Orient* (vol. 2; Louvain, 1960) 208-23.

WOLFGANG HAGE

Subculture

1. In the 1920s scholars in the United States noted the development of relatively independent subcultures that were clearly different from the dominant → culture, as, for example, in the spheres of criminality, in a youth culture among high school and college students, or in a culture of poverty among less qualified industrial workers and ethnic groups that were discriminated against (→ Industrial Society; Minorities; Poverty). As an analytic term, however, the word first came into use in the 1950s. Public usage suggests that the connotation of the term is negative, applying it to groups living on the edge of → society and opposing the central values of the dominant, "official" culture.

2. Sociological research has shown, however, that the conduct of subcultural groups does not have to be opposed to the basic values of society. A charge made against advocates of the main culture is that they do not take seriously their own declared values but make → compromises or get their priorities wrong.

But an accusation against subcultures is that they parasitically rate too highly a specific cultural value and destroy social unity. If the activities of a group programmatically aim at the symbolic destruction of existing → norms, opposing custom, demonstratively setting sanctions at naught, or throwing scorn on the symbols of society, then what we really have is a → counterculture. But even in this case we cannot judge the conduct by existing norms, for the champions of the main culture are not aware of their deepest values and → norms, and the subcultures tend to stress difference, disagreement, and even confrontation to rally what is very often their weak support.

Only the relative → autonomy of the subculture and its dissociation from the functioning and authoritative orders of society (→ Authority) make possible the development of its own cognitive and communicative abilities (→ Cognition; Communication) and its own forms of expression and relationship to the age. We can speak of a subculture in the true sense only when the → socialization of the members has achieved its own form of administration and its own mode of action. For this purpose it needs an institutional point at which to anchor itself (e.g., youth cultures in a school, a sports club, a group at church, in politics, or at work; → Institution). It also needs its own resources.

3. Compared with the dominant social structure, a subculture may involve social regression in the sense that, in place of functional criteria of → organization, it stresses inborn qualities of age, gender, race, region, or outlook, and its form of organization is as a rule primitive and determined by the → masses. Yet we must not overlook the positive element of a new social development, for as the members create what may be a symbolic (→ Symbol) but still an independent social recognition, they can free themselves from the chains of a dominant culture and eventually create new social contacts and cultural identities. Subcultures are a field of changing experiments in society.

4. As traditional differences fall away and the imprint of subcultures, mediated by the → mass media, → tourism, and migration, is today much the same internationally, the character of national cultures (→ Nation, Nationalism) is declining. Life is becoming pluralistic, and society multicultural or transcultural (→ Pluralism 1). The forms of cultural practice are losing their authority. But this means that the term "subculture" is losing its analytic value (e.g., in relation to class and social stratum; → Youth). Where we once had a youth culture, we now have cliques. We have multiple memberships that adjust to the situation.

The idea of a subculture now has a more "expressive" character. It dissolves into various scenarios by which people show themselves and forge new contacts or demonstrate a selected collective → identity. At the same time, in → politics, city planning (→ City), or social work (→ Social Education), the term still retains an ideological function (→ Ideology).

Bibliography: D. O. ARNOLD, ed., *The Sociology of Subcultures* (Santa Barbara, Calif., 1970) • D. BAACKE, *Jugend und Jugendkulturen* (3d ed.; Weinheim, 1999) • R. H. BALMER, *Mine Eyes Have Seen the Glory: A Journey into the Evangelical Subculture in America* (3d ed.; New York, 2000) • A. FURLONG and I. GUIDIKOVA, eds., *Transitions of Youth Citizenship in Europe: Culture, Subculture, and Identity* (Strasbourg, 2001) • K. GELDER and S. THORNTON, eds., *The Subcultures Reader* (London, 1997) • C. JENKS, *Subculture: The Fragmentation of the Social* (London, 2005) • D. MUGGLETON, *Inside Subculture: The Postmodern Meaning of Style* (New York, 2000) • J. M. YINGER, "Contraculture and Subculture," *ASR* 25 (1960) 625-35.

WALTER BÜHL

Subintroductae

Subintroductae are life partnerships of male and female ascetics without sexual contact (→ Asceticism; Sexuality). The Greek name for such persons is *syneisaktoi/ai* or *epeisaktoi/ai* (= brought together; led in); the English noun derives from Lat. *virgo subintroducta*. This kind of "spiritual → marriage" was found in the → early church in the third century (there is no reference in 1 Cor. 7:36-38) and was at first rejected as an offense against ecclesiastical order (Cyprian *Ep.* 64; 13.5; 14.3; Synod of Elvira, can. 27; Synod of Ancyra, can. 19; Council of Nicaea, can. 3; → Councils of the Church). But though the practice seemed to be so incriminating, it became widespread, as we learn from → Jerome (ca. 345-420, *Ep.* 22.14), Ambrose (ca. 339-97, *Ep.* 70), Basil of Ancyra (d. ca. 365, *On Virginity*), and especially → Chrysostom (ca. 347-407), who wrote two works in opposition.

The origins of this practice lie in premonastic asceticism when male and female ascetics lived with their families and sought help and spiritual contact with those like-minded (→ Monasticism). From the fourth century onward, urban asceticism fostered similar conditions that promoted spiritual friendships of this kind.

→ Celibacy of the Clergy; Religious Orders and Congregations

Bibliography: H. ACHELIS, *Virgines Subintroductae* (Leipzig, 1902) • P. BROWN, *The Body and Society: Men, Women, and Sexual Renunciation in Early Christianity* (New York, 1988) • E. A. CLARK, "John Chrysostom and the Subintroductae," *CH* 46/2 (1977) 171-85 • K. ELM and M. PARISSE, eds., *Doppelklöster und andere Formen der Symbiose männlicher und weiblicher Religiosen im Mittelalter* (Berlin, 1992) • R. RADER, *Breaking Boundaries: Male/Female Friendship in Early Christian Communities* (New York, 1983) • R. E.

REYNOLDS, "Virgines subintroductae in Celtic Christianity," *HTR* 61 (1968) 549-66.

KARL SUSO FRANK†

Subjectivism and Objectivism

1. Terms
2. Subjectivism versus Objectivism
3. Ways Beyond the Impasse

1. Terms

The subject-object distinction and relationship is an important topic in → philosophy. In their relationship, the *subject* is *the one engaged* in knowing, believing, experiencing, and acting. As the first-person standpoint, as the I, the subject is consciously aware of something. The *object* is *what* the subject is aware of, by knowing, believing, feeling, experiencing, or acting upon it. The object is what the subject takes to be the case. So defined, subject and object are mutually related.

"Subjectivism" and "objectivism," however, are positions that focus on one side or the other of the relation and make that side the determining feature of philosophical reflection. They also raise the issue of whether, or how, subject and object exist independently, apart from standing in the subject-object relation.

2. Subjectivism versus Objectivism

Subject and object are basic elements in systems of → epistemology, as well as of → metaphysics, → ethics, → aesthetics, and other branches of philosophy. Subjectivism in epistemology reduces the truth of our judgments or convictions to the subjective certainty with which we hold or affirm them. Objectivism, in contrast, regards their truth as a function of circumstances that exist unconnected to our subjective → experience, certainty, or affirmation.

Subjectivists think that ethical → norms do no more than indicate behaviors of which people approve, and that aesthetic qualities are the aspects of things that people deem pleasurable. Objectivists, in contrast, say that appropriate moral and aesthetic judgments recognize, and conform to, inherent characteristics of morality and beauty as such, features that exist apart from our recognition of them, and which we are obliged to acknowledge and respect.

Metaphysics typically extends this distinction to all areas. To the metaphysical subjectivist, the structures and norms of the experienced world are generated by the subject's own consciousness. To the objectivist, they are real apart from their being experienced; they are the truth about things that we are challenged to discover.

Subjectivism is open to the charge of → relativism because it offers no safeguard against diverse subjects making different judgments about → truth and other important matters. Objectivism can be accused, in turn, of relying on controversial assumptions or speculative hypotheses about "the way things really are."

Subjectivism holds that the only thing known directly is the state of the subject's consciousness. The existence and nature of what presumably gives rise to that consciousness is just something assumed. The ancient Greek Sophists count as subjectivists because they regarded objects of experience as phenomena whose significance is determined by the subject. Protagoras (ca. 485-ca. 410 B.C.) taught that "man is the measure of all things — of things that are, that they are, of things that are not, that they are not."

Modern subjectivism declares that mental states (ideas and representations) are the only things directly given in our consciousness. The objects mental states purport to be about are not so given. It follows, then, that our judgments about objects are subjective in nature, a view clearly expressed in *psychologism*.

In the 20th century, *behaviorism* rejected as unscientific the self-conscious ego postulated by psychologism, by traditional philosophical psychology and its epistemology. What, then, does an expression such as "I believe that . . ." actually signify? Who or what believes, feels, or initiates an action? Scientific explanation of behavior has no place for a subjective ego, as a supposedly nonphysical agent of belief and action. Behaviorists declare that first-person pronouns have no referent other than the speaker's physical organism and its actions. While language usage may seem subjective, it is not indicative of a metaphysical subject or self but is just another kind of behavior.

Proponents of objectivism assert that the relativistic consequences of subjectivism leave no place for strictly universal judgments or the affirmation of eternal truths, for the latter presuppose the reality of objective standards and ideals, such as the Platonic Ideas, to which our correct judgments are said to conform. Denying independent reality leaves us merely with human conventions that are arbitrary, of restricted application, and subject to change. Denial of universality poses serious difficulties for epistemology as well as for ethics.

The extreme libertarian thought of Ayn Rand (1905-82), which espouses laissez-faire → capitalism and considers selfishness as a virtue, dubs itself "the philosophy of objectivism," although it has elements that are atypical of objectivism as such.

3. Ways beyond the Impasse

Efforts have been made to overcome the mutual opposition of subjectivism and objectivism as one-sided positions. Some sought to transcend the subject-object split by positing a *suprarational intuition,* a self-attesting insight into truth that calls for no further grounding. Examples include the pronouncements of certain mystics, the ascent to the One in the philosophy of Plotinus (ca. 205-70), and "intellectual intuition" in the early thought of F. W. J. Schelling (1775-1854).

Another approach proceeds from the contention that the subject's reality is not exhausted in its acts of experiencing, nor the object's reality wholly comprised in the events of its being experienced. Instead, the subject and object poles together are *constituents of a nexus of being* that extends beyond the givens in self-conscious experience. The philosophy of Nicolai Hartmann (1882-1950) took this route, in part, by acknowledging ideal objects over and above the spatiotemporal objects of experience, but it required a hypothetical metaphysical structure to do so.

Transcendental philosophy treats the object of experience, not as something subsistent as such on its own, but instead as a phenomenal object. Immanuel Kant (1724-1804; → Kantianism) depicted it as a phenomenon or experienced object constructed from sense experience by the subject's prescriptive forms of spatiotemporal intuition and categories of the understanding. More recent transcendental philosophy does not take phenomena to be conditioned by the subject's inherent mental faculties but instead views them as dependent on interpretations that are made within an adopted categorial framework.

To the extent that something can be an object for consciousness only when in dependence on a subject, we can rule out naive objectivism. In transcendental philosophy, however, the subject also no longer enjoys its traditional status as something graspable independently, on its own account. We can still draw useful distinctions between the contrasting stances of subjectivity and objectivity. Yet those distinctions are relativized by the fact that we cannot speak of a subject or of an object by itself, without the concurrent moment of their mutual relationship in experience.

A far-reaching consequence of transcendental philosophy is that objects can be experienced only within a theoretical framework. This consequence alters the meaning of "objectivity," because objects are no longer truly "things in themselves." Objects are theory-dependent and, in that sense, are phenomena.

Bibliography: H. ALBERT, *Treatise on Critical Reason* (Princeton, 1985) • N. GOODMAN, *Ways of Worldmaking* (Indianapolis, 1978) • N. HARTMANN, *Grundzüge einer Metaphysik der Erkenntnis* (4th ed.; Berlin, 1949) • I. KANT, *Critique of Pure Reason* (Cambridge, 1998) • K. POPPER, *Objective Knowledge* (Oxford, 1972) • G. PRAUSS, *Einführung in der Erkenntnistheorie* (Darmstadt, 1980) • W. RÖD, *Erfahrung und Reflexion* (Munich, 1991) • B. RUSSELL, *Meaning and Truth* (London, 1940) • B. SKINNER, *Beyond Freedom and Dignity* (New York, 1971).

ROBERT F. BROWN

Sublimis Deus

In May and June 1537, Pope Paul III (1534-49) issued three important statements on the missionary situation in America (→ Mission 3.4): the → bulls *Sublimis Deus* (*SD,* also called *Unigenitus* and *Veritas ipsa*) and *Altitudo divini consilii (ADC),* along with *Pastorale officium (PO),* which served as an executing brief for *SD.* The bull *ADC* was of a legal and disciplinary nature, settling the strife about baptism between the → Franciscans and → Dominicans in Mexico. *SD* related to the debated issue of the humanity of the Indians and to the central economic problem of an emerging colonial society, namely, how to use the working power and possessions of the Indians (through enslavement and the *encomienda* system of tributary labor), a process that would essentially involve their mass extermination (→ Colonialism; Slavery). The degrading of the human rights of the Indians, in which church officials took part such as Tomás de Ortiz (d. 1542; see Report on Chiribichi on the coast of Cumaná/Venezuela [1524], which has often been improperly generalized) or the Dominican provincial of Mexico, Domingo de Betanzos (1480-1549), resulted in their being exploited over a long period of time.

In contrast, *SD* served as a Magna Carta of Indian human → rights by affirming that Indians, like all others, are able to believe, and thus come under the baptismal mandate of Matt. 28:19: *Euntes ergo docete omnes gentes* (Go therefore and make disciples of all nations). Even as heathens, they are not on any pretext to be robbed of their freedom and their possessions (→ Natural Law). They must "be invited to faith in Christ by the proclaiming of the gospel and the example of a good life." *PO* threatens to excommunicate automatically all those who act differently (→ Excommunication).

It is not clear how these affirmations can be made compatible with the content of the bull *Inter cetera* (1493) of Alexander VI (1492-1503), which viewed the Spanish crown as the basis of the enterprise of conquest and colonization. Implicit here was Aristotle's (384-322 B.C.) thesis that some peoples are so primitive that they are by nature adapted to serve as slaves (*Pol.* 1.3-6; → Aristotelianism). The Spanish jurist and humanist Juan Ginés de Sepúlveda (1490-1573) referred to this belief in his *Democrates alter* (1544/45) in order to justify Spain's colonial rule over the Indians and its concept of civilization.

SD took its initiative from the Dominicans. Bernardino de Minaya (ca. 1484-1566) journeyed to Rome from Mexico on this matter. He was influenced to some extent by the missionary treatise of Bartolomé de Las Casas (1484-1566) *De unico vocationis modo omnium gentium ad veram religionem* (The only way to draw all people to a living faith). Minaya probably gave a copy of this work to the pope and helped influence the bull. A role was also played by the first Mexican bishop, Dominican Julián Garcés (1457-1547), who had his seat at Tlaxcala and who had written to the pope in 1535, making it clear that he saw the Indians as rational beings.

Garcés took a bold line and violated Charles V's understanding of → patronage to go over the head of the emperor directly to the pope, which Minaya also did, following the recommendation of the regent, Empress Isabella of Portugal. This was done, however, without the approval of the president of the Indian Council, Cardinal García de Loaysa, O.P., archbishop of Seville, who at that time had a negative view of the intellectual capabilities of the Indians. For this reason, Minaya had apparently seen to it that *PO* was sent to Cardinal Juan Pardo de Tavera (1472-1545), archbishop of Toledo and president of the Council of Castile.

Loaysa incited Charles I of Spain (1516-56), who was also Emperor Charles V (1519-56), to intervene against the *PO* at Rome and to prevent Minaya from returning to Mexico. The bull remained in force, but those who opposed it were not automatically excommunicated. The practical intention behind *SD* was to initiate new laws, but they were never fully put into effect. In daily practice, Americans would always treat Indians in a way that fell short of the church's teaching and legal theorizing.

→ Human Dignity; International Law

Bibliography: G. GUTIÉRREZ, *Dios o el oro en las Indias. Siglo XVI* (Lima, 1989) • L. HANKE, "Pope Paul III and the American Indians," *HTR* 30 (1937) 65-102 • A. DE LA HERA, "El derecho de los Indios y la libertad a la fe. La bula 'Sublimis Deus' y los problemas que la motivaron," *AHDE* 26 (1956) 89-181 • A. LOBATO CASADO, "El obispo Garcés, O.P., y la bula 'Sublimis Deus,'" *Los Dominicos y el Nuevo Mundo. Actas del I Congreso Internacional* (Madrid, 1988) 739-95 • J. METZLER, ed., *America pontificia. Primi saeculi evangelizationis, 1493-1592* (2 vols.; Rome, 1991) 1.364-66 • S. A. ZAVALA, *Repaso histórico de la bula "Sublimis Deus" de Paulo III, en defensa de los indios* (Mexico City, 1991).

HANS-JÜRGEN PRIEN

Subsidiarity

According to the principle of subsidiarity, a higher-level authority will assume only those tasks that a subordinate authority cannot perform. This principle underlies the traditions of an organic-federalist doctrine of society, of → liberalism, and of Roman Catholic social teaching (→ Social Ethics). This social teaching relates the individual to society by way of the principle of → solidarity and, by the principle of subsidiarity, establishes the truth that → society serves the individual.

Because the human person is both the agent and the goal of all society, subsidiarity asserts that it is "a grave evil and disturbance of right order to assign to a greater and higher association what lesser and subordinate organizations can do. . . . Every social activity ought of its very nature to furnish help to the members of the body social, and never destroy and absorb them" (*Quadragesimo anno* [*QA*] 79 [1931]; → Social Encyclicals). A "liberal" interpretation of this section of the text (emphasizing *gravissimum principium* as "most [*not* very] weighty principle") stresses the negative-avoiding aspect, while a "socialist" interpretation (emphasizing *subsidium*, "help," in the last sentence) stresses the positive-promoting aspect. The → teaching office (§1) presently lays stress on the → autonomy of the intermediary groups (called "the 'subjectivity' of society" in *Centesimus annus* 13 [1991]).

When used in criticism of the church, the subsidiarity principle is a weapon against Roman centralism (→ Roman Catholic Church). Protestant → ethics can adopt Roman Catholic social principles as pragmatic rules, not ontological principles (→ Ontology). A "graduated order" (*QA* 80) of relations based on proximity to the person no longer holds good because modern → society allows for so many different functions (→ Modern Period).

In a free order the principle of subsidiarity promotes the autonomy and abilities of social groups and → institutions, though there is always the danger that groups will just serve their own ego. The principle favors participatory modes of decision and helps to orient social measures toward self-help. In the European Union it can allocate responsibilities and jurisdiction to the level of the member states, where cultural diversity is supported and competition for improved performance is fostered (→ Achievement and Competition). The principle of subsidiarity also allows for necessary international decisions, particularly in the interest of effective environmental politics.

Bibliography: S. Beretta, "Wealth Creation and Distribution in the Global Economy: Human Labor, Development, and Subsidiarity," *Communio* 27 (2000) 474-89 • H. Lecheler, *Subsidiarität im künftigen Europa* (Cologne, 1991) • A. Leys, *Ecclesiological Impacts of the Principle of Subsidiarity* (Kampen, 1995) • J. L. O'Donovan, "Subsidiarity and Political Authority in Theological Perspective," *Bonds of Imperfection: Christian Politics, Past and Present* (Grand Rapids, 2004) 225-45 • P. E. Sigmund, "Subsidiarity, Solidarity, and Liberation: Alternative Approaches in Catholic Social Thought," *Religion, Pluralism, and Public Life* (ed. L. E. Lugo; Grand Rapids, 2000) 205-20 • T. Strohm, "Die unerwartete Renaissance des Subsidiaritätsprinzips," *ZEE* 45 (2001) 64-72.

WALTER SCHÖPSDAU

Subsistence Economy → Development 1; Industrial Society; Third World 1

Substance Abuse

1. Alcohol
2. Tobacco
3. Drugs

The abuse of illegal drugs, prescription drugs, alcohol, and nicotine is an international problem of overwhelming scope. Although such activities have historically been considered vices and socially unacceptable in the United States and many other countries, some of them have increasingly become more tolerated, although regulated, but in some instances are still legally prohibited. At least until the mid-20th century, Protestant America strongly discouraged drug and alcohol abuse and the use of tobacco

products, and even today it is thought appropriate to tax those substances that are not prohibited to support social programs in what is called a "sin tax." As historian John C. Burnham demonstrates, all of these issues have been subjects of vigorous public debate for most of U.S. history. In many ways, the debate is more intense today than it has been for several decades. Tobacco use, in particular, has gone from being deplored in U.S. society, to becoming respectable, to again being disreputable.

1. Alcohol

Alcohol use has been legal almost everywhere in the United States since the repeal of the 18th Amendment in 1933, although its sale is still heavily restricted by age of consumer, place and time of sale, whether it may be consumed in public, and in other ways. It is aggressively marketed in electronic, print, and outdoor advertising media. In the United States, beer manufacturers alone spend $634 million per year on television and radio advertising, while in Great Britain over £200 million per year is spent advertising alcoholic beverages of all types. In both countries, about two-thirds of adults drink alcohol, many to excess. Approximately one in eight American drinkers are alcoholic or experience problems that are due to alcohol.

The effects of alcohol abuse on behavior and health are well documented. In the United States 17.4 percent of individuals between 18 and 25 years of age meet federal standards for alcohol dependence or abuse. In 1998 the estimated cost of alcohol abuse in the United States was $185 billion, according to the National Institute on Alcohol Abuse and Alcoholism of the National Institutes of Health. These costs include alcohol abuse services and health care, accidents and crime, and lost earnings. There are annually nearly 20,000 alcohol-induced deaths, not including accidents or homicides. Alcohol is involved in the majority of violent crimes and sexual assaults and almost half of all property crimes.

American activists, mostly Protestants, began the so-called temperance movement in the 19th century to battle the ills associated with alcohol abuse, particularly in the institution known as the saloon. They succeeded in securing the passage of the 18th Amendment, abolishing the manufacture and sale of alcohol, which was in effect from 1920 until 1933, when it was repealed by the 21st Amendment. Alcohol use is still opposed by many American denominations, notably the United Methodists (→ Methodism), Southern → Baptists, → Assemblies of God, and many smaller evangelical bodies. Even church groups considered tolerant of alcohol, such as the Episcopal Church and the Evangelical Lutheran Church of America, have issued policies that strongly caution against the abuse of alcohol. Many churches of all denominations are active in ministry to alcohol abusers, including sponsorship of chapters of Alcoholics Anonymous.

2. Tobacco

Tobacco is widely used in the United States and around the world. It is consumed mostly in the form of cigarettes, but also in pipes, cigars, and in smokeless forms. In the United States, almost 21 percent of adults smoke cigarettes, and 5.5 percent smoke cigars. Cigarette smoking, which is estimated to take 440,000 lives per year in the United States, is linked to cancer, respiratory diseases, and cardiovascular disease. Other countries are facing the same losses, with 110,000 smoking-related deaths per year in Germany, 106,000 per year in the United Kingdom, 45,000 in Canada, and 19,000 in Australia.

Smoking tobacco, and in particular cigarettes, has been a popular practice both in the United States and the world for many years. Smoking long was ubiquitous, and people went unchallenged as they smoked in offices, airplanes, restaurants, hospital rooms, and seemingly everywhere else. It was depicted favorably on television and the movies as a sophisticated and acceptable activity, from Robert Young in *Father Knows Best* lighting up a cigarette after a long day of work, to the celebrity endorsements of cigarette brands by such major entertainment figures as Desi and Luci Arnez, Ronald Reagan, Perry Como, and John Wayne.

Although it was vigorously condemned along with other vices in evangelical churches, few outside of these circles were concerned about it. Evangelical, fundamentalist, and Pentecostal condemnation of tobacco was based, not primarily on health concerns, but as opposition to "worldliness" and as an aspect of a "separated" lifestyle that was thought to characterize a true Christian, a position recently reaffirmed by the Assemblies of God, which notes that "the church has opposed the use of tobacco because it is a habit that is harmful to a Christian's testimony as well as to a Christian's body, which is the temple of the Holy Spirit."

Cigarette smoking has not always been socially or even legally acceptable in the United States. Tobacco use had been seen as a vice, a dangerous and unclean habit to be discouraged at all levels, and in fact was illegal or strongly discouraged in many states. In the early 20th century 43 out of the 45 U.S. states had laws restricting cigarettes. In 1927 Kansas became the last state to lift the prohibition of the manufacture and sale of cigarettes.

The use of tobacco was linked to all sorts of moral, spiritual, and physical ailments in popular publications of the early 20th century. Smoking was particularly discouraged among young males and among women of all ages. Soldiers fighting in World War I, however, received cigarette rations, and many returned home as smokers. Smoking continued to be glamorized in the 1920s, and the sons of these soldiers were themselves sent overseas to fight yet another world war and again came home smoking. Smoking came to be considered sophisticated, manly, and assertive, a practice acceptable to men and women alike, if not for children. Fueled by aggressive, expensive, and ubiquitous advertising, by movies and television, the use of tobacco, particularly in cigarettes, became glamorized and acceptable. By the mid-20th century, the zenith of smoking in the United States, 80 percent of American men between the ages of 18 and 64 were tobacco users.

By the 1940s smoking had become so acceptable that even Emily Post, the arbiter of American etiquette, defended smoking and advised nonsmokers to "learn to adapt themselves to existing conditions . . . and when they come into contact with smokers, it is scarcely fair that the few should be allowed to prohibit the many from the pursuit of their comforts and their pleasures" (quoted in C. Borio, chap. 6, 1940-09). Smoking had become well established in American society, a situation that changed only by the end of the 20th century.

Smoking, as a matter both of personal choice and of public policy, has come under strenuous attack in recent decades, in the United States and elsewhere. Official federal opposition to smoking began in 1959 with a warning from the surgeon general. Today, tobacco use is under increasing attack, and new restrictions arise on a regular basis to place the user more and more on the defensive as the practitioner of a "dirty habit." Increasingly, smokers are banished to isolated areas far from polite society to practice their vice in social isolation. Also increasingly, municipalities and even states are imposing stringent bans on smoking in such public places as restaurants, workplaces, and jails, and even outdoor facilities such as ballparks and music venues. Even in Europe, smoking bans are becoming more widespread, including the well-known and surprising case of the Irish pub becoming smoke-free as of March 2004.

Opponents of smoking, such as philosopher Robert Goodin, defend their position on the basis of scientific reports suggesting that even secondhand smoke, also known as environmental tobacco smoke (ETS), is harmful to nonsmokers. Furthermore, since in Goodin's view smoking is not a voluntary activity but an addictive behavior, the legitimate liberty of those who smoke is not infringed by restricting their smoking. Those who continue to defend smoking, such as Jacob Sullum, do so on the basis of a commitment to individual liberty, coupled with skepticism about the scientific basis of the government's conclusions about the hazards of ETS.

3. Drugs

The United States is engaged in a "war on drugs," and many other nations are also wrestling with an immense traffic in illegal drugs, as well as dealing with the consequences of widespread drug abuse. In the United States the White House Office of National Drug Control Policy estimates that the abuse of illegal drugs cost its users $57.3 billion between 1988 and 1995, divided among cocaine ($38.0 billion), heroin ($9.6 billion), marijuana ($7.0 billion), and other illegal drugs and legal drugs used illicitly ($2.7 billion). The National Institute on Drug Abuse estimated that the economic cost to society from drug abuse and dependence was over $143 billion in 1998. Drug dependence is defined by three characteristics: (1) use of the drug over a period of time; (2) experiencing difficulty in stopping the use of the drug, with attendant personal sacrifices to keep using it; and (3) suffering if the user is forced to stop using the drug, known as the withdrawal syndrome.

The illegal use of psychoactive drugs is widespread in the United States. Some 70 million Americans age 12 and over have tried at least one or more prohibited drugs for the purpose of getting high. Commerce in illegal drugs involves vast sums of money; it rivals the total sales of the largest American corporations and surpasses the total earnings of American farmers. Although drug abuse is an international problem, the United States consumes most of the world's illegal drugs.

In the United States, addiction to narcotics was prevalent in the 19th century, when there were virtually no legal controls on such substances, and opium, cocaine, and morphine could be obtained in patent medicines without a prescription. In 1900 there were more narcotics addicts, in proportion to the population, than there are today. In 1914 the Harrison Act made it illegal to obtain narcotics without a prescription, and by the end of World War II the number of narcotics addicts had dropped substantially. Very few Americans at that time used cocaine, heroin, hallucinogens, or other such drugs, which remained the case until the 1960s, when the

drug subculture emerged, which glamorized drug use and regarded it as an act of defiance of the establishment (→ Counterculture). The use of recreational drugs increased from that point on.

In 1970 Congress passed the Comprehensive Drug Abuse Prevention and Control Act, which became a model for most state laws. This act distinguishes between categories of drugs based on their potential for abuse and their medical usefulness. Drugs with a high potential for abuse and no accepted medical use, such as heroin, LSD, and marijuana, are not legally available. Drugs with high abuse potential but medical usefulness, such as morphine, cocaine, methaqualone, the amphetamines, and short-acting barbiturates, are tightly controlled and available only by prescription. Medically useful drugs with significant, but lower, abuse potential, such as tranquilizers, are also controlled somewhat more loosely by prescription.

American drug policy has been based largely on a punitive model, and today one in four prisoners is being punished for a drug offense. Less effort has been invested in treatment and prevention efforts. The dangers of drug abuse are well known, and it has claimed numerous celebrities as victims, including Jimi Hendrix, John Belushi, Janis Joplin, and Kurt Cobain. Yet drug abuse remains prevalent in society.

Americans exhibit a wide range of viewpoints about the acceptability of the use of various drugs, legal and illegal. Robert M. Veatch has argued that one's position on the ethics of drug use depends on one's philosophical outlook. He has identified five basic perspectives on drug use:

1. A "wisdom of nature" ethic: accepts drug use if the drugs are "natural" and if they facilitate natural functioning.
2. Protestant: reflects a worldview often called the → Puritan ethic, which exalts work and social contribution; to the extent drug use serves those ends, it is acceptable.
3. Neo-Protestant: seeks a religious experience in the use of drugs.
4. Protean: seeks new experiences through drugs.
5. Therapeutic: advocates drug use to treat what have been identified as clinical ailments.

All branches of Christianity condemn drug abuse; the diversity of positions found on the permissibility of the use of tobacco and alcohol are not replicated in this area. While such groups as the Latter-day Saints (→ Mormons) and the Seventh-day → Adventists condemn the use even of caffeine, most accept it, along with that of prescription medications. The illegality of illicit drug use, along with attendant physical harms and associated behavior problems, has earned it strong condemnation by all churches. To some extent, these messages are being heeded by young people; research indicates that teenagers who are more religiously involved are less likely to use drugs, or for that matter cigarettes or alcohol, than other youth. Of young people aged 12 to 17 who believe that their religious beliefs influence their life decisions, 7.0 percent have used illicit drugs in the previous month, compared with 18.1 percent of those who do not have this belief. Of those who regard religion as important in this way, 7.9 percent report binge drinking in the previous month, versus 17.8 percent of the other group. A similar contrast exists in cigarette use, with 7.9 percent versus 20.2 percent. Churches of all types support ministry to those who have become enslaved by substance abuse, and claims are made that faith-based rehabilitation programs have a better long-term success rate than secular programs.

The abuse of various substances that affect mood, perception, and behavior continues to be a besetting problem of the affluent West, as well as much of the rest of the world. While the United States continues its "war on drugs," the European Union reports, "The drugs phenomenon is one of the major concerns of the citizens of Europe and a major threat to the security and health of European society. The EU has up to 2 million problem drug users. The use of drugs, particularly among young people, is at historically high levels" (European Council). To deal with this problem the European Union in 2005 adopted "EU Drugs Action," a multifaceted program to reduce drug abuse in Europe. In the United States, Europe, and elsewhere, interdiction, criminalization, therapy, rehabilitation, and moral teaching working together may help to limit drugs from damaging even more lives.

→ Behavior, Behavioral Psychology, 2.4; Health and Illness

Bibliography: G. Borio, Tobacco Timeline (Tobacco.org: Tobacco News and Information) http://www.tobacco.org/resources/history/Tobacco_History.html • J. C. Burnham, Bad Habits: Drinking, Smoking, Taking Drugs, Gambling, Sexual Misbehavior, and Swearing in American History (New York, 1994) • G. L. Dillow, "Thank You for Not Smoking: The Hundred-Year War against the Cigarette," American Heritage 32/2 (1981) 94-107 • European Council, EU Drugs Action Plan (2005-2008) (2005) http://ec.europa.eu/justice_home/fsj/drugs/fsj_drugs_intro_en.htm • General Council of the Assemblies of God, "Alcohol, Tobacco, and Drugs," http://ag.org/top/beliefs/charctr_08_drugs.cfm • R. E. Goodin, No Smoking: The Ethical Issues (Chicago, 1990) • H. J. Harwood, Updating Estimates of the Economic Costs of Alcohol Abuse in the United States: Estimates, Update Methods, and Data (Bethesda, Md., 2000) http://pubs.niaaa.nih.gov/publications/economic-2000/index.htm • Office of Applied Studies, "Youths' Religious Participation by Demographics and Substance Use: Tables 3.44A to 3.47B," 2004 National Survey on Drug Use and Health: Detailed Tables (Washington, D.C., 2004) http://www.oas.samhsa.gov/nsduh/2k4nsduh/2k4tabs/lotsect3pe.htm#relig • Office of National Drug Control Policy, The Economic Costs of Drug Abuse in the United States, 1992-1998 (Washington, D.C., 2001) http://www.whitehousedrugpolicy.gov/publications/pdf/economic_costs98.pdf • W. Rhodes, S. Langenbahn, R. Kling, and P. Scheiman, What America's Users Spend on Illegal Drugs, 1988-1995 (Washington, D.C., 1997) • J. Sullum, For Your Own Good: The Antismoking Crusade and the Tyranny of Public Health (New York, 1998) • R. M. Veatch, "Drugs and Competing Drug Ethics," Hastings Center Studies 2/1 (1974) 68-80 • A. J. Weaver and J. Garbarino, "Can a Spiritual Connection Help Immunize Youth against the Deadly Effects of a Toxic Society? Religion Can Help Protect Teens from Harmful Influences They Encounter," Science and Technology News, November 1, 2000, http://www.stnews.org/package-11-2363.htm.

David B. Fletcher

Sudan

	1960	1980	2000
Population (1,000s):	11,165	18,681	29,823
Annual growth rate (%):	2.03	2.78	2.17

Area: 2,503,890 sq. km. (966,757 sq. mi.)

A.D. 2000

Population density: 12/sq. km. (31/sq. mi.)
Births / deaths: 3.25 / 1.08 per 100 population
Fertility rate: 4.23 per woman
Infant mortality rate: 64 per 1,000 live births
Life expectancy: 57.0 years (m: 55.6, f: 58.4)
Religious affiliation (%): Muslims 71.7, Christians 16.1 (Roman Catholics 9.1, Anglicans 4.2, Protestants 1.4, other Christians 1.4), tribal religionists 11.1, nonreligious 1.0, other 0.2.

1. General Situation
2. Religious Situation

1. General Situation

In terms of both history and population, the former British colony and present Republic of the Sudan is closely connected to Egypt, which ruled it jointly with Britain as a condominium from 1899 until the 1950s. Set in the northeast of Africa, Sudan lies partly in an arid zone and partly in a subtropical rain forest.

The main source of life is the Nile, which flows right through the Sudan. In 2003 the population was estimated at 34.9 million, most of them in the North, where Khartoum is the capital. There are Arabic-speaking Muslims in the North (46 percent of the total population) and Christians and adherents of African religions in the South. The most numerous of the residents in the South are the Dinka (12 percent), Azande (6 percent), Nuer (5 percent), and Shilluk (2 percent). The North also has a population mix that includes traditionally Islamic Sudanese Arabs and ethnic tribes more recently converted to Islam. For historical reasons the two regions have had different social and economic patterns and find it difficult to integrate as a single state.

Agriculture is the most important way of making a living. Under → colonialism Sudan became a great producer of cotton, and then in the 1970s it tried unsuccessfully to become a breadbasket for the financially involved states of the Persian Gulf. In its politics of development, Sudan relies for the most part on vast projects like the Gezira scheme for cotton, the Kenana Sugar Project, and the Jonglei Canal, which is being used to drain the swamps in the South. Since the 1990s it also has relied on steadily expanded petroleum production.

Unrest marks the postcolonial period, stemming essentially from two causes. The first is the opposition between two politically active Muslim orders: the pro-Egyptian Khatmiyya and the nationalist Umma Party, whose leaders take up the cause of the Mahdis who in 1881 revolted against Egyptian rule (esp. Muḥammed Aḥmad [1844-85], known as al-Mahdī). Issues here are the degree of cooperation with Egypt, the process of Islamization, and economic development.

The second cause is the conflict between the North and the South since the 1950s, or between Arab-Muslim and non-Arab-Muslim African population groups. It is based on divergent social and economic development and the racism of the Arabs and expresses itself in the demands of the South for autonomy, as well as in forced Islamization. These problems evoked the change from parliamentarianism to a military government under Gaafar al-Nimeiri (1969-85), a change now associated with years of unrest.

In the early 1980s the Muslim government began Islamization of the laws, instituting → Shariʿa law in the North in 1990 (→ Islam 4). This step increased tensions between North and South and led to a second civil war, following the first civil war (1955-72), which had been concluded with the Treaty of Addis Ababa. After the deposing of Nimeiri, attempts to rebuild civic life took place but were broken off in 1989 by the military coup led by Omar Hasan Ahmad al-Bashir. As a result of growing local opposition and foreign pressure (including U.S. accusations of supporting internal terrorism), al-Bashir developed a presidential system by 1996 and accomplished his goal of unification with the South, aided by foreign mediation. After 2003, however, a conflict developed in the western region of Darfur between Arab militias, supported by the government, and the non-Arab African population. In its wake, at least 200,000 people were killed between 2003 and 2005. Two million others fled (→ Refugees), mostly to Chad, which caused a severe regional crisis. A peace agreement in May 2006 failed, for it was signed by only one of the three rebel groups involved. The situation deteriorated further, despite mediation efforts by the African Union and the United Nations.

Since its independence in 1956, Sudan has had to struggle with growing economic difficulties (esp. debt and drought), which continually give the country a low credit rating and regularly lead to massive famines.

2. Religious Situation

Religiously, Sudan is divided. → Sunni Muslims of the Malikite persuasion are predominant in the North. The various brotherhoods — Khatmiyya, Mahdiyya, Sanussiyya, Quadiriyya, Shadhiliyya, and Tijaniyya — all have great influence. Toward the end of the 1980s 73 percent of the population were Muslims. In the South, however, there are many Christians, and 16.7 percent of the population belong to traditional African religions (see → Guinea 2). These believe in the existence of one God — Nhialic (Dinka), Mbori (Azande), or Kwoth (Nuer). → Magic and → witchcraft play only a minor role among the Nuer, Shilluk, and Dinka, though they are more important for the Azande. Ancestor worship is not significant. The Shilluk idea of a divine king resembles what we find in ancient Egypt (→ Africa 2; Egyptian Religion).

The Christian portion of the population (estimated variously from 9 to 20 percent or more) derives its faith from the work of various missions. All the Christian congregations were devastated by the first civil war but had begun to rebuild by 1972. Two-thirds of the Christians belong to the nine dioceses of the → Roman Catholic Church, which has archbishops in Khartoum and Juba. About one-third are Anglicans (→ Anglican Communion) in an autonomous province (1976) with four dioceses; previously they were under the archbishop of Jerusalem. Much smaller percentages of the people belong to the Orthodox faith, either Armenian, Coptic, Ethiopian, or Greek. The Sudanese Council of Churches (→ National Councils of Churches) represents Christians externally, promotes their cooperation, and since 1972 has done church reconstruction in the South.

Bibliography: D. B. Barrett, G. T. Kurian, and T. M. Johnson, *WCE* (2d ed.) 1.698-703 • I. M. Dau, *Suffering and God: A Theological Reflection on the War in Sudan* (Nairobi, 2002) • E. E. Evans-Pritchard, *Nuer Religion* (Oxford, 1956) • L. C. Harris, *In Joy and in Sorrow: Travels among Sudanese Christians* (Nairobi, 1999) • A. H. Idris, *Sudan's Civil War: Slavery, Race, and Formational Identities* (Lewiston, N.Y., 2001) • D. H. Johnson, *The Root Causes of Sudan's Civil Wars* (Bloomington, Ind., 2003) • R. Lobban et al., *Historical Dictionary of the Sudan* (3d ed.; Lanham, Md., 2002) • G. Meyer, *War and Faith in Sudan* (Grand Rapids, 2005) • G. R. Warburg, *Islam, Sectarianism, and Politics in Sudan since the Mahdiyya* (London, 2003) • R. Werner et al., *Day of Devastation, Day of Contentment: The History of the Sudanese Church across 2000 Years* (Nairobi, 2000).

Regina Wegemund

Suffering

1. Term
2. Religious Explanations
3. Theological Data
   3.1. OT
   3.2. NT
   3.3. Church History
   3.4. Third World Theologies
4. Pastoral Aspects

1. Term
The term "suffering" describes the involvement of all → life in finitude and vulnerability. As a rule, distinction is made between social, psychological, intellectual, and physical dimensions. Each affects the sufferer as a whole. → Anxiety and grief are mainly but not exclusively emotional. In some recent discussions suffering has been more fully ascribed to organic and inorganic → nature.

Theologically, the experience of suffering calls for discussion in the doctrine of → God. The question of God's part in suffering is linked to the relation between suffering and → guilt and finally to the possibilities of removing suffering.

2. Religious Explanations
Religious explanations of suffering can hardly be seen as a challenge to fight suffering by removing the objective causes and conditions but rather as a call to endure it by distancing oneself from it. In → Hinduism it is a means to bear and master the personal → *karman* and in this way, by → incarnation, to achieve a less painful existence, and finally to attain to the union of the individual soul *ātman* with the world soul *brāhman*. → Buddhism finds redemption from suffering only in a radical detachment from life and the will to live, which alone can lead to painless *nirvāṇa*. The hope of a life without constant disruption by suffering has here been so fully abandoned that even the desire or thirst for it is combated as a basic root of suffering. In → Islam, too, only the martyr's total despising of the world can lead for certain to the end of suffering in the hereafter. The strict concept of the absoluteness and omnipotence of Allah leads here to the idea that Allah created suffering as a test of true belief.

Neither in the monistic Asian religions nor in the strictly dualistic Islam (→ Monism; Dualism) does there seem to be any life-affirming → hope of an end to suffering. But this hope is the theme of Christian → eschatology. In spite of the sinfulness of the world (→ Sin), we find here a hope for the end of suffering, thanks solely to God's loving relationship to the world as it finds expression in the doctrine of the → Trinity and → Christology (→ Love). A future end of suffering by God's own act may thus be anticipated in an ethics of → healing.

3. Theological Data
3.1. *OT*
Affirmation of life is to the fore in the OT, and it leads to explicit complaints to → Yahweh regarding suffering (see esp. the Psalms). In explanation the authors of the OT use the ancient Near Eastern model of the relation between a sinful act and the ensuing suffering, though they do not always link Yahweh directly to this → causality. In the later Wisdom literature the innocent who suffer raise the question of → theodicy (as in Job), to which the OT gives an ambivalent answer. Suffering may thus come indirectly from Yahweh but also directly, whether as a test (Job) or as an expiatory → punishment for human apostasy or transgression of the

law (Exod. 16; 21:18-22; Prov. 3:11-12; 13:24; Job 5:17, etc.). The latter view underlies the idea of the vicarious expiatory suffering of the → Servant of the Lord (→ Atonement).

In spite of the numerous OT texts in which suffering is interpreted as expiatory, it may be doubted whether one may infer a general → responsibility of God for the world's suffering. In Job and Ecclesiastes this thought is cautiously questioned, and the → prophets Hosea and Jeremiah at least soften it when they say that God himself suffers when he punishes. The OT nowhere engages in basic reflection on the attitude of Yahweh to suffering.

3.2. *NT*
The NT views suffering mainly as an experience of Jesus' → disciples as they testify in an ungodly world (→ Discipleship). The starting point of theological reflection is Christ's → passion. The NT looks back from this event on suffering as a basic fact of life as a whole. There is thus no essential connection with guilt. At least guilt does not arise as a model for understanding the experience of suffering that can be generalized and that is irreversible (Luke 13:1-5; John 9:3). Instead, suffering as the general suffering of → creation (Rom. 8:18-22) cannot now be willed by God and is borne indeed by God in Christ.

Nevertheless, the NT does speak of expiatory suffering and therefore incidentally of the link between suffering and guilt, which the atoning death of Christ has removed on our behalf. In → Paul especially the "for us" of the death of Jesus is central if it is to be shown that peace with God is established for us and not won by us. Here, too, the coming of this peace is not related to physical death alone but to the participation of believers in Christ's destiny of suffering as one who was rejected in a world that is hostile to God (2 Cor. 5:15; see esp. G. Ebeling, 206-7).

3.3. *Church History*
The belief that in this suffering with the world God does not perish, but that his re-creative love in → solidarity with the world remains intact as the basis of the → promise of overcoming suffering, is an important foundation for later Trinitarian discussion. Efforts are made here to distinguish between God's grief at the world and the suffering of Christ. In this regard reference was made to the Greek idea of God's impassibility (*apatheia;* note the debate with Patripassianism in the 3rd cent. and the Christological controversies of the 4th and 5th cents. and the 16th cent.).

Martin → Luther (1483-1546; → Luther's Theology) attempted finally to make Christology fruitful expressly for talk about God, and in theological de-bate he even ventured to speak about the death of God (see the Christological disputation with C. Schwenckfeld, WA 39/2.92-121). Appealing to the Christologically anchored doctrine of the communication of the divine and human attributes of Christ, Lutheran theology inclines to soften the Trinitarian concern for nuanced talk about God, as does also Anglican theology (e.g., J. B. Mozley). The reason for this approach may lie in a different view of God's presence from that of the → Middle Ages and the → early church.

In pre-Reformation theology interest in redemption went hand in hand with talk about God or Christ as the Victor over suffering (→ Salvation). God's presence, for example in → worship or especially in the → Eucharist, was sought in a non-suffering atmosphere of unity by which one would feel prepared to endure suffering. The suffering experienced in the world would follow the model of Christ on the cross (note medieval depictions of the passion) but could be felt as a transitional stage to the redeemed state of union with God.

With the → Reformation came a shift of perspective to the extent that an experience of God's hidden presence was felt in the suffering itself (→ Theologia crucis). In this regard the Reformers followed medieval → mysticism. Meister → Eckhart (ca. 1260-ca. 1328) could already call the experience of union with God a God-suffering by which suffering would finally be done away with (A. Haas).

3.4. *Third World Theologies*
In modern → Third World theology this theology of suffering has again been vigorously adopted and at times linked to indigenous cultural traditions (→ Acculturation; Contextual Theology). Two different trends may be seen in the theologies of Asia and Africa. In → *African* theology, which must be distinguished from South African black theology, → initiation suffering is often to the fore, especially in the Roman Catholic sphere. Suffering matures us for a new stage of life with new tasks. The Roman Catholic theologian Charles Nyamiti, adopting this model, tries to understand Christ's passion as an inner-Trinitarian initiation process.

In *Asian* conceptions (→ Asian Theology), in even closer relation to talk about God, suffering is linked to a theology of the pain of God (K. Kitamori, J.-Y. Lee, C.-S. Song; see also J. Moltmann). A special focus along these lines may be seen in the South Korean minjung theology, when, on the basis of political and social oppression and of opposition to it (Korean *han*, variously translated "grief," "regret," or "pathos"), it tries to interpret suffering directly as an experience of God's presence.

South African black theology views suffering primarily as the suffering of God's witnesses and can thus relativize the two trends mentioned. Suffering is neither solely a basic anthropological fact, as in the reference to initiation suffering, nor is it solely a way of experiencing God, as on the Asian approach. Suffering is here a necessary experience in the setting up of God's new order. Hence the two aspects can be integrated.

Especially Latin American → liberation theology since the beginning of the 1970s, as also some Euramerican theology (see D. Sölle), has loudly objected against such a view of suffering. Against traditional theology, it protests that this view, with its nonbiblical spiritualizing of redemption, casts a veil over the concrete forms and social presuppositions of suffering (→ Poverty), thereby stifling action.

4. Pastoral Aspects

Whereas in approaches along the lines of liberation theology, politically caused collective suffering is the starting point of discussion, in → pastoral care (of the sick) and → medical ethics, suffering is more commonly dealt with in terms of individual sickness or physical or mental impairment (→ Persons with Disabilities). In this context at least, differentiations are needed in the concept that must also be taken into account in systematic theology. In modern medicine and → psychiatry, along with great successes in fighting pain, there are growing tendencies to value the healing function of accepted suffering. In distinction from a masochistic love of suffering, there is developing a branch of research that aims to show how much can be learned from those who suffer (E. Lindemann, D. von Engelhardt; see earlier V. von Weiszäcker). Modern thinking on the function of penance in the → Roman Catholic Church (→ Penitence) understands this insight in the context of mastering suffering.

The necessary nuances in the concept that are apparent from these examples might be summed up under such contrasting terms as avoidable and unavoidable suffering or deserved and undeserved suffering. Christian ethics, especially Protestant, has perhaps too often seen suffering as exclusively deserved or unavoidable (see in criticism D. Sölle). Nevertheless, in view of incurable illnesses and handicaps, it would not be any great help to construe the overcoming and healing of suffering exclusively as its setting aside.

Bibliography: On 1, 2, 3.1-3: J. W. Bowker, *Problems of Suffering in Religions of the World* (Cambridge, 1970) • G. Ebeling, *Dogmatik des christlichen Glaubens* (vol. 2; Tübingen,1982) §19B • P. L. Gavrilyuk, *The Suffering of the Impassible God: The Dialectics of Patristic Thought* (New York, 2004) • A. M. Haas, *Gottleiden–Gottlieben. Zur volkssprachlichen Mystik im Mittelalter* (Frankfurt, 1989) esp. 127-52 • S. Hauerwas, *Naming the Silences: God, Medicine, and the Problem of Suffering* (Grand Rapids, 1990) • W. McWilliams, *Where Is the God of Justice? Biblical Perspectives on Suffering* (Peabody, Mass., 2005) • J. K. Mozley, *The Impassibility of God* (Cambridge, 1926) • D. Ngien, *The Suffering of God according to Martin Luther's "Theologia crucis"* (New York, 1995) • B. D. Smith, *Paul's Seven Explanations of the Suffering of the Righteous* (New York, 2002) • M. Stoeber, *Reclaiming Theodicy: Reflections on Suffering, Compassion, and Spiritual Transformation* (New York, 2005) • A. J. Tambasco, ed., *The Bible on Suffering: Social and Political Implications* (New York, 2002).

On 3.4 and 4: D. von Engelhardt, *Mit der Krankheit leben* (Heidelberg, 1986) • G. Gutiérrez, *On Job: God-Talk and the Suffering of the Innocent* (Maryknoll, N.Y., 1987) • K. Kitamori, *Theology of the Pain of God* (Richmond, Va., 1965) • J. Y. Lee, *God Suffers for Us* (The Hague, 1974) • E. Lindemann, *Beyond Grief* (New York, 1979) • J. Moltmann, *The Trinity and the Kingdom* (Minneapolis, 1993) 36-76 • A. G. Nnamani, *The Paradox of a Suffering God: On the Classical, Modern-Western, and Third World Struggles to Harmonise the Incompatible Attributes of the Trinitarian God* (Frankfurt, 1995) • C. Nyamiti, "Christ's Resurrection in the Light of African Tribal Initiation Ritual," *PastOrS* 3 (1979) 4-13 • D. Sölle, *Suffering* (Philadelphia, 1984) • C.-S. Song, *The Compassionate God* (Maryknoll, N.Y., 1982) • D. Tutu, *Hope and Suffering* (Grand Rapids, 1984) • V. von Weizsäcker, *Pathosophie* (2d ed.; Göttingen, 1967) • A. A. Yewangoe, *Theologia Crucis in Asia: Asian Christian Views on Suffering in the Face of Overwhelming Poverty and Multifaceted Religiosity in Asia* (Amsterdam, 1987).

Ulrike Link-Wieczorek

Sufism

1. Early Islamic Mystics
2. The Sufi Path to Friendship with God
3. Spread and Growth
4. Spiritual Lineages and Orders
5. Expansion of Influence

"Sufi" and "Sufism" are terms adopted from Arabic. The word ṣūfī, most probably from Arab. ṣūf, "wool," originally designated those who wore woolen garments — specifically, ascetics who wore wool as a sign of their renunciation of this world. From the middle of the ninth century, however, *ṣūfī* came to be used increasingly as a technical term to designate a group of people who belonged to a clearly identifiable social movement in lower Iraq, especially Baghdad, based on a distinct type of mystical → piety. The most prominent members of this movement were Abū Saʿīd al-Kharrāz (d. 899 or a few years earlier), Abū l-Ḥusayn al-Nūrī (d. 907), and Junayd al-Baghdādī (d. 910). In time, the Baghdad mystics adopted the name *ṣūfī* and began to use it for themselves; the word then no longer signified "wool-wearing renunciant" but came to be applied exclusively to the mystics of Baghdad. This new, distinctive form of pious living was in turn dubbed *taṣawwuf*, "living as a *ṣūfī*."

1. Early Islamic Mystics

While Sufism was taking shape in Baghdad, individuals and social groups with similar views and practices were to be found among Muslim communities in other locations, even though these latter were not initially known as Sufis. Most notable among these were Sahl al-Tustarī (ca. 818-96) in lower Iraq, al-Ḥakīm al-Tirmidhī (d. probably between 905 and 910) in central Asia, and a group of mystics in northeastern Iran who were known as the "People of Blame" (the Malāmatiyya). These mystics differed from Baghdad Sufis and from each other in thought and practice, but they gradually blended with the mystics of Baghdad, and in time they too came to be identified as Sufis. The origins of these originally distinct Muslim mystic groups are obscure, and the issue of the possible influence of earlier religious traditions, most notably Christian → asceticism, on the emergence of Islamic → mysticism remains unresolved.

The early Muslim mystics were most concerned with obtaining experiential knowledge *(maʿrifa)* of God's unity. In the Sufi perspective, human beings, viewed as God-servants, had experienced proximity to their Lord before the beginning of time, when all human beings, in spirit, stood witness to God's lordship on the Day of the Covenant (Qurʾān 7:172), and they were promised an even more intimate closeness to him at the end of time in → paradise. While on earth, however, they had to strive to preserve and renew the memory of their primordial proximity to their Creator by turning their backs to everything other than God and by living their lives in constant recognition of his presence. In practice, this orientation meant training and domestication of the lower self through continuous cultivation of the heart. The latter was understood as the spiritual organ of God's presence in the human person, and

its chief sustenance was remembrance or mention of God through "invocation" *(dhikr)* and "hearing/witnessing God in poetry and music" *(samāʿ)*.

2. The Sufi Path to Friendship with God

Paradoxically, the journey *(sulūk)* toward the Lord started only when the Sufis realized their own weakness as an agent and acknowledged God as the only true actor in the universe. This journey was normally envisaged as a path *(ṭarīq or ṭarīqa)* marked by various stations *(maqām)* and states *(ḥāl)*. Closeness to God was thought to entail a sharp turn from the lower concerns of this world *(dunyā)* toward the realm of ultimate matters *(ākhira)*, a movement away from the lower self *(nafs)* toward the inner locus of God's presence *(qalb)*, but it proved difficult to characterize the final encounter with God located at the end of the journey. While some, like Kharrāz and Nūrī, described the highest stage of intimacy with God as the dissolution of all self-consciousness, others like Junayd viewed the ultimate goal as a "reconstituted" self, a human identity recomposed in the image of God after being thoroughly deconstructed during the Sufi journey. All agreed, however, that the ultimate Sufi experience was to be viewed as the passing away or reabsorption of the created human being into the only true/real *(ḥaqq)* being of God and, most emphatically, not as a divinization (→ Theosis) of the human. The Sufi could, so to speak, flow into God, but movement in the other direction was off-limits, or at the very least extremely limited, since such a flow from the divine into the human could pave the way to divinization of the human and thus lead to the suspect, even heretical, doctrines of incarnation and inherence *(ḥulūl)*.

Whatever their approach to the thorny issue of encounter with the divine, those who shared the common aim of drawing close to God through experiential knowing enjoyed a special camaraderie with one another in the form of circles of fellowship, mutual mentoring, and relationships of master and disciple (→ Spiritual Direction). Not all human beings ever became wayfarers, let alone grew close to God: that privilege was, it seems, reserved for the few "friends of God" *(walī*, pl. *awliyāʾ)*, who were highly conscious of their special status and viewed themselves as the spiritual elect. Many "friends," much like the prophets, saw themselves as God's special agents among humans, rendered distinct by their special status as intermediaries between the divine and the human planes of being. In their view, they channeled God's mercy to humankind and served to increase God-consciousness among the otherwise heedless and self-absorbed human race through their personal example and their tireless advocacy of God's cause in human affairs.

The special status of the friends manifested itself in a number of practices that simultaneously underscored their distinctness from common believers and served to forge bonds of fellowship, loyalty, and mutual allegiance among the spiritual elect. They began to assemble in certain places of congregation and to travel in groups, developed distinctive prayer rituals in the form of the invocation and listening to poetry and music that frequently led to rapture or → ecstasy *(wajd),* and adopted special initiation practices, notably investiture with a white woolen robe *(khirqa).*

3. Spread and Growth
During the course of the 10th century, Sufism spread to regions beyond Iraq and blended with indigenous mystical trends elsewhere. Its diffusion throughout Muslim communities went apace with the emergence of a normative Sufi tradition, as evidenced clearly in the appearance of a specialized literature that was self-consciously about Sufis and Sufism. Two major genres grew out of historical reports about individual Sufis: the survey and the biographical compilation. These two genres were sometimes combined together in the form of discrete sections in a single work, and the material they conveyed was compiled and packaged in various ways to serve different but related functions: pedagogical guidance of those who aspired to become Sufis, pious commemoration of past masters, the building of corporate solidarity among Sufis, and confident self-presentation and self-assertion vis-à-vis other groups competing for authority within Muslim communities.

The specialized Sufi literature of the 10th and 11th centuries was produced by Sufis of two divergent orientations: the "traditionalists," who were averse to all scholarship that assigned a prominent role to human → reason, and the "academic" Sufis, who, in contrast, were aligned with legal and theological scholarship. The latter approach, popularized by Abū Ḥāmid al-Ghazālī (d. 1111) in his seminal work *Iḥyā' 'ulūm al-dīn* (Bringing the religious sciences to life), gradually but surely assumed authoritative status throughout all Muslim communities, especially among educated elites.

4. Spiritual Lineages and Orders
The shaping of Sufism as a distinct tradition was evident equally in the formation of "spiritual lineages" *(silsila)* around major Sufi masters, who placed a special emphasis on training disciples. Such spiritu-

ally linked communities took some time to develop, and the different stages of this development are difficult to document. Increasingly, aspirants who were accepted as novices by a sheikh were "initiated" not only into Sufism but also into a particular lineage held together by bonds of loyalty and devotion extending from the novices and experienced disciples to the master, and by bonds of guidance and protection running in the other direction. The aspirants submitted to the authority of the master with complete trust; in return, the master pledged to guide them to their goal and to protect them from dangers on the road of spiritual development. This "director-novice" relationship (often known as *ṣuḥba*) was increasingly solemnized through initiation and graduation ceremonies that involved elements such as an oath of allegiance *(bay'a)* and a handclasp during the initial instruction of the *dhikr* formula, as well as the bestowal of a "certificate of graduation" *(ijāza)* accompanied by special insignia, most notably a cloak *(khirqa),* when the novices attained their goal.

The rise to prominence of the director-novice relationship led to the gradual formation of spiritual lineages, some of which were powerful enough to spawn actual social communities held together through devotion to a particular master. Perhaps the most visible social manifestation of these new spiritual families and the main social locus for the formation of communities around them was the growing social visibility of the Sufi lodge, which by the end of the 11th century grew into a durable social institution from its tentative beginnings more than a century earlier. With the establishment of lodges as prominent social institutions, Sufi spiritual lineages were slowly but surely being woven into the fabric of the greater society around them.

Remarkably, the ascendancy of training masters who increasingly came to preside over communities of Sufis resident in lodges coincided with the rise to prominence among Muslims of cults of saints. Originally based on belief in the existence of a divinely appointed company of saints, cults of saints began to take shape already during the 9th and 10th centuries, and there is little doubt that they were in full bloom by the 11th century, when clear reflections of this popular practice began to appear in intellectual life. In practical terms, the saint cults manifested themselves as an ideological and ritual complex organized around the basic concept of spiritual power *(baraka)* and the ritualistic performance of visiting tombs and other holy places *(ziyāra;* → Pilgrimage). Even though Sufis by no means had a monopoly on popular sainthood in this period, they easily formed the majority of the saints.

Through this conjunction of the Sufi and the popular spheres of sainthood, Sufism gradually ceased to be a form of piety that appealed almost exclusively to the urban middle and upper-middle classes and began to spread through the whole social canvas of premodern Islamic societies, from political elites to wage earners in urban centers to peasants and nomads in the countryside. Sainthood increasingly came to be defined almost exclusively in Sufi terms, and Sufi masters began to exercise considerable power in all spheres of social life.

From the 12th century onward, when Sufism became mainstream, the Sufi presence in Islamic societies took the form of distinct social groupings generally known as orders (ṭarīqa, pl. ṭuruq). These were concrete, institutional mappings of spiritual lineages onto the social fabric in the form of networks of lodges. Often built and maintained as pious foundations (waqf), these lodges frequently doubled as tomb-shrines that evolved into centers for saint cults. Since the 12th century, orders of local, regional, and international scope have proliferated in all Muslim communities. The most widespread and durable among these have been the Qādirī, Kubrawī, Shādhilī, Naqshbandī, and Khalwatī orders, followed by such regional orders as the Chishtī and the Mevlevī. The orders represent an extremely wide range of Sufi activity at different levels of institutionalization, and they continue even now to define Sufism among Muslims.

5. Expansion of Influence

The 12th century formed a watershed also for the spiritual, intellectual, and artistic landscape of Sufism. Up until that point, Sufis had largely maintained an inward orientation. However, the alignment of this distinct form of piety with legal and theological scholarship opened the floodgates through which legal, theological, and philosophical thinking could flow into Sufism. Indeed, from the end of the 11th century, Sufis began to open up to all the different intellectual discourses that were available in Islamic societies, and not only legal, theological, and philosophical speculation but also the whole array of "occult sciences" — including interpretation of → dreams and other → visionary experiences, as well as divination and prognostication — gradually found their way into Sufi thought. At the same time, Sufism blended with other forms of piety such as messianism, apocalypticism, and esoterism.

The expansion of the scope of Sufi thought and practice to all levels and aspects of social and intellectual life in this period also resulted in an unprecedented literary and artistic florescence. Cultivation of poetic and musical expression, which had been a special feature of Sufism from its very beginnings, now reached new artistic heights in all the different linguistic and musical traditions prevalent in Muslim communities. This confluence of Sufism with all other major intellectual, artistic, and spiritual trends conspired to produce a stellar array of seminal Sufi figures during this period, of whom Abū Madyan (d. 1197), Najm al-Dīn Kubrā (d. 1221), Ibn al-ʿArabī (d. 1240), and Jalāl al-Dīn Rūmī (d. 1273) are prominent examples.

The almost complete blending of Sufism into all forms of social and cultural life from the 12th century onward makes it practically impossible to write the history of Sufism from this point onward as if it were a self-contained tradition of mystical thought and practice, since in a very real sense all subsequent Islamic history was at least colored if not permeated by Sufi themes and practices. Today Sufism continues to be a vibrant mode of piety in Muslim communities throughout the globe. Although Sufi thought and practices have come under heavy and sustained criticism from many rationalizing Muslim modernists who view mystical piety as antithetical to "development and progress," Sufi orientations remain attractive to a broad array of Muslims who cherish this spiritually and artistically rich aspect of their religious tradition. Traditional Sufi orders are active in practically all Muslim-majority settings, and new orders continue to appear with some frequency. Clearly, the Sufis have succeeded in conveying the significance and urgency of their central concern, which was to obtain experiential knowledge (maʿrifa) of God's unity by distilling the reality of the Islamic profession of faith "There is no god but God" into their daily lives, and doing so for the great majority of their fellow Muslims from all walks of life.

→ Islam; Islamic Philosophy

Bibliography: J. BALDICK, *Mystical Islam: An Introduction to Sufism* (New York, 1989) • W. C. CHITTICK, *Sufism: A Short Introduction* (Oxford, 2000) • C. W. ERNST, *The Shambhala Guide to Sufism* (Boston, 1997) • A. KARAMUSTAFA, *Sufism: The Formative Period* (Edinburgh, 2007) • A. D. KNYSH, *Islamic Mysticism: A Short History* (Leiden, 2000) • S. H. NASR, ed., *Islamic Spirituality* (2 vols.; New York, 1987-90) • J. RENARD, *Historical Dictionary of Sufism* (Toronto, 2005); idem, *Seven Doors to Islam: Spirituality and the Religious Life of Muslims* (Berkeley, Calif., 1996) • A. SCHIMMEL, *Mystical Dimensions of Islam* (Chapel Hill, N.C., 1975) • M. J. SEDGWICK, *Sufism: The Essentials* (Cairo, 2000).

AHMET T. KARAMUSTAFA

Suicide

1. Basic Insights

Certain basic insights must precede any thinking about suicide and about the possibility of helping in suicide crises. We must start by recognizing that suicide is a possibility known only to human beings, but a familiar one in all ages and cultures (→ Anthropology). Since it is part of the human condition, however, all attempts to eliminate it totally (e.g., by legislation, ethics, or counseling) are doomed to failure. We must admit that the ability to take one's own life is cherished by many people as a final form of action, even though they never make use of it. Obvious ways of committing suicide, such as by hanging, poison, or shooting, may be concealed in socially accepted forms of behavior (e.g., overwork, anger, or reckless driving).

In theological → ethics consideration of suicide has moved away from biblical examples (V. Lenzen, 65ff.) as concepts of ourselves and of God have changed, along with our feeling for life. No theological ethics can rule out the final possibility expressed as a question by K. → Barth (1886-1968; → Dialectical Theology): "Who can say that it is absolutely impossible for the gracious God Himself to help a man in affliction by telling him to take this way out?" (CD III/4, 410). At the same time, → life is not ours to control. From all this it follows that if we want to keep a person from suicide, we must be ready to become involved in that person's life. To think only in terms of preventing a suicide is not to think deeply enough (→ Grace 2).

2. Paradigm Shift

E. Ringel presented the thesis that a presuicidal syndrome (including psychological and situational pressure, turning of → aggression against oneself, and involuntary fantasies of suicide), which is open to diagnosis, always precedes suicide. This view brought about a paradigm shift that affects theological ethics as well, namely, that suicide is the conclusion of a sick development and hence is not to be condemned morally.

After World War I the practice of not burying suicides in consecrated ground (1917 → CIC 1240; cf. 1983 CIC 1184) was largely changed, although Vatican II still judged that "wilful suicide" is a scandal and militates "against the honor of the creator" (Gaudium et spes 27). The penal measures of the 1917 CIC rested on the verdict of the Greek philosophers Plato (427-347 B.C.; Leg. 9.872-73) and Aristotle (384-322; Eth. Nic. 3.11 and 5.15; → Greek Philosophy) and were given a theological basis by → Augustine (354-430, → Augustine's Theology).

Theologically, the sickness thesis, although attractive, is not wholly adequate.

3. Suicidological Theories

Because life is at issue, we must consider various aspects in the case of suicide and yet also see them together: the phenomenology of suicide and attempted suicide (act, method, accompanying circumstances, statistics), the psychological and psychosocial dimensions, the ethical-moral dimension, and the legal issues in specific cases. These aspects may be differentiated in analysis, but at many points they merge into one another.

To prevent suicide, suicidological theories (C. Reimer) are also important insofar as we can use them in analyzing the above aspects. At issue are medical and psychological diagnoses (→ Psychiatry) that demand medical treatment, usually in connection with → psychoses and → depressions. As regards the aggressive components of suicide, psychoanalysis draws on the thesis of S. Freud (1856-1939; also of K. Abraham) that suicide unconsciously involves an act of murder and the expiatory reaction of self-murder (→ Atonement). With respect to the narcissistic aspect, psychoanalysis finds important the thesis of H. Henseler that suicide is an escape from an intolerable sickness in feelings about oneself (→ Narcissism). Also in this connection we should note the thesis of the parasuicidal gesture or pause (W. Feuerlein), which has no self-destructive purpose.

In the field of → sociology or → social psychology, É. Durkheim (1858-1917; → Sociology of Religion 2.2), on the basis of empirical material, argued in 1897 that we must view suicide as a reaction to social conditions and developments and distinguish typologically between altruistic, egoistic, anomistic, and fatalistic suicide. It is clear that the inclination toward suicide and the desire for it work together by a common psychopathological dynamic. Externally similar acts, as many see them, are self-sacrifice (e.g., the biblical Samson; → Sacrifice 2) and martyrdom, but to group these as suicide is a mistake, even if suicidal inclinations may be associated with them in specific cases.

4. Motives

Decisive for surviving the crisis is the investigation of the (dominant) motives in order to understand the subjective point of the action of suicide and to make effective intervention. Asking what the trigger is will often offer a clue to the reason.

1. The aim may be to prevent something happening, to escape from further troubles, worse illnesses, threats to self-image and self-meaning, with perhaps a desire to submerge or "explode."
2. Or the aim may be to reach a goal that can be reached in no other way, to attain rest, peace, shelter, warmth, coolness, etc.
3. Another aim is to punish oneself or another by the act (the aggressive component predominant).
4. Suicide may result from pressure, as when "a wayfarer is set upon by thieves" (M. → Luther; see WA.B 10.25 and Lenzen, 207ff.; → Luther's Theology), in which case the suicide might be the victim of intolerable pain at some great loss, a radical sickness, or the recognition of guilt (e.g., Judas), all of which can kill as does a sword.
5. We then have individual or collective → grief (J. Baechler, 92-93, on the "Jewish mourning suicide"), world-weariness, despair of life (J. Améry), and the sting of the absurd (A. Camus), all of which can provoke to suicide. Here we should note the wish not to have been born or to return as quickly as possible to the place from which we came (Sophocles, *Oedipus at Colonos*, 1224-38; likewise also Jer. 20:17 and Plato *Phd.* 62).

Once the motive is known, there is the possibility of seeking means to help potential suicides to find the life they seek (see 6).

5. Evaluations and Implied Norms

All evaluations of suicide rest on → norms and value systems. It is therefore important that the one who is under an individual or collective suicidal compulsion thinks in the same way as the one who does the evaluation. We can achieve understanding only if there is some approximation of values to shape the criteria.

If we look at suicide victims in terms of the context of events in their lives, a *nomos* (law) of an individual biography will be followed. If we assess in terms of sociopsychological norms, then what counts is the social *nomos*. If we see suicide as the last act in a theologically constructed nexus of action and consequence, then we have a theonomous view; theocratic laws (→ Theocracy) that claim validity in every sphere of life can accept no other *nomos*. The account of the life will take shape accordingly, as in the interpretation of the death of Saul in 1 Samuel 31, 2 Samuel 1, and 1 Chronicles 10. Finally, if we see suicide as an expression of personal freedom, it would seem to be autonomously justified (→ Stoicism).

Value systems may apply individually or collectively. Suicides may be commanded or forbidden by individual *nomoi* according to the situation (note the accounts of mass suicide in early Judaism, esp. Josephus on Masada and Jotapata; see Lenzen, 113ff.). Thus we should not apply theonomous sanctions (e.g., forbidding churchyard burial) if relatives hold a socionomous view or respect the individual's situation (e.g., the burial of Ahithophel in 2 Sam. 17:23).

6. Why Live?

Only those who allow that the desire to stay alive is by no means self-evident or a matter that can be legally enforced can intervene in a suicidal crisis with the shared question, What might keep the suicide alive? This is the decisive question in theological ethics because it takes into account the nexus of life that binds together both the one under threat and the one who might help. At issue here is a "center of life" (Jörns, 1979, 88ff.) that will enable people to resist destructive tendencies. A related matter is the possibility of releasing pent-up aggressions.

If we start with the thesis that life means communicating, then all its relationships (to others, to God, to ideas, to → animals, etc.), as well as the → forgiveness of → guilt that God and others grant, work against suicide. For they produce a feeling that life has meaning, weight, even glory (Heb. *kābôd*, Gk. *doxa*), that we can "count" for others, and that life as it is need not threaten us with destruction. Against this background we can see in suicide a "paradoxical" attempt to return to a (preindividual) stage of life in which our own lives unquestionably had meaning and were protected. Suicide can be prevented when help is given toward continuation of the search for life with means that maintain life.

Fluctuating statistical statements about suicide in so-called risk groups tell us where life is felt to be most unprotected in a given society. All suicides (U.S. average: 32,000 per year, according to the Suicide and Crisis Center, Dallas, Tex.) and attempted suicides (U.S. average: 730,000 per year) are cries for help that the churches in particular must hear and respond to with → proclamation, → pastoral care, and → diakonia. Listening, being there, accompanying, and assisting are methods that all Christians can use along with those who offer special services in the pastorate or in telephone ministry or → counseling.

Proclamation must have the courage to publicly distinguish the means used to maintain life from those by which we die spiritually — before further victims of a humane-appearing neutral worldview (→ Relativism; Worldview) and an actual practice of indifference force activity that is irremediable. If faith is to draw a definite line against suicide, it must respond to the often despairing search for life by seeing to it no less definitely that those who are born into this life not only have an abstract right to life (→ Abortion) but find people who will accept them with attentive love on their journey into life and bear them witness concerning the future of a life with God that can never be lost. Part of opting for life in this way is a recognition that guilt usually arises through seeking more from life than we have at any given time. The message of the acceptance of sinners in Christ must address this twofold need in order to save life.

→ Crisis Intervention; Dying, Aid for the; Euthanasia; Pastoral Care of the Dying

Bibliography: A. Alvarez, *The Savage God: A Study of Suicide* (New York, 1972) • J. Améry, *On Suicide: A Discourse on Voluntary Death* (Bloomington, Ind., 1999) • J. Baechler, *Suicides* (New York, 1979) • M. P. Battin, R. Rhodes, and A. Silvers, eds., *Physician-Assisted Suicide: Expanding the Debate* (New York, 1998) • N. Biggar, *Aiming to Kill: The Ethics of Suicide and Euthanasia* (Cleveland, 2004) • B. A. Brody, ed., *Suicide and Euthanasia: Historical and Contemporary Themes* (Boston, 1989) • *Crisis: The Journal of Crisis Intervention and Suicide Prevention* (Toronto, 1980-) • É. Durkheim, *On Suicide* (trans. R. Buss; London, 2006; orig. pub., 1897) • G. Evans and N. L. Farberow, *The Encyclopedia of Suicide* (2d ed.; New York, 2003) • H. Henseler, *Narzißtische Krisen. Zur Psychodynamik des Selbstmordes* (4th ed.; Wiesbaden, 2000) • K.-P. Jörns, *Nicht leben und nicht sterben können. Suizidgefährdung, Suche nach dem Leben* (Göttingen, 1979; 2d ed., 1986); idem, "Suizidverhinderung und Menschenwürde," *ThPr* 21 (1986) 255-63 • V. Lenzen, *Selbsttötung. Ein philosophisch-theologischer Diskurs mit einer Fallstudie über Cesare Pavese* (Düsseldorf, 1987) • K. Menninger, *Man against Himself* (New York, 1938; repr., 1963) • I. Orbach, *Children Who Don't Want to Live: Understanding and Treating the Suicidal Child* (San Francisco, 1988) • C. Reimer, *Suizid. Ergebnisse und Therapie* (Berlin, 1982) • E. Ringel, *Der Selbstmord. Abschluß einer krankhaften psychischen Entwicklung* (9th ed.; Frankfurt, 2005) • E. Schneidman, *The Suicidal Mind* (New York, 1996).

Klaus-Peter Jörns

Summa

1. Term
2. The Classic Questions-Summas
3. The *Summa theologiae* of Thomas Aquinas

1. Term

"Summa" was first used for a comprehensive literary work in the 12th century. We can hardly use it, however, for the totality, crown, or summary of what is done without further definitions and synonyms such as *compendium, epitome, summula,* and others. The traditional medieval use occurs in the title of P. → Melanchthon's (1497-1560; → Reformers 3.1.1) *Corpus doctrinae Christianae;* according to the 1571 edition, it is "a *summa* of Christian doctrine in a short, plain, and basic collection."

Summas were a specific phenomenon of university life but were not used in teaching in the Middle Ages. They are found in every faculty but reached their fullest development in 13th-century theology. Unlike *sententiae* or *quaestiones,* "summa" was not a technical term. It appeared in titles but had no relation to the original aims of the author. It could be used in commentaries for the Apostles' Creed but might also be used for the exposition of a discipline, though not with encyclopedic fullness. It might also be a compilation, a compendium, a selection, the presentation of part of a discipline, or even a list of biblical "distinctions" (such as the *Summa Abel* of Peter the Chanter [d. 1197]). We also find summas of summas (e.g., the *Summa de creaturis* of Albertus Magnus [ca. 1200-1280], treating fully of creation, matter, time and eternity, angels, and much more).

2. The Classic Questions-Summas

We use the term "summa" today with reference to the classic *quaestiones-summas* of the High Middle Ages (→ Middle Ages 1; Scholasticism). The distinctive feature of these works is that the authors are not content to offer a cursory commentary on the text of the dominant *Sentences* (1155-58?) of Peter Lombard (ca. 1100-1160; → Patristics, Patrology, 2). These "sentences," even those of Lombard, could also be called summas, but the authors, according to their interests, created organically and coherently constructed summas on the text, often thought of as introductions. These summas form the high point of the Scholastic method, even though the great theologians still used the traditional form of a "sentence" commentary (of which over 1,000 are known).

What becomes increasingly clearer in the process was the influence of one's own reason over the authority of the binding text, so that more room is given to the thinking of the theologian, even within the context of the authoritative text (→ Hermeneutics). From the *lectio* (reading) arise *quaestiones disputatae* (i.e., questions about all aspects of the doctrine and calling for arguments both for and against), which become the literary form of the summa. The principle of construction *(ordo disciplinae)* shows the originality of the author.

Though the structure is the same, the medieval summa does not form a rationalistic systematizing (→ Rationalism). The thought of a derived discipline, which may be seen in Aquinas's aim of justifying the Aristotelian ideal of scholarship (→ Aristotelianism), fails to meet the modern ideal of a closed, universal, logically consistent system (→ Social Systems) and does not serve as a principle that gives order to the summa.

3. The *Summa theologiae* of Thomas Aquinas

Thomas Aquinas's incomplete *Summa theologiae* *(STh)* is the most famous of the summas. Aquinas (ca. 1225-1274; → Thomism) thinks of theology as the science of God, rather than the science of revelation *(revelabilia* [what can be won by natural reason or revealed] instead of *revelata* [what has been revealed]). He uses a twofold *exitus-reditus* formula: the movement of creation *from* God, and that of salvation *to* God (→ Creation; Salvation; Salvation History).

Aquinas's so-called *Summa contra gentiles* (often, though wrongly, called *Summa philosophica)* was obviously not originally a summa. Even in the *STh* the word *theologiae* does not go back to Aquinas. (The term is dubious, since in the document itself Thomas does not call his subject matter *theologia* but *sacra doctrina.* The popular designation *theologica,* although very old, lacks a historical foundation.)

The *STh* met with resistance at first but finally replaced the *Sentences* as an official instructional text. This development began in Germany in the 15th century. According to P. Classen, the first known intervention of a political agency into the teaching in a German university aimed at hindering the introduction of Thomist theology at the University of Cologne. In 1512 Konrad Köllin (ca. 1476-1536), a prominent jurist and an opponent of the doctrine of marriage held by Martin → Luther (1483-1546; → Luther's Theology), published a very influential commentary on the *STh.* The best-known commentary comes from Luther's opponent Thomas Cajetan (1469-1534). Aquinas's summa continued its victorious march through the universities in the 16th century, for Thomistic theology had decisive influence on the Council of → Trent. A

Thomas renaissance began in the middle of the 19th century (→ Neoscholasticism), and in the 20th, many teaching texts were written in the spirit of Thomas Aquinas.

→ Dogmatics 2

Bibliography: F. C. BAUERSCHMIDT, ed., *Holy Teaching: Introducing the Summa theologiae of St. Thomas Aquinas* (Grand Rapids, 2005) • P. M. CANDLER, *Theology, Rhetoric, Manuduction; or, Reading Scripture Together on the Path to God* (Grand Rapids, 2006) • P. CLASSEN, "Libertas scolastica–Scholarenprivilegien. Akademische Freiheit im Mittelalter," *Studium und Gesellschaft im Mittelalter* (ed. S. Fried; Stuttgart, 1983) 238-84 • M. GRABMANN, *Die Geschichte der scholastischen Methode,* vol. 2, *Die scholastische Methode im 12. und beginnenden 13. Jahrhundert* (Berlin, 1956; orig. pub., 1911) 13-25, 476-563.

WILLIAM J. HOYE

Summum bonum → Good, The

Sunday

1. History and Development
2. Present Situation and Problems

1. History and Development

Sunday is the day of the → resurrection of Jesus and his manifestation as the living Lord to his → disciples (Matthew 28; Luke 24; John 20). This basic message is the inalienable foundation of the Christian recognition of this day. It is the day of the gathering of the → congregation for → proclamation and for the → Eucharist (1 Cor. 16:2; Acts 20:7-12). Participation in Sunday → worship was for the first Christians an obvious expression of their life "in Christ" (→ Primitive Christian Community).

From the second century, except in Palestine, there are reports of Sunday observance in all churches. These are always linked to references to, or explicit explanations of, the Eucharist, around which Christians assemble. Since Sunday was a working day, believers gathered late in the evening or early in the morning. → Justin (ca. 100-ca. 165) refers to initiation on Sundays (*1 Apol.* 65; → Baptism). In his *Traditio apostolica* (ca. 215), Hippolytus (ca. 170-ca. 236; → Early Church) mentions as part of the Sunday eucharistic celebration both baptism (§§20-21) and the → ordination of bishops, priests, and deacons (§§2-9). Around 300 the Council of Elvira in Spain expelled for a short time Christians who lived in the → city and were not present at wor-

ship on three consecutive Sundays (can. 21; →
Church Law).

In 321 Constantine (306-37) decreed that
Sunday be a day of rest for all judges, citizens,
tradesmen, and merchants. This ruling made the
Sunday worship of the church much easier, and it
gave time for refreshment. The duty to participate in
Sunday worship was repeatedly stated as a law in the
following centuries. → Scholasticism found a basis
for this duty in the fourth commandment (→
Decalogue) and in the natural law that we must
honor God by visible celebration.

In the late → Middle Ages Sunday worship became a church law that brought members under
penalty of a mortal → sin. The → Roman Catholic
Church maintained this obligation formally in 1918
→ CIC 1248 and 1983 CIC 1246-47. The churches
of the → Reformation (→ Lutheran Churches; Reformed and Presbyterian Churches), however, did
not follow this legalizing of Sunday worship. All the
→ Reformers, however, sharpened the call of duty
to hear the → proclamation of God's Word and to
join in receiving the Eucharist.

The worship mentality and practice of believers,
however, has lost a focus on the Sunday celebration
of the Eucharist in almost all churches, with instruction taking its place. Since the legal pressure is not
so high in Europe and the large Protestant denominations in North America, participation in Sunday
worship is less strong than in the Roman Catholic
Church. Since Wilhelm Löhe (1808-72) and others,
the → liturgical movement, especially in the 20th
century, rediscovered the essential meaning of the
full divine service for Sundays. The → Old Catholic
Churches recognize the duty of celebrating the Eucharist on Sunday but, unlike the Roman Catholic
Church, have not made it binding on one's → conscience. The Eastern churches (→ Orthodox
Church) cling to the one eucharistic celebration
each Sunday, which is an obligation but is not made
a legal duty.

The combination of "Sunday observance" and
"the day of rest" began in the sixth century, influenced by the command to rest. The command not to
work on Sundays does less to make possible the celebration of the Eucharist than to ensure rest in accordance with the Sabbath legislation.

2. Present Situation and Problems

The present situation in the churches is marked, in
Europe at least, by a diminishing number who
gather for divine service on Sundays. At the same
time, especially in countries with technologically
highly developed industries (→ Technology), dis-

cussion of Sunday as a normal working day (with
other days off) is in full swing. The churches' task in
this process is, on the one side, to protect the traditional function of Sunday both as a day of worship
and as a day of rest and, on the other, to care for
those who have to work (e.g., in public-service jobs,
as well as those with responsibilities in transportation, hotels, and restaurants) by offering them divine service on days that come as close as possible to
Sunday.

→ Church and State; Church Year; Economic
Ethics; Sunday School

Bibliography: A. M. ALTERMATT and T. A. SCHNITKER,
eds., *Der Sonntag. Anspruch–Wirklichkeit–Gestalt*
(Würzburg, 1986) • S. BACCHIOCCHI, *From Sabbath to
Sunday: A Historical Investigation of the Rise of Sunday
Observance in Early Christianity* (Rome, 1977) • D. A.
CARSON, ed., *From Sabbath to Lord's Day: A Biblical,
Historical, and Theological Investigation* (Grand
Rapids, 1982) • M. J. DAWN, *Keeping the Sabbath
Wholly: Ceasing, Resting, Embracing, Feasting* (Grand
Rapids, 1989) • W. J. SHERZER and P. R. COONEY,
"Sunday," *NCE* (2d ed.) 13.606-9 • J. WILKE, ed., *Mehr
als ein Weekend? Der Sonntag in der Diskussion*
(Paderborn, 1989).

THADDEUS A. SCHNITKER

Sunday School

1. History
2. Spread
3. Later Development
4. Ecumenical Engagement

1. History

The Sunday school movement began around 1780
in Great Britain and quickly led to the formation of
independent regional and interdenominational societies. In 1785 William Fox (1738-1826), a Baptist,
founded the Society for the Establishing and Maintaining of Sunday Schools in Great Britain. The
London Sunday School Union took its place in
1803. In 1843 the Church of England Sunday School
Institute of the Anglican Church (→ Anglican
Communion) was founded. The First Day Society
(1791) and American Sunday School Union (1821)
were the first Sunday school organizations in North
America. Regional unions arose first in Europe (e.g.,
the Erste Hamburger Sonntagsschulverein, in 1824),
most of them during the second half of the 19th
century, such as the unions in the Netherlands
(1865), Finland (1888), and Norway (1889).

The English publisher Robert Raikes (1736-

1811), from Gloucester, is customarily looked upon as the actual father of the Sunday school movement. His role, though, was more to provide the publicity and popularity that the already-existing Sunday "charity schools" needed to help them flourish.

2. Spread

The Sunday school movement aimed from the first to alleviate the needs of children (→ Childhood) in → industrial societies and in the process also addressed pedagogical tasks (→ Poverty; Literacy; Pedagogy). It was led by laity from the start, with volunteer workers playing an essential role. The movement spread quickly within Great Britain and then beyond the British Isles: Sunday school work began in Wales in 1785 and, a year later, in Ireland. Around the turn of the century the Roman Catholic Church in England also took up Sunday school work, with the teaching of Christian doctrine.

The British Sunday school became quickly known in Germany (1825, through J. H. Wichern; → Revivals 2.5), as well as in Scandinavia. The concept of the Sunday school is so flexible that it can be adopted by various churches without difficulty and can be shaped to their specific needs. In the course of the 19th century in Germany, the tasks gradually became designated as children's worship.

In spite of its European origins, the Sunday school was adopted in North America in 1786. Up until 1880 it was the most widely accepted form of Protestant education in the United States, and even today, to some extent, it replaces the religious education that is lacking in the public schools (→ School and Church).

3. Later Development

After World War II, Sunday school work experienced a considerable upswing all around the world. The reason was partly the strong reconstruction of church work and the increase in the birth rate, as well as an increase in lay activity (→ Lay Movements). The following phenomena are typical for Sunday school work and children's worship: a decrease in the average age of volunteers; a steady development of new curricula, including on the international level; and an intensified reference to educational work and the → worship life of the church. In many churches, weekday activities for children have broadened the Sunday school, or also replaced it.

Since the 1960s participation in the Sunday school has diminished, except in developing countries and in the younger churches. Reasons include the sharp decline in the birth rate in many countries, competition to the Sunday school from other forms of education in virtually all churches, and declining interest in promoting the Sunday school.

→ Catechesis; Christian Education; Congregation; Development 2-3; Pastoral Care of Children; Socialization 2

Bibliography: A. M. BOYLAN, *Sunday School: The Formation of an American Institution, 1790-1880* (New Haven, 1988) • P. B. CLIFF, *The Rise and Development of the Sunday School Movement in England, 1780-1980* (Nutfield, Redhill, Surrey, 1986) • J. FERGUSON, ed., *Christianity, Society, and Education: Robert Raikes, Past, Present, and Future* (London, 1981) • W. B. KENNEDY, *The Shaping of Protestant Education: An Interpretation of the Sunday School and the Development of Protestant Educational Strategy in the United States, 1789-1960* (New York, 1966) • R. W. LYNN and E. WRIGHT, *The Big Little School: Two Hundred Years of the Sunday School* (2d ed.; Birmingham, Ala., 1980) • D. C. WYCKOFF, ed., *Renewing the Sunday School and the CCD* (Birmingham, Ala., 1986).

PERTTI LUUMI

4. Ecumenical Engagement

From the beginning, the Sunday school movement was a typically → Protestant phenomenon, but ecumenical contacts arose early, and it was increasingly integrated into the various churches. During the 19th century, missionary involvement spread the Sunday school to the mission fields (→ Mission), where it was the first step toward the starting of day schools (→ Mission Schools).

At the first World Sunday School Conference, in London in 1889, there were 845 participants, mostly from North America, the United Kingdom, and Ireland, but 15 mission reports from abroad were also read. The World Sunday School Convention was then founded to arrange further conferences, to propagate Sunday schools worldwide, and to pass on information regarding them. Between 1889 and 1958 there were 14 such conferences, each with the aim of discussing the goals, theory, and practice of the instruction given to children, young people, and finally adults. Approaches were also made to a theology of → unity ("by fact, by labor, by love") that would influence the emerging ecumenical movement (→ Ecumenism, Ecumenical Movement). Changes came in name and structure. At Rome in 1907 "Convention" in the name was changed to "Association."

In 1947 a new name was chosen: the World Council of Christian Education and Sunday School Movement. This council had its own publications and regional structures, and it worked more and more closely with the ecumenical movement (→ World Council of Churches [WCC]). Finally in 1971 at Lima, Peru, it voted to become a part of the WCC under its program of education and renewal. Regional alliances (e.g., the European Conference on Christian Education) continue but, in some cases, have undergone renewal.

Since 1971 only one worldwide conference on Sunday school questions has been held, which was the 200th anniversary celebration of the Sunday school — in Evian, France, in 1980.

Bibliography: U. BECKER, "Ecumenical Formation," *A History of the Ecumenical Movement*, vol. 3, *1968-2000* (ed. J. Briggs, M. A. Oduyoye, and G. Tsetsis; Geneva, 2004) 175-93 • J. T. HÖRNIG, *Mission und Einheit. Geschichte und Theologie der amerikanischen Sonntags-schulbewegung im neunzehnten Jahrhundert unter besonderer Berücksichtigung ihrer ökumenischen Relevanz und ihres Verhältnisses zur Erweckungsbewegung* (Maulbronn, 1991) • G. E. KNOFF, *The World Sunday School Movement: The Story of a Broadening Mission* (New York, 1979).

ULRICH BECKER and PERTTI LUUMI

Sunna

"Sunna" (Arab. *sunnah*, "custom, way") emerged as a central normative concept for Muslims within the first two centuries of → Islam. While the → Qur'an speaks of the "Sunna of God" and the "Sunna of the early generations," Muslim scholars of the early period focused primarily on the Sunna of the Prophet Muḥammad (ca. 570-632). Many of these scholars went to great lengths to collect reports, called hadith (sing. and pl.; Arab. *ḥadīth*, "speech, report"), of his actions and statements and of the practices that received his tacit approval. Each hadith consists of a chain of authorities (*isnād*) and a text (*matn*).

By the early 9th century, thousands of hadith had been evaluated by a modest number of hadith critics and put into books arranged either by topic (*muṣannaf*) or by prophetic Companion (*musnad*). Two of these hadith books — the Ṣaḥīḥs of al-Bukhārī (810-70) and of Muslim ibn al-Ḥajjāj (ca. 817-75) — have long been recognized by Sunni Muslims as the most authoritative collections of prophetic Sunna, and four others that had been compiled in the 9th century achieved canonical status by the 13th century. Numerous noncanonical Sunni hadith collections from the 9th and 10th centuries also have survived (→ Sunnism, Sunnis).

The Sunna of Muhammad, as recorded in the hadith, exerted a major impact upon the legal, ethical, theological, and mystical (→ Mysticism) dimensions of Islam. Muḥammad ibn Idrīs al-Shāfiʿī (767-820) is usually considered the preeminent champion of the legal authority of hadith among the famous early jurists, although Mālik ibn Anas (ca. 715-95) and Aḥmad ibn Ḥanbal (780-855), two jurists of comparable stature, were generally held to be better transmitters and critics of hadith than al-Shāfiʿī. Later Sunni legal theorists grounded the probity of prophetic Sunna in the creedal principle that Muḥammad had been "protected from sin" (*maʿṣūm*), but they disagreed as to whether his actions had to be considered obligatory, recommended, or merely acceptable, and whether Muḥammad's actions took precedence over his statements in cases where a contradiction between the two was reported.

Shiite Muslims also have treasured prophetic Sunna (→ Shia, Shiites). The largest group of Shiites, the Imamis (or Twelvers), has its own books of Sunna, four of which are considered canonical. Imami Shiite hadith (or *akhbār*) differ structurally from Sunni hadith because of the Imamis' core belief that all 12 imams were, like the Prophet, "protected from sin"; consequently, the isnads of their hadith must trace back only to one of the first 11 imams, whereas for Sunnis, every isnad must go back to the Prophet via one of his Companions (*ṣaḥāba*). Thus, while books on Imami Shiite legal theory share a common set of discussions on Sunna with their Sunni counterparts, most of the Imami Shiite hadith corpus is not considered to meet the minimal requirements for authenticity in the eyes of Sunni scholars, since its isnads rarely go back to Muhammad with uninterrupted chains of transmitters. Likewise, Shiite scholars dismiss most Sunni hadith as inauthentic because of their general rejection of the religious probity of the Companions of the Prophet and other early transmitters found in Sunni isnads.

Western scholarship on Sunna has revolved overwhelmingly around the question of whether the vast corpus of Sunni hadith is authentic and can be used as a source for the history of the first century of Islam. In general, Western scholarship since Ignaz Goldziher (1850-1921) has taken a pessimistic view of hadith as accurate reports of prophetic practice, although there is much agreement that this material is useful for understanding Islam in the eighth century. Much fruitful research remains to be done on the development and influence of hadith literature from the ninth century to the present, especially since one of the most popular books in the Muslim world today is al-Nawawī's (1233-77) collection of hadith called *Riyāḍ al-ṣāliḥīn*, or *Gardens of the Righteous*.

Bibliography: W. A. GRAHAM, *Divine Word and Prophetic Word in Early Islam* (The Hague, 1977) • G. H. A. JUYNBOLL, *Muslim Tradition: Studies in Chronology, Provenance, and Authorship of Early Ḥadīth* (Cambridge, 1983) • H. MOTZKI, ed., *Ḥadīth: Origins and Developments* (Brookfield, Vt., 2004) • NAWAWĪ, *Riyāḍ-us-Sāliheen* (Gardens of the Righteous) (2 vols.; trans. M. Amin and A. Usamah bin Razduq; New York, 1999) • M. Z. SIDDIQI, *Ḥadīth Literature: Its Origin, Development, and Special Features* (2d ed.; Cambridge, 1993).

SCOTT C. LUCAS

Sunnism, Sunnis

1. Term
2. Historical Overview
3. Theology
4. Institutions
5. Scholars
   5.1. al-Ṭabarī
   5.2. Ibn Ḥazm
   5.3. al-Ghazālī
   5.4. Ibn ʿArabī
   5.5. Rūmī
   5.6. al-Nawawī
   5.7. al-Taftāzānī
6. Modern Developments

1. Term

The terms "Sunnism" and "Sunni" are anglicizations of Arab. *ahl al-sunnah* (the people of the → Sunna [lit. "custom, way"]) or *ahl al-sunnah wa-l-jamāʿa* (the people of the Sunna and community). In most of the Islamic world, "Sunni" has been synonymous with "Muslim." The vast majority of Muslims have always been Sunnis, and nearly all sectarian groups, with the exception of the main body of Shiites, dwindled to small numbers or became extinct.

Compound expressions that contain the word "Sunna" appear with some frequency in the ninth century C.E., primarily in the writings of scholars of hadith (sing. and pl.; Arab. *ḥadīth*, "speech, report") — that is, the men who collected, sorted, and critically evaluated tens of thousands of reports of what Muḥammad (ca. 570-632) purportedly said, did, or tacitly approved. A few hadith found in ninth-century collections even report that the Prophet identified "the people of the Sunna and community" as the only sect of → Islam to enjoy salvation.

Although the term "Sunni" does not appear to have been used with any regularity during the first two centuries of Islam, Sunnis of the ninth century devoted most of their energies to promoting the authority of the teachings of the Prophet and the earliest religious authorities of Islam, known as the Companions and the Successors.

The open attitude of Sunni scholars toward their predecessors (and contemporaries) who had regularly found themselves on the opposite sides of religious practices, beliefs, and even the battlefield is the essence of the word "community." This meaning is lost in the conventional term "Sunni" yet is preserved in Marshall Hodgson's (1922-68) expression "Jamāʿī-Sunnīs" (Sunnis of the Community), which has yet to find currency among Western scholars of Islam.

2. Historical Overview

2.1. The formative period of Sunni Islam can be dated to the 9th and 10th centuries. During this time, hadith scholars produced over a dozen large volumes that recorded the teachings of the Prophet, his Companions, and the reliability of hundred of transmitters of this material. Second, legal schools coalesced around the teachings of Abū Ḥanīfah (699-767), Sufyān al-Thawrī (716-78), Mālik ibn Anas (ca. 715-95), al-Shāfiʿī (767-820), Ibn Ḥanbal (780-855), Ibn Rāhawayh (ca. 782-853), Dāwūd al-Ẓāhirī (ca. 815-84), and al-Ṭabarī (ca. 839-923). Four of these schools — Hanafi, Maliki, Shafiʿi, and Hanbali — developed individual legal methodologies, attracted deeply loyal followers, and collectively maintained their privileged positions as the sole surviving Sunni schools of law until this day.

The third major trend in this period was the emergence of the two great schools of → speculative theology *(kalām)*, grounded in the writings of their eponyms, al-Ashʿarī (873-935) and al-Māturīdī (before 873-944). An important third school of theology that survived alongside and in tension with these two schools was that of the hadith scholars, who insisted upon the curtailment of speculative theology beyond the literal word of the → Qur'an and hadith.

The fourth facet of Sunni Islam that took root in these centuries is the mystical tradition (→ Mysticism), known as *taṣawwuf,* or → Sufism. Many of the famous early masters, such as al-Muḥāsibi (ca. 781-857) and al-Junayd (ca. 840-910), were squarely in the Sunni fold.

Finally, the Abbasid Caliphate in Baghdad (from 750; also, from 836 to 892, in Sāmarrāʾ) provided a high degree of political unity during the first half of this period, before degenerating into a powerless symbolic authority over the course of the tenth century, when the term "caliph" was adopted by the Isma'ili Shiite dynasty of the Fatimids in North Africa and the local Sunni rulers of the southern half of the Iberian Peninsula.

2.2. While the traditions of Sunni hadith scholarship, law, and theology continued to develop over the centuries following the formative period, the seminal new development of Sufi brotherhoods emerged only in the course of the 12th and 13th centuries. Major transregional orders based upon the spiritual exercises and teachings of 'Abd al-Qādir al-Jīlānī (1077/78-1166) and Shihāb al-Dīn al-Suhrawardī (1145-1234) in Iraq, Abū al-Ḥasan al-Shādhilī (1196/97-1258) in Morocco, Mu'īn al-Dīn al-Chishtī (ca. 1141-1236) in North India, and many others emerged throughout the Muslim world. These orders rapidly developed the institutional structure of the *khānqāh,* or Sufi lodge, which became a regular feature of Muslim society. The popular veneration of saints (Arab. *awliyā',* "friends of God") grew alongside the high literary tradition of the Sufi orders, and soon shrines or tombs became ubiquitous throughout the Muslim world.

2.3. By the 14th century, most educated Sunnis belonged to one of the four legal schools, were affiliated with one of three theological schools, and were initiated into any number of Sufi brotherhoods. In many parts of the Muslim world, the choice of legal school would be largely predetermined by geography. For example, in Sumatra and Java, one would be a Shafi'i, whereas in Mali one would almost certainly be a Maliki. This pattern continued largely uninterrupted until the arrival of European imperial powers, which, by the First World War, occupied most of the lands in which Sunni Muslims were a majority of the population, from Senegal to what is today Indonesia. The introduction of European educational and political institutions in the Muslim world severely undermined the madrasa (*madrasah,* "place of study"), or traditional Sunni legal college (see 4.2), and the rapid rise of secular nationalism and Salafi Islamism (see 6) in the early 20th century significantly challenged the esoteric metaphysics and practices of many of the established mystical orders.

3. Theology

Three topics are prominent in Sunni theology: divine attributes, divine power, and the supremacy of the first four political successors to Muḥammad. Sunni theologians as a rule affirm a plurality of attributes by which God describes himself in the Qur'an and hadith. Hadith-scholar theologians,

sometimes called Traditionists, affirm all of God's attributes and reject interpreting them or reducing them to a specific number. Ash'arī theologians regularly restrict the number of eternal attributes that are "neither God nor other than God" to seven: knowledge, power, life, will, seeing, hearing, and speech. Adherents of the Māturīdī school, such as al-Nasafī (ca. 1068-1142), identify additional divine attributes beyond the "Ash'arī seven," such as creating, desiring, doing, and sustaining. A final hallmark of Sunni theology concerning the divine attributes is the insistence that the Qur'an is the eternal speech of God and cannot be considered to have been created at any point in time.

The second major topic common to all three Sunni schools of theology is the insistence that God is the sole creator of all things and actions in the universe (→ Creation). Unlike the Mu'tazila and most Shiites, who believed that humans create their own actions, Sunni theologians argued that certain qur'anic verses, such as "He created all things" and "there is no God but He, Creator of all things" (6:101-2), did not allow for the possibility of any rival creators to God. Despite their firm belief that humans cannot create their own acts without divine intervention, theologians from all three Sunni schools devised theories stipulating that human beings bear complete → responsibility for their voluntary actions. These theories can be seen as defensive efforts against the accusations issued by Mu'tazila and Shiites that Sunnis had in fact stripped humans of all responsibility for their actions.

The third major topic stressed in Sunni creeds from the earliest days was the affirmation that the historical sequence of the first four caliphs corresponds to their respective merits. In other words, Abū Bakr (ruled 632-34) was the greatest Muslim after Muḥammad, followed by 'Umar (634-44), followed by 'Uthmān (644-56), and then 'Alī (656-61). Anyone who advocated that 'Alī was the most elevated Muslim after the Prophet was declared by Sunni religious authorities to be a Shiite (from *shī'at 'Alī,* "the party of 'Alī"; → Shia, Shiites). Sunnis also enforced categorically the principle that, in the words of al-Nasafī, "only good should be spoken of the Companions of Muḥammad." The treatment of the Companions of Muḥammad is probably the most acrimonious difference between Sunnis and Shiites, since there is a long history of Shiites degrading (and at times cursing) the overwhelming majority of Muḥammad's Companions for their failure to recognize 'Alī's purported claim to religiopolitical authority immediately following the death of Muḥammad.

4. Institutions

4.1. Three institutions warrant consideration in this brief survey of Sunnism. The first is the caliphate, a system of government at whose head is the caliph, or vicegerent of God on earth. From its humble origins after the death of Muḥammad in 632, the caliphate grew rapidly in stature concomitantly with the major conquests of Egypt, Syria, Iraq, and Iran during the reigns of ʿUmar and ʿUthmān. The significance of the first four caliphs, whom Sunnis call "rightly guided," in the formation of Sunni dogma has already been noted. Sunnis historically remained loyal to the caliph, regardless of his personal qualities or behavior. The first Umayyad caliph, Muʿāwiya (ruled 661-80) is credited in the Sunni tradition with permanently transforming the caliphate into a hereditary kingship.

The longest-lasting caliphate was that of the Abbasids, who seized power from the Umayyads in 750 and wielded real political power from their capital in Baghdad (and briefly Sāmarrāʾ) until the early 900s. By 945 the caliph had lost all political power but retained symbolic prestige among Sunnis, which lasted long beyond the infamous Mongol sack of Baghdad in 1258. This prestige derived from the sterling reputations of the first caliphs and the Sunni ideal of a unified Muslim community under a single ruler. A new line of purely ceremonial Abbasid caliphs was supported by the staunchly Sunni rulers of Egypt almost immediately after the catastrophic events of 1258.

The final Ottoman sultans also adopted the title of caliph in order to bolster their support from Sunnis worldwide; one interesting consequence of this decision was the rise of a caliphate movement in far-off India in the early 20th century in support of the Ottomans. The caliphate was officially abolished by Mustafa Kemal Atatürk (1881-1938) in 1924. At least one contemporary Sunni political organization, Ḥizb al-Taḥrīr (the Party of Liberation), has as its central platform the restoration of this institution.

4.2. A second significant institution is the legal college, or madrasa. It appears to have emerged with the arrival of the Seljuk Turks in northeastern Persia, starting in the mid-11th century, and spread rapidly throughout the entire Middle East. All four Sunni schools of law succeeded in establishing independent madrasas, although it became common for patrons to endow legal colleges in which jurists from all four schools taught. The madrasa was the heart of the classical Muslim educational system, replete with endowed professorships for Arabic grammar, Islamic law, and, in due time, additional religious disciplines of legal theory, theology, and

hadith studies. It remained largely unrivaled until the arrival of European missionary schools in the 19th century. (Today, the term "madrasa" is used more commonly to refer to primary and secondary schools than colleges.)

4.3. A third noteworthy institution is that of the canonical hadith collections. Sunni scholars ultimately settled upon six books that had been compiled in the ninth and early tenth centuries as the most authoritative reference works for accessing the Prophet's Sunna, and they were unanimous from an early date that the collections of al-Bukhārī (810-70) and of Muslim ibn al-Ḥajjāj (ca. 817-75) were the most authoritative of all. It is not uncommon for classical scholars to declare that the hadith books of these two scholars are the most important books after the Qurʾan itself. By the late classical period, Sunnis from all four legal schools could agree upon the superiority and significance of these two hadith collections, and their lofty reputations remain intact even after a century of critical attacks on the authenticity of their contents by numerous Westerners and Western-educated Muslims.

5. Scholars

Much of the articulation of Sunni Islam derived from the work of gifted individual scholars who often operated with minimal institutional support. Since the founders of the legal schools have already been discussed in the article → "Shariʿa" (§3) and the Sunni philosopher (and major Maliki jurist) Ibn Rushd (1126-98) was covered in the article → "Islamic Philosophy" (§4.6), an additional seven major Sunni scholars of the classical period who profoundly shaped the Sunni tradition are introduced here.

5.1. al-Ṭabarī

Muḥammad ibn Jarīr al-Ṭabarī composed a massive universal history, *The History of the Messengers and Kings,* as well as an equally large qurʾanic commentary. He lived much of his life in Baghdad, where he founded a short-lived legal school. His history remains the preeminent source for our knowledge of early Islamic civilization and has received a complete annotated translation into English.

5.2. Ibn Ḥazm

Ibn Ḥazm (994-1064) was an iconoclastic scholar in Islamic Spain who challenged the mainstream Sunni legal schools on methodological grounds by arguing that all sacred law had to be grounded upon the Qurʾan and sound prophetic hadith. He also criticized many biblical stories that contradicted the parallel accounts in the Qurʾan and wrote an important treatise on love, translated as *The Dove's Neck-*

Ring. His legal thought later influenced modern Sunni reformers such as Rashīd Riḍā (1865-1935) and Muḥammad Asad (né Leopold Weiss, 1900-1992).

5.3. *al-Ghazālī*

Abū Hāmid al-Ghazālī (1058-1111) was an outstanding professor of Islamic law who wrote a major refutation of aspects of Ibn Sīnā's → metaphysics entitled *The Incoherence of the Philosophers.* He cured a deep spiritual crisis of his own by relinquishing his academic post and living among the Sufi mystics, an experience that led him to write inspirational books such as *Revival of the Religious Sciences* (in Arabic) and *The Alchemy of Happiness* (in Persian).

5.4. *Ibn ʿArabī*

Muḥyī al-Dīn Ibn ʿArabī (1165-1240) was one of the most prolific and controversial Sufis in Islamic history. He grew up in Islamic Spain, migrated east to Mecca and Anatolia, and ultimately settled in Damascus. Several of his most radical premises, such as the claim that all creation is both God and simultaneously not-God, expressed in verse and prose, were condemned by many later Sunnis, but his reputation as the "Greatest Master" survived. His most influential book, *The Bezels of Wisdom,* has received over 100 commentaries by both Sunni and Shiite mystics and has been translated into English.

5.5. *Rūmī*

Jalāl al-Dīn Rūmī (ca. 1207-73), one of the greatest Persian poets and Sufi masters, lived most of his life in Konya, in what is now central Turkey. Rūmī's thousands of verses advocate a deep love of God and teach that the human situation is akin to "a donkey's tail tied to an angel's wing." Hundreds of his poems, including his 25,000-line *Masnavi,* have been translated into English, along with a collection of his discourses. The Mevlevi Sufi order, often referred to in the West as the Whirling Dervishes, grew out of his teachings and employs his poetry set to music in its ceremonies.

5.6. *al-Nawawī*

Yaḥyā ibn Sharaf al-Nawawī (1233-77) was an exceptional Syrian scholar of hadith and Islamic law whose works were highly respected at both the scholarly and the popular levels. On the scholarly level, he played a major role in reorganizing the classical Shafiʿi legal school; his collection of 40 hadith and a substantially larger book of hadith arranged according to ethical topics, *Gardens of the Righteous,* remain highly popular among Sunnis to this day.

5.7. *al-Taftāzānī*

Saʿd al-Dīn al-Taftāzānī (1332-90) was a central Asian scholar who composed works that rapidly came to serve as a core curriculum for aspiring religious scholars. These books, which often took the form of abridgments or commentaries on earlier works, addressed logic, Arabic linguistics, Sunni theology, and legal theory; they also drew on both Ashʿarī and Māturīdī positions, as well as those of the Shafiʿis and Hanafis.

6. Modern Developments

Three key catalysts of change within Islam during these past five centuries were (1) the increasing institutionalization of the Ottoman Empire; (2) the spread of Islam in West Africa, South Asia, and Southeast Asia; and (3) the rise of European powers, which ultimately conquered much of the Muslim world (→ Colonialism). Although European interference played a major role in Sunni developments, especially over the past two centuries, it is clear that a purely internal reorientation appeared in the 18th century. Scholars such as Shāh Walī Allāh (1702/3-62) of Delhi, Muḥammad Ibn ʿAbd al-Wahhāb (1703-92) of central Arabia, and al-Shawkānī (1760-1834) of Yemen challenged prevailing theological and even legal paradigms in unique ways.

One methodology common to many of these scholars entailed a new emphasis on the study of the hadith canon and the opinions of the earliest authorities in Islam, known as the *salaf.* This reevaluation of the tradition is often described as Salafi Islam, an expression that has become confusing because of its application both to Sunnis perceived of as being liberal, such as Muḥammad ʿAbduh (1849-1905) of Egypt, and to those considered ultraconservative, such as the so-called Wahhabis of the modern kingdom of Saudi Arabia. The term also refers on occasion to the Hanbali school, which historically emphasized hadith, discouraged speculative theology, and produced some of the heroes of Salafi Islam, such as Ibn Taymiyya (1263-1328) and Ibn ʿAbd al-Wahhāb. It is also applied at times to 20th-century sociopolitical organizations, such as the Muslim Brotherhood, that declare Islam to be a comprehensive ideology that is the only solution for a litany of modern Muslim problems, including tyranny, inequality, corruption, and political impotence. The most notorious ideologue of the Muslim Brotherhood remains Sayyid Quṭb, who was executed by President Nasser of Egypt in 1966.

One prominent theme in 20th-century Sunni discourse has been that of reform. Numerous Western-educated Muslim scholars and intellectuals have called for a reassessment of the inherited tradition, especially in the legal sphere. Major writers in this vein include the South Asians Muhammad

Iqbal (1877-1938) and Fazlur Rahman (1919-88), the Indonesian Nurcholish Madjid (1939-2005), the Algerian Mohamed Arkoun, the Syrian Muhammad Shahrour, the Sudanese ʿAbdullahi An-Naʿim, the Moroccan Fatima Mernissi, and the Americans Amina Wadud and Kecia Ali.

While the ideas of reformers and ideologues are certainly significant, the vast majority of observant Sunnis should probably be classified as traditional Muslims who endeavor to harmonize inherited beliefs and practices with modern social and economic realities. Institutions located in the sphere of traditional Sunnism range from al-Azhar University in Cairo to the Nahdlatul Ulama (Renaissance of Islamic Scholars) in Indonesia, the world's largest Muslim organization. Since most efforts to "Islamize" society from above have had very limited success, it seems safe to say that the future of Sunni Islam will largely be determined by the vast community of traditional believers across the globe whose daily interactions with contemporary ideas and practices ensure the continuing vitality of this 1,400-year-old tradition.

Bibliography: D. W. BROWN, *Rethinking Tradition in Modern Islamic Thought* (Cambridge, 1996) • R. W. BULLIET, *Islam: The View from the Edge* (New York, 1994) • F. DENNY, *An Introduction to Islam* (3d ed.; New York, 2006) • M. HODGSON, *The Venture of Islam* (3 vols.; Chicago, 1974) • M. Z. SIDDIQI, *Ḥadīth Literature: Its Origin, Development, and Special Features* (2d ed.; Cambridge, 1993) • W. M. WATT, trans., *Islamic Creeds: A Selection* (Edinburgh, 1994).

SCOTT C. LUCAS

Superintendent

In 1527, at the time of the → visitation throughout electoral Saxony, the consistory appointed certain pastors as "superintendents" over specific districts. In other territorial churches "inspectors" were also instituted. To them were given the episcopal tasks (→ Bishop, Episcopate) of → ordination and visitation. The Rhenish Westphalian order used the term "preses" in a similar synodical structure (→ Synod).

Superintendents, appointed by synods or congregations, both represent and coordinate. The appointment is only for a time and goes along with pastoral duties. Through wider contacts and → information, they are better equipped than other church officials to coordinate, counsel, and resolve conflicts. Their position gives rise to problems, since they must both offer pastoral care and give leadership. Deputies offer necessary collegial support.

Superintendents had a role in the Church of Scotland, being appointed from 1560 to travel through, and set in order, the ten districts of the church. In the U.S. United Methodist Church, district superintendents are pastors exercising spiritual leadership in the various church districts. In southern Germany the superintendent is called a dean, and in northern Germany, a provost. A general or regional superintendent exercises similar duties in a larger sphere. We find the same functions in the Roman Catholic dean, the Reformed → moderator, the Anglican rural dean, and the Orthodox archpriest. British Methodists use the term "superintendent minister" for the head administrator of each circuit (i.e., subdivision of a district).

→ Church Government

Bibliography: G. DONALDSON, *The Scottish Reformation* (Cambridge, 1960) 108-29 • J. KIRK, *Patterns of Reform: Continuity and Change in the Reformation Kirk* (Edinburgh, 1989) 154-231 • M. H. LEIFFER, *The Role of the District Superintendent in the Methodist Church* (Evanston, Ill., 1960) • T. C. O'BRIEN, ed., "District Superintendent" and "Superintendent (Lutheran); Superintendent (Methodist)," *CDWC* 268 and 736 • A. STEIN, *Evangelisches Kirchenrecht* (3d ed.; Neuwied, 1992) 144-45; idem, "Seelsorgerliche Schweigepflicht und kirchenämtliche Dienstpflicht," *PTh* 85 (1988) 84-95.

ALBERT STEIN†

Superstition

1. Term
2. Source
3. In Religious Life
4. Psychoanalytic Theories
5. Pastoral Care

1. Term

The term "superstition" does not originally belong to either → theology or → religious education but to everyday speech. It is thus an evaluative word for a semi- or pseudoreligious attitude that is soon left behind as infantile or outdated but that some groups classify as a faith.

In her detective story *Light Thickens* (New York, 1982), New Zealand mystery novelist Ngaio Marsh tells of an actress whose conduct bears all the typical marks of superstition. She had developed a private ritual for when she returned to her apartment. Out of her handbag she would take a crucifix, "which she kissed and laid on the table near a clove of garlic and her prayerbook. She . . . put on her spectacles, crossed herself, and read aloud the ninety-first Psalm." After crossing herself again and laying down the prayerbook, she put the crucifix "on the prayerbook, and, after a slight hesitation, the clove of garlic at the foot of the crucifix" (p. 15).

2. Source
Superstition goes hand in hand with fear of unknown → evil and leads to the use of magical objects and rites. It often causes shame because it is known to be unscientific and infantile, and it is disparaged as such. It springs from childish wishful thinking, which tries to exorcise evil with magical means and rob it of its power. B. Wilson thus relates it to → popular religion, which seems better adapted to give security than "developed" religions. Yet one cannot speak of true → magic in this regard, for magic, especially in the Bible, means the worship of false gods that are not regarded as legitimate in a given social structure.

3. In Religious Life
Superstition has always accompanied the religious life. → Exorcism is an example. The veneration of → relics likewise often has superstitious traits. → Astrology is an instance of a culturally acceptable form of superstition. In spite of strong religious, intellectual, and cultural resistance, superstition permeates religious life.

Psychologically, superstition can be related to the antithesis between authentic (intrinsic) and conventional (extrinsic) → religion, for this distinction mirrors the difference between the existential loneliness of the individual cast back on the self and conventional everyday religion, with its rites that alleviate the difficulty of personal decision (A. Gehlen). In this sense superstition is a means of release at the individual level. As in childhood, the individual in fear of evil finds support in objects that serve as transfer objects.

4. Psychoanalytic Theories
Some modern psychoanalytic theories throw light on superstition. Thus E. Fromm (1900-1980) refers to → neurosis as a private religion, giving as examples → ancestor worship, → totemism, → fetishism, ritualism, and rites of ritual purity. For him some individual and collective forms of superstition, like → fascism, are neurotically determined. The term thus takes on a wider meaning.

C. G. Jung (1875-1961) calls superstition an inferior form of dealing with → archetypes, that is, a lower form of religious experience. Being related to → anxiety, it must, according to Jung, be regarded as neurotic and demands "mastering of the shadow."

5. Pastoral Care
In theology, and especially in → pastoral care, the important thing in dealing with superstition is first to learn from the humane sciences to give the term a broader meaning and to understand it better by including it with forms of neurotic action like ancestor worship, compulsive action (fascism in the collective sense), and primitive mythology (C. G. Jung). Then a distinction needs to be made between neurotic forms of superstition and those that are culturally accepted. The task in pastoral care is to find suitable methods of dealing with superstitious people both individually and in groups. Help can be found in → social education and → adult education. The best option is to combine theoretical explanation on the one side with an educational treatment of collective fears on the other.

In individual care the pastor must learn how to discover the underlying anxiety and then how to help to bring it to expression. In this manner he or she can prepare the ground for adequate care. Modern cults (e.g., satanic cults) represent a real problem today. Religious psychology has unfortunately not done much research on them, so that in pastoral dealing with the cults the need is to create trust, to explain, and sometimes to give → spiritual direction. In any case, as regards the collective forms of superstition, we need to see how it ties in with the social situation and then take steps to change it.

Bibliography: E. Fromm, *Psychoanalysis and Religion* (New York, 1972) • A. Gehlen, *Man, His Nature and Place in the World* (New York, 1988) • G. Holtz, *Die Faszination der Zwänge. Aberglaube und Okkultismus* (Göttingen, 1984) • C. G. Jung, *Psychology and Alchemy* (Princeton, 1968) • S. A. Vyse, *Believing in Magic: The Psychology of Superstition* (New York, 1997) • B. Wilson, *Religion in Sociological Perspective* (Oxford, 1982).

HEIJE FABER†

Supervision

1. Term
2. Theme, Goals, and Methods
3. In the Church
4. Administrative vs. Clinical Supervision
5. Associations

1. Term
"Supervision" designates a form of professional career → counseling. Since conditions and demands are changing so rapidly in many fields, it makes sense as a lifelong learning process. The term itself

arose in industry and government administration (→ Economy; Bureaucracy). A supervisor sees to it that the necessary tasks are carried out. Social work (→ Social Education) and → psychotherapy then adopted the word, and soon it was recommended for almost every professional field, not just the psychosocial. We find *individual* supervision, which is oriented to the doctor-patient model; → *group* supervision (a homogeneous group of workers in the same profession); and *team* supervision (a cooperative team of various professions within a single structure, such as a clinic).

2. Theme, Goals, and Methods

The theme of supervision is the interplay between the supervisees, their roles and fields of service, and their clients. Because of concentration on this complex interplay, as seen through the perception of the supervisee, supervision differs from instruction in praxis, from psychotherapy, from organizational advising, and from coaching (which is a goal-oriented leadership training).

The goals of supervision are to contribute to a clarification of the relationship between occupational role and personal → identity in a given institutional framework (→ Institution; Organization), to teach improved cooperation with professional colleagues through → conflict resolution and review of job descriptions, to improve → communication and interaction with the respective clientele through the practice of improved perception of self and others, and thereby in the end to contribute to an improvement of work as a whole and to the psychological health of those being supervised.

These goals are to be reached through a multiplicity of methods from the fields of psychotherapy and the applied social sciences (e.g., communication theory and group dynamics). More recently, approaches from systems therapy and constructivism are giving new impetus to supervision. The optimization of the effectiveness of occupational activity should not, however, become the decisive standard of measurement. In spite of the asymmetrical supervisory relationship, the → dialogue carried out in this process must in principle be "authority-free" and subject oriented.

3. In the Church

Within the churches, supervision is winning recognition, since the traditional forms of → theological education do not sufficiently equip graduates for work and ministry in a complex pastoral office (→ Pastor). The specific feature of so-called pastoral supervision (or, better, supervision in the realm of the church) consists of reflection on the meaning of → faith and of one's personal sense of religion, on one's sense of meaning in the church context and its effect on professional praxis, and on one's professional self-understanding.

4. Administrative vs. Clinical Supervision

Supervision arose originally in the Anglo-Saxon world, first, as noted, in the form of instruction and oversight in business and government, and then in social organizations as a form of control, help, and advice for colleagues in social work and in psychotherapeutic education (control analysis). A distinction must still be made between administrative and clinical supervision. Administrative supervisors are experienced practitioners in their respective occupational areas who also include supervision as a part of their duties. Clinical supervisors aim at the personal handling of occupational problems.

5. Associations

The training of supervisors usually takes place on the job and in private institutions. In Germany the most important occupational organizations with corresponding standards of education and of quality are the Deutsche Gesellschaft für Supervision (German Association for Supervision) and, in the area of the church, the Deutsche Gesellschaft für Pastoralpsychologie (German Association for Pastoral Psychology).

In the churches, pastoral supervision is one of the widely spread and accepted forms of occupational qualification and problem solving in the context of → Clinical Pastoral Education. Professional organizations in the United States such as the Association for Clinical Pastoral Education (Decatur, Ga.) and the American Association of Pastoral Counselors (Fairfax, Va.) provide standards of professional education and quality.

→ Pastoral Care; Psychology; Vocation

Bibliography: N. Belardi, *Supervision und Praxisberatung* (Stuttgart, 2006) • L. D. Borders and L. L. Brown, *The New Handbook of Counseling Supervision* (new ed.; Mahwah, N.J., 2005) • W. R. DeLong, "From Object to Subject: Pastoral Supervision as an Intersubjective Activity," *JPCCo* 66 (2002) 51-61 • R. Ekstein and R. S. Wallerstein, *The Teaching and Learning of Psychotherapy* (2d ed.; New York, 1972) • P. Hawkins and R. Sholet, *Supervision in the Helping Professions* (3d ed.; Maidenhead, Eng., 2006) • M. Klessmann, "Pastorale Supervision? Die Bedeutung theologischer Feldkompetenz für Supervision im Raum der Kirche," *WzM* 56 (2004) 377-90 • H. Möller, *Was ist gute Super-*

vision? Grundlagen, Merkmale, Methoden (2d ed.;
Stuttgart, 2003) • A. Schreyögg, *Supervision. Ein
integratives Modell* (4th ed.; Wiesbaden, 2004; orig.
pub., 1991) • D. A. Steere, *The Supervision of Pastoral
Care* (Louisville, Ky., 1989) • F. Ward, *Lifelong Learning:
Theological Education and Supervision* (London, 2005).

Michael Klessmann

Supralapsarianism → Predestination

Suriname

	1960	1980	2000
Population (1,000s):	290	355	452
Annual growth rate (%):	2.72	1.20	1.00

Area: 163,820 sq. km. (63,251 sq. mi.)

A.D. 2000

Population density: 3/sq. km. (7/sq. mi.)
Births / deaths: 1.84 / 0.54 per 100 population
Fertility rate: 2.10 per woman
Infant mortality rate: 20 per 1,000 live births
Life expectancy: 72.7 years (m: 70.2, f: 75.1)
Religious affiliation (%): Christians 50.9 (Roman
Catholics 23.5, Protestants 17.6, unaffiliated 7.6,
marginal 1.2, other Christians 0.9), Hindus 18.3,
Muslims 13.1, new religionists 4.9, nonreligious 4.8,
spiritists 3.7, tribal religionists 1.8, Baha'is 1.7, other
0.8.

1. Historical Context
2. Churches
3. Other Religions

1. Historical Context

Suriname, on the northeastern coast of South
America, was colonized in 1651 by Englishmen
from Barbados in search of fertile land for plantation agriculture. In 1667 the colony was captured by
the Dutch and since then until independence in
1975 — with a short interruption between 1804 and
1816 — has been a Dutch colony (→ Colonialism).

Enslaved Africans were brought in until the
1820s to work on the plantations (→ Slavery). Resistance to enslavement led to flights into the deep interior, resulting in the establishment of Maroon
communities. Beginning in 1853, Chinese indentured laborers were recruited, and after emancipation in 1863, also from India (1873-1917) and Java
(1890-1939). Most of the indentured laborers did
not renew their contracts after expiration but settled

in the colony. Other free immigrants followed, resulting in what has been termed a plural society
(R. A. J. Van Lier), with many ethnic groups.

In the decades after emancipation plantation
agriculture declined, giving way to small-scale
farming (esp. of rice) and, later, the mining of gold
and bauxite, which is today the largest foreign exchange earner. Since the 1980s oil has been growing in importance.

According to the 2004 census, the population is
approximately 490,000. Ethnically, the largest percentage are of African origin (35 percent, with 16
percent Maroons), followed by Indian (29 percent),
Javanese (15 percent), mixed (14 percent), indigenous (Amerindians, 4 percent), and others (including Lebanese and Chinese, 3 percent). Two-thirds of
the population lives in or around the capital,
Paramaribo. Many languages are spoken, but Dutch
is the official language, and Sranan, a creole language, the lingua franca.

After World War II a decolonization process
started, with elections under universal suffrage held
for the first time in 1949, bringing into power →
political parties along ethnic lines (E. Dew). Home
rule followed in 1954, and independence in 1975.
Political polarization and dissatisfaction among
noncommissioned officers in the army resulted in a
military coup in 1980. The military regime lost the
initial support it had because of infighting, which
led to a lack of support for the regime's reform policies. The arbitrary execution of 15 opponents on
December 8, 1982, caused the suspension of Dutch
development aid. This suspension, combined with
falling bauxite prices, resulted in a heavy loss of government income, giving way to heavy monetary financing and then high inflation rates, causing social
unrest. → Democracy was restored in 1987, but
guerrilla warfare initiated by relatively deprived Maroon former soldiers resulted in civil war, which
ended only in 1992. Since then, the country has enjoyed relative political stability, with elections held
every five years. The economy, however, continues
to be fragile.

2. Churches

The 2004 census showed that 49 percent of the population were Christians (not specified by denomination). → Anglicanism arrived with the first English
settlers, but after the Dutch conquest the Dutch Reformed Church became the established church. In
1735 → Moravians came in as settlers, albeit under
heavy resistance from the Dutch Reformed Church.
Not until 1765 did they receive permission to do
mission work among the enslaved, but only if the

slave owners did not object. In 1741 Lutherans were allowed to hold worship services (→ Lutheran Churches). → Roman Catholics were only sporadically allowed by the Dutch Calvinist republic to give pastoral care to their adherents, but they also received permission to set up a leprosarium far away from Paramaribo, where Peter Donders (1809-87, beatified in 1982) was the pastor.

The missionary endeavors of the Moravians were numerically not successful until the 1830s, when government restrictions were relaxed. In the following decades and up to 1863, a large number of the enslaved embraced Christianity. After constitutional reform in the Netherlands (1848), freedom of religion was guaranteed (→ Religious Liberty), and the Catholics entrusted Suriname to the Congregation of the Redemptorists (1866). The educational systems of Moravians and Catholics became very important as instruments of social mobility for the former slaves among the Afro-Surinamese (H. Jap-A-Joe, P. Sjak Shie, and J. Vernooy). Both also started missions among the indentured laborers and their descendants, as well as → medical missions among Maroons and indigenous. In 1958 the apostolic vicariate was proclaimed a diocese, and in 1962 the Moravian Church became a Unity Province in the Unitas Fratrum.

Dutch Reformed and Lutherans remained "white planter churches" until the late 19th century but are now fully "Surinamized." In the first decades of the 20th century several new denominations arrived in Suriname (Baptist, African Methodist, Salvation Army, and Seventh-day Adventist), but each of them stayed small. In the 1960s → Pentecostalism was introduced and spread very quickly, also gaining influence among the Moravians and in the Roman Catholic Church. Their number in various small congregations is estimated at 12 percent of the total number of Christians in Suriname (Jap-A-Joe 2005).

Even though the churches sometimes openly criticize the government, the relationship between → church and state is quite good. Teachers in the Moravian and Catholic schools are paid by the government.

In 1943 the Committee of Christian Churches (Catholic, Moravian, Reformed, and Lutheran) was founded in reaction to perceived moral decadence during the war years. Still existing today (now including Salvation Army and Anglicans), it was one of the founding members of the → Caribbean Conference of Churches. Moravians, Reformed, and Lutherans have operated a hospital in Paramaribo since 1958, to which also patients of the Medical Mission, since 2000 a joint venture of Moravians and Catholics, are referred in case of hospitalization. Also, all denominations (including Pentecostals) participate in a → Bible Society, which has operated since 1963.

3. Other Religions

Interaction between Africans and Europeans resulted in a creolization process from which new cultures, including new religions, came forth in the New World (S. W. Mintz and R. Price). In Suriname, this process led to the emergence of Winti, a religion with a pantheon of spirits *(winti)* and other intermediate beings that can be invoked and eventually take possession of human beings. Christianity and Winti have influenced each other in various ways. Until 1973 Winti was banned by law as idolatry, but many Afro-Surinamese practiced both, and increasingly there are public manifestations of this religion and discussions among and with theologians about their complementarity or incompatibility.

→ Hinduism and → Islam, introduced with indentured laborers from (former British) India, are today the second (23 percent) and third (16 percent) largest religions according to the 2004 census. Islam was also introduced in its Javanese form with indentured labor from Indonesia. Both are organized in "orthodox" and "liberal" associations recognized by the state and, like the churches, receive financial support. Since the 1960s both have had educational systems with elementary and junior secondary schools, with teachers on the government payroll.

The Inter Religious Council, which includes Roman Catholics, Hindus, and Muslims, has functioned since the 1980s. Moravians and other Protestant churches are still reluctant to participate, but there is increasing cooperation in interreligious committees dealing with social issues such as HIV/AIDS (→ Theology of Religions).

Bibliography: E. Dew, *The Difficult Flowering of Suriname: Ethnicity and Politics in a Plural Society* (2d ed.; Paramaribo, 1996) • H. Jap-A-Joe, "Afro-Surinamese Renaissance and the Rise of Pentecostalism," *Exchange* 34 (2005) 134-48 • H. Jap-A-Joe, P. Sjak Shie, and J. Vernooy, "The Quest for Respect, Religion, and Emancipation in Twentieth-Century Suriname," *Twentieth-Century Suriname: Continuities and Discontinuities in a New World Society* (ed. R. Hoefte and P. Meel; Kingston, Jam., 2001) 199-219 • S. W. Mintz and R. Price, *The Birth of African-American Culture: An Anthropological Perspective* (Boston, 1992) • R. A. J. Van Lier, *Frontier Society: A Social Analysis of the His-*

tory of Suriname (The Hague, 1971) • J. Van Raalte, *Secularisatie en zending in Suriname, over het secularisatieproces in verband met het zendingswerk van de Evangelische Broedergemeente in Suriname* (Wageningen, 1973) • J. Vernooij, *De Rooms-Katholieke Gemeente in Suriname. Handboek van de geschiedenis van de Rooms-Katholieke kerk in Suriname* (Paramaribo, 1998).

Harold Jap-A-Joe

Swaziland

	1960	1980	2000
Population (1,000s):	326	560	984
Annual growth rate (%):	2.51	2.95	2.61

Area: 17,364 sq. km. (6,704 sq. mi.)

A.D. 2000

Population density: 57/sq. km. (147/sq. mi.)
Births / deaths: 3.40 / 0.79 per 100 population
Fertility rate: 4.07 per woman
Infant mortality rate: 56 per 1,000 live births
Life expectancy: 62.5 years (m: 60.2, f: 64.8)
Religious affiliation (%): Christians 86.9 (indigenous 56.5, Protestants 13.8, unaffiliated 8.6, Roman Catholics 5.6, Anglicans 1.7, other Christians 0.7), tribal religionists 10.7, nonreligious 1.2, other 1.2.

1. General Situation
2. Religious Situation

1. General Situation

The Kingdom of Swaziland borders South Africa on the north, west, and south, and Mozambique on the east. Politically, the country has a dual monarchy, with the king ruling in conjunction with the queen mother. Executive power is vested in the king, who rules in consultation with the Cabinet, headed by the prime minister; the Libandla, or bicameral Parliament; and the Swazi National Council, which advises the king on all matters and speaks in particular for traditional Swazi customs and values. The legal system also operates on a dual basis, with statutory courts using laws from the South African, Dutch, and Roman systems, and traditional courts following Swazi traditional law.

Economically, Swaziland's small, open, and export-driven economy (mainly sugar, wood pulp, cotton yarn, and citrus and canned fruit) has both a direct and an indirect impact on growth prospects. The drop in commodity prices and the weakening of its currency do not bode well for the kingdom, which already faces a reduced rate of foreign direct investment, which in turn aggravates the already serious level of → unemployment. Unfavorable weather conditions and an increasing inflation rate have further compounded the problems.

In 2007 the Swazi population was estimated at 1,133,000. Swazis are essentially homogeneous, descending from southern Bantu who migrated south from central Africa during the 15th and 16th centuries; together with the Xhosas and the Zulus, they belong to the Nguni subgroup. The Swazi's ancestors, the Nkosi Dlamini, broke away from the mainstream of Nguni migrants during the 16th century and entered what today is Mozambique.

Led by King Ngwane III of the Nkosi Dlamini clan in the mid-18th century, the people later moved into the region of the Pongola River in southern Swaziland, where they absorbed the Nguni and Sotho clans already living there, bringing them under Dlamini dominance. By 1750 they settled near the south of Swaziland, now known as Hluti, under Ngwane III. The country actually derives its name from late King Mswati I, who ruled in the early-to-mid 16th century. ("KaNgwane" is an alternate name for Swaziland, now popularly known as ESwatini.) "Dlamini" remains the surname of the royal family, while *Nk(h)osi* means "king."

In 1910 Swaziland became a British protectorate (→ Colonialism) and in 1968 gained its independence. After independence there was a time of political tension. In 1973 King Sobhuza II (ruled 1921-82) repealed the constitution, declared a state of emergency, dismissed Parliament, and ruled by absolute decree. The king formed the Royal Constitutional Commission to propose an alternative to the parliamentary system.

2. Religious Situation

Christianity was introduced in Swaziland in 1844. Christian → missions have played an important role in Swaziland's political, as well as religious, history. This role was exemplified by the initial Swazi invitation to the Wesleyans to establish a mission in Mahamba, not only to proselytize the people but also to establish a missionary area. James Allison established the first Wesleyan mission at Mahamba in 1844. Thereafter a group of African evangelists reestablished the Wesleyan station at Mahamba in 1882. Meanwhile, other missions were establishing themselves in Swaziland, following the Wesleyans' Lead. The Anglican Society for the Propagation of the Gospel, under Joel Jackson, established a mission at Ndlotane in 1871, and in 1881, at the invitation of King Mbandzeni (1875-89), they built a school at Luyengo (→ British Missions).

Under the direction of Christopher Watts, the Anglicans opened a school for European children. In 1887 the Berlin (Lutheran) Mission Society built a station at Nduma in the shadow of Ngwenya Mountain (→ German Missions). In 1890 the South African General Mission founded a station at Bethany, west of modern Manzini, near the banks of the Lusushwana River. William Dawson of the Scandinavian Alliance Mission (Evangelical Alliance Mission) established its initial station at Bulunga in central Swaziland in 1892 (→ Scandinavian Missions). One of its missionaries, Malla Moe, started a second mission at Bethel near Hluti in southern Swaziland in 1898. It became an occasional haven for British forces during the Anglo-Boer War (1899-1902). In 1912 the Roman Catholic Mission was established at Mbabane (→ Catholic Missions).

In 1925 the Church of the Nazarene, under Dr. David Hynd, established a mission at Bremersdorp (Manzini). Hynd, a surgeon, began construction of the Raleigh Fitkin Memorial Hospital on government-furnished land nearby, opening it in 1927. Hynd also established Swaziland's first teacher training college and first nursing college (→ Medical Missions).

It is estimated that 86 percent of Swazis are Christians, most Protestant or indigenous Christians, with 5 percent Roman Catholics; 11 percent are → tribal religionists. In general, the approach of the Christian missionaries has ignored, misconstrued, and misconceived the positive aspects of traditional beliefs, customs, and institutions that they encountered in traditional Swazi society, which has been stable (P. Kasenene). Missionaries would have had more positive responses if they had better understood the Swazi religion and way of life and used it as the starting point for evangelization. Even today, the church is well advised to examine Swazi culture in order to discover the values and customs that can form the basis for a more genuinely Swazi Christianity.

Bibliography: D. B. Barrett, G. T. Kurian, and T. M. Johnson, *WCE* (2d ed.) 1.707-10 • A. R. Booth, *Swaziland Tradition and Change in a Southern African Kingdom* (Boulder, Colo., 1983) • M. Z. Booth, *Culture and Education: The Social Consequences of Western Schooling in Contemporary Swaziland* (Lanham, Md., 2004) • P. Kasenene, *Swazi Traditional Religion and Society* (Mbabane, Swaziland, 1993) • J. S. M. Matsebula, *A History of Swaziland* (2d ed.; Cape Town, 1976)

Sibongile C. Nxumalo

Sweden

	1960	1980	2000
Population (1,000s):	7,480	8,310	8,898
Annual growth rate (%):	0.67	0.10	0.20

Area: 449,964 sq. km. (173,732 sq. mi.)

A.D. 2000

Population density: 20/sq. km. (51/sq. mi.)
Births / deaths: 1.17 / 1.08 per 100 population
Fertility rate: 1.87 per woman
Infant mortality rate: 5 per 1,000 live births
Life expectancy: 79.4 years (m: 77.1, f: 81.6)
Religious affiliation (%): Christians 68.0 (Protestants 93.3, Roman Catholics 2.0, Orthodox 1.6, other Christians 1.9), nonreligious 17.8, atheists 11.8, Muslims 2.1, other 0.3.

1. Church and Nation
2. Roman Catholic and Lutheran
3. Revival Movements
4. Immigration
5. Church and Ecumenism
6. Church and State

1. Church and Nation

Sweden is situated in northern Europe, sharing political and religious experience with its neighboring Nordic countries and churches. To counter the Viking → paganism of these countries, the Diocese of Hamburg-Bremen in Germany sent → missionaries, first and foremost among them Anskar (801-65), who came twice to Sweden, in 830 and 852. The Christian mission, coming both from Germany and Britain, was not particularly successful until 1000, when the first King Olof was baptized. Although there were many connections to the east through Russia, very few Christian influences from the Orthodox Church prevailed; most reached Sweden from Germany and, to a lesser extent, from Britain.

This pattern was followed through the whole second millennium, and Sweden is thus a part of Christian Europe in its structures of church and nation. A diocesan structure — with → bishop, chapter, and → cathedral — was established early and still exists today. Uppsala became the see of the archbishop in 1164, although Lund in southern Sweden, originally part of Denmark, had an archbishop as early as 1103. Lund became integrated into Sweden in 1658. Its 11th-century cathedral is the oldest in Sweden and has the country's finest Romanesque architecture. Medieval cathedrals and rural parish churches dominate the landscape and are largely in use by local congregations. Parish structures have been preserved, and records are extant of all clergy since medieval times.

2. Roman Catholic and Lutheran

2.1. Roman Catholic culture dominated Sweden as the kingdom was centralized. A common law was accepted, and local → slavery was abolished. From 1143, starting with French → Cistercians, several monasteries and cloisters were established, the most famous being the Order of St. Birgitta, the Bridgettines, at Vadstena. Birgitta (or Bridget, ca. 1303-73) is the only canonized Swede and the only Swedish founder of a → religious order. She is now honored as an ecumenical bridge-builder.

In the early 16th century there was a political union between the Nordic countries, but strife led to wars in which bishops became warlords, which in turn led to a movement to cut ties to Rome and the powerful bishops that had been placed in Sweden. This political reality contributed to a climate that enabled the Lutheran → Reformation to be quickly accepted. Another such reality was the influence of many Germans in the port cities, who were the first to welcome the ideas from Wittenberg. The liberation leader Gustav Vasa (1496?-1560) became king in 1523, winning independence from Rome. As king, he gave full support to the first religious reformers, the brothers Olaus Petri (1493-1552), who had studied at Lutheran Wittenberg, and Laurentius Petri (1499-1573). Stockholm became the political capital, and from its cathedral (Storkyrkan), the new tunes of the Reformation were heard. In 1523 Olaus Petri became dean of the cathedral, and he used Swedish in the service instead of Latin. A hymnbook and the first translation of the NT into Swedish were printed (→ Bible Versions 4.4).

In this situation, the king managed by sheer royal might to establish the church as a → state church. He acquired church land and riches, arguing that the property of the church was really the property of the people whom he represented; cloisters were confiscated and used for other purposes. He appointed bishops and recruited staff from Germany to copy the rule of the German princes. Simultaneously, however, there were balancing powers. Sweden's Parliament (Riksdagen) had its roots in the early 15th century. The four estates that formed the Parliament (clergy, nobility, burghers, and freeholding farmers [peasants], who formed the majority of the population) assembled from what is now middle Sweden and from Finland, which was then part of the realm. Swedish peasants have taken part in all parliamentary decisions regarding church matters since the

Diet of Västerås in 1527, when, albeit in vague terms, the Reformation was formally adopted.

It took the rest of the 16th century for the Reformation to take root in all of Sweden and Finland. The main architect of this accomplishment was Laurentius Petri, who served for 42 years as archbishop of Uppsala (1531-73). He and the reforming church provided balance to the more powerful king. He managed to keep the church's traditions and preserved as much as possible of its order (→ Church Orders). Thanks to his endeavors, much of the church's liturgical life and its understanding of the roles of bishops and clergy in the ecclesiastical order were preserved. The Swedish Reformation was not as drastic as in other parts of Europe — for example, iconoclasm was unheard of. Because of this continuity, especially the maintenance of the Church of Sweden's understanding and practice of episcopacy, → ecumenical dialogue — notably with Anglicans and Roman Catholics in the 20th century — found a common platform.

In 1593 a special synod met in Uppsala to confirm the basis for the Evangelical Lutheran Church in the Kingdom of Sweden. The foundation rests on Scripture, the Word of God; the three early ecumenical creeds; and the Augustana, the unaltered → Augsburg Confession of 1530. The doctrine therein expressed is the foundation for the Church of Sweden, not a king, parliament, or synod. With these decisions the 70-year period of Reformation came to an end. In 1595 the last nuns left Vadstena. Hereafter it was regarded as almost treasonous for a Swedish citizen not to be Lutheran in confession.

The uniformity of the church was enhanced through better education both for → clergy and the population at large. Through the university-educated clergy, present in every parish in the realm, a church culture developed that was in close conformity to the common life of household agriculture. The parish pastor was an agriculturalist among farmers, and his wife and daughters were examples for the parishioners. The household is key to understanding this period, during which most things were organized according to the teaching of the three estates, as expressed in Martin → Luther's Small Catechism of 1529. All the rites of life from baptism to burial were common to all. State and church became intertwined. The parish priest systematically examined young and old from every household in knowledge of the Bible and understanding of the → catechism. He was also a guardian of private and public morality, particularly that of → marriage. Additionally, the church took responsibility for keeping population records, which show an amazingly high literacy rate, particularly among women, even before primary education became compulsory. These records have always been public in archives, but now they are available also on the Internet.

The king of Sweden saw himself as a chief defender of Protestantism in Europe against Roman Catholicism. The → Thirty Years' War, fought largely on German soil, was central to this Swedish involvement. For this reason Gustavus II Adolphus (1594-1632) entered the war at the same time as Sweden became a great power. The Treaty of Westphalia of 1648, including its affirmation of the Peace of Augsburg of 1555 (→ Augsburg, Peace of), is a watershed for Protestant Europe. In central and northern Europe, small Protestant nation-states like Sweden could now develop their own realms into efficient states in a time of peace with one unified church cooperating with the state. The powers of pope and emperor were definitely broken for northern Europe (→ Empire and Papacy).

A parenthesis in this trend was the conversion to Roman Catholicism of Queen Christina (1626-89). She was the daughter of the Lutheran hero Gustavus II Adolphus. Well educated by European scholars, among them the philosopher René Descartes, she felt locked in as queen in Stockholm. In 1654 she abdicated in favor of her cousin Charles X Gustav (1622-60), who continued the warring habits of the emerging great power, and Christina converted afterward on her journey to Rome. In the Basilica of St. Peter in Rome, she has been awarded a prominent place.

2.2. As a great power, Sweden expanded its realm in conflict with the Danish king, German principalities, Russian czars, and Polish kings. Sweden, however, with a population of less than two million, could not produce enough human and material resources to sustain expansion, finally crumbling in 1721. During this period, the Church of Sweden established new dioceses, particularly in the border areas close to Denmark, and two dioceses in Finland. For the conquered territories — present-day Estonia, Latvia, and Ingria (a district of early Russia where St. Petersburg was later founded) — the king appointed Lutheran superintendents to supervise religious life. Swedish → church law was also established, and in all these territories universities were founded: Turku (Swed. Åbo) in Finland and Tartu (Ger. Dorpat) in Estonia; the University of Greifswald in Pomerania was also regarded as a Swedish university. Around 1700 the region around the Baltic Sea was regarded as Lutheran, and the aim of the kings was to make it totally Swedish, to the exclusion of Russian Orthodoxy and Roman Catholicism. The Swedish king lost these areas in the 18th century and all of Finland in 1809 to the Russian czar. The religion of these Baltic territories, however, has basically remained Lutheran.

Another Swedish venture was the establishment in 1638 of New Sweden, a settlement along the Delaware River in the Mid-Atlantic Coast in North America. One of its Swedish pastors, John Campanius (1601-83), translated Martin Luther's Small Catechism into the language of the Algonquin Indians, also producing a written vocabulary of their language. Holy Trinity, or "Old Swedes," a stone church built in 1699 outside Wilmington, Delaware, is one of the oldest churches in continuous use in the United States; it is now a parish of the Episcopal Church. The settlement was lost to the Dutch in 1655, but a small Swedish population long remained, leaving its traits in religion and culture.

2.3. Lutheran → orthodoxy (§1) was dominant when Sweden was considered a great power. It went hand in hand with the powerful kings, adhering strictly to the → confessions. Compulsory confirmation for both boys and girls was introduced at the beginning of the 18th century. Seating in church service was according to the homesteads and also according to social class. Quotations from the OT were more frequent in sermons than from the NT.

A reaction to these practices was expressed in → Pietism. Ideas of Pietist August Hermann → Francke (1663-1727) in Halle reached Sweden around 1700 both from theologians and from Swedish soldiers. Pietism was accepted by many when peace reached Sweden in the 1720s. For political reasons Lutheran orthodoxy prevailed and attempted to curb Pietism (e.g., through a law that outlawed religious meetings without an ordained minister officiating). Through the → Moravians, the pietistic ideas never faded away, but they were never officially adopted in Sweden.

One person influenced by this spirituality was Emanuel Swedenborg (1688-1772), son of a bishop and a highly regarded mineralogist. He was also one of the first phrenologists. He received a revelation in 1744 and thereafter began communicating with the spirit world, writing his observations in *Spiritual Diary* (5 vols.; ET London, 1883-1902). His brand of spiritism found followers in England, America, and South Africa (→ Swedenborgianism).

2.4. In the mid-19th century many revolts against the society and its traditions occurred, often in the form of popular revival movements (→ Revivals). A few adherents of these movements remained in the Lutheran Church, but most left the established church to form new, largely anticlerical denominations (see 3).

Two revival movements led by clergy remaining inside the Lutheran Church, each lasting to this day, were found in the northernmost and southernmost parts of the country. In Lapland, where the Sami live with their reindeer-based culture, the pastor of Karesuando, Lars Levi Laestadius (1800-1861), experienced a personal conversion. Its repercussions were felt all over the northern parts of Sweden, Finland, and Norway, particularly among the Sami people; it found most adherents in Finland. For its followers this revival meant a break with one's sinful past and a strict observance of the law. Spiritual expressions, loud in tone, became common in public worship. The Laestadians were loyal to the Church of Sweden but always critical of clergy and bishops who did not adhere to the → Word of God as they understood it.

A revival movement in southern Sweden found its inspiration through the preaching of Henrik Schartau (1757-1825), dean of the cathedral in Lund. His sermons had a distinct style, always divided into three parts, with an equal stress on law and gospel (→ Law and Gospel). Schartau's astute psychological understanding of the human person showed itself in his teaching concerning the five stages every Christian should go through, an *ordo salutis* (→ Order of Salvation). Schartau's view of the preacher as a "right teacher" was a key element in his thinking. Particularly on the west coast of Sweden, where many fishermen lived and still live, this revival has adherents to the present day.

2.5. A doubling of the population in the 19th century led to massive migration from the old rural parishes into the nearby small towns, each marked by a new railway station. Industrialization reached Sweden late, but the country's abundant forests, iron ore, and waterfalls allowed it to produce an abundance of cheap electricity, which helped transform the country from a rural and static society into a modern urban industrial nation (→ Industrial Society). This urbanization created new social organizations, often called people's movements. The main ones, existing even today, are the temperance movement, the trade union movement, and the revival movement. Often temperance and revival movements enlisted the same persons. These movements, in opposition to the establishment, including the clergy-led Lutheran Church, made such an impact that they became well represented in Parliament, a result of the gradual introduction of free, democratic suffrage.

Simultaneously, in a huge exodus, more than one million Swedes left their homeland for the United States and a few other countries. From the 1840s this mass exodus found its way largely to Minnesota and other northern and central U.S. states. Many — but not all — of the immigrants founded Swedish-speaking Lutheran congregations and schools, clinging fast to the faith of their homeland, based on the Lutheran Augsburg Confession (Confessio Augustana). In 1860 they established the Augustana Synod. Although there were few differences in doctrine between the new Swedish-American church and the Church of Sweden itself, there were great differences in views regarding the ministry, participation of laypeople, and other aspects of church practice. In the new country the historic episcopate was thought to be too hierarchical and was avoided; pietism was the norm, and freedom and equality were the hallmarks.

3. Revival Movements

3.1. The key terms "freedom" and "equality" also applied to the revival movements in Sweden. In opposition to the established order, they reached a peak in membership around 1900. Most of these movements found their inspiration in the Anglo-Saxon world. From American and British personalities, Swedes were introduced to Methodists (→ Methodist Churches), → Baptists, Scottish → Congregationalists, and, later on, the → Salvation Army, → Mormons, → Jehovah's Witnesses, and others. Baptists and Methodists organized themselves in Sweden, but with ties to their international sister churches. They were legally labeled "foreign" religions when Swedish citizens were allowed to withdraw from the state church and join them.

The largest revival movements tried to be as Swedish as possible in organization. They were often led by ministers who had left the Lutheran Church. One revival movement close to the Lutheran Church and evangelical in character — stressing conversion, Bible reading, and fellowship — was led by Carl Olof Rosenius (1816-68), a lay preacher who had been influenced by British Methodists. In 1856 his followers organized themselves in Stockholm as Evangeliska Fosterlands-Stiftelsen (EFS, The Swedish Evangelical Mission). Most adherents were small landowners from the northern and southern parts of the country, but many clergy also joined. In contrast to other revival movements, the EFS sought to be loyal to king, country, and the established church. Their lay preachers were successful in forming many voluntary associations (peaking in about 1920), and chapels were built in many places. In 1866 their missionary zeal resulted in the first evangelical mission to Eritrea and Ethiopia. One result of this effort was the Ethiopian Evangelical Church Mekane Yesus, formed in 1959 from the EFS and other groups (over 4.5 million members in 2006).

3.2. In 1878 Svenska Missionsförbundet (The Swedish Covenant Church) broke away from the EFS, led by the theologians P. P. Waldenström (1838-1917) and E. J. Ekman (1842-1915). The two advocated congregationalism and the active participation of laypeople (→ Lay Movements). Many of their followers were great entrepreneurs and politically liberal, and many were in Parliament. One of its laypersons, editor C. G. Boberg (1859-1940), in 1885 wrote the well-known hymn "How Great Thou Art." The doctrinal break with EFS was over their different understandings of the atoning role of Christ. The break with the Church of Sweden was over the issue of Holy Communion. The Swedish Covenant Church had a peak in membership around 1930, with 160,000 active members and many adherents; in North America the Evangelical Covenant Church, formed in 1885 as an offshoot of this revival, has more than 700 congregations.

3.3. The biggest revival movement in 20th-century Sweden was the Pentecostal movement (→ Pentecostalism). From the Asuza Street Revival in Los Angeles it found its way to Sweden via Oslo, Norway (→ Theology of Revival 8). It was first established in 1913 in Stockholm as an independent congregation after a break with the Baptist Union. Its founder was Lewi Pethrus (1884-1974). In the middle of the 20th century it had around 100,000 members. Its mission efforts reached Brazil and Burundi and later on scores of other countries around the world. Pethrus founded a newspaper and publishing and music companies. In 1964, in reaction to the lax moral codes being accepted by Swedish society at that time, he started Kristdemokraterna (Christian Democrats), a political party.

At the beginning of the 20th century the traditional revival movements were at a peak. Gradually, though, they turned into institutional churches, with stricter demands for → theological education and with the use of worship that was more liturgical. As voluntary organizations they were large and influential, demanding that the privileged state church become a → free church like theirs. The religious map of Sweden resembled that of the United Kingdom, quite unlike its Scandinavian neighbors, where the revival movements stayed inside the Lutheran churches.

4. Immigration

4.1. In 1786 a law was passed allowing Jews for the first time to settle in the country's four major trading cities, where synagogues were built. Most Jews assimilated into Swedish society. In the 19th century many Jews from eastern Europe, however, were denied entry. → Anti-Semitism found its way into films and cartoons in the 1930s. Currently, there are approximately 22,000 Jews in Sweden, of whom approximately 10,000 participate in Jewish religious life.

With its policy during World War II of non-alignment and neutrality, the Swedish government has faced criticism for its inaction toward the → Holocaust. In contrast, the heroic rescue by Swede Raoul Wallenberg (1912-47?) of tens of thousands of Hungarian Jews in the final months of the war has been widely lauded, as has the Swedish Red Cross's "white bus" operation saving Scandinavian and other prisoners from concentration camps in northern Germany.

4.2. At the end of World War II, 30,000 Estonians and Latvians fled Soviet occupation and at great risk crossed the Baltic Sea to Sweden. Estonian and Latvian "churches in exile" were organized with the support of Church of Sweden. Another refugee group of 8,000 Hungarians fled after the 1956 revolution and were welcomed to a homogeneous Swedish society not yet accustomed to receiving refugees. The Lutherans among these Hungarians were assisted by the Church of Sweden, and they never formed their own church. They kept close relations with Bishop Lajos Ordass (1901-78) during the years before and after his imprisonment in Hungary. In 1928 Ordass had studied in Sweden; he spoke Swedish and maintained contact with Swedish church leaders and others.

A Finnish congregation has existed in Stockholm since 1533. In the 1960s, at the peak of industrial growth in Sweden, half a million Finns migrated and joined the Swedish labor force. In recent decades the Church of Sweden has carried out a special ministry to the more than 400,000 Finns in Sweden, 80 percent of whom are Lutherans.

4.3. The → Roman Catholic Church in Sweden increased from 5,000 members in 1900 to 160,000 a century later, largely due to immigration. Since → Vatican II there has been a new openness to Catholicism, and many Swedes have converted (→ Conversion 2), among them several well-known intellectuals and theologians. The Roman Catholic cathedral is in central Stockholm, and the Catholic → hierarchy was reestablished in 1953. Since 1998, for the first time since the Reformation, the Roman Catholic bishop of Stockholm is himself Swedish, Anders Arborelius. In 2004 there were 41 parishes and 151 priests (73 diocesan and 78 religious) in the Catholic Church in Sweden, with 214 sisters in Roman Catholic orders.

4.4. A new influx of refugees to Sweden began arriving in 1970. By 2000, their numbers had reached one million, presenting a major challenge to Sweden as a homogeneous welfare state. Sweden first welcomed political refugees from dictatorial regimes, such as those in Greece, Chile, South Africa, and the Communist countries. The next wave came from Muslim and mainly Middle East countries. Several Oriental and Eastern Orthodox churches were established, as well as large Muslim communities; mosques now mark urban landscapes (→ Islam).

The largest and most visible Christian community of immigrants is the → Syrian Orthodox Church in Södertälje, which numbers 28,000 members and has its own bishop. The Greek Orthodox Church has around 17,500 adherents. In recent years the Serbian (23,000 members), Russian, and Romanian Orthodox churches have increased their membership. Smaller churches of Coptic, Armenian, and Ethiopian Orthodox serve their members in the largest cities, in many cases conducting church services in buildings offered by the Church of Sweden (→ Orthodox Church; Oriental Orthodox Churches).

5. Church and Ecumenism

The religious landscape in Sweden, as well as the Church of Sweden itself, changed immensely during the 20th century. From its uniformity, shaped by a rural culture and a homogeneous population, as well as by its unity in doctrine, morality, and liturgy, the church has been deeply challenged by the diversity of → modernism. The establishment of free churches and the antichurch rhetoric of the early socialists and radical liberals around 1900 reduced church attendance to a record low level. The social factor of migration made many people feel uprooted, and in the new environment they never found their way to the church. In this situation, two factors heavily influenced 20th-century church life: the ecumenical movement and the changing relationship between church and state (see 6).

5.1. Nathan → Söderblom (1866-1931) was the outstanding Swedish church leader of the modern age. As a student leader when the → World Student Christian Federation was founded in Vadstena in 1895, he became modern and ecumenical in outlook. His theology of revelation helped him and the Church of Sweden accept its tradition as episcopal and Lutheran and destined him to be a bridgebuilder between different ecclesial traditions. In his outlook he was French from his studies, German in his scholarly criticism, and Anglican in liturgy and ecclesiology. To his dismay his three beloved countries started World War I in 1914. He was appointed archbishop in May 1914 as the nations marched toward war. In 1925, after the war, he managed to draw together many churches as host to the first Universal Christian Conference on → Life and Work. Many Protestant church leaders from Europe and the United States attended. This event marked a new age of → ecumenism.

Söderblom had many followers in Sweden, particularly among students in Uppsala who formed the Young Church movement. Three of his sons-in-law became bishops, and one of them, Yngve Brilioth (1891-1959), became archbishop of Uppsala (1950-58).

5.2. Swedish bishops and theologians acted in the spirit of Nathan Söderblom and participated actively in the modern ecumenical movement. In 1933 the Swedish Ecumenical Council was founded. One of its first statements was a letter to the Evangelical Church in Germany criticizing the anti-Semitic Aryan laws that had been passed by the new Nazi regime.

In 1931 Erling Eidem (1880-1972) succeeded Söderblom as archbishop, serving until 1950. During his time a new hymnbook was adopted (1937), as well as a new liturgical order (1942). His hardest test came from the German church. Some scholars have condemned him for being too diplomatic, although this approach was perhaps determined by the Swedish government's policy of strict neutrality at the beginning of the war. Eidem made an official visit to Berlin in November 1942 to install a new vicar in the Swedish church in Berlin. This visit was at the highest diplomatic level, and Swedish officials recorded Eidem's speeches, which included severe criticism of the German authorities. During the war years, the foreign policy of the Church of Sweden was conducted by the Nordic Ecumenical Institute in Sigtuna. This institute played host to a remarkable but unfruitful 1942 meeting between Bishop G. K. A. Bell (1883-1958) of Great Britain and Dietrich → Bonhoeffer (1906-45) of Germany. The institute kept in close contact with both the WCC-in-formation in Geneva and the resistance movements in Germany and Norway.

Before and during World War II, a small minority (2 percent) of Swedish clergy, as well as a few teachers of theology, were accused of being too friendly to Nazism. The strong German influence in theology perhaps helps explain their reluctance to break decisively with Nazism. There has never been a formal investigation of this issue, although historians have debated it for decades. In Sweden as a whole, Nazi political parties never gained more than 0.7 percent of the votes in free elections.

The Nordic Ecumenical Institute was founded in 1940 in Sigtuna by Manfred Björkquist (1884-1985), a vigorous lay leader in the church and a prolific entrepreneur. The Sigtuna Foundation became an inspiration for many lay academies in Europe as a center for dialogue with the world of culture. In 1942 Björkquist was appointed bishop by the government for the newly established Diocese of Stockholm, which required rapid ordination to the priesthood.

During the war years the Church of Sweden was held in great esteem by the people, and attendance at services was at its highest. In 1942 university theologians, including some bishops, published an important ecclesiology that had international ecumenical importance: *This Is the Church.* As part of his important studies of the Anglican Church and its theology, Yngve Brilioth in 1930 published *Eucharistic Faith and Practice: Evangelical and Catholic,* a major inspiration to the Swedish liturgical renewal of the mid-20th century, a movement that has transformed worship life from cathedrals to rural churches. The High Church movement was led by rural clergy who introduced what was basically Anglo-Catholic worship. Foremost among the leaders of this movement was Gunnar Rosendal (1897-1988).

Other Swedish systematic theologians were largely represented by Lundensian theology, which had a particular methodology of "motif research." Anders Nygren (1890-1978) in 1930 and 1936 published his major work *Agape and Eros,* which became a basic textbook for a generation of clergy in Sweden and was translated into English, German, Spanish, and Chinese. Gustaf Aulén (1879-1977) was known to the larger public for his resistance to Nazi Germany. Theologians around the world valued his major works, which included *The Faith of the Christian Church* (1923), *Christus Victor: An Historical Study of the Three Main Types of the Idea of the Atonement* (1931), and *Jesus in Contemporary Historical Research* (1973). As a colleague of Nygren and Brilioth, Aulén and his prolific theological writing, which stresses → liturgy and particularly its music (→ Church Music), made its mark on church life. All three of these theologians became bishops, one of them archbishop, in the Church of Sweden.

5.3. After World War II the Church of Sweden, led by Archbishop Eidem, actively participated in the formation of the → World Council of Churches at its first assembly in Amsterdam in 1948 and has remained committed to the council's work ever since. All of the Swedish archbishops since 1948 have been members of the WCC Central Committee. The Mission Covenant Church of Sweden is also an active member. The Swedish Baptist Union and the Methodist Church in Sweden participate in the WCC via their international bodies.

Eidem also played an active role in the formation of the → Lutheran World Federation after World War II. He hosted a preparatory meeting in Uppsala in July 1946 that was particularly difficult in that it brought together church leaders whose countries in many instances had recently been at war with each other. It was decided to hold the first assembly of the LWF in Lund in July 1947. The grand theologian of the University of Lund and the future bishop of that diocese, Anders Nygren, was elected the first president of the LWF. At the same time a Swedish church-related funding agency, Lutherhjälpen, was established to aid the relief and development efforts of Lutheran churches throughout the world (→ Relief and Development Organizations). Lutherhjälpen became a major nongovernmental organization for development, especially under the leadership of Åke Kastlund (1916-99).

In 1968 the Fourth Assembly of the WCC took place in Uppsala, probably the largest church assembly of the century for Sweden. The event was marked by cries for social justice and calls that authoritarian structures be crushed. → Liberation theology took the stage, a new paradigm especially for churches in Africa, Asia, and Latin America — and for Christians in Sweden as well. This theological movement had great influence in Sweden for the rest of the 20th century. The "'68 Generation" took over, shaping a new role for traditional mission and aid organizations. A special emphasis was put on southern Africa, with Christian activist organizations in Sweden making common cause with the anti-apartheid movement. During this period churches clearly had considerable effect on policies of the Swedish government in respect to the → Third World.

Practically all Swedish churches started foreign mission organizations in the 19th century. In 1946 a total of 477 Swedish men, 433 married women, and 380 unmarried women were registered as missionaries. Since the middle of the 19th century their supporters had largely been women's groups, organized in every congregation and parish as sewing associations. Their handicrafts have traditionally been sold at church auctions for the support of missions within Sweden and the world.

After World War II this widespread support for international solidarity gave Sweden a high profile in international affairs, particularly at the → United Nations, where in 1953 the Swede Dag Hammarskjöld (1905-61) was unexpectedly appointed its second secretary-general. He served the organization during a difficult period of the cold war, when independence was coming to many Third World countries. In his political negotiations for peace and development, he was driven by an inner conviction, based largely on his intense readings of the Christian mystics. His personal diaries were found after his death in Ndola, Zambia, in an airplane crash when trying to negotiate a cease-fire in the Congo. These notes were published in Swedish in 1963 as *Vägmärken* and in English in 1964 as *Markings;* it has thus far gone through 38 editions. Hammarskjöld's deep faith and his sparse way of expressing his convictions astonished much of the secularized cultural elite, though in 1954 he had been a main speaker at the WCC Assembly in Evanston, Illinois.

6. Church and State

Sweden became Christian around the year 1000, accepted the Reformation shortly after 1500, and then during the 20th century worked at separating its church-state ties, which was finally achieved in 2000. Several factors contributed to this separation: the demand for religious liberty from the free churches was strong, and the Social Democratic Party, from its beginning in 1889, had a plank in its platform calling for separation. When the party came to power in 1936, however, it never challenged the church as such but focused rather on reforming the education system, thus freeing it from church control and influence. At the same time, a very public philosophical debate on science and theology tended to discredit theologians in general ($\rightarrow$ Church and State).

In 1957 the Synod of the Church of Sweden became the subject of controversy when it rejected the $\rightarrow$ ordination of women. Parliament protested this action and called a new Synod in 1958, which, under considerable pressure, approved ordination. The first three women were ordained on Palm Sunday of 1960. Foremost among them was Margit Sahlin (1914-2003), a theologian who had a doctorate in French literature. She had created a lay academy and a community of sisters and was an esteemed spiritual leader. Thereafter many more women were ordained. By 2006 around 40 percent of all clergy in the Church of Sweden were women.

6.1. In recent decades various committees produced proposals for new church-state relations, to little effect. Simultaneously, however, the political parties wanted increased control over the church because of the resistance against female pastors, which also existed in some revival movements. A "conscience clause" had been included for bishops and clergy who remained opposed to female pastors. This provision, however, was overruled by the government, which in 1982 passed a church ordinance making it illegal for any ordained minister to refuse to cooperate with clergy of either sex.

In 1951 a law was passed on religious freedom granting members of free churches or of no church to leave the Church of Sweden without repercussion and also to be released from the obligation to pay church taxes. Many were astonished that 95 percent of the population remained in the state church and paid the church tax. Most members of free churches have chosen to remain members of the Church of Sweden. The gradual decrease in church membership can be attributed to the effects of general $\rightarrow$ secularization.

6.2. In 1982 a partial separation between church and state took place. The Church Synod was enlarged both in size and mandate, and a national Church Board was also created. It took another 15 years, however, to solve the problem of how a "free" Church of Sweden should be governed and financed. In the meantime most of the secular functions of the church were transferred to the government, including responsibilities for education and the keeping of public records. Before the new millennium the Parliament made a change in the Swedish Constitution stating that the Church of Sweden is one of several *registrerade trossamfund* (recognized faith communities). The law also stipulates that the Church of Sweden should be democratic, episcopal, and evangelical Lutheran — with a national provenance. This law is actually a summing up of the church's history as described in this article.

The separation, which finally took place in 2000, was financially favorable for the church. The national internal revenue system continues to calculate and collect all church fees, which equal approximately 1 percent of a person's working income. When this separation took place, the Church Synod produced a new ordinance replacing all former church regulations. In summary, it stresses the democratic nature of all decision-making bodies at parish, diocesan, and national levels. This emphasis has resulted — with continued debate — in the political parties taking a more active interest in church decision-making processes. For 1,000 years the organization of the church has been territorial, and, in conformity with the Swedish way, it has emphasized the collective, not the individual. Today many parishes are merging with neighboring parishes in order to have enough material and human resources to keep a church building and to conduct regular worship.

The episcopal structure of the church is intact, although the age of authoritarian bishops is over. The focus of the → mass media does remain, however, on the bishops, particularly the archbishop, who in fact has become much more of a spokesperson for the whole church than had previously been the case. The internationally recognized theologian Krister Stendahl (b. 1921) was bishop of Stockholm from 1984 to 1988 and received considerable media attention. Two women bishops have been elected: Christina Odenberg, who served from 1997 to 2007 in the Diocese of Lund, and Caroline Krook, whose service in the Diocese of Stockholm began in 1998. In 2007 the Diocese of Lund elected another woman, Professor Antje Jackelén, as bishop.

6.3. Since 1993 the Swedish Ecumenical Council has been organized according to four church families — Lutheran, free churches, Roman Catholic, and Eastern and Oriental Orthodox — which reflects Sweden's new religious landscape. Pentecostals have traditionally chosen to stay outside the council but now are considering membership. New congregations like Livets Ord (Word of Life) in Uppsala, inspired by Oral Roberts and also by a theology of prosperity, have traditionally been critical toward the established church leadership in Sweden, but they are now joining local ecumenical bodies. The ecumenical bodies have characteristically been advocates for the poor, opponents of apartheid, and, more recently, proponents for a fair reception of → refugees. In recent years, divisions within these bodies have arisen over biblical interpretation, moral issues, and same-sex unions. In 2006 the Synod of the Church of Sweden approved the introduction of an act of church blessing for same-sex unions.

One strong ecumenical achievement in Sweden has been the hymnbook (Psalmboken) of 1986, which replaced the hymnal of 1937. Its first 325 hymns are common to eight different denominations, including the Roman Catholic Church. Toward the end of the 20th century new hymns were produced at an unprecedented rate; the most prolific hymn writer in the 20th century was Anders Frostensson (1906-2006; → Hymnody). Another project, ecumenical in nature with Jewish participation, was Bibel 2000, a new authorized translation of the Bible, initiated and financed by Parliament. (Since 1541 all official Swedish Bible translations have been sponsored by king and nation.)

The theological faculties of Uppsala and Lund were officially tied to the Church of Sweden when Nathan Söderblom, Anders Nygren, and others held chairs. Since 1970, however, there has been a separation. At the same time, more colleges and universi-

ties have been established across the country, and it is now possible to engage in the academic study of religion at 15 institutions of higher learning, 5 of which offer doctorates in theology. In recent years feminist studies have had a breakthrough. Overall, the general theological tendencies have been similar to those of other Western countries.

6.4. The Church of Sweden was very much involved in the formation of the → Porvoo Common Statement (1992), an ecumenical agreement that has been signed by most evangelical Lutheran churches of the Baltic and Nordic regions, as well as by the Anglican churches in Europe. It stresses the role of episcopacy in the church, as well as the apostolic succession of clergy, and declares that a pastor in one church is recognized for service in another. In 2003 the Church of Sweden also signed an agreement with the Evangelical Church of Germany. These agreements underscore the influence on Sweden from churches of others countries.

Sweden had a population of nine million in 2005, close to seven million of whom were members of the Church of Sweden. Since its separation from the state almost 1 percent of its members leave the church each year. The Church of Sweden consists of 1,820 territorial parishes in 13 dioceses; many small parishes are merging with larger ones, so that number is diminishing. There are slightly more than 3,800 clergy, of whom 1,600 are women. Ordained deaconesses and deacons number about 1,500, of whom 200 are men. Around 100,000 babies are born in Sweden annually, 70,000 of whom are baptized in the Church of Sweden. Each year 22,000 weddings, 50 percent of all marriages in the country, take place in churches. In 2006 the confirmation of young persons was down to 36 percent, or 46,000. Of all who died in 2006, approximately 83 percent, or 77,000, were buried according to the rites of the Church of Sweden.

Bibliography: G. AULÉN, *Christus Victor: An Historical Study of the Three Main Types of the Idea of the Atonement* (New York, 1969; orig. pub., 1931); idem, *Dag Hammarskjöld's White Book: An Analysis of "Markings"* (Philadelphia, 1969); idem, *The Faith of the Christian Church* (2d ed.; trans. from 5th Swed. ed.; Philadelphia, 1960); idem, *Jesus in Contemporary Historical Research* (trans. from 2d Swed. ed.; Philadelphia, 1976) • Y. BRILIOTH, *Eucharistic Faith and Practice: Evangelical and Catholic* (London, 1930) • O. P. GRELL, *The Scandinavian Reformation: From Evangelical Movements to Institutionalisation of Reform* (Cambridge, 1995) • D. HAMMARSKJÖLD, *Markings* (New York, 1964) • N. HOPE, *German and Scandinavian Protestantism,*

1700-1918 (Oxford, 1995) • L. Lindberg and G. Nilsson, eds., *Modern svensk teologi–strömningar och perspektivskiften under 1900-talet* (Stockholm, 1999) • C. H. Martling, *Fädernas kyrka och folkets. Svenska kyrkan i kyrkovetenskapligt perspektiv* (Stockholm, 1992) • R. Murray, ed., *The Church of Sweden: Past and Present* (Malmö, 1960) • A. Nygren, *Agape and Eros* (London, 1982; orig. pub., 1930-36); idem, ed., *This Is the Church* (Philadelphia, 1952; orig. pub., 1943) • L. Österlin, *Churches of Northern Europe in Profile: A Thousand Years of Anglo-Nordic Relations* (Norwich, 1995) • B. Ryman et al., *Nordic Folk Churches: A Contemporary Church History* (Grand Rapids, 2005) • B. Sundkler, *Nathan Söderblom: His Life and Work* (Lund, 1968) • L. Tegborg, ed., *Sveriges kyrkohistoria* (8 vols.; Stockholm, 1998-2005).

Björn Ryman

Swedenborgianism

Denominations that include "New Church" or "New Jerusalem" in their names, found mostly in Britain, the United States, and South and West Africa, all go back to the Swedish "visionary" (so I. Kant) Emanuel Swedenborg (1688-1772), the first in the → modern period to present revelations from the spirit world. As a brilliant scientist, engineer, and inventor, Swedenborg was one of the leading thinkers of his age. He had doubts, however, regarding whether we can truly grasp reality with scientific means, which brought to the surface his repressed religious endowments (→ Religion, Personal Sense of). In 1736 he began to have → dreams and → visions (including, in 1744, a vision of his own calling, followed by "heavenly journeys"; → Occultism). Swedenborg rejected the Pauline and Reformation doctrine of → grace and → justification, expounding instead his own visionary, speculative, and totally unorthodox theology, which the various forms of Swedenborgianism have adopted in some 30 volumes.

The basic principle is the law of correspondence between the (real) spiritual world and the phenomenological physical world that we perceive with the senses. The leading motif is the all-embracing → love of God. Swedenborg reached the conclusion that there is no → resurrection to the → last judgment, that at → death we live on in the spirit world in a form based on our conduct in life, which may be clarified but can no longer change. Impressed by the dogmatic rigidity and profound decline of the Church of Sweden, he prophesied a "new church," the "crown of all previous churches," and he offered Christianity, the *vera christiana religio,* as a disclosure of the "spiritual meaning" of verbally inspired (→ Inspiration) Holy Scripture. He saw in this → revelation the promised return of Christ (→ Eschatology; Promise and Fulfillment).

Swedenborg had neither followers nor pupils but exerted great influence, first by his religious → worldview, which encompassed → immanence and transcendence and was in contrast to both the traditional Christian view and that of the prevailing → Enlightenment. His visions also were influential, as was his apparent proof of the existence of spiritual entities that can enter into contact with us (→ Spiritism).

The first New Jerusalem Church arose in London in 1787. In the United States the first congregation gathered in 1792, and in 1817 the various U.S. congregations formed the General Convention of the New Jerusalem, which later became a member of the U.S. → National Council of Churches (1967). A stricter episcopalian group split off from the General Convention in 1897. The movement spread more extensively in South Africa (esp. Pretoria), Ghana, and Nigeria. There were some adherents in Germany in the middle of the 19th century; the New Church was founded in Berlin only in 1900.

Writings and lectures propagate Swedenborg's ideas. We thus find the Swedenborg Society in England, the Swedenborg Foundation in the United States, and the Swedenborg-Gesellschaft in Switzerland. Often the members engage in social and humanitarian activities. In Britain and America the Swedenborgians joined in the fight against → slavery. They also played a part in the formation of the West African state of Liberia in 1848/49.

At present there are only a few congregations. Numbers worldwide total 25,000-30,000 members (2007), a few thousand each in the United States and the United Kingdom, a few hundred each in Australia and Germany, and most of the others in Africa.

→ Esotericism; Sect; Theosophy

Bibliography: Primary sources: Arcana Coelestia: A Disclosure of Secrets of Heaven Contained in Sacred Scripture (trans. L. H. Cooper; West Chester, Pa., 2007-; earlier ed. 8 vols.; trans. J. H. Elliott; London, 1949-73) • *New Century Edition of the Works of Emanuel Swedenborg* (25 vols.; ed. J. Rose; West Chester, Pa., 2000-[2015 projected]) • *The Spiritual Diary of Emanuel Swedenborg, Being the Record during Twenty Years of His Supernatural Experience* (5 vols.; trans. G. Bush and J. H. Smithson; London, 1883-1902).

Secondary works: E. J. Brock, ed., *Swedenborg and His Influence* (Bryn Athyn, Pa., 1988) • A. M. T. Dibb, *Servetus, Swedenborg, and the Nature of God* (Lanham,

Md., 2005) • G. F. DOLE et al., *Emanuel Swedenborg: Essays for the New Century Edition of His Life, Work, and Impact* (West Chester, Pa., 2005) • C. S. SIGSTEDT, *The Swedenborg Epic: The Life and Works of Emanuel Swedenborg* (New York, 1952) • W. VAN DUSEN, *The Presence of Other Worlds: The Psychological/Spiritual Findings of Emanuel Swedenborg* (2d ed.; West Chester, Pa., 2004).

HANS-DIETHER REIMER†

Switzerland

	1960	1980	2000
Population (1,000s):	5,362	6,319	7,412
Annual growth rate (%):	1.77	0.67	0.43

Area: 41,284 sq. km. (15,940 sq. mi.)

A.D. 2000

Population density: 180/sq. km. (465/sq. mi.)
Births / deaths: 1.02 / 0.92 per 100 population
Fertility rate: 1.53 per woman
Infant mortality rate: 5 per 1,000 live births
Life expectancy: 79.1 years (m: 75.8, f: 82.3)
Religious affiliation (%): Christians 88.3 (Roman Catholics 47.5, Protestants 42.5, indigenous 2.2, marginal 1.6, unaffiliated 1.0, other Christians 0.6), nonreligious 6.9, Muslims 2.8, atheists 1.2, other 0.8.

1. General Situation
  1.1. Structure of the State
  1.2. Religious Profiles
  1.3. Church-State Relationships
2. Churches
  2.1. Roman Catholic
  2.2. Evangelical Reformed
  2.3. Orthodox
  2.4. Christian Catholic
  2.5. Free and Minority Churches
3. Ecumenism
4. Other Groups
5. Non-Christian Religions
  5.1. Judaism
  5.2. Islam
  5.3. Hinduism, Buddhism, and Sikhism

1. General Situation

1.1. Structure of the State

The official name of Switzerland, the Swiss Confederation, shows that the nation has no linguistic or cultural uniformity. The constitution recognizes German, French, and Italian as official languages; in 1938 Rhaeto-Romance was added as a national language. Of the 7,288 million inhabitants (2000 census) 63.7 percent speak German, 20.4 percent French, 6.5 percent Italian, 0.5 percent Rhaeto-Romance, and 9.0 percent other languages.

With its 1848 constitution Switzerland became the first European nation with a democratic form of federal government (→ Democracy), which affects church life as well. Voters may take the initiative in many matters that are under parliamentary control. The 26 member states, or cantons, in which municipalities have many responsibilities with corresponding financial control, may choose their own forms of government.

Industrialization (→ Industrial Society) and the free admission of immigrants brought about a mixing of population after the middle of the 19th century, which began to change the denominational boundaries, though not the main church relationships. Thus in 2000 the overwhelming majority of the Swiss citizens, as well as the population as a whole, declared themselves as belonging to one of the two main confessions: Protestant (Swiss: 42.7 percent; all residents: 35.3 percent) or Roman Catholic (Swiss: 41.2 percent; all residents: 41.8 percent). Also 16.1 percent of Swiss citizens belonged to other groups. Considering the population as a whole, 22.9 percent belonged to other religious groups or to no group: 11.1 percent declared no faith, 4.3 percent were Muslim, 1.8 percent Orthodox, 0.2 percent Christian Catholic (Old Catholic), 0.2 percent Jewish, 1.0 percent other churches and religious communities, and 4.3 percent did not respond to the question.

Links between denominational adherence and social and cultural characteristics are declining. Thus no special connection can be seen between church adherence and language. But there is a relation to the economic situation in the cantons. The more developed cantons are still mostly Reformed, while the less developed are Roman Catholic.

1.2. Religious Profiles

Cultural division according to denomination plays a diminishing role. Sociological research (→ Sociology of Religion) into cultural diversity and national identity has shown an increasing trend both toward → syncretism and toward many different forms of religious orientation, ranging from the strictly Christian to those that are religiously diffuse, even though the population is still Christian in the main. We find the same syncretistic forms and contents in the contemporary religious life of the church members responsible for the church organizations.

Worth noting are the relations between religious orientation and strength of denominational adherence, including churchgoing. Polls show that 10 percent of Protestants are "exclusive Christians" (i.e., holding exclusively Christian beliefs), compared with only 3 percent of Roman Catholics. The category "generally religious Christians" (i.e., Christian beliefs, but with some syncretism) applies to 34 percent of Roman Catholics but only 18 percent of Protestants. The distinction applies only to Sunday churchgoers, so that religious orientation depends partly on churchgoing and partly on adherence.

The two churches are much alike in both losing members; we might speak of a national shift from a denominational to a generically religious orientation. What counts is no longer so much one's denominational alignment but the firmness of one's church anchoring, the closeness of a person's relation to the churches being linked to various patterns of thought and conduct, especially ethical and religious convictions. Religious orientation tends to show a distinction only for the more evangelical Protestants and the more Catholic Roman Catholics; for the majority, however, one's religion and church are concerns that are more pragmatic than theological.

1.3. Church-State Relationships

There is full → religious liberty in all cantons, with all issues of institutional relations left to the cantons (→ Church and State). The constitution guarantees freedom of faith, → conscience, and → worship, and any provision regarding these matters is designed to ensure religious peace. The cantons set up relations within their own borders in keeping with these provisions, and all of them except Geneva and Neuchâtel recognize as corporations in public law both the Reformed and the Roman Catholic churches, some also the Christian Catholic Church (→ Old Catholic Churches 3). Geneva recognizes these churches officially, and in Neuchâtel they are institutions of public interest.

The cantonal state church order, as a whole, is characterized by the two large churches having public and legal recognition. This recognition has developed in three, historically conditioned forms:

1. In cantons that were at one time Reformed (Appenzell–Outer Rhodes, Basel-Land, Bern, Schaffhausen, Vaud, and Zurich), there is a relatively close connection between church and state. The churches are governed by public law, and the canton contributes to the budget of the churches.

2. In cantons that were once Roman Catholic (Appenzell–Inner Rhodes, Fribourg, Jura [before 1978, a Catholic area in the canton of Bern], Lucerne, Nidwalden, Obwalden, Schwyz, Solothurn,

Ticino, Uri, Valais, and Zug), as well as in Basel-Stadt (at one time Reformed), the churches, in particular the Roman Catholic Church, are granted broad autonomy.

3. In cantons with confessional parity (Aargau, Glarus, Graubünden, Saint Gall, and Thurgau), the state has created analogous, autonomous structures for both of the large churches.

Modern development is in two different directions. On the one hand, there are attempts to legally recognize other faith communities (thus in the cantons of Basel-Stadt, Bern, Fribourg, and Saint Gall, Jewish congregations are given equal status with the cantonal churches). On the other hand, moves toward a disentangling or separation of church and state are being undertaken by freethinkers and increasingly also by right-wing conservatives. (In 1980 a national referendum on separation was heavily defeated in all cantons, with 78.9 percent voting against it.)

The official recognition of a church in a canton means that there is a church tax, although in Geneva and Neuchâtel this is a voluntary tax that the state helps to collect (→ Church Finances). Other matters in which there is government involvement include cantonal support, pastoral appointments, → religious education in state schools, pastoral care in state institutions such as the army and hospitals (→ Military Chaplaincy; Pastoral Care of the Sick), and theological faculties at certain universities. The Universities of Basel, Bern, Lausanne, and Zurich have Protestant-Reformed faculties, as do, with special agreements between church and state, the universities of the "separation cantons" Neuchâtel and Geneva. The universities of Fribourg and Lucerne have Roman Catholic faculties, while the theological faculty in Chur and the theological faculty of Lugano are church establishments. At the University of Bern, the Christian Catholics and the Protestants are united in the Old Catholic and Protestant Theological Faculty. The various universities mentioned here are cantonal institutions; in addition, the federal government operates institutes of technology in Zurich and Lausanne.

2. Churches

2.1. Roman Catholic

A distinctive feature of the → Roman Catholic Church in Switzerland is that it has its own law as well as state law, for its members are also members of a public corporation (see 1.3). The competence of the corporation covers only financial and administrative matters in the "parishes." On the national level a conference unites the cantonal corporations.

In contrast, the hierarchical structure involves six dioceses directly responsible to Rome (Basel, Chur, Lugano, Saint Gall, Sitten, and the single diocese "Lausanne, Geneva, and Fribourg"). Two other districts (the territorial abbeys of Maria Einsiedeln and Saint Maurice) are represented on the Schweizer Bischofskonferenz (SBK, Swiss Bishops' Conference). The bishops concerned meet to deal with affairs limited to the linguistic regions. Commissions of the SBK handle matters of national concern.

Catholicism as the social form of the church, and particularly the Catholic associations, has found itself in profound change since 1950/1960. The large organizations with wide support such as the Swiss Caritas Association (cantonal Caritas offices and Caritas of Switzerland) and the Fastenopfer–Katholisches Hilfswerk Schweiz (Lenten Offerings–Swiss Catholic Charity Work) are not endangered.

Although the membership of → religious orders has declined, these orders still have an important position in the church. On the national level, they come together in the Conference of the Unions of Religious Orders and Secular Institutes in Switzerland (KOVOSS/CORISS). The association of male orders, the Union of the Major Superiors of Swiss Religious (VOS/USM) has 1,648 members. The women's orders are organized in various associations: Union of the Mother Superiors of German-Speaking Switzerland and Liechtenstein (VONOS), with 2,397 members; Union of the Mother Superiors of the Contemplative Orders of German-Speaking Switzerland (VOKOS), with 578 members in 38 convents; Union of the Major Superiors of French-Speaking Switzerland (USMSR), with 850 members in 32 congregations; Union of Contemplatives of French-Speaking Switzerland (UCSR), with 12 communities; and Association of the Religious Diocese of Lugano (ARL), with 526 members in 37 communities. The Working Group of the Secular Institute of Switzerland (AGSI) has 330 members.

2.2. *Evangelical Reformed*

The Evangelical Reformed Church (→ Reformed and Presbyterian Churches) consists of the synodically organized cantonal churches and the self-governing congregations. Though most of the activity takes place in the congregations, the whole is greater than the sum of the parts. A free-church branch (see 2.5) contributes to the variety, as do various initiatives, acts, and organizations that encompass several congregations.

To be mentioned in this regard is the Schweizerischer Evangelischer Kirchenbund (SEK, Federation of Swiss Protestant Churches, formed in 1920),

which carries out its tasks partly in its own bodies and partly in organizations connected with it. Representatives from the 26 member churches meet twice a year in the Assembly of Delegates; the Diaconia and the Women's Conference are independent specialized areas. The elected executive body of the Assembly is the board of the SEK, which oversees an administrative office. Within the framework of the administrative office, specialized work is carried out by the Central Services Department, the Church Relations Division, the Communications Department, and the Institute of Theology and Ethics.

Since 2004 the Hilfswerk der Evangelischen Kirchen Schweiz (HEKS, Relief Work of the Swiss Protestant Churches, founded in 1945) and Bread for All (BFA) have existed in the form of foundations. In these agencies, as also in Fondia–Stiftung zur Förderung der Gemeindediakonie im SEK (Fondia–Foundation for the Promotion of Congregational Social Work in the SEK), the SEK board and Assembly have functioned as organs of the foundation. Responsibility for matters pertaining to each language region is handled by corresponding church conferences with their own institutions (e.g., the Conference on Liturgy in German-Speaking Switzerland).

2.3. *Orthodox*

Russians founded the first Orthodox congregation in Bern in 1816 (→ Orthodox Church), but up to World War I the few members were mostly diplomats, merchants, immigrants, and visitors. Persecutions in Armenia (→ Armenian Apostolic Church) and Russia brought more members, and then a relatively large surge came with the arrival of immigrant workers (e.g., from Yugoslavia after 1960).

As of 2000, there were 131,851 Orthodox Christians living in Switzerland. In 1966 the Orthodox Center of the Ecumenical Patriarchate was founded in Chambésy, near Geneva; it was followed in 1982 by the founding of the Metropolitanate of the Ecumenical Patriarchate for Switzerland. Greek Orthodox Church congregations exist today in almost all of the large cities of Switzerland. Serbian Orthodox make up the largest Orthodox community in Switzerland. There are also congregations of Romanian Orthodox churches, along with Coptic and Armenian Apostolic.

2.4. *Christian Catholic*

The Christian Catholic Church consists of one diocese with 36 parishes and 13,312 members (2000 census). This church forms a national church in a → diaspora situation. We cannot ignore it, in view of its ecumenical and diaconal involvement.

2.5. *Free and Minority Churches*

Some 6 percent of Swiss Protestants belong to some kind of → free church. This number includes cantonal church members who belong to the Evangelical Alliance. Also included are adherents of the free churches, mostly Pietist, Baptist, or Pentecostal, which together form the Verband evangelischer Freikirchen und Gemeinden in der Schweiz (VFG, Swiss Federation of Protestant Free Churches and Fellowships; → Baptists; Evangelical Movement; Pentecostal Churches). This association embraces approximately 600 groupings with about 150,000 members and friends. The French-speaking congregations and agencies are brought together in the Fédération Romande d'Églises et d'Oeuvres Évangéliques (FREOE, French-Speaking Federation of Protestant Churches and Works).

For the free churches, the Theological Seminary of Bienenberg (TSB) and the Theologisch-Diakonische Seminar Aarau (TDS) together offer a curriculum at the master's level; the master of arts in pastoral ministries is offered by the University of Wales (U.K.). The Staatsunabhängige Theologische Hochschule Basel (STH, Basel Independent Theological Seminary) is one of many evangelically oriented places of training.

3. Ecumenism

The SEK was formed in 1920 out of the Conference of Cantonal Churches. With a goal of promoting the international relations of Swiss Protestantism, it brought the Swiss Reformed Church into the ecumenical movement. Although representatives of the Swiss churches attended the founding meeting of the → World Alliance of Reformed Churches in London in 1875, it was only in 1925 that the Swiss Reformed Church joined this international body. Some Swiss theologians took part in the preparatory work for the founding of the → World Council of Churches, and in 1940 the Swiss Reformed Church decided, with some hesitation, to become a member. It now participates in other ecumenical organizations, such as the → Leuenberg Agreement, the Community of Protestant Churches in Europe, the → Conference of European Churches (CEC, including its Church and Society Commission, formerly the European Ecumenical Commission on Church and Society), and the → World Association for Christian Communication. With the new openness of the Roman Catholic Church to → ecumenism, the ecumenical movement has taken on great significance in Switzerland. There is now a commission for Protestant–Roman Catholic Dialogue.

As a member of the Union of Utrecht (→ Old Catholic Churches 4), the Christian Catholic Church has been ecumenically committed from the outset and belongs to both the WCC and the CEC. It now has less tense relations with the Roman Catholic Church as a result of → Vatican II. In 1965 its bishop and synod set up a commission for dialogue with the Roman Catholic bishops' conference.

The main relations of the Roman Catholic Church are with other churches in Switzerland, but by means of the Council of European Bishops' Conferences it also has dealings with the CEC. Following Vatican II, through commissions on dialogue and shared working groups, it institutionalized its connections with the SEK and the Christian Catholic Church.

In 1971 the three national churches joined with the free churches in the Arbeitsgemeinschaft christlicher Kirchen in der Schweiz (AGCK, Working Community of the Christian Churches in Switzerland). Methodists, Baptists, and the → Salvation Army were founding members on the free-church side. The Lutherans formed the Alliance of Evangelical Lutheran Churches in 1973 (→ Lutheran Churches 2.3). The Reformed and Roman Catholic Churches have constituted commissions for dialogue with the Orthodox. The SEK also works with the VFG, the FREOE, and the Swiss Evangelical Alliance.

4. Other Groups

Of the many other religious groups in Switzerland, mention must be made of → Jehovah's Witnesses and → Mormons. In 1955 the Mormons built the first Mormon temple on European soil at Zollikofen, a village in the canton of Bern. In 2000 the Jehovah's Witnesses had approximately 30,000 members, the Mormons, 7,000.

5. Non-Christian Religions

The principal non-Christian religious groups in Switzerland are Jews, Muslims, Hindus, Buddhists, and Sikhs. An overview of the many other, mostly small religious associations and communities sharing a worldview is not possible.

5.1. *Judaism*

Approximately three-quarters of the 17,914 Jews in Switzerland belong to one of 24 religious communities (→ Judaism). Of these, 18 are together in the all-Swiss umbrella organization of Jewish congregations, Der Schweizerische Israelitische Gemeindebund (SIG, Swiss Federation of Jewish Communities). The largest Jewish congregations are found in Zurich, Geneva, and Basel. In some cantons, such as Basel-Stadt, Bern, Fribourg, and Saint Gall, the Jewish congregations are considered to be on an equal basis with the state churches. In other cantons, they are smaller associations that strive for an equal position. The Swiss Talmudic College (Yeshiva) is located at Kriens, near Lucerne. The SIG is represented on dialogue commissions with the larger Christian churches (→ Jewish-Christian Dialogue).

5.2. Islam

By 2000 the number of Muslims (→ Islam) living in Switzerland had increased to 310,807, fed originally by the immigration of Yugoslavian and Turkish guest workers, along with the stream of asylum-seekers from various countries. In all, 36,481 Muslims possess Swiss citizenship (i.e., Swiss citizens who have converted to Islam, plus those becoming citizens through naturalization or marriage), with 56 percent coming from the former Yugoslavia (Kosovo-Albanians and Bosnians), 20 percent from Turkey (one-half or more of whom are Alevites), 4 percent from North Africa, 3 percent from Lebanon, and 15 percent from black Africa and Asia. Besides the Sunni majority (75 percent), about 12,000 Shiites, primarily from Iran, live in Switzerland.

According to its own information, this multifaceted Islam was organized in 2005 into approximately 50 associations (including youth and women's centers and charitable groups), as well as around 130 culture centers and places for prayer (49 are Albanian, 31 Turkish, 26 Arabic, and 21 Bosnian). These associations, however, are linked only partially and only regionally. Even the two largest organizations, which designate themselves as Swiss — Liga der Muslime der Schweiz (Swiss Muslim League) and Muslime, Musliminnen in der Schweiz (Swiss Muslim Men and Women), a service organization, both of which were founded in 1994 — are not extensive umbrella organizations. Besides them, other umbrella organizations cross over borders of language and culture.

5.3. Hinduism, Buddhism, and Sikhism

The number of Hindus in Switzerland amounts to around 38,000 persons; nine out of ten are of foreign extraction (→ Hinduism). In 2005 there were 17 Hindu-Tamil temples.

Four-fifths of the approximately 20,000 to 25,000 Buddhists in Switzerland are refugees and immigrants from Asian countries. At the end of the 1990s there were somewhat more than 100 Buddhist groups, centers, conference centers, and monasteries (→ Buddhism). Special mention must be made of the Tibetan Buddhist monastery in Rikon, in the canton of Zurich.

It is estimated that over 500 → Sikhs live in Switzerland.

Bibliography: U. Altermatt, *Katholizismus und Moderne. Zur Sozial- und Mentalitätsgeschichte der Schweizer Katholiken im 19. und 20. Jahrhundert* (Zurich, 1989) • D. B. Barrett, G. T. Kurian, and T. M. Johnson, *WCE* (2d ed.) 1.713-18 • M. Baumann and J. Stolz, eds., *Eine Schweiz–viele Religionen. Risiken und Chancen des Zusammenlebens* (Bielefeld, 2007) • J. M. Gabriel and T. Fischer, eds., *Swiss Foreign Policy: 1945-2002* (Basingstoke, 2003) • B. Gordon, *The Swiss Reformation* (New York, 2002) • P. Johnston and R. W. Scribner, *The Reformation in Germany and Switzerland* (Cambridge, 1993) • L. Karrer, *Katholische Kirche Schweiz. Der schwierige Weg in die Zukunft* (Fribourg, 1991) • D. Kraus, *Schweizerisches Staatskirchenrecht. Hauptlinien des Verhältnisses von Staat und Kirche auf eidgenössischer und kantonaler Ebene* (Tübingen, 1993) • *Schweizer Lexikon 91 in sechs Bänden* (6 vols.; Lucerne, 1992-93) • J. Stolz and O. Favre, "The Evangelical Milieu: Defining Criteria and Reproduction across the Generations," *SocComp* 52 (2005) 169-83 • R. S. Wallace, *Calvin, Geneva, and the Reformation* (Grand Rapids, 1988) • R. Weibel, *Schweizer Katholizismus heute. Strukturen, Aufgaben, Organisationen der römisch-katholischen Kirche* (Zurich, 1989) • J. H. Yoder, *Anabaptism and Reformation in Switzerland* (Kitchener, Ont., 2004) • *Zeitschrift für Schweizerische Kirchengeschichte* (Fribourg, 1907-).

Rolf Weibel

Syllabus of Errors

The term "Syllabus of Errors" traditionally refers to the 80 statements that were published with the → encyclical *Quanta cura* by → Pius IX (1846-78) on December 8, 1864 (DH 2901-80). They form a climax in the controversies of the → Roman Catholic Church with the intellectual movements of the age, which were a particular concern of the pope in drawing up his Syllabus. It represents, as Cardinal I. Antonelli wrote in an accompanying letter to the → bishops, a "Syllabus" of "the most conspicuous errors and false doctrines of this especially unhappy age," which "our most holy Lord, Pius IX . . . has never ceased by his Encyclical Letters and Allocutions held in Consistories, and by publishing other Apostolic Letters and Allocutions to proscribe and condemn." There is nothing materially new in the list, but it gathers together what the pope had been calling errors from the days of his initial encyclical, *Qui pluribus* (1846), in which, for example, he had condemned → Bible societies and also for the first time → Communism (→ Marxism; Marxism and Christianity).

In *Quanta cura* Pius IX listed the various errors under ten heads (R. J. Deferrari):

→ pantheism, → naturalism, and absolute → rationalism
modified rationalism
indifferentism, latitudinarianism
→ socialism, communism, secret societies, biblical societies, clerico-liberal societies
errors concerning the church and its rights
errors concerning civil society, viewed both in themselves and in their relation to the church
errors concerning natural and Christian → ethics (→ Natural Law)
errors concerning Christian → marriage
errors concerning the civil power of the Roman Pontiff
errors which are related to modern → liberalism.

For example, it rejected the separation of → church and state, civil marriage, divorce (→ Marriage and Divorce), and the freedom of worship and opinion (→ Rights; Religious Liberty [Modern Period]), along with the whole idea that the Apostolic See would do best to free itself from all secular government. The final statement sums up the heart of the pope's concern in listing the 80 points, namely, to oppose with all possible force the view that "the Roman Pontiff can and should reconcile and adapt himself to progress, liberalism, and the modern civilization."

The Syllabus prepared the ground for → Vatican I by attempting to bring to an end the debate with liberalism. Seen as a war cry to the modern world (→ Modernity), especially if the statements are viewed without reference to their context, the Syllabus ran up against strong opposition, especially in France, where F. A. P. Dupanloup (1802-78) tried to give it a weaker interpretation. But the pope praised only a strict exposition, such as that by Clement Schrader (1820-75). The Syllabus was one of the actions of the papacy that, toward the end of the 19th century, brought the Roman Catholic Church into an intellectual ghetto. Historical developments, especially the loss of the → Papal States in 1870, also contributed (→ Vatican; Kulturkampf), but the main reason lay with doctrinal developments, especially the dogmatizing of papal → infallibility (→ Teaching Office; Neoscholasticism; Ultramontanism).

At the end of the development stood something that in form, content, and significance was very like the beginning in 1864, namely, the decree of the Congregation of the Holy Office (now the Congregation for the Doctrine of the Faith) called *Lamen-*

tabili (July 3, 1907; DH 3401-66), which condemned "the errors of the Modernists" (→ Modernism) in 65 propositions. A little later, on September 8, 1907, the encyclical *Pascendi* of Pius X (1903-14; DH 3475-3500) was indeed almost a new Syllabus. In this process a new dimension was gained that only the resolutions of → Vatican II would finally overcome theologically, although it still has its impact as an undercurrent (→ Traditionalist Movement).

→ Antimodernist Oath

Bibliography: J. B. Bury, *History of the Papacy in the Nineteenth Century* (ed. R. H. Murray; London, 1930; aug. ed., New York, 1964) lects. 1-2, pp. 1-46 • R. J. Deferrari, trans., *The Sources of Catholic Dogma* (30th ed. of H. Denzinger, *Enchiridion symbolorum;* St. Louis, 1957) • F. Dupanloup, *La convention du 15 septembre et l'encyclique du 8 décembre* (Paris, 1865) • W. F. Hogan, "Syllabus of Errors," *NCE* (2d ed.) 13.651-55 • C. Schrader, *Der Papst und die modernen Ideen* (Vienna, 1865) • H. Wolf, "Der syllabus errorum (1864)," *Kirche im 19. Jahrhundert* (ed. M. Weitlauff; Regensburg, 1998) 115-39.

Hubert Kirchner

Symbol

1. Term
2. In Philosophy
3. In Theology
4. Liturgical Aspects

1. Term

"Symbol" (Gk. *symbolon,* Lat. *symbolum*) is a broad term with various senses and applications. Symbols are like → signs in that they represent, or refer to, something that is other, or more, than themselves. The category of symbols is usually said to overlap that of signs. Some interpreters use the two terms almost interchangeably; others treat symbols as special kinds of signs with characteristics of their own. Still others seek to distinguish clearly between the two (→ Sign 1).

Symbols and signs point beyond themselves. The conventional kind of sign usually has a single or uniform → meaning. A red, octagonal road sign signals the motorist to stop. The word "dog," whether written or spoken aloud, indicates a certain type of animal. Other objects or terms could have served these signifying purposes just as well, had society chosen to use them instead.

Many symbols, however, are capable of multiple meanings. Their physical characteristics, whether as object or as executed action, are often especially suited to the meanings that the symbols convey, namely, suited to that to which the symbol points. For instance, the United States flag consists of stripes and stars, standing respectively for the original colonies and the current number of states. Flags of some Muslim-majority countries display the crescent moon and star, symbolism associated with → Islam. For citizens of these countries, substitution of other elements on their flags would not convey the same messages. Paul → Tillich (1886-1965) states in his *Dynamics of Faith* (1957) that a religious symbol participates in the reality of that to which it points and is in that respect irreplaceable (p. 42).

2. In Philosophy

There is widespread disagreement among philosophers as to the appropriate uses of the term "symbol." How broad or narrow is the range of kinds of things that should be called symbols? To what extent is a symbol like or unlike what it symbolizes? Does a symbol convey a specific, clear-cut meaning or message, or is its communication instead open to multiple interpretations? That there is no philosophical consensus about the nature and function of symbols is no excuse for dropping the effort to define and explain symbols rationally. To do so would hand over the topic to some congenial mode of irrationality, as the proponents of esoteric positions do.

Alfred North Whitehead (1861-1947) engaged the term most broadly, as a synonym for "sign." G. W. F. Hegel (1770-1831), however, in his posthumously published *Lectures on Aesthetics,* treated symbolism as just the preliminary stage of the classical era and opposed its extension to all the subsequent domains of mythology and art. Johann W. Goethe (1749-1832), as well as the neo-Kantians after him, presented a broader theory of symbolism. For him, a symbol is something particular that directly represents or indicates something general or universal, such that everything that takes place can count as symbolic. He sharply distinguished symbolism from → allegory, for allegory is arbitrary and contingent, and it presupposes that the meaning behind it is already known apart from the allegory itself.

In his *Critique of Judgment* (1790), Immanuel Kant (1724-1804; → Kantianism) treated symbols as sensible intuitions subordinate to a priori concepts, intuitions that indirectly present those concepts. They are just analogies to abstract ideas, without possessing an essential likeness to them, since for Kant intuitions and concepts are distinctly different kinds of mental elements. While Kant took a broad view of the indicative capacities of symbol, he nevertheless regarded symbols as a special instance of signs. The semiology of the linguist Ferdinand de Saussure (1857-1913) is in the same vein. In his doctrine of signs, a symbol presents something analogically and inadequately, whereas a linguistic sign, as signifier, is inextricably linked to what it signifies (→ Linguistics 2.2). More recently, Umberto Eco (b. 1932) has treated symbols thematically as part of the doctrine of signs.

In modern symbolic logic, each symbol is assigned a specific meaning and is employed unambiguously in formal arguments. At the other extreme is the outlook of German → Romanticism, one of whose central figures, G. F. Creuzer (1771-1858), held that symbols represent the world of ideas in veiled forms. Often they are embedded in esoteric doctrines such as those of the ancient mystery cults and must be uncovered and interpreted. Insofar as a symbol exhibits more content than its explicit form expresses, it therefore makes us think.

Ernst Cassirer (1874-1945) was the founder of a wide-ranging and thoroughgoing "philosophy of symbolic forms." He did not restrict symbolism to any one domain of the human spirit, to specific features of → epistemology, → logic, or → aesthetics. Instead, he made it central to a philosophy of → culture. His beginning point was the basic ability of human beings to recognize and create symbols. This ability consists in enhancing or fulfilling a sensible reality with ever more constitutive meanings. It is the foundation of all higher symbol systems, such as those of art, religion, and science. He viewed the symbol not as a substance but as a mental or spiritual configuration produced by human subjects.

Critics objected that Cassirer gave the term "symbol" too broad an application. His reply drew upon a threefold distinction with regard to the symbolic function. First, there is the capacity for symbolic expression. Examples of its use include → myth, in which an image is not a presentation of something but is that thing essentially, and the human body as understood in more recent theology to be itself a symbolic reality. Second, there is the function of symbolic presentation as exemplified in the linguistic symbol-system, which does not simply mirror actuality but produces it. Third, there is the function of symbolic meaning as in symbolic logic, where a symbol represents a universal, objective circumstance or relationship.

Cassirer's follower Susanne Langer (1895-1985) regarded the use of symbols as an essential mental activity that not only records sensory data, as in empiricist epistemologies, but also undertakes permanent "symbolic transformations." She distinguished *presentational* symbols, in which specific sensory contents or objects directly present themselves (including music and "life symbols," which underlie sacraments and myths), from *discursive* symbols, most notably language, which consists for the most part of general references and presents circumstances and relationships in a temporal sequence.

According to this philosophy of symbolic forms, a human being is not just a "rational animal," as Aristotle said, but is a "symbolizing animal," inasmuch as we dwell permanently within our symbols, including our prelinguistic symbols.

Bibliography: A. Bucher, *Symbol–Symbolbildung–Symbolerziehung* (St. Ottilien, 1990) • R. Carnap, *Introduction to Symbolic Logic and Its Application* (New York, 1958) • E. Cassirer, *An Essay on Man: An Introduction to a Philosophy of Human Culture* (New Haven, 1944); idem, *The Philosophy of Symbolic Forms* (3 vols.; New Haven, 1953) • F. G. Creuzer, *Symbolik und Mythologie der alten Völker* (Leipzig, 1810; repr., 6 vols., New York, 1978) • U. Eco, *Semiotics and the Philosophy of Language* (Bloomington, Ind., 1984) • I. Kant, *Critique of Judgment* (New York, 1951) • S. Langer, *Philosophy in a New Key: A Study in the Symbolism of Reason, Rite, and Art* (Cambridge, Mass., 1942) • M. Merleau-Ponty, *Phenomenology of Perception* (New York, 1962) • P. Ricoeur, *Freud and Philosophy: An Essay on Interpretation* (New Haven, 1970) • P. Tillich, *Dynamics of Faith* (New York, 1957) • A. N. Whitehead, *Symbolism: Its Meaning and Effect* (Cambridge, 1928).

Anton A. Bucher and Robert F. Brown

3. In Theology

Philipp Marheineike (1780-1846) gave the name "symbolics" to the discipline of confessional theology. His *Christliche Symbolik* (1810) shows that the use of the term for the teachings of various → denominations extends back to the → Reformation era. It also projects the term back to the → early church, to the relation of "symbol" to "confession" understood as the profession of faith. It is evident that the early church preserved the original Greek sense of symbolic understanding, and this understanding underwent specific modifications in the three disciplines of confessional theology, sacramental theology, and → Christology.

3.1. The most ancient baptismal confessions underlie the → Apostles' Creed *(symbolum apostolicum)* and are exemplary for this confessional theology. Prominent in them are the two distinctive marks of this symbolism: indication of a nexus of meaning for the believer, and the establishment of that nexus. As made visibly concrete by the baptismal rite, the confession symbolizes membership in the community of those who are bound together by the *credo* it expresses, and it at the same time renews this bond. This sense of symbol as confessional formula goes back as far as → Tertullian (ca. 160-ca. 225), as seen in his *Adv. Marc.* 5.1.

Debates in the first four or five centuries of the life of the church concerning the two natures of Christ involved controversies about the status of symbols in the early formulations of Christian → theology. Theologians who during this period adopted various forms of subordinationism, usually ascribing less reality to the human nature of Christ than to his divine nature, often held, as in → Docetism, that the divine Logos simply took up a human body or the appearance of a human body without a human soul. The historical Jesus, in this view, symbolized God's saving deed in such a way that the symbol and what it symbolizes are not one and the same. In contrast, theologians — largely in agreement with → Athanasius of Alexandria (ca. 297-373) — maintained instead that the Logos became actual flesh, that Christ is the incarnate God, and that Christians must believe this doctrine. The symbolic meaning of Christ's saving deed, in this view, lies in the substantial identity in him of God and humanity. Docetism thus viewed God as basically a *deus absconditus,* a remote deity, whereas the Alexandrians stressed a *deus revelatus* (→ Alexandrian Theology).

From the beginning, those who tended to hold to the symbolic meaning of the → incarnation have affirmed that Jesus represents the unity of redeemed humanity with God. But how radically is this unity to be understood? It is well established that advocates of a "real presence" (in Christological, eucharistic, and baptismal doctrine) are closer to the ancient pre-Christian understanding of symbol than their opponents. They affirm that the symbol creates a nexus of meaning or a commonality by means of its palpable presentation.

3.2. Post-Reformation controversies in much of Protestantism about the correct understanding of the sacrament, both within and between denominations, passed over directly into controversies about the meaning of the symbol concept itself. Is the symbol in the narrow sense to be understood exclusively as a sign pointing to something else that is not present, something the sign itself cannot replace? If so, then it underscores the qualitative difference and insuperable distance between the sign and what it symbolizes. In contrast to this stand, both the Roman Catholic and the Lutheran eucharistic doctrines uphold the "real presence" in the symbol itself of what it symbolizes, namely, the body of Christ in the bread and his blood in the wine (→ Eucharist).

3.3. The issue of symbols has received extensive attention in the 20th century, quite apart from theology, without contributing much to the precision of the concept as theology employs it. Noteworthy, however, is theology's renewed focus on the concept of symbol beyond the scope of those theological disciplines to which symbolics has belonged since the onset of the 19th century — that is, the confessional statements of churches. Prominent examples of this focus are found in the Protestant thought of Paul → Tillich (1886-1965) and the Roman Catholic theology of Karl → Rahner (1904-84). They agree, across confessional lines, on the Christological foundation of the theological concept of symbol. For both, Christ is the perfect symbol of the human situation.

Rahner regards Christ as the primal symbol of God's grace as it is directed to humanity. In this sense, Christ is to be understood as the primal sacrament. Theological symbolics exhibits the common ground among denominations, as well as their differences. Rahner seeks to reinforce the reality-content of the symbol concept more strongly than does Tillich, by giving it ontological significance. He says that, of itself, the concrete existence of the symbol is necessarily symbolic only because it "expresses" itself necessarily, in order to find its own proper being. So understood, the symbol is a "real-symbol," both a reality and a symbol. This interpretation has stronger links with the original meaning of *symbolon* than the Protestant tradition could have.

Also pertinent for theological symbolics is the thought of Ernst Cassirer (1874-1945). His *Philosophy of Symbolic Forms* is devoted to the concept of symbol and the constitutive role of symbols in culture. Cassirer locates → myth and → religion, alongside the triad of language, knowledge, and art, as the five primal forms of spirit, the forms in which the cultural energies of history manifest themselves. He speaks of "symbolic forms" because of the diverse historical efficacy of symbols as they give rise to different cultures. For instance, archaic myths have a significance completely different from that of the political myths of modern totalitarian systems. Yet both kinds of myth symbolize a quite specific form of cultural self-understanding. In the ancient sense, symbols are signs that are meaning-generating, or *poesis*. This mythical consciousness brings its experience of the world's meaning to expression via histories of the gods and via ritual pre-

sentations indicative of magical causality. Thus it creates for itself its world. Symbols are acts that bestow meaning. Without them, there can be no consistent experience of the world.

The history of symbols, from the earliest times to the currently most abstract mathematical symbols used to express scientific knowledge, can be understood as a kind of genealogy of cultural history. Myth and religion belong both to the beginnings of this cultural history and to the contemporary world. Cassirer's thought calls for theological symbolics to be ever attentive to the connection of signs with *poesis* in symbolism and shows that there is no truth to be sought that transcends symbolic forms.

Bibliography: E. CASSIRER, *The Philosophy of Symbolic Forms* (3 vols.; New Haven, 1953); idem, *Symbol, Myth, and Culture: Essays and Lectures of Ernst Cassirer* (ed. D. Verene; New Haven, 1979) • E. JÜNGEL and K. RAHNER, *Was ist ein Sakrament?* (Freiburg, 1971) • H. LOOF, *Der Symbolbegriff in der neueren Religionsphilosophie and Theologie* (Cologne, 1955) • K. RAHNER, "The Theology of the Symbol," *Theological Investigations* (vol. 4; Baltimore, 1966) 221-52 • E. SCHILLEBEECKX, *Christ: The Christian Experience in the Modern World* (New York, 1980) • P. TILLICH, "The Nature of Religious Language," *Theology of Culture* (New York, 1964) 53-67; idem, *Systematic Theology* (3 vols.; Chicago, 1951-63).

ENNO RUDOLPH

4. Liturgical Aspects

4.1. Christian → worship as a whole is a symbolic event linked to the actualizing in faith of the mystery of the death and resurrection of Jesus Christ. → Liturgy is a symbolic expression of the way God deals with humanity in creation.

The Word lives in visual or tangible signs. In line with the views of Paul → Tillich (1886-1965) and Karl → Rahner (1904-84; see 2.3), contemporary Protestant and Roman Catholic theologians often consider the → sacraments as symbols. The Catholic sacramental theologian Louis-Marie Chauvet (Paris) and the Reformed theologian Henry Mottu (Geneva) both see in the sacraments a symbolic expression of God's action in salvation and of his alliance with humans. For Chauvet, the divine humanity of God finds symbolic expression in the sacraments.

Christian liturgy as a whole integrates cultural and religious symbols, such as → light or → fire, that belong to specific cultures or epochs and that have undergone constant development. Christian confessions give a special sense to the adopted symbols (→ Spirituality) and at times give them a new form. Each liturgical symbol carries its own reference, for example, the → sign of the → cross (as a gesture or figure), the use of → water at baptism, the liturgical colors (in the vestments of ministers, in room or object decoration, in abstract stained-glass windows), and liturgical floral decorations (→ Iconography; Church Architecture; Church Year 3.1; Paraments; Symbolism of Animals).

4.2. The older churches and the younger churches (→ Third World 2) take different approaches to symbols. A special Protestant tradition, particularly within the Reformed context (→ Reformed and Presbyterian Churches), gives the spoken message (→ Preaching) precedence over all symbols. The Eastern and Roman Catholic liturgies (→ Worship 2-3) make rich use of varied symbols, including those that often recover OT images. The churches in Asia, Africa, and Latin America (→ Worship 5) have come to terms with the symbols of their own cultures and traditional religions. All Christian churches today must rethink the symbolic significance and shape of their liturgies in light of postmodern society.

4.3. Liturgical symbols must be appropriate to the gospel and accessible to modern men and women. It is also important that symbols should be ecumenically recognizable. In symbolic communication there need be no gap between → tradition and openness to new experience. Symbols used in Christian worship, especially those from the Bible, carry a clear eschatological reference (→ Eschatology) and are critical vis-à-vis an outdated form of devotional life. An arbitrary use of symbols that has constantly plagued the liturgy (e.g., the use of modern didactic symbols) must be avoided, along with symbolic objects or actions that contribute nothing to the meaning of → revelation. Worship is not a symbolic dealing with cosmic powers. Liturgical symbols are neither archetypes nor decoration but serve the commemoration of Christ and the kingdom of God.

Bibliography: L.-M. CHAUVET, Symbol and Sacrament: A Sacramental Reinterpretation of Christian Existence (Collegeville, Minn., 1995) • P. CRAIG-WILD, Tools for Transformation: Making Worship Work (London, 2002) • R. GUARDINI, Sacred Signs (rev. ed.; trans. G. Branham; Wilmington, Del., 1979; orig. pub., 1927) • N. MITCHELL, "Sign, Symbol," The New SCM Dictionary of Liturgy and Worship (ed. P. Bradshaw; London, 2002) 438-40 • H. MOTTU, Le geste prophétique. Pour une pratique protestante des sacrements (Geneva, 1998) • K. RICHTER, Feste und Brauchtum im Kirchenjahr. Lebendiger Glaube in Zeichen und Symbolen (Freiburg, 1992) • D. SARTORE, "Segno, simbolo," Liturgia (ed. D. Sartore, A. M. Triacca, and C. Cibien; Milan, 2001) 1853-64 • P. TILLICH, Symbol und Wirklichkeit (3d ed.; Göttingen, 1986) • R. VOLP, ed., Zeichen. Semiotik in Theologie und Gottesdienst (Munich, 1982).

BRUNO BÜRKI

Symbolism of Animals

1. Cultural History
2. Old and New Testaments
3. Early Church
4. Middle Ages
5. Catalog of Symbols
   5.1. Christ
   5.2. Mary
   5.3. Virtues and Vices
   5.4. The Devil and Demons

1. Cultural History

1.1. Stone Age engravings and paintings on rock walls and caves include portrayals of → animals, whose significance goes beyond the pictured life-forms. The naturalistic portrayal of hunting animals expresses the effort of the ancient hunter, by means of the images, to gain power over the animal by casting a hunting spell on it (→ Magic) and to utilize the animal's strength and power by worshiping it. In the cultures of shepherding and animal husbandry, the fertility of bull, cow, or sheep motivates the depiction and veneration of animals. The cow as a symbol of life-containing power is recognized, for example, by Zoroastrianism (→ Iranian Religions 7.1) and still today by → Hinduism. The motive can also be reverence when animals are experienced as manifestations of the holy (e.g., in the Indo-Germanic area the horse was a holy animal; → Sacred and Profane). Awe and fear can also be motives for treating animals symbolically when they are encountered as life threatening and as the embodiment of demonic powers (e.g., the dragon, which embodies → evil and chaos, iconographically portrayed in Babylonian composite figures as a mixture of → serpent and bird, or lion and bird).

The complex relationship between animal and human, whether individual or social group, is characteristic of → tribal religions (→ Totemism); on the basis of the group's assumed relationship with the animal species (and evolution from it), a certain animal or a kind of animal is stylized to be the symbol of the clan, tribe, or local group. The religious significance of animals is reflected in figures of gods in animal form (often on the painted ceramics of Indians) and in epiphanies of gods (e.g., the Indian god Vishnu comes to earth, among others, as a fish, a turtle, and a lion). Impressive evidence of this development is offered by → Egyptian religion (see 1.2). In a word, the animals symbolize human weaknesses and vices.

1.2. The oldest Egyptian art evolved from Stone Age cliff drawings. Later, the animal portrayals lost their symbolic character. In burial sites in the Old Kingdom (2750-2250 B.C.) they witness to the wealth of the deceased owner. Yet at this time the sky-god Horus is encountered in the form of a falcon that touches the earth with the tips of its wings.

The actual worship of animal gods began in the late period of Egyptian culture (633-325 B.C.), when almost all of the old gods were portrayed in connection with an animal. Beside Horus there are, among others, the ram-headed Amon, the jackal-headed Anubis, the lion-headed Sekhmet, and the ibis-headed Thoth. God and animal enter into a magic connection in which the characteristics of the animal determine the essence of the god.

1.3. The ancient Greek world had a critical and unsympathetic view of the Egyptian animals; Greek gods had anthropomorphic or anthropopathic characteristics (→ Greek Religion). Yet the Greeks also had composite animal beings that possessed no sacred meaning but had a mostly negative connection to humans. Thus, for example, Siren, half-human and half-bird, bewitches Odysseus; or Cerberus, a three-headed dog, watches over the realm of Hades and is conquered by Heracles. The Minotaur, a being with a human body and a bull's head, sits in the center of a labyrinth and swallows the virgins who are sacrificed to him. Demeter and Poseidon, both horse-shaped, come from the Indo-Germanic region.

2. Old and New Testaments

The OT contains a richness of animal species, although no animal cult. Animals are observed on the basis of their (partly assumed) biological and "personal" characteristics. The → dove, for example, can announce the end of the flood with its sense of orientation (Gen. 8:8-12), show sadness with its cooing (Isa. 38:14), and be a pet name for a loved one (Cant. 1:15; 2:14). The lion is the symbol of terror-inducing power (Ezek. 1:10; 1 Macc. 3:4), can be defeated by prayer (Ps. 91:13), arouses amazement because of its courage and its strength (Prov. 30:30 and elsewhere), serves as a model (Gen. 49:9), and acts as the executor of divine judgment (1 Kgs. 13:24). The eagle symbolizes, among other things, speed

(2 Sam. 1:23), youthful strength (Ps. 103:5), care for one's young (Deut. 32:11), and divine power (Ezek. 1:10). The bull or ox embodies fertility (e.g., Deut. 28:4), as well as power (e.g., Ps. 22:12); its image is part of the furnishings of the temple (1 Kgs. 7:25; cf. the golden calves of Exod. 32:4 and 1 Kgs. 12:28). The deer, which thirsts for water, is a sign of the soul that longs for God (Ps. 42:1).

The NT takes up the animal comparisons of the OT, occasionally with a wider meaning. The lion can be compared with the → devil (1 Pet. 5:8) but also can point to the victorious Christ (Rev. 5:5). The → serpent — taking up Gen. 3:1-15 (→ Protevangelium) — becomes the symbol of the devil (Rev. 12:9), but because of its cleverness, it is also a model for Jesus' → disciples (Matt. 10:16). As a hen with her brood, Christ will gather the children of Israel (Matt. 23:37). The simple dove (Matt. 3:16) becomes, in particular, the symbol of the → Holy Spirit.

3. Early Church

The first Christians used animals as symbols for their faith. From the first to the fourth centuries, the → fish was particularly often portrayed, apparently due to its Greek name, ichthys, and the acrostic connected with it: Iēsous Christos Theou Huios Sōtēr (Jesus Christ, Son of God, Savior). Clement of Alexandria (ca. 150-ca. 215) names the fish and the dove as proper images for the signet rings of Christians (Paed. 3.59). He also gives an index of animals with their symbolic meaning (birds: sensuousness; serpent: betrayer; lion: violent one; swine: wasteful one; wolf: robber).

The early Christian Physiologus (author unknown; chronology debated, but perhaps end of the 2d cent.), which is based on ancient animal lore, describes animals and fabled beings with their characteristics and occasionally mentions a Christian meaning. In numerous, widely spread translations this book and its contents profoundly influenced → Christian art, especially of the Middle Ages. In Contra Celsum → Origen (ca. 185-ca. 254; → Origenism) apparently refers to the Physiologus (4.74-79; see also 4.87) as he discusses ancient zoology, remarking that the statements about the animals are valid also for the humans they represent.

In his Formulae spiritualis intelligentiae, Eucherius of Lyons (d. ca. 450) offers a record of all of the Christian → symbols, together with an allegorical biblical → exegesis (chap. 4). The medieval bestiaries — collections of known animals, as well as fabled animals and composite beings — offer allegorical or moralizing commentary on the various creatures, sometimes including reference to their Christian meaning.

Next to fish and dove, the peacock and the phoenix occupy the most important positions in animal portrayals in early Christian art, being the symbols of eternal life and → resurrection. The peacock is found on grave monuments and in → catacombs, often in illustrations of → paradise. Its flesh was considered imperishable. Legend tells of the phoenix that, shortly before its death, it built a wooden nest that was ignited by the sun and in which it burned up. Out of the ashes a new bird emerged. Deer, lamb, and lion (see 2) are early Christian symbols of Christ. The symbols of the four Evangelists — angel (Matthew), lion (Mark), bull or ox (Luke), and eagle (John) — were already known by → Irenaeus of Lyons (ca. 130-ca. 200) and Hippolytus (ca. 170-ca. 236).

4. Middle Ages

The art of the Romanesque and Gothic periods (→ Christian Art 3) makes use of a number of animals, fabled as well as composite beings, whose symbolism can be explained only in part. Many ornamental animal portrayals on capitals and tympana may be pure decoration, or they may in their abstraction to braided bands, knots, or demonic masks have an apotropaic meaning for averting evil. A new naturalistic interest in the environment led to the emergence in the 13th century of a series of animal portrayals that possessed only a limited symbolic character, even if they illustrate the Christian doctrine of salvation as a "mirror of nature." The vast majority of medieval animal representations symbolize either persons or characteristics (e.g., attributes of saints, heraldic animals; → Saints, Veneration of); animal fables serve to interpret basic ethical positions. Early Christian animal symbolism refers mostly to Christ or God; in the Middle Ages the field is widened and at the same time gives animals an ambivalence, which often allows them to appear with contradictory tendencies.

After the Middle Ages the symbolism of animals no longer played any major role. The → Renaissance transformed ancient animal motifs into ornamental forms of embellishment. Only in the emblematics of the 17th and 18th centuries can one see in small measure the continuation of the medieval symbolism of animals.

5. Catalog of Symbols

5.1. *Christ*

Pure symbols of Christ (→ Images of Christ) are the bull, dolphin, eagle, fish, griffin, hart, lamb, pelican, phoenix, and unicorn.

5.2. *Mary*

Symbols of Mary were chosen mostly from the sphere of plants and flowers (→ Mary, Devotion to). Animals from the *Physiologus* that were symbols of Christ, however, also served as symbols for Mary: the lion (which awakens its young), ostrich (which allows its eggs to incubate in the sun), phoenix, and pelican. The most important source is *Defensorium inviolatae virginitatis beatae Mariae* of the Viennese Dominican Franz von Retz (ca. 1343-1427).

5.3. *Virtues and Vices*

The same animals have often been used as symbols of either virtue or vice: the dog (loyalty, but also envy and anger), eagle (justice, but also pride and immoderation), lion (persistence, moderation, and strength, but also cruelty), peacock (immortality, but also pride and arrogance), and rooster (vigilance, but also unchastity).

The following animals are symbols solely of virtue: bees (eloquence, industry), camel (mercy, obedience), dove (modesty, harmony, chastity), pelican (willingness to make sacrifices, love), phoenix (hope), and unicorn (virginity).

Animals serving as symbols for vices are the ape (miserliness, unreliability), bear (unchastity, anger), cat (laziness), fly (sin), fox (injustice), owl (lack of faith), panther (desire, lasciviousness), rabbit (lust), and swine (unchastity, immoderation).

5.4. *The Devil and Demons*

As symbols of the devil and → demons, certain animals appear in various connections. Most often used are the ape, asp and basilisk, bat, bear, boar, buck, cat, centaur, chimera, crocodile, dog, donkey, dragon, fox, frog, goat, griffin, hedgehog, leopard, scorpion, serpent, siren, sphinx, toad, whale, and wolf.

→ Iconography; Images

Bibliography: L. Charbonneau-Lassay, *The Bestiary of Christ* (trans. D. M. Dooling; New York, 1992) • K. J. Dell, "The Use of Animal Imagery in the Psalms and Wisdom Literature of Ancient Israel," *SJT* 53 (2000) 275-91 • F. D. Klingender, *Animals in Art and Thought to the End of the Middle Ages* (London, 1971) • B. C. Raw, "The Archer, the Eagle, and the Lamb," *JWCI* 30 (1967) 391-94 • L. Réau, *Iconographie de l'art chrétien* (3 vols. in 6; Paris, 1955-59) • B. Ross, *The Inheritance of Animal Symbols in Modern Literature and World Culture* (New York, 1988) • B. Rowland, *Animals with Human Faces: A Guide to Animal Symbolism* (Knoxville, Tenn., 1973) • J. Tresidder, ed., *The Complete Dictionary of Symbols* (San Francisco, 2005) s.v. "Animals" • C. E. Watanabe, *Animal Symbolism in Mesopotamia* (Vienna, 2002) • H. B. Werness, *The Continuum Ency-*

clopedia of Animal Symbolism in Art (New York, 2004) • T. H. WHITE, ed., *The Book of Beasts: Being a Translation from a Latin Bestiary of the Twelfth Century* (new ed.; Phoenix Mill, Eng., 1992)

HELGA NEUMANN

Synagogue

1. Term
2. Origins
3. Temple and Synagogue
4. Function
5. Architecture
6. Furniture
7. Worship
8. Synagogue and Church

1. Term

Synagōgē is a Greek term meaning "gathering, conventicle," used first by Philo (15-10 B.C.–A.D. 45-50), then by Josephus (ca. 37-ca. 100), and also in the NT for a place of gathering. The Hebrew equivalent is *bēt ha-kĕneset* (Aram. *bē kĕništā*), meaning "community house" or "house of the assembly" (from the root *kns*, "assemble"). In the Egyptian → diaspora and in Josephus we also find the term *proseuchē*, "place of prayer." Other terms such as *sabbateion* (house in which a → Sabbath service was held) are infrequently used.

M. Luther's (1483-1546) translation *Judenschul* in the NT is based on Yid. *Schul,* while the term "temple" for this institution arose as recently as Reform → Judaism in the 19th century.

2. Origins

Obscurity surrounds the origin of the synagogue. Nehemiah 8 and 9 depict a ritual that is parallel to synagogue worship. Egyptian inscriptions bear witness to the existence of places of prayer in the third century B.C., though they are not called synagogues. An inscription from Jerusalem (before A.D. 70) refers to Theodotus, a priest and head of a synagogue and a grandson of a head of a synagogue, who built the synagogue. Early rabbinic sources (→ Mishnah and Tosepta) refer to a congregation *(kĕneset)* with members *(bĕnē ha-kĕneset),* a head *(rōš ha-kĕneset),* an official *(ḥazzan ha-kĕneset),* and a building *(bēt ha-kĕneset).*

By rabbinic tradition the synagogue existed since the days of → Moses. Various hypotheses in modern research can be summarized as follows: the origin of the synagogue is be dated to the time (1) before the Babylonian exile (→ Israel 1), (2) during the Baby-

lonian exile, (3) of the Hellenistic diaspora, or (4) of the → Pharisees in Palestine.

As regards the preexilic origin, L. Löw (1811-75) derived the synagogue from the *bêt hā`ām* of Jer. 39:8 and from gatherings for prayer that replaced local sacrifices, following the reforms under Josiah. He found references to this institution in Ps. 74:8 and Job 30:23.

Second, regarding the exile in Babylon, I. Elbogen (1874-1943) saw the synagogue as replacing the → temple and thus making the religious survival of the exiles possible. This view is favored by many scholars.

M. Friedländer (1844-1919), however, regards the synagogue as an original creation of the Hellenistic diaspora designed both for prayer and for instruction.

Finally, S. Zeitlin (1892-1976) puts its origin in the early days of Pharisaism in Palestine, when sporadic political gatherings gave way to regular local meetings for the reading of Scripture and prayer during the times of sacrificial offerings in the temple. In his view the Hebrew term precedes the Aramaic and Greek ones. For non-Jews, who saw the synagogue simply as a place of prayer, *proseuchē* made its function as an assembly invisible.

Variations of this date have been suggested, for example, by S. B. Hoenig, who regards the destruction of the second temple as the time when the need for a synagogue arose.

3. Temple and Synagogue

In discussions of the origins of the synagogue, its relation to the temple plays an important role. On the one hand, it should not be overlooked that lay worship, with → prayer and the reading of Scripture, stands in contradiction to the temple sacrifices, which had to be offered by the → priests. Synagogue worship could take place without either rabbis or priests. The priestly blessing recited in the synagogue (Num. 6:24-26) forms an exception, since only a descendant of a priest could recite it in its original wording.

On the other hand, there are points of contact between the synagogue and the temple. Prayers as well as sacrifices were offered up in the temple worship. Morning and afternoon prayers in the synagogue took place at the same time as sacrifices offered in the temple. Some synagogue prayers (e.g., the *hôšă`nā*) seem to have originated in the temple, while other synagogue prayers found their way into the temple service. Analogies between the two were suggested some time after the destruction of the temple, when increasingly the synagogue took its place. Yet in spite of similarities, the synagogue still had its own character as a lay institution.

4. Function

As early sources such as Philo, Josephus, the NT, the Mishnah, and the Tosepta attest, the congregation met in the synagogue for daily prayer, Sabbath worship, festivals (→ Jewish Practices), judicial purposes, and various community functions. Instruction, when not given in a school, could also take place in the synagogue, and so too could → circumcision. The synagogue could also serve as a hostel for Jews on a journey. The synagogue occupied a central position in Jewish society. Often more than one synagogue served a single Jewish community.

5. Architecture

Any room, even in a private house, could serve as a synagogue if it was large enough for the minyan (ten adult men) to meet there for public → worship. The gathering of the people made the room into a synagogue. In itself it was not sacred but, rather, profane (→ Sacred and Profane). A synagogue did not require any special architectural features. Even meeting places constructed for non-Jewish use could be adapted to this purpose. The lack of characteristic architectural features is perhaps the reason why today it is difficult to identify some archaeological sites as synagogues. The three earliest ones — at Gamla (1st cent. B.C. or 1st cent. A.D.), at Herodium, and at Masada (1st cent. A.D.) — are recognized as such only through seats along the walls and spaced pillars that held up the roof. All three are places of assembly.

We do not know of any synagogues in Israel dating to the two centuries that followed. Many synagogues in Galilee (Chorazin, Capernaum) and on the Golan Heights dating from the third to the sixth centuries are architecturally similar. A front entrance with usually three portals faces Jerusalem and resembles pagan temples. Seats are lined along the walls behind a row of pillars. The architectural elements are richly decorated.

Another type of synagogue building appears in Israel in the sixth century: a three-naved → basilica with an apse on the side facing Jerusalem (Bet Alfa). The decoration consisted of mosaics. Side by side with purely geometric ornamentation, we also find depictions of plants, → animals, biblical scenes, and cultic objects (menorah, Torah shrine, incense shovels, etrog and lulav), as well as the zodiac with Helios driving a chariot. This type resembles church buildings of that time.

Yet some synagogues differ from both these types. They are often broad houses with niches for the Torah scrolls on the side facing Jerusalem (Eshtemoa).

The diaspora synagogues are widespread and varied, as we learn from remains in Italy (Ostia), Syria (Dura-Europos), Asia Minor (Sardis), and Tunisia (Hammam Lif).

The various inscriptions in Greek, Hebrew, and Aramaic show that donors supported the construction of synagogues.

In the Middle Ages we find two-naved buildings resembling a refectory up to the 16th century (Worms and Prague). Beginning with the Jewish emancipation in Germany in the 19th century, monumental synagogues were built, often in Moorish style. On the night of November 9/10, 1938, the so-called Reichskristallnacht (Crystal Night), almost all synagogues in Germany were damaged or destroyed (→ Anti-Semitism, Anti-Judaism; Holocaust).

Hardly any rabbinic prescriptions exist for the structure of a synagogue. The prescription that the entrance should be facing east seems to apply only to locations east of the Jordan. A setting near water or at the highest point of a city was preferred, but often not realistic. Especially Christian and Islamic governments restricted the building of synagogues, when they did not actually forbid them. In the Middle Ages a pole was fixed on the roof of the synagogue, which was higher than the surrounding houses. The floor of the synagogue was lowered beneath street level in fulfillment of the verse "Out of the depths I cry to you, O Lord" (Ps. 130:1). Prayer was conducted toward Jerusalem (Dan. 6:10), though the building itself required no direction.

It is debated whether men and women were seated separately in antiquity, an arrangement that dates only from the Middle Ages. Curtains or latticework was used for the division, and we find not only galleries but special rooms for women, or even women synagogues (Worms). But though these synagogues had a prayer leader, they were not separate institutions but were attached to male synagogues. In today's more liberal synagogues the separation of men and women has been abandoned.

6. Furniture

The two essential items of furniture in a synagogue are a Torah shrine (*'ărôn ha-qōdeš*, lit. "sacred ark") in which the scrolls necessary for worship are kept and a lectern (the bimah, or almemar) for the reading of Scripture and for use by the prayer leader. Until the → modern period the lectern was the central point around which the seats were arranged. In the 19th century the interior of the synagogue became oriented to the Torah shrine, which was located on the side facing Jerusalem. The shrine was originally portable and was brought in for worship. Later it had a fixed place in a niche on the wall or in an apse facing Jerusalem. It was made of wood or of stone and was covered by a curtain. The scrolls of the Torah were draped in special wraps and decorated with crowns (→ Liturgical Vessels 2). A pointer was used for reading so that a human finger would not pollute the sacred scrolls.

An eternal lamp burns in commemoration of the menorah, the sevenfold temple candelabra (Lev. 24:2). According to the → Talmud, imitation of the temple candelabra is forbidden in metal, but in ancient Israel reproductions in stone were widespread, and today we once again find examples of the menorah in synagogues. The head of the synagogue has a special seat, which in earlier times was called the seat of Moses. The narthex contains a place in which to wash hands before prayer.

7. Worship

The most important parts of threefold daily worship (Dan. 6:10) are the Shema (*šěma*ʿ, "hear," Deut. 6:4-9; 11:13-21; Num. 15:37-41; → Jewish Theology 1) and the Prayer of the Eighteen Benedictions, which consists of 18 (or 19) parts and is said standing. Psalms and other prayers are also recited. Readings from the Pentateuch occur three times in the week: on Monday, Thursday, and the Sabbath. Worship on the Sabbath and at feasts differs from that on weekdays. It is accompanied by religious poetry (*piyyûṭîm*), the Prayer of the Eighteen Benedictions is reduced to seven parts, and a sermon by the rabbi could be delivered. An additional prayer takes place in the afternoon.

Many parts of the liturgy are of great antiquity and go back to the days of the Second temple. An effort in the 9th and 10th centuries to impose uniformity on the many versions of the prayers was only partially successful. The prayers have always been fluid, and individual congregations have had their own distinctive uses. Reform Judaism attempted to renew the rite in the 19th century by altering and shortening the prayers to make them more suitable for modern times. Native languages were used in prayers along with Hebrew and Aramaic, which had been dominant for hundreds of years, and → organs and choirs were introduced.

8. Synagogue and Church

In the → early church the word "synagogue" was used to denote Judaism, in contrast to *ekklēsia*, the → church. The two words "synagogue" and "ecclesia" have since stood for the tense relationship between Judaism and Christianity, even though essentially, as we see from the LXX translation of the OT, they represent the same thing.

→ Liturgy 1.2

Bibliography: G. H. COHN and H. FISCH, eds., *Prayer in Judaism: Continuity and Change* (Northvale, N.J., 1996) • I. ELBOGEN, *Jewish Liturgy: A Comprehensive History* (Philadelphia, 1993) • S. FINE, *This Holy Place: On the Sanctity of the Synagogue during the Greco-Roman Period* (Notre Dame, Ind., 1997); idem, ed., *Sacred Realm: The Emergence of the Synagogue in the Ancient World* (New York, 1996) • J. GUTMANN, comp., *The Synagogue: Studies in Origins, Archaeology, and Architecture* (New York, 1975); idem, ed., *The Dura-Europas Synagogue: A Re-evaluation (1932-1992)* (Atlanta, 1992) • C. H. KRINSKY, *Synagogues of Europe: Architecture, History, Meaning* (New York, 1985) • L. I. LEVINE, *The Ancient Synagogue: The First Thousand Years* (New Haven, 2000) • B. OLSSON and M. ZETTERHOLM, *The Ancient Synagogue from Its Origins until 200 C.E.* (Stockholm, 2001) • J. J. PETUCHOWSKI, comp., *Understanding Jewish Prayer* (New York, 1972) • L. I. RABINOWITZ et al., "Synagogue," *EncJud* 15.579-629 • A. RUNESSON, *The Origins of the Synagogue* (Stockholm, 2001) • W. SCHRAGE, "Συναγωγή κτλ.," *TDNT* 7.798-852 • D. URMAN and P. V. M. FLESHER, eds., *Ancient Synagogues: Historical Analysis and Archaeological Discovery* (Leiden, 1995).

GOTTFRIED REEG

Synaxarion

From the word *synagō,* "collect," the synaxarion is a collection for the → church year of short lives and notices of the → saints (§5.1) that, in the Eastern churches, can be used either in public → worship or privately (→ Orthodox Christianity; Orthodox Church). From the 9th century onward, the literary genus of the synaxarion has merged into that of church calendars and martyrologies (→ Martyrs; Martyrs, Acts of the). There are examples in Byzantium and Italy and Greece, and also in the Near East, though usually in translation from the Greek.

Modern Greek usage has added the texts to the → liturgical books (Menaion, Triodoon, and Pentecostarion), where they occur in morning prayer between the kontakion and the seventh ode of the nine-ode canon, introduced by the iambic distichs of Christopher of Mytilene (11th cent.).

The Slavic Menaions did not have any synaxarion, but a new edition published by the Moscow Patriarchate beginning in 1978 (→ Patriarch, Patriarchate) offered some new, short lives that could be added to the liturgical texts for individual days. Not to be confused with synaxaria are the menologions, which are longer lives of the saints collected for private use in relation to the church year. In Russian these are called prologues and, since the 16th century, also reading Menaions.

→ Monasticism

Bibliography: J. E. KLENTOS, "Byzantine Liturgy in Twelfth-Century Constantinople: An Analysis of the Synaxarion of the Monastery of the Theotokos Evergetis" (Diss., University of Notre Dame, 1995); idem, "The Synaxarion of Evergetis: Algebra, Geology, and Byzantine Monasticism," *Work and Worship at the Theotokos Evergetis, 1050-1200* (ed. M. Mullett and A. Kirby; Belfast, 1997) 329-55 • MAKARIOS OF SIMONOS PETRA, *The Synaxarion: The Lives of the Saints of the Orthodox Church* (6 vols.; Ormylia [Chalcidice], Greece, 1998-) • J. NORET, "Ménologes, synaxaires, ménées. Essai de clarification d'une terminologie," *AnBoll* 86 (1968) 21-24 • *The Synaxarion of the Monastery of the Theotokos Evergetis* (2 vols.; trans. R. H. Jordan; Belfast, 2001-5) • W. VANDER MEIREN, "Précisions nouvelles sur la généalogie des Synaxaires byzantins," *AnBoll* 102 (1984) 297-301.

PETER PLANK

Syncretism

1. Term
2. Symbiotic and Synthetic Syncretism
3. Christianity and Syncretism

1. Term

The term "syncretism" (Gk. *synkrētismos*) appears first in the *Moralia* (490ab) by Plutarch (ca. 46-after 119). Popular opinion or perhaps Plutarch himself derived the term on the basis of a false etymology from the Cretans, who in times of danger would set aside all differences in order to make common cause against the enemy. The term appears first in its theological meaning in the late → Middle Ages (→ Erasmus), where it means the mixing together of various confessionally related doctrines that originally did not belong together. Not until the modern age is it used to describe the blending and equating of various religious systems.

The term has never been value-neutral, even though research into the religions, as at Göttingen, has tried to make it so. Modern discussion of systems (→ Social Systems) makes it plain that even → religious studies cannot avoid a self-referential

framework (A. Feldtkeller) and that the use of the term "syncretism" always reveals something at the same time about the speakers and their own system of thought. This is particularly true up to the present in the theological use of the term. It was above all H. Kraemer (1888-1965), who in his book *The Christian Message in a Non-Christian World,* written for the World → Missionary Conference (§2.3) at Tambaram, India (1938), used the term in an exclusively negative sense, denoting an illegitimate intermingling of heterogeneous elements. The term became one of conflict (H. Brandt; see also W. A. → Visser 't Hooft), and it is still used by evangelicals against supposed liberal movements within the → World Council of Churches and against its concept of → dialogue.

In the → history-of-religions school a more positive use was found for the term. H. Gunkel (1862-1932), R. Bultmann (1884-1976; → Dialectical Theology; Existential Theology), and others viewed Christianity itself as a syncretistic religion and saw here a strength rather than a weakness, for syncretism denotes the inner dynamic of a religion and its possibility of synthetically incorporating important elements from other religions. In this sense, W. Pannenberg also considers the term positive.

In recent times voices have been heard in the → Third World that we should construe the term in a new way dogmatically: on the one hand, in order to limit the claims to universality by Western Christianity; on the other, to legitimate the attempt by the Third World churches to seek their own form, which would be the result of encounter with a non-Christian context. M. M. Thomas (1916-96) speaks of a "Christ-centered syncretism"; L. Boff interprets syncretism by means of the concept of condescension and thus comes very near to the idea of inculturation.

The Frankfurt group Theologie Interkulturell (founded in 1985) attempts afresh to bring into dialogue the various uses of the term in religious-historical and ecumenical research (H. P. Siller). We find here noteworthy approaches and intersections, even though no final consensus has been envisioned or achieved. All the participants believe, however, that in the future there must be more clearly differentiated levels on which the term is used, whether collective, biographical, semantic, theoretical, or practical.

2. Symbiotic and Synthetic Syncretism

Contrary to the Göttingen Research Group (which includes C. Colpe, U. Berner, and G. Wiessner), which undertakes a differentiation of the term so that all the variables of the mixing of religions fit into a systematic theoretical framework, it is advisable to understand the term in a wider sense. In doing so, however, both the theoretical and the practical levels must be equally considered. Two basic models of syncretism can be distinguished, which we might call symbiotic and synthetic (G. Mensching, T. Sundermeier).

2.1. *Symbiotic syncretism* involves the process in which primary cultures and their religions are overlaid and ruled by differentiated, superior societies. Within the context of cultural contacts, migrations, conquests, → colonialism, and mission efforts by world religions, this process is unavoidable but remains ambivalent (→ Colonialism and Mission). Since in smaller societies we cannot distinguish religion from the society, culture and religion go hand in hand (→ Tribal Religions). Thus the higher religion does not simply replace the previously existing one; rather, it selectively integrates, rejects, or reinterprets elements of the traditional religion. The more successful the process is, the more vigorously will the new religion establish itself as the religion of the people.

The way Muḥammad integrated pre-Islamic religion and its rites into the religion of revelation in Mecca (→ Islam) is as vivid an example as the absorbing of elements of Germanic religion into northern European Christianity. Israel, too, adopted Canaanite rites and ideas into its religion (→ Judaism; Tribes of Israel). The process of integration usually takes a long time, but at times it can take a dramatically rapid course. It involves several levels. → Language must be adapted insofar as it affects the theological or philosophical system. → Rites that bear on the cult are also affected, as are → ethics. Symbiotic merging can also bring changes to individuals, thus affecting the biographical, as well as the collective sphere.

In the area of ritual, the traditional religions prove themselves to be the most resistant. The overlaying ones, though, can adjust themselves by taking over rites and festivals in the annual or lifelong cycles, integrating them with new meaning into their own systems. The Jewish calendar of festivals (→ Jewish Practices) and those of Christianity (→ Church Year) are examples, as are Buddhist feasts in Thailand and Sri Lanka. Christianity made a feast of the sun into a celebration of the birth of Christ (→ Christmas).

This process of integration is ambivalent insofar as nothing from the outset indicates which religion will be dominant. On Bali the invading → Hinduism was able to survive in that it took over and integrated essential elements of the traditional Balinese tribal religion. By contrast, the tribal religions on Sumatra adopted the cosmological elements of Hinduism, but the latter could not establish a foothold. New religious movements in Africa, Melanesia, and Indonesia are contemporary examples of symbiotic syncretism; in isolated cases the prior religion reasserts itself anew, although broadly Christianity remains the "victor," albeit in changed form.

2.2. Whereas symbiotic syncretism occurs vertically between a subsidiary primary religion and an overlaying secondary religion, *synthetic syncretism* refers to a horizontal encounter of equal systems involving urban or transnational world religions. In theory, an integration of entire systems is conceivable (U. Berner), but in fact syncretism takes place here on the elementary level as well. A classical example in the ancient world involves parallel gods and their intermingling (→ Greek Religion; Roman Religion).

The motives behind this kind of syncretism may vary according to the age or the society. Mercantile interests lay behind pre-Hellenic syncretism, political and legal interests behind Roman syncretism. In the case of → Gnosticism we may see subversive motives on what Colpe has called the left spectrum of syncretism. Like the → mystery religions, Gnosticism served to effect new social orders in the breaking apart of the prior ancient world. In more recent religious history, we might mention Baha'i or the → New Age movement. The latter, however, forms an extreme example of a very arbitrary selectionism that hardly fits the criteria for the adoption and exchange of elements of different religions.

More recent religious movements (→ New Religions) have arisen around a clearly defined center that gathers the various elements into a new, homogeneous entity. Examples include the → Unification Church in Korea and Japanese → sects such as Tenrikyo and Rissho Koseikai (→ Japan 5.2). The Latin American religious movements Makumba, → Umbanda, and Candomblé should not be mentioned here, for they belong in the area of symbiotic syncretism.

3. Christianity and Syncretism

If we agree with N. → Söderblom (1866-1931) in making a typological distinction between prophetic and mystical → religion, we can note that prophetic religions are generally more afraid of losing their identity through syncretism. Mystical religions appear more generous and → tolerant, for they are convinced that the reality behind all forms of religion is one and the same. Confessions, a canonical scripture, and teaching concerning the founder and his life belong to prophetic religions and resist syncretistic alienation. So, too, does the legal establishment of their institutions and the fixing of their liturgical and ritual practice.

If we ask whether Christianity has been a syncretistic religion, the answer depends on whether we interpret the term more narrowly or more broadly. Many researchers incline to protect Christianity against this "reproach" (Colpe, Visser 't Hooft, H.-W. Gensichen). They have adopted a narrow view that we may identify with synthetic syncretism, and they call symbiotic syncretism inculturation, as Kraemer tended to do. This position is based upon a narrow idea of revelation that emphasizes more strongly the distance from other religions than their connectedness, however that is understood (→ Revelation; Truth).

If, however, we take a broader and even inclusive view of revelation like → Vatican II, K. → Rahner (1904-84), L. Boff, or W. Pannenberg, the idea of syncretism loses some of its negative edge. With an open spirit one can accommodate the other religions, which are understood variously as a redemptive-historical preparation for revelation (→ Salvation History), as a work of the → Holy Spirit, or in other ways. Hence it is possible to take over what is true and holy in them, and even to incorporate what is alien by reinterpretation, without having to fear that one's own religion is subject to change or jeopardy. A wide margin exists for what is compatible and for what may be assimilated.

The study *Religionen, Religiosität und christlicher Glaube* (Religions, religiosity, and Christian faith, 1991), presented by the United Evangelical Lutheran Church in Germany (VELKD) and the → Arnoldshain Conference, goes in a different direction. It assigns other religions to the first article of the creed and thereby to God's action in the world. Since the → gospel is a part of the Trinitarian action of God (→ Trinity), it can neither separate itself from other religions nor identify with them, but it involves itself with the others, just as God in Christ entered into the world of religion. It will undergo necessary changes in its passage through the world and its cultures and languages. Inculturation and symbiotic syncretism are inevitable and necessary. The changeability of the gospel does not mean, however, the giving up of its identity, which in each setting must be constantly rewon by reorientation to its origin. Arbitrariness, which is inherent to synthetic syncretism, is not an option; it would lead to a shift of the basic axes (R. Hummel). A constructive dialogue among the religions, in which the encounter of truth claims leads to new recognition of truth, is a theological imperative.

→ Acculturation; Contextual Theology; Mission; Relativism; Theology of Religions

Bibliography: U. BERNER, "Der Begriff 'Synkretismus'–ein Instrument historischer Erkenntnis?" *Saec.* 30 (1979) 68-85; idem, *Untersuchungen zur Verwendung des Synkretismus-Begriffes* (Wiesbaden, 1982) • L. BOFF, *Church, Charism, and Power: Liberation Theology and the Institutional Church* (New York, 1985) • H. BRANDT, "Kontextuelle Theologie als Synkretismus? Der 'neue Synkretismus' der Befreiungstheologie und der Synkretismusverdacht gegenüber der Ökumene," *ÖR* 35 (1986) 144-59 • C. COLPE, "Vereinbarkeit historischer und struktureller Bestimmungen des Synkretismus," *Synkretismus im syrisch-persischen Kulturgebiet* (ed. A. Dietrich; Göttingen, 1975) 15-37 • C. CORNILLE, ed., *Many Mansions? Multiple Religious Belonging and Christian Identity* (Maryknoll, N.Y., 2002) • A. FELDTKELLER, "Der Synkretismus-Begriff im Rahmen einer Theorie von Verhältnisbestimmungen zwischen Religionen," *EvT* 52 (1992) 224-45 • H.-W. GENSICHEN, "Der Synkretismus als Frage an die Christenheit heute," *EMZ* 23 (1966) 58-69 • J. GORT et al., eds., *Dialogue and Syncretism: An Interdisciplinary Approach* (Grand Rapids, 1989) • R. HUMMEL, "Reizwort Synkretismus," *MdEZW* 49 (1986) 252-59 • K. KOYAMA, "A Theological Reflection on Religious Pluralism," *ER* 51/2 (1999) 160-71 • H. KRAEMER, *The Christian Message in a Non-Christian World* (London, 1938) • G. MENSCHING, "Synkretismus," *RGG* (3d ed.) 6.563-66 • H. P. SILLER, ed., *Suchbewegungen. Synkretismus–kulturelle Identität und kirchliches Bekenntnis* (Darmstadt, 1991) • W. C. SMITH, *Towards a World Theology: Faith and the Comparative History of Religion* (Philadelphia, 1981) • T. SUNDERMEIER, "Inkulturation und Synkretismus," *EvT* 52 (1992) 192-208 • M. M. THOMAS, "The Absoluteness of Jesus Christ and Christ-Centered Syncretism," *ER* 37 (1985) 387-97 • W. A. VISSER 'T HOOFT, *No Other Name: The Choice between Syncretism and Christian Universalism* (Naperville, Ill., 1963).

THEO SUNDERMEIER

Syncretistic Controversy

The syncretistic controversy was the longest and last theological debate in the so-called confessional period (→ Catholic Reform and Counterreformation 1.2). In it, doctrinal views traceable to Philipp → Melanchthon (1497-1560, positions polemically labeled Philippism or → crypto-Calvinism), coupled with the attempt to search for the → truth held in common by all three Christian churches in order to arrive at a fundamental minimum common ground, collided with a strict → Lutheranism that was faithful to the → Formula of Concord, uncompromising in defense of its own truth, and compelled to draw lines of division. The originally positive concept of → syncretism was applied negatively to the union theologian Georg Calixtus (1586-1656) in the middle of the 17th century, in connection with the → Gnesio-Lutheran skepticism toward Jakob Andreae's (1528-90) first attempt at a formula of concord.

Calixtus had provided confessionally conscious Lutherans with numerous causes for criticism, expressed by Balthazar Mentzer (1616/20), the Jena theologians (1621), and Statius Buscher (1640). Arising out of humanistic roots (→ Humanism), Reformed impressions, and contemporary observations (→ Thirty Years' War), Calixtus and likeminded Lutherans proceeded from the hypothesis of a biblically based fundamental consensus of the first five centuries, somewhat like the style of the → Apostles' Creed (the *consensus antiquitatis*), and had as its goal confessional → tolerance through the setting aside of nonfundamental special doctrines.

The basic cause of the syncretistic controversy, carried out on both sides with princely support, was the Reformed-friendly religious policy of the Great Elector (Frederick William, 1640-88); the catalyst was the Colloquy of Thorn (Pol. Toruń), held in 1645 to bring about the reconciliation of the Polish Protestants with the Catholics, in which Georg Calixtus took part as a Lutheran Prussian delegate. The undertaking, which failed because of the inflexibility of all participants, led to a three-phase literary war against syncretism, which ended only after the decease of the main Lutheran protagonist, Abraham Calovius (1612-86).

The first phase (1645-56), which began in Königsberg (Johann Latermann) and lasted until the death of G. Calixtus, saw strict Lutheranism (in Königsberg, Danzig, Wittenberg, Leipzig, Dresden, Hamburg, Celle, and Strasbourg) turning against irenic teachers in Helmstedt and Königsberg. Fearing for its identity, these Gnesio-Lutherans issued numerous writings about the controversy. Nonetheless, the inclusion of the Reformed in the Peace of Westphalia in 1648 could not be hindered, nor could general acceptance be reached of Calovius's *Consensus repetitus fidei vere Lutheranae* (Repeated consensus of the truly Lutheran faith, 1655), which condemned union theology, along with its presuppositions.

The second phase (1661-69) of the syncretistic controversy broke out following the 1661 Colloquy of Kassel, carried out with limited success between Hessian Reformed and Lutherans of the Helmstedt school at the University of Rinteln. It grew even more serious after an eight-month-long conference in Berlin, which failed in 1663, and after which the great hymn writer Paul Gerhardt (1607-76) lost his position because of his rejection of the elector's prohibition against using the pulpit for polemics. In addition, Wittenberg was excluded as a university for future Brandenburg theologians. The Helmstedt position was represented, among others, by Friedrich Ulrich Calixtus (1622-1701), son of Georg, as well as the polymath Hermann Conring (1606-81). Ernest the Pious of Saxe-Gotha (1640-75) and his Jena theologians exerted themselves as mediators, but to no result.

At the same time that Philipp Jakob Spener (1635-1705), in his *Pia desideria* (Pious desires, 1675; → Pietism), rejected the one-sided polemical theology (→ Polemics), Calovius kindled the controversy in 1675 again, which introduced its third and final phase (1675-86). The centennial celebration of the Book of Concord in 1680 did not culminate, however, in the victory of → orthodoxy (§1) over union theology. Calovius summarized his unchanged standpoint in 1682 in his richly documented *Historia syncretistica*. Confrontation and hindrances to communication among the three confessional churches continued to exist for a century. Yet the moderate Calixtinism influencing all of northern Germany preserved a trace of the ecumenicity of Christianity (→ Oikoumene).

The outcome of the syncretistic controversy was inconclusive. The ahistorical and ancient principle of → tradition advocated by union theology was opposed by the Lutheran tradition of *viva vox evangelii* (living word of the gospel) and by the confessional writings (→ Confessions and Creeds). Similarly, the effort to bring about interconfessional reconciliation was opposed by the decisive rejection of compromise in dogmatic matters and the commitment to confessional boundaries. The present-day ecumenical discussion could derive impulses from both positions (→ Ecumenical Theology).

→ Augsburg Confession; Ecumenism, Ecumenical Movement

Bibliography: G. CALIXTUS, *Werke in Auswahl* (4 vols.; Göttingen, 1970-82) • A. CALOV, *Wiederholter Consens des wahren lutherischen Glaubens* (Wittenberg, 1666) • W. C. DOWDING, *The Life and Correspondence of George Calixtus* (Oxford, 1863) • C. G. FRY, "Three Lutheran Fathers of the Seventeenth Century," *ConJ* 5/4 (1979) 133-40 • W. GASS, *Georg Calixt und der Synkretismus*

(Breslau, 1846) • S. GÖRANSSON, "Schweden und Deutschland während der synkretistischen Streitig-keiten, 1645-1660," *ARG* 42/1-2 (1951) 220-43 • E. L. T. HENKE, *Georg Calixtus und seine Zeit* (2 vols. in 3; Halle, 1853-60) • I. MAGER, "Brüderlichkeit und Einheit. Georg Calixt und das Thorner Religions-gespräch 1645," *Thorn. Königin der Weichsel, 1231-1981* (ed. B. Jähnig and P. Letkemann; Göttingen, 1981) 209-38; idem, *Georg Calixts theologische Ethik und ihre Nachwirkungen* (Göttingen, 1969) • A. C. PIEPKORN, "Calixt(us), George" and "Calov(ius), Abraham," *ELC* 1.349-50 and 352-53 • H. SCHÜSSLER, *Georg Calixt, Theologie und Kirchenpolitik. Eine Studie zur Öku-menizität des Luthertums* (Wiesbaden, 1961) • H. STAEMMLER, *Die Auseinandersetzung der kursäch-sischen Theologen mit dem Helmstedter Synkretismus* (ed. J. A. Steiger; Waltrop, 2005).

INGE MAGER

Synergism

1. Concept
2. Early Church
3. Reformation and Seventeenth Century
4. Methodism
5. Ecumenical Relations

1. Concept

"Synergism" (from Gk. *synergeō*, "work together") denotes all theological positions that teach a co-operation of human beings with divine → grace, so that both their own action and divine grace are the cause of their → justification (§2). In contrast to this view are theological systems that regard human beings as incapable of → salvation because of their corruption through original → sin (§3.2) and the bondage of their will. These systems assign justifica-tion solely to grace on the basis of divine → predes-tination (monergism). In → ethics, in reflection on the psychological side of → conversion and the → experience of grace, and in criticism of magical ideas of grace and conversion, human action de-mands notice. Such factors can lead to a synergism, as can consideration of the various degrees of suc-cess of the offer of grace among different people.

2. Early Church

In the debate between → Augustine (354-430; → Augustine's Theology 5) and Pelagius (ca. 354-after 418; → Pelagianism 2-3), the interplay of faith or grace and works became the main point. Augustine argued that divine grace always precedes all that we ourselves plan or do, whereas the Pelagians con-tended that we can fulfill the → law of God and the commands of Christ even without grace. The ethical seriousness of the doctrine lies here.

For Eastern theologians the relation between the grace of God and human works was beyond ques-tion (→ Grace 2.2): they took it that God and hu-mans work together. The necessary saving work that we ourselves do as "colaborers with God," which has social and ethical consequences (→ Salvation 3.3), does not diminish the equally necessary saving grace of God.

Later, Lukáš of Prague (ca. 1460-1528; → Bohe-mian Brethren) argued against Martin → Luther (1483-1546; → Luther's Theology 3.1) that "good works" correspond to the *nuda lex* (bare law) of Christ (→ Law 3.3) and are to be fulfilled in the working out of our redemption. The law of Christ is the measure of faith, the formal principle of the church, and must be worked out by everyone in civil life.

3. Reformation and Seventeenth Century

In the Reformation controversies (→ Reformers) the theologians who were reproached as synergists were accused of Pelagianism or semi-Pelagianism. They taught that fulfilling the law of God brings people into the → kingdom of God (§2), as the → gospel does (→ Law and Gospel), or that we may start our → faith and carry it on to the end by our own willpower. In contrast to the doctrines of hu-man nature as corrupted through original sin, of the bondage of the will, and of predestination (so Lu-ther and John → Calvin), the Council of → Trent taught the freedom of the will, with justification re-quiring one's "giving free assent to and cooperating with . . . grace" (N. P. Tanner, 2.762; DH 1525). The Reformed side thus accused it of synergism. In post-Reformation Roman Catholic systems of grace, → Molinism went the furthest in emphasizing the free-dom of the will, illustrating it in the picture of two horses that together pull a ship.

Synergism in the narrower sense arose among Philippists in the 16th and 17th centuries (→ Crypto-Calvinism), departing from Luther's view of the position of humans in the process of conversion. Philipp → Melanchthon (1497-1560) at first agreed with Luther's *Bondage of the Will* that we are wholly passive in justification and divine → predestination (§3). He later gave up this position, however, be-cause it seemed to him to lead to → fatalism and moral laxity. Following → Erasmus (1469?-1536), Melanchthon understood free will as our ability to turn to grace. He spoke of three factors that work together in the event of conversion: the → Word of

God (§3), which calls to salvation; the → Holy Spirit (§2), who moves us to faith; and the Yes of the human will. God draws, but he draws those who are willing; he effects salvation if the free will is in agreement or does not reject it.

J. Pfeffinger (1493-1573) and V. Strigel (1524-69) systematized this position in the sense of three independent causes. It is as though *I would sit* next to a rich man in an inn, and *he would give* a pound, and *I would give* a penny.

The Gnesio-Lutherans N. Amsdorf (1483-1565) and M. Flacius (1520-75), however, taught the pure doctrine of Luther (→ Luther's Theology 4.4) in both form and content. They would not reject the concept of the bondage of the will, the original corruption of human nature, or predestination. In this connection Flacius accused the theologians he criticized for being synergists. He argued that the human being reacts to his or her justification like a stone or a block of wood. The person is thus wholly passive and, even worse, is a child of the → devil, defined by original sin and thus an enemy of God. There is no free will to salvation; we are free only to sin. Grace must convert not only the passive and neutral but also the one who opposes. The high point of this bitter synergistic controversy, which took place also in the political arena, was reached in the Weimar Disputation (August 1560) between Flacius and Strigel, which, despite the superior dialectical ability of Flacius, remained unresolved.

The → Formula of Concord repudiates the synergism of the Philippists. According to it, we do not have the capability to turn ourselves to grace. Yet it does not accept the formulation of Flacius that original sin is the nature or the essence of the human being. Through and in the working of grace, however, one can be capable of one's own consent of the will. The Formula of Concord, however, to a large extent followed Melanchthon's position on predestination, which meant that the problem of synergism remained basically unresolved.

4. Methodism

For John → Wesley (1703-91; → Methodism 3; Methodist Church 3.2), grace or faith and works, as well as God's rule and human freedom, belong unconditionally together. In God's work of → reconciliation with us in Christ, we participate with our own efforts (repentance, faith, and conversion), and in our salvation we are always on the way of increasing knowledge (holy life, growth, and maturity of faith). Methodist "synergism" is grounded in the conviction that in the justification begun in the new birth (the beginning of the divine work), there will have to be

"appropriate fruits." In the process of personal salvation, whose goal is "complete → sanctification" through the cooperation between God and the human being, the attained salvation is to be visibly and controllably preserved and developed.

In the same way, the divine and human interaction in one's lifestyle may represent and attest to the presence of the grace of God, Christ, and the Spirit. Good works are not the basis of salvation, but they bear witness that believers are chosen by God (→ Assurance of Salvation). A person, however, can admittedly refuse or turn away from the "received grace." This grace therefore needs constant appropriation, for which Methodism has developed rules. The task of concretely developing faith (sanctification) in every area of human life (the "social confession") has given to Methodist "synergism" the characteristic feature of sociopolitical activism.

5. Ecumenical Relations

In the ecumenical discussion, standpoints on the doctrine of justification have come much closer together (→ Ecumenical Dialogue). In the document *Justification by Faith* (1985), a statement from U.S. Lutheran–Roman Catholic dialogues, extensive convergences on the question of justification were attained. According to the statement under the heading "The condemnations . . . which no longer apply to our partner today" (K. Lehmann and W. Pannenberg, 168-74), "the condemnatory pronouncements formulated in the sixteenth-century Confessions about the doctrine, form, and practice of the Roman Catholic Church are no longer applicable to today's partner" (p. 168). Cooperation, therefore, "cannot be a matter of controversy, if it means that in faith the heart is involved, when the Word touches it and faith is created" (p. 182). This position was affirmed officially by the churches in the signing of the → Joint Declaration on the Doctrine of Justification (1999) between the → Roman Catholic Church and the → Lutheran World Federation, in which both sides declared that "a consensus in basic truths of the doctrine of justification exists between Lutherans and Catholics," and that the remaining differences "do not destroy the consensus regarding the basic truths" (§40).

In Orthodox theology, the doctrine of *synergeia* is not placed in the framework of the idea of human merits. Rather, it appears in the context of our free involvement in God's work of salvation and our cooperation in the process of the divinization *(theōsis)* of humanity. Thus the concepts of justification and of → theosis show themselves to be open to each other.

In the ecumenical movement the cooperation of

God and human beings relates to our concern to make the → unity (§1) of the church visible as God has given it (→ Ecumenism, Ecumenical Movement). In addition, it relates to the permanent task of doing justice, notwithstanding a one-dimensional understanding of → salvation (§7), to the social reference of the gospel and the → discipleship of Christ in the workaday "crisis scenario" of the world.

→ Economic Ethics; Liberation Theology; Political Theology 2; Social Ethics

Bibliography: H. G. Anderson, T. A. Murphy, and J. A. Burgess, eds., *Justification by Faith* (Minneapolis, 1985) esp. 15-74 • P. Ferry, "Confessionalization and Popular Preaching: Sermons against Synergism in Reformation Saxony," *SCJ* 28 (1997) 1143-66 • R. Flogaus, "Einig in Sachen Theosis und Synergie," *KuD* 42 (1996) 225-43 • W. Klaiber, *Wo Leben wieder Leben ist* (Stuttgart, 1984) • K. Lehmann and W. Pannenberg, eds., *The Condemnations of the Reformation Era: Do They Still Divide?* (Minneapolis, 1990) • The Lutheran World Federation and The Roman Catholic Church, *Joint Declaration on the Doctrine of Justification* (Grand Rapids, 2000) • M. D. Meeks, ed., *What Should Methodists Teach? Wesleyan Tradition and Modern Diversity* (Nashville, 1990) • C. Moeller and G. Philips, *The Theology of Grace and the Oecumenical Movement* (London, 1961) • E. Mühlenberg, "Synergia and Justification by Faith," *Discord, Dialogue, and Concord: Studies in the Lutheran Reformation's Formula of Concord* (ed. L. W. Spitz and W. Lohff; Philadelphia, 1977) 15-37; idem, "Synergism in Gregory of Nyssa," *ZNW* 68 (1977) 93-122 • T. Nikolaou, "Participation in the Mystery of the Church," *GOTR* 28 (1983) 255-76 • O. H. Pesch and A. Peters, *Einführung in die Lehre von Gnade und Rechtfertigung* (3d ed.; Darmstadt, 1994) • O. Ritschl, *Dogmengeschichte des Protestantismus* (vol. 2/1; Leipzig, 1912) • U. Swarat, J. Oeldemann, and D. Heller, eds., *Von Gott angenommen–in Christus verwandelt. Die Rechtfertigungslehre im multilateralen ökumenischen Dialog* (Frankfurt, 2006) • N. P. Tanner, ed., *Decrees of the Ecumenical Councils* (2 vols.; Washington, D.C., 1990) • J. Wesley, "On Working Out Our Own Salvation," *Wesley's Works* (3d ed.; vol. 6; Kansas City, Mo., 1979) 506-13.

Peter Neuner

Synod

1. Term

The word "synod" (Gk. *synodos,* "on the way together") was common already in classical Greek. In the apocryphal NT it occurs in *Prot. Jas.* 15.1 and is parallel to → "synagogue." As a term originally with the same meaning as "councils," it has gained currency since the → Reformation. It refers to church bodies that meet relatively regularly and that, through duly authorized members, advise the church on matters of → faith, order, and government. In many church constitutions today, synods are collegial authorities by which members of the community consider the legal affairs of their union and thus help to share in its leadership (H. Frost, 173-74).

We must distinguish between synods of ordained ministers (bishops or clergy) and synods in which lay members have an equal say (→ Clergy and Laity 4). We must also distinguish between synods that give counsel to a higher authority (e.g., synods in the territorial churches or Roman Catholic bishops) and synods that have a binding right of decision in their own domain, and between synods of the whole → church and synods at a lesser level (diocesan or deanery synods).

2. Historical Presuppositions

The historical and theological presupposition for the formation of synods in the Reformation churches was not so much the concept of the priesthood of all believers (→ Priest, Priesthood, 4) but the doctrine of the Reformed ministry and the corresponding understanding of → church discipline. In the 19th century the older Reformed doctrine was partially overshadowed by the thought that all members of the church should be represented on the synods (→ Church Government 5.1). A typical feature of this view, which rests on a secular democratic principle (→ Democracy; Secularization), is that all parties should take part in elections.

During the → church struggle in Germany, one of the distinctive concerns was that, in both theory and practice, there should be a purely spiritual self-understanding of the synod that did not give way to the principle of the sharing of power or to the power of the majority.

Members of a synod are not summoned to promote their own opinion at any cost. Rather, all of them, according to their vows, should stand in the service of their one Lord (G. W. Heinemann, 669).

3. Place in Denominations

3.1. *Roman Catholic Church*

The 1983 → CIC defined the bishops' synod as a gathering that is selected to help the → pope to preserve and promote the faith, morals, and discipline of the church in its work in the world (cans. 342-48). Diocesan synods, according to 1983 CIC 460-68, exist to give advice to bishops (→ Diocese), being called by him and consisting of leading clergy and laity. Bishops must approve of and publish resolutions of the synod (can. 466), though they also determine what will be the items on the agenda.

3.2. *Orthodox Church*

Synods have always had the highest standing in the → Orthodox Church. The bishops of an autocephalous church (→ Autocephaly) together form the Holy Synod of the → hierarchy, which is responsible for deciding all basic questions. The president is the chief bishop, the "first among equals." Ongoing matters are left to the permanent synod, a council of bishops.

For many years a Holy and Great Council (Synod) has been planned that would unite all the Orthodox churches (→ Pan-Orthodox Conferences) and that would give advice on an issue that has not yet been solved, namely, what part the laity should play in the life and leadership of the church.

3.3. *Reformed Churches*

The first Reformed synod took place in Paris in 1559 and adopted the Gallican Confession. Since that time the synodical principle has been a distinctive feature of the → Reformed churches. Reformed theology lays special emphasis on the fact that synods find a basis in both → Christology and pneumatology (→ Holy Spirit). It stands by the principle that the participation of the laity makes a synod a *collegium qualificatum* (according to the Duisburg general synod of 1610).

The Church of Scotland set up provincial synods in 1562; in 1579 it divided the synods into presbyteries and placed congregations under a kirk session. But the later unions of 1900 and 1929 did not adhere to this system, and the synods have since been abolished. From the 16th century the Reformed churches in the Netherlands have had a synodical constitution with an emphasis on regional gatherings (the "classes"). The different models of

the Reformed type of synodical government in Europe have spread to the Reformed churches in North America, Latin America, Asia, Africa, and the Pacific countries.

An important principle is that after each session of the synod the tasks of leadership should be placed for the time being in the hands of a moderator, who has usually presided over the synod and who is responsible for carrying out what the synod has decided. Even where Reformed churches have bishops, as in Hungary, the bishops simply have the office of presiding over synods and carrying out their wishes.

During the German church struggle the structures of the church were profoundly altered by political inroads, and the so-called free churches were called upon to claim that to them alone had been given the true leadership of the church. The Confessing Synods (→ Confessing Church) renewed the older Reformed tradition, and in spite of (or perhaps because of) their formally revolutionary approach, they exerted a great influence on the reconsideration of the nature of the synod in the time that followed (Frost, 495-97).

3.4. *Lutheran Churches*

Up to 1918 the German → Lutheran churches did not entrust their leadership to synods. Where synods existed (as clergy gatherings) they simply served to give advice to the governments of the churches (→ Church Government 2.2).

During the 19th century a synodical system developed in the American Lutheran churches (Ohio Synod in 1818, Buffalo Synod in 1845, Missouri Synod in 1847, etc.). In these we find a combination of episcopalianism and → congregationalism. For the time being, Lutherans living in the land of the Reformation failed to see the advantages of this system. A synodical system came only after the breakup of the territorial system.

Today a synodical episcopate has become the norm in → Lutheranism. The main features are that the bishop is appointed for life by the synod, though he can also be recalled for unworthy ethical or doctrinal conduct or for sickness. The bishop has responsibility for → visitation, for → ordination, and for scriptural teaching and → proclamation. He serves as a pastor of pastors, promotes the fellowship of the congregations in their life and work, and represents the congregations. The synod has the right of legislation, and the president or a special body has the task of implementing the decisions made. The bishop can veto these decisions and those of a consistory set up by the synod. Either he or an authority set by the synod both summons and conducts it. Almost all the Lutheran churches have accepted this arrangement of an episcopal leader and a synod composed of clergy and laity.

3.5. *Anglican Communion*

The worldwide → Anglican Communion looks for leadership, not to a synod, but to the Lambeth Conferences, though these have no legislative authority. Along with the Lambeth Conference, an Anglican Consultative Conference has also been meeting every two years since 1971, and this body includes the laity. Not being related to the state, Anglican churches outside England have more easily been able to develop synodical forms of leadership.

The Church of England has its own synodical system (→ Church 3.3.3). From early times the provincial synods (or "convocations") of Canterbury and York played a role in the church (except for over a hundred years after 1717, when they were never summoned). The task of the convocations is to give advice on doctrine and practice. In addition, there are also diocesan, deanery, and congregational synods to discuss various matters. From 1919 to 1969 the whole church also set up a national synod — the Church Assembly — that could offer proposals that Parliament could either accept or reject, but not amend, and that were then passed on for approval by the Crown. In 1970 a General Synod adopted the tasks of the Church Assembly, and though the convocations still meet, the General Synod has taken over most of their tasks. This synod consists of the House of Bishops, the House of Clergy, and the House of Laity. In matters relating to doctrine, worship, or the sacraments, it can discuss only the version accepted by the House of Bishops.

3.6. *Free Churches*

The → free churches have always valued the laity and given them a share in leadership. For reasons of distinction from the mainline churches, however, they do not call their governing systems synods, even though they are structurally the same. Under the influence of Congregationalism the governing bodies are usually called Assemblies or Conferences. Many of the younger churches also follow a free-church structure (→ Third World 2). The various → national councils of churches, as well as the → Christian Conference of Asia, are supreme ecumenical governing bodies that, even more strongly than the classic synods in Europe, foster interdenominational → dialogue and develop their own conference theology (by means of proposals, consensus texts, and efforts to achieve reception).

4. Synods in Church Unions

Synods have played a part in all church unions (→ Union) since the 19th century. When it was desired to unite the Lutherans and the Reformed in Germany, synods were called at Idstein for Nassau in 1817, at Kaiserlauten for the Palatinate in 1818, and at Berlin for Prussia in 1846. Constitutionally, all the union churches are governed by synods made up of both clergy and laity. A model that looks even beyond the sphere of union may be found in the Rhenish-Westphalian constitution of 1835, which set up a government by presbytery and synod at every level from the congregation to the church as a whole.

In connection with the many efforts toward unity in German Protestantism in the 19th century, a call came for a national synod, which did not materialize. The German Protestant Church Alliance did not have a governing synod between 1922 and 1933, but the churches and other societies found a means to assemble at the Protestant church conferences. The Lutherans objected to the use of the word "synod" on the ground that a synod can be summoned only by a confessionally united church and not by a union of confessionally disunited churches. Though the national synod (1933) that was dominated by the → German Christians had a devastating effect, the Evangelische Kirche in Deutschland (EKD, Evangelical Church in Germany) set up a synod after 1945, and the United Evangelical Lutheran Church is also governed by a synod. The → Reformed Alliance expresses its own ecclesiological self-understanding by not using "synod" for its synodical form of leadership, referring instead to a Chief Assembly.

Currently, the Synod of the EKD discusses issues affecting the church and passes resolutions on them. It has nine permanent committees, which include "Scripture and the Proclamation of the Gospel," "Social Services, Mission, and Ecumenical Relations," "Education and Young People," and "The Environment." Members serve six-year terms on the Synod, which convenes yearly for a session lasting several days.

5. Problems in the Theology of the Church

During recent decades the whole oikoumene has reached a virtual consensus that synods are the proper way to rule the churches, or should at least share in that rule. Even churches based on the principle of a → hierarchy must increasingly give ear to the demand for synodical participation. Churches that have had synods for generations should also pay attention to the problems of theology and ecclesiology that call for attention if there is to be further development of the synodical principle.

5.1. *Synod and Ministry*

Everyone who is part of a synod holds a special office in the church. When synods meet, it must be recalled how this office relates to the other offices in the church, especially the office of proclaiming the Word and administering the → sacraments. The answer to this question has ramifications for the mode of the calling of synods (e.g., the selection of members) and for basic matters of the order of synods (who will preside, how to find consensus, how to put decisions into effect). Solutions must be sought that, despite similarities to parliamentary gatherings, demonstrate that synods are a special phenomenon of the liturgical fellowship of the church.

5.2. Synod and Law

In practice, legislating for the church is of great importance in synods (→ Church Law 5). Though synods may bear responsibility for legislation in many different ways, one must recall that the united will of the church, which comes to expression in a resolution by a synod, must not thrust the church into an unevangelical legalism or rob Christians of the → freedom (§2.9) that is given by the gospel. Though there will be many forces working to secure compliance, the fact remains that the law of the church is a spiritual law, a law of love (→ Church Law 3).

5.3. Synod and Doctrine

Among the early Reformation insights was that of M. → Luther (1483-1546; → Luther's Theology) that decisions on doctrinal questions should be made by the Christian community itself (*LW* 39.305-14). If the congregations give synods the task of deciding on necessary doctrinal developments or opening up new questions, one must recall that every synod is subject to Holy Scripture as its "standardizing norm" (*norma normans;* → Teaching Office 2). Strict adherence to this basic rule is very difficult in some of the doctrinal decisions that must be taken today. We must seek solutions that, in spite of their unavoidable reference to contemporary challenges, demonstrate that the doctrine of each individual church pays attention to the tradition of the whole church and seeks both ecumenical fellowship and consensus.

Bibliography: H. Frost, *Strukturprobleme evangelischer Kirchenverfassung* (Göttingen, 1972) • G. W. Heinemann, "Synode und Parlament," *EK* 4 (1971) 668-69 • P. I. Kaufman, *Church, Book, and Bishop: Conflict and Authority in Early Latin Christianity* (Boulder, Colo., 1996) • D. C. Kessler and M. Kinnamon, *Councils of Churches and the Ecumenical Vision* (Geneva, 2000) • W. Maurer, "Typen und Formen aus der Geschichte der Synode," *SThKAB* 9 (1955) 78-99 • N. Närger, *Das Synodalwahlsystem in den deutschen evangelischen Landeskirchen im 19. und 20. Jahrhundert* (Tübingen, 1988) • T. C. O'Brien, ed., "Synod," *CDWC* 739-40 •

R. C. Wiederaenders, ed., *Historical Guide to Lutheran Church Bodies of North America* (2d ed.; St. Louis, 1998).

Joachim Mehlhausen†

Synoptics

1. The Problem
2. Solutions
3. The Two-Source Theory
4. The Synoptic Gospels

1. The Problem

The first three canonical → gospels — those traditionally attributed to Matthew, Mark, and Luke — are referred to as the Synoptic gospels (from Gk. *synoptikos* = *syn* [with] + *optikos* [relating to sight]) in recognition of the marked similarities in the wording and sequence of their common material. Together these similarities, which extend to occasional verbatim agreement, suggest some sort of literary relationship. The challenge of determining the precise nature of the relationship has come to be known as the Synoptic problem (→ Literature, Biblical and Early Christian, 2).

2. Solutions

The most widely accepted solution is called the *two-source theory,* according to which Matthew and Luke used Mark as their principal source. This view originated with K. Lachman in 1835 and was later developed by such interpreters as C. G. Wilke (1838), H. J. Holtzmann (1863), and especially B. H. Streeter (1924). The two-source theory also proposes that, in addition to Mark, both Matthew and Luke used a common written source, not utilized by Mark, containing mostly Jesus' sayings in Greek — dubbed → Q, for Ger. *Quelle,* "source" — as well as their own unique source materials, whether oral or written, designated "M" and "L."

Besides the two-source theory, a variety of other proposals have been put forward. G. E. Lessing (1776) and J. G. Eichhorn (1796) argued for an *Urevangelium* written in Aramaic that was translated into Greek before undergoing various revisions, while J. G. von → Herder (1796) and J. K. L. Gieseler (1818) posited a common oral tradition eventually put into writing. F. → Schleiermacher (1817) suggested that numerous short memorabilia composed by Jesus' disciples were the ultimate basis of the three gospels. Following → Augustine, B. C. Butler (1951) maintained that Mark abridged Matthew, while Luke used both Matthew and Mark.

The main competitor to the two-source theory, however, is the *Griesbach hypothesis* (so called after a prominent advocate, J. J. Griesbach [1789]), according to which Matthew wrote first, Luke relied on Matthew, and Mark utilized both Matthew and Luke. This view still has adherents today, such as W. R. Farmer and D. L. Dungan, but has not won wide support.

3. The Two-Source Theory

Though the two-source hypothesis is not without its difficulties (e.g., those passages in which Matthew and Luke agree in their wording against Mark), four main arguments support Markan priority.

Length. Although Mark is the shortest of the three Synoptic gospels, it does not look like the work of a condenser. In almost all of the material it shares with Matthew and Luke, Mark's version is longer. It is therefore likely that Mark was written first and that Matthew and Luke omitted some of Mark's redundancies and inconsequential details.

Language. Mark's diction is often poor or conveys difficult ideas, and its style is often inelegant or awkward. By contrast, passages in Matthew and Luke usually have a better style and clearer wording; this linguistic feature favors the conclusion that Matthew and Luke improved Mark, rather than the opposite idea that Mark worsened their style.

Patterns of agreement. In cases where two of the gospels agree in their wording against the third, it is very rare for Matthew and Luke to share the wording of a Markan passage with Mark differing; Mark is therefore the probable source for the accounts.

Narrative sequence. Even the traditions common to Matthew and Luke but not found in Mark point to Mark as a source for Matthew and Luke. When Matthew and Luke preserve material in the same order, it is almost always with material that is also found in Mark, whereas non-Markan matter preserved in Matthew and Luke (e.g., the → Lord's Prayer and → Beatitudes) is almost always located in different places within their respective narratives. The best explanation of this phenomenon is that Matthew and Luke each used Mark as one of their sources but also used a different source with material that had no narrative framework, material that they inserted into the framework provided by Mark.

Aside from Markan priority, the use of Q by Matthew and Luke forms another key element of the two-source theory. By definition, Q contains non-Markan materials common to Matthew and Luke. The existence of Q is posited chiefly on the basis of the implausibility of either Matthew or Luke using the other as a source. Doubts about whether a "say-ings gospel" like Q would have been composed in early Christian circles were laid to rest with the discovery of the *Gospel of Thomas,* which comprises exclusively sayings attributed to Jesus. The precise extent and wording of Q remain unclear; the issue is complicated by two factors. First is the existence of so-called Markan overlaps — sayings that both Mark and Q contained, as seems indicated by alternate versions of the same sayings that appear twice in both Matthew and Luke (e.g., Matt. 13:12 and Luke 8:18, derived from Mark; and Matt. 25:29 and Luke 19:26, drawn from Q). Second is the possibility that some M and L passages are actually Q passages, in which case Q was utilized at times by only Matthew or only Luke (e.g., Luke 3:10-14; 7:3-6; Matt. 5:5, 7-9, 19, 21-30). Although the existence of Q is almost universally accepted, debate continues over whether supposed redactional layers of Q can be correlated with stages in the history of a Q community.

4. The Synoptic Gospels

The Gospel of Mark was likely written around the time of the first Jewish revolt against Rome (A.D. 66-70/73) in a predominantly Gentile Christian community undergoing or facing the prospect of → persecution, either in Rome or the near vicinity of Palestine (e.g., Syria). The anonymous author collected a variety of oral and written materials about Jesus, imposed a narrative framework upon them, and shaped them in accord with his theological interests, thereby inventing the gospel genre. Most of Mark's source materials appear to have come by way of oral tradition, but candidates for written sources include the group of controversy dialogues gathered in 2:1–3:6, one or two collections of miracles stories incorporated into chaps. 4–8, an apocalyptic discourse adapted in chap. 13, and a passion narrative reworked in chaps. 14–15.

The Gospel of Matthew was written within a decade or two after Mark for a predominantly Jewish community of believers who were in tension with synagogue-based Pharisaic Judaism, probably somewhere in Upper Galilee or Lower Syria. Matthew incorporates almost all of Mark's contents but revises and expands it considerably with Q and M material, most of it sayings and → parables of Jesus. Among Matthew's most notable expansions are its birth and infancy narratives (chaps. 1–2), sayings fashioned into five discourses (chaps. 5–7; 10; 13; 18; 24–25), and new material relating to Jesus' resurrection and post-Easter appearances (27:52-53, 62-66; 28:11-20). Matthew follows the general outline of Mark but, besides adding sayings material, rearranges and abridges Markan passages, improves

Mark's diction and style, corrects occasional inaccuracies, enhances the portrait of the disciples while darkening the profile of the Jewish leaders, and rewords or omits passages that imply a lack of ability or authority on Jesus' part.

The Gospel of Luke, which has its sequel in the Book of Acts, contains some of the finest Greek in the NT. Judging by its redactional changes to Mark, it was likely written for a Gentile community of Christians living in a large urban area somewhere outside Palestine, probably around the same time as Matthew (ca. A.D. 80-90). Luke incorporates only about half of Mark's contents, alternating it with Q and L material. Though Luke changes Mark less frequently than Matthew does, the kinds of alterations Luke makes resemble those of Matthew's redaction (improvements in style, rearrangement of material to suit emphasis or theme, changes in characterization, abbreviation or omission of details deemed irrelevant or uncongenial). Its major changes to Mark include the addition of infancy narratives for both → John the Baptist and → Jesus (chaps. 1–2), the inclusion of special material in 6:20–8:3, the omission of the material in Mark 6:45–8:26 and 9:41–10:12, the expansion of Jesus' journey to Jerusalem with Q and L material (9:51–19:44), and the incorporation of stories relating to Jesus' postresurrection appearances and ascension (24:13-53).

Most scholars continue to understand the Synoptics as works written in and for particular Christian communities, whose needs and challenges had a part in influencing each evangelist's particular handling of his material. Recently, however, R. Bauckham and other scholars have insisted that all of the canonical gospels were written with the intention of being circulated among and outside all the churches. Although this view has drawn needed attention to such neglected issues as ancient book production and circulation, as well as to the networks of communication linking early Christian groups, it has so far not succeeded in overturning the current paradigm.

Bibliography: R. BAUCKHAM, ed., *The Gospels for All Christians: Rethinking the Gospel Audiences* (Grand Rapids, 1998) • A. BELLIZONI, ed., *The Two-Source Hypothesis: A Critical Appraisal* (Macon, Ga., 1985) • R. A. BURRIDGE, *What Are the Gospels? A Comparison with Graeco-Roman Biography* (2d ed.; Grand Rapids, 2004) • D. L. DUNGAN, *A History of the Synoptic Problem: The Canon, the Text, the Composition, and the Interpretation of the Gospels* (New York, 1999) • W. R. FARMER, *The Synoptic Problem: A Critical Review of the Problem of the Literary Relationships between Matthew, Mark, and Luke* (New York, 1964) • H. KOESTER, *Ancient Christian Gospels: Their History and Development* (Philadelphia, 1990) • K. F. NICKLE, *The Synoptic Gospels: An Introduction* (rev. ed.; Louisville, Ky., 2001) • J. M. ROBINSON, P. HOFFMAN, and J. S. KLOPPENBORG, eds., *The Critical Edition of Q* (Minneapolis, 2000) • E. P. SANDERS and M. DAVIES, *Studying the Synoptic Gospels* (London, 1989) • R. H. STEIN, *Studying the Synoptic Gospels: Origin and Interpretation* (2d ed.; Grand Rapids, 2001).

DANIEL C. HARLOW

Syria

	1960	1980	2000
Population (1,000s):	4,561	8,704	16,126
Annual growth rate (%):	3.10	3.56	2.46

Area: 185,180 sq. km. (71,498 sq. mi.)

A.D. 2000

Population density: 87/sq. km. (226/sq. mi.)
Births / deaths: 2.92 / 0.45 per 100 population
Fertility rate: 3.58 per woman
Infant mortality rate: 28 per 1,000 live births
Life expectancy: 70.2 years (m: 67.9, f: 72.7)
Religious affiliation (%): Muslims 87.7, Christians 9.0 (Orthodox 5.8, Roman Catholics 2.2, other Christians 0.9), nonreligious 3.1, other 0.2.

1. History, Population, and Religious Communities
2. Christian Churches
3. Non-Christian Religions
4. The State and Religion

1. History, Population, and Religious Communities

Al-Jumhūrīya al-ʿArabīya al-Sūrīya, or the Syrian Arab Republic, is the northern part of the territory that, prior to the breakup of the Ottoman Empire, was called Greater Syria (Bilād al-Shām), an area that included not only modern Syria but also Lebanon, Jordan, and Palestine and Israel. The country's geographic location at the intersection of three continents has had a great effect on Syria's history. From ancient times, under Roman and Byzantine sovereignty, Syria was an important node of international trade, military activities, and religious and intellectual movements; early Christian history is firmly rooted in Syrian lands. After the Islamic conquest Syria became the political, religious, and cultural center of the Umayyad Caliphate (661-750), with its capital in Damascus, and remained under Muslim sovereignty, except in part during the period of the → Crusades in the 12th and 13th centuries. In 1516 Syria became an Ottoman province and remained so until 1920, when it became part of a French League of Nations mandate after World War I and the collapse of the Ottoman Empire. Syria achieved full political independence in April 1946, when the last French troops left its borders.

In 2005 Syria had a population of some 19 million, including about 400,000 Palestinian → refugees (according to the U.N. Relief and Works Agency for Palestinian Refugees in the Near East). The high density of population decreases gradually from the coastal areas toward the Euphrates valley and on to the arid inner countryside. Though it has often been seen as one of the peculiarities of Syria, a multiconfessional state, that the ruling family comes from a marginal Shiite group, the Alawites, it remains uncertain to what extent confessional ties of the ruling elite direct internal politics (→ Shia, Shiites). Almost 90 percent of the population is Muslim, with 74 percent Sunnis and 16 percent other Muslim groups, including Alawites (11 percent), Twelver Shiites (less than 3), Druze (1.7), Ismailis (1.0), and Yazidis (0.1). However, with the increasing number of Iraqi refugees — approximately 450,000, according to the U.N. High Commissioner for Refugees, of Christian but mostly Muslim, Shia and → Sunni, background — these figures are likely to change.

Estimates of the Christian population in 2005 varied between 6.5 and 10 percent, reflecting a slow but constant decrease because of demographic reasons, emigration, and only inconsequentially conversion. Early in the 1920s Christians amounted to about 30 percent of the population, and still 10-13 percent until the 1990s. (It is difficult to obtain exact figures or estimates, as in the 1960s the secular Ba'th Party discontinued registering confessional affiliation in census figures.) In 2005 the Greek → Orthodox Church was dominant, with approximately 37 percent of all Christians, followed by the → Oriental Orthodox churches with 23 percent, the → Uniate churches with 22 percent, and the → Nestorian Church with 2.3 percent. Ethnically, Syria is rather homogeneous: most Christians and almost all Muslims are Arabs (some 90 percent). → Kurds compose the next largest ethnic group (about 8 percent). Also present, especially in the north and northeast, are Armenians, Turks, Circassians, and a very small group of Jews.

2. Christian Churches

The diversity of Christian → denominations in Syria, 11 in all, bears witness to the divisions in the fifth and sixth centuries among the Oriental churches, which originated in Antioch, now in modern Turkey. The *millet* organization (→ Islam 2) under Ottoman rule guaranteed non-Muslim religious communities in the "territory of Islam" the status of *dhimmī*, that is, possessing religious → autonomy in questions of cult and civil law. During the four centuries of Ottoman rule, the Christian population tripled, rising to 30 percent of the population. In the 1860s, however, Syria saw some brief but violent anti-Christian riots spreading in major Syrian cities. The Ottoman reform edicts of 1839 and 1856 (the Tanzimat, or period of reform) stressed the equality of all Ottoman subjects, regardless of religious affiliation, before the law and in paying taxes, and they provided for greater representation in governmental positions and military service.

Since the → Middle Ages, but especially since the 19th century, Christians in Syria have been in close contact with Europe. Often having a relatively higher educational standing, they have played a prominent role in the process of modernization, cultural revival, and development of nationalist ideas from the 19th century onward and have occupied a strong position in trade, industry, and culture. Because of greater economic opportunities, approximately two-thirds of the Christian population live in urban centers, especially in Homs, Latakia, Damascus, and Aleppo, cities with large Christian congregations.

2.1. The *Greek Orthodox Church* is the largest and oldest Christian denomination, with about 503,000 members (figures throughout are from the period 2000-2005), and stands under the → patriarch of Antioch and All the East, who resides in Damascus. There are six dioceses (Damascus, Homs, Hama, Latakia, Aleppo, and Hauran); the largest congregation is in Latakia. The origins of the church go back to the schism between the churches of the East and the West (1054), although the actual division between the Eastern and Western churches is much older (→ Heresies and Schisms 3). Following ancient Byzantine practice, the adherents of the church refer to themselves as *rūmī*, or Roman Orthodox. Since the latter part of the 19th century, patriarchs of Antioch have been exclusively Arab, rather than Greek, as had previously been the case.

2.2. *Oriental Orthodox churches* are represented by the → Armenian Apostolic Church, whose three dioceses in Syria are attached with the catholicos in Echmiadzin, Armenia, and in Sis-Antelias, Lebanon (figures on adherents vary between 112,000 and 160,000), and the → Syrian Orthodox (Jacobite)

Church (89,000 adherents), whose patriarch has resided in Damascus since 1959. In 2000 in a move to avoid nationalist overtones, the Holy Synod of the church changed its name to the Syriac Orthodox Church.

2.3. Among the so-called → *Uniate churches,* with obedience to Rome, the largest group is the → Melchites (also called the Greek Catholic Church), with between 118,000 and 240,000 adherents. Others are the Maronites (estimates vary between 28,000 and 60,000 adherents), who today are found mainly in Lebanon, but also in Syria, with a large congregation in Aleppo; the Armenian Catholic Church (25,000-30,000 adherents), with its catholicos in Beirut; the Syrian Catholic Church (22,000 adherents), with its patriarch in Lebanon; and since 1952 the Uniate Assyrian Church, or Chaldean Church (ca. 22,000 adherents).

2.4. The *Nestorian Church* (the Holy Apostolic Catholic Assyrian Church of the East) in Syria consists mostly of Christians who fled Iraq, from around Mosul, after the persecution and massacres of the 1930s.

2.5. Smaller Christian groups include the → *Roman Catholic Church* and the many *Protestant groups.* The latter, products of 19th-century Anglo-American → missionary work, are organized mainly as the Union of Armenian Evangelical Churches and the National Evangelical Synod of Syria.

2.6. Historically among the churches, which differ significantly in → liturgy, canonical regulations, leadership, and language (Syriac and Aramaic are used as the liturgical language of various Syriac denominations), tensions have developed, partly because of the opposition of the Byzantine church to the Crusaders. Yet all the churches belong to the → Middle East Council of Churches (MECC), having joined at the Beirut general meeting of 1990. The MECC is concerned with ecumenical relations among the churches of the Middle East.

3. Non-Christian Religions

3.1. Among the *Muslims* there is less confessional division. As carriers of the Ottoman heritage, in which Sunni Islam was the state religion, the Sunnis are the largest segment. They are not, however, a socially homogeneous group covering geographically the entire country, with the exception of regions in which Alawites, Druze, and Ismailis originally resided.

While the Ismailis do not play any distinctive role in Syria, the Alawites (official name Nuṣairī), who dwell in the Nuṣairīyah Mountains of northwest Syria, constitute the majority of the population in the governorate of Latakia. After centuries without any political influence, today they occupy the leading positions of power in the country (see 4). Historically isolated and poor, the Alawites split in the ninth century from Shia Islam, but as they adopted elements of other religions in their theology, orthodox Muslims have tended to regard them as heretics.

3.2. The *Druze,* who live mostly in the Hauran Mountains, are another esoteric sect, emerging in the 11th century from the Ismailis. They are officially considered a Muslim sect, but they differ widely from orthodox Islam on matters of religious thought, doctrine, and practice. Druze play an important political role in → Lebanon (§3), but in Syria they have no special significance.

3.3. The small *Jewish community* is found for the most part in Damascus and Aleppo. In 1943 it numbered some 30,000, but today, through emigration resulting from ongoing conflicts in the Middle East, it has shrunk to less than 4,000 (→ Judaism).

4. The State and Religion

4.1. Although it is the dominant religion, Islam is not a state religion in modern Syria. The Syrian state observes a clear separation between state and religious institutions, although the state oversees the Muslim cult through the *awqāf* (religious endowment) minister, head of a special department. Constitutionally, all citizens are equal before the law and have full → religious liberty, though the demographic dominance of Muslims is reflected in an additional clause stating that the president of the republic must be a Muslim and that one of the main sources of Syrian legislation is Islamic jurisprudence. In matters of family law, however, except for inheritance, Christians, Jews, and Druze follow their respective canonical laws. Based on a certain understanding of religious proportion, Christians find representation among cabinet ministers, in the army, and in the Ba'th Party.

The constitution gives extraordinary powers to the president, who from 1971 to 2000 was Ḥāfiẓ al-'Asad, an Alawite. Upon his death he was succeeded by his son, Bashār al-'Asad. Officially a republic, Syria in fact is an authoritarian regime. The decisive political factor in Syria today is the Ba'thist military and security forces.

4.2. Since the military coup d'état of 1963, the laicist Arab Socialist Resurrection Party (Ba'th Party) has been in power. The Greek Orthodox Syrian Michel Aflaq (1910-89), who founded the party in 1947, conceived it as an avant-garde group that would initiate a comprehensive nationalization program, in accordance with its political goals of Arab unity, → freedom, and → socialism.

4.3. The Syrian government today maintains good relations with minorities, especially Christians. In contrast, it rigorously persecutes militant Muslim movements that are opposed to its secular program (→ Secularization) or to what it perceives as an Alawite regime. The bombing of the city of Hama in February 1982, where Sunni Muslim Brotherhood militants were entrenched, marked a turning point in the state's rigorous persecution of militant Muslims who are active inside Syria.

With the spread of global Muslim → fundamentalism, the secular Syrian state has taken a strong stand against radical religious movements, while at the same time, for regional strategic reasons, Syria became a strong supporter of the Lebanese Hezbollah (Arab. *Ḥizb Allāh,* "Party of God"), a radical Shiite movement and an ally of Iran. In addition, the Syrian state has of late been encouraging a variety of state-sponsored clerics and Muslim organizations with a conservative religious profile.

The so-called Damascus spring (July 2000–February 2001), triggered by the inauguration of the young president Bashar al-Asad and the promise of greater economic liberalization and political reform, did not lead to significant changes.

4.4. Although not involved directly, Syria since the 1990s has found itself in the midst of regional political upheavals that have strong religious overtones. A series of drastic developments has negatively affected the previously decisive political weight that Syria exercised in the region. Most significant among these developments are the end of the Lebanese civil war through the Taif Accord of October 1989 and the ending in March 2005 of Syria's 30-year presence in Lebanon; the unresolved conflict between Palestine and Israel and the series of hitherto failed peace talks, from which Syria has been excluded since 2000; and the American-led wars against Syria's neighbor Iraq (supported by Syria in 1991 as part of a Western-Arab alliance but opposed by Syria in 2003). All of these events, along with the hitherto unsuccessful internal reform efforts, have caused severe internal and external pressure on the government. Internationally, Syria has been greatly isolated, despite its efforts and collaboration with Western countries to counter militant Islamism after the events of September 11, 2001, and to deal with internal challenges by Islamic opposition groups and secular critics alike.

Bibliography: R. T. Antoun and D. Quataert, eds., *Syria: Society, Culture, and Polity* (Albany, N.Y., 1991) • R. B. Betts, *Christians in the Arab East: A Political Study* (rev. ed.; Atlanta, 1978) • A. Böttcher, *Syrische Religionspolitik unter Asad* (Freiburg, 1998) • K. Cragg, *The Arab Christian: A History in the Middle East* (Louisville, Ky., 1991) • N. van Dam, *The Struggle for Power in Syria: Politics and Society under Asad and the Ba'th Party* (3d ed.; London, 1996) • P. Fargues, "The Arab Christians of the Middle East: A Demographic Perspective," *Christian Communities in the Arab Middle East: The Challenge of the Future* (ed. A. Pacini; Oxford, 1998) 48-66 • R. M. Haddad, *Syrian Christians in Muslim Society: An Interpretation* (Westport, Conn., 1981; orig. pub., 1970) • A. Hourani, *Syria and Lebanon: A Political Essay* (London, 1946) • E. Kienle, ed., *Contemporary Syria: Liberalization between Cold War and Cold Peace* (New York, 1994) • A. Pacini, *Les communautés chrétiennes dans le monde musulman arabe* (Beirut, 1997) 59-78 • R. G. Rabil, *Syria, the United States, and the War on Terror in the Middle East* (Westport, Conn., 2006) • P. Seale, *Asad of Syria: The Struggle for the Middle East* (Berkeley, Calif., 1989).

Nadia Al-Bagdadi

Syrian Orthodox Church

1. History
2. Faith and Worship
3. Ecumenical Relations

1. History

The Syrian Orthodox Church of Antioch, sometimes referred to as the Syriac Orthodox Church, one of the → Oriental Orthodox family of Eastern churches, traces its history back to the see established by the apostle → Peter in Antioch. Located in the valley of the Orontes River, → Antioch served as a vital crossroads of the Euphrates and the Mediterranean and was an important center of international trade and culture. The Patriarchate of Antioch claims the greatest antiquity of all the churches of Christendom. The Acts of the Apostles (11:26) confirms that the disciples of Christ were first called Christians in Antioch. According to ancient tradition, Peter, chief of the apostles, established the Holy See of Antioch and became the first Patriarch of Antioch and All the East, presiding over the see from A.D. 33 to 40, prior to his departure for the west. The Patriarchate of Antioch held ecclesiastical authority over all the territory between the Mediterranean Sea and the Persian Gulf, this jurisdiction being confirmed by both the Council of → Nicaea (325) and the Council of Constantinople

(381). This authority was later to extend even as far as India by the church's → missionary endeavors. By the tenth century, the patriarchate held ecclesiastical authority over 20 metropolitanates and more than 100 bishoprics.

1.1. Around the beginning of the fourth century, because of administrational difficulties stemming from the size of the Antiochene Patriarchate, the Catholicate of the East was established at Seleucia-Ctesiphon, about 30 km. (20 mi.) southeast of modern Baghdad, as a Patriarchal Vicariate to minister to the needs of the faithful of the bishoprics within the Persian Empire and Iraq. This catholicate eventually fell victim to political → persecution at the hands of the Persian emperors and came under the jurisdictional control of the → Nestorian church. In 559 Ahudemmeh was elevated to the office of metropolitan of the East, establishing a new catholicate that remained until the death of Catholicos Behnam IV in 1859, when the jurisdiction was abolished by the Holy Synod of the church. Among the sites of this catholicate were the Iraqi cities of Tikrit and Mosul, as well as the neighboring Monastery of St. Matthew. In 1964 His Holiness Patriarch Ignatius Yacoub III (1957-80) granted formal patriarchal approval for a Catholicate of the East in India.

The Syrian Orthodox Church participated in the ecumenical councils of Nicaea (325), Constantinople (381), and → Ephesus (431) and fully accepted the teachings professed by these councils. However, the church rejected the decisions of the Council of → Chalcedon (451), specifically concerning the council's profession of two separate and distinct natures in Christ. Because of this disagreement and also because of political suppression, the Syrian Orthodox Church of Antioch suffered significant persecution and hardship.

The city of Edessa (modern Urfa, Turkey) was an important center of Syrian Orthodoxy in the early centuries of the church. The capital of an independent kingdom until 214, it served as a center for early Syriac-speaking Christianity and culture. A site of early church martyrs and a center of strong opposition to the Christology of the Council of Chalcedon, it remained a metropolitan see of the Syrian Orthodox Church until the early 20th century.

1.2. In 518 Patriarch Severus of Antioch (d. 538) was forced into exile and established his residence in Egypt, where he labored to keep the Syrian Church of Antioch alive. By 542 only three bishops remained free to serve the needs of the church. During this extremely critical period, a dedicated and reli-

gious monk of the church, Jacob Baradaeus (ca. 500-578), visited Constantinople and won the support of Empress Theodora, herself believed to have been the daughter of a priest of the Syrian church. She in turn extended to him the protection of the royal throne. Jacob was now consecrated as a general metropolitan by Patriarch Theodosius, Coptic pope and patriarch of Alexandria, and was authorized to strengthen and restore the persecuted churches of the patriarchates of both Antioch and Alexandria. Motivated by tremendous Christian zeal, Jacob, assisted by three fellow bishops, visited the faithful throughout the entire Middle East, Asia Minor, and even Ethiopia, rebuilding and expanding the church. Because of the many efforts of Jacob to preserve and strengthen the church, the Syrian Orthodox Church has been and is often referred to as the Syrian Jacobite Church.

Following the exile of Patriarch Severus, the Syrian Orthodox Patriarchate moved its headquarters to various locations, including the Monastery of St. Barsauma, near Malatya, Turkey, and to Diyarbakir, also in Turkey. Eventually, the see was established at the Za'faran Monastery, near Mardin, Turkey. In 1933 it was relocated to Homs, Syria, where it remained until 1959, when the patriarchate was transferred to Damascus.

On the eve of the Muslim conquest of the Middle East, the Syrian Orthodox Church of Antioch was once again a victim of persecution at the hands of the Byzantines. Constantinople recognized and approved of only the Byzantine (Melchite) patriarch of Antioch. In his *History of Eastern Christianity,* A. S. Atiya states that "the Jacobites under Muslim rule attained a degree of religious enfranchisement they had never had with their Byzantine co-religionists" (p. 193). A spirit of religious tolerance and justice also characterized the early years of Muslim occupation. Indeed, under both the Umayyad (661-750) and Abbasid (750-1258) caliphates, Syrian Orthodox enjoyed positions of great influence and prestige as private tutors, advisers, and physicians to various caliphs. During this period the Arabs profited from the vast cultural achievements and learning of the Syrian Church of Antioch. The Fathers of the Syrian church, knowledgeable in both classical Greek and Arabic, in addition to Syriac, provided the Arabs with the first Arabic translations of the wisdom of the ancient Greeks in such areas as astronomy, mathematics, medicine, and philosophy. Following the → Crusades, however, Islamic religious → tolerance in general gave way to alienation and even open persecution. This situation was further aggravated by the Mongol invasions, which brought devastation to the Syrian Orthodox Church in much of eastern Turkey, Iraq, and northern Syria.

1.3. By the 13th century, the Syrian Orthodox Church of Antioch numbered approximately 20,000 parishes, in addition to hundreds of monasteries and convents, especially in the region of southeastern Turkey known as Tur 'Abdin. The church had likewise established a history of great educational and cultural institutions, including the famous schools of Antioch, Nusaybin, and Edessa. The Syrian Orthodox Church provided the world with eminent scholars in such fields as astronomy, law, literature, medicine, music, philosophy, and theology. Among the church's foremost scholars are such individuals as Ephraem Syrus (d. 373), Jacob of Sarug (d. 521), Philoxenus of Mabbug (d. 523), Jacob of Edessa (d. 708), Moses bar Kepha (d. 903), Dionysius bar Salibi (d. 1171), and Gregorius Bar Hebraeus (d. 1286). The tragedies and difficulties mentioned in the previous paragraph brought to a sad end the growth and cultural achievements of the Syrian church.

The following years were further aggravated by divisions resulting from both internal strife and missionary endeavors among the faithful of the Syrian Orthodox Church, first by Roman Catholic sources and later, to a lesser degree, by Protestant missionaries. By 1783 a permanent line of Syrian Catholic patriarchs had been established and officially recognized by Rome. By the end of the 19th century, a number of Protestant missionary schools were active in areas of significant Syrian Orthodox population. During this same period Syrian Orthodox faced persecution at the hands of local Ottoman authorities and Kurdish tribal leaders. This tragic situation continued into the early 20th century, resulting during these years in the massacre of an estimated quarter of a million faithful, with others being forced to flee as refugees into various parts of the Middle East and elsewhere.

1.4. Since 1980 the Syrian Orthodox Church of Antioch has been under the spiritual direction of His Holiness Moran Mor Ignatius Zakka I Iwas, the 121st Patriarch of Antioch and All the East and the supreme head of the Universal Syrian Orthodox Church. The church numbers approximately three million faithful, who reside principally in the Middle East, India, Europe, and the Americas, with growing communities in both Australia and New Zealand. The church operates parochial schools, theological seminaries, hospitals, and orphanages in various locations.

2. Faith and Worship

2.1. The basic beliefs of the Syrian Orthodox Church of Antioch are established on Holy Scripture and are embodied in the → Niceno-Constantinopolitan Creed. As noted previously, the church professes the faith of the first three ecumenical councils. The Council of Nicaea condemned → Arianism and declared that Jesus Christ, the Son of God, is consubstantial with the Father. The Council of Constantinople upheld the divinity of the → Holy Spirit, while that of Ephesus both condemned Nestorianism, which held that there were two distinct persons in Christ, a human and a divine, and upheld the Virgin Mary as truly the mother of God (→ Mary in the New Testament).

Syrian Orthodox profess Mary to be truly the bearer of God *(Yoldath Aloho),* having carried Jesus in her womb and having given birth to Christ, God truly incarnate. The church teaches that Mary remained a virgin her entire earthly life and will remain so forever but that she was born with the sin of Adam and Eve, being purified from all sin by the Holy Spirit at the moment of Christ's → incarnation.

2.2. The church likewise rejected the → Monophysite teaching of Eutyches (d. 454), which affirmed one nature in Christ, but only one of divinity, not humanity. On the contrary, Syrian Orthodox believe that Christ is of one nature, but being, as expressed by → Cyril of Alexandria (d. 444), fully divine and fully human in the unique oneness of his person and nature, without mixture, diminution, or confusion.

Syrian Orthodox faithful also believe that Jesus Christ entrusted the Holy Church to the care and fatherly administration of the → apostles and, most specifically, to Peter, the chief of the apostles. The church accepts the tradition of apostolic succession and looks upon the Syrian Orthodox Patriarch of Antioch and All the East as the true successor of Peter, the first patriarch of the Holy See of Antioch, acknowledging Peter's successors to the throne of the Holy See of Antioch as the supreme head of the Universal Syrian Orthodox Church. Since the late 13th century, these successors have been given the name "Ignatius," in addition to their name of episcopal consecration, in remembrance of Ignatius of Antioch, martyred about 107, the third successor to the patriarchal throne.

2.3. The Syrian Orthodox Church practices the seven → sacraments of → baptism, chrismation, the Holy → Eucharist, repentance (→ Penitence), → marriage, holy orders, and → anointing of the sick. At baptism, the Syrian Orthodox Church places the one to be baptized into the water of the font and pours the baptismal water over the candidate three times in the name of the Holy Trinity. The baptismal font is often referred to by the church as both the womb, in that in it the candidate is born to a new life, and the tomb, referring to Christ's tomb, through which Jesus passed from death to life. To Syrian Orthodox, baptism is the mystery of the second birth by water and the Holy Spirit for the washing away of sin and the endowment with the life of grace and the inheritance of everlasting life and the → kingdom of God. By baptism, one becomes a member of Christ's body, the church.

Chrismation and the Holy Eucharist are immediately administered to the new Syrian Orthodox Christian following the candidate's baptism. Concerning the Holy Eucharist, given under both species to the faithful, Syrian Orthodox believe that the bread and wine of the Holy Liturgy truly become the body and blood of Christ during the consecratory portion of the liturgy, though remaining under the appearance of bread and wine.

The official liturgical language of the church is classical Syriac, though vernacular languages are permitted. Although the official calendar of the church is the Julian, the church in India observes Easter according to the Gregorian date.

Candidates for the priesthood are permitted to marry but must do so before their ordination to the diaconate. Candidates for episcopal consecration are selected from the monastic clergy and are consecrated by His Holiness the patriarch, assisted by at least two metropolitans. The Holy Synod, which is composed of the church's hierarchy and is the official administrative body of the church, elects the → patriarch to the throne.

Regarding the liturgical life of the Syrian Orthodox Church, the liturgical year begins on the eighth Sunday before Christmas and is divided into seven seasons of seven weeks each, including the annunciation period; the nativity and epiphany; the Great Lenten Fast and Holy Week; the resurrection, ascension, and Pentecost; the apostles; the transfiguration; and finally the cross (→ Church Year). Wednesdays are dedicated to the Virgin Mary, Fridays to the Holy Cross, Saturday to the departed, and Sunday to the resurrection. The annual fasts are Nineveh (3 days), Lent and Holy Week (48 days), the Apostles (3 days), the Virgin Mary (5 days), and Christmas (10 days). In addition, → fasting is required every Wednesday and Friday throughout the year, with the exception of the 50 days from Easter to Pentecost.

The central portion of the church's eucharistic liturgy is the → anaphora, with more than 80 in existence. Among the most commonly used are those of St. James of Jerusalem, Bar Salibi, St. Peter, and the Twelve Apostles. There are seven canonical office hours each day, beginning with Vespers *(ramsho)* and continuing with Compline *(soutoro)*, Matins *(lilio)*, Lauds *(safro)*, Terce *(tloth sho'een)*, Sext *(felgeh dyawmo)*, and None *(tsha sho'een)*.

3. Ecumenical Relations

The Syrian Orthodox Church is an active member of the → World Council of Churches, the → Middle East Council of Churches, and the → National Council of the Churches of Christ in the U.S.A., as well as a founding member of Christian Churches Together in the U.S.A.

In addition to ecumenical contacts and efforts as a family member of the Oriental Orthodox churches, the Syrian Orthodox Church of Antioch in recent decades has played a significant role in the ecumenical life of the Christian church. In their Common Declaration of 1984, Patriarch Ignatius Zakka I and Pope John Paul II (1978-2005), among other matters, considered their two churches so close as to include cooperation in → pastoral care and a degree of sacramental sharing. Likewise in 1991 an agreement was achieved between the Syrian Orthodox Church of Antioch and the Greek Orthodox Patriarchate of Antioch, expressing that both churches share one common faith, that further efforts should be made to manifest in reality the oneness of the two churches, and that the liturgical and patristic traditions of both churches should be respected and fostered.

Bibliography: A. S. ATIYA, *A History of Eastern Christianity* (new ed.; Millwood, N.J., 1991) • S. P. BROCK, *A Brief Outline of Syriac Literature* (Kottayam, India, 1997) • C. CHAILLOT, *The Syrian Orthodox Church of Antioch and All the East* (Geneva, 1998) • J. W. ETHERIDGE, *The Syrian Churches* (London, 1846) • A. FORTESCUE, *The Lesser Eastern Churches* (London, 1913; repr., Piscataway, N.J., 2001) • W. HAGE, *Die syrisch-jakobitische Kirche in frühislamischer Zeit nach orientalischen Quellen* (Wiesbaden, 1966) • J. JOSEPH, *Muslim-Christian Relations and Inter-Christian Rivalries in the Middle East: The Case of the Jacobites in an Age of Transition* (Albany, N.Y., 1983) • P. KADAVIL, *The Orthodox Syrian Church: Its Religion and Philosophy* (Puthencruz, India, 1973) • P. KAWERAU, *Die jakobitische Kirche im Zeitalter der syrischen Renaissance. Idee und Wirklichkeit* (Berlin, 1955) • O. H. PARRY, *Six Months in a Syrian Monastery* (London, 1895; repr., Piscataway, N.J., 2001) • C. SELIS, *Les Syriens orthodoxes et catholiques* (Turnhout, 1988) •

H. Southgate, *Narrative of a Visit to the Syrian Jacobite Church of Mesopotamia* (New York, 1856; repr., Piscataway, N.J., 2003) • W. Wright, *A Short History of Syriac Literature* (London, 1894; repr., Piscataway, N.J., 2001).

JOHN P. MENO

Syrian Orthodox Churches in India

1. Organization
2. History
3. Liturgical Worship
4. Ecumenical Relations
5. Institutions

1. Organization

There are two Syrian Orthodox churches in India:

1. an → autocephalous church, acknowledging no other → authority over it, known as the Malankara Orthodox Syrian Church, or the Indian Orthodox Church, with membership officially estimated at 2.5 million; and
2. an autonomous church, acknowledging the authority of the Syrian → patriarch in Damascus, known as the Malankara "Jacobite" Syrian Orthodox Church, with membership estimated at 1.2 million.

The two churches are identical in faith, both following the Oriental Orthodox tradition. Both acknowledge Thomas the apostle as patron saint and founder of the Indian church. Both are headed by a catholicos of the east and an episcopal synod.

The autocephalous Malankara Orthodox Syrian Church (#1) is governed by a Holy Episcopal Synod of 24 bishops, presided over by His Holiness Moran Mar Baselios Mar Thoma Didimos (elected 2005), catholicos of the east, resident in Kottayam, Kerala. In Kerala there are dioceses of Angamaly East, Angamaly West, Chengannur, Idukki, Kandanad East, Kandanad West, Kochi (Cochin), Kollam, Kottayam, Kunnamkulam, Malabar, Niranam, Sulthan Bathery, Thiruvananthapuram (Trivandrum), Thrissur (Trichur), and Thumpamon, and other dioceses in Chennai (Madras), Kolkata (Calcutta), Mumbai (Bombay), and New Delhi for the rest of India. There is also a diocese for Europe and Canada, and another for the United States.

The catholicos of the patriarchal group, recognizing the Damascus Patriarchate (#2), is His Beatitude Mar Baselios Thomas I (elected 2002), with offices in Ernakulam, Kerala. He is assisted by a total of 22 other bishops; there are dioceses of Angamaly,

Greater India, Kandanad, Kochi (Cochin), Kollam, Kottayam, Malabar, Niranam, Thrissur (Trichur), and Thumpamon in India itself, as well as dioceses in Europe and the Middle East, and archdioceses for North America and the Knanaya community.

2. History

The church in India traces its origin to the apostle Thomas, one of the Twelve. According to tradition, Thomas landed in Muziris (Cranganore) on the Kerala coast in A.D. 52 and was martyred in Mylapur, near Madras, around A.D. 72 (→ Martyrs). Most scholars agree that the church existed in India from the 2d century, and by the 4th century the evidence is clear and documented. By the 8th century these "Thomas Christians" were in full communion with the Assyrian Church of the East (→ Nestorians), under a metropolitan who occupied the tenth place in the Assyrian hierarchy, and there were occasional contacts with the West Syrian Church as well.

After the arrival of the Portuguese colonizers at the end of the 15th century, there was increasing pressure to adopt Roman Catholic customs, culminating in the Synod of Diamper (1599; → Pope, Papacy), when a number of Latin practices were formally imposed. This resulted in a major revolt against Roman authority in 1653 (Coonan Cross) and a division in the community, with the anti-Catholic party establishing a connection with the Syrian Orthodox Church. The West Syrian → liturgy was subsequently introduced among the Orthodox and slowly took root.

Under British colonial-missionary influence (→ Colonialism and Mission), many Orthodox joined the Anglican Church (→ Anglican Communion), and a reformed branch of the Syrian Orthodox called the Mar Thoma Syrian Church came into existence in the middle of the 19th century. To counter these influences within their church, the Syrian Orthodox in India appealed to the Syrian Orthodox patriarch of Antioch for assistance, and at a synod held at Mulanthuruthy in 1876 they were received under his direct jurisdiction. In 1912, however, a group rebelled against the patriarch's authority, declared itself autocephalous, and announced the reestablishment of the ancient Catholicosate of the East in India. The rest remained loyal to the Syrian patriarch. The two factions were reconciled in 1958, following a Supreme Court of India judgment that the Syrian patriarch had no temporal authority in India. They split again in 1972, following the Syrian patriarch's consecration of an Indian bishop.

In June 1995 the Supreme Court of India rendered a decision that (1) upheld the constitution of the church that had been adopted in 1934 and made it binding on both factions; (2) stated that there is only one Orthodox church in India, currently divided into two factions; and (3) recognized the Syrian Orthodox patriarch of Antioch as the spiritual head of the universal Syrian Church, while affirming that the autocephalous catholicos has legal standing as the head of the entire church, and that he is custodian of its parishes and properties. The implementation of this decision has been resisted, however, and the division remains.

These Orthodox churches today represent a minority of the descendants of the original Thomas Christians. More than half belong to one of the three Catholic churches: the Syro-Malabar (E. Syrian), Syro-Malankara (W. Syrian), and Roman (or Latin). In addition, there is a distinct ethnic community known as the Southists, or Knanaya. Its origins have been traced to a group of 72 Jewish Christian families who immigrated to India from Mesopotamia in the year A.D. 345. The descendants of these ancient immigrants, who are endogamous and now number about 300,000, have their own dioceses in both the Malankara Syrian Orthodox Church and the Syro-Malabar Catholic Church.

3. Liturgical Worship

Both groups of the Indian Syrian Orthodox use the West Syrian liturgical tradition. The authorized languages of worship today are Syriac, Malayalam, Tamil, Hindi, and English, depending on the congregation. There are a hundred different eucharistic anaphorae available, but fewer than half a dozen are in actual use. The → Anaphora of St. James in Syriac is different from that in Greek, but both are derived from the worship of the original apostolic community in Jerusalem (→ Eucharist).

4. Ecumenical Relations

The Malankara Orthodox Syrian Church was a founding member of the → World Council of Churches. Both of the Syrian Orthodox churches in India have separate bilateral dialogues with the Catholic Church that meet annually, and both participate in the international dialogue between the Catholic Church and the Oriental Orthodox churches as a group. There have also been dialogues with the Mar Thoma Syrian Church and evangelical churches in India.

5. Institutions

The Malankara Orthodox Syrian Church maintains an Orthodox Theological Seminary in Kottayam (founded in 1815) and St. Thomas Theological Seminary (founded in 1995 in Bhilai, moved to Nagpur in 1999). The Sophia Center, which is adjacent to the seminary in Kottayam, has facilities for conferences, seminars, and classes. It is used mostly for training courses for the laity and also hosts meetings of the Holy Synod of Bishops.

The Malankara Syrian Orthodox Church opened a new facility for its seminary in Ernakulam in 1990. It will eventually include on its grounds a theological college, library, chapel, auditorium, printing press, hostel for students, and residences for monastic communities, thus serving as a major center of the church's activities. A new administrative headquarters of the church, the Patriarch Ignatius Zakka I Iwas Centre, was consecrated in September 2004. It is situated at Puthenkurishu in Ernakulam District, Kerala.

Both churches are heavily involved in → education, health care, and assistance to the poor. Each administers a significant number of hospitals, high schools, colleges, and orphanages and oversees spiritual organizations for young people and other groups. Both churches also foster the monastic tradition, with communities of both men and women taking an active part in church life.

Bibliography: C. V. CHERIYAN, *Orthodox Christianity in India: A History of the Malankara Orthodox Church* (Kottayam, 2003) • P. GREGORIOS, *The Orthodox Church in India* (Kottayam, 1982) • G. MENACHERY, ed., *St. Thomas Christian Encyclopaedia* (2 vols.; Trichur, 1973-82) • P. J. PODIPARA, *The Thomas Christians* (Bombay, 1970) • J. THEKKEDATH, *History of Christianity in India* (vol. 2; Banglore, 1982) • P. VERGHESE, *Die Syrische Kirchen in Indien* (Stuttgart, 1974).

PAULOS GREGORIOS† and RONALD G. ROBERSON

Systematic Theology

1. Term
2. Legitimacy
3. Rise and Development of Themes
4. Types
5. Task

1. Term

The attempt is made here to describe systematic theology by comparing its understanding in Protestant and in Roman Catholic thought.

1.1. The term "systematic" as an attribute of theology is often viewed as unfortunate because it seems to imply that the full → truth of the living God can be summarized in a system. The Anglican

Church (→ Anglican Communion) did not use it for fear of theological system-building, but in Roman Catholic theology it encompasses the various disciplines of → dogmatics, → fundamental theology, → moral theology, and → canon law. In Protestant theology K. → Barth (1886-1968) and his disciples avoided it totally, but P. → Tillich (1886-1965) consciously chose it, as have also W. Pannenberg, G. Kaufman, G. Wainwright, and others.

In → theological education in the Western world and other places, however, the term is commonly used for the fourth of the five classic theological disciplines: OT studies, NT studies, historical theology, systematic theology (dogmatics and ethics), and practical theology (religious education, homiletics, counseling, church administration, church law, etc.). The dispute over its appropriateness among theological authors in this discipline reflects basic decisions concerning its task. Is it an orderly summation and explication of the church's → dogmas? or a systematization of the main themes of → biblical theology? or an exposition of → faith, in dialogue with → philosophy? Does it center on the self-understanding of the believers and the various theories of interpretation and communication (→ Hermeneutics), or does it explore the function of the language of faith? Behind these alternatives lurk two perennial questions: First, is the bearer of faith the church (so the Roman Catholic tradition) or the individual (the tendency in Protestantism, though Barth, for example, viewed dogmatics as always *church* dogmatics)? Second, are theological statements true (→ Truth) merely on the grounds of → faith ("fideism"), or are there other legitimations?

While early Jewish thought (→ Mishnah; Talmud) did not strive to systematize the content of the → Torah and the → Halakah, there is no question that the fathers of the → early church in fact pursued systematic approaches in emphasizing central themes of faith and the church's teaching (e.g., redemption, salvation, the → incarnation, the → Trinity, → Christology, → the church, → eschatology, and → the sacraments). The selection of such themes marked the beginning of what later made theological systems possible. The → councils of the church promulgated dogmas, accepted by the church in East and West. The works of individual authors enjoyed enormous respect. Later systematic theology thus contained what may be called officially elaborated, as well as privately elaborated, elements. Although the early fathers' view of God's history with Israel and with humankind after the coming of Jesus Christ (→ Salvation History) resembles a system, one could not call their writings systematic theology in the strict sense.

The dogmas and excerpts (the so-called catenae) of the important fathers were transmitted into the → Middle Ages and were collected in books of "sentences" long before the great systematically structured summae by the famous "doctors of the church" in the time of → Scholasticism arose. Now the great themes were subdivided into many *loci* (main themes and subthemes, proof texts for further arguments). While the Reformers, especially Martin → Luther (1483-1546; → Luther's Theology), at first saw no reason for developing a total systematic presentation of the faith, we find early forms of such in the last versions of John → Calvin's (1509-64; → Calvin's Theology) *Institutes of the Christian Religion* of 1559 and also of Philipp → Melanchthon's (1497-1560; → Reformers 3.1.1) *Loci communes* of 1521-59. Truly systematic elaborations of the total content of theology came (here as before, not without the influence of Aristotle's thought) in the 16th and 17th centuries, in the era of → orthodoxy (§§1-2; see 2.1.2).

"System" can (though it does not have to) denote a full, complete, enclosed, and describable set of statements or doctrines that are seen in interdependence. But it may also be an "open system" (of which natural scientists speak), an orderly view of the internal biblical contents, the unity of → theology in its different disciplines, the methodical closure or association with different open systems, and so forth. If theology is not treated in a merely historical or practical manner but is seeking the *grammar* of the ways of speaking of God and thus ultimately of the truth, then systematics is proper to it. The description "systematic theology" is then justified, including both dogmatics and → ethics. In this sense systematic theology, for all the differences both intercultural and confessional, is a useful designation in theological education. It signals — perhaps better than the term "dogmatics" — that the many elements of biblical and church tradition are not unrelated entities and, furthermore, that believers are not to "believe in" doctrines but are to use them for their studies and dialogues in matters of faith.

1.2. In modern Roman Catholic theological teaching the term "systematic theology" is used in a rather similar way. Today's post–Vatican II authors do not merely seek data given by historical methods but analyze the orderly flow between the exegetical findings of Scripture, the historical positions of tradition, and the present situation with its questions. In practice, however, many still tend merely to enumerate historical positions before dealing with systematic problems, a tendency that is due to the Catholic concept of tradition. Thus, as some critical authors today claim, the classic distinction between biblical, historical, systematic, and practical disciplines, resting on certain methodological differences, distorts the reality insofar as the impact of such different interests among scholars with their historical methods may produce unfortunately autonomous results. They may make it difficult to see the whole of God's truth in a wide perspective. (There is no denying that this tendency exists also in Protestant theology; see 4.3, on "monothematic theologies.")

The individual disciplines in Roman Catholic theology have different goals and, accordingly, use different methods. The primary concern of → fundamental theology is reflection on the possibilities of faith in the sense of understanding God's revelation as this is possible for human → reason. Fundamental theology must then deal with questions of philosophical and theological → epistemology (i.e., what counts as knowledge) and integrate them with the → philosophy of religion and the study of religion (→ Religious Studies). The basis of dogmatics is the word of revelation, which, directed by the question of our human being, unfolds itself to us in our historical traditions, constantly raising new questions. (On the new form of the dogmatic method, → Vatican II; see 3.2.)

Today, the understanding and methods of moral theology are open to question. Some argue (materially) that our conduct should be according to the content of the biblical writings, but others argue (formally) about the motivating force of the action, whose determinative impulse is autonomous, that is, with reference only to human reason. Both sides agree that moral theology has to do with an interdisciplinary conversation with the social and natural sciences (e.g., → ecology, → medical ethics, and → psychology). Likewise, the discipline of → social ethics occurs in dialogue with → sociology and deals with the principles and contents of Christian-motivated action in → society (→ Economy; Family; State; Work).

2. Legitimacy

2.1. In the following we discuss the problem of systematizing the content of a nonsystematic (i.e., the biblical) tradition, the question of the difference between overarching and dependent sentences and their claim for truth, the authority of church doctrine in Protestant and Roman Catholic traditions, and finally the question whether systematic theology is to be ruled by a single guiding principle.

2.1.1. Are systematizations legitimate? The Torah (including the Halakah) and the Prophets (→ Prophet, Prophecy, 2) include no self-conscious theology, let alone any systematic theology. The same applies to the NT, with its stories of Jesus, its → parables, the stories of Acts, and the Epistles, except perhaps for Galatians and Romans. Theologians must thus always face the critical question of what right they have to try to systematize the very different passages of the Bible, with their unsystematic stories, metaphors, and symbols. Biblical exegesis has left this critical question open since its beginning some 250 years ago. Its early pioneers (e.g., J. S. Semler and J. P. Gabler) attempted a biblical theology along with pure exegesis, one built on *sacrae notiones,* the inner thematic themes of the Bible, which they thought it was their task to discover. In fact, systematic theology in every epoch has ultimately followed the implied themes (though no longer called *notiones*). But these themes must be rediscovered in their biblical roots to show the autonomy, or lack of it, of their concepts, which can be seen as "implicit axioms" (D. Ritschl).

It may be granted that the general theme of the Bible, the saving will of God, is set forth in the election of Israel, the history of salvation, the → incarnation, the outworking of the eternal divine decrees, and the setting up of the → kingdom of God. If so, can these comprehensive themes become the fundamentals for systems, so that special theories can be built upon them? If these themes, presented in the Bible in picture language, in symbols and stories, are veritable summations of the "contents" of faith, capable of being formalized in condensed and fixed sentences, and if they become subjects of constant and ongoing reinterpretation, then indeed a multistoried construct comes in sight having the appearance of a "house" of knowledge and truth.

Two questions arise. First, is the mere process of interpreting the sentences again and again in the community of the believers more important than the insight that the sentences are true? This point could be argued. And second, are they hierarchically ordered, so that some of them are basic, while others are derived from basic truths? The importance of ongoing reinterpretation and dialogue is undisputed and plays a central role in ecumenical relations. The concept of a → hierarchy, however, not only of themes but also of truths (Y. Congar), is more difficult. Is the semiotic system (i.e., the total of Christian truths) like a building, concerning which we would have to decide whether it is a true picture of the truth of God (→ Ontology) or merely a helpful construct that decisively integrates the themes of faith? Unquestionably, theologians have always operated with derivations of sentences, claimed to be true, from overarching assertions and themes. Are they considered true in the sense of giving us objective information, or could they be seen as intentions, conclusions from faith-experience, ways of speaking? If so, they would go along with certain attitudes of believers, questions of lifestyle and conviction. Moreover, are the derivations of lesser truth than their overarching sentences, or do they merely represent special truths, historically grown, of certain traditions and denominations? → Ecumenical dialogue (→ Ecumenical Theology; Ecumenism, Ecumenical Movement) in fact mainly focuses on such derived sentences and doctrines and, arising from them, the believers' lifestyle, piety, and personal convictions.

We must be cognizant of the fact that sentences of systematic theology, as distinct from exegetical or historical observations, always carry the inner logic of "if . . . then" or "this is so because . . ." sentences — that is, they always reflect the logic of conditions and (permissible) conclusions from premises. Obviously, different denominational traditions (as well as different authors within a given tradition!) "permit" different derivations and conclusions. These basic figures of thought are not merely part of theoretical or academic theology, although they are characteristic of it. They are noticeable also when practical questions of piety and lifestyle are being examined theologically. Those who perform such theological examination need not be professional systematic theologians. Members of local churches or of ecumenical study groups can constructively participate and thus be engaged in systematic theology.

Two ways to claim legitimacy for constructing systems seem possible and have always been at work in history. The first type is based on what is claimed to be revealed as supernatural truth (→ Revelation 2), especially in Eastern Orthodoxy (e.g., D. Staniloae; → Orthodox Christianity). It is understood as God's gift, which is revealed in unchangeable dogmas. This figure of thinking is also found in Roman Catholic teaching. Despite its supernatural character, analogies (→ Analogy) will have to be drawn with, for example, the human experience of receiving a gift in order to make clear what is meant by the use of such language with reference to what God has given. It is interesting that supernaturally oriented theologies (in → Scholasticism and → fundamentalism) always include reflections on the parallel between the language of → faith and human → experience (→ Natural Theology). This connection is shown in the great → summae of theology in the Middle Ages or in Protestant orthodoxy. At the ex-

treme case, theology is viewed as *theologia revelata;* that is, the very words of doctrine come, so to speak, directly from God.

The second type, found since the → Enlightenment and in most theological works today, can in principle be focused on a clearly arranged structuring of the content of faith in its classic "closed" language-system, as well as its later semiotic articulations. It too will relate its findings and propositions to everyday human language and experience, but it will not claim that they are experienced as part of a universally structured ontological system in which God is at the peak and all the rest secretly or openly part of him. It will constantly analyze and discuss the relation between God-language and our human experience of the world we live in. It will do so by bearing in mind the biblical witness, but a mere sentencelike arrangement of quotations from the Bible and the church's tradition would by no means be considered as a theology helpful for the church and the society believers live in.

It is clear that the first type follows the idea of enclosing the truth of God in a rational and ontic system, which, it is readily admitted, humans can understand only partially. If there is an extreme stress on the supernatural, a loss of human reason occurs, and faith becomes something outside reason. (Today, many believers and nonchurched people in Western culture in fact share this understanding: God's sphere is restricted to the extraordinary, the tsunami, an accident, a miracle.) The second type carries the danger of a surrender to human preference, even if carefully and critically analyzed. It is vulnerable to the "anything goes" of → postmodernism and an openness in principle to → pluralism. Sound theology, it seems, is positioned between these two extremes.

2.1.2. Protestantism, in theology as well as in the churches, has always maintained a principled and critical attitude to a systematization of the → gospel, which derives from its constant reference to the importance of the Bible. Protestants have produced many theological systems, however, in both the Lutheran and Reformed traditions, especially in the late 16th and 17th centuries. Were these systems mere intellectual experiments of little interest to the church's believers, or was more at stake? The leaders of both Protestant traditions accepted without any reservation the first four ecumenical councils of the early church, with their implicit systematics, and then in their "confessional writings" (a technical term) — addressed to the emperor or the city authorities and, of course, to their own members — achieved early expressions of relatively full summaries and systematizations of the faith. The Lutherans were first with the → Augsburg Confession of 1530 (with which, incidentally, Calvin also agreed), followed by other confessional statements that were collected in 1580 in the Book of Concord, aiming at one doctrine and unity of doctrine *(una doctrina, unitas doctrinae)* in architecturally structured themes.

The → Reformed, in contrast, prepared separate books of → confession in the various regions or countries in which Reformed churches had come into being: Geneva, Zurich, Basel, France, Scotland, Hungary, and others — altogether nearly 60 documents. These confession books, however, have enjoyed different degrees of respect in the Reformed churches across the years. In Switzerland the 16th-century confessional works are given much less value than, for example, the → Westminster Confession (1647) in the many Presbyterian churches today. In the Third World, strict adherence to the Westminster Confession is typical of churches in East Asia and is clearly due to the influence of American missionary activities in the late 19th and early 20th centuries. It is not typical, however, of African Presbyterian churches that have grown out of Swiss, German, and British missions. In recent decades such African "mainline" churches have often given way to the countless African → Independent Churches, where "independent" can be understood as having no concern for the traditional European books of confession.

Similarly, the Lutheran confessional writings are given a different value in German-speaking churches than in Scandinavia or in → Lutheran churches in the United States. But even there the final collection of documents in the Book of Concord is hardly considered the ultimate authority in matters of doctrine in today's mainline Lutheranism. There are, however, interesting exceptions. Some conservative Lutheran churches (e.g., U.S. Missouri Synod Lutherans, Lutherans in South Australia) have their roots in protest movements against the formation of the union of Lutherans and Reformed in Prussia after 1817, the 300-year commemoration of the beginning of the Reformation in Germany. (The Prussian royal family was Reformed, as were the French Huguenots who had settled in Prussian cities.) Large numbers of believers emigrated and upheld the full number of confession books as their authoritative standards until today. Until very recently, they have hesitated to cooperate in the ecumenical movement.

2.1.3. The question remains open whether a single guiding principle in theology allows the unfolding of a special kind of theological system — a monothematic legitimacy, as it were. Luther serves as an example. His refraining from systematic theology (→ Luther's Theology 1) has been variously interpreted in terms of his background in → nominalism and his passionate adoption of the *sola Scriptura* principle. In fact, we have no systematic presentation of the faith except for his → catechisms (§2) and the Schmalkaldic Articles (1537; → Confessions and Creeds 2). We cannot conclude, however, that he did not read off any superior principle from the gospel. He found such a principle in the → justification of the sinner, the perspective from which he interpreted every conceivable topic of theology. Calvin, in contrast, even in the final edition of his *Institutes,* did not adhere to any one principle. Early attempts to show that his theology centers on the concept of the glory of God *(gloria Dei)* or on predestination have now been abandoned. These two examples show that a leading principle in interpretation of the biblical writings and of faith to shape a systematic theology is possible but not necessary.

In the 16th century the → proclamation of the gospel could be understood as teaching *(doctrina),* which made the modern distinction between *kērygma* (proclamation, preaching) and *didachē* (teaching) unnecessary. Despite this broad conception of *doctrina,* Protestant tradition always had a tendency to view the proclaimed Word as God's work *(opus Dei)* and doctrine as human work *(opus hominum),* a distinction of weighty consequences. This tendency explains why in the Protestant churches the confessionally specific writings, as well as the great books of systematic theologians, were treated as theological teaching but were not respected as definitive doctrines of the church. In Protestantism all the books on systematic theology carried the air of privacy.

2.2. According to the Roman Catholic understanding, the legitimacy of systematic theology depends on the attempt to clothe proclamation within the limits of human knowledge and language in the total context of the → tradition of faith. It may be seen as a continuation of what was done in the NT. The risen and newly present Christ (→ Jesus) was present on the road to Emmaus, and "beginning with Moses and all the prophets, he interpreted to them the things about himself in the scriptures" (Luke 24:27). Typological exegesis (→ Bible Exegesis 2.1.1; Typology) in times past strengthened the tendency to speak about a given *analogia fidei* (see Rom. 12:3; → Analogy 3). Individual statements of faith can be made only with reference to the theological whole. The reference in → Vatican I to the *nexus mysteriorum* (DH 3016) also must be considered, namely, that a personal factor, the Christ-event, forms the connection between the mysteries of faith and, additionally, permits different and gradually differentiated statements of faith. (Note the reference to the hierarchy of truths in *Unitatis redintegratio* [*UR*] 11.) The faith that demands rational insight *(fides quaerens intellectum)* finds in Jesus Christ the revealed mystery of God (Col. 2:2). The founding of faith in the personal being of Jesus Christ carries an ultimate system-critical attitude.

In books on → neoscholastic literature (though not much used today), there is a distinction between the positive, or given, and the speculative, which is a reflection, a mirroring, of what faith knows. This difference goes back to the medieval distinction between authority *(auctoritas)* and reason *(ratio)*. In addition to the data of the first biblical witnesses, it continues in the postapostolic period and can be regarded as a further positive factor in the fellowship of faith and confession (→ People of God). It is a testimony to the experienced working of God in historical events and initiates the process of a faith tradition, a process of Christian knowledge as a personal event — that is, the experience of God in Christ Jesus and the attested certainty of his living presence by the Spirit. The positiveness of the good news contained in the Gospels (see John 21:24) forms the basis of theology as the witness of faith. Believers have confidence in the testimony. Speculative systematic theology follows the concern to bring the truth of the gospel to light by showing its coherence.

The distinction between the positive and the speculative awakens the suspicion that there are objective data apart from subjective questions and prior understandings. Nevertheless, it is a reminder of the fact that the *mysterium* of God is prior to all theological analysis (→ Roman Catholic Church 2).

3. Rise and Development of Themes

3.1. We may discuss the rise and development of themes in systematic theology in the following ways.

3.1.1. It is important to realize that the biblical stories (the exodus, conquest, exile, and Jesus' → passion; → Israel 1) and all other stories are not like single unrelated blocks but are capable of being summarized and connected with one another, as well as with thoughts not contained in them (J. Barr, S. Hauerwas, D. Ritschl, and others). This connection happens frequently within the biblical writings and has produced standardized forms of faith language (→ Literature, Biblical and Early Christian, 1-2). Summations of such — for example, on the exodus of Israel, above all on the passion of Jesus in the Pauline epistles and later in the Apostles' Creed —

can lead to derivations that can be understood only by those who know the summarized story (e.g., "he died for the sins of the world" or the "blood of Jesus"). Early forms of doctrines can grow from such derivations of a single story or of several related stories or of a combination of stories and quoted texts. An example is the exodus, which ultimately leads to the theological doctrine of the *providentia Dei* (→ Providence) or to the *gubernatio Dei*. Summaries and derivations from the texts of the crucifixion and resurrection lead to themes like → salvation, → forgiveness, and new → life (§1).

We can see this process clearly in the writings of the second-century fathers (→ Church Fathers 2). Ignatius (ca. 35-ca. 107) has the circular model of the procession of the Logos from the Father and his return to the divine unity following his accomplishment of salvation. → Irenaeus (ca. 130-ca. 200) extended this model by bringing in history. Combined derivative sentences from summarized theological themes were gradually worked out and together constituted the components of early theology. To be sure, alongside this abstract depiction of the rise of themes, attention should be paid to the concrete causes for such statements — for example, the defense against → Gnosticism or against the attacks of philosophers (→ Apologetics), as well as catechetical and related tasks in the church. It took centuries for systematic theology to develop. The first example is the *De principiis* of the great biblical theologian → Origen (ca. 185-ca. 254; → Origenism). Listening to innumerable Bible stories, he gained a comprehensive vision of the saving ways of God to us and of our ways to him that anticipates the great works of the Middle Ages or even of G. W. F. Hegel (1770-1831; → Hegelianism).

3.1.2. The church fathers were slow to develop systematic theology. → Augustine (354-430; → Augustine's Theology) wrote his *Enchiridion* in 423, but it can hardly be called a systematic theology. → John of Damascus (ca. 655-ca. 750; → Orthodox Christianity 5) in the East, however, brought the writings of the Greek fathers systematically together in his famous *De fide orthodoxa*. Much later came Peter Lombard (ca. 1100-1160; → Scholasticism) in the West with his *Sentences,* a collection of classic quotations whose influence can hardly be overestimated. His sequence of Trinity, doctrine of God, angels, sin and grace, Christology, ethics, and sacraments has come down, with modifications, across the centuries to Roman Catholic and Protestant systematic theology.

Two problems, however, are created: first, the need to justify the sequence in which the great themes are handled; second, the decision that just these and no others make up the sum total of systematic theology. Does the Bible not offer more than the classic themes, or less, or others? Do we really need a doctrine of → creation and one of the new creation? Must → justification and → sanctification be distinct, forgiveness and → soteriology, election (→ Predestination) and providence, ecclesiology (→ Church) and the sacraments? Yet, it is of some ecumenical value that even today similar themes in similar sequence make up the theological systems in all mainline denominations. So the discovery was welcome that the structure of the ten-volume *Loci theologici* of 1622 by the Protestant J. Gerhard resembles the plan of Thomas Aquinas's *Summa theologiae* of the 13th century (R. P. Scharlemann). Even if today Protestant authors rarely follow in their works the classic themes and sequence, the knowledge of them connects theologians all over the world.

3.2. Most Protestant works on dogmatics gave up the traditional adherence to the classic sequence of themes in the early 19th century. In Roman Catholic theology this change occurred much later. An openness to a less stringent order in dealing with the themes and subthemes of systematic theology has become visible in modern times.

3.2.1. In Roman Catholic theology, especially since → Vatican II, the arrangement of the themes of systematic theology is seen primarily as an attempt to approach in orderly fashion, using different perspectives and questions, the one theme: the self-revelation of God attested in the Bible (see 2.2). Fundamental theology thus expounds the Christian faith (in conversation with other religions; → Dialogue 2.2) as the church's knowledge grounded in the history of revelation. In dogmatics the sequence of tractates (doctrine of God, Christology, pneumatology, doctrine of grace, ecclesiology [→ Church 3.2], sacraments, and eschatology) was borrowed from medieval patterns and rests finally on the ancient creeds. Moral theology and social ethics distinguish between basic and principal questions and specific answers to actual problems.

3.2.2. More recent Roman Catholic theology sees the basic principle in the rule of analogy of the Fourth Lateran Council (see DH 806; → Councils of the Church 3). It states that on the basis of the greater dissimilarity between Creator and creature, all seemingly similar features, as well as sentences in picture language about them, can at best be a shadow experience. Affirmative theology is always negative as well, never stating its true object, and in going beyond itself reaches in its knowledge true ig-

norance (*docta ignorantia*, Nicholas of Cusa; → Negative Theology).

The development was this: Under the impact of Aristotelianism, Scholasticism consolidated itself and formed its method. In the face of strongly different questions, arguments were developed that opposed accepted positions. A short text from Scripture or tradition led to the corpus of arguments with highly speculative claims. The train of thought was interrupted by a use of objections to the previously grounded answer. This method, which led to theological conclusions, was sharply criticized by the humanists (→ Humanism 1.1) and the Reformers. In the newly constructed systematic theological method after the Reformation (→ Catholic Reform and Counterreformation), Melchior Cano (ca. 1509-60) played a leading role. Unlike the Reformers, he argued that the concept of the *locus theologicus* must be seen as a place *(locus)* of demonstrating a particular truth, a source of theological perception.

Not until the 19th-century movement of neo-scholasticism were the sayings of the church's → teaching office (§1) conceived as *norma proxima* and the sayings of Scripture and tradition as *normae remotae* — that is, the teaching office in Rome was "closer" to the believers than Scripture. A threefold step was worked out: (1) pointing to the promulgation of the teaching office of the church, (2) turning to its basis in Scripture and tradition, and (3) then moving to speculative reflection.

This method was severely shaken by the crisis of → modernism at the beginning of the 20th century, which claimed a new approach to biblical exegesis and history of dogma (→ Dogma, History of). After the first sharp rejection by the Vatican of the new idea of the history of truth, this thought, grounded in the 19th-century Tübingen School and in the works of J. H. → Newman, achieved a broader acceptance at Vatican II and found its way into the approved documents (*Gaudium et spes* [*GS*] 62). The new understanding of revelation developed in the document *Dei Verbum* regarding its personal character (in place of the instructive and theoretical form previously favored), and the recognition of the (older church's) communio-ecclesiology, especially in *Lumen gentium* (→ Catholicism [Roman] 3; Church 3.2), produced nothing less than a post-conciliar systematic theology. It was of great significance that amid individual documents the so-called transcendental anthropological turn in Catholic theology occurred, beginning with a reception of the works of Karl → Rahner (1904-84; → Transcendental Theology; see *Nostra aetate* 1). To proclaim God as the answer to the human question opened up new ways of thought within Catholic theology but also in dialogue with other religions. Moreover, the council recognized the autonomy of the (natural) sciences and their methods (*GS* 36 and elsewhere).

The leading ideals of the council, *ad fontes* and *aggiornamento,* worked themselves out in the new definition of dogmatic method (see *Optatam totius* [*OT*] 16). In plain contrast to the threefold step of neoscholasticism, it demanded that first we should set out the themes of Scripture, then we should discuss in what ways they have been handed down in the church's tradition (using speculative perception and searching in → liturgy and the church's life), and at last we should study to see God's revelation worked out in human problems and questions. The reform of the dogmatic method, as shown in many of the texts (*GS* 10, 21-22, 46; *OT* 14, 16; *UR* 11), focuses on the Christological center of theology (→ Christology 4). This turn is of high ecumenical significance. The task of philosophical and theological disciplines is to open up the mystery of Christ, which goes through human history (*OT* 14).

4. Types

4.1. In classic Protestant systematic theology, or dogmatics, the Reformed B. Keckermann (1571-1609) and the Lutheran G. Calixtus (1586-1656) promoted a new conception. They saw no sense in a synthetic way of approach that allowed deductions from the prior statements about God and thus made theology a *scientia* or *scientia speculativa.* Armed philosophically with Aristotle (384-322 B.C.; → Aristotelianism; Greek Philosophy 6), they looked back analytically from the end of the ways of God, so that theology became a practical undertaking looking ahead to salvation *(disciplina operatrix).* Salvation is prepared by God *(finis externus),* and the way to it by faith *(finis internus)* is told by theology, which, in practical terms, can be a system.

With the analytic method a way is opened up in principle to make → faith the object of systematic theology. In the history of → Pietism (→ Methodism), along with the theological history of F. D. E. → Schleiermacher's *Glaubenslehre* (1821-22; ET *The Christian Faith*) and his successors in the 19th century, there emerged an impressive array of fundamental theological works (in American theology leading all the way to E. Farley's works). The earlier school, with its synthetically oriented authors who used the local method, that is, the ordered arrangement of great themes, along with the lesser themes (*loci* in → Melanchthon's sense), had some interesting followers. Now, however, the influence of

Schleiermacher (1768-1834; → Schleiermacher's Theology) became predominant. It is questionable, however, whether the common interpretation of 19th-century Protestant theology as an almost linear continuation of Schleiermacher's anthropological emphasis can be upheld. Countless studies in 19th-century theology have shown that, besides the so-called → mediating theology, there were more than simply Schleiermacherians and conservatives.

Nonetheless, the massive protest of K. Barth (→ Dialectical Theology) demolished any type of anthropocentric doctrine. This protest was much more effective in the German-speaking sphere (partly because of the church's experiences in the Nazi era) than in the English-speaking world. (Furthermore, in Britain and the United States, Brunner's influence was stronger than Barth's.) There, as in other theological centers of the → Third World, theology was still viewed as a doctrine of faith, while conservative circles — under the influence of their "classics" (like J. → Edwards and the "Princeton theology") — saw their task in the continuation of pre-Kantian orthodoxy (→ North American Theology). Such circles, sometimes tied to → fundamentalism, exist also in many parts of the → Third World, for example, in Korea and Protestant schools in Latin America, where, in some places, they seem to exist alongside → liberation theologians.

Between the alternatives of viewing theology as a doctrine of faith and as a doctrine of the Word of God was the theology of Tillich, which thematically and systematically describes both revelation and the questions of humanity as delineated and grounded in philosophy. Hermeneutic systematic theology, as developed by G. Ebeling (1912-2001), John Macquarrie (1919-2007), R. Smith, and others (→ Hermeneutics 3.3), avoided this alternative by focusing, against the background of → existential philosophy, on understanding the biblical → kerygma. It did so by existentially interpreting the Word of God in such a way that a new self-understanding occurs. R. Bultmann's (1884-1976) exegetical and systematic works prepared the way, systematized by E. Fuchs (1903-83).

Although it seemed at first that the Barthian and Bultmannian schools would remain in hostility forever, the influence of great writers such as D. → Bonhoeffer (1906-45), whose authority today apparently grows, and important authors in the United States (e.g., L. Gilkey, R. R. Niebuhr, V. A. Harvey, R. L. Hart, J. M. Robinson, R. W. Funk, and the series "New Frontiers in Theology," esp. vol. 2, *The New Hermeneutic* [New York, 1964]) presented a wide spectrum of new insights and methods, so that the enmity between the two streams is perhaps melting away. In the German-speaking sphere this change is in part due to the work of E. Jüngel and others in their interpretation of revelation, the resurrection of Jesus, and time and the future.

4.2. Since approximately 1970 the antagonism between "doctrine of faith" and "doctrine of the Word of God" theologies has given way to another tension in the house of theology, namely, the difference between a hermeneutical outlook and an analytic mode of approach. The former appeared earlier and is still noticeable today, but the latter departs from the hermeneutical approach and seeks the ultimate synchronic constitution of a subject in relation to its truth and credibility. Thus the task of theology (or preaching) is not to "make relevant" ancient texts for today. With analytic questioning, new horizons of meaning open up ecumenically. Its representatives (G. Sauter, D. Ritschl, et al.) see speech about God rather than God as the theme of systematic theology. Thus the critical function of the analytic philosophy of language (→ Analytic Philosophy) carries as much weight in theology as does the impact of the so-called philosophy of science *(Wissenschaftstheorie).* (The latter has also been of concern to W. Pannenberg.)

A critical analysis of what actually happens when ecumenical groups utter doctrinal sentences has led G. A. Lindbeck to the stimulating thesis that these and other theological-religious statements are best understood when seen as the product of the cultural-linguistic context from which they came. This concept is tested by reviewing some general assertions regarding Christology, unsurpassability, dialogue, and other topics. Lindbeck finds "steering devices" behind these utterances and reflects upon them in his "rule theory" of doctrine. (G. Wainwright, in *EvT* 46 [1986] 555-61, compares this approach with the similar concept of semiotic systems and implicit axioms in D. Ritschl's *Logic of Theology.*) C. Schwöbel and others see in Lindbeck's approach a quasi-postmodern preference of searching for the cultural-linguistic embeddedness of theological sentences rather than for their truth.

The possibility of total and all-embracing systems in which deduced conclusions make up a rational network is denied for theology. In the place of apodictic theses that are accepted as ultimate grounds there is an analysis of "discovery-contexts" *(Entdeckungszusammenhänge)* and "disclosure/reasoning-contexts" *(Begründungszusammenhänge).* Here "steering devices" for biblical and later theological sentences come into sight, providing regulative sentences (see 2.1.1 for implicit axioms). Revelation is no longer seen as a historical event of the past but is understood as re-recognition of past experiences of faith, thus placing weight on the memory of the church. Here thoughts of Pannenberg's merge with the position of analytically oriented authors. It is interesting that many of the modern writers, continuing both the impulse of the Barthian school and the analytic method, have contributed constructively to new and important studies on the → Holy Spirit (J. Moltmann, M. Welker) and on the doctrine of the → Trinity (Moltmann, R. W. Jenson, C. Gunton, Elizabeth A. Johnson, C. Schwöbel, R. von Sinner; on the Roman Catholic side, L. Boff, B. Forte, et al.).

4.3. With the gradual fading of the comprehensive claims of hermeneutical systematic theology (→ Hermeneutics 3.4), there appeared in the second half of the 20th century a blossoming of monothematic discourses, though some were devoted to a kind of hermeneutical method. They may be grouped as follows:

1. *Theological themes of overarching importance* were seen as the very center of the gospel. Examples are books on hope by J. Moltmann (1964), on → Jewish-Christian dialogue by P. M. van Buren and F. W. Marquardt, on the exodus/liberation motif by various liberation theologians, or on (Roman Catholic and Anglican) sacramental theologies (→ Sacramentality). Their themes were seen as dominating the whole field, the *cantus firmus* of Christian thought, as it were.

2. Similarly, we have a *concentration on a single great theme* at the expense of all the others in the Christian tradition, as in many liberation theologies.

3. We then find an approach to *a perspective that thus far had not been a theme in Christian tradition or systematic theology at all,* such as → feminist theology today or the → Social Gospel a hundred years ago. These positions characteristically interpret the whole of theology in the light of a single perspective. Some advocates of this approach have at times claimed to represent a theology that is "inductive," as distinct from "deductive." With the latter term they mean to characterize critically all classic theology of the past. It has been shown above that this assessment is erroneous.

The first and third models can, however, lead with their one-sided approach to a broad treatment of the other themes, as is shown in some of the feminist theologies. They thus give up their monothematic character. (We must of course distinguish monothematic theologies from monographs, in which, as a rule, the theme is not absolutized.)

4.4. British systematic theology, which features Anglican, Reformed, and Roman Catholic thinking in close contact, finds itself, more strictly and to a higher degree than German theology, in critical debate with a more than 2,000-year-old religious-philosophical tradition. With the rise of analytic philosophy (B. Russell et al.), however, the dialogue with philosophy faded away and seemed silent until the exchange began again with J. Wisdom (1904-93), R. M. Hare (1919-2002), and later authors. It has been very well documented (by A. Flew, A. MacIntyre, W. A. de Pater, F. Ferré, and the American J. A. Martin). T. F. Torrance took a somewhat different approach, continuing the Scottish Reformed and the Barthian traditions with important and highly influential works of his own. (Torrance's philosophical partner was the natural scientist M. Polanyi.) D. MacKinnon (1913-94), an Anglican Scot teaching in England, was the respected teacher of a great number of leading theologians in England.

The more recent works of S. Sykes, (Archbishop) R. Williams, D. Ford, C. E. Gunton, and others have (untypical of English theology) taken up intense contact with Continental theology. This group of systematicians has contributed much to the ecumenical cause, while their erstwhile partners in analytic philosophy preferred the purely academic world for their activities. (Their debate, incidentally, was received in Continental theology only at a later date, esp. by J. Track and I. U. Dalferth.)

5. Task

5.1. In taking up the challenge of modern "philosophy of science" *(Wissenschaftstheorie)*, theology had to demonstrate once more its academic character as a genuine discipline of knowledge — that is, it had to provide avenues of thought that show its claims are true. But voices are still heard that strongly challenge this claim. Undoubtedly, the exegetical and historical disciplines of theology can claim to be scientific in method and execution, and they enjoy international reputation in academic institutions (→ University), even where theology works only in relatively isolated divinity schools at universities or in church-related seminaries and colleges. In British and continental European universities it enjoys some respect more for traditional reasons and out of regard for the disciplinary expertise of its proponents than for its own sake.

Because of the origin of theology in → devotion, → prayer, and confession and its turning into → doxology, it must make use of classes of sentences that are only in part capable of scientific (i.e., generally demonstrable) verification. The claim of plausi-bility seems not to be as respectable as the claim of generalizable truth. If the search for the regulative principles, or the grammar of the speech of faith (implicit axioms), has a certain scientific character, the basic statements about God's love and his will, the heart of theology, are wisdom rather than academic learning or knowledge. (Theology shares this fate in part with philosophy, also with medicine, at least with its psychosomatic wing.)

5.2. Roman Catholic theology understands itself as a discipline that, in Aristotelian fashion, can offer knowledge about self-understanding and whose reasons can be proved by rational argument and win over others who maintain a detached, reflective mood. On the basis of Aristotle, Thomas Aquinas (ca. 1225-74) discussed the way in which theology can be shown to have a scientific character, which is also of significance to the modern understanding of systematic theology.

As distinct from philosophy, which works solely with the means of human reason, theology *(sacra doctrina)* has its basis in the revelation of God *(Summa theol.* I, q. 1, art. 1c. and art. 8c.). The Word of God is the criterion of truth, the argument that gives theology its scientific character (M. Seckler, "Theologie als Glaubenswissenschaft," *HFTh* 4.192). In our day, there is a clear tendency to see systematic theology as an attempt whose presupposition is the self-declaration of God and whose goal is the proclamation of God (J. Werbick, "Prolegomena," *Handbuch der Dogmatik* 1.11-23). Its hermeneutical principle, the Word of God, is the formal and material principle of systematic theology. It indeed deals with specific questions (the tractates of dogmatics), but it conceives of them ultimately as unfolding a general theme: the dialogically argumentative description of faith in God, whose source is not human reason but the given presence of God.

Systematic theology presupposes the faith that it reflects. The personal event of belief in the being of the one who gives himself to faith *(fides qua creditur)* precedes all concern for an appropriate systematic exposition of the contents of faith *(fides quae creditur)*. The thought is current in the Roman Catholic sphere that the subject of theology is not the individual believer but the church, the totality of believers *(congregatio fidelium)*. In scientifically theoretical discourse the language of theology as a whole will express the conviction that the faith will essentially be social and ecclesial inasmuch as it awakens experiences of God in the community. It is expounded in the Word and is delivered to the living people of God. Theology is ecclesial because it has an intrinsic relation to the basic actions and life of the church (i.e., in liturgy, martyrdom, diakonia, etc.). In this sense theology also has a critical function over against the church insofar as it measures church life by the standards of biblical revelation.

Like non-European Roman Catholic theology, European theology too is increasingly confronted by the fact that fewer and fewer people in the European sphere adhere to an unquestioning Christian faith (→ Catholicism [Roman]). Rather, the church must lead the way to faith. The strongly demanded mystagogical quality of systematic theology could be gained by an intensified regard for the liturgy of the church, in which God's promise is heard in the Word proclaimed and the mystery of faith is illumined in the celebration of the sacraments (→ Liturgy 2.2.1). The common sending to evangelize (→ Evangelism 2) joins together the systematic theologies of the various denominations in the ecumenical enterprise (→ Ecumenism, Ecumenical Movement).

5.3. European church leaders and theologians argue that theology has a responsibility not only for the church but also for the society the church lives in. (By "theology" they mean systematic theology, including ethics.) This insistence on its "public responsibility" may have historical reasons, related to the juridically established character of the major denominations. But it is interesting to remember that Reinhold → Niebuhr (1892-1971) had similar ideals, and it is not surprising that many politicians of his day read his works (→ Political Theology).

Theology's responsibility for the church is undisputed. Churches without doctrines are lacking helpful orientation and are in difficulty, as history demonstrates. The claim of having no need for theology on account of having a direct access to the Bible has proved to be very risky. An explanation for such refutation of theology may lie in the widespread but erroneous idea that doctrines should be believed in. They are, however, no more than rules for dialogue about the faith, lines of orientation in the midst of countless unanswered questions. It is of great importance to realize that systematic theology is only for practical and didactic reasons a separate academic discipline. In fact it operates in every conclusion drawn from the Bible, in every sermon preparation, counseling session, and sociopolitical engagement. History shows what happens when believers and church leaders act without thinking theologically. The professional, academic language of systematic theologians is certainly not meant to become the idiom of all believers, nor are preachers expected to preach theology in their sermons. But every intelligent utterance in matters of faith, even by the uneducated, is a hidden version of theology.

→ Language and Theology; Philosophy and Theology

Bibliography: Late 20th-century systematic theologies: G. EBELING, *Dogmatik der christlichen Glaubens* (3 vols.; Tübingen, 1979; 3d ed., 1987-93) • W. HÄRLE, *Dogmatik* (3d ed.; Berlin, 2007) • R. JENSON, *Systematic Theology* (2 vols.; New York, 1997-99) • G. D. KAUFMAN, *Systematic Theology: A Historical Perspective* (New York, 1968) • J. MACQUARRIE, *Principles of Christian Theology* (2d ed.; New York, 1977) • W. PANNENBERG, *Systematic Theology* (3 vols.; Grand Rapids, 1991-98) • D. RITSCHL, *The Logic of Theology: A Brief Account of the Relationship between Basic Concepts in Theology* (Philadelphia, 1987; orig. pub., 1984) • T. SCHNEIDER et al., ed., *Handbuch der Dogmatik* (2 vols.; Düsseldorf, 1992; 2d ed., 1995-2000) • G. SIEGWALT, *Dogmatique pour la catholicité évangélique. Système mystagogique de la foi chrétienne* (5 vols.; Geneva, 1986-2006) • D. STANILOAE, *The Experience of God: Orthodox Dogmatic Theology* (2 vols.; Brookline, Mass., 1994-2000) • H. WAGNER "Fundamentaltheologie," *TRE* 11.738-52 • G. WAINWRIGHT, *Doxology: The Praise of God in Worship, Doctrine, and Life; A Systematic Theology* (New York, 1980).

Anglicanism: CHURCH OF ENGLAND, DOCTRINE COMMISSION, *Christian Believing* (London, 1976) • S. SYKES, *Unashamed Anglicanism* (Nashville, 1995) • R. WILLIAMS, *On Christian Theology* (Oxford, 2000).

Methodism: W. KLAIBER and M. MARQUARDT, *Living Grace: An Outline of United Methodist Theology* (Nashville, 2001).

Theological method, hermeneutics, philosophy of science: E. FARLEY, *Ecclesial Reflection: An Anatomy of Theological Method* (Philadelphia, 1982) • G. D. KAUFMAN, *An Essay on Theological Method* (3d ed.; Atlanta, 1995) • R. LUNDIN, C. WALHOUT, and A. C. THISELTON, *The Promise of Hermeneutics* (Grand Rapids, 1999) • W. PANNENBERG, *Theology and the Philosophy of Science* (Philadelphia, 1976) • H. PEUKERT, *Science, Action, and Fundamental Theology: Toward a Theology of Communicative Action* (Cambridge, Mass., 1984) • G. SAUTER et al., eds., *Wissenschaftstheoretische Kritik der Theologie* (Munich, 1973) • R. SCHAEFFLER, *Glaubensreflexion und Wissenschaftslehre* (Freiburg, 1980).

Language and culture: P. L. HOLMER, *The Grammar of Faith* (San Francisco, 1978) • G. A. LINDBECK, *The Nature of Doctrine: Religion and Theology in a Postliberal Age* (Philadelphia, 1984) • J. A. MARTIN, *The New Dialogue between Philosophy and Theology* (New York, 1966) • D. TRACY, *The Analogical Imagination: Christian Theology and the Culture of Pluralism* (New York, 1981).

Special approaches: F. S. Fiorenza, *Foundational Theology: Jesus and the Church* (New York, 1984) • G. Gutiérrez, *A Theology of Liberation: History, Politics, and Salvation* (Maryknoll, N.Y., 1988) • E. A. Johnson, *She Who Is: The Mystery of God in Feminist Theological Discourse* (10th anniv. ed.; 2002) • C. M. LaCugna, ed., *Freeing Theology: The Essentials of Theology in Feminist Perspective* (San Francisco, 1993) • P. M. Van Buren, *A Christian Theology of the People Israel* (3 vols.; New York, 1980-88).

General and specific topics: C. E. Gunton, *Theology through the Theologians* (London, 1996) • P. C. Hodgson and R. H. King, eds., *Christian Theology: An Introduction to Its Traditions and Tasks* (new ed.; Minneapolis, 1994); idem, ed., *Readings in Christian Theology* (Philadelphia, 1985) • E. Jüngel, *God as the Mystery of the World: On the Foundation of the Theology of the Crucified One in the Dispute between Theism and Atheism* (Grand Rapids, 1983) • D. Ritschl and M. Hailer, *Diesseits and jenseits der Worte. Grundkurs christliche Theologie* (Neukirchen, 2006) • R. P. Scharlemann, *Thomas Aquinas and John Gerhard* (New Haven, 1964) • C. Schwöbel, *Gott in Beziehung. Studien zur Dogmatik* (Tübingen, 2002) • M. Welker, *God the Spirit* (Minneapolis, 1994).

Dietrich Ritschl, with Dorothea Sattler

Systems Theory → Social Systems

T

Tabernacle

1. OT
2. Christian

1. OT

"Tabernacle" is a rendering of *'ōhel mô'ēd*, "the tent of meeting." We find it in Exod. 33:7-11; Num. 11:14-17, 24b-30; 12:4-5a, 6-8, 10, traditions that were inserted into the Yahwist source (→ Pentateuch) and likely were pre-Deuteronomistic. This tent-sanctuary stood outside the camp and was a place of → revelation at which → Yahweh declared his will after the → theophany at → Sinai, so that those who received the Spirit became → prophets. In Deut. 31:14-15 it was also the place at which → Joshua became → Moses' successor. It later came to be located by the Deuteronomist at Shiloh (Josh. 18:1; 19:51; 1 Sam. 2:22), and then by the Chronicler at Gibeon (1 Chr. 16:39; 21:29; 2 Chr. 1:3).

In the Priestly source this tent-sanctuary, as the setting for the → sacrifices that God ordained at Sinai, stood in the middle of the camp. With it begins the cult, which is indispensable for → atonement. In the Priestly writings of the Sinai narrative found in Exodus 25–27 and 36–38, the mediation of the cult replaces divine revelation. The cult looked forward to the sacrifices in the → temple at → Jerusalem with such things as the → ark, the cherubim, the table, and the → altar. In exilic or early postexilic times, however, people looked forward, not to a new temple, but to the presence of the cult in the Word, thus ensuring the forgiveness of sins and the assurance of the divine presence.

Bibliography: V. FRITZ, *Tempel und Zelt. Studien zum Tempelbau in Israel und zu dem Zeltheiligtum der Priesterschrift* (Neukirchen, 1977) • K. KOCH, "אֹהֶל *'ōhel;* אָהַל *'āhal*," *TDOT* 1.118-30 • C. R. KOESTER, *The Dwelling of God: The Tabernacle in the OT, Intertestamental Jewish Literature, and the NT* (Washington, D.C., 1989) • J. MORGENSTERN, *The Ark, the Ephod, and the "Tent of Meeting"* (Cincinnati, 1945) • S. WESTERHOLM, "Tabernacle," *ISBE* 4.698-706.

VOLKMAR FRITZ

2. Christian

In the Roman Catholic Church, the tabernacle (Lat. *tabernaculum*, "hut, tent") is an ornamented receptacle for the consecrated eucharistic elements. Like the → ark of the covenant in the tent of meeting (see 1) in the wilderness, it embraces the presence of the Lord (see Ps. 43:3 and 1983 CIC 938).

Originally the elements were kept in the → sacristy. From the tenth century, according to Regino von Prüm (d. ca. 915), they were kept outside the → Mass for adoration. Then in 1215 the Fourth Lateran Council demanded rules against profanation of the elements (→ Sacred and Profane). The tabernacle as a fixed shrine was developed to protect the Eucharist, including against theft and other antireligious purposes. Interest in defending the doctrine of the Mass against medieval opposition movements that denied transubstantiation (→ Eucharist 3.2.2) also promoted the development of the tabernacle.

There are often lavish containers for the sacrament, frequently wall tabernacles and tabernacles on the high altar. In 1563 the Council of → Trent wrote that the tabernacle should be placed on the → altar. → Baroque forms of the altar, with flaming suns, columns, pilasters, and figures, express a sacramental answer to the Reformation rejection of the sacrificial character of the Mass (M. → Luther) or to the real presence (U. → Zwingli, H. Bullinger; → Luther's Theology 4.5; Zwingli's Theology).

→ Liturgical Vessels

Bibliography: J. Braun, *Der Christliche Altar in seiner geschichtlichen Entwicklung* (Munich, 1924) • A. A. King, *Eucharistic Reservation in the Western Church* (New York, 1965) • H. von Meurers, "Altar and Tabernacle," *LJ* 3 (1953) 10-28 • J. B. O'Connell and F. R. McManus, "Tabernacle," *NCE* (2d ed.) 13.726 • A. Reinle, *Die Ausstattung deutscher Kirchen im Mittelalter* (Darmstadt, 1988) 24-31.

Gerlinde Strohmaier-Wiederanders

Taboo

The concept of taboo (Tongan *tabu*) holds a high place in Polynesian religious systems. Without experiences of *tabu,* we have no suitable word for translation. "Forbidden" or "holy" might seem to work, but they do not fit properly; it is closer to the unholy, violation of which causes shock.

A look at the original meaning of *tabu* is helpful. In Polynesia, *tabu* was and is transferred by touch and harms those who are weaker. For this reason the people avoid stronger taboo and protect the weak from their taboos. Special *tabu,* necessary for sowing seed, building boats, burials, and so forth, is later dissolved. Burials and graves, holy places and things, → priests and the firstborn, and every man to some degree, especially his body and blood, constantly give off *tabu.* Prisoners of war lose their *tabu* and become → slaves. (Missionaries have sometimes mistakenly translated *tabu* as "holy." Thus the Bible becomes the *paipera tabu* [taboo book]; Sunday, the *rā tabu* [taboo day]; and *tabu — tabu — tabu* appears on → altar coverings.) *Noa* (i.e., freed from *tabu,* common, profane), the counterforce, extinguishes *tabu.* To have one without the other would bring about disaster instead of benefit.

Closely related to both is *mana,* the power for blessing that heals individuals, society, its land, and its actions. Human beings are responsible for this power, for its growth or decline. They thus have good reason to deal carefully with it. *Tabu* serves *mana* as a powerful protection, but *noa* holds security and freedom in balance.

→ Cultic Purity; Sacred and Profane

Bibliography: R. B. Browne, ed., *Forbidden Fruits: Taboos and Tabooism in Culture* (Bowling Green, Ohio, 1984) • M. Douglas, *Purity and Danger: An Analysis of the Concepts of Pollution and Taboo* (London, 2005; orig. pub., 1966) • S. Freud, *Totem and Taboo* (trans. J. Strachey; London, 2001; orig. pub., 1913) • H.-J. Greschat, *Manu und Tapu* (Berlin, 1980) • J. Irwin, *An Introduction to Maori Religion* (Bedford Park, Austral., 1984) • J. Prytz Johansen, *The Maori and His Religion in Its Non-ritualistic Aspects* (Copenhagen, 1954) • J. Singer, *Taboo in the Hebrew Scriptures* (Chicago, 1928).

Hans-Jürgen Greschat

Taiping Rebellion

1. Name and Origin
2. Establishment of the Heavenly Kingdom of the Great Peace
3. Historical Action as Interpretation of the Vision
4. Holy Scriptures and Program
5. Collapse of the Kingdom

1. Name and Origin

The Chinese Taiping Rebellion rested on a → vision of its originator, Hung Hsiu-ch'üan (Hong Xiuquan, 1814-64), in the year 1837. The term *t'ai-p'ing* (great peace) adopted a utopian ideal (→ Utopia) that went back to the third century B.C. In the vision an "old man" charged Hung to chase out the → "demons" from earth and heaven who had caused human beings to forget their Creator. The finding of a book containing Bible verses and evangelical tracts verified for him the genuineness of the vision.

Putting his mission into action, Hung in 1842 initiated the God Worshipers Society in Kuang-tung (Guangdong) and Kuang-hsi (Guangxi), and these groups identified as demons the images in local temples and began to destroy them. With his cousin Hung Jen-kan (Hong Rengan, 1822-64), who became Taiping prime minister in 1857, he went for three months in 1847 to the American Baptist missionary I. J. Roberts (1802-71) in Canton to work out more details of the doctrine.

2. Establishment of the Heavenly Kingdom of the Great Peace

The God Worshipers Society was only one of the many religiously inspired movements of South China at this time. It was unique, however, in its radical break from traditional Chinese religions (→ Confucianism; Taoism) and in its wish to destroy them. It was unique also in its turning to Western → monotheism in the middle of the Opium Wars (1839-42, 1856-60) and of growing hostility to the West. It was also unique in its opposition to the Manchu regime, which was regarded as ethnically and culturally foreign. The Taiping Rebellion found recruits originally from the marginalized Hakka, and then later from rural young people, from miners, and finally from city workers.

The decisive turning point that changed it from a movement against idolatry to a movement directed against the Manchu government came in 1848, when the Manchus were defined as demons and a military revolt took place. Relying on divine intervention and the support of evangelical missionaries (→ Mission 3.4, 3.5; Revivals), who had dreams of massive, sudden conversions of persons prepared by the Holy Spirit (just like Cornelius in Acts 10), the Taiping rebels stormed northeast to Nanking, which they took in 1851, and which they made into their capital, renaming it New Jerusalem.

3. Historical Action as Interpretation of the Vision

Hung's vision was the symbolic text for all aspects of this movement, which simply put the vision into action. It did so in respect of the military strategy as a fight against demons. It did so also in respect of its policy in condemning Confucianism (while adopting acceptable parts); in forbidding → Buddhism, → Roman Catholicism, and Taoism as demonic idolatry; in opposing the Manchus, who, by worshiping the lamaistic black dragon deity (→ Tibetan Religions), were viewed as worshipers of Satan; in giving a high place to women, who in heaven would play an active role in the battle and who were thus recruited into their own army, separate from the men's army; and in prohibiting opium as the "old man" had demanded. The clothing of the leaders and the architecture of the Nanking palace were also an imitation of the heavenly original.

The members of the movement also found a model in the march of the Israelites through the wilderness and in John Bunyan's (1628-88; → Devotional Literature 2.3) classic, translated into Chinese as *The Pilgrim's Progress to Salvation Directed* (1851). By → glossolalia the heavenly Father and the heavenly Older Brother (i.e., Jesus, with Hung Hsiuch'üan viewing himself as the younger brother of Jesus) were also able to give leadership. Like Christian in Bunyan, and like the children of Israel, the movement refused to cooperate with other sects working against the Manchu government if they did not show themselves ready for conversion.

4. Holy Scriptures and Program

With commentaries on the OT and NT, the movement also had its own testament, including an account of Hung's vision, the minutes of later heavenly interventions, and a list of books of moral instruction and state doctrine. They linked the tracts of evangelical missionaries to the publishing strategies of popular Chinese sects. (The missionaries, though, did not give them any theological leadership.)

The aim of the movement was not to convert China to a new God but to bring back the god Shang-ti, who had been honored in antiquity. Their political and social teaching would have divided the land between men and women (→ Social Ethics 5) and, by providing security to everyone, would have initiated a change that would make a true Christian life possible.

5. Collapse of the Kingdom

No further advance was made after the capture of Nanking. The Manchu regime was able to assemble regional Chinese armies that in 1862 surrounded the heavenly capital, recapturing it in July 1864. The reason for the success of the movement, obedience to the writings prescribed in the vision, was also the cause of its collapse.

The missionaries of the great mainline denominations who took the place of revivalist missionaries found in this rebellion a Chinese counterpart of → sects they had had to combat at home. The doubly blasphemous claim of a Chinese man to bring in the millennial kingdom as the second son of God was seen as justifying the action taken by England and France against the Taiping Rebellion.

The movement affected many portions of South China. It was the largest and most deadly rebellion in the 19th century, claiming the lives of about 30 million people.

→ Charismatic Movement 2; Mission 3.4; New Religions

Bibliography: Y. W. Jen, *The Taiping Revolutionary Movement* (New Haven, 1973) • P. Kuhn, *Origins of the Taiping Vision: Cross-cultural Dimensions of a Chinese Rebellion* (The Hague, 1977) • F. H. Michael, *The Taiping Rebellion: History and Documents* (3 vols.; Seattle, Wash., 1966-71) • J. Spense, *God's Chinese Son: The Taiping Heavenly Kingdom of Hong Xiuquan* (New York, 1996); idem, *The Taiping Vision of a Christian China, 1836-64* (Waco, Tex., 1998) • S.-y. Teng, *The Taiping Rebellion and the Western Powers* (Oxford, 1971) • R. G. Wagner, *Reenacting the Heavenly Vision: The Role of Religion in the Taiping Rebellion* (Berkeley, Calif., 1982).

RUDOLF G. WAGNER

Taiwan

	1960	1980	2000
Population (1,000s):	10,792	17,642	22,401
Annual growth rate (%):	2.07	1.38	0.70
Area: 36,179 sq. km. (13,969 sq. mi.)			

A.D. 2000

Population density: 619/sq. km. (1,604/sq. mi.)
Births / deaths: 1.47 / 0.61 per 100 population
Fertility rate: 1.80 per woman
Infant mortality rate: 32 per 1,000 live births
Life expectancy: 71.0 years (m: 69.2, f: 73.0)
Religious affiliation (%): Chinese folk religionists 50.1, Buddhists 20.8, Taoists 10.0, Christians 7.1 (indigenous 2.2, Protestants 1.8, unaffiliated 1.6, Roman Catholics 1.3, other Christians 0.2), new religionists 6.9, nonreligious 4.2, other 0.9.

Overview
1. History
2. Religious Situation
   2.1. General Features
   2.2. Christianity
        2.2.1. Roman Catholic Church
        2.2.2. Presbyterian Church in Taiwan
        2.2.3. Other Christian Groups
   2.3. Ecumenical Relations
3. Church and State
4. Prospects

Overview

The Republic of China (ROC) on the Island of Taiwan (formerly Formosa), once the stronghold of the Kuomintang (KMT, or Nationalist Party), has evolved into a democracy with an elected president, national and local legislatures, and elected national, provincial, county, city, and town officials. Since 2000 the head of state has been Chen Shui-bian, a member of the Democratic Progressive Party.

Administratively, Taiwan is divided into 18 counties, five municipalities (Chiayi, Hsinchu, Keelung, Taichung, and Tainan), and two "special municipal-

ities" (Kaohsiung and Taipei, the capital). About 25 percent of the island is under agriculture. Industry has blossomed during recent decades, in 2005 employing an estimated 36 percent of the population. A wealthy industrial society has come into being, the per capita gross domestic product being $29,000 in 2006. Taiwan maintains a trade surplus; in 2007 it had the world's fourth largest reserves of foreign exchange and gold.

Statistics collected by the Ministry of Information from religious groups indicate that, as of March 2003, some 15.85 million people in Taiwan were members of one or more religious groups. Altogether, 33,026 temples and churches serve the spiritual needs of the people in Taiwan.

1. History

Taiwan has experienced numerous migrations and invasions over its long history: from archipelago Southeast Asia (the aborigine populations), from the Dutch East Indies (the Dutch East India Company; → Colonialism), from defenders of the Ming Dynasty once based in Fujian Province (the warlord/pirate Koxinga [Cheng Ch'eng-kung] and his heirs), from the Ch'ing Dynasty (the Manchu-led government that conquered, expanded, and controlled China from 1644 to 1912), from the post-1869 imperial Japanese (who made Taiwan a colony after the Sino-Japanese War of 1895 and controlled and reshaped the island until 1945), and finally from mainland China (the Nationalist Chinese, who came in 1945 and took control of the island). The Nationalists misruled the island, which led to a revolt that began on February 28, 1947, by local Taiwanese angry at the despotic and corrupt Nationalist bureaucrats and military forces. The Chinese governor responded by shooting unarmed civilians who had gathered to protest recent police brutality. Eventually more than 30,000 Taiwanese lost their lives as the Nationalists consolidated their control of the island.

In 1949 the Nationalists lost control of the Chinese mainland and that year brought their government to Taiwan, making it the home in exile of the ROC. The Americans who had supported the regime on the mainland then agreed to defend it and bankroll it in its new and smaller home. The American government continues to be deeply involved in Taiwanese affairs.

Christianity arrived in the 17th century when Taiwan was occupied by the Dutch (1624-61) in southwestern Taiwan and when Catholic missionaries, under the Portuguese, attempted to take control of the northeastern region of the island (→ Catholic

Missions). The Dutch Reformed Mission, working under the protection of the Dutch East India Company, worked hard among the Minnan-speaking immigrants from Fujian Province but made little if any headway. They did, however, gain converts among the Plains Aborigines and developed a small community of believers during their nearly 40 years of control of the island. These missionaries also recorded what they had seen and done, and thus we have a valuable and detailed look at this island during its first encounter with the West. The community died out when the Dutch were forced from the island by the forces of the Ch'ing rebel Koxinga, whose family then controlled the island for the next 20 years.

When the Ch'ing took over and began to expand the Chinese areas of settlement of the island, they allowed no Westerners to return, neither merchants nor → missionaries. The next time Western Christians were able to come back to the island was in the 19th century under the protection of the Western powers that had defeated Ch'ing military forces and forced open the Chinese coast to Western diplomats, merchants, and missionary orders. Taiwanese cities in the north (Tansui) and in the south (Tainan) were designated as treaty ports after the signing of the treaties of Tien-tsin (1858) and Peiking (1860).

2. Religious Situation

2.1. General Features

Each invasion of the island since the early 1600s brought with it a change of regime and a transformation of political, economic, social, cultural, and religious systems. In this atmosphere of change, religious systems and religious communities began to develop and take on their own distinctive Taiwanese flavor.

The Chinese religious tradition and the Taiwanese variant of that tradition are not easily compared with Western traditions. While formal structures do exist (large and small → churches, → denominations, organized → sects, schools, and temple communities), scholars of Chinese/Taiwanese religion note its fluidity and its ability to adapt to changing environments and circumstances. They also note that the basic role → religion plays in daily life is rather different from that known in the West. The neat categories of belief and observance that we find in the West break down, and there is more interplay of various traditions in the lives of individuals.

Over 90 percent of the population of Taiwan define themselves as adherents of what we could call simply the Chinese/Taiwanese religion. If forced to pigeonhole themselves, they might say they were Taoist or Buddhist. Others might say that they are believers in one of the major or minor gods in the Chinese/Taiwanese pantheon (e.g., Kuan-kung, Kuanyin, Mazu, Pao-sheng Ta-ti, or Wang-yeh). Yet another growing body of individuals might state that they are members of major cults of Japanese/Chinese-style → new religions (e.g., Hai Zih Dao, Mahikarikyo, Ta-yi Chiao, Tien-te Chiao, Yi-Kuan Tao, and a host of other such groups or religious communities). To complicate matters further, most Taiwanese would also consider themselves as Confucian — that is, believers in the sociocultural system defined by the Great Sage, K'ung Ch'iu (551-479 B.C., called K'ung Fu-tzu [i.e., "Master K'ung"], Latinized as Confucius), by his circle of followers and disciples in the years from 500 B.C. to about 300 B.C., and then by the philosophers, political and social thinkers, and government personnel who helped rework the core tradition to fit the different conditions that evolved in dynastic China in the following two millennia.

New and dynamic forms of → Buddhism have evolved such as Pure Land/Chan Buddhism, practiced in the Fo-kuan Shan temple, and megatemples can be found in Kaohsiung and other areas of Taiwan, as well as in Los Angeles and New York City. The Tzu Chi (or Buddhist Compassion Relief) Foundation has been powerful in bringing laywomen into a socially active form of female-led Buddhism that has reached the United States.

→ Taoism continues to be important, and the Taiwan Yearbook 2006 tells us that a number of important popular syncretistic movements have evolved as well. I-Kuan Tao (Unity Sect) is perhaps the most famous and studied of these. We also find Muslims (→ Islam), along with other small religious groups. In 2002 there were 53,000 Muslims and six mosques in Taiwan.

2.2. Christianity

The various ethnic groups show wide variation in their embracing of Christianity. Around 80 percent of the mountain tribes are Christian, versus 10 percent of the mainland Chinese now in Taiwan and only 2-3 percent of the native Taiwanese.

The 12 mountain tribes, who were the original inhabitants and today number approximately one million, have their own set of distinctive religious systems, which are usually termed → animistic. By the 1990s, however, a very large majority of these peoples had converted to Roman Catholicism or to mainline and sectarian forms of Protestantism.

In 2000 some 70 denominations and many independent churches were at work in Taiwan. The largest Protestant missions were the → Baptists, the Overseas Missionary Fellowship (OMF), and The Evangelical Alliance Mission (TEAM). All the Protestant churches together numbered over 400,000 members. The → Roman Catholic Church had 300,000 members.

With pastoral work and evangelizing, the churches engage in educational work (from kindergartens to universities) and medical work (hospitals and care of the elderly and the handicapped; → Medical Missions). Active in diaconate are Lutheran World Relief (→ Lutheran Churches 6.3; Lutheran World Federation), Christian Children's Fund, and World Vision (→ North American Missions 4). The churches also take steps to protect the environment and to humanize labor. They make effective use of the → mass media. The Taiwanese → Bible Society also does good work in both Chinese and other Taiwanese languages.

2.2.1. *Roman Catholic Church*
After the 19th-century treaties were signed, Catholic missionaries returned to Taiwan, establishing themselves in the north in 1859. This presence grew over the years, especially after the Nationalists' retreat to Taiwan in 1949. An apostolic see was established, and a number of the major Catholic missionary orders resettled on the island. → Jesuits continued their work in education, and Maryknollers, transplanted from Fujian and Guangdong Provinces, began to work again among people who were similar in culture and language to those they had worked with in the Chinese mainland (→ Religious Orders and Congregations 1.5.2). Maryknollers worked in vocational training and in language research and instruction as part of their focused effort to work among the aborigine population. Other orders also entered Taiwan and became involved in establishing and staffing universities. The Vatican, however, desiring better relations with the People's Republic of China (PRC), has downplayed formal relations with the government on Taiwan. This decision has somewhat alienated Taiwanese Catholics.

In 2004 the Roman Catholic Church in Taiwan was organized in seven dioceses and 453 parishes, served by 717 priests. The church operates one university in Taiwan, the Fu Jen Catholic University (founded in 1925).

2.2.2. *Presbyterian Church in Taiwan*
British Presbyterians arrived in 1865 from their base in Hsia-men (Xiamen) in southern Fujian Province, where they had developed a Romanization system for the Minnan dialect spoken by the majority of the Chinese who had been migrating to the island since the 1600s. The Presbyterians began to establish

themselves in the oldest of Taiwanese cities, Tainan, where they continue to work to this day. They were able to make converts among the Minnan (Taiwanese) Chinese and also among the aborigine populations that lived in the mountains east of Tainan. They planted churches, built secular schools and seminaries, developed a mission press, and built hospitals, where they practiced Western medicine. These efforts led to a community of Taiwanese believers in what became the Southern Synod of the Presbyterian Church of Taiwan (→ Reformed and Presbyterian Churches).

Members of the Canadian Presbyterian Church settled in northern Taiwan and began their own mission work in the mid-1870s. Here, led by the dynamic George Leslie MacKay (1844-1901), they founded a mission station in the port town of Tamsui and then expanded their efforts into the Taipei basin. They did medical work and dentistry, set up middle schools and a high school, and were able to plant churches among the area's population. After surviving the Japanese takeover of the island and the Taiwanese revolts that followed in its wake, they were able to serve as intermediaries between the Japanese and the Taiwanese and expand their presence in Japanese-controlled Taiwan. They provided education and medical services that the Japanese did not adequately give to the island's Han and aborigine populations. These efforts heightened the church's visibility, and it grew during these years. By the early 1900s a northern presbytery had been established, and a northern seminary was training pastors and lay workers.

The two synods came together in 1951. The church — the Presbyterian Church in Taiwan (PCT) — is the largest Protestant church on Taiwan. It is Taiwanese-run and maintains close relations with the worldwide Presbyterian community and the → World Council of Churches (WCC). It has a General Assembly, two synods, and 16 presbyteries. In 2000 it had 240,000 members, of whom 60 percent are Taiwanese and Hakka from northern China. From 1949 to 1960 the church grew rapidly as → evangelism flourished among the minority of mainland Chinese, although the Taiwanese were for the time being neglected. Then after 1960 attempts were made to evangelize the Taiwanese (74 percent of the population), the Hakka (14 percent), and the aborigines who lived in the mountains of the island's interior and along its rugged eastern coast. What differentiates the PCT is its deep sense of selfhood and its commitment to bearing witness to the political and social evils its sees in its homeland. It has been willing to confront the KMT-dominated state (see 3).

2.2.3. *Other Christian Groups*

The Presbyterians were not the only churches on the island during the Japanese period and afterward. Missionaries from the American Holiness Church, who began their work in Japan, moved to the central Taiwanese city of Taichung and established a presence there (→ Holiness Movement). In the 1920s an indigenous Chinese charismatic church that had been founded in Shan-tung (Shandong) on the Chinese mainland began mission work on Taiwan and gained a strong following. This group, the Jen-yessu Chiao-huei (True Jesus Church), continued to grow after the Japanese occupation. In the early 21st century, this church was one the largest of the totally Chinese/Taiwanese-controlled churches on the island.

After the end of World War II and the worst years of retrocession and the Nationalist resettlement (1945-51), many of the Western church missions that had been active on the Chinese mainland moved to the safe and open-to-Christians island of Taiwan. A missionary invasion of sorts thus took place, and Taiwan became an overchurched, but far from Christian, island. Southern Baptists, Lutherans, Methodists (→ Methodist Churches), → Assemblies of God and other Pentecostal churches, Quakers (→ Friends, Society of), and → Mennonites, as well as the → Mormons, all began work on the island. Over the decades the presence of these various churches became increasingly visible in the expanding cities of the island. → Conversions (§1) and → church growth did not match the growing numbers of missionaries who now called Taiwan their home.

Another major indigenous church with mainland roots, the Little Flock, inspired by Watchman Nee (1903-72), came after 1945. Nee himself did not come to Taiwan, but this group began to challenge the equally aggressive and highly independent True Jesus Church for Taiwanese souls. This struggle continues to this day, with each church having its own very visible centers in Taipei and in Taichung, along with churches in many other cities and towns.

A rather radical and anti-KMT rival to these churches is the charismatic New Testament Church. This was also a church indigenous to China, with roots in Shanghai and Hong Kong; it is led on the island by their prophet Elijah Hong. Based in a mountain stronghold in Tainan country, the church carried on a long struggle with the ROC government before it was negotiated by the sociologist and activist Chu Hai-yuan of the Institute of Sociology/Academia Sinica. It remains to this day a small but vocal and very distinctive independent church with a strong orientation to biblical inerrancy.

2.3. *Ecumenical Relations*

Despite many attempts, there is no ecumenical church council in Taiwan (→ National Christian Councils). In 1954 a union was organized, the Taiwan Missionary Fellowship, with 80 members (including the Presbyterians, Methodists, Lutherans, Anglicans, Baptists, and evangelicals). There is also an association of Chinese Lutheran churches in Taiwan (1979).

One reason for this lack of common church council is the split between churches that work with the *waishenren* (mainlanders) and those who work with the people who were on Taiwan before 1945 — the *bendiren* (Taiwanese- and Hakka-speaking Han Chinese) and the *yuan-chu-min* (aborigines). There is also a political difference, for the PCT is a liberal church that supports Taiwanese selfhood, while the other major churches, all much smaller than the PCT, back the KMT and are primarily Waishenren. The Presbyterians tend to work with the indigenous churches that worked with the Taiwanese and the aborigines, such as the True Jesus Church, though such contacts are more informal, given the fierce independence of the indigenous churches. The True Jesus pastors also have contacts with Maryknoll brothers, for members of that order work with Taiwanese and aborigines and were supporters of Taiwanese selfhood in the bitter political struggles of the 1970s and 1980s. Although most Catholics and Protestants did not work together, the Maryknollers and the PCT did maintain contact during the 1970s and 1980s, given their shared politics and devotion to the Taiwanese and their struggle for political → rights and democratization.

Such churches as the Southern Baptists are also more conservative politically and did work with the Nationalist regime. The pastor of former president Chiang Kai-shek (1887-1975) was Chou Lien-hua, an American-trained Southern Baptist pastor. Chou spoke at Chiang's funeral and at the funeral of his son Chiang Ching-kuo, 13 years later.

The Roman Catholic Bishops' Conference includes a commission for Christian unity and religious → dialogue. The church takes part in the work of the Federation of Asian Bishops' Conferences. Some Protestant churches are also active in the work of the → Christian Conference of Asia.

3. Church and State

Taiwan is a secular state and guarantees → religious liberty. By its strong nationalism and anti-Communism, which has somewhat softened (in 1987 a security council replaced the state of emergency, and → political parties were allowed), it has come into conflict with the churches, especially with the Presbyterians, whose members are mostly Taiwanese and who work strongly in the Taiwanese independence movement (T'ai-tu). The Roman Catholics, unlike the Protestants, have not been actively in dialogue with the government, but the Maryknollers were politically active, and some were expelled from the ROC in the late 1970s because of their work with Taiwanese political activists. Since 1972 certain key Protestant churches, however, have a clear public profile on the basis of their contextual ecclesiology (→ Contextual Theology).

The Presbyterians have published several statements on political and social questions such as security, human rights, self-determination, and the right to vote. They have also challenged the KMT with public petitions and have called on the WCC and the U.S. → National Council of Churches to support the rights of the Taiwanese ethnic majority, who have challenged the minority Waishenren-led KMT government. A number of important leaders of the Tangwai (lit. "outside the party") movement, a group of Taiwanese political leaders and organizers of the 1970s and 1980s, were Presbyterians. Some of the leaders of the PCT were jailed for aiding and abetting the Tangwai in the struggles against the KMT regime in the late 1970s and the early 1980s. The twin daughters and the mother-in-law of the prominent Tangwai attorney Lin Yi-hsiung were murdered in their apartment in the spring of 1980 as Lin was standing trial for treason and insurrection. As of 2007, the murderers had not been found. The Lin family apartment was given to the PCT and is now an important church that is located a mile or so away from the PCT headquarters in the south-central part of Taipei.

Since 1984 there has been an unofficial quota for missionaries, and churches have been discouraged from political engagement. No religious activity in schools or military buildings is allowed. The churches are not required to register, but a careful watch is kept on their activities. The Ministry of Social Services oversees religious matters.

4. Prospects

That the churches are seen as alien is a great obstacle to evangelization. So too is the growing pragmatism and commercialization. Chiang Kai-shek (ROC president 1948-75) was a Christian, as was President Lee Teng-hui (1988-2000), which has brought Christianity greater visibility. The work of the Presbyterians in the struggles of the 1970s and 1980s centered on political and social justice did much to increase the visibility and prominence of the Christian faith among the average citizens of Taiwan.

Taiwan may seem open to the → gospel, but given the renewed strength of the popular religious tradition, the syncretistic sects, and the social-activist forms of Taiwanese Buddhism, a breakthrough seems unlikely to come from either the Roman Catholics or the Protestants. Since 1990/91 a process of Chinese reunification has been much discussed, but little has been done on the government-to-government level. Taiwan, however, has become both a customer of and an investor in the PRC, and in 2006 there were one million Taiwanese living in the PRC. While China and Taiwan have very different ideas of what form a reunited China should take, it is clear that economic and people-to-people contact is on such a high level that a new vision of a greater southeastern China has now become more viable. In this new very dynamic and potentially crisis-ridden environment, the churches need to find a new role politically, ecclesiologically, and pastorally.

Bibliography: D. B. Barrett, G. T. Kurian, and T. M. Johnson, *WCE* (2d ed.) 1.723-26 • D. Bays, ed., *Christianity in China: From the Eighteenth Century to the Present* (Palo Alto, Calif., 1996) • S. Chandler, *Establishing the Pure Land on Earth: The Foguang Buddhist Perspective on Modernization and Globalization* (Honolulu, 2004) • P. Clart and C. Jones, eds., *Religion in Modern Taiwan: Tradition and Innovation in a Changing Society* (Honolulu, 2003) • A. R. Gates, *Christianity and Animism in Taiwan* (San Francisco, 1979) • Huang Po-Ho, *A Theology of Self-Determination* (Tainan, 1996) • J. Johnston, *China and Formosa: The Story of the Mission of the Presbyterian Church of England* (London, 1897) • C. B. Jones, *Buddhism in Taiwan: Religion and the State, 1660-1990* (Honolulu, 1999) • M. A. Rubinstein, "The NT Church and the Taiwanese Protestant Community," *The Other Taiwan: 1945 to the Present* (ed. M. A. Rubinstein; Armonk, N.Y., 1994) 445-73; idem, *The Protestant Community in Modern Taiwan* (Armonk, N.Y., 1991) • C.-m. P. Wang, "Christianity in Modern Taiwan," *China and Christianity: Burdened Past, Hopeful Future* (ed. S. Uhalley Jr. and X. Wu; Armonk, N.Y., 2001) 321-44 • C.-f. Yü, *Kuan-yin: The Chinese Transformation of Avalokiteâsvara* (New York, 2001).

Murray A. Rubinstein and Roman Malek

Taizé Community

The founder and first prior of the ecumenical community of Taizé was Roger Schutz (1915-2005), born in Switzerland as the son of a Reformed pastor. After studying theology, he bought a house in 1940 in Taizé, near Cluny in Burgundy, started regular worship there (→ Hours, Canonical), and took in refugees. The first Protestant brothers joined him in 1942, the first Roman Catholics in 1969. In 2005 the community included more than 100 brothers, Roman Catholic, Anglican, and Protestant.

Entry into Taizé involves vows binding one to community life (→ Monasticism) and → celibacy. Fraternities exist in many lands at places of need. Since 1966 the Roman Catholic Soeurs de St. André have been among the many visitors, most of whom are youthful. A Council of Youth was held in 1974, and since 1982 it has found a continuation both in Europe and abroad as the "pilgrimage of trust on earth" (→ Transdenominational Movements), which has the goal of deepening the inner life and → solidarity with the human family. Every summer the council attracts nearly 100,000 teenagers.

Taizé has kindled worldwide a sense of → unity and offers a model of community life that knows no borders (→ Ecumenism, Ecumenical Movement). It is represented on many commissions set up by the → World Council of Churches and the → Vatican. It very early sought communion with the pope as the "universal pastor." It finds the source of growing Christian unity in the → Eucharist, at which Roman Catholics and Protestants receive communion according to their own traditions. In 1990, at its 50th anniversary, almost all church governing bodies recognized what Taizé had done. Prayer (→ Liturgy), → Bible study, stillness, conversations, and work fill up the day. With simple means, and very tentatively, Taizé is for many people a place of reconciliation, sharing, and celebration (→ Worship).

In August 2005, in a shocking moment for the Taizé Community, Brother Roger was stabbed to death by a mentally unstable woman during the Taizé evening prayer service. His successor is Brother Aloïs (b. 1954), a German Roman Catholic.

→ Ecumenical Dialogue; Religious Orders and Congregations

Bibliography: O. CLÉMENT, *Taizé, a Meaning to Life* (Chicago, 1997) • M. FIDANZIO, ed., *Brother Roger of Taizé: Essential Writings* (Maryknoll, N.Y., 2006) • J. L. GONZÁLEZ-BALADO, *The Story of Taizé* (rev. ed.; London, 2003) • J. M. KUBICKI, *Liturgical Music as Ritual Symbol: A Case Study of Jacques Berthier's Taizé Music* (Louvain, 1999) • *Praise God: Common Prayer at Taizé* (trans. E. Chisholm; New York, 1977) • BROTHER ROGER, *Parable of Community: The Rule and Other Basic Texts of Taizé* (New York, 1981) • K. SPINK, *A Universal Heart: The Life and Vision of Brother Roger of Taizé* (rev. ed.; London, 2006).

JAKOB FREY†, with THE EDITORS

Tajikistan

	1960	1980	2000
Population (1,000s):	2,083	3,953	6,398
Annual growth rate (%):	3.75	2.89	1.90

Area: 143,100 sq. km. (55,300 sq. mi.)

A.D. 2000

Population density: 45/sq. km. (116/sq. mi.)
Births / deaths: 2.82 / 0.64 per 100 population
Fertility rate: 3.57 per woman
Infant mortality rate: 51 per 1,000 live births
Life expectancy: 68.5 years (m: 65.7, f: 71.4)
Religious affiliation (%): Muslims 85.5, nonreligious 10.6, Christians 2.1 (Orthodox 1.6, other Christians 0.6), atheists 1.4, other 0.4.

1. General Situation
2. Religious Situation

1. General Situation

The Republic of Tajikistan, in central Asia, has its longest border with Afghanistan to the south. It also borders China to the east, Kyrgyzstan to the north, and Uzbekistan to the west. The Pamirs and the Tian Shan Mountains dominate the country, with more than half its territory lying above 3,000 m. (10,000 ft.). Only 6 percent of its land is arable. Economically, it is the poorest member of the → Commonwealth of Independent States.

Ethnically, about 65 percent of the population are Tajiks, speaking an eastern dialect of Persian. One-quarter of the people are Uzbeks, a Turkic group, with 3-4 percent Russians and the rest primarily a variety of other Turkic groups (Kyrgyz, Tatar, and Turkmen). Tajiks are descendants of the Sogdians and Bactrians, eastern Iranian inhabitants of central Asia, and of the Persian-speaking Samanid Empire (875-999).

In the mid-19th century, Tajikistan came under Russian rule. A brief period of greater freedom occurred after the Russian revolution in 1917, but soon the Soviets had reestablished control. In 1924 Tajikistan became an autonomous Soviet socialist republic within Uzbekistan; in 1929 the Tajik Soviet Socialist Republic was proclaimed (→ Soviet Union).

Tajikistan declared its independence on September 9, 1991, just before the final breakup of the

USSR. A costly civil war ensued, ultimately claiming an estimated 55,000 lives, with former Communists fighting against Islamists and secular democrats. A pro-Communist regime ultimately triumphed. President Emomali Rahmon (b. 1952) has been in office since November 1994. In 2003 voters approved constitutional changes that could allow Rahmon to serve as president until 2020.

2. Religious Situation

Very little is known about the nature of a Christian presence in Tajikistan between the 8th and 10th centuries, when it constituted part of the hinterland for the episcopal sees along the Silk Road, where nearby Samarqand (now in Uzbekistan) was the cathedral city. The region, thinly settled, came under the influence of → Islam at least by the 12th century and remained so till the → secularization attempts during the era of the Soviet Union. At present, the citizens of Tajikistan enjoy constitutional freedom of religion (→ Religious Liberty). Fear of radical Islam, however, leads the government to closely monitor, and sometimes restrict, religious activity.

In Dushanbe, the capital of Tajikistan, an Evangelical Christian–Baptist (ECB) congregation started in 1929 but was closed by 1937 when Stalinist religious persecution reached central Asia. There was a new beginning in 1944, when the congregation in Dushanbe was registered. By 1958 over 200 people were attending services, representing 16 nationalities; there was also an afternoon service in German, reflecting the influence of Soviet Germans who had been forcibly resettled there during World War II. A new church building was completed in 1981, and there were several other meeting points not far from Dushanbe. During the mid-1990s there was a growth of neo-Protestant groups (→ Baptists, → Evangelicals, and → Pentecostals), plus active mission work by the Bible League and the indigenous Nadezhda (hope) Mission from Kyrgyzstan. Around 1996 repressions against believers started, an Orthodox scholar speaking of a "massive antireligious campaign 1998-1999" (N. Mitrokhin, 541).

The → Russian Orthodox Church also increased its presence in Tajikistan after 1944, when more immigrants from Russia and Ukraine, many of them sent there involuntarily during the era of purges, were able to assemble for worship. By 1990 there were six Orthodox parishes in Tajikistan, with a cathedral church in Dushanbe. Two of the parishes were in Dushanbe, two in northern Sughd Province (formerly Leninabad Oblast, Khudzhand and Chkalovsk), and two in the southern regions (Qŭrghonteppa [Kurgan-Tyube] and Tursunzade).

But within a decade the majority of Slavic-speaking Orthodox believers had immigrated to Russia, leaving only pensioners and military personnel.

Although the cathedral church in Dushanbe had a membership list of 5,000, even at the Easter liturgy in 2002 only 600 attended, with the usual attendance around 400. According to Nikolai Mitrokhin's findings, which included personal visits and interviews in 2002, the Russian Orthodox Church in Tajikistan had 6 parishes with 800 parishioners, the → Roman Catholic Church (largely for Soviet German settlers) had 3 parishes with 200 parishioners left, and Lutherans met in one congregation of 50 members (→ Lutheran Churches 2.5). The neo-Protestant churches included Evangelical Christian–Baptists (11 congregations, 700 members), Nadezhda Mission (12 congregations, 1,500 members, many Tajik-speaking), Sonmin (a Korean Presbyterian mission with 5 congregations, 1,500 members), and 500 → Adventists in 6 congregations.

→ Persecution of Christians 4.1

Bibliography: K. ABDULLAEV and S. AKBARZADEH, *Historical Dictionary of Tajikistan* (Lanham, Md., 2002) • R. R. HANKS, *Central Asia: A Global Studies Handbook* (Santa Barbara, Calif., 2005) • *Istoriia evangel'skikh Khristian–Baptistov v SSSR* (History of the Evangelical Christian–Baptists in the USSR) (Moscow, 1989) official history • L. JONSON, *Tajikistan in the New Central Asia: Geopolitics, Great Power Rivalry, and Radical Islam* (London, 2006) • N. MITROKHIN, *Russkaia Pravoslavnaia Tserkov. Sovremennoe sostoianie i aktual'nie problemy* (Russian Orthodox Church. Contemporary status and problems) (Moscow, 2006) 538-43 • M. H. RUFFIN and D. C. WAUGH, eds., *Civil Society in Central Asia* (Seattle, Wash., 1999). A Web site operated by Forum 18 (www.forum18.org) regularly features reports of religious rights violations in Tajikistan.

WALTER SAWATSKY

Talmud

1. Origin
2. Features
3. Development
4. Commentaries

1. Origin

The Talmud (Heb. *lmd,* "learn, teach"), strictly *talmûd tôrâ,* "study/teaching of the → Torah," is the main work of rabbinic literature. It consists of the → Mishnah (the earliest authoritative rendering of Jewish oral laws, mostly in Hebrew) and the Gemara

(Aram. *gemar*, "study, complete," a rabbinic commentary on the Mishnah, largely in Aramaic).

As rabbinic learning (→ Rabbi, Rabbinism) developed differently in its two geographic centers, the teaching tradition gave rise to two different versions of the Talmud. The Palestinian Talmud (PT, often but incorrectly called the Jerusalem Talmud) emerged from the study houses of Palestine at Caesarea, Sepphoris, and Tiberias, while the academies of Babylonia at Nehardea, Pumbedita, and Sura gave us the Babylonian Talmud (BT). There are, however, Babylonian traditions in the former, and Palestinian traditions in the latter.

2. Features

In structure and basic content the Talmud conforms to the Mishnah with its orders and tractates, though the inner arrangement differs considerably, and there are also substantial differences in detail between the two Talmuds. Thus the PT has Gemara only on the first four orders (apart from two tractates of the fourth order) and several chapters of a tractate on the sixth order, whereas the more voluminous BT lacks Gemara on the first and sixth orders, as well as several tractates of the second, fourth, and fifth orders. Though geared in structure to the Mishnah and organized as a discussion of it, the Gemara in both PT and BT also contains an abundance of traditional material that goes far beyond mere explanation or commentary upon the Mishnah, so that in part the two have the function of a kind of thesaurus or → encyclopedia, offering highly diverse, even seemingly disparate materials derived from manifold sources (Mishnah, Baraitot, Midrashim). Unlike the Mishnah and its almost exclusively → Halakic traditions, the Gemara of both Talmuds, but especially the PT, incorporates many → Haggadic traditions.

3. Development

The material in the Talmud was collected over several centuries and found expression in forms we are only just beginning to understand. Like all rabbinic literature, the Talmud cannot be ascribed to individual authors but consists of traditions and quotations, some anonymous, some ascribed to named individuals, which are arranged into thematic discourses according to a system of rules not yet fully understood. Traditionally viewed as a kind of shorthand record of discussions actually held in the study houses, these discourses have increasingly come to be seen as literary fictions that were created at the level of redaction, when bits of communication that had originated at different times and places were framed into a coherent whole. Hence we must distinguish between a diachronous Talmud, manifest in historically distinguishable textual units that have been subjected to much textual and redactional criticism, and a synchronous Talmud as a body of text in existence at a given time and preserving a uniform level of meaning.

Since the Talmud conveys itself only but does not reveal anything about itself, we can answer questions of how the text was committed to writing and redacted, if at all, only from the text itself. Results thus far rule out that we are dealing with the work of one redactor, as was once thought. We are rather to think of a redaction stretched out over a long period and following a variety of criteria. For the PT this process came to a close around the first half of the fifth century; for the BT, toward the end of the sixth and beginning of the seventh century. Research into these issues has long been hampered by the lack of a critical edition. Only in the 1990s were the most important textual witnesses of the PT made available in a synoptic edition.

4. Commentaries

While the BT enjoyed a quasi-canonical authority (→ Canon 1.2) early on, the PT received less attention and was seen only as a parallel or explanation of the BT. Thus, works commenting on the PT as an independent work emerged relatively late. The earliest commentary on individual tractates that has been preserved was written by Shlomo Sirillo (d. ca. 1558) in or about 1530. Shmuel Ashkenazi (ca. 1525-95) prepared commentaries on the Haggadic portions in 1590, and Joshua Benveniste (ca. 1590-1665) did so on the Halakic portions of 18 tractates. Likewise in the 17th century, the commentary of Elijah ben Loeb of Fulda (ca. 1650-1720) initiated increased study of the PT in eastern Europe. In the 18th century, Elijah Gaon of Vilnius (1720-97) put the study of the PT on a new basis when he tried to elucidate it as an independent work without having recourse to the BT. The commentaries most commonly used to this day are those of David Fränkel (1704-62, the teacher of Moses Mendelssohn) and Moshe Margolies (d. 1780). Modern research has greatly profited from the work of Saul Liebermann (1898-1983) and Louis Ginzberg (1873-1953).

The BT has been made the subject of commentaries since it came into being; it has formed the center of rabbinic learning for centuries and up until today. Many of the first expositions found their way into legal records, Halakic compendiums, and proto-introductions to the Talmud. Of almost all the commentaries written before the 10th century, only scattered citations have been preserved. The first surviving commentaries are those of Gershom ben Judah of Mainz (ca. 960-1028/40) and Ḥananel ben Ḥushiel of Kairouan (990-1053). The 11th century also saw the commentary of Rashi (Rabbi Shlomo Yitzḥaqi, 1040-1105), whose work continues to command great authority, even though hundreds of commentaries have been written since. Commentators after Rashi are divided into "early" (*rîšônîm*, up to the 15th cent.) and "late" (*'aḥărônîm*, from the 15th cent. to our own time).

→ Judaism 2

Bibliography: Translations: I. Epstein, ed., *Hebrew-English Edition of the Babylonian Talmud* (30 vols.; London, 1965-89) • J. Neusner, ed., *The Talmud of the Land of Israel* (35 vols.; Chicago, 1982-93) • A. Steinsaltz, ed., *The Talmud* (21 vols.; New York, 1989-99).

Secondary works: J. Z. Abrams, *The Babylonian Talmud: A Topical Guide* (Lanham, Md., 2002) • E. Bashan, "Talmud, Babylonian," *EncJud* 15.755-67 • B. Bayer, "Talmud," *EncJud* 15.750-55 • L. Jacobs, *Structure and Form in the Babylonian Talmud* (New York, 1991) • J. N. Lightstone, *The Rhetoric of the Babylonian Talmud: Its Social Meaning and Context* (Waterloo, Ont., 1994) • L. Moscovitz, *Talmudic Reasoning: From Casuistics to Conceptualization* (Tübingen, 2002) • J. Neusner, *The Reader's Guide to the Talmud* (Boston, 2001); idem, ed., *The Talmud: Law, Theology, Narrative; A Sourcebook* (Lanham, Md., 2005) • S. Safrai, ed., *The Literature of the Sages,* pt. 1, *Oral Tora, Halakha, Mishna, Tosefta, Talmud, External Tractates* (Philadelphia, 1987) • P. Schäfer, ed., *The Talmud Yerushalmi and Graeco-Roman Culture* (3 vols.; Tübingen, 1998-2002) • P. Schäfer and H.-J. Becker, eds., *Synopse zum Talmud Yerushalmi* (7 vols.; Tübingen, 1991-2001) • H. L. Strack and G. Stemberger, *Introduction to the Talmud and Midrash* (trans. M. Bockmuehl; Minneapolis, 1992; orig. pub., 1887).

Margarete Schlüter

Tanzania

1. General Situation
2. Christian Churches
3. Ecumenical Relations
4. Church and State
5. Non-Christian Religions

1. General Situation

The United Republic of Tanzania, on the coast of East Africa, is primarily an agrarian country; approximately 70 percent of the population is rural.

	1960	1980	2000
Population (1,000s):	10,205	18,581	33,687
Annual growth rate (%):	2.87	3.18	2.71

Area: 942,799 sq. km. (364,017 sq. mi.)

A.D. 2000

Population density: 36/sq. km. (93/sq. mi.)
Births / deaths: 3.91 / 1.20 per 100 population
Fertility rate: 5.06 per woman
Infant mortality rate: 72 per 1,000 live births
Life expectancy: 53.8 years (m: 52.4, f: 55.2)
Religious affiliation (%): Christians 50.9 (Roman Catholics 26.7, Protestants 12.9, unaffiliated 6.4, Anglicans 4.2, indigenous 2.2, other Christians 0.1), Muslims 31.7, tribal religionists 15.5, Hindus 1.0, other 0.9.

Tanzania has a spectacular landscape of mainly three physiographic regions: the islands and the coastal plains to the east; the inland, saucer-shaped plateau; and the highlands. Mount Kilimanjaro (highest peak: 5,895 m. / 19,341 ft.), in the northeast corner of the country, is the highest point in Africa.

Present-day Tanzania was formed by the union of two sovereign states: Tanganyika, which achieved independence from Britain in December 1961 and became a republic the following year, and the island Republic of Zanzibar, off the coast of Tanganyika, which became an independent sultanate in December 1963 and a republic a month later. The two joined as the United Republic of Tanzania on April 26, 1964. The government is a unitary republic consisting of the Union Government and the Zanzibar Revolutionary Government (the latter retaining considerable local autonomy).

Approximately 120 ethnic groups live in Tanzania, where large centralized kingdoms such as those found in precolonial West Africa did not exist. Over 90 percent of the population belongs to Bantu-speaking groups. Many Hamitic peoples live in the north, such as the Masai and Wakwavi or Parakuyo. The Swahili-speaking population of the East Coast and in Zanzibar is shaped by the early influence of Arab cultures. The large number of ethnic groups in Tanzania has not been divisive. Swahili (with English, the national language) has spread through the entire country and is today its most important unifying element. The other ethnic groups living in Tanzania include the economically powerful Asians (esp. Indians), Arabs, and Europeans.

Jakaya Mrisho Kikwete, president of Tanzania since December 2005, ran on a campaign of "New Vigour, New Zeal, and New Speed" and seeks to provide better life for all Tanzanians through economic reforms and the reduction of poverty. The present government seeks to build on the country's record of political stability by creating a more favorable climate for attracting foreign investors, plus developing its mineral resources (esp. diamonds, gold, and gemstones) and its largely untapped tourism sector.

2. Christian Churches

Approximately one-half of the population of Tanzania are Christians; of that number, about two-thirds are Roman Catholic, and one-third Protestant. Overall, the Christian churches in Tanzania have contributed much to the formation of many aspects of contemporary life, affecting the whole population equally. Sometimes there are reservations, however, concerning the historical and current role of the churches in society, due in part to the mixed record of the churches in dealing with questions of economic and social justice.

2.1. As early as the 16th century, missionaries from Portugal attempted to found a church in Tanzania. By the 17th century the work no longer existed, but in 1848 a further attempt was made as missionaries in Bagamoyo took up their work on the coast. The mission station at Bagamoyo became a refuge center for slaves (→ Slavery) on the coast who were living in misery or who had fled from Zanzibar. The first converts came from this group. They were settled in areas around Bagamoyo known as Christian Communities. Many later became itinerant preachers as new mission stations were opened in the interior of the country. Roman Catholic missionaries settled chiefly along the coast, especially in Pugu, where they founded one of the most respected upper schools in Tanzania, as well as in the southern highlands and the Kilimanjaro region.

Today the *Roman Catholic Church* has spread through the entire land; many Roman Catholic mission societies are at work in the country. The pioneer missions are the Holy Ghost Fathers, the White Fathers, the Benedictines, and the Franciscans. The church, whose leadership is Tanzanian, is now divided into two provinces. Particular emphasis is laid on church renewal and development.

2.2. The second largest church is the *Church of the Province of Tanzania*, the fruit of a mission work built by Anglicans (→ British Missions). In 1864 the Universities' Mission to Central Africa (UMCA) took up their work in Zanzibar, which then was extended in 1875 to the mainland. The UMCA founded a well-known upper school, as well as a teacher training school in Minaki. In 1965 the UMCA united with the Society for the Propagation of the Gospel to form the United Society for the

Propagation of the Gospel. These two movements belonged to the Catholic wing (High Church) of the → Anglican Communion (§1.2), which was dominant in southern Tanzania. From 1878 on, missionaries from the Church Missionary Society, from the tradition of the Protestant wing (Low Church), arrived from Great Britain, Australia, and later New Zealand. They began their work in central Tanzania, with Dodoma as its center.

In the colonial period the Anglican Church played a relatively larger political role than did other churches. Its cathedral in Dar es Salaam became the church of the regent, whose oath of office was administered by the bishop of the Anglican diocese. The Anglican Church dedicated itself to medical care and the school system. In 1970 the Anglican church of Tanzania became autonomous (i.e., a full province of the Anglican Church).

2.3. The third largest church is the *Evangelical Lutheran Church of Tanzania* (ELCT; → Lutheran Churches). Its history begins with the arrival of German missionaries toward the end of the 19th century, when Tanzania was under German rule (→ German Missions). The first mission society was the Evangelical Mission Society, or Berlin III, which began work in Dar es Salaam in 1887 and was later reorganized and became Bethel Society, working in Usambara, Digo, and Bukoba. In 1891 the Berlin Mission Society, or Berlin I, began work in the southern highlands, and in 1893 the Leipzig Mission Society began work in Kilimanjaro and spread to the Pare Mountains, Meru, Arusha, and Ruruma in Singida Region.

When the German missionaries had to leave the country during World War I, the Augustana Lutheran Church of America, which had had its own mission area in the center of Tanzania before the war, sent personnel into the orphaned mission areas (→ North American Missions). At the outbreak of World War II, the German mission work was again interrupted, and the National Lutheran Council of America sent help. Before and after the war, Scandinavian Lutherans helped as well; Swedish and Danish missionaries took over the mission work in Bukoba and its environs (→ Scandinavian Missions). In 1963 the various Lutheran churches joined together and founded the ELCT. It offered medical work and was also substantially involved in the building of schools (lower and upper schools and teacher training), which today, however, are under the government.

2.4. In the year 2000 several smaller churches had approximately a half million members each. The largest two were the *Africa Inland Church,* the fruit of mission work by the Africa Inland Mission (from 1908), and the *Pentecostal Churches in Tanzania,* started by Pentecostals from Sweden, Canada, and the United States, who were at work in Tanzania since the 1930s.

The → *Moravian Church in Tanzania* was founded by German missionaries in 1891. This church is located mostly in the west and southwest and is mainly involved in medical work. The *Seventh-day Adventist Church* stems from German → Adventists, who in 1903 founded a church in Tanzania. Other churches are the *Tanzania Assemblies of God* (from 1930) and the *New Apostolic Church.* There are numerous → Independent Churches, although fewer than in many other African countries.

3. Ecumenical Relations

The Tanganyika Missionary Council was formed in 1936, which made the cooperative work of the various missions possible. In 1948 it became the Christian Council of Tanganyika, and in 1964 the Christian Council of Tanzania (CCT; → National Councils of Churches). Its members include the Lutherans, → Anglicans, → Moravians, → Salvation Army, and → Baptists. In the decade of the 1960s, conversations were held concerning a unification of the churches, but in 1968 they ended in failure.

The Roman Catholic Episcopal Commission for Ecumenism has established good contacts with the various Protestant churches. An example of interconfessional cooperation is the shared leadership of religious radio programming. In addition, there is a general curriculum for religious teaching in the schools. At the large religious celebrations there are common services of worship. Julius K. Nyerere, Tanzania's first president (1964-85) after independence and an active Catholic, mediated among the churches. The Education Act of 1969, which gave the Tanzanian government oversight of all the schools, was a side effect of the upturn in ecumenical cooperation.

The CCT and the Tanzanian Bishops' Conference meet regularly in order to discuss matters of mutual interest. This cooperation is visible also at the level of village congregations.

4. Church and State

No clear-cut policy has been formulated governing the relation between → church and state in Tanzania. The primary interest of the government since independence (1961) has been the securing of national unity. The state guarantees the protection of human rights, as well as equal justice for all, regard-less of race, religion, or social rank. No religion is privileged or seen as the state religion. Each Tanzanian citizen has free choice of religion. All religious groups must officially register.

The churches in Tanzania recognize today that they are placed in a special cultural context. They must learn to express themselves in a way that is relevant for the present cultural and political environment, though without completely conforming to it. The significance of the church in today's society is not identical with that of the mission societies of the colonial period (→ Colonialism and Mission). The churches have gained a new understanding of what they can do in the specific social, ecumenical, and political development of the nation.

As late as 1970, the Christian churches in Tanzania carried responsibility for the leadership of two-thirds of the lower and upper schools, for which their annual financial contribution was estimated to be nearly $10 million. That year the schools were taken over by the Ministry of Education, which led to certain tensions, but not to a break.

The Tanzanian churches decided, as an alternative, to support work dealing with agriculture and water supply, as well as technical education. They were financially supported by European and American churches, as well as the → Lutheran World Federation. The development work (→ Development 1) of the churches was not only appreciated by the government but supported by the population. The churches recognized that they should contribute to the process of national reconciliation. They also saw the necessity of strengthening their own → unity. They seek no close connection with the government. Moreover, they have made an effort to show themselves independent regarding political ideologies.

5. Non-Christian Religions

Religions other than Christianity that are practiced in Tanzania are → Islam, traditional African religion (→ Guinea 2), → Hinduism, and → Bahai. The last two are found exclusively among the Asian population, who are for the most part descendants of contracted workers who came from India in the early 20th century.

Islam shows a notable strength, especially in the coastal region of Tanzania and the island group Zanzibar, whose inhabitants are predominantly Muslim. The organizing authority over the various groups of Tanzanian Muslims is the National Muslim Council of Tanzania, which is recognized by the government. For the most part, there is harmony between Muslims and Christians, as well as some shared religious programs. Under the colonial government, contacts between the two communities were discouraged; today, though, Christians are active in areas that were formerly almost exclusively Muslim.

The traditional religions have remained vital, especially among certain peoples in the south and west of Tanzania, and they continue to have an influence on the country's culture. The so-called Ujamaa program of Tanzania (a project of resettling peasants in villages in order to practice collective farming) is partially derived from African religious concepts. The traditional religions are based on the values of the community (→ Tribal Religions). In the earlier rural congregations, taking part in the religious rites was an element of communal membership. Under the Ujamaa program, with its emphasis on social factors, the traditional ties of family and tribe were extended to the entire people.

Bibliography: W. B. Anderson, *The Church in East Africa, 1840-1994* (Dodoma, Tanz., 1977) • D. B. Barrett, G. T. Kurian, and T. M. Johnson, *WCE* (2d ed.) 1.729-33 • A. Hastings, *A History of African Christianity, 1950-1975* (Cambridge, 1979) • E. Hillman, *Toward an African Christianity: Inculturation Applied* (New York, 1993) • A. A. Lema, *The Influence of Christian Mission Societies on Education Policies in Tanganyika, 1868-1970* (Hong Kong, 1980) • G. H. Maddox and J. L. Giblin, eds., *In Search of a Nation: Histories of Authority and Dissidence in Tanzania* (Oxford, 2005) • J. S. Mbiti, *African Religions and Philosophy* (2d ed.; London, 1990) • J. K. Nyerere, *Ujamaa—Essays on Socialism* (London, 1971) • L. Rasmussen, *Christian-Muslim Relations in Africa: The Cases of Northern Nigeria and Tanzania Compared* (London, 1993) • M. Wright, *German Missions in Tanganyika, 1891-1941* (Oxford, 1971).

Anza A. Lema† and Joseph Parsalaw

Taoism and Chinese Popular Religion

1. Taoism

Taoism (often "Daoism," reflecting the modern pinyin method of transliterating Chinese), the in-

digenous higher religion of China, has traditionally been divided into a "philosophical" and a "religious" aspect but is better understood as consisting of three strands: literati, communal, and self-cultivating.

1.1. *Literati Taoists*

Literati Taoists are members of the educated elite who focus on Taoist ideas as expressed by the ancient thinkers. They use these concepts to create → meaning in their world and hope to exert some influence on the political and social situation of their time, contributing to greater universal harmony, known as the state of Great Peace *(taiping).* The lineage and legitimacy of such literati Taoists comes from devotion and dedication to the classical texts, which they interpret in commentaries and essays, and whose metaphors they employ in stories and poetry. Part of the tradition since its inception, literati Taoists appear throughout Chinese history among commentators to the texts, patriarchs of religious schools, thinkers of Confucian or Buddhist background, and academics today (→ Confucianism; Buddhism).

1.2. *Communal Taoists*

Communal Taoists, too, are found in many different positions and come from all levels of → society. They are members of organized Taoist groups that have priestly hierarchies, formal initiations, regular rituals, and prayers to the gods. Some communal Taoists organizations are tightly controlled fraternities with secret → rites and limited contact with the outside world. Others are part of ordinary society, centered on neighborhood temples and concerned with the affairs of ordinary life, which they manage with the help of rituals, prayers, and moral rules. Historically, they have been documented from the second century A.D. onward and have shown a high degree of continuity over the millennia.

1.3. *Self-Cultivating Taoists*

The third group of Taoists focus on self-cultivation and are known as practitioners of *yangsheng,* or nurturing life. They too come from all walks of life, but rather than communal rites, their main concern is the attainment of personal health, longevity, peace of mind, and spiritual → immortality — either in mystical oneness with Tao or through visions of and interaction with the gods. They tend to pay little attention to political involvement, and their organization depends strongly on the master-disciple relationship. Their groups can be small and esoteric, with only a few active followers (as certain Taiji lineages), large and extensive with leanings toward organized religion (as the contemporary Falun Dafa), or vague and diffuse with numerous people practicing a variety of different techniques (as in modern Qigong).

Interconnected from the beginning, these three types of Taoism, although distinct in their abstract description, are not mutually exclusive in practice. On the contrary, as contemporary practitioners often emphasize, to be a complete Taoist one must follow all three paths: studying → worldview and being socially responsible, performing rituals and praying to the gods, and undertaking self-cultivation for health and spiritual advancement.

2. Chinese Divine Beings

Chinese popular religion, in ancient times as much as today, consists of the belief in a multitude of divine beings and the practice of rites and ceremonies to keep in good standing with them. Divine entities can be divided into three groups: nature gods, ancestors and gods derived from ancestors, and ghosts and demons.

2.1. *Nature Gods*

Nature gods are the deities of heaven and earth, stars and planets, rivers and lakes, mountains and fields, rain and wind, lightning and thunder, and so on (→ Nature Religion). They are seen as semianthropomorphic or semibeastly (water-related deities tend to be dragons, for example) and ranked in a hierarchical system of command, with heaven at the top and the various other gods below. So, for example, the deities of the five sacred mountains would outrank those of lesser peaks, and the dragon king of the Eastern Sea would be higher in status that his counterpart in a mere lake or river. Nature gods have a great impact on human life in that they determine the fertility of the land, the amounts of rain and sunshine, the occurrence of disasters (floods, earthquakes, landslides), as well as the harmony of society and the selection of the ruler. They are propitiated through regular seasonal sacrifices offered at special nature altars and performed by all, from the king and high nobility on down to the common peasant — each according to his or her station. Heaven and earth, for example, should be worshiped particularly by the central king or emperor, while the various gods of mountains, fields, and waterways have to be taken care of by the local people.

In addition to this basic nature pantheon, Han cosmologists added several new figures. Most important among them were the Five Emperors *(wudi)* as representatives of the cosmic powers of the five phases, each worshiped in his respective season and with his matching colors, numbers, tones, and so on. They also established a central deity known as the Great One (Taiyi) to hold a position in their cen-

ter and rank slightly above them in a higher form of the Yellow Emperor. This Great One was associated closely with Tao, which also became a deity in the Han dynasty and was worshiped in the figure of the saintly Laozi (Lao-tzu, fl. 6th cent B.C.), now equipped with supernatural and cosmic powers. There was therefore a tendency in popular and official religion to add human-form representations of abstract cosmic entities to the basic pantheon of nature-based gods.

2.2. *Ancestors*

Another major group of deities were the ancestors, defined as deceased immediate relatives in the male line plus their spouses, usually venerated up to five generations (→ Ancestor Worship). Their worship was central in ancient China, and especially prominent in the Shang, the earliest Chinese dynasty (1766-1122 B.C.), whose people believed that most events in life were caused by either the goodwill or the curse of an ancestor and whose calendar (the ten-day week) was set up to allow regular sacrifices to all of them.

Since the Warring States period, ancestors have been understood to exist in two parts, their *hun* and *po* souls, which would separate at death and go different ways. The *hun*, or spiritual part, would move on into an ancestral heaven and could be accessed through worship of the ancestral tablet at home. The *po*, or material part, went into the grave, where it had to be supplied with a legal contract to the land of the grave as well as with goods and proper care to prevent it from coming back as a ghost. Grave contracts have been found in tombs from the early centuries A.D., when grave goods consisted of meals, gifts, texts, and personal belongings. Today, grave goods are mostly paper replicas of desirable items. Ancestors were and are believed to be conscious and knowledgeable of their descendants' affairs. They require regular supplies of food, wine, incense, and incantations, and they will in due return send good fortune and provide protection. The relationship is strictly reciprocal, for disasters and illnesses in life are often attributed to neglect of one's ancestral duties.

While most ancestors in their concern and influence are strictly limited to their own family, some people are considered too meritorious and too beneficial for society to be limited to serving one family only. By popular consent, and ratified in a lengthy process of official recognition, such ancestors are made into popular gods who serve one specific community or grow to become national deities. Two well-known examples are the city god of Shanghai, Qin Yubo, a meritorious local official of the 14th century who was promoted to his supernatural position upon popular petition, and the wealth god Guandi, originally a military general of the 3d century who was first locally and then nationally worshiped and whose temple is found in most major Chinese cities.

The popular gods who grew from ancestors are also ranked in an organized hierarchy and divided into separate departments under the rule of the central Jade Emperor (Yuhuang), the personification of heaven. One department is of particular importance to people since it supervises humanity, keeping track of people's good and bad deeds and adding to or subtracting from the time of one's life span. This so-called Department of Destiny is run by the Ruler of Fates (Siming), a deity first documented in manuscripts from the fourth century B.C. and still important today. Proper behavior on earth and regular worship of these deities will ensure good fortune and prosperity for generations to come.

2.3. *Ghosts and Demons*

A third group of supernatural entities prominent in Chinese popular religion are ghosts and → demons, for the most part defined as the unhappy or discontented dead. Some are people who died violently and who have come back to wreak vengeance; others are ancestors who have been neglected by their families and are hungry and in search of sustenance; yet others are mutant animals, creatures that have somehow gained the power to change their shape and cause trouble. To deal with these, people take basic precautions such as hanging demon-dispelling branches (preferably peach wood) or talismans over their doors, muttering spells against ghosts whenever they enter an unknown area, or performing a → divination before venturing out. Once a demon or ghost has made itself known, more active measures are taken, such as throwing a slipper at it, holding up a mirror, which will reveal its true, hideous shape, or calling it by its name. Normally, it can stand none of these acts and will vanish forthwith. Sometimes, however, more extensive rites of → exorcism are necessary, or perhaps a shamanic séance in which the demon is called out, identified, and properly vanquished (→ Shamanism).

3. Taoism and Popular Religion

All these deities have been part of Chinese popular religion since antiquity and have required various forms of care through worship and veneration or preventative rites and exorcisms. They have played an important part also in Taoism.

→ Popular religion enters the Taoist sphere with the early Taoist communities in the second century A.D. They participated actively in popular religious culture and adopted its key features, with two differences. First, they added a different type of deity to the pantheon, one that was not based on nature or a dead person and whose key characteristic was to be utterly beyond the relationship of common mutuality. This type of divinity is represented by the immortals who were originally humans but whose transformation into spirit beings did not involve the separation of the two souls and who thus bypassed → death as commonly understood. These divinities also included personifications of major cosmic forces, such as Lord Lao as the personification of Tao, the Queen Mother of the West as the representative of cosmic yin, and the Lord King of the East, who stood for cosmic yang. They were considered to be of higher purity and thus greatly superior to the gods derived from dead people.

The second difference that emerged among early Taoists and that has persisted to the present day was that they rejected shamanic trances, blood sacrifices, and orgiastic fertility rites, replacing them with written communications to the gods. Expressing their prayers and wishes in petitions, memoranda, and announcements, they established a formal line of communication with the otherworld, in which the master functioned as an otherworldly official himself, carrying the seals and powers of divine appointment. All this, moreover, they placed into the larger social agenda of transforming the world to a new level.

Bibliography: D. K. JORDAN, *Gods, Ghosts, and Ancestors: The Folk Religion of a Taiwanese Village* (Berkeley, Calif., 1972) • L. KOHN, *Daoism and Chinese Culture* (Cambridge, Mass., 2001) • D. L. OVERMYER, *The Religions of China: The World as a Living System* (San Francisco, 1986) • M. PUETT, *To Become a God: Cosmology, Sacrifice, and Self-Divinization in Early China* (Cambridge, Mass., 2002) • M. SHAHAR and R. P. WELLER, eds., *Unruly Gods: Divinity and Society in China* (Honolulu, 1996).

LIVIA KOHN

Teaching Office

1. Roman Catholic

As it now exists, the Roman Catholic doctrine of the church teaching office is a mixture of early and medieval elements given a distinctive profile by → Reformation controversies and influenced especially by modern secular absolutism. It can be regarded as neither free from contradictions nor as uncontested.

1.1. *History*

In its doctrine of the teaching office, a dogmatic exposition of Scripture enables the → Roman Catholic Church to appeal to specific NT passages (e.g., Matt. 16:16-17, 18-19; John 21:15-19), even though this exposition cannot stand up to modern historical-critical investigation (→ Exegesis, Biblical). Dogmatic historical writing (→ Historiography) also enables the church to amend actual relations in the life of the early church — for example, in matters of the ministry and the primacy of the Roman bishop (→ Pope, Papacy) — in such a way that the desired result is achieved for its teaching office.

The following historical developments have been decisive for the shape taken by the teaching office today. First, we have the monarchical episcopate and its understanding of itself, which owed its first development as a mono-episcopate to the battle against → Gnosticism. Then, we have the assimilating and structuring of the church and its ministry (→ Offices 1; Church Government) along the lines of the government and official → hierarchy of the → Roman Empire when Christianity became the state religion.

Third came the doctrine of the two powers that rule this world: the sacred authority of the → bishops *(auctoritas sacrata pontificum)* and the power of the king *(potestas regalis)* from the days of Gelasius I (492-96; *QGPRK* 462 and DH 347). This doctrine — focused now on the *one* bishop and the *one* pontiff — was stabilized and enforced by the donations of land made to the Roman bishop by Pepin (754) and Charlemagne (774). Fourth was the development of this teaching into the doctrine of the two kingdoms and then the theory of the two swords (Peter Damian [1007-72]; *QGPRK* 546).

Fifth came the long struggle for supremacy between popes and emperors, contrary to the intentions of the doctrine of the *two* powers, and culminating in the → bull *Unam sanctam* (1302) of Boniface VIII (1294-1303; → Empire and Papacy). In this bull the pope as the vicar of Christ raised the claim that, for the sake of their → salvation, all human beings must be subject to the Roman pontiff (*QGPRK* 746 and DH 870-75). The pope received all power from Christ; the emperor receives his secular power now from the hand of the pope.

Sixth, and against this background, there developed the idea of two classes within the church: the higher class of clergy and the lower of laity (→ Clergy and Laity). In keeping with the medieval ideas of order, the relation of laity to clergy was solely one of subordination (i.e., of lower to higher), in order that the order of the universe might be upheld (*QGPRK* 746). The papal claim, which could not be made good in the secular political sphere, was thus successfully internalized in the church itself. The result has been, even to this day, to give the church and its teaching office their essential structure and constitution, the semantic pillars of which derive from the political controversies between the popes and the emperors. The concept of two teaching offices in Thomas Aquinas (ca. 1225-74; → Thomism) — that of the bishops and popes *(magisterium cathedrae pastoralis)* and that of the doctors and professors of theology *(magisterium cathedrae magistralis)* (*Contra impug.* 2; *Quod.* 3, q. 4, art. 1[9]; *Sent.* 4.19.2.2, q. 3, sol. 2, ad 4) — has not thus far found acceptance. The tendency to do away with all originally independent offices, incorporating them into that of leadership, was promoted with great success. Only theology managed to resist, and it too runs up against a claim to absolute supremacy (M. Seckler).

Seventh, we must also take into account the battle of several papal jurisdictions during the Great Schism (1378-1417; → Heresies and Schisms 3), the ending of these by late medieval → conciliarism, and the defaming of conciliarism by the newly enhanced power of the papacy.

Eighth, and no less significant for the present profile of the teaching office, was the formalistic use of the teaching office in the Reformation period, which prevented it from properly taking up many very weighty and justifiable material issues and thus from acting in a way that would have been profitable to Christianity as a whole.

Ninth, princely absolutism after the religious civil wars of the 17th century, when it had been ended by the French → Revolution, then served as a model for the church and its teaching office in the 19th and 20th centuries. It created the setting for concrete acceptance of the teaching office and led in particular to the dogmatic definitions of → Vatican I (1869-70) that dealt with papal jurisdictional primacy and papal → infallibility in solemn ex cathedra pronouncements on doctrinal and moral questions.

1.2. *Doctrine and the Teaching Office*

The doctrine of the church's teaching office is embedded in that of the → church and its constitution. The teaching office is in the hands of the bishops as the teachers and pastors of their local churches (though individually they do not have infallibility) and of the whole body of bishops, along with the papacy and the pope. Distinction is made between the *ordinary teaching office,* expressed in → encyclicals, decrees, statements, admonitions, addresses, pastoral letters, → catechisms, and so forth, and the *extraordinary teaching office,* bindingly expressed in solemn ex cathedra pronouncements by the pope, in solemn conciliar decrees (→ Councils of the Church), and in doctrine agreed upon by all the bishops and the pope.

Those who oppose either the ordinary or the extraordinary teaching office (even though it is not infallible) must reckon with actions and proceedings against them. The local bishop can initiate such action at the national bishops' conference, which must then take the case to Rome if no clarification is achieved. But the → curia may also initiate an action directly itself. The carrying out of the proceedings against an "accused" party is, even today, closer to an → inquisition than an orderly judicial proceeding, despite many legal improvements. For those accused of → heresy or deviation, the proceedings themselves are murky. The accused are denied access to documents, their prosecutors are the judges, and they do not know who the witnesses are. Such actions in the teaching office fall short of what is universally felt to be just.

In the context of ecclesiology, especially acute themes regarding the teaching office are the church's teaching authority, binding doctrine, authentic teaching, infallibility, condemnation of false doctrine, and disciplining of (often allegedly) false teachers. From this ecclesiological standpoint the church's teaching office moves in the thematic field of → revelation, Holy Scripture, tradition, and binding exposition. → Vatican II dealt with both the dogmatic place and the thematic range of the teaching office in the dogmatic constitutions on the church *(Lumen gentium, LG)* and on divine revelation *(Dei Verbum, DV).*

1.3. *Doctrine of the Teaching Office*

1.3.1. In *LG* the doctrine of the church teaching office may be found in the part dealing with the church's hierarchical structure, which in the main follows the traditional line. As successors of the → apostles, bishops have the Lord's commission to teach all nations and to proclaim the → gospel to every creature (*LG* 24). In this respect the body of bishops, the College of Bishops, has authority only in conjunction with the bishop of Rome as Peter's successor and head of the college. "The Roman Pontiff, by reason of his office as Vicar of Christ, namely, and as pastor of the entire Church, has full, supreme and universal power over the whole Church, a power which he can always exercise unhindered. The order of bishops is the successor to the college of the apostles in their role as teachers and pastors. . . . Together with their head, the Supreme Pontiff, and never apart from him, they have supreme and full authority over the universal Church" (*LG* 22).

The bishops are "authentic teachers, that is, teachers endowed with the authority of Christ," and they are to be honored as witnesses to divine and catholic → truth. Believers must consent to a statement of their bishop on doctrinal and moral matters that is uttered in Christ's name and show it a religiously based → obedience. Furthermore, "this loyal submission of the will and intellect must be given, in a special way, to the authentic teaching authority of the Roman Pontiff, even when he does not speak *ex cathedra* in such wise, indeed, that his supreme teaching authority be acknowledged with respect, and that one sincerely adhere to decisions made by him, conformably with his manifest mind and intention." The pope has infallibility when as the supreme pastor and teacher "he proclaims in an absolute decision a doctrine pertaining to faith or morals." Acts of this kind are "irreformable by their very nature and not by reason of the assent of the Church" (*LG* 25).

The bishops also enjoy such infallibility when as a college, and in agreement with the pope, they unanimously and definitively issue a specific judgment on a matter of faith and morals. This is especially true when they do so in an ecumenical council. The doctrine to be defined is set forth in accordance with revelation. "This revelation is transmitted integrally either in written form or in oral tradition through the legitimate succession of bishops and above all through the watchful concern of the Roman Pontiff himself; and through the light of the Spirit of truth it is scrupulously preserved in the Church and unerringly explained. The Roman Pontiff and the bishops . . do not, however, admit any new public revelation as pertaining to the divine deposit of faith" (*LG* 25).

1.3.2. In *DV* (chap. 2) the issue is the interrelation of Scripture, tradition, and the teaching office in connection with the handing down of revelation. Two contrary positions in the understanding of tradition are interwoven in the one word "tradition." In the one position, apostolic preaching, as the apostolic tradition now enshrined in Holy Scripture, has absolute priority over the postapostolic churchly teaching tradition in which the apostolic tradition must be handed down and expounded. This position comes to clear expression in the statement that "this Magisterium is not superior to the Word of God, but is its servant" (*DV* 10). This view could fundamentally be brought into agreement with Reformation positions.

The other position, as formulated at the Council of → Trent (DH 1501), is that the scriptural apostolic tradition (i.e., Holy Scripture) and the oral apostolic tradition (i.e., postapostolic church tradition) do not differ in rank. Here holy tradition (i.e., the church's doctrinal tradition) and Holy Scripture are not differentiated but are closely bound together; indeed, "both of them, flowing out from the same divine well-spring, come together in some fashion to form one thing, and move towards the same goal" (*DV* 9). It may thus be said that, "in the supremely wise arrangement of God, sacred Tradition, sacred Scripture and the Magisterium of the Church are so connected and associated that one of them cannot stand without the others" (*DV* 10). Here there is no longer any trace of the supreme normative role of Scripture *(norma normans non normata)*.

1.3.3. Both *LG* and *DV* speak in an unusually idealistic way of the church's teaching office. Vatican II, however, missed the opportunity of wrestling with wrong decisions by the teaching office, of correcting them, and of showing realistically how the teaching office, with the assistance of the Holy Spirit, "listens to [the Word of God] devotedly, guards it with dedication and expounds it faithfully" (*DV* 10). These just-cited sentences from *DV* 10 conceal many serious, flawed decisions of the teaching office with regard to proceedings involving complaints over doctrine and judgments.

The tendency to greatly extend the universal papal primacy of doctrine, unrestrictedly and right up to the point of papal infallibility, and no less extensively to claim primacy in jurisdiction, has characterized development in recent years (at least since the 1983 CIC). In this development, many paths of renewal that would have been practicable through Vatican II have until now not been followed ecclesially. In view of the massive threat to the internal peace of the church posed by the Roman teaching office, the Cologne Declaration (1989) by more than 200 German, Austrian, Swiss, and Dutch theo-

logical professors drew attention to the danger. Many professors in Spain, Italy, France, Belgium, Latin America, and the United States supported the declaration or spoke out on the theme themselves. In obvious reaction the magisterium issued a statement in its document of May 24, 1990 ("Instruction on the Ecclesial Vocation of the Theologian"), in which it stated even more sharply the traditional doctrine of the teaching office, would not recognize the right of theologians to dissent even from noninfallible doctrines and doctrinal decisions, and demanded the subordination of theology to the teaching office.

In this situation involving church jurisdiction, nothing has changed to this date. The theological debate over the papal teaching office, however, has not come to a standstill. John Paul II (1978-2005), in his encyclical *Ut unum sint* (1995), invited the non–Roman Catholic churches to "engage with me in a patient and fraternal dialogue on this subject" (§96; see also §89), which includes the primacy of doctrine (§95). The theological debate that this invitation unleashed is in full swing; it has not been concluded either within the Roman Catholic Church or ecumenically.

1.4. *Theological and Ecumenical Problems*

In its present form the doctrine of the church teaching office expresses an ecclesiology that centers solely on Rome (→ Church 3.2). The koinonia *(communio)* ecclesiology of the early church, which Vatican II rediscovered and tried to make fruitful for the renewal of the church, has not yet penetrated into the concept of the teaching office. Vatican II simply put the two types of ecclesiology — Rome centered and *communio* centered — alongside one another without mediation. The two concepts, however, are not materially compatible. How a teaching office can have a place in *communio* ecclesiology needs to be worked out in a completely new way.

The current serious theological defects in the doctrine of the church's teaching office are indicated by this question: How is a church teaching office possible that takes seriously the gifts of the Spirit granted to each baptized person; that respects the maturity and personal responsibility of all believers, along with their insights into the faith; that takes into full account the *sensus fidelium* and the growing theological competence of numerous laypeople, women as well as men; and that abandons a paternalistic attitude?

Non–Roman Catholic churches find the Roman teaching office in its present form to be contrary to the spirit of the → gospel and the spirit of the → early church. An attentive listening to the biblical, historical, and material arguments from all of Christendom and their open discussion within the Roman Catholic sphere could lead to insights that could introduce the opening of what was formerly closed, bringing change, renewal, revision, and the beginning of the removal of historical baggage. Since hope is the hallmark of a Christian, this process could perhaps lead to a common, ecumenical form of church doctrinal teaching that, according to *DV* 10, could truly be understood as the result of devoted listening, dedicated guarding, and faithful exposition of the → Word of God (→ Ecumenism, Ecumenical Movement).

→ Church Discipline; Church Law; Excommunication; Polity, Ecclesiastical

Bibliography: *On 1.1:* A. DULLES, "The Magisterium in History: A Theological Reflection," *ChiSt* 17 (1978) 264-81 • B. LAURET and P. EICHER, "Lehramt," *NHThG* 2.438-50 • N. LÜDECKE, *Die Grundnormen des katholischen Lehrrechts in den päpstlichen Gesetzbüchern und neueren Äußerungen in päpstlicher Autorität* (Würzburg, 1997) • H. J. POTTMEYER, *Unfehlbarkeit und Souveränität. Die päpstliche Unfehlbarkeit im System der ultramontanen Ekklesiologie des 19. Jahrhunderts* (Mainz, 1975) • K. SCHATZ, *Vaticanum I. 1869-1870* (3 vols.; Paderborn, 1992-94) • M. SECKLER, *Die schiefen Wände des Lehrhauses. Katholizität als Herausforderung* (Freiburg, 1988) • B. TIERNEY, *Origins of Papal Infallibility, 1150-1350: A Study on the Concepts of Infallibility, Sovereignty, and Tradition in the Middle Ages* (Leiden, 1988).

On 1.2-3: "The Cologne Declaration: Authority out of Bounds," *Commonweal,* February 24, 1989, 102-4 • CONGREGATION FOR THE DOCTRINE OF THE FAITH, "Instruction on the Ecclesial Vocation of the Theologian," *OR(E),* July 2, 1990, 1-4 • R. R. GAILLARDETZ, *Teaching with Authority: A Theology of the Magisterium in the Church* (Collegeville, Minn., 1997) • A. GREELEY, "Information Deficit: Why the Church's Hierarchy Isn't Working," *Commonweal,* March 12, 2004, 14-15 • JOHN PAUL II, *Encyclical Letter "Ut unum sint": On Commitment to Ecumenism* (Washington, D.C., 1995) • H. KÜNG and J. MOLTMANN, eds., *The Right to Dissent* (Edinburgh, 1982) • J. B. METZ and E. SCHILLEBEECKX, eds., *The Teaching Authority of Believers* (Edinburgh, 1985) • H. J. POTTMEYER, *Towards a Papacy in Communion: Perspectives from Vatican Councils I and II* (New York, 1998) • J. PROVOST, K. WALF, and J. A. GARDINER, eds., *Power in the Church* (Edinburgh, 1988) • J. RATZINGER, *Principles of Catholic Theology: Building Stones for a Fundamental Theology* (San Francisco, 1987) • F. A. SULLIVAN, *Magisterium: Teaching Authority in the Catholic Church* (New York, 1983).

On 1.4: J. BROSSEDER, "Ökumenische Probleme der Dogmatischen Konstitution Dei Verbum des Zweiten Vatikanischen Konzils," *Das Zweite Vatikanische Konzil und die Zeichen der Zeit heute* (ed. P. Hünermann; Freiburg, 2006) 270-82 • J. BROSSEDER and W. SANDERS, eds., *Der Dienst des Petrus in der Kirche. Orthodoxe und reformatorische Anfragen an die katholische Theologie* (Frankfurt, 2002) • P. EMPIE, ed., *Papal Primacy and the Universal Church* (Minneapolis, 1974); idem, ed., *Teaching Authority and Infallibility in the Church* (Minneapolis, 1979) • H. FRIES and K. RAHNER, *Unity of the Churches: An Actual Possibility* (Philadelphia, 1983) • GROUPE DES DOMBES, *"Un seul Maître" (Mt. 23,8). L'autorité doctrinale dans l'Église* (Paris, 2005) • W. KASPER, *Leadership in the Church: How Traditional Roles Can Serve the Christian Community Today* (New York, 2003) • H. KÜNG, *Infallible? An Unresolved Enquiry* (exp. ed.; New York, 1994) • K. LEHMANN and W. PANNENBERG, eds., *The Condemnations of the Reformation Era: Do They Still Divide?* (Minneapolis, 1990) • NATIONAL COUNCIL OF CATHOLIC BISHOPS (U.S.A.), "Doctrinal Responsibilities: Approaches to Promoting Cooperation and Resolving Misunderstandings between Bishops and Theologians," *Origins* (Washington, D.C.), June 29, 1989, 97-110 • H. J. POTTMEYER, "Recent Discussions on Primacy in Relation to Vatican I," *Il ministero petrino. Cattolici e ortodossi in dialogo* (ed. W. Kasper; Rome, 2004) 227-47 • J. R. QUINN, *The Reform of the Papacy: The Costly Call to Christian Unity* (New York, 1999) • T. P. RAUSCH, *Catholicism in the Third Millennium* (2d ed.; Collegeville, Minn., 2003); idem, *Towards a Truly Catholic Church: An Ecclesiology for the Third Millennium* (Collegeville, Minn., 2005) • G. WENZ, *Kirche. Perspektiven reformatorischer Ekklesiologie in ökumenischer Absicht* (Göttingen, 2005).

JOHANNES BROSSEDER

2. Protestant

2.1. Concept

In the Protestant tradition we find both a broader and a narrower concept of doctrine. It is presupposed that the doctrine and the life of the church must be distinguished for the sake of the latter. As in the NT, → "proclamation," "witness," → "confession," and "doctrine" are almost interchangeable terms (cf. Matt. 4:17 with 7:28; Mark 1:14, 27 and John 7:16-17 with CA 7, in which we have an equation of pure teaching and preaching). In the narrower sense doctrine involves the theological attempt to put the content of proclamation in speech that is relevant to a particular time but still scriptural.

In keeping with this sense is the self-understanding of the Reformation confessions as outlines of doctrine (see Rom. 6:17, also *doctrinae forma* in Formula of Concord SD, introduction, "Binding Summary") that are made "at various times" (Formula of Concord Ep., introduction §8). Such outlines might not always be necessary but are required from time to time in order to distinguish true teaching from false. (In its early history the church had to deal with → Gnosis, → Montanism, → Arianism, and → Pelagianism. Later, the Reformers disputed Roman Catholicism, → Anabaptists, → anti-Trinitarians, and various controversies within Protestantism itself.)

2.2. *Enforcement*

The term "teaching office" has to do with the standard of true or pure or correct doctrine in the church, with the authority behind it, and the means to enforce it. In the Reformation view, the means of preserving pure doctrine for the church include teaching obligations and → ordination vows. The church authorities oversee these obligations in different ways, even to the point of removal from the office of public preaching by a formal action.

2.3. *Criteria*

Regarding the standard of church teaching, there is unanimity in the Reformation tradition in citing Holy Scripture as "the only judge, rule, and guiding principle" (Formula of Concord Ep., introduction §7). Against the enthusiasts, emphasis is put on the relation between letter and spirit. Internal conflicts in Scripture (e.g., between Paul and James) are set aside in the interests of the doctrine of verbal → inspiration.

The eroding of the older doctrine of verbal inspiration by historico-critical research (→ Exegesis, Biblical) led to detailed doctrinal conflicts, especially in the second half of the 19th century, but did not affect in principle the Reformation position. In the older → orthodoxy the confessions gradually became a secondary standard (*norma normata*, ibid.) of doctrine. With the rise of confessionalism in the 19th century (→ Denomination 4; Union), they came into even stronger use in identifying true doctrine.

2.4. *Authorities*

The material equation of proclamation and teaching in the NT shows who is finally the real subject of true doctrine, according to the Protestant understanding. In the last resort, the → Holy Spirit is the teaching office (John 14:26; 16:13). According to the NT, *all* Christians can have the gift of teaching and testing, of examining and judging the spirits, for all receive the Spirit (cf. Matt. 28:19-20 with John 20:22; 1 Cor. 2:15; 1 Thess. 5:19-20, etc.) and thus share in the threefold → office of Christ as prophet (teacher), priest, and king. For this reason M. → Luther (1483-1546; → Luther's Theology) stated that "a Christian assembly or congregation has the right and the power to judge all teaching and to call, appoint, and dismiss teachers" (1523, *LW* 39.305-14). The only differences as regards the teaching office are thus in terms of task and function.

In principle, the following groups function in the Protestant church as what we might call the penultimate authority in the teaching office. First, those who are ordained (→ pastors and their assistants) teach as they proclaim and instruct. Then, theological teachers (on theological faculties and in church schools) discharge the teaching office by investigating the → truth of doctrine. Today the promotion of → consensus in church teaching and the tackling of contemporary problems (e.g., → atheism or → secularization) are special tasks of academic theology. Finally, church leaders (e.g., → bishop and → superintendent; → Synod) exercise the teaching office by seeking continuity with valid doctrine, by deciding doctrinal questions in an orderly way, by attempting to preserve true doctrine through → visitations, and by taking action against false doctrine. Materially, the yearly Methodist Conference (→ Methodist Churches) sees to the fulfillment of these same functions.

2.5. *Means*

From what has been said about the norm and standard of the teaching office, it follows that the means to establish true doctrine in the church cannot be legal, as it is in the → Roman Catholic Church (see 1). The truth itself, making its own way, usually proves to be the decisive means. Doctrinal decisions are binding in virtue of the witness of Scripture, supported by the church's confession and the consent of the church. Extensive theological discussion may at times be needed, for church leaders and synods may also be mistaken in assessing what is true doctrine or false.

2.6. *Freedom*

Since the Reformation churches themselves originated out of the opposition of doctrinal authorities to the truth (W. Härle), and since they are convinced that the final judge of church doctrine is the Holy Spirit, they treasure freedom of teaching as a supreme good. At the same time, the Reformation tradition has never hesitated to pinpoint and reject false teaching. On the Reformation view this judgment is to be done "not with human power but with God's Word alone" (CA 28.21). Thus Luther said that "burning heretics is contrary to the Holy Spirit"

(WA 1.624.35-36). The → Reformers agreed, though, that when false teachers threaten public order or even shatter it, they should be punished.

Up to the 20th century the Protestant church exercised discipline according to → church law (→ Church Discipline; Excommunication). Thus the older dogmaticians, in their doctrine of the ministry, had a section on deposition, as well as calling, of pastors. But a change came in the 19th and 20th centuries with the separation of discipline relating to doctrine from discipline relating to manner of life. The Prussian Union Church broke new ground in 1910 with its heresy law. The prehistory, passage, and only two applications of this law brought to light differing positions on the question (debated by R. Sohm, M. Rade, and A. von Harnack). Most of the German territorial churches have now adopted corresponding procedures.

2.7. Processes

2.7.1. A first form of procedure is that of pastoral admonition and counseling. True doctrine does not consist merely of quoting Scripture and reciting confessional statements but of concretely expounding, relating, and applying Scripture and the confession. In this regard wrestling with the world, with the spirit of the time, and so forth plays a central role. The venture of new inquiry into the content of doctrine raises the possibility of heresy or error (→ Heresies and Schisms). On the Protestant view, then, there is always a need for doctrinal supervision by the church (whether → congregation, superintendent, bishop, or synod). Every visitation, assessment of preaching, or act of oversight on a superintendent's part, every pastors' conference, can be a form of doctrinal supervision. As a rule, too little use is made of such procedures.

2.7.2. Then we have doctrinal processes in the case of teachings that, while they may or may not scandalize the congregation, depart persistently and publicly from Scripture and the confession. At the request of the congregation the doctrine of an ordained minister is examined and assessed as to its agreement with the valid confession. German regulations that call for note are those of 1956 (rev. 1983), 1976 (Baden), and 1979 (Hesse and Nassau). A model was adopted by the → Arnoldshain Conference of 1975. In each case a long procedure is envisioned with a preceding theological discussion and study leave. It is assumed that efforts at a consensus may fail. Written and oral statements both have a place, with a view to some collegial decision before the hearing. This will state whether the proclamation and teaching of the minister concerned, in efforts to make application to the contemporary

scene, are incompatible with the decisive content of the biblical message according to the Reformation understanding (Arnoldshain). If a majority decides that they are incompatible, ordination privileges and office will be forfeited, but financial provision will be made to help the minister concerned into a new line of work.

The free churches (→ Baptists) have no regular procedures, but a two-thirds majority of the annual conference can dismiss a pastor when there is gross neglect of pastoral duties or when life and conduct are incompatible with the office (i.e., when mediation is no longer possible or a pastor has lost the chance of using it). All decisions exclude from the office of public proclamation but not from the church or → salvation. They are themselves subject to the Spirit, who guides into all truth.

In the → Orthodox Church and the → Anglican Communion, doctrinal deviation, as a violation of official spiritual duties, can lead to administrative and disciplinary procedures.

Bibliography: Christian Believing: A Report by the Doctrine Commission of the Church of England (London, 1976) • I. U. Dalferth, "Wissenschaftliche Theologie und kirchliche Lehre," *ZTK* 85 (1988) 98-128 • E. Geldbach, *Ökumene in Gegensatzen* (Göttingen, 1987) • G. A. Lindbeck, *The Nature of Doctrine* (Philadelphia, 1984) • J. Moltmann, H. Küng, and M. Lefébure, eds., *Who Has the Say in the Church?* (Edinburgh, 1981) • R. R. Osmer, *A Teachable Spirit: Recovering the Teaching Office in the Church* (Louisville, Ky., 1990); idem, *The Teaching Ministry of Congregations* (Louisville, Ky., 2005) • C. M. Robeck Jr., "An Emerging Magisterium? The Case of the Assemblies of God," *Pneuma* 25/2 (2003) 164-215 • W. Strietzel, "Disziplinarrecht der deutschen evangelischen Landeskirchen," *JusEcc* 34 (1988) 208-66 • W. A. Visser 't Hooft, *Teachers and the Teaching Authorities* (Geneva, 2000) • World Council of Churches, Commission on Faith and Order, "How Does the Church Teach Authoritatively Today?" *ER* 31 (1979) 77-93.

Wilhelm Hüffmeier

Technology

1. Social Sciences
2. Theological Ethics

1. Social Sciences

1.1. Technology is and has always been part of human → culture. The first tools appeared between two and three million years ago. Toolmaking devices were developed some 15,000 years ago in the Neolithic period, after the end of the last Ice Age. Some cultures then used farming and breeding technologies to create permanent settlements. The so-called higher cultures developed organized technological systems of transportation, irrigation, mining, taxation, writing, and religious and city architecture. Following Max → Weber (1864-1920), many social scientists list instruments of governance such as → law and → organization as technologies and regard immaterial technologies of social control as parallel to the material technologies used to master → nature. In short, technology is the source as well as the product of differentiated social life.

1.2. The universality of technology makes it difficult to define. It may refer to actual physical artifacts of engineering, to the processes by which these artifacts were created, or to the intellectual approach to solving problems that results in such artifacts. Nevertheless, one can identify four interwoven approaches. First, the classic approach stresses the finding and using of means to do things from the standpoint of instrumental action (A. Gehlen; → Action Theory).

In the second approach, goals and means are interchangeable: In doing something, every goal can become a means for achieving a further goal. Likewise every means can be turned into a goal for itself. Thus a definition in terms of → institutions has been found helpful (S. C. Gilfillan). The technical development of a → society thus runs parallel to the development of institutions that preserve and advance technological knowledge.

Third, many basic technologies are so consistent with societal structures that the terminology of means and ends needs to be expanded to a theory of technological media (W. Rammert). Historical examples are the spread of writing and → money. Today we would include all technological infrastructures such as systems of commerce, → mass media, and Internet systems.

Fourth, a nuanced view of technology shows that with different emphases, technology always has three aspects: the transforming of nature, social control, and individual competencies. A musical performance uses musical instruments, demands orchestral organization, and requires individual exercise or training. Production, too, depends upon technological means but also on the organizing of labor and on individual → work (→ Vocation). The linking of the instrumental, organizational, and methodological components has given rise to an approach in terms of sociotechnical systems (G. Ropohl; → Social Systems).

1.3. A consideration of the historical semantics of technology enriches sociological research into technology. The focus here is society's changing understanding and evaluation of what it regards as technological. The oldest sources in the West are the works of Homer, at the end of the eighth century B.C. (→ Greek Religion 2). In the *Iliad* the story of the Trojan horse figures as an example of a clever invention that was also a trick. In the *Odyssey* the hero overcomes many unusual situations by his inventiveness, combined with unscrupulous courage. The word "mechanics" (Gk. *mēchanē*, "cunning") thus carries two almost contradictory meanings.

In addition to this emphasis on clever applications, the myths of → creation encircling Prometheus (first found in Hesiod ca. 700 B.C.) underlie the view that technological aptitude is a basic human condition (*conditio humana*). The fire lit by Prometheus is a symbol that the human race must constantly use this aptitude. In his *Prometheus Bound* Aeschylus (525-456) calls fire the teacher of all technology (*didaskalos technēs*, 110).

According to Plato (*Prot.* 319ff.), Protagoras (ca. 485-ca. 410 B.C.) claimed that this basic anthropological aptitude extends to political technology in that the discovery and upholding of legal relations has a conventional technological character (→ Law and Legal Theory). The earliest medical schools at Cos and Cnidus, known from the Corpus Hippocraticum (Hippocrates, ca. 460-ca. 377), show for the first time that medical technology involves scholarly training and professional control. The Hippocratic writings also discuss whether technology works against or in accordance with nature. They thus open up a discussion of the legitimate limits of technology.

1.4. In the early → modern period the idea that social → progress was advanced by technological inventions became a theme of its own. F. Bacon (1561-1626) was the first technological optimist in this regard. Interest now shifted from the structure to the dynamics of technology. In the 16th and 17th centuries an expression of this shift was concern for the logic and art of invention, which were seen as applying the power of invention to the procedures of invention itself. Here technology could be an expression of nature's beauty or God's will. But it could also be a demon or an artistic abomination (J. Ruskin). Another expression of this dynamic involved the setting up of research institutions in which the natural sciences became the inventive resource for technological progress.

An effective combination of science and technology came only in the 19th century, initially in the fields of organic chemistry, electricity, and medicine. Technical research in state and industrial organizations became increasingly independent of academic research. The first to analyze the importance of technical dynamics on the development of the → industrial society was K. → Marx (1818-83; → Marxism).

1.5. Paradoxically, humanity's continually increasing technological success has changed the original optimism of progress into a kind of evolutionary → fatalism (→ Evolution). Society fears that it is becoming irrevocably dependent on a foreseeable but no longer controllable dynamic. This fatalism relates not only to material technology but also to self-perpetuating rationalization that seemingly no tradition can withstand (see J. Ellul and L. Mumford).

Since throughout human history many cultures have been responsible for deforestation, overpasturing, erosion, and pollution of the → environment, it is difficult to claim that preindustrial societies had a higher regard for nature. The point is, however, that the risks have increased today because of technology's extreme depth of intrusion into nature and the broad extent of its effects. Many applications of technology pose ecological problems for world society that place humankind in an evolutionarily unparalleled situation (→ Environmental Ethics). Global climate change (→ Ecology) is caused by the excessive use of energy. Increases in population come about because of medical progress and agricultural technology. Many forms of life are being lost, along with the genetic potential for new life forms.

Chemical compounds with not very well known side effects are invented on an ever increasing scale. Large installations in the nuclear and chemical industries have the potential for catastrophic accidents. Since all material technology sooner or later is turned into waste, unsolved problems of waste management are handed over to the next generation. Equally challenging is the pressure exerted upon societies as they increasingly face new technologies and the serious nature of such issues as → unemployment, migration, and inner-city slums (→ Poverty).

1.6. Sensitivity to these pressures in terms of the changing of values and the development of alternative technologies can long be seen in citizens' initiatives, in → social movements, and in Green parties. Commissions have been formed on assessing the effects of the new technologies. Ordinances have been issued on limiting environmental hazards. Regulations restricting military weapons have been signed (→ Weapons of Mass Destruction). All these devel-

opments point to the fact that industrial societies are not unaware of the problems that technology has caused. Science, too, takes account of risks, tries to minimize harmful effects of technology, does research into the → future, carefully observes genetic technology (→ Genetic Counseling), and uses processes of mediation to test the ways in which new technologies will affect society and the environment.

Thus far, however, the imperative of economic growth (→ Economy) continues to drive technology and the global spread of industrialization. In the future, it will not be enough simply to analyze and control the consequences of individual technologies. A more normative approach is needed that would instrumentalize the principles that technology is not the only answer to humankind's needs and that nature itself must be respected first, and not as an afterthought. The future task of thinking about technology is that of a constructive integration of technology into the complex cycles of nature itself, with the two ideals of limiting energy consumption to the use of renewable sources and developing waste management that does not burden generations to come. Recent years have shown success in putting into political action small aspects of the ecological challenge to technology. However, the pathway toward a comprehensive and worldwide change in the technological perspective has yet to be taken.

Bibliography: A. BORGMANN, Technology and the Character of Contemporary Life: A Philosophical Inquiry (Chicago, 1984) • J. ELLUL, The Technological Society (New York, 1964); idem, The Technological System (New York, 1980) • A. FEENBERG, Transforming Technology (New York, 2002) • A. GEHLEN, Man, His Nature and Place in the World (New York, 1988) • S. C. GILFILLAN, The Sociology of Invention (Cambridge, Mass., 1970) • J. HENDERSON, The Globalisation of High Technology Production (London, 1989) • W. KROHN and G. KRÜCKEN, eds., Riskante Technologien. Reflexion und Regulation (Frankfurt, 1993) • C. MITCHAM, Thinking through Technology (Chicago, 1994) • L. MUMFORD, The Myth of the Machine, vol. 1, Technics and Human Development; vol. 2, The Pentagon of Power (New York, 1967-70); idem, Technics and Civilization (New York, 1934) • T. PETERMANN, ed., Technikfolgen-Abschätzung als Technikforschung und Politikberatung (Frankfurt, 1992) • W. RAMMERT, Technik aus soziologischer Perspektive (Opladen, 1993) • G. ROPOHL, Eine Systemtheorie der Technik (Munich, 1979) • J. RUSKIN, The Seven Lamps of Architecture (London, 1988; orig. pub., 1849) • P. WEINGART, ed., Technik als sozialer Prozeß (Frankfurt, 1989) • L. WINNER, Autono-

mous Technology: Technics-out-of-Control as a Theme in Political Thought (Cambridge, Mass., 1977); idem, *The Whale and the Reactor: A Search for Limits in an Age of High Technology* (Chicago, 1986).

WOLFGANG KROHN, with ROBERT FORTNER

2. Theological Ethics

2.1. Technology is a theme in theological ethics (1) as a dimension of the modern world that calls for understanding and response, (2) as a phenomenon whose effects impinge on human → freedom and call for the acceptance of → responsibility (see 1.5), and (3) as a reality that relates to social justice by affecting the way in which the goods of this world are distributed among individuals, cultures, and regions. These ethical themes raise questions of human compatibility, of compatibility with → nature, and of international commitment in a world dominated by technology (T. Strohm).

2.2. Theologically, the entry of the machine age in the 19th and early 20th centuries met with two responses: an inner aversion (A. Rich) that rejected it as a new instance of the fall of humanity, and the welcoming of a phenomenon that could enhance life through extending human capacity to control its own destiny (→ Industrial Society). In the first instance, the apparent increase in human power was understood to be a loss of the freedom granted at creation, which was now subjected in every sphere, even in → leisure time, to the machine. The social stresses caused by the changes in industrial structure, and the way in which the automated production that technology brought meant alienation in daily life, even carried with them eschatological perspectives (S. Giedion, D. Riesman, A. W. Gouldner; → Eschatology). In the second instance, the positivist tradition fully endorsed technology, even saying in religious terms that God willed the machine (→ Positivism). The changing of the world by technology had a special impact upon 20th-century philosophy (M. Heidegger, A. Gehlen, H. Marcuse, C. P. Snow, et al.). The precarious position of humanity vis-à-vis technology lay behind such movements as → expressionism and → existentialism.

In theology H. Lilje (1899-1977) was one of the first to attempt a new approach. Clearly, what is said about technology had its roots in contemporary → anthropology and its hermeneutical ramifications, for example, whether we have power to act, whether we are sinful or justified, whether we are rulers or stewards of nature, whether we are little more than another type of creature. The works of J. Ellul (1912-94), who could not equate technology

and human freedom, and E. Dessauer (1881-1963), who on a neo-Thomist basis regarded technology as a continuation of creation, along with the research of H. Goedeking (1964), considered these issues as crucial to adequate human response to the machine. W. Barrett (1978) considers the emphasis on increasing control of technology through the application of technique to be an illusion (also M. Stanley).

→ Vatican II regarded → progress in technology as part of a changing world (*Gaudium et spes* 5 and 54). But in all spheres research and development must support the creation-appropriate → autonomy of all earthly realities in a truly scientific way and in accordance with moral norms. The laity has a special responsibility to develop the goods created by technology "according to the plan of the creator and the light of his word," which should "be more suitably distributed among all men" and "be conducive to universal progress" (*Lumen gentium* 36.2). The view of Marxist schools (→ Marxism) was that human needs could be satisfied by the achievements of technology if we have a truly scientific conviction and accept the core principle of hope. The main thrust of a liberal economic order (→ Achievement and Competition; Consumption) and the overextension of limited resources in centrally governed societies, however, came up against the ecological movement (→ Ecology; Economic Ethics), again making a unified response to technology problematic.

2.3. One of the great themes of ethical discourse in the 1970s and 1980s was the antithesis between technological possibilities and human capacity, or the breadth of what can be done by technology and human responsibility for the consequences. Human self-denial was no longer a detailed matter vis-à-vis a single technology that was judged to be a worldwide threat but was now regarded as something that all people had to understand if they were to craft a sustainable future. Ethical statements were still usually made relative to individual technologies, such as nuclear or genetic technology or the technologies of → information and → communication, but these statements were made in order to show how relevant the whole subject was.

On a theological basis the churches sometimes tried to give direction for dealing with technology, even though they ran into passionate disputes and had to extend their range of knowledge. The spheres of technology could not be allowed an autonomy of their own (L. Winner). Nuclear power might seem to offer inexhaustible supplies of energy, but its military use was a threat to all life on earth (→

Weapons of Mass Destruction), and incalculable risks threatened even its civil use. Genetic and biotechnological research also carried with it a threat to all human, animal, and plant life (→ Medical Ethics 3.2). The technology of communication and information certainly opened up new dimensions for worldwide human understanding and control (J. R. Beninger), but it also carried with it new forms of dependence and loss of reality.

The "imperative of responsibility" of H. Jonas (1903-93) issued a general summons to → asceticism. Against this view the position was advanced that further technological progress will eliminate the dangers and give a better estimate of the consequences. Either way, in the technical world of work today, we are all affected in many ambivalent ways by technology. Technology, according to M. McLuhan, extends human capability. It challenges → creativity or smothers it. Its threats are always with us. But any individual technology may be replaced or may prove to be socially unacceptable, and as a result we may lose our jobs (→ Unemployment).

2.4. There is an unequal division between North and South (and also between men and women) in the development of technology and its use. The North is vastly superior in key technologies and in knowing how to use them (see 1.1). Since the end of → colonialism, only East Asia has been able to keep up and even to forge ahead in specific sectors. Latin America, Africa, the Near East, and South Asia have fallen behind.

Both Europe and North America have voiced basic criticism of technology. Judgments coming from the North — for example, that in the world of → Islam modern technology would oppose the so-called Middle Ages — totally misjudge the differentiated approaches that Islam developed.

In the attempt to arrive at independence, great technological projects have been attempted, the use of which increases dependence. Producing more energy (e.g., by hydro or nuclear power) and increasing agricultural production (by machines and artificial fertilization) are now often viewed with skepticism as no more than a "conformist technology."

In the 1970s and 1980s the → World Council of Churches made this issue a subject of discussion and invited theologians of the South to participate (e.g., see Bena-Silu and B. C. E. Nwosu). A high point was reached at the 1979 Church and Society conference held in Cambridge, Massachusetts, at the Massachusetts Institute of Technology. Today it has been seen that biotechnology has life-threatening consequences when applied to agriculture in the South (e.g., in the use of so-called patented plants).

2.5. Technology is a matter of growing complexity. Ethical warnings and restrictions seem to be simply reactive in the face of incalculable threats and the global demand for innovation. The hope remains that research and technology, when based on an ethically reflected and intercultural → consensus, will seek righteous goals that do not lead us away from nature but press "forward to nature" (A. Feenberg).

Bibliography: On 2.1-2: W. Barrett, *The Illusion of Technique: A Search for Meaning in a Technological Civilization* (Garden City, N.Y., 1978) • F. Dessauer, *Streit um die Technik* (Frankfurt, 1963) • J. Ellul, *The Technological Society* (New York, 1964; orig. pub., 1954) • S. Giedion, *Mechanization Takes Command* (New York, 1948) • H. Goedeking, "Die Auffassungen der modernen Technik, ihr Wandel und ihre Aufnahme in der Theologie" (Diss., Münster, 1964) • A. W. Gouldner, *The Dialectic of Ideology and Technology* (New York, 1976) • M. Heidegger, *Die Technik und die Kehre* (Pfullingen, 1962) • H. Lilje, *Das technische Zeitalter. Versuch einer biblischen Deutung* (Berlin, 1928) • A. Rich, *Christliche Existenz in der industriellen Welt* (2d ed.; Zurich, 1964) • D. Riesman, *The Lonely Crowd: A Study of the Changing American Character* (New Haven, 1973) • C. P. Snow, *The Two Cultures and the Scientific Revolution* (2d ed.; Cambridge, 1965) • M. Stanley, *The Technological Conscience: Survival and Dignity in an Age of Expertise* (New York, 1978) • T. Strohm, "Denken und Handeln. Aspekte ethischer Orientierung in der wissenschaftlich-technischen Zivilisation," *Alltagswelt und Ethik* (ed. K. Ebert; Wuppertal, 1988) 85-105.

On 2.3-5: Bena-Silu, "Nuclear Technology Today," *Nuclear Energy and Ethics* (ed. K. Shrader-Frechette; Geneva, 1991) • J. R. Beninger, *The Control Revolution: Technological and Economic Origins of the Information Society* (Cambridge, Mass., 1986) • A. Feenberg, *Critical Theory of Technology* (Oxford, 1991) • I. Illich, *Tools for Conviviality* (New York, 1973) • H. Jonas, *The Imperative of Responsibility: In Search of an Ethics for the Technological Age* (Chicago, 1984) • M. McLuhan, *Understanding Media: The Extensions of Man* (Cambridge, Mass., 1994) • B. C. E. Nwosu, "Issues and Experiences concerning Nuclear Energy and Nuclear Proliferation," *Nuclear Energy and Ethics,* ed. Shrader-Frechette • K. Shrader-Frechette, ed., *Nuclear Energy and Ethics* (Geneva, 1991) • L. Winner, *Autonomous Technology: Technics-out-of-Control as a Theme in Political Thought* (Cambridge, Mass., 1978) • Wolrd Council of Churches, *Faith and Science in an Unjust World* (2 vols.; Geneva, 1980).

Jürgen Stein, with Robert Fortner

Teleological Argument → God, Arguments for the Existence of

Teleology

1. Nature and Origins of Teleology in Classical Philosophy

Teleology, from Gk. *telos* (end, aim, goal) and *logos* (science, study), refers to the systematic reflection upon purpose and purposive activity in the universe; it is most commonly used to refer to observable design or purpose in the universe. In Plato's (427-347 B.C.) *Phaedo,* Socrates cautions against purely naturalistic or mechanistic accounts of natural activity and occurrences that overlook the purposiveness of the natural order and fail to recognize the telos of the universe as determined by transcendent reality, the Forms. In Plato's *Republic,* book 1, Socrates moves from the observed function of human organs to the conclusion that the human soul, too, has a natural function and that → happiness, the telos of human beings, consists of living purposively to fulfill the function of the → soul. In *Philebus,* Plato's Socrates poses the question, "Are we to say that the universe, this 'whole,' as it is called, is controlled by irrationality, randomness and → chance [a view held by Democritus and other atomists]? Or are we to say the opposite, as our predecessors did, that it is governed by intellect and the coordination of a wonderful → reason?" (28D). The *Timaeus* presents Plato's most developed teleology. There he introduces a supremely good "craftsman" who causes the universe, employing a mental model of the universe in his creation of things. For Plato, then, an ultimate reality that transcends the empirical world has ordered the universe and, as a part of this ordering, directs human beings by their natures toward the achievement of the telos of the human species. The order of the universe, dependent as it is upon a transcendent reality, is not, however, dependent upon a personal being, as Christians and other theists insist.

Aristotle (384-322 B.C.), too, believed the universe to be shot through with purpose, although, unlike Plato, he believed that the purposiveness of the universe can be explained naturalistically. Change in the universe is explained in terms of four causal elements:

material cause — the matter or stuff that changes;

formal cause — an inborn principle of change that makes a thing what it is changing into;

efficient cause — that which initiates the process of change; and

final cause — the ultimate goal or end toward which the change is directed.

Aristotle thought of living things in a process of development from potentiality to actualization of the form inherent within them. The acorn will be formed into an oak tree, its final cause, thus actualizing its potential and realizing its form. And so it is for all living things. "Everything that comes to be moves toward a principle, i.e., an end. For that for the sake of which a thing is, is its principle, and the becoming is for the sake of the end; and the actuality is the end; and it is for the sake of this that the potentiality is acquired" (*Meta.* 1050a5-10). Aristotle further believes that the only coherent account of why there is in the universe the movement from potentiality toward actuality is the necessary existence of an "unmoved mover" — that is, pure actuality, or God. This God is not a personal being but "thought thinking itself throughout all eternity." (For this Thought to think of things other than itself would be to introduce potentiality into pure actuality.) Things move toward their final ends out of "love" for, or in imitation of, pure actuality.

According to Aristotle, human beings, like all other living things, are in the process of realizing their telos — the telos for human beings being *eudaimonia,* that is, happiness, well-being, or flourishing. The happy or flourishing person is one who, throughout a lifetime, possesses the → virtues or excellences of the human being. Happiness is constituted by the possession of the virtues. Some human excellences are *moral* virtues, which Aristotle characterizes as qualities that enable us to respond to the world obediently to reason; others are *intellectual* virtues, excellences of reasoning and understanding, both practically and theoretically. In his most significant work on ethics, the *Nicomachean Ethics,* Aristotle seems to suggest that, as great and important as possession of the moral virtues may be, genuine happiness and fulfillment will be achieved best not in a life of action but in a life of → contemplation, in a life of study and rational engagement: "For what is proper to each thing's nature is supremely best and most pleasant for it; and hence for a human being the life in accord with understanding will be supremely best and most pleasant, if understanding, more than anything else, is the human being. This life, then, will also be happiest" (1178a5-9).

The → Stoics, too, embraced a teleological metaphysic, although one decidedly more deterministic than that of Plato and Aristotle. The Stoic "God," or eternal reason, a divine fire infused in everything that exists, is an uncreated and indestructible first principle of the universe working its intentions upon the other first principle, matter. Everything that happens is an expression of this eternal reason working itself out in matter. The wise person, or Stoic sage, orders his or her emotions and actions in accordance with the *logos* of things, eliminating passions of attachment to that which is outside his or her control.

Plotinus (ca. A.D. 205-70) and other Neoplatonic philosophers likewise understood the universe to be characterized by purpose and design. Ultimate reality — the One, God, Unity — is necessarily generative. Perfect being thus "overflows," from which comes "Intellect." From this "Divine Mind" emanates "World Soul," which contemplates Intellect as it both organizes and informs material reality. Finally, when being is exhausted, when every possible degree of being is realized, we find matter, the privation of being. Even as there is a movement "outward" from the One, so there is a second movement. Soul, according to Plotinus, yearns to return to its origin in the One.

2. Christian Theology and Classical Teleology

Early Christian thinkers were not surprised to find their view of order, design, and purpose in the universe shared by others. God created all things ex nihilo and actively sustains the universe and its order. The apostle Paul had written that "ever since the creation of the world his eternal power and divine nature, invisible though they are, have been understood and seen through the things he has made" (Rom. 1:20), echoing the psalmist who sang, "The heavens are telling the glory of God; and the firmament proclaims his handiwork" (Ps. 19:1). At the same time, Christian theologians told a story of a divine ordering of things that is not transparent, that cannot be observed in the natural order.

Accordingly, the story of the universe is in fact the story of God realizing God's own intentions for the creation. God had freely created the universe in order to enjoy the internal harmony of his → creation, as well as the harmony of all things with God.

But humans rejected God's ordering of creation, and disharmony and disorder came to characterize the world lovingly created by God. → Salvation history is the story of God's intervention in order to restore and re-create the harmonious order he intends for creation. The election of Israel, the election of Jesus the Christ, and the election of the church are all parts of the story of this process of redemption and re-creation, according to Christian thinkers. The end of God's creative, sustaining, and redemptive work, as → Athanasius (ca. 297-373) put it, is that "we might be made divine," and to this end, the Word became man (*De incar.* 54). The culmination of the redemptive process — an end Christians believe is yet to be fully realized, although it has been achieved through the death and resurrection of Jesus Christ — is the new heaven and new earth foretold in Revelation 21.

Christian thinkers have thus found themselves, like → Augustine (354-430) and Thomas Aquinas (ca. 1225-74), on the one hand largely sympathetic to the teleological outlook of ancient → Greek philosophy, while at the same time realizing that the design and purpose apparent in the workings of the universe do not fully disclose, and may in fact distract from, God's final purpose. In historical periods in which a teleological outlook has been dominant — roughly the 3d through the 15th centuries, for example — Christian thinkers like Aquinas have been happy to explore along broadly Aristotelian lines the ways in which God realizes a part of his purpose for creation as beings follow their own natures, their own natural appetites or inclinations (see, for example, *Summa theol.* I of II, q. 94; → Scholasticism). But following the collapse of confidence in Aristotelian accounts of final causes in the early 16th century, Christian thinkers tended to abandon any teleology in their philosophical theology and to concentrate instead on theological → eschatology. A notable exception to this trend is Jonathan → Edwards's (1703-58) magisterial *Dissertation concerning the Ends for Which God Created the World,* published posthumously in 1765.

3. Teleology and Contemporary Philosophical Theology

3.1. Teleological Arguments for the Existence of God

Teleology continues to play a significant role in contemporary philosophical theology, although in a highly truncated form when compared to its place in medieval thought. A classic proof for God's existence is the analogical teleological argument, one version of which appears in David Hume's (1711-

76) *Dialogues concerning Natural Religion* (1779; →
God, Arguments for the Existence of, 2.5). In simple
form, the argument is that, reflecting upon the orderly working of the universe, we can see that the
universe is like a machine, and since machines are
products of intelligent design, we may conclude that
the universe has an intelligent designer, that is, God.
Hume's criticisms of this version of the argument
are devastating. First, Hume challenged the analogy.
Natural growth and development suggest an organic rather than a mechanical analogy for the universe. Second, even if we conclude that the universe
is the product of an intelligent designer, we are not
warranted in identifying this designer with the
Christian God. Like other designers of machines,
the designer of the universe may have been a team
rather than a single individual, may be limited in
knowledge and power, may have died, and so on.
Immanuel Kant (1724-1804), while agreeing with
Hume on the failure of natural teleological arguments to establish the existence of God, nevertheless
believed that natural teleological arguments coupled with moral teleology — human beings as rational agents bound by a moral law — "are very important, since they support the practical reality of
the idea of God" (*Critique of Judgment*, §§88, 456).

More recent versions of the teleological argument are probabilistic in character, inferring that an
intelligent designer probably exists, given the im-
probability of the random or chance occurrence of
the conditions that make possible the variety and
kinds of life that currently exist. In the words of
some contemporaries, "The fact that appealing to
purposive ordering best explains a number of ante-
cedently improbable conditions lends credence to
the contention that a more probable explanation of
the universe appeals to the activity of a purposeful
being" (M. Peterson et al., 106). Intelligent-design
theory may be understood as an application at the
microlevel of the macrolevel probabilistic teleological argument.

3.2. *Teleology and Moral Theory*
Following the 16th-century attacks upon Aristotelian philosophy and the flourishing of post-
Darwinian evolutionary theory (→ Evolution), teleological theories of morality — that is, those that
identify some telos to which human moral agents
should aim — might be thought unsalvageable. Yet
teleological moral theories are arguably among the
most powerful moral theories currently available. In
his groundbreaking *After Virtue* (1982), Alasdair
MacIntyre argued that morality makes little sense
apart from the assumption that morality is the
means by which humans move from the condition

we are currently in to a state in which we realize our
telos. At the time of writing that book, MacIntyre
believed the telos of human beings could be inferred
only from sociological rather than biological observations, that is, from the types of activities social
groups of human beings engage in. More recently,
MacIntyre has shown an openness to more biological, neo-Aristotelian construals of the human telos,
such as that suggested by Philippa Foot. Foot argues
that the good for human beings is what is necessary
or useful in achieving our telos, that is, to successfully engage in the range and type of activities typical of our species at some given time. Christian
moral thinkers sympathetic to such teleological accounts face the challenge of coordinating the demands of our natural telos with the moral content
of the Christian Scriptures.

Bibliography: R. M. ADAMS, *Finite and Infinite Goods: A
Framework for Ethics* (New York, 1999) • A. H.
ARMSTRONG, *An Introduction to Ancient Philosophy*
(London, 1947) • J. EDWARDS, "Concerning the End for
Which God Created the World," *Ethical Writings* (ed.
P. Ramsey; New Haven, 1989) • P. FOOT, *Natural Good-
ness* (Oxford, 2001) • R. C. KOONS, *Realism Regained:
An Exact Theory of Causation, Teleology, and the Mind*
(New York, 2000) • A. MACINTYRE, *After Virtue* (Notre
Dame, Ind., 1982); idem, *Dependent Rational Animals*
(Chicago, 2001) • M. PETERSON, W. HASKER,
B. REICHENBACH, and D. BASINGER, *Reason and Reli-
gious Belief* (3d ed.; New York, 2003) • K. WARD, *Reli-
gion and Creation* (Oxford, 1996).

THOMAS D. KENNEDY

Television → Mass Media

Temple

1. Religious History
2. OT

1. Religious History
1.1. Temples are places to worship → God (§1)
or the gods. Their construction and artistic furnishings reflect the basic cosmological and mythical
ideas of a religion. Especially the way of distinguishing the → sacred and the profane, which is not always as clear and simple as in the case of the Greek
temenos or the Roman *templum,* is demonstrated by
the shape of the temple. In many cases, as in the
East, we find concentric spheres of the sacred, culminating in the holiest place of all (→ Sanctuary). A

path leads from the outer secular sphere through intervening rooms to the central place, which contains a statue or representation of the deity. Distinguishing between sacred and profane is fundamental for the whole culture. The temple that represents deity is a religious manifestation of the divine.

Religions of the Word — → Judaism, Christianity, and → Islam — do not have a statue of God (→ Images) as a central cultic picture because God reveals himself in the Word (→ Revelation). In prophetic Zoroastrianism → fire represents supreme deity. The cultic religions of the Greco-Roman world and the Orient have statues in which the deity manifests itself.

1.2. In the *Greco-Roman sphere* (→ Greek Religion; Roman Religion) the temple is a sacred, restricted site established by → theophanies and similar manifestations. It carries a central cultic symbol but may also have other statues of deity and may also picture scenes that are from mythology (→ Myth 2.1).

In late antiquity what were formerly open and light-filled temples became rooms enclosed behind walls set behind pillars. We see here a change in views of the cosmos. In the age of city-states the cosmos had been a bright sphere in which to live; the light helped people to find their way in the world. But later the cosmos became the sphere of the dominion of dark cosmic powers. Only beyond this sphere was the kingdom of light and salvation. This change in relation to the cosmos affected the construction of the Hellenist temple (→ Hellenistic-Roman Religion), especially in the dark, underground cultic sites of the → mystery religions (e.g., Mithraism).

1.3. In → *Egyptian religion* the temple developed in the Old Kingdom as a monument decorated with rich symbolism. An enclosed courtyard and inner cove were constitutive, and a strong wall was built around the whole temple. The entrance was through high pylons, and then through intervening rooms to the central holy place, where a cultic statue was located. The sun temples are a separate category, and so too are the burial temples of the kings. The temple for worship understands itself as the *axis mundi,* the primary island of cosmogonic time, according to directions for the building of temples.

1.4. In → *Babylonian and Assyrian religions,* along with the Sumerian and Akkadian, the temple is so strongly linked to the spatial presence of deity that an alienation or destruction of the temple can lead to lamentation and religious disorientation (see the Babylonian laments). We must distinguish here between the steplike temples on high terraces

that were built from 2000 B.C. onward (the ziggurats) and lower temples. Whereas the high temple was the dwelling place of deity, the second type was the place of manifestation. Of central significance was the temple for the important New Year festival. This was the place for the holy wedding of the king and the goddess, represented here by a priestess.

1.5. In the area of *Iran* (→ Iranian Religions), Herodotus reports (*Hist.* 1.131) that the Persians had neither temples nor depictions of the gods. Yet the songs (*Gāthās*) of Zoroaster disclose (*Yasna* 28.1-3) that in earlier times ceremonial processions were held around an → altar.

Beginning in the Achaemenid dynasty, it became customary to build temples to fire as an orthodox reaction to the introduction of the Babylonian temple cult of lesser deities (e.g., Anahita). The altar to fire could make one a child of the supreme god Ahura Mazda, who could not be represented cultically (*Yasna* 25.7). Parthian East Iran set up temples in memory of the dead or on behalf of their souls (*fravāshi*s). Later iconoclasm led to the widespread replacing of images by temples to fire.

1.6. Of the temples in *Asia Minor,* we know most about those of the Hittites. The best-known shrine of the Hittites is Yazılıkaya (Turk. "inscribed rock"), a sanctuary near Boğazköy, in north-central Turkey, with its capital, Hattusha. Various temples from the 14th and 13th centuries B.C. have been excavated.

1.7. In *Syria and Palestine* the earliest temples go back to the Bronze Age. We find great variety in construction, reflecting different cultic influences. A basic distinction is between broad temples and long temples.

1.8. In the *Germanic sphere* an open place for worship was predominant. The few archaeological remains (e.g., in Iceland) show that temples consisted of two areas: the larger one for those who gathered for the sacrifice, and the smaller for the cultic image. The Celts, too, favored temples for open worship.

1.9. In *India and Southeast Asia* the symbolism of temples is very complex. Cosmological and especially soteriological concepts come to expression in the most important architectural elements (→ Soteriology). → Hinduism has temples that clearly show the way from the outer wall to the inner core, in accordance with the hierarchical principle of its thinking. But there was not only a way to the center, with its statue or symbol of the deity. There was also a way upward to the topmost point of the temple, where there was a vessel containing amrit (Skt. *amṛta*), the drink of immortality and the symbol of salvation. One must tread this way in meditation.

→ Buddhism distinguishes between the stupa, a half-circular image crowned by covers and resting on a round or square pedestal, and the gathering place of monks, which also serves cultic ends. The stupa was originally a place for → relics, then for the image of Buddha, and finally for a representation of nirvana. It was also a cosmological symbol.

1.10. In *central and eastern Asia,* to which Buddhism spread, we find the stupa often in a cultic cave. The stupa was the source of the pagoda, which developed as a Buddhist sanctuary. Indigenous religions such as → Taoism, → Confucianism, and → Shinto had their own cultic buildings.

1.11. In *America* Peruvian temples and the step-like high temples of Mexico are the best known. Their forms suggest cosmological symbolism. Important temples were erected to the sun and moon, as well as to other deities.

1.12. The → tribal religions of *Africa* demonstrate that the cultic place displays a specific structure that was related to the ordered life of the tribe. Among the Mbanderu in Namibia and Botswana, for example, the sanctuary was traditionally round, for the circle had symbolic significance. It symbolized the unity of life that is protected against the threatening world without. This view is basically valid also for other tribes. Thus sanctuaries in West Africa are often set in an enclosed clearing, within which is a hut where the priest can make contact with the spirits, as well as a heap of stones or an altar for public sacrifices.

Bibliography: On 1.1: J. G. DAVIES, *Temples, Churches, and Mosques: A Guide to the Appreciation of Religious Architecture* (Oxford, 1982) • H.-J. KLIMKEIT, ed., *Götterbild in Kunst und Schrift* (Bonn, 1984) • A. T. MANN, *Sacred Architecture* (Rockport, Mass., 1993) • H. W. TURNER, *From Temple to Meeting House: The Phenomenology and Theology of Places of Worship* (The Hague, 1979).

On 1.2: T. DERKS, *Gods, Temples, and Ritual Practices: The Transformation of Religious Ideas and Values in Roman Gaul* (Amsterdam, 1998) • G. GRUBEN, *Die Tempel der Griechen* (4th ed.; Munich, 1986) • V. J. SCULLY, *The Earth, the Temple, and the Gods: Greek Sacred Architecture* (rev. ed.; New Haven, 1979) • L. M. WHITE, *Building God's House in the Roman World: Architectural Adaptation among Pagans, Jews, and Christians* (Baltimore, 1990).

On 1.3: R. B. FINNESTAD, *Image of the World and Symbol of the Creator: On the Cosmological and Iconological Values of the Temple of Edfu* (Wiesbaden, 1985) • W. M. F. PETRIE, *The Pyramids and Temples of Gizeh* (London, 2003; orig. pub., 1883) • F. TEICHMANN, *Der Mensch und sein Tempel: Ägypten* (3d ed.; Stuttgart, 2003) • R. H. WILKINSON, *The Complete Temples of Ancient Egypt* (New York, 2000).

On 1.4: S. B. DOWNEY, *Mesopotamian Religious Architecture: Alexander through the Parthians* (Princeton, 1988) • K.-H. GOLZIO, *Der Tempel im alten Mesopotamien und seine Parallelen in Indien* (Leiden, 1983) • G. J. P. MCEWAN, *Priest and Temple in Hellenistic Babylonia* (Wiesbaden, 1981) • B. MENZEL, *Assyrische Tempel* (2 vols.; Rome, 1981) • L. WOOLLEY, *The Ziggurat and Its Surroundings* (London, 1939).

On 1.5: K. ERDMANN, *Das iranische Feuerheiligtum* (Leipzig, 1941; repr., 1969) • R. GHIRSHMAN, *Persian Art: The Parthian and Sasanian Dynasties* (New York, 1962) • J. M. ROSENFIELD, *The Dynastic Arts of the Kushans* (Berkeley, Calif., 1967).

On 1.6: H. H. ANDERSEN, *The Barbar Temples* (Århus, 2003) • D. C. HOPKINS, ed., *Across the Anatolian Plateau: Readings in the Archaeology of Ancient Turkey* (Boston, 2002) • R. NAUMANN, *Die Architektur Kleinasiens. Von ihren Anfängen bis zum Ende der hethitischen Zeit* (Tübingen, 1971).

On 1.7: A. ALT, "Die Verbreitung und Herkunft des syrischen Tempeltypus," *Kleine Schriften zur Geschichte des Volkes Israel* (3 vols.; Munich, 1953-59) 2.100-115 • P. W. HAIDER, M. HUTTER, and S. KREUZER, eds., *Religionsgeschichte Syriens. Von der Frühzeit bis zur Gegenwart* (Stuttgart, 1996) • H. SCHMÖKEL, ed., *Kulturgeschichte des Alten Orient. Mesopotamien, Hethiterreich, Syrien-Palästina, Urartu* (Augsburg, 1995).

On 1.8: H. JANKUHN, ed., *Vorgeschichtliche Heiligtümer und Opferplätze in Mittel- und Nordeuropa* (Göttingen, 1970).

On 1.9: A. L. DALLAPICCOLA, with S. Z.-A. LALLEMANT, eds., *The Stupa: Its Religious, Historical, and Architectural Significance* (Wiesbaden, 1979) • V. DEHEJIA, *Early Buddhist Rock Temples: A Chronology* (Ithaca, N.Y., 1972) • S. KRAMRISCH, *The Hindu Temple* (2 vols.; Delhi, 1996) • M. W. MEISTER, with M. A. DHAKY, eds., *Encyclopaedia of Indian Temple Architecture* (Philadelphia, 1983ff.) • G. MICHELL, *The Hindu Temple: An Introduction to Its Meaning and Forms* (Chicago, 1988) • H. VON STIETENCRON, "Orthodox Attitudes towards Temple Service and Image Worship in Ancient India," *CAsJ* 21 (1977) 126-39.

On 1.10: W. H. M. CREEMERS, *Shrine Shinto after World War II* (Leiden, 1968) • *The Great Eastern Temple: Treasures of Japanese Buddhist Art from Tōdai-ji* (organized by Y. Mino; Chicago, 1986) • E. LIP, *Chinese Temples and Deities* (Singapore, 1986) • R. T. PAINE, *The Art and Architecture of Japan* (Baltimore, 1974) • A. C. SOPER, *The Evolution of Buddhist Architecture in Japan* (New York, 1978).

On 1.11: C. B. Donnan, ed., *Early Ceremonial Architecture in the Andes: A Conference at Dumbarton Oaks, 8th to 10th October 1982* (Washington, D.C., 1985) • F. S. Murphy, *Dragon Mask Temples in Central Yucatan (1952-1972)* (Hong Kong, 1988) • B. Olmedo Vera, *Los templos rojos del recinto sagrado de Tenochtitlan* (Mexico City, 2002).

On 1.12: T. Sundermeier, *Die Mbanderu. Studien zu ihrer Geschichte und Kultur* (St. Augustin, 1977) 136-50.

Hans-Joachim Klimkeit†

2. OT

Israel had several → sanctuaries prior to the building of the temple in → Jerusalem. Temples existed at Shiloh and Nob according to 1 Samuel 1–3 and 21:1-9. After the division of the kingdom, Jeroboam I set up sanctuaries at Bethel and Dan (1 Kgs. 12:28-33; Amos 7:13). Archaeology has unearthed a temple at Arad (Tell ʿArad) dating from the middle period of the → monarchy. In the Hellenistic period the → Samaritans founded their own cult at Gerizim and set up a temple (see 2 Macc. 6:2; Josephus *Ant.* 12.5.5). Outside → Palestine the Jews built a temple on Elephantine, an island in the Nile, to which there are many references in Aramaic papyri. After being expelled from Jerusalem, the Zadokite → high priest Onias built a temple after the Jerusalem pattern at Leontopolis (Tell el-Yehūdīye; Josephus *Ant.* 13.3.1-2; 13.10.4; *J.W.* 7.10.2-3). In the Hellenistic period there were temples also at Lachish (Tell ed-Duweier) and at Beersheba (Tell es-Sebaʿ), discovered by archaeologists. The main biblical emphasis, however, is on the temple at Jerusalem.

2.1. The general term for the temple is *bêt YHWH* or *bêt ʾĕlōhîm*, the "House of Yahweh" or "house of God." We find these descriptions in 1 Kgs. 7:12, 40, 45, 51; Zech. 8:9; Neh. 6:10, and elsewhere. Another term, *hêkāl*, has been borrowed from Akkad. *ēkallu* (from Sumer. *e-gal*); it appears in 2 Kgs. 23:4; 24:13; Isa. 6:1; Jer. 7:4; 24:1; 50:28; 51:11, and other places. These terms suggest that the temple is the dwelling place of God on earth.

Under the influence of Priestly thinking (→ Priest 2), the temple is also known as the sanctuary, as in Ps. 74:7 or Ezek. 44:1. This term, based on the root *qdš*, "holy," marks the temple off from the profane world round about it. It relates to the special quality of the building and its precincts. Because God is special, a sphere of divine holiness must be made for him on earth that demands a response of → cultic purity (→ Sacred and Profane).

2.2. The building of the temple and environs is described in 1 Kings 6 in connection with the building of → Solomon's palace. Though there is some lack of clarity in detail, the outline is plain enough. The temple consists of a long building with a vestibule (*ʾûlām*) and inner sanctuary (*dĕbîr*). This inner sanctuary is known as the holiest of all. The temple was 20 cubits broad, 60 cubits long, and 30 cubits high. The entrance, or vestibule, projected 10 cubits from the front, and the sanctuary, presumably built of wood, had the shape of a cube of 20 cubits. Two pillars probably stood in the entrance hall; the extensively described renovation appears to be literarily and architecturally an emendation. Two cherubim in the sanctuary seem to have been part of a throne, and the → ark symbolized the presence of → Yahweh in the holy of holies (1 Kgs. 8:1-11). The temple was within the grounds of the royal palace, and it was surrounded by a court (see 1 Kgs. 6:36; 7:12; Jer. 36:10). The first temple was a royal sanctuary of the official cult, and the king was in a sense the supreme priest. Vessels included the necessary → altar in the courtyard and other bronze vessels, like the sea and ten basins on movable stands (1 Kgs. 7:23-47).

The structure type is what is called an *antentempel*, the oldest form of the ancient Greek temple, which has a portico with two pilaster-like doorjambs. This type of construction developed in the second millennium in northern Syria as a cultic building and is also found in the first millennium at Tell Taʿyinat, in the Hatay Province of modern Turkey; the form was probably transmitted to Israel via the Phoenicians. It is unlikely that Israel took over an older structure, given the form of the newly erected palace complex.

2.3. The dedication of the temple in 1 Kgs. 8:12-13 shows that it was meant to be a concrete dwelling place. Yahweh of course dwelt in → heaven, but the temple was a setting for the divine presence. It is not clear, however, whether he would be permanently present or would be present only at moments of → theophany.

The presence of God made the temple in effect the center of the world, and Jerusalem the city of God (see the songs of Zion). The temple was not merely a place for → sacrifice and worship, but in view of the presence of Yahweh, it had a unique position of cosmic significance. It would also be a motif in battle and a defense against invasion. In the cultic reforms of Hezekiah and Josiah, it was shown to have a radically unique quality as compared with other sanctuaries. The presence of God in the temple gave it a distinctive function as a bulwark, for Yahweh oversaw the place of his dwelling.

2.4. The temple took seven years for Solomon to build and was consecrated in the 13th year of his reign (1 Kgs. 6:37–7:1). It stood until the conquest of Jerusalem by Nebuchadnezzar in 587 B.C. A second temple on the same site and using the same measurements was built under Darius (Ezra 6:3), but what had formerly been the palace precincts now became the courts of the temple. The expansion meant the distinguishing of further entrances, demanding different types of purity. The dedication took place in 515 B.C. The ark had been lost in the Babylonian invasion (cf. Jer. 7:14), and so the inner sanctuary of the temple was empty.

Herod the Great (ruled B.C. 37-4; → Herod, Herodians) engaged in a vast reconstruction of the temple. He rebuilt the vestibule and put a new wall around the precincts, which still today encloses the temple area. He also built new courts. We find descriptions of Herod's temple in Josephus *J.W.* 5.5.1-6 and in the Mishnah tractate *Middot*. The capture of Jerusalem by Titus in A.D. 70 meant the complete destruction of this temple; it was never rebuilt.

The site of the temple has not yet been fixed and demands full archaeological investigation. Whether or not it encircled the rock that stands under the cupola of the Dome of the Rock is uncertain. Outside staircases in the south led up to the two southern gates, and inner stairs led up from there to the temple courtyard. The temple could also be approached to the west by outside staircases and a bridge.

2.5. The transition of the temple into large designs of an ideal conception began during the exile. In the so-called constitutional draft in Ezekiel 40–48, a temple sanctuary is designed that would meet priestly demands for the preservation of cultic purity by consisting of two forecourts separated from each other and secured by massive gates. The sanctity of the temple could also be protected by a special building to the rear. In the Priestly source (→ Pentateuch), the instructions for the tabernacle at → Sinai (Exodus 25–31; 35–40) locate the cultic building back in the period before the conquest, while simultaneously spiritualizing it in the sense of a word-event. This idea is taken up in the *Temple Scroll* of → Qumran (11QTemple) and expanded into a major design of the ideal sacrificial cult.

→ Jesus (Mark 11:15-17) advocated the purity of the temple as the place of the divine presence and made a plea for unconditional holiness. But he also replaced the temple as the site of worship. The post-Easter → congregation (§1) is itself the temple in which God dwells (see 1 Cor. 3:9, 16-17; 2 Cor. 6:16-17; Eph. 2:19-22). Stephen argued that "the Most High does not dwell in houses made with human hands" (Acts 7:48), and John equates Jesus himself with the temple (John 1:14; 2:19-21). In contrast, → Judaism expects the beginning of God's reign with the rebuilding of the temple (see 4 Esdr. 10:27-59; → Apocalyptic 2; Eschatology 1).

→ Jewish Theology

Bibliography: T. A. Busink, *Der Tempel von Jerusalem, von Salomo bis Herodes* (2 vols.; Leiden, 1970-80) • D. V. Edelman, *The Origins of the "Second" Temple: Persian Imperial Policy and the Rebuilding of Jerusalem* (London, 2005) • V. Fritz, "Der Tempel Salomos im Licht der neueren Forschung," *MDOG* 112 (1980) 53-68; idem, *Tempel und Zelt: Studien zum Tempelbau in Israel und zu dem Zeltheiligtum der Priesterschrift* (Neukirchen, 1977) • S. Goldhill, *The Temple of Jerusalem* (Cambridge, Mass., 2005) • R. Hayward, ed., *The Jewish Temple: A Non-biblical Sourcebook* (New York, 1996) • C. M. McCormick, *Palace and Temple: A Study of Architectural and Verbal Icons* (Berlin, 2002) • Y. Yadin, ed., *The Temple Scroll* (3 vols. in 4; Jerusalem, 1977-83).

Volkmar Fritz

Temple Society

1. The Temple Society is a small Christian fellowship that was apocalyptic at first but then became interested in social and international reforms. It stands for a Christianity free of → dogma; its main concern is setting up the → kingdom of God on earth by creating a Christian outlook and a Christian society (first focused on → Palestine) under the symbol of the → temple (§2; see Eph. 2:21).

2. The society was founded by a Württemberg Pietist (→ Pietism 2.7), theologian C. Hoffmann (1815-85), and he was closely identified with its early beginning and development. Coming to Marbach in 1856 to meet with "friends of Jerusalem," he had the goal of starting Christian fellowships in the Holy Land. His church, the Lutheran Landeskirche of Württemberg, dismissed him in 1859, and in 1861 he founded the Deutscher Tempel (German Temple) as an independent religious society reacting to the current political and ecclesiastical crisis.

In 1868 Hoffmann went to Palestine with G. D. Hardegg (1812-79), and the two started settlements in Haifa, Jaffa, Sarona (the present-day government precinct in Tel Aviv), Jerusalem, and Bethlehem of the Galilee. These colonies made a great cultural contribution to the development of Palestine (esp.

in commerce, agriculture, and health) and helped prepare the way for later Jewish settlers.

3. In the course of its history the society has had to overcome many internal and external tensions and crises. After World War II its settlement work in Palestine came to an end, and new communities were established in Australia and Germany. There are now two legally independent organizations: the Temple Society in Australia, with some 700 members, and the Tempelgesellschaft in Deutschland, with about 180 members, mostly in Württemberg.

The society's largely rational understanding of the Christian faith focuses on the → gospel, on the ethics of → love, and on social reconstruction. → Jesus is a model and teacher, not the Son of God or Savior of the world. A commitment to the → confessions of the → early church and the → Reformation is expressly rejected, as is the celebration of the → sacraments of → baptism and the Lord's Supper (→ Eucharist), which, next to the Word of God, are constitutive of the church. Worship of God is by → devotion and by concentrating on everyday demands. In 1976 the society joined the Bund für Freies Christentum.

Bibliography: C. Hoffmann, Occident und Orient (Stuttgart, 1875) • P. Lange, ed., Templer-Handbuch. Texte und Informationen zum Verständnis der Tempelgesellschaft (Stuttgart, 1992) • P. Sauer, The Holy Land Called: The Story of the Temple Society (Melbourne, 1991) • Temple Society of Australia, Memories of Palestine: Narratives about Life in the Templer Communities, 1869-1948 (Bentleigh, Austral., 2005); idem, Temple Society: Statement of Identity, Faith, and Practical Concerns (Bentleigh, Austral., 2000).

Reinhard Hempelmann

Temple, William

William Temple (1881-1944) was one of the most distinguished archbishops of Canterbury of the past millennium. He was the first churchman since the → Reformation to be a national leader and a world figure. His main distinction was that of a Christian leader and statesman, especially in the areas of social concern, the ecumenical movement, and Christian thought. He was a superb popular preacher and teacher. Although he published 37 books, he was more a thinker than a scholar; in the 20th century he put Christianity on the map for many.

Temple was born in the Bishop's Palace in Exeter and lived most of his life, at the heart of the English establishment, in episcopal palaces. After schooling at Rugby he studied classics, literature, and philosophy at Balliol College, Oxford, where he was influenced by the → idealism of Edward Caird (1835-1908), to whom he later dedicated his Gifford Lectures. There he also became concerned with social and political issues through his friendship with the Christian socialist R. H. Tawney (1880-1962). After a brief stint as a lecturer in philosophy at Oxford, Temple was elected president of the Workers' Educational Association. Because of his new socialist convictions, in the tradition of F. D. Maurice (1805-72), Charles Kingsley (1819-75), and Tawney, he was placed on a list of dangerous characters by the British government during World War I.

After some doubts about the virgin birth and the bodily resurrection of Jesus were resolved, Temple was ordained in the Church of England in 1908 and became headmaster of Repton School. This period saw the publication of his first two books, *The Faith and Modern Thought* (1910) and *The Nature of Personality* (1915), which was an elaboration of a fundamental category in his philosophy and theology. In 1914 he became the rector of St. James' Church, Piccadilly, London, his one parochial post.

In 1916 he married Frances Anson, who shared his social concerns. The same year he resigned from St. James to become the leader of the Life and Liberty Movement, which was dedicated to achieving the autonomy of the Church of England from Parliament. In 1919 it achieved its goal with the establishment of the Church Assembly. Temple fought hard and successfully for the inclusion of women in the Assembly, believing that deaconesses were ordained ministers and that women should be ordained to the priesthood, although that step should be postponed for strategic reasons. During this period he published two small books, *Church and Nation* (1915) and *Plato and Christianity* (1916), and also his first major treatise, *Mens Creatrix* (1917), in which he argues that the → incarnation supplies the central point at which the sciences of knowledge, art, morality, and religion meet and find their unity.

After turning down two academic posts, Temple became canon at Westminster. In 1921 he was consecrated → bishop of Manchester, a midland industrial diocese and one of the largest in the Church of England. Here his involvement in the social witness of the church was deepened. He chaired a group that planned the 1924 Conference on Politics, Economics, and Citizenship, whose goal was to seek the will and purposes of God in public life. This international and ecumenical conference drew 1,500 delegates and had a major impact on the developing ecumenical movement. During a coal stoppage that led to a general strike in 1926, Temple served on a committee of churchmen that mediated between the mine owners and the labor unions. This intervention failed, and Prime Minister Stanley Baldwin rebuked the committee for interfering in something that was not the church's business. Temple responded that it was exactly the church's business and elaborated on this conviction in a book entitled *Essays in Christian Politics* (1927). One result of these events was a remarkable change in the attitude of organized labor toward the churches.

In 1924 Temple published his most extended theological treatise, *Christus Veritas,* in which his aim was to present a "Christo-centric → metaphysics." It was a sequel to *Mens Creatrix* and followed a similar method in treating metaphysical issues, the central Christian affirmations, and finally the former again in the light of the incarnation. The failure of Parliament to ratify the 1928 revision of the → Book of Common Prayer was a great disappointment to Temple, since he had labored on the revisions and argued for it successfully in the Church Assembly. This setback caused him to conclude that disestablishment of the church was not too great a price to pay for the church's freedom.

In 1929 Temple was enthroned as archbishop of York. He served 13 years in that Northern Primacy, his longest service in one post, and it was jammed with activity. He was at the height of his powers and quickly became a world figure. He chaired the Council of the new British Broadcasting Corporation (BBC), was a member of the Privy Council, preached at the disarmament conference in Geneva in 1932, wrote a dozen books, delivered the Gifford Lectures (1932-34), lectured in the United States, played a key role in the ecumenical movement, and managed to visit almost all of the 457 parishes in his diocese.

Temple was the first archbishop ever to deliver the famed Gifford Lectures at Glasgow University. Published in 1934 under the title *Nature, Man, and God,* they constitute the fullest statement of his → natural theology, or → philosophy of religion. They consist of an extended argument for → theism, beginning with the picture of the world offered by → science and concluding with the demand for a special revelation of the transcendent and immanent God. He considered subtitling it "A Study in Dialectical Realism," for it represents his movement from the idealism of Caird toward the → realism of Alfred North Whitehead (1861-1947). Its underlying vision is that of the "sacramental universe." In 1925 Temple became chairman of the Archbishops' Commission on Doctrine, whose charge was to assess and moderate the tensions between different schools of thought in the Church of England. Its final report of 1938, *Doctrine in the Church of England,* is a monument to the gifts and wisdom of its chairman.

Temple's labors and travel for the ecumenical movement were among his prime concerns during the York primacy. He had learned the ropes at the World Missionary Conference at Edinburgh in 1910 (→ Missionary Conferences 2), where he was a steward; at the first World Conference on → Faith and Order, at Lausanne in 1925; and at the International Missionary Conference in Jerusalem in 1928. In 1929 he became chairman of the global Faith and Order Continuation Committee, and in 1937 he chaired the second World Conference on Faith and Order, at Edinburgh. That same year the two branches of the ecumenical movement, Faith and Order and → Life and Work, committed themselves to union, and Temple became chairman of the committee charged with the writing of a constitution for the incipient → World Council of Churches. With World War II intervening, the council was not officially convened until 1948, in Amsterdam, in the fourth year after his death. In his sermon of 1942 at his enthronement as archbishop of Canterbury, Temple famously described the modern ecumenical movement as "the great new fact of our era."

Temple's involvement in the social witness of the church came to its climax in 1941 in the notable Malvern Conference of the Church of England, which he chaired. Its purpose was to explore social reconstruction and the ordering of a new society based on Christian principles. Temple drafted the final report, "The Life of the Church and the Order of Society," which supported a moderate socialist approach to economic issues. The conference sparked a storm of controversy, and conservatives on both sides of the Atlantic denounced Temple as a confused and dangerous radical. The English genius was demonstrated the next year when the Conservative prime minister, Winston Churchill, sent Temple's name to the king as the next archbishop of Canterbury. George Bernard Shaw quipped, "An Archbishop of Temple's enlightenment is a realized impossibility."

Temple was enthroned at Canterbury in January 1942 in the midst of war, and many of his activities as primate dealt with the wartime struggles of his compatriots. He supported a negotiated peace and opposed the policy of unconditional surrender. At the same time, he managed to finish *Christianity and Social Order* (1942), his last book, which argued the church's right and duty to interfere in social issues and presented the principles upon which such interventions should be made. The gout from which he had suffered since childhood increased in severity during the war years, and his continuous labors for church and nation finally ceased with his death in October 1944.

→ Ecumenism, Ecumenical Movement

Bibliography: A. E. Baker, *William Temple and His Message* (London, 1946) • J. D. Carmichael and H. S. Goodwin, *William Temple's Legacy: A Critical Assessment* (London, 1963) • R. Craig, *Social Concern in the Thought of William Temple* (London, 1963) • J. Fletcher, *William Temple, Twentieth-Century Christian* (New York, 1963) with complete, annotated bibliography of Temple's writings • F. A. Iremonger, *William Temple, Archbishop of Canterbury: His Life and Letters* (London, 1948) • J. Kent, *William Temple: Church, State, and Society in Britain, 1880-1950* (Cambridge, 1992) • W. R. Matthews et al., *William Temple: An Estimate and an Appreciation* (London, 1946) • J. Padgett, *The Christian Philosophy of William Temple* (The Hague, 1974) • R. H. Preston et al., *Archbishop William Temple: Issues in Church and Society Fifty Years On* (Manchester, 1994) • A. M. Ramsey, *From Gore to Temple* (London, 1960) • A. M. Suggate, *William Temple and Christian Social Ethics Today* (London, 1987) • F. S. Temple, ed., *Some Lambeth Letters* (Oxford, 1963) • O. C. Thomas, *William Temple's Philosophy of Religion* (London, 1961).

Owen C. Thomas

Temptation

1. Term
2. In the Bible and Theology
3. In Counseling

1. Term

The → Reformation shaped the use of the German term *Anfechtung*, which is often translated as Eng. "temptation." There is no clear equivalent for it in Hebrew, Greek, or Latin (which has *tentatio* and *afflictio*). Other modern languages lack an exact equivalent, and in everyday speech it is rarely used any longer in a religious connection.

1.1. In today's humanistically oriented terminology, the term "temptation" (even more so *Anfechtung*) is inadequately characterized. It carries with it the sense of → conflict, though this term is inadequate unless it relates specifically to → faith. It also involves crisis, although in modern parlance this word tends to be used for a temporary breakdown in orientation that either inner developmental pro-

cesses or external factors appear to make necessary. "Crisis" may accompany the question of → guilt and → meaning of life and relates implicitly to a theological understanding. The same applies to a term like "frustration."

1.2. Even the traditional term *Anfechtung* hardly covered all that the Reformation had in view; "temptation" *(Versuchung),* as far as it denotes being led astray in a partial (e.g., moral) sense, comes short of it. → "Doubt," however, names primarily the intellectual aspect. Within the framework of the problem of → theodicy, the experience focuses on philosophical or critical religious aspects outside the individual existential context.

1.3. For Reformation theology, temptation (and esp. *Anfechtung*) means the believer's experience not only of God's absence but of God's ultimate opposition to him or her, which removes the basis of the believer's existence and eternal blessedness. This experience found pregnant expression in Jesus' cry of dereliction on the cross, "My God, my God, why have you forsaken me?" (Mark 15:34).

2. In the Bible and Theology

For the → Reformers the great example of temptation in the OT was not so much Job, who with God's consent was tested by Satan with excessive → suffering, but → Abraham, whom God himself tested by telling Abraham to offer his own son (Gen. 22:1-14), and who obeyed. S. → Kierkegaard (1813-55) followed this biblical and Reformation line by writing his "Panegyric upon Abraham" (at the beginning of his *Fear and Trembling*). What Job endured as a righteous sufferer was only superficial compared to what Abraham experienced as the father of faith. When the NT writes about the meaning of suffering and temptation (2 Cor. 4:7-12; 12:1-10; Jas. 1:2, 12), it is partly under the influence of OT → Wisdom literature, although sometimes with an → apocalyptic thrust (see the → Lord's Prayer request in Matt. 6:13; also Matt. 26:41; Luke 8:13).

2.1. For M. → Luther "temptation" becomes a full-scale assault *(Anfechtung)* when it threatens to shake believers in their relation to God. True temptation came to Christ, not when the → devil tempted him in the wilderness, but when he met the → wrath of God in Gethsemane and on the cross and thus became the epitome of the assailed human being. It is precisely the believer who must concede to the → law that reveals → sin and accuses him or her, and thus to the wrath of God directed toward the believer. It is here, according to Luther, that temptation becomes the most profound and dangerous. For Luther the devil was the author of temptation only superficially and instrumentally, although he did use it to pursue his own radically ungodly purposes. In truth, temptation comes from God.

But this fact also brings to light the limit of temptation. For Christ has met the demands of the law and taken upon himself the opposition of divine wrath against sin, and he let himself be tempted in this way, all of which shows us that when we are tempted, we can flee "against God to God" (WA 5.204), live in "comforted → despair" (WA.B1, no. 11), and even "sin boldly" (WA.B2, no. 424). The temptation that threatens believers is dialectically aligned with the saving action that is concealed under what appears to be its opposite.

2.2. This position, taken from the NT, presents itself in a garb that is mythologically colored and pervaded by theistic implications (→ Theism). K. → Barth (1886-1968) could adopt it in modified form (*CD* II/1, 247-50; IV/1, 610-14). P. → Tillich (1886-1965), in contrast, mediates it with an experience of existential threat and loss of meaning that no longer needs to be articulated theistically. He speaks of a "courage to be" that proves itself. In this way he detached the problematic of temptation from what seemed to him to be too close a link with sin and → forgiveness, thereby enabling a connection to a humanistic approach that is now adopted especially in → pastoral care.

3. In Counseling

The medieval and Reformation discussions of temptation carry a rich awareness of the psychological distinctions in people and of the dangers that these involve (see the writings of Jean Gerson [1363-1429]). Luther's pastoral counseling shows that he was fully aware of the psychosomatic implications of temptation (WA.B5, no. 1670). More important both for him and for the tradition that followed him are the spiritual aids that enable us to overcome temptation: Word and → sacrament, especially penance (→ Penitence) and → confession of sins, mutual → counseling, → hymns, and → prayer.

Present-day pastoral care of a greater psychological and theological competence will try not to confuse the psychosomatic presuppositions and the theological interpretation of temptation, but also not to neglect one aspect in favor of the other. In this way it will help to make it possible to perceive temptation as such and to make it fruitful for the deepening of faith and the Christian life.

Bibliography: H.-M. Barth, *Der Teufel und Jesus Christus in der Theologie Martin Luthers* (Göttingen, 1967) • L. A. Coser, *The Functions of Social Conflict*

(Glencoe, Ill., 1956) • C. W. Hovland, "Anfechtung in Luther's Biblical Exegesis," *Reformation Studies* (FS R. H. Bainton; Richmond, Va., 1962) 46-60 • E. Jüngel, *Anfechtung und Gewißheit des Glaubens oder wie die Kirche wieder zu ihrer Sache kommt. Zwei Vorträge* (Munich, 1976) • C. H. Ratschow, *Der angefochtene Glaube. Anfangs- und Grundprobleme der Dogmatik* (5th ed.; Gütersloh, 1983) • D. P. Scaer, "The Concept of Anfechtung in Luther's Thought," *CTQ* 47 (1983) 15-30 • H. Seesemann, "Πεῖρα κτλ.," *TDNT* 6.23-36 • D. K. Switzer, *The Minister as Crisis Counselor* (Nashville, 1974) • H. Thielicke, *Between God and Satan* (Grand Rapids, 1958); idem, *Theologie der Anfechtung* (Tübingen, 1949) • P. Tillich, *The Courage to Be* (New Haven, 1953) • M. Weinrich, "Die Anfechtung des Glaubens. Die Spannung zwischen Gewißheit und Erfahrung bei Martin Luther," *Jesus Christus als die Mitte der Schrift* (ed. C. Landmesser; Berlin, 1997) 127-58.

Hans-Martin Barth

Ten Commandments → Decalogue

Teresa of Ávila

Teresa of Ávila (1515-82, also known as St. Teresa of Jesús, Teresa of Ahumada, and Teresa of the Cross) was a Spanish mystic, a Carmelite nun, and a reformer of orders (→ Religious Orders and Congregations 1). Teresa came from a family of *conversos* (her grandfather was converted from Judaism to Christian faith in 1485) who purchased their title of nobility. According to her autobiography, *Vida,* or *Libro de las misericordias del Señor* (1565, Book of the mercies of the Lord), Teresa, as a child in 1522, wanted to flee to the Moors with her brother Rodrigo in order to suffer martyrdom at their hands. In 1531 she entered the Augustinian convent Santa Maria de Gracia in Ávila but the next year returned to her parents' home. In November 1535 she secretly entered the Carmelite Monastery of the Incarnation in Ávila, whose 180 nuns were not cloistered. After the mishandling of a heart and chest affliction in 1539, Teresa was in a coma for four days, from which she only very slowly recovered. She learned from books about the elevation of the soul to God, while she often felt a lack of understanding from her father confessors of the → Franciscan, → Dominican, and → Jesuit orders.

In 1554 Teresa had her first mystical experiences, which she interpreted as her → conversion, and then, sometime between 1556 and 1560, her "mystical betrothal." Even when her father confessor directed her to cease the practice of the prayer of the heart, she had mystical experiences that were considered to be demonstrations of the grace of Christ. For example, she once felt as though she had been pierced by a seraph with a golden lance, which was interpreted as → stigmatization.

Teresa's intention to return to the original rule of the Carmelite order led to the founding of the convent of St. Joseph on August 24, 1562, in Ávila; in 1563 Teresa became its prioress. There were 13 nuns living there, strictly cloistered and in complete → poverty (§§4-5). As innovations Teresa established three scourgings weekly and the wearing of sandals *(Carmelitae discalceatae)*. In 1565 the Constitutions of the convent were approved by Pius IV (1559-65). In April 1567 the general of the Carmelite order, Giovanni Battista Rossi (Rubeo), granted Teresa the task of founding more convents.

In 1560 Teresa had a vision of → hell in which she felt what she would face because of her sins if God did not save her. Corresponding pains of hell, according to Teresa, would have to be borne by "Lutherans" (Teresa's collective term for all those who had deviated from Catholic doctrine), whom Teresa wanted to save. In 1572 Teresa experienced her "spiritual marriage" while receiving the → Eucharist.

She reported on her founding of 18 convents of → Discalced Carmelite women in *Libro de las fundaciones* (Book of the foundations), written between 1573 and 1582. Through John of the Cross (1542-91), with whom she had been working since the beginning of October 1567, she proposed the reform of the male Carmelite order. Also as prioress she reformed her mother monastery from 1571 to 1573, with John as her father confessor.

In 1575 → Inquisition proceedings were opened against Teresa. When her orthodoxy was substantiated in 1579, her mystical teachings, as well as the Discalced Carmelite order, could spread, and Gregory XIII (1572-85) authorized the formation of a special province. Teresa died in the monastery in Alba that she had founded.

Teresa's writings were first printed in 1588 by Luis de León in Salamanca. Besides biographical and mystical writings, Teresa left behind writings about monastery reform, poems, and 440 letters. In 1614 she was beatified, and in 1622 canonized (her feast day is October 15). In 1970 Teresa was further recognized as a doctor of the church, the first woman to be so honored.

Teresa developed her teaching on interior → prayer not only in her *Vida* but also in a guide for her sisters, *Camino de perfección* (The way of perfec-

tion, 1566), and especially in *Castillo interior, o, Las moradas* (Interior castle, or, The mansions, 1577). In these writings she describes the soul as the vassal of the almighty King, who awaits it in the inner chambers of a crystal castle. The gate to the castle is prayer. Praying, the soul ascends through seven chambers to arrive at full reunion with God, which is a divine grace. The sign of the reality of the vision is tears, in which the awakened one is found "washed." Characteristic of Teresa's teaching is not only intensive self-observation but also a certain ambivalence. On the one hand, she emphasizes the *cooperatio* between the human and God; on the other hand, divine grace (→ Synergism).

Bibliography: Primary sources: The Complete Works of Saint Teresa of Jesus (3 vols.; trans. E. A. Peers; London, 1946) • *The Life of Saint Teresa of Avila* (trans. J. M. Cohen; London, 1957) • *Obras completas* (4th ed.; ed. E. de la Madre de Díos and O. Steggink; Madrid, 1974).

Secondary works: J. BURGGRAF, *Teresa von Avila. Humanität und Glaubensleben* (Paderborn, 1996) • E. CARRERA-MARCÉN, *Teresa of Avila's Autobiography: Authority, Power, and the Self in Mid-Sixteenth-Century Spain* (London, 2005) • E. W. T. DICKEN, *The Crucible of Love: A Study of the Mysticism of St. Teresa of Jesus and St. John of the Cross* (New York, 1963) • E. HOWELLS, *John of the Cross and Teresa of Avila: Mystical Knowing and Selfhood* (New York, 2002) • E. A. PEERS, *Handbook to the Life and Times of St. Teresa and St. John of the Cross* (Westminster, Md., 1954); idem, *Mother of Carmel: A Portrait of St. Teresa of Jesus* (London, 1945) • R. WILLIAMS, *Teresa of Avila* (Harrisburg, Pa., 1991).

ANGELIKA DÖRFLER-DIERKEN

Terre des Femmes

According to its Web site, Terre des Femmes (TdF) is "a non-profit human rights organisation that supports women and girls through international networking, public relations, campaigns, case-by-case assistance, and by promoting individual projects." TdF was founded in Lausanne in 1981. Up to 1990 the organization consisted of a board along with active local volunteer groups. In 1990 it succeeded in establishing an office in Tübingen financed by the Labor Office. This arrangement laid the foundation for the establishment of a national headquarters with paid staff.

According to the Universal Declaration of Human Rights of 1948, women and girls have the right to self-determined lives characterized by → freedom and dignity. TdF works to advance these human →

rights. The organization engages itself in particular with issues such as female genital mutilation, forced marriage, honor killing, forced → prostitution, domestic violence in Germany, exploitation of textile workers, and sex trafficking, including rape. TdF networks with other national and international organizations and is itself a member of numerous organizations, including the Human Rights Forum and the Clean Clothes Campaign, which aims at improving working conditions in the garment and sportswear industry worldwide.

In many cities in Germany, TdF is represented by local groups, whose work is accomplished by volunteers. In cooperation with the national headquarters, they inform the public about the exploitation, mistreatment, and persecution of women. In addition, three times a year TdF publishes the journal *Menschenrechte für die Frau* (Human rights for women), which reports on current human rights violations against women worldwide.

On November 25, the international day "No to Violence against Women," TdF initiates a two-year campaign theme. For November 2004-6 the theme was "No to Crimes in the Name of Honor"; for 2006-8, "No to Domestic Violence." In 2008-10, TdF will specifically address female genital mutilation.

TdF produces educational materials for schools and youth centers regarding prevention of abuse and offers educational events on themes such as forced marriage. In individual cases where threatened women and girls are seeking help, TdF offers assistance with counseling, legal representation, and local shelters. With the help of a rapid distribution system, TdF sends hundreds of protest letters to governments, authorities, and responsible parties in order to save or improve the lives of individual women.

In Tanzania, Kenya, and Burkina Faso, TdF supports local self-help projects, one example of which is the work against female genital mutilation.

→ Health and Illness; Human Dignity; Sexism 4.1; Torture; Women's Movement

Bibliography: TERRE DES FEMMES, *Schnitt in die Seele. Weibliche Genitalverstümmelung–eine fundamentale Menschenrechtsverletzung* (Frankfurt, 2003); idem, *Tatmotiv Ehre* (Tübingen, 2004); idem, *Widerstand ist ein Geheimnis des Glücks. 20 Jahre Terre des Femmes* (Tübingen, 2001).

BRITTA HÜBENER

Terre des Hommes

The Swiss journalist Edmond Kaiser (1914-2000) founded Terre des Hommes in 1960 as a program to help Algerian children (→ Childhood). Subsequently, other Terre des Hommes groups were created. In 1966 they joined together to form the International Federation of Terre des Hommes (IFTDH), a network of 11 autonomous national, mainly European, organizations. The international secretariat is in Geneva.

The mission of the IFTDH is to support children, avoiding all racial, religious, political, cultural, or gender-based discrimination. To this end, the Terre des Hommes organizations develop programs to improve the living conditions of disadvantaged children in their own environment (including families and communities), and they advocate for justice and the implementation of children's → rights. Three-quarters of their funds come from private donations.

More than 1,000 partner organizations and self-help groups in approximately 65 countries engage in projects of health, nutrition, education, child protection, child participation, women's rights, community-based → development (§1.4), and caring for internally displaced persons and → refugees. Through press and public relations work, as well as special campaigns, the IFTDH also aims to change economic and political structures and to bring about a reform of → lifestyle in the North that will be in favor of the children of the South.

Bibliography: Examples of Terre des hommes publications: M. DOTTRIDGE, *Kids as Commodities? Child Trafficking and What to Do about It* (Geneva, 2004) • *A Lifeline for Children / Terre des hommes* (Lausanne, 1990) • P. MCCARRICK, *A Study on Street Children in Ho Chi Minh City* (Hanoi, 2004) • M. VAN REISEN and A. STEFANOVIC, *Lost Kids, Lost Futures: The European Union's Response to Child Trafficking* (Geneva, 2004). See also www.terredeshommes.org.

PETER STRACK

Terrorism

4.3. Nonviolent
5. Biblical Reflections

1. Term

Lacking clear definition, the term "terrorism" has become a weapon itself, brandished by → nations and nonstate groups alike as a propagandistic label for their adversaries. The last decades of the 20th century saw the rise of efforts to clarify the concept. According to one scheme, *terrorism* is violence perpetrated by groups without a → state to sanction their violence, *reign of terror* is a state's violent repression of its own citizens, and → *war* is a state's violence against foreign adversaries.

Such attempts at definitional clarity raise new problems, however, for they do not distinguish between terrorists and "revolutionaries," or terrorists and "resistance fighters." Are George Washington and the French resistance to be counted in the ranks of terrorists? If not, how should we distinguish them? If the state can be guilty of a reign of terror but not of terrorism, how should we understand the accusation "state sponsorship of terrorism"? While governments may sharply distinguish "war" from "terrorism," is such a distinction meaningful to the victims of either one? Furthermore, what of those once labeled terrorists who succeed in achieving their goals (i.e., in becoming "governments")? Examples include Zionists in British-occupied Palestine, the African National Congress in South Africa, and Fatah and Hamas in the Palestine Authority.

The use of "terrorism" in English is due in part to its popularization by Edmund Burke (1729-97), a champion of tradition. Burke was horrified by events across the Channel, where, he believed, French revolutionaries were destroying not only the monarchy but traditional values as well (→ Revolution 2.4). As historian Crane Brinton notes, many revolutions are followed by a period of "terror" in which those who were so recently subversive of state authority but who now control that authority become keen to sniff out suspects who might in turn subvert them. Such was certainly the case in revolutionary France, with the guillotine bloodied and Robespierre (1758-94) embracing the term *terroriste* as virtuous. While Burke renounced these revolutionary terrorists, their terrorism was actually the product of a new state that wielded a degree of centralized authority unmatched by anything the French monarchy had ever attained. Thus, even though the terrorists now led the government of France, Burke contributed to a view of terrorists as those who are opposed to government and order.

Today's terrorism experts are far from unified on a common definition of their subject. One of the most prolific of these, Walter Laqueur, has said, "Terrorism is like pornography. No one can really define it, but everyone recognizes it when they see it" (D. J. Brown and R. Merrill, 179). Is it to be seen in the ashes of the Twin Towers on September 11, 2001? Is it to be seen in the ashes of Hiroshima on August 6, 1945?

2. History

Most histories of terrorism assert that it is not a phenomenon of the modern era alone. These histories often cite the → Zealots and the Sicarii of first-century Judea. The Sicarii were named for the type of dagger (Lat. *sica*) they used to attack Jewish religious officials who collaborated with Roman occupiers. Another group given prominent attention is the 12th-century Islamic Fedayeen (Arab. *fidāalīyīn*, "ones who are ready to sacrifice their life") of the → Shia Ismaili sect. The Fedayeen attacked both Christian → Crusaders and Sunni rulers with such ferocity that it was alleged that they were *ḥashshāshīn* (Arab., "those who use hashish," and the source of Eng. "assassin"). Thugs (from Hindi *ṭhag*, "thief") are a third example: devotees to the Hindu goddess Kali who, on feast days, would kidnap people for human sacrifices to the goddess.

In the modern era many historians point to three periods of terrorist activism. The first, in the late 19th and early 20th centuries, is associated with → anarchism. During this period Europe and North America were rocked by a wave of assassinations with alleged links to the anarchist movement. The victims included Russian czar Alexander II (1881), French president Sadi Carnot (1894), Spanish prime minister Antonio Cánovas del Castillo (1897), Austrian empress Elizabeth (1898), Italian king Umberto I (1900), and U.S. president William McKinley (1901). In many nations, anarchists guilty and innocent were imprisoned, executed, or deported.

The second period of terrorist activism, the mid-20th century, is associated with anticolonial struggles (→ Colonialism). Here the question of whether the label "terrorist" is to be applied only to nonstate actors emerges with special relevance. The rise of a plethora of terrorist groups in the various anticolonial struggles is not owing to any greater propensity for violence among colonized people. Rather, any armed resistance at all in a colonial context can be labeled terrorism. And so, we are told, groups ranging from the Mau Maus of Kenya to the Zapatistas of Mexico engaged in terrorism, not because of any particular level of violence they employed, but because of their political status (or lack thereof).

In the third period, the present, terrorism is said to be associated with ethnonationalist and religious movements. Examples of groups with ethnonationalist inspiration are separatist groups such as the Basque ETA and the Kurdish PKK. Examples of those claiming religious inspiration include Aryan Nations, Aum Shinrikyō, and al Qaeda. Nationalist and religious motivations commingle in movements such as the predominantly Muslim Moro separatist group in the Philippines.

What accounts for the change in terrorist tactics from the anarchists' assassinations of selected political leaders to today's indiscriminate slaughter of civilians in suicidal attacks? Have terrorists become more desperate, or are they merely imitating trends among the powers that be? In the bloody trench warfare of World War I, nearly 90 percent of all casualties were combatants, and 10 percent were civilians. For World War II and the wars of today, however, those percentages have been almost reversed. We have all become fair game — and not only for the "terrorists."

3. Causes

Since 2001, several schools of thought have arisen regarding the cause of contemporary manifestations of terrorism. Some of the proposed causes are mutually compatible; others are not (e.g., the first conflicts with the last two).

3.1. *Evil People*

The proclamations of political leaders on terrorism are rife with dualistic caricatures of good versus evil. Such statements resonate among people who are beset by fear in the immediate aftermath of violence. If the source of terrorism is evil people, then the solution is simple. In the words of Jerry Falwell, "You've got to kill the terrorists before the killing stops. . . . If it takes ten years, blow them all away in the name of the Lord" (CNN interview, October 24, 2004).

Speaking before Congress on September 20, 2001, President George W. Bush posed the rhetorical question, "Why do they hate us?" His answer: "They hate our freedoms." The president later expressed his exasperation with such hatred: "I just can't believe it, because I know how good we are" (C. Johnson, ix). Despite the rhetoric of some 19th-century nihilists, practitioners of terror today do not say, "We love evil and hate the good." Indeed, most acts of terrorism have been accompanied by demands, justifications, and rationales that, at least to their authors, are cogent. Al Qaeda operatives have claimed that their war against America is

sparked by the occupation of Islamic holy sites by armed infidels (i.e., the U.S. troops based in Saudi Arabia at the beginning of the 1991 Gulf War). As they swap dualistic demonizing, all sides risk emulating one another not only in rhetoric but also in deed.

3.2. *Religion*

Religious extremism is a second explanation for terrorism. The same Western media that carry frequent references to "Islamic terrorists," however, largely avoid the phrase "Christian terrorists." Yet, terrorist groups have in fact associated themselves with Christianity (e.g., Ku Klux Klan, Christian Army of God), as well as with every other major religion, including Hinduism (Tamil Tigers), Sikhism (Dal Khalsa, "Army of the Pure"), and Judaism (Mivtzan Elohim, "Wrath of God"). Among new religions, Aum Shinrikyō's Shoko Asahara, mastermind of the sarin gas attack on the Tokyo subway in March 1995, drew from an eclectic mix of Buddhist, Hindu, and Christian beliefs.

This model cannot account, however, for the contemporary and historical groups that have been either without religious orientation or zealously atheistic — for example, the 19th-century Narodnaya Volya (People's Will) in Russia or the 20th-century Baader-Meinhof Gang and Red Army Faction in Europe and the Túpac Amaru Revolutionary Movement and the Shining Path of Latin America. Indeed, in a model proposed by Claire Sterling and endorsed by the Reagan Administration in the 1980s, terrorism was generated by an international network based in Moscow and had nothing at all to do with religion.

In discourse about religion and terrorism, the focus too often settles on an → Islam viewed very homogeneously. To regard Islam as a monolithic reality, however, is akin to refusing to differentiate among Amish farmers, snake-handling Pentecostalists, and the College of Cardinals. It is worth noting that Abdul Ghaffar Khan (1890-1988), one of the great Muslim leaders of the 20th century, was a pacifist who led the nonviolent struggle for independence in the northwest provinces of India (→ Pacifism).

3.3. *Clash of Civilizations*

A third model sees the cause of terrorism in a so-called clash of civilizations. While religion is certainly a component of the civilizations that are purportedly clashing in this model, additional political, economic, and technological elements enter into the conflict. It is claimed that environments favorable to the generation of terrorism are created when traditional values and cultures are undermined, and such is the inevitable consequence of global → capitalism and technological development. In some versions of this model (e.g., that espoused by S. P. Huntington), "the West" is depicted in a favorable light as "the free world" now under assault.

One serious shortcoming of this model is its failure to account for the fact that the relationship between the West and terrorists is not simply one of clashing. In some cases, the former has sponsored the latter.

3.4. "Blowback"

Nation-states have sponsored an assortment of groups that have subsequently been identified as terrorist organizations. Clear examples have included the periodic support for Amal and Hezbollah by Iran, the sponsorship of several groups in Namibia and Mozambique by apartheid-era South Africa, and the organization and funding of the Contras in Nicaragua by the United States.

"Blowback" — the negative effect one receives from one's own weapons — refers here to foreign-policy decisions and military actions by one nation that at a later time can have unintended negative consequences harmful to that nation. Many of the leading groups that are identified today as terrorist organizations (notably the Afghan Taliban, the Algerian Islamic Salvation Army, the Chechen branch of the Muslim Brotherhood, the Philippine Abu Sayyaf, and al Qaeda itself) either originated from or were bolstered by Mujahideen "freedom fighters" who had been covertly recruited, trained, and funded by the United States in the 1980s. In an effort to defeat Soviet forces in Afghanistan, the U.S. Central Intelligence Agency (CIA) recruited fighters from predominantly Muslim countries around the globe. The tactics of these "freedom fighters" included attacks on schools, hospitals, and civilian airliners. Once the Soviets were defeated, however, the Mujahideen returned to their homes and began to engage in forms of violent activism not sanctioned by the United States. At that point the United States started calling them "terrorists," no longer "freedom fighters." In 1998, when President Clinton ordered cruise-missile strikes against "terrorist training camps" in Afghanistan following attacks on U.S. embassies in Africa, the United States was destroying some of the very camps that its own CIA had built. The blowback model contends that, like Dr. Frankenstein, like Dr. Moreau, the superpowers are creating their own monsters.

3.5. Festering Injustice

A fifth explanation for terrorism is festering injustice in the societies of the terrorists. Terrorism has been called a tool of the weak. The assertion is that those who lack the ability to deliver explosions by cruise missiles and B-1 bombers will find other means of delivery, including on the bodies of suicide bombers. Thus, victims of oppression are susceptible to the allure of terrorism.

This model fails to explain, however, why people who have so recently conspired in planning terrorism are of middle- or upper-class background (e.g., Osama bin Laden), although it is true that many of those who do their violent bidding have lived in conditions of → poverty and oppression. We cannot say that poor people are more prone to acts of violence than are the rich, but it is clear that ignoring long-standing grievances and injustice creates vulnerabilities that violent actors on all sides can exploit.

Does our current focus on terrorism distract us from greater horrors? Each year 40 million people die from starvation and diseases related to hunger. To match that toll, terrorists would have to crash 320 filled-to-capacity jumbo jets every day; half of the passengers would have to be children (D. Berrigan, 96).

4. Responses

How should people and governments respond to terrorism? Three models have been proposed: judicial, military, and nonviolent.

4.1. Judicial

The proponents of this response maintain that terrorism is organized crime and that participants ought to be apprehended to face criminal proceedings. It is the response most frequently employed against domestic terrorism. In response to the 1995 attack on the Murrah Building in Oklahoma City, Oklahoma, rather than bombing the headquarters of right-wing militia groups in Idaho and Montana, state and federal governments apprehended suspects and tried them. In some domestic settings, elements of both judicial and military responses are employed (e.g., the British response to the IRA in Northern Ireland).

While the U.S. government has adopted a military response in its "global war on terror," it has frequently counseled other governments to exercise restraint when responding to terrorist attacks. On December 13, 2001, over a dozen people were killed when the Indian parliament building was besieged by attackers with ties to militant groups in Pakistan. In view of the nuclear danger in any military conflict between India and Pakistan, the United States (then engaged in bombing Afghanistan) urged India to seek extraditions and adopt a law-enforcement approach toward its attackers.

4.2. Military

How does one fight a war against an abstraction like terrorism, the very definition of which involves subjectivity? Is it a case of trying to mix apples and oranges to militarily oppose an adversary whose weapons might be passenger jets, fertilizer bombs, and home-brewed nerve agents? Did the United States and Britain opt for a military response to terrorism because it had been judged that it would be effective, or because the military is the one resource these superpowers have in abundance (thus, the tail wagging the dog)? How does one ascertain when victory is won over terrorism? Is such a war perpetual?

If one measure of success in the war on terrorism is a decrease in terrorist attacks, the evidence from the years since September 11, 2001, has not been reassuring. Since that date, terrorist attacks have increased dramatically from Bali to Morocco, from Kenya to Iraq, from Jordan to the U.S. Postal Service. Like terrorism itself, the war on terrorism has taken a horrible toll in human lives. The September 11 toll of 3,000 lives was exceeded by the number of noncombatant deaths in the first few weeks of the war in Afghanistan.

What of war's toll on human → freedom? The war on terrorism has led the United States to form alliances with regimes (e.g., in Tajikistan and Uzbekistan) whose human-rights records are no better than that of Saddam Hussein in Iraq. Furthermore, considering the camps for unlawful combatants, the use of torture, the extraordinary renditions (i.e., the "outsourcing" for torture), the detentions without charge, and the surveillance, one must wonder whether the obsessive quest for security is not already depriving citizens of the dignity and freedom that terrorists alone could never take away (→ Human Dignity; Rights).

4.3. Nonviolent

Taking seriously the equivalence of violent "freedom fighters" and "terrorists," proponents of a nonviolent response to terrorism endorse a full cessation of the international arms trade (of which the United States accounts for a majority) and an end to the covert operations that train, arm, and fund violent movements worldwide. In addition, the advocates of nonviolence argue that the superpowers must begin the process of disarming themselves of weapons of mass destruction. Nations are fallible entities; whatever weapons they possess will inevitably fall into the hands of others (→ Disarmament and Armament).

Governments around the world have proclaimed, "We do not negotiate with terrorists!" although the significance of the U.S. proclamation was cast in doubt by the Iran-Contra scandal. Nonviolence requires a contrary proclamation, one requiring → dialogue; if talking is proscribed, then violence is one of the few remaining options for engagement. Peace organizations that have attempted to foment dialogue between adversaries include Peace Brigades International (formed in 1981), Witness for Peace (1983), Voices in the Wilderness (1996), and Nonviolent Peaceforce (2002). Christian Peacemaker Teams (founded in 1988 by three historic → peace churches) have interfered with real and potential violence in Colombia, Israel, Palestine, Iraq, and elsewhere. In Iraq the group has worked in coordination with Muslim Peacemaker Teams (2005). The Peaceful Tomorrows group, started in February 2002 by family members of those killed in the September 11 attack, urges that resources be diverted from the military to fund humanitarian relief and cultural exchanges between the common people whose leaders are at odds (→ Peace Movements).

In the aftermath of governmental reigns of terror, truth and reconciliation commissions have emerged as a powerful tool in forestalling cycles of violent retaliation. The first commission was led by Archbishop Desmond Tutu in South Africa, where it made a major contribution to averting the retaliatory bloodbath that some feared would accompany the end of apartheid. A truth and reconciliation commission has also been tried in El Salvador and elsewhere.

5. Biblical Reflections

During the heyday of the British Empire, the Englishman John Nelson Darby (1800-1882) developed a detailed theology of the "rapture," according to which believing Christians would be whisked up into the clouds to meet Jesus, thus being spared from suffering the tribulation of the final days (→ Apocalypticism 4.5; Dispensationalism 1). From their celestial perches, the righteous could observe those who would suffer terror down below. It is a theology befitting empire, with its notion that those who are well-situated should not have to suffer along with lesser mortals.

Terrorism, however, did not first strike America in 2001. There is a long history of terrorism being visited on Native Americans, African Americans, and others deprived of lofty perch. September 11 reminded the rest of America that neither military might nor presumed righteousness offers exemption from suffering the fate that others elsewhere have long endured. In Romans 8:18-39 Paul urges believers not to try to escape the groanings of creation but to join in them and make of them a prayer for redemption.

But what about the → wrath and terror of God? In view of the biblical accounts of God being roused to anger, are there ever instances in which people may enlist as instruments of divine terror? Although the Revelation of John is perhaps the bloodiest of biblical texts, it is essential to note that the sources of the bloodshed are Empire and Beast. God's victory is won by → resurrection — first and foremost, the resurrection of the slaughtered Lamb (Rev. 5:9; 12:10-11). The only weapons in the arsenal of the Lamb are the sword of his mouth, that is, the Word of God (2:16; 19:15), and the blood of the martyrs (14:13-20), which is pressed out in mighty torrents to intoxicate the powerful and to mark their fall. Those who had thought that bloodshed would be their security find it to be their undoing. The outcome of Revelation is not destruction but a new heaven and new earth, which may explain why John of Patmos can record with such assurance, "Do not be afraid" (1:17; 2:10).

From the slaughter of the innocents to the crucifixion, the life of Jesus was surrounded by terror. But to the shepherds in the field (Luke 2:10) and to the women at the empty tomb (Matt. 28:5), the angels said, "Do not be afraid." Beyond the choice of terrified flight or brutal fight, the biblical word offers a third response to fear — to → love in the face of it. Martyrs aplenty may be created by all of the shock and awe and the acts of terrorists petty and great, but death itself cannot stand in the presence of the resurrected Lamb. Do not be afraid indeed!

Bibliography: S. K. ANDERSON and S. SLOAN, *Historical Dictionary of Terrorism* (2d ed.; Lanham, Md., 2002) • M. BENJAMIN and J. EVANS, eds., *Stop the Next War Now: Effective Responses to Violence and Terrorism* (San Francisco, 2005) • D. BERRIGAN, *Lamentations: From New York to Kabul and Beyond* (Chicago, 2002) • C. BRINTON, *The Anatomy of Revolution* (rev. ed.; New York, 1965) • D. J. BROWN and R. MERRILL, eds., *Violent Persuasions: The Politics and Imagery of Terrorism* (Seattle, Wash., 1993) • T. G. BROWN, ed., *Getting in the Way: Stories from Christian Peacemaker Teams* (Scottdale, Pa., 2005) • J. K. COOLEY, *Unholy Wars: Afghanistan, America, and International Terrorism* (3d ed.; London, 2002) • M. DANNER, *Torture and Truth: America, Abu Ghraib, and the War on Terror* (New York, 2004) • J. ELLUL, *Apocalypse: The Book of Revelation* (New York, 1977) • J. FERGUSON, *War and Peace in the World's Religions* (New York, 1978) • L. GRIFFITH, *The War on Terrorism and the Terror of God* (Grand Rapids, 2002) • E. S. HERMAN and G. O'SULLIVAN, *The "Terrorism" Industry: The Experts and Institutions That Shape Our View of Terror* (New York, 1990) • B. HOFFMAN, *Inside Terrorism* (rev. ed.; New York, 2006) • S. P. HUNTINGTON, *The Clash of Civilizations and the Remaking of World Order* (New York, 1996) • C. JOHNSON, *Blowback: The Cost and Consequences of American Empire* (New York, 2004) • M. JUERGENSMEYER, *Terror in the Mind of God: The Global Rise of Religious Violence* (3d ed.; Berkeley, Calif., 2003) • W. LAQUEUR, *The New Terrorism: Fanaticism and the Arms of Mass Destruction* (New York, 1999) • R. J. LIFTON, *Destroying the World to Save It: Aum Shinrikyō, Apocalyptic Violence, and the New Global Terrorism* (New York, 1999) • L. NAPOLEONI, *Terror Incorporated: Tracing the Dollars behind the Terror Networks* (New York, 2005) • E. W. SAID, *Covering Islam: How the Media and the Experts Determine How We See the Rest of the World* (rev. ed.; New York, 1997) • C. STERLING, *The Terror Network: The Secret War of International Terrorism* (New York, 1981) • D. TUTU, *No Future without Forgiveness* (New York, 1999) • R. WILLIAMS, *Writing in the Dust: After September 11* (Grand Rapids, 2002) • S. ŽIŽEK, *Welcome to the Desert of the Real! Five Essays on September 11 and Related Dates* (New York, 2002).

LEE GRIFFITH

Tertiaries

From the 13th century male and female tertiaries have existed within → religious orders. They are a closely related "third," or lay, order (besides the "first" and "second" orders, usually referring respectively to orders of men and of women; → Clergy and Laity). They came into being in the 12th and 13th centuries when popular religious movements grew up in the towns. They are parallel to the 12th-century *conversi* (i.e., lay brothers) of the older orders, but adapted now to the city orders, especially the mendicants, which became common from 1200 onward. Tertiaries depended critically on the rise of penitent and religious-social societies among city dwellers, especially in Upper Italy.

A third order first arose when the Lombard Humiliati, an Italian penitential movement, was organized in 1201 by → Innocent III (1198-1216) in three orders. Under the leadership of its priestly order, married members, who were the first to give rise to the movement, were organized as the third order. The second order was made up of celibate men and women living in separated convents.

The development of autonomous brotherhoods and sisterhoods was further promoted by the penitential preaching of → Francis of Assisi (1181/82-1226), who took up the work in an orthodox way that had been developed by lay movements that were heretical or denounced as such (→ Waldenses). We find similar movements among the → Dominicans. Francis drew up general rules of life for his followers. The third → Franciscan rule of order, confirmed by Nicholas IV (1288-92), goes back to a text written during the papacy of Gregory IX (1227-41), although an earlier form may have appeared in 1221. Corresponding associations under the supervision of the Dominicans appeared as early as the 1230s.

In the second half of the 13th century the male and female penitents developed their own convent communities. The → Augustinians, Carmelites, and others soon had their own lay orders as well (the → Benedictines only in the 19th cent.). From the 15th century onward we have tertiary unions or → congregations.

The whole movement developed when city populations who were loyal to the church took up the idea of brotherhoods and sisterhoods after the crisis of → heresies around 1200. The → Reformation and the French → Revolution resulted in the elimination of orders, including tertiaries, in the affected territories. Yet we find in Protestantism similar impulses (→ Religious Orders and Congregations 4) among the → Anabaptists, the → Puritans, and the Pietists (→ Pietism).

In the → Roman Catholic Church the tertiary movement received new life in the 19th and 20th centuries in connection with the charitable, educational, and missionary work of the orders and has now spread across the whole world. "Secular tertiaries" can now be attached to any order, and the church can also use independent lay associations for various devotional and social types of activity (1983 CIC 676, 710-30). Especially under the name of St. Francis there are hundreds of tertiaries worldwide in what are often local societies, most of them for women, though they do not all bear the name of tertiaries. We find the same among the Dominicans, Augustinians, and other orders.

→ Communities, Spiritual

Bibliography: P. FOLEY, *Three-Dimensional Living: A Study of Third Orders Secular* (Milwaukee, Wis., 1962) • M. J. HEIMBUCHER, *Die Orden und Kongregationen der katholischen Kirche* (2 vols.; 3d ed.; Munich, 1965) • F.-D. JORET, *Dominican Life* (Westminster, Md., 1947) • G. G. MEERSSEMAN, *Dossier de l'Ordre de la pénitence au XIIIe siècle* (2d ed.; Fribourg, 1982) • R. PAZZELLI, *St. Francis and the Third Order* (Chicago, 1989) • K.-V. SELGE, "Humiliaten," *TRE* 15.691-96.

KURT-VICTOR SELGE

Tertullian

Quintus Septimius Florens Tertullianus (ca. 160-ca. 225) was an African → church father who wrote primarily in Latin. Texts available for a reconstruction of Tertullian's biography include, next to his own writings, accounts by Eusebius (ca. 260-ca. 340) and → Jerome (ca. 345-420). It has been shown, however, that information from the fourth-century authors should not be used uncritically. From his own writings it appears that Tertullian's father possibly was in the military, and one could add Jerome's account that his father was a *centurio proconsularis,* thus a centurion in the *cohors I urbana* in Carthage. It is highly likely that his son Tertullian belonged to the aristocracy and was perhaps at first a non-Christian. A stay in Rome is substantiated, but otherwise Tertullian appears to have lived in the North African provincial capital of Carthage; according to Jerome, he was born there.

A particular "juristic" influence on Tertullian's terminology is not observable; this applies also to the expressions *meritum* and *satisfactio/satisfacere.* Thus the frequently alleged identification of Tertullian with a contemporaneous Roman lawyer of the same name, from whom five brief fragments have been handed down, is unlikely. The widely held assumption that Tertullian was a rhetorically schooled advocate *(causidicus)* is improbable as well. In any case, Tertullian is stylistically one of the best representatives of the Second Sophistic movement, although he protested against the classical system of education ("What has Athens to do with Jerusalem, what has the academy to do with the church?"). In the most cultivated Latin he articulates drastic → polemics but also intellectually clever allusions. Church Latin owes to Tertullian a large number of new expressions, for example, the word *trinitas* (→ Trinity). His authorship of at least two Greek texts indicates that he had been thoroughly educated. The members of his family were schooled and literarily active as well. Tertullian was married and before 203 wrote two books entitled *Ad uxorem* (To my wife).

Around 205 (or perhaps 207) he joined a movement that differed from customary Carthaginian Christianity, particularly in its ethical rigor. This movement was initiated by Montanus (fl. 2d cent.) and his prophetesses but had changed since its origin. One cannot really speak of Tertullian's converting to → Montanism, since he was the one who initiated and carried out the process of separation. Although this development marked Tertullian as a heretic, it does not obscure the fact that ever since

→ Cyprian (ca. 200-258), Tertullian's theology, by virtue of its language and its content (esp. the doctrine of the Trinity and → Christology), set the standard for Christian Latin literature of the late classical period and continued to be influential. His literary production in the years between 196 and 212 is reliably documented. He is not believed to have become a presbyter.

There are 31 works of Tertullian extant, along with several fragments; their chronology is debated. They are usually divided into either pre-Montanist and Montanist writings or separated into three groups according to their content:

1. The apologetic works include the double work *Ad nationes* and *Apologeticum,* in which the → prosecution of Christians is shown to be illegal; also *De testimonio animae* (→ Apologists; Apologetics)
2. The "dogmatic" writings consist of general antiheretical literature *(De praescriptione haereticorum),* including works against individual → Gnostics *(Adversus Valentinianos),* Marcion (→ Marcionites), and deviant Christological doctrines *(Adversus Praxean).* In this group also is the first Christian writing about the → soul *(De anima).*
3. Writings on "practical-ascetic" questions include a warning about visits to the theater *(De spectaculis)* and against military service *(De corona). De monogamia* condemns second marriages, which were permitted by the church, as adultery; *De virginibus velandis* calls for the veiling of women.

Bibliography: Primary sources: CChr.SL 1/2 • *CPL* 1-31 • *SC* 173, 273, 280, 310, 316, 319, 332, 343, 365, 368, 394, 399, 424, 439, 456, 483 • *StPM* 5 (1956) • *VCSup* 1 (1987).

Secondary works: W. Bähnk, *Von der Notwendigkeit des Leidens. Die Theologie des Martyriums bei Tertullian* (Göttingen, 2001) • T. D. Barnes, *Tertullian: A Historical and Literary Study* (2d ed.; Oxford, 1985; orig. pub., 1971) • R. Braun, *Deus Christianorum. Recherches sur le vocabulaire doctrinal de Tertullien* (2d ed.; Paris, 1977; orig. pub., 1960) • G. D. Dunn, *Tertullian* (London, 2004) • G. Hallonsten, *Überprüfung einer Forschungstradition,* vol. 1, *Satisfactio bei Tertullian;* vol. 2, *Meritum bei Tertullian* (Malmö, 1984-85) • E. F. Osborn, *Tertullian, First Theologian of the West* (Cambridge, 1997) • D. L. Rankin, *Tertullian and the Church* (Cambridge, 1995); idem, "Tertullian's Vocabulary of the Divine 'Individuals' in 'Adversus Praxean,'" *SE* 40 (2001): 5-46 • G. Schöllgen, *Ecclesia sordida? Zur Frage der sozialen Schichtung frühchristlicher Gemein-den am Beispiel Karthagos zur Zeit Tertullians* (Münster, 1984).

Christoph Markschies

Thailand

	1960	1980	2000
Population (1,000s):	26,392	46,718	60,495
Annual growth rate (%):	2.99	1.80	0.69
Area: 513,115 sq. km. (198,115 sq. mi.)			

A.D. 2000

Population density: 118/sq. km. (305/sq. mi.)
Births / deaths: 1.58 / 0.70 per 100 population
Fertility rate: 1.74 per woman
Infant mortality rate: 25 per 1,000 live births
Life expectancy: 70.0 years (m: 67.0, f: 73.2)
Religious affiliation (%): Buddhists 84.8, Muslims 6.9, nonreligious 2.2, tribal religionists 2.2, Christians 1.9, other 2.0.

1. General Features
2. History
3. Buddhism
4. Christianity
    4.1. Roman Catholicism
    4.2. Ecumenical Protestantism
    4.3. Evangelical Protestantism
5. Christian Theology

1. General Features

Thailand is a constitutional monarchy whose ruler, King Bhumibol Adulyadej (on the throne since 1946), is deeply revered by the nation. The official census of 2000 showed a population of 60,606,947, of which 68.9 percent was rural. By 2006 the population was estimated to be nearly 65 million, and the growth rate had dropped to 0.68 percent, from 2.76 percent in 1960. Economically, Thailand is a free-market nation, and its economy grew between 4.4 percent and 6.9 percent per year in the years 2003-5. → Unemployment is less than 2.0 percent (2005 est.), and roughly 10 percent of the population lives under the → poverty line (2004 est.).

Geographically, Thailand includes a large central rice plain and numerous mountainous regions. It is divided into four geographic and cultural regions: North, Northeast, Central, and South. The climate varies from tropical to subtropical. The nation is rich in natural resources, including especially fertile farmland. Environmental degradation, especially pollution and deforestation, is a major issue.

Thailand was known as Siam until 1939, when its

name was changed to its present, more "modern" name. After World War II, the name reverted to "Siam" but was again changed, this time permanently, in 1949.

2. History

In prehistoric times, the area occupied by modern-day Thailand was sparsely populated until the spread of rice growing and the production of bronze (ca. 3000 B.C.). Beginning in roughly the 6th century B.C., groups of Mon-Khmer peoples spread throughout the area from the south and east, while Tai peoples infiltrated from the north. After centuries of cultural mingling, Thai culture and language became increasingly dominant in the Chaophraya basin. Chiang Mai emerged as a major Thai kingdom, called Lan Na, in the north in the 13th century, and in the late 14th century Ayutthaya became the dominant kingdom in the south. While Lan Na fell under Burmese control, Ayutthaya in the 17th century ruled a prosperous, powerful state that had close trading ties with Europe. It developed a "feudal" patron-client social structure grounded on an unusually high reverence for the monarchy.

In 1767 Ayutthaya fell to the Burmese, and in 1782 King Yotfa (1782-1809) founded the Chakri Dynasty, with its capital in Bangkok. He also established formal suzerainty over Chiang Mai and the other northern principalities. During the reigns of King Mongkut (1851-68) and King Chulalongkorn (1868-1910), Thailand adapted to and survived the onslaught of European → colonialism and emerged as a modern nation-state. In 1932 a revolution ended the absolute monarchy and led to a long era of military political domination. Japan occupied Thailand during World War II. During the cold-war era, Thailand was a close ally of the United States and, for some years, experienced rapid economic growth. While it has taken important strides toward democratic rule, Thailand still wrestles with globalization, poverty, racism, corruption and cronyism, military interference in politics, and environmental degradation.

3. Buddhism

→ Buddhism arrived in Thailand in the 5th century, and Theravada Buddhism was reintroduced from Sri Lanka in the 13th century. It became the state-supported faith of all of the Thai states, mixing classical Buddhism with Brahmanism and local beliefs in spirits. Buddhism flourished during several periods, including the 15th century in Chiang Mai and the 17th century in Ayutthaya. While tied closely to the patronage of the ruling class, it also often served as a moral check on that class. Popularly, it provided

society with a religious and moral framework and with values and was a key center of social life. In the 19th century it became even more closely tied to the government, and in the 20th century it lost its ability to influence political life. → Secularism, political control, and corruption have weakened Buddhism's influence in Thai society, but at the same time several reform sects have sought to regain its classical purity as a religious faith.

Buddhism is anchored in the Buddhist orders (sangha), which are under the control of the supreme patriarch. Buddhist religious instruction is given in the public schools. The over 30,000 monasteries are centers of religious activities; they teach a Buddhist lifestyle, promote cultural and social development, and serve as sites for festivals.

4. Christianity

Christian → missions have played an important role in the modernization of Thailand, including in medicine, education, and the importation of new technologies such as printing. While only a small fraction of lowland ethnic Thais are Christians, there are growing numbers of tribal Christians, who now account for one-half or more of the Christian population. Thai Christianity today is split into three large streams.

4.1. *Roman Catholicism*

The first Roman Catholic → missionaries to Thailand arrived in Ayutthya in 1567 (→ Catholic Missions). By 1662 there was a Christian community of roughly 2,000 believers, mostly foreigners, in Ayutthya. In 1662 the Missions Étrangères de Paris sent three missionaries to Ayutthya, including an apostolic vicar. French missionaries in Ayutthya held a synod in 1664 aimed at expanding and solidifying Catholic work and opening a seminary. In 1669 a papal bull, *Speculatores*, was issued giving the apostolic vicars full authority over all Catholics in Ayutthya, which they had not had before. That same year the mission opened its first hospital (→ Medical Missions), and the work of the mission prospered. By 1674 there were roughly 600 Thai Catholics. In 1688, however, the apparently pro-Catholic King Narai of Ayutthya was deposed, Catholic missionaries were expelled, and a severe oppression of Christianity followed.

Matters did not improve until the establishment of the Chakri Dynasty. In 1785 King Yotfa (Rama I) invited Catholic missionaries to return to Siam. By 1875 the Siam Mission had roughly 10,000 Christians, 20 European missionaries, and 8 Thai priests. From this point onward, the mission's work continued to grow rapidly. In 1885 it established its first

Western-style school in Bangkok — Assumption College. St. Louis Hospital was founded in 1898. After 1910 Catholic work began to spread quite rapidly into new areas of the country, particularly in the north. In 1965 the Vatican established two archbishoprics in Thailand, Bangkok and Thare-Nongaseng, and in 1983 Archbishop Joseph Kiamsun Nittayo was consecrated as Thailand's first cardinal. By 2000 there were roughly 300,000 Catholics in Thailand.

4.2. Ecumenical Protestantism

The first two Protestant missionaries, sent by the London Missionary Society, arrived in Bangkok in 1828 (→ British Missions). The American Baptists and the American Board of Commissioners for Foreign Missions (ABCFM) both established a permanent presence in the early 1830s. In 1840 the American Presbyterians sent their first missionary couple to Bangkok, and in 1847 they established the Siam Mission. These early missions suffered under repression, as well as severe limitations in resources and personnel.

The ABCFM mission ended in 1849, and its chief missionary, Dan B. Bradley, subsequently founded a small mission under the American Missionary Association, which ended with his death in 1873. The Baptist mission ended in 1893. The Presbyterians survived until governmental repression ended in 1851 and then established several stations in central and southern Thailand. In 1867 they founded a second mission in northern Thailand, which gained a much larger number of converts and founded stations in all of the major centers in the north. In 1920-21 the two missions formed the American Presbyterian Mission.

The Presbyterians dominated Protestant missionary and church life from the 1860s until after World War II. Besides conducting church work and evangelism, they created extensive educational and medical networks. In 1934 they formed the Church of Christ in Thailand (CCT). In 1957 the Presbyterian mission transferred all of its work to the CCT. The Disciples of Christ mission followed suit in 1961. By 2006 the CCT numbered over 100,000 communicant members. Numerous ecumenical missions from Europe, Asia, the Pacific, and East Asia worked with the CCT, including the American Baptist Convention and the German Marburger Mission.

4.3. Evangelical Protestantism

Evangelical Protestantism has its roots in the work of several Presbyterian missionaries and Thai church leaders. It gained momentum from two visits by the Chinese evangelist John Sung in 1938 and 1939. After World War II a number of evangelical bodies established work in Thailand, including the Overseas Missionary Fellowship, the Southern Baptist Convention, and several Pentecostal groups. While the Southern Baptists established an independent Baptist denomination, many of the other missions and their churches created a loosely structured evangelical alliance, which in 1967 became the Evangelical Fellowship of Thailand (EFT), a "congress" of missions and churches.

Although the EFT has been noted for its commitment to → evangelism, numerical success among lowland Thais has remained limited. → Pentecostal churches, however, have had an impact on the life of Thai Protestant churches generally and have established several megachurches, especially the New Hope Church and the Rom Klao Church, which have branch congregations in several areas.

5. Christian Theology

Indigenous theological reflection in Thailand resides almost entirely in the practice of faith and grows, in important part, from a blend of Thai religious consciousness and Western missionary religious thought. It is not systematic in a formal, Western sense. K. Koyama calls it "kitchen theology," or one that is hidden away from the eyes of formalist theology. Among Thai Catholics, there has been a drive, especially since Vatican II, to incorporate indigenous ceremonies, local cultural forms, and Buddhist institutional forms, as well as to address pressing social issues (→ Acculturation).

Thai Protestants have been reluctant to engage in overt indigenization and betray a far less dialogic attitude toward Thailand's other faiths than do Catholics. The relationship of Thai religious consciousness and Western (missionary) theology has been more problematic for Protestants, especially because of missionary strictures against → "syncretism." Even so, Protestants blend their Thai-Western heritage in a variety of creative ways. They express their "Thai side" by being less dualistic and exclusivist than missionary thought allows, and they express their missionary heritage through their reluctance to participate in Buddhist institutional and ceremonial life.

Both Catholic and Protestant, lowland and tribal Christians particularly reflect the spiritualist ("animistic," so called) component of Thai religious consciousness. God is the divine Protector, to whom they must give undivided loyalty and trust if they are to merit divine protection. The First Commandment is thus of central importance, especially among Protestants.

Bibliography: Historical works: D. Abeel, *Journal of a Residence in China, and the Neighboring Countries* (2d ed.; New York, 1836) • M. Backus, ed., *Siam and Laos as Seen by Our American Missionaries* (Philadelphia, 1884) • A. J. Brown, *The Expectation of Siam* (New York, 1925) • M. L. Cort, *Siam; or, The Heart of Further India* (New York, 1886) • W. C. Dodd, *The Tai Race* (Cedar Rapids, Iowa, 1923) • G. H. Feltus, *Samuel Reynolds House of Siam, Pioneer Medical Missionary, 1847-1876* (New York, 1924) • C. Gutzlaff, *Journal of Three Voyages along the Coast of China in 1831, 1832, and 1833* (London, 1834) • G. B. McFarland, ed., *Historical Sketch of Protestant Missions in Siam, 1828-1928* (Bangkok, 1928) • D. McGilvary, *A Half Century among the Siamese and the Lao* (New York, 1912) • R. E. Speer, *Report of Deputation . . .* (New York, 1916) • J. Tomlin, *Missionary Journals and Letters* (London, 1844).

Modern works: H. Grether, "The Cross and the Bodhi Tree," *TToday* 16/4 (1960) 446-58 • A. P. Hovemyr, *In Search of the Karen King* (Uppsala, 1989) • L. Judd, *Chao Rai Thai: Dry Rice Farmers in Northern Thailand* (Bangkok, 1977) • K. Koyama, *Water Buffalo Theology* (London, 1974) • D. C. Lord, *Mo Bradley and Thailand* (Grand Rapids, 1969) • Seri Phongphit, *The Relation between the Catholic Church and Thai Society from 17c. to Today* (Tokyo, 1985) • H. R. Swanson, *Khrischak Muang Nua: A Study in Northern Thai Church History* (Bangkok, 1984) • Wan Petchsongkram, *Talk in the Shade of the Bo Tree* (Bangkok, 1975) • K. E. Wells, *History of Protestant Work in Thailand, 1828-1958* (Bangkok, 1958).

Dissertations: Y. Hayami, "Ritual and Religious Transformation among the Sgaw Karen of Northern Thailand" (Brown University, 1992) • P. J. Hughes, "Christianity and Culture: A Case Study in Northern Thailand" (Southeast Asia Graduate School of Theology, 1983) • Maen Pongudom, "Apologetic and Missionary Proclamation" (University of Otago, 1979) • Nantachai Mejudhon, "Meekness: A New Approach to Christian Witness to the Thai People" (Asbury Theological Seminary, 1997) • Surachai Chumsriphan, "The Great Role of Jean-Louis Vey" (Pontifical Gregorian University, 1990) • H. R. Swanson, "Prelude to Irony" (Melbourne College of Divinity, 2003).

HERBERT R. SWANSON

Thanksgiving Day → Harvest Festivals

Theism

1. Term
2. In Philosophical and Religious Systems
3. How Many Gods?

1. Term

Basic to theism is the distinction between God and the world. According to the various ways of seeing the relation between transcendent primal being and the contingent universe, we find different forms of theism. In a narrower sense, theism is the view in which God is conceived of as a free personal being who is characterized by a creative relationship to creation (→ God 3.4-6). The express referring of this personal being to his world distinguishes theism from → deism.

1.1. *Deism,* too, differentiates the world from its underlying cause. Deists are open to the idea that the relation between God and the world may be either necessary or free. They may think of the first cause as one that sets the world going and then leaves it to work out its own development (God as the clockmaker).

Before the 18th century the terms "theism" and "deism" were largely synonymous, but then a distinction came to be made. I. Kant (1724-1804; → Kantianism) regarded deism as a → transcendental theology that uses purely transcendental terms to explain God by pure reason. He opposed it to a → natural theology that, in using the method of analogy, derives the existence of a supreme intelligence as the creator of the world from the fact of the actual constitution of human beings. Kant thought of such a view as theistic. The origin of the world is a being that, by reason and freedom, encloses the primal ground of all other beings in itself. In contrast, a deistic view thinks of God only as the first cause of all else.

1.2. If both deism and theism rest on the distinction of God and the world, → *pantheism* to some degree levels down the theistic distinction. In pantheistic systems the transcendence of God dissolves into immanence through its identification with the course of temporality as its proper mode of being (→ Time and Eternity; Eschatology). No room is left for the → absolute. The absolute comes to full fruition in the world. For pantheism, the world is therefore the site of the manifestation of God. It represents for the Creator himself a necessary aspect of his self-actualization (→ Hegelianism).

2. In Philosophical and Religious Systems

2.1. One of the main concerns of F. W. J. Schelling (1775-1854; → Idealism) in combating the pantheistic systems of B. Spinoza (1632-77; → Spinozism) and G. W. F. Hegel (1770-1831) was to be open to both aspects, the transcendence and the immanence of God, so as to maintain the freedom of God relative to his → creation. The main problem with his → *panentheism* is not the way he thinks of the relation between freedom and → nature (Kant) but the way in which he relates divine freedom to human freedom. Schelling thus confronts the basic insight that a → religion of freedom must always consider that God as a free being can create only free creatures. Only a free creature could be an adequate image of God, and only in God was this possible.

The cleft between God and the world is sharpened in the → existential theology of R. Bultmann (1884-1976) and the → dialectical theology of K. → Barth (1886-1968) by an emphasis on the absolute freedom of God over the world, so that the necessary relation between the Creator and his creation is loosened.

→ *Atheism* replies to this elimination of the link between the creator and its creation by celebrating it as a form of liberating human freedom. The handing over of transcendence to human subjectivity gives self-importance to emancipated and enlightened humans. Either individuals or the species may autopoietically legislate for themselves in order to realize human autonomy (→ Anthropology 4.2). Pantheism eliminates the absolute, but here we find a multiplication of the absolute in a plurality of absolute free subjects.

2.2. Along these lines we find the derived absolute that is significant for Mahayana → Buddhism. The ground of the world transcends every possible epoch but in such a way that it communicates itself to humans, so that the absolute becomes innerworldly present in the very moment of its epiphany — a singular moment in which the Eternal has been temporalized in time.

2.3. The theistic tradition of → Hinduism combines the derived absolute of Buddhism and the Christian doctrine of creation. It acknowledges Isvara as the creator of the world, who, as the self-consciousness of Brahma and with the help of his *śakti* power, infinitely brings to manifestation the involved potency of his existence. By the *śakti* power of Isvara, Brahma, the transcendental being *(sat)*, will evolve divine forms out of the material cosmos *(prakṛti)* in which he is involved thereby. The powers liberated by Isvara in its divine embodiment therewith become themselves a derived absolute.

3. How Many Gods?
We thus have the question of the number of gods.

3.1. → *Polytheism* honors many gods influencing the world. The Greek concept of Olympus offers a good example.

3.2. → *Monotheism,* which is upheld by → Juda-

ism, Christianity, and → Islam, rejects any such plurality of gods. It stresses the fact that there is only one God, who stands above all creaturely comparison (ontological difference). We may know God only as he reveals himself. For Christianity this → revelation culminated when God became incarnate in Jesus Christ (→ Christology; Incarnation). This God is the Mediator who by the life and death of Jesus bridged the gulf between himself and us, by the renewing power of the Holy Spirit reconciling creation to the Father in order that we may all be perfect, even as the Father in heaven is perfect (→ Trinity).

→ God Is Dead Theology

Bibliography: P. A. BERTOCCI, "Theism," *EncRel(E)* 14.421-27 • P. FORREST, *God without the Supernatural: A Defense of Scientific Theism* (Ithaca, N.Y., 1996) • H. FUHRMANS, *Schellings Philosophie der Weltalter* (Düsseldorf, 1954) • A. GHOSE, *The Life Divine* (New York, 1953) • G. W. F. HEGEL, *The Christian Religion: Lectures on the Philosophy of Religion, Part 3* (Missoula, Mont., 1979) • N. KRETZMANN, *The Metaphysics of Theism: Aquinas's Natural Theology in "Summa contra gentiles" I* (Oxford, 1997) • J. L. MACKIE, *The Miracle of Theism: Arguments for and against the Existence of God* (Oxford, 1982) • J. S. MILL, *Three Essays on Religion* (New York, 1874; repr., New York, 1969) • P. K. MOSER and P. COPAN, eds., *The Rationality of Theism* (London, 2003) • K. NISHITANI, *Was ist Religion?* (2d ed.; Frankfurt, 1986) • S. RADHAKRISHNAN, *Indian Philosophy* (London, 1923) • F. W. J. SCHELLING, *Of Human Freedom* (Chicago, 1936; orig. pub., 1809) • R. SWINBURNE, *The Coherence of Theism* (Oxford, 1993) • B. WELTE, *Religionsphilosophie* (Freiburg, 1978).

ARNO BÖHLER

Theocracy

1. OT Background
2. Early and Medieval Church
3. Modern Period
4. Theocracy, Establishment, and Civil Religion
5. In Islam

1. OT Background
As the word itself suggests, "theocracy" is a form of government in which, literally, "God rules." As the term has historically been employed, it has been used to describe geopolitical governments in which the civil magistrates are expected to use their powers to promote obedience to the laws of God, or at least some of those laws.

The purest expression of theocracy is found in

ancient → Israel (§1), where the theocracy is instituted by God himself at Sinai, when through Moses he delivers a → covenant that charters the infant nation. → Yahweh is Israel's God, and his laws are Israel's laws: "For what other great nation has a god so near to it as the LORD our God is whenever we call to him? And what other great nation has statutes and ordinances as just as this entire law that I am setting before you today?" (Deut. 4:7-8; → Law 1).

This Israelite theocracy reflected the conviction that the entire created order is a theocracy in the literal sense of God ruling directly without any human intermediary: "Heaven is my throne and the earth is my footstool" (Isa. 66:1). The same God who creates the various aspects of the created order issues commands to each in the very process of creating: "Then God said, 'Let there be light'; and there was light" (Gen. 1:3). Humans were created to rule the creation on God's behalf, exercising "dominion over the fish of the sea and over the birds of the air and over every living thing that moves upon the earth" (Gen. 1:28). When Adam and Eve revolted, they were banished from this literally understood theocracy, from the presence of the God whose rule they had rejected. Later, God reestablished in one small part of his creation another theocracy — Israel.

2. Early and Medieval Church

The first known use of the term "theocracy" was by Josephus (ca. 37-ca. 100), who used it to describe to his Greco-Roman audience the distinctive nature of the ancient Jewish government: "Some peoples have entrusted the supreme political power to monarchies, others to oligarchies, yet others to the masses. Our lawgiver, however, was attracted by none of these forms of polity, but gave to his constitution the form of what — if a forced expression be permitted — may be termed a 'theocracy' [*theokratian*], placing all sovereignty and authority in the hands of God" (*Ag. Ap.* 2.17).

The → early church was not theocratic, and could not have been so, because it was a geopolitical minority. With the conversion of Constantine (ruled 306-37) to Christianity at the Milvian Bridge in 312, however, the new historical possibility arose of blending the powers of the church and the powers of the state, which ultimately produced what is called "Christendom" or, often by opponents, "Constantinianism." Various forms of theocracy — some milder, some more zealous — characterized Western Christian nations from Constantine until the → Enlightenment, although the earliest ecclesiastical statements appear to have resisted such, favoring instead the Augustinian notion of → two

kingdoms (→ State Church 3). Pope Gelasius I (492-96), for instance, in a letter he sent in 494 to Emperor Anastasius (491-518), stated that the emperor should submit to the church in ecclesiastical matters, and the bishops should submit to the emperor in temporal matters.

As the term "theocracy" developed, it was used in a less technical sense to describe governments or theories of government that required obedience to the moral laws of God, if not other ceremonial or sacramental laws. During the later Middle Ages, the various → Papal States subordinated the civil authority to that of the Roman → pope, and in the Byzantine world the emperor was similarly expected to protect and preserve the church, while ordering society according to God's laws. The purest expression of what may have previously been more implicit appeared in *Unam sanctam* (1302), a bull of Boniface VIII (1294-1303) that articulated the idea of the pope's dual jurisdiction, both priestly and royal, over both the ecclesiastical and the civil realms. Such a clear and explicit statement attracted critical attention, and the doctrine was opposed by such individuals as Marsilius of Padua (ca. 1280-ca. 1343), whose *Defensor pacis* (1324) was condemned in 1326 by John XXII (1316-34), and → William of Ockham (ca. 1285-1347) throughout his *Opera politica*, who in consequence was excommunicated and is sometimes referred to as the first Protestant.

In → Protestantism the Geneva of John → Calvin (1509-64) was theocratic in the sense that the civil magistrate could and did punish people for violations of things taught in the Christian Scriptures. The same was true in other Protestant states and, later, in the Massachusetts Bay Colony.

3. Modern Period

In the early American republic, contemporary with and informed by the Enlightenment, the churches themselves began to self-consciously resist theocracy and to separate church from state, a movement that no less a theologian than Princeton's Charles Hodge (1797-1878) justly declared to be the one distinctive contribution of the American churches to Christian theology (→ Church and State). He famously asserted: "The NT, therefore, does not teach that the magistrate is entitled to take care that true religion is established and maintained; that right men are appointed to Church offices; that those officers do their duty. . . . If to this it be added that experience teaches that the magistrate is the most unfit person to discharge these duties; that his attempting it has always been injurious to religion, and inimical to the rights of conscience, we have reason to rejoice in the recently discovered truth, that the Church is independent of the state, and that the state best promotes her interests by letting her alone" (pp. 117-18).

American Presbyterians, for instance, in 1787/88 changed the entire chapter of the English → Westminster Confession of Faith of 1647 on the civil magistrate, removing from his arena of responsibility any specific obligation to establish the Christian church, and they also modified that confession's Larger Catechism, q. 109, removing from the list of sins forbidden in the second commandment the clause "tolerating a false religion," which, in the language of the 17th and 18th centuries, referred to civil magistrates who permitted false religions to exist unmolested in their realm. By 1787 American Presbyterians no longer considered such toleration to be a sin, because by this time American Presbyterians were rejecting the notion of theocracy. They returned to and embraced the Augustinian notion (reiterated by Marsilius, Ockham, and later, John Locke [1632-1704]) that the church's power is spiritual, not coercive, and therefore distinct from that of the state. That a culture founded without religious props from the civil government could nonetheless be so significantly religious in practice confounded Alexis de Tocqueville (1805-59) and not a few other observers of American culture since.

Such action reflected the earlier testimonies of William Penn (1644-1718) and Roger Williams (ca. 1603-83), who had labored for → religious liberty in the American colonies. Indeed, other communions, both in the colonies and in Europe, also accepted the separation of church and state, though not all took the express action of changing their standards to articulate the change. By the middle half of the 19th century, disestablishment was the de facto reality of Western Christianity outside of the Vatican state, though many European governments, such as those of England, the Nordic countries, and much of Roman Catholic southern Europe, retained the de jure notion of the monarch's or government's duty to protect and defend an established church, clearly giving legal preference and protection to these "state," "folk," or "national" churches.

By the middle of the 20th century, with cultural progressives tending to attain power in many mainline American churches, the former separation of church and state began to disappear, as many churches became much more aggressive in using their powers to shape both public opinion and government policies. Initially, the more conservative American Christians objected to this blurring of church and state, but eventually many of them decided to join the movement, for the so-called culture wars of the late 20th century led to a number of evangelical Christians in America becoming more willing to repudiate their heritage in order to approve a somewhat more direct relation between the state and religion, if not between the state and any particular church. During this period, for instance, the movement known as Christian Reconstruction arose, attempting to "reconstruct" America under biblical laws. There were debates about whether the pledge of allegiance should contain the phrase "under God," each Christmas season witnessed heated debates on the propriety of manger scenes on public properties, and in 2003 Judge Roy Moore of Alabama made a public issue of disobeying a court order to remove a monument of the Mosaic Decalogue from his courthouse. Many reacted to this trend with deep concern (e.g., Kevin Phillips, a noted journalist and political commentator).

4. Theocracy, Establishment, and Civil Religion

There is a conceptual continuum from theocracy, through establishment, to → civil religion, as one moves from a purer to a more diffuse relation between state and church without entirely severing religious values from the public square. In a theocracy, the laws of a particular deity or religion are the laws of the civil entity; in a state with an established religion, such laws are not civil laws, but the civil power supports and aids one religion over others; in civil religion, there is no official relation between the civil and ecclesiastical spheres at all, but there may be attitudes and values in the public arena that are influenced and informed by a religious heritage.

Historically speaking, the theocracy of the medieval West gave way to the various European established religions of the Renaissance and Reformation eras, which in turn gave way to the various civil religions that emerged after the Enlightenment. Even in nations that self-consciously distinguish between church and state, such as the United States, civil religion continues, as citizens tolerate public reference to values and attitudes that originally derive from religious sources. The biblical quotations and allusions of Abraham Lincoln (1861-65) in his Second Inaugural address (1865), as well as those of → civil rights leader Martin Luther → King Jr. (1929-68), have become an ordinarily acceptable part of American public life and discourse. To be sure, the so-called creed, upon which G. K. Chesterton (1874-1936) asserted that the American republic was founded, was not any particular ecclesiastical creed but, rather, what Richard E. Wentz has called the "cluster of ideas and convictions, the special practices, and the sense of peoplehood that belong to America" (p. 57).

Bibliography: M. ANGROSINO, "Civil Religion Redux," *AnthQ* 75 (2002) 239-67 • R. BEINER, "Machiavelli, Hobbes, and Rousseau on Civil Religion," *RP* 55 (1993) 617-38 • R. N. BELLAH, "Civil Religion in America," *Daed.* 96 (1967) 1-21 • T. C. HALL, "Christianity and Politics IV: Politics and the Reformation," *BW* 41 (1913) 229-35 • C. HODGE, *Discussions in Church Polity* (New York, 1878) • M. KAMRAVA, *The Political History of Modern Iran* (Westport, Conn., 1992) • K. PHILLIPS, *American Theocracy: The Peril and Politics of Radical Religion, Oil, and Borrowed Money in the Twenty-first Century* (New York, 2006) • S. RUNCIMAN, *The Byzantine Theocracy* (London, 1977) • D. L. WEBSTER, "On Theocracies," *AmA* 78 (1976) 812-28 • G. WEILER, *Jewish Theocracy* (Leiden, 1988) • R. E. WENTZ, *The Culture of Religious Pluralism* (Boulder, Colo., 1998).

T. DAVID GORDON

5. In Islam

Governments in Islamic societies have not generally been theocratic, if by that is meant that political authority is concentrated in a person or persons who have a special charisma, a pronounced sacerdotal function, the ability to bind subjects by means of pronouncements on doctrine, or whose leadership is connected in some critical way with the salvation of the community (→ Islam). For the most part, Islamic societies have been governed, as are most today, by governments that claim varying degrees of legitimacy through their support of religious figures and institutions that are to some extent separate from the institutions of political authority (e.g., Egypt, Pakistan, Saudi Arabia). There are, however, important exceptions to this general description, including the early Islamic community and Shiite states.

5.1. The Prophet Muḥammad (ca. 570-632) acquired political authority after his move from Mecca to Medina in 622. His successors were first called caliphs (Arab. *khalīfah*, "successor") — a qur'anic term applied to → Adam and King → David, who are God's trustees on earth — and later added the title "commander of the faithful" *(amīr al-mu'minīn)*. The so-called orthodox, or "rightly guided," caliphs ruled from Medina (632-61), the Umayyad caliphs from Damascus (661-750), and the Abbasid caliphs from Baghdad (750-1258).

All the caliphs were rulers in fact until the mid-ninth century, when the Abbasid empire fragmented and the central Islamic lands came to be ruled in many cases by various Turkic groups. Dis-

putes, occasionally violent, over legitimacy of rule during the orthodox and Umayyad periods led to theological speculation about the ruler's piety, but dissatisfaction with the caliphs caused the resulting ideas about right conduct and → sin to become generalized and applicable to Muslims at large (e.g., as Islamic law). Those who engaged in such speculation emerged as the scholarly institution of the ulema (*'ulamā'*, "scholars"), whose own religious authority, over the course of the eighth and ninth centuries, came to rival and ultimately to eclipse that of the caliphs. The caliphs, whose importance continued to be recognized by Sunni political theorists such as al-Māwardī (d. 1058), remained as figureheads into the Ottoman period, when the title was assumed by the Ottoman sultans. The office was ultimately abolished in 1924 by Mustafa Kemal Atatürk (1881-1938) in connection with the founding of the Turkish Republic (→ Turkey 2).

→ Sunni Muslims revered their earliest history, in which political and religious authority were fused in the person of Muḥammad and his immediate successors, as a myth of the unity of the primeval Muslim community. The relatively swift decline of the caliphs' religious authority and its replacement by that of the ulema, who continued to emphasize the simultaneous momentousness and remoteness of that golden age, has presented a structural barrier to the realization of theocratic government in Sunni Islam, if not always to the yearning for it (including among some contemporary jihadists). One early movement, the Kharijites, made the entire community charismatic and every member potentially suitable to rule but excluded sinners, making the latters' property and lives forfeit and their families subject to enslavement. Although the early Sunnis were less militant than the Kharijites, the Kharijite example illustrates how the diffusion of authority, as among the Sunni ulema, could lead to a certain egalitarianism.

There have been exceptions, however, to the general Sunni reluctance to welcome charismatic rule, such as the Almoravids (1062-1147) and the Almohads (1130-1269) in Spain and North Africa and, in the 19th century, the caliphs of Sokoto (northern Nigeria and the Niger valley) and the revolt of the Mahdi (*mahdī*, "one rightly guided" — a messiah figure) against British rule in the Sudan (1880-90s). Also, both Morocco and Jordan remain monarchies whose rulers claim descent from the Prophet's family, though in both cases the associated claim of charisma, while more than implicit, is relatively modest (less so in Morocco), and religious authority remains firmly lodged with the ulema.

5.2. For Shiites, matters were different (→ Shia, Shiites). They held that the wrong persons had succeeded to the caliphate after Muḥammad, and they thus formed and clung to a utopian ideal of the ruler, called an imam (*imām,* "leader"), who combined absolute political and religious authority. ʿAlī ibn Abī Ṭālib (d. 661), Muḥammad's cousin and son-in-law, was the fourth of the Sunnis' "rightly guided" caliphs, but the Shiites consider him their first imam and believe that his immediate succession to Muḥammad had been divinely decreed and expressly confirmed by Muḥammad. The imams who succeeded ʿAlī were held to be descended from him and Muḥammad's daughter Fatima (Muḥammad had no sons). The Shiite imams enjoyed, in theory, a more robust connection to the supernatural than did the Sunni caliphs.

Various Shiite groups achieved political power and formed states governed by imams, the most important of which were the Fatimids and the Safavids. The Fatimids (named after Muḥammad's daughter) came to power in North Africa in the 9th century, founded Cairo in the late 10th century, and ruled Egypt and Syro-Palestine until the late 12th century as the main rivals to the Abbasid caliphs. Among their various offshoots today are the followers of the Aga Khan.

In 1500 a messianic movement came to power in Iran and founded the Safavid state, which patronized Imami (Twelver) Shiite ulema. When the state crumbled in 1722, the structure of scholarly authority remained and gradually evolved into that of modern Imami Shiism, more hierarchical than that of the Sunni ulema, but still characterized by the diffusion of authority. The complete failure of the Imami Shiite ideal of the charismatic ruler, where the advent of the true imam was postponed until the end of time, left the Shiites in some ways freer to experiment than the Sunnis. In 2007 the only real theocracy in the Muslim world was the Islamic Republic of Iran, which presents a fascinating mix of clerical and democratic rule. Its eclecticism is already foreshadowed in the political writings of the architect of the Islamic revolution in Iran, Ayatollah Khomeini (1900?-1989), who held that only religious scholars were entitled to rule an Islamic state. It is an experiment that is difficult to imagine being undertaken by Sunnis.

Bibliography: A. BLACK, *The History of Islamic Political Thought: From the Prophet to the Present* (Edinburgh, 2001) • C. E. BOSWORTH, *The New Islamic Dynasties: A Chronological and Genealogical Manual* (Edinburgh, 1996; repr., 2004) • P. CRONE, *God's Rule: Government and Islam* (New York, 2004) • H. HALM, *Shiʿism* (2d ed.; Edinburgh, 2004) • R. KHOMEINI, *Islam and Revolution* (Berkeley, Calif., 1981) • AL-MĀWARDĪ, *The Ordinances of Government* (Reading, 1996) • R. P. MOTTAHEDEH, *The Mantle of the Prophet: Religion and Politics in Iran* (Oxford, 2000) • A. A. SACHEDINA, *Islamic Messianism: The Idea of Mahdī in Twelver Shīʿism* (Albany, N.Y., 1980); idem, *The Just Ruler (al-sultān al-ʿādil) in Shīʿite Islam: The Comprehensive Authority of the Jurist in Imamite Jurisprudence* (New York, 1998) • W. M. WATT, *Muhammad: Prophet and Statesman* (Oxford, 1961).

JOSEPH LOWRY

Theodicy

1. Term

The ancients wondered about the reasons for → evil in the world, about its causes. In the Bible, Job wrestled with why he had undeserved miseries heaped upon him. In his dialogue *The Nature of the Gods,* Cicero asked why, if the gods care for human beings, the good fail to prosper or bad people not come to grief (3.79). There Cotta, Cicero's spokesperson for → Skepticism, who attacks the → Stoic belief in → providence, declares that "divine providence is either unaware of its own powers or is indifferent to human life. Or else it is unable to judge what is best" (3.92). Cotta also dismisses the Epicurean sidestepping of the issue, in their depiction of the gods as blissfully uninvolved with the world.

How the divine can be compatible with the existence of evil in the world has perplexed profound thinkers and ordinary people right down to the present day. *When Bad Things Happen to Good People* (1981), by Harold Kushner, is a recent best-seller. The issue is especially acute for monotheistic belief in a good and just Creator who cares for the world. It is a perennial topic for both → philosophy of religion (§4) and → systematic theology.

"Theodicy" combines the Greek words *theos* ("god") and *dikē* ("judgment" or "justice") and literally means "justification of God." In practice, the term refers to the believer's justification for maintaining faith in a good and powerful deity, in light of the evil in the world.

2. The Theodicy Dilemma and Strategies for Response

2.1. *The Dilemma*

The critic of religion typically poses the theodicy challenge as a dilemma for the believer, as a forced choice between two alternatives. Given the fact of evil in the world, either (1) God can prevent evil but does not do so and thus is not good, or (2) God wants to prevent evil but cannot and so is not (all-) powerful. This challenge works best against monotheistic belief in a good and powerful God who creates the world and providentially cares for it by governing it justly. In fact the challenger would like the believer to find both options unattractive, and so to renounce belief in God altogether. The believer's counterstrategy is to reject the terms in which the dilemma is posed, by modifying one of its alternatives to make it compatible with religious belief.

Some clarifications are needed at this point. First, participants in the debate must agree that evil is actual in the world, not just an illusion or the apparent result of our misperceiving the way things really are. This requirement excludes from the debate some Eastern philosophies and perhaps → Christian Science. But mainstream → Judaism, Christianity, and → Islam fall directly in the critic's crosshairs. Second, "evil" refers neutrally to circumstances that reasonable persons might well wish did not exist, such as → suffering (including animal pain), disease, → death, and harm from natural disasters. It does not include "sin," a category with controversial content, since it is theologically defined by particular authorities that others need not acknowledge. Third, to be effective, the challenge does not require belief in literal omnipotence; it applies also to a creator simply said to be very powerful. Fourth, statement (1) makes the assumption that a perfectly good being will act to prevent evil when it is capable of doing so.

Philosophers find it helpful to distinguish two kinds of evil. *Natural* or *physical evil* results from the regular, lawlike operations of nature (as in disease, hurricanes, and earthquakes). It is normally said to be nobody's fault. *Moral evil* is a deliberate act of omission or commission by a person with free will who could have chosen to act otherwise. The free act is regarded as responsible for the evil, as its decisive cause. There are in-between cases such as illness resulting from reckless exposure of oneself to disease by one's own choice, and being found not guilty of a crime by reason of insanity. But the distinction works for the most part and is useful for handling the relation of God to evil differently for each kind of evil.

2.2. *Strategies of Believers*

Mainstream monotheists cannot accept statement (1) as it stands, namely, that God does not prevent evil because he is not good (i.e., is evil himself). They also cannot say that there is no evil or that evil is an illusion or that God's power is so slight that he cannot thwart evil if he chooses to. How, then, do believers respond to the theodicy challenge?

One approach is present in the framing story in Job, where evil is God's test of one's → faith, except that (unlike for Job) the rewards for passing and punishments for failing are justly meted out mainly in the afterlife. This answer may satisfy the believer, but it has no probative value for others. It is useless as an apologetic because it rests on two assumptions one is not obliged to accept, namely, that there is an afterlife where persons continue to exist as the same persons they were in this life, and that the afterlife does consist of just rewards and punishments for individuals.

Another approach is to contend that a good and powerful God has sufficient reasons for not preventing evil, reasons that do not compromise divine goodness. In one version, the believer simply accepts this contention as a revealed truth that God's reasons are beyond human comprehension. It involves another assumption with no apologetic force, one that looks like special pleading, like stubbornness in the face of facts to the contrary. A second version proposes specific reasons the critic might find plausible. Examples of plausible reasons are given in what follows.

3. Theodicies and Critics in History

We consider here just a few of the many philosophers and theologians who have tackled this issue down through the centuries.

The → church fathers and the medieval theologians typically held that the world as originally created by God was wholly good and that its disorder and evil came about as a consequence of Adam's fall. In Gen. 3:17 God says to disobedient → Adam, "Cursed is the ground because of you." → Augustine (354-430), Thomas Aquinas (ca. 1225-74), and others are emphatic that death and all bodily defects are consequences of the original sin. The lot of the natural world is so interlocked with that of Adam, who names the animals and is custodian of all of nature (Gen. 1:26-29; 2:19-20), that the consequences of Adam's evil deed afflict all of nature too. This view prevailed up through the → Reformation era because nearly everyone took the Genesis account to be historically accurate. According to it, natural evil is simply the by-product of Adam's moral evil and calls for no further explanation. Belief in Adam's moral evil and the inherited sin of his descendants rests on the authority of → revelation, hardly a rationale plausible to critics or nonbelievers.

The context of the theodicy challenge to faith shifted in the 17th century with the advent of the new cosmology, of modern science, and specifically the work of Isaac Newton (1642-1727). The ensuing → Enlightenment era no longer depicted nature as God's original handiwork spoiled by → sin but envisaged it as a great machine, designed and operated by divine reason according to uniform and understandable laws. The new challenge for faith was to explain why natural evils occur as by-products of the rational world-system operating exactly as God designed it.

The German philosopher G. W. Leibniz (1646-1716) declared in his *Theodicy* (1710) that "this is the best of all possible worlds." He argued that God brought into being the richest ensemble of coexisting creatures that he possibly could, selected from the range of candidates open to his choice. God did so with foreknowledge of what any of the possible ensembles with their individual members would be like, were that ensemble to be created. The optimism of Leibniz precluded any objection to religious faith based on actually existing natural evils, because this world is said to be better than any other world that might have been, and its existence is better than if there were no world at all. His view proved less convincing to many after the devastating Lisbon earthquake of 1755, which killed tens of thousands. Voltaire (1694-1778) ridiculed it via the humorous pontification of Pangloss, the starry-eyed tutor in his novel *Candide* (1759).

The posthumous *Dialogues concerning Natural Religion* (1778), by David Hume (1711-76), criticized the design proof for God's existence by enumerating features of the world that should not exist, had it been created by a good, powerful, and intelligent deity. Two bear directly on theodicy. One is pain (rather than just a lessening of pleasure) as the stimulus for an organism to seek to remedy disease or injury. The other is nature governed by uniform general laws, the operations of which often clash with human needs, whereas nature could have been punctuated by frequent favorable accidents or miracles.

In the 19th century the speculative thought of G. W. F. Hegel (1770-1831; → Hegelianism), especially his lectures on world history, portrayed the world spirit's arduous journey through the harsh conflicts and vicissitudes of the ages to its contemporary attainment of full self-consciousness and the realization of political freedom. These lectures conclude with the declaration that this historical process is "the true theodicy," that it shows that "what has happened, and is happening every day, is not only not 'without God,' but is essentially his work." This Hegelian perspective was soon overshadowed by Darwinism, which for many, though not for Charles Darwin (1809-82) himself, rendered belief in God untenable, not just irrelevant for understanding natural events and processes.

4. Twentieth-Century Issues

Various → analytic philosophers revitalized interest in theodicy. Antony Flew argued that an omnipotent, omniscient deity would foreknow what any free-willed person he might decide to create would choose in life if actually created. Such a deity, if good himself, would select for his creation only those persons who, if created, would always freely choose what is morally good. Flew contended that the fact of moral evil in the world shows that there is no such good Creator.

Alvin Plantinga responded to Flew's argument by adverting to Leibniz. Plantinga said that, in creating a richly varied world, God must select for creation a set of "possible persons" who would be mutually compatible ("compossible") in the specifics of a particular world. To change one person is to change the world in that respect. (For instance, a world in which I existed but never had the specific sister I do have in this world would be a different world, and I would to that significant extent be different in it too.) Plantinga argued that there may not have been available for God's choice a possible world that is both richly varied in its members and contains only persons who, if created, would always freely choose what is morally good. That we don't have such an actual world is no refutation of belief in a good and powerful God; the burden of proof lies on the critic to show that such a world is indeed available for God to choose. Scholars disagree as to the effectiveness of Plantinga's response to Flew's challenge.

In *Evil and the God of Love* (1966), John Hick advocated, in response to Hume and Flew, a "soul-making" theodicy. Hick said that God's goal is character development, and meaningful character traits are not God-given natural attributes. We acquire and reinforce our character traits by our free choices. For instance, choosing to face hazards steadfastly is what makes one actually brave rather than untested or cowardly. A suitably challenging environment and free will are requisite for character development to occur. The physical environment must be governed by uniform natural laws, though their operations sometimes result in mishap, suffering, even death for us or for others. Reckless or harmful behavior must have consistent natural consequences not averted by divine intervention (miracles) if free human beings are to learn and grow. If I do you deliberate bodily harm, God will not erase the injury so that I escape guilt feelings or legal action or the moral disapproval of others. Hick held that our actual world is, on average, suitably challenging, but not overly so, for "soul-making" to occur, although some people indubitably face more hazards and suffering than do others. Therefore the natural and moral evils of our actual world are no disproof of a good and powerful God.

A different tack by critics employs the *falsifiability principle* borrowed from scientific procedures. A meaningful scientific hypothesis makes testable assertions about how things occur in the observable world. Scientists typically confirm hypotheses, not directly, but by exhausting all attempts at disproving them. A religious belief, like any other, is meaningful only if it can specify possible circumstances that, were they to occur, would show the belief to be mistaken. An alleged belief compatible with any and every possible worldly outcome is nonspecific, thus meaningless and so no belief at all. In everyday life the mark of sanity is holding beliefs that square with experienced facts, specific beliefs about the world that pass this test. A meaningful religious belief should not be held in the face of overwhelming evidence to the contrary. The theodicy critic says that belief in a good and powerful God is falsifiable or testable (meaningful) and is actually falsified (disproved) by the evils in the world.

Richard Rubenstein argued, in *After Auschwitz* (1966), that the ruthless extermination of six million Jews by the Nazis disproved the biblical portrait of a providential God of history. Such a God, if he existed, would have intervened before the → Holocaust of his "chosen people," the Jews, had reached this magnitude. Rubenstein focused on the innocents who perished, not on the subsequent gain of Israel as a homeland for other Jews who survived. Their suffering is especially poignant because, unlike Christianity, traditional → Judaism has no explicit doctrine of assured individual survival in an afterlife, where recompense for undeserved suffering could occur.

A notable response to Rubenstein came from Emil Fackenheim (1916-2003) in lectures published as *God's Presence in History* (1968). He argued that God's "saving presence" (as seen in the exodus) was not experienced by Jews during the Holocaust, but God's "commanding presence" (as at Sinai) was, and it continues to be felt. God commands: "Thou shalt survive as Jews." God commands Jews to maintain their religious identity despite this monstrous evil perpetrated against them by others, else the forces that sought to eradicate Jews and Judaism will have triumphed after all.

Debates about theodicy continue among believers and unbelievers alike. In a series of philosophical articles about natural evil, William Rowe disputes religious belief. On behalf of faith, Marilyn McCord Adams wrestles with the enigma of moral evil. David Griffin approaches the topic from a process perspective that accepts some limits on divine power (→ Process Theology). Many others have addressed the theodicy task from a theological perspective, including C. S. Lewis (1898-1963), Dorothee Sölle (1929-2003), and Jürgen Moltmann. Theodicy remains a perennial concern for thoughtful religious commitment.

Bibliography: M. ADAMS, *Horrendous Evils and the Goodness of God* (Ithaca, 1999) • M. ADAMS and R. ADAMS, eds., *The Problem of Evil* (Oxford, 1990) • S. DAVIS, ed., *Encountering Evil: Live Options in Theodicy* (Edinburgh, 1981) • E. FACKENHEIM, *God's Presence in History: Jewish Affirmation and Philosophical Reflections* (New York, 1968) • A. FLEW, "Divine Omnipotence and Human Freedom," *New Essays in Philosophical Theology* (ed. A. Flew and A. MacIntyre; London, 1955) 144-69 • P. GEACH, *Providence and Evil* (Cambridge, 1977) • D. GRIFFIN, *God, Power, and Evil: A Process Theodicy* (New York, 1990) • G. HEGEL, *The Philosophy of History* (trans. J. Sibree; rev. ed.; New York, 1900) • J. HICK, *Evil and the God of Love* (New York, 1966; 2d ed., 1977) • D. HUME, *Dialogues concerning Natural Religion* (New York, 1948) • H. KUSHNER, *When Bad Things Happen to Good People* (New York, 1981; repr., 2001) • G. LEIBNIZ, *Theodicy* (trans. E. Huggard; Indianapolis, Ind., 1966) • C. S. LEWIS, *The Problem of Pain* (New York, 1979) • J. MACKIE, "Evil and Omnipotence," *Mind* 64 (1955) 200-212 • J. MOLTMANN, *The Crucified God: The Cross of Christ as the Foundation and Criticism of Christian Theology* (New York, 1974) • A. PLANTINGA, "The Free Will Defense," *God, Freedom, and Evil* (New York, 1974) 29-33 • B. REICHENBACH, *Evil and a Good God* (New York, 1982) • W. ROWE, "Evil and Theodicy," *PhTop* 16 (1988) 119-32 • R. RUBENSTEIN, *After Auschwitz* (Indianapolis, 1966) • D. SÖLLE, *Suffering* (Philadelphia, 1975) • W. SPARN, *Leiden, Erfahrung und Denken* (Munich, 1980).

ROBERT F. BROWN

Theogony

"Theogony" (Gk. *theogonia,* "birth of the gods"), the title of an epic poem by Hesiod (ca. 700 B.C.), refers to the origin of the gods. Many of the almost 300 gods whose names and qualities Hesiod gives in this work make up the world, so that a theogony is also a cosmogony. When the world is constituted, it is ruled by the great gods (Uranus, Cronus, Zeus). Hesiod makes use here of the concept that northern Syria and Asia Minor employed: a succession of gods instead of a genealogical list or an anthropomorphizing of divine families (Alalu/Anu [heaven], Kumarbi, and Teshub among the Hurrians; Hypsistus/Elioun, Uranus, Cronus/Elus, and Zeus/Baal for Philo of Byblos). We see here a step toward linking historical reminiscences to earthly periods. These periods were represented in universal history by the gods, who previously had represented only individual peoples, but the victories of these peoples were now regarded as the victories of their gods over other gods. Thus the conflict between generations of the gods played a role in theogony (→ Greek Religion).

Before and after Hesiod, wonder-workers like Aristeas of Proconnesus (after mid-7th cent. B.C.) and priests like Epimenides (fl. 6th cent. B.C.?) composed orphic rhapsodies. Plato (427-347; → Platonism) understood by "theogony" the conception or birth of a god (*Leg.* 886C). The genealogical principle in explanation of the world still played a role in Neoplatonism and → Gnosticism. Theogony also carried an epistemological meaning in crystallizing what contingent historical events might signify and offering a deductive explanation by means of a mythical genealogy.

→ God 1; Greek Religion; Myth, Mythology

Bibliography: C. COLPE, "Heidnische, jüdische und christliche Überlieferung in den Schriften aus Nag Hammadi V," *JAC* 19 (1976) 120-38; idem, "Die Zeit in drei asiatischen Hochkulturen (Babylon–Iran–Indien)," *Die Zeit* (ed. A. Peisl and A. Mohler; Munich, 1983) 225-56 • F. M. CORNFORD, "A Ritual Basis for Hesiod's Theogony," *The Myth and Ritual Theory* (ed. R. A. Segal; Malden, Mass., 1998) 147-72 • HESIOD, *Theogony* (ed. M. L. West; Oxford, 1966) • K. STODDARD, *The Narrative Voice in the Theogony of Hesiod* (Leiden, 2004) • N. WYATT, "The Theogony Motif in Ugarit and the Bible," *There's Such Divinity Doth Hedge a King: Selected Essays of Nicolas Wyatt on Royal Ideology in Ugaritic and OT Literature* (Aldershot, 2005) 147-72.

CARSTEN COLPE

Theologia crucis

1. Term and Development
2. Aspects in Twentieth-Century Theology
3. The Cross as Fact and as Symbol

1. Term and Development

The *theologia crucis,* or theology of the cross, focuses on the saving significance of the → cross of Christ (→ Salvation 3-7). With its roots in Paul, it has taken a central place in Western devotion and theology ever since the Middle Ages (esp. with → Anselm's satisfaction theory; → Soteriology 2.2). The central role of the cross finds expression in → church architecture, in → Christian art, in music (→ Theology and Music), and in → spirituality.

1.1. Martin → Luther (1483-1546; → Luther's Theology) worked out the concept of *theologia crucis* in three writings in 1518: the Hebrews lectures (*LW* 29.130, 146), the theses for the Heidelberg Disputation (*LW* 31.39-41), and the explanation of the 58th of his 95 theses on → indulgences (*LW* 31.225, 227). In returning to the opposition that Paul establishes between cross and wisdom (esp. in 1 Cor. 1:18–2:8), Luther in his Heidelberg theses 19-21 was sharply critical of a speculative reconstruction of the doctrine of the cross after the manner of the Scholastics (→ Scholasticism). Such reconstructions Luther called theologies of glory, which he considered "enemies of the cross of Christ" (Phil. 3:18) because, trusting in the divine gift of wisdom, they try to know the invisible through the visible and engage in scholastic rationalization (→ Natural Theology). The only one who "deserves to be called a theologian" is the one who "comprehends the visible and manifest things of God through suffering and the cross" (thesis 20; G. Forde, 77). From the law such persons know that human nature is subject to sinful corruption (→ Sin 1). In despair they therefore humble themselves under the word of the cross of Christ. We find God's essence, not in the glory of → creation, but hidden *sub contrario specie* in Christ's suffering on the cross.

The theology of the cross found a systematic place primarily in Luther's → epistemology as he contrasted → revelation and → faith with → reason, a humble yielding to the event of the cross with self-glorifying religious philosophy, the wisdom of the cross with the wisdom of the world. The theology of glory is an attitude toward knowledge of God that corresponds to the righteousness of works, but the theology of the cross is in keeping with the message of Christ because only from the → grace (§4.1) of → justification (§2.2.2) can it show the knowledge of

God to be possible. The dialectic of God's revelation and concealment (→ God 7.1.2) — namely, the message of the God who works in hidden fashion through Christ's passion — not only constitutes the content of the Christian knowledge of God but determines its hermeneutic fulfillment. Theology is itself "crucified theology" (K. → Rahner). As we know God in this way, we existentially equate ourselves with the cross in our own → suffering as we judge ourselves in repentance (→ Penitence). God is present and active in our weakness. The servanthood of Christ is a model for believers (WA 40/1.283). Only this knowledge of God makes → discipleship possible, that is, a life that accords with the power of God in weakness, with the wisdom of God in folly, with the proper works of God in our improper works, and so forth. → Baptism (§1) brings to light the significance of this Christian way of life, for according to Romans 6 it represents our constant dying and rising again with Christ (WA 5.534).

1.2. In a broader sense the term "theology of the cross," which is not so prominent in the later Luther, can be restricted neither in time to a specific phase of Luther's work nor in content to his theological hermeneutics. We might see in it a principle of the total theology of Luther (E. W. von Loewenich), for the message of the cross as the event of God's judgment and grace stands for the unmerited justification of the sinner. Here, then, we find that which distinguishes Reformation theology from Roman Catholic theology.

Concentration of the theology of the cross upon the individual appropriation of salvation was undoubtedly responsible for a lack of interest in social ethics. This imbalance became apparent when Luther met the demands of the peasants for social justice with a reference to the theology of the cross (→ Peasants' War).

1.3. The reception of the *theologia crucis* is a subject that goes beyond the bounds of the present article. In older Protestant → orthodoxy (§1) it was conceptualized in the doctrine of Christ's priestly work. But as in Luther himself, it had greater resonance in devotion (→ Piety 1) than in theology, of which → Pietism is a good example. The summons to discipleship of the cross carried its own problems as a glorifying of suffering (see 3). Certain passages in Luther support this view by speaking of → punishment (§2) and the cross, and even → death itself as our greatest treasure (*LW* 31.225).

2. Aspects in Twentieth-Century Theology

Several approaches in 20th-century theology lay stress on the theology of the cross.

2.1. The theology of the cross is *a corrective to hermeneutical triumphalism.* In his Christocentric hermeneutics K. → Barth (1886-1968; → Dialectical Theology 1) radicalized Luther's rejection of natural theology by relating the total theory of theological knowledge to the thought behind the theology of the cross (*CD* II/1, §§25-27). We can know God only as we reflect on the revelation of God in Christ, and God himself makes this knowledge possible. In the knowledge of revelation the theology of glory relates to the resurrection of Christ *(theologia resurrectionis),* and the theology of the cross is praise of what Christ has done for us through his cross and passion. This attack on an abstract glorifying of the cross as the saving event apart from the resurrection not only puts the cross of Christ in its proper place but also undermines any glorifying of the suffering of Christians (*CD* IV/1, 557-59; → Martyrs; Persecution of Christians).

2.2. The theology of the cross is also seen as *an expression of God's compassion.* For Luther, God remained above the passion, but a "theology of the pain of God" (K. Kitamori) sees God himself suffering in the Incarnate and thus challenges the impassibility of God. In his theology of the cross J. Moltmann thinks the Trinitarian God was not just acting and suffering at the cross; rather, the crucifixion of Jesus is put in the very being of God himself, so that we have "the crucified God." Such an intra-Trinitarian history of the cross has direct political ramifications.

2.3. The theology of the cross has also been *a prophetic protest against oppression and social injustice.* Luther saw in the cross the symbol of suffering, which prepares for the reception of justification but never constitutes it. Yet in Latin American → liberation theology (J. Sobrino), Korean minjung theology (→ Contextual Theology), → black theology (T. A. Mofokeng), and → feminist theology (E. Moltmann-Wendel), the cross stands for the overcoming of suffering that is due to unjust relations. The early Christian symbol of the cross is a sign of victory over ungodly power and violence. The liberation for new life effected in this judgment involves critical and liberating practice in the fight against hostile structures and in active → solidarity with those who suffer from them.

2.4. The theology of the cross is *a corrective against church triumphalism.* In his 1539 work *Von den Räten und der Kirche* (On the councils and the church), Luther regarded the cross as one of the marks of the church, the power simply to proclaim the → gospel (*LW* 41.164-65). Adopting this line of thinking, the church in its → proclamation and practice must see itself on the way of a discipleship of the cross and thus must renounce both political claims and the claims to theological absoluteness, setting conformity with the Crucified above every hostile structure, even at the cost of its own self-preservation (see F. Fleinert-Jensen and J. Vercruysse).

3. The Cross as Fact and as Symbol

Such varied use of different forms of a theology of the cross is an indication of the tenacity and power of this portion of the NT message. As with any such influential doctrine, its widespread application can become so general a symbol that the specificity of its original reference becomes ancillary to other agendas. The danger is obviated, however, when the more specific form of Pauline teaching as recovered and reinterpreted by Luther is kept in mind. To rule out a misuse of the theology of the cross to legitimate or even impose new suffering, we must distinguish between the cross as the execution of Jesus, in which it stands for meaningless wrongdoing (as epitomized in the → Holocaust; → Theodicy), and the Pauline "word of the cross" (1 Cor. 1:18 RSV) as a synonym for the gospel, that is, for the hope, grounded in the resurrection, that all the forces that do violence to God's creation will be overcome.

Bibliography: N. CAMERON, ed., *The Power and Weakness of God* (Edinburgh, 1990) • A. DETTWILER and J. ZUMSTEIN, eds., *Kreuzestheologie im Neuen Testament* (Tübingen, 2002) • F. FLEINERT-JENSEN, *Das Kreuz und die Einheit der Kirche. Skizzen zu einer Kreuzestheologie in ökumenischer Perspektive* (Leipzig, 1994) • G. O. FORDE, *On Being a Theologian of the Cross: Reflections on Luther's Heidelberg Disputation, 1518* (Grand Rapids, 1997) • A. L. GARCIA and A. R. VICTOR RAJ, eds., *The Theology of the Cross for the Twenty-first Century: Signposts for a Multicultural Witness* (St. Louis, 2002) • M. J. GORMAN, *Cruciformity: Paul's Narrative Spirituality of the Cross* (Grand Rapids, 2001) • K. KITAMORI, *Theology of the Pain of God* (Richmond, Va., 1965) • W. VON LOEWENICH, *Luther's Theology of the Cross* (Minneapolis, 1976; orig. pub., 1929) • T. A. MOFOKENG, *The Crucified among the Crossbearers: Towards a Black Christology* (Kampen, 1983) • J. MOLTMANN, *The Crucified God: The Cross of Christ as the Foundation and Criticism of Christian Theology* (New York, 1974) • E. MOLTMANN-WENDEL, "Is There a Feminist Theology of the Cross?" *God—His and Hers* (by E. Moltmann-Wendel and J. Moltmann; New York, 1991) 77-91 • D. NGIEN, *The Suffering of God according to Martin Luther's "theologia crucis"* (New York, 1995) • W. PLACHER, *Narratives of a Vulnerable God* (Philadelphia, 1994) • J. SOBRINO, "Le ressuscité est le crucifié" and "La mort de Jésus et la libération dans l'histoire," *Jesus et la libération en Amérique Latine* (ed. J. Nieuwenhove; Paris, 1986) 233-90 • M. M. SOLBERG, *Compelling Knowledge: A Feminist Proposal for an Epistemology of the Cross* (Albany, N.Y., 1997) • D. TIDBALL, *The Message of the Cross: Wisdom Unsearchable, Love Indestructible* (Downers Grove, Ill., 2001) • E. VALTINK, ed., *Das Kreuz mit dem Kreuz. Feministisch-theologische Anfragen an die Kreuzestheologie* (2d ed.; Hofgeismar, 1990) • J. VERCRUYSSE, "Luther's Theology of the Cross: Its Relevance for Ecumenism," *CPUB* 35 (1989) 2-11; idem, "Luther's Theology of the Cross at the Time of the Heidelberg Disputation," *Greg.* 57 (1976) 523-48 • R. WETH, ed., *Das Kreuz Jesu. Gewalt, Opfer, Sühne* (Neukirchen, 2001) • A. A. YEWANGOE, *Theologia Crucis in Asia: Asian Christian Views on Suffering in the Face of Overwhelming Poverty and Multifaceted Religiosity in Asia* (Amsterdam, 1987).

REINHOLD BERNHARDT and
DAVID WILLIS-WATKINS

Theological Education

Overview
1. Historical Patterns and Precedents
2. Around the World
3. Challenges for the Future

Overview

Instruction or teaching has always been foundational for the Christian faith. Jesus Christ was himself called *rabbi*, teacher. Philip ran to the Ethiopian enunch, a court official of the Candace of Ethiopia, who said to him: "How can I [understand], unless someone guides me?" (Acts 8:31). In the earliest Christian communities, adults preparing for → baptism, the catechumens, received oral instruction ("catechism," from the Greek meaning "to make to hear," and hence "to instruct") on basic Christian beliefs. The pattern of educating the faithful in preparation for key moments in the life of faith — baptism, → confirmation, first communion, personal profession of faith, and so forth — was further developed in the third century by Hippolytus of Rome (ca. 170-ca. 236) and in the fourth century by → Augustine of Hippo (354-430), and this practice subsequently shaped centuries of Christian → catechesis.

This foundational and continuing tradition of instruction in the Christian faith is particularly pertinent for a discussion of theological education in two regards. First, the focus is on the whole → people of God. Second, the focus of instruction on key moments in the life of faith shows clearly that learning is a lifelong endeavor; it does not begin and end with → baptism. The significance of these two characteristics will be explored in section 3 below.

1. Historical Patterns and Precedents

The notion of advanced theological studies may have initially emerged as early as the 5th century at the Christian school in Alexandria. Advanced theological studies emerged in the West in 13th-century → universities such as Bologna, Paris, Oxford, and Cambridge. These universities grew out of and reflected the ecclesiastical institutions of the day. For example, the authority of teachers was indicated by their sitting, as did bishops, in thrones (whence reference to professorial "chairs"), and the lecture had a liturgical cadence and character not unlike the sermon. It was in these universities that theology found a place along with two other disciplines of advanced studies: → canon law and medicine.

This threefold disciplinary pattern was replicated in Reformation-era Protestant universities such as Marburg, Königsberg, Tübingen, Berlin, Wittenberg, and Württemberg, which were founded to raise an educated ministry. It was thought that a ministry that was well trained humanistically and theologically could more effectively lead the laity, through → preaching and teaching, in Christian faith and life. Nonetheless, it took a long time to establish educational standards and enforce them, resulting by the middle of the 16th century in two tiers of ministry, one academically trained and one untrained.

Two → Enlightenment-era developments in Berlin, the first envisioned by W. von Humboldt (1767-1835) and the second by Friedrich D. E. → Schleiermacher (1768-1834), were significant for the shaping of contemporary theological education: (1) greater emphasis on rational results and formal skill in argument and novelty than on the study of traditional texts in the quest for truth, and (2) a correlative emphasis on specialization. What followed was the description of → theology as a positive science with clearly delineated fourfold theological disciplines, namely, biblical studies, church history, → systematic theology, and → practical theology. This fourfold delineation continues to be replicated in theological schools in many regions of the world.

A somewhat distinct pattern of theological education took shape in the universities of Great Britain. In the oldest medieval universities of Oxford and Cambridge a more monastic model, centered on the tutorial, continued to predominate. Also characteristic of this model was a first degree followed by a more advanced course of study for a master's or doctor's degree, including degrees in law, medicine, or theology. Many graduate degrees were therefore professional degrees that prepared students for a particular vocation. This point will also be more fully addressed below in section 3.

Through the medieval era, Roman Catholic education produced, on one hand, learned theologians trained in universities and, on the other, local clergy whose preparation was informal apprenticeship in the administration of → sacraments. The Council of → Trent established designated institutions for the education of clergy. Indeed, the term "seminary" itself comes from the Tridentine canon that directed bishops of major sees to establish colleges for the training of persons dedicated to the service of the church, so that the college would be a "perpetual seed-plot of ministers of God" (23d sess., can. 18). The Tridentine seminary did not aim to be a school of advanced theological studies but focused on the practical preparation of students in ecclesiastical knowledge and formation in → piety. This model continued into the 20th century.

2. Around the World

In most regions of the world Protestants train their ministers in denominational or ecumenical colleges, seminaries, or divinity schools. For example, there is a United Theological College in Bangalore (India), Harare (Zimbabwe), Kingston (Jamaica), and Limuru (Kenya). Other ecumenical theological seminaries include the Comunidad Teológica in Mexico and Chile, the Instituto Superior Evangélico de Estudios Teológicos in Buenos Aires (ISEDET), the Near Eastern School of Theology in Beirut (Lebanon), the Pacific Theological College in Suva (Fiji), and the Seminario Bíblico Latinoamericano in San José (Costa Rica). Some colleges that were founded as denominational schools became ecumenical, for example, the Lutheran schools in Hong Kong (Tao Fong Shan), in Makumira, Tanzania, and in São Leopoldo, Brazil, as well as the Methodist university in Mutare, Zimbabwe. A few theological colleges, with the addition of other colleges or faculties, became private Christian universities. In still other instances, especially in countries to which English-speaking missionaries went (Ghana, India, Kenya, Namibia, Nigeria, South Africa, Zimbabwe), state universities have departments of religion that train teachers or offer courses for graduates of theological colleges. Protestants and Roman Catholics teach in these departments, and Islamic courses are often also offered.

These theological colleges, seminaries, and schools were predominantly founded by Western missionaries in the 19th and 20th centuries. Accordingly, they are shaped by Western models of theological education. Today, however, the curricula of these colleges, seminaries, and schools are also shaped by contextual realities and pastoral practice in their diverse settings. Extension programs enable teachers to interact with students in their own settings. Adult and lay education courses are provided. Basic courses of study typically involve four or five years and include practical field assignments for six months or a year. Women teachers and students are by now present, and women's programs have been introduced. Moreover, there are societies of women theologians in most regions of the world.

Churches in countries to which Western missionaries went are flourishing, churches in the West struggle. This fact poses challenges for theological education in Europe and, perhaps especially, in North America, where a sharper separation of church and state has traditionally tied theological schools more closely to churches than in the European state church system. From a historical perspective, however, contemporary challenges to theological education in North America are not altogether unprecedented.

Until the early 19th century, the pattern of theological education in North America was the English tutorial pattern. There were differences; for example, the American tutor was an ordained clergyman whose work with a student training for ministry was limited to time taken away from pressing parish duties. Moreover, students studied with tutors in remote rural parishes without benefit of a community of tutors and students with diverse perspectives. By 1800 it was a system ready for change.

What followed was the founding of denominationally related theological schools, for example, Andover (Congregational, in Massachusetts, 1808), Princeton (Presbyterian, in New Jersey, 1812), Harvard Divinity (Unitarian, now interdenominational, in Massachusetts, 1816), Colgate (Baptist, now ecumenical, in New York, 1817), General (Episcopal, in New York, 1819), Yale Divinity (Congregational, in Connecticut, 1822), Gettysburg (Lutheran, in Pennsylvania, 1825), the Reformed at Mercersburg (now United Church of Christ, Lancaster, in Pennsylvania, 1825), Garrett Biblical (United Methodist, in Illinois, 1856). These were but the forerunners of a greater wave of seminaries comparable, although on an even larger scale, to the wave of universities in late medieval Europe. There was another significant difference along with the larger scale: in the United States in the 19th and 20th centuries, denominationalism was the driving force that monastic orders and state churches once had been ($\rightarrow$ Denomination). In time, the denominational diversity came to include Roman Catholics, the historic African American churches, the historic peace churches, evangelicals born of revivalism, Pentecostals, fundamentalists, and Greek and Russian Orthodox — in all, accounting for well over 300 accredited theological schools in North America.

Meanwhile, in continental Europe theological faculties arose at several by-then established universities, for example, at the Swiss universities of Basel, Bern, Lausanne, and Zurich, or the Dutch universities of Amsterdam, Groningen, Leiden, and Utrecht, where students still study today. Likewise, students preparing for ordination in Scandinavia study at state university faculties, for example, in Copenhagen, Århus, Oslo, Lund, and Uppsala. In eastern Europe, Lutheran and Reformed theological academies offer theological degrees. As a stricter separation of $\rightarrow$ church and state has been introduced on the European continent, church-related academies, colleges, and seminaries also emerged.

3. Challenges for the Future

While challenges differ from region to region, at least one challenge is common: finances adequate to fund theological education. Reasons for this challenge have already been suggested: the numerical, and consequently financial, decline of church life in North America; stricter church-state separation and a consequent diminishment of state funds for churches in Europe; endemic economic injustice in many African, Asian, Latin American, and Pacific countries, and the consequent financial straits of the churches that support theological schools. There are exceptions to the financial challenges that face theological schools; for example, some seminaries in the United States are well endowed and therefore better able to weather the vagaries of demographic and economic trends. But financial challenges are not new. Seminaries and divinity schools have typically been comparatively small, inadequately funded institutions that have served rather limited constituencies.

This reality indicates another challenge: traditionally it has been thought that theological education is for the purpose of preparing women and men for ordained ministry in the churches. As time has passed, this focus has increasingly limited the pool of candidates from which to recruit prospective students. Theological schools are now turning attention to the *laos*, the whole people, thereby harkening to the earliest Christian centuries and echoing → Vatican II's emphasis on the church as "the people of God," as well as the primacy accorded "the whole people of God" in the → Faith and Order ecumenical text *Baptism, Eucharist, and Ministry* (1982). This renewed focus may restore an understanding that theological education is first and foremost embedded in the life of faith and is therefore a lifelong process. Refocusing theological education in these ways may more broadly engage the priesthood of all believers as they seek to live their faith not only in the church but in the world.

This focus could lead to a reconsideration of the fourfold theological curriculum as defined in 19th-century Berlin. As the education of the whole people of God increasingly becomes the focus for seminaries and divinity schools, theological education may also increasingly prepare students, whether preparing for lay or for ordained ministry, to address economic, political, scientific, and social issues of the day for the sake of Christian witness in the world. The emerging dialogue between theology and the arts — film, media studies, graphic arts, music, literature, poetry, and dance — is also becoming incorporated into curricula as the Christian community finds new ways of being in the world. Finally, as consciousness of the reality that Christians in every region live in a richly interreligious world is growing, theological education is making interfaith studies and → dialogue integral to curricula.

These challenges are all compounded by the profile of many, if not most, students coming to seminary in most regions. Long-standing patterns of theological education, particularly that of an advanced degree following a baccalaureate degree, are breaking down as students who enroll tend to be older and have degrees not designed to prepare them for theological study. In addition, these students have multiple, often competing, commitments to careers, families, and so on and find it difficult to negotiate the demands of graduate studies. This factor in turn raises again a centuries-old conflict within theological education: is it graduate study or professional formation? Or both? The curricular and other implications of this discussion will be significant for the future.

Each of these challenges will be most fruitfully faced by ecumenical dialogue and cooperation across regions. Since its formation in 1948 the → World Council of Churches (WCC) has facilitated the foundation of regional and continental associations of theological schools, for example, the Association for Theological Institutions in Eastern Africa (Nairobi), the Conference of African Theological Institutions, the Association of Theological Education in South-East Asia (Singapore), the South Pacific Association of Theological Schools, the Melanesian Association of Theological Schools, the Asociación de Seminarios e Instituciones Teológicas for Argentina and the South, and the Asociación Latinoamericana de Instituciones de Educación Teológica Ecuménica Lationoamericano. These associations create contacts, engage in scholarly exchange, compare curricular offerings and examinations, hold theological conferences, edit theological journals, and more. Members are from colleges, seminaries, Christian universities, and departments of religious studies.

The WCC also has a theological education subunit that financially supports programs and projects, particularly in the east and south, and provides resources for conferences and publications. Theological education for the churches, for the whole people of God, was the focus of attention in the 1990s.

Some associations predate the WCC, for example, the Association of Theological Schools in the United States and Canada, founded in 1918. While this association serves some of the functions noted above, a primary responsibility is the accreditation of member seminaries: Protestant, Roman Catholic, evangelical, Pentecostal, and Eastern Orthodox. Likewise, the → World Evangelical Alliance has its own associations in diverse regions that primarily serve as accrediting bodies.

Bibliography: E. Farley, *The Fragility of Knowledge: Theological Education in the Church and University* (Philadelphia, 1988) • J. C. Hough and J. B. Cobb Jr., *Christian Identity and Theological Education* (Chico, Calif., 1985) • L. G. Jones and S. Paulsell, eds., *The Scope of Our Art: The Vocation of the Theological Teacher* (Grand Rapids, 2002) • D. H. Kelsey, *Between Athens and Berlin: The Theological Education Debate* (Grand Rapids, 1993) • S. Oxley, *Creative Ecumenical Education: Learning from One Another* (Geneva, 2002) • M. L. Warford, ed., *Practical Wisdom: On Theological Teaching and Learning* (New York, 2004) • H.-R. Weber, *A Laboratory for Ecumenical Life: The Story of Bossey* (Geneva, 1996) • B. G. Wheeler and E. Farley, eds., *Shifting Boundaries: Contextual Approaches to the Structure of Theological Education* (Louisville, Ky., 1991) • A. Wingate, *Does Theological Education Make a Difference? Global Lessons in Mission and Ministry from India and Britain* (Geneva, 1999).

Melanie A. May

Theology

1. Concept

Theology is nowadays mostly understood as the enterprise of rendering account for statements of faith in → God, undertaken in the community of → faith by disciplined thought and with reference to God's → revelation. Concepts of God and revelation can thereby themselves become problematic, and given forms of church fellowship (→ Church; Denomination), questionable. Some find that it better suits the task to engage in theology as an academic discipline (→ Theological Education) without any essential church connection. From the point of view of the common history and subject matter, a critical tension may sometimes exist between these two orientations, but scarcely any necessary contradiction.

Theologia and related words first appeared in → Greek philosophy, and Christian writers showed hesitation in taking them over (→ Philosophy and Theology 2). Greek → church fathers use them to designate such diverse matters as the doctrine of God, (mystical) knowledge of God, naming of God, praise of God, and acknowledgment of the divinity (say of Jesus Christ or the Holy Spirit). A distinction is frequently made between *theologia* as the doctrine of God and *oikonomia* as God's plan of salvation (→ Order of Salvation 1.1). It was in the 12th century, and in the West, that the word "theology" was first used in the comprehensive sense customary today. What it refers to had existed earlier.

2. Theology, Church, Science

2.1. Theology comes to expression in various dimensions of church life and ministry, where it also finds corroboration in various ways. In the → confession of faith, it places itself before the God of whom and from whom it must speak in sincerity: It acknowledges God and commits itself afresh to God.

The work performed by theology is put to the test in → proclamation (→ Preaching) and praise (→ Doxology), as one experiences whether one can also answer before human beings, the → congregation, and God for what it has tested, clarified, and elaborated. In diaconal service (→ Diakonia), the range of its vision is measured by the rule of love. The daily life (→ Everyday Life) of the congregation tests theology's openness for realities of → society, history, → politics, and → nature (→ Environment 2). Its conception of how far the message of → salvation reaches (→ Gospel) must prove itself in → pastoral care, → evangelism, → dialogue (§2.2) with other religions (→ Theology of Religions), and the struggle for social and economic justice (→ Social Ethics; Economic Ethics). But whether or not theology stands such a test itself becomes a question that one can answer only in faith, and it is possible to give an account of any such answer only theologically.

This circle of theological critique and church practice is, however, incapable of final justification within itself. Theology joins the church in its confession of → sin, in laying hold of God's → promise, in waiting for God's justifying absolution (→ Justification), and in prayer for → grace and illumination. For, in the final instance, theology experiences verification only through God's own → Word and Spirit.

2.2. No theology may claim for itself such validation by God's judgment. Theology's dependence on this validation does not therefore obviate the necessity for it to render account as far as humanly possible of its own subject matter and path to knowledge. Before any → apologetics, it is a matter of the integration of the → truth (§2) believed with other perspectives that believers share with their contemporaries (→ Pluralism 2). Modern theology furthermore consists of a complex of individual disciplines, each with its own principles and goals, about which it is necessary to maintain communication and understanding. Theology is also undertaken in each case from the point of view of particular → traditions, perspectives, and experiences. Theologians belong to different → confessions, → cultures, generations, and schools and therefore need to debate with each other what they have in common and wherein they differ. Each form of theology must thus answer to others regarding its way of seeing things and its procedure (see 4.1). In view of the multiplicity of churches and the present empirical picture of the church in the changing reality of life (→ Church 5), theology must also critically consider its role and its capacity for contributing to Christian life today and to the human search for truth (→ Ecumenical Theology; Church 5.4).

2.3. From all these aspects the problem arises of theology's character as an academic discipline or science: How can its presuppositions and methods be so presented that they may also be recognized by those who do not believe and think in the same ways as the theologians engaged in it? This problem also affects the question of Christian theology's truth claim in various regards. First, out of the emerging truth claims of regional and local theologies (→ Contextual Theology) depending on specially constituted human → experience, the need arises to mediate between universal and regional truth claims within the framework of the pluralistic theological cosmos (see 4.3).

Second, daily encounter with practices of non-Christian religions and trends in their thought (in Africa and Asia, also in European and Anglo-Celtic areas) challenges theology to enter into discussion with other religions (→ Buddhism and Christianity; Hinduism and Christianity; Islam and Christianity). Within the framework of a plurality of → religions, one's own truth claim must be legitimated vis-à-vis that of others.

Third, with its truth claim, theology runs up against those of other sciences, which also compete in setting orientation points (→ Meaning) for human life (→ Worldview). Here, in the framework of contemporary research and thought, theology is compelled to account for its content and claims in sufficiently grounded and comprehensible ways (see 4.2; → Philosophy and Theology; Science and Theology).

3. Types

The beginnings of theology may be traced back to the handiwork of different biblical writers (e.g., → Deuteronomistic History; Prophets 2; Paul, and many others). In the course of the history of church and theology, various important types of theology have developed.

3.1. *Early Church*

The → early church was characterized by the predominance of → Platonism. Its theology was concerned above all with → *cognition, insight, and wisdom.* Only the Intelligible that transcends the visible world and makes it possible has true being and can thus be truly known, and this concept is now to be understood as the God of the biblical revelation. Faith is grounded on → authority, but the believer is supposed to attain to the → love and knowledge of God in this life, and hereafter, to the beatific vision (→ Happiness 2.2).

In a discussion of theology as *de divinitate ratio sive sermo* (an account or discourse about divinity),

→ *Augustine* (354-430; → Augustine's Theology) carries out an immanent criticism of philosophical teachings on God, but he also offers the Christian faith as the most satisfactory doctrine of the true God. In this way, Platonism is both linked with a doctrine of the → Trinity and also surpassed by it, while faith first comes to perfection through the knowledge or wisdom it leads on to.

Educated in philosophy and strongly involved in the life of the church, → *Origen* (ca. 185-ca. 254; → Alexandrian Theology; Origenism) dedicated himself to research and teaching. He engaged in text-critical, exegetical, hermeneutical, and dogmatic studies and cultivated dialogue with Jews (→ Judaism), → Gnostics, and heathen. In biblical → exegesis (§2.1), he sought, on the basis of what is unambiguously attested, to establish a clear yardstick for further investigations, but also to determine the moral or spiritual meaning behind the literal. For that project, he had to develop hermeneutical rules (→ Hermeneutics 2.2). Origen has often been accused of excessive speculation, with which his use of → allegory has been associated. His concept of → truth and the relation between → faith (§3.4) and cognition (→ Epistemology 2.2) remain generally problematic.

The theology of the Greek → church fathers found its conclusion in → *John of Damascus* (ca. 655-ca. 750). John wrote as his chief work *Pēgē gnōseōs* (Source of knowledge), which consists of three parts: a → dialectic, a history of → heresies, and an "exact reproduction of the orthodox faith." He sometimes emerges as an original thinker (→ Images 3.2). Above all, he wants to present the tradition and teaching of the orthodox church. He portrays the "orthodox faith" in accordance with a thematic scheme and handles the material with systematic ability. In the doctrine of God, he prefers → apophatic theology.

3.2. *Early Scholasticism*

In early → Scholasticism, *thinking* became the most important element in theology. A fresh revival of → Aristotelianism brought, for a start, changes in method (→ Dialectic 1.1; Logic 2.1).

→ *Anselm of Canterbury* (1033-1109; → Scholasticism 4.1) understands his theology as an independent, rational exploration and substantiation of what revelation sets forth for belief (*fides quaerens intellectum*, faith in search of understanding). This ambitious program means a speculative attempt at developing in thought what the church has determined on the basis of Scripture. In this way, Anselm counters the criticisms leveled by the so-called dialecticians at contradictions in the tradition. The problems that have been identified here — such as the → autonomy of → reason, the establishing of what is believed otherwise than in revelation, and the ontological proof of God (→ God, Arguments for the Existence of, 2.1) as an empty tautology — are to be understood only from the goal of appropriation and the Platonic presupposition that all knowledge comes to a peak in the knowledge of God as the being that exists of necessity. The believer therefore should and may also strive toward God with the aid of reason.

Peter Abelard (1079-1142; → Scholasticism 2.3) also gives the central position to reason, although rather as the capacity for dialectical inquiry, questioning, and decision. From the leading contemporary authorities he collected opposing theses to particular questions in order to settle the contradictions dialectically. Going on from that work, *Gilbert de la Porrée* (1076-1154) completed the development of the *quaestio* as a form through which the pros and cons of any issue at all could be debated and a decision reached about them.

3.3. *High Middle Ages*

The theology of the High → Middle Ages (§§1.3.1, 2.3.3) strove to accumulate theological *knowledge* in great collections and → summas. These works are as a rule conceived in accordance with an *exitus-reditus* scheme, which follows the threefold pattern of (1) God, (2) all things issuing from God by creation and fall, and (3) all things returning to God, although partly there are other arrangements.

In his *Sententiarum libri quatuor* (Four books of sentences), *Peter Lombard* (ca. 1100-1160) collects pronouncements of church fathers, reports contemporary opinions on doctrine, and discusses disputed questions. Combining the dialectical method of the Lombard's teacher Abelard with the theological position of *Hugh of St.-Victor* (1096-1141), these books became the classic presentation of 12th-century theology. By their restrained treatment of such a rich collection of material, they were suited to be the theological textbook for following generations.

Thomas Aquinas (ca. 1225-74; → Thomism; Scholasticism 4.3) realized the desired global view by integrating Aristotelian philosophy into theology. Distinctions between *esse* (being) and *essentia* (essence; → Ontology) and between → nature and the supernatural make it possible for him to limit the immanence of Aristotle's understanding of existence, to interpret the latter's philosophical *theologia* completely transcendently (→ Transcendentals), and to coordinate it with theology's *sacra doctrina*. This *sacra doctrina* comprises knowledge of God and of all things as related to God. It represents a de-

rived science, for the revealed articles of faith from which it draws deductions are established by the higher *scientia* of divine self-knowledge. For the same reason, it must count as the most valuable of all sciences and the highest degree of wisdom *(sapientia)*.

3.4. *Scotus and Luther*

It is inevitable that such magnificent syntheses soon come to be disputed. *John Duns Scotus* (ca. 1265-1308; → Scotism; Scholasticism 4.2; Nominalism) raises the objection against the Thomist *analogia entis* (analogy of being; → Analogy 2) that, lacking any point of comparison between creaturely and divine being, one must understand the concept of being univocally. Thomas's proofs of God (→ God, Arguments for the Existence of, 2.2) thus become ineffective. Duns bases his own proofs on a univocal concept of being. He declares various conclusions of Anselm's and Thomas's not to be cogent: God is not determined by logical necessity, but by God's own loving will. Emphasis on the human will also shifts the human being closer to the center of theology and brings out the character of theology as a practical science.

Martin → *Luther* (1483-1546; → Luther's Theology) sees not only the medieval synthesis of faith and works but also that of faith and reason radically called into question by the → gospel, for reason is unable to hold itself neutral out of the dialectic of → law and gospel, faith and unbelief. As the reason of the fallen human being, it is determined by the unfree will and is dependent on → grace (§4.1). As creaturely reason, it must let itself be confined within its limits. Theology must free itself in principle from Aristotle (384-322 B.C.) in order to serve the → Word of God alone.

3.5. *Reformation-Based*

While Luther himself did not attempt any full presentation of Protestant faith in the grand style, the reconstruction of theology on the basis of the Reformation soon commenced. Coming from → humanism, *Philipp* → *Melanchthon* (1497-1560; → Reformers 2.1.1) combined a keen eye for Protestant concerns with a deep interest in education. By 1521 he had already written the first edition of his *Loci communes,* a sequence of the chief theological concepts needed for the study of Scripture. The "speculative" doctrines of the Trinity and incarnation were not discussed there but, rather, anthropological and soteriological themes in accordance with law and gospel. The later editions of the *Loci,* from 1535 on, developed into a complete presentation of theology. Biblical and early church doctrines are treated in accordance with the *exitus-reditus* scheme (see 3.3).

The theology of *John → Calvin* (1509-64) grew to maturity in the course of his work as reformer, preacher, and exegete. Reciprocal influence occurred between his sermons, commentaries, and *Institutes*. After the first edition of the *Institutes,* which in form resembles Luther's catechisms (→ Catechism 2), subsequent editions were increasingly given further chapters, up to a complete restructuring in 1559. Now the → Apostles' Creed, which for Calvin has four parts, provides the framework for the whole. The other elements are all systematically built into that structure.

In the old Protestant → orthodoxy (§1) of the 16th and 17th centuries, Protestant doctrine was systematically developed, partly in controversy with Catholic, sectarian, and other Protestant opponents. The connection with patristic theology (→ Patristics, Patrology) was above all elaborated. A doctrine of → inspiration was developed and placed at the start of most presentations of theology, but a preoccupation with "clear" proof-texts tended to hinder careful exegesis. Aristotelian philosophy increasingly regained influence but was in some places repressed by Ramist criticism (P. Ramus [1515-72]; → Orthodoxy 2.1) or replaced by → Cartesianism. Among the Lutherans, *Johann Gerhard* (1582-1637) with his *Loci theologici* followed the later Melanchthon in abandoning the topical method in order to bring out the inner connections in the material. For Reformed theology, Calvin's *Institutes* provided the chief model.

3.6. *Modern Period*

The theology of the → modern period saw the → Enlightenment as having set it the task, on the one hand, of asserting the continuing validity of theology and belief in God and, on the other, of defining anew their relation to the other factors in human life (→ Physicotheology) or to the other academic disciplines. *Friedrich Daniel Ernst → Schleiermacher* (1768-1834; → Schleiermacher's Theology) seeks in exemplary fashion to revive a sense for → religion in the spirit of → Romanticism. Statements of faith become expressions of immediate self-awareness, by which the human being is supposed to become aware, on the one hand, of reality as a whole and, on the other, of God in the feeling of utter dependence. Schleiermacher designates Christian theology as a "positive" science, which becomes useful and necessary through its relation to the Christian form of the awareness of God. It becomes a science by starting above Christianity with → ethics as "the science of the principles of history," which brings out the characteristics and possible differentiations, not only of academic and political communities, but also of religious ones.

Since that time, many have asserted that talk about God is a meaningful subjective statement, whether as expression of a value judgment (A. Ritschl), of the → assurance of salvation (F. H. R. Frank, L. Ihmels, W. Elert), or of existential self-understanding (R. Bultmann; → Existential Theology; Theology in the Nineteenth and Twentieth Centuries 1.2). Theology's scientific character then depends on its use of recognized methods or on some particular → ontology. Confining oneself to Christianity could be explained as a value judgment or a faith decision or by reference to the peculiar nature of the subject matter.

3.7. *Twentieth Century*

The following types of theology were to be noted in the 20th century.

3.7.1. *Karl → Barth* (1886-1968; → Dialectical Theology) requires theology to orient itself on Jesus Christ as the revealed Word of God. He accordingly defines it as "the service by particular human beings of God's revelation taking place in the forms of conceptual thinking in some particular here and now" ("Kirche und Theologie," 653) or "the Christian Church's scientific self-examination with regard to the . . . talk about God peculiar to itself" (*KD* I/1, 1). Barth does not submit the concepts he uses to clarification in advance, but only as they are employed in lines of thought that follow God's self-declaration. His theology sets out from the togetherness of God and the human being in Jesus Christ, to which the Scriptures witness, and so initially proceeds analytically, with the contrast of cross and resurrection providing the basis for distinctions. For syntheses, Barth performs dialectical *Aufhebungen* (canceling or suspending, lifting up, preserving), on the model of the *assumptio carnis* in the → incarnation. The → analogy (§3) stands as the most important tool in the service of understanding. Questions to be directed at Barth concern the danger of a → positivism of revelation, the apparent difficulty of assessing how he draws analogies, and his perhaps not always successful connection with nontheological reality.

3.7.2. Partly in connection with dialectical theology, an effort arose in the 1920s no longer to view the Scriptures as chiefly the object of theological research, but above all to bring out their own theology (or theologies). Despite a number of significant achievements, the ensuing movement soon petered out. From it, there remains an ecumenically expanded community of scholars among whom the question of a → *biblical theology* (§2) remains a live issue. Different new approaches pursue such questions as: Is there a demonstrable unity of Scripture as a whole or even just of the OT, or is it possible to determine a center for the one or the other? Does the OT find its continuation only in the New, or only in the → Talmud, or are the claims of Christians and Jews equally true and equally problematic? What does the amalgamation of precisely these, and only these, writings as the → canon mean for biblical exegesis? What is the significance of their obviously close relation to other factors in the history of religion and culture? In addition, the relation of projects in biblical theology to → dogmatics (§7.3.4) and → systematic theology remains unclear.

3.7.3. According to *Paul* → *Tillich* (1886-1965; → Existential Theology 3.1; God 7.2), theology is concerned with a methodical interpretation of the content of the Christian faith. This project requires a method of correlation by which one sets "situation" and "message" (→ Kerygma) or "human existence" and "divine self-revelation" in relation to each other as question and answer. *David Tracy,* in contrast, defines the two poles as "common human experience and language" and "Christian texts." He investigates the former phenomenologically for their "religious dimension," but the latter, historically and hermeneutically. The metaphysical (→ Metaphysics), which already emerges in Tillich as the goal of the analysis of human existence, is brought into play by Tracy only when the results of a correlation are to be verified.

3.7.4. In the 1960s *Wolfhart Pannenberg* sought, in association with *Ulrich Wilckens* and *Rolf and Trutz Rendtorff,* to overcome the "kerygma theology" of Barth and Rudolf Bultmann (1884-1976) by a new conjunction of theology and history (*Revelation as History* [1961]). In revelation, as more generally, the meaning of an event can be read out of the event itself if one just views the latter in context. Theological statements refer to the meaning of particular historical events as such. But to recognize the revelation of God in the Christ-event, one must consider it in the framework of history as a whole. This perspective is possible because Christ's → resurrection, which is in principle historically verifiable, anticipates the end of history.

3.7.5. Pannenberg later defines theology as the science of God. As the reality that conditions everything and is also implied in → philosophy, God is initially given only as a problem or for subjective religious → experience (§2). As part of → *religious studies,* theology asks about what faith in God relates to. Christian theology represents a branch of such general theology. One must ask whether both of these new approaches do not partly involve confusion of categories and necessarily remain unstable.

3.7.6. → Process theology connects with *Alfred North Whitehead's* (1861-1947) → process philosophy, which seeks to understand reality not in terms of either substances or states but in the conceptuality of becoming. In the process of transformation, something new often arises that does not allow itself simply to be traced back to earlier stages. Whitehead thinks of God both as the enabling ground of all processes and as a sensitive participant who in them is himself just coming to be.

Charles Hartshorne (1897-2000), *Schubert M. Ogden, John B. Cobb,* and others develop in different directions a philosophical theology from Whitehead's thinking. On the basis of this theology, it is claimed, we can think of God and the world together in a quite different way from classical, patriarchally conceived → theism and can also appropriate biblical and patristic → Christologies in new ways and include problems of → nature and the → environment.

3.7.7. The reference, meaning, and logic of the language of faith and theology are now frequently investigated in debate and conjunction with → *analytic philosophy* (→ Language and Theology). This line of inquiry can be seen as the task of a special philosophical theology, but it also may appear as a method of dogmatics or systematic theology. Above all, the aim is to clarify the status, significance, and connection of theological statements by some kind of reference to experienced reality. This approach does not by any means need to obliterate the peculiarity of talk about God.

3.7.8. The *question of method* (→ Systematic Theology; Philosophy of Science) was raised afresh at different points in the last century. While the historical-critical method was initially still dominant in Protestant theology, dialectical theology restricted its area of competence by new initiatives in dogmatics and → hermeneutics (§2.2), but it later acquired heightened ecumenical significance, above all as it spread into Roman Catholic biblical scholarship (→ Exegesis, Biblical, 2.1.6). The fact that it still forms the basis of exegetical and historical disciplines says nothing for the scientific character of theology as a whole, which depends on systematic theology or → dogmatics. Pannenberg's and *G. Ebeling's (1912-2001)* new impetuses sought, by development of → hermeneutics (§3.3), to provide fresh foundations for the universality of historical science, as earlier asserted by *Ernst* → *Troeltsch* (1865-1923), in Pannenberg also with recourse to *G. W. F. Hegel* (1770-1831; → Hegelianism). The result might have been a historical theology capable of verifying itself and scarcely still susceptible to criticism, but instead we still face unanswered questions about the relations of historical inquiry and hermeneutics, hermeneutics and reality.

Barth admits the question of theology's scientific character only from the point of view of how it accords with its own subject matter. Against this position, *Heinrich Scholz* (1884-1956) declares that he knows of no criterion for establishing what is appropriate to a given subject matter. Barth is unwilling to comply even with Scholz's first, minimal postulates on how Protestant theology could be possible as a science, because for him revelation is a matter of God's free grace: "It is precisely appropriateness to the subject-matter in this annoyingly indefinite sense" that gives most general expression to the rule that theology must adhere to (*KD* I/1, 7).

In view of the history of theology in the German → church struggle, the demonstration of scientific character in relation to a discipline's own subject matter deserves a degree of respect. Yet it can at most secure a discipline's independence, but not set it in relation to other sciences. In order to do so, attempts have been made to determine the nature of theology by establishing connections elsewhere. Both an ontological basis and an analytic method may be drawn from philosophies like existentialism (e.g., Bultmann; → Existential Theology 2; Existential Philosophy), personalism (F. Gogarten, E. Brunner), or the → idealism (§5) of Friedrich Wilhelm Joseph von Schelling (1775-1854; Tillich, J. Macquarrie). In a different way, *Thomas Forsyth Torrance* has attempted to use developments in the natural sciences and philosophy (above all in M. Polanyi; → Epistemology 2.3.3) to overcome the subject-object model and the → dualism it entails and once again to reunite theology with other sciences. Emphasis on the criterion of relatedness to the subject matter testifies to a leaning toward the side of objectivity.

Of longer duration than such attempts was, after the experiences of the Third Reich and World War II (→ Modern Church History 1.4.3), the turn to → *Marxism* and the social sciences (→ Sociology): theology must no longer allow itself to be measured only by internal criteria but also empirically by its effects in → society (J. Moltmann; → Social Science 4; Liberation Theology). In the face both of this thrust and of the still broad front of hermeneutical theology, *Dietrich Ritschl, Gerhard Sauter,* and others employ the methods of → phenomenology and analytic philosophy (→ Language 2) to clarify the foundations, logic, truth, and validity of talk about God in the present in relation to modern theories of science. In this context, there also arises the pro-posal that theology should not understand itself as a science but as wisdom, not as *sapientia* in the sense of the Platonic or Aristotelian concept of science, but as practical wisdom growing out of experience. Others again are on the lookout for a new theological paradigm similar to paradigm change in the natural sciences (→ Science and Theology; Christianity; Relativity Theory; Quantum Theory).

4. Current Requirements
4.1. *Integration*
The problem of a theological method remains so urgent because theology must develop new ways of bringing divergent positions into relation with each other. Both the question of → truth (§2) and self-criticism are most adversely affected, not just by open contradictions, but by ways in which different theological orientations, schools, and disciplines, as well as → denominations, close themselves off from each other (→ Feminist Theology; Pluralism 2.2.3).

4.2. *Interdisciplinarity*
In order to test and take responsibility for Christian talk about God in relation to human beings, history, and the world, theology must enter into → dialogue with other disciplines. From the beginning, theology had a relation to → philosophy (and theology), and its separate disciplines have long had relations with other sciences. They have too often taken an apologetic, eclectic, or even dilettantish approach at the expense of the exactness of theological statements and their coherence with the current state of knowledge in other areas of experience and research. Theology must instead seek interdisciplinarity.

This stance in no way requires it to depart from its own standpoint but to persist in careful listening and to formulate its own questions and proposals in relation to the standpoint of its dialogue partners. For example, theology cannot allow the social sciences to tell it who the human being now is. Rather, its task is to work out by interdisciplinary means both a modern view of the human being and a theologically responsible expression of the promise of God's → salvation (§7.4) for the modern human being (→ Anthropology 3, 4.2; also → Social Ethics; Economic Ethics; Environmental Ethics 2).

4.3. *Intercultural Theology*
Intercultural theology (→ Culture and Christianity 4; Ecumenical Theology 2; Theology of Religions) asks (1) how gospel and faith may be carried over from one → culture to another, (2) how an indigenous theology is to be developed in critical engagement with a dominant foreign one, and (3) how understanding is to be fostered between theologies from different cultures. Objectively, culture means

the physical, intellectual, and spiritual environment, to the extent that it has been shaped by human beings; subjectively, it means ways of experiencing and behaving, perceiving, and expressing, handed down in a society and acquired by individuals. The intercultural question is therefore unavoidable, comprehensive, and hard to grasp. It even arises from the tension between theology that conforms to a dominant high culture and forms of piety (→ Spirituality) practiced in particular subcultures.

The issue of intercultural theology has become urgent, especially since World War II in former missionary and colonial territories (→ Colonialism and Mission), and forms an essential task of the → Ecumenical Association of Third World Theologians and various conferences of Third World theologians (→ Third World Theology). When faith and a Christian congregation arise through missionary work, it is, on the one hand, an instance of → acculturation and, on the other, the beginning of the integration of Christianity into the indigenous culture ("inculturation"). The new indigenous theologies are grounded in experiences within their own cultures and oppose foreign domination by the received → European theology (→ Contextual Theology; Biblical Theology 2). They are related in differing degrees to further efforts at the preservation of cultural identity. They wish to be appropriate to the spiritualities and ethos of their own congregations and to serve their growing missionary work. Urgent questions can thereby arise about the extent to which, and the basis on which, a particular theology should criticize its own context and enter into current social problems.

In the face of the many new initiatives springing from many different cultures and subcultures of Africa, Asia, and South America, there immediately also arises the question of intercultural understanding in the camp of the new theologies. This issue demands rather more than simply their original orientation each in its own context, together with critical distance vis-à-vis Western theology. Aylward Shorter takes up a proposal of Tanzanian bishop Joseph Blomjous (1908-92) that, to emphasize partnership and mutuality, one should speak of "interculturation" rather than "inculturation." For, although the Christian heritage contains indispensable elements, it is essentially historically conditioned and multicultural, and not to be captured in the form of one universal Christian culture (→ Pluralism 2.2.2). Even the continued existence of the → Roman Catholic Church as a "universal subculture" would not be something to welcome. The one → church subsists primarily in relatively autonomous individual churches (→ Catholicism [Roman] 2.3). In each of them different cultures are brought together, and they should determine as much as possible for themselves by → councils of their own. Intercultural theology thus also poses far-reaching questions for → church government.

→ African Theology; Asian Theology; Fundamental Theology; Latin American Theology; North American Theology

Bibliography: K. Barth, *CD* I/1-2; idem, *Evangelical Theology: An Introduction* (London, 1963); idem, "Kirche und Theologie" (1925), *Gesamtausgabe* III, *Vorträge und kleinere Arbeiten, 1922-1925* (ed. H. Finze; Zurich, 1990) 644-82 • H. Berkhof, *Two Hundred Years of Theology* (Grand Rapids, 1989) • I. U. Dalferth, *Theology and Philosophy* (Oxford, 1988) • A. Dulles, *The Craft of Theology* (New York, 1992) • G. Ebeling, *The Study of Theology* (Philadelphia, 1978); idem, "Theologie I: Begriffsgeschichtlich," *RGG* (3d ed.) 6.754-69 • E. Farley, *Ecclesial Man* (Philadelphia, 1975); idem, *Ecclesial Reflection* (Philadelphia, 1982) • C. Geffré and W. G. Jeanrond, eds., *Why Theology?* (London, 1994) • J. L. González, *A History of Christian Thought* (3 vols.; 2d ed.; Nashville, 1987) • P. C. Hodgson, *Winds of the Spirit: A Constructive Christian Theology* (Louisville, Ky., 1994) • P. C. Hodgson and R. H. King, eds., *Christian Theology: An Introduction to Its Traditions and Tasks* (2d ed.; Philadelphia, 1989) • R. W. Jenson, *Systematic Theology* (vol. 1; New York, 1997) • H. Küng and D. Tracy, eds., *Paradigm Change in Theology: A Symposium for the Future* (Edinburgh, 1989) • A. McGrath, *Christian Theology: An Introduction* (3d ed.; Oxford, 2001) • J. Milbank, *Theology and Social Theory* (Oxford, 1990) • L. Newbigin, *Foolishness to the Greeks: The Gospel and Western Culture* (Grand Rapids, 1986) • W. Pannenberg, *Systematic Theology* (vol. 1; Grand Rapids, 1991); idem, *Theology and the Philosophy of Science* (London, 1976) • H. Peukert, *Wissenschaftstheorie–Handlungstheorie–Fundamentale Theologie* (Frankfurt, 1978) • D. Ritschl, *The Logic of Theology* (Philadelphia, 1987) • D. Ritschl and M. Hailer, *Diesseits und jenseits der Worte. Grundkurs Christliche Theologie* (Neukirchen, 2006) • G. Sauter, *Gateways to Dogmatics: Reasoning Theologically for the Life of the Church* (Grand Rapids, 2003); idem, *Vor einem neuen Methodenstreit in der Theologie?* (Munich, 1970); idem, ed., *Theologie als Wissenschaft. Aufsätze und Thesen* (Munich, 1971) • H. Scholz, "Wie ist eine evangelische Theologie als Wissenschaft möglich?" *ZZ* 9 (1931) 8-53 (repr., *Theologie als Wissenschaft*, ed. Sauter, 221-64) • H. Schwarz, *Theology in a Global Context* (Grand Rapids, 2005) • A. Shorter, *Toward a Theology of Inculturation* (Maryknoll, N.Y., 1988) • C. S. Song,

Theology from the Womb of Asia (Maryknoll, N.Y., 1986) • T. F. TORRANCE, *The Ground and Grammar of Theology: Consonance between Theology and Science* (new ed.; Edinburgh, 2001; orig. pub., 1980); idem, *Theological Science* (Edinburgh, 1996; orig. pub., 1969) • D. TRACY, *Blessed Rage for Order: The New Pluralism in Theology* (Minneapolis, 1975).

JOHN MICHAEL OWEN

Theology and Music

Overview
1. Liturgy and Devotion
2. The Material and Social World
3. Musical Models

Overview

On the night he was betrayed, Jesus and his disciples broke bread together, prayed, and sang (Matt. 26:30; Mark 14:26). Ever since then, these three activities have continued to mark Christian gatherings. The ubiquity of music in Christian worship, and indeed in human society, has encouraged many theologians to give this practice their careful attention.

Recent musicology has drawn attention to the diverse social functions of music, both in and beyond the culture of the West. Similarly, the dialogue between theology and music has taken many different forms, and the partners in that dialogue have played varying roles. This article surveys highlights from that conversation.

Broadly speaking, this theological reflection has been carried out with reference to three spheres. The first is that of *liturgy and devotion*. Music, in other words, has been a concern of so-called → practical theology, and through appeal to Scripture or theological principles, theologians have commended or condemned various uses of music within Christian → worship. The second sphere is that of *the material and social world,* that is, objects and actions. Music is a universal human practice; moreover, it is one by which human beings interact with the created world (in the form of wood, string, vibrating air, etc.). Recognizing these two features of music, some theologians have considered what music might tell us about the shape of created reality, and about humanity's way of being within it. Third is *the conceptual sphere*. As a phenomenon with strikingly distinctive characteristics, music has the potential to enrich and extend the theologian's conceptual vocabulary. Attending to music and the way it works may help us to think in creative ways about issues such as biblical → hermeneutics, the charac-

ter of interpersonal relationships, and the relationship of causes to their effects.

1. Liturgy and Devotion

1.1. The early church was decidedly ambivalent in its reflection on musical practice. On the one hand, music was generally acknowledged as a legitimate expression of Christian → devotion. Singing was encouraged in corporate worship: "Let them arise therefore after supper and pray; let the boys sing psalms and the virgins also. And afterwards let the deacon, as he takes the mingled chalice of oblation, say a psalm from those in which the Alleluia is written" (Hippolytus *Trad. apos.* 25). → Athanasius (ca. 297-373) commends the "melodious reading" of the Psalms as "a sign of the well-ordered and tranquil condition of the mind" (*Ep. Mar.* 29; *PG* 27.40-41). John → Chrysostom (ca. 347-407) even contends that "nothing so arouses the soul, gives it wing, sets it free from the earth, releases it from the prison of the body, teaches it to love wisdom and to condemn all the things of this life, as concordant melody and sacred song composed in rhythm" (*In Ps.* 41.1).

On the other hand, these commendations are tempered by warnings and restrictions. Instrumental music, often associated with prostitution and Bacchic celebrations in pagan culture, regularly comes in for special censure. Gregory of Nazianzus (329/30-389/90) contrasts the debauched musical celebrations of "the Greeks" with appropriately sober Christian psalmody. "First brethren, let us celebrate the feast, not with carnal rejoicing . . . nor with carousing and drunkenness, nor surrounded by the sound of auloi and percussion; for this is the manner of the monthly Grecian rites. . . . Let us take up hymns rather than tympana, psalmody rather than shameful dances and songs, a well-rendered applause of thanksgiving rather than theatrical applause, meditation rather than debauchery" (*Or. theol.* 5.35; *PG* 35.708-9).

In book 10 of his *Confessions,* → Augustine (354-430) agonizes over the place of music in the church's worship, and the following passages nicely capture the early church's ambivalence. Augustine can attest from his own experience that music is a powerful aid to devotion. He believes that in song "our souls are moved and are more religiously and with a warmer devotion kindled to piety" (10.33.49). Sometimes, however, Augustine realizes that he is not meditating on the meaning of the words being sung but simply enjoying the sensual beauty of the melody. When this happens, "I confess myself to commit a sin deserving punishment, and then I would prefer not to have heard the singer" (10.33.50). His concern, then, is that music has the potential to lead the listener to privilege the "lower" faculties of sense and passion over the "higher" faculty of → reason.

1.2. Later theological pronouncements on musical practice often echo Augustine: music is a valuable addition to the → liturgy when practiced within certain restraints. The musical innovations of the 14th century (the growth of musical polyphony often characterized as the Ars Nova, or "New Art"), for instance, raised serious concerns for church officials, precisely because of the way these new musical practices appealed to the emotions and drew attention to the musical performance itself. John XXII's (1316-34) bull of 1323-24 warned against the practices of "certain disciples of the new school." In contrast to the sobriety and restraint of plainsong, in this new practice "the voices incessantly rock to and fro, intoxicating rather than soothing the ear, while the singers themselves try to convey the emotion of the music by their gestures." "Nevertheless," the pronouncement continues, "it is not our wish to forbid the occasional use of some consonances, which heighten the beauty of the melody" (quoted in *Music in the Western World*, 71).

1.3. Among the → Reformers of the 16th century, both Martin → Luther (1483-1546) and John → Calvin (1509-64) recognized and celebrated the virtues of music and, like Augustine, specifically noted its power to arouse the emotions in worship. One of Luther's most recognizable reforms, one that clearly emerged from his broader theological stance, was the initiation of congregational singing, using the vernacular. Calvin's congregations likewise sang in the vernacular, though these tunes were monophonic and unaccompanied. Calvin believed that music "has the greatest value in kindling our hearts to a true zeal and eagerness to pray." Nevertheless (citing Augustine), "We should be very careful that our ears be not more attentive to the melody than our minds to the spiritual meaning of the words" (*Inst.* 3.20.32).

Luther was far less troubled about letting the ears run ahead of the mind. For Luther, music itself — even apart from any religious text — gives testimony to a delightful and well-ordered creation. "From the beginning of the world it has been instilled and implanted in all creatures, individually and collectively. For nothing is without sound or harmony. . . . Let this noble, wholesome, and cheerful creation of God be commended to you. . . . At the same time you may by this creation accustom yourself to recognize and praise the Creator" (*LW* 53.322, 324).

Of all the magisterial reformers, Ulrich → Zwingli (1484-1531) had by far the most restrictive view of music. At his insistence all choral and instrumental music was eliminated from the church in Zurich. This move did not arise from an antipathy toward music — ironically, Zwingli himself was an exceptionally gifted musician. Rather, this policy was the expression of a profound suspicion of the liturgical practices of the medieval church. This suspicion was joined to a hermeneutic that dictated that any practice not explicitly commanded by Scripture be forbidden.

Though Zwingli's proscriptions on music were severe, they were not altogether out of step with contemporary concerns about liturgical excesses. In fact, the Council of → Trent (1545-63) addressed many of the same apprehensions voiced by Zwingli. Trent warned against any gratuitous displays of musical virtuosity, or indeed any music intended simply to please the ear. The council also urged caution in the use of vocal polyphony, lest the profusion of vocal parts obscure the text being sung (22d sess., "Decree concerning the Things to Be Observed, and to Be Avoided, in the Celebration of Mass"). Notably, the counterreformers did not follow Luther and Calvin in advocating congregational song in the vernacular.

1.4. Things did not change for most Roman Catholic worship until the end of the 19th century. Throughout the 20th century Rome actively sought to include the laity more fully in the music of the liturgy, beginning with the efforts of Pius X (1903-14) and culminating in → Vatican II. The reforms of Vatican II in particular brought about rapid and massive changes in worship practice. The liturgy very quickly came to include not only congregational singing in the vernacular but songs in the style of contemporary folk, pop, and rock music.

Various forms of popular music — rock, jazz, folk, and others — have had a massive and controversial influence on 20th-century Protestant worship as well (→ Hymnody). Beginning in the 1980s, North American churches were racked and sometimes split by disagreements over music, debates often collectively characterized as worship wars. These battles pitted defenders of "traditional worship" (i.e., hymns) against proponents of "contemporary worship" (i.e., pop and rock choruses). Several theologians have assessed and written about these developments and debates, including Don Saliers, Robert Webber, and Cornelius Plantinga and Sue Rozeboom.

1.5. These discussions represent an attempt to discern the appropriate relationship between the shape of Christian worship and the idiom of the surrounding → culture. This issue is significant at this juncture in church history, for at the start of the 21st century there is a growing recognition that Christian musical worship takes place in a diverse array of cultural and geographic settings. The story of Christian song includes not only J. S. Bach (1685-1750) and Isaac Watts (1674-1748) but also contemporaries Pablo Sosa (Argentina), I-to Loh (China), and Patrick Matsikenyiri (Zimbabwe). C. Michael Hawn has written about these and other non-Western musicians and the worshiping communities they represent. In the West as well, Christian worship takes place within many cultural settings, an important one of which is considered in James Abbington's *Readings in African American Church Music and Worship* (2002).

2. The Material and Social World

2.1. Not all theological engagement with music has focused on liturgy or issues of musical practice. Some have believed that music might provide distinctive insight into some aspect of human experience, or even into the structure of reality. This idea predates Christianity, being associated particularly with Pythagoras (ca. 580-ca. 500 B.C.) and Plato (427-347). Christian writers such as Boethius (ca. 480-524, *De institutione musica*), Cassiodorus (ca. 490-ca. 585, bk. 2 of *Institutiones divinarum et humanarum litterarum*), and Isidore of Seville (ca. 560-636, bk. 3 of *Etymologiarum sive Originum libri xx*) all made explicit use of the Pythagorean tradition in their writings on music. By far the most creative and theologically profound adaptation of this tradition, however, is that found in Augustine's treatise *De musica* (PL 32.1081-1194).

De musica, a dialogue in six books, is an early work of Augustine's (composed between 387 and 391). Perhaps most striking to the modern reader is how, over the course of these six books, *De musica* progresses steadily from music theory to → metaphysics, with the musical material of the first five books providing the foundation for the philosophical and theological reflections of book 6. The central category throughout is proportion, or *ratio* — the proper relationship of different things to one another. Different rhythms, the dialogue explains, arise and take on their distinctive qualities according to how individual pulses (or beats) are ordered in relationship to one another. (Thus, *long-long-short* and *short-long-long* are two different rhythms. The distinctive character of each arises from the proportion and interrelationship of its elements, "short" and "long.") Similarly, different meters arise and take on their distinctive qualities as rhythms are

ordered in various relationships to one another. Moreover, in a remarkable discussion of music perception, book 6 demonstrates that even to hear music as music, one must both perceive (proportional) order and (proportionally) order perception. Music, for Augustine, is *scientia bene modulandi,* "the knowledge of maintaining right measure."

Augustine recognizes something of fundamental importance in this discussion. When one considers music carefully, one comes to realize "what proportion is and how great is its authority in all things" (1.12.23). One's very salvation, in fact, lies in being an "ordered soul" — keeping mind, body, soul, God, self, and neighbor in right order and relationship: "That soul keeps order that, with its whole self, loves Him above itself, that is, God, and fellow souls as itself. In virtue of this love it orders lower things and suffers no disorder from them" (6.14.46). Augustine articulates this same idea some years later in his description of the Heavenly City: "The peace of all things lies in the tranquility of order, and order is the disposition of equal and unequal things in such a way as to give to each its proper place" (*De civ. Dei* 19.13). Music enacts this proper "disposition of equal and unequal things" in time and space, in which we delight and participate when we listen to it.

2.2. Throughout the Middle Ages *De musica* remained a popular and influential work, while during the modern era it came to occupy a far less prominent position within Augustine's oeuvre. Since the 1980s, though, it has once again attracted scholarly attention. Within the Radical Orthodoxy school, John Milbank and Catherine Pickstock have both drawn upon *De musica* in articulating a "musical ontology," one that acknowledges difference while striving toward harmony. For Milbank, "Christianity is peculiar because while it is open to difference . . . it also strives to make of all these differential additions a harmony, 'in the body of Christ,' and claims that if the reality of God is properly attended to, there can be such a harmony. And the idea of a consistently beautiful, continuously differential and open series is of course the idea of 'music'" (pp. 227-28).

2.3. British theologian Jeremy Begbie has also devoted serious and sustained attention to music as a feature of the created world. In particular, Begbie's work reflects a desire "to theologize not simply *about* music but *through* music" (1997, 687). Such an interaction allows the possibility that music may raise new questions, offer unexpected approaches to old problems, or open up distinctive aspects of experience.

Begbie has applied this method most systematically to the issue of time. Our musical experience of temporality differs in significant respects from our experience of "clock time," and by attending carefully to music, Begbie suggests, we may develop a fuller and richer understanding of temporality. This enriched understanding may in turn allow us to see old theological issues in a new light. "Music offers a particular form of participation in the world's temporality and in so doing, we contend, it has a distinctive capacity to elicit something of the nature of this temporality and our involvement with it. . . . The experience of music can serve to open up features of a distinctively theological account of created temporality, redeemed by God in Jesus Christ, and what it means to live in and with time as redeemed creatures" (2000, 6-7). John Polkinghorne in his study of → eschatology (2003) has made a similar appeal to the distinctive qualities of musical time.

2.4. Another strand of the theological tradition has been drawn to music not because of what it may disclose about the material or temporal world but because of what it may reveal about the inner world of human religious experience. This is one of the central themes of Friedrich → Schleiermacher's (1768-1834) *Christmas Eve,* a work that Richard Niebuhr believed discloses "the specific genius" of → Schleiermacher's theology (p. 68). In this short dramatic dialogue, the characters consider the suggestion that "it is precisely to the religious feeling that music is most closely related" (p. 46). In the course of a Christmas Eve together, the friends who populate Schleiermacher's dialogue discover that there is indeed no more apt expression of piety than music. Music, like religion, is both profoundly meaningful and ineffable. In song, as in piety, we feel deeply, and we come to grasp intuitively those truths that refuse to be boundaried by concepts. Karl → Barth (1886-1968) summarizes the message of the dialogue: "Exactly because of its lack of concepts, music is the true and legitimate bearer of the message of Christmas" (1962, 157).

This line of thinking has been explored in more recent theological literature as well. "Music and religion are realms of experience veiled in mystery," writes Albert Blackwell, "where verbal descriptions and cultural analyses are desirable and valuable but are finally inadequate and cannot substitute for the primary experiences manifested most fully in intuition and immediate feeling" (p. 24).

3. Musical Models

Theology, like all thought, is dependent upon imagery, → metaphor, and models. Since the patristic era, music has enriched the conceptual vocabulary of theology, enabling scholars to articulate various sorts of ideas, theories, and theological convictions.

A number of early theologians (again, in ways that echo the Pythagorean tradition) appeal to the metaphor of musical harmony. Musical harmony provides a sounding image of a well-ordered cosmos, of right relations in human society, of right relationship between humanity and God. Thus, for instance, Clement of Alexandria contemplates a musical universe, writing that Christ "ordered the universe concordantly and tuned the discord of the elements in a harmonious arrangement, so that the entire cosmos might become through its agency a cosmos" (*Protr.* 1.5.1; *PG* 8.57). Likewise, Ambrose can speak of a symphonic church: "For this is a symphony, when there resounds in the church a united concord of differing ages and abilities as if of diverse strings" (*In Ps.* 41.2; *PG* 55.158). In each case, the experience of musical harmony powerfully embodies a reality that is difficult to conceive in spatial or visual metaphors, namely, a reality that has its being in the coincidence of both difference and unity; of both "diverse strings" and "a united concord." For this reason David Bentley Hart suggests that "the image of cosmic music is an especially happy way of describing the analogy of creation to the trinitarian life" (p. 276).

This capacity of music to make theological realities powerfully manifest in sound was also recognized by Karl Barth, who suggested that Mozart's music sounds out "parables of the kingdom of heaven" (1986, 57). In a personal address to Mozart, Barth wrote: "Whenever I listen to you, I am transported to the threshold of a world which in sunlight and storm, by day and by night is a good and ordered world. . . . With an ear open to your musical dialectic, one can be young and become old, can work and rest, be content and sad: in short, one can live" (22). Through Mozart's music, Barth contends, we hear the appropriate timbre of creation rendering praise to God: not heroic, heavenly praise, but finite, humble, and creaturely praise. Precisely in its finitude this praise articulates the joy and freedom of the creature who is not God's rival but the recipient of his → grace. In Mozart "the sun shines but does not blind, does not burn or consume. Heaven arches over the earth, but it does not weigh it down, it does not crush or devour it. Hence earth remains earth, with no need to maintain itself in a titanic revolt against heaven" (35). In its freedom "Mozart's music renders the true *vox humana*" (54).

Jeremy Begbie enlists music in an exposition of the Chalcedonian affirmation that the human and divine natures of Jesus Christ have their being "without confusion, without change, without division, without separation; the distinction of natures being in no way annulled by the union, but rather the characteristics of each nature being preserved and coming together to form one person and subsistence" (→ Chalcedon, Council of). He observes that sounding phenomena — musical polyphony in particular — may offer a more helpful and appropriate model for these affirmations than visual or spatial analogies (2001). In the visual field, for instance, space can typically be shared only by means of exclusion (as when one object blocks another from view) or confusion (as when red and blue are mixed, producing purple). When musical notes are played together, however, the sounds coinhabit the same resonant field; they sound through one another rather than remaining "separate." At the same time, the distinctiveness of each individual note within the sonority is preserved ("without confusion," as it were; the distinct character, pitch, and timbre of each "being in no way annulled by the union"). Begbie's point in such commentary is not to "explain" Christ's person through music. Rather, he shows how a musical conceptuality allows one to avoid the difficulties that may arise through a tacit reliance upon visual or spatial metaphors.

Bibliography: J. ABBINGTON, ed., *Readings in African American Church Music and Worship* (Chicago, 2002) • AUGUSTINE, *De musica* (trans. R. C. Taliaferro; New York, 1947) • K. BARTH, *Theology and Church: Shorter Writings, 1920-1928* (trans. L. P. Smith; London, 1962); idem, *Wolfgang Amadeus Mozart* (trans. C. K. Pott; Grand Rapids, 1986) • J. S. BEGBIE, *Resounding Truth* (Grand Rapids, 2007); idem, "Sound Mix," *Beholding the Glory: Incarnation through the Arts* (ed. J. Begbie; Grand Rapids, 2001) 138-54; idem, "Theology and the Arts: Music," *The Modern Theologians: An Introduction to Christian Theology in the Twentieth Century* (ed. D. F. Ford; Oxford, 1997) 686-99; idem, *Theology, Music, and Time* (Cambridge, 2000) • J. S. BEGBIE and S. R. GUTHRIE, eds., *Musical Theology* (Grand Rapids, 2007) • A. L. BLACKWELL, *The Sacred in Music* (Cambridge, 1999) • BOETHIUS, *Fundamentals of Music* (trans. C. M. Bower; New Haven, 1989) • Q. FAULKNER, *Wiser Than Despair: The Evolution of Ideas in the Relationship of Music and the Christian Church* (Westport, Conn., 1996) • J. GELINEAU, *Voices and Instruments in Christian Worship: Principles, Laws, Applications* (trans. C. Howell; Collegeville, Minn., 1964) • D. B. HART, *The Beauty of the Infinite: The Aesthetics of Christian Truth* (Grand Rapids, 2004) • C. M. HAWN, *Gather into One: Praying and Singing Globally* (Grand Rapids, 2002) • J. MACKINNON, *Music in Early Christian Literature* (Cambridge, 1987) • J. MILBANK, "'Postmodern Critical Augustinianism': A Short *Summa* in Forty-two Responses to Unasked Questions," *MoTh* 7/3 (1991) 225-37 • *Music in the Western World: A History in Documents* (selected and annotated by P. Weiss and R. Taruskin; New York, 1984) • R. R. NIEBUHR, *Schleiermacher on Christ and Religion* (London, 1964) • C. PICKSTOCK, "Soul, City, and Cosmos after Augustine," *Radical Orthodoxy: A New Theology* (ed. J. Milbank, C. Pickstock, and G. Ward; London, 1999) 243-77 • C. PLANTINGA Jr. and S. A. ROZEBOOM, *Discerning the Spirits: A Guide to Thinking about Christian Worship Today* (Grand Rapids, 2003) • J. POLKINGHORNE, *The God of Hope and the End of the World* (New Haven, 2003) • E. ROUTLEY, *The Church and Music: An Enquiry in the History, the Nature, and the Scope of Christian Judgment on Music* (London, 1950) • F. SCHLEIERMACHER, *Christmas Eve: Dialogue on the Incarnation* (trans. T. N. Tice; San Francisco, 1990; orig. pub., 1806) • P. WESTERMEYER, *Te Deum: The Church and Music* (Minneapolis, 1998) • A. WILSON-DICKSON, *The Story of Christian Music* (Minneapolis, 1996).

STEVEN R. GUTHRIE

Theology in the Nineteenth and Twentieth Centuries

1. Protestant Theology

1.1. *Theology in Confrontation with the Enlightenment, Romanticism, and Materialism*

1.1.1. *Theology in Relation to Church and State*

Despite the many similarities and convergent tasks that connected Protestant theology in many countries in the 19th and 20th centuries, there were significant differences, dependent on the relation of theology, church, and state or society.

In central Europe and Scandinavia, theology was mostly an integral part of the state universities, except for countries where Protestants were a minority. Where religious education was taught in state schools, teachers were trained in the universities or state-founded seminaries. In Germany, theology, jurisprudence, and medicine were considered "positive sciences" for training students to serve the needs of the people, alongside philosophy as "speculative science" and the "natural sciences."

Another important factor was the founding of new universities that included theology as an integral part of the curriculum (Berlin, 1810; Breslau, 1811; Bonn, 1819). Also, there was a reform of universities, especially in Prussia, in consequence of the development of education that resulted from the movement to overcome the political crisis caused by the rule of Napoleon, which had implemented cultural, legal, and administrative principles of the

French Revolution. → Practical theology was installed as a new academic discipline within theology; at least today in England and Scotland, it is often combined with social ethics. Students of Protestant theology were trained in Latin, Greek, and Hebrew and were required to have a basic philosophical knowledge that was provided by the departments of philosophy. The rise of historical studies during the 19th century supported interdisciplinary exchange with historians, with Protestant theologians contributing remarkable editions of biblical and early-church texts. In 1900 E. → Troeltsch (1865-1923) noted the deep gap between "historical" and "dogmatic" method in theology at the end of the century; in his judgment, only the historical method was appropriate in the academy; for him, "dogmatic" was related to ecclesial devotion, which could hardly be represented in the university (*Religion in History* [1989] 11-32).

New faculties of Protestant theology, sometimes independent, were established in Vienna (1821), Budapest (1855, a Reformed academy), Paris (1879), Prague (1920), Warsaw (1920), Rome (1922, the Waldensian faculty), and Bratislava (1934). As alternatives to faculties dominated by "liberal" theologians, the Free University of Amsterdam was founded in 1880 under the influence of A. Kuyper (1837-1920; see 1.2.4), the Menighetsfakultet in Oslo in 1908, and the Kirchliche Hochschule in Bethel, Germany, in 1905.

Another significant development was the transformation of strictly "confessional" traditions. "Protestant" was often replaced by "evangelical" (Ger. *evangelisch* vs. *evangelikal,* the latter synonymous with "fundamentalist") in order to mark a common heritage of Lutherans and Calvinists, based on the immediate, individual relationship of the faithful to God, in opposition to the Roman Catholic Church, its hierarchical structure, and its claim of privilege to mediate salvation. Often the Reformation was claimed as the liberating force initiating the spirit of the modern age.

The separation of church and state in the United States caused denominations to organize the training of theologians independently, and, for better or worse, the teaching of theology was often influenced by church policy. Sometimes political interests forced unions, for example, the → Union, a merger of Lutherans and Reformed since 1817 in the Prussian and other territories, today called Union evangelischer Kirchen (UEK). In Germany this union caused the development of denominational minorities, since the other German territorial churches remained intact. When Prussia accepted the Union, the Old Lutherans mounted a confessional movement beginning in Silesia and eventually split off. In 1838 Saxon Lutherans, protesting against a rationalistic church government, emigrated to North America. Under the leadership of C. F. W. Walther (1811-87; see 1.2.6), who desired to repristinate Lutheran → orthodoxy (§1), they founded in 1847 the church now known as the Lutheran Church–Missouri Synod.

Outside of Germany revivalist churches advocated a separation of church and state and → religious liberty (Modern Period 4) and focused their attention on the lives of believers in the congregations. In Holland confessionally minded groups separated from the national church. Groups opposed to radical liberalism split off from the Protestant church in France, and a moderately liberal Église libre (→ Revivals 2.3) struggled for independence. A. R. Vinet (1797-1847) upheld this view with his theory of two societies, church and state. Protest against the undue influence of the state led to the foundation of the → free church as a new church type in Scotland. In England → Methodism (§1) had sought to revive the Church of England but had to develop its own congregational structures (→ Methodist Churches 2.1).

1.1.2. *The Independence of Religion and Religious Subjectivity*

Protestant theology on the European continent was shaped by the demise of → rationalism, followed by the ascent of German → idealism (§§3-7), which understood itself as a second period of the German → Enlightenment, led by I. Kant (1724-1804; → Kantianism), J. G. Fichte (1762-1814), G. W. F. Hegel (1770-1831; → Hegelianism), and F. W. J. Schelling (1775-1854). By critically adapting idealism, theology tried to avoid → empiricism and to escape → materialism (§5).

The theology of F. D. E. → Schleiermacher (1768-1834) asserted the existence of an independent realm for religion as a self-sustaining perception of eternity, to be distinguished from both speculation and action (*On Religion: Speeches to Its Cultured Despisers* [1799; ET 1958]). He also replaced the traditional structure of Christian doctrine (→ Dogmatics), which had mostly arranged topics *(loci)* in an order following a scheme that was quasi–salvation historical (from creation to consummation), with religion or revelation as opening topics, followed by the doctrine of God and the → Trinity. Instead, Schleiermacher reconstructed a principle to be developed into a concise system. This change can be studied best in comparison with the thought of A. J. L. Wegscheider (1771-1849), who published the last work of Christian doctrine tied to rationalism that followed the traditional order of topics (*Lehrbuch der christlichen Dogmatik* [first in Latin, 1815; in German in 2 vols., 1831-34]). Schleiermacher instead based his *Christian Faith* (2 vols., 1820-21; 2d ed., 1830-31; ET 1928) on pious self-consciousness and its experiential transition from sin to grace (→ Experience 2). All topics of his theology unfold this systematic principle. Schleiermacher thus proposed a theology structured by a stringent system that was based on a religious subjectivity embedded in a community. The community, the church, possesses a common perception that is an integral part of its cultural environment and must be developed accordingly. Church leadership needs theology because it makes possible the conjunction of various forms of piety (*Brief Outline of the Study of Theology* [2d ed., 1830; ET 1966, §5]).

Among several well-known theologians, as F. Zimmer recorded in *Bibliothek theologischer Klassiker* (vol. 1, 2d ed., 1888), the writings of Schleiermacher were regarded as of special value for the Christian life and the ministry of the church, even though his reinterpretation of Christian truth plainly differed from the teaching of the Lutheran Reformation and ignored the debates between Lutherans and Reformed (→ Schleiermacher's Theology).

Schleiermacher understood religious subjectivity as determinative of "immediate self-consciousness," "of being absolutely dependent, or, which is the same thing, of being in relation with God" (*Christian Faith,* 2d ed., §§3-4). He shared the idealistic understanding that human beings are steadfastly related to an external reality that religion calls "God." Human beings intuitively perceive themselves as "given," and reflection on this givenness discloses a human freedom that is not conditioned by the nexus of cause and effect. This conception became widely significant for German Protestantism in the 19th century.

The various influences of German idealism may be seen in → speculative theology. The right wing of Hegel's theological disciples (K. Daub [1765-1836], P. K. Marheineke [1780-1846], and later, partly, I. A. Dorner [1809-84]) adopted a thesis from Hegel's philosophy of religion. They argued that, in the form of images and ideas, religion expresses the same truth that philosophy conceptualizes in the higher form of absolute knowledge. That is, a speculative reconstruction of the dogmatic tradition results in an apparent harmony between philosophy and Christianity. The Trinity, the divine humanity of Christ, and reconciliation are regarded as concepts that are both deeply speculative and devotional. The speculatively developed unity of deity and humanity is given in the person of Jesus.

The Hegelian left wing (L. Feuerbach [1804-72], D. F. Strauss [1808-74], and B. Bauer [1809-82]) linked themselves politically to the liberal or radical democratic opposition and thought that the truth of the absolute idea was represented only inadequately in religion. The true content of religion needs a conceptual form, which Strauss tried to work out radically. His basic thought was that the idea of Christianity cannot be realized in only one person, the person of Jesus. What faith says about Jesus applies in truth to humankind as a whole. In humankind, deity and humanity are one; the Infinite has become finite. What was divinely miraculous in the appearance of Jesus was inspired by popular myths (*The Life of Jesus, Critically Examined* [2 vols., 1835-36; ET 1846]; → Hegelianism 2). Christian dogma involves its own immanent criticism and progressive resolution (*Christliche Glaubenslehre* [2 vols., 1840-41]). Feuerbach was even more radical in his denial that the absolute differs from the human. In *The Essence of Christianity* (1841; ET 1854), he claimed that the concept of God is merely a projection of the infinity of humanity, which represents our true human nature. We must free ourselves from the perversion of religion by love for the human race (→ Anthropology 4.2; Hegelianism 3; Philosophy of Religion 3.1; Religion, Criticism of, 1.2.1).

In Denmark, S. → Kierkegaard (1813-55) passionately rejected speculative attempts to harmonize idealistic philosophy and Christianity. He attacked the Hegelian system on the grounds that subjectivity (i.e., the person exposed to God), not objectivity, is truth and that the system of religious speculation lacks ethics. In his own experiences Kierkegaard discovered the profundities of human existence. Sin cannot be a function in the world process as a mere negation to be overcome by progressive synthesis. It shows human existence to be ungodly, and only divine grace can save us from it. Christ's disciples exist simultaneously with Christ, and only here is the door opened up for unconditional obedience to the will of God — as exemplified by Abraham's willingness to sacrifice his son Isaac. The language of faith is not subject to immediate communication, and faith cannot be acquired by religious self-reflection but is due to the basic decisions that confront humans. Kierkegaard influenced → dialectical theology, → existentialism and → existential theology, and, most recently, deconstruction.

Kierkegaard harshly criticized N. F. S. → Grundtvig (1783-1872; → Denmark 1.2.3), who was influenced at first by the Enlightenment and Romanticism but who later turned toward an orthodox Lutheran theology, with the congregation as the focal point. He worked by means of sermons and hymns, many of which are still sung today. The center of his theology was the doctrine of creation, combined with an awareness of what was naturally human. With a concept of the people that was shaped by Romanticism, Grundtvig helped to found adult education centers. He had little immediate influence outside Denmark, but his influence is still evident in Denmark.

Idealism could finally lead to radical → individualism (§3.3), as the later Strauss (*Der alte und der neue Glaube* [1872]) and B. Bauer show, arguing that Christ is merely the product of subjective religious consciousness. Hegelianism also found an echo in the Scottish theologian J. Caird (1820-98), for whom the affinity of the divine and the human was a key to the incarnation. In the United States W. E. Channing (1780-1842), a Unitarian, attempted a synthesis of idealistic immanentism (→ Immanence and Transcendence 4) and Christian doctrine.

The development of the German Enlightenment differed significantly from the English and French Enlightenment, which also influenced North American Protestantism. New England transcendentalism integrated idealistic elements, but the dominant rational orthodoxy, oriented to Scottish common-sense → realism, advocated a natural theology that attempted to mediate between revelation and reason (→ North American Theology 3). → Utilitarianism gained a hold in England, calling into question the speculative approaches of German idealism. Empiricism and → positivism were also anti-idealistic intellectual forces. In southwestern Germany (Swabia), theologians like F. C. Oetinger (1702-82) developed a biblical realism that remained uninfluenced by the Cartesian dichotomy of thought and being (→ Cartesianism). J. T. Beck (1804-78) taught the organic emergence of the kingdom of God on earth, which cannot be produced by human activism. Following J. A. Bengel (1687-1752) and others, Beck stressed the inner unity of Scripture. With these emphases and through his counseling, he influenced biblical theologians like M. Kähler (see 1.3.4) and the NT scholar A. Schlatter (1852-1938), who also taught systematic theology.

1.1.3. *History as the Remedy of Theology*

In 1806 the so-called Holy Roman Empire came to an end, and beginning in 1803, state authorities took possession of many properties, mainly of the Roman Catholic Church. This transfer of property, called → secularization, was followed by the transformation and reconstruction of religious values by philosophers, politicians, writers, and other shapers of public opinion. Many Christians welcomed this process, hoping it would gain new plausibility and increased relevance for Christianity.

In order to avoid the loss of intellectual credibility, as well as of academic and public influence, Protestant theology intensified its study of history, much in line with the Reformers' criticism of church tradition, which was not regarded as faithful to the gospel. The Enlightenment had enlarged and radicalized this attitude to historical-critical analysis and reconstruction. Tradition as such had been suspect of being oppressive or misleading as long as it could not be evaluated and proved reliable. Enlightened philosophers and theologians had often judged tradition on rationalistic grounds, that is, with reference to perennially valid values. The later Enlightenment called for a penetrating and more sophisticated perception of history — namely, history as the comprehensive realm of humanity ("world history") and driven by processes that are "law governed"; these laws must be grasped in order to act according to the flow of universal history.

The turn to history in the first decades of the 19th century was sometimes accompanied by → Romanticism. This complex movement combined aesthetic elements with those that were social and psychic, holding critically that at least parts of the past were neglected (specifically, by rationalism). It tried to revitalize religion by reviving the richness of feeling, following Schleiermacher. Nevertheless, much of the theological interest in history was shaped by a rationalistic reconstruction of past developments.

This theological approach to history was ambiguous — both critical and affirmative — and the problem was how to balance the two. Often the results of historical-critical reconstruction did not cover the breadth of experiences in thinking as they had been formulated in Christian doctrine. In consequence, theologians were sometimes tempted to rely on simplified religious ideas regarded as universal, at least in the European or North American contexts. More elaborated historical knowledge should offset this loss of spiritual substance. Historical theology therefore advanced to the center of theological research and education, true to the historical consciousness that was the dominant spirit of the age. Eventually, at the end of the century, it led to a → historicism (§§1-2) marked by a total relativism that could no longer be controlled by true historical reflection.

In these circumstances Protestant theology contributed important historical studies that often caused controversies. F. C. Baur (1792-1860), for instance, was able to uncover rich historical detail while at the same time achieving comprehensive, conceptual understandings (→ Historiography 3.6). His early works were oriented to the theology of Schleiermacher, and he set aside supernatural explanations in order to view Christianity in the perspective of universal history. In his monographs on the history of the early church, Baur used Hegel's principle that progress rests on dialectical antitheses in summing up all church history. Religious and political developments resulting from a sense of autonomy were seen as a legitimate continuation of a Reformation religion of freedom. Baur pointed to the antithesis between the Reformed concept of predestination (objective) and the Lutheran concept of faith (subjective). He valued this antithesis as an essential feature of Protestantism, and therefore he opposed the way in which it had been leveled down by theologians close to the Church of the Union. In treatises on the history of the doctrine of reconciliation (1838) and on the Trinity and incarnation (1841, 1843), Baur described a conceptual development of the history of ideas driven by objectivity and subjectivity. In 1844 he excluded the Gospel of John as a source of the life of Jesus.

Baur's successor C. H. Weizsäcker (1822-99; *Das apostolische Zeitalter* [1886]) and H. J. Holtzmann (1832-1910; *Lehrbuch der neutestamentlichen Theologie* [1897]) argued for a two-source theory for the → Synoptic gospels and for the priority of Mark. J. Wellhausen (1844-1918) developed the analysis of the Pentateuch (e.g., in his *Geschichte Israels* [vol. 1, 1878]; → Pentateuchal Research 1.1), laid further foundations for the critical investigations of the Gospels, and became a renowned Arabist scholar. E. Schürer (1844-1910) explored → Judaism in the Hellenistic age (*Neutestamentliche Zeitgeschichte* [1874] and *The History of the Jewish People in the Age of Jesus Christ* [3 vols., 3d and 4th eds., 1901-9; ET 1973-87]) and, together with A. Harnack (1851-1930; since 1914, A. von Harnack), in 1876 founded the *Theologische Literatur-Zeitung*. This period of historical theology reached its peak with Harnack (see 1.3.2).

1.2. Restoration, Liberalism, and Theologies of Mediation

1.2.1. Revival, Revision, and Reaffirmation

The so-called → restoration (§4) in central Europe after the defeat of Napoleon (1813/14) was mostly a self-identification with the "natural" flow of history, something to be distinguished from the development of constructive ideas to be put into effect. Restoration tried to stabilize institutional structures, such as the binding force of church confessions, in order to establish church life and theology. Here the German state supported the regional church(es), and reciprocally the church(es) the state.

An important factor was the move of → Pietism (§2.10) toward such restoration tendencies. Early Pietism had been a sibling of the Enlightenment as far as the critique of "orthodox theology" (Protestant scholasticism) and ossified church structures was concerned. After the French Revolution, however, and influenced by various forms of awakening and revivalism, Pietism increasingly tended toward restoration; in addition, Pietism often moved beyond church institutions, becoming an international movement. Paradoxically, Pietism on the European continent was sometimes also shaped by English and North American kindred influences that moved in an antirestoration direction.

In religious life a romantic-idealistic outlook prevailed. Awakenings (→ Revivals 2.5) also influenced German theology for many decades. With his *Die Lehre von der Sünde und vom Versöhner* (1823), F. A. G. Tholuck (1799-1877) offered a devotional tractate that formulated the consciousness of → sin in a way typical of revivalism — the personal surrender of the self to God on the basis of the atoning work of Christ was seen as the way to redemption, which had to be upheld against pantheism (in criticism of Hegel and Schelling; → Soteriology 2.5). J. A. W. Neander (1789-1850), a converted Jew, supported the awakening, uniting an enlightened historical interest and a feeling of romanticism with a sense of the organic processes of development.

E. W. Hengstenberg (1802-69) combined revivalist piety and restoration politics. He was a descendant of Prussian nobility and, beginning in 1827, had a great influence on church and theology as editor of the *Evangelische Kirchenzeitung*. He aimed to combat rationalistic criticism and to defend the older Protestant legacy.

Revivalism, supported by an expectation of the coming of God's kingdom in the near future, increased the spread of Christianity in domestic culture and in the world (→ Mission). This eschatology was not identical with → millenarianism (§6) but pointed rather to the integral and cosmic dimension of salvation (e.g., J. C. Blumhardt [1805-80]). Some circles debated "universal restoration," a homecoming of all people to God, even though such views went against traditional church doctrine (→ Apocatastasis).

The United States experienced the First Great

Awakening (mid-18th cent.) and, after the Revolutionary War (1775-83), the Second Great Awakening (1795-1835), with various denominations, parties, and reforming groups addressing nonbelievers and people who were not integrated in churches, in both urban and rural settings. The awakenings shared the optimistic views of postmillennialism, did evangelistic work in the expanding West, opposed the domination of tradition, were open to the many possibilities of a democratic life, and addressed the social needs of an industrial society (→ Modern Church History 2.4).

Many North American theologians struggled with the awareness of sin (→ North American Theology 2.2). N. W. Taylor (1786-1858), a leading figure at Yale Divinity School (founded 1822), combined an Arminian stress on human freedom with a decisive emphasis upon → conversion. C. G. → Finney (1792-1875), president of Oberlin College in Ohio, called for a personal contribution to the process of conversion by the addition of perfectionist traits to (self-) → sanctification (→ Perfection 5.1). His thought of a sinless life, corresponding to Christ's saving work and the divine act of grace, inspired many 19th-century groups that were aiming at full sanctification (→ Holiness Movement 3).

In *The Mystical Presence* (1846), J. W. Nevin (1803-86) represented a romanticizing theology that sought to preserve the spirit of the → Heidelberg Catechism (1563) and highlighted the presence of God in the church and the sacraments. With P. Schaff (1819-93), who favored a union of Lutherans and Reformed (and perhaps also Roman Catholics; see Schaff's *Principle of Protestantism* [1844]), Nevin was an advocate of the Reformed Mercersburg theology, which, although it was in direct encounter with rational orthodoxy, had little influence. In 1870 Schaff became professor at Union Seminary in New York. In addition to his *History of the Christian Church* (6 vols., 1882-92) and *Creeds of Christendom* (3 vols., 1877), he participated in the revision of the King James Version of the Bible and in 1888 founded the American Society of Church History (→ North American Theology 4.3).

1.2.2. Mediation

Several types of → mediating theology (§§2-3) joined in efforts to mediate Christian tradition to the spirit of the present age. Mediation in both a wider sense and a moderate form meant an increased study of Christianity as a historical phenomenon, especially of the influences of leading philosophical ideas on the development of Christian theology. This study was designed to reformulate theology in basic agreement with contemporary philosophical conceptions. Radical forms of this theology adopted speculative systems, especially of the philosophy of history, in order to construct theology.

The slogan "mediation" as the basic interest of a theological school and of church politics derives from a program of the periodical *Theologische Studien und Kritiken* (1828-1938). This mediating theology was initially an attempt to form a synthesis of modern scientific study, which had related Christianity to the cultural process, with revivalist supernatural ideas of salvation and revelation. Secondarily, however, the term also denoted an effort to bring together motifs of Hegel and Schleiermacher. Mediating theology linked concentration on the nature of Christian faith in revelation with openness to new forms of cultural creativity. In his *Life of Jesus* Strauss had not been able to introduce new systematic concepts in relation to critical questions. Mediating theologians, however, followed new paths in exegesis (e.g., Holtzmann and Weizsäcker) and historical theology (e.g., K. A. von Hase [1800-1890] and K. R. Hagenbach [1801-74]). In debates about church politics they were in favor of the Union and a presbyterial constitution (→ Elder 2). In efforts at gaining independence from the state, they were unable to prevail and made alliances with liberal and even conservative political forces.

C. Ullmann (1796-1865) tried to prove historically that the objective significance of Christ's saving work was the essence of Christianity (*The Sinlessness of Jesus* [1828; ET 1858]), which he highlighted as the common ground in every theological discord. C. I. Nitzsch (1787-1868) was significant not only for his support of the institution of presbyteries in the western part of the Church of the Union but also theologically for his *System of Christian Doctrine* (1829; ET 1849) and *Praktische Theologie* (3 vols., 1847-67). This group of theologians followed Schleiermacher by taking the religious life as a matter of priority for theological instruction. But they did not share Schleiermacher's attacks on church doctrine, which they accepted for the most part on objective grounds. A. Twesten (1789-1876) and the followers of Schleiermacher who differed from him upheld the OT and the doctrine of the Trinity. These theologians in fact sought to embrace the pluralistic life of the culture with the essence of Christianity.

Mediating theology in a wider sense was influenced by speculative theology on the one side and by "awakening theology" on the other. The periodicals *Deutsche Zeitschrift für christliche Wissenschaft und geistliches Leben* (1850-61; J. Müller and J. A. W. Neander) and *Jahrbücher für deutsche Theologie* (1856-78; T. Liebner and I. A. Dorner) combined intellectual and ecclesial reflection. J. Müller (1801-78) was closer to revivalism in his rejection of the way philosophy and → pantheism (§§2-3) relativized the antithesis of good and evil (*The Christian Doctrine of Sin* [2 vols.; 5th ed., 1867; ET 1868]). He was willing to go along with J. Böhme (1575-1624) and Kant in explaining the origin of evil. On the other side of the spectrum stood persons who were more under the influence of Hegel and Schelling, such as T. Liebner (1806-71) and I. A. Dorner, who tried to show the emergence of faith in his *System of Christian Doctrine* (2 vols., 1879-81; ET 4 vols., 1888-91). Dorner's idea of God's unchangeableness also found interest in North American theology.

Beck and J. P. Lange (1802-84) tried to mediate between → biblical theology and the concept of salvation history. R. Rothe (1799-1867) belonged to this wider circle. Methodologically oriented to Hegelian dialectics, he elaborated his speculative system of God-consciousness in *Theologische Ethik* (3 vols., 1845-48; 2d ed., 5 vols., 1867-71). Here he argued that God as absolute person unfolds God's self in the development of religion and morality, so that nature becomes more and more spiritual as a religious and moral world takes shape. This was the theoretical background of his approach to political commitment and programmatic involvement in the Deutscher Protestantenverein (German Protestant Union, 1863). In his view the Reformation initiated an era in which church and state no longer confronted one another as religious and moral institutions (→ State Ethics 3). The decline of clearly differentiated forms of the church in the modern age should be viewed not as degeneration but as a step toward the → kingdom of God (§3.2.6). Rothe regarded this development as the ideal for the organism of a Christian state, in which a free religious self-determination would cooperate with a communal moral sense (*Theologische Ethik* [2d ed., §§579-81]; → Liberal Theology 2.4.3).

1.2.3. *Lutheranism*

The Lutheran territorial churches in Germany developed neo-Lutheranism (→ European Theology [Modern Period] 1.2.1.1), which in the 1840s and 1850s again took up the confessions of the Lutheran Reformation (→ Confessions and Creeds 2) and reaffirmed Scripture as their norm (C. Harms [1778-1855]). Treatises on the nature of the church by W. Löhe (1808-72), A. Harless (1806-79), F. Delitzsch (1813-90), and T. Kliefoth (1810-95) largely ruled out the critical function of the distinction between the → church (§2.2.7.1) as the hidden work of God and the empirical church. Instead, they stressed the objectivity of the → sacraments (§2.4.1)

and → ministry (§3.1). Reflecting the realism of the age, A. F. C. Vilmar (1800-1868) emphasized that the Word and sacrament instituted by God are based on Christ's presence and that ministering them is Christ's own ministry (*Die Theologie der Thatsachen wider die Theologie der Rhetorik* [1856]). Viewing the sacraments as constitutive means of grace was in opposition to the views of the Reformed in the Union. He also pursued his theological intentions as a politician and a social scientist.

The most influential movement in Lutheranism was the so-called Erlangen theology (represented by the *Zeitschrift für Protestantismus und Kirche* [1838-76]), which opposed most of these conservative tendencies. Influenced by the awakening but with a modern view of history, this movement tried to reassert traditional teaching. In his *Einleitung in die Dogmengeschichte* (1839), Kliefoth based his theory of the development of dogma on the biblical witness to Christ. He argued that in each age a specific dogma (e.g., Christology, anthropology, soteriology) would become the organizing dogmatic center; ecclesiology was the center for the 19th century (*Acht Bücher von der Kirche* [1854]). J. C. K. von Hofmann (1810-77) based his system on the inner experience of the new birth. He held that theology must deal with this experience and its historical presuppositions and consequences. At the same time, theology is to reflect the whole of biblically based teaching (*Weissagung und Erfüllung* [2 vols., 1841-44] and *Der Schriftbeweis* [3 vols., 1852-55]) by giving a new interpretation to traditional doctrine; for example, the immanent Trinity is the prototype of God's love for us. Christ obeys God in an absolute way that we cannot achieve, and therefore he is the origin of the new humanity bound by love. Hofmann also introduced the term *Heilsgeschichte* (→ Salvation History 1). F. H. R. Frank (1827-94) drew conclusions from the experiences of rebirth and sanctification for the knowledge of faith. He sought a stronger speculative system, but one that embraces all the traditional doctrinal contents as an objective basis of faith. G. Thomasius (1802-75) tried to reformulate the doctrine of the two natures of Christ (→ Christology 2.1) by giving full stress to the humanity of Jesus. In his main work, *Christi Person und Werk* (3 vols., 1852-61), he reinterpreted the traditional doctrine of *kenōsis* by claiming that renunciation of the divine attributes of omnipotence, omniscience, and omnipresence was not an act of the God-man but an act of the preexistent divine Logos, and only through this self-emptying did he become a human being. W. F. Gess (1819-91) argued in a similar way (→ Kenosis 3).

F. J. Stahl (1802-61) — in *Die Philosophie des Rechts* (2 vols., 1830-37), *Die Kirchenverfassung nach Lehre und Recht der Protestanten* (1840), and *Die lutherische Kirche und die Union* (1859) — presented a restoration concept of the Christian state that supported church law. He asserted that Holy Scripture orders the → confessions as acts of the church, but in opposition to arbitrary innovations and semidemocratic decision making, he declared that the confessions were the irrefutable basis of the Lutheran church, which must be enforced by an authoritative → teaching office (§2).

1.2.4. *Calvinism*

J. → Edwards (1703-58; → Theology of Revival 4.2; Revivals 2.1) combined elements of Calvinistic tradition with Locke's epistemology. He emphasized divine sovereignty and majesty, as well as the "sense of the heart," stressing that sinners depend wholly on God's work of atonement and redemption. Edwards initiated the tradition of New England theology, which took up the same themes and problems (→ North American Theology 1.2). His disciples, like the New Divinity theologians J. Bellamy (1719-90) and S. Hopkins (1721-1803), subtly modified their master's views, while T. Dwight (1752-1817), president of Yale College (1795-1812), accentuated experience in matters of salvation.

In a critical reaction from Andover Seminary (founded 1808), A. Park (1808-1900) opted for a "moderate Calvinism" by stressing both divine sovereignty and human possibilities. He was too liberal for the conservative Calvinism of Princeton Seminary (founded 1812), ably represented by A. Alexander (1772-1851) and C. Hodge (1797-1878; see 1.2.6; → North American Theology 2.3). The Unitarians, transcendentalists, and confessionalists (→ North American Theology 4) also shaped American Protestantism, along with the various forms of the New England theology. All these movements emphasized the need for a renewed Christian life, which corresponded to the individualism of the age.

In Scotland, as well as in England in a challenge to the Anglicans, political and social involvement developed along with a desire to re-Christianize the masses (→ Revivals 2.2). T. Chalmers (1780-1847) championed a restored Calvinistic tradition. He was active in both theology and society, impelled by a strict faith, a fervor for Presbyterianism, and an older Reformed social activism. Protesting against interference of the state, he and many others left the national church and in 1843 founded the Free Church of Scotland. In France and Switzerland Protestant congregations expanded on a traditional Reformed basis (→ Revivals 2.3). In Holland protest

against the spirit of the age (I. Da Costa [1798-1860]) led to the founding of an antirevolutionary party (→ Revivals 2.4).

Where → Calvinism had influenced church life and theological reflection, as well as culture and society, a strong ethical interest and pragmatic views were evident, in keeping with the Reformed openness to "worldly" questions and experiences. On the one hand, this approach favored theological liberalism, but on the other, it made way for neo-Calvinist conceptions, so that lively debates ensued.

In French-speaking theology the school of the Geneva Oratoire tried to renew → Calvin's theology through the works of H. A. C. Malan (1787-1864), L. Gaussen (1790-1863), and J. H. Merle d'Aubigné (1794-1872). Calvinistic orthodoxy, endorsed by the theological faculty of Montauban (refounded in 1808 and including D. Encontre [1762-1818] and G.-A. de Félice [1803-71]), contrasted with the teaching of both Lausanne (A. Vinet; see 1.1.1) and Strasbourg and its more modern critical approach.

In the Netherlands the liberal Groningen school was opposed by ethical orthodoxy (N. Beets [1814-1903], D. Chantepie de la Saussaye [1818-74], and the journal *Ernst en vrede* [since 1853]). This orthodoxy tied in with classic Calvinism, but it also tried to mediate between revelation and a natural knowledge of God, between the gospel and human needs. Its individualism and its restraint on matters of church polity and Christian politics gave rise to the Confessionelen, a politically active group whose leading representatives were G. Groen van Prinsterer (1801-76) and P. J. Hoedemaker (1839-1910). Ecclesiological and Christological concepts here gave rise to theocratic views.

A. Kuyper stood under the influence of van Prinsterer's antirevolutionary party ("against revolution, the Gospel!"). He assembled the Reformed in a church committed to the Bible and the confession (the independent Gereformeerde Kerken [1892]; → Confessions and Creeds 3; Netherlands 2.2) and founded Christian schools and the Free University of Amsterdam. With his strong theology of election (→ Predestination), he and H. Bavinck (1854-1921), who also taught at the Free University, supported confessional Reformed theology (→ European Theology [Modern Period] 1.2.4). The desire for a return to Calvinistic teaching led to the formation of the Old Reformed Church in 1834.

1.2.5. *Liberalism*

The term "liberal" was and is ambiguous (→ Liberal Theology 1). It is often used with either programmatic or polemical intention, depending on the user's point of view. In addition, there are significant differences between England and the United States, on the one hand, where liberalism has been a politically distinctive phenomenon that is reflected in religion and culture (→ Liberal Theology 2), and central Europe, on the other hand. In Europe liberal church politics fought against rigid church structures, but political liberalism was not unified, with differing voices at best concurring in respect to the self-determination of the individual. Regarding theology, a common denominator could be found in a basically critical attitude toward traditions, which were viewed as repressive and dividing. Often the Reformation was regarded as half-hearted because it held on to the authority of the Bible. Dogmatic theology was refused because it complicated the simplicity of the original message of Jesus, supported church authority, and burdened religious life with needless intellectual problems and outdated quarrels.

The constitutions of the universities granted liberty to any research and teaching that met academic standards, which seemed to be fulfilled best in historical theology. Dogmatic or systematic theology was accepted insofar it was allied with the historical reconstructions of the philosophy of religion. But often dogmatics and practical theology were suspected of primarily serving the church — that is, a particular interest instead of a general religious consciousness alive in culture.

It would be misleading to derive the labels "liberal" and "conservative" from political standpoints. Often "liberal" theologians applauded conservative politics, and "conservatives" sympathized with progressive ideas. Sometimes something that was announced as progressive turned out to be regressive, and liberality itself could be conservative in respect to the continuity of culture.

Central European liberalism was basically interested in relations between the many historical forms of Christianity. Their reconstruction, it was held, should lead to the "essence" of Christianity. This effort was critically supported by the liberation of the idea of Christianity from its mythical forms. The bases of liberalism were the idea of development and the concept of religion itself. Christianity had to be seen in the general context of the intellectual and cultural world (→ Culture 1-2; Culture and Christianity 1-2) but also in the world of historical religions (→ Phenomenology of Religion). Under the influence of Schleiermacher and Hegel a basic feature of liberalism was interpreting Protestantism in terms of its nature or principle. From this principle the unity of theology was derived, even in all its variety.

In church politics liberal theology had only a limited influence in Germany. After 1830, however, and in more moderate form, it had an increasing impact on the liberal regimes and church politics of Switzerland, especially when in 1845 the historic confessions ceased to be binding (→ Liberal Theology 2.3). Of great significance were Alexander Schweizer (1808-88; *Die Christliche Glaubenslehre* [2 vols., 1863-72]) and A. E. Biedermann (1819-85). The latter especially, despite his speculative systematics, recognized the autonomy of various forms of the religious life (*Die freie Theologie* [1844] and *Christliche Dogmatik* [1869; 2d ed., 2 vols., 1884-85]).

In France the theologians who contributed to the Strasbourg *Revue de théologie et de philosophie chrétienne* (since 1850) — for example, E. Reuss (1804-91), T. Colani (1824-88), and E. Scherer (1805-89) — were acquainted with the works of German liberal theologians. In his *Vues sur le protestantisme en France* (1829), S. Vincent (1787-1837) mediated the theology of Schleiermacher and tried to give a new self-consciousness to his church (the "church in the wilderness").

In the Netherlands J. H. Scholten (1811-85; → European Theology [Modern Period] 1.2.4) advocated the empirical speculative method that had led the Groningen theology (see 1.2.4) in a modern, humanistic direction.

In England S. T. Coleridge (1772-1834), T. Arnold (1795-1842), C. Kingsley (1819-75), and J. F. D. Maurice (1805-72) pioneered theological liberalism, which was open to the theory of → evolution (§1), historical criticism, and social involvement (→ Liberal Theology 2.1). J. B. Lightfoot (1828-89), B. F. Westcott (1825-1901), and F. J. A. Hort (1828-92) treated theology historically. Philosophical theology, beginning with J. Ward (1843-1925), considered the basic problems of philosophy from a Christian angle.

1.2.6. *Between Liberalism and Fundamentalism* In North American Protestantism T. Parker (1810-60), who was linked to the radicalism of Strauss, helped to introduce liberal theology. A central figure in this effort was also H. Bushnell (1802-76; → Liberal Theology 2.2.1). The → Unitarians and Universalists (→ Universalism, Universalists) played a role as liberalism was developed by various theologians. In the final decades of the 19th century radical liberalism in North America was characterized by empiricism and pragmatic optimism. Traditionalism in the southern states and orthodox Lutheranism stood opposed to both liberalism and the → Social Gospel. The cities of the North also saw the rise of → fundamentalism, which attacked liberalism theologically in the churches and also protested against the public loss of Christian faith and values. In general, however, American Protestantism was still largely open to the ideals, forms of thinking, and anthropological concepts of the Enlightenment, even when that Protestantism opposed historical-critical → exegesis, criticism of the tradition, or the theory of evolution. Various theological schools developed, often localized at theological seminaries; their interactions reveal the variations of North American theology at this time.

A leading liberal was W. A. Brown (1865-1943) of Union Theological Seminary in New York (→ North American Theology 5.4). His *Christian Theology in Outline* (1906) represented a specifically American form of theology that found a place for both native revivalist theology and German liberalism. His main themes were the personality and teaching of the historical Jesus and the transformation of the lives of his followers, the moral value of repentance, the practical proofs of faith, and involvement in movements to reform the social order. For Brown, denominational barriers were hindering the work of the churches (*The Church: Catholic and Protestant* [1935]). Brown was an ecumenical pioneer (*Toward a United Church* [1946]), working to bring together the → Life and Work and → Faith and Order movements (see 1.6.6).

From his pulpit in Brooklyn, L. Abbott (1835-1922) disseminated the idea that evolution is God's way of working and that we should seek God both in history and in the individual soul (*Theology of an Evolutionist* [1897]). B. P. Bowne (1847-1910) at Boston University learned from experience and the "common world" that the ego is the source and norm of knowledge and of an understanding of God. Reality is constituted by the "Creator-Person" (i.e., God) and by "created persons" (→ North American Theology 5.4), ideas that Bowne developed into an influential philosophy of religion focusing on persons (*Personalism* [1908]).

Pragmatism appealed to experiences and found God's presence in existence and actual events ("piecemeal supernaturalism"). With echoes of both Edwards and Schleiermacher, W. James (1842-1910) at Harvard stirred up a good deal of interest in contemporary culture (→ Experience 2; Psychology of Religion). He developed and popularized the basic ideas of the philosophy of C. S. Peirce (1839-1914; → Pragmatism 2), adopted psychological theories (*The Principles of Psychology* [1890]), and examined the nature and epistemological status of religious phenomena (*The Varieties of Religious Experience* [1902]). J. Royce (1855-1916; → North American

Theology 5.3), also at Harvard, did not regard an empirical basis as sufficient for religion; rather, it needs a metaphysical system. Individuals and their experiences must be viewed as manifestations of an absolute will (*The World and the Individual* [2 vols., 1900-1901], which promoted a voluntaristic → idealism [§10]). In his last main work, *The Problem of Christianity* (1913), Royce found in the church, sin, and penitence specifically Christian ideas, which he saw illustrated in the "beloved community," the place of love and loyalty.

D. C. Macintosh (1877-1948; → North American Theology 5.4), at Yale, advocated a different form of liberalism, namely, religious realism, in which religious experience is perceived in (objective) empirical categories and the Godhead is sought on "the far side" of subjective consciousness. We also find a "realistic liberalism" at Chicago Divinity School, where H. N. Wieman (1884-1975) linked his empirical theology in part with what was later called → process theology (§2; see 1.6.8). His colleagues S. Mathews (1863-1941) and S. J. Case (1872-1947) used modern scientific methods in studying faith, convinced that in this way they would discover and present the central values of the Christian tradition and apply them in answering contemporary questions (see Mathews's *Faith of Modernism* [1914]).

"Traditional" theologians either showed contempt toward these developments or used dogmatic propositions to counter the contemporary tendency to put Christianity in a philosophical dress so as to trace religious aspects of philosophy, to use scientific methods in theology, and to verify theological concepts pragmatically. Fundamentalism reacted by defending essential truths and also by starting a movement that cut across all denominations, even to the point of founding the World Christian Fundamentals Association (1919).

Princeton Seminary was a stronghold of Calvinism (see 1.2.4). C. Hodge, who taught doctrine there from 1822 to 1878, combined in his *Systematic Theology* (3 vols., 1872-73) → Calvin's theology, the → Westminster Confession, the Reformed scholasticism of F. Turretin (1623-87; → Orthodoxy 2.3.2), and Scottish commonsense realism. Against the facts of science, this Old Princeton theology set the facts of Scripture ("a storehouse of facts"). Convinced of the infallibility and divine authority of the Bible as the Word of God given by the inspiration of the Holy Spirit, it maintained that all biblical statements are free from error and that one can therefore spread the Christian religion by rational arguments ("mission to reason") and defend it against every foe ("apologetic religion"). C. Hodge, his son A. A. Hodge

(1823-86), and his successor at Princeton, B. B. Warfield (1851-1921), supported this view in opposition to contemporary modernism and relativism.

Protesting the modernist influence after World War I in the Presbyterian Church, J. G. Machen (1881-1937) of Princeton took up the cudgels in his *Christianity and Liberalism* (1923) and *The Attack upon Princeton Seminary* (1927). In 1929 he and others founded Westminster Theological Seminary in Philadelphia, and Machen became the leading defender of fundamentalism. Opposing → modernism in a way similar to that of the Roman Catholics, the fundamentalists laid down six fundamentals in the 12-volume paperback series *The Fundamentals* (1910-15): the infallibility of Scripture, the deity of Jesus, the virgin birth, the atoning sacrifice of Christ, the resurrection of the body, and Christ's return (→ Evangelical Movement 3). The group was particularly opposed to the theory of evolution because its scientific method seemed to call into question the dogmatic system. The aim was to protect the authentic historical identity of Christianity and to maintain it against churches that were committed to progress.

A particular form of fundamentalism emerged in → dispensationalism. Developed by Brethren leader J. N. Darby (1800-1882), it found a sequence of saving dispensations in history that would come to an end in apostasy because those who were called did not meet up to their responsibilities. Therefore the church dispensation, which replaced the Jewish dispensation, would no longer exist. The true church stands above the denominations, separates itself from the world, and expects the return of Christ prior to the millennial kingdom (→ Apocalypticism 4.5). Along with belief in inspiration, an eschatological element was an essential feature in the rejection by dispensationalism of the dominant belief in progress and cultural optimism, as well as in the negation of all efforts to achieve the unity of the church (→ International Council of Christian Churches).

American Lutheran confessionalism represented by C. P. Krauth (1823-83) at Gettysburg (Pennsylvania) Seminary, C. F. W. Walther at Concordia Seminary in St. Louis, and J. M. Reu (1869-1943) at Wartburg Seminary in Dubuque (Iowa) stood aloof from questions of the age. With constant support from immigrants, the Lutheranism of the time was concerned about its own affairs, especially matters of church polity and approaches to other denominations.

1.2.7. Social Tasks

The primary interest of many theologians of the 19th century was in serving the religious needs and related intellectual conflicts of the middle class, which was dominant in the prevailing culture. The period from 1870 to 1914 was often called the later middle-class age, which was especially true for Germany. In this age, social politics and the state's weaving of a security net of welfare were designed to prevent socialist or even communist rebellion. In former times, social work had often been one of the tasks of the church. During the 19th century much impressive social-welfare work was established or initiated, not always by church administration, but generally by committed church laypeople. This endeavor was mostly inspired by ideas of restoration (see 1.2.1). Prominent figures were J. H. Wichern (1808-81), F. von Bodelschwingh (1831-1910), and A. Stoecker (1835-1909).

In French Protestantism a Christian social movement led by T. Fallot (1844-1904) took issue with the church's failures in social matters. In England Kingsley and Maurice contended for "Christian socialism" (→ Religious Socialism 1), and the Methodists and others played a key role in the labor movement.

In the United States the Social Gospel movement was active at first through programmatic publications but quickly turned to radical activities as the social consequences of industrialization were perceived (W. Gladden, *Working People and Their Employers* [1876]). The main goal was God's kingdom on earth, now understood in moral and largely evolutionary terms rather than those of Puritanism or Pietism. Social change was the new version of conversion. Five fundamentals were sought: social justice, common rights of property, industrial democracy, closer equality, and cooperation (H. W. Ward, ed., *The Social Creed of the Churches* [1912]). Toward the end of the 19th century, the Social Gospel began to organize politically and to have an influence on the seminaries. In the 20th century it became the official position of many American churches (→ Modern Church History 2.6.3). The Baptist W. → Rauschenbusch (1861-1918) was instrumental in the leadership of early phases of the movement (*Christianizing the Social Order* [1912]; → Liberal Theology 2.2.5; North American Theology 5.2).

In Germany the Evangelisch-soziale Kongreß (Protestant Social Congress), founded in 1890, aimed at reconciliatory policies but had little political influence because it was perceived as being too academic in its discussion of structural and legal changes. In Switzerland → religious socialism (§§3-4) held out hope for the kingdom of God as it was proclaimed by C. Blumhardt (1842-1919), who aligned himself with the Social Democrats. H. Kutter (1863-1931) thought that God's revolution worked through this party (*Sie müssen* [1903]), and L. Ragaz (1868-1945) argued that belief in the → kingdom of God (§3.2.6) would accomplish global change. K. → Barth and E. Brunner (see 1.4.2) were at first influenced by this movement. In his German days P. → Tillich (1886-1965), who emigrated to the United States in 1933, held similar ideas. The German defeat in 1918 was viewed as the *kairos* for the socialist reconstruction demanded by Jesus' → Sermon on the Mount.

1.3. *Various Groundings of Theology*

In the second half of the 19th century, there was a growing need to clarify the foundation of Christian faith, often identified with the quest for religious perception in general.

1.3.1. *Ethical Theology*

A. Ritschl (1822-89) was the most prominent German theologian of his time. He had studied under F. C. Baur, but in the second edition of his *Entstehung der altkatholischen Kirche* (1857) he adopted a less critical stance regarding studies in history compared to speculative understanding. History had to be reduced to the essence of its ethical energies of formation. Regarded as the leader of German → liberal theology (§2.4.4), Ritschl was rather conservative with respect to politics. In his main work, *The Christian Doctrine of Justification and Reconciliation* (3 vols., 1870-74; 3d ed., 1888-89; ET, vol. 1, 1872; vol. 3, 1900 [vol. 2, untranslated]), he developed a Christocentric theology of revelation from the standpoint of the Christian community. Transforming Kant's epistemology (i.e., we can know things only through their effects on us and our response to them), he advocated a knowledge of God that is historically attested in the Bible and appropriated by a "value judgment" (→ Kantianism 1).

Ritschl's system opposed all metaphysical tasks and might be illustrated as an ellipse whose foci are → reconciliation (§4) and the kingdom of God. There is nearly no place for the → wrath of God. → Justification (§2.3.2) is the creative judgment of God that opens humanity for God's kingdom. Against Pietism Ritschl viewed this kingdom as a human organization motivated by love, so that individual piety plays a lesser part. A decisive point is the orientation of the will by reconciliation, so that it fulfills one's vocation *(Beruf),* with God's purpose for the world as the final goal. A combination of Prussian sternness and an optimistic spirit marked Ritschl's conception. He gave a new impetus to the ethicizing of Protestantism.

Followers of Ritschl were J. Kaftan (1848-1926), J. Gottschick (1847-1907), M. Reischle (1858-1905), and W. Herrmann (see 1.3.3), along with many exegetes and historians. Ritschl's theology made an impact, too, upon some Scandinavian and American theologians. The organ for his circle was the *Zeitschrift für Theologie und Kirche,* founded in 1891.

1.3.2. *Culture Protestantism*

A. von Harnack was an outstanding church historian, as well as an able organizer of scholarship in his capacity as director of the Prussian State Library and president of the Kaiser-Wilhelm-Gesellschaft, the most important foundation for research in Germany at that time. He was the widely respected hero of → Culture Protestantism (§2), which merged religious subjectivity, cultivated piety, and liberal attitudes. In *Lehrbuch der Dogmengeschichte* (3 vols., 1886-90; 5th ed., 1931; ET *History of Dogma* [from 3d ed., 7 vols., 1896-99]), he critically evaluated the Hellenistic "metaphysical" elements of the Christian tradition and reduced "dogma" to the pure and nondogmatic form as he found it in Luther and → anti-Trinitarianism. His lectures on the essence of Christianity (ET *What Is Christianity?* [many eds.]) were published in 1900 and represented the liberal Protestant program at the turn of the century. With their stress on humanity they formed a counterpart to *Welträtsel* (1899; ET *Riddle of the Universe* [1929]) of the Darwinist E. Haeckel (1834-1919). In his work Harnack promoted what he called a return to the simple teaching of Jesus, which he identified as the fatherhood of God, divine providence, ourselves as God's children, and the infinite value of the human soul. Religion is the soul of morality (love), and morality is the body of religion. Jesus proclaimed the gospel; he was not its object.

Other important church historians were A. Hauck (1845-1918), who edited the distinguished third edition of the *Realencyclopädie für protestantische Theologie und Kirche* (1896-1913), K. Müller (1852-1940), F. Loofs (1858-1928), R. Seeberg (1859-1935), and A. Ritschl's son O. Ritschl (1860-1944). The journal *Die Christliche Welt* (1886-1941), similar to the *Christian Century* in the United States (since 1900), epitomized Culture Protestantism as it addressed educated people who were active in politics, society, and church.

1.3.3. *Internalization*

Partly following Ritschl, W. Herrmann (1846-1922) based his *Communion of the Christian with God, Described on the Basis of Luther's Statements* (1886; ET 1971) on the *Erleben* (experience) of Jesus' "inner life," that is, an experience that is not subject to empirical scrutiny. Here the perception of justification is transformed into a new sense of personal consciousness of truth freed from metaphysics. It converges with the Kantian-Prussian sense of duty, whose basis is credibility. Individuals truly find their personal and moral life when they are converted by the inner life of Jesus. This change frees them for their own thinking and action in their secular occupations. Along these lines Herrmann opposed both the Roman Catholic faith in authority and pietistic → biblicism. He was a teacher of K. Barth and R. Bultmann and also had an impact upon the Swedish theologians E. Billing (1871-1939), A. Runestam (1887-1962), and A. Nygren (1890-1978).

1.3.4. *Soteriology*
M. Kähler (1835-1912) was an antagonist to Ritschl. He was the only theologian who centered his lifework on a biblical-theological doctrine of justification (*Die Wissenschaft der christlichen Lehre* [3 vols., 1883]). Justification is, according to the gospel, the receiving of God's sovereign reconciling action toward humanity, accomplished by the obedience of Jesus Christ to the First Commandment. Kähler's friend H. Cremer (1834-1903) published a biblical-theological dictionary of NT Greek in relation to Hebrew and Hellenistic texts.

In some respects, Kähler was a pioneer of the new theological beginning after the First World War. He focused on Christ as the *sōtēr*, the Savior, and he was a strong influence on P. Tillich's Christology, which saw Christ as the "new being." Kähler also emphasized the kerygmatic character of the gospel in distinction from its historical reconstruction, which influenced R. Bultmann.

1.3.5. *Facing Historicism*
Troeltsch, a friend of sociologist M. → Weber (1864-1920), interpreted church history as marked by different ethical attitudes toward society. In his view churches try to adjust to common values and therefore abandon subversive hopes; in contrast, sects orientate themselves by an eschatology that denies the present state of affairs (*The Social Teachings of the Christian Church* [1912; ET 1931]). Troeltsch stood for a liberalism that advances culture by its critique of outdated traditions and by affirming creative impulses, which ensure steady development. Progressive revelation shapes religious history, represented best in Christianity in its correspondence with the ongoing evolution of Western culture (*The Absoluteness of Christianity and the History of Religions* [1902; ET 1971]). Revelation within history corresponds with an unconditional affection of the human spirit to the divine ("religious a priori"), which fulfills itself in all cultural spheres. Troeltsch represented an early German version of → public theology.

Troeltsch was also the theoretician of the → history-of-religions school, which interpreted Jesus Christ solely in the terms of his own time und religious culture. J. Weiss (1863-1914), a son-in-law and disciple of Ritschl, drew attention to apocalyptic features in his *Jesus' Proclamation of the Kingdom of God* (1892; ET 1971). A. → Schweitzer (1875-1965) realized that no biographical reconstruction of Jesus' life could represent his message for our time because of his misguided expectation of the imminent end of the world (*Von Reimarus zu Wrede. Eine Geschichte der Leben-Jesu-Forschung* [1906; ET *The Quest of the Historical Jesus* (1910)]). He also asserted, however, that we share with Jesus an enthusiastic and heroic view of the world.

1.4. *Crises, Confrontations, and Breakthroughs*
1.4.1. *A Turning Point*
World War I clearly caused a major crisis all over Europe, including in the church and the academy. In Germany the Weimar Constitution of 1919 separated church and state, but faculties of theology remained parts of the universities. The collapse of nearly all areas of culture compelled many to ask which bases of the culture that were hitherto thought to be valid and capable of development could survive in the new situation. The war also abruptly brought to an end the widespread optimism based on a trust that God could be encountered within the developments of history. In his treatise *Marcion: The Gospel of the Alien God* (2d ed., 1924; ET 1990), Harnack asserted that the loving God of salvation is not responsible for the misery of creation; his activity is to save the perverted world.

R. Otto (1869-1937) tried to establish theology on the paradoxical experience of God as the Wholly Other, the *mysterium tremendum et fascinans*. He thought of this experience as the core of all religion, which comes to universal fulfillment in Christianity (*Das Heilige* [1917; ET *The Idea of the Holy* (1923)]). Here Luther's dialectics of → law and gospel (§1.2) was linked with the history of religion and the theology of experience.

The Swedish scholar and archbishop N. → Söderblom (1866-1931) had thought along the same lines as early as 1914. Söderblom became a leading figure of the ecumenical movement (→ Ecumenism, Ecumenical Movement, 2.6.2.3), which seemed to him and others a sufficient answer to the cultural and religious crisis.

1.4.2. *Dialectical Theology*
→ Dialectical theology — a movement from 1922 to 1933 led by K. Barth (1886-1968), E. Brunner (1889-1966), R. Bultmann (1884-1976), F. Gogarten (1887-1967), and others — vehemently criticized

Culture Protestantism as represented by Harnack and Troeltsch and, in general, → liberal theology (§2.4.5). This movement's rejection of any view of a continuing cultural progress of Christianity was a result of its radical reflection upon the "impossible possibility" of doing theology in general. Barth referred both to the critique by Franz Overbeck (1837-1905) of any synthesis of Christianity and contemporary culture and to his observation that the radical eschatology of Jesus and his followers had been lost even by early Christianity (*How Christian Is Our Present-Day Theology?* [2d ed., 1903; ET 2005]). In his correspondence with his former teacher Harnack (1923), Barth rejected the evaluation of the essence of Christianity by historical reconstruction.

According to Barth, theology always depends on God's effective Word: God has spoken, and God's First Commandment is the axiom of theology. Bultmann's theology centered on the → kerygma (§3), the Word of the cross. God's speaking, his sovereign initiative addressing people "here and now," is the vivid beginning of theology. The starting point of theology requires a critique of all attempts to recall ancient religious experiences and to relate them to the present time, focusing on analogies and similarities of religious subjectivity. The task of theology is therefore to serve God's speaking, to refer to God's self-revelation in Jesus Christ, which endures through time, since God's Word is external to all time and to every human self-reference. Every scientific grounding of theology is excluded.

Dialectic theology also stressed the view that theology as situated in the university is a self-sufficient and coherent academic discipline, not subordinate to the study of religion and its history. Bultmann tried to combine without confusion comparative studies of biblical texts and other religious sources, especially Hellenistic ones, with a strictly theological explanation of the kerygmatic message of the NT. The independence of religion no longer seemed sufficient for establishing theology within the academy.

1.4.3. *The Luther Renaissance*

Another program to reform theology was the Luther renaissance, which centered particularly on the "young Luther," trying to demonstrate the continuity between his insights and the philosophy of religion of German idealism. K. Holl (1866-1926) explained Luther's inner tension between God's judgment and grace in Kantian terms of a religion of conscience (→ Kantianism 1). Fichte's view of the radically independent personality who internalizes God's will through constant moral activity molded the theology of E. Hirsch (1888-1972). Hirsch also

translated and interpreted Kierkegaard's writings and held to a nationalistic contextual theology. He stated that the crisis of 1918 led to the "German year" of 1933, when Hitler seized power, as God's gracious intervention, which he saw as providing a rebuilding of the German state and culture (*Die gegenwärtige Lage im Spiegel philosophischer und theologischer Besinnung* [1934]). God's law discloses itself in the reality that surrounds human life, especially in political structures; in this way it challenges human responsibility nurtured by the conscience that is informed by the inwardly received gospel. Hirsch thus eliminated Luther's basic distinction between → law and gospel (§1.3).

Quite another type of Luther scholarship was carried on by R. Hermann (1887-1962), who explored the temporality of the human creature ("I am my time") and related self-perception to prayer, where God's gracious time and justifying promise embrace the time that was lost to sin (*Luthers These "Gerecht und Sünder zugleich"* [1930]). He was the teacher of H. J. Iwand (1899-1960), who later followed Barth in the → church struggle (§3). He, along with H. Vogel (1902-89), became a leading theologian in the Confessing Church, and his work was formative for → preaching in Germany.

In Sweden the Luther renaissance was more interested in church reform. Its most important representative was E. Billing, who taught that the atoning work of Christ creates confidence for the personal struggle of faith and is the center of the drama of salvation. On this basis he sought an ecclesiology that promotes the people's church (*folkkyrkan)*, largely as an alternative both to the High Church movement and to the sects.

1.4.4. *Agreement and Dissent*

In the 1920s the theological breakthrough revolving around Barth in Germany was noticed and acclaimed especially in Switzerland, the Netherlands, Scotland, Hungary, and Czechoslovakia. In France renewed interest in Calvinism fostered E. Doumergue's (1844-1937) biography of Calvin (7 vols., 1899-1927). A. Lecerf (1872-1943) was both a rigid Calvinist and a meticulous observer of contemporary thought. P. Maury (1890-1956) introduced the theology of Barth, especially through the journal *Foi et vie*. Barth found a quick entry into the Netherlands through the writings of T. L. Haitjema (1888-1972; *Karl Barths "Kritische" Theologie* [1926]) and K. H. Miskotte (1894-1976). He also found a critic in G. C. Berkouwer (1903-96), who opposed him in his *Karl Barth* (1936) but who still learned a great deal from him for his own dogmatic work (see 1.5.3). Lutheran and Reformed theologians also drew on the works of Barth in many countries, for example, R. Hauge (1903-67) in Norway and N. H. Søe (1895-1978) in Denmark. The Danish movement around the journal *Tidehverv* (turn of the times) in the 1920s followed Kierkegaard, Barth, and Bultmann.

Scotland had a pioneering Barth in P. T. Forsyth (1848-1921), who, with learning and passion, proclaimed the priority of God and the supreme greatness of both God's wrath and God's love as revealed on Golgotha. H. R. Mackintosh (1870-1936), who had studied under W. Herrmann and translated Schleiermacher, was another theologian who came under Barthian influence in his later years. G. T. Thomson initiated a translation of Barth's *Church Dogmatics* that was continued under the leadership of T. F. Torrance (b. 1913) and G. W. Bromiley (b. 1915). This effort helped to give new vitality to the church's thought and work in Scotland, as well as in other English-speaking countries.

Not all Scottish theologians, however, were under Barth's influence. J. Denney (1856-1917) was not, who had earlier expounded Romans (1900) and written *The Death of Christ* (1903). J. Baillie (1886-1960) was both an apologist and an ecumenist, and his brother, D. M. Baillie (1887-1954), wrote one of the most significant works on Christology of the day (*God Was in Christ* [1948]). The Baillies welcomed Barth with reservations, just as they were indebted to their legacy from Calvin, but they still pursued their own paths. In England and the United States reservations toward Barth at first prevailed.

Brunner was much respected abroad because of his modified affirmation of → natural theology (§2.2; *Nature and Grace* [1934; ET 1946]), which was strictly rejected by Barth (*No!* [1934; ET 1946]). Brunner also conceived of a doctrine of revelation based on dialogue and, furthermore, projected an ethics of "the orders [*Ordnungen, Stände*] of society," which include family, state, and economics (*Wahrheit als Begegnung* [1938; ET *The Divine-Human Encounter* (1943)], *Das Gebot und die Ordnungen* [1932; ET *The Divine Imperative* (1937)], and *Gerechtigkeit* [1943; ET *Justice and the Social Order* (1945)]).

In Sweden G. Aulén (1879-1977) referred to Luther in picturing history as a drama in which the love of God was victorious against the forces of evil, and he found an inward reflection of this drama in steadfast and courageous faith. Talk of God's love, furthermore, is symbolic, so that space is left for historical criticism. Love creates and directs fellowship. The incarnation and crucifixion of Jesus achieve reconciliation, which through faith leads to love as

active concern for the neighbor, the critical principle of action.

The methodological work of A. Nygren (1890-1978) had a formally critical basis in philosophy, which describes the conditions of the possibility of religious and moral experience. The content of such experience derives either from God or from our own authority; therefore, this content must be found by historical evaluation. In Christianity this dominant motif is divine *agapē* love, in contrast both to the Jewish *nomos* (law) and to the Greek *erōs* love. For Christians, human love is due directly to God, which constitutes an ethics of motive (selfishness spoils every other type). Nygren's sharp antithesis between *agapē* and *erōs* underlay his criticism of the social Darwinism of National Socialism. The historicist tendency of the Lund school (Aulén, Nygren, and R. Bring [1895-1990]) laid the ground for the positivist inclinations of the next generation of Swedish theologians (see 1.6.4).

German Lutherans who were conservative both theologically and politically, including W. Elert (1885-1954) and P. Althaus (1888-1966), did not accept dialectical theology. Both of these scholars were suspicious of the Reformed elements in Barth's way of doing theology and rejected his doctrine of the exclusiveness of the revelation in Christ. Althaus pointed to a primordial revelation in nature and history to which both heart and conscience bear witness. This position agrees with an ethics of duty that receives its content from the command of God given by the third (ethical) use of the → law. To find it, we are referred to the orders of creation, though they came under the influence of sin. Elert argued against the exclusiveness of a view of the Christian kerygma that alone can create faith; for him, the gospel must be accompanied by the law as a word of judgment (→ Law and Gospel 4.1).

1.4.5. The Clash with National Socialism

As a result of the political reorganization in Germany after World War I, a revision of the relationship of → church and state (§2.5), as well as a reorientation of the church, was urgently needed, especially in the structure of the Protestant territorial churches (Landeskirchen) and by endeavors for establishing their institutional unity. In consequence of the National Socialist proposal to establish this unity in a Reichskirche based on a nationalistic religion, church leaders and theologians were challenged to clarify the nature of the life and organization of the church. The answer was given by the → Barmen Declaration (1934), which also led to a substantial theological consensus (→ Church Struggle 3). It was much more than a front line against the → German Christians (Deutsche Christen) and their nationalistic contextual theology, which stressed the unity of race and German cultural history. The Nazi regime silenced and expelled critical voices in the churches and in the faculties of theology, mostly systematic and practical theologians. During the church struggle the Confessing Church (Bekennende Kirche) founded seminaries that could exist only illegally. Two journals close to the Confessing Church were founded: *Evangelische Theologie* in 1934, and *Verkündigung und Forschung* in 1940.

In 1934 W. Elert composed the Ansbacher Ratschlag in reply to the Barmen Declaration, in which he linked the law of God to the people as a nation, to race, and to family as natural orders. F. Gogarten welcomed the totalitarian execution of the "law of the people" by the National Socialist state. The neo-Lutheran → two-kingdoms doctrine, as promoted, for example, by Troeltsch, had divided reason and faith: reason is responsible for the well-being of the world, and faith grasps salvation. This dichotomy caused confusion among German confessional Lutherans, as well as among liberals. Luther's doctrine of the two "rules" or sovereignties (Ger. *Regimente*) of God — the spiritual ruling, carried to faith by the proclamation of the gospel, and the worldly ruling, limited by God's preservation of the creation, governed by law and power to protect the helpless and to serve the needs of the people — inspired the resistance of the Norwegian bishop E. Berggrav (1884-1959) against the Nazi collaborator V. Quisling.

1.4.6. *After the Great Depression*

The crisis in the aftermath of World War I was delayed in the United States. The outcome of the war seemed to support belief in progress. Social problems increased, but the Social Gospel seemed able to address them. It was the economic crisis of 1929, the Great Depression, that called this optimism into question. R. → Niebuhr (1892-1971), teaching at Union Theological Seminary in New York, saw the situation most clearly (*Moral Man and Immoral Society* [1932]). In his view the root of social problems is individual egoism increasing to collective egoism, which can be overcome only by a relative justice, by a fluid balancing of power in which freedom and equality are in equilibrium. Love needs expression through institutions. Niebuhr reinforced his analysis by an Augustinian and Lutheran doctrine of sin as hubris, but also by adopting K. Mannheim's (1893-1947) universal concept of ideology that accompanies all claims to absolute knowledge made in the various interests of power. A failure to achieve a

social actualization of love causes unavoidable guilt, which forces humans to choose lesser evils and always to stand in need of divine forgiveness. In society knowledge of our own errors should lead us to forgive the errors of others and to promote tolerance (*The Nature and Destiny of Man* [2 vols., 1941-43]). Based on his modified two-kingdoms doctrine, Niebuhr was in favor of America's entering the war in 1941. He was an enormous influence on theological and political thinking in the United States.

His younger brother, H. R. Niebuhr (1894-1962), who taught at Yale Divinity School, tried to achieve a synthesis of Barth and Troeltsch. As a church sociologist (*The Kingdom of God in America* [1937] and *Christ and Culture* [1951]) and ethicist, he viewed the present situation in the light of the revelation of Christ but also from the angle of the experiencing subject and the circumstances of his or her life. For an interactive society he developed an ethics of → responsibility (§3) that addresses individuals as consenting to God's acting in history and relates them to other people and to a common "cause" (J. Royce). Niebuhr stressed particularly a Calvinistic shaping of society (*The Responsible Self* [1963]).

1.4.7. *Uniting Tendencies and Growing Pluralism*

World War I had helped the North American Lutherans to come together (United Lutheran Church, 1918; National Lutheran Council, 1918; American Lutheran Church, 1930; → Lutheran Churches 3.1). Unions were taking place also in other denominations, although at this same time pluralism was growing. The Holiness and → Pentecostal churches, along with other groups (e.g., → Jehovah's Witnesses), were also growing by leaps and bounds, and so too, as African Americans moved into industrial cities, were → black churches (§1.5), which took up the struggle against racial discrimination. Secularization and pluralism began to have an impact upon social and cultural life, though the number of church members remained stable. Private religion was on the increase, but so too was → civil religion (§3). These factors all posed a great challenge to the North American Protestant churches and were an occasion for theologians to think about a new political Christian realism.

1.5. *Continuation and Revision*

1.5.1. *New Beginning or Reconstruction?*

No theological breakthrough took place after 1945 similar to that which occurred in the decade after World War I. Most theologians tried to continue the theology that had proved itself under challenging or oppressing circumstances, although clarifications and critical adjustments were needed. In the Stuttgart Declaration (October 1945) prominent German Protestant church leaders confessed the guilt of the German people and church; many wounds needed healing. In Germany the reorganization of the faculties of theology was pressing and was guided largely by the idea of resuming traditions that seemed not to have been affected by the ideological turmoil of the preceding 12 years. Only gradually was communication restored between German theologians and those of other countries, and communication by theologians in Eastern Europe with colleagues in the West was restricted during the first decades of the cold war. In addition, theologians in Poland, Czechoslovakia, and Hungary were often afraid of Western liberal tendencies, which were considered devastating to an already endangered church life.

The division of Europe and the cold war affected theology and the churches in many ways. In the East some church officials and theologians affirmed the political changes and accepted the goals of building up socialism. In Hungary, after the 1956 uprising had gone wrong, a "theology of service" called for the support of socialism as obedience to Christian faith because ultimate social justice and world peace were equated with the kingdom of God. Critical Hungarian voices such as I. Török (1904-96) and E. Vályi-Nagy (1924-93) were suppressed. In Czechoslovakia J. Hromádka (1889-1969), who had taught in Princeton during the German occupation of the Czech Republic, stressed the involvement of church and theology in critical social, even socialistic, engagement and was one of the founders of the Prague Christian Peace Conference. In Hungary (E. Kocsis [b. 1926]) and East Germany (H. Müller [b. 1925]), there were some attempts to construct theology in accordance with socialism, but with very limited success. In West Germany the left wing of the former Confessing Church opposed the ties of the government to Western nations, especially to the United States, and searched for reconciliation with the people of the East and for a recognition of urgently needed national changes, even revolutionary ones (→ Darmstadt Declaration, 1947).

1.5.2. Secularism

After 1948 the sometimes fierce debate on → "demythologizing" was the dominating topic in Germany and beyond. The controversy between Barthians and Bultmannians intensified. Barth accused Bultmann of a relapse into a neo-Protestant subjectivity that reduces the extent of God's revelation to the liberating change of human self-understanding. Bultmann and his followers found Barth's theology lacking hermeneutical clarification, maintaining an outdated realism.

In 1951 the publication of the letters and papers from prison of D. → Bonhoeffer (1906-45), who was executed because of his resistance against the Nazi regime, intensified the awareness of progressing → secularization and → secularism, fueled especially by his statement about a → religionless Christianity. F. Gogarten (*Despair and Hope for Our Time* [1953; ET 1970]) interpreted this idea in a twofold way: on the one hand, secularization is a replacement of the mythological order of the world, leading to true "worldliness" (and thus it is a Christian heritage); on the other hand, it is a transformation of Christian conceptions into secularism, that is, the substitution of contingent history for the idea of progress joined with utopian thinking that distorts pure hope.

In his dissertation, *Sanctorum Communio* (1930), Bonhoeffer had first elaborated the social dimension of the reality centered in Christ, which is Christ living as community. In *Ethics* (1949; new ed., 1992; ET 1995, 2005) he emphasized the point that Christ has also bound himself to all the reality of the world, which is how we should understand the mandates of church, state, family, and culture (→ Social Ethics). The orders of creation are subject to changing social structures, and Christ vicariously bears our guilt. In his letters and papers from prison Bonhoeffer stated that Christ cannot be known externally and that religion must come under criticism. We modern people must live before God as if God were not there.

In the 1960s this line of thinking was radicalized in the United States by → God-is-dead theology, which asserted either a death of the cultural self-evidence of the consciousness of God (G. Vahanian [b. 1927]) or God's dying on the cross for the sake of the liberation of humanity (T. J. J. Altizer [b. 1927]). The Anglican J. A. T. Robinson (1919-83) saw similarly radical consequences for "God talk" in a secularized society (→ Theology in the Nineteenth and Twentieth Centuries 4.2.5). The German D. Soelle (1929-2003), who had studied under Gogarten, held that Jesus was acting for God and asks us to do the same by taking over God's suffering and compassion.

1.5.3. Theology between or beyond Historicism and Existentialism?

In the 1950s and 1960s attention was more often paid to Barth's firm stand criticizing political and ecclesial restoration, to his tendency to check the credibility of theological statements by ethical options, or to his critique of church practices (e.g., infant baptism) than to other details of his voluminous, although incomplete, *Church Dogmatics* (4 parts in 12 vols., 1932-67; ET 1936-77). Here he started with the perception of the Word of God as God's self-revelation in Jesus Christ, the biblical witness, and the proclamation of the church (→ Theology 3.7.1). Barth characterized the Trinity as God's active relations and election as the sovereign activity of God's grace prior to all time. Christian thinking, to Barth, must therefore be judged by God's revelation in Christ. Moreover, Barth's comprehensive discussion of creation, anthropology, and providence; of the various aspects of reconciliation, justification, and sanctification; of the church and its mission; and of Christian faith, love, and hope enriched many theologians, pastors, and laity in their spiritual and intellectual lives and in their work and ministry. His work attracted a remarkably lively ecumenical and international response.

Reacting to Barth, the Dutch G. C. Berkouwer analyzed what he saw as an imbalance of the doctrines of grace and sin in Barth's work (*The Triumph of Grace in the Theology of Karl Barth* [1954; ET 1956]). His fellow countrymen K. H. Miskotte and O. Noordmans (1871-1956) presented the combination of pastoral theology and intense theological meditation in the proven Dutch Reformed tradition. H. M. Kuitert (b. 1924), a disciple of Berkouwer, based theology on a human searching for God by experiencing meaning and acting meaningfully.

In Denmark R. Prenter (1907-90) combined the reception of Lutheran confessions with biblical-theological insights in his dogmatics (*Creation and Redemption* [2 vols., 1951-53; ET 1967]). K. E. Løgstrup (1905-81) developed his reflection on revelation in debate with Kierkegaard and Grundtvig (see 1.1.2), adopted a phenomenologically based ethics of spontaneous life-expression (*The Ethical Demand* [1956; ET 1971]), and presented a descriptive philosophy of creation that interprets basic experiences (e.g., the annihilation that is part of creation and the irreversibility of time) in a religious and Christian way. With his work, which embraced many fields of learning, as well as art and literature, Løgstrup influenced Danish culture.

The Swede G. Wingren (1910-2000) criticized Barth from a viewpoint that is characteristic of a strand of Scandinavian theology, namely, one that connects the dramatic elements of patristic theology and Luther's theology and embeds the doctrine of salvation in the task of the church to preserve the endangered creation by God's law (*Theology in Conflict: Nygren, Barth, Bultmann* [1954; ET 1958], *Creation and Law* [1958; ET 1961], and *Gospel and*

Church [1960; ET 1964]; → Law and Gospel 4.2). The German Lutheran C. H. Ratschow (1911-99) carried on a dialogue between German and Scandinavian theologians. He also gathered a group of German Lutheran theologians who cooperated in producing a series of handbooks of systematic theology. The topics were developed by comparing the theology of the Reformers with representative recent conceptions. Ratschow also called for Christian theology to give greater attention to the world religions (→ Theology of Religions).

In the late 1950s and 1960s → hermeneutics promised to offer a link between all areas of theology, in Germany often according to the scheme "from (biblical) text to preaching" (→ Proclamation 5). There were various threads. In Germany E. Fuchs (1903-83; *Hermeneutik* [1954]) and G. Ebeling (1912-2001; *Word and Faith* [vol. 1, 1960; ET 1963] and *Introduction to a Theological Theology of Language* [1971; ET 1973]) were close to Bultmann and took up the ontology of language of the later M. Heidegger (1889-1976), showing that the kerygma evokes a "language-event." E. Jüngel (b. 1934), a disciple of Fuchs, has tried to mediate between Bultmann and Barth. J. Macquarrie (1919-2007) transferred Heidegger's existentialism to English and North American theology (*Principles of Christian Theology* [1966]).

In the United States H. Frei (1922-88) at Yale developed hermeneutics further toward a profound → narrative theology (§2). The Lutheran R. F. Thiemann has argued that God's promise acts in the biblical narrative in such a way that God encounters the reader or hearer, causing the shattering of his or her contextual self-understanding and creating a new context; text and context are dialectically and asymmetrically related (*Revelation and Theology: The Gospel as Narrated Promise* [1985]). The relation between the theology of revelation and narrative theology also has forged links between British and German theologians (*Revelation and Story: Narrative Theology and the Centrality of Story* [ed. J. Barton and G. Sauter, 2000]).

The Mennonite G. D. Kaufman (b. 1925) at Harvard understands the term "historicist" as giving tools to Christian theology to interpret the meaning of history and human "historicity" as supported by the concepts of the Christian tradition (*Systematic Theology: A Historicist Perspective* [1968]). As a point of orientation Kaufman takes the central Christian symbol "God" and relates it to images of God based on human experience (*The Theological Imagination: Constructing the Concept of God* [1981]). In the radically new situation of the nuclear age, theology can be appropriate only as "imaginative construction." We must have a view of God as the reality that has brought us into life and that constantly upholds us (*Theology for a Nuclear Age* [1985] and *In the Face of Mystery: A Constructive Theology* [1993]).

1.5.4. *Philosophical Theology*

When the German translation of P. → Tillich's (1886-1965) *Systematic Theology* (3 vols., 1951-63) was published, it seemed to be the golden mean between Barth und Bultmann (→ Theology 3.7.3). But Tillich's refusal to identify with either neoorthodoxy or liberalism in the United States was misunderstood when simply transferred to the debate in Germany. Tillich, however, brought some aspects of a North American critical theology of culture (see 1.4.6) to Europe. While under the influence of Bultmann and his school, nearly all the philosophical interest of theologians was concentrated on the existentialism of M. Heidegger. Tillich again opened up the critical reception of German idealism, especially to its religious philosophy of history (F. W. J. Schelling). He based his theology on a philosophy of religion that combined idealism and existentialism; for Tillich, all being derives from the ground of being and symbolically points to it (→ Symbol 2.3). Within the "theological circle," however, the insights of reason raise questions, and faith responds to them. This correlation rests on an ontological correlation of being and self-being (i.e., God). All that is, has its foundation in God but has become alienated from God, and only the love of God set forth in Christ can bring reconciliation. When people share in the new being in the Spirit, whatever they do is entangled in ambiguity, and the solution may be found symbolically at each moment *(kairos)* but will finally come only in the *eschaton*.

1.5.5. *Biblical Theology*

In the period after World War II the OT gained new significance, having often been neglected and even despised, above all in Germany during the Third Reich. The German Christians had repudiated the OT, and Bultmann later interpreted it as a "document of failure" in the quest for salvation; he followed an extreme Lutheran division of law and gospel. A fresh look at the OT, especially its stories and its prophecy, led to a discovery of its importance for theology in general (G. von Rad [1901-71] and W. Zimmerli [1907-84]; in the Netherlands, A. A. van Ruler [1908-70]). OT research became an inquiry that was innovative for many fields of theology. It also influenced systematic theologians (e.g., W. Pannenberg) who wanted to overcome the ban

against a theology of history invoked by dialectical theology. In the Netherlands van Ruler promoted a theology of Christian culture with reference to theocracy and the activity of the Holy Spirit.

As understood by von Rad and others, → biblical theology (§§1.3.3-4) to a certain extent showed itself to be a rehabilitation of the conception of salvation history (Heilsgeschichte). It fostered an approach to the unity of the Bible as canon (B. S. Childs [1923-2007]), understood as the set of texts the early church received as the reliable and binding testimony of God's faithfulness. The canon therefore is and remains the primary source for the life of the church and its search for truth. The procedure of distinguishing canonical texts from noncanonical ones was not an arbitrary decision of the early church (e.g., as a means of establishing its own authority) but a faithful recognition of the complex coherence of human answers to God's revelation. M. Noth (1902-68) and H. W. Wolff (1911-93) established the Biblischer Kommentar–Altes Testament (Biblical Commentary of the OT, since 1955). In 1986 an international editorial board started the *Jahrbuch für Biblische Theologie*. F. Mildenberger (b. 1929) integrates biblical theology in his *Biblische Dogmatik* (3 vols., 1991-93).

1.5.6. *Eschatology*

New interest in → eschatology (§§3.4 and 7) was partially stimulated by new insights into the theology of the OT. O. Cullmann (1902-99) advocated an eschatology based on salvation history that was understood as a linear passage of time planned by God for the purpose of carrying out God's plan for salvation (*Salvation in History* [1965; ET 1967]). W. Pannenberg (b. 1928) is interested in an apocalyptic view of "universal history"; he interprets the Easterevent as the proleptic revelation and historical validation of the meaning of history (*Revelation as History* [1961; ET 1968] and *Grundzüge der Christologie* [1964; ET *Jesus, God and Man* (1968)]; → Theology 3.7.5). Pannenberg and NT scholar E. Käsemann (1906-98), a disciple of Bultmann, and others like Cullmann have rejected Bultmann's interpretation of salvation as the new self-understanding of the faithful (→ Eschatology 7.3), which seems to dissolve all contents of Christian hope. It also destroys an awareness of real history, viewed by Käsemann and J. Moltmann (b. 1926) as driven by dramatic tensions and clashes that cause real catastrophes. Moltmann has been stimulated also by A. A. van Ruler and by the neo-Marxist philosopher E. Bloch (1885-1977), who in his *Principle of Hope* (1969; ET 1986) had affirmed that the God of the exodus will lead us out of the misery of the present to the promised land of ultimate justice, fulfilled life, and reconciliation of humanity with nature.

In his influential *Theology of Hope* (1964; ET 1967), Moltmann interpreted God's promises as goals given and supported by God to be seized in "real possibilities" as chances to revolutionize social life and political structures. Salvation and happiness, the kingdom of God and → utopia, are combined on a Trinitarian basis, namely, God in the crucified Christ has taken to God's self the plight of the world (see 1.5.7). G. Sauter (b. 1935) argues that God always reserves further action for himself in the future and yet casts a hint of that future action into the present as promise (*Zukunft und Verheißung* [1965] and *Eschatological Rationality* [1993]).

In the United States, C. E. Braaten (b. 1929) has called attention to the relation of eschatology and history (*The Future of God: The Revolutionary Dynamics of Hope* [1969]), and R. W. Jenson (b. 1930) has stated that Barth's later theology was missing a leading eschatological directive (*God after God: The God of the Past and the God of the Future* [1969]); both scholars together wrote *The Futurist Option* (1970). The English Methodist G. Wainwright (b. 1939), who is teaching at Duke Divinity School (Durham, N.C.), has explored the eschatological dimension of the Eucharist (*Eucharist and Eschatology* [1971]).

1.5.7. Divergences in Christology

After 1953, inquiries about the "historical Jesus" became a prevailing tendency in reflections on → Christology (§6.2; see J. M. Robinson [b. 1924], *A New Quest of the Historical Jesus* [1959]). Dialectical theology had rejected this question as misleading in any attempt to recognize, for memory or proclamation, the kerygmatic Jesus Christ. Bultmann had stated that only the facts of Jesus' having come and his death on the cross were both historically reliable and theologically sufficient grounds for Christian theology. Now G. Ebeling and E. Fuchs, followers of Bultmann, asked for more clues and found them in the *Verhalten* of Jesus, that is, in Jesus' understanding of his existence — for example, in expressions of his special relationship to God like prayer and authoritative proclamation, in his freedom and acts of love. This approach was reminiscent of W. Herrmann (see 1.3.3) and his attempt to outline a specific encounter with Jesus that is *geschichtlich* (a Ger. expression similar to "historic," to be distinguished from "historicist") but must not be historically objectified or psychologically explained.

Another Christological approach was a Trinitarian "theology of the cross," highlighting God's identification with the crucified and seemingly God-forsaken Jesus. Here God reveals God's self in a way that sets aside theistic as well as atheistic views (E. Jüngel, *God as Mystery of the World* [1977; ET 1983]). Also the crucifixion has been interpreted as God's compassion with human suffering (J. Moltmann, *The Crucified God* [1972; ET 1974]). The English Baptist P. Fiddes argues that God involves God's self in human suffering (*The Creative Suffering of God* [1992]).

Partly influenced by an intensified → Jewish-Christian dialogue, → messianism (§1) is regarded as a common ground of Judaism and Christianity (e.g., J. Moltmann, *The Way of Jesus Christ: Christology in Messianic Dimensions* [1989; ET 1990]), expecting the consummation of the unredeemed and perverted world (see 1.6.7).

1.6. Doing Theology under New Conditions and Requirements?

1.6.1. Reflecting the "Context" of Doing Theology

In the 1960s a wave of protest, radical criticism, and emancipation shook Mexico, the United States, and western Europe. It influenced theology in many, often indirect ways. Social relations were integrated into historical research, and psychology and psychoanalysis interpreted piety and theological ideas by reconstructing often-hidden personal motivations, interests, and conflicts. Linguistics expanded or even substituted for hermeneutics. Reception theories (→ Literary Criticism 11) enriched and sometimes confused biblical interpretation, homiletics, and Christian education.

The civil rights movement and various other liberating tendencies in U.S. society brought about a turning point in the relationship between North American and European, especially German, theology. A new sensitivity for the "context" of doing theology arose in theology. It was, and is, directed toward particular cultural heritages, toward race and gender, and toward facing the impact of economic conditions and the structure of social life on Christian theology. In some respects this movement placed social theory and linguistic studies ahead of philosophy as the first and foremost dialogue partner of theology in the academy. At the same time, the interest of North American theologians in having exchanges with their European counterparts, which had been shaping theology in the United States for more than two centuries, declined. The last representative document of the former exchange were the three volumes *New Frontiers in Theology: Discussions among Continental and American Theologians* (1959-63), edited by J. M. Robinson and J. B. Cobb (b. 1925). Since the 1960s theology in the United States has become more self-confident and self-sufficient. It has started to encourage and to shape theology in the so-called → Third World.

Sociopolitical analysis, programs of social ethics, and → political theology (§5; J. Moltmann, D. Soelle) seemed to supersede not only the existentialism of Bultmann and his school but the existentialist mood that had shaped Western culture for more than four decades. For a relatively short period in the 1960s, there was a halting dialogue between → Marxism and Christianity (§§3-6), abruptly ended in 1968 by the violent Soviet suppression of the "Prague Spring" and the Czech struggle for democracy. A so-called hermeneutic of suspicion inveighed against "ideological" prejudices, replacing any hermeneutic of understanding and renewing the former criticisms of religion (→ Religion, Criticism of, 1).

Reflection on contextual conditions of doing theology (→ Contextual Theology) became especially relevant. P. L. Lehmann (1906-94) introduced the term "context" into Christian ethics, asking, "What am I, as a believer in Jesus Christ and as a member of his church, to do?" (*Ethics in a Christian Context* [1963] 25). Lehmann argued that every faithful answer requires a perception of God's work in its whole scope. But soon the term "context" was interpreted as a particular environment, often called a "situation," but then, more inclusively, the world as a whole, especially conditions of oppression that call for radical changes. "Context" characterized the quintessence of the interrelationships of life and activity that illuminate and determine all ways of thinking, reflection, and expression, as well as all sorts of texts. In this way "contextual theology" significantly changed biblical studies, historical theology, Christian ethics, and all fields of practical theology, not only in North America, but all over the world. It promised to restructure theology from the ground up and to provide a new way of doing theology in general.

1.6.2. *Theology and the Humanities*
In respect to the relation between theology and other sciences, there has been widespread suspicion that theology has not been able to address the whole scope of human reality and has lost contact with basic elements of the human experience. Some solitary voices had pleaded for a combination, for example, of psychology of religion and systematic theology (G. Wobbermin [1869-1943], *Systematische Theologie nach religionspsychologischer Methode* [3 vols., 1913-25]) or of psychoanalysis and pastoral counseling (O. Pfister [1873-1956], *Analytische Seelsorge* [1927]), and Tillich had pointed to the importance

of psychotherapy for pastoral care. But the demarcation of theology from other sciences had mostly been clear and undisputed.

Now, however, there seemed to be an urgent need for an "empirical" foundation, especially of theological ethics and practical theology. Since the 1970s much has been borrowed from social sciences (→ Sociology), → pedagogy (§3), → psychology (§5), → psychoanalysis, and → psychotherapy, though often without adequate theoretical reflection (→ Everyday Life 3; Sociology of Churches; Sociology of Religion). Often the alleged results of the humanities were adapted and reformulated using a semireligious language. For example, the nondirective psychotherapy of C. R. Rogers (1902-87, *Client-Centered Therapy* [1951]) was sometimes simplistically accepted by theologians and pastors, first in the United States, then in Western Europe. Pastors were often unable to see the difference between the church's task of pastoral care and therapeutic efforts. A more nuanced discussion of pastoral care was required, and a way had to be found to relate it to the theoretical presuppositions of S. Freud, C. G. Jung, and others (see D. van Deusen Hunsinger, *Theology and Pastoral Counseling: A New Interdisciplinary Approach* [1995]; → Pastoral Care 3 and 5; Pastoral Psychology).

Other branches of theology were also subject to change through their contact with other disciplines. Biblical exegesis started to deal with sociological and psychological theories (→ Depth-Psychological Exegesis; Sociohistorical Exegesis). Systematic, ethical, and ecclesiological discussion gave attention to → functionalism and the structural theory of systems. A linguistic turn since the 1970s radicalized hermeneutics (→ Linguistics 4).

1.6.3. *Theology under Discussion*
The tendencies as outlined above in 1.6.1 and 1.6.2 caused an enormous diversity of understandings of Christian theology. Is it an academic field where conceptions are represented as related to gender, race, different environments, and so forth? In the United States and Europe, God-is-dead theology understood itself as a response to secularism, reducing the theological spectrum (T. Altizer, *The Gospel of Christian Atheism* [1966]). → Black theology was linked to the black power movement and was embedded in the → black churches (§1.6; J. H. Cone [b. 1938], *Black Theology and Black Power* [1969]; → North American Theology 10.1). It castigated discrimination against blacks and relativized the dominant white theology.

→ Feminist theology (§2) radically opposed white male theology and the patriarchalism of the biblical and Christian heritage (E. Schüssler-Fiorenza [b. 1938], *In Memory of Her: A Feminist Theological Reconstruction of Christian Origins* [1983]). It saw itself as part of → liberation theology (S. D. Welch, *Communities of Resistance and Solidarity: A Feminist Theology of Liberation* [1985]), where liberation was understood as the claim of all people who are or feel oppressed by the status quo of culture, social life, economic conditions, and, last but not least, traditional academic standards and hierarchical structures.

Since the 1970s the so-called New Christian Right has taken issue with a society that had adjusted the Christian faith to a secular worldview ("The Hartford Appeal for Theological Affirmation" [1975], *Against the World for the World* [ed. P. L. Berger and R. J. Neuhaus, 1976]; → Conservatism 2.1 and 2.3). The New Evangelicals (e.g., H. J. Ockenga [1905-85] and C. F. H. Henry [1913-2003]) were also at work theologically and organizationally to make their voices heard and to influence the public (→ Electronic Church). The Pentecostal churches and the → charismatic movement (§§2-3) highlighted spiritual experiences and demonstrated an "oral culture" and theological deficiencies (K. McDonnel, *The Holy Spirit and Power* [1975]). These trends were taken up in other parts of the world, although not nearly as extensively as in the United States.

These particular theologies differed primarily in their views about how to do theology. "Doing theology" became an often-controversial theme, especially between theologians coming from different parts of the world (e.g., at ecumenical consultations held 1972-74 in Bossey, Switzerland, and published in *Doing Theology Today* [ed. C.-S. Song, 1976]). When Christian theology was explained as merely a function of cultural or culture-critical processes, it could be subordinated under other academic disciplines such as, for example, sociology of religion or political science. The result of this tendency is that theology itself could eventually be replaced, as has begun to happen in the United States and Great Britain, where departments of theology or chairs for teaching theology in departments of religion or in colleges founded by churches have been integrated into departments of the academic or comparative study of religion (→ Theological Education). In Sweden dogmatics was allied with philosophy of religion and at times merged into the study of the "philosophy of life" *(livsåskådning)*, which goes beyond Christianity. In addition, the growing interest in comparative studies seemed to support a revitalization of religion outside the churches, either in

discovering a new awareness of transcendence (P. L. Berger [b. 1929], *A Rumor of Angels: Modern Society and the Rediscovery of the Supernatural* [1969]) or in reclaiming "religion" as a universal phenomenon grounded in the basis of humanity (→ Religion 2.1).

The loss of theology as a coherent and unifying academic discipline, which has had negative consequences for church leadership and other areas, has been harshly criticized, for example, by T. C. Oden (b. 1931) in *Requiem* (1995). In Germany the Wissenschaftliche Gesellschaft für Theologie (Academic Society for Theology) was founded in 1974 as a forum that supports the exchange of theological inquiry.

1.6.4. The Foundations, Structure, and Character of Theology

Partly provoked by the unclear state of doing theology, the debate resumed on theology as a self-sufficient, independent academic discipline and as a science in a broad sense open for dialogue with other sciences. Sometimes it followed the questions debated early in the 20th century (see 1.4.2), but now there were various gateways. In interdisciplinary work, especially in the field of → language and theology, methodology began to play a major role (→ Philosophy of Science 2-3; Theology 3.7.8). → Analytic philosophy (§2.3) was authoritative in the debate in Sweden (A. Nygren, *Meaning and Method* [1972]; → European Theology [Modern Period] 1.2.3.3), as well as for studies in religious → language (I. U. Dalferth, *Theology and Philosophy* [2d ed., 2001]). This approach stood in opposition to hermeneutical theology in its existentialistic version. Simultaneously, G. Ebeling began to advance hermeneutics toward a → fundamental theology (§4) and a systematic theology based on the "basic situation" of humans, found in the elementary human relation to God's speaking, in which language exercises its threefold function: to contradict, to promise, and to correspond (*Dogmatik des christlichen Glaubens* [3 vols., 1979]).

W. Pannenberg attempts to integrate data from the humanities into a comprehensive religious awareness (*Anthropology in Theological Perspective* [1983; ET 1985]), which must be distinguished from the perception of God as explained in a Trinitarian-structured theology (*Systematic Theology* [3 vols., 1988-93; ET 1991-99]). Other major works of systematic theology also reflect on God's "triune identity" (the title of a 1982 work by R. W. Jenson; see also his *Systematic Theology* [2 vols., 1997-99]) or choose a Trinitarian approach (T. C. Oden, *Systematic Theology* [3 vols., 1987-94]). In the United States inquiries into the linguistic constitution of theology have led to a debate on "foundationalism" and "antifoundationalism" (see S. Grenz and J. Franke, *Beyond Foundationalism: Shaping Theology in a Postmodern Context* [2000]; F. L. Shults, *The Postfoundationalist Task of Theology: Wolfhart Pannenberg and the New Theological Rationality* [1999]).

The North American discussion concerning "postliberal" or "postmodern" theology has emerged as another significant development (→ Postmodernism 3). Both liberalism and modernity are viewed as quasi-totalitarian conceptions of a unified cultural world scientifically established. In opposition to constructive postmodern thinking, as in → process philosophy (§3) and → process theology (§3), a destructive postmodern model has developed that rejects any idea of nonlinguistic reality. M. C. Taylor's *Deconstructing Theology* (1982) finds no place for otherworldly transcendence. God has fully incarnated himself into the material of this world and is now present in speech, for example, in the metaphor of pain, so that theology must deal with mourning.

D. Allen (b. 1933, *Christian Belief in a Postmodern World* [1989]) and others, however, are convinced that the end of modernity provides a new openness for faith as a legitimate and reasonable basis for religious conviction. The New Zealand theologian S. Patterson argues that language as an entity in itself links the nature of theology and the nature of reality (*Realist Christian Theology in a Postmodern Age* [1999]). G. Lindbeck (b. 1923) has produced a major statement concerning postliberal theology (*The Nature of Doctrine: Religion and Theology in a Postliberal Age* [1984]). Reflections on postliberal theology have also been directed to the often-questioned location of theology in the academy (e.g., H. Frei, *Types of Christian Theology* [1992]).

At the same time, renewed attention has been paid to path-breaking conceptions of the past. It is supported and enriched by extensive editions of the works of Schleiermacher (since 1980), Troeltsch (since 1998), Barth (since 1971; ET since 1981), Tillich (since 1959; see also his 6-vol. *Main Works / Hauptwerke* [1987-98], a selected edition in English and German), and Bonhoeffer (1986-99; ET since 1996). The *Zeitschrift für dialektische Theologie*, which began in 1985, shows the range of advanced Barth studies in many countries, including the United Kingdom and the United States (G. Hunsinger, *How to Read Karl Barth* [1991] and B. L. McCormack, *Karl Barth's Critically Realistic Theology* [1995]).

1.6.5. *Trends in Theological Ethics*

After the political and intellectual turmoil of the 1930s and 1940s, and despite the military and moral victory over fascism, it was still unclear how a concise and consistent Christian contribution to the often-confused moral orientation of many people would look. The situation in Germany was especially difficult. German Christians under the Nazi regime had discredited the neo-Lutheran two-kingdoms doctrine. Barth's Christological grounding of ethics as a part of his *Church Dogmatics* seemed to be the only credible option left; it operated with "analogies," with human action "corresponding" to the features of God's revelation in Christ (e.g., reconciliation). But H. Thielicke (1908-86) argued that even under National Socialism there had often been ambiguous situations of conflict in which people unavoidably incur guilt, for which they need forgiveness but also must be ready for → compromise (§2; *Theological Ethics* [4 vols., 1958-64; ET, 2 vols., 1966-69]). Like his teacher P. Althaus (see 1.4.4), Thielicke referred to the "orders," but only as God's precautionary means of preserving the endangered creation. In contrast, E. Wolf (1902-71) interpreted marriage, vocation, property, church, and the state as "institutions" that give opportunity to obey Christ's sovereign rule over the world, a rule that calls people to follow him toward the coming kingdom of God (*Sozialethik* [1975]).

Up to the 1970s there was an intense debate about a revision of the → two-kingdoms doctrine in other countries also (see U. Duchrow, ed., *Zwei Reiche und Regimente* [1977]). A careful analysis of this doctrine, as well as of the conception "kingship of Christ," showed that these are not conflicting theories but, rather, complementary aspects of the relation between Christian living as formed by God's creation and being dependent on God's judging and saving action (J. Rogge and H. Zeddies, ed., *Kirchengemeinschaft und politische Ethik* [1980]).

In the 1960s a general move toward social ethics developed, concentrating both on social conditions as determinative of human life and on the expectations of changing those conditions. The formation of society was seen as one of the universal tasks of ethics, together with an intensified witness of social care, justice, and political involvement. In this way social ethics became programmatic, and any field of theological reflection was forced to take this perspective into account. Institutions for research and teaching in theological social ethics were established in order to intensify communication with the social sciences. The Societas Ethica was founded in 1964 as an ecumenical European society for ethics that is following that tradition. T. W. Ogletree (*Hospitality to the Stranger* [1985]) has stated that the task of ethics is to show the moral structure of life processes. G. Winter (*Elements for a Social Ethic* [1966]) has insisted on the "we" reference, in which persons must take responsibility for the consequences of what they do. H. R. Niebuhr (see 1.4.6) had earlier made a plea for an ethics of → responsibility (§3). The Anglican J. Fletcher (1905-91) argued for the same in his *Situation Ethics* (1966) and *Moral Responsibility* (1967), but with utilitarian components. He argued that acts that obey the commandment of love, which links self-realization with the good of the neighbor (→ Solidarity 3), will be justified in the end by the success of their deeds. Fletcher also provoked a debate about the relation of norms and situation. These are two aspects that, perhaps under different labels (e.g., principles or values vs. contexts), need to be investigated.

The ongoing and often controversial debate shows that theological ethics must find its contours in a field of tensions between various positions (→ Ethics 7.1-2). Some adopt the basic concept of a Christian ethical tradition within the wider context of society and politics and attempt to prove that tradition to be the general and even universal ground for any ethics. Here the endeavor is to connect the Christian tradition with universal theories of action and other general theoretical elements of moral theory. At the same time, this ethical approach attempts to provide the basic context for any theology or even to offer an "ethical theology" that intends to impinge on all theological issues, transforming the content of Christian faith into an ethical one. For example, T. Rendtorff (b. 1931) understands ethics (*Ethics* [2 vols., 1980-81; ET 1986-89]) as the theory of a religiously based lifestyle. W. Schweiker has written *Responsibility and Christian Ethics* (1995) and *Power, Value, and Conviction: Theological Ethics in the Postmodern Age* (1998).

A different approach to ethical reflection is taken by those who look for the Christian life as it exists within the Christian community, from where witness is made in the various social and political contexts. The task of ethics is to elaborate and reconsider what Christians are to do and what Christian life is about within the established framework of the Christian faith. Ethics is to be understood as the implications of the Christian faith as articulated in the context of the teaching of the church. P. Lehmann perceives messianic Christology and ecclesiology as calling for participation in God's revolutionary action (*Ethics in a Christian Context* [1963]). And in *The Transfiguration of Politics* (1975) he discusses the basic problems of political ethics by elaborating a theological hermeneutics of the political. In *The Decalogue and a Human Future* (1995) he has the subtitle *The Meaning of the Commandments for Making and Keeping Human Life Human*. In his *Ethics from a Theocentric Perspective* (2 vols., 1981-84), J. M. Gustafson (b. 1925) deals with the questions What does God enable us to do? What does God want us to be, and in what given orders of human life? S. Hauerwas points to the Christian community as the genuine place of God's acting, the location for learning to wrestle with social conditions (*Character and the Christian Life* [1975], *A Community of Character: Toward a Constructive Christian Social Ethic* [1981], and *The Peaceable Kingdom* [1983]).

A tension remains between these two approaches. On the one hand, we have an attempt to offer Christian ethics itself as a universal context for understanding human life; on the other hand, there is a focus on the witness of a Christian life as it is lived in the community of the church. This tension was and is modified by varying ways of understanding the witness of Christian life — not in contrast or even in opposition to society and politics, but rather in discerning the implications of Christian witness in the context of society and its politics. In this perspective ecclesiology — the church itself, in its presence and with its witness for society and politics — becomes a basic issue.

1.6.6. *Ecumenical Tasks*

The tribulations and persecutions in totalitarian states and the consequences of World War II have brought together many Christians of different traditions and helped to reach mutual understandings. These experiences of ecumenical understanding and agreement paved the way in many fields for extensive communication between Christians in the last third of the 20th century. At significant points these contacts helped to overcome the East/West confrontation. In addition, the mass migration after the war changed many traditional confessional borders and forced people to take note of other ecclesial traditions. Transdenominational encounters enriched the participants, and intercultural exchanges helped to widen horizons and increase insights. Bilateral and multilateral dialogues have furthered the work of theological research and teaching by taking up theological and ecclesiological differences. Milestones in these developments were the First Assembly of the World Council of Churches, in Amsterdam in 1948 (→ Ecumenism, Ecumenical Movement, 2.6.3.1); the agreement between the Lutheran, Reformed, and United churches in Germany concerning the → Eucharist (§1.1), the Arnoldshain Theses (1957), which became a model for further understanding between church communities on the basis of the perception of Jesus Christ as both giver and gift; and the → Leuenberg Agreement of 1973/74, which established mutual recognition of sacraments and ministries between many European Protestant churches.

The ecumenical movement has also stimulated most theological disciplines. The Faith and Order Commission has dealt with matters of doctrine, sacraments, ministry, and church unity; Life and Work has attended to tasks of social ethics (→ Ecumenism, Ecumenical Movement, 2.6.2.3-4). As early as the 1930s studies related to the Bible and ecclesiology, as well as analyses of the social and political situation, focused on the essence and obligations of the church. Discussing the church's function in society, J. H. Oldham (1874-1969) suggested that the concept of a responsible society could be advanced by → "middle axioms," which would mediate theological judgments and moral decisions (*The Church and Its Function in Society* [1937]). A basic condition of the church's unity was the tension between institution and event, as J.-L. Leuba (1912-2005) demonstrated in a biblical-theological study (*L'institution et l'événement* [1950]). Y. Congar (1904-95) wrote on disunity from a Roman Catholic standpoint (*Chrétiens désunis. Principes d'un oecuménisme catholique* [1937]); in contrast, H. Berkhof (1914-95) wrote about the catholicity of the church (*Katholiciteit der Kerk* [1962]). Berkhof's main work (*Christian Faith* [1973; ET 1979]) linked the Reformed tradition with insights from other churches. The theological and practical relevance of → liturgy for church renewal and unity was a matter of great concern to J.-J. von Allmen (*Essai sur le Repas du Seigneur* [1966]).

Vatican II (1962-65) initiated an opening of theological discourse (→ Ecumenical Dialogue) between Roman Catholics and other ecclesial bodies. Now there were efforts to communicate and even cooperate, instead of unhelpful talk about "the other." In 1973 J. Feiner and L. Vischer edited *Neues Glaubensbuch. Der gemeinsame christliche Glaube* (ET *The Common Catechism: A Book of Christian Faith* [1975]), which brought together contributions of Protestant and Roman Catholic theologians who corrected, improved, and complemented one another. The same way of working has been used since 1975 (preparatory work since 1969) in the German Protestant-Catholic commentary of the NT (Evangelisch-katholischer Kommentar zum Neuen Testament [EKKNT]), which also includes significant examples of the history of interpreting the Bible.

Ecumenical institutes (→ Ecumenical Theology 1.2) were established to promote exchange of views and to support joint study and research. Difficult matters were handled at interdenominational consultations and at world conferences (→ World Council of Churches 7). One of the most important of these issues was work by Faith and Order that resulted in the 1982 Lima Declaration, *Baptism, Eucharist, and Ministry* (→ Baptism 2.3; Eucharist 1.3 and 5.2.2; Ministry, Ministerial Offices, 5.5). A German ecumenical discussion group tested the condemnations of doctrine of the 16th century, put divergences in a historical perspective, and stated that they cannot longer separate churches (K. Lehmann and W. Pannenberg, eds., *The Condemnations of the Reformation Era: Do They Still Divide?* [ET 1990; K. Lehmann, M. Root, and W. Rusch, eds., *Justification by Faith: Do the Sixteenth-Century Condemnations Still Apply?* (exp. ET, 1997)]).

Although the 1963 Helsinki Assembly of the → Lutheran World Federation had unsuccessfully attempted to invoke the doctrine of justification as an answer to the universal human quest for meaning, the → Joint Declaration on the Doctrine of Justification of the Lutheran World Federation and the Roman Catholic Church, signed in 1999, states that justification is a dynamic and decisive action of the triune God who judges and saves. God liberates the sinner from the power of hostility against God's creative will and, at the same time, unites the justified person with Christ. Some Lutherans, to be sure, had reservations about this agreement. A protest initiated by a circle around G. Ebeling, who suspected that the joint declaration involved a renunciation of the Reformation view of justification by faith alone, was accepted by a minority of German theologians. This debate has fostered an interest in the doctrine of justification.

There are different ideas within the ecumenical movement as to whether it is aiming at → consensus (§4), at convergence, or at → conciliarity. Ecumenical encounters have also inspired self-reflection on the part of individual traditions and new assessments of confessional distinctiveness, such as the two-volume Lutheran *Christian Dogmatics* (ed. C. E. Braaten and R. W. Jenson, 1984); E. W. Gritsch and R. W. Jenson, *Lutheranism* (1976); C. E. Braaten, *Principles of Lutheran Theology* (1983; 2d ed., 2007); *Toward the Future of Reformed Theology* (ed. D. Willis and M. Welker, 1999); and *Reformed Theology: Identity and Ecumenicity* (2 vols., ed. W. M. Alston and M. Welker, 2003-7).

1.6.7. *Christianity and Judaism*

Reflection on the → Holocaust has raised the question whether Christian theology can simply continue its way of thinking without responding to the anti-Semitic and anti-Judaic tendencies in European culture, not only in Germany, but also, for example, in Austria, Poland, and Russia. Though there are differing assessments of the Holocaust as a crucial event or a turning point in history, this reflection is much more weighed down in Germany by the pressure of the past than in England and North America. Among Jewish thinkers the Holocaust led to new theological reflections on God's acting in history (e.g., E. Berkovits [1908-92], *Faith after the Holocaust* [1973]; M. L. Morgan, *Beyond Auschwitz: Post-Holocaust Jewish Thought in America* [2001]). But this type of response to the Holocaust almost vanished within Christian theology and narrowed mainly to the question of the nature of the witness to God's presence in the people of Israel (C. Münz, *Der Welt ein Gedächtnis geben. Geschichtstheologisches Denken im Judentum nach Auschwitz* [1995]).

In Germany there had been a rare → Jewish-Christian dialogue in the first half of the 20th century, involving, for example, M. Buber (1878-1965), F. Rosenzweig (1886-1929), and K. L. Schmidt (1891-1956). A new approach was attempted beginning in the 1950s that stressed the continuity between the Old and the New Testaments (now often called the First and the Second Testaments). There was a growing tendency to place the presence of Jews and of their faith within Christian theology. Others viewed Christianity as a branch of Judaism or even as a Jewish sect.

Faced with the Jewish presence (→ Judaism 5; Jewish Philosophy 6; Jewish Theology 4) and the persistent → anti-Semitism and anti-Judaism that culminated in the Holocaust, Jewish-Christian dialogue has become convinced that it is essential that Christian theology find a place for the faith and presence of Jews within Christian theology (P. Van Buren [1924-88], *Discerning the Way: A Theology of the Jewish-Christian Reality* [1980] and *A Christian Theology of the People Israel* [1982]). Even more radically, F.-W. Marquardt (1928-2002), who had studied under H. Gollwitzer (1908-93), pleaded for a start "from scratch" to rebuild Christian theology on the basis of a continuing learning from faithful Jews, their traditions, and their piety (*Von Elend und Heimsuchung der Theologie* [1988] and *Das christliche Bekenntnis zu Jesus dem Juden* [2 vols., 1990-91]).

Playing an influential role in this whole discussion has been the biblical paradigm of God's covenant (C. S. McCoy [1923-2002], *When Gods Change: Hope for Theology* [1980]; B. Klappert [b. 1939], *Miterben der Verheißung* [2000]), an issue that had been prominent in the theology of salvation history, as well as in that of K. Barth (→ Covenant 3.1.3–3.2). In 1980 the Synod of the Evangelical Church of the Rhineland in Germany stated that God has adopted Christians into his covenant with Israel. In 1996 the Synod added to its church order the witness to "God's faithfulness, which clings to his election of his people Israel. With Israel it hopes for new heavens and a new earth." G. Lindbeck has initiated ecclesiological studies that respect God's election of Israel, as reflected by Paul in Romans 9–11 (*The Church in a Postliberal Age* [2003]; → Church 2.1.3).

In this overall context, every claim of the distinctiveness of Christianity can easily give rise to suspicions of anti-Semitism. To avoid this suspicion, many have championed a radical revision of anti-Judaistic tendencies in Christian theology, including Christological dogma and the doctrine of the Trinity.

1.6.8. *Philosophy and Theology*
Process theology adopted the speculative and empirical system of A. N. Whitehead (1861-1947), which integrated modern scientific knowledge, insights of the humanities, and aspects of the social sciences. It viewed reality as an open process whose particular concretions are interdependent, with God's self as the center. In God's primordial nature God differs from the world, but in God's consequent nature God is the creative principle of the interactions that take place in the world. This concept inspired two generations of theologians. The Chicago school, led by S. Mathews (see 1.2.6) and C. Hartshorne (1897-2000), first understood Christianity as a social movement. Then H. N. Wieman turned to Whitehead's religious philosophy and, according to the manner of American liberalism, interpreted God as the process of human good. From this school came the process theologians J. B. Cobb, S. M. Ogden (b. 1928), and D. D. Williams (1910-73). In Germany M. Welker incorporates modified impulses of Whitehead's philosophy into biblical-theological interpretations of God's creativity in creation and through the manifold manifestations of the Holy Spirit (*God the Spirit* [1992; ET 1994]).

Process theology does not think of God as an almighty superpower but emphasizes God's persuasive energy that creates free humans. We are neither isolated individuals nor like robots only following orders, but we are made for harmonious mutual relations. Since, left to ourselves, we do not by nature live according to our calling, we may do so by sharing in God's perfect manifestations in Christ. God's love is the basis of human creativity and enjoyment, which arises through mutual love both for God and for ourselves. Here we see a concern to overcome the dichotomy of nature and spirit. Interdependence of humanity and nature carries with it important environmental implications (→ Environment 2).

E. Farley (b. 1929) is a philosophical theologian who, using the → phenomenology (§2) of E. Husserl (1859-1938), developed a new theological approach to the reality and truth of faith (*Ecclesial Man* [1975], *Ecclesial Reflection* [1982], and *Theologia* [1983]). In the first volume of his systematic theology (*Good and Evil* [1990]), he dealt with the fundamental anthropological themes of tragedy, evil, and sin, showing how these can be changed into the situation of faith. Also oriented to phenomenology were the French philosopher P. Ricoeur (1913-2005; → Narrative Theology 3) and the Jewish philosopher E. Lévinas (1905-95), who influenced many theologians in both North America and Europe.

Philosophical Investigations (1953, pub. posth.) and other treatises of L. Wittgenstein (1889-1951) enriched the observation of religious language and communication in church and theology, as shown, for example, in the works of G. Lindbeck (see 1.7.3) and of the English philosopher of religion D. Z. Phillips (1934-2006; *The Concept of Prayer* [1965], *Faith and Philosophical Enquiry* [1970], and *Faith after Foundationalism* [1998]). The reception of analytic philosophy (Philosophy and Theology 5) was different. It convinced P. Van Buren that any talk of God would be invalid, and Christianity could therefore rely only on ethical affirmations (*The Secular Meaning of the Gospel* [1963]). J. A. Martin (1917-2007) wrote *The New Dialogue between Philosophy and Theology* (1966) and presented different methods for examining theological argumentation. I. U. Dalferth and others who participated in the dialogue with British philosophers of religion have used analytic insights for clarifying the logic of the language of theology (see 1.6.4). More recently, younger theologians have shown an increased interest in the thinking of C. Peirce (see 1.2.6).

1.6.9. *Theology in Dialogue*

As noted above (see 1.6.2), a change has taken place regarding the relation between theology and other sciences. Yet seldom is there a real dialogue, for theologians often try to develop their positions simply by broadening their horizons through elements adopted from other sciences. In some respects, the relationship between the natural sciences and theology is an exception, and there are significant differences between interdisciplinary conversations in the United States and Great Britain, on the one hand, and central Europe, on the other, partly due to divergences concerning the epistemology of "nature" and what can be "naturally" perceived. In Great Britain

and the United States, the prevalent opinion denies that there must be a clash of theology of nature with → natural theology (§3), while on the Continent a sharp dividing line has largely prevailed.

In order to overcome this division, the German theologian K. Heim (1874-1958) attempted to evaluate convergences in the worldviews of theology and basic theories of physics. After World War II, theologians and physicists started a dialogue in Göttingen and focused on the ethical implications of nuclear physics. Since 1979 the dialogue in the United States has intensified (→ Science and Theology 4-5), debating cosmology, as well as moral obligations. Most recently, eschatology has become a uniting topic (*The End of the World and the Ends of God* [ed. J. Polkinghorne and M. Welker, 2000]).

Other opportunities for dialogue have appeared that would be worthwhile to consider more extensively. The often-underestimated interrelation of theology and literature is most cultivated and advanced in Great Britain and North America; the writers F. O'Connor (1925-64), J. Updike (b. 1932; *Roger's Version* [1986]), and J. Irving (*A Prayer for Owen Meany* [1989]) allude to theological topics. In Germany J. Klepper (1903-42) reflected in his fiction and poems what he had learned from his teacher R. Hermann (see 1.4.2); the poet R. A. Schröder (1878-1962) was a member of the Confessing Church and revived attention to the vivid links between Christian traditions and Western higher education. The British J. S. Begbie discusses the relationship of several diverse fields in his *Theology, Music, and Time* (2000).

1.7. *Theology in Transition*

1.7.1. *Plurality and Pluralism*

At the turn of the millennium, Protestant theology faces new challenges and tasks worldwide, including regarding its identity. How can this identity be described — by evaluating the essence of Christianity? Is it sufficient to be related to a Christ-event that can be historically investigated? Its meaning could be demonstrated, perhaps even its universal relevance, by its perception of humanity in its religious dimension or by contextually interpreting the substance of experiences provided by the Christian tradition. Or is this identity external, interwoven with the work of the triune God, with God's promises? If so, theology can only point to its grounding and, in so doing, confidently serve rather than secure its continuity. Or can the warrant of its identity be an ethical one — for example, a Christian contribution to gain peace, justice, and the fullness of life? These values are presumably universal and therefore possible answers to the challenges caused by globalization.

Contextual varieties have led to a plurality of theologies. This plurality can be fruitful when it helps achieve mutual enrichment. But an establishment of basically divergent or even contradicting theologies (→ Pluralism 3) would be a disaster for the Christian witness to the world, which by definition is based on the unity of faith.

In addition, institutional differences exist. In Germany, the Netherlands, and Switzerland the number of teaching personnel at faculties of theology has been reduced, due partially to a shrinking number of students and a decline in church membership. In Hungary schools of theology were reopened after the fall of Communism; seminaries in other Eastern European countries were reintegrated in universities. Universities in the European Community will be reformed toward the English and North American system of studying. It is an open question whether and to what extent this transformation will shape theological education, research, and publications.

In Asia, Africa, and South America, theological education shares many opportunities and difficulties with the European and North American system, especially when it is integrated into the academy. But it is also challenged by its own cultural environment, especially if its culture rests on a long-standing tradition of higher education, such as Confucianism in China and Korea. Here theology must find its way, examining its own cultural tradition, as well as European theology, which was shaped by Greek and Roman antiquity, forming this heritage right at the beginning of Christianity and throughout its history.

Theologians of the Third World often, and vigorously, oppose → European theology (§2.1) and its North American development. They view it merely as a monolithic Western imperialistic tradition and not as a continuing and (admittedly) difficult process of searching in faith and hope for consensus. European theology is often criticized as intellectualistic and not sufficiently rooted in a spirituality that can broaden the horizon of theological rationality. Training in theology by institutions close to the church, as is usual in the Third World, may stimulate other ways to do theology in an academic setting. For example, the South African J. de Gruchy (b. 1939) suggests a "hermeneutical spiral" in doing theology. The discipline starts "with the witness of the church in the world, then proceeds to reflect critically on that witness both through reflection on the Scriptures and through an analysis of what is happening in the world," thus making Christian action "more faithful to the gospel and more relevant to the needs of the world" ("The Nature, Necessity, and Task of Theology," *Doing Theology in Context: South African Perspectives* [1994] 10). De Gruchy, however, takes little account of former expressions of Christian thought.

Many theologians in the Third World are demanding an "indigenous theology" that corresponds to the Third World's sociocultural contexts (→ Acculturation). This claim is often intensified by the accusation that European and North American theology has blended the gospel with the Western context. These critics thus regard Western theology as foreign and its importation as causing an alienation from their roots. Here we must not fail to differentiate the essential strangeness of the gospel to all cultures from forms of cultural distinctiveness that arise as the gospel is incorporated into a culture. This strangeness must be reflected and clarified. Only by means of this differentiation can we avoid a → syncretism of Christianity and indigenous religions (or cultural phenomena with quasi-religious demands), which would destroy the distinctiveness of the Christian faith.

Sometimes a "mild" syncretism tries to adapt Christianity to the context of indigenous religions by reducing theology to topics that seem familiar to the surrounding religious milieu. Frequently the classic → Christology (§2.1) — Christ as truly divine and truly human — is felt to be disturbing and is repressed (e.g., in India) in favor of the veneration of creation and of a holistic view of the Holy Spirit.

North America, with its intermingled nationalities, cultural and ethnic identities, religious convictions, and denominations, has long known plurality and has valued it as an element of → equality (§2.7) and → freedom. Theological particularity and diversity, even religious pluralism, have been given high marks, as represented, for example, by the American Academy of Religion (AAR). This trend became influential during the last four decades. It has been balanced, however, by a strong confidence in universal cultural values, especially in the broad range of human rights cultivated in democracy and supported by rules of argumentation and by coping with conflicts.

In discussing particularistic perspectives, some simplified labeling is needed in order to identify them and to show their distinctive characteristics. We must use typologies if we are to bring out complex multiplicities and also delineate main attributes. We can refer, for example, to postliberal, revisionist, and nonapologetic positions (W. Placher, *Unapologetic Theology: A Christian Voice in a Pluralistic Conversation* [1989]) or to antimodern, modern, or postmodern trends (D. Tracy, *Blessed Rage for Order: The New Pluralism in Theology* [1975], *The Analogical Imagination: Christian Theology and the Culture of Pluralism* [1981], and *Plurality and Ambiguity: Hermeneutics, Religion, Hope* [1987]). Or we can represent the aims as (1) being true to Christian identity by reference to Scripture, revelation, confession, and so forth; (2) trying to show the rationality of faith in relation to modern understanding; or (3) focusing on the applicability and social relevance of the Christian faith. With such parameters we can indicate the problems that give rise to individual theologies and determine their perspectives. In addition, however, the charge of relativizing the truth may also be brought against it (A. Bloom, *The Closing of the American Mind* [1987]). The problem will not go away: how theologically can we receive and apply pluralistic culture?

The attitude of many Christian theologians living in the Third World toward other religions often differs from those in Europe and North America because they experience these religions both as integrated wholes and as complex entities. Their view may therefore differ significantly from comparative studies of religion in the First and Second Worlds, which often tend to use grandiose schematizations. Comparative studies of religions are not always helpful for a dialogue, which needs partners rooted in their specific religious identities.

A pluralistic culture requires a sense of the relativity of theological knowledge and of the historicity of truth claims. The exclusiveness of Christianity must thus prove itself in relation to other religions. Discussion in Protestant theology of religious pluralism has challenged the relation between Christianity and other religions and has given a new emphasis to this problem in → religious studies (§4) and in the → philosophy of religion (→ Religion 2.6). The question is not so much one of interaction as that of basic positions. Pluralists treat all religions as equal and avoid any claim to absoluteness, but inclusivists, while respecting other religions, regard the Christian religion as supreme and normative. J. Hick and P. Knitter (*The Myth of Christian Uniqueness: Toward a Pluralistic Theology of Religion* [1987]), however, have spoken of a Copernican turning point. Hick postulated the one reality, which he did not identify as a personal God, and took it that the practical aim of all religions is to transform human I-centeredness into reality-centeredness. Among others, S. M. Heim (*Is Christ the Only Way? Christian Faith in a Pluralistic World* [1985] and *The Depth of the Riches: A Trinitarian Theology of Religious Ends* [2001]) has defended,

against the view of Hick and others, the absolute uniqueness of Jesus Christ as the living authority that transcends all other norms. The values of other religions must all be incorporated in the universal person of Christ.

The Christian reference to salvation that is linked to Jesus Christ and that relies on the ongoing story of Christ raises a universal claim that may be viewed from different angles, as is debated in ecumenical discussions (→ Salvation 7) and shown by experiences in Africa, Asia, and Latin America (→ Salvation 6). The impact of this debate on commitment to mission and on its strategy may be seen in the further controversy between those who have largely retreated on mission and those who call upon the churches for a more urgent commitment (the latter include L. → Newbigin [1909-98], D. J. Bosch [1929-92], J. R. W. Stott [b. 1921], J. Verkuyl [1908-2001], and D. A. McGavran [1897-1990]).

1.7.2. *Theology and Culture*

Cultural sciences serve like an umbrella over all academic disciplines that are oriented to history in its widest sense (→ Culture 1; Culture and Christianity). Seen from this point of view, theology is like all phenomena of history related to culture. But as contextual theology tries to derive theology from specific contextual conditions, the theology of culture understands theology merely as a function of culture — as either a stabilizing or a transforming (or perhaps even revolutionary) force. The former rests on a view of traditional religious values or even a divine constitution of social and economic structures; the latter emerges from a theologically motivated protest against the status quo.

The theology of culture is often traced back to liberalism. Liberalism remained an unbroken option for North American theology (see P. Hodgson, *Liberal Theology: A Radical Vision* [2007]; → Liberal Theology 3), even as a bridge between Protestants and Roman Catholics who share the same idea of an alliance between theology and culture (see 1.2.5). In Germany, however, liberal theology as a creative intellectual movement died after the clash of Culture Protestantism and dialectic theology. During the European crises caused by totalitarian attitudes, liberalism could not always make the urgently needed rigid theological decisions. So far, liberalism is linked with the ethos of tolerance as one pillar of democratic culture. Protestant churches and theologians generally agree and are supportive, but tolerance is multifaceted politically, as well as in religious matters (→ Tolerance 2.2 and 3).

Strictly speaking, the theology of culture views culture as the subject of theology; to put it more precisely, salvation occurs outside the Christian church. Here we may consider → civil religion (§2) as it has been cultivated in the United States. This socioreligious construct does not have any real equivalent in Europe because of far-reaching differences in the relation between church and state. The same is true regarding public theology, although there previously were somewhat similar efforts in Europe. Originally a fruit of American civil religion, public theology points increasingly to the religious mind of a cross-cultural public. In Germany there were attempts to revitalize former tendencies, for example, by the founding of the German Troeltsch Society in 1981 (T. Rendtorff; → Liberal Theology 3). But the situation in the last decades of the 19th century and today are hardly comparable. Similarly, Schleiermacher's theory of theology as aiming at church leadership (see 1.1.2) has recently been recalled as serving the converging scope of a diverse, common Christian consciousness (e.g., E. Herms). Today this idea is also often linked with an understanding of the church as a congregational joining together of persons who are individually faithful to God — a view that can have an antiecumenical effect.

1.7.3. Church and Theology

From the 1930s to the 1960s a consensus existed concerning theology as a function of the church, serving the church's memory and accounting for its hope (e.g., Barth, Bonhoeffer, Brunner, Tillich). This understanding varied, depending on the evaluation of the primary tasks of the church, with Barth, Bonhoeffer, and Brunner stressing the church's proclamation in its broadest sense. Today, though, the church often appears as a function of religious, ethical, or political aims. These aims are claimed to be theologically identified — but according to the prevailing pluralistic view, these aims seldom include one that is properly theological.

Most contemporary theologians understand their theological work as related to the church, mostly to a particular denomination; representatives of theology of culture share this understanding, although more indirectly, mediated by public discourse. Distinct from this general attitude, there have been recent attempts to recognize the life of the church itself as the starting point for theology and leading to its subject matter. For example, G. Wainwright (*Doxology: A Systematic Theology* [1980]) and E. Schlink ([1903-84], *The Coming Christ and the Coming Church* [1961; ET 1967] and *Ökumenische Dogmatik* [1983]) focused on doxology; S. Hauerwas perceives the liturgy as a fountain for Christian ethics (*In Good Company: The Church as*

Polis [1995]); G. Lindbeck has investigated the process of learning the language of faith as the precondition for every approach to Christian theology and for understanding Christian responsibility (*The Nature of Doctrine: Religion and Theology in a Postliberal Age* [1984]; → Postmodernism 3.2.3); and G. Sauter describes doctrinal statements as an explanation of the inner grounding and intrinsic rationality of church practices (*Gateways to Dogmatics: Reasoning Theologically for the Life of the Church* [1998; ET 2003].)

→ Dogmatics 2.2-7; Ethics 6; European Theology (Modern Period) 1.2.1-4; Exegesis, Biblical, 1.3 and 2.1.5; Lutheranism 3; North American Theology; Reformed Tradition 4.3-4; Systematic Theology; Theology

Bibliography: K. BARTH, *Protestant Theology in the Nineteenth Century: Its Background and History* (new ed.; Grand Rapids, 2002) • H. BERKHOF, *Two Hundred Years of Theology: Report of a Personal Journey* (Grand Rapids, 1989) • D. FORD, ed., *The Modern Theologians: An Introduction to Christian Theology in the Twentieth Century* (2d ed.; Cambridge, Mass., 1997) • E. HIRSCH, *Geschichte der neuern evangelischen Theologie im Zusammenhang mit den allgemeinen Bewegungen des europäischen Denkens* (5 vols.; Gütersloh, 1949-54) • M. KÄHLER, *Geschichte der protestantischen Dogmatik im 19. Jahrhundert* (2d ed.; ed. E. Kähler; Wuppertal, 1989) • E. LESSING, *Geschichte der deutschsprachigen evangelischen Theologie von Albrecht Ritschl bis zur Gegenwart* (vols. 1-2; Göttingen, 2000-2004; vols. 3-4 forthcoming) • J. C. LIVINGSTON, *Modern Christian Thought* (2d ed.; 2 vols.; Upper Saddle River, N.J., 1997-2000) • J. MACQUARRIE, *Twentieth-Century Religious Thought* (4th ed.; London, 1988) • W. PANNENBERG, *Problemgeschichte der neueren evangelischen Theologie in Deutschland. Von Schleiermacher bis zu Barth und Tillich* (Göttingen, 1997) • G. SAUTER, *Protestant Theology at the Crossroads: How to Face the Crucial Tasks for Theology in the Twenty-First Century* (Grand Rapids, 2007) • H. SCHWARZ, *Theology in a Global Context: The Last Two Hundred Years* (Grand Rapids, 2005) • C. WELCH, *Protestant Thought in the Nineteenth Century* (2 vols., New Haven, 1972-85).

GERHARD SAUTER

2. Roman Catholic Theology

2.1. Modern Questions

The long struggle within Roman Catholic theology and thought to transform classical and modern forms of human intelligence and reason to become compatible with Christian → revelation and → faith was gradually clarified in the middle of the

20th century. With the contributions of such diverse theologians and philosophers as J. Maréchal (1878-1944), E. Stein (1891-1942), B. Lonergan (1904-84), K. → Rahner (1904-84), A. MacIntyre (b. 1929), C. Taylor (b. 1931), D. Tracy (b. 1939), J.-L. Marion (b. 1946), K. Wojtyla (1920-2005; John Paul II), and J. Ratzinger (b. 1927; Benedict XVI), the classical methodology, which was based almost totally on → logic and syllogism, as well as on the Cartesian separation of subject and object, was changed. It was accomplished by the critical appropriation of Christian → humanism, as represented by J. Maritain (1882-1973); of personalism, as represented by E. Mounier (1905-50); of the phenomenological school, as represented by M. Scheler (1874-1928) and E. Stein; and of cognition theory, with the interrelated operations of human consciousness and of "conscious intentionality," as represented by J. Maréchal, K. Rahner, and especially B. Lonergan. In different but related studies they contributed to a more differentiated integrity of subject and object and of metaphysics and history.

This methodological perspective sheds new light on the work of 19th- and 20th-century Catholic theologians. Some scholars were able to make small breakthroughs, while others, sensing that the intellectual achievements in the areas of doctrinal theology were not fully mediated, did not succeed in bringing the substance of knowledge that had been realized in the classical methodologies into conversation with those of the modern era. R. Garrigou-Lagrange (1877-1964) and others perceived this failure as thwarting the church's responsibility to bring the fullness of the tradition into the modern academy, with its focus on the role of historical consciousness, → hermeneutics, and → dialectics, both in developing further critical knowledge of the past and in advancing the tradition into the new cultural and intellectual context that the church had to engage. The methodological perspective thus helps to shed light on the broad historical dimensions of the church in its former responses to wider political and cultural situations, both positive and negative, as well as to the then-new fields of the humanities such as → history, → sociology, → economics, and cultural analysis (→ Culture). In a sense, the methodological perspective recasts the difficulties in the relation of → theology with the other disciplines, presenting them as influenced both by philosophical wisdom and by the encounter between church and culture (→ Culture and Christianity).

Throughout the 18th and 19th centuries, various political and cultural events and turmoil engulfed Europe (e.g., the → French Revolution, Napoleonic wars, and the breakup of the Holy Roman Empire; → Modern Church History 1.3). During this same period the modern church faced questions and problems for which it had either only partial (and therefore not systematically satisfactory) responses or only the unintegrated insights of the classical engagements with prior culture. In some cases the response of the church was simply to retreat from the world and its problems, gathering into small enclaves in order to maintain its classical identity in the face of the hostile cultural winds that often threatened either the church or, indeed, all religion. Such intentions were evident in the writings of Voltaire (né F.-M. Arouet, 1694-1778), P.-S. de Laplace (1749-1827), and K. → Marx (1818-83). In contrast, there was clear empirical evidence of the ways that Christianity had benefited not only the religious life of Europe but also its secular institutions such as education, medicine, social organizations, and human services, as was studied by the sociologist P. Le Play (1806-82) and later by Lord Acton (J. E. E. Dalberg, 1834-1902) and the cultural historian C. Dawson (1889-1970). But even within this situation, as difficult as it was, a more engaging theology was advanced by scholars seeking to incorporate the new, but not yet fully critically argued, insights of the age. At that time, theology for the → Roman Catholic Church, as well as for the Protestant churches, was Eurocentric, with different foci in Germany, France, England, Spain, and Italy.

Some of the ideas were dialectically engaged in critical polemics by Roman theologians, often in Vatican congregations (→ Curia 1.2.2). In addition, the Index Librorum Prohibitorum (List of Prohibited Books) was developed as a way of warning Catholics about books that lacked a proper integration of classical teachings and modern ideas. (This reaction has certain parallels in secular scholarship, as when the academy rejects unintegrated knowledge of scientific hypotheses and theories. For example, Newtonian scientists resisted and, for a significant time, blocked the insights of Albert Einstein or Max Planck from German universities.) Placing books or the whole of an author's writings on the Index meant that no Roman Catholic could read them (→ Censorship) without the advice and direction of one who was aware of the issues involved. The aim was to avoid destructive consequences for the church and its life. The Index remained in use until 1968, being abandoned only after → Vatican II (1962-65). By that time more Catholics were going to colleges and universities in Europe and the Americas. (In England, Catholics were not permitted to enroll in universities until 1829, when Parliament passed the Emancipation Act.)

2.1.1. *Enlightenment Theology*

At the beginning of the 19th century an → Enlightenment theology permeated Roman Catholic intellectual life. Philosophers and theologians engaged in constructive debate with thinkers like R. Descartes (1596-1650; → Cartesianism), himself a Catholic who sought to overcome the skepticism of his time, as well as with G. W. Leibniz (1646-1716; → Philosophy of Nature 2.2), C. Wolff (1679-1754; → Ontology), and I. Kant (1724-1804; → Kantianism). Efforts by the church and its theologians to uphold the relationship of faith and reason within the intellectual framework of the Enlightenment meant that faith, → reason, and → piety were placed in the context of new criteria that demanded that all religious claims be purged of superstitious elements (→ Superstition) and that all → miracles, including those contained in Scripture, be brought under the domain of the new → rationalism.

The new rationalism itself, we now know from the advance of methodological insights, had no room for the kind of knowledge that could include the intentional levels of meaning that → symbols and → myths carry, and it posed serious problems in the interpretation of Scripture for both Protestants and Catholics. One example is the so-called Jefferson Bible of the third American president (entitled *The Life and Morals of Jesus of Nazareth* [1804]), which purged from Scripture all supernatural mysteries. The difficulty in scriptural theology was one of both hermeneutics and → ideology.

As T. Jefferson's (1743-1826) work makes clear, there was, furthermore, a major difficulty in the relationship between doctrine and the foundations of Christian ethics or → virtue. Part of what was needed in a new methodology was the clarification of a foundation, based both on Scripture and on human intelligence, regarding natural virtue and its relationship to Christian virtue (→ Ethics 4). Casuistic distinctions that had once been helpful in relating principles to particular actions, especially for confessors (→ Casuistry 3), needed to be set into the broader framework of the self-sacrificing love (*agapē*) of the Christian spiritual life, while also pointing out the actions and ways of life that could destroy Christian faith itself.

Scholars such as the church historian J. J. von Döllinger (1799-1890), the biblical scholar J. F. von Allioli (1793-1873), and the moral and pastoral theologian J. M. Sailer (1751-1832) deserve mention for having introduced new data that needed to be integrated with the classical methods. Sailer — influenced by Kant, J. G. Hamann (1730-88), J. G. → Herder (1744-1803), F. Fénelon (1651-1715), and J. K. Lavater (1741-1801) — placed particular focus on the interiority of the Christian believer and on the affections of the heart and, with great pedagogical skill, contributed important, though partial, insights to the renewal of theology (→ Pastoral Theology 2.2). There was also an emphasis on serious religious interiority in the tradition that focused most particularly on piety shaped by attention, for example, to the → "Sacred Heart of Jesus." This particular Roman Catholic response to the crises and consequences of the French Revolution and Napoleonic tyranny was especially fostered by young French Jesuits.

2.1.2. *The Tübingen School*

While individuals were making their contributions to what would lead to methodological breakthroughs, centers began to form where a number of people gathered to take up different parts of the whole field of theology. One of these was at Eberhard Karls University of Tübingen, a "school" that had a broad and lasting influence. It focused on the general relation between religion and → experience, and on the more particular Christian concern of the relationships between experience, reason, and faith. In debates with Protestant theologians, some of the Catholic scholars began to give more attention to issues of methodology, leading to new developments in the areas of → exegesis and history that were based on insight into the historicity of revelation and theology, as well as on a search for unity in both historical and speculative work.

Furthermore, the → Romantic movement within Enlightenment thought brought a distinctive concern for wholeness and the organic (→ Apologetics; Organism 3.8). J. S. von Drey (1777-1853) and others recognized that this emphasis fit in rather more fully with the Catholic sense of → sacraments and a broader → sacramentality than did the Enlightenment forms of rationalism. He was influenced both by F. W. Schelling (1775-1854) and by F. D. E. → Schleiermacher (1768-1834; → Schleiermacher's Theology). Drey regarded the idea of the → kingdom of God (§3.2) as the basic principle of doctrinal and systematic theology, and he attempted to link the objective truth of faith to human subjectivity (→ Subjectivism and Objectivism). He was interested in the dialectics of opposites and in → mysticism and historicity. In → moral theology J. B. Hirscher (1788-1865) pointed to the limitations of conceptualism, which had infused the scholastic theological enterprise (→ Scholasticism).

J. A. Möhler (1796-1838) was also both influenced by, and a critic of, Schleiermacher and Sailer. In his studies Möhler presented an organic theological model of the church in which the → Holy Spirit is the principle of the unified mystical body, somewhat in line with formulations of the early → church fathers in their theological reflections on Scripture. Perhaps the most evident influence of Schleiermacher on Möhler's work is found in his notion that faith is an intuitive understanding and experience. In this regard, Möhler barely avoided fideism, since he could not explain the deeper relations of the structure of knowledge to the gift of faith (see 2.1.4.2). Today the J. A. Möhler Institute at Paderborn continues to publish his work and to link it with that of later thinkers, both Catholic and Protestant. It is an important center for ecumenical theological collaboration.

The speculative thought of J. E. von Kuhn (1806-87) drew on the work of G. W. F. Hegel (1770-1831; → Hegelianism), particularly his → phenomenology. Along with other aspects of → idealism, Kuhn dealt with the relation between faith and knowledge, nature and grace, and tradition and progress, always with a concern for mediation between faith and the modern consciousness. In confrontation with D. F. Strauss (1808-74), Kuhn attempted to address the problems of revelation and myth. Relating dialogically to the movements of the day, F. A. Staudenmaier (1800-1856) considered Christianity to be a system of absolute truth; he explored the finiteness of human self-awareness in its efforts to appropriate such truth.

2.1.3. *Romanticism, Liberalism, Hermesianism*

As noted above, the thinking and experience of Romanticism provided a new sense of the religious and the holy, in opposition to the rigid rationalism of the Enlightenment. Romanticism, furthermore, sought a deeper reconciliation of faith, reason, experience, and feeling. The main centers in Europe for such work were at Münster, Munich (under Sailer's influence), and Vienna. At Munich the lay theologian F. von Baader (1765-1841), who was influenced by J. Böhme (1575-1624; → Mysticism 2.5.2), found himself in a close relation to the Romantic elements in Hegel. He and other scholars were interested in a philosophy of life and in feelings, with a variety of ethical implications, but these feelings were not always tied to the traditions of Christian virtue as related to grace. They began to accept some of the positions of the emerging social critics and spoke of the need for a greater openness to intellectual research and study within the church.

In the French-speaking world, many scholars developed what can be called a Catholic liberalism

(→ Catholicism [Roman] 1.2.5). This "school" was clear on the importance of dogmatic theology and doctrine, yet it simultaneously promoted both individual and social freedom of thought and action. H.-F.-R. de Lamennais (1782-1854) and J.-B.-H. Lacordaire (1802-61) may be mentioned for their ability to interrelate aspects of Catholic doctrine and commitment to a life of charity and also to programs that engaged the political and cultural currents of the time (→ Catholicism [Roman] 1.2.3). The Romantic emphasis on feeling and its general appreciation of an imagination and action that could remove itself from the exercise of authentic reason, in part because Romanticism was itself a reaction to the model of reason as rationalism in both philosophy and theology, aroused concerns among some Roman Catholic theologians and led to a resistance to such theology for its lack of clarity in mediating the tradition. Gregory XVI (1831-46) expressed this particular concern in his encyclical *Mirari vos* (1832).

Further condemnation of Romantic theologies came in Gregory's brief *Dum acerbissimas* (1835), which was directed against the views of G. Hermes (1755-1831). "Hermesianism" was rejected specifically in a decree issued by Gregory in 1836 as lacking a full account of the objectivity of human knowledge, which was crucial for knowing not only revelation but also secular realities. Challenged by Kantian idealism, Hermes proposed an → epistemology that attempted to resolve the relationship of faith, knowledge, and doctrine. In his use of the writings of Kant and J. G. Fichte (1762-1814), Hermes tried to find intellectual support for faith, while criticizing those thinkers in their limited explanations of reason. Kant had raised doubts about faith, and Hermes set about trying to overcome these doubts in a new critique of Kant, but he also found the notion of intellectual proofs posed by scholastic thought to be unimpressive. Subjecting faith to methodical doubt, he regarded faith as the final goal of → philosophy, thus making it appear as if all was determined by reason, with no need for → grace. Through disciples he had a short-lived influence. In 1860 many who supported Hermes were removed from their professorships on the order of Johannes Cardinal von Geissel (1796-1864) of Cologne. (In German universities it was necessary to receive episcopal approval to teach on Catholic theological faculties.)

2.1.4. *The Development of Partial Integrations and the Internal Catholic Dialectic*

Toward the end of the 19th century and in the early 20th century, an increasing number of scholars began to add to the critical appropriation of modern philosophical work, relating it to the insights of classical thought.

2.1.4.1. B. Bolzano (1781-1848), who had studied mathematics and the philosophy of religion at Prague, had an influential following that promoted his ideas for the reform of the church and its theology. While he was faithful religiously, his intellectual training led him to follow a rationalist path similar to that of Hermes (→ Logic and Theology 2.6).

Concerned to narrow the broadening gap between scientifically assured knowledge and faith, and at the same time to combat → pantheism, A. Günther (1783-1863) advanced a new theory of self-awareness. He had some academic influence in Austria and argued for more freedom for reflection within the church, but he came under condemnation in the brief *Eximiam tuam* (1857) of Cardinal von Geissel, an opponent of G. Hermes.

At Munich, M. Deutinger (1815-64) was a critic of rational-idealistic philosophy and also of Scholasticism.

F. Pilgram (1819-90) was interested in questions of ecclesial fellowship like those later developed by R. Guardini (1885-1968; see 2.4.1), who had a considerable influence at Vatican II.

J. Frohschammer (1821-93) of Munich was more radical in his rationalism and in a sense brought Günther's views into the open. He thought that the religion of Jesus had been falsified by church theory and practice. His hypotheses were condemned in 1862 (DH 2850-61).

Under the influence of Kant and theologians from the Tübingen school, H. Schell (1850-1906) of Würzburg wrestled dialogically with modern errors that threatened to destroy religion, the church, and theology itself (→ Catholicism [Roman] 1.2.6). With a dynamic personalist view of God and the Trinity, he attempted to bring the structure of → dogma into line with the existential self-actualization of humanity. He had many ideas for the reform of the church, but his works were considerably truncated, especially in his teaching on the supernatural dimension of faith.

2.1.4.2. In France it might be said that the great advances in natural science and the philosophical influences of Cartesianism initiated Enlightenment rationalism. A commitment to reason is manifest in the works of the philosophes, as well as in thinkers and planners of social philosophy such as the Utopians. A. Comte (1798-1857; → Positivism) renounced all theology and → metaphysics, and J.-E. Renan (1823-92) eliminated the divine nature of Christ, returned to → Arian views, and was also a social Darwinist in his theories of nature and race.

Theology, however, adopted → restoration theories such as → Ultramontanism, which arose as an integralist view of the papal office, always central to Catholic life and thought, as a revealed voice of authority in matters involving the church and theology. Some thinkers sought to expand the role of the office of Peter to cover all matters, not just those limited to the intrinsic truths of revelation and faith. One thinker who developed this response to the prevailing rationalism and its political consequences was J. de Maistre (1753-1821), whose theocratic ideas (→ Theocracy 2) were influential and not really addressed until → Vatican I.

Likewise, one who tried to intellectually meet secularist → positivism was L.-E. Bautain (1796-1867), professor of philosophy and rector of the theological faculty at Strasbourg, who taught that all knowledge is reached only through divine revelation. Linked to the Tübingen school, he sought to ground theology on an antirationalist, mystical intuitionism (→ Intuition), which he held to be the basis of faith and theology. This form of fideism had been first noted and rejected in 1348 in the works of Nicholas of Autrecourt (ca. 1299-ca. 1369). In 1840, and again in 1844, Bautain was required to subscribe to certain theses on the proper relationship of faith and reason that had been presented by theologians in Rome (DH 2751-56).

2.1.4.3. The political movement of national unification in Italy involved an anticlericalism that was similar to French and German → secularism. → Pius IX (1846-78), who succeeded Gregory XVI, was favorable to the political movements for liberation that were underway in Italy, and he supported developments that could promote → human dignity in ways that the older regimes had not accomplished. Problems arose, however, when he was expected to approve a violent overthrow of Austria and to surrender all of the → Papal States — regions that had been given to the Holy See by kings and princes over the prior centuries. In an important way, the very hatred that lived within the new → liberalism led him to become a critic of its vision and plans.

Italian theology at the time had scholars well trained in neoscholastic developments within Thomism (→ Neoscholasticism), but few scholars showed much interest in → modernity or history or a mediating synthesis. V. Gioberti (1801-52) upheld a doctrine that was intuitionist. An immediate apprehension of God, he claimed, makes human knowledge possible.

This "ontologism" also had advocates in France and Belgium, who, in the age of L. Feuerbach (1804-

72) and Marx, were trying to avoid a complete break between human knowledge and transcendent reality (→ Immanence and Transcendence 4). All works promoting this ontologism were put on the Index in 1852, and a decree condemning the "ontologists" was issued in 1861 (DH 2841-47).

A. Rosmini-Serbati (1797-1855), who was faithful to the church, sought to advance a modern personalist → anthropology that would take seriously some of the Enlightenment's insights into both history and the human subject (→ Self). He found the conceptualism of Scholasticism enormously limiting and was interested in contributing to a reform of theology and church that would be supported by a broad range of religious sources. He engaged his followers, the Rosminians, in an academic debate with Thomists and only with difficulty escaped being listed among the ontologists. His thought was actually more closely aligned with certain Platonic understandings of human "ideas of the infinite" held to be innate in our own consciousness. As the sense of a universal openness to God came to be understood as present in Thomistic philosophy and in the larger tradition, it is not surprising that the fathers at Vatican II developed a deeper appreciation for Rosmini-Serbati's work.

2.1.4.4. Unlike the experience of theological faculties in the universities in the German-speaking realm, those in the Mediterranean world and the Anglo-Saxon spheres were relatively free of philosophical conflict. Spain and Portugal were different from the rest of Europe from the time of the Reformation and the emergence of the → baroque period. From the end of the 18th century, scholars there had promoted neoscholasticism, and it remained influential in both countries, as well as in Latin America, until well into the 20th century. In England and Ireland Roman Catholics, as noted above (see 2.1), were not permitted by the government to attend any of the national universities until the Emancipation Act of 1829.

In these circumstances, the conversion of J. H. → Newman (1801-90) was fortuitous, leading to emphasis on the historical formation of ancient doctrine through the questions raised by particular theologians and the use of their underlying hermeneutics and philosophies. In his Anglican days Newman had shown great interest in the philosophy of antiquity and in the history of dogma (→ Dogma, History of). He had also attempted to give theology a new foundation in the → Oxford Movement, arguing that in fact there was more of a broad Christian consensus on the question of → justification than was acknowledged. His conversion to Roman Catholicism in 1845 did not change his concern for the historicity of the faith. He affirmed the instinctive ability of human reason to accept convincing conclusions, and he found in → conscience a personal center of truth and morality. On these grounds he acknowledged a *consensus fidelium*. He also understood the importance of the laity in the formation of doctrine, as was clear in the Trinitarian and Christological affirmations of the fourth and fifth centuries (→ Clergy and Laity). The fact that he was attacked for his criticisms of the conceptualism of Scholasticism isolated him from many in the church. Yet in 1879 he was named a → cardinal of the church by Leo XIII (1878-1903). Newman's influence was of great importance in the development of the methodological insights that prepared the way for Vatican II. He was of particular importance to the Canadian theologian B. Lonergan, who acknowledged Newman's role in opening his own mind to the implications of development. As a result, Lonergan was able to intellectually integrate the metaphysical and the historical, the classical and the modern.

2.2. Official Reactions, Neoscholasticism, Historical Research

2.2.1. Official Reactions

For the most part, the church's → teaching office (§1) saw in the spirit of the age a decline in the clarity of the classical accounts of Christian truth and life. It often responded with condemnation, which created more of a negative dialectic within the church. Yet, strangely enough, without the limit of a negative dialectic, the true advances that were needed would never have occurred. But given that Roman Catholic tradition and mediation are different from the vision of many Reformation churches, religious and cultural concerns were connected not only to issues of faith but also to a necessary clarification of what human intelligence and the order of consciousness actually are. In the church's own specific context, the ecclesial authorities and theologians proved unable to effect the transposition from a classical to a historical account of consciousness, which came only later in the 20th century.

As can be seen from the data presented above, the patterns of theological conflict rested between faith and reason, and then within each of those realms. What really was the way reason performed and faith was given, and how were they nourished, protected, and advanced? Pius IX's encyclical *Quanta cura* (1864), with the attached → Syllabus, is a typical example of how the struggle remained clear: theology had to serve the church, not the Enlightenment, which (as is now evident) has fallen into massive disrepair and has been almost totally abandoned by the postmodern world. It was important that Roman Catholic theology used neoscholasticism to immunize dangerous tendencies, ideas, and methods, which slowly prepared the way for its scholars to make the pertinent adaptations that would bring together ancient and modern insights.

2.2.2. *Neoscholasticism*

From the time of Renaissance humanism, the church criticized the concepts, contents, and methods of Scholasticism. From 1567, however, when Pius V (1566-72) proclaimed Thomas Aquinas a doctor of the church, papal favor had been extended to Scholasticism because of its comprehensiveness and understanding of faith and reason. Thomism had been accepted in the medieval universities during the 14th century, as is clear from the 1348 General Chapter of the Dominicans. At certain times special focus was given to the value of Thomism, as for example in M. Cano's (ca. 1509-60) *De locis theologicis libri XII* (pub. 1563). While Scholasticism had long been a source of theological scholarship, it was not the only source; Aquinas himself prepared and used biblical commentaries and also cited materials from the church fathers in all his articles in the *Summae*. Later thinkers did not return to the sources that Aquinas used and to which he himself was indebted. It is interesting that even many 19th- and 20th-century scholars did not notice this variety of sources in their critiques of Scholasticism.

While Kuhn, Günther, Deutinger, and Schell attacked the objectivism of Scholasticism, they were in fact objecting to its conceptualism. It appeared to them to give the role of the subject no explicit place in the knowledge of truth. As with all classical thought, it was nonhistorical. They saw it as undervaluing the → autonomy of human → freedom as it engaged the very questions of freedom, conscience, and virtue within the realm of metaphysical thought, although by doing so, it gave a more substantive meaning to freedom.

B. Welte (1906-83) characterized neoscholasticism as almost always including a "both-and," as worked out by Aquinas in his two *Summae*. It principally stressed the outward and objective elements of faith and the → sacraments. It did not speak much of the human subject, yet it was formed only by a human subject, Aquinas himself; it was his personal appropriation of Aristotle's intellect and of the Scriptures, with all of their interiority, as well as outward substantive expression. For such thinkers Scholasticism emphasizes the central authority of the church at the expense of individual theological freedom. Unfortunately, many who condemn Scho-

lasticism for its classical methodology have never read the full range of Aquinas's work, especially his many biblical commentaries. There the place of the subject and its engagement with history is very clear, and the hermeneutic is the *sensus plenior* (fuller sense) of Catholic biblical theology.

Within the church's ordering of philosophy and theology, neoscholasticism had an almost exclusive influence (→ Thomism). Yet in his encyclical *Aeterni Patris* (1879), Leo XIII referred only briefly to the theology of Aquinas; his interest was in social philosophy and the Christian renewal of the church.

The main modern stress on the philosophical and theological contributions of Aquinas came under the influences of Pius X (1903-14), Benedict XV (1914-22), and Pius XI (1922-39). Interestingly, in the encyclical *Studiorum ducem* (1923), Pius XI introduced a greater pluralism by indicating that the Catholic theological tradition was moving through its own slow change in the relationship between classical and modern historical methods.

→ Pius XII (1939-58) also made significant advancement in promoting the engagement with the more recently developed critical scriptural methodology in his 1943 encyclical *Divino afflante Spiritu.* Furthermore, in his encyclical on the church, *Mystici Corporis Christi* (1943), he brought the new theology forward to reflect on biblical sources for ecclesiology. Thus he made major preparations, from within the Petrine office, for the insights that would develop in the preparations for Vatican II.

Vatican II made only occasional references to Aquinas. For Paul VI (1963-78), who was deeply trained in the work of neoscholastic thought through the writings of Jacques Maritain (1882-1973), the teaching of Aquinas had lasting worth, but he was not considered the church's only teacher.

The main center of neoscholastic Thomism today is the Accademia Romana di S. Tommaso d'Aquino, which since 1974 has published the journal *Studi tomistici.* Also pursuing critical research in neoscholasticism is the Pontifical Lateran University and the Pontifical University of St. Thomas, known as the Angelicum, which is administered by the Dominicans. The → Codex Iuris Canonici gives prominence to Aquinas as a teacher (1983 CIC 252).

In his 1998 encyclical *Fides et ratio,* John Paul II (1978-2005) pointed to the long and important tradition of Thomistic philosophy and theology as helping the church to differentiate elements of the fully revealed mystery of the divine Trinitarian life; the creation, fall, and redemption; Christ and the church; and the promise of eternal life as a participation in the divine life. He also encouraged the study and appropriation of other philosophical schools that offer critical insights into the new questions of our time. Formed in the neoscholasticism of the early 20th century, the phenomenology of M. Scheler, and the personalism of E. Mounier (1905-1950), he was also a serious reader and commentator on the writings of Edith Stein. John Paul II thus played a key role in encouraging the transformation of the old thinking into the forms of the new philosophical and theological insights for Catholic learning. He canonized Stein as a saint in 1998, her religious name being Teresa Benedicta of the Cross.

Benedict XVI (2005-) adds another dimension to this transformation. His work is profoundly influenced by → Augustine (354-430) and Bonaventure (ca. 1217-74) and is in dialogue with Hans Urs von Balthasar (1905-88). Benedict's theological education was in a context that was historical, biblical, and ecumenical in character. From Augustine he learned the ongoing dialogues of the various forms of → Platonism with cultures; from Bonaventure, the importance of history as it had been developed by the early → Franciscans, particularly Joachim of Fiore (ca. 1135-1202); and with von Balthasar, founder of the journal *Communio,* he shared a commitment to ongoing theological research. His many contributions include the further integration of historical and doctrinal theology, an awareness of the danger of philosophical → relativism, the need for interreligious → dialogue, and the importance of such dialogue in the formation of humanity in different cultures.

2.2.3. *Historical Research*

The development of historical scholarship, combined with biblical studies and neoscholasticism, gave history an increased and important role in 19th-century Roman Catholic theology. New editions of the Fathers and the schoolmen, as well as work done in → archaeology and medieval studies, were undertaken by various scholars. They gave greater attention to Augustine's theology, Platonic and Neoplatonic elements in early Christian theology, and ancient and medieval mysticism. Many theological centers published academic series and journals — for example, the Dominican study center at Le Saulchoir, Belgium, beginning in 1905; the Medieval Academy of America, from 1925; and the Pontifical Institute of Medieval Studies, Toronto, from 1929. The growth of scholarship since the methodological transpositions that occurred during the period from 1960 to 1980 has led to an explosion of institutes and specialized centers of research in biblical studies, → patristics, doctrine and systematics, → liturgy, moral theology, and → ecu-

menical theology, with historical research playing a role in all of these fields.

2.3. *Modernism and Antimodernism*

The attention paid by theologians and other academics to contemporary moods and to the question whether the faith could be held in concert with scientific findings finally produced what Pius X in 1907 called → modernism. The essential themes that occupied the modern discussion included the possibilities and limitations of divine revelation, the inspiration of the Bible, the uniqueness of religious knowledge, the person of Jesus and his relation to the church and its institutions, the nature of the sacraments, the strength of church tradition, the boundaries of the development of dogma, and the authority and leadership of the church's teaching office. Since the church's antimodernist measures, established by Pius X in 1910, had in a sense preserved central elements of the Christian reality during a time of turmoil (→ Antimodernist Oath), they were removed as methodological transpositions were achieved, and a broad range of theological questions were worked through in the 1940s and 1950s. The developments of those years were assembled and integrated in Vatican II. The use of the Antimodernist Oath was rescinded in 1967 by the Vatican's Congregation for the Doctrine of the Faith.

2.4. *Signs of Renewal*

2.4.1. *Cultural Catholicism*

One of the manifestations of Catholic life, nourished by the liturgical and sacramental life of the church, as well as by the biblical and historical studies that were developing, is the emergence of Catholic imagination and scholarship. The fields of history and literature took the lead in France (→ Catholicism [Roman] 1.2.4), as manifested in the *Renouveau catholique,* with religious and theological implications for the whole church. In Germany articles on similar matters of liturgy, history, and theology for intelligent Catholics appeared in the journal *Hochland.*

The extensive work of R. Guardini was a striking example of how much this religious and theological renewal could achieve. Avoiding secondary literature and exegetical findings, he produced thoughtful meditations and relevant educational expositions, trying to point to both Roman Catholic and broader Christian elements in his interpretations of the major Christian figures in intellectual history. His work was especially important in giving rise to a new awareness of the church and the role of the laity in its life. In general, Guardini produced one of the early syntheses of the many developments in theology that were underway.

2.4.2. *Movements*

Many developments and movements contributed to the renewal of theology in these two centuries. The → liturgical movement, with its contribution to the study of → liturgics (§5), prepared the ground for the renewal of worship and prayer that was undertaken by Vatican II.

A profound return to Scripture, even if it went slowly because of the need to temper the sometimes extraordinary self-confidence of thinkers such as A. Loisy (1857-1940), was established — albeit in a dialectical way because of the seemingly intractable methodological problems — by Leo XIII in his encyclical *Providentissimus Deus* (1893). Then, 50 years later, as a result of the careful work of many biblical scholars, Pius XII in *Divino afflante Spiritu* presented a more positive expression of the scholarly developments that had taken place by encouraging greater use of modern scholarship. Another significant milestone was the achievement of M.-J. Lagrange (1855-1938) in founding the École Biblique in Jerusalem in 1890. His work was especially important in that it related the historical-critical method to the traditional *sensus-plenior* hermeneutic of Catholic theology. He also began conversations with Protestant biblical scholars. After Vatican II, Roman Catholic scholars joined with scholars from the Reformation traditions in interdenominational and international cooperation (→ Exegesis, Biblical, 2.1.6).

The modern ecumenical movement (→ Ecumenism, Ecumenical Movement, 2.6-7), which dates from the World Missionary Conference in Edinburgh in 1910 and which Roman Catholics for a long time called the → Una Sancta movement, was at first treated with great reservation by the teaching office. This position is evident in the 1928 encyclical of Pius XI *Mortalium animos* and in the 1949 instruction of Pius XII *Ecclesia catholica*. Yet at the same time, individuals in several places were engaged in mutual conversations on Scripture and the life of the churches in relationship to the culture (→ Ecumenical Theology 2). The Malines Conversations, held between 1921 and 1925 in Malines, Belgium, were convened by Joseph Cardinal Mercier (1851-1926) and Viscount Halifax (1839-1934). Considerable ecumenical work was done in Holland, particularly during World War II, and a group of Dutch nuns, the Ladies of Bethany, established a house in Rome, Foyer Unitas, specifically for offering housing and hospitality to members of the Reformed churches who went to Rome in the interest of church unity. The Vatican II Decree on Ecumenism, *Unitatis redintegratio* (1964),

shepherded untiringly by Augustin Cardinal Bea (1881-1968), resulted in the institutional commitment of the Roman Catholic Church to work with other Christian churches and communities for the visible unity of the church (→ Ecumenical Dialogue). The creation of the Secretariat (from 1988, Pontifical Council) for Promoting Christian Unity by Paul VI institutionalized the ecumenical mission of the church. This commitment was expressed even more fully in John Paul II's encyclical *Ut unum sint* (1995).

Many other theologians helped to forge the methodological breakthrough by promoting it in specific areas of theological learning. By doing so, they sparked a considerable flowering of conversations within Catholicism itself, as well as in the ecumenical reexamination of many common theological questions. Both this serious internal study and the ecumenical encounters benefited greatly from common developments in biblical theology. The other sources that were recovered were the writings of the early fathers of the church (→ Patristics, Patrology, 2). French theologians took a considerable lead in a number of movements and scholarship. Perhaps one of the best known was the controversy over → Nouvelle théologie, which came to a head in 1950 and led to Pius XII's encyclical of that year *Humani generis*. This controversy involved such theologians as R. Garrigou-Lagrange, H. de Lubac (1896-1991), and Y. Congar (1904-95), as well as the series of patristic texts "Sources chrétiennes," begun in 1943 by the Jesuits de Lubac, Jean Daniélou, and Claude Mondésert. In 1938 H. Rahner (1900-1968) and other Innsbruck theologians began to develop a kerygmatic theology that contributed to the pneumatologically renewed ecclesiology of Vatican II (→ Church 3.2).

As a result of the declaration of Vatican II *Nostra aetate* (1965), special dialogues were established with → Judaism and other world religions. Again it was Cardinal Bea who guided the discussions at the council, with the bishops voting to accept this dialogue as an important part of the church's relationship to all peoples. The Secretariat for Non-Christians (1964; from 1988: Pontifical Council for Interreligious Dialogue) was established, as was the Commission for Religious Relations with the Jews (1974). Both of these offices have published important pastoral and theological materials.

2.5. *Openness to the World*

Toward the end of the 19th century, moral theology was confronted with questions and problems that a conceptualist reading of → natural law could not fully address. Teachers in moral theology took varying approaches to their subject: some invariably referred back to revealed biblical injunctions (e.g., F. X. von Linsenmann [1835-98], F. Tillmann [1874-1953], and B. Häring [1912-98]); some were preoccupied with basic discussions of moral norms and responsible Christian service to the world (e.g., T. Steinbüchel [1888-1949] and F. Böckle [1921-91]); and others dealt with moral foundations and consequences (e.g., J. Fuchs [1912-2005]). In → social ethics (§1.4.1) O. von Nell-Breuning (1890-1991) and various moral theologians who were sensitive to modern economic and political issues made substantial contributions. The so-called → social encyclicals of the late 19th and 20th centuries were often responses to particular world events that led to the disordering of systems of justice. They include *Rerum novarum* (1891), *Quadragesimo anno* (1931), *Mater et magistra* (1961), *Populorum progressio* (1967), *Laborem exercens* (1981), *Sollicitudo rei socialis* (1987), and *Centesimus annus* (1991). We could also include the apostolic letter *Octogesima adveniens* (1971). On the integration of natural law and history, and on particular matters of morality and the proper formation of conscience, two encyclicals of John Paul II stand out: *Veritatis splendor* (1993) and *Evangelium vitae* (1995).

Openness to the world and its relative autonomy may be seen elsewhere in Roman Catholic theology. Theologians paid special attention to the conditions of faith and the reasons for the lack of faith in much of the Western world. A dialogue with → Marxism began in France in 1967 (→ Marxism and Christianity), and similar conversations were held with representatives of → existentialism, with the advocates of technological progress (→ Technology), and with humanists. Some theological efforts arose seeking to interrelate issues raised by Marxist ideology and political praxis, especially → liberation theology in Latin America. Here theologians struggled with the opposition between the Marxist view of history and society and the Christian view. While some interesting insights arose in this theology regarding the meaning and mystery of → suffering and redemption, its misunderstanding of the church's role in what are secular political fields was strongly criticized and in some places condemned. Among the values that this school has brought to the church's attention are the problems of institutional poverty and the structures of injustice. The most active South American authors are G. Gutiérrez (b. 1928), L. Boff (b. 1938), and J. L. Segundo (1925-96). A more balanced form of → political theology has been formulated by the German J. B. Metz (b. 1928).

2.6. *Vatican II*

With great intensity and breadth the Second Vatican Council took up the thinking and the results of the various Roman Catholic renewals. It provided an occasion for all who had labored in the work of theology, philosophy, and history to speak openly about their discoveries, and it created a place and time for a synergy that has helped the church reappropriate its tradition and relate it to those of other Christian communities and other religions. It made theological consultants (the *periti*) available to the bishops, and they provided the necessary resources needed for the church to approach the various cultures in which it lives. The council began to develop more concrete understandings of how to identify what is of value and what is destructive in culture. The *Catechism of the Catholic Church,* published in 1992, is a resource that makes available much of the council's wisdom. It is unique among → catechisms in that it integrates the church's doctrinal, historical, moral, and spiritual traditions into a coherent whole.

Vatican II, with both its achievements and its limitations, was a continuation of the church's life, not a revolutionary event that cast aside all history and tradition. The ancient questions remain at the core of the modern situation, in which theologians continue to reappropriate new resources for the benefit of the church's identity, its important dialogues with other Christians, and its reflection concerning the mediation of the mystery of the Trinity and the redemption offered by Christ and the church to other religions and to contemporary cultures.

Bibliography: Nineteenth (and twentieth) century: R. Cessario, *A Short History of Thomism* (Washington, D.C., 2005) • E. Coreth et al., eds., *Christliche Philosophie im katholischen Denken des 19. und 20. Jahrhunderts* (3 vols.; Graz, 1987-90) • R. Corrigan, *The Church and the Nineteenth Century* (Milwaukee, 1938) • H. Daniel-Rops, *The Church in an Age of Revolution, 1789-1870* (London, 1965) • W. Dantine and E. Hultsch, "Lehre und Dogmenentwicklung im Römischen Katholizismus," *HDThG* 3.289-423 • E. Hocedez, *Histoire de la théologie au XIXe siècle* (3 vols.; Brussels, 1947-52) • D. Mercier, *Cardinal Mercier's Philosophical Essays: A Study in Neo-Thomism* (ed. D. A. Boileau; Herent, Belg., 2002) • C. F. Montalembert, *Catholic Interests in the Nineteenth Century* (London, 1852) • T. M. Schoof, *A Survey of Catholic Theology, 1800-1970* (New York, 1970) • G. Schwaiger, "Die katholischen Kirche in der geistigen Strömungen des 19. Jahrhunderts," *In Verantwortung für den Glauben* (ed. P. Neuner and H. Wagner; Freiburg,

1992) 119-33 • E. Vilanova, *Historia de la teología cristiana,* vol. 3, *Siglos XVIII, XIX y XX* (Barcelona, 1992) • B. Welte, "Zum Strukturwandel der katholischen Theologie im 19. Jahrhundert," *Auf der Spur des Ewigen* (Freiburg, 1965) 380-409.

Twentieth century: G. Bitter and G. Miller, eds., *Konturen heutiger Theologie* (Munich, 1976) • A. Darlap, "Zur Rekonstruktion der Theologiegeschichte des 20. Jahrhunderts," *ZKT* 107 (1985) 377-84 • C. Geffré, *A New Age in Theology* (New York, 1974) • R. Gibellini, *La teologia del XX secolo* (Brescia, 1992) • A. Grillmeier, *Christ in Christian Tradition* (2d ed.; Atlanta, 1975) • G. Kaufmann, ed., *Tendenzen der katholischen Theologie nach dem Zweiten Vatikanischen Konzil* (Munich, 1978) • B. J. F. Lonergan, *Insight: A Study of Human Understanding* (New York, 1957); idem, *Method in Theology* (New York, 1972) • G. A. McCool, *The Neo-Thomists* (Milwaukee, Wis., 1994) • J. L. McKenzie, *Authority in the Church* (Garden City, N.Y., 1966) • J. Macquarrie, *Twentieth-Century Religious Thought: The Frontiers of Philosophy and Theology, 1900-1960* (New York, 1963) • K. Rahner, *Hearer of the Word: Laying the Foundation for a Philosophy of Religion* (New York, 1994); idem, *Spirit in the World* (New York, 1994) • J. E. Ratté, *Three Modernists: Alfred Loisy, George Tyrell, William L. Sullivan* (New York, 1967) • R. Schaeffler, *Die Wechselbeziehung zwischen Philosophie und katholischer Theologie* (Darmstadt, 1980) • R. P. Scharlemann, ed., *Theology at the End of the Century* (Charlottesville, Va., 1990) • L. Scheffczyk, "Grundzüge der Entwicklung der Theologie zwischen der Ersten Weltkrieg und der Zweiten Vatikanischen Konzil," *HKG(J)* 7.263-301 • O. Schroeder, *Aufbruch und Mißverständnis. Zur Geschichte der reformkatholischen Bewegung* (Graz, 1969) • E. Stein, *Finite and Eternal Being: An Attempt at an Ascent to the Meaning of Being* (Washington, D.C., 2002) • G. Thils, *Orientations de la théologie* (Louvain, 1958) • H. Vorgrimler and R. Vander Gucht, eds., *Bilanz der Theologie im 20. Jahrhundert* (4 vols.; Freiburg, 1969-70).

ARTHUR L. KENNEDY

3. Orthodox Theology

3.1. *Revival of the Tradition*

In addition to ending the long reign of the Byzantine Empire, the fall of Constantinople in 1453 silenced a long and vibrant intellectual tradition in the Orthodox Christian East, whose last notable theologian was Gregory Palamas (ca. 1296-1359; → Palamism). It took nearly 400 years before a revival occurred in Russia, which is discernible in part with the establishment of the intellectual academies of the → Russian Orthodox Church at St. Petersburg (1809),

Moscow (1814), Kiev (1819), and Kazan (1842). After the fall of the Ottoman Empire, theological faculties were established in traditional Orthodox cities, including Athens (1837), Iaşi (1860), Czernowitz (1875), Bucharest (1884), Belgrade (1920), Sofia (1923), and Thessalonica (1942).

A movement to return to more authentic forms of the Orthodox spiritual and theological traditions began in the late 18th century with the Slavonic translation of the → Philocalia compiled by Nicodemus of the Holy Mountain (ca. 1749-1809), which was followed by a series of Russian translations of Eastern patristic texts. The revival of the Orthodox intellectual tradition, however, is also indebted to individual thinkers who were not affiliated with the emerging theological institutions of higher learning in traditional Orthodox countries and who, in fact, were reacting to the theology emerging from these institutions. Although the theological academies throughout the Orthodox world did play an indispensable role in the revival of the Orthodox intellectual tradition, especially in their creative appropriation of the Philocalia and in the production of translations of patristic texts (→ Patristics, Patrology), they were established on the models of German universities, and much of the theological work produced by the faculty of these theological schools was considered primarily imitative of the Protestant and Catholic scholastic manuals (→ Scholasticism).

3.2. *Russian Sophiology*

3.2.1. *Vladimir Solovyov*

Early 19th-century Russia saw the emergence of an intellectual tradition that was rooted in the Orthodox theological and liturgical tradition but that also sought to engage the modern philosophical currents streaming into Russia, especially German → idealism. From this particular trajectory emerged what is referred to as the Russian school. The best-known and most influential scholar of the Russian school is Vladimir Sergeevich Solovyov (1853-1900), considered to be the father of Russian → Sophiology. Two ideas were central to Solovyov's thought: the humanity of God *(bogochelovechestvo)* and Sophia. The fact that both these concepts remained central to Russian religious philosophy allows Rowan Williams to claim, echoing Whitehead's remark on Plato, that the whole of Russian religious thought is but a footnote to Solovyov.

Solovyov's concept of the humanity of God is related to the Orthodox dogmatic principle of the divine-human union in Christ. Solovyov, however, was far from a dogmatician. His philosophy attempts to express the Orthodox principle of the divine-human union in Christ in the categories of German idealism, particularly the philosophy of Friedrich Wilhelm Joseph von Schelling (1775-1854). Although he appropriates the philosophy of Schelling, Solovyov in his philosophy offers a unique synthesis of the Orthodox affirmation of divine-human communion and German idealism, which was marked by attempts to criticize the inadequacies of modern philosophies. The humanity of God forms the basis for Solovyov's attempt to conceptualize a God who is both transcendent of and immanent to creation (→ Immanence and Transcendence). For Solovyov, affirming the humanity of God means that → creation is intrinsic, not extrinsic, to the life of God. God relates to creation from all eternity, and creation exists in the life of God insofar as God's life is the reconciliation of all opposites: the material and the spiritual, freedom and necessity, the finite and the infinite. Creation is a movement of recovery of the original unity that is manifested in the God-man — Christ. Solovyov expresses this particular understanding of the God-world relation with the concept of Sophia, and by so doing gives birth to the Sophiological tradition of the Russian school. God is Sophia, which means that God eternally relates to creation, and creation itself — that is, created Sophia — is a movement of reconciliation toward divine Sophia.

As a result of the particular understanding of God's relation to the world that is implied in his Sophiology, Solovyov had a higher estimation of secular knowledge than the more extreme Orthodox → Slavophiles of his time. Yet Solovyov was critical of the determinism and meaninglessness of the → materialism of modern → atheism. His Sophiology was a *via media* between extreme ideas and currents of thought prevalent throughout 19th-century Russia, which included rationalism and materialism, freedom and necessity, modern atheism and Orthodox Slavophile nationalism. The identification of the humanity of God with Sophia allows Solovyov to affirm that all of created reality reflects the divine Sophia and is the movement of created Sophia toward the unity of all in God, who is divine Sophia.

3.2.2. *Sergei Bulgakov*

Although the thought of the Russian school bears the stamp of Solovyov's Sophiology up until the 1917 revolution, it was Sergei Nikolaevich Bulgakov (1871-1944) who advanced the most sophisticated development of Solovyov's thought. Bulgakov was more conversant than Solovyov with the Eastern patristic tradition, and his Sophiology is expressed explicitly in the idiom of the traditional theological dogmas and categories of the Orthodox tradition.

Bulgakov was a convert from → Marxism to Orthodoxy (→ Orthodox Christianity) and was eventually ordained in 1918. After being exiled from Russia in 1922, Bulgakov in 1925 became the cofounder and first dean of the St. Sergius Orthodox Theological Institute in Paris. Bulgakov was active in the ecumenical movement and was one of the most prominent spokespersons of Orthodoxy to the Western world (→ Ecumenism, Ecumenical Movement).

The most developed form of Bulgakov's Sophiology appears in his dogmatic trilogy *On Divine Humanity* (*O bogochelovechestve*, 1933-45), which is only now being completed in English translation. Bulgakov follows Solovyov in identifying the humanity of God with Sophia and affirms the core meaning of Solovyov's Sophiology — God is always God for "me" (i.e., for creation). God's being is not dependent on creation, nor is God exhausted in God's relation to creation; but God's being is such that God *is* the God who creates and redeems creation. Bulgakov affirms the distinction between the world that God relates to from all eternity and the created world, but it is impossible for humans to think of God as not eternally relating to the world.

Unlike Solovyov's, Bulgakov's Sophiology is more explicitly Trinitarian and appropriates traditional Trinitarian language. Sophia is identified with being, the *ousia*, but as such, *ousia* comes to mean much more than that which the persons of the → Trinity possess in common. God in God's being exists as the Creator and Redeemer of the world. *Hypostasis* does not simply indicate that which is particular in the three persons of the Trinity. The divine Sophia does not exist monistically but as Trinity. For Bulgakov, the relations between the Trinitarian persons are best understood in terms of → kenosis, as a movement of self-giving and self-receiving that has the capacity to overflow and reflect itself in the creation of the world. This kenotic movement is the source of the world and is reflected in the world, especially in the → incarnation and crucifixion of Christ. Anticipating later → liberation theology, Bulgakov argues that the crucifixion of Christ reveals the kenosis of each of the persons of the Trinity, which includes the cosuffering of the Father with the Son. Always participating in the divine Sophia, the world as created Sophia is moving toward the unity of all in God's life, which is given in and made possible by the kenosis of the Son and completed by the → Holy Spirit.

The mark of German idealism, particularly the philosophy of Schelling, is evident on Bulgakov's theology, but equally as evident is his embeddedness within the Orthodox patristic and dogmatic tradition. Like Solovyov's, his own understanding of the

God-world relation allows him to have a more positive estimation of nontheological disciplines. Moreover, Bulgakov identified problems within the patristic tradition that the resources of German idealism could assist in resolving. The Fathers did not have the last word for Bulgakov, and as they used the philosophical categories of their time, so must theology today make use of modern → philosophy to continue to extract the implications of the divine-human communion in Christ.

3.3. *The Neopatristic School*

Sophiology did not survive in any influential form past Bulgakov. Its demise is partly due to the explicit refutation of Sophiology by Orthodox thinkers in the Russian diaspora whose own understanding of Orthodox theology would come to be known as the neopatristic school. Although this school has roots in the translations of the Eastern patristic texts in Russia, it is most associated with Georges Florovsky (1893-1979) and Vladimir Nikolaevich Lossky (1903-58). Both Florovsky and Lossky were part of the 1935 "Sophia Affair" — the accusation of Bulgakov's theology as heretical by both the Moscow Patriarchate and the rival émigré synod of the Russian Orthodox Church (eventually known as the Russian Orthodox Church Outside Russia, or ROCOR).

During the time of the Sophia Affair, Florovsky was professor of patristics at St. Sergius, and he later served as dean of St. Vladimir's Orthodox Theological Seminary in Crestwood, New York (founded 1938). Florovsky framed the debate with Russian Sophiology in terms of the relation between theology and philosophy. For Florovsky, → theology must be rooted in the language and categories of the Eastern patristic texts. He coined the phrase "neopatristic synthesis," also asserting that such a synthesis must retain the Hellenistic contours of patristic thought. Florovsky argued that any attempt to de-Hellenize the language of the → church fathers would only distort their theology and divide the church.

Lossky was also a part of the Russian émigré community in Paris, but he was never affiliated with St. Sergius. He contributed a pamphlet to the Sophia Affair, *Spor o Sofii* (The debate on Sophia), that he produced for the Brotherhood of St. Photius and that rejected Bulgakov's attempt to unite certain aspects of German idealism with dogmatic Orthodox theology. For Lossky, however, the debate with Sophiology was not primarily about the relation between theology and philosophy; it was about conceptualizing the transcendent and immanent God. Both Bulgakov and Lossky share a similar starting point in theology: the principle of divine-human communion, that is, → *theōsis*. They both agree that divine-human communion is not simply the goal of the Christian life but the very presupposition, the first principle, in all theological thought. Their debate over the relation between theology and philosophy is really a disagreement over the implications of the affirmation of divine-human communion.

3.4. *Apophatic Theology*

For Lossky, much like Bulgakov, the divine-human union in Christ is the starting point for theological thinking about God. Insofar as this union is one between two opposites, between what is God and what is not God, it is beyond the grasp of human → reason, whose capacity for understanding is restricted to created reality. While human reason functions on the basis of the law of noncontradiction, the incarnation demands that theology be antinomic — that is, it must affirm the nonopposition of opposites. Theology's function is to give expression to the divine-human communion in Christ, which reveals the antinomic God — the God who is radically immanent in Christ and whose very immanence reveals God's radical transcendence. Its purpose is not to attempt to resolve the → antinomy through reason but to stretch language so as to speak of the divine-human communion in Christ in such a way that it guides one toward true knowledge of God, which is mystical union with God beyond reason. Theology is → apophatic, by which Lossky means two things: that language is inadequate to represent the God beyond all representation, and that true knowledge of God consists in experience of God and not in propositions rooted in human logic.

The affirmation of the God who is beyond being yet radically immanent to creation is the basis for the essence/energies distinction. The essence of God refers to God's transcendence, while the energies refer to God's immanence and the means for communion with God. True knowledge of God consists in participation in the energies of God, which are uncreated. The crystallization of the essence/energies distinction can be traced to Gregory Palamas. Lossky, together with Florovsky and John Meyendorff (1926-92), presented the essence/energies distinction as uniquely characteristic of and central to Orthodox theology. Its centrality is affirmed by virtually every 20th-century Orthodox theologian, including the Romanian Dumitru Staniloae (1903-93), the most famous outside the Russian and Greek orbits, and it is the reason why Orthodox theology today is often referred to as neo-Palamite. The distinction was also used in polemics against → neoscholastic understandings of created grace.

For Lossky, the truth of the essence/energies distinction lies in its antinomic character: it expresses the transcendent and immanent God without attempting to resolve the antinomy. The essence/energies distinction also constitutes Lossky's response to Bulgakov's Sophiology. The attributes of God, such as Sophia, are identified with God's energies and not with God's essence, since the latter is beyond all being and thus unknowable. Lossky also argues that the logic of apophaticism, of affirming the incomprehensibility of God's essence, requires a strict division between *theologia,* or knowing God in Godself, and *oikonomia,* knowing God as God relates salvifically to the world. To think of God as eternally relating to the world, as Bulgakov does, is to transgress this apophatic boundary and to negate the otherness between the world and God, which is the very basis for a divine-human communion based on love and freedom.

In addition to the essence/energies distinction, an additional antinomy is foundational for theology: God as Trinity. For Lossky, the revelation of God as Trinity is a "primordial fact" given in the incarnation. The goal of theology is not to explain how God is Trinity but to express the antinomy. The patristic categories of *ousia* and *hypostasis* are given in the tradition in order to express what is common and incommunicable in God as Trinity.

The Trinitarian categories, however, also provide the foundation for an understanding of personhood that is defined as irreducible uniqueness to and freedom from nature (→ Self). → Salvation as the event of → mystical union through participation in the divine energies means a realization of true personhood in which the human person is irreducible to the common human nature and thus unique, but also free in transcendence from the limitations of human nature to experience what is other than creation — the God beyond being. For Lossky, this mystical experience of God occurs though union with the deified nature of Christ and through the power of the Holy Spirit. Lossky was also a vehement opponent of the → *filioque,* which he interpreted as the natural result of the rationalization of the doctrine of the Trinity.

3.5. *John Zizioulas*

Beginning in the 1960s, the work of Lossky and Florovsky had a significant influence on a group of young theologians in Greece, most notably Nikos Nissiotis (1925-86), Christos Yannaras (b. 1935), and John Zizioulas (b. 1931). Elements of Lossky's theology, such as apophaticism, the essence/energies distinction, and the theology of personhood, are evident in Yannaras's major work of 1970, forthcoming in English translation as *Person and Eros.*

The most influential of these theologians is John Zizioulas, who has synthesized the eucharistic theology of Nicolas Afanasiev (1893-1966) and Alexander Schmemann (1921-83) with the theology of personhood of Lossky via Yannaras. Zizioulas was a student of Florovsky when the latter was a professor at the Divinity School of Harvard University; he also taught dogmatics at Holy Cross Greek Orthodox School of Theology (founded 1938) in Brookline, Massachusetts, before taking academic positions in the United Kingdom. In 1986 he was named titular metropolitan bishop of Pergamon.

Zizioulas, like Bulgakov and Lossky, affirms the principle of divine-human communion as the starting point of all theology, but unlike Lossky, who emphasizes the ascetic, mystical ascent to God, Zizioulas argues that the experience of God is communal in the event of the → Eucharist (§3.1). According to Zizioulas, the early Christians experienced the Eucharist as the constitution of the community by the Holy Spirit as the eschatological body of Christ. This experience of Christ in the Eucharist is the basis for the patristic affirmation of the divinity of Christ and the Spirit and, hence, of the affirmation of God as Trinity.

Zizioulas's emphasis of the experience of God in the *hypostasis,* or person, of Christ has at least two implications. First, it is a noticeable break with the virtual consensus in Orthodox theology on the use of the essence/energies distinction for expressing Orthodox understandings of salvation as the experience of the divine life.

Second, it is the foundation for what Zizioulas calls an "ontological revolution," insofar as it reveals God's life as that which itself is constituted in freedom and not necessity. If the Eucharist is the experience of God, and if such an experience is for created reality the freedom from the tragic necessity of death inherent to created existence, then God exists as this freedom from necessity, even the necessity of God's nature, since God gives what God *is.* The freedom of God from the necessity of God's nature is the meaning of the patristic assertion of the monarchy of the Father — the Father "causes" the Son and the Spirit and, in so doing, constitutes God's life as Trinity through a movement of → freedom and → love. With the doctrine of the Trinity, for the first time, otherness, relation, uniqueness, freedom, and communion become ontologically ultimate.

This understanding of divine-human communion in the life of the Trinity through the *hypostasis* of Christ also grounds Zizioulas's theology of personhood. Person is an *ecstatic* being — that is, free from the limitations of created nature; it is also a *hypostatic* being — that is, unique and irreducible to nature. This freedom and irreducibility is possible only in relation to God the Father through Christ by the Holy Spirit, because it is only in the eternal relations of love that one is constituted as a unique and free being — that is, a person. Zizioulas maintains the building blocks of Lossky's theology of person, but with an emphasis on relationality and in a decidedly non-apophatic approach. Zizioulas's theology of personhood is the organizing principle for this theology, and it is evident in his theology of → ministry, his ecclesiology (→ Church), and his theology of the → environment.

3.6. *Issues for the Future*

At least three central issues face Orthodox theology in the future. One is the centrality of the essence/energies distinction for expressing the transcendence and immanence of God, as well as the compatibility of this distinction as the language of divine-human communion with the language of the Trinity. Otherwise put, if the language of the Trinity is the language of divine-human communion, as Zizioulas argues, then what does this imply for understanding the essence/energies distinction?

A second issue is the question of the patristic interpretation of *hypostasis* and whether the contemporary Orthodox theology of personhood, which is arguably one of the most distinctive contributions of modern Orthodox theology, is a logical development of patristic thought. This particular understanding of *hypostasis* has been challenged by, among others, John Behr, an Orthodox patristic scholar and dean of St. Vladimir's Orthodox Theological Seminar. It has often been accused of being under the influence of French existentialism.

Finally, the revival of Russian Sophiology, especially that of Bulgakov, and its impact on the engagement of Orthodox theology with nontheological currents of thought must be studied. The Russian school was actively engaged in social issues, and its influence is evident in the work of Mother Maria Skobtsova (1891-1944), who died in a German concentration camp for protecting Jews, and of Elizabeth Behr-Sigel (1907-2005), who wrote extensively on gender issues and women's → ordination (§7.4). Engagement in social issues is noticeably absent, however, in the neopatristic school. The challenge for Orthodox theology is to retrieve what is best in the Russian and neopatristic schools in order to produce a theology that is simultaneously mystical and prophetic.

Bibliography: J. BEHR, *The Nicene Faith* (Crestwood, N.Y., 2004) • E. BEHR-SIGEL, *The Ministry of Women in the Church* (Redondo Beach, Calif., 1991) • S. BULGAKOV, *The Friend of the Bridegroom: On the Orthodox Veneration of the Forerunner* (Grand Rapids, 2003); idem, *On Divine Humanity*, vol. 1, *The Lamb of God;* vol. 2, *The Comforter;* vol. 3, *The Bride of the Lamb* (Grand Rapids, 2007, 2004, 2002; orig. pub., 1933-45); idem, *Toward a Russian Political Theology* (Edinburgh, 1999) • G. FLOROVSKY, *The Collected Works of Georges Florovsky* (14 vols.; Belmont, Mass., and Vaduz, Lichtenstein, 1972-89) • D. B. HART, *The Beauty of the Infinite: The Aesthetics of Christian Truth* (Grand Rapids, 2003) • V. LOSSKY, *In the Image and Likeness of God* (Crestwood, N.Y., 1974); idem, *The Mystical Theology of the Eastern Church* (Crestwood, N.Y., 1976); idem, *Orthodox Theology: An Introduction* (Crestwood, N.Y., 1978) • J. MEYENDORFF, *A Study of Gregory Palamas* (Crestwood, N.Y., 1964) • C. MILLER, *The Gift of the World: An Introduction to the Theology of Dumitru Stăniloae* (Edinburgh, 2000) • A. PAPANIKOLAOU, *Being with God: Trinity, Apophaticism, and Divine-Human Communion* (Notre Dame, Ind., 2006) • A. SCHMEMANN, *The Eucharist* (Crestwood, N.Y., 1988) • M. SKOBTSOVA, *Mother Maria Skobtsova: Essential Writings* (Maryknoll, N.Y., 2003) • V. SOLOVYOV, *The Justification of the Good: An Essay on Moral Philosophy* (2d ed.; Grand Rapids, 2005); idem, *Lectures on Divine Humanity* (Hudson, N.Y., 1995) • D. STANILOAE, *The Experience of God: Orthodox Dogmatic Theology* (2 vols.; Brookline, Mass., 1994-2000) • P. VALLIERE, *Modern Russian Theology: Bukharev, Soloviev, Bulgakov; Orthodox Theology in a New Key* (Grand Rapids, 2000) • C. YANNARAS, *Elements of Faith: An Introduction to Orthodox Theology* (Edinburgh, 1991); idem, *On the Absence and Unknowability of God: Heidegger and the Areopagite* (Edinburgh, 2005); idem, *Person and Eros* (Brookline, Mass., forthcoming; orig. pub., 1970) • J. ZIZIOULAS, *Being as Communion: Studies in Personhood and the Church* (Crestwood, N.Y., 1985); idem, *Communion and Otherness: Further Studies in Personhood and the Church* (London, 2006).

ARISTOTLE PAPANIKOLAOU

4. Anglican Theology

4.1. *Nineteenth Century*

4.1.1. *The Church of England and Anglicanism*

Until at least the middle of the 19th century, the term "Anglican" meant little more than "English": Anglican theology was simply the theology of the Church of England. It would be anachronistic and misleading to speak of Anglican theology except in relation to England until after about 1850. However, with the spread of the English church across the British Empire and the development of national churches, "Anglicanism" began to describe the form of church polity associated with the English church, particularly the principles of the autonomy of national churches and the importance of the historic episcopate. While the Church of England continued to be intimately connected to the state through political, educational, and economic privileges, most churches outside England were forced to survive without the official support or protection of the British monarch. Consequently, much of the political theology of the Church of England, which had dominated theological discussion from the → Reformation until the 19th century and which survived well into the 20th century, was irrelevant to a situation where Anglicanism was simply one denomination alongside others. This was true not only of most missionary contexts but also of the (Protestant) Episcopal Church of the United States, which split from the Church of England with American independence.

As national churches developed, there was an increasing perception that theological and ethical disputes between the different churches required some sort of global decision-making body. This situation led the archbishop of Canterbury to call a meeting of Anglican bishops from across the world at his official residence at Lambeth in 1867. The subsequent Lambeth Conferences, held about every ten years since, have resulted in an increased sense of pan-Anglican identity, defined more in terms of polity than in terms of English customs or origin. However, the emphasis on national independence ("provincial autonomy"), together with the lack of canonical authority for the central instruments of communion, raises questions for any international sense of Anglicanism (→ Church 3.3).

4.1.2. *Theological Institutions*

Anglican theology was intimately connected with the history of the two ancient English universities of Oxford and Cambridge, which were responsible for the education of nearly all graduate clergy. Between 1834 and 1863, about half of all graduates were ordained. For much of the century, until 1871, both universities were Anglican institutions, although Cambridge allowed non-Anglicans to matriculate, but not to graduate without subscribing to the → Thirty-nine Articles of Religion. Theology, however, did not become an undergraduate discipline at either university until the 1870s, and even then it was not highly regarded by either tutors or undergraduates; most clergy were educated in other subjects, taking a modest amount of compulsory theology as part of the examination process (which survived in Oxford until the 1930s). Charles Simeon (1759-

1836), the Cambridge church leader of the early part of the century and a prominent Evangelical, held that mathematics was far more important for clergy than the intellectual study of the Scriptures. Although a number of other Anglican institutions emerged in the 19th century, including Lampeter (1822), King's College London (established in 1829 as a counterfoil to the secular University College), and Durham (1832), most graduate → clergy were still educated at the ancient universities (→ United Kingdom 1.7).

The teaching of the compulsory courses in → theology was in the hands of the professors, who, at least at the beginning of the century, were not held in particularly high esteem. It was only later that college tutors became closely involved with the mentoring and coaching of undergraduates. This collegiate relationship became of central importance in the Oxford theological revival of the 1830s. While there was much theological discussion in England, it tended to emerge in controversies outside the universities. Theological debate was frequently occupied with the defense of the Anglican establishment, often on the High Church Tory model, with its love for order. Charles Daubeny (1745-1827), archdeacon of Salisbury, offers a good example of this style of theology. His theological justification of the church-and-state settlement, based on a high view of authority in both spheres, was written while he was working in a parish. The wide dispersion of Anglican theological debate throughout the country was reinforced by the system of patronage, which meant that the universities were able to appoint clergy (often married fellows [academics]) to about 1,000 parishes by the end of the century. University networks thus moved far outside the universities themselves, and theological and academic controversies reached the grass roots. Patronage, especially under Simeon's influence, became an important tool to ensure the propagation of Evangelicalism, which also initiated many theological and polemical organizations to promote activism at home and overseas, including the Society for the Abolition of the Slave Trade (1787), the Church Missionary Society (1799), and the Church's Ministry among the Jews (1809; → British Missions).

Clergy were often highly educated and continued to be involved in academic politics before the university reforms of the 1850s. The → university functioned as an extended community rather than simply a gathered institution of scholars and students. Given this context, English theology lacked the systematic structures of its German counterpart — most theologians were broadly educated "amateurs" occupied with many tasks in church and beyond. Anglican theology was consequently seldom systematic but far more often historical and polemical. It was characterized by occasional writings and sermons rather than lengthy systematic exposition, although many of the important lectures, especially the key Bampton Lectures in Oxford, were in fact more systematic in tone. Throughout the century a vast amount of important theological and historical work was undertaken in parsonages or rectories, including, for example, the massive *History of the Papacy* (5 vols.; 1882-94) of Mandell Creighton (1843-1901).

Crucial for the development of Anglican theology was the rise to prominence of Oriel College, Oxford, particularly under Provosts Edward Copleston (1776-1849), later bishop of Llandaff, and Edward Hawkins (1789-1882). A group of clergy gathered there known as the Noetics, who were loosely united around a defense of the rationality of Christianity on Latitudinarian lines; there was an uneasy alliance between those of different political views against dissenters and Unitarians. Most famous of the Noetics was R. D. Hampden (1793-1868), appointed amid controversy as regius professor of divinity in 1836. Although there was much movement of scholars between parishes and the common room, there was nevertheless enough coherence and intellectual stability to attract bright young tutors, among them John Keble (1792-1866), John Henry → Newman (1801-90), R. Hurrell Froude (1803-36), and Edward Bouverie Pusey (1800-1882), all of them later leaders of the → Oxford Movement. An earnest morality rooted in Bishop Butler's Aristotelianism shaped the wider Oxford scene, which helped reinvigorate the professoriate, leading to a renewed sense of seriousness and improved discipline. Professors included Charles Lloyd (1784-1829), who was influential for the leaders of the Tractarians. By 1847 the number of theology professors in Oxford had doubled to six; unlike their colleagues in most other disciplines, they gave well-attended and often influential lectures.

4.1.3. *The Oxford Movement*
It was partly through opposition to Catholic Emancipation in 1829 that some of the Oriel fellows reacted against what they regarded as a threat to the Anglican establishment of both Parliament and university. In 1833 John Keble preached a sermon before the Oxford judges in which he accused the government of "national apostasy" in its policy of trying to amalgamate a number of Irish bishoprics. This criticism led quickly to the production of Tracts for the Times, a series of 90 tracts published between 1834 and 1841. Many of them emphasized the doctrine of the apostolicity of the church, including Newman's famous Tract 1, against the perceived failures of the government.

While much of the theology of the Tractarians was characterized by polemic and controversy, they nevertheless revived Anglican theology, primarily through their patristic scholarship, which followed in the path of earlier generations of Oxford scholars. This emphasis led to the publication of a significant number of translations (the Library of the Fathers, from 1838). Tractarian theology, which regarded the end of the development of doctrine in the fifth century, pointed to the → early church rather than the Reformation as the source of theology. Some, especially Keble and Froude, explicitly attacked the Reformation heritage of the Church of England. From 1841 another publishing project, the Library of Anglo-Catholic Theology, led to reprints of the major writings of the 17th-century High Church Anglican divines, many of whom had emphasized sacramentalism and the independent ecclesiastical authority exercised principally by → bishops. As a counterblast a group of more Protestant-minded clergy republished the texts of the → Reformers through the Parker Society.

Some of the Oxford men converted to Roman Catholicism, including Newman and W. G. Ward (1812-82). After Newman's conversion, Pusey, regius professor of Hebrew, became the undisputed leader of the Anglo-Catholics until his death. As an OT scholar he maintained a strict theory of verbal → inspiration, alongside an exact knowledge of → patristics and opposition to the use of secular reason in theology.

From midcentury, dissatisfaction with the state of the universities as Christian institutions led some High Church bishops, including Samuel Wilberforce (1805-73), bishop of Oxford, who founded a diocesan seminary near his palace in Cuddesdon, to establish "theological colleges" to ensure orthodox theological formation among clergy. Later in the century Evangelicals founded their own institutions to counter the increasing Anglo-Catholic influence of the colleges. From the 1850s much energy was expended on ritualistic controversies and in battles between the church parties. As so often in the past, Anglican theology was expressed in debates over architecture, aesthetics, and liturgy as much as through doctrine.

4.1.4. *Broad Churchmen*
The impact of Oriel can also be detected in the work of Thomas Arnold (1795-1842), who had come under the influence of the Noetics. A first-class classi-

cal scholar and acquainted with German historical scholarship, Arnold went on to become headmaster of Rugby School in 1827, transforming the standards of English secondary education through the application of a "Socratic" method. In this system, which quickly spread to other schools, theology was understood as part of the general quest for truth. This goal was reached through → education and discipline of the mind as humans progressed from childhood to adulthood. Such an understanding of education resulted in an undogmatic and historical approach to religion, a progressive view of → revelation, and a broad understanding of a "national" and comprehensive church.

This approach proved extremely influential in later generations, with many leading theologians serving time as schoolmasters. Indeed, three archbishops of Canterbury in the 19th century (and two in the 20th) had been headmasters of major public schools. This humanist tradition, which was dubbed "Broad Church," continued in later generations through the work of Arnold's biographer, A. P. Stanley (1815-81), Oxford professor of ecclesiastical history and afterward dean of Westminster, as well as Frederick Temple (1821-1902), headmaster of Rugby and later archbishop of Canterbury, and Benjamin Jowett (1817-93), master of Balliol. The latter two figures helped mediate German liberal critical scholarship into English theology, which raised suspicion among many more conservative figures. In particular, Pusey, who had developed a thorough understanding of German theology in his pre-Tractarian days, later disowned its critical spirit and was hostile to the campaign for a joint Anglican and Prussian bishopric in Jerusalem. The collected volume *Essays and Reviews* of 1860, which made a serious effort to reconcile the claims of Christianity with those of general science, marked the high point of a critical Broad Church theology. Jowett's view that the Bible should be read "like any other book" was opposed both by Evangelicals and by Anglo-Catholics, causing more of a theological stir than Darwin's *Origin of Species,* published in the previous year.

Cambridge moved in a different direction from Oxford, although there were many contacts between the two universities. Arnold, for instance, had been influenced by the enigmatic poet and philosopher Samuel Taylor Coleridge (1772-1834), who had also made his mark on Cambridge theology, especially mediated through Julius Hare (1795-1855), archdeacon of Lewes. Hare was a classical historian and translator of Barthold Niebuhr's *History of Rome* (3 vols., 1811-32), as well as one of the few authors

with a serious interest in the German Reformation. He had shared his work of translation with another Cambridge man, Connop Thirlwall (1797-1875), bishop of St. David's, who had also translated F. D. E. → Schleiermacher and who as a parish priest had written the massive *History of Greece* (8 vols., 1835-44).

Hare's lectures were attended by F. D. Maurice (1805-72), who had been educated in law at Cambridge as a Unitarian before his conversion to the Church of England. Maurice, whose theology developed through sermons and polemicizing, shared in a form of → Platonism that stressed the ultimate unity of → church and state. Polymathic and complex in his writing style, Maurice has proved difficult to categorize and does not fit neatly into any church party; what he resisted most was a conception of the church that was set against the world and that defined the church as a tightly bounded system. He saw such dogmatic systems as the main error both of Evangelicals and of Tractarians. An emphasis on cooperation rather than competition led to the development of Christian socialism in the late 1840s and the establishment of the Working Men's College in 1854. His view that punishment was not everlasting led to his dismissal in 1853 from his post at King's College London. Nevertheless, Maurice was appointed to a professorship in Cambridge in 1866. He remained influential on later generations, including Michael Ramsey in the 20th century.

4.1.5. *Developments Later in the Century*

With the death of Pusey in 1882, there was no obvious successor to take on the mantle of Anglo-Catholic conservatism. Even the Oxford institution established to perpetuate his memory (and his library), Pusey House, soon came under the influence of the more open-minded Charles Gore (1853-1932). In 1889 Gore edited a volume of essays, → *Lux Mundi,* which sought to embrace a modest amount of scientific scholarship. This book paved the way for what Gore called "liberal Catholicism," which characterized much 20th-century Anglican scholarship. Gore emphasized the importance of the → incarnation, advocating a strongly kenotic theory of God's presence in Christ (→ Kenosis). At the same time, however, he maintained a high view of the → ministry and a strong belief in apostolic succession, which brought him into conflict with J. B. Lightfoot (1828-89), who maintained a more functional approach to ministry. Gore, together with Westcott in Cambridge and his friend Henry Scott Holland (1847-1918), who became Oxford regius professor, also played a central role in the revitalization of Christian socialism, by which was meant the application of Christian principles to society. Like many of his colleagues, Gore was influenced by the emergent → idealism that began to dominate Oxford philosophy in the final years of the century through the teaching of T. H. Green (1836-82) and Edward Caird (1835-1908).

In the second half of the 19th century, Cambridge theology moved in a different direction from Oxford theology. Love of classical literature and mathematics, which had been learned in the reformed public schools and as undergraduates, led many scholars to develop a meticulous attention to textual scholarship, especially the philology of the NT and other writings from the early church. In particular, J. B. Lightfoot, B. F. Westcott (1825-1901), and F. J. A. Hort (1828-92) — sometimes referred to as the Cambridge triumvirate (the first two of whom became successive bishops of Durham) — contributed to critical editions, including a NT text that became the basis for the Revised Version of the Bible (→ Bible Versions). Their cautious and thorough scholarship also produced many biblical commentaries and was regarded by some as overturning some of the more radical NT scholarship coming out of Germany. Their mutual friend Edward White Benson (1829-96), first headmaster of Wellington and first bishop of Truro and later archbishop of Canterbury, shared their fondness for textual and historical research, adopting a similar approach in his study of → Cyprian and in his solutions to the liturgical controversies in the 1880s. For Benson the antiquity of a practice, whether in defining the relationships between bishops or in determining the permitted trappings of the liturgy, proved its legitimacy.

A Cambridge mathematician who made his mark on Anglican theology in the 19th century was J. W. Colenso (1814-83), who was consecrated the first bishop of Natal in Southern Africa in 1853. His acceptance of universal redemption, his relatively tolerant attitudes toward the beliefs and practices of the Zulus, including polygamy, and his critical commentaries on the Pentateuch and Joshua created an enormous storm both in Southern Africa and in England. He was deposed in 1863 by Robert Gray (1809-72), bishop of Cape Town, but appealed to the British Crown, which overturned the decision. One result of the disputes was the convening of the 1867 Lambeth Conference to discuss relations between provinces and bishops.

Under the influence of the American theologian William Reed Huntington (1838-1909), who in *The Church Idea* (1870) sought principles for reuniting the different factions of the Episcopal Church after the Civil War, the nature and basis of the → Angli-

can Communion were clarified at the 1888 Lambeth Conference, where the assembled bishops adopted the so-called Chicago-Lambeth Quadrilateral. This document grouped the essentials of Anglicanism under four headings: acknowledgment of Scripture, acceptance of the catholic creeds, necessity of the sacraments of → baptism and → Eucharist, and the "historic episcopate," adapted to local circumstances. Within this framework there was a wide field for maneuver for the national churches. Indeed, there were great differences between the national churches, partly due to the theological emphases of the missionary societies originally responsible for planting Anglicanism, which mirrored partisan disputes in England.

4.2. *Twentieth Century*
4.2.1. *Idealism*

Although at the beginning of the 20th century there was a greater consciousness of the global nature of Anglicanism, for the most part this globe still revolved around Canterbury; most bishops were still educated in England and sent out to serve overseas (→ United Kingdom 1.8). Local Anglican theologies emerged only very slowly in different parts of the Communion. Even though the Anglican Communion later established an Inter-Anglican Theological and Doctrinal Commission, most of its work was concerned with working out principles for communion and conflict resolution rather than → systematic theology. The first American Episcopalian theologian of global stature was William Porcher DuBose (1836-1918), who exercised a modest influence outside the United States, including on the Oxford Lady Margaret Professor of Divinity William Sanday (1843-1920). Like his English counterparts, DuBose sought to learn from science and idealist philosophy.

The dominance of philosophical idealism continued to shape theology in the early years of the 20th century. This tendency was perhaps most clearly displayed in the writing of J. R. Illingworth (1848-1915), who gathered around him a number of influential writers of the *Lux Mundi* circle who met regularly in his country parsonage. Illingworth's writing stresses the incarnation, but also the → Trinity as the symbol of the perfect personality. A more idiosyncratic and Platonic variety of idealism was maintained by William Ralph Inge (1860-1954), the "gloomy dean" of St. Paul's Cathedral in London, who had worked in both Oxford and Cambridge. Drawing on a classical education and deeply influenced by neo-Platonist mysticism in both the early church and the Anglican tradition, Inge emphasized the "indestructible and eternal" values of

Goodness, Beauty, and Truth immanent in the world of space and time.

The most important figure in 20th-century Anglican theology, as well as the most influential church leader for over 20 years, was William Temple (1881-1944), who ended his career as archbishop of Canterbury. He also drew on idealism in his earlier works, asserting the rational principle behind the universe, along with the unification of all thought and experience. Divine and human personality, immanence and transcendence, were thus intimately related. Later in his career Temple moved away from this relatively optimistic idealism, gradually adopting a position closer to the Christian realism of the American Reinhold → Niebuhr (1892-1971). Temple chaired the committee that produced the 1938 report *Doctrine in the Church of England,* which attempted a theological synthesis between different parties and schools of thought but which had little coherence or lasting influence. Temple also formulated theological principles for Christian social action, retaining a strong sense of the unity of all thought and the need to work with other disciplines. His *Christianity and Social Order,* published in 1942, made an important contribution to the development of the welfare state. Social theologians, including Ronald Preston (1913-2001), who taught in Manchester, continued Temple's program of serious engagement with economic and social thought. Temple's influence can also be seen in the influential Church of England report *Faith in the City* (1985).

Others theologians, including Leonard Hodgson (1889-1969), an Oxford professor who had worked also in New York, followed a path similar to Temple's, avoiding party issues and engaging in Christian → apologetics. Some later Anglican theologians continued to draw on philosophy, including Austin Farrer (1904-68), whose work showed great originality (and few footnotes) in its treatment of the great themes of theology, and Ian Ramsey (1915-72), who worked from within the analytic tradition of linguistic philosophy (→ Language and Philosophy). Others drew on → process philosophy, including John Macquarrie (1919-2007), who taught in New York and Oxford, and Norman Pittenger (1905-97), who taught in New York and Cambridge.

4.2.2. *Controversies*

Alongside such philosophical theology, English scholarship was transformed through its increasing encounter with Continental thought, particularly in biblical studies. Sanday commented on developments in German scholarship, gradually moving toward a liberal position himself and becoming more skeptical about miracles. He introduced a research seminar, the first of its kind in English theology, members of which produced a number of important collected volumes. The publication of one of these collections in 1912, *Foundations,* edited by B. H. Streeter (1874-1937), created a major controversy, primarily on account of Streeter's own essay, which questioned the historicity of the → resurrection, using the findings of modern science and psychology. The ensuing conflict crossed continents, indicating something of the global nature of Anglicanism. Streeter's opinions so incensed Frank Weston (1871-1924), bishop of Zanzibar and a pupil of Charles Gore and author of an important work on → Christology, that shortly before World War I a pamphlet war erupted in which Sanday, who came to Streeter's defense, and Gore were the major protagonists. Weston's anxiety was that the watering down of belief acceptable in the ivory towers would prove ineffective in the competitive missionary field.

The style of thought that sought a unity between science and theology became associated with the (Modern) Churchmen's Union, led by Henry Major (1871-1961), which organized an annual conference. The conference held at Girton in Cambridge in 1921 provoked bitter controversy. J. F. Bethune-Baker (1861-1951), Cambridge Lady Margaret Professor, a patristics scholar, and Hastings Rashdall (1858-1924), dean of Carlisle, historian, and idealist philosopher, appeared to deny the truth of the incarnation. → Liberal theology seemed suspect to many of more orthodox views, including Darwell Stone (1859-1941), principal of Pusey House in Oxford and one of the most influential Anglo-Catholic theologians of the time. Bishop E. W. Barnes of Birmingham (1874-1953) continued to fly the liberal flag later in the century, although the historical scholarship in his *Rise of Christianity* (1947) was modest and confused, and his persecution of Anglo-Catholics in his diocese did little to help the modernist cause. Nevertheless, various forms of liberal → modernism, some more scholarly than others, continued to exert an influence on Anglican theology throughout the century. Similar controversies over the incarnation and resurrection reemerged at several points throughout the century, involving, for instance, some of the essays published in *The Myth of God Incarnate* in 1977 and some remarks on the resurrection made by David Jenkins (b. 1925) while bishop of Durham.

4.2.3. *The Triumph of Anglo-Catholicism*

Weston's notoriety and eloquence made him the natural leader of the Anglo-Catholics after World War I, when Anglo-Catholicism began to move into a predominant position in the Church of England. This dominance was particularly true in Oxford through such figures as N. P. Williams (1883-1943), Lady Margaret Professor of Divinity from 1927. In 1933 he published the collection *Northern Catholicism,* which functioned as a manifesto for non-Roman national catholic churches. A more liberal variety of Anglo-Catholicism found expression in characteristic Anglican fashion through another collection that drew mainly on Cambridge scholars, *Essays Catholic and Critical* (1926), edited by E. G. Selwyn (1885-1959). Selwyn became dean of Winchester and edited the journal *Theology,* which represented liberal catholicism throughout much of the century under successive editors.

Interest in ministry and → sacraments proved a particular Anglo-Catholic emphasis, producing major works of liturgical scholarship. These included A. G. Hebert's (1886-1963) *Parish Communion* (1936), Gregory Dix's (1901-52) *Shape of the Liturgy* (1945), and the volume of essays *The Apostolic Ministry* (1946), edited by Kenneth Kirk (1886-1954), bishop of Oxford. One of the most insightful discussions in this area, however, was Michael Ramsey's (1904-88) volume *The Gospel and the Catholic Church* (1936), which, unlike most Anglo-Catholic writing, shows the strong influence of Continental → Protestantism. Even beyond narrowly Anglo-Catholic circles there was important work produced in these areas, including Oliver Chase Quick's (1885-1944) *Christian Sacraments* (1927).

4.2.4. *Outside Influences*
On the whole, Anglican theology after World War I was relatively isolated from Continental influences. In particular, both Anglo-Catholicism and Evangelicalism were usually hostile to what they regarded as rationalist German thought. World War I put an end to some of the more significant dialogues between Anglican and German theologians, represented by Sanday in Oxford and F. C. Burkitt (1864-1935), a NT scholar in Cambridge. Nevertheless, a number of theologians continued to be closely acquainted with German, French, and Swedish thought. These included Alec Vidler (1899-1991), who mediated much modernist Roman Catholic thought into England, and A. G. Hebert, who was responsible for organizing translations of a number of important Swedish writings, including *Christus Victor* of Gustav Aulén (1879-1977). In a different vein, the Anglo-Catholic Eric Mascall (1905-93), an idiosyncratic Oxford philosophical theologian, helped explain transcendental Thomism to an English audience, although his broader influence was marginal.

Increasing ecumenical contact, especially after the appeal to work with other churches made at the Lambeth Conference of 1920, meant that some theologians and church leaders began to debate with German Protestant thought after World War I. These included Sir Edwyn Hoskyns (1884-1937), of Corpus Christi College, Cambridge (the only college, according to Streeter, in Oxford or Cambridge that took the teaching of theology seriously). Hoskyns knew the German scene intimately, sent his students to study at German universities, and translated Karl → Barth's *Römerbrief* in 1933. Similarly, though separately, George Bell (1883-1958), afterward bishop of Chichester, knew the German theological scene through a number of conferences. He befriended Dietrich → Bonhoeffer (1906-45) and also got to know Nathan → Söderblom (1866-1931) of Sweden. Bell was a major influence behind the foundation of the → World Council of Churches after World War II.

Anglicans were in the forefront of → ecumenical dialogue for much of the century, which included entering into successful union schemes, the most important perhaps being the → Church of South India. Anglican diversity has contributed much to → ecumenical theology through the Anglican–Roman Catholic International Commission (ARCIC) dialogues and many other bilateral conversations with other churches.

4.2.5. *After World War II*
Following World War II, Anglican theology began to move in different directions. On the one hand, figures like Michael Ramsey, professor in Durham and Cambridge before his appointment as a bishop, and Alan Richardson (1905-75), professor of theology in Nottingham and afterward dean of York, were influenced by the → "biblical theology" movement, retaining a strong interest in history and in the authority and unity of Scripture, while also maintaining the proper place of reason in theology. On the other hand, by the 1960s a number of theologians, particularly associated with Cambridge, were calling for a modernization of theology and reform of the liturgy and were questioning the traditional approach to Christian morality. This found publication in the collected volumes *Soundings* (1962) and *Objections to Christian Belief* (1963), both edited by Alec Vidler. These books looked toward the reconciliation of modern thought and theology.

Also in 1963 the bishop of Woolwich, John Robinson (1919-83), published *Honest to God,* which sold over a million copies and brought theological discussion to the popular press. It drew heavily on German sources, particularly Rudolf Bultmann

(1884-1976), Paul → Tillich (1886-1965), and Bonhoeffer, popularizing their thought and calling for the recognition of the presence of God outside the churches by demythologizing traditional forms of language about God. There were large numbers of responses from across the theological spectrum, including a hostile but intelligent criticism from Michael Ramsey, by then archbishop of Canterbury, as well as one of the leading Evangelicals, James Packer (b. 1926). *Honest to God* provided one response to the increasing secularization of society and the seeming irrelevance of traditional forms of Christianity. Its aim of secularizing religion shows close similarities to the death-of-God theology developed in the United States (→ God Is Dead Theology). Another Cambridge figure, the Scottish Episcopalian Donald Mackinnon (1913-94), who was particularly influential as a teacher, not least of future archbishop Rowan Williams, emphasized the tragic character of theology, drawing on both philosophy and Continental thought to offer a critique of the optimistic theology of the earlier liberal Anglican settlement, with its understanding of the unity between church and state.

From the mid-1960s there was a significant decline in the influence of Anglican theology in the universities and also in the country at large. This decline had been under way from the end of the 19th century with the growth of non-Anglican colleges, in both Oxford and Cambridge, as well as the opening up of university theology positions to non-Anglicans, especially in the newer universities. The relatively benign moderately liberal consensus that had dominated the churches between the wars and into the early years of the welfare state, exemplified by William Temple's writings, did not survive the onslaughts of the 1960s. Anglican theology became increasingly polarized, especially after the revival of Evangelicalism after the Keele Conference of 1967, where leaders, including John Stott (b. 1921), sought to engage with church structures and the contemporary world. The Evangelical influence on Anglican theology has increased substantially since the 1960s, particularly in the 1990s, when George Carey was archbishop of Canterbury. Widely read Evangelical theologians include Alister McGrath in Oxford, N. T. Wright, bishop of Durham, and David Ford in Cambridge. Anglican Evangelicals have moved into the theological mainstream and have come to dominate the majority of the remaining theological colleges (→ United Kingdom 2.6.2).

More liberal-minded theologians, including the patristic scholars Geoffrey Lampe (1912-80) and Maurice Wiles (1923-2005), continued to produce controversial volumes. Often there was little consensus in the church at large, as is shown by the failure to reach a consensus over *Christian Believing,* a report of 1976. Partisanship and controversy characterize contemporary Anglicanism both in England and elsewhere. Perhaps most important, the decline in candidates for ordination in England led to the closure of a number of theological colleges from the 1970s, which was followed by the closure of a number of theology departments during the 1980s. The Church of England monopoly on Oxford and Cambridge has been almost completely removed, which means that the traditional institutional basis for Anglican theology has collapsed. Shorn of their links with the churches, most theological departments, including those of Oxford and Cambridge, have been forced to question the relevance of their traditional curriculum, and most have expanded into the field of → religious studies. Nevertheless, some English theologians have sought to develop a more coherent and distinctly "Anglican" theology, notably Stephen Sykes, professor at Cambridge and Durham and bishop of Ely.

While many Anglicans are active in theology, it is not clear that there were distinctive Anglican theological movements at the end of the 20th century. This lack of an explicit confessional identity is exemplified by Rowan Williams, professor in Oxford and, since 2002, archbishop of Canterbury. A major theologian, he nevertheless draws on a huge variety of writers from many different traditions. At the same time, however, a large number of theologians from outside England and the United States are emerging as global figures in the Anglican Communion, which in time is likely to replace the English hegemony over Anglican theology. → Contextual theologies, which have developed in recent years, point to a very different future for Anglican theology, in complete contrast to earlier models.

Bibliography: I. Bradley, *The Call to Seriousness: The Evangelical Impact on the Victorians* (London, 1976) • O. J. Brose, *Frederick Denison Maurice: Rebellious Conformist* (Athens, Ohio, 1971) • P. Butler, ed., *Pusey Rediscovered* (London, 1983) • O. Chadwick, *The Mind of the Oxford Movement* (London, 1960); idem, *The Victorian Church* (2 vols.; London, 1966-70) • K. Clements, *Lovers of Discord: Twentieth-Century Theological Controversies in England* (London, 1988) • I. Ellis, *Seven against Christ: A Study of Essays and Reviews* (Leiden, 1980) • R. J. Helmstadter and B. Lightman, eds., *Victorian Faith in Crisis: Essays on Continuity and Change in Nineteenth-Century Belief* (London, 1990) • P. Hinchliff, *God and History: As-*

pects of British Theology, 1875-1914 (Oxford, 1992) • I. KER, *John Henry Newman* (Oxford, 1988) • T. A. LANGFORD, *In Search of Foundations: English Theology, 1900-1920* (New York, 1969) • J. R. MOORE, *The Post-Darwinian Controversies* (Cambridge, 1979) • R. MORGAN, ed., *The Religion of the Incarnation: Anglican Essays in Commemoration of Lux Mundi* (Bristol, 1989) • E. NICHOLSON, ed., *A Century of Theological and Religious Studies in Britain* (Oxford, 2003) • P. NOCKLES, *The Oxford Movement in Context: Anglican High Churchmanship, 1760-1857* (Cambridge, 1994) • A. M. RAMSEY, *From Gore to Temple: The Development of Anglican Theology between Lux Mundi and the Second World War, 1889-1939* (London, 1959) • B. M. G. REARDON, *Religious Thought in the Victorian Age: A Survey from Coleridge to Gore* (2d ed.; London, 1995) • A. M. G. STEPHENSON, *The Rise and Decline of English Modernism* (London, 1984) • S. SYKES and J. BOOTY, eds., *The Study of Anglicanism* (London, 1988) • P. TOON, *Evangelical Theology, 1833-1856: A Response to Tractarianism* (London, 1979) • F. M. TURNER, *Contesting Cultural Authority: Essays in Victorian Intellectual Life* (Cambridge, 1993) • G. WAINWRIGHT, ed., *Keeping the Faith: Essays to Mark the Centenary of Lux Mundi* (Philadelphia, 1988) • C. WELCH, *Protestant Thought in the Nineteenth Century* (2 vols.; New Haven, 1972-85).

MARK D. CHAPMAN

Theology of History

1. Definition

In general, the term "theology of history" denotes an express theory of history (beginning, end, course, unity, subject) in relation to God's activity, or the theological interpretation of history (its totality, meaning, epochs, and present state). More broadly, it denotes the various efforts to relate history to religious themes. Specifically, it involves relating history to God's own being and history (→ Trinity). Since concepts of its nature and validity are themselves historical, the borders are fluid.

2. Modern Theology of History

Today the presupposition that all reality is historical gives the theology of history two characteristics. First, Christianity is regarded as factually historical but is also thought to have what is essentially its own (religious) relation to history. Second, theology reflects itself historically, so that the theology of history also gives theology its own basis.

3. Issues

All forms of the Christian theology of history relate to, and are made possible by, the fact that Christianity is a religion of historical revelation and is to be explicated as such. Hence Christian thinking must deal with the theology of history. Important motivations and questions, resulting from ideal types, either collectively or individually shape its development.

3.1. The Historicity of Jesus

A basic condition of the possibility of any Christian theology of history is belief in the person and history of → Jesus as the self-revelation and → incarnation of God and as the definitive salvation-event. The historicity of → revelation and redemption has triggered reflection on the theology of history as nowhere else.

3.2. The Historicity of Christianity

As an independent continuation of the history of the faith of → Israel, Christianity grew up in a historical context. In → Paul this fact led to a kind of theology of history (Romans 4 and 9–11). Yet things are more complex, for theology of history is constitutive for the OT itself (→ Promise and Fulfillment), so that one can view OT theology as a theology of historical traditions (G. von Rad; → Deuteronomistic History; Chronicles, Books of), and the theology of history might even be restricted exclusively to → Judaism (K. Löwith).

3.3. Salvation History

From the NT references to the OT (→ Typology), there has resulted an especially influential type of theology of history that describes God's plan of salvation (Eph. 1:10), his saving action from → creation to the consummation (→ Eschatology). Along with early sketches (→ Irenaeus), we find this form of salvation history in covenant theology (J. Cocceius; → Covenant 3), in biblical theology (J. T. Beck, J. C. von Hofmann), and in modern versions of these (K. → Barth, O. Cullmann), all of them focusing on the supernatural work of salvation (the early Barth's *Urgeschichte*) within world history.

3.4. *Eschatology*

The eschatological outlook of Jesus motivated thinking about the theology of history from the very beginning. Thus we find discussion of → apocalyptic, the Pauline doctrine of the change in aeons, the problem of the → parousia, the empirical continuation of history (Luke and Acts, with their idea of the center of time), and Christian end-time speculation. All these themes have made a great historical impact (Joachim of Fiore, J. A. Bengel; → Millenarianism).

3.5. *Apologetics*

In presenting Christianity as the true philosophy as compared with Jewish → monotheism and Hellenistic religious philosophy, the → early church had to do work in the theology of history (→ Justin Martyr, Clement of Alexandria). A special question here was that of the difference between the particularity of the → church and the universality of → salvation (→ Origen and the question of universalism; → Apocatastasis).

3.6. *Political History*

The spread and consolidation of Christianity in the → Roman Empire necessitated discussion of the relation of church history to the → state and political history. → Augustine's (354-430) great contribution *The City of God* (→ Augustine's Theology) was the basis of the classic theological → philosophy of history. The true dynamic of history lay here in the antithesis of the two cities, the purely historical difference between church and state being less important (→ Progress). Along different lines the historical work of Eusebius of Caesarea (ca. 260-ca. 340) tried to demonstrate the theological status of church history.

3.7. *Secular History*

In contrast to the medieval unity of the biblical → worldview and the depiction of world history (chronology, division into periods), the 16th century brought a cautious detaching of secular history (R. Reiniccius [Reineck], J. Bodin) as a separate theological theme.

3.8. *Philosophy of History*

From a Christian standpoint the modern emancipation of philosophical thinking about history (G. B. Vico, Voltaire, I. Kant, F. Schiller) brought new basic problems but also resulted in new syntheses (G. E. Lessing, J. G. → Herder, G. W. F. Hegel). The relation of the theology of history to the philosophy of history is an ongoing topic. A new type has come in mo-

dernity with the adoption of the abiding theological presuppositions and implications of the philosophy of history (Löwith) or of historiography (L. von Ranke, J. G. Droysen). The theology of history has sometimes taken up the themes of world history (A. Toynbee, R. G. Collingwood, E. Voegelin), sometimes becomes expressly a theology of the history of the cosmos (P. Teilhard de Chardin), or in an ecumenical context (W. → Temple, H. Berkhof), has linked up with the history of human civilization.

3.9. *Theodicy*

From the time of G. W. Leibniz (1646-1716) and the criticisms of Voltaire (reacting to the 1755 Lisbon earthquake), the desire to vindicate God in face of the → evil in history has produced fresh answers that necessarily take the form of a theology of history (see Kant). Hegel (1770-1831) made a final effort to fuse the modern philosophy of history with the Christian concept of → providence. He viewed → reason in history as the self-unfolding of the → absolute and progress in the consciousness of → freedom (→ Hegelianism).

3.10. *Historical Research*

The clearer understanding of reality as wholly historical led historicocritical theology into the problem of → historicism (E. → Troeltsch, F. Meinecke). The theology of history had to face new questions regarding the theological conditions of historical work (G. Ebeling) or of the history of theology (E. Hirsch) or in debate with historical → relativism (Troeltsch, W. Dilthey) or pluralism (Troeltsch). In rather a different direction, it also had to deal with the historical nature of understanding (→ Hermeneutics), which could broaden out into an understanding of the theology of history as a history of tradition (T. Rendtorff).

3.11. *Secularity*

The phenomenon of secularity (→ Secularization) also triggered reflection on the theology of history (F. Gogarten). It could be set within a comprehensive concept of the history of Christianity (R. Rothe, Rendtorff) or grounded in intellectual history (→ God Is Dead Theology).

3.12. *Political Theology*

In the 20th century, as theology had vital experience of the tie to history in situations of collapse (World War I, the rise of Nazism in 1933), certain concepts with their own theological categories came into the theology of history (P. → Tillich: kairos and demonism; E. Hirsch, C. Schmitt). Along these lines the theology of history still has an impact on → political theology (→ Liberation Theology; Theology of Revolution) and engages in the venture of interpreting the times.

3.13. *Social Ethics*

The problems of religion and social politics that arise in modern → industrial society under the sign of → democracy and secularity led R. → Niebuhr to construct a "dramatic" theology of history. Such a theology tried empirically and critically to see social progress within a dialectical theological framework in which the Christian perception of history and → society includes the category of → sin, as well as categories of → love and → righteousness (applied Christianity).

3.14. *Thinking about the Future*

The theme of eschatology and the concept of → utopia gave a new form to the theology of history with E. Bloch's (1885-1977) theology of hope (J. Moltmann, J. B. Metz). W. Pannenberg has done the most comprehensive work in the theology of history as a basic systematic discipline. Rejecting models of progress and → teleology, he has presented history as a whole as the process of God's eschatological self-revelation anticipated by the resurrection of Jesus.

In a more radical Christian conception of time and eternity, God's own being is also thought of historically. Although eternally the same, it has a history in time. The theology of history thus takes on here a thoroughly principled form.

Bibliography: H. U. von Balthasar, *A Theology of History* (New York, 1963) • E. Breisach, *Historiography: Ancient, Medieval, and Modern* (3d ed.; Chicago, 2006) • R. K. Bultmann, *History and Eschatology* (Edinburgh, 1957) • H. Butterfield, *Christianity and History* (New York, 1950) • J. Daniélou, *The Lord of History: Reflections on the Inner Meaning of History* (Cleveland, 1958) • P. O. Lewry, *The Theology of History* (Notre Dame, Ind., 1969) • K. Löwith, *Meaning in History: The Theological Implications of the Philosophy of History* (Chicago, 1949) • C. T. McIntire, ed., *God, History, and Historians: An Anthology of Modern Christian Views of History* (New York, 1977) • J. Moltmann, "Theology of History," *Experiences in Theology* (Minneapolis, 2000) chap. 4 • R. Niebuhr, *Faith and History: A Comparison of Christian and Modern Views of History* (New York, 1949) • W. Pannenberg, ed., *Revelation as History* (New York, 1968) • H. Thielicke, *Geschichte und Existenz* (2d ed.; Gütersloh, 1964) • E. Troeltsch, *Religion in History* (Minneapolis, 1991).

Joachim Ringleben

Theology of Religions

1. Term
2. Content
3. Problems
4. Dialogue and Mission

1. Term

Theology of religions is a relatively new theological discipline that "attempts to account theologically for the meaning and value of other religions" (V.-M. Kärkkäinen 2003, 20). It studies the various religious traditions from the perspective of Christian faith and its foundational affirmation concerning Jesus Christ. Other terms have been suggested: "theologies of religions" (P. F. Knitter) or "theology of religious pluralism" (J. Dupuis). Yet "theology of religions" has gained an established status as a general title for this field of study.

Because of globalization, migration, and urban multicultural developments, most people live in multireligious situations. This factor stimulates reflection on how religions can exist side by side or together. All religions are thus challenged to review their own perspective on how their faith relates to other faiths; one can thus also find theology of religions from Buddhist, Hindu, or Islamist perspectives. Christian theology of religions, which reflects theologically on what it means for Christians to live with and relate to people of other faiths, is the most developed type of theology of religions partly because of developments within Christian mission.

2. Content

Christianity was born and is today mostly living in situations where different religions exist in multireligious contexts. That is, religious pluralism has followed Christianity throughout its existence. Christianity emerged from its Jewish roots into a kaleidoscopic world of religious views in the Hellenistic and Roman cultures. Its missionary proclamation of the true and living God manifested in Jesus Christ was pursued outside Israel in a world of many cultures and religions. The NT bears witness to the early church's encounter and controversy with these other cultures and religions. Acts speaks of Paul's encounter with the pantheon of Greek gods in Athens (Acts 17:22-34), and in Rom. 1:18-25 he writes of the hidden God known to all creatures. The eternal power and deity of God may be rationally perceived by those who look to his creation; their conscience tells them what God wants from them because the law is written "on their hearts" (Rom. 2:15). Paul also pointed to the negative aspects of religions: the conversion of the Thessalonians meant a turning from idols to serve the true God (1 Thess. 1:9); the Colossians had been transferred from the dominion of darkness to the light

(Col. 1:13), implying that their former religion was devoid of truth.

The assertion of → Cyprian (ca. 200-258) that *extra ecclesiam nulla salus est* (outside the church there is no salvation) has molded the Christian attitude for centuries. After Christianity was made a legal religion by Constantine (ruled 306-37), it eventually achieved a monopoly, and other religions were not allowed to exist.

In the course of history a number of models for how different religions could coexist have been attempted. In order to prevent war in lands of the Reformation, it was deemed advantageous to let the ruler of a land decide the faith of the land by the principle of *cuius regio eius religio* (lit. "whose the region, his the religion"). The introduction of human rights with the Enlightenment — with the most important right being that of religious freedom, including the right to change religion or to have none — established the foundations for modern plural societies. In the 20th century the rapid development of modern communication and intercultural exchange in the wake of globalization has increased the mobility of religions and cultures; as a consequence, plurality now reigns. The modern world is thus polycentric, and monistic constructions such as Christian exclusivist claims come under criticism. How to stake the claim for Christianity's absoluteness and universality is at the core of a contemporary theology of religions that can be developed only dialogically, recognizing and respecting the religious "other."

Only in the 20th century was theology of religions developed as an independent systematic theological discipline. The German theologian Ernst Troeltsch (1865-1923) argued in *Die Absolutheit des Christentums und die Religionsgeschichte* (1901; ET *The Absoluteness of Christianity and the History of Religions* [1971]) for the standard view, which followed main Christian attitudes toward other religions at that time. In his later essay "The Place of Christianity among the World Religions" (1923), Troeltsch abandoned his earlier position and opted for the very different view that Christianity is "absolute" for Christians and that the other world faiths are likewise "absolute" for their own adherents. This made him, several decades later, an influential voice of so-called pluralist theory (J. Hick, W. C. Smith, P. F. Knitter, A. Race).

In contrast, the Swiss theologian Karl → Barth (1886-1968) rejected the idea of general revelation and stated that all religions stand in contrast to divine revelation, which alone is the basis for true religion. Following Barth, the Dutch missiologist Hendrik Kraemer (1888-1965), well known for his *Christian Message in a Non-Christian World* (1938), stated that God has revealed "the way, and the truth, and the life" (John 14:6) in Jesus Christ, which God wills to be known through the whole world. The influence of Barth and Kraemer led to a so-called exclusivist attitude toward other religions, which can explain why theological conversations with other religions were in fact rare for Protestants up to the middle of the 20th century.

Under the influence of Roman Catholic theologian Karl Rahner (1904-84), Vatican II (1962-65) inaugurated a new line of thought in the Roman Catholic Church. In *Nostra aetate,* the Declaration on the Relation of the Church to Non-Christian Religions, the council provided an open and a more inclusive attitude toward other religions. Rahner's notion of "anonymous Christians" attracted broad interest in academic theology. Other Catholic theologians have broadened the scope of this approach and talked about the "unknown Christ" (Raimundo Panikkar), "ways of salvation" (Hans Küng), and "mediation of salvation" (Gustave Thils). John Paul II (1978-2005) furthered interreligious relations by spectacular events (common prayer in Assisi and visiting a mosque in Damascus), while Benedict XVI (2005-) caused an uproar in the Islamic world by ill-considered remarks about Muhammad in his talk at the University of Regensburg on September 12, 2006.

Within the ecumenical movement, especially after the integration of the International Missionary Council into the World Council of Churches (WCC, at the Third Assembly, at New Delhi in 1961), there has been both a focus on mission and an interest in developing good relations to people of other faiths. The WCC Office of Interreligious Relations has increasingly focused attention on global problems regarding "justice, peace, and the integrity of creation" (from the 1983 Vancouver assembly) as issues for interreligious dialogue, leaving theological problems unresolved but providing helpful guidelines for a dialogue for life.

3. Problems

The standard typology divides the theology of religions into *exclusivism* (Christ is the only way of salvation, and all must therefore come to Christ), *inclusivism* (Christ is the way, but God is determined to save everyone through Christ, even those far outside the church), and *pluralism* (Christ is a way to God, but God saves people in other ways as well). The most widespread attitude today within the theology of religions is the third, and its main spokesperson is John Hick, a British philosopher of religion who has spent much of his career in the United States. In Hick's view, the shift in focus from a Christocentric to a theocentric perspective is "a Copernican revolution," for it allows all religions to be seen as traveling on paths of equal value to the ultimate ("the Real"), or as planets circling around the "sun" of absolute truth.

For Christianity, the central issue for a theology of religions is that of Jesus Christ. The conviction permeates the Bible that "there is salvation in no one else, for there is no other name under heaven given among mortals by which we must be saved" (Acts 4:12); Jesus said clearly, "I am the way, and the truth, and the life. No one comes to the Father except through me" (John 14:6). But the NT also underscores God's desire that all men and women be saved, most pointedly in 1 Tim. 2:4, which affirms that God "desires everyone to be saved and to come to the knowledge of the truth." The heartbeat of the loving, caring God is to save all of his creation, to bring that creation into an eternal communion with him.

The tension between the affirmations of God's universal will to save all and the NT texts that state that salvation is only through Christ can be resolved when we see the foundation of salvation as exclusive but as realized only in the inclusive message that it is for all to accept in faith. Radical trust in God's saving acts leads to the relativization of all religious claims to truth and absoluteness. This (self-) relativization, also of the Christian faith, makes way for *mission* as witness to God's saving acts as the only cause for salvation, for *tolerance* because the justified sinner himself or herself is carried by God's own tolerance, for *dialogic praxis* that recognizes God's truth in all religions, and for *cooperation* in all dialogically established goals for the betterment of all who are included in the grace of God (Christoph Schwöbel).

4. Dialogue and Mission

Theology of religions comes to the forefront in actual interreligious dialogue in which the dialogue partners share experiences and proclaim or give witness to the truth found in their traditions. When a bridge is established, the traffic can go both ways and conversions happen. A tension has thus been perceived between dialogue and mission. This need not be the case, as there is no mission without dialogue, and no dialogue without giving witness to what is believed (mission). Christian theology of religions and missiology have much in common in that each takes its starting point in the observation of religious plurality and reflects on how to understand and respond to the reigning religious diversity. In a globalized world and amid the attractions of religious pluralism, "theology of religions and missiology must provide a responsible answer, in a culturally appropriate manner, to the question why one should adopt the claims of the Christian gospel rather than other available religious alternatives" (H. Netland 2005, 151-52).

Increasingly there is a focus on a Trinitarian and pneumatological foundation for a contemporary theology of religions. This trend is evident not only within evangelical and broadly Protestant theology (Kärkkäinen, A. Yong, M. Heim) but also in Roman Catholic contributions (Dupuis, G. D'Costa). "Perichoretic communion" is the key to understanding the triune God. The Trinity thus allows for genuine diversity and unity, where the "Other" is encountered in a mutually learning yet challenging atmosphere. Trinitarian theology of religions invites us to "relational engagement" (D'Costa) and furthers a genuine openness toward other religions, where diversity can be celebrated under the one God.

Bibliography: G. D'Costa, *The Meeting of Religions and the Trinity* (Maryknoll, N.Y., 2000) • J. Dupuis, *Christianity and the Religions: From Confrontation to Dialogue* (Maryknoll, N.Y., 2002); idem, *Toward a Christian Theology of Religious Pluralism* (Maryknoll, N.Y., 1997) • J. Hick, *A Christian Theology of Religions: The Rainbow of Faiths* (Louisville, Ky., 1995) • V.-M. Kärkkäinen, *An Introduction to the Theology of Religion* (Downers Grove, Ill., 2003); idem, *Trinity and Religious Pluralism: The Doctrine of the Trinity in Christian Theology of Religions* (Burlington, Vt., 2004) • P. F. Knitter, *Introducing Theologies of Religions* (Maryknoll, N.Y., 2002) • H. Kraemer, *The Christian Message in a Non-Christian World* (London, 1938); idem, *Religion and the Christian Faith* (London, 1956) • H. Küng et al., *Christianity and World Religions: Paths of Dialogue with Islam, Hinduism, and Buddhism* (Maryknoll, N.Y., 1993) • V. Mortensen, ed., *Theology and the Religions: A Dialogue* (Grand Rapids, 2003) • H. Netland, *Encountering Religious Pluralism: The Challenge to Christian Faith and Mission* (Downers Grove, Ill., 2001); idem, "Theology of Religions, Missiology, and Evangelicals," *Miss.* 33 (2005) 141-58 • R. Pannikar, *The Trinity and the Religious Experience of Man* (Maryknoll, N.Y., 1973) • A. Race, *Interfaith Encounter* (London, 2001) • C. Schwöbel, *Christlicher Glaube im Pluralismus. Studien zu einer Theologie der Kultur* (Tübingen, 2003) • A. Yong, *Beyond the Impasse: Towards a Pneumatological Theology of Religions* (Grand Rapids, 2003).

VIGGO MORTENSEN

Theology of Revival

Overview

The English word "revival," together with its foreign equivalents (Ger. *Erweckung,* Fr. *réveil,* Sp. *avivamiento,* Chin. *fen xing,* Kor. *bu hung*), refers to a period of time in which a community of Christians undergoes renewal and revitalization. It has been defined as "a period of religious awakening: renewed interest in religion," with "meetings often characterized by emotional excitement"; also, "revivalism" is "the spirit or kind of religion or the methods characteristic of religious revivals" *(Webster's Third New International Dictionary).* To call a religious gathering a revival is to suggest that an *intensification of experience* has occurred. The fact that numbers or multitudes attend a religious service does not make it a revival as such. What distinguishes a revival from the ordinary course of affairs is a deepening of religious feeling and expression. Revivals are thus *corporate, experiential events.*

At least since the mid-1700s, reports of Christian revivals from differing geographic regions and cultural groups have shown common themes. Participants in revivals speak of their vivid sense of spiritual things, great → joy and → faith, deep sorrow over → sin, passionate desire to evangelize others (→ Evangelism), and heightened feelings of → love for God and fellow humanity. In times of revival, people often crowd into available buildings for religious services, filling them beyond capacity. Services may last from morning until midnight. News of a revival usually travels rapidly, and sometimes the reports of revival — in person, print, or broadcast media — touch off new revivals in distant localities. During a revival, clergy and other Christian workers may receive many requests for their services. Sometimes people openly confess their sins in public settings. Another mark of revivals is generosity — individuals willing to give their time, money, or resources to support the work of the revival. Revivals are often controversial, with opponents and proponents who vehemently criticize one another. Antirevivalism typically arises in the wake of revivals. Often there are unusual bodily manifestations in revivals, such as falling down, rolling on the ground, involuntary muscle movements, laughing, shouting, and spiritual dancing. Another common feature in revivals is the occurrence of so-called signs and wonders, such as the → healing of the sick, prophecies, → visions or → dreams revealing secret knowledge, deliverance or → exorcism from the power of Satan and the demonic, and speaking in tongues (→ Glossolalia).

1. Significance and Scope of the Term

Having characterized the term "revival," it is necessary to explore the significance and scope of the phrase "theology of revival." First, the descriptions of experiences that commonly occur during Christian revivals are intertwined with intellectual formulations of belief or doctrines. The first-person narratives of the revival tradition make constant reference to the Christian doctrines of God, God's love, the → Trinity, the divinity of Jesus, Jesus' atoning death, Jesus' second coming (→ Eschatology), the → Holy Spirit, faith, repentance, holiness (or → sanctification), and so forth. Christian revival experiences are thus closely linked with theological ideas and teachings.

Second, most revivals have included → preaching

as a key element, and "theology of revival" might appropriately refer to the explicit or implicit → theology contained in sermons associated with revivals. Different revivals have had different messages. Some have been known for a strongly penitential atmosphere (→ Penitence) and heavy emphasis on sin and the → confession of sins, while others have been characterized by joy and even hilarity. The public preaching during a time of revival might center on → conversion, confession of sins, holiness or sanctification, the call to → unity among Christians, → consecration for God's service, deliverance from addiction or habitual sin, healing of the sick, or manifestations of God's power in signs and wonders. Theology of revival may be a *preached* theology.

Third, Christian revivals not only contain explicit or implicit doctrinal content but also have frequently served as a basis and provocation for theological reflection. Theological themes that have often been discussed in the wake of Christian revivals include the nature of sin, the meaning of faith and repentance, the place of → prayer in triggering revival, the signs or marks of true conversion, the significance of bodily manifestations in the midst of revivals, spiritual discernment and the distinction between genuine and counterfeit → spirituality, the activity and effects of Satan and the → demonic, the dangers of religious fanaticism, the role of laypersons and especially the issue of lay preaching or exhorting (→ Lay Movement), the role of women in the church, the limits of ministerial authority, the resolution of → conflicts between ministers and laypeople, the possible grounds for ministers or laypersons to separate from congregations or denominations that oppose revivals, the need for new associations and collaborations among proponents of revival, the challenges of practicing the Christian faith in a rigorous and authentic fashion, and the call for social reform and social justice.

Because Christian revivals have been a notable feature in the growth and expansion of Christianity throughout Latin America and the Caribbean, sub-Saharan Africa, Asia, and Oceania in the 19th and 20th centuries, it would be inappropriate to limit the theology of revival to writings produced in Europe and North America, or to theological reflections that have been occasioned by spiritual awakenings within the so-called Western world. Especially during the last century, crucial developments have occurred outside of Europe and North America, and a growing literature treats Christian revivals within non-Western contexts. Since the *content* of a given theology of revival emerges from the *context* of a particular revival, this article will give attention to the shifting historical

and cultural contexts in which thinkers have reflected on revivals during the last 300 years. The idea of revival has special pertinence and application for → Protestantism beginning in the 1700s, and though renewal movements in early and medieval Christendom, as well as in modern → Roman Catholicism, show affinities with the Protestant revival, the discussion here will primarily focus on Protestant Christianity, together with its daughter traditions such as → Pentecostalism, the Charismatic Renewal (→ Charismatic Movement; Charismatic Religion), and nondenominational and parachurch movements.

2. Pietism and the Pietist Tradition

In continental Europe during the decades following the Peace of Westphalia (1648), a number of Protestant leaders spoke of listlessness and torpor in the churches. Congregations were clergy-centered, and ministers gave lengthy sermons with overriding stress on correct doctrine. Johann Arndt's *True Christianity* (1606-9) was an early sign of German Lutheran interest in the cultivation of the interior life. Philip Spener (1635-1705), regarded as the father of the Pietist movement, wrote an influential preface to Arndt's work, *Pia desideria* (1675), later republished separately. Spener laid out a renewal program centering on prayer and devotional reading of the Bible outside the context of Sunday worship. He called for a "reformation of life" to complement the reformation of doctrine that had occurred during the 1500s.

Since the 1800s, and especially through the influence of Albrecht Ritschl's hostile study *Geschichte des Pietismus* (3 vols., 1880-86), the word → "Pietism" became associated with emotionalism, subjectivism, moralism, legalism, separatism, and other-worldliness. Yet Spener's original program for church-based renewal had many positive aspects, not least that it sought spiritual transformation in the lives of individuals and congregations without producing separation or schism in the church.

Spener defined a Pietist as a person who "uses all his energy to improve the church." This energy was focused on small gatherings of believers known as *collegia pietatis* (colleges of piety) or *ecclesiola in ecclesia* (little churches within the church). Spener had read widely in Christian literature, and it is possible that his idea for small groups, or conventicles, had been taken over from English → Puritanism, though the Continental Reformer Martin → Bucer (1491-1551) had also suggested this idea. The deadness of the churches, Spener thought, was in part a consequence of the deadness of the ministers themselves, who needed awakening. The sharp division of clergy from laity was also unhelpful (→ Clergy and Laity). Spener believed that not all elements of Lutheran → orthodoxy (§1) were equally important, and a distinction needed to be made between primary and secondary doctrines. The Bible was to be read in a devotional way, not merely to establish theological doctrines. The Pietists stressed conversion, or the new birth, and published personal stories that often included a dramatic struggle to come to repentance (Ger. *Bußkampf;* → Penitence).

Through Spener's disciple August → Francke (1663-1727), long associated with Halle University, Pietism became linked with philanthropic work and foreign → missions. In New England, Cotton Mather (1663-1728) promoted a church renewal agenda that mirrored that of Spener and Francke, with whom he corresponded. A later exponent of Pietism was the nobleman, Christian activist, and early ecumenist Count Nicholas von → Zinzendorf (1700-1760), who opened his estate (called Herrnhut, lit. "under the Lord's watch," or "on watch for the Lord") to Pietist → Moravians and made it a place for prayer and foreign missionary outreach. Reformed Pietists in Germany (such as Friedrich Adolph Lampe [1683-1729]) and Reformed Pietists in the Netherlands (including Jodocus van Lodenstein [1620-77] and Willem Teellinck [1579-1629]) shared much in common with German Lutheran Pietists.

W. R. Ward's erudite volume *The Protestant Evangelical Awakening* (1992) traces the beginnings of the 18th-century evangelical movement in continental Europe not to church leaders like Spener but to a grassroots movement in Lower Silesia (i.e., Germany) among Protestant populations that had undergone "forcible catholicisation." Following Swedish military intervention in 1707-8, a "revolt of the children" in Silesia featured daily prayer and singing in open-air services *(Feldgottesdiensten),* inasmuch as the Catholic authorities had confiscated the Protestant church buildings. Revival services flourished and spread, despite political opposition. A similar pattern, as Ward notes, was seen among other groups of harassed Protestants, such as the Swedish prisoners of war in Russia during 1707-22 and among the Salzburg exiles in 1731-32. Such "revivalism" was "a response of those . . . who not only had no time for programmes of church renewal to succeed, but for the most part had no institutional church to renew" (p. 136).

Scandinavia during the 1800s developed a rich Pietist tradition that existed in both the state Lutheran churches and the free churches. In Norway the preaching of Hans Nielsen Hauge (1771-1824) led a church renewal movement that became controversial because of its reliance on lay preachers. By the early 20th century the restrictions on → lay preaching had been relaxed in Norwegian Lutheranism.

Many practices originating in the Pietist program for church renewal — the formation of small groups, stress on private prayer and Bible reading, call for individual conversion experience, sharing of personal testimonies, insistence that ministers be spiritually qualified, and emphasis on experience rather than doctrine alone — were later carried into → Methodism, the American Great Awakening and Second Great Awakening, and into global evangelicalism, with its many parachurch organizations (e.g., missionary societies, social reform organizations, and campus fellowship groups). Though Pietism did not display the full set of characteristics associated with Christian revivals since the early 1800s, its theological stress on conversion was a key ingredient within an emerging theology of revival.

3. Puritanism in the 1600s

3.1. *England*

In England, the Puritan movement anticipated Pietism by several decades in its promotion of church-based reform and renewal. Like Pietists, → Puritans sought to cultivate the interior life through prayer, Scripture reading, and disciplined living. They also laid great emphasis on the doctrine of conversion. Yet Puritanism differed from Pietism in a number of respects, partly because of the differing ecclesial situation in England, with its established → Anglican Church, and also because of differing theological emphases in → Calvinism as compared with → Lutheranism. Certain issues debated by Puritans and their opponents in the Church of England were not major concerns for Continental Pietists, such as the proper form of → church government (e.g., episcopacy, presbyterianism, or congregationalism), the use of physical gestures in → worship (e.g., genuflection or kneeling), the revision of the → liturgy, and the suitability of artwork in church sanctuaries (→ Icon; Iconography 2). Perhaps more than the Pietists, the Puritans understood the Christian life in strenuous terms, as a struggle of God's chosen few against the world, the flesh, and the devil. Their sense of an all-encompassing divine providence led them to concern themselves with God's work in the world at large, including the home, school, marketplace, and town meeting.

Characteristic of the Puritan outlook was a pronounced concern with self-deception and the danger of hypocrisy. Mere outward conformity to Christian principles was no guarantee that a person had achieved regeneration. In an effort to transcend hypocrisy, Puritanism became preoccupied with a search for signs to indicate the presence of → grace. This focus engendered a tendency toward prolonged and profound self-scrutiny. Through unrelenting introspection one might be able to strip away the onionskins of vain and self-flattering hopes and at last discern a core of sincere and unhypocritical faith.

Just as important to the Puritans as self-scrutiny was the "morphology of conversion," described by Edmund Morgan as a scheme of experience in which each spiritual stage might be distinguished from the next, allowing a person to check his or her eternal condition by a set of recognizable signs. While the details of this morphology varied from one Puritan author to another, the general assumption was that a sinner would receive grace only after becoming aware of spiritual impotence and utter helplessness before God. One had to receive and embrace the bad news regarding one's sinfulness before one could grasp the good news of God's pardoning love. "Humiliation" or even "terror" had to precede conversion. The Puritan author William Perkins (1558-1602) laid out no fewer than ten steps by which a lost sinner moved from spiritual insensibility toward uneasiness, anxiety, futile self-effort, resignation, and, at last, a cautious, chastened hope in God's mercy.

The 17th-century Puritan theology of conversion presumed that → assurance of one's salvation could be obtained and maintained only through struggle. Unlike most revival preachers of the 1800s and 1900s, the Puritans did not imagine that a well-grounded hope in God's favor could be based on a passing experience or a momentary decision to respond to an evangelistic appeal. The Puritans, by and large, were skeptical regarding reports of instantaneous conversion, for they thought of the soul's salvation as a lengthy and difficult ordeal.

A complication in the Puritan theology of revival, as Charles Lippy has explained, was its grounding in the thought of John → Calvin (1509-64), especially as mediated through the writings of Calvinist theologians such as Perkins and William Ames (1576-1633). The difficulty was to reconcile human decision-making, responsibility, and covenant keeping with the notion of divine → predestination. Strict Calvinists — maintaining the famous "five points" formulated at the Synod of Dort in the Netherlands in 1618-19 — used the term "limited atonement" to imply that the beneficial and salvific effects of Christ's death applied only to the elect. Such a Calvinistic theology of revival was characteristic not only of 17th-century American Puritans such as John Cotton, Richard Hooker, Solomon Stoddard, and Increase and Cotton Mather, but also of 18th-century American preachers and teachers such as Jonathan → Edwards, Jonathan Dickinson, Gilbert Tennent, Samuel Davies, Samuel Blair, the Anglican Devereaux Jarratt, and the Baptist Isaac Backus, as well as 19th-century American revivalists such as James McGready, Asahel Nettleton, and Bennett Tyler.

Another implication of Calvinistic predestination was that humans did not enter into salvation simply as a result of their own volition. Why, then, would preachers like Edwards and Nettleton urge their listeners to seek conversion? In actuality, what they urged was not so much a choosing of salvation as a looking into one's soul to see if there were signs that God had already bestowed salvation. Through introspection, one could discern the incipient signs of grace. Nonetheless, Calvinistic theology held that unconverted persons could dispose or prepare themselves for divine grace through use of the so-called → means of grace, that is, attendance at worship, listening to sermons, personal prayer, Bible reading, and the keeping of a spiritual journal. This call to prepare oneself for conversion in these ways was later referred to as preparationism. Though seemingly in tension with the doctrine of predestination, preparationism balanced out the Puritan stress on God's sovereignty by insisting that there was something that human beings could and should do while they were waiting on God to grant his converting grace.

3.2. New England

In colonial New England, where Puritanism achieved its most concentrated expression during the 1600s, pastors from time to time had noted sparks of increased interest in religion, times of "harvest" when larger than usual numbers of new people came under the church's care. Often those earlier harvest times occurred after preachers offered jeremiads — sermons bemoaning an apparent decline of commitment to God and warning of dire consequences that would follow from disobeying God's commands. For New England Puritans, perceptions of decline were consistent with their interpretation of the Bible, particularly of the Hebrew Scriptures. In the saga of ancient Israel, Puritans found precedents for their own experience of a cyclic pattern of heightening and declining spiritual life in their communities. God had entered into a → covenant with the Hebrew people at → Sinai, promising blessing so long as the people remained faithful. So, too, God entered into a covenant with Puritan Christians, likewise promising blessing so long as the people remained faithful to their commitments to God and their covenant with God.

Following an OT pattern (see Joshua 24), 17th-century Puritan communities periodically renewed their pledge to follow God and God's ways — something like a repetition of vows by a long-married couple. This step was sometimes referred to as "owning the covenant," and it suggested a corporate rather than an individualistic model of how God related to Christian people. Colonial pastor Increase Mather (1639-1723), for example, preached a sermon entitled "Returning unto God the Great Concernment of a Covenant People" (1680), which was accompanied by a church covenant stating that "we do give ourselves unto . . . God" and "we do also give up ourselves one unto another, in the Lord." To be committed to God was also to be committed to the community. With its corporate process of covenant renewal, Puritanism differed from the more individualistic theology of revival that became prominent during the 1700s and subsequently.

4. The Evangelical Awakening in Britain and the Great Awakening in America

The transatlantic religious revolution that became known as the Evangelical Awakening in Britain and the Great Awakening in America burst forth in the mid-1730s and early 1740s. Its leading personalities included George → Whitefield (1714-70), Jonathan Edwards (1703-58), and the brothers John (1703-91) and Charles (1707-88) Wesley. Each had distinctive gifts — Whitefield the "Grand Itinerant" and comparable orator; Edwards the pastor, author, and theologian of Christian revival; Charles Wesley the hymn writer; and John → Wesley the itinerant preacher and Methodist organizer. By most measures, Edwards stands out as the most influential of all authors on the topic of Christian revival. He is also the observer, analyst, theoretician, and theologian with whom all later authors on revival have had to grapple. Because of the wide diffusion of global evangelicalism (→ Evangelical Movement) and Pentecostalism, Edwards's ideas are arguably more influential today than ever before.

A forerunner of the Great Awakening in America was Theodorus Frelinghuysen (1691-1747), who spent his early life in Germany and the Netherlands and then immigrated to America in 1720 as a Dutch Reformed minister among Dutch immigrants in New Jersey. Shortly after arriving in America, Frelinghuysen became known for his intense piety and probing sermons, and for speaking out against gambling, drunkenness, and nominal Christianity

among the Dutch. He became intensely controversial after he warned his congregants against partaking of the Lord's Supper unless they exhibited clear evidences of conversion.

4.1. *Whitefield*

Beginning in the late 1730s, George Whitefield's preaching had an extraordinary effect on both sides of the Atlantic in catalyzing and solidifying what was perceived to be a single revival movement, or "work of God," in far-flung locations. Whitefield's fervent and often extemporaneous sermons turned biblical narratives into a kind of actor's script, so that Whitefield became, in Harry Stout's phrase, "the divine dramatist." In London he is estimated to have preached to as many as 20,000 at one time, and in Boston and Philadelphia during 1740-41 his crowds may have included as many as 15,000 persons. While Whitefield's role in the awakening of the 1740s is well known, hundreds of lesser known and unknown local pastors and lay exhorters were inspired by Whitefield and the spiritual climate of that time to preach revival sermons in local parishes and other locations. In this way the Great Awakening came not only to the venues where Whitefield preached but to hundreds of towns and hamlets throughout Britain and the American colonies.

The town of Cambuslang, Scotland (located on the outskirts of Glasgow), was the scene of a dramatic episode in Whitefield's ministry. A sacramental season, or "holy fair" — for Scottish Presbyterians a days-long outdoor event, with preaching followed by reception of the Lord's Supper — began quietly under the leadership of William M'Culloch (1691-1771) but then became increasingly enthusiastic. Weeping, trembling, outcries, pain, and even nosebleeds were reported, and the event came to a climax as Whitefield arrived and preached to an estimated 30,000 hearers in August 1742. Debates over the unusual phenomena at Cambuslang were repeated in the aftermath of the Cane Ridge Revival in Kentucky in August 1801. Like the revival at Cambuslang, that at Cane Ridge began during a Presbyterian sacramental season and led to tears, outcries, and fainting. The significance of bodily manifestations became an ongoing theme in the literature of Christian revivals.

4.2. *Edwards*

An early sign of the emerging 18th-century revival tradition was the Northampton (Mass.) Awakening of 1734-35, led by the town's pastor, Jonathan Edwards, and resulting in the conversion of several hundred people in this town. In 1733-34 the young people of Northampton began to show "flexibleness" in yielding to the pastor's spiritual advice, and then the sudden deaths of two flourishing youths brought a deep seriousness to the whole community. Edwards observed that his sermon series on the doctrine of → justification had a notable impact. Soon there were signs of spiritual interest springing up throughout the town, as well as arising independently at various localities that had not been in communication with one another. By the spring of 1735 the town, Edwards wrote, "seemed to be full of the presence of God," and nearly everyone was preoccupied with God and the issue of salvation. Yet the atmosphere of revival quickly dissipated when a man in despair over his lack of a conversion experience — Edwards's own uncle — took his own life. Though Edwards saw his uncle's melancholic temperament as a contributing factor in the suicide, he also claimed that Satan had driven his uncle to a desperate act to hinder God's work in the revival.

Just as important, in the long run, as the 1734-35 revival itself was Edwards's description of the event in his *Faithful Narrative of the Surprising Work of God* (1737). Edwards's account combines acute psychological observation with brilliant inference and theological analysis. Description and interpretation mesh. Nothing quite like it had been written before, and for this reason Edwards's *Faithful Narrative* might be regarded as the first full-fledged revival narrative. Edwards's observations showed him that conversion took place in different ways and showed a "vast variety." The older Puritan morphology of conversion, specifying definite stages of conversion that everyone had to undergo, did not match up with converts' lived experience. Edwards made note of the extraordinary experiences that some people had undergone in the midst of the Northampton revival, including visions of God, of Christ on the cross, and of the fires of → hell. With his customary caution, Edwards neither accepted these experiences as revelatory nor rejected them as delusory. Instead, he generally held them as due to the activity of the imagination while someone was in a state of spiritual and emotional arousal.

In his 1741 Yale College commencement address, "Distinguishing Marks of the Work of the Spirit of God," and in his full-length treatise *Some Thoughts on the Revival* (1742), Edwards responded to critics of the Great Awakening who attacked the revival and saw nothing good in it. Edwards believed that critics of the revival had gone astray, first, by judging the revival a priori (i.e., with presuppositions about how a revival could or should take place); second, by not using the Bible as a whole as their rule for judging; and, third, by not distinguishing the good from the bad in the revival. *Some Thoughts* asserted that

critics must not pass judgment on a revival as a whole because it had negative aspects; the fire and fervor of revival was bound to bring with it a measure of extremism. Furthermore, Edwards reasoned that no one should dictate in advance how God might act in the midst of a revival. If God chose to accomplish his purposes through lowly people, then it was incumbent on the leaders to acknowledge the revival and not oppose it. Even the "rash zeal" of younger believers might be a rebuke to the pride and spiritual coldness of older Christians. Edwards, however, also took aim at the "excesses and extravagances" of the prorevival party. He was especially critical of those who believed that they were invulnerable to error, and he identified "spiritual pride" as a common source of error. People undergoing ecstatic experiences could become convinced that God was guiding their every thought, interpret their passing impressions as divine revelations, and thus become immune to criticism. This dangerous attitude led to all manner of rash behavior, and it could be avoided only through an attitude of → humility. Taken as a whole, *Some Thoughts* exhibited openness and caution in nearly equal measure.

Edwards's later publications contributed further to his many-sided theology of Christian revival. A sermon series from the 1730s, posthumously published as *History of the Work of Redemption* (1774), offered a narrative of world history from creation to consummation in which alternating phases of revitalization and declension brought the church ever closer to the culmination of God's purposes. Progress was linear, and yet the church's advance did not occur without ups and downs. The picture portrayed in this treatise was — as Perry Miller noted — "Northampton writ large," or Edwards's attempt to generalize the revival experiences of his own parish.

Edwards's *Religious Affections* (1747) continued and completed many ideas treated in his earlier works on the revival. Though Edwards was preoccupied with the old Puritan issue of assurance of salvation, he rejected the idea that conversion always followed a given pattern. Assurance of salvation was not based on experiences of terror and comfort that follow a given sequence. Instead, Edwards highlighted the centrality of the "affections" in spiritual life and found the sign of truly gracious affections to lie in their objective, God-centered character and their tendency to engender "holy practice."

In *Humble Attempt* (1748) Edwards promoted the transatlantic "concert of prayer," in which congregations in far-flung locations united to pray for revival on the same day of the month. This work had notable historical influence in promoting prayer for revival in the 1700s and 1800s and, since the 1980s, has reemerged as a seminal work in the contemporary international Christian prayer movement. Finally, Edwards's *Life of Brainerd* (1749), though not specifically addressed to the topic of revival, helped to instill the idea that spiritual awakening might be rooted in the self-sacrificial life of a dedicated individual.

4.3. *Chauncy*

While Jonathan Edwards judged the Great Awakening to be, on the whole, "a glorious work of God," Boston Congregationalist pastor Charles Chauncy (1705-87) held an opposing view. "Religion, of late," he wrote, "has been more a commotion in the passions, than a change in the temper of the mind." His sermon "Enthusiasm Described and Cautioned Against" (1742) argued that many who participated in the revival mistook their own passions for supernatural guidance. These "enthusiasts" were caught up in a false spirituality characterized by bodily convulsions, freakish conduct, imagined favor with God, and a dismissal of rational thought. Strengthening Chauncy's case against the revival was the outlandish behavior of James Davenport (1716-57), known for singing in the streets, preaching for as long as 24 hours at a time, and, in one notorious episode, calling for a public bonfire in which his followers burned their clothes and other finery to purify themselves of worldliness.

Chauncy's book *Seasonable Thoughts on the State of Religion in New England* (1743) interpreted the awakening in terms of emotionalism, religious excess, social disorder, and a breakdown of proper relations between ministers and their flocks. Itinerant preachers like Whitefield were "busie-bodies" who had no right to invade other ministers' parishes. Even worse, itinerant preachers opened the door to unqualified lay exhorters who did much harm. By setting laypeople against their ministers, the revival preachers sowed "the seeds of contention and separation." The practice of "uncharitable judging" had begun with Whitefield, who set a negative example.

Chauncy's prioritization of → reason over affections marked a difference between his position and that of Edwards, who viewed the affections and the reason as coequal elements in human personhood. The Edwards-Chauncy debate during the Great Awakening was probably the most influential public controversy over religious revivals in American history, and echoes of their arguments from the 1740s could be heard throughout the 1800s and 1900s. The controversy of the 1820s and 1830s regarding revival preacher Charles → Finney repeated many themes debated in the 1740s.

4.4. *Wesley*

John Wesley was the father of the Methodist movement and later the → Methodist Church, a grandfather (through his teaching on sanctification) of the → Holiness movement of the 1800s, and, in effect, a great-grandfather of the Pentecostal movement that emerged from the Holiness movement. Wesley had a brief and troubled stint as a minister in the American colony of Georgia, returned to England, and then underwent conversion or spiritual renewal (scholars have debated which category to use) at Aldersgate in London in 1738. Though Wesley was not Edwards's peer as a theological author, his sermons and autobiographical writings contain an implicit theology of revival that emerged from his wide reading of the → church fathers, Anglican and Puritan authors, and Catholic mystics; from his contact with Moravians Pietists; and from his experience as an itinerant preacher over a period of 50 years. Among the characteristics of Wesley's theology of revival were his stress on the believer's assurance of salvation through "the witness of the Spirit" (see Rom. 8:16), his evangelical → Arminianism, his doctrine of "entire sanctification," and what might be called his openness to bodily and charismatic manifestations.

Though Wesley's encounters with Moravians in America and England were a factor in his attainment of personal assurance of salvation, he later parted company with the Moravians because of their teaching on "stillness," the idea that believers should do nothing but wait on God to act in their lives. His sermon "The Means of Grace" (1739) set forth the idea — akin to earlier Puritan preparationism — that practices such as prayer, Scripture reading, listening to sermons, and partaking of the Lord's Supper are "the ordinary channels whereby [God] might convey to men, preventing, justifying, or sanctifying grace."

Before Wesley, Arminian theology — as summarized and repudiated in the Synod of Dort's "Five Points" in 1618-19 — was generally associated with enlightened or rationalistic thinkers who questioned not only Calvinist tenets but other Christian doctrines as well. Wesley showed that it was possible to combine an evangelical and evangelistic stress on Christ and salvation — and even a robust doctrine of original sin — with a principled rejection of Calvinist positions on unconditional election, limited atonement, the unfree will, and the perseverance of the saints. For Arminian Methodists, who traced their roots to John Wesley, humans were indeed mired in sin. Yet if humans freely chose to disobey God's will, they must also freely choose to accept the salvation offered to all through the atoning death of Christ for all people. When Arminians spoke of divine predestination, they described it as conditional rather than unconditional. That is, those chosen for salvation were persons whom God foreknew would choose to accept the Christian gospel. According to this conditional concept of predestination, God's choice is contingent on human choice, rather than vice versa.

For Wesley, there was no way to reconcile the Bible's open-ended invitations — "whosoever will, let him take the water of life freely" (Rev. 22:17 KJV) — with the seemingly closed system of predestinarianism. Calvinism was a form of → fatalism and, as such, inconsistent with the evangelistic imperative of the NT. Wesley's vitriolic assault on Calvinism in his sermon "Free Grace" (1740) created a rift with his fellow revivalist, the Calvinist George Whitefield, and the two men remained in a respectful and yet uneasy coexistence in later years because of their theological disagreements. During the so-called Antinomian Controversy of 1770-76, Wesley's close associate John Fletcher (1729-85) charged Calvinists with teaching a form of theological fatalism that discouraged holy living and good works. While Wesley's Arminian theology of revival has prevailed among Methodists, Holiness teachers, Pentecostals, and many Baptist and nondenominational groups, the Calvinist position continues to be represented by an outspoken and articulate minority. The theological conundrum of Calvinism versus Arminianism is still a live issue within the theology of revival.

Wesley is also known for his teaching on holiness, contained in his treatise *A Plain Account of Christian → Perfection* (1777), which argued that it is possible for a Christian believer in the present life to become free from sin, or at least free from all conscious and deliberate sinning against God. Wesley referred to this state variously as "entire sanctification" or "perfect love." Though he never claimed that he himself had attained this state, Wesley was willing to accept the claims of certain followers to have done so. Wesley regarded entire sanctification as Methodism's defining doctrine, though many non-Methodist theologians have attacked it as unbiblical, self-delusory, and tending toward fanaticism. The Methodists themselves began to deemphasize entire sanctification by the early 1800s, and outside of stricter Wesleyan circles, this doctrine largely dropped out of circulation among 20th-century Methodists. Nonetheless, altered forms of the original Wesleyan teaching endured in 19th-century Holiness teaching and 20th-century Pentecostalism.

In effect, Wesley replaced a two-stage Puritan and Pietist pattern for spiritual life (from unconverted to converted) with a three-stage pattern (from unconverted to converted, and from converted to sanctified; → Order of Salvation). The general idea of a "second blessing" coming subsequent to conversion is found in Phoebe → Palmer's "altar theology," the Holiness movement's idea of sanctification through faith, Asa Mahan's "baptism of the Holy Ghost," and the Keswick Convention's imperative of surrender and consecration to God. During the 1890s, radical Holiness teachers sought a clear, biblical sign of the "second blessing." The theology of revival — and, indeed, world Christendom — was changed forever when early Pentecostals identified speaking in tongues as the necessary outward sign (or "initial evidence") of attaining this higher spiritual level.

Also significant for subsequent developments in revivalism, and especially Pentecostalism, was Wesley's relatively open attitude toward the bodily, emotional, and charismatic manifestations that occurred in revivals. During the 1740s Jonathan Edwards had acknowledged that some converts displayed bodily effects and even experienced trances and visions, and yet he warned believers not to identify their unusual experiences with the movement of the Holy Spirit. To interpret one's subjective ideas and impressions as God-given was, for Edwards, to fall into "enthusiasm." In contrast, Wesley, while denouncing "enthusiasm," tended to accept visionary experiences as God-given so long as their content was consistent with biblical teaching and brought spiritual edification to the persons who experienced them. This more open posture — which a Calvinist critic might call indiscriminate — became characteristic of the Methodists into the early 1800s, the Holiness movement of the later 1800s, and the 20th-century Pentecostal and charismatic revivals. Indeed, among charismatic thinkers since the 1980s there has been a school of thought that maintains that charismatic phenomena such as speaking in tongues, prophetic utterances, healings of the sick, and casting out of demons, so far from being an embarrassment or theological problem for revivalism, function as the means whereby God confirms the authenticity of the preached gospel.

With regard to emotional expression in worship, the ethos of Wesleyan revival services differed from the constrained, dignified atmosphere that was characteristic of Calvinist revivals. The "shouting Methodists" of the early 1800s, and the later Holiness or Pentecostal "holy rollers" in both Caucasian and African-American congregations, insisted that a genuine experience of God's glorious presence called for exuberant, bodily response. George W. Henry's *Shouting: Genuine and Spurious* (1859), published in the context of the Methodist camp-meeting revivalism of the mid-1800s, defended the practice of shouting during worship and was reprinted in 1903 by Holiness shouters in Chicago to defend their oft-criticized practices.

5. The Second Great Awakening in North America

At the beginning of the 19th century, revivals again revitalized North American religious life. They came first in the camp meetings that erupted in southern frontier regions of Kentucky and Tennessee, the campus revivals that occurred at Hampton-Sydney College in Virginia and Yale College in Connecticut, and the urban revivals that swept through the emerging factory towns of upstate New York. So powerful were the New York State revivals that some later referred to the area as the "burned-over district." Theologically, these revivals signaled a shift away from the thinking that underlay the 18th-century revivals. By the time this Second Great Awakening (1795-1835) ebbed, most evangelical Protestants based their summons to conversion on Arminian notions of free will and attached less importance to Calvinist ideas of predestination. That Arminian approach was especially associated with the Methodists and with many — though not all — of the Baptists who reaped a harvest of new members in these revivals of the early 1800s.

Even at Yale College — long a stronghold of Jonathan Edwards's theology — divinity professor Nathaniel William Taylor (1786-1858) in the 1820s and 1830s began to promote a "New Haven Theology" that modified Edwardseanism in the direction of Arminianism. Holding a libertarian notion of the will, Taylor maintained that humans have "power to the contrary" to avoid sin. This teaching ran counter to the basic concept of the will offered in Jonathan Edwards's *Freedom of the Will* (1754), according to which "the will always is as is the greatest apparent good," and a person's underlying "motives" actuate his or her behavior (→ Self). According to Edwards, a sinner with no "natural necessity" would still have a "moral necessity" of continuing in sin unless God conferred grace. In contrast, because of his stress on the human will as a self-determining entity, Taylor held that "sin is in the sinning" and that original sin should not be thought of as an inherent corruption in human nature. Taylor's views were strongly opposed by Bennet Tyler (1783-1858), later associated with Hartford Seminary; during the pre–Civil War era this conflict became known as the Taylor-Tyler debate.

5.1. *Finney*

The single best-known preacher of the Second Great Awakening in America was Charles Grandison Finney (1792-1875), who adapted frontier camp-meeting techniques for his urban revivals and forever altered the ethos of the American revival tradition by placing at its center the personality and the influence of the revivalist himself. Finney's theological position, though probably only minimally influenced by Nathaniel William Taylor, tended in the same direction as Taylor's. Finney admitted to being ignorant of Calvinistic doctrine as taught in the → Westminster Confession (1648), even though he had been ordained to serve as a Presbyterian minister in New York State.

Finney prayed by name for sinners to respond to the gospel call and urged those who were uncertain about their spiritual state to come forward to the "anxious bench" and there to wrestle spiritually until they came to assurance of salvation. In Finney's day, there was intense debate — known as the "new measures" controversy — over the use of the "anxious bench" and the allegedly crude and impudent language that Finney and his followers used in prayer and in preaching. Echoing earlier arguments from the 1740s, revivalist Asahel Nettleton (1783-1844) in the 1820s held that Finney's young and inexperienced disciples showed contempt for pastors who were their seniors, even as they invaded congregations and sowed confusion. Finney's practice of allowing women to pray aloud in mixed gatherings of men and women was also controversial.

From the 1840s onward, Finneyite revivalism became closely associated with a number of social reform movements and social crusades in America, including abolitionism and antislavery, temperance, anti-Masonry, and women's rights. Finney once famously declared that, if all God's people exerted themselves, the millennium might arrive in three months. His revival theology tended toward melioristic → optimism, which was a function of his belief in each person's inherent power to repudiate sin and choose righteousness. Theological critics — with some justification — accused Finney of reviving the ancient → Pelagian heresy that humans could obey God without any special gift of divine grace. With Asa Mahan (1799-1889), his colleague at Oberlin College, Finney developed a distinctive "Oberlin Theology" that adapted the Wesleyan notion of entire sanctification.

5.2. *Theological Issues*

Religious revivals in the 19th century raised a number of theological issues.

5.2.1. One concerns *whether humans themselves*

can generate a genuine revival. If revivals are the work of God, it would seem that God must determine when and where they occur. But if spiritual revitalization may be stimulated by the proper use of means given by God, then revivals may occur as humans choose to employ those means. Finney defended the latter position, arguing in his influential and controversial *Lectures on Revivals of Religion* (1835) that revivals occur through human initiative when the God-given means to promote them are properly used. He provocatively asserted in his first lecture that a revival is "not a miracle." Finney's Calvinist critics sometimes compared genuine revivals to a summer rainstorm that arrives unpredictably. A farmer might plant seed and prepare the soil, but he had to wait for rain to fall. Without the rain, there would be no crop to harvest. An adjective commonly invoked in Calvinist revivals was "surprising," as in the title of Jonathan Edwards's *Faithful Narrative of the Surprising Work of God* (1737). In Finney's theology of revival, by contrast, the spiritual outcome was less surprising, more predictable, and more a matter of human planning and control.

The decline of Calvinism and the rise of Arminianism in the early 1800s resulted in part from the congruence of Arminian → individualism with the spirit of American → democracy. The political ideology of the new republic elevated ordinary people and assigned to them the power to govern themselves through elected representatives. Analogously, the emerging theology of revival empowered individuals to search their souls, cast aside sin, and freely accept the gift of grace. Calvinism had had a pessimistic understanding of human nature according to which people cannot extricate themselves from the state of sin, and God must initiate the process of salvation. By contrast, Arminianism was more optimistic because it held that humans could choose to leave behind their sinful condition through a free choice to repent of sin, believe the gospel, and accept salvation.

With his use of the "anxious bench," Finney foreshadowed the invitation of Billy Sunday (1862-1935), a revivalist active in the late 19th and early 20th centuries, to hit the "sawdust trail" of his makeshift tabernacles and come forward to shake his hand as a sign of repentance. He also anticipated the invitation of 20th-century evangelist Billy Graham (b. 1918) to come forward to signal having made a decision for Christ. Finney, Sunday, and Graham assigned greater importance to individual choice than was the case in the earlier Calvinist theology of revival. The work of the revivalist, on this view, was to stir humans to make a decision to accept God's free gift of grace.

5.2.2. Another question for 19th-century revivalism was *the relationship between spiritual nurture* (esp. during → childhood) *and the conversion experiences that occur in the midst of revivals.* The Connecticut Congregationalist pastor Horace Bushnell (1802-76) penned a classic critique of revivalism entitled *Christian Nurture* (1847, rev. 1860). Bothered by his inability to stimulate revivals in his congregation, Bushnell argued that if Christian parents and the church nurtured young children in the faith, they would grow up never thinking of themselves as anything other than Christians. A dramatic conversion experience would be unnecessary.

In many respects Bushnell anticipated the work of psychologist and philosopher William James (1842-1910), who in his *Varieties of Religious Experience* (1902) identified two types of religious personalities. The twice-born type was the one who underwent a classic conversion, such as that proffered in revivals, and adopted a religious worldview. The once-born type was one for whom such an experience seemed to be superfluous.

5.2.3. In 19th-century revival literature, a number of authors returned to themes that Edwards had probed earlier, especially regarding the evaluation of *involuntary phenomena* of those experiencing revival. In dialogue with Edwards's position, they inquired into the cause, meaning, and value of the powerful emotions, bodily manifestations, and visionary experiences that occurred in the midst of revivals. The Cane Ridge Revival of 1801 became notorious because of the unusual and even grotesque bodily manifestations it provoked — including "jerking," "dancing," and "barking," all of which seemed to happen involuntarily. In response to the revivals occurring just after 1800, John Cree and others in *Evils of the Work Now Prevailing* (1804) argued against Edwards's position and maintained that the work of the Holy Spirit properly centered on the human reason and not on the emotions or imagination. Grant Powers's *Essay upon the Influence of the Imagination on the Nervous System, Contributing to a False Hope in Religion* (1828) — a pioneering work in the → psychology of religion — argued that the new bodily manifestations did not comport with biblical teaching, created "false hopes in religion" for those who underwent them, and could be explained in terms of changes within the "arterial system" or "animal functions."

Powers's psychological musings on revival were a foreshadowing of Frederick Davenport's *Primitive Traits in Religious Revivals* (1905), perhaps the first attempt at a completely naturalistic explanation for religious revivals. Davenport maintained that revivals typically affected "the nervously unstable, the suggestible, [and] the inexperienced" rather than "the dignified and intelligent people of judgment and standing." He asserted the superior rationality of white male adults as compared with children, women, and nonwhites. Davenport sought to explain revivals in terms of environmental factors (e.g., the dangers of frontier life) and the dynamics of crowd psychology or "hypnotic suggestion." Though his views might find few defenders today, his discussion raised important questions about the involuntary phenomena often observed among participants in revivals.

5.2.4. A factor that became increasingly prominent in revivalism during the later 1800s and early 1900s was → *apocalypticism.* In the later decades of the 19th century, revivalist Dwight L. → Moody (1837-99) was drawn to the premillennial and dispensationalist eschatology of British Bible teacher John Nelson Darby (1800-1882). This approach presumed that history was divided into epochs, or dispensations, in which God offered humanity a way to salvation, followed in each instance by human failure and divine judgment. Darby claimed that the present era, or "church age," was the sixth of the seven dispensations to occur before God's final judgment. Especially important to Darby's thought were the apocalyptic prophecies of the Bible that he saw as keys to unlocking the meaning of historical events. A sense of urgency followed from Darby's teachings, for time was short to bring souls to salvation.

This premillennial and dispensationalist approach to Scripture buttressed revivalism's fervent calls for conversion, particularly after the 1909 Scofield reference edition of the King James Bible disseminated Darby's views widely and they became central to 20th-century American → fundamentalism. The continuing influence of → dispensationalism in evangelical and revivalist Christianity today may be seen in Hal Lindsey's *Late Great Planet Earth* (1970) and in Tim LaHaye's *Left Behind* (1996-) fiction series, one that in less than ten years had collectively sold more than 60 million copies.

5.2.5. Some interpreters of the American revival tradition have viewed it as essentially Protestant in its theology and practices. To be sure, revivalists have often downplayed the role and efficacy of the sacraments (e.g., baptism and Eucharist) and promoted an individualistic version of Christianity. Yet Jay Dolan, in his *Catholic Revivalism* (1978), demonstrates that 19th-century Catholic parish missions shared many characteristics with Protestant revivals during the same period, including fervent preaching, calls for repentance, and emotional exu-

berance. Instead of conducting an altar call, the parish mission preacher summoned lapsed Catholics to the sacrament of penance (i.e., reconciliation) and so encouraged the sort of spiritual rededication that also occurred in Protestant revivals.

Parish missions have continued among Catholics to the present day, though with less stress on sin and repentance than formerly. Moreover, the emergence of the Catholic Charismatic Renewal (beginning in 1967) and its official sanction by the Vatican and Catholic bishops have demonstrated that revivalist fervor need not be antithetical to the church structures and sacramental practices of Roman Catholicism.

6. The Holiness Movement in Transatlantic Perspective

As early as the 1820s, some of the stricter Methodists in America sensed that, as their church gained numbers and influence, it was beginning to lose its distinctive teaching on sanctification. The Holiness movement (Ger. *Heiligungsbewegung*) sought to restore the centrality of sanctification to Methodism and in time brought teaching on sanctification to many non-Methodist Protestants as well.

6.1. *Palmer*

One of the pioneers of the Holiness movement was the American Methodist laywoman Phoebe Worrall Palmer (1807-74), who began to hold "Tuesday Meetings for the Promotion of Holiness" in 1835 with her sister Sarah Lankford in the common parlor of the New York City home shared by their families. By 1839 the meetings were frequented by non-Methodists and included men as well as women. From 1859 to 1863 Palmer and her husband lived and ministered in England, often under the sponsorship of the Evangelical Alliance (→ World Evangelical Alliance 1). She used the imagery of the first → Pentecost to describe her wonder at the spiritual dynamism and nonsectarianism that marked her meetings. By 1867 Palmer's leadership had given way to an association of Methodist pastors who — with growing numbers of Presbyterians, Baptists, Congregationalists, and other non-Methodists — adapted the traditional format of the camp meeting for new purposes and led the movement into a major phase of expansion.

Theologically, Palmer's revival services were based on a "shorter way" to sanctification, also referred to as an "altar theology." Since God commands holiness of heart and life for all believers, and since God commands nothing without intending that it be fulfilled, Palmer reasoned that God will inwardly cleanse all seekers after sanctification at the moment that they consecrate themselves at the "altar" and accept by faith the fact of their sanctification. Having met God's conditions by coming to the "altar" and believing, the sanctified believer was to testify publicly to the reality of his or her sanctification, even in the absence of any distinct experience confirming a change of state. While 18th-century Methodist revivals generally involved powerful emotions, Palmer's approach to sanctification was more subdued and allowed Holiness teaching to influence better-educated and genteel persons who were put off by the raucous emotionalism of the original Methodists. Some regarded the "shorter way" as a drastic departure from the teaching of John Wesley, though Palmer argued for its compatibility with both the Bible and Wesley. Because of its emphasis on testifying publicly to one's sanctification, some have compared it to 20th-century Pentecostalism, and especially to the idea of the so-called positive confession — namely, that God's blessings are received and held only through the process of verbalizing them.

6.2. *The Smiths*
Hannah Worrell Smith (1832-1911) and her husband, Robert Pearsall Smith (1827-98), second-generation Holiness teachers, carried the Holiness message across the Atlantic. Born into wealthy Quaker families in Philadelphia (→ Friends, Society of), the Smiths professed conversion in the Revival of 1857-58 and entered Holiness ministry following their attendance at a Methodist camp meeting in 1867 in which both professed to have received the "second blessing" of sanctification. By the 1870s, Hannah Smith had become active in the summer Holiness meetings sponsored by Lord and Lady Mount Temple at their Broadlands estate in Hampshire, England. Intended for university students who had responded to Robert Smith's meetings in Oxford and Cambridge, these retreats attracted an eclectic group. Amanda Berry Smith (1837-1915) — not a blood relative — was another prominent Holiness teacher in North America, England, India, and Africa, and the first African-American woman with an international ministry.

Robert Smith's whirlwind 1875 tour through Europe's established and → free churches culminated in the Convention for the Promotion of Scriptural Holiness, held in May in Brighton, England, with thousands of delegates from churches on both sides of the Atlantic and the English Channel. This gathering marked an apogee for the Smiths. While in Brighton, there were unsubstantiated rumors about Robert Smith's personal conduct that led to the Smiths' return to America and their withdrawal

from itinerant Holiness preaching. Nonetheless, Hannah Smith's *Christian's Secret of a Happy Life* (1875) became the best-selling Christian devotional volume of the 19th century.

In the 1880s and 1890s the Holiness movement — now overlapping with the "Higher Life" movement (after the title of a book by William Boardman) and the "Keswick" movement (after the site of an annual convention in England, beginning in 1875) — left its imprint on the *Gemeinschaftsbewegung* (→ Fellowship Movement) among German Pietists and on the architects of the American revival tradition such as Dwight L. Moody and Reuben A. Torrey (1856-1928). Thus Holiness teaching entered 20th-century American fundamentalism, along with its better-known role in the origins of Pentecostalism.

6.3. *Perfectionism*
Theologically speaking, the Holiness teaching offered by the Smiths and the Higher Life and Keswick teachers combined a number of elements. One was the Wesleyan idea of salvation as a present experience, epitomized in Robert Smith's declaration while in Germany: *Jesus erretet mir jetzt!* (Jesus saves me *now*). Another stress was on faith as the means of sanctification. On the question of "indwelling sin" or a "sin nature" within the believer, mainstream Holiness teaching tended toward "counteractionism." According to this view, the sin nature continued to exist after the experiences of conversion and sanctification. Like a stone tied to a piece of wood and floated above the bottom of a pond by the wood's buoyancy, the sin nature was counteracted by the believer's new nature in Christ (→ New Self) without being destroyed. Certain Holiness teachers, however, tended toward the "eradicationist" idea that the sanctification experience removed one's underlying tendencies to sin.

The most incisive and prolific critic of Holiness teaching was Princeton Seminary professor Benjamin Breckenridge Warfield (1851-1921), whose two-volume *Perfectionism* (1931-32) reprinted the many articles he had authored on this topic. He advocated a Calvinistic, activistic notion of the Christian life and faulted Hannah Smith for what he took to be the → quietism and passivity implied in her teaching on sanctification and attributable to her Quaker upbringing. "Perfectionism," in Warfield's account, was the viewpoint that "those who have been justified by faith may attain sanctification also with equal immediacy by an equally simple exercise of faith" (2.513). In response, he argued that the idea of "sanctification by faith" is untrue to biblical teaching and to everyday experience, which both show that genuine holiness is attained only through struggle and suffering. Warfield noted, with satisfaction, that the leading German exponent of Holiness teaching, Theodor Jellinghaus, had muted certain aspects of the doctrine of sanctification in successive editions of *Das völlige, gegenwärtige Heil durch Christum* (Complete, Present Salvation through Christ, 1880) and later had even published a full retraction of his earlier views in *Erklärungen über meine Lehrirrungen* (Explanations regarding My False Teachings, 1912).

7. Global Developments, 1800-1910

7.1. *Pacific Islands*

In the 1800s and early 1900s Christian revivals swept across the Pacific Islands (→ Oceania), with the result that eventually more than 90 percent of the indigenous population became at least nominally Christian. The means by which many came to profess the Christian faith has been variously called a group conversion or a people movement, and the process of conversion in this region might suggest that a revised theology of revival — differing from those developed in the modern West — may be needed to understand what transpired there.

Modern Western thinkers tend to see the individual person, or perhaps the nuclear family, as the fundamental social unit. It is often forgotten that the Christianization of ancient Germanic and Slavic peoples typically hinged on a ruler's conversion, like that of the Russian Prince Vladimir, baptized in 988 (→ Germanic Mission; Slavic Mission; Russian Orthodox Church 1). When a leader converted, so did the tribe or extended family associated with him. Moreover, a people's entry into the new faith frequently involved a contest and competition between the old gods and the new God, and between the traditional priests or shamans and the Christian emissaries. In eighth-century Germany, Boniface is said to have convinced the pagans of the superior power of his God when he chopped down Thor's sacred oak tree and suffered no retribution for doing so.

The Pacific Islands during the 1800s offered a number of analogous cases. In Fiji, Tonga, and Samoa the public destruction of fetish objects was the decisive turning point in a people's entry into the Christian faith. King Pomare II (d. 1821) of Tahiti ate the sacred turtle without any of the accompanying rituals that would have made it a licit act. He also took the traditional temple pillar and showed contempt for it by setting it up as a post in his kitchen. In Alan Tippitt's analysis, the people movements in the Pacific Islands were often group decisions in which a ruler did not act alone but con-

sulted the ruling elders, and sometimes many others as well. The destruction of the fetish objects was accomplished in a public ceremony in which the people at large played a role. Christian revivals in the Pacific Islands thus challenge the notion that a faith decision must be solitary and that revivals happen through an accumulation of individual choices.

7.2. *Wales*

In 1900 Wales was one of the most religiously devout nations in Europe, with its churchgoing population divided almost equally between four major groups — the Anglican Church of Wales, Congregationalists, Calvinistic Methodists, and Baptists. A strong Welsh revival tradition harkened back to the mid-1700s awakenings, a national revival in 1859, and local revivals in the later 1800s. Church services centered on the preacher, who was expected to meet exacting standards of public oratory and, if possible, to go into *hwyl* — an inspired manner of preaching that congregations encouraged with their verbal affirmations and responses during the sermon.

Beginning in diverse locations, and then expanding widely, a powerful revival took hold of Wales in 1904-5, resulting in an estimated 100,000 conversions. This Welsh revival had a strong lay orientation, featuring impromptu worship services with impassioned singing, public testimonies, fervent prayer, and intense emotionalism. No one seemed to be orchestrating the services, which lasted for up to 12 or even 16 hours at a stretch, day after day. By early 1905 the Welsh newspaper reports focused on a young theology student and former coal miner, Evan Roberts (1878-1951), who came to symbolize the revival as a whole, though evidence indicates that the revival was already in progress in numerous locations before Roberts had begun his preaching expeditions.

Roberts exhibited a mystical bent and remains a mysterious figure in many respects. For a decade before 1904, he had often stayed up nights reading about past revivals and praying for revival to come again. By his account, just months prior to the outbreak of revival, he had awakened in the early hours each night to experience several hours of unspeakable bliss in the presence of God before going back to sleep. Roberts became convinced that revival was coming soon to Wales. God, he said, had disclosed to him the number of converts in the impending revival — 100,000 — and he felt compelled to ask for this exact number in his prayers. In a state of spiritual desire approaching agony, Roberts asked God to "bend" him and make him an instrument of revival, and thereafter he began to travel throughout Wales in late 1904 in the company of some younger women who assisted, prayed, and sang at his services.

As Roberts's meetings grew in numbers and in emotional intensity, his behavior became unpredictable. In January 1905 Peter Price published a piece in the *Western Mail* declaring that a "double revival" was in progress — one genuine and the other, led by Roberts, a counterfeit revival. Roberts did not respond publicly to this attack, though it stung him deeply. On February 20, 1905, he halted a service with the declaration that several people present were disobeying the Spirit and that the service could not go on until they had confessed and repented. The following night he declared that a "lost soul" was at the meeting, with no hope of salvation. While his first campaigns had stressed God's love, he became more peremptory and prone to reliance on allegedly supernatural guidance. On April 7, 1905, he seemed to be in torment in the meeting and declared that someone was attempting to hypnotize him. Soon Roberts ceased from itineration, and in 1906 he went to stay in the home of Mrs. Jessie Penn-Lewis (1861-1927) and thenceforth all but vanished from public life. By 1912 he spoke of "gathering the whole world under the wings of my prayers," explaining that he was able to accomplish far more by his prayers than would be possible through preaching.

In *War on the Saints* (1912), a book coauthored with Penn-Lewis, Roberts offered his retrospective judgment on the Welsh Revival. Without denying the revival's benefits, Roberts argued — in a fashion ironically reminiscent of Peter Price's critique — that the genuine revival had been accompanied by false, counterfeit, and, indeed, demonic manifestations. The problem was that Christians unaccustomed to the supernatural realm accepted everything of a paranormal character as coming from God. Flashes of insight, visions of Christ, and streams of words or ideas that appeared in the mind were often produced by evil spirits: "The teachings of the deceiving spirits in this form are so natural in appearance that they seem to come from the man himself, as the fruit of his own mind." Even "honest souls" could be deceived. Danger lurked when believers adopted a passive posture, waiting for something special to happen and hoping for supernatural manifestations, which the devil could mimic. Evil spirits might give counterfeit guidance through sudden impulses or audible voices, and this experience could lead believers into foolish, unyielding obstinacy and fanaticism. In the 1730s Jonathan Edwards had attributed his uncle's suicide to the devil's influence, yet Roberts's *War on the Saints* developed a

theory of diabolical influence more elaborate than Edwards's. Roberts's decision to withdraw from public sight, though unusual for a 20th-century Protestant, was not without precedent. Like the monks of ancient Egypt and Syria (→ Stylites; Monasticism), Roberts found his calling in removing himself from the world in order to battle against evil spirits and to promote God's kingdom through incessant prayer.

Reports on the Welsh Revival of 1904-5 spread rapidly throughout the world, raising the spiritual expectations of Protestant Christians in many nations and helping to trigger revivals in Pune, India (at a Christian girls' school), in Korea (among Methodist and Presbyterian missionaries and Korean converts), and in the United States — in Wilkes-Barre, Pennsylvania (where many Welsh resided), and in Los Angeles, California (in a largely African-American Holiness congregation).

7.3. *Korea*

The incipient revival in Korea, which had begun in Wonsan in 1903 among a gathering of Methodist missionaries and Korean converts, reached a new level of intensity after the report of the Welsh Revival came to Korea and the Koreans offered fervent prayers for a full-blown revival there. Centering on the city of Pyongyang, the so-called Great Revival of 1907 affected the whole of Korean Protestantism and laid the foundation for the later exponential expansion of Christianity in Korea (→ South Korea 3). A hallmark of this revival was the public confession of sins — itself a countercultural act in Korean culture — followed by the → reconciliation of enemies, restitution of stolen goods, and repudiation of such culturally tolerated practices as concubinage and opium smoking.

During the 1907 revival and subsequently, Korean Protestants have been known for their intensive Bible study and distinctive prayer practices, including unison prayer (wherein all pray aloud at once), daybreak prayer (involving a large proportion of each church's membership), all-night prayer, and fasting prayer. Beginning in the 1930s and 1940s, the custom of the "prayer mountain" took shape in Korea. Believers retreated into small cells in a mountain to pray and fast, sometimes for as long as 40 days at a time.

Pentecostalism entered Korea in 1928, and its remarkable growth in the later 20th century is associated especially with the pastor Yonggi Cho (b. 1936) and his mother-in-law and prayer supporter, Ja-Sil Choe (1915-89). Cho's Yoido Full Gospel Central Church in Seoul has more than 700,000 members (as of 2007) and is presently the world's largest

Christian congregation. Cho's personal theology has been influenced by the so-called prosperity theology of such American teachers as Kenneth Hagin Sr., Kenneth Copeland, and perhaps Oral Roberts. Cho's book *Triple Salvation* (1977) is based on the idea that God intends to give believers prosperity in their soul, healing in their body, and blessing in their varied life activities.

8. Pentecostal, Charismatic, and "Third Wave" Theologies of Revival

Many of the Christian revivals of the last century have occurred within Pentecostalism (since 1901) and its daughter traditions — the Charismatic Renewal (since the 1960s) and the neocharismatic, or so-called Third Wave, movement (since the 1980s). While the theologies of revival associated with each of these movements show significant variations, there are common features that distinguish a Pentecostal-charismatic perspective on revival from that of most non-Pentecostals. The defining features include a basically Arminian (or non-Calvinist) theology of the divine-human relationship (according to which God is ready to confer blessings but awaits those who ask and "tarry" for them), an emphasis on visible manifestations of God's supernatural presence (e.g., divine healing, prophecy, visions, casting out demons, and speaking in tongues), and a teaching regarding a "baptism of [in] the Holy Spirit" that comes subsequent to conversion. Another common theme in earlier Pentecostal theology is premillennial eschatology and a heightened anticipation of Christ's imminent return (→ Parousia).

8.1. *Emphasis on Power*

The 18th-century Wesleyan and 19th-century Holiness movements, as noted above, were grounded on the idea of an "entire sanctification," "perfect love," "perfection," or "second blessing" that came after conversion. Before his death in 1785, the early Methodist theologian John Fletcher began to use the phrase "baptism of [in] the Spirit" to describe the experience of sanctification. The titles of Asa Mahan's books *The Scripture Doctrine of Christian Perfection* (1839) and *The Baptism of the Holy Ghost* (1870) signaled a shift in terminology and conceptuality. Until the mid-1800s, the transatlantic Holiness movement interpreted sanctification primarily in terms of purity of heart and action. Yet by the late 1800s there was a transition from purity to power, that is, a preoccupation with visible manifestations of God's power in Christian life and service. William Arthur, in *The Tongue of Fire* (1856), argued that the Christian church needed a fresh, "Pentecostal" manifestation of the Spirit's power.

In parallel with the stress on spiritual power was a profusion of books during the 1880s and 1890s on the Holy Spirit and a resurgence of interest in divine healing and other spiritual phenomena. By 1900 many Holiness ministers were preaching a twofold message of "salvation for the soul" and "healing for the body." Some missionary leaders suggested that miraculous manifestations — such as speaking in tongues — might accompany the preaching of the gospel and usher in a vast harvest of new souls for the church.

8.2. *Glossolalia*

The early Pentecostal movement took shape during the first decade of the 1900s against this backdrop of an intensified supernaturalism and a quest for definitive marks of the Spirit's power. In December 1900 the white Holiness preacher Charles Parham (1873-1929) asked the students in his small Bible college in Topeka, Kansas, to search the Bible to find a spiritual phenomenon that might serve as a clear sign of the Spirit's presence. When Parham's students identified speaking in tongues as the sign in question, and when Agnes Ozman (1870-1937) and others in the school began to speak in tongues on January 1, 1901, Parham began to teach publicly that tongues-speaking is the "Bible evidence" of baptism in the Spirit. He further claimed that he and his pupils were witnessing an "end times" restoration of God's supernatural power, rivaling the manifestation of the Spirit during the apostolic era. Parham held that the glossolalia he witnessed was xenolalia, or a supernaturally conferred ability o speak actual human languages, and a divine enablement for foreign missionaries, who would no longer need to acquire language facility through painstaking formal instruction. Despite contravening evidence from early Pentecostal missionaries, Parham maintained this view throughout his life.

Parham's African-American disciple William Seymour (1870-1922) embraced Parham's view of Spirit baptism and initiated early Pentecostalism's major revival at the Azusa Street Mission in Los Angeles (1906-9). Seymour provoked Parham's opposition, however, when he brought whites, blacks, and Latinos into a single spiritual community in violation of the racial protocols of the Jim Crow era (→ Racism). For Seymour, speaking in tongues was an outward act that could be counterfeited by those who lacked the Holy Spirit. A clearer sign of the Spirit's presence was the remarkable breaking down of social barriers at Azusa Street, so that, in the words of Frank Bartleman, "The color line was washed away in the blood [of Jesus]." While most white Pentecostals during the 20th century held to some version of Parham's "Bible evidence" (later known as "initial evidence"), black Pentecostals often interpreted tongues speaking as only one of a number of possible manifestations of the Spirit.

From the outset, Pentecostals showed an openness to divine healing, visions, prophecies, and other signs of God's immediate presence, and they later used the term "full gospel" to refer to churches in which these varied manifestations were welcomed and encouraged. Pentecostals and the later charismatics generally held that believers without this "full gospel" dimension lacked power and effectiveness in Christian service, and this claim helps to account for the controversy that has often surrounded Pentecostalism. The preachers Billy Graham and Oral Roberts (b. 1918) illustrate two versions of revival ministry. The two men have preached an almost indistinguishable "salvation" message, and yet Roberts as a "healing-evangelist" couples his call to conversion with the laying on of hands for healing the sick and for casting out demons. Other notable healing evangelists have included Maria Woodworth-Etter (1844-1924), Francisco Olazábal (1886-1937), and Aimee Semple McPherson (1890-1944).

8.3. *Apostles and Prophets*

The so-called Latter Rain revival that began in 1948-49 in Saskatchewan, Canada, represented a return to the fervor of early Pentecostalism, and yet it created controversy when its leaders taught that the NT gifts of apostleship (→ Apostle, Apostolate) and prophethood (→ Prophet, Prophecy) were being given again to the church, thus challenging the prevailing authorities in Pentecostalism. The Latter Rain revival featured extended → fasting and praying, lasting for days and even weeks at a time. Its teaching regarding contemporary apostleship as a restoration of the "fivefold ministry" (involving apostles, prophets, evangelists, pastors, and teachers; see Eph. 4:11) became a staple idea among neo-charismatics in the 1990s and especially in the so-called Apostolic Movement, led by C. Peter Wagner (b. 1930).

8.4. *Charismatic Renewal*

Before about 1960, Pentecostal phenomena in the Christian world were almost entirely confined to Pentecostal denominations that came into existence when the Holiness churches and other Protestant bodies rejected these phenomena and their related theologies of Spirit baptism. Yet during the 1960s and 1970s, the Charismatic Renewal brought tongues-speaking and a teaching on Spirit baptism to growing numbers of Episcopalians, Presbyterians, Methodists, Lutherans, and, beginning in 1967, Roman Catholics. By the 1990s even the Southern Baptists, who had long been vocal critics of Pentecostalism, had growing numbers of ministers and missionaries who at least covertly spoke in tongues and accepted charismatic teachings.

The charismatic movement differed theologically from the old-line Pentecostalism, inasmuch as most charismatics held that the Holy Spirit was at work outside, as well as inside, the "Spirit-filled" community. Charismatics saw continuity between Pentecostal and non-Pentecostal Christians. Some refused to say that they had "received" the Spirit in their experience of Spirit baptism, preferring to speak of the "release" of the Spirit, who had already been conferred in the experience of conversion (the evangelical Protestant model) or else in the sacrament of → baptism (the Roman Catholic, or High Church, model). Since many charismatics deemphasized or questioned the Pentecostal doctrine of "initial evidence," the boundaries distinguishing charismatics from noncharismatics became blurry.

8.5. *"Third Wave"*

During the 1980s and 1990s the boundaries of the "Spirit-filled" movement became yet more indistinct as growing numbers of Christians — some associated with John Wimber (1934-97) and his → Vineyard Church — experienced charismatic manifestations such as speaking in tongues, divine healing, and prophetic ministry and yet rejected the "initial evidence" doctrine and did not think of themselves as Pentecostals or charismatics. Wimber popularized the idea of "power evangelism," according to which the verbal proclamation of Christ needs to be accompanied by tangible signs and wonders of God's presence, such as divine healing. Inasmuch as Wimber's 1980s movement differed from the earlier Pentecostal and charismatic movements, missionary theorist C. Peter Wagner dubbed it the "Third Wave" of the Holy Spirit. Yet the new movement brought controversy. A revival of prophetic ministry among the "Kansas City Prophets" in the mid-1980s and a major outbreak of revival in Toronto during the mid-1990s — involving prolonged laughter and even animal sounds — provoked Wimber's opposition, even though both developments had direct ties to the Vineyard Church.

Probably no one during the last generation has had a more widespread or many-sided influence on the theology of revival than C. Peter Wagner, who during his long career has been successively associated with the church-growth school at Fuller Seminary (1960s and 1970s), the so-called Third Wave movement (1980s), the resurgent interest in "spiritual warfare" (1990s), and the Apostolic (or New

Apostolic) movement (since the late 1990s). Beginning from the assumption that quantitative and qualitative growth is normative for churches, Wagner investigated congregations around the globe and found that the strongest growth occurred in regions where ministry included signs and wonders (→ Church Growth). This insight, embodied in Third Wave congregations, led to worship services that regularly included prayer for physical and emotional healing. During the 1990s Wagner's teaching on "spiritual warfare" reflected the influence of the Argentine ministers Carlos Annacondia, Omar Cabrera, and Claudio Freidzon, whose ministries included mass exorcistic ceremonies and fervent prayer for victory over evil spirits. Wagner's books offered prayer-based strategies for identifying "territorial spirits," whose malign presence hindered the church's ministry and whose removal could trigger spiritual awakening. Along similar lines, George Otis Jr. produced the documentary video *Transformations* (2002), demonstrating that unified prayer among Christians could bring revival and social reform even to such an unlikely location as Cali, Colombia — once Latin America's major center for illegal drug trafficking.

9. Twentieth-Century Revivals

9.1. *Africa*

The Christian population of sub-Saharan Africa has grown from only a few million in 1900 to perhaps 400 million by the year 2000. This astonishing expansion included thousands of African Indigenous Churches (AICs) that sprang up alongside of Western-led missionary congregations or split off from them (→ Independent Churches). In general, African cultures presume that "salvation" does not pertain merely to a spiritual dimension of human life but rather includes bodily health, family relations, social harmony, financial prosperity, and general human wellness. The failure of Western missionaries to appreciate and respond to this aspect of African cultures was a major reason for the emergence of the AICs. Because of the perceived split between body and soul in Western teaching and practice, an African who had joined a Western-led church congregation to receive "spiritual" salvation sometimes returned to an indigenous healer whenever bodily needs were paramount (e.g., if illness struck a member of the family). Another common feature of African cultures involves belief in the presence of malign, unholy forces associated with → witchcraft or sorcery. A major function of African traditional religions, from time immemorial, has been to protect against evil spirits. If one begins

with these two assumptions — that salvation means personal and family wellness, and that evil forces stand against the experience of this wellness — then revival, healing, and social restoration may be expected as the outcome when evil forces are removed.

The theology of revival, in most African contexts, thus includes a call to remove evil spirits, curses, and sorcery as a precondition for spiritual advancement. Nigeria has prayer villages, where individuals or entire families can undergo spiritual diagnosis to discern demons, which are then neutralized through prayer. The teaching on spiritual warfare by C. Peter Wagner is akin to the African perspective, and books, tapes, and videos by Western Pentecostal and neocharismatic teachers have had a notable impact in Nigeria, South Africa, and elsewhere on the continent. In the AICs of South Africa the healing process may involve spiritual preparation by the healer and the use of physical media. The healer must be pure before healing others, and the process often begins with prayer and fasting. The colors of clothing may be related to certain activities. White is for visions, while blue or red is for healing. Water or bathing is very important and is a part of the process of purification. Traditional medicines are compounded of ash, sugar, salt, seawater, and other ingredients; some are given to induce vomiting as a way to expel evil. Information on patients comes through dreams or visions, and candles are lit to clarify the visions. Praying can occur during dancing, and singing may be a way of invoking the Holy Spirit. Cords, flags, and staves are all symbols of protection.

One major movement in Africa, known as the East African Revival, may be regarded as an extension of the British Holiness movement associated with the Keswick conventions. By the 1920s, some East Africans were only nominally Christian and had professed the faith for the sake of social advancement. Yet a 1929 meeting in Kampala, Uganda, between Joe Church (1899-1989), a Cambridge-educated missionary doctor stationed in Rwanda, and Simeoni Nsibambi (1897-1978), a young African, resulted in spiritual revitalization for both men. The revival that followed was a call for Africans and missionaries alike to enter into a deeper consecration to God. After the revival spread quietly in the early 1930s, ecstatic manifestations such as trances, weeping, and shaking commenced in Rwanda in 1936, and within a year the movement spread to Burundi, Uganda, and Kenya. By 1939 the revival reached Tanzania, southern Sudan, and eastern Zaire (today the Democratic Republic of the Congo). Throughout the 1940s and 1950s, revival teams and conventions spread the message to other parts of Africa and to members of various denominations. Public confessions of sins and public declarations of spiritual victory in Christ were common features. Tension resulted when Africans, now calling themselves *balokole* (saved ones), suggested that the missionaries themselves needed to be revived. Within the Anglican Church, the danger of schism loomed large during 1941-44, yet no major division ensued. Though some have interpreted the East African Revival along the lines of the African Indigenous Churches, Brian Stanley has called it an "African initiative within a European tradition," that is, a genuinely African movement that took its ethos from British Holiness teaching. The practice of publicly declaring one's experiences was likely indebted to the influence of Frank Buchman's (1878-1961) Oxford Group, which Joe Church encountered at Cambridge University in 1920-21.

9.2. *China*

China experienced a revival in Manchuria during 1908 through the mediation of missionary Jonathan Goforth (1859-1936), who had been involved in the Korean Revival of 1907 and who wished to see it spread to China. Beginning in 1927, Shantung Province witnessed revival that involved sudden conversions, powerful emotions, and bodily manifestations. As in Korea, the Chinese revivals involved public confession of sins. Yet in early 20th-century China, as Chun Kwan Lee notes, there was polarization between a conservative-revivalist and a liberal-ecumenical school of thought. The conservatives promoted revival with a consistent soteriological message of deliverance from sin through Christ. They viewed revival as a unique work of the Holy Spirit. Despite the anti-Christian movements of the 1920s, revival regained momentum in China during the 1930s. Conservatives such as John Sung (1901-44), Wang Ming-tao (1900-1991), and Watchman Nee (1903-72) interpreted revival in terms of what Lee calls "a theology of spiritual pursuit." This involved a commitment not to social change but rather to a solitary pursuit of faith and holiness. By contrast, the liberal-ecumenical school promoted social involvement by participating in movements of social change and social reconstruction, both before and after 1949.

Since the Communist revolution, the unregistered → house churches (with perhaps 70 million members as of 2007) have carried the fervor of revival into every region of China. During the anti-Christian persecutions of the 1960s and 1970s, there were reports of signs and wonders among believers, including the healing of sicknesses and extraordi-

nary escapes from prison and persecution in response to prayer. Beginning in the 1980s, Dennis Balcombe, a Bible smuggler turned charismatic advocate, introduced tongues speaking into the house churches, and today it is estimated that about half of all the unregistered congregations could be classified as charismatic. Yet the "Statement of Faith of Chinese House Churches" (1998), endorsed by a number of leaders of unregistered churches, declares that tongues-speaking is neither required nor forbidden. Some revivalistic practices in the house churches are controversial, such as the noisy worship of the "Shouters" and the tears of repentance during the gatherings of the "Weepers."

9.3. *Indonesia*

In Indonesia a Christian revival occurred following the failed Communist coup of 1965. The revival in its origins was associated with the Indonesia Evangelists' Institute at Batu Malang, East Java, and it was especially strong in Timor from 1965 to 1969, with as many as 200,000 conversions reported there. This revival had a strong lay orientation, and rather than centering on a professional evangelist, it involved groups of Christians coming together to witness to, and to experience, God's power. Teams of believers went out to the villages under the leadership of a person who claimed to have been led by the Holy Spirit. The Spirit revealed the names or faces of those who were to be included in the team as the leader's assistants. The teams ranged in size from 3 or 4 to possibly 20 or more. They included young people and schoolteachers and were often led by simple, uneducated folk, in many cases women, though they also included church elders, deacons, and pastors as members. Where they went and what they did was wholly dependent on the direct guidance of the Spirit, usually revealed through prayer. The teams spent hours each day in prayer for guidance and for power. Many healings of the sick and sudden conversions were reported. The implicit theology of revival in Indonesia centered on the equality of all believers under God and the need for moment-by-moment guidance from the Spirit.

10. Conclusion

The preceding examination of the Christian theology of revival has demonstrated the wide variations that have emerged since the 1600s in differing regions (Europe, North America, Latin America, Africa, Asia, and Oceania) and in diverse theological traditions (Roman Catholic, Lutheran, Reformed, Methodist, Holiness, Pentecostal, charismatic, and neocharismatic). Some of the authors noted above have interpreted revival as a quiet, inner, individualistic experience of God's presence, while others associate it with the crusading zeal of social reformers, with the spirit of fellowship that breaks down racial and social barriers, or with supernatural signs and wonders such as speaking in tongues and deliverance from evil spirits. In his foundational text *Faithful Narrative* (1737), Jonathan Edwards referred to revivals as a "surprising work of God," and one of the commonalities amid the plurality of reflections on revival is a sense that the work of the Holy Spirit is both powerful and unpredictable. If the human experience of God's grace is inherently diverse and variegated, then it would stand to reason that no theology of revival — if attuned to the particularities of experience — can ever be complete, final, or unrevisable. A Christian theology of revival will always be unfinished business.

Bibliography: On 1-6 (pre–20th cent.): F. ACKVA, J. VAN DEN BERG, M. BRECHT, and K. DEPPERMANN, eds., *Der Pietismus im achtzehnten Jahrhundert* (Göttingen, 1995) • G. A. BENRATH and M. SALLMANN, eds., *Der Pietismus im neunzehnten und zwanzigsten Jahrhundert* (Göttingen, 2000) • J. VAN DEN BERG and M. BRECHT, eds., *Der Pietismus vom siebzehnten bis zum frühen achtzehnten Jahrhundert* (Göttingen, 1993) • J. DOLAN, *Catholic Revivalism: The American Experience, 1830-1900* (Notre Dame, Ind., 1978) • J. EDWARDS, *The Works of Jonathan Edwards,* vol. 4, *The Great Awakening* (ed. C. C. Goen; New Haven, 1972) • C. G. FINNEY, *Lectures on Revivals of Religin* (ed. W. G. McLoughlin; Cambridge, Mass., 1960; orig. pub., 1835) • P. FLEISCH, *Die Pfingstbewegung in Deutschland. Ihr Wesen und ihre Geschichte in fünfzig Jahren* (Hannover, 1957) • C. LIPPY, "Theology of Revivals," *Encyclopedia of Religious Revivals in America* (2 vols.; ed. M. J. McClymond; Westport, Conn., 2007) 1.434-38 • M. J. McCLYMOND, "Issues and Explanations in the Study of North American Revivalism," *Embodying the Spirit: New Perspectives on North American Revivalism* (ed. M. J. McClymond; Baltimore, 2004) 1-46; idem, ed., *Encyclopedia of Religious Revivals in America* (2 vols.; Westport, Conn., 2007) • E. MOLLAND, *Church Life in Norway, 1800-1950* (trans. H. Kaasa; Minneapolis, 1957) • P. VAN ROODEN, "The Concept of an International Revival Movement around 1800," *PuN* 16 (1990) 155-72 • W. R. WARD, *The Protestant Evangelical Awakening* (Cambridge, 1992) • B. B. WARFIELD, *Perfectionism* (2 vols.; New York, 1931-32) • A. WEMYSS, *Histoire du réveil, 1790-1849* (Paris, 1977).

On 7-10 (20th cent.): D. AIKMAN, *Jesus in Beijing: How Christianity Is Transforming China and Changing the Global Balance of Power* (Washington, D.C., 2003) • F. L. COOLEY, "The Revival in Timor," *The Gospel and Frontier Peoples: A Report of a Consultation, December 1972* (ed. R. P. Beaver; South Pasadena, Calif., 1973) 205-30 • D. G. JACOBSEN, *Thinking in the Spirit: Theologies of the Early Pentecostal Movement* (Bloomington, Ind., 2003) • R. T. JONES, *Faith and the Crisis of a Nation: Wales, 1890-1914* (trans. S. P. Jones; ed. R. Pope; Cardiff, 2004) • I.-J. KIM, *History and Theology of Korean Pentecostalism: Sunbogeum (Pure Gospel) Pentecostalism* (Zoetermeer, 2003) • CHANG KI LEE, *The Early Revival Movement in Korea (1903-1907): A Historical and Systematic Study* (Zoetermeer, 2003) • CHUN KWAN LEE, "The Theology of Revival in the Chinese Christian Church, 1900-1949: Its Emergence and Impact" (Diss., Westminster Theological Seminary [Chestnut Hill, Pa.], 1988) • T. S. LEE, "Born-Again in Korea: The Rise and Character of Revivalism in (South) Korea, 1885-1988" (Diss., University of Chicago, 1996) • M. J. McCLYMOND, "We're Not in Kansas Anymore: The Roots and Routes of World Pentecostalism," *RelSRev* 31 (2005) 163-69 • G. C. OOSTHUIZEN, *The Healer-Prophet in Afro-Christian Churches* (Leiden, 1992) • B. STANLEY, "The East African Revival: African Initiative within a European Tradition," *ChM* 92 (1978) 6-22 • A. R. TIPPITT, *People Movements in Southern Polynesia: Studies in the Dynamics of Church-Planting and Growth in Tahiti, New Zealand, Tonga, and Samoa* (Chicago, 1971) • C. P. WAGNER, *Warfare Prayer: How to Seek God's Power and Protection in the Battle to Build His Kingdom* (Ventura, Calif., 1992); idem, ed., *Engaging the Enemy: How to Fight and Defeat Territorial Spirits* (Ventura, Calif., 1991) • C. P. WAGNER and J. THOMPSON, eds., *Out of Africa: How the Spiritual Explosion among Nigerians Is Impacting the World* (Ventura, Calif., 2004).

MICHAEL J. McCLYMOND

Theology of Revolution

1. Historical Context
2. Theological Discussion
3. Reception

1. Historical Context

The theology of revolution has been a theme for discussion when there have been political and social conflicts, when there has been awareness of the conditioning social structures, and when the church and theology have taken these factors into account (→ Modern Church History 1.4.4; Modern Period; Peace; Pluralism; Righteousness; Justice; Secularization; Society; Third World; War). Facing global situations that, instead of overthrowing unfairness and injustice, did more to stabilize or even sharpen them, the churches from the mid-1960s were challenged by current events and their own self-understanding to ask what their contribution would be to the urgent social changes that were needed. The concept of a responsible society, which had been advocated by theology, and especially by → social ethics, since the first two General Assemblies of the → World Council of Churches, in Amsterdam in 1948 and Evanston in 1954, and which on the basis of Anglo-Saxon doctrines of → natural law called for a fundamental democratization of society (with control of armed power, broad participation in the processes of decision, social equality, etc.), was now increasingly falling into difficulties.

The Geneva World Conference on Church and Society in 1966 initiated a significant change. Thus far the theological problem of → revolution had dealt only with legitimacy and the ethical question of reaching a judgment, but now → theology began to take up the full problem (→ Christology 5; Eschatology 7.4; Ethics 5.4; God 7.2) in a way that, in view of its practical implications (e.g., financial support for armed liberation movements in Africa, the fight against → racism), caused serious interecumenical tensions and proved to be a grave test for the ecumenical movement, setting "ecumenicals" especially against "evangelicals" (→ Ecumenism, Ecumenical Movement; Evangelical Movement). God's presence was sought and found not primarily in traditional structures of created reality but in the changing of prevailing social relations, that is, in revolution. The American theologian R. Schaull, who had been involved in revolutionary activities in Latin America, spoke at this conference, and with an appeal to P. L. Lehmann's theory of theological ethics and H. Marcuse's understanding of society, formulated as a new social and ethical strategy the theology of revolution, that is, change not merely by small steps but by a rapid and, if necessary, violent step that had the aim of shaking up society (even via guerrilla warfare). The Fourth Assembly of the WCC, at Uppsala in 1968, had a full discussion of this theme. The following experiences formed a background.

The North American → civil rights movement (→ Black Theology; Modern Church History 2.7) had used nonviolent methods in opposing social injustice, but it had run up against an established society that showed little interest in political or social changes and had resisted all attempts to bring them about. This movement had thus come to see its own impotence. The conclusion many people drew was that social change was impossible without a massive use of force.

In Latin America (→ Latin American Theology 4-5) it was clear that social reforms could not alter economic and political structures (→ Dependence). The opinion therefore grew that a revolution was needed on the part of intellectual groups, for the masses of the people were not able to carry through any revolution (C. Torres, Che Guevara; → Liberation Theology).

The Vietnam War had revealed, on the one side, the brutal capability and yet also the impotence of a great power (the United States) and, on the other side, the corresponding possibilities of revolutionary guerrilla warfare. These experiences found expression in the theories of a revolutionary changing of a stagnant society (Mao Tse-tung on cultural revolution and on the idea of permanent revolution; → Revolution 3.1.4).

2. Theological Discussion

2.1. The theology of revolution harks back to earlier Christian traditions (→ Religious Socialism; Social Gospel). It could appeal to the revived eschatological character of Christianity (the theology of → hope; Eschatology 7.4). It was designed to protect against an ideological misuse of → faith (→ Ideology) as a means to support the legitimacy of "ontocratic authorities" who claimed they had divine support. It could go back to the God of the Bible (→ God 4.2 and 5.2) in favor of revolutionary social change. A characteristic of God is his power to change things (Psalm 9; 72; 146; Luke 1:52-53). The Jewish-Christian tradition has the power to engage in revolutionary situations. Theology can see God acting dynamically. It can evoke symbols like the exodus, the exile, the crucifixion, the resurrection, and transcendence (→ Immanence and Transcendence) that show God at work on humanity's behalf. It tries to relate → salvation history and liberation history (→ Salvation 5.7 and 6.7; Emancipation). Christian → ethics (§7) must be politically concerned, and messianology is central. The figure of the Messiah (→ Messianism) is the measure by which God humanizes human life.

Transcendence is another basic concept in revolutionary theology. It can bring together a neo-Marxist (→ Marxism 1.2.5) social philosophy and theology. It involves striding across the present to the future, and vice versa. The transcendence of the → kingdom of God is not otherworldliness. It is a radical and total rejection of the existing world system and a striving for a new reality (H. Gollwitzer).

2.2. Over against the ecumenical world, the theology of revolution received little development and had little influence among Roman Catholics. We might refer to individual theologians such as J. Comblin and G. Girardi. The encyclical *Populorum progressio* (1967) of Paul VI (1963-78) also contains some references to the use of force and revolution in §§30-31 (→ Social Encyclicals).

Protestants in the Calvinist tradition do not absolutely oppose revolution. They can point back to Reformation Scotland and Holland, and the American churches might refer to the American Revolution. They insist, however, that a stand against tyranny should be taken by those who are themselves responsible leaders, that mob action should be avoided, that all terrorist acts must be shunned, and that the goals should be Christian rather than ideological. In the main, this approach is largely one of theory, not practice.

Many evangelicals contend that churches, as such, should stay out of politics. They condemn guerrilla activities that bring suffering on the innocent. The churches should focus their attention on the preaching of the gospel, which will ultimately bring with it social change. Individuals can work through the system for economic and political reform. If evangelicals have thrown their weight behind the status quo, it is often because the theology of revolution has been advocated by Marxist-leaning revolutionaries, whose proposals will do little to bring real development to the countries concerned. Their opposition to the theology of revolution also insists that those who adopt it have ignored the situation in Marxist lands, where tyranny was most apparent.

3. Reception

The theology of revolution provoked quick reaction and violent criticism, for revolutionary enthusiasm conceals serious defects. A biblical → hermeneutic and an understanding of → revelation that sees revolutionary events as direct revelation comes under attack, as does the inadequate Christological dimension. An introduction of Christ crucified rules out both a one-sided, triumphalist messianism and a short-sighted view of political action. The new → political theology and liberation theology (→ Black Theology), which arose independently of the theology of revolution, yet at much the same time in the 1960s, have had a bigger influence in the long run and have done much more to shape the response of Christianity and theology to the social challenges of the day.

Bibliography: J. COMBLIN, *Théologie de la pratique révolutionnaire* (Paris, 1974); idem, *Théologie de la révolution. Théorie* (Paris, 1970) • J. G. DAVIES, *Christians, Politics, and Violent Revolution* (London, 1976) • G. GIRARDI, *Faith and Revolution in Nicaragua: Convergence and Contradictions* (Maryknoll, N.Y., 1989) • J. P. GUNNEMANN, *The Moral Meaning of Revolution* (New Haven, 1979) • F. HOUTART, *The Church and Revolution* (New York, 1971) • F. HOUTART and A. ROUSSEAU, *L'église, force anti-révolutionnaire?* (Brussels, 1973) • A. T. VAN LEEUWEN, *Development through Revolution* (New York, 1970) • P. L. LEHMANN, *The Transfiguration of Politics* (New York, 1975) • K. RAHNER, "On the Theology of Revolution," *Theological Investigations* (vol. 14; Baltimore, 1976) 314-30 • WORLD CONFERENCE ON CHURCH AND SOCIETY, *Official Report* (Geneva, 1967).

GIANCARLO COLLET

Theophany

Theophany in the OT denotes the direct manifestation of God in the earthly sphere.

1. From the days of Jeremiah, "theophany" has been a term for God's visible coming with power and the accompanying earthly or cosmic reactions of terror. In the veneration of God the oldest manifestation is in the earthquake, when in giant human form God strides across the mountains (Mic. 1:3-4 and Amos 4:13). Clouds are viewed as the dust that is stirred up by him (Nah. 1:3; Ps. 18:9). We find ideas similar to those relating to Baal, the god of the tempest: Yahweh displays his power in the storm, with the clouds as his chariots (Deut. 33:26; Ps. 68:4, 33-34; cf. Job 38–41); he fights the chaos of the primeval sea with the voice of his thunder and the arrows of his lightning (Hab. 3:8-15; Ps. 18:13-15; in the context, enemy peoples); and his shining forth (*yp'* Hiph.), initially without reactions of terror, leads to → war (Deut. 33:2; Ps. 80:1-2). Yahweh's *kbwd* (glowing coals and smoke) can also come forth in a theophany (Ps. 18:8-13). The → fire of Yahweh's mouth consumes his enemies (Ps. 18:8; 50:3). A host of → angels (§1) may accompany him (Deut. 33:2? but not Joel 2:10-11 or Zech. 14:5; with a different function, *1 Enoch* 1:9).

The earth and the mountains are terrified (Ps. 97:4-5), and the sea flees (Ps. 18:7-15; Nah. 1:4; the conflict with chaos); the nations are astounded (Jer. 10:10; Ps. 99:1; either from the chaos conflict or from a shaking of earth and the mountains), and after the exile, the → heavens are shaken (Joel 2:10; *1 Enoch* 102:2). Yahweh comes forth from → Sinai and the surrounding mountains (Deut. 33:2; Judg. 5:4-5), later, from Zion (Amos 1:2; Ps. 50:2) or from heaven (Isa. 26:21; *1 Enoch* 1:3-4). Sometimes he aims at Zion (Isa. 31:4; Zech. 2:10-11).

The function of a theophany is widely diverse: God seeks to prove his power (Ps. 29; 99:1), war against his foes (Judges 5; Isa. 66:15-16), attack → Israel (Isa. 31:1-4; Joel 2:1-17), accuse Israel (Psalm 50; see also Mic. 1:2-16), carry out the → last judgment (*1 Enoch* 1:9; Isa. 66:18 LXX; see also Mal. 3:1-5), bring → creation to order (Ps. 96:13; 98:9), and set up his dwelling in the → temple and bring salvation (Zech. 2:10-13).

2. There are many references to the theophany at Sinai. According to Exod. 24:9-11, God dwells at Sinai; → Moses goes up to see him there and escapes death in so doing. In 33:18, 21-22 Moses sees God's glory on Sinai, in v. 19 his goodness, in vv. 20 and 23 only his back. In 33:19-20 and 34:2, 5 (cf. Neh. 9:13), Yahweh comes down from heaven to Sinai and gives Moses a fleeting glimpse. In Exod. 19:18-19 and 20:21 (E?), God's presence at Sinai is recognized only by thunder, lightning, clouds, and earthquakes. Moses alone can draw near, and he hears God in the thunder (cf. Deut. 4:11-12). In Exod. 24:15-18 (P?) God's glory is concealed in the clouds on the mountain, but the Israelites see the fire. The original Sinai theophany was added later to the making of the covenant and the divine legislation (→ Covenant 1.3.2).

3. Yahweh's entry into the temple or the → tabernacle (§1) may be recognized by a cloud, as in 1 Kgs. 8:10-11 and Exod. 40:34-35 (cf. Gen. 15:17 and the pillar of cloud and fire in Num. 9:15-23).

4. From father gods functioning as protecting tribal gods, Yahweh gradually came to appear as a normal human being in encounters with individuals (Gen. 16:13; 32:25; later a messenger of God in 16:7; 18:2; in E, from heaven, 21:17; 22:11).

5. In visions of prophetic calling (→ Prophet, Prophecy, 2), Yahweh is seen on a throne with winged serpents (Isa. 6:1-4) or on a heavenly chariot of fire and white gold (Ezekiel 1). In prophetic theophanies we hear only of the receiving of a word (Jer. 1:4). In → dreams God may give direct instructions (Gen. 20:3-7), may manifest himself and give promises (28:10-22), or may symbolically intimate the future (37:5-11; Daniel 2). A dream theophany occurs in 1 Kgs. 3:2-15.

6. Theophanies rarely occur in other natural phenomena. We find, for example, a burning bush in Exod. 3:2-4 and wind in 2 Sam. 5:24 and 1 Kgs. 19:11. Is Yahweh also to be seen in the cult in the (disguised) priest (Gen. 26:24; Ps. 50:7)?

7. The OT shows, in total, that Yahweh was considered as having human form (as were, often, the Canaanite gods). The calves in 1 Kgs. 12:28 were only Yahweh's pediment; the snake in the temple (2 Kgs. 18:4), only a substitute symbol. Archaeology has little to tell us about these theophanies, for no iconography has come from a (semi-)nomadic people that did not use images. The imageless cult (with → images [§2] banned from the 7th cent.) did not, however, totally rule out depictions of Yahweh. Not until the era of Hellenistic philosophy (→ Hellenism 2.4 and 3.1) were visualizations of God rejected (Aristobulus, Fragment 2; Philo).

Bibliography: ANEP, figs. 464-573, esp. 490, 493, 500-501 • AOB, figs. 299-366, esp. 326, 339-40 • F. M. CROSS, *Canaanite Myth and Hebrew Epic* (Cambridge, Mass., 1973) 91-111, 147-77 • O. KEEL, *Gods, Goddesses, and Images of God in Ancient Israel* (Minneapolis, 1998); idem, *Jahwe-Visionen und Siegelkunst* (Stuttgart, 1977) • C. KLOOS, *Yhwh's Combat with the Sea: A Canaanite Tradition in the Religion of Ancient Israel* (Amsterdam, 1986) • M. C. A. KORPEL, *A Rift in the Clouds: Ugaritic and Hebrew Descriptions of the Divine* (Münster, 1990) • J. J. NIEHAUS, *God at Sinai: Covenant and Theophany in the Bible and Ancient Near East* (Grand Rapids, 1995) • G. W. SAVRAN, *Encountering the Divine: Theophany in Biblical Narrative* (New York, 2005) • A. SCRIBA, *Die Geschichte des Motivkomplexes Theophanie* (Göttingen, 1995).

ALBRECHT SCRIBA

Theosis

1. Patristic and Eastern Orthodox Theology
    1.1. Term
    1.2. Historical Development
    1.3. Christology and Pneumatology
2. Western Theological and Ecumenical
    Developments
    2.1. The Western Tradition
    2.2. Luther Research in Finland
    2.3. Other Traditions
    2.4. The Wider Significance of *Theōsis*

1. Patristic and Eastern Orthodox Theology
1.1. *Term*

The Gk. term *theōsis* (deification, divinization) became a common term in Greek Christian theology (→ Orthodox Christianity 7) under which to describe God's economy with us and the world and to show the world what its final destiny is (→ Order of Salvation 1.1). In its proper use, *theōsis* cannot be equated with other terms in Western theology like → "justification," "redemption" (→ Soteriology), → "reconciliation," or → "sanctification." It can be understood only in relation to the total theological structure of Greek Orthodox theology, and for this reason it is best not to translate it.

1.2. *Historical Development*

In the history of Greek theology, the tradition and experience of human and cosmic → salvation (§2) in Jesus Christ have been developed in terms of deification, in distinction from the orientation to juridical themes common in the West. Gregory of Nazianzus (329/30-389/90) introduced *theōsis* into theological language. Its meaning, however, had been indirectly present from the second century (Ignatius, → Justin, Tatian, Theophilus of → Antioch), and it had become a direct part of Christian awareness and faith from the days of → Irenaeus (ca. 130-ca. 200; see his *Adv. haer.* 3.19.1), Clement of Alexandria (ca. 150-ca. 215; → Alexandrian Theology 2.3), and → Origen (ca. 185-ca. 254; → Origenism).

It was the achievement of → Athanasius (ca. 297-373) to unite *theōsis* closely with the → incarnation of the preexistent Logos (→ Christology 2.2.2). Along these lines, the great → Cappadocians (Basil, Gregory of Nazianzus, and Gregory of Nyssa) linked *theōsis* to the deity and work of the Holy Spirit. → Cyril of Alexandria (ca. 375-444; → Alexandrian Theology 3.2) then linked it to the → sacraments of → baptism and the → Eucharist (→ Eucharistic Ecclesiology). Through the writings of Dionysius the Pseudo-Areopagite (fl. ca. 500) and their commentator Maximus the Confessor (ca. 580-662; → Light 3.3.2), *theōsis*, borrowing and newly expounding the Neoplatonic tradition (→ Platonism 3), then reached its fullest development, and in this form it was received by → John of Damascus (ca. 655-ca. 750; → Orthodox Christianity 5) as the firm tradition and legacy of the Greek church. Gregory Palamas (ca. 1296-1359; → Palamism) gave it a final focus by relating it to the traditional distinction between the *ousia* (being, essence) of God and his uncreated energies.

In large measure, *theōsis* draws on the → ascetic, hymnographic (→ Hymn), and liturgical tradition (→ Liturgy 2) of the Greek church. In many different ways, then, believers are brought into the living stream of the *theōsis* tradition.

Biblically, the term is based on our creation in the image of God (→ Anthropology 3.3) and on the many NT references to our divine origin (e.g., Acts 17:27-29), our sonship in Christ (Gal. 3:26), the demand to be perfect as God is perfect (Matt. 5:48; → Discipleship; Perfection), the new nature of the Christian as participation in the divine nature (2 Pet. 1:4; → New Self), and so forth.

In the theology of the Greek fathers (→ Church Fathers), *theōsis* is not defined. It is a gracious historical and eschatological gift of God to those who are worthy (→ Eschatology 4). It is described only doxologically (→ Doxology) and liturgically as "being as much as possible like and in union with God" (Pseudo-Dionysius, 198). What is clear here is that it does not mean being absorbed into the divine or losing our human nature (→ Ontology 3). It is gracious union with the personal God along the lines of 1 Cor. 15:28. It is not an inherent potency in us but is due wholly and utterly to divine → grace (§2; Maximus). It does not imply any participation in the uncreated and ineffable nature of God but only in his uncreated energies, that is, in the perfect life of the → Trinity.

1.3. *Christology and Pneumatology*

Theōsis takes on its real sense in connection with → Christology (§3). It relates first to the human nature of Jesus Christ, which in unmixed and inseparable union with the divine nature is deified by the communication of attributes (the doctrine of perichoresis; → Grace 2.1). The divine qualities are essentially lent to it. But because Jesus Christ has taken to himself a true human nature, all people are truly received in him and become potential participants in his deified human nature; as Gregory of Nazianzus put it (*Or. theol.* 43.48), a person is "bidden to be a god" *(theos einai kekeleusmenos)*. The famous formula of Athanasius runs like a scarlet thread through Greek theology: "God became human in order that we might be made god" (*De incar.* 54). In *theōsis*, believers can share, by grace and participation, in that which God is by nature.

Theōsis thus has clear pneumatological (→ Holy Spirit 2.4), ecclesiological (→ Church 3.1), liturgical, and ascetic dimensions. By his → incarnation Jesus Christ has deified the whole of human nature. He accomplished *theōsis* by his → cross, by his → resurrection, and by → pentecost. Personal appropriation is solely by the gracious working of the Holy Spirit in individual believers. It may be achieved through participation in the sacraments of baptism and the → Eucharist, that is, in the gracious life of the church (which, according to Gregory Palamas, is the real "koinonia of *theōsis*"). It thus presupposes the willing "synergy" of the free will (→ Grace 2.2; Synergism 2). Believers, with the help of the Holy Spirit, may thereby achieve purification and → virtues, namely, the perfection of God and his deifying → love.

A basic part of the *theōsis* tradition is its universal, cosmological, and eschatological aspects. It embraces the whole world, the whole cosmos. It is presently received as the gracious → experience of the divine, uncreated light, but it will be fulfilled in the → kingdom of God as the face-to-face vision of the Trinitarian God. By *theōsis,* we ourselves become → immortal, that is, no longer creaturely.

Bibliography: P. B. T. BILANIUK, "The Mystery of Theosis or Divinization," *OCA* 195 (1973) 337-59 • D. B. CLENDENIN, "Partakers of Divinity: The Orthodox Doctrine of Theosis," *JETS* 37 (1994) 365-79 • J. GROSS, *The Divinization of the Christian according to the Greek Fathers* (Anaheim, Calif., 2002; orig. pub., 1938) • V. LOSSKY, *In the Image and Likeness of God* (Crestwood, N.Y., 1985); idem, *The Mystical Theology of the Eastern Church* (Crestwood, N.Y., 1976; orig. pub., 1957); idem, *The Vision of God* (Crestwood, N.Y., 1973) • M. LOT-BORODINE, *La déification de l'homme selon la doctrine des pères grecs* (Paris, 1970) • G. I. MANTZARIDES, *The Deification of Man* (Crestwood, N.Y., 1984) • P. NELLAS, *Deification in Christ: Orthodox Perspectives on the Nature of the Human Person* (Crestwood, N.Y., 1987) • PSEUDO-DIONYSIUS, *The Complete Works* (trans. C. Luibheid; New York, 1987) • R. SAARINEN, "Theosis," *TRE* 33.389-93 • C. STAVROPOULOUS, *Partakers of Divine Nature* (Minneapolis, 1976) • R. WILLIAMS, "Deification," *DCS* 106-8.

JOHANNES PANAGOPOULOS†

2. Western Theological and Ecumenical Developments

2.1. *The Western Tradition*

Although *theōsis* has never been a concept totally foreign to the theology of the Christian West — references can be found in → Tertullian (*Apol.* 11.1-10; CChr.SL 1.107-8) and → Augustine (*Enarr. in Ps.* 49.2.5-15, 29-35; CChr.SL 38.575-76), among others — it was the medieval mystical tradition, especially under the influence of → Bernard of Clairvaux (1090-1153), that rediscovered and enthusiastically embraced the idea. While the term *theōsis* occurs rarely in Thomas Aquinas (ca. 1225-74; → Thomism), Martin → Luther (1483-1546; → Luther's Theology), or John → Calvin (1509-64; → Calvin's Theology), the corresponding idea was more often expressed with concepts such as union (with God), participation (in God), glorification, restoration of the image of God, and the symbolism of marriage.

Until recent times, the Eastern Orthodox and pa-

tristic idea of *theōsis* has been viewed with suspicion in the West for a number of reasons, such as its association with the medieval and 16th-century enthusiastic and apocalyptic groups, with some Christian movements considered marginal by the mainstream (e.g., the 20th-cent. Chinese preachers Watchman Nee and Witness Lee), with non-Christian groups such as the → Mormons, and more recently with the → New Age movements with their Eastern religious influences. Church historian Adolf von Harnack (1851-1930) bluntly called *theōsis* a pre-Christian (*unterchristlich*) idea (pp. 238-39).

Protestant suspicion of the idea of deification has also to do with basic differences in theological outlook: Eastern Orthodox theology has been considered to affirm too positive an → anthropology and understanding of the role of the human will and divine-human synergy (G. Kretschmar).

2.2. *Luther Research in Finland*

Beginning in the late 1970s, a new paradigm of Luther studies in Europe, specifically in Finland, has arisen to challenge the standard opinion that the Orthodox and Lutheran views of → salvation are not only different from, but also antagonistic to, each other. Tuomo Mannermaa and his pupils at the University of Helsinki (also S. Peura) have argued that *theōsis* was one of the ideas in Luther's → soteriology and that the Reformer's own view of → justification was based on the idea of the presence of Christ in the believer (*in ipsa fide Christus adest*) through the → Holy Spirit. The presence of Christ leads to renewal and good works. This interpretation challenges the more forensically oriented view of justification that came to the fore in later → Lutheranism, largely as expressed in the Book of Concord. While Luther used the term "deification" only 32 times (e.g., WA.B 5.415.45), other terms such as "union" and "participation" were more often used by him to express the same idea.

The impetus for this new perspective on Luther's theology arose out of the ecumenical contacts between Orthodox and Lutheran churches, initially between the → Russian Orthodox Church and the Lutheran Church of Finland (R. Saarinen). At the same time, this new interpretation of Luther has also significantly influenced the Lutheran and Roman Catholic dialogue concerning justification (→ Joint Declaration on the Doctrine of Justification). In general, this new paradigm for Luther's view of salvation as both justification and deification has received a critical, at times even hostile, reception among German-speaking scholars but has been embraced by many of their American counterparts.

2.3. Other Traditions

The idea of deification can also be found in the writings of the other major Protestant Reformer, John Calvin (C. Mosser). Similarly, the idea is found in → Anglicanism and → Methodism (A. M. Allchin), → Anabaptism (T. Finger), and → Pentecostalism (E. Rybarczyk). Theologians and writers as diverse as Jonathan → Edwards (1703-58), Augustus Hopkins Strong (1836-1921), C. S. Lewis (1898-1963), and even some American evangelicals have embraced the view.

In modern Roman Catholicism the revival of Catholic mystical theology at the end of the 19th century, as well as the recovery by theologians such as Karl → Rahner (1904-84) of the idea of → grace as the presence or indwelling of God, points toward deification. Similarly, Rahner's transcendental anthropology and Christology, as well as Hans Urs von Balthasar's (1905-88) theology of divine beauty and its communication to humans in Christ, reflect the Orthodox idea of divinization.

2.4. The Wider Significance of Theōsis

Apart from significant ecumenical advancements, the significance of the ancient soteriological concept of *theōsis* has recently been acknowledged in relation to other religions and cultures and to contemporary worldviews. It has been suggested, for example, that *theōsis* may provide a challenging encounter with the African (Bantu) concept of "vital participation" (H. Schönherr, 160) and that deification may help clarify the Christian scientific understanding of → creation and → evolution (J. Polkinghorne, 103).

Bibliography: A. M. ALLCHIN, *Participation in God: A Forgotten Strand in Anglican Tradition* (Wilton, Conn., 1988) • D. BIELFIELDT, "The Ontology of Deification," *Caritas Dei. Beiträge zum Verständnis Luthers und der gegenwärtigen Ökumene* (ed. O. Bayer, R. W. Jenson, and S. Knuuttila; Helsinki, 1997) 90-113 • S. H. BLACKBURN, "Death and Deification: Folk Cults in Hinduism," *HR* 24 (1985) 255-74 • C. E. BRAATEN and R. W. JENSON, eds., *Union with Christ: The New Finnish Interpretation of Luther* (Grand Rapids, 1998) • M. CHRISTENSEN, "Theosis and Sanctification: John Wesley's Reformulation of a Patristic Doctrine," *WTJ* 31 (Fall 1996) 71-94 • T. FINGER, *A Contemporary Anabaptist Theology: Biblical, Historical, Constructive* (Downers Grove, Ill., 2004) 136-56 • R. FLOGAUS, *Theosis bei Palamas und Luther* (Göttingen, 1997) • A. VON HARNACK, *What Is Christianity?* (London, 1904; repr., New York, 1957) • V.-M. KÄRKKÄINEN, *One with God: Salvation as Deification and Justification* (Collegeville, Minn., 2004) • G. KRETSCHMAR, "Die

Rezeption der orthodoxen Vergöttlichungslehre in der protestantischen Theologie," *Luther und Theosis. Vergöttlichung als Thema der abendländischen Theologie* (ed. S. Peura and A. Raunio; Helsinki, 1990) 61-80 • M. C. MCDANIEL, "Salvation as Justification and Theosis," *A Lutheran-Orthodox Dialogue* (ed. J. Meyendorff and R. Tobias; Minneapolis, 1992) 67-84 • T. MANNERMAA, *Christ Present in Faith: Luther's View of Justification* (Minneapolis, 2005; orig. pub., 1989) • C. MOSSER, "The Greatest Possible Blessing: Calvin and Deification," *SJT* 55 (2002) 36-57 • F. W. NORRIS, "Deification: Consensual and Cogent," *SJT* 49 (1996) 411-28 • S. PEURA, *Mehr als ein Mensch? Die Vergöttlichung als Thema der Theologie Martin Luthers von 1513-1519* (Stuttgart, 1994) • J. POLKINGHORNE, *Reason and Reality: The Relationship between Science and Theology* (Philadelphia, 1991) • E. RYBARCZYK, *Beyond Salvation: Eastern Orthodoxy and Classical Pentecostalism on Becoming like Christ* (Carlisle, 2004) • R. SAARINEN, *Faith and Holiness: Lutheran-Orthodox Dialogue, 1959-1994* (Göttingen, 1997) • H. SCHÖNHERR, "Concepts of Salvation in Christianity," *ATJ* 12/3 (1983) 159-65.

VELI-MATTI KÄRKKÄINEN

Theosophy

1. Features
2. History
3. Theological Evaluation
4. Theosophical Societies

In distinction from Indian or pseudo-Indian theosophical societies (see 4) of the Blavatsky type, theosophy in the traditional sense represents the concern in all religions to penetrate the deepest mysteries of the deity. In the → early church and the Middle Ages "theosophy" was another term for → theology. It came to be restricted to special kinds of Christianity only in the 18th century and now applies analogously to non-Christian phenomena.

1. Features

As distinct from → metaphysics and → philosophy, theosophy relies generally on → revelation. If this is not found in the Bible or some other writing, it lies for pansophists, for example, in the "book of nature." We move on from God to the world, which is pantheistically understood as the development or unfolding of the Godhead (→ Pantheism).

Unlike theologians, theosophists not only proceed rationally with knowledge resting on their own convictions (→ Epistemology) but look with vision in facing their problems, the vision being inborn, trained by schooling, or resting on inspiration. Linking knowledge to the divine being, this vision is superior to all other forms of knowledge and, according to → Gnostic models, leads theosophists on to → salvation.

The ultimate theosophist vision is a total vision that often has theogonic elements (→ Theogony) and is always cosmogonic, cosmological, → anthropological, and → eschatological. In the Christian sphere answers are often given to questions of the → sin of Lucifer (→ Devil) or of → Adam, the nature of → evil, the natural divine likeness, and the androgynous character of the first pair, questions that official church teaching has neglected or ignored. Theosophy investigates the relation of the deity to → creation and with its help plunges into the hidden secrets of nature and humanity.

Unlike speculative → mysticism, theosophy makes no clear-cut distinction between spiritual and material phenomena. Its confusing images are features of reality and are more than → symbols. The rationally indecipherable ambiguity of its symbolism gives all theosophy from the outset a character that makes light of dogmas and confessional limitations.

2. History
Since theosophy actualizes hidden divine relations in the cosmos, its development has been historically esoteric (→ Esotericism). It came into Christianity from other religions but found a basis in 1 Cor. 2:10. We find traces of theosophy in the Alexandrians Clement (ca. 150-ca. 215) and → Origen (ca. 185-ca. 254). Forms of theosophy with a Gnostic tinge may be found in Neoplatonism (→ Platonism) and the Hermetic literature (→ Alchemy).

Paracelsus (1493-1541) showed theosophist leanings, as did pansophists, → Rosicrucians, Christian cabalists, and the no less theosophically inclined Jewish cabalists (→ Cabala; Jewish Philosophy). In reaction to Reformation → orthodoxy (§1) in the 17th and 18th centuries, theosophy also influenced J. Böhme (1575-1624), E. Swedenborg (1688-1772; → Swedenborgianism), and F. Baader (1765-1841). It also found support among the Russian religious philosophers N. A. Berdyaev (1874-1948), S. N. Bulgakov (1871-1944), and V. S. Solovyov (1853-1900; → Sophiology). We also find well-known variations of theosophy in Brahmanism, in early → Hinduism, and in the wisdom schools of → Buddhism.

3. Theological Evaluation
To decipher the world by primary models concealed in the deity is an unending task, given the infinity of God. In a day when even the elementary rules of dogmatic speech are vulnerable, and when even those who have taken the magic out of the world would like it to be restored, the basic theosophical conviction of a revelation that is not yet complete poses a demand for church theologians but one whose extent is beyond all imagining.

In a reply of the Holy Office made by Benedict XV (1914-22) in July 1919, the teachings of the theosophical societies were judged to be incompatible with the doctrine of the → Roman Catholic Church (DH 3648).

→ Anthroposophy; Astrology; Masons; Spiritualism; Syncretism

Bibliography: B. F. Campbell, *Ancient Wisdom Revived: A History of the Theosophical Movement* (Berkeley, Calif., 1980) • M. Carlson, *"No Religion Higher Than Truth": A History of the Theosophical Movement in Russia, 1875-1922* (Princeton, 1993) • J. Dixon, *Divine Feminine: Theosophy and Feminism in England* (Baltimore, 2001) • A. Faivre, *Theosophy, Imagination, Tradition: Studies in Western Esotericism* (Albany, N.Y., 2000) • J. Godwin, *The Theosophical Enlightenment* (Albany, N.Y., 1994) • O. Hammer, *Claiming Knowledge: Strategies of Epistemology from Theosophy to the New Age* (Boston, 2001) • R. Steiner, *Theosophy: An Introduction to the Supersensible Knowledge of the World and the Destination of Man* (4th ed.; London, 2005; orig. pub., 1910).

Karl Hoheisel

4. Theosophical Societies
4.1. The first theosophical society was founded in New York City in 1875 by Henry Steel Olcott (1832-1907), an American Civil War officer and later a lawyer, and Helena Petrovna Blavatsky (née Hahn, 1831-91), a Russian spiritualist and author. Olcott was influenced by → spiritualism, and Blavatsky, a gifted medium, had been interested in → occult phenomena since childhood. She wanted to assemble theosophical truths (see 1) and make available a higher knowledge of the divine, particularly through spiritualist elements.

The revelation of spiritualist fraud at that time caused Blavatsky and Olcott to move their Theosophical Society to India. The two arrived there in 1879 and in 1882 established their center at Adyar, near Madras. From that point, Buddhist wisdom teachings, especially Tibetan and partly also Hindu, dominated the theological "secret doctrine" (Blavatsky, *The Secret Doctrine* [3 vols.; Madras and Wheaton, Ill., 1987; orig. pub., London, 1888]; → Buddhism, Tibetan Religions; Hinduism). In addition, the practice of clairvoyance, seen especially in Tibetan Buddhism, was declared a fundamental human characteristic that could be reawakened through theosophical methods. In a vision, the initiated person becomes part of the threefold (or "trinitarian") self-unfolding of the absolute (being, spirit-matter/life-form, world spirit), which forms the basis of the universe, of history, and of the ever newly embodied human being (→ Immortality 1).

In 1885 Blavatsky traveled to Germany, where she founded an esoteric school in 1889 (→ Esotericism). Its "secret doctrine" was reworked into an esoterically formed Hinduism by Blavatsky's protégée, Annie Besant (née Wood, 1843-1937), who in 1907 became the international president of the Theosophical Society in Adyar, a position she held until her death.

4.2. The theosophical movement spread quickly at first in Asia, America, and Europe. But soon it divided, not least because of the introduction of an exclusive inner circle and theocratic methods of rule. In the United States the Universal Brotherhood and Theosophical Society was established, as well as the Theosophical Society Point Loma–Covina [Calif.]. In addition, a theosophical Liberal Catholic Church (first initiated by the theosophist C. W. Leadbeater in England in 1916) arose in Los Angeles, joining traditional Catholic forms of worship with the reception and passing on of spiritual gifts and practicing → Gnostic mystery teachings (→ Mystery Religions). In 1941 the church divided over how closely the group should be aligned with theosophy.

In Germany Franz Hartmann (1842-1912) challenged the claim to leadership of the Adyar center and in 1897 established the International Theosophical Brotherhood, which existed alongside the German section of the Theosophical Society. Rudolf Steiner (1861-1925), who had been general secretary since 1902, separated from the Theosophical Society, along with most of the German members, and in 1912 established the Anthroposophical Society (→ Anthroposophy).

The European Federation of the Theosophical Society unites over 20 national societies of the Theosophical Society in Adyar; its International Theosophical Center is located in Naarden, Netherlands. Most of the members of the Theosophical Society (Adyar) live in → India, the next highest number in the United States. Esoteric-Gnostic groups basing themselves on the foundations of theosophy include the → New Thought movement, the German secret society Fraternitas Saturni, and the circle around the journal *Weltspirale*.

Bibliography: E. A. Greenwalt, *The Point Loma Community in California, 1897-1942: A Theosophical Experiment* (Berkeley and Los Angeles, 1955) • L. H. Leslie-Smith, ed., *The Universal Flame: Commemorating the Centenary of the Theosophical Society* (Wheaton, Ill., 1975) • H. Mynarek, *Mystik und Vernunft: Zwei Poler einer Wirklichkeit* (Olten, 1991); idem, *Religiös ohne Gott?* (Düsseldorf, 1983); idem, *Die Vernunft des Universums* (Munich, 1988) • J. Ransom, *A Short History of the Theosophical Society* (Adyar, India, 1938; repr., 1989) • E. B. Sellon and R. Weber, "Theosophy and the Theosophical Society," *Modern Esoteric Spirituality* (ed. A. Faivre and J. Needleman; New York, 1992) • A. Taylor, *Annie Besant: A Biography* (New York, 1992) • P. Washington, *Madame Blavatsky's Baboon: A History of the Mystics, Mediums, and Misfits Who Brought Spiritualism to America* (New York, 1995).

Hubertus Mynarek

Thessalonians, Epistles to the

1. General Features

In 316 b.c. Cassander, the king of Macedonia, founded Thessaloniki at the head of the Thermaic Gulf, naming it after his wife, Thessalonike, the daughter of Philip II and half sister of Alexander the Great. The city became one of the great ports on the Aegean. When the Romans conquered Macedonia at the battle of Pydna at the end of the Third Macedonian War (168), they divided the former kingdom into four districts and named Thessaloniki capital of the second. Various Macedonians organized unsuccessful rebellions against Roman domination. As a result, Rome opted to convert Macedonia from a vassal state into a province and made Thessaloniki its capital (146), since the city had maintained loyalty to Rome. The construction of the Via Egnatia (146-120) from the Adriatic, through Thessaloniki, and on to Byzantium further enhanced the fortunes of the city.

Many Romans emigrated to Thessaloniki and became benefactors; in return, the council and citizens established a priesthood to honor the goddess Roma and Roman benefactors. After Brutus and Cassius assassinated Julius Caesar (44 B.C.), Thessaloniki sided with Octavian and Mark Antony, who, at the battle of Philippi (42), defeated the assassins. In return, Mark Antony granted Thessaloniki free-city status. The city also aligned with Octavian in his fight against Mark Antony at the time of the battle of Actium (31). Thessaloniki honored Julius Caesar and Augustus (Octavian) by erecting an imperial temple. Strabo called the city the metropolis ("mother city") of Macedonia, and Cicero commented that it was at the heart of the Roman power. The city was securely loyal to Rome and celebrated the fruit of its strong relationship with the imperial power (→ Roman Empire; Roman Religion).

2. 1 Thessalonians

2.1. *Occasion*

According to Acts 17:1-9, the apostle → Paul traveled from Philippi to Thessaloniki (doubtless on the Via Egnatia) on his second missionary journey, being accompanied by Silas, also known by his Latin name Silvanus, and Timothy (see 1 Thess. 1:1; 2:1-2; and Acts 16:1-3; 17:14-15). While Acts 17:1-5 focuses upon the proclamation of the → gospel to Jews and Gentile God-fearers attached to the → synagogue, 1 Thess. 1:9 indicates that the majority in the church were Gentiles converted from idolatry. Acts 17:5-10 records the hasty departure of the apostolic company from the city, suggested also by 1 Thess. 2:17 ("we were made orphans by being separated from you").

Paul attempted to return to Thessaloniki but, when thwarted, sent Timothy to strengthen the church and find out whether they had continued in the gospel, given the social ostracism these recent converts endured (2:14–3:5). Paul wrote 1 Thessalonians upon Timothy's return when he brought news of the congregation's → faith, → love, and endurance produced by → hope (3:6-10; 1:3). If Paul penned the letter from Corinth (see Acts 18:5), the date of composition would likely be around A.D. 50-51.

2.2. *Content*

The letter opening (1:3-10) is a thanksgiving to God for the → conversion (§1) of the Thessalonian believers. Here Paul presents the main themes of the letter, including the coming of the gospel, their response to it, the character of the heralds, suffering, mission, and eschatological hope, which the author frames in terms of an imperial → parousia (1:9; see 2:19; 3:13; 4:15-17; 5:23).

The body of the letter begins with an apologetic defense of the messenger's character (2:1-12), a section sometimes interpreted as → parenetic in which the apostle presents himself as a moral example (A. J. Malherbe). Paul distanced himself from the practices of the popular philosophers by declaring that he preached despite having endured great opposition and that his message, methods, and motives were honorable. In 2:13–3:13 the apostle recounts his plans to provide continuing pastoral care for the church, including his own attempts to get back to Thessaloniki; Timothy's mission, return, and report; and Paul's prayers to visit the church.

Although Timothy reported good news (3:6-8) about the church's faith, love, and steadfastness, some in the church had dismissed Paul's commands about sexual morality (4:1-8). They also inquired, perhaps by letter carried by Timothy, about fraternal love (4:9-12), the destiny of the deceased in Christ (4:13-18), and the time of the day of the Lord (5:1-11). The final issues Paul addresses in the body of the letter focus upon the emergent leadership in the church (5:12-13), the refusal of the *ataktoi* (here best translated "disorderly," i.e., those not following the community rule) to abandon their status as dependent clients (v. 14; see also 2 Thess 3:6-15), proper relationships within and outside the church (5:14-15) and with God (vv. 16-18), and the reception and evaluation of prophecy (vv. 19-22; → Prophet, Prophecy). The letter closing includes a prayer for their → sanctification, as well as greetings and a blessing (vv. 23-28).

2.3. *Authorship*

Pauline authorship of 1 Thessalonians (1:1; 2:18) was never doubted in the early church. Eusebius classified it as one of the undisputed letters (*Hist. eccl.* 3.3.5), and allusions to the book appear as early as the *Didache,* Ignatius, and the Shepherd of Hermas. → Tertullian commented that even Marcion accepted the letter (*Adv. Marc.* 5.15). It appears in the Muratorian Canon, and → Irenaeus quotes 5:23, attributing the words to Paul (*Adv. haer.* 5.6.1).

Doubts regarding authorship surfaced in the 19th century because of the letter's apparent lack of doctrinal depth as compared to the undisputed Paulines and because of the way it merely echoed Paul's writings (F. C. Baur). Contemporary scholarship, however, stands firmly with the early church in regarding the letter as authentic.

Current questions about authorship touch upon the role of Silvanus and Timothy in the composition (1:1; cf. 2:18; 3:5; 5:27, where Paul steps out from the authorial community) and the authenticity of the anti-Jewish polemic in 2:14-16 (cf. Romans 9–11).

3. 2 Thessalonians

3.1. *Occasion*

The similarity of the themes treated in 1 and 2 Thessalonians suggests that the second letter was written not long after the first but at a time when the situation of the church had deteriorated. We do not know how the apostle became apprised of developments in the congregation. Second Thessalonians could have been written during the same 18-month period when Paul was in Corinth after the founding of the Thessalonian church (Acts 18:11). In that case, the letter would have been written either in late A.D. 50 or in 51.

3.2. *Content*

Although some topics from 1 Thessalonians do not reappear in this letter, such as the character and absence of the apostles, → sexuality, church leadership, and fraternal love, three previous concerns receive considerable attention: persecution (1:3-12), the day of the Lord (2:1-17), and the topic of → work (3:6-15).

The letter begins with a thanksgiving (1:3-4) that underscores the church's faith, love, and perseverance in the face of social rejection (cf. 1 Thess. 1:3; 3:6-8; 5:8). The → persecution that the believers endured since first hearing of the gospel (1 Thess 1:6; 2:14; 3:2-4) continued unabated and even intensified. For their cause in → suffering for the kingdom, Paul recalls the coming judgment of God and the vindication of the believers (2 Thess 1:5-10). He prays that the Lord would be honored and would honor them (1:11-12).

A teaching that threatened to destabilize the church was propagated among the Thessalonians, namely, that the day of the Lord had already come or was right at hand (2:1-2). Paul responds to this destabilizing teaching by mentioning two events that would precede that day: "the rebellion" and the revealing of "the man of lawlessness" (v. 3 RSV). He does not indicate whether a political or a religious rebellion against authority is in view, but in Jewish literature the term frequently refers to → apostasy. The second event preceding the day of the Lord is the revelation of the "man of lawlessness," whose doom is sure (vv. 3-12). This figure demands worship in the temple as a god, evoking the image of the imperial cult in Thessaloniki (v. 4; G. L. Green). The "temple" has often been interpreted as the Jerusalem temple. This agent is held back or restrained from being revealed by some power (vv. 6-7), which has been variously identified as the state, the emperor, the church, the proclamation of the gospel, God the Father, the Holy Spirit, or even Paul. C. H. Giblin, however, argues that this figure is not antithetical to the man of

lawlessness but, rather, anticipates his coming ("the mystery of lawlessness is already at work"). While others will be deceived (vv. 9-12), Paul thanks God for the church and calls them to adhere to the received → tradition (vv. 13-17; cf. 2:5).

After asking for prayer for the mission and protection, and assuring the church of God's protection (3:1-5), the apostle addresses the problem of work (3:6-15). He previously taught them by word and example (3:7-10), but some continued to be "disorderly" by not living according to the apostolic rule (3:6, 11; cf. 1 Thess. 4:11-12; 5:14). The Thessalonians' ardent eschatological expectation may have been the reason they abandoned work (2:1-2), but others interpret the passage within the framework of the patron-client relationship (B. W. Winter, Green). Paul encourages benefaction but calls the believers to abandon their status as dependent clients and to institute disciplinary measures for those who continue to act disorderly (3:10-15).

3.3. *Authorship*

The introduction of the letter includes the names of Paul, Silvanus, and Timothy (1:1), and Paul left an authenticating note at the end of the letter in his own hand (3:17). The early church unanimously accepted the letter as authentic, with early witnesses alluding to it (Ignatius, → Justin Martyr) and even attributing quoted sections to Paul (Polycarp, Irenaeus, Clement of Alexandria).

Questions about authenticity arose in the 19th and 20th centuries (W. Trilling, J. A. Bailey). Similarity of style and form to 1 Thessalonians and the lack of characteristic Pauline theological themes are adduced as arguments. These differences, however, are not sufficiently marked to warrant rejection of the traditional ascription (Green, Malherbe).

4. Special Problems

4.1. *The Order of the Letters*

The canonical order of the letters was determined principally on the basis of their respective lengths. But, according to C. A. Wanamaker, 2 Thessalonians may have been the first letter to the church, since the persecutions in 1 Thessalonians appear to be past (2:14; 3:4), whereas those in 2 Thessalonians are a present reality (1:4-7). Also, the purpose of Timothy's mission and 2 Thessalonians were the same, making it likely that Paul's associate took 2 Thessalonians with him (cf. 1 Thess. 3:2, 3 and 2 Thess. 2:17, 2). The problem of the disorderly in 2 Thessalonians (3:6-13) appears to have subsided, and Paul needs simply to gives the church a reminder in 1 Thessalonians (4:11; see also the teaching on eschatology in 2 Thess. 2:1-12 and 1 Thess. 5:1). The authenticating note in 2 Thessalonians (3:17) would make more sense in a first correspondence.

The majority of contemporary scholars, however, do not find these arguments persuasive and point to Paul's reference to a previous letter (2:15), which is most likely 1 Thessalonians. Moreover, the most recent events recalled in 1 Thessalonians are the apostolic visit and the conversion of the church (chaps. 1–3).

4.2. *Rhetorical or Epistolary Analysis?*

Scholars continue to be divided over the question of whether the letters should be analyzed according to the canons of ancient (oral) rhetoric as taught by Aristotle and Cicero (F. W. Hughes, P. K. Jewett, Wanamaker), or whether their structure should be analyzed according to standards of epistolary theory (Malherbe, Green, J. A. D. Weima). Traditional analysis of the letters has been strictly topical (F. F. Bruce). The question posed is what model best helps us understand Paul's strategy to persuade the Thessalonian believers (K. Donfried and J. Beutler).

Bibliography: Commentaries E. Best (BNTC; Peabody, Mass., 1986) • F. F. Bruce (WBC; Nashville, 1982) • M. Dibelius (HNT; 3d ed.; Tübingen, 1937) • E. von Dobschütz (KEK; Göttingen, 1909) • J. E. Frame (ICC; Edinburgh, 1912) • V. P. Furnish (AbNTC; Nashville, 2006) • B. R. Gaventa (Interp.; Louisville, Ky., 1998) • G. L. Green (PNTC; Grand Rapids, 2002) • T. Holtz, *Der erste Brief an die Thessalonicher* (EKKNT; Neukirchen, 1990) • A. J. Malherbe (AB; New York, 2000) • I. H. Marshall (NCBC; Grand Rapids, 1983) • M. J. J. Menken, *2 Thessalonians* (NTR; London, 1994) • G. Milligan (London, 1908) • L. Morris (NICNT; Grand Rapids, 1991) • E. J. Richard (SacPa; Collegeville, Minn., 1995) • B. Rigaux (EtB; Paris, 1956) • W. Trilling, *Der zweite Brief an die Thessalonicher* (EKKNT; Zurich, 1980) • C. A. Wanamaker (NIGTC; Grand Rapids, 1990).

Other works: J. A. Bailey, "Who Wrote II Thessalonians?" *NTS* 25 (1978-79) 131-45 • R. Collins, *The Thessalonian Correspondence* (Louvain, 1990) • K. Donfried, *Paul, Thessalonica, and Early Christianity* (Grand Rapids, 2002) • K. Donfried and J. Beutler, eds., *The Thessalonians Debate* (Grand Rapids, 2002) • K. Donfried and I. H. Marshall, *The Theology of the Shorter Pauline Letters* (Cambridge, 1993) • C. H. Giblin, *The Threat to Faith* (Rome, 1967) • H. Hendrix, "Thessalonicans Honor Romans" (Diss., Harvard University, 1984) • G. S. Holland, *The Tradition That You Received from Us: 2 Thessalonians in the Pauline Tradition* (Tübingen, 1988) • F. W. Hughes, *Early Christian Rhetoric and 2 Thessalonians* (Sheffield, 1989) • P. K. Jewett, *The Thessalonian Correspondence* (Philadelphia, 1986) •

A. J. Malherbe, *Paul and the Thessalonians* (Philadelphia, 1998) • A. Smith, *Comfort One Another: Reconstructing the Rhetoric and Audience of 1 Thessalonians* (Louisville, Ky., 1995) • T. Still, *Conflict at Thessalonica: A Pauline Church and Its Neighbors* (Sheffield, 1999) • J. A. D. Weima, *Neglected Endings: The Significance of the Pauline Letter Closings* (Sheffield, 1994) • B. W. Winter, *Seek the Welfare of the City: Christians as Benefactors and Citizens* (Grand Rapids, 1994).

Gene L. Green

Third World

1. Political, Economic, Social, and Cultural Problems
   1.1. Term, Criteria, Groups
   1.2. Rise
   1.3. Economy
   1.4. Political Systems
   1.5. Culture and Education
   1.6. Health
   1.7. Religion
   1.8. Hunger and Poverty
   1.9. Human Rights
   1.10. Women
   1.11. Theories
   1.12. Limitation of the Concept
2. Churches
   2.1. Survey
   2.2. Status
   2.3. Indigenous Christianities
   2.4. Social and Economic Context
   2.5. Religious and Cultural Context
   2.6. Ecumenism
   2.7. A "New Christendom"?

1. Political, Economic, Social, and Cultural Problems

1.1. *Term, Criteria, Groups*

1.1.1. The African Caribbean (Martinique) doctor and freedom fighter Frantz Fanon (1961) is thought to have been the author of the term "Third World." He based it on the Third Estate (i.e., the commoners) in the French Revolution and denoted by it the colonized and underdeveloped countries. I. L. Horowitz (1966) and then D. Nohlen and F. Nuscheler (1982) studied the significance of the term both practically and in terms of the theory of development. P. Worsley (1964) found in it an attempt by the independent liberal Left to find a third way as compared to the capitalist and Communist parties, and to forge a free bloc internationally over against both the United States and its allies on the one side (the First World) and the USSR and its allies on the other (the Second World).

In practice, this attempt suffered defeat at the Bandung Conference of Afro-Asian countries in 1955. Latin America came under the Rio Pact of 1947 (inter-American aid), and the Organization of American States (OAS), founded in 1948, and J. F. Kennedy's Alliance for Progress were both set up strictly for the Western Hemisphere in response to the Cuba crisis of 1961/62. From the very first, the term is thus a political one. The growing gulf between the Western industrial lands (→ Industrial Society) and the developing lands (→ Development) led in 1964 to the first U.N. Conference on Trade and Development (UNCTAD) and to the rise of what is now a common economic criterion for the Third World.

The "Group of 77," a delegation founded in Algiers in 1967 in connection with UNCTAD and representing developing countries that came into being through decolonizing, numbers 130 member states (2007) and has given the Third World an economic self-awareness similar to that of the industrial countries. Thus political and economic criteria for membership of the Third World differ. *Political criteria* are the experiences of → colonialism and neocolonialism, modernization directed from outside, commonly the result of a strategy of catching up oriented to the industrial nations, with a view to becoming independent of these nations. *Economic criteria* are the degree of industrialization, the per capita income, and the urban-rural curve in production (structural heterogeneity).

1.1.2. Especially since the fixing of oil prices in 1973 and 1974 by the Organization of Petroleum Exporting Countries (OPEC), there has been a division in the Third World. The Group of 77 and the movement to be independent of blocs, to which a high majority percent of the developing nations belong, represent the Third World over against the industrialized nations. They are recognized to be representative by almost all the countries of the Third World.

The United Nations distinguishes three categories of countries needing special attention. The *Least Developed Countries* (LDCs), or Fourth World (50 countries in 2007), are defined by a low-income criterion (annual gross national income per capita of under $750 per year), a human resource weakness criterion (based on indicators of nutrition, health, education, and literacy), and an economic vulnerability criterion (based on five factors, including agriculture, exports, and natural disasters). Another is

Landlocked Developing Countries (31 countries, 16 of them also LDCs), which have no direct access to the sea and are hampered by their insularity. Third are the *Small Island Developing States* (37 U.N. members, 12 of which are also LDCs, plus 14 states or territories that are not U.N. members), which struggle with their environmental and social fragility and often extreme economic vulnerability.

1.1.3. Some Third World countries have banded together because of common economic interests, for example, the 13 OPEC countries in 1960, and 58 states of Africa, the Caribbean, and the Pacific (the ACP states), which in 1975 and 1979 in Lomé, Togo, signed a commercial agreement with the ECC. (In 2007 the ACP comprised 79 states.) The term "Threshold Countries" is used for the more industrialized states of the Third World whose industrial production and foreign trade might rise but who still suffer severely from the urban-rural ratio (e.g., Brazil, Mexico, and South Korea).

1.2. *Rise*

The last five centuries shaped the history of the Third World. The colonial policies of the European states arose out of a profound connection between a Christian sense of mission, a civilizing belief in election, and overseas trading interests. The needs of the colonial powers determined the economy of the colonies as these powers sought economic expansion in tropical areas or zones other than their own. This goal is clear in the colonizing of South America by Portugal and Spain in the 16th century, which went hand in hand with missionary work (→ Mission). At first commercially and then politically, Great Britain and Holland pursued colonial policies in India and Indonesia. In the relatively brief period of German colonialism in East Africa, Togo, Cameroon, and Southwest Africa (1884-1918), the social and economic problems linked to industrializing, along with nationalism and an expansionist policy of emigration, proved decisive.

1.3. *Economy*

The main feature of the economy of the Third World is the export of raw materials to the industrial countries. Third World trade became dependent on one or only a few raw materials in the colonial era. Production varies from year to year, and prices fluctuate accordingly. Long-term planning was impossible. Increased production of the same raw material often leads to a glut, so that the price falls. Only when there is a shortage do prices rise, as in the case of oil in 1973/74. The worldwide recession of 1974/75 brought them down again. The cost of goods produced in the industrial countries rose from the 1950s much more sharply than that of raw materials in the Third World, so that the terms of trade (i.e., the relation between the prices of exports and those of imports) steadily worsened. Julius Nyerere, the president of Tanzania (1964-85), offered as an example the fact that a meat factory that cost $1.8 million to build in Tanzania in 1972 cost $7.1 million two years later. For him, in real terms, what originally cost 7,000 tons of sisal to erect, two years later cost almost 24,000 tons of sisal. Many countries of the Third World have thus come to rely on hard-cash crops like tobacco and coffee so as not to be at the mercy of fluctuations in price. But in the process they have had to neglect subsistence farming, which has increased malnutrition among the population.

In raw materials and finished goods a few concerns dominate the world market. Thus, for example, in the 1980s three banana companies controlled 70 percent of the market in 16 industrial countries, and one European coffee concern controlled 50 percent of the market in the eight largest consumer countries of Europe. These leading concerns fix the prices on the world market and shut out smaller rivals.

In industrial production European and North American companies exploit the low standard of living — specifically, the cheap labor — in the Third World and locate mass production plants there (e.g., for automobiles, textiles, and consumer goods). Urban areas are favored, which leads to migration to the cities, increased poverty as those seeking work live in city slums, and the neglect of agricultural production and subsistence farming. In industrial countries the relocation of factories in the Third World causes → unemployment. The lands that multinational concerns prefer are those in which unions are controlled or forbidden, so that wages stay low. In many countries (e.g., Nigeria and Brazil), two-thirds and more of industry is in foreign hands. Even where Third World governments view this situation with concern, they often have to bow to the upper classes who have shares in foreign companies.

The six UNCTAD conferences between 1964 and 1983 did not succeed in securing the agreement of the industrial countries to the demands of the Third World, especially the Group of 77, which asked for adjusting the prices of raw materials to those of finished goods, making official agreements to circumvent multinational concerns, and setting up banks of raw materials to prevent price fluctuations. UNCTAD V in Manila (1979) particularly disillusioned the Third World. It showed how much the Third World needed a force to counterbalance the industrial interests represented by the International Monetary Fund (IMF), the General Agreement on Tariffs and Trade (GATT), and the world economic summit of the most important industrial countries. At UNCTAD V the Group of 77 could not get the industrial nations to agree to its thesis of the interdependence of monetary, commercial, and industrial decisions that disregarded Third World interests. UNCTAD VI in Belgrade (1983) accomplished even less. The industrial countries were unwilling to compensate the Third World for falls in the prices of raw materials (between 1980 and 1983, $17 billion), nor were they prepared to reduce the huge debts owed by the developing countries ($895 billion in 1984). A new global economic order is not yet in sight.

1.4. *Political Systems*

Though the nations of the Third World face common tasks, their political systems vary greatly. Quick technological progress and forced industrialization in the Third World usually come at the cost of democratic rights and freedoms. This reality is all the more tragic because a concept of development restricted to economic growth helps to validate military and one-party dictatorships as more favorable to development and to disqualify democratic procedures and orders as harmful to development. The basic principle is that development must come first, then political freedom.

At a personal, economic, and military level, especially by commercial and military agreements, the United States and the USSR during the years of the cold war played a vital role in shaping the world's political systems, thereby spreading the East-West conflict to the Third World. The authoritarian regimes in Asia and Latin America bear witness to this influence, especially the Association of Southeast Asian Nations (ASEAN, founded 1967) and the Organization of American States (OAS). So did the corresponding Communist groupings (e.g., COMECON, 1949-91). The Non-Aligned Movement (begun in 1961 and, in 2007, including 118 member states, almost all from the Third World) simply tries to oppose domination by outsiders and bloc politics, but also to stop the militarization that, in the service of a bloc, often endangers democratic rights and human development.

The Third World includes several different forms of government. The main types are (1) quasi-feudal regimes (e.g., Saudi Arabia), (2) authoritarian regimes with republican leanings (common in Latin America), (3) military dictatorships (Latin America, Southeast Asia, Africa), (4) one-party dictatorships (esp. in Africa), (5) parliamentary democracies (e.g., India), and (6) Communist "people's republics" (e.g., North Korea, China).

1.5. *Culture and Education*

1.5.1. The more pronounced a policy of development oriented to economic growth, the more the sociocultural dimension comes to the fore. Industrialization has alienated and destabilized many countries of the Third World from the cultural standpoint. Cultural identity once seemed to many experts to be hostile to progress, but now it is the starting point for self-focused development and a necessary framework for a sensible labor policy, especially in rural areas. Yet the preservation of cultural identity cannot be used as an alibi for withholding overdue economic and political rights from the Third World.

Language and history, essential factors of cultural self-discovery, do not permit a dogmatic or romantically cultural insistence on an authentic or "real" national and cultural identity or on a cultural objectivism that makes all intercultural dialogue artificial. Yet language and history do sharpen awareness of the dynamism and breadth of a culture and its link to communal life. Multicultural life in concert, in early Christianity as also today, opens the door to a mutual participation that includes joint responsibility for the world as a whole and transcends cultural barriers (H.-W. Gensichen). But this cooperation is true and dynamic only when groups in the Third World, which have hitherto had no voice and remained unheard, are allowed to speak, and when discriminated peoples whose history seems to be forgotten can take up and shape their own history. The abstract languages of the West should abandon their absolute claim to superiority over all cultures, and the West should cease making the arrogant assumption that it can describe the history of the Third World as objectively as it does its own.

1.5.2. Education in the Third World, insofar as it is also regarded as sensitization to social action ("conscientization," P. Freire), has two things in view: to link up with the immediate sociocultural environment, and to influence a just shaping of communal life. In the attempt to achieve → literacy, it must overcome the deeply rooted pessimism and fatalism that is often observed in the basic attitude of illiterates, and it must promote an ability to take responsibility for the → environment and for other people. Freire's method is simply to find questions and choose words that relate especially to everyday life and local and national problems. Thus words like "house," "land," and "work" point to housing problems, dependence on large landowners, and unemployment. Freire's concept corrects and supplements the more formal education of European origin that also obtains in the Third World, questioning it especially as a means of individual progress.

Related to ideological ends, formal education hardly guarantees the wealthier of a job (there is a high rate of unemployment in the academic world), and it certainly does not meet the needs of the majority of the people. Improved primary and adult education especially needs to be developed in rural areas, if possible in a practical way that will enhance the individual responsibility of families and villages that are outside the traditional system. Village centers along these lines are already helping greatly to overcome illiteracy. The U.N. Organization for Education, Science, and Culture (UNESCO) calls people illiterates when they cannot read or write simple statements about their everyday life (an estimated 781 million people, 64 percent of them women, were illiterate in 2007).

1.6. *Health*

The World Health Organization (WHO) and the ecumenical Christian Medical Commission (→ Medical Ethics 2.1; Medical Missions 4) have worked for years to change existing health systems — from the largely curative medicine of the West and the building of city hospitals to basic health services and preventive medicine in the villages. As yet, medical care in the Third World is not an integral part of national life and development. Especially in Africa a synthesis of traditional and modern medicine is sought. The aim is to incorporate the traditional village "medicine man," who knows precisely the social and psychological causes of sickness, to use healing herbs, and to keep the sick close to their relatives in village hospitals. In 1975 the WHO specified that aid should be given as close to the home of the sick as possible, and that those who give it need not be experts, the more important point being that they know and understand the people who are sick.

1.7. *Religion*

Some 75 percent of the people of the Third World belong to one of the six great religions — → Buddhism, Chinese religions (→ Taoism), Christianity, → Hinduism, → Islam, and, in extremely low numbers, → Judaism. The religions of South and East Asia have remained more localized than Christianity, though offshoots have gained some influence in the West. The expansion of Christianity, especially in Africa (by 2000 it was approaching 50 percent of the total population), can no longer be ignored. In Africa and the Pacific region → tribal religions have not lost their influence relative to the life cycle of smaller societies. Their significance lies especially in the sphere of what T. Sundermeier has called "primary religious experience," which by means of rites and the language of symbols contributes to the unity of the individual, the group, and the environment — in contrast to the great literary religions, which put the individual before society. Even in societies where world religions have established themselves strongly, the older forms of religion continue to survive, their values often incorporated into the world systems in a variety of ways, for example, in attitudes to a potentially malign spirit world and in therapeutic understandings. Paradoxically, however, the overt practice of indigenous religion as an all-embracing religious system has often been compromised and is relegated to the realm of the private and secretive.

The aim of religious → dialogue can perhaps be understood as not so much to preserve the religions as to serve the future of humanity. Religions and ideologies easily cause divisions. They must view themselves critically so as to be able to make a common contribution to the well-being of human society (→ World Council of Churches [WCC] guidelines for dialogue). The times have gone when it was thought that religions hamper development and their contribution to human identity was overlooked. The Third World is seeking to foster the social and political influence of the individual religions on behalf of a just world order. Two dangers arise: (1) the restriction of a religion to a single nation and its dogmatic revitalization; (2) the disqualification of religious minorities and tribal religions.

1.8. *Hunger and Poverty*

According to the U.N.'s Food and Agriculture Organization, more than 800 million people in the world are chronically undernourished, that is, have calorie-protein intake levels below the minimum considered necessary for normal growth and work. Every day, more than 25,000 people die of starvation. F. M. Lappé and J. Collins have calculated that 3,000 calories of grain are grown on earth per person per day, which would be enough to feed everybody well. R. Strahm has shown that 35 percent of the grain is fed to animals to produce meat and milk, yet 7 calories of grain can produce only 1 calorie of meat. India has such a surplus of grain that when the United States put an embargo on wheat sales to the USSR in 1980, it could export 12 million tons of wheat to the Soviets and still send some 56 million marks' worth of grains to West Germany as animal feed every year.

To fight → hunger in the Third World a multiple strategy is needed: the restoring of fair distribution, a return to the subsistence farming that larger farms have crowded out, a better use of native farming methods, and a reduction of food exports in ex-

change for industrial imports. The vagaries of climate and the growth in population are less responsible for hunger in the Third World than is unfair distribution. The growing concern about environmental issues and global warming put new, often unrealistic demands on Third World countries, where long-term concerns about global warming and the sustainability of the planet are likely to be seen as failing to answer immediate and pressing needs, and as hypocritical, given the fact that the origins of the overexploitation of the environment lie overwhelmingly in the First World, and that the first to suffer will be the poor of the Third World, who have contributed least to the problem.

1.9. *Human Rights*

Violations of human rights in the Third World are usually due to the fact that the striving for development that promotes self-help efforts on the part of the poor and oppressed creates conflict with the mostly economic interests of a dictatorship or of those who hold political power. The dismantling of unions and credit associations in favor of small farmers, landless day workers, slum dwellers, and factory workers without rights often leads to confrontations with moneylenders, big landowners, and industrialists. Most of the people of the Third World are not asking for individual or civil → rights but for social rights, especially the right of national self-determination, since problems like the industrializing of the Third World by the industrial nations and the exploitation of raw materials from the Third World can be solved only at the international level. When the WCC held a consultation on human rights in 1974, it took into account the fact that a controlled redistribution of resources must be part of the structure of human rights if all peoples are to enjoy the minimal presuppositions of such rights.

The export of armaments (→ Disarmament and Armament) to the Third World is very important in the discussion of human rights. In lands that are undergoing rapid industrialization (e.g., South Korea, Philippines, Paraguay, Chile) and are thus experiencing severe social tensions, the regimes have invoked the doctrine of national security to suspend human rights and justify the torturing (→ Torture), deporting, and interning of the "domestic enemy." This battle supposedly validates the costly purchase of arms from the industrial countries, for which exports have to pay.

For the churches the question of human rights came to a head in the white → racism found in South Africa, to which theological errors contributed. In 1969 the WCC started a program to combat racism and created a special fund to help organizations that are pledged to fight it (→ Racism, Program against). In 1977 the → Lutheran World Federation made racism a confessional matter (→ Status confessionis).

1.10. Women

As much as 80 percent of the people of the Third World live in rural areas, and over half of them are women. They almost all work as housewives and in the subsistence sphere. For the rest, they are cheap, underpaid, or nonpaid workers in the production of goods or in agriculture to supplement the wages of their husbands. In industry they receive only about half the wages of men, and in agriculture, often less. Not only do they suffer most from social and economic oppression; they also suffer from patriarchal traditions (→ Sexism). Most of them can get neither schooling nor vocational training, and they have little say in family planning and birth control. They often have to stay at home in the villages to care for children and the elderly when their husbands go off to the cities looking for work. The feminizing of poverty is a common theme in the Third World as the gap increases between what women do and the rewards they receive, and women do not have the social power connected to the possession of money. Because low pay deprives them of dignity, there is too little protection at work, and since education is too costly for the family, many young women are enticed into → prostitution, usually in the illusory hope that it will quickly bring them wealth and standing. Many representatives of what are regarded as economically privileged lands, especially Europeans, North Americans, and Japanese, are involved in prostitution tourism in Asia.

The United Nations has held a number of world conferences on women, including in 1975 (Mexico City) and in 1985 (Nairobi). In between came the "Decade of Women," yet these programs did not succeed in removing patriarchal obstacles. There is no doubt that for a long time women have been promoting development in the Third World, for they literally bear the burden of it. Yet they still do not fully enjoy its fruits. As Nairobi pointed out, they will not do so as long as they do the work of men but still accept their mastery. The Fourth World Conference on Women, held in Beijing in 1995, proved particularly controversial in its assertion of women's rights over their own bodies. Statements about abortion, birth control, and lesbian rights were contested by many religious bodies, Muslim, Roman Catholic, and conservative Protestant.

1.11. Theories

A common feature of the countless memoranda on the Third World is that they all arise out of some guiding interest, usually ideological or economic, and they all use some country, region, or continent as an example. At present one may distinguish between *theories* that give the Third World a definite role in world events and *models* that try to solve the phenomenon of underdevelopment.

The definition of "Third Estate" supports theories that involve the Third World in class conflict relative to → capitalism; they point to the growing gap between industrial and developing countries (A. Sauvy and, to some extent, G. Myrdal). The "Third Worldism" of S. Amin, which is oriented to a theory of imperialism and to China, takes the view that the domination of the First and Second Worlds, and the city centers of the Third World that represent them, will not be destroyed at their core but only on the margins in the village hinterland, where the weakest live. This is the aim of the bloc-free states and the Group of 77, whose members are mostly agrarian countries of those that are least developed.

Attempts to explain and overcome underdevelopment are related. There are three primary approaches. First, the strategy of economic catching up to the industrialized nations, especially in the first decade of development, followed a model of *stages between traditional society and the age of mass consumption* (W. W. Rostow). After the 1960s the industrial and developing nations began to take into account the enormous damage that this strategy was causing to the bulk of the Third World population (Pearson Report). The industrial nations accepted the limits of growth (Club of Rome) but found it hard to understand why transferring their own development to the Third World was not historically possible and made no economic sense. Closely related to the strategy of catching up are models that blame the Third World itself for underdevelopment and its reproduction (e.g., the theory of the vicious circle of poverty).

Second, the difference between the poor and the rich in the Third World has given rise to the theory of *dual economic systems and societies:* a feudal sector with little division of labor and a subsistence economy stands over against a capital-intensive economy oriented to imported norms (J. H. Boeke, with Indonesia as an example; also B. Higgins). But this theory overlooks the interdependence of the two sectors even in more feudal societies.

Finally, the theory of dependence (first adopted in Latin American, A. G. Frank) regards *underdevelopment and development as two dimensions of one and the same historical process.* The lands of the Third World are the economic periphery, and the dominant lands are the center. Along similar lines is J. Galtung's theory of structural imperialism, which points especially to the difference of interests and structural power between the center and the periphery. These theories have gained much support in the Third World. In some economic spheres a number of lands have dissociated themselves from the industrial countries (D. Senghaas) to lessen external dependence and to shape living and working conditions more justly and in better adjustment to their own context.

1.12. *Limitation of the Concept*

The collapse of Communism as a system has cast in doubt the conceptual utility of a "third world," now that the "second world," that of eastern Communism, appears to have collapsed in face of the triumph of the "first world" — western Capitalism. The idea of a "third way" between capitalism and Communism remains elusive. Moreover, the countries of the old Third World continue to diversify both economically and in their sociopolitical view of the world. The Asian tiger economies evidence vigorous patterns of private entrepreneurship, alongside corporate and state forms of capitalism. The latest Asian tiger is China itself, which has managed to incorporate aggressive forms of capitalism into its system while retaining a Communist, centralized political system. The unprecedented growth of the Chinese economy at the beginning of the 21st century is having a profound impact on the nature of the world economic system. The enlargement of scale involved by the entry of the Chinese consumer into the world market has profound effects for the understanding of growth on a global scale, as well as potentially catastrophic implications for the environment. In different ways, the Indian economy is also showing enormous growth, with particularly profound effects on global communication technology.

If China and India are competing on a world scale and challenging the hegemony of the old centers of industrial capitalism, other parts of the Third World appear to be falling off the map of a world economy: failed states, areas of chronic instability, of declining agriculture and deindustrialization, of hyperinflation and intolerable debt, of civil war and refugees. An ironic term, "Fourth World," is sometimes used to describe these most impoverished countries, many of them in Africa.

Another phenomenon that has challenged the utility of the concept "Third World" has been the rise of an Islam characterized by radical opposition to the imperialism of Western countries, as expressed economically, religiously, and culturally. This opposition is most strongly associated with the rise of militant forms of Islam, associated in the popular mind with al Qaeda and the attack of September 11, 2001. But even in an earlier, post–Second World War generation, modernist forms of Islam (i.e., those forms of Islam that wanted traditional religious authority to modernize and accept many of the values of secular societies) argued that Islam offered an alternative to the two rival political blocs of the cold war. Islam, embodied in its strong sense of the community, the *umma,* and the teachings of the → Shari'a (adapted for modern conditions), offered a form of economic management that was a third way.

In the last decades of the 20th century this kind of modernism has been discredited in the eyes of many Muslims, to be replaced by a more assertive form of Islam that is more concerned to attack the basic presuppositions — religious, cultural, political, and economic — of Western society. This critique is associated with various kinds of Salafi Islam, that is, an Islam that advocates an unapologetic adhesion to traditional beliefs and values. The term *salafi* is to be preferred to more pejorative epithets such as "extremist" or "fundamentalist." Samuel Huntington has characterized this development as a "clash of civilizations," which he sees as replacing the old clash between the blocs of capitalism and Communism, in which the so-called Third World looked on from the sidelines. But the concept of a clash of civilizations is itself open to criticism as part of a neoconservative reassertion of the primacy of American values.

2. Churches
2.1. *Survey*

By "Third World churches" we understand (1) those churches that arose out of the missionary work of European and North American churches and that have since become independent or local churches; (2) → independent churches, especially in Africa, which often arose in juxtaposition to the missionary churches; (3) the ancient Orthodox churches (→ Orthodox Christianity; Oriental Orthodox Churches), especially in Egypt, Ethiopia, and India, which became native churches in the first three centuries of the Christian era, long before Catholic and Protestant missions; and (4) the growing global Pentecostal movement, which made particularly spectacular gains throughout the Third World in the last quarter of the 20th century. The phrase "Third World" here points to the autonomy, context, and problems of these churches and aims to prevent our looking at them in terms of their European origin and stressing their dependence on the original centers in the Northern Hemisphere, as terms like "missionary churches" or "younger churches" do.

2.2. *Status*

When the → International Missionary Council adopted the term "younger churches" at Jerusalem in 1928, many of those concerned rejected it as disparaging. Yet it remained in use up to the mid-1970s. For the Third World churches, Jerusalem 1928 was the beginning of a struggle for their independence, for World War I and its consequences had brought a break between Christianity and Western civilization.

There had already been some moves toward independence, for example, in India through the Danish Halle Mission (→ German Missions) and its concern for a native church in the early part of the 18th century, or through the Italian Jesuit R. de Nobili (1577-1656) in the 17th century when he tried to build up a Christianity with an Indian stamp. Another Italian Jesuit, M. Ricci (1552-1610), a missionary in South China from 1583 to 1610, had also related his message to → Confucianism, and this effort had produced a church with a Chinese character by the middle of the 18th century. It is true that from 1622 the papal Congregation for the Propagation of the Faith put overseas mission fields directly under Roman jurisdiction or Iberian supervision, but earlier influences had freed the mission from colonial interests, as for example in the instruction issued by the congregation in 1659 that told missionaries to plant the faith in a way that would not despise or destroy the usages and customs of any people but would leave them intact.

In the 19th century the British and American missionary leaders R. Anderson (1796-1880), H. Venn (1796-1873), R. Allen (1868-1947), and J. M. Davis (1875-1960) discussed the problem from the standpoint of missionary methods, urging that the mission fields should become independent as quickly as possible in finance, government, and evangelization. Anderson and Venn wanted "self-support, self-government, and self-propagation." In Korea the Presbyterian China missionary J. L. Nevius (1829-93) also moved toward the creation of an "independent, self-supporting, and aggressively missionary church."

The German missionary theorists G. Warneck (1834-1910), B. Gutmann (1876-1966), and C. Keysser (1877-1961) did not seek the economic self-sufficiency of the Third World churches but spiritual independence and national rootage. The national churches that they sought, even when it was a matter of autonomous churches, had little connection with the → state churches of Europe. They did not have the character of mainline churches, nor did they have any agreed relation with the state (→ Church and State) that would give them equal status. They were not legal corporations but voluntary associations. They often operated schools and hospitals and theological seminaries taken over from the missionary societies or the mother churches. They were more or less independent of the churches of Europe and North America.

Where a complete break came, it was influenced by social and political changes (e.g., in Cuba and Burma, 1960-65). The WCC World Conference on Mission and Evangelism at Bangkok in 1973 suggested a "moratorium," that is, a cessation of help from the First World in both money and personnel, but the missions did not accept this suggestion. Yet the Third World churches learned to say no when what was offered was detrimental to their independence (*Empty Hands* [1980]). Increasingly their goal is to strengthen contacts with one another and to confirm their spiritual links to the First World churches, but to break away economically so as to achieve a balance of giving and receiving.

2.3. *Indigenous Christianities*

Except in the Philippines and Latin America, the Third World churches tend to be a minority in their societies, or at least exist in a situation of religious pluralism. In Africa some 46 percent of the total population belong to the Christian churches, but in all Asia less than 10 percent, and in south-central Asia less than 5 percent. Exceptional in Asia are the growing churches of South Korea, with 20 million Christians (40 percent of the population), 4 million of whom are Roman Catholics.

Church members may not be defined as middle class, but there is a strong aspiration toward lifestyles that might be so described. Like their parents, they have been educated in church schools or schools shaped by Western missions. As minorities they are a focus for critical forces when there are political, social, racial, or religious threats to → human dignity in state and society. Thus members of the lower classes (e.g., landless workers, slum dwellers, and people groups that suffer from discrimination) feel drawn toward the churches or, when these withhold their support, toward the basic movements that are under Christian influence and often interreligious but that do not fit into the framework of traditional church membership (e.g., → Urban Rural Mission). Already in the 18th century some missions were supporting human rights, for example, the ending of → slavery in West Africa and equal rights for the untouchables (→ Caste) in India.

African Independent Churches like the → Kimbanguists (now one of the largest denominations in the Democratic Republic of the Congo) have often appealed to marginalized peoples. But this is also true of many of the mission-established churches, such as the Lutherans of the Chagga area of Tanzania, Anglicans in Uganda, and Roman Catholics in Igboland and Buganda.

The worldwide advance of Pentecostalism is also complex. Some have seen its impact on parts of the Third World as a new form of imperialism, the triumph of American values, material, and ideas. Certainly the globalized nature of American culture is often in evidence in the use of electronic music and technology. But Pentecostal churches also well evidence the triumph of the local. Typically they are built up by local individuals, often tapping into the resources of American or other Northern technologies, but nevertheless utilizing these resources to satisfy local needs and aspirations. Pentecostalism confronts the reality of traditional worldviews, not by ignoring or sidestepping the issues that those views raise, as they see the mission churches doing, but by taking them seriously and offering solutions, for example, in gaining power over evil spirits and in enabling the individual to triumph over negative forces. In this respect the Pentecostal movement repositions Christianity so that it speaks to worldviews marginalized or rejected by modern Western Christianity, which had seemed to triumph in the Third World.

2.4. *Social and Economic Context*

The Third World churches have not merely recognized the urgency of social questions with their charitable enterprises, but they are increasingly gathering the poor — a two-thirds majority in the Third World — into their ranks (e.g., in the → base communities in Latin America). They are rediscovering their social context, the misery of the very poorest in rural areas and in the slums of the cities. They tie their church growth closely to the work of → development in their communities and also to social help toward self-help for the poorest. The new work of the so-called → contextual theologies has made the question of social justice the starting point of theological reflection. Representatives of indigenous theology (indigenization) aim even more strongly at cultural accommodation.

The → Ecumenical Association of Third World Theologians (EATWOT), which was founded in 1976 at Dar es Salaam, Tanzania, finds in the various approaches of → liberation theology an invitation to the poor to shape their own history in liberating practice and to bring about change from below. The World Missionary Conference at Melbourne in 1980 discussed the "theology of the poor," and the Sixth Assembly of the WCC, at Vancouver in 1983, committed itself ecumenically to justice and → peace, arguing that it is God's way to share power with us, whereas injustice corrupts the powerful and mars the weak. The WCC program of transnational corporations is a concrete part of the ecumenical effort to give the Third World the right to determine its own affairs, and it has commanded support, for example, from German missionary societies (1981).

2.5. *Religious and Cultural Context*

From the very first, Western missions faced alien values and categories of thought, which shaped their attitudes. Religion was a primary form of cultural expression, including the → tribal religions of Africa, with their sense of community; Indian cultures; and the great religions Islam, Buddhism, and Hinduism. The Third World churches are now trying to adjust to their background by means of indigenous theology (e.g., → African Theology) and the increasing inculturation of → worship, church life, art, music, and theological training (e.g., with the help of the WCC's Theological Training Fund, 1958-77; → Acculturation). They have left behind the colonial identification of faith and civilization (→ Colonialism and Mission). Yet they are hesitant to try to set up a national form of Christianity, for in the past such attempts have failed, in Asia but also in the Middle East and North Africa, because of the surrounding stable cultures and religions.

By long historical experience with their identity, Third World churches are rooted in the cultural traditions of their countries, so that their witness to those of other faiths is no longer a one-way street "from us to them," but also a listening to the witness "from them to us" in an attempt to find God's creative working among those of other faiths (see the Vancouver report "Witness in a Divided World" [1983]). The Third World churches appealed to the 1958 International Missionary Council, at Accra, Ghana, which warned against equating the *missio Dei*, in which we believe, with the mission of the church, which we organize and which asked for participation in the former: "Mission is Christ's mission, not ours."

As regards the contextualization of the → gospel (→ Biblical Theology 2), three tasks arise. First, in evangelizing, the Third World churches realize that they are directed above all to "God's favorites" (Charles Avila), that is, to marginal groups that are excluded from community life both culturally and religiously. Second, in the process of → secularization and urbanization (→ City) and the related ongoing intercultural and interreligious encounter, the Third World churches must contribute to the building up of a "just, participatory, and sustainable society," to "nation building" (WCC Central Committee, Jamaica, 1979). Finally, the Third World churches must engage in → dialogue with individuals and groups of other religions in various forms of neighborly contact and mutual respect ("Dialogue in Community," WCC Central Committee, Geneva, 1977). Of supreme importance in all this is that each religious society should have the freedom to bear its own witness to its faith and to define itself (WCC "Guidelines for Dialogue," 1979).

The thesis of "Christ-centered syncretism" (M. M. Thomas) helps the Third World churches to differentiate faith and culture, yet it also strengthens them in finding contextual expressions of the faith by recognizing in Christ the link between each and all.

2.6. *Ecumenism*

The majority of Third World churches still reflect the denominational and confessional diversity of North America and Europe. But by living among those of other faiths, they are finding their way more rapidly and intensively than First World churches to a unity of faith and confession, even though this unity is not unconditionally expressed in organizational terms. Already before the First World Missionary Conference, at Edinburgh in 1910, there were international and interdenominational → missionary conferences in the Third World. Today only a few Third World churches have reached the final ecumenical goal of organic → union in a given region (→ Church of South India in 1947, Church of North India and the Church of Pakistan in 1970), according to the proposal of the First World Conference on Faith and Order, at Lausanne in 1927. Whereas Presbyterians, Congregationalists (→ Congregationalism), and Methodists (→ Methodist Churches) are pressing for church union, → Baptists, Lutherans (→ Lutheran Churches), and Anglicans (→ Anglican Communion) do so less enthusiastically. Nearly all → denominations take part in negotiations for union, but many are hesitant to conclude them because they do not want to have to forge a new denominational identity.

Almost all the Third World churches have conciliar fellowship (Nairobi, 1975) at the national level. This creates an umbrella for cooperation in the form of → National Councils of Churches (or Christians), to which the local Roman Catholic churches also belong. Continental bodies correspond to these national groups, for example, the → Christian Conference of Asia (CCA, founded in

1959 as the East Asia Christian Conference), the → All Africa Conference of Churches (AACC, founded in 1963), the → Pacific Conference of Churches (PCC, founded in 1966), the → Middle East Council of Churches (MECC, founded in 1964), the → Caribbean Conference of Churches (CCC, founded in 1973), and the → Latin American Council of Churches (CLAI, founded in 1982, after many initial efforts and working closely with local Catholic churches). The main task of national and continental councils is to look beyond their organizational forms and to strengthen spiritual fellowship among the members ("spiritual ecumenism"), keeping step with the resultant ecclesiological changes in them. In Africa and Asia Western missionary societies cannot be members, even though their regional bodies were often precursors of the councils.

Five changes and new beginnings may be seen in the ecumenical profile of Third World churches. First, many local Roman Catholic churches want greater autonomy on the one side and, on the other, the possibility of ecumenical openness to non–Roman Catholic denominations. Second, base communities and Christian base movements in Latin America and Asia are increasingly separating from the established churches. Third, Chinese Christians, also the churches in Cuba and Burma, show how the period after a break with outside missionary work has helped to strengthen, and to shape productively, the independence of the churches. Fourth, the cleft between conservative evangelicals (→ Evangelical Movement) and the Third World churches that want ecumenical renewal has become less fixed, since several evangelical Third World churches take part in interchurch and ecumenical projects and in local struggles for social justice. The main tension today in Third World churches is between those that are growing independently and those that still have a Western orientation. Finally, independence comes to expression increasingly in new interpretations of the Christian faith, as for example in the confessions of the Lutheran Batak Church in 1951 or the Presbyterian Reformed Church in Cuba in 1977. As regards the basis of individual contextual confession, it seems that negotiations for union will bring changes in the preliminary hermeneutical decisions.

2.7. A *"New Christendom"?*

A number of missiologists and church historians have noted a profound shift in the relationship between the Christianity of the "global North" and the "global South" (terms that are to some extent replacing language of "First World" and "Third World" in the vocabulary of some Christian circles). Andrew Walls and Lamin Sanneh have both noted that the center of gravity of Christianity has moved south and that the assumption that Christianity can be defined by its Western theological and ecclesiological presuppositions and the biblical → hermeneutics of the academy and seminary can no longer be taken for granted.

Increasingly, the churches of the South want to assert their expressions of Christian faith as having a validity of their own. In *The Next Christendom: The Coming of Global Christianity,* Philip Jenkins explores the implications of this trend for what he sees as a reassertion of more conservative expressions of religion, which accept a world of → magic and supernaturalism and advocate stricter forms of morality than are common in the increasingly liberal and secular forms of Christianity in the North (Jenkins 2002, 2006). The crisis in the worldwide Anglican Communion over → homosexuality can be seen as a particularly acrimonious example of this dichotomy between Christian values shaped in the West by → Enlightenment and liberal democratic values and a much more assertive and uncompromising expression from Christians in the Third World. In the Anglican case the arguments have taken the form of a strong desire to escape the "Anglo-Saxon captivity of the church" (Ward 2006, chap. 15).

Nevertheless, it would be oversimplistic to see the Christianity of the South as "fundamentalist" or monochrome, or even to think that there is a concerted rejection of Enlightenment values. The work of liberation theologians and such biblical scholars as R. S. Sugirtharajah emphasize that there is also a biblical hermeneutic at work in many parts of the Third World that is anything but conservative and reactionary; rather, it is radical and tends toward liberation and the assertion of human values.

→ Asian Theology; Black Theology; Latin American Theology; Third World Theology

Bibliography: On 1: S. AMIN, *Accumulation on a World Scale: A Critique of the Theory of Underdevelopment* (2 vols.; New York, 1974) • J. H. BOEKE, *Economics and Economic Policy of Dual Societies, as Exemplified by Indonesia* (New York, 1953; repr., 1978) • F. FANON, *The Wretched of the Earth* (trans. R. Philcox; New York, 2004; orig. pub., 1961) • A. G. FRANK, *Capitalism and Underdevelopment in Latin America: Historical Studies of Chile and Brazil* (New York, 1967); idem, *Dependent Accumulation and Underdevelopment* (London, 1978) • P. FREIRE, *Pedagogy of the Oppressed* (30th anniv. ed.; New York, 2000) • J. GALTUNG, "A Structural Theory of Imperialism," *Approaches to Peace* (ed. D. P. Barash; New York, 1999) 42-44; idem, *Strukturelle Gewalt* (Reinbek, 1975) • H.-W. GENSICHEN, *Mission und Kultur* (Munich, 1985) • *The Group of 77 at the United Nations* (ed. M. Ahmia; Oxford, 2006) • B. HIGGINS, "The Dualistic Theory of Underdeveloped Areas," *EDCC* 4/2 (1956) 99-115 • I. L. HOROWITZ, *Three Worlds of Development: The Theory and Practice of International Stratification* (Oxford, 1966) • S. HUNTINGTON, *The Clash of Civilizations and the Remaking of World Order* (New York, 1996) • G. T. KURIAN, ed., *Encyclopedia of the Third World* (4th ed.; 3 vols.; New York, 1992) • F. M. LAPPÉ, J. COLLINS, and P. ROSSET, *World Hunger: Twelve Myths* (2d ed.; New York, 1998) • G. MYRDAL, *Asian Drama: An Inquiry into the Poverty of Nations* (3 vols.; New York, 1968); idem, *The Challenge of World Poverty: A World Anti-poverty Program in Outline* (New York, 1970); idem, *Economic Theory and Underdeveloped Regions* (London, 1957) • D. NOHLEN and F. NUSCHELER, eds., *Handbuch der Dritten Welt* (8 vols.; 3d ed.; Bonn, 1992-94) • W. W. ROSTOW, *The Stages of Economic Growth: A Non-Communist Manifesto* (3d ed.; Cambridge, 1990; orig. pub., 1960) • A. SAUVY, *Le "Tiers-Monde." Sous-développement et développement* (Paris, 1961) • D. SENGHAAS, *Weltwirtschaftsordnung und Entwicklungspolitik. Plädoyer für Dissoziation* (Frankfurt, 1977) • R. H. STRAHM, *Warum sie so arm sind. Arbeitsbuch zur Entwicklung der Unterentwicklung in der Dritten Welt* (9th ed.; Wuppertal, 1995) • T. SUNDERMEIER, "Die 'Stammesreligionen' als Thema der Religionsgeschichte," *Fides pro mundi vita. Missionstheologie heute* (ed. T. Sundermeier; Gütersloh, 1980) • P. WORSLEY, *The Third World* (2d ed.; London, 1967; orig. pub., 1964).

On 2: A. ANDERSON, *An Introduction to Pentecostalism: Global Charismatic Christianity* (Cambridge, 2004) • D. B. BARRETT, G. T. KURIAN, and T. M. JOHNSON, *WCE* (2d ed.; 2 vols.) • P. BEYER, *Religion and Globalization* (London, 1994) • P. BEYERHAUS, *The Responsible Church and the Foreign Missions* (London, 1964) • W. BÜHLMANN, *The Missions on Trial: Addis Ababa, 1980; A Moral for the Future from the Archives of Today* (Slough, Eng., 1978) • A. CAMPS, *Partners in Dialogue* (Maryknoll, N.Y., 1983) 157-232 • CHRISTIAN CONFERENCE OF ASIA, *Christianity in Asia: North-East Asia* (ed. T. K. Thomas; Singapore, 1979); idem, *Towards the Sovereignty of the People: A Search for an Alternative Form of Democratic Politics in Asia; A Christian Discussion* (Singapore, 1983) • S. COLEMAN, *The Globalization of Charismatic Christianity* (Cambridge, 2000) • J. HAYNES, *Religion in Third World Politics* (Boulder, Colo., 1994) • P. JENKINS, *The New Faces of Christianity: Believing the Bible in the Global South* (Oxford: 2006); idem, *The Next Christendom: The Coming of Global Christianity* (Oxford, 2002) • S. J. SAMARTHA, *Courage for Dialogue: Ecumenical Issues in Inter-religious Relationships* (Geneva, 1981) • L. SAN-

NEH, *The Changing Face of Christianity: Africa, the West, and the World* (Oxford, 2005); idem, *Encountering the West: Christianity and the Global Cultural Processes* (London, 1993) • R. S. SUGIRTHARAJAH, *The Bible and the Third World: Precolonial, Colonial, and Post-colonial Encounters* (Cambridge, 2001); idem, ed., *The Postcolonial Biblical Reader* (Oxford, 2006) • K. WARD, *A History of Global Anglicanism* (Cambridge, 2006) • WORLD COUNCIL OF CHURCHES, *Dialogue in Community* (Geneva, 1977); idem, *Empty Hands: An Agenda for the Churches; A Study Guide on the Ecumenical Sharing of Resources* (Geneva, 1980); idem, *Voices of Unity* (ed. A. J. van der Bent; Geneva, 1981).

WOLFGANG GERN, with KEVIN WARD

Third World Theology

1. Description
2. Common Features
3. Themes
   3.1. A Posture of Resistance
   3.2. A Method of Subversion
      3.2.1. Africa
      3.2.2. Asia
      3.2.3. Latin America
      3.2.4. Feminist Theology
   3.3. Preferential Options
   3.4. Salvation as Liberation, Humanization, and Integrated Life
   3.5. Third World Christologies
4. Prospect

"Third World theology" identifies a cluster of Christian theologies that emerged over the last few decades that has generally remained on the periphery of Western discourse. This → theology encompasses vast though diverse communities of "little voices" that are strategically and globally banded together in order to claim a larger role in theological formulation. These communities are united by bonds of common affliction, intertwined with stirrings of shared hope, and energized by a growing recognition that theological formulations are intimately related to overall human transformation. This theology is thus an arena for inscribing Christian → faith, → hope, and → love as they lead to abundant life for all human beings, especially the oppressed, the poor (→ Poverty), and the excluded. Sometimes systematic, oftentimes audacious, it is always rooted in the existential experience of communities usually excluded from conventional theological discourse.

1. Description

These emergent and collaborative movements have consciously chosen for themselves the term "Third World theology." A common context among various global theological collectives has forged this identity. Amid the divergences, there are several key commonalities.

Historically, the → "Third World" label brings together countries that have experienced imperialistic political domination. It connects peoples that were previously colonized and exploited by the Euramerican nations. The first joint statement of the → Ecumenical Association of Third World Theologians (EATWOT) gives paramount importance to the commonality of the colonial past: "The principal cause of the modern phenomenon of the underdevelopment of the peoples of the Third World is the systematic exploitation of their peoples and countries by European peoples. From the end of the fifteenth century, a large-scale and unprecedented expansion of the European peoples brought most of the rest of the world under their military, economic, political, cultural, and religious domination" (S. Torres and V. Fabella, 260).

Geographically, the term "Third World" denotes the countries of the global South, excluding Australia and New Zealand.

Socioeconomically, the term refers to countries and peoples that are poor and underdeveloped. Their economic standard of living is low, and they are technologically less advanced; in most cases, their economies are agrarian. The Third World is thus a confederation of peoples who not only are poor and underdeveloped but who will certainly remain so as long as the exploitative global structure remains as is, presently advantageous to the developed nations.

Politically, the term highlights the so-called nonaligned countries that were sandwiched between the capitalist and Communist power blocs. (The connotation of this political reality is questionable, however, in light of the overtly socialist rhetoric of Third World theology.)

Theologically, the label "Third World" refers to the countries and peoples "from the underside of history," that is, the peoples known to be preferred by God. In summarizing the various connotations of this term, one must be deeply aware of the creative potential that emanates from the ambiguities of such an identity. Sergio Torres stresses the impact of subjugation in his editorial for the first issue of *Voices from the Third World*: "Even if the term 'Third World' is ambiguous, we consider it a relevant way of defining the countries and the peoples that have been colonies, have been oppressed and are still poor and underdeveloped" (December 1978, p. 1). Virginia Fabella alludes to the possibilities of agency for such oppressed peoples, noting that "Third World" also "connotes a growing historical force that is threatening the present international order (or disorder)" (Fabella and Torres, xii). Clearly imbued with historical, geographic, socioeconomic, political, and theological commonalities, Third World theology signifies a dynamic, active, and constructive movement of globally subjugated peoples as they move toward a role as subject, not object.

2. Common Features

Third World theology is a broad and diverse body of thought that endeavors to produce an alternate discourse to the self-proclaimed universality of expansionist Western theology. It generates collective, contextual, critical, and constructive reflections on God, the world, and human beings from the experience of oppressed and excluded peoples, primarily from Africa, Asia, and Latin America, in dialogue with African Americans and native communities in their own homelands or displaced from their territories by Western colonizers. Grounded in Jesus Christ, Third World theology is a faith-based reflective activity that seeks both to be in consonance with the actions of God in the world and to be in service to working and worshiping oppressed and poor people as they search for life in all its fullness.

Third World theology is *collective* in character. It unites community solidarity and free association for a common purpose and moves away from thinking that only religiously inspired and academically trained individuals do theology (→ Clergy and Laity). Collective collaboration synchronizes the body politic in its forward movement toward the will of God and the hopes of all human beings.

Contextuality is stressed in Third World theology. It asserts that theology is more a reflection on or about God than God's own reflection concerning God's very being. Theology in the former sense cannot be an apolitical and ahistorical discipline. It seeks to be relevant to human life in the world and, even if it is rooted in God, seeks to be fruitful in specific contexts. Historical context is therefore placed in the foreground and positively embraced in Third World theology.

Such theology is also a *critical* enterprise, in two senses. It is important and crucial; it likewise requires judicious discernment.

Finally, Third World theology is *constructive*, which assumes an element of human responsibility, emphasizing the creative and noncircular nature of

theological activity. Yet this construction is also a reaction and a response to God's activity. In this sense faith precedes theological construction. Theology is thus not merely an imaginative projection, a fascinating journey of fantasy. Rather, it concretely creates new modes of relationship by taking seriously connectivity with God and the rest of the human family.

In light of the frequent misrepresentation of Third World theology as merely a theology of human work that dispenses with God's grace, it is important to reiterate its dependence on the economy of God's gracious and free activity. A twofold, intertwined energy drives Third World theology: the free working of a loving God, and the faithful striving of peoples for the "fullness of life" promised as a gift by God. The relationship between these two forces is complex. On the one hand, they cannot be fully collapsed into each other; on the other hand, they work collaboratively for the purpose of bringing abundant life for all. Life in all its fullness is the object and activity both of God (→ grace) and of striving people (→ work). The faithful collaboration of striving peoples, which is sustained by the gracious energy of God, becomes both the launching pad and the landing ground for theology. Fullness of life as the objective of Christian theology involves holiness, freedom, justice, and peace. In the Christian vision this fullness is represented by the gift and demands of the → kingdom of God.

3. Themes

Explicating the main theological characteristics of Third World theology involves selective generalization of trajectories and themes. In what follows I attempt to fuse together aspects of process, content, and categories so as to offer a comprehensive understanding of Third World theology.

3.1. *A Posture of Resistance*

From its inception, Third World theology has favored an oppositional form of theological discourse. The long history of Western-based and European-led theological co-option, which has assumed it could lead the global Christian community into a universal orthodoxy, needed to be opposed. Third World theology has not wished to surrender to the unitary theological project of Western theology, which in effect deprives peoples of the Third World of the responsibility and joy of articulating their own experience of God, the world, and creation.

Third World theology also aims to disrupt and dismantle the master narrative of Western Christian theology. The initially dialectical rather than dialogic tenor of Third World theology was more than a reflection of Marxist theory. A calculated deconstruction of Western theological models that bolstered the status quo was necessary in order to disrupt their purpose and rupture their logic, as well as unmask the will to power behind them.

3.2. A Method of Subversion

Third World theology challenges the accepted methods of Western theological schools, suggesting that a radical methodological inversion is needed to extract the riches that can be gained from Third World peoples. In order to bring into conscious view the world that they inhabit and seek to transform, Third World theology strongly advocates beginning all theological reflection from a discernment of their people's particular historical contexts. In contrast to Western theology, whose starting point is Holy Scripture, Christian tradition, or universal human reason, Third World theology arises out of the experience of the oppressed and excluded peoples in their specific historical contexts. This approach thus shifts the burden of doing theology from faithful transportation of the content of the Christian message to the life-giving possibilities of such a gospel for a specific people in a particular historical context (→ Contextual Theology).

This methodological inversion saves theology from giving undue importance to the received faith of Christianity, which arrived in the Third World with Western teachers and preachers and which is assumed to transcend all historical contexts. Instead, the realities and experiences of local people are lifted up as the historical locus for theology. Such theology tends to be realistic and practical in that it does not unduly concern itself with the restoration or reclamation of the supracultural revealed faith that exists either in the rationality of the Western theorists or in the intentionality of the original writers of Scripture.

The varying contextual dynamics in the diverse regions of the Third World clearly influence the subject and substance of theological content, as does the common thread of → feminist theology.

3.2.1. Africa

The complex process of Western colonization made Africa anthropologically weak and self-doubting (→ Colonialism). The slavery of peoples, demonizing of communities, prejudice against races, and colonization of civilizations was supported by a certain theological legitimation on the part of the victors. The African context has thus necessitated a theology that restores African dignity and humanity; an ethnographically sensitive approach to theology is needed that will restore the cultural identity of its peoples.

3.2.2. Asia

Asian Christians have found themselves theologically estranged from the majority of their neighbors, who live contentedly in commitment to other religious traditions. Their historical context obliges them to work toward a theology that is passionately Christian and respectfully interreligious (→ Theology of Religions). An imperialistic view toward other religions cannot be maintained within the bonds of intimate community in Asia. R. S. Sugirtharajah has observed, "The basic thrust now is not the declaration of the gospel in an Asian [or Indian] style but discerning it afresh in the ongoing broken relationships between different communities and between human communities and the created order. The task is seen not as adapting the Christian gospel in Asian idioms but as reconceptualizing the basic tenets of the Christian faith in the light of Asian realities" (*Frontiers,* 5). Third World theology in Asia needs to take into consideration the fact that Christians are a small minority giving account of their faith and practice in a continent that is more than 90 percent non-Christian.

3.2.3. Latin America

Theologians in Latin America have found that taking that continent's historical context seriously means that they cannot ignore the church's complicity in the historic mission of Spain and Portugal. The irony of → colonialism in Latin America is the expansion of a wealthy church situated in the midst of an ever-increasing mass of oppressed and impoverished people (→ Colonialism and Mission). The nature of theology as inclusive and reflective of the "concrete faces of the poor" has become a crucial part of this reclamation of the Latin American historical context.

3.2.4. Feminist Theology

Each of these geographic regions shares a context of patriarchy. For centuries, cultural and religious traditions have upheld deeply embedded patriarchal privilege in gender relations, which affects women both in the church and in society at large. From the outset, Third World theology built a powerful movement to challenge the legitimacy of Western forms of theology that were also patriarchal. The theological voice of Third World women, which is powerful and well coordinated, has contributed substantially to the growth and spread of feminist/womanist theology in non-Western regions. As Ursula King has noted, "Feminist theology in the Third World must be understood within the larger context of both feminist theology and liberation theology as well as that of a distinct Third World theology" (p. 8).

3.3. *Preferential Options*

Third World theology weaves together the perspective of → liberation theology, which advances the interests of the poor; the findings of theological contextualization, which taps into the insights of culturally and religiously marginalized peoples; and the viewpoints of anti-imperial cultural studies, which seeks to overcome the disservice done to the Third World through the process of "Orientalism."

3.3.1. → Vatican II (1962-65) can be said to have opened the door of the → Roman Catholic Church to the possibility of liberation theology. It prophetically criticized the disparity between the rich and poor, giving rise to talk of a "preferential option for the poor." Soon after, in 1968, the Medellín Conference of Latin American Bishops made concrete the affirmation of the council and laid a solid foundation for liberation theology (→ Latin American Councils 2.4). The conference sought to present "the face of the authentically poor, missionary, and Paschal church, without ties to any temporal power and boldly committed to the liberation of the whole human being and of all human beings" (G. Gutiérrez, "Option," 35).

An emphasis on the contextualization of theology, ministry, and mission was initiated by the → World Council of Churches beginning in 1972, when the Theological Education Fund launched its program "Ministry in Context." This was a global effort to take seriously the obligation to incorporate the emerging demands and needs of the Third World into theological education. According to J. Parratt, "Contextualisation was understood as a critical assessment of the peculiarity of the Third World contexts in which Christian theology had to be worked out" (*Introduction,* p. 8).

Edward Said's masterpiece *Orientalism* (1978) uncovered a complex process in the generation, accumulation, and dissemination of knowledge that valorized the self-image of the West and denigrated the image of the non-West. In the guise of objective scholarship entire bodies of knowledge (anthropology, philology, religious studies, philosophy, and literature) functioned to enhance the West as the subject of human history and the non-West as the objects of that universal agency. Said, through a comprehensive and critical reading of Oriental studies, concluded that in the end Orientalism had meticulously created both a fictitious image of the West as subject and a misleading description of non-Western cultures and peoples as object. Third World theologies thus became conscientized to the fact that the process of Western colonization over them was more than just economic, political, and

military. Knowledge systems worked powerfully to justify the often human but sometimes divine logic of colonization. In his early work, while Said did an exceptional job of pointing to the active, concerted, and comprehensive scheme of Western-driven Oriental studies, he failed to highlight the strategies of resistance that these were met with in the non-Western world.

Third World theology is a fine example of a broad forum among peoples treated as outsiders by the regimes of Orientalism in which there is both a coordinated effort to resist such hegemonic knowledge systems and also a deliberate endeavor to collect and gather up the constructive and substantive body of self-representational local knowledge. The burgeoning and influential field of postcolonial studies arose from this impetus of Third World theology. Its attack on the knowledge systems of Western forms of theology and its creative reinterpretation of various hybrid narrations of local theologies is sustained, comprehensive, and skillful.

3.3.2. Putting together these three strands, we might say that Third World theology is characterized by its preferential option for those who are treated as "others." The economically poor, the culturally marginalized, the epistemologically excluded have together forged a global community of theological discourse. This community of Third World theologians has become a reflective, resistive, and assertive site wherein the "absent ones" make their presence heard and felt.

The nature of such a preferential option for the poor, the marginalized, and the excluded has been an ongoing debate within Third World theology itself. Is this an ontological affirmation, which claims that the "othered" are more organically related to God and God's activity in the world? An affirmative answer to this question would imply that God is revealed through Scripture as being on the side of the excluded rather than with the self-assured, the rich, and the ones who lord it over others. Elsa Tamez speaks in favor of this view: "God takes sides and comes on the scene as one who favors the poor, those who make up the masses of the people. The Bible makes perfectly clear this divine prediction and option for the poor" (p. 194).

Or is this option at heart an epistemological assertion maintaining that knowledge of God is more apt to be devoid of vested interest, and thus more pure, when it emanates from the "othered"? Taking this trajectory would lend credence to the effort of Third World theology to mine the wisdom of those treated as outsiders. Such an effort becomes an apt method to know and serve God without succumbing to the human tendency to fabricate a god that serves the interests of the rulers of the world.

Or, finally, is this preferential option much more of a missiological contention, one that impels the church to be about the business of serving the poor? In this case, the preferential option of God is linked with the church's preferential love for the poor.

3.3.3. There is a dialectic involved in the missiological mandate of working for the poor, since Christ is manifested through the poor (the poor as a sacrament of God), and the church as the body of Christ serves the last and the least. In his encyclical *Sollicitudo rei socialis* (1987), John Paul II (1978-2005) interpreted this preferential love for the poor along missiological lines. Alluding to "the characteristic themes and guidelines dealt with by the Magisterium in recent years," he identifies one of them as "the option or love of preference for the poor. This is an option, or a special form of primacy in the exercise of Christian charity, to which the whole tradition of the Church bears witness. It affects the life of each Christian inasmuch as he or she seeks to imitate the life of Christ, but it applies equally to our social responsibilities and hence to our manner of living, and to the logical decisions to be made concerning the ownership and use of goods" (§42). Third World theologians have generally considered this encyclical missiological because it implies the preferential sending out of the church to promote the gospel of salvation/liberation.

3.4. *Salvation as Liberation, Humanization, and Integrated Life*

3.4.1. In order to move reflection on → salvation, which is taken to be the heart of the Christian gospel, away from the otherworldly, soul-focused, and individual-fixated interpretations of Western theology, Third World theology confidently reconfigures this term according to its own differing contexts and existential requirements. Latin American and black American theologies have been the most noticeable in interchanging the terms "salvation" and "liberation." Liberation has thus been posited as being synonymous with salvation in Christian theology. "Liberation is not only *consistent with* the gospel but *is* the gospel of Jesus Christ" (J. H. Cone, 1).

Reflecting on the historical shift in this important terminology, Gutiérrez comments, "Liberation has been a key term in the experience of the Latin American people for some years now. At the economic and political level, it expresses a breach with compromise and reformism. But the term 'liberation' also means, at the theological level, an effort to cut to the very roots of the social injustice rampant in our part of the world — to go all the way to an

understanding of the notion of salvation in present historical conditions, as a free gift of the Lord who becomes flesh in the life of a people fighting for its human dignity, and its status as offspring of God" ("Liberation," 41; → Social Ethics).

3.4.2. God's activity of salvation has also been interpreted in relation to the common quest for humanization. In many parts of the Third World, the political, economic, social, and cultural revolutions taking place under the banner of nationalism have been taken to be expressions of human beings seeking a fuller and richer human life. It is within the context of this quest for humanization in Africa, Asia, and Latin America that the presence and working of Christ's salvation is located and interpreted. In suggestive but little-known works, the Indian theologian, ecumenist, and statesman M. M. Thomas (1916-96) made this link brilliantly. He identified a broad and influential spirit of social, economic, and political revolution at work among non-Western communities, which Christian theology needs to recognize and integrate. Thomas noted that the overall situation through the mid-20th century in many colonized regions was one of struggle for humanization. He connected the theological goal of Christian salvation with the native people's legitimate objective of humanization. Search for fuller humanity has motivated these native collectives in their resistance against domination and their advancement of liberation. (In itself, humanization cannot be categorically identified with the process of salvation. Salvation as the gift of God in Jesus Christ, however, modifies and qualifies all humanization movements.)

3.4.3. In his "planetary theology," Tissa Balasuriya explores the idea of salvation being "integral liberation." This concept envisions a harmonious order that integrates all aspects of life: the individual, societies, cultures, religions, and other elements of the cosmos. In construing the content for these pivotal terms, there has been much stress on the comprehensive, social, and integral dimensions of life. "More simply, the theology of liberation is reflection on the life of the Christian community from a standpoint of its contribution to liberation. 'Life' here is a richer and more flexible concept than that of 'praxis,' which is an external activity of historical transformation" (L. Boff and C. Boff, 14). The widely circulated 1968 *Statement of the Indian Theological Association* put the matter of liberation as follows: "Liberation is understood as integral. It begins here and moves towards the New Age. It is liberation of the whole person and the entire social order from everything that oppresses and alienates.

Person and society are not extrinsic to each other. They are interior, each to the other, and they are together. Liberation therefore cannot be purely individualistic, spiritual or psychic; it will necessarily be social and political."

Three aspects of this integral nature of liberation can be noted. First, liberation consciously includes all people, particularly the people on the fringes of society. It becomes inevitable, then, that theology is intertwined with the concerns of the poor, women, the alienated, the oppressed, and the excluded. Second, liberation is comprehensive because it is no longer confined only to the spiritual and religious realms of human life. Instead, it enfolds and encompasses the social, political, and economic realms of communities and nations. Third, this unitary focus is expressed in theology by a stress on the cosmic dimension of liberation, without negating its individual and communitarian implications.

3.5. *Third World Christologies*

Third World theology has generated a host of creative and disparate Christological representations. On the one hand, the historical Jesus has been patterned as the sole basis and criterion for doing Christian theology in order to ward off the defacing and hegemonic consequences of dominant Western theologies. On the other hand, the spacious cosmic Christ is reclaimed generously in order to remember and reintegrate local and native cultural and religious experiences/traditions that reappropriate the subjectivity of Third World communities.

Latin American theologians (e.g., Leonardo Boff, José Míguez Bonino, and Jon Sobrino) have been the most cogent and systematic in promoting a historicist turn in Third World Christology. They have advocated this approach because of the historical drift in Western theology, which filled → Christology with coercive power through its call for submissive believing. Given this context, the starting point for liberation Christology ought to be the historical → Jesus in his totality. In the words of Sobrino, "It is the historical Jesus who enlightens us with regard to the basic meaning of the task as well as his personal way of carrying it out. Liberation theology is concentrated in Christology insofar as it reflects on Jesus himself as the way to liberation" (*Christology*, 37).

This emphasis was also adopted by African and Asian theologians. Three trajectories mark this turn to the historical Jesus. First, since the historical Jesus is situated with the poor and the excluded, Third World theology has valorized its own existential situation. The human Jesus was the Human One from God who was and thus continues to be in solidarity with the poor, the colonized, the minjung, the Dalit, and the outcaste. In the words of the South African theologian James R. Cochrane, Jesus is "where the people are; he is 'down below' on their piece of earth" (p. 26). C.-S. Song also situates the historical Jesus at the place of the poor and the oppressed: "The real Jesus is the love of God that creates miracles of life in the world. He is the pain of God mingled with the pain of humanity. He is the hope of God that people manifest in the midst of despair. He is the eternal life of God that people live in spite of death. . . . The real Jesus is the light of God's salvation that men, women and children kindle in the darkness of hell. The real Jesus is the power of God's truth that people manifest in the face of the power wielded by the powers and principalities of this world. Jesus is the story of such people. And being the story of such people, Jesus is the story of God" (*Jesus*, 14).

Second, the emphasis on the identity of Jesus is seen more as relational than as ontological. Jesus' relationship with God, the world, and various communities constitutes his very being. How Jesus restores this relationship in community is a key question in contexts around the world: in Africa (with attention to → ancestors and ethnic and national identities), Asia (religious, → caste, and ethnic communities), and Latin America (relations between rich and poor that are just). Sobrino initiated a discussion that shifts Jesus' identity from the realm of substance to one of relationality. For him, Jesus' self-consciousness must be seen not so much in absolute terms as in relational terms. Jesus did not come merely for self-disclosure or simply for transferring knowledge about God. Rather, his self-consciousness communicated a distinct relationship to the kingdom of God.

Third, in Third World theology the praxis of Jesus appears more significant than his being and teaching. Persons are judged by what they do for the people. An interesting set of questions by a Masai elder illustrates this point: "You have spoken well, but I want to learn more about this great person Jesus Christ. I have three questions about him: First, did he ever kill a lion? Second, how many cows did he have? Third, how many wives and children did he have?" (D. Stinton, 105).

Almost counter to this purposeful move toward the historical Jesus, Third World theology also extols the potentialities of the cosmic Christ. Much of this reclamation of such a spacious, cosmic Christ comes from contextual experimentation in Africa and Asia, rather than from the liberation theologians of Latin America. The purpose of such a Christological move stems from the need to ascribe theological value to the religion, culture, and history of their forebears and also to tap into the surplus divine resources that emanate from their own community experiences that are not consciously connected with the historical Jesus. In a Trinitarian framework, the cosmic Christ suggests three theological theses that help validate the religious, cultural, and historical sources of local communities:

1. The cosmic Christ is the incarnational dimension of God through the origin, sustenance, and fulfillment of the cosmos. The cosmic Christ is thus before any experience of, or formulation concerning, Jesus Christ.
2. The cosmic Christ unites all of creation (Col. 1:15-20). Even if religions divide on the basis of the names of God (e.g., Jesus vs. Krishna vs. Buddha), Christ mediates cosmic solidarity and unity.
3. The cosmic Christ is thus a principle of mediation. The Christic principle makes all human beings accessible to God (incarnational) and unifies human beings for God.

This approach to Christology has been helpful in restoring identities to Third World communities that were fragmented or overpowered because of colonial Christianity. The cosmic Christ frees local communities to grant theological value to experiences of the divine that have nourished their lives before they accepted Jesus as Lord. Such religious wisdom as the movement of the cosmic Christ can illuminate aspects of Jesus that may not be explicit in what can be known of the historical Jesus. Mercy Amba Oduyoye of Ghana is thus able to reclaim the traditional cultural figure of Agyenkwa to throw light on the idea of Jesus as Rescuer: "The *Agyenkwa,* the one who rescues, the one who holds your life in safety, takes you out of a life-denying situation and places you in a life-affirming one. The Rescuer plucks you from a dehumanizing ambience and places you in a position where you can grow toward authentic humanity. The *Agyenkwa* gives you back your life in all its wholeness and fullness" (*Beads and Strands,* 18).

This accent on the cosmic Christ also permits Third World theologians working in religiously plural settings to utilize and celebrate the sustaining and redeeming religious and cultural sources that may not have parallels in the life, death, and resurrection of the historical Jesus. The Christ-dimensions of God are held to be vaster and broader than the Christ-dimensions of Jesus. To put it differently, there is some "Godness" beyond Jesus that is theologically grounded in the cosmic Christ and testifies to activities of the Divine that existed before and exists after the historical Jesus. The spirit of such an open and broad Christology is captured in Stanley Samartha's words: "Christians are moving toward a position of relational distinctiveness of Christ. It is relational because Christ does not remain unrelated to neighbors of other faiths, and distinctive because without recognizing the distinctiveness of the great religious traditions as different responses to the Mystery of God, no mutual enrichment is possible" (pp. 76-77).

4. Prospect

In the 21st century, as in the closing decades of the 20th, peoples, ideas, and systems continue to expand. Nevertheless, in the present globalized world, the question of the feasibility of the Third World itself is highly relevant. Is the Third World witnessing a fragmentation into a multitude of socioeconomic and religiopolitical bits and sound bites, or are new and unexpected forms of solidarity being forged among the excluded and oppressed peoples of that world? Three factors suggest that Third World theology is indeed poised to move forward in support of a growing solidarity.

One factor is the discontent of countless local communities in the Third World with globalization. To be sure, some privileged regimes herald globalization as the engine of the new age, pushing for a single global system of economics, communication, and culture. As communities across the Third World respond negatively to these forces of globalization, forms of a prophetic theology will arise that will forge a different world under a just and inclusive God.

A second factor is the work of women's networks all over the Third World, which continues to inspire an effective mobilization of movements for liberation. This linkage is already producing new theological insight, an unyielding collective determination for progress, and innovative strategies designed to dismantle the religious and theological ideologies, as well as the social, political, and economic structures, of African, Asian, and Latin American patriarchy.

The final factor is the creative coming together of the spirituality of the disinherited with the existential pain that marks the spirit of the cosmos, which continues to provide a trajectory for theology and ethical praxis. A willingness to appreciate the wisdom of other religious traditions, along with the embracing of a deeper view of environmental responsibility (or so-called ecosophy; → Environmental Ethics), provides a new and important locus for genuinely creative learning in the Third World.

We have reason to be confident, then, in saying that, in continuity with the formation and formulations of Third World theology in the 20th cen-

tury, this theology will persist in the coming decades in its vocation of registering and circulating
alternate theological conversations and configurations of liberation.

Bibliography: Introductory: K. C. ABRAHAM, ed., *Third
World Theologies: Commonalities and Divergences*
(Maryknoll, N.Y., 1990) • J. H. CONE, *A Black Theology
of Liberation* (New York, 1970) • V. FABELLA and
S. TORRES, ed., *Irruptions of the Third World* (Mary-
knoll, N.Y., 1983) • V. FABELLA and M. A. ODUYOYE,
*With Passion and Compassion: Third World Women
Doing Theology* (Maryknoll, N.Y., 1988) • D. W. FERM,
ed., *Third World Liberation Theologies: A Reader*
(Maryknoll, N.Y., 1986); idem, ed., *Third World Libera-
tion Theologies: An Introductory Survey* (Maryknoll,
N.Y., 1988) • C. KELLER, M. NAUSNER, and M. RIVERA,
eds., *Postcolonial Theologies: Divinity and Empire* (St.
Louis, 2004) • U. KING, ed., *Feminist Theology from the
Third World: A Reader* (London, 1994) • J. PARRATT,
ed., *An Introduction to Third World Theologies* (Cambridge, 2004) • L. RUSSELL, P. KWOK, A. M. ISASI-DIAZ,
and K. G. CANNON, eds., *Inheriting Our Mothers' Garden: Feminist Theology in Third World Perspective*
(Philadelphia, 1988) • R. S. SUGIRTHARAJAH, *The Bible
and the Third World: Precolonial, Colonial, and
Postcolonial Encounters* (Cambridge, 2001) • E. TAMEZ,
"Good News to the Poor," *Third World Liberation Theologies: A Reader,* ed. Ferm, 189-96 • S. TORRES and
V. FABELLA, eds., *The Emergent Gospel: Theology from
the Underside of History* (Maryknoll, N.Y., 1978).

Africa: K. APPIAH-KUBI and S. TORRES, eds., *African Theology en Route* (Maryknoll, N.Y., 1979) •
A. BOESAK, *Farewell to Innocence* (Maryknoll, N.Y.,
1977) • E. BOULAGA, *Christianity without Fetish: An African Critique and Recapture of Christianity* (Maryknoll, N.Y., 1984) • J. R. COCHRANE, *Circles of Dignity:
Community Wisdom and Theological Reflection* (Minneapolis, 1999) • K. DICKSON, *Theology in Africa* (London, 1983) • R. GIBELLINI, *Paths of African Theology*
(Maryknoll, N.Y., 1994) • J. S. MBITI, *African Religions
and Philosophy* (London, 1969) • C. NYAMITI, *Christ as
Our Ancestor: Christology from an African Perspective*
(Harare, 1984) • M. ODUYOYE, *Beads and Strands: Re-
flections of an African Woman on Christianity in Africa*
(Maryknoll, N.Y., 2004); eadem, *Hearing and Knowing:
Theological Reflections on Christianity in Africa* (Mary-
knoll, N.Y., 1986) • J. PARRATT, *Reinventing Christian-
ity: African Theology Today* (Grand Rapids, 1995) •
J. POBEE, *Toward an African Theology* (Nashville, 1979)
• D. STINTON, "Africa, East and West," *Introduction to
Third World Theologies,* ed. Parratt, 105-36 • G. O.
WEST and W. DUBE, eds., *The Bible in Africa: Transac-
tions, Trajectories, and Trends* (Leiden, 2000).

Asia: T. BALASURIYA, *Planetary Theology* (Mary-
knoll, N.Y., 1984) • V. FABELLA, *Asia's Struggle for Full
Humanity: Towards a Relevant Theology* (Maryknoll,
N.Y., 1980) • K. KOYAMA, *Water Buffalo Theology*
(Maryknoll, N.Y., 1974) • C. H. KYUNG, *Struggle to Be
Sun Again* (Maryknoll, N.Y., 1990) • P. KWOK, *Dis-
covering the Bible in the Non-biblical World* (Maryknoll,
N.Y., 1995) • A. PIERIS, *Toward an Asian Theology of
Liberation* (Maryknoll, N.Y., 1988) • S. J. SAMARTHA,
*One Christ–Many Religions: Toward a Revised Christol-
ogy* (Maryknoll, N.Y., 1991) • C.-S. SONG, *Jesus, the
Crucified People* (Nashville, 1993); idem, *Tell Us Our
Names: Story Theology from an Asian Perspective*
(Maryknoll, N.Y., 1984); idem, *Third-Eye Theology:
Theology in Formation in Asian Settings* (Maryknoll,
N.Y., 1979) • R. S. SUGIRTHARAJAH, *Asian Biblical Her-
meneutics and Postcolonialism* (Maryknoll, N.Y., 1988);
idem, ed., *Frontiers in Asian Christian Theology:
Emerging Trends* (Maryknoll, N.Y., 1994) • M. M.
THOMAS, *The Christian Response to the Asian Revolu-
tion* (Lucknow, 1967); idem, *Risking Christ for Christ's
Sake: Towards an Ecumenical Theology of Pluralism*
(Geneva, 1987); idem, *Salvation and Humanization*
(Bangalore, 1971).

Latin America: J. ANA, *Good News to the Poor: The
Challenge of the Poor in the History of the Church*
(Maryknoll, N.Y., 1979) • L. BOFF, *Jesus Christ Libera-
tor: A Critical Christology for Our Time* (Maryknoll,
N.Y., 1978) • L. BOFF and C. BOFF, *Liberation Theology:
From Dialogue to Confrontation* (San Francisco, 1986) •
J. MÍGUEZ-BONINO, *Doing Theology in a Revolutionary
Situation* (Philadelphia, 1975); idem, *Toward a Chris-
tian Political Ethics* (Philadelphia, 1983); idem, ed.,
Faces of Jesus: Latin American Christologies (Maryknoll,
N.Y., 1984) • R. GIBELLINI, ed., *Frontiers of Theology in
Latin America* (Maryknoll, N.Y., 1979) • G. GUTIÉRREZ,
"Liberation and the Poor: The Puebla Perspective,"
Third World Liberation Theologies: A Reader, ed. Ferm,
22-63; idem, "Option for the Poor," *Systematic Theol-
ogy: Perspectives from Liberation Theology* (ed. J. Sobrino and I. Ellacuría; Maryknoll, N.Y., 1996); idem,
The Power of the Poor in History: Selected Writings
(Maryknoll, N.Y., 1983); idem, *A Theology of Libera-
tion: History, Politics, and Salvation* (Maryknoll, N.Y.,
1973) • J. L. SEGUNDO, *The Liberation of Theology*
(Maryknoll, N.Y., 1976); idem, *A Theology for the Artisans of a New Humanity* (Maryknoll, N.Y., 1974) •
A. SHORTER, *Toward a Theology of Inculturation* (Maryknoll, N.Y., 1988) • J. SOBRINO, *Christology at the Crossroads* (Maryknoll, N.Y., 1978); idem, *Jesus the Liberator:
A Historical-Theological View* (Maryknoll, N.Y., 1993).

SATHIANATHAN CLARKE

Thirty Years' War

1. Historical Survey
   1.1. Bohemian-Palatine War (1618-23)
   1.2. Danish–Lower Saxony War (1623-29)
   1.3. Swedish War (1630-35)
   1.4. Swedish-French War (1635-48)
2. Consequences for the Church

1. Historical Survey

The term "Thirty Years' War," first used shortly after 1648, denotes the series of political and military engagements that had its focus in central Europe from 1618 to 1648 but that affected the whole of Europe in its complexity, course, and consequences. At the beginning of the 17th century France was still resisting Hapsburg encirclement, the Estates-General were battling for freedom against Spain (though there was a 12-year truce starting in 1609), and the Nordic kingdoms of Denmark and Sweden were struggling for supremacy and trade in the Baltic. These and other conflicts helped to destabilize Europe politically.

Further potential for conflict existed in Germany through the dynastic crisis in the Hapsburg dynasty and the ongoing disintegration of the empire, in which the struggle of the two confessions for the correct interpretation of the Peace of Augsburg (1555; → Augsburg, Peace of) and the struggle for power between the emperor and the individual states played a leading part. In 1608 the Protestants demanded a solemn reaffirmation of the peace, while the Roman Catholics demanded the restoration of church possessions seized after 1552. These demands led to the division of the Diet and the formation of protective alliances: the Protestant Union (1608) and the Catholic League (1609).

1.1. *Bohemian-Palatine War (1618-23)*

The immediate cause of the Thirty Years' War was the so-called Defenestration of Prague (May 23, 1618), which plunged the Bohemian nobility into revolt. In the background were the conflicts with Ferdinand II (1578-1637), king of Bohemia from 1617 and champion of the Counter-Reformation (→ Catholic Reform and Counterreformation) and of absolutism. Ferdinand passed Catholic measures that came into collision with the confessional and political concessions that had been achieved by the Letter of Majesty issued by Emperor Rudolf II on July 9, 1609, during the fraternal dynastic strife between Rudolf II (1552-1612) and Matthias (1557-1619). Important, too, was the struggle between the modern princely state and the estates movement, with its claim to liberty.

Ferdinand II was deposed on August 22, 1619, and Frederick V, elector Palatine (1596-1632) and head of the Protestant Union, was elected king of Bohemia on August 26/27. Ferdinand was then elected Holy Roman emperor on August 28, and in the battle against the Bohemian revolt, which had support in Moravia and in Upper and Lower Austria, he could rely on help from Maximilian I of Bavaria (1573-1651), the Catholic League, Spain, and electoral Saxony. Under pressure from England and France, the union remained neutral. Frederick's regime, which had no great support in Bohemia and no decisive military help from abroad, collapsed after the battle of White Mountain, near Prague (November 8, 1620).

Austrian general Wallenstein (1583-1634) perhaps gained the most from the social reconstruction that followed. Alien troops (from Spain and the Catholic League) plundered the Palatinate, its ruler was outlawed (January 22, 1621), and Maximilian I took over the electoral dignity and seized the Upper Palatinate (as a pledge). The proscribed ruler and allied troops continued the fight in northern Germany, where Count Tilly (1559-1632) pursued them with troops from the league, defeating Christian of Brunswick (1599-1626) at Stadtlohn, west of Münster, on August 6, 1623.

1.2. *Danish–Lower Saxony War (1623-29)*

Various factors led to a continuation of the war, especially the justifiable fear of recatholicizing measures as a result of the presence of imperial troops and troops of the Catholic League in the north, along with the resumption of hostilities between Spain and the Estates-General after the expiration of the 12-year truce. Supported by a European coalition (the Hague Alliance [December 9, 1625] between England, the Estates-General, Denmark, and some Protestant princes), Christian IV of Denmark (1577-1648) intervened. Ferdinand II then accepted Wallenstein's offer to equip an imperial army at his own expense and to finance it by contributions. This development put Ferdinand in a position to move forcefully in the empire and his hereditary lands. Tilly defeated Christian IV at Lutter am Barenberge, Lower Saxony (August 27, 1626).

The determined advance of Wallenstein and his military victories in 1627, 1628, and 1629 led to the conquest of all of northern Germany and much of Denmark, resulting in the Peace of Lübeck (May 22, 1629) with Denmark. Already the emperor had issued the Edict of Restitution (March 6, 1629), which had restored all church properties taken over since 1552 that did not depend directly on the empire, and established unrestricted validity for the exemption in favor of the church. This restitution was the catalyst for growing opposition to the emperor and Wallenstein on the part of the princes, the decisive signal for a move against the Hapsburgs on the part of France under Richelieu (1585-1642), and an instrument of propaganda in preparing the way for Swedish intervention. The edict persuaded Sweden to intervene both to defend Protestantism and to safeguard and extend its sway in the Baltic.

1.3. *Swedish War (1630-35)*

The initial great military successes of Gustavus II Adolphus of Sweden (1594-1632) were aided by differences among the Catholic opponents and the opposition of the imperial estates. At the Electoral Diet at Regensburg (July 3–November 12, 1630), the electoral princes secured the dismissal of Wallenstein. With French help (Treaty of Bärwalde, January 23, 1631), though only reluctantly supported by most of the Protestant princes, Gustavus, with a united Swedish and Saxon force, defeated the armies of the empire and the league under Tilly at Breitenfeld, eastern Germany (September 17, 1631). Northern and central Germany and much of the empire came under Swedish control, and Sweden sought an alliance with the Protestant princes.

After further successes in Bavaria early in 1632, Gustavus was forced to retreat to the north by Wallenstein, whom Ferdinand recalled in the emergency. Gustavus was killed at Lützen, southwest of Leipzig, on November 16, 1632. Swedish chancellor Count Oxenstierna (1583-1654), who until 1648 was the decisive figure in Swedish policy, managed to restrict the damage done by the death of the king by uniting four North German principalities and Brandenburg in the Heilbronn Alliance (April 23, 1633), though Sweden and the allied troops met with a decisive defeat at Nördlingen, Bavaria, on September 5/6, 1634. Sweden now lost its dominant influence, but Wallenstein, found guilty of high treason at a secret trial in Vienna, was murdered in Eger (modern-day Cheb, Czech Republic) on February 25, 1634.

These developments opened the door to the Peace of Prague on May 30, 1635. This agreement did not formally repeal the Edict of Restitution, but it did put a 40-year limit on the restoration of church territories taken over since 1552 on the basis of the confessional situation on November 12, 1627 (the "normal year"). The treaty also forbade the princes to make alliances and the emperor to have supreme command over an imperial army. Most of the princes, except for those who were outlawed, accepted the peace, but it did not bring pacification because it was not enforceable against Sweden and France.

1.4. *Swedish-French War (1635-48)*

After Nördlingen, France began to be militarily and politically dominant. With its declaration of war on May 19, 1635, the European dimension of the war on Spain broadened. The Hapsburgs had been victorious up to the mid-1630s, but the rest of the war was marked by victories for Sweden, France, and their allies. Only by the inclusion of France and Sweden could the lengthy negotiations that began in 1643/44 lead finally to the Peace of Westphalia on October 24, 1648. This agreement set up a community of equal, sovereign European states in place of the former ecclesiastical and religious unity.

Constitutionally, the new feature was the recognition, insisted upon by France and Sweden, that all the states of the empire represent the empire no less than the emperor, and that all are independent members of a European congress. The Osnabrück Treaty granted them the *ius pacis et belli* and ratified their right to make foreign alliances so long as they were not directed against the emperor or the empire. In general, the supreme power of the emperor now shifted to the states, which were assured of a voice in all imperial affairs. Sweden took over part of Pomerania with Rügen, the secularized bishoprics of Verden and Bremen, also Wismar; it thus became an imperial state. France achieved full sovereignty over all Hapsburg possessions and rights in Alsace, over the bishoprics of Metz, Toule, and Verdun, also over Breisach, and permanent rights of occupation in Philippsburg. Bavaria retained the electoral privilege, along with the Upper Palatinate. An eighth electorate was created for the Rhenish Palatinate. The confessions and religious parties received legal parity, including the Reformed. Except in the Upper Palatinate and the hereditary imperial lands, 1624 was the cutoff date for the possession of ecclesiastical lands, which restricted the right of rulers to engage in reform.

It has been estimated that during the war Germany lost 40 percent of its population, though the figure varies from region to region and locality to locality. The economic consequences were equally severe.

→ Nation, Nationalism; State Ethics

Bibliography: R. G. Asch, *The Thirty Years War: The Holy Roman Empire and Europe, 1618-1648* (New York, 1997) • K. Bussmann and H. Schilling, eds., *1648, War and Peace in Europe* (3 vols.; Münster, 1998) • P. D. Lockhart, *Denmark in the Thirty Years' War, 1618-1648* (Selinsgrove, Pa., 1996); idem, *Frederik II and the Protestant Cause: Denmark's Role in the Wars of Religion, 1559-1596* (Leiden, 2004) • H. Lutz, *Reformation*

und Gegenreformation (5th ed.; Munich, 2002) •
G. Mortimer, *Eyewitness Accounts of the Thirty Years
War, 1618-48* (New York, 2002) • G. Parker, ed., *The
Thirty Years' War* (2d ed.; London, 1997) • J. V.
Polišenský, *The Thirty Years War* (Berkeley, Calif.,
1971); idem, *War and Society in Europe, 1618-1648*
(Cambridge, 1978) • B. C. Pursell, *The Winter King:
Frederick V of the Palatinate and the Coming of the
Thirty Years' War* (Aldershot, 2003) • K. Repgen,
"Dreißigjähriger Krieg," *TRE* 9.169-88 • C. V. Wedg-
wood, *The Thirty Years War* (New York, 2005; orig.
pub., 1939).

Klaus Malettke

2. Consequences for the Church

In the first stage the Thirty Years' War was a religious war, an extension of the conflicts between Roman → Catholicism and → Calvinism in western
Europe (Huguenot wars, the Dutch War of Independence), the Lutherans being neutral. In the later
phases political interests became paramount. The
futile protest of the pope against the Peace of
Westphalia showed that the European state system
had freed itself from the church.

The Thirty Years' War did not alter the climate
between the three confessions, for polemics continued into the postwar period. The confusion of war
produced plans for the reuniting of the confessions
(J. A. Comenius, J. Duräus, G. Calixtus), but these
came to nothing. After the intervention of Gustavus
Adolphus, the two Protestant confessions drew
close, but only for a short time (Leipzig Colloquy,
1631).

Sermons, → devotional literature, and → hymns
(esp. by Paul Gerhardt and Johannes Heermann)
treated the Thirty Years' War as a divine punishment
and a sign of the end time. In the Reformed
churches especially, chiliastic hopes were aroused
(J. H. Alsted and J. A. Comenius; → Millenarianism). The war gave an added edge to radical criticism from the spiritualism of the so-called left wing
of the Reformation (Christian Hoburg, *Heutiger
langwieriger verwirreter Teutscher Krieg* [Today's in-
terminable, confused German war, 1644]). Friedrich
von Logau wrote a satirical verse acknowledging the
presence of Papists, Lutherans, and Calvinists but
asking where Christianity was to be found. Such
doubts, nurtured by the war, undermined the foundations of confessional Christianity and prepared
the way for the → Enlightenment.

Works of complaint and calls for reform (esp. by
J. V. Andreä and J. M. Meyfart) bear witness to the
collapse of church morality and discipline during
the war. After the war German authorities tried to
reconstruct the territorial churches by disciplinary
measures (with Württemberg taking Geneva as a
model). → Pietism was a reaction against the attempt of the absolutist state, which was developing
in Germany after the war, to achieve a true Christianity by social discipline.

Bibliography: R. Bireley, *The Jesuits and the Thirty
Years War* (New York, 2003); idem, *Religion and Politics
in the Age of the Counterreformation: Emperor Ferdinand II, William Lamormaini, S.J., and the Formation of
Imperial Policy* (Chapel Hill, N.C., 1981) • O. Clemen,
Volksfrömmigkeit im Dreißigjährigen Kriege (Dresden,
1939).

Johannes Wallmann

Thirty-nine Articles

1. Origins in the English Reformation
2. Post-Reformation Developments and
   Controversies
3. The Episcopal Church in the U.S.A.

1. Origins in the English Reformation

Since the time of the → Reformation, the Thirty-
nine Articles have been the authoritative, official
standard of doctrine for both → clergy and laity in
the Church of England. By conceptualization and by
formulation, they are the legacy of Archbishops
Thomas → Cranmer (1489-1556) and Matthew
Parker (1504-75). Earlier precursors were the Ten
Articles of 1536, the Thirteen Articles of 1538, and
the Six Articles of 1539, as well as the Bishops' Book
of 1537 and the King's Book of 1543. Then in 1553,
toward the end of the reign of Edward VI (1547-53),
42 articles compiled by Cranmer were ratified in
Latin and English versions, but these were probably
neither accepted nor enforced because of the king's
death and the accession of Queen Mary (1553-58).
At the beginning of the reign of Queen Elizabeth I
(1558-1603), the articles were revised, largely by
Archbishop Parker, and were ratified by Convocation in 1563. They totaled 38 at this point and were
in Latin. In 1571 they were followed by an English
version, to which was added a further article (no. 29,
which had been proposed but was rejected in 1563),
making the final Anglican collection of 39, which
was passed by Parliament and made binding on the
clergy in 1571.

The act of Parliament in 1571 provided by stat-
ute law (13 Eliz. I, c. 12), reinforced by a supplementary act of the Canterbury Convocation the same
year, that for the future the Thirty-nine Articles
were to be "subscribed" by all candidates for → or-

481

dination, as well as by any person admitted to any benefice with cure of souls. (The York Convocation did not formally accept them until 1605.) Also, the final 1571 revision of the articles took place in the very year following the papal → excommunication of Queen Elizabeth and the withdrawal of all persons of Roman obedience from the Church of England. Shortly after the Convocation's action in 1571, moreover, about a hundred Puritan clergy were deprived of their livings for failure to subscribe to all of the 39.

Among the topics covered by the articles are "the sufficiency of the Holy Scriptures for salvation" (no. 6), "the → justification of man" (11), "good works" (12), "→ sin after baptism" (16), "→ predestination and election" (17), "the → authority of the church" (20), "the authority of general councils" (21), "→ purgatory" (22), "the → sacraments" (25), "the unworthiness of the ministers, which hinders not the effect of the sacraments" (26), and "the → marriage of → priests" (32). The articles do not constitute a creed but summarize positions taken by the Anglican Church on questions of doctrine under controversy at that time; they were deliberately formulated to be inclusive of a number of different viewpoints.

2. Post-Reformation Developments and Controversies

For some three centuries, from the later 16th to at least the later 19th, the Thirty-nine Articles have defined the authorized doctrinal standard for the Church of England and implicitly for much of the rest of the → Anglican Communion, even though there have been recurring disputes about their correct interpretation, their intention, their enduring validity, and their modern relevance. Without question, though, there has been a progressive Anglican detachment from them as a test of doctrinal orthodoxy.

2.1. The form of subscription was formalized, in an attempt to quell public dissent, by the Thirty-sixth Canon of 1604. In 1628 King Charles I (1625-49) stipulated that the articles were to be taken only in their "literal and grammatical sense." This Declaration of 1628 was frequently but not invariably placed at the beginning of the articles printed within Prayer Books of the Church of England on into the later 20th century, although it ceased to have legal or constitutional force after the year 1662, since it was not contained in the copy of the 1662 Prayer Book appended to the Act of Uniformity of that year. It was fairly successful, though it never gained the force of law. In the 1660s a new, 40th article was seriously proposed, on the duty of subjects to their sovereign.

Some authorities of the Church of England held the necessity of a very precise assent to the articles, while others, such as the 17th-century archbishops William Laud (1573-1645), James Ussher (1581-1658), and John Bramhall (1594-1663), argued that clergy were not bound to agree on every point but merely to refrain from public dissent. A well-known protest against any subscription at all, to be replaced by a simple declaration of belief in the Bible, was formulated in the Feathers Tavern Petition of 1772, but it was firmly rejected by Parliament.

2.2. The next major controversy over the articles in the Church of England was generated in the → Oxford Movement, by the publication in 1841 of Tract 90, "Remarks on Certain Passages in the Thirty-nine Articles," written by John Henry → Newman (1801-90). Whereas pre-Tractarian High Churchmen had held to a strict interpretation of the articles, for example against the Latitudinarians of the 18th century, Newman was the first major writer of his school of thought to hold the view that the literal words of the articles, with any reasonable interpretation that they might bear, were what was binding, and not the historic views of those who shortly after the Reformation had composed them. "It is a duty which we owe both to the Catholic Church and our own," Newman said, "to take our reformed confessions in the most Catholic sense they will admit; we have no duties towards their framers." The stipulation that enjoined their "literal and grammatical sense" (p. 83), he observed, was added at a time when the leading English churchmen were known for their Catholic views and could not therefore be used to support a Protestant rather than a Catholic interpretation. Newman's Tract 90 is perhaps the most famous, but both before and after him over the course of history nearly 200 Anglican theologians have published their own separate and individual commentaries upon the articles, representing a wide spectrum of viewpoints.

2.3. Still other quarters of the English church had concerns over the articles in the mid-19th century, those within the Broad Church movement regarding them as overly dogmatic and unnecessarily divisive. Thomas Arnold (1795-1842), the headmaster of Rugby, as well as others, argued that "conformity to our Liturgy . . . is a much better test to require than subscription to our Articles" (p. 121). In the later 19th century, when the Chicago-Lambeth Quadrilateral was being formulated, the articles were not mentioned within it, although the Lambeth Conference of 1888 did modify the 1886 Chicago form of the Quadrilateral by adding phraseology from the articles to the first three of its four points.

All told, with such challenges from various quarters, one can say that whereas at the beginning of the 19th century there was a broad acceptance of the importance of the articles and a measure of agreement on their "literal and grammatical sense," by the end of that century there was not. With this loss of consensus, their public role began to change and diminish. A report to the same Lambeth Conference of 1888 recognized that "some modification of these Articles may . . . naturally be expected on the part of newly-constituted Churches" (R. T. Davidson, 174), as the Anglican Communion was expanding geographically. In its resolution 19 the same conference allowed that such newer Anglican churches "should not necessarily be bound to accept in their entirety the Thirty-nine Articles of Religion" (p. 124).

2.4. With certain variants, the form of subscription provided in the canon of 1604 was retained until 1865, when a less stringent declaration of "assent" was approved by the two Convocations and confirmed under royal letters patent. Thereafter, the requirement was no longer "subscription" but rather an "assent" that they contained the doctrine of the Church of England and were "agreeable to the Word of God."

More recent alteration has further weakened this requirement. *Doctrine in the Church of England,* a report of the Archbishops' Commission on Christian Doctrine published in 1938, commented of them: "They are not a complete confession of faith, but a declaration of the position adopted by the Church of England at a critical moment in relation to the chief controversies of that moment" (p. 9). Still, every new incumbent on the first Sunday when he officiated in his parish was required to read aloud the Thirty-nine Articles to the congregation and his declaration of assent to them, adding after the words "Articles of Religion" the words "which I have now read before you." And church members, by the canons of 1604, were still bidden not to attack them.

2.5. The ancient universities of Oxford and Cambridge, moreover, as bodies of ecclesiastical foundation, also required subscription to them of all their students and teachers well into the 19th century. Beginning in 1581, subscription was required at the time of matriculation at Oxford, and before proceeding to a degree at both Oxford (since 1576) and Cambridge (1616/1623), such requirements being finally removed by formal legislation in 1854 and 1871.

2.6. The Articles of the Church of England were adopted by the Convocation of the clergy of the Church of Ireland in synod at Dublin in 1634. The two churches were united in 1801, and the articles were endorsed again by the clergy and laity in Dublin in 1870.

The Scottish Church accepted them in 1804 but in 1980 removed reference to them from its canons and abolished the forms of assent associated with them.

2.7. As of the time of this writing, most, though not all, churches of the Anglican Communion still retain the articles in their constitutions, and many of them still require some form of ministerial assent or subscription, either explicit or implicit. Churches that have actually revised the articles include the Church of the Province of New Zealand and the Episcopal Church in the U.S.A. The Church of India, Pakistan, Burma, and Ceylon and the Church of the Province of Central Africa have omitted them from their doctrinal basis, and in the Church of the Province of East Africa each diocese may decide for itself.

The Churches of Kenya and Tanzania make the articles an option that individual dioceses may adopt. Kenya and Tanganyika indicate that although the articles are not mentioned among their fundamental clauses, this does not "preclude their use" at a diocesan level. West Africa and Nigeria refer to the articles as expressing the faith of the Church of England, which contributed much to their own development, but they do not see them as authoritative in their own life. In Japan they are no longer appealed to. In the provinces of Australia and Uganda, however, they are still given prominence, and in Ireland, Wales, Canada, Nigeria, and Uganda they are still regarded as statements of doctrine.

2.8. The 1888 Lambeth Conference, in its resolution 19, declared explicitly that new Anglican provinces need not "be bound to accept in their entirety the Thirty-nine Articles," but the resolution also stated that, as a condition of "complete intercommunion" with existing Anglican bodies, "and especially of their receiving from us Episcopal Succession," new provinces must give "satisfactory evidence that they hold substantially the same doctrine as our own, and that their Clergy subscribe Articles in accordance with the express statements of our own standards of doctrine and worship" (Davidson, 124). A related report submitted to this same 1888 Lambeth Conference also commented that although the Thirty-nine Articles are "statements of doctrine, for the most part accurate in their language and reserved and moderate in their definitions . . . , the Articles are not all of equal value. . . . They are not, and do not profess to be, a complete statement of Christian doctrine. . . . From the temporary and local circumstances under which they were composed, they do not always meet the requirements of Churches formed under wholly different conditions" (p. 174).

A deliberate attempt to demote the articles was made at the Lambeth Conference of 1930, where the report of a committee defined the authority of the Anglican Communion in an ecclesiastical and doctrinal sense without reference to the articles. Describing "the doctrines and ideals for which the Church of England has always stood," the report proceeded to say: "What are these doctrines? We hold the Catholic faith in its entirety: that is to say, the truth of Christ, contained in Holy Scripture; stated in the Apostles' and Nicene Creeds; expressed in the Sacraments of the Gospel and the rites of the Primitive Church as set forth in the → Book of Common Prayer with its various local adaptations; and safeguarded by the historic threefold Order of the Ministry" (Conference of Bishops, 144).

2.9. In the Church of England, the 1968 report of the Archbishops' Commission on Christian Doctrine, "Subscription and Assent to the Thirty-nine Articles," had recommended that the articles be always printed in the same volume as the Book of Common Prayer and the Ordinal. This recommendation was not sustained, however, by the 1968 Lambeth Conference that followed it, although the main conclusions of the report were accepted. That same Conference of 1968 in its resolution 43 voted that each province of the Anglican Communion should (1) consider whether the articles needed to be bound up with the Prayer Book, (2) no longer require "assent" to the articles from ordinands, and (3) ensure that "subscription" to the articles, when still required, should be given only in light of the full range of the inheritance of faith and within their historical context.

In 1975 a new Declaration of Assent was stipulated in the Church of England, replacing the oath of subscription to the Thirty-nine Articles and the related Royal Declaration of 1628 (which after 1975 was no longer contained in Prayer Books of the Church of England) by a less specific but more all-embracing declaration of "loyalty."

3. The Episcopal Church in the U.S.A.

For the Episcopal Church in the U.S.A., the Constitution that was voted at its first General Convention in 1789 provided for Articles of Religion that should be in use whenever they might be adopted, but they were not at that time included within the Prayer Book because of various disagreements. Some objected to the use of such terms as "priest" in the articles as being overly clerical or dogmatic, whereas

others, such as Bishop Samuel Seabury (1729-96), thought the articles seemed too Calvinistic. The official decision to adopt them finally came at the General Convention of 1801, but with some modifications of the English Thirty-nine Articles. These included the entire omission of number 21 and revisions to numbers 8 and 35-37 (nos. 21, 36, and 37 being altered to reflect political changes, no. 8 being altered to reflect the American church's decision to drop the → Athanasian Creed, and no. 35 reflecting the uncertain status of the homilies).

An attempt just three years after 1801, at the General Convention of 1804, to make a specific subscription to the articles compulsory upon the clergy by canon law failed, the reason being given that inasmuch as the articles were listed in the church's Constitution as being already part of the Prayer Book, the general oath of conformity to the "doctrine, discipline, and worship of the Protestant Episcopal Church," already required to be taken before ordination, was deemed sufficient. The decision for the articles in 1801 was not implemented in printings of the American Prayer Book until 1803, and it is significant that the articles were then placed directly after the Psalter and just in front of the Ordinal, thus possibly indicating some prior doctrinal responsibility placed upon the clergy, rather than at the end, as had been customary in the Church of England. In some printings of the American Prayer Book subsequent to 1803, however, they were still not included at all. Later, apparently in 1886, the decision was made to move their location to the very end of the American Prayer Book, which can first be clearly seen in the Standard Prayer Book of 1892.

By action of the General Convention of 1829, the articles were incorporated into the Constitution of the Episcopal Church, and they were soon being appealed to as the church's doctrinal position, even though in the Episcopal Church no subscription to them, nor even assent, has ever been required. Charles P. McIlvaine (1799-1872), bishop of Ohio, appealed to them in 1841 in his attack on the *Tracts for the Times* (1833-41) over the doctrine of justification. And in the Tractarian controversy of 1844 at the General Theological Seminary in New York, one of the questions asked was, "What [is taught] concerning the obligation of a clergyman of this Church to be conformed in doctrine to the Thirty-nine Articles in their literal and grammatical sense?" (*Journal*, 232-33). In a famous case in 1860, Bishop Manton Eastburn (1801-72) of Massachusetts refused to ordain a certain William Reed Huntington (1838-1909), later author of the famed Chicago-Lambeth Quadrilateral, for one whole year, on the ground that he had stated his disbelief in article 4, on the bodily resurrection of Christ.

Although the location of the articles was fixed at the very end of the American Book of Common Prayer after 1892, there nonetheless were proposals to omit the articles from the Constitution in several later General Conventions, beginning with an attempt led by the same William Reed Huntington in 1907, and also in 1928, but none succeeded until 1988. The committee on amendments of the Convention of 1907, which recommended omission, produced a lengthy report on their status and purpose. The General Convention of 1925 gave its first vote to remove them from the Prayer Book, but the 1928 Convention restored them. Finally, with the Prayer Book revision of 1979, the same Articles of 1801 were removed to the newly created "Historical Documents" section at the back of the book in their amended American form, with, however, the full original 1571 English texts being supplied in italics. No explanation was given there beyond that of their adoption in 1801, with their divergences from those of 1571 noted in italics after each article that was altered.

Specific reference to the articles was finally deleted from the Episcopal Church's Constitution by action of the General Convention of 1988. It may be reasonably inferred, however, that their inclusion among the "Historical Documents" already since 1979 is to be seen in a positive rather than a negative sense, more as a matter of acknowledgment than of disapproval, for the historical documents are evidently not an index of forbidden treatises that the Episcopal Church condemns but, rather, a collection of important documents that the church clearly deems to be of definite, if unspecified, historic significance.

Bibliography: T. ARNOLD, *The Miscellaneous Works of Thomas Arnold, D.D.* (New York, 1845) • W. BEVERIDGE, *Ecclesia Anglicana Ecclesia Catholica; or, The Doctrine of the Church of England Consonant to Scripture, Reason, and Fathers: In a Discourse upon the Thirty-nine Articles* (new ed.; Oxford, 1840) • E. J. BICKNELL, *A Theological Introduction to the Thirty-nine Articles* (3d ed.; rev. H. J. Carpenter; London, 1955; 1st ed., 1919) • E. H. BROWNE, *An Exposition of the Thirty-nine Articles, Historical and Doctrinal* (7th ed.; London, 1865) • CONFERENCE OF BISHOPS OF THE ANGLICAN COMMUNION, *The Lambeth Conference, 1930* (London, 1930) • R. T. DAVIDSON, comp., *The Five Lambeth Conferences, 1867, 1878, 1888, 1897, and 1908* (London, 1920) • *Doctrine in the Church of England: The Report of the Commission on Christian Doctrine Appointed by the Arch-*

bishops of Canterbury and York in 1922 (London, 1938) • W. H. GRIFFITH THOMAS, *The Principles of Theology: An Introduction to the Thirty-nine Articles* (2d ed.; London, 1930) • C. HARDWICK, *A History of the Articles of Religion* (rev. ed.; Cambridge, 1859) • W. R. HUNTINGTON, "The Articles of Religion from an American Point of View," *HibJ* 5/4 (1907) 808-20 • *Journal of the General Convention, 1844* (n.p., n.d.) • B. J. KIDD, *The Thirty-nine Articles* (2 vols.; London, 1911) • J. G. MORRIS, *The Augsburg Confession and the Thirty-nine Articles of the Anglican Church* (Gettysburg, Pa., 1878) • J. H. NEWMAN, *Tract Ninety: Remarks on Certain Passages in the Thirty-nine Articles* (1841; repr., London, 1933) • O. M. T. O'DONOVAN, *On the Thirty-nine Articles: A Conversation with Tudor Christianity* (Exeter, 1986) • S. C. PASCOE, *The Thirty-nine Articles: Buried Alive?* (Dallas, 1998) • P. TOON, "The Articles and Homilies," *The Study of Anglicanism* (rev. ed.; ed. S. W. Sykes, J. Booty, and J. Knight; London, 1998) • W. G. WILSON and J. H. TEMPLETON, *Anglican Teaching: An Exposition of the Thirty-nine Articles* (Dublin, 1962).

J. ROBERT WRIGHT

Thomism

1. St. Thomas Aquinas
  1.1. Terminology
  1.2. Life
  1.3. Writings
  1.4. Theology
    1.4.1. *Sacra doctrina*
    1.4.2. Trinity and Creation
    1.4.3. Law and Grace
    1.4.4. Christ and His Sacraments
  1.5. Philosophy in Theology
2. The Thomist tradition

1. St. Thomas Aquinas
1.1. *Terminology*

The term → "Thomism" can refer both to (1) the theology and philosophy of St. Thomas Aquinas (ca. 1225-74) himself, the most influential of all scholastic theologians, and to (2) the very substantial theological and philosophical tradition of interpretive commentary on Aquinas, which began almost immediately after his death and continues today (see 2). The extent to which Thomism (2) reflects Thomism (1) — the extent to which the commentary tradition embodies and develops the mind of Thomas or departs from his views — remains a contested question. This article will focus chiefly on Aquinas himself.

1.2. *Life*

Thomas was born in 1224 or 1225 in Roccasecca, about midway between Naples and Rome, the youngest son of an Italian noble family. He was sent when still quite young to the nearby Benedictine abbey of Monte Cassino as an oblate (ca. 1230), and from there to Naples for further study in the fall of 1239. In Naples he may first have encountered the natural philosophy and metaphysics of Aristotle ($\rightarrow$ Aristotelianism), and he certainly met members of the Order of Preachers (Dominicans), which he entered in April 1244. The Dominican Order had been founded barely a generation earlier (1215), and Thomas's family sharply opposed this unexpected turn in his life. For a time they held him under a kind of house arrest in the family castle, but his resolve to be a friar remained unbroken, and he left for Paris in the fall of 1245 for study with Albert the Great (ca. 1200-1280), the leading intellectual figure among the $\rightarrow$ Dominicans at that time.

Until 1251 or 1252 Thomas was Albert's student and, later, his assistant, first in Paris and then, from 1248, in the new Dominican *studium* (house of studies) in Cologne. From 1251/52 Thomas was back in Paris, where he probably produced his first theological writings, "cursory" lectures on Isaiah and Jeremiah, and was at work on the primary task required of those who wished to rise to the rank of master in theology: teaching and writing on the four books of the *Sentences* of Peter Lombard (ca. 1100-1160). He became a master in September 1256, giving two inaugural lectures on the interpretation of Scripture.

Having become a theological master, Thomas held a succession of teaching posts until the end of his life. From 1256 to 1259 he was regent-master of theology in Paris, where he began work on the *Summa contra Gentiles* ($\rightarrow$ Summa), and from 1261 to 1265 he taught as lector in the Dominican priory in Orvieto, Italy. (Thomas's exact whereabouts between mid-1259 and mid-1261 remain obscure.) From Orvieto he went to Rome in 1265 to teach in the modest Dominican *studium* that had just been established at Santa Sabina, beginning work there on the *Summa theologiae,* and from 1268 to 1272 Thomas was in Paris as regent-master of theology for a second time. Leaving Paris in the spring of 1272, Thomas was sent to Naples in order to set up a new Dominican house of studies there. While saying Mass on December 6, 1273, Thomas underwent, according to eyewitnesses, "an astonishing transformation" and famously told his secretary, Reginald of Piperno, that he could write no more, since "everything I have written seems to me as straw in com-

parison with what I have seen" (J.-P. Torrell, *Person,* 289). He did, however, write a bit more before his final illness and death on March 7, 1274, at the Cistercian monastery of Fossanova, where he had stopped on his way to the Second Council of Lyons.

1.3. *Writings*

In Thomas's time the three statutory responsibilities of a theological master were *legere, disputare, praedicare:* to read and interpret Scripture, to resolve disputed questions, and to preach the gospel. All three of these activities were in fact ways of being engaged with the Bible. The master's basic teaching responsibility was direct commentary on the Bible, while the scholastic questions he had to resolve arose first of all from the reading of the Bible ($\rightarrow$ Scholasticism 2.3), as, in a different way, did the content of his $\rightarrow$ preaching. In this comprehensive sense Thomas's proper academic title was "master of the sacred page" *(magister in sacra pagina).* His writings can be grouped under the three headings of his teaching activity.

1.3.1. Thomas commented on the Bible more extensively than any other scholastic theologian of the Middle Ages. In addition to the "cursory" commentaries on Isaiah and Jeremiah/Lamentations from Thomas's time as a biblical bachelor, he wrote, among the OT books, a full commentary on Job and on Psalms 1–54 (left incomplete at his death). Thomas's writings on the NT are extensive. While in Orvieto he composed for Pope Urban IV (1261-64) a *Glossa continua* on the four gospels, a running commentary extensively based on the writings of the Greek and Latin fathers (the *Catena aurea*). He also left substantial expositions of Matthew and John, and a detailed commentary on the entire corpus attributed to Paul in the Vulgate, from Romans to Hebrews. Much of this material comes to us, like many literary products of the medieval universities, in the form of *reportationes,* versions of the master's lectures prepared by his assistants or students.

In addition to his interpretation of the Bible, Thomas composed detailed commentaries on *The Divine Names* of Pseudo-Dionysius, the *Liber de Causis* (Book of causes, author unknown), and Boethius's short treatise *De Hebdomadibus* (on the philosophical problem of participation), all of which attest to his interest in Neoplatonism and its theological uses. Aquinas also commented on many of the works of Aristotle during an astonishing period of sustained productivity from 1267 to the end of his life. Thomas produced complete commentaries on the *De Anima, Nichomachean Ethics, Physics, Metaphysics,* and *Posterior Analytics,* and incomplete or fragmentary ones on the *Politics, On Interpreta-*

tion, and several shorter works. In writing extensively on Aristotle, Thomas follows and develops the pattern of his teacher Albert the Great, though the practice of commenting closely on the text of Aristotle was already underway in the Paris arts faculty in the 1230s. Aquinas largely keys his interest in Aristotle to his own theological work. Thus his commentary on the *De Anima* is contemporary with the composition of the questions on the human creature in the *Summa theologiae* (*Summa theol.* I, qq. 75-102), and that on the *Ethics* with the vast → moral theology of the *Summa theol.* (most of II-II). Aquinas evidently regarded the mastery of these Aristotelian treatises as a necessary part of his own theological enterprise, and he regularly adapted their teaching to his own purposes.

1.3.2. Teaching in the medieval university took place largely by the argumentative resolution of questions held up for dispute. Aquinas's three large synthetic works all reflect this scholastic theological procedure: the *Scriptum* on Lombard's *Sentences,* the *Summa contra Gentiles* (*Summa c. Gent.*), and the *Summa theol.,* which Thomas began to write after he abandoned the project of a second commentary on Lombard. Like most of the medieval "commentaries" on the *Sentences*, Aquinas's *Scriptum* is not primarily an interpretation of Lombard's text but a massive collection of disputed questions suggested by Lombard and debated in medieval classrooms, with only a vestige of true commentary (the *expositio textus* at the end of each distinction). Aquinas's *expositio* on Boethius's *De Trinitate* (ca. 1258), important for his understanding of the nature of → theology and the structure of scientific knowledge, follows the same pattern. While the *Summa c. Gent.* is composed in chapters and not in the arrangement of questions and answers familiar especially from the *Summa theol.,* the basic structure of objections, explanatory arguments, and replies often remains visible among the chapters. The same can be said for the incomplete *Compendium theologiae* (1265-67), a brief explanation of the Christian faith organized around the → Apostles' Creed and the Our Father (→ Lord's Prayer, The).

In the same scholastic vein Thomas published four sets of disputed questions, products of his teaching activity in Paris and Rome: *De veritate* (On truth, 1256-59, by far the largest collection, embracing 29 questions divided into over 250 articles), *De potentia* (On the power of God, 1265-66), *De malo* (On evil, ca. 1269-71), and *De virtutibus* (On the virtues, 1271-72). He also produced single disputed questions on the → soul (*Quaestio disputata de anima,* 1265-66), on the spiritual properties of an-

gels and human beings (*De spiritualibus creaturis,* 1267-68), and on the → incarnation (*De unione Verbi incarnati,* 1272). The collections of disputed questions take their names from the title of the first question in the set, but each covers a variety of topics (e.g., important developments in Thomas's teaching on grace are to be found in *De veritate,* and on the → Trinity in *De potentia*).

These works also show Thomas at his most argumentatively involved, with the number of objections and replies sometimes running to 30 or more, in addition to the main body of the article, by contrast with the three to which he generally limits himself in the *Summa theol.* (which Thomas, after all, regards in the prologue to the work as an introduction to sacred doctrine for "beginners," though his beginners already had a substantial formation in philosophy and biblical studies). Still greater variety is to be found in Thomas's *Quodlibetal Questions,* products of his two Paris regencies. In the seasons of Lent and Advent public debates were held in which the participants could pose to the theological master any question they liked, from the minutely practical to the speculatively arcane, for resolution in the proper scholastic manner. This was a challenge that many masters were reluctant to take up more than once; Thomas did it 12 times.

Even when Thomas did not use a standard scholastic literary format, his writings can often be understood as the resolution or determination of disputed questions. This is true for his defenses of the mendicant life, his treatises concerning the unity of the intellect (*De unitate intellectus contra Averroistas,* 1270) and the eternity of the world (*De aeternitate mundi,* probably 1271, though perhaps as early as the late 1250s), and the expert opinions on various questions requested of Thomas by friends, religious superiors, and (on a few occasions) the nobility. Of these expert opinions the most extensive are the *Contra errores Graecorum* (1263-64), *De rationibus fidei ad Cantorem Antiochenum* (ca. 1265), *Expositio super primam et secundam Decretalem ad Archidiaconum Tudertinum* (ca. 1261-65), and *Responsio ad magistrum Ioannem de Vercellis de 108 articulis* (ca. 1265-67). Only rarely did Thomas compose a treatise that was neither occasioned by an unresolved question nor cast in the form of a question in dispute. Of these the best known is the influential early treatise *De ente et essentia* (On being and essence, ca. 1252-56).

1.3.3. Only a small number of authentic sermons by Thomas are known to us. The vast academic literary output we have thus gives a misleading impression when it comes to the importance of preaching in Thomas's vocation as a mendicant and a theological master. Among his surviving sermons are series on the Great Commandment and the Ten Commandments *(Collationes in decem praecepta)*, the Apostles' Creed *(Collationes Credo in Deum)*, the Our Father *(Collationes in orationem dominicam)*, and the Hail Mary *(Collationes in salutationem angelicam)*. These would have been preached in Aquinas's own Neapolitan dialect, but we have them only in Latin versions prepared by his secretaries. Thomas composed the Office and the Mass for Corpus Christi at the time Urban IV declared this a feast of the universal church (1264), including the sequence *Lauda, Sion,* and the Eucharistic hymn *Pange lingua;* he is the author of other well-known prayers and hymns, very probably including *Adoro te devote.*

1.4. *Theology*
1.4.1. *Sacra doctrina*

Thomas's concept of "holy teaching" *(sacra doctrina)* embraces more than we customarily mean by "theology." The most basic propositions of Scripture, creed (→ Confessions and Creeds), and → liturgy belong to *sacra doctrina,* as do the most complex elaborations of Christian teaching. Aquinas makes no radical distinction between theology as a spiritual enterprise and theology as an academic responsibility but instead sees sacred doctrine as all of a piece. Human beings need this holy teaching, which lies beyond the reach of natural → reason and → philosophy, for their salvation. God has made us for a purpose that exceeds all the capacities of the nature he has given us, namely, the most intimate possible creaturely share in his own life through the face-to-face vision of him. In order for us to know our true purpose, God must teach us about himself as the goal for which we were made. Sacred doctrine is this teaching, revealed by God and unfolded by receptive human intelligence out of love for God *(Summa theol.* I, q. 1, art. 1 — here ground is already laid, at the outset of the *Summa theol.,* for the long debate among Thomists about the relationship between nature and grace, or the supernatural).

If the purpose of *sacra doctrina* is → salvation, it has the form of a science, and its method is argument. Thomas realizes that the notion of a science in Aristotle's *Posterior Analytics* must be adapted in order to describe the enterprise of Christian theology, especially because the first principles of an Aristotelian science are supposed to be self-evident, whereas those of sacred doctrine — the saving truths God reveals, summarized in the articles of the creed — are not. But he thinks this adaptation can be accomplished without destroying Aristotle's idea of a science *(Summa theol.* I, q. 1, arts. 2-5; → Scholasticism 2.4). While Christian theology accepts its first principles on the authority of God, who alone can teach them to us, it seeks an understanding of the truths God teaches and all that these truths imply for our knowledge of the real, by way of rigorous argument. In sacred doctrine only an argument based on Scripture can have the force of necessity, but arguments derived from the teachings of both the → church fathers and the pagan philosophers, while their force is at best probable, can be useful as well. They help us to understand the mysteries God reveals by appeal to what is better known to us, to derive new knowledge from the teachings of the faith, and to defend the faith against any objection brought in the name of reason (art. 8).

1.4.2. *Trinity and Creation*

As Aquinas sees it, "The Christian faith consists above all in the confession of the holy Trinity, and it glories especially in the cross of our Lord Jesus Christ" *(De rationibus fidei,* prooem.). The doctrine of God lies at the heart of *sacra doctrina,* whose overarching aim (or "formal object," in Aquinas's terminology) is to know God, and all other things in relation to God *(Summa theol.* I, q. 1, art. 7). But the God whom sacred doctrine seeks to know is the Trinity, and it seeks to understand all things in relation to this triune God and his works of → creation and salvation in Christ. In the *Summa theol.* Thomas's questions on the Trinity (I, qq. 27-43) are directly preceded by a series of questions on God's existence and essence (qq. 2-26; other works organize these issues differently). This classic account of the transcendent divine essence — of God's simplicity, goodness, infinity, eternity, and unity, and of the perfections belonging to his intellect and will — is not meant to be taken as Aquinas's doctrine of → God, to which the questions on the Trinity would form a separate Christian addition. Rather, the questions on the divine essence are a necessary prelude to the treatment of the Trinity. They identify the features of that unique essence that are common to the three persons, as the Father eternally imparts the essence to the Son by generation, and Father and Son eternally impart it to the → Holy Spirit by what Aquinas calls "common spiration."

Aquinas's Trinitarian theology was a contested position in the vast medieval debate about the Trinity, but it has since come to be widely viewed as the standard scholastic position on the subject, with its detailed account of the divine persons as "subsistent relations" numerically distinct from each other but not distinct from the one divine essence and (thus) the one God (*Summa theol.* I, qq. 28, 39-40), and its modest but lucid use of the idea that the Son comes forth from the Father as his Word by way of the divine intellect, and the Holy Spirit comes forth from the Father and the Son as their Love by way of the divine will (qq. 27, 41); this is sometimes called "the psychological analogy."

The rest of Christian "holy teaching" (and, in particular, the rest of the *Summa theol.*) is concerned with creation: with the coming forth from the triune God of all that is not God (I, qq. 44-119) and with the return of creatures to God, above all the attainment by fallen human beings through God's saving work of the end for which they were originally made (the whole of pts. II and III). Aquinas's understanding not only of God's essential powers but of God as Trinity stamps his entire account of creation and its return to God. The processions of the Son and the Spirit (→ Filioque) from the Father are the original pattern for all creation (I, q. 45, arts. 6-7), and in particular for the human soul, which is made in the image of the Trinity (I, q. 93). And Aquinas's question on the missions of the divine persons (I, q. 43, which considerably distills the more elaborate account in *Scriptum*, bk. 1) serves as the hinge that joins the entire account of the return of creatures to God (e.g., all of *Summa theol.* II and III) to the doctrine of God itself. The salvation of sinful humanity, and with that the return of creatures to God from their greatest distance, takes place precisely by the missions of the Son in his incarnation and of the Holy Spirit in sanctifying grace.

1.4.3. *Law and Grace*

For rational creatures to return to God, they not only have to know the triune God as the aim of life, they have to know what to do in order to reach that aim, and they need the power to do it. They need both → law (*Summa theol.* I-II, qq. 90-108) and → grace (qq. 109-14), which must alike come from God, since both have a role in bringing us to a goal beyond the natural capacities of our mind and will. In fallen creatures grace not only must elevate human beings above their natural powers but must heal the wound of → sin. Thus the effects of grace are, first, the → justification of sinners (the greatest work of God; q. 113, art. 9) and, second, the meriting of further grace and ultimately of full and beatifying union with God (q. 114). Merit itself is always a result of grace, and the grace of justification can never be merited but can only be given freely (→ Justification 2.2.4).

The gift of grace in the depths of the soul yields the "theological virtues" of → faith, which believes

what God teaches about himself (*Summa theol.* II-II, qq. 1-16); → hope, which relies on his help to attain an end beyond its own power (qq. 17-22); and → love *(caritas),* which clings, with the intimacy of friendship, to the triune God as the highest good (qq. 23-46). For Aquinas the Christian life consists in the exercise, not only of these theological virtues, but also of distinctively Christian versions, transformed and perfected by grace, of the ancient moral virtues of prudence, justice, courage, and temperance (qq. 47-170). Thomas thus offers a remarkably rich and nuanced account of the shape of a life on its way home to God.

Particularly in his later writings, Aquinas develops a robustly Augustinian theology of grace, to which he gives novel articulation by the extensive deployment of Aristotelian concepts (esp. of nature, efficient and formal causality, and habit or disposition). His kind of Augustinianism sharply resists any suggestion that divine grace and human freedom are in competition with one another, or that God is in any sense morally responsible for human evil (→ Augustine's Theology).

1.4.4. *Christ and His Sacraments*

→ Jesus Christ and his → sacraments are the subject of the third and final part of the *Summa theol.,* left unfinished at Thomas's death (though full treatments of the sacraments and → eschatology may be found in *Summa c. Gent.* bk. 4, and esp. in the massive bk. 4 of the *Scriptum*). In recent times the fact that Aquinas holds his → Christology for the last part of the *Summa theol.* (again, other works are organized differently) is sometimes taken as an indication that he thinks it to be of only secondary importance in a theological understanding of God and his works. But the opposite is the case. The incarnation of the Word, and "those things which the incarnate Son of God did and suffered in the human nature united to him" (*Summa theol.* III, q. 27, prooem.), are the climax of the work. As Thomas elsewhere insists, "The chief doctrine of the Christian faith is the salvation accomplished by the cross of Christ" (*Super 1 Cor.* 1.3 [§45]). Since "Christ as man is our way to God" (*Summa theol.* III, prologus), the human creature's return to God, to which the entire second part of the *Summa theol.* is devoted, wholly depends on the actions and passions of the incarnate Word and on the sacraments he established in order to incorporate us here and now into himself and his saving work.

Like many scholastic theologians Aquinas gives a full-bodied account of the Word's incarnation, freely undertaken by God out of his goodness in order to rescue humanity from sin (though the incarnation of God also confers benefits, extending to the deification of humanity [→ Theosis], which go beyond repairing the damage done by sin; *Summa theol.* III, q. 1). Aquinas interprets incarnation as the subsistence of the one person of the Word in complete human as well as divine natures, a personal union of natures adequate to verify the statements "God is this man" and "This man is God" (qq. 2-26). He charts new ground in scholastic theology by offering, in the *Summa theol.,* a detailed account of Christ's scripturally narrated deeds and sufferings and their saving significance, from the sanctification of his Virgin Mother to his future return in sovereign judgment (qq. 27-59). Special emphasis falls on Christ's → passion, death, and → resurrection (qq. 46-56), and Aquinas has a highly developed interest in the prefigurative economy of salvation (i.e., the history of Israel) and its intimate connection with the saving shape of Christ's own life. He devotes a whole question, for example, to → circumcision as a genuine sacrament of the "old law," which anticipates baptism (q. 70).

The sacraments derive their saving power from the passion and resurrection of Christ, upon which the salvation of the world entirely depends. In Christ's passion is poured out the grace of salvation and all the virtues and gifts that go with it, and Christ's saving grace reaches us in his sacraments. Aquinas refuses to play off the saving sufficiency of Christ's passion against the saving effect of the sacraments; instead, he sees the seven sacraments as the richly various means by which Christ joins us to himself, especially to his cross and resurrection, for our salvation. This union takes place above all in the → Eucharist, where Christ joins us most intimately to himself, sustaining our bodily pilgrimage by his real bodily presence with and in us (*Summa theol.* III, q. 75, art. 1; see qq. 60-84).

1.5. *Philosophy in Theology*

Even when his work does not explicitly fall under the heading of sacred doctrine (e.g., in commenting on Aristotle), Thomas always speaks and writes as a theological master, or as he puts it in the first line of the preface to *Summa theol.,* as a "teacher of Catholic truth" *(catholicae veritatis doctor)*. For Thomas, therefore, no statement can be true, whatever its seeming reasonableness, that fails to be at least consistent with the revealed principles of sacred doctrine (*Summa theol.* I, q. 1, art. 6). Aquinas thus does not do philosophy in the typical modern sense, where unaided reason is capable of establishing the truth of statements in a fashion beyond correction from any other source, and in particular from claims, such as those of Christian doctrine, that are above reason. Nonetheless there is much in Aquinas of evident philosophical interest, though it generally must be pieced together from writings whose theological purpose philosophy must, in the end, always serve.

Probably best known today among the philosophical aspects of Aquinas's thought is his proofs for the existence of God ("the five ways"; *Summa theol.* I, q. 2, art. 3; → God, Arguments for the Existence of). The effectiveness of these arguments remains debated, both as to their persuasiveness and as to their status — what they actually try to show. Thomas numbers the existence of God among the "preambles" to the articles of Christian faith, those truths God reveals but that are also knowable by reason from the created world. For some modern interpreters this means that the proofs of God's existence are the cornerstone of a robust → natural theology, for which most of the Christian doctrine of God, up to the threshold of the Trinity, is rationally demonstrable. But for Aquinas himself the demonstrability of God's existence is itself first of all a teaching of Christian faith (Romans 1), and it is not clear that he expects the range of reason, especially in its fallen condition, to extend nearly so far as modern natural theology sometimes supposes.

Thomas's idea of analogical predication comes to the fore in his treatment of language about God ("the divine names"; *Summa theol.* I, q. 13, esp. arts. 5-6). But → analogy plays a wide role for him, and it is sometimes regarded not only as a logical and linguistic tool but as a basic metaphysical principle in his thought. Aquinas sees the analogical predication of perfection terms (like "good" and "wise") as an alternative both to equivocation in our talk of God, which would empty it of any discernible content, and univocal predication, which would fail to respect God's transcendence. Here too, long-running interpretive disputes have arisen, especially between those who think the point of analogy for Thomas is to generate definite concepts of God's unique perfections and those who think its point is that we can have no such concepts, and who take analogy more as part of Thomas's warrant for a coherent → negative theology, broadly in the tradition of the mystic Pseudo-Dionysius (5th/6th cents.).

For some interpreters Aquinas's primary philosophical contribution lies in the area of → metaphysics, and especially in his treatment of being (→ Ontology). From his early treatise *On Being and Essence,* Aquinas argues that the existence *(esse)* of a created reality is irreducibly distinct from its essence *(essentia)*. What a thing is, its essence or nature and its individual properties, fails to account for the mysterious fact that it is there at all, that it exists. Here Aquinas develops ideas not only from Aristotle and Boethius but from medieval → Jewish philosophy (Maimonides [1135-1204]) and → Islamic philosophy (esp. Avicenna [980-1037] and Averroës [1126-98]) to take an original — and, for some, supremely important — philosophical position.

Here as elsewhere (e.g., his Christological account of what individuates a created nature, or his eucharistic treatment of substance, dimension, and space), Thomas's philosophical innovations are at the service of his theological commitments. The distinction of existence from essence enables him to radicalize the Christian doctrine of creation ex nihilo. On the one hand, it clarifies the pure contingency of creatures, who owe to God's free creative act not only what they are but, at every moment, that they are at all. On the other hand, it deepens our appreciation of God's transcendence. God is not only the highest essence, the one who fully includes all perfections only partially realized in creatures, he is the one whose essence is itself the pure act of existence, who is being itself, subsisting (*ipsum esse subsistens; Summa theol.* I, q. 3, arts. 3-4; q. 4, art. 2). God's being is thus not simply higher than that of creatures but lies on an utterly different plane (→ Immanence and Transcendence).

Especially in recent times Aquinas's moral theory has been the subject of philosophical interest in its own right. Attention has ranged from the conceptual underpinnings of his ethics to the content of particular virtues, including especially the complex accounts Aquinas offers of the human act, the intimate unity of body and mind in action, human action as inherently directed to happiness (and not simply to the multiplication of choices), the intertwining of → virtue and law in morality, and the content and justification of natural law.

2. The Thomist Tradition

Here we can give only a brief sketch of Thomism, the complex tradition of interpretation and commentary to which Aquinas's writings have given rise over more than seven centuries (see R. Cessario, F. Kerr, Torrell, *Aquinas's Summa*).

Already within a dozen years of his death there was legislation in the Dominican order mandating the study of Thomas and the advocacy of his theology by teachers in the Dominican *studia*. This arose in part from an effort to resist the suggestion that Thomas's teaching was implicated in the Paris and Oxford condemnations of 1277 and was also part of the Dominican response to early attacks by → Franciscan theologians on their master. The Dominicans

thus began to rally behind Thomas at an early point, but by the early 14th century considerable controversy arose within the order over the interpretation of Thomas and the extent to which Dominican theologians needed to agree with him. This controversy centered especially on Durand of Saint-Pourçain (ca. 1275-1334), who often followed Thomas but who also openly disagreed with him, for example, on the way the mind forms concepts and on the usefulness of psychological ideas in Trinitarian theology. Durand was opposed most of all by Hervaeus Natalis (1250/60-1323), eventually master general of the Dominicans. This conflict resulted in renewed and more strictly enforced legislation requiring fidelity to the teaching of Thomas within the order, though debate naturally continued as to just what this fidelity involved.

Outside the Order of Preachers, Thomas's teaching continued to be widely criticized, especially among leading Franciscan theologians such as Duns Scotus (ca. 1265-1308), Peter Auriol (ca. 1280-1322), and William of Ockham (ca. 1285-1347). Thomas's canonization in 1323 made it impossible to suggest that his teaching was actually heterodox, as earlier Franciscans had sometimes done (particularly regarding his view that the rational soul is the single substantial form of the human being), but among the Franciscans and others in the first half of the 14th century, he generally came to be regarded as a figure from an earlier time, and his views as often outmoded. Against this background John Capreolus (ca. 1380-1444) composed his *Defensiones theologiae divi Thomae Aquinatis,* a massive argument on behalf of Thomas's positions against his 13th- and 14th-century critics, and itself a Thomistic work of abiding influence. Characteristically, it follows the order of Peter Lombard's *Sentences,* which remained the basic text for university theology, though Capreolus displays a wide acquaintance with Thomas's works.

First in Cologne and then in Italy, Dominican theologians in the 15th century began to teach from the *Summa theologiae* rather than the early *Scriptum* on Lombard, which had been the norm up to that time. Early in the 16th century Thomas de Vio Cajetan (1469-1534) published the first complete commentary on the *Summa,* proceeding article by article through the entire work. Cajetan's commentary was very widely circulated, not least through its inclusion in the first complete printed edition of Thomas's works (1570). It can be said to inaugurate the classic period of Thomas commentary among the Dominicans, including Francisco de Vitoria (ca. 1480-1546), Dominic de Soto (1494-1560), Melchior Cano (ca. 1509-60), and Domingo Báñez (1528-1604).

By this time Thomas had been appropriated as the basic theological and philosophical resource by the Society of Jesus, and the → Jesuits Francisco Suárez (1548-1617) and Gabriel Vázquez (1549-1604) produced extensive and influential commentaries on the *Summa,* often in debate with Thomas's Dominican interpreters. Carmelite theology was also extensively engaged with Aquinas, most notably in the enormous *Cursus theologicus summam theologicam angelici doctoris D. Thomæ complectens,* published anonymously by the Discalced Carmelites of Salamanca between 1600 and 1725. Naturally, these interpreters of Aquinas sought not only to be faithful to what Thomas said but to address the theological issues and controversies of their own time. The same goes for the Dominican John of St. Thomas (1589-1644), who cast his interpretation of Aquinas in the form of "disputations" oriented to contested questions of his day (some of which were, of course, perennial). Many Thomists followed his lead, well into the 18th century. Then as now, how to discern legitimate applications of Thomas to new problems from distortions of his teaching was much disputed.

The intellectual changes wrought by the → Enlightenment, and even more the institutional upheaval of the French Revolution and its aftermath, led to a partial eclipse of Thomism in the early 19th century. But by the middle of the 1860s a considerable revival was underway, first in Rome, and then in Spain, France, and Germany. This Thomist revival received great impetus from Leo XIII's (1878-1903) encyclical *Aeterni Patris* (1879), the chief interest of which was "the restoration of Christian philosophy," and more broadly of a Christian social order, according to the teaching of Thomas (→ Scholasticism 2.9). From this renewal of Thomism and Leo's initiative sprang the critical "Leonine" edition of Thomas's works, and also the multiplication of systematic theological treatises (or "manuals") organized according to the order of the *Summa theologiae,* though sometimes more engaged with the commentary tradition than with the text of Thomas himself; among the last of these is the *Sacrae Theologiae Summa* of the Spanish Jesuits, which went through multiple editions into the early 1960s. But the Thomist revival also led to efforts to impose a certain kind of Thomism on Catholic theology by enlisting the authority of the church's → teaching office; the most significant of these was the "24 Thomistic Theses" of 1914 (DH 3601-24). Though never entirely successful, these efforts came

to be widely perceived as an authoritarian restriction of legitimate theological freedom for the benefit of a single theological school. They are no doubt at least partly responsible for the disregard in which Thomas himself came to be held for a time after → Vatican II.

While Roman Catholic theology was beginning to chafe under school Thomism, however, an explosive growth in the historical-critical study of Thomas was underway at the hands of M. Grabmann (1875-1949), M.-D. Chenu (1894-1989), É. Gilson (1884-1978), and others. This determination to understand Aquinas in his own historical context was largely responsible for ending the "manualist" dominance in the interpretation of Thomas. It did not, however, put an end to more speculative interpretations of Aquinas aimed at contemporary theological and philosophical problems. The last 75 years have seen many efforts to understand Aquinas in dialogue with modern currents of thought, including Kant and post-Kantian → idealism (the "transcendental Thomism" of K. → Rahner [1904-84] and, in a different way, B. Lonergan [1904-84]); → existentialism (Gilson and J. Maritain [1882-1973]); and, more recently, → analytic philosophy (e.g., D. Burrell, H. Goris, E. Stump). Equally, after a brief period of relative neglect following Vatican II, Aquinas has once again come to the forefront of theological interest, mainly, but not only, among Roman Catholic theologians.

Bibliography: Primary sources: The critical edition of Thomas's works, still far from complete, is *Sancti Thomae Aquinatis doctoris angelici Opera omnia iussu Leonis XIII, P. M. edita, cura et studio Fratrum Praedicatorum* (Rome, 1882-), the "Leonine" edition. Most of Thomas's works are available in English translation, the major exception (apart from a few fragments) being the *Scriptum* on Peter Lombard's *Sentences.* For a detailed list of the writings of Aquinas, including all modern Latin editions and available translations for each work, as of 2005, see G. EMERY, "Brief Catalogue of the Works of Saint Thomas Aquinas," in Torrell, *Person,* 330-61. To Emery's list should now be added L. E. BOYLE and J. F. BOYLE, eds., *Thomas Aquinas: Lectura Romana in primum Sententiarum Petri Lombardi* (Toronto, 2006).

On 1.2-3, including general works on Aquinas's thought: M.-D. CHENU, *Toward Understanding Saint Thomas* (Chicago, 1964) • B. DAVIES, *The Thought of Thomas Aquinas* (Oxford, 1992) • N. KRETZMANN and E. STUMP, eds., *The Cambridge Companion to Aquinas* (Cambridge, 1993) • J.-P. TORRELL, *St. Thomas Aquinas,* vol. 1, *The Person and His Work;* vol. 2, *Spiritual*

Master (Washington, D.C., 1996-2003; vol. 1, rev. ed., 2005) • J. P. Wawrykow, *The Westminster Handbook to Thomas Aquinas* (Louisville, Ky., 2005) • J. A. Weisheipl, *Friar Thomas d'Aquino: His Life, Thought, and Works* (2d ed.; Washington, D.C., 1983).

On 1.4: J. A. Aertsen, *Nature and Creature: Thomas Aquinas's Way of Thought* (Leiden, 1988) • H. Bouillard, *Conversion et grâce chez s. Thomas d'Aquin* (Paris, 1944) • D. B. Burrell, *Aquinas: God and Action* (Notre Dame, Ind., 1979) • G. Emery, *The Trinitarian Theology of Saint Thomas Aquinas* (Oxford, 2007); idem, *Trinity in Aquinas* (Ypsilanti, Mich., 2003) • H. J. M. J. Goris, *Free Creatures of an Eternal God: Thomas Aquinas on God's Infallible Foreknowledge and Irresistible Will* (Nijmegen, 1996) • J. Y. B. Hood, *Aquinas and the Jews* (Philadelphia, 1995) • G. Lafont, *Structures et méthode dans la "Somme théologique" de Saint Thomas d'Aquin* (Paris, 1961; repr., 1996) • B. J. F. Lonergan, *Grace and Freedom: Operative Grace in the Thought of St. Thomas Aquinas,* (Toronto, 2000); idem, *Verbum: Word and Idea in Aquinas* (Toronto, 1997) • B. D. Marshall, "Quod scit una vetula: Aquinas on the Nature of Theology," *The Theology of Thomas Aquinas* (ed. R. Van Nieuwenhove and J. P. Wawrykow; Notre Dame, Ind., 2005) 1-35 • O. H. Pesch, *Thomas von Aquin. Grenze und Größe mittelalterlicher Theologie* (3d ed.; Mainz, 1995) • L.-T. Somme, *Fils adoptifs de Dieu par Jésus Christ. La filiation divine par adoption dans la théologie de saint Thomas d'Aquin* (Paris, 1997) • J.-P. Torrell, *Aquinas's Summa: Background, Structure, and Reception* (Washington, D.C., 2005); idem, *Le Christ en ses mystères. La vie et l'œuvre de Jésus selon saint Thomas d'Aquin* (2 vols.; Paris, 1999) • R. Van Nieuwenhove and J. P. Wawrykow, eds., *The Theology of Thomas Aquinas* (Notre Dame, Ind., 2005) • J. P. Wawrykow, *God's Grace and Human Action: 'Merit' in the Theology of Thomas Aquinas* (Notre Dame, Ind., 1995) • T. G. Weinandy, D. A. Keating, and J. P. Yocum, eds., *Aquinas on Doctrine: A Critical Introduction* (London, 2004); idem, eds., *Aquinas on Scripture: An Introduction to His Biblical Commentaries* (London, 2005).

On 1.5: C. Fabro, *Participation et causalité selon S. Thomas d'Aquin* (Louvain, 1961) • É. Gilson, *The Christian Philosophy of St. Thomas Aquinas* (New York, 1956) • T. S. Hibbs, *Dialectic and Narrative in Aquinas: An Interpretation of the "Summa contra Gentiles"* (Notre Dame, Ind., 1995) • R. M. McInerny, *Aquinas and Analogy* (Washington, D.C., 1996) • J. Maritain, *The Angelic Doctor: The Life and Thought of Saint Thomas Aquinas* (New York, 1931) • R. Pasnau, *Thomas Aquinas on Human Nature: A Philosophical Study of Summa theologiae 1a, 75-89* (Cambridge, 2002) • S. Pinckaers, *The Sources of Christian Ethics* (Washington, D.C.,

1995) • S. Pope, ed., *The Ethics of Aquinas* (Washington, D.C., 2002) • E. Schockenhoff, *Bonum hominis. Die anthropologischen und theologischen Grundlagen der Tugendethik des Thomas von Aquin* (Mainz, 1987) • E. Stump, *Aquinas* (New York, 2003) • D. Turner, *Faith, Reason, and the Existence of God* (Cambridge, 2004) • R. A. te Velde, *Participation and Substantiality in Thomas Aquinas* (Leiden, 1995) • J. F. Wippel, *The Metaphysical Thought of Thomas Aquinas* (Washington, D.C., 2000).

On 2: R. Cessario, *A Short History of Thomism* (Washington, D.C., 2005) • L. Feingold, *The Natural Desire to See God according to St. Thomas Aquinas and His Interpreters* (Rome, 2001) • I. Iribarren, *Durandus of St. Pourçain: A Dominican Theologian in the Shadow of Aquinas* (Oxford, 2005) • F. Kerr, *After Aquinas: Versions of Thomism* (Oxford, 2002) • H. de Lubac, *The Mystery of the Supernatural* (2d ed.; New York, 1998).

Bruce D. Marshall .

Three-Self Patriotic Movement

The "three-self" principle among Protestants goes back to the mid-19th century and the thought of the Englishman Henry Venn (1796-1873, secretary of the Church Missionary Society from 1841) and the American Rufus Anderson (1796-1880, secretary of the American Board of Commissioners for Foreign Missions, 1826-66). It denotes the goal that mission churches should as soon as possible become "self-supporting, self-governing, and self-propagating." As the Communist Party established its control of China between 1949 and 1951, the three-self concept became a handy device to induce the Protestant churches to comply with the directives and goals of the new regime.

In 1949 there were fewer than a million Protestants in China, but they were an influential group, with respected colleges and universities and with important links to foreign organizations and foreign governments. From the new government's point of view, it was imperative that the foreign ties of Chinese Protestants be severed and that they be brought into compliance with state policies and aims. This task was accomplished in a series of steps that was traumatic for the remaining foreign missionaries and for many Chinese Christians as well. In 1950 Premier Zhou Enlai (1898-1976) and Wu Yaozong (Y. T. Wu, 1893-1979), a → YMCA national officer and editor of the Protestant magazine *Tianfeng,* created a document referred to as the Christian Manifesto, which pledged its signers to eradicate remaining imperialistic foreign influences in the Chinese church and pursue the "three-self" principles as an independent and fully Chinese religious community. Between 1950 and 1954, allegedly 400,000 Chinese Protestants signed the manifesto.

By 1951, with the Korean War raging and simultaneously an internal campaign against "counterrevolutionaries" escalating, peremptory expulsion of foreign → missionaries and extension of control over Protestants were pursued, sometimes with tactics such as public denunciation meetings. This was done under the aegis of the party's United Front Work Department (UFWD), whose responsibility it is to create interfacing directive agencies between all social groups and the state, and of the Religious Affairs Bureau (RAB), a government agency responsible for monitoring and directing all religious groups. Thus was created in 1951 the Chinese Protestant Aid-Korea Resist-America Three-Self Reform Movement, intended to gather all Protestants under its banner. Clearly heavily politicized, as its title alone indicates, this organization was resisted by many evangelical groups who feared what the term "reform" might mean for them. Thus by 1954 and the convening of the first National Christian (Protestant) Conference, the organization, now officially headed by Y. T. Wu, was renamed the Chinese Christian Three-Self Patriotic Movement (TSPM). Among its vice-chairs were a respectable number of evangelical leaders, such as Chen Chonggui (Marcus Cheng, 1883-1963) and Jia Yuming (1880-1964).

From 1954 to the 1960s, the TSPM was a faithful implementer of party policy, overseen by both the UFWD and the RAB. The TSPM cooperated with the state in the elimination of some of the evangelical groups that, for political or theological reasons, refused to join or even recognize the religious authority of the TSPM and the state. Several respected Protestant leaders, including some independent figures and churches without any foreign ties at all, such as Wang Mingdao (1900-1991), Watchman Nee (Ni Tuosheng, 1903-72), the Jesus Family, and the True Jesus Church, were persecuted, with the leaders imprisoned and the churches dismantled. The TSPM's actions in the 1950s rightly or wrongly earned it the lasting enmity of many Chinese Protestants, which explains some of the animosity toward the TSPM in certain sectors of the Chinese church even today.

Several leading members of the TSPM itself spoke out against repressive government religious policies in a period of openness in spring 1957, and all were punished for their efforts. Wu himself remained in charge, but with the frenzied national

scene of the late 1950s and early 1960s, the TSPM looked superfluous because Christianity seemed to be withering, along with other religions, leaving little use for → "religion" at all. During the Cultural Revolution (1966-76), the TSPM was disbanded, as were all other religious groups, as well as the RAB itself. There seemed no purpose for the RAB, since all religions were now banned and all religious organizations had officially ceased to exist.

In the reorientation of national policy after the death of Mao Zedong (1893-1976) and the rise to top power of Deng Xiaoping (1904-97) in late 1978, the UFWD resuscitated the RAB, and in 1979 it reestablished the TSPM. Wu had just died, and the new TSPM head was Bishop Ding Guangxun (K. H. Ting, b. 1915), who had risen through the ranks of the organization in the 1950s, becoming principal of Nanjing Theological Seminary in 1953; he was consecrated → bishop of Zhejiang in 1955. Bishop Ting was also made president of the China Christian Council (CCC), a new body created in 1980 to work in tandem with the TSPM and to shoulder some of the task of liaison with local churches, leaving the TSPM with more "political" functions. When Ting led delegations of Chinese Christians abroad from the early 1980s on, they were always CCC delegations. Nevertheless, from national down to local levels, there is great overlap between leadership personnel of the two organizations. Ting retired from both church positions in 1997 but retained his headship of Nanjing Seminary, as well as his high posts in both the National People's Congress and the Chinese People's Political Consultative Conference, prestigious state forums in which at times he has been able to speak effectively on behalf of the Chinese Protestant community.

Two hallmarks of the TSPM since the 1980s have been the remarkable growth of the Chinese Protestant community and, at the same time, a polarization of that community. There are over 13,000 churches registered with the TSPM, with perhaps 18 million believers, and over 20 seminaries and Bible schools. They enjoy substantial protection from harassment by authorities. The unregistered sector of Protestants, however, is far larger, with even faster growth, although it is subject to persecution and suppression at times. A substantial number of these Protestants in autonomous Christian communities (often called, somewhat misleadingly, → "house church" or "underground" Christians) have negative perceptions of the TSPM that range from suspicious to actively hostile. Some of this negativity dates back to events of the 1950s, and some is due on the part of some Christian groups to opposition on theological grounds to any state or party relationships. The frequent charge of theological → liberalism or deficiency of faith in the TSPM is largely off the mark. Like all Chinese churches, TSPM churches are strongly evangelical, as are the great majority of their → pastors. Open displays of Pentecostal behaviors, however, are very seldom seen in the TSPM churches, since these are quite beyond the understanding of the state officials in the RAB (now called the State Administration of Religious Affairs), with whom the TSPM must interact.

Early in the 21st century, it seems to some that the TSPM, still saddled with the burden of its past record of close and willing cooperation with the regime, is too compromised, bureaucratic, and ossified to play the role of representing all Protestants. It seems unlikely that Chinese Protestantism, with its great variety, can be so represented by any one organization. Thus some Chinese Christians argue that the TSPM is obsolete and should be scrapped in favor of a conscious state and party pullback from the use of such an instrument for monitoring the Protestant community, or any religious community.

Bibliography: D. AIKMAN, Jesus in Beijing: How Christianity Is Transforming China and Changing the Global Balance of Power (Washington, D.C., 2003) • T. A. HARVEY, Acquainted with Grief: Wang Mingdao's Stand for the Persecuted Church in China (Grand Rapids, 2002) • A. HUNTER and K.-K. CHAN, Protestantism in Contemporary China (Cambridge, 1993) • F. P. JONES, ed., Documents of the Three-Self Movement (New York, 1963) • J. KINDOPP and C. L. HAMRIN, eds., God and Caesar in China: Policy Implications of Church-State Tensions (Washington, D.C., 2004) • D. E. MACINNIS, Religion in China Today: Policy and Practice (Maryknoll, N.Y., 1989); idem, Religious Policy and Practice in Communist China: A Documentary History (New York, 1972) • P. L. WICKERI, Seeking the Common Ground: Protestant Christianity, the Three-Self Movement, and China's United Front (Maryknoll, N.Y., 1988).

DANIEL H. BAYS

Tibet

1. General Situation
2. Buddhism
3. Christianity

1. General Situation

1.1. Geographically, Tibet lies on the highest plateau on earth, between the 28th and 36th north parallels. Its average altitude is 4,000-5,000 m. (13,000-16,500 ft.). The Himalayas to the south, the Ladakh and Karakoram Ranges to the west, and the Kunlun Shan and Tanggula Ranges to the north form its frontiers. The melting snows from the East Tibetan highlands are the water source of the Yellow, the Yangtze, and the Mekong Rivers. The high steppes and semiwilderness of North Tibet are home to nomads who raise yaks. The south and east are richer in water, and agriculture is predominant in a mixed economy.

1.2. The Tibet region includes the current Tibet Autonomous Region (TAR), as well as several autonomous prefectures and counties in Gansu, Qinghai, Yunnan, and Sichuan Provinces of China bordering TAR. There are 5.4 million Tibetans living in China, with 2.4 million in TAR and 2.9 million in other autonomous prefectures and counties. There are about 110,000 Tibetan in diaspora, with the majority of them in India (85,000) and Nepal (14,000), and smaller numbers in Bhutan, Sikkim, and elsewhere.

The Tibetan language, with its many dialects, belongs to the Tibetan-Burmese family of languages. The written language developed in the seventh century and is still unchanged. There are three major Tibetan dialects: Weizang, Kang, and Amdo, plus a number of subdialects. The Chinese government designated the Weizang dialect used in Lhasa as the official Tibetan language, and this dialect is commonly used in TAR and among Tibetans in the diaspora.

1.3. In the beginning of the seventh century King Songtsän Gampo (Srong-brtsan-sgam-po, ruled 629-50) established the Tubo regime and made Losha (now Lhasa) the capital. Gradually Tibet became a vassal state under the various Chinese dynastic rulers.

During the Republican Era of China (1911-49), the Tibetan local government (Kasha) was under the authority of the Commission for Tibetan and Mongolian Affairs of the Republic of China, albeit enjoying a high degree of autonomy. The Chinese government subsequently established the Qinghai and Xikang Provinces and transferred part of the Tibetan region to the Gansu, Yunnan, Sichuan, and Xikang Provinces. In 1951 the newly established central government of the People's Republic of China reached a 17-article agreement with the Tibetan local government whereby the Tibetans would enjoy a large measure of autonomy but be subject overall to the Chinese. In 1956 a preparatory committee for the TAR was formed. Tensions rose as a land-reform campaign was launched that greatly reduced the privilege and wealth of the aristocratic classes and the monasteries (→ Monasticism).

In 1959 some Tibetans organized an uprising in the TAR against Chinese government rule. The Chinese suppressed this rebellion and later established the TAR in 1965. After the unsuccessful uprising, 80,000 Tibetans, together with the 14th Dalai Lama, Tenzin Gyatso (b. 1935), fled to India, where they established the Central Tibetan Government, now situated at Dharamsala, India, trying to seek the independence of Tibet.

In 1993 the Dalai Lama publicly abandoned the idea of an independent Tibet, as far as its defense and external relations were concerned, in favor of Tibetan autonomy. Since then there have been continuous negotiations with the Chinese government on the political future of Tibet that would include an accommodation between the ideas of Chinese sovereignty and Tibetan autonomy.

2. Buddhism

2.1. King Gambo introduced the Mahayana form of → Buddhism from India to Tibet in the seventh century, with resistance from the priests of the local Bon religion, the ancient religion of the Tibetans (→ Tibetan Religions). There were periods of rivalries between these two religions, and each integrated elements from the other. With the diminishing of the Bon religion by the tenth century, Buddhism became the dominant religion and developed into several sects reflecting various political loyalties and doctrinal emphases. The form of Tibetan Buddhism popularly known as Lamaism was adopted later also in Mongolia.

2.2. Tibetan Buddhism includes several major sects, including Nyingma (Red), Sakya (Flower), Kagyu (White), and Gelug (Yellow). The native Bon religion, which has also absorbed some elements of Buddhism, is still active today among a small population of Tibetans and is known as the Black Sect.

The system of learning is divided into two stages: the Open School and the Secret School. A student enters into a monastery to learn the scriptures and relevant doctrines, leading to the examination for the title *gebshe*. After a monk receives such a title, he can enter the Secret School, where he will receive instruction from a master. Slight variations in the formats of these two schools exist among the various sects.

2.3. Tibetan Buddhism believes in → reincarnation of the Buddha. The reincarnated Buddhas are venerated as the Living Buddha, with the reincarnated Dalai Lama as the supreme spiritual leader and the reincarnated Panchen Lama (both Gelug Sect) as the second most important religious authority.

Controversy has surrounded the selection of the next Panchen Lama. In May 1995 the exiled Dalai Lama selected the six-year-old Gedhun Choekyi Nyima as the reincarnated Panchen Lama, while in November 1995 the Chinese government recognized another six-year-old child, Gyaincain Norbu, as the next Panchen Lama, who was chosen in a draw of lots under the supervision of the Chinese authorities.

2.4. During the Cultural Revolution (1966-76) the Chinese authorities destroyed or damaged almost all the 6,000 monasteries and nunneries and suppressed virtually all religious activity in the Tibetan region. Since 1980 monasteries began to be rebuilt and religious activities were gradually resumed, all under the control of the Chinese government. There are now about 1,700 Tibetan monasteries and nunneries and 40,000 Tibetan monks and nuns in the TAR, and at least 1,500 monasteries and nunneries and 60,000 monks and nuns outside the TAR within regions in China. There are also about 200 Tibetans monasteries and nunneries in India, Nepal, and Bhutan, as well as several hundred Tibetan Buddhist centers all over the world.

3. Christianity

3.1. The Jesuit António de Andrade (1580-1634) came to Tibet in the early 17th century, followed by other → missionaries. A church was built in Lhasa in 1726, and several Tibetans were baptized. Later the Christians were persecuted, the church was destroyed, and the missionaries fled Tibet.

Protestant and Catholic missionaries resumed their work in Tibet in the mid-19th century. French missionaries successfully established several Catholic communities in the early 20th century in the Diqing area, with more than 1,500 Catholics; they were met with strong resistance from the local lamas. Some priests and Tibetan Catholics were → martyred.

Protestant missions had a few Tibetan converts in Lintan County of Gansu Province and a handful of converts in Wexi County of Diqing. The Tibetan NT has been available since 1885; the translation of the complete Bible into Tibetan was finished in 1948.

3.2. Currently the → Roman Catholic Church has a parish in Yanjing of the TAR, with about 800 Tibetan Catholics. There are also several Catholic parishes in the Diqing Tibetan Autonomous Prefecture of Yunnan, with about 7,500 in Deqin County and 2,000 in Shangri-la (formerly known as Zhongdian) County. There is at least one Tibetan priest and several Tibetan nuns serving the Tibetan Catholic community.

3.3. There is a Tibetan Protestant Church in Lintan County of the Gannan Tibetan Autonomous Prefecture of Gansu, which was started in the 1920s. There are at least two small Tibetan fellowships in Naqu Prefecture of the TAR, and several Christian meeting points (some with several hundred people attending every Sunday) in Lhasa and Rikaze of the TAR, attended mostly by Han Chinese. Beginning in 1990, Lisu Christians from Wexi County of Diqing sent missionaries to the Tibetan areas within the prefecture, and currently there are at least 12 new churches in Deqin County, mostly with mixed congregations of Lisus and Tibetans. A few dozen Tibetan Christians have attended local Bible schools and pastoral training institutes. Also some individual Tibetan converts are attending churches in Qinghai.

Bibliography: C. I. BECKWITH, *The Tibetan Empire in Central Asia* (Princeton, 1987) • K.-k. CHAN, "The Tibetan-Protestant Community in China," *News and Views* (Hong Kong Christian Council), fall 2004, 9-11 • P. HATTAWAY, *Operation China: Introducing All the Peoples of China* (Pasadena, Calif., 2000) • G. N. PATTERSON, *Tibet in Revolt* (London, 1960) • B. SAUTMAN and J. T. DREYER, eds., *Contemporary Tibet: Politics, Development, and Society in a Disputed Region* (Armonk, N.Y., 2006). For current information about Tibet from the points of view of the Government of Tibet in Exile and of the People's Republic of China, see, respectively, http://tibet.com and http://en.tibet.cn.

KIM-KWONG CHAN

Tibetan Religions

1. Before Buddhism
2. Buddhism
3. Popular Religion

1. Before Buddhism

Because of incomplete sources and disputed interpretation, our knowledge of pre-Buddhist religious ideas and practices in Tibet is very defective. Most of the known rituals (→ Rite), concepts of faith, and → myths are connected to the person of the king. Different rituals related to royal tombs, processions, sacrifices (of "holy sheep"; → Sacrifice 1), and burials were directed by the → priests (§1.2, *bon-po*) and ritual specialists *(gsen)*. We know of an eschatological cosmology (→ Creation 1) with a cyclic idea of → time and also of a pantheon on three levels: heaven for the gods *(lha),* earth for humans *(mi),* and the underworld for water spirits *(klu).* We can-

not rule out influences from western (Iran?) and eastern (China), but simply to refer to this religion as → shamanism is misleading. Shamanist features occur for the first time in the practices of the Buddhist *snags-pa* (see 2.2). Many of the later characteristics (see 3) are undoubtedly old, but we have few sources. It is certainly not possible to distinguish what came in from outside.

Probably by the 7th century A.D. a coherent ideology of sacral kingship had developed that was called *gtsug* or *gtsug-lag* (law of the gods). Later sources call this most ancient religion *bon*. We must distinguish it from the Buddhist tradition (from the 11th cent.) of the *bon-po* (priests), whose teaching is also called *bon* and that viewed itself as the inheritor of the older *bon* religion, looking, not to Buddha, but to the teacher gShen-rab as its founder (→ Buddhism 3.1).

2. Buddhism

The normative religion of Tibet is Buddhism, which was fully accepted in the 8th century. Buddhism suffered reverses during the 9th century but was revived at the end of the 10th century. In the 11th century many schools developed that gave Tibetan Buddhism its doctrine and organization.

2.1. The Tibetan schools, or *lugs* (methods), represent different theoretical expositions and practices on the basis of the same authoritative source. In monastic rules they follow the ancient Vinaya (lit. "discipline") of Mūlasarvāstivādin, while their philosophical teachings and spiritual aims depend on Indian, especially Mahayana, Buddhism, and the religious practice rests on Vajrayana Buddhism, or Tantrism. Differences arise over the degree of emphasis given to specific traditions and over the choice of the spiritual teacher to follow. Along with the different directions given by different teachers, influential monasteries and their opinions also had a say. The following are the most important schools.

2.2. Rnying-ma-pa (Nyingmapa) is the only tradition that can be traced back to the early Tibetan Buddhism of the monarchy. Within it *sngags-pa* stressed magical ritual, and *rdzogs-chen-pa* stressed Tantric ways of meditation.

Bka'-gdams-pa (Kadampa) derives from the Indian scholar Atīśa (982-1054) and stresses the way of bodhisattva, the authority of the Prajñāpāramitā-sutras, and the theory of Mādhyamaka teachings. It recognizes but restricts the tantras. Its founder was 'Brom-ston, a student of Atīśa, who in 1056 founded the monastery of Rwa-sgreng (Reting) at Lhasa.

Ka'rgyud-pa (Kagyupa) may be traced back to Mar-pa (1012-96) and the Indian tantric masters *(siddha)* Tilopa and Nāropa. Stress falls on experiences of → yoga (*mahāmudrā*, "great seal") and tantric practices. Mi-la ras-pa (Milarepa, 1040-1123) bears witness to this in his famous mystical songs. Various schools were founded by the doctor Sgam-po-pa (1079-1123) and his 12th-century disciples 'Bri-gung-pa, Stag-lung-pa, 'Brug-pa, and Karma-pa.

Sa-skya-pa (Sakyapa) took its name from the monastery Sa-skya (Sakya, 1073). 'Brog-mi (992-1072) was the founder of this school, which adopted tantric traditions. The monastery quickly became a center for great scholars (esp. Sa-skya Pandita [1182-1251]), and during the Mongol period it became the political center of Tibet. At the beginning of the 14th century a branch school issued a collection of the Tibetan canon in two divisions, Bka'-'gyur (Kanjur), a collection of the sayings of Buddha, and Bstan-'gyur (Tanjur), a collection of translations of expository texts.

Dge-lugs-pa (Gelukpa) derived from a reforming movement in the school of Bka'-gdams-pa. The founder was Tsong-kha-pa (1357-1419), who insisted on → celibacy, collected a great → summa (the *Lam-rim chen-mo*) of religious practices, and regulated tantric studies. Philosophically, he followed the Prāsangika direction of the Madhyamaka. His students founded large monasteries around Lhasa. After the 15th century this school was also active politically. In the 16th century a Mongol prince gave one of its successors the title "Dalai Lama" (teacher of the ocean of wisdom). The Mongols (→ Mongolia 2) were open to mission and adopted Tibetan Buddhism. Under the fifth Dalai Lama, Ngag-dbang-rgya-mtsho (1617-82), Lhasa finally became the political center of Tibet. A city arose (related to the Potala Palace and Monastery, occupied in 1643), the Dalai lama came to be seen as a reincarnation of his predecessor and ultimately of Bodhisattva Avalokiteśvara, the patron of Tibet, and as ruler over a politically united Tibet. The relation of the Dalai Lama to the Chinese emperor, which was modeled on the Mongol monarchy under the Manchus (after 1644), was understood as that of spiritual teacher to secular protector and patron. Without suppressing the other schools, the Dge-lugs-pa (the school of virtue) was the most important.

2.3. Along with monastery traditions Tibet also saw wandering tantric yogi or masters *(siddha)* who imparted mystical experiences and worked miracles by magical practices and often extreme asceticism. Instead of the long path to meditative perfection (→ Meditation) and the discipline of Mahayanist bodhisattva, they taught the shortcut of a radical breakthrough to liberation and the actualizing of the true nature of existence.

3. Popular Religion

Among the people, and along with Tibetan Buddhism, we also find a complex network of ideas and practices. Pre-Buddhist traditions live on in Tibetan popular religion, even though they are now related to Buddhist ideas and practices. Such practices as winning merit, ritual transformation, → pilgrimages, and → visions are plainly Buddhist, but they are linked to local cults, holy mountains, domestic gods, personal gods, a threefold cosmos, predictions, and healings (with oracles and mediums) that contain many non-Buddhist elements. The many numina (expressions of deity) and dealings with them are seen by Buddhism as connected with the this-worldly sphere *('jig-rten-pa)* and thus have their place. They do not conflict with the higher religion, which points us beyond this world.

Bibliography: C. A. Bell, *The Religion of Tibet* (Oxford, 1931) • A. Cadonna and E. Bianchi, eds., *Facets of Tibetan Religious Tradition and Contacts with Neighbouring Cultural Areas* (Florence, 2002) • M. C. Goldstein and M. T. Kapstein, *Buddhism in Contemporary Tibet: Religious Revival and Cultural Identity* (Berkeley, Calif., 1998) • S. G. Karmay, *A General Introduction to the History and Doctrines of Bon* (Tokyo, 1975) • S. G. Karmay and Y. Nagano, eds., *New Horizons in Bon Studies* (Osaka, 2000) • P. Kvaerne, "Tibetan Religions," *EncRel(E)* 14.497-504 • D. L. Snellgrove, *Indo-Tibetan Buddhism: Indian Buddhists and Their Tibetan Successors* (2d ed.; Boston, 2002) • D. L. Snellgrove and H. E. Richardson, *A Cultural History of Tibet* (3d ed.; Bangkok, 2003) • L. Sopa and J. Hopkins, *Practice and Theory of Tibetan Buddhism* (London, 1976) • G. Tucci, *The Religions of Tibet* (trans. G. Samuel; Berkeley, Calif., 1980) • M. L. Walter, "Tibetan Religions: History of Study," *EncRel(E)* 14.504-7.

Ernst Steinkellner

Tillich, Paul

Paul Johannes Tillich (1886-1965) was a German theologian and philosopher of → culture who, beginning in 1933, made the United States his home. Tillich was born in Starzeddel, Brandenburg, Prussia, on August 20, 1886. He was the son of a Lutheran pastor who in 1900 was appointed to the Consistory in Berlin. Following his final school examinations, Tillich studied → theology and → philosophy in Berlin, Tübingen, and Halle (1904-9).

In his first year of studies Tillich began, on his own, to read F. W. J. Schelling, about whom he later wrote two works: his dissertation at the University of Breslau (1910) and his theological licentiate at Halle (1911). In August 1912 he was ordained to the pastorate of the Protestant St. Matthew's Church in Berlin. From 1912 to 1914 he was deputy clergyman in the worker's quarter of Moabit, in Berlin. Here he began work on his habilitation thesis, writing for the University of Halle on the concept of the supernatural prior to F. D. E. → Schleiermacher (finished 1916).

With the outbreak of World War I in August 1914, Tillich volunteered for military duty. On September 28, 1914, he married Margarete Wever; this marriage lasted until 1921, when it was ended by divorce. From October 1, 1914, until 1918, Tillich served on the western front (France) as an army chaplain. After only a few weeks, the war had already sobered him. He now recognized that genuine theological thinking could happen only in the "boundary experiences" of life. Soon he also saw that the → war was no longer a struggle of independent peoples but, in the end, a → class struggle. He welcomed the → revolution of 1918 and the Weimar Republic and was a founding member of the Kairos Circle, a well-known group of Berlin religious socialists who published their ideas in the journal *Blätter für religiösen Sozialismus* (1920-27).

From 1919 to 1924 Tillich was adjunct professor at the University of Berlin. During this time he married Hannah Werner. As professor of systematic theology at the University of Marburg (1924-25), he was strongly influenced by the thinking of his colleagues Rudolf Otto (1869-1937) and Martin Heidegger (1889-1976). From 1925 to 1929 Tillich was professor of philosophy and → religious studies at the Technical University of Dresden. In 1926 his first large public success came with the appearance of *Die religiöse Lage der Gegenwart* (ET *The Religious Situation* [1956]). In the same year his daughter, Erdmuthe, was born. From 1927 to 1929 he taught systematic theology at the University of Leipzig.

Through his publications, Tillich acquired the reputation of a theologian who attempted to correlate the Christian answer in all areas of modern culture with existential questions. This approach was clear in his works *Über die Idee einer Theologie der Kultur* (1919; ET *Visionary Science: A Translation of Tillich's "On the Idea of a Theology of Culture"* [1987]), *The Religious Situation,* and *Protestantisches Prinzip und proletarische Situation* (The Protestant principle and the proletarian situation).

In 1929 Tillich accepted a call to the University of Frankfurt and took over a professorate of philosophy and → sociology, succeeding Max Scheler (1874-1928). It was here that his controversy with National Socialism reached its zenith, especially through his contacts with Jewish students and colleagues at the Institute for Social Research (Max Horkheimer, Theodor W. Adorno as postdoctoral researcher) and through his demand (as dean of the philosophical faculty) that National Socialist students who were inciting discord should be expelled from the university. In *Die sozialistische Entscheidung* (1932, forbidden in the Third Reich; ET *The Socialist Decision* [1977]), Tillich differentiated between → religious socialism, dogmatic → Marxism, and romantic and revolutionary → conservatism (i.e., National Socialism). In April 1933 his authorization to teach was withdrawn, whereupon he emigrated with his family to the United States. With the help of Reinhold → Niebuhr (1892-1971), he was given a chair of philosophy and systematic theology at Union Theological Seminary in New York. Later he became a professor at Harvard University (1955-62) and at the Divinity School of the University of Chicago (1962-65). During the Hitler era, he maintained his contacts in Europe and Germany.

In America, Tillich quickly became known through his courses, books, sermons, and energetic lecture activity. His own experience of life on the border between → faith and → doubt, → church and → society, home and the foreign, which he described in *Auf der Grenze* (1936; ET *On the Boundary* [1966]), and his affirmation of the meaning of existence even over against nonexistence, which he portrayed in *The Courage to Be* (1952; Ger. trans. *Der Mut zum Sein* [1953]), one of the most influential and most widely read theological books of the 20th century, evidently filled a gap in contemporary American culture — particularly the interest in the connection between theology and → psychology. Tillich's idea of faith as that which concerns us unconditionally, of God as the unconditional or the ground of being, of sin as the estrangement or separation from this ground, and redemption as the overcoming of this alienation through the experience of new being in Christ — these are the themes that constantly return in his three-volume *Systematic Theology* (1951-63; Ger. trans., 1956-66).

Tillich received numerous international honors, including the Peace Prize of the German Book Trade (1962). His trips to Japan (1960) and to Israel and Egypt (1963), as well as his book *Christianity and the Encounter of the World Religions* (1963; Ger. trans., 1964), show the direction of his theological thinking in the last years of his life.

Bibliography: Primary sources: Gesammelte Werke (14 vols.; ed. R. Albrecht; Stuttgart, 1959-75) • *Main Works = Hauptwerke* (6 vols.; ed. C. H. Ratschow; Berlin, 1987-92).

Secondary works: J. L. Adams, eds., *The Thought of Paul Tillich* (San Francisco, 1985) • W. Pauck and M. Pauck, *Paul Tillich: His Life and Thought,* vol. 1, *Life* (New York, 1976) • A. J. Reimer, *The Emanuel Hirsch and Paul Tillich Debate: A Study in the Political Ramifications of Theology* (Lewistown, N.Y., 1989); idem, *Paul Tillich: Theologian of Nature, Culture, and Politics* (Münster, 2004); idem, "Prayer as *Unio mystica:* Tillich's Concept of Prayer in Contrast to Barth's Christological Realism and Hirsch's Pietistic Personalism," *Das Gebet als Grundakt des Glaubens* (ed. W. Schüßler and A. J. Reimer; Münster, 2004) 109-35 • M. K. Taylor, *Paul Tillich: Theologian of the Boundaries* (London, 1987).

Journals: DIALOG. Mitteilungsblatt der Deutschen Paul-Tillich-Gesellschaft (1989-) • *Newsletter: North American Paul Tillich Society* (Charlottesville, Va.) (1975-).

A. James Reimer

Time and Eternity

1. Philosophy

A philosophical discussion of time faces the task of inquiring into the original, objectively first, and fundamental experience of time, of reflecting on its multiplicity, and then of defining it. It should not be forgotten that time, for its part, has its own temporal and historical conditions. The relationship of time and being, the distinction between time and the temporal, and the fact that those who try to understand time are in time themselves must all be focal points in the discussion.

1.1. *Gnostic Philosophy and Thomas Aquinas*

Classical → metaphysics (→ Philosophy of Nature 2), which investigates time in the tension between being and consciousness, defines time as a sequence of nows (illustrated by a timeline). The being that underlies movement and becoming is the temporal. Seen from this perspective, time, in which all movement occurs, appears constant. Yet the constant belongs also to the becoming: what is constant (no matter how long the period of time) becomes older. For the now is always an other; it proceeds inexorably from the not-yet to the no-longer. One must thus distinguish between a twofold passing: the passing of the temporal in time, and the passing of time itself (the image of "time flying"). The temporal stands in opposition to the eternal as *being* in its authentic sense, which excludes all becoming and all time from itself. It cannot be said either of the → future or of the past that it *is* — the one is not yet, the other is no longer — but also the present now is not in its authentic sense but *is* only in that it passes. The temporal now *(nunc praeteriens)* is to be distinguished from the eternal and persistent now *(nunc stans)* that neither comes nor goes.

Plato (427-347 b.c.; → Platonism) defines time as an image that is "eternal but moving according to number [in the heavens], while eternity itself rests in unity" *(Ti.* 37D). In that the temporal is seen as being in its inauthentic sense (nonbeing as *mē on),* it stands in danger of being ontologically devalued. (From the purview of classical metaphysics, history appears as a lessening of being and a dispersion of unity; the goal of history consists in its own overcoming, the annulment of time.)

Aristotle (384-322 b.c.; → Aristotelianism; Experience 1) characterizes time from the viewpoint of the problem of movement as "the [measured] number of motion in respect of 'before' and 'after'" *(Ph.* 4.219b) and, together with the measurement of time, introduces the problem of the relation of time and → soul (§2). After Aristotle, the contrast between time and eternity governs the approach to the problem of time, along with the fact that it can be measured and the question whether it is subjective or objective (→ Subjectivism and Objectivism).

"Eternal" can be understood in two ways. Less strictly, it is endless temporal duration *(sempiternum);* more strictly, it is the nontemporal divine present *(aeternum).* For Boethius (ca. 480-524; → Platonism 4), God's eternity rests on his full and perfect life *(Consol.* 5.6.4). Thomas Aquinas (ca. 1225-74; → Thomism) differentiates between the temporality of material being *(tempus)* and the temporal character of the imperishable though changeable being of the pure spirits *(aeviternitas, aevum).* In the typical modern discussion of "eternal" or "rational truths" (→ Modernity), the meaning of the eternal as rational becomes mixed together with the eternal as endless abiding. "Eternity" here means that which is always valid so long as time endures.

1.2. *Further Development*

A central point for → Augustine (354-430; → Augustine's Theology) was that time can be measured and that it also relates to the soul or consciousness (→ Anthropology 2.3). We can measure only that which is present. For the soul, the past is present in memory, the present is what exists for the moment, and the future is known by expectation (*Conf.* 11.20.16). Time is the unity of future, present, and past and, as such, is the threefold self-extension of the spirit (11.26.33). This approach tends to break apart the interlocking of time and space and places time in the consciousness that understands time. In modernity, it leads to the complete subjectivization of time.

That time exists for the subject means that it also exists through the subject. I. Kant (1724-1804; → Kantianism) viewed time as a form of pure perception for the inner sense. It enables us to see sensory matter successively. Time possesses "empirical reality," that is, objective validity, but only as "transcendental ideality." Without the viewing subject (for whom the temporal succession appears), there is also no time — it neither exists in itself, nor does it define the things themselves (*Critique of Pure Reason,* A32ff., B49ff.). It has no existence if we do not take into account the conditions of the subject who perceives it (A36, B52).

I. Newton (1642-1727), in contrast, maintained the idea of absolute time, convinced that the measurement of a process is possible only if we presuppose that time flows at an equal rate and is not dependent on movement.

G. W. Leibniz (1646-1716) saw the essence of time in a relationship, in the ordering of succession, which is based on God's idea of time (→ God 3).

H. Bergson (1859-1941) shifted attention away from time as measurable succession to the experience of time. Time as duration (*durée*) is the real time that shapes all life. As such, it is psychological time. This living time, which triumphantly persists from youth to maturity, is grounded in the primal unchangeability and uniqueness of both individual and supraindividual history.

E. Husserl (1859-1938) distinguished measurable "objective" time from the temporality of inward time-consciousness. Awareness that experiences are temporal is the presupposition on which awareness of objective time rests. Remembrance of the past and expectation of the future are based on the just now (retention) or on the presentness of the immediate ("protention"). Time exists in the unity of attention (dedication to the directly present), retention, and protention.

For M. Heidegger (1889-1976), time understood as a measurable procession of nows belongs to the popular understanding of time. It involves blindness to cosmic time and its typical structural elements of significance, precalendrical datability, tension, and openness. Cosmic time is grounded in the ecstatically horizontal temporality of existential time. Time is the unity of coming to oneself (the primal future), coming back to oneself (the primal past), and letting things happen (the primal present).

1.3. *Views*

Natural science and history operate with a chronometric concept of time. Time is viewed as a procession of nows and is discussed under the limited view of its availability and measurability. Time itself is not measured but is always only a period of time, with a periodic process producing the standard for measurement. (Even the theory of → relativity discusses time purely in view of its measurability when it makes the defining of the simultaneity of two events dependent on contingent conditions.) Historical time is, in contrast, a homogeneous procession of nows through, among other things, substantive principles of distribution that arise from, and reflect, a sociocultural understanding of time (e.g., time before or after Christ's birth, historical divisions into epochs). When the calendar recognizes sacred times (→ Church Year), it keeps alive, in the form of mythical speech, the consciousness of the divine foundational beginnings of everything temporal (→ Creation 2).

The philosophical question of time cannot simply adopt the scientific or historical view. Every measurement of time rests on an understanding that cannot be reduced to a chronometric concept. (The presence of the subject, to which each time specification remains necessarily related, is not a "now" proceeding from a "not-yet" into a "no-more.") A chronometric view thrives on the possibility that the relation between time and subject will not be discussed, so that methodologically no account will be given of the basic experience of time, of time as a gift.

Measurement of time takes place in time. It is a way of having time, and it rests on the gift of time. The dimensions of time must be seen along these lines. We control time (the present), but it is a pure gift (the future), and it partly conditions us (the past). Historical time manifests itself accordingly as the time of ever-opening possibilities and challenges us to grasp them responsibly (the present as *kairos*).

Relating time to the consciousness does not have to mean subjectivization. It can mean an awareness of absence that irresistibly impels those who investigate time. Awareness of our own origins is a constitutive part of this investigation and cannot be exchanged for the idea of a world from which we are absent. Our own origin is something we can have, but not something we can have *had*. It is not a fact belonging to the past. The root of the philosophical question of time is the question of a present that has neither the form of a passing now nor that of an ecstatically temporal present.

Bibliography: H. Bergson, *Time and Free Will: An Essay on the Immediate Data of Consciousness* (Mineola, N.Y., 2001; orig. pub., 1889) • F. H. Bradley, *Appearance and Reality* (Oxford, 1968; orig. pub., 1893) • P. C. W. Davies, *About Time: Einstein's Unfinished Revolution* (New York, 1995) • A. Grünbaum, "The Nature of Time," *Frontiers of Science and Philosophy* (ed. R. G. Colodny; Pittsburgh, 1962) 147-88; idem, *Philosophical Problems of Space and Time* (2d ed.; Boston, 1973) • M. Heidegger, *Being and Time* (Albany, N.Y., 1996; orig. pub., 1927) • E. Husserl, *On the Phenomenology of the Consciousness of Internal Time* (Boston, 1991; orig. pub., 1928) • E. Lévinas, *Time and the Other, and Additional Essays* (Pittsburgh, 1987) • H. Reichenbach, *The Direction of Time* (Berkeley, Calif., 1958); idem, *The Philosophy of Space and Time* (New York, 1958) • C. M Sherover, *Heidegger, Kant, and Time* (Bloomington, Ind., 1971) • J. J. C. Smart, ed., *Problems of Space and Time* (New York, 1964) • C. F. von Weizsäcker and E. Rudolph, eds., *Zeit und Logik bei Leibniz* (Stuttgart, 1989).

Günther Pöltner

2. Systematic Theology

2.1. *Time*

2.1.1. Asking what time is, → Augustine (354-430) stated that we know it but cannot explain it (*Conf.* 11.14). He associated the basic experience of passing moments to that of flowing streams. One moment passes into another. We experience the present but also think of a past and a future.

In this direct sense theology speaks also of God's work in the world. The fact of temporal being is one of the conditions of → creation (§3); it is a constitutive part of God's own working within it. He gives us time as living space. The cycle of nature makes life possible, but so does its imposed limitation, with birth at the one end and → death at the other (C. Westermann, J. Barr; see also K. → Barth). In creation we experience God through temporal events. God allots us our own time (Eccl. 3:1-11). He accompanies his people in a history of → promise and fulfillment. Such an understanding of time is also needed in → pastoral ministry, especially to the dying (→ Pastoral Care; Pastoral Care of the Dying).

2.1.2. Christians also must understand time as it relates to the divine economy of creation and redemption (→ Soteriology) and → sanctification (§3;

→ Trinity), and indeed of all the divine actions in history as events succeed one another. Even up to the 19th-century → theology of history (O. Cullmann; → Religious Socialism), the idea was not questioned that God is teleologically leading history up to its final consummation (→ Evolution; Salvation History; Teleology). A basic belief in → progress (→ Optimism and Pessimism) overlaid the everyday experience of time and its sense of perishability.

In the 20th century, however, Protestant theology was afflicted by doubt. Can we really speak of a divine future and a prophetic time (J. Moltmann; → Predestination; Providence)? We perhaps detect the problem in the tendency to focus on → Christology. (§6) and on an eschatological view of the → incarnation as the final event of past history (see esp. Anglican and Roman Catholic theology; on this point, G. Müller-Fahrenholz). In post-Christian → feminist theology a protest is made against all past Christian theology and ethics (D. Hampson and R. Radford Ruether). → Existential theology and mystical theology objected to an enclosing of God in linear history (M. von Brück; → Mysticism).

2.1.3. Though oriented to temporal sequence, salvation history can also grasp a concept of external time. Everyday experience, however, thinks in terms of an inner time that is the context of external time. An experience of the power of time results (R. Schulte). The temporal sequence that manifests external time is inexorable. In contrast, the great statements of Christian faith tell us that God fills up external time. The event of → forgiveness nondeterministically replaces the old creation by the new (Rom. 8:19-23). Future consummation takes place already in the present as the old structure is renewed. The sequence of past, present, and future is asymmetrically conditioned by a divinely filled future that invades the present and can renew the past. In this sense, and not through constantly recurring natural cycles of time, creation is a continuous creation *(creatio continuata)* governed by divine providence (O. Weber).

The NT refers to a present that is filled with the divine future of → reconciliation, in which God will be "all in all" (1 Cor. 15:28). As the "now," it is the beginning of the consummation (→ Eschatology 2). The now of the coming of Jesus opens up the beginning of the new aeon. It is the now of the moment of decision that is demanded of all of us (Rom. 13:11). We should understand along these lines both the phrase "day of the Lord" in the OT and the term *kairos* as the right time in the NT (M. Plathow, H. Weder). On this messianic understanding of time, past and future are not successive. The tenses merge into one another (Moltmann). A linear view of time, such as that of the earlier works of J. Mbiti (→ Eschatology 6), brought the Christian concept into opposition to traditional African thinking. But it suppresses the eschatological openness to the future at the end of time, in which Christian → hope finds its sustenance (for Japan, K. Koyama).

2.1.4. K. Barth (1886-1968) suggested a general shortening of perspectives when he construed time as the time that is given by God in the revelation through Christ. Our only time is this time, which stands apart from the empty continuum of external time, our lost time. The temporality of creation is not a determinative condition for the possibility of the divine work of salvation. It is simply a vessel that God fills when he turns to us. It is thus fulfilled time (*CD* I/2, §14; III/2, §47; → Covenant 3).

Theologians influenced by Barth entered into a lively dialogue with natural scientists, who had developed a view of time based on the → quantum theory, for this view differed similarly from seeing time in tenses and also opened up the future (G. Howe, H. Nebelsick). The thought of a river of time and Isaac Newton's (1642-1727) theory of absolute time were both now found to be unusable. Time is an open system. The past does not just disappear, nor does it determine the future. New things are always awaited and can be achieved (G. Picht, K. Müller). T. F. Torrance, influenced by M. Polanyi, welcomes the new knowledge. He regards the incarnation ontologically as the future of God's revelatory entry into the time and space of this world, which declared itself in dialogue with the nondualistic theories of science and which in them, as also in creation, demonstrates the rationality of God.

2.2. Eternity

A result of these discussions is that the eternity of God cannot be thought of apart from a reference to time. The picture of God living in perpetual duration is no longer usable, now that criticism of the classical axiom of divine apathy has established itself (for a radical view, see → process theology). Christians must still talk of the providence of God and of God as the Lord of time (see Barth's subsection "Jesus as the Lord of Time," *CD* III/2, §47). They relate the work of reconciliation to the foreshortening of times (Moltmann). Both Jews and Christians pray to God (→ Prayer) as the one who takes the past up into his future and who works it out in the present. They also believe that with their limited lives they will in this way find entry into the eternal life of God.

Bibliography: In English: J. Barr, *Biblical Words for Time* (London, 1962) • W. L. Craig, *Time and Eternity: Exploring God's Relationship to Time* (Wheaton, Ill., 2001) • O. Cullmann, *Christ and Time: The Primitive Christian Conception of Time and History* (Philadelphia, 1964; orig. pub., 1946) • G. J. DeWeese, *God and the Nature of Time* (Aldershot, 2004) • D. Hampson and R. Radford Ruether, "Is There a Place for Feminists in a Christian Church?" *NBl* 68 (1987) 7-24 • K. Koyama, "Will the Monsoon Rain Make God Wet? An Ascending Spiral View of History," *Waterbuffalo Theology* (Maryknoll, N.Y., 1974) 27-42 • J. Mbiti, *NT Eschatology in an African Background* (Oxford, 1971) • J. Moltmann, *The Coming of God: Christian Eschatology* (Minneapolis, 1996) • H. P. Nebelsick, *Theology and Science in Mutual Modification* (New York, 1981) • E. Pannenberg, "Eternity, Time, and Space," *Zygon* 40 (2005) 97-106; idem, "Zeit und Ewigkeit in der religiösen Erfahrung Israels und des Christentums," *Grundfragen systematischer Theologie* (2 vols.; Göttingen, 1967-80) 2.188-206 • T. Peters, *God as Trinity: Relationality and Temporality in Divine Life* (Louisville, Ky., 1993) esp. 146-87 • M. Polanyi, *Personal Knowledge: Towards a Post-critical Philosophy* (2d ed.; London, 1962) • G. Theissen, *Biblical Faith: An Evolutionary Approach* (London, 1964) • T. F. Torrance, *Space, Time, and Incarnation* (London, 1969) • S. de Vries, "Time in the Bible," *Times of Celebration* (ed. D. Power; Edinburgh, 1981) 3-13 • O. Weber, *Foundations of Dogmatics* (2 vols.; Grand Rapids, 1981-83) 1.455-60.

In German: M. von Brück, "Zeitlichkeit und mystische Einheitserfahrung," *EvT* 49 (1989) 142-60 • G. Howe, *Die Christenheit im Atomzeitalter* (Stuttgart, 1970) • A. M. K. Müller, *Die präparierte Zeit* (Stuttgart, 1972) • G. Müller-Fahrenholz, *Heilsgeschichte zwischen Ideologie und Prophetie* (Freiburg, 1974) • G. Picht, *Mut zur Utopie* (Munich, 1969) • M. Plathow, "Zeit und Ewigkeit," *NZSTh* 26 (1984) 95-115 • E. Rudolph, *Zeit und Gott bei Aristoteles. Aus der Perspektive der protestantischen Wirkungsgeschichte* (Stuttgart, 1986) • R. Schulte, "Zeit und Ewigkeit," *CGG* 22.121-86 • H. Weder, *Gegenwart und Gottesherrschaft* (Neukirchen, 1993).

Ulrike Link-Wieczorek

Timothy, Epistles to → Pastoral Epistles

Tithe

1. To tithe is to give a portion (ideally one-tenth) of the produce of an agrarian society for religious purposes, especially the upkeep of the priesthood. The

tithe may consist of fruits of the field or animals from the herd. The recipients were, besides the local clergy, the → bishop, the poor, and the church building and program. Tithes could sometimes go to laypersons who had bought the right to them (→ Proprietary Church; Clergy and Laity).

2. The tithe belongs to → Yahweh, according to Lev. 27:30-33. Details are given in Deut. 14:22-29. The tithe might be spent on joyful meals on → pilgrimage, but it was also used to support the Levites, as well as "the resident aliens, the orphans, and the widows in your towns" (v. 29; see also Num. 18:21-24; Neh. 13:5, 12).

There are parallels, for example, in Babylonian religion. The Islamic *zakāt* (→ Islam 3.4), however, is simply a tax for the poor.

3. Not found in the → early church, the tithe first became legally binding in the Frankish kingdom by the Second Synod of Mâcon (A.D. 585) for the replacement of church property co-opted for the equipping of vassals. Further development came during the → Middle Ages (§1.2.3), and a papal tithe of the clergy was introduced. During the → Peasants' War (1524-25) a new ordering of the tithe was attempted: it should be used, in accordance with Scripture and with the agreement of the congregation, partially for the support of the → pastor and otherwise to aid the poor and defend the country (the Twelve Articles, no. 2).

The → Puritans (John Selden) contested its basis in sacred law, and the tithe increasingly became a feudal privilege. In France civic leaders and peasants called for its repeal, which, along with the repeal of other privileges, took place in 1789 (French → Revolution [§3]). Otherwise the tithe was discontinued in the process of ending rural serfdom and property levies.

England ended compulsory tithing only in 1936, although hints of it are recognizable even today in the country's system of taxation. In the realm of the church, the concept of withholding a percentage of one's income (e.g., for diaconal purposes) is still argued for and, to a lesser extent, is realized.

In many → free churches (e.g., the → Baptists), the voluntary giving of one-tenth of one's personal income is considered part of the normal spiritual practices of church members.

4. Many churches, especially in the United States, advocate voluntary tithing. Some claim that a tenth of one's income should go to the local church and that free gifts beyond the tithe should support other causes. One-tenth of a church's income might also go to the diocese. Usually the tenth is not regarded legalistically. It is a percentage (before or after taxes) at which church members should aim. The financial stability and even wealth of many U.S. churches depend upon the voluntary tithing principle.

Bibliography: R. W. Frazier, *The Tithe Act, 1936, and the Rules Thereunder* (London, 1936) • E. Le Roy Ladurie and J. Goy, *Tithe and Agrarian History from the Fourteenth to the Nineteenth Centuries* (Cambridge, 1982) • P. K. Meagher and D. Dietlein, "Tithes," *NCE* (2d ed.) 14.90-92 • J. Selden, *The History of Tithes* (London, 1618).

                                                    Jürgen Stein

Titus, Epistle to → Pastoral Epistles

Tobacco → Substance Abuse

Togo

	1960	1980	2000
Population (1,000s):	1,514	2,615	4,676
Annual growth rate (%):	1.44	2.93	2.63
Area: 56,785 sq. km. (21,925 sq. mi.)			

A.D. 2000

Population density: 82/sq. km. (213/sq. mi.)
Births / deaths: 3.98 / 1.36 per 100 population
Fertility rate: 5.58 per woman
Infant mortality rate: 78 per 1,000 live births
Life expectancy: 51.6 years (m: 50.3, f: 53.0)
Religious affiliation (%): Christians 49.4 (Roman Catholics 35.7, marginal 9.0, Protestants 6.8, indigenous 2.6, unaffiliated 1.9), tribal religionists 30.8, Muslims 19.0, other 0.8.

1. Statistics
2. Protestant Groups
3. Roman Catholic Church
4. Church and State
5. Islam
6. Traditional Religion

1. Statistics

The Togolese Republic, on the south coast of West Africa, has a population of 5.6 million (2005), nearly half of whom are less than 15 years of age. The people are divided into 45 language groups, including Ewe (44 percent) in the south and Kabye (or Kabré, 14 percent) in the north. Lomé (800,000), on the Atlantic Ocean, is the capital, the largest city, and the main port.

2. Protestant Groups

The Evangelical Presbyterian Church of Togo (Église Évangélique Presbytérienne du Togo, EEPT), which developed out of the work of the North German Mission (→ German Missions 1), has 300,000 members (2006). In all, 101 pastors and 579 catechists serve in 579 congregations. Most of the members belong to the Ewe and Akposo tribes in the southwest, but some belong to the Kabye tribe in the north and to the Aja and Ehve tribes in the southeast. The EEPT takes the lead in the Communauté Évangélique d'Action Apostolique (CEVAA; → French Missions) and is a member of the → All Africa Conference of Churches.

2.1. The story of EEPT began in 1847 with work that Lorenz Wolf started among the Ewe in Peki (now in Ghana). The first congregation in what is now Togo was formed in 1893. German colonial rule (→ Colonialism), which had begun in 1884, ended in 1914 when Britain and France invaded and divided the country. The French mandate covered what is now Togo.

2.2. After the expulsion of the German missionaries, the church stayed united despite the division of the country. The Evangelical Ewe Church was formed in 1922 at Kpalimé. Leaders were Andreas Aku (ca. 1863-1931, president and later moderator) and Robert Baeta (1883-1944, secretary of the synod). Division of the country did not prevent cooperation. The EEPT is still joined synodically to the Evangelical Presbyterian Church of Ghana and uses the same Bible translation and → hymnal. With the help of the Paris Mission, it organized its own system of theological training in 1929 and also began the → evangelism of the Kabye. In 1959 the EEPT placed the workers of the Paris Mission and of the U.S. United Church of Christ (which had begun work in Togo in 1955) under the Bureau Executif (moderator, secretary, and a nontheologian). A Comité Synodal of 28 members acts alongside the Bureau Executif.

2.3. The North German Mission started a new work of evangelization and development in 1960, which led to many new congregations being formed between 1962 and 1970. Work began among the Konkomba in the northwest in 1984. Bread for the World and other organizations helped to build schools, a large hospital, many regional clinics (→ Medical Missions), and a program of adult education. It also strengthened the structure of EEPT. Agricultural centers became important, for most of

Togo's inhabitants are farmers. Only 20 percent of the land is fertile. It is possible to work another 40 percent, but the rest is infertile. Too much financial support is received from foreign organizations. Programs for development and the general budget are financed in good part with subsidies, mostly furnished by Germany. In 2001 the EEPT became one of the supporting churches of the North German Mission.

2.4. The EEPT tries to interpret the gospel in an integrated manner. The synod formulated its own four-sentence → confession in 1971.

2.5. The Methodists (Église Protestant Méthodiste au Togo; → Methodist Churches) came to Togo around 1870. This church had 10,000 members in 2005; the majority of them, who belong to the Mina people, live by the coast. It works closely with the Methodist Church of Benin. The EEPT has good ecumenical relations with the Methodists, with the → Assemblies of God, who began work in 1940, and with other Christian groups.

2.6. Since 1990, Pentecostal congregations have been established in increasing numbers and are experiencing rapid growth. Their membership numbers are difficult to ascertain statistically. Other groups in Togo that to one degree or another have been syncretistically influenced are insignificant.

3. Roman Catholic Church

The → Roman Catholic Church is by far the largest Christian community in Togo, with some 1.4 million members. The African Mission Society began this work in 1892, and after 1921 Divine Word missionaries continued it. An excellent school system supports it. National pastors and foreign missionaries are at work in seven → dioceses. In many programs of development it works closely with the EEPT.

4. Church and State

After World War II many Christians actively sought independence. Pastors risked imprisonment if they preached on the biblical concept of → freedom and applied it to political independence. Tensions between → church and state were heightened when Sylvanus Olympio (1902-63), the first president elected after Togo's independence on April 27, 1960, was assassinated. A declaration of the synod of EEPT critically stressed the coresponsibility of Christians for the well-being of the country and for the right of criticism.

A military dictatorship under Gnassingbé Eyadéma came into power in 1967, a regime that was charged with violations of human and civil →

rights. In 1975, following the example of → Zaire (§1.2), the regime aimed at *authenticité*. Citizens now had to have only genuinely African names and had to renounce all others, even biblical names. The freedom of the press and opposition parties came under a ban in October 1990. Bloody repression did not stop the *Conférence Nationale Souveraine*, at which the EEPT issued a confession of guilt. The military regime intensified its pressure, and a nine-month-long general strike ensued. Massacres caused many people to seek refuge in neighboring countries. Ethnic pressure and corruption marked the election to Parliament, but though the opposition triumphed, Eyadéma remained in power.

Eyadéma consolidated his power through manipulated elections and through changing the constitution. When he died in 2005, many Togolese gained new hope. The Roman Catholic Church, the Methodists, and the EEPT, with their ecumenical partners, advocated for democracy and the retention of human rights publicly and in conversation with responsible politicians. Unfortunately, these efforts were in vain. Following apparently falsified elections, human rights suffered severely, and there was mass flight from the country. Eyadéma's son, Faure Gnassingbé, became the new president.

5. Islam
Approximately one million Muslims (→ Islam), mainly → Sunnis (→ Sunna) of the Malikite rite, are found among the Kotokoli, Bassari, Chakosi, and Fulbe tribes. The first → mosque was built at Sokodé in 1820. In 1973 the Union Musulmane du Togo was founded. Helped by aid from Libya and Egypt, it builds mosques and qur'anic schools.

6. Traditional Religion
→ Nature religions are widespread in Togo, claiming about 1.5 million members. Many of these religions claim *authenticité*. Various cults gather around leader figures (esp. prophetesses and those in the media), particularly in Lomé and the surrounding districts. Belief in a creator God (called Mawu in Ewe, Eso in Kabye) is accepted by many Christians, along with generally traditional lifestyles.
→ African Theology

Bibliography: D. B. BARRETT, G. T. KURIAN, and T. M. JOHNSON, *WCE* (2d ed.) 1.739-42 • H. W. DEBRUNNER, *A Church between Colonial Powers: A Study of the Church in Togo* (London, 1965) • G. L. JONES, "Training Leaders concerning Spiritual Issues for the Growth of the Church in Togo, West Africa" (Diss., Fuller Theological Seminary, 1993) • B. MEYER, "Christianity and the Ewe Nation: German Pietist Missionaries, Ewe Converts, and the Politics of Culture," *JRA* 32/2 (2002) 167-99 • P. NUGENT, *Smugglers, Secessionists, and Loyal Citizens on the Ghana-Togo Frontier: The Life of the Borderlands since 1914* (Athens, Ohio, 2002) • E. SCHÖCK-QUINTEROS and D. LENZ, eds., *150 Years of North German Mission* (Bremen, 1989) • S. SIDZA, "Islam in Togo," *BICMR* 7 (1989) 1-26 • E. VIERING, *Togo singt ein neues Lied* (Erlangen, 1969).

ERICH VIERING

Tolerance

1. Term
2. Political Tolerance
3. Religious Tolerance

1. Term
Tolerance is, according to its literal sense, "bearing" (Lat. *tolero,* "carry, bear, tolerate"). At a first level, this means to accept others, including something that is different. On a secondary level, there is the added point of seeing the existence of others as valid, as well as their special features within defined arrangements, without being significantly concerned about, or striving for, integration. In a further step, others — strangers — are accepted, along with their particularities. Finally, one consciously encounters others with a readiness and expectation to be enriched by them and their differentness.

Extreme, "pure," unlimited tolerance can, however, be unconsciously transformed into the opposite insofar as it allows everyone and everything to be valid without distinction — even intolerance. If all differences are equally valid, then nothing is really endured any longer. Unlimited tolerance is more than a structured society that engages in vital differences of opinion can stand. It becomes a repressive tolerance that suppresses the search for → truth.

2. Political Tolerance
Unlike the idea of tolerance in the personal sense, with its various levels of realization, the term "tolerance" in the political realm has achieved a clear profile in determining the relation between the state and religious communities (→ Church and State). Here it means accepting basically different opinions or convictions in the framework of a legally secured coexistence. Those who are different are "borne with" as long as they can be "endured" and insofar as they do not permanently disturb society. Toler-

ance becomes a documented legal right that can also be sued for under law. For the sake of the higher, mostly political, interests of the state, a juxtaposition or a cooperation may be granted within a limited scope (e.g., the English Toleration Act, passed in 1689, granting freedom of worship to → Dissenters). Only in this sense can the term be rather precisely used, in meeting the problems and opportunities of coexistence with the help of historical experiences.

2.1. Imperial Rome offers us a classic example (→ Roman Empire). Subjugated peoples and foreign religions (often the same thing) were tolerated insofar as they could fit into the state and its relatively flexible religious structure. The state was able to allow differing subordinate cults because its unity appeared to be sanctioned in the person of its ruler, while republican structures were suppressed. While Jews and Christians rejected the cult of the emperor, they came into conflict with a tolerance that they must have seen as hostile to their faith. The more a state is bound to one religion in order to attain political consolidation (e.g., Japanese Shinto as a state religion), the more it tends to be intolerant of all who are different.

2.2. In Europe tolerance was politically recognized during the time of the → Enlightenment, again, however, often at the price of the state taking on absolutistic characteristics (→ State 2). In this case the unity embodied in the person of the ruler could accept no rival. Under this structure, faith communities that previously had lesser rights now received attested rights (e.g., the *Toleranzpatent* of the Austrian emperor Joseph II in 1781).

Tolerance, which was the force behind the U.S. Constitution of 1787, had still other roots. North America was the promised land of tolerance for all those who had fled from intolerant Europe on religious or political grounds. The demand for tolerance in the Declaration of Independence was linked to a nominal separation of church and state and the rejection of the Anglican state church of the former colonial rulers, or of other established churches. The later history of the United States shows how precarious the equilibrium has remained between the democratic rationale and tolerance, for in order to grant far-reaching tolerance, the state has taken on secondary religious characteristics (→ Civil Religion). However, functions of the state such as education and the legal system are endangered if tolerance means that all the various ways of life, all kinds of liberation movements (including → terrorism), and global conformism are seen to be of equal value.

These days, Islamic critics of Western civilization reject tolerance that thinks of values in relative terms only. They especially regard boundless freedom of speech as often offending their moral principles.

2.3. The democratic constitutional state (→ Democracy), which rests upon tolerance, can grant it only to those who acknowledge the principles and rules of interaction of the state. It must oppose every totalitarian claim (→ Totalitarianism). Unrestricted → pluralism jeopardizes tolerance too. Under the guise of tolerance, intolerance intervenes, demanding that each and all should be recognized under the pressure to treat all equally (→ Equality). The demand for tolerance thus cannot be unlimited and unconditional, otherwise it would have to cancel itself out. Tolerance may tolerate no intolerance. The same is true also for the position of a religious community within a state and in relation to it (→ Religious Liberty). Rigorous → fundamentalism that seeks to impose its own values is hard to reconcile with democratic principles (→ Rights).

3. Religious Tolerance

As regards religious tolerance, we must distinguish between the religious sources of tolerance and the practice of tolerance of a → religion, both inwardly and outwardly.

3.1. How far a religion is ready for tolerance, or accepts it as a duty, will in fact depend on the binding character of its statements. If the religion has to do essentially with guidance for living (e.g., → Buddhism, → Hinduism, Christian ethics), then hardly any claims arise on the clarification of more comprehensive convictions, which makes tolerance easier. The relativity of the human capacity for knowledge (Voltaire, G. E. Lessing), emphasized in → humanism and the Enlightenment, also led to tolerance, to a respect of the → conscience as the site of moral decisions, whose ultimate basis is unfathomable and thus could not be regulated, certainly not religiously. The efforts toward → peace and the overcoming of religious disputes (→ Dialogue 2; Confessions 2) also encouraged a readiness for tolerance for the benefit of religious nonconformists (Nicholas of Cusa, J. Kepler).

Martin → Luther (1483-1546; → Luther's Theology) thought differently. The only basis of tolerance is that, when missing the tolerance of God, all human lives would break under the weight of their own guilt. Trust in God's tolerant mercy is rooted in the assurance of → faith and thus is not at human disposal. Although → love cannot be separated from faith, being the fruit of this trust, it cannot be generous enough. Christian tolerance thus belongs to love, not to faith. Under this understanding, the scope of tolerance is significantly broadened, but not at the expense of avoiding conflicts of faith. Love of the → neighbor cannot involve tolerance that is mere acceptance of those who think differently or who are ready for → compromise at any cost. It brings all coexistence and interaction under God's judgment.

3.2. Religions that emphasize orthodoxy and test it by some obligatory interpretation of their sacred texts or their doctrine are often considered to be intolerant because they seem to espouse an exclusive claim to truth: The god whom they worship is the only God for all. The binding commandment for Jews (→ Judaism), Christians, and Muslims (→ Islam) to serve no other gods than the one God (Exod. 20:3; → Monotheism) allows for no tolerance of other gods. But intolerance toward others can be required only if they distort or contend against the true worship of God.

It is said in Acts 4:12 that → salvation may be found only in Jesus Christ, but this exclusive confession of Christ as Savior is put forward by way of invitation, not exclusion (→ Mission; Dialogue 2; Salvation 7.4; Theology of Religions). The universality of the God who is proclaimed does stand in tension with the limited number of those who believe in him. If we fail to endure this tension, intolerance results. The reason for the tension is grounded, as Christians see it, in the way God is hidden in what he does (→ God 7.2). His acts far exceed all boundaries of human acceptance or rejection.

3.3. Judaism, Christianity, and Islam know well the command for tolerance toward the alien (→ Xenophobia), yet they interpret it differently, which is often dependent on the political conditions under which tolerance will be practiced. Christianity, after it had struggled for and achieved tolerance with the Edict of Milan (313), did not always grant this tolerance to other religions and persecuted digressions from its own orthodoxy (→ Inquisition). Within Islam, Jews and Christians experience tolerance theoretically as second-class believers. Religious tolerance in the State of → Israel (§2) is limited with regard to Jewish Christians.

Bibliography: A. G. Fiala, *Tolerance and the Ethical Life* (New York, 2005) • Y. Friedmann, *Tolerance and Coercion in Islam: Interfaith Relations in the Muslim Tradition* (New York, 2003) • G. G. Ghantous, *Tolerance, Religious Brotherhood, and Freedom: Resolving Disputes according to the Holy Scriptures; The OT, the NT, the Koran, Prophetic Teachings, Court Rulings, Tribal Reconciliation, Cultural Tales, Issues and Comments, Meetings and Contacts with Religious, Social, and Political Figures* (Jerusalem, 2004) • H. R. Guggisberg, *Religiöse Toleranz* (Stuttgart–Bad Cannstatt, 1984) • B. Häring, *Tolerance: Towards an Ethic of Solidarity and Peace* (New York, 1995) • B. Lobet, *Tolérance et vérité* (Paris, 1993) • S. B. Lubarsky, *Tolerance and Transformation: Jewish Approaches to Religious Pluralism* (Cincinnati, 1990) • H. Lutz, ed., *Zur Geschichte der Toleranz und Religionsfreiheit* (Darmstadt, 1977) • G. Mensching, *Tolerance and Truth in Religion* (University, Ala., 1971) • T. Rendtorff, ed., *Glaube und Toleranz. Das theologische Erbe der Aufklärung* (Gütersloh, 1982) • P.-A. Stucki, *Tolérance et doctrine* (Lausanne, 1973) • R. P. Wolff, B. Moore, and H. Marcuse, *A Critique of Pure Tolerance* (Boston, 1965).

Gerhard Sauter

Tongues, Gift of → Glossolalia

Tonsure

Tonsure (Lat. *tondeo,* "shave, shear") is the cutting of the hair as a sign of → penitence, → grief, or subjection. It occurs both before Christianity and outside it. Monks (→ Monasticism) are characterized by tonsure, as were secular → priests (§3) and other clergy. The ceremony of tonsure became part of admission to the clergy under → Gregory the Great (590-604; → Clergy and Laity). During the High Middle Ages the different styles of tonsure for monks and clergy became interchangeable.

In the → Roman Catholic Church candidates for the clergy (bishops, priests, deacons) no longer have to receive the tonsure (after 1972) but are accepted by the → bishop in a ceremony of reception. The older monastic orders in the various churches of the West still retain a form of tonsure (→ Religious Orders and Congregations). In the → Orthodox Church tonsure is required for clergy at their first ordination.

Three types of tonsure have been used: the Eastern (shaving the whole head), the Western (shaving the crown, with a fringe symbolizing the crown of thorns), and the Celtic (shaving the hair in front, from ear to ear).

Bibliography: A. A. Häussling, "Tonsur," *LTK* 10.250-51 • R. Mills, "The Signification of the Tonsure," *Holiness and Masculinity in Medieval Europe* (ed. P. H. Cullum and K. J. Lewis; Cardiff, 2004) chap. 8 • T. J. Riley, "Tonsure," *NCE* (2d ed.) 14.110.

Thaddeus A. Schnitker

Torah

"Torah" (*tôrâ*, pl. *tôrôt*) derives from Heb. *yrh, hôrâ,* "show, direct, instruct." In a more general sense it means "teaching"; in a narrower sense, → "law." It can denote either a single instruction, as in Lev. 6:9, 14 (MT: 6:2, 7), or more generally a collection of commands. Only in the latter sense can a specific group such as the → Decalogue be considered as a Torah, although it is not exclusively called by this word. "Torah" further denotes the → Pentateuch (*ḥummāš),* the five books of Moses, whose unfortunate Greek and Latin renderings (*nomos* and *lex*), however, are inappropriate insofar as Genesis, for example, can hardly be characterized as law. In later times, "Torah" was used for Prophets and Writings — that is, for the whole Hebrew Bible. The → Wisdom literature identifies Torah with preexistent (Prov. 8:22-31) wisdom (*ḥokmâ;* Sir. 24:1-12, 23-34).

Rabbinic → Judaism (→ Rabbi, Rabbinism) regarded the Torah, which was created before the creation of the world, as a blueprint of creation used in its construction (*Gen. Rab.* 1:1; *m. 'Abot* 3:14). It is thus constitutive to its existence (*m. 'Abot* 1:2; *b. Pesaḥ.* 68b), and its observation is a sine qua non for the consummation of all history in messianic times. While the preexistence of the Torah was contested by several medieval Jewish philosophers (→ Jewish Philosophy), the → cabalists accepted it as fundamental and integrated it into their systems. For example, some of them equated the primal Torah with the second *sefira,* the emanation of divine wisdom. When read as a connected series of alphabetic letters, rather than according to the existing word divisions, thought to represent the world of history and the commandments, the text of the Torah could also be conceived as the actual mysterious, ineffable, and inexpressible name of God. According to one form of eastern European → Hasidism, the Torah, prior to creation, was only a chaotic conglomerate of letters, which were combined into meaningful sequences recounting each historical event only as that event unfolded.

Since the divinely willed fulfillment of the statutes and commands in the Torah can be achieved only by its divinely legitimated adaptation to changing circumstances, early rabbinic Judaism conceived of a twofold Torah, written and oral, with the latter a commentary on the former. This concept has been quintessential to almost all trends within Judaism for centuries and, to some extent, up to the present day. It rests on a literalist reading of the dichotomy in Exod. 34:27, where Moses is told to write down these words (the written Torah), for in accordance with them ("on the mouth of these words," the oral Torah) God has made a covenant with Israel (*b. Giṭ.* 60b). Both forms of the Torah, then, were revealed by God at → Sinai, and both have become Israel's responsibility. Indeed, at times the oral Torah could be regarded as more important, for in the last resort the written Torah could be lived only by means of the oral as it found development in the tradition formed by judges and scholars in rabbinic literature. Originally, perhaps, the twofold Torah related primarily to the field of → Halakah, but it was later taken up by the rationalistic thinking of the philosophers and the mystical and esoteric speculations of the cabalists. At all times, then, we find a highly dynamic understanding of the Torah. Though given once and for all, the Torah finds endless meanings as it is adapted to the living conditions of history.

→ Jewish Theology

Bibliography: Sources: The Chumash: The Torah; Haftaros and Five Megillos, with a Commentary Anthologized from the Rabbinic Writings (11th ed.; ed. N. Scherman; Brooklyn, N.Y., 2000) • *The Contemporary Torah: A Gender-Sensitive Adaptation of the JPS Translation* (ed. D. E. S. Stein; Philadelphia, 2006) • *The Metsudah Chumash/Rashi: A New Linear Translation* (trans. A. Davis; 5 vols.; Hoboken, N.J., 1994-97) • *Midrash Bereshit Rabba: Critical Edition with Notes and Commentary* (ed. J. Theodor and C. Albeck; Jerusalem, 1996; orig. pub., 1903).

Secondary works: S. CARMY, ed., *Modern Scholarship in the Study of Torah* (Northvale, N.J., 1996) • J. MAIER, "Torah and Pentateuch," *Biblische und judaistische Studien* (ed. A. Vivian; Frankfurt, 1990) 1-54 • M. J. MULDER, ed., *Mikra: Text, Translation, Reading, and Interpretation of the Hebrew Bible in Ancient Judaism and Early Christianity* (Peabody, Mass., 2004; orig. pub., 1988) • J. NEUSNER, *The Oral Torah: The Sacred Books of Judaism* (Atlanta, 1991); idem, *Torah: From Scroll to Symbol in Formative Judaism* (Atlanta, 1988) • L. I. RABINOWITZ and W. HARVEY, "Torah," *EncJud* 15 (1973) 1235-46 • S. SAFRAI, ed., *The Literature of the Sages,* pt. 1, *Oral Tora, Halakha, Mishna, Tosefta, Talmud, External Tractates* (Philadelphia, 1987) 35-119 • G. SCHOLEM, "The Meaning of the Torah in Jewish Mysticism," *Essential Papers on Kabbalah* (ed. L. Fine; New York, 1995) 179-211.

MARGARETE SCHLÜTER

Torture

It is difficult to give a single definition of torture, since people are so different as regards threshold of pain, psychological makeup, and social and cultural conditioning. Nevertheless, certain essential features of torture are part of any definition: (1) it always involves at least two persons, one of whom is in the physical power of the other; (2) it involves acute pain or anguish, physical, mental, or spiritual; (3) its aim is to subdue and break the victim; (4) it is a systematic action with a rational purpose; and (5) it is done by, or at the command of, an official of the state.

1. After a long history of torture, in all nations and cultures, and after many attempts to justify its use, the view has now established itself that torture cannot be justified and is thus to be renounced without exception. The Universal Declaration of Human → Rights (1948) makes this point in its article 5, which states that "no one shall be subjected to torture or to cruel, inhumane, or degrading treatment or punishment."

On December 9, 1975, the General Assembly of the United Nations adopted the Declaration on the Protection of All Persons from Being Subjected to Torture and Other Cruel, Inhuman, or Degrading Treatment or Punishment. In its first article, it defined torture as "any act by which severe pain or suffering, whether physical or mental, is intentionally inflicted by or at the instigation of a public official on a person for such purposes as obtaining from him or a third person information or confession, punishing him for an act he has committed or is suspected of having committed, or intimidating him or other persons. It does not include pain or suffering arising only from, inherent in or incidental to, lawful sanctions to the extent consistent with the Standard Minimum Rules for the Treatment of Prisoners." In addition, "torture constitutes an aggravated and deliberate form of cruel, inhuman or degrading treatment or punishment."

Despite this total prohibition and general evaluation of torture, it is still practiced in most countries. → Amnesty International (AI) reported that, from the beginning of 1997 to mid-2000, state officials in more than 150 countries allegedly used torture. In about half of these nations, reports of torture were widespread or persistent. AI has alleged that in order to conceal torture, more subtle forms are now used that are designed to make proof impossible. With scientific help, psychological torture has been developed, which uses psychological and psychopharmacological treatment, deprivation techniques, communication techniques, interview techniques, and conditioning techniques. Perversely, some scientists speak about "cleaner" torture.

The psychology of torture has concluded that acts of torture are by no means manifestations of abnormal character traits of psychopathic personalities. Tests have shown that several social factors play a part in predisposing persons to practice torture: subservience to people in → authority, use of excessive punishment, the repression of nonmoral impulses, prejudices and intolerance (→ Tolerance) toward → minorities, strict conformity to group norms, and a tendency to depersonalize relationships.

On December 12, 1984, the United Nations unanimously adopted the Convention against Torture and Other Cruel, Inhuman, or Degrading Treatment or Punishment," which 152 countries had signed or ratified as of 2006. The convention represents a compromise between different views of torture and punishment (e.g., the Islamic and Christian). Since recognized mechanisms to enforce it are not contemplated, it will do little to do away with torture.

In 1987 the Council of Europe adopted a parallel European Convention for the Prevention of Torture, which has practical measures in view. At their heart is an independent delegation that has the authority to pay periodic visits to all places where people are for any reason held in captivity — for example, prisons, police posts, courts, and institutions in which there is internment for medical or educational reasons. Such a system of visitation means that no torture could be inflicted with the certainty of going undetected. Along similar lines AI has a 12-point program for the prevention of torture and calls upon all governments to enforce it.

2. On into the later Middle Ages the Christian churches both justified and promoted torture. It played a prominent part in the trials of witches and heretics (→ Inquisition; Witchcraft 2). But it was then officially proscribed and abolished in the age of the → Enlightenment.

Today Christian → theology is of the opinion that, in view of the torture and death that Jesus suffered on the cross, no one should be subjected to torture. Christian → ethics repudiates and condemns every form of torture. In the future it is important that the Christian churches play an active part in the formation of public opinion with a view to strengthening the will of politicians to do away with torture.

→ Force, Violence, Nonviolence; Human Dignity

Bibliography: AMNESTY INTERNATIONAL, *Stopping the Torture Trade* (New York, 2001); idem, *Torture Worldwide: An Affront to Human Dignity* (New York, 2000) • A. BOULESBAA, *The U.N. Convention on Torture and the*

Prospects for Enforcement (The Hague, 1999) • M. D. Evans and R. Morgan, *Preventing Torture: A Study of the European Convention for the Prevention of Torture and Inhuman or Degrading Treatment or Punishment* (New York, 1998) • H. Frenz, "Nur zaghaft gegen Folter," *dü* 1 (1986) • J. K. Harbury, *Truth, Torture, and the American Way: The History and Consequences of U.S. Involvement in Torture* (Boston, 2005) • C. Ingelse, *The U.N. Committee against Torture: An Assessment* (Boston, 2001) • M. B. Merback, *The Thief, the Cross, and the Wheel: Pain and the Spectacle of Punishment in Medieval and Renaissance Europe* (Chicago, 1999) • J. Perry, *Torture: Religious Ethics and National Security* (Maryknoll, N.Y., 2005).

Helmut Frenz

Totalitarianism

1. Term
2. Antitotalitarianism in the 1930s
3. The Cold War and the Scholarship of Totalitarianism
4. Totalitarianism and the Christian Church
5. Totalitarianism after 1989

1. Term

The term "totalitarianism" has been used by politicians and intellectuals to label and analyze the ideological dictatorships of the 20th century, in particular Nazi Germany and the Soviet Union under Josef Stalin (1879-1953). Applied normatively and descriptively, "totalitarianism" denotes the monopoly of power by a single, revolutionary party that advocates the transformation of society (→ Revolution), politicizes every sphere of life, delineates internal and external enemies, and compels obedience through the use of terror (→ Terrorism). A regime is totalitarian, therefore, in its program for the total remaking of → state, → society, and → culture; its demands for total loyalty; and its attempts at the total domination of its citizens.

The word "totalitarianism" originated in the 1920s among opponents of Italian → Fascism, who applied the concept *sistema totalitaria* to Mussolini's (1883-1945) attempts at unrestricted political power, as well as to the ambitions of the Fascist movement for social, cultural, and moral change. The Fascists themselves soon appropriated the term. They interpreted totalitarianism, in contrast to parliamentary → democracy, as a vigorous political program: a dynamic union of party, state, and society that would achieve the total transformation of Italy. Supporters of the Nazi party in Germany also adopted the term to express their aim of the total state *(der totale Staat),* although party ideologues insisted that Nazism was not comparable to movements in other nations.

2. Antitotalitarianism in the 1930s

In the 1930s intellectuals fleeing Nazi-ruled Germany introduced the concept of totalitarianism to England and the United States. Initially, neo-Marxist academics such as Theodor Adorno (1903-69) and Herbert Marcuse (1898-1979) applied the term only to Germany and Italy, arguing that similarities between Nazi and Fascist totalitarianism indicated fundamental problems in European politics, liberal → capitalism, and bourgeois culture. By the late 1930s, other intellectuals on the political Left began comparing the Soviet Union to Germany and Italy under the rubric of totalitarianism. Two of the most notable literary critics of totalitarianism — Arthur Koestler (1905-83) and George Orwell (1903-50) — were supporters of → socialism who saw Stalin's rule as similar to Hitler's (1889-1945). Koestler's novel *Darkness at Noon* (1940) was a direct condemnation of the Stalinist terror, while Orwell's *Nineteen Eighty-Four* (1949) was a universal warning of a totalitarian future. The novel reflected Orwell's fear that totalitarianism threatened to take hold around the world after World War II.

In addition to critics on the Left, advocates of political and economic → liberalism, many of whom were also émigrés from Nazi-ruled Europe, applied "totalitarianism" to the dictatorships of Europe. Management expert Peter F. Drucker (1909-2005), economist Friedrich Hayek (1899-1992), sociologist Raymond Aron (1905-83), and philosophers Eric Voegelin (1901-85) and Karl Popper (1902-94) offered studies of the economic, social, and psychological roots of the totalitarian movements. Particularly provocative were the analyses of Hayek, who excoriated any economic planning as the first step toward totalitarian rule, and of Popper, who condemned Plato as the original proponent of the utopian, collectivist state as opposed to the "open society."

3. The Cold War and the Scholarship of Totalitarianism

World War II brought a tempering of rhetoric associating the Soviet Union with Nazi Germany, but with the opening of the cold war, American and British policymakers openly branded the Soviet state as totalitarian. In his 1946 "Iron Curtain" speech, Winston Churchill (1874-1965) warned of totalitarian rule in Eastern Europe, and President

Harry Truman (1945-53) declared in 1947 that U.S. foreign policy was aimed at the defense of "free peoples" against "totalitarian regimes." To better understand and combat the totalitarian threat, American scholars undertook comparative historical and social scientific studies of Soviet Russia, Nazi Germany, and Fascist Italy, as well as the newly Communist states of Eastern Europe and China. Political scientists Carl D. Friedrich (1901-84) and Zbigniew Brzezinski held that communist and fascist forms of totalitarianism were similar in their basic features: an → ideology offering a vision of a new society, a single mass party led by one man, a system of terror effected through party discipline and secret police, party-state monopoly over mass communications (→ Mass Media) and the use of force, and central control of the economy. Friedrich and Brzezinski drew comparisons to other dictatorships of the time, such as Franco's (1892-1975) Spain and despotic governments of the past, but they maintained that totalitarian regimes, owing to the characteristics above, along with their use of technology in exerting control and their democratic pretensions, were novel developments.

The most respected academic study of totalitarianism published in the 1950s remains *Origins of Totalitarianism* (1951) by Hannah Arendt (1906-75). Although critics then and now fault the empirical substance of her comparative study, Arendt's interpretations of the psychological, sociological, and cultural roots of totalitarian movements were novel and insightful: the atomization of society as a precondition for building mass movements; the scientific claims of the party, which are later twisted into emotional myths; and the confusing shapelessness of the actual governing system. More than a scholarly analysis, Arendt's book was an unequivocal moral statement about the threat of totalitarian regimes: "The totalitarian attempt at global conquest and total domination has been the destructive way out of all impasses. Its victory may coincide with the destruction of humanity; wherever it has ruled, it has begun to destroy the essence of man" (viii). The culmination of totalitarian rule was the concentration camp, where these regimes were able to exercise total and dehumanizing domination over the individual.

In the 1960s the rhetoric of totalitarianism declined. The period of détente brought an easing of anti-Soviet propaganda. Meanwhile, scholars studying the Soviet Union and Eastern European Communist states discovered far greater complexity in party leadership, bureaucratic behavior, and state-society relations than totalitarian theories of the 1950s would suggest, even in the Soviet Union under Stalin. At the same time, scholars of Nazi Germany on both sides of the Atlantic offered similar revisions, describing the system of the Third Reich as "polycratic," not autocratic.

While scholars of Germany and the Communist states debated the appropriateness of the totalitarian model, intellectuals living in (or exiled from) the Soviet Union and Eastern Europe used the term to characterize their societies. Russian Nobel Prize–winners Aleksandr Solzhenitsyn (b. 1918) and Andrei Sakharov (1921-89), exiled Polish poet Czesław Miłosz (1911-2004) and philosopher Leszek Kołakowski, and Yugoslav dissident Milovan Djilas (1911-95) described the Communist regimes, even in the post-Stalin period, as totalitarian in their centralization of → power and suppression of individual freedoms.

In post-Mao China as well, dissident Wei Jingsheng has warned against totalitarian power. And Czech playwright Václav Havel, in "The Power of the Powerless" (1978), described the later development of the Communist states as "posttotalitarian." The prefix "post-" did not suggest that the system was no longer totalitarian; instead, it was totalitarianism made routine, a governing system built on lies, rather than a leader's charisma or revolutionary ideology. Havel's contribution to dissident thought was his emphasis on the moral corruption resulting from the system's pervasive lies and his call for resistance by "living in truth."

The testimony of dissidents, particularly Solzhenitsyn's *Gulag Archipelago,* published in the West in 1973, prompted some Western European and American intellectuals to readopt the language of antitotalitarianism. With increased tensions between the Soviets and the West in the early 1980s, the term also reappeared in political rhetoric. President Ronald Reagan (1981-89) described the Soviet Union as a totalitarian state and, famously, as "an evil empire." His foreign policy revived another feature of 1950s thinking: the distinction between totalitarian Communism and authoritarian states. Reagan's ambassador to the United Nations, Jeane Kirkpatrick, argued that personal dictatorships and military regimes allowed for the existence of markets and traditional social classes, as well as demonstrating the potential for reform, something Communism was unable to do. The distinction was significant, as it allowed the Reagan administration to take an assertive policy against the perceived Communist threat by providing military and financial support to illiberal regimes in Asia, Africa, and Latin America.

4. Totalitarianism and the Christian Church

The responses of church leaders and individual Christians to the totalitarian regimes varied from open support and pragmatic accommodation to distrust and dissent. In Fascist Italy, Catholic politicians recognized Mussolini's designs for political and social control, but church hierarchs, including Pope Pius XI (1922-39), initially were supportive of the government. For Mussolini, and later Hitler, the → Roman Catholic Church was a serious obstacle; Catholic schools, trade unions, and other organizations were potentially troublesome units outside the power of the "total state." When both dictators moved against these institutions in the 1930s, Pius XI denounced the regimes' accumulation of power and assaults against the church. His encyclical *Mit brennender Sorge* (1937) delivered a direct theological response to totalitarian rule: "Whoever exalts race, or the people, or the State, or a particular form of State, or the depositories of power, or any other fundamental value of the human community . . . above their standard value and divinizes them to an idolatrous level, distorts and perverts an order of the world planned and created by God" (§8).

European Protestants, notably Karl → Barth (1886-1968) and Paul → Tillich (1886-1965), also denounced the idolatry of state and leader at the center of totalitarianism. In Germany, however, Protestants were deeply divided, with two minority movements — the pro-Nazi → "German Christians" and the → Confessing Church, which included supporters and opponents of the government — competing for authority in the institutional church. Nazi leaders successfully used rhetoric of moral regeneration and anti-Communism (and sometimes even explicitly Christian language) to gain support from Protestants. Dietrich → Bonhoeffer (1906-45) offers a singular example of a heroic stance against the Nazis, yet even his writings offer no theological dissection of the totalitarian state or a direct, developed argument for resistance.

Whereas the Nazi movement envisioned a "positive Christianity" that would integrate church and nation, the Soviet Union and, after 1948, the Communist states of Eastern Europe proposed an avowedly atheist program. Nevertheless, the Communist party-states did allow for the functioning of churches, with varying degrees of state intervention and repression. Under Stalin's rule, the → Russian Orthodox Church was brought to the threshold of extinction before the German invasion of 1941 inspired a nationalist alliance of church and state. In Eastern Europe, Czechoslovakia and Romania were most aggressive in imprisoning clergy and confis-

cating church property. In Poland and Yugoslavia, in contrast, the Catholic Church maintained an active role in society.

In the early years of the cold war, the trial of Hungarian primate József Mindszenty (1892-1975) galvanized Western Christian opinion against Communism. Some Christians living under Communist rule, however, found theological justification for their cooperation in the building of socialism. But by the 1970s and 1980s, when Communism was morally bankrupt and stagnant, Christians took important roles in opposition movements in Poland, Czechoslovakia, East Germany, and Romania, building networks that ultimately broke the power of the regimes in 1989.

5. Totalitarianism after 1989

The collapse of the Soviet bloc in 1989-91 has not brought the end of totalitarianism. Although specialists of Nazi and Soviet history still debate the term, historians acknowledge the parallels between the revolutionary dictatorships and their long shadow over the 20th century. The academic journal *Totalitarian Movements and Political Religions* began publication in 2000 in order to study totalitarianism in the last century and the present.

A common question today is whether Islamist terrorist movements can be viewed as totalitarian (→ Islam). Some commentators, Left and Right, have already applied the term, citing the Islamists' disregard of individual → rights, hostility to free expression, and "cult of death." But the importance of the term today is not so much in what it denotes as what it connotes: the most violent and repressive regimes of the 20th century, regimes that were opposed by the full resources of the Western democracies. It is therefore implied that the only proper response to totalitarianism today must likewise be condemnation and opposition.

Bibliography: H. Arendt, *The Origins of Totalitarianism* (New York, 1951) • P. Berman, *Terror and Liberalism* (New York, 2003) • C. J. Friedrich and Z. Brzezinski, *Totalitarian Dictatorship and Autocracy* (Cambridge, Mass., 1956) • E. Gentile, "The Sacralization of Politics: Definitions, Interpretations, and Reflections on the Question of Secular Religion and Totalitarianism," *TMPR* 1 (2000) 18-55 • A. Gleason, *Totalitarianism: The Inner History of the Cold War* (Oxford, 1995) • F. A. Hayek, *The Road to Serfdom* (London, 1944) • I. Kershaw and M. Lewin, eds., *Stalinism and Nazism: Dictatorships in Comparison* (Cambridge, 1997) • J. J. Linz, *Totalitarian and Authoritarian Regimes* (London, 2000) • H. Maier and M. Schäfer, eds., *Totalitarismus und politische Religionen. Konzepte des Diktaturvergleichs* (3 vols.; Paderborn, 1996-2003) • R. J. OVERY, *The Dictators: Hitler's Germany and Stalin's Russia* (London, 1994) • S. PAYNE, *A History of Fascism: 1914-1945* (Madison, Wis., 1995) • K. POPPER, *The Open Society and Its Enemies* (London, 1945) • L. SCHAPIRO, *Totalitarianism* (London, 1972).

BRUCE R. BERGLUND

Totemism

Totemism was a scientific illusion that long dominated → ethnology until C. Lévi-Strauss (b. 1908) finally disproved it in 1962. The idea derived from the word *ototeman* in the Algonquin languages of North America and was given academic status by J F. McLennan (1827-81) in 1869. In 1910 J. G. Frazer (1854-1941) gave it wider currency. Three elements summarize totemism: (1) unilineal descent groups (clans); (2) emblems (totems) such as animals, plants, and, more rarely, other natural phenomena such as wind, the four points of the compass, or everyday objects; and (3) the concept of a relationship between the totem and the members of the group. Also in 1910 A. Goldenweiser (1880-1940) denied the existence of totemism as a unified phenomenon, seeing only a collection of individual features. But the international journal *Anthropos* entitled its volume 9 (1914) *Problem des Totemismus,* and the word "totemism" achieved academic status on a larger scale.

J. G. Frazer abandoned his earlier view of a religious relationship between people and totems in favor of a sociological relationship. É. Durkheim (1858-1917) did not find any cult of → animals but thought the totem marked off sacred territory. Ethnology at the time believed that → society as a whole was integrated into clans and that totems symbolized a coordinated system of relationships. This collective → representation (§2) was more important than the relation between the individual totem and the related clan members. The so-called *individual* totem, or individual relationship between the person and the totem that implied the special protection of the totem genre, was regarded by Durkheim as a secondary appearance; he regarded the totem of the sexes (or *sex* totem) as the connection between the individual totem and the *clan* totem. Independently of the evolutionary views of the day (→ Evolution), he regarded the symbolic character (→ Symbol) of the totem as decisive. The sober secular world was divided off from the ecstatic sacred world as two separate domains. The latter would be expressed among Australians during the so-called rites of procreation *(intichuma),* when the group members came together for mimetic → dances and consumed a totem animal.

The Australian ethnologist A. P. Elkin (1891-1979), however, pointed out that the term "totemism" covers many heterogeneous forms. He tried to save many different kinds of totemism — for example, dream totemism, in which the protective nature of dreams plays an important role for individuals. In 1929 A. R. Radcliffe-Brown (1881-1955) used functionalism in favor of this interpretation, giving specific value to the type of animal chosen. In 1951, however, he made use of structuralism to show that the relations between the species mediate both similarities and differences, both friendship and conflict, so that the animal world is given the form of social relationships such as we find in human society. Such an interpretation depends upon our giving specific meanings to the totem categories. By means of a special nomenclature of animal and plant names, contrary principles would be joined together like formally separated groups that became a society through marriage relationships. Lévi-Strauss next demonstrated (1963) that the names did not refer to feared or admired or desired creatures; rather, they portrayed group relationships. Animals and plants served as totems not because they were "good to eat" but because they were "good to think."

What 19th-century scholars, in the guise of scientific objectivity outside of their own moral world, wanted to relegate to *nature,* to alleged *natural peoples,* was in reality the expression of the universal exercise of classification through the logic of opposites and interactions, as well as of inclusion and exclusion. What was observed as totemism were *culturally* constituted groups in a structure that made use of → categories borrowed from → nature in order to illustrate a closed and sensible whole. The artificial character of a totem was then demonstrated in the inversion that described reproduction: whereas natural species reproduce only internally, the totem group named after a species is regularly exogamous, or dependent upon others according to the rule of exogamous marriage.

Bibliography: É. DURKHEIM, *Les formes élémentaires de la vie religieuse. Le système totémique en Australie* (Paris, 1912; ET *The Elementary Forms of the Religious Life* [New York, 2001]) • A. P. ELKIN, "Studies in Australian Totemism: The Nature of Australian Totemism," *Oceania* 4 (1933/34) 113-31 • J. G. FRAZER, *Totemism and Exogamy* (4 vols.; London, 1910; repr., 1968) •

A. Goldenweiser, "Totemism, an Analytical Study," *JAF* 23 (1910) 179-293 • R. A. Jones, *The Secret of the Totem: Religion and Society from McLennan to Freud* (New York, 2005) • C. Lévi-Strauss, "The Bear and the Barber," *JRAI* 93 (1963) 1-11; idem, *Le totémisme aujourd'hui* (Paris, 1962; ET *Totemism* [Boston, 1963]) • J. F. McLennan, "The Worship of Animals and Plants," *Fortnightly Review* 6 (1869) 407-582 and 7 (1870) 194-216 • A. R. Radcliffe-Brown, "The Comparative Method in Social Anthropology," *JRAI* 81 (1951) 15-22; idem, "The Sociological Theory of Totemism" (1929), *Structure and Function in Primitive Society* (Glencoe, Ill., 1965) 117-32 • R. Wagner, "Totemism," *EncRel(E)* 14.573-76.

Georg Pfeffer

Tourism

1. Term
2. Growth and Forms
3. Issues

1. Term

Tourism comprises both the demand for tourist facilities and the supply of these facilities. On the demand side, according to the World Tourism Organization (WTO), tourism means leaving one's own locality for the purposes of relaxation, enjoyment, social or business activity, or other reasons, and doing so for a period of less than one calendar year. On the supply side, tourism implies the totality of services catering to tourist demand.

2. Growth and Forms

Worldwide, tourism (in terms of both numbers of tourist arrivals and volume of the tourist industries) has grown rapidly in the last 150 years as both Western and many non-Western societies have been modernized and industrialized (→ Industrial Society; Service Society). More → leisure, a higher standard of living, urbanization (→ City), increasing mobility, better means of travel, and increased horizons because of the new information technology (→ Mass Media) have all combined to open up many parts of the world to tourism.

A series of crises and disasters with worldwide repercussions since the late 1990s (notably the attacks of September 11, 2001, and the 2004 Asian tsunami) did not impede tourism growth but led to a reconsideration of growth as the norm. Sustainable → development has come to be a major preoccupation of both antitourism activists, local communi-

ties and governments of receiving countries, and the main actors in the tourism industry (e.g., WTO, Pacific Asia Travel Association, national tourism boards, airlines, tour companies, other industry stakeholders), leading to a steady development of new forms of tourism. They include ecotourism, special-interest tourism, nature-based tourism, community-based tourism, rural tourism, responsible tourism, soft tourism, educational tourism, heritage tourism, and solidarity tourism, all distinguished from mass tourism (M. Mowforth and I. Munt).

Tourism thus takes many forms. Being a consumer good, it has diversified to cater to rather diverse tastes and expectations. People travel on vacation, for cultural reasons, for health, for shopping, for sporting events, for conventions, for economic and business reasons, for religious and spiritual enhancement, for emotional and sexual satisfaction, and simply to see other countries (V. L. Smith, E. Cohen). Modern consumerism has also contributed to the transition from the essentially penitential purposes of the medieval pilgrimage to the rise of the varied spiritualities of contemporary religious tourism, the growing prominence of which contradicts popular notions of secularization (W. H. Swatos and L. Tomasi; → Consumption).

Up to the middle of the 20th century, travel was largely limited to the upper classes, but mass tourism in the 21st century includes all the social classes in industrialized countries (J. Dumazedier, D. MacCannell, J. Urry) and, to an increasing degree, the new middle classes in the newly industrializing countries (K. B. Ghimire). Tourism can no longer be organized within national boundaries but has become a transnational undertaking.

3. Issues

During the last few decades, more and more developing countries have discovered international tourism as an engine of economic growth (J. Brohman). The prospect of obtaining prosperity — by providing jobs, bringing in money, and leading to the development of the economy in peripheral fields — has enticed national governments to actively promote international tourism by taking a liberal stance toward tourism development and lifting legal restrictions on foreign investments.

While these policies have been successful in terms of an actual increase of international arrivals, resulting in resort-based mass tourism in many developing countries, tourism has not brought about the projected prosperity. International mass tourism has caused serious problems. Being organized and exploited by a foreign-based tourism industry, international tourism greatly benefits transnational corporations, whereas local people often pay a high price. Local communities may be dispossessed from their agricultural lands and relocated if they are seen as standing in the way of large tourism developers. For local people, the economic benefit of tourism is small, for the jobs created are mostly seasonal, and the jobs themselves demand few qualifications and are not well paid. The growth of the gross national product and foreign exchange, the creation of jobs, and the improvements that come in transportation and medical care can easily be negated by instability in the job market, by inflation, by the importing of Western consumer goods for tourists, and by the damaging of subsistence strategies. Tourism can also do harm to the → environment and threaten wildlife (→ Ecology). Yet it has also led to the creation of national parks and wilderness areas, to a heightened sense of the → environment, and to the protection of nature and plant and animal species.

Tourism goes hand in hand with political processes and is easily affected by political instability (L. K. Richter). Tourism is implicated in nation-building enterprises or political showcasing (H. Dahles). It may contribute to → democracy, but it may just as well work in favor of unjust relations and the suppression of ethnic and religious → minorities (M. Picard and R. E. Wood). Whether it can make a positive contribution to development depends largely on how stable a country is. Where tourism is not controlled, it creates social problems such as → prostitution and trafficking in women and children (through sex tourism), drug abuse, and health problems, of which HIV/AIDS may be the most alarming.

A central theme of academic research and writing in the field of tourism studies has been the relationship between cultural change and → identity. There is a strong interest in cultural and ethnic tourism and therefore in the impact of tourism on local communities, particularly issues having to do with their increasing "touristification" and the invention of traditions in response to the needs and interests of the tourist market. The most famous example may be the Kecak dance in Bali, which was designed only a few decades ago for tourism performances.

Views of globalization held in the 1990s contended that processes of global change would culminate in a world → culture in which traditional → societies lose their autonomy and cultural identity, threatening to become a homogeneous nexus of social forms that have been uprooted both spatially

and culturally. Recent writings, however, point out that ethnic identity is not fixed and bequeathed from the past but instead is constantly reinvented or symbolically constructed, and often contested (Picard and Wood). Processes of globalization interact with local agencies in generating the cultural diversities on which tourism thrives.

When a region is opened up for tourists, communal organizations should see to it that existing social, religious, and moral relations and practices remain intact. Tourism can help to overcome national and nationalistic → prejudices, but it must also work against the loss of identity that arises when commercial considerations affect tradition and culture. Tourists and tourist organizations must accept the fact that host communities are not passive recipients but a proactive force in the making of their own culture as a tourist product. Only along these lines can tourism help forward the lasting social, economic, ecological, and political development of a country and contribute to the growth of a truly multicultural society.

Bibliography: J. BROHMAN, "New Directions in Tourism for Third World Development," *Annals of Tourism Research* 23 (1996) 48-70 • E. COHEN, "The Sociology of Tourism," *ARSoc* 10 (1984) 373-92; idem, "Towards a Sociology of International Tourism," *SocRes* 39 (1972) 64-82 • H. DAHLES, *Tourism, Heritage, and National Culture in Java: Dilemmas of a Local Community* (Richmond, Surrey, 2001) • J. DUMAZEDIER, *Toward a Society of Leisure* (New York, 1967) • K. B. GHIMIRE, ed., *The Native Tourist: Mass Tourism within Developing Countries* (London, 2001) • D. HARRISON, ed., *Tourism and the Less Developed Countries* (New York, 1992) • D. MacCANNELL, *The Tourist: A New Theory of the Leisure Class* (3d ed.; Berkeley, Calif., 2000) • A. MATHIESON and G. WALL, *Tourism: Economic, Physical, and Social Impacts* (London, 1982) • M. MOWFORTH and I. MUNT, *Tourism and Sustainability: Development and New Tourism in the Third World* (London, 2004) • R. O'GRADY, *Third World Stopover: The Tourism Debate* (Geneva, 1981) • M. PICARD and R. E. WOOD, eds., *Tourism, Ethnicity, and the State in Asian and Pacific Societies* (Honolulu, 1997) • L. K. RICHTER, *The Politics of Tourism in Asia* (Honolulu, 1989) • V. L. SMITH, *Hosts and Guests: The Anthropology of Tourism* (Philadelphia, 1977) • W. H. SWATOS and L. TOMASI, *From Medieval Pilgrimage to Religious Tourism: The Social and Cultural Economics of Piety* (Westport, Conn., 2002) • J. URRY, *The Tourist Gaze: Leisure and Travel in Contemporary Societies* (London, 1990) • WORLD TOURISM ORGANIZATION, *Yearbook of Tourism Statistics, 1999-2003* (Madrid, 2005).

HEIDI DAHLES

Tradition

1. Society and Religion

From about 1960, tradition has been a much-discussed theme in → theology, in the → church, and in the humanities and social sciences. Its usual definition as the acts and process of handing down *(traditio)*, as well as what is handed down *(traditum)*, has developed in quite varied ways. Against a frequently narrow and negative understanding of the term, it is now emphasized that both individual life and social life always stand in a given tradition that maintains its → identity and continuity. Human historicity implies tradition. Tradition is the transgenerational process by which → society reproduces itself. It is a constitutive part of → culture and civilization.

In the sphere of the → religions, tradition may be maintained, changed, or discarded. It is kept alive by the transmission of → rites, → myths, → symbols, stories, doctrine, cult, and custom, but also by the Holy Scriptures and their exposition. As such, it is an essential element in all religion. It forms the basis of religious life and helps to shape it as it passes on from one generation to another.

2. The Old and the New Testaments

2.1. The books of the OT grew out of the varied oral traditions of divine → revelation given to earlier generations. → Exegesis (§1) has found many levels of tradition in the OT and many forms in which it has found expression. Traditions were kept alive by the cult, → law, → Wisdom literature, etiological tales, stories, and the sayings of the → prophets. They were tied to specific objects and places. They might be transferred (Israel's tradition adopted by Judah), altered (David connected with the Psalms), and related to new events (new interpretation of the exodus experience). But through the cultic creeds (Deut. 6:20-24; 25:5-9; Josh. 24:2-13) and, for example, the ritual of the → Passover (Deut. 6:20-25; 16:1-8) and other traditions, the revealing and saving work of God was handed down from past to present.

2.2. Tradition was constitutive also for primitive Christianity because it tied believers to the Christ-event, which revealed and communicated to them the → salvation of God. It was passed on and applied to them as the → kerygma, as the → gospel. The oral tradition of the sayings and history of → Jesus took written form through a complex process, and in this way the original content of the gospel was safeguarded. Various elements of tradition found their way into the NT writings. The received tradition of the gospel (1 Cor. 15:1-2) was handed down in confessional (1 Cor. 15:3-5; Rom. 1:1-4; 4:24-25; 10:8-9; 1 Pet. 3:18) and liturgical (1 Cor. 11:23-26) formulas, in → hymns (Eph. 5:14; Phil. 2:5-11; 1 Tim. 2:5-6; 3:16; 1 Pet. 1:20), in catechetical instruction (Rom. 6:16-19), in references to dominical sayings (1 Cor. 7:10; 9:14; 11:23-25; 1 Thess. 4:15), and in traditional customs (1 Cor. 11:3-16; → Exegesis, Biblical, 2).

The process of handing down the gospel involved the task of making critical distinctions. We find this in the case of Jesus himself, with whom the New had appeared: "But I say unto you" (Matt. 5:22, 28, 32, 34, 39, 44). But Jesus could still place himself in the traditional nexus of fulfilling OT → promises and seeing his own destiny along these lines. Freedom from tradition may be seen in the many ways in which the one Christ-event (e.g., cross and → resurrection, humiliation and exaltation) is handed down and in the development of the original confession of Christ (e.g., through connecting the incarnation with the preexistence of the Son of God, as in Rom. 1:1-4; → Christology 1).

As the apostolic witnesses died (→ Apostle, Apostolate) and errors arose (→ Heresies and Schisms 2.2), the living tradition *(paradosis)* became a fixed teaching *(parathēkē)*. We can see this development in the NT in the chain of tradition of Luke 1:1-4 (see also Acts 20:17-35), in reference to the teaching and tradition that had been there from the beginning and had to be maintained, such as in 1 John 1:1-4; 2:7, 13-14, 24. The essential contents of the apostolic tradition had now become doctrine and order and were to be observed in obedience to authorized ministers (→ Pastoral Epistles).

3. The Early Church and Middle Ages

The → early church understood tradition as a means of preserving and defining the basic contents of the faith and as a means to promote the coherence of the growing Christian churches. → Irenaeus (ca. 130-ca. 200) and → Tertullian (ca. 160-ca. 225) thought that a true apostolic tradition could be guaranteed by a succession of → bishops bearing witness to the true faith. They linked this personal testimony to churches of apostolic foundation, from which other churches developed and shared their apostolicity (→ Church 2.2). The establishment and reception of the NT → canon (§2) also helped to preserve the apostolic tradition, and so too did the summaries of Christian teaching (the → confessions and creeds, → ecumenical symbols, conciliar decisions, etc.), which Irenaeus, Tertullian, → Origen (ca. 185-ca. 254; → Origenism), Hippolytus (ca. 170-ca. 236), and Novatian (ca. 200-257/58) referred to as the canon, or → rule of faith.

This rule of faith was a key to the exposition of Scripture (so → Augustine; → Augustine's Theology 8). According to Vincent of Lérins (d. before 450) in his *Commonitorium* (2.3; 29.41), true tradition is that which has been believed everywhere *(ubique)*, always *(semper)*, and by all *(ab omnibus)*. Remaining in the → truth (§2) of the tradition once handed down requires the presence and guidance of the → Holy Spirit.

In the development of → dogma in the → Middle Ages, this idea went hand in hand with the idea of the → inspiration of → councils and dogma itself. The Middle Ages also advanced the thought of individual apostolic traditions that were unwritten and that would add to the authority of the papal → teaching office (§1). Increasingly, an undifferentiated mixture of apostolic and ecclesiastical traditions emerged, against which medieval reforming movements waged a vigorous protest (→ Wycliffe, John; Hussites; Middle Ages 1.4.4).

4. Orthodoxy

The tradition that constitutes the theology, → spirituality, and life of the → Orthodox Church embraces Holy Scripture, the decisions of the seven ecumenical councils, the consensus of the church fathers, and, in a broader sense, writings of individual Fathers, → liturgies, orders, and the spiritual forms in which the ancient church expressed itself. Orthodox theologians emphasize today that, notwithstanding the fact that tradition is closed in content, a critical distinction must be made between the basic Tradition and church traditions. Tradition as a living experience of the Holy Spirit in the church must always be open to new interpretations.

5. The Reformation

The Reformers radically opposed the symbiosis of Scripture, apostolic tradition, church traditions, and the church's teaching office. They did so in their struggle for unconditional recognition of the free → grace of God in Jesus Christ. Scripture alone must hold a normative position and have critical authority (→ Reformation Principles) over the church, over its → proclamation and teaching, and over its orders and ways of life. It was not as a collection of writings that Scripture was supreme but as an authentic testimony to divine revelation and → salvation in Jesus Christ. Contrary to → Puritanism, which allowed in the church only what was explicitly commanded in Scripture, the Reformation, particularly in its Lutheran form, in no way rejected tradition in the sense of human statutes. Controversial theology (→ Polemics) involved many clichés, but after these have been transcended, a differentiating "yes" and "no" can be given to Tradition and traditions. Accordingly, the dogma of the early church continues to be binding.

Later doctrinal affirmations, as well as patristic writings, may also strengthen one's own confession (e.g., in the → Augsburg Confession) and its continuity with the true apostolic tradition if they are in agreement with the gospel. Church traditions may also be adopted in modified form (e.g., in the liturgies and the episcopal ministries of Scandinavia or the Church of England; → Anglican Communion). But traditions that obscure the unconditional grace of God must be discarded. It is thus possible to keep or restore a tradition that is in accordance with the gospel, but a break must be made with traditions that enslave. The Reformation also advanced new confessional traditions (→ Confession of Faith) that claimed to embody the one apostolic tradition.

6. Trent to Vatican II

The Roman Catholic reply to the Reformers' alleged rejection of all church traditions was considered at the fourth session of the Council of → Trent, on April 8, 1546. There it was stated that the truth and teaching of the gospel are contained both in "written books" *(libris scriptis)* and in "unwritten traditions" (*sine scripto traditionibus;* DH 1501). The discussion following Trent was strongly determined by the formulation in the preliminary draft, whereby the gospel is contained partly in the scriptural text and partly in the unwritten traditions. From the one source of the gospel, which flows into two channels (Trent), emerged the idea of two sources of revelation, where tradition supplements and interprets insufficient Holy Scriptures. Vatican I took up Trent again by referring as follows to the contents of the word of God: "All those things are to be believed which are contained in the word of God as found in scripture and tradition" (DH 3011). Prior to Vatican II this two-source theory found much support.

The dogmatic constitution *Dei Verbum* (1965; *DV*) of Vatican II wished to carry forward Trent as well as Vatican I, but also to overcome the post-Tridentine narrowings through the reception of Reformation and ecumenical insights. Primarily, tradition is the faith of the church lived out under the Spirit's guidance and handed down in the church's life, teaching, and liturgy (*DV* 8). Holy Scripture is part of the nexus of tradition. In it God has given the church a norm for all time. Tradition is also the church's hermeneutical category (preserving, handing on, updating). The → teaching office is the organ for its binding exposition.

7. Theology and Ecumenical Dialogue

In 1963, before *DV*, the Fourth World Conference on Faith and Order, at Montreal, had reached an ecumenical convergence of understanding about tradition and its relation to Scripture. So far, though, it has not yet found reception in many churches, apart from its extremely lively discussion in the Roman Catholic Church. The new approach, and the embodying of Scripture in the process of tradition, has come to expression in the following oft-quoted statement from Montreal 1963: "We exist as Christians by the Tradition of the Gospel (the *paradosis* of the *kerygma*) testified in Scripture, transmitted in and by the Church through the power of the Holy Spirit. Tradition taken in this sense is actualized in the → preaching of the Word, in the administration of the → Sacraments and → worship, in Christian teaching and theology, and in → mission and witness to Christ by the lives of the members of the Church" (G. Gassmann, 11).

This all-embracing and dynamic understanding of tradition has now become determinative. For example, a similar Roman Catholic formulation defines tradition as "the continuing process of the self-communication of God in the Christ-event through the Holy Spirit in the medium of the proclamation of the church" (*Handbook of Catholic Theology*, 715). The problem is that tradition, "the faith of the Church through the ages" (Lima Document, Preface), is always accessible to us only in the church's confessional traditions. The task for all the churches is thus to permanently renew their own traditions in line with the apostolic tradition, to which a normative witness is given by Holy Scripture. In this way the tradition of the gospel, based on the revelation of God, centered on the saving work of Jesus Christ, and communicated by the Holy Spirit, will thus become a true reality of faith that frees from all restrictive and outmoded traditions and thus opens the way for a common Christian life and confession.

Bibliography: *Roman Catholic*: E. CATTANEO, *Trasmettere la fede. Tradizione, scrittura e magistero nella Chiesa; Percorso di teologia fondamentale* (Milan, 1999) • M. KELLY-ZUKOWSKI, *The Role of Tradition in Modern Catholic Ecclesiological Problems: The Ordination of Women and the Interpretations of Catholic Truths* (San Francisco, 1998) • K. RAHNER and J. RATZINGER, *Revelation and Tradition* (New York, 1966) • J. E. THIEL, *Senses of Tradition: Continuity and Development in Catholic Faith* (New York, 2000).

Orthodox: G. FLOROVSKY, *Bible, Church, Tradition: An Eastern Orthodox View* (Belmont, Mass., 1972) • T. Y. MALATY, *Tradition and Orthodoxy* (Alexandria, 1979) • K. WARE, "Tradition and Traditions," *DEM* (2d ed.) 1143-48.

Early church and Middle Ages: G. EBELING, *Word of God and Tradition: Historical Studies Interpreting the Divisions of Christianity* (Philadelphia, 1968) • R. ENO, *Teaching Authority in the Early Church* (Wilmington, Del., 1984) • B. GERHARDSSON, *Tradition and Transmission in Early Christianity* (Lund, 1964) • K. F. MORRISON, *Tradition and Authority in the Western Church, 300-1400* (Princeton, 1969) • R. L. WILKEN, *Remembering the Christian Past* (Grand Rapids, 1995) • D. H. WILLIAMS, *Evangelicals and Tradition: The Formative Influence of the Early Church* (Grand Rapids, 2005).

Other works: D. BROWN, *Tradition and Imagination: Revelation and Change* (Oxford, 1999) • Y. CONGAR, *The Meaning of Tradition* (New York, 1964) • O. CULLMANN, *La tradition. Problème exégétique, historique et théologique* (Neuchâtel, 1953) • H. G. GADAMER, *Truth and Method* (New York, 2004; orig. pub., 1960) • G. GASSMANN, ed., *Documentary History of Faith and Order, 1963-1993* (Geneva, 1993) • B. P. GAYBBA, *Tradition: An Ecumenical Breakthrough? A Study of a Faith and Order Study* (Rome, 1971) • R. R. GEISELMANN, *The Meaning of Tradition* (New York, 1966) • J. C. K. GOH, *Christian Tradition Today: A Postliberal Vision of Church and World* (Louvain, 2000) • S. HOLMES, *Listening to the Past: The Place of Tradition in Theology* (Grand Rapids, 2002) • S. KAPPEN, *Tradition, Modernity, Counterculture: An Asian Perspective* (Bangalore, 1998) • D. S. KNIGHT, ed., *Tradition and Theology in the OT* (Philadelphia, 1977) • E. LANNE, *Tradition et communion des églises. Recueil d'études* (Louvain, 1997) • J. P. MACKEY, *Modern Theology of Tradition* (New York, 1963) • P. S. MINEAR, ed., *The Old and the New in the Church: Two Interim Reports on Tradition and Traditions and on Institutionalism and Unity* (Minneapolis, 1961) • J. PIEPER, *Überlieferung. Begriff und Anspruch* (Munich, 1970) • P. C. RODGER and L. VISCHER, eds., *The Fourth World Conference on Faith and Order: Montreal 1963* (New York, 1964) • H. C. SKILLRUD, J. F. STAFFORD, and D. MARTENSEN, eds., *Scripture and Tradition,* (Minneapolis, 1995) • D. WIEDERKEHR, ed., *Wie geschieht Tradition?* (Freiburg, 1991).

GÜNTHER GASSMANN

Traditionalist Movement

1. Background
2. Marcel Lefebvre
3. Critique

1. Background

The traditionalist movement within the → Roman Catholic Church is essentially a reaction to → Vatican II (1962-65) and postconciliar developments. More or less significant parts of the Catholic faithful (differing in various countries but overall only a small minority) hold to the idea that with the council and the reforms associated with it, the Catholic Church broke with the central content of the faith tradition, which the church alone can preserve (→ Tradition 6). The attention that the movement enjoys within the church, even in the highest circles, is greater than its real strength might warrant.

Traditionalism today owes its origin to Vatican II, but it ties in with earlier traditionalist tendencies. The core of antirationalist traditionalism in the 19th century (Joseph de Maistre, Louis G. A. de Bonald, Félicité R. de Lammenais; → Ultramontanism) was the view that a knowledge of metaphysical → truths is something to which human → reason cannot attain. Truths are given in the form of primal revelation that human beings must hand down with the decisive help of human → authority (→ Revelation 2.5). → Faith as the Roman Catholic Church advocates it is the content of what we believe is true (→ Catholicism [Roman] 3).

2. Marcel Lefebvre

An important champion of the postconciliar traditionalist movement in the Roman Catholic Church was Archbishop Marcel Lefebvre (1905-91), who on November 1, 1970, in Fribourg, Switzerland, founded the Priestly Society of St. Pius X. A member of the central commission to prepare for Vatican II, he was archbishop of Dakar (Senegal) and then in 1962 became bishop of Tulle in France and also was superior general of the Holy Ghost Fathers (1962-68). Dissatisfied with the progress of the council, he helped to found the Coetus Internationalis Patrum (International group of fathers), a group of ultraconservative members of the council who sought unsuccessfully to turn the progress and decisions of the council in their own direction. Rejecting the council's decisions and the reforms in liturgy made after the council (→ Liturgy 3.2), Lefebvre — with church approval — opened a seminary in 1970 in Ecône, Switzerland. In 1975, however, the new bishop of Fribourg suppressed the institution. Since Lefebvre continued to ordain → priests when expressly forbidden to do so, in 1976 a *suspensio a divinis* (1917 CIC 2279.2.2) was issued that forbade him to engage in any acts of ordination, a prohibition that he consistently ignored.

On June 30, 1988, the traditionalist movement entered on a new phase as, contrary to church law, Lefebvre consecrated four priests of the Society of St. Pius X as bishops. Intensive but unsuccessful efforts had been made by the Vatican Congregation for the Doctrine of the Faith (→ Curia 1.2.2) to reach agreement with Lefebvre prior to this consecration. Then on July 1, 1988, the Vatican congregation decreed that Lefebvre, the co-consecrators, and the four bishops themselves were excommunicated (→ Excommunication). In the → motu proprio *Ecclesia Dei,* issued July 2, John Paul II held out to supporters of Lefebvre who did not want to follow him into schism a chance to correct their relationship with the Roman Catholic Church. Also in October 1988 a papal commission instituted the Priestly Fraternity of St. Peter, a community of priests granted the right to follow the traditional (i.e., Tridentine) liturgy of the Roman Rite.

It is doubtful how far nonschismatic traditionalism may be regarded as an expression and part of the legitimate church plurality.

3. Critique

Even though it is a widespread idea that the central concern of the traditionalist movement is to keep Latin in the liturgy and to cling to preconciliar or Tridentine rites (→ Mass 2.3.1), the leading members of the movement took a much wider view. They advocated an unhistorical absolutizing of a specific and relatively early and limited part of the church's tradition. They believed that an antimodernist (→ Modernism), antidemocratic, and antiecumenical portion of the tradition is permanent, and by it they measure all else. A key question for them is their relation to the → teaching office (§1). On the one side they have a decided belief that → obedience (§4) to the teaching office is mandatory, but on the other side they see that they are forced into areas in which they renounce those who are now in charge of the teaching office and instead follow their own consciences. Extremists such as the so-called Sedevacantists (Lat. *sede vacante,* "while the seat is vacant") solve the problem by declaring that the chair of Peter has been vacant since the death of → Pius XII (1939-58).

The concerns of the traditionalist movement are to be distinguished from neoconservative or fundamentalist tendencies within the Roman Catholic

Church, even if the boundaries are fluid. Parts of the traditionalist movement belong, on the one hand, to the most determined defenders of the pronouncements of the church's teaching office with fundamentalist leaning, while, on the other hand, traditionalists reject decisive parts of official church or conciliar doctrine, such as the acknowledgment of the → freedom of religion and conscience.

In more than one way the traditionalist movement is like → fundamentalism. Traditionalists share with fundamentalists an aversion in principle to modern freedoms, share an unhistorical view of the tradition of faith, but also adopt modern means in pursuit of their aims. Like fundamentalists, they shun uncertainty by not entering into → dialogue with contemporaries that might relativize the truth claims of the faith. They advocate a hermeneutically naive and outdated view of God, order, and authority.

Bibliography: Y. Congar, Challenge to the Church: The Case of Archbishop Lefèbvre (Huntington, Ind., 1976) • M. W. Cuneo, The Smoke of Satan: Conservative and Traditionalist Dissent in Contemporary American Catholicism (New York, 1997) • W. D. Dinges, "Roman Catholic Traditionalism," America's Alternative Religions (ed. T. Miller; Albany, N.Y., 1995) 101-7; idem, "'We Are What You Were': Roman Catholic Traditionalism in America," Being Right (ed. M. J. Weaver and R. S. Appleby; Bloomington, Ind., 1995) 241-69 • W. D. Dinges and J. Hitchcock, "Roman Catholic Traditionalism and Activist Conservatism in the United States," Fundamentalisms Observed (ed. M. Marty; Chicago, 1991) 66-141 • H. Küng, "Against Contemporary Roman-Catholic Fundamentalism," Fundamentalism as an Ecumenical Challenge (ed. H. Küng and J. Moltmann; London, 1992) 116-25 • M. Lefebvre, Open Letter to Confused Catholics (Kansas City, Mo., 1986) • Priest, Where Is Thy Mass? Mass, Where Is Thy Priest? The Seminary Interviews (2d ed.; Kansas City, Mo., 2004) • A. Schifferle, Das Ärgernis Lefebvre. Informationen und Dokumente zur neuen Kirchenspaltung (Fribourg, 1989); idem, Marcel Lefebvre. Ärgernis und Besinnung (Kevelaer, 1983).

Klaus Nientiedt

Transcendence → Immanence and Transcendence

Transcendental Meditation

1. Founder
2. Theory and Practice
3. Goal

Transcendental Meditation (TM) is a spiritual, neo-Hindu movement (→ Hinduism).

1. Founder

The founder of TM was Mahesh Prasad Warma (b. 1911 or 1918). He was initiated into the traditions of → meditation by Himalayan and South Indian masters. The last of these, and the most influential, was Shankara (700?-750?). When Mahesh had developed his own method, Transcendental Meditation (TM), he put "Maharisha" (great seer) before his name and "Yogi" (one who practices → yoga) after it.

In Madras on January 1, 1958, Mahesh founded the Spiritual Regeneration Movement in order to make TM better known. He also traveled to Indo-China, Singapore, Hong Kong, Hawaii, San Francisco, and then on to Germany in 1960. TM became the name both of the movement and of the teaching of Maharishi Mahesh Yogi (MMY).

By 1975 five organizations had been formed. In the same year MMY announced the beginning of the age of enlightenment, which would begin at specific times in the various continents. MMY nominated a world government from existing groups. They would achieve success if 1 percent of the world's population learned meditation. Since there is no means of verifying this percentage, there is no way of giving statistical results.

2. Theory and Practice

According to MMY's theory, in TM the conscious spirit attains to the transcendental sphere of the absolute being of nonmanifested nature that does not reveal itself otherwise. The spirit transcends all borders of intellectual experience, surpasses everything relative, and achieves a state of pure consciousness or absolute being known as self-consciousness (Science of Being, 249).

Help is given to the spirit by mantras, which work magically, but may also be used as formulated prayers, and which are code words for the diverse forms of consciousness allotted to the five stages of life (ages 5-25, 26-34, 35-44, 45-54, 55 and over). The mantras are linked to the seven chakras (energy centers) of the human body and in this way ought to be opened up and developed for their further activity. A personal mantra is given to each individual on initiation. It is supposedly unlike any other, serves for recognition, but must be kept secret. The deities and forces of Hindu mythology reside, in a nonclassical way, in the various spheres of life and energy. To those who are aware of it, this shows that the character of transcendental meditation is Indian.

Meditation on the mantra for 20 minutes twice a day seems in fact to be an attenuated procedure adapted to the lesser Western attention span. Its therapeutic value is disputed. Whether what are called *siddhi* capabilities (invisibility, ability to fly, seeing through eyelids or various obstacles) can be experienced, as promised and taught, seems at best to be a matter of chance and in most cases self-deception. Since TM participants share their experiences, it has become clear that many mantras agree with one another and that their number constitutes only a small portion of the 60 million available in Sanskrit literature, and thus the central point of the whole practice has irrevocably lost its significance.

3. Goal
In 1994 the way to the "age of enlightenment" was by vowing personal commitment to MMY as the only guru. In this way Swami Brahmananda Sarasvati (1870-1953) lost his position as the guru who had first stood alongside of, then was secondary to, MMY. Transcendental meditation is thus rightly named a → religion. Its active members form centers that promote a world plan.

The plan aims at new institutions until there are enough for the redemption of the world. Intellectually, there is little concern for proper medicine, nourishment, politics, ecology, science, and so forth to reach this goal. They simply are all to be in accord with TM. Its basic principles must be made generally evident even to the most hesitant. To do this, from resorts to universities, as many different institutions need to be founded, registered, financed, and established eschatologically as possible, demanding uncompromising input and gifts and resources from entrepreneurs.

It is hard to say which type of person will see here a call and find material blessing in seeking the world's salvation along these lines, and which will come to the conclusion that, by following TM, they would be making a radical mistake.

Bibliography: K. A. GERBERDING, *How to Respond to Transcendental Meditation* (St. Louis, 1977) • F.-W. HAACK and T. GANDOW, *Transzendentale Meditation. Maharishi Mahesh Yogi, Maharishi Veda* (6th ed.; Munich, 1992) • D. P. KANELLAKOS and J. S. LUKAS, *The Psychobiology of Transcendental Meditation: A Literature Review* (Menlo Park, Calif., 1974) • M. MAHESH YOGI, *Science of Being and Art of Living: Transcendental Meditation* (New York, 1963; repr., 1995) • M. ROTHSTEIN, *Belief Transformations. Some Aspects of the Relation between Science and Religion in Transcendental Meditation (TM) and the International Society for Krishna Consciousness (ISKCON)* (Århus, 1996) • P. RUSSELL, *The TM Technique: An Introduction to Transcendental Meditation and the Teachings of Maharishi Mahesh Yogi* (3d ed.; Boston, 1978).

CARSTEN COLPE

Transcendental Philosophy

1. Term
2. Between Idealism and Realism
3. Metatheoretical Dimension
4. Connections with Other Philosophical Currents

1. Term
The meaning of the term "transcendental philosophy" in the 19th and 20th centuries derives from I. Kant (1724-1804; → Kantianism), who in the introduction to his *Critique of Pure Reason* (1st ed., pp. 11-12) used "transcendental" to refer to all knowledge that is occupied not so much with objects as with the mode of our knowledge of objects, insofar as this mode is possible a priori. A system of such concepts might be called transcendental philosophy. Although the older meaning of the term (i.e., transcendental = transcendent) can also be found, he sharply distinguished the older meaning from the newer one, according to which transcendental philosophy does not have the task of passing judgments on real objects (including transcendent real objects) and of proving them; rather, it analyzes the conditions of the objective validity of judgments. Consequently, transcendental philosophy differs fundamentally from particular sciences.

From the transcendental point of view, objective knowledge is possible because the conditions under which objects are given coincide with the conditions under which we have knowledge of them. In order to substantiate this coincidence, Kant assumed that objects are constituted by means of subjective forms of perceiving and judging — namely, space, time, and categories; these forms belong necessarily to the object, insofar as it is constituted by the subject. For example, judgments concerning geometric relations apply to things because objects of outer sense are constituted by means of the a priori intuition of the structure of space, which, according to Kant, is the structure of Euclidean geometry. Besides space, → time, and categories (e.g., → Causality), as well as the principles of pure understanding (e.g., the principle of causal determination), there are elements of the theoretical framework within which data are constituted as objects of nature. Since the object that can be perceived and known depends a priori on the above-mentioned conditions, human knowledge is restricted to phenomena; things in themselves cannot be known.

2. Between Idealism and Realism

According to Kant, objects are real if considered from the empirical point of view, and ideal if considered within the framework of transcendental philosophy. Thus the traditional opposition between → subjectivism and objectivism is overcome. Similarly, Kant tried to reconcile realism with idealism. Realism is right, insofar as the forms of objective knowledge presuppose a content that is given by the thing in itself (i.e., by something that exists independently from the subject). Idealism is right, insofar as the spatiotemporal and categorial form of the object has to be reduced to the subject.

J. G. Fichte (1762-1814; → Idealism 4) went further than Kant by abandoning the idea of a thing in itself and holding that objects are posited by the ego not only with regard to their form but also with reference to their matter. The opposite view was taken by authors such as E. von Hartmann, A. Riehl, and H. Albert, who argued in favor not only of the existence, but of the recognizability, of things in themselves, whereas Kant denied that they might be known in their contents. Transcendental realism is therefore just as incompatible with Kant's transcendental idealism as is absolute idealism.

3. Metatheoretical Dimension

Already in Kant the theory of objective knowledge is supplemented with metatheoretical considerations — for example, with regard to the relationship between metaphysical dogmatism and criticism (*Critique of Pure Reason*, 2d ed., p. 16). From the metatheoretical point of view, theories of objective knowledge may be compared with respect to their explanatory power. Critical philosophy today has the task of developing the metatheoretical aspect of transcendentalism.

4. Connections with Other Philosophical Currents

Although transcendental philosophy differs fundamentally from scientific theories, attempts have been made to connect it with particular sciences. Thus J. F. Fries (1773-1843) linked it to psychology (or anthropology), and K. R. Popper (1902-94) related it to an evolutionary → epistemology. Neo-Kantianism (→ Kantianism 3) rejected such attempts but limited transcendental philosophy to a theory of scientific knowledge — an unacceptable restriction, according

to M. Heidegger (1889-1976; → Existentialism). A remarkable synthesis between transcendentalism and phenomenology was created by E. Husserl (1859-1938). Husserl characterized transcendental philosophy as egology; it has the task of analyzing the object-constituting acts of the pure ego.

During the second half of the 20th century, critical philosophy was influenced by linguistic philosophy (→ Language 5). According to linguistic philosophy, objects are not formed through space, time, and categories but are constituted within the framework of a language (or a system of symbols in general). The linguistic variant of critical philosophy can lead to an idealistic position, but for the most part it is realistic (→ Linguistics 3).

Another view was adopted by transcendental pragmatists, who tried to link transcendental philosophy to → pragmatism, though differing from classic pragmatism in its belief in absolutely true principles (in contrast to pragmatistic fallibilism). Most advocates of linguistic analysis (→ Analytic Philosophy 2.3) are in fact opposed to the Kantian type of transcendental philosophy, but some of them — for example, Wilfrid Sellars (1912-89) and Hilary Putnam (b. 1926) — touch on certain ideas of transcendentalism.

Bibliography: H. Albert, *Kritik der reinen Erkenntnislehre* (Tübingen, 1987) • E. Cassirer, *The Philosophy of Symbolic Forms* (4 vols.; New Haven, 1953-96) • S. G. Crowell, *Husserl, Heidegger, and the Space of Meaning: Paths toward Transcendental Phenomenology* (Evanston, Ill., 2001) • J. G. Fichte, *Foundations of Transcendental Philosophy* (Ithaca, N.Y., 1992; orig. pub., 1796/99) • J. F. Fries, *Neue Kritik der Vernunft* (3 vols.; Heidelberg, 1807) • E. Husserl, *The Crisis of European Sciences and Transcendental Phenomenology* (Evanston, Ill., 1970); idem, *Ideas Pertaining to a Pure Phenomenology and to a Phenomenological Philosophy* (The Hague, 1980) • H. Lauener, *Offene Transzendentalphilosophie* (Hamburg, 2002) • H. Lenk, *Interpretationskonstrukte* (Frankfurt, 1993); idem, *Philosophie und Interpretation* (Frankfurt, 1993) • J. Mohanty, *The Possibility of Transcendental Philosophy* (Dordrecht, 1985) • K. R. Popper, *Objective Knowledge* (Oxford, 1972) • G. Prauss, *Die Welt und wir* (2 vols. in 4; Stuttgart, 1990-2006) • H. Putnam, *Reason, Truth, and History* (Cambridge, 1981) • A. Riehl, *Der philosophische Kritizismus, Geschichte und System* (3d ed.; 3 vols.; Leipzig, 1924-26) • T. Rockmore and V. Zeman, eds., *Transcendental Philosophy and Everyday Experience* (Atlantic Highlands, N.J., 1997) • W. Röd, *Erfahrung und Reflexion. Theorien der Erfahrung in transzendentalphilosophischer Sicht* (Munich, 1991) • W. Sellars, *Science and Metaphysics:*

Variations on Kantian Themes (London, 1968) •
G. ZÖLLER, *Fichte's Transcendental Philosophy: The
Original Duplicity of Intelligence and Will* (Cambridge,
1998).

WOLFGANG RÖD

Transcendental Theology

1. Origin
2. Distinctiveness
3. Development
4. Criticism

1. Origin

Transcendental theology originated when Roman
Catholic Christians wrestled with the transcendental philosophy of I. Kant (1724-1804; → Kantianism). Initiated by the Belgian Jesuit J. Maréchal
(1878-1944), it used the → metaphysics of Thomas
Aquinas (ca. 1225-74; → Thomism) in expansion of
the transcendental method of Kant. In this way it
hoped to justify the traditional doctrine of God
philosophically. This transcendental Thomism established as a starting point something that Kant
neglected, namely, an absolute acceptance of being.
Many advocates of this approach did only philosophical work (e.g., J. B. Lotz), but the initiators,
and the German Jesuit K. → Rahner (1904-84) in
particular, developed it in a way that was specifically
theological.

Recognizing without reservation the → truth
(§2) of → philosophy, transcendental theology attempted to give a view of Christian → faith that
would be in keeping with modern thought. Insofar
as faith demands it, this theology worked out its
own philosophy. But unlike F. D. E. → Schleiermacher (1768-1834; → Schleiermacher's Theology),
who regarded philosophy as more comprehensive
than theology, philosophy was now only one element in theology, which posits its own → truths
(§3). Under the influence of M. Heidegger (1889-
1976; → Existentialism), Rahner interpreted the being of Aquinas as knowability (which Aquinas,
though, saw as truth). Metaphysics thus became
epistemology.

2. Distinctiveness

Transcendental theology accepts unlimited transcendence in the unchangeable transcendentality of
the human consciousness, as well as an inner relationship between humanity and God that is open to
us as the ineffable goal of the transcendence of the
human spirit. It thus seeks to reflect on the contents
of → revelation that are related to the transcendentally unavoidable truths of faith but are mediated in
history. It pays special attention to the possibility of
achievement under conditions contributed by believing subjects themselves.

The crucial distinctiveness concerns the decision of interpreting reality in such a way that its nature is related to the consciousness. Rahner included matter itself, which he called "frozen spirit."
Against the background of reality, theology must
see itself as → anthropology and vice versa. Christianity is an event of consciousness, and the relationship with God has the character of transcendental → experience. We are by nature hearers of
the Word. We ourselves are the question, and revelation, which is not attainable transcendentally but
strictly historically, is the answer.

3. Development

Nearly all areas of systematic theology begin with
transcendental reflection. Transcendental theology
can be considered as its own theology, not as part of
theology. God is primarily the absolute mystery. By
its very nature the human spirit transcendentally
seeks God, though it cannot comprehend him. →
Salvation means fulfillment of the human striving
for finality; it is the eschatological and saving self-
impartation of God.

→ Hermeneutics teaches transcendental theology that the truths of faith have no content. They
can be mythological (→ Existential Theology; Language and Theology) only insofar as they are not interpreted with reference to transcendentally accessible reality. All the statements of faith simply develop
this basic thought. Thanks to the transcendental approach we can compress all Christian teaching (→
Dogmatics) into short formulas. Faith is coextensive
with acceptance of our own existence (→ Faith
3.5.7.4).

In transcendental → Christology Jesus Christ
embodies the fulfillment of teleologically developing
human nature and its meaning on the one side (→
Teleology), and the concrete pronouncing of the self-
impartation of God on the other. The historical
event of the ultimate and absolute bearer of salvation
is transcendentally unavoidable but corresponds to
our transcendental hope of → resurrection.

Since the substance of Christianity lies in the
present but eschatological experience of God (→
Eschatology 7), ecclesiology (→ Church 5.4) cannot
be the core of theology. Ecclesiology rests on two
transcendental principles, namely, historicity (e.g.,
dogmas) and sociability (e.g., on ministry; →
Church 1). The transcendental depth of the church's

teaching makes it possible for transcendental theology to accept an anonymous Christianity outside of explicitly church-based Christianity.

4. Criticism

Criticism by the → teaching office (§1; see the 1993 encyclical *Veritatis splendor*) of a purely transcendental concept of freedom did not affect Rahner, who always stressed the concrete dimension of → freedom. Transcendental theology was itself concerned with overcoming heretical ontologism (→ Ontology) and → modernism. Philosophical and theological critics focused on the neglect of specific areas of reality (e.g., practice, intersubjectivity), on the unattainability of transcendental analysis (a common complaint against idealism), and on the understanding of Aquinas (e.g., viewing reflection only secondarily).

→ Immanence and Transcendence

Bibliography: M. F. Fischer, *The Foundations of Karl Rahner: A Paraphrase of the Foundations of Christian Faith* (New York, 2005) • T. F. Guenther, *Rahner and Metz: Transcendental Theology as Political Theology* (Lanham, Md., 1993) • W. J. Hoye, *Gotteserfahrung? Klärung eines Grundbegriffs der gegenwärtigen Theologie* (Zurich, 1993) 112-70 • A. Losinger, *The Anthropological Turn: The Human Orientation of the Theology of Karl Rahner* (New York, 2000) • O. Muck, *The Transcendental Method* (New York, 1968) • K. Rahner, *Foundations of Christian Faith: An Introduction to the Idea of Christianity* (New York, 1978); idem, *Hearer of the Word: Laying the Foundation for a Philosophy of Religion* (New York, 1994; orig. pub., 1941); idem, *Spirit in the World* (New York, 1994; orig. pub., 1939); idem, "Transzendentaltheologie," *SM* 4.986-92.

William J. Hoye

Transcendentalism

Transcendentalism was a 19th-century American philosophy that emphasized the unity of spirit and → nature. Its most renowned spokesman was Ralph Waldo Emerson, who called it "the Saturnalia or excess of Faith." That which is "popularly called Transcendentalism among us," he wrote, "is → Idealism; Idealism as it appears in 1842" (Emerson, 198, 193).

Rather than being a well-organized and clearly defined movement, transcendentalism was instead the name given to a loosely knit group of authors, preachers, and lecturers bound together by their opposition to certain beliefs and practices. The transcendentalists shared a disdain for Unitarian orthodoxy (→ Unitarians), a desire to free American culture from bondage to dead → traditions, and a faith in the vast potential of democratic life in America (→ Democracy). Situated in and near Concord, Massachusetts, between 1835 and 1860, the transcendentalists formed a loose federation of kindred spirits rather than a disciplined, narrowly defined group.

Emerson (1803-82) was clearly the central figure of transcendentalism; the publication of his *Nature* in 1836 marked the beginning of the movement. The next two decades were to see numerous additional works from Emerson and poems, essays, and books from other transcendentalists, such as Orestes Brownson (1803-76), Margaret Fuller (1810-50), Theodore Parker (1810-60), and Henry David Thoreau (1817-62). These figures and others formed a discussion group called the Transcendental Club, published a literary journal, *The Dial*, and established a → utopian experiment in communal living at Brook Farm, in West Roxbury, Massachusetts.

What bound the members of the group together was a common heritage in Massachusetts Unitarianism, which each of them subsequently rejected. They objected to the Unitarian commitment to certain particulars of Christian → dogma, including belief in the uniqueness of Jesus and the efficacy of the → sacraments. According to Emerson, instead of preaching "a faith like Christ's in the infinitude of man," the church "has dwelt, it dwells, with noxious exaggeration about the *person* of Jesus"; it preaches "not the doctrine of the → soul, but an exaggeration of the personal, the positive, the ritual." Emerson challenged his audience to "dare to love God without mediator or veil" by seeking direct access to the Deity unmediated by Scripture or tradition (pp. 88, 81, 89).

The transcendentalists also decried the sterility of Unitarian belief and practice. In one sense they were trying to recapture the fervor of the original → Puritan enterprise, which had been effectively pushed to the periphery of American religious experience by the end of the 18th century. Although transcendentalism did not live up to the expectations of its adherents — many of whom anticipated nothing less than a millennial regeneration of American life through the application of idealist principles — the movement has had a lasting impact. In the years immediately preceding the Civil War, several transcendentalists were important figures in the abolitionist movement, and in the decades to follow, widely divergent figures found inspiration in the transcendentalist protest against society and the past. For instance, Henry Ford

(1863-1947), who once said that "history is more or less bunk" and who declared Emerson's essays his favorite reading, dwelt upon the transcendentalists' disdain for convention and their exaltation of self-reliant power. For their part, Mahatma Gandhi (1869-1948) and Martin Luther → King Jr. (1929-68) drew deeply upon the moral and spiritual resources of Thoreau's celebrated essay "Civil Disobedience" (1849).

Perhaps even more significantly, transcendentalism marked the first sustained attempt in American history to retain the experience of the Christian faith without the substance of Christian belief. By claiming the essential innocence of human nature, by substituting a direct intuition of God for the substance of → revelation, and by foreseeing a glorious future for humanity, the transcendentalists gave life to → romantic notions of human nature and destiny that have been a central part of the modern American experience.

Bibliography: L. BUELL, *New England Literary Culture: From Revolution through Renaissance* (Cambridge, Mass., 1986) • R. W. EMERSON, *Essays and Lectures* (ed. J. Porte; New York, 1983) • F. O. MATTHIESSEN, *American Renaissance: Art and Expression in the Age of Emerson and Whitman* (Oxford, 1941) • P. MILLER, ed., *The Transcendentalists: An Anthology* (Cambridge, Mass., 1941) • B. PACKER, "The Transcendentalists," *The Cambridge History of American Literature* (vol. 2; ed. S. Bercovitch; Cambridge, 1994) 329-604 • R. C. RICHARDSON, *Emerson: The Mind on Fire* (Berkeley, Calif., 1995) • A. ROSE, *Transcendentalism as a Social Movement, 1830-1850* (New Haven, 1981).

ROGER LUNDIN

Transcendentals

Deriving from Lat. *transcendens* (stepping over), the word "transcendentals" was used by the Scholastics (→ Scholasticism) for that which is far above ordinary → categories. In reality, we find transcendentals in both Plato (427-347 B.C.; → Platonism) and Aristotle (384-322 B.C.; → Aristotelianism) as initial forms of being. We can define what is, in terms of its goodness, truth, or unity. Special features of transcendentals are that they lie beyond the ability of categories to predicate and that they are also mutually convertible: *ens et unum, verum, bonum, pulchrum convertuntur* (being and one, the true, the good, the beautiful are interchangeable).

Thomas Aquinas (ca. 1225-74; → Thomism) listed five transcendentals: *res, unum, aliquid,*

verum, and *bonum* (being, oneness, otherness, truth, and goodness). Their particularity consists in the fact that, in contrast to categorial statements, they predicate being in an analogous manner and not univocally (→ Analogy).

Immanuel Kant (1724-1804; → Kantianism) accepted the five as a basis when discussing the categories (*Critique of Pure Reason,* §12). But Kant also offered a new definition of the word "transcendental." In the sense of his transcendental philosophy, "transcendental" did not mean "something passing beyond all experience, but something that indeed precedes it *a priori,* but that is intended simply to make cognition of experience possible. If these conceptions overstep experience, their employment is termed transcendent" (*Prol.,* app., 130). For Kant, the antithesis of transcendental is empirical (a posteriori). The transcendent is that which is beyond all → experience and lies outside the world that we can know by the senses. Its antithesis is the immanent (→ Immanence and Transcendence).

→ Transcendental Philosophy; Transcendental Theology

Bibliography: J. A. AERTSEN, *Medieval Philosophy and the Transcendentals: The Case of Thomas Aquinas* (New York, 1996) • I. KANT, "Prolegomena to Any Future Metaphysics," *Immanuel Kant's "Prolegomena to Any Future Metaphysics": In Focus* (ed. B. Logan; London, 1996) 27-138 • J. MALPAS, ed., *From Kant to Davidson: Philosophy and the Idea of the Transcendental* (New York, 2003) • A. B. WOLTER, *The Transcendentals and Their Function in the Metaphysics of Duns Scotus* (St. Bonaventure, N.Y., 1946). See also the bibliographies in "Transcendental Philosophy" and "Transcendental Theology."

HEIMO HOFMEISTER

Transdenominational Movements

When persons of differing denominations or traditions follow a specific form of Christian faith and life and develop that form in such a way that, irrespective of their church allegiance, they are at one, a transdenominational movement has come into being. It is to be noted that the modern ecumenical movement is by definition a movement of churches, not of individual persons, and hence does not qualify as a transdenominational movement (→ Ecumenism, Ecumenical Movement). The reason for the growth and persistence of these movements is often the sense that there are serious defects in the life of existing churches or that those churches are unable to respond to new challenges. These movements are thus innately and intentionally movements of church renewal.

The phrase "transdenominational movements" came into vogue during the 1970s, but the phenomenon was not new. The 16th-century → Reformation itself may be seen as such a movement insofar as it originated with the presentation of particular proposals to the church catholic concerning the → gospel, with no initial intent to form new ecclesial institutions. The 19th century saw such movements as → revivalism, the Evangelical Alliance (→ World Evangelical Alliance), and the → liturgical movement. The 20th century saw the → evangelical and → charismatic movements, the movement of → evangelical catholicity, and movements of social action (→ Social Movements) that adopt particular positions for work in society or the natural environment. In recent times, transdenominational movements have also formed around specific ethical, social, or even political positions, such as, for example, Christian movements that champion particular positions regarding → abortion or human → sexuality. There are also programmatic movements, often short-lived, such as the so-called emerging church movement. In point of fact, these movements point to the reality that there is often greater unity between persons of differing denominations than between persons within the same denomination.

Phenomenologically, however, these movements bear plain analogies to → denominations (§§2, 4.3). First, they stand for a specific concern of Christian faith, life, or → piety. Second, they have specific biblical reasons supporting their concerns. Finally, they often transcend national, geographic, and cultural boundaries. The sharpest difference from denominations is that they are movements. Even if they develop institutional forms, they have little interest in institutions per se. They seek to form groups and fellowships and do not wish to become denominations or churches.

Finally, their character as movements is the basis of their relation to the → churches. As movements of renewal, they are plainly critical, and tensions can and often do arise. But since they largely work apart from existing churches and do not seek to become churches themselves, their relation to the churches is fundamentally positive. Yet while the churches recognize these movements and their concerns and leave room for their existence and work, the fact remains that in a number of instances movements have become institutionalized as denominations, as is true in the case of the → Holiness movement and, in a certain way, the Pentecostal movement (→ Pentecostalism). There is, accordingly, always the

potential in transdenominational movements of schism and division. Ambivalence also characterizes the relation of these movements to the ecumenical world, since in crossing denominational frontiers, they potentially also give rise to new polarizations.

Bibliography: W. J. ABRAHAM, *The Logic of Renewal* (Grand Rapids, 2003) • R. H. CULPEPPER, *Evaluating the Charismatic Movement: A Theological and Biblical Appraisal* (Valley Forge, Pa., 1977) • H. MEYER, "Transkonfessionelle Bewegungen–Hoffnung oder Gefahr?" *ÖR.B* 32 (1978) 34-62 • T. C. ODEN, *The Rebirth of Orthodoxy: Signs of New Life in Christianity* (San Francisco, 2003); idem, *Turning Around the Mainline: How Renewal Movements Are Changing the Church* (Grand Rapids, 2006) • W. O. THORNTON, *Radical Righteousness: Personal Ethics and the Development of the Holiness Movement* (Salem, Ohio, 1998).

HARDING MEYER, with NORMAN A. HJELM

Transfiguration of the World

The patristic tradition (→ Patristics, Patrology) always related the doctrine of → creation (§4) to → Christology and ecclesiology (→ Church). Only thus could it be properly seen as a statement of faith (→ Dogmatics 1.2.5). It found fuller development only during the Arian controversy (→ Arianism). Against the Arians → Athanasius (ca. 297-373) made a radical distinction between the eternal begetting of the Son (→ Christology 2.1, 2.2, and 3) and the temporal making of creatures. Christ as Son is consubstantial with the Father (→ God 6). Creation was made ex nihilo — that is, it is a work, not of God's nature, but of his free will and → love (→ Grace 2). The distinction between eternal begetting and temporal creation, or between God's nature and God's will, became one of the most distinctive features of Greek patristic theology. It had a bearing not only on the world's origin but also on its final goal.

The chief expositors of patristic cosmology were Basil of Caesarea (ca. 330-79; *Hex.*), Dionysius the Pseudo-Areopagite (ca. 500; *De cael. hier.*), Maximus the Confessor (ca. 580-662; *Ambigua*), → John of Damascus (ca. 655-ca. 750; *De fide orth.*), and Gregory Palamas (ca. 1296-1359; *Capita physica, theologica*, etc.; → Palamism; Hesychasm). Christ, the mighty → Word of God, is both the Creator and the goal of everything creaturely. All things were made with a view to union with him (Col. 1:16-17). Maximus brilliantly expounded these thoughts. All things have their own logos, but this logos is enclosed by the divine and personal Logos, Jesus Christ (→ Holy Spirit 2). Christ is at work as the point at which the supreme Logos and human → reason meet. God's "logic" in creation impels it toward unity with the divine Logos, in which it finds its true nature. The inner thrust toward union with Christ explains the movement of time (→ Time and Eternity).

This Christological logic also has ecclesiological and anthropological dimensions. Creation is an indivisible totality, which the church and individuals (→ Anthropology 3.3) reflect. Humanity is called upon to uphold the divine order. It must praise God as Creator. By work, art (→ Aesthetics), → technology, and science, it can actualize the dynamic of God's philanthropy. Along these lines the transfiguration of the world is set in the context of a cosmologically oriented ecclesiology. Above all, the incarnate Logos (→ Incarnation) has fully assumed our human nature and divinized it in his own person (→ Theosis). It is itself the body of the incarnate Logos. By his cross (→ Theologia crucis) and → resurrection, he finally redeemed the world from its death-dealing enemy, so that it is no longer subject to the fate of corruptibility. It has achieved a "spiritual substance" that points it to its glory as God's world.

The church's → liturgy functions in this way on the world's behalf. The bread and wine of the → Eucharist (§3.1; → Eucharistic Ecclesiology) are seen by the church as representing the world. In the grace of the Spirit (→ Trinity) the church blesses everything in the world in all its spheres. It thus gives them the power by which they may be transfigured. The → kingdom of God is manifested in the church. The church's liturgical consummation anticipates the eschatological transfiguration (→ Salvation 3). Icons specifically express this connection (→ Icon; Iconography). They show how the whole material world depicts and anticipates the beauty and glory of God's kingdom. A redeemed creation is one of the elements in God's redeeming work (→ Soteriology).

→ Orthodox Church; Orthodox Christianity

Bibliography: H. U. VON BALTHASAR, Cosmic Liturgy: The Universe according to Maximus the Confessor (San Francisco, 2003) • W. BEINERT, Christus und der Kosmos (Freiburg, 1974) • G. FLOROVSKY, "The Concept of Creation in Saint Athanasius," StPatr 6 (1962) 36-57 • M. KADAVIL, The World as Sacrament: Sacramentality of Creation from the Perspectives of Leonardo Boff, Alexander Schmemann, and Saint Ephrem (Dudley, Mass., 2005) • C. MILLER, The Gift of the World: An Introduction to the Theology of Dumitru Stăniloae (Edinburgh, 2000) • A. RIOU, Le monde et l'église selon Maxime le Confesseur (Paris, 1973) • S. ROSE, Genesis, Creation, and Early Man: The Orthodox Christian Vision (Platina, Calif., 2000) • D. STĂNILOAE, The Experience of God, vol. 2, The World: Creation and Deification (Brookline, Mass., 2000).

JOHANNES PANAGOPOULOS†

Transubstantiation → Eucharist 3.2

Transylvania → Romania

Trauma

"Trauma," which derives from the Greek word for wound, hurt, or defeat, denotes either physical-organic injury (e.g., to the skull or brain) or psychological hurts that are more than the ego can cope with and that plunge one into a helpless panic, for example, the sexual seduction of children (→ Childhood), which S. Freud (1856-1939) regarded as the decisive factor in → neurosis. When Freud abandoned this monocausal hypothesis in favor of an unconscious infantile fantasying, he still did not contest the pathogenic role of traumatizing in actual life.

Psychologically, no "objective" internal or external event can cause trauma (e.g., an early loss or an alcoholic father). What counts is only the relation between the event and the experience. A specific event becomes a trauma for someone when measures to avert it or transform it fail. Traumatic effects from drastic "life events" or from psychosocial chronic stress ("strain-trauma") therefore cannot be purely extrospectively ascertained (e.g., through questionnaires or tests); statistical studies are meaningful only in connection with empathetically achieved clinical findings, for example, how early separation or hospitalization was subjectively managed ("separation trauma").

S. Ferenczi (1873-1933) related the genesis of trauma to childhood abuse as follows: The incompatibility of the adult's sexual passion (→ Sexuality) with the child's seeking of tenderness leads to confusion in feelings and language between both. Since the adult denies the event, the overstimulated child, confused by fear and feelings of guilt, is left with only the "introjection" of the imposed self-image of a "bad child." This unconscious inner subjugation as victim is also observed in those who experience torture.

If we approach trauma psycho-economically as

the sudden breaking down of barriers, a twofold differentiation is possible. First, with development interference the environment is chronically ill-adapted to the needs of the child. Repeated micro-experiences of neglect cause "cumulative trauma" (M. R. Khan). Second, psychological neuroses as inward → conflicts do not result directly from traumas but are attempts to avoid traumas. For the most part, all factors are present in psychological disturbances, particularly when early traumatic → anxiety is unavoidable. As an analogy to birth — the prototype of a violent flood of stimulation to which the unprotected child is exposed (O. Rank's "birth theory") — separations and losses are experienced traumatically because these catastrophic anxieties cannot be changed into signals that warn the ego in dangerous situations against the helplessness that was previously experienced.

We find "traumatic neurosis" when traumatic disasters take place (accidents or war neuroses) of which we know the exogenous cause but cannot experience it emotionally. We find this kind in the extreme traumatization of surviving concentration camp prisoners (with a cumulative trauma in the second generation) and in victims of persecution. Here any psychological structure capable of being processed breaks down. All attempts at overcoming (e.g., by somatization or acting) end in a fatal "compulsive repetition" that envisages the traumatic scene in ever new ways ("fate neurosis"), which Freud postulates as a "death drive." Alternatively, it can be understood as an attempt to actualize, and thus retroactively manage, the divided emotions of aversion and grief that the traumatically overstimulated ego cannot cope with. Without help, however, the constantly new variations of the trauma must fail in their goal of emotionally living through incomprehensible experiences.

Therapy and → pastoral care cannot heal the wound or the cumulative trauma of misused religious → education. But they can translate into psychologically understandable reality the hurts that life may bring, which pastoral theology refuses to recognize as judgments from God. In this way they can be helpful to healing and acceptance.

Bibliography: J. C. ALEXANDER, Cultural Trauma and Collective Identity (Berkeley, Calif., 2004) • M. EHLERT and B. LORKE, "Zur Psychodynamik der traumatischen Reaktion," Psyche 42 (1988) 502-32 • S. FERENCZI, "Confusion of Tongues between the Adult and the Child," IJPsa 30 (1949) 225-30; idem, Selected Writings (ed. J. Borossa; London, 1999) • M. R. KHAN, "The Concept of Cumulative Trauma," The Psychoanalytic Study of the Child 18 (1963) 286-306; idem, The Privacy of the Self: Papers on Psychoanalytic Theory and Technique (New York, 1974) • J. LAPLANCHE and J.-B. PONTALIS, The Language of Psycho-Analysis (New York, 1974) • W. MERTENS and B. WALDVOGEL, eds., Handbuch psychoanalytischer Grundbegriffe (2d ed.; Stuttgart, 2002) • O. RANK, The Trauma of Birth (New York, 1952) • L. TERR, Too Scared to Cry: Psychic Trauma in Childhood (New York, 1990) • R. J. URSANO and A. E. NORWOOD, eds., Trauma and Disaster Responses and Management (Washington, D.C., 2003).

HERIBERT WAHL

Trent, Council of

1. Prior History
2. Tasks and Conditions
3. Course
4. Results
5. Significance

The Council of Trent (1545-63, with two breaks of several years each; → Councils of the Church 4) was the official answer of the → Roman Catholic Church to the → Reformation and its questions to theology, its preaching, and its ecclesiology. By means of definitions, judgments, and reforming decrees, and in spite of interruptions and internal worries, the council brought about a limited but effective renewal of the church (→ Catholic Reform and Counterreformation) and created presuppositions for self-assurance and resolution that initiated a new stage in its history.

1. Prior History

In 1518 Martin → Luther (1483-1546; → Luther's Theology) appealed for the convening of a general council (WA 2.36-40), and he did so again in 1520 (WA 7.75-82, Ger. 85-90). He believed that a valid council, assisted by the Holy Spirit, was superior to the → pope. He renewed the earlier conciliarist arguments (→ Conciliarism), ignoring prohibitions of such appeals (by Martin V [1417-31] and Pius II [1458-64], the latter in his 1460 bull Execrabilis; DH 1375). He disregarded the claim that the pope is superior to councils (made by Leo X [1513-21] in his 1516 bull Pastor aeternus; DH 1445). Luther not only wanted a council to undertake the reforming of the church publicly but felt that the Christian church as a whole should be the true agent behind the council. His appeal gained popular support.

After Nürnberg in 1523 the German Diet repeatedly called for a "free Christian council" in accordance with Luther's intentions, not accepting the pope as judge but viewing the council itself as a Christian assembly subject to the Reformation principle of Scripture and the church. The threat that a German council might be held to resolve regional problems had to be taken seriously by both pope and emperor. Charles V (1519-56), convinced of the need for major church reform, saw in a council the most appropriate instrument for his ecclesiastical policies if he was to preserve the empire intact, achieve church unity, and thus be able to marshal all his forces against the Turkish menace. Clement VII (1523-34), however, sought to evade these demands. He feared the strengthening of conciliarist traditions that had already been overcome and the related weakening of his own position in actual conflict with the emperor (→ Empire and Papacy).

It was left to Paul III (1534-49) to initiate a change. He gave new life to the college of → cardinals by appointing those who favored reform (e.g., G. P. Caraffa, G. Contarini, J. Sadoleto), and in June 1536 he summoned a council at Mantua for May 1537. A commission of cardinals listed abuses that were in need of church reform. Political circumstances, however, meant a postponing of the council, then its relocation at Vicenza, and finally its suspension in May 1539. Protestants rejected the invitation. The plan foresaw a council *iuxta morem ecclesiae consuetum* (though this was not included in the invitation), which meant that subjection to the pope was presupposed. France was also in opposition.

In 1542 further steps were taken, but the outbreak of the fourth war between Charles V and Francis I (1515-47) intervened. A fresh invitation went out for May 1545. According to the 1544 bull *Laetare Hierusalem,* Trent, on the borders of the empire in what is now northwestern Italy, was the site selected. External conditions, though, were still not favorable. The pope wanted to restrict imperial influence as much as possible, and a united approach to Protestants was prevented. Francis had suffered a military defeat and, by the Treaty of Crépy (1544), was forced to attend, but he had no inclination to promote the council and its aims.

2. Tasks and Conditions

The council was given a threefold task: restore church unity, reform the church, and free Christians from the yoke of unbelief. It did not achieve any of the aims. The liberation of southeastern Europe from Turkish domination, which reached its climax with the armistice of 1544, played no great role in the council.

External influences repeatedly forced the council to break up, so that the question arises whether the interrupted council was restarted or whether in each case a new council was formed. Furthermore, the order of business showed no clear design; only after discussion did the council hit upon a clear-cut theological line. The delegates were not representative, and the papal legates took the lead. The Protestant estates of the empire had rejected an invitation to be present at the Diet of Worms in the summer of 1545. The invitation sent by both pope and emperor was a serious threat, for the emperor had accepted reforming measures only until a council met, and the state of peace would soon be at an end. Theologians like Philipp → Melanchthon (→ Reformers 2.1.1), in memoranda that rejected the council, stated that they were ready, at the emperor's request, to come to the council and give reasons for their teaching (CRef 6.45).

3. Course

3.1. The *first period* (December 1545–March 1547) began by discussing the agenda. Paul III objected to the decision that doctrine and reform would be handled together, but he was overruled. The first topics concerned Scripture and → tradition, original → sin, → justification, and the → sacraments (general sacramental teaching, → baptism, and → confirmation). The first treatment of a reform proposal focused on the duty of bishops to reside in their dioceses and led to a fundamental debate that threatened the unity of the council.

The Schmalkaldic War began in July 1546. The emperor and the pope defeated the Protestant princes and forced them to accept the council. Before the victory was won, however, a new, serious division arose between the emperor and the pope regarding the methodology of the council. An outbreak of typhus at Trent brought welcome relief. The council had to move to Bologna, within the → Papal States.

Rome seemed to be writing off Germany, and the unity of the empire was under threat. The emperor sought his own solution. After his victory against the Schmalkaldic League, he imposed the Augsburg Interim of 1548, which involved many concessions to Rome. The rump council at Bologna discussed the sacraments but did not publish any findings. During the second half of 1548 it began to dissolve. Paul III died in November 1549.

3.2. Julius III (1550-55) reconvened the council at Trent. This *second period* lasted less than a full year (May 1551–April 1552). On the basis of preliminary work done at Bologna, it published decrees on the individual sacraments (Eucharist, penance, and extreme unction). Reforming decrees dealt with details regarding the episcopal office.

As a result of the Schmalkaldic War, representatives of the Protestant states attended (from Württemberg, Strasbourg, and Saxony). In January 1552 they presented documents prepared earlier (the Württemberg Confession and the Saxon Confession) and presented orally their basic demands. But no true negotiations took place, for meanwhile the so-called Princes' Revolution, under Elector Maurice of Saxony (1541-53), was now threatening the south, endangering the council itself. Even before the Saxon delegates had arrived, the council was suspended at the end of April 1552. The "council of union" was shattered even before it had begun.

3.3. Julius was followed by Marcellus II (1555), whose pontificate lasted only three weeks. The election of Paul IV (1555-59) kindled fresh hopes, for he had advocated reform. He set up a reforming commission and considered calling a new council at Rome instead of reconvening at Trent. Paul IV's stern measures (Index; → Inquisition 2), however, shocked the Reformers and ruled out any continuation of the council.

Pius IV (1559-65), the fourth new pope since the opening of the council, finally initiated the *third and concluding period* (January 1562–December 1563). The situation in France was a compelling factor. In spite of serious persecutions under Henry II (1547-59), the movement of reform had been gaining ground in France. The early death of the king had brought a period of peace, but a national council was summoned in the summer of 1561, at which church reform would be discussed, along with a general discussion of religion. Rome was alarmed, even though no concrete results were achieved.

Reforming proposals regarding the duty of bishops to reside in their dioceses were postponed once again. The papacy did not accept the idea that this was a matter of divine law but saw it rather as an attack on its own authority. Decrees were passed about Communion in both kinds, the → Mass as a sacrifice, and the use of the vernacular. In the autumn of 1552 a French delegation under Cardinal C. Guise (1524-74) gave added strength to the "episcopalistic" faction. The result was a hardening of the fronts as the secular powers (Emperor Ferdinand I and King Philip II of Spain) responded. The diplomatic skill of Cardinal G. Morone (1509-80), the new president of the council after the death of the legates E. Gonzaga (1505-63) and G. Seripando (1492/93-1563), made compromise possible and saved the situation. Decrees about orders were now passed, and further decisions were made con-

cerning → marriage, → purgatory, veneration of the → saints, reform of the orders (→ Religious Orders and Congregations 1), → indulgences, → fasting, and the Index. The council fathers signed the documents on December 4, 1563, and the work of the council was done. Pius IV ratified the decisions on June 30, 1564, in the bull *Benedictus Deus* (backdated to January 26, 1564). The Reformers had taken no part in this final period but heavily criticized what was done (R. Kolb).

4. Results

The doctrinal decrees answering Reformation questions covered all the main points of the controversy: Scripture and → tradition (→ Canon; Revelation 2; Reformation Principles) as the basis of → faith (§3.4.4) and doctrine (→ Teaching Office 1), → justification (§2) as the central Christian teaching *(articulus stantis et cadentis ecclesiae,* "the article by which the church stands or falls"), and the → sacraments (§2.4.3) as, along with → proclamation, the most important spheres of church ministry.

4.1. The decree concerning the sources of revelation (*CT* 5.91-92; DH 1501-8) declares that the Apocrypha is part of the biblical → canon (§2.2), that equal reverence is to be given to Scripture and to tradition, and that the Vulgate (→ Bible Versions 2) constitutes the authentic form of the text.

4.2. The decree concerning original sin (*CT* 5.238-40; DH 1510-16; → Sin 3.2.4) says that all hereditary guilt is forgiven at → baptism and that the concupiscence that remains is not really → sin, contrary to the Lutheran view (→ Sin 3.3). The question of the immaculate conception of Mary was raised in this connection (→ Mariology 1.3.3, 2.4), but no dogmatic definition was established.

4.3. A comprehensive decree concerning justification (*CT* 5.791-99; DH 1520-83) tried to deal with Reformation insights by rejecting nominalistic theses that dealt with the possibility of human merit in a full sense (→ Nominalism; Grace 3.2). Whether or not it went halfway by accepting a "merit of congruity" is disputed even today. The decree did not reject the "faith alone" of the Reformers (→ Reformation Principles), but it stressed the need "to make preparation and be disposed by a movement of [one's] own will" (can. 9) and thus to play one's part in conjunction with the God upon whom one calls (can. 4). It did not agree that faith is trust in the divine mercy (→ Faith 3.4.3), and it also rejected the link that the Reformers perceived between faith and → assurance of salvation (can. 13). Justification includes "sanctification and renewal of the inward being by a willing acceptance of the grace and gifts whereby someone from being unjust becomes just" (chap. 7), and it is augmented by good works before God (can. 24).

4.4. Decrees about the sacraments (DH 1600-1630, 1667-1719, 1738-59, 1763-78, 1797-1812) confirm traditional teaching both in general and in detail, and they reject Reformation insights. Real presence is accepted, along with the eucharistic sacrifice and transubstantiation (→ Eucharist 3.2.1-2). The cup is withheld from the laity. The obligation of penance (→ Pentinence 3) was upheld, and the seven sacraments were seen to be true sacraments instituted by the historical Jesus (→ Sacrament 2.4.3). The decree on → ordination (*CT* 9.620-22; DH 1763-68) left open the question of divine law, that is, the relation between episcopal and papal authority (cans. 6, 8).

4.5. The reforms were in the main pastoral (→ Pastoral Care). They fell short of expectations but did impose stricter norms. Cardinal Morone's reforming program was especially significant (*CT* 9.623-30). The position of the → bishop was strengthened. → Residence was a divine command (can. 1), and the bishop should not be greedy. Provincial and diocesan synods were instituted, as were diocesan seminaries. The reading of Scripture and preaching were promoted. The decree *Tametsi* (*CT* 9.966-71; DH 1813-16) was important in developing the law of marriage.

5. Significance

The council, which ended 27 years after it was first summoned, concentrated on internal church reforms. Defense was the guiding principle, given the fear that secular powers might intervene. It rightly sought to pose both internal and external questions and to come up with new answers. But it did not really face the challenge of the Reformation. In doctrine it took into account and, to varying degrees, wrestled with the positions of the Reformers, and it did some correction (e.g., with indulgences), but it kept strictly to traditional principles. The political decisions of the Peace of Augsburg were confirmed in the religious sphere (→ Augsburg, Peace of).

The Roman church achieved confessional status at Trent. Two documents that appeared after Trent — the *Professio fidei Tridentina* (1564; → Creed of Pius IV) and the → Catechismus Romanus (1566) — gave visible expression to this fact. Along these lines the council helped to solidify Reformation positions. M. Chemnitz (1522-86) critically examined the results of the council in his *Examen concilii Tridentini* (4 vols., 1566-73; ET *Examination of the Council of Trent* [St. Louis, 1971-86]) and worked

out his own position in response. Controversy with the decrees and canons of Trent promoted the development of "Lutheran Scholasticism" (→ Orthodoxy 1).

Interchurch → dialogue (§2.3.1; → Ecumenical Dialogue) after → Vatican II has involved a wide discussion of how far-reaching and how valid the decisions and anathemas of Trent are. The most extensive results, not undisputed, have come from a group in Germany, the Ecumenical Study Group of Protestant and Catholics Theologians, who have found a common basic understanding of the → gospel and of the gift of the → sacraments (§3.2). The group noted that "neither the Protestant Confessions, nor even the decrees and canons of the Council of Trent, may be read primarily as texts directed against the genuine doctrine of the other side" (K. Lehmann and W. Pannenberg, 21).

The attempt in this sense to summarize definitively the results of the theological dialogue about the doctrine of justification on several levels led in 1995 to a "Joint Declaration" of the Lutheran World Federation and the Roman Catholic Church. It mentions a "consensus on the basic truths of the doctrine of justification," and both churches are encouraged to mutually recognize that the doctrinal judgments of the 16th century on this subject no longer apply to either partner. In spite of some strongly controversial discussions (on the Catholic side, with direct reference to the permanent validity of the Tridentine decrees), this declaration was affirmed by both churches on October 31, 1999, with the ceremonial signing of a "joint declaration" — until then a unique result in the course of ecumenical theological dialogue (→ Joint Declaration on the Doctrine of Justification). Because of the diversity of theological approaches, however, there remain wide divergences, especially on the points that were hotly contested in the 16th century (esp. *simul iustus et peccator, sola fide*, and the criteriological significance of the doctrine of justification). The anticipated outworking and preservation of this → consensus in the life and teaching of the churches has not yet become evident.

Bibliography: G. Alberigo and I. Rogger, eds., *Il Concilio di Trento nella prospettiva del terzo millennio* (Brescia, 1997) • B. Brenner, "Gemeinsame Erklärung zur Rechtfertigungslehre," *KJ 1998* • *CT* • H. Jedin, *Crisis and Closure of the Council of Trent: A Retrospective View from the Second Vatican Council* (London, 1967); idem, *A History of the Council of Trent* (2 vols.; St. Louis, 1957-61); idem, "Trent, Council of," *NCE* (2d ed.) 14.168-76 • R. Kolb, "The German Lutheran Reaction to the Third Period of the Council of Trent," *LuJ* 51 (1984) 63-95 • K. Lehmann and W. Pannenberg, *The Condemnations of the Reformation Era: Do They Still Divide?* (trans. M. Kohl; Minneapolis, 1990) • The Lutheran World Federation and The Roman Catholic Church, *Joint Declaration on the Doctrine of Justification* (Grand Rapids, 2000) • G. Maron, "Das Konzil von Trient in evangelischer Sicht," *MdKI* 46 (1995) 107-14 • O. H. Pesch, "Kernpunkte der Kontroverse: Die antireformatorischen Lehrentscheidungen des Konzils von Trient (1545-1563)–und die Folgen," *Zur Zukunft der Ökumene: Die Gemeinsame Erklärung zur Rechtfertigungslehre* (ed. B. J. Hilberath and W. Pannenberg; Regensburg, 1999) 24-57 • D. N. Power, *The Sacrifice We Offer: The Tridentine Dogma and Its Reinterpretation* (New York, 1987) • P. Prodi and W. Reinhard, eds., *Il Concilio di Trento e il moderno* (Bologna, 1996) • W. Reinhard and H. Schilling, eds., *Die katholische Konfessionalisierung* (Gütersloh, 1995) • G. Schreiber, *Das Weltkonzil von Trient* (2 vols.; Freiburg, 1951) • R. Stupperich, "Die Reformation und das Tridentinum," *ARG* 47 (1956) 20-63 • A. Tallon, *La France et le Concile de Trente, 1518-1563* (Paris, 1997) • N. P. Tanner, ed., *Decrees of the Ecumenical Councils* (2 vols.; Washington, D.C., 1990) 2.657-799.

HUBERT KIRCHNER

Tribal Religions

1. History of Research and Definition
2. Features
3. Tribal and Other Religions

1. History of Research and Definition

The religions of so-called primitive peoples, which G. W. F. Hegel (1770-1831; → Hegelianism; Idealism 6) would not recognize as religion according to his definition, became an object of research in the 19th century, not on their own account, but to offer material for wide-ranging theories and to provide an answer to the question of the origin of religion as such. The presuppositions of the → Enlightenment and the concept of → evolution included the idea that these religions were at the lowest stage of what was regarded as the progressive course of the → history of religion.

A. Lang (1844-1912) and W. Schmidt (1868-1954) took an opposite view. They tried to show that at the first there was a belief in God that regressively declined into idolatry. É. Durkheim (1858-1917) and the contribution he made to ethnosociology (followed by B. Malinowski and his school) repre-

sented a big step forward. Under the influence of psychoanalysis, depth psychology, and structural theorizing (→ Structuralism), newer research has embraced studies of individual religions. Through symbol research, these efforts have led to the comparison of many religious ideas, notwithstanding the differences, and, avoiding improper reduction, have demonstrated common structures and convictions among them. The understanding thus arose that we are dealing here with religions in the full sense of the word. They constitute a kind of basic religiousness and are, as a "primary religious experience" (T. Sundermeier), the basis of the world religions that have come to overlay them, with whom they merge into the prevailing folk religion (→ State Church).

There is as yet no agreement on what tribal religions should be called. Some suggest "the religions of nonliterary cultures," or "nature religions." Yet the term "tribal religion" is particularly apt because it takes seriously the deep integration of religion and society under territorial conditions. Some terminological uncertainty remains, however, because the term "tribes" denotes ethnic units that may range from very small numbers (e.g., in the Amazon basin and Brazil) to the kingdoms of Africa that had over a million people. Yet even in the latter cases the religion shows something of the structure of smaller tribal societies.

2. Features

2.1. We always must consider *the inner structure of a smaller society* when looking at its religion. The unity of the territory determines tribal religion. Special features in the environment affect the total culture and therefore the religious symbolism. The east-west axis and the way the sun rises and sets are determinative directions. Events come from the east, which holds good even when it is known that they come from the north. The east symbolizes the dawn and a new beginning. The sea can be a threat and thus stands for → evil, but it can also be a source of nourishment and thus be a symbol of → life.

Geographic location determines the understanding of life. The "navel" of the world is localized, whether we be in Greece, India, Africa, Indonesia, or Israel. The land possesses mythical features (→ Myth, Mythology). It is the gift of the ancestors or of God, belongs to the whole tribe, and cannot be alienated. The Europeans disregarded this religious and legal principle in the colonial period (→ Colonialism), which became the cause of many revolts and ecclesiastical separations (→ Colonialism and Mission).

2.2. *Social unity* corresponds to territorial unity. It may not be comprehensible, but it is known in some way as deriving from the ancestors and mythically and genealogically represented by the chieftain or king. The chieftain counts as a father and is usually addressed as such. Society centers on the extended family, a feature that is constitutive for religion. Often the term "person" applies only to one's own group.

A strong network of social relations intersects society. No one can leave this network unless one moves away, falls into a false and unsocial line of conduct, or changes one's religion. This generalization continues in effect in the → modern period. No one can stand alone; all people are in relation. To destroy the relation, which applies to → animals as well, as seen in → totemism, is to undercut humanity.

2.3. All members of the tribe participate in its *one common life*. They have inherited it, and they pass it on to coming generations. No one must break the chain. Childlessness is not merely a scandal but also involves guilt. A large number of children is a sign of blessing, for life means increase. Life cannot end at death. It lives on in ancestors in a changed form that is partly stronger and partly weaker (→ Ancestor Worship). A relation to ancestors is a social task and not merely a religious exercise.

With some exceptions, this task is inherent in tribal religions. It is a basically conservative attitude that has various consequences. We see them in the structure of how houses and villages are laid out, with an altar to ancestors in the middle or with reflection of a human body visible in some way. Where ancestor worship is strong, there is a cosmological orientation. Individuality in the building of houses is unthinkable. The life of ancestors may be seen in children or grandchildren. It can be said that they return in the grandchildren (West Africa), yet there is no real thought of reincarnation or of the Asian notion of belief in → karma.

Small societies do not allow of pluralism. Their uniformity makes for instability and cannot protect them from internal or external threats. Only one culture and one model of ethical conduct are possible. Orientation must be given to the conduct of the ancestors, who will bless or punish if their commands are kept or ignored. The heart of a religiously sanctioned → ethics is good social behavior and respect for the neighbor, which means recognizing the neighbor's place in the hierarchically integrated society. In common action, in assisting or feasting, the supreme aim is → peace, or harmonious human relations. Peace or harmony counts much more than → truth or justice (in the Western sense). Those who stir up strife are in the wrong, even though their cause is just. The Asian ethical principle of "saving face" has its root here. Wicked deeds, and even evil itself, come from the heart. This idea is at the root of belief in witches and magicians. Tribal religions, though, are not dualistic (→ Dualism).

2.4. A definition of religion that does not include tribal religion is wide of the mark, for we cannot separate religion from society. One can be born into religion without any choice, unless we have cultural contact with other peoples or engage in → mission that brings about the downfall of society as well as religion. Tribal religions are *by nature opposed to mission,* for they have validity only in the tribe and include ancestor worship, tribal tradition, and tribal ethics. Rites in the annual or life cycle (rites of passage, rites for the seasons, rites for rain or at times of drought, rites of birth, puberty, marriage, and death; → Initiation Rites), along with communal undertakings (the hunt, harvest), are central means of presenting religion and its symbolic mediation. They are the cement of society. Addressed to the people, they include the invisible world of ancestors and spirits, and even deities if a pantheon is in view, though not God.

God is too great and infinite to be brought into the little things of daily life (→ Spirituality 2.1). He is not honored in the cult, but he is invoked in many tribal religions in extraordinary circumstances. God is the last horizon of reality and cannot be crossed. Rites are religious constants and may persist even with a change of culture, or as a religion is subjected to inculturation. Myths are variable. For their part, symbols retain their religious significance. What may confuse outsiders is clear to those who know.

Symbols are constituted by a network of → analogy that orients African, Indonesian, and South American tribal religions to the human body; in contrast, North American Indian and East Asian tribal religions are oriented to the cosmos. In the one case nature is seen in human terms; in the other, in cosmological terms. The latter results in a stronger openness to mystical experiences, which are alien to African religions.

3. Tribal and Other Religions

In many cases tribal religions have remained isolated, but in other cases they have changed through contacts with other cultures. The religions of Indonesia came under Hindu influence, and those of the Sudan under Egyptian influence (more than was once believed). → Islam and Christianity have prevailed over tribal religions and had great missionary success.

Tribal religions, however, are not suppressed. They show great resistance in new religious movements. They possess a religious legacy that world religions overlook or try to defeat at their own peril. As Christianity and its symbols have been essentially influenced and changed when passing through the Greek, Roman, and Germanic worlds, so it will be again in the process of inculturation in the so-called → Third World if the strength of the churches' faith can accept, without fear of → syncretism, an indigenous and independent form of Christianity in the new situation with a new symbolic expression. The so-called African → Independent Churches are forerunners in this process.

Bibliography: *American Tribal Religions* (12 vols.; Lincoln, Nebr., 1977-87) • M. CHARLESWORTH et al., eds., *Aboriginal Religions in Australia* (Aldershot, 2005) • W. R. COMSTOCK, *The Study of Religion and Primitive Religions* (New York, 1972) • E. E. EVANS-PRITCHARD, *Theories of Primitive Religion* (Oxford, 1965) • F. GÖLZ, *Der primitive Mensch und seine Religion* (Gütersloh, 1963) • *International Encyclopaedia of Tribal Religion* (ed. S. M. Channa; New Delhi, 2000) • E. JENSEN, *The Iban and Their Religion* (Oxford, 1974) • J. S. MBITI, *African Religions and Philosophy* (London, 1969); idem, *Concepts of God in Africa* (London, 1970) • H. NEVERMANN et al., *Die Religionen der Südsee und Australiens* (Stuttgart, 1968) • H. RÜCKER, *"Afrikanische Theologie." Darstellung und Dialog* (Innsbruck, 1985) • W. SCHMIDT, *Der Ursprung der Gottesidee* (12 vols.; Münster, 1912-55) • T. SUNDERMEIER, *The Individual and Community in African Traditional Religions* (Hamburg, 1998); idem, *Nur gemeinsam können wir leben. Das Menschenbild schwarzafrikanischer Religionen* (3d ed.; Hamburg, 1997) • J. J. WAARDENBURG, *Classical Approaches to the Study of Religion* (New York, 1999) • F. WHALING, ed., *Contemporary Approaches to the Study of Religion* (2 vols.; New York, 1983-85) • I. WULFHORST, ed., *Spirits, Ancestors, and Healing: A Global Challenge to the Church* (Geneva, 2006) • D. ZAHAN, *The Religion, Spirituality, and Thought of Traditional Africa* (Chicago, 1979).

THEO SUNDERMEIER

Tribes of Israel

1. History and Results of Research
2. Before Nationhood
3. The Tribes and the Young Nation
4. The Twelve-Tribe System

1. History and Results of Research

From Numbers to 1 Kgs. 11:30, Israel is portrayed as a community of 12 tribes. Discrepancies in the lists (either with Levi and Joseph, the sons of → Jacob, or without Levi and with Ephraim and Manasseh, the grandchildren of Jacob), as well as an older system of 10 tribes of Israel (Judges 5 [without Judah, Simeon, Gad, and Manasseh, but with Machir and Gilead]; 1 Kgs. 11:31) plus Judah (1 Kgs. 11:32), show the 12-tribe system to be a recent, theoretical construct (see 4). In their material culture and linguistically, the tribes of the 12th through the 9th centuries B.C. formed no unity. What they had in common was their origin in the agricultural colonization of the territory, which at the end of this period belonged to the nations of Israel and Judah (→ Israel 1.2).

The point of departure for research since 1976 is the archaeological discoveries in the highlands of Palestine and their socioanthropological interpretation (→ Archaeology). The consensus of those involved in this study is that the new tribes were of a double origin: on the one hand, migrants who were agricultural underlings in the Late Bronze Age city-states that were breaking apart (→ City 1); on the other hand, autochthonous "local nomads" (the Shasu of Egyptian texts) from the mountains, with no interclan tribal organization. The tribes exhibited a developed class society with an egalitarian ideology, not a "segmentary-egalitarian" society (W. Dostal); Heb. *šebeṭ*, "staff" (as a sign of power), has "tribe" as a derived meaning.

By means of property and prestigious possessions (Judg. 5:10; 12:14), a tribal aristocracy set itself apart from free tribal members who possessed land, had a duty to serve militarily, and had the right to vote in the tribal council — over against members who were personally free but not able to vote (the *gērîm*, or sojourners) and slaves, who were not free (see also J. W. Rogerson). This social stratification is found with consistency in the Song of Deborah, the narratives of the Book of Judges, the → Book of the Covenant (Exod. 20:22–23:19), and archaeological findings.

The research of the late 19th century assumed the unified immigration and settlement of nomadic tribes from the desert (→ Nomads). M. Noth (1902-68) was the first to recognize the formation of tribes by new settlers in the various tribal territories. A. Alt (1883-1956) had already identified the process of the "conquest of Israel" with the transformation of the Palestinian highlands from an expansive unsettled area in the Late Bronze Age to the heartland of the states populated by agricultural clans of the first century B.C. Israel's need for unity before the formation of the nation led Noth to the formulation of his so-called amphictyony hypothesis, according to which the 12 tribes maintained a common central holy place (→ Sanctuary 2). Objections to an empirically unverifiable nomad concept such as offered by Alt and Noth led American researchers to suggest a "revolutionary" origin of Israel — a peasant uprising against the feudal power of the Canaanite cities that was supposedly nurtured by → monotheism as an antiurban → ideology. This concept also does not correspond with the sources.

The aforementioned explanatory attempts have a common motivation: to allow the central theologoumenon of the OT — → Yahweh as the God of Israel, and Israel as the → people of God — to define this history from the very beginning. It may be posited in response that this formula loses nothing of its normative character for → church and → Judaism if one derives it from theological reflection on the history of the 10th to the 5th century B.C.

2. Before Nationhood

The catastrophe of "first Israel," brought on by Pharaoh Merneptah in 1208 B.C., when he led a military campaign into Canaan, may perhaps be connected to the tribes of *Levi* and *Simeon*, which are historically no longer accessible (the tribe of Levi in the 12-tribe system is an occupational group, and Simeon's settlement area in the south is a geographic fiction; S. Mittmann). The village colonization of the area, which had previously been populated only by nomadic farmers and herdsmen who lacked any tribal relationship beyond their clans, began in the mountains of Ephraim, the territory of the "first Israel" in the 12-tribe system — that is, after the catastrophe of 1208 (and possibly also at the same time in the northern part of the Lower Galilee and in Gilead). It then spread by the end of the 11th century into the Upper Galilee and Judah, and in the 10th century into the southern part of Lower Galilee (*Issachar;* see I. Finkelstein, R. Frankel).

The driving power of the village colonization must have been the villages themselves (esp. the technical knowledge of agriculture), whereby new settlements carried the process forward (B. Mershen and E. A. Knauf). The original local nomadic population was integrated into satellite settlements of the large villages; for numerical reasons alone, it could neither initiate nor maintain the process of settlement. The breaking up of the Late Bronze Age economic system with the resulting crises, unrest, and threats to survival in the older settled territory on the plains gives sufficient reason for the process of colonization (R. B. Coote and K. W. Whitelam).

Tradition reflects the dual origin of the tribes of Israel, perhaps even in the names of the primal mothers *Leah* ("cow," referring to the raising of cattle by the plow farmers) and *Rachel* ("ewe," referring to the local nomads). The emigrants from the Caananite city-states had experienced an "exodus out of Egypt," for these states stood until the first half of the 12th century under Egyptian colonial rule. The formation of agricultural tribes ensued, bringing increasing population pressure in the newly settled territory, which called for a political organization for mutual support against their neighbor.

Of the tribal names, *Ephraim, Benjamin, Naphtali, Gilead,* and *Judah* are territorial designations, thus documenting the priority of territory over the political unifications of its inhabitants. The lack of distinct personal names among the tribal designations (a possible exception is Manasseh; see below) points to the fact that, in contrast to surviving Bedouin tribes, the person-associated tribe centered around a chief's clan played no role in the names' origins, in contrast to agricultural/territorial tribes.

The primary tribe of biblical Israel is *Ephraim*, located on the highlands of Ephraim. *Manasseh* in its northern part had secondarily broken away from Ephraim (hence the name "who makes forgotten"). *Pirathon* in the area of Manassite clans is still located, according to Judg. 12:15, "in the land of Ephraim." The Song of Deborah in Judg. 5:14, 17 recognizes *Machir* in the west and *Gilead* in the east but not Manasseh.

Later Machir becomes a son of Manasseh and a father of Gilead (Gen. 50:23; Num. 26:29, among others). Because of the mention of Issachar in Galilee (Judg. 5:15), the battle of Deborah, as well as the Song of Deborah, can be dated not before the 10th and not later than the 9th century B.C. The Galilean tribes *Issachar* (see Judg. 10:1) and *Asher* (see 1 Chron. 7:30-40; D. V. Edelman) also came out of Ephraim (unlike the native Galileans *Zebulun* and *Naphtali*). Evidence that the process of tribal formation had its center in the highlands of Ephraim is shown also by the tribal name "Benjamin" (lit. "the southerner"), for Benjamin was once the southernmost of the Israeli tribes. Not until the end of the 11th century did the process of settlement reach *Judah*, whose name has the same etymon as the Benjaminic clan name "Ehud" (*yhd;* see Arab. *wahda,* "gorge").

In view of the assumed emigration from Asher and Issachar to Galilee and the Ephramitic-Manassitic-Benjaminic colonization in East Jordan, the wandering saga of *Dan* in Judges 17–18 is perhaps historical (H. M. Niemann), although it may well stand behind the existing polemic against the northern kingdom of Israel. In East Jordan the native Gileadites (Judg. 5:17; 10:3–12:7) received an influx from Ephraim/Manasseh (Josh. 17:14-18) and Benjamin (1 Chron 8:1-3; see possibly also Judg. 21:8-14, with 1 Sam. 11:3-4). *Reuben* appears to have been a cattle-raising tribe on both sides of the north end of the Dead Sea (Judg. 5:15-16; Num. 26:6-7; Josh. 15:6; 18:17; Num. 32:37-38) that died out either in or soon after the tenth century (Deut. 33:6). *Gad* is well known from the Mesha legend inscription (KAI 181.10), yet Mesha considered the tribe to be Moabite, whose territory had been under Israeli occupation under Omri. (For a similar fate, note the Alsatians in Europe between 1871 and 1945.)

3. The Tribes and the Young Nation
The tribes were not a unified cultural people (any more than Franconia, Saxony, and Bavaria in the 6th-8th cents. could understand themselves as German). Ad hoc associations existed, though, between neighboring tribes (e.g., see Judg. 6:35; 7:23; historical records indicate, however, that they did not exist from earliest times). The path to Israel's nationhood led to expanded chieftaincies. In the beginning there were figures such as Gideon of Abiezer (Judg. 8:4-27*) or Jephthah of Gilead (Judg. 11:1-11; similarly, the rise of David). Tribal leaders/local rulers indeed existed among the so-called minor judges. If a tribal aristocrat succeeded in becoming the ruler of a town (Judges 9, Abimelech and Shechem; see later → Saul and Gibeon, → David and Hebron, → Solomon and → Jerusalem), a "tribal nation" arose that either broke apart over the conflict between nation and tribe or, over a period of time, devalued (but did not remove) the tribal structures. Saul achieved the first comprehensive chieftancy (with Benjamin, Ephraim, and Gilead; see Edelman). If one can designate his predecessors (anachronistically?) as rulers *in* Israel, then Saul can be called the first ruler *over* Israel. This achievement cannot be taken away from the ruler whom tradition labels a failure. Saul's death on the battlefield did not endanger the survival of his creation (as little as the death of Cyrus the Great ended the Persian kingdom).

The gradual increase of nationhood in central Palestine between the 11th and 9th centuries was financially as well as structurally necessitated by the pronounced economic upturn in the world. Saul's son Ishbaal already reigned over an Israel that, from Saul onward, included Galilee (*ăšûrî*, "Asher-tribe") and the plain of Jezreel (2 Sam. 2:9). It is the Israel of the Song of Deborah (Judges 5), which, with its praise of the tribes struggling against Sisera (an Illyrian name with a Philistine expansion; see Saul's battles and the rise of David) and its scorn for those tribes holding back from the battle, presents itself as a piece of courtly propaganda, revealing its "Israel" (as all later biblical Israels) as a postulate.

It is characteristic for a tribe early in the process of becoming a → state to demand loyalty to "the [warrior-]people of Yahweh" (Judg. 5:11, 13) rather than to the ruling house (E. R. Service; see, however, religious → pluralism [§2] in the Early Iron Age in Palestine; O. Keel and C. Uehlinger). A paradigmatic example of secondary state formation is offered by David, who, as a Philistine vassal of Ziklag, united the tribes of late Judah (Judah [from Benjamin], Caleb [native? Judg. 1:12-15], Kenites [1 Sam. 30:27-31], and Jerahmeelites [local nomads of the Negev]) by means of bribery (Judah, Jerahmeelites, Kenites: 1 Sam 30:27-31) or violence (Caleb: 1 Samuel 25; 2 Sam. 2:1-4 [a war report]; David's capital, Hebron, was a Calebite center) and makes them subjects of a tribal kingdom. In Judah's case, state formation and tribal formation coincided.

4. The Twelve-Tribe System
The prophecy of Ahijah of Shiloh, which possibly goes back to the tenth century (H. Weippert), still recognizes *ten tribes plus one* (1 Kgs. 11:31-32). → Isaac's fatherhood of Jacob/Israel and Esau/Edom, along with the situation of Judah being centrally located between both neighbors, perhaps mirrors also a lordship claim of Judah over Israel that goes back to the time of David. Judah, however, stood in the shadow of Israel (possibly as a vassal; J. M. Miller and J. H. Hayes) from the end of the formation of the Israeli state under Omri until the appearance of the Assyrians in the southern Levant. In the *12-tribe system* with Judah, one of the sons of Jacob, one can see the Israeli expression of the power relationships of the ninth-eighth centuries that Judah took over with the inheritance and claims of Israel under Hezekiah (→ Israel 1.5).

→ Literature, Biblical and Early Christian; Moses; Sinai; Tribal Religions

Bibliography: R. B. Coote, *Early Israel: A New Horizon* (Minneapolis, 1990) • R. B. Coote and K. W. Whitelam, *The Emergence of Early Israel in Historical Perspective* (Sheffield, 1987) • H. Donner, *Geschichte des Volkes Israels und seiner Nachbarn in Grundzügen* (vol. 1; Göttingen, 1984) • W. Dostal, *Egalität und Klassengesellschaft in Südarabien. Anthropologische Untersuchungen zur sozialen Evolution* (Horn, 1985) • D. V.

EDELMAN, "Saul," *ABD* 5.989-99 • I. FINKELSTEIN, *The Archaeology of the Israelite Settlement* (Jerusalem, 1988); idem, "The Emergence of Israel in Canaan: Consensus, Mainstream, and Dispute," *SJOT* 5/2 (1991) 47-59 • R. FRANKEL, "Galilee," *ABD* 2.879-95 • C. H. J. DE GEUS, *The Tribes of Israel: An Investigation into Some of the Presuppositions of Martin Noth's Amphictyony Hypothesis* (Assen, 1976) • N. K. GOTTWALD, *The Tribes of Yahweh: A Sociology of the Religion of Liberated Israel, 1250-1050 B.C.E.* (Sheffield, 1999; orig. pub., 1979) • O. KEEL and C. UEHLINGER, *Göttinnen, Götter und Gottessymbole* (Freiburg, 1992) • N. P. LEMCHE, *Early Israel* (Leiden, 1985) • B. MERSHEN and E. A. KNAUF, "From Ǧadar to Umm Qais," *ZDPV* 104 (1988) 128-45 • J. M. MILLER and J. H. HAYES, *A History of Ancient Israel and Judah* (Philadelphia, 1986) • S. MITTMANN, "Ri. 1,16f und das Siedlungsgebiet der kenitischen Sippe Hobab," *ZDPV* 93 (1977) 213-35 • H. M. NIEMANN, "Dan," *NBL* 1.382-83 • M. NOTH, *Das System der zwölf Stämme Israels* (Stuttgart, 1930) • J. W. ROGERSON, "Was Early Israel a Segmentary Society?" *JSOT* 36 (1986) 17-26 • E. R. SERVICE, *Origins of the State and Civilization: The Process of Cultural Evolution* (New York, 1975) • T. L. THOMPSON, *Early History of the Israelite People* (Leiden, 1992) • H. WEIPPERT, "Die Ätiologie des Nordreiches und seines Königshauses (I Reg 11,29-40)," *ZAW* 95 (1983) 344-75.

ERNST AXEL KNAUF

Trinidad and Tobago

	1960	1980	2000
Population (1,000s):	843	1,082	1,341
Annual growth rate (%):	1.23	1.71	0.99
Area: 5,128 sq. km. (1,980 sq. mi.)			

A.D. 2000

Population density: 261/sq. km. (677/sq. mi.)
Births / deaths: 1.72 / 0.61 per 100 population
Fertility rate: 2.10 per woman
Infant mortality rate: 12 per 1,000 live births
Life expectancy: 74.6 years (m: 72.5, f: 77.2)
Religious affiliation (%): Christians 65.3 (Roman Catholics 30.5, Protestants 14.2, Anglicans 12.1, indigenous 3.3, unaffiliated 3.0, marginal 1.5, other Christians 0.8), Hindus 22.1, Muslims 7.1, nonreligious 2.1, spiritists 1.3, Baha'is 1.2, other 0.9.

1. General Situation
2. Christians
   2.1. Roman Catholics
   2.2. Anglicans
   2.3. Spiritual Baptists
   2.4. Other Protestant Bodies
3. Other Living Faiths

1. General Situation

The Republic of Trinidad and Tobago is an archipelago nation in the southern Caribbean off the coast of Venezuela. A former British colony independent since 1962, the country consists of two main islands, of which Trinidad is the larger at 4,828 sq. km. (1,864 sq. mi.) and with 96 percent of the population; Tobago is the smaller at 300 sq. km. (116 sq. mi.), and 21 other islands complete the chain. Eighty percent of its heterogeneous population are of African or Indian descent, while the rest are of diverse or mixed European, Chinese, Arab, Syrian, and Lebanese descent. Once an agricultural colony that produced sugar and cacao, the country now derives its revenue principally from oil and → tourism. It has produced a host of well-known cultural figures, including V. S. Naipaul, Eric Williams, and C. L. R. James.

The islands were inhabited by Arawak and Carib peoples when Columbus claimed them for Spain in 1498 (→ Colonialism). As with most of their other New World possessions, Spanish colonizers on Trinidad forced the Amerindians into the *encomienda* system of tributary labor on plantations and ranches. As a result of disease and forced labor, the indigenous population declined steadily through the 16th and 17th centuries, though the last native resistance was not put down until 1699. Many Arawaks converted to Christianity. The Spanish colonial presence on Trinidad remained relatively weak during the 18th century, and a "Cédula [bill, warrant] of Population" issued in 1783 by the Spanish king opened the colony to non-Spanish Catholic immigrants, particularly French and Irish. Britain finally occupied it in 1797 during the Napoleonic Wars. Tobago, meanwhile, passed between Dutch, British, and French possession before being annexed by the British in 1790.

To regenerate the plantation economy, the British imported large numbers of enslaved Africans into the colonies during the decade before the end of the transatlantic slave trade in 1807, and sugar production soared. At the time of slave emancipation in the British colonies in 1838, Trinidad and Tobago between them held some 26,000 slaves (→ Slavery; Wilberforce, William). To augment the labor supply, the British imported more than 150,000 people from India to work as indentured servants, though some eventually repatriated. Immigrants from other British Caribbean colonies also added to the population. Labor disputes between employers and workers of African and Indian descent remained a feature of the islands' colonial economy well into the 20th century. Trinidad and Tobago were consolidated into a single colonial administration in 1889 and remained together with the coming of independence.

2. Christians
2.1. *Roman Catholics*
Despite two centuries of English rule, the early Spanish, French, and Irish colonial presence has left a strong enduring → Roman Catholic legacy, particularly in Trinidad. French parish priests ministered to many slaves, and the church provided school for newly freed people after emancipation. According to a church report in 1835, Trinidad's population of 41,000 included 35,000 Catholics. The church has continued to play a central role in the nation's cultural and political life, with almost one-third of the population claiming a Catholic affiliation. The church maintains a strong network of schools and churches throughout Trinidad, particularly in the capital, Port of Spain. After the → Vatican II reforms of 1965, Archbishop Gordon Pantin, a charismatic, populist native of Trinidad, guided the church into the modern era until his death in 1999.

2.2. *Anglicans*
The British brought the → Anglican Church to Tobago in 1790 and to Trinidad in 1797. Though originally reserved for British settlers, the church later opened its doors to slaves and then the free black population. The Diocese of Trinidad and Tobago was incorporated into the church in the Province of the West Indies in 1883. Today the diocese encompasses 91 congregations and about 90,000 members.

2.3. *Spiritual Baptists*
Also known as the Shouter → Baptists, the Spiritual Baptists, composed principally of black working-class worshipers, combine the Baptist faith with strong elements of West African practice, particularly a Yoruba-derived emphasis on spirit possession, characterized by shouting, shaking, and speaking in tongues (→ Glossolalia). Baptist missionaries introduced the faith in the early nineteenth century, and it became indigenized by the Shouters. A 1921 ban on the church was overturned in 1951, and it remains popular on Trinidad.

2.4. *Other Protestant Bodies*
The first Methodist society was established in Port of Spain in 1809, drawing mainly from the enslaved and free black population, whose descendants continue to form its principal membership (→ Methodist Churches). The → Moravians established a

mission to slaves on Tobago in the late 18th century, and mission schools helped in the transition to freedom. By 1847 the church claimed some 2,000 members, and the mission spread to Trinidad in the late 19th century. Missionaries from the Presbyterian Church of Canada arrived on Trinidad in the 1860s to work among indentured Indian laborers, and the island remains home to several Presbyterian congregations and numerous schools (→ Reformed and Presbyterian Churches). Seventh-day → Adventists arrived in the late 19th century and remain a visible presence with schools, mission work, and assistance in drug rehabilitation and AIDS programs. In recent years, the → Pentecostal, → Jehovah's Witnesses, and Latter-day Saints (→ Mormons) movements have gained significant numbers of adherents.

3. Other Living Faiths
The nation's ethnic and cultural diversity, particularly on Trinidad, has given rise to distinctive Trinidadian inflections of several major religious traditions. The heavy influx of Indian laborers from South Asia in the 19th century introduced → Hinduism into Trinidad, where several varieties are still practiced by nearly a quarter of the population. A Trinidadian form of worship has deemphasized traditional Hindu folk practices in favor of a more congregation-centered ritual orthodoxy in line with Christianity.

→ Islam, first introduced by enslaved West Africans in the 18th century, also remains a significant legacy of Indian immigrants, though it too has developed a Caribbean flavor. The Hosay festival, for example, is an adaptation of a Shiite ritual from Iran and Iraq, by way of India, that now marks Indo-Trinidadian ethnic and religious identity.

The Orisha cult, once more commonly known as Shango (the Yoruba god of lightning and thunder), remains a popular expression of West African Yoruba practice, sometimes tinged with Protestant, Catholic, and Hindu influences.

Bibliography: M. BAUMANN, "Trinidad and Tobago," *RelW* 4.1297-99 • B. BRERETON, *A History of Modern Trinidad, 1783-1962* (Kingston, Jam., 1981) • S. R. CUDJOE, *The Intellectual Tradition of Trinidad and Tobago in the Nineteenth Century* (Amherst, Mass., 2003) • L. HORNE, *The Evolution of Modern Trinidad and Tobago* (Chaguanas, Trinidad and Tobago, 2003) • A. KHAN, *Callaloo Nation: Metaphors of Race and Religious Identity among South Asians in Trinidad* (Durham, N.C., 2004) • F. J. KOROM, *Hosay Trinidad: Muharram Performances in an Indo-Caribbean Diaspora* (Philadelphia, 2003) • K. A. LUM, *Praising His*

Name in the Dance: Spirit Possession in the Spiritual Baptist Faith and Orisha Work in Trinidad, West Indies (Amsterdam, 2000) • S. MacDonald, *Trinidad and Tobago: Democracy and Development in the Caribbean* (New York, 1986) • G. E. Simpson, *Religious Cults of the Caribbean: Trinidad, Jamaica, and Haiti* (3d ed.; Rio Piedras, P.R., 1980) • E. Williams, *From Columbus to Castro: A History of the Caribbean, 1492-1969* (New York, 1970; repr., 1984).

Jon F. Sensbach

Trinity

Overview
1. Development, Eastern Orthodox Tradition, and Roman Catholic Tradition
    1.1. Beginnings
        1.1.1. Trinity Arises from Christology
        1.1.2. Sporadic Developments
    1.2. Consolidation through Controversy and Council
        1.2.1. Nicaea (325)
        1.2.2. Constantinople (381)
    1.3. The Cappadocians
        1.3.1. *Hypostasis* and *Ousia*
        1.3.2. *Perichōrēsis*
    1.4. The *Filioque* Controversy
    1.5. Augustine
    1.6. Boethius
    1.7. Richard of St.-Victor
    1.8. Thomas Aquinas
2. The Protestant Tradition and Contemporary Ecumenical Discussion
    2.1. The Reformation through Schleiermacher
    2.2. The Twentieth Century: Barth and Rahner
    2.3. Trinitarian Language
    2.4. The Challenge of "Three in One"
    2.5. Trinitarian Challenges to Traditional Assumptions
    2.6. The Trinity and Relationality
    2.7. Recent Issues
        2.7.1. Contexts and Pluralism
        2.7.2. The Trinity, Christian Experience, and the Naming of God
        2.7.3. The Trinity and Human Beings

Overview

The Trinity, as it came to be understood in the formative period of both the Greek and Latin churches, is a uniquely Christian doctrine and one whose sheer difficulty indicates that the → God under discussion cannot be fully grasped by the human mind. One of the early benefits, and yet an additional diffi-culty, of conceiving God as Trinity was the gradual emergence of the concept of *person* (→ Self). In both the divine case and the human case, "person" has its own mystery and eludes strict definition.

The Trinity is one of the beliefs that arise from the → incarnation of Christ. Besides → Jesus' own teachings, the incarnation itself reveals much about the human relation to God. It says that transcendence is capable of → immanence, that God is capable of humanity. It rocks the staid assumptions of human orthodoxy, even as it gives rise to a new orthodoxy based on a Trinitarian understanding of God. Thus as Thomas Aquinas comments on → Augustine, "When we speak of the Trinity, we must proceed with care and with befitting modesty. As Augustine says, 'Nowhere is error more harmful, the quest more toilsome, the finding more fruitful'" (*Summa theol.* I, q. 31, art. 2, citing Augustine, *De Trin.* 1.3).

1. Development, Eastern Orthodox Tradition, and Roman Catholic Tradition

1.1. *Beginnings*

Christian → monotheism is marked by an inescapable tension between belief in divine unity and the concomitant belief that this oneness is shared as Father, Son, and Spirit — as Trinity. Trinitarian doctrine is unique to Christianity. It sets the Christian understanding of monotheism apart from the earlier appearing → Judaism and the later appearing → Islam. To some the Trinity appears as an outright contradiction of monotheism, but the inherent tension of claiming monotheism and Trinity has spawned creative exploration of personhood, interrelatedness, and an ongoing investigation of how unity and diversity can be thought together.

1.1.1. *Trinity Arises from Christology*

The Trinitarian conception of God first arises from the question of Jesus' relationship to God the Father. At the foot of the Mount of Transfiguration, Jesus himself provokes the earliest Christological development by asking, "Who do people say that I am?" (Mark 8:27; → Christology). The disciples variously reply that he is one of the prophets, Elijah, or John the Baptist. But Jesus asks more pointedly, "But who do you say that I am?" and Peter declares that Jesus is the Messiah (v. 29). In a crescendo of revelatory events, Jesus is first transfigured (Mark 9:2-3), and then two celestial visitors, Elijah and Moses, appear (v. 4). But the final and full revelation of Jesus' identity is voiced at the top of the mountain by God the Father: "This is my Son, the Beloved; listen to him!" (v. 7). While Matthew's gospel differently reports that Peter is the first to confess that Jesus is the Son, in both cases the question of the identity of Jesus becomes thematic among his earliest followers.

Nonetheless, the question was left to be answered: What does it mean that Jesus is called Son and, in the Gospel of John, Logos? How is Jesus' sonship to be differentiated from that of his followers, who also address God as Father (Matt. 6:9; Rom. 8:14-15)?

1.1.2. *Sporadic Developments*

For almost 300 years after Jesus' death on the cross, a variety of Trinitarian or proto-Trinitarian views were put forward, but none was systematically articulated, and there was no formal consensus or clearly formed church doctrine. Yet from this period of sporadic development some creative terms, images, and concepts began to emerge, even if some of these were occasionally at odds with later orthodoxy.

Given the Great Commission to "make disciples of all nations, baptizing them in the name of the Father and of the Son and of the Holy Spirit" (Matt. 28:19), it is not surprising that numerous post-apostolic writers sometimes place the three together. (See, for example, *1 Clem.* 46.6; *Did.* 7; and *Mart. Pol.* 14.1-3.) These groupings typically appear in prayers or baptismal formulas.

However, when attempting the far more difficult task of clarifying the relationships among Father, Son, and Spirit, some either blur the distinction between Son and Spirit (e.g., *Herm. Sim.* 9.1.1 and *2 Clem.* 14.4) or even speak of the Son as an angel (→ Justin Martyr *Dial.* 56.4). Others, such as → Origen (ca. 185-ca. 254) in *Comm. in Ioan.* 13.25 and → Tertullian (ca. 160-ca. 225) in *Adv. Prax.* 9, variously suggest a subordinate position for the Son and Spirit.

In a problematic proposal, Sabellius (fl. 220) argues that the Father, Son, and Spirit are not distinct persons; instead, they are modes or aspects of the one divine person. While Sabellianism, also called monarchianism or modalism, avoids the subordination of the Son to the Father, it does so only at the cost of removing the distinct personality of the Son. Hence, it is the Father who suffers on the cross under a different name (Patripassianism). Sabellius was condemned by Pope Callistus I (217-22).

Apart from Sabellius, many of the writers during this period pointed the way forward with helpful images that were later taken up and systematized. Thus → Justin Martyr (ca. 100-ca. 165) compares the Word of the Father to the light from the sun; while the sun and its light are distinct, they are also "indivisible and inseparable" (*Dial.* 128). Significantly, the Council of → Nicaea later declared the Son to be "God from God, light from light."

The earliest Greek use of the term "Trinity" *(trias)* occurs in the work *Ad Autolycum* (2.15), by Theophilus of Antioch (d. ca. 185). The earliest Latin use *(trinitas)* is by Tertullian (*Adv. Prax.* 2, 8), who is also the first to use the formula "one substance, three persons." As noted above, however, Tertullian does not provide a consistent articulation of Trinitarian relationships among equals.

1.2. *Consolidation through Controversy and Council*

The question of Christ's relation to the Father became urgent when Arius (ca. 280-336; → Arianism), a presbyter who was probably of Libyan descent, explicitly denied the equality of the Son with the Father and, in so doing, attracted many followers. Once Arius provoked the question, the disputes among Christians became so pronounced that the recently converted Roman emperor Constantine (ruled 306-37) called together a council at Nicaea to resolve the dispute. In the presence of Constantine, a sizable number of bishops (tradition holds that it was 318) gathered to address the question of the Son's relation to the Father. Their proceedings are now recognized as the first ecumenical → council of the church.

1.2.1. *Nicaea (325)*

Arius and his followers evidently contended about the Son that "there once was when he was not" (anathema appended to the council's Profession of Faith). Believing that the Son came into being from nonbeing, the Arians could revere the Son as "the firstborn of all creation" (Col. 1:15), but they could not affirm equality between the Son and the Father. To the Arian mind, the Son could be the most exalted of creatures, but having been born, whether such birth is called "begotten" or "made," the Son could not be God without compromising divine transcendence.

A key presupposition of all parties to the debate is what is called "divine simplicity." This commonly held, even unquestioned, doctrine indicates an infinite, perfectly seamless unity within the divine being. Where human beings think one thing at a time, do one thing at a time, and cumulatively synthesize things, God is always already an intensively infinite unity. If the Father and Son were understood as equally God, then the Arians feared that the unity of divine simplicity would be broken by the distinction between them. Arius is really raising a common-sense objection: a truly simple being does not undergo change; the Son undergoes change in the incarnation and throughout the mortal life and death of Jesus; therefore the Son cannot be equal to the unchanging Father — the true God. Where Arius would subordinate the Son to the Father, and where Sabellius would see the Father, Son, and Spirit as merely different modes of the same being, they hold in common the desire to protect divine unity, or simplicity.

→ Athanasius (ca. 297-373), who became the most famous defender of orthodoxy, does not dispute the tenets of divine simplicity, but he does contend that the Son is begotten in eternity; the Son is "from the substance of the Father" *(homoousios),* and thus the Son is fully equal to the Father. The Council of Nicaea condemned the views of Arius and affirmed those that become associated with Athanasius. Crucially, the adoption of the term *homoousios* (same substance, or consubstantial) set the church on the road to its full-fledged Trinitarian doctrine. While it is unclear who first introduced the term into the council's proceedings, *homoousios* has never left its defining place in Christian theology.

To argue that the Son and Father are of the same substance while also arguing for divine simplicity sets up the problem of belief and explanation that has endured for Trinitarian theology. This doctrine goes against the grain; it asks us to hold the logic of divine simplicity or monotheism in tension with real distinctions among Father, Son, and Spirit. Having taken this route, the church refused a "restful," easy understanding of God; instead, Trinitarian doctrine demands that we try to think something that is greater than our current capacity to understand. Undertaking this apparent impossibility has proved salutary in two ways: first, it reminds us that the God about whom we are speaking is in crucial ways unlike anything else that the human mind may attempt to understand; second, the attempt to understand God as Trinity has led to some very creative developments, especially the concept "person."

The acceptance of the full equality of Son and Father soon engendered further debate about how they are to be distinguished, as well as how the humanity of the Son who had lived among us was to be understood. For Athanasius, understanding the power and depth of God's activity on our behalf was at stake. Driven by soteriological concerns, Athanasius perceived that the gift of the Son incarnate solved problems that humanity had caused itself but could not solve itself: "The Word of God was not changed, but . . . took a human body for the salvation and well-being of man, that having shared in human birth, He might make man partake in the divine and spiritual nature" (*Vita Ant.* 74). Appealing to something more than common sense, Athanasius insists upon both unity and distinction when considering the Father and Son. He thus cites Jesus'

statement "The Father and I are one" (John 10:30) but also elaborates, "The Father is Father and is not also Son, and the Son is Son and not also Father; but the nature is one" (*Contra Arian.* 23.4).

Notwithstanding the considerable advancements made by Athanasius and those who joined him, Nicaea left some important matters unsolved and unclear. While the council declared that the Son is "consubstantial with the Father" *(homoousion tō patri),* its closing anathemas appear to equate the terms *hypostasis* and *ousia.* Eventually, however, creating a distinction between these terms is crucial to further development of the concept of the Trinity. And the promulgation of Nicaea only states belief in the Holy Spirit without further elaboration. The focus of this Nicene Council was to establish a unified understanding of the Son's relation to the Father. Its success in solving this first issue led to other questions that others would later address.

1.2.2. *Constantinople (381)*

Although no written record of the council that met at Constantinople in 381 is extant, a synodical letter in 382 by the bishops who met there lays out their doctrinal decisions. Here again the Trinitarian consolidation is generated by controversy, as the bishops responded to a list of what were deemed heretical teachings, including those of earlier and later types of Arians, Sabellians, and Pneumatomachi, who denied the divinity of the → Holy Spirit. The letter claims continuity with Nicaea, but it significantly declares that we should "believe in the name of the Father, the Son and the holy Spirit: believing also, of course, that the Father, the Son and the holy Spirit have a single Godhead and power and substance, a dignity deserving the same honour and a co-eternal sovereignty, in three most perfect hypostases, or three perfect persons" (N. P. Tanner, 28). Defending an "uncreated and consubstantial and co-eternal Trinity," the bishops now unhesitatingly couple the claim of a single Godhead with three persons (three *hypostaseis*).

1.3. *The Cappadocians*
1.3.1. *Hypostasis and Ousia*

Once the church came to understand the oneness and equality of Father, Son, and, eventually, Spirit, the problem became how to distinguish the three. The solution, which is already apparent in the synodical letter of Constantinople, had come from the → Cappadocian Fathers: Basil, known as the Great (ca. 330-79), Gregory of Nazianzus (329/30-389/90), and Basil's younger brother, Gregory of Nyssa (ca. 330-ca. 395). In the Cappadocian solution, God is one *ousia* ("substance," "essence," or "being") equally and fully expressed in three *hypostaseis,* Father, Son, and Spirit. For the first time, the previously synonymous terms *ousia* and *hypostasis* are significantly differentiated by using *hypostasis* to refer to the distinctive aspect of each member of the Trinity and *ousia* to refer to that which is common. The Cappadocians' innovative use of terms is all the more remarkable when we notice that one of the anathemas appended to the earlier Profession of Faith at Nicaea (but not mentioned by any later council) was against those who contend that the Son of God is "from another *hypostasis* or *ousia*" than the Father.

New understandings generally require new terms, or at least new uses of older terms. Thus Basil, distinguishing *hypostasis* from the more general term *ousia,* defines the former as "that which, through the specific qualities evident in it, restricts and defines in a certain object the general and indefinite" (*Ep.* 38). Basil argues that each *hypostasis* possesses common qualities like infinity, incomprehensibility, being uncreated, and being uncircumscribed by space, but each *hypostasis* can also be distinguished by origin, relatedness, and how it is known by creatures.

A concomitant benefit of the Cappadocian distinction is that *hypostasis,* now translated into Latin as *persona,* begins a long Christian development of the concept of person — as understood both in God and among human beings. In fact, the development of the concept of person is the linchpin of the evolving understanding of the Trinity, as well as the eventual understanding of Christology settled upon at the Council of → Chalcedon (451). Such articulation as the mystery of the Trinity allows requires that one not push a position too hard. Any explanation of the Trinity must locate itself in the tension between the infinite unity of the divine nature or substance and the distinctiveness of Father, Son, and Spirit. To refuse the distinctiveness leads to some form of modalism, as in the case of Sabellius. To overemphasize the distinctiveness falls into tritheism, which all the ancient Fathers avoided.

From the time of the Cappadocians, we can say the following about the divine persons: "person" distinguishes, relates, and unifies. It distinguishes because, in spite of the common possession of the divine nature, the Father is not the Son, and the Spirit is neither Father nor Son. "Person" relates through eternal origin. The Son is the only begotten. To be Son or Father is inherently relational. Likewise, the Spirit proceeds from the Father and, controversially, from the Son (see 1.4). In any case, the Spirit is sent by the Son and represents the Son (John 16:7, 14-15). Finally, this term unifies because, notwithstanding the distinct relations of ori-

gin, each of the Father, Son, and Spirit is fully united to the infinite entirety of the divine substance, so that each of the Father, Son, and Spirit is God. As Gregory of Nazianzus says, "Each of the Trinity is in entire unity as much with himself as with the partnership" (*Or. theol.* 31.16).

1.3.2. *Perichōrēsis*

The inherently relational identity of the Trinitarian God was colorfully illustrated among the Greek fathers and the subsequent tradition by the term *perichōrēsis* (Lat. *circumincessio*). While there is some dispute about how best to understand the term, which some have translated as "rotation" or "alternation," the weight of evidence points to "interpenetration" or "coinherence." Gregory of Nazianzus was apparently the first to use the term theologically, but Basil implies something quite similar.

Arguing that the Spirit is the Spirit of the Son, and that the Son is the Son of the Father, and that the three share everything of the divine nature in common, Basil offers this illustration: "And since He is the Spirit of Christ and from God, as Paul says [Rom. 8:9], just as he who has grasped one end of a chain also draws along with him the other end, so he who draws the Spirit . . . through Him draws along both the Son and the Father" (*Ep.* 38). Of the three divine persons, Basil argues, "There is observed a certain uninterrupted sharing in them . . . the intelligence does not tread on a gap between the Father and the Son and the Holy Spirit. For, there is nothing which intrudes itself between these persons" (ibid.). With such illustrations, Basil and his fellow Cappadocians at least give the church a way to articulate and defend its belief that God is one being in three persons.

1.4. *The Filioque Controversy*

The doctrine that the Spirit proceeds "from the Father *and from the Son* [= Lat. *filioque*]" has historically caused great friction between the Orthodox East and the Latin West. While the Eastern → Orthodox churches have more or less consistently rejected it, except that many Orthodox would allow that the Spirit proceeds from the Father *through* the Son, the Latin West has variously adopted the double procession of the → *filioque*. It appears in numerous occasional letters and writings, such as the sixth-century Spanish version of the Nicene Creed and the synodical letter of Pope Martin I (649-55) to Constantinople (649). In arguments of Photius (ca. 810-ca. 895) against Rome (867 and 879), the critique of *filioque* played a central role. In the Great Schism of 1054, arguments for and against *filioque* were used by the opposing sides. Later, *filioque* was declared to be a dogma of the Western church by the Fourth Lateran Council (1215), the Second Council of Lyons (1274), and the Council of Florence (1438-45). When *filioque* was confirmed at Florence in 1439, some Greeks were in attendance, but no real consensus of the broader church was established.

In the more conciliatory period since → Vatican II, Roman Catholics and Orthodox have reached agreement that both *filioque* and the Orthodox understanding of the procession of the Holy Spirit are admissible theologoumena that are not church-dividing ("The Filioque" [2003]).

1.5. *Augustine*

The development of the articulation of the Trinity is characterized by complex interrelationships between the Eastern Greek-speaking church and the Latin West, where → Augustine (354-430) has become a benchmark. Through the centuries both his accomplishments and his limitations have continued to play central roles. Generally, his purpose is to defend the church's evolving Nicene theology, that is, the equality of the three Trinitarian persons against the semi-Arian Homoians (those who claimed that the Son was only *like* in essence to the Father), on the one hand, and against the Sabellians, on the other. Like that of so many others, Augustine's thinking is guided by such church doctrine as had already been established, as well as by the metaphysical presupposition of divine simplicity. Given his commitment to the equality of the three persons, his problem is how to articulate any distinction among them that does not violate divine simplicity. Augustine is well aware of the difficulty and danger of saying anything about the Trinity: "I will be attempting to say things that cannot altogether be said as they are thought by a man — or at least as they are thought by me" (*De Trin.* 5.1.1).

In attempting to avoid confusing or mixing up the persons, and likewise to avoid distinctions that imply any disparity (which would fall prey to the Arian objections concerned with maintaining divine simplicity), Augustine conceives a new understanding of the category of relation. He argues against the Arians that there is absolutely no modification of the Father's being in relation to the Son because the Father is always, eternally Father and the Son is always, eternally Son. Against Sabellian modalism he significantly adds: "Every being that is called something by way of relationship is also something beside the relationship" (*De Trin.* 7.1.2).

The heart of Trinitarian articulation hinges upon how "person" is understood, and Augustine insists that relations alone do not constitute the divine persons. Problematically, he consistently thinks of person in substance terms, often referring to "three substances or persons" (*De. Trin.* 7.4.9). As he himself confesses, the difficulty arises because he is not sure what to make of the Cappadocian distinction between *hypostasis* and *ousia,* both of which had earlier been translated into Latin as *substantia* (substance) but were now being distinguished as "person" and "substance" (see 1.3.1 above). Although Augustine distinguishes person (i.e., "something singular and individual") from nature (something held in common), he still hesitates to apply this distinction to God (*De Trin.* 7.6.11). He is clearer about the distinction when applied to humanity, as he asks in *Confessions,* "Who am I, and what am I?" (9.1.1).

Augustine's most controversial strategy is to develop → analogies of the Trinitarian God from *within* the human image. Rather than turn to relations among humans, Augustine explores human interiority as the image and analogue of the divine persons. While Augustine's turn to the interiority of the human image has been criticized, it should be noted in his defense that, before he does so, he first sets out an explicitly relational framework that links human beings with God and with one another. Thus, just as the Holy Spirit conjoins the Father and the Son, "we are bidden to imitate this mutuality by grace, both with reference to God and to each other, in the two precepts on which the whole law and the prophets depend [Matt. 22:40]" (*De. Trin.* 6.5.7). Hence, by loving God with the heart, soul, and mind, and by loving our neighbor as ourselves, an external relational framework is first established for the subsequent interior exploration of human consciousness.

In any case, Augustine famously develops a series of triadic phenomena of the human mind. He warns that because of divine simplicity, "the Trinity as a thing in itself is quite different from the image of the Trinity in another thing" (*De. Trin.* 15.22.42). He holds that → love is the key to understanding the Trinity, and that all love has a triadic unity, involving "the lover, what is being loved, and love" (8.10.14, an image that Plotinus had earlier used). Turning to the human image, he distinguishes and yet relates mind, its knowledge of itself, and its love of itself, which are "three somethings, and these three are one thing, and when they are complete they are equal" (9.4.4). In the human analogue, phenomenal diversities are unified and equal as they are enacted. The triad within the human mind can likewise be portrayed as self-memory, self-understanding, and self-willing (10.10.16). Augustine more or less equates self-willing to self-loving and then describes the triad as "the mind remembering itself, understanding itself, loving itself." This triad is "a trinity, not yet God of course, but already the image of God" (14.8.11). But for Augustine the chief capacity of the human mind is to know God, and its full act is to remember, understand, and love God, who has created it (14.12.15). Nonetheless, Augustine cautions that these human analogues are like the Pauline mirror in which we see only dimly (1 Cor. 13:12). The persistent presupposition of divine simplicity keeps all similarities between God and humans embedded in even greater dissimilarity.

1.6. *Boethius*

Like Augustine, Boethius (ca. 480-524) exerted great influence in subsequent centuries, especially through his oft-cited definition of "person" as an "individual substance of a rational nature" *(Contra Eutychen)*. Given the centrality of "person" in any explication of the Trinity, Boethius's importance in the medieval era is hard to overestimate. However, while Boethius accomplished a great deal in a great many areas, his definition, which was clearly presented and clearly argued in a Christological work, turns out to be more of a burden than a help for understanding the Trinity. Less well known but undoubtedly more fruitful than his celebrated definition is his use of *incommunicabilis* (unique, unrepeatable, nontransferable to another) to explicate the meaning of "person." *Incommunicabilis* suggests that the meaning of personhood is its ultimate particularity; "Plato-ness" *(Platonitas)* cannot be possessed by anyone except Plato *(In librum de interpretatione)*. The concept of *incommunicabilis* was used to great effect by those who follow, especially Richard of St.-Victor and Aquinas.

In Boethius's major work on the Trinity *(De Trinitate)*, "person" is, with one exception, conspicuously absent. Boethius, like Augustine, understandably translates *hypostasis* as "substance," but doing so prevents him from capitalizing on the new distinction by the Cappadocians between *hypostasis* and *ousia*, where the former signifies *persona* (person), and the latter signifies being or substance. As a result, Boethius's Trinitarian argument is hardly successful. The problem is that a successful account must articulate the tension between divine unity (simplicity) and the diversity of persons, but Boethius's diversity is so tame that the tension gives way in favor of divine unity.

In some ways regressing from Augustine's insights on divine relations, Boethius addresses divine diversity under the title of relations and not persons. His discussion is dominated by two considerations: divine simplicity and the Aristotelian categories, especially the categories of substance and relation. Thinking of God not just in substance terms but

even beyond substance *(ultra substantiam)*, he declares: "Relation . . . cannot be predicated at all of God" *(De Trin.* 4). Since Boethius does in fact attribute some sort of relations to God, his intention is to exclude relations in terms of God's actual being. As Boethius puts it: "Father, Son, and Spirit are not predicated of the divinity in a substantial manner, but in some other way. . . . It is evident that these terms are relative [*ad aliquid*], for the Father is someone's Father, the Son is someone's Son, the Spirit is someone's Spirit. *Hence not even Trinity is predicated substantially of God*" *(Opus. sac.* 2, emphasis added). Caught between the language that the church had already adopted for the Trinity and the metaphysical presuppositions of simplicity and Aristotelian categories, Boethius, like many who follow him, cannot quite seem to articulate a suitable portrayal.

1.7. *Richard of St.-Victor*

Reflections on love by Richard of St.-Victor (d. 1173) present an original and creative approach to understanding human and divine persons and thereby contribute to a greater understanding of the Trinity. In many ways a mediating figure between the Greek and Latin traditions, much of Richard's work seems quite harmonious with contemporary sensibilities. While influenced by Augustine's Trinitarian understanding of lover, beloved, and love, Richard's Trinitarian thought shifts the metaphysical focus from individual substance to interpersonal love.

Richard's argument for the Trinity bears some formal resemblance to → Anselm's ontological proof for the existence of God (→ God, Arguments for the Existence of, 2.1), which begins by asserting that God is "that than which nothing greater can be conceived." Thus presupposing that God infinitely is all things that it would be better to be than not to be, Richard lays out his argument in several stages, which, greatly simplified, are as follows.

First, presupposing that God can lack nothing of the highest good, Richard argues that supreme good requires supreme love. But since love cannot exist all by one's self, there must be more than one person. Second, Richard argues that there must be equality, that God must have someone of equal dignity to love: "But a person who was not God would not be of equal dignity with a divine person" *(De Trin.* 3.2). Thus he argues that the fullness of love in the divine being requires a relationship between divine persons of fully equal dignity. Richard's third and final step is to argue that "shared love" *(condilectus)*, which it is better to have than not to have, can exist in the divinity only if there are three persons and not merely two. Essentially, his argument is that, without the personalization of the Spirit, divine love would be incomplete. In its actualized perfection, however, the divine love of Father and Son cannot be limited to divine concept or subjectivity. Hence, the shared love between Father and Son is objectively, not just subjectively, real. The Father and the Son love the love; they love the *person*, the Spirit.

Moreover, Richard unequivocally adopts the term *persona*, rejects using "substance" to explain the divine persons, and instead develops *incommunicabilis* as virtually coterminous with "person." Richard notes that with some words, like "animal" or "man," a substance is implied with a property common to all animals or all men; but with the word "person," our attention is directed to what is "individual, unique, incommunicable" (*De Trin.* 4.6). "Person" is thus used to signify a "who" and not a "what"; it signifies what is incommunicable, unrepeatable, and nontransferable. Thus each of the divine persons "is an incommunicable existence of a divine nature" (4.23).

By his argument for the existence of three persons within the Trinity, his critique of terms traditionally used to understand "person," and his creative use of *incommunicabilis,* Richard's work is another benchmark in the developmental understanding of the Trinity. A century later, Aquinas, even though he believed that Richard too emphatically tried to prove that God is Trinity, frequently cited and adopted key provisions of Richard's work.

1.8. *Thomas Aquinas*

In his great medieval synthesis of Christian theology, Thomas Aquinas (ca. 1225-74) actually solves one of the great problems that had befuddled earlier thinkers in the West, namely, how the troublesome category of relation could be successfully applied to the Trinitarian God without violating divine simplicity. In the Aristotelian schema that Aquinas inherits, relation is the weakest and most elusive of the categories. In the creation, its reality is not in either of the things being related but is a directedness toward the other, a "betweenness." But a unique situation arises in the divine case, where the real relations of the Father, Son, and Spirit are a "between" that is also a commonly possessed "in." The real relations are between the persons *in* the commonly shared, identical divine nature. Hence, the "processions" used to describe the eternal origin of the Son and Spirit are not movements toward something different. They are, uniquely, within the identity of the same divine nature (*Summa theol.* I, q. 28, art. 1).

Directly addressing what others had ignored or obscured, Aquinas turns the requirements of simplicity to advantage. Within the simplicity of the divine being, where the being of God is distinct from all else that is, relations have a reality that they cannot have within the creation. Within the divine being, relations are not appendages — which simplicity precludes. Rather, Aquinas boldly makes the pivotal move: "In God, relation and essence do not differ from each other, but are one and the same" (ibid., q. 28, art. 2). Hence, in terms of divine simplicity, relations *within* God are coterminous with the divine being itself. Applying the requirements of simplicity to a Trinitarian framework, the weakness has become a strength. There is no way to avoid predicating relation of a Trinitarian God, and as Aquinas has shown, no reason to avoid doing so. By taking the requirements of divine simplicity and applying them to Trinitarian faith and, vice versa, by thinking Trinitarian relationship in terms of simplicity, Aquinas adds "relation" to the short list of terms that can literally be applied to the being of God.

Bibliography: Augustine, *The Trinity* (trans. E. Hill; ed. J. E. Rotelle; Brooklyn, N.Y., 1991) • "The Filioque: A Church-Dividing Issue? An Agreed Statement of the North American Orthodox-Catholic Theological Consultation" (October 25, 2003) www.scoba.us/resources/filioque-p01.asp • R. P. C. Hanson, *The Search for the Christian Doctrine of God: The Arian Controversy, 318-381* (Edinburgh, 1988) • V. Harrison, "Perichoresis in the Greek Fathers," *SVTQ* 35 (2006) 53-65 • J. N. D. Kelly, *Early Christian Creeds* (New York, 1960) • B. Lonergan, *The Way to Nicea: The Dialectical Development of Trinitarian Theology* (London, 1976) • V. Lossky, *In the Image and Likeness of God* (ed. J. H. Erickson and T. E. Bird; Crestwood, N.Y., 1985) • G. O'Collins, *The Tripersonal God: Understanding and Interpreting the Trinity* (New York, 1999) • R. E. Olson and C. A. Hall, *The Trinity* (Grand Rapids, 2002) • J. Pelikan, *The Christian Tradition: A History of the Development of Doctrine,* vol. 1, *The Emergence of the Catholic Tradition (100-600)* (Chicago, 1971) • P. A. Rolnick, *Person, Grace, and God* (Grand Rapids, 2007) • N. P. Tanner, *Decrees of the Ecumenical Councils* (2 vols.; London, 1990).

Philip A. Rolnick

2. The Protestant Tradition and Contemporary Ecumenical Discussion

2.1. *The Reformation through Schleiermacher*

The dominant strands of the Protestant → Reformation did not dramatically rethink the doctrine of the Trinity. Article 1 of CA (→ Augsburg Confession) presents the doctrine of the Trinity as an issue that is not contested between the Roman theologians and the → Reformers. Martin → Luther

(1483-1546; → Luther's Theology), John → Calvin (1509-64; → Calvin's Theology), and Philip → Melanchthon (1497-1560), each in his own way, sought to guard against making the Trinity an object of empty speculation that would distract from the saving knowledge of God in → Jesus Christ. The first → systematic theology of the Reformation, Melanchthon's *Loci communes* of 1521, explicitly declined to discuss the Trinity. When Melanchthon in later editions came to speak more of the Trinity, like Luther and Calvin he concentrated on the economic Trinity (the Trinity revealed and experienced in the economy of salvation) as opposed to the immanent Trinity (the divine Three independent of the economy of salvation).

The Reformers' allergic reaction to Trinitarian speculation bespeaks a complex theological relation to experience. On the one hand, the Reformers insisted that the bedrock for Christian faith is not human religious → experience but God's → promises. On the other hand, they rejected as irrelevant and indeed dangerous Trinitarian theories that lost touch with the experience of God-given salvation.

The → Enlightenment, with its attack on claims that rested on an appeal to an authority other than → reason, forced a rethinking of the doctrine of the Trinity. One response was to marginalize the doctrine. A different response came from the German Lutheran philosopher G. W. F. Hegel (1770-1831), whose philosophical reconceptualization of the doctrine of the Trinity was meant to demonstrate not only that the doctrine did not conflict with reason but that it was the very ground of contemporary reason's insistence on rejecting → dogmatism. A third response came from Friedrich → Schleiermacher (1768-1834; → Schleiermacher's Theology), the great theologian of the Prussian Union between Lutheran and Reformed. Schleiermacher claimed that the doctrine of the Trinity belonged to the unfinished business of the Reformation: applying fundamental Reformation insights would yield a significantly different doctrine. Although Schleiermacher wrote a long essay on the Trinity, the fact that he accorded only a few pages to the doctrine at the very end of his magnum opus, *Der christliche Glaube* (The Christian Faith), has led to the frequent charge that he minimized the doctrine's importance.

2.2. The Twentieth Century: Barth and Rahner

The 20th century, particularly in its second half, brought a renaissance of attention to Trinitarian theology. The first major move in this direction was the decision of Karl → Barth (1886-1968) to make the doctrine of the Trinity a gateway to his *Church Dogmatics*. He placed his major treatment of the doctrine in the prolegomena, which he entitled "The Doctrine of the Word of God." Within the overall doctrine of the Word, Barth has "The Triune God" as the first of three subsections in "The Revelation of God." For Barth the doctrine of the triune → God was not just part of the content of revelation; it described the structure of revelation itself: (1) God is the revealer, the one who reveals; (2) God is the one through whom revelation occurs; (3) God is the one revealed by the event of revelation (→ Word of God 3).

The Roman Catholic theologian Karl → Rahner (1904-84) took a second major step when he insisted that, despite its official doctrinal status, the doctrine of the Trinity made little or no practical difference in the lives of most Christians. Rahner thought that this irrelevance stemmed from the fact that the distinction between the economic Trinity and the immanent Trinity too often had widened into a division. As an antidote he asserted the identity of the economic and the immanent Trinity. Rahner's axiom has become one of the touchstones of much of the contemporary revival of Trinitarian reflection. At the same time, Rahner did not want to abolish the distinction between the immanent and the economic Trinity. For Rahner, this distinction serves to maintain the truth that God's activity in the economy of salvation is free (→ Freedom 2). As Barth put it, the Trinity is the God who loves in freedom.

Both Barth and Rahner held that "person" (from Lat. *persona*), the traditional term in the so-called Western church for the divine Three, had become seriously misleading. While originally designating a theater mask and then a role and hence an identity, in contemporary usage "person" (→ Self) had come to denote a subjective center of consciousness. With that understanding of "person," the claim that God is three persons stands in grave danger of degenerating into tritheism. Barth proposed as an alternative the phrase "mode of being" *(Seinsweise);* Rahner proposed "mode of subsisting" *(Subsistenzweise).*

2.3. Trinitarian Language

As with the language of "person," so the category "substance" in the traditional Western (Latin-based) Trinitarian formula "one substance, three persons" has met with criticism. Eastern Orthodox theologians have claimed that it places an impersonal category at the heart of divine being (→ Orthodox Christianity). Modern Western thought has valued highly the freedom and creativity more evident in the category of subject than in that of substance. Emblematic is Hegel's program to think Spirit not just as substance but as subject. One upshot is that many contemporary Western theologians prefer the Greek term for the divine unity, *ousia*, over the Latinate "substance."

A number of contemporary thinkers, such as Wolfhart Pannenberg and Robert Jenson, have become wary of speaking as God as subject, for fear that such terminology replaces the Trinity of → salvation history with a Trinity modeled on the complex dynamics of human subjectivity (→ Subjectivism and Objectivism). Antonio González in turn has criticized Pannenberg's retention of the language of subject for the divine Three. González, who prefers the term "agent," worries that "subject" implies a substrate underlying an action or event. Theologians such as González and Jenson argue that the doctrine of the Trinity pushes us to think of God's being as event. Along this line, the old Trinitarian vocabulary of *perichōrēsis* or *circumincessio,* describing the mutual indwelling of the divine Three, has gained new life in the contemporary discussion. Some theologians, such as González, Leonardo Boff, and Patricia Wilson-Kastner, equate the divine *ousia* with the *perichōrēsis.*

2.4. The Challenge of "Three in One"

The teaching that God is three in one poses the theological challenge of how to relate God as three to God as one. Théodore de Régnon (1831-93) suggested that so-called Western theology traditionally moves from the one to the three, since Latin philosophy moves from the nature to the agent, while so-called Eastern theology moves from the three to the one, since → Greek philosophy moves from the agent to the nature. Whatever the historical validity of that distinction may be, Eastern Orthodox theologians have frequently complained that Western theology privileges God as one over God as three. A significant strand of the contemporary Trinitarian renaissance in Western theology has been a critique of the primacy of God as one over God as three. Karl Rahner criticized Thomas Aquinas (ca. 1225-74) for placing his treatment *De Deo uno* as a block before his treatment *De Deo trino.* Boff and Jürgen Moltmann have both sought to describe the Trinity as a model community or society. The emphasis of their so-called social Trinitarianism on God as three has been so strong that some critics have wondered whether the result was closer to tritheism than to Trinitarian monotheism.

Rahner also challenged the habit of placing the doctrine of the Trinity within the doctrine of God, over against the doctrines of Christ and of the Spirit. This is a consequence of Rahner's basic axiom, that there is not some immanent Trinity "behind" the God self-revealed in the economy of salvation. Among recent Trinitarian theologians, Robert

Jenson has notably followed Rahner's lead on this point, placing the doctrines of Christ and of the Spirit within the larger topic of the triune God.

The German Lutheran theologian Wolfhart Pannenberg has argued that Barth privileges the one over the three by letting the model of individual self-consciousness structure his conception of the Trinity. The use of analogies based on self-consciousness for talking about the Trinity goes back to → Augustine (354-430) and also plays a central role in Hegel's Trinitarian philosophy. Pannenberg instead proposes developing the doctrine of the Trinity from the personal relation between Father and Son (→ Christology). This starting point has the advantage of keeping personhood at the heart of God, an emphasis advanced by Eastern Orthodox theologians such as John Zizioulas. At the same time, Pannenberg's proposal seeks to incorporate mutual relationality at the core of the divine, an emphasis that may be neglected in Eastern Orthodox insistence on the monarchy of the Father.

2.5. Trinitarian Challenges to Traditional Assumptions

Barth insisted that, in the triune God, the classical ontological opposition between being and becoming was incorrect. This point had already been central to Hegel's appropriation of Trinitarian thinking a century earlier. The rejection of the dichotomy of being and becoming is now a shared feature of many contemporary Trinitarian thinkers — not only those who are heavily influenced by Barth, such as Moltmann, Jenson, and Eberhard Jüngel, but feminist Trinitarians such as Elizabeth Johnson and Catherine LaCugna, process Trinitarians such as Joseph Bracken, and those seeking to reconceptualize the Trinity within classical categories of Asian thought, such as Jung Young Lee.

Closely related to the question of the relation between being and becoming is the question of a theology of → time. Moltmann, Pannenberg, Jenson, and also Ted Peters have all reconceived God's relation to time in a way that rejects a simple opposition between eternity and time, emphasizing instead the eschatological character of the triune God. For all of them, the future becomes the preeminent mode of time for Christian faith.

Renewed reflection on the Trinity has also led many recent theologians to question traditional doctrines of God's immunity to → suffering. Here again Hegel lurks in the background, with his talk of a "speculative Good Friday," by which Spirit becomes itself through suffering its own negation. Moltmann's *Crucified God* has been especially influential, along with further Trinitarian elaboration in

Moltmann's *Trinity and the Kingdom of God*. Important contributions on this theme have also come in Jüngel's *God as Mystery of the World* and Heribert Mühlen's essay "The Mutability of God as Horizon of a Future Christology." These works were all preceded by Kazoh Kitamori's *Theology of the Pain of God* and Dietrich → Bonhoeffer's (1906-45) *Letters and Papers from Prison*.

2.6. The Trinity and Relationality

Throughout its history, Trinitarian theology has stimulated creative reflection on the ontological status of relation. At the time of the development of the doctrine of the Trinity, Greek philosophy assumed that substance and relation were two distinct and unmixable ontological categories. Substance was being that perdured independent of relation. Augustine remained dissatisfied with any term to describe the divine Three, because they seemed to be both substance and relation. Thomas Aquinas straightforwardly stated the Trinitarian innovation over against the Greek ontology, defining the Trinitarian persons as "subsistent relations." They are not relations composed of independent substances that have ontological priority over the relations; the relations themselves are ontologically fundamental. At the same time, Aquinas denied that God had a "real" relation to → creation. His point was that God is not affected by, not dependent upon, and not vulnerable to creation.

On the contemporary scene, relationality plays a primary role in the Trinitarian thought of theologians as diverse as the German Lutheran Wolfhart Pannenberg, the Roman Catholic feminist Elizabeth Johnson, the evangelical Baptist Stanley Grenz, and the Methodist process feminist Marjorie Suchocki (the latter three all from North America). Theologians who question the doctrine of divine immunity to suffering, such as those mentioned above in this article, are by implication challenging Aquinas's denial that God has a real relation to the world. The incarnate Word is the presence of God in finite vulnerability — even to the suffering and death of the cross. In general, the emphasis on the fundamental status of relation well positions Trinitarian theology to engage the contemporary movements of thought that privilege relation, whether ecological, feminist, process, or many of the developments in 20th-century physics.

The past century has seen increased theological interaction between Eastern Orthodoxy, on the one hand, and → Protestantism and Roman → Catholicism, on the other. Among contemporary thinkers, the Greek theologian John Zizioulas and the Romanian theologian Dumitru Staniloae (1903-93) have especially influenced Trinitarian theology in the so-called Western church. The fourth-century → Cappadocian theologian Gregory of Nyssa (ca. 330-ca. 395), long a fundamental figure in Orthodox theological and ecclesial life, has become a favorite influence on contemporary theologians as diverse as the Anglican feminist Sarah Coakley and the Lutheran antifeminist Robert Jenson. The traditional Orthodox emphasis on the personal relations of the divine Three over against the supposed primacy of one divine substance in Western Trinitarianism fits well with the widespread contemporary appreciation of relationality. At the same time, some Western Trinitarians worry whether patriarchy is necessarily built into the Orthodox emphasis on the Father as the source of divinity for the other persons.

2.7. Recent Issues

2.7.1. Contexts and Pluralism

Recent years have seen the publication of major works in English seeking to rethink the doctrine of the Trinity in cultural contexts quite different from the Latin-based "Western" church and the Greek-based "Eastern" church. For example, Jung Young Lee employs yin-yang symbolism to fashion a broadly conceived theology of the Trinity in Asian perspective. Nozomu Miyahira uses the Japanese value of concord to elaborate a more specific inculturation in his work subtitled *A Japanese Perspective on the Trinity* (→ Asian Theology).

Trinitarian thought is also playing a rich role in theological reflection on religious pluralism. Historically, the doctrine of the Trinity has been one way to insist on the falsehood of divergent theological claims. In this view, → Judaism and → Islam are right in their monotheism, but wrong in their failure to recognize the Trinity. Within Christianity, the denial of the Trinity is seen as a heresy, punishable in the extreme case by death, as in the execution of Michael Servetus (ca. 1511-53) in Calvin's Geneva. By contrast, contemporary thinkers such as Raimundo Panikkar, Mark Heim, Gavin D'Costa, and Rowan Williams have used the doctrine of the Trinity for more positive assessments of religious pluralism from a Christian perspective (→ Theology of Religions).

2.7.2. The Trinity, Christian Experience, and the Naming of God

Many theologians have sought to bridge the chasm lamented by Karl Rahner between the doctrine of the Trinity and Christian experience. While the young Melanchthon thought that exploration of the doctrine of the Trinity was irrelevant to knowledge of the saving benefits of Christ, contemporary theology is producing manifold attempts to free the doctrine of the Trinity from its reputation as abstruse and impractical. Catherine LaCugna, Ingolf Dalferth, and David Cunningham, to name but a sampling, have all explicitly insisted on the practicality of the doctrine of the Trinity. Paul Fiddes has written a book subtitled *A Pastoral Doctrine of the Trinity,* and Ruth Duck and Patricia Wilson-Kastner have coauthored *Praising God: The Trinity in Christian Worship.* James Buckley and David Yeago have edited a collection of essays by nine different authors on how church practices form their participants in knowledge of the triune God. González and Boff have both authored major works on the Trinity that grow out of, and seek to support, church-based liberation movements of socioeconomically marginalized people in Latin America (→ Liberation Theology; Latin American Theology).

One specific practical issue that has received much attention in recent Trinitarian theology is the naming of God in worship. → Feminist theology has challenged the dominant, even exclusive use of male language and imagery to refer to God. The traditional Trinitarian language of "Father, Son, and Holy Spirit" has been one object of this critique. Elizabeth Johnson and other theologians have argued for the use of multiple names and images for God in a way that does not abandon traditional male imagery but removes it from a position of dominance. It is generally assumed in this approach that all names for God are metaphoric (→ Metaphor). In Johnson's case this position is partially grounded in the insistence of Aquinas, grounded in God's self-revelation to Moses in Exodus 3, that God's ontological status is not that of a being, even the supreme being, but rather that God is being itself. Since God transcends the status of any particular being, God also transcends the status of any particular naming (→ Immanence and Transcendence).

Opponents have insisted that the language of "Father" has unique and irreplaceable status because of Jesus' own prayer practice. An essential point of Trinitarian theology is that God both transcends any particular being and is present with and for us in the finite flesh of Jesus of Nazareth. Our invocation and naming of the triune God is faithful only when it participates in Jesus Christ's own invocation and naming of God.

At this point there is a temptation for the dialogue to degenerate into polemics. One way to avoid that failure is to ask, as Johnson does, how "Father" functions as name and symbol, both in the Bible and in our own times and places. To take but one angle of such an approach, one could ask: What is the relation between Jesus' invocation of God as Father and his charge to call no one on earth "father" (Matt. 23:9)? What is the relation between Jesus' presentation of God as Father and the conspicuous absence of fathers from the list of blessings his followers will receive both in this age and in the age to come (Mark 10:29-30)? What difference does it make when Christians, as adopted siblings of Jesus, invoke God as Father yet also call others on earth "father"?

2.7.3. *The Trinity and Human Beings*

A different kind of practical concern is the question of how human beings are located in relation to God in our practice of Trinitarian theology. Does the placement of the Trinity as the object of Christian theological reflection already risk a misleading representation of our relation to God? God is not just over against us as the object of our thought. God is also nearer to us than we are to ourselves, as Augustine said. The Eastern Orthodox emphasis on deification *(→ theōsis)* has long conceived of salvation as participation in the life of the triune God. An increasing number of Western theologians have been highlighting the claim that we theologize in a sense from within the Trinity. For instance, Catherine LaCugna has called attention to a typical Trinitarian doxological form in the early centuries of the church, in which prayer and praise was "to the Father, through the Son, in the Spirit." The subsequent ascendency of the doxological form that gives glory "to the Father and the Son and the Spirit" effectively asserted the equality of the three persons but diminished the sense of Christian life as participation in the life of the triune God.

Another way of locating believers in our practice of Trinitarian theology is through the insistence of Ingolf Dalferth and Joe Jones that the doctrine of the Trinity specifies the grammar of Christian belief (→ Exegesis, Biblical; Hermeneutics). The purpose of this grammatical emphasis is not to distance us from God, as if theology were imprisoned in its own language and grammatical rules. On the contrary, Dalferth says that the doctrine of the Trinity reminds us that we never know God at arm's length, that if we try to take the position of a detached observer in relation to God, we are not really dealing with God. Put differently, the doctrine of the Trinity clarifies the notion that talk about "God" without confession, doxology, and repentance is not really talking about God.

Bibliography: Historical works; authors mentioned first in 2.1-2: K. BARTH, *CD* I/1, *The Doctrine of the Word of God* (New York, 1936) • J. MEYENDORFF, *Byzantine Theology: Historical Trends and Doctrinal Themes* (New

York, 1979) • W. Pauck, ed., *Melanchthon and Bucer* (Philadelphia, 1969) • K. Rahner, *The Trinity* (New York, 1997) • F. D. E. Schleiermacher, *The Christian Faith* (2 vols.; New York, 1963; orig. pub., 1821-22; rev., 1830-31).

Authors mentioned in 2.3-4: L. Boff, *Trinity and Society* (Maryknoll, N.Y., 1988) • A. González, *Trinidad y liberación. La teología trinitaria considerada desde la perspectiva de la teología de la liberación* (San Salvador, 1994) • R. W. Jenson, *Systematic Theology,* vol. 1, *The Triune God* (New York, 1997); idem, *The Triune Identity: God according to the Gospel* (Philadelphia, 1982) • E. A. Johnson, *She Who Is: The Mystery of God in Feminist Theological Discourse* (New York, 1993) • W. Pannenberg, "Die Subjektivität Gottes und die Trinitätslehre. Ein Beitrag zur Beziehung zwischen Karl Barth und der Philosophie Hegels," *Grundfragen systematischer Theologie. Gesammelte Aufsätze II* (Göttingen, 1980) 96-111; idem, *Systematic Theology* (vol. 1; Grand Rapids, 1991) • J. D. Zizioulas, *Being as Communion: Studies in Personhood and the Church* (Crestwood, N.Y., 1993); idem, "The Doctrine of the Holy Trinity: The Significance of the Cappadocian Contribution," *Trinitarian Theology Today: Essays on Divine Being and Act* (ed. C. Schwöbel; Edinburgh, 1995) 44-60.

Authors mentioned in 2.5-6: D. Bonhoeffer, *Letters and Papers from Prison* (New York, 1972) • J. A. Bracken and M. H. Suchocki, eds., *Trinity in Process: A Relational Theology of God* (New York, 1997) • S. Coakley, "The Trinity, Prayer, and Sexuality," *Feminism and Theology* (ed. J. M. Soskice and D. Lipton; Oxford, 2003) 258-67 • E. Jüngel, *God as the Mystery of the World: On the Foundation of the Theology of the Crucified One in the Dispute between Theism and Atheism* (Grand Rapids, 1983); idem, *God's Being Is in Becoming: The Trinitarian Being of God in the Theology of Karl Barth* (Grand Rapids, 2001) • K. Kitamori, *Theology of the Pain of God* (Richmond, Va., 1965) • C. M. LaCugna, *God for Us: The Trinity and Christian Life* (San Francisco, 1991) • J. Y. Lee, *The Trinity in Asian Perspective* (Nashville, 1996) • J. Moltmann, *The Crucified God: The Cross of Christ as the Foundation and Criticism of Modern Theology* (London, 1974; repr., Minneapolis, 1993); idem, *The Trinity and the Kingdom of God: The Doctrine of God* (London, 1981; repr., Minneapolis, 1993) • H. Mühlen, *Die Veränderlichkeit Gottes als Horizont einer zukünftigen Christologie. Auf dem Wege zu einer Kreuzestheologie in Auseinandersetzung mit der altkirchlichen Christologie* (Münster, 1969) • D. Staniloae, *The Experience of God* (Brookline, Mass., 1994).

Authors mentioned in 2.7: J. J. Buckley and D. S. Yeago, eds., *Knowing the Triune God: The Work of the Spirit in the Practices of the Church* (Grand Rapids,

2001) • D. S. Cunningham, *These Three Are One: The Practice of Trinitarian Theology* (Oxford, 1998) • I. U. Dalferth, *Der auferweckte Gekreuzigte. Zur Grammatik der Christologie* (Tübingen, 1994) • G. D'Costa, *The Meeting of Religions and the Trinity* (Maryknoll, N.Y., 2000) • R. C. Duck and P. Wilson-Kastner, *Praising God: The Trinity in Christian Worship* (Louisville, Ky., 1999) • P. S. Fiddes, *Participating in God: A Pastoral Doctrine of the Trinity* (Louisville, Ky., 2000) • S. M. Heim, *The Depth of the Riches: A Trinitarian Theology of Religious Ends* (Grand Rapids, 2001) • N. Miyahira, *Towards a Theology of the Concord of God: A Japanese Perspective on the Trinity* (Carlisle, Cumbria, 2000) • R. Panikkar, *The Trinity and the Religious Experience of Man: Icon–Person–Mystery* (Maryknoll, N.Y., 1973) • R. Williams, "Trinity and Pluralism," *On Christian Theology* (Oxford, 2000) 167-80.

John F. Hoffmeyer

Trito-Isaiah → Isaiah, Book of, 2

Troeltsch, Ernst

Ernst Troeltsch (1865-1923) was a Protestant theologian, philosopher of → culture, and politician. His theological/philosophical works, although many-faceted, were characterized by one theme: given the historicist insight that all historical reality is relative, with the resulting loss of normative validity (→ Relativism), he sought to identify new, binding values in historically given cultural contexts.

Troeltsch, born on February 17, 1865, in (Augsburg-) Haunstetten, was the eldest son of the medical doctor Ernst Troeltsch. His family belonged to the well-educated middle class and had interests in the history of nature and culture. Following his schooling in a humanistic upper school *(Gymnasium)* and then military service, Troeltsch graduated from a philosophical preparatory course at the Roman Catholic Lyceum in Augsburg. In 1884 he began studies in theology and philosophy in Erlangen, Berlin, and Göttingen, and he attended several lectures in history and economics. The late-idealist G. Class and the theological neo-Kantian A. Ritschl were his most important teachers. In 1888 Troeltsch passed his first church examination and began a vicariate in Munich.

In 1891 Troeltsch completed his habilitation at the University of Göttingen with a dissertation entitled "Vernunft und Offenbarung bei J. Gerhard und Ph. → Melanchthon" (Reason and revelation in

J. Gerhard and P. Melanchthon). In this theological and cultural-historical work Troeltsch, as the systematician among the proponents of the → history-of-religions school then active in Göttingen, defended the thesis that the ethical challenges of modern society were not to be resolved by resorting to the class ethics of so-called Old Protestantism. Following a short tenure as adjunct lecturer in Göttingen, he was called in 1892 to a chair of → systematic theology in Bonn. Here Troeltsch wrote a metacritique of the modern critique of religions and developed, in interdisciplinary exchange, the theological program that functioned as the historical and cultural study of Christianity. In 1894 Troeltsch was called to be the regular professor of systematic theology in Heidelberg.

As a result of numerous highly regarded studies of cultural history, as well as → fundamental theology — some authored in close interaction with M. → Weber, including *Die Absolutheit des Christentums und die Religionsgeschichte* (1902; ET *The Absoluteness of Christianity and the History of Religions* [1971]) and *Die Soziallehren der christlichen Kirchen und Gruppen* (1912; ET *The Social Teaching of the Christian Churches* [1931]) — Troeltsch rapidly became well known outside the field of theology. This activity, however, resulted in widespread rejection by conservative theological and church circles. Although completely open to modern → historicism, Troeltsch did not advocate unlimited relativism; rather, he taught the "highest validity" of Christianity as a personal religion of redemption. As a reform-oriented follower of the constitutional monarchy, Troeltsch was initially committed to F. Naumann's National Social Association, and then to the National Liberal Party. From 1910 to 1915 he represented his university in the Upper House of the state of Baden and was involved with the National Liberals in local Heidelberg politics.

After a call to a theological and philosophical chair in Berlin in 1909-10 failed to materialize because of church opposition, Troeltsch was able to make the shift in 1915 to a chair in "cultural-, historical-, and societal-religious philosophy and the Christian history of religion." He was happy to be able to leave behind the intellectual narrowness of an increasingly clerical theological enterprise, although he continued to take part in theological discussion. In Berlin he was more actively involved as a scholar-politician than he had been in Heidelberg. Together with scientists and politicians such as H. Delbrück, F. Meinecke, and W. Rathenau, Troeltsch advocated for a democratization of the empire and a peace based upon mutual understand-

ing. He was thus a public advocate for the Volksbund für Freiheit und Vaterland (People's Association for Freedom and Fatherland). He interpreted World War I as a cultural conflict imposed upon Germany in which it was important that the specifically German concept of → freedom should be defended. After the defeat and the revolution, Troeltsch worked in the left-liberal, middle-class German Democratic Party as a delegate to the constitution-drafting Prussian National Assembly, as well as undersecretary for church and cultural affairs under K. Haenisch. He became very influential as a journalist through his "Spectator Letters," in which he analyzed the politics and culture of the revolutionary period.

In terms of his intellectual production, Troeltsch focused in his Berlin period on the development of an original historical methodology and the search for new and compelling European cultural values in a pluralistic time that was characterized by the loss of unambiguous perceptions and fixed ethical orientations (*Der Historismus und seine Probleme* [1922; ET *Christian Thought, Its History and Application* (1923)]). Shortly before the beginning of a lecture trip to England, Troeltsch died — on February 1, 1923, just before his 58th birthday.

Karl → Barth's treatment of Troeltsch, which has been criticized as almost slanderous (G. Rupp), destroyed his continuing influence in Germany, except for the continued interest of especially Trutz Rendtorff and Friedrich Wilhelm Graf, who are now editing a critical edition of Troeltsch's collected works. Troeltsch's reception in the United States, however, was wide and deep. The translation of his *Social Teaching of the Christian Churches* in 1931 became the basis of many courses in → social ethics and thus set the terms of debate in American Protestantism for much of the century. It shaped the programs at Yale under H. Richard Niebuhr, at the University of Chicago and later Harvard under James Luther Adams, at Union Theological Seminary under Reinhold → Niebuhr and later Roger Shinn, and at Boston University under Walter Muelder — and under their students in many other places.

Bibliography: Primary sources: The Absoluteness of Christianity and the History of Religions (Louisville, Ky., 2006; orig. pub., 1902; first Eng. ed., 1971) • *Christian Thought, Its History and Application* (New York, 1957; orig. pub., 1922; first Eng. ed., 1923) • *Kritische Gesamtausgabe* (20 vols.; ed. F. W. Graf et al.; Berlin, 1998ff.) • *The Social Teaching of the Christian Churches* (2 vols.; Louisville, Ky., 1992; orig. pub., 1912; first Eng. ed., 1931).

Secondary works: M. Chapman, *Ernst Troeltsch and Liberal Theology: Religion and Cultural Synthesis in Wilhelmine Germany* (Oxford, 2001) • S. Coakley, *Christ without Absolutes: A Study of the Christology of Ernst Troeltsch* (Oxford, 1988) • H.-G. Drescher, *Ernst Troeltsch: His Life and Work* (Minneapolis, 1993) • F. W. Graf, "Ernst Troeltsch (1865-1923)," *Klassiker der Theologie,* vol. 2, *Von Richard Simon bis Karl Rahner* (ed. F. W. Graf; Munich, 2005) 171-89 • F. W. Graf, R. Anselm, J. Dierken, and G. Pfleiderer, eds., *Troeltsch-Studien, Neue Folge* (Gütersloh, 2005ff.) • F. W. Graf and H. Ruddies, *Ernst Troeltsch Bibliographie* (Tübingen, 1982) • *Mitteilungen der Ernst-Troeltsch-Gesellschaft* (Munich, 1982ff.) • H. Renz and F. W. Graf, eds., *Troeltsch-Studien* (12 vols.; Gütersloh, 1982-2004) • G. Rupp, *Culture-Protestantism: German Liberal Theology at the Turn of the Twentieth Century* (Atlanta, Ga., 1987; orig. pub., 1977).

Friedrich Wilhelm Graf and
Max L. Stackhouse

Troparion → Hymnody

Trust

1. Psychological and Theological Aspects
2. Social Aspects

1. Psychological and Theological Aspects

1.1. The term "trust" proves, especially since E. Erikson's (1902-94) creation of the concept of "primal trust" (→ Ego Psychology; Identity), to be a mechanism for reducing both social (N. Luhmann) and theological complexity. It describes "the basic process between man and God. Man's relationship to God stands and falls therefore with trust in God" (E. Jüngel, 196). As a central category of theological → anthropology, it is based on the psychological idea that the infant in its first year lives in a symbiosis with the mother that is supported by the infant's innate "basic trust" (Erikson). The task of religious formation would be to detach this basic trust "from its initial connection with the parents and to give it a new direction" (W. Pannenberg, 227).

Empirical research of infancy (→ Childhood) has proved the symbiosis model, which forms the basis for this concept of trust, to be untenable. The infant is no longer seen as a predominantly passive being who receives maternal care but as an interactive partner of both parents, with differentiated competencies. With this new view of the infant it can be seen that both in the symbiosis model and in the concept of "basic trust" that evolved from it, the patriarchal model of the relationship of the sexes is implicated. Thus, with the extensive absence of the father, the woman is seen exclusively as mother, and consequently the subjectivity of the mother is denied (J. Benjamin). Furthermore, the symbiosis model neglects the entire range of unconscious fantasies of the infant (S. Isaacs), which contain archaic attacks as well as primitive imaginings of love in connection with both parents, mother as well as father. It is these extremely vital internal pictures of the unconscious fantasy life, extraordinarily frightening to the adult imagination, which constitute the inner world of humans (H. Beland). These archaic, unconscious fantasies are symbolized in the world of apocalyptic images (→ Apocalypticism).

1.2. Criticism of the symbiotic model requires a revision of the theological concept of trust. The OT word group *amn,* from which the → "Amen" at the end of a → prayer derives, corresponds to the Greek concept *pistis* (faith, trust). The Heb. *amn* designates the child in arms; its theological context, however, is the → covenant between → Yahweh and → Israel, which is oriented toward shalom (→ Peace 2.1.1), toward the intersubjectivity of both covenant partners, and it intends a relationship of trust supported "with all your heart, and with all your soul" (Deut. 6:5).

In the NT → Paul refers the *pistis* concept to the connection between cross and → resurrection (Rom. 10:9). With Paul, as well as the writers of the → Synoptics, trust refers to the miraculous activity of God (→ Miracle), in which trusting humans participate (Mark 11:22-23; 1 Cor. 12:8-11), which brings new → life out of → death.

Psychoanalytic assumptions (→ Psychoanalysis) correspond to this miracle of trust: the child from the beginning of its life attacks its primary attachment figures in its unconscious fantasies, in "merciless love" (D. W. Winnicott), which is the expression of its innate bodily vitality, and imagines in its early fantasy life to have destroyed the parents. If the parents neither take revenge nor deny the attack but rather "survive" it, then this infinitely repeated experience of interaction constitutes the basis of the ability to trust and to experience a feeling of → guilt. Put theologically, → sin (put psychologically, → aggression) destroys the relationship supporting the subject — before this relationship "resurrects," in transformed form, through the survival of the early attachment figures, as an action *extra nos* (outside ourselves). "God cannot be God unless he first becomes a devil. We cannot go to heaven unless we first go to hell. We cannot become God's children until we first become children of the devil" (M. → Luther, *LW* 14.31). Trust thus becomes the sensibility for history: the subject sees what it has done to other subjects in the past and out of this painful insight develops hope for future opportunity for reparation.

1.3. Psychological insights into the absolutely constitutive role of early interpersonal relationships, which are the basis of trust, have an important result for → pastoral care, as well as for → religious instruction. They can see their basic anthropological assumptions pre-formed in the interpersonal experiences of relationship that are differentiated at the beginning of life and guided by unconscious fantasies. In these early relational fantasies the ability to trust arises first through the experience that the understanding of the needs of the child, which are articulated in motor-sensory ways, is accomplished in the personality of the adult reference person *(extra nos)*. The child grasps this external ability to comprehend early in the first year, always by means of its vital bodily impulses.

Seen from the perspective of the *parents,* the development of the ability to trust is grounded in the kind of behavior that offers the vital child sufficient opportunity for reparation (Winnicott). This can be done only by parents who do not see themselves — as in the symbiosis model — as functional objects of children's needs but who see themselves as their child's subjective interactive partner and who thus accept that their child is equipped in the same measure from the beginning of life with competence to interact. Seen from the perspective of the *child,* the ability to trust presupposes the acceptance of its personal vitality, including those elements attacking the other subject (Benjamin). It forms the basis of a theological anthropology, according to which trust represents the result of successful human experiences of aggression, a result that one constantly questions one's entire life.

Bibliography: H. BELAND, "Die unbewußte Phantasie. Kontroverse um ein Konzept," *Unbewuße Phantasien. Neue Aspekte in der psychoanalytischen Theorie und Praxis* (ed. H.-V. Werthmann; Munich, 1989) 73-92 • J. BENJAMIN, *The Bonds of Love: Psychoanalysis, Feminism, and the Problem of Domination* (New York, 1988) • M. DORNES, *Der kompetente Säugling. Die präverbale Entwicklung des Menschen* (Frankfurt, 1993) • E. H. ERIKSON, *Childhood and Society* (2d ed.; New York, 1978; orig. pub., 1950) • S. ISAACS, "The Nature and Function of Phantasy," *Developments in Psycho-Analysis* (ed. M. Klein, P. Heimann, and S. Isaacs; London, 1952) 67-121 • E. JÜNGEL, *God as the Mystery of the World* (Grand Rapids, 1983) • N. LUHMANN, *Vertrauen. Ein Mechanismus der Reduktion sozialer Komplexität* (4th ed.; Stuttgart, 2000; orig. pub., 1968) • M. S. MAHLER, F. PINE, and A. BERGMAN, *The Psychological Birth of the Human Infant: Symbiosis and Individuation* (New York, 1975) • W. PANNENBERG, *Anthropology in Theological Perspective* (Philadelphia, 1985) • H. RAGUSE, *Psychoanalyse und biblische Interpretation. Eine Auseinandersetzung mit Eugen Drewermanns Auslegung der Johannes-Apokalypse* (Stuttgart, 1993) • M. WEIMER, "'Wir setzen uns mit Tränen nieder. . . .' Die Zerstörung des Objekts und die Wiederherstellung des Subjekts," *WzM* 43 (1991) 222-38 • D. W. WINNICOTT, *Playing and Reality* (New York, 1971); idem, *Through Paediatrics to Psycho-analysis* (New York, 1975).

MARTIN WEIMER

2. Social Aspects

2.1. The growth of → fascism was an express reason for political → psychology to investigate how models of personality develop and spread in political, economic, and social contexts. Recalling psychoanalytic theories (→ Psychoanalysis) about the parental training of young children, T. W. Adorno (1903-69) described the "authoritarian personality," which is inclined to hierarchical and conformist patterns and treats foreigners with hostility. Such conditions both nurture and influence this personality. H. D. Lasswell (1902-78) compares the "authoritarian character" and the "democratic character" in a variety of possible → socialization experiences. A characteristic of the democratic personality is that, with the relatively balanced psychological structure of an "open ego," it is basically trusting of fellow citizens.

Trust is one of the principles of a constitutional state (→ Democracy; State). Both individually and collectively this kind of state rests on confidence that the judicial system and the administration will function satisfactorily. Yet where a depoliticized citizenry has too great a trust that the state will function constitutionally, belief in the state can have domesticating effects (→ State Ethics; Totalitarianism).

2.2. A functional-structural system theory (→ Social Systems 1.3) that considers the reduction (or selection) of all the possible experiences and actions within the human potential of life and tradition regards trust as an elementary fact of social living (N. Luhmann). As confident expectation, trust can embrace and reduce the complexity that the freedom of others enhances. Personal trust relative to the freedom of action bridges over the element of uncertainty regarding what we may expect from others.

Broadened into "system trust," it refers to other personalities as systems of activity and to the social dimensions of human actions and experiences. To decide for trust, and to give it, augments the potential of action and reduces the complexity of the environment, and also of the alternatives of expectation, so that life can be lived without taking too many risks. In social life looking to people is not a good reason for trust; their complexity makes too great a demand. Trust can find a footing here only in the working of the more general media of → communication, → money, truthfulness, and → power.

Trust must be learned and tested and will also prove to be uncertain and enchaining. Its functional counterpart is the distrust that is found in the strategies of conflict or resignation. Distrust also simplifies, but it demands more information. By itself it restricts the possibility of unprejudiced investigation and the related learning.

2.3. Ethical reflection into the role that the presence of others has on one's own action treats the expectation of trust as a tacit obligation that is already in force in dealings among people and that is subject to explicit commands (K. E. Løgstrup). Like such things as sincerity, mercy, or sympathy, trust is a spontaneous feeling relative to others. It promotes community life. To act with mutual trust expresses the inner dimension of trust. Its outer dimension consists of acting in a trustworthy world. Trust expects justice for all. It comes to expression in a just society in which justice is a basic constitutional element and where trust assumes an intrinsically social form.

Bibliography: T. W. Adorno, *The Authoritarian Personality* (New York, 1950) • K. S. Cook, ed., *Trust in Society* (New York, 2001) • T. C. Earle and G. T. Cvetkovich, *Social Trust: Toward a Cosmopolitan Society* (Westport, Conn., 1995) • H. D. Lasswell, "Democratic Character," *Political Writings* (Glencoe, Ill., 1951) 465-525 • K. E. Løgstrup, *The Ethical Demand* (Philadelphia, 1971) • N. Luhmann, *Trust and Power: Two Works* (New York, 1979) • G. Möllering, *Trust: Reason, Routine, Reflexivity* (Boston, 2006).

Jean-Marie Charpentier

Truth

1. Biblical Aspects

1.1. OT

The Heb. word for truth is *'emet,* indicating something firm, reliable, and trustworthy or durable. True words or events may be denoted (Deut. 22:20; 1 Kgs. 10:6), or authentic guarantees (Josh. 2:12). The truth may be that of a → revelation (Dan. 10:1) or of wisdom (Prov. 22:21). The antithesis is what is false, deceptive, or unstable. Those who tell the truth are people of truth (Gen. 42:16). The reference may be to the truth of their statements or to their inner truthfulness (1 Kgs. 17:24).

The word *'emet* often occurs for the truthfulness of God and is sometimes translated "faithfulness" (e.g., Exod. 34:6). God is true to his → promises. He will not depart from or change the truth (Ps. 111:7-8). His work in → creation is "true," as are all his ordinances (v. 7), in both cases in the sense of being reliable (see also Ps. 19:9). They faithfully reveal God's will to humans. God himself is the true God, in contrast to idols, which are a sham. Idols involve those who worship them in untruth (see Rom. 1:18). Truth can apply to doctrines. A true religion is oriented to the true God (Deut. 18:22; Jer. 10:10), and the true → Word of God underlies it (Ps. 119:160).

1.2. NT

Gk. *alētheia* (lit. "unveiled") in the NT takes up the points of the OT in its own way. A thing is true if it is valid or normative and genuine. But it is also true if it is reliable, if one can count on it, either because of itself or because the one who says or does or underlies it is honest and sincere (2 Cor. 7:14). Truth reveals or discloses reality. Jesus is said to be the true vine (John 15:1) and, more important, the truth in person (John 1:9; cf. v. 17). Truth can also involve accuracy of statement (Mark 12:14). The

Pharisees spoke the truth in this passage, even if they did not mean it. Jesus himself taught the way of God truthfully.

Applied to teaching, truth involves both true information and true belief (cf. 2 Cor. 13:8). The → preaching of the → gospel is truthful preaching (2 Cor. 6:7). True faith relates to God's revelation in Jesus Christ. As the household of the living God, the church is "the pillar and bulwark of the truth" (1 Tim. 3:15). Christians do not follow erroneous or deceptive views; they are established in the truth (2 Pet. 1:12).

The Word of God, living and active, is the basis of theological truth. In John's gospel Jesus is the → incarnation of the Logos, who was with God and is God (John 1:1). He is the embodiment of truth, especially God's truth and Word: "I am the way, and the truth, and the life" (John 14:6). Jesus is truth, and Jesus knows the truth and speaks the truth (John 8:14-18). To know Jesus is to know God the Father, and so to know ultimate truth. Jesus is made known by the Spirit, who is the Spirit of truth (John 14:16-17). The Spirit guides believers into all truth (John 16:13); his witness is true (1 John 5:6). To worship in the Spirit is to worship in truth (John 4:24). The Father, as well as the Son and Spirit, is truth. Jesus prays that the Father will sanctify his followers by the truth, for "your word is truth" (John 17:17). Here truth is personal, not propositional, and is lived out in personal relationships.

1.3. Ethics and Truthfulness

To follow after the God who is truth is to live as → disciples of truth, to live in truthfulness. Being true suggests honesty and integrity (Ps. 51:6). Telling the truth is an expression of integrity (Ps. 15:2), as is the faithful fulfilling of one's obligations (v. 4). A truthful person will not bear false witness (Exod. 20:16). God is truth, and therefore the opposites of being true (engaging in lying, falsehood, deception) are excluded from his kingdom (Rev. 21:8, 27).

Truth is called forth by God from his people. God's disclosure of himself in his created works ought to have been enough to lead people to the true God, but various forms of idolatry put error in the place of truth. This culpable error goes hand in hand with even more culpable deception, as the wicked suppress the truth (Rom. 1:18-32; 1 Tim. 4:1-2). Similar error and similar deception keep the wicked from grasping the saving self-revelation of God in Jesus Christ. Even more culpable is the hypocrisy that makes a show of commitment to God without any real substance.

Truth is demanded in relation to others. In every kind of personal dealing God expects his human creatures to speak the truth insofar as their tangled relationships allow. God thus expects our truthfulness in social contexts. Life in society becomes impossible if lying, falsehood, and disinformation constantly replace the truth. What would legal systems be without the undertaking to speak the truth, the whole truth, and nothing but the truth? What becomes of scholarship if truth does not prevail over both error and deception? How can a business prosper if it does not live up to its promises and obligations? How can citizens have confidence in their governments if rulers and politicians play fast and loose with the truth? And what happens to international relationships if nations engage in all kinds of underhand activities, cheating, and lying, and entering into treaties only with a view to breaking them? In ancient Israel the → prophets underscored the need for truth and faithfulness in many of these spheres of life, and every nation and culture still has need of prophets to demonstrate how lying poisons human life in society and to insist once again upon both the ethical and the practical value of the truthfulness that God has commanded.

In our fallen society truth necessarily comes under pressure, especially when it enters into conflict with other responsibilities. In personal dealings we must speak the truth, but only with love (Eph. 4:15). To be completely honest can at times be hurtful. On a wider canvas, speaking the truth may indeed do harm to others. Should Christians tell the truth when doing so would betray our friends, perhaps whom we are hiding from evil forces? A classic example of this dilemma from the last century was the German Jews, who often were not protected by their Christian neighbors. Was not the sin of lying a lesser sin than that of betrayal to almost certain death? Truthfulness is thus a central virtue, but not the highest principle in Christian ethics, which must remain love. Still, we should follow the rule of truth in all possible situations, praying that we are not trapped in difficult moral dilemmas.

Nevertheless, so far as our fallen world permits, the God of truth expects truth from his creatures. He expects them to engage in an intellectual search for truth that is ready to forsake error when the truth is revealed. He expects them to enlist in an ethical search for truth that will do everything possible to avoid every form of falsehood or deception. He expects them to commit themselves to a religious search for truth that will lead them to himself, the God of truth.

Bibliography: J. M. G. BARCLAY, *Obeying the Truth: Paul's Ethics in Galatians* (Minneapolis, 1991) •

K. Barth, *CD* IV/3, §70.2 • G. W. Bromiley, "Truth," *ISBE* 4.926-28 • W. Brueggemann, "Truth-Telling as Subversive Obedience," *The Ten Commandments* (ed. W. P. Brown; Louisville, Ky., 2004) 290-99 • C. Helmer and K. de Troyer, eds., *Truth: Interdisciplinary Dialogues in a Pluralistic Age* (Louvain, 2003) • A. Jepsen, "אָמַן *'āman*" VI-IX, *TDOT* 1.309-23 • P. D. Kenneson, "Truth," *Handbook of Postmodern Biblical Interpretation* (ed. A. K. M. Adam; St. Louis, 2000) 268-76 • A. G. Padgett and P. R. Keifert, eds., *But Is It All True? The Bible and the Question of Truth* (Grand Rapids, 2006) • G. Quell et al., "Ἀλήθεια κτλ.," *TDNT* 1.232-51.

The Editors

2. Philosophical Aspects

2.1. *Meaning*

As noted in section 1, Eng. "truth" translates Gk. *alēthēs* and Heb. *'emet,* as well as Lat. *veritas.* It carries such senses as "being reliable, credible, honest." The truth opens up reality to us, or mediates reality through words or another medium such as visions. Theories of truth in Western philosophy typically focus on statements, rather than persons, art, or other true things; another long tradition, however, thinks of truth in terms of being.

2.2. *Definition*

There is no one fully accepted definition of truth in → philosophy. One quite early definition is also the one most commonly accepted for statements (or propositions), namely, the realist, or "correspondence," theory of truth (→ Realism). Aristotle (384-322 b.c.; → Aristotelianism) defined truth for statements as "to say of what is that it is, and of what is not that it is not" (*Meta.* 4.7). Plato (427-347; → Platonism) held a very similar view in his dialogue *The Sophist* (263B), but in his developed theory of Forms (or Ideas) he connected truth more fully with an intellectual intuition of the true and eternal Forms as the basic structures of reality (*Rep.* bk.10). This alternative, powerful tradition in the West connected truth with being, or what is (→ Ontology).

2.3. *History and Theories*

2.3.1. *Realism*

More generally in ancient → Greek philosophy from Parmenides (ca. 540-after 480 b.c.) to Plotinus (a.d. ca. 205-70), truth was connected to being. This agreement had its basis in the relationship of being and thought and, for some, in the divine mind, soul, or Logos that permeates the cosmos. Christian theology adopted this tradition, for example, in → Augustine. It saw in God himself (→ God 7) the supreme ground of truth. The Ideas, or Forms, which Platonism viewed as the basis of being, could now

be identified as the divine mind and ascribed to God the Creator. As such, God both is the source of all created truth and is himself the ultimate truth. The Holy Spirit has created both the things we know and our minds that know them, and so the Spirit is rightly named the Spirit of truth.

Thomas Aquinas (ca. 1225-74; → Thomism) combined the Aristotelian and Platonic traditions, which were broadly accepted for much of the classical and medieval periods. He developed the Aristotelian view in a slightly different direction, seeing truth as "the conformity of thing and intellect [*adaequatio rei et intellectus*]" (*Truth* 1.1) or, otherwise expressed, "the conformity [*conformitatem*] of intellect and thing" (*Summa theol.* I, q. 16, art. 2). Aquinas held that truth could also be found in things to the degree that they are related to intellect (divine or human), and so truth finds its complete fulfillment in the process of conformity (adequation) between being and mind. Either the things we know or the things we say can thus be true, but for Thomas the proper sense of truth must include the intellect. As a Christian thinker he also argued that God is the first truth and the final end of all our seeking after the truth.

Much of the Western tradition broadly accepted the Aristotelian or another realist, or correspondence, theory of truth. J. Locke (1632-1704), for example, held that truth and falsity properly belong to propositions, although he allowed for mental or verbal propositions. He defined truth as the conformity between the ideas (verbal or in the mind) and real things (*Essay* 2.32, §1; 4.5, §11).

Also during the → Enlightenment, the critical philosophy of I. Kant (1724-1804; → Kantianism) took a new direction by placing truth in the context of the a priori conditions of the intellect, which make knowing possible. Thus Kant argued that "conformity with the laws of understanding is the formal element in all truth" (*Critique of Pure Reason,* B350).

After the Kantian turn to the mind as active in knowing, G. W. F. Hegel (1770-1831; → Hegelianism) returned to the idea of the truth of being in a new way. For Hegel, truth was the unity of concept and reality in the Idea. But ideas do not exist in isolation. The full truth could be known only in the whole, and the whole is completed (both logically and historically) only in absolute spirit or mind.

2.3.2. *Truth as Created*

A quite different path after Kant was taken by F. → Nietzsche (1844-1900), the grandfather of → postmodernism. He took Kant in a radical direction, arguing that we cannot in fact verify the conditions under which we can know the truth. All language is metaphoric at base, and truth as such is the creation of the "true" philosopher. Since truth is "a mobile army of → metaphors," Nietzsche would have us abandon the will for truth in favor of the will to → power ("On Truth and Lies"; also *Beyond Good and Evil,* 211). We might say that this approach anticipates the postmodern view that there simply is no truth in the realist sense; rather, we ourselves make the truth (see 2.3.7 and comments on Foucault)

2.3.3. *Pragmatic Theories*

The impossibility of finding an objective and universal basis for the realist theory led in the United States to more pragmatic theories of truth, especially with the philosophers C. S. Peirce (1839-1914) and W. James (1842-1910). For the → pragmatist, "an idea is something that tends to guide or to plan a mode of action" (Royce, 369). While James held that statements actually become true to the extent that they are validated in practice and experience, Peirce held the more modest view that the meaning of a scientific statement (and its ultimate truth) is an ideal result of the sum of its practical consequences over an indefinite period of scientific investigation.

2.3.4. *Coherence Theory*

A coherence theory was developed about this same time by idealist followers of Hegel such as F. H. Bradley (1846-1924) in England. Since truth is most manifest in a harmonious system of ideas, the truth of a simple idea or belief is fully displayed only when it is part of an entire system of beliefs or statements that is consistent, comprehensive, and harmonious.

2.3.5. *Logical Positivism*

The development of early → analytic philosophy on the Continent led to a consideration of linguistic truth that is closely related to empirical verification. Members of the Vienna Circle, in particular, strove to make clear the difference between meaningful and senseless language, based upon empirical verification for simple sentences. This test, known as the verification criterion of meaning, was made popular in the English-speaking world by A. J. Ayer (1910-89) in his *Language, Truth, and Logic* (1938). This school was generally called logical → positivism or logical empiricism. This program excluded from meaningful language (and thus from truth or falsehood) both theological and moral truth-claims.

This position, however, did not long survive philosophical critique, especially from the later L. Wittgenstein (1889-1951). After arguing for a "picture theory" of truth for simple propositions in his *Tractatus Logico-Philosophicus* (1921), the later Wittgenstein in his *Philosophical Investigations* (1953) insisted that → meaning can be found only

in the use of language by a community of speakers practicing a large variety of "language games," which are rooted in the various "forms of life" humans engage in as part of their everyday existence. He came to think that any proposed theory for truth was misguided (see 2.3.7).

Another movement beyond positivism arose from a 1963 paper on realism by M. Dummett (b. 1925) that inaugurated the current conversation about truth in terms of realism and "antirealism." According to this approach, (1) a realist theory of truth accepts the principle of bivalence for sentences about a specific domain of inquiry (i.e., these sentences are either true or false), and (2) their truth or falsity is not a matter of what evidence we happen to have (i.e., it is not based on verification). Many philosophers now prefer to speak of a "realist" theory of truth, avoiding the somewhat misleading term "correspondence."

2.3.6. *Truth as Unconcealment*

About this same time, as logical positivism was developing, the German philosopher M. Heidegger (1889-1976) worked toward reclaiming a conception of truth as the disclosure of being — that is, as dis-covery, or unconcealment. For Heidegger, truth is primarily an event of the unconcealment of being, the event of which clears a space for the coming together of thinking and being. Truth applies to statements only in a derivative sense. This theory has been the starting place for much of the Continental discussion concerning truth.

Heidegger's student H.-G. Gadamer (1900-2002) brought an appreciation for tradition, community, and preunderstanding to his philosophy of language and his view of truth, especially for → hermeneutics and the human sciences. For Gadamer, human consciousness is effective-historical, and → language is the inevitable context, or "horizon," in which the self, the world, and the words of others (texts) come together. Truth for this mode of understanding cannot be found in a simple logical method (such as propositional verification or natural explanation) but, rather, in the "fusion of horizons" between the thought and life of readers today and that of the author/text from the past. Gadamer was influenced by Wittgenstein to speak of the "play" of language in the event of truth, as humans encounter and seek to understand the world and the words of others.

2.3.7. *Truth and the Hermeneutics of Suspicion*

Recent postmodern and poststructuralist theories, especially in France, have called into question any account of truth as normally understood. For example, M. Foucault (1926-84), who was in debt to Nietzsche, analyzed truth claims historically and sociologically as power-moves made by individuals or institutions to prop up the status quo and maintain their power. One thinks immediately of George Orwell's prophetic novel *1984* (1949) and the role of the Ministry of Truth in his imagined (but all too realistic!) totalitarian state. While not holding to any system or single viewpoint, Foucault came to believe that any claim for universal or absolute truth is either completely naive or very suspicious. In fact, much of the postmodern attitude can be characterized as a hermeneutics of suspicion applied to any and all claims to truth.

Contemporary philosophers of many kinds have found the definition and conception of truth so conflicted and complex that some despair of finding any adequate definition that will fit every domain of inquiry. For example, A. Tarski (1901-83) developed a definition of truth that is widely accepted for symbolic logic, but its usefulness outside that domain is highly contested. Some, like the later Wittgenstein, think that any developed theory of truth is a confusion and unnecessary. This is sometimes called a redundancy or a deflationary notion of truth, both of which seek to argue that any developed theory of truth is in fact unnecessary (or just plain wrong). Whatever one's philosophical preferences, the idea of truth is under serious stress at the beginning of the 21st century.

3. Theological Aspects
3.1. *The Issue*
Christian theologians have long identified God and the truth, based firmly on the biblical witness (see 1). Nevertheless, the proper way to understand this basic insight theologically and to relate it to Christian life, witness, and worship has been the subject of profound reflection and serious difference among theologians over the centuries. The question for theology is thus that of the relationship of the truth of God in Christ, the living Word, to our everyday truths and to truth as understood in → science and philosophy. Because the first of these three areas of truth has to do with God and salvation, → theology can never approach the question of truth in a merely abstract manner but knows that this quest involves worship, witness, and the transformation of our selves and communities by the → Word of God.

3.2. *Historical Development*
Following the Middle Ages, the → Reformation based its call to transform Christianity and the church upon an appeal to Scripture as the Word of God. Truth was thus connected to the Word and the promises of God. M. → Luther (1483-1546) typi-

cally understood truth in terms of the Word of God, the promises of God, the gospel, and so also as Jesus Christ. The Scriptures became the written form of this Word, made known to → faith (e.g., *Lectures on Galatians, LW* 26.53-73). J. → Calvin (1509-64) could likewise state that "it pleased the Lord to hallow his truth to everlasting remembrance in the Scriptures alone" (*Inst.* 1.7.1). The Scriptures are, for the → Reformers, truly understood through faith and the illumination of the Spirit, not by purely worldly analysis of the text.

This evangelical emphasis on Christ as truth, known in the Scriptures by the illumination of the Spirit and the presence of the living Word, was transformed in the development of Protestant scholastic theology in the 17th and 18th centuries. Returning to a method grounded in Aristotelian philosophy and logic, these theologians blended a view of truth as grounded in Scripture with a propositional understanding of truth. F. Turretin (1623-87), speaking of the "truth of propositions," stated that "divine revelation dictates axioms or sentences of faith to us in the Scriptures" (*Institutes* 1.8.11). Over against this rationalizing understanding of theological truth, the Pietists (→ Pietism) and → evangelicals like P. Spener (1635-1705) and J. → Wesley (1703-91) sought to return to scriptural truth, but they supplemented it with an emphasis on spiritual life and experience. Thus Wesley could name the goal of his preaching as "the true, scriptural, experimental religion" (preface to his *Sermons*). In both of these movements, however, this emphasis on "experiment," or → experience, was strongly subordinate to the truth of Scripture.

A very different appeal to experience was made by F. D. E. → Schleiermacher (1768-1834), the father of Protestant → liberal theology. Influenced by Kant and the → Romantic movement, Schleiermacher turned toward human consciousness as the illuminating principle of religious truth. Like Hegel, he adopted a coherence theory of truth, but of a different sort. In → dogmatics, truth is sought in a system of theology that is clear and comprehensive in its harmony. But the root of the knowledge of God is not so much God's Word as our consciousness of God, our feeling of absolute dependence upon One who is the ground of the world and the self but yet who is beyond all creation. Christ thus gives the church the truth in the historical perfection of his God-consciousness.

Over against this liberal tradition in theology, K. → Barth (1886-1968) and other dialectical or neoorthodox theologians in the early 20th century rediscovered the emphasis of the Reformation on the Word of God. Barth understood God's Word as the truth for the church and for any scientific theology that hopes to be Christian (*CD* I/1, 3-5). His Christocentric approach to theology found the Word of God (and so the truth) first in the living Word, Jesus Christ, and only secondarily in Scripture as the primary human witness to Christ. The Word of God is an event, a personal encounter, and so this truth is neither a possession nor a proposition. Just how this understanding of truth connects to the truth of philosophy and the sciences has been a significant issue for Barth and his followers and was, for example, the main source of his break with E. Brunner (1889-1966).

The development of → existentialism in philosophy created an opportunity to rethink the philosophy of Aquinas in contemporary terms. The neo-Thomistic movement among predominantly (but not exclusively) Roman Catholic thinkers (e.g., É. Gilson [1884-1978], J. Maritain [1882-1973], and K. → Rahner [1904-84]) accepts the idea of degrees or hierarchy in the truth, rooted mainly in the thought of Aquinas, but with important themes also taken up from Continental philosophy. A central point in this view goes back to Augustine, namely, that God has placed in every human mind a thirst for truth, a questing and searching after the truth of life and of being, which can find its true end and fulfillment only in God.

For example, H. U. von Balthasar (1905-88) in his work *Truth of the World* (1947) accepted Heidegger's understanding of truth as unconcealment, attaching it to the Greek word for truth *(alētheia)*. This understanding of truth can accommodate both philosophy and science, rightly understood, especially when combined with the Hebrew term *'emet,* which he associates with trust and truthfulness. These two concepts are blended together by von Balthasar and connected to his vision of God as the ultimate truth. Human existence is an open questioning after truth, a search for something in which to trust at a deep level in our lives. Only God, as the highest and deepest truth, can finally and completely fulfill our profound intellectual and existential longings.

3.3. *Current Debates*

The postmodern turn in the late 20th century has raised in a powerful way the question of truth, not excluding the truth of theology. Each of the various theories concerning theological truth that we have covered has its defenders today, including those of a propositional approach. Several major voices seek to break new ground, while also incorporating key ideas from the past.

The late pope John Paul II (1920-2005) drew upon the neo-Thomistic tradition in his important encyclical on theology and philosophy *Fides et ratio* (1998). On this basis he opened this document as follows: "Faith and reason are like two wings on which the human spirit rises to the contemplation of truth; and God has placed in the human heart a desire to know the truth — in a word, to know himself."

The Lutheran theologian W. Pannenberg (b. 1928) has long made truth an important theme in his theology. Taking a somewhat Hegelian approach, Pannenberg argues that truth today is always partial, always part of a larger communal and historical process that can find its fullness only eschatologically (apocalyptically). Over against Barth, Pannenberg brought theological truth more openly into conversation with science and critical history. Although broadly coherentist in his theory of truth, Pannenberg grounds theological truth in God's revelation in history. For him the truth of God and his "lordship" are open to question in historical contingency — a contingency made most evident in the cross. Because God is God of the whole world and of universal history, in principle Christian truth should be open to the whole world and to truth found in any religion or academic discipline, while at the same time being grounded in biblical revelation.

E. Jüngel (b. 1934), another Lutheran in Germany, takes a very different direction with a many-faceted theology of truth. Deeply influenced by Heidegger and hermeneutic philosophy, as well as by Luther and Barth, Jüngel argues against a correspondence theory of truth and proposes that we understand gospel truth as a kind of interruption — an event that breaks open the ordinary flow of life, a crisis that opens up a space for transformation. He finds a human analogy for this event in → death. Since all human being is being-toward-death (Heidegger), death provides an analogy to gospel truth as an interruption in our lives that forces us to face the truth about our own being. The "interruption" of the everyday world that we experience in the face of great beauty in art is another example.

Turning to theology, Jüngel holds that the → parables of Jesus that open up his hearers to the kingdom of God are similar to this event of interruptive truth. This theology of truth leads Jüngel to insist that metaphor, not proposition, is the fundamental character of linguistic truth for God's Word and is closer to the narrative and history that are characteristic of human encounter with the Word. Jüngel also turns this "interruptive" concept around to God's very existence, arguing that in the "interruption" of the cross, in the death of God, God embraces nonbeing within the triune life and overcomes it (in the resurrection), thus making gospel truth and life for sinners. Here Jüngel appeals to Luther's theology of the cross (→ Theologia crucis) as grounds for this view of truth within the → Trinity, an openness within God that leads finally to our → justification and transformation in the life of faith.

In America a broadly postmodern theology, which G. Lindbeck (b. 1923) has termed "postliberal," appropriates the philosophy of Wittgenstein and the hermeneutics of Barth to create another kind of → narrative theology. Lindbeck argued in *The Nature of Doctrine* (1984) that theological truths should not be understood as propositions (premodern) or as "experience-expressive" statements (modern, i.e., liberal Protestant) but as a regulative "grammar" for faith-communities, which he called the "cultural linguistic" understanding of doctrine. On this view, doctrines are verified (shown to be true) in the praxis of those communities as they conform to the Word of God. A number of recent theologians have embraced this approach, broadly speaking, along with a narrative theology and hermeneutics, while modifying Lindbeck's understanding of doctrinal truth to some degree (e.g., B. Marshall, W. Placher, and K. Vanhoozer).

Theologies that more openly embrace postmodern thought, especially of the French variety, are exemplified by two conflicting trends. What we might call "deconstructive" theologians explore what is left of spirituality or religion after the loss of God, an essential or transcendent self, and any universal meaning to human existence. Meaning is created by individuals in the struggles of life. M. C. Taylor and D. Cupitt exemplify this kind of postmodern "a/theology," which jettisons any conception of a genuine or realist truth coming to humans from God in the Christian witness to God's Word and instead embraces the death of God (→ God Is Dead Theology).

Another way to develop a postmodern theology, however, would be to accept a claim to profoundly Christian notions and practices — such as the → incarnation, the Trinity, celebrating the → sacraments, and living a holy life of love as disciples of Christ — and to use the tools of postmodern philosophy to defend/explain them against secularity (→ Secularism). In such an approach the postmodern would be celebrated, even as it is radically transformed in the light of Christ. The modernist claims to rational truth and secular reason are rejected,

along with any claim to own truth or possess mastery over reality. Examples of this kind of positive Christian postmodern thought can be found in the English movement calling itself "radical orthodoxy" or in a number of French postmodern Christian philosophers exemplified by J.-L. Marion and M. Henry. How influential or even coherent such approaches to theological truth may be is an open question at the start of the 21st century.

3.4. Conclusion

Given this amazing diversity of views, no consensus or even majority report is possible regarding Christian theological truth. A few salient points may be highlighted for continued reflection and debate.

1. Christian thought cannot be happy with just a propositional notion of truth, since we embrace Jesus as the truth, the way, the life, and the living Word. Yet a complete abandonment of realist notions for theological truth, including propositional truth, may be equally dangerous to a vital faith.
2. Christian truth is grounded in an appeal to special revelation, and because this truth is God's Word, it will necessarily involve the believer and the church in personal and communal transformation but also in linguistic communication that makes (sometimes implicit) truth claims.
3. Jesus Christ and the Word of God, including cross and resurrection, lie at the heart of the Christian community and our tradition of inquiry into truth.
4. As a truth-seeking community, our witness is open to public inspection by intelligent people of goodwill from every faith or none, and we should be able to state as clearly as possible our understanding of religious truth.
5. At the same time, the proclamation of the → gospel as the Word of God will inevitably lead to critique and even condemnation of aspects of every human → culture and philosophy because of the ubiquity of sin, folly, and human pretension — not excluding the church or the theologian.

What seems clear is that attempts to ground the truth or Word of God upon rational and broadly nonreligious grounds have been a dead end for theism in general and theology in particular. Theology begins with many basic beliefs, some of which cannot be proved to be true, especially to the skeptical-rationalist mind. Rather, the truth of God remains beyond human grasp as the free Word from God, which enters into human existence in judgment and salvation.

→ Philosophy and Theology

Bibliography: Philosophical: W. ALSTON, *A Realist Conception of Truth* (Ithaca, N.Y., 1996) • A. J. AYER, *Language, Truth, and Logic* (London, 1938) • F. H. BRADLEY, *Essays on Truth and Reality* (Oxford, 1914) • M. DUMMETT, *Truth and Other Enigmas* (London, 1978) • M. FOUCAULT, *The Foucault Reader* (New York, 1984) • H.-G. GADAMER, *Truth and Method* (2d ed.; New York, 1997) • M. HEIDEGGER, *The Essence of Truth* (New York, 2002; orig. pub., 1949); idem, "On the Essence of Truth" (1943), *Basic Writings* (New York, 1977) 111-38 • M. HENRY, *I Am the Truth* (Stanford, Calif., 2003) • W. JAMES, *The Meaning of Truth* (New York, 1909) • W. KÜNNE, "Wahrheit VI.C: Analytische Philosophie; Oxforder Neu-Hegelianismus; Pragmatismus," *HWP* 12.115-23 • J. MEDINA and D. WOOD, eds., *Truth* (Oxford, 2005) • F. NIETZSCHE, *Beyond Good and Evil* (New York, 1966; orig. pub., 1886); idem, "On Truth and Lies in a Nonmoral Sense" (1873), *Philosophy and Truth* (London, 1979) 79-97 • A. G. PADGETT, "Dialectical Realism in Theology and Science," *Science and the Study of God* (Grand Rapids, 2003) 22-45 • C. S. PEIRCE, *The Essential Peirce* (2 vols.; ed. N. Houser and C. Kloesel; Bloomington, Ind., 1992-98) • N. RESCHER, *The Coherence Theory of Truth* (Oxford, 1973) • J. ROYCE, "Error and Truth," *ERE* 5.366-73 • A. TARSKI, *Logic, Semantics, Metamathematics* (Oxford, 1956) • THOMAS AQUINAS, *Truth* (3 vols.; Chicago, 1952-53) • L. WITTGENSTEIN, *Philosophical Investigations* (3d ed.; Oxford, 2001); idem, *Tractatus Logico-Philosophicus* (London, 1947).

Theological: historical developments: H. U. VON BALTHASAR, *Theo-Logic,* vol. 1, *Truth of the World* (San Francisco, 2000) • E. BRUNNER and K. BARTH, *Natural Theology* (London, 1946) • E. GILSON, *The Spirit of Mediaeval Philosophy* (London, 1936) • E. JÜNGEL et al., "Wahrheit," *RGG* 8.1246-59 • C. LANDMESSER et al., "Wahrheit / Wahrhaftigkeit II-V," *TRE* 35.340-78 • J. MARITAIN, *Degrees of Knowledge* (London, 1937) • J. MÖLLER, "Truth I: Philosophical," *SM* 6.308-13 • K. RAHNER, *Spirit in the World* (New York, 1968; orig. pub., 1939) • F. D. E. SCHLEIERMACHER, *The Christian Faith* (2 vols.; New York, 1963; orig. pub., 1821-22) • P. J. SPENER, *Pia desideria* (Philadelphia, 1964; orig. pub., 1675) • F. TURRETIN, *Institutes of Elenctic Theology* (3 vols.; Phillipsburg, N.J., 1992-97; orig. pub., 1679-85) • J. WESLEY, *The Works of John Wesley,* vols. 1-4, *Sermons* (Nashville, 1984-90).

Theological: current debates: J. P. CASE, "The Death of Jesus and the Truth of the Triune God in Wolfhart Pannenberg and Eberhard Jüngel," *JCTR* 9 (2004) 1-13 • D. CUPITT, *Mysticism after Modernity* (Oxford, 1998) • G. HYMAN, *The Predicament of Postmodern Theology* (Louisville, Ky., 2001) • E. JÜNGEL, *Theological Essays* (2 vols.; Edinburgh, 1989-95) • C. LANDMESSER, *Wahrheit*

als Grundbegriff neutestamentlicher Wissenschaft (Tübingen, 1999) • G. LINDBECK, *The Nature of Doctrine* (Philadelphia, 1984) • J.-L. MARION, *God without Being* (Chicago, 1991) • B. MARSHALL, *Trinity and Truth* (Cambridge, 2000) • J. MILBANK and C. PICKSTOCK, *Truth in Aquinas* (London, 2001) • J. MILBANK, C. PICKSTOCK, and G. WARD, eds., *Radical Orthodoxy: A New Theology* (London, 1999) • W. PANNENBERG, *Systematic Theology* (vol. 1; Grand Rapids, 1991); idem, "What Is Truth?" *Basic Questions in Theology* (vol. 2; Philadelphia, 1976) 1-27 • W. PLACHER, *Unapologetic Theology* (Louisville, Ky., 1989) • M. C. TAYLOR, *Erring: A Postmodern A/theology* (Chicago, 1984) • K. VANHOOZER, *The Drama of Doctrine: A Canonical-Linguistic Approach to Christian Theology* (Louisville, Ky., 2004); idem, ed., *The Cambridge Companion to Postmodern Theology* (Cambridge, 2003).

ALAN G. PADGETT

Tunisia

	1960	1980	2000
Population (1,000s):	4,221	6,448	9,837
Annual growth rate (%):	1.85	2.57	1.60
Area: 164,150 sq. km. (63,378 sq. mi.)			

A.D. 2000

Population density: 60/sq. km. (155/sq. mi.)
Births / deaths: 2.16 / 0.56 per 100 population
Fertility rate: 2.59 per woman
Infant mortality rate: 31 per 1,000 live births
Life expectancy: 70.9 years (m: 69.6, f: 72.2)
Religious affiliation (%): Muslims 98.9, other 1.1.

1. General Situation
2. Religious Situation

1. General Situation

The Tunisian Republic, located in North Africa between Algeria in the west and Libya in the southeast, borders the Mediterranean. Mountains in the north overlook a hot, dry central plain that merges into the Saharan desert in the south.

In the 12th century B.C., the Tunisian coast was colonized by the Phoenicians. They built the city of Carthage (near the modern capital, Tunis), from where the brilliant general Hannibal invaded Italy in 218 B.C. Carthage eventually fell to the Romans in 146 B.C., and the area, the "Province of Africa," became one of the granaries of Italy.

In the new millennium, the Christian message spread quickly, prompting Carthage's famous son

→ Tertullian (ca. 160-ca. 225) to boast in the year 197, "We have left nothing to you but the temples of your gods" (*Apol.* 37). → Martyrs of this period included Perpetua and Felicitas (d. 203). Bishop → Cyprian (ca. 200-258) had a key role in developing responses to Roman → persecution. However, the Vandal invasion of 439 weakened the orthodox church, and the Arab conquest in 648 began the supremacy of → Islam. The Ottoman Turks were ruling when a French occupation army of 30,000 soldiers arrived in 1881. Tunisia remained a French protectorate until 1956.

In Tunisia 18.7 percent of the land is arable, enabling a significant agricultural sector, which employs 22 percent of the workforce. Mining, energy, manufacturing, and → tourism are the other major industries. Increasing privatization has brought foreign investment, resulting in economic growth. In 2006 the GDP per capita was estimated at $7,768. France, Italy, Germany, and Spain are Tunisia's major import and export partners. A Human Development Index of 0.76 in 2006 shows a significant rise from 0.52 only 30 years ago.

Arabic and French are the main languages of the 10 million people of Tunisia, with French and Islamic law blending to form the legal system.

Politically, there is a strong predilection to the status quo. In over 50 years of independence and republican democracy, there have been only two presidents: Habib Bourguiba (1957-87) and Zine El Abidine Ben Ali (1987-), who was reelected for a fourth term in 2004 with nearly 95 percent of the vote. Ben Ali's party — the Rassemblement Constitutionnel Démocratique (RCD, Democratic Constitutional Rally) — holds 80 percent of the seats in the Chamber of Deputies.

2. Religious Situation

The Tunisian constitution (1959, amended 1988 and 2002) declares Islam as the official state religion. Freedom of religion is allowed, as long as it does not conflict with public order. Nominally, 98 percent of the population are adherents, mostly of the Sunni Malikite school. The president must be a Muslim. Political parties based on religion are prohibited, and the wearing of the *hijab* (Islamic headscarf) is restricted. Mosques are controlled and subsidized by the government, which also appoints the grand mufti. Bureaucratic barriers are placed in the way of those who convert from Islam to another religion, although no statutory prohibitions exist. Social pressure against leaving Islam is strong.

Islamists are closely watched and sometimes prosecuted. Between 10,000 to 15,000 members of the Hizb al-Nahda (Renaissance party) have had their identity cards revoked, preventing legal employment. An estimated 600 are in prison for association with this fundamentalist group. → Amnesty International has highlighted human → rights abuses, as well as intimidation of those trying to draw attention to Tunisia's human rights problems.

There are about 1,500 Jews and several synagogues in Tunisia (→ Judaism). They are partly funded by the government, which pays the stipend of the chief rabbi.

Tunisia is home to about 2,500 practicing Christians, including several hundred local adherents, according to the 2004 U.S. Department of State Religious Freedom Report. Proselytizing is forbidden, and there are some restrictions on Christian activities, with visas for foreign workers occasionally being revoked. The → Roman Catholic Church operates 11 churches, 9 schools, several libraries, and 2 clinics. Protestant, → Anglican, and → Orthodox churches conduct services in various locations.

Bibliography: L. ANDERSON, *The State and Social Transformation in Tunisia and Libya, 1830-1980* (Princeton, 1986) • D. B. BARRETT, G. T. KURIAN, and T. M. JOHNSON, *WCE* (2d ed.) 1.749-52 • G. A. GEYER, *Tunisia: A Journey through a Country That Works* (London, 2003) • P. HOLMES-EBER, *Daughters of Tunis: Women, Family, and Networks in a Muslim City* (Boulder, Colo., 2003) • K. J. PERKINS, *A History of Modern Tunisia* (New York, 2004).

BERNARD J. POWER

Turkey

	1960	1980	2000
Population (1,000s):	27,509	44,438	65,732
Annual growth rate (%):	2.49	2.50	1.39

Area: 779,452 sq. km. (300,948 sq. mi.)

A.D. 2000

Population density: 84/sq. km. (218/sq. mi.)
Births / deaths: 2.03 / 0.64 per 100 population
Fertility rate: 2.30 per woman
Infant mortality rate: 36 per 1,000 live births
Life expectancy: 70.5 years (m: 68.0, f: 73.2)
Religious affiliation (%): Muslims 97.1, nonreligious 2.1, other 0.8.

1. 1453-1918
2. Mustafa Kemal (Atatürk)
3. World War II and the Cold War
4. The Kurdish Minority

The Republic of Turkey, with a population of 71 million (July 2007), is the most populous country in the Middle East. Modern Turkey is a new creation, arising out of the Anatolian remnants of the Ottoman Empire after World War I.

1. 1453-1918

Constantinople, the one-time capital of the Eastern → Roman Empire, was conquered in 1453 by Turks, who renamed it Istanbul. It became the capital of the Ottoman Empire, which at its peak was one of the largest empires in the world. From the 17th century, decline came about for internal and external reasons: failure to modernize, coupled with increasing encroachment from the West. In the 19th century a modernization program was initiated (the *tanzimat*, "reorganization," lasting 1839-76), but dependency on Europe nevertheless increased. The 1908 "Young Turk" revolution forced a constitution on the Ottoman Empire, and Sultan Abdülhamid II (1876-1909) was forced to abdicate in favor of Mehmed V (1909-18), who followed a nationalistic Turkic policy opposing ethnic minorities (esp. Armenians and Greeks) and foreign involvement. During World War I, Turkey ruthlessly repressed a number of these ethnic groups; Armenians in particular suffered greatly, with over 1 million killed in a deliberate policy of → genocide. During the war Turkey sided with Germany.

2. Mustafa Kemal (Atatürk)

The 1920 Treaty of Sèvres led to a widespread sense of humiliation, but Mustafa Kemal (also known as Atatürk, lit. "father of the Turks," 1881-1938), a military leader, deposed the sultan and declared the republic on October 29, 1923. He became the first president and renegotiated the treaty.

Kemal pursued a rapid modernization program. He abolished the caliphate (the traditional religious and political leadership of the Islamic community), separated religious offices and the state, replaced the Arabic script with a Latinized alphabet, changed the nonbusiness day from Friday to Sunday, and sought to prevent women from wearing the Islamic headscarf in public. Kemal wanted to create a modern, secular, democratic state based on his definition of Turkish identity — and this was to be the only identity people living in the Anatolian heartland would need. The six founding principles — nationalism, statism, revolutionism, populism, republicanism, and secularism — became known as Kemalism and form the core of Turkey's identity. By law, the military is responsible for protecting the constitution and the country's unity, which has led to significant military involvement in politics.

3. World War II and the Cold War

During World War II, Turkey attempted to stay neutral, signing a nonaggression pact with Germany in 1941, but in 1945 it joined the Allies. After the war Turkey became a U.S. ally and allowed U.S. forces to be based on its soil, opposing the Soviet Union; Turkey joined the → United Nations in 1945 and NATO in 1952. The United States encouraged multiparty rule, and in the 1950 election the opposition Democratic Party won. While more parties developed and political diversity grew, military coups took place in 1960, 1971, and 1980, ostensibly to protect the state; in each case political power was eventually restored to civilians. Relations with Greece, never easy since the forced transfers of Greek and Turkish populations after World War I, worsened with Turkish involvement in Cyprus in 1974, resulting in Turkish troops remaining in the north of the island.

After the 1980 coup, which was followed by considerable repression, a new constitution was implemented (1983) that sought to ease European criticism and pave the way for full membership of the European Community (associate membership had been granted in 1963). Economic liberalization in the 1980s (on IMF/World Bank guidelines) was not matched by corresponding political changes, and it was 1995 before further integration took place, with a customs union agreement.

4. The Kurdish Minority

Meanwhile, Abdullah Öcalan's Kurdish Workers' Party (PKK), an ethnic secessionist group founded in 1970, launched insurgency attacks on Turkish forces. Turkey, under the unitary state principle, had for decades engaged in a form of cultural extermination of Kurdish culture and language, prohibiting most forms of expression, and now responded with escalation; the conflict caused widespread devastation and tens of thousands of deaths.

Turkey engaged in only a limited way in the 1990-91 conflict over Iraq, closing off an oil pipeline from Iraq via Turkey to the Mediterranean and allowing U.S. forces to fly from Turkey, but not itself participating directly in the attacks. This hesitance was partly out of concern for the Kurdish reaction. → Kurds are spread across Turkey, Syria, Iraq, and

Iran, and there was no desire to inflame Kurdish sensibilities yet further.

5. Modern Political Developments

By 1993, economic liberalization had resulted in a huge deficit, but Tansu Çiller, Turkey's first woman prime minister (1993-96), sought to hasten privatization in an attempt to rescue the economy on free-market principles, which resulted in widespread social protests. In a related development, the elections of December 1995 saw the Islamic Welfare Party become the largest party in Parliament. Coalitions of the secular parties initially prevented the Welfare Party from achieving power, but these arrangements did not last, and eventually, in June 1996, Necmettin Erbakan became head of government. The rise of this party appeared to contradict the secularist principles of Kemalism, and in 1997 the military again intervened: Erbakan's party was outlawed, and he and a number of others were banned from politics for several years. The replacement party, the Islamic Virtue Party (PIV), sought to continue promoting Islamic ideals in the political sphere. The PIV was banned in 2001 (by which time it had become the main opposition party); its members formed a new party, Saadet (meaning "happiness" or "prosperity").

The attempts to crush the PKK, meanwhile, met with some successes, in part through Turkish incursions into northern Iraq (1997), but especially through the capture of Öcalan (1999) with the help of Greece, leading to considerable improvements in Turkish-Greek relations. Öcalan was sentenced to death, and the June 1999 elections brought a new government — including an ultraright party, among others — committed to destroying the Kurdish guerrillas. Greece, which had previously vetoed Turkish and Cypriot approaches to the European Community/Union, withdrew its objections, and in 1999 Turkey was invited to join the EU, with various reforms expected, including improvements in human → rights. Öcalan's death sentence was initially postponed, and the European Human Rights Court was consulted; in 2002 Turkey abolished the → death penalty, and Öcalan's sentence was commuted to life imprisonment. Since 2000 the PKK has called several cease-fires, but all have broken down, partly as a result of internal PKK divisions, and partly because the Turkish government refuses to accept them.

The prospect of EU membership has become one of the main driving forces behind Turkey's internal and foreign politics. The integration into the EU has promoted market liberalization and attempts to make Turkey more economically compat-

ible with the EU, but the extremely slow progress on human rights and full democratization processes has repeatedly hindered smooth progression (e.g., only in 2001 was the Kurdish language finally permitted in the media, and full legal equality for women was implemented only the following year). Doubts expressed by some European leaders regarding Turkey's suitability for EU membership (sometimes crudely caricatured as a "Muslim" state joining a "Christian" Europe) has contributed to many Turks' increasing disenchantment with the ponderous accession process. Nonetheless, in 2007 Turkey announced that it is committed, regardless of its membership status, to achieve EU standards in all areas by 2013, the earliest date at which membership could now be expected.

6. Middle East Politics

Turkey's politics within the Middle East are also replete with uncertainty. Attempts to engender solidarity with other Turkic states to the east largely failed, though a new Baku-Tbilisi-Ceyhan oil pipeline (opened May 2006) marks a notable level of economic and strategic cooperation.

Military and other agreements with Israel from the late 1990s soured already complex relationships with the Arab states, in particular with its neighbor Syria. Turkey and Israel share a number of commonalities, from an affinity to the West to a perception of threat from Arab neighbors and a common sense of difference in the Middle East. Turkey's recent pursuit of closer relations with Israel appears to have contradicted a general desire to avoid involvement in internal Middle Eastern affairs. It needs to be seen, however, as part of a reassessment of Turkey's foreign-policy needs in the post-Soviet era, as well as a result of Turkey's Middle Eastern politics being an extension of its pro-Western orientation, which is visible also in economic terms. In 2005 the primary export markets were all Western: Germany (12.9 percent), United Kingdom (8.1), Italy (7.6), United States (6.7), and France (5.2).

The 2003 U.S.-led invasion and subsequent occupation of Iraq was not supported by Turkey (e.g., refusing the use of its air bases), and concern about the creation of a Kurdish state in Iraq, with corresponding instability within Kurdish areas in Turkey itself, makes it wary of Iraq disintegrating on ethnic lines. (Despite these worries, by 2007 three-quarters of all cargo to U.S. troops in Iraq was going through southern Turkey.) In the recent years of Islamic-dominated governance, it is possible to discern more interest and empathy with Middle Eastern neighbors and causes, and indeed in 2007 Prime

Minister Recep Tayyip Erdoğan declared that Iraq had replaced the European Union as Turkey's top priority item. The polls reflect these sentiments: a 2007 poll showed Iran's favorability ranking to be at 46 percent, similar to that of the United States a few years ago. (In 2007 the U.S. ranking was languishing around single digits.)

7. Sociopolitical Challenges

Economic and demographic change in Turkey presages unknown factors in the political direction of the country. For example, a quarter of the population is under 15 years old, and rapid urbanization (3.1 percent growth a year [2000]) is leading to an increase in urban → poverty, as agriculture, previously a mainstay of the economy, gradually is reduced in significance. Turkey lacks significant natural resources, which, coupled with recent disastrous economic policies and therefore minimal capital investment, means that urban industrialization has been limited. Pollution is also a problem; for example, Istanbul's air already has high levels of sulfur dioxide, while the Sea of Marmara is contaminated with mercury.

Turkey's secular foundations have been severely tested by the rise of Islamic parties, which have succeeded in a certain level of Islamization of Turkey (limited acceptance of headscarves, some funding of Islamic schools, etc.), though it can also be argued that the Islamic parties have driven democratization further than the Kemalist parties, not least through reducing the rampant corruption at higher levels of government. The state's unitary foundations ("Turkish" as a complete identity) are also called into question by the existence of minorities, especially Kurds, but also others. The presence of Kurds (20 percent of the population) questions primarily the ethnic, while the presence of non-Muslims questions the secular, but gradually Islamizing, nature of the state. Major ethnic or religious minorities include Arabs (2 percent), Georgians (0.5), Circassians (0.5), Armenians (0.3), and → Roma, Jews, and Greeks; assimilation is relatively high.

There are numerous forms of discrimination in employment and social fields (e.g., restrictions on the use and teaching of minority languages), which are only slowly being addressed, partially under EU-driven reforms. Related to these discriminatory practices is a strident campaign, pursued internationally, of denial of the Armenian genocide. The 2007 murder of the moderate, Turkish-Armenian journalist Hrant Dink by an ultranationalist activist, while widely condemned by many Turks, is indicative of the difficulty of reconciling divergent histori-

cal and contemporary understandings of Turkishness with Kemalist principles. (The notorious art. 301 of the Turkish Penal Code, which criminalizes offenses against "Turkishness," symbolizes this difficulty; novelist Orhan Pamuk was threatened with prosecution under 301 until he was awarded the Nobel Prize for literature in 2006, when the charges were suddenly dropped.)

In many ways, Turkey's challenges in the coming years center on the nature of the Kemalist state itself: how it deals with its religious and ethnic minorities, the place of the economically and socially marginalized, the locus of religion in politics, the acknowledgment of the Armenian genocide, and how the state incorporates its interests in both Europe and the Middle East.

8. Religious Situation

Although Turkey is a secular state, → Islam dominates: approximately 80 percent are Sunni, 14 percent Alevi (a Shia sect), 6 percent other Shia, and 0.2 percent Christian.

Several Christian denominations are found in Turkey. The Greek Orthodox, → Armenian Apostolic Orthodox, and Syriac Orthodox churches perhaps represent the most politically significant communities, though in terms of numbers, the churches themselves give the following figures (2007): Armenian Orthodox, 65,000-70,000; → Syrian Orthodox, 15,000; Armenian Catholic, 5,000; Greek Orthodox, 3,200; Arab Orthodox in Antioch, 2,500; Syrian Catholic, 2,200; Chaldeans 1,700; Latins, or Roman Catholics, 1,500. Although Anatolia was a target of substantial Protestant missionary activity in the 19th century, in 2005 there were only about 2,700 regularly attending Protestant churchgoers in 96 churches or house groups, and another 280 in other gatherings (60 percent of these are from Muslim backgrounds, including Alevi). In general, no church has fared as well under the Turkish republic as it did under Ottoman rule. For example, the Greek → Orthodox Church now maintains only a minimal number of priests under four metropolitans in Turkey, while the Syriac patriarchate, which had been based in Mardin (southeastern Turkey) from the 13th century, was forced to move to Homs, Syria, in 1933. (Since 1959 the patriarchate has been in Damascus.)

Bibliography: Christianity in Turkey: A. S. ATIYA, A History of Eastern Christianity (new ed.; Millwood, N.Y., 1980) • H. HOLLERWEGER, Tur Abdin. Lebendiges Kulturerbe / Living Cultural Heritage / Canlı Kültür Mirası (Linz, 1999) • T. WARE, The Orthodox Church (2d ed.; Harmondsworth, 1993).

Other topics: W. L. CLEVELAND, *A History of the Modern Middle East* (3d ed.; Boulder, Colo., 2004) • W. HALE, *Turkish Politics and the Military* (London, 1994) • D. JUNG, with W. PICCOLI, *Turkey at the Crossroads: Ottoman Legacies and a Greater Middle East* (London, 2001) • D. McDOWALL, *A Modern History of the Kurds* (London, 1996) • R. OWEN and Ş. PAMUK, *A History of Middle East Economies in the Twentieth Century* (London, 1998) • N. POPE and H. POPE, *Turkey Unveiled: A History of Modern Turkey* (Woodstock, N.Y., 1997; repr., 2004) • E. J. ZURCHER, *Turkey–a Modern History* (3d ed.; London, 2004).

MICHAEL MARTEN

Turkmenistan

	1960	*1980*	*2000*
Population (1,000s):	1,594	2,861	4,479
Annual growth rate (%):	3.41	2.42	1.82

Area: 488,100 sq. km. (188,500 sq. mi.)

A.D. 2000

Population density: 9/sq. km. (24/sq. mi.)
Births / deaths: 2.58 / 0.69 per 100 population
Fertility rate: 3.21 per woman
Infant mortality rate: 51 per 1,000 live births
Life expectancy: 66.3 years (m: 63.1, f: 69.4)
Religious affiliation (%): Muslims 88.0, nonreligious 8.0, Christians 2.9 (Orthodox 2.3, other Christians 0.6), atheists 1.0, other 0.1.

1. General Situation
2. Religious Situation

1. General Situation

Turkmenistan, in west-central Asia, borders the Caspian Sea to the west. Its neighbors are Kazakhstan (northwest), Uzbekistan (north and northeast), Afghanistan (southeast), and Iran (south). The Kara-Kum (Garagum) Desert, covering 80 percent of the country, extends from the Caspian to the Amu Dar'ya (ancient Oxus) River in the east. Dunes rise to the Kopet-Dag Mountains in the south; the eastern part of the country is plateau. Only 4.5 percent of the land is arable. Turkmenistan is an important supplier of natural gas, petrochemicals, and raw cotton, with its main customers the Ukraine, Iran, Italy, Turkey, Russia, and the United States.

By the 11th century, the area was inhabited by a collection of Turkmen tribes and clans. Over the centuries, various empires came and went, with Turkmen raiders on horseback notorious for prey-

ing on passing caravans. Russian czarist troops decisively defeated the Turkmen in 1881 and made the area part of Russian Turkestan. In 1924 the Turkmen Republic was proclaimed one of the 15 republics of the → Soviet Union.

On October 27, 1991, as the USSR was breaking up, the Supreme Soviet of Turkmenistan declared its independence and elected Saparmurat Niyazov (1940-2006) president. Niyazov had been first secretary of the Communist Party of Turkmen SSR since 1985 and, at the time, was chairman of the Supreme Soviet. He was popularly elected president in June 1992 (there were no other candidates), and the next year he took the name "Turkmenbashi," or "Leader of the Turkmen." Until his death, he ruled as an autocratic dictator, increasingly establishing a cult of personality around himself. (Niyazov wrote *Ruhnama*, a national epic that became the object of indoctrination across the country. He had copies placed in mosques and churches; applicants for a driver's license had to pass an exam on its teachings. In 2005 physicians were ordered to swear an oath to Turkmenbashi, which replaced the Hippocratic Oath.) The post-Niyazov government has not signaled any clear change from past policies.

2. Religious Situation

The Turkmen constitution provides for freedom of religion and does not establish a state religion, although the government has encouraged some aspects of Muslim culture, and President Niyazov himself made the → pilgrimage to Mecca and sponsored the construction of numerous → mosques. All religious groups with five or more members must register with the government. As of January 2006, only 11 groups were registered: Sunni → Islam (→ Sunnism, Sunnis), the → Russian Orthodox Church, and nine minority religious groups. Unregistered groups are prohibited from gathering publicly, proselytizing, or disseminating religious materials.

As early as 1890, a small Evangelical fellowship started in Ashgabat (Ashkhabad), the capital, when F. S. Ovsiannikov, a Russian convert to Christianity through Mennonite influence in the province of Samarqand, his birthplace, came to live there. Within two years a small congregation, consisting of Molokans (Bible-centered Christians descending from so-called Spiritual Christian Russian peasants, who refused to join the Russian Orthodox Church in the 1600s), Baptists, and Armenian Evangelicals were meeting, led by Isai Tumaniants, with worship conducted in both Russian and Armenian. Another congregation started in 1892 in the village of Keltichivar (later named Kurapatkinski), 20 km. (12 mi.) away, consisting mostly of Baptists. More Russian families from Tver', a region of the Russian Empire, immigrated in 1896. By 1912 there were 100 members. This group continued till 1937, when all meeting places were closed. Gradually after 1944 believers gathered in small groups, meeting more formally after 1948, but only in 1981 was it possible to meet in Ashgabat in a private home, reconstructed as a meeting house. By 1989 one Turkmen preacher was leading a group.

In Turkmenistan, according to data from 2003, there were 13 Russian Orthodox parishes. All activities of neo-Protestants were banned, and there followed arrests, fines, and the deportation of all persons with foreign passports (including those with Russian or Ukrainian passports). Yet for the Russian Orthodox, the dwindling number of Russian and Ukrainian residents meant that by 1997, when Nikolai Mitrokhin visited all the functioning parishes, there were essentially only 6 parishes: Ashgabat (450 adherents, meeting in two churches), Turkmenbashi (before 1993, named Krasnovodsk; 50), Nebitdag (20), Turkmenabat (formerly Chärjew/Chardzhou, 40), Mary (formerly Merv, 50) and Bairamaly (30). Between 1996 and 1999 there were efforts to start a parish paper, a women's society, and some charity projects, but by 1999 "all organized missionary and diaconal activities in the parishes had become practically impossible" (N. Mitrokhin, 543). In 2002 the Turkmen authorities banned subscriptions to the *Journal of the Moscow Patriarchate*.

In 2007 Forum 18 News Service (Oslo) presented a summary of numerous repressions against Turkmen-language Christians. In the village of Dogryyol, 25 km. (16 mi.) from Turkmenabat, houses of believers were raided, and in public meetings the members were threatened with having their children expelled from school and their utilities (electricity, gas, and water) cut off if they refused to stop attending the Protestant services. Other congregations in Turkmenabat and Dashoguz (formerly Tashauz) were harassed, and in Turkmenbashi the Baptist pastor Vyacheslav Kalataevsky was given a three-year labor camp sentence on May 14, 2007. Visits at the time by representatives of the Organization for Security and Cooperation in Europe, who expressed concern about religious intolerance, appeared to be ignored.

→ Persecution of Christians

Bibliography: R. ABAZOV, *Historical Dictionary of Turkmenistan* (Lanham, Md., 2005) • S. N. CUMMINGS and M. OCHS, "Turkmenistan: Saparmurat Niyazov's Inglorious Isolation," *Power and Change in Central Asia* (ed. S. N. Cummings; London, 2002) 115-29 • A. L. EDGAR, *Tribal Nation: The Making of Soviet Turkmenistan* (Princeton, 2004) • R. R. HANKS, *Central Asia: A Global Studies Handbook* (Santa Barbara, Calif., 2005) • *Istoriia evangel'skikh Khristian–Baptistov v SSSR* (History of the Evangelical Christian–Baptists in the USSR) (Moscow, 1989) official history • N. MITROKHIN, *Russkaia Pravoslavnaia Tserkov. Sovremennoe sostoianie i aktual'nie problemy* (Russian Orthodox Church. Contemporary status and problems) (Moscow, 2006) 538-43 • M. H. RUFFIN and D. C. WAUGH, eds., *Civil Society in Central Asia* (Seattle, Wash., 1999) • S. TURKMENBASHY, *Rukhnama: Reflections on the Spiritual Values of the Turkmen* (Ashgabat, 2005). • A Web site operated by Forum 18 (www.forum18.org) regularly features reports of religious rights violations in Turkmenistan.

WALTER SAWATSKY

Twelve, The

1. The Twelve (*hoi dōdeka:* in Mark 3:14-16; 4:10; 6:7 and par., 9:35; 10:32 and par., 11:11; 14:10 and par., 17 and par., 20, 43 and par.; Luke 8:1; 9:12; John 6:67, 70-71; 20:24; Acts 6:2 and 1 Cor. 15:5), or the 12 disciples (*dōdeka mathētai:* in Matt. 10:1; 11:1; and 20:17), are the NT group of 12 men whom Jesus selected from the large number of his → disciples to be his more specific followers. Later these 12 were also called → apostles (Matt. 10:2 and par.; Luke 22:14; cf. Mark 14:17; Matt. 26:20; Rev. 21:14; also Mark 6:7/30 and par.; Acts 1:2, 13, 21-26). This is, however, a secondary construction. The reference to the Twelve alongside the apostles in 1 Cor. 15:5, 7 shows that a distinction may be made historically between the two groups, even though they overlap, as in the case of → Peter.

2. The NT has four lists with the names of the Twelve: in Mark 3:16-19; Matt. 10:2-4; Luke 6:14-16; and Acts 1:13. Mark lists Simon Peter, → James and John the sons of Zebedee, Andrew, Philip, Bartholomew, Matthew, Thomas, James the son of Alphaeus, Thaddaeus, Simon the Cananaean, and Judas Iscariot. All four lists agree in naming Peter first and Judas the traitor last, which is doubtless intended as a judgment. Acts 1:13 does not mention Judas. He had been banished from the group (1:18; see mention of "the 11 [disciples]" in Matt. 28:16 and Luke 24:9, 33), and by lot his place was taken by Matthias (Acts 1:21-26).

Some of the names and the pairings differ in the

various lists. For Philip, see the lists in Matthew and Acts. Thaddaeus is not mentioned in Luke or Acts. Instead we have "Judas son [brother?] of James." Thus far no fully satisfying explanation of this discrepancy has been offered.

3. It has been suggested that the Twelve developed only after → Easter, with a projection back to the time of Jesus (e.g., G. Klein, 34ff.; W. Schmithals, 58ff.; L. Schenke, 76). In view of the close connection between Jesus and Judas (Mark 14:10, 20, 43), however, we may confidently assert that → Jesus himself selected the Twelve.

The appointment of the Twelve is then understandable as a symbolic action (see M. Trautmann; → Symbol) that expresses the orientation of Jesus' → proclamation to the gathering of *all* of → Israel (§1). In that the → number 12 stands as a symbol for the number of the → tribes of Israel, the Twelve represent the end-time → people of God, whose restitution formed part of Israel's eschatological → hope (cf. Rev. 21:12-14 and Isa. 11:12; Ezek. 11:17 and 20:41; 4 Ezra 13:39-50; *2 Apoc. Bar.* 78; Rev. 7:4-8; → Eschatology 1). We read in Matt. 19:28 that they will reign in the renewed → kingdom of God, though doubt has been cast on the authenticity of this saying.

After Easter, with Peter in the lead, the reconstituted Twelve probably formed a kind of senate for the → primitive Christian community that arose in → Jerusalem after the → resurrection. They did so, however, for only a relatively short time. They had a place in the pre-Pauline tradition (1 Cor. 15:5), but their role was no longer normative when → Paul first visited Jerusalem (ca. A.D. 35), for according to Gal. 1:18-19, Paul met with only the "apostles" Peter and "James the Lord's brother," who had not been one of the Twelve. After the replacement of Judas (Acts 1:15-26) and the execution in A.D. 44 of James the son of Zebedee (12:2), Luke has nothing more to tell us about the Twelve. The apostles in a more general sense had now taken their place as the Christian message of → salvation had spread abroad, as new forms of organization were demanded, and as Christian mission expanded beyond Jerusalem and Israel. Even in Jerusalem itself "the Seven" had already emerged as leaders of the Hellenists (Acts 6:3, 5; 21:8).

4. Peter, of course, had already given a lead in the mission to the Gentiles (Acts 10–11). We also read of his activity in Corinth (1 Cor. 1:12), and a fairly credible tradition associates him with Rome (see 1 Peter). John, too, is reported to have been a teacher of Polycarp at Ephesus (Papias). Less reliable traditions link members of the Twelve to other areas of mission, for example, Andrew to Asia Minor or Achaia, and Thomas as far afield as India.

Bibliography: R. BROWNRIGG, *The Twelve Apostles* (London, 1974) • G. KLEIN, *Die zwölf Apostel* (Göttingen, 1961) • R. P. MEYE, *Jesus and the Twelve* (Grand Rapids, 1968) • K. H. RENGSTORF, *Apostleship* (London, 1952) • J. ROLOFF, *Apostolat, Verkündigung, Kirche* (Gütersloh, 1965) • L. SCHENKE, *Die Urgemeinde* (Stuttgart, 1990) 75-78 • W. SCHMITHALS, *The Office of Apostle in the Early Church* (Nashville, 1969) • M. TRAUTMANN, *Zeichenhafte Handlungen Jesu* (Würzburg, 1980) 167-233 • W. TRILLING, "Zur Entstehung des Zwölferkreises," *Die Kirche des Anfangs* (ed. R. Schnackenburg, J. Ernst, and J. Wanke; Leipzig, 1977) 201-22.

MICHAEL WOLTER

Twelve Prophets, Book of the → Minor Prophets

Two-Kingdoms Doctrine

1. Historic Roots
   1.1. Biblical Traditions
   1.2. Augustine
   1.3. Medieval Application of Augustine
2. Reformation Positions and Fronts
   2.1. Luther
   2.2. Zwingli
   2.3. Calvin
3. Ecclesiastical and Political Significance in the Nineteenth and Twentieth Centuries
4. Contemporary Significance

The term "doctrine of the two kingdoms" has come to designate a much-controverted and many-faceted complex of ideas regarding one or more of the following relationships: God and evil, God and the world, faith and works, the spiritual or sacred aspects of human life and its earthly or profane aspects, as well as the institutions of church and state. The term arose out of 19th-century discussions of the respective responsibilities of → church and state, particularly in Germany, and out of efforts to formulate an evangelical ethic for the 20th century, particularly in Scandinavia. The disputes regarding the doctrine have arisen out of Martin → Luther's concepts of two kingdoms, although parallel ideas have existed throughout Christian history. Because Luther used the phrase "two kingdoms" for the distinction of God's rule and Satan's rule and for the distinction of church and state, as well as the distinction between human relationships with God (the heavenly kingdom) and with other human beings (the earthly kingdom), some scholars have substituted "two realms" for this last concept in their analysis of Luther's thought. In his formulation Luther was giving his own interpretation to a matter with which every religious tradition wrestles in its own way: the explanation of the relationship between → sacred and profane realms.

1. Historic Roots

1.1. *Biblical Traditions*

Throughout the OT, beginning with Genesis 1, it is clear that God is the ruler of the universe that he created. That all creatures owe their origin to him through the act of → creation establishes the priority of his person, power, and rule within his cosmos. He repeatedly renewed his claim upon his people, overcoming what separated them from his rule through his promise to remain their God (Gen. 3:15) and liberating them from their captors in the exodus and the return from exile. The prophets described God's final deliverance and restoration as the reestablishment of his rule over the peoples of the earth (Isaiah 9; Daniel 2; Micah 4). Jesus defined his message as the good news of God's → kingdom (Luke 4:43); his coming into the world to drive out demonic rule heralded the advent of God's kingdom (Matt. 12:28). This rule of God advanced on the strength of the → proclamation of Jesus' disciples (Luke 9:2, 60; 16:16). Paul defines → salvation as being placed in the kingdom of God's Son (Col. 1:13). At the same time, this establishment of God's rule through his Word did not exclude another use of the term: for the future rule of God (or Christ) over all things at and after the consummation of this existence (Mark 14:25; Luke 13:29).

Within his relationship to human creatures, God exercises his lordship over all things in two ways. The relationship with them involved first the mutual love of the Creator with these creatures, comparable to that between parent and child. The children, however, were not only to trust their God, they were also created to fulfill his expectations for their actions. Thus, God's → covenants with them always involved both his promise to remain faithful to them and his expectations for their performance of the actions he designed as appropriate for their humanity. His rule in regard to his people came through (1) his word of promise, an action of God governing the relationship between Maker and human being, and (2) his word of command, specify-

ing human actions and particularly governing the relationships between his human creature and the rest of creation, including relationships of human beings with one another.

These commands addressed individual human living within the context of the community and the institutions, or "orders," God fashioned to expedite good human living. Thus, God's commands established and continue to govern family, political life, economic activity, and other social relationships. In the world polluted by sin and evil, God reestablished his rule in the vertical dimension of human life, that is, the relationship of love and trust with him, only through the word of promise. In relationships within the horizontal dimension of human life, the word of command is carried out through the promise of reward and the threat of → punishment with those not moved by the love of God. In that dimension God permits the use of coercion (Rom. 13:1-7, along with OT examples).

1.2. *Augustine*

→ Augustine (354-430; → Augustine's Theology) composed the most formidable and influential attempt to interpret these two dimensions of human life in the early church. He confronted the attacks of pagan writers who held the church responsible for the fall of Rome (410) in *De civitate Dei* (On the city of God, written 413-27). He distinguished two forms of governing: God's and the devil's. Their "cities," as forms of rule, referred fundamentally not to two kinds of institutions but rather to two kinds of people — the godly, rational people who act out of love for God, and sinners who act out of selfishness and pride. Both "cities" are at work in the world, and both can establish some kind of necessary order and protection through political institutions. In spite of hypocrites and heretics in its midst, the church, as God's congregation of the elect, does represent and project true justice, above all in and through its monastic communities. In this way it serves the need for political order, which is fundamentally the responsibility of the state. In seeking the good world, the state suppresses → paganism and heresy but does not truly resemble God's kingdom.

1.3. *Medieval Application of Augustine*

Augustine's heirs in succeeding generations appropriated his thought in their own situations. In the Christendom of western Europe, as papacy and empire wrestled with their respective competencies in both spiritual and temporal matters (→ Empire and Papacy), theories of the relationship of two powers *(potestates),* swords *(gladii),* or kingdoms *(imperia)* provided tinder for intellectual discussions that played themselves out in part in sharp political, and sometimes military, confrontation. Questions of how God's rule is actualized in the world focused on the institutions of church and state. Papal advocates argued from the 12th century that God had given both swords to the → pope, who in turn dispensed governance of secular affairs to temporal princes. Their opponents contended that just as God had given the pope supremacy over the church, he had given the emperor temporal power directly. Related disputes took place over the responsibilities of temporal rulers for the church in their lands.

In the → Investiture Controversy (1075-1122), the clash regarding the rights of temporal princes over ecclesiastical appointments and related matters of church governance, the church temporarily won, but in the end lost, the battle for its independence as an institution in relationship to the state. Papal claims that rulers had to subject themselves to the papacy in order to be saved, made explicitly by Boniface VIII (1294-1303) in *Unam sanctam* (1302), failed to reestablish the hegemony that only a very few earlier popes (such as → Innocent III [1198-1216]) had been able to exercise. To the end of the Middle Ages most Western Christian thinking on God's rule was channeled into questions regarding church and state.

In Eastern Orthodoxy the power of the Byzantine emperors over the church was quite complete. To the end of the empire, in 1453, the emperors understood their role as both sacral and secular.

2. Reformation Positions and Fronts

The → Reformation benefited from a special form of the late medieval development of greater princely exercise of spiritual responsibilities, particularly in German principalities and cities and in the kingdom of England. More important theologically was the reinterpretation initiated by Martin Luther (1483-1546; → Luther's Theology) of how God exercises his rule in the world. Luther expanded the agenda of discussion by considering under this topic how God provides for his world and how he establishes and maintains his → church through the creation and sustenance of faith in his own people.

2.1. *Luther*

2.1.1. Luther used the term *zwei Reiche* (two kingdoms) in several different ways, thus causing subsequent confusion in some of his interpreters. It could occasionally refer to church and state as institutions, but most often it signified either the polarity of God's rule and Satan's rule or God's own two ways of governing his world: through the gospel of Christ, which establishes the vertical relationship between believer and God, and through the → law,

which regulates the horizontal relationships among human beings and in the world. In recent years some scholars have substituted the German *Regiment* ("realm" or "sphere") for "kingdom" to designate the last of these definitions.

This distinction of God's two ways of governing his world is not, strictly speaking, one doctrinal topic among many in Luther's thought but instead functions as a general presupposition or framework for the application of other topics to human life. In this regard it is closely related to, but not identical with, Luther's distinction of God's two words through which he acts and addresses human beings, → law and gospel, and his distinction of the two elements that constitute what it means to be human: the passive righteousness by which God gives his chosen people new life, and the active righteousness by which they render him obedience.

2.1.2. Luther began to develop the distinction between the two realms in the early 1520s, particularly in *Von weltlicher Obrigkeit* (1523; ET "Temporal Authority: To What Extent It Should Be Obeyed," *LW* 45.75-129), using it in discussions of ethical issues. On the basis of his reading of Scripture, he placed all power ultimately in God's hands and rejected the equation of godly only with sacred activities. He affirmed that people of faith employ all of life as structured by God, in both sacred and profane spheres, in a godly way. The power to restore human beings to communion with God lies in the gospel of Christ, which gives new birth to sinners through the forgiveness of sins in → baptism and other forms of God's Word (→ Word of God). Luther labeled this realm the "right-hand," "spiritual," or "heavenly" realm. Only Christians experience this form of God's rule.

The power to regulate and direct human activities in this world constitutes the second "kingdom" or "realm." He labeled this realm the "left-hand," "temporal," or "earthly" realm. Fundamental to understanding his view of the latter are his concept of civil or civic righteousness and his appropriation of medieval social theory, which divided human life into three "estates" (Ger. *Stände*, Lat. *status*), or walks of life. This civic righteousness is practiced by unbelievers on the basis of the law of God that is written into their nature. Luther believed that in life's horizontal dimension those who are not righteous through faith in Christ may still live lives closely corresponding to his standards for ethical behavior. Christians can therefore live under and cooperate with unbelieving rulers and others outside the church in seeking justice and order in social life.

All human beings live by God's creation and command in the situations, or estates, of *oeconomia* (family and economic life), *politia* (political, social life), and *ecclesia* (the empirical church, or some other form of religion). Within each of these estates individuals exercise an *Amt* (office; Lat. *officium*), which embraced for Luther both the specific roles within society and the functions involved in carrying out these responsibilities. Believers perceive these roles and functions as callings (Ger. *Beruf,* Lat. *vocatio*) from God. It must be noted that the institutional church is part of the "left-hand realm," even if its primary tasks carry out God's "right-hand" rule. Luther argued for the integrity of each of these estates and their institutions. He strove to liberate the state from ecclesiastical control, and the church from the tyranny of the secular government, while advocating cooperation between the two institutions.

Luther originally followed the medieval pattern of assigning each individual to only one of the three estates. Later he spoke of every Christian's calling in each of them. The reformer viewed the family as the fundamental walk of life, upon which all others were dependent, and he praised family life over celibacy and exalted ecclesiastical callings. In his Small Catechism the "Household Chart" for "all kinds of . . . walks of life" models its instruction for daily life after the monastic ideal, with the family replacing the monastic community as the seat of the highest praise of God (→ Vocation).

2.1.3. Luther's political theory, developed out of and expressed in the terminology of two "realms" or "kingdoms," has caused controversy in the discussions of the last century, in part because popular myths misrepresenting what he wrote have gained more attention than his own texts. His political statements must be interpreted against the background and setting in which they developed. He grew up in a peasant mining village where princely power was exercised on behalf of the community; he did not experience the more republican forms of government in larger towns around him. He spent his career in the proximity and service of a princely court. His deep fears of disorder and chaos, common in his time, especially after peasant revolts in the 1500s and 1510s, shaped his desire for strong government. Nonetheless, from the beginning of his career to its end he supported passive resistance to anti-Christian and unethical decisions by secular governments, in accordance with the biblical word "we must obey God rather than any human authority" (Acts 5:29).

Luther's initial reluctance to grant any right of active, armed resistance gave way to the concession of that right to "lesser magistrates." He became convinced of the ethical propriety of such resistance in specific situations on the basis of arguments that the German political system permitted it and also because of his own understanding of God's two realms. When government officials do not obey God and usurp the responsibilities entrusted to others — for example, to the leaders of the church in spiritual matters — necessary means of correction may be undertaken by the lesser magistrates. Luther believed that while coercive force is appropriate for upholding justice in horizontal relationships, only the sword of the Holy Spirit, the Word of God, may exercise power in the vertical dimension of life. He therefore argued against attempts to convert people by force to the Christian faith. Johann Brenz (1499-1570) and others among his followers argued similarly against the use of persecution.

2.1.4. Luther's understanding of the two realms underlies Philip → Melanchthon's (1497-1560) presentation of the relationship of church and state in the → Augsburg Confession of 1530, articles 16 and 28. Melanchthon posited the integrity of the institutions of both church and state and the holiness of the secular callings of believers, as well as a concept of civil righteousness.

After the deaths of Luther and Melanchthon, Lutheran theologians structured much of their ethics on the basis of the concept of God's calling to service in the three estates, but they did not make the larger framework of the distinction of the two realms a dogmatic topic in itself, resulting in the loss of its effective use. The Lutheran churches of the late 16th and 17th centuries worked as partners with and branches of secular government in Germany and the Nordic countries. However, the general opinion that pastors and professors were merely instruments of state power ignores the fact that these theological leaders within Lutheran churches repeatedly exercised sharp critiques of their rulers. The examples of opposition to Calvinist absolutist princes in Lippe and Prussia are only the most prominent instances of frequent lay and clerical opposition to governmental policies by Lutherans in the late 16th and 17th centuries. The connections between church and state became ever more problematic by the beginning of the 18th century. The theory that God had given secular rulers the calling to exercise care for the religion of their people gave way to other theories, above all "territorialism" (i.e., by natural law, secular government must use the church to support the welfare of the entire state) and "collegialism" (rulers administer the church on behalf of the people as a community formed by free association of the people).

2.2. *Zwingli*

Ulrich → Zwingli (1484-1531; → Zwingli's Theology) formulated his concept of the relationship between spiritual and secular powers in a very different situation than Luther faced. The Swiss form of political governance required him to concentrate more on practical questions and less on the theological base on which they were answered. Zwingli's understanding of the righteousness of God and the understanding of the civic community in Switzerland led him to teach that God's demands for human righteousness, as found in the Decalogue and the Sermon on the Mount, govern civic as well as individual activities. Zwingli therefore directed civic authorities in the Swiss cantons to reform both church and state and individual believers to obey God and secular government, insofar as the latter submitted to God's law. Scholars accent elements of Zwingli's understanding of the structure of society differently, but it is clear that he placed the activities of the church, particularly → church discipline, under the administration of the civil authorities, while at the same time holding those authorities to a strict adherence to God's law enunciated by the pastors of the church. Thomas Erastus (1524-83) developed his plan for placing → church government under the direction of Christian secular authorities (Erastianism) under the influence of Zwingli's practice in Zurich.

2.3. *Calvin*

John → Calvin (1509-64; → Calvin's Theology) emphasized the concept of the kingdom of God and confessed God's sovereign rule over all of human life. Although he did not use Luther's distinction of God's two realms as a working framework, his reading of Luther as well as the medieval milieu (and many other Christian thinkers, along with Aristotle and Cicero) led him to insist upon the integrity of both the institution of the church and the institution of secular government, each totally subject to God's commands and each dedicated by God to specific tasks in human society. However, he believed that church and secular authorities should work closely together in maintaining Christian standards in society. The secular government is established by God to support pure doctrine and public morality, and it must use the church effectively to uphold both (see esp. *Inst.* 4.20). Christians must submit to God-ordained government but are also obligated by God to protest against abuses of power by the secular authorities.

Calvin's successor, Theodor → Beza (1519-1605), using particularly the argument of the Lutheran Magdeburg Confession (1550), developed this idea further into a justification of active resistance by lesser magistrates within the context of the persecution of Calvinists in France. Theories of the right to resist were further developed by other French Calvinist theologians, including Philippe Duplessis-Mornay (1549-1623). English Puritans adapted these theories to support their revolt against Charles I of England in the mid-17th century.

3. Ecclesiastical and Political Significance in the Nineteenth and Twentieth Centuries

In the course of the 19th century the use of the term "two kingdoms" had largely disappeared from the language of Lutheran theologians, and the concept "kingdom of God" took on a wide variety of ramifications, particularly in → Culture Protestantism in Germany. It occurred, for example, in the thought of Albrecht Ritschl (1822-89), who anticipated the advancement of an earthly kingdom of God through German Protestantism and other Christian churches. In some popular arguments, particularly in Germany, Luther's view of the two realms was cited in defense of the proposition that the state had its own laws to govern its conduct and that the standards of the Bible and the church for human behavior did not apply to the conduct of state affairs.

Particularly with the rise of National Socialism, this argument had sinister implications. Although some Luther scholars (e.g., Emanuel Hirsch) remained loyal to the Hitler regime, others abandoned their early support of the Nazi government and criticized its policies (e.g., Paul Althaus and Werner Elert). Others, such as Hermann Sasse (1895-1976), Dietrich → Bonhoeffer (1906-45), and Walther Künneth (1901-97), from the beginning of the Hitler era used Luther's concept of the two realms as the basis for sharp censure of Nazi ideology, particularly its racial theories. Luther's understanding of God's lordship over all of human life and his distinction of the two realms also shaped the thinking of leading political figures in the resistance against Hitler — in Norway and Denmark, as well as in Germany. Furthermore, this distinction provided a foundational element for Bonhoeffer's ethical reflection.

Reformed systematician Karl → Barth (1886-1968) charged that the Lutheran distinction of the two realms supported the idea that the state is autonomous and may act independently of God's law. Even before the rise of National Socialism he advocated overcoming the dualism between this world and the kingdom of God that he found in Lutheran social-ethical writings. In the → Barmen Declaration of 1934 he and other prominent Reformed and Lutheran theologians declared that there is no other Lord apart from Jesus Christ and that God does rule in both church and society.

In Scandinavia, particularly under the leadership of Einar Billing (1871-1939), Gustaf Aulén (1879-1977), and Gustaf Wingren (1910-2000), use of the distinction between two realms, with specific reference to Luther, developed in a significantly different intellectual environment. These scholars explored the ethical implications of Luther's concepts of order for both individual and social ethics. In North America this Swedish scholarship has been used, along with fresh Luther research, in formulating approaches to a series of urgent ethical questions by Karl Hertz, William H. Lazareth, and Robert Benne. Since 1951 the North American discussion of questions relating to the rule of God within human society has been shaped by *Christ and Culture,* a seminal work by H. Richard Niebuhr (1894-1962). (Niebuhr's description of Luther's distinction of the two realms as "paradox," however, does not accurately convey the Reformer's perception of God's working in different ways within the vertical and horizontal dimensions of human life.)

Karl Barth carried on vigorous disputes with Lutherans, including Althaus and Elert, and with his Reformed colleague and fellow founder of the so-called dialectical theology movement, Emil Brunner (1889-1966), concerning the concept of the "orders of creation." "Order" in this case refers to the fundamental situations or structures of human life that God has built into humanity, including family, state, and the empirical church. Brunner argued that these orders are inherent in human existence and thus shape daily life. He was concerned to create points of contact with those outside the Christian faith and to argue for an ethic based on human reason apart from revelation, although he held revelation as necessary for saving faith in Christ. He held that these orders, the reality that God fashioned when he created the human creature, still provide the foundation for moral conduct for Christians and non-Christians alike, even despite sin and evil. In contrast, Barth insisted that Scripture alone constitutes the basis of Christian ethical thinking.

The term "theology of orders" has been put to use with differing definitions and for different purposes. Some, such as Ernst → Troeltsch (1865-1923), criticized the idea for dividing Christian personal → ethics, based on the Christian tradition and held inwardly, from → social ethics, determined by publicly identifiable values. He believed that this division led to quietist indifference and subservience to secular authority. Others have argued that the sense of order in creation, expressed in the "orders" or "estates," do provide common ground for Christian social action in cooperation with those outside the church.

4. Contemporary Significance

The term "two kingdoms" will continue to generate controversy because of its many divergent uses in the past. Continuing study of Luther's own writings, however, which are usually regarded as the basis for the distinction between the two realms of God, shows that this distinction sets forth certain cardinal principles for a useful understanding of how God conducts his rule within human societies.

4.1. God rules all of his creation, and no element of it is autonomous or independent in relationship to him. Every human being in every action is to be held responsible for living according to his plan.

4.2. Human creatures relate to God primarily through the love and trust he creates in them. He "rules" in the lives of faith-filled people through the personal relationship that stems from his → love as it has been revealed in Jesus Christ, whose death and resurrection effect the restoration of sinners to life. Furthermore, God has created relationship among fellow humans based on their performance of deeds of love. The exercise of humanity in relationship to God centers on trusting him and enjoying his parental love. The exercise of humanity in relationship to the creation, particularly other human beings, consists of deeds of love performed in obedience and service to God and for the sake of the welfare of his creatures.

4.3. God has established structures for human life — that is, situations in which life is lived in relationships of mutual support with other people. These situations take concrete form in → institutions, such as → family, forms of government, economic organizations, and religious groups. God has designed these institutions to enable individuals to perform specific activities for the common welfare of all, although some are more immediately related to the individual than to the society. When an institution interferes with the activities and responsibilities assigned by God to other institutions, the lives of those involved usually suffer. That is true, for instance, when churches try to dictate policies to secular governments or when secular governments try to control religious activities.

The state exists to promote the welfare of its people in specific historical situations that may call for more or less support of ecclesiastical institutions and activities. The church exists to bring the Word of

God into people's lives, which always requires forthright moral proclamation of God's will, also within the hearing of secular authorities. A total separation of the message of the church from the policies of a state is impossible. Some ideological force will fill the vacuum, for societies' governing institutions need principles, values, and laws to guide them. But the assumption of power over other institutions brings with it the danger of wreaking havoc in both the one exercising power and the one subject to it.

4.4. This principle of the integrity of institutions opens every human organization to the criticism of God's law, and at the same time it liberates the Christian participant from being tyrannized by those institutions, whether state, church, or any other. In the 21st century some Christians live in nation-states experiencing resurgent nationalism or other ideologies (→ Nation, Nationalism), which on occasion require something akin to religious commitment or openly demand the association of citizenship with another religion or secularist ideology. The distinction between God's two realms enables Christians to recognize the blessings of God's gift of one's native culture and the validity of its government's claims for obedience, while also allowing for the rejection of false religious claims that that government may make. Similarly, the distinction of God's two realms helps ecclesiastical institutions perceive when true service to God should lead them to submit to secular governments and when they should not.

4.5. Bonhoeffer's distinction between the ultimate and penultimate, which itself arises from the distinction of the two realms, assists Christians in recognizing that the relationship with God through faith in Christ forms the center of what it means to be human and that all earthly relationships are secondary. Many of these secondary relationships, however, including responsibilities and commitments within economic, political, cultural, and familial spheres of life, are *pen*ultimate (lit. "almost" ultimate) and command the attention and dedication of individual and collective commitment and action.

Bibliography: General: R. ANSELM, W. HÄRLE, and M. KROEGER, "Zweireichlehre," *TRE* 36.776-93 • U. DUCHROW, *Christenheit und Weltverantwortung. Traditionsgeschichte und systematische Struktur der Zwei-Reiche-Lehre* (2d ed.; Stuttgart, 1983) • W. ELERT, *The Christian Ethos* (Philadelphia, 1957; orig. ed., 1940) • K. HERTZ, ed., *Two Kingdoms and One World* (Minneapolis, 1971).

Patristic: R. MARKUS, *Saeculum: History and Society in the Theology of Saint Augustine* (Cambridge, 1970) •

J. O'MEARA, *Charter of Christendom: The Significance of the City of God* (New York, 1961) • J. VAN OORT, *Jerusalem and Babylon: A Study into Augustine's City of God and the Sources of His Doctrine of the Two Cities* (Leiden, 1991).

Reformation: P. ALTHAUS, *The Ethics of Martin Luther* (Philadelphia, 1972); idem, *Grundriß der Ethik* (Erlangen, 1939) • J. BOHATEC, *Calvins Lehre von Staat und Kirche* (Breslau, 1937) • T. BRADY, "Luther and the State: The Reformer's Teaching in Its Social Setting," *Luther and the Modern State in Germany* (ed. J. Tracy; Kirksville, Mo., 1986) 31-44 • W. D. J. CARGILL THOMPSON, *The Political Thought of Martin Luther* (Sussex, 1984) • H. DIEM, *Luthers Lehre von den zwei Reichen* (Munich, 1938) • J. ESTES, *Peace, Order, and the Glory of God: Secular Authority and the Church in the Thought of Luther and Melanchthon, 1518-1559* (Leiden, 2005) • G. W. FORELL, *Faith Active in Love: An Investigation of the Principles Underlying Luther's Social Ethics* (New York, 1954) • W. F. GRAHAM, *The Constructive Revolutionary: John Calvin and His Socio-economic Impact* (Atlanta, 1971) • R. KINGDON, "The First Expression of Theodore Beza's Political Ideas," *ARG* 46 (1955) 88-100; idem, *Geneva and the Consolidation of the French Protestant Movement, 1564-1572* (Madison, Wis., 1967) • W. LAZARETH, *Christians in Society: Luther, the Bible, and Social Ethics* (Minneapolis, 2001) • J. H. LEITH, *John Calvin's Doctrine of the Christian Life* (Louisville, Ky., 1989) • H. SCHILLING, *Konfessionskonflikt und Staatsbildung* (Gütersloh, 1981) • G. SEEBASS, "An sint persequendi haeretici? Die Stellung des Johann Brenz zur Verfolgung und Bestrafung der Täufer," *Die Reformation und ihre Außenseiter* (Göttingen, 1997) 283-335 • G. WINGREN, *Luther on Vocation* (Philadelphia, 1957) • J. WITTE, *Law and Protestantism: The Legal Teachings of the Lutheran Reformation* (Cambridge, 2002) • E. WOLGAST, *Die Wittenberger Theologie und die Politik der evangelischen Stände. Studien zu Luthers Gutachten in politischen Fragen* (Gütersloh, 1977).

Modern: K. BARTH, *CD* III, IV • R. BENNE, *Ordinary Saints: An Introduction to the Christian Life* (2d ed.; Minneapolis, 2003); idem, *The Paradoxical Vision: A Public Theology for the Twenty-first Century* (Minneapolis, 1995) • D. BONHOEFFER, *Ethics* (Minneapolis, 2005) • E. BRUNNER, *The Divine Imperative: A Study in Christian Ethics* (Philadelphia, 1947; orig. ed., 1932) • M. HONECKER, *Konzept einer sozialethischen Theorie* (Tübingen, 1971) • R. KOLB, "Niebuhr's 'Christ and Culture in Paradox' Revisited," *LQ*, n.s., 10/4 (1996) 259-79 • H. R. NIEBUHR, *Christ and Culture* (New York, 1951) • U. SIEMON-NETTO, *The Fabricated Luther: The Rise and Fall of the Shirer Myth* (2d ed.; St. Louis, 2007).

ROBERT KOLB

Typology

1. Term
2. Examples
3. In Salvation History
4. Commentary

1. Term

Typology derives from Gk. *typtō,* "strike." The *typos* is what is struck, a seal or mold, which is then used for a model or pattern. As in the case of sealing, also printing or typing, it may refer both to the mold and to the impress. Typology has this basic meaning in view. In the Bible, OT events, institutions, or persons may be patterns or prototypes *(typoi)* that prefigure the NT events, institutions, or persons that deepen and fulfill them and that are called antitypes *(antitypoi).* A specific view of salvation history underlies typology. Later typology became a hermeneutical methodology in exposition of OT texts (→ Exegesis, Biblical, 2.1).

Along with typology the NT also uses comparisons, allegories, and biblical proofs. → Allegory differs from typology in assuming that the texts have a hidden and spiritual meaning that needs to be brought to light. But allegorical and typological modes of exposition frequently overlap (e.g., Gal. 4:21-31), so that a clear distinction is not always possible. The type and antitype may share only a few elements, sometimes only one. The antitype provides the starting point, for from it alone can we see what the preceding prototype signifies.

→ Paul was the first to use the term in this way (Rom. 5:14; 1 Cor. 10:6, 11 [*typikōs*]). The term *antitypos* occurs in 1 Pet. 3:21 (". . . this prefigured"). The words have rather a different sense in Exod. 25:40 and Heb. 8:5 ("pattern") and 9:24 ("copy"). Since the NT does not expressly use the term for typological correspondence, we cannot always say for certain what is a mere comparison with the OT, not typology. In these cases we may speak of typological motifs and relations.

2. Examples

A few clear NT examples may be given. In 1 Cor. 5:7 Christ is the antitype of the Passover lamb, for his death has power to bring salvation and forgiveness in a way that far surpasses what the Passover lamb did. In 1 Cor. 10:1-13 the manna and water that God gave his people in the wilderness are types of the → Eucharist and → baptism, which give life to the saved eschatological community. In Gal. 4:21-31 Paul shows that the two wives of → Abraham, Hagar and Sarah, are types denoting, on the one hand,

bondage under the law and, on the other, freedom for the eschatological community. In Rom. 5:12-21 Christ as antitype reverses the role of Adam the type. Adam brought judgment on humanity, but Christ has brought salvation. Christ transcendently reverses what Adam did.

In John 3:14 the crucified Son of Man is the antitype of the serpent in the wilderness set up by → Moses. The ark and the flood are types of baptism in 1 Pet. 3:20-21.

Typology is used extensively in Hebrews. In chapters 3–4 Israel's wilderness wandering is a type of the wandering of the saved community toward its eschatological resting place. In 8–10 the Levitical priesthood is a type of Christ, who as the heavenly → high priest offers the once-for-all sacrifice that does away with the OT cult. A theological basis for typology is offered in 1:1-2.

3. In Salvation History

The most important root that gives rise to the view of → salvation history underlying typology is to be found in Deutero-Isaiah (→ Isaiah, Book of, 3). Isaiah shows how the return from exile corresponds to and indeed surpasses the exodus, for no haste will be required, all hindrances will be removed, and God himself will lead the returning Israelites home. In the intertestamentary period typology in the narrower sense is used only in relation to → eschatology (L. Goppelt). It has a primary eschatological relevance in the NT, too. God's final, eschatological action will enhance and exceed his action in the OT.

The → early church gave typology an important role in its exposition of the OT and detected many more types than we can find in the NT. Thus → Justin Martyr (ca. 100-ca. 165; *Dial.* 42.4) applied all the accounts of what Moses did to Christ. The → Reformers had little use for allegory, but typology played a big role in their exposition, although doctrinally they restricted themselves to NT examples.

4. Commentary

Modern theology takes various views of typology. G. von Rad (1901-71), W. Eichrodt (1890-1978), H. W. Wolff (1911-93), and L. Goppelt (1911-73) defend its validity. K. → Barth (1886-1968), influenced by W. Vischer (1895-1988), could make what seems to be almost excessive use of it in his *Church Dogmatics* II/2. For various reasons, however, many scholars opposed typology. R. Bultmann (1884-1976) regarded it as cyclic, with a focus on repetition rather than fulfillment. For F. Baumgärtel (1888-1981) types have no existential meaning for Christians, and the underlying view of salvation history has no validity. A common objection is that typology is subject to caprice rather than method.

Typological motifs that have no NT foundation abound. Research has shown, however, that there are a great number of typological motifs in the NT itself. These motifs accompany typology in the strict sense, and along with it they express in open or hidden form the inalienable Christian insight that there is close correspondence between what God did for Israel and what he does for his eschatological people, and that God's work in history reached its climax and fulfillment in the coming of Jesus Christ.

→ Hermeneutics

Bibliography: F. BAUMGÄRTEL, Verheißung. Zur Frage des evangelischen Verständnisses des Alten Testaments (Gütersloh, 1952) • G. W. BUCHANAN, Typology and the Gospel (Lanham, Md., 1987) • R. BULTMANN, "Promise and Fulfilment" (1949), Essays: Philosophical and Theological (London, 1955) 182-208 • J. DANIÉLOU, From Shadows to Reality: Studies in Biblical Typology of the Fathers (London, 1960) • R. M. DAVIDSON, Typology in Scripture: A Study of Hermeneutical ΤΥΠΟΣ-Structures (Berrien Springs, Mich., 1981) • W. EICHRODT, "Ist die typologische Exegese sachgemäße Exegese?" TLZ 81 (1956) 641-54 • E. E. ELLIS, The OT in Early Christianity: Canon and Interpretation in the Light of Modern Research (Tübingen, 1991) • L. GOPPELT, Typos. The Typological Interpretation of the OT in the New (Grand Rapids, 1982) • G. W. H. LAMPE and K. J. WOOLLCOMBE, Essays on Typology (Naperville, Ill., 1957) • I. H. MARSHALL, ed., NT Interpretation: Essays on Principles and Methods (Grand Rapids, 1977) • H. W. WOLFF, "Zur Hermeneutik des Alten Testaments," EvT 16 (1956) 337-70.

HANS-PETER MATHYS

U

Ubiquity

1. In the context of Christian theology, ubiquity, or the teaching that God is everywhere (Lat. *ubique*), is related to the distinction between God and the world (i.e., God's transcendence). The omnipresence of God shows clearly that the divine transcendence (→ Immanence and Transcendence) does not mean that the Creator is alongside the creature but involves the direct permeation of every creature by the Creator, who has given it its being and maintains it in being (*conservatio;* → Creation). → Pantheism, which stresses the unity of God with the world, does at least resist the idea of God at a spatial distance from the world.

→ Scholasticism spoke of the divine presence through his effects, through his present action, and through the giving of existence. It regarded God's ubiquity as his "repletive" presence. God fills the world so that we cannot anywhere exclude him. He is wholly present in every part of each specific space (*circumscriptive* or *definitive*), but in such a way that he still permeates and fills all creation (*repletive*). His presence thus excludes "local motion" (*motus localis;* see P. Lombard *Sent.* 1.37.164-72; Aquinas *Summa theol.* I, q. 8; G. Biel, *Collectorium ca. Quattuor libros* 1.37.2.4, where there is a definition of modes of presence).

2. Ubiquity is a predicate of God alone. In the debates between M. → Luther (1483-1546; → Luther's Theology) and U. → Zwingli (1484-1531; → Zwingli's Theology) about the possibility of the real presence of Christ's body and blood at the → Eucharist (§3.3), which was later renewed by Reformed and Lutheran dogmaticians, the question concerned the ubiquity of the human nature of Christ. The Reformed agreed with Zwingli that the distinction of Christ's divine and human natures remains, in spite of the unity of person. They claimed that both Scripture and the creeds stated that between the ascension and the return, the humanity of Christ is at the right hand of the Father. They could argue, as did J. Hooper (ca. 1495-1555) and M. V. Coverdale (1488?-1569), that omnipresence is incompatible with true humanity. They rejected a eucharistic presence of Christ's body and blood that was a presence only of substance without accidents. They believed, however, that by the incomprehensible working of the Holy Spirit, believers can spiritually feed on Christ's body and blood, so that, as J. → Calvin (1509-64; → Calvin's Theology) paradoxically put it, "the whole Christ is present, but not in his wholeness" (*Inst.* 4.17.30).

With Luther, the champions of Lutheran → orthodoxy (§1) argued for a real and not merely a verbal communication of attributes (→ Christology 2.4.4), so that with the unity of person there is a unity of attributes. The attributes of the one nature are shared with those of the other. Ubiquity can thus be referred to Christ's human nature (Luther, "Confession concerning Christ's Supper" [1528], *LW* 37.214-32). A distinction must of course be made between Christ's universal presence in all things and his presence to salvation in the → sacraments, in which he imparts himself to sinners (*pro me;* "That These Words of Christ, 'This Is My Body,' etc., Still Stand Firm against the Fanatics" [1527], *LW* 37.68-69).

Distinction also had to be made by Lutherans regarding the ubiquity of Christ's human nature after the second eucharistic controversy and J. Brenz's (1499-1570) conflict with Wittenberg Philippism (H. C. Brandy, 11-69; → Crypto-Calvinism) about a strict application of the *genus maiestaticum* to the communication of attributes. This point, too, gave rise to domestic Lutheran disagreements, for example, about "ubivolipresence" (Christ is present everywhere he wishes to be; M. Chemnitz) and restriction of ubiquity to the Eucharist (see also the debate between Tübingen and Giessen; T. Mahlmann, J. Baur).

→ Christology 1.4; God 7; Kenosis 2

Bibliography: J. Baur, *Luther und seine klassischen Erben* (Tübingen, 1993) 117-44, 204-89 • D. G. Bloesch, *God the Almighty: Power, Wisdom, Holiness, Love* (Downers Grove, Ill., 1995) esp. 79-102 • H. C. Brandy, *Die späte Christologie des Johannes Brenz* (Tübingen, 1991) • W. Farley, "Works and Grace: Reflections on Religious Practice and the Ubiquity of God," *TToday* 52 (1996) 449-57 • A. G. Jorgenson, "Luther on Ubiquity and a Theology of the Public," *IJST* 6/4 (2004) 351-68 • T. Mahlmann, *Das neue Dogma der lutherischen Christologie* (Gütersloh, 1969).

Notger Slenczka

Uganda

1. General Situation
2. Religious Situation
   2.1. Indigenous Beliefs
   2.2. Christian Churches
   2.3. Ecumenical and Interreligious Relations

1. General Situation

1.1. The Republic of Uganda lies on the equator on an elevated plateau between the eastern and western branches of the Great Rift Valley, with mountains soaring to 5,119 m. (16,795 ft.) toward its southwest border. It is landlocked and shares borders with Kenya on the east, Democratic Repub-

	1960	1980	2000
Population (1,000s):	6,562	13,120	22,459
Annual growth rate (%):	4.08	2.36	2.95
Area: 241,040 sq. km. (93,070 sq. mi.)			

A.D. 2000

Population density: 93/sq. km. (241/sq. mi.)
Births / deaths: 4.75 / 1.80 per 100 population
Fertility rate: 6.47 per woman
Infant mortality rate: 101 per 1,000 live births
Life expectancy: 44.2 years (m: 43.2, f: 45.1)
Religious affiliation (%): Christians 89.3 (Roman Catholics 47.4, Anglicans 29.2, unaffiliated 6.1, indigenous 3.5, Protestants 3.0, other Christians 0.2), Muslims 5.3, tribal religionists 3.7, other 1.7.

lic of Congo on the west, Sudan on the north, and Tanzania and Rwanda on the south. Nearly one-sixth of its territory is covered with water. Uganda has many rivers and streams, as well as ten lakes, including Lake Victoria, from which the Nile River flows westward and northward across the country. The climate is mild and makes possible a wide range of agricultural products, including plantain, cassava, and a large variety of tropical fruits and cereals like millet, sorghum, and maize for home consumption, with coffee, tea, sugar, and cotton for both domestic consumption and export.

In 2006 the population was estimated at 27 million. There are over 70 ethnic and linguistic groups, the largest being the Baganda; other major groups are the Banyoro, Batooro, Basoga, Lugbara, Acholi, Banyankole, Bakiga, and Iteso. During the colonial period (1894-1962; → Colonialism) and since independence (1962), English has been the official language. Kiswahili, which is prevalent in eastern and central Africa and which extends to the southern regions of the continent, claims over 150 million speakers and is generally spoken and understood in Uganda as well. Uganda is home also to some small immigrant communities of Asians, mainly Indians and Pakistanis, and some Europeans.

1.2. Hunters and gatherers inhabited Uganda in the Middle Stone Age. Later came peoples of the Bantu language group, who brought agricultural and metal-working skills. They evolved centralized political systems that reached a peak in the 15th-century Kitara Empire under rulers known as the Bacwezi. This empire collapsed and was replaced in the 17th century by indigenous kingdoms of the Baganda, Banyankole, Banyoro, and Batooro. In 1832 and 1844 Arab traders arrived in the western, West Nile area and in the central Buganda area.

In 1894 Britain took over the country as the

Uganda Protectorate and began to rule indirectly through traditional kings and chiefs. In the course of time, the people agitated for and received complete independence.

1.3. In 1971 the army chief, Idi Amin, took over power as president of the nation, ousting Prime Minister Milton Obote. During Amin's eight-year reign, relations deteriorated considerably between the various ethnic groups. Many religious leaders criticized the regime for abuse of human → rights and called upon it to provide peace and security for the people. In 1975, believing that saboteurs were masquerading as missionaries, Amin closed 27 Christian → denominations. He maintained only four religious organizations in the country: the Church of Uganda (→ Anglican), the → Roman Catholic Church, the → Orthodox Church, and the Muslims (→ Islam). Before and during that period, many thousands of people were killed (estimates range from 100,000 to 500,000), and tens of thousands were forced to flee as → refugees. Religious leaders also were imprisoned, and some were killed, including Archbishop Janani Luwum of the Church of Uganda and Father Clement Kiggundu of the Roman Catholic Church.

After Amin was ousted in 1979, Obote returned as president in 1980. Many Ugandans, however, believed that he came into power only through rigged elections, and civil unrest continued. He was opposed by many Ugandans, and especially by the National Resistance Movement, a broad-based and nonpartisan political group that finally came into power in 1986, the year in which Yoweri Museveni took power.

Uganda's location in the Great Lakes region makes it prone to various conflicts. Violent armed struggles continued from the late 1980s to the present, especially in the northern part of the country, with the disruption spreading from the Acholi area of the Lord's Resistance Army, under Joseph Kony, to areas of Lango, Teso, and parts of the West Nile, especially Adjumani District. For many decades, the acquisition of small arms and light weapons has compounded problems, especially in Karamoja and neighboring areas. Also, for many years refugees have been fleeing into Uganda from nearby Sudan, Democratic Republic of Congo, and Rwanda.

In 1993 President Museveni restored the Kingdom of Buganda, followed by the Kingdoms of Bunyoro and Tooro. The restoration of the institutions of cultural leaders is important, especially in motivating people to participate actively both in the building of peace and in the fight against ignorance and especially the HIV/AIDS pandemic.

Uganda has enjoyed a measure of success in dealing with its HIV/AIDS problem. These positive results have come as a result of a policy of transparency and of the many initiatives taken by the state and by the national, social, and religious leaders at all levels in sensitizing the citizens concerning the reality of the pandemic and of how to humanly fight it through the strategies of abstinence, being faithful, and (where accepted) the use of condoms.

In 2006 there were one million internally displaced persons in Uganda, living in camps. In addition, there are numerous other conflicts such as those in Kibaale District involving the *bafuruki* (immigrants) and the original inhabitants.

1.4. In northern Uganda alone, peace mediation efforts have been continuous since 1986. Since then, there have been 24 insurgencies countrywide. In light of such proneness to violence, systematic efforts have evolved over the years that aim to strengthen the hand of policymakers and practitioners in peace building and conflict resolution (→ Force, Violence, Nonviolence). One of the most important initiatives is that of Makerere University, which in 2003 launched a master's-level Peace and Conflict Studies program in its Department of Religious Studies.

Through the concerted efforts of this program, in conjunction with NGOs, civil society organizations (CSOs), and the Deutscher Entwicklungsdienst Project, Makerere University has produced a Peace and Conflict database of 856 relevant documents. The documents show the efforts made toward solving the national problem of insurgencies, conflicts, and civil strife and, positively, toward helping people practice the philosophy of waging peace (→ Peace Research; Peace Education). People are taught, since man's inhumanity to man is most often expressed through acts committed out of philosophical and religious ignorance, that they have the resources in their own minds and hearts to fight against these negative elements. For the sake of waging peace, people are sensitized to cease condoning any act of violence or destruction. They are being made aware of their responsibility to end the perverse cycle that is sacrificing the lives of their own children. Makerere and many other organizations around the country are committed to educating the people at all levels and to implementing such a philosophy in their respective spheres.

So far, 150 people have graduated from the Makerere program, and in 2006 another 70 were registered in it. Graduates are deployed throughout the country as teachers, administrators, NGO and CSO project operators, social workers, and religious counselors. Collectively, these workers are pursuing welfare programs and training sessions that target the entire educational system and the whole gamut of national stakeholders.

2. Religious Situation
2.1. *Indigenous Beliefs*
Several religions coexist in Uganda. When Islam and Christianity were introduced in the country starting in 1832, it was on the foundation of what is described as Ugandan or African traditional religion (→ Tribal Religions), which is the teaching inherited from God, the Teacher of teachers and source of all truth. This religion or teaching touches on all aspects of life. The various indigenous peoples express it differently, depending on their cultural and educational backgrounds, but in general it is estimated that they are in agreement on more than 90 percent of the content and general structure of their belief. At the core is belief in the existence of God and in the world of the souls and of the environment. The latter is known by many different names: Emagombe (among the Buganda), Kuzimu (among the Bunyoro and Tooro), Owa Nyamuteza (among the Ankole), Piny Polo (among the Acholi), Babuga (among the Madi), and many others.

In Uganda there are innumerable names for God that describe his being, nature, activities, and relationship with his entire → creation. He is known as the Master Creator (as Katonda by the Luganda, Ruhanga in western Uganda, and Were in parts of eastern Uganda). More commonly, though, he is known as the Giver of Life, the Father and/or Mother of the people (as Isebantu or Ihnebantu by the Lusoga), and thus the Parent of humankind. As for his character, Ruhanga is the most loving, just, honest, truthful, and compassionate (and many other attributes). He is the role model for all human beings; people are meant to resemble him. In worship of him people offer daily prayers, invocations, sacrifices, and offerings.

When people — as all do — depart from the visible physical world to the invisible spiritual world of the souls, according to the laws established by the Creator of the universe, they remain viewed as honorable members of their families, clans, and communities. We have many reports from those still alive of their experiences with those who have passed on before, including daily communications through dreams, visions, auditions, and spirit possession in which they "see" and "hear" the dead.

Furthermore, many religious activities are performed to sustain relationships with spirit persons, such as offering them flowers, commemorative offerings of food and drink on family altars, making contact through mediums, and executing the wishes of the departed → ancestors. Such actions are deemed to be the highest duty of filial piety, incumbent on all descendants. As part of their happy responsibility, the departed ancestors shower their descendants on earth with all kinds of help, guidance, support, education, and protection.

In addition, people recognize the existence of mystical powers in nature, manifested variously as electricity, poisonous substances, lightning, wind, and storms. They also recognize the existence of people who think, speak, and do evil to others. These persons, generally called witches and sorcerers (*barogo*, among the Runyoro), choose to misuse the powers in nature (→ Witchcraft). Such manifestations of evil are never condoned.

In Uganda the preservation and passing on of human life has always been regarded as a core duty and responsibility bestowed upon all people by the Master Creator since time immemorial. Accordingly, people also carry out rituals, ceremonies, and celebrations in connection with the major stages in life such as conception, birth, marriage, and death, as well as initiation or puberty → rites. People recognize and especially cherish three donations from God, the Giver of all things, namely, love, life, and lineage. None can exist without the other. The emphasis, however, is on the lineage, or blood relationship (*oruganda,* among the Runyoro), which as the thread of life binds people to their ancestors for generations, even for thousands of years. Blood relationships and kinship ties are thus central, forming the basis of social relations that extend from the earthly environment to that in the world of the souls.

Despite the arrival of the new religions in Uganda, the traditional teachings remain alive everywhere, for they have many areas of compatibility with → Islam and Christianity. Its roots lie very deep in the Master Creator himself; it is not about to disappear or get wished off.

2.2. *Christian Churches*
Members of the Church Mission Society, missionaries of the Anglican Church, arrived in Uganda in 1877 (→ British Missions 1.2.3), followed in 1879 by the White Fathers of the Roman Catholic Church (→ Catholic Missions 5). The 1880s were times of interreligious wars, persecutions, and martyrdoms involving Anglicans, Catholics, Muslims, the British, the French, and African kings and people. The aftermath of conflicts, hostilities, and hatreds lingered on for a number of years. Christianity, though,

spread very rapidly in Uganda, helped by work in schools, hospitals, and other social services (→ Medical Missions). In 1900 only 7 percent of the people were Christian; by 1990 the percentage had risen to 80 percent.

In 1961 the Anglican Church established the autonomous Province of Uganda, embracing Rwanda, Burundi, and Boga-Zaire; later it became the Church of Uganda. The Anglican community has been strongly influenced by the East African revival movement, or *Balokole* (Luganda, meaning "saved people"), which initially started in Rwanda in 1927 but then spread into Uganda and other East African countries (→ Revivals). The movement contains many groups, but all remain within the church.

The Roman Catholic Church has been even more successful than the Anglicans. Besides the White Fathers, other Catholic men's and women's orders have been active in Uganda. Mill Hill priests arrived in 1895; Mill Hill sisters, in 1902. Both Catholics and Anglicans are strongly represented throughout the country, and both are in charge of schools and hospitals and engage in social services and the work of development.

Protestant churches include the Seventh-day → Adventists (who arrived in Uganda in 1926), the → Salvation Army (1931), the Pentecostal → Assemblies of God (1935), the Full Gospel Churches of Uganda (1959), and smaller denominations of American or European origin.

→ Independent (Indigenous) Churches were first formed in 1914, when the Society of the One Almighty God split from the Anglican Church. Another division occurred in 1929, led by Reuben S. S. Mukasa Spartas (1899-1982), which later called itself the African Greek Orthodox Church. It was admitted into the Greek Orthodox communion in 1946, but a new schism occurred in 1955. A number of small independent churches have come to Uganda from nearby Kenya.

2.3. *Ecumenical and Interreligious Relations*

Ecumenical relations have meant much in Uganda. They are formed against the background of religious diversity that has existed ever since the arrival of Islam and Christianity. A given clan or blood lineage may thus include traditionalists, Muslims, and Christians. This mixture is similar to that within families, for the system of exogamous marriages in the country manifests a great deal of blood mix. Among the Baganda, for example, there are 56 clans *(ebika);* among the Banyoro/Batooro, 83; among the Luos, 99. Blood mix through intermarriage is the norm. For many, in fact, one is cul-

turally not allowed to marry from one's blood lineage and that of one's mother. To view → ecumenism as spiritual blood-mix is thus a ready comparison that is well understood and culturally encouraged. Early → missionaries to Uganda discouraged such relations on pain of condemnation. This kind of teaching contributed to the bloody religious wars and conflicts. In recent decades, however, attitudes and religious teachings have been rapidly changing.

As evidence of this change, in 1963 the Church of Uganda, the Roman Catholic Church, and the Orthodox Church founded the Uganda Joint Christian Council, which fosters cooperation in educational and medical services, in Bible translations and distribution, in the press, and in local relations. Some of the smaller Christian groups have come together in the Ugandan Association of Evangelicals. There is also the Interreligious Council of Uganda, which specifically brings together Muslims and Christians for educative seminars, discussions, conferences, and the like. It is very valuable in its determination to bring unity, harmony, and peace among the people of faith in God.

In 1971 the government under Idi Amin established the Department of Religious Affairs to oversee relations between religious bodies and the state. Amin was also instrumental in establishing the Muslim Supreme Council, similar to the Joint Christian Council.

The majority of Ugandan Muslims are → Sunnis. Historically, the Indian Muslims have been largely Ismailis. In all, 23 different Muslim sects were present in Uganda in 2006. Other Indians living in Uganda have been → Hindus, mostly those who live in cities and towns. There are also some → Sikhs in Uganda, and well as → Baha'is, who have a large temple in Kampala.

Since the period of reconstruction after Idi Amin was ousted in 1979, Christian and Muslim organizations have generally been actively involved in reconciliation and the rebuilding of social services. The religious organizations continue to get help from both local and foreign sources for these activities. A century ago Christians and Muslims were opponents and suffered martyrdom, but now they work together in defense of human rights and in economic, social, political, and spiritual reconstruction.

It is hoped that, as time goes on, Uganda will overcome all negative religious differences and that the old jealousies and latent animosities based on wrong teachings will be no more. The Department of Religious Studies at Makerere University in Kampala, along with many of the 16 new universities in the country, continues to carry out intensive study of the major religions, focusing on the high percentage of beliefs held in common between them and, in this way, contributing to interreligious understanding and the waging of peace.

Bibliography: A. B. T. Byaruhanga-Akiiki, *Religion in Bunyoro* (Nairobi, 1982) • M. Fortes and G. Dieterlen, eds., *African Systems of Thought* (London, 1964) • H. B. Hansen, *Mission and State in a Colonial Setting: Uganda, 1890-1925* (London, 1984) • K. M. Justice, *New Religious Movements and the Catholic Church in Uganda* (Stavanger, Norw., 2003) • B. D. Kateregga, "Islam in Dialogue with People of Faith: Insights from Traditions," *Interreligious Dialogue: Voices from the Frontiers* (ed. D. M. Bryant and F. Flinn; New York, 1989) 109-18 • A. M. Lugira, *Ganda Art: A Study of the Ganda Mentality with Respect to Possibilities of Acculturation in Christian Art* (Kampala, 1970) • P. A. Musana, "New Religious Movements in Post-independent Uganda" (Diss., Makerere University, 2000) • C. Noll, "The Betrayed: An Exploration of the Acholi Opinion of the International Criminal Court," *JThWS* 24 (2007) • L. Pirouet, *Black Evangelists: The Spread of Christianity in Uganda, 1891-1914* (London, 1978); idem, ed., *A Dictionary of Christianity in Uganda* (Kampala, 1969) • J. V. Taylor, *The Growth of the Church in Buganda* (London, 1958) • Y. Tourigny, *So Abundant a Harvest: The Catholic Church in Uganda, 1879-1979* (London, 1979) • A. D. T. Tuma and P. Mutibwa, eds., *A Century of Christianity in Uganda, 1877-1977* (Nairobi, 1978) • F. B. Welbourn, *East African Rebels: A Study of Some Independent Churches* (London, 1961). See also the Peace and Conflict database, produced by the Deutscher Entwicklungsdienst Project, in collaboration with the Civil Peace Project, Makerere University, Kampala.

A. B. T. Byaruhanga-Akiiki

Ugarit

Excavations from 1929 at Ras Shamra, 12 km. (8 mi.) north of Latakia on the coast of Syria, have brought to light the existence of the city-state of Ugarit. Ugarit was the center of a thriving economy. People lived there from the seventh millennium B.C. (Prepottery Neolithic), but the urban culture dates from the Bronze Age. In the 12th century B.C. various factors combined to overthrow it.

The discovery of the Ras Shamra clay tablets was epoch making, for they were in a form of writing that was totally unfamiliar before 1929. The monuments derive from the 15th to the 13th centuries B.C. Besides a few other languages, the largest share of the writing consists of Babylonian cuneiform script, used for several languages, and a new writing called cuneiform alphabetic, a consonantal script that was used for the people speaking Northwest or North Semitic (→ Hebrew language), though Hurrian is also found.

These excavations gave rise to a new branch of Near Eastern research, namely, Ugaritology. Among other things the finds have produced original textual material bearing on Canaanite religion. Voluminous → myths bear witness to the religious experience of the inhabitants, whose existence was guaranteed by the recitation of myths in the cult. Two epics that center on the question of dynastic succession aim to safeguard law and custom. They show how the welfare of the state depended on the relation of the king to the gods.

The texts have promoted and enriched OT scholarship (→ Exegesis, Biblical, 1.4), for Israel, though it did not live in the same place or time, had acquaintance with the same Canaanite world. The texts have confirmed, altered, or even corrected certain cultural, linguistic, and literary insights. The witness from Ugarit shows that faith in → Yahweh, in the course of history, had some resemblance to belief in the gods El and Baal. Nevertheless, we are not to equate Yahweh and El, for from the outset Yahweh had traditional qualities that differentiate him from these deities.

Bibliography: A. Caquot and M. Sznycer, *Ugaritic Religion* (Leiden, 1980) • A. Curtis, *Ugarit (Ras Shamra)* (Grand Rapids, 1985) • G. R. Driver, *Canaanite Myths and Legends* (2d ed.; ed. J. C. L. Gibson; Edinburgh, 1978) • O. Eissfeldt, "Kanaanäisch-ugaritische Religion," *HO* 1.8.1 (1964) 76-91 • C. H. Gordon, *Ugaritic Textbook* (Rome, 1965) • O. Loretz, *Ugarit und die Bibel. Kanaanäische Götter und Religion im Alten Testament* (Darmstadt, 1990) • I. Márquez Rowe, *The Royal Deeds of Ugarit: A Study of Ancient Near Eastern Diplomatics* (Münster, 2006) • J. Obermann, *Ugaritic Mythology: A Study of Its Leading Motifs* (New Haven, 1948) • G. del Olmo Lete, *Canaanite Religion: According to the Liturgical Texts of Ugarit* (Bethesda, Md., 1999) • G. del Olmo Lete and J. Sanmartín, *A Dictionary of the Ugaritic Language in the Alphabetic Tradition* (2 vols.; Leiden, 2004) • D. Pardee, *Ritual and Cult at Ugarit* (ed. T. J. Lewis; Leiden, 2002) • W. G. E. Watson and N. Wyatt, eds., *Handbook of Ugaritic Studies* (Leiden, 1999) • N. Wyatt, *The Mythic Mind: Essays on Cosmology and Religion in Ugaritic and OT Literature* (London, 2005); idem, *Religious Texts from Ugarit* (2d ed.; London, 2002).

Wolfram Herrmann

Ukraine

	1960	1980	2000
Population (1,000s):	42,783	50,044	50,801
Annual growth rate (%):	1.16	0.36	−0.36

Area: 603,700 sq. km. (233,100 sq. mi.)

A.D. 2000

Population density: 84/sq. km. (218/sq. mi.)
Births / deaths: 0.99 / 1.40 per 100 population
Fertility rate: 1.38 per woman
Infant mortality rate: 15 per 1,000 live births
Life expectancy: 70.3 years (m: 65.6, f: 75.0)
Religious affiliation (%): Christians 82.7 (Orthodox 55.1, indigenous 15.8, Roman Catholics 11.1, Protestants 2.7, other Christians 0.6), nonreligious 11.2, atheists 3.9, Muslims 1.8, other 0.4.

1. The Principal Christian Groups
2. History
   2.1. Christian Roots
   2.2. Orthodox–Roman Catholic Separation
   2.3. Eastern Rite Catholics (Uniates)
3. Twentieth-Century Developments
4. Current Tensions

In Christian history the Ukraine played a central role during the Slavicization of Eastern Christianity. It also played a key formative role as home of the largest and most active Greek, or Eastern Rite (Uniate), Catholic Church. Since Ukraine's reemergence as a sovereign country in August 1991, there has been a struggle within Orthodoxy between those asserting an → autocephalous patriarchate for Ukraine (the Ukrainian Orthodox Church–Kievan Patriarchate [UOC-KP], led since 1995 by Patriarch Filaret) and those seeking to remain an integral and influential part of the → Russian Orthodox Church (the Ukrainian Orthodox Church–Moscow Patriarchate [UOC-MP], led since 1992 by Metropolitan Volodymyr). Heads of both now-separate churches maintain headquarters in Kiev, the Ukrainian capital city. In like symbolic fashion, the leading hierarch of the Ukrainian Catholic Church, Cardinal Lubymyr Husar, moved his headquarters in 2005 from L'viv — the region with greatest concentration of Uniate faithful — to Kiev, assuming the title of patriarch (→ Uniate Churches). The fourth largest church in Ukraine today, the Union of Evangelical Christian → Baptists, has maintained its administrative center in Kiev. Nowhere does this Baptist Union constitute a majority of the population, but it is more evenly distributed across all 27 *oblasty* (provinces) of the country than are the various Orthodox and Uniate parishes, perhaps more so than even the Pentecostals, another free church Protestant tradition now claiming nearly as many members (→ Pentecostal Churches; Pentecostalism).

1. The Principal Christian Groups

In a nominal sense, the UOC-MP claims nearly half the population of nearly 50 million. It has 10,384 parishes, which is only slightly fewer than the 11,525 parishes now registered in the sprawling Russian Federation (pop.: 150 million). The UOC-KP, canonically unrecognized by Moscow or by the → Ecumenical Patriarchate, claims 3,395 parishes. The Ukrainian Autocephalous Orthodox Church (UAOC) has 1,156 parishes. The Greek Catholic (Uniate), with 3,340 parishes, represents 10 percent of the population, with another million in 863 Roman Catholic parishes. The Baptist Union has 2,517 registered congregations, the Pentecostals 1,597. In terms of active participation in religious practice, the Orthodox rate lowest and the free churches highest, an indication that counting parishes or congregations is an uneven measure of religious influence.

Geographically, Ukraine's 27 *oblasty* constitute the same territory as the Ukrainian Soviet Socialist Republic (1945-91). The eastern half, long designated "new Russia" after Russia claimed it from the Ottoman Empire in 1776, was peopled by peasants from other regions and drew even more during the industrial boom of the early Soviet period. Linguistically, Russian was the official language. After 1990 Ukrainian became the official language and was taught in the schools, yet even in 2007 the eastern half spoke mainly Russian, whereas western provinces were forgetting Russian, since the predominant foreign language learned was English. Diverse views on the reality of Ukraine range from intense nationalism (perhaps most strongly asserted by immigrants to Canada and the United States) to those stressing the inseparability of Russia, Belarus, and Ukraine.

The general public remains insufficiently aware of the realities of religious → pluralism, because of uneven public education. Nevertheless, the social and political influence of religion is such that today politicians are taking the trouble to cultivate the goodwill of all of these major churches, quite in contrast to the Soviet years. Orthodox culture permeates through the symbolism of its buildings, feast days, and popular definitions of what is essential to being Ukrainian. The Uniates have played a symbolic role for suppressed Ukrainianism, though

Uniatism also signified strong links to Rome. The Baptists and the Pentecostals, in contrast, have a reputation for high-intensity → piety, expressed in regular and frequent worship attendance. Their worship and church programs are democratic and modern. Known for demanding high moral standards of all members, they have also shown greater interest in social reforms during the latest period of greater freedom of religion, so far expressed through projects to care for orphans, seniors, and street people, as well as through poverty assistance. → Worship in all of these churches is currently conducted in Ukrainian or Russian, depending on the social context.

2. History
2.1. *Christian Roots*
Ukraine's official Christian history started in 988, when Grand Prince Vladimir (ruled 985-1015) of what was then known as Rus ordered the people into the Dnieper River in Kiev for a mass baptism. The *Primary Chronicle* (compiled in Kiev in the early 12th cent.) records a story of Vladimir making a deliberate choice of the best religion by sending emissaries to explore Judaism, Islam, Roman Catholicism, and Byzantine Orthodoxy. The emissaries' report rejected → Judaism as too legalist, → Islam as dirty and uncouth (as experienced in the Khazar kingdom to the east), and → Catholicism as too cold and formal (as experienced in Cologne in winter). But when the emissaries got to the Hagia Sophia cathedral in Constantinople, they felt themselves transported to heaven; never had they experienced such beauty — the iconography, frescoes, and grandeur of the liturgy spoke to all five senses.

Christianity had preceded the first baptism, as has often been true of other "firsts." The Slavs have long claimed that the apostle Andrew, the first missionary (who brought his brother Peter to Jesus), raised the cross of Christ on the shores of the Black Sea. In 325 a bishop sent missionaries to the area between the Danube and the Caucasus, to what the chronicler called the "Hunnic-Turkic migrants." There also was the tradition of mission to the Slavs by Cyril (ca. 827-69) and Methodius (ca. 815-85), and of Clement of Ochrid (ca. 840-916) shaping what became known as the Cyrillic script (→ Slavic Mission). The extensive translation output of the Preslav school (in eastern Bulgaria) established the script that the Ukrainians and Russians later adapted. There had been earlier ties to Byzantium, and Vladimir's mother, Olga, was a Christian.

Christianity took root and spread, only in part because of its being the new official religion. Hermit monks, starting with Anthony, who founded the Kievskaia Pecherskaia Lavra (Kiev Monastery of the Caves) on the hills outside Kiev in 1051, and Theodosius, as its organizer, set the standards for the piety of the next several centuries. In his own → spirituality, Theodosius made the kenotic ideal pivotal (following the → kenosis of Christ). It was expressed in three cardinal Christian virtues: poverty, humility, and agape love. The Christianity of Rus has been characterized as a religion of → ethics. Nonresistance is the theme associated with the first two saints, Boris and Gleb (early 11th cent.), so revered by the people and in 1071 canonized by the church. It was their death that was remembered, rather than their pious lives. Boris consciously chose not to resist the aggression of his older brother Sviatopolk in a succession struggle, and Gleb was still a boy when he was caught in a boat and his throat was cut by his cook. In his classic work on Russian spirituality, Georgy Fedotov (1886-1951) concluded that "the act of nonresistance is a national Russian feature, an authentic religious discovery of the newly converted Russian Christians. . . . Through the lives of the holy sufferers as through the Gospels, the image of the meek and suffering Savior entered the heart of the Russian nation as the most holy of its spiritual treasures" (1.104).

This era ended in 1237 with the invasion of the Mongols, who leveled Kievan Rus, scattering the survivors westward and northward. Until the defeat of the Mongols in 1448, Orthodox Christianity was still able to function, although under constraints. Clergy were forced to pray for the khan but were spared some of the exorbitant taxes extracted from the princes in annual submission rites in Sarai. This era of difficulty enabled the flourishing of → monasticism, especially also the new → Hesychasm. The Mongol era is thus associated with Sergius of Radonezh (ca. 1314-92), with other missionary monks like Cyril of Turov (ca. 1130-82) and Stephen of Perm (1340-96), and with iconographers like Theophanes the Greek (ca. 1330/40-1405) and Andrei Rublev (b. 1360 to 1370, d. ca. 1430).

2.2. *Orthodox–Roman Catholic Separation*
The tensions between → Byzantium and → Rome after the schism of 1054 were played out in the territory of Ukraine. When Byzantium became surrounded by the expanding Ottoman Empire, and even its regular contacts with the Orthodox church under Mongol overlordship were imperiled, its patriarch agreed to a council with the papal (not conciliar) side of the → Roman Catholic Church, a council later known as the Council of Florence (1439; → Councils of the Church 3). That council

ended with a reunion of the churches, on the principle of acceptance of papal supremacy and a series of compromises that included granting local rites (rather than Latin) in worship and giving clergy the right to marry.

Once the Byzantine and other Eastern delegations returned home, however, they rejected what they called a forced union. Isidore (ca. 1385-1463), metropolitan of Kiev, a signatory of the union who was made a cardinal by the pope, returned home to find himself rejected. He ended his days as a papal legate, attempting to foster the union on the western edge of Slavic lands. Even the ecumenically open Alexander Schmemann (1921-83) spoke of the Council of Florence as "cowardly error" and "complete capitulation to Rome" (p. 254).

This perceived "sacrifice of Orthodoxy" stimulated support for the rise of the bishop in Moscow to leadership, first autocephaly (1448), in light of the fall of Constantinople to the Ottomans (1453), and then the claim to the Patriarchate of Moscow and all Russia in 1589, which was soon recognized by the Eastern patriarchates. This occurred during the Time of Troubles (1598-1613), when the Catholic Polish-Lithuanian commonwealth threatened to control Muscovy. In the end, the Russian patriarch, Philaret (ca. 1553-1633), crowned his son Michael (czar 1613-45) to establish the Romanov line. Eventually the Russian Empire came to dominate what was left of Lithuania and Poland.

2.3. *Eastern Rite Catholics (Uniates)*

For the story of the Eastern Rite Catholics (Oriental in rite and canon, but Roman in ecclesial allegiance), there followed the more important Union of Brest (1596), which marked the new beginning of Uniate churches in Slavic territory. A conflict arose in western Ukrainian territory between Uniate bishops and local Orthodox priests. Then in 1620 a visiting Orthodox patriarch, Theophanes of Jerusalem, secretly ordained seven bishops for Orthodoxy. Out of this context emerged Peter Mogila (1596-1646), a graduate of the Sorbonne (Latin educated) but Orthodox, who started a Latin school in Kiev and, in a confession attributed to him, left a theological legacy for Orthodoxy in Ukraine more consciously influenced by Catholic theology. Till the end of the 18th century the school in Kiev supplied educated bishops for Russian Orthodoxy as a whole. (Ukrainian-origin clerics were disproportionately strong on the Holy Synod.) Feofan Prokopovich (1681-1736), for example, after schooling in Kiev, studied at a Uniate college in Rome, where he learned to dislike the papacy. His influence in drafting the spiritual regulation that was to guide the

Russian Holy Synod (1721-1917) reveals the way Western ideas mixed with those of Eastern Orthodoxy.

During the reign of Alexander I (1801-25) the Uniates, strongly guided for a time by the Bazilian order of monks, experienced extensive tolerance. At the same time, Roman Catholics inside the empire (in Polish and Lithuanian territories), through the skilled leadership of Archbishop (soon Metropolitan) Siestrzencewicz-Bohusz (1731-1826), a Lithuanian aristocrat, gained great influence. His work somewhat replaced the influence of the → Jesuits, banned at this time, who had trained many Russian aristocrats between 1773 and 1820. By 1825 the number of Uniate parishes had increased to 1,466, which was 50 percent more than the number of parishes under the control of the Roman Catholic metropolitan.

Apparently because of insufficiently pro-Russian sympathies during the Polish uprising of 1830-31, the Uniates were forced in 1839 to be absorbed into Orthodoxy. It was a political interference resisted by the faithful. Such a forced integration was repeated with more tragic consequences in 1946, thereafter making the Uniate church the largest illegal church in the Soviet Union till 1989. Those memories of underground resistance fueled the recovery of Eastern Catholics in the post-Soviet era. It fostered the conviction that Catholic opposition to Communism in Poland had been the right approach to → revolution, and it helps explain the pro-Western or anti-Russian orientation of the western part of the Ukraine.

3. Twentieth-Century Developments

Two interrelated developments in the 20th century left a lasting impression. One was the lopsided predominance of Christians in the western part of the USSR. When the Soviet Union withdrew from World War I in early 1918 (Brest-Litovsk), it agreed to a boundary that left much of western Ukraine, Catholic Lithuania, and the Baltic states independent or under Polish control. Between 1918 and 1945 this area became one of free religious practice and growth, in particular of Baptist and Pentecostal churches. Incorporated into the USSR in 1945, these annexed territories contained well over half of all the practicing Christians now in the USSR. These believers now experienced the Stalinist repressions that during the 1930s had resulted in an astounding number of → martyrs (several million killed, millions more in the gulag). Repressions included forcible resettling of millions from the Ukraine to the eastern regions of exile (Siberia and central Asia).

An unintended consequence was the spread of Christian practice, the Roman Catholic Church claiming rights (esp. after 1990) to supply priests or missionaries for its people as far away as Magadan, on the Sea of Okhotsk, on the eastern edge of Russia. Baptists and Pentecostals with experienced leaders trained in the interwar years provided leadership to church growth across the eastern half of the USSR. Similarly, better trained priests from Orthodox churches served their people in central Asia and Siberia. For evangelical Protestants, the resettlements also account for the unusually active missionary outreach from Ukraine to places like Yakutia and Vladivostok since 1990, for these groups already had contacts in these places. The evangelical Protestants, still with half their number in Ukraine and compared with Protestants in the rest of the former Soviet Union, established a disproportionately high number of theological schools, publishing ventures, and missionary societies.

The second, more fateful development was a Uniate and Roman Catholic Church that had regained ground in the interwar years, with well-trained clergy, but that became a persecuted church in the period from 1945 to 1990. The Uniates were officially united to Russian Orthodoxy in 1946, a coerced union orchestrated by the KGB. Father Havryil Kostel'nyk (1886-1948) was forced (by holding a child hostage) to call a church council for January 1946. Metropolitan Josyf Slipyi (1892-1984) and all the bishops had just been arrested. Two unmarried priests were hastily consecrated bishops, a "pseudocouncil" met in March 1946, annulled the Union of Brest, and joined the Moscow Patriarchate. Then later the KGB covered their tracks by eliminating Kostel'nyk in a drive-by shooting. Russian Orthodox leaders were pressured to bless the union and tried to see it as just retribution for the forced union of Florence of 1439. There were many clashes (including physical violence) during the post-Soviet years over access to church buildings and other property.

4. Current Tensions

Attempts at Catholic–Russian Orthodox rapprochement after 1990 began with a rejection of the Uniate option as a basis for full recognition of each other as sister churches (Freising 1990 and Balamond 1993). This was followed by Rome's renewed effort to provide → pastoral care and → missionaries for the diaspora across Ukraine and Russia, and then by the naming of bishops, which resulted in a virtual breakdown of relations. The Moscow Patriarchate publicly requested John Paul II not to visit Ukraine, but he did so anyway, in June 2001. Tensions were easing at the time of his death (2005), and regular meetings of a Catholic–Russian Orthodox consultation resumed. Ukrainian Greek Catholic leaders, however, felt slighted and remained worried. The persistent efforts of Uniate ecumenists, supported by their synod and patriarch, to seek dialogue with the Moscow Patriarchate were rebuffed. As late as 2003 Patriarch Alexis II still insisted that the L'viv Council of 1946 dissolving the Uniates was canonical.

Confessional pluralism has thus had a long, contorted history in Ukraine. An even greater pluralism today remains contested.

Bibliography: Orthodoxy: S. K. Batalden, ed., *Seeking God: The Recovery of Religious Identity in Orthodox Russia, Ukraine, and Georgia* (De Kalb, Ill., 1993) • N. Mitrokhin, *Russkaia Pravoslavnaia Tserkov. Sovremennoe sostoianie i aktual'nie problemy* (Russian Orthodox Church. Contemporary status and problems) (Moscow, 2006) a sociological study, with latest statistics on Ukraine • D. Pospielovsky, *The Orthodox Church in the History of Russia* (Crestwood, N.Y., 1998) • A. Schmemann, *The Historical Road of Eastern Orthodoxy* (ed. L. W. Kesich; Crestwood, N.Y., 1977) • A. Yurach, "Orthodoxy and the 2004 Ukrainian Presidential Electoral Campaign," *RelStSo* 33/4 (2005) 367-86.

Catholics, Ukrainian and Roman: B. R. Bociurkiw, *Ukrainian Churches under Soviet Rule: Two Case Studies* (Cambridge, Mass., 1984); idem, *The Ukrainian Greek Catholic Church and the Soviet State (1939-1950)* (Edmonton, 1996) • S. Keleher, "Response to Sophia Senyk, 'The Ukrainian Greek Catholic Church Today: Universal Values versus Nationalist Doctrines,'" *RelStSo* 31/3 (2003) 289-306 (a broad rehearsing of the debates and evidence for the role of the Ukrainian Greek Catholic Church and its forced absorption into the Moscow Patriarchate in 1946) • S. Plokhy, *The Cossacks and Religion in Early Modern Ukraine* (New York, 2001) • P. Ramet, ed., *Catholicism and Politics in Communist Societies* (Durham, N.C., 1990); idem, ed., *Eastern Christianity and Politics in the Twentieth Century* (Durham, N.C., 1988).

Protestants/evangelicals and new religions: L. Filipovich, "Tendencies of Change and Growth of New Religious Movements in Ukraine," *RelEE* 19/5 (1999) 29-44 • S. P. Ramet, ed., *Protestantism and Politics in Eastern Europe and Russia: The Postcommunist Eras* (Durham, N.C., 1992) • W. Sawatsky, *Soviet Evangelicals since World War II* (Scottdale, Pa., 1981) • W. Sawatsky and P. F. Penner, eds., *Mission in the Former Soviet Union* (Schwarzenfeld, Ger., 2005) • C. Wanner, "Advocating New Moralities: Conversion to Evangelicalism in Ukraine," *RelStSo* 31/3 (September 2003) 273-88 • S. I.

Zhuk, *Russia's Lost Reformation: Peasants, Millennialism, and Radical Sects in Southern Russia and Ukraine, 1830-1917* (Baltimore, 2004).

General studies and other topics: W. van den Bercken, "Theological Education for Laypeople in Russia, Belarus, and Ukraine: A Survey of Orthodox and Catholic Institutions," *RelStSo* 32/3 (September 2004) 299-311 • G. Fedotov, *The Russian Religious Mind* (2 vols.; Cambridge, Mass., 1946-66) • H. Fild, *Zwischen Odessa und Kasachstan. Aspekte Zum Weg der Deutschen Evangelischen und Katholischen Gemeinden in der Ukraine* (2d ed.; Erlangen, 1996) • L. Filipovich and A. Koɪodny, "Theology and Religious Studies in Post-Communist Ukraine: Historical Sources, Modern Status, and Perspectives of Cooperation," *RelEE* 23/6 (2003) 1-20 • G. A. Hosking, ed., *Church, Nation, and State in Russia and Ukraine* (New York, 1991) • A. Kolodniy, "Traditional Faith in Ukraine and Missionary Activity," *RelEE* 20/1 (2000) 20-45 • S. Plokhy and F. E. Sysyn, *Religion and Nation in Modern Ukraine* (Edmonton, 2003) • S. P. Ramet, *Nihil Obstat: Religion, Politics, and Social Change in East-Central Europe and Russia* (Durham, N.C., 1998).

Walter Sawatsky

Ultramontanism

In the 18th century the term "Ultramontanism" (Lat. "beyond the mountains," here meaning the Alps) came into polemical use to describe a European Roman Catholicism that was oriented to the → pope. The movement developed historically in reaction to national church movements such as → Gallicanism, and theologically in opposition to the theses of Justinus Febronius (pseud. of J. N. von Hontheim [1701-90]) that would exalt the rights of → bishops at the expense of the papacy (→ Episcopacy 1). Those who supported papal → infallibility and papalism were Ultramontanists. Most of the interest centered on the relations between the church and the → curia. National concerns also played a part, for it was assumed that the Ultramontanists could not be good citizens (→ Nation, Nationalism).

The word quickly became a fighting slogan when the 19th-century political → restoration after the overthrow of Napoléon (→ Romanticism) heightened ecclesiastical and intellectual tensions, especially in France. As secular support for the freedom of the church collapsed, many circles, especially among the clergy, began to look almost automatically to their spiritual center at → Rome, to the pope (→ Roman Catholic Church 1). The popes them-selves made greater efforts to achieve universal control of the church. Tension developed between (1) the national states as these became increasingly liberal (→ Liberalism) and thought of the churches as national and (2) theological concerns to uphold traditional doctrine, especially in ecclesiology (→ Dogma). J. M. de Maistre (1753-1821) saw in an absolute and infallible pope the crown of Catholicism (*Du Pape* [1819]). H. F. R. Lamennais (1782-1854) thought that the church alone was the source of → truth and → authority but that there could be no church without the pope as the supreme court of appeal. The movement of liturgical renewal started by P. Guéranger (1805-75) also directed the attention of masses of believers directly to Rome.

In Germany various events such as the church controversy in Cologne after 1835 brought about a mobilization of the laity, which assumed direct political form (Centrum Party) and allowed Ultramontanism to become a problem of → church and state (→ Kulturkampf). Further theological as well as intellectual developments led to the Ultramontanist movement becoming an ecclesiological system, solidified in the sense of the statement of 1788 that "only what is Ultramontanist is Catholic" (H. Raab, 173; → Syllabus; Neoscholasticism), as it was then promulgated as official teaching in the decisions of Vatican I. New approaches did not appear until Vatican II, with its emphasis on a *communio* ecclesiology (→ Church 3.2). They have come, however, to little effect.

Bibliography: P. Bryne, "American Ultramontanism," *TS* 56 (1995) 301-26 • K. Buchheim, *Ultramontanismus und Demokratie. Der Weg der deutschen Katholiken im 19. Jahrhundert* (Munich, 1963) • J. B. Bury, *History of the Papacy in the Nineteenth Century* (London, 1930) • R. F. Costigan, *Rohrbacher and the Ecclesiology of Ultramontanism* (Rome, 1980) • A. Gough, *Rome and Paris: The Gallican Church and the Ultramontane Campaign, 1848-1853* (Oxford, 1986) • R. Lill, "Der Ultramontanismus," *Kirche im 19. Jahrhundert* (ed. M. Weitlauff; Regensburg, 1998) 76-94 • M. Mergel, "Ultramontanism, Liberalism, Moderation," *CEurH* 29 (1996) 151-74 • F. Nielsen, *The History of the Papacy in the XIXth Century* (2 vols.; New York, 1906) • H. J. Pottmeyer, *Unfehlbarkeit und Souveränität. Die päpstliche Unfehlbarkeit im System der ultramontanen Ekklesiologie des 19. Jahrhunderts* (Mainz, 1975) • H. Raab, "Zur Geschichte und Bedeutung des Schlagwortes 'ultramontan' im 18. und frühen 19. Jahrhundert," *HJ* 81 (1962) 159-73 • J. Von Arx, ed., *Varieties of Ultramontanism* (Washington, D.C., 1998) • C. Weber, "Ultramontanismus als katholische Fundamentalismus," *Der Katholizismus im Umbruch zur Moderne* (ed. W. Loth; Stuttgart, 1991) 20-45.

HUBERT KIRCHNER

Umbanda

Umbanda is a new and consciously syncretistic (→ Syncretism) religion of Brazil. It is also a name for religious groups of Afro-Brazilian origin. Indian spirituality and elements of → popular Catholicism (worship of the saints) contribute to it, along with → spiritism, which is widespread in Brazil. The basis and historical starting point, however, are the structurally different African traditions of the originally northern Brazilian Candomblé (priestly type, West African religions) and the southern Macumba (healer type, Bantu religions), which came together under the mantle of the slave veneration of saints (→ Slavery) and achieved recognition with the granting of religious liberty in 1892. With the spread across all Brazil, many different religious elements were adopted, and after 1930 white Brazilians who had a tradition of spiritism tried to provide an integrated theoretical superstructure. The number of cultic sites *(terreiros)* and practitioners is difficult to estimate. In the 1960s there were 50,000 *terreiros,* a number that by the early 1980s had risen to 300,000. Perhaps half or more of the total Brazilian population take part at some level.

Umbanda sees itself as *the* → religion, not only because it exists in all religions, but above all because it stands above all religions and races, uniting them all. It is thus the religion of the future. Olorun (Father God) is the supreme being and the source of all salvation. He is in command of all good powers *(orishas)* and with their help can lead people to salvation. The chief of these powers is Oshala (Jesus Christ), who with Olorun works through the oracle-*orisha* Ifa (Holy Spirit). Ifa spiritually empowers people, giving them assurance of the presence of the *orishas* and helping them toward self-perfection as the salvation that is sought. The *orishas* are integrated into seven *linhas,* which form seven *falanges.* The *linhas* are led by Oshala (Christ), Yemanja (Mary), Oshun (John the Baptist), Oshossi (St. Sebastian), Shango (St. Jerome), Ogum (St. George), and Omolu (St. Cyprian).

Alongside them we find the *eshus,* or spirits of evil, which can be overcome with the help of the *orishas* (esp. in the cult). Dealings with the *orishas* helps to preserve or restore salvation and also to secure and enhance it. Umbanda is a this-worldly system aiming at salvation here and now. For this reason the cult is a saving action in the presence of the *orishas,* who manifest themselves through mediums *(filhas-* and *filhos-de-santo).* Conducting the cult is the task of the *alufá,* or *babalorisha* (priest) or *iyalorisha* (priestess), who have gone through all the rites of initiation. Their chief tasks are to "open the *terreiros*" and to identify and interpret the *orishas* and saints who are revealed there. They can diagnose various ills and offer therapy. They act as both mediums and cultic functionaries. The cult includes → dances, → offerings (of food, drink, and animals), signs (oracles), preaching, liturgical songs, joint prayers, prayers at the altar, and pictures of the *orishas.*

Umbanda is not highly organized, though efforts have been made to form village unions. Meetings take place at the individual *terreiros,* each of which has its own cultic hierarchy. At the head is a president who represents the congregation to outsiders. Then there are the priests and priestesses. Next are the *ogans,* who direct the liturgical offerings. Then come the *filhas-* and *filhos-de-santo,* next the *indiciandos* (those waiting for initiation), then the *noviços* (novices), and finally the *sambas* and *cambones* (helpers). The congregation divides itself sharply between members and clients in need of help. The calendar is based on the Roman Catholic → church year.

Bibliography: R. BASTIDE, *The African Religions of Brazil: Toward a Sociology of the Interpenetration of Civilizations* (Baltimore, 1978) • D. D. BROWN, *Umbanda: Religion and Politics in Urban Brazil* (New York, 1994) • F. G. BRUMANA, *Spirits from the Margin: Umbanda in São Paulo; A Study in Popular Religion and Social Experience* (Uppsala, 1989) • H. H. FIGGE, *Geisterkult, Besessenheit und Magie in der Umbanda-Religion Brasiliens* (Freiburg, 1973) • U. FISCHER, *Zur Liturgie des Umbandakultes* (Leiden, 1970) • R. FLASCHE, *Geschichte und Typologie afrikanischer Religiosität in Brasilien* (Marburg, 1973) • Y. MAGGIE, "Afro-Brazilian Cults," *EncRel(E)* 1.102-4 • A. DO NASCIMENTO, *Orixás: Os deuses vivos da Africa / The Living Gods of Africa in Brazil* (Rio de Janeiro, 1995) • L. WEINGÄRTNER, *Umbanda. Synkretistische Kulte in Brasilien–eine Herausforderung für die christliche Kirche* (Erlangen, 1969).

RAINER FLASCHE

Una Sancta Movement

1. Name
2. History
3. Importance and Influence

1. Name

In Germany the Una Sancta movement — one of ecumenical awakening between the rise of National Socialism ($\to$ Fascism) and $\to$ Vatican II — was specifically ecclesiological, spiritual, and dialogic, and it embraced Protestant and Roman Catholic theologians, pastors, and laity, both men and women. In the worldwide 20th-century ecumenical movement the Una Sancta movement was part of the surge of interdenominational efforts that had arisen in the 19th century and that sought to renew the historical shape of the church so that it would be, as the $\to$ Niceno-Constantinopolitan Creed put it, the one *(una)*, holy *(sancta)*, catholic, and apostolic object of Christian belief ($\to$ Church 1.1). The programmatic use of "the slogan *una sancta*" (A. Deissmann) was typical of ecumenical efforts based on the underlying conviction (1) that the one church as the Spirit-inspired body of Christ, resting on the one inalienable sacramental reality of baptism ($\to$ Sacramentality), is still existing, even though it is divided into separated $\to$ denominations; (2) that the catholicity of the church is fully actualized in none of these denominations; (3) that the various confessional branches of the church need to come to "corporate" unity; and (4) that something essential is lacking in the $\to$ oikoumene without the $\to$ Roman Catholic Church and some form of a universal ministry of $\to$ unity ($\to$ Pope, Papacy).

The Roman Catholic Church, however, claimed to be the only true church and would not participate in the ecumenical movement (encyclical *Mortalium animos* [1928]). In its view, unity would come only through individual $\to$ conversions (§2) to Rome. Only after Vatican II were other denominations seen as ecclesial societies leading to salvation ($\to$ Ecumenism, Ecumenical Movement).

2. History

2.1. The Anglo-Catholic movement in the 19th century ($\to$ Oxford Movement) held a so-called branch theory that led to the founding of the *Union Review* (1856) and the Association for the Promotion of the Union of Christendom (1857). (By this theory, separated churches are like branches of Christ's one true church; in order to realize the whole apostolic tradition, they must come together as "united but not absorbed churches.") These efforts came to an end in 1864, when Roman Catholics were forbidden to participate. In 1888 the bishops of the $\to$ Anglican Communion (§4.1) published the Lambeth Quadrilateral (referring to Scripture, creeds, the sacraments of baptism and Eucharist, and

the historic episcopate) as the basis of unity. This move had repercussions in both France (see 2.3) and Germany (see 2.4).

2.2. All these efforts contributed to making a visible church $\to$ unity (§1) the goal of the ecumenical movement. This focus could be seen at the World Conference on Faith and Order in Lausanne (1927), which M. J. Metzger (1887-1944), then coordinator of the Una Sancta movement, attended as a Roman Catholic observer. Indeed, the Universal Christian Conference on Life and Work at Stockholm (1925) had borne witness to the same aim. Archbishop N. $\to$ Söderblom (1866-1931), the initiator of this conference, had coined the phrase $\to$ "evangelical Catholicity" ($\to$ Catholic, Catholicity, 3.2), comparing the three great confessional traditions — Roman Catholic, Orthodox, and Protestant — to the testimonies of the apostles Peter, John, and Paul.

From 1917 onward Metzger became one of the leaders of the international $\to$ peace movement and made contact with the founder of the $\to$ International Fellowship of Reconciliation, F. Siegmund-Schultze (1885-1969), who worked very closely with Söderblom in preparing for the Stockholm conference. Like Siegmund-Schultze, Metzger first focused on social work, and from there he came to work for peace and for ecumenical unity. For Metzger, these two things were not to be divided in the "peace in Christ's kingdom." In 1944 his proposal for peace led to his execution by the National Socialist regime.

2.3. For the Una Sancta movement, several effective incentives also came from France. First, Belgian cardinal D. Mercier (1851-1926) organized the Mechlin Conversations (1921-25), unofficial discussions between Anglicans and Roman Catholics about ecumenical reunion. Second, Russian Orthodox emigrants living in France conceived of the church as *sobornost* ($\to$ European Theology [Modern Period] 1.2.6). Third, the Benedictines of the "union monastery" of Amay (founded in 1925, moved to Chevetogne in 1939) were working for the recognition of the Orthodox tradition in the Catholic Church, publishing the periodical *Irénikon*. Fourth, in 1935 P. Couturier (1881-1953) issued a call for common $\to$ prayer (esp. in the ecumenical week of prayer) for the coming of the visible unity of the kingdom of God in the nature and in the time that Christ wants. Finally, Y. M.-J. Congar (1904-95) pleaded in his "Principles of a Catholic Ecumenism" for a catholicity that would recognize the positive worth of all confessions.

2.4. The German High Church movement (from 1918) sought to restore the catholicity of the early church in the Lutheran church. The result was the formation of the High Church Ecumenical Association, which sought conversations with Roman Catholics. A. von Martin edited the journal *Una Sancta* (1924-27). After reintegration into the High Church Union, and under the leadership of F. Heiler (1892-1967), its goal was a Protestant as well as an ecumenical catholicity. *Die Hochkirche* was the periodical, changed in 1934 to *Eine heilige Kirche.* Parallel movements were the Berneuchener Circle, formed in 1923 and led by K. B. Ritter and W. Stählin and, after World War II, the struggle of H. Asmussen (1898-1968), who edited the periodical *Die Sammlung* from 1954 to 1963. Protestant communities and fraternities were also formed.

Forerunners on the Roman Catholic side, supported by the journals *Hochland* and *Stimmen der Zeit,* were many movements of church renewal, as well as the biblical and → liturgical movements and the revision of the Catholic understanding of Martin → Luther (1483-1546) and of the → Reformation (J. Lortz). Furthermore, there was a rising consciousness that the catholicity in the Roman Catholic Church was realized only in a "narrowly catholicistic" manner (A. Rademacher).

Initiated by Heiler and sponsored by Bishop N. Bares (1871-1935), a first conversation was held between Protestant and Roman Catholic theologians at Berlin-Hermsdorf in 1934. L. Jaeger (1892-1975), archbishop of Paderborn and after 1943 the representative of the German Bishops' Conference on questions of reunion, now made it his aim to promote ecumenical discussion. In 1946 he started the Ecumenical Working Circle of Protestant and Catholic Theologians (the so-called Jaeger-Stählin Circle), and in 1957 he founded the Johann Adam Möhler Institute in Paderborn, which took over the journal *Catholica* (founded by R. Grosche in 1932).

3. Importance and Influence

The many local Una Sancta circles were centers of → local ecumenism where Protestants and Roman Catholics met freely and could openly discuss denominational misunderstandings and prejudices. They focused on what is common to all believers. They also joined in prayer as a sign of "hoping against hope" (Rom. 4:18). They believed, too, that the struggle for unity must include a struggle for holiness in the form of repentance, humility, respect, and love. Metzger, untiringly active in lecturing and writing, was at the heart of Una Sancta. He set up Christkönigshaus (House of Christ the King) at Meitingen in 1928. In 1938 he named the Una Sancta movement the Fraternity of Una Sancta — not an organization, but an expression of reawak-

ened consciousness of fraternity in Christ as transcending all differences. The circular letters since 1946 collected by M. Laros were developed, beginning in 1953, in concert with the Ecumenical Institute of the Benedictine abbey of Niederaltaich (Abbot E. Heufelder), into *Una Sancta,* a periodical of ecumenical conversations edited at first by D. Sartory, then by A. Ahlbrecht (1963-67) and G. Voss (1968-2002), and now by E. Dieckmann.

The experiences shared in the period of National Socialism, World War II, and the postwar disruptions, as well as the increasing number of → mixed marriages, brought about a new interest in the Una Sancta movement. But criticism also arose. Protestants feared hidden → proselytism; Roman Catholics, indifference. In 1948 Rome more sternly forbade Roman Catholics to participate in ecumenical gatherings. They were afraid of a Una Sancta movement that was "running wild." Yet how far ecumenism had advanced at the grass roots even before Vatican II became evident from the success of the Una Sancta event at the 1960 World Eucharistic Congress, in Munich. After Vatican II, Christians with experience in the Una Sancta movement were especially valuable members of the new ecumenical bodies in the churches. But also in the future the official ecumenical bodies in the churches will have to be in dialogue with the ecumenical experiences of grassroot groups. Thus, as a follow-up to the Una Sancta movement, the Arbeitsgemeinschaft ökumenischer Kreise (Council of ecumenical groups) was set up in 1969.

Bibliography: Y. Congar, *Divided Christendom: A Catholic Study of the Problem of Reunion* (London, 1939) • H. Hartog, *Evangelische Katholizität. Weg und Vision Friedrich Heilers* (Mainz, 1995) • M. Laros, *Schöpferischer Friede der Konfessionen. Die Una-Sancta-Bewegung, ihr Ziel und ihre Arbeit* (Recklinghausen, 1950) • J. Lortz, *The Reformation in Germany* (2 vols.; London, 1968) • H. Petri, "Die römisch-katholische Kirche und die Ökumene," *HÖ* 2.95-135 • L. J. Swidler, *Bloodwitness for Peace and Unity: Life of M. J. Metzger* (Denville, N.J., 1977); idem, *The Ecumenical Vanguard: The History of the Una Sancta Movement* (Pittsburgh, 1966) • G. H. Tavard, *Two Centuries of Ecumenism* (Westport, Conn., 1978; orig. pub., 1960).

Gerhard Voss

Unction → **Anointing**

Underworld → **Hell**

Unemployment

1. Definition and Causes
2. Level, Distribution, and Effects
3. The Church and Unemployment

1. Definition and Causes

Those who are over a certain age (often the maximum age of mandatory school attendance), who are totally without work, and who are available for work and actively seeking it are considered unemployed by the International Labor Organization (ILO) and most countries collecting statistics on unemployment. Those who work at all for pay (and often those who work without pay in family businesses) are considered employed. The unemployment rate is the number of unemployed as a percentage of the total number of those employed and unemployed (→ Work).

Although unemployment can exist in all types of economies, including both market and centrally controlled economies and heavily industrial, service, and agricultural economies, its existence in market-dominated, industrial/service economies receives the most analysis by economists. In such economies they often distinguish between different types of unemployment, caused by different factors (→ Industrial Society; Service Society).

Frictional unemployment (i.e., of people temporarily between jobs or searching for new ones) exists because it takes a person who is out of work time to find and start a job, even when a suitable job is available for the person. This type is usually of short duration.

Structural unemployment exists when those looking for jobs are for some reason not suitable to employers looking for workers (e.g., they may not have the desired skills, experience, location, age, sex, or race). This mismatch between available workers and employers' demands may be caused by technological change, international trade patterns, demographic changes, lack of education and training required for the available job openings, and discrimination (→ Racism). This type tends to be long-term unemployment, often lasting more than a year, because it takes time for workers to change their characteristics to meet the demands of employers (if indeed they can) or for employers to adjust their demands to the available supply of workers.

Cyclical (also called *demand-deficient*) *unemployment* occurs when total demand for goods and services in the economy is not sufficient to require employment of all those wishing to work who are not structurally or frictionally unemployed. The amount of this type varies over the business cycle, rising in recessions. It often is long-term unemployment, lasting more than six months or a year for those who suffer from it.

2. Level, Distribution, and Effects

The level of unemployment varies across countries and over time. In the United States the average annual unemployment rate between 1995 and 2005 was about 5 percent. Rates varied during the same period for other high-income countries, with Japan, Luxembourg, the Netherlands, Norway, and Switzerland having rates in the range of 3-4 percent. Higher average unemployment for high-income countries existed in Germany (8 percent), France (10 percent), and Spain (13 percent). (Comparisons here are not necessarily precise, for differences exist in the definitions of "unemployment" used in the various countries.)

Although the unemployment rates in recent decades in high-income countries have not reached the levels of 25 percent or more that occurred in many countries in the 1930s during the Great Depression, many, including the United States, have had rates above 10 percent within the last 25 years. These measured unemployment rates underestimate the problem because they do not include those who are underemployed (e.g., those who desire full-time work but have only part-time work and those who are working in jobs where they are less productive and earn less than they are capable of). In general, unemployment rates are higher for those under 25, those with low levels of education, those who are sick or disabled, and ethnic minorities than for other workers.

Unemployment data for low-income countries is less complete and reliable. By the definitions used in high-income countries, unemployment may be low, since without a social safety-net those without formal employment must engage in some type of informal self-employment (e.g., peddling) in an attempt to earn enough to survive and thus would not be counted as unemployed. But studies of urban unemployment plus underemployment in a number of low-income countries have led to estimates above 30 percent, and there is also much underemployment in rural areas. (The high rates of absolute → poverty in many low-income countries are indirect evidence of high levels of underemployment.)

Unemployment has serious effects on the individuals suffering from it, on their families, and on society as a whole. Economists usually concentrate on the loss of production for the society and the loss of income for the family. The loss of production for society is of more concern for low-income societies, which often cannot produce enough for the basic needs of all of their people, than it is for affluent societies, which can meet all needs if they choose to do so. Long-term unemployment causes particularly severe economic hardship for the families of those who suffer from it, especially in many low-income countries and countries such as the United States, which provide less protection from loss of income and medical care through government social-insurance programs than do most western European countries. But long-term unemployment can have other serious effects as well, for it contributes to higher levels of stress and stress-related diseases, many psychological problems, divorce, and crime.

3. The Church and Unemployment

Statements by both Protestant and Roman Catholic churches emphasize the importance of work for human beings (e.g., see M. Stackhouse et al., chap. 10). Work is a God-given way for people to provide for their families and contribute to the community, to which all human beings are called. It is also an opportunity to reflect the creative God, in whose image they have been made. Thus it is unjust when people are deprived of the opportunity for work that can adequately provide for their families. Church statements call on governments to provide opportunities for employment under conditions of dignity for all and to provide economic support for families when unemployment prevents them from supporting themselves (→ Human Dignity). They also call upon those who control property and thus are able to provide employment opportunities to do so in a just manner.

Churches and other Christian organizations are also involved in directly addressing the problem of unemployment and underemployment in diverse ways. They work to alleviate the economic hardships of unemployment and underemployment by assisting those in need to gain access to food, shelter, medical care, and other necessities when the government does not provide them. And they work to help the unemployed and underemployed to find and keep employment that will provide for their families and support their communities. In high-income countries this help often takes the form of counseling, training, help in job searches, mentoring, and contacting potential employers to encourage them to hire those who have been unemployed or underemployed for long periods of time, or who have other barriers to employment. In low-income countries this aid often takes the form of assisting in the creation of opportunities for more-productive self-employment, for example, through training, formation of cooperatives, and microlending.

→ Economic Ethics

Bibliography: John Paul II, *On Human Work: Laborem Exercens* (Washington, D.C., 1981) • B. Kaufman and J. L. Hotchkiss, *The Economics of Labor Markets* (7th ed.; Mason, Ohio, 2006) information on high-income countries • M. Stackhouse et al., eds., *On Moral Business: Classical and Contemporary Resources for Ethics in Economic Life* (Grand Rapids, 1995) esp. chap. 10 • M. Todaro and S. C. Smith, *Economic Development* (9th ed.; Boston, 2005) information on low-income countries • United Nations Development Program, *Human Development Report, 2006* (New York, 2006). Statistics on unemployment and related topics can be found at the Web sites of the U.S. Department of Labor, Bureau of Labor Statistics (http://www.bls.gov/) and the ILO (http://www.ilo.org/global/What_we_do/Statistics/lang--en/index.htm).

George Monsma

UNESCO

The founding of the United Nations Educational, Scientific, and Cultural Organization (UNESCO) was proposed in 1943 by the Conference of Allied Ministers of Education, which was meeting to seek ways of rebuilding the systems of education crippled by the war. The UNESCO charter was signed in London by 37 countries on November 16, 1945. Its model was the International Committee of Intellectual Co-operation, which the League of Nations had organized in January 1921.

As of October 2005, UNESCO had 191 member states and 6 associate members. Because of tensions between → states, unavoidable considering the cultural diversity of its members, the occasional withdrawal of members was understandable (e.g., South Africa in 1956, Portugal in 1972, the United States in 1984, the United Kingdom in 1985, and Singapore in 1986; the U.K. rejoined in 1997, the U.S. in 2003).

Bodies of UNESCO are the General Conference (comparable to the General Assembly of the → United Nations), which meets every two years; the Executive Board, whose 58 members are elected by the General Conference; and the Secretariat, consisting of the director-general and the staff whom he appoints (in July 2005, it numbered over 2,100 civil servants).

The activities of UNESCO are distinguished by an unusual breadth. The three areas alluded to in its name each have economic, political, and legal aspects. Under → *education* belong efforts to promote education as a fundamental human right (→ Rights) and to improve its quality. Under *science* are programs that address the environment and that promote ethical norms in scientific development. Under → *culture* belong efforts to foster cultural diversity, → pluralism, and → dialogue, as well as, under the heading of → *communication,* to promote universal access to information. (In 1978 UNESCO tried unsuccessfully to create a "New World Information Order," which some member-states saw as an attack on freedom of the press.)

The furthering of education, science, and culture in developing countries makes UNESCO an important organization of development aid (→ Development 1.4). During the East-West conflict UNESCO mediated contacts between the political blocs. Today the connection between North and South (→ Third World) within the scope of the global U.N. system stands in the forefront.

Bibliography: M. CONIL-LACOSTE, *The Story of a Grand Design: UNESCO, 1946-1993* (Paris, 1994) • S. DUTT, *The Politicization of the United Nations Specialized Agencies: A Case Study of UNESCO* (Lewiston, N.Y., 1995) • S. SPAULDING and L. LIN, *Historical Dictionary of the United Nations Educational, Scientific, and Cultural Organization (UNESCO)* (Lanham, Md., 1997) • C. WELLS, *The UN, UNESCO, and the Politics of Knowledge* (New York, 1987).

OTTO KIMMINICH† and THE EDITORS

Uniate Churches

1. Phenomenon
2. Ecclesiology
3. Present Status

1. Phenomenon

So-called Uniate Churches are churches of Eastern Christendom that are in communion with the Roman Catholic Church. The term "uniate" was first used by those opposed to the Union of Brest-Litovsk (1595/96), which brought many Ukrainian Orthodox believers into allegiance with Rome. The churches thus united with Rome, which prefer to call themselves Eastern Catholic (EC) churches, belong to various traditions, following Byzantine, Coptic, Syrian, and other rites.

The several EC churches of the Byzantine tradition, which were given the designation "Greek-Catholic" by the Austrian government in 1773, share similar rites, but they each possess their own national traditions and also have national names. The EC churches differ in size, origin, development, and extent of Latinization (→ Roman Catholic Church 1.3). Failure to observe the distinctions among the EC churches has caused misinterpretations and has led to unfounded accusations among the confessions.

The present EC churches come from one of several Eastern traditions, are bound to the pope as the successor of Peter, and confess a post-Tridentine ecclesiology. In October 1990 John Paul II (1978-2005) promulgated the Codex Canonum Ecclesiarum Orientalium (CCEO, Code of Canons of the Eastern Churches), a common canon law for the EC. Additional accords exist between specific churches.

2. Ecclesiology

2.1. Churches have always made efforts toward → union after division. They could achieve it if they felt themselves equal and if their diverging ideas led to a synodically endorsed synthesis. Often they avoided arduous debate. The historically more powerful church decided unilaterally how agreement would proceed and demanded that the other churches conform. Ecumenism calls this process "Uniatism."

This tactic has been used often since the time of Justinian I (527-65). Following Justinian's victory over the Vandals and the advance of Byzantine armies into Syrian and Armenian territory, the dogmatic formulas (→ Dogma) of the imperial church were forced upon the → heterodox, and in this way a kind of unity was achieved. The consequences were schisms (→ Heresies and Schisms 3) among the Armenians, whether conquered or not. Unions of ancient Oriental Christians with the Byzantines or Latins meant the introduction of the Christological terms of the ecumenical → councils (notably → Chalcedon and → Ephesus) in both liturgy and preaching. The → Crusaders regarded common church customs as the way of ending all schism and required the Greeks to adopt Latin rites, or at least gave them Latin bishops. To have a Latin bishop meant to be "Uniate." But their successors (e.g., native Latin Christians of → Palestine) are no longer today counted as "Uniate" because of extensive Latinization (→ Israel 3.1.2).

2.2. At first Uniatism recognized the ecclesial dignity of churches that became obedient, even if their insights were neglected and alien views were accepted. After the Council of → Trent, however, Roman Catholics began to question the legitimacy of sacramental administration by → bishops and → priests who were not subject to the pope and made a plea for full union with Rome that would confer this legitimacy. These appeals generated indignant responses and were never acquiesced to entirely by any church; there were only partial unions with boundaries that separated dioceses, parishes, and families. Finally, as Roman Catholics wholly disputed the ecclesial existence of the Eastern fellowships, and as the Greek → patriarchs in 1756 declared the baptism of the Roman Catholic Church to be invalid, both sides felt obliged to seek to win over as many as possible from the other.

In the 19th and 20th centuries Roman Catholics founded several small Uniate churches through proselytism. For its part, the Russian Orthodox Church proselytized among the Uniate churches of the East Syrians in Iran and, following the divisions in Poland, among the Uniates there.

2.3. The clear division between EC and Orthodox churches came only later. Well into the 18th century, Roman Catholic missionaries helped to care for Orthodox Christians in Muslim states. They regarded all monks and clergy, even the bishops and priests of churches regarded as schismatic, as part of the one church under their care. The legal order that exists today, which forbids cooperation between the Orthodox and the EC, was instituted in the 18th century. The slow alienation is in contrast to the rapid growth of new churches after Protestant missionaries began work in the Middle East, after Anglicans offered aid to the Thomas Christians of India, and after Russian missionaries went to the East Syrians (→ India 3; Iraq 3; Iran 2).

2.4. To heal the wounds of Uniatism, the seventh plenary session of the Joint International Commission for Theological Dialogue between the Roman Catholic Church and the Orthodox Church, meeting June 17-24, 1993, issued the Balamand Agreement. In it they jointly declared that Uniatism "can no longer be accepted either as a method to be followed nor as a model of the unity our Churches are seeking" (§12). It grants, though, that "the Eastern Catholic Churches, . . . as part of the Catholic Communion, have the right to exist and to act in response to the spiritual needs of their faithful" (§3).

3. Present Status

3.1. Under the conditions of early-modern thinking on → church and state (§1), and on the basis of the decisions of the Council of Ferrara-Florence (1438-ca. 1445; → Councils of the Church 3), the Synod of the Kiev Metropolitanate (then comprising Poland and Lithuania) in 1595 asked for full communion with the Roman Church. Rome did not regard this request as a step by an autonomous

sister church but as a desire by the Ruthenians (Ukrainians and White Russians) for entry into the Roman Church. The difference between application and response provoked resistance, and the metropolitanate broke apart. Instead of full unity, a part of the Ruthenian church transferred to the Roman side in a partial union, and in Poland-Lithuania a clear division arose immediately between EC Christians and the Orthodox. With Russia's expansion, many EC were helped by the state to be united with the church of the czar's empire, something their ancestors had never done. The EC church was able to continue its existence only in the Austrian portion of Poland.

J. Stalin (1879-1953) repressed the EC Christians brutally but could not eradicate them, which was seen clearly when religious freedom came after the end of the Soviet Union and the Ukraine Greek Catholic Church was able again to operate publicly. With approximately 5.5 million members, it is today the largest of the EC churches.

3.2. On the basis of the conciliar decree of Ferrara-Florence, toward the end of the 17th century the Romanian dioceses of Transylvania belonging to the Austrian Empire sought union with the Roman Church (→ Romania 2.1). Because, by Austrian law, this move would have brought social and political emancipation, the Transylvanian estates were opposed to a full union. In Vienna, where the union was negotiated by the primate of Hungary, the thinking of Trent was widespread. The result was a partial union and confrontation with the Orthodox.

3.3. The Arab-speaking EC church of the Melchites is organized as a patriarchate. The Melchites came into being after the Council of Chalcedon. The EC Melchites arose from a divided election in the Orthodox Patriarchate of Antioch 1724. A candidate supported by many Catholic missionaries was voted the Orthodox patriarch. The defeated candidate, however, sought papal confirmation. He received it in 1744 and became the first patriarch of the EC Melchite church.

3.4. Because of changes in borders and national allegiances, it is hardly possible to list the EC churches of the Byzantine Rite. In any case, some of them are very small and cannot really be counted as specific churches. Many — for example, the Greek Byzantine Catholic Church — do not go back to a union agreement but were created for individual converts from the Orthodox Church after the pope allowed them to ordain bishops.

3.5. The Maronite Church is the only Eastern church that preserved its tradition and yet made full union with Roman Catholicism. From the days of the Crusades it has been in unbroken communion with Rome. It is organized as a patriarchate.

3.6. When the Portuguese arrived in India, the Thomas Christians from South India, coming from an East Syrian tradition (the Malabars), entered into full union with them (now the Syro-Malabar Catholic Church). Yet because of a strong pressure to Latinize, part of the church broke away. It accepted bishops of the West Syrian Patriarchate rather than from the East Syrian patriarchate, to which their ancestors were subject. They gradually became accustomed to the West Syrian rite. In 1930 some of them entered into union with Rome as the Syro-Malankara Catholic Church.

3.7. In the 16th century a reforming group of Eastern Syrians (→ Nestorians) sought papal consecration for its bishops. Since then, one part of the East Syrian church, the Chaldeans, has been in union with Rome. The Chaldean Catholic Church is organized as a patriarchate. The Eastern Syrian church that is not allied with Rome is called the Assyrians.

3.8. Other EC churches of the old Eastern tradition include the Coptic Catholic Church, which was honored with a patriarchate in 1895, despite having only a few believers; the (West) Syrian Catholic Church, which resulted from a disputed election in 1781/82 for the Patriarchate of the Syrian Orthodox Church; the Armenian Catholic Church, also a patriarchate; and the Ethiopic Catholic Church, a metropolitanate since 1961.

The Mechitarists are instructive for the history of the EC churches. Mechitar of Sebaste (1676-1749), an Armenian priest, founded the order in Venice "for all Armenians" with the blessing of Pope Clement XI (1700-1721), according to the rule of St. → Benedict. Later a first Armenian Catholic bishop was appointed, to whom the Mechitarists submitted, and they became an order of the EC churches.

Bibliography: General: K. HITCHINS, *A Nation Discovered: Romanian Intellectuals in Transylvania and the Idea of Nation, 1700-1848* (Bucharest, 1999) • J. MARTE, ed., *Internationales Forschungsgespräch der Stiftung PRO Oriente zur Brester Union* (Würzburg, 2004) • G. NEDUNGATT, ed., *A Guide to the Eastern Code: A Commentary on the Code of Canons of the Eastern Churches* (Rome, 2002) • R. G. ROBERSON, *The Eastern Christian Churches* (6th ed.; Rome, 1999) • J. L. ROCCASALVO, *The Eastern Catholic Churches: An Introduction to Their Worship and Spirituality* (Collegeville, Minn., 1992) • D. SCHÖN, *Der Codex Canonum Ecclesiarum Orientalium und das authentische Recht im christlichen Orient* (Würzburg, 1999) • E. C. SUTTNER,

Die Christenheit aus Ost und West auf der Suche nach dem sichtbaren Ausdruck für ihre Einheit (Würzburg, 1999); idem, "Kircheneinheit im 11. bis 13. Jahrhundert durch einen gemeinsamen Patriarchen und gemeinsame Bischöfe für Griechen und Lateiner," *OS* 49 (2000) 314-24; idem, "Metropolit Petr Mogila und die 1644 verfaßte 'Sententia cuiusdam nobilis Poloni graecae religionis' über die Einigung der Kirchen," *OS* 50 (2001) 106-16 • T. R. WEEKS, "Between Rome and Tsargrad: The Uniate Church in Imperial Russia," *Of Religion and Empire: Missions, Conversion, and Tolerance in Tsarist Russia* (ed. R. P. Geraci and M. Khodarkovsky; Ithaca, N.Y., 2001) 70-91.

On the Ukrainian Greek Catholic Church: B. R. BOCIURKIW, "The Ukrainian Catholic Church in the USSR under Gorbachev," *Problems of Communism* 39 (1990) 1-19 • M. MARYNOVYCH, *An Ecumenist Analyzes the History and Prospects of Religion in Ukraine* (L'viv, 2004) • T. M. NÉMETH, *Eine Kirche nach der Wende. Die Ukrainische Griechisch-Katholische Kirche im Spiegel ihrer synodalen Tätigkeit* (Freistadt, 2005) • O. TURIJ, *Griechisch-Katholiken, Lateiner und Orthodoxe in der Ukraine: Gegeneinander, Nebeneinander oder Miteinander?* (L'viv, 2001). For current information, see www.ugcc.org.ua/eng/ugcc_structure.

ERNST C. SUTTNER, with THE EDITORS

Unification Church

1. History
2. Beliefs
3. Appeal
4. Critique

1. History

The Unification Church is one of the most well-known and controversial new religious movements (→ New Religions). It is led by Korean native Sun Myung Moon, who was born on January 6, 1920. He was influenced in his youth both by traditional Christian churches and by several indigenous Korean religious movements (→ South Korea 2). Moon's disciples believe that Jesus appeared to Moon on April 17, 1935, and that Moon was asked to fulfill the mission of Jesus.

Moon has been married twice. His first marriage lasted over ten years (1943-53), and Moon has one child from this union. In 1960 he married Hak Ja Han, his current wife. Mrs. Moon was born on January 6, 1943, and has given birth to 13 children. Their marriage is viewed by Unification members as the fulfillment of the marriage supper of the Lamb

(Rev. 19:9). Unificationists refer to Moon as True Father and his wife as True Mother; together they are known as True Parents.

Moon officially launched the Holy Spirit Association for the Unification of World Christianity in 1954, after a decade of persecution, including imprisonment in North Korea. Young Oon Kim, one of the most important Unification theologians, was sent to the United States of America as a missionary in 1959. The church received scrutiny for its giant rallies at Madison Square Garden (September 18, 1974), Yankee Stadium (June 1, 1976), and the Washington Monument (September 18, 1976). By this time Moon was probably the most visible target of the anticult movement. Large Unification weddings have also received considerable attention over the years. These are indicative of the significance that Moon attaches to the concept of the new family under God.

The U.S. government charged Moon with income-tax evasion on October 15, 1981. Though powerful religious groups protested Moon's indictment, the Korean leader was found guilty and sentenced to 18 months in prison. He began his term in a prison in Danbury, Connecticut, in the summer of 1984 and was released from a Brooklyn halfway house on August 20, 1985. Immediately after serving his sentence Moon became more explicit about his messianic status (→ Messianism).

Moon's followers were elated with Moon's meetings with Mikhail Gorbachev on April 11, 1990, and with North Korean leader Kim Il-sung in November 1991. These strategic meetings were viewed as evidence of Moon's complete supremacy over Communism. Moon took credit both for the fall of the Berlin Wall in 1989 and for the victory of the Coalition forces in the Persian Gulf War in 1991. These events are interpreted as major fulfillments of Moon's completion of God's final dispensation for humanity through him. The movement was reshaped in 1994 to focus on the unity of religions and the importance of the → family, expressed in a new title for the movement: Family Federation for World Peace and Unification.

In 1998 Nansook Hong, Moon's former daughter-in-law, published a devastating memoir about life inside the church. Titled *In the Shadow of the Moons,* Hong accused her former husband, Hyo Jin Moon, of adultery, drug addiction, and physical and emotional abuse. Furthermore, in her most serious charge, she claimed that Sun Myung Moon had an illegitimate child who was raised by another Unification family. Unification leaders have officially denied this allegation.

2. Beliefs

The Unification Church is committed to → monotheism but does not adopt a Trinitarian understanding of God (→ Trinity). Moon teaches that Satan seduced Eve sexually and then she engaged in sex with Adam before the providential time allowed by God. Moon's private teachings about Jesus build upon explicit views given in *Divine Principle* (the Unification Bible) that Jesus was not sent to die on the cross but that the ideal plan for Jesus was to have found a true Eve to restore humanity. The fact that Jesus was not married during his earthly life led to the necessity of a new messiah. Unificationists claim that Moon presided over a marriage ceremony for Jesus at one of the church's mass weddings.

Moon contends that Jesus is the product of a sexual relationship between Mary and Zechariah, the father of John the Baptist. According to Moon, Mary never told Joseph who the real father was of Jesus. Moon states that Mary and Joseph purposefully left the 12-year-old Jesus behind in Jerusalem when they were visiting at Passover. Moon explicitly teaches that Jesus failed in several crucial ways. In fact, God has been liberated by Moon from the failures of past prophets, including Jesus. Moon's sermons contain frequent observations about his superiority to all of humanity.

Since 2000 Moon has challenged the traditional Christian view of the cross, calling for churches to take down their crosses. This campaign is being carried out through the American Clergy Leadership Conference, based in Washington, D.C. Ceremonies to remove the cross of Jesus are highlighted in Unification publications and defended on the basis both of God's original ideal and of the desire to remove a major stumbling block to Jews and Muslims.

Since 1995 Unification members have been participating in renewal and liberation workshops at a Unification retreat center at Chung Pyung Lake in Korea. These are led by Mrs. Hyo Nam Kim, who claims to receive messages from Moon's deceased mother-in-law, who is given the honorific title of Dae Mo Nim. Disciples are urged to liberate their ancestral lineage from demonic influence and from the toll of human iniquity that plagues generations. One workshop announced the cost of liberating both sides of a family (though only for the first generation) as $1,400.

For the last two decades Moon has placed great emphasis on direct revelation from the spirit world (→ Spiritism). This has included claims of supernatural messages from Heung Jin Nim, Moon's son, who died in January 1984 as a result of a car accident. Revelations are also claimed from Moon's mother-in-law and from Dr. Sang Hun Lee, who was a prominent Unification scholar. Unificationists believe that Lee, in his postmortem state, revealed details of a meeting he conducted in the spirit realm on Christmas Day 2001 with the leaders of the five major religions. The fathers of → Buddhism, → Hinduism, → Confucianism, and → Islam met with Jesus to proclaim their total alignment with True Parents. This document was translated from Korean into English and then published in July 2002 in some of the major newspapers of the world under the title "A Cloud of Witnesses."

3. Appeal

Converts to the Unification Church have often been introduced to Sun Myung Moon through an extensive series of lectures about the Divine Principle. This apologetic would leave the impression, especially among the uninformed, that the Unification → ideology was rooted in careful biblical study and the unfolding of progressive revelation. Moreover, Unificationists have always believed that Moon's life and mission clearly duplicated that of Jesus.

Moon has obviously gained credibility through his many educational, media, political, and religious organizations. He achieved significant attention when he founded the *Washington Times* in 1982 as he was facing income-tax charges by the U.S. government. He also owns the *Segye Times* (Korea) and the *Middle East Times* (Cairo) and in 2000 took over United Press International (UPI). Moon is the founder of the International Conference on the Unity of the Sciences, the Professors World Peace Academy, the Summit Council for World Peace, and the World Media Conference, among other educational and political enterprises.

The direct appeal of the Unification Church lies in the power of a → utopian vision fostered by a dedicated and committed following. The movement's announced message is one of radical love for God, professed allegiance to Jesus Christ, openness to all religions, and deep commitment to solving the world's problems. In spite of his egocentrism and his anti-Christian teachings, Moon has inspired a generation of highly moral and loving disciples.

Both the endorsement of Moon by the world's elite and the persecution of Moon by his detractors are viewed as proof that the spirit world is behind the Korean prophet. The long-standing focus on messages from that world serves as ongoing reinforcement for Moon's claim to be the second coming of Jesus Christ. It will be fascinating to witness how the Unification movement adapts to new or competing revelations after Moon's death.

The Unification Church attracts a large following in both South Korea and Japan, with membership likely in the hundreds of thousands. The movement has received widespread media attention in the United States, Canada, and Europe, but the numbers of followers are not proportional. There are less than a thousand followers in Canada, and only a few thousand in both the United States and Europe. Nevertheless, the movement attracts a large number of people to its various academic, social, and religious programs.

4. Critique

Unification doctrine is clearly distinct from orthodoxy Christianity. Traditional Christian notions of God, Christology, and soteriology have obviously been abandoned under a new Moon-centered ideology. For over 30 years Christian scholars of new religions have objected to Moon's transparent distortions of Scripture and the Christian tradition.

There is no reason to adopt many of the standard anticult lines against Moon. Eileen Barker has shown that his movement cannot be explained as a case of brainwashing. Moon himself said that if he could brainwash people, he would go visit the editors at the *New York Times*. By all accounts, Moon is sincere in his beliefs and has worked effortlessly to build his religious empire. His sincerity, however, cannot explain his deviations from the clear teachings of the Christian gospel as expressed in the NT and in the creeds of the church catholic. Furthermore, Moon's ego and narcissistic tendencies have been evident in his countless statements of conceit, false prophecies, and claims that defy belief. Moon is one of the few religious leaders in history to claim that he is the liberator of God.

Bibliography: Primary sources: HOLY SPIRIT ASSOCIATION FOR THE UNIFICATION OF WORLD CHRISTIANITY, *Divine Principle* (5th ed.; New York, 1977); idem, *The Tradition* (New York, 1986) • M. INGLIS and M. L. MICKLER, eds., *Forty Years in America: An Intimate History of the Unification Movement, 1959-1999* (New York, 2000) • S. H. LEE, *Life in the Spirit World and on Earth* (New York, 1998) • S. M. MOON, Sermons, www.tparents.org/lib-moon-talk.htm.

Secondary works: E. BARKER, *The Making of a Moonie: Choice or Brainwashing?* (Oxford, 1984) • J. A. BEVERLEY, "Spirit Revelation and the Unification Church," *Controversial New Religions* (ed. J. R. Lewis and J. A. Petersen; New York, 2005) • R. E. BUSWELL, ed., *Religions of Korea in Practice* (Princeton, 2007) • G. D. CHRYSSIDES, *The Advent of Sun Myung Moon: The Origins, Beliefs, and Practices of the Unification*

Church (New York, 1991) • N. Hong, *In the Shadow of the Moons: My Life in the Reverend Sun Myung Moon's Family* (Boston, 1998) • M. Introvigne, *The Unification Church* (Salt Lake City, 2000).

James A. Beverley

Unio mystica → Mystical Union

Union

1. Term
2. Examples in Church History
3. Situation Today

1. Term

As a model of church → unity and unification, *union* has a long history. Various forms of union have taken place, so that a single definition is hardly possible.

1.1. From the Middle Ages different unions have been contracted between the → Roman Catholic Church and parts of the → Orthodox Church that have integrated Orthodox Church structures into the worldwide Roman Catholic Church (note the union bull of Clement VIII in 1595, *Magnus Dominus et laudabilis:* "we receive, unify, attach, annex, and incorporate"; see N. Thon, 394). The Orthodox Church retained the liturgical features that gave it identity but, as a particular church, acknowledged papal supremacy (see 2.1 below; → Pope, Papacy; Uniate Churches).

1.2. The → Reformation attempted unification by upholding or restoring church unity through → consensus (§3) on the basis of the confession and common doctrine (see 2.2). Concord could be established, for example, with reference to eucharistic teaching (→ Eucharist), and mutual recognition was sealed by intercommunion (see the Concord of Wittenberg, 1526; → Confession of Faith 2). Union was intended, though the term was not used.

1.3. In 19th-century Germany (see 2.4) union was a matter of administration, consensus, or confession. These were different stages of union, varying according to the degree of unification and the existence of a common, explicit confession.

1.4. Other terms for coming together are "alliance," which is usually used for Christians (not churches) joined together in the fellowship of Christ's church (→ World Evangelical Alliance); "agreement," which denotes a common understanding of the → gospel and creates and estab-

lishes presuppositions for church unity (e.g., the → Leuenberg Agreement); "church fellowship," which denotes the fellowship of different denominational churches in witness and service on the basis of an agreed understanding of the gospel (→ Unity 3); and "church federation," which presupposes intercommunion and makes possible common activities at different levels, though largely leaving intact the identities of the respective churches (→ Unity 2.1).

1.5. "Union churches" is a phrase often used for various forms of united (or uniting) churches (→ Church of South India).

2. Examples in Church History

2.1. The schism between West and East from 1054 (→ Heresies and Schisms 3) was not the first schism to show how acute the problem of unity was. The problem had been there from the very first. In 1054, however, the divide entered a new stage when through geography, theology, and bitter experience, especially on the part of the Orthodox (particularly because of the Fourth → Crusade, which conquered Constantinople in 1204), it was given greater emotional depth. The divisions of an earlier period now seemed to be inconsequential. Union now became the main aim of the Latin church.

In 1181 the Maronites of Lebanon joined the Roman Church for various political reasons, and they have remained true to Rome to this day (→ Lebanon 2.1). The small Armenian princedom of Cilicia joined Rome in 1198, and the union lasted for 117 years. An attempt was made at union with the Bulgars in 1204, but with no practical success. At the Council of Lyons in 1274, an effort at union was made through the Eastern emperor Michael VIII Palaeologus (1259-82), which also was unsuccessful. The emperor could not make his agreement acceptable at home. The church rejected it and excommunicated the emperor. The efforts at Florence in 1439 (→ Councils of the Church 3; Reform Councils 2.3) seemed to hold out greater hopes of success. The two parties met as equals and reached agreement on several disputed questions of doctrine and church law. The Orthodox accepted the primacy of the pope, with the addition that the rights and privileges of the → patriarch of the East be observed. Yet this effort also failed because large portions of the Orthodox church (esp. in Russia) rejected the agreement. Rome thus paid more attention to winning over partial churches, whose members now are preferably called Eastern Catholic Christians. The Union of Brest-Litovsk (1595/96) brought in large parts of the → Russian Orthodox Church that were then in Poland-Lithuania and that went along with the agreement that had been reached at Florence. In direct connection with this union, other portions of the Orthodox Church in Carpatho-Ukraine and Croatia also joined with Rome.

But this mode of promoting union failed as a means of restoring general unity between the Western and Eastern churches. It did not promote unity between sister churches but brought about divisions that resulted in further hardening. So-called uniatism is one of the issues that seriously imperils current relations between Rome and Orthodoxy.

2.2. It soon became evident that special ways and means were required if the various expanding streams of the Reformation movement were to be brought together. For one thing, there were no decision-making bodies present, and corresponding criteria first needed to be developed. An increasingly important role was played by the various theological conferences, held in connection with the new pressure to justify the faith to the political bodies of the empire, while structural questions of external church unity at that early time did not present a problem and remained largely unperceived.

Union was sought by Martin → Luther (1483-1546; → Luther's Theology) and Ulrich → Zwingli (1484-1531; → Zwingli's Theology) at Marburg in 1529. Philip, landgrave of Hesse (1518-67), sponsored the consultation. The aim was a theological understanding in the interests of a common confession, but much wider ramifications could also be expected. Disagreement over the → Eucharist (§3.3) led to the failure of this effort.

The untiring activity of M. → Bucer (1491-1551; → Reformers 3.2), however, led to partial success seven years later. The Lutherans on the one side and the preachers of southern Germany on the other reached the understanding that we know as the Concord of Wittenberg (1536; → Confessions and Creeds 3.1) and protected Lutheranism against a threatened split, though at the cost of a sharper division from the Swiss Reformation and its more Zwinglian eucharistic teaching. This was not union in the true sense, but it prepared the way for future unions.

2.3. The Consensus Sandomiriensis (or Concord of Sandomierz), in 1570, formed the basis of the first authentic union on Reformation soil. By the terms of this agreement, the Lutherans, the Reformed, and the → Bohemian Brethren in Poland accepted intercommunion on the basis of the Second → Helvetic Confession, extracts from the → Augsburg Confession, and other formulas. This union did not last long, but it showed that the thought of union lived on in → Protestantism as an instrument whereby the inalienable unity of the church could be preserved, even though the Reformation had brought with it many types of churchmanship. G. Calixtus (1586-1656), P. J. Spener (1635-1705), G. W. Molanus (1633-1722), and G. W. Leibniz (1646-1716) were some of the individuals who worked hard in this direction.

The → Moravian Brethren, founded in 1727 by Count Nikolaus → Zinzendorf (1700-1760), climbed a step higher. Those fleeing from Moravia (the Bohemian Brethren) joined with Lutherans and Reformed to create a fellowship whose feature was constant → love for all the children of God. For his confession Zinzendorf offered his *Tropentheorie* (from *tropoi paideias theou*, "ways of God's upbringing"), according to which no → tradition should predominate. Members ought not to be concerned about where they came but about what they should bring. The "Ground of the Unity," formulated in 1957, found a place for the confessions of the early church and also for the great Reformation confessions.

2.4. On similar grounds → Pietism and the → Enlightenment were concerned about unifying the German churches at the beginning of the 19th century. As in the case of Zinzendorf, mildness and moderation led on to → tolerance. A conviction arose that the true unity of the church does not rest on similar theological views but on biblical faith in Jesus Christ. Written confessions fulfill an important function by formulating agreements, but they have their limits. As the Prussian Report of 1817 said, union does not mean that the Reformed should become Lutherans or vice versa, but that they both become a revivified evangelical Christian church in the spirit of their Founder (G. Ruhbach, 34).

The 1834 Prussian order again stated that there would be no abandonment of previous confessions. Union was built on mildness and moderation, which would no longer allow differences in doctrine to stand in the way of external fellowship (ibid., 37). The confessions agreed on basic matters.

In the 20th century organic unity follows this model. It usually calls for a common declaration of faith, agreement on the → sacraments and ministry, and a uniform organic structure (→ United and Uniting Churches).

3. Situation Today

Union falls within the scope of ecumenical efforts. → Ecumenism developed as such only in the 19th century, but in different forms it has always been inherent in the church. Union is the attempt to draw out the implications of the church and to accept → responsibility in the face of contemporary challenges and of the church's own concern to achieve both inner and outer unity in witness, ministry, → mission, → diakonia, → proclamation, → pastoral care, and daily living. Theology is involved — the theology of the unity of the church amid the tensions of unity and → truth (§2), truth and confession, and unity and diversity (→ Church 1.4.2). Union as a model of church unity tries to give answers and also to be an answer, paying heed to the limits of knowledge (and of each confession) and to the need for constant recourse to the true centers of faith (though using the help of the confession).

→ Church 5; Denomination 3; Ecumenical Theology; Ecumenism, Ecumenical Movement, 2; Pluralism 2

Bibliography: K. BARTH, *The Church and the Churches* (Grand Rapids, 2005) • G. GASSMANN and H. MEYER, *The Unity of the Church: Requirements and Structure* (Stuttgart, 1983) • K. M. GEORGE, *Church of South India: Life in Union, 1947-1997* (Delhi, 1999) • J. W. GRANT, *The Canadian Experience of Church Union* (London, 1967) • R. GROSCURTH, ed., *What Unity Implies* (Geneva, 1969) • G. F. MOEDE, ed., *The COCU Consensus: In Quest of a Church of Christ Uniting* (Princeton, 1985) • G. RUHBACH, *Kirchenunionen im 19. Jahrhundert* (Gütersloh, 1967) • D. K. SAHU, *The Church of North India: A Historical and Systematic Theological Inquiry into an Ecumenical Ecclesiology* (New York, 1994) • F. SCHLINGENSIEPEN, ed., *Union und Ökumene. 150 Jahre Evangelische Kirche der Union* (Berlin, 1968) • N. THON, ed., *Quellenbuch zur Geschichte der Orthodoxen Kirche* (Trier, 1983).

HUBERT KIRCHNER

Unitarians

1. Term
2. Sources
   2.1. Poland and Transylvania
   2.2. British Isles
   2.3. United States
3. The Transcendentalists
4. Religious Humanism
5. International Developments
6. Recent Developments

1. Term
The name "Unitarian" implies oneness — in particular, the oneness of God. On occasion, this name has been used to identify any monotheistic faith (→

Monotheism), but more usually it refers to a diverse group of churches and religious movements in continental Europe, the British Isles, and North America that emerged, for the most part, from various branches of Reformed Protestant Christianity. Sometimes these churches and movements have used the Unitarian name, while at other times they have deferred on the grounds that, contrary to their noncreedal nature, the name would seem to imply a fixed doctrinal position. The British Unitarian James Martineau (1805-1900) made a sharp distinction between personal belief and the undesirable application of the same belief to a corporate context, stating in 1888, "If anyone, being a Unitarian, shrinks on fitting occasion from plainly calling himself so, he is a sneak and a coward; if being of our catholic communion, he calls his chapel or his congregation Unitarian, he is a traitor to his spiritual ancestry and a deserter to the camp of its persecutors" *(National Conference).*

For contemporary Unitarians, faith is a matter of personal responsibility within the context of active religious communities. Not only do Unitarians draw on Jewish and Christian teachings about responding to God's love by loving their neighbors as themselves, but they often draw as well on wisdom from other world faiths, and on insights from → science, → humanism, or earth-centered → spiritualities.

2. Sources
The Unitarian movement has two main sources. One is an original protest against favoring church creeds and human → confessions of faith (e.g., the 1647 → Westminster Confession) over the scriptural text, coupled with a later recognition that Scripture itself is inevitably subject to rational interpretation and to human understanding. The second is a parallel protest against the Christian Trinitarian understanding of God as both a → Trinity of persons and a Unity of substance, which is a developed understanding doubtfully sustained by the earliest NT evidence. Proto-Unitarians have therefore sometimes been referred to as → Anti-Trinitarians.

Two particular events gave form to these twin sources: the recognition by → Erasmus (1469?-1536) that the so-called Johannine comma (1 John 5:7: "There are three that testify in heaven: the Father, the Word, and the Holy Spirit") was a late, probably ninth-century addition to the Latin biblical text; and the burning at the stake of Michael Servetus (ca. 1511-53) in Geneva for anti-Trinitarian → heresy. These two occurrences led to widespread debate throughout Europe concerning the Trinitarian doctrine.

2.1. *Poland and Transylvania*

In the following years organized anti-Trinitarian synods emerged within the Reformed Christian churches of both Poland/Lithuania and Hungary. In Poland the synod's official designation was "The Minor Reformed Church," but its adherents were frequently known as → "Socinians," or followers of Faustus Socinus (1539-1604), an Italian refugee who became their principal theologian and who considered Jesus as servant *(servatore)* rather than Savior *(salvatore)*. Polish scholars referred to them as *Arianie,* in association with the early Christian Arian heresy (→ Arianism). Only in their diaspora, following their expulsion from Poland in the mid-17th century, did Polish Socinians begin using the name "Unitarian."

In Hungary, especially in Transylvania (now in northwestern Romania), the adherents of the anti-Trinitarian Reformed synod were early called Unitarians by the orthodox Trinitarians, who were anxious to denigrate them as fellow travelers with the Moslem Turks. They did so in the Consensus Ministrorum in Hungaria Orthodoxorum contra Unitarios Transylvanos (Agreement of the Orthodox ministers in Hungary against the Transylvanian Unitarians, 1569). Later, the anti-Trinitarians chose to wear the name "Unitarian" with pride, in their Confessio Fidei secundum Unitarios (A confession of faith according to Unitarians, 1638). Despite much → persecution during the Austrian oppression of the 18th century and then during the Communist ascendancy of the 20th, this Hungarian-speaking Unitarian church continues with a strong and faithful witness today.

2.2. *British Isles*

The earliest churches in Britain emerged from a 16th-century movement made up of → Puritans dissatisfied with the Henrican reform of the → Roman Catholic Church in England. At this stage, strictly orthodox in doctrine, these Puritans desired further reform, primarily in a Genevan direction. The Cromwellian Commonwealth of the 17th century gave hope to many of them, but a promised comprehension was dashed when, in 1662, the restored King Charles II (1660-85) caused them to be ejected from the Church of England for nonconformity.

During the 18th century, and now partly legitimized, these → dissenters from the Church of England divided into Evangelical and Rational branches, with adherents of the latter preferring scriptural authority — rationally understood — to creedal statements and confessional subscription. In Ireland, similar "nonsubscribing" trends within Presbyterian churches led in the same direction.

Without adopting the "Unitarian" name as such, Rational Dissenters and Nonsubscribing Presbyterians (also referred to as Arians or semi-Arians) found much in common with a vigorous and distinctly Unitarian movement of tract and debating societies that knew Unitarian teachings from the writings of Polish Socinians and the "Unitarian" name from traveling Hungarian students. John Biddle (1615-62), sometimes referred to as the father of English Unitarianism, organized a Unitarian society in Commonwealth London (1651-52) and published an English translation of the Polish Socinians' Racovian Catechism. When Henry Hedworth (1626-1705) wrote, "I will therefore present to the reader a short account of these men's opinions concerning Christ, who, for distinction sake call themselves Unitarians to distinguish them from other Christians that hold three persons and one essence of God and are therefore denominated Trinitarians" (*Controversie Ended* [1672]), he was using the word "Unitarian" for the first known time in English print.

Late in the 18th century this underground Unitarian movement emerged into the open. Its leaders were the minister-scientist Joseph Priestley (1733-1804) and the established church rector Theophilus Lindsey (1723-1808). Lindsey attempted but failed to gain legal relief for Anglican Unitarians, so in 1774 he opened his own distinctly Unitarian church on Essex Street, London, where today's British Unitarian headquarters are still located. The Unitarian Society published books and tracts, while the Unitarian Fund sponsored missionary activity throughout the British Isles, including Wales, where a distinctly Welsh-speaking Unitarian movement was supported by the bard and "antiquarian" Iolo Morganwg (1747-1826, also known as Edward Williams). The British and Foreign Unitarian Association (B&FUA) was founded in 1825 as an association of churches and individuals but later, because of the reluctance of many — including James Martineau — to describe their churches as Unitarian, became just an organization for individual members. Later a National Conference of congregations was established that in 1928 amalgamated with the B&FUA to form the present General Assembly of Unitarian and Free Christian Churches. Its double-barreled name reflects the traditional reluctance of some churches to identify themselves with a doctrinal name.

2.3. *United States*

A similar reluctance to use the Unitarian name is associated with the Unitarian movement that emerged among the standing-order churches established in New England by Elizabethan Puritan refugees from

England. A preference by some for scriptural authority — rationally interpreted — together with the independent polity of Massachusetts town churches, especially those in and around Boston and its environs, enabled doctrinal development along lines similar to Great Britain's Rational Dissenters. A leading representative liberal was Charles Chauncy (1705-87), who wrote, "There is the religion of the understanding and judgement, and will, as well as of the affections; and if little account is made of the former, while great stress is laid upon the latter, it can't be but people should run into disorders" (*Seasonable Thoughts on the State of Religion in New England* [Boston, 1743] 422).

Pamphlet wars broke out, with the evangelicals accusing the liberals of being closet Unitarians. As long as they could, the "Boston liberals" denied this charge, since they had no wish to be associated with such philosophically determinist English Unitarians as Joseph Priestley, Thomas Belsham (1750-1829), and others. Emigrating British Unitarians tended to steer clear of New England and settle further south in the mid-Atlantic states.

In the midst of these debates William Ellery Channing (1780-1842), while originally reluctant to accept the Unitarian name, proffered a blend of Christianity that was at the same time both reasonable and unitarian and that provided the New England liberals with a focused response to the evangelical onslaught. Channing's "affirmative philosophy of human development or self-culture" (D. Robinson, 229) was also significant for Unitarians beyond America, making him perhaps the most significant Unitarian anywhere.

3. The Transcendentalists

Within this new liberal matrix there emerged the intuitive transcendentalist philosophy linked to Germany through Ralph Waldo Emerson's (1803-82) friendship with Thomas Carlyle (1795-1881). In Britain the transcendentalist writings of Channing, Emerson, and Theodore Parker (1810-60) greatly influenced many and contributed to James Martineau's articulating a new Unitarian rationale of religious authority based on the enlightened human conscience.

In Germany, during the turmoil that followed the 1848 German revolution, Parker was read by Johannes Ronge (1813-87), a Roman Catholic priest who resigned the priesthood and established the Catholic reform movement Deutschkatholizismus. This movement subsequently amalgamated with the Protestant Lichtfreunde (Friends of light) to form the German Free Religious movements.

The transcendentalists also brought to early Unitarian attention the scriptures of non-Christian faiths. As early as 1828 a solitary Unitarian missionary effort in India led to a disruption between the Unitarian Christians of Calcutta and their Hindu members, who realized they could establish their own Unitarian movement — the Brahmo Somaj (Society of God) — within the religious and cultural confines of → Hinduism. Also in Britain from the mid-1850s there are instances in Unitarian worship of readings being given from other than Christian sources. In America the Free Religious Association was established in 1865 specifically to break free from the Christian "Unitarian orthodoxy" of Henry Whitney Bellows (1814-82) and the National Conference.

4. Religious Humanism

In the expanding American Midwest, "free religion" and → transcendentalism drew Unitarians away from the specifically Christian center favored by New England Unitarians toward a somewhat broader theistic and ethical foundation. This step paved the way in turn for a movement of "religious humanism," whose protagonists preferred a language of faith using exclusively this-worldly and nonsupernaturalist terms. Many religious humanists signed Humanist Manifesto I (1933) and thereby initiated a vigorous debate between theists and humanists, which, after three decades of controversy, resolved itself in a middle-ground denominational norm of "naturalistic theism." For much of the later 20th century, however, religious humanists dominated the leadership of the American Unitarian Association (1825) and its successor, the Unitarian Universalist Association, formed in 1961 by consolidation with the Universalist Church of America (→ Universalism, Universalists).

These vigorous humanist-theist debates were influential elsewhere in the English-speaking world. In Great Britain, however, the sustenance of church life during two world wars and the contemporary → secularism of western Europe have probably been of greater concern than vigorous theological debate. Nevertheless, the inclusive Unitarian approach to faith practices provides a positive position from which to engage with today's multifaith and multicultural society.

5. International Developments

Following the Parliament of the → World's Religions, held in Chicago in 1893, the Council of Unitarian and Other Liberal Thinkers and Workers was formed in 1900 (now known as the International Association for Religious Freedom [IARF]). Since the council from the start embraced the Hindu Brahmo Somaj, IARF claims to be the world's first international interfaith organization (→ Theology of Religions).

IARF's first international congress was held in London in 1901, and others followed at frequent intervals. Attending its 1910 congress in Berlin were two European Protestant pastors, Norbert Capek (1870-1942), who went on to develop a new Unitarian movement in Czechoslovakia (1922), and Rudolf Walbaum (1869-1948), who wrote a significant essay "Was ist der Unitarismus?" (1915) and in Germany, following World War II, organized the Deutsche Unitarier Bund (1948).

Increasingly, however, during the late 20th century, the interfaith aspects of IARF's work grew, with special emphases upon issues of religious freedom. Eventually the particular needs of the specific Unitarian and Universalist and Unitarian-Universalist IARF member communities were transferred to the International Council for Unitarians and Universalists (ICUU, 1991). Individual Unitarian Christians in mainline European Protestant churches, however, were less comfortable with this change, since for them it appeared to reflect the shift — which James Martineau had feared — from "Unitarian" as the name of a personal faith stance to "Unitarian" as the name of a church. Thus, for example, the Non-Subscribing Presbyterian Church of Ireland has associations with the IARF but not with the ICUU.

6. Recent Developments

Recent developments include the accession to ICUU of Spanish-speaking groups in the Philippines and in South America with Roman Catholic, rather than Protestant, backgrounds. There also is growing cooperation through the partner church movement, which links Unitarian and Unitarian Universalist congregations in North America and the British Isles with Unitarian congregations in Transylvania, the Philippines, and India.

Among Unitarians and Unitarian Universalists worldwide, there is presently a strong recovery of the language of spirituality and the holy as being essential components of religious community. Faced worldwide with growing movements within every faith tradition of scriptural literalism and religious extremism, the Unitarian and Unitarian Universalist movement offers a moderate and imaginative spiritual alternative that seeks to be faithful to its own Judeo-Christian heritage but also sympathetic to the common core of compassionate religion characteristic of world faith traditions and attuned to the best insights of scientific exploration.

Bibliography: G. Bolam et al., The English Presbyterians from Elizabethan Puritanism to Modern Unitarianism (London, 1968) • D. E. Bumbaugh, Unitarian Universalism: A Narrative History (Chicago, 2000) • R. Henry, Norbert Fabián Capek: A Spiritual Journey (Boston, 1999) • P. B. Hewett, Unitarians in Canada (Toronto, 1995) • A. M. Hill, "Unitarier," TRE 34.332-39 • A. M. Hill, J. McAllister, and C. Reed, eds., A Global Conversation: Unitarian/Universalism at the Dawn of the Twenty-first Century (Prague, 2002) • C. A. Howe, A Short History of Unitarianism in Europe (Boston, 1997) • S. Kot, Socinianism in Poland (Boston, 1957) • S. Lavan, Unitarians and India: A Study in Encounter and Response (Boston, 1977) • National Conference of the Members and Friends of Unitarian, Liberal Christian, Free Christian, Presbyterian, and Other Non-subscribing or Kindred Congregations: Report of the Conference Held at Leeds, April, 1888 (London, 1888) • D. Robinson, The Unitarians and the Universalists (Westport, Conn., 1985) • E. M. Wilbur, A History of Unitarianism, vol. 1, Socinianism and Its Antecedents; vol. 2, In Transylvania, England, and America (Boston, 1945-52) • C. Wright, A Stream of Light: A Sesquicentennial History of American Unitarianism (Boston, 1975).

ANDREW M. HILL

United and Uniting Churches

1. History and Statistics
2. Typology
3. Motivating Factors
4. Ecclesiological Identity
5. Alternatives to Organic Union
6. Relationships Worldwide
7. Challenges and Vision

United churches are those formed through the → union of two or more existing churches to produce a new, autonomous church. In a united church the separate identities of the uniting churches have been brought together such that all members share an agreed basis of faith and form a single eucharistic fellowship; all have become responsible for one another within one ecclesial community; all members and ministers are recognized as members and ministers of that church with a defined place in its life of → worship, → mission, and service (→ Diakonia); and decision-making bodies have been agreed upon to deliberate and act on behalf of the whole church. These features of united churches find expression in such direct, visible ways as the holding of property, control of funds, and exercise of → church discipline (ICUUC, Fifth, 13).

1. History and Statistics

Beginning with the Old Prussian Union of 1817 and existing mainly at the national level, united churches have been formed from various combinations of Protestant (esp. → Reformed, → Congregational, → Methodist, Disciples of Christ (→ Christian Church [Disciples of Christ]), → Lutheran, → Baptist, and → Brethren) and → Anglican churches. Reformed and Congregational churches have entered into the largest number of unions. The broadest diversity so far brought into union is seen in the Church of North India (formed in 1970), incorporating Anglican, Baptist, Brethren, Congregational, Disciples, Methodist, and Presbyterian elements. United churches thus form a very diverse group linked not so much by a uniform ecclesiology or form of church life as by a commitment to visible, structural (rather than merely "spiritual") unity and by the actual experience of entering into, and living within, union.

As of 2006, united churches numbered about 60 worldwide. But as many of these bodies have incorporated churches themselves formed through earlier unions, the extent of union activity over the past two centuries has been much greater than this number suggests. (For example, the U.S. United Methodist Church brought together the Methodist Church — formed from 3 churches in 1939 — and the Evangelical United Brethren, itself the fruit of a union in 1946.) Approximately 45 percent of united churches today are found in Europe, 20 percent in Asia, 12 percent each in Africa and North America, 5 percent each in the Caribbean and the Pacific, and 1 percent in South America.

Uniting churches are those actively involved in a process toward union. As of 2006, almost 40 churches were known to be involved in 16 such union processes worldwide, including 6 in Africa, 5 in Asia, 4 in North America, and at least 1 in Latin America. The most diverse of these is Churches Uniting in Christ (since 2002, in the United States), which includes no fewer than 9 churches as full members: African Methodist Episcopal, African Methodist Episcopal Zion, Christian Church (Disciples of Christ), Christian Methodist Episcopal, Episcopal, International Council of Community Churches, Presbyterian Church (USA), United Church of Christ, and United Methodist. In addition, 2 churches are "partners in mission and dialogue": Evangelical Lutheran Church in America and → Moravian Church (Northern Province).

Recent unions include the United Church in Jamaica and the Cayman Islands (1992), the Uniting Presbyterian Church in Southern Africa (1999), and

the Protestant Church in the Netherlands (2004). It should be remembered that some already united churches identify themselves as "uniting" to stress their openness to possible future unions (e.g., the Uniting Church in Australia, 1977).

2. Typology

Despite the variety and complexity of the church union movement, patterns can be discerned in the union processes undertaken over the past two centuries. A generally accepted schema groups united churches into the following five categories (adapted from M. Cressey, 59-61):

1. The original unions in Germany, Austria, and Czechoslovakia, which united Reformed and Lutheran elements. Characteristic of the 19th and early 20th centuries, these began with the Old Prussian Union (1817) and continued in the Evangelische Kirche der Union, now within the Union of Evangelical (Protestant) Churches in the Evangelical Church in Germany (→ Germany 2.2). These unions have been ecclesiologically significant as forerunners of Reformed-Lutheran rapprochement (see the → Leuenberg Agreement, 1974). The most recent full union — the Protestant Church in the Netherlands (2004) — incorporates Reformed and Lutheran churches (→ Netherlands 2.4).

2. Unions beginning with the United Church of Canada (1925) and found mainly in North America, the United Kingdom, and Australia. This category includes unions formed from various combinations of churches, most commonly Presbyterians, Congregationalists, Methodists, and Disciples of Christ. The most recent developments in this group are the union of the Congregational Union of Scotland with the United Reformed Church (2000), and continuing work toward union by the U.S. group Churches Uniting in Christ.

3. Unions formed throughout the 20th century from missionary-founded churches of the denominations mentioned in 2 in Asia (The Church of Christ in Thailand, 1934), Africa (The United Church of Zambia, 1965), and the Caribbean (The United Church in Jamaica and the Cayman Islands, 1992). Recent moves include the Covenant of Partnership (looking toward eventual union) between the United Church of Christ in the Philippines and the Iglesia Philipina Independiente (1999).

4. Unions so far limited to the Indian Subcontinent. Beginning with the → Church of South In-

dia (1947), these have incorporated Anglican churches and, therefore, episcopal structures of governance (→ Episcopacy). The Communion of Churches in India (linking the Church of South India, Church of North India, and Mar Thoma Church, with a view to possible union) was inaugurated in 2003.

5. Intraconfessional unions, that is, of churches within the same confessional tradition, such as the Evangelical Lutheran Church in America (1988). The most recent example is the formation of the Uniting Presbyterian Church in Southern Africa (1999), formed from the multiracial, but mainly white, Presbyterian Church of Southern Africa and the black Reformed Presbyterian Church in Southern Africa.

3. Motivating Factors

Many factors have contributed to the rise of the church union movement.

3.1. Most fundamentally, churches unite because they are convinced that, in their situation, union best reveals the reconciling power of the gospel and enables their witness and service to the world. As the Church of South India commented about its union in 1947, the churches entered union not because it seemed convenient or clever but because they were convinced it was the will of God.

Historically, several more specific factors may be identified. First was the → missionary movement and its growing conviction that division among the churches hindered their witness to the gospel and impaired their own lives as churches. Then as mission-founded churches moved toward independence and autonomy as local expressions of the one gospel, the divisions among them began to appear increasingly artificial and unnecessary. The Tranquebar conference of church leaders in India in 1919 stated: "We believe that the challenge of the present hour . . . calls us to mourn our past divisions and turn to our Lord Jesus Christ to seek in Him the unity of the body expressed in one visible Church. . . . We find ourselves rendered weak and relatively impotent by our unhappy divisions — divisions for which we were not responsible, and which have been, as it were, imposed upon us from without" (quoted in S. C. Neill, "Plans," 473). Many unions in the Southern Hemisphere have thus been motivated by the desire to offer an autonomous, locally based witness to the gospel. This witness has taken visible form as several separate, mission-founded churches have united in a single, locally led and locally trained church.

3.2. A second motivating factor was the relativiz-

ing of denominational differences experienced by some church leaders during extreme circumstances, particularly of the Second World War. In Malaysia, → ecumenism "was born in the common experience of Christian leaders interned in Changi Prison during the Second World War. Their denominational differences had centred on varying interpretations of baptism, communion, etc. When there was no bread, no cup, no wine to be had, when the only water for baptism was that from the toilet in their cell, they experienced their primal unity as Christians rather than their separate identities as Anglicans or Methodists" ("Survey of Church Union Negotiations," 1986, 456-57).

Not all such experiences translated directly into church union processes, but for some leaders this was indeed an impulse to overcome the historic and nonessential matters that kept their churches divided.

3.3. A third factor was the growth of the ecumenical movement. At the local and national levels, increasing ecumenical contacts and experience helped to break down barriers of misunderstanding and unfamiliarity among churches. Internationally, the series of → Faith and Order world conferences and the Assemblies of the → World Council of Churches (WCC) focused attention on the goal of Christian unity and provided ecclesiological categories that helped churches reflect together on the nature of the unity they were seeking. And not least, the increasing experience of common → Bible study nurtured a new awareness of the gospel imperative for unity.

3.4. Some factors motivating the search for union have been social and psychological. Many denominations, especially in countries marked by immigration, were rooted in distinctive ethnic or language populations. As later generations assimilated into the wider culture, such denominations often found they had less reason to exist as separated churches. (These factors were important in the experience of Lutheran churches in the United States.)

3.5. Other factors have been economic. Besides the biblical, ecclesiological, and missional grounds for union, some churches have argued that union will enable a more efficient use of financial and other resources.

3.6. Finally, external factors have played a role in some unions. For example, the Kyodan (United Church of Christ in Japan, 1941) was formed by the government for political reasons during the Second World War. Strikingly, the experience of union has almost always led such churches to remain united, even when the original external motivation no longer exists.

4. Ecclesiological Identity

Church union is fundamentally an ecclesiological act. As the great Asian ecumenist D. T. Niles said at the WCC's founding Assembly (Amsterdam 1948): "No schemes of union had come about: *the churches had united*" (WCC, *First Assembly*, 62, emphasis mine). They have understood themselves as the most complete expression of "organic union," as proposed at the Second World Conference on Faith and Order (Edinburgh 1937), a union aiming for "the unity of a living organism, with the diversity characteristic of the members of a healthy body" and able to "take up and preserve in one beloved community all the varied spiritual gifts which [God] has given us in our separations" (p. 252). United churches express a radical vision of mutual accountability within the body of Christ, an accountability so complete that it cannot be expressed through relationships among separate ecclesial bodies but only within a single church.

United churches have embraced the words of the WCC's New Delhi Assembly (1961): "The achievement of unity will involve nothing less than a death and rebirth of many forms of church life as we have known them" (p. 117). They have endorsed a kenotic ecclesiology whereby the divided denominations have "died" to their separate identities in order to "rise" to new life together within a single new, united church. Between the WCC's New Delhi and Nairobi (1975) Assemblies, no fewer than nine church unions came into being. The Nairobi statement on "conciliar fellowship" speaks of "local churches truly united" (p. 60), for which the united churches provided a clear model.

At the time of union most united churches have stressed that their new identity is itself provisional. In this way they express a readiness to grow and develop through entering further unions in the future, as noted above in the case of the Uni*ting* Church in Australia.

The same readiness appears in the continuing integration of the varied ecclesial traditions that have been brought into the union. United churches enter union with a high, but not necessarily complete, level of agreement on essential matters of faith and practice. Rather than seeking full formal agreement before union, they have preferred to resolve some significant (though not fundamental) issues of understanding and practice after, rather than before, the act of union. This choice reflects their conviction that some matters are best resolved within the context of shared life within the new united church — not only through discussions in theological committees, but as these issues are actually experienced within the one church body and in the life of local congregations. As these churches have lived out the implications of unity, they have sought to integrate diverse ecclesiological positions and practices (e.g., the decision within the United Reformed Church in the United Kingdom to integrate, within each congregation, such diverse practices as believer's and infant baptism).

The most significant of these reconciliations theologically and ecclesiologically is certainly the incorporation of the office of → bishop into the life of united churches in India, Pakistan, Sri Lanka, and Bangladesh. In adopting bishops, these churches appeared to pave the way for a wave of reconciliations of many other divided church structures throughout the world. In practice, however, this result has proved elusive; so far, unions including episcopal oversight are limited to the Indian Subcontinent.

As fruits of reconciliation between divided churches, united churches have also made an important witness to the power of the gospel to heal historic, social, and cultural divisions. A powerful example of this healing is the formation of the Uniting Presbyterian Church in Southern Africa in 1999, which brought together two Reformed churches, one predominantly white and one black, that had been divided a century before in order to ensure the separation of the races. It was clear to these divided churches that, in the context of a South Africa struggling to overcome the vestiges of apartheid, nothing less than *full organic union* would do: no amount of common worship, joint parishes, joint programming, partnerships, or pastoral exchanges would match the witness that would be offered through the full structural integration of these racially divided church bodies. This witness is captured in the following comments made in preparation for the Seventh International Consultation of United and Uniting Churches: "It is sometimes forgotten that the goal of church union is not to unite church bureaucracies; nor are they merely for the sake of efficiency or, indeed, survival. Church unions are not the end, but the beginning, of a process whose goal is to heal wounds, to witness to the justice and reconciliation effected by Christ (in both the church and in the world!), and to enable more effective witness and service to the world." As Alastair Rodger wrote, "This union is a step in faith. It does not mean that the old divisions and all the hurts, suspicions and fear that go with them have suddenly been overcome, but it does demonstrate a willingness to allow God to take us a stage further in the healing process" ("Survey" 2000, 29).

Church unions are affected not only by theological but also by nontheological factors. Memories of earlier divisions between the churches involved, as well as differing social and cultural perspectives, complicate the union process, even where no significant theological and eccesiological differences are involved. Unions within the same confessional family may thus prove as difficult as, or even more difficult than, those involving churches from different confessional families.

All church unions, whether between or within confessional families, have significant practical, financial, and legal implications as churches integrate their resources and administrative structures. This process engages all the human issues of uniting clergy and staff, buildings, seminaries, diaconal facilities, pension plans, and all the other dimensions of church life. Such nontheological factors are perhaps the greatest reason why church union processes falter or are never undertaken.

As church unions are completed, it often happens that small groups in one or more of the uniting churches decide to remain outside the union, thus disclosing divisions that have not yet been reconciled within one of the uniting churches. Yet these churches have not been willing to deny the call to union. Indeed, sometimes the union process has clarified divisions and thus helped toward their longer-term resolution.

5. Alternatives to Organic Union

Before reaching full organic union, many uniting churches express their unity in Christ through partnerships, partial-recognition agreements, or in other ways. Examples are the creative partnership between the Disciples of Christ and the United Church of Christ (Crow, "Ecumenical Partnership"), as expressed in a common agency through which the two churches exercise their world → mission mandate, as well as other approaches to shared church life, such as the Local Ecumenical Partnerships in the United Kingdom and the Cooperating Parishes in Aotearoa–New Zealand (H. Cross, D. Lendrum, P. Smetana, M. Tanner). Prominent among these wider options is the process of Churches Uniting in Christ (United States), which seeks to manifest the unity of its member churches through their common confession, worship, life, and action rather than through the fusion of their church structures.

6. Relationships Worldwide

Despite their identity as a distinct group of churches, the united and uniting churches have not formed a → Christian World Communion, fearing that this

action would make them effectively another → denomination and lessen their interest in working for further union. Rather, they have preferred that the Faith and Order Commission of the WCC serve as their common reference point. This relationship has been inscribed in the bylaws of Faith and Order, which has supported the united and uniting churches by publishing surveys of church union negotiations at approximately two- to three-year intervals in the *Ecumenical Review* and by organizing a series of international consultations of united and uniting churches (ICUUC, beginning in 1967) for reflection on issues of unity in relation to the life of the church and its mission and witness today.

Because of their origin among churches with diverse confessional identities, the united churches face special issues in relating to the Christian World Communions. These relationships may offer powerful signs of reconciliation and recognition. For example, because the united churches from the Indian Subcontinent have incorporated fundamental elements of the Anglican heritage — especially the episcopally ordered ministry — bishops from those churches have been accepted as full members at the Lambeth Conference. Some Christian World Communions, particularly the Disciples Ecumenical Consultative Council and the → World Alliance of Reformed Churches, have encouraged their member churches around the world to enter local church unions.

In the Southern Hemisphere financial and personal ties may foster dependence on "parent" mission-sending churches in the North. Although not unique to united churches, the issue is often particularly acute for them, since they relate not just to one but to several mission-sending churches and confessional bodies.

7. Challenges and Vision

Crucial issues facing united and uniting churches today include (1) how much agreement is essential for union, what structures best serve each new united church, and how to relate full structural union to other efforts to make unity more visible (e.g., through church partnerships, recognition agreements, or common parishes); (2) how to ensure that union actually leads to more effective mission; and (3) what the distinctive identity is of united churches and how it can be strengthened for more effective mission and service.

The most difficult theological and ecclesiological issue facing united and uniting churches is that of incorporating episcopal order into church unions. This difficulty is vividly illustrated in the most recent Survey of Church Union Negotiations, with its reports from South Africa, Scotland, Wales, and the United States ("Survey" 2006, 5-10, 42-53). Despite the earlier examples from the Indian Subcontinent, in each of these places an effort — sometimes very creative — to incorporate episcopal structures of governance has come to grief.

Recent developments are testing the meaning of "unity" itself as churches are identifying themselves as being "united" — without, however, any signs of structural integration or apparent change in their lives ("Survey" 2006, 23-27, on the Reformed and Lutheran churches in Alsace-Lorraine, France). How far may churches, still structurally divided, claim to be "united"? What does the "unity" of the church mean today, and how far do all the churches remain committed to the goal of unity? These questions press not only the united and uniting churches but the ecumenical movement as a whole.

When Lesslie → Newbigin, a great pioneer of church union in India, returned from India to England in 1974, he encountered several kinds of culture shock, both in the church and in society. He wrote with penetrating insight about the pain of moving from ministry and life in a united church to a church and cultural situation in which unity could not be expressed in the same inclusive way: "For twenty-seven years I had been a bishop in the Church of South India. . . . For all these years we had been living in a fellowship where the treasures of the Anglican, Methodist and Reformed traditions were all ours to share. Now we faced the painful necessity of choosing which slot to go into" (p. 243).

Newbigin found a happy home within a united church, the United Reformed Church in the United Kingdom, that brought together Reformed and Congregational (and later Churches of Christ/Disciples of Christ) traditions. But he missed the broad inclusiveness of the Indian union with its Anglican, Methodist, and Reformed traditions. Following Newbigin, we could summarize the vision of the united and uniting churches as follows: that having to decide which church "slot" to go into will become a thing of the past and that, within one church, the generous range of expressions of the Christian faith and life will be freely available to all.

Bibliography: Reports of WCC Assemblies and Faith and Order meetings: First: *The First Assembly of the World Council of Churches* (ed. W. A. Visser 't Hooft; London, 1949) • Third: *The New Delhi Report* (ed. W. A. Visser 't Hooft; London, 1962) • Fifth: *Breaking Barriers, Nairobi 1975* (ed. D. M. Paton; Geneva, 1976) • *The Second World Conference on Faith and Order* (ed.

L. Hodgson; New York, 1938) • *Minutes of the Meeting of the Standing Commission on Faith and Order, Faverges, Haute-Savoie, France, 2006* (Geneva, 2006) bylaws, 119-25.

ICUUC reports: International Consultation of United and Uniting Churches: Fifth, *Living Today towards Visible Unity* (ed. T. F. Best; Geneva, 1988); Sixth, *Built Together: The Present Vocation of United and Uniting Churches (Ephesians 2:22)* (ed. T. F. Best; Geneva, 1995); Seventh, *"With a Demonstration of the Spirit and of Power"* (ed. T. F. Best; Geneva, 2004) • H. Cross, "Local Unity Where There Is No National Church Union: For Example, Local Ecumenical Partnerships," ICUUC, Sixth, 106-11 • P. A. Crow Jr., "Ecumenical Partnership: Emerging Unity between the Disciples of Christ and the United Church of Christ," ICUUC, Sixth, 112-19; idem, "Reflections on Models of Christian Unity," ICUUC, Fifth, 21-38 • D. Lendrum, "The Negotiating Churches Unity Council (NCUC): Aotearoa/New Zealand," ICUUC, Sixth, 94-99 • P. Smetana, "Agreement between the Reformation Churches in Europe: The Leuenberg Agreement," ICUUC, Sixth, 137-41 • M. Tanner, "The Porvoo Agreement," ICUUC, Sixth, 142-47.

Other works: T. F. Best, "Unionen, Kirchliche, II: Weltweit," *RGG* (4th ed.) 8.751-54 • N. K. Clifford, *The Resistance to Church Union in Canada, 1904-1939* (Vancouver, B.C., 1985) • M. Cressey, "Where and Whither? An Interpretive Survey of United and Uniting Churches, with a View to Their Contribution to the Fifth World Conference on Faith and Order, to Be Held in 1993," *Minutes of the Meeting of the Faith and Order Standing Commission, Rome, Italy, 1991* (Geneva, 1992) 57-64 • H. P. Douglas, *A Decade of Objective Progress in Church Unity, 1927-1936* (New York, 1937) • F. Engel, *Australian Christians in Conflict and Unity* (Melbourne, 1984) • M. Kinnamon, "United and Uniting Churches," *DEM* 1164-68 • S. C. Neill, "Plans of Union and Reunion, 1910-1948," *A History of the Ecumenical Movement,* vol. 1, *1517-1948* (ed. R. Rouse and S. C. Neill; 3d ed.; Geneva, 1986) 445-505 and 787-91; idem, *Towards Church Union, 1937-1952: A Survey of Approaches to Closer Union among the Churches* (London, 1952) • L. Newbigin, *Unfinished Agenda: An Autobiography* (Geneva, 1985) • "Reunion," *ODCC* 1390-92 • B. Sundkler, *Church of South India: The Movement towards Union, 1900-1947* (London, 1954). Since 1952 the "Survey of Church Union Negotiations" has appeared at approximately two- to three-year intervals in *ER*, most recently in the following issues: October 1986, April 1989, January 1992, January 1995, April 1997, January 2000, July 2002, and July/October 2006.

Thomas F. Best

United Arab Emirates

	1960	1980	2000
Population (1,000s):	90	1,015	2,444
Annual growth rate (%):	9.38	8.49	1.69

Area: 83,600 sq. km. (32,280 sq. mi.)

A.D. 2000

Population density: 29/sq. km. (76/sq. mi.)
Births / deaths: 1.83 / 0.33 per 100 population
Fertility rate: 3.12 per woman
Infant mortality rate: 12 per 1,000 live births
Life expectancy: 75.9 years (m: 74.9, f: 77.7)
Religious affiliation (%): Muslims 74.6, Christians 12.1 (Roman Catholics 5.5, Orthodox 3.3, indigenous 2.1, other Christians 1.2), Hindus 7.7, Baha'is 2.3, Buddhists 2.0, other 1.3.

1. General Situation
2. Religious Situation

1. General Situation

Few countries have undergone the dramatic changes experienced by the United Arab Emirates (UAE) in the last quarter of the 20th century. Located between Saudi Arabia and Oman on the northeast part of the Arabian Peninsula, its seven constituent emirates (Arab. *emir,* "prince"), or states, are Abu Dhabi, Ajman, Dubai, Fujairah, Ras al-Khaimah, Sharjah, and Umm al-Quwain. They have undergone remarkable economic and social development, being transformed from a population of indigent nomads into prosperous modern communities. Once known as the Pirate Coast, these neglected desert sheikhdoms were called the Trucial States prior to 1971 because of treaties signed with Britain in the 19th century.

A flat, barren coastal plain merges into rolling sand dunes, with some mountains in the east. The desert landscape (only 0.77 percent of the land is arable), low rainfall, and harsh climate had prevented the development of much agriculture. Trading, pearling, and fishing were the major industries until the discovery of oil over 30 years ago. A Human Development Indicator of 0.839 (in 2004) indicates high life expectancy, literacy, education, and a good standard of living, which places the UAE among the top 50 nations in the world from an economic and social perspective.

The Al Nahyan clan of Abu Dhabi and the Al Maktoum clan of Dubai exercise hereditary control of the presidency and premiership respectively of the UAE. Rulers of the seven emirates form the Supreme Council, which also elects the Council of Ministers. → Political parties are banned. The Federal National Council (FNC), drawn from all the emirates, reviews proposed laws, but it cannot change or veto them. In December 2006, in a first experiment in guided → democracy, 20 of the FNC's 40 members were elected. Of a potential 300,000 voters, 6,689 citizens (including 1,189 women), chosen by the rulers of the UAE, were allowed to vote. One of the elected members was a woman.

Only about 15 percent of the UAE's population of 4.5 million are Emirati citizens. A massive influx of expatriates has enabled the oil industry to operate, along with the expansion of commercial services and some industrial development. Half of the population are South Asian (including 1.2 million Indians), 23 percent are other Arab or Iranian, and the remainder are other expatriates (including Westerners and East Asians). The outward impression is that of a melting pot of nationalities working well together in a progressive and affluent society.

Human → rights concerns center on the trafficking and abuse of women, often under the guise of domestic employment, and the exploitation of poor Asian construction workers. There is a media ban on public criticism of the ruling families.

Petroleum dominates the economy, with oil and gas providing about 33 percent of the gross domestic product (GDP), but international banking and trade, financial services, regional corporate headquarters, and tourism are also important. The open economy has resulted in a high productivity (GDP per capita is estimated at $49,500) and a trade surplus. Oil production is around 2.4 million barrels per day.

An extensive and imaginative building and infrastructure program, aided by political stability, a low crime rate, and the absence of terrorist attacks, has attracted much foreign capital and investment. Desalinated water from the Arabian (or Persian) Gulf has turned the desert sands in urban areas into green parkland and enabled an agricultural sector employing 7 percent of the labor force and producing 2.3 percent of the GDP. Shopping centers abound, and duty-free shopping is popular. High-profile entertainment and international sporting events, such as golf, tennis, and racing, have been successful because of world-class venues and good organization. Some world-renowned universities have established campuses in the UAE. Despite its location in the otherwise volatile Middle East, the UAE has managed to maintain internal stability and good international relationships, with its near-neighbor Iran being a possible exception.

2. Religious Situation

Archaeological remains of pre-Islamic sites have been discovered in the UAE, indicating the presence of Christian communities in the sixth and seventh centuries. The Arab military conquests brought → Islam in the eighth century, and its practice in the UAE has been total until recent years. Nearly all Emirati citizens are Muslims, approximately 85 percent of whom are → Sunni, and the remaining 15 percent are → Shia. Although no official figures are available, it is estimated that approximately 55 percent of the foreign population is Muslim, 25 percent is Hindu (→ Hinduism), 10 percent is Christian, 5 percent is Buddhist (→ Buddhism), and 5 percent belong to other religions, including Parsi, → Baha'i, and → Sikh. Although Islam is the official religion, the constitution provides for religious freedom in accordance with established customs.

There are at least 31 Christian churches in the country, built on rent-free land donated by the ruling families of the emirates. Christian services are well attended, and Bibles and Christian literature are allowed. Hindu and Sikh temples function from rented commercial properties, and meetings in private homes are allowed. Religious groups openly advertise their events in the press. The UAE is seen as a model of religious → tolerance in the Islamic world. Proselytizing among the Muslim population, however, would result in expulsion for those involved, while conversion to Islam is encouraged by various means.

Bibliography: I. al-Abed and P. Hellyer, *The United Arab Emirates: A New Perspective* (London, 2001) • C. M. Davidson, *The United Arab Emirates: A Study in Survival* (Boulder, Colo., 2005) • G. R. D. King, "A Nestorian Monastic Settlement on the Island of Sir Bani Yas, Abu Dhabi: A Preliminary Report," *BSOAS* 60/2 (1997) 221-35 • D. Potts, H. Al Naboodah, and P. Hellyer, eds., *Archaeology of the United Arab Emirates* (London, 2003).

Bernard J. Power

United Kingdom

	1960	1980	2000
Population (1,000s):	52,372	56,330	58,336
Annual growth rate (%):	0.74	0.10	0.07

Area: 244,110 sq. km. (94,251 sq. mi.)

A.D. 2000

Population density: 239/sq. km. (619/sq. mi.)
Births / deaths: 1.16 / 1.09 per 100 population
Fertility rate: 1.79 per woman
Infant mortality rate: 6 per 1,000 live births
Life expectancy: 77.9 years (m: 75.3, f: 80.6)
Religious affiliation (%): Christians 82.3 (Anglicans 42.1, unaffiliated 15.8, Roman Catholics 9.7, Protestants 8.4, indigenous 4.5, marginal 1.1, other Christians 0.8), nonreligious 12.0, Muslims 1.9, atheists 1.5, other 2.3.

1. Historical Development

The United Kingdom of Great Britain and Northern Ireland is constituted from four major units: England, Scotland, Wales, and Northern Ireland. Each of these regions has had a distinct history, both secular and ecclesiastical. The present article deals with the first three of these regions, collectively known as Great Britain until the 17th century, when the part of Ireland that became "Northern Ireland" in 1920 began to develop a distinctive religious identity. From that point the article also includes material on this region, which will be referred to anachronistically as Northern Ireland throughout.

1.1. Early Christianity in the United Kingdom

The arrival of Christianity in the geographic area comprising Great Britain was intimately linked to the position of the southern two-thirds of the region as a province of the → Roman Empire. Probably arriving first with Roman soldiers and traders, Christianity may have been present as one option among many in the religious landscape by the second or third century — if later, then it must have made quite rapid progress, since the existence of an apparently well-organized episcopal system is attested by the presence of British bishops at the Council of Arles in 314 (→ Episcopacy). The development of Christianity in Britain, however, was disrupted by the collapse of Roman administration in the early fifth century and the rise to political and cultural dominance of pagan settlers from northern Europe — the peoples who later became known as the English. Considerable British populations may have continued to exist in areas dominated by the English, and some of these people may have been Christians, but an organized British church is visible only in regions (esp. in Wales and Strathclyde) where English power had not been established.

Despite its reduced scope, the British church nevertheless played an influential role in the region, especially as a source of Christian influence on its neighbors. This influence can be seen in the work of Patrick (mid or late 5th cent.) in establishing Christianity among the Irish, and Ninian (5th or 6th cent.) among the Picts of what is now southern Scotland, and British Christians may also have been a significant source of religious influence among their eastern neighbors, the English. The best-recorded vehicles of Christian influence among the English, however, are the missions of Celtic monks and of → missionaries dispatched by Rome. The Celtic monks were based initially in the part of modern Scotland settled by Scots from Ireland, their primary center being the great monastery of → Iona, founded by Columba in 563. They were at their most influential in the northern English kingdom of Northumbria, where they established a base at Lindisfarne under the leadership of Aidan (d. 651) in the 630s. The Roman missions made greatest headway in the southeast of the country, especially in the kingdoms of Kent and East Anglia and among the East Saxons, whose capital was in London. The two missions both made progress unevenly through the seventh century, and by the 680s the last of the English kingdoms, Sussex, had adopted the "new religion." Disputes over practice (esp. the correct method for determining the date of → Easter) between the Irish and Roman churches were decided in favor of the latter at the Synod of Whitby in 664.

By the early 8th century, English Christianity was equipped with a diocesan system and a network of → monasteries, the best known of which, like Lindisfarne and Jarrow, were considerable centers of scholarship. The latter produced, inter alia, the most important source for early English Christianity — the *Ecclesiastical History* of Bede (ca. 673-735). The English church was also capable of mounting its own missions to continental Europe — notably that of Boniface (ca. 675-754) among the Germans. However, the extent to which Christian beliefs and practices had spread beyond the local elites to the people more generally at this date is difficult to determine, and the degree of personal attachment to the faith is unknowable. Moreover, much of the infrastructure, both political and ecclesiastical, that had been established in the 7th and 8th centuries was destroyed in the ninth by the Vikings and had to be reestablished in the 10th century by the kings of Wessex, who gradually expanded their realm to include the whole of England. They reestablished dioceses and promoted reformed → Benedictine monasticism. At a local level Christianity was probably promoted by a system of → "minsters," or mother churches served by the monks, with outlying chapels at which services might be held on an occasional basis. The late 10th and 11th centuries, however, seem to have seen the development, out of this earlier arrangement, of the parish system, which became the basis of English Christianity for the next millennium.

1.2. *Medieval Christianity*

The world of British Christianity was profoundly affected by the Norman invasion (1066) and conquests of the 11th century. The English diocesan system was overhauled, and many cathedral churches were established on new sites. The primacy of the archbishop of Canterbury was firmly established and, by the middle of the 12th century, had been extended to Wales. At a local level the parochial system was consolidated, and the Middle Ages as a whole saw the further elaboration of stone-built parish churches, which remain a prominent feature of the English landscape. The 11th and 12th centuries also saw a significant period of monastic growth, with many major houses being established under royal or private patronage, especially by the → Cistercians.

The church was open to Continental influences such as the regulation of diocese and parish by the Fourth Lateran Council (1215) and the growth of the new preaching orders, especially the → Dominicans and → Franciscans. In some respects, however, it also remained an insular institution exhibiting a good deal of independence and strongly influenced by royal power. In Scotland the influence of Celtic Christianity remained strong in the 11th century, but the Scots church was gradually recast in the 12th and 13th to approximate more to continental European norms with the development of → cathedrals and parish kirks, as well as the introduction of reformed → religious orders and friars. This process culminated in 1472 in the elevation of the bishop of St. Andrews to metropolitan status.

By the 15th century the church throughout Britain was the dominant cultural institution, closely integrated into royal government, a major landowner, enjoying a monopoly in the sphere of education, and able to command considerable support among the laity. Its presence, thanks to → monasticism and the parish system, extended to virtually every corner of the land and, as the church's penitential system became more elaborate in the late Middle Ages, tending to become ever more omnipresent in the lives of Britons.

It seems also, with one major exception, to have produced a largely orthodox society — that exception being the followers of John → Wycliffe (ca. 1330-84), the Lollards. Wycliffe, a leading light in the University of Oxford in the second half of the 14th century, engaged in attacks on a number of key doctrines, including the → sacraments and the → authority of the church. He also emphasized the importance of access to the Bible and encouraged the production of a vernacular English version — positions for which his followers suffered executions for heresy in the 15th century and which had a wider influence on the Continent, especially in Bohemia (→ Bible Versions 4; Hussites).

1.3. Reformation

The Lollards were, however, never more than marginal to English religious life, and in the early 16th century, England remained powerfully attached to the → Roman Catholic Church. Its king, Henry VIII (1509-47), was linked by marriage to the strongly Catholic Hapsburgs, and his personal adherence to the church was symbolized by the pope's decision to award him the title "Defender of the Faith" in recognition of an anti-Lutheran defense of the seven sacraments issued over the king's name. Churchmen, like Thomas More (1478-1535), dominated the intellectual life of the nation and played a major role in affairs of state, and at a popular level the church was well keyed in to the rhythms of communal life by means of its sacraments and → sacramentals. Numerous guilds, fraternities, and saints' cults catered for a lively popular → piety that continued to flourish into the Reformation era.

The defenses of the English church against the penetration of the Protestant → Reformation were weakened, however, by the failure of the king's marriage to produce a male heir. Unable to procure an annulment of his marriage from a Hapsburg-dominated papacy, Henry responded by repudiating the authority of the pope over the church in England and Wales and substituting the authority of the Crown. Influenced by pro-Protestant advisers under the patronage of his new queen, especially Thomas Cromwell (ca. 1485-1540), Henry then introduced significant changes into the church. Monasteries were dissolved, some → images were removed from churches, and an authorized translation of the Bible in English was introduced. The

king remained conservative in relation to doctrine, however, and little was achieved on this front until after Henry's death in 1547.

During the minority of Henry's son, Edward VI (1547-53), the government was under the control of determined Protestants, and a more thoroughgoing process of Protestant reformation got underway. The doctrine of → purgatory was denounced, and the chantries associated with the penitential system were dissolved. An English → liturgy was introduced, along with the Forty-two Articles (1553) — a confession of faith in the Reformed tradition.

Edward's early death and the eventual succession of his Catholic half-sister Mary (1553-58) saw many of these changes go into reverse, along with the planned introduction of a number of features of the Continental Catholic reformation, for example, a system of seminaries. There is no evidence that these changes were unpopular among the mass of the population, but Mary's marriage to the Spanish Philip II (1556-98) and her government's execution of both prominent and obscure Protestants were unpopular.

Mary's reign, however, was also cut short by early death, and the succession and subsequent long reign of her Protestant half-sister Elizabeth I (1558-1603) paved the way for the ultimately Protestant direction of the Church of England. A revised English prayer book was introduced, and a moderately Reformed confession of faith — the → Thirty-nine Articles (1563, rev. 1571) — was issued. The Act of Uniformity (1558) imposed fines on all those refusing to attend their parish church. The resulting Church of England was clearly a member of the family of churches of the Reformation, but it retained a number of conservative features in its liturgy and its structure, especially concerning bishops and cathedrals. This aspect was comforting to conservatives, who might otherwise have chosen in greater numbers to throw in their lot with the illegal Roman church. It was frustrating, however, for those Protestants who desired a more thoroughgoing reformation, the more determined of whom came to attract the pejorative label → "Puritan." Such frustration grew during the course of the reign as it became apparent that Elizabeth would countenance no further alterations to the church settlement. The Elizabethan settlement, however, also found a number of distinguished defenders, especially the bishops John Jewel (1522-71) and Richard Hooker (ca. 1554-1600).

Those desiring a more Genevan-style church needed to look no further than the neighboring kingdom of Scotland. There the Reformation, which had begun in earnest a little later than in England, was effectively consolidated under the ecclesiastical leadership of John → Knox (ca. 1513-72) in the early 1560s. The Scottish church had a Calvinist confession of faith and an essentially Presbyterian style of church order (→ Reformed and Presbyterian Churches). Under James VI and I (of Scotland, 1567-1625, and of England, 1603-25), both the English and Scottish churches retained their reformed confessional stances, but the Scots polity was modified to include bishops. The most long-lasting product of James's reign was his sponsorship of a revised English translation — the "Authorized Version" (1611) — of the Bible, the preferred text for the majority of English-speaking Christians well into the 20th century.

Perhaps the most fateful of James's measures, however, was his encouragement of the "plantation of Ulster," the settlement of English and Scots Protestants in the north of Ireland, as a means of securing what had previously been a notably rebellious province to the English crown. This process eventually gave Northern Ireland a substantially different religious culture from the rest of Ireland. Elsewhere, although the Church of Ireland — a Protestant episcopalian body like the Church of England — became the church established by law, Roman Catholicism remained the religion of the majority of the people. In Northern Ireland, however, while Roman Catholicism remained a powerful presence, → Protestantism came to dominate, though the Protestants were themselves divided between adherents of the established church (often descended from English settlers) and the Presbyterians (mainly descended from Scots settlers), who represented the larger of the two groups.

1.4. Civil War

The 17th century saw a further series of revolutions in British religion. The first, introduced by royal policy, was the spread of so-called Arminian ideas and practices in the English church. The Arminians, most notably William Laud (archbishop of Canterbury, 1633-45), challenged the broad Calvinist consensus of the Jacobean church and were also characterized by their support for *de jure divino* kingship and their emphasis on "the beauty of holiness." The latter was manifested in a return to a more ceremonial style of worship, with uniformity enforced by royal and episcopal power. This attempted Arminian revolution provoked opposition in England, especially from those who viewed it as a step back toward popery, and fury in Scotland when, in 1639, the king attempted to impose similar measures on the Scottish church (→ Arminianism; Calvinism).

Religious discontent was thus one of the most powerful factors leading first to a breakdown of royal authority and finally to civil war. The years of civil war (1642-49) and the Commonwealth (1649-53) and Protectorate (1653-58) that followed were a period of rapid change. An assembly of divines meeting at Westminster under the auspices of Parliament produced a new and more thoroughly Reformed statement of doctrine — the Westminster Confession (1648) — and a Directory of Public Worship, which officially replaced the Book of Common Prayer in 1645 (→ Westminster Assembly and Confession). Under Oliver Cromwell (1599-1658), the Church of England was to all intents and purposes abolished, and while the parish system was continued, many ministers were replaced by men of Presbyterian or Independent leanings. The civil war also saw a flourishing of sectarian religion, including → Baptists and Quakers (→ Friends, Society of), and also more extreme millenarian groups like the Diggers and the Muggletonians. In Ireland the civil wars and Cromwellian settlement resulted in a further strengthening of the position of the Protestants and sharpened divisions between them and their Catholic neighbors.

1.5. Toleration

The end of the Protectorate saw the return of the Stuart dynasty and full-blooded episcopalianism throughout England, Scotland, Wales, and Ireland. Although Charles II (1660-85) may himself have favored a measure of toleration of minority religious views, the parliaments of the 1660s restored the Church of England and made conformity to its doctrine and discipline as embodied in the prayer book of 1662 compulsory. They also equipped it with a raft of coercive legislation aimed at stamping out opposition. Around 2,000 ministers left or were expelled from the church for Nonconformity in the first two years of Charles II's reign, and many of them set up Presbyterian, Independent, or Baptist congregations meeting illegally and often secretly, especially in urban areas. In England such groups were vulnerable to → persecution, and many Nonconformists died in prison.

In southern Scotland, where militant Presbyterians attempted armed resistance, the new religious settlement was imposed with even greater ruthlessness. Under Charles's brother and successor James II (1685-88), a committed Roman Catholic, the regime destabilized and after only three years was overthrown by James's Protestant son-in-law William of Orange (1689-1702), supported by leading elements of the British nobility and disaffected Anglican churchmen — an event generally known as the Glorious Revolution. In Scotland the Episcopalians remained strongly committed to the ousted senior branch of the Stuart line and were effectively proscribed. This proscription paved the way for the restoration of a national church on Presbyterian lines that dominated the Scots religious scene for the next century and a half.

In England and Wales the new regime produced in 1689 one of the most significant changes in the legal framework for religious observance since the Reformation — the Act of Toleration. Technically, the act was limited in its scope, simply providing freedom of worship for Trinitarian Protestants by releasing them from the penalties attached to Nonconformity. It did provide legal recognition, however, for a plurality of → denominations — a fundamental component of the modern religious landscape. Even more fundamentally, it effectively rendered unenforceable the laws requiring that all should attend their local parish church. Religious adherence thus ceased to be a matter of legal obligation and began its long and slow movement into the realm of personal choice (→ Religious Liberty [Foundations] 3). In Scotland dissent took the form of Presbyterian splinter groups from the national church that grew in the following century to considerable numbers in some Scots towns.

In Ireland, which saw significant fighting between the supporters of William and of James, the role played by the Protestants of Northern Ireland in resistance to, and the ultimate overthrow of, the latter strengthened yet again their sense of separate identity. There the events of the Glorious Revolution and especially the resistance of the city of Londonderry and William's victory at the battle of the Boyne (1690) provided the basis for a set of historical traditions, memories, festivals, and iconography that could be appropriated as the means of articulating that sense of identity. In the 21st century, July 12 remains a public holiday in Northern Ireland in memory of the Boyne, murals of William are visible in many predominantly Protestant areas, and Orange marches, which in aggregate represent possibly the largest folk festival in the United Kingdom, are prominent parts of the Northern Irish scene, especially in the month of July.

1.6. Eighteenth-Century Church

After the tumult of the 16th and 17th centuries, the first half of the 18th century appears as a period of relative calm. The Roman Catholics, while perennially suspected of disloyalty and operating outside the law, were given de facto toleration and probably maintained their numbers, though at less than 2 percent of the population in England and Wales and even less in Scotland, they were relegated to the margins of British religious life. Despite achieving legal toleration, the → Dissenters experienced a period of numerical decline, especially among the most widespread groups: the Presbyterians and the Quakers. The established churches, in contrast, experienced a period of relative stability, and though their accepted levels of pastoral vigor may have been low by Victorian standards (and so often criticized by later generations of churchmen), there is little sign that they were unacceptable to the bulk of parishioners.

In the second half of the century, however, there was a distinct quickening of pace associated with the impact of the evangelical → revivals. In England and Wales these movements found their majority of early supporters in the Church of England, with the Dissenters (esp. Baptists and Independents) falling under evangelical influence relatively late in the century. In Scotland the earliest supporters were in small breakaway Presbyterian groups, but evangelical influence soon spread to the established church. Wherever it took root, 18th-century evangelicalism represented a reassertion of the Reformation doctrine of → salvation by → grace through → faith and the priority of active measures to promote the → gospel.

In England and Wales perhaps the most prominent consequence of the spread of evangelicalism was the growth of the Methodist movement, which, while operating under the umbrella of the established church, essentially developed its own parallel organization. Converts were joined together for mutual support in small groups called classes or societies, which were visited by leaders of the movement — especially John → Wesley (1703-91) and George → Whitefield (1714-70), who itinerated throughout the country and further afield. Unable to find enough ordained clergy to assist him in running the burgeoning movement, Wesley in particular proceeded to break with Anglican tradition by allowing laypeople to play a leading part in the movement, including as preachers. This development placed considerable strain on the Anglican identity of the Methodist movement, which, after Wesley's death, gradually separated from the established church to form a new Nonconformist denomination (→ Methodism; Methodist Churches). The Welsh branch of the movement, which was predominantly Calvinist in theology, followed a similar trajectory in the early 19th century.

In addition to its advocacy of justification by faith, the priority of → evangelism, and lay activism, the evangelical revival made a significant contribution to the character of British Christianity by its championing of the use of hymns in worship (→ Hymnody). Evangelicals were also the major sponsors of the → Sunday school movement, which became, in aggregate, Britain's most popular religious institution in the next century.

In Northern Ireland, the late 18th century was perhaps most notable for a temporary realignment in religious politics, with some Catholics and Presbyterians (both excluded from the privileges of Establishment) making common cause in the Society of United Irishmen — originally a Presbyterian and republican organization that sought greater recognition for the rights of the Irish as a nation. Sectarian divisions reemerged, however, in the wake of an abortive revolutionary uprising in 1798 that also prompted legislation for the union of Ireland with Great Britain to form the United Kingdom in 1800.

1.7. Nineteenth-Century Church

The 19th century saw the further growth of diversity in British religion both by the development of new tendencies within existing denominations and by the creation of new ones. For the Church of England the first half of the century was a period of considerable structural change, with parliamentary legislation being used to redistribute resources and remodel the diocesan system in an attempt to reequip the church to deal with rapid population growth and industrial urbanization (→ Industrial Society). The evangelicals continued to increase in influence within the church, pioneering new forms of urban ministry and beginning the process of the launching of Anglicanism as a worldwide faith by their advocacy of cross-cultural missionary activity (→ British Missions). They also engaged in a wide variety of projects of social reform — from abolishing the slave trade (→ Slavery; Wilberforce, William) to attempts to improve conditions in factories.

From the middle of the century, however, the influence of evangelicals began to wane with the resurgence of two other strands of Anglicanism. The first of these strands comprised the → Oxford Movement and its Anglo-Catholic successors. They represented a reemphasis of the importance of the church as a divine institution and gradually moved away from established Anglican positions on the nature of the → sacraments, the use of religious ritual, and the identity of the church. Under their influence a significant body of Anglicans began for the first time since the 16th century to view their church as Catholic rather than Protestant. They also promoted changes in the architecture and layout of churches and in the conduct of worship that fundamentally altered the experience of Sunday church-

going. The second was a liberal Protestant movement that sought to align Christianity more closely with developments in modern thought. This issue became particularly important in the light of the challenge posed to traditional conceptions of the Christian faith by developments in biblical criticism, physical science, and ethics.

In England the early strength of evangelicalism was even more significant among the Protestant Nonconformists, especially the Independents, Baptists, and also the Methodists, who divided into a number of competing churches in the course of the century, the most important of which were the original Wesleyan Methodist Church and the more revivalist Primitive Methodists (→ Evangelical Movement). Taking advantage of the flexibility of their structures and impelled by a clear evangelical theology, Nonconformist churches expanded rapidly, especially among the working and middle classes of early industrial England. By 1851 the first religious census revealed that they accounted for nearly half of all church attendances in England.

In Wales the evangelical Nonconformist churches were even more successful and had already so outstripped the Church of England that they virtually replaced it as the Welsh national expression of Christianity. In Scotland the growth of evangelicalism within the national church lent a new energy to its mission, especially in the growing urban centers of lowland Scotland and the dispersed rural communities of the highlands and islands. However, it also tended to focus attention on a significant point of dispute within the church over the role of private patrons, who often tended to favor liberally inclined ministers, even when an evangelical was the popular choice. The failure of attempts to remedy this grievance led to the most spectacular religious division of the 19th century, the Disruption (1843), when over a third of the ministers and nearly half of the members separated from the establishment to form the Free Church of Scotland.

Both among Protestant Nonconformists in England and Wales and among Presbyterians in Scotland, the second half of the century saw a liberalization of the evangelical theology and culture inherited from the first half, so that liberal Protestantism came to occupy a greater place in the denominational mix (→ Liberal Theology). The main exceptions to this rule are the denominations newly formed in the second half of the 19th century such as the → Salvation Army.

The final great change in the ecology of religion in Britain was the resurgence of the Roman Catholic Church, fueled largely by substantial immigration from Ireland into the urban centers of England and Scotland. In Northern Ireland, Irish Protestants, and especially the Presbyterians, although energized by the influence of evangelicalism, which produced a widespread revival in the region in 1859, felt increasingly marginalized by assertive Roman Catholicism in Ireland and especially by its association with Irish nationalism, which threatened to leave them as a minority in an independent Ireland. They increasingly saw their security in maintaining the union with Great Britain and thus opposing calls for Irish independence.

1.8. *The Twentieth Century*

1.8.1. As the 20th century opened, the majority of British churches were still growing in numerical terms, though in aggregate they were growing considerably less strongly than the population as a whole. The first years of the century also witnessed one of the most spectacular religious revivals of the post-Reformation period — the Welsh Revival of 1904-5, in which around 100,000 converts professed faith in less than two years.

In the Church of England the early 20th century saw the apogee of Anglo-Catholic influence, especially in the years after the First World War, when their strength was manifest at a series of well-attended Anglo-Catholic congresses. Many Anglo-Catholic practices had been absorbed into the mainstream of the Church of England, and their ideas strongly influenced the production of a new prayer book for the church in 1928, though its adoption was halted by a belatedly mobilized Protestant majority in Parliament. The same period also witnessed a renewed confidence in the independent authority of the church, resulting in calls for a greater say in its own government, a development conceded in the Enabling Act of 1919, which established a church assembly, with episcopal, clerical, and lay representation.

With conservative evangelical voices in recession, the other major influence on the church came from its liberal wing, which included not only the more radical liberals associated with the Modern Churchmen's Union but also substantial liberal groups within both the Anglo-Catholic and evangelical wings of the church. Partly because of this influence, the interwar period was also notable for a renewal of the social vision of the church. New ideas came from a variety of directions, including Christian Socialists, but perhaps the figure most associated with this development was William → Temple (archbishop of York, 1929-42; archbishop of Canterbury, 1942-45). Particularly notable was his chairmanship of the interdenominational Conference on Politics,

Economics, and Citizenship in 1924, which paved the way for increasingly close attention to social problems, and his publication of *Christianity and Social Order* in 1942, which popularized the notion of the welfare state.

While both world wars had posed serious difficulties for the churches, these did not appear to be insuperable, and the 1950s saw a brief period of boom for the established churches in both England and Scotland, with active membership, as measured by communicant figures, on the increase. The same period also saw a resurgence of conservative evangelical influence in the church, with missions by the American evangelist Billy Graham (b. 1918) attracting episcopal support, evangelical organizations exercising increasing influence on university campuses, and the emergence of a new generation of leaders — most notably John Stott (b. 1921), the rector of All Souls Langham Place in London. Further energized from the 1970s by the spread of the → charismatic movement, evangelicalism became again one of the most dynamic features of the British religious landscape.

1.8.2. Outside the established churches, the first half of the century was notable for denominational consolidation, with various nonestablished Scots Presbyterian groups coming together to form the United Free Church in 1900 and then reuniting with the Church of Scotland in 1929, while a similar process among the various branches of Methodism culminated in the formation of a single Methodist Church in 1932.

In many respects the years between the first and second world wars might be seen as the high point of Protestant Nonconformity — most of the major churches reached their largest absolute size in the late 1920s or early 1930s, and their dominant position in Wales was finally recognized by the disestablishment of the Anglican church there in 1920. However, they did not share in the modest boom experienced by the established churches in the 1950s and were already beginning slowly to shrink before more serious decline set in during the 1960s and 1970s.

The Roman Catholic Church also grew strongly in the early 20th century, attracting support from a wide constituency, including a strong working-class base and prominent members of the interwar intelligentsia. It found its role in British society increasingly secure and began to resemble more closely the other mainstream churches, especially after the reforms promoted by the Second → Vatican Council (1962-65).

The cultural changes of the latter third of the

century — including the widespread questioning of a whole set of inherited values, practices, and institutions; the arrival of mass → consumerism; and large-scale commercial → leisure — produced a difficult climate for all the British churches. One popular response to this challenge was a renewed attempt to redefine Christian belief in the light of modern culture, most popularly by Bishop John Robinson (1919-83), whose radical work *Honest to God* (1963) became a best-seller in the 1960s. The more active sections of British Christianity continue to struggle strenuously with the issue of how to present the faith in a period of cultural change, but only a few churches — initially the Catholics and latterly mainly theologically conservative but culturally innovative evangelicals and charismatics — have found the means to prosper in the new climate.

1.8.3. In Ireland the early years of the century saw considerable political turmoil, in which competing religiocultural identities played a key role. As Irish Home Rule appeared increasingly likely to be granted by the Westminster parliament, so Unionist sentiment among the Protestant majority in Northern Ireland became more strident, with the more militant preparing for armed resistance. When the union was finally dissolved in 1920, the six counties of Northern Ireland were excluded from the new Irish Free State and granted their own devolved government in Belfast. This was a self-consciously Protestant state for a Protestant people, and the discontent of a substantial Nationalist minority with their position in, and treatment by, that state ultimately fueled protest and violence.

By the mid-1970s terrorism by both "Nationalist" and "Loyalist" paramilitary groups had become commonplace in Northern Ireland and, in the case of the former, sometimes spread to mainland Britain. "Nationalists" came largely (though not exclusively) from the Catholic community, and "Loyalists" almost entirely from the Protestant community, and so even though those religious affiliations often served more as a cultural identity than a spiritual one, the conflict effectively had a sectarian dimension. However, a political agreement reached in 1998 has led to a virtual cessation of intercommunal terrorist activity (→ Terrorism). While much suspicion and hostility remains, the 21st century has begun much more peacefully in Ireland than did the 20th.

2. The Present Situation

Throughout Great Britain, the majority of the population retains some degree of identification with the mainstream Christian churches, especially the established national churches in England and Scot-

land. More than 80 percent of the population identifies itself as Christian, and only 5 percent as belonging to other faiths. The largest of these is → Islam, which accounts for roughly 2 percent of the population, mostly first- and second-generation immigrants from South Asia. There are also substantial communities of → Sikhs and → Hindus and a long-established Jewish community. The remainder of the population mostly identifies itself as nonreligious.

This widespread identification with Christianity does not, however, translate into active → church membership. In Scotland a church census of 2002 estimated that 11.2 percent of the population attended church on an average Sunday, though in the more conservative religious culture of the western highlands and islands, this figure rose to around 40 percent. In England the 2005 church census suggested that only about 6.5 percent of the population were engaged in regular weekly attendance, a decline from around 10 percent in 1989 and a little under 8 percent in 1998. Such statistics are complicated, however, by evidence of a change in patterns of churchgoing, with a higher proportion of the population attending church on a fortnightly or monthly basis.

2.1. Established Churches

A particular characteristic of the British religious landscape is the continued existence in England and Scotland of established national churches. These provide a symbolic relationship between religion and the state and guarantee to a limited extent the public role of religion in Britain, though not religious influence on state policy. According to the church census of 1998, the Church of England remains the largest church in England in terms of the number of its congregations and the second largest in terms of aggregate attendance at just under a million. In 2005 it retained this position, though regular weekly attendance fell to around 870,000.

Three major tendencies can still be identified within the church. First, in 1992 the conservative Catholic wing suffered a blow with the decision to ordain women to the priesthood. A number of conservative Anglo-Catholics left the Church of England to join the Roman Catholic Church, and special arrangements have been made for the episcopal oversight of churches unable to accept the new arrangements. Although many Anglo-Catholic congregations remain within the church, there has been a tendency among this group toward a theological convergence with the liberal wing, so that the term "liberal Catholic" provides the best description of a large grouping of congregations within the church.

This is the sector of the church that has fared worst in terms of numerical decline in recent years.

By contrast, the evangelical congregations have tended to decline more slowly, maintain their numbers, or grow; as a group, they actually increased the total size of their membership between 1989 and 1998, so that they accounted for 31 percent of all Anglican attendances, and they continued to decline much less slowly in the early years of the 21st century, so that in 2005 they represented some 34 percent of Anglican attendances. Part of this success may be put down to the energy provided by the charismatic movement and a greater willingness to engage with popular culture. It also relates to the greater priority given by the most conservative evangelical churches to evangelism and their enterprise in developing new ways of approaching it — for example, the popular Alpha and Emmaus courses.

Third, the Church of England has maintained its commitment to a parochial presence throughout the whole of the country, despite the pressure created by declining resources. It also continues to exhibit a strong social conscience, as witnessed by its strong support of relief organizations such as Christian Aid and Tear Fund. The major challenges facing the church in the 21st century are likely to be the continued growth of theological diversity focused on issues like the church's attitude to homosexual practice and its capacity to direct its resources away from managing decline and into promoting growth.

The Church of Scotland, within which a liberal and an evangelical wing can also be discerned, shares many of the same problems as the Church of England. It remains the church with which the majority of Scots claim an identity and, especially during the recent debates over political devolution in Scotland, displayed a continuing ability to serve as a locus of national identity. It also remains the largest church in Scotland, in terms of both the number of its congregations and the number of its active church members, accounting for 40 percent of regular weekly attendance in 2002. At the same time, the church has continued to decline in absolute terms (by some 22 percent between 1994 and 2002), and its capacity to utilize its traditional parish structures as a basis for mission is likely to become an increasingly urgent issue.

2.2. Roman Catholics

Viewed from a British perspective, the Roman Catholic Church has more regular attenders than any other religious body on the island. In 1998 its regular weekly congregations, though declining in absolute terms, outnumbered those of the Church of England by around 250,000, and they accounted for about a third of the total attendance. However, they seem to have fared rather more badly in the present century, with the 2005 census suggesting an average weekly attendance of 893,000 — only 23,000 more than the Anglicans. In Scotland in 2002 the Roman Catholics accounted for some 35 percent of all attendances — not far behind the Church of Scotland. Although there has been a small continuing Roman Catholic presence in Britain since the Reformation, the majority of Catholics are descendants of 19th-century migrants from Ireland, supplemented by more recent immigrants, especially from central Europe.

Religious/ethnic tensions of the kind usually associated with Northern Ireland sometimes have the capacity to reemerge — most prominently in Glasgow, where they also are associated with support for the two major soccer teams. Nevertheless both the Catholic community and its church are to all intents and purposes more fully integrated into mainstream British society than ever before, to the extent that traditional Protestant objections to the visit of John Paul II (1978-2005) to Britain in 1982 appeared simply eccentric. The church has not been free from controversy, however, and like the other mainstream churches has suffered a significant decline in regular weekly attendance, possibly exacerbated by less strict enforcement of the obligation to attend mass.

2.3. Traditional Nonconformist Churches

Easily the largest of the traditional Protestant Nonconformist churches is the Methodist Church, which, though a relatively minor presence on the Scottish scene, is the third largest denomination in England, with nearly 380,000 regular weekly attenders in 1998. Methodism, however, is also suffering from rapid numerical decline, losing regular worshipers almost as fast as the Church of England; the 2005 census indicated that numbers had fallen to just over 289,000. The United Reformed Church, a largely English denomination formed in 1972 from a union of Presbyterians, Congregationalists, and Churches of Christ, has followed a similar trajectory to the Methodists and suffered significant numerical decline in the 1990s, which seems to have accelerated in the early 21st century. Its aggregate total of weekly attenders was estimated at over 149,000 in 1989, 121,700 in 1998, and only 69,900 in 2005. Both of these denominations are ones in which mainstream and charismatic evangelicalism have a small and declining presence, but even some of the longer established, mainly white → Pentecostal churches where evangelicalism is much more prominent have suffered some numerical decline in this period. The decline of traditional Protestant Nonconformity has been particularly significant for Wales, where it has continued to supply the place occupied in other parts of Britain by the established churches.

There are two main exceptions to this trend among mainstream Protestant Nonconformist churches. First are the black-majority Pentecostal churches, which include some of the largest individual congregations in the country, like Kensington Temple and the Kingsway International Christian Centre, both located in London (→ Black Churches 2.1.3). Second is the case of the Baptists, the only traditional Nonconformist denomination in which a majority of worshipers attend churches identifying with mainstream evangelicalism. The Baptists not only held their own in both England and Scotland but actually achieved modest growth throughout the 1990s, and though they have lost numbers in the early 21st century, they have done so much more slowly than other Nonconformists. Overall, the traditional Nonconformist churches still occupy a significant place within the landscape of English Christianity. On the basis of current trends, however, this position is likely to diminish in the 21st century, with the exception of the black-majority Pentecostal and Baptist churches.

2.4. New Churches

The major exception to the overall pattern of numerical decline in British Christianity at the turn of the 21st century is to be found in the "new churches." This label covers a wide range of bodies from the black-majority churches to charismatic churches with their origins in the 1970s and later, like New Frontiers, the → Vineyard churches, and the London branch of the Hillsong Church, which originated in Sydney, Australia. What they share in common is the location of the vast majority of their congregations on the evangelical and usually the charismatic evangelical end of the British Christian spectrum. They also share a recent history of sustained growth. Numbers attending new church congregations grew from around 167,000 in 1989 to over 230,000 in 1998 — a growth rate of 38 percent. If current trends continue, the new churches could expect to become more significant in aggregate than the Methodist Church early in the 21st century. Such churches share not only a recent history of numerical growth but also a greater expectation of growth in the future than their traditional or mainstream neighbors and have displayed considerable energy and skill in pursuing it.

2.5. Northern Ireland

Within the United Kingdom, Northern Ireland remains remarkable for the extent to which its population continues to associate with the churches and to participate in their activities. At the 2001 census, for example, over 85 percent of the population identified themselves with one or the other of the churches (45 percent Protestant and 40 percent Catholic). The Roman Catholic Church is the largest body, followed by the Presbyterian Church in Ireland (21 percent), the Church of Ireland (15 percent), and the Methodists (4 percent). The remainder is made up of smaller bodies, including Free Presbyterians, Baptists, and Pentecostals. As a result of relatively low immigration rates, only 1 percent of the population of Northern Ireland identified with a non-Christian religion — a significant contrast with mainland Britain.

The figures for identification with Christian churches may even be an underestimate, since approximately half of the remaining 15 percent comprises people who did not state their religion, as opposed to identifying themselves as having no religion. This last group has grown considerably since 1961, when only 384 people from a total population of around 1.5 million identified themselves as → atheists or having no religion, to around 9 percent in 2001, but this figure still remains much lower than in the rest of the United Kingdom.

The above figures represent cultural identification with the churches that are strengthened in Northern Ireland because of their association with national and political identities. Regular church attendance, however, has undergone a process of decline. In the late 1960s around 95 percent of Catholics and 46 percent of Protestants attended church on a weekly basis; in 2004 these figures had dropped to 60 percent and 34 percent respectively.

Perhaps more striking, however, is the continuing strength of churchgoing in Northern Ireland when compared with the rest of the United Kingdom. In 1999, for example, it was calculated that 57 percent of the population of Northern Ireland attended church at least once a month, as compared with 13 percent in Great Britain. Only 18 percent of the Northern Irish population never attend church, and religion remains a key influence on the culture to an extent unknown on the mainland.

One feature that Northern Irish Christianity shares with British Christianity is the tendency for the growing churches to be disproportionately concentrated in the evangelical sector. Evangelical churches, both of a traditional and of a charismatic variety, have been particularly effective in attracting younger people in the cities and include some of Northern Ireland's most dynamic congregations — for example, the Christian Fellowship Church in Belfast.

2.6. Relationships and Prospects

2.6.1. Perhaps one of the most notable features in the modern British religious scene is a change in the nature of ecumenical endeavor between churches. → Ecumenism in the late 19th and 20th centuries was dominated by the prospects of corporate reunion, a goal that continues to provoke interest. The Church of England has been particularly active in promoting conversations to this end, and it seems not unlikely that some form of reunion with the Methodist Church might be achieved in the current century. However, the creation in 1990 of a new set of ecumenical instruments — "Churches Together," with individual bodies for England, Scotland, and Wales — has tended to focus attention less on grand schemes and more on local conversations and cooperation; in many places these initiatives have provided common ground for both Catholics and Protestants. This issue is of particular importance in Northern Ireland.

For the growing evangelical constituency in the churches, the resurgence of the Evangelical Alliance (a body founded in 1846 as a link between evangelicals in various churches, both in Britain and overseas; → World Evangelical Alliance) has helped different denominational representatives of the movement to draw closer together, as have a series of large-scale annual festivals such as Spring Harvest and New Wine. The latter, however, while bringing together different denominational expressions of evangelical Christianity, may also have the effect of reinforcing fault lines within the movement — for example, between charismatic and Reformed evangelicals.

The most problematic religious relationships in modern Britain are no longer the product of conflicts between groups of Christians but of difficulties in reaching an accommodation with more recent arrivals on the religious scene, especially Islam. This issue has become particularly prominent in places where it is reinforced by ethnic tensions and on a public level by the association of some forms of Islam with political terrorism. In seeking to address this issue, the public role of religion in society has become the subject of renewed debate, with consequences for other religious groups especially in educational and social policy and the promotion of a new criminal offense of incitement to religious hatred. It seems unlikely that this issue will become any the less urgent or more easily resolvable in the near future.

2.6.2. Two clear impressions emerge from any review of the modern religious landscape of Britain. The first is the overall impression of continued numerical decline. This is not so apparent in rela-

tion to the broad sense of identity between the vast bulk of the British population and the Christian faith, though that attachment is likely to become ever more attenuated as fewer Britons experience meaningful contact with a church. It is readily apparent, however, in relation to the numbers of people attending church or (where this is a valid category) coming into membership. This is a particular problem for the long-established mainstream churches and especially the established national churches, with their substantial material and cultural investment in a parish system. If resources — in terms of regular worshipers and therefore of finance and active participation — continue to decline, the commitment to such an arrangement will prove ever more difficult to sustain. At the same time, there is clear evidence that the churches are unlikely to remain content simply to manage decline, and a number of programs have been developed in the new century in order to address the problem. One prominent example is Fresh Expressions, a joint Anglican and Methodist enterprise that aims to support, encourage, and develop local initiatives in finding new ways of configuring the church to reach groups for whom traditional forms have proved inadequate.

The second is the broad exception to the overall pattern of decline presented by evangelicalism. This impression clearly should not be represented in absolute terms — some liberal and Catholic congregations are experiencing growth, and some evangelical congregations are in decline — but it is evident that at present the vast majority of growing churches are located at some point on the evangelical spectrum, mostly at its more conservative and charismatic end. Evangelicalism as a whole has grown from 30 percent of English churchgoers in 1989 to 40 percent in 2005. If this trend continues for any significant length of time, it will certainly change the character of English Christianity, possibly recapturing, in a contemporary mode, the enterprise and activity of the period 1750-1850. Something of this potential is already apparent in churches like Holy Trinity Brompton, which, by pioneering the Alpha course and similar initiatives, has begun to exert an influence far beyond its immediate locality. Whether a British Christianity in which expansionist evangelicalism was the dominant component would then be capable of reversing the trend to numerical decline is perhaps the most intriguing question for British Christianity in the 21st century.

Bibliography: D. W. BEBBINGTON, Evangelicalism in Modern Britain: A History from the 1730s to the 1980s

(London, 1989) • P. BRIERLEY, *"Christian" England: What the 1989 English Church Census Reveals* (London, 1991); idem, *The Tide Is Running Out: What the English Church Attendance Survey Reveals* (London, 2000) • C. G. BROWN, *Religion and Society in Scotland since 1707* (Edinburgh, 1997) • G. DAVIE, *Religion in Britain since 1945: Believing without Belonging* (Oxford, 1994) • S. GILLEY and W. J. SHEILS, eds., *A History of Religion in Britain* (Oxford, 1994) • K. HYLSON-SMITH, *Christianity in England from Roman Times to the Reformation* (3 vols.; London, 2001); idem, *The Church in England from Elizabeth I to Elizabeth II* (3 vols.; London, 1997) • P. MITCHEL, *Evangelicalism and National Identity in Ulster, 1921-1998* (Oxford, 2003) • C. MITCHELL, *Religion, Identity, and Politics in Northern Ireland* (Aldershot, 2006) • G. PARSONS, ed., *The Growth of Religious Diversity: Britain from 1945* (2 vols.; Manchester, 1994); idem, ed., *Religion in Victorian Britain* (4 vols.; Manchester, 1998) • M. WATTS, *The Dissenters from the Reformation to the French Revolution* (Oxford, 1978) • J. WOLFFE, *God and Greater Britain: Religion and National Life in Britain and Ireland, 1843-1945* (London, 1994).

MARK SMITH

United Nations

1. Origins
2. Organs
3. Significant Activities of Concern to the Churches
4. Assessment

1. Origins

The concept of an association of all the nations of the world to keep the peace and promote international cooperation seems to have originated with British foreign secretary Edward Grey (1905-16) and was promoted during World War I by U.S. president Woodrow Wilson (1913-21) in his statement of war and peace aims (the Fourteen Points). A commission at the Paris Peace Conference of 1919 drafted the covenant for the League of Nations (LN, Société des Nations), and it was included in all the peace treaties. The LN, with headquarters in Geneva, then convened in January 1920, and its secretariat, council, and assembly engaged in a wide range of activities to foster international harmony. Various ecumenical organizations, such as the U.S. Federal Council of Churches, the → YMCA/YWCA, and the → Life and Work movement supported the vision of the LN. It was crippled from the outset, however, because it seemed to be an organization that the victors created to maintain a postwar status quo, while the United States rejected both the Versailles Treaty and League membership. The Soviet Union joined only in 1934, while Japan and Germany withdrew in 1933. Unable to halt aggression by either the Axis powers or the Soviet Union, it became dormant after the outbreak of World War II. It formally dissolved on April 18, 1946, and transferred its mission to the United Nations (U.N.).

Through the Declaration of the United Nations (January 1, 1942), the United States, Great Britain, the Soviet Union, China, and 26 other countries formally allied to combat the Axis powers. At various conferences during the war the four great powers considered the idea of a new international body to replace the failed LN. In 1944 at Dumbarton Oaks (Washington, D.C.), a provisional structure for the United Nations Organization (UNO) was worked out. At the San Francisco conference, April 24–June 26, 1945, the draft was extensively rewritten, and the final version was unanimously approved by representatives from 50 nations. Known as the Charter of the United Nations, it was then ratified by the five permanent members of the Security Council (China, France, Great Britain, the Soviet Union, and the United States) and a majority of the other signatories and went into force on October 24, 1945. Included in the Charter were the Statutes of the International Court of Justice, the successor to the Permanent Court of International Justice (1922), with its seat in The Hague, Netherlands. Through a donation from John D. Rockefeller Jr. (1874-1960), the U.N. headquarters was built on an 18-acre site in New York City.

By not including it in any peace treaty, the drafters of the U.N. Charter avoided the mistake that undermined the League of Nations. The Charter also tied the U.N. ("UNO" fell into disuse by the 1950s) to the peoples of the member nations and expressed several far-reaching aims: "to save succeeding generations from the scourge of → war . . . ; to reaffirm faith in fundamental human → rights, in the dignity and worth of the human person . . . ; to establish conditions under which justice and respect for the obligations arising from treaties and other sources of → international law can be maintained; and to promote social progress and better standards of life in larger freedom." The U.N. committed itself to maintaining international peace and security and promoting the economic and social advancement of all peoples. At the same time, the Charter affirmed the equality and sovereign independence of the member states and specified that the U.N. could not intervene in their internal affairs.

2. Organs

As of 2007, there were 192 members of the U.N. It is financed through an elaborate formula of contributions from the members. The principal organs are the General Assembly (the main deliberative body, in which every member has one vote), Security Council (five permanent members with veto power and ten temporary seats rotated among the other members; it has authority to take concrete actions to uphold peace and security), Secretariat (the executive agency, whose general secretary is elected by the General Assembly upon the recommendation of the Security Council), Economic and Social Council (promotes international economic and social cooperation and development), and International Court of Justice (the primary judicial organ). A Trusteeship Council oversaw the decolonization of the 11 dependent territories that were under the international trusteeship system created by the U.N. Charter as a successor to the LN mandate system, but it suspended operations in 1994 after the last territory became independent.

There are approximately 20 autonomous specialized agencies, programs, and funds that relate to the U.N. through the Secretariat, such as the Food and Agriculture Organization, World Health Organization, International Labor Organization, U.N. Conference on Trade and Development (UNCTAD), U.N. Children's Fund (UNICEF), and U.N. Educational, Scientific, and Cultural Organization (→ UNESCO). Two nonmember states, the Holy See and → Palestine, have "observer" status, as do some 60 intergovernmental organizations, nongovernmental organizations (NGOs), and entities whose statehood or sovereignty are not precisely defined. They have the right to speak at General Assembly meetings but cannot vote. The Economic and Social Council has granted "consultative" status to over 2,700 NGOs. They are divided into three categories — general, special, and roster — depending on the significance of the contributions they can make within their competence to the work of the council, its subsidiary bodies, or other U.N. bodies. Many religious bodies hold this status, for example, the → Baptist World Alliance, Catholic Relief Services, Commission of the Churches on International Affairs (CCIA) of the → World Council of Churches, Franciscans International, Greek Orthodox Archdiocesan Council of North and South America, → Lutheran World Federation, Mennonite Central Committee, Pax Christi International, → Salvation Army, and → World Evangelical Alliance.

3. Significant Activities of Concern to the Churches

The U.N. is an extraordinarily complex organization whose bureaucracy deals with a myriad of concerns — peacekeeping, decolonization, economic development, commerce, environmental protection, caring for children, combating hunger and disease, and refugees. The ongoing Palestine question and the defusing of small wars around the globe have been of great interest to the churches. From its founding in 1946, the WCC's CCIA worked closely with various U.N. bodies (esp. the U.N. High Commissioners for Refugees) in dealing with → refugee problems and supported U.N. efforts to foster decolonization, combat → racism, and promote economic development and environmental protection.

Of paramount significance was the matter of human rights. Various church representatives (mainly from the United States) lobbied in San Francisco for including a general affirmation in the Charter, the National Catholic Welfare Conference issued "A Declaration of Human Rights" in 1947, and the CCIA, under its first director, American Lutheran O. Frederick Nolde (1899-1972), mobilized some 42 NGOs to persuade the Economic and Social Council to draft an all-encompassing statement. The final version, known as the Universal Declaration of Human Rights, was adopted and proclaimed by the General Assembly on December 10, 1948. Declaring that "all human beings are born free and equal in dignity and rights," the 30 articles include almost every imaginable aspect of human rights, including religious freedom: "Everyone has the right to freedom of thought, conscience and religion; this right includes freedom to change his religion or belief, and freedom, either alone or in community with others and in public or private, to manifest his religion or belief in teaching, practice, worship and observance" (art. 18; → Religious Liberty).

Although this document was essentially declaratory and had no binding status in international law, it was the first time that the international community had agreed to expressing human rights in a way that included universally acceptable norms. In 1968 the U.N. International Conference on Human Rights decided that the declaration "constitutes an obligation for the members of the international community." It was subsequently expanded by two treaties: the International Covenant on Civil and Political Rights, and the International Covenant on Economic, Social, and Cultural Rights (adopted 1966, ratified 1976). The U.N. Commission on Human Rights, founded in 1947 (replaced by the U.N. Human Rights Council in 2006) and overseen by the

U.N. High Commissioner for Human Rights, is responsible to monitor and call attention to human rights abuses. The overlapping responsibilities of the human rights bureaucracy, membership of countries in the commission/council who themselves engage in notorious human rights violations, and the politicization of the agency have undermined the U.N.'s effectiveness in the human rights field.

Also of significance to the churches is the Millennium Development Goals (MDGs), a set of time-bound goals and targets for combating poverty, hunger, disease, illiteracy, environmental degradation, and discrimination against women. They were agreed to at a special U.N. summit meeting in New York in September 2000 and affirmed by the General Assembly. The eight goals to be achieved by 2015 are:

1. eradicate extreme → poverty and → hunger
2. achieve universal primary → education
3. promote gender equality and empower women
4. reduce child mortality
5. improve maternal → health
6. combat HIV/AIDS, malaria, and other diseases
7. ensure environmental sustainability (→ Environment)
8. develop a global partnership for → development.

A set of specific objectives has been identified to achieve each of the goals. The MDGs are intended to be a framework for the entire U.N. system to work together toward a common end, and the U.N. Development Group is charged with keeping them at the center of the world body's focus. Reports are issued each year detailing what has been accomplished so far.

4. Assessment

The lofty vision of the U.N.'s founders of ushering in an era of world → peace was never fulfilled. The cold war hamstrung much of its peacekeeping efforts, and its effectiveness was largely limited to defusing smaller conflicts. It did, however, provide a forum for the newly emerging nations to assert their interests and was a critical force in the ending of → colonialism. It afforded space for the NGOs, including church-related and faith-based groups, to exercise influence. In the long run, the U.N.'s efforts to keep the issues of human rights and economic development in the foreground of global concern may be its most enduring achievement.

Bibliography: P. ALSTON, *The United Nations and Human Rights: A Critical Appraisal* (Oxford, 1992) • D. A. BELL and J. M. COLCAND, *Ethics in Action: The Ethical Challenges of International Human Rights Organizations* (New York, 2007) • A. J. VAN DER BENT, *A Brief History of the WCC's Commission of the Churches on International Affairs* (Geneva, 1986) • J. FOMERAND, *Historical Dictionary of the United Nations* (Lanham, Md., 2007) • P. M. KENNEDY, *The Parliament of Man: The Past, Present, and Future of the United Nations* (New York, 2006) • J. MAHONEY, *The Challenge of Human Rights* (Malden, Mass., 2007) • O. F. NOLDE, *The Churches and the Nations* (Philadelphia, 1970) • J. S. NURSER, *For All Peoples and All Nations: The Ecumenical Church and Human Rights* (Washington, D.C., 2005) • J. S. ROSSI, *Uncharted Territory: The American Catholic Church at the United Nations, 1946-1972* (Washington, D.C., 2006) • T. G. SCOTT, *The Rise and Fall of the League of Nations* (London, 1973) • G. WEISS, *UN Voices: The Struggle for Development and Social Justice* (Bloomington, Ind., 2005) • WORLD COUNCIL OF CHURCHES, *The Role of the World Council of Churches in International Affairs* (Geneva, 1999). The U.N. Documentation Centre, New York, provides online access (at www.un.org/documents/) to the texts of most official documents produced by the principal organs of the U.N. system.

RICHARD V. PIERARD

United States of America

	1960	1980	2000
Population (1,000s):	186,158	230,406	277,825
Annual growth rate (%):	1.41	0.97	0.71

Area: 9,529,063 sq. km. (3,679,192 sq. mi.)

A.D. 2000

Population density: 29/sq. km. (76/sq. mi.)
Births / deaths: 1.32 / 0.87 per 100 population
Fertility rate: 1.96 per woman
Infant mortality rate: 6 per 1,000 live births
Life expectancy: 77.4 years (m: 74.2, f: 80.6)
Religious affiliation (%): Christians 85.4 (indigenous 29.0, Protestants 24.7, Roman Catholics 22.2, unaffiliated 10.9, marginal 4.1, Orthodox 1.6, other Christians 0.8), nonreligious 8.6, Jews 2.0, Muslims 1.4, other 2.6.

1. Christian Churches
   1.1. Indian Churches
   1.2. Roman Catholic Church
   1.3. Black Churches
      1.3.1. Baptists
      1.3.2. Methodists
      1.3.3. Pentecostals

1. Christian Churches

1.1. *Indian Churches*

The story of Christianity in the United States of America should begin with reference to the → conversion of Native Americans, long called Indians. Most of the conquerors and settlers claimed to have interest in converting the Indians by baptizing them and leading them to faith (→ Mission). However, a combination of several factors kept the Indians from being receptive to attempts at conversion. First, they had suffered terribly in acts of "Indian removal," especially from the eastern states to barren lands in the Great Plains and the Southwest. Second, they saw that the Christian mission agencies were giving low priority to work among Indians, especially as opportunities for overseas missions developed in the 19th century. Third, many of the approaches, particularly the often harsh treatment of Indian children in mission schools, left them with negative views of Christians and their gospel. Finally, the beliefs and rituals of Indians appeared to be quite incompatible with those who represented the biblical traditions. So there was resistance.

After five centuries many Native Americans still practice their ancestral non-Christian faiths or blend them with Christian features in the largely non-Indian denominations to which they belong (→ Syncretism). The single notable exception is the Native American Church, which, founded in 1906, numbers around 250,000 adherents and is known to the larger public chiefly for legal discrimination against its sacramental activity. The latter involves the chewing of peyote seeds, which is deemed illegal because of the psychedelic effects it induces. For the most part one pursues the story of Native American religion through the life of denominations that Indians do not control.

In the final third of the 20th century a nondenominational Indian → spirituality evolved that has evoked admiration and imitation in non-Indian circles (→ New Religions) because of its concern for the → environment (→ Nature 2). Some non-Indian devotees of → New Age and other experimental spiritual movements have been drawn to some Indian practices (e.g., "Sweat Lodge" rituals), but most of these practices are disdained by Indians.

1.2. *Roman Catholic Church*

The Roman Catholic Church commands the loyalty of about one out of four U.S. citizens. In Arizona, New Mexico, and Texas the explorers and conquistadores were accompanied by missionary priests who aimed to convert the Indians and who resisted their enslavement (→ Colonialism; Colonialism and Mission 2; Slavery 1). The mission stations provided a refuge against the worst excesses of the conquest (→ Reductions; Asylum). The Roman Catholics came early to Florida, but there were few Roman Catholics originally in the 13 eastern colonies. The grand exception was the founding of Maryland as a "proprietary colony" by British converts to Roman Catholicism, but their rule was relatively brief.

A change came only in the middle of the 19th century, when immigration from Ireland and continental Europe swelled Roman Catholic ranks. The permanent Roman Catholic story began with the founding of St. Mary's in Maryland (1634); the hierarchy started only with the election of Bishop John Carroll (1735-1815) of Baltimore in 1789, the year of the writing of the U.S. Constitution. In 1829, again at Baltimore, the convening of the First Provincial Council advanced the hierarchy that eventually came to shape and govern Roman Catholics in all 50 states (→ Synod 3.1; Councils of the Church).

Roman Catholicism today is dominant throughout New England, which had first been settled by anti-Catholic Puritan Protestants. It is also predominant in the industrial cities bordering on the Great Lakes, in most metropolitan areas, in the Southwest with its Hispanic populations, and in the most populated state, California, in none of whose counties is there a larger church than the Roman Catholic. Long resident in a kind of physical and cultural → ghetto, and placed there both by Protestant opposition and by its own choice to prosper in this setting, Roman Catholicism is today well integrated into most features of American life, as evidenced and symbolized by the election of the Roman Catholic J. F. Kennedy to the U.S. presidency in 1960 and by the political power of Roman Catholics, especially in the larger cities. Only on a few social issues is a vote representative of a Catholic base or bloc evident, as in the case of opposition to legalized abortion and the marriage of homosexuals and lesbians. For the rest, Catholic votes blend in with those of their non-Catholic neighbors, who line up politically on regional and other grounds, rarely reflective of religious interests. The Catholic Church itself is ecumenically active, and since Vatican II (1962-65) it has been generally congenial toward non–Roman Catholic neighboring churches.

Doctrinally, the American Roman Catholic Church has developed no distinctives but has been instinctively loyal to Rome, which counts on it for financial and moral support. At the same time, it has contributed greatly toward the global understanding of Catholicism. The American Catholic Church has adopted the separation of → church and state (§2.3) and the development of modern voluntary organizations and lay support. It took over Protestant models of → evangelism in integrating European immigrants. In most cases, Catholics tended to form "ethnic parishes," in which Germans could worship with Germans, Hispanics with Hispanics, and the like. Church officials discouraged the formation of the ethnic parishes, but they formed anyhow, very often because members of various ethnic groups lived near each other, whether or not their church was central to their identity. The church also undertook educational and medical work, using the → religious orders of men and women for this purpose. A network of schools, colleges, universities, and hospitals was created, with the local congregations at the center.

The National Catholic Welfare Council and the Bishops' Program did more for industrial workers than Protestants did (but note the → Social Gospel). On several occasions in the 19th and 20th centuries, the laity sought democratic leadership on a Protestant model through "lay trusteeism," though this movement was suppressed. The conversions of Protestants seeking a spiritual home made Roman Catholicism at once both attractive and dangerous. Members of anti-Catholic movements like "nativism" feared that subservience to the Vatican would threaten American security and freedom (→ Prejudice). Roman Catholics could not understand this accusation and enthusiastically and patriotically adjusted to American society. The isolation, caused in part by Protestant misunderstanding, finally ended, especially after Vatican II.

Roman Catholics historically have thrown much of their support to the Democratic Party, but at the turn of the 21st century the pattern was growing more complex, and they were not reflexive followers of Democratic Party leaders; many cooperate with conservative factions, for example, in opposing → abortion. Also around the turn of the century the church was suffering a shortage of priests and members of religious orders. It also had to deal with a "priestly abuse" scandal, when hundreds of priests were found to have violated church and civil law by abusing children and youth of both sexes.

1.3. Black Churches

The already mentioned Protestant character of the colonies (see 1.2) had reference originally to white populations, not Afro-Americans, though the latter were present as early as 1619. Most of the black immigrants had been brought to the colonies by force, and they were for the most part slaves until the Emancipation Proclamation of 1863. Even later they still had to lead segregated lives (→ Racism), which applied to their churches and denominations as well. Almost 10 percent of the American people today identify with the → black churches (§1), organized chiefly in Baptist, Methodist, and Pentecostal denominations.

1.3.1. Baptists

Rival bodies named the National Baptist Convention, United States of America (the statistics are always regarded as unreliable, but they give some sense of the size of each, in this case with 8 million members), and the National Baptist Convention of America (over 3.5 million members) go back to the 18th century. The National Baptist Convention was organized in 1895 and remained a single body until 1915. Many other smaller Baptist groups also exist. The organizational life of the black Baptist denominations parallels that of white Baptists. They have no separate doctrinal patterns and are noncreedal. The black churches have carried over aspects of African religion or forms of worship developed under slavery and in recent decades have affirmed their distinctive roots (→ Afro-American Cults).

1.3.2. Methodists

Two Methodist bodies predominate in the second largest cluster of black churches. The African Methodist Episcopal Church is the result of a separation in the Philadelphia church in 1787 and was formally organized in 1816. It leads a separate life from the African Methodist Episcopal Zion Church, which began when black members withdrew from a church in New York City and founded their own church. Both bodies attracted free blacks in the slave era and prospered under the rather formally structured patterns of Methodist polity, which is connectional, as opposed to either hierarchical or purely congregational. The leaders intentionally replicated the modes of largely white Methodist bodies but, like the Baptists, preserved and developed distinctive patterns of worship.

1.3.3. Pentecostals

Fast growing are the black Pentecostal churches (→ Pentecostalism 2.2; Black Churches 2), whose roots go back to the very founding of Pentecostalism early in the 20th century. There are dozens of such bodies, many of them gathering their congregations in humble storefront churches, but the largest is the Church of God in Christ (1907; → Churches of God). Like the black Baptists and Methodists, these churches are biblically conservative, but they have features that characterize Pentecostal bodies everywhere, including the enjoyment of gifts of the Spirit such as → glossolalia, prophesying, and → healing. Like the other four largest Afro-American churches, they can claim a membership in millions, in this case between five and six million. One recent trend finds more and more African Americans forming megachurches, large congregations that reflect values of commercial society, especially as they advertise their programs and build auditoriums to attract large congregations and to advance television ministries. In almost all cases, the black congregations are politically involved, especially in issues that affect their own areas of their cities.

1.4. *Protestant Churches*

1.4.1. *In the Original Colonies*

Several Protestant churches have been at work from colonial days.

1.4.1.1. In the southern colonies *Anglicanism* (→ Anglican Communion) came in with the first settlers in 1607, and it became the established church with the privileges of a state church (→ Church and State 1). Episcopalians also settled in northern colonies like New Netherland, which became New York. Because this branch of the Church of England was so often identified with Britain during the War of Independence, it did not thrive for a time. In 1789, however, it was reorganized as the Protestant Episcopal Church in the United States of America, with its own episcopal structure (→ Bishop, Episcopate). It has long been a leader in the international Anglican Communion, though ties with Episcopal or Anglican churches in places like Africa have become strained, especially when Americans elected an openly gay bishop in August 2003 and supported the ordination of gay and lesbian candidates who were openly in same-sex relationships. Though numerically outstripped by rival Baptist and Methodist movements, and with a membership thinly spread in most states, the Episcopal Church has become a national presence.

1.4.1.2. → *Congregationalism* (§2) was the established church in the northern or New England colonies (apart from Rhode Island). It remained so until well into the 19th century (see 1.4.1.1), even though the Baptists and Methodists had more members. This church was a collection of locally autonomous yet loosely associated congregations resulting from Puritan migrations (→ Puritans), beginning with the Plymouth Colony of 1620 and the Massachusetts Bay Colony of 1630. Under the influence of the → revivals, Baptists who split off from the official Congregational Church and moved into the South set up their own churches (see 1.4.1.3). Today the word "Congregational" survives in the name of congregations who refused to join a union of most Congregational churches with the Evangelical and Reformed Church (1957) to form the United Church of Christ.

1.4.1.3. Among the *Baptists,* the Northern Baptists, now called the American Baptist Churches U.S.A., can trace their organizational roots to 1814, when they founded the American Foreign Mission Society. In their present form they were organized in 1907. They claim lineage to the First Baptist Church in Providence, Rhode Island (1639), the only New England colony that had no established church. Many Baptists developed life independently of their parent (the Congregationals) as a result of colonial era disputes about → religious liberty, → church discipline, and adult → baptism (§3.1). Those who moved south and adopted revival styles grew more rapidly than did the northern branch, which includes a spectrum of viewpoints, some of them liberal.

The conservative Southern Baptist Convention is the largest Protestant church in the country and is today increasingly a national presence. It had its roots in the work of New England revivalists (see 1.4.1.2) and English Dissenters but, unlike the → Mennonites, had no connection with European → Anabaptism. Disputes over slavery led to division from the North in 1845. Through the ensuing century and a half it had little to do with the northern and other more moderate and liberal counterparts. While it is noncreedal, it has adopted expressive statements that have been increasingly used to regularize belief, especially since an extremely conservative or fundamentalist (→ Fundamentalism) element came to dominate the denomination after the 1970s. Such conservatives also linked with fundamentalist and strict evangelicals in other denominations and became notably active in Republican Party activities and support. The Southern Baptist Convention emphasizes both biblical infallibility and the independence of local congregations, and it aggressively promotes international missionary work.

1.4.1.4. *Reformed churches* include the Reformed Church in America, the oldest church in the tradition of the pioneers who founded what is now New York (1628; → Reformed and Presbyterian Churches 4.2). Historically, most of the members have been of Dutch descent. They accept the confessions of the 17th century, though interpretations vary. The conservative Christian Reformed Church in North America was founded by Dutch immigrants in 1857.

Presbyterian Churches arose in part through a desire by some New England Congregationalists to link their congregations, but primarily under the influence of Scottish-Irish and Scottish immigrants, who settled inland, often up against the ranges of mountains such as the Appalachians, when they could settle the West. The Presbyterian Church (U.S.A.) is the largest Reformed church. It resulted from a merger of northern and southern denominations that had separated as a result of doctrinal disputes and the controversy over → slavery (§2), taking different sides in the Civil War. All Presbyterians, whether in this largest group or in the Presbyterian Church in America, which broke away in 1973 in reaction to → liberalism in the main body, trace their roots to the organization of the presbytery in Philadelphia in 1706. In → polity they are presbyterian and synodical. Along with Episcopalians, members of the United Church of Christ, and other bodies that came to be called "mainline Protestant," they suffered decline in the closing decades of the 20th century.

1.4.1.5. The *Quakers,* or Society of → Friends, were brought to Pennsylvania by William Penn (1644-1718). They were a minority movement in the other colonies. A nonsacramental church that stresses simplicity, silence, and responsiveness to the Spirit, they are also committed to → pacifism, at least in moderate forms.

1.4.2. *Arising Later*

Other Protestant groups derive from mergers, splits, or immigration.

1.4.2.1. The United Methodist Church was formed in 1939 when branches in the North and the South came together after an almost century-long separation (→ Methodist Churches 3.4). The smaller United Brethren Church joined the union in 1968. The United Methodist Church has lost members in recent decades but still numbers about eight million members. A well-organized connectional body, it coordinates efforts through a polity in which bishops are regarded as beneficial *(bene esse),* rather than essential *(esse).* Methodism, which had John → Wesley (1703-91) as its founder, also includes many conservative Wesleyan, Holiness, and Nazarene Churches. It is out of the → Holiness movements that much of early Pentecostalism issued. Meanwhile, the United Methodist majorities advocated a "pluralist" approach to doctrine and

discipline, accents that also led to reaction by more conservative Wesleyans.

1.4.2.2. Next in size are the → *Lutheran churches,* the largest Protestant body deriving from European, especially German and Scandinavian, roots. They replicated many features of the European Lutheranism of the immigrants. Only in the second half of the 20th century did many follow the European practice and have → bishops, who are of the *bene esse* of the church and who do not see themselves in the apostolic succession as being *(esse)* of the essence of the church. Some Lutheran groups call their synodical leaders presidents rather than bishops. Because the Lutherans came from so many nations, spoke so many languages, and were so divided in their understanding of polity and doctrine, Lutheran history includes a crazy quilt of separate and often merging churches. The largest group is the Evangelical Lutheran Church in America, created in 1987 by a merger of bodies, some of which were organized in Pennsylvania in 1748. Next largest is the conservative Lutheran Church–Missouri Synod, formed by immigrants to the Midwest in the 19th century and organized in 1847. Both these churches, along with the Wisconsin Evangelical Lutheran Synod and still smaller bodies, are responsive to the 1530 → Augsburg Confession and other 16th-century Lutheran formulations, though they differ about ecumenical relations (→ Ecumenical Dialogue; Ecumenism, Ecumenical Movement), the → ordination (§7.4) of women, and biblical interpretation, since all but the Evangelical Lutheran Church in America oppose ecumenical engagements and the ordination of women.

1.4.2.3. The → *Christian Church (Disciples of Christ)* is a native growth with Presbyterian and Baptist roots. It was organized in a union of Christians and Disciples in 1832. It is congregational in outlook, practices adult → baptism (§3.2), is determinedly anticreedal, and intends to be governed only by loyalty to the Bible (→ Biblicism). Ultraconservative and ultracongregational groups formed the → Churches of Christ, when the Disciples allowed for more liberal interpretations. The Churches of Christ have a headquarters and issue some periodicals, but they have no coordinating organization.

1.4.2.4. A very large number of Americans belong to *conservative* or *evangelical churches* (→ Evangelical Movement 3). Along with conservative Baptist, Reformed, Methodist, and Lutheran churches, we find many smaller churches (usually Baptist) and also the much larger Pentecostal, Holiness, Nazarene, and Adventist groups. Moderately conservative is the small Evangelical Covenant

Church, which had its roots in Swedish → Pietism (§2.8). Also of Swedish origin is the Evangelical Free Church of America, which was founded in 1884.

Three groups helped to form the → Church of the Nazarene. Of Wesleyan descent, it stresses the entire → sanctification of personal life and the experience of the Holy Spirit, though without glossolalia.

The largest of the Pentecostal Churches is the → Assemblies of God, which was formed in 1914 and had about two million members in the early years of the new century. It is one of the most rapidly growing denominations in the United States. A revivalist, conversion-minded group, it cherishes physical evidence of the presence of the Holy Spirit, especially speaking in tongues.

The → Adventists (→ Sabbatarians) differ from other conservative groups. Founded in 1863 after the failure of Christ to return according to prophecy in the 1840s, the Seventh-day Adventist Church teaches strict → Sabbath observance, has distinctive views of the second advent (→ Millenarianism 6), is known for its devotion to health (vegetarianism), and operates outstanding hospitals worldwide.

1.4.2.5. Many groups and sects stand outside Christian orthodoxy.

Not all → Unitarians regard themselves as Christian (some are humanists), but there is a Christian wing within the Unitarian Universalist Association of Congregations in North America, which was formed in 1963 when the American Unitarian Association (1825) joined forces with Universalism (1793). There is great latitude in the expressions of belief and practice, from secular humanist to liberal Protestant forms.

The → Mormons are the fastest-growing among the larger bodies in the United States, whence thousands of Mormon missionaries leave to gain converts in many areas of the world. They are rooted in revelations experienced by Joseph Smith (1805-44) in the 1830s, texts that are gathered in the *Book of Mormon.*

Jehovah's Witnesses (organized in 1884 as Zion's Watch Tower Tract Society) insist on their own Bible translation (→ Bible Versions) and have developed a doctrinal position at all points at variance with all other Christian groups.

The Church of Christ, Scientist (1879; → Christian Science) is similarly independent. The canonical text in this tradition is founder Mary Baker Eddy's (1821-1910) *Science and Health: With Key to the Scriptures.* The accent in Christian Science is on healing, its practices based in a metaphysic shared by no other church body.

Mention should also be made of Indian religions

(see 1.1) and also of Afro-American and Afro-Caribbean cults (→ Voodoo) that make use of biblical elements but are not in any sense Christian.

1.5. *Orthodox Churches*

Of the → Orthodox churches the → Russian Church did missionary work in Alaska prior to its purchase by the United States. It also started other congregations on the West Coast (Seattle, Portland, San Francisco). A bigger influx came from Greece; the Greek Orthodox Diocese of North and South America was founded in 1922. Immigrants from Armenia, Romania, and many other countries flooded into the industrial cities of the East and Midwest. Rivalries and disputes afflicted the various groups in the 20th century, for example, between the Russian Orthodox Church outside Russia (founded at Istanbul in 1920, but with headquarters in the United States from 1950) and the Russian Orthodox Church at work in the Soviet Union, or between the Balkan Orthodox churches during the days of National Socialism and the Soviet occupation. Though their numbers are similar to those of the Jews, the Orthodox churches are perceived as exerting little influence on American political and cultural life. Their ecumenical involvement, however, is increasing, even if ethnic differences are still important.

2. Ecumenical Work and Parachurch Organizations

2.1. Ecumenical organizations are similar to those in other countries. The → World Council of Churches has the support of many Christian bodies. The Federal Council of Churches was organized in 1908, which became the → National Council of Churches in 1950. This body is responsible to 35 member denominations but is shunned by conservative evangelicals. It does its work through many kinds of cooperative agencies and programs. The competing → National Association of Evangelicals includes not only 60 cooperating denominations but various other agencies, schools, and voluntary organizations. It was founded in 1942. Early in the 21st century attempts were being made to enhance cooperation in work and witness among the conciliar and evangelical bodies. The American Council of Christian Churches (1941) represents a stricter and more militant type of → fundamentalism. The → Roman Catholic Church participates in → Jewish-Christian dialogue and other ecumenical activities but does not belong officially to any ecumenical organization.

Most denominations offer theological training in their seminaries. Theological faculties were formerly strongly denominational but have now become more ecumenical at the greater universities (→ North American Theology). Evangelical seminaries are often multidenominational. In general the seminaries, while remaining staunchly conservative in doctrine, have shown greater openness than before in regard to experimenting with curriculum, → theology, education, and church practice.

Part of the complex character of American church life is the mixture of competition and cooperation among denominations. For some of the members ecumenical cooperation must be based on reasoned doctrinal grounds, while for others, practical agreement for common action is sufficient.

2.2. Parachurch agencies, which grew out of 19th-century voluntary organizations, offer many opportunities for Christian involvement. Included here are the American Bible Society (1816; → Bible Societies), Church Women United, Churches Uniting in Christ (founded in 1962 as the Consultation on Church Union in an effort to unite denominations, with name change in 2002), Christian participation in the National Conference for Communities and Justice (founded in 1928 as the National Conference of Christians and Jews, with name change in 1999), and the National Religious Broadcasters, an evangelical group. We might mention some others such as Inter-Varsity, Campus Crusade, Leprosy Mission, Prison Fellowship, Billy Graham Evangelistic Association, World Impact, and World Vision. Christians also cooperate in missionary work around the globe (→ North American Missions). Sociologists observe that for many Christians these interdenominational or parachurch agencies have more appeal than do the historic church bodies.

3. Non-Christian Religions

Up to 10 percent of the population are members of non-Christian religious groups or are atheists (→ Atheism).

3.1. *Judaism*

About 2-3 percent of the people are Jews (→ Judaism 4). Jews arrived in the colonies in 1654. In the 21st century they fall into three groups: Reform, which is more liberal; Conservative, a historical school that blends traditionalism with accommodation to America; and Orthodox, which works strenuously to promote strict observance and historic textual interpretation. Judaism is chiefly an urban phenomenon. It has a bigger influence than its numbers would indicate (→ Zionism).

3.2. *Islam*

→ Islam enjoys rapid growth both in its classic form and in natively developed versions like the Nation of Islam, which has its own scriptures, as well as the →

Qur'an (→ Crisis Cult). Estimates of the number of Muslims in the United States range from two million to as high as five million. While long perceived as marginal to other believers, after the 1990s Islam came to be the subject of much scrutiny and controversy because of Muslim participation in terrorist activities that affect the United States.

3.3. *Others*

From the beginning (note the arrival of the Shakers from England in 1774), America has seen scores, if not hundreds, of innovative groups that the majority regard as exotic, esoteric (→ Esotericism), and even threatening. In the late 1960s and the early 1970s there was a flowering of especially youth groups in the → counterculture (→ Youth Religions). These drew attention, not for their numbers, but for the way they indicated restlessness and rejection of traditional faith and as examples of widening options in religion. At first called cults, they were later named New Religious Movements. Many of them faded, and some disappeared in the course of the years.

4. Church and State

The separation of → church and state guaranteed by the U.S. Constitution represents a significant model of church-state polity. Most of the colonies originally had established churches (see 1.4.1) with special privileges, but these could not survive as immigrants came with their different ecclesiastical and confessional backgrounds. Voluntary church life, which in Rhode Island, Pennsylvania, and New York meant the absence of dependence upon the state, proved that church life independent of government support could prosper and be relied upon.

Philosophical and practical factors played their part. While almost all the "founding fathers" of the nation remained members of Christian church bodies, many combined their participation with accents from the philosophy of the → Enlightenment (§1) and British → deism, which had helped to shape the religion of men like George Washington (1732-99), John Adams (1735-1826), Thomas Jefferson (1743-1826), and James Madison (1751-1836). God was for them the God of → reason, not → revelation (§2). Nature as well as Scripture served to reveal God. Natural law, rights, and reason underlay civil morality and government. In contrast, the sectarian and dogmatic teaching of the competing churches was to be fenced off or rejected. The founders and the distinctive church bodies, some of them quite conservative, often allied in promoting religious liberty.

The practical factor was that religion should not form an obstacle to commerce, travel, and mobility between the colonies, which would soon become states. Congress realized that it could not form a nation with a national religion, an official establishment. The Bill of Rights (1789) therefore stipulated that "Congress shall make no law respecting an establishment of religion, or prohibiting the free exercise thereof." These 16 words spelled doom for the residual establishments, for example, Connecticut or Massachusetts, where in any case revivalism was quickly making the established churches into minorities.

The Constitution gives no preference to any faith, but it also allows no interference. In 1802 Jefferson coined the phrase "a wall of separation between church and state," but in actual practice the metaphor of the wall is not a satisfying image for the reality of church-state relations, and the U.S. Constitution and the Bill of Rights make no mention of such a barrier. If there is a wall, it has always been permeable. James Madison spoke more accurately of a line of distinction. The churches have always had a good deal of political influence, for example, in their opposition to slavery, in banning alcohol, in promoting voting rights for women (→ Sexism 1), in the → civil rights movement, in taking up the question of → conscientious objection (→ War), and in other social questions (→ Social Ethics 2; Substance Abuse). Furthermore, the freeing of churches from taxation indirectly represents financial largesse that is more generous than the tax support offered in many state churches. Congress and state legislatures authorize government payment of military and legislature chaplains. Churches cannot financially support candidates for public office in overt ways, but many do so covertly or allusively. Similarly, churches are not to set the curriculum taught in public schools (→ Education 2), but many organize to exert influence. Some problems remain, for example, whether to demand, permit, or deny school prayers, but, while religion-and-public-schools will never be a zone of quiet consensus, by and large most Americans are content with the separation and see religion prospering because of it.

The church's sanctioning of → civil religion and church participation in state ceremonies is a striking expression of religious life in the United States. Note should also be taken of the holiday of Thanksgiving, of presidential prayer breakfasts, of prayer fellowships, and of church support for various local concerns. Invocation of God is almost a fixed item on the agendas of many events and ceremonies.

No less striking is the involvement of many evangelicals through nondenominational groups such as the Moral Majority and Christian Coalition. These cut across the denominations, represent theologi-cally and politically conservative Protestantism, and took on great significance during and after the 1980s and 1990s, especially in regard to education and the question of abortion. In many ways they now have a greater influence than that of politically involved Afro-Americans, Jews, Roman Catholics, and liberal Protestants.

Bibliography: Edited volumes: S. E. Ahlstrom, ed., Theology in America: The Major Protestant Voices from Puritanism to Neo-Orthodoxy (Indianapolis, 2003; orig. pub., 1967) • E. S. Gaustad and M. A. Noll, eds., A Documentary History of Religion in America (3d ed.; 2 vols.; Grand Rapids, 2003) • A. Heimert and A. Delbanco, eds., The Puritans in America: A Narrative Anthology (Cambridge, Mass., 1985) • A. Heimert and P. Miller, eds., The Great Awakening: Documents Illustrating the Crisis and Its Consequences (Indianapolis, 1967) • R. R. Ruether and R. S. Keller, eds., Women and Religion in America (3 vols.; New York, 1981-86) • J. Wilson and D. L. Drakeman, eds., Church and State in American History (Boston, 1987).

Monographs: S. E. Ahlstrom, A Religious History of the American People (New Haven, 1972) • H. W. Bowden, American Indians and Christian Missions (Chicago, 1981) • J. Butler, Awash in a Sea of Faith: Christianizing the American People (Cambridge, Mass., 1992) • J. Dolan, The American Catholic Experience: A History from Colonial Times to the Present (Garden City, N.Y., 1985) • E. S. Gaustad and P. L. Barlow, New Historical Atlas of Religion in America (New York, 2001) • R. T. Handy, A Christian America: Protestant Hope and Historical Realities (New York, 1984) • J. Hennessey, American Catholics: A History of the Roman Catholic Community in the United States (New York, 1981) • C. E. Lincoln and L. H. Mamiya, The Black Church in the American Experience (Durham, N.C., 1990) • W. G. McLoughlin, New England Dissent, 1630-1833: The Baptists and the Separation of Church and State (2 vols.; Cambridge, Mass., 1971); idem, Revivals, Awakenings, and Reform, 1607-1977 (Chicago, 1978) • S. E. Mead, The Lively Experiment: The Shaping of Christianity in America (New York, 1963) • P. Miller, Errand into the Wilderness (Cambridge, Mass., 1956) • H. R. Niebuhr, The Kingdom of God in America (Chicago, 1937); idem, The Social Sources of Denominationalism (New York, 1929) • M. A. Noll, America's God: From Jonathan Edwards to Abraham Lincoln (New York, 2002); idem, A History of Christianity in the United States and Canada (Grand Rapids, 1992) • V. Synan, The Holiness-Pentecostal Tradition: Charismatic Movements in the Twentieth Century (2d ed.; Grand Rapids, 1997).

Martin E. Marty

Unity

On the basis of the biblical witness, and with the early → creeds, Christianity confesses *one* → church. From the beginning of the church, theological reflection has been concerned about the church's unity, and ecclesiastical and theological history has sought to maintain or regain it. With the rise of the ecumenical movement, the struggle for unity became a dominant feature of church history in the 20th century, and it will continue to be an urgent task in the 21st century.

1. Terminology

This new and intensive attention to one of the essential marks of the church, which embraces all aspects of church teaching, theological reflection, and church life, could not proceed from an agreed understanding of unity. The term "unity" in fact has many meanings, and Christianity, which is marked by division into denominations and by a multiplicity of theological positions and social and cultural contexts, understands the term in various ways. Phrases like "the unity of the church or of Christians" or "ecclesiastical or Christian unity" need closer definition, which ecumenical discussion aims to provide.

In such discussion the concept of visible unity is to the forefront. It stands opposed to an idea of invisible unity and presupposes that unity must take concrete, recognizable, and effective forms. At the same time, it indicates that the ecumenical task is to make unity visible. Unity does not have to be created or established, for it is the gift of the triune God to his church and is thus an object of → faith and → confession. In basic outline it is experienced already in Christian fellowship and → solidarity.

2. First Concepts or Models

At the beginning of the ecumenical movement there were no concepts or models of unity. There was only a painful sense of the divisions of Christianity and an awareness that unity was needed for the sake of credible witness to the world and common service in it. As discussions began, it was quickly seen that it was necessary to reflect on goals in order to hold together and integrate the many ecumenical efforts and give them a common orientation. In this first phase of ecumenical discussion (1910-37) there were various concepts or models of unity, which are still influential.

2.1. *Federation of Churches*

First comes that of a federation or alliance of churches with various structures and tasks. Representatives of the Protestant and Orthodox churches found in this conception an expression of an already existing spiritual unity in faith in the one Lord and also a basis for common action in what were now seen to be worldwide social, missionary, and evangelistic tasks. A step was seen here on the path toward a more comprehensive unity, and it was taken in federations of churches of the same or similar (e.g., Reformation) traditions. It also was taken in the formation of many councils, associations, and conferences of churches of different traditions at various levels: ecumenical (e.g., the → World Council of Churches [WCC]), continental (e.g., Conference of European Churches), national (e.g., National Council of the Churches of Christ in the U.S.A.), regional, and local.

2.2. *Spiritual Unity*

In contrast to a federative model, representatives from Pietist circles (→ Pietism) within the churches stressed the spiritual unity that is already present based on common affirmation of God's → revelation according to the witness of Holy Scripture and on the joint commitment of personal → faith in Jesus Christ as Lord and Savior. Mutual respect and cooperation in a federation would thus be an adequate expression of this unity. This view, which in effect meant acceptance of the status quo, is often presented even now, though with other arguments.

2.3. *Pulpit and Altar Fellowship*

Pulpit and altar fellowship is regarded as a form of unity by those (esp. in → Lutheran churches) who see it as the result of an achieved agreement in basic convictions of faith and who thus, with reference to the → early church, champion an indissoluble relation between eucharistic and ecclesial fellowship (→ Eucharist 5). Also here, a federation would provide an adequate structural model for a fellowship of this kind.

2.4. *Organic Unity*

Anglicans especially advocate an organic or corporate unity, and this idea has achieved some priority in the → Faith and Order movement (→ Anglican

Communion). It stresses the fact that unity must take visible and therefore structural forms, as may be seen in the NT and the early church, and it results from an understanding of the church as an → organism, as the body of Christ. The forms include eucharistic fellowship and a commonly recognized → ministry (being part of the apostolic succession of the episcopate; → Bishop, Episcopate). Adopting this view would mean bringing so far independent churches into a unified church on the regional or national level. This has been achieved in various reunions (→ United and Uniting Churches; Church of South India) and is sometimes still a goal.

3. Development of Concepts and Models

After the founding of the WCC in 1948, discussions of unity and concrete efforts to achieve it became more intense. The entrance of the → Orthodox churches brought new accents when they came out of their isolation in 1961, as did the membership of a growing number of → Third World churches. → Vatican II brought the → Roman Catholic Church into the ecumenical movement, which contributed to the initiation of a great number of bilateral dialogues between → Christian World Communions and their member churches. This interaction led to new forms of the ecumenical search for unity besides those undertaken by the WCC.

In spite of the ecclesiological neutrality imposed on the WCC by the Toronto Declaration of 1950 (which declared that the WCC as such and officially affirms no specific doctrine of the church or of the nature of church unity), the WCC Assembly in New Delhi in 1961 gave a first description of the unity of the church, which has become one of the most important statements of the ecumenical movement: "We believe that the unity which is both God's will and his gift to his Church is being made visible as all in each place who are baptized into Jesus Christ and confess him as Lord and Saviour are brought by the Holy Spirit into one fully committed fellowship, holding the one apostolic faith, preaching the one Gospel, breaking the one bread, joining in common prayer, and having a corporate life reaching out in witness and service to all and who at the same time are united with the whole Christian fellowship in all places and all ages in such wise that ministry and members are accepted by all, and that all can act and speak together as occasion requires for the tasks to which God calls his people." Adopted here is the concept of organic unity, even though the form of structural implementation is left open.

3.1. *Conciliar Fellowship*

The WCC Assembly at Nairobi in 1975 received afresh the New Delhi concept and connected it with the conciliar and universal dimension of unity set forth at the Uppsala Assembly in 1968. According to Nairobi, "The one Church is to be envisioned as a conciliar fellowship of local churches which are themselves truly united." This conciliar fellowship finds its basis and expression in a common confession of the apostolic faith (→ Apostles' Creed); in the mutual recognition of the apostolicity and catholicity of the participating churches and their members, sacraments, and ministries; in eucharistic communion; in witness and service in the world; and in conciliar gatherings and decisions at every level. These elements, along with an added renunciation of mutual condemnations (1978), are now regarded as indispensable for the achievement of church unity. The development of the idea of visible organic unity is now tied to the structural model of united churches and the surrender of prior denominational identities.

3.2. *Unity in Reconciled Diversity*

Increasingly in bilateral ecumenical conversations the aspect of surrendering confessional identities and the question of goals have led representatives of Christian World Communions to introduce the concept of "unity in reconciled diversity" into ecumenical discussion. Here the determinative idea is that, in the perspective of universal denominational traditions, there can be unity not only on the basis of unified metadenominational local churches but also where confessional traditions and identities are preserved even structurally. This understanding presupposes that in the process of ecumenical → dialogue the given confessional differences are renewed and changed in such a way as to lose their divisive character and hence to be reconciled.

The elements essential to the visible unity sought in this way are the same as in the concept of conciliar unity. Accordingly, conversations between representatives of these two concepts led to the agreement that these two concepts are not to be seen as alternatives but rather as complementary. The concept "unity in reconciled diversity" has been welcomed by the → Lutheran World Federation and other Christian World Communions, and its thrust has been integrated into related concepts such as "communion of communions," "church fellowship," "full communion," and "sister churches."

3.3. *Koinonia, Communion*

A further significant step in outlining the nature of the unity we seek was taken by the Seventh Assembly of the WCC, meeting in 1991 at Canberra. The assembly statement "The Unity of the Church as Koinonia: Gift and Calling" stands in obvious continuity with earlier statements but situates its formulations in a wider, comprehensive salvation-historical, ecclesiological, and historical context. The central section of the statement formulates the conditions and expressions of church unity: "The unity of the church to which we are called is a koinonia given and expressed in the common confessions of the apostolic faith; a common sacramental life entered by the one baptism and celebrated together in one eucharistic fellowship; a common life in which members and ministries are mutually recognized and reconciled; and a common mission witnessing to the gospel of God's grace to all people and serving the whole of creation. The goal of the search for full communion is realized when all the churches are able to recognize in one another the one, holy, catholic and apostolic church in its fullness." The statement further says that unity must be expressed through conciliar forms of life and should always include legitimate diversity. Finally, the statement challenges the churches to draw concrete consequences from the convergences and agreements that have been reached. The Canberra statement, being so far the most comprehensive official WCC description of church unity, has been reaffirmed and further expanded by the statement "Called to Be the One Church" of the Ninth Assembly of the WCC, in 2006 at Porto Alegre, Brazil.

Several decisions of churches after 1991 to enter into full church fellowship or full communion are in accordance with the basic lines of the Canberra statement, for example, the declarations of full communion between the Anglican and most Lutheran churches in northern Europe (Porvoo Declaration of 1992), between the Anglican and Lutheran churches (but not Missouri-Synod Lutherans) in the United States and Canada (2003), and between the Evangelical Lutheran Church in America and three Presbyterian churches in the United States (1997) and the Moravian Church in America (1999). Even where such declarations have not yet been possible, many churches have been enabled through the ecumenical movement to achieve preliminary forms of visible unity by overcoming past enmities and moving toward better mutual understanding, theological agreements, exchange, cooperation, and solidarity.

4. Methods and Basic Orientations
Questions of method are playing an increasingly important part in ecumenical discussion and theology. Overall, the following common convictions and expectations have emerged:

The spiritual dimension (e.g., → prayer, → worship, and sharing joys and sorrows) is of fundamental importance in all efforts toward unity.

These efforts have their place in the life and work of the churches, as well as in theological dialogue.

Accordingly, we must hold together in these efforts the theological, ecclesiological, missionary, and social-ethical motives for unity.

We must not overlook the bearing of so-called nontheological or nondoctrinal factors on the disunity and unity of the churches.

Theological dialogue aims at → consensus and convergence, though different ideas may obtain regarding the degree of agreement and approximation necessary for unity (e.g., in the question of ministry).

There is agreement, however, that consensus and convergence are promoted by fellowship actually experienced and remain dependent on → reception by the churches in order to make further steps to fellowship possible.

In general, full communion (e.g., conciliar fellowship or unity in reconciled diversity) can be achieved only by a series of intervening steps (association of churches, councils, eucharistic hospitality, covenants).

Several common basic orientations also shape the quest for unity.

Unity is not uniformity but must include a diversity of theological views and of forms of ecclesiastical and Christian life (→ Pluralism 2)

Unity is not to be sought for its own sake but with reference to the mission and task of the church of Jesus Christ.

Unity and church renewal are in an indissoluble mutual relation.

All achievements of unity are provisional and stand under the caveat of eschatological consummation (→ Eschatology).

This consummation will embrace both the church and all humanity, and therefore the striving for unity must be seen in the perspective of God's plan of → salvation for the whole human race (→ Order of Salvation).

→ Ecumenical Theology; Ecumenism, Ecumenical Movement

Bibliography: Primary sources: T. F. Best and G. Gassmann, eds., *On the Way to Fuller Koinonia: Official Report of the Fifth World Conference on Faith and Order* (Geneva, 1994) • J. A. Burgess and J. Gros, eds.,

Growing Consensus: Documents from Church Conversations in the United States (New York, 1993) • G. GASSMANN, ed., *Documentary History of Faith and Order, 1963-1993* (Geneva, 1993) • *Growth in Agreement: Reports and Agreed Statements of Ecumenical Conversations on a World Level* (ed. H. Meyer and L. Vischer; New York and Geneva, 1984) • *Growth in Agreement II: Reports and Agreed Statements of Ecumenical Conversations on a World Level, 1982-1998* (ed. J. Gros, H. Meyer, and W. G. Rusch; Geneva and Grand Rapids, 2000) • JOHN PAUL II, *Encyclical Letter "Ut Unum Sint": On Commitment to Ecumenism* (Washington, D.C., 1995) • C. S. SONG, ed., *Growing Together into Unity: Texts of the Faith and Order Commission on Conciliar Fellowship* (Madras, 1978) • L. VISCHER, ed., *Documentary History of the Faith and Order Movement, 1927-1963* (St. Louis, 1963) • *What Unity Requires: Papers and Report on the Unity of the Church* (Geneva, 1976).

Secondary works: P. J. ACHTEMEIER, *Quest for Unity in the NT Church: A Study in Paul and Acts* (Philadelphia, 1987) • C. E. BRAATEN and R. W. JENSON, eds., *Church Unity and the Papal Office: An Ecumenical Dialogue on John Paul II's Encyclical "Ut Unum Sint"* (Grand Rapids, 2001); idem, eds., *In One Body through the Cross: The Princeton Proposal for Christian Unity; A Call from an Ecumenical Study Group* (Grand Rapids, 2003) • *Church and World: The Unity of the Church and the Renewal of Human Community* (Geneva, 1990) • Y. CONGAR, *Diversity and Communion* (London, 1984) • G. GASSMANN and H. MEYER, *The Unity of the Church: Requirements and Structure* (Geneva, 1983) • G. GASSMANN and J. RADANO, eds., *The Unity of the Church as Koinonia: Ecumenical Perspectives on the 1991 Canberra Statement on Unity* (Geneva, 1993) • R. GROSSCURTH, ed., *What Unity Implies: Six Essays after Uppsala* (Geneva, 1969) • S. HARRISON, *Conceptions of Unity in Recent Ecumenical Discussion: A Philosophical Analysis* (Oxford, 2000) • H. MEYER, *That They All May Be One: Perceptions and Models of Ecumenicity* (Grand Rapids, 1999) • J. MÍGUEZ BONINO, *Conflicto y unidad en la iglesia* (San José, C.R., 1992) • G. MÜLLER-FAHRENHOLZ, *Unity in Today's World: The Faith and Order Studies on "Unity of the Church, Unity of Humankind"* (Geneva, 1978) • C. PODMORE, ed., *Community, Unity, Communion* (London, 1998) • J. F. PUGLISI, ed., *Liturgical Renewal as a Way to Christian Unity* (Collegeville, Minn., 2005); idem, ed., *Petrine Ministry and the Unity of the Church: Toward a Patient and Fraternal Dialogue* (Collegeville, Minn., 1999) • G. RUGGIERI and M. TOMKA, eds., *The Church in Fragments: Towards What Kind of Unity?* (Maryknoll, N.Y., 1997) • W. A. SAAYMAN, *Unity and Mission: A Study of the Concept of Unity in Ecumenical Discussion since 1961 and Its Influence on the World Mission of the Church* (Pretoria, 1984) • G. THILS, *Histoire doctrinale du mouvement œcuménique* (new ed.; Paris, 1962) • J.-M.-R. TILLARD, *Church of Churches: The Ecclesiology of Communion* (Collegeville, Minn., 1992).

GÜNTHER GASSMANN

Universalism and Particularism

1. Terms
2. In Philosophy
3. In Theology

1. Terms

In philosophy, a *universal term* refers with the same meaning to each member of a class of objects. Common nouns provide the clearest examples of universal terms. For instance, "dog" refers to each animal that belongs to one of several wild species of canines or the various domestic breeds that derived from them. The correlative *universal concept* is the thought or idea that we think when correctly understanding and using the universal term. Dictionary definitions give us the → meanings of terms by stating the shared essential characteristics of the kinds of things to which they refer.

Medieval philosophy affirmed four universal features shared not just by members of one class of things but by every being that exists, whether divine or created. These wholly *universal properties,* called the → transcendentals (because they transcend, or cut across, all class distinctions), are oneness (unity), truth, goodness, and beauty.

Philosophies that seek to be systematic and comprehensive typically stress the universal or shared features of things. In doing so, they downplay the unique or idiosyncratic features that make individuals stand out from others of their kind. They exhibit a universalizing or generalizing tendency, one that is to be expected when seeking to grasp the big picture, to comprehend the whole.

Philosophers do not routinely speak of *particularism,* yet we can regard the opposite to the universalizing tendency as tantamount to it. Philosophers of this opposite sort more often speak of what they call the concrete, unique, or individual features of things, features that they choose to emphasize.

In theology some revealed truths are said to be *universal* because they apply to all persons and all times. Also, *universalism* in theology is the belief that all persons will ultimately receive salvation (→ Universalism, Universalists). Perhaps beliefs in a "chosen people" or a "saved remnant" amount to a type of particularism, although theologians do not ordinarily use that term for them.

2. In Philosophy

Plato (427-347 B.C.; → Platonism) made the issue of universal terms central to his dialogues. His eternal, unchangeable Ideas sustain the individual beings that are imperfect instantiations, in space and time, of those Ideas. When we correctly think and speak about the kinds of things that make up the experienced world, we do so in virtue of knowing the eternal Ideas. These Ideas are also the basis for our ethical and aesthetic concepts.

Much of the history of → philosophy after Plato consists of debates about the nature and status of the abstractions that give rise to universal terms and concepts. "To abstract" means "to draw out," specifically, to single out some elements of things for attention, while omitting from consideration their other features. For instance, the ensemble of properties in the concept "dog" does not include specification of a particular color or size. The main controversy concerns whether the basis for a universal concept has an independent reality that we just recognize when we have knowledge, or instead is our own mental construct, formed by us from our sensory experiences of things.

Aristotle (384-322 B.C.; → Aristotelianism) thought that universal properties exist right in the objects of sense experience. The mind constructs a universal concept by abstracting from sense experience the properties shared by individuals, which are the essential or defining characteristics of that kind of thing. These universal properties are real in the sensed objects and are replicated in the mind's concept. They are not also real in an independent, eternal realm, as they are for Plato.

Medieval philosophers adopted diverse positions on universals, as interpretations of Plato or Aristotle, positions variously called → realism, → nominalism, and conceptualism.

In the modern era, the philosophies of → rationalism and → empiricism introduced further modifications. Although leaning toward Plato, rationalists treated the mind's universal concepts as our direct cognition of nonsensory structures of the world itself, rather than as our apprehension of eternal entities in a separate realm altogether. Empiricists said that general concepts arise from the natural affinity or association, in our thought, of similar features drawn from our repeated sensory experiences. → Kantianism sought synthesis of the two positions, but its transcendental perspective was soon challenged by its successors.

Particularism is the opposite to stressing the universal or shared features of things. Even empiricism, though rooted in individual sense experiences, ultimately is interested in the general ideas that emerge from sensation rather than in the particular sensed objects themselves. So we could say that none of the dominant philosophies considered so far is an actual instance of particularism. All dwell on the status of universal terms and concepts and brush aside the particular object of experience once it has served its purpose.

In his lectures on the history of philosophy, G. W. F. Hegel (1770-1831; → Hegelianism) spoke disparagingly of "the particular." He says there that self-developing reason is not abstract but instead is the concrete universal. Reason is to be sought, not in such particulars of culture as the ephemera of clothing fashions or in the inconsequential details of the lives of historical figures, but instead in actual human achievement.

Emphasis on the particular aspects of life tends to be expressed in different terminology. Søren → Kierkegaard (1813-55) regarded "the existing individual" as the proper focus of philosophical and religious thought, in his deliberate attack on Hegel's preference for "world-historical" figures as the embodiment of the spirit of an entire age. Existential philosophy scrutinized specific life experiences in order to disclose what it is to be a free human being (→ Existentialism). But even those authors who advocate the centrality of the particular aspect of things must end up expounding it as a general or shared, if not truly universal, facet of human experience, or else the analysis would be of no relevance to their readers. What is philosophically noteworthy about the particular aspect as such is its significance for me and for others, its indication of some broader meaning or purpose.

3. In Theology

Dogmatic theology in traditional Christianity commonly affirms *universal propositions*. A central example is, "Everybody except Jesus [and Mary, for Roman Catholics] is a sinner in need of salvation." Another, now less acceptable to many, is, "Outside the church there is no salvation." Such affirmations, and others of more restricted scope, are said to be based on → revelation. There obviously are important disagreements among denominations, among liberal and conservative groups, as to how many, and which, affirmations of universal or limited scope form the indispensable core of the faith.

Universalism is the belief, held by some down through the centuries, that everyone eventually will be saved. The heterodox church father → Origen (ca. 185-ca. 254; → Origenism) was a universalist in this sense. The universalist movement of 17th- and

18th-century Britain and America was influenced in part by European → Pietism.

Christians who reject universalism point to general biblical statements about everlasting punishment for the unredeemed, as well as to such passages as the parable of Dives and Lazarus (Luke 16:19-31) that suggest there are indeed individuals in a place of torment from which there is no release.

Despite his Calvinist roots, Karl → Barth (1886-1968) is thought by some to have left open the possibility of universal salvation through Christ, although he did not expressly affirm it, since for him all ultimately depends on the decision and grace of God.

Bibliography: J. COLLINS, *The Mind of Kierkegaard* (Chicago, 1953) • G. W. F. HEGEL, *Lectures on the History of Philosophy* (3 vols.; London, 1892; repr., 1995) • J. H. RANDALL JR., *Aristotle* (New York, 1960) • D. ROSS, *Plato's Theory of Ideas* (Oxford, 1951) • R. SOLOMON, *From Rationalism to Existentialism: The Existentialists and Their Nineteenth-Century Background* (New York, 1972) • A. WOOZLEY, "Universals," *EncPh* 8.194-206.

ROBERT F. BROWN

Universalism, Universalists

1. History
   1.1. Origins and European Development
   1.2. In Great Britain
   1.3. In North America
2. Universalism and Unitarianism
3. Growth and Special Interests
   3.1. Theological Education
   3.2. Women
   3.3. Creedalism
   3.4. Expansion to Asia
   3.5. Redefinitions
4. The Unitarian Universalist Association

Universalism, the view that all souls eventually will be saved by, reconciled with, or restored to God, has been a belief of many Christians since the time of the earliest churches. This doctrine, like → Pelagianism, was such a natural way of thinking about → soteriology that it has always remained an option in folk and heterodox religion. It has often been deduced from the infinite → love and the overwhelming power of God.

1. History
1.1. *Origins and European Development*
Although forms of universalism were advocated by some → church fathers, including Clement of Alex-

andria, → Origen, and Gregory of Nyssa, it was never generally accepted as early church doctrine, and sporadic attempts were made to have it condemned. There is no continuous intellectual tradition of universalism from ancient times. Universalist works of scholarship in the 19th century, such as *Ancient History of Universalism* (1829), by Hosea Ballou II (1796-1861, first president of Tufts College), traced the doctrine through the ages to supply apologists with an answer to the question of why, if universalism is correct, no one of importance had thought of it before then.

During the → Reformation, universalism was a feature of certain forms of Pietist → Anabaptism. Some of these universalists advocated radical interfaith toleration, embracing Jews, Muslims, pagans, and even demons in the scheme of → salvation. → Pietism was brought from Germany to the mid-Atlantic states of the United States in the early 18th century. Not all of these Anabaptist immigrants were universalists, nor was this doctrine often the distinctive feature of their religion.

One of the earliest explicitly universalist preachers in America was Georges de Benneville (1703-93), who had lived among the Pietists in Germany and continued to work alongside Dunkers and other Pietists after he arrived in Pennsylvania in 1741. One of these German immigrants published a translation into English of *The Everlasting Gospel* (ca. 1700) of George Klein-Nicolai (Paul Siegvolk), which later influenced American Universalists, including Elhanan Winchester (1751-97). Winchester, a Calvinist Baptist from New England, came to doubt his church's teaching on salvation while evangelizing in South Carolina and in 1781, after settling among the → Baptists of Philadelphia, openly espoused universalism.

1.2. *In Great Britain*
Organized Universalism began in England with the Calvinistic Methodist James Relly (1722-78), author of *Union* (1759). According to *Union,* Christ made a full → atonement for all of humankind on the cross. There was no → punishment from God in the afterlife, only self-inflicted suffering by not-yet-reconciled souls. A handful of Rellyan congregations survived into the early 19th century.

The most important convert to Relly's brand of Universalism was the evangelist John Murray (1741-1815), who emigrated to the American colonies in 1770. There in 1774 he met a group of → Congregationalists in Gloucester, Massachusetts, who were already in possession of Relly's *Union.* Together, in 1779, they founded the Independent Church of Christ in Gloucester, the first Universalist church in the United States.

Between 1787 and 1794 the American Elhanan Winchester visited England. He gathered a congregation in London, published *Dialogues on Universal Restoration* (1788), and converted his successor, William Vidler (1758-1816). Under Vidler the Universalists first associated with the General Baptists, then, as they also disbelieved in the → Trinity, became Unitarian. They fueled Unitarian growth and provided British Unitarian leadership in the early 19th century. The Scottish Universalist Convention, founded by James Ure Mitchell (1833-1905), welcomed the American missionary Caroline Soule (1824-1903). Her ordination by the convention in 1880 was the first ordination of a woman in the United Kingdom. The Scottish churches eventually became Unitarian.

1.3. *In North America*

The liberal Boston Congregationalist minister Charles Chauncy (1705-87) became convinced of universal salvation in the 1750s. Thinking the world not ready for such doctrine, he refrained from publishing *The Mystery Hid from Ages and Generations* until 1784. The book was, in part, a response to John Murray's Rellyan theology. Chauncy argued that many people would require long periods of divine punishment in the afterlife in order to work out their salvation, but that the all-powerful God would ultimately succeed in his benevolent purpose. His emphasis on the reformatory nature of punishment convinced other liberal Congregationalists to cease preaching eternal punishment, though they remained unconvinced that all would be saved. When they became → Unitarians in the early 19th century, these liberals distanced themselves from universalism, not wishing to give orthodox Congregationalist apologists further ammunition against them. Chauncy's *Mystery*, meanwhile, had joined Winchester's *Dialogues* as required reading for Universalists.

Universalism in rural New England was largely an indigenous reaction against the extremes of → Calvinism, both in its established (Congregationalist) and separatist (Baptist) forms. Indeed, the conflict between Congregationalists and Baptists, especially in frontier towns unguided by Boston-educated clergy, led many people, including Caleb Rich (1750-1831), to wonder if both "orthodoxies" might be equally wrong. Two sets of visions, in 1773 and 1778, taught Rich, first, that no one would be condemned to everlasting punishment, and then that all would be saved. His ministry converted and inspired a new generation of evangelists. The earliest churches, alongside Murray's churches in Gloucester and Boston, were gathered in the rural towns

of Oxford and Milford, in central Massachusetts. The work of the rural evangelists was reinforced by Winchester's tours through New England in 1785 and 1794.

At a meeting in 1785 in Oxford, Massachusetts, Murray instructed Universalists how to organize legally so that members of their societies would be exempt from the established Congregational (or Standing Order) parish taxes. The first sustained Universalist organization was the Philadelphia Convention (1790-1809). The New England General Convention, founded in 1793, was the seed from which the national denomination eventually grew. The most celebrated of its annual conventions was held in 1803 in Winchester, New Hampshire.

This 1803 convention adopted the so-called Winchester Profession, which reads in whole: "We believe that the Holy Scriptures of the Old and New Testaments contain a revelation of the character of God and of the duty, interest and final destination of mankind. We believe that there is one God, whose nature is love, revealed in one Lord → Jesus Christ, by one → Holy Spirit of Grace, who will finally restore the whole family of mankind to holiness and happiness. We believe that → holiness and true → happiness are inseparably connected, and that believers ought to be careful to maintain order and practice good works; for these things are good and profitable unto men." This statement was understood not as a creed but as one of general → consensus. It was adopted to make Universalism more like other denominations in the eyes of the law. A liberty clause was appended, allowing churches to make additions to the statement as long as they did not contradict the general profession.

Universalist state conventions began to organize in the 1820s. When the national General Convention was established in 1833, the state organizations retained most of the power, including that of licensing and disciplining ministers. The General Convention did not begin to develop guiding authority until a generation later.

2. Universalism and Unitarianism

Beginning in 1795, Hosea Ballou (1771-1852, great-uncle of Hosea Ballou II) introduced and popularized Unitarianism among Universalists. In his *Treatise on Atonement* (1805), Ballou rejected the idea, retained by Relly, that God needed to be reconciled to humanity, arguing instead that humanity needed to be reconciled to God. According to Ballou, Christ was incarnated to demonstrate divine love; it was up to every person to respond. This doctrine became nearly universally popular among Universalists.

Ballou went too far, though, according to some of his peers, when he began to preach that everyone would be saved immediately after death.

The followers of Ballou struggled for control of the denomination with a faction called the Restorationists, who, like Winchester and Chauncy, envisioned a purgatorial and educational period of limited "future punishment." Ballou's party won a political victory, largely because Ballou was personally supported by the majority of those who disagreed with him theologically.

In 1831 some of the Restorationists withdrew and formed the Massachusetts Association of Universal Restorationists. This tiny sect, many of whose members served Unitarian churches, lasted a decade, until its membership fragmented over issues of social reform. The proportion of Universalists who held Ballou's doctrine of the afterlife, never more than half, began to decline soon after the schism. By 1878, when the Universalist ministers of Boston issued a statement affirming that repentance and salvation are not limited to this life, American Universalists were almost unanimously Restorationist in belief.

3. Growth and Special Interests

Universalists were as energized and divided by 19th-century social reform movements as other American denominations. Although they did not speak with a single voice, many Universalists were ardent supporters of temperance, abolition, → peace, worker's → rights, woman's rights, and other causes. Among the most notable were Benjamin Rush (1745-1813), a pioneer in the treatment of mental illness; Adin Ballou (1803-90), who founded a socialist and pacifist utopian community in Hopedale, Massachusetts; Charles Spear (1803-63), opponent of capital punishment; Mary Livermore (1820-1905), abolitionist and woman's rights advocate; and Clara Barton (1821-1912), battlefield nurse and founder of the American Red Cross.

In the latter years of the 19th century, Spiritualism (→ Spiritism), perceived as a reform because it was held to be a science of the afterlife, captured the imagination of Universalists. Séance reports confirmed Universalist, especially Restorationist, eschatology. More than other issues, such as that of slavery, Spiritualism divided local Universalist churches. By the late 19th century, however, as the claims of mediums were increasingly repudiated by science, Universalists became disillusioned and lost interest.

There had been an exponential growth in Universalist numbers during the period 1810-30. By the end of the 1840s, however, the number of churches had stabilized at just over a thousand. This represented a decline relative to the growing American population. In the 20th century even the absolute numbers would drop. Various reasons have been offered for this decline. One is the gradual liberalization of theology in many mainstream American Protestant denominations, to which the advocacy of universal salvation may have contributed. There was no longer a need for a church built around this single doctrine. As Universalists became more conservative in the second half of the 19th century, the theological and liturgical differences between their churches and those of Congregationalists and Baptists began to disappear. Also, as standard-bearers of liberal Christianity (→ Liberal Theology), Universalists faced increasing competition from Unitarians, who began to endorse universal salvation themselves. Unitarians had been slower than the Universalists to establish themselves in the American West, but after the mid-19th century Unitarian efforts were more widespread and organized. By then, taking a critical approach to the Bible, Unitarians appealed more to radical Christians and → freethinkers.

3.1. *Theological Education*

Hosea Ballou and many early evangelists, most of whom were converted Baptists, had opposed the formal → theological education of the ministry. After this generation passed away, Universalists, many of whom had promoted public education, organized their own universities and seminaries, including Tufts College (1854, the Crane Divinity School started in 1869), Lombard College (1857, the Ryder Divinity School was added in 1881), and St. Lawrence University and Theological School (1858, the latter known as Canton Theological School). Of the three seminaries, only the second one survives today, merged with a Unitarian school (Meadville Lombard Theological School, Chicago).

3.2. *Women*

The Universalists were pioneers in welcoming women into the ministry. Lydia Jenkins (ca. 1825-74) began preaching and was given fellowship in the 1850s. Olympia Brown (1835-1926), a graduate of St. Lawrence, was ordained in 1863. In 1871 Universalist women formed the Women's Centenary Association (later the Association of Universalist Women), the first permanent and independent national organization of church women in the United States.

3.3. *Creedalism*

In 1870 the Universalists began to treat the 1803 Winchester Profession, without its liberty clause, as a → creed, making it a requirement for ministerial fellowship. In 1872 a Minnesota minister, Herman

Bisbee, was removed from fellowship by his state convention because he had "uttered doctrines subverting Christianity, and entirely contrary to the principles of the Universalist Church." The Universalists defended their stance by saying, "A church without a creed is smitten with paralysis, is in a false position before the world."

After much debate, in 1899 the Universalist General Convention ended the experiment with creedalism by adopting a set of principles and a new liberty clause. The principles were "The Universal Fatherhood of God; the spiritual authority and leadership of His Son, Jesus Christ; the trustworthiness of the Bible as containing a revelation from God; the certainty of just retribution for sin; the final harmony of all souls with God."

In response to new developments in science, theology, and biblical criticism and to the → Social Gospel and humanistic movements, the Universalists in 1935 adopted another new statement, the Washington Avowal: "We avow our faith in God as Eternal and All-Conquering Love, in the spiritual leadership of Jesus, in the supreme worth of every human personality, in the authority of truth known or to be known, and in the power of men of goodwill and sacrificial spirit to overcome all evil and progressively establish the kingdom of God." Once again there was a liberty clause.

3.4. *Expansion to Asia*

American Universalist missionaries arrived in Japan in 1890. They founded a small seminary, ran a "School of Liberal English," and sponsored the Blackmer Home in Tokyo, a residence for girls pursuing education. In all of these activities Universalists emphasized service rather than conversion. These activities were broken off by World War II and were not afterward resumed. By this time, however, the Universalist Church of Japan had been founded. The Universalist Church of the Philippines was organized in 1954.

3.5. *Redefinitions*

The greatest Universalist theologian of the 20th century, Clarence R. Skinner (1881-1949), revisioned Universalism in a this-worldly fashion. The kingdom of heaven, he thought, was to be realized on earth by expanding human sympathy and understanding and by adopting ideal ways of human interaction such as → pacifism and → socialism.

Yet another way of redefining Universalism — as the gathering together of the best ideas of all world religions — was undertaken in the 1950s at the Universalist Charles Street Meeting House in Boston during the influential ministry there of the Unitarian Kenneth Patton (1911-94). Although the Meet-

ing House itself is defunct, its worship and the ideas of its pastor have influenced later Unitarian Universalist liturgy and hymnody.

4. The Unitarian Universalist Association

Although union with Universalists had been considered by the National Conference of Unitarian Churches in 1865, it was not until 90 years later that the two denominations began to make plans for merger. Meanwhile, during 1925-27, the Universalists had seriously considered an overture made to them by the Congregationalists. Worried about loss of their identity, concerned about Congregational plans to unite with other more conservative denominations, and simultaneously wooed by the Unitarians, who feared the loss of a potential partner for themselves, the Universalists let this opportunity pass. Negotiations between the Universalist Church of America and the American Unitarian Association begun in 1956 resulted in the creation in 1961 of the Unitarian Universalist Association of Congregations in North America (UUA). The group today comprises just over 150,000 members and about 1,000 congregations.

Since 1961 some Universalists have expressed regret at this consolidation. Unitarian culture, history, and theology predominated, and many Unitarian Universalists needed to be reminded not to simply call themselves "Unitarian." Conservative Universalists watched with concern as the majority of Unitarian Universalists moved steadily away from Christianity. In recent years, however, there have been attempts to revive Universalism as a distinctive identity or dimension within Unitarian Universalism. Old and new specifically Universalist organizations have been activated. Making creative interpretations of this tradition, some people have cast Universalism as the mystical and emotional side of Unitarian Universalism. This stance has allowed Unitarian Universalists to criticize what they perceive as the excessive intellectualism of the Unitarian heritage and to organize support for new spiritual pathways they are eager to explore.

There are also universalists outside the Unitarian Universalist Association, sometimes identifying themselves as "universalist Christians," often in basic agreement with historic faith statements of the Universalists. As has been the case for centuries, universalism continues to be rediscovered and adopted by individuals and groups within various sects and denominations.

Bibliography: General histories: R. EDDY, *Universalism in America* (2 vols.; Boston, 1884-86) • C. A. HOWE, *The*

Larger Faith (Boston, 1993) • R. MILLER, *The Larger Hope* (2 vols.; Boston, 1979-85) • G. H. WILLIAMS, *American Universalism* (Boston, 2002).

European Universalism: J. W. HANSON, *Universalism in the First Five Hundred Years of the Christian Church* (Boston, 1899) • A. HILL, "The Obscure Mosaic of British Universalism," *TUHS* 23/1 (2003) 421-44 • G. H. WILLIAMS, *The Radical Reformation* (Philadelphia, 1962).

American Universalism: J. BUESCHER, *The Other Side of Salvation* (Boston, 2004) • E. CASSARA, *Hosea Ballou: The Challenge to Orthodoxy* (Boston, 1961) • M. HARRIS, *Historical Dictionary of Unitarian Universalism* (Lanham, Md., 2004) • P. HUGHES, "The Origins of New England Universalism: Religion without a Founder," *JUUH* 24 (1997) 31-63 • D. ROBINSON, *The Unitarians and the Universalists* (Westport, Conn., 1985) • E. ROBINSON, "The Universalist General Convention: From Nascence to Conjugation," *JUHS* 8 (1969-70) 44-93 • W. R. ROSS, *The Premise and the Promise: The Story of the Unitarian Universalist Association* (Boston, 2001) • C. WRIGHT, *The Beginnings of Unitarianism in America* (Boston, 1955).

PETER HUGHES

University

1. Term and Founding
2. Universities before 1945
3. Technical and Other Colleges
4. Idea and Ideology
5. Universities after 1945
6. The Common Structure of Universities

1. Term and Founding

From the → Middle Ages onward, universities have been cooperative amalgamations of teachers and students devoted to scholarship *(universitas magistrorum et scholarium)*. The learned academies of Greece (→ Greek Philosophy), of the → Roman Empire, and of → Islam were predecessors. The church's monasteries and schools played a part in preserving the early scholastic tradition (→ Monasticism).

As an independent search for knowledge grew, it involved a desire to link → faith to → reason and → science. → Scholasticism led to the formation of the first church-related universities. Bologna (1119) and Paris (1175) came first and provided a model for all future continental European universities. Oxford (13th cent.) and Cambridge (1226) later became a pattern for much of the Anglo-Saxon world.

In their desire to communicate knowledge, the universities established faculties of classical learning (→ theology, law, medicine) and of liberal arts (arithmetic, geometry, astronomy, music, → rhetoric, and dialectics). The aim was to promote intellectual growth, but also to train students for the professions (→ Vocation). Over the centuries the latter aim proved predominant.

2. Universities before 1945

Princes who wished to enhance their power and prestige set up the first universities in the Holy Roman Empire, beginning with Prague (1348), Vienna (1365), and Heidelberg (1385). The → Renaissance, → humanism, and → Reformation universities pushed Scholasticism into the background. Training in canon law and medicine came to the fore in the 16th century. From the 16th to the 18th century reason liberated itself from faith and from the church's authority, and then the freedom and → autonomy of scholarship and its relation to the state became central issues in the age of enlightened despotism (→ Modern Church History 2.2).

Halle was founded in 1694 under the influence of → Pietism, → rationalism, and Prussian views of the state. Göttingen (1736) aimed at a union of research and teaching. W. von Humboldt (1767-1835) organized Berlin (1810) to advocate the idealistic philosophy of F. Schelling, J. G. Fichte, F. D. E. → Schleiermacher, and H. Steffens (→ Idealism). Humboldt had in view a *universitas literarum* that would gather together all knowledge. Reactionary regimes (→ Restoration), however, soon cut short the new freedom.

In the 19th and 20th centuries the foundation of new universities — Bonn (1818), Strasbourg (1872), Frankfurt (1914), and Hamburg (1919) — followed the models of Halle and Göttingen. They stressed the autonomy of research and competent teaching. Members of the faculties were respected scholars, with philosophy as the basis.

3. Technical and Other Colleges

The universities fairly quickly linked the communication of knowledge to commercial practice. Industrialization (→ Modern Period 3) resulted in the development of technical colleges that put scientific knowledge to practical use. At first a distinction was made between universities and technical colleges, but this distinction was abandoned or modified in the 20th century.

4. Idea and Ideology

Since the days of Humboldt there has been a developing challenge to enlist science in the service of truth, to insist on the freedom of research and teaching, and to bring together teachers and students in a common search for truth. Teachers, according to Fichte, should be morally good and should use their scholarship in ways that will help the community. The vaunted freedom of universities has its limits, of course. Some universities are state institutions and are subject to legal requirements. The training of pastors, attorneys, and physicians is under external control. Even private universities, if they receive government grants, are in some sense subject to the → state.

Notwithstanding the influence of Humboldt, the German universities came under the sway of reactionary and finally anti-Semitic conservatism. The rigorously ascetic thinking of M. → Weber (1864-1920) could not prevent many professors from endorsing the expansionist war aims of 1914, rejecting the Weimar democracy (→ Modern Church History 1.4), and even backing Hitler and cooperating in National Socialism, the Holocaust, and the disastrous war that ended in 1945.

5. Universities after 1945

The efforts of socialism to take over the university system proved unsuccessful. Denazification was pursued in West Germany after 1949. Most of the students who thronged the universities were now career oriented, as was understandable for those who had survived World War II and later the Korean War. The number of universities also increased, especially, for instance, in Great Britain, where university degrees had previously been available only for the few. Women also came into the universities, especially as the courses in theology, law, and medicine became available to them.

Student unrest during and after the 1960s shattered the traditionally hierarchical structure of the universities. Secularization and political correctness also made an impact, posing their own challenges to academic freedom. The universities fell under the sway of bureaucracy as they developed in size and as budgetary pressures mounted. A struggle also took place between the demands of research and the claims of teaching, which in many cases left able teachers at a disadvantage compared with those who could publish books or academic articles or make new scientific discoveries.

Nations have become dependent on the universities for the training of leaders in all areas of life and also for the research that is done by universities and that underlies industrial and technological progress. Universities depend on governments in some measure to meet their financial needs. This mutual interdependence has much in its favor, though it can also pose serious dangers.

6. The Common Structure of Universities

The faculties and curricula of the universities have changed with intellectual, cultural, social, economic, and political changes. Scholarship itself has also undergone development. Yet, except for a few variations, the universities have remained the same in their characteristic structures through their long history.

6.1. The first structural element, that of *a corporate life of teachers and students,* was taken over from the monastery schools. Material care was provided, but far greater importance attached to the living of a common life. In some British and American schools this tradition is still to some extent maintained, but in the larger universities it can be so only to a limited degree. It has usually become impossible in many → Third World universities.

6.2. A second structural element that is hardly contested is *universities as independent corporations,* with certain privileges in the setting of curriculum, in the owning of property and endowments, in the making of statutes, and in economic and personnel matters. On much of mainland Europe, apart from Roman Catholic and private schools, most of the universities are state controlled.

In England, Oxford and Cambridge and their colleges are independent corporations. As population expanded in the 19th century, new universities were founded (Durham, London, Manchester, etc.), and further expansion came in the 20th century. Of Scotland's four original universities, Edinburgh owed its origin to the city. New universities were added as the 20th century brought a new demand for university study and government grants could be secured.

The familiar British pattern has been followed in British dominions and the former colonies. The founding of Harvard (1636) and Yale (1701) took place in the colonial period, but American independence brought with it both population growth and a demand for more universities, met in part by Christian denominations, by private donors, and by the states.

France, Spain, and Italy have universities that reach far back into the Middle Ages (e.g., Paris, Toulouse, Salamanca, Padua, and Naples), but new developments have also come in the modern period. Incidentally, universities were first thought of either as guilds of masters or as guilds of students (Bologna). The idea of a guild of masters was triumphant in the main, but students have always found difficulty in being reduced to too inferior a status.

6.3. The third structural element is *full-scale autonomy* as regards both teaching and research. Included here is not merely the organization of faculties and curriculum but also the holding of examinations, the granting of degrees, the appointing of professors, and the controlling of research. Research projects, though undertaken with aid from the government or private corporations, still are under the supervision of the university.

6.4. The fourth structural element is *the universal validity of the knowledge to be acquired*. Already in the 12th century universities were in communication with one another. We find both cooperation and learned rivalry in the different exchanges and disputations. Lectures, seminars, tutorials, and examinations aim at the establishment of agreed knowledge. Both teachers and students visit other schools and may exchange one university for another. More recently the coming together of the European states and intensified global interaction at the political, economic, cultural, and especially academic levels has made it possible for even freer exchanges and a more broadly based sharing in the research fields.

After World War II the number of universities and of students attending them underwent a tremendous increase on a worldwide scale. Differences exist, of course, in the level of achievement, in size, in the departments that are offered, and in the possibilities of research. Care must therefore be exercised in comparing colleges and universities both nationally and internationally.

→ Distance Education; Education; Theological Education

Bibliography: Encyclopedic works: The Encyclopedia of Higher Education (4 vols.; ed. B. R. Clarke and G. R. Neave; New York, 1992) • *Higher Education in the United States: An Encyclopedia* (2 vols.; ed. J. J. F. Forest and K. Kinser; Santa Barbara, Calif., 2002) • *International Dictionary of University Histories* (ed. C. Summerfield and M. E. Devine; Chicago, 1998) • *International Higher Education: An Encyclopedia* (2 vols.; ed. P. G. Altbach; New York, 1991) • *World of Learning* (London, 1947- ; 56th ed., 2006) annual.

Historical studies: A. B. Cobban, *The Medieval Universities: Their Development and Organization* (Methuen, N.J., 1975) • W. J. Courtenay and J. Miethke, eds., *Universities and Schooling in Medieval Society* (Boston, 2000) • A. Maierù, *University Training in Medieval Europe* (trans. D. N. Pryds; Leiden, 1994) • H. Rashdall, *The Universities of Europe in the Middle Ages* (new ed.; 3 vols.; ed. F. M. Powicke and A. B. Emden; New York, 1987) • H. de Ridder-Symoens, ed., *Universities in the Middle Ages* (Cambridge, 1992) • H. Robinson-Hammerstein, ed., *European Universities in the Age of Reformation and Counter Reformation* (Portland, Oreg., 1998).

United States: W. Clark, *Academic Charisma and the Origins of the Research University* (Chicago, 2006) • A. Duke, *Importing Oxbridge: English Residential Colleges and American Universities* (New Haven, Conn., 1996) • D. J. Frank and J. Gabler, *Reconstructing the University: Worldwide Shifts in Academia in the Twentieth Century* (Stanford, Calif., 2006) • H. D. Graham and N. Diamond, *The Rise of American Research Universities* (Baltimore, 1997) • C. L. Jackson and E. F. Nunn, *Historically Black Colleges and Universities: A Reference Handbook* (Santa Barbara, Calif., 2003) • A. Levine, ed., *Higher Learning in America, 1980-2000* (Baltimore, 1993) • G. M. Marsden, *The Soul of the American University: From Protestant Establishment to Established Nonbelief* (New York, 1994) • S. E. Morison, *The Founding of Harvard College* (Cambridge, Mass., 1995; orig. pub., 1935).

Germany: D. Fallon, *The German University: A Heroic Ideal in Conflict with the Modern World* (Boulder, Colo., 1980) • M. J. Hofstetter, *The Romantic Idea of a University: England and Germany, 1770-1850* (New York, 2001) • T. A. Howard, *Protestant Theology and the Making of the Modern German University* (New York, 2006) • R. M. O. Pritchard, *The End of Elitism? The Democratisation of the West German University System* (New York, 1990) • F. K. Ringer, *The Decline of the German Mandarins: The German Academic Community, 1890-1933* (Hanover, N.H., 1990; orig. pub., 1969).

Britain, France, Italy: L. W. B. Brockliss, *French Higher Education in the Seventeenth and Eighteenth Centuries* (New York, 1987) • A. B. Cobban, *The Medieval English Universities: Oxford and Cambridge to c. 1500* (Berkeley, Calif., 1988) • G. E. Davie, *The Democratic Intellect: Scotland and Her Universities in the Nineteenth Century* (Edinburgh, 1961) • P. F. Grendler, *The Universities of the Italian Renaissance* (Baltimore, 2002) • H. Silver and S. J. Teague, *The History of British Universities, 1800-1969, Excluding Oxford and Cambridge: A Bibliography* (London, 1970).

Other studies: R. L. Geiger, *Private Sectors in Higher Education: Structure, Function, and Change in Eight Countries* (Ann Arbor, Mich., 1986) • K. Jaspers, *The Idea of the University* (ed. K. W. Deutsch; Boston, 1959) • T. J. Murphy, *A Catholic University: Vision and Opportunities* (Collegeville, Minn., 2001) • J. Ortega y Gasset, *Mission of the University* (trans. H. L. Nostrand; London, 1998) • S. Rothblatt and B. Wittrock, *The European and American University since 1800* (New York, 1993) • W. Rüegg, ed., *Universities in the Nine-*

teenth and Early Twentieth Centuries (1800-1945) (Cambridge, 2004) • UNESCO, *The Virtual University: Models and Messages, Lessons from Case Studies* (ed. S. D'Antoni; Paris, 2006).

DIETRICH GOLDSCHMIDT† and WOLFGANG
VORTKAMP, with THE EDITORS

Upanishads

1. The Upanishads (Skt. *upa-ni-ṣad,* "set down close by," in which students sit at the feet of their teachers, who by mystagogic instruction *[rahasya]* lead them to personal experience) are the heterogenous Sanskrit literature of → Hinduisim, which, as the Vedanta (lit. "end of the Veda"), contain the Samhitas (the four great collections of Vedic writings: Rig-veda, Sama-veda, Yajur-veda, and Atharvaveda) and the Aranyakas (lit. "forest treatises": spiritual commentaries on the Vedas deriving from the *vānaprasthas,* or forest-dwelling hermits). Some of the teachers *(guru)* are known from the texts (e.g., Uddalaka, Sandilya, Sanatkumara, Gargi, Kausitaki, Yajnavalkya, and his wife Maitri).

The classical Upanishads were written during the period from the 8th to the 2nd century B.C. Later works that go by the title, which were influenced by → Yoga, the Tantras, and even → Islam, date from the 10th century A.D. and later. It is hard to give an exact dating, which depends on comparisons of style and on how far → Buddhism may have had an influence.

2. Like Buddhism, the Upanishads abandon the sacrificial rituals of the Brahmans in favor of spiritual self-knowledge, so that as an esoteric tradition they became the main source of the wisdom → mysticism of later Hinduism (the *jñāna-mārga,* "path of knowledge"). Though sociologically dependent on the Kshatriya → caste, which accepted women as teachers of wisdom, they offered an ideal for the Brahmans, though without being identified with the caste, for being a Brahman is not a matter of birth but a quality of the person (Chāndogya 4.4). In the later Muktika Upanishads there are 108 classical Upanishads, and some say as many as 235.

We may distinguish among the Upanishads in terms of relative age. First are the early, pre-Buddhist Upanishads (Chāndogya, Bṛhadānyaka, Aitareya, Taittirīya, Kauṣītaki, and, somewhat later, Kena and Īśa). They press on from cosmological to anthropological questions and interpret the Vedic

gods as forces that are subject to the absolute and neutral *brahman.*

Then there are intermediate Upanishads (Kaṭha, Muṇḍaka, Śvetāśvatara, and Mahānārāyaṇa), which are under the influence of the Sankhya philosophy and of Buddhism and gradually find a supreme personal God in place of the neutral absolute.

We then have later Upanishads (Praśna, Māṇḍukya, and Maitrāyaṇī), in which we find distinction from Buddhism. Finally, we find very late Upanishads (2d cent. B.C.), which are modeled on the main religious trends of Hinduism (Saivism, Vaishnavism, Shaktism, and Yoga).

3. The Upanishads include the → philosophy of nature, → anthropology, → psychology, the → hermeneutics of myths, → epistemology, and → astrology. They often use dialogues that lead to debates. They are full of symbols, analogies, parables, and aphorisms. They deal with the nature of the world and humanity, which in the early Upanishads is often identified with the element of space *(ākāśa),* with vital energy *(prāṇa),* and finally with the self *(ātman,* originally linked to breath). Atman, the source of human consciousness, is equated with the cosmic absolute, the quintessence of universal energy *(brahman).* Atman and *brahman* are interchangeable and are beyond time. In seeing and thinking, seers transcend empirical reality as that which truly is *(satya),* knowledge *(jñāna)* of which is transformative. It gives liberation *(mokṣa)* from the circle of birth *(saṁsāra),* which is marked by the uncertainty of the self-engendered effects of thought and action *(karman).*

Four great sayings *(mahāvākyāni)* state this line of thought:

1. *Prajñānam brahma,* "Consciousness is Brahman."
2. *Aham brahmāsi,* "I am Brahman."
3. *Ayam ātmā brahma,* "This self is Brahman."
4. *Tat tvam asi,* "Thou art that"; that which holds reality together is also the essence of humanity (Chāndogya 6.9.1ff.).

This transcendent reality can be described only apophatically, since it has no attributes *(nirguṇa)* and transcends speech and the related dualities *(neti . . . neti,* "either . . . or"; Bṛhadāraṇyaka, 4.4.22ff.).

4. Bādarāyaṇa's Brahma Sutra attempts in 550 aphorisms to systematize the related but contradictory teachings of the Upanishads. This work gave rise to a great flood of commentaries *(bhāṣya)* and helped to form the four most important schools of the Vedanta that are still normative in India:

1. Advaita (nondualism), championed especially by Śankara (d. ca. A.D. 750)

2. Visistadvaita (modified nondualism), especially Rāmānuja (d. 1137)

3. Dvaita (dualism), especially Madhva (d. ca. 1278)

4. Bhedabheda (unity of opposites), especially Nimbārka (fl. 12th or 13th cent.?).

Bibliography: Texts: The Early Upanisads: Annotated Text and Translation (trans. P. Olivelle; New York, 1998) • *The Principal Upanishads: A Poetic Transcreation* (trans. A. Jacobs; New York, 2003) • *The Thirteen Principal Upanisads: Translated from the Sanskrit, with an Outline of the Philosophy of the Upanishads and an Annotated Bibliography* (2d ed., rev.; trans. R. E. Hume and G. C. O. Haas; Delhi, 1995) • *The Upanishads* (trans. V. J. Roebuck; London, 2003).

Secondary works: K. B. ARCHAK, *Philosophy of Realism: A Study Based on Chāndogya Upanisad* (New Delhi, 2003) • M. VON BRÜCK, *The Unity of Reality: God, God-Experience, and Meditation in the Hindu-Christian Dialogue* (New York, 1991) • R. GOTSHALK, *The Beginnings of Philosophy in India* (Lanham, Md., 1998) • Y. GRINSHPON, *Crisis and Knowledge: The Upanishadic Experience and Storytelling* (New Delhi, 2003) • J. MEHLIG, *Weisheit des alten Indien* (vol. 1; Leipzig, 1987) • P. C. MUKHOPADHYAY, *Journey of the Upanisads to the West* (Calcutta, 1987) • M. L. PANDIT, *Philosophy of the Upanishads: A Christian Understanding* (Delhi, 1978) • R. D. RANADE, *A Constructive Survey of Upanishadic Philosophy* (2d ed.; Bombay, 1968) • P. SEN, *God's Love in Upanishad Philosophies* (Bombay, 1995) • V. K. SUBRAMANIAN, *The Upanishads and the Bible* (New Delhi, 2002) • K. WARD, "The Upanishads," *Religion and Creation* (Oxford, 1996) 77-108.

MICHAEL VON BRÜCK

Upper Volta → Burkina Faso

Urban Rural Mission

1. Since 1978 the Urban Rural Mission has been a working group of the Commission on World Mission and Evangelism (CWME) of the → World Council of Churches (WCC; → Ecumenism, Ecumenical Movement 4.1); it arose out of the Urban Industrial Mission (UIM) and the Rural Agricultural Mission (RAM). A literal translation of the name can lead to misunderstanding, because goals, target groups, and work methods clearly differ from traditional "city mission" and "village mission" (→

Evangelism 1.3). URM belongs to the WCC team Mission and Ecumenical Education. A working group of representatives from the various URM regions (Africa, Asia, Europe, Latin America, Middle East, and North America), as well as members of the CWME and staff, oversee international cooperation and direct the program. The work varies according to region.

In Europe there is the European Circle of Community and Justice in Mission/Urban Rural Mission, with which migrant organizations and "Formation for Mission" also cooperate. The European Working Community of Church and Labor (European Contact Group, ECG) works together in the WCC with the Commission on Justice, Peace, and Creation and is an associate member of the → Conference of European Churches (CEC). Both work "from below" with the victims of economic and social injustice and of violence, increasingly with women, the unemployed, and ethnic → minorities. The URM circle approaches its work in terms of a theology of mission, while the ECG is more oriented to social ethics. Under the influence of globalization new forms of work are being developed, for example, "Good Work Projects." In these, the increasingly difficult problems of inequalities, exclusion, part-time work, and outsourcing are being concretely addressed. In its engagement URM works in churches and labor unions but must also contend with opposing church interests.

2. The URM seeks to remedy unjust social and economic structures. Its aim is a just → society that is freed from competitive strife (→ Industrial Society), that acknowledges the divine likeness of all people, and that gives aid to the exploited and dispossessed. The URM encourages "the people," that is, slum dwellers, industrial workers, farmers, agricultural laborers, fishermen, artisans, immigrant workers, victims of the → tourism industry, and natives. Training and the exchange of experiences are its methods. The people it helps tell their own stories. They thus engage in "analysis from below." By mutual reflection and action they overcome their isolation, find → solidarity, and receive empowerment.

3. The basis of URM is the divine mission for fullness of life (John 10:10). Justice is a presupposition. Justice involves fellowship with God, with fellow humans, and with → nature (→ Environment). The emphasis falls on the founding, upbuilding, and organizing of community. All people have dignity, powers, and gifts (→ Human Dignity), and → responsibility falls upon them all to give shape to

God's → creation. The URM focuses on the suffering, the poor, and the dispossessed, seeking to make them participants so that they too may achieve fullness of life. "Mission" here means intervening for their rights in Jesus' name. The churches are challenged to take the URM and its struggle seriously, to give it concrete support, and to endorse both its theology and its mission.

Bibliography: Für eine Zukunft in Solidarität und Gerechtigkeit. Wort des Rates der Evangelischen Kirche in Deutschland und der Deutschen Bischofskonferenz zur wirtschaftlichen und sozialen Lage in Deutschland (Hannover, 1997) • J. KLUTE, H. SCHLENDER, and S. SINAGOWITZ, eds., *Gute Arbeit, Good Work* (Münster, 2004) • H. SYMANOWSKI, *Kirche und Arbeitsleben: getrennte Welten? Impulstexte aus 1950-2000* (Münster, 2005) • WORLD COUNCIL OF CHURCHES, "Mission from the Perspective of People in Struggle: Conference Communiqué, Accra, Ghana, May 1-7, 2004," Urban Rural Mission, http://www.wcc-coe.org/wcc/what/mission/accra-urm2004.html; idem, *Urban Rural Mission Reflections '93* (Geneva, 1994).

CHRISTA SPRINGE

Uruguay

	1960	1980	2000
Population (1,000s):	2,538	2,914	3,274
Annual growth rate (%):	1.19	0.64	0.55
Area: 176,215 sq. km. (68,037 sq. mi.)			

A.D. 2000

Population density: 19/sq. km. (48/sq. mi.)
Births / deaths: 1.64 / 1.04 per 100 population
Fertility rate: 2.19 per woman
Infant mortality rate: 16 per 1,000 live births
Life expectancy: 73.3 years (m: 70.0, f: 76.5)
Religious affiliation (%): Christians 65.3 (Roman Catholics 78.7, marginal 3.8, Protestants 3.8, indigenous 1.5, other Christians 1.5), nonreligious 26.9, atheists 6.2, Jews 1.2, other 0.4.

1. General Situation
2. Christian Groups
   2.1. Roman Catholic Church and Society
   2.2. Non–Roman Catholic Churches
   2.3. Others
3. Interdenominational and Ecumenical
   Organizations
4. Non-Christian Religions

Uruguay is a relatively small country situated in the southeast section of South America. It is bordered by Brazil (east and north) and Argentina (west) and has a large coastline on the Atlantic Ocean and the Río de la Plata (or River Plate, south and west). Its capital city, Montevideo, founded in 1724, has 47 percent of the total population. Overall, there is a high rate of urbanization (93 percent in 2003).

1. General Situation

1.1. Before European colonization, tribes of hunter-gatherers belonging to different native cultures lived in the southern region of the continent, including within the area presently known as Uruguay. In the latter, most of the native tribes belonged to what is known as the Charrúa Nation, whose people have been described as strictly nomadic, able to survive in difficult conditions, and strongly independent. The Charrúa suffered under the European settlers, being killed or integrated into the colonial cultures. In 1831 most of those remaining were invited to a meeting with the settlers and then massacred at Salsipuedes Creek by a group led by the nephew of Fructuoso Rivera, who had recently become the first president of Uruguay.

In colonial times Uruguay, known then as Banda Oriental ("eastern stripe," meaning the eastern shore of the Río de la Plata), was a relatively unimportant territory among Spain's possessions at the time of the Spanish domination (viceroyalty) of the Río de la Plata (→ Colonialism). This situation changed drastically when the Portuguese claimed the area for themselves, arguing that this territory was the natural southern border of Brazil. On the east bank of the river the Portuguese founded Colônia do Sacramento, opposite Buenos Aires in Argentina, and the area became the scene of continuous dispute between Portugal and Spain.

In the context of the Napoleonic wars, people in the Spanish colonies revolted against Spain, a struggle that ended in 1824 with the collapse of the Spanish colonial system in South America. Since it was an imperial border, Uruguay was invaded by, and then annexed to, Portugal in 1820, only five years after local revolutionaries took control of Montevideo. Military hostilities then erupted between Brazil (heir of the Portuguese authorities) and the United Provinces of the Río de La Plata. With the intervention of the British Foreign Office, an international conference was held, one outcome of which was the creation of Uruguay in 1828 as what historians have called a buffer state.

In 1828 Uruguay had 60,000 inhabitants. Through immigration, coming at first mainly from Spain and Italy, and then from other European countries, the population grew to around one million at the turn of the 20th century.

At the very beginning, two political parties arose in the Republic — the Blancos (whites) and the Colorados (reds) — with two conflicting points of view for the emerging nation. Civil wars between the two groups, usually with the involvement of Brazil and Argentina, were the rule during the first decades of independence. By the end of the 19th century, these two opposing regimes were firmly in place, making the country virtually ungovernable. In 1903 newly elected president José Batlle y Ordóñez (1856-1929, pres. 1903-7 and 1911-15) used military means to end the stranglehold of the parties.

In the beginning of the 20th century the rural gaucho population was mostly domesticated and expropriated so that large estates could be formed, which increasingly reached the world market with their products. Progressive social legislation introduced by Batlle y Ordóñez led eventually to an enormous increase in the civil service, which became increasingly difficult to finance. At the same time, under the leadership of Batlle y Ordóñez, the country began a process of modernization, which included industrial development and a major growth in national production. This growth stimulated immigration and led to a significant increase in population. These circumstances allowed Uruguay to pioneer development of the first welfare state in Latin America.

1.2. Uruguay went through a period of significant economic growth and prosperity during World War II and the postwar years. A new crisis of development in the 1960s produced galloping inflation and elicited social protest, which took shape in urban guerrillas known as the Tupamaros. Despite its long tradition of political stability, in 1973 Uruguay suffered a military coup d'état, Parliament was dissolved, trade unions were declared illegal, and any protest or political activity contrary to decrees of the military was regarded with suspicion. A military dictatorship ruled the country until 1985. This period was marked by unlimited → censorship of individuals and organizations, illegal imprisonments, disappearance of persons, extreme social controls, political exile, and a long list of human-rights abuses. Appealing to the need for "national security," the military government set up a police state, repressing all criticism and resorting to unrestricted physical and psychological → torture against left-wing groups and anyone else deemed an enemy of the state.

The persistent economic crisis made it difficult, if not impossible, for the military regime to achieve any social legitimacy. By 1984 the military government called for restricted general elections, and by 1985 the democratic rule of law was gradually restored. Immediately after the release of political prisoners in 1985, the new legislature passed an amnesty law that absolved the armed forces of any wrongdoing, which was ratified by referendum in 1989.

1.3. Since the return of → democracy, Uruguay has had free elections every five years. The two traditional parties, which are among the oldest on the continent, alternately controlled the government of Uruguay up to 2005. Then the left-wing coalition Frente Amplio (lit. "broad front"), founded in 1971, took control of the government for the first time. Some ministers of this new government had been guerrilla fighters in the 1960s.

In 2002 the country faced a difficult economic crisis, caused, on the one hand, by a decline in beef exports to North America because of an outbreak of foot-and-mouth disease and, on the other hand, by Argentine withdrawals from Uruguayan banks. The gross domestic product shrank, and unemployment rose to over 20 percent. The country was on the brink of bankruptcy, but implementation of an economic program based on significant international loans led to a process of recovery.

Since 1991 Uruguay has been a full member of Mercosur (for *Mer*cado *Com*ún del *Sur,* or Southern Common Market), a regional trade agreement involving Brazil, Argentina, Uruguay, Venezuela, and Paraguay as full members. Representing more than 300 million people, Mercosur aims to promote free trade and the free circulation of goods, peoples, and currency.

2. Christian Groups

2.1. *Roman Catholic Church and Society*

2.1.1. Uruguay was originally a parish of the See of Buenos Aires and only after a long time developed its own structures. Not until 1815 did the → Roman Catholic Church create the general vicariate of Montevideo, which became an apostolic vicariate in 1832 and a diocese in 1878. In 1897 the third bishop created a province with two suffragan bishops. But development was slow, because the state held patronage. The 1830 constitution had made Roman Catholicism the state religion (→ State Church). The formation of a diocese was an independent step, taken only later, but it was also costly, for ministers of state, who were Freemasons, perceived a threat to the laity if the church became too strong.

→ Freethinking, → rationalism, and deistic

moralism influenced the elite, while the general public adhered to a → popular Catholicism. The Romantic spiritualism of "Catholic Freemasonry" allowed Christianity to maintain its role in society, but it kept the → Jesuits from promoting → Ultramontanism. In 1861 the church leadership was confronted with the secularizing and laicizing tendencies of the state. Finally, in 1919, → church and state parted company. Henceforth the Roman Catholic Church would have the character of a corporate body. Religious liberty was guaranteed, and freedom from taxation was granted to all religious institutions.

In the 1880s → secularism was adopted by the university elite, and → deism evaporated into agnosticism and even → atheism and → materialism. For his secular policies Batlle had to depend on the anticlericalist views of Italian immigrants and the traditionally liberal Colorados. In 1919 anticlericalism led to a reform of the calendar, with Christmas becoming "Family Day," and Holy Week, "Tourist Week." Protestants supported the anticlerical policies, believing that it was a good opportunity to reduce the privileges of the Roman Catholic Church and ultimately to gain equal rights with the Catholics. Diaconal work was initiated in 1919.

Roman Catholicism unsuccessfully tried to exert political influence through its own party (Unión Cívica, later Christian Democrat), which never gained more than 6 percent at the polls. Social and political consciousness was enhanced by → Vatican II and the Medellín Conference (1968; → Latin American Councils 2.4). In 1975 the bishops' conference issued a letter that President Juan María Bordaberry (1973-75) tried to suppress, calling for an amnesty for political prisoners and an end to torture. Even during this time, though, the church was able to continue its apostolic, educational, and diaconal work. In 2005 it had 2.3 million nominal members in 10 dioceses and 226 parishes, served by 464 priests (198 diocesan, 266 religious) and 76 permanent deacons.

2.1.2. Religion has been in the private sphere since 1918, when church and state were separated under a new national constitution. In Uruguay it has been commonly held that religion will disappear with the advance of science, for it has been identified with superstition and ignorance. In the 1960s, however, religious topics and defenders returned to the public sphere, but the secular nature of the state did not change.

The French word *laïcité* (Sp. *laicidad*) is the word used most frequently when describing the religious identity of Uruguay. At the beginning of the 20th century, it meant neutrality and prejudice against religion, which is seen as associated with oppression and imposed uniformity (→ Religion, Criticism of). Nowadays, however, the significance and connotations of religion have changed, giving it a changed value in the public square. Uruguayans thus need to attempt a new definition of *laicidad*. No one is arguing for a return to a confessional state, but religion is clearly everywhere, and cultural diversity is seen as valuable.

Throughout Uruguay, Roman Catholic schools account for 10 percent of the education. The Catholic University of Uruguay, administered by the Jesuits, was founded in 1985. In addition, an important number of social services are provided by the Catholic Church throughout the country.

In Uruguay 82 percent of the population believe in God. Only 47 percent, however, are both believers and members of the Roman Catholic Church, which is the lowest percentage in South America. Except for Cuba, Uruguay has the highest percentage of atheists and nonreligious in all Latin America and the Caribbean.

2.2. Non–Roman Catholic Churches

2.2.1. Other churches arrived with 19th-century immigration. Serving mostly ethnic groups, these churches include the → Armenian Apostolic Church, Greek → Orthodox Church, two → Russian Orthodox churches, Ukrainian Orthodox Church, → Anglican Church (from 1850), Evangelical Waldensian Church (formed in 1858 by Italian → Waldensian immigrants, now Spanish-speaking), → Mennonites (Germans, Poles, and Russians), New Apostolic Church (largely from German immigrants), and River Plate Evangelical Church (work beginning in 1857, with congregations in Montevideo, Nueva Helvecia, and Paysandú, and many daughter churches).

2.2.2. The first church formed by Anglo-Saxon missionary work was the Evangelical Methodist Church, whose roots go back to J. F. Thompson, who was sent out from the United States in 1838, and Pastor T. Wood, who founded it in 1878. Wood also helped to establish schools that later came under the leadership of the Crandon Institute, one of the most important educational institutions in Uruguay. With 47 congregations and about 6,000 members, the → Methodist Church accomplishes high-quality social and economic work and has been a leader in Latin America's Protestantism. Pastor Emilio Castro, a member of the Uruguayan Methodist Church, served as general secretary of the → World Council of Churches (1985-92).

The → Plymouth Brethren (→ Darbyism), which

arose in opposition to the Anglican establishment, came to Uruguay in 1882. The Baptist Convention, based on missionary work by U.S. Southern Baptists, arrived in Montevideo in 1911 and was strengthened by Slavic Baptist immigrants. The → Salvation Army began a mission in 1890. The → Adventists came in 1895. They maintain a high school, a seminary, and an agricultural school in the province of Canelones. Many smaller churches and missions exist that cannot be enumerated here.

2.2.3. → Pentecostal churches first gained a footing in Uruguay in the 1940s but have grown more than most of the other Protestant churches. The strongest churches are the Asambleas de Dios (1944; → Assembleias de Deus no Brasil), the Iglesia de Dios (1940, Cleveland), and, in more recent years, the neo-Pentecostal Iglesia Universal del Reino de Dios (Universal Church of the Kingdom of God), founded in Brazil by Bishop Edir Macedo. Together with a number of smaller neo-Pentecostal churches, the Iglesia Universal has a noteworthy presence in Uruguayan society.

2.3. *Others*

The Church of the Latter-day Saints (→ Mormons) has existed in Uruguay since 1942, and the → Jehovah's Witnesses since 1923.

3. Interdenominational and Ecumenical Organizations

Until its suppression after the military coup d'état of 1973, the central administration of the Movimiento Iglesia y Sociedad en América Latina (ISAL = Church and Society in Latin America, a branch of the World Council of Churches) was based in Montevideo, where it published the journal *Cristianismo y sociedad*. The Federación de Iglesias Evangélicas del Uruguay (FIEU) is a church council of the Evangelical Waldensian Church of the River Plate, Hungarian Reformed Church, Mennonites, Methodist Church of Uruguay, River Plate Evangelical Church (Lutherans), Salvation Army, and United Evangelical Lutheran Church. The Roman Catholic Church has a national commission for → ecumenism, with an ecumenical center coordinating efforts. Jews and Christians of all denominations participate in the Confraternidad Judeo-Christiana, founded in 1964.

Formed in 1984, the Servicio Ecuménico para la Dignidad Humana (SEDHU, Ecumenical Service for Human Dignity) includes the Anglican Church of Uruguay, Evangelical Church of the River Plate (Lutherans), Evangelical Waldensian Church, Franciscan Center (Catholics), Methodist Church of Uruguay, Roman Catholic Church of Montevideo,

and the → YMCA. The service promotes human dignity in working with refugees.

4. Non-Christian Religions

After World War I many Jews from eastern Europe and the Middle East came to Uruguay. Jews also fled Germany and Hungary after 1936. In Uruguay in 2000 they numbered 60,000 and are strongly secularized, bound together by cultural rather than religious ties (→ Judaism).

Afro-Brazilian cults such as → Umbanda, Quimbanda, and Candomblé have been spreading widely across the country.

The → Unification Church International has its main South American headquarters in Uruguay. It operates a bank and a hotel, publishes a paper, and has other commercial organizations. Other sects and religious organizations are relatively unimportant.

Other religions present in Uruguay, though in no great numbers, are → Baha'i, → Buddhism, and → Islam.

Bibliography: D. B. Barrett, G. T. Kurian, and T. M. Johnson, *WCE* (2d ed.) 1.790-93 • D. Bazzano et al., *Breve visión de la historia de la iglesia en el Uruguay* (Montevideo, 1993) • G. Caetano and R. Geymonat, *La secularización uruguaya (1859-1910)* (2 vols.; Montevideo and Buenos Aires, 1993-97) • G. Caetano and J. Rilla Manta, *Historia contemporánea del Uruguay* (2 vols.; Montevideo 1994; 2d ed., vol. 2, 2005) • CEHILA, *Historia General de la Iglesia en América Latina,* vol. 9, *Cono Sur (Argentina, Chile, Uruguay y Paraguay)* (Salamanca, 1994) • N. Da Costa, *Religión y sociedad en el Uruguay del siglo XXI* (Montevideo, 2003); idem, ed., *Laicidad en América Latina y Europa* (Montevideo, 2006) • C. Ehrick, *The Shield of the Weak: Feminism and the State in Uruguay, 1903-1933* (Albuquerque, N.M., 2005) • J. C. Elizaga, *Las sectas y las nuevas religiones a la conquista del Uruguay* (Montevideo, 1988) • W. J. Giménez Casco, *San Cono. Fenómeno religioso de un país* (Montevideo, 1994) • D. R. Kohut, *Historical Dictionary of the "Dirty Wars"* (Lanham, Md., 2003) • P. Lapadjián, *Huellas de una iglesia. La Iglesia Evangélica y su desarrollo en Uruguay* (Montevideo, 1994) • A. Moro and M. Ramírez, *La Macumba y otros cultos afrobrasileños en Montevideo* (Montevideo, 1981) • B. Nahum, *Manual de historia del Uruguay* (2 vols.; Montevideo, 1996) • T. Sansón, *El catolicismo popular en Uruguay* (Montevideo, 1998) • J. L. Segundo and P. Rodé, *Presencia de la iglesia* (Montevideo, 1969).

Hans-Jürgen Prien, Carlos Zubillaga, and Néstor Da Costa

USSR → Commonwealth of Independent States; Russia; Soviet Union

Usury

Adopting ancient cultural traditions (Babylon, Egypt, Rome) and Jewish rulings (e.g., Exod. 22:25; Deut. 23:19-20), the → early church took up the question of usury. On the basis of Luke 6:35 ("lend, expecting nothing in return"), John → Chrysostom (ca. 347-407) and → Augustine (354-430) demanded full prohibition. The Council of → Nicaea (325) forbade it absolutely for clergy. In the Carolingian capitularies we also find an absolute prohibition at the Synod of Paris in 829. Contemporary theology followed suit, and Lateran II (1139) confirmed it (→ Councils of the Church). It then came into classic → canon law (→ Corpus Iuris Canonici).

The changed economic situation in the High Middle Ages (capital investment and → money as a factor not merely in consumption but also in production) then required rethinking. Roman law was adopted, allowing gain from a loan to compensate for the loss. Thomas Aquinas (ca. 1225-74) renewed the prohibition but allowed exceptions (*Summa theol.* II of II, q. 78). In → church finance a legal place was found for the purchase of annuities and mortgages and for juridical persons.

The tendency both to continue the prohibition and yet to adjust to economic development governed → church law in the centuries that followed and may be seen in 1917 CIC 1543. There is no express prohibition in 1983 CIC, but canon 1259 allows capital increase, or return, "by every just means of natural or positive law permitted to others."

Among the Reformers M. → Luther (1483-1546) at first favored an absolute prohibition of usury, but P. Melanchthon (1497-1560), M. → Bucer (1491-1551), and J. → Calvin (1509-64) took a more modern view (→ Calvin's Theology). Protestant → social ethics today accepts the real economic function of money in the life of society but points out that it must have a servant role.

→ Economic Ethics

Bibliography: S. L. Buckley, *Teachings on Usury in Judaism, Christianity, and Islam* (Lewiston, N.Y., 2000); eadem, *Usury Friendly? The Ethics of Moneylending–a Biblical Interpretation* (Cambridge, 1998) • E. Kerridge, *Usury, Interest, and the Reformation* (Aldershot, 2002) • O. I. Langholm, *The Aristotelian Analysis of Usury* (Bergen, Norw., 1984) • B. N. Nelson, *The Idea of Usury* (2d ed.; Chicago, 1969) • W. Stützel and H.-H. Schrey, "Kapital und Zins," *ESL* 622-73 • P. A. Wee, "Biblical Ethics and Lending to the Poor," *ER* 38 (1986) 416-30.

Herbert Frost†

Utilitarianism

1. Term
2. Utilitarian Philosophy
3. Applications

1. Term

Utilitarian philosophy is primarily an ethical system of principles for determining what is morally right. Francis Hutcheson (1694-1746) is one of its precursors. The principal founders of utilitarianism were the British philosophers Jeremy Bentham (1748-1832) and John Stuart Mill (1806-73).

Hutcheson was perhaps the first to state a version of the principle of utility, according to which the morally right alternative is the one that results in the greatest overall → happiness. Bentham may have used the term "utilitarianism" informally, but Mill was the first to employ it in publications for this philosophy.

Popular usage treats the adjective "utilitarian" much more loosely, as applicable to any procedures or objects that prove useful in accomplishing a task or achieving a goal. As such, the term functions as a synonym for "practical" or even "pragmatic," although the philosophy known as → pragmatism differs in important ways from utilitarianism.

This discussion is about the ethical philosophy of utilitarianism, with mention of its applications in → economics, decision theory, and game theory. Utilitarianism shares with religious → ethics a concern for issues of public policy and for the moral standing of individual interests in comparison to those of others or of society as a whole. But it is not itself a religious philosophy.

2. Utilitarian Philosophy

Bentham held that pleasure and pain are decisive factors in human action. Pleasure is the only good thing, pain the only evil. Happiness results from the experience of pleasure and the absence of pain. Actions by individuals or governments that maximize happiness are right actions. Bentham proposed a calculus for comparing the anticipated quantity, intensity, and duration of pleasures and pains likely to result from alternative courses of action. His calculus for right action sought to consider not just sensual pleasures but higher ones too, such as aesthetic or intellectual satisfactions, and even pleasure derived from observing the happiness of others.

Mill's *Utilitarianism* (1863) built upon the ideas of Bentham, and of his own father, James Mill (1773-1836). His principle of utility holds that a morally right action is one that maximizes human welfare. A person not only can take pleasure in the general welfare but also *ought to be motivated* to promote it. We are morally obliged to so act that the consequences, compared to those of alternative actions, contribute to the greatest overall happiness. Policies of governments and social institutions should meet this standard too.

Distinctions among different types of utilitarianism emerged as others refined the thought of Bentham and Mill. *Act utilitarians* determine what is morally right by applying the principle of utility directly to individual actions, taken singly. *Rule utilitarians* determine what is morally right indirectly, by applying the principle of utility to the choice, or justification, of moral rules, which are then used directly for deciding on the right action. For instance, an act utilitarian would say that lying is morally right if doing so maximizes happiness. In contrast, a rule utilitarian would say that it is never morally right to violate a "justified" moral rule, such as the rule prohibiting lying.

There are also other distinctions within utilitarianism. Some view pleasure mainly in hedonistic terms, whereas others give differential weighting to the intrinsic qualities of different pleasurable objects or experiences. Consider, for example, the pleasure of viewing fine art compared with the pleasure from a cartoon. If not all pleasures such as these ought to be deemed equivalent, then perhaps enjoying fine art ranks higher, despite what those enjoying the cartoon might think. Most utilitarians do not believe that individuals are always the best judges of what promotes their happiness; for instance, drug addicts are not.

Utilitarianism is a normative ethics that states how people and institutions ought to act. It is an alternative to other normative moral systems, such as → Kantianism and natural-law ethics. Some, however, who are not themselves philosophers, reinterpret utilitarianism as simply descriptive of how pleasure-seeking beings do in fact act. This distinction between *ought* and *is* with respect to human behavior is an important one for philosophy and is also relevant to the intersection of utilitarianism with modern capitalist economics.

Utilitarianism has been an extremely influential philosophy since its inception. Prominent utilitarians in the latter half of the 20th century include

Richard Brandt (1910-97) and R. M. Hare (1919-2002). In *A Theory of Justice* (1971), John Rawls (1921-2002) provoked great interest by how he opposed his own natural rights or contractarian theory of society to classic utilitarianism.

Utilitarianism is sometimes criticized for lacking the kind of moral absolutes by which practices such as → slavery or → genocide would always be wrong, despite their utility alleged by some. The requisite response would have to show that no social system employing such abhorrent practices has ever maximized utility for its overall membership.

3. Applications

Utilitarianism is an influential moral theory in the burgeoning field of applied ethics, most especially in debates about distributive justice, which concerns principles and practices governing the availability of opportunities and resources to the various groups and individual members of society. The utility principle has direct relevance to moral stances on, for instance, affirmative action, tax policies that redistribute wealth, and the social allocation of very expensive or limited medical resources.

Advocates of market → capitalism typically espouse a descriptive application of utilitarianism. They argue that the level of demand for particular products and services directly reflects the extent of people's willingness to purchase them at current prices. It directly reveals their own judgments as to what best produces happiness for them, given their available financial resources. A normative appeal to utilitarianism emerges with the further contention that nonmonopolistic competition among producers is the optimal (thus, morally correct) avenue to efficiencies yielding maximum choice and benefit to consumers, in the form of the best and most economical products.

A major flaw of Communist economies, with production decisions made centrally by the state, is that by utilitarian measures they fail to deliver sufficient happiness and well-being to their people. Yet advocates of → socialism or of an extensively regulated capitalism can also draw upon utilitarianism. They argue that the greater happiness calls for a managed economy reflecting a concept of fairness, one that seeks to avert the misery of socially disadvantaged persons who would otherwise be left to shift for themselves ineffectually in a wholly competitive world.

Decision theory also draws in part upon utilitarianism. Rational decision-making involves more than just calculating the likelihoods of various possible outcomes. It also takes into account the degree of desirability of each possible outcome (in utilitarian terms, how much happiness it will yield if it occurs). For instance, my decision as to which horse I bet on to win depends not just on its chances of winning but also on the prospective payout if it does. Utilitarianism is not the only resource decision theory employs in judging the benefits of alternative outcomes, but it plays a significant role in doing so.

Game theory involves decision making in circumstances with multiple participants, where the likely actions of all the interacting competitors must be anticipated, along with one's own. Checkers is fairly straightforward, because each of the two competitors has the same specific goal. Other endeavors are more complex, with varying circumstances, rules, and procedures. For instance, a trader on the stock market does not know the individual competitors yet must make decisions based on their likely behavior, by anticipating their expectations and desires and the trading strategies they will employ in seeking to satisfy them.

Bibliography: E. Albee, *A History of English Utilitarianism* (New York, 1902) • K. Baier, *The Moral Point of View* (Ithaca, N.Y., 1958) • J. Bentham, *An Introduction to the Principles of Morals and Legislation* (London, 1789) • R. Braithwaite, *Theory of Games as a Tool for the Moral Philosopher* (Cambridge, 1955) • R. Brandt, *Morality, Utilitarianism, and Rights* (Cambridge, 1992) • R. Hare, *Moral Thinking: Its Levels, Method, and Point* (Oxford, 1981) • D. Haslett, *Capitalism with Morality* (Oxford, 1994) • F. Hutcheson, *Inquiry into the Original of Our Ideas of Beauty and Virtue* (4th ed.; Glasgow, 1938) • S. Kagen, *The Limits of Morality* (Oxford, 1989) • J. Mill, *Utilitarianism* (London, 1863) • M. Resnick, *Choices: An Introduction to Decision Theory* (Minneapolis, 1987) • L. Selby-Bigge, *The British Moralists* (2 vols.; Oxford, 1897) • H. Sidgwick, *Outlines of the History of Ethics* (London, 1946) • J. Smart, *An Outline of a System of Utilitarian Ethics* (Melbourne, 1961) • L. Stephen, *The English Utilitarians* (London, 1900) • S. Toulmin, *The Place of Reason in Ethics* (Cambridge, 1951) • J. Von Neumann and A. Morgenstern, *Theory of Games and Economic Behavior* (Princeton, 1944; repr., 2004).

Robert F. Brown

Utopia

1. Term

"Utopia," a word that has found much use in political and social discussion, was originally a geographic metaphor. Then in France it denoted fictional reforms that were not practicable. T. More (1478-1535) combined the two uses in his *Utopia* (1516; see 2.1). His ideal state was located on a newly discovered island named Utopia (made up of Gk. *ou* and *topos,* meaning "nowhere"). The term achieved common usage in works describing ideal constitutions (novels about the state, as R. von Mohl called them in 1845). Independent of its literary model, the word also figured in conflicts against Communist and socialist ideas that were dismissed as impractical.

In the 20th century K. Mannheim (1893-1947) and E. Bloch (1885-1977) attempted to use the term positively (see 5.1), borrowing from the → millenarianism of the → Anabaptists. The utopian, they claimed, is a dimension of human awareness, an expression of the collective mentality, an element in social criticism. Up to the 1970s the use of the term in this sense spiraled. Art, for example, was given a utopian role (G. Ueding).

In literary criticism, however, a reaction set in. Attention was drawn to the history of the term, to its role in literature, and to its contextual use. The collapse of the socialist states (→ Socialism) brought a questioning of the ideal of utopia in terms of the philosophy of history. How can there be a convergence of utopia and history?

2. Political Utopias

2.1. More, a British stateman who, as a martyr for the truth, was beatified in 1886 and canonized in 1935, depicted a political utopia in his work *De optimo reipublicae statu deque nova insula Utopia* (On the best state of a republic and on the new island of Utopia, 1516). The introduction contains a dedication to the humanistic circle around → Erasmus (1469?-1536). In the first book a fictitious world traveler, in a dialogue, criticizes England and Europe both politically and socially. In the second book he offers the fictional countermodel of Utopia, with its identical 54 cities, its constitution, its social structure, its culture (oriented to antiquity), its foreign policy, and its religion. He lauds the social justice that obtains in this utopian state. The second book was written first, so that we should focus, not on the introduction, but on the interrelation of the two books and the conclusion. More wanted contemporary humanism to engage in a consistent discussion of social problems. By making moral ideals (justice, equity, the public good) into social →

norms, he hoped to initiate a debate about social norms on a humanistic basis (→ Humanism 1.1).

2.2. The discursive and normative openness of More's *Utopia* is limited by its reception as a countermodel to existing society. Only the German and English translations of it, which are associated with the → Reformation in Basel and England, treat it as a foundational catalog of what could be done by way of municipal and national reforms (→ City; State). Contemporaries understood the socially regulative interpretation of *Utopia,* with its orientation to social consensus and integration, as an antifeudal (→ Feudalism) alternative to the territorial rule of princes. In 1555 C. Stiblin, in his *De Eudaemonensium republica,* described a utopia that, under a feudal model, projected a normative system under state control. Officials would undergo humanistic training, and the people would be under their discipline. The *Gargantua* (1534) of F. Rabelais (ca. 1483-1553) offered a third variant, which engaged in playful criticism of the institutionalism of *Utopia* and highlighted → individualism as the basis of social life.

As thought experiments, these utopias were secular and rational responses to the social and intellectual revolutions that took place in the 16th century. They differed radically from the current religious utopianism of T. → Müntzer (ca. 1489-1525; → Anabaptists 2.1), which united mystical and chiliastic elements, opposed the secularizing tendencies of the time, and sought to bring to fruition the → kingdom of God on earth (→ Millenarianism 5).

3. Religious Utopias

In his work *Reipublicae christianopolitanae descriptio* (A description of the Christian republic, 1619), J. V. Andreae (1586-1654) favored a religious utopia. He was influenced both by later humanism (neo-Stoicism; see *Civitas solis* [City of the sun, 1611, 1621] by T. Campanella [1568-1639]) and by early Pietism (J. Arndt [1555-1621]; → Pietism 2). His aim was to Christianize both individuals and society. In contrast to the 16th-century utopias, Andreae sought to redefine utopian possibilities by relating individuals to inward Christian commitment. Individuals who are Christ's disciples will fit easily into society because they have an individual moral disposition that is universally valid and not because they belong to a utopian city. Andreae used chiliastic allusions for his utopia (Christianopolis = New → Jerusalem = → Augustine's *Civitas Dei*), but natural → science was also an important new coordinate. The stress on natural science may be found, too, in the *Nova Atlantis* (1620) of F. Bacon (1561-1626).

4. The Enlightenment

Perspectives are displaced in → Enlightenment utopias such as that of L. S. Mercier (*L'an deux mille quatre cents quarante* [The year 2440, 1771]). We now have utopias in time instead of space, and from the standpoint of literary structure the allegorical novel has replaced dialogue. The futuristic utopias of the 19th century (H. de Saint Simon's *Nouveau Christianisme* [New Christianity, 1825], C. Fourier's *Le nouveau monde industriel* [The new industrial world, 1829], R. Owen's *The New Moral World* [1836], W. Morris's *News from Nowhere* [1891]) advocate a secularized → eschatology that depicts utopia as the final goal of a linear historical process culminating in human → emancipation.

The first half of the 20th century brought a crisis to the belief in → progress and opposition to utopian ideas. *The Brave New World* (1932) of A. Huxley (1894-1963) and *Nineteen Eighty-four* of G. Orwell (1903-50) pour scorn on exaggerated technological and democratic thinking and its authoritarian implications for the state.

5. More Recent Concepts

During the 19th and 20th centuries a narrow → philosophy of history and a foreshortened view of utopias had a great influence, both positively and negatively, on philosophical and sociological discussion.

5.1. In the 19th century, criticism of utopias began when K. → Marx (1818-83) and F. Engels (1820-95) rejected the early socialist utopias as outdated thinking that ignored the historic role of the proletariat (→ Marxism). Economic knowledge alone will help us to understand the development of societies and will show us that → socialism is historically inevitable. Socialism could not be regarded as a regime of → freedom leading to utopia.

E. Bloch held a more positive view of utopian thinking in his work *Das Prinzip Hoffnung* (The principle of hope, 1954-59). He found for it both a subjective and an objective → ontology. What we are not yet aware of is mediated by what has not yet come. → Nature participates in the realm of freedom, so that a reconciliation of nature and humanity will be achieved.

5.2. The ontological categories of Bloch were taken up into theology by J. Moltmann in his *Theologie der Hoffnung* (Theology of hope, 1966). Moltmann tried to show that eschatology has an immanent dimension that affects the → future. He found it difficult, however, to retain its eschatological quality.

Bloch's view of utopia came under criticism from

K. R. Popper (1902-94) and H. Jonas (1903-93). From the standpoint of the philosophy of history, Popper raised the formal objection that this view involves → totalitarianism. Jonas (→ Responsibility 4) had anthropological objections. Its anthropocentricity gives humanity a special place in nature and involves the exploitation of all other creatures (→ Anthropology 4).

5.3. The collapse of the socialist states and the disowning of Marxist utopias have had a big impact upon modern discussion. It is thought that utopias are necessarily totalitarian. The rejection, however, is based on philosophically and historically foreshortened views of utopia. A new and more classically based understanding now calls for consideration. This approach will see a regulative principle (R. Saage) in utopias and hence a means by which we can discuss the norms of social life and various new orientations. This modern use of the utopian model need not take the form of literature. It can find expression in scientific essays or in critical reports. Utopia as a regulative principle can also be of theological significance, either by following Andreae's classic spatial model or by introducing newer theological movements (e.g., → feminist theology and → liberation theology) that critically propose new norms and aim at social reform.

→ Golden Age

Bibliography: Texts: J. V. ANDREAE, Christianopolis (trans. E. H. Thompson; Boston, 1999; orig. pub., 1619) • F. BACON, New Atlantis (1626) and The Great Instauration (1620) (rev. ed.; Arlington Heights, Ill., 1989) • Famous Utopias: Being the Complete Text of Rousseau's Social Contract, More's Utopia, Bacon's New Atlantis, Campanella's City of the Sun (New York, 1901) • A. HUXLEY, Brave New World (1932) and Brave New World Revisited (1958) (New York, 2004) • T. MORE, A fruteful, and pleasaunt worke of the beste state of a publyque weale, and of the newe yle called Vtopia, written in Latine by Syr Thomas More knight, and trans. into Englyshe by Raphe Robynson citizein and goldsmythe of London . . . (London, 1551); idem, Utopia (trans. P. Turner; New York, 2003; orig. pub., 1516) • G. ORWELL, Nineteen Eighty-four (New York, 2003; orig. pub., 1949) • PLATO, Republic (trans. C. D. C. Reeve; Indianapolis, 2004) • J.-J. ROUSSEAU, The Social Contract; and, The First and Second Discourses (ed. S. Dunn; New Haven, 2002; orig. pub., 1762) • B. F. SKINNER, Walden Two (Norwalk, Conn., 1995; orig. pub., 1948) • C. STIBLIN, De Eudaemonensium republica (ed. L. Firpo; Turin, 1959; orig. pub., 1555) • H. G. WELLS, A Modern Utopia (London, 2005; orig. pub., 1905); idem, The Open Conspiracy: H. G.

Wells on World Revolution (ed. W. W. Wagar; Westport, Conn., 2002; orig. pub., 1928).

Secondary works: E. BLOCH, The Principle of Hope (trans. N. Plaice et al.; 3 vols.; Cambridge, Mass., 1986; orig. pub., 1954-59); idem, The Spirit of Utopia (trans. A. A. Nassar; Stanford, Calif., 2000; orig. pub., 1918) • D. P. CHATTOPADHYAYA, Sociology, Ideology, and Utopia: Socio-political Philosophy of East and West (New York, 1997) • G. CLAEYS, ed., Utopias of the British Enlightenment (New York, 1994) • D. DAWSON, Cities of the Gods: Communist Utopias in Greek Thought (New York, 1992) • M. HOLLOWAY, Heavens on Earth: Utopian Communities in America, 1690-1880 (2d ed.; New York, 1966) • L. HÖLSCHER, "Utopie," GGB 6.733-88 • R. JACOBY, Picture Imperfect: Utopian Thought for an Anti-Utopian Age (New York, 2005) • R. S. JOHNSON, More's Utopia: Ideal and Illusion (New Haven, 1969) • K. MANNHEIM, Ideology and Utopia: An Introduction to the Sociology of Knowledge (New York, 1968) • F. E. MANUEL and F. P. MANUEL, Utopian Thought in the Western World (Cambridge, Mass., 1979) • J. MOLTMANN, Theology of Hope (London, 2002) • K. R. POPPER, The Open Society and Its Enemies (6th ed.; New York, 2002) • L. SARGISSON, Contemporary Feminist Utopianism (New York, 1996) • Q. SKINNER, The Foundations of Modern Political Thought (New York, 1978) • M. WINTER, Compendium Utopiarum. Typologie und Bibliographie literarischer Utopien (Stuttgart, 1978-).

BIRGIT BENDER-JUNKER

Uzbekistan

	1960	1980	2000
Population (1,000s):	8,559	15,952	25,018
Annual growth rate (%):	3.57	2.61	1.82

Area: 447,400 sq. km. (172,700 sq. mi.)

A.D. 2000

Population density: 56/sq. km. (145/sq. mi.)
Births / deaths: 2.58 / 0.62 per 100 population
Fertility rate: 3.13 per woman
Infant mortality rate: 39 per 1,000 live births
Life expectancy: 68.8 years (m: 65.8, f: 71.9)
Religious affiliation (%): Muslims 78.5, nonreligious 17.0, atheists 2.7, Christians 1.3, other 0.5.

1. General Situation
2. Christian Presence

1. General Situation

A long-gone grand civilization of Muslim culture is evoked for most Westerners by naming Uzbekistan's cities Tashkent, Samarkand, and Bukhara. Even during the Soviet era, when Uzbekistan was often combined with several other "-stans" as central Asia, tourists were shown a tent *(urta)* commemorating the well where Job of the OT had lived.

Much of the country's terrain is desertlike; in recent decades the rapid drying up of the Aral Sea on its western border contributed to an economic crisis, already severe following the breakup of the → Soviet Union. Uzbekistan had served as cotton producer through massive irrigation, but it was dependent on other republics for resources.

As the 1990s developed, the official claim of Uzbekistan being a Muslim society took on problematic meanings as not only Christian communities experienced increased loss of rights and even outright → persecution but so too did the more active Muslim communities that were fostering Islamic renewal.

2. Christian Presence

The Christian history in the territory of Uzbekistan can be divided into three rather distinct periods: ancient pre-Islamic Christianity, especially along the Silk Road to China; the introduction of Christianity by settlers in the late 19th century and existing on the frontiers of the Russian and Soviet empires; and finally, in the post-Soviet era, small communities living in a survivalist mode, with limited contact abroad.

2.1. What is generally referred to as the → Syrian Orthodox Church, which spread from a major theological center in Edessa (modern Urfa, formerly part of Persia) as far as India and China, also included the → Nestorian Church, whose monks and intrepid merchant travelers were especially active missionaries. Following an edict of toleration (409) by Shah Yazdegerd, the East Syrian Orthodox Church held a synod of bishops in 410 that included bishops from as far away as Samarkand. The 200 surviving letters of missionary-minded Nestorian patriarch Timothy (served 780-823) include correspondence with the Turkic people of north-central Asia. In 781 the episcopal see of Samarkand was elevated to metropolitan status, indicating that there were other bishops in the region overseeing numerous parishes.

After 1295, with the conversion of Mongol ruler Ghazan to → Islam, a sustained era of decline of Christianity set in. Ghazan ordered the destruction of numerous churches and synagogues, and soon Muslim mobs had caused the violent deaths of many Christians.

Christianity, according to Samuel Moffett, numbered around 12 million when the decline set in, but

it was a Christian community stretched across vast territories, very hard to maintain, at least when compared with an equivalent number within the Byzantine world and that of Rome. In addition to the communication challenges and the difficulties of nurturing such a variety of cultures, including those in Uzbek territories, the cultural growth of Islam from the 7th century forward eventually starved the roots. The wholesale massacres under Timur (Tamerlane, 1336-1405) at the beginning of the 15th century essentially ended the Christian story in central Asia.

2.2. Starting around 1880, scattered settlements of Russians, Ukrainians, and other nationalities arrived in Uzbekistan. A small number were there because of the then-current apocalyptic expectation that the Lord would return at some point in the east. For example, a Mennonite leader named Klaas Epp (d. 1921), who, like others, had been influenced by the Pietist writings of Heinrich Jung-Stilling (1740-1817) while still living in Germany, was able to organize a trek of several hundred families to central Asia. Leaving their newly established German Mennonite colonies around Saratov (Volga), Epp and his group crossed the Kyzyl Kum Desert and settled finally in the village of Ak Mechet in Uzbekistan. Not only was it a costly venture (many children perished along the way), but the dual motives for the trek became more distinct by 1882, when a larger group led by Elder Peters, seeking to escape Russia's imperial military reach, sought a peaceful life in the Tokmak River valley of Kyrgyzstan. A smaller chiliast group led by Epp settled in Ak Mechet, Uzbekistan, living in great penury until most families had found sponsorship to Kansas in the United States.

Others came to Uzbekistan as a result of Russian harrassment of sectarians. As early as 1896 an evangelical community had formed in Tashkent. It maintained its existence as part of the Evangelical Christian Baptist Union (ECB) and continues up till the present, along with a theological seminary it founded around 2000. During the Khrushchev campaign against religious practice (1959-64), more believers came to Uzbekistan, hoping for less severe conditions. In 1961 there was a split within the ECB community to form the Council of Churches of ECB (CCECB).

By 1988 the central ECB church in Tashkent had 1,300 members, another congregation nearby had 300, and the CCECB congregation had 150. Other major locations for congregations included Fergana (500 members), of whom the majority were German. Already by 1988 there were worship services in Fergana offered in Tajik by a convert.

Russian Orthodox worship also began as a result of the expanding frontier, and an episcopal see was established in Tashkent. Its membership consisted mostly of Slavic settlers who had known Orthodoxy, though it was significantly expanded as a result of Soviet-forced resettlements of purged elements, including also the workers army during World War II that focused on canal building.

In the most recent statistics available, there were 32 registered parishes of the → Russian Orthodox Church in Uzbekistan, compared with 23 ECB congregations, 18 → Pentecostal, and 10 → Adventist. In addition, there were 47 registered Korean Presbyterian congregations, for the minority of Koreans who had been living in the region for decades. In contrast, almost 2,000 Muslim communities were registered.

The liturgy of the Russian Orthodox in two major parishes in Tashkent was attended weekly by about 1,000 and 200 respectively. Fewer attended in Fergana (150) and Navoi (120), and a mere 15 came once a week to worship in Bukhara, a few more in Karshi, and only 5 in Termez. In Easter 2002, however, 300-400 attended the paschal liturgy in Termez (N. Mitrokhin, 545-46).

2.3. Soon after 1991, when Uzbekistan became a sovereign state as part of the → Commonwealth of Independent States, there was rapid out-migration of Slavic and German nationalities, especially from the Fergana region, where there had been riots and a massacre. There are also increasingly regular reports of arrests, fines, or acts of vandalism (apparently sanctioned by local authorities) against → Baptists, → Pentecostals, and → Jehovah's Witnesses.

In 2006-7 the spokespersons for the state's religious affairs office began pushing for legal measures to protect Islam and disenfranchise Christians. The Uzbek law on religious associations is the most repressive of any, banning the religious activity of any organization not registered with the justice agencies. In practice, the authorities resist registration (the Jehovah's Witnesses in Tashkent have been refused eight times). The criminal and administrative codes also prohibit → proselytism and missionary activity. Finally, public intolerance of Muslims converting to Christianity accounts for the murder of several Protestant believers in 2005.

Bibliography: R. C. FOLTZ, *Religions of the Silk Road: Overland Trade and Cultural Exchange from Antiquity to the Fifteenth Century* (New York, 1999) • R. R. HANKS, *Central Asia: A Global Studies Handbook* (Santa Barbara, Calif., 2005) • D. T. IRVIN and S. W. SUNQUIST, *History of the World Christian Movement* (2 vols.; Maryknoll, N.Y., 2001) • *Istoriia evangel'skikh Khristian–Baptistov v SSSR* (History of the Evangelical Christian–Baptists in the USSR) (Moscow, 1989) official history • N. MITROKHIN, *Russkaia Pravoslavnaia Tserkov. Sovremennoe sostoianie i aktual'nie problemy* (Russian Orthodox Church. Contemporary status and problems) (Moscow, 2006) • S. H. MOFFETT, *A History of Christianity in Asia* (2 vols.; rev. ed.; Maryknoll, N.Y., 1998-2005) • E. PRIES, "Revisiting the Russian Mennonite Trek to Central Asia," *CGRev* 9/3 (1991) 259-76 • M. H. RUFFIN and D. C. WAUGH, eds., *Civil Society in Central Asia* (Seattle, Wash., 1999) • A. SHIELDS, *Creating Enemies of the State: Religious Persecution in Uzbekistan* (New York, 2004). A Web site operated by Forum 18 (www.forum18.org) regularly features reports of religious rights violations in Uzbekistan.

WALTER SAWATSKY

V

Vatican

1. Place-Name
2. Incorrect Usage

1. Place-Name

The "Vatican" was the name of a hill (the Mons Vaticanus) on the right bank of the River Tiber in → Rome. From the 2nd century onward it was revered as the burial place of the apostle → Peter. Constantine (306-37) built St. Peter's Church there, and in the 15th century it became the residence of the pope. It was expanded in the 15th to 17th centuries to become the largest palatial complex in the world. It includes today, in addition to the papal residence, the Vatican archives, library, and museums.

2. Incorrect Usage

In everyday (but incorrect) usage the "Vatican" denotes the → pope and the Roman → curia; the Holy See, which acts in the name of the church; and the state called Vatican City.

2.1. The Roman curia consists of all the officials that assist the pope in his leadership of the church. It was founded by Pope Sixtus V (1585-90) in 1588 and was reformed by Pius X (1903-14) in 1908, by Paul VI (1963-78) in 1967, and by John Paul II (1978-2005) in 1988 on the basis of the new → Codex Iuris Canonici (CIC; → Curia 1.1). The Secretariat of State is located in the Apostolic Palace (→

Curia 1.2.1), and other officials in various Roman buildings, some at a considerable distance from the Vatican.

2.2 The "Holy See" (Sancta Sedes) and "Apostolic See" (Apostolica Sedes) are terms used for the pope, the secretariat, and other institutions (1983 CIC 361). It is a title denoting the pope's "full, supreme, and universal power over the whole Church" (*Lumen gentium* 22.2) as "the visible head of the whole Church" (18.2), the legal successor of Peter as bishop of Rome (→ Pope, Papacy, 1.2.1), and the office of "the first of the Apostles" (1983 CIC 331).

Personifying the apostolic see of St. Peter (see the letter *Regi Regum* of Leo II; DH 562) in a supreme → representation of the church, the "Holy See" can also be a legal term for the church and its corporation. In international law the pope and the Holy See stand for the → Roman Catholic Church as a supranational institution that also has diplomatic dealings with other states and international organizations.

2.3. Vatican City (It. Stato della Città del Vaticano) is the smallest state in the world (0.44 sq. km. / 109 acres). It lies within → Italy ($1.2) and embraces the Basilica of St. Peter, St. Peter's Square, and the Vatican palaces and gardens. Various official buildings and the papal summer residence of Castel Gandolfo also enjoy extraterritorial privileges.

Vatican City is not just a remnant of the → Papal States, which came to an end in 1870. It was created by the Lateran Treaty of December 11, 1929, as a constitutional monarchy. It gives the Holy See an international status and gives the popes secular as well as spiritual sovereignty, though the relation between Vatican City and the Holy See is under academic discussion. In Vatican City the pope has legislative, executive, and judicial powers; a papal commission oversees the government. Diplomatic exchanges are arranged by the Holy See in the name of the church and by Vatican City.

Bibliography: J. L. ALLEN JR., *All the Pope's Men: The Inside Story of How the Vatican Really Thinks* (New York, 2004) • *AnPont* • P. HEBBLETHWAITE, *In the Vatican* (Bethesda, Md., 1986) • J.-P. D'ONORIO, *Le pape et le gouvernement de l'Église* (Paris, 1992) • J. M. PACKARD, *Peter's Kingdom: Inside the Papal City* (New York, 1985) • T. J. REESE, *Inside the Vatican: The Politics and Organization of the Catholic Church* (Cambridge, Mass., 1996) • H. SCHMITZ, *Kurienreform* (2 vols.; Trier, 1968-75) • *The Vatican Library: Its History and Treasures* (ed. A. M. Stickler and L. E. Boyle; Yorktown Heights, N.Y., 1989) • B. WALL, *The Vatican Story* (New York, 1975).

ERWIN GATZ

Vatican I and II

1. Vatican I (1869-70)
    1.1. Preliminaries
    1.2. Course
    1.3. Effects
    1.4. Doctrinal Pronouncements
2. Vatican II (1962-65)
    2.1. Preliminaries
    2.2. Course
    2.3. The Council's Pronouncements
    2.4. Effects
    2.5. Further Reflections
        2.5.1. Ecumenical Implications and Steps
        2.5.2. The Unfolding of Tradition

1. Vatican I (1869-70)

1.1. *Preliminaries*

Within the Roman Catholic tradition, the First Vatican Council is considered the 20th general council of the church, the first to be convened in the 324 years since the Council of → Trent (1545-63). In the history of the church, this was the longest period between ecumenical → councils. Given this length of time in which the church had not engaged in a systematic reflection on its own teaching and → tradition, and given the enormous intellectual, political, economic, social, and cultural changes that had

taken place over these three centuries, we must consider carefully the relations of the → Roman Catholic Church to → culture and history from the mid-16th to almost the beginning of the 20th century as we try to understand Vatican I (→ Catholicism [Roman] 1.2; Modern Church History 1.3).

Francis Bacon (1561-1626) was of great importance in the shaping of that culture. His work built on a vast array of studies in what would later be called the natural sciences, and especially on the gradual emergence of the empirical method as it was being drawn during the late 15th and early 16th centuries from the classical philosophical writers in their treatises on nature and medicine. Pope Nicholas V (1447-55), who in 1448 brought classical codices together to form the Vatican Library, also had promoted the work of a wide range of scholars who were assembling both empirical data and the theories of the ancients.

Bacon did something similar, explaining the new method in his *Novum Organon* (1620), doing so with an angry attack against the classical method, which had actually led scholars toward the empirical method. He also introduced a break in the form of classical knowledge that remains a significant and unresolved problem for Western culture and that influences various fields of knowledge as they even now struggle to integrate facts and values. Bacon broke apart the classical form of human explanation by eliminating the connection that the ancients had always maintained in their claim that full knowledge of an essence, or nature, was gained by an understanding of the four causes of anything — material, formal, efficient, and final (→ Causality). Bacon argued that the final cause (the ends or purpose of an event) had no place in empirical method and left it as a remnant for theology to work out. The new *organon* became in fact the source of the new authority; according to Bacon, its own final cause is → "power."

Adding to these complications, Western philosophical traditions, with which Roman Catholic theology was and is so interrelated, had been undergoing a long struggle to establish the claims and limits of knowledge, from R. Descartes (1596-1650; → Cartesianism) to B. Spinoza (1632-77; → Spinozism); to clarify the meaning of the social character of human life, especially the understanding of political freedom and of natural law, through the work of T. Hobbes (1588-1679) and J. Locke (1632-1704); and to take account of the idealist programs for knowledge, faith, and history of I. Kant (1724-1804; → Kantianism) and G. W. F. Hegel (1770-1831; → Hegelianism). F. → Nietzsche

(1844-1900), it should be noted, was only beginning his academic career, being appointed professor at Basel in 1869, the year Vatican I commenced.

If the context for the council had been shaped only by the philosophers, it would still be an enormous project to take the measure of their contribution. Other intellectual, social, spiritual, and cultural movements needing integration, however, also occurred during these centuries. In light of the great effort to integrate all knowledge with the flood of new data and hypotheses that were building on one another in the emergence of the new human sciences from philosophical studies (e.g., the development of → economics from moral philosophy in the writings of A. Smith [1723-90] and the development of → sociology from political philosophy in the work of A. Comte [1798-1857; → Positivism 1-2]), it was a daunting task indeed to incorporate biblical knowledge and knowledge grounded in faith and in a tradition that was everywhere considered naive and suspect. The modern social, economic, cultural, and educational controls of meaning were increasingly institutionalized, with J.-J. Rousseau's (1712-78) plan for the education of Émile becoming a model.

These debates, coupled with the emergence of the empirical method within the natural sciences, meant that assumptions and proposals about the relationships between reason and faith had shifted radically since the Council of Trent. They indeed had shaken not just Catholicism but the whole of the Western world, including Protestantism, as evidenced in F. D. E. → Schleiermacher's (1768-1834) quest for religious foundations and knowledge in an intuition of faith and life. In a profound sense the moves from older thought forms and methodologies, when introduced into the new academic and political life, were not perceived or accepted as developments from within traditions but rather as revolutions from beyond traditions, revolutions that were seeking to overthrow all past history. Hegel had tried to address this issue in *Phenomenology of Mind* (1807), but this effort was followed by the broad revolutions that began throughout Europe in 1848.

It is no wonder, then, that the church was on the defensive intellectually, politically, and ecclesiastically, for where once a philosophical tradition would have been able to mediate its new insights to its older ones, the tradition itself had become revolutionary and no longer dialectical. In the first half of the 19th century, the European structure of the tradition had been severely shaken by the French → Revolution (§2.4) and the Napoleonic wars (→ Sec-

ularization 1.4). The postrevolutionary states attempted to make the church dependent on the state or civil societies (→ Church and State 1.2). The anticlerical and antichurch intentions of the revolutions (→ Liberalism) were not just an intellectual and political threat to the church's principles, constitution, and activity, but they opposed its very history and purposes. → Concordats made by the → Papal States gave the papacy some modest political grounds for protecting the faith of the community over against policies that would tear it apart. These minor successes, offset by weakness within the church because of decades-long efforts by national leaders to control the appointment of → bishops who would agree with their views (the states thus virtually becoming fifth columns within the church) placed a great burden on the papal office.

Paradoxically, the authority of the popes and their influence within the church were actually enhanced by this turn of events (→ Pope, Papacy, 1.5), as many faithful favored a stronger, more centralized authority for the Holy See. This tendency, or → Ultramontanism, was part of a dynamic tension within Roman Catholicism itself, placing an emphasis on the universal dimension of the church in contrast to the emphasis on local character and rule that more liberal members of the church preferred. Ultramontanism thus stood in opposition to the movements that were attempting to define the church in limited local spheres, namely → Gallicanism and the episcopalianism of the empire. In a word, the Ultramontane movement sought to strengthen the jurisdictional primacy of the papacy by supporting a clear statement of what many in the Catholic tradition considered as having been the practice of the church from the earliest days: the doctrine of papal → infallibility (§3). Strongly opposed to the intellectual confusion and political chaos of the revolutionary attacks of → modernity (→ Restoration 4), some Ultramontanists called for the church and its theologians to address the issues of the church's identity on its own terms, not those of the secularists (→ Catholicism [Roman] 1.2).

The conflicts that existed in academic dialectics regarding the relationship of faith and reason thus provoked a growing sense that the authority of Scripture and, for Catholics, the authority of the teaching office of the church needed to be clarified. This need was deeply sensed by Gregory XVI (1831-46) and → Pius IX (1846-78). In promulgating *Ineffabilis Deus* (1854), the dogma of the immaculate conception (→ Mariology 1.3.3 and 2.4), namely that Mary was conceived without original sin, Pius IX made known his consultations with theologians and bishops, as well as the requests of clergy and laity for some affirmation by the teaching office of what all believed. He also added, "We concluded that we should no longer delay in decreeing and defining by our supreme authority the Immaculate Conception of Our Blessed Virgin."

Similarly, the 1864 → Syllabus of Errors, an attachment to Pius IX's encyclical *Quanta cura*, pointed with some concern to the modern error of denying the transcendent and supernatural dimensions of existence. This list directly challenged the teaching of some seminary professors of theology, who were teaching future pastors a kind of → naturalism (→ Modernity 2.1) and liberalism. Such internal opposition to modern secular positions created a Roman Catholic voice in the broad dialectic of which the late → Enlightenment was so proud, and it helped to discipline intellectuals and theologians who might have misunderstood the Catholic vision within the dialectic itself. Interestingly, while these broad debates were under way, there was a little-noticed Catholic expansion of evangelization and a churchwide commitment to personal piety and to missionary activity (→ Evangelism; Catholic Missions; Religious Orders and Congregations 1).

1.2. *Course*

Preparations for Vatican I began in 1865, as a considerable number of → cardinals and → bishops were consulted. In June 1868 the bull *Aeterni Patris* announced that the council would commence at St. Peter's Basilica on December 8, 1869, the feast of the immaculate conception. The opening celebration had 725 bishops present, out of the 1,056 bishops worldwide. One-third of the bishops present were Italian, and they exercised significant leadership and had considerable influence. → Ecumenism had not developed in either Protestant or Catholic communities, so no Protestants were present. (In 1868 the apostolic letter *Iam vos omnes* was sent to Protestant leaders, inviting them to return to the Roman Catholic Church.)

The council had available to it 51 studies or schemata, prepared by five preparatory commissions, only a few of which were discussed at the 89 general sessions. There were three dogmatic proposals, and two of them were given primary emphasis. One was related to the issue of Catholic theologians using the methodologies of modern rationalism in presenting teachings about the relationship of faith and reason; the other was a consideration of the church of Christ. The third proposal, on Christian marriage, was not discussed because of the brief time that the council met. The Franco-Prussian War, the withdrawal of French troops from Rome, and the entrance into Rome in 1870 of the Italian army of the Risorgimento (resurgence) made things too difficult for the council to continue. Two dogmatic → constitutions (§1) resulted: *Dei Filius,* on the Catholic faith (April 24, 1870); and *Pastor aeternus,* on the church of Christ (July 18, 1870).

The preparations and the course of the council were sometimes overshadowed by controversies surrounding papal infallibility. Fears existed in some local dioceses and parishes of the political repression that might follow if primacy was promulgated openly. In France, then the numerically largest Roman Catholic country, an Ultramontanist view was very much favored by significant groups of both the laity and the younger clergy. On February 6, 1869, the Italian Jesuit journal *Civiltà cattolica* published correspondence from French Catholics that distinguished between liberals and other Catholics and that seems to have led to further agitation for opposing the proposal to proclaim infallibility a dogma of the church. The article divided Roman Catholics into three groups: those favoring the proclamation of papal infallibility, those against it, and those who believed it to be correct but thought the time was not opportune for its proclamation.

In Germany additional controversy arose when I. von Döllinger (1799-1890), professor of church history at the University of Munich, wrote five essays published in *Allgemeine Zeitung* against both the Syllabus and the doctrine of infallibility. His book *Der Papst und das Konzil* (1869) was the major German statement of opposition. The social and economic thinker among the bishops, W. E. von Ketteler (1811-77) of Mainz, did not believe that the time for a definition was opportune; he advocated a very limited doctrinal infallibility for the pope, subject to the unanimous agreement of the bishops' college.

There were three groups among the bishops at the council. First were the resolute supporters of infallibility, led by H. E. Manning (1808-92) of Westminster, England, and I. von Senestrey (1818-1906), of Regensburg, Germany. Then came those who thought the time inopportune, mostly bishops from Austria-Hungary and Germany, with several others from France, the United States, and elsewhere. Finally, there was a large group that did not object to the dogma but wished to avoid extreme formulations.

As a result of the cultural crises that the church was facing within the disorder of the European world, which was not necessarily evident to the local churches, Pius IX's response became clearer. As it became evident that the political turmoil in Italy would limit the time for the council, the pope first sought to add a chapter on papal infallibility to the schema on the church, but soon he decided that the time was so short that papal infallibility should be discussed first and as a constitution of its own. The bishops accepted this idea, and the minority group of bishops was not able to postpone the adoption of a definition of infallibility, although they were helpful in clarifying the precise nature of the Petrine office in the exercise of its ministry. Immediately after papal infallibility was defined, most of the delegates had to leave Rome because of the Italian occupation of the city. The pope adjourned the council on October 20, 1870.

1.3. Effects

Many bishops were not happy with various aspects, particularly the timing of the new definition of infallibility, even though upon the conclusion of the discussion they finally gave it close to a full acceptance, with a vote of 433 in favor, and 2 opposed. Reception in some parts of the church was slow, especially where there had been some opposition before the beginning of the council. Less than 100 years later, Vatican II would expand the ecclesial context of the church and the role of its bishops in relation to the Petrine office (see 2.3) and deepen the sense of the mystery of the whole church.

Taken out of its ecclesiological context, the definition of papal infallibility and its catechetical exposition became an ecumenical stumbling block, and it must be admitted that often neither Roman Catholics nor Protestants understand what the precise papal office (→ Pope, Papacy, 2.2.2) and its limits are. Many persons have interpreted it crassly in terms of the modern notion of a mere *libido dominandi* (lust for power).

A number of Döllinger's followers left the Roman Catholic Church over this issue and established a body known as the → Old Catholic Church, although Döllinger himself did not become a member. A few bodies in Europe, notably Prussia and some cantons in Switzerland, passed measures against the church (→ Kulturkampf). The Austrian government withdrew from its concordat with the Vatican.

1.4. Doctrinal Pronouncements

The Dogmatic Constitution on the Faith *(Dei Filius)* deals mainly with the themes of → fundamental theology and the meaning of revelation. In opposition to → pantheism, → materialism, → atheism, and → rationalism, it expounds the Christian doctrine of → God. Rejecting fideistic traditionalism and religious intuitionism, it affirms the possibility of a true knowledge of God's existence by reason (→

Epistemology 2.2; Faith 3.5.4). Resisting erroneous Kantian (G. Hermes [1775-1831]) and idealistic (A. Günther [1783-1863]) influences on Roman Catholic theology, it points to the genuinely mysterious and supernatural character of → revelation (§2.5), though arguing that revelation can be shown to have a rationally credible context, which supporting theological efforts make clear. Finally, the constitution stands for the legitimate and proper freedom of scholarship and explains why scholarship and revelation can sometimes seem to be at odds with each other. It employs and recommends the classical forms of apologetics in the → neoscholasticism of the day. In many ways it proved to be helpful in preparing the way for the scholarship that later enabled theologians to address methodological foundations (→ Theology in the Nineteenth and Twentieth Centuries 2).

The Dogmatic Constitution on the Church *(Pastor aeternus)* has four chapters dealing with the Petrine primacy and its institution, its continuation in the office of bishops, the jurisdictional primacy of these bishops, and their infallible → teaching office (→ Bishop, Episcopate, 2; Ministry, Ministerial Offices, 1 and 5.6). It is mostly directed against → conciliarism, Gallicanism, Febronianism, and the concept of a state church (→ Church and State 1). Papal primacy means full, supreme, and direct jurisdictional leadership over the universal church. It does not conflict, however, with the position of bishops as "true pastors" in the churches.

The council did not define the rights of primacy. In its application to the teaching office, it articulated for the church the very infallibility that the church and its councils had previously claimed for the Petrine ministry, as exercised ex cathedra on matters of faith and morals and only within the solemn intention of making a doctrinal definition. *Pastor aeternus* also conferred on the holder of the papal office the title "eternal pastor" (→ Pastor 2).

2. Vatican II (1962-65)

2.1. Preliminaries

We could say that Vatican I, through its understanding of the apostolic office of Peter, brought the church to an articulation of its authority in respect to Scripture and the church itself and thus provided resources for the church to meet the crisis of Europe that Edmund Husserl (1859-1938) described in *Die Krisis der europäischen Wissenschaften und die transzendentale Phänomenologie* (1936; ET *The Crisis of European Sciences and Transcendental Phenomenology* [1970]). Vatican II, originating at the behest of John XXIII (1958-63), who announced it in 1959 and convened it in 1962, had two basic intentions: (1) an *aggiornamento* (renewal) of the church's life and presence in the world, and (2) Christian unity, which could now be pursued in light of foundational scholarship since the work of Vatican I. Barriers from the viewpoint of European liberalism were removed in some measure, in that the church had expanded enormously because of its missionary activity and evangelization, and by the 1960s the church was not concerned solely with European problems. Two world wars had revealed deeply serious problems in Enlightenment rationalism. It was now the church's task to bring all its work up to date to meet the new challenges.

The church, in effect, was seeking to define its place and mission in the modern world and was now dealing with a fuller and more complex understanding of itself (→ Roman Catholic Church 2 and 4) and the world. The council belonged to its time, and its judgments and decisions brought forth developments that changed the face of the church in promoting further dimensions of the mystery entrusted to it by Christ. The scriptural movement (→ Exegesis, Biblical, 2.1.6; Bible Societies 4), → liturgical movement (§2), → ecumenical movement (§4.4), → social movement (§3.5), movements of → youth and the laity (→ Lay Apostolate), the rediscovery of the → church fathers, and the rescuing of theology from the grip of the conceptualism of neoscholasticism were all part of the varied contribution made by theologians, scholars, bishops, pastors, and laypersons. The result was the spiritual enlivening of the *communio,* or → *koinonia.* An optimistic and even utopian view of the future, so characteristic of the Western world in the early 1960s, influenced the church's sense of itself and its tasks.

A historic epoch had ended in 1958 with the death of → Pius XII (1939-58), whose pontificate had been the high-water mark of a universal church centralized in Europe. Pius XII, however, made no small contribution to the new council's coming into being; he himself had begun consultations regarding calling a council himself, one that would assemble with a fuller sense of the universality, the → oikoumene, of the church. But then the charismatic John XXIII was elected, and suddenly on January 25, 1959, the feast of St. Paul, to the surprise of almost everyone, he announced that a general council would be held, to be devoted to the pastoral concerns of the church.

2.2. Course

2.2.1. Preparations began in 1959 with the establishment of a general secretariat and commissions composed of bishops, superiors of religious orders, heads of → universities and theological faculties, and other consultants. The commissions and secretariat received a wide variety of proposals, the most important being those on revelation, the church, liturgy, and Christian unity (→ Curia 1.2.4; Ecumenism, Ecumenical Movement, 1.4). Altogether 73 schemata were produced, 4 of which were of central interest in that they addressed issues that had been limited to very brief discussions at Vatican I.

On November 11, 1962, John XXIII opened the council at St. Peter's Basilica with a notable address that enunciated both the openness of, and expectations for, the council. In attendance were 2,540 voting delegates; an average of about 2,000 attended the 168 general congregations and 10 public sessions. The composition of the council reflected the enormous growth of the church in the → Third World over the past century, as native bishops made evident the new face of the universal church. One-third of the bishops came from Europe, one-third from the Americas, and one-third from other continents. Over 200 theologians served as *periti,* or consultants, who were chosen either by the secretaries of commissions or by their own local bishops. Also present were 93 official observers from 18 non–Roman Catholic churches who had been invited by the Holy See and by their presiding bishops or judicatories: Anglicans, Lutherans, Reformed, and Orthodox (→ Anglican Communion; Lutheran Churches; Reformed and Presbyterian Churches; Orthodox Church). After some initial hesitation, representatives of both the → Ecumenical Patriarchate of Constantinople and the Moscow Patriarchate (→ Russian Orthodox Church) also attended.

John XXIII died in 1963, after the first session of the council, and Paul VI (1963-78) presided over the remaining sessions (September 1963–December 1965). At the outset, the schemata that reflected neoscholasticism were generally acknowledged to be incomplete and unsatisfactory; the particularly problematic schema on revelation was returned to its committee with a request for a thorough rewriting. After some struggles, disagreements, and considerable reworking of the texts, those that expressed reforming concerns were adopted, and in time a number of bishops who had been in opposition accepted the changes.

The council affirmed the celebration of the Eucharist and the recitation of the breviary, and a broader experience of a common life of prayer and charity was of considerable assistance in fostering understanding and respect for differing views. The general theme of *aggiornamento* also helped the fathers to present church renewal in the light of the church's origins, the promotion of Christian unity, and → dialogue with the modern world. Those of both majority and minority views often used some of the formulations of Vatican I as a basis for their positions. One of the ways that internal disunity was met and doctrinal continuity not only preserved but enhanced was through finding ways that different concerns could be expressed in certain of the texts, even when they were in tension with one another.

Paul VI closed the council on December 8, 1965. At a major celebration on December 7 the mutual sentences of → excommunication between Rome and Constantinople, dating back to 1054, were lifted.

2.2.2. The council accepted four constitutions:

Sacrosanctum concilium, On the Sacred Liturgy (*SC;* → Liturgy 3.2; Mass 2.3.2; Roman Catholic Church 3; Worship 2.2)

Lumen gentium, On the Church (*LG;* → Catholicism [Roman] 3; Church 3.2; Ecumenism, Ecumenical Movement, 1.4.5; Mariology 1.4 and 2.5; Roman Catholic Church 2.1; Teaching Office 1.3)

Dei verbum, On Divine Revelation (*DV;* → Dogma 3.3; Exegesis, Biblical, 2.1.6; Salvation History 4.2; Teaching Office 1.3; Word of God 3)

Gaudium et spes, On the Church in the Modern World (*GS;* → Human Dignity 2.1; Peace 2.3.3; Roman Catholic Church 4).

Nine decrees were also adopted:

Inter mirifica, On the Means of Social Communication (*IM;* → Christian Communication 1; Communication 4)

Orientalium ecclesiarum, On the Catholic Eastern Churches (→ Uniate Churches)

Unitatis redintegratio, On Ecumenism (*UR;* → Codex Iuris Canonici 3; Ecumenism, Ecumenical Movement, 1.4.5; Eucharist 5.1.2; Roman Catholic Church 7.1)

Christus Dominus, On the Pastoral Office of Bishops in the Church (→ Curia 1.1)

Optatam totius, On the Training of Priests

Perfectae caritatis, On the Renewal of Religious Life (→ Monasticism 5.6; Religious Orders and Congregations 1.6)

Apostolicam actuositatem, On the Apostolate of Lay People (→ Catholic Action; Lay Apostolate; Roman Catholic Church 4.4)

Ad gentes divinitus, On the Church's Missionary Activity (→ Catholic Missions; Mission 3.5.3)

Presbyterorum ordinis, On the Ministry and Life of Priests (→ Celibacy of the Clergy; Worker-Priests 4)

Also, three declarations were passed:

Gravissimum educationis, On Christian Education

Nostra aetate, On the Relation of the Church to Non-Christian Religions (*NA;* → Buddhism and Christianity; Jewish-Christian Dialogue; Roman Catholic Church 7.2; Theology of Religions 2)

Dignitatis humanae, On Religious Liberty (*DH;* → Religious Liberty [Modern Period] 4.1).

All 16 documents were promulgated by Pope Paul VI at different times during the council.

2.3. *The Council's Pronouncements*

The theological teachings of Vatican II are focused primarily on the church itself, its relationship to God, and its relationship to the world in its various manifestations. The principal expressions of the council are pastoral, and no dogmas were defined during the years that it met. The structure of the council can be envisioned in a number of ways. One such way is through its understanding of the mystery of the church in its constitution and mission. Thus *LG* and *GS,* both drawing considerably on the encyclical *Mystici corporis* (1943), are serious examinations of the church's self-understanding as the body of Christ and its mission to the world; these themes serve as an axis. Developments include the definition of the church as the → people of God, all those baptized into the mystery of redemption, with a focus on the priesthood of all believers (→ Priest, Priesthood, 4); the church's mission (→ Clergy and Laity 2.1); and the charisms (→ Charisma) of the church, not as a closed → society, but as a sacrament of the union of humanity with God and with the church itself (→ Roman Catholic Church 2; Sacramentality 2). In this view of the church, dialogue with all people of goodwill is central. The fact is underlined that the church should not be overly centralized but is a fellowship of believers in particular dioceses who are under the pastoral care and teaching office of the local bishop, who together with other bishops forms a collegiality of pastoral care and governance that exists under the headship of the bishop of Rome (→ Church 3.2.2; Hierarchy 1; Roman Catholic Church 5 and 7.2).

The Dogmatic Constitution on the Church, *Lumen gentium,* addresses a number of important matters regarding the church's existence, order, and mission. It is here that the phrase "people of God" is used to identify the whole of the church in its unity with Christ through baptism, and the people are thus opened to a participation in the divine life of Father, Son, and Spirit. Through the gift of Christ and their life in the church and world, they both share in and carry forward the mystery of divine love and salvation. This document also takes up the work of Vatican I on the topic of the Petrine office and papal infallibility, placing it in the fuller context of the whole church. It also identifies the body of bishops, successors to the apostles, as persons who are in essential unity and who share in the teaching office (*LG* 18). "The college or body of bishops has . . . no authority unless united with the Roman Pontiff, Peter's successor, as its head" (22). Together, the body of bishops and the pope have full teaching authority in defining faith and morals and thus authority to proclaim the mysteries handed over and entrusted to them by Christ for the purpose of teaching the mystery of the saving love of God to the world. Furthermore, they are not only to celebrate the sacraments, they are also to make certain that the → preaching of the gospel "has pride of place" (25). The document further notes: "Although the bishops, taken individually, do not enjoy the privilege of infallibility, they do, however, proclaim infallibly the doctrine of Christ on the following conditions: namely, when, even though dispersed throughout the world but preserving for all that amongst themselves and with Peter's successor the bond of communion, in their authoritative teaching concerning matters of faith and morals, they are in agreement that a particular teaching is to be held definitively and absolutely" (25). Finally, *LG* integrates authority with revelation, asserting that when the pope and the bishops together with him "define a doctrine, they make the definition in conformity with revelation itself" (25).

The liturgical constitution (*SC*) follows much the same lines. The liturgy is for the celebration of the worship and glory of God alone; it is at the center of a gathering of the whole congregation with the priest celebrant, who offers the rites of the church in the place of the local bishop. The constitution on revelation (*DV*) deals with fundamental theology. Revelation is the self-communication of the triune God, which is mediated in time through the teaching of the church as it speaks the truth in every new situation and age. Scripture and tradition are not two sources of revelation. Revelation itself is the source of all saving → truth (§3). In the relation between Scripture and tradition, precedence goes to Scripture, with a clear understanding of the apostolic tradition as the bearer of what Christ taught in his person and life. The church's teaching office does not control the Word of God but sees to its faithful transmission and to ways of developing an understanding of its teaching and meaning.

The decrees and declarations deal with specific concerns or tasks, and they propose matters of basic policy and pastoral practice. The most important of these are the decree on ecumenism (*UR*), which brought Rome institutionally into the ecumenical movement; the declaration on the church's relation to Jews and non-Christian religions (*NA*); and the declaration on religious liberty (*DH*). These documents express three important things for the church: the desire and need to listen to others more carefully, the dignity of all human beings in conscience and freedom, and the willingness to learn about others' and one's own tradition in a way that permits conversation and dialogue in which persons are respected by being accepted as belonging to God and, in the case of ecumenism, of belonging to Christ in common fellowship and koinonia.

2.4. *Effects*

The reception of the council and the appropriation of its theological and pastoral reflections continue today and will continue to make their marks on the tradition of Catholic life and thought. It is not surprising, however, that such a major undertaking within the church would have some difficulties. The sense that the council could be understood as modern culture understands changes — namely, as a revolution — has had some unfortunate consequences, perhaps most notably and strangely a reversion to the loss of the sense of divine transcendence, as well as a loss of the integrity of faith and reason, which had been the concern of Vatican I.

During his papacy, John Paul II (1978-2005) addressed this tendency in a number of his encyclicals. Even more, however, the fundamental "spirit of Vatican II" was found in his constant outreach to peoples of all nations and religions. He also brought the council's vision into the structure of → church law and in large measure into the curia and the college of cardinals. His particular attention to evangelization, both of persons and cultures, brought the church into fuller awareness of the multiple levels of dialogue that are required for the present time. This point is best articulated in the encyclical *Ut unum sint* (1995; §§21-40) and the earlier document *Dialogue and Proclamation* (1991), promulgated by the Pontifical Council for Interreligious Dialogue. While many postconciliar institutions and regulations reflect tensions that have not yet been resolved, it is nevertheless clear that one of the most important effects of Vatican II has been the growth of Roman Catholic awareness that its commitment to the ecumenical task is constitutive of its very existence.

The relation of the Roman Catholic Church with the Jewish people has also flourished over the decades since Vatican II. Joint dialogues exist with the Reform and Conservative bodies of the Jewish community. Issues involving Catholic catechesis regarding the Jews, the horror of the Shoah (→ Holocaust), and the State of Israel are now, along with more theological topics, serious issues of conversation between Catholic and Jewish scholars.

There has also been growth in the dialogues with world religions, most especially with → Islam. These conversations assume two different forms: direct dialogues with local imams on religious and pastoral issues, and three-way conversations between Jews, Muslims, and Christians (i.e., so-called Abrahamic religious dialogues).

2.5. Further Reflections

2.5.1. Ecumenical Implications and Steps

The modern ecumenical movement can be said to have begun with the World Missionary Conference held in Edinburgh in 1910. The → World Council of Churches (WCC) itself was not established until 1948, although steps toward its establishment had been taken before World War II by both the → Faith and Order and the → Life and Work movements. As a result of Vatican II, the Roman Catholic Church committed itself institutionally to the ecumenical movement 17 years after the founding of the WCC. In reality, 17 years is not a very long time, considering the centuries of mutual condemnations that Christian churches had imposed on one another. Often during those centuries the self-definitions of the churches emphasized what and whom they were against rather than more positive ecclesial characteristics. In the mid-20th century it became clear that this was not a sufficient manner of reading the will of Christ or of responding to the Holy Spirit. In this transformation of spirit and action, the churches were granted a fuller life with Christ and together, and thus they became mediators to each other of their own traditions and gifts.

The *aggiornamento* of Vatican II put an end to apologetic confrontations and to strategies in opposition to the ecumenical movement. New ecclesial offices were now needed to carry forth the mission of the Roman Catholic Church as affirmed at the council. The primary office for this purpose was the Secretariat for Promoting Christian Unity, which had originally been established in 1960 in preparation for the council. Paul VI made the secretariat permanent and appointed Cardinal Augustin Bea (1881-1968) as its first president. In 1988 John

Paul II elevated it to a pontifical council, which made it clear that ecumenism had become institutionally established in the church. Also in 1960, and also contributing to the church's ecumenical involvement, was a confidential meeting held in Milan between Cardinal Bea and W. A. → Visser 't Hooft (1900-1985), general secretary of the WCC, for the purpose of inviting official observers to attend the Vatican Council.

The *Ecumenical Directory* of 1967-70, with a revised edition, *Directory for the Application of Principles and Norms on Ecumenism* (1993), offers guidance to the church at large in applying Roman Catholic principles of ecumenism. After the council various forms of cooperation were initiated with the WCC (→ Ecumenism, Ecumenical Movement, 2.7.1; SODEPAX). The ecumenical commitment of the church is also evident in bilateral and multilateral dialogues between ecclesial bodies (→ Ecumenical Dialogue), in joining or working with → national councils of churches, in local contacts and experiments (→ Local Ecumenism), and in exchanges in theological research (→ Ecumenical Theology).

This process of appropriation and mutual understanding rests on a common conviction in both the WCC and the Roman Catholic Church that each must seek the unity of the church. This commitment involves an ecumenical realism that often oscillates between a broad vision and a more cautious upholding of confessional identity (→ Confession of Faith 5). National bishops' conferences have had a significant role in developing ecumenical relations and theology, particularly in England, France, Germany, India, and the United States, where commitments to ecumenical and interreligious dialogue have assisted the universal church in advancing the project of Vatican II. The common and mutual reception in October 1999 of the → Joint Declaration on the Doctrine of Justification by the Roman Catholic Church and the churches of the → Lutheran World Federation was a major advance for both communions, having been prepared for by serious theological dialogue in both national and international spheres that lasted several decades. Fruitful ecumenical dialogue has also occurred in the Anglican–Roman Catholic International Commission, which addressed the place of Mary in the ecclesiology of both communions in an agreed statement entitled *Mary: Grace and Hope in Christ* (2005).

John Paul II strongly affirmed the Roman Catholic ecumenical commitment in *Ut unum sint* by endorsing and expanding the Catholic position along the lines of Vatican II, speaking of the "fruits of dialogue" thus far. Yet he also emphasized the confessionally inviolable elements in the Roman view of unity. Sacramental and hierarchical fellowship ($\rightarrow$ Roman Catholic Church 1.2) presupposes the acceptance of the "whole truth" (§36) and "true consensus of faith" (79), especially on such matters as Scripture and tradition, the doctrine of the Eucharist, ordination as sacraments (deacon, priest, and bishop), the church's teaching office, Mary as the mother of God, and the primacy of the bishop of Rome. In an unexpected turn, he called for and welcomed an ecumenical discussion of the concrete form and exercise of Petrine primacy and its role in promoting Christian unity (96). Clearly, the consequences of Vatican II continue, and the council offers guidance in matters never imagined before.

2.5.2. *The Unfolding of Tradition*

The Second Vatican Council's engagement with the world, in the sense of the *aggiornamento* that was the underlying vision of John XXIII when he convened the event, can in a certain way be found by the appropriation of developments within the theological and philosophical disciplines, as augmented by the new human and social sciences that were so alien to Vatican I.

In 13 of the 16 documents of Vatican II there is some reference to the importance of the church engaging "culture." No precise definition of culture is given, other than that it is a way of life and that there are "a plurality of cultures" (*GS* 53). This sense of the variety of cultures has helped considerably in overcoming the limitation of the classical tradition concerning culture, namely, that there is only one authentic culture.

The modern study of culture had barely begun at the time of Vatican I, which obviously limited that council's understanding of the church and its mission. Missionary expansion and the establishment of new dioceses in Africa and Asia had taken hold by the start of Vatican II, a fact that transformed the council's understanding of the church. One can find an interesting instance of the tensions brought by evangelization and missionary expansion in the history and debates surrounding *Ad gentes divinitus*, the Decree on the Church's Missionary Activity. On the one hand, there was concern that the church be united and universal in its expansion, and on the other hand, that the local dioceses have their bishops and clergy appointed from within their own communities of faith. That discussion extended well after the council. The contemporary importance of culture is now everywhere evident as the church develops aspects of its self-understanding that came to light only through the conflicts, debates, and formulations that transpired during the council.

The council does not stand as a revolution in the church's life so much as the unfolding of its tradition. It is clear that engagement with cultures employs a hermeneutic that moves not only from the past to the present but also from the present back to the past. Both of these movements are a part of what Benedict XVI (2005-) calls the "hermeneutic of reform." In a speech given to the members of the curia on December 22, 2005, he referred to the twofold hermeneutic that interpreted the meaning of the council between 1965 and 2005. The first he named "a hermeneutic of discontinuity and rupture," and the second, "the 'hermeneutic of reform,' of renewal in the continuity of the one subject-Church which the Lord has given to us." Thus it will always be possible to draw on already-known resources that may well be valuable for dealing with situations of need in respect to the church's mission. To be sure, when the hermeneutic moves from the present back to the past, as has occurred in debates over $\rightarrow$ liberation theology, with its values as related to issues of justice and poverty and its dangers in resting its claims in Marxist terms and visions, it may well seem that there is a *renversement,* or repudiation of the council. Such a hermeneutic of tradition, or "reform," may cause some to be concerned about the return of the church to a conceptualist reading of itself and the world. In fact, however, the church draws on this hermeneutical mode when some issue arises that needs clarification or when it seeks to bring forth a genuine unity with those who had resisted positions taken at Vatican II. The conflict over liberation theology led to such a clarification of its premises, and thus when Benedict XVI visited Brazil in May 2007, it was commonly agreed that liberation theology, albeit without assumptions of Marxist ideology, is a considerable gift to local churches throughout Latin America.

In the same vein, in 2000 the Congregation for the Doctrine of the Faith (CDF), in response to certain situations in the church, particularly in Asia, issued *Dominus Iesus,* subtitled "On the Unicity and Salvific Universality of Jesus Christ and the Church." This document affirmed for the church much of what the ancient creeds proclaimed about Jesus Christ as the one and only Savior. The document, however, could well have been more attentive to other documents that had been developed with the Vatican's Pontifical Councils for Promoting Christian Unity and for Interreligious Dialogues. The purpose of *Dominus Iesus* was not to void progress but again to bring the foundation of the church's faith to the attention of the whole community. Similarly, one finds this hermeneutic at work in the moto proprio *Summorum pontificum* of July 2007. This document sets rather careful boundaries to its permission to celebrate the Eucharist using the Latin missal of Pius V (1566-72) as an exception to the use of the vernacular missal of Paul VI. In this situation the church is responding from its heritage to those who continue to find this eucharistic celebration from the tradition fruitful for their lives of worship and holiness.

Likewise, in the CDF's "Responses to Some Questions regarding Certain Aspects of the Doctrine of the Church" (June 2007), which is focused on the meaning of the Latin term *subsistit* (subsists) in three documents of Vatican II, there is a repetition and emphasis on what these documents teach regarding the Roman Catholic Church and also regarding the graces and gifts found in Reformation churches and communions. The document is similar to what is also reflected in John Paul II's *Ut unum sint*, and its views have been widely discussed in international and national ecumenical dialogues over the decades since Vatican II. Nevertheless, leaders of Orthodox and Reformation churches have responded to Cardinal Walter Kasper (b. 1933), president of the Pontifical Council for Promoting Christian Unity, with disappointment and concern. It must be admitted that the CDF document does not indicate how much the Roman Catholic Church has learned from the faith, theology, and worship particularly of Protestant traditions, something that the church has actually been doing since Vatican II. In years to come, it is hoped that greater sensitivity will mark such statements, which would only increase ecumenical reception.

Bibliography: Infallibility and Vatican I: R. F. COSTIGAN, *The Consensus of the Church and Papal Infallibility: A Study in the Background of Vatican I* (Washington, D.C., 2005) • J. J. KIRVAN, ed., *The Infallibility Debate* (New York, 1971) • H. KÜNG, *Infallible? An Unresolved Enquiry* (exp. ed.; New York, 1994) • *Das ökumenische Concil vom Jahre 1869* (3 vols.; ed. M. J. Scheeben; Regensburg, 1869-71) • G. SCHNEEMAN and T. GRANDERATH, eds., *Acta et Decreta Sacrosancti Oecumenici Concilii Vaticani* (Freiburg, 1892).

Vatican II: G. ALBERIGO and J. A. KOMONCHAK, eds., *History of Vatican II* (5 vols.; Maryknoll, N.Y., 1995-2006) • G. ALBERIGO, J.-P. JOSSUA, and J. A. KOMONCHAK, eds., *The Reception of Vatican II* (Washington, D.C., 1987) • R. M. BROWN, *Observer in Rome: A Protestant Report on the Vatican Council* (Garden City, N.Y., 1964) • G. CAPRILE, *Il Concilio Vaticano II* (5 vols.; Rome, 1966-69) • A. FLANNERY, ed., *Vatican Council II: The Conciliar and Post Conciliar Documents*

(2 vols.; Collegeville, Minn., 1992) • H. FRIES and O. H. PESCH, *Streiten für die eine Kirche* (Munich, 1987) • M. GREENE, ed., *The Layman and the Council* (Springfield, Ill., 1964) • A. HASTINGS, ed., *Modern Catholicism: Vatican II and After* (London, 1991) • F.-X. KAUFMANN and A. ZINGERLE, eds., *Vatikanum II und Modernisierung. Historische, theologische und soziologische Perspektiven* (Paderborn, 1996) • H. KÜNG, *The Council, Reform, and Reunion* (New York, 1962) • R. LATOURELLE, ed., *Vatican II: Assessment and Perspectives; Twenty-five Years After (1962-1987)* (New York, 1989) • G. A. LINDBECK, *The Future of Roman Catholic Theology: Vatican II–Catalyst for Change* (Philadelphia, 1970); idem, ed., *Dialogue on the Way: Protestants Report from Rome on the Vatican Council* (Minneapolis, 1965) • E. LORA et al., eds., *Enchiridion Vaticanum* (22 vols.; Bologna, 1976-2006) • E. SCHLINK, *After the Council* (Philadelphia, 1968) • K.-V. SELGE and G. MARON, *Evangelischer Bericht vom Konzil* (4 vols.; Göttingen, 1963-66) • K. E. SKYDSGAARD, ed., *The Papal Council and the Gospel: Protestant Theologians Evaluate the Coming Vatican Council* (Minneapolis, 1961) • A. STACPOOLE, ed., *Vatican II Revisited: By Those Who Were There* (Minneapolis, 1986) • T. F. STRANSKY and J. B. SHEERIN, eds., *Doing the Truth in Charity: Statements of Pope Paul VI, Popes John Paul I, John Paul II, and the Secretariat for Promoting Christian Unity, 1964-1980* (New York, 1982) • W. A. VISSER 'T HOOFT, "WCC–Roman Catholic Relations: Some Personal Reflections," *ER* 37 (1985) 336-44 • A. WENGER, *Vatican II* (4 vols.; Paris, 1963-66).

ARTHUR L. KENNEDY

Vedic Religion → Hinduism

Venezuela

	1960	1980	2000
Population (1,000s):	7,579	15,091	24,170
Annual growth rate (%):	3.64	2.54	1.82
Area: 912,050 sq. km. (352,144 sq. mi.)			

A.D. 2000

Population density: 27/sq. km. (69/sq. mi.)
Births / deaths: 2.28 / 0.47 per 100 population
Fertility rate: 2.72 per woman
Infant mortality rate: 19 per 1,000 live births
Life expectancy: 73.7 years (m: 70.9, f: 76.7)
Religious affiliation (%): Christians 94.9 (Roman Catholics 92.7, Protestants 2.3, marginal 1.8, indigenous 1.7, unaffiliated 1.3, other Christians 0.1), nonreligious 2.0, spiritists 1.1, other 2.0.

1. Country, Society, Economy

The Bolivarian Republic of Venezuela comprises three different geographic regions: the Andes to the west, forested in the valleys; the wide grassy plains *(llanos)* in the central part; and the Guiana mountains south of the Orinoco River.

1.1. On the foundation of approximately 12,000 Spanish immigrants, their black slaves (whose number is difficult to estimate; → Slavery), and the original, native population, a "new people" of approximately 800,000 individuals was formed by 1810. In 1980 this population consisted predominately of mestizos (64 percent), with → minorities of whites (20 percent), Afro-Americans and mulattoes (10 percent), and Indians (3.5 percent). A macho image extolled virility, and in 1967 only 47 percent of the children were legitimate. In 1975 the number of those under 19 years old was about 57 percent. A population explosion lifted the number of inhabitants from 12 million in 1975 to 21 million in 1995.

Oil was discovered at the end of the 19th century, which started an economic upswing that led to tremendous growth of the cities. Between 1936 and 1980 the number of city dwellers rose from 35 percent to 81 percent. Urbanization brought open or concealed unemployment, the rise of the proletariat, and a great increase in poverty.

1.2. Costly but inappropriate development projects, expensive state bureaucracy, and neglect of the production of foodstuffs combined with corruption to produce a crisis in the 1980s. The radical steps taken by President Carlos Andrés Pérez (1989-93) evoked massive demonstrations and riots on February 27, 1989 (the so-called *caracazo*), the suppression of which resulted in over 3,000 deaths. A military rebellion then followed by sections of the army under the leadership of Hugo Chávez Frias, first lieutenant of the paratroopers, and in May 1993 the president was forced out on corruption charges.

In December 1994, in the midst of recession, inflation, and drug racketeering, the Christian Socialist Rafael Caldera Rodríguez (b. 1916, president 1969-74) was chosen to be president again, this time as the country's "saving hero." His term in office was disappointing, both because of his suspected senility and because of increasing evidence that the corrupt and inefficient political system was disintegrating.

1.3. Hugo Chávez, who had been granted amnesty by Caldera, was elected to the presidency by a large majority in December 1998 and immediately began an extensive program of reform. A new constitution was affirmed by the people in 1999. Incorporating plebiscite elements and strengthening the rights of the Indians, it changed the name of the country to República Bolivariana de Venezuela. In reference to the national hero, Simón Bolívar (1783-1830), and other idols of the war of independence, Chávez put in place a Left-nationalistic program that targeted social reform in the domestic realm and the economic integration of Latin America internationally through the Mercosur (for Mercado Común del Sur, or Southern Common Market), in a clear distancing from the U.S. project to widen the ALCA (Área de Libre Comercio de las América, or Free Trade Area of the Americas [FTAA]).

The long-standing conflict that arose internally with the oligarchic forces of the large landowners, middle-class businessmen, and the United States (due largely to good connections with Fidel Castro's Cuba) led to a series of actions against Chávez. These included a series of strikes against Chávez in 2001 because of the planned agricultural reform; a coup supported by the United States in April 2002, which failed two days later; a lengthy general strike in 2003; and an equally unsuccessful plebiscite to remove Chávez from office in August 2004.

Since Venezuela must import two-thirds of its food supply because the large landowners produce very little for internal consumption and fail to use all of their land (5 percent of the farmers possess over 80 percent of the agriculturally productive land), Chávez began again to plan for land reform following the 2004 referendum. His government was aided by growing oil production, the loyalty of a large majority of the military to the constitution, and the fact that the president had come to be seen as a messiah by the impoverished masses. While Chávez accused the United States of state terrorism, Pat Robertson, an evangelical commentator who had supported Bush in the 2004 presidential election, called on television in August 2005 for the assassination of the Venezuelan head of state.

In response to threats from the United States, which he provokes through his friendship with Fidel Castro, Chávez went on the offensive with a massive armament and, in 2006, an ever more aggressive rhetoric, which climaxed in his U.N. speech in September, in which he described Bush as the devil. Chávez's interference in the Peruvian election, however, was counterproductive and helped Alán García attain a majority in the July 2006 voting. Chávez's proposed gas pipeline to Argentina is technically problematic and ecologically harmful. Rather than being satisfied with having a leading role in Latin America, Chávez seems to want to become the leader of global opposition to the United States. The declared darling of the Left in Latin America has become a bogeyman of the conservatives, who see in him a dangerous dictator. Not surprisingly, tensions have increased with the conservatively governed neighboring state of Colombia.

2. History and the Roman Catholic Church

2.1. In 1507 the first Spaniards reached the island of Cubagua on the north coast of Venezuela. The native population was then estimated at between 100,000 and 300,000, mostly concentrated along the coast and in the highlands. The inhabitants spoke many different languages. Just in the plains of what later became Caracas, 30 different people groups were living. The missionaries could not master all the different tongues and tried to make Spanish a common language.

For many years European → colonialism was at its worst in Venezuela. Slave expeditions under Spanish captains worked along the Caribbean coast, followed by French, English, and Dutch pirates. Pearl fishing led to the extirpation of the Indians on the island of Margarita. Mainland Indians were decimated by forced labor as porters or in gold prospecting.

In 1528, when Emperor Charles V (1519-56) lacked the capital to conquer and colonize further territories, he sought help from the German commercial houses of the Welsers and the Ehingers. They signed a treaty with Charles, agreeing to finance naval expeditions to "Little Venice" (the greater part of what was later called Venezuela), with the goal of exploiting the land. These commercial houses founded a company to pursue these goals, whose first governor was Ambrosius Ehinger (Alfinger/Dalfinger, d. 1533). Ehinger and subsequent governors were more interested, however, in finding the El Dorado and getting its gold than in developing the territory. Ehinger arrived in 1528 with 281 colonists, followed in 1530 by Nikolaus Federmann (1505-42) and 147 German soldiers and miners. Georg Hohermuth von Speyer (1498-1540) arrived in 1535 as the new governor. Philipp von Hutten (ca. 1511-46) accompanied him with another 600 men. Many of the colonists perished in exploring the country and searching for El Dorado. The Dominican Antonio de Montesinos (ca. 1486-1540), sent by Charles V to protect the Indians, was probably murdered toward the end of the year 1540 by the soldiers.

The administration of the Welser company under Ehinger suffered from chaotic circumstances and from the increasing animosity of the Spaniards. It ended in 1546, when Francisco de Caravajal assumed the governorship under dubious circumstances. Governor Bartholomäus Welser and Hutten were leading an expedition in the interior in 1545, and on their return the following year, Caravajal had them assassinated, along with two of their followers. When news of this event reached Europe, it caused a great stir, and the emperor himself led the investigation. Carvajal was sentenced to death and executed. Failure to find gold meant that little was done after the first wave to set up cities at the coast, in the valleys of the Andes, or in the central cordillera. Only in 1777 was Venezuela organized with its present borders (designated a *capitanía general*), and not until 1803 was it united ecclesiastically as an archbishopric.

2.2. The first Venezuelan diocese was established at Coro in 1531. It was removed to Caracas between 1613 and 1637. The bishoprics of Mérida and Santo Tomás de la Guyana (now Ciudad Bolívar) followed in 1777 and 1790. Bishop Pedro de Agreda (1560-79), who laid the foundations for the church and its mission, founded a seminary (which became a university in 1725), set up a synod, and worked to protect the Indians. The Constituciones Sinodales, which a diocesan synod under Diego de Baños y Sotomayor (1648-1706) adopted in 1687, regulated the church and much of society until 1904. Protection was given to the Indians and slaves. Several → religious orders did missionary work: the → Augustinian Eremites came before 1650, the → Franciscans and Capuchins from 1650 to 1818, and the → Jesuits and → Dominicans after 1700.

In 1654 all further military conquests were forbidden, and the missionaries tried to gather the scattered Indians peacefully into → reductions, where they could be easily evangelized and put to work. Because the settlers were few and the roads were poor, the isolated reductions villages became especially significant religiously, politically, and economically. The danger of ethnic wars and surprise attacks meant that the Capuchins, Dominicans, and Jesuits relied on military help at the reductions. Only the Franciscans rejected military help. In theory the reductions were supposed to become missionary parishes after ten years, but the process took much longer, was only partially successful, and could have negative consequences. West African slaves soon replaced the Indians in diving for pearls and in work on the sugar and later the cocoa plantations. The church never took much care of them. In 1681/82 the Capuchin Francisco de Jaca (1645-89) pleaded for their emancipation, but without success.

2.3. The long and gruesome struggle for independence (1810-21) under Francisco de Miranda (1750-1816) and Simón Bolívar (1783-1830) shook the Roman Catholic Church to its foundations. In 1812 a destructive earthquake shattered Caracas, which the Royalists saw as a judgment from heaven on the Patriots. Independence came in 1821, but so too did a breakdown in public order and the economy. Church buildings were in ruins, there were few pastors, and the reductions had been largely devastated. Catholicism had been the ideology of colonial rule, winning over the Indians by promising them a better future in the hereafter. A religious mood of resigned piety had developed that did not worry about earthly possessions. When the reductions collapsed, only a diffuse → syncretism remained.

In 1830 Greater Colombia was dissolved, and Venezuela finally became an independent state. The emancipation of slaves in 1854 led to a decline in agricultural production. The process of becoming a state resulted in civil strife. Finally a moderate federalism won the day in 1864, with the creation of the Estados Unidos de Venezuela. From 1870 to 1945 the presidents were de facto military dictators. Ever since independence, the state was clearly supreme in its relation to the church. Lay leaders were influenced by → utilitarianism and → rationalism.

To attract immigrants, religious liberty was adopted in 1834. An Anglican chapel was set up in Caracas in the same year. → Tithes had been abolished in 1833. The state financed Roman Catholicism and in 1857 pledged to defend it. → Positivism influenced the university, which was reopened in 1863, and the → Masons were also active. The two together advocated a belief that was little more than → deism.

2.4. With the coming of the → Syllabus (1864) and the dogma of papal → infallibility (1870), President Antonio Guzmán Blanco (1870-77), in a campaign resembling the German → Kulturkampf, gave prominence to anticlericalism, secularized the possessions of nunneries, prohibited church schools, attached the diocesan seminary to the university, abolished church courts, initiated the secular registration of births, weddings, and deaths, secularized cemeteries, and expelled Archbishop Silvestre Guevarra y Lira (1852-82, in exile since 1870), who had resisted him. During his second term in office (1879-84), Guzmán was on better terms with the Vatican. He allowed the orders to take up their Indian mission work.

In 1900 the church seminaries were reopened.

The Jesuits returned in 1905, and other orders followed. Church schools were reopened. President Juan Vicente Gómez (in office three times 1908-35) did much to improve relations between church and state. In 1920 Rome appointed a → nuncio and after 1927 increased the number of bishoprics. The military dictatorships, especially that of Marcos Pérez Jiménez (1948-58), brought even further improvement. More dioceses were formed, foreign clergy were admitted, and the Virgin of Coromoto became the patron saint of Venezuela. The conclusion of the modus vivendi in 1964 freed the Catholic Church from the yoke of patronage but evoked the protests of the Protestant churches, which sought a separation of church and state. Roman Catholicism showed its growing political power when the Christian Socialist Rafael Caldera was elected president in 1968.

Rome now had 24 dioceses and four apostolic vicariates for the Indian mission fields. There were 39 bishops, 894 secular priests, and 5,410 monks and nuns. The church had built up an imposing structure but not on a firm foundation, for 65 percent of the priests and 83 percent of those in orders were from abroad. A ministry after the spirit of Medellín (1968; → Latin American Councils 2.4) that would build up the church from below was still awaited in Venezuela.

2.5. Beginning with the presidency of Hugo Chávez, there have been constant tensions between the → Roman Catholic Church and the → state. In the spirit of John Paul II, the papal nuncio André Dupuy bolstered the traditionalists, who were somewhat tied to Opus Dei, at the Conferencia Episcopal Venezolana (CEV, Venezuelan Episcopal Conference; → Traditionalist Movement). The new constitution of 1999, which has been criticized for various reasons by politicians and economists, was rejected by Cardinal Balthasar Porras, archbishop of Mérida and president of the CEV (since 1999), who was reproached for his sympathy to Opus Dei. His objections were based upon provisions of the new constitution that extended the freedom of cults, diminished the state support for the Catholic Church (according to an agreement with the Vatican in 1964, the state would finance the building of churches and subsidize the CEV and the exclusively Catholic → military chaplaincy), and did not designate any religion as official. These provisions, which corresponded with an old proposal of the Protestant churches, now gave Protestants equal legal status with Catholics; for the first time they received equal access to the means of communication and education. A large majority of members of its 2,000 congregations apparently voted for Chávez in the 2004 referendum.

A polarization has appeared in the Roman Catholic Church between the traditionalist leadership of the CEV and a large number of priests and nuns who did not support a general public strike in 2002. The church leadership, though, took the lead in supporting this antigovernment action: Cardinal Ignacio Velasco, the archbishop of Caracas, was the first, and Porras the second, to sign the decree that was to legalize the ephemeral state strike. Chávez, who has often attracted notice by his verbal excess in attacking the Roman Catholic Church, has been somewhat more restrained since his two-day imprisonment in conjunction with the coup attempt of 2002, although Porras and his like-minded fellows engineered the holding of the 2004 referendum, whose clear goal was to force Chávez out of office.

Benedict XVI ended this course of confrontation by dispatching a friendly nuncio in the person of Monsignor Giacinto Berlocco. He also had the leadership of the CEV replaced through new elections and Porras replaced as its leader by the moderate Ubaldo Santana, archbishop of Maracaibo. Furthermore, in 2005 he appointed Jorge Urosa, another moderate, archbishop of Caracas and, a year later, elevated Urosa to cardinal.

3. Protestantism

A few German Lutherans were present during the early period of the Welser administration. The limited religious tolerance of the 19th century principally favored foreign Protestant residents. In spite of freedom of worship granted in 1911, foreigners who wished to enter the country for the purpose of religious work continued to be prohibited, so that Protestant work was greatly restricted. The 1961 constitution eliminated the restrictions. Before 1970 Venezuela, along with Ecuador and Paraguay, had the fewest number of Protestants. The spread of the → Pentecostal churches, however, has now raised the number of Protestants to about 5 percent, but of these only 1 percent belong to mainline denominations. Non–Roman Catholics fall into three groups.

3.1. First are foreign and immigrant congregations. The Anglicans (→ Anglican Communion) came in 1832, the Lutherans (→ Lutheran Churches) after 1870. After World War II a flood of Hungarians, southern Europeans, Latvians, and Scandinavians increased the number of Lutheran congregations. Members of the U.S. Missouri Synod also came on the scene. Spanish-speaking Venezuelans also belong to these churches. Six → Orthodox churches and a small Armenian church also deserve mention.

3.2. The oldest strongly rooted national churches were founded at the end of the 19th century and in the early days of the 20th, being formed by the work of the → Bible societies and various missions. The Plymouth Brethren began work in 1883, the Presbyterians (→ Reformed and Presbyterian Churches) in 1897, the → Adventists in 1910, the → Baptists in 1924, and the Evangelical Free Church Association in 1920. The last group now has a seminary along with the → Christian and Missionary Alliance, which began work in 1969. The Iglesias Nativas Venezolanas de Apure, or Bethel Church, founded in 1925, is the strongest indigenous body, with as many members as the Roman Catholics have in the sparsely populated state of Apure. The Pentecostal churches, with the Asambleas de Dios (→ Assembleias de Deus no Brasil), started work in 1916 but gained in strength after World War II and now numbers about 70 percent of all Protestants.

Beginning in 1990, neopentecostals have been active in Venezuela. The Iglesia Universal del Reino de Dios, in particular, with its explosive growth, has realigned the numbers along the fundamentalist spectrum. It speaks to the destitute masses (if not exploits them) with its healing services and its theology of prosperity. The Pentecostal churches have found fertile soil among the religiously and socially uprooted underclass in both country and city, offering them a restricted worldview.

3.3. Finally, we have the work of a whole series of missionary societies and faith missions. The New Tribes Mission (NTM) began work in 1946 among tribes in the Orinoco and Amazon valleys, competing with Roman Catholicism. Its more legalistic and Puritanical ethics has divided Indian societies and weakened their resistance to exploitation. After 1980 it came under challenge because of its fusion with U.S. economic interests. In October 2005 Chávez announced the expulsion of approximately 160 members of the NTM working among 12 different ethnic groups. As early as the beginning of the 1970s, the Congreso Indígena de Venezuela accused the NTM of ethnocide in not respecting indigenous cultures.

Among sects we need mention only → Jehovah's Witnesses, which in 2000 had over 200,000 adherents, making it one of the largest non-Catholic denominations in Venezuela.

4. Ecumenical Groups

On the national level the evangelical and fundamentalistic churches have formed various associations. The Anglicans, Lutherans, Presbyterians, and some

Pentecostals belong to the → Latin American Council of Churches (CLAI). The Roman Catholic Bishops' Conference has a Secretariado de la Fe (Secretariat of faith) that deals with ecumenical issues. On the initiative of Christians of various confessions, an *Acción Ecuménica* was founded in Caracas. It provides a center for meeting and does development and social work.

5. Non-Christian Religions

In addition to indigenous religions, → Judaism, and → Baha'i (which grew from 6 to 166 congregations between 1964 and 1973), we also find → Afro-American cults (e.g., Cuban Santeria and the María Lionza cult, both of which blend African, indigenous, and Catholic beliefs). The → Umbanda cult has spread from Brazil and is now highly significant.

→ Latin American Theology; Social Ethics 3; Spirituality 3

Bibliography: D. B. Barrett, G. T. Kurian, and T. M. Johnson, *WCE* (2d ed.) 1.798-802 • P. da Costa Gómez, *El Espíritu Santo. Protagonista y guía de la primera evangelización de Venezuela y de la América Hispana* (Caracas, 1999) • J. Denzer, *Die Konquista der Augsburger Welser-Gesellschaft (1528-1556)* (Munich, 2005) • J. Eastwood, *The Rise of Nationalism in Venezuela* (Gainesville, Fla., 2006) • J. Friede, *Los Welser en la conquista de Venezuela* (Caracas, 1961) • H. González, *Iglesia y estado en Venezuela* (Caracas, 1973) • N. Kozloff, *Hugo Chávez: Oil, Politics, and the Challenge to the United States* (New York, 2006) • D. H. Levine, *Popular Voices in Latin American Catholicism* (Princeton, 1992); idem, *Religion and Politics in Latin America: The Catholic Church in Venezuela and Colombia* (Princeton, 1981) • R. Madry Galíndez, *Montes de Oca. El obispo mártir* (Valencia, 1997) • A. Micheo, *Proceso histórico de la iglesia venezolana* (Caracas, 1983) • G. Ocando Yamarte, *Cuatro gemelas: Coro, Cumaná, San Cristóbal, Valencia; I Congreso de Historia Eclesiástica Tachirense* (San Cristóbal, 2000) • A. Pollack-Eltz, *Estudio antropológico del Pentecostalismo en Venezuela* (Caracas, 2000); idem, *Maria Lionza. Mito y culto venezolano* (Caracas, 1985); idem, *Religiones afroamericanas hoy* (Caracas, 1994); idem, *Umbanda en Venezuela* (Caracas, 1993) • G. Simmer, *Gold und Sklaven. Die Provinz Venezuela während der Welser-Verwaltung (1528-1556)* (Berlin, 2000) • M. Watters, *A History of the Church in Venezuela, 1810-1930* (Chapel Hill, N.C., 1933; repr., New York, 1971); idem, *Telón de fondo de la iglesia colonial en Venezuela* (Caracas, 1951).

Hans-Jürgen Prien, Jochen Streiter, and Pedro Trigo

Vestments

1. Apparel outside of Worship
2. Liturgical Apparel
   2.1. Eastern Church
   2.2. Roman Catholic Church
      2.2.1. Undergarments
      2.2.2. Outer Garments
      2.2.3. Prerogatives
      2.2.4. Insignia
   2.3. Protestant Churches

1. Apparel outside of Worship

Outside of the worship service, clergy from the Eastern Church usually wear a black cassock (full-length garment buttoned in the front) or the appropriate garments for an order.

For the garments of Roman Catholic clergy, the only two considerations are that they must be "suitable ecclesiastical garb according to the norms issued by the conference of bishops," and they must be "according to legitimate local customs" (1983 CIC 284). Orders require that the apparel of the order be constantly worn. The Roman Pontificate defines the following colors for collar, cassock, cincture (cord girdle), and pileus (small skullcap): black for → priests, purple for → bishops, red and green for → prelates (formerly bishops' colors), crimson for → cardinals, and white for the → pope.

There was never the same sort of requirements for Protestant clerical garb. Into the 19th century, though, Lutheran clergy wore, as daily garb, a black cassock or the so-called German robe (from which the so-called Luther robe arose), at times with bands. Today in Europe this Luther robe (with and without bands) is often used for special occasions.

2. Liturgical Apparel

The various pieces of clothing worn by the clergy for official liturgical activities are called liturgical vestments. They are customary in the → Orthodox Church, in the → Roman Catholic Church, and in the various churches of the → Reformation. In the OT, such as Exod. 28:2-43 and 39:1-31, there are reports of special clothing for the worship service worn by priests and the → high priest. There is no reference to special liturgical garb in the NT.

The main liturgical garments of the Eastern Church and of the Roman Catholic Church derive, in all probability, from the distinguished patricians of antiquity; in the early Middle Ages between the fourth and ninth centuries, these garments gradually became the worship apparel of the priests. Certain vestments correspond to the steps of consecration with which the ordinand is first clothed during the ordination. The color of the individual liturgical vestments are oriented, especially in the West, to the → church year. The following sections consider the most important liturgical vestments of the individual churches.

2.1. Eastern Church

In the Eastern Church the → deacon wears the *sticharion* (a long white silk robe), the *orarion* (narrow stole wrapped around the left shoulder), and *epimanikia* (cufflike sleeve holders). The priest wears the sticharion (with narrow sleeves, however), the *epitrachelion* (sewn-together stoles), the *zone* (belt), the epimanikia, and the *phelonion*, which is the special vestment for the Mass, more similar to the Roman choir gown than to the Roman chasuble.

The higher clergy wear, in addition, the *hypogonation* (rectangular piece of silk that hangs down from the belt), and bishops wear over the Mass vestments the *omophorion* (shoulder cloth corresponding to the Roman pallium). Signs of the bishop are the *pectoral cross,* the *panagia* (medallion usually depicting the Blessed Virgin holding the Christ child), the *miter* (helmetlike head covering), and the *pateritsa* (pastoral staff).

There is no fixed canon for colors. Clergy serving simultaneously often wear differently colored apparel. Light colors (white and green) are preferred for high festivals (esp. Easter), and dark colors (purple, blue, dark red, black) for services of penance and mourning.

2.2. Roman Catholic Church

The Roman Catholic Church has the most complicated vestment regulations. Since → Vatican II, they have been governed by *Sacrosanctum concilium,* the Constitution on the Sacred Liturgy, 122-30, especially 128.

2.2.1. Undergarments

Garments worn underneath the outer garments are the *amice* (or *humeral veil*), a rectangular linen cloth placed around the neck, shoulders, and chest and fastened with two cords around the hips; the *fanon,* or circular shoulder cloth of the pope; the *alb,* a full-length gown out of white linen or hemp; and the *cincture,* the belt, usually made from linen, which goes over the alb and around the hips. The *subcinctorium* is a strip of cloth, like a *maniple,* fastened on the left side to a cincture (today worn only by the pope as decoration at a pontifical mass). The wide-sleeved white *surplice* (from Lat. "over the fur"), originally worn in the cold northern regions, is knee-length and similar to an alb. The narrow-sleeved *rochet,* similar to the surplice, may be worn only by bishops, prelates, and specially designated clergy.

2.2.2. Outer Garments

Of the outer garments, the *chasuble* (or *planeta*) is the special garment worn by the priest during the → mass, a poncholike wrap that falls over chest and back, usually made from costly silk and bearing symbols. Typical for the silk *dalmatic* (outer garment for deacons) and *tunic* (for subdeacons) are wide, vertical bands on front and back connected with a diagonal strip. The *cope* (also *cappa,* a mantel for incense, vesper, and choir) is a full-length cape open in the front, secured often with a richly decorated fastening at the chest; the back has a sewn-on hood or a cloth peak.

2.2.3. Prerogatives

A bishop's prerogative is the wearing of silk gloves and pontifical hose and shoes (only at pontifical masses, not for masses for the dead or on Good Friday). The pope's *tiara* is the liturgical head covering; it comes to a peak and is adorned with three crowns. The *miter* is worn by the pope and by cardinals, bishops, → abbots, and specially designated prelates. It is furnished with two bands that hang down over the back. The *pileus* (also called a *soli Deo*), the small, round skullcap, is white for the pope, red for cardinals, purple for bishops, but otherwise black. These colors also differentiate the level of office when the *biretta* is worn. The biretta is a stiff, four-sided hat with three or four curved upper sections; a tassel is in the center.

2.2.4. Insignia

Liturgical insignia include the *maniple,* a small strip of cloth corresponding to the color of the chasuble, worn by the subdeacon over the alb and the left forearm, with ends hanging down. The *stole* is a longer, wider strip of cloth in the color of the chasuble and bearing three crosses. The deacon wears it hanging over the left shoulder; the priest wears it around his neck and crossed over the chest; the bishop wears it with both ends open and hanging down. The *pallium,* a ring-shaped white strip of wool, is worn around the shoulders, from which a strip descends on chest and back. It is a special pontifical ornament of the pope, the archbishop, and certain bishops who have been recognized with it. Additional pontifical insignia are the bishop's ring and staff, the pectoral cross, and the archbishop's processional cross.

2.3. Protestant Churches

Today in the Protestant church in Germany the black gown with bands or ruff is worn almost exclusively. In North America, Lutherans (→ Lutheran Churches) — but also many other Protestants — made a profound change from the black "Geneva gown" to the cassock and stole (worn over a surplice), to alb with stole. Increasingly, chasuble and choir gown are worn.

In the Protestant churches of Asia and Africa, the attire mostly reflects the missionary background. In Africa, however, there existed a strong movement toward the historical Western vestments, especially on the part of bishops; in Asia, the attire was adapted to the climate: white is preferred over black.

The Lutheran reformers were completely open on the use of liturgical vestments because they were regarded as → adiaphora (CA 26.40-45; CA Apol. 7.34, 45; 24.52, et al.). In contrast, Ulrich → Zwingli (1484-1531) and John → Calvin (1509-64) pressed rigorously to end the practice. The Lutheran reformers turned away only from the overemphasis on vestments by the Roman Catholics; they also disapproved of the radical rejection of them by the enthusiasts, especially Thomas → Müntzer (ca. 1489-1525). Thus within → Lutheranism the academic gown or the cassock continued to be worn until the 18th century — for the → sermon and the → liturgy, especially for Communion, along with the alb, chasuble, stole, and surplice or cope. Then, in the 18th century, because of criticism by Enlightenment theologians and → rationalism, the old apparel from the Lutheran → worship service was suppressed in German regions as being "Catholic."

In connection with the renewal of liturgy and → parament use, Wilhelm Löhe (1808-72) sought to reintroduce the old liturgical vestments (esp. white, the color of joy). In the course of the → liturgical movement since World War I, various groups (F. Heiler, the High Church movement, St. Michael's Brotherhood, among others) have worked for the regaining of liturgical dress for the Protestant worship service (W. Lotz). After World War II numerous Protestant communities began to use liturgical vestments (alb, stole, choir gown). In addition, frequent ecumenical contacts furthered the congregations' appreciation for a richer liturgical apparel. Since about 1980, the wearing of white alb with stole, especially for celebratory worship services, has been "on trial" or fully allowed, with the approval of the church council/presbytery, but with the principled retaining of the black cassock.

For women pastors there is no binding rule on vestments.

→ Custom

Bibliography: B. D. B. BAUMGARTEN, Vestments for All Seasons (Harrisburg, Pa., 2002) • E. HOFHANSL, "Gewänder, liturgische," TRE 13.159-67 • W. LOTZ, Das hochzeitliche Kleid. Zur Frage der liturgischen Gewänder im evangelischen Gottesdienst (Kassel, 1949) • C. C. MAYER-THURMANN, Raiment for the Lord's Service: A Thousand Years of Western Vestments (Chicago, 1975) • J.-C. NOONAN and J. P. FOLEY, The Church Visible: The Ceremonial Life and Protocol of the Roman Catholic Church (New York, 1996) • H. NORRIS, Church Vestments: Their Origin and Development (Mineola, N.Y., 2002; orig. pub., 1950) • D. PHILIPPART, ed., Clothed in Glory: Vesting the Church (Chicago, 1997) • A. C. PIEPKORN, The Survival of the Historic Vestments in the Lutheran Church after 1555 (St. Louis, 1956).

JOACHIM HEUBACH†

Vicar-General

According to the 1983 CIC, the vicar-general is the permanent representative of the diocesan → bishop in administering the → diocese. He is appointed by the bishop (can. 477.1). If he is not himself an auxiliary bishop, his office terminates with a vacancy in the see. It may also be suspended by the diocesan bishop (481, along with 409.2).

In his role as representative, the vicar-general has ordinary executive authority. By virtue of his office he can perform any administrative act that legally is the responsibility of the "local ordinary" (134.2), as long as the diocesan bishop has not reserved for himself or one or more bishop's vicars such an act relating to a geographic or administrative area or to a certain group of persons (479). This authority may be delegated by "special mandate" (134.3), but it is often granted "for all cases" (137).

The vicar-general and assistant bishops come directly under the diocesan bishop and must keep him informed and give an account to him (480).

Bishops may be appointed to the office and retain it during a vacancy, while → priests may be named for a period and lose the office when there is a vacancy (477.1).

→ Ministry, Ministerial Offices

Bibliography: D. V. FLYNN, "Vicar-General (Syncellus)," NCE 14.639-41 • É. FOURNIER, Le vicaire général au moyen âge (Paris, 1923) • H. MÜLLER, "Die Diözesankurie," HKKR 364-73.

WERNER BÖCKENFÖRDE†

Viet Nam

1. General Situation
2. History
   2.1. Vietnamese Dynasties (939-1945)
   2.2. French Colonization (1862-1954)

	1960	1980	2000
Population (1,000s):	34,743	53,711	80,549
Annual growth rate (%):	1.97	2.18	1.51

Area: 331,041 sq. km. (127,816 sq. mi.)

A.D. 2000

Population density: 243/sq. km. (630/sq. mi.)
Births / deaths: 2.15 / 0.63 per 100 population
Fertility rate: 2.53 per woman
Infant mortality rate: 32 per 1,000 live births
Life expectancy: 69.4 years (m: 66.9, f: 71.6)
Religious affiliation (%): Buddhists 48.4, nonreligious 13.8, new religionists 11.5, tribal religionists 8.8, Christians 8.3 (Roman Catholics 6.8, other Christians 1.4), atheists 7.1, other 2.1.

2.3. Viet Nam War (1956-75)
3. Non-Christian Religions
4. Christianity
    4.1. Roman Catholics
    4.2. Protestants

1. General Situation

The Socialist Republic of Viet Nam, in southeast Asia, is bordered on the west by Cambodia and Laos, on the north by China, and on the east by the China Sea. Its two principal geographic regions, the Red River delta in the north and the Mekong River delta in the south, are connected by a narrow, mountainous strip. Its capital is Hanoi, though Ho Chi Minh City (formerly Saigon) is the largest city. In 2007 the population was estimated at 85 million.

Though there are 54 ethnic groups, the population is largely homogeneous, with the Viet, also known as the Kinh, forming 86 percent of it. Their language, which belongs to the Austroasiatic family but with heavy borrowings from Chinese, is the national language. Chinese characters *(chu nho)* were used for communication, especially during the Chinese millennium-long domination. From the 13th century an adaptation of the Chinese characters was introduced known as the demotic script *(chu nom)*. Both scripts were replaced at the beginning of the 20th century by a romanized script with Latin letters and diacritical marks devised in the 17th century by Catholic → missionaries, principally Alexandre de Rhodes, and now serving as the national script *(chu quoc ngu)*.

Politically, Viet Nam is a single-party → state, with the Communist Party controlling the government. Economically, since 1986 Viet Nam has been taking steps toward a market economy. In January 2007 it formally joined the World Trade Organization.

2. History

Popularly, the Vietnamese claim to have descended from a marriage between a dragon lord and a heavenly goddess and often boast of a four-millennia-old civilization. However, archaeological discoveries of bronze drums date the beginning of their history to the 13th-century-B.C. Dong Son culture. Viet Nam was occupied by the Chinese four times for a total of one thousand years: the Former Han dynasty (111 B.C.–A.D. 40), the Later Han and the Wei-Jin dynasties (43-544), the Sui and T'ang dynasties (603-936), and the Ming dynasty (1406-27).

2.1. *Vietnamese Dynasties (939-1945)*

Rebellion against Chinese domination took place frequently, most notably under the leadership of three women, namely, the two Trung sisters (A.D. 40) and Trieu Au (A.D. 248). Long-lasting independence was achieved only in 936 by Ngo Quyen, who founded the Ngo dynasty (939-67), to be followed by those of the Dinh (968-80), the Le (980-1009, often referred to as the Tien [Anterior] Le), the Ly (1009-25), the Tran (1225-1400), the Ho (1400-1406), the Le (1428-1527, founded by Le Loi, and often referred to as the Hau [Posterior] Le), and the Mac (1527-32).

After the Mac, Viet Nam was divided into two parts: the north, governed by the Trinh lords (1533-1789), and the south, by the Nguyen lords (1558-1775). Between 1627 and 1672 there were seven civil wars between the Trinh and the Nguyen, ending finally in a truce. In 1771 three brothers known as Tay Son led a rebellion, and one of them, Nguyen Hue, who took the name of Quang Trung, succeeded in reuniting both parts of the country. The Tay Son reign (1778-1802) was short-lived. A descendant of the Nguyen lords, Nguyen Anh (whose imperial name is Gia Long) defeated the Tay Son and founded the Nguyen dynasty — the last Vietnamese dynasty — which ended in 1945 with the abdication of Emperor Bao Dai.

Toward the end of the 16th century Viet Nam began expanding its southern border (the so-called Southern March [*nam tien*]), annexing the Cham kingdom and part of the Khmer kingdom of Cambodia.

2.2. *French Colonization (1862-1954)*

When Nguyen Anh attempted to defeat the Tay Son and the Trinh lords, he was assisted by French bishop Pierre Pigneau de Béhaine (1741-99), who lobbied the French government to supply him with troops and arms. When Nguyen Anh's successors, especially Tu Duc (1829-83), persecuted French missionaries and Vietnamese Catholics, France used the occasion as a pretext for the conquest of Viet Nam. In 1858

France attacked Da Nang, and by 1875 it had turned the south of Viet Nam (Cochin China) into a colony. In 1884 it made the rest of the country (Annam and Tonkin) into a protectorate (→ Colonialism).

Among the many Vietnamese nationalists fighting against French domination, Ho Chi Minh (1890-1969), who adopted Marxist Leninism for its anticolonialist stance, is no doubt the most prominent. When Japan, which had defeated the French, surrendered to the Allied forces, Ho declared independence from French rule on September 2, 1945, and formed the Democratic Republic of Viet Nam (DRV). Soon a nine-year war broke out between France and the DRV, which ended in 1954 after the French defeat at Dien Bien Phu. The Geneva Accords recognized the DRV, divided Viet Nam temporarily into two parts at the 17th parallel, and called for national elections in 1956 to decide about the unification of the country.

2.3. *Viet Nam War (1956-75)*
The general elections never took place. In 1955 Ngo Dinh Diem proclaimed the Republic of Viet Nam, with himself as president. The United States, under Presidents D. Eisenhower and J. F. Kennedy, supported his government with financial aid and military advisers. Diem's government, however, failed to carry out the reforms deemed necessary, and on November 1, 1963, with Kennedy's approval, Diem was assassinated in a coup. With the removal of Diem and finding no viable replacement, the United States took on an increasing role in the war against the Communist north. The so-called Viet Nam War ended in April 1975 with the victory of the Communist DRV, and in 1976 the country was reunified under the name of the Socialist Republic of Viet Nam.

3. Non-Christian Religions
In Viet Nam, → Buddhism, → Confucianism, and → Taoism are often referred to as the Triple Religion *(tam giao)*. Viet Nam also has an indigenous religion, consisting mainly in the worship of spirits, especially the → ancestors. Humans are said to possess three superior souls *(hon)* and seven inferior souls *(phach,* or *voc* or *via)*. While the inferior souls perish with death, the three *hon* survive. For the benefit of the dead, it is essential that funeral rites are correctly carried out. Those without proper funerals become *ma* (ghosts) or *qui* (demons), whereas those with proper burials become *than,* that is, benevolent spirits.

Buddhism entered Viet Nam as early as the second century A.D. It came first from India in the form of Theravada, and later from China and central Asia in the form of Mahayana. From the 11th and the 15th centuries, under the Ly and Tran dynasties, Buddhism established itself as a powerful political and cultural force as it was patronized by these dynasties and as Buddhist monks played a key role in the social, political, and cultural life of the independent nation. By this time there were two strands of Buddhism. One is the "old" popular Buddhism, which since the second century had amalgamated various religious beliefs and practices of indigenous religion, Confucianism, and Taoism; the other is the "new" court Buddhism, which was cultivated by the elite and was more indebted to Chinese patriarchal → Zen, whose literary masterpiece is *Thien Uyen Tap Anh* (Outstanding figures in the Vietnamese Zen community).

Confucianism was introduced into Viet Nam from the beginning of the Chinese domination. A humanistic religion or religious → humanism, Confucianism emphasizes moral self-cultivation to achieve the ideal human person *(quan tu)*. This ideal is realized by the practice of five → virtues: *nhan* (benevolence), *le* (propriety), *nghia* (righteousness), *tri* (wisdom), and *tin* (loyalty). These five virtues must inform five social relationships that entail reciprocal obligations, namely, those between king and subject, husband and wife, parent and child, older and younger siblings, and friends. While Buddhism teaches the way to personal enlightenment, Confucianism provides a system of education, a moral code, and rituals for the family and the state. From the time of the Ly dynasty (1009-25), Confucianism, with its *ngu kinh* (five classics) and *tu thu* (four books), has formed the subject of examinations for civil service. The ideal of *quan tu* constitutes the norm of behavior. Among the many rituals, ancestor worship is the most sacred, as it is the exercise of the most fundamental virtue, namely, *hieu thao* (filial piety). On the state level, the most solemn ceremony is the *te nam giao* (sacrifice at the South Gate), which is offered to Heaven, Earth, and Spirits and officiated by the emperor himself in the name of the nation.

While Confucianism finds ready acceptance among the educated elite, Taoism, which came to Viet Nam at the same time as Confucianism, is widespread among the common people, not so much as a philosophical system as a complex of religious beliefs and practices. Central to philosophical Taoism is the concept of *tao* (way). It holds that the universe *(vu tru)* is a complex of ever-changing and interdependent events that happen spontaneously or noncoercively *(tu nhien)* according to their dynamic nature, "going out" and "returning" to themselves in the rhythm of mutually entailing opposites *(am-duong)*. As a religious system, Taoism introduces to Viet Nam its pantheon of spirits (the highest of whom is Ngoc Hoang, or the Jade Emperor) and a set of magical, alchemical, and meditative rituals with the purpose of achieving longevity and → immortality. Most popular among the common people are the practice of worshiping the titulary spirits of the village at the *dinh* (the village administrative building and temple), recourse to mediums, and → divination.

It is to be noted that in Viet Nam these three religions, though distinct from each other in terms of philosophical doctrines and at times vying with each other for political prominence, are deeply intertwined with each other in practice, with heavy mutual borrowings and extensive amalgamation with the indigenous religion. Officially, of the three only Buddhism is recognized as a religion, whereas Confucianism and Taoism, without a hierarchical organization, are regarded as more cultural than religious traditions.

4. Christianity

There is evidence that Christianity first entered Viet Nam at the beginning of the 16th century, with Christian missions per se being initiated only in 1615.

4.1. *Roman Catholics*

Until 1659 the bulk of missionary work was carried out by the Jesuits, of whom the most famous was Alexandre de Rhodes (1593-1660; → Catholic Missions). In 1645 de Rhodes went to Rome to lobby for the establishment of a → hierarchy in Viet Nam. As a result, in 1658 Alexander VII (1655-67) appointed François Pallu bishop of Tonkin and Pierre Lambert de la Motte bishop of Cochinchina. Missionary work in the next two centuries, though greatly increased by the arrival of → Dominicans, → Franciscans, → Augustinians, Carmelites, and especially the members of the Missions Étrangères de Paris, met with grave difficulties. These difficulties stemmed from the political rivalry between the Trinh and Nguyen lords, the *padroado* system, Rome's condemnation of ancestor veneration, and, above all, → persecution by the Nguyen emperors. An estimated 130,000 missionaries and Vietnamese Catholics were killed, of whom 117 were canonized by John Paul II (1978-2005) in 1988.

The church expanded rapidly in the 20th century. In 1933 Nguyen Ba Tong was consecrated the first Vietnamese bishop. In 1934 the first Indochinese council was held in Hanoi, with the participation of 20 bishops, 5 religious superiors, and 21 priests. Unfortunately, no sooner had the church be-

gun its expansion than the country was engulfed in its war of independence against France. As a result of the 1954 Geneva Accords, which turned the north over to the Communists, 650,000 Catholics fled to the south. In 1960 John XXIII (1958-63) established the Vietnamese hierarchy, dividing the church into three ecclesiastical provinces: Hanoi, Hue, and Saigon. Unfortunately, the subsequent war between the north and south significantly hampered church development.

For two decades (1954-75), cut off from the church in the south and the Church of Rome, persecuted by the Communist government, and devastated by the departure of a great number of clergy and laity in 1954, the church in the north barely survived. With its educational and social institutions confiscated by the government and its clergy practically under house arrest, the church was forced to limit its activities to sacramental celebrations and popular devotions. In contrast, during the same period, the church in the south enjoyed much freedom and growth. It was strengthened by the influx of Catholics from the north and benefited from the reforms of → Vatican II. Thanks to its numerous first-rate educational, health-care, and social institutions, the church exercised a great influence on the society.

Following the reunification of the country under the Communist government in 1976, the church met with severe difficulties. Its educational and social institutions were confiscated, and almost all of its religious organizations were disbanded. A number of priests were sent to "reeducation" camps. Though sacramental celebrations were permitted, the functions of the clergy were severely limited. The number of priestly ordinations was restricted, and episcopal appointments must have the government's approval.

Beginning in 1988, the government adopted a more relaxed attitude toward the church. The Vietnamese Episcopal Conference was reinstituted and was allowed to hold regular meetings. Diplomatic relations with the Vatican were established, and negotiations for more religious freedom were conducted (→ Religious Liberty). Six major seminaries were allowed to reopen. Besides these official seminaries, there are several underground centers where thousands of seminarians are trained. In recent years, the government permitted a number of priests and religious to go abroad for higher studies. Even though the government still controls religious institutions, the trend is toward a greater autonomy for the church's internal affairs. Currently, the Catholic Church has 26 dioceses, and Catholics make up about 6 percent of the total population.

4.2. *Protestants*

Known in Vietnamese as Dao Tin Lanh (religion of the good news), → Protestantism entered Viet Nam in 1911 with the coming of the Canadian missionary R. A. Jaffray (1873-1945). Under the auspices of the → Christian and Missionary Alliance (C&MA), mission was initiated in Da Nang (central Viet Nam), in Hai Phong and Hanoi (North Viet Nam), and in Saigon and My Tho (South Viet Nam). The first task was to translate the Bible into Vietnamese. In 1921 a Bible school was established in Da Nang with the purpose of providing the Vietnamese with a thorough grounding in the Bible and training them for → evangelism. Membership grew rapidly, and in 1927 the Evangelical Church of Indochina was founded (later known as the Evangelical Church of Viet Nam), with the goal of becoming self-supporting and self-governing. At the end of World War II, the C&MA turned its attention to the tribal peoples in the central highlands of Viet Nam, Laos, and Thailand. Two Bible schools were established for the tribes, one in Da Lat, and the other in Banmethuot. Among the tribes the Koho were the most receptive to evangelization. Another very important school, the Bible and Theological Institute, was founded in Nha Trang.

From the beginning, the C&MA understood its mission to be exclusively spiritual, that is, to preach the gospel of Jesus Christ. However, after the partition of the country in 1954 and with a million → refugees from the north (among whom were 1,000 members of the C&MA), the C&MA and its offspring, the Evangelical Church of Viet Nam, were challenged to expand their mission to include social and educational services. A leprosarium and two hospitals were opened (→ Medical Missions), with the help of the Mennonite Central Committee. After the Communist takeover, the church suffered grievously. All foreign missionaries were repatriated, 100 churches were closed, 90 pastors were sent to reeducation camps, and 3 pastors were killed. In addition, almost all the tribal churches were shut down, and their pastors were persecuted. In spite of tremendous difficulties, however, the Evangelical Church of Viet Nam remains vibrant; its membership is estimated at one million.

Bibliography: L. CADIÈRE, *Résumé d'histoire d'Annam* (Qui Nhon, 1911) • V. JAMES, "American Protestant Missions and the Vietnam War" (Diss., University of Aberdeen, 1989) • A. LAUNAY, *Histoire de la mission en Cochinchine, 1658-1823. Documents historiques;* vol. 1, *1658-1728;* vol. 2, *1728-1771;* vol. 3, *1771-1823* (Paris, 1924) • LE HOANG PHU, "A Short History of the Evangelical Church of Viet Nam (1911-1965)" (2 vols.; diss., New York University, 1972) • MINH CHI, HA VAN TAN, and NGUYEN TAI THU, *Buddhism in Vietnam* (Hanoi, 1993) • C. T. NGUYEN, *Zen in Medieval Vietnam: A Study and Translation of the Thien Uyen Tap Anh* (Honolulu, 1997) • NGUYEN KHAC VIEN, *Viet Nam. Une longue histoire* (Hanoi, 1993) • P. C. PHAN, *Mission and Catechesis: Alexandre de Rhodes and Inculturation in Seventeenth-Century Vietnam* (Maryknoll, N.Y., 1998) • F. ROMANET DU CAILLAUT, *Essai sur les origines du Christianisme au Tonkin et dans les autres pays annamites* (Paris, 1915).

PETER C. PHAN

Vigil → Church Year 4.2; Holy Week 6

Vineyard Christian Fellowships

The Vineyard church movement began in Southern California and appealed primarily to post–World War II Baby Boomers who felt dissatisfied with what they perceived as the routinization and cultural irrelevance of evangelical churches. Kenn Gulliksen, a leader in the → Jesus People movement of the 1960s, started the first Vineyard in Los Angeles in 1974 as a home → Bible study group under the umbrella of Calvary Chapel. In 1977 John Wimber, former jazz musician and manager of the Righteous Brothers, started a similar Calvary Chapel group in Yorba Linda, California. In 1982 the founder of Calvary Chapel, Chuck Smith, criticized Gulliksen's and Wimber's emphasis on the public use of the gifts of the Holy Spirit and encouraged them to form a separate movement, the leadership of which quickly passed to Wimber. Incorporated in 1985, the Association of Vineyard Churches is today a rapidly growing, international church-planting movement.

Like other leaders in the "third wave" → charismatic movement (with "first wave" referring to the Pentecostal movement of the early 1900s, "second wave," to the charismatic movement of the 1960s), Wimber saw the Vineyard as an optimal middle way between evangelicalism (→ Evangelical Movement) and → Pentecostalism — grounded in the Bible and open to the → Holy Spirit. Wimber claimed that, before having any supernatural experiences, he became convinced by the Bible's teachings on the → kingdom of God that all the biblical gifts of the Holy Spirit should still be active in the church. Wimber reported that it took ten months of preaching on → healing and praying for the sick in obedience to the Bible's commands before his team witnessed their first miraculous healing; subsequently, claims of supernatural healing became a hallmark of the Vineyard.

Wimber taught that ten essential emphases constituted the Vineyard's spiritual "genetic code": accurate Bible teaching, contemporary → worship, gifts of the Holy Spirit in operation, active small groups, ministry to the poor, physical healing, church planting and world → missions, → unity with the whole body of Christ, evangelistic outreach, and equipping the saints for ministry. Emphasizing the priesthood of all believers (→ Priest, Priesthood, 4), Wimber encouraged lay Christians to do all that Jesus and his early disciples did, proclaiming and demonstrating the kingdom of God by healing the sick, casting out demons (→ Exorcism), and caring for the poor. Leading what became known as the "signs and wonders" movement, Wimber taught that spiritual gifts such as healing and prophecy are tools for "power evangelism": demonstrating the presence and power of God in order to overcome resistance to the gospel, resulting in conversions to Christianity. As an adjunct instructor at Fuller Theological Seminary in the 1980s, Wimber's course "Signs and Wonders and Church Growth" set school attendance records until the administration canceled it because of controversial "laboratory" sessions in which students prayed for each other.

Vineyard churches attracted adherents, many of whom switched from evangelical churches, by cultivating an innovative style that combined biblical primitivism (→ Biblicism) with a postmodern concern for verification of → truth through personal → experience, in reaction against the emphasis on propositional theology typical of Enlightenment-oriented evangelicalism. Rejecting a rigid sacred/secular divide (→ Sacred and Profane), Vineyard congregations typically dress informally, meet in nontraditional buildings such as warehouses and schools, and sing contemporary worship songs to the accompaniment of rock bands as the words are projected on overhead screens. Characteristically, Vineyard songs are intimate addresses of worship to Jesus rather than songs about God; Vineyard music is today sung in churches of many denominations around the world.

In January 1994 the Toronto Airport Vineyard Fellowship began a series of renewal meetings, dubbed the "Toronto Blessing," that have since birthed a global missionary movement. Toronto pastors John and Carol Arnott had invited Randy Clark, the pastor of a small Vineyard church in St. Louis, to preach a four-day sermon series. As participants in the Toronto meetings experienced unac-

customed manifestations that they attributed to the Holy Spirit, such as laughing, shaking, falling, and claims of miraculous healings, the nightly services were extended for days, weeks, months, and years, becoming the longest protracted meeting in North American history. More than a decade later, the frequency and size of the meetings had diminished, but not disappeared. An estimated three million people from around the world, representing nearly every stream of the Christian church, have undertaken pilgrimages to Toronto searching for physical healing or spiritual renewal, and many have claimed that when they returned home, they brought the revival fires with them. One such pilgrim was Heidi Baker — a self-described "burned-out" American missionary to Mozambique. After visiting Toronto in 1996, Baker reported that the ministry that she and her husband, Rolland, led grew from two churches and an orphanage to 7,000 churches and homes for 3,000 orphaned children.

Meanwhile, Wimber, alarmed by what he considered exotic and extrabiblical practices, "disengaged" the Toronto church from the Vineyard movement. Christian pilgrims nevertheless continued traveling to Toronto, and Clark, who founded a missions organization named Global Awakening, regularly took teams of volunteers influenced by Toronto to conduct meetings in 40 countries. As Clark's teams preached and prayed for the sick and those thought to be demonized, they attracted as many as 100,000 people at a time, many of whom reportedly experienced conversion, healing, and deliverance.

Wimber died in 1997 at age 63, after a decade-long struggle with health problems, including heart trouble, cancer, stroke, and a brain hemorrhage. Todd Hunter succeeded Wimber as national director of the Association of Vineyard Churches–U.S.A., but he stepped down from his position in 2000 in order to plant culturally relevant churches targeted to Generation X. He was succeeded by Berten Waggoner.

There are currently more than 600 Vineyard churches in the United States and roughly the same number in other countries, including Canada, the United Kingdom, other countries of Europe, South Africa, and Australia; well over 100,000 people attend Vineyard services on any given Sunday. In the United States 95 percent of Vineyard pastors are Caucasian, but a significant number of Latinos/as and Asian Americans are members. The movement's worldwide impact is much broader than these numbers would suggest. During the 1980s the Vineyard influenced an estimated 10,000 Catholic, Anglican, evangelical, and mainline churches through international "equipping seminars." Wimber's numerous books, especially *Power Evangelism* (1986) and *Power Healing* (1987), encouraged many to expect church growth through signs and wonders. Although the Vineyard now identifies itself as a → denomination and has not forged many formal ecumenical ties, the movement has informally encouraged churches of many denominations to invite the Holy Spirit's presence through intimate worship and expectant → prayer.

Bibliography: R. BAKER and H. BAKER, *There Is Always Enough: God's Miraculous Provision among the Poorest Children on Earth* (Grand Rapids, 2003) • G. CHEVREAU, *Catch the Fire: The Toronto Blessing; An Experience of Renewal and Revival* (London, 1994) • R. CLARK, *There Is More! Reclaiming the Power of Impartation* (Mechanicsburg, Pa., 2006) • B. JACKSON, *The Quest for the Radical Middle: A History of the Vineyard* (Cape Town, 1999) • P. KENNEDY, "Satisfied Customers: Miracles at the Vineyard Christian Fellowship," *MHRC* 1/2 (1998) 135-52 • D. MILLER, *Reinventing American Protestantism: Christianity in the New Millennium* (Berkeley, Calif., 1997); idem, "Routinizing Charisma: The Vineyard Christian Fellowship in the Post-Wimber Era," *Pneuma* 25/2 (2003) 216-39 • R. D. PERRIN, "Signs and Wonders: The Growth of the Vineyard Christian Fellowship" (Diss., Washington State University, 1989) • R. D. PERRIN and A. L. MAUSS, "Saints and Seekers: Sources of Recruitment to the Vineyard Christian Fellowship," *RRelRes* 33/2 (1991) 97-111 • A. M. SÁNCHEZ-WALSH, *Latino Pentecostal Identity: Evangelical Faith, Self, and Society* (New York, 2003).

CANDY GUNTHER BROWN

Violence → Force, Violence, Nonviolence

Virgin Birth

1. Bible
2. History
3. Criticism

1. Bible

Virgin birth is the usual way of referring to what is more accurately called the virginal conception of → Jesus. According to the accounts by Matthew (1:18-25) and Luke (1:26-38), the conception of Jesus was the direct creative act of the → Holy Spirit without the cooperation of a male partner. The use of Isa. 7:14 LXX by Matthew brought an apologetic feature into the discussion.

Only in the 19th century was it realized how ambivalent the Hebrew is. Whether the tradition was familiar to other NT writers is open to question. Rom. 1:3 insists on the descent of Jesus from → David "according to the flesh," which some scholars see as an indication that → Paul did not know the tradition. Gal. 4:4-5, sometimes adduced as evidence that he did, can hardly be conclusive.

John 1:13 exists in a variant form with pronoun and verb in the singular ("[He] who was born, not of blood or of the will of the flesh or of the will of man, but of God"), but the attestation of this reading is poor, depending almost entirely on Latin sources. It is probably an apologetic emendation. The suggestion has even been made that the original plural form *does* witness to John's knowledge of the story but represents a tacit polemic against it: Jesus' status does not depend on signs and wonders or on his fulfillment of prophecy; the real "divine birth" is the → regeneration of believers.

2. History

2.1. The virginal conception emerges as a well-known and significant item of belief in the second century. Ignatius of Antioch (ca. 35-ca. 107) mentions it as one of "three mysteries" (referring to Jesus' conception, birth, and death) that were "wrought in the stillness of God," the significance of which was hidden from the prince of this world (*Eph.* 19.1). For Ignatius, what matters is not so much the → miracle in itself but the notion of a cosmically decisive event taking place in secrecy and obscurity or humiliation. That is, it is part of his "theology of humility," the exaltation of God's silent but real activity over the elaborate but fruitless and empty conceptualizations of the heretical world picture (→ Heresies and Schisms).

→ Justin (ca. 100-ca. 165) concentrates on the aspect of fulfillment of prophecy and also adduces pagan myths of divine birth as distorted and diabolically inspired adumbrations of the true narrative of the Gospels (*1 Apol.* 54).

→ Irenaeus (ca. 130-ca. 200) uses the story in two ways in his typological reflections: → Mary, as obedient virgin, reverses the effects of Eve's choice as disobedient virgin; and the new → Adam must be born from a virgin, just as the first Adam came from the virgin earth (*Demon.* 33), a metaphor paralleled in pre-Christian Jewish sources but perhaps mediated to Irenaeus by Gnostic texts. Here the virginal conception is seen in the context of the overarching doctrine of recapitulation — the exact reworking, in the events of salvation, of the pattern of events in creation and the fall.

2.2. The same period also saw the development of a legend of painless birth (*Asc. Isa.* 11:8-14; *Odes Sol.* 19:6-9; see also the strange views of the Valentinians on Christ's birth) and — related to this — of Mary's virginity *in partu* (i.e., during the delivery of Jesus; *Prot. Jas.* 19-20). The idea of a perpetual virginity evolved in the Eastern Christian world (the brothers of Jesus are → Joseph's children by an earlier marriage; *Prot. Jas.* 9), and by the end of the patristic period the teaching of Mary's virginity before, during, and after Christ's birth *(ante partum, in partu,* and *post partum)* was established in East and West, with contrary opinions being fiercely attacked (e.g., → Jerome's polemics against Helvidius and Jovinian).

Initially, the creedal phrase "born of the Virgin Mary" (→ Apostles' Creed) served primarily to secure the affirmation that Jesus had a real, physical human birth (→ Docetism). Later, though, the belief in virginal conception was to some extent reinforced by, and used to validate belief in, the supreme value of virginity for Christians. More widely and more important, however, Mary's virginity was appealed to in illustrating the Christological paradox: Jesus was *born* like us, yet miraculously *begotten* (→ Christology).

This rhetorical disjunction of features in the story of Jesus — designed to underline the distinction of the two natures — was typical of Antiochene Christology (→ Antiochian Theology) and was used in the *Tome* of → Leo I (440-61). Maximus the Confessor (ca. 580-662) developed it in the seventh century with his differentiation between *logos* and *tropos hyparxeōs:* Jesus is by nature human, the *logos* or generic structure of his humanity being like ours, but the *tropos* (mode) of his coming into being, and of his life, is divine. The virginal conception does not compromise the fullness of his humanity but points to the divinity of the *hypostasis* united to human nature.

3. Criticism

3.1. Apart from some Jewish-Christian groups (e.g., the → Ebionites; → Jewish Christians) in the early period, no one raised serious doubts about the virginal conception prior to the rise of critical scholarship. M. → Luther (1483-1546; → Luther's Theology) and U. → Zwingli (1484-1531; → Zwingli's Theology) even accepted the common belief in Mary's perpetual virginity, which Protestantism generally abandoned only in the 19th century. At that time increasing awareness of literary and narrative conventions in the earliest Christian period also led many scholars to be skeptical of the historical foundations of the whole story.

However, even it if is granted that the Evangelists clearly employ the techniques of → Midrash, the problem of the ultimate provenance of the tradition remains unsolved. Parallels with Greek and Egyptian legends of divine intervention in the birth of kings or heroes are slight and inconclusive; much has been made of Hellenistic Jewish stories of God's miraculous intervention in the conception of → Isaac and other holy men, but there is no exact correspondence to the idea of *virginal* conception. The tradition is likely to be early and Syro-Palestinian, but it evidently enjoyed limited circulation. It may depend on recollections of unusual or obscure circumstances surrounding the birth of Jesus; critical scholarship in itself cannot finally determine the question of historicity.

3.2. It should be recognized that the virginal conception has never been consistently used by theologians as strict *evidence* for the divine sonship of Jesus. The doctrine of the → incarnation does not entail acceptance of the full historicity of Matthew 1 or Luke 1. Modern theologians have disagreed about the dogmatic significance of these texts. K. → Barth (1886-1968) considered the virginal conception an essential witness to the creative freedom of God and the passivity of the sinner in the event of revelation and reconciliation. E. Brunner (1889-1966) accepted the miracle of Christ's birth as an act of God but saw in the tradition of the virginal conception a biological interpretation of the basic fact, which had perhaps been brought in secondarily by mistake. W. Pannenberg (b. 1928) concludes that the virginal conception contradicts belief in the preexistence of the Son.

Roman Catholic exegetes have increasingly accepted the position that the story has no evidential significance but do not agree on the possibility or necessity of supporting it. (R. Brown treats the texts skeptically but leaves open the possibility that we should confess the virgin birth as a reality revealed to the faith of the church.) Orthodox theology (→ Orthodox Christianity) has not yet entered the discussion and for the most part clings to the thought of Maximus the Confessor regarding the theological significance of the miracle. It has also not yet contributed any inquiry into the question of Mary's perpetual virginity.

The central affirmation of the narratives remains vital for Christian doctrine, namely, that the *whole* course of the life of Jesus is grace and gift and that, at the same time, the grace of God calls forth and works with human obedience. Mary's declaration (Luke 1:38) establishes her as a paradigm of discipleship.

→ Kenosis; Mariology

Bibliography: ANSELM, *Why God Became Man; and, The Virgin Conception and Original Sin* (trans. J. M. Colleran; Albany, N.Y., 1969) • K. BARTH, *CD* I/2 • T. D. BOSLOOPER, *The Virgin Birth* (Philadelphia, 1962) • R. E. BROWN, *The Birth of the Messiah* (London, 1977); idem, *The Virginal Conception and Bodily Resurrection of Jesus* (New York, 1973) • E. BRUNNER, *The Mediator: A Study of the Central Doctrine of the Christian Faith* (London, 1934) • H. CAMPENHAUSEN, *The Virgin Birth in the Theology of the Ancient Church* (Naperville, Ill., 1964) • M. DIBELIUS, "Jungfrauensohn und Krippenkind" (1932), *Botschaft und Geschichte* (vol. 1; Tübingen, 1953) 1-78 • G. LÜDEMANN, *Virgin Birth? The Real Story of Mary and Her Son Jesus* (Harrisburg, Pa., 1998) • J. G. MACHEN, *The Virgin Birth of Christ* (New York, 1930).

ROWAN D. WILLIAMS

Virtue

1. Approaches
2. The Recovery of Virtue
3. Virtue and Scripture

1. Approaches

→ Ethics is often thought of as a battleground between two competing notions of the → good. The first strives to find a universal foundation by identifying *actions* that are always right or always wrong. This approach is sometimes called deontological ethics (→ Deontology). But debate starts as soon as someone utters the words "it depends." It is constantly pointed out that an action that in some circumstances may be very fitting may in other circumstances be disastrous. For example, if a Nazi guard were to ask, "Are there Jews living in this house?" it seems absurd to maintain a rule that holds that it is always wrong to lie. Hence a second notion of the good concentrates on good *outcomes*. An action is not right or wrong in itself; it is to be judged right or wrong in the light of the likely results of that action. This is sometimes called consequential ethics (or utilitarian ethics, when the criterion is the greatest happiness of the greatest number). The debate between the two reached its height in the 1960s with the publication of Joseph Fletcher's *Situation Ethics* (1966), an extreme version of consequentialism.

A third approach has become much more common in the last 30 years. This focuses not on actions or on consequences but on good *people*. Contemporary philosophers and theologians increasingly point out that the good life is not about finding rules or guidelines that everyone can follow, regardless of other commitments or convictions, but about shaping the character of people so that they do the "right" thing out of habit, hardly noticing that they have done so. Thus ethics becomes less about quandaries than about training, less about scratching the head in a crisis than about developing character and learning to take the right things for granted. In contrast to what is sometimes called decisionist ethics, this approach is known as virtue (or character) ethics.

2. The Recovery of Virtue

Perhaps the single book that best represents this trend in the last generation to reorient ethics to character rather than decision is Alasdair MacIntyre's *After Virtue* (1981). MacIntyre has a very negative understanding of the contemporary moral climate: ethical theories that have emerged as attempts to offer value-free, neutral approaches to resolving quandaries are portrayed as part of the problem; the problem is that people have become detached from their roots and are at the whim of emotional manipulation. MacIntyre proposes a return to Aristotle, whose ethics steers a path between two extremes (→ Aristotelianism). On the one extreme is behaviorism, according to which all human actions are determined by external forces or stimuli (→ Behavior, Behavioral Psychology). On the other extreme is → voluntarism, which posits a → self abstracted from all context — bodily, societal, historic — which simply governs ethical activity. Aristotle sees ethics as a mean between these two extremes, and sees character as the name of that mean.

Like deontological ethics, virtue ethics has a profound sense of things one should not do. Like consequentialism, virtue ethics has an eye to the future. But the future for virtue ethics is a teleological one — that is, one concerned with the ultimate end or purpose of a person (their *telos* ; → Teleology). And the things they should or shouldn't do are assessed not by whether those actions are right or wrong in themselves but by whether such actions would contribute to the formation of a good person. Moral formation is always the key. For example, virtue ethics does not say, "Murder is wrong," but asks, rather, "How could killing be described as being a reconciling presence in the life of my neighbor?" Aristotle sees virtue as moral action that leads to → happiness, which is essentially something that one seeks for oneself and not for another.

Aristotle, following Plato, perceives four inherent virtues: prudence, justice, courage, and temperance. These are all means between extremes. → Stoicism also placed a high value on virtue. Thomas Aquinas incorporated Aristotle's ethics into his notion of virtue. To the four cardinal virtues he added the three theological virtues: → faith, → hope, and → charity (or love). MacIntyre's very influential argument rests on an assumption that Aquinas's incorporation of Aristotle into a theological scheme was comprehensive and appropriate.

The theologian most associated with the recent recovery of virtue is Stanley Hauerwas. In a series of books beginning with *Vision and Virtue* (1974), he redirected the focus of Christian ethics from the action performed to the person performing the action. This is the heart of his whole theological program, which has led him to emphasize the distinctiveness of the → church and the importance of practices such as → worship that shape the character of Christians. Like MacIntyre, Hauerwas has written of the importance of narrative for setting an indispensable context for understanding character ethics. In Hauerwas's case this narrative is unapologetically the Christian narrative, notably the story of → Jesus.

3. Virtue and Scripture

Hauerwas's achievement has been to overcome much of the deep suspicion Protestants have had toward the notion of virtue. For centuries, a significant number of Protestants have assumed that since → salvation is by → grace alone through → faith alone, any suggestion that a Christian can grow toward perfection through the Holy Spirit building up his or her character in virtue is highly suspicious. The contemporary emphasis on virtue arises partly out of the failures of Protestants to treat the Bible as a rule book offering clear instructions for life in the contemporary world. Virtue ethics sees the Bible more as a training manual that shapes the character of Christians and empowers them to act faithfully in new and challenging circumstances. In that sense the Bible is less a script for a drama than a school for faithful improvisation.

Rather than search the Bible for references to the term "virtue," theologians sympathetic to virtue ethics are more likely to identify ways in which Jesus is normative for ethics or to point out Paul's notion of → sanctification. Once released from the assumption that Scripture is primarily concerned with providing universal moral rules, theologians are free to discover the enormous possibilities for engaging with questions of character in narrative passages like the story of Joseph or the Book of Esther.

Bibliography: Aristotle, *Eth. Nic.* • J. F. Fletcher, *Situation Ethics: The New Morality* (Philadelphia, 1966; repr., 1997) • S. Hauerwas, *The Peaceable Kingdom: A Primer in Christian Ethics* (Notre Dame, Ind., 1983; 2d ed., London, 2003); idem, *Vision and Virtue: Essays in Christian Ethical Reflection* (Notre Dame, 1974; repr., 1981) • A. MacIntyre, *After Virtue: A Study in Moral Theory* (Notre Dame, Ind., 1981; 2d ed., 1984) • S. J. Pope, ed., *The Ethics of Aquinas* (Baltimore, 2002) • J. Porter, *The Recovery of Virtue: The Relevance of Aquinas for Christian Ethics* (Louisville, Ky., 1990) • Thomas Aquinas, *Summa theol.* I of II, qq. 49-58; II of II, qq. 1-170 • S. Wells, *Improvisation: The Drama of Christian Ethics* (Grand Rapids, 2004).

Samuel Wells

Visions

1. Cultures that have loanwords from Lat. *visio* (a seeing, view) often use them for visionary hallucinations. Such a vision, which takes place when the person is awake, is not a → dream. Psychokinetic phenomena may accompany it, and it may include paranormal information. If the visionary is religiously inclined, it might seem to contain a → revelation. The vision itself is not a revelation and must be interpreted. The visionary might be the interpreter, or some other person might be. Interpretation imparts mystical knowledge, falling between the rational and the occult (→ Occultism).

2. A vision might depict an episode or a series of episodes. Its content might have personal or social significance. Means can be sought to inculcate a disposition that favors recurrent visions. Psychedelic drugs (→ Substance Abuse), drumming, rattling, various breathing techniques, and → fasting make brief spontaneous visions possible. Such means are also used for sequential visions, along with meditative rituals (→ Meditation), and the longest possible shutdown of the sensory apparatus that visions need.

Pure visions seldom occur. They come for the most part under → parapsychology and might include auditions. As visions fade, the visionary experience is often felt to denote sickness or depression (the sickness of shamans). We do not know the physiological cause. More rarely a vision is pleasant, euphoric, and joyful. In this case a cerebral synthesis of beta-endorphins is at work quite apart from the vision itself. A visionary can act as a healer, but only on his or her own responsibility.

3. Types of society and the forms of visions have something in common, although there are no strict rules of interdependence. It is striking, however, how powerfully early cultural forms persist in more elaborate forms; in them visions form a kind of connection between highly differentiated mystical systems and a subtle → mysticism. The contents of visions are consistent with the surroundings of the vision recipient. The ability, occasion, and value of seeing visions soon became institutionalized, and seers developed. The seer then became the → prophet or diviner.

Externally, the ontogenesis of the vision contains phylogenetic elements. For example:

- Helpful spirits are seen in the vision. Sometimes an organ appears at a different location from the body (soul journeys; hunters and gatherers).
- Protective spirits are closely linked to the various stages of life (horticulturalists).
- Contact is made with the "masters" of bodies of water, mountains, woods, and animals (nomadic shepherds).
- Visionary experiences range beyond what an institution guarantees (farmers).
- Of the earlier forms, only possession remains (city dwellers).

Such phylogenetic remnants are naturally never completely met in one individual and can also be completely absent. The last instance appears to be favorable for the emergence of visionary experiences involving color, as a kind of compensation.

4. We cannot plainly relate or culturally date the earliest religious use and interpretation of visions. Their main occurrence was where technology was least developed (most clearly in → shamanism), and they became more specific and marginal with advances in nutrition, social organization, and writing. In such circumstances vision mysticism was preserved in the greatest variety in India (Vishnuism). Seers (e.g., Cassandra, Calchas, Tiresias) functioned at the courts of Greek nobles. In Israel direction and goals were sought from seers (Numbers 22–24; 1 Sam. 9:9). The prophets were mostly called by an audible voice, but we also find visions in Amos 7–9 and Isaiah 6. Visions take a literary form in Ezekiel and Zechariah. Both real and literary visions occur in → apocalyptic (Daniel and Revelation).

Pneumatic experiences and dependence on Scripture influenced the attitude of the → primitive Christian community to visions. So did the circumstances of the time. Hellenistic → mysticism (§1.2.6) had a growing impact (see Dionysius the Pseudo Areopagite [ca. 500]). A visionary tradition was maintained in the Byzantine church (→ Mysti-

cism 2.3.2). → Augustine (354-430; → Augustine's Theology) referred to three types of visions: sensory, spiritual, and intellectual. Medieval mysticism retained this distinction, especially among women mystics such as Mechthild of Magdeburg (ca. 1207-ca. 1282), with her love for God. Helfta, near Eisleben, was a cloister of visionaries (K. Ruh) to which Gertrud (1256-ca. 1302) belonged. Protestantism in general shows little understanding of visions of this type, though founders of messianic movements may still lay claim to visions.

→ Mystical Union

Bibliography: BRIDGET OF SWEDEN, *The Revelations of St. Birgitta of Sweden* (trans. D. Searby; New York, 2006) • M. Fox, *Illuminations of Hildegard of Bingen* (Rochester, Vt., 2002) • F. D. GOODMAN, "Visions," *EncRel(E)* 15.282-88 • L. IRWIN, *The Dream Seekers: Native American Visionary Traditions of the Great Plains* (Norman, Okla., 1994) • W. JAMES, *The Varieties of Religious Experience* (Centenary ed.; New York, 2002) • *Mechthild of Magdeburg: Selections from "The Flowing Light of the Godhead"* (trans. E. A. Andersen; Cambridge, 2003) • S. NIDITCH, *The Symbolic Vision in Biblical Tradition* (Chico, Calif., 1983) • J.-D. PLÜSS, *Therapeutic and Prophetic Narratives in Worship: A Hermeneutic Study of Testimonies and Visions* (New York, 1988) • K. RAHNER, *Visions and Prophecies* (New York, 1963) • K. RUH, *Geschichte der abendländischen Mystik* (4 vols.; Munich, 1990-99) • P. H. WIEBE, *Visions of Jesus: Direct Encounters from the NT to Today* (New York, 1997) • U. WIETHAUS, *Ecstatic Transformation: Transpersonal Psychology in the Work of Mechthild of Magdeburg* (Syracuse, N.Y., 1996).

CARSTEN COLPE

Visitation

1. Biblical
2. Ecclesiastical

1. Biblical

The words "visit" and "visitation" often indicate divine involvement with humans, sometimes by way of → theophany. God not only observes human life, he also acts in our world. God's visitation may bring blessing to God's own people or to the whole earth (Ps. 65:9). More often, divine visitation punishes offenses, as in Job 35:15 and Ps. 59:5 (KJV). The → Decalogue contains the familiar reference to God "visiting the iniquity of the fathers upon the children" (Exod. 20:5 RSV). Isaiah 26:14 (RSV) tells us that God will visit with destruction.

The idea of visitation for → punishment disappears in the NT. Jesus bewails the fact that the people of Jerusalem did not know or recognize the time of their visitation. The coming of the → gospel is seen as God's visitation (see Luke 19:43-44; Acts 15:14 RSV). An exception is 1 Pet. 2:12 (marg.), for it refers to the future day of visitation. The Greek word used in the LXX is *episkeptomai*, which the NT applies to divine visitation and to human oversight of community life. The latter meaning is the basis for ecclesiastical forms of visitation (see 2).

Bibliography: J. ROHDE, "'Ἐπισκέπτομαι, ἐπισκοπέω," *EDNT* 2.33-34.

GEOFFREY W. BROMILEY

2. Ecclesiastical

Ecclesiastical visitation is a legally institutionalized mode of inspecting → congregations, deaneries, and church operations for the sake of examining their spiritual state and physical condition. Through visitations ecclesiastical authorities ensure that the → Word of God (§3) is proclaimed, that the → sacraments are rightly administered, and that the laity are duly shepherded. The visitors (→ bishops, → superintendents, archdeacons, etc.) hold regular visits and may be accompanied by theologians and others. (Historically, visitors were sometimes accompanied by secular authorities.) Visitors aim to offer spiritual and practical help within the constitutional framework of the church. The specific form of visitation, the questions asked or the procedure followed, varies from place to place and from time to time. Visitations may be more personal and pastoral, more congregational and missionary, or more concerned with local or national questions. Visitors almost always inspect worship and youth work. They converse with ministers and church councils. They inspect the running of the parish, including the physical state of church buildings. Visitors usually compile a report of their findings and present recommendations for improvement.

Visitations originated in NT days, although apostolic visits lacked the legal character typical of later visitations. → Paul oversaw the congregations that he had founded through letters, messengers, and personal visits. He sought → unity in the → faith (§3.5.1), purity of teaching, → holiness of life, and strengthening against → persecution. In the postapostolic age oversight of churches developed within the metropolitan areas (→ Church Government 2.1).

Visitations fell out of use until Carolingian times, when secular authorities made visitations the duty of bishops. In conjunction with → confirmation, the bishop investigated the condition of the local congregation. Over the Middle Ages, however, the ecclesiastical rights of bishops declined, and visitations disappeared.

In the 16th century the practice of visitations revived, in both Catholic and Protestant churches. Martin → Luther (1483-1546) called for visitations with a spiritual and pastoral emphasis. In 1527-29 he led a visitation of electoral Saxony at the request of the Saxon elector, Johann the Steadfast. Luther and Johann's cooperation became typical for Protestant territories, where secular and religious authorities worked together to carry out visitations. The results of the Saxon visitation showed that few laypeople understood Christian doctrines; in response, Luther composed his Large and Small → Catechisms (1529). In Catholic areas the Council of → Trent instructed bishops to complete a visitation at least every two years (24th sess., "Decree on Reformation," chap. 3). Bishops had sole responsibility for visitations in Catholic areas, unlike Protestant areas, where religious and secular authorities shared the responsibility. Visitation records from the 16th and 17th centuries have become particularly valuable source material for historians in recent years, as they provide unique insight into church practice and popular belief.

With the rise of the Enlightenment thinking, state-sponsored visitations ceased in Protestant areas. The custom was occasionally revived, albeit without secular oversight. → Revivals in the 19th century introduced visitations that aimed for religious and moral renewal. The → Confessing Church gave visitations a fraternal character.

The Protestant churches now stress the → partnership aspect of visitations. Visitation is not a controlling act by the authorities but an occasion for self-examination. Visitations also continue in Catholic regions. The 1983 → Codex Iuris Canonici describes visitation as an episcopal duty (can. 396). Visitations strive to uphold the unity of the church and its → proclamation. They often emphasize → church growth.

Bibliography: C. R. CHENEY, *Episcopal Visitation of Monasteries in the Thirteenth Century* (2d ed.; Philadelphia, 1983) • J. A. GOODALE, "Rethinking the Rural Reformation: New Strategies for Reading the Saxon Visitation Transcripts" (Diss., UCLA, 1995) • F. KRAUSE, *Visitation als Chance für Gemeindeaufbau* (Göttingen, 1991) • J. OBERSTE, *Die Dokumente der klösterlichen Visitationen* (Turnhout, 1999) • M. PLATHOW, *Lehre und Ordnung im Leben der Kirche heute. Dogmatische, rechtstheologische und pastoraltheologische Überle-*

gungen zu den Lebens- und Visitationsordnungen unserer evangelischen Kirche (Göttingen, 1982) • A. L. SLAFKOSKY, *The Canonical Episcopal Visitation of the Diocese: An Historical Synopsis and Commentary* (Washington, D.C., 1941).

JÖRG WINTER and MARY NOLL VENABLES

Visser 't Hooft, W. A.

1. Early Life
2. Before the Provisional Committee
3. 1938-48: The WCC in Process of Formation
4. 1948-66: The General Secretary
5. Legacy

1. Early Life

Willem Adolf Visser 't Hooft (1900-1985) — known to all as Wim — is often characterized as the person who shaped much of the modern ecumenical movement. Also, though, he himself was deeply shaped by that same movement (→ Ecumenism, Ecumenical Movement).

Born September 20, 1900, in Haarlem, the Netherlands, Visser 't Hooft grew up in a family that was closely associated with the legal profession, his grandfather having been presiding judge of the district tribunal in Haarlem, and his father a lawyer. He was a voracious reader and linguistically accomplished from his youth, studying Latin, Greek, German, French, and English. He had a special interest in Dutch literature of the late 19th century.

Initially, it was intended that the young Visser 't Hooft would study law. In the early 1920s, however, he studied the second edition of Karl → Barth's *Epistle to the Romans* (1922) and then struck a deal with his father that he would alternate his studies year by year between the study of law (→ Law and Legal Theory) and the study of → theology. Soon, however, he found law to be extremely dull in comparison with theology and thereafter devoted himself entirely to theological studies, pursuing his work at Leiden University. In 1924, after much involvement in the Dutch Student Christian Movement, he took a position on the Boys' Work staff of the World Committee for the → YMCA in Geneva, Switzerland. To the end of his life, his residence remained in Geneva.

In 1924 Visser 't Hooft married Henriette Philippine Jacoba Boddaert. They had three children and nine grandchildren. She died in 1968, having been a close companion and challenging intellectual partner for the years of their marriage.

2. Before the Provisional Committee

Visser 't Hooft's introduction to the wider ecumenical movement came in 1925, when he was appointed an alternate delegate for the YMCA to the Universal Christian Conference on Life and Work held in Stockholm, a conference presided over by the ecumenical pioneer Nathan → Söderblom (1866-1931), primate of the Church of Sweden. The next year he became personal assistant to John R. → Mott (1865-1955), another founder of the modern ecumenical movement and then general secretary of the → World Student Christian Federation (WSCF).

In 1925 Visser 't Hooft made his first visit to the United States, traveling with Mott in preparation for the World Conference of the YMCA, which was to be held in Helsinki in 1926. In the United States he became intrigued by questions of → social ethics (§2) as manifested both in American society and in the churches. This interest led to his doctoral dissertation, entitled "The Background of the → Social Gospel in America," which he defended in 1928 at Leiden. His work was both appreciative and, somewhat under the influence of the young American theologian Reinhold → Niebuhr (1892-1971), critical. In his *Memoirs* (1973) he pointed to one sentence from the dissertation as shaping his own development: "May we not expect that as Americans try to dig deeper, listening to the voice of Christ and translating it into a language of their own, America will find a deeper and more genuinely Christian message?" (p. 27).

In 1932 Visser 't Hooft succeeded Mott as general secretary of WSCF. In that capacity he began a lifetime of world travels, beginning that year with a journey to India to help organize Christian students there. In 1936 he was ordained a pastor in the National Protestant Church of Geneva.

The year 1937 was one of great ecumenical importance, and Visser 't Hooft found himself in the midst of formative activity. He participated in two international ecumenical meetings: → Life and Work, held at Oxford as the Second World Conference on Church and State, where he was a member of the steering committee; and → Faith and Order, held in Edinburgh, where he served on the executive committee. Before these two meetings a small gathering of 35 church leaders and officers of ecumenical organizations met at Westfield College, London, to explore the establishment of a global council of churches. William → Temple (1881-1944), then archbishop of York, chaired the meeting. It was proposed that Visser 't Hooft be named the chief staff person for the "World Council of Churches in Process of Formation." The sole objection to this proposal was that, since he was at that time only 36 years old, he lacked the experience and stature for so daunting a responsibility. Temple took the lead, however, in arguing that despite his youth, the Dutch churchman had the requisite knowledge, experience, and skills for the task.

The Oxford meeting of Life and Work enthusiastically accepted the idea of forming a → World Council of Churches (WCC); the Faith and Order conference at Edinburgh was initially somewhat less enthusiastic, fearing that its theological and ecclesiological concerns would be compromised by association with Life and Work and its sociopolitical vocation. A conference at Utrecht in the Netherlands in May of 1938, however, succeeded in drafting a proposed constitution for a WCC. At Utrecht the most intense discussions centered on the formation of a basis for the projected council. It was felt that theological clarity was required for such a basis, and it was agreed to define the forthcoming organization as "a fellowship of churches which accept our Lord Jesus Christ as God and Saviour." In this context, Visser 't Hooft accepted the position of general secretary of the World Council of Churches in Process of Formation.

3. 1938-48: The WCC in Process of Formation

The original hope was that the WCC would be formally constituted in 1941 or 1942. World War II intervened, however, which made establishing a global organization of churches impossible. Visser 't Hooft found himself in Geneva with a staff of but five persons, but his role not only in preparing for the founding of the WCC but in being a point of communication between the churches of the world was considerable.

Some biographers have pointed to his speech at the First World Conference of Christian Youth, held in Amsterdam in 1939, as providing a kind of leitmotiv for his work during the war. He reminded the 1,500 participants in that conference that their task would be to communicate to Christian youth all over the world that "it is inevitable that unity will prove to be stronger than diversity." He challenged the delegates to reject "that deepest of all conservatisms, to accept the spiritual status quo of the world," and to see "the dimensions of the plan of God who thinks in terms of the whole world."

Visser 't Hooft turned down an opportunity to establish his office in the United States, being convinced that Geneva, even under difficult circumstances, provided the best location for keeping open lines of communication, some secret, between churches. He was able to keep remarkable contact

with the German church, and in 1941 he twice received visits from Dietrich → Bonhoeffer (1906-45), who informed him of conspiracies in Germany against Adolf Hitler. Until 1944 he was also able to travel to London to meet with church leaders who were shaken by the war, concerned about the fate of → refugees and resistance movements, and beginning preparations for reconstruction after the war.

The general secretary was involved in many wartime activities, which included rescuing Jews and others from Nazi Germany, working to alleviate the conditions in which refugees and prisoners were forced to live, and smuggling information into and out of the Netherlands and other countries for the use of governments-in-exile in London. As the war came to a close, two projects occupied him greatly, besides preparing for the establishment of the WCC. First, he gave great support to the Evangelical Church in Germany when, in October 1945, it promulgated the remarkable Stuttgart Declaration, which, on behalf of the church, acknowledged guilt and accepted responsibility for its weakness during the Nazi regime. Accompanying the declaration, German Bishop Theophil Wurm (1868-1953) notably confessed, "We accuse ourselves for not witnessing more courageously, for not praying more faithfully, for not believing more joyously, and for not loving more ardently. Now a new beginning is to be made in our churches." Second, Visser 't Hooft was much occupied with the establishment in 1947 of the Bossey Institute, near Geneva, which became an influential ecumenical training ground for church leaders from all parts of the world. The institute was founded largely with a gift of $1 million from the philanthropist John D. Rockefeller Jr. (1874-1960).

4. 1948-66: The General Secretary

In August 1948, after a ten-year delay, the First Assembly of the WCC was convened. In all, 351 delegates from 147 churches throughout the world gathered to form the WCC. Under the leadership of W. A. Visser 't Hooft, the theme "Man's Disorder and God's Design" was considered in four sections, which can be seen as precursors of central themes in his leadership of the WCC for the next 18 years: (1) The Universal Church in God's Design, (2) The Church's Witness to God's Design, (3) The Church and the Disorder of Society, and (4) The Church and the International Order.

The ecumenical breakthroughs that occurred during Visser 't Hooft's tenure as WCC general secretary were considerable: the establishment of the Geneva secretariat, which by the end of his service numbered over 350 persons; the growth in member churches from the 147 at Amsterdam to around 235 by 1968; the development of extensive programs of service to refugees and programs for → Third World development; and the holding of several global conferences on the church's vocation of → mission and → evangelism, stimulated by the incorporation of the → International Missionary Council into the WCC in 1961.

Of particular importance were advances and remarkable contacts between the WCC and, first, the world of Eastern and Oriental Orthodoxy (→ Orthodox Church; Oriental Orthodox Churches) and, later, the → Roman Catholic Church. Visser 't Hooft was able, in 1959, to convince Patriarch Alexis (1945-70) of the → Russian Orthodox Church that churches were called to overcome what by then had become the globe-threatening East-West divide. At the WCC Assembly in New Delhi, 1961, nearly all large Orthodox churches were in attendance.

The story of the WCC's increasing contact with the Roman Catholic Church is primarily one of the personal relations between Visser 't Hooft and, initially, Augustin Cardinal Bea (1881-1968), the first president of the Vatican's Secretariat (later Pontifical Council) for Promoting Christian Unity, which was established by Pope John XXIII (1958-63) in 1960, and then with Jan Cardinal Willebrands (1909-2006), successor to Cardinal Bea. In 1965, at the then-new headquarters of the WCC in Geneva, Cardinal Bea announced the formation of a Joint Working Group between Geneva and Rome, an early fruit of ever-growing contacts between the post–Vatican II Roman Catholic Church and the WCC. In retirement, in 1969 and 1984, Visser 't Hooft participated in the official visits of Popes Paul VI (1963-78) and John Paul II (1978-2005) to the Ecumenical Center, the headquarters of the WCC in Geneva.

During his 18 years of service as WCC general secretary, W. A. Visser 't Hooft launched countless programs and initiatives — including serious ecumenical theological and ecclesiological studies on the unity of the church and its mission — which defined the global program of the council. He was in fact one of the parents of the modern ecumenical movement through one of its instruments, the World Council of Churches.

5. Legacy

Visser 't Hooft's legacy cannot be measured by the awards he received, although he received more than a dozen honorary degrees and other honors. They included the Grand Cross of the Order of Merit (West German government, 1957), Officer of the Legion of Honor (France, (1959), Cross of the Great Commander of the Holy Sepulchre (from the ecumenical patriarch in Constantinople, 1963), the Family of Man Award (United States, 1966), and election as Honorary Fellow of Hebrew University in Jerusalem (1972).

Nor can his legacy be measured by his literary output, although he published some 15 books in several languages and left an estimated 50,000 letters and some 1,500 items under his name in printed or duplicated form. The fact that among his published books the remarkable study *Rembrandt and the Gospel* (1957) received high praise from scholars outside the church and theological community is a testimony to the breadth of his learning. His establishment in 1948 of the quarterly *Ecumenical Review* has provided a major location for serious and creative ecumenical reflection.

To be sure, there has been strong criticism of Visser 't Hooft, namely, that his leadership style was often abrasive; that his theology was Eurocentric, elitist, and dated; and that he lacked genuine empathy with the struggles of the Third World (although he did play a role in the decolonization of Dutch East Indies). On the second point, one of his colleagues who admired him deeply, Philip Potter (b. 1921), who himself became a successor as WCC general secretary, once wrote, "What strikes one is that despite these events [the flames of World War II], neither Visser 't Hooft nor many of his contemporaries have really been able to shake off the European Christendom triumphalism of the pre–First World War" (pp. 378-79). Such a critique is certainly important in our day, yet it cannot dislodge the foundations laid by Visser 't Hooft and the other ecumenical pioneers.

In sum, Visser 't Hooft's legacy can perhaps best be measured by the growth and depth of what is simply called "the modern ecumenical movement." That movement surely includes the WCC, but Visser 't Hooft knew well that the movement, with all its flaws and accomplishments, was larger than a single institution, even as he knew that the various streams reflected a deep underlying unity. His extreme dedication to the unity and mission of the church remains a foundation stone for the future of the movement he helped shape.

Wim died in his home outside Geneva in 1985, just three days after he had completed the second draft of *Teachers and the Teaching Authorities: The "Magistri" and the "Magisterium."* This work addresses a question that occupied him throughout his life: Who has the authority to speak for the churches in → ecumenical dialogue?

Bibliography: Primary sources: The Genesis and Formation of the World Council of Churches (Geneva, 1982) • *Has the Ecumenical Movement a Future?* (Belfast, 1974) • *Memoirs* (London, 1973) • *No Other Name: The Choice between Syncretism and Christian Universalism* (London, 1963) • *The Pressure of Our Common Calling* (New York, 1959) • *Rembrandt and the Gospel* (London, 1957) • *Teachers and the Teaching Authorities: The "Magistri" and the "Magisterium"* (Geneva, 2000).

Secondary works: A. VAN DER BENT, ed., *Voices of Unity: Essays in Honour of Willem Adolf Visser 't Hooft on the Occasion of His Eightieth Birthday* (Geneva, 1981); idem, ed., *Willem Adolf Visser 't Hooft, 1900-1985: Fisherman of the Ecumenical Movement* (Geneva, 2000) • F. C. GÉRARD, *The Future of the Church: The Theology of Renewal of Willem Adolf Visser 't Hooft* (Pittsburgh, 1974) • R. C. MACKIE and C. C. WEST, eds., *The Sufficiency of God: Essays on the Ecumenical Hope in Honor of W. A. Visser 't Hooft* (London, 1963) • J. R. NELSON, ed., *No Man Is Alien: Essays on the Unity of Mankind* (Leiden, 1971) • P. A. POTTER, "But Still It Moves: A Review of the *Memoirs* of W. A. Visser 't Hooft," *ER* 25 (1973) 378-79.

NORMAN A. HJELM

Vitalism

1. "Vitalism" (Ger. *Lebensphilosophie,* "philosophy of life"), a term used in several senses, designates:

1. an individual → philosophy, mostly unexpressed and with indefinite general principles, in which → persons or → groups find their → identity (→ Worldview);
2. a philosophy of vitalist biology, especially H. Driesch's (1867-1941) philosophy of the organic, in which he advanced, in opposition to the mechanism of physics and the → evolutionary theory of C. Darwin (1809-82), the creative totality of the organic;
3. from the 18th century onward, a pragmatic "direction to live rationally" (so C. A. Crusius, *Anweisung, vernünftig zu leben* [1744]) in the tradition of → moralism, with a view to the → aesthetic and religious deepening and perfecting of individual and cultural life along the lines of poet- and confessor-philosophy (e.g., R. W. Emerson and G. Santayana in the United States, L. Tolstoy, F. Dostoyevsky, V. S. Solovyov, and N. Berdyaev in Russia); and
4. trends in German and French philosophy that stress, over against the dogmatic claims of an all-pervading and all-dissolving → Enlightenment, the totality, impermeability, → creativity, and individuality (→ Individualism) of life.

Vitalism in the last sense goes back to F. H. Jacobi (1743-1819), J. G. Hamann (1730-88), and J. G. → Herder (1744-1803; → Classicism), who opposed the transcendental → idealism of I. Kant (1724-1804; → Kantianism), in which they found life deprived of the forces of → faith, → language, and history (→ Philosophy of History). Even Kant's solution to the problems of the beautiful, creative, and organic in his *Critique of Judgment* (1790) they found inadequate. F. Schelling (1775-1854), J. G. Fichte (1762-1814), and G. W. F. Hegel (1770-1831; → Hegelianism) were all stimulated, therefore, to a reconciliation of life and system. In his lectures on the philosophy of life (1827), F. von Schlegel (1772-1829) made a fresh attack on that kind of philosophical systematics.

Often, however, the term "vitalism" is used only for a philosophical trend of the period from 1880 to 1930, which was more influenced by A. Schopenhauer (1788-1860) than by the philosophers named above. The proponents in this case were W. Dilthey (1833-1911), F. → Nietzsche (1844-1900), H.-L. Bergson (1859-1941), G. Simmel (1858-1918), L. Klages (1872-1956), and O. Spengler (1880-1936). Guided by → experience of the individual life of the soul, of the organic, of art, religion, and history, this vitalism tried to set aside all abstract constructions and to understand life in terms of itself (Dilthey).

2. For Dilthey and Nietzsche, who did not call themselves vitalists, "life" at its core was a critical term for the conditions and limitations of rationality (→ Reason). Thought cannot get behind life (Dilthey). Reality, which thinking filters through an apparatus of simplification, is indescribably more complicated (Nietzsche). Thinking involves a limited perspective that changes with the conditions of life. Given conditions shrink the horizon (Nietzsche). They are a totality that makes thinking possible but also limits it, so that it cannot fully grasp life.

In vitalism, "life" is a term for totality. Philosophy cannot master it in terms of idealism and historicism alone (H. Schnädelbach, 146). Nevertheless, Bergson, Klages, and Spengler again make life a specific metaphysical subject (→ Metaphysics) that can be experienced with absolute certainty in "intuition" (Bergson) and to which spirit is by nature antithetical (Klages). By setting thought, which is abstract, rigid, and fixed, in opposition to life and experience, which are concrete, temporal, and creative, these thinkers themselves think abstractly.

Vitalism later became very popular. With its criticism of the rationalizing and bureaucratizing (→ Bureaucracy) of life, it made an impact in literature (esp. in A. Gide, M. Proust, T. Mann, R. M. Rilke, and S. George) and on more popular writing. In Germany it also influenced the youth movement and → pedagogy. Its fervent polemic, its often crude dichotomies, and its fresh objectifying of life soon brought it into academic discredit (H. Rickert). Its "metaphysics of the irrational" was accused of preparing the way intellectually for → fascism (G. Lukács).

Modern assessments, however, lift Dilthey, Nietzsche, and Simmel out of "the vague, vitalistically toned productivity of life or the stream of consciousness" (J. Habermas, 143). Its acceptance in opposition to the prevailing positivism and neo-Kantianism led to the rise of → existentialism and philosophical → anthropology, with which vitalism merged. Together with → pragmatism, which was in many ways related to vitalism, these streams contributed to modern philosophy a theme that is still growing in intensity, that of the opposite of reason or of the incommensurable.

→ Romanticism; Spinozism; Subjectivism and Objectivism

Bibliography: K. ALBERT, *Lebensphilosophie. Von den Anfängen bei Nietzsche bis zu ihrer Kritik bei Lukács* (Freiburg, 1995) • F. BURWICK and P. DOUGLASS, eds., *The Crisis in Modernism: Bergson and the Vitalist Controversy* (Cambridge, 1992) • H. DRIESCH, *The History and Theory of Vitalism* (London, 1914); idem, *The Science and Philosophy of the Organism* (2d ed.; London, 1929; orig. pub., 1908) • F. FELLMANN, *Lebensphilosophie. Elemente einer Theorie der Selbsterfahrung* (Reinbek, 1993) • H. H. FREYHOFER, *The Vitalism of Hans Driesch: The Success and Decline of a Scientific Theory* (Frankfurt, 1982) • J. HABERMAS, *The Philosophical Discourse of Modernity: Twelve Lectures* (Cambridge, Mass., 1987) • K. LORENZ, "Vitalism," *The Natural Science of the Human Species* (Cambridge, Mass., 1996) 185-94 • G. LUKÁCS, *The Destruction of Reason* (Atlantic Highlands, N.J., 1981) • H. RICKERT, *Die Philosophie des Lebens. Darstellung und Kritik der philosophischen Modeströmungen unserer Zeit* (Tübingen, 1920) • H. SCHNÄDELBACH, *Philosophy in Germany, 1831-1933* (Cambridge, 1984) chap. 5, "Life" • M. A. WEINSTEIN, *Structure of Human Life: A Vitalist Ontology* (New York, 1979).

WERNER STEGMAIER

Vocation

1. Term
2. Old and New Testaments
3. Early Church
4. Middle Ages
5. Luther and Other Reformers
6. Modern Period

1. Term

The word "vocation," deriving from the Latin verb *voco,* "call," is nearly interchangeable with "calling." In popular usage "vocation" designates a secular job or career. Sometimes the term is limited to specific jobs, to service-oriented professions like social work, or to professions holding higher social status, such as medicine or law. "Vocation" is also used to designate the occupations of pastor, priest, nun, or monk. These popular uses restrict and secularize the more expansive and religiously charged meanings of vocation in earlier eras, and especially the era of the Protestant → Reformation.

2. Old and New Testaments

In the Bible, "vocation" primarily means the call to become a member of the → people of God and to take up the duties that pertain to that membership. Secondarily, it refers to special tasks, offices, or places of responsibility God assigns to particular individuals.

Terms for vocation permeate the Old and New Testaments. Gk. *kaleō* and its variants mean either "name" or "invite, call, summon." The two sets of meanings are not entirely separate, because in the Bible one's name frequently sums up the divinely given purpose or identity to which God calls that person. Heb. *qāhāl* refers to the people God has called together for service. The → Septuagint translates *qāhāl* with Gk. *ekklēsia,* which in the NT usually has the meaning "church," or, from the etymology (*ek,* "from, out of," and *klēsis,* "calling"), "called-out ones." God calls Israel and the church out of the world to minister to God in → worship and sends them back into the world to serve the world in God's name. Individuals have their callings within the corporate calling of God's people. The NT describes vocation as a "heavenly calling" (Heb. 3:1) and a "holy calling" (2 Tim. 1:9). It is the call that all Christians have in common.

In both the OT and the NT, God also calls particular individuals to specific tasks and offices. In the NT, church-related roles such as → prophet, → pastor, evangelist, and → deacon are vocations. There is debate about whether the NT provides a basis for

Martin → Luther's view of one's job or one's station in life as a vocation (see 5). The only place in the NT where *klēsis* (derived from *kaleō*) might have this meaning is 1 Corinthians 7:17-24, where Christians are exhorted to "abide with God" in the "calling" (*klēsis*) in which they were when they were "called" (*kaleō*, vv. 20, 24 ASV). Here "calling" refers to "condition" (so NRSV) in life, namely, being married or unmarried, circumcised or uncircumcised, slave or free. The main point is that the call to become a Christian relativizes differences in → class, status, or position. In his *Kirchenpostille* (1522; WA 10/1.308) Luther translates *klēsis* in 7:20 as *Beruf* (occupation). Though this rendering may not be fully justified, the larger NT insistence that believers lead a life "in the Lord" and "worthy of the calling to which you have been called" (Eph. 4:1) confers vocational meaning upon life in home and society, as well as in churches (see Eph. 4:2–6:9). "In the Lord" and "for the Lord" qualify every job, social role, and task, making it a vocation.

3. Early Church

During first three centuries after Christ, Christians formed a small, sometimes persecuted minority within the → Roman Empire. Vocation was understood largely as a call away from a fallen world structured by empire. Early church leaders condemned occupations tied to the imperial cult, such as municipal offices and the military, as well as those expressing Greco-Roman cultural values, such as acting and teaching. In many churches renouncing these professions was a condition of → baptism. The call of Christ often meant breaking ties with family and friends; it diminished one's social status and was costly. But household roles and social occupations not directly incompatible with discipleship were locations for living out the Christian vocation. As in the NT, the call relativized and subtly subverted life in the world.

After Constantine legalized Christianity in 313 (Edict of Milan) and Theodosius II later established it as the only acceptable religion of the empire (ca. 438), being a Christian elevated one's economic and social standing. Christianity became more worldly and less costly. Christians saw the empire as God's servant. Political positions, such as ruler, soldier, and municipal officer, were now affirmed as legitimate occupations for Christians. Monastic movements emerged during these years, partly in response to this comfortable and compromised Christianity. After his conversion → Augustine embarked on a path that led him to become → priest and → bishop, forsaking marriage and rejecting his former occupation of rhetorician as a "chair of lies." In this context "vocation" came to mean an invitation to enter into a religious life apart from the world.

4. Middle Ages

The association of vocation with → monasticism persisted into the Middle Ages after the fall of the Roman Empire. Knights and nobles served worthy purposes, higher than those of the peasants and craftsmen. But only priests, monks, and nuns had vocations. In the later Middle Ages "vocation" became an optional invitation to live according to 12 "evangelical counsels," which went beyond God's commandments and were summed up in the vows of poverty, chastity, and obedience. Although the → Franciscans, → Dominicans, and other → religious orders were very active in serving the needs of society, monastic values came to prize the contemplative life above the active life. On this view it was not so much wrong to take up secular work, to marry and have children, as it was spiritually inferior to the vocations of priest, monk, or nun.

5. Luther and Other Reformers

Luther (1483-1546; → Luther's Theology) revolutionized the medieval notion of vocation. In keeping with his view of the priesthood of all believers (→ Priest, Priesthood, 4), Luther insisted that every Christian has a vocation and that every legitimate social sphere can become a calling if by faith one serves one's → neighbor through it. God calls princes, soldiers, farmers, spouses, household servants, and more to their stations in life. God prizes the work of the cobbler as much as that of the preacher. Like his contemporaries, Luther distinguished a spiritual calling (*vocatio spiritualis*) from one's outward calling (*vocatio externa*) Unlike his contemporaries, however, he insisted that all believers received both forms of God's call. Though distinct, the two forms are not two separate callings. They are two sides of the one call (*generalis vocatio*), in which God comprehensively claims the whole person.

The effect of this teaching was to infuse secular life with religious meaning and to challenge value structures based on wealth, prestige, and power. Contrary to both the Roman Catholic teaching of his day and to the popular advice of moralists, for Luther, a father changing his infant's dirty diapers is doing the holy work of angels and should imagine he is holding the baby Jesus in his hands.

Insofar as the priesthood and religious orders had become corrupt and turned away from the concrete needs of people, Luther grouped these occupations with those of thieves and pimps as occupations that could not be vocations. With these exceptions, Luther believed that the broader structures of social life — domestic, economic, and political — were ordained by God and served to meet human need. For Luther, God milks the cows through the milkmaids; the duties of one's stations are positive expressions of the will of God. The broader social orderings were not subject to the systematic critique to which he subjected the → Roman Catholic Church of his day. In spite of this optimism, Luther insisted that God looks not to the works of one's callings but to the obedience or disobedience to God's commandments in the midst of those works. One cannot assume that following the duties of one's stations is always in accord with God's will and commandments.

John → Calvin (1509-64; → Calvin's Theology) and → Puritan thinkers refined the Luther's doctrine of vocation. They retained Luther's idea that vocation includes all social spheres. Calvin distinguished occupation from vocation more consistently than did Luther, insisting that believers look to God's call in all their occupations. William Perkins (1558-1602) and Richard Baxter (1615-91) continued the basic lines set out by Luther and Calvin but, unlike them, begin to give more sustained attention to the relation of vocation to what moderns would call career choice.

6. Modern Period

Max → Weber's (1864-1920) influential study *Die protestantische Ethik und der Geist des Kapitalismus* (1905; ET *The Protestant Ethic and the Spirit of → Capitalism* [New York, 1930]) traces the process by which the Puritan emphasis upon labor as a calling contributed to the rise of → capitalism and the modern secular preoccupation with → work. Luther's "outward calling" increasingly became separated from the "spiritual calling." By seeking assurance of grace in the success and diligence of work, while at the same time emphasizing the virtues of thrift that led to amassing capital, Calvinists prospered. As they prospered, they lost the religious aspects of work as vocation. The work itself came to take on idolatrous proportions. Upward social mobility and increased freedom replaced service to one's neighbors as the goal of work. The result was the primacy of the economic domain, the secularization of vocation, and the restriction of vocation to paid work.

In the 20th century there were numerous calls to recover the early Reformers' notion of vocation,

both in Europe and North America. Neoorthodox theologians in Germany opposed using the idea of vocation to support conformism and an idolatrous sense of Germany's destiny. Dietrich → Bonhoeffer (1906-45) and Karl → Barth (1886-1968) shifted the theological basis of vocation from creation and providence, doctrines central for theologians supporting Hitler, to Christology. Emil Brunner (1889-1966) kept vocation based in creation orders but, in a revised way, intended to resist conformism. Some, like Jacques Ellul (1912-94), rejected the association of modern industrialized and technologized work with vocation. But most theologians called for its renewal. All strove to resist simplistic equations of God's call with the demands of one's station. Their aim was to reverse the secularization of vocation, re-emphasizing its comprehensive grasp not only of paid work but of all social spheres, and to recover the religious dynamism of the original idea.

Since the 20th century, Roman Catholic teaching about vocation has essentially agreed with that of Protestantism. Though it might not often refer to labor as a vocation, it is clear that for Catholic teaching paid work participates in God's creative and redemptive purposes. Engaging in work constitutes part of the image of God in human beings. Papal encyclicals explicitly designate domestic roles as vocations (e.g., Leo XIII, *Rerum novarum* [1891]; John Paul II, *Laborem exercens* [1981] and *Centisimus annus* [1991, on the 100th anniversary of *Rerum novarum*]). Though popular Catholic usage still tends to use "vocation" and "calling" to refer to a religious occupation, the official teaching has clearly expanded their meaning to embrace all of life.

The doctrine of vocation is deeply linked with other central Christian ideas and has profound practical implications for the Christian life. God, as Creator and Redeemer, is the one who calls people to faith and new life. The call of the Redeemer must reshape life amid the varied vocations God assigns to all people as provident Creator. The doctrine of vocation presupposes that divine → providence, rather than fate or → chance, has shaped each individual's life so that the varied social locations are assigned by God as specific places for expressing love for God and neighbor. God's continuous creative activity is expressed through the acts of care, mercy, and justice undertaken amid one's callings.

Though there may be rare exceptions, God's call and callings are mediated. Creation itself is calling (Ps. 19:1-4). Jesus called the → Twelve (Mark 3:13-19 and par.). Ananias prayed for Saul, restoring his sight and filling him with the Spirit (Acts 9:10-19). God's call comes through the preaching and teaching ministry of the church. It often is experienced in discernment of needs, gifts, and opportunities for service.

The idea of vocation can become either a catalyst or an opiate. Strands of Luther's idea of vocation were twisted to support social conformity and resistance to change. The opposition of Luther (and Calvin) to restlessness and meddling in the affairs of others can slide into passive acceptance of one's own limited lot in life. But it can also be used to restrict totalitarian impulses in ways that challenge the status quo. Their high regard for authority can be used to justify mindless submission, but their ideas of vocation also contained explicit and implicit challenges to authorities who required disobedience to the will of God. As the call of the Creator and Redeemer, vocation opposes sinful, corrupt practices and institutions and demands reform, withdrawal, or resistance. The Christian must be "in but not of" this world insofar as it is fallen but also must support and reform this world insofar as it is created good and is being redeemed.

Bibliography: E. BILLING, *Our Calling* (Philadelphia, 1964) • P. MARSHALL, *A Kind of Life Imposed on Man: Vocation and the Social Order from Tyndale to Locke* (Toronto, 1996) • P. S. MINEAR, ed., *Work and Vocation: A Christian Discussion* (New York, 1954) • W. C. PLACHER, ed., *Callings: Twenty Centuries of Christian Wisdom on Vocation* (Grand Rapids, 2005) • D. J. SCHUURMAN, *Vocation: Discerning Our Callings in Life* (Grand Rapids, 2004) • M. VOLF, *Work in the Spirit: Toward a Theology of Work* (New York, 1991) • G. WINGREN, *Luther on Vocation* (Philadelphia, 1957).

DOUGLAS J. SCHUURMAN

Voluntarism

1. Term
2. History
   2.1. Ancient Greece to the Reformation
   2.2. Modern Period

1. Term
The term "voluntarism" derives from Lat. *voluntas,* "will." The correlative term *voluntarius* refers to acting of one's own accord. In everyday language, a voluntary decision or act is one free from coercion or external causation. More robust types of voluntarism assert that free acts are not determined even by a person's innate desires or characteristics, although freedom of choice may be circumscribed by the range of alternatives apparent to or deemed feasible by the chooser.

Empiricists who affirm that desire or passion is not under the control of reason are sometimes said to be voluntarists in a weaker sense. The following discussion, however, focuses on those who give prominence to free will as such.

Voluntarism and → determinism (and intermediate positions) offer competing accounts of the basis for decisions and actions. Debates about voluntarism occur in → psychology and, most especially, in → philosophy and → theology. They concern the nature and freedom, not just of the human will, but also of God's will. If will is primary and thus constitutive of not only the acts but also the very being of one who wills, is this also true of God?

2. History
2.1. *Ancient Greece to the Reformation*
Plato (427-347 B.C.) and Aristotle (384-322) concentrated on intellect and its objects and thus gave little attention to will. The ethical subjectivism of Protagoras (ca. 485-ca. 410) held that "man is the measure of all things." Plato countered that will serves our nonrational or desiring nature, which is properly controlled by knowledge of the Good. Under the constraint of such knowledge, a person chooses only what is good, since evil results from ignorance. Aristotle was perplexed by the phenomenon of *akrasia* (weakness of will), wherein a person deliberately chooses the worse of the known options (as in selecting unhealthy food). In the ancient world, the topic of will came to prominence only in conjunction with religious belief in culpable sin that is rightly punishable by a just God.

→ Augustine (354-430; → Augustine's Theology), the principal architect of the doctrine of original → sin, held that while human beings have free will in everyday matters, they are beset with an inherited sin and thus are unable to love and obey God as Adam and Eve could before the fall. The redeemed are given a new → freedom *(libertas)* that renders them able not to sin in this life, and unable to sin in heaven. Augustine's theology involves a robust voluntarism, a fully free and responsible human will, but only before the fall and not after it.

Peter Damien (1007-72) declared that the laws of logic for the creation are decreed to be what they are by God's omnipotent will and could have been different had God willed other laws instead. According to his extreme voluntarism, theological dialectic (reasoning) is of no value in understanding revealed → dogma. God can will even to change past events so that they become other than what they have already been.

Thomas Aquinas (ca. 1225-74; → Thomism)

sought to restrict voluntarism with respect to the deity by teaching that God wills his own goodness with necessity and wills other things (the creation) in accord with his goodness (*Summa theol.* I, q. 19). Because God's will is an attribute of (and hence subordinate to) his perfect being, God is not free to be other than he is. God is not, however, obliged to will created things to be perfect too but only to make them good in their appropriate kind and degree. Such a God is incapable of willing evil.

→ William of Ockham (ca. 1285-1347) and other late medievals said that God is free to will anything not involving logical contradiction, that God has *potentia absoluta* (absolute → power). God's *potentia ordinata* enacts what he actually chooses to will for the creation. We know those ("arbitrary") decrees from Scripture. Somewhat in this vein is the "divine command" theory in recent theological ethics, which holds that we know which acts are morally good or evil only because God tells us so, not in virtue of that being discoverable rationally, apart from revelation.

Martin → Luther (1483-1546; → Luther's Theology) took an Augustinian stance on human freedom in *The Bondage of the Will* (1525, *LW* 33), a rebuttal to the optimistic humanism of → Erasmus (1469?-1536). For Luther, God's own will, however, is inscrutable, and we should not inquire whether it is limited in any way. Most pre-Enlightenment Christianity, Protestant and Roman Catholic alike, accepted an original human freedom in Adam yet affirmed the sinful will's need for transformation by grace. Only later and more liberal forms questioned the assumptions about the will underlying the doctrine of original sin.

2.2. Modern Period

In the modern era various philosophers espoused forms of voluntarism, with or without reference to religion.

René Descartes (1596-1650) thought that God could have willed different laws of logic and mathematics than the ones he actually decreed for the world. The Cartesian Occasionalists declared that the sole causal agent is God's will, which directly produces all phenomena, without use of secondary or created causes.

In going beyond the moral philosophy of Immanuel Kant (1724-1804), J. G. Fichte (1762-1814) portrayed the free self-positing of the I, or individual subject, as determining both the theoretical structures of its knowledge and the practical sphere of its ethical endeavor. Its freedom is qualified only by the need of free subjects to coexist in community. Arthur Schopenhauer (1788-1860) treated Kant's

"thing-in-itself," or fundamental reality, as will. He stated that individual striving results in a suffering remedied only by passive aesthetic experience and the cessation of desire. The later philosophy of F. W. J. Schelling (1775-1854) located will at the center of human personality as a person's free and primal self-determination as good or evil (disordered). His *Ages of the World* (1811-15) depicted God as dynamic and consisting of two poles, as an ultimate will and as God's own structured being that this divine will freely and timelessly brings about. This portrait vividly contrasts with mainstream theology's conception of an eternal, immutable, necessary divine perfection.

Søren → Kierkegaard (1813-55) espoused the infinite passion of → faith, construed as a leap of the will unsupported by reason, and titled one of his religious works *Purity of Heart Is to Will One Thing* (1846). Friedrich → Nietzsche (1844-1900) took an opposite course, rejecting religious belief in free will as a device of theologians to convince believers of their culpable sinfulness before God, a belief he dismissed as "an insanity of the will." He simultaneously extolled "the will to power" as vital human energy rooted in one's instinctive, biological nature.

William James (1842-1910) endorsed "the will to believe" as a legitimate — indeed essential — factor in responsible decisions to adopt, and live by, religious, moral, and personal commitments. Jean-Paul Sartre (1905-80), an atheistic existentialist, declared that the person or subject is radically free and self-creating, that one's concrete existence comes about through one's free choices made from among the possibilities of which one is aware. His is an extreme voluntarism, in opposition to all philosophies and sciences that seek to objectify human beings, to treat them as "things."

Bibliography: Primary sources: Augustine, "On Free Will," *Augustine: Earlier Writings* (Philadelphia, 1953) • D. Erasmus, *Discourse on Free Will: Erasmus-Luther* (London, 2005) • J. Fichte, *The Vocation of Man* (LaSalle, Ill., 1965) • W. James, *The Will to Believe, and Other Essays in Popular Philosophy* (New York, 1897) • S. Kierkegaard, *Purity of Heart Is to Will One Thing* (New York, 1948) • M. Luther, *Martin Luther: Selections from His Writings* (ed. J. Dillenberger; New York, 1961) • F. Nietzsche, *The Will to Power* (New York, 1967) • Ockham, *William Ockham: Predestination, God's Foreknowledge, and Future Contingents* (New York, 1969) • Peter Damien, "On Divine Omnipotence," *Medieval Philosophy: From St. Augustine to Nicholas of Cusa* (ed. J. F. Wippel and A. B. Wolter; New York, 1969) 143-52 • Plato, *Protagoras* (Oxford, 1991)

• J.-P. SARTRE, *Being and Nothingness* (New York, 1956)
• F. SCHELLING, *Schelling: The Ages of the World* (New York, 1942; repr., 1967); idem., *Schelling: Of Human Freedom* (Chicago, 1936) • R. TAYLOR, ed., *The Will to Live: Selected Writings of Arthur Schopenhauer* (New York, 1962) • THOMAS AQUINAS, *Summa theologiae: Parallel Latin and English Text* (61 vols.; London, 1964-81).

Secondary works: V. J. BOURKE, *Will in Western Thought* (New York, 1964) • R. F. BROWN, *The Later Philosophy of Schelling: The Influence of Boehme on the Works of 1809-1815* (Lewisburg, Pa., 1977) • E. GILSON, *The Christian Philosophy of St. Augustine* (New York, 1983) • A. MELE, *Irrationality: An Essay on Akrasia, Self-Deception, and Self-Control* (Oxford, 1987).

ROBERT F. BROWN

Voodoo

Voodoo, or *vodun* (as it is often known in African countries), is a religion of Caribbean origin, developed in Haiti by peoples of African descent in response to the social, political, economic, and religious oppression consequent on transatlantic → slavery. It originated largely against the background of both the remembered religious past of the slaves, primarily from Dahomey (since 1975, named Benin), and the rites of the → Roman Catholic Church as propagated by the Spanish and French. It may be seen as an attempt to answer the age-old questions of the meaning and purpose of life, and of how to survive in the present.

Voodoo apparently began to take shape in the 18th century, following the French Code Noir (Black Code), which prescribed → baptism into the Roman Catholic faith for all slaves and at the same time outlawed all other public forms of religious expression. Borrowing and reinterpreting the religious symbols of the dominant society and of African religious expression, voodoo is a religion of both protest and appeasement. As such it is both a source of societal and personal healing and also a tool used by leaders of political and social revolt.

Since voodoo cannot be controlled, it has been held in suspicion by many governments, even when practiced by them. It has no hierarchy and is a movement of the "spirit" dependent on psychological trance for its messages and on oral tradition for the perpetuation of its rituals. It is a way of living; its devotees find in it serviceable answers to the events of every day. The seemingly syncretistic nature of its religious practices (→ Syncretism), the absence of centralized authority, its secrecy, and its location in the underclass invite active opposition from the state, as well as from Roman Catholic and Protestant churches.

Voodoo shares with Christian faith a concern for → revelation and intercession. There is a belief in one God, who is the supreme deity and to whom worship and reverence are due. This God is distant, however, and must be approached via intermediaries called *loa*s. These are spirit beings who do the bidding of humans in prayer, somewhat similar to the → saints in Roman Catholic theology. For instance, the *loa legba*, who is the "spirit of openings," is equated with St. Peter, "the keeper of the keys." The voodoo belief in the human → soul is somewhat akin to the ideas of the OT. The life-force of an individual is considered permanent, continuing after physical death in a form that would allow the slave to return to Africa. Here there is much in common with the understanding of the ancestor in African religion. The dead are therefore central to voodoo, and in some areas their intercessory functions are considered only slightly less important than those of the *loa*s, although the value put upon the dead is dependent upon the manner and interpreted cause of their death.

Voodoo, in common with all religions, has both social functions and taboos. Its celebrations are times for music, storytelling, card playing, eating, and dancing, times in which the devotees and the deity participate. Flower arrangements, paintings and drawings, numbers, "spiritual writings," and pictures of Roman Catholic saints are present on the voodoo altar and provide a mystical location for the intersection of the visible and invisible worlds. This nexus can have a positive or negative value as these altar objects act as either → sacrifice or → taboo and are believed to grant tangible benefits to the devotee either as reward or protection from peril.

In recent years voodoo has accompanied Haitian immigrants to the United States and Europe, undergoing significant adaptation and modification in each place. In Haiti itself, urbanization, the dominant cultural influence of → Protestantism and evangelicalism (→ Evangelical Movement) during the U.S. occupation (1915-34) and afterward through mission agencies, the dissemination of Western medicine, and the increasing inclusion of the black underclass in government and church leadership have caused the importance of voodoo to diminish. It nevertheless remains an exotic tourist attraction and the subject of novels and films. As with all religions, its vestiges remain faithful to its deepest nature as a means for protest and survival, albeit hidden in remote hills and underdeveloped slums and valleys.

Bibliography: L. G. Desmangles, *The Faces of the Gods: Vodou and Roman Catholicism* (Chapel Hill, N.C., 1992) • M. Fernández Olnos and L. Paravisini-Gebert, *Creole Religions of the Caribbean: An Introduction from Vodou and Santería to Obeah and Espiritismo* (New York, 2003) • L. Hurbon, *Dieu dans le vaudou haïtien* (Port-au-Prince, 1987) • J. J. Jean, *God in the Haitian Voodoo Religion* (Pittsburgh, 2004) • M. S. Laguerre, *Voodoo Heritage* (Beverly Hills, Calif., 1980) a classic book of songs used in the rituals • C. Michel and P. Bellegarde-Smith, eds., *Vodou in Haitian Life and Culture: Invisible Powers* (New York, 2006) • G. M. Mulrain, *Theology in Folk Culture: The Theological Significance of Haitian Folk Religion* (Frankfurt, 1984) • M. Riguad, *Secrets of Voodoo* (trans. R. B. Cross; New York, 1970) • G. E. Simpson, *Black Religions in the New World* (New York, 1978); idem, *Religious Cults of the Caribbean: Trinidad, Jamaica, Haiti* (3d ed.; Rio Piedras, P.R., 1980).

HORACE O. RUSSELL

Vow

1. Term
2. Biblical Aspects
3. In Theology
4. Current Discussion

1. Term

Very much like an → oath, a vow is a solemn promise to do or not to do something. In the history of religion it had its origin in the *do-ut-des* concept of → sacrifice (i.e., reciprocity): it was made in order to make the deity kindly disposed or to secure divine help in an emergency. To be distinguished from a vow that is conditioned on a reciprocal act on the part of the deity is the unconditional vow; when such a vow is valid for all time, it is called eternal.

2. Biblical Aspects

In Israel the place of the vow was between sacrifice and → prayer. It frequently occurs in the OT, almost always in the positive form of a promise to do something. Its frequency suggests popular → piety but is also based on Israel's → covenant relationship with God and expresses its certainty of being heard. Vows of renunciation (→ Asceticism) are uncommon. Significant in this connection is the vow of the → Nazirites (Judges 13–15; 1 Samuel 1; Numbers 6).

If there is some progressive questioning of the vow in the OT, it was unchallenged at → Qumran and became a fixed element in later Jewish practice, two tractates of the → Mishnah and the → Talmud being devoted to it.

The NT presupposes Jewish practice but sharply criticizes its casuistry. We see an example in the condemnation by → Jesus of the vow that relieves of the duty of supporting parents (Mark 7:9-13). As Jesus sees it, this practice is totally contrary to the OT precept.

We find an example of the Nazirite vow in the → primitive Christian community (Acts 21:23). There is allusion to → Paul's taking of this vow in Acts 18:18, and he adopted a nuanced position vis-à-vis celibacy according to 1 Cor. 7:25-31. In the early Christian ethics of → discipleship, Paul's example led to the point at which the vow seemed to open up the possibility of a stricter following of Jesus.

3. In Theology

In the theology of vows in the early church, which related mostly to → celibacy for the sake of the kingdom of heaven (→ Marriage), the vow was regarded as a dedication of life and consecration to God that involved a → perfection above the mere performance of duty and that gained special merit. → Poverty, chastity, and → obedience were the classic themes (Matt. 19:21; 19:12; 16:24). These were achieved by free decision in the community life of → monasticism.

This step of a specific act of honoring God and ensuring → salvation ran up against the theological opposition of M. → Luther (1483-1546; → Luther's Theology) in *De votis monasticis iudicium* (On monastic vows, 1521; WA 8.573-669). Luther's objection was closely linked to his doctrine of → faith, which he developed over against works righteousness. Like CA 27, Luther was also opposing legalism — in particular, the inadequately defined relation between baptism and the monastic vow (B. Lohse).

John → Calvin (1509-64; → Calvin's Theology) dealt with the issue of vows in *Inst.* 4.13.1-21.

In the → Orthodox Church there is not only the monastic vow but also the marriage vow, in which the partners swear lasting fidelity to one another, the special vow taken by → priests, and the → starets vow.

4. Current Discussion

Controversial discussion today is guided on the one hand by the Roman Catholic definition of the vow in 1983 → CIC 1191.1 as "a deliberate and free promise made to God about a possible and better good [*bonum melius*]." On the other hand, we have the more open attitude on the Protestant side that does not totally rule out vows but integrates them theologically as a part of → sanctification (the baptismal vow, the confirmation vow, the ordination vow, the vow on taking up a church office), though with no expectation of a performance of more than is required. With due regard to the moral freedom of those who take a vow, the vow as an act of confirmation gives public evidence of a serious will to engage in an activity related to the community or to accept more fully a Christian lifestyle.

→ Ordination; Pilgrimage

Bibliography: T. W. Cartledge, *Vows in the Hebrew Bible and the Ancient Near East* (Sheffield, 1992) • G. Lanczkowski et al., "Gelübde," *TRE* 12.300-316 • B. Lohse, *Mönchtum und Reformation. Luthers Auseinandersetzung mit dem Mönchsideal des Mittelalters* (Göttingen, 1963) • M. R. E. Masterman, "Vow (in the Bible)," *NCE* (2d ed.) 14.590-91 • H. Thielicke, *Theological Ethics* (2 vols.; Philadelphia, 1966-69) 2.376-405 • B. B. Thurston, *Religious Vows, the Sermon on the Mount, and Christian Living* (Collegeville, Minn., 2006) • A. Wendel, *Das israelitische-jüdische Gelübde* (Berlin, 1931).

Karl Schwarz

Vulgate → Bible Versions

W

Waldenses

1. Description
2. History
3. The Modern Period
4. Churches
   4.1. Extent
   4.2. Theology
   4.3. Organization
   4.4. Relations with the State
   4.5. Ecumenical Contacts

1. Description

From the Middle Ages the Waldenses have been a unique historical movement of evangelical protest that has had a changing and painful history right up to our own period (see 4). The movement has been called "a body with two souls." The medieval history of the Waldenses up to 1532 continues to influence the thinking of the group. For 350 years the Waldenses formed a widespread if scattered community in southern, central, and eastern Europe. Its survival is remarkable when we consider the steps taken to eradicate it as heretical and the severe persecutions it endured, especially in Italy and the Duchy of Savoy, which was so loyal to the papacy. The Waldenses have not forgotten their past, even if their more modern history is determinative for today's Waldensian congregations.

2. History

The English cleric Walter Map (ca. 1140-ca. 1209) stated that the Waldenses had no fixed abode but wandered two by two through the land with bare feet and in woolen clothes, just as the apostle had done. Naked, they followed the naked Christ. Map had met the Valdesi in Rome and gave this description in his *De nugis curialium* (ed. M. R. James; Oxford, 1914). In 1179 the Waldenses had come to the Third Lateran Council, where they urgently requested Alexander III (1159-81) for permission to preach.

2.1. The name "the Poor Men of Lyons" carries a reference to the city that was the home of the Waldenses' founder, Valdes (Valdensis, Valdes, Gualdensis, and, later, Waldo; ca. 1140-ca. 1217). Valdes's Christian name, Peter, is not mentioned in the early records but was probably added in the 14th century in order to give apostolic credibility to the movement and to show that Valdes rather than the → pope was the true successor of → Peter. Valdes was a well-to-do merchant who was led to renounce his riches when convicted by the saying of Jesus in Matt. 19:21. Jesus' → Sermon on the Mount and the commissioning of the disciples showed Valdes that he must take up → preaching in native tongues.

The apostolic life was one of poverty and preaching (→ Discipleship 2.1; Poverty 3-5), which characterized the movement. It aimed to restore to the church its long-forgotten apostolic lifestyle. Radical poverty rather than preaching of the Word was the cause of a dispute between "the Poor Men of Lyons" and "the Poor Men of Lombardy," who had founded "worker congregations" in Upper Italy. The Donatism (→ Donatists 3) of the latter was hotly contested by the former. A meeting at Bergamo in 1218 brought some measure of unity but also recognized the division and the tensions to which it gave rise.

2.2. We learn from the early portrayal of the Waldenses what they took to be the meaning, content, and range of a "free preaching" of the → Word of God (libere praedicare verbum Dei). Such preaching, which was not offensive, was for them the core of their life and teaching. Nevertheless, the Council of Verona (1184) objected to their preaching and placed it under the ban of the church (→ Excommunication).

Waldensian preaching was free in many ways. Both men and women, both → clergy and laity, could preach. When accused of preaching without episcopal commission (→ Missio canonica), Valdes replied that he must obey God rather than men (Acts 4:19). Preaching of the Word of God was also not tied to specific times, places, or liturgical rituals (→ Liturgy). Itinerant preaching gave the Word mobility in apostolic fashion (Matt. 10:5-15). The Waldenses preached on the streets, in marketplaces, and in private houses. Also, the words and acts of Jesus and the apostles rather than hagiography (→ Lives of the Saints) formed the theme of their proclamation. They learned the biblical Word in their heart and stored it up in their memory so that they could give it to people literally in their everyday, native speech, not in Latin. Finally, it was preaching without commentaries (sine glossa). It enabled Valdes to preach the Word without ecclesiastical or academic interpretation, just as similar ideas freed → Francis of Assisi (1181/82-1226; → Franciscans 1) some 30 years later.

2.3. A special feature of the medieval Waldenses was that they not only freely preached the Word but also tried to follow literally the Sermon on the Mount. Their refusal to take → oaths was of great sociopolitical consequence, for it challenged the religiously based unity of social institutions. Voluntary poverty also offered a spiritual challenge to the dominant economic structures (E. Buonaiuti), as refusal to take the oath ran contrary to the existing political order (A. Molnár). Religious dissidents thus came to be seen as political rebels.

The Waldenses also rejected the → Donation of Constantine as a sign and cause of the secularization of the church. In 1458 the Waldensian bishop in Germany, Friedrich Reiser (1400-1458), told the → Inquisition that by the grace of God he was the bishop of the faithful in the church of Rome that spurned the Donation of Constantine. His criticism of the "Constantinian" church was theological as well as ethical. The Waldenses' biblicism also taught them to reject such traditional doctrines as → purgatory, veneration of the → saints, and all prayers, masses, and almsgiving on behalf of the dead.

2.4. The Waldenses saw themselves as the "good part" of the universal church, in distinction from the "church of the wicked" (ecclesia malignantium, Ps. 25:5 Vg; cf. "company of evildoers," 26:5 NRSV), which was alive and at work and even in control. They were constituted of full members (perfecti) and sympathizers (amici). Typical features were their meetinghouses (hospitia), their workers' societies in northern Italy that supported the itinerant preachers (laborancium congregaciones), and their schools (scholae), which met in private houses and in which all — men and women, poor and rich — could teach and learn by both day and night.

For many years some groups (e.g., in France) accepted as valid the → sacraments dispensed by Roman priests, but most of the Waldenses adopted a Donatist position and would not accept Roman Catholic sacraments. During the days of persecution, when they had to work out their theology, the evangelistic itinerant preachers also distributed the sacraments. In this way they became a church within the church. The → Eucharist, or love feast, as some called it, involved the blessing of bread, wine, and fish, not as an atoning sacrifice, but as a commemoration of the Lord's Supper (non in sacrificium vel holocaustum, sed in memoriam dominice cene, as a statement from 1320 reads). The Waldenses also had a foot-washing ceremony on Maundy Thursday (John 13:1-17).

2.5. Not surprisingly, 50 years after their origin the Waldenses ran into severe persecution, according to the records of the Inquisition. A → crusade launched against → Islam also had heretics as its target: first the Cathari (→ Heresies and Schisms 2.3), then the Waldenses and others. Despite constant threats, however, the Waldenses spread throughout France, northern Spain, Italy, Switzerland, Germany, Austria, Bohemia, Moravia, and Hungary. The spiritual exchanges of the so-called Waldensian Hussite International, which developed with the rise of the closely related → Hussites in the 15th century (A. Molnár), enriched and strengthened the Waldenses theologically.

But persecution grew more fierce, and a new and bloody crusade took place in 1488. The Waldenses found a fortress in the Cottian Alps. At the

Synod of Chanforan (1532) the western group, though not unanimously, accepted the Swiss → Reformation (see 4.2). Some itinerant preachers maintained contact with the → Bohemian Brethren. Elsewhere in Europe the end came for the medieval Waldenses either through persecution or through gradual dissolution.

3. The Modern Period

The Reformation brought great changes for the Waldenses, a kind of death and resurrection. Their teaching, lifestyle, worship, spirituality, and congregational life were all profoundly transformed. Yet they still gave primacy to Scripture. This is the point of contact between the medieval and the modern Waldenses.

3.1. The Waldensian congregations became a small → Reformed church. In 1555 they built their first three churches and began holding their own services of public worship. They abandoned what J. → Calvin (1509-64) had criticized as a Nicodemus-like position (see John 3:1-10). New persecutions began, which in 1545 caused a bloodbath among the Waldenses in Provence, and which in 1560 wiped out all Waldenses congregations in Calabria. In 1560 Duke Emmanuel Philibert (1553-80) led a war against Waldenses in Piedmont and Savoy, which ended with the Treaty of Cavour (1561). For about a century thereafter, the existence of Waldensian congregations was recognized. For the first time, though, the principle of → *cuius regio eius religio* had been broken in Europe.

In 1655 a new and gruesome persecution was launched that horrified Protestant Europe (see Milton's famous sonnet "On the Late Massacre in Piedmont" [1655], commemorating the Easter massacre that year of Waldenses). With the revocation of the Edict of Nantes in 1685 (→ Huguenots), Duke Victor Amadeus II of Savoy (1675-1730) in 1686 ordered the Waldenses to either recant or emigrate. A spontaneous armed revolt was suppressed, the Waldensian valleys were devastated, and the Waldenses suffered exile or imprisonment in Piedmont.

In 1689 one group under Henri Arnaud (1641-1721) fought their way back to their native valleys, and some months later the duke welcomed them back in peace. But refugees from the French valleys sought new homes in Württemberg, Hesse, and Baden.

3.2. After bloody persecution came legislative discrimination. In 1848, however, King Carlo Alberto of Piedmont (1831-49) granted the Waldenses all civil and political rights. The freedom of

religious → tolerance was the second major turn in their history. The unification of the kingdom of Italy then opened up for them a field of fruitful endeavor. Finding adherents in all parts of the country, they formed congregations and built churches both in the important cities and in outlying villages. Throughout Italy the Waldensian church became a scattered → diaspora community, though it was still a people's church in the Alpine valleys. The founding of a theological seminary at Turin in 1855 furthered the process of its rooting in Italian culture. This seminary moved to Florence in 1860 and to Rome in 1922. In the late 19th and early 20th centuries many Waldenses had to emigrate for economic reasons, mostly to Uruguay or Argentina (see 4.1).

The Concordat of 1929 (→ Italy 1.2) left a place for the Waldenses, and the 1948 constitution granted them → religious liberty. But it was the 1984 agreement between the Italian government and the church that allowed the Waldenses to achieve their goal: to live and work in freedom as a Protestant church (see 4). Vatican II changed the religious situation. Protestant believers were treated as "separated brethren" rather than as an offensive, alien body (*Unitatis redintegratio* 3). The → pluralism (§1) of the culture and public opinion helped contribute to this end. Despite their differences, modern Waldenses share much in common with the → Roman Catholic Church. We could call the situation one of dialectical ecumenism.

Bibliography: G. Audisio, *The Waldensian Dissent: Persecution and Survival, c. 1170-c. 1570* (New York, 1999) • E. Cameron, *The Reformation of the Heretics: The Waldenses of the Alps, 1480-1580* (Oxford, 1984); idem, *Waldenses: Rejections of Holy Church in Medieval Europe* (Malden, Mass., 2000) 11-60 • R. Cegna, *Medioevo cristiano e penitenza valdese* (Turin, 1994) • G. Gonnet and A. Molnár, *Les Vaudois au Moyen Âge* (Turin, 1974) • G. G. Merlo, *Valdesi e valdismi medievali* (Turin, 1991) • A. Molnár, *A Challenge to Constantinianism: The Waldensian Theology in Middle Ages* (Geneva, 1976); idem, *Die Waldenser. Geschichte und europäisches Ausmaß einer Ketzerbewegung* (Göttingen, 1980) • A. Molnár, A. Armand-Hugon, and V. Vinay, *Storia dei Valdesi* (3 vols.; Turin, 1974-80) • C. Papini, *Valdo di Lione e i "poveri nello Spirito." Il primo secolo del movimento valdese, 1170-1270* (Turin, 2002) • P. Ricca, ed., *Valdesi, metodisti e pentecostali in dialogo* (Turin, 2002) • K. H. Ruggiero, *And Here the World Ends: The Life of an Argentine Village* (Stanford, Calif., 1988) • P. Stephens, *The Waldensian Story: A Study in Faith, Intolerance, and Survival* (Lewes, Sussex,

1998) • G. Tourn, *The Waldensians: The First Eight Hundred Years (1174-1974)* (New York, 1980).

Paolo Ricca

4. Churches

4.1. *Extent*

The modern Waldensian churches are just a remnant of what was once a significant European movement. During the 16th and 17th centuries, after becoming linked to the → Reformation, they survived in only two Alpine valleys close to the Italian-French border. By the early 19th century they were reduced to 13 congregations located in a very small area of western Piedmont (in the Valli Valdesi, or Waldensian Valleys), stifled by very oppressive state legislation.

For Italy the 19th century was one of liberal revolution. Quite paradoxically, Piedmont became the center of this revolution, which in less than 20 years unified the entire country. On February 17, 1848, the Waldenses received basic civil rights, followed by a growing religious freedom. In the same period a movement of Waldensian expansion took place, with immigrant congregations being formed in Uruguay and Argentina under the name Iglesia Evangélica Valdense del Rio de la Plata. In → Italy (§2) → evangelism led to the formation of many new Waldensian congregations, from Piedmont to Sicily, from Venice to Rome. Today one-third of the church members and two-thirds of the pastors do not come from Waldensian stock but are children or grandchildren (sometimes great-grandchildren) of converts from Roman Catholicism (→ Conversion 2) or from nonbelief.

Over the years Italian Methodists (→ Methodism; Methodist Churches) grew closer to the Waldenses. In 1979 a covenant of integration was accepted, and Waldenses and Methodists merged in the Chiesa Evangelica Valdese, Unione delle Chiese Metodiste e Valdesi. A famous member of the united church, Professor Giorgio Spini (1916-2006), was a Methodist; his son Valdo Spini, a well-known socialist politician, is Waldensian.

Today the number of church members declines, but the number of sympathizers slowly increases; many of them are disappointed Roman Catholics or secularists abandoning → atheism. They join the Waldensian church after a time of biblical preparation.

In Italy in 2006 the Evangelical Waldensian Church had 19,600 full members (of whom 17,000 were Waldenses, and 2,600 Methodists). There were 2,700 children and teenagers under catechetical instruction, and 3,300 additional persons were considered adherents or sympathizers. The 138 congregations (39 of them Methodist) are served by 95 pastors (of whom 21 are women). The seminary in Rome (Facoltà Valdese di Teologia) has 5 full-time professors and about 30 students (many of them non-Italians). Extension classes also minister to the laity, with strong interest on the part of Pentecostals and members of other → free churches. The seminary publishes the theological quarterly *Protestantesimo*.

The Waldensian publishing house, Casa Editrice Claudiana, is in Turin. The historical society Società di Studi Valdesi is in Torre Pellice, in the heart of the Waldensian Valleys, together with the Waldensian Cultural Center, which oversees a library of 80,000 volumes and the archives of many Italian Protestant churches. In addition, the church sponsors five youth centers, a high school, five bookshops connected with the Claudiana, eight homes for the aged, and other social institutions like the Centro Diaconale "La Noce" in Palermo and the Servizio Cristiano in Riesi, Sicily.

Also in 2006 the Waldensian church in South America numbered 11,000 members, with 24 pastors ministering to 31 congregations.

4.2. *Theology*

The theological position of the Waldenses has changed over the years. In the Middle Ages the Waldenses were a popular protest movement seeking to follow the → Sermon on the Mount. They strongly criticized the use of violence (→ Force, Violence, Nonviolence) and adopted a life of → poverty. Then in 1532, at the Synod of Chanforan, they accepted Reformation theology (→ Reformation 4.13); between 1550 and 1560 the Waldensian theology became thoroughly Calvinist. The Waldensian confession of faith, issued during a terrible persecution in 1655, is a summary of the Confession of La Rochelle (1571), which is a modified form of the Gallican Confession (1559) of the French Calvinists. The confession of faith is now interpreted in the light of the → Leuenberg Agreement and has been accepted also by the Italian Methodists. New pastors sign it on the day of their ordination. The 19th-century *risveglio* (revival), as well as → liberal theology, had an impact on Waldensian thinking, though not undermining its Reformed foundation.

From the 1930s to the 1960s the theology of Karl → Barth (1886-1968; → Dialectical Theology) was extremely influential. It was, and still is, regarded as a biblical → orthodoxy that is open to dialogue with contemporary culture and to political engagement. Barthianism therefore became the theology of antifascist Waldensians and Methodists, many of whom took an active part in the armed resistance movement in 1943-45. The → Barmen Declaration is viewed as the best 20th-century confession of faith.

Barthianism continued as the theology of the Waldensians and Methodists who wanted to be socialist without denying a Christocentric faith. Their dialogue with → Marxism was largely influenced by the theology of H. Gollwitzer (1908-93; → Marxism and Christianity 3). Then came a pacifist era (still under Gollwitzer's influence), which was followed by a strongly feminist phase (→ Feminism; Feminist Theology). Today the greatest theological concern comes from the challenge of a multicultural society (→ Pluralism).

Not all Waldenses and Methodists adopted a Barthian or post-Barthian orientation. They all agreed, however, that they must develop a → political theology that respects the separation of → church and state. The Intesa (i.e., agreement) reached on February, 21, 1984, with the Italian state gives appropriate expression to this separation.

4.3. *Organization*

4.3.1. In → church government the Waldensian churches are presbyterian, but with a congregationalist accent. Local congregations still enjoy a good deal of autonomy — the larger ones own their own buildings, choose their own pastors, and are responsible for → evangelism in the areas around them.

Congregations in the same region (e.g., Sicily or Tuscany) are connected in a *circuit* (a Methodist feature that was adopted also by the Waldenses as part of the Covenant of Integration). The circuit helps the local congregations in matters of → pastoral care, preaching, and evangelism. Three to six circuits constitute a *district*, which handles only administrative matters.

On the national level, the Synod, composed of some 80 pastors and 100 lay members, holds a key position as the church's highest judiciary. Through full and vigorous debate, it adopts church positions on all internal and external issues, including theology. The Synod, which meets yearly, ordains new pastors and gives the highest level of visibility and cohesion for the Waldensian and Methodist diaspora. Each year the Synod elects an executive committee, the Tavola Valdese (Waldensian table, or board), composed of pastors and lay members, Waldensians and Methodists. In August 2005 Maria Bonafede became moderator of this board, the first woman to be elected to this position. The Synod also elects a Methodist Committee (Opera per le Chiese Metodiste che sono in Italia), which deals with ecumenical and economical concerns of the Methodist congregations.

4.3.2. Italian Waldensian and Methodist pastors receive their training at the Facoltà Valdese di Teologia. In South America, Waldensians receive pastoral training in the Protestant Seminary ISEDET, in Buenos Aires, Argentina.

The body of pastors *(corpo pastorale),* which is responsible for the theological life of the church, enjoys high prestige. The pastors discuss all doctrinal, cathechetical, and liturgical matters (→ Catechism; Liturgy; Teaching Office 2), as well as supervise candidates for the ministry and nominate the professors of theology. Final confirmation of all these matters, though, comes from the Synod.

4.3.3. The Waldensian Church of the Rio de La Plata has its own synodical meeting, which elects its own board (the Mesa Valdense) and moderator. Issues of doctrine, organization, and intercommunion are settled through concurring decisions of the Italian and South American synodical meetings.

4.4. *Relations with the State*

The law adopted by the Italian Parliament on August 11, 1984, on the basis of the 1984 Intesa, governs the relationship between → church and state. It gives full recognition to the "autonomy and independence" of the Waldensian church and regulates church weddings and pastoral care in prisons, hospitals, and other institutions.

A new Intesa reached in 1993 makes it possible for Italians to devote 0.8 percent of their personal taxes to the Waldensian church for social, cultural, and humanitarian work. Of this money, at least 30 percent is devoted to social initiatives in the Third World (usually in cooperation with the social agencies of larger Protestant churches). In 2006 the 19,600 Waldensians and Methodists were surprised to see that 204,000 Italians chose to devote their *otto per mille* (0.8 percent) to the Evangelical Waldensian Church. Such a figure attests to the relatively large national influence of this small church.

4.5. *Ecumenical Contacts*

The Waldensian and the Methodist churches were founding members of the → World Council of Churches and of the → Conference of European Churches. They are also members respectively of the → World Alliance of Reformed Churches and of the → Methodist World Council. They both also belong to the Community of Protestant Churches in Europe.

The Waldensian and Methodist churches belong to the Federazione delle Chiese Evangeliche in Italia. Founded in 1967, this federation includes Baptists, Lutherans (→ Lutheran Churches 2.3), the → Salvation Army, and other bodies. The federation is responsible for Protestant radio and television programs. In 2006 the Sunday Protestant radio service had 1.5 million listeners, and the twice-monthly Protestant TV program attracted 600,000 viewers. Today a very important work of the federation is its Servizio Rifugiati e Migranti (Office for refugees and immigrants). Its importance is rapidly increasing, for Italy is becoming a country of immigrants (→ Refugees). Many of them are Protestant and relate naturally to the various Protestant churches (esp. Pentecostal, Adventists, Baptists, Methodists, and Waldensian). The future of Italian Protestantism is no doubt multicultural.

Waldensians and Methodists have a special relationship with the → Baptists. The Synod and the Baptist General Assembly met jointly in 1990, 1995, 2000, and 2007. An official document was approved that declares full mutual acknowledgment of each other's pastors. Since 1993 the two parties have jointly published the weekly magazine *Riforma*. → Youth work has been united since 1969 in the Federazione Giovanile Evangelica Italiana and has a common monthly, *Gioventù evangelica*.

Dialogue is sought with the → evangelical movements (mostly Pentecostal), which now constitute the majority of the 400,000 Italian Protestants. A common statement of Trinitarian theology was issued in 2002 in cooperation with some of the Pentecostal groups, and in 2006, a statement on the authority of the Bible.

Relations with the → Roman Catholic Church are complex. Waldensians and Methodists are indeed not ready to accept papal authority, Marian devotion (→ Mariology), or the political power of the church. Furthermore, despite the Barthian orthodoxy of the Waldensian church, it is open to discussion regarding the modern issues of bioethics and → euthanasia, of the remarriage of divorced persons, and of → homosexuality. Such openness has caused some ecumenical tensions. Nevertheless, biblical ecumenism is cultivated both at the grass roots and at an academic level. An ecumenical translation of the Bible (the TILC, or Traduzione in lingua corrente) has been a great success (→ Bible Versions). Furthermore, an agreement about → mixed marriages has been worked out and officially approved by the Synod and by the Roman Catholic Conferenza Episcopale Italiana (2000).

Bibliography: S. AQUILANTE, F. BECCHINO, G. BOUCHARD, G. TOURN, and L. VIOLANTE, *Chiese e Stato nell'Italia che cambia. Il ruolo del protestantesimo* (Turin, 1998) • P. BILLER, *The Waldenses, 1170-1530: Between a Religious Order and a Church* (Aldershot, 2001) • G. BOUCHARD, *I valdesi e l'Italia* (2d ed.; Turin, 1990) • G. BOUCHARD and G. TOURN, *Turin and the Olympic Valleys: History of a Protestant Witness* (Turin, 2006) • E. CAMERON, *The Waldenses: Rejections of Holy Church in Medieval Europe* (Oxford, 2000) • R. GEYMONAT, *El templo y la escuela. Los Valdenses en el Uruguay* (Montevideo, 1994) • P. RICCA, ed., *Valdesi, metodisti e pentecostali in dialogo* (Turin, 2002) • G. SPINI, *Risorgimento e protestanti* (3d ed.; Turin, 1999) • G. TOURN et al., *You Are My Witnesses: The Waldensians across Eight Hundred Years* (Turin, 1989) • *The Waldensians: Eight Centuries of Witness* (DVD; text by G. Bouchard; directed by P. E. Landi; Turin, 2006).

GIORGIO BOUCHARD

Wandering Jew

Legend has it that when Jesus was exhausted on his way to the cross, a certain Jew refused him rest and has thus been condemned to wander forever until the → last judgment.

The legend occurs for the first time in a Bologna chronicle of the 13th century. In the centuries that followed, not least under the influence of growing → anti-Semitism in the Middle Ages, it spread in various forms to southern and western Europe. In these forms the Jew was called Buttadeus, Boutedieu, and similar names. He then became "Ahasuerus" in a historically significant *Brief Description and Account of the Wandering Jew* (1602). This pamphlet, which probably came from Gdańsk, told of a meeting of Paul von Eitzen (1522-98), a Lutheran theologian and later general superintendent, with Ahasuerus in Hamburg. The use of the name of the Persian king of Esther, Ahasuerus (= Xerxes), for the wandering Jew undoubtedly reflects hostility to the Jews, for the king appears in a bad light in the → Talmud and → Midrash. Ahasuerus then figured in scores of folk stories in the next centuries and became a popular figure in literature, especially that of → Romanticism. Even to the present, many poems, plays, and novels have been written about him, often satirically. Finally, the first films about Ahasuerus came out in 1926 (France) and 1935 (England).

From a critical standpoint, one may discern obvious anti-Semitic tendencies in the writings about Ahasuerus, and one must be on the watch for them even when they are not apparent. From a theological standpoint, one must note that the Jesus of the legend, who curses his opponent, does not correspond to the Jesus of the Bible, who commands → love for enemies and the → forgiveness of offenses and who suffered on the cross "for our sins."

Bibliography: G. K. ANDERSON, *The Legend of the Wandering Jew* (Providence, R.I., 1965) • G. HASAN-ROKEM and A. DUNDES, eds., *The Wandering Jew: Essays in the Interpretation of a Christian Legend* (Bloomington, Ind., 1986).

WOLFGANG G. RÖHL

War

Few issues have spurred Christian reflection and concern with such recurring intensity as the problem of war. From early Christians who pondered whether it was permissible to take up arms under Roman authority, to Christians in the 21st century vexed by problems associated with humanitarian interventions and the use of force in the global "war on → terrorism," Christianity presents no united front in its support of, or opposition to, war in general or any particular war. War has played a prominent part in the history of Christianity, during which various wars have been evaluated in terms of crucial religious teachings and enduring moral traditions. War has also provided illuminating modes of understanding political life and the human condition more generally. Technological advancements in the nuclear age and political changes in an era of globalization have produced challenges that highlight the need for continued religious reflection and further development of the traditions that animate such reflection. The following discussion cannot encompass fully the complex and variegated Christian experience of war, but we can gain some purchase on this subject by exploring some of the terminological, thematic, and typological problems of war and by examining certain political events and moral moments that have shaped what we might call the Christian conscience of war and peace. Surveying war's secular features will be important to this task, for Christian considerations of war always exist in some relation or opposition to secular understandings of war.

1. Terminology, Themes, and Conceptual Problems

In common parlance, war is often conceived as the collective pursuit and conduct of organized armed struggle or military combat operations against a government, nation, or people. War, in this sense, is an inherently political and public activity, distinct from individual or private acts of violence. Political theory going back to Thucydides (ca. 460-ca. 400 B.C.) thus associates war with the life of governments and political communities. Even religiously inspired forms of combat (as when God called Moses and Joshua to battle) signify the inescapable political dimensions of religious communities. In modern times, the view of Prussian general and strategist Carl von Clausewitz (1780-1831) that war is merely the continuation of politics by other means has shaped much military and political thinking on the subject. Modern warfare's pursuit of political ends has increasingly relied upon the highly controlled and organized application of military force, notwithstanding the perennial "fog of war," from which no battlefield in history has been immune.

There are, nonetheless, quite apolitical and orderless notions of war. Thomas Hobbes (1588-1679), for one, likened war to a prepolitical state of nature — a chaotic state of all against all where life is "solitary, poore, nasty, brutish, and short" (*Leviathan*). As evidence, witness the anarchic aftermath when governments dissolve. Politics, through the creation of a sovereign state, helps people escape the state of war. Yet even for Hobbes, states still inhabit a state of nature vis-à-vis one another, since no suprasovereign authority possesses the force needed to prevent them from resorting to war. War, then, is a liminal activity or sign of when politics succeeds or fails.

Traditional forms of war begin with an open declaration and end with a formal treaty. Sandwiched between periods of peace, war demarcates when the guns are angry and aglow. Because the world has never been without war or threat of war, however, war may come to be seen as a normal part of the human condition, empirically speaking, so much so that peace often is defined with respect to its own aberration: peace is the absence of war. Christianity, however, begins not with the aberration of war but with → peace (§1) as the normative condition of human life. The Christian measure of peace is not simply some intermittent silence of the guns but the pursuit and achievement of justice, order, and right relationship to God. Morally and theologically speaking, peace is a → norm for the way life ought to be. For the Christian conscience, this ethical norm always remains definitively prior, notwithstanding war's abiding historical reality.

Political notions of war entail a rather minimalist account of peace, which pales in contrast to Christian tenets of peace, considered both individually and collectively. For the individual Christian, peace involves moral values and social conditions richer and more robust than the mere absence of armed conflict. In the Hebrew Scriptures and the NT alike, peace is tied to pursuits of → righteousness, to → obedience and gratefulness to God, to loving God and one's → neighbor — friend, stranger, or enemy — and to → forgiveness (Isa. 57:19-21; Jer. 6:12-15; Luke 10:25-37; 2 Tim. 2:22). Peace is also intimately bound up with the cause of political order and justice, as suggested by John Paul II's refrain "No peace without justice" in his 2002 World Day of Peace message. Neither political stability nor social harmony can be assured when gravely unjust conditions threaten to give way to strife. One ought not shroud injustice under the banner of peace, lest the people cry "'peace, peace,' when there is no peace" (Jer. 6:14; 8:11). Justice, then, must be a constituent of true peace, as when → Augustine (354-430) speaks of one who, having "learnt to prefer right to wrong and the rightly ordered to the perverted, sees that the peace of the unjust, compared with the peace of the just, is not worthy even of the name of peace" (*De civ. Dei* 19.12). In short, the language of peace and the language of justice cannot be severed.

While Christians generally share a common commitment to peace, Christian differences over war hinge largely on different interpretations of violence and nonviolence. Pacifists unconditionally renounce war as an extreme form of violence (→ Pacifism); war constitutes perhaps the gravest departure from the life of peace that Jesus led and called his followers to emulate (Matt. 5:9). Jesus' teaching — resist not, turn the other cheek — is a command, not a suggestion; forswearing war is a central, nonnegotiable facet of Christian discipleship (v. 39). The sincere pacifist recognizes that when violence is inflicted upon oneself or others, a faithful Christian refuses to return violence for violence.

Historically, most Christians have not seen war and peace as diametrically opposed, for they are often related in more complex ways than may at first appear. Whereas pacifists make no distinctions between the end of peace and nonviolence as its means, nonpacifist Christians believe that war can be a morally justifiable instrument to bring about peace, particularly a just peace worthy of the name. Seen in this context, the Christian resort to war may be a civic obligation. (During the → Crusades and at certain moments in the European wars of religion, it was also a religious duty.) While Christians today generally renounce war on behalf of religion, they also generally believe that the civic call to arms should not ask them to compromise their religious faith or allegiance (→ Conscientious Objection).

Pacifist and nonpacifist positions alike are grounded on religious footing, but they differ over whether such a religious foundation allows or prohibits Christians from participating in or supporting war. Differences between pacifist and nonpacifist accounts of violence sharpen over the question of violent force and political legitimacy. Pacifists are apt to measure force or war along a scale of violence without making distinctions concerning the parties that employ force. Christian faithfulness, pacifists maintain, entails embracing Jesus' teachings over civic or state responsibilities to support or wage war. Nonpacifists, however, are more inclined to prescind the legitimate use of coercive force by civil magistrates, governments, and those charged with the community's protection from the violent crimes and actions of those who lack such public authority. In this sense, war that is justly waged by a legitimate authority may be destructive but is not violent; that is, it does not violate the moral-political order but, rather, upholds it by restraining those who do, by protecting citizens, and by preserving peace. (Of course a public authority's abuse or misuse of force in the service of an unjust cause also violates the moral-political order.) This approach tends to view force and war as morally neutral tools of coercion, albeit the most acute forms on a spectrum of coercive measures; the moral value of such measures is determined with respect to legitimate political authority, the pursuit of justice, and limits that govern the use of force. Other nonpacifists tend to think of political force as tragic, a lesser evil than that which its use intends to oppose.

Finally, the word "war" sometimes refers colloquially to a struggle or cause involving great mobilization of effort (e.g., the so-called war on poverty). While such usage is not treated here, it should be noted that, even when actual warfare or combat is not involved, Christians have routinely used war imagery and metaphors to express faith commitments or to exert them in the face of contending beliefs:

"army of piety" (→ Origen), *miles Christi* (medieval and later callings to be a soldier of Christ), the "mighty fortress" of God (M. → Luther), or even the modern Campus Crusade for Christ (→ Student Christian Movements).

2. Typologies

One may conceive and catalog war in many ways, since no single typology is fully adequate or coherent. A common *legal approach* distinguishes wars of aggression from wars of self-defense. → International law generally defines aggression with respect to actions that endanger international peace or that threaten the rights and security of an individual nation. International law has generally viewed war in a state-centered manner — involving hostile activities conducted by → states against other states. As evidence, consider resolution 3314 of the 29th session of the U.N. General Assembly: "Aggression is the use of armed force by a State against the sovereignty, territorial integrity or political independence of another State, or in any other manner inconsistent with the Charter of the United Nations" (December 14, 1974). Legally defined acts of aggression and war include armed attack, military bombardment, invasion or occupation, territorial annexation and blockade, and material support of other states or armed groups that carry out such acts.

However tidy such distinctions may appear, it is not always clear what is aggression and what is self-defense; certainly the different sides involved in any given conflict often contest how the terms are applied. The United States justified its preemptive war against Iraq in 2003 on grounds of self-defense. Iraq also invoked self-defense to justify military resistance to the invasion. In other circumstances, the same nation that develops nuclear weapons to defend itself may be charged with threatening behavior by its neighbors.

Alongside such legal categories are *ethical typologies,* the most common of which, as discussed by secular political philosopher Michael Walzer and many Christian ethicists, consists of "just" versus "unjust" wars. Such a determination is made through a form of ethico-political reasoning that applies moral criteria to assess the justice of waging war *(ius ad bellum)* and the justice of war's conduct *(ius in bello;* see 4.3). Ethical and legal reasoning often overlap and also may overlap with religious reasoning. In some cases, though, a *religious typology* transcends legal or ethical categories. For example, those invoking holy war, crusade, or jihad have made appeals based upon religious principles or in defense of common religious identity. In such cases,

a religious call to arms can displace the language of justice or trump secular legal norms that forbid violent means in the service of holy pursuits.

A *political typology* based upon the causality of war could include the following: wars over disputed territories (e.g., Kashmir; Israel/Palestinian territories), wars for or against independence and succession (e.g., the U.S. Revolutionary War and Civil War), or "great power" wars (e.g., Napoleonic wars), where political dominance is pursued or balance of powers is sought. (A single conflict indeed could involve several types of war.) Sometimes particular methods or tactics become defining features (e.g., nuclear war, guerilla war, terrorism) that overshadow other aspects. In some cases, the ideological character of war, while present in most forms of armed conflict, becomes so global or intense that it becomes all-encompassing to the point of engulfing lesser, regional conflicts. Such ideological battles may be secular in nature (e.g., the cold war between democratic and Communist nations) or tied to religion (as with the "global war against terror," which ostensibly targets militant Islamists).

Christians or governments representing Christian-majority populaces have been involved in all of these kinds of wars and the various typologies they represent. Undertaking the messy business of cataloging wars requires prudence in considering these (and surely other) ways of framing the problem, for a given war can cut across any single typology and involve several typologies at once. Europe's "wars of religion" well illustrate this point. The → Thirty Years' War, which ravaged Catholic and Protestant polities in Europe from 1618 to 1648, involved wars for independence or autonomy (the Dutch, from Spain; Switzerland and the Protestant German princes, from the Holy Roman Empire), as well as "great power" political struggles to diminish Hapsburg dominance and achieve political balance on the Continent. The confessional divisions between Catholics and Protestants (and among Protestants) fueled religious tensions and gave the war its ideological character. After prolonged years of bloodshed and financial ruin, the Thirty Years' War ended with the Peace of Westphalia (1648) and an international "constitution" that enshrined the very principles of sovereignty and prohibitions against aggression that ultimately would form the basis of modern-day international law and its attendant legal definitions of war.

3. Scripture and War

Christian consideration of war emerges against the backdrop of the portrayal of war in the Hebrew Scriptures. One finds clear statements of God's historical participation in war, including guidance and direction of Israel's political leaders (Numbers 31; Joshua 5–7). God issues very specific commands to Moses and Joshua to wage particular battles (e.g., in Midian, Jericho, and Ai), to employ specific strategies or methods (e.g., ambush), and to divide the spoils of battle in certain ways. These examples provide the most striking images of holy war — war waged explicitly on God's authority, for divine purposes — and are confined to specific periods of Jewish history. Examples of holy war appear nowhere in the NT. Holy war has endured, however, as an important mode of interpretation as Christians have discerned themes in war of chosenness, → covenant, → providence, jeremiad, and sacred history first chronicled in early Hebrew stories of battle.

For Christians, divinely commanded holy wars were succeeded by Jesus' preaching of nonviolence, love for one's enemies, and care for the poor, downtrodden, and defenseless. Jesus' life and ministry — his teachings extolling peace, his refusal to defend himself, his willingness to suffer violent death at the hands of the Romans, and his call to followers to be faithful → disciples — have inspired Christians who view war as fundamentally irreconcilable with their faith.

The NT, however, provides no record of Jesus' specific beliefs about the legitimacy or illegitimacy of war as a public or political activity. Some Christians have taken this silence as evidence that Jesus did not intend to proscribe Christian participation in war. In support of this view, some may refer to Jesus' encounter with the centurion, wherein Jesus extols the centurion's faith yet expresses no disfavor for his profession (Matt. 8:5-13). Jesus' teaching about "Caesar's coin" (Matt. 22:15-22) suggests that the state has a legitimate, though carefully delimited, authority to which Christians are bound; such authority presumably includes the lawful use of force. Similarly, while not addressing war per se, Paul professes that the state's authority, instituted by God, includes "the sword" of coercion through which justice is administered (Rom. 13:1-7).

4. Christian Encounters with War
Several key moments in the history of Christianity illustrate the contested and variegated approaches to war that Christians have adopted across the ages. Such debate makes it possible to speak of different Christian perspectives, if not traditions, of war and peace.

4.1. *Early Church*
The Christian experience of military service and war dates back to early days of the faith. The first

Christians, by virtue of their persecution by Roman authorities and their marginalized civil status, were often disinclined, if not ineligible, to serve in the military. From the writings of → Tertullian (ca. 160-ca. 225), we see that service in the Roman army presented considerable challenges to Christian faith. Christians considered idolatrous pagan practices that were part of Roman military service such as the taking of → oaths, the wearing of a crown, and participation in ungodly sacrifices and ceremonies. Tertullian did believe, though, that Christians could be good citizens by praying for their governments and their political leaders. Origen (ca. 185-ca. 254) counseled in kind, though his prohibition on Christian military service was tied not to the idolatry of military life but to the Christian commitment to higher laws and spiritual forms of → piety that transcend participation in violent earthly struggles.

There is little information about the precise number of early Christians who took up arms, though many Roman soldiers converted to Christianity while maintaining their military profession. The apparent lack of early Christian participation in the military is often adduced as an argument for the pacifist character of early Christianity. Some go on to argue that this era of Christian pacifism represents Christianity in its purest form, before it "lapsed" into a legal religion with the conversion of Roman emperor Constantine in 312, following his vision of the cross at Milvian Bridge, and then under later emperors became the state religion. Others, however, argue that Christians served in the military well before the time of Constantine. Historian James Turner Johnson suggests that there were significant numbers of Christian soldiers by the late second century, and perhaps tens of thousands of Christians distributed in the Roman army at the dawn of the fourth century before Constantine's conversion. The range of interpretations of early Christian ethics reveals ongoing struggles over the essence of Christianity and whether its true form requires a reversion to a pre-Constantinian ethic in which persecution is preferred over power. This pacifist position has been adopted by various → Anabaptists in history, as well as by leading contemporary Christian pacifists such as Stanley Hauerwas.

4.2. *Augustine*
The skepticism that some early Christians showed toward war or military service must be weighed against the writings of → church fathers such as Ambrose of Milan (ca. 339-97) and especially his student Augustine of Hippo, who is widely recognized as the forefather of the just-war tradition. Plato (427-347 B.C.), Cicero (106-43 B.C.), and other

pagan writers had earlier articulated certain moral instructions with regard to war. Augustine borrowed some ideas from them, while recasting existing pagan norms of his day within a Christian theological framework.

On the individual level, Augustine counseled nonresistance, hence nonviolence; he worried that inordinate desires even to preserve one's own life could arouse sinful dispositions in the individual, which could lead further to evil deeds. Augustine knew well the horrors of war and counseled against both the lusts that incite war and the lusts that war itself incites. Yet he also understood the reality of evil in the "earthly city" and the role of the state to confront such evil and render protection (including, in his day, protection of the church). Augustine spoke eloquently of the rueful and necessary duty of statesmen to wage just wars against forces that threatened life and resorted to violence. For Augustine, war is always tragic, undertaken out of sorrowful recognition of the injustice that necessitates it and the horrors and cruelty that often attend it (*De civ. Dei* 19.7).

What was prohibited for the private individual was permitted for the soldier, who acted in a public capacity; Augustine presumed that a legitimate political authority stood a better chance of restraining inordinate, willful desires, in part by channeling them toward a collectively just civic cause. Augustine contended that God uses political authority in general to achieve minimal levels of order, justice, and peace in the earthly realm. That war could serve as an acceptable means of achieving a peaceful or tranquil order *(tranquilitas ordinis)* attests to the always limited and imperfect measure of peace and justice one finds on earth; perfect peace and true justice, however, await in the Heavenly City.

4.3. *Just-War Thinking and the Middle Ages*
Throughout the Middle Ages, as further occasions arose for the use of force, theologians, canon lawyers, and political thinkers returned to Augustine, in some cases to deepen, in others to expand, Christian tenets of just war. In particular, Thomas Aquinas (ca. 1225-74; → Thomism) codified Augustine's views, elaborating more fully the three central conditions for a just war: sovereign (i.e., legitimate) authority, just cause, and right intention. For Thomas, peace is the only proper intention of war (*Summa theol.* II of II, q. 40, "On War").

Other leading Catholic thinkers followed suit, including Dominican Francisco de Vitoria (ca. 1480-1546) and Jesuit theologian Francisco Suárez (1548-1617). These Spaniards found inspiration from Thomistic methods and insights, furthering just-war thinking as they addressed questions about the lawful conditions, limits, and conduct of war. Extending Aquinas's treatment of morality and war beyond the traditional contours of Christendom to non-Christian peoples and lands, especially in the New World, they reinforced existing moral principles, urging that the rights and protection of the innocent be extended to the "other." Natural law and human law, Vitoria implored, "are not destroyed by want of faith." That is, the "primitive" or "pagan" religious status of non-Christians cannot be considered adequate reason to conquer them or deprive them of their lands. The limits and rules of war, Vitoria and Suárez believed, were not uniquely Christian but were part of the law of nations *(ius gentium)*, knowable by reason, accessible to all peoples, and in conformance with → natural law. Their views were central in showcasing the universal character and protections of just-war thought. These just-war thinkers, especially given later developments by the important Dutch jurist Hugo Grotius (1583-1645), codified and secularized what were often deemed Christian ethical tenets by transforming them into essential cornerstones of modern international law. Just war, as a form of moral discourse, displayed certain common features throughout the centuries, though it would wax and wane many times before one could begin to speak of it as an enduring, evolving, and resilient "tradition" of war and peace.

The contribution of Christian thought to moral and political instruction about war did not, however, prevent Christian abuses. The Crusades, waged from the 11th to the 13th centuries, fit neatly within the logic of just-war thinking at the time. They were, in fact, a special type of just war — a holy war — that seemed to meet the three *ad bellum* conditions: they were declared by a religious authority (the → pope), waged not simply for a just but also for a righteous cause (defense of the Holy Land), and waged out of love for beleaguered Christian compatriots, if not for Christ himself. Theologians such as Ivo of Chartres (ca. 1040-1115), → Bernard of Clairvaux (1090-1153), and Thomas Aquinas supported various Crusades not merely on limited just-war grounds but on full-fledged religious grounds. What eventually distinguished the Crusades was the belief that war could be a form of penance that possessed a salvific quality. This view that war could be holy or righteous seems hard to square with the angst voiced by Augustine. The Crusades thus signaled a new turn — but not for the better, as non-Christians and Christians now generally agree.

Just war has often been associated with Roman

Catholicism, given its indebtedness to natural-law thinking and to leading Catholic thinkers in the tradition. But insofar as Augustine was also a forefather of → Lutheranism and → Calvinism, so too were Martin Luther (1483-1546), John → Calvin (1509-64), and other Protestants keen to accept Augustine's moral justification for war. For Luther, just wars may be indispensable tools of the prince, whose mandate, under God, is to punish the wicked, protect the upright, and preserve peace. Luther makes it clear that war must always be the *last resort*, another tenet found in the just-war tradition; those who too precipitously wage war, Luther warned, will find defeat in God's wrath ("Whether Soldiers, Too, Can Be Saved," *LW* 46.87-138). Luther has been criticized for demanding subjects' uncritical obedience, even at the expense of great → suffering under absolutism, a view based largely on his support in putting down the Peasants' War (1524/25).

Calvin, like Luther, believed that God fully ordains the power of the sword, evoking his obsession with order and fearing the chaos that sin can unleash. Calvin firmly upheld the lawfulness of force to preserve tranquility, suppress sedition, and punish crimes (*Inst.* 4.20.11). Yet Calvin's → political theology has been attributed to supporting revolution, as it leaves room for the overthrow of greater magistrates by lesser magistrates. Moreover, Calvin's Puritan devotees, such as his fellow Genevans and followers of Oliver Cromwell (1599-1658) in England, viewed the sword as integral to the formation of holy commonwealths.

Not all Protestants sought to reconcile the use of force with their religious principles. Radical Reformers → Menno Simons (1496-1561) and Michael Sattler (1490?-1527) led Anabaptist communities that renounced all war and violence, doing so at great peril to themselves and their followers, given the persecution they experienced at the hands of both Catholics and other Protestants. Not all Anabaptists, however, were pacifists. Thomas → Müntzer (ca. 1489-1525) associated war with the coming of the last days, preaching in his "Sermon to the Princes" that "the sword is necessary to wipe out the godless."

4.4. *Peace of Westphalia*
The great schisms within Christianity following the Protestant Reformation erupted into their most destructive form during the Thirty Years' War, which engulfed nearly all of Europe. Peoples and polities pursued religious independence under the protection of the state (usually through the formation of official state churches). These tumultuous times also witnessed Protestant rulers and regions align-

ing to check the power of the Hapsburg dynasty, which was backed by the → Roman Catholic Church and the Holy Roman Empire. Religious freedom and freedom of conscience were at stake, especially for Protestants, though more than a few political interests were also at stake, including power, property, wealth, influence, and collective identity. But after 30 bloody years (including protracted efforts to end the war), Europe breathed a collective sigh of relief as representatives gathered in Westphalia to sign the peace treaties.

With this peace emerged a modern patchwork of sovereign nation-states, which gradually replaced the medieval feudal antecedent. Unified Christendom gave way to the separate nations of Europe, whose borders represented new political and religious divisions. Yet the agreement allowed Roman Catholics and Protestants — or at least Catholic and Protestant states — to live side by side in relative peace. Henceforth, Europe made a firm commitment to secular statecraft, namely, to keep religion and politics separate and to disqualify religious beliefs or differences from being causes for war. Through the Crusades and the wars of religion, Christianity had apparently learned its lesson. War might not be eliminated, but it could be limited to secular, or "penultimate," concerns. In political language, it meant that wars would be waged to defend state sovereignty, preserve national security, and protect economic and political interests. Some resisted this political turn toward realism at the expense of religious or moral reflection. Others, like religious humanist Desiderius → Erasmus (1469?-1536), followed later by rationalist Immanuel Kant (1724-1804), rejected the inevitability of war under the crude framework of political statecraft, instead proposing a vision of sustainable, if not perpetual, peace.

The moral, the religious, and the political often intermingle during times of war, as the U.S. Civil War (1861-65, fought over secession and, by extension, → slavery) ably demonstrates. Religion rose to the fore in arguments supporting and opposing slavery, as well as in Union and Confederate political rhetoric. Lincoln knew that both sides could not be right, yet he cautioned that religious differences and appeals to righteousness exacerbate war, famously affirming, "I am not much concerned to know whether God is on our side. What I want to know is whether we are on God's side" (quoted in S. Mathews, "Religion and War," *BW* 2 [1918] 176). Refining the Westphalian settlement, Abraham Lincoln sought to limit religion's propensities for war, while still acknowledging the place of religious reflection and judgment in fostering political humility and reconciliation. After all, he believed, both sides pray to the same God, incur divine judgment, and suffer from the same "mighty scourge of war" (Second Inaugural Address).

4.5. The World Wars

Some have traced direct connections between the Peace of Westphalia and later European efforts to limit wars, including the Hague Peace Conferences (1899, 1907); the Treaty of Versailles (1919), which ended World War I and delineated the League of Nations; the Kellogg-Briand Pact (1928), which called for the renunciation of war "as an instrument of national policy" (art. 1); and even the 1945 charter that formed the → United Nations. All of these efforts to outlaw, prevent, or contain war were marked by failures, not just in Christian-dominated Europe, but on a global scale among other nations and alliances. But Europe had fairly well succeeded at keeping religion at bay. In fact, by the time General Dwight Eisenhower (1890-1969) spoke of the Atlantic campaign in World War II as a "crusade through Europe," the religious connotations had all but dissolved.

The rise of 20th-century → totalitarianism and → fascism in Germany, Italy, and Japan and, later, Communism (→ Marxism) in the → Soviet Union and Eastern Europe illustrated clearly that religion was no longer the paramount threat it once was. If anything, extreme → secularism supplanted the religious bogeyman of medieval and early modern times. In some cases, Christian responses to these pagan or atheistic movements were often capitulatory, such as the agreements reached by Protestant and Catholic churches with Adolf Hitler; in other cases, "seditious," wherein figures like Dietrich → Bonhoeffer (1906-45), Paul → Tillich (1886-1965), and Karl → Barth (1886-1968) in Germany or Karol Wojtyla/Pope John Paul II (1920-2005) of Poland challenged, to varying degrees, oppressive authoritarian regimes that, they believed, violated the moral mandates of the state and were founded on falsehoods (if not false religions) that were anathema to Christian belief.

4.6. The Cold War

The second half of the 20th century was dominated by the cold war standoff between, on the one hand, the United States, Western Europe, and their allies and, on the other, the Soviet Union, Eastern Europe, and their allies. The threat of atomic warfare and the strategy of deterrence effectively limited an all-out nuclear exchange between these two sides (→ Weapons of Mass Destruction). The 1962 Cuban missile crisis, which saw a face-off between U.S. and Soviet ships, brought the two sides to the brink of direct engagement, including the very real possibility of a follow-on nuclear attack, before the Russian navy eventually turned back. This encounter tested and affirmed the deterrence theory of mutual assured destruction (MAD), the clear risks of which, realists argued, would prevent nuclear exchanges. The idea that the arms race could be managed so as to avoid actual use of nuclear weapons did not appease many Christian efforts to slow or halt the buildup.

The cold war also witnessed numerous hot campaigns and proxy wars in Asia, Africa, Latin America, and the Middle East, where democratic-backed and Communist/socialist-backed forces sparred. These engagements ranged from covert operations to all-out conflicts such as the war between North and South Korea (which, technically speaking, continues, since the two sides signed an armistice, not a peace treaty) and the protracted and bloody combat in Viet Nam (which, due to its gradual escalation, the U.S. Congress never declared a war, despite the nearly 60,000 U.S. servicemen killed there). The dissolution of the Soviet Union in 1991 not only thawed cold war tensions but also melted the geostrategic balance of powers that, despite many regional struggles, had prevented World War III from breaking out and had preserved relative stability in international relations since the end of the Second World War.

5. Restrictions in War

Various efforts to end war — whether through peace or through more war itself — have so far proved unsuccessful. But there have been important and effective measures to limit war's sufferings and cruelties. Ancient and feudal chivalric codes sought to prescribe general principles that would govern combat and ensure that justice was applied even to one's enemy. Cicero extols warriors whose honor and honesty extended so far that, upon being captured and conditionally released, they freely returned to their captors to undergo sentences of → torture and execution. Augustine spoke movingly of the respect that pagans afforded to those who took refuge in → sanctuaries (§3). This innovation contrasted with other practices in the ancient world, as chronicled by Thucydides and even the Hebrew Scriptures, wherein military victors slaughtered all men of fighting age and enslaved (if not killed) the women and children.

Medieval innovations such as the Peace of God (declared in 975 at the Council of Le Puy), the Truce of God (promulgated in 1027 by the Council of

Toulouges), and bans on bows, arrows, crossbows, and siege weapons by the Second Lateran Council (1139) all sought to restrict further the excesses of war within Christendom. (Beyond Christendom, however, these restrictions often did not apply.) The Peace of God declared that monks, priests, and pilgrims, as well as church property, should be spared injury and destruction in combat. The Truce of God, although less successful, identified certain days and occasions (e.g., holy days and church feasts) when battle was to be forsworn. While calling a "time out" during war seems odd by some standards, echoes of it have survived in the modern era. On Christmas Day 1914, during World War I, German and French troops emerged from their respective trenches and met peacefully in the no-man's-land between enemy lines. As recently as Easter 1999, U.S. president Bill Clinton was criticized for not halting military operations against Serbian forces during the NATO air campaign in Kosovo. According to then secretary of state Madeline Albright, the allies decided that recognizing Easter with a "no fly" day inappropriately privileged a (Latin) Christian holiday over against holidays celebrated by other religions in the region.

The most significant set of limitations on war involve those associated with the Geneva Conventions. These conventions refer, not to a single document, but to a compilation of treaties and agreements, the first of which was drawn up in 1864 at an international meeting in Geneva. There, representatives set out provisions for the care of sick and wounded soldiers in combat. These measures built upon an important development a year earlier when Genevan Jean-Henri Dunant (1828-1910) helped form the International Committee of the Red Cross, a neutral organization devoted to making war less inhumane. Other conventions were added later, such as the 1899 Hague Conventions, which extended the 1864 provisions to maritime warfare and also prohibited the use of expanding bullets. The 1925 Geneva Gas Protocol prohibited poison and asphyxiating gases in the wake of World War I, in which mustard gas and chlorine gas had been used to hideous effect. The four Geneva conventions of 1949 updated and reaffirmed earlier conventions concerning the treatment of (1) wounded soldiers and (2) those wounded and shipwrecked at sea; it also added provisions for (3) prisoners of war and (4) civilians under enemy control. Two additional protocols were added in 1977: one extended Geneva protections to civilian personnel and objects from direct attack; the other expanded the laws of international conflict to civil conflicts. A third protocol ratified in 2005 created an additional distinctive emblem — a "red crystal" (resembling a diamond) — that provides the same protections as those traditionally associated with sectarian symbols such as those used by the Red Cross or the Red Crescent.

Most nations are signatories to these conventions, and while they are not universally respected, they have significantly reduced the overall suffering experienced in war. Moreover, even when violations of laws of war do occur, it is only through the existence of international norms that a violation or breach can even be declared. Without laws of war, there could be no war crimes. National militaries have also enshrined these laws of war into military law. For example, the U.S. military's Uniform Code of Military Justice provides for the prosecution and punishment of war crimes committed by American members of the armed forces. These international and national laws of war dovetail with just-war principles regarding *noncombatant immunity,* set out by writers such as Gratian (d. by ca. 1160), Vitoria, and Grotius, which prohibit the intentional targeting of civilians. Another key just-war principle is *proportionality,* which restricts the use of excessive force (more than is needed to accomplish a particular objective) and prohibits tactics wielded with cruel or vengeful intent to increase suffering.

According to most just-war thinkers, the Allied use of incendiary, or "terror," bombing in 1945 against the German cities of Dresden and Berlin and against Tokyo was a direct violation of noncombatant immunity. This was particularly the case in Germany, since many munitions factories and other war-making industries were located in the city outskirts, away from the population centers in the heart of the cities. Proportionality was also compromised, since the turning point in the Allied defeat of Germany preceded the bombing campaign; the use of force exceeded that which was necessary to win the war. Many have argued that retribution, more than military necessity, inspired the firebombing of these cities. Similarly, the use of atomic bombs against Hiroshima and Nagasaki violated the just-war principle of noncombatant immunity, since these weapons intentionally targeted densely populated Japanese cities and did not seek to isolate military targets. Most Americans, however, including many Christians, stood behind President Harry Truman's decision to use the bomb to end the war, which it successfully did. Truman's remark that he "didn't hesitate a minute" and "never lost any sleep" over his decision to bomb Japan is at odds with the Christian conscience that laments the horror of war. Ethical debates over the only wartime use of atomic weapons continue today.

In the nuclear age, some, like the U.S. Conference of Catholic Bishops, argued vociferously against reliance on nuclear weapons. Given their overwhelmingly destructive impact, nuclear weapons, even when used in a deterrent capacity, may tend to violate *in bello* provisions of immunity and proportionality and hence cannot be defended on just-war grounds. The bishops advocated test-ban treaties, deep cuts in the nuclear arsenal, and a strategy of progressive disarmament that rejected the pursuit of nuclear superiority and the strategy of MAD. Others such as Protestant just-war thinker Paul Ramsey (1913-88) argued that, however disastrous nuclear warfare might be, to bow out of the arms race would be politically and morally irresponsible and therefore at variance with just-war thinking. Ramsey overcame certain Catholic just-war reservations by arguing that noncombatants may never be the *intended* target of attack, whether of conventional or of nuclear weapons. Military targets, however, enjoy no such immunity. The fact that many civilians might die as a result of nuclear attacks on military targets, though tragic, was not itself a violation of *ius in bello* principles.

Since the 1990s, significant advances in weapons technology, facilitated particularly by the global positioning system (GPS), lasers, and other means of munition precision guidance, have improved the capacities of technologically sophisticated militaries to discriminate between military and nonmilitary targets. While certain munitions such as land mines and unexploded cluster bombs continue to pose threats to civilians who happen upon them, increased weapons accuracy overall has reduced inadvertent civilian casualties and "collateral damage" to civilian infrastructure and has offered tremendous ethical advances over the tactics, weapons, and ethical considerations deployed in World War II and Viet Nam. At the same time, such technological advancements, which also improve mission effectiveness, have been countered by "asymmetric warfare" techniques, which explicitly violate rules of war, both as prescribed by just-war principles and as established in international law. Such use of "low technology," evident in wars in the Balkans, Iraq, and Lebanon (2006), seeks to counter military superiority by using "human shields" and protected sites (e.g., hospitals, churches, mosques, civilian homes) as protective cover for military personnel and their operations. Noncombatants often bear grave costs in conflicts involving insurgents. Finally, the age of global, real-time communications, embedded reporters, and digital cameras has placed members of the armed forces under increased scrutiny, allowing the world to watch how they conduct military operations — from bombing campaigns to urban combat to the capture and treatment of POWs. This near real-time access to the battlefield has not eliminated all war crimes or atrocities, but it has helped to hold accountable those who are caught on film.

6. Post–Cold War "Wars" and Prospects for the Future

6.1. *The Balkans*

The end of the cold war aroused the slumbering forces of nationalism (→ Nation, Nationalism), tribalism, and terrorism, which had often been contained by authoritarian states that enjoyed the support of Western or Soviet backing. In the 1990s Western Europe witnessed in its backyard the violent disintegration of Yugoslavia, a multiethnic state long held together by Communist strongman and president Marshal Tito (1892-1980). When Communism collapsed there, ethnic differences surged to the fore, compounded by attendant religious tensions among Serbian and Montenegrin Orthodox, Croatian and Slovenian Catholics, Bosnian Muslims, and Macedonians Orthodox and Muslims. All sought independence — in some cases nationhood, in others, simply freedom from oppression.

The nationalist Slobodan Milošević (1941-2006) became the major force behind the move to create a greater Serbia, at great expense to those, particularly Muslims, who were forcibly removed from their lands. As images unseen since World War II of mass murder, concentration camps, and ethnic cleansing flashed across television screens, much of the world wondered, Could → genocide really be happening again? The world waited for someone to do something — perhaps as U.S. and U.N. troops had intervened in Somalia in 1992, when warring clans used food as a weapon, inducing famine and massive suffering. Western powers dawdled and dithered over Bosnia but finally took action in 1995, giving way to the Dayton Accords, which ended hostilities. Later, in 1999, with the Balkan crisis still simmering, the province of Kosovo became the next site of ethnic cleansing, as well as a full-fledged, 78-day humanitarian military intervention. As Czech president Václav Havel said of the NATO-led effort, "This is probably the first war that has not been waged in the name of 'national interests,' but rather in the name of principles and values. If one can say of any war that it is ethical, or that it is being waged for ethical reasons, then it is true of this war." The use of military force, it seemed, could be more moral than a decision to forgo war. Critics, however, interpreted U.S./NATO unwillingness to use ground forces — and the fact that the allies incurred no casualties — as a commitment to "combatant immunity"; correlatively, reliance upon air power entailed bombing many fixed, "dual-use" sites rather than Serbian ground forces actually carrying out ethnic cleansing.

6.2. Rwanda and Sudan

As Serbian nationalism ripped apart the Balkans, African tribalism was ravaging → Rwanda (§1). In 1994 the Hutu government orchestrated a nation-wide campaign to annihilate members of the Tutsi tribe in a brutal genocide carried out primarily by machete. (Moderate Hutus, including those who tried to protect Tutsis, were also killed.) The last gasps of the 20th century — the age of genocide — were full-scale attacks that took only 100 days to wipe out three-quarters of a million people or more. Officials in the United States and in the United Nations, including Kofi Annan, who later served as secretary-general, failed to act, despite knowledge of the actions that were about to occur. The inaction could be attributed to fresh memories of gut-wrenching scenes from Somalia — of U.S. soldiers caught up in clan warfare, killed and dragged through the streets by the very people they thought they came to help. Genocide never again? Think again.

In the 21st century deadly African tribalism reared its head once more as Arab militias, backed by Sudan's government, began to undertake ethnic cleansing of native African tribes in the western region of Darfur. Although over 200,000 have died in Darfur and millions have been displaced, other nations have generally been hamstrung by the Sudanese government's insistence that allowing U.N. peacekeepers into the Darfur amounts to Western or colonial meddling in Sudanese internal affairs. Meanwhile, Christians on the political left and right — in addition to people of other faiths or no faith at all — have protested that the lives at stake in Darfur are certainly more sacred than Sudan's sovereignty.

In all of these humanitarian catastrophes, the faces of war rarely involved nations' forces squaring off against one another. Much more frequently, militias and irregular armed forces battled one another, sometimes directly attacking civilian populations; where conventional militaries were involved, they often intervened on behalf of noncombatants. Many Christians and just-war thinkers have viewed humanitarian intervention as a textbook example of the moral use of force. But one need not be Christian or appeal to just-war reasoning to share the de-

spair, outrage, and sense that something must be done. Some skeptics have worried about violating the principle of nonintervention accorded to sovereign nations (an idea preserved in the U.N. charter), though others, including former secretary-general Annan, have pointed out that the United Nations also must defend those whose human → rights are wantonly violated.

Finally, many of the "just causes" invoked by Western nations in post–cold war uses of force involved actions taken on behalf of Muslim populations: Kuwait in the Persian Gulf War, Somalia, and Bosnia and Kosovo in the Balkan crises. Some have seen a continuation of this trend in military actions on behalf of Muslims in Afghanistan and Iraq. But others have viewed these actions as expressions of Western hostility toward Muslim countries. Some have even viewed them as evidence of a new form of religious warfare — a Western/Christian crusade against Muslims or a global "clash of civilizations" between Western and Islamic nations and peoples (→ Islam).

6.3. Terrorism and the "War on Terrorism"

As national and tribal warfare were tearing asunder parts of Europe and Africa, anti-Western forces were quietly plotting in parts of the Middle East and Afghanistan, animated by a violent strain of Islamic extremism. The militancy of groups such as al Qaeda was augmented by widespread resentment among many Muslims for Western support that, throughout the cold war, had propped up corrupt, unrepresentative Arab governments. The terrorist attacks of September 11, 2001, involving the hijacking of civilian airliners by 19 al Qaeda radicals, who flew planes into the New York City World Trade Centers and into the Pentagon, became the first of a series of assaults in many countries against Western targets (in Bali, Madrid, and London). However, Muslims in Jordan, Afghanistan, and, especially, Iraq (among other places) have suffered terribly from terrorists attacks by Islamic extremists.

In response to the September 11th attacks, a "global war on terror" was unleashed, the first salvo of which was the U.S.-led military overthrow of the Taliban in Afghanistan and the routing of al Qaeda in October 2001. Just-war reasoning again came into play, and many Christians, joined by others, saw the war against Afghanistan as just: the U.S. government (unlike al Qaeda) was a legitimate political authority charged with protecting its citizens, if necessary, through the use of force; the U.S. military reprisal was in direct response to a blatant act of aggression; and overthrowing the Taliban and thwarting al Qaeda was deemed essential to preventing future attacks. Not all Christians, however, supported this position. Pacifists and others who oppose all or most forms of war dissented.

Far more controversial in the United States and around the world was the U.S.-led invasion of Iraq and the overthrow of Saddam Hussein in 2003. The stated reason for the invasion was Saddam Hussein's violation of numerous U.N. resolutions dating back to the Persian Gulf War and, particularly, his presumed possession of weapons of mass destruction (WMD), which, the United States and the United Kingdom feared, could easily be passed on to terrorists. The preemptive use of force was declared to prevent this threat from materializing further. Another goal, it seemed, was to implant a democratic government in the heart of the Middle East. Following the fall of Saddam, though, no WMD were found. Four years after the invasion, despite the eventual formation of a fragile democratic government, coalition forces were still struggling to bring order to the country; to stanch a seemingly intractable insurgency, and to end intense sectarian conflict, if not civil war, among Iraqi Sunni and Shia.

Support for the Iraq invasion among Christians, as with the general populace, divided largely along liberal and conservative lines, though diminishing support across many groups characterized the occupation as it continued. Moral discourse about the Iraq War generally has been overtaken by more realist concerns (including Christian realist concerns like those voiced by Reinhold → Niebuhr in his day) about the limits of American power and influence and the hazards of excessive optimism concerning the task of spreading democracy.

While military operations abroad proceeded apace, the "war on terror" in the United States and other countries gave way to vast new "homeland security" efforts (esp. the protection of transportation facilities, population centers, and other potential, high-value targets), law enforcement measures (including wiretapping and monitoring of bank activity), and various legal-judicial measures (permitting the designation of enemy combatants, the indeterminate holding of enemy detainees, and the creation of military tribunals). Many actions taken by the United States, particularly those involving expanded executive powers, have been very controversial. Debates over the violation of civil liberties, coercive interrogation, extradition, torture, and the abuse of detainees have been fueled by widespread uncertainty, fear, and disagreement over the way to prosecute this "new kind of war."

We began by noting the significance of war terminology. Many people contest the very designation of a "war on terror," instead likening the effort to defeat Islamic radicalism to domestic law-enforcement strategies. Those who agree with President George W. Bush, who has championed a "war on terror," share with al Qaeda leader Osama bin Laden and his supporters the notion that "global war" accurately describes the nature of this violent conflict, one that could last several decades and claim thousands, if not millions, of lives before it ends. Many Christians, especially in Western countries, seek to diminish the religious overtones of this struggle, owing to the secular sensibilities of their Westphalian heritage. Al Qaeda militants, however, strive for support of Muslims for their cause, in part by seeking to absorb regional conflicts in Afghanistan, Iraq, Lebanon, and elsewhere into the rubric of a worldwide religious war.

Bibliography: Historical studies: R. Bainton, *Christian Attitudes toward War and Peace: A Historical Survey and Critical Re-evaluation* (Nashville, 1979) • L. S. Cahill, *Love Your Enemies: Discipleship, Pacifism, and Just War Theory* (Minneapolis, 1997) • S. A. Garrett, *Ethics and Airpower in World War II: The British Bombing of German Cities* (New York, 1993) • J. T. Johnson, *The Holy War Idea in Western and Islamic Traditions* (University Park, Pa., 1997); idem, *Just War Tradition and the Restraint of War: A Moral and Historical Inquiry* (Princeton, 1981); idem, *The Quest for Peace: Three Moral Traditions in Western Cultural History* (Princeton, 1987) • P. Ramsey, *The Just War: Force and Political Responsibility* (new ed.; Lanham, Md., 2002); idem, *War and the Christian Conscience: How Shall Modern War Be Conducted Justly?* (Durham, N.C., 1961) • J. Riley-Smith, *The Crusades: A History* (2d ed.; New Haven, 2005) • F. H. Russell, *The Just War in the Middle Ages* (Cambridge, 1977) • M. Walzer, *Just and Unjust Wars: A Moral Argument, with Historical Illustrations* (3d ed.; New York, 2000).

Edited collections: J. D. Carlson and E. C. Owens, eds., *The Sacred and the Sovereign: Religion and International Politics* (Washington, D.C., 2003) • J. B. Elshtain, ed., *Just War Theory* (New York, 1992) • A. F. Holmes, ed., *War and Christian Ethics: Classic and Contemporary Readings on the Morality of War* (2d ed.; Grand Rapids, 2005) • M. Howard, G. J. Andreopoulos, and M. R. Shulman, eds., *The Laws of War: Constraints on Warfare in the Western World* (New Haven, 1994) • T. Nardin and D. Maple, eds., *The Ethics of War and Peace* (Princeton, 1996).

Contemporary issues: Catholic Church. National Conference of Catholic Bishops, *The Challenge of Peace* (Washington, D.C., 1983) • D. Charles, *Between Pacifism and Jihad: Just War and Christian Tradition* (Downers Grove, Ill., 2005) • J. B. Elshtain, *Just War against Terror: The Burden of American Power in a Violent World* (New York, 2004) • M. IGNATIEFF, *Virtual War: Kosovo and Beyond* (New York, 2000); idem, *The Warrior's Honor: Ethnic War and the Modern Conscience* (New York, 1997) • J. T. JOHNSON, *The War to Oust Saddam Hussein: Just War and the New Face of Conflict* (Lanham, Md., 2005) • R. B. MILLER, *Interpretations of Conflict: Ethics, Pacifism, and the Just-War Tradition* (Chicago, 1991) • J. H. YODER, *Nevertheless: The Varieties and Shortcomings of Religious Pacifism* (rev. ed.; Scottdale, Pa.:, 1992).

JOHN D. CARLSON

Watchtower Society → Jehovah's Witnesses

Water, Holy

1. All religious cultures have regarded water as both alive and cleansing (→ Sacred and Profane). From the outset, Christianity used this natural element as a → symbol for basic salvation. In John 3:5 water is the means by which, in → baptism, God imparts the grace of → regeneration.

2. Early in the third century, → Tertullian (d. ca. 225) referred to the consecration of baptismal water (*De bapt.* 4.4). In both East and West, prayers of consecration had a threefold character. They included → *exorcism*, asking that the evil spirits who dwelled in the water might be expelled; *anamnesis*, recalling what God did with water, especially at the Red Sea; and *epiclesis*, calling upon the Holy Spirit to sanctify the water, into which oil and chrism were also mixed.

Reformation churches that retained consecration followed the Lutheran model and its reference to the flood. Along with the anamnesis, prayer was also offered for the baptismal candidates. Liturgical reforms after 1960 (→ Liturgy 1) led Roman Catholics, Old Catholics, Lutherans, and Anglicans to adopt texts thanking God for what he did through water in → salvation history and praying that the → Holy Spirit would act upon the candidates in and by the water. Both Eastern and Western prayers of consecration stress the meaning of baptism and are thus an important source for baptismal theology.

3. Consecrated water finds another use in the → Roman Catholic Church. A practice developed in the eighth century of sprinkling holy water on the congregation each Sunday. The water is kept in stoups near the main church doors. The texts now in use (→ Benedictions) carry the thought of protection but also recall baptism (cf. the → sign of the cross). The pastoral hope is that the use of holy water will help parishioners to remember their own baptism and also spur them on to observe their baptismal promises.

→ Incense; Sacramentality

Bibliography: A. FRANZ, *Die kirchlichen Benediktionen im Mittelalter* (vol. 1; Freiburg, 1909) 43-220 • E. J. GRATSCH, "Water, Liturgical Use of," *NCE* (2d ed.) 14.660-62 • A. A. KING, *Holy Water: A Short Account of the Use of Water for Ceremonial and Purificatory Purposes in Pagan, Jewish, and Christian Times* (London, 1926) • L. L. MITCHELL, "Thanksgiving over the Water in the Baptismal Rite of the Western Church," *Sacrifice of Praise* (ed. B. D. Spinks; Rome, 1981) 229-44.

THADDEUS A. SCHNITKER

Way of the Cross → Stations of the Cross

Weapons of Mass Destruction

1. Terminology
2. Chemical Weapons
3. Biological Weapons
4. Nuclear Weapons
5. The Ethical Debate
   5.1. Just-War Theory
   5.2. Ethical Questions
6. Present Needs

1. Terminology

"Weapons of Mass Destruction" (WMD) is a term coined at the beginning of the atomic era that soon came to refer to nuclear, biological, and chemical (or "NBC") weapons. The term has a history of usage in U.N. documents and arms-control debates. Yet because "WMD" was used by politicians and the media to describe Saddam Hussein's purported weapons programs and to justify the invasion of Iraq in 2003, some people argue that the term clouds ethical and political deliberation. Rather, nuclear weapons should be held in a separate category because only they are destructive on a massive scale. Others hold that it is meaningful to think of nuclear, biological, and chemical weapons in the collective category of WMD because all three types of weapons are difficult to limit to legitimate military targets; by design, they are harmful to civilians.

This article assumes it is possible to think of WMD in both ways: as a collective category of unrestrained weapons, of which nuclear weapons should cause particularly urgent moral and political concern. The use and even the mere possession of WMD is of great concern to Christianity and other religious traditions. The great world religions, as well as various philosophical schools, espouse ethical principles that can be used to condemn the use of WMD (→ Ethics). More contested in these traditions is how the world can actually reach the goal of eliminating WMD.

2. Chemical Weapons

Although all three types of WMD are predominantly modern weapons, there are precedents for biological and chemical weapons in the history of warfare, for militaries and their sponsoring regimes have ever innovated in order to gain an edge over their enemies. Chemical weapons refer to chemical concoctions added to existing weapons (such as arrows and bombs) to make them more deadly or to increase the suffering of the targeted people. Originally, but less commonly now, the term can refer to poisons delivered to an enemy outside of regular weapons technologies. The poisoning of the enemy's food and water supplies can be considered a rudimentary form of chemical warfare. As far back as the seventh century B.C., some ancient Greek city-states mutually agreed to forbid the poisoning of water supplies as a method of → war. Poison-tipped arrows can also be considered an early chemical weapon.

The modern era of chemical weapons dates to World War I (1914-18). The French and British used projectiles filled with poison and liquefied chlorine, and the Germans fired canisters of mustard gas. Soldiers on all sides had to scramble to put on gas masks, lest their eyes and lungs get chemically burned (direct exposure to any of these poisons could cause death). The most notorious recent uses of chemical weapons demonstrate that both nations and terrorist groups can be a threat: Iraq killed tens of thousands of Kurds by chemical-gas weapons in 1988, and the radical-Buddhist terrorist cult Aum Shinrikyo released sarin gas in a Tokyo subway in 1995, killing 12 people and making hundreds sick.

3. Biological Weapons

Biological weapons refer to methods of delivering disease-causing agents during war. The spreading of disease into an enemy army or population was difficult to conceive of before the germ theory of disease was understood in the 19th century. Still, in a sad chapter of history, the spreading of smallpox from the European colonizers to the indigenous peoples of the Americas was a kind of inadvertent biological warfare, as it made the Native Americans highly susceptible to military conquest. In 1763 Lord Amherst and other British commanders considered infecting the Native American tribes they were fighting by giving them smallpox-contaminated blankets. At least one commander did so, but with uncertain results.

Biological weapons have generally proved difficult to develop, which did not stop many → nations from scientifically exploring their feasibility in the 20th century. As far as is known, the only use of biological weapons in modern warfare was by Japan during World War II (1939-45). Scientific units of the Japanese Imperial Army, including the infamous Unit 731, tested biological weapons on prisoners of war, killing at least 1,000 subjects. A bubonic plague epidemic in China and Manchuria was caused or advanced by dropping plague-infested fleas from planes. Japan also dropped infected food and clothing from planes, an act reminiscent of Lord Amherst. Japanese troops contaminated wells and streams with anthrax, cholera, dysentery, and typhoid cultures. Estimates of the deaths caused by the diseases resulting from these infestations range from tens of thousands up to 200,000.

Although difficult to disperse broadly, biological weapons may be attractive to terrorist groups and cults, owing to the rudimentary technology involved. The Aum Shinrikyo cult tried several times without success to release botulin toxin around Tokyo. The distribution of anthrax spores through the U.S. mail just after September 11, 2001, is a case of successful biological → terrorism with a low technological threshold, as five people were killed simply by opening letters.

4. Nuclear Weapons

Nuclear weapons are the preeminently modern weapon. The nuclear era was inaugurated with the U.S. bombings of Japan in August 1945. The single bomb dropped on Hiroshima on August 6 completely devastated four square miles in the center of the city, killed 66,000 people immediately, and injured 69,000 more. Three days later, Nagasaki was struck with a second and larger atomic bomb, killing 39,000 and injuring a further 25,000. Many more civilians died before the end of the year, and thousands lived with ill-health effects for the rest of their lives. Japan quickly surrendered, ending World War II. Most Americans considered the death and destruction worth the goal; American policy-makers believed that by ending the war quickly, the atomic bombs saved hundreds of thousands of American and Japanese soldiers from dying during a U.S. invasion of Japan. This claim remains contested by historians (G. Alperovitz; W. D. Miscamble). The human cost is clear.

But any ethical — not to mention historical, military, or political — assessment of the use of nuclear arms must also consider the implications of crossing the nuclear divide. It led swiftly to an arms race between the United States and the Soviet Union, which, at its height, had each nation aiming tens of thousands of strategic nuclear warheads at each other. Crossing the nuclear divide also enticed other nations to seek nuclear arms in the process known as nuclear proliferation. The "nuclear club" of nations now includes the United States, Russia, United Kingdom, France, China, Pakistan, and India. (South Africa had some weapons in the 1980s.) Israel is an undeclared nuclear-weapons state. North Korea claims to have tested a nuclear bomb in 2006, which seems to be true; what weapons it has is unclear, but it openly seeks to develop them. Iran and other nations may also be seeking to develop or acquire them. The initial use of nuclear weapons by the United States may not have prevented this proliferation, but it gave impetus to the cold war buildup, and it makes it more difficult today for the United States to take the moral high road in the drive for → disarmament.

5. The Ethical Debate

Was the ending of the Second World War worth the massive killing and devastation caused by the atomic bombs? Is it even proper to ask that question, for isn't the direct killing of civilians immoral? Aren't nuclear weapons impossible to use without intentionally killing civilians? If so, shouldn't the nations recognize this fact and rid themselves of these weapons immediately? These ethical questions, which were raised by the original atomic bombings, lie at the heart of the debate over WMD. For simplicity, they are reduced here to the issues of (1) the possible ethical use of WMD, (2) the ethical status of holding WMD as a deterrent, and (3) the ethical imperatives concerning the nonproliferation of WMD.

Before addressing these questions, ethical tools must be at hand. There are many religious traditions treating the ethics of war, and there is much variety and disagreement within each tradition. Presented here are the major trends within Christianity and a few instructive differences from other traditions.

5.1. *Just-War Theory*

The major ethical framework on war in Christianity is the just-war theory (→ War 4.3). This theory was taken over from its roots in classical Roman political thought by Ambrose and → Augustine in the fourth and fifth centuries and then developed by a number of Roman Catholic and Protestant theologians in the West. Starting in the late Middle Ages, a secularized strand of the tradition became incorporated into the developing body of → international law. The tradition comprises several criteria against which to judge a case for going to war or to judge an ongoing or completed war. A nation must meet all the criteria for going to war *(ius ad bellum)* before starting military actions, and it must rigorously abide by the criteria for fighting in war *(ius in bello)* throughout the campaign. Failure to do so makes the nation's actions immoral.

Just-war theory has its critics. Christian pacifists and other types of pacifists (→ Pacifism) criticize it for being too supportive of what they see as an immoral activity, while realists think that it is dangerous to moralize about war, which should instead be amoral and pragmatic choices nations make to defend their own interests.

Nonetheless, many religious traditions have either a version of just-war theory (so → Judaism and → Islam) or teachings on the ethical conduct of political life that are analogous to various just-war principles (so → Buddhism and → Confucianism). Most secular philosophical systems — any that are not guided solely by ethics of consequentialism, → pragmatism, or → realism — affirm the just-war framework. Just-war principles are affirmed by the American military and the militaries of Western nations and are woven into military training. Furthermore, the principles governing the conduct of war have guided the development of modern international conventions to restrain and eliminate some forms of WMD. Just-war theory thus provides a framework that helps secure interreligious and international agreement on some basic regulations of WMD.

The just-war tradition's commentary on WMD begins with their inherent destructiveness to civilians. The ethics of WMD fall largely under the two major *ius in bello* principles. The first is *discrimination*, sometimes called noncombatant immunity, which means that those who are not fighting in a war are technically "innocent" of aggression and therefore must not be intentionally targeted. In addition, the weapons used in war must be able to discriminate between military and nonmilitary targets. The second principle is *proportionality*, which says that the methods and strategies for fighting a war, including the weapons used, must not cause more overall harm than the moral benefit expected from the war.

The discrimination principle has the virtue of being crystal clear about the immorality of intentionally targeting noncombatants. It is qualified only by the principle of double effect, which allows for "foreseen but unintended" loss of civilian life if an army is aiming at military targets. Even though double effect, if used to rationalize, may erode protection for civilians, discrimination has generally set a clear line for not drawing civilians into battle, and it was a principle largely adhered to until the total warfare of World War II. In the Middle Ages, church councils and theologians also used these principles to forbid the use of new weapons technologies, such as crossbows, although with little success.

5.2. *Ethical Questions*

5.2.1. The first ethical question is, *May we ever use WMD?* The just-war tradition is generally opposed. One can easily see that a broadly destructive weapon such as a strategic nuclear weapon (a high-yield weapon targeted on a foreign city) would, if used, kill thousands and thousands of innocent civilians, as did the U.S. bombings of Hiroshima and Nagasaki. Just-war thinkers in every tradition agree that any use of a strategic nuclear weapon on a population center violates the principle of discrimination. Furthermore, most would say that the extensive and long-term devastating effects of radioactive weapons on infrastructure, culture, public health, and the → environment would, in most conceivable instances, violate proportionality.

Two just-war qualifications, though, might open the door to nuclear use. First, some just-war thinkers, especially those leaning toward realism, argue that *discriminate* uses of a nuclear weapon could pass muster. They have in mind so-called tactical nuclear weapons (low-yield weapons meant for a battlefield) and nuclear-tipped conventional bombs that could penetrate a bunker buried deep underground. Christian ethicist Nigel Biggar contends that such uses could be acceptable, although leaders should probably still hold back from crossing the nuclear threshold, considering the potentially destabilizing effects (a proportionality concern).

Second, could the stakes of a war ever be so great that nuclear weapons could be used as a last resort? Secular just-war thinker Michael Walzer has advanced the controversial criterion of a "supreme emergency," which would allow a nation to violate ethical rules of war when its very existence is at stake. He thinks this criterion did not apply for the United States at Hiroshima, but it did when Britain firebombed German cities in 1943-44 with a cumulative effect similar to that of atomic bombs. Christian ethicists Paul Ramsey and Reinhold → Niebuhr

and Christian just-war theorist James Turner Johnson have also, in various ways, left the door open to the use of nuclear weapons, even when their use would harm population centers.

Other religious traditions do not have a developed body of commentary on the use of WMD, but when scholars representing the religious traditions apply teachings about war and political order to this contemporary issue, the weight of the argument goes against the use of WMD. Exceptions are attitudes favoring the procurement and use — at least second use or defensive use — of WMD in the politicized versions of → Hinduism and → Islam (see essays in S. H. Hashmi and S. P. Lee).

As for the use of chemical and biological weapons, although neither category is as destructive of noncombatant life, just-war thinkers and most other ethical and religious commentators have been opposed to their use. Though there are differences between the two categories and different histories of each, there is a near-universal revulsion against them. Chemical weapons are not necessarily indiscriminate, in that they can be aimed narrowly at opposing soldiers. But their wide use in World War I revealed the extra pain they could cause, and thus they quickly came to be seen as unnecessarily cruel (ignoring the ironic point that there is no pleasant way to be killed in war). The nations of the world, recovering from the horrors of the First World War, expanded the bans on chemical weapons in the Geneva Convention of 1925 and, in the Chemical Weapons Convention of 1997, called for their complete elimination. Most just-war thinkers and others thus believe that chemical weapons should never be used, in part out of respect for international law, and in part to strengthen the climate of international cooperation, which could lead to further and more effective arms limitation conventions.

Biological weapons are different in that, if they were made effective, they would be very hard to control. Like nuclear weapons, they are inherently indiscriminate, and any conceivable use of them seems to violate proportionality. For instance, if a nation successfully introduced the smallpox virus into an enemy population, a pandemic could ensue, harming even the group that started it. The effects of dying from diseases such as smallpox and anthrax have also been seen as terribly cruel. Again, the nations of the world mostly agree; almost all have signed the Biological Weapons Convention of 1975.

5.2.2. The second ethical question considered here is, *May we hold WMD as a deterrent?* The generally negative judgment on the first question does not mean that just-war theory and religious traditions necessarily answer this second question in the negative. The secular theory of realism has often set the terms of this debate, asking pointedly whether, in a dangerous world where some nations hold WMD, it is not prudent to hold enough weapons that will deter other nations from attacking us. Many just-war thinkers have agreed, even claiming that it was ethically responsible, even if not ethically ideal, for the United States to hold nuclear weapons as a deterrent against the USSR during the cold war.

Christian just-war thinkers generally were and remain less comfortable than secular thinkers with nuclear deterrence. Since deterrence relies on a nation's implied threat to use the weapons if it is attacked, deterrence relies on the implied threat to kill the innocent. A further worry is that should any mistake occur on either side, such as an accidental launching, the nuclear powers would slide down a path that leads to killing millions of innocent people. Still, Christians, both laity and church leaders, have advocated stances across a spectrum: pacifists such as the → Mennonites advocate unilateral nuclear disarmament (→ Peace Churches); the U.S. Methodist bishops (→ Methodist Churches) have condemned nuclear deterrence; the U.S. Catholic bishops (→ Roman Catholic Church) have argued for temporary deterrence as a step toward disarmament; many American Christians think that the American nuclear deterrent is ethically necessary in a dangerous world; and many evangelical and Pentecostal Christians believe that nuclear weapons are foreordained in God's plan for the end of the world. It is fair to say that the extensive traditions of ethical reasoning in Christianity weigh against nuclear deterrence on anything but a provisional basis, while popular Christianity — especially in the United States and especially among evangelicals and Pentecostals with a dispensationalist understanding of the end time — accepts or even encourages the holding of nuclear arms (→ Evangelical Movement; Pentecostalism; Dispensationalism).

Most other religious traditions (with exceptions similar to those found in Christianity) can be straightforwardly interpreted as criticizing nuclear deterrence but begrudgingly accepting it in situations such as the cold war. This is true of the internal logic of the traditions that accept something like a just-war framework, and it is a judgment that scholars discern in these traditions (Hashmi and Lee). Several well-known religious leaders (e.g., the Dalai Lama, Pope Benedict XVI, Daisaku Ikeda) and progressive religious organizations and interreligious bodies criticize deterrence forthrightly, but many other bodies lend tacit support to the deterrence status quo by not criticizing it directly. Still, the religious traditions for the most part recognize that nuclear deterrence is potentially dangerous and implies a destructive mentality.

In various ways, the world's major religious traditions, even those holding a just-war ethic, promote visions of positive → peace. It is therefore heartening, if ironic, that there seems to be more universal agreement against the use and development of biological and chemical weapons. This situation is ironic because nuclear weapons remain the greatest threat to the world. This situation is understandable because the world is, fortunately, in a situation where biological and chemical weapons are not widespread or numerous, so it is simply prudent to try to get every nation out of the race to acquire them. (It is probably also the case that the great powers do not see much strategic advantage in these weapons, so it is easier to sacrifice them.) But the situation is heartening if the broader agreement against biological and chemical weapons could leverage stronger religious advocacy against nuclear weapons.

5.2.3. We come, then, to the final ethical question: *How morally imperative is it to prevent proliferation of WMD and to disarm those nations now in possession?* This question is a large and politically complicated one, given the mistakes and misrepresentations made by American and British leaders regarding Iraq's purported WMD programs (leading to international resentment against these two nations), the limited leverage that the international community can hold over a nation with nuclear ambitions, and the total lack of leverage it can hold over terrorist groups with WMD ambitions. Generally speaking, most religious and secular ethics of war argue against any further proliferation of WMD to new nations or to nonstate groups (i.e., so-called horizontal proliferation). The exceptions are that the politicized versions of Islam want their favored governments (Iran, for instance) to join the nuclear club. Many ordinary believers and a good number of leaders in several religions tend not to criticize their favored governments who already possess the bomb. International law allows an asymmetry: the 1968 Nuclear Nonproliferation Treaty forbade proliferation only to those states that did not have the bomb at that time. The resulting situation leads to envy among some nations who wish to join the powerful club and to inevitable hypocrisy among the nuclear powers who do not disarm themselves but say it is wrong for any other nation to acquire nuclear capacity. In fact, this asymmetry has proved to be no deterrent, for the nuclear club continues to expand.

It is therefore not enough to say that proliferation of WMD should stop where it is now. Ethical commentators argue that horizontal proliferation must be reversed through disarmament and that vertical proliferation (the increasing numbers of weapons by current possessors) must be reduced through arms control. Nuclear arms control was the major focus of ethical commentators during the cold war era. Fortunately, the end of the cold war allowed both the United States and Russia to make deep cuts in strategic arms. After the deep cuts of the late 1980s and 1990s, however, these nations became complacent about going further. Views about the urgency and methods of disarmament are related to views of deterrence. Since the United States and Russia still believe in the need for deterrence, they do not want to disarm. In the eyes of North Korea and presumably other nations, however, the nuclear club's possession of arms makes these nations insincere advocates for nonproliferation. It is critical, then, that strategies for nonproliferation and for responding to breaches are crafted so that they are in the interests of all states. Otherwise, these strategies will rightly be seen as attempts by the states that are currently powerful to retain their military superiority. The same reasoning applies to the proliferation of biological and chemical weapons.

6. Present Needs

An urgent task at the beginning of the 21st century is to build up institutions with the potential to foster trust among nations, in turn enabling states to reach weapons-control agreements that reliably provide for both verification and responses to breaches. Genuine security from the use of WMD will become possible and lasting only if the much broader problems of war and injustice are simultaneously addressed. It is necessary to diffuse and prevent military conflicts around the globe. Conflicts in which hundreds of thousands of civilians die in conventional wars fought with conventional weapons every year are not only injustices crying out to heaven (see Gen. 4:10), but they greatly increase the risk of some party using WMD. To prevent such scourges from occurring in the first place, nations must commit to working through international institutions, abiding by agreements and norms of international law, promoting techniques of negotiations and conflict resolution, and supporting human rights and the development of civil society, especially in war-torn regions. These tasks are among the ten practices that constitute "just peacemaking theory," an exciting and promising project developed by a team of ethicists, theologians, and

political scientists, including both pacifists and just-war thinkers (G. Stassen).

The role of religious groups in addressing the challenges of WMD might seem indirect, even irrelevant. But religious traditions shape the cultures of nations and thus certainly have important roles to play in building the international culture of trust that is needed. Religious groups should bring the specific commentaries of their traditions to bear on the ethical questions of WMD and should urge their adherents to work through the political process in favor of WMD nonproliferation and disarmament. In the United States, Canada, Great Britain, and elsewhere, religious bodies (particularly Catholic, Protestant, and Jewish) have lobbied governments and developed policy statements with some good results, especially when they have partnered with other organizations. In the years ahead, other religious traditions will come to develop a higher profile in public policy work; all of these religious groups can be helped by drawing on their best scholars and their most upstanding public leaders.

To spread ideas is important, but religions perform an even greater service when they model trust and cooperation in their relations with other religions and groups. In the last decade, for example, religious leaders (such as East Timorese bishop Carlos Filipe Ximenes Belo and Bishop Desmond Tutu) and religious agencies (such as the Plowshares Institute, Christian Peacemaker Teams, and the international development agencies of various churches and religions) have made tangible contributions to peace. By forsaking the extremists and fundamentalists in their midst and by building trust with other communities, religions can help ease the tensions that encourage nations to seek false security in the possession of WMD.

→ Peace Movements; Peace Research

Bibliography: G. ALPEROVITZ et al., *The Decision to Use the Atomic Bomb and the Architecture of an American Myth* (New York, 1995) • N. BIGGAR, "Christianity and Weapons of Mass Destruction," *Ethics and Weapons of Mass Destruction: Religious and Secular Perspectives* (ed. S. H. Hashmi and S. P. Lee; Cambridge, 2004) 168-99 • D. L. CLOUGH and B. STILTNER, *Faith and Force: A Christian Debate about War* (Washington, D.C., 2007) • S. H. HARRIS, *Factories of Death: Japanese Biological Warfare, 1932-1945, and the American Cover-up* (rev. ed.; New York, 2002) • S. H. HASHMI and S. P. LEE, eds., *Ethics and Weapons of Mass Destruction: Religious and Secular Perspectives* (Cambridge, 2004) • A. MAYOR, *Greek Fire, Poison Arrows, and Scorpion Bombs: Biological and Chemical Warfare in the Ancient World*

(Woodstock, N.Y., 2003) • R. B. MILLER, ed., *War in the Twentieth Century: Sources in Theological Ethics* (Louisville, Ky., 1992) • W. D. MISCAMBLE, *From Roosevelt to Truman: Potsdam, Hiroshima, and the Cold War* (Cambridge, 2006) • G. STASSEN, ed., *Just Peacemaking: Ten Practices for Abolishing War* (2d ed.; Cleveland, 1998) • M. WALZER, *Just and Unjust Wars: A Moral Argument, with Historical Illustrations* (4th ed.; New York, 2006).

BRIAN STILTNER

Weber, Max

Max Weber (1864-1920), born on April 21 in Erfurt, was a legal scholar, historian, and sociologist. His father was a lawyer and politician, and early in his life Weber already had a wide array of intellectual and political interests. Through his deeply religious mother he came under the influence of the → Puritan tradition, which showed itself in his strong orientation to → achievement. By the age of 13 he had already written two historical treatises. He studied law, along with history, economics, and philosophy, in Heidelberg and Berlin. After fulfilling his military service, he passed his law examinations in Göttingen in 1886. From 1887 to 1891 he practiced law in Berlin, and he continued to serve his profession on occasion through the years (→ Law and Legal Theory). Weber's doctoral thesis was entitled "Die Geschichte der Handelsgesellschaften im Mittelalter" (The history of commercial partnerships in the Middle Ages), and his habilitation thesis was "Die römische Agrargeschichte und ihre Bedeutung für das Staats- und Privatrecht" (Roman agrarian history and its significance for public and private law). In 1888 he became a member of the Verein für Socialpolitik (Union for social policy), and in 1889, under the influence of his mother, a member of the Evangelisch-Soziale Verein (Protestant social union). In both groups he worked on the situation of the Junkers and agricultural workers east of the Elbe. At this time, Weber was a proponent of nationalism and imperialism. This orientation came to the fore most strongly in his inaugural lecture in Freiburg, where in 1894 he had been called to be professor of economics. In 1897 he transferred to Heidelberg.

In 1893 Weber married Marianne Schnittger. In 1897 a long-standing tense relationship with his father led to severe disagreements, and shortly thereafter his father died without there being any reconciliation. Probably as a result of this experience Weber suffered a physical and psychological breakdown, and in 1903 he had to ask to be released from his position. Weber later enjoyed a more productive period, during which he worked on the phenomenon of → religion. In his methodological publications, *Gesammelte Aufsätze zur Wissenschaftslehre* (1922; ET *The Methodology of the → Social Sciences* [New York, 1968]), in which he addressed *Verstehen* (understanding), *Idealtypus* (the ideal type), and *Wertfreiheit* (value-neutrality), he set religion and other historical phenomena in a position between history and a positivistically understood → sociology. Personally, he described himself as "religiously unmusical." In 1904 he became, along with Werner Sombart and Edgar Jaffé, editor of the *Archiv für Sozialwissenschaft und Sozialpolitik* (Archive for social science and social policy), in which he published the first version of *Die protestantische Ethik und der Geist des Kapitalismus* (1905; ET *The Protestant Ethic and the Spirit of → Capitalism* [New York, 1930]). In that work he expressed his pessimism about Western → culture, in which individual freedom was increasingly being suppressed through → bureaucracy (which he called "the iron cage").

Weber traveled widely and maintained many contacts, among others, with Karl Jaspers, Robert Michels, Georg Simmel, György Lukács, and Ernst Bloch. Beginning in 1909, Weber was the editor of *Grundriß der Sozialökonomik* (Outline of social economics). During this time many contributions emerged that were published posthumously in *Wirtschaft und Gesellschaft* (1922; ET *Economy and Society* [2 vols.; Berkeley, Calif., 1978]). After 1910 Weber worked on the phenomenon of → charisma, which he saw as the only (in the end, ineffective) counterweight to bureaucratization. His Puritan activism was gradually replaced by an interest in eroticism as a sphere of freedom and protest, a focus that had to do, it is supposed, with his intimate relationships with Mina Tobler and Else Jaffé, which, however, did not jeopardize his platonic marriage.

During World War I Weber served as an officer in the Reserve Hospital Commission in Heidelberg and took part in the peace negotiations in Versailles. During this time he involved himself intensively in political debates, where he often took a position against the kaiser. He laid out his political ideas in *Politik als Beruf* (1919; ET *Politics as a Vocation* [Philadelphia, 1965]) and testified to his basic scientific position in *Wissenschaft als Beruf* (1917; ET *Science as a Vocation* [London, 1989]). In 1919 he returned to the professorate (in Munich). On June 14, 1920, he died as a result of a lung infection, leaving uncompleted a compilation of his complete works.

Only after his death did Weber's significance become recognized. Today his reputation transcends the boundaries of the scientific community. This recognition is largely due to his far-reaching analysis of the problems of Western culture, an analysis that today, to a large degree, is still relevant.

Bibliography: Primary source: H. Baier et al., eds., *Max Weber–Gesamtausgabe* (Tübingen, 1981ff.).

Secondary works: E. Baumgarten, *Max Weber, Werk und Person* (Tübingen, 1964) • R. Bendix, *Max Weber: An Intellectual Portrait* (new ed.; Berkeley, Calif., 1977; orig. pub., 1960) • M. B. Green, *The von Richthofen Sisters: The Triumphant and the Tragic Modes of Love; Elsa and Frieda von Richthofen, Otto Gross, Max Weber, and D. H. Lawrence, in the Years 1870-1970* (New York, 1974) • A. Mitzman, *The Iron Cage: An Historical Interpretation of Max Weber* (New Brunswick, N.J., 1985; orig. pub., 1970) • Marianne Weber, *Max Weber: A Biography* (New York, 1975; orig. pub., 1926).

Leo Laeyendecker

Wedding Ceremony

1. Liturgical Aspects
   1.1. History
   1.2. The Present
2. Pastoral Aspects

1. Liturgical Aspects

1.1. *History*

1.1.1. In all cultures → marriage has a cultic side. State regulations, tradition, and custom — in all their variety — determine how the wedding ceremony is to be performed. In the → early church the → bishop had to know when a marriage was taking place (Ignatius *Pol.* 5.2). The *oblatio* (bread and wine) that the bridal pair gave for the → Eucharist served as *confirmatio matrimonii* (confirmation of marriage; → Tertullian *Ad. uxor.* 2.8). Two rites were used in the fourth and fifth centuries: *velatio* (the → vow) and *benedictio* (the → blessing). Both took place in the church and were accompanied by the Eucharist. Originally, the liturgy adopted pagan rites such as crowning the bridal pair and joining their right hands.

Weddings, however, were also an act in private law. Roman law adopted the principle of *consensus facit nuptias* (mutual consent makes the marriage). The bride's father would go along with the consent. German law distinguished between private engagement and public wedding. For the latter the bride had to have someone she could trust to give her away, which might be the → priest. The rite often took place at the church door (*in facie ecclesiae,* "in

the presence of the congregation"). The mass then took place in the church.

In the Middle Ages the priest would personally serve as the guarantor of public weddings. His function thus changed from that of blessing to that of binding, using the words *ego coniugo vos* (I unite you). The development was essentially complete by the 12th century. A tendency to include weddings in church services, still at the door, may be noted (e.g., at Arles, ca. 1300). Marriage also had come to be regarded as a → sacrament (→ Marriage and Divorce 1.3). The Gregorian Sacramentary (with elements going back to → Gregory the Great [590-604]) had introduced the motif of the blessing of → paradise into the reading at weddings (Ephesians 5; → Marriage 1.2.2). → Scholasticism and → mysticism built on these tendencies, reaching a conclusion in 1563 at the Council of → Trent in the decree *Tametsi* (DH 1813-16).

1.1.2. Martin → Luther (1483-1546; → Luther's Theology) rejected the idea of marriage as a sacrament. In his "Order of Marriage for Common Pastors" of 1529, he accepted the division of weddings into two parts (*LW* 53.110-15). At the entrance to the church the priest would ask for consent and wed the two in the name of the triune God, and then in the church there would be a → proclamation of the Word of → law and → promise and the blessing. The prayer of blessing was to the effect that marriage denotes "the sacramental union of thy dear Son, the Lord Jesus Christ, and the church, his bride" (p. 115). The → church orders combined the two parts in a regular service in the church.

In the 18th century a change took place. The minister now married the pair before the altar. In Germany civil marriage became obligatory in 1875, and so Protestants see in the church ceremony only a proclaiming and a blessing, though they insist that a public declaration of consent be made before a priest.

Other countries have different laws. England requires that banns of marriage be published on three successive Sundays so that any objections may be made, that the bridal pair themselves be asked to admit any impediment, that they then declare their consent, that they symbolize it by giving and receiving a ring and joining hands, and that they then receive from the minister not only a blessing but a pronouncement that they be man and wife together. The state recognizes church weddings so long as notification is given.

1.2. *The Present*

Protestants and Roman Catholics both understand marriage as something instituted by God at → creation (§4.5). They also recognize the importance of publicly declared consent. Christians can truly carry out what was instituted at creation, however, only in → faith, for marriage is the mystery of the fellowship that Christ has with the church as his bride. Marriage is thus part of the order of salvation (→ Soteriology), even though Protestants construe the word "sacrament" more narrowly and do not use it of marriage. Weddings, however, come very close and may perhaps be called sacramental rites.

Wedding ceremonies often include the Eucharist as a reminder that the sacrifice of Christ is the source of mutual love and that Christian marriage has its place in congregational life. Roman Catholics place weddings within the Mass after the reading of the Gospel and the homily and before "the prayer of the faithful" (*Sacrosanctum concilium* 78.1). Bishops may develop their own wedding rites corresponding to usages in their own lands (77.3). According to the *Ordo celebrandi matrimonium* (1969), they must leave room for a declaration of consent and a blessing.

In the → Orthodox Church the wedding liturgy contains prayers, intercessions, readings (Eph. 5:20-33; John 2:1-11, etc.), the vows, the wedding itself, in which the priest sets a crown over the bridal couple, as in the early church, and finally the Eucharist. Marriage is one of the sacraments and is accomplished liturgically.

→ Family 2

Bibliography: Liturgical texts: Agende für evangelisch-lutherische Kirchen und Gemeinden, vol. 3, pt. 2, *Die Trauung* (new ed.; Hannover, 1988) • Book of Common Prayer • EVANGELICAL LUTHERAN CHURCH IN AMERICA, *Life Passages: Marriage, Healing, Funeral* (Minneapolis, 2002) • *Lutheran Book of Worship Liturgies* (electronic ed.; Minneapolis, 1997) • *Manual on the Liturgy: Lutheran Book of Worship* (ed. P. H. Pfatteicher and C. R. Messerli; Minneapolis, 1979) • *Ordo celebrandi matrimonium* (Vatican City, 1969; ET *The Celebration of Marriage* [Dublin, 1980]).

Other works: H.-H. JENSSEN, "Die kirchliche Trauung I: Geschichte und Theologie," *HLit* (3d ed.) 509-19 • "Marriage," *A New Dictionary of Liturgy and Worship* (ed. J. G. Davies; London, 1986) 349-64 • J. MEYENDORFF, *Marriage: An Orthodox Perspective* (3d ed.; Crestwood, N.Y., 2000; orig. pub., 1970) • A. RAES, *Le mariage. Sa célébration et sa spiritualité dans les églises d'Orient* (Paris, 1959) • C. H. RATSCHOW et al., "Ehe / Eherecht / Eheschließung," *TRE* 9.308-62 • K. RICHTER, "The Liturgical Celebration of Marriage: The Problems Raised by Changing Theological and Legal Views of Marriage," *The Future of Christian Mar-riage* (ed. W. Bassett and P. Huizing; New York, 1973) 72-87 • K. RITZER, *Formen, Riten und religiöses Brauchtum der Eheschließung in den christlichen Kirchen des ersten Jahrtausends* (2d ed.; Münster, 1981) • M. SEARLE and K. W. STEVENSON, *Documents of the Marriage Liturgy* (Collegeville, Minn., 1992) • S. A. STAUFFER, ed., *Baptism, Rites of Passage, and Culture* (Geneva, 1998) • K. W. STEVENSON, *Nuptial Blessing: A Study of Christian Marriage Rites* (London, 1982); idem, *To Join Together: The Rite of Marriage* (New York, 1987).

OTTFRIED JORDAHN

2. Pastoral Aspects

2.1. Weddings and other church → occasional services apply to turning points in life. The turning points are ambivalent. They give much → joy and → hope but also are beset by uncertainty and → anxiety regarding the future. The presence of the → congregation gives the event an official character and expands it by a common invoking of God. Even if one of the marriage partners does not belong to the church, by taking part in a church wedding, the partner shows some respect for the numinous. As M. → Luther said in the preface to his "Order of Marriage for Common Pastors" (1529), "Whoever desires prayer and blessing from the pastor or bishop indicates thereby . . . into what peril and need he enters and how greatly he stands in need of the blessing of God and common prayer for the estate which he enters" (*LW* 53.113). The reasons given for a church wedding, which often have to do with solemnity at this high point in life, do not make of the → pastor a mere adornment but are an expression of the human longing for the numinous.

2.2. The → vows are real vows before God, as the couple promise that they will stand by one another through thick and thin, loving one another and respecting one another. Unforeseeable and difficult changes in life situation and spiritual estrangement may plague the new relation right on through to old age (→ Lifestyle). Some churches accept the possibility of divorce and remarriage.

2.3. Wedding counseling can explain the prerequisites of Christian marriage. Ideally, it touches on (1) what it means to "leave father and mother"; (2) what becoming "one flesh" signifies, that is, physical union (→ Sexuality), the sharing of all goods, and, finally, the responsibility for having a child together; (3) the concept of → faithfulness, which embraces the entirety of both partners; (4) the cultivation of the common life, in view of the possible employment of both partners; and (5) mutual acceptance of each other, just as each one is.

Counseling for a wedding will aim at joy and → responsibility and dispel fears. The atmosphere in which it is given plays an essential role. It must not be bureaucratic. Care must be taken that there are no interruptions, and the couple must not feel that they are under cross-examination. The couple must state their wishes, so far as the church allows, regarding the forms of the ceremony: music, texts, inclusion of parents or friends, and so forth. The pastor should go as far as possible in meeting these wishes. But the symbolism (→ Symbol) remains important: meeting at the church door, escorting to the chancel steps, the exchange of rings, the prayer of intercession, and the meaning of the blessing. Stress should be laid on the vows, and especially on the addition "with God's help."

The couple may also give suggestions as to the content of the wedding address. The pastor should be ready to give advice and counsel. A group of two or three couples may be assembled for this time of preparation. Enough time should be given. Where no set readings are appointed, a list of suitable texts may be proposed. The pastor should be visited at least six or eight weeks before the wedding.

2.4. Some Protestant pastors are ready to marry divorced persons on the condition that they accept their own role in the failure of the past marriage and are ready to learn from the experience, that they have received God's → forgiveness, and that they themselves are ready to forgive. The thought in Rev. 21:5 is often quoted: "See, I am making all things new," as a basis whereby the pardoning → grace of God can give a new beginning when we so often fail. Roman Catholics, however, with many others, are strongly opposed to remarriage after divorce.

2.5. Mixed marriages may sometimes take place when pastors of different denominations share in the ceremony (so-called ecumenical weddings). Even Roman Catholics are prepared for this type of ceremony. They insist, however, that the service be either Roman Catholic or non–Roman Catholic, not a hybrid. If the couple desires a nuptial mass, exceptional circumstances may be needed. The Protestant partner does not have to agree that the children will be brought up as Roman Catholics. The Roman Catholic partner, however, must do all that he or she can to have the children receive Roman Catholic baptism and instruction (1983 CIC 1071.2, 1086.2, 1125, 1164; → Mixed Marriage 2).

2.6. The blessing of same-sex partnerships should then be allowed if in these partnerships the same presuppositions as those for a church wedding are valid: partnership in responsibility before God without temporal limitation, in faithfulness and

tenderness. A wedding ceremony, though, cannot be carried out, since the heterosexual marital relationship includes also the continuation and preservation of the → creation (i.e., procreation). The biblical record leads one to consider that the Bible is viewing the social situation of antiquity (young boys used for pleasure, heathen cults).

Modern-day biological knowledge about → homosexuality points to an activation of characteristic control centers in the brain during pregnancy (L. Kaplan). Through the spiritual and physical burdening of the mother during pregnancy, a lowering of the testosterone level can occur, whereby the libido of the fetus can be decisively influenced. Other occurrences of organic brain and psychological etiology, as well as hereditary elements, can also be influential. A reversal of sexual behavior can have negative effects. The theological judgment of homosexuality or lesbianism will need to take these results of clinical research into consideration.

Bibliography: A. Cornes, *Divorce and Remarriage: Biblical Principles and Pastoral Practice* (Grand Rapids, 1993) • L. Kaplan, *Das Mona-Lisa-Syndrom. Männer, die wie Frauen fühlen* (2d ed.; Düsseldorf, 1990) • M. G. Lawler, *Ecumenical Marriage and Remarriage: Gifts and Challenges to the Churches* (Mystic, Conn., 1990) • D. Mack and D. Blankenhorn, eds., *The Book of Marriage: The Wisest Answers to the Toughest Questions* (Grand Rapids, 2001) • W. P. Roberts, ed., *Divorce and Remarriage: Religious and Psychological Perspectives* (Kansas City, Mo., 1990) • H.-J. Thilo, *Ehe ohne Norm? Eine evangelische Eheethik in Theorie und Praxis* (Göttingen, 1978).

Hans Joachim Thilo†

Wesley, John

John Wesley (1703-91), the principal founder of the Methodist movement within the Church of England, was born at the Epworth rectory on June 17, 1703 (Julian calendar). He was the 15th of the 18 or 19 children of Samuel and Susanna Wesley.

Nominated for the Charterhouse School in London by the Duke of Buckingham, Wesley studied at this institution from 1714 to 1720, at which point he matriculated at Christ Church, Oxford, where he received his baccalaureate degree in 1724. The next year Wesley's religious interests grew more serious, and he was ordained a → deacon, and in 1728 a → priest, by Bishop John Potter (ca. 1674-1747) of Oxford, who eventually became the archbishop of Canterbury.

Wesley was elected a fellow of Lincoln College,

Oxford, in 1726. During the period between August 1727 and November 1729, however, John Wesley actually spent much time away from the university in the parishes of Epworth and Wroot assisting his elderly father. The dutiful son was eventually called back to the university in 1729 by Dr. Morley, the rector of Lincoln College, who maintained that "the interests of the College and the obligation of the statutes" necessitated his return to tutorial duties.

By the spring of 1729 John Wesley's younger brother, Charles (1707-88), had experienced a "religious reformation" that resulted in serious study and regular church attendance with another student, William Morgan. Within a few months of John and Charles's return to Oxford in the fall of 1729, Robert Kirkham also began associating with this emerging group, whose visible activities resulted in a variety of names given briefly such as the Holy Club, Bible Moths, Sacramentarians, and, by 1732, the name that eventually stuck, Methodists. Over the next two or three years, as many as four dozen persons participated in the activities of various related cell groups throughout the university, including James Hervey (1714-58) and George → Whitefield.

Shortly after the death of their father in 1735, John and Charles Wesley, along with Benjamin Ingham and Charles Delamotte, embarked on a missionary journey to the colony of Georgia. John later confessed to a friend that his chief motivation for undertaking this arduous task was to save his own soul: "I hope to learn the true sense of the Gospel of Christ by preaching it to the heathen." En route to Georgia their ship, *The Simmonds,* was buffeted by powerful Atlantic storms. Wesley, who was quite fearful, even admitting his reluctance to die, marveled at the serenity of the → Moravian community on board, who calmly sang on in the midst of such terror. That evening Wesley recorded in his journal: "This was the most glorious day which I have ever hitherto seen."

When John Wesley returned to England in 1738 (Charles had already preceded him), he continued his contacts with the Moravian community and helped to form a religious society at Fetter Lane in London with Peter Böhler (1712-75), a young Moravian leader. Under Böhler's spiritual direction, on May 24, 1738, Wesley experienced — while listening to Martin → Luther's "Preface to the Epistle to Romans" being read at a religious society meeting in Aldersgate Street — the power and peace, the → happiness and → holiness, for which he had so longed: the new birth (→ Regeneration), with its accompanying mark of freedom from the power of → sin, as well as the → assurance that his sins were for-

given and that he was therefore no longer a servant but a child of God.

Emboldened by his evangelical → conversion, Wesley continued to preach → justification by → grace through → faith alone in a forthright manner, with the result that many Anglican churches eventually closed their doors to him. A new avenue for ministry, however, was opened by George Whitefield (1714-70), who persuaded the reluctant Wesley to preach outdoors in Bristol in April 1739. The response to Wesley's field preaching was so great that he established a preaching house at Bristol in 1739, known as the New Room, as well as the Foundery in London during that same year, to garner the fruit of the beginnings of the evangelical → revival. In 1742 the third major center of → Methodism was established further north at Newcastle upon Tyne.

During the 1740s the institutional structure of Methodism began to take shape with the employment of John Cennick and Thomas Maxfield as lay preachers; with the establishment of the class meeting, first in Bristol in 1742 and then elsewhere; and with the institution of the first Methodist conference, which was held at the Foundery in London in June 1744. In these conferences Wesley and those assembled invariably emphasized the three grand doctrines of Methodism, namely, (1) repentance (the "porch" of religion; → Penitence), (2) justification by faith alone (the "door" of religion), and (3) → sanctification, or holiness ("religion itself").

Ever concerned with the indigent and outcasts of 18th-century Britain, Wesley sought money from the rich for the poor, collected clothing on their behalf, established a medical dispensary, gave loans to those in need, visited the sick and dying, helped to provide housing for widows and orphans, supported education at the Kingswood School and elsewhere, preached against the dangers of riches, and wrote forcefully against the horrible institution of American → slavery, "the vilest that ever saw the sun."

As principled in many respects as his father, Samuel, and his mother, Susanna, John Wesley boldly distinguished the Methodism that was under his care from several other 18th-century religious movements: from the Calvinistic Methodism of George Whitefield, with the publication of the sermon "Free Grace" in 1739; from Moravian quietism, with the reading of a paper at the Fetter Lane Society on July 20, 1740; from nominal Christianity in the form of a staid and churchly Anglicanism, with the preaching of "Scriptural Christianity" before the university at St. Mary's, Oxford, on August 24, 1744; and once again from Calvinistic Methodism with the publication of the Conference Minutes of 1770 and the *Arminian Magazine,* beginning in 1778.

Wesley sought "to spread Scriptural holiness across the land" by underscoring the importance of entire sanctification, or perfect → love, in his sermon "The Circumcision of the Heart," produced in 1733, and in his treatise *A Plain Account of Christian Perfection,* published in 1766. Carefully defining Christian → perfection in the light of Scripture, Wesley maintained that this Christian doctrine, witnessed to by early Greek fathers, Catholic mystics, and Caroline Anglicans, represented the actualization by grace through faith of the twofold great commandment of Jesus Christ: to love God with all one's heart and one's → neighbor as oneself.

Wesley made provision for the continuance of Methodism in England after his death by signing the Deed of Declaration in 1784, which made the Legal Hundred (i.e., the Methodist conference) the heir of Wesley; and in the United States of America, by ordaining Richard Whatcoat (1736-1806) and Thomas Vasey (ca. 1746-1826), and by setting apart Thomas Coke (1747-1814) to ordain Francis Asbury (1745-1816) and others for ministry in the New World.

Leaving behind nearly 75,000 Methodists in the United Kingdom, having traveled over 250,000 miles in ministry, and having preached more than 40,000 sermons, John Wesley died in his 88th year on March 2, 1791, in London, exclaiming to the faithful beside his bed a truth that had characterized his entire ministry, "The best of all is, God is with us!"

Wesley's life and thought were not widely known among other theological traditions until the 20th century, when Albert Outler (1908-89), the dean of Methodist historians, rediscovered Wesley in the context of the many theological traditions (e.g., Eastern fathers and Anglican authors) that streamed into his thought. In addition, Outler and others were instrumental in establishing the Bicentennial Edition of Wesley's works (Nashville, 1984-), a critical edition that continues to offer the contemporary scholarly community the writings of Wesley with proper contextualization, helps, and introductory essays.

Bibliography: Primary sources: A Plain Account of Christian Perfection (ed. W. R. Ward and R. P. Heitzenrater; Philadelphia, 1990) • *Poetical Works of John and Charles Wesley* (ed. G. Osborn; 13 vols.; Salem, Ohio, 1992) • *The Works of John Wesley,* vol. 1-4, *Sermons* (ed. A. C. Outler; Bicentennial Ed.; Nashville, 1984-87) • *The Works of John Wesley,* vol. 9, *The Methodist Societies I: History, Nature, and Design* (ed. R. E. Davies; Bicentennial Ed.; Nashville, 1989) • *The Works of John Wesley,* vol. 11, *The Appeals to Men of Reason and Religion and Certain Related Open Letters* (ed. G. R. Cragg; Bicentennial Ed.; Nashville, 1975) • *The Works of John Wesley,* vols. 18-24, *Journals and Diaries I-VII* (ed. W. R. Ward and R. P. Heitzenrater; Bicentennial Ed.; Nashville, 1988-2003) • *The Works of John Wesley,* vols. 25-26, *Letters I-II* (ed. F. Baker; Bicentennial Ed.; Nashville, 1980-82) • *The Works of Rev. John Wesley* (ed. T. Jackson; 14 vols.; London, 1829-31).

Secondary works: W. R. CANNON, *The Theology of John Wesley, with Special Reference to the Doctrine of Justification* (Lanham, Md., 1984) • G. S. CLAPPER, *John Wesley on Religious Affections: His Views on Experience and Emotion and Their Role in the Christian Life and Theology* (Metuchen, N.J., 1989) • K. J. COLLINS, *A Real Christian: The Life of John Wesley* (Nashville, 1999) • R. P. HEITZENRATER, *Wesley and the People Called Methodists* (Nashville, 1995) • D. S. LONG, *John Wesley's Moral Theology: The Quest for God and Goodness* (Nashville, 2005) • T. C. ODEN, *John Wesley's Scriptural Christianity: A Plain Exposition of His Teaching on Christian Doctrine* (Grand Rapids, 1994) • A. C. OUTLER, *Theology in the Wesleyan Spirit* (Nashville, 1975) • C. WILLIAMS, *John Wesley's Theology Today* (Nashville, 1960).

KENNETH J. COLLINS

Western Sahara

	1960	1980	2000
Population (1,000s):	32	142	289
Annual growth rate (%):	8.57	3.70	2.58
Area: 266,769 sq. km. (102,680 sq. mi.)			

A.D. 2000

Population density: 1/sq. km. (3/sq. mi.)
Births / deaths: 2.86 / 0.76 per 100 population
Fertility rate: 3.51 per woman
Infant mortality rate: 53 per 1,000 live births
Life expectancy: 63.9 years (m: 62.3, f: 65.6)
Religious affiliation (%): Muslims 99.3, other 0.7.

1. General Situation
2. Religious Situation

1. General Situation

1.1. The Western Sahara is a territory in northwestern Africa inhabited by the Saharawi people. It comprises the Saqīyat al-Ḥamrāʾ and Wādi al-Dhahab regions (known as Saguía el Hamra and Río de Oro by the Spanish colonial regime). Western Sahara is administered primarily by Morocco, whose claim to the territory is disputed by the Polisario front (from Sp. [Frente] *P*opular de *L*iberación de

Saguía el Hamra y Río de Oro, the Popular Front for the Liberation of Saguía el Hamra and Río de Oro), which declared the independence of the Saharawi Arab Democratic Republic (SADR) in 1976. SADR is diplomatically recognized by 45 nations and the African Union; an additional 37 states previously recognized the SADR, but 24 of these nations have withdrawn their recognition, and 13 others have suspended it. On the other side, 25 nations, including the Arab League, recognize Morocco's claim to sovereignty over the territory. The → United Nations brokered a cease-fire in 1991, but their Mission for the Referendum in Western Sahara (MINURSO) has been stalemated by irreconcilable Moroccan and Polisario views concerning who is Saharawi (and thus eligible to vote for self-determination of the territory) and their refusal to submit to a referendum out of fear that it might go against their competing goals of exclusive sovereignty. Algerian backing of the Polisario since the beginning has heightened regional tensions in the Maghreb, effectively disabling L'Union du Maghreb Arabe (UMA, the Arab Maghreb Union) and leading some to claim that it is a proxy conflict for Morocco-Algerian tensions.

The Western Sahara, formerly known as the Spanish Sahara, is a hot, flat desert region at the western extreme of the Sahara, extending to the Atlantic. The territory is rich in minerals, with one of the largest deposits of phosphate in the world, which is extracted and transported to the coast on a conveyor belt that is 100 km. (62 mi.) long, the longest in the world. Significant deposits of iron, copper, and zinc are also found. Uranium and oil may also be present, though rights to their exploitation are a source of dispute. The Atlantic coast of this region has some of the most abundant fishing waters in the world, which are exploited by international fishing vessels (chiefly Spanish, Scandinavian, and East Asian) through agreements with Morocco, including extensive export of fish oil by Norwegian fisheries. Several oil companies initiated talks with Morocco concerning possible reserves in Western Sahara but backed off at U.N. and U.S. insistence that Morocco does not have the legal authority to commercially exploit natural resources in the territory. Many see Algerian potential for oil export through Western Sahara as a chief motivating factor for support of the Polisario.

1.2. The Western Sahara has been inhabited by a mixed Berber-Arab population of nomadic clans (→ Nomads) since the Beni Hassan Arabs intermarried with the Sanhaja Berbers, whose 11th-century Almoravid Empire controlled areas from Spain to Senegal. The current family tribal groups (Raguibāt, Oulād Delīm, Tekna, etc.) speak Hassaniya, the Beni Hassan dialect of Arabic, also spoken in Mauritania. The nomadic socioeconomic structure led to scant accumulation of capital outside of herds, and few permanent edifices.

At the 1884 Berlin Conference, Spain claimed the area as a protectorate (→ Colonialism). Their rule lasted until 1975, when 350,000 unarmed Moroccans marched on the southern border carrying green flags, known as the Green March. The Madrid Accords, reached a week later on November 14, divided Western Sahara between Morocco and Mauritania. Many of the Saharawis fled from the Moroccan and Mauritanian troops to Tindouf, Algeria, where they became → refugees.

The Polisario first fought the weaker Mauritania, which in 1979, crushed by a protracted and unconventional war, evacuated Western Sahara and abandoned its territorial claims. Morocco then extended its claims to the part that Mauritania had renounced, despite continued Polisario resistance, which received backing from Algeria. Morocco staked off increasingly large territorial claims with a huge sand-berm wall enclosing the "useful triangle" (of Laâyoune, Smara, and the phosphate mines of Bou Craa [Boukra]) first in 1982. By 1987 Morocco had built a sixth wall that enclosed over 90 percent of the territory, including its most inhabitable areas, and extending over 2,700 km. (1,675 mi.), making it the second longest wall in the world, after the Great Wall of China, and the longest continuous wall.

Since brokering the cease-fire in 1991, MINURSO has focused on negotiating a referendum for Saharawi self-determination, which by 2000 reached an impasse over the status of refugees and Moroccans living in Western Sahara. At this point U.N. special envoy James Baker proposed a new plan that would make Western Sahara an autonomous region for a five-year transitional period, after which a vote for self-determination would occur, with enfranchisement of both refugees and Moroccans still inhabiting the territory. The first draft, keeping security and foreign policy within Morocco's sphere's of power, was rejected by the Polisario and Algeria, while the second, which proposed a transitional government, the "Western Saharan Authority," for the interim period, was rejected by Morocco.

After the rejection of the Baker plan, Morocco has been even less willing to negotiate, and many believe the two sides have come to an impasse. The U.N.'s mandate for MINURSO, scheduled to end on April 31, 2007, without any measurable progress in recent negotiations, was renewed at the last minute by an agreement between Morocco and the Polisario to talk directly and negotiate unconditionally once again.

1.3. Because of the protracted nature of the conflict, a large number of Saharawis have lived in exile for 20 years or more, with over 100,000 (estimates are as high as 175,000) living in Tindouf, and some children having never set foot in the Western Sahara. Cuba has welcomed many Saharawi children in their schools, and many are in school in Cuba away from their families for 12 years or more; others have won scholarships to study in Spain. Because of the heavy emphasis on education and extensive literacy programs in the refugee camps, Saharawis are highly literate, mostly in Spanish and Arabic.

2. Religious Situation

Almost 100 percent of the population are Sunni Muslims (→ Islam; Sunnism, Sunnis). In the colonial period Spanish Catholicism attracted only the Spanish community (→ Roman Catholic Church). It is possible that some Saharawis who have grown up in Cuba or Spain have had contact with Christianity. There is a Roman Catholic cathedral in Laâyoune and another (possibly inactive) church building in Dakhla, the southernmost city before the Mauritanian border. The abandoned settlement of Lagouira, which is on the Saharan side of the Ras Nouadhibou, at the Mauritanian border, also had a church, which is deserted.

Bibliography: "Morocco and Polisario Agree [to] Talks," *BBC News,* April 30, 2007, http://news.bbc.co.uk/2/hi/africa/6610191.stm • D. NOHLEN and F. NUSCHELER, eds., *Handbuch der Dritten Welt* (vol. 6; 3d ed.; Bonn, 1993) • A. G. PAZZANITA, ed., *Historical Dictionary of Western Sahara* (3d ed.; Lanham, Md., 2006). • U.S. CONGRESS, HOUSE, COMMITTEE ON INTERNATIONAL RELATIONS, *Getting to "Yes": Resolving the Thirty-Year Conflict over the Status of Western Sahara* (Washington, D.C., 2006). Two MINURSO Web sites provide helpful information: http://www.minurso.unlb.org and http://www.un.org/Depts/dpko/missions/minurso/.

JOEL MITCHELL

Westminster Assembly and Confession of Faith

1. The Westminster divines were summoned to meet by the Long (English) Parliament on June 12, 1643. In November 1640, following the Bishops'

Wars between England and Scotland, King Charles I (1625-49) had recalled Parliament. In 1641 the General Assembly of the Church of Scotland had appealed for greater uniformity of doctrine and worship, and now the English Parliament took up the theme, requiring a defense and clarification of the worship and order of the Church of England and urging closer relations between the English, Scots, and Continental → Reformed churches.

Despite the king's refusal to assent to the bill of October 15, 1642, which required the convening of an assembly of divines, and despite the royal proclamation of June 22, 1643, prohibiting any such assembly, the first session took place on July 1 in Henry VII's chapel in Westminster Abbey (hence the assembly's name, though it subsequently met in the Jerusalem Chamber).

By October 12, 1643, the → Thirty-nine Articles of the Church of England had been revised with a view to excluding Arminian, Pelagian, and Romanist interpretations; but meanwhile, on August 17 and September 25, respectively, the Scottish and English Parliaments had signed the Solemn League and Covenant, which provided the assembly with added impetus and an extended brief.

The assembly appointees consisted of 10 members of the House of Lords, 20 members of the House of Commons (including John Selden [1584-1654]), and 121 divines. There were Episcopalians such as Bishop Ralph Brownrig (1591-1659) of Exeter and Archbishop James Ussher (1581-1656) of Armagh, neither of whom attended, and Bishop Thomas Westfield of Bristol (1573-1644), who attended the first meeting only; Erastians such as John Lightfoot (1602-75); and English Presbyterians such as Edmund Calamy (1600-1666), Peter Sterry (1613?-72), Anthony Tuckney (1599-1670), and William Twisse (1578?-1646). In addition, there were 11 Independents/Congregationalists, including William Bridge (1600?-1670), Jeremiah Burroughes (1599-1646), Thomas Goodwin (1600-1680), Philip Nye (1596?-1672), and Sidrach Simpson (1600?-1655), all of whom had signed *An Apologeticall Narration* (1643), in which they advocated their favored polity. Finally, there were eight commissioners who, on August 19, 1643, were deputed to attend by the General Assembly of the Church of Scotland. They included Robert Baillie (1599-1662), George Gillespie (1613-48), Alexander Henderson (ca. 1583-1646), Samuel Rutherford (ca. 1600-1661), and three ruling elders. The assembly met on 1,163 occasions between 1643 and February 22, 1649; it was convened periodically until 1653 but was never officially terminated.

2. The assembly produced the Directory for Public Worship (1645), Form of Church Government (1645), Larger Catechism (1647), and Shorter Catechism (1648). It also approved the Psalter of Francis Rous (1579-1659). The Westminster Confession was completed on December 4, 1646, revised, and then was approved by the General Assembly of the Church of Scotland and by the English Parliament on August 27, 1647, and June 20, 1648, respectively.

If, as we have seen, the assembly divines did not work in sociopolitical isolation, neither were they in a theological void. Behind them lay not only more than a century of Reformed theological activity but also an Augustinian influence that had been spread in England through the writings of → Anselm (1033-1109) and Thomas Bradwardine (ca. 1295-1349), the activities of John → Wycliffe (ca. 1330-84), and such contributions as Ussher's Irish Articles of 1615. All of this combined to ensure an emphasis in the Westminster documents upon God as sovereign Lord of → creation and → salvation, upon his providential governance of all things, and upon the sinfulness of a humanity whose dire condition could be remedied only by sovereign → grace freely bestowed. The → Puritan emphasis upon holy living as the fruit of salvation is also strongly present; indeed, two-thirds of the confession is concerned with it. Given the relatively varied theological and ecclesiastical interests at work in the assembly, the resulting works display a remarkable degree of consistency and clearly manifest the authors' concern to match detailed study of Scripture with the use of right reason, and to allow Scripture to be self-interpretative. Parliament, however, required the addition of "proof texts" to the confession.

3. Like some, but not all, other Reformed → confessions, the Westminster Confession opens with a chapter on Holy Scripture. There follow statements on God, the → Trinity, → creation, → providence, the fall, the → covenant(s) of work and of grace, → Christology, free will, the application of redemption, the divine law and its implications for → worship, civic life and → marriage, the → church, the → sacraments, → church order, and → eschatology.

Some have detected an unresolved tension in the confession between the ordered view of the world as expounded by 17th-century scientists and the posited providential interventions of a sovereign God. Some have branded the confession scholastic, and its construal of the covenant as contractual, while others have argued that the confession's federal theology mitigates more rationalistic interpretations that envisage decrees as enacted by inscruta-

ble will. Yet again, the nature-grace dichotomy on which the confession is said to turn prompts some to conclude that the biblical view of the headship of Christ is obscured.

4. Needless to say, the Independent commissioners were not satisfied with the polity delineated in the confession. In Cambridge, Massachusetts, the → Congregationalists heartily endorsed the substance of the Westminster Confession, and in their Cambridge Platform (1648) they set down their principles of church order. A decade later, the English Independents published the Savoy Declaration of Faith and Order (1658), a modification of Westminster that includes a substantial new chapter 20, "Of the Gospel, and of the extent of the Grace thereof," as well as 30 appended articles on church government. This work was done by a group including Bridge, Goodwin, and Nye, who had been Westminster commissioners, but which now had the added weight of John Owen (1616-83) and the inspiration of John Cotton (1585-1652), formerly of Boston, Lincolnshire, subsequently (from 1633) of Boston, Massachusetts. The Particular Baptists followed in Savoy's wake with the Second London Confession of 1677 (superseding that of 1644), in which they did not restrict the Lord's Supper to those who had been baptized by immersion and greatly expanded the Westminster chapter on the church to accommodate their views on church polity. Thus the major bodies that were not legally tolerated in England expressed their considerable unity in doctrine.

With the restoration of the English monarchy in 1660, the hope of Presbyterians that their order might become established was seriously wounded; but in Scotland it was otherwise. By 1711 the expression of opinions contrary to the Westminster Confession and Catechisms was forbidden, and in that year subscription formulas for use at ordinations and inductions were introduced. This pattern was reproduced in the several regions of the world in which Presbyterianism took root.

5. With the passage of time, and prompted by alterations in biblical and theological understanding that in turn led to debates concerning subscription, Declaratory Acts were passed that revised the formulas of subscription. That of the United Presbyterian Church of Scotland (1879), for example, proved to be a catalyst of others.

At the present time some Presbyterian churches still require subscription to the Westminster Confession on the part of ministers and elders, though even some of the most conservative Presbyterian churches have concluded that the identification of the pope with the antichrist is not biblical, accurate, or kind. In other Presbyterian churches the doctrines of Westminster are adhered to with greater or lesser degrees of firmness, and a number have adopted new confessional statements to supplement or replace Westminster. In the united churches (e.g., in the United Kingdom, Canada, and Australia; → United and Uniting Churches) into which the Westminster Standards have flowed, they tend to find themselves, together with Congregational, Methodist, or other appropriate texts, honored as part of the united church's heritage, rather than instrumental in shaping its current thought.

In the face of glib talk about confessions as such being "guardians of the faith," the contrary English and American experiences constitute a cautionary tale. Whereas (for a variety of complex reasons) most English Presbyterians had become unitarian by the end of the 18th century, American Unitarianism came largely out of Congregationalism (→ Unitarians).

It is a moot point whether there is today sufficient doctrinal consensus within the Reformed family at large to render the writing of a declaration of the things commonly believed among a practical possibility. We could well ask whether it matters, and whether it would help or hinder → ecumenism?

Bibliography: S. W. CARRUTHERS, *The Everyday Work of the Westminster Assembly* (Philadelphia, 1943); idem, *The Westminster Confession of Faith* (Manchester, 1937) • G. H. CLARK, *What Do Presbyterians Believe? The Westminster Confession, Yesterday and Today* (rev. ed.; Unicoi, Tenn., 2001) • J. H. GERSTNER, *A Guide: The Westminster Confession of Faith; Commentary* (Signal Mountain, Tenn., 1992) • A. I. C. HERON, ed., *The Westminster Confession in the Church Today* (Edinburgh, 1982) • J. H. LEITH, *Assembly at Westminster: Reformed Theology in the Making* (Richmond, Va., 1973) • A. F. MITCHELL, *The Westminster Assembly: Its History and Standards* (Philadelphia, 1897) • A. F. MITCHELL and J. P. STRUTHERS, eds., *Minutes of the Sessions of the Westminster Assembly of Divines While Engaged in Preparing Their Directory for Church Government, Confession Faith, and Catechism (November 1644 to March 1649)* (Edinburgh, 1874) • R. S. PAUL, *The Assembly of the Lord: Politics and Religion in the Westminster Assembly and the "Grand Debate"* (Edinburgh, 1985) • P. SMITH, *The Westminster Confession: Enjoying God Forever* (Chicago, 1998).

ALAN P. F. SELL

Westphalia, Peace of → Thirty Years' War

Whitefield, George

A contemporary of John and Charles Wesley and Jonathan → Edwards, George Whitefield (1714-70) was the Great Awakening's leading figure in both Britain and North America. A dynamic preacher with a gift for dramatic storytelling, he drew immense crowds throughout a 33-year ministry. Though his gifts were remarkable, his lasting impact came through his emphasis on the new birth (→ Regeneration) and → justification by → faith.

Born of humble parentage, Whitefield paid for his Oxford schooling by working as a servant. At Oxford he joined a small group of devout students derisively called the Holy Club or Methodists for their rigorous self-discipline. Reading Henry Scougal's *Life of God in the Soul of Man,* he became convinced of the necessity of being born again, and after a harrowing season of searching, "the weight of sin went off, and an abiding sense of the pardoning love of God . . . broke in upon my disconsolate soul!" (*Journals,* 58). Ordained by the Church of England in 1736, he quickly gained fame as a preacher with his zeal, his eloquence, and his character. He was offered a curacy in London but instead made plans to join John Wesley, already overseas, as a missionary to the new colony of Georgia. (Delayed for nearly a year, Whitefield's ship set sail only after Wesley had already arrived back in England.) By the time Whitefield returned to England late in 1738, publication of his sermons brought him before the public eye and into storms of controversy.

England was in desperate need of a spiritual revival, with the chaplain to the king writing in 1732, "An open and professed disregard of religion is become . . . the distinguishing character of the age" (quoted in J. C. Ryle, 6). This was despite the vast majority of its citizens having been baptized into the Church of England. Not surprisingly, Whitefield's emphasis on the new birth angered some, including the bishop of London, Edmund Gibson, who argued that England was a Christian land with no need for extraordinary aids from the → Holy Spirit. Whitefield replied, "There are thousands and ten thousands in his Majesty's dominions, as ignorant of true and undefiled religion as ever the heathen were" (*Works,* 4.138). As he later recorded, "The first quarrel many had with me was because I did not say that all people who were baptized were born again" (*Eighteen Sermons,* 351). Sadly, the publication of his journals in 1738 gave his detractors further offense. Still in his early 20s, Whitefield could be read as self-congratulatory in his accounts of the success of his → preaching. Branded as an enthusiast and → antinomian, Whitefield was accused of emphasizing a felt experience of → conversion over the evidence of "the degree and measure of goodness to which they have arrived in this life" (quoted in R. Seagrave). Whitefield was quick to point out that this view amounted to justification by works, and the flurry of books and pamphlets generated brought these doctrinal debates before the English-speaking world. (Of 200 anti-Methodist publications during 1739 and 1740, fully 154 were aimed specifically at Whitefield.) Very publicly at odds with several of England's leading establishment clergy, he was invited to preach to many → dissenting groups. Though he never left the Church of England, his warm ecumenism also characterized his ministry.

Whitefield's first trip to the American colonies began his calling as an itinerant. He kept up an astonishing pace, traveling 14 times to Scotland, crisscrossing England, Ireland, and Wales; it is estimated that he preached over 15,000 times, or over 450 times per year during his public ministry. He sailed to colonial America seven times, becoming their best-known public figure until George Washington. The range of his voice was phenomenal, with Benjamin Franklin calculating that Whitefield could be heard by a staggering 30,000 people at once. The crowds could not be contained indoors, so he often preached outside in the open air. Unusual for his day, it was an effective evangelistic strategy, drawing many who would not usually enter a church, particularly among the poor.

Ever faithful to the → Thirty-nine Articles (in theory, required of all Anglican clergy), Whitefield countered much opposition by appealing to these often-ignored doctrinal standards. Here, concise summations of original → sin (art. 9), justification by faith (11), and aspects of the new birth as opposed to baptismal regeneration (25 and 27) may be found. It was his acceptance, though, of article 17, on election and → predestination, that led to a rift with John Wesley, who took a modified → Arminian view. Estranged for a season and never united again in ministry, their friendship was eventually restored, though their debate has had a profound effect on evangelicalism that continues to this day.

It has been said that Whitefield planted and Wesley reaped, for despite his immense effectiveness as a preacher, it was others who built churches from the new converts. Some may be tempted to compare the effectiveness of the two and repeat the story of a discouraged Whitefield saying, "All my disciples are as a rope of sand." Yet his effect on literally millions of hearers changed the religious landscape of his day, and his unique gifting and his untiring energies were greatly used for the furtherance of the → kingdom.

Bibliography: Primary sources: Eighteen Sermons (London, 1771) • *Journals* (Edinburgh, 1976) • *Letters of George Whitefield for the Period 1732-1742* (Edinburgh, 1976) • *Works* (6 vols.; Edinburgh, 1771-72). Gillies, *Memoirs,* has sometimes been printed as a seventh volume.

Secondary works: J. BELCHER, *George Whitefield: A Biography, with Special Reference to His Labors in America* (New York, 1857) • A. DALLIMORE, *George Whitefield: The Life and Times of the Great Evangelist of the Eighteenth-Century Revival* (2 vols.; London, 1970-80) • J. GILLIES, *Memoirs of the Life of the Reverend George Whitefield* (London, 1772); idem, comp., *Historical Collections Relating to Remarkable Periods of the Success of the Gospel* (Edinburgh, 1981; orig. pub., 1754) • E. S. NINDE, *George Whitefield, Prophet-Preacher* (New York, 1924) • T. PRINCE, *The Christian History Containing Accounts of the Revival and Propagation of Religion in Great Britain and America for the Years 1743-1745* (Boston, 1743-45) • R. O. ROBERTS, *Whitefield in Print: A Bibliographic Record of Works by, for, and against George Whitefield* (Wheaton, Ill., 1988) • J. C. RYLE, *The Christian Leaders of the Last Century* (Moscow, Idaho, 2002; orig. pub., 1869) • R. SEAGRAVE, *Remarks upon the Bishop of London's Pastoral Letter* (Philadelphia, 1740) • J. TRACY, *The Great Awakening: A History of the Revival of Religion in the Time of Edwards and Whitefield* (Boston, 1842) • L. TYERMAN, *Life of the Rev. George Whitefield* (2 vols.; London, 1876-77) • J. B. WAKELEY, *Anecdotes of the Wesleys* (10th ed.; London, 1878).

ROBERT OWEN ROBERTS

Wilberforce, William

William Wilberforce (1759-1833), a lay evangelical leader and → slavery abolitionist, was born in England in the seaport of Hull, Yorkshire, on August 24, 1759, into a wealthy mercantile family. As a boy he came under strong Christian influence from an uncle and aunt with whom he lived for a period following his father's premature death in 1768. He was subsequently educated at Pocklington School and St. John's College, Cambridge.

In September 1780 Wilberforce was elected a member of Parliament for Hull, and in 1784 for the more prestigious county constituency of Yorkshire. As a financially independent, highly intelligent, and well-connected young man, he had the prospect of a glittering conventional political career. In 1785, however, he went through a period of spiritual crisis and → conversion, leading, under the influence of Isaac Milner (1750-1820) and John Newton (1725-1807), to distinctively → evangelical convictions. As a consequence, he committed himself in the later 1780s to work for the abolition of the slave trade, and for moral and spiritual reformation at home.

Wilberforce's first major speech on the slave trade was delivered in May 1789. He established himself as the key leader of the campaign in Parliament, complementing the work of others, such as Thomas Clarkson (1760-1846), who gathered information and mobilized public opinion. Debates were increasingly overshadowed by political insecurity and international instability following the French → Revolution (§2.4). Hence although in April 1792 the House of Commons agreed in principle to the gradual abolition of the trade, it proved impossible to turn this decision into enforceable legislation. For the next decade Wilberforce kept the issue alive, until from 1804 onward success was at last in sight. The act abolishing the slave trade in British colonies and ships was eventually passed in 1807, the fruit of 18 years' work.

Meanwhile, Wilberforce pursued his parallel concern for the re-Christianization of British national life. He was instrumental in persuading King George III (ruled 1760-1820) to issue in 1787 the Proclamation for the Encouragement of → Piety and → Virtue, and he then set up a society to further its implementation. His most important contribution in this sphere of action came in 1797 with the publication of *A Practical View of the Prevailing Religious System of Professed Christians in the Higher and Middle Classes of This Country, Contrasted with Real Christianity.* The work was a searching critique of nominal religious observance and a characteristically evangelical appeal to his readers to recognize their inherent sinfulness and to obtain → salvation by placing their → faith in Jesus Christ. There was also a significant patriotic dimension, as Wilberforce fervently believed that a turning to real Christianity was essential if the nation was to avoid the political and social convulsions currently sweeping France. The *Practical View* had a substantial impact and did much to renew spiritual interest and commend evangelicalism to the British elite. It also strengthened the position of evangelicals in the Church of England, to which Wilberforce was firmly committed.

The 1790s and early 1800s were the heyday of the so-called Clapham Sect, in which Wilberforce and his close friend Henry Thornton (1760-1815) were the leading figures, named after the village near London where several of them made their homes. This group of able and influential evangelical laymen played an important role in supporting the antislavery campaign and other evangelical political causes, as well as stimulating the formation of major organizations such as the Church Missionary Society (1799; → British Missions) and the British and Foreign → Bible Society (1804).

After 1807 Wilberforce campaigned for the effective implementation of the abolition of the slave trade and for its extension to the jurisdictions of other nations. In 1813 he helped to secure official sanction for Christian missionary activity in India. By the 1820s advancing years and declining health were limiting his activities, but he remained a revered evangelical figurehead. In 1823-24 he played an important part in launching the campaign for the abolition of slavery itself in British dominions, which was eventually successful in July 1833, a few days before his death.

Wilberforce married Barbara Spooner in 1797 and was a devoted family man who had two daughters and four sons. His third son, Samuel (1805-73), successively bishop of Oxford and of Winchester, became one of the leading figures in the early Victorian Church of England.

Wilberforce's legacy is a complex one. In spiritual and moral terms he was a trenchant critic of complacency and → compromise with the secular world. In political terms, though, his instincts were conservative, and especially as he grew older, he was perceived as insensitive to the injustices of his own society, even as he condemned the oppression of the slaves in the West Indies. He continues to inspire evangelicals who strive for spiritual renewal, for the transformation of contemporary society, for racial equality, and for justice to the developing world. While, however, his career can indeed yield important insights for contemporary activists, care needs to be taken to avoid anachronistic or distorted interpretations.

Bibliography: Primary sources and biography: From Enlightenment to Romanticism: Anthology I (ed. I. Donnachie and C. Lavin; Manchester, 2003) • *A Practical View of the Prevailing Religious System . . .* (1797; repr. as *A Practical View of Christianity* [ed. K. C. Belmonte; Peabody, Mass., 1996]) • *Private Papers of William Wilberforce* (ed. A. M. Wilberforce; London, 1897) • R. WILBERFORCE and S. WILBERFORCE, *The Life of William Wilberforce* (5 vols.; London, 1838; repr., Freeport, N.Y., 1972).

Secondary works: R. ANSTEY, *The Atlantic Slave Trade and British Abolition, 1760-1810* (London, 1975)

• I. BRADLEY, "The Politics of Godliness: Evangelicals in Parliament, 1784-1832" (D.Phil. thesis, University of Oxford, 1974) • E. M. HOWSE, *Saints in Politics: The "Clapham Sect" and the Growth of Freedom* (London, 1971) • J. R. OLDFIELD, *Popular Politics and British Anti-Slavery: The Mobilisation of Public Opinion against the Slave Trade* (Manchester, 1995) • J. POLLOCK, *Wilberforce* (London, 1977) • J. WOLFFE, *The Expansion of Evangelicalism: The Age of Wilberforce, More, Chalmers, and Finney* (Downers Grove, Ill., 2007).

JOHN WOLFFE

William of Ockham

1. Life
2. Ockham's "Razor"
3. God's Omnipotence and Freedom

1. Life

William of Ockham (ca. 1285-1347) was born in Ockham, a village in Surrey southwest of London, and entered the → Franciscan Order near the age of 14. Presumably, he was educated in the liberal arts at the Franciscan *studium* (house of studies) in London before being sent to Oxford in 1309 to study → theology. William probably lectured at Oxford on the Bible from 1315 to 1317, and on the *Sentences* of Peter Lombard (ca. 1100-1160) from 1317 to 1319. He thus fulfilled all the requirements to become a master of theology, but he never served as the Franciscan regent master at Oxford, either because others were in line before him or because of the criticisms of his theology by the chancellor of the university, John Lutterell (d. 1335). Instead, Ockham went back to the Franciscan *studium* in London, where he reworked somewhat his *Commentary on Book I of the Sentences* and wrote commentaries on some of Aristotle's works on logic and on his *Physics*, produced his monumental *Summa logicae*, and argued his *quodlibet* questions (i.e., questions on any subject the listeners might choose). His close Franciscan associates at London were his main critic, Walter Chatton (ca. 1290-1343), and Adam Wodeham (ca. 1300-1358), a loyal follower.

At the instigation of Lutterell, who charged him with heresy, Ockham was called to Avignon by Pope John XXII (1316-34). He spent five years in exile there while his case was being examined. At Avignon he joined Michael of Cesena (ca. 1270-1342), the general minister of the Franciscans, in his dispute with the → pope over the nature of apostolic → poverty (§5). In 1328 William, Michael, and a num-

ber of other Franciscans fled first to Genoa and then to Pisa, where they received an invitation from the pope's opponent, Emperor Louis IV of Bavaria (1314-47), to settle in Munich. Ockham spent the last 20 years of his life in Munich, writing on apostolic and Franciscan poverty, his *Questions on the Power of the Pope,* and other political writings. He died unrepentant in Munich in 1347 and was buried in the recently removed Franciscan cemetery of the Church of St. Anna.

2. Ockham's "Razor"

Ockham is most famous for the use of his "razor," that is, the principle of parsimony formulated by Aristotle in book 1 of the *Physics:* "It is better to assume a smaller and finite number of principles" (188a17-18). In his philosophical writings, William applied this principle of parsimony to the ten kinds of predicates affirmed or denied of realities according to Aristotle in his *Categories:* "substance, quantity, quality, relation, place, time, position, state, action, or affection" (1b25-26). For Ockham, there was no need to posit realities for each of these ten predicates. Some qualities in fact do signify realities distinct from the substances of which they were affirmed or denied. When we say "Socrates is white," Socrates is a substance, and white is a reality distinct from Socrates' substance; this whiteness is a reality, that is, a quality that inheres in him. If Socrates is white and Plato is white, they are alike in their color, but their likeness or similarity is not itself a quality inhering in each of them. They are qualitatively alike simply because they both are white and not because similarity exists as a quality in each of them.

Individual substances likewise are realities, but there is no need, according to Ockham, to posit any universal reality to explain how Socrates and Plato are essentially alike. There is no common reality "man" existing in each individual man that makes them alike. Parallel to the case of their qualitative similarity, they do not need some essential similarity existing in each of them to explain their essential likeness. They are essentially alike independently of any operation of our minds. Just being men is the foundation for their essential similarity. Ockham, in his *Summa logicae,* goes through each of the → categories, attempting to show how they can be understood without multiplying extra realities. He then applies his conception of the categories in all his other works.

Ockham frequently found that, in dealing with Aristotle's natural philosophy, for example, many of his contemporaries fell prey to a reifying temptation. They did so by contending that "sudden change," "motion," "time," "action," and "affection" signified realities distinct from individual substances and inhering qualities. Words, especially when they are put in noun forms, he argued, often deceive us into thinking there are separate realities corresponding to them. "Sudden change" is not a reality on its own; it does not signify anything that does not last or endure through time, but it signifies that some enduring substance acquires or loses something (a form) all at one time and not part before part or part after part (→ Nominalism).

In theology, likewise, Ockham warns us to be careful regarding the realities described by our words. William attempts at times to show how a predicate can be really affirmed of a subject, even though such a predicate does not signify something really and subjectively inhering in the thing signified by the subject. He argues, for example, that "creativity is not really in God, although God is really creative . . . because if it were really in God, He would have something in Himself which He previously did not have, since before the creation of the world this was a false proposition 'Creativity is really in God.'" Much of Ockham's philosophy and theology deals with restating or decoding philosophical and theological statements to bring out exactly what realities these statements are signifying.

3. God's Omnipotence and Freedom

3.1. One of the chief truths that affects Ockham's basic intellectual framework and plays an important role in the application of his "razor" is God's omnipotence and freedom, on which he concentrates intensely. One conclusion he draws from his view of divine omnipotence is that the world is not produced by God necessarily. → Creation is essentially a free production flowing from God's wisdom and love. William accepts the technical scholastic explanation of the freedom of creation by distinguishing between God's absolute power and God's ordained → power. These are not, for him, two distinct powers or competing sources of action in God. Alexander of Hales (ca. 1185-1245) and Bonaventure (ca. 1217-74), before William, indicated that this distinction does not imply a contrast between ordered power and disordered power. Shortly after them, Richard of Middleton (ca. 1249-?1302) claimed that the distinction serves the purpose of simply saying, "Given that God has freely placed a certain order among creatures, it is manifest that there is an infinite number of other possible and perfectly good things that could have been chosen by God, absolutely speaking."

From these Franciscan predecessors Ockham thus learned that all things that God does, he does by his well-ordered or ordained power. God's absolute power is not a disorderly or arbitrary power; indeed, it is not a power at all but rather is an expression that explains how God could have done things differently or chosen another way, indeed another world. Absolute power expresses the other possible directions that God's actual or ordained will might have chosen. It is in this sense that the world and everything about it could have had another order. The actual or chosen order still has laws, but such necessary, or rather habitual, dimensions of created reality have been freely chosen by God. They are thus only contingently or conditionally necessary. Aristotle's philosophy, according to Ockham, attempts to deal with the way nature functions, though nature does not function in this way with absolute necessity. Any statements regarding the created world that suggest absolute necessity must be adjusted.

3.2. More generally speaking, William's conceptions of philosophy and theology were very much fostered by the debates concerning the scientific character of these disciplines that took place over the preceding century. During that period theologians attempted to respond to the challenge of Aristotle's claim that → philosophy is the fundamental intellectual discipline. For Ockham, philosophy is Aristotle's corpus or, more generally, pagan thought. Most often he criticizes some of his contemporaries' understanding of the Aristotelian corpus of writings and, at times, he challenges Aristotle himself when Aristotle, unaware of divine revelation, presents created reality as following absolutely necessary laws.

By Ockham's time, the term "theology" had taken on three basic meanings: the study of Scripture within the framework of the teachings of the faith handed down by the church; the understanding of that same faith that could be brought about by rational reflection and argumentation related to its central teachings; and, finally, the further development of that faith by means that would bring out or make explicit what was seen as presumed or implicit in the teachings of the Scriptures. The first understanding of theology he accepts without challenge. The latter two forms of theology were, in his era, called declarative and deductive theology. Declarative theology, following an Augustinian path, attempts to bring understanding to the truths accepted on God-given faith and pushes in the direction of a unified philosophical-theological vision of reality.

Ockham, while supporting the unified form of Christian knowledge that declarative theology fosters, criticizes Peter Auriol's (ca. 1280-1322) presentation of such theology as wisdom, since many elements of declarative theology represent opinions that could be erroneous. Deductive theology, following more the Aristotelian direction of deductive science fostered by Thomas Aquinas (ca. 1225-74) and his followers, such as Richard of Middleton, extends the truths that must be necessarily accepted as certainly revealed by God. Ockham does not object to the deductive method as such, but he does oppose those who make the claim that such conclusions are science, since science means "based on evidence." Just as the premises or principles are accepted on faith, so are the conclusions drawn from them. As he argues, "It is no more derogatory to say that conclusions are not known in an evident way than it is derogatory to the dignity of the knowledge of the principles [or articles of the creed], that they are not known in an evident manner" (Ockham, "Sent. I, q. 7" [ed. St. Bonaventure, N.Y., 1967] 1.199). William practices both declarative and deductive theology, but he is very hesitant when it comes to attributing to them the titles "wisdom" or "science" in the strict sense of these terms.

3.3. As mentioned above, many of the discussions carried on in Ockham's writings are explicitly treated within the framework of the distinction between God's absolute and ordained power. For instance, in his discussion of grace in distinction 17 of his *Commentary on Book I of Peter Lombard's Sentences,* Ockham follows the treatments of John Duns Scotus (ca. 1265-1308; → Scotism) and Peter Auriol in the same location. Scotus distinguishes between actual and sanctifying grace and describes the latter as a created habit that is a free gift of God inhering in the soul that makes the graced person dear to God. From Scotus's viewpoint God, as omnipotent, by his absolute power could accept a soul without the created habit of charity being present in it. From the viewpoint of God's established order, however, → grace or → charity as a quality in the soul is necessary for meriting eternal life.

Peter Auriol, Ockham's chief opponent on this issue, argues against Scotus, claiming that for a soul to be loved and dear and accepted by God for eternal beatitude, it is necessary that some absolute created habit of grace inform the soul, so that without such a form a soul cannot, even by God's absolute power, be dear to God. This form itself is necessarily dear to God, and likewise so is a soul that is informed by such a form. The result is that when this form is present, the soul cannot not be dear to God, even by his absolute power. Ockham criticizes Auriol's position for establishing something as necessary when it is not absolutely necessary. Operating within the framework of God's absolute power, Ockham argues that someone can be dear to and accepted by God for eternal life without an inhering supernatural form and that no matter what kind of supernatural form might be posited in the soul, the soul can still be not accepted by God. In the actual order God has established, however, it is the habit of grace inhering in the soul that makes a person dear to God and capable of performing acts that can merit eternal life.

Here, as in so many places in his philosophical and theological writings, Ockham shows his tendency to challenge necessities that are presented as absolute. He tries to establish, where possible, a portrait of God's omnipotence and freedom in regard to an essentially contingent created world that manifests an order; it is not a self-contained order, however, but one set by God's wisdom and love.

If we were to compare Ockham to other medieval authors, we would note that Thomas Aquinas accepted the distinction between God's absolute and ordained power, as did his contemporary Bonaventure and other 13th-century theologians. Aquinas's orientation, however, was much more aimed at actuality, so the thrust of his philosophy and theology headed in the direction of the order ordained by God. Duns Scotus reacted to the intellectual world slightly later at Oxford and Paris. If the condemnations of 1267 are any indication, the Averroistic interpretation of Aristotle tended to stress the uncreated eternal character of the world and the necessary nature of its laws (→ Islamic Philosophy 4.6). Scotus countered this approach by stressing the distinction between God's absolute and ordained power, underlining the freedom with which God created. Fire burns, but as the Book of Daniel (chap. 3) tells us regarding the three burning boys in the furnace, it does not necessarily burn. It burns by God's free will. Ockham tried to achieve a further balance of divine freedom and the necessity of nature within this context that he inherited from Scotus.

Bibliography: Primary sources: A Compendium of Ockham's Teachings: A Translation of the Tractatus de principiis theologiae (trans. J. Davies; St. Bonaventure, N.Y., 1998) • *The De sacramento altaris* (trans. T. B. Birch; Burlington, Iowa, 1962) • *Guillelmi de Ockham Opera philosophica et theologica* (17 vols.; ed. G. Gál et al.; St. Bonaventure, N.Y., 1967-88) • *Guillelmi de Ockham Opera politica* (3 vols.; ed. J. G. Sikes and H. S. Offler; Manchester, 1956-74) • *A Letter to the Friars Minor, and Other Writings* (ed. A. S. McGrade and J. Kilcullen; Cambridge, 1995) • *Predestination, God's*

Foreknowledge, and Future Contingents (2d ed.; trans. M. M. Adams and N. Kretzmann; Indianapolis, 1983) • *Quodlibetal Questions* (2 vols.; trans. A. J. Freddoso and F. E. Kelly; New Haven, 1991) • "Using and Enjoying" (*Sent.* I, dist. 1, qq. 1-6), *Ethics and Political Philosophy* (trans. A. S. McGrade et al.; Cambridge, 2001) 349-417.

Bibliography: J. P. BECKMANN, *Ockham Bibliographie, 1900-1990* (Hamburg, 1992).

Secondary works: M. M. ADAMS, *William Ockham* (2 vols.; Notre Dame, Ind., 1987) • J. P. BECKMANN, *Wilhelm von Ockham* (Munich, 1995) • R. GUELLUY, *Philosophie et théologie chez Guillaume d'Ockham* (Louvain, 1947) • M. KAUFMANN, *Begriffe, Sätze, Dinge, Referenz und Wahrheit bei Wilhelm von Ockham* (Leiden, 1994) • V. LEPPIN, *Geglaubte Wahrheit. Das Theologieverständnis Wilhelms von Ockham* (Göttingen, 1995) • A. MAURER, *The Philosophy of William of Ockham in the Light of Its Principles* (Toronto, 1998) • A. PELLIGRINI, *Statuto epistemologico della teologia secondo Guglielmo di Occam* (Florence, 1995) • P. VIGNAUX, *Justification et prédestination au XIVᵉ siècle* (Paris, 1934).

STEPHEN F. BROWN

Wine

1. OT
2. NT
3. Church History

1. OT

Viniculture finds early attestation in Israel. Along with grain and oil, wine symbolized agrarian prosperity (Hos. 2:8; Gen. 27:28; Deut. 7:13, etc.). The spies who investigated the promised land brought back giant grapes (Num. 13:21-27) to show what wealth God had promised his people. The autumn harvest was a time of rejoicing (Isa. 16:9). Wine was an everyday drink and was generally judged positively (Judg. 9:13; Ps. 104:15; Deut. 8:7-10). It was a gift of God that brought joy (Judg. 9:13; Eccl. 9:7). But warnings against intoxication had to be given (Amos 6:6; Isa. 5:11-12, 22; 28:1, 7; → Prophet, Prophecy, 2). The → Wisdom literature viewed wine as a divine gift that could be misused (Sir. 39:25-27; see also Prov. 23:20, 30-31). Priests had to accept temporary abstinence (Lev. 10:8-10; Ezek. 44:21). The → Nazirites (Num. 6:2-4; Judg. 13:4) and Rechabites (Jeremiah 35) were total abstainers in their protest against a more cultivated lifestyle.

In the cult, wine served as a drink offering (Exod. 29:38-41; Num. 15:5; → Sacrifice 2). The red color

of wine in antiquity carried associations with blood offerings (Gen. 49:11: "the blood of grapes"; see also Sir. 50:15). Early → Judaism found a place for wine in celebrating the → Sabbath and also at the → Passover (*Jub.* 49:6; *m. Pesaḥ.* 10:1).

Wine also found a broad metaphoric use in Israel. It was a symbol of the time of → salvation (§1.2) with its great abundance and its days of festal joy. Mountains would "drip with wine" (Amos 9:13); the coming messianic ruler would "wash his garments in wine" (Gen. 49:13); God would provide costly wine at his eschatological banquet for the nations (Isa. 25:6). Israel is depicted as a vine that God has planted (Isaiah 5; Ps. 80:8-13); it is a choice vine (Jer. 2:21). Yet the association between wine and blood also gave rise to the thought of divine judgment (→ Last Judgment 2.1) as a cup that God hands to the enemies of his people (Isa. 63:1-6; cf. Rev. 14:19-20).

2. NT

At the festive meals that → Jesus celebrated with his disciples, wine was drunk to symbolize the joy that the imminent approach of God's kingdom brought with it (Mark 2:19; cf. John 2:1-10). We see here a contrast with the Naziritic → asceticism of John the Baptist (Matt. 11:18-19).

Wine carried an even greater symbolism relative to the time of salvation as it was used at the Last Supper (→ Eucharist 2). In the eschatological saying as the last cup was handed round (Mark 14:25), Jesus promised the recipients a visible consummation of their fellowship with him as the rule of God achieved final fulfillment. He was able to give this → promise because, as he said, he would lay down his life "for many" (v. 24). The wine symbolized his blood that would be outpoured. It was a realistic symbol of his death.

The NT also adopts the thought of God's people as a vine. In John 15 Jesus compared himself to the vine and his followers to the branches. The branches must remain in the vine and they must be pruned if they are to be fruitful. Only fellowship with Jesus himself gives believers the status of branches.

3. Church History

Except in a few cases, wine has always been a constituent part of the → Eucharist (§4.3). (Water was used in Communion in the ancient → Syrian Orthodox Church.) Churches in the East use red wine because of its symbolic power, but white wine, which is more easily cleansed, is used in the West. Water is often added to symbolize the two natures of the God-man (→ Christology 2.1; see John 19:34).

A question in Asia and Africa is whether wine must be used, for in some places bread and wine are not staple products. In some situations, the use of alcohol is also a problem. Perhaps exceptions are permissible so long as good reasons are given. We must remember, however, that the Eucharist is a gift of Jesus and is not at our disposal. Administrative changes should not be made arbitrarily. We should see, too, that not to use wine is to abandon both the symbolism and the reality.

Bibliography: J. L. BERQUIST, *Ancient Wine, New Wineskins: The Lord's Supper in OT Perspective* (St. Louis, 1991) • W. DOMMERSHAUSEN, "Der Wein im Urteil und Bild des Alten Testaments," *TTZ* 84 (1975) 253-60 • R. FRANKEL, *Wine and Oil Production in Antiquity in Israel and Other Mediterranean Countries* (Sheffield, 1999) • S. H. GRIFFITH, "Spirit in the Bread; Fire in the Wine: The Eucharist as 'Living Medicine' in the Thought of Ephraem the Syrian," *MoTh* 15 (1999) 225-46 • C. T. SELTMAN, *Wine in the Ancient World* (London, 1957) • C. E. WALSH, *The Fruit of the Vine: Viticulture in Ancient Israel* (Winona Lake, Ind., 2000).

JÜRGEN ROLOFF†

Wisdom Literature

1. Term
2. Books
3. Setting
4. Influences
5. Forms and Genres
6. Ideology
7. Later Developments
8. NT and Church

1. Term

The Hebrew word *ḥokmâ* originally meant technical and intellectual understanding resting on → experience. While statutes were associated with the priests, and the → Word of God with the → prophets, counsel typified the wise (Jer. 18:18). The quest for wisdom involves reflection on universal human concerns: the place of humanity within the world, especially the potential and limitations of the individual. In the Bible, it is the attempt to ascertain the meaning of life, to explore its difficult and painful mysteries, to engage in the relentless search for God, and to discover God's will as crucial to human welfare. One cannot truly be wise without a relationship with God; ultimately, the most important goal in life is to fear God and obey him (Eccl. 12:13-14; Sir. 1:20).

2. Books

The canonical and deuterocanonical works of the OT (→ Canon) that teach a basically sound and successful attitude to both God and society are called Wisdom books because the terms "wise" and "wisdom" play a central role in them and because they set forth a lifestyle that is based on wisdom. → Solomon is depicted as a king whom God had granted wisdom (1 Kgs. 3:11-12; 4:29-34; 10:1-7, 23-25; 2 Chr. 1:7-12; 9:1-7, 22-24), and tradition associated him with the books of Proverbs (1:1; 10:1; 25:1), Ecclesiastes (1:1, 12ff.), Wisdom (9:7-8), and the Song of Songs (1:1; 3:11). Job is also a Wisdom book, as is Sirach (Ecclesiasticus).

Also belonging to this category are some of the Psalms (e.g., 1; 32; 39; 49; 73; 128; and alphabetic psalms such as 9/10; 25; 34; 37; 119). Wisdom influences may be detected in the prophets as well (Isa. 28:23-29). Certain scholars also put in this category the Joseph story (Genesis 37–50), the beginning and end of Job (1:1–2:10; 42:11-17), Jonah, Ruth, the stories of Daniel and his three friends (Daniel 1–5), some aspects of Esther, and Tobit (4:3-19; 12:6-15). A reflection on the way on which contemporary wisdom viewed nature and peoples might be found in Genesis 1 and 10, and in Job 38–41.

3. Setting

Wisdom writings have been identified throughout the ancient Near East and Egypt. Biblical sayings, teachings, and dialogue find their equivalents in Sumerian, Akkadian (*TUAT* 3/1), and Egyptian (*AEL* vols. 1-3; *BAW.AO; TUAT* 3/2) works. There is no indisputable biblical or archaeological evidence of the existence of a school in either the preexilic or postexilic period (see Jer. 9:23-24; Ezek. 7:26). Only in about 190 B.C. do we first read of a *bet* → *midrash,* or "house of instruction" (Sir. 51:23). Sirach seems to have been a priestly writer who as a scribe, working with other scholars, supervised the sons of the upper classes in Jerusalem.

One theory is that Job and Proverbs 1–9 are a literary echo of the practical wisdom offered by fourth- or third-century scribes. Unlike the proverbs of Egypt (→ Egyptian Religion), only in some cases are the sayings and teachings of Mesopotamia and Israel addressed to specific groups or ages. Thus the fatherly proverbs of Proverbs 1–9 aim at adolescents. A scribal calling comparable to that of Egypt (*AEL* 2.168-78) is found only in Sir. 38:24–39:11.

4. Influences

Geographically and politically, Israel was always under the divergent influences of Egyptian, Mesopotamian, Persian, and Hellenistic cultures (→ Hellenism), and we must take these influences into account regarding Wisdom as well. The second half of the second millennium saw a movement of Akkadian literature from Asia Minor to Egypt (see the texts in North Canaanite → Ugarit). Parallels with Ugaritic poetry (*TUAT* 3/1.140-43) show that the wise men of Israel borrowed from Canaan.

Egyptian Wisdom also had an impact under the monarchy, as illustrated by Prov. 22:17–24:22, whose structure and themes are dependent on the teaching of Amenemope (*TUAT* 3/2.222-50). But these Words of the Wise are also related to Aramaic Wisdom (3/2.320-47). We detect the influence of the Akkadian poem *Ludlul bēl nēmeqi* in the structure of Job, with its complaints and answers, which contain a song of praise to the Lord of Wisdom (3/1.110-35) and the complaint of a sufferer with a prayer to Marduk (3/1.140-43). Possibly Job took its dialogue form from the so-called Babylonian Theodicy (3/1.143-57). Ecclesiastes shows the poetry and philosophy of Hellenism at work (→ Greek Philosophy), as do Sirach and Wisdom, though these last two have evident apologetic features.

5. Forms and Genres

In the OT the various forms of Wisdom sayings are called *māšāl*. They may derive from common observations and individual experiences (1 Sam. 4:20; Gen. 35:17; Isa. 28:20), which could then be generalized and applied in solving verbal conflicts (Judg. 8:2, 21; 1 Kgs. 20:11).

The basic forms of proverbs are brief statements or pronouncements, comparative ("better than") sayings, number sayings, admonitions, counsels, warnings, congratulations, and didactic questions. Pronouncements in synonymous (Prov. 5:15; Job 5:2; Sir. 14:4) or synthetic (Prov. 21:21-31; Eccl. 6:7; Sir. 13:20; Wis. 1:3) parallelism state matters either by positive or negative contrast (Prov. 1:7; Eccl. 5:11; Sir. 13:21). Comparative sayings tell us what is good or helpful and then what is better (Eccl. 7:1-8; Prov. 15:16-17; Sir. 20:31; Wis. 4:1). Number sayings denote objects with one or more common features and list what is common to them (Prov. 30:15-31). Warnings and counsels usually say why they are to be followed and emphasize the good or bad results of observance or nonobservance (Prov. 3:1-2; 7:2; Ps. 37:37; Eccl. 5:1; vs. Prov. 22:22-23; 27:1; Eccl. 5:2; Sir. 6:1-2; 27:17). The strongest form of motivation is that God will bless those who do what is suggested, rewarded in congratulatory formulas resembling → beatitudes (Prov. 3:13; Job 5:17; Ps. 1:1; Sir. 14:1-2). Didactic or rhetorical questions that rest on

accepted religious or ethical presuppositions expect agreement (Amos 3:3–6:14; Isa. 40:12-31; 50:1-3; Job 8:11; Eccl. 6:12; 8:4; Sir. 25:11).

Wisdom genres also include fables from the → animal or vegetable world that are applied to human situations (Judg. 9:8-15; 2 Kgs. 14:9; see *TUAT* 3/1.41-43). Riddles demonstrating authenticity are also found (Judg. 14:14, 18; see *TUAT* 3/1.44-46). Other genres include illustrations (Job 33:14-18; see *TUAT* 3/1.174-80), personal testimonies (Prov. 4:3-9; 30:1-3; Eccl. 1:12-18; Ps. 37:25, 35-36), and → parables (Isa. 28:23-28; Eccl. 9:14-16).

Literary forms include collections of proverbs (Prov. 10–15; 16:1–22:16; 25–29; see *TUAT* 3/1.23-40, 163-68; *BAW.AO* 193ff., 257ff.) and of teaching material (Prov. 1–9; 22:17–24:22; 24:23-34; 31:1-9; see *BAW.AO* 101ff., 196ff., 292ff. and *TUAT* 3/2.195-221). Typically, this teaching is introduced by a call for attention (Prov. 4:1; 5:1) or a prologue or opening formula (Prov. 1:1-7; 22:17-21; see *TUAT* 3/2.225-26) and concluded with a recapitulation (Prov. 1:19; Job 8:13; Eccl. 7:23-24; Sir. 1:10; Isa. 17:14b). Reflection on a matter (Eccl. 3:10-15) and a theological summary (Prov. 30:1-14) are specific forms of instruction. Job uses the genre of controversy or → dialogue (Job 3–31[37]; see *TUAT* 3/1.91-102, 143-57, 158-63 and *AEL* 1.163-69, 169-84).

6. Ideology

The basic thinking of proverbs, like that of myth, is aspective rather than constructive. It is situational rather than rigid for every circumstance. The wise person has a store of wisdom gained from experience and knows which way of behaving is appropriate to the situation.

Primary human experience shows that a socially righteous life brings happiness and personal well-being. The theory of retribution underlies most of the Wisdom writings. Doing good leads to pleasure, the greatest ethical goal (→ Ethics 1.3). In the OT the theological foundation is that → Yahweh is the Lord of destiny who guides the universe and will grant long → life and prosperity to the righteous and faithful (Prov. 3:13-18). The sayings of the wise, therefore, take a sober look at human conduct, contrasting the ways of the wise with those of fools (Prov. 3:35; 10:1; Eccl. 2:14) and those of the devout and righteous with those of the unjust and ungodly (Prov. 3:33; 4:18-19; 10:3, 6-7, 11, 20-21; 11:5-31; Ps. 37:8-40; Wis. 2:10–3:12). Wisdom demands a choice between the way of evil and the way of uprightness (Proverbs; Psalm 1). An ideal person will be God-fearing, self-controlled, and diligent, always acting, speaking, or being silent at the right time (Prov. 3:5-10; 15:23; 18:13; 21:23; 24:30-34; Eccl. 9:10; Sir. 1:11-20; 4:20-31; 20:1-8). Patience, hope, trust, and other virtues are essential factors of character in order for God to maintain moral order, including justice.

7. Later Developments

Faced with increased diversity and the dissolution of a kinship-based society, the wise in Israel increasingly came to regard as only conditionally valid the basic principle that faithfulness brings happiness. Their primary focus became an intensification of basic integrity (Prov. 16:16, 19; 17:1; 19:1; 28:6). A broader notion of individual destiny during the late Persian period produced a more skeptical attitude (Job 21; 24:1-4, 10-12). Hence the wise pointed to the divine wisdom that transcends human intellect and is thus hidden (Job 28; 38–39; Eccl. 8:10-15; Sir. 11:18-26; 16:15-23; Wis. 2:1–3:12). Foremost, they demanded fear of God, "the beginning of wisdom" (Prov. 1:7, 29; 9:10; 14:27; 15:16; 19:23; Eccl. 12:13).

In the age of → Hellenism the sages related these developments to a common belief in fate (Eccl. 3:1-15; see 1QS 3:13–4:26). This gave rise in Judaism to belief in (1) the responsibility of humans to conduct themselves with trust in the righteousness of God and (2) the dogma of divine → forgiveness (Job 34:10-15; Ps. 145:8-20), in some cases linking these with the wisdom of God's created order (Prov. 3:13-26; 8:22-36; → Creation). The sufferings of the innocent were viewed as a means of divine correction and ultimately part of one's complete instruction for life (Job 5:17-27; 33:8-33; Prov. 3:11-12). Stability was achieved when it was realized that sinfulness (→ Sin 1) is inherent in humankind (Job 4:12-21; 15:14-16; Ps. 51:5; 1QS 11:14-17). Wisdom was now expressly equated with devotion to the Law (Ps. 1; 19:7-11; 119). Study of the → Torah was regarded as the true source of wisdom (Sir. 24:23, 25-29) and demanded discipline (21:11), leading students to the fear of the Lord, which is both the crown and the root of all wisdom (1:18, 20).

8. NT and Church

Wisdom influences can be discerned throughout the NT, from the parables of Jesus to the Gospel of John and Paul's first letter to the Corinthians. The Epistle of James especially reflects the ethos of Hebrew Wisdom traditions (Jas. 3:13-14, 17-18). James identifies himself as a teacher (3:1) and connects Christian virtue with wisdom (3:13-18); the letter stresses the seriousness, care, and moral integrity required for that endeavor.

In the Greco-Roman world, *sophia* occurs as a synonym for → "philosophy" in general or for reasoned rhetoric. Paul views the natural or worldly "wisdom of this age" (1 Cor. 2:6) as inferior to the "wisdom of God" (Rom. 11:33; Eph. 3:10), revealed in the cross (1 Cor. 1:23-24, 30; → Theologia crucis). The capacity to discern the workings of the Divine in the midst of daily life is superior to the technical competence of knowledge without faith (1 Corinthians 1–3, esp. 1:20, 25; 3:19; 13:2). James, too, contrasts wisdom "from above" with a wisdom that is "earthly, unspiritual, devilish" (Jas. 3:15).

The NT testifies to Jesus Christ as the very embodiment of God's wisdom (1 Cor. 1:30). He grew up in wisdom (Luke 2:40-51) and is the one "in whom are hidden all the treasures of wisdom and knowledge" (Col. 2:2-3). To seek true knowledge is to seek a deepening relationship with Jesus Christ.

The early church viewed the Wisdom books as guidance for an obedient life. Emphasis on the teachings of Jesus provided the foundation for later concern for ethics, practical or pastoral theology, philosophical theology, and other disciplines.

Wisdom is a gift from God (Eph. 1:17; Jas. 1:5). It urges believers to walk in the "way" that leads to → life in the fullest sense, experiencing a vital relationship to the Lord, knowing and doing the truth. For Christians, the teachings of the sages as embodied by Christ are a call to moral action, including honesty, diligence, self-control, and a sense of responsibility. Morality and wisdom cannot be separated.

Bibliography: H. W. BALLARD and W. D. TUCKER, eds., *An Introduction to Wisdom Literature and the Psalms* (Macon, Ga., 2000) • D. BERGANT, *Israel's Wisdom Literature: A Liberation-Critical Reading* (Minneapolis, 1997) • J. BLENKINSOPP, *Wisdom and Law in the OT: The Ordering of Life in Israel and Early Judaism* (rev. ed.; New York, 1995) • W. P. BROWN, *Character in Crisis: A Fresh Approach to the Wisdom Literature of the OT* (Grand Rapids, 1996) • J. CRENSHAW, *OT Wisdom* (rev. ed.; Atlanta, 1998) • K. J. DELL, *Get Wisdom, Get Insight: An Introduction to Israel's Wisdom Literature* (Macon, Ga., 2000) • D. J. ESTES, *Handbook on the Wisdom Books and Psalms* (Grand Rapids, 2005) • J. G. GAMMIE and L. G. PERDUE, eds., *The Sage in Israel and the Ancient Near East* (Winona Lake, Ind., 1990) • H. GESE, *Lehre und Wirklichkeit in der alten Weisheit* (Tübingen, 1958) • M. HENGEL, *Judaism and Hellenism* (Philadelphia, 1974) • O. KAISER, *Der Gott des Alten Testaments* (3 vols.; Göttingen, 1993-2003); idem, *Introduction to the OT* (Minneapolis, 1975) • W. G. LAMBERT, *Babylonian Wisdom Literature* (Oxford, 1960) • M. LICHTHEIM, *Late Egyptian Wisdom Literature in the*

International Context (Freiburg, 1983) • D. F. Morgan, *Wisdom in the OT Traditions* (Atlanta, 1981) • R. E. Murphy, *The Tree of Life: An Exploration of Biblical Wisdom Literature* (2d ed.; Grand Rapids, 1996) • M. Noth and D. W. Thomas, eds., *Wisdom in Israel and in the Ancient Near East* (Leiden, 1969) • G. von Rad, *Wisdom in Israel* (London, 1962) • O. S. Rankin, *Israel's Wisdom Literature* (Edinburgh, 1936) • F. K. D. Römheld, *Die Weisheitslehre im Alten Orient* (Munich, 1989) • S. Weeks, *Early Israelite Wisdom* (New York, 1994) • R. N. Whybray, *The Intellectual Tradition in the OT* (New York, 1974) • R. L. Wilken, ed., *Aspects of Wisdom in Judaism and Early Christianity* (Notre Dame, Ind., 1975) • J. G. Williams, *Those Who Ponder Proverbs: Aphoristic Thinking and Biblical Literature* (Sheffield, 1981).

Otto Kaiser, with Allen C. Myers

Witchcraft

1. Biblical
2. Historical
3. Anthropological
4. Neopagan

"Witchcraft" is a word that history and usage have stretched beyond a single meaning. Jeffrey Burton Russell distinguishes three types of witch: "the sorcerer who practices the simple magic found worldwide; the heretic who allegedly practiced diabolism and was prosecuted during the witch hunts; the neopagan. They have little in common other than the name 'witch'" (J. B. Russell and B. Alexander, 193). We can add to Russell's typology a fourth classification, that of the biblical witch. Each of these categories has its own history and definition.

1. Biblical
Biblical references to witches or witchcraft are hard to apply with precision today because the biblical translators were naming ancient occult practices with terms taken from the theological controversies of their own day (the KJV was produced at the height of the English witch craze; see 2), and they were not always consistent in the way they did it. The various Hebrew and Greek words used — translated "witch" or "witchcraft" nine times in the KJV (1611), five times in the ASV (1901), and once in the NRSV (1989) — appear to refer to various forms of sorcery or malevolent → magic, possibly involving drugs. Sorcery in that sense is part of some, but by no means all, modern witchcraft.

The Hebrew word most often translated "witch(craft)" or "sorcerer/sorcery" is *kāšap* (e.g., Exod. 22:18; Deut. 18:10; 2 Chr. 33:6; Nah. 3:4). The root perhaps derives from a word that means "cut (up)" and may refer to drugs or medicinal plants sliced and shredded into a magical brew. The OT references may thus be to one who deals in medicines, potions, or poisons for occult purposes.

In the NT, Gk. *pharmakeia* and related forms refer to sorcery (Gal. 5:20 [KJV "witchcraft"]; Rev. 9:21; 18:23; 21:8; 22:15). Again, the central notion seems to be the occult use of drugs and potions.

Thus, while biblical pronouncements on the subject have an indirect relevance to modern witchcraft (and → occultism generally), the way the term was translated does not lend itself to scholarly precision or shed much light on the neopagan witchcraft we see today (see 4).

2. Historical
What is known as historical witchcraft had a limited life span. It began in Europe in the 11th century, flourished during the → Middle Ages, and finally ended in America in 1692. It is also called European, classic, dualistic, or diabolical witchcraft.

The academic view of historical witchcraft has undergone several major revisions over the last hundred years. At the beginning of the 20th century, historians largely discounted witchcraft as a fantasy of the → Inquisition, a product of the superstitious, Roman Catholic "Dark Ages." Then in 1921 Margaret Murray (1863-1963) startled scholars with a sensational new theory in her book *The Witch-Cult in Western Europe*. Murray argued that "witchcraft" was the Inquisition's term for an older, pre-Christian, fertility religion that had once pervaded Europe — in other words, that witchcraft was really leftover → paganism, as demonized by Christianity. Murray's view eventually became generally accepted (her article "Witchcraft" appeared in the *Encyclopedia Britannica* from 1929 until 1968). Murray's ideas helped fuel the rise of neopagan witchcraft during its formative years of the 1950s by (falsely) lending credibility to its claims of ancient lineage. However, her increasingly extreme opinions and increasingly careless scholarship caused the Murrayite thesis to be challenged and then rejected outright by scholars after her death (see Russell 1972, 36-37).

Today, historians approach the subject in several ways. One group, currently the most influential, emphasizes the social history of witchcraft, especially the social pattern of witch-accusations. Those historians generally assume that witchcraft per se never really existed and attribute the widespread belief in witchcraft to ignorance, superstition, and a Freudian dynamic of psychological projection. Another group of historians emphasizes the history of ideas, arguing that the concept or stereotype of witchcraft developed gradually from ideas that were assembled over centuries. Those historians conclude that (1) a stereotype of witchcraft evolved, derived in part from ancient ideas; (2) no one ever embodied the stereotype completely; (3) some people probably embodied some parts of the stereotype; and (4) the general belief in witchcraft disappeared when the → Enlightenment changed the prevailing worldview and turned the witchcraft stereotype into a → superstition.

According to Jeffrey Burton Russell (1972, 23), the stereotype of witchcraft was composed of elements drawn from five sources: (1) folk fertility religion, (2) low magic and sorcery, (3) → spiritism and demonology, and (4) Christian (Gnostic) heresy. The amalgam of those four was then interpreted and defined by a fifth element — Christian (scholastic) theology.

As the stereotype came together and was defined by scholastic theology, witchcraft began to be viewed as a → heresy; by 1235 it was being targeted by the Inquisition. By 1300, as the medieval synthesis began to unravel, witchcraft and witches, real or imagined, became the focus of popular anxieties, occasional pogroms, and, increasingly, theological concern.

However, it was the conflicts and anxieties unleashed by the → Reformation and the Counter-Reformation (→ Catholic Reform and Counter-reformation), coupled with the new technology of the printing press (mid-15th cent.), that turned Europe's sporadic witch-fears into the widespread and lethal witch-panic that raged from 1500 to 1700 and killed upwards of 60,000 victims. By 1500 the stereotype of witchcraft was fully developed; standard accusations included invoking and rendering obscene homage to the → devil, promiscuous sexual orgies, infant sacrifice by burning, → cannibalism of the sacrificed infant, flying through the air and performing black magic by the power of demons, changing visible shape by diabolical illusion, and so forth.

But by 1650 the mania had begun to burn itself out. In America the witch trials (1692) in Salem, Massachusetts, were the figurative last gasp of the European witch craze, which had largely died out in Europe several decades earlier. After 1700 witchcraft is heard from again only "in legend, literature and jest" (Russell and Alexander, 123).

3. Anthropological

Scholars of anthropology frequently refer to "witches" and "witchcraft" in their studies of primitive and tribal societies. The usage arose because E. E. Evans-Pritchard (1902-73), a leading scholar of primitive religion, distinguished between three kinds of magic among the Azande (sing. Zande) of southern Sudan: (1) benevolent magic; (2) malicious magic, or sorcery, which is learned and is performed by external means; and (3) a power to harm by internal, "psychic" means, inherited without learning or external methods. Evans-Pritchard called this third kind of magic "witchcraft." The distinctions are valid, but the terminology is arbitrary.

Today, many anthropologists use "witchcraft" in a broader sense to mean ordinary, malevolent, "black" magic (i.e., sorcery), particularly when it involves spirit-helpers or familiars. Sorcery of this kind was only one component of European witchcraft and is even less a component of neopagan witchcraft; studies of tribal "witchcraft" are therefore only indirectly relevant to either historical or modern witchcraft. From our standpoint, such studies serve mainly as a reminder that sorcery and black magic are indeed universal phenomena that appear in all times, in all societies, and among all classes of people.

4. Neopagan

About 250 years after historical witchcraft ceased to exist, neopagan witchcraft appeared. Also known as modern or religious witchcraft, it took form in England in the 1940s as the creation of one man. But as it grew, and especially when it came to the United States in the 1960s, neopagan witchcraft mushroomed into a populist magical mystery cult that has become one of the most dynamic and rapidly growing spiritual movements in America.

Modern witchcraft has its deepest roots in the → Romantic movement of the early 19th century. In 1828 Karl Jarcke (1801-52), a German legal scholar, proposed the idea that witchcraft was actually a form of leftover, degenerated paganism. Jarcke was trying to defend Roman Catholicism by discrediting witchcraft as an antisocial cult, but his concept lacked factual support. Nevertheless, it was picked up and turned on its head by French historian Jules Michelet (1798-1874), one of the 19th century's most vocal opponents of Christianity. In his 1862 work *La sorcière* (ET *Satanism and Witchcraft: A Study in Medieval Superstition* [1939]), Michelet argued that witchcraft was indeed a surviving pagan fertility-religion but that, far from being an antisocial cult, it alone had nurtured the spirit of freedom against what he saw as the medieval darkness and repression of the → Roman Catholic Church.

Michelet's idea, despite its continuing lack of evidential support, was then developed by one of his disciples, Charles Godfrey Leland (1824-1903), in his 1899 book *Aradia; or, The Gospel of the Witches.* Margaret Murray's work (see 2), while not building directly on Michelet, seemed to validate the same idea from a different direction. In that way, the belief that historical witchcraft was really a surviving form of pre-Christian paganism became the "charter myth" of neopagan witchcraft, and the idea was central to modern witchcraft's sense of its own religious identity until it was definitively discredited during the 1970s (R. Kieckhefer).

The man who brought together the various ideas and created the religion of modern witchcraft was Englishman Gerald B. Gardner (1884-1964). Gardner was widely traveled and spent much of his adult life in the Far East, where he became familiar with many systems of occultism and religion. After his return to England in 1936, he claimed to have discovered a secretive, surviving remnant of the "Old Religion." Because the witchcraft laws then in effect would have subjected him to legal penalties, Gardner first presented his ideas in a novel, *High Magic's Aid* (1949), but after these laws were repealed in 1951, he wrote of it directly in *Witchcraft Today* (1954) and *The Meaning of Witchcraft* (1959), now considered to be the founding texts of modern witchcraft.

Today, Gardner's story is widely regarded as an invention, even by many modern witches, and it is clear that the identification of witchcraft with pre-Christian paganism is historically untenable. Nevertheless, the thesis was considered tenable in the early days of the movement, when it mattered, and helped the movement to become established and self-sustaining.

Gardner called his witch-religion "wicca" (from OEng. *wicce,* "witch"), and the term has become a general designation for all forms of modern witchcraft, even those that developed independently of Gardner's direct influence. Gardner's own movement (sometimes called Gardnerian witchcraft) successfully promoted itself in Britain during the 1950s as the authentic version of witchcraft, then exported itself to America in 1962, when Raymond and Rosemary Buckland established a Gardnerian coven in Long Island, New York.

In the United States the movement has converged uniquely with a series of powerful cultural trends — first with the → counterculture of the 1960s, and then with some of the movements that emerged from it, especially → feminism, environmentalism, and self-help psychology. American witchcraft harnessed the cultural momentum of those trends to give itself a social, cultural, and spiritual presence that is increasingly robust and increasingly global in scope. The movement has also grown significantly by using the tool of the Internet, both for internal networking and for external publicity. Popular entertainment (including movies, TV, and the wildly successful Harry Potter books) has likewise contributed strongly to the new image and appeal of modern witchcraft. Today, the number of people participating in the movement is credibly estimated at between 1 and 1.5 million.

Modern witchcraft has no central authority and is therefore difficult to define; its common threads are less in the details of belief and practice than they are in a sense of agreement on attitude, outlook, and perspective. Witchcraft begins by asserting itself against the rejected background of the main → culture. Its identity is proclaimed in terms of its difference from, and its opposition to, the Christian-based culture and religion(s) of the West. Margot Adler describes witchcraft's religious outlook in four major points, which can be summarized as (1) → animism/polytheism/pantheism, (2) feminism, (3) "there's no such thing as sin" (her formula), and (4) spiritual reciprocity (i.e., people receive what they mete out to others) (p. viii).

Neopagan witchcraft is a new religion of nature worship and has no connection with its historic namesake, either in its beliefs or its practices. Modern witches are attempting to re-create a modern version of paganism, and their efforts have also sparked the wider neopagan movement, which includes those dedicated to reviving or reconstructing ancient Egyptian, Norse, Greek, and Roman religions.

Bibliography: M. ADLER, *Drawing Down the Moon: Witches, Druids, Goddess-Worshippers, and Other Neo-Pagans in America Today* (2d ed.; Boston, 1986) • D. E. AUNE, "Magic," *ISBE* 3.213-19 • R. BRIGGS, *Witches and Neighbors: The Social and Cultural Context of European Witchcraft* (2d ed.; Oxford, 2002) • N. COHN, *Europe's Inner Demons: An Enquiry Inspired by the Great Witch-Hunt* (New York, 1977) • E. E. EVANS-PRITCHARD, *Witchcraft, Oracles, and Magic among the Azande* (Oxford, 1950) • R. HUTTON, *The Triumph of the Moon: A History of Modern Pagan Witchcraft* (Oxford, 2000) • R. KIECKHEFER, *European Witch Trials: Their Foundations in Popular and Learned Culture, 1300-1500* (Berkeley, Calif., 1976) • S. A. NIGOSIAN, *Occultism in the OT* (Philadelphia, 1978) • J. B. RUSSELL, *Witchcraft in the Middle Ages* (Ithaca, N.Y., 1972) • J. B. RUSSELL and B. ALEXANDER, *A History of Witchcraft: Sorcerers, Heretics, and Pagans* (2d ed.; London, 2007).

BROOKS ALEXANDER

Women's Missions

Women's work as a calling for unmarried women in the sphere of Protestant world → mission developed only in the 19th century. The wives of missionaries had been performing certain tasks alongside their husbands, but it became clear that there was also a need for women to minister to women. For cultural and religious reasons narrow limits were often set for male → missionaries in women's work. But women especially needed to be told about the liberating and life-changing power of the gospel. Education would give women a new dignity. They also had a big part to play in church organizing and → church growth.

At first, independent women's work met with misunderstanding, opposition, and criticism, for vocational → work by women was unusual, and such work abroad seemed to be especially venturesome. The calling of women was associated with the desire for → emancipation, for the Christian world regarded → marriage as the divinely planned → vocation of women.

The first breakthroughs came in the United States in 1819 with the founding of the Methodist Women's Society and in England in 1827 with the commissioning of a woman missionary by the London Missionary Society. A pioneering event in the German-speaking world was the "appeal to women in Germany and Switzerland" issued in 1841 by Wilhelm Hoffmann (1806-73) of Basel. The great readiness of women to work in missions to pagans quickly found expression in missionary societies for women, for example, the Morgenländische Frauenmission (Oriental women's mission) in 1842 and Theodor Fliedner's (1800-1864) Kaiserwerther Orientwerk in 1851. In 1900 the Frauenmissionsgebetsbund (Women's missionary prayer league) was founded with a view to winning women for mission and finding them financial and spiritual support at home. Women first went out in great numbers in the → China Inland Mission. After long hesitation most missionary societies included branches for women's work or for nursing work. New societies were later founded to deal specifically, for example, with the handicapped, prostitutes, and other groups of women. The → Roman Catholic Church began to use nuns and women's societies in the 19th century, and today it has far more women at work than priests or members of the male orders.

Women are at work in → medical mission, education (schools for girls), and evangelistic and pastoral work among women. The great growth of women's work and appreciation of its importance have led the churches to appoint commissions to report on it (e.g., in Germany the commission Frauen in der Mission of Evangelisches Missionswerk). The aim is to keep women's work in touch with all aspects of world mission. Conferences are held for missionaries on leave, and opportunities are given for the exchanging of experiences, with input from women who belong to churches in other continents and whose witness regarding situations in which Christians are in a minority or in a battle for economic survival or under political repression constitute a challenge to missionary life and work. In the past, women's missions have brought vital changes in women's relations, and in solidarity with their sisters around the world (→ Ecumenism, Ecumenical Movement), they struggle against ongoing forms of → prejudice, oppression, and discrimination from which women suffer worldwide (→ Catholic Missions 5).

→ Ordination 7.4; Sexism; Third World 1.10

Bibliography: R. P. BEAVER, *All Loves Excelling: American Protestant Women in World Mission* (Grand Rapids, 1968) • A. DRIES, "American Catholic Women Missionaries, 1870-2000," *EncWRNA* 2.843-50 • M. T. HUBER and N. C. LUTKEHAUS, eds., *Gendered Missions: Women and Men in Missionary Discourse and Practice* (Ann Arbor, Mich., 1999) • H. B. MONTGOMERY, *Western Women in Eastern Lands: An Outline Study of Fifty Years of Woman's Work in Foreign Missions* (New York, 1911; repr., 1987) • D. L. ROBERT, *American Women in Mission: A Social History of Their Thought and Practice* (Macon, Ga., 1996); eadem, "Protestant Women Missionaries: Foreign and Home," *EncWRNA* 2.834-42; eadem, ed., *Gospel Bearers, Gender Barriers: Missionary Women in the Twentieth Century* (Maryknoll, N.Y., 2002) • H. THOMÄ, *Frauen unterwegs in die Zukunft* (Stuttgart, 1968) • R. TUCKER, *Guardians of the Great Commission: The Story of Women in Modern Missions* (Grand Rapids, 1988).

ELISABETH OTTMÜLLER

Women's Movement

1. Central Themes
2. Interlocking Inequalities
3. History
4. Diversity within the Movement

The women's movement seeks broadly to achieve → equality, justice, and self-determination for women. → "Feminism," or the theory and organized activity that promotes the full equality of women, often focuses also on other oppressed groups. The women's movement within Christianity consists of individuals for whom their Christian faith is central to their identity and the source of their feminist convictions. This position is in contrast to that of secular feminists, who might or might not practice a religion but for whom religion is immaterial to or compartmentalized away from their fight against → sexism. What Christianity contributes to feminism is a challenge to patriarchy as perpetuated in the church; conversely, feminism transforms Christianity into a reconstructed community closer to the ideal of the body of Christ.

1. Central Themes

The diverse groups within the religious women's movement draw together in a set of common concerns. They note that, according to the gender-role expectations in the dominant form of Christianity, men must be the strong leaders and actors in the public sphere and engage in domination over women, whereas women must be the nurturing supporters in the private sphere, oppressed into passivity and treated as inferiors. Christian feminists counter this prevailing patriarchal oppression of women with several strategies.

First, feminist theologians highlight the female imagery used in the Bible to describe → God (§7). From the feminine Wisdom (Gk. Sophia and Heb. Hokmah), who delighted God with her play before → creation, to → metaphors of God as a mother eagle, a midwife, and a baker woman, Christian feminists counter the notion that God is literally or metaphorically only male; instead, God both transcends and includes all human genders. Similarly, Christian feminists argue for inclusive language to refer to God, explaining how destructive it can be to women to refer to God exclusively as "he," which came about simply because in the Hebrew of the OT, all nouns and all second- and third-person pronouns have grammatical gender, even though most things referred to by these words (objects, concepts, and God) clearly have no actual gender. Some Christian feminists choose to balance out the usage by speaking of God exclusively as "she" or by using the altered spelling "Godde," while others in their writing avoid gender-specific pronouns completely.

A second strategy against patriarchalism is to highlight the positive stories that do exist in the Bible and in the records of the → early church. The Bible indeed is the source of inspiring stories of women who overcame gender oppression, such as → Mary Magdalene, who was among the first to visit the empty tomb after Jesus' resurrection and to deliver the news to the male disciples. Jesus' own revolutionary treatment of women is held up as a model for today's gender relationships. In addition, Christian feminists celebrate little-known female characters in the Bible such as Priscilla and Phoebe, whose existence is not often acknowledged in patriarchal sermons. Paul's companion Thecla, not mentioned in the canonical texts, and Emperor Constantine's mother, Helena (ca. 255-ca. 330), are two examples of women of the early church whose stories have been recovered and brought to prominence. Phyllis Trible's classic study *Texts of Terror: Literary-Feminist Readings of Biblical Narratives* (1984) deconstructs the biblical dark side, stories that have been used to send silencing and threatening messages to women in the patriarchal paradigm of the church.

Finally, Christian feminists reinterpret individual passages in the Bible, especially in the → Pentateuch and in the letters of → Paul, that have been used to prevent women from speaking, teaching, and leading in the church and living in equal relationships in the home. To do so, Christian feminists marshal the tools of the classical Greek and Hebrew of the original Bible authors, along with cultural knowledge of ancient Palestine and surrounding areas, to provide sociological context, historical accounts of the patriarchal beliefs of the church fathers, and even personal experiences of prayer and prophecy (→ Sociohistorical Exegesis). These alternative readings challenge prevailing interpretations of Scripture that ostensibly call for women's subordination. And Christian feminists point to Scriptures that support full equality as part of God's plan for all humanity, primarily: "There is no longer Jew or Greek, there is no longer slave or free, there is no longer male or female; for all of you are one in Christ Jesus" (Gal. 3:28).

Grounded in these reinterpretations of the Bible, Christian feminists have taken positions in favor of women's → ordination (§7.4), lay leadership, teaching, and prophesying in the church. The Christian feminist lens also is important for → everyday living, providing perspectives on the controversies of → abortion, → poverty, → war, domestic violence, and mothering.

2. Interlocking Inequalities

Christian feminism does not focus solely on gender equality, since sexism is inextricably linked within religion to other oppressions based on race (→ Racism), social class (→ Classism), disability, sexual orientation, and environmental destruction (→ Environmental Ethics). Authors Delores Williams and Katie Geneva Cannon have articulated an African-American perspective on feminism and Christianity called womanism. Mujerista theology foregrounds the voices of Hispanic Christian feminists like Ada María Isasi-Díaz and Ana Castillo. Asian women's theology is epitomized by the work of Kwok Pui-lan and Chung Hyun Kyung.

Rosemary Radford Ruether is also a forerunner in Christian approaches to ecofeminism, arguing that the flora and fauna of the earth are a key part of the divine creation and deserve careful attention. Joan Chittister argues that what Christian feminists can add to the move toward environmental preservation is a challenge to the language of domination and subjugation of the earth as interpreted in Genesis.

Advocating for the full inclusion of gay, lesbian, bisexual, and transgender people in ordained leadership and church participation remains controversial, but some Christian feminists embrace sexual identity as part of the larger feminist struggle (→ Homosexuality). Organizations such as Christian Lesbians Out (founded in 1990) and SoulForce (1998) believe that the Bible offers good news to all people, regardless of sexual orientation or gender expression.

3. History
Individual female prophets, abbesses, and authors have utilized Christian arguments in favor of gender equality for hundreds of years. According to Rosemary Radford Ruether, women like → Hildegard of Bingen (1098-1179), → Julian of Norwich (ca. 1342-after 1416), and Christine de Pisan (1364-ca. 1430) served as isolated voices who spoke out for women, although in their time they could not articulate the revolutionary transformation necessary to overturn their patriarchal church cultures.

Critical mass began to build in the first wave of feminism in the United States, in which leaders Sarah (1792-1873) and Angelina (1805-79) Grimké, Lucretia Mott (1793-1880), Sojourner Truth (ca. 1797-1883), Elizabeth Cady Stanton (1815-1902), Susan B. Anthony (1820-1906), Antoinette Brown Blackwell (1825-1921), Frances Willard (1839-98), and Anna Howard Shaw (1847-1919) applied the knowledge of biblical justifications for equality they had gained in the struggle for abolition to women's suffrage. For these women, their Christianity and their activism for social justice reinforced each other.

Christian feminism was somewhat separated out of the second wave of U.S. feminism, which occurred in the 1970s, either by radical feminists leaving it behind completely or by moderate liberal feminists focusing on legislative and judicial routes to justice centered on the Equal Rights Amendment. Secular feminists were inspired by Betty Friedan's *Feminine Mystique* (1963), Robin Morgan's *Sisterhood Is Powerful* (1970), Kate Millett's *Sexual Politics* (1970), and the birth of Gloria Steinem's *Ms. Magazine* (first regular issue, July 1972). Christian feminism became a discrete strand within the multifarious women's movement, focusing on the church as a site of both oppression and possible liberation. In this period, thanks to the growth of new university and seminary programs in women's studies and → feminist theology, the isolated foremothers of religion in the feminist movement were drawn out of obscurity.

Second-wave Christian feminists opposed the complementarian movement, as typified by Marabel Morgan's *Total Woman* (1973), which asserted that women are intended by God for a separate sphere of influence — home and family — which complements the men's sphere of public leadership and work. Complementarians maintain that a wife's submission to her husband, when done openly and correctly, leads to satisfaction and godliness and is freeing rather than oppressive.

Many believe that U.S. feminism is currently experiencing a third wave, namely, young women born after the initial successes of the second-wave activists of the 1970s. Third-wave feminists are particularly interested in celebrating overlapping identities, including religious beliefs. They are also concerned with expressions of religious faith in film, television, music, and the Internet. The very notion of Christian churches has been expanded with access to online communities and religion blogs. Secular third-wave feminism is focused on issues of the body, and young Christian women are using that focus to interrogate Christian practices such as → fasting, chastity, sexual abuse ignored or sanctioned by the church, → abortion, contraception, sexual orientation, and gender identity.

4. Diversity within the Movement
There is significant variation within Christian feminism. Some post-Christian feminist theologians (who typically prefer the spelling thealogians, emphasizing the feminine aspect of the Divine), such as Mary Daly and Carol Christ, believe that the Christian church is inherently sexist and cannot be reformed. They thus conclude that the only option

is to leave Christianity in favor of more woman-friendly religious practices.

Catholic theologians Rosemary Radford Ruether and Elisabeth Schüssler Fiorenza represent others who agree that some aspects of Christianity are irrevocably oppressive but who argue that there is a viable core of Scripture and church community that can be recovered to support Christian equality. The Women-Church Convergence (active as Women of the Church Coalition since the 1970s, but operating under its present name since 1983) provides for them an alternative liturgical *ekklesia* that values mutuality and egalitarianism. Advocates of women-church concentrate on passages in the Bible that depict women as dignified and worthy creations of God.

Still others with evangelical approaches to reading Scripture believe that the entire Bible can still be revered because, if interpreted correctly, it supports full human self-determination. The Evangelical and Ecumenical Women's Caucus (1974) and Christians for Biblical Equality (1987) provide organizational support for this reformist position, articulated in the works of Virginia Ramey Mollenkott, Letha Dawson Scanzoni, Nancy A. Hardesty, Gilbert Bilezikian, and Paul King Jewett. They believe the Bible itself is not patriarchal; instead, patriarchy has produced the preferred interpretations of the Bible, which need reconstruction according to their true egalitarian meaning.

Christian feminists practice solidarity with feminists of other religions. Both globally and within the United States itself, Christian feminists are participating in the process of examining the patriarchal structures within all religions and finding the liberating possibilities in other religious communities.

Jewish feminists Judith Plaskow and Blu Greenberg have been vocal about the need to eradicate → anti-Semitism in Christian feminism, while also working within → Judaism to transform its sexist elements. Riffat Hassan of Pakistan has engaged in significant dialogue with Christian feminists about women in → Islam. In the Muslim tradition, Hassan finds the interpretations of the → Qur'an and the hadith, the accounts of the actions and sayings of the Prophet Muhammad, controlled by powerful male interpreters. Yet Hassan has also discovered within the Qur'an an affirmation of the absolute equality of women and men before God. Likewise, Leila Ahmed of Egypt challenges Western stereotypes about Muslim women's oppression, and Amina Wadud, professor of Islamic studies, provides nonsexist reinterpretations of the Qur'an and calls for the revision of the patriarchal elements of → Shari'a, the sacred Islamic laws of everyday living.

Although Christian feminists have the most in common with their monotheist sisters, they also communicate with feminists of → Hindu, → Buddhist, → Baha'i, and neopagan traditions to help uncover the sexism within religious practice, and also to reveal the seeds of liberation in each faith community.

Bibliography: C. P. Christ and J. Plaskow, eds., *Womanspirit Rising: A Feminist Reader in Religion* (San Francisco, 1979) • E. S. Fiorenza, *In Memory of Her: A Feminist Theological Reconstruction of Christian Origins* (New York, 1983) • A. M. Isasi-Díaz, *En la Lucha = In the Struggle: A Hispanic Women's Liberation Theology* (Minneapolis, 1993) • P. K. Jewett, *Man as Male and Female: A Study in Sexual Relationships from a Theological Point of View* (Grand Rapids, 1975) • G. Lerner, *The Majority Finds Its Past: Placing Women in History* (New York, 1979) • V. R. Mollenkott, *Women, Men, and the Bible* (Nashville, 1977) • S. F. Parsons, ed., *The Cambridge Companion to Feminist Theology* (Cambridge, 2002) • J. Plaskow, *Standing Again at Sinai: Judaism from a Feminist Perspective* (San Francisco, 1990) • R. R. Ruether, *Sexism and God-Talk: Toward a Feminist Theology* (Boston, 1983); eadem, *Women-Church: Theology and Practice of Feminist Liturgical Communities* (San Francisco, 1985) • L. D. Scanzoni and N. A. Hardesty, *All We're Meant to Be: A Biblical Approach to Women's Liberation* (Waco, Tex., 1974) • A. Sharma, ed., *Women in World Religions* (Albany, N.Y., 1987) • P. Trible, *Texts of Terror: Literary-Feminist Readings of Biblical Narratives* (Philadelphia, 1984).

Alena Amato Ruggerio

Word of God

1. OT
2. NT
3. Systematic Theology
   3.1. Biblical Background
   3.2. Historical Development
   3.3. A Contemporary Understanding

1. OT

1.1. As Israel began to develop a Word-of-God theology, it had at its disposal important predecessors, especially in Mesopotamia rather than Egypt. Praising the word of the gods was common in Mesopotamia, and it was thought that the divine will was communicated by → prophets (§1.2). Yet Egypt proved to be a fruitful starting point for reflections on creation by the Word, which occurred in various cosmogonic systems. The divine Word found personification in various deities. In literature dealing with death we find divine words, magical words, and oracular words, which in essence are interchangeable (→ Egyptian Religion 1.2 and 2).

1.2. Israel was late and selective in making use of Egyptian models in its theology of → creation. But development of God's speech as his Word may be traced largely to eighth-century prophecies of judgment (→ Prophet, Prophecy, 2.3). It is by his Word (which also can be in the plural) that God will demonstrate his presence in prophecy. The Word is almost never linked with the name, itself a form of God's presence. In prophecy the Word stands for God's concrete resolve (for judgment). The name is a sign of God's cultically mediated salvific presence and is of little importance for the prophets.

Israel did not use a specialized terminology. The everyday usage, *děbar YHWH* (word of the Lord), is used over 200 times. Typical are the formulas "thus says [*ʾāmar*] Yahweh" or "the declaration [*něʾum*] of Yahweh." Stress might fall on the event, as in "the Word of the Lord came," which points to the fact that the prophets were communicating God's Word to Israel. The semantic range of *dābār* (word, object, event; cf. Egypt. *md.t*) is in keeping with the prophetic claim.

As spoken by the prophets, the Word of God creates a reality that neither the prophet nor his listeners can escape. Amos thus experienced the powerful character of the Word of God (Amos 3:8). Later editors themselves give witness to the fact that the "word" appears as a visionary reality (1:1) and report its shockingly threatening inescapability (7:10-17). When God sends a word upon Israel (Isa. 9:8), it is like a consuming fire or a hammer that shatters rocks (Jer. 5:14; 23:29).

1.3. Jeremiah is likewise the prophet who, in his book and along with his Deuteronomistic editors, articulates the ambivalence and the misuse of the Word of God by false prophets. The Word of God (also in the plural) is laid upon the prophet's lips in a vision of calling (1:9, 12; see also Ezek. 3:1-3). In the seventh century B.C. it had become the quintessence of the prophetic message (Jer. 18:18). It grasped the prophets (esp. Jeremiah), causing them both pleasure and pain (15:16; 20:8-9). The pain was exacerbated by the prophets of salvation, who contradicted the message of judgment and thus challenged the validity of the message delivered by the writing prophets (23:9-22; 27–28; Ezekiel 13).

1.4. At approximately the same time as Jeremiah (7th/6th cent. B.C.) and the Book of Jeremiah (6th cent.), the crisis of the prophetically transmitted Word of God is documented through Deuteronomy (13:2-5; 18:13-22). Deuteronomy, in reaction to this crisis, became epoch-making for the theology of the Word of God in two respects: through the understanding (1) that →Moses communicated the Word (more often "words") of God and (2) that this communication was in the form of law, which must be obeyed. The many commands found compendious form in the "ten commandments" (4:13; 10:4), the → Decalogue (5:5-21), which is also called "the Word[s] of Yahweh" (5:5). One may keep "the words of this law" (17:19; 27:3, 8, 26; 28:58; 29:29, etc.) because it "is very near to you; it is in your mouth and in your heart for you to observe" (30:14; see also v. 11). God himself will see to it that all the words proclaimed by his prophets will be fulfilled. Fulfillment is a mark of true prophecy (18:21-22; see also Jer. 28:9).

The shift of the powerful character of the Word of God into historically verifiable fulfillment was an essential, driving force of the portrayal by DtrP, who added a prophetic layer of redaction to the historically oriented DtrH (1 Kgs. 12:15; 15:29; 16:11-12; 2 Kgs. 9:26; 10:17; 24:2, etc.).

The abiding validity of the Word of God, confirmed in DtrH by both past and present, may be seen in Deutero-Isaiah (→ Isaiah 3.2), where it also affects the future. God's Word has creative power. In days of hopeless instability, it comes with a message of comfort and → promise (Isa. 40:6-8; 55:10-11, etc.).

The Priestly writing connects with such writings in its creation narrative Gen. 1:1–2:4a (→ Pentateuch; Primeval History [Genesis 1–11]). In connection with other structural elements, the sovereignty of God's action in creation is established through a report of God's Word (1:3, 6, 9, 11, 14-15, etc.), which, in combination with the corresponding report of God's deed that follows, apostrophizes the powerful character of his Word.

1.5. The → Wisdom literature, oriented to experience, finds no place for reflection on the Word of God, but such reflection is found in the Psalms, which sporadically includes the various traditions and also at points develops the theology of the Word of God. Psalm 19 refers to the heavens, which declare what God has done through his Word (vv. 1-4), and also extols the law (vv. 7-11) but deliberately avoids the traditional linking of this law to the Word of God.

The Word of God figures in other psalms that stress its nature as both → power and → promise relative to creation, history, and the law (33:4-6; 105:8, 19, 42 ["his holy promise"]; 119 throughout, etc.). → Hope rests upon the Word of God and its constant renewal (119:74, 81, 114, 147; 130:5, etc.). Here the Word of God has almost the same function as the name of God. It promises that God is present, so that in Psalm 56, in an exaggerated but logical way, the Word is extolled in a manner appropriate only to God himself.

Bibliography: F. R. Ames, "דבר," *NIDOTTE* 1.912-14 • J. Bergman, H. Lutzmann, and W. H. Schmidt, "דָּבַר *dābhar;* דָּבָר *Dābhār,*" *TDOT* 2.84-125 • T. E. Fretheim, "Word of God," *ABD* 6.961-68 • G. Gerleman, "דבר *dbr* word," *TLOT* 1.325-32 • K. Hoheisel, "Wort Gottes im Judentum," *Götterbild in Kunst und Schrift* (ed. H.-J. Klimkeit; Bonn, 1984) 81-92 • D. G. Kibble, "The Jewish Understanding of the OT as the Word of God," *EvQ* 51 (1979) 145-55 • H. Ringgren, *Word and Wisdom* (Lund, 1947) • J. N. Sanders, "Word, The," *IDB* 4.868-72 • H. Spieckermann, "Rede Gottes und das Wort Gottes in den Psalmen," *Neue Wege der Psalmenforschung* (ed. K. Seybold and E. Zenger; Freiburg, 1994) 157-73 • A. Thiselton, "The Supposed Power of Words in the Biblical Writings," *JTS* 25 (1974) 283-99 • C. Westermann, *Elements of OT Theology* (Atlanta, 1982) 15-34.

Hermann Spieckermann

2. NT

2.1. The NT writings use the phrase "word of God" (Gk. *logos* [*tou*] *theou/kyriou,* and occasionally *rhēma* [*tou*] *theou*) in different contexts.

Clearly in the foreground in Acts and the Pauline corpus, the Word of God is *the Christian message of salvation* (Luke 8:11; Acts 4:29, 31; 1 Cor. 14:36; 2 Cor. 2:17; Col. 1:25; 2 Tim. 2:9; Heb. 6:4-5; 1 Pet. 1:23; Rev. 1:2; 20:4, etc.). It refers also to the preaching of → Jesus (see 2.3 and 2.4). Materially, the meaning is the same in texts that speak of the "word" of → *proclamation* (Matt. 13:18-23; Mark 2:2; Gal. 6:6; Phil. 1:14, etc.).

The term "Word of God" also carries a reference to *the prophets* (Luke 3:2; see 1; → Prophet, Prophecy, 2) and to *God's word of creation* in Genesis 1 (Heb. 11:3; 2 Pet. 3:5, 7; John 1:1; → Creation 2). *OT quotations* are also cited as the Word given by God himself (e.g., Mark 7:13 and par.; John 10:35), through mediators (angels: Acts 7:53; Heb. 2:2; or through prophets: Matt. 1:22; 2:15; 2 Cor. 6:16; Heb. 8:8; 10:15; see also Luke 1:70 and Heb. 1:1). The → Holy Spirit (§1) mediated the Word of God in quotations from the Psalms (Acts 4:25; Heb. 3:7-8; 9:8, etc.). Hebrews 4:4 refers to Gen. 2:2 as the Word of God. The author of Hebrews regarded all Scripture as the Word of God (→ Inspiration).

2.2. → Paul viewed his preaching as the Word of God because God was at work by means of it. Word and deed go together and cannot be separated. The preaching of the → apostle is the Word of God because it refers to the death and → resurrection of Jesus Christ as the sole event by which God has brought → salvation to the world. In content the Word of God is nothing other than "the message about the cross" (1 Cor. 1:18; → Theologia crucis) or "the word of Christ" (Rom. 10:17; see also 1 Thess. 1:8; Col. 3:16; 2 Thess. 3:1; → Christology 1) or "the message of → reconciliation" (2 Cor. 5:19; → Soteriology) or "the word of life" (Phil. 2:16; see also 1 John 1:1; → Life 1).

If it is to be the Word of God, preaching must be tied to these themes; preachers and their message must not depart from them (see 1 Cor. 1:18–2:5; → Rhetoric 1). Because the preaching of Christ is the Word of God in this sense, it is highly effective. It is an event in which God is at work. The Word of God posits, rather than constitutes, reality (Rom. 9:6, 28). As the Word of God, the → gospel preached by Paul does not just communicate God's work of salvation. It is God himself who both brings and effects salvation as his Word awakens → faith and thus leads believers to appropriate it (see 1 Thess. 2:13; Rom. 10:8-11; Heb. 4:12; Jas. 1:21; 1 Pet. 1:23).

2.3. Luke found the Word of God in the preaching of Jesus (Luke 5:1; 8:21; 11:28). In Acts 10:36, with this meaning in view and with an appeal to Ps. 107:20, he refers to the sending of the Word (see Ps. 147:15, 18; Jer. 49:5 and 50:1 LXX [= 42:5 and 43:1 MT]). In Acts Christian → missionaries proclaim the message of salvation as the Word of God (see 2.1). Luke insists, however, that they do so in continuity with the preaching of Jesus and that only in virtue of this continuity is their message the Word of God. God's Word is always a telling forth of the salvation that has been achieved by Jesus Christ (Acts 8:25; 10:36; 13:5, 7, 44; 17:13, etc.). This identity sets the Word of God over those who proclaim it, making them its "servants" (see Luke 1:2; Acts 6:2, 4).

For Luke, too, God's Word is a powerful word (see Acts 6:7; 12:24; 19:20). The metaphors that speak about its growing, increasing, and strengthening follow OT usage, which employs similar terms when referring to → blessing or to the fulfillment of God's → promises (e.g., Gen. 1:22, 28; 9:1; 17:20; 28:3; Exod. 1:7, 20; Jer. 3:16; 23:3, etc., with reference to the chosen people). By emphasizing the Word of God, Luke makes it clear that, with the spread of the Christian message of salvation overcoming all resistance, God's blessing is transmitted and his promise is fulfilled, for in it God himself is at work through his Word. Thus for Luke the Word of God being heard in the proclamation of Christ is the impetus of → salvation history, and the Christian → congregation itself is the *creatura verbi*.

2.4. In John's Gospel the Word of God forms an integral part of → Christology (§1.4). The Prologue (1:1-18) sets the direction for the rest of the presentation. Jesus Christ is the preexistent Logos, who participates in the being of God himself. God made the world with him, and the Word gives it → light and → life (vv. 1-4). He came into the world, and his → incarnation means no less than the self-revelation of God (v. 14).

The sayings of Jesus are thus the Word of God. God has sent him (3:34; 5:38; 8:26, etc.). He also has the power appropriate to the Word (6:63, 68; 12:48, etc.). The special emphasis of Johannine Word-of-God Christology comes out in the fact that, as the one who proclaims this Word, he points to himself as its content. He comes from God, and in his sayings and works, which are → "signs" pointing to the Word (2:23; 3:2; 6:14, 30; 7:31, etc.), God reveals himself and is also at work: "The Father and I are one" (10:30; see also 12:44-45; 14:9-11). The Evangelist can thus call for belief *(pisteuō)* and abiding *(menō)* in the Word or the words of Jesus and also in Jesus Christ himself, which also means in God (cf. 5:38, 46-47; 15:4, 7 with 2:22; 8:31 with 3:15-18; 6:29, 56; 12:44, etc.; see also 1 John 2:14, 24).

This merging of Word and person involves the world in which Jesus is both the messenger and the message (himself the Word) in a true crisis. Believers "hear" the sayings of Jesus as the Word of God, "receive" him as the authentic representative of God, and experience eschatological salvation through the Word (5:24; 6:63, 68-69; 8:51-52; → Eschatology 2). This insight, however, is denied to unbelievers (see 8:37-47), who are judged by the same Word itself (12:47-48; see also 3:18-19).

Bibliography: K. BARTH, *The Word of God and the Word of Man* (New York, 1957) • G. BORNKAMM, "God's Word and Man's Word in the NT," *Early Christian Experience* (New York, 1969) 1-13 • R. E. BROWN, "The Word," *The Gospel according to John* (Garden City, N.Y., 1966) 519-24 • R. BULTMANN, "The Concept of the Word of God in the NT," *Faith and Understanding* (ed. R. W. Funk; Philadelphia, 1987) 1.286-312 • T. FRETHEIM and K. FROEHLICH, *The Bible as Word of God in a Postmodern Age* (Minneapolis, 1998) • G. FRIES, "Λόγος: Classical," *NIDNTT* 3.1081-87 • E. FUCHS, "Neues Testament und Wort Gottes," *TLZ* 97 (1972) 1-16 • O. HOFIUS, *Paulusstudien* (2 vols.; Tübingen, 1989-2000) 1.148-74 • G. KITTEL, "Λέγω κτλ. D: Word and Speech in the NT," *TDNT* 4.100-143 • B. KLAPPERT, "Λόγος: NT," *NIDNTT* 3.1106-17 • A. THISELTON,

"The New Hermeneutic," *NT Interpretation* (ed. I. H. Marshall; Grand Rapids, 1977) 308-33.

MICHAEL WOLTER

3. Systematic Theology

Christians confess and believe that the Word of God — that is, the gospel, or good news, of the life, death, and → resurrection of → Jesus of Nazareth — brings → salvation to all people. Furthermore, they affirm that Jesus himself is the "Word of God," the revelation of God's true identity, in human form.

3.1. *Biblical Background*

This understanding of the Word of God draws on OT depictions of God interacting in concrete and palpable ways with a variety of figures in the history of Israel — from → Abraham, → Moses, and → David to the prophets and psalmists. In the OT, God's Word enacts both liberation and a → covenant. It judges, calls for repentance, and promises salvation, culminating not only in Isaiah's vision of God's creative word bringing about a new heaven and a new earth for all history and nature but also in the link (drawn in → Wisdom literature) between God's distinct word for Israel and a universal wisdom accessible to all people in creation.

In the NT the → Synoptic gospels describe how Jesus proclaimed the Word of God — calling people to repent and "believe in the good news" of God, since "the time is fulfilled, and the kingdom of God has come near" (Mark 1:15; also Matt. 4:12-17; Luke 4:14-15). In the power of the Spirit that also inspired Israel's prophets, Jesus brought good news to the poor, release to the captives, sight to the blind, and freedom to the oppressed (Luke 4:18; Isa. 58:6; 61:1-2) — healing people's diseases, exorcising demons, and forgiving sins. Soon after his death, Jesus' followers proclaimed that his name brought "repentance and forgiveness of sins . . . to all nations" (Luke 24:47) and that after his crucifixion at the hands of the religious and political authorities, God raised him from the dead as "Lord and Messiah" (Acts 2:36).

The apostle → Paul, who had encountered Jesus only after Jesus' resurrection, linked these events with an apocalyptic in-breaking of God's new age of the Spirit (→ Holy Spirit; Trinity). He proclaimed that all people could be saved ("there is no distinction between Jew and Greek") if they confessed and believed "the word [that] is near you, on your lips and in your heart," that "Jesus is Lord" and that "God raised him from the dead" (Rom. 10:8-13). Paul proclaimed this gospel "in fear and in much trembling," not with "lofty words or wisdom," so that the cross might not be "emptied of its power." Though a "stumbling block" and "foolishness" that is "hidden to the rulers of this age," this message calls out a new people from among those who are not wise or powerful or noble, using what is "low and despised . . . things that are nothing to reduce to nothing things that are" (1 Cor. 1:18–2:5).

Finally, this Word is not only a subversive message but a person who embodies the reality of God. In John's gospel, Jesus is the Word who was "with God" and "was God" — the embodiment of God's glory, "full of grace and truth," who reveals the "Father's heart" (John 1:1-18). This Word is the world's light and life, the source of all its truth and love, and can be described by such commonplace → symbols as water, bread, wine, a door, a vine, blood, and fish.

3.2. *Historical Development*

3.2.1. Early Christian theologians expanded on these understandings of the Word of God. Drawing on Philo of Alexandria (b. 15-10 B.C., d. A.D. 45-50), who related Jewish conceptions of God's Word as personified wisdom (Prov. 8:1-31), and on Greek philosophical conceptions of the Logos as the intelligible principle ordering the cosmos, Justin Martyr (ca. 100-ca. 165) argued that the latter prepared the way for belief in Christ as the Logos in a manner similar to the way OT prophecies prepared for the reception of Jesus as Messiah. In contrast to Marcion (d. ca. 160), who rejected the authority of the OT for Christians, Irenaeus (ca. 130-ca. 200) developed an understanding of God's economy of salvation in history — that God has been carrying out an infinitely wise plan of salvation from the beginning of time, preparing the human race, educating it and bringing it to maturity for Jesus Christ, who will sum up in himself all of nature and history (→ Order of Salvation).

In their Trinitarian theologies, the → Cappadocians — Gregory of Nazianzus (329/30-389/90), Gregory of Nyssa (ca. 330-ca. 395), and Basil the Great (ca. 330-79) — stressed God's mystery; God's depths and mysterious darkness cannot be plumbed, even though the enlivening action of the Spirit enables us, through the Word, to penetrate the mysteries of the Father and Son more deeply. Early church theologians also elaborated on the Spirit's activity in enabling us to interpret God's Word. → Augustine (354-430) in particular developed an understanding of how the Spirit illuminates the "letter" of Scripture, enabling humans to experience its truth more deeply in their innermost selves *(De doc. Christ.),* a theme that would have pervasive influence on later medieval mystics.

The early church developed a canon of Scripture that consolidated the authoritative apostolic witnesses to the import of Jesus' life, death, and resurrection. Christian communities have continued the proclamation of these apostolic witnesses in their public → worship, celebrating the risen presence of Jesus in their midst with the sacrament of bread and wine (→ Eucharist). They believe Jesus, the living Word, is a → sacrament who embodies the way of life Christians are to enact by the power of the Spirit — forgiving sins, healing, loving others, and enacting God's reign of justice and mercy.

3.2.2. Different Christian traditions have emphasized different aspects in their witness to Jesus as living Word. The traditions of Eastern Orthodoxy (→ Orthodox Christianity) focus on how Jesus as Logos is a → theophany in human form that leads to our divinization (→ Theosis). The traditions of the West, following Augustine, focus on how Jesus as Word is God's personal gift of → grace leading to → faith. Among them, → Roman Catholics stress both that Scripture must be interpreted in relation to tradition and that the Word is always embodied as sacrament and incarnational presence. → Protestants, in turn, stress how the Word of God expressed in Scripture must govern church practice, arguing that the sacraments of bread and wine are given meaning only by the proclamation of the gospel that brings faith.

3.2.3. The → Reformation stressed the importance of the Word of God. For Martin Luther (1483-1546; → Luther's Theology), this Word is the gospel of God's Son made flesh that saves, frees, and feeds human souls ("The Freedom of the Christian," *LW* 31.327-77). This Word has efficacy as the law that convicts persons of sin and as the promise that offers the → forgiveness of sin. As it forgives and justifies believers, the Word communicates to them all that belongs to it — especially God's → righteousness. The purpose of → preaching this Word is not simply to present historical facts or the laws of human tradition but to bring about faith in Christ — that is, to effect what is said in his name. John → Calvin (1509-64; → Calvin's Theology) also stressed the importance of preaching the Word but highlighted both the inspired character of the written text of Scripture and the inner testimony of the Spirit in self-authenticating the Word's truth in human hearts.

3.2.4. After the Reformation, Protestant orthodoxy tended to equate the Word of God with the text of Scripture itself. In turn, biblical scholars who used methods of historical criticism to study Scripture as an ancient manuscript caused many to question how Scripture could continue to be God's

Word if its contents could be analyzed merely as historical phenomena. Friedrich Schleiermacher (1768-1834; → Schleiermacher's Theology) offered one response, partly inspired by Pietist and earlier mystical attention to the internal experience of the Word. He emphasized the inner experience of faith, generated by the church's preaching, within Christian consciousness and human experience as it communicates to them the power of Christ's God-consciousness. In contrast, Karl → Barth (1886-1968) stressed the objective and critical character of God's Word in the church's preaching of Scripture as apostolic witness. He argued that the church's → proclamation of the gospel of Jesus Christ justifies and sanctifies human beings precisely because it proclaims God's objective speech and action in Jesus Christ, which addresses them as a transcendent word of judgment and grace.

Since Barth, the plethora of academic approaches to the study of the Christian Bible have only continued to expand — from forms of grammatical and historical criticism, social history, biblical archaeology, and form criticism (including redaction, tradition, and canonical criticism) to more recent approaches drawing on methods from psychology and psychoanalysis, sociology, and anthropology to a range of narrative and rhetorical criticisms (including reader response, structuralism and semiotics, and deconstructionism) and ideology and liberationist critiques.

Two other developments have enriched the Christian theological understanding of Scripture as the Word of God — increased ecumenical work among Roman Catholic and Protestant biblical scholars, especially after → Vatican II, and increased attention to the global character of Christianity and thus of the importance of reading the Bible from Asian, African, and Latin American perspectives, as well as from European and North American standpoints. Far from detracting from the power of the Word of God, which Christians believe is expressed in the canonical witness of Scripture, this plethora of approaches has opened up fresh insights into its distinctive character.

3.3. A Contemporary Understanding

Four themes can be identified as central to a contemporary Christian understanding of the Word of God.

3.3.1. First, Christians affirm that this Word is uniquely and absolutely revealed or manifested in the humanity — the life, death, and resurrection — of Jesus Christ. Early Christians interpreted the significance of Jesus' life, death, and resurrection in terms of the OT's expectation of a messianic age of the Spirit for all creaturely existence. They proclaimed that Jesus ushers in a new creation for all of history and nature. Faith in the gospel of Jesus Christ justifies all people, bestowing on them God's righteousness and promise of the Spirit. Sin, suffering, evil, demonic powers, death, and all other forces that oppress creaturely existence have been overcome in Jesus' death and resurrection. By faith in the gospel of Jesus Christ humans can, in spite of evidence to the contrary, live in the "already but not yet" character of this new creation (→ Eschatology).

This Word is not only a future hope. It is also a message that God has taken a human form, becoming flesh in Jesus of Nazareth. In full union with God and as God, Jesus incarnates divine truth and love (→ Incarnation). Furthermore, by assuming creaturely humanity, Jesus encompasses all humanity within himself and redeems it. The person and message of Jesus Christ creates and reconciles a new humanity within history out of people of all races, ethnicities, and classes and thus is expressed in all the diversity and forms this new humanity takes (→ New Self). Christians can proclaim this Word with freedom and creativity — like Paul, they become "all things to all people" (1 Cor. 9:22), or as at Pentecost, they speak God's Word in a diversity of languages and forms of cultural expression (Acts 2:11).

3.3.2. Second, the Word of God is an inherently historical word. Unlike Eastern spiritual traditions and Greek philosophy, which discern truth in what is here and now, Christian faith proclaims → truth by narrating events that have occurred in the past and that engender a new future for its hearers. It is true that the gospel of Jesus Christ announces that God's salvation has come for people here and now. When the gospel is preached, people repent, have their sins forgiven, and are adopted as God's children. Nonetheless, this message cannot be divorced from the central events in Jesus' life — birth, baptism, temptations, preaching and teaching, healings and exorcisms, conflict with religious authorities and attention to outcasts, crucifixion, and resurrection appearances. It cannot be divorced from Israel's great events (the call of Abraham, exodus, the monarchy, exile, and restoration) and institutions (covenant, law, and temple), even if it reinterprets them. Christians even recount how the gospel of Jesus Christ spread, by the power of the Spirit, from Jerusalem, Judea, and Samaria to "the ends of the earth" (Acts 1:8), as well as describing early church struggles over incorporating Gentile converts into the Christian community (see Acts 15; Galatians) and other conflicts that characterized early congregational life (e.g., in 1 Corinthians).

Christians believe that this message, in all its historical particularity, opens up a new future to those who believe in it, even if the promise of a new creation is both "already here" but has "not yet" arrived. They believe that persons now, like the early Christians, can live out of this new future, even if they still live in a world that suffers, is held in the grip of unjust and sinful forces, and still groans in expectation of an eschatological future (Romans 8).

3.3.3. Third, the Word of God is a dialogic word. The Word made flesh is the Son who abides in deep communion with the Father, an abiding that grounds the possibility of true community among human beings (John 17). This Son, Jesus, gathers around him a community of friends whom he sees, loves, and calls to follow him. People either accept or reject him and his message; if they accept it, they are to see and respond to the world and other people differently (2 Cor. 5:16; Matthew 25). What they receive in believing his message is his own inheritance as God's Son — the Spirit who enables them to address God intimately and discern the very mysteries of God's own life (1 Cor. 2:6-13; Gal. 4:6; Romans 8). This Spirit leads believers to do things they normally would not be able to do, even causing them to change deeply ingrained beliefs and practices (Acts 15).

The dynamic character of the Word of God in its interaction with human beings has precedent in the OT, which conveys how God encounters individuals in theophanies that have import for their communities. Interpreted in relation to previous traditions that narrate God's engagement in history, these events demonstrate that how persons interact with this Word — whether in faithfulness or in rebellion — affects how it influences their lives. The OT even depicts instances where God repents or changes what he said he would do, depending on how human beings respond (e.g., Gen. 18:22-32).

3.3.4. Finally, the Word of God is ultimately about God and how Jesus as the Word made flesh enables humankind to participate in God's Trinitarian life. The Gospel of John is the most explicit on this point, telling that the Word, which is the Son, not only reveals the Father but also enables humans to abide in the unity he shares with his Father. Paul also speaks of how the gospel of Jesus Christ not only justifies but also adopts us as God's children, enabling us to share in the Spirit's life. Because of that life, the gospel of Jesus Christ is always a generative word. It enacts a new creation that causes us to view the world and other human beings in a radically different light. It undoes our preconceived categories — even what we perceive to be God's signs

or wisdom — with the stumbling block and foolishness of its message of the cross. It forgives sin and restores broken circumstances, shifting perspectives on life so that things are seen from the Spirit's standpoint and not simply from that of egocentric human preoccupations. This Word cannot be controlled or manipulated for our purposes, but we can participate in its generative life as we live by faith in its truth and love.

Bibliography: H. U. von Balthasar, *Word and Revelation* (New York, 1964) • K. Barth, *Church Dogmatics,* vol. 1, *The Doctrine of the Word of God* (Edinburgh, 2004; first ET, 1936-56) • J. Barton, ed., *The Cambridge Companion to Biblical Interpretation* (Cambridge, 1998) • A. Dulles, *Models of Revelation* (New York, 1983) • S. Escobar, *The New Global Mission: The Gospel from Everywhere to Everyone* (Downers Grove, Ill., 2003) • H. Frei, *The Eclipse of Biblical Narrative: A Study in Eighteenth- and Nineteenth-Century Hermeneutics* (New Haven, 1974) • T. E. Fretheim, "Word of God," *ABD* 6.961-68 • D. H. Kelsey, *The Uses of Scripture in Modern Theology* (Harrisburg, Pa., 1999; orig. pub., 1975) • R. Latourelle, "Revelation," *DFTh* 905-50 • J. Levenson, *The Hebrew Bible, the OT, and Historical Criticism: Jews and Christians in Biblical Studies* (Louisville, Ky., 1993) • D. McKim, *Historical Handbook of Major Biblical Interpreters* (Downers Grove, Ill., 1998) • P. Ricoeur, "Towards a Hermeneutic of the Idea of Revelation," *Essays on Biblical Interpretation* (ed. L. Mudge; Philadelphia, 1980) 73-118 • E. Schillebeeckx, *Revelation and Theology* (London, 1967) • F. Schleiermacher, *The Christian Faith* (Edinburgh, 1999; orig. pub., 1821-22) • R. Williams, "Trinity and Revelation," *On Christian Theology* (London, 2001) chap. 9.

Lois Malcolm

Word Square

A word square is a set of equal-length words, arranged in the pattern of a square, that read the same horizontally and vertically. The earliest example, which uses the magic formula *sator arepo tenet opera rotas,* was found on graffiti in Pompeii, dated a.d. 50-79, and uses *rotas* first. In later antiquity it appears on amulets, papyri, ostraca, and inscriptions. In the Middle Ages we find it mostly in Western and Byzantine codices, but also on a pavement mosaic in the Church of Pieve Terzagni at Cremona (ca. 11th cent.).

The palindromic structure gives the formula its magical quality, for reading it backward (which, it was believed, would break a magic spell) does not

change its wording. Various modes of its use in → magic bear witness to the transition from late antiquity to the early modern period, for example, to exorcise, heal, and ward off → evil. The obscurity of the text, often translated as "Arepo the sower holds the wheels with difficulty," has given rise to many interpretations in philological research. Anagrammatic interpretations such as *petro et reo patet rosa sarona* (The Rose of Sharon is still open to Peter, even though he is guilty; cf. Cant. 2:1) are much debated, as is also the arrangement of letters as a "Pater noster" cross (→ Lord's Prayer; Cross) beginning and ending with *a* and *o*, corresponding to Gk. → alpha and omega.

Since the formula has verbal affinities to the → vision of the divine throne chariot in Ezek. 1:15-21, a Jewish origin has been conjectured. Modern research, however, traces the word square back to pagan antiquity. Thus far the attempt to find in it a magical or symbolic number square by assigning a numerical value to the letters has not gained acceptance (→ Number; Symbol). In view of the many inscriptions to charioteers in the context of the earliest examples from Pompeii, a link has been seen to the circus. A persuasive interpretation sets the square in the light of Stoic thinking (→ Stoicism), linked to the boustrophedonic, or "furrowing," reading (successive lines read in opposite directions) and eliminating the Ephesian word "arepo": *Sator opera tenet, tenet opera sator*. In this form the

saying reflects Stoic belief in a Creator God who keeps the world continuously in being.

Those who advocate an origin of the formula in pagan antiquity tend to seek that origin, whether in time or space, apart from ancient monuments. Thus it has been traced to the first century B.C. in → Alexandria or to circles in Rome in the last days of the republic (→ Roman Empire), which inclined to magical practices, as we see in the case of P. Nigidius Figulus (fl. 98-45 B.C.). The name "Arepo" has always been an expository crux. It has recently been equated with the Egyptian sky-god Horus (= Gk. Harpo[crates]; → Egyptian Religion 1). We perhaps best explain the word square in terms of Roman field measurements and their emphasis on the cross axle (*cardo* and *decumanus*), which is reflected by the central cross *tenet* in the formula.

Modern scholars integrate the magic square into the history of visual poetry and place it between the crossword labyrinth of the *Tabulae iliacae* (carved stone plaques in Rome, between 50 B.C. and A.D. 50) and the *Carmina quadrata* (poems in the shape of rectangles) of the fourth-century Latin poet Publius Optatianus Porfyrius. Fascination with magic, based on the many ways of understanding the *sator* square, did not end with the Middle Ages but extended into the modern period. Athanasius Kircher (1602-80) took it up in his book *Arithmologia, sive de abditis numerorum mysteriis* (Rome, 1665, pp. 220-21).

Even today, high value is still set on this word square by writers and artists. The Brazilian Osman Lins (1924-78) used the square and a superimposed spiral in structuring his novel *Avalovara* (1973), and the New York Fluxus artist Dick Higgins integrated it into his painting *La Melancolia* (1983), in which there is allusion to A. Dürer's (1471-1528) *Melencolia I* (1514).

Bibliography: D. ATKINSON, "The Origin and Date of the 'Sator' Word-Square," *JEH* 2 (1951) 1-18 • R. CAMMILLERI, *Il quadrato magico* (Milan, 1999) • U. ERNST, *Carmen figuratum. Geschichte des Figurengedichts von den antiken Ursprüngen bis zum Ausgang des Mittelalters* (Cologne, 1991) • F. FOCKE, "Sator Arepo. Abenteuer eines magischen Quadrats," *WüJA* 3 (1948) 366-401 • C. D. GUNN, "The Sator-Arepo Palindrome: A New Inquiry into the Composition of an Ancient Word Square" (Diss., Yale University, 1969) • H. HOFFMANN, "Satorquadrat," PWSup 15.477-565 • H. LAST, "The Rotas Sator Square: Present Position and Future Prospects," *JTS*, n.s., 3 (1952) 92-97 • W. O. MOELLER, *The Mithraic Origin and Meanings of the Rotas-Sator Square* (Leiden, 1973) • W. C. SCHNEIDER, "Sator Opera Tenet–Poro Aras, 'Der Sämann erhält die Werke–Du aber pflügst.' Eine Deutung des Sator-Quadrats," *Castrum Peregrini* 189/90 (1989) 101-24.

ULRICH ERNST

Work

1. Term
2. Biblical Description
3. Middle Ages and Reformation
4. Modern Period

1. Term

In a broad sense, work is "any activity by man, whether manual or intellectual, whatever its nature or circumstance" (John Paul II, *Laborem exercens* [1981], introductory blessing). More narrowly, "work" refers to activity undertaken as a means to some other end and so is distinct from hobbies, which are done for their own sake. The English term "labor" perhaps derives from Lat. *labo,* "stumble under a burden."

Western thinkers have proposed a variety of definitions of work. Plato and Aristotle associated work with toil required to provide necessities of life. They held that some people were "natural slaves," whose paucity of reason suited them, like animals, for burdensome labor. The work of → slaves provided the freedom for the political and contemplative activity of the leisured class, who developed reason and deliberation and so achieved the highest degree of human fulfillment.

2. Biblical Description

Biblical depictions of work combine positive features with recognition of work's futility. God's benediction stands over human beings as they are "fruitful" and "multiply" and "have dominion" over central aspects of → creation (Gen. 1:28). Before the fall, Adam was to name animals and till the garden, symbolizing the inherent goodness of human work. Human beings are "like God" in their creative and productive work; their work is a participation and continuation of the work of the Creator. This feature gives work and the worker dignity, as was stressed in *Laborem exercens*. In many ways humans live in order to work.

But people also work to live. The work intended by the Creator to be humanity's glorious expression of God's image warps into meaningless toil as a result of → sin (Gen. 3:17-19). Futility and vanity plague human labor in the world after the fall. God's

commandments include → Sabbath rests, in part to mitigate the toilsome burden of daily work. God's redemption holds the promise of removing the cursed futility from work, restoring it to meaningful labor in the Lord (1 Cor. 15:58).

3. Middle Ages and Reformation

Monastic communities link prayer and work, often stressing the dignity of human labor (→ Monasticism). In the High Middle Ages Thomas Aquinas (ca. 1225-74; → Thomism) prized contemplation of God over the active life, combining Aristotelian and Christian themes. Though love of neighbor made the active life more necessary in some contexts, → contemplation, considered in itself, was the highest form of human activity.

Martin → Luther (1483-1546; → Luther's Theology) and John → Calvin (1509-64; → Calvin's Theology) reversed the medieval understanding of work. Both considered work a crucial part of Christian → vocation. Calvin stressed the activity of God in governing and redeeming the world; Christians most image God when they too are actively engaged in their work. Luther and Calvin stressed serving God, not by idly contemplating God's nature, but by serving the needs of neighbors. In serving others, Christians serve Christ incarnate in the needs of neighbors.

→ Puritans emphasized the importance of work even more strongly than did Calvin and Luther. Though not the cause of one's election, diligence and success in one's work were seen as signs of God's election. Idleness and sloth were to be avoided at all cost. As Max → Weber (1864-1920) has shown, the Puritan stress on diligence and frugality was a major cause of the rise of modern → capitalism, in which Calvinism's "ascetic worldliness" richly prospered. Over time, the religious aspects of work as vocation fell away, and prosperity in one's work became an end in itself. The terms "vocation," "calling," and "profession" continue to be used for one's work, but in a thoroughly secularized way. Adam Smith's (1723-90) optimism that an "invisible hand" would cause pursuit of self-interest to benefit others replaced Calvinist faith in divine → providence.

4. Modern Period

The rise of industrial capitalism brought about dehumanizing working conditions, which Karl → Marx (1818-83) criticized as "alienated labor" (→ Industrial Society). Capitalism removes control of the means of production from workers and objectifies labor, transforming it into a commodity worth only its exchange value. Capitalism destroys workers' humanity and turns other communal institutions, such as → marriage and → family, into articles of commerce and instruments of labor. Behind Marx's critique is an Edenlike ideal of labor that is creative, liberating, and communally constructive. Marx taught that a global → revolution was necessary to take the means of production away from capitalist owners and return them to laborers.

Roman Catholic social teaching since Leo XIII's encyclical *Rerum novarum* (1891) has stressed the dignity of human labor while criticizing both Marxist and capitalist extremes (→ Social Encyclicals). The Catholic Church teaches that every person has a God-given right to meaningful work. Workers have a right to a just wage, defined as a wage sufficient for a head of a household to support that household in a modest way and to set some aside for retirement. People also have a right to private → property, though that right is not absolute but limited by "the universal destination of material goods" (John Paul II, *Centesimus annus* [1991], chap. 4). In the late 20th century Roman Catholic teaching acknowledged the greater effectiveness of free markets and capitalism as compared with state-controlled economies but also conveyed a powerful ethical critique of the abuses and dangers of capitalism. Through its principles of → subsidiarity and → solidarity, Catholic teaching urges the state to promote productive economies while protecting human → rights and promoting the common good.

Several influential social forces converged in the 20th century to shape human work and are likely to continue to affect work in the 21st century. Feminist movements criticize the devaluation of domestic work and demand that all forms of "paid-work" be open to women's participation. The rise of computers, the Internet, and the information age may reshape the way the "public-private" worlds have been divided under industrialism. Globalization tends to relativize limits to corporate power imposed by nation-states, markets, and work forces. Longer life spans and expanded retirement years challenge the almost idolatrous value ascribed to career and paid work, inviting a reassessment of traditions stressing the importance of leisure for human flourishing. The persistence of → unemployment and abject → poverty cry out for justice in work and the distribution of resources.

Bibliography: G. BAUM, *Work and Religion* (New York, 1980) • L. HARDY, *The Fabric of This World: Inquiries into Calling, Career Choice, and the Design of Human Work* (Grand Rapids, 1990) • JOHN PAUL II, *On Human Work: Laborem Exercens* (Washington, D.C., 1981) • J. PIEPER, *Leisure: The Basis of Culture* (New York, 1963) • S. TERKEL, *Working* (New York, 1972) • M. VOLF, *Work in the Spirit: Toward a Theology of Work* (New York, 1991) • M. WEBER, *The Protestant Ethic and the Spirit of Capitalism* (Los Angeles, 1998; orig. pub., 1905) • G. WINGREN, *Luther on Vocation* (Philadelphia, 1957).

DOUGLAS J. SCHUURMAN

Worker-Priests

1. The movement of worker-priests *(prêtres-ouvriers)* arose in France in 1943 in connection with the process of → secularization, which was pushing Christianity into the private sphere, and the development of a working class that, under the influence of → Marxism, regarded the → church as a capitalistic and bourgeois institution. Paternalistic ideas could not bridge the deep cleft between the proletariat and the church.

Based upon a programmatic approach to → pastoral care in a social setting (→ Catholic Action), the Jeunesse Ouvrière Chrétienne (JOC, Young Christian Worker), founded in 1925 by the priest J. Cardijn (1882-1967), commenced an apostolate among young workers. Then in the 1930s theologians like M.-D. Chenu (1894-1989) began to reflect on the working world, class consciousness, and economic change and increasingly gave their teaching work a missionary direction.

2. None of these efforts could change the alienation of workers and the indifference of much of the population. This was the conclusion of a decade of experience as two chaplains of JOC, H. Godin (1906-44) and Y. Daniel (1909-86), laid it out in a white paper to Cardinal E. C. Suhard (1874-1949, published under the title *La France, pays de mission?*). Their decisive insight was that France, "the oldest daughter of the church," had become a missionary country, socially if not geographically. They urged that → priests should be freed from regular pastoral duties, that they should be allowed to live as workers among workers, and that they should form small cells among the workers. This realistic report attracted considerable attention, meeting with tentative agreement, but also arousing vocal objections. Yet Cardinal Suhard was impressed, and he became the patron of the experiment of worker-priests, the Mission de Paris.

3. Already in 1941, J. Loew as a longshoreman in Marseilles had gained experience for pastoral work

among the proletariat. Beginning in 1942, the seminary of the Mission de Paris in Lisieux trained priests for pastoral care among dechristianized sectors of the population. A year later priests presenting themselves as civilian workers were sent to their compatriots in German labor camps, while the *frères missionaires des campagnes* began work among the agricultural proletariat of France.

The experiment of the Mission de Paris began in January 1944, when seven priests went into the working-class quarters of Paris. The work was soon extended to other industrial cities. In a few months the number of priests rose to 20, and it reached 100 by 1952. The worker-priests adopted working-class → lifestyles, took part in efforts to raise wages, in strikes, and in political demonstrations, agitated with the Communist union Confédération Générale du Travail (CGT), won much sympathy among the people, but also ran into severe criticism and came under violent attack.

4. The Roman → curia prepared to end the experiment of worker-priests in September 1953. It laid down conditions if the mission was to continue, limiting manual work to three hours a day, forbidding trades union and political activity, and demanding reentry into priestly fellowship. Only half the worker-priests obeyed. As a modified form, the French bishops founded the Mission Ouvrière in 1957, but two years later Rome forbade any factory work for priests. In the meantime the Decree on the Ministry and Life of Priests, *Presbyterorum ordinis* (1965), of → Vatican II declared that priests, in the context of their apostolate, could "engage in manual labor and share the lot of the workers," if it seemed appropriate to the responsible authority (§8).

During the council, in October 1965, the French bishops also initiated a new phase, the mission of "working priests" (now called *prêtres au travail*). They allowed a small number of selected and specially trained priests to do paid full-time work for a limited time in the context of their continuing apostolate and in close connection with the pastoral clergy. By the early 1980s there were approximately 800 such working priests in various jobs. They were loosely connected with one another but resisted any attempt at institutionalizing.

5. Stimulated by the French experiment, priests in other countries (esp. Italy) entered the working world. It is of interest that in the → Third World the priests earned their living by working with their hands. Although the standards of *Presbyterorum ordinis* 8 and of 1983 CIC 286 allow for the possibil-

ity of worker-priests, the only consequence of the French experiment was that workers increasingly became the object of pastoral activism coming from the outside, but otherwise they were left to the lay apostolate. Thus the so-called workers question is recognized as a task of the church, but not resolved.

It may be noted that the problem of secularization and the rift between workers and the church has become a problem of the very existence of priests. As worker-priests went into the secular world of workers and ran the risk of a laicizing of priestly life, the identity of the priest became the main theme for the → teaching office. Fundamentally, the concept of worker-priests is more in keeping with the Roman Catholic than the Protestant view of the office and image of the pastor, although there has also been a movement of "pastor-workers." The course of events surrounding the worker-priests has helped to promote the modern debate about the office of the priest.

Bibliography: Primary sources: H. GODIN and Y. DANIEL, *La France, pays de mission?* (Paris, 1943; ET included in M. Ward, *France Pagan? The Mission of Abbé Godin* [New York, 1949]) • J. LOEW, *Journal d'une mission ouvrière, 1941-1959* (Paris, 1959) • H. PERRIN, *Priest-Workman in Germany* (trans. R. Sheed; London, 1947).

Secondary works: O. L. ARNAL, *Priests in Working-Class Blue: The History of the Worker-Priests (1943-1954)* (New York, 1986) • A. DANSETTE, *Destin du catholicisme français, 1926-1956* (Paris, 1957) • L. ERLANDER, *Faith in the World of Work: On the Theology of Work as Lived by the French Worker-Priests and British Industrial Mission* (Stockholm, 1991) • M. LABOURDETTE, *Le sacerdoce et la mission ouvrière* (Paris, 1959) • J. MANTLE, *Britain's First Worker-Priests: Radical Ministry in a Post-war Setting* (London, 2000) • G. SIEFER, *The Church and Industrial Society: A Survey of the Worker-Priest Movement and Its Implications for the Christian Mission* (London, 1964).

JEAN-MARIE CHARPENTIER

World Alliance of Reformed Churches

The World Alliance of Reformed Churches (WARC) first met at a conference in Edinburgh in 1877 as the Alliance of the Reformed Churches throughout the World Holding the Presbyterian System. Previously in London in 1875 representatives of 21 churches had decided to form such an organization. It is the oldest international confessional alliance of churches (→ Denomination). At first it had Anglo-Saxon countries at its center, though some European churches were also charter members. After World War II most of the Reformed churches of Europe and many from Africa, Asia, Latin America, and the Pacific joined it (→ Reformed and Presbyterian Churches 4). At the General Assembly at Nairobi in 1970, a union was formed with the International Congregational Council (founded 1891), and the present name was adopted.

The basis of the WARC is not acceptance of specific confessional documents (→ Confession of Faith) but a Reformed understanding of the → church (§3.5): "The one foundation of the church is Jesus Christ, the Lord, in whom God's Word became flesh and to whom the Scriptures bear witness; and the church on earth, though composed of many members, is one body in the communion of the Holy Spirit, under the leadership of the Lord Jesus Christ" (Preamble to the Constitution). Any church is eligible for membership "whose position in faith and → evangelism is in general agreement with that of the historic Reformed confessions; and which recognizes that the Reformed tradition is a biblical, evangelical, and doctrinal ethos, rather than any narrow and exclusive definition of → faith and order" (art. 2.1.4-5). → United and uniting churches that share this understanding of the nature and calling of the church can also be members, since membership does not rule out belonging to other denominational alliances.

As a family of Reformed churches, the WARC seeks to promote fellowship among its members by sharing information and mutual support and by helping its members to share their Reformed heritage ecumenically. In 2006 the alliance comprised 218 churches (58 from Africa, 57 from Asia, 40 from Europe, 25 from Latin America, 14 from the Pacific, 12 from North America, 8 from the Caribbean, and 4 from Middle East), representing some 75 million Christians in all.

The chief organ is the General Council, which meets every seven to eight years. The last two meetings have been in Debrecen, Hungary (1997), and in Accra, Ghana (2004). An executive committee directs the work of the WARC between council meetings and holds an annual conference. It consists of the president, six vice-presidents, representatives of the major regions, and 32 elected members. The permanent business is run by the executive officers, who are the general secretary, the general treasurer, and the executive secretaries of departments (there are four: Theology, Cooperation and Witness, Partnership of Women and Men, and Finance) and committees, as deemed necessary. The general sec-

retariat is located at the ecumenical center at Geneva. To promote and deepen member cooperation and fellowship, five areas have their own leaders, assemblies, and working committees: Southern Africa, Caribbean and North America, Europe, Latin America, and Northeast Asia. In addition, there exists a similar regional body: the Alliance of Reformed Churches in Africa. The WARC publishes *Reformed World,* a quarterly journal, and *Update,* a newsletter.

A central aim is to make relevant the Reformed tradition and to revitalize and deepen the fellowship of the churches, especially as regards the often small, minority churches outside the West, which are concerned to give their own witness to the faith in their own context (→ Contextual Theology) and in so doing need the fellowship and support of churches in other lands. A further concern is to promote interdenominational → unity, as well as unity with other churches. To that end the WARC engages in → dialogue conversations with the → Anglican Communion, the → Baptist World Alliance, the Disciples of Christ, the → Lutheran World Federation (→ Lutheran Churches), the → Mennonites, the → Orthodox Church (Patriarchate of Constantinople), the → Roman Catholic Church, and the → World Methodist Council.

Apartheid as a racist structural element (→ Racism) of the Reformed Churches in South Africa presented a special challenge to the WARC. At Ottawa in 1982 the General Council condemned apartheid as a → sin and a theological error, and it further declared that it was a matter of a → *status confessionis.* It suspended the membership of the two South African churches concerned until they made it clear by both word and deed that they were renouncing apartheid.

The WARC has also worked on other themes, including the fellowship of men and women; → mission and evangelization in the context of various cultures; justice, → peace, right, and might; and human and civil → rights. Recently the focus has been directed also to topics, such as the confession of faith, that relate to the larger issues of worldwide economic injustice and environmental destruction (→ Environmental Ethics).

Bibliography: "The Ecumenical Role of the World Confessional Families in the Ecumenical Movement" (1974), *WCC Exchange* (Geneva) 3/2 (1977) • J. W. DE GRUCHY and C. VILLA-VICENCIO, eds., *Apartheid Is a Heresy* (Cape Town, 1983) • M. PRADERVAND, *A Century of Service: A History of the World Alliance of Reformed Churches, 1875-1975* (Grand Rapids, 1975).

Publications from the series "Studies from the World Alliance of Reformed Churches" (Geneva): *Colloquium 2000: Faith Communities and Social Movements Facing Globalization* (2002) • *Confessions and Confessing in the Reformed Tradition Today* (1982) • *Covenanting for Peace and Justice* (1989) • *Eldership in the Reformed Churches Today* (1991) • *Gospel and Cultures: Reformed Perspectives* (1996) • *Islam in Africa* (1995) • *Justification and Sanctification in the Traditions of Reformation* (1999) • *Oriental Orthodox–Reformed Dialogue: The First Four Sessions* (1998) • *Reformed Theology and the Jewish People* (1986) • *Rights of Future Generations, Rights of Nature: Proposal for Enlarging the Universal Declaration of Human Rights* (ed. L. Vischer; 1990) • *Towards a Common Understanding of the Church* (1991) Reformed–Roman Catholic dialogue • *Towards Closer Fellowship* (1988) Reformed-Disciples dialogue.

JOACHIM GUHRT

World Association for Christian Communication

1. The Early Years
2. WACC and the Right to Communicate
3. WACC beyond 2005

1. The Early Years

The World Association for Christian Communication (WACC) is among the earliest expressions of the ecumenical movement. It is nearly as old as the → World Council of Churches (WCC), for its history begins with an informal international conference on religious broadcasting held in Chichester, England, in October 1950. The two world wars had exposed in stark relief the dark side of broadcasting as a tool for propaganda and nationalism. The church leaders and Christian broadcasters who met in Chichester, and then in April 1953 in Bossey, Switzerland, were determined to redeem broadcasting. This determination led to the establishment of the World Committee for Christian Broadcasting (WCCB), which was entrusted with the "use of radio and TV for the proclamation of the Christian message." At the second world congress of the WCCB, held in New Delhi in November 1961, the organization was renamed the World Association for Christian Broadcasting (WACB).

The formation of two committees contributed to the strengthening of ecumenical cooperation in global communication. One was the Radio, Visual Education, and Mass Communication Committee, formed in 1948 in the United States under the aegis

of the → National Council of the Churches of Christ; the other was the WCC-sponsored Coordinating Committee for Christian Broadcasting (CCCB), which was specifically established in 1959 to support radio ministry — in particular, the → Lutheran World Federation's (LWF) Radio Voice of the Gospel, broadcasting from Addis Ababa, Ethiopia.

By the late 1960s, acknowledgment of the potential of communications in global ministry and recognition of the need for media-ministry support in the developing world led to closer cooperation between the CCCB and the WCCB. This development culminated in a merger, followed by the establishment of the World Association for Christian Communication in Oslo, Norway, in June 1968. While WACC's credentials as a forum for, and as a supporter of, Christian broadcasting had already been established, it had less experience in other areas of communications.

WACC's media mandate was subsequently expanded by the organization's merger with the Agency for Christian Literature Development in May 1975 in London. This merger led to the formation of the new WACC, with an expanded international focus on the training of professional communicators, electronic media, the regionalization of WACC, and support for Christian literature and periodicals. Headquarters for the organization was in London.

2. WACC and the Right to Communicate

2.1. Until 1975, WACC's mission *of* communication and *to* communication was actualized through support for global, media-based mission and → evangelism initiatives. A number of factors, external and internal, including ecumenical support for global peace and justice initiatives, the influence of → liberation theology, and an emphasis on the → Social Gospel, led to the employment of staff committed to a broader understanding of mission. The publication of the WACC journal *Media Development* stimulated a new understanding of the mission of → Christian communication. The establishment of participatory, decision-making processes by WACC's Central Committee then led to power-sharing between the executive and officers and to the involvement of the regional representatives of WACC in decision making. This understanding was profoundly influenced by WACC's involvement in global communication advocacy, particularly its espousal of the right to communicate as described in the "New World Information and Communication Order" proposed within the → United Nations.

WACC's commitment to the right to communicate earned the organization a certain critical notoriety in ecumenical circles, although public support for a "wider ecumenism" secured its reputation in secular, activist, and academic circles. This commitment to a wider → ecumenism has been routinely contested by WACC's membership, particularly by those who believe that the mission of Christian communication ought to translate mainly into support for church communication structures, church-based projects, and communication support for evangelism. The composition of WACC's membership has also changed over the years, with an opening up of membership to people belonging to other faith communities. While this decision has provoked intense debate, it has offered the organization opportunities to clarify the larger meaning of communicating Christ in and to the oikoumene (→ Theology of Religions).

2.2. The right to communicate highlighted the need for WACC to move beyond an instrumental understanding of → communication and to the recognition of communication as fundamental to life and → human dignity, the basis for meaning, relationships, and community. This new understanding became the basis for WACC's "Christian Principles of Communication," a statement adopted by the WACC Central Committee in 1989 that captured WACC's philosophical and theological position on Christian communication. "Christian Principles of Communication" affirms that communication creates community, communication is participatory, communication liberates, communication supports and develops cultures, and communication is prophetic. These principles, translated into the support of many projects located in different parts of the world, particularly in the developing world, included popular theater, cinema, community radio, gender and media justice, participatory communication, media literacy, and church-based media and communication.

2.3. Immediately after the first World Congress on Christian Communication, organized by WACC and held in Manila in 1989, WACC's Central Committee recommended that the organization augment its projects portfolio with a sector dedicated to studies and advocacy. By then, WACC had already been recognized for its commitment to research — primarily through its flagship quarterly journal *Media Development,* a book series with Sage Publishers that led to the publication of numerous academic works on communication, and its support for research, including projects on intercultural communication, communication in → theological education, and women and media (→ Mass Media). The

last two areas subsequently became virtually synonymous with WACC.

While communication and theological education led to the introduction of communication as a subject of study in theological seminaries around the world, the women-and-media program not only resulted in gender equity within WACC's internal structures but led to a global program that explores issues related to gender and media justice. The Women Empowering Communication Conference, sponsored by WACC in Bangkok in 1994, was a landmark event that brought together more than 400 women and media scholars and activists. In 1995 the women's program launched a Global Media Monitoring project, a global study on the media reporting of gender issues on a single day, an initiative that was repeated in 2000 and 2005.

By 2005, WACC had organized three global congresses (Manila, 1989; Metapec, Mexico, 1995; and Amsterdam, 2001). It also had supported an innumerable number of projects related to every conceivable area in communication from traditional communication to electronic networking, and it had completed three five-year study-and-advocacy programs based on workshops and publications on subjects ranging from media ethics to the relation of science and new technologies to faith.

3. WACC beyond 2005

With its small staff and its access to regular sources of funding, the WACC (unlike the WCC and other ecumenical agencies) was not faced with the prospect of downsizing until relatively recently. Rising overheads in London and cuts in funding from ecumenical agencies, with a subsequent impact on the WACC program budget, resulted in the Central Committee recommending an integrated program strategy based on an incorporation of its projects and research sectors, a reduction in the size and frequency of its governance meetings, a cutting back on its administrative staff, and the relocation of its administrative office to Toronto, Canada. WACC began functioning out of its Toronto office in September 2006. WACC's fifth global congress is scheduled to be held in Cape Town, South Africa, in 2008.

WACC has played an important role in bringing key issues in global communication to the attention of the ecumenical movement. It has had enduring partnerships with the WCC, the LWF, the World YWCA, and numerous regional and national ecumenical groups and churches, including Orthodox and Roman Catholic. In addition, it has forged strong links with a number of secular, nonfaith groups. It now occupies a unique position in the ecumenical movement and remains the only ecumenical agency dedicated to communication support. It has been in the forefront of global communications advocacy and has been described as a transnational moral lobby.

While WACC has played a pivotal role at the forefront of ecumenical communication, its future, like that of very many ecumenical agencies, seems less assured. There was a time when WACC was the sole ecumenical Christian body in the business of supporting church and nonchurch communication projects. That is no longer the case. Today, there are a number of specialized, media-support organizations, and WACC's role as a clearinghouse for media and communication projects is increasingly upstaged by bilateral denominational support for media and other projects.

Rather ironically, the ecumenical movement has downgraded communication precisely at a time when knowledge and communication in a globalized world have become vital to human survival. This in itself is a serious concern. Communication is more than "image" and "technique," technology and skills. It is also essentially about meaning and mediation, process and content. The ecumenical movement needs to renew its commitment to a deeper and wider expression of ecumenical communication, which is more relevant today than ever.

→ Third World

Bibliography: C. J. ARTHUR, *The Globalization of Communications: Some Religious Implications* (Geneva, 1998) • M. GALLAGHER, *Gender Setting: New Agendas for Media Monitoring and Advocacy* (London, 2001) • F. KÜRSCHNER-PELKMANN, *Die Mauern des Schweigens brechen. Schritte auf dem Weg zu einer demokratischen Medienkultur* (Zurich, 2005) • P. LEE, *Communication for All: New World Information and Communication Order* (Maryknoll, N.Y., 1986); idem, ed., *Communication, Reconciliation: Challenges Facing the Twenty-first Century* (Geneva, 2001); idem, ed., *The World Association for Christian Communication, 1975-2000: "A Labour of Love"* (London, 2000) • K. LOWE, *Opening Eyes and Ears: New Connections for Christian Communication* (Geneva, 1983) • J. E. MCELDOWNEY, ed., *Fram: A Report on the Oslo Assembly, June 1968* (London, 1968) • P. MALONE, *Can Movies Be a Moral Compass?* (London, 2005) • D. S. PLOU, *Global Communication: Is There a Place for Human Dignity?* (Geneva, 1996) • P. SOUKUP, *Communication and Theology: Introduction and Review of the Literature* (London, 1983) • C. VALLE, *Communication and Mission: In the Labyrinth of Globalisation* (London, 2002).

PRADIP THOMAS

World Council of Churches

1. Membership
2. Basis
3. Early History
4. Foundation
5. Organization
6. Structure
7. Activities
8. Assemblies
9. Future

The World Council of Churches (WCC) is an international organization, a fellowship of churches, headquartered in Geneva, Switzerland. By its own self-identification, it is not a church. In 2007 the WCC's membership included 348 church bodies in some 120 countries. Many churches in the → Pentecostal and → evangelical traditions are not members of the WCC. It has been estimated that less than one-half of the non-Orthodox and non–Roman Catholic churches in the world belong to the WCC. The → Roman Catholic Church is not a member of the council, although it actively participates in a number of WCC programs and sends observers to key WCC events. Thus, although the scope of WCC membership is extensive and varied, it is limited. This fact suggests that we cannot simply equate the WCC with the global ecumenical movement.

1. Membership

Membership in the WCC is open to churches of at least 25,000 members; churches of more than 10,000 but less than 25,000 members may be considered "associate member churches," with limited rights to participate in the life of the WCC. Churches seeking membership must have a viable life and organization, as well as positive ecumenical relations with other churches in their own country. They are asked to give an account of how their faith and witness relate to the → Niceno-Constantinopolitan Creed and must practice → baptism in the name of the triune God. Churches are voted into membership by a WCC Assembly or the Central Committee. The WCC has no provision for suspending or removing churches from its membership. In the course of the WCC's history, a few churches have withdrawn, and contact has been lost with some others, largely because of political events. The governing documents of the WCC also provide that associate councils, regional ecumenical organizations, and → Christian World Communions may send delegated representatives to the Assembly and advisers to meetings of the Central Committee.

2. Basis

The WCC constitution indicates that a precondition for membership is agreement with the basis of the council. The original basis was drafted prior to the council's founding in 1948 and then accepted at the First Assembly, which met in Amsterdam. This basis was reformulated at the Third Assembly of the WCC, in New Delhi in 1961, and still remains in force: "The World Council of Churches is a fellowship of churches which confess the Lord Jesus Christ as God and Saviour according to the Scriptures and therefore seek to fulfil together their common calling to the glory of the one God, Father, Son, and Holy Spirit."

This basis is regarded as less than a → confession of Christian faith, certainly not a creed, but more than a formula. Its purpose is to serve as a point of reference for member churches. The basis offers no judgment on churches that accept it. Member churches have the freedom to interpret the basis in their own way. This view of the basis was affirmed by the so-called Toronto Statement, properly entitled "The Church, the Churches, and the World Council of Churches," received by the Central Committee in that city in 1950.

Antecedents to the basis are to be found in the 19th-century work of the → Young Men's Christian Association, the → Young Women's Christian Association, and the → World Student Christian Federation. Influences from the 20th century include the invitation to the First World Conference on → Faith and Order and, perhaps more directly, the encyclical of the Ecumenical Patriarchate of Constantinople of 1920, which urged a "koinonia" (fellowship) of churches.

3. Early History

The more remote origins of the WCC lie in the 19th century, when various denominational organizations sought to bring a number of different Christians together in meetings to discuss the mission of the church. For example, the Baptist missionary William Carey (1761-1834) proposed the calling of a missionary conference of all denominations to meet in Cape Town, South Africa, in 1810. The hope was that such a conference would meet every ten years. But this and similar efforts in that century bore little fruit.

Such hopes for pan-Christian contacts were also expressed in the early 20th century in an encyclical of Joachim III (1834-1912), the ecumenical patriarch of Constantinople, and in the efforts of Spencer Jones (1857-1943) in England, Paul Wattson (1863-1940) in the United States, and Paul Couturier

(1881-1953) in France to establish the Week of Prayer for Christian Unity.

A key event was the World Missionary Conference, which met in Edinburgh in 1910 and led to the formation of the → International Missionary Council in 1921. The Edinburgh Conference was a precursor to the formation of two global movements: → "Life and Work," to work for peace and justice, and → "Faith and Order," to address the theological issues that divide the churches. Both movements held a number of international conferences in the 1920s and 1930s.

4. Foundation

One result of this ecumenical activity during the first decades of the 20th century was the recognition that greater coordination among the various components of the ecumenical movement was desirable. Although little occurred between 1928 and 1932, it was becoming clear to some in 1933 that Faith and Order, as well as Life and Work, could accomplish more as parts of a single organization. Critical meetings were held in Princeton, New Jersey, in 1935 and at Westfield College in London in 1937. Plans were drawn up for the integration of the two into a World Council of Churches. The possibility of such a council was discussed in 1937 in Oxford at a Life and Work conference, and the same year in Edinburgh at a Faith and Order conference. Both movements gave their approval, and a conference was held at Utrecht in 1938 to draw up a constitution for a world council.

The Utrecht meeting established a provisional committee responsible for the "World Council of Churches in the Process of Formation." It named William Temple (1881-1944) of England as chairman and Willem A. → Visser 't Hooft (1900-1985) of the Netherlands as general secretary. In the same year the International Missionary Council decided not to become part of the process leading to the WCC. In 1939 this provisional committee made plans for a constituting assembly to meet in 1941. World War II delayed these plans, however, although the "WCC in formation," with Visser 't Hooft headquartered in Geneva, was active in many areas during the war, including chaplaincy and assistance to Jews and other → refugees.

The provisional committee met in 1946 and 1947 to renew plans for a constituting assembly. It was decided to hold this event in Amsterdam in 1948. After considerable discussion, the decision was reached to send invitations to individual → denominations at the national level. World confessional bodies, national councils of churches, and other international groups were invited to send nonvoting representatives to Amsterdam.

On Monday, August 23, 1948, the founding of the WCC "was declared to be and is hereby completed" by delegates representing 147 churches. The message of the Assembly noted the conviction of the delegates: "Here at Amsterdam we have committed ourselves afresh to Him and have covenanted with one another in constituting this WCC. We intend to stay together."

This first Assembly defined in a general manner the tasks and responsibilities of the new organization. It made decisions about budget, policies, and programs, and it authorized itself to issue statements to the churches and to the world, with specific limits on the nature and authority of such statements. The Amsterdam Assembly elected Visser 't Hooft as the first general secretary of the WCC.

The constituting Assembly of the WCC brought Faith and Order and Life and Work as organizations and movements into one new organization and structure. In 1961, at the New Delhi Assembly, the International Missionary Council, which had earlier declined an invitation to be part of the WCC, joined the WCC. It became part of the council's structure as the Commission on World Mission and Evangelism.

5. Organization

The constitution of the WCC allots the legislative and executive functions and decisions of the organization to the Assembly, to the Central Committee, and to officers and subordinate entities within a General Secretariat. The Assembly is the highest legislative body of the WCC; it determines policies and reviews and implements programs. An Assembly ordinarily is held once every seven years, and its voting delegates are selected by the member churches on the basis of a formula. The Assembly elects no more than eight WCC presidents to represent various regions of the world. The Assembly also elects from the delegates at the Assembly a Central Committee of not more than 150 members. The Central Committee, headed by an elected moderator, is the main continuation body between Assemblies, meeting about once every 12 months. It implements Assembly policies and programs, adopts the budget, and elects an Executive Committee of approximately 25 persons. The Executive Committee usually meets twice a year. Since 2006 there has also been a Permanent Committee on Consensus and Collaboration, at least half of whose membership must be from Orthodox churches.

The composition of these organs of the WCC has changed through the years as the council became less Euro–North Atlantic centered, as more national churches from outside of Europe or North America, with their own indigenous leadership of → clergy and laity, joined the WCC. Since the 1960s efforts have been made by the WCC to ensure as much balance as possible in the Assemblies and on the various committees and structures between women and men, adults and youth, clergy and laity. Some member churches have resisted these efforts, although an examination of the membership of the Assembly and committees over the years will demonstrate increased numbers of women, youth, and laity involved in the work of the WCC.

The general secretary of the WCC is elected by the Central Committee and reports to it. This person is the chief executive of the council and the head of the staff responsible for the ongoing work of the organization. The general secretaries of the WCC have been Visser 't Hooft (1948-66), Eugene Carson Blake of the United States (1966-72), Philip Potter of Jamaica (1972-84), Emilio Castro of Uruguay (1984-92), Konrad Raiser of Germany (1993-2003), and, since 2004, Samuel Kobia of Kenya.

6. Structure

In the course of growing in understanding its work and in confronting differing emphases in the ecumenical movement, the WCC has fairly often changed its organizational structure. The tasks of reconstruction after World War II, the tensions of the cold war, the independence of new nations in Asia, Africa, and Latin America, and the increasing recognition of the results of worldwide injustices and inequities in wealth have had considerable impact on the WCC and, on the whole, have deepened the commitment of its member churches to stay together.

The Amsterdam Assembly (1948) established 12 departments. This arrangement was changed at the Evanston Assembly (1954) with the creation of four divisions, each with a number of departments. This structural plan continued through the New Delhi Assembly (1961), although the entrance of the International World Mission Council at that time brought its own structural alterations. The Uppsala Assembly (1968) authorized a major restructuring that brought simplification and coordination to the WCC. Three administrative units were formed: (1) Faith and Witness, (2) Justice and Service, and (3) Education and Renewal. This arrangement, with some adjustments, continued through and after the Canberra Assembly (1991). The Harare Assembly (1998) put a new structure in place that was influenced by a "Common Understanding and Vision" study process. This structure called for the WCC to have four clusters, composed of a number of teams: (1) Relations, (2) Issues and Themes, (3) Communication, and (4) Finances, Services, and Administration.

More recently, as a result of discussions at the Porto Alegre Assembly (2006), interest in spirituality and ecumenical formation, concerns for global justice, and prophetic witness have influenced the structuring of the WCC. Since Porto Alegre the council has functioned with a General Secretariat, units for communication and public relations, and for financial services and administration. It now works within six program sectors: (1) the WCC and the Ecumenical Movement in the 21st Century; (2) Unity, Mission, Evangelism, and Spirituality; (3) Public Witness: Addressing Power, Affirming Peace; (4) Justice, Diakonia, and Responsibility for Creation; (5) Education and Ecumenical Formation; and (6) Interreligious Dialogue and Cooperation. These programs each have a director and management teams to carry out their work. There is also an associate general secretary for programs.

7. Activities

It is difficult to describe in small compass the activities of this pan-Christian, multinational organization, with a history at this writing of almost 60 years. Some of the activities of the WCC have been with it from its foundation; others have been added because of the needs of member churches and the needs and demands of a world that has changed profoundly since 1948. Proponents of the WCC have tended to view all of these activities as responsive to the teachings of Scripture and the challenges facing the modern ecumenical movement. Persons more critical of the WCC have asked whether a number of these activities have distracted the council from the goal of the visible unity of divided churches. Nevertheless, virtually all acknowledge that the WCC has altered in positive ways the relationships between divided churches and addressed many of the burning social and political issues of the world in the 20th and 21st centuries.

The WCC has been responsible for a number of international conferences on Faith and Order, including at Lund (1952), Montreal (1963), and Santiago de Compostela (1993). Likewise, the WCC has sponsored a number of conferences on world mission, including at Bangkok (1973), Melbourne (1980), San Antonio, Texas (1989), and Athens (2005).

Key documents for ecumenical work have arisen in the context of WCC activity. These include *Mission and Evangelism: An Ecumenical Affirmation* (1961) and *Baptism, Eucharist, and Ministry* (1982). The latter has become the most widely circulated text of the modern ecumenical movement.

The WCC has promoted special emphases such as the Ecumenical Decade in Solidarity with Women (1988-99) and the Ecumenical Decade to Overcome Violence (2001-10); a study process entitled "Towards a Common Understanding and Vision of the World Council of Churches," which reported in 1998 to the Harare Assembly; the Special Commission on Orthodox Participation in the WCC, which reported to and influenced the Porto Alegre Assembly in 2006; and the Joint Consultative Group with Pentecostals, which began its work in 2005.

Over the years the WCC has also instituted programs such as the controversial → Program to Combat Racism, as well as the less-contentious Commission on Churches' Participation in Development, Christian Medical Commission (→ Medical Missions), Dialogue with People of Living Faiths and Ideologies, and Justice, Peace, and the Integrity of Creation.

Since → Vatican II, relationships between the Roman Catholic Church and the WCC have strengthened. A joint working group between the two meets regularly to take into account past developments and to chart new areas of endeavor. The Harare Assembly (1998) called on this group "to continue its effort to understand past difficulties and open ways towards new perspectives and possible positive initiatives."

A significant WCC enterprise is the Ecumenical Institute at the Château de Bossey, near Céligny in Switzerland. This institute has the special function of providing graduate training in ecumenical studies. It also is a venue for specific consultations. The institute at Bossey has played a leading role in forming future generations of ecumenical leaders. At Bossey and in Geneva the WCC administers an impressive ecumenical library, whose holdings include comprehensive WCC documentation and other ecumenical literature.

Over the years, because of its interest in interchurch aid, service to refugees, and issues of → peace, → war, and social justice, the WCC has maintained observer status at the → United Nations and its related agencies.

In all these activities the WCC offers to its member churches an opportunity for common witness and united action. The WCC explicitly refrains from legislating for, or speaking on behalf of, the churches. Exceptions to this provision are provided by the WCC constitution, which itself has been approved by the council's membership.

8. Assemblies

One of the most effective places for the member churches of the WCC to learn to know each other, to cooperate, and to provide for common witness has been the WCC Assembly, which occurs approximately every seven years. Including the foundation of the WCC in 1948, nine assemblies have been held.

First Assembly, Amsterdam, Netherlands, 1948, with the theme "Man's Disorder and God's Design." This gathering marked the formal establishment of the WCC, the creation of its initial structure, and the ownership of the churches assembled of the modern ecumenical movement.

Second Assembly, Evanston, Illinois, United States, 1954, with the theme "Christ — the Hope of the World." This Assembly reflected a growing theological maturity within the WCC as it grappled with the stated Christological theme. It also took up issues of social and economic concern, as well as the responsibility of Christians for peace and justice.

Third Assembly, New Delhi, India, 1961, with the theme "Jesus Christ — the Light of the World." This meeting saw the integration of the International Missionary Council into the WCC as its Commission on World Mission and Evangelism. It expanded the WCC basis by adding the phrase "according to the scriptures" and the Trinitarian formula. The New Delhi Assembly received a number of Orthodox churches into the WCC's membership and advanced an enduring vision of church fellowship, koinonia, "in all places and in all ages."

Fourth Assembly, Uppsala, Sweden, 1968, with the theme "Behold, I Make All Things New." This Assembly has often been viewed as the most activistic and politically conscious Assembly in the WCC's history. It affirmed that more dialogue with the world is needed, youth should be given a more active role in the life of the WCC, and more attention should be given to the poor of the world (→ Poverty). With such emphases the Uppsala Assembly is often regarded as the opening of a new chapter in the development of the ecumenical movement.

Fifth Assembly, Nairobi, Kenya, 1975, with the theme "Jesus Christ Frees and Unites." This gathering discussed how evangelism relates to involvement in economic and social problems, and it sought to provide theological support, based on faith in the triune God, for such involvement. It stressed the need for interfaith dialogue and the search for a participatory and sustainable society.

Sixth Assembly, Vancouver, Canada, 1983, with the theme "Jesus Christ — the Life of the World." This Assembly has been seen as the most representative assembly of the WCC, with 30 percent of the delegates women, 13 percent youth, and 46 percent laity. A highlight was a eucharistic celebration using the liturgy from the important 1982 Faith and Order conference at Lima, Peru. It set as a WCC priority the commitment to "justice, peace, and the integrity of creation."

Seventh Assembly, Canberra, Australia, 1991, with the theme "Come, Holy Spirit — Renew the Whole Creation." This meeting brought a new emphasis with its theme on the → Holy Spirit and its formulation as a prayer. It revealed the challenges of linking theology and experience. The Assembly gave attention to the situation of indigenous peoples, and its discussions on → Eucharist, ministry, and ecclesiology revealed in bold relief the deep differences between churches in the ecumenical movement.

Eighth Assembly, Harare, Zimbabwe, 1998, with the theme "Turn to God — Rejoice in Hope." This Assembly was conspicuous for its lack of attention to the issue of the visible unity of the church. The largest Assembly in the council's history, it celebrated the 50th anniversary of the WCC and recommitted itself to continue the ecumenical journey. It utilized "padares," meeting places in some 400 locations that provided a setting for grassroots discussion and reflection on a number of topics, not all of which were part of the official agenda of the Assembly.

Ninth Assembly, Porto Alegre, Brazil, 2006, with the theme "God, in Your Grace, Transform the World." This was the first WCC Assembly held on the South American continent. The most notable feature was a major change in the way in which WCC business is to be conducted. Instead of strictly following rules of parliamentary procedure (deemed as Western and largely unusable to many from the Third World), a process of decision making by consensus was initiated, with a series of amendments to the governing documents of the WCC. This new process of decision making was not designed to totally displace the making of some decisions by vote, but it did mark a significant departure from previous practice. Spirituality and ecumenical formation, global and prophetic justice emerged as critical issues for future WCC work.

9. Future

As the WCC entered the 21st century, it had a rich history and a number of significant accomplishments. It also was facing a number of serious challenges, which included continuing financial limitations, the preoccupation of many of its member churches with internal matters (including survival!), a general loss of ecumenical energy, and a rising disinterest in the gift and quest of the visible unity of divided churches. An open question remains as to whether the new process of decision making by consensus will be workable and remove some of the tensions within the life of the WCC. Furthermore, there is a deepened need for dialogue with other world religions, not least in light of global tension and hostility. And the opportunity for the WCC to work more closely with the Christian World Communions, perhaps including joint assemblies in the future, may open a new chapter of ecumenical activity. All these issues notwithstanding, the WCC in the early years of the 21st century represents an impressive and noble experiment of ecumenical commitment on behalf of its member churches.

→ Ecumenism, Ecumenical Movement

Bibliography: R. S. Bilheimer, *Breakthrough: The Emergence of the Ecumenical Tradition* (Grand Rapids, 1989) • J. Briggs, M. A. Oduyoye, G. Tsetsis, eds., *A History of the Ecumenical Movement,* vol. 3, *1968-2000* (Geneva, 2004) • H. E. Fey, ed., *A History of the Ecumenical Movement,* vol. 2, *1948-1968* (Philadelphia, 1970) • M. VanElderen and M. Conway, *Introducing the World Council of Churches* (Geneva, 2001) • W. A. Visser 't Hooft, *The Genesis and Formation of the World Council of Churches* (Geneva, 1982); idem, *The Ten Formative Years, 1938-1948: Report on the Activities of the World Council of Churches during Its Period of Formation* (Geneva, 1948). See also minutes of the successive meetings of the Central Committee (1948 to present), preparatory documents and reports of each WCC Assembly, and reports of the Central Committee to each Assembly.

William G. Rusch

World Evangelical Alliance

Overview
1. History
2. Theological Basis
3. Commissions
4. Ecumenical Relations

Overview

The World Evangelical Alliance (WEA) is an association of 128 national evangelical alliances, grouped, for administrative purposes, into seven regional associations (Africa, Asia, Caribbean, Europe, Latin America, North America, and South Pacific). The North America branch comprises the Evangelical Fellowship of Canada and, in the United States, the

→ National Association of Evangelicals. In 2006 the WEA also included 8 affiliate members (independently incorporated organizations that work in harmony with WEA structures and serve the WEA constituency) and 109 associate members (independent organizations with their own specific ministries and accountability, an international scope of ministry, and the capacity to serve in and beyond the WEA community).

The effectiveness of the WEA lies in its emphasis on → prayer, spiritual renewal, → discipleship, personal piety, and commitment to the historic tenets of evangelical Christianity. By stressing the role of the local church, global → missions, and compassion for the poor and oppressed, it integrates → evangelism and church planting into the holistic mission of the church. Through its networking ability, the WEA is a major force in evangelical → ecumenism.

The word "evangelical" is used to denote those Christians who, regardless of their denominational affiliation or conciliar connection, hold a conservative view of Scripture and stress the importance of personal faith in Christ and of engaging in evangelism. The WEA estimates there are about 420 million evangelicals in the world.

1. History

The Evangelical Alliance (EA) was founded in London in 1846 to foster Christian unity in a spiritual rather than institutional sense and to provide channels of cooperation for carrying out the mission of the church. A voluntary alliance of individuals and not a confederation of churches, it promoted unity through mutual love and evangelical affirmations. The EA, which consisted of autonomous national branches rather than an overarching world body with a secretariat, sponsored 11 international conferences between 1851 and 1907, each bringing Christians together from various countries for fellowship and sharing of ideas.

The branches formed in Britain and Europe remained active until the present, whereas the U.S. branch (formed in 1867) faded out of existence early in the 20th century. Other EA activities included sponsoring an annual universal week of prayer; furthering missionary work; publishing *Evangelical Christendom* (1847-1954), a journal that reported on revivals and other Christian activities; fostering religious liberty for → persecuted Christians; and producing a multilingual hymnbook. In 1912 the EA in Britain incorporated itself as the World's Evangelical Alliance (British Organisation), but it had no jurisdiction over the other national EAs.

The international thrust of the EA faded during the years after World War I, but a new movement for evangelical unity arose in the United States in reaction to alleged failures of liberal ecumenism. This interest led to the formation of the National Association of Evangelicals (NAE) in 1942-43. After World War II evangelicals on both sides of the Atlantic sensed the need for closer ties, and at meetings at Hildenborough Hall in Kent, England, and at Gordon Divinity School in Boston in 1950, the matter was intensely discussed. The NAE also formed a Commission on International Relations, which sent two of its leaders on a world tour to explore possibilities for united action. This effort led to the International Convention of Evangelicals, held in August 1951 at the Woudschoten Hostel near Zeist in The Netherlands, which created an organization named World Evangelical Fellowship (WEF).

The conferees adopted a statement of faith and a constitution; established commissions for evangelism, missions, literature, and "Christian action" (defense of → religious liberty); and chose a slate of officers, with British army general Sir Arthur Smith as president and F. Roy Cattell of London and J. Elwin Wright of Boston as cosecretaries. The office would be in London. John Stott closely linked the purposes of the new WEF to the gospel, wishing to see the fellowship contribute to the furtherance and defense of the gospel, encourage conformation to the gospel, and provide a source of fellowship in these tasks. Over the years the group's purpose statement was expanded, now stating: "The WEA exists to foster Christian unity and to provide a worldwide identity, voice and platform to Evangelical Christians. Seeking empowerment by the Holy Spirit, they extend the Kingdom of God by proclamation of the Gospel to all nations and by Christ-centered transformation within society."

The national fellowships continued to maintain their autonomy, and they became members of the new WEF by subscribing to the statement of faith. However, there was considerable tension between the Europeans and the Americans over fears of → fundamentalism, especially over the issues of biblical infallibility and ecumenical relationships. In fact, representatives from several European countries met in Germany in 1952 and formed a separate European Evangelical Alliance. The breach with the WEF was not fully healed until 1968.

In August 1953 the first General Council meeting of the WEF took place in Clarens, Switzerland, and the organization was now on a relatively stable footing, although it repeatedly faced financial difficulties in the ensuing years. The most serious crisis was in 1985, but the efforts of its dynamic treasurer, British lawyer John E. Langlois, rescued it from becoming insolvent. In 1953 the British organization reverted to its original name of Evangelical Alliance, and as part of a restructuring in 2001-2, the WEF reclaimed the name "World Evangelical Alliance."

At first, WEF activities included sponsoring publications, scholarships for theological students, and meetings of evangelical leaders and serving as a conduit for exchange of information and ideas among church and mission society leaders and parachurch ministries. Over the years these tasks expanded to include social witness and the promoting of religious freedom. Beginning in 1956, the General Assembly met every six years (later four) in various countries. It elected a president (now chairman) and an Executive Council (now International Council), and a small staff carried out the day-to-day activities. The chief executive officer, known as a secretary or director, continued to serve his own agency, and the office moved as the location of the director changed. In 1986 the office was relocated in Singapore, but it was closed some years later and is now in Canada. In 1974 Waldron Scott (from the U.S.) was appointed the first full-time general secretary (later international director). His successors were Wade Coggins (U.S., 1980), David Howard (U.S., 1982), Agustin (Jun) Vencer (Philippines, 1992), Gary Edmonds (U.S., 2002), and Geoff Tunnicliffe (Canada, 2005).

2. Theological Basis

The statement of faith adopted in 1951 continues in effect. It affirms (1) the divine inspiration, infallibility, and supreme authority of Holy Scripture; (2) the eternally existent divine → Trinity; (3) Christ's → virgin birth, sinless human life, performance of miracles, vicarious and atoning death, → resurrection, → ascension, mediatorial work in heaven, and personal return in power and glory (→ Parousia); (4) the → salvation of lost and sinful humans through the shed blood of Christ by faith apart from works, and → regeneration by the Holy Spirit; (5) the indwelling → Holy Spirit, who enables the believer to live a holy life and to witness and work for Christ; (6) the spiritual unity of all believers in the church, the body of Christ; and (7) the final resurrection of both the saved and the lost — the former to life, and the latter to damnation.

3. Commissions

In addition to the work of the national alliances and fellowships, the WEA carries on much of its activities through its six commissions. The Missions

Commission facilitates the advancement of national mission movements by providing opportunities for mission leaders to collaborate on initiatives and share resources, sponsoring conferences, and publishing the magazine *Connections*. The Religious Liberty Commission monitors infringements of religious freedom and, through its aggressive advocacy efforts, strives to help all people, especially Protestants, to exercise their faith without oppression or discrimination. Because the WEA's constituent bodies represent 150 million Christians in 115 countries, its voice demanding the religious freedom enshrined in the U.N.'s Universal Declaration of Human Rights is heard.

The Theological Commission, led by Bruce Nicholls, Bong Rin Ro, Peter Kuzmic, Rolf Hille, David Parker, and others, networks and promotes → theological education around the globe and publishes the *WEA Theological News* (a global newsletter), the journal *Evangelical Review of Theology,* a monograph series, and the proceedings of various task forces and consultations. In 1980 it launched an independent accrediting body for theological schools, the International Council for Evangelical Theological Education. The Women's Commission encourages evangelical women to identify and maximize their gifts and endeavors to empower and mobilize them to meet the unique needs of women around the world.

The Youth Commission fosters the building of youth ministry networks and publishes the magazine *Network* (→ Youth Work). The Information Technology Commission applies technology for the dissemination of information and sharing of resources within the WEA constituency to enable the global church to be more effective in its public witness.

4. Ecumenical Relations

The WEA is strongly interested in spiritual unity, which it regards as essential to the well-being of the church. Organizational or conciliar unity is not a high priority, which has been a matter of tension within the group from the very beginning. It draws its constituents from both established and independent churches, and some of its members are active in their own denominations. From time to time WEA commissions have participated in consultations with the → World Council of Churches, and some contacts are maintained between the WEA and the → Roman Catholic Church.

The relationship with the → Lausanne Committee for World Evangelization, essentially a rival organization created in 1974 after the International Congress on World Evangelism, was at times problematic. Although there was cooperation in sponsoring conferences and overlap between personnel, some questioned the need for two world evangelical bodies. Both groups seem to have put the past behind them and are now working together more closely on matters of mutual concern.

Bibliography: E. BEYREUTHER, *Der Weg der Evangelischen Allianz in Deutschland* (Wuppertal, 1969) • W. H. FULLER, *People of the Mandate: The Story of the World Evangelical Fellowship* (Grand Rapids, 1996) • H. HAUZENBERGER, *Einheit auf evangelischer Grundlage. Von Werden und Wesen der Evangelischen Allianz* (Giessen) • D. M. HOWARD, *The Dream That Would Not Die: The Birth and Growth of the World Evangelical Fellowship, 1846-1946* (Exeter, 1986) • P. D. JORDAN, *The Evangelical Alliance of the United States of America, 1847-1900* (New York, 1982) • B. J. NICHOLLS, "World Evangelical Fellowship," *A Dictionary of Asian Christianity* (ed. S. W. Sunquist; Grand Rapids, 2001) 899-901 • D. PARKER, *Discerning the Obedience of Faith: A Short History of the WEA Theological Commission* (Bangalore, India, 2005) • N. M. RAILTON, *No North Sea: The Anglo-German Evangelical Network in the Middle of the Nineteenth Century* (Leiden, 2000) • I. RANDALL and D. HILBORN, *One Body in Christ: The History and Significance of the Evangelical Alliance* (Carlisle, 2001) • W. SCOTT, ed., *Serving Our Generation: Evangelical Strategies for the Eighties* (Colorado Springs, Colo., 1980). The WEF/WEA records are located in the Billy Graham Center Archives, Wheaton, Illinois.

RICHARD V. PIERARD

World Methodist Council

1. The World Methodist Council (WMC) is a global council of → Methodist and United churches that link their beginnings to the 18th-century awakening in England that was associated with the work of John → Wesley (1703-91). The WMC was organized in 1881 with the aim of strengthening members in their → faith and → love for Jesus Christ, in proclaiming the → gospel, and in serving Christ with a catholic spirit in the Wesleyan manner.

2. World Methodists today affirm the primacy and authority of Scripture and join with other Christians in confessing the faith expressed in the creeds of the → early church (→ Confessions and Creeds). Through the council, churches in the Wesleyan tradition listen and learn from one another and engage

in mutual support and united witness in the ministry of making → disciples of Jesus Christ. The WMC endeavors to strengthen international ties; promote peace, justice, and unity; clarify theological and moral standards; and identify priorities for the Methodist movement.

At the beginning of the 21st century the WMC, which has its administrative offices at Lake Junaluska, North Carolina, links Methodist and United churches in over 130 countries, with a membership close to 40 million and a constituency of more than 75 million persons. Sizable growth in churches, as well as in membership, continues to occur in Africa, Asia, and South America.

3. WMC decisions are made by agreement of the vote of 500 elected representatives from member churches. The council meets every five years to survey its program, to elect officers and transact necessary business, to organize committees, and to convene a World Methodist Conference.

The 2006 conference marked the 125th anniversary of the World Methodist Council. This meeting, held in Seoul, Korea, at the Kum Nan Methodist Church sanctuary, accommodated 10,000 worshipers. A historic event was the signing of the → Joint Declaration on the Doctrine of Justification, on July 23, 2006, by the WMC, the → Lutheran World Federation, and the → Roman Catholic Church. Also of note was a service of worship at the Demilitarized Zone attended by hundreds of conference participants.

Between quinquennial meetings the council's standing committees — Ecumenics and → Dialogue, → Education, → Evangelism (which includes the World Methodist Evangelism Institute), Family Life, Social and International Affairs, → Theological Education, → Worship and → Liturgy, and → Youth — are active in their respective areas of responsibility, as are the ongoing Operational Committees of Finance, Nominating, Program, and World Exchange. A new "Achieving the Vision" endowment fund has been established. The goal of $20 million and the theme were developed as WMC members planned and participated globally and ecumenically in the 2,000th anniversary of the birth of Jesus Christ.

These committees meet biennially with elected Executive Committee members from member churches and with council officers. The WMC constitution provides for the election of eight presidium members (which shall include clergy, laywomen and laymen, and youth), plus a chairperson, vice-chairperson, and treasurer to be elected as officers. They meet annually to conduct necessary business transactions, along with the general secretary, past chairpersons, and the presidents of women's and men's groups.

Affiliated organizations are the World Federation of Methodist and Uniting Church Women, the World Fellowship of Methodist and Uniting Church Men, and the World Methodist Historical Society. International Publishing and Oxford Institute of Methodist Theological Studies are two important special committees.

4. WMC officers receive nominations submitted by individuals and by churches for persons or groups that may be considered as recipients for the annual presentation of the World Methodist Peace Award, which was inaugurated in 1976 at the council meeting in Dublin, Ireland. Recipients are chosen for their courage, creativity, and consistency in making exceptional contributions to the cause of reconciliation and peace. Past recipients include Saidie Patterson, Northern Ireland (1977); Tai-Young Lee, Korea (1984); Jimmy Carter, United States (1985); Elias Chacour, Galilee, Israel (1994); members of St. Egidio Community, Rome (1997); Grandmothers of Plaza de Mayo, Argentina (1999); Nelson Mandela, Republic of South Africa (2000); and Joe Hale, Brighton, England (2006).

5. The council readily acknowledges that Methodists form only a part of the church universal. As a part of the larger church, WMC members are committed to seek new understandings and promote mutual trust with all other Christians. One vehicle for achieving this end is bilateral church-to-church dialogues, in which the WMC has been active with several other → Christian World Communions, or "families of churches." Such conversations have been held in meetings between the council and the Lutheran World Federation (1979-84), the → World Alliance of Reformed Churches (1992-96), and the → Anglican Communion (1992-96). The International Joint Commission for Dialogue between the Roman Catholic Church and the World Methodist Council has met regularly and has reported to the council and to the Vatican since 1967. The WMC began formal conversations with the → Salvation Army in 2003. Steps taken to begin formal conversations with the Orthodox through the Ecumenical Patriarchate, affirmed by the council meeting in Rio de Janeiro, 1996, are under discussion with → Orthodox Church officials. Unity among the world's 2.0 billion Christians (2000) is an urgent and continuing concern.

Bibliography: *God in Christ Reconciling: Nineteenth World Methodist Conference, Seoul, Korea, 2006* (Waynesville, N.C., n.d.) • S. J. JONES, *The Evangelistic Love of God and Neighbor: A Theology of Witness and Discipleship* (Nashville, 2003) • D. L. MCKENNA, *What a Time to Be Wesleyan! Proclaiming the Holiness Message with Passion and Purpose* (Kansas City, Mo., 1999) • G. WAINWRIGHT, "Methodists and Roman Catholics: Bilateral Dialogue in a Multilateral Context," *Ecclesiology* 2 (2005-6) 285-305; idem, *Methodists in Dialogue* (Nashville, 1995).

FRANCES M. ALGUIRE

World Student Christian Federation

1. Foundation to World War I
2. Between Wars: A Changing Profile
3. 1956-64: "The Life and Mission of the Church"
4. 1968: Student Revolt
5. New Dynamism in a Changing Context

The World Student Christian Federation (WSCF) is a federation of some 100 national Christian student organizations spread over all continents. The member organizations, usually called → Student Christian Movements (SCMs), represent a diversity of Christian communities within institutions of higher education, including confessional, inter-confessional, and fully integrated ecumenical groups. The WSCF functions today primarily through its six regional units, which are linked together through its interregional office at the Ecumenical Center in Geneva. The main unifying link and the governing body of the whole WSCF is the General Assembly, a meeting of delegates from each member organization that convenes every four years.

1. Foundation to World War I

The WSCF was founded in July 1895 at Vadstena, Sweden. It brought together Christian groups that had sprung up in → universities and colleges in North America, northern Europe, and the Far East under the influence of the interdenominational youth movement and of the missionary awakening of the 19th century. Its predecessor organizations were the → Young Men's and → Young Women's Christian Associations (YMCA, YWCA) and the Student Volunteer Movement for Foreign Missions (SVM). The overarching thrust of the new organization was in "leading students to become disciples of Jesus Christ." The catchphrase "the evangelization of the world in this generation" described well the original ethos. Universities and colleges were considered "strategic points in the world's conquest."

The chief architect and the first general secretary of the WSCF was John R. → Mott (1865-1955), a young lawyer from the United States. Earlier he had emerged as an influential leader in both the YMCA and the missionary movement. He was the unquestioned leader and strategist of the new organization formed in Vadstena by six representatives of Christian student organizations from Germany, Great Britain, Norway, Sweden, and the United States. Mott was the leading figure of the WSCF until 1920, when the → International Missionary Council (IMC) was founded and when his role widened in the ecumenical and international missionary movements. Until 1920 the offices of the WSCF were in New York, when it was moved to Geneva.

Under Mott's leadership the scope of the federation began to expand rapidly in Europe, Asia, the Middle East, and North America. He and his colleagues were instrumental, through extended travels, in presenting the Christian message to students and in enlisting leaders for emerging Student Christian Movements. The influence of the movement was felt across the continents in universities and colleges that lived in very different social and religious environments. The pre–World War I colonial framework of much of the world provided favorable conditions for the expansion of the Christian student movement to universities in so-called non-Christian lands.

It was the deliberate decision of Mott and his cofounders to give space for diverse expressions of Christian witness in different national and cultural contexts and to rely in all member movements, old and new, on local "native" leadership. This principle stood in sharp contrast to the policies of mission organizations of the time, and it generated new nuances and emphases for Christian witness and for the task of the federation. It opened doors for theological and cultural → pluralism and led the WSCF to reject the model of a unified, one-issue parachurch movement, thus becoming a forerunner of interconfessional and multicultural → ecumenism.

Already at the turn of the century some European movements, inspired by the → Social Gospel, brought issues of social responsibility to the agenda of the WSCF. Some movements, especially in the Balkans, came into confrontation with vocal anti-Semitic tendencies in universities and their surrounding societies. North American movements brought the issue of racial justice from their own experience as a concern for the whole of the federation. The expansion of the WSCF to the Near East and to imperial Russia produced new relationships with Orthodox Christians, thereby leading to a broadened understanding of the ecumenical, interconfessional nature of Christian witness. In this era *Ut omnes unum sint* ("That all may be one") was adopted as the motto of the federation. The main themes of the modern ecumenical movement were sown in the work of the WSCF in its pioneering years. These seeds produced a rich harvest for the wider ecumenical movement and for the formation of the → World Council of Churches (WCC) between the two world wars.

The work of the first two decades of the WSCF culminated in a global conference at Lake Mohonk, New York, June 2-8, 1913. Attended by 320 participants from 42 countries, this event illustrated the expansion of the Christian movement among students to virtually every country in which there was a university. The influence of the worldwide Christian student movement among students and university teachers was then at its peak of visibility.

The outbreak of war in 1914 drastically limited the international activities of the WSCF for the ensuing five years. International conferences and committee meetings came virtually to a halt. Nevertheless, WSCF activity continued vigorously through many of its national movements and through increased visits by WSCF leaders. The SCMs in the countries hardest hit experienced a boost in their life as communities, since they had to rely on personal communication with their members, many of whom were in trenches or facing other hardships. Furthermore, the movement continued to spread to countries and universities outside the immediate war zones. The general secretary, based in New York, shrewdly used all possibilities to travel, even to the warring parties, while also extending his visits to areas less touched by the war. One area in which the federation experienced a significant expansion in those years was Latin America.

The WSCF community was soon also faced with the plight of → refugees, whose numbers increased rapidly. Student refugees were a special challenge to university communities in central Europe and in Britain. Their numbers grew to thousands. Among them were a great variety of nationalities, including Armenians, Belgians, Lithuanians, Poles, Russians, Serbs, and Turks. With its national movements the WSCF was active in organizing special relief actions for student refugees. Ministry to prisoners of war emerged as an additional concern. At the end of the war these actions led to the founding of European Student Relief (1920), later renamed International Student Service, and finally, in a restructured form

and independent of the WSCF, the World University Service (WUS).

The war experience deeply affected the prevailing mood in European universities and among students all over the world. A wave of pessimism, even → nihilism, replaced the cultural and colonial → optimism characteristic of the prewar Western world. New voices from colonized regions arose to challenge Western domination, and new political ideologies, especially Marxism and various forms of nationalism, gained ground. The Russian revolution had a profound global impact. The Indian independence movement led by Mahatma Gandhi (1869-1948) posed questions to Christian leaders about the claims of the Christian religion to universality.

2. Between Wars: A Changing Profile

The profile of the WSCF was drastically changed during the post–World War I era. The prominent French ecumenist and WSCF leader Suzanne de Diétrich (1891-1981) described the years 1920 to 1928 of the federation as an era of the search for identity. Political and spiritual changes felt acutely in the academic world shook the global Christian student movement as well. The inherited theological basis and the missionary vision of the prewar WSCF no longer unified Christian students or provided a convincing rationale for common tasks. The old and the new collided at the international gatherings of the WSCF. Theological trends — the Social Gospel movement, theological → liberalism, and neoorthodoxy, together with the evangelical emphases of the missionary movement — had set the tone for the theological and spiritual search within the WSCF through the 1920s. But these trends no longer prevailed, and the ensuing spiritual and intellectual turmoil led several evangelical leaders and students to distance themselves from the WSCF, since in their view its Christian witness had been weakened. As a result, evangelical student organizations grew especially in Britain and in continental and northern Europe. This development led in 1946 to the founding of the International Fellowship of Evangelical Students (IFES).

The leadership of the WSCF changed thoroughly after 1920. The pioneers of the WSCF moved with John R. Mott to new tasks in churches and in the emerging ecumenical movement, although Mott remained chairman of the federation until 1928. Henri-Louis Henriod (1897-1969) from Switzerland became general secretary (1920-32). Francis P. Miller (1895-1978) of the United States succeeded Mott as the chairman (1928-38). Willem A. → Visser't Hooft (1900-1985) of the Netherlands joined the staff and was elected general secretary in 1932. He was succeeded by Robert C. Mackie (1899-1984) of Scotland (1938-49). The new leaders faced an erosion of the theological and missionary consensus of the pre–World War I era and the search for new directions. In addition, the federation ran into financial difficulties when the pre–World War I generation of individual supporters of the movement was no longer there. A transition into a new era was inevitable.

A new shift in the life of the WSCF took place when the chairman, Francis Miller, convened a "Message Commission" and when the young Dutch theologian W. A. Visser 't Hooft, later the key architect of the WCC and its first general secretary, took over the day-to-day leadership of the federation and was soon made general secretary (1932-38). The plan of Miller and Visser 't Hooft was to gather the top minds of the Christian student movement and the emerging ecumenical movement to give shape to a comprehensive, theologically well-founded vision of the mission of the church in an increasingly threatened and dangerous world. The Message Commission functioned as an ecumenical think tank of 20-25 of the top minds of SCM leaders and contemporary theologians. As a result, in the 1930s the WSCF focused more on biblical renewal and the spread of an ecumenical commitment to mission.

The seeds were also sown for contacts with Roman Catholic student organizations between the two world wars. Pax Romana, a Roman Catholic student and university organization, was founded in 1920, and it became the main counterpart to the WSCF until the turbulent late 1960s.

The WSCF quarterly *Student World*, founded in 1908, rose under Visser 't Hooft's editorship to become a tool of the whole ecumenical movement. It covered, besides the topics of the Message Commission, most of the key themes with which Christian students and church leaders had to wrestle: → Marxism, nationalism (→ Nation, Nationalism), Nazism, → racism, the threat of a new world → war, concerns for → peace and → disarmament, and the role of Christian community as a social conscience. The journal was published without interruption until 1969, when it was brought to a halt under the antiestablishment pressures of the time.

The climax of the WSCF in the 1930s was the World Christian Youth Conference in Amsterdam, July 24 to August 2, 1939, cosponsored by the worldwide Christian youth organizations. It brought together 1,500 youth and students from all continents under the theme "Christus Victor." This became a signal event to transmit Christian hope and commitment to witness for the generation of young people who were to be torn from one another by another world war, which broke out only a month after the conference.

The war years again stopped much of the international activity of the WSCF as such, but just as during the previous war, so this time also the national SCMs were injected with a fresh determination. For the WSCF leaders, crossing the borders in 1939-45 was even more complicated than it had been in 1914-18. Nevertheless, limited communication was maintained even across the battle lines. In addition to the traditional links, the federation pursued contacts with its member movements involved in resistance movements in Germany and in Nazi-occupied countries and territories.

Outside the warring countries the expansion of Christian student movements continued, especially in Latin America and in several of the African countries that had institutions of higher education. The number of WSCF staff was reduced to a minimum. The general secretary, Robert Mackie, worked out of Toronto, while a modest office remained in Geneva.

3. 1956-64: "The Life and Mission of the Church"
In the first decade after World War II the WSCF experienced significant growth and consolidation of its member movements. The rediscovery of the Bible, Christian responsibility for the university and society, goals and emphases for relevant theological training, and Christian participation in the struggles for independence in Asia and in Africa emerged as central themes of WSCF conferences and activities. The concern for world mission reemerged in the context of the ending of colonial order and under the impact of the expanding influence of Marxism, notably in eastern Europe and in China. → Evangelism continued as an overarching concern of the SCMs as they encountered new social and intellectual frontiers of mission. Such leaders of the WSCF as John and Marie-Jeanne Coleman of Canada, Suzanne de Diétrich of France, Robert Mackie of Scotland, Philippe Maury of France, D. T. Niles of Sri Lanka, M. M. Thomas of India, and K. H. Ting of China made a tangible impact on the tone and emphases of the WSCF in the postwar era.

The perception that the world had entered a new era with the end of World War II gave new directions for Christian student activity. The agenda of the WSCF soon widened to include the impact of the cold war, threats to peace, nuclear armament, the imposed isolation of peoples of socialist countries, national liberation movements, the longing for a world order based on respect for human →

rights, and the ending of discrimination and oppression.

In 1956 the General Committee of the WSCF launched an eight-year program "Life and Mission of the Church." It was the last comprehensive program of the federation that united member movements on all the continents with many key leaders of churches and mission organizations. Together they faced, region by region and worldwide, crucial issues of the contemporary mission of the church. The program consisted of a series of six regional conferences on mission issues and an ambitious world teaching conference, held in Strasbourg, France, in 1960. The teaching conference brought together some 700 participants from all continents with a group of ecumenical and mission leaders as resource persons. The intention was to challenge the current generation of SCM leaders from passivity and traditionalism to active service in mission in varied contemporary contexts. The conference with its thorough preparatory studies made a substantive contribution to the wider ecumenical mission enterprise.

The Strasbourg conference led, however, to unforeseen results among Christian students and the WSCF as a whole. The current generation was not ready to accept the teachings of the previous generation on the mission of the church. They were determined to scrutinize their own perceptions about the state of the world and the failures of the church. Senior leaders and respected theological authorities at the conference were puzzled by this seemingly widespread rejection of the suggested ecumenical consensus on mission.

Two speakers, however, were able to catch the interest of critical students: the Dutch missiologist J. C. Hoekendijk (1912-75) and the American missionary-scholar Richard Shaull (1919-2002). Hoekendijk presented the formula for mission "Christ–world–church" as a corrective to the assertion that Christ's mission was entrusted to the church, which was sent into the world. Shaull, in turn, stirred his audience by claiming that the church's structures had become obsolete and that the concept of mission presupposed by traditional mission organizations of historic churches was no longer valid. He called for a Copernican revolution in the church's understanding of mission. These two presentations presaged two major themes that influenced the ecumenical movement in subsequent years: (1) the Christ-event interpreted as a secular event, the point of departure for secular theology, and (2) Christ breaking the walls that bar the church from sharing the destiny of the oppressed, the → theology of revolution. These themes were to make

a major impact on the WSCF at the end of the 1960s.

The Life and Mission of the Church program came to a conclusion in 1964 at the General Committee of the WSCF at Embalse Río Tercero, Argentina, with the document *Christian Community in the Academic World.* This marked the beginnings of concrete efforts by the WSCF to develop a comprehensive ecumenical strategy for the academic world. The strategy was to integrate student-based concerns, pastoral services, social action, and worship as expressions of Christian presence, a witness of a united Christian community. The main tools for this effort were six regional strategy consultations organized in 1966-68 and cosponsored by regional ecumenical church organizations. These consultations were important steps toward more formal regionalization of the work of the WSCF.

4. 1968: Student Revolt

The year 1968 became a turning point for the WSCF. Rising student activism had already made an impact on many member movements, most markedly in the United States, where the rising → civil rights movement converged with the protest movement against the Viet Nam War and with the student rebellion against authoritarian university structures. The ecumenical student movement in the United States came to identify itself largely with the "New Left." The National Student Christian Federation (NSCF) decided to reorganize itself by 1966 to become the University Christian Movement (UCM), which was to be a fully integrated ecumenical, grassroots-based, radical action organization. The newly founded organization collapsed, however, in 1969.

Parallel developments took place in Europe, where protests against the Viet Nam War began to spread alongside protests against authoritarian trends in universities and in Western society at large. These developments produced a major explosion in France, the Paris revolution of 1968, in which protesting students established a brief alliance with labor organizations. In addition to the revolutionary occupation of several French universities by rebelling students, a nationwide students' and workers' strike was organized that nearly toppled the French government. Direct action and participatory democracy were the trademarks of the movement. The same stir swept over universities in most of Western Europe, in parts of Latin America, and also in Asia, most notably Japan.

This revolutionary ferment found its way to most SCMs in these regions. It was felt in the WSCF, which was preparing a world student conference to be held in Finland in July 1968 before its General Assembly. The student conference was hard hit by the turbulence of the revolutionary movement. A vocal part of the some 300 delegates wanted revolutionary change and protested against the student-led steering group. Pitted against one another were a radical, New Left, neo-Marxist alliance of Christian students and an alliance of those who wanted their response to the current social, political, and university issues to arise out of the tradition of the church and the heritage of the SCM. The split that divided the conference foreshadowed the deep internal division that emerged in the WSCF in following years.

The actions of the 1968 General Assembly turned the WSCF from a world organization to an interregional federation. The restructuring was completed in 1973. Since then each region has had its own programs, governing structure, office, and staff. The regional offices are today located in Nairobi, Hong Kong, Budapest, Buenos Aires, Beirut, and Toronto, with the interregional office remaining in Geneva. The main functions of the interregional office have been to organize assemblies and Executive Committee and officers' meetings, maintain communication between the regional units, and administer a central budget.

In the aftermath of the revolutionary period of the late 1960s, the constituency and the programs of the WSCF shrank sharply. A number of the formerly large member movements in Europe lost many of their branches and turned into small one-issue groups. The American movement was in disarray from 1969 until 1990, although senior members and campus ministry agencies made several efforts to revive it. In North America only the Canadian SCM and the denominational Lutheran Student Movement of America survived the crisis without discontinuity.

5. New Dynamism in a Changing Context

Since 1990 signs of a new dynamism have begun to emerge. New movements from the former Eastern Europe, Africa, and the Middle East have joined the WSCF. General Assemblies have indicated a sense of global vision and initiated common program emphases for the federation as a whole. Centennial celebrations in 1995 gave rise to a wave of new support from senior friends and church institutions. The journal *Student World* was resuscitated in 2003. The annual celebration of the Universal Day of Prayer for Students has taken on a new meaning. The desire to play an active role within the ecumenical movement has become manifest. In 2006 the WSCF

constituency consisted of about 100 national Christian student communities and organizations in more than 80 countries.

A statement of vision for the WSCF was adopted at the 2004 General Assembly, meeting in Thailand. It expresses a joint commitment to → dialogue, ecumenism, social justice, and peace. It emphasizes the need of critical thinking and of constructive global transformation. It provides space for prayer and celebration, for theological reflection and the study of social and cultural processes, and for expressing solidarity across boundaries of culture, gender, and ethnicity. It affirms the calling of the WSCF to participate in prophetic witness to church and society.

The WSCF has gone through major transformations from its early years until today. In its beginning it represented a mass movement for evangelization and ecumenical commitment. It grew to become an important tool for the worldwide growing together of churches and for serving as a testing ground for the future work of the WCC. It strove to be an instrument for a comprehensive and united witness of the church within the academic world. The revolutionary era of the late 1960s brought a change of direction that prompted the WSCF to accept a more limited and more modest role among the actors in mission and ecumenical endeavors. The WSCF of today, even though it represents a minority of Christian students, is self-consciously a pioneering worldwide community of Christian students, intellectuals, and social activists who are committed to building on its distinct heritage within the church, to working together with people sharing similar concerns, and to exploring new ways for ecumenical witness in the rapidly shifting context of the world.

Bibliography: J. COLEMAN, *The Task of the Christian in the University* (Geneva, 1947) • S. DE DIÉTRICH, *World Student Christian Federation: Fifty Years of History, 1895-1945* (Geneva, 1993) • C. LEDGER, ed., *World Student Christian Federation: A Community of Memory and Hope* (Geneva, 1992) • R. LEHTONEN, *Story of a Storm: The Ecumenical Student Movement in the Turmoil of Revolution, 1968 to1973* (Grand Rapids, 1998) • J. B. LINDNER, A. I. COX JR., and L.-M. DELLOFF, *By Faith: Christian Students among the Cloud of Witnesses* (New York, 1991) • J. R. MOTT, *The World's Student Christian Federation: Achievements of the First Quarter-Century of the World's Student Christian Federation and Forecast of Unfinished Tasks* (Geneva, 1920) • P. POTTER and T. WIESER, *Seeking and Serving the Truth: The First Hundred Years of the World Student Christian Federation* (Geneva, 1996) • P. ROSSMAN, *Ecumenical Student*

Workbook (New York, 1949) • R. ROUSE, *The World's Student Christian Federation: A History of the First Thirty Years* (London, 1946) • C. P. SHEDD, *Two Centuries of Student Christian Movements* (New York, 1934) • K. UNDERWOOD, *The Church, the University, and Social Policy* (2 vols.; Middletown, Conn., 1969).

RISTO LEHTONEN

World Vision → Relief and Development Organizations

World's Religions, Parliament of the

1. The First World Parliament, 1893
2. Significance
3. The Council for a Parliament of the World's Religions
4. Subsequent World Parliament Events

1. The First World Parliament, 1893

The first World's Parliament of Religions was convened in Chicago in 1893 in conjunction with the Columbian Exposition, which was celebrating the 400th anniversary of Columbus's voyage to the Americas. By every measure, this parliament was a religious event of unprecedented scope and genuine originality. It was the first convention of its kind, attracting 400 official delegates from around the world, together with 150,000 visitors from the general public. This 17-day event opened on September 11 in the newly built Memorial Art Palace, now the Art Institute of Chicago. Nearly 200 speakers represented and discussed the beliefs of an impressive variety of the world's religions, including → Buddhism, → Confucianism, → Hinduism, → Islam, Jainism, → Judaism, Parseeism, → Shinto, and → Taoism, as well as Eastern Orthodoxy (→ Orthodox Christianity), Protestant Christian denominations (→ Protestantism), and → Roman Catholicism. It was the beginning of an interreligious movement that came to prominence in the last decades of the 20th century (→ Theology of Religions).

Despite this broad array of participating religions, American Christians delivered a majority of the platform presentations at the parliament. Indeed, one legacy of the event was that it became one of the harbingers of the modern ecumenical movement, bringing face-to-face, often for the first time, representatives of many Christian groups. The emerging pluralistic religious landscape of North America was also evident at the parliament, where Jewish leaders took their places alongside Protestants and Catholics. Missing from this array of religious diversity in 1893 were significant numbers of Muslims and people from indigenous traditions. Only in the modern phase of the parliament movement would they be present in more substantial numbers.

Primary attention at the first parliament focused on the encounter between East and West personalized in the presence of three "modern religious reformers" from Asia: Swami Vivekananda (1863-1902) of India, Anagarika Dharmapala (1864-1933) of Ceylon (now Sri Lanka), and Shaku Soyen (1859-1919) of Japan. They came with a dream to "Easternize" the West and in the process succeeded in altering the intended outcome of the parliament itself. Charles Bonney (1831-1903), a Chicago lawyer who served as president of the World's Congresses Auxiliary, and John Henry Barrows (1847-1902), a prominent Presbyterian minister who chaired the parliament, eloquently championed the goals of the charter: "To unite all Religions against irreligion . . . and to provide for a World's Parliament of Religions, in which their common aims and common grounds of unity may be set forth" (R. H. Seager, *Dawn*, 9).

The real theological perspective that developed during the parliament, however, was not the unfolding of an overarching unity among the religions gathered but the "revelation of the plurality of the religious forces in the world at large" (ibid.). This change in the intended outcome of the parliament was the result of the opportunity the World's Parliament of Religions provided to Asians "to speak to the public about their faiths in their own voices unencumbered by either the idealism of western liberals or the judgments of Christian missionaries" (E. J. Ziolkowski, 201).

2. Significance

The significance of the parliament is a subject of renewed inquiry in current religious studies. Three positive contributions of the 1893 event are generally recognized: (1) its strong stimulus to the study of comparative → religions, (2) the impetus it provided for formal dialogue between religions, and (3) the boost it gave to the Christian ecumenical movement (→ Ecumenism, Ecumenical Movement). Today the 1893 parliament is widely regarded as the first exercise in globalization and multiculturalism among religions. It is remarkable that the event was even convened at all and that this historic assembly stands at the forefront of the most important and conspicuous developments that occurred in the religious world in the 20th century.

There is considerable speculation about why an event of the magnitude and significance of the World's Parliament of Religions was virtually forgotten in the West for more than 60 years, while it remained vivid in the memories of many religious people in other parts of the world, especially in the East. Reasons suggested include the observation that the modern religious reformers who came to the parliament from Asia with their doctrine of a universal religion were lionized in their native lands in the wake of their success in Chicago, while this same doctrine was discouraged, if not repressed, in Christian circles in the decades following the assembly. Whatever the reasons, the 1893 World's Parliament of Religions is now remembered, at least in scholarly circles, because of the work of University of Chicago scholars Martin E. Marty and Joseph Kitagawa, who laid the foundations for a pluralist-oriented study of American religions. Significantly, the parliament was included in the 1987 edition of *The Encyclopedia of Religion,* edited by Mircea Eliade (1907-86).

3. The Council for a Parliament of the World's Religions

This renewed awareness of and interest in the 1893 parliament corresponded with the dramatic influx of people into America from Asia and other parts of the world following the passage of the historic U.S. Immigration Act of 1965. This legislation, together with other influences of the emerging age of globalization, became fertile ground for two monks from the Vivekananda Vedanta Society of Chicago who in 1988 suggested holding a centennial celebration of the World's Parliament of Religions. This suggestion resulted in the formation of the Council for a Parliament of the World's Religions (CPWR), the host organization for three parliament events in the next two decades.

The subtle change in the name of the new council — from World's Parliament of Religions to Council for a Parliament of the World's Religions — shifted the emphasis from an accent on the global nature of the event itself to the more egalitarian inclusion of all the world's religions and spiritual traditions. The change also reflects a significant shift in the vision of the council organizers. The intention that motivated the founders of the first parliament, namely, to demonstrate the superiority of Christianity, was entirely gone. Not only was the new council representative of the world's religious and spiritual traditions, but the reasons for calling a centennial parliament were now shaped by the spirit of the emerging interreligious

movement. Today the mission of the CPWR is "to foster dialogue and cooperation between the world's religious and spiritual communities and to encourage their engagement with other guiding institutions in pursuing a vision of a more just, peaceful and sustainable world" (CPWR case statement, 2006).

4. Subsequent World Parliament Events

The CPWR has convened three parliament events in the past two decades.

- 1993: The Chicago Centennial. This event attracted 8,000 participants from around the world, the largest interreligious gathering in history. Observers and participants hailed it as a pivotal event that gave the interreligious movement global prominence.
- 1999: a parliament in Cape Town, South Africa, with the theme "A New Day Dawning." Nelson Mandela (b. 1918) praised the role of the interreligious movement for its part in the historic struggle to overcome apartheid. Also, 7,000 participants joined in an inaugural march commemorating World AIDS Day.
- 2004: a parliament in Barcelona, Spain, with the theme "Pathways to Peace: The Wisdom of Listening, the Power of Commitment." Attended by 9,000 participants, this event examined the changing realities for religions in the world after September 11, 2001 (New York and Washington attacks) and after March 11, 2004 (Madrid train bombings), a world now of violent religious extremism (→ Terrorism).

While each of these parliament events has been uniquely shaped by the host city and by current events, the general format has been similar: plenary sessions featuring addresses by global leaders, topics of current religious concern, and colorful religious, musical, and cultural presentations. Throughout the weeklong periods, hundreds of dialogue groups, panels, workshops, and performances were scheduled according to such program rubrics as "intrareligious," "interreligious," and "engagement." Assemblies of religious and spiritual leaders meeting in conjunction with the parliaments have provided settings to explore new dimensions of the interreligious movement. In 1993 the assembly debated a document entitled "Toward a Global Ethic: An Initial Declaration." In 1999 the assembly extended the global ethic emphasis by applying it to other social institutions in a document entitled "A Call to Our Guiding Institutions." In 2004 the assembly took a different tack, engaging religious leaders, scholars, and activists in a process that resulted in over 500 commitments being made to address four compelling issues of human suffering: increasing access to clean water, eliminating international debt for developing countries, alleviating the plight of → refugees, and overcoming religious violence (→ Force, Violence, Nonviolence).

Three principles guide the current work of the CPWR: (1) promoting interreligious harmony rather than unity among religions, (2) seeking convergence on issues rather than consensus on issues of religious concern, and (3) working to facilitate relationships among religions rather than building formal organizational structures. The council works cooperatively with all other interreligious organizations, seeking to serve the movement as a whole by convening periodic parliament events, building a global network of Partner Cities, supporting the development of local interreligious organizations, and engaging in partnerships with other institutions that help fulfill its goals.

The council intends to convene a fifth Parliament of the World's Religions in 2009. Among its emerging foci, the council seeks to engage the international economic development community in a relationship with world religious bodies to address the U.N. Millennium Development Goals to eradicate extreme → poverty.

Bibliography: J. H. Barrows, ed., *The World's Parliament of Religions: An Illustrated and Popular Story of the World's First Parliament of Religions, Held in Chicago in Connection with the Columbian Exposition of 1893* (2 vols.; Chicago, 1893) • J. Beversluis, ed., *Sourcebook of the World's Religions: An Interfaith Guide to Religion and Spirituality* (Novato, Calif., 2000) • D. F. Burg, *Chicago's White City of 1893* (Lexington, Ky., 1976) • W. R. Houghton, ed., *Neely's History of the Parliament of Religions and Religious Congresses at the World's Columbian Exposition* (3d ed.; Chicago, 1893) • J. M. Kitagawa, *Religions of the East* (Philadelphia, 1968) • H. Küng and K.-J. Kuschel, *A Global Ethic: The Declaration of the Parliament of the World's Religions* (New York, 1993) • M. E. Marty, *The Fire We Can Light: The Role of Religion in a Suddenly Different World* (Garden City, N.Y., 1973) • R. H. Seager, *The World's Parliament of Religions: The East/West Encounter, Chicago, 1893* (Bloomington, Ind., 1995); idem, ed., *The Dawn of Religious Pluralism: Voices from the World's Parliament of Religions, 1893* (LaSalle, Ill., 1993) • E. J. Ziolkowski, ed., *A Museum of Faiths: Histories and Legacies of the 1893 World's Parliament of Religions* (Atlanta, 1993).

WILLIAM E. LESHER

Worldview

1. Term

The term "worldview" covers many different ways of viewing the world. It is used for views, pictures, images, concepts, and orientations toward the world, as suggested by the various Ger. terms *Weltanschauung, Weltansicht, Weltbeschreibung, Weltbild,* and *Weltorientierung.* Note also the Fr. *science générale* (C. H. Saint-Simon [1760-1825]), *esprit positif* (A. Comte [1798-1857]), and *conscience collective* (É. Durkheim [1858-1917]), as well as the Eng. "outlooks on life" (J. Dewey [1859-1952]).

1.1. Model of Interpretation

The term "worldview," or *Weltanschauung,* serves as a designation for an all-encompassing model of interpretation that helps individuals to give their own → meaning and purpose to the world that surrounds them. In German a distinction may be made between *Weltanschauung* and *Weltbild* ("world picture" or "world image"), the latter referring to an institutionalized, collective system of worldviews available to anyone in the society, from which an individual selects the "pictures" that make up that individual's specific worldview.

1.2. Patterns of Interpretation

People need patterns of interpretation because we are beings who seek meaning (→ Anthropology 4) and question the meaning of our → experiences and the phenomena surrounding them. The patterns of interpretation differ from each other in extent and depth. For many experiences and phenomena, a reference to daily routine suffices (→ Everyday Life); for others, a scientific interpretation is called for (e.g., in the case of illness, a medical interpretation is informative; → Health and Illness). With the question of a "final" meaning, however, only a religious or nonreligious worldview (→ Religion) can offer a solution.

Like most patterns of interpretation, the worldview has a cognitive and a normative aspect (→ Cognition; Norms). It informs about how the world functions and indicates how one should correspondingly behave. No single worldview is created out of nothing. One is born into a → family, in which the parents make their own worldview manifest through their way of thinking and behavior and verbalize it through → language (→ Education; Socialization). The child first adopts and follows such patterns; at a later age, more or less critical questions arise and lead to moments of personal life formation (→ Identity). According to the persuasiveness of the arguments and the power and influence of those who pass on existing patterns of interpretation, the individual will construct his or her own worldview and — through new experiences, → conflicts, and so forth — possibly (and perhaps repeatedly) reconstruct it. The result, which is usually provisional, is offered to the following generation as a model. The worldview is seldom idiosyncratic enough that it is not shared with other (relevant) worldviews; it has at the same time an individual and a collective aspect. Occasionally, worldviews are determined by → ideologies and → prejudices.

1.3. Worldview and World Pictures

A continuing interaction exists between individually shaped worldviews and institutionalized world pictures. World pictures grow out of communicatively shared worldviews. They are reflected and systematized by "experts" and presented as more or less closed patterns of interpretation. They are selectively processed in the worldview. When the resulting modifications converge to some degree and become collectively visible in sufficient mass, changes in world pictures are possible. The speed of such changes, however, depends on the influence wielded by the official proponents of the worldview.

1.4. Social Factors

In a closed society with a dominant world picture (→ Totalitarianism) or a → ghettolike environment (→ Fundamentalism), the individual will find little room to visibly make use of a deviating pattern of interpretation. In an open and pluralistic society (→ Pluralism 1) characterized by great mobility and where differing world pictures are available in books, → mass media, and public discussion (→ Communication), the individual will more easily be able to overcome the limits of his or her own environment.

In modern society (→ Modernity 4) individual → autonomy has increased so sharply that a specific world picture can no longer be forcibly im-posed; on the contrary, individual freedom of choice (→ Freedom 1-3) makes it possible to put together a worldview from the "supermarket" of worldviews according to one's own needs (→ Consumption 2). Furthermore, the worldview is an object of permanent reflection (H. Schelsky). The perverse result of such reflection is the fragmentation of world pictures.

Bibliography: P. L. BERGER, *The Sacred Canopy: Elements of a Sociological Theory of Religion* (Garden City, N.Y., 1967) • W. DILTHEY, *Weltanschauungslehre,* vol. 8 of *Wilhelm Diltheys gesammelte Schriften* (5th ed.; Stuttgart, 1977) • R. DORAN, *Birth of a Worldview: Early Christianity in Its Jewish and Pagan Context* (Lanham, Md., 1999) • *Kursbuch der Weltanschauungen* (Frankfurt, 1981) • T. LUCKMANN, *The Invisible Religion: The Problem of Religion in Modern Society* (New York, 1967) • K. MANNHEIM, "On the Interpretation of 'Weltanschauung,'" *Essays on the Sociology of Knowledge* (London, 1952) 33-83 • D. K. NAUGLE, *Worldview: The History of a Concept* (Grand Rapids, 2002) • M. SCHELER, *Problems of a Sociology of Knowledge* (London, 1980; orig. pub., 1926) • H. SCHELSKY, "Ist die Dauerreflexion institutionalisierbar?" *ZEE* 1 (1957) 153-74 • A. SCHÜTZ and T. LUCKMANN, *The Structures of the Life-World* (2 vols.; Evanston, Ill., 1973-89) • E. TOPITSCH, *Erkenntnis und Illusion. Grundstrukturen unserer Weltauffassung* (2d ed.; Tübingen, 1988) • R. WUTHNOW, *The Consciousness Reformation* (Berkeley, Calif., 1976).

LEO LAEYENDECKER

2. History

2.1. Biblical

2.1.1. OT

According to the worldview of the OT, like that of the Near East in general, the → heavens, the earth, and the underworld were different regions. This view, which corresponds to the daily experience of the world, was no longer a mythical depiction (→ Myth). In the beginning Gen. 1:9-13 tells us that the earth rose out of the waters. According to Ps. 24:2, God "founded it on the seas, and established it on the rivers." Ps. 75:3 and Job 9:6 state that it rests on pillars; earthquakes result when these are shaken. But in Job 26:7 the earth is stretched out "over the void" and is hanging "upon nothing."

If the earth is circular, the → people of God dwell at its center (Ezek. 38:12; see also Judg. 9:37 RSV). The → temple (§2) on Zion is at its heart. Around the earth are the threatening floods of chaos. Over it, in the shape of a bell, is the overarching firmament of heaven, which separates the waters into two parts (Gen. 1:7). The upper waters are kept back, allowing living things and people to flourish on the earth. When the "windows of heaven" are opened, life-giving rain descends (Mal. 3:10), but so too do destructive floods (Gen. 7:11-12; Isa. 24:18). The firmament contains the sun, moon, and stars, lights that the nations around Israel regarded as deities (Gen. 1:14-18). These lights follow the paths that → Yahweh appointed for them. The vault rests on "the pillars of heaven" (Job 26:11; cf. Ps. 104:3, "the beams of your chambers"), that is, high mountains that mark the horizon.

The outlook on time corresponds to that on space. The world does not follow a circular course. It had a beginning, which was also the beginning of history (→ Creation 2; Salvation History). This history is progressive and is depicted in various ways. In 1 Enoch 72–82, written in the fourth or third century B.C., there is a detailed "astronomical" account. → Apocalyptic (§2) uses vivid colors to describe the end of the world (Daniel 7–12). Hellenistic → Judaism introduced expansive cosmological speculations and depictions of the end-time events that would transform the world (→ Eschatology 1).

The OT depictions of the world act as a means to express the true doxological and theological interests of the text and also to proclaim the → promises of God and their fulfillment. The different notions are all vivid and defy comparison and systematization. They do not claim to offer full or uniform teaching about the world.

2.1.2. NT

In the NT we find the same direct sensory observation as we do in the OT. Along with OT views of world, we find the current ideas of Near Eastern Judaism and → Hellenism. The NT has no systematic cosmological interest but uses these ideas as means by which to proclaim the fact that Jesus Christ is Lord of the world (→ Christology 1) and that it is integrated into and subject to his dominion.

As in the OT, "heaven and earth" constitute the world (Matt. 5:18). A distinction is made between heaven, earth, and the underworld (Phil. 2:10; Rev. 5:13 also adds "the sea"), but they are all parts of creation. The comprehensive Greek term *kosmos* can be used, and *aiōn* is also used for → time (1 Cor. 1:20). The firmament is up above, but it now has several layers, and the heavenly world of → light is a subject of his own. Heaven is the dwelling place of God. After his → ascension Christ sits there on his throne at God's right hand. He will stay there until the consummation (Acts 3:21). Heaven is a place of blessedness (Matt. 5:12).

After a delay, the return of Christ will come "from heaven," and with him the end of the world will come (→ Eschatology 2; Parousia). According to 2 Pet. 3:7 fire will bring the world to an end. "A new heaven and a new earth" (Rev. 21:1) are awaited, the new creation of God. This is a consistent Christian → hope (→ Eschatology 1.3, 4.1.4, 6.2.1, 7.4; Golden Age 2). The time and shape of the world are thus relativized and provisional (1 Cor. 7:31); God has granted them for → life in this world. Human concepts of the world are not an independent biblical theme but are used as a means of conveying the message to all humankind.

2.1.3. Openness to the World

The biblical worldview is thus historically an open one. The world is God's, but it is also ours and shares our history. Human → sin has falsified it. We draw our being from it, and we are fully entangled in its relationships. It exercises demonic power over us. The world has become "this world" (1 Cor. 3:19). The primitive Christian confession that Jesus Christ is Lord (Phil. 2:11) and that the world is his (John 12:31; see also 1:11) means that believers in him, though threatened by this world, are sustained by the Creator's → grace and → love. This protection frees them for appropriate action. Even in → death the Creator is present, who gives being to nonbeing (Rom. 4:17).

Christian openness to the world, which sees God's work in the categories of the world and can claim the world for God's own actions, includes especially the possibilities of → reconciliation and → forgiveness. It finds demonstration in the hope that awaits the divine future, in spite of all appearances to the contrary. This hope works itself out in the love that constantly seeks to reshape human relationships and indeed all those within the whole creation. The Christian view of the world is neither optimistic nor pessimistic. It is realistic. It attempts in gratitude to do all that can possibly be done to preserve and promote good life.

2.2. Ancient and Medieval

2.2.1. Philosophical Description

Historical openness to the world as shown by Christian faith competed with the immanent sense that → nature and history are closed. This was the view of Greek and Roman philosophy (→ Greek Philosophy). Aristarchus of Samos (ca. 310-230 B.C.) had already put the sun at the center of the world. The idea that the earth moves, however, could not be reconciled with the dominant philosophy of Aristotle.

Aristotle (384-322 B.C.; → Aristotelianism) viewed things differently. Around an unmoved center, sublunary elements (earth, air, fire, water) are placed. Empirically, they are constantly admixed. Heaven is a qualitatively different region. Here the moon and the planets Mercury, Venus, Mars, Jupiter, and Saturn, with the sun in their middle, all have their appointed movements. In the form of interacting crystal spheres, they are concentrically coordinated with the earthly sublunary sphere, moving around a central point.

Along these lines the → philosophy of nature (§1) explained the movements of the planets (→ Nature 1.1). Each sphere was kept in motion by an immaterial unmoved mover. The whole system was enclosed by the sphere of fixed stars, through which the first and supreme Mover, as *actus purus* (pure action), foreordained eternal and unchangeable cosmic movement.

2.2.2. *Mathematical Description*

In physical terms, however, it quickly became apparent that this philosophical description of the cosmos did not fit with the empirical data. Alongside it, then, we find the mathematical system of Ptolemy (fl. A.D. 127-45). Ptolemy used combinations of uniform circular movement to describe the movements of the planets. The planets circle around the earth. The earth, however, is not the mathematical center of these movements. It is close to the center of the cosmos. The observed recurrent and looped movements of the planets were seen as epicycles that follow their own primary courses in accordance with their central points.

2.2.3. *Medieval Views*

These ideas all presuppose → axioms of uniformity of movement and perfect circularity. Plato (427-347 B.C.; → Platonism) had advanced these axioms on both mathematical and religious grounds. This type of cosmology and astronomy had a decisive influence on the Western understanding of the world. The perfect hierarchical structure (→ Hierarchy 1.1) of the Aristotelian cosmos formed a basis for medieval views of the world (→ Middle Ages). It could find a place for Christianity and influence it in specific ways, though naturally Christianity could also modify the cosmology.

The cosmos, the life on earth, and the church were all tied together in a fixed structure. Nature and the supernatural could all find expression on earth, in the sublunary world, and in heaven. We find depictions of the celestial spheres on → cathedral entrances, and these lead on to the higher world that is present already in the → sacraments.

2.3. *Modern*

2.3.1. Late medieval → nominalism made the concept of God absolute (→ God 7.1.1.5). It gave → reason, however, free play in investigating relations on earth. Thus a new beginning came for → science. The Reformers, going back solely to Scripture (→

Reformation Principles), and especially to the Pauline doctrine of → justification in examining salvation and their sense of the world, opened up the world to human formation and to a fulfilled, good life. → Salvation, as the assurance of life through the gift of God's grace in Jesus Christ, always precedes what we ourselves do and is beyond human attainment. This view has consequences for a new understanding of the world.

The freeing of reason shattered the closed nexus of Aristotle's view of the cosmos. N. Copernicus (1473-1543), seeing in the sun a symbol of God the Father (an idea from Nicholas of Cusa [1401-64]), made it the center of the earth's movement. He no longer viewed the earth as the center of the cosmos. J. Kepler (1571-1630) traced the courses of the planets and found them to be ellipses. Their mathematical relationships were musical intervals in the cosmic harmony. T. Digges (d. 1595) pointed beyond the fixed stars to a vast stellar plurality (in *A Prognostication of Right Good Effect* [new ed., 1576]).

2.3.2. The postulate that there are infinite worlds (G. Bruno [1548-1600]) meant that our world could no longer be treated as a finite and self-enclosed totality. A dynamic nexus replaced a static structure. The fixity of → ethics went the same way as the hierarchy of being. Mathematical and physical sciences came to be taken for granted. The world was now seen as a nexus of causes like a machine (→ Philosophy of Nature 4-5). God was its maker. The concept of God degenerated to become a rational principle that had little to do with the reality denoted by theology. → Theology and science parted company.

2.3.3. A new start came with the idealist → philosophy of nature (→ Idealism), which for a time bore fruit in theology. The mystical and theosophical tradition (Paracelsus, J. Böhme, F. C. Oetinger; → Mysticism 2.5.2; Theosophy) promoted the concept of evolution. → Marxism, Darwinism (→ Evolution 2), and → psychoanalysis (S. Freud), by adopting a mechanistic view of the world, focused on specific elements of reality in the sociological, biological, and psychological spheres (→ Sociology; Life 2.1; Psychology). Their one-sided and this-worldly ideologization (→ Ideology), however, discredited them and concealed the elements of truth in their systems. Theology has tried to relate these elements of truth to the world as we experience and understand it, including also the facing of religious phenomena (→ Science and Theology).

2.3.4. Modern atomic research (→ Quantum Theory) has outdated the earlier mechanistic theories. Without the subject there can be no objective knowledge. A "picture" of the world (see 1.3) cannot be an objectifying description of the world's reality. The relations that we can depict mechanistically hold good only in statistical experience. They are not iron laws. Specific experiences are complementary. They cooperate as depictions, even though they might seem to exclude one another. For example, light may be seen as the movement of both particles and waves. Full description depends on what might seem to be logically contradictory data. Mathematical depiction has made older portrayals of the world impossible. Equations have replaced pictures in the abstract search for a comprehensive theory, a "theory of everything."

2.3.5. Cybernetics (N. Wiener) provided a decisive standpoint for understanding the world. It deals with the structuring and regulating of → technology in such spheres as biology, sociology, and psychology and specifically interrelates these different spheres of knowledge. It views the world as a monstrously complicated web of mutually reacting circles, of news items, of information, and of data that define that which interacts at the nuclear level, right on up to human → communication in both time and space.

Information theory underlies the project of artificial intelligence. It thus enables us to achieve decisive knowledge about the structure of our world, and more especially of living creatures and human → behavior. A characteristic model of technology is the learning automaton, which can become a paradigm of self-organization.

2.3.6. Causally, the world is the plaything of the technological reason that so greatly transforms it. This reason has created the world and society of modern industry (→ Industrial Society). Computer technology has quickened the pace of transformation and brought widespread changes. What was once ascribed to the divine sphere now belongs to our human world, which biological evolution views as a part of natural history. On this basis Teilhard de Chardin (1881-1955; → Evolution 3.2.3) found in nature, spirit, and religious → revelation the totality of a world that by the divine energy of love is infinitely complex but yet is moving as a whole toward the divine Omega. This thought has had a widespread influence upon modern views of the world. Similar approaches may be found in various authors and their fields of study (e.g., B. Rensch, C. Bresch, E. Jantsch).

Modern worldviews have developed under the increasing input of human reason. In light of the stated and constantly expanding problems of the → future of humanity, it is essential that plans should be made to deal with these issues. If such plans are to succeed, the → peace of the world must be a condition, which depends upon a humane and meaningful integration of all parts of the world's population, particularly the so-called → Third World. Steps must especially be taken to deal with the rapid increase of global population and its ongoing interconnections.

2.4. *Christian Perspective*

In this situation true → piety is to be found in its "worldliness," that is, in relevance to today's world. Worldly talk about → God (§7.2) involves a close intertwining of God and the world, though not adopting a concept of God as part of the world's reality. If Christians are to show that God is the Creator, they cannot flee out of the world. The world is now an adult world, a "world come of age" (D. → Bonhoeffer). Christians are responsible to it and for it.

Listening to the → Word of God, Christian faith sees that God's love is addressed to this world. Faith operates as the world is sustained by God. Giving itself to the world involves openness. Genuine openness to the world can both change and conserve it, without making conservation a principle. The goal of Christian ethics is to transform the world in love. Yet it still lets the world be the world. It does not ascribe absoluteness to its own view of the world. It continually tests afresh the content of authentically human conduct.

Bibliography: J. D. BARROW, *Theories of Everything: The Quest for Ultimate Explanation* (Oxford, 1991) • G. BÖRNER, J. EHLERS, and H. MEIER, eds., *Vom Urknall zum komplexen Universum. Die Kosmologie der Gegenwart* (Munich, 1993) • J. DILLENBERGER, *Protestant Thought and Natural Science* (Garden City, N.Y., 1960) • G. DUX, *Die Logik der Weltbilder* (3d ed.; Frankfurt, 1990) • N. H. GREGERSEN and U. GÖRMAN, eds., *Design and Disorder: Perspectives from Science and Theology* (London, 2002) • A. H. GUTH, *The Inflationary Universe: The Quest for a New Theory of Cosmic Origins* (Reading, Mass., 1997) • S. K. HENINGER JR., *The Cosmographical Glass: Renaissance Diagrams of the Universe* (San Marino, Calif., 1977) • *Der Himmel* (= *JBTh* 20 [2005]) • J. HÜBNER, I.-O. STAMATESCU, and D. WEBER, eds., *Theologie und Kosmologie. Geschichte und Erwartungen für das gegenwärtige Gespräch* (Tübingen, 2004) • B. JANOWSKI and B. EGO, eds., *Das biblische Weltbild und seine altorientalischen Kontexte* (Tübingen, 2001) • G. H. VAN KOOTEN, *Cosmic Christology in Paul and the Pauline School* (Tübingen, 2003) • A. KOYRÉ, *From the Closed World to the Infinite Universe* (Baltimore, 1957) • A. O. LOVEJOY, *The Great Chain of Being* (Cambridge, Mass., 1936) •

H. P. Nebelsick, *Circles of God: Theology and Science from the Greeks to Copernicus* (Edinburgh, 1985); idem, *The Renaissance, the Reformation, and the Rise of Science* (Edinburgh, 1992) • J. Polkinghorne and M. Welker, *Faith in the Living God* (London, 2001) • C. Southgate, ed., *God, Humanity, and the Cosmos* (2d ed.; London, 2005) • P. Teilhard de Chardin, *The Human Phenomenon* (Brighton, 1999; orig. pub., 1955) • S. Toulmin and J. Goodfield, *The Fabric of the Heavens: The Development of Astronomy and Dynamics* (Chicago, 1999; orig. pub., London, 1961) • A. N. Whitehead, *Science and the Modern World* (New York, 1925; repr., London, 1975) • N. Wiener, *Cybernetics; or, Control and Communication in the Animal and the Machine* (2d ed.; New York, 1961).

JÜRGEN HÜBNER

Worldwide Church of God

1. Founder and Successors
2. Distinctive Beliefs
3. Remaking of the Church

The Worldwide Church of God (WCG), founded in 1933, is a North American → Adventist church that strongly emphasizes biblical prophecy. Although it deviated from Protestant orthodoxy in a number of ways, a major doctrinal and organizational transformation occurred in the late 1980s and early 1990s that converted it into an evangelical denomination. Subsequently, a number of schisms resulted in an exodus of half its adherents. The most recent (2004) estimated membership is 63,000 worldwide.

1. Founder and Successors

The WCG was virtually the personal extension of its founder, Herbert W. Armstrong (1892-1986). Born to a Quaker family in Des Moines, Iowa, he was a high school dropout and worked in sales and advertising. After bouncing from job to job, he relocated to Salem, Oregon, in 1924. Influenced by his devout wife, Loma, he underwent a → conversion experience and became an ardent Bible student. Among the doctrines he discovered were the seventh-day Sabbath, the validity of Mosaic practices, → baptism by immersion, and British-Israelism. In 1927 he was immersed by a Baptist pastor and soon after joined the small Church of God (Seventh Day) because it took a → Sabbatarian stance. The church ordained Armstrong in 1931, and he went from leading a small congregation to radio preaching. In 1933 he inaugurated the *Radio Church of God* and in

1934 began a publication that soon took the name *The Plain Truth*. He claimed that God had called him to be a → prophet and that the first preaching of the true gospel since A.D. 69 was now taking place. Although at first he directed his message to the churched, by 1937 he was reaching a much wider audience. Denominational leaders feared that he was moving beyond the church's doctrines and authority and revoked his ministerial credentials in 1938.

In the early 1940s Armstrong renamed his program *The World Tomorrow* and shifted his base from Oregon to Pasadena, California. Both the program and magazine engaged in extensive prophetic speculation. In 1947 he founded a liberal arts school (Ambassador College) and, later, branch campuses in St. Albans, England (1960), and Big Sandy, Texas (1964). Both by radio and by print Armstrong became an internationally known figure, and in 1968 he renamed his organization the Worldwide Church of God. He now proclaimed himself as the apostle-messenger of the last days and his group as the Philadelphia church described in Revelation 3. Although he ruled the WCG with an iron hand, successful marketing strategies and the loyalty of its staff enabled substantial growth, and the radio program and publications brought in millions of dollars.

During the 1970s the church was rocked by financial and sexual scandals and damaging exposés by critics, and a power struggle between the elder Armstrong and his heir apparent, son Garner Ted (1930-2003), led to the latter's expulsion in 1978. In 1985 the ailing founder appointed longtime loyalist Joseph Tkach Sr. (1927-95) as pastor general of the WCG. After Armstrong's death, however, Tkach began questioning basic WCG doctrines, and by 1995 the church was in great disarray. His son Joseph Tkach Jr. (b. 1951) succeeded him as pastor general and continued the reform process.

2. Distinctive Beliefs

Although the WCG affirmed many traditional Christian views and Armstrong claimed his doctrines were based solely on the Bible, it taught some clearly unorthodox positions. Armstrong rejected the Trinity as a single deity, holding that God the Father is part of a "divine family" with → Jesus Christ, and the → Holy Spirit is not a person but a force emanating from God. → Salvation is a sixfold process involving repentance, faith, baptism, receiving the Holy Spirit, obedience to his chosen apostle, and resurrection — and is not fully achieved until the future. A person who missed the chance to believe in this life would be given a second chance in the hereafter. The idea of an everlasting → hell for unbelievers was rejected, while → heaven would be eternity on earth with Christ. A core emphasis was British-Israelism — that Anglo-American people are the literal descendants of the ten "lost tribes" of Israel, thus making them God's chosen people.

Members were expected to conform to OT law, including strict Sabbath observance, the → dietary rules, and the seven Jewish festivals (Christmas and Easter were proscribed as pagan holidays). Those who did not keep the Sabbath were not acknowledged as Christians. The three ordinances of baptism, → foot washing, and the Lord's Supper were practiced. → Tithing of up to 30 percent was commanded, "worldly" lifestyles were proscribed, and divorce was not permitted. Seeking medical treatment, bearing arms, and voting were not allowed. Congregations generally worshiped in homes or rented facilities and were subject to control from Pasadena. Those who deviated from obeying the leaders were "disfellowshipped" (i.e., excommunicated).

3. Remaking of the Church

Under the leadership of the Tkaches, the WCG went through a metamorphosis from a cultic fringe → sect to a doctrinally orthodox evangelical church. In 1997 it was formally received into the → National Association of Evangelicals. The church now affirmed the → Trinity and → salvation by → grace, renounced the OT covenant laws, and recognized as Christians those who did not observe the Sabbath. British-Israelism was repudiated. The rigid tithing requirement and other forms of legalism were shelved.

The rapid changes led to unprecedented turmoil in the WCG. This included a dramatic drop in finances that required closing Ambassador College, dismissal of staff, sharply cutting back on radio and television programming, and selling off assets. In 1996 the Tkaches founded Plain Truth Ministries, which now functions as a separate media agency under WCG auspices. The Armstrong faithful left, mainly for various splinter groups, of which in the 1990s there may have been as many as 300. A few disaffected went to Garner Ted Armstrong's earlier schism, the Church of God International (1978), while a large number gravitated to the Philadelphia Church of God (Edmond, Okla., 1989), which aggressively maintains Armstrong's legacy through publications and a college. Other noteworthy successor bodies include the Global Church of God (1992), United Church of God (1995), and Restored Church of God (1999).

Most scholars regard this transformation of the WCG as one of the truly remarkable stories in recent religious history. Although it still holds to seventh-day worship and does not accept the eternal damnation of the unsaved, it has in virtually every other way become a normative evangelical church (→ Evangelical Movement). Rarely has a body whose belief system was at such variance with accepted orthodoxy undergone such a radical reversal in direction.

Bibliography: H. W. Armstrong, *Autobiography* (Pasadena, Calif., 1986) • P. W. Benware, *Ambassadors of Armstrongism* (Nutley, N.J., 1975) • J. M. Feazell, *The Liberation of the Worldwide Church of God* (Grand Rapids, 2001) • J. Hopkins, *The Armstrong Empire* (Grand Rapids, 1974) • D. LeBlanc, "The Worldwide Church of God: Resurrected into Orthodoxy," *CRJ* 18 (Winter 1996) 6-7, 44-45 • L. Nichols and G. Mather, *Discovering the Plain Truth: How the Worldwide Church of God Encountered the Gospel of Grace* (Downers Grove, Ill., 1998) • R. V. Pierard, "The Contribution of British-Israelism to Antisemitism within Conservative Protestantism," *Holocaust and Church Struggle: Religion, Power, and the Politics of Resistance* (ed. H. G. Locke and M. S. Littell; Lanham, Md., 1996) 45-68 • J. Tkach Jr., *Transformed by Truth* (Sisters, Oreg., 1997) • R. A. Tucker, "From the Fringe to the Fold," *ChrTo*, July 15, 1996, 26-32.

Richard V. Pierard

Worship

1. NT and Early Church
 1.1. Term and Usage
 1.2. Temple and Synagogue Worship in
   NT Days
 1.3. Primitive Christian Worship
 1.4. Worship in the Early Church
 1.5. The Fourth Century as a Turning Point
2. Western Tradition
 2.1. Medieval Developments
 2.2. Roman Catholic Liturgical Reform
 2.3. The Reformation and Its Fruit
  2.3.1. The New View of Worship
  2.3.2. Luther's Reforms
  2.3.3. Other Reformers
  2.3.4. Developments in England
  2.3.5. Developments in the United States
 2.4. Protestant Liturgical Reform
  2.4.1. Germany
  2.4.2. United States
  2.4.3. Significant Books

1. NT and Early Church

1.1. *Term and Usage*

The term "worship" (from "worth-ship") has established itself as a general word for the service that is rendered to God in praise, → prayer, → proclamation and hearing of the Word, and administration of the → sacraments. An older term is "divine service" (cf. the German *Gottesdienst,* which M. → Luther used as a technical term for gatherings for worship), though along with its specific use this term has a broader reference to Christian life and → diakonia. A common phrase today for gatherings for worship is "worship service." Alternative terms are "common prayer," → "liturgy," and, with a more specific reference to Holy Communion, → "Eucharist" and → "anaphora." Scholars also use the word "cult."

1.2. *Temple and Synagogue Worship in NT Days*

As regards → temple worship, the changes that the basic concept of → sacrifice underwent in → Israel's history are important. First, Semitic → nomads offered sacrifices when changing pastures at the full moon early in the year. The blood was poured out as God's portion, and the flesh was eaten on departure. In the → Passover meal, whose link to the exodus is obvious, the people enjoyed fellowship with God. The sacrifice became a sacrament in which God protects (Exod. 12:13-14) and seals (24:8, 11) the conclusion of the → covenant. With cultic centralization at the Jerusalem temple, slaughtering elsewhere was secularized, and thus the sacramental dimension was taken out of the → everyday.

Later, another sacrifice, the whole or burnt offering, was set up along with agricultural feasts and customs when Israel took over the land of Canaan. The gift to God rather than the fellowship received with him now came to the fore. In the later monarchy consecration, homage, submission, repentance, thanksgiving, and prayer expressed themselves thus in the daily morning and, later, evening sacrifices of the temple.

Still later, after the exile, the emphasis lay on the thought of → atonement, which reached a climax in the great Day of Atonement (Leviticus 16). The sin offering would placate God's wrath and also restore the sinner to a state of → cultic purity. Earlier ideas were less prominent except on such occasions as the Passover. The development from the idea of the God who enters into fellowship with his people in judgment and → grace, by way of that of acknowledgment by gift, to a preeminent act of atonement explains the indispensability of the cult, whose functions corresponding to legal actions could take over when the temple was destroyed.

The theory that the "word worship" of the → synagogue, which knew no sacrifice and was tied to no place, initiated "heart worship" (I. Elbogen, 3), making the temple no more than a preliminary stage to the true worship of obedience to the → Torah (→ Law 1), can be proved from neither the history nor the liturgy of the synagogue. The origin of the synagogue is obscure. It probably developed in the Babylonian diaspora or in postexilic Palestine. (The first archaeological evidence dates from the third century B.C. in inscriptions from near Alexandria and Arsinoë in Faiyûm.)

The thesis that the institution of *ma'amadot,* or local gatherings, led to that of the synagogue (J. J. Petuchowski, 15) has much to commend it and would confirm the close connection between synagogue and temple. At the time of the second temple the priesthood (→ Priest, Priesthood) was divided into 24 companies, each of which served a week in the temple and was allotted its own territory. The divisions sent delegations to be present at the sacrifices as ma'amadot, or assistants. Then at the time of the daily sacrifice, Jews at home began to gather for the reading of Scripture and prayer. Out of these practices the local synagogue might have developed. It then made its way back into the temple. The Mishnah (*Tamid* 5/6) tells us that the priests interrupted the morning offering to recite the Shema, the → Decalogue, and the prayers that are found in the later synagogue liturgy. From about A.D. 60 Joshua ben Hananiah tells of morning, musaf (i.e., "additional"), and afternoon services on the Feast of Tabernacles, the first after and the other two before the relevant sacrifices (Elbogen, 198).

After the destruction of the temple the biblical accounts of sacrifices found their way into the synagogue liturgy and were interpreted as substitute offerings ("God accepts the reading as though they brought sacrifices to me" [*b. Ta'an.* 27b]). The Prayer of the Eighteen Benedictions includes, "Restore the service to the inner sanctuary of your house; receive in love and favor both the offerings of Israel and their prayer" (17th benediction). The Aaronic blessing also found a place in synagogue worship. Already before NT days the reading of the law and the prophets and the Targum (trans. into Aramaic), preaching, confession of the one God, prayer (chiefly praise, the *berakot*), and the singing of psalms were constituent elements of synagogue worship.

1.3. Primitive Christian Worship

Apart from meetings in homes, the primitive Christian community took part daily in temple/synagogue worship (Acts 2:46; 5:42). Because of the criticism of the temple cult by Jesus (Mark 13:2; 14:58, etc., the cleansing of Mark 11:15-17, and Jesus' claim to have authority to forgive sins, which made the offerings superfluous, Mark 2:5-11 and par.; Luke 7:48-49), it did so mainly because it found opportunities for Christian proclamation in the temple and synagogue (F. Hahn, "Gottesdienst," 31, according to Acts 3:1, 11-26; 5:12-16, 42). Yet even the word-worship of the synagogue could not offer a liturgical home to Christians, for the first sermon of Jesus in Nazareth (on Isa. 61:1-2: "Today this scripture has been fulfilled," Luke 4:21) and the authority proclaimed in his healings and his attitude to the Sabbath (Mark 1:23-27; 3:1-6) had not met with faith. It was only a matter of time until there was a full break with the synagogue, the abandoning of

the → Sabbath, and the exclusive observance of "the first day of the week" (Acts 20:7, also 1 Cor. 16:2), "the Lord's day" (Rev. 1:10; *Did.* 14.1); these changes all took place toward the end of the first century.

In terminology, too, the NT underlines the break with the worship tradition of the OT and Judaism and a new beginning. In worship the first Christians did not use traditional cultic and hierarchical terms like "priest" and "sacrifice." Where these occur, they denote the one sacrifice of the one → high priest (Eph. 5:2; throughout Hebrews) or, in a completely noncultic way, the love of others in → discipleship (Rom. 12:1; Phil. 2:17; Heb. 13:16) or dedication in the apostolic ministry of witness (2 Tim. 4:6). Only the sacrifice of praise (Heb. 13:15, based on Ps. 50:23) retains a liturgical reference. In his community Jesus is the only sacrifice and the only priest.

On the basis of his eschatological message (→ Eschatology) of the cross, the → resurrection, and the event of → Pentecost, a wholly new worship was instituted that none of the traditional terms could denote and that was characterized by the congregation assembling in the name of Jesus (P. Brunner, 84-93). In spite of closeness to the Jewish tradition of prayer and points of contact with the synagogue liturgy (reading, preaching, praise), we thus must emphasize what is eschatologically new and unique in Christian worship, the decisive starting point for this being the Last Supper of Jesus with his disciples. At any rate, the basic form of primitive Christian worship was the gathering to celebrate the Lord's Supper (Hahn, "Gottesdienst," 30, 33).

The traditional thesis that justification for the post-Reformation separation of a ministry of preaching and the → Eucharist lies in the existence of two different forms of worship in the NT — the one deriving from the synagogue worship tradition, the other from the institution of Jesus — has proved to be untenable in modern exegesis (at first O. Cullmann, then G. Kretschmar, Hahn, et al.). In place of the Jewish (and pagan) cult Christ instituted a table fellowship within which the proclamation of the Word to the community took place (H. W. Heidland). Alongside this was the service of baptism and also missionary preaching. Other meetings are to be regarded as complementing the basic eucharistic structure or as singling out specific elements of this structure, and they are always to be related to it.

1.4. Worship in the Early Church

The NT contains many liturgically structured texts, for example, the Aramaic cries "Abba" (Gal. 4:6; Rom. 8:15; Mark 14:36) and "Marana tha" (1 Cor. 16:22; Rev. 22:20; cf. *Did.* 10.6), Hebrew elements

("Hallelujah," "Hosanna," → "Amen"), the → Lord's Prayer, → hymns (Phil. 2:6-11; Col. 1:15-20; 1 Tim. 3:16; John 1:1-18), confessional kerygmatic formulas (1 Cor. 15:3-5; 11:23-26; Rom. 4:25, etc.), three canticles (Luke 1–2), → doxologies, → acclamations, and greetings of peace. It refers to readings of Scripture (1 Tim. 4:13), sermons (1 Cor. 12:8-11; 14:16, etc.), and the reading and exchanging of apostolic letters (1 Thess. 5:27; Col. 4:16). Pneumatic fullness and vitality mark Corinthian worship (1 Corinthians 12; 14). Passages like *Did.* 9; 10; 14 and *1 Clem.* 59:2–61:3 and other descriptions complete the picture.

From the later second century → Justin Martyr (ca. 100-ca. 165) gives us a comprehensive view of early Christian worship (*1 Apol.* 61, 65-67) — it included readings, preaching, intercession, and eucharistic liturgy. Then at the beginning of the third century we have the *Apostolic Tradition* of Hippolytus (ca. 170-ca. 236). Since the liturgies that soon thereafter were becoming known from other areas and in other languages display the same basic structure, we may assume that the tradition had a very early origin. To be sure, some scholars think that there was greater variety in early liturgical practice (P. Bradshaw). Nevertheless, the tradition of Hippolytus (with the addition of the Sanctus) was determinative later in both East and West. We must remember that in the first three centuries the liturgy was mostly extemporaneous, and the use of models did not restrict the freedom that, according to *Did.* 10.7, → prophets usually enjoyed in the community.

Four changes from primitive Christian worship may be seen in the pre-Nicene period. First, the so-called agape meal dropped away. Originally the meal came between the bread and the cup, but all the liturgies known to us bring these together. They are both taken up, thanks is pronounced for them, the bread is broken, and both elements are then distributed (i.e., the "four-action shape"; see G. Dix, 48-50). The growth of the church and the transition from evening celebration of the Eucharist in a house to celebration on Sunday morning hardly explain this change, nor can we suppose that the sense of koinonia had dwindled at this period. What we have is a (possibly very early) theological decision that follows upon separation from the traditional cult. Bread and wine as Christ's body and blood are the eschatological gift to the community of the new covenant, whereas the agape is part of the dispensable framework of ancient custom.

Second, the cultic language that the NT deliberately avoided quickly made its way back into liturgical usage. The Eucharist is already a sacrifice in *Did.*

14.1-2. The epiclesis in Hippolytus requests the sending of the Spirit "on the church's holy oblation." Reduced confrontation with Judaism, as well as the need to find Christian worship prefigured in the OT, might have caused this change.

Third, a related change was the increasing development of an institutionalized leadership. → Bishops and priests were more and more separated from the rest of God's people. Yet in pre-Nicaean times the Eucharist was still an action of the whole congregation. All took communion, including the sick, who were served by the → diaconate. Daily prayer, viewed as the prayer of the whole church, was developed in the fourth century into daily matins and vespers.

Finally, the original opening of worship to unbelievers (1 Cor. 14:23-25; 16:22; cf. *Did.* 10.6b) was replaced by a strict division between the worship of catechumens and that of the faithful.

1.5. *The Fourth Century as a Turning Point*

As the church suddenly became the state church instead of a persecuted church, extraordinary changes took place that to some extent still affect us today. The basic eschatological orientation of worship with the celebration of the whole salvation-event on each → Sunday as a little Easter gave place to the domestication of the church in the world, the development of the → church year, the building of large churches, and a public cult that borrowed from the ceremonial of the imperial court. The end of the threat of paganism made possible the appropriation of pagan feasts and their filling out with a new Christian content (→ Christmas; cf. Epiphany). Sacred sites could be taken over for churches, along with many rites and practices. The battle against → heresies could become a public one in which both sides used hymns and altered texts. As congregations grew, their splitting up was delayed, and in daughter churches bishops took precedence over priests. This step led to the quenching of spontaneity and extemporization and the creation of fixed liturgies. The separate development of the common inheritance in East and West also took place at this time.

Especially, however, there is growing interest in a *moment of consecration* in the eucharistic liturgy, which the East locates in the epiclesis (→ Eucharistic Prayer), as effecting the transformation (Cyril of Jerusalem *Cat.* 23.7). With a good theological instinct, but with a similarly restricted approach, the West under Ambrose (ca. 339-97) and → Augustine (354-430) fixed on the actual words. As Augustine put it, "The adding of the word to the elements makes the sacrament" (*In Evang. Johan.* 80.3).

Worship

The East found a way out of the restriction by identifying the elements with the (offered up) Christ in the introduction (Proskomidia) and venerating them. The resurrection then took place with the prayer of epiclesis (Theodore of Mopsuestia *Cat. serm.* 5-6). In this way the prolonged consecration, in a dramatic celebration of the paschal mystery, embraces the whole service (see H.-C. Schmidt-Lauber, 156ff.).

Bibliography: P. F. Bradshaw, *The Search for the Origins of Christian Worship: Sources and Methods for the Study of Early Liturgy* (2d ed.; New York, 2002) • P. Brunner, *Worship in the Name of Jesus* (St. Louis, 1968) • T. K. Carroll and T. Halton, *Liturgical Practice in the Fathers* (Wilmington, Del., 1988) • O. Cullmann, *Early Christian Worship* (London, 1953) • G. Dix, *The Shape of the Liturgy* (2d ed.; London, 1945) • I. Elbogen, *Jewish Liturgy: A Comprehensive History* (Philadelphia, 1993; orig. pub., 1913) • W. Elert, *Eucharist and Church Fellowship in the First Four Centuries* (St. Louis, 1966) • E. Ferguson, ed., *Worship in Early Christianity* (New York, 1993) • F. Hahn, "Gottesdienst III: NT," *TRE* 14.28-39; idem, *The Worship of the Early Church* (Philadelphia, 1973) • H. W. Heidland *Wesen und Wert des Gottesdienstes* (Frankfurt, 1974) • L. W. Hurtado, *At the Origins of Christian Worship: The Context and Character of Earliest Christian Devotion* (Grand Rapids, 2000) • G. Kretschmar, "Abendmahlsfeier I: Alte Kirche," *TRE* 1.229-78 • J. J. Petuchowski, "Zur Geschichte der jüdischen Liturgie," *Jüdische Liturgie* (ed. H. H. Henrix; Freiburg, 1979) 13-32 • H.-C. Schmidt-Lauber, *Die Eucharistie als Entfaltung der verba testamenti* (Kassel, 1957) • K. W. Stevenson, *The First Rites: Worship in the Early Church* (Collegeville, Minn., 1989) • P. Wick, *Die urchristlichen Gottesdienste. Entstehung und Entwicklung im Rahmen der frühjudischen Tempel-, Synagogen- und Hausfrömmigkeit* (Stuttgart, 2002).

Hans-Christoph Schmidt-Lauber

2. Western Tradition
2.1. *Medieval Developments*

Many details about the evolution of Christian → liturgy in the Latin West during the first millennium remain obscure or unknown, but some facts seem indisputable, among them: (1) the liturgical language of the Roman Rite shifted from Greek to Latin in the late fourth century; (2) the basic shape of the Roman eucharistic liturgy (a Liturgy of the Word, followed by a Liturgy of the Table, with communion) was probably in place by the time of Pope Gelasius I (492-96); (3) many Western churches — for example, those of Gaul, Spain, northern Italy

(Milan), and the British Isles — maintained their own liturgical traditions, distinct from Roman usage in both texts and ritual forms; and (4) no single manner of celebrating sacraments (e.g., → baptism, → confirmation, → Eucharist) and daily → prayer (the "Divine Office" or "Liturgy of the Hours"; → Hours, Canonical) was adhered to by all churches in Europe before the year 1000.

Still, the influence of Roman liturgical practice slowly spread across the Continent, particularly during the period between → Gregory I (590-604) and → Gregory VII (1073-85). This spreading was partly due to a gradual standardization of liturgy in the city of Rome itself (where parish ceremonies and music often differed from what was done at papal liturgies), and partly due to the activity of → pilgrims, who brought Roman customs back with them to northern Europe. Eventually, powerful monarchs such as Charlemagne (ruled 768-814) sought greater liturgical uniformity within their territories by importing practices (texts, chants, ritual customs) from Rome. Charlemagne requested a copy of the principal Roman liturgical book (known as the Gregorian, or Hadrianum, sacramentary) in order to regularize ritual practice in his kingdom, which Hadrian I (772-95) sent to him around 790. Charlemagne discovered that it lacked material for some of the celebrations familiar to Frankish Christians, and so a supplement was added to the Hadrianum to supply this defect. This supplemented, hybrid sacramentary eventually made its way back south across the Alps, where it in turn influenced liturgical practice in Rome itself. The medieval Roman liturgy is thus a hybrid rite — a blend of Romano-Frankish (or Romano-Germanic) customs.

Such hybridization characterizes virtually all the → liturgical books we have that provide any evidence for the medieval Roman Rite. These include (1) *sacramentaries* (containing material for use by → priests or → bishops presiding at rites such as Eucharist or baptism), represented, for example, by its Verona ("Leonine"), Gelasian, and Hadrianum versions; (2) *Ordines Romani* (booklets containing directions for liturgies such as papal Masses, baptism, ministerial → ordinations, coronations, and → funerals); and (3) *pontificals* (directions for rites at which a bishop presides; the oldest of these is the Romano-Germanic Pontifical of Mainz, from ca. 950). All these books, containing old Roman material *as altered and expanded on Franco-German soil,* eventually reshaped the medieval Roman liturgy itself.

A great champion of this (now hybridized) Roman Rite was Gregory VII, whose reform of church life included a deliberate effort to suppress indigenous ritual practice that departed from Roman custom (e.g., the Mozarabic liturgy of the Iberian Peninsula). While the Gregorian reform was significant, its reach should not be exaggerated. Despite early medieval efforts to Romanize the liturgy throughout the Latin West, local variation continued to flourish in dioceses and monastic communities (such as the → Benedictines, → Cistercians, and Carthusians). Even within fairly small nations such as England, varying diocesan "usages" or "uses" (e.g., those of Sarum, Lincoln, York, and Hereford) continued until the period of the Reformation. These usages followed the basic Roman liturgical pattern but included both ceremonial and textual variations.

The medieval period witnessed not only an evolution in liturgical forms but parallel developments in popular attitudes toward the church's → rites. The relative simplicity and terseness of the old Roman liturgy were transformed by an ever-greater ritual complexity. The reception of communion by laypersons at the Eucharist declined (in 1215, the Fourth Lateran Council decreed that all Christians must receive at least once a year). Controversies about the Eucharist (e.g., about how Christ is present in the sacramental bread and wine) may also have contributed to shifts in popular piety and participation, as did the rise of the *devotio moderna*.

Meanwhile, the older liturgical books described above gradually yielded to more portable formats, such as the *missale plenum* (complete missal) for celebration of the Eucharist and the *breviarium* (breviary) for use in celebrating the daily Divine Office. Beginning with the reforms of → Innocent III (1198-1216), the missal and breviary (along with the pontifical) — *as they were used by the Roman →curia and papal household* — were revised, standardized, and then carried all over Europe by mendicant friars (e.g., the → Franciscans). These books formed the basis of the "modern" Roman Rite, such as we find it in the 1570 Missale Romanum (→ Mass 2.3.1), reformed after the Council of → Trent and used until the time of the Second Vatican Council (1962-65).

2.2. Roman Catholic Liturgical Reform

The 1570 Missale Romanum, which reformed the Roman eucharistic liturgy after Trent, gave the Western Latin church what earlier reformers, such as Gregory VII, had sought but failed to achieve: a unified liturgy. Only liturgical traditions that were over 200 years old (e.g., the rite of Milan and the order for praying the Divine Office in Benedictine monastic communities) were allowed to continue.

In the bull that accompanied his reformed version of the Breviarium Romanum in 1568, Pius V (1566-72) laid down the basic norm that was to shape Roman liturgy for the future: "To one God, with one and the same formula, prayers and praises are to be addressed."

2.2.1. The 20th century, however, witnessed the birth of a liturgical renewal movement, based on a new understanding of worship within Roman Catholicism (→ Liturgical Movement). Pioneers in this movement were the Benedictine abbeys of Solesmes, Beuron, Maria Laach, and Mont-Cesar (in the person of Lambert Beauduin, who organized the first Liturgical Weeks in Europe). Also notable were the contributions of Pius Parsch (1884-1954), an Augustinian canon of Klosterneuburg and an apostle of liturgy that fostered direct participation by laypeople. In the United States this movement took hold largely through the work of Benedictine Virgil Michel (1890-1938), who in 1926 launched the liturgical journal *Orate Fratres* (now called *Worship*) at St. John's Abbey, Collegeville, Minnesota.

The movement to restore the liturgy had also been gaining momentum at the papal level. Pius X (1903-14) gave a decisive push in 1910 with his call for frequent communion and his concept of active participation — themes the Second Vatican Council would later adopt. In 1947 → Pius XII's (1939-58) encyclical *Mediator Dei* took up the concerns of the liturgical movement but also counseled gradualism in introducing liturgical changes. Pius's own liturgical reforms began with small steps: restoration of the → Easter Vigil (1951), revision of → Holy Week (1955), and relaxation of the eucharistic fast and approval of evening → Mass (1957).

2.2.2. The great breakthrough came at → Vatican II, whose *Sacrosanctum concilium* (*SC,* 1963), the Constitution on the Sacred Liturgy, developed a dialogic understanding of worship in which both priest and people have essential roles to play. It defined liturgy as "an exercise of the priestly → office of Jesus Christ" for our "sanctification," and therefore also as a "public worship" that "is performed by the Mystical Body of Jesus Christ, that is, by the Head and his members" (7). It spoke, too, of worship as a dialogue between God and people: "In the liturgy God speaks to his people, and Christ is still proclaiming his Gospel. And the people reply to God both by song and prayer" (33). Above all, the council insisted, "In the restoration and promotion of the sacred liturgy the full and active participation by all the people is the aim to be considered before all else" (14).

The council recognized the legitimacy of various

liturgical traditions (*SC* 4), permitted the use of the vernacular languages (36, 54), and commissioned a comprehensive revision of all liturgical books (21). Communion in both kinds was allowed and encouraged, preaching was made obligatory at Sunday Mass, the general prayer of the church was reinstated, and concelebration rather than single (or private) celebration of the Eucharist was recommended. Ritual reforms for all the other → sacraments were also decreed, as well as thorough revisions of occasional services (e.g., funerals), the Liturgy of the Hours, the → church year, → church music, and sacred art and architecture (→ Christian Art). Instead of imposing "a rigid uniformity" in ritual, the council sought to respect the diverse cultural riches of the "various races and nations," incorporating these "intact" into the liturgy itself, "if possible" (37).

2.2.3. The first fruit of Vatican II's liturgical reform was the Roman Missal of 1970, with its new "order of Mass." The basic shape of the rite remained (Liturgy of the Word, followed by the eucharistic Liturgy of the Table), but the lectionary for Sundays and weekdays was completely revised (→ Readings, Scripture). On Sundays three readings (Hebrew Bible, Christian Testament, and Gospel) replaced the old system of two readings ("epistle" and "gospel"); moreover, different readings were provided for each of three yearly cycles, thereby offering worshipers a much richer sampling of biblical texts. The rite of "preparation of gifts" (formerly called the offertory) was greatly simplified in the 1970 missal, and three new eucharistic prayers were added to the old Roman Canon (now called → Eucharistic Prayer I).

As noted above, the postconciliar "order of Mass" emphasizes the full, conscious, and active participation of all present, each person doing "all and only" those tasks that belong to him or her. Since Vatican II, Catholics at Mass regularly bring the gifts of bread and wine to the altar (along with offerings for the poor), serve as liturgical ministers (e.g., readers, altar servers, eucharistic ministers), sing or say all the parts assigned to them, and typically receive communion in both kinds, from elements consecrated at the Mass that they are attending. Even though Latin may still be used in the postconciliar Eucharist, the overwhelming majority of Catholics experience Sunday liturgy in vernacular languages they can readily hear, understand, and respond to.

Among the other sacraments and occasional services, the first postconciliar revisions to appear were those for the baptism of children (1969), marriage (1969), and funerals (1969, rev. 1985). These were followed by new rites for adult initiation (1971), → pastoral care of the sick (1972), and the sacrament of reconciliation, or penance (1973). The new Rite of Christian Initiation for Adults restores the ancient Christian catechumenate and allows for a unified, integral celebration of initiation (baptism, followed immediately by confirmation/chrismation and Eucharist); it has become a significant feature of parish life in many parts of the United States.

A revised (and simplified) format for the Liturgy of the Hours ("Divine Office") appeared in 1971. For many centuries, this daily cycle of prayers — attached to fixed times (morning, noon, evening, night, etc.) — was considered a clerical responsibility. The postconciliar reform makes it clear that "public and common prayer by the people of God" belongs to all and is one of the "primary duties of the church" (General Instruction of the Liturgy of the Hours, 1). Instead of the traditional sequence of canonical hours (Lauds, Prime, Terce, Sext, None, Vespers, Compline, and Vigils or Matins), the revised rite includes Morning Prayer, Midday Prayer, Evening Prayer, and a daily "Office of Readings" (a form for night prayer is also provided).

Further changes to all these rites have continued to appear over the past 40 years. Translations into modern vernaculars continue to be revised, and the 1970 Roman Missal itself has undergone three major revisions (most recently, in 2002).

Bibliography: General: P. BRADSHAW, *Early Christian Worship: A Basic Introduction to Ideas and Practice* (London, 1996); idem, *The Search for the Origins of Christian Worship: Sources and Methods for the Study of Early Liturgy* (2d ed.; New York, 2002); idem, ed., *The New Westminster Dictionary of Liturgy and Worship* (Louisville, Ky., 2002) • Y. BRILIOTH, *Eucharistic Faith and Practice: Evangelical and Catholic* (London, 1953) • A. J. CHUPUNGCO, ed., *Handbook for Liturgical Studies* (5 vols.; Collegeville, Minn., 1997-2000) • G. DIX, *The Shape of the Liturgy* (London, 1945) • A. GERHARDS and B. KRANEMANN, *Einführung in die Liturgiewissenschaft* (Darmstadt, 2006) • C. JONES, G. WAINWRIGHT, E. YARNOLD, and P. BRADSHAW, eds., *The Study of Liturgy* (rev. ed.; New York, 1992) • A.-G. MARTIMORT, ed., *The Church at Prayer* (4 vols.; Collegeville, Minn., 1986-88) • F. C. SENN, *Christian Liturgy: Catholic and Evangelical* (Minneapolis, 1997); idem, *The People's Work: A Social History of the Liturgy* (Minneapolis, 2006) • R. F. TAFT, *Beyond East and West: Problems in Liturgical Understanding* (2d ed.; Rome, 1997) • G. WAINWRIGHT, *Doxology: The Praise of God in Worship, Doctrine, and Life* (New York, 1980) • G. WAIN-

WRIGHT and K. B. WESTERFIELD TUCKER, eds., *The Oxford History of Christian Worship* (New York, 2006) • J. F. WHITE, *Christian Worship in North America: A Retrospective, 1955-1995* (Collegeville, Minn., 1997); idem, *Introduction to Christian Worship* (3d ed.; Nashville, 2000).

On 2.1-2: A. BUGNINI, *The Reform of the Liturgy, 1948-1975* (Collegeville, Minn., 1990) • E. DUFFY, *The Stripping of the Altars: Traditional Religion in England, 1400-1580* (2d ed.; New Haven, 2005) • T. J. HEFFERNAN and E. A. MATTER, eds., *The Liturgy of the Medieval Church* (Kalamazoo, Mich., 2001) • INTERNATIONAL COMMISSION ON ENGLISH IN THE LITURGY, *Documents on the Liturgy, 1963-1979: Conciliar, Papal, and Curial Texts* (ed. T. C. O'Brien; Collegeville, Minn., 1982) • J. A. JUNGMANN, *The Mass of the Roman Rite: Its Origins and Development* (2 vols.; Westminster, Md., 1992; orig. pub., 1951) • N. D. MITCHELL, *Cult and Controversy: The Worship of the Eucharist outside Mass* (Collegeville, Minn., 1982) • E. PALAZZO, *A History of Liturgical Books: From the Beginning to the Thirteenth Century* (Collegeville, Minn., 1998) • M. RUBIN, *Corpus Christi: The Eucharist in Late Medieval Culture* (New York, 1991) • S. VAN DIJK and J. H. WALKER, *The Origins of the Modern Roman Liturgy* (Westminster, Md., 1960) • C. VOGEL, *Medieval Liturgy: An Introduction to the Sources* (Washington, D.C., 1986) • J. F. WHITE, *Roman Catholic Worship: Trent to Today* (2d ed.; Collegeville, Minn., 2003).

NATHAN D. MITCHELL

2.3. The Reformation and Its Fruit

With its new understanding of worship, the → Reformation set in motion decisive forces that would affect much more than its own age or merely the Protestant world.

2.3.1. The New View of Worship

In Reformation theology, worship is controlled by the doctrine of → justification as God's work, as his service to us, to which we can respond only with prayer, praise, thanksgiving, and a lifestyle in keeping with the → gospel (Rom. 12:1). Martin → Luther (1483-1546) defined it thus: "Our dear Lord himself may speak to us through his holy Word and we respond to him through prayer and praise" (Torgau, 1544; *LW* 51.333). Worship is a word-event developed in → proclamation and → sacrament (CA 5); it is a dialogic event in which God always has the initiative (Word and response).

The Reformation thus reversed the role of the → priest. He no longer makes an offering to God in the name of the congregation but becomes the spokesperson of God proclaiming God's promise to the congregation. Luther, then, could already ask for a

table-altar behind which "the priest should always face the people" (German Mass, 1526; *LW* 53.69). The priest does not offer the Mass to God for special intentions but administers the gifts of God to God's people. The acceptable idea of sacrifice was the form of a sacrifice of praise, perhaps in → eucharistic prayers other than the Roman Canon (CA Apol. 24.19ff.) but certainly in → canticles and → hymns throughout the liturgy.

2.3.2. Luther's Reforms

The real brunt of Luther's assault on the sacrifice of the Mass was the votive Mass, in which the Mass was offered for special intentions *(vota)* not covered by the all-sufficient atoning sacrifice of Christ. Votive Masses and private Masses (i.e., Masses with no congregation present) were promptly abolished. Communion under both kinds was restored, and efforts were made to put the Mass and other liturgical services into the vernacular language, a change that required vernacular translations of the Bible.

The Lutheran Reformation retained the tradition of the Western Mass. It sought to purge out from this tradition elements that were contrary to the gospel, such as the changing of the divine *beneficium* or *sacramentum* into a human *sacrificium* (V. Vajta, 43ff.). All words in the canon or collects that referred to sacrifice "simply must and shall be done away with" (1522, *LW* 36.254). The canon itself was condemned root and branch: "As a mere human word it gives place to the gospel and the Holy Spirit" (1521, WA 8.448); "let us, therefore, repudiate everything that smacks of sacrifice, together with the entire canon" (1523, *LW* 53.26). In the *Formula Missae et Communionis* (1523; "An Order of Mass and Communion for the Church at Wittenberg," *LW* 53.15-40), the order of Mass remained unchanged up to the offertory. The offertory prayers were eliminated. The words of institution were attached to the preface so that they would be sung aloud rather than recited silently, as in the pre-Reformation silent canon. The Sanctus and Benedictus followed the Verba, at which point Luther retained the elevation of the Host. This was followed by the → Lord's Prayer, Pax, and Agnus Dei, during which the elements were administered. This order of Communion also served as the model for the Swedish Mass (1531) of Olavus Petri (1493-1552).

In the German Mass of 1526 (*LW* 53.51-90) Luther laid down the principles of a valid liturgical order. → Freedom (the exercise of which "is up to everyone's conscience and must not be cramped or forbidden") has its limit in → love ("we must make sure that freedom shall be and remain a servant of love and of our fellow-man"). Love leads to being "of one mind." Finally, Luther mentions order, which for him is "an external thing" that has no validity in or of itself (pp. 61, 90). These principles explain the great variety of Protestant → church orders and practice. Liturgical law became a cooperative matter, and the validity of an order depended on its reception by local congregations.

The emphasis on the *verba testamenti,* which we find in the fourth century and which became increasingly stronger in the West, reached a climax in the German Mass. As regards their liturgical function, Luther understood them (1) as words with which Christ instituted the supper; (2) as words, with the recitation of which the Lord himself consecrates bread and wine; and (3) as words of witness that proclaim the Lord's atoning sacrifice. Luther related the words as thus understood directly to communion apart from the eucharistic prayer, which showed what for him was constitutive of the supper (T. Knolle, "Luthers Reform der Abendmahlsfeier," *Schrift und Bekenntnis* [ed. V. Herntrich and T. Knolle; Hamburg, 1950] 88ff.). In the process he completely lost the ancient thanksgiving within which the dominical sayings had been embedded. But he pointed out that the whole Mass is pervaded by praise and thanksgiving — "and we have kept these parts also in our Mass" (i.e. Kyrie, Gloria, Credo, Sanctus and Benedictus, Agnus Dei; *LW* 53.21). The eucharistic elements of thanksgiving, anamnesis, and epiclesis also found a new place in the congregational chorale, the sermon, and the admonition to Holy Communion.

Luther's orders carried great weight in the orders of Mass specified in the authorized church orders that began to appear from 1526 on. The orders prepared by Johannes Bugenhagen (1485-1558; e.g., Brunswick, 1528; Denmark-Norway, 1537) were much influenced by Luther's German Mass and link the words of institution to reception of communion. Another group of → church orders (e.g., Brandenburg-Nuremberg, 1533; Mark Brandenburg, 1540) placed the Verba after the Preface and Sanctus, followed by the Lord's Prayer, Pax, and Agnus Dei. Generally the Lutheran church orders also retained the historic → church year calendar and lectionary, abolishing only many of the post-NT saints' days, and also retained the prayer offices of Matins and Vespers. Lutheran orders of service provided for both congregational singing of vernacular hymns (many composed by Luther himself) and for Latin choir music.

2.3.3. *Other Reformers*

Ulrich → Zwingli (1484-1531) undertook reformed orders of worship for Zurich in the same years as Luther (Latin, 1523; German, 1525). He set the pattern for Reformed worship by providing continuing reading of Scripture with exegetical preaching and Holy Communion celebrated four times a year — on → Easter (also Maundy Thursday and Good Friday, to accommodate the whole community), → Pentecost, → Christmas, and the autumn festival of Zurich's patron saint. Generally, these were the only festivals observed in the Reformed calendar. Worship in Zurich was devoid of congregational singing or choir music.

An important mediating center of liturgical reform was Strasbourg, under *Martin → Bucer* (1491-1551). The order of the German Mass at Strasbourg (1524, through various editions up to 1537) followed the historic order of the Mass more closely than Zwingli's order. It provided for congregational singing of German metrical psalms and canticles. Communion was celebrated every Sunday at the cathedral and monthly in parish churches. Bucer had weddings celebrated at the Sunday Communion Service so that brides and grooms could receive communion with the congregation, but he avoided the idea of the private votive Mass.

John → Calvin (1509-64) came to Strasbourg in 1538 and was assigned by Bucer to minister to the French-speaking congregation. He used a slightly modified form of the Strasbourg German service and took this with him back to Geneva in 1542. Calvin's order of worship for Geneva had a → confession of sin and words of → assurance, metrical psalm, free prayer, sermon, intercession, Lord's Prayer in paraphrase, and → blessing. Sunday worship with sermon and Eucharist was Calvin's ideal, which he could not achieve in Geneva, since the Reformed quarterly Communion schedule was already established. His service of communion is in the Reformed tradition, mediated through Strasbourg, with some changes: following the Ante-Communion, the prayer for the church, Lord's Prayer, Apostles' Creed, words of institution according to 1 Corinthians 11, admonition, prayer of consecration, distribution, Psalm 138, thanksgiving prayer, and blessing. A notable contribution to Protestant worship was the Geneva Psalter, in which Louis Bourgeois (ca. 1510-after 1561) and others set 150 metrical psalms to elegant French chansons.

During the Marian → persecution of Protestants in England (1553-58), *John → Knox* (ca. 1513-72) settled in Geneva and ministered to English exiles. From there he took a form of the Genevan service back to Scotland in 1560, where it was included in the *Book of Discipline* in 1562. There is thus a line of succession in Reformed worship from Strasbourg to Geneva, thence to Scotland and eventually the Netherlands.

2.3.4. *Developments in England*

The Anglican Church took its own way in the → Book of Common Prayer (→ Anglican Communion). Thomas → Cranmer (1489-1556) was strongly influenced by German church orders, as well as the reformed Roman Breviary (1535, 1536) of Cardinal Quiñones (d. 1540), in the preparation of a totally English-language Book of Common Prayer in 1549. Following the Calenburg-Göttingen Church Order, Cranmer blended Matins and Lauds into a single order for Morning Prayer, and Vespers and Compline into a single order of Evening Prayer. He derived the course of psalmody and lectionary for daily prayer from the Quiñones Breviary. The order for Holy Communion followed the medieval Mass, with a revised eucharistic prayer. Collects were translations of medieval prayers, especially from the Sarum Use. Cranmer also translated Luther's German litany and drew on German orders of Holy Baptism.

This prayer book, accompanied by royal injunctions in 1550 that altered the space of worship in England by abolishing stone altars and setting wooden communion tables lengthwise in the chancels, was significantly revised in 1552 in a more Reformed direction, under the influence of Bucer (who was given a professorship at Oxford). Especially noteworthy was a new introductory penitential rite in the Communion Service that used the Kyrie as a response to the recitation of the Decalogue, and a new arrangement of the Communion rite in which the prayer of consecration ended with the words of institution, followed by the administration of the sacrament to communicants gathered in the chancel, in the order and style of Luther's German Mass. At Knox's insistence, an infamous "black rubric" was added at the last minute before publication to explain that kneeling for communion does not imply an adoration of the earthly elements.

The 1552 prayer book was short-lived because of the death of Edward VI (1547-53) and the ascendency of the Catholic Mary Tudor (1553-58). At Mary's death, the Protestant Elizabeth I (1558-1603) succeeded to the throne and, through the Act of Uniformity (1559), effected a *via media* between the 1549 and 1552 prayer books, especially in the words of administration of the sacrament, that tried to comprehend both Anglicans and → Puritans. There were minor changes in the prayer book in 1604 under James I (1603-25). A High Church party during the reign of Charles I (1625-49), led by Arch-

bishop William Laud (1573-1645), tried to restore east-wall altars and gave encouragement to the bishops in the Church of Scotland to restore features of the 1549 Communion Service in its 1537 prayer book.

Resistance to these changes in Scotland led to an invasion of England and precipitated the English Civil War. With the Presbyterian party in control of the House of Commons, the Book of Common Prayer was abolished by Parliament in 1645 and replaced by a Directory of Worship, which remained the official Anglican order of worship during the Puritan Commonwealth (1649-60). The Directory provided an outline of worship, with suggestions for content rather than a set of texts.

At the restoration of Charles II in 1660, the prayer book was also restored in 1662, with a few changes but few concessions to the dissenters. This prayer book remained the official rite of the Church of England until the late 20th century. Anglican worship during the period between 1559 and the late 19th century consisted of Morning Prayer, Ante-Communion, and Evening Prayer. Holy Communion was celebrated at least quarterly or monthly.

2.3.5. *Developments in the United States*

In 1786 the Episcopal Church in the U.S.A. received orders from the nonjuring Episcopal Church of Scotland upon the consecration of Bishop Samuel Seabury (1729-96). The American Book of Common Prayer (1790) departed from the English Prayer Book principally in adopting the form of the Communion Service used in the Episcopal Church in Scotland, which restored the eucharistic order of 1549 via 1537 and the Scottish "wee bookies" (pamphlets). In this order the preface and Sanctus (without the Benedictus) was followed by a prayer of thanksgiving, including the institution narrative, an anamnesis and oblation, an epiclesis, and a petition to receive the benefits of Christ's passion through this sacrament, leading to the Lord's Prayer. The prayer of humble access preceded the administration of the elements. Nevertheless, the English pattern of Morning Prayer, Ante-Communion, and Evening Prayer continued in the U.S. Episcopal Church.

The Wesleyan Movement in Britain and the United States desired more frequent Communion, using the order of the English Prayer Book as set out by John → Wesley (1703-91). The people attracted to → Methodism were generally the urban poor, and John and Charles Wesley (1707-88) engaged them in vigorous singing, personal testimonies, and spontaneous prayer in class meetings. In North America, Methodist circuit riders brought the sacrament to scattered settlements on the frontier. Since celebrating Holy Communion was contingent on the availability of ordained ministers, the Agape Meal was often celebrated instead of Holy Communion. The Disciples of Christ (→ Christian Church) emerged under the principle that the Lord's Supper should be celebrated every Lord's Day, and lay elders were set aside to preside at the sacrament as a matter of principle. Methodist and Disciples worship was heavily influenced by revivalism during the 19th century (→ Revivals; Theology of Revival 4.4).

The original frontier camp meetings were designed by Presbyterian ministers James McGready (ca. 1758-1817) and Barton W. Stone (1772-1844) to imitate the Scots Presbyterian "communion seasons." What emerged from the camp meetings, as stylized by Charles G. → Finney's (1792-1875) "new measures," was a new order of worship that included preliminaries (songs, testimonies, offering), proclamation of the Word (reading of Scripture and "message"), and response (the prayers of the "anxious bench" for those who made a decision for Christ).

Churches in the Reformation tradition — Lutheran, Episcopal, Reformed, and Presbyterian (→ Reformed and Presbyterian Churches) — mostly resisted the influence of revivalism and instead worked toward recovering their historic traditions. The most scathing critiques of revivalism came from the faculties of Princeton Theological Seminary and the Mercersburg Seminary of the German Reformed Church, where John Nevin (1803-86) pronounced the "new measures" heresy because they promoted → Pelagianism.

2.4. *Protestant Liturgical Reform*

The age of → orthodoxy was one of teaching and rigidity of form, but with a rich musical life culminating in the → church music of J. S. Bach (1685-1750). → Pietism inclined to personal → piety and small groups that discussed the sermons. In the → Enlightenment the congregation became the general public, and the preacher the pulpit orator. The concern of → rationalism was for the instruction and moral betterment of the people by the religious teacher. This period has often been called one of decline (P. Graff), yet there was new thinking even in the Enlightenment and then in its vanquisher, F. D. E. → Schleiermacher (1768-1834; → Schleiermacher's Theology). King Frederick William III (1797-1840) issued a new liturgical order for Prussia (1822ff.). Lutheran liturgical restoration under the influence of Wilhelm Löhe (1808-72) of Neuendettelsau and the → liturgical movements of → liberalism (J. Smend, F. Spitta) characterized the 19th century. The 20th century provided a new

stimulus for liturgical renewal. New orders were thus prepared in Germany after World War II.

2.4.1. *Germany*

The 1960s saw a dissatisfaction with restorationist forms that found expression in alternative models, variations and supplements, situational approaches, and house worship (→ House Church). At the same time came the discovery and investigation of the nonverbal element, of → speech, → sign, ritual, and → communication by symbol (pastoral anthropology), and of the diaconal dimension of worship (pastoral liturgics; → Pastoral Psychology). Comprehensive German revision began about 1970, and the paper *Versammelte Gemeinde* (Gathered community) came out in 1974. This showed that all traditional and new forms have the same basic structure of opening, invocation, proclamation/confession of faith, supper, and dismissal. A group from East and West Germany began work on a revised form, with a view to preparing a draft of Renewed Agenda in 1988.

2.4.2. *United States*

A comparable story is told in American → Lutheranism. The first Agenda prepared by Henry Melchior Muhlenberg (1711-87) and adopted by the Ministerium of Pennsylvania in 1748 was a classic Lutheran order of Ante-Communion and Holy Communion. It began to break down in the early 19th century under the combined impact of rationalism and revivalism. Massive immigration from Lutheran countries to North America in the mid-19th century brought agendas that were closer to classic Lutheran church orders. In the 1880s the eastern synods embarked on the Common Service in the English language, which would restore worship consistent with the 16th-century church orders and provide for greater participation of the people. The Common Service (1888) won widespread acceptance and was included in the hymnals of various → synods.

The high point of liturgical restoration was the *Service Book and Hymnal* (1958), used by eight Lutheran denominations that subsequently merged into three. But a desire for more contemporary expressions surfaced only a few years after the publication of the *SBH*. It led in 1966 to the formation of the Inter-Lutheran Commission on Worship at the invitation of the Lutheran Church–Missouri Synod, which included representatives of the largest three Lutheran denominations in North America. This work led to the *Lutheran Book of Worship* (1978) and the Missouri Synod *Lutheran Worship* (1982).

In a similar pattern there was a gradual retrieval of older texts and practices in the American Book of Common Prayer in 1892 and 1928. The Oxford and Cambridge ecclesiological movements of the 19th century exerted a profound influence on parish worship and architecture in the Episcopal Church in the U.S.A. in terms of recovering High Church ceremony and neo-Gothic buildings, accoutrements, and vestments (→ Oxford Movement). More significantly, the celebration of Holy Communion became more frequent by the end of the 19th century, although it was often a Low Mass at an 8:00 A.M. service, with morning prayer and sermon at 11:00 A.M. The Standing Liturgical Commission of the Episcopal Church began to issue *Prayer Book Studies* after 1950, with a view toward a major revision of the prayer book. By the 1960s, because of widespread cultural changes, American Lutherans, Episcopalians, Methodists, and Presbyterians were ready to move in the direction of renewal rather than restoration.

2.4.3. Significant Books

Of great influence on liturgical renewal was the work of Swedish bishop Yngve Brilioth (1891-1959, *Eucharistic Faith and Practice: Evangelical and Catholic* [1927]) and Anglican Benedictine Dom Gregory Dix (1901-52, *The Shape of the Liturgy* [1945]). Brilioth held that the Eucharist could not be reduced to one idea or to one set of ideas in logical combination. He saw the elements of thanksgiving, fellowship, commemoration, and sacrifice present in the whole eucharistic tradition, with the dimension of mystery infusing each of these aspects with the depth of the real presence of Christ. Dix held that the search for an original apostolic eucharistic text was fruitless and suggested that what the eucharistic tradition held in common were the actions of the Eucharist rather than texts. From the seven actions in the four NT institution narratives, he derived four: taking, blessing, breaking the bread, and eating and drinking, which evolved into the offertory, great thanksgiving, fraction, and administration of communion.

To the work of Brilioth and Dix should be added that of Geoffrey Wainwright (*Eucharist and Eschatology* [1971; 3d ed., 2003]), who showed that the eschatological motifs of the messianic feast, the second coming of Christ, and the firstfruits of the kingdom pervaded early Christian eucharistic celebrations. These studies were foundational for the Lima Declaration *Baptism, Eucharist, and Ministry* (1983), prepared by the → Faith and Order Commission of the → World Council of Churches. This declaration finds thanksgiving, anamnesis, epiclesis, communion, and eschatology the fundamental dimensions of the Eucharist, and which introduces a mutual exchange of experiences.

These studies profoundly influenced the major American Protestant worship books of the late 20th century: *Lutheran Book of Worship* (1978), *The Book of Common Prayer according to the Use of the Episcopal Church* (1979), *The United Methodist Book of Worship* (1988), and *The Presbyterian Book of Common Worship* (1993). The ecumenical convergence in these worship books is remarkable. They reflect an ecumenical ordo of gathering, word, meal, and sending. They use common English liturgical texts that have been shared with English editions of the Roman Missal and a three-year common lectionary for Sundays and festivals that is based on the three-year Roman Lectionary for Sundays and festivals (→ Readings, Scripture). Subsequent supplementary resources in these denominations to address issues of cultural diversity and inclusive language have clearly been designed to build on and not depart from these pioneer resources in liturgical renewal. The most important result of Protestant liturgical renewal has been the recovery of the premier place of → baptism as initiation into the Christian community and the celebration of Holy Communion as the chief liturgy on Sundays and festivals.

Bibliography: H. DAVIES, *Worship and Theology in England* (5 vols.; Princeton, 1961-75) • P. GRAFF, *Geschichte der Auflösung der alten gottesdienstlichen Formen in der evangelischen Kirche Deutschlands* (2 vols.; Göttingen, 1921-39; repr., 1994) • M. J. HATCHET, *Commentary on the American Prayer Book* (New York, 1981) • C. HEFLING and C. SHATTUCK, eds., *The Oxford Guide to the Book of Common Prayer: A Worldwide Survey* (Oxford, 2006) • J. MELTON, *Presbyterian Worship in America: Changing Patterns since 1787* (Richmond, Va., 1967) • H. O. OLD, *The Patristic Roots of Reformed Worship* (Zurich, 1975); idem, *The Reading and Preaching of the Scriptures in the Worship of the Christian Church* (5 vols.; Grand Rapids, 1998-); idem, *Worship That Is Reformed according to Scripture* (Atlanta, 1984) • I. PAHL, *Coena Domini. Die Abendmahlsliturgie der Reformationskirchen* (2 vols.; Fribourg, 1983-2005) • P. H. PFATTEICHER, *Commentary on the Lutheran Book of Worship* (Minneapolis Fortress, 1990) • L. D. REED, *The Lutheran Liturgy* (rev. ed.; Philadelphia, 1959) • B. D. SPINKS, *Freedom or Order? The Eucharistic Liturgy in English Congregationalism, 1645-1980* (Allison Park, Pa., 1984); idem, *From the Lord and "the Best Reformed Churches": A Study of the Eucharistic Liturgy in the English Puritan and Separatist Traditions, 1550-1633* (Rome, 1984) • G. STILLER, *Johann Sebastian Bach and Liturgical Life in Leipzig* (ed. R. A. Leaver; St. Louis, 1984) • V. VAJTA, *Die Theologie des Gottesdienstes bei*

Luther (2d ed.; Göttingen, 1954) • K. B. Westerfield Tucker, *American Methodist Worship* (New York, 2001) • J. F. White, *Christian Worship in North America: A Retrospective, 1955-1995* (Collegeville, Minn., 1997); idem, *Protestant Worship: Traditions in Transition* (Louisville, Ky., 1989) • J. H. Yoder, *The Politics of Jesus: Vicit Agnus Noster* (2d ed.; Grand Rapids, 1994).

Frank C. Senn and Hans-Christoph
Schmidt-Lauber

3. Orthodox Tradition

3.1. *History, Practice, Environment*

The Orthodox tradition of worship is practiced by more than 200 million Christians worldwide, several million of whom are in the West. Its codification took place via Constantinople (Byzantium, present-day Istanbul), whence it spread and came to dominate Greece, the Balkans, Ukraine, Belarus, Russia, and parts of the Middle East. Previously, it even dominated regions of southern Italy. (The Armenian, Coptic, Ethiopian, Syrian "Jacobite," and Malankara traditions, referred to as → Oriental Orthodox, are each markedly different from the Eastern Orthodox, or Byzantine, tradition and are not treated here.)

The eucharistic service ("Divine Liturgy") and other sacramental rites (called "Mysteries") underwent a steady evolution until 1453, when Constantinople fell to the Ottoman Turks. But the Liturgy of the → Hours (nine services, with Vespers and Matins being the most prominent) has had a more volatile history: much of the indigenous Constantinopolitan Rite was supplanted after the 13th century by monastic elements derived from Palestine.

The liturgical calendar, with its movable and fixed cycles, was also sequentially codified in Constantinople, though every local Orthodox church has added saints and commemorations of its own. The propers for the movable cycle, which begins at Easter, are found in the Octoechos, Triodion, and Pentecostarion, those for the fixed cycle are in the 12-volume Menaion, with September the first month. In addition to these texts, the most important are the Gospel and Epistle books, with their one-year lectionary cycle; the Psalter, divided into 20 sections for liturgical use; the Horologion, for the ordinary of the Hours; and the Euchology, or Hieraticon, for the Eucharist, sacraments, and other occasional rites.

The eucharistic rite used throughout most of the year is the Divine Liturgy of St. John → Chrysostom (ca. 347-407), while ten times per year the Divine Liturgy of St. Basil the Great (ca. 330-79) is pre-

scribed. The → anaphoras (great → Eucharistic prayers) of both of these liturgies were edited to a greater or lesser extent by the two saints. Both formularies are composed of three parts: a nonpublic preparation of bread and wine, followed by a liturgy of the → Word ("of the catechumens") and liturgy of the → Eucharist ("of the faithful"). A third eucharistic rite, the Liturgy of the Presanctified Gifts, erroneously attributed to Pope → Gregory the Great (ca. 540-604), is celebrated on weekdays of Lent with bread consecrated the preceding Sunday.

Generally, the Orthodox have fostered linguistic and musical indigenization of their worship. This variety of languages and musical styles is the main characteristic that distinguishes East Slavic worship, for example, from Greek or Arabic forms. However, the interior structure of the church building, as well as utensils and vestments, remains quite similar throughout Orthodoxy. Even the → iconography, if painted according to canonical norms, is more similar than different in the various local churches. These paintings, which are considered visual epiphanies, not merely decoration, are regularly censed, venerated, and carried in procession.

The church building is divided into three parts: (1) a sanctuary, reserved for the clergy and separated by an → iconostasis, or icon screen; (2) a nave, for the laity (and singers wherever congregational singing has fallen into desuetude, as is generally the case); and (3) a vestibule (narthex), in which certain lesser offices or parts of services are occasionally celebrated. → Processions around or beyond the church are also prescribed several times per year and, until the Ottoman period, were a more frequent part of the tradition.

3.2. *The Theology and Spirit of Orthodox Worship*

Orthodox worship is viewed as a copy of the heavenly liturgy and thus redolent with the aura of the Book of Revelation and the Epistle to the Hebrews. Two "movements" typify its ethos, or spirit. The first is an eastward dynamic (churches are traditionally built facing east), with both → clergy and laity facing that direction during much of the service. Early Christians believed that Christ, the Sun of Justice, would return in glory from the east. The focus proceeds even beyond the → altar, as gestures of worship are also directed at the space behind the holy table (positioned in the middle of the sanctuary) as if to point toward the heavenly and the eschaton. The fact that the sanctuary is segregated from the congregation by a wall of icons, with the clergy as leaders "preceding" the assembly on the other side of the wall, also evokes the sense of an eschatological journey. The congregation is spatially reminded that their life as church transcends this assembly and this place.

The second movement characterizing the ethos of Orthodox worship is one of descent. Not only is the nave covered by a dome filled with an → icon of Christ the All-Ruler (Pantocrator) descending, as it were, into the assembly, but the clergy regularly come down from the sanctuary into the midst of the faithful to bring Communion, the gospel book, icons, and so forth for distribution and veneration.

The engagement of all of the senses, as well as the inclusion of so many symbols, gives Orthodox worship a strong cosmic quality. Building on the conviction that Christians have become "participants of the divine nature" (2 Pet. 1:4), Orthodox worship aims to intensify this participation and extend it to all of creation. The Greek patristic theology of divinization (→ Theosis) is thus a key theological inspiration. Constantinople's status as an imperial capital also contributed to the development of a ritual opulence.

Another constant of Orthodox worship is the inextricable link between crucifixion and resurrection. In hymnography and symbols, Christ's suffering is viewed from the perspective of his victory. The eucharistic elements, for example, are considered the risen body and blood of Christ, and the anaphora of Basil the Great even takes the liberty of adding "and resurrection" to the Pauline text "as often as you eat this bread and drink the cup, you proclaim the Lord's death until he comes" (1 Cor. 11:26).

The Mother of God and the saints are also prominent in the calendar and liturgical texts. Depicted on icons positioned at ground level throughout the church, the saints are considered living, present members of the worshiping community. Their ascetic struggles are a recurring theme in hymnography, and liturgical → fasting remains a central aspect of → spirituality. Orthodox are expected to abstain from all food and drink from midnight in preparation for the Eucharist, celebrated at least every Sunday. Most Wednesdays and Fridays, as well as four periods of the year, are — in principle — devoted to fasting. Worship services during these periods are suitably adapted. This is especially the case during Lent, called the Great Fast, when on weekdays prostrations to the ground are repeatedly performed.

Orthodoxy stresses continuity between the patristic era and modernity. Indeed, the → Renaissance, → Reformation, and → Enlightenment were experienced only derivatively in the East. Orthodox consciousness thus remains theocentric in a way that can seem odd in the West, where the "turn to the

subject" has come to dominate culture. This continuity has profoundly influenced Orthodox worship: liturgical texts exude a strong theocentrism, and liturgical change is downplayed.

3.3. *Adaptation*

The official Orthodox liturgical books continue to replicate the contents of editions first printed in the 16th century. Unofficially, however, one finds usages — especially in the case of the Hours — that depart significantly from the prescriptions of these books. "Liberals" and "conservatives" divide according to their relative regard for the official editions, though all Orthodox adhere to some ordo (or, in Greek, *typicon*). Departures from the *typicon* are then explained as "local usage." Nonetheless, these departures are rarely spontaneous, and such local usages thus constitute in effect a parallel ordo. The difficulty of calling a → Pan-Orthodox council means that liturgical adaptation will probably continue to evolve without broader coordination. While this process guarantees a certain organicity to the process, it also perpetuates adaptations not always consistent with sound theological and historical principles.

In the West, Orthodox liturgical adaptation is limited to adopting the local language, singing a (very small) percentage of newer, indigenous musical compositions, and abbreviating the offices.

Bibliography: Aimilianos of Simonopetra, *The Church at Prayer: The Mystical Liturgy of the Heart* (Athens, 2005) • K. Anatolios, "Heaven and Earth in Byzantine Liturgy," *Antiph.* 5 (2000) 21-28 • J. Corbon, *The Wellspring of Worship* (New York, 1988) • *The Divine Liturgy of Our Father among the Saints, John Chrysostom* ([ed. E. Lash]; Oxford, 1995) • T. Pott, *La réforme liturgique byzantine. Étude du phénomène de l'évolution non-spontanée de la liturgie byzantine* (Rome, 2000) • L. Safran, ed., *Heaven on Earth: Art and the Church in Byzantium* (University Park, Pa., 1997) • A. Schmemann, *For the Life of the World: Sacraments and Orthodoxy* (Crestwood, N.Y., 1973); idem, *Liturgy and Tradition: Theological Reflections of Alexander Schmemann* (ed. T. Fisch; Crestwood, N.Y., 1990) • H.-J. Schulz, *The Byzantine Liturgy: Symbolic Structure and Faith Expression* (New York, 1986) • R. F. Taft, *Beyond East and West: Problems in Liturgical Understanding* (2d ed.; Rome, 1997); idem, *The Byzantine Rite: A Short History* (Collegeville, Minn., 1992).

Peter Galadza

4. Free Church Tradition
4.1. *General Characteristics*
Of all the Protestant liturgical traditions, the free church tradition is hardest to define. Yet in some

countries, such as the United States, it has more adherents than any other Protestant tradition. Furthermore, the free church tradition has had decisive influence, pulling worship in Reformed, Methodist, and even Lutheran traditions into its orbit. Two characteristics seem to typify free church worship: a strong desire to be free to reform worship completely according to God's Word (i.e., a strong biblicism) and commitment to congregational autonomy in the ordering of worship. Service books are usually nonexistent except for → hymnbooks. In general, most free church → congregations observe the → Eucharist as an occasional rather than a weekly celebration.

4.2. *Original Free Church Worship Tradition*

Historically, there are three main sources of the free church tradition: European → Anabaptists, English → Puritans, and American frontier denominations. Each, in its origins, stressed → biblicism; each has practiced congregational → autonomy.

The Anabaptist groups of the 16th century show both widespread diversity but some common features: opposition to infant → baptism, the concept of a pure church of committed believers, resistance to the fixed liturgies of the state churches, and usually a memorialistic approach to the Lord's Supper (or Lord's Memorial). Some, such as Balthasar Hubmaier (1485-1528), produced liturgies; most preferred unwritten and informal services. Hymnody was a prominent part of worship for most congregations. Controversies arose over the use of the ban to ensure the purity of disciplined congregations of baptized believers (→ Church Discipline).

A second source of the free church tradition is English Puritanism at the end of the 16th and beginning of the 17th centuries. The influence of the Anabaptists is apparent among some early English → Baptists, but the main body of Puritanism increasingly demanded worship reformed according to its own interpretations of the → Word of God. Completion of the → Reformation supposedly meant abolition of ceremonies and practices for which scriptural warrant could not be found. The monument of this movement is the Westminster Directory for the Public Worship of God, adopted by Parliament in 1645 as a replacement for the → Book of Common Prayer. Worship in the churches of England and Scotland was governed by this directory's collection of rubrics. No fixed formularies were provided. Congregations were allowed considerable freedom to order their worship on a local basis but within specified national guidelines. Thus, all worship could be made "agreeable to God's Word."

Great growth in the free church tradition was ex-

perienced in America on its western frontier. The 19th century saw the beginnings of new → denominations, such as the Disciples of Christ (→ Christian Church), which also resolved to follow Scripture alone in worship. In their view, such a commitment eliminated the use of creeds (→ Confessions and Creeds) and infant baptism but led to a weekly Eucharist, usually led by laypeople. Other groups, such as the Baptists, expanded rapidly in this period. There was a proliferation of new denominations such as → Adventists, → Mormons, and Holiness churches, with worship almost always reflecting free church characteristics.

An important phenomenon of the 19th century was the gradual reshaping of the Reformed (→ Reformed and Presbyterian Churches) and Methodist (→ Methodist Churches) traditions in America, so that Sunday worship, except for their occasional celebrations of the sacraments, moved to imitation of free church worship. The revival movement generally proved stronger than the historic patterns of worship of these traditions, and the usual Sunday service tended to conform to a threefold shape: music and → prayer, evangelistic reaching and preaching, and a gathering of converts. By the mid-19th century, the free church pattern had been largely reinterpreted in the direction of freedom to do what worked — for example, that which produced converts. This functionalism outweighed the earlier biblicism.

4.3. *New Developments*

Recent developments have seen some free church congregations affected by the ecumenical and liturgical currents of the era after → Vatican II. Probably the most widespread of the reforms has been adoption of the ecumenical lectionary and the consequent commitment to a closer following of the → church year. There has also been, in a few sectors, an effort to move beyond the prevailing sacramental theology and practice (largely shaped by Enlightenment rationalism) to a deeper sacramental life. This development is reflected in some American denominations (such as the United Church of Christ) in the publication for voluntary use of eucharistic and baptismal rites not unlike those of Anglicans and Lutherans. Local autonomy is zealously guarded, but this position includes the possibility of appropriating from other traditions just as surely as ignoring them. In general, pastors feel free to order worship according to local preferences. The "pastoral prayer" is prepared locally and usually is the chief prayer of the service. Hymnody, choral music, and → preaching are usually important parts of the service. A maximum of freedom is possible in adapting the style of these components to the specific occasion and local culture.

→ Church 3.6; Church Growth

Bibliography: D. ADAMS, *Meeting House to Camp Meeting* (Austin, Tex., 1981) • R. S. ARMOUR, *Anabaptist Baptism* (Scottdale, Pa., 1966) • J. BISHOP, *Methodist Worship in Relation to Free Church Worship* (New York, 1975) • H. DAVIES, *Worship and Theology in England* (6 vols. in 3; Grand Rapids, 1996; orig. pub., Princeton, 1961-75); idem, *The Worship of the American Puritans, 1629-1730* (New York, 1990); idem, *The Worship of the English Puritans* (Morgan, Pa., 1997; orig. pub., London, 1948) • C. J. ELLIS, *Gathering: A Theology and Spirituality of Worship in Free Church Tradition* (London, 2004) • G. F. SNYDER and D. M. MCFARLANE, *The People Are Holy: The History and Theology of Free Church Worship* (Macon, Ga., 2005) • G. WILLIAMS, *The Radical Reformation* (3d ed.; Kirksville, Mo., 1992).

JAMES F. WHITE†

5. Africa
5.1. *Framework*
As the highest form of religious expression, worship presupposes the existence of a deity, as well as the need and value of acknowledging the worth of the deity and of offering one's homage or adoration. It stems from a sense of allegiance owed to this being that is wholly other and that has manifested or revealed itself to humans, often in the form of deliverance or liberation. Worship usually requires the creation of sacred spaces — shrines, mosques, temples — where believers in the deity can express their faith through → prayer, thanksgiving, → sacrifice, and petition for protection.

Worship is expressed in three principal ways: (1) verbally, through words of praise and acknowledgments; (2) through gestures, such as bowing, genuflecting, arm-raising, kneeling, and prostration; and (3) through giving of material substances such as sacrifices and offerings. For example, in Psalm 116 the psalmist, after having experienced Yahweh's deliverance, acknowledges in words his love for the Lord (v. 1). These words are followed by a gesture ("I will lift up the cup of salvation," v. 13), and then by the giving of some material substance ("I will pay my → vows to the LORD in the presence of all his people," v. 14). Although worship can take place privately, this last phrase underscores the importance also of corporate worship.

In the Christian Scriptures, such worship is due to God alone, who is acknowledged as the One in whom "we live and move and have our being" (Acts 17:28). Unlike the gods of other peoples, which are all "idols," Israel's God, Yahweh, "made the heavens" (Ps. 96:5). That is, worship is offered to that which is ultimately *real*. The first four commandments of the Decalogue deal with human relationship to God and affirm that cultic allegiance is owed to him and him alone, since he brought them "out of the land of Egypt" (Exod. 20:2), which is associated with their bondage, servitude, humiliation, and loss of destiny. In other words, in worship the people of Israel were expected to celebrate God because of their encounter with him as their source of deliverance and → salvation; indeed, they were to "tell of his salvation from day to day" (Ps. 96:2). The NT continues this relationship between deliverance and worship: since we have been "rescued from the hands of our enemies," we may now "serve him without fear, in holiness and righteousness before him all our days" (Luke 1:74-75).

5.2. *Worship as Service*
The duty of service, mentioned in Luke 1:74, is taken for granted by the commandments (→ Decalogue). That is, worship has a moral dimension ("in holiness and righteousness") and an expectation of human response (e.g., see Isa. 6:3-9; John 4:23-24). The idea of service is significant when understood against the backdrop of African interpretations of worship. The vernacular word for worship in African languages usually can also be translated "serve." Worship in the African context thus presupposes that a person owes allegiance to a deity as the source of being and sustenance, who must be served actively in worship. In many places, Africans go to shrines to acknowledge the gods of their → ancestors, particularly during festive occasions, and they approach their gods through traditional priests, seeking forgiveness for their sins, cures for their ills, answers to their questions, and guidance for their lives.

5.3. *Corporate Worship*
Corporate worship in traditional Africa is very expressive and involves much drumming and dancing (→ Dance). African Initiated Churches have retained these celebratory forms of religious expression, with their worship tending to be very dynamic, expressive, exuberant, and spontaneous (→ Independent Churches). Much of it blends features of worship in the Psalms and in the worship of African traditional religions, which incorporates drumming, dancing, hand-clapping, and different types of spontaneous movements (→ Tribal Religions).

5.4. *African Worship and Pentecostalism*
The oral nature of African worship also corresponds with elements of Pentecostal expression. Pentecostal spirituality is characterized by bodily movements,

voluble praise, clapping and swaying, personal testimonies, speaking in tongues, loud and piercing cries, weeping, spontaneous singing and prophecies, and prayers for → healing (J. K. Asamoah-Gyadu). Western mission Christianity often takes a very liturgical, subdued, and ordered approach to Christian worship, but African worship is more experiential and emotional. For this reason Pentecostal worship in particular has proved very attractive in African contexts. → Pentecostalism is an experiential religion par excellence, and this stream of Christianity challenges us to recognize the importance of the emotional and nonrational in a fully integrated faith and life and to give place to these less structured and less predictable elements in worship (J. D. G. Dunn).

Like Pentecostalism, worship in African-initiated Christianity is always a felt experience; in this respect, the continent has chosen a different path from that taken by Western → mission Christian worship, which is shaped by its → Enlightenment worldview. In the African worldview, what is primarily real is the spiritual. The African Christian by extension lives in a universe where the presence of the triune God is perceived to be actively impinging upon human life, and to this presence the believer is called to *respond* in worship. In the African Christian context worship is thus holistic and is defined by "vital participation" in the life of a God who is holy and who is present in the power of the Holy Spirit (K. Bediako). That presence, African Christianity teaches, must be felt and experienced when his people meet.

→ African Theology

Bibliography: J. K. Asamoah-Gyadu, "'Signs of the Spirit': Worship as Experience in African Pentecostalism," *JACT* 8/2 (2005) 17-24 • K. Bediako, "Worship as Vital Participation: Some Personal Reflections on Ministry in the African Church," *JACT* 8/2 (2005) 3-7 • J. D. G. Dunn, "'Ministry and the Ministry': The Charismatic Renewal's Challenge to Traditional Ecclesiology," *Charismatic Experiences in History* (ed. C. M. Robeck Jr.; Peabody, Mass.; 1985) 81-101 • D. Horton, *The Meaning of Worship* (New York, 1959) • E. B. Idowu, *Olódùmarè: God in Yoruba Belief* (New York, 1963) • R. P. Martin, *The Worship of God: Some Theological, Practical, and Pastoral Reflections* (Grand Rapids, 1982) • J. S. Mbiti, *African Religions and Philosophy* (2d ed.; Oxford, 1990) • J. K. Olupona, "Africa, West (Survey)," *The New International Dictionary of Pentecostal and Charismatic Movements* (rev. ed.; ed. S. M. Burgess and E. M. van der Maas; Grand Rapids, 2002) 11-21; idem, ed., *African Spirituality: Forms,* *Meanings, and Expressions* (New York, 2000) • M. H. Shepherd, ed., *Worship in Scripture and Tradition* (New York, 1963) • N. Smart, *The Concept of Worship* (London, 1972) • M. Stringer, *A Sociological History of Christian Worship* (Cambridge, 2005) • E. Underhill, *Worship* (New York, 1937) • G. Wainwright, "Christian Worship: Scriptural Basis and Theological Frame," *The Oxford History of Christian Worship* (ed. G. Wainwright and K. B. Westerfield Tucker; Oxford, 2006) 1-31 • J. F. White, *A Brief History of Christian Worship* (Nashville, 1993) • S. J. White, *Groundwork of Christian Worship* (Peterborough, 1997) • N. T. Wright, *For All God's Worth: True Worship and the Calling of the Church* (Grand Rapids, 1997).

J. Kwabena Asamoah-Gyadu

6. Asia

Asia is a vast area culturally and geographically, with great diversity in language, culture, and history. It shows equal diversity in its various practices of Christian worship.

6.1. Roman Catholic → missionaries arrived in China as early as the 16th century, and Protestant missionaries came in the early 19th century. In the face of → Buddhism, → Confucianism, → Taoism, and many forms of → shamanism, all missionaries had to face questions of how to translate Christian terms of theology and worship, how much to embrace of the local cultural and linguistic elements, and whether to allow local rituals and ceremonies that were widely practiced (Hae Jung Park, Kyeong Jin Kim).

In many cases Protestant churches forbade the use of traditional forms and symbols of worship, including candles, incense, and prostration. (Seung Nam Kim's work on mask dancing attempts to recover traditional Korean theater arts for liturgical application.) An issue faced by both Catholic and Protestant churches has been → ancestor veneration, a factor in China, Japan, Korea, and Viet Nam (P. C. Phan).

For Protestant missionaries, → preaching was prominent in church life, an emphasis that continues to shape Asian Protestant worship (Eun Chul Kim, E. M. Kim).

6.2. The recent history of Asian worship can be studied region by region, for which we now have more resources than ever before (S. W. Park, A. J. Chupungco, S.-J. Joo and K. J. Kim). In February 1987 and February 1991 the Asian Institute for Liturgy and Music, centered in Quezon City, Philippines, hosted an Asian workshop on liturgy and music. This event brought together Asian church musicians and pastors, who shared in joint worship and table fellowship (both → Eucharist and daily meals) and in examining the worship resources in each country. The workshop was hosted by I-to Loh and the → World Council of Churches, who were interested in gathering authentic expressions of music and prayer from each cultural group in Asia. These workshops led to the publication of *Sound the Bamboo*. (See also studies by Swee Hong Lim and I. P. Chun.)

Another regional gathering was the Institute for the Study of Religion and Theology, held in August 1989 at Sogang University, a Jesuit institution in Seoul. The study text from this gathering appeared in *Ritual Meals and the Eucharist,* published by the institute for the 44th International Eucharistic Congress, held in Seoul in October 1989. The congress discussed the communion aspect of Korean meal rituals. The Eucharist, with its elements of fellowship, is like many other religious practices that share the life in food. Asian philosophy, as well as religious symbols generally, includes many other attempts to define the holy with respect to God and humankind (Kee-Yeon Cho).

In their rich symbolism, → baptism and the Eucharist cry out for a greater inculturation of the powerful symbols existing in the Asian context. In Christian worship, more attention is needed on the → sacraments, along with the gestures and movements of public worship, as well as the theological interpretation of each (Soon Whan Kim, Ho Nam).

The *Korean Hymnal* (1983) was published as an ecumenical effort, seeking to embrace and serve an estimated 10 million Protestants in Korea. A new edition (2006) is now in print, but copyright disputes among the affiliated denominations have so far hindered distribution (P. Huh; see also the Methodist and Presbyterian versions of *Come, Let Us Worship*).

Churches in Asia value ecumenical direction, even as they are much affected by globalization, which promotes the increased use of English and the adoption of Western values. Local churches, however, also tend to resist change as strongly as ever, leaving open the question of how progress will be made (Deok-Weon Ahn).

Bibliography: Hymnals: Alleluia Aotearoa: Hymns and Songs for All Churches (ed. J. Murray; Christchurch, N.Z., 1993) • *CCA Hymnal* (ed. D. T. Niles; Kyōto, 1964) • *Come, Let Us Worship: Korean-English Presbyterian Hymnal and Service Book* (ed. P. Huh; Louisville, Ky., 2001) • *Come, Let Us Worship: Korean-English United Methodist Hymnal* (ed. D. Won; Nashville, 2001) • *Hymns from the Four Winds* (ed. I-to Loh; Nashville, 1983) • *Liturgical Music II* (ed. I-to Loh; Tainan, Taiwan, 1984) • *New Songs of Asian Cities* (2d ed.; ed. I-to Loh; Tainan, 1973) • *Sound the Bamboo: CCA Hymnal 2000* (ed. I-to Loh; Hong Kong, 2000).

Dissertations and other studies: Deok-Weon Ahn, "Ecumenism, Inculturation, and Postcolonialism in Liturgy, Based on the Responses of the Younger Churches to 'Baptism, Eucharist, and Ministry' (BEM)" (Diss., Drew University, 2004) • Kee-Yeon Cho, "Worship as a Cosmic Event of Communion and Union: Christian Worship from an East Asian Perspective" (Diss., Drew University, 1996) • I. P. Chun, *Asian Music Studies* (Seoul, 2001) • A. J. Chupungco, "Mission and Inculturation: East Asia and the Pacific," *The Oxford History of Christian Worship* (ed. G. Wainwright and K. B. Westerfield Tucker; New York, 2006) 661-77 • P. Huh, "Creating Bilingual Worship Services in Korean and English," *Call to Worship* 37/4 (2003-4) • S.-J. Joo and K. J. Kim, "The Reformed Tradition in Korea," *Oxford History of Christian Worship,* ed. Wainwright and Westerfield Tucker, 484-91 • Eun Chul Kim, "Preaching in the Korean Protestant Church (1884-1945): A Study in Light of John Calvin's Understanding of Word and Sacrament" (Diss., Drew University, 2001) • E. M. Kim, *Preaching the Presence of God: A Homiletic from an Asian-American Perspective* (Valley Forge, Pa., 1999) • Kyeong Jin Kim, "The Formation of Presbyterian Worship in Korea: A Historical and Theological Study of Early Korean Presbyterian Worship, 1879-1934" (Diss., Boston University, 1999) • Seung Nam Kim, "Contribution of Korean Traditional Theater to Liturgical Expression" (Diss., School of Theology at Claremont, 1992) • Soon-Whan Kim, "The Symbolic Dimensions in the Korean Protestant Worship and Its Relationship with the Inculturation of the Eucharistic Elements" (Diss., Drew University, 1996) • Swee Hong Lim, "Giving Voice to Asian Christians: An Appraisal of the Pioneering Work of I-to Loh in the Area of Congregational Song" (Diss., Drew University, 2006) • Ho Nam, "Liturgical Inculturation in the Marriage and the Funeral Rites of Korean Protestants" (Diss., Drew University, 1999) • *The Oxford History of Christian Worship* (ed. G. Wainwright and K. B. Westerfield Tucker; New York, 2006) • Hae Jung Park, "Understandings of the Lord's Supper in the Methodist Churches in Korea, 1885-1935" (Diss., Drew University, 2004) • S. W. Park, *Report from Asia,* special issue of *Reformed Liturgy and Music* (Louisville, Ky., 1995) • P. C. Phan, "Culture and Liturgy: Ancestor Veneration as a Test Case," *Worship* 76 (2002) 403-30 • S. Sunquist, *A Dictionary of Asian Christianity* (Grand Rapids, 2001).

Paul Junggap Huh

7. Latin America

Pre-Tridentine and Tridentine Roman Catholic worship, adapted to the realities of the New World, predominated in Latin America for more than three centuries, beginning with the invasion by Spain and Portugal in the 15th century. During this period there were only rare incursions of Protestant worship.

In 1555 Calvinist immigrants from France established themselves in Guanabara Bay, to the east of Rio de Janeiro. Internal theological differences, however, brought the project to an end a few years later. Between 1612 and 1615 French Calvinists made other attempts to begin settlements in Latin America, this time in São Luís do Maranhão, Brazil, as well as in Haiti, in Guadeloupe, in Martinique, and in the French Guyana. And then in 1624 Dutch Calvinists disembarked in northeast Brazil, in Bahia, where they were eventually suppressed by the Catholic hegemony. → Calvinists persisted with their worship on some islands of the Caribbean and in Suriname.

Only in the 19th century was the hegemony of Catholic worship broken by the coming of English and German immigrants to Latin America, especially Anglicans, Lutherans, and Reformed. In the latter half of the 19th century a second type of Protestant worship arrived in Latin America. Coming mostly from U.S. → missionaries, it included worship by Methodists, Presbyterians, Episcopalians, Congregationalists, and Baptists. Another significant event in the 20th century was the advent of → Pentecostalism and neo-Pentecostalism.

Latin American worship is therefore an extremely complex subject. The various traditions vary widely from each other and in general began on the continent with a mentality of opposing all other Christian worship traditions present, and especially the Roman Catholic (C. J. Hahn, "Observações," 45-46). Furthermore, we lack any comprehensive study of Latin American Christian → liturgy, which should include an analysis of new, emerging liturgical practices and a search for the roots of the current stagnation in liturgical renewal.

7.1. *Roman Catholicism*

Roman Catholic worship was brought to the Latin American continent as part of the Iberian program of conquest and colonization. In this program the royal and the papal power, the patronage regime, was a single force. With rare exceptions, the Europeans made no effort to include indigenous religious expression in Catholic worship. Where clergy were not present, however, grassroots Catholic worship services and devotional expressions developed that were extremely syncretistic and in clear opposition to the Romanized Catholic worship. These new forms arose either as a form of resistance or simply as a way of expressing basic religious devotion.

Only with the Second → Vatican Council (1962-65), which sanctioned what had already been developing in the so-called → liturgical movement, was space opened up for Latin American forms in the official Roman Catholic worship. The inculturation included local language, music, symbols, and other native cultural expressions. The opening to this reality culminated with the Conferência Episcopal Latino-americana (CELAM, → Latin American Council of Bishops), in their meetings at Medellín, Colombia (1968), and Puebla, Mexico (1979; → Latin American Councils 2.4-5), and with the birth of → liberation theology and its project of ecclesial → base communities. Liturgy came to be seen as "the announcement of liberation," as well as "the denouncement of death in all of its forms: oppression, hunger, extreme poverty exploitation and extermination of the poor" (I. Buyst, 73). A very concrete example of this social dimension of liturgy is found in the Central American Masses, especially the Nicaraguan People's Mass (1968), the Nicaraguan Peasant Mass (1975), and the Salvadorean People's Mass (1980; J. M. Vigil and A. Torrellas). This social tendency seems to be dormant currently, giving place to a more Romanized tendency of worship.

7.2. *Historic Protestantism*

7.2.1. *Anglicanism*

Anglican worship was introduced in Jamaica in 1665, and in the Bahamas in 1731 (→ Anglican Communion). With the increase of commerce with the English, strengthened mainly by the Napoleonic wars, Anglicans arrived in practically all the countries of Latin America, but without any missionary interest. "Their grand worship services brought comfort and spiritual encouragement to the many English-speaking businessmen and to their families when they arrived at the ports of Rio, Santos, and Recife, as well as to the growing city of São Paulo" (C. J. Hahn, *História*, 72).

The first Anglican house of worship in Latin America was dedicated in Rio de Janeiro in August 1819. The immigrants brought with them the → Book of Common Prayer from 1549, which by 1861 had been partially translated into Portuguese. A full translation was done in 1893, based primarily on the prayer book of the Episcopal Church in the United States. In Argentina, Paraguay, Bolivia, and Chile, Anglican congregations followed the English Book of Common Prayer.

Now, as in the past, Latin American Anglicanism is based on the Book of Common Prayer. This holding on to liturgical tradition today, however, makes it difficult to have an Anglican renewal and a dialogue with the local cultures. The Anglicans in Latin America experienced nothing like Henry VIII's break with Rome, which led to the rise of a new prayer book stemming from the work of Thomas → Cranmer and his collaborators with regard to the medieval liturgical books. In Latin America, though, we have not seen contextualization but transplantation — in fact, an "acritical transplant" (J. Maraschin, 52).

7.2.2. Lutheranism, Calvinism, and United Churches

The Lutheran, Calvinist, and United congregations in Latin America emerged in the 19th century with the arrival of German-speaking immigrants from Germany, Austria, Switzerland, and the Volga region in Russia. They settled mainly in Brazil, Argentina, Chile, Uruguay, and Paraguay. Because of the denominational diversity of their origins, they adopted the name "evangelical" to identify themselves in their new places. The differences among them are reflected in their respective manners of worship and in the specific details of the various calendars, catechisms, hymnals, vestments, and liturgical symbols.

The United Church of Prussia strongly influenced many Latin American churches, sending pastors and resources to emerging congregations in Brazil (the Evangelical Church of Lutheran Confession in Brazil, IECLB, begun in 1823); in Argentina, Uruguay, and Paraguay (the Evangelical Church of the River Plate, IERP, begun in Argentina in 1843); and in Chile (the Evangelical Lutheran Church of Chile, IELCH, begun in 1846). In the IECLB and in the IERP, the Prussian calendar (the Kirchenagenda für die Hof- und Domkirche in Berlin) of 1822 was officially adopted, translated into Portuguese in 1930 and into Spanish in 1979. In the Spanish-speaking countries the book *Culto Cristiano* (Christian worship) was produced in 1964, with orders of worship, prayers, psalms, and hymns. This book has come to be used in practically all Lutheran congregations on the continent.

Lutherans from the U.S. Missouri Synod have been present on the continent since 1900. In some countries (Cuba, Mexico, El Salvador, and Panama), they came through missionary efforts (→ North American Missions). In others (Guatemala, Venezuela, Chile, Uruguay, Paraguay, Argentina, and Brazil) they established themselves in the crisis situations of already existing German congregations, especially during the World War II era. Their worship

is characterized by strict confessionality and an adaptation of the Missouri Synod liturgy.

The transplant process of liturgy and hymns of these churches has begun to break down more recently with a process of liturgical renewal, materialized primarily in the *Livro de culto* (Book of worship, 2003) of the IECLB and in the *Pequeño manual de liturgia* (Small liturgy manual, 2000) of the IERP. The worship service has come to be understood as the place where God meets his community, and as a consequence this worship reflects the reality and the culture of this community. Worship also is *anamnese,* or the retelling of the salvation story. Christian worship ritualizes the past and anticipates the future in the present of God's history.

The biblical and historical perspective, as well as the life experience of the first communities in Latin America, is beginning to have fundamental importance in molding the Christian worship service. We thus have the unfolding of a true process of inculturation of the liturgy that takes into account the reality of the people, their time and their place, their human, psychological, social, and cultural needs in the face of God's "project," the gospel of Jesus Christ, celebrated in the worship of the church. The Latin American Lutheran Consultation on Liturgy, meeting in 1986 in Caracas, Venezuela, made an important contribution to this trajectory. In addition, the studies of the → Lutheran World Federation on worship and → culture have contributed much to liturgical renewal and its inculturation (S. A. Stauffer).

7.3. Mission Protestantism

7.3.1. Congregationalism

Congregationalists established themselves in Jamaica in 1837, in Brazil in 1855, and later in other countries (→ Congregationalism). In Brazil a Congregationalist church was established in 1858 by Robert Reid Kalley (1809-88), an independent Scottish medical missionary. They remained Calvinist and Presbyterian in their doctrine but maintained the independence of each local church. In liturgy Kalley defended "home worship services," which later, under the leadership of João M. G. dos Santos, took on a Baptist model, without any established liturgical order, which in a certain way came to be the dominant pattern of the evangelical worship of the mission churches on the continent. The home worship came to include Sunday schools, a clear expression of a lay church and a great contribution to worship in this context.

Another important contribution were the hymns written by Kalley's wife Sarah Poulton Kalley (1825-1907). Henriqueta Rosa Fernandes Braga became

Sarah Kalley's successor in the development of music in the Congregational Church. The hymns are characterized by their revival content and individualistic spirituality.

7.3.2. Presbyterianism

Presbyterian missions came from the United States to Jamaica in 1800, to Colombia in 1856, to Brazil in 1859, to Mexico in 1872, to Guatemala in 1882, and to Trinidad in 1886. The worship became characterized by liturgical improvisation, similar to Kalley's home worship.

The first Synod of the Presbyterian Church, which met in 1888, adopted an amended form of the Guide for Public Worship from Westminster as the official document of the church. The first serious liturgical problem that confronted the Presbyterian mission in Brazil concerned the practice of rebaptism of those converted from Roman Catholicism. The controversy led to a schism of the church in 1903 in Rio de Janeiro, out of which emerged the Independent Presbyterian Church.

7.3.3. Methodism

The work of the mission of the Methodist Church began in Antigua in 1760, in Jamaica in 1789, in Trinidad in 1809, in Argentina and Uruguay in 1867, in Mexico in 1873, in Peru in 1888, and toward the end of the 19th century in Costa Rica, Panama, and Bolivia. The Methodist Church in Brazil emerged from the missionary work of J. J. Ransom in 1876, among lay groups who were reading the Bible on their own. Ransom prepared the book *O culto dominical* (Sunday worship, 1978) for these groups based on the liturgical proposals of John → Wesley (1703-91) and the Book of Common Prayer. Just as in the United States, so in Brazil the Methodist Church developed with evidence of its Anglican and → Puritan ancestors. Ransom's book gave place to the canons of the Methodist Church of Brazil (1950), in which 2 of its 239 pages are dedicated to public worship. The liturgy of the → Eucharist and → baptism carefully follows the Methodist ritual of North America.

In 1962 the *Hinário evangélico com antífonas e orações* (Evangelical hymnal with antiphons and prayers) was published by the Evangelical Confederation of Brazil, with a new edition published in 1964 that contained instructions for the worship service. Worship is a duty imposed by the conscience of the human being and by the Scriptures, and it is a moment of learning and witness. At present, the Methodist Church in Latin America is seeking to grasp more fully the reality of the context of its churches and to engage more deeply in discussions of this topic with other → denominations.

7.3.4. Baptists

→ Baptists first appeared in Jamaica in 1814, in Brazil in 1881, and in Bolivia in 1898. Baptist worship, similar to the Presbyterian, is marked by more spontaneity. In 1926 in Brazil they published the first *Manual das igrejas* (Manual of the churches). They have also published song books such as *Cantor cristão* (Christian singer, 1924) and *Hinário para o culto cristão* (Hymnal for Christian worship, 1991). According to the *Manual,* any local group of believers can construct a church and elect their pastor, and baptism is the public profession of faith of the believer. This model has spread through various new evangelical churches on the continent.

7.4. Pentecostalism

Pentecostal worship in Latin America emerged within the active mission congregations on the continent, often as a protest against the institutional control of the missionary work or because of tension between the different economic classes, or tension between rationalism and emotionalism (H.-J. Prien, 823). Pentecostal worship is also a result of the missionary movement coming from the United States, which has had great numerical success. The liturgical expression of Pentecostalism is very pertinent to the present and deserves fuller study.

Pentecostal worship has influenced all other forms of Protestant and Catholic worship in Latin America. This influence is evident especially in the neo-Pentecostalism of the Igreja Universal do Reino de Deus (the Universal Church of the Kingdom of God), a fast-growing group that in 2006 had 6 million followers in Brazil and congregations in 114 other countries (L. S. Campos). Pentecostal worship has deeply incorporated the impoverished strata of the population of the continent, and it contributes liturgically by giving value to feelings, bodily movement, and the ritual enactment of health. Overall, it is a truly indigenous expression of → Protestantism in Latin America.

7.5. Current Issues

The denominational and liturgical diversity on the Latin American continent is a key factor that has so far largely hindered the development of → ecumenical dialogue. Such dialogue should aim to formulate a → contextual theology that elaborates an authentically Latin American liturgy and worship. One could therefore say that the most relevant issues for worship are contextualization and liturgical renewal, the missionary dimension and the social commitment of liturgy, ecumenical dialogue itself, and the interchange of experiences and the elements and forms of worship.

Important initial steps in ecumenical dialogue

include the work of the Rede Latino-Americana de Liturgia (Latin American liturgy network) and of the Conselho Latino-Americano de Igrejas (CLAI, → Latin American Council of Churches), through the encounters, workshops, bulletins, and Internet resources it sponsors. At the academic level, meetings in São Leopoldo, Brazil, in October 2006 of the Comunidade de Educação Teológica Ecumênica Latino-Americana e Caribenha (CETELA, Latin American and Caribbean ecumenical community of → theological education) included a liturgy seminar with the title "Liturgy and Pastoral Work."

Liturgical renewal is occurring mostly in the adaptation of some of specific elements, mainly hymns, and it is still very dependent on the traditions of the countries of origin. In the effort to differentiate oneself from the Roman Catholic liturgy, Latin American Protestant writers often fail to consider elements from the tradition of the primitive church and even from the biblical tradition, which could provide an authentic basis for a healthy liturgical renewal in the Latin American context. The practices of popular religiosity, present throughout the Latin culture (→ Popular Catholicism), especially elements proceeding from the indigenous and African cultures, are still generally considered profane and pagan and needing to be combated and exterminated (M. de Barros Souza, 97-108; Buyst, 65-67; Prien, 809-48). In contrast, charismaticism — which is essentially antiliturgical, extremely individualistic, and patterned according to the models of the First World — grows rapidly and is influencing all Christian denominations (→ Charismatic Movement; Charismatic Religion).

Within the aspect of contextualization and liturgical renewal, it is increasingly necessary that worship respond to the reality of Latin American cities and metropolises, for worship to a great extent still reflects an agrarian and peasant reality. The reality of the → youth, the means of → communication that they have dominion over, the use of images, bodily movements, music, and rhythms — all these are factors that the celebrations of popular religiosity and the Pentecostal movements have in some way contributed to. It is vital for renewal and contextualization to abandon clericalism and to invest in the work of liturgical teams so as to return worship to the community.

Music is doubtless the element that has developed the most, reflecting the contents relevant to the context, as well as the authentically Latin American rhythms, sounds, styles, and instruments. If liturgy as a whole can integrate reality like music has, we Latin Americans will indeed be on the way to a

worship that is more committed to our culture, our social problems, and our confessional differences. We will be, in fact, developing a liturgy that contextualizes, in the present, the greatness of Christ's work.

Bibliography: M. de Barros Souza, *Celebrar o Deus da vida. Tradição litúrgica e inculturação* (São Paulo, 1992) • I. Buyst, *Como estudar liturgia. Princípios de ciência litúrgica* (2d ed.; São Paulo, 1990) • L. S. Campos, *Teatro, templo e mercado. Organização e marketing de um empreendimento neopentecostal* (2d ed.; Petrópolis, 1999) • E. L. Cleary, "The Transformation of Latin American Christianity, c. 1950-2000," *The Cambridge History of Christianity,* vol. 9, *World Christianities c. 1914-c. 2000* (ed. H. McLeod; Cambridge, 2006) 366-84 • H. R. Fernandes Braga, *Música sacra evangélica no Brasil. Contribuição à sua história* (Rio de Janeiro, 1961) • C. J. Hahn, *História do culto protestante no Brasil* (São Paulo, 1989); idem, "Observações sobre os cultos evangélicos no Brasil," *Simpósio* (São Paulo) 11 (1973) 44-48 • N. Kirst, "Liturgia," *Teologia prática. No contexto da América Latina* (ed. C. Schneider Harpprecht; São Leopoldo, 1998) 119-42; idem, ed., *Coleção Miriã 1. Cantos litúrgicos da América Latina* (São Leopoldo, 2001) • J. Maraschin, *A beleza da santidade. Ensaios de liturgia* (São Paulo, 1996) • R. R. Martini, *Livro de culto* (São Leopoldo, 2003) • S. de Barros Monteiro, *O cântico da vida. Análise de conceitos fundamentais nos cânticos da Igreja Evangélicas no Brasil* (São Bernardo do Campo, 1991) • H.-J. Prien, *La historia del cristianismo en América Latina* (Salamanca, Sp., 1985) • P. Sosa, ed., *Todas las voces* (San José, C.R., 1988) • S. A. Stauffer, ed., *Baptism, Rites of Passage, and Culture* (Geneva, 1999) • U. Teixeira, "Liturgia Metodista em América Latina," *La tradición protestante en la teología latinoamericana* (ed. J. Duque; San José, C.R., 1983) 287-302 • S. Tesche, *Vestes litúrgicas. Elementos de prodigalidade ou dominação?* (São Leopoldo, 1995) • J. M. Vigil and A. Torrellas, eds., *Misas centroamericanas. Transcripción y comentario teológico* (Managua, Nicaragua, 1988) • W. Wachholz, "Mainline Protestants in Latin America," *The Oxford History of Christian Worship* (ed. G. Wainwright and K. Westerfield Tucker; New York, 2006) 651-60.

Júlio Cézar Adam

8. United States and Canada
8.1. *Worship in American and Canadian Society*

Christian worship entered the New World via the devotions of European explorers in the 16th century and then, in the century following, by the liturgical practices of → clergy and devout laity in

Roman Catholic, Anglican, Dutch Reformed, and Puritan/Congregational settlements. Immigrant Christians to the United States and Canada still bring with them their → prayers and → customs for worship in the 21st century, some of which bear the marks of North American and European → missionaries, while others show signs of indigenous development in the country of origin. The kaleidoscope of Christian worship in North America ever changes with the influx of foreign believers, as well as with theological, liturgical, and cultural shifts introduced from within and outside the continent. More than 200 distinct ecclesiastical groups may be identified in the United States and Canada (and certain bodies are found in both countries); they are generally of Orthodox, Catholic, Anglican, Lutheran, Reformed, Methodist, Baptist, Anabaptist, Pentecostal, and Independent types. At one extreme the worship practices of a particular group may be relatively stable and largely uniform; at the other, there may be a wide range of diversity within a single denomination.

Christianity played a significant role in the founding and growth of the United States and Canada, with bodies in the latter more willing to keep ecclesiastical ties with the countries of origin — and, consequently, with the worship of the → Book of Common Prayer of the Church of England and the rites of French Roman Catholicism. In the United States, founded in the spirit of liberty and dissent, worship practices were sometimes new experiments or variations upon established older patterns. In different times and to different degrees, the expression of the Christian faith in community worship and private devotion was an important component of the social fabric of these two nations. For a time, laws prohibited labor or commerce on → Sunday, the principal day of Christian worship: the social expectation in these "Christian nations" was that persons would attend worship in the church of their choice on Sunday morning. Respect for non-Christian religions and growing → secularism in both countries eventually led to the removal of Sunday restrictions. Nevertheless, by the first decade of the 21st century, approximately one-quarter of Christians in the United States regularly attend worship; roughly another quarter identify themselves as attenders but are not as scrupulous in their attendance. The percentages are reduced for Christians in Canada. When compared to worship attendance in the late 19th century, these numbers are small, yet they exceed attendance in western Europe, though lag behind when set against Asia and Africa, where the churches are growing.

8.2. *Historical Developments*
8.2.1. *Sixteenth and Seventeenth Centuries*

Liturgical practices brought from the land of origin were transplanted into, but also sometimes adapted to, the new environment. Roman Catholic missionaries, Spanish in the region of the Rio Grande in the south and French around Quebec in the north, maintained familiar Latin formularies and customs for their respective European constituencies. Occasionally, with approval or not, they conflated Christian observances with native religious traditions (e.g., ceremonies related to the yearly cycle) and made innovative substitutions when usual supplies were unavailable. Because the Anglican Book of Common Prayer presupposed a geographically limited parish system, adjustments were sometimes required in remote settings for the rites of → baptism, the churching of women, and the burial of the dead (→ Funeral). The absence of a resident Anglican bishop in North America made episcopally administered → confirmations and → ordinations impossible, which led in 1789 to the creation of a distinct prayer book for the Protestant Episcopal Church in the newly independent United States.

Instead of liturgical formularies or prayer books, English Puritans in the New England colonies preferred their worship to follow what they perceived as divine directives in the Bible and called their gathering space a "meetinghouse," since the assembly was the "church." While all adhered to the divine decree of keeping Sabbath, each congregation had the freedom to order its own worship. The regular Sunday service usually consisted of long-familiar components, namely, prayer, the reading of Scripture, and psalm singing (scripturally supplied texts), along with biblical exposition, exhortation, and → preaching; the Lord's Supper was observed infrequently (→ Eucharist). Some Christians in New England found certain → Puritan practices, such as infant baptism, unscriptural and joined with immigrant Baptists in beginning new settlements in which only professing believers were baptized and worship focused simply on prayer and the reading and exposition of Scripture.

Other immigrant clergy and laity also brought their accustomed texts, songbooks, and practices for worship. French, Dutch, and German Reformed used orders inspired directly or indirectly by John → Calvin's (1509-64) *La forme des prières et des chants ecclésiastiques* (1542). Irish, English, and Scottish Reformed worship showed the influence of John → Knox's (ca. 1513-72) *Forme of Prayers* (1556) and the instructions in the Westminster Directory for Public Worship (1642). Reformed metrical psalters in various versions and languages crossed the Atlantic with their owners. Lutherans from Germany and Scandinavia retained for worship their regional resources, including → hymnals (→ Hymnody).

8.2.2. *Eighteenth Century*

Immigrant worship practices continued to be introduced throughout the 18th century, but also during this time new forms emerged on North American soil, many of which were influenced by the European movements of → Pietism, → rationalism, and liturgical orthodoxy. The primacy of Scripture, the expression of fervent faith, and spiritual accountability both personal and corporate were characteristics of Pietism that were brought to bear on worship and fueled the two Great Awakenings. Rationalism, with its focus on reason and the intellect, saw worship principally in terms of learning and edification. Liturgical orthodoxy sought to preserve or restore a denomination's rites and liturgical/sacramental theology of generations past. All three movements contributed to the interest in lively and edifying preaching as the focus of worship, including both the evangelical sermons of a George → Whitefield (1714-70) and the reasoned and impassioned discourses of → Unitarians.

New resources produced within the American colonies included a hymnbook for private and social (but not liturgical) use entitled *Collection of Psalms and Hymns,* which was brought out in 1737 for the Anglican community in Georgia by John → Wesley (1703-91), a priest of the Church of England and eventual leader of the Methodist movement. In 1784 Wesley published an abridgement of the 1662 Book of Common Prayer called *The Sunday Service of the Methodists in North America;* also in 1784 the Methodist Episcopal Church came into being. A large part of Wesley's book, however, was soon laid aside, given the Methodist preference to "pray with the eyes closed." Henry Melchior Muhlenberg (1711-87) drew upon older materials in the creation of a Lutheran *Agende* (worship book) and hymnals that appeared in German- and English-language versions. The Lutheran Ministerium of Pennsylvania in 1748 approved Muhlenberg's *Agende* for use, but the text was never printed, being circulated only in handwritten copies until a published revision appeared in 1786. Among the Reformed, the Dutch Reformed Church in New York in 1767 issued English versions of prayers and selected rites from their inherited liturgy, while the Presbyterian Church in the United States authorized a Directory for Worship in 1788 that contained suggestions and models for prayers and services rather than explicit liturgical texts.

Worship practices were also employed that did not need written texts. Love feasts, inspired by the ancient Christian agape meal and consisting of prayer, song, testimonies, the sharing of simple food and drink, and the collection of alms, were taken up by the → Moravians and then by Methodists. Preaching and prayer services in the open air and in frontier regions required the "lining out" of hymns and psalms so that all could participate. The secret worship of slaves in "hush arbors" included the rhythms of speech, sequences of "call and response," and the spontaneity of song and physical movement that connected them with their roots in Africa.

8.2.3. *Nineteenth Century*

The Second Great Awakening, at the turn into the 19th century, gave rise to the days-long, residential, and outdoor camp meeting, for which the expected result of the several services of preaching, prayer, and song was the conversion of unbelievers and the recommitment of lukewarm believers. In urban settings the worship style of the camp took place as protracted meetings or revivals. Worship was planned and measured according to its effectiveness in yielding warmed hearts, a liturgical pragmatism that influenced the shape of worship for numerous Protestant groups for generations: "preliminaries" would be followed by the centerpiece sermon and a call for commitment. Liturgical space for these communities focused upon the pulpit.

While Methodists, Baptists, and independent groups utilized the methods of revivalistic worship — with a normative Sunday practice of prayer, Scripture reading, preaching, singing, and only an occasional celebration of Holy Communion — other groups sought to recover older texts and practices. The Oxford (Tractarian) and Cambridge movements within the Church of England had an effect upon Anglican liturgical and sacramental theology, church architecture, ceremonial, and music in North America. Historical and theological studies of the Reformed liturgy by the German Reformed John Williamson Nevin (1803-86) and the Presbyterian Charles Baird (1828-87) contributed to the creation of the controversial yet influential "Mercersburg Liturgy." Lutherans drew upon Reformation and pre-Reformation liturgical texts, as well as older forms of rendering German chorales, in their efforts of revision; the "Common Service" of 1888 was a product of this endeavor. By the end of the 19th century, even some of the so-called → free churches were looking to their liturgical past to shape their worship. Simple revivalistic patterns became more complex as orders of worship expanded to include the responsive reading of the Psalms, creeds or affirmations of faith, and the use of church choirs. The African Methodist Episcopal Church's authorized structure for worship in the late 19th century shows this move toward complexity, while its long-established preferences in preaching and music styles were maintained. Local congregations within these "free" groups often fiercely defended their liberty to conduct worship as conscience and preference dictated.

Some changes in worship practice in the late 19th century were the direct result of technological advances. The slowing or curtailing of the process of fermentation addressed concerns about temperance present in many churches and resulted in the substitution of the "unfermented juice of the grape" for Communion wine. The discovery of germs as a source of contagion prompted some denominations to serve their grape juice in individual cups rather than in the customary single common cup. The development of the mimeograph, an inexpensive process to duplicate paper copies, gave pastors and worship leaders the capability to print their own orders of service.

8.2.4. *Twentieth Century*
The largely European ecumenical and liturgical movements begun in the 19th century influenced North American worship in the 20th. In 1908 the Federal Council of Churches of Christ in America was founded, and although Roman Catholics and Orthodox did not participate, there was involvement by representative Baptists, Episcopalians, Lutherans, Methodists, and Reformed, as well as by smaller groups such as the Society of Friends. The Committee on Worship of the Federal Council was instrumental in encouraging serious reflection on worship practices within and across those bodies, and in 1937 it published *The Christian Year* as a means of introducing the Christian calendar to congregations unfamiliar with it (→ Church Year). Intentionally ecumenical worship books were produced during the 1930s as a result of the council's work, and a denomination's new resources for worship were often compiled after consultation with the leaders and books of other Christian groups.

For Roman Catholics in the United States, the → liturgical movement largely had its base at St. John's Abbey in Collegeville, Minnesota, under the initial leadership of the monk Virgil Michel (1890-1938), who, during the 1920s and 1930s, urged the renewal of the liturgy through recognition of the inseparability of worship and social justice. By the 1940s American Protestants were aware of Roman Catholic interest in reform (as well as of some unauthorized experiments) and were engaged in renewal of

their own; for example, the Episcopal Church's Associated Parishes for Liturgy and Mission and the Methodist Church's Order of St. Luke were both founded in 1946 and were committed to the informed and more frequent observance of the → Eucharist.

Liturgical revision in the aftermath of the Second → Vatican Council (1962-65) reached far beyond the → Roman Catholic Church. In the climate of reinvestigation and recovery of the practices of Christian antiquity, new Protestant liturgical texts and worship books were developed that shared commonalities in structure and content with their Catholic counterparts, though these have not always replaced the previous worship practices of a congregation. Since Canada and the United States could no longer be identified as Christian nations, of particular concern were processes and rites for Christian formation and initiation. The comprehensive Roman Catholic Rite of Christian Initiation of Adults inspired the production of comparable resources in certain Protestant groups, including the → Mennonite Church in both nations.

Despite the liturgical ferment in the late 20th century, worship within some churches remained relatively unchanged from prior generations but often with a single exception: the introduction of new styles of music with Christian texts and, to accompany them, musical instruments not previously utilized. Once forbidden from worship as "secular" musical forms, and not without ongoing controversy, gospel, blues, jazz, folk, rock, and rap styles made their way in different times and places into the worship space. While the liturgical movement generated an approach to worship that drew upon ancient liturgical practices, the underground folk mass of the 1960s in many respects laid the groundwork for the culturally attentive and music-driven "contemporary worship" that also crossed ecclesiastical boundaries in the late 20th century. Typified by prayer, preaching, and praise-band-accompanied "sets" of songs sung more often by select singers than the congregation, practices of "contemporary worship" perhaps are an unconscious recovery of the worship design of 19th-century revivalism.

8.3. *New Developments*
The 21st century has witnessed the continuation and ongoing development of the previous century's worship renewal, including, in addition to so-called contemporary worship (with the substyles of "praise and worship" and "blended worship") and the products of the liturgical movement, approaches to worship arising out of the → feminist and liberation movements (with concerns for lan-

guage and issues of leadership and participation) and the global Christian music movement. In reaction to the renewal, there have been efforts to recover past forms. For example, although the Tridentine Mass never fully disappeared in North America, its frequency of celebration appears to be on the increase. A compromise with such stylistic diversity (and controversy) may be found in the "emerging worship" movement, which urges both faithfulness toward church traditions and respect for the local context, attention to ecumenicity and multiculturalism, and use of a variety of art forms, as well as electronic technologies.

Bibliography: J. ABBINGTON, ed., *Readings in African American Church Music and Worship* (Chicago, 2001) • K. BLACK, *Worship across Cultures: A Handbook* (Nashville, 1998) • W. R. BLOTT, *Blessing and Glory and Thanksgiving: The Growth of a Canadian Liturgy* (Toronto, 1998) • M. W. COSTEN, *African American Christian Worship* (Nashville, 1993) • H. DAVIES, *Worship of the American Puritans, 1629-1730* (New York, 1990; repr., Morgan, Pa., 1999) • T. HARDING and B. HARDING, *Patterns of Worship in the United Church of Canada, 1925-1960* (Toronto, 1995) • M. J. HATCHETT, *Commentary on the American Prayer Book* (New York, 1981; repr., San Francisco, 1995) • A. C. LOVELAND and O. B. WHEELER, *From Meetinghouse to Megachurch* (Columbia, Mo., 2003) • J. MELTON, *Presbyterian Worship in America: Changing Patterns since 1787* (Richmond, Va., 1967; repr., Eugene, Oreg., 2001) • K. F. PECKLERS, *The Unread Vision: The Liturgical Movement in the United States of America, 1926-1955* (Collegeville, Minn., 1998) • M. PROCTER-SMITH and J. R. WALTON, eds., *Women at Worship: Interpretations of North American Diversity* (Louisville, Ky., 1993) • R. W. QUERE, *In the Context of Unity: A History of the Development of the Lutheran Book of Worship* (Minneapolis, 2003) • L. D. REED, *The Lutheran Liturgy* (rev. ed.; Philadelphia, 1947; repr., 1959) • K. B. WESTERFIELD TUCKER, *American Methodist Worship* (New York, 2001) • J. F. WHITE, *Christian Worship in North America, a Retrospective: 1955-1995* (Collegeville, Minn., 1997).

KAREN WESTERFIELD TUCKER

Wrath of God

1. OT

1.1. Using anthropomorphic or anthropopathic language, many religions described their gods in human terms; they could thus see them as wrathful. Fear of divine wrath was undoubtedly one of the main motivations behind the development of → religion and also of the cult. Israel was close to its neighbors in this regard, as may be seen from an inscription of King Mesha of Moab (mid-9th cent. B.C.), who, speaking of the long-standing oppression of Moab by King Omri of → Israel (§1.5), attributes it to the wrath of Chemosh, the Moabite god (*KAI* 181.5; *TUAT* 1.647; cf. 2 Kgs. 3:27).

1.2. Mention of the wrath of God is characteristic of the OT, which refers three times more often to divine wrath than to human wrath. The terminology used is quite varied. As nouns we find *'ap* (strictly "nose, nostrils"), *ḥārôn* ("burning"; *ḥărôn 'ap*, "blazing anger"), *ḥēmâ* ("heat"), *zā'am* ("cursing, denunciation"), *qeṣep, 'ebrâ* ("excess, surge"), and *za'ap* ("rage"). Verbs are *ḥrh* ("break out, be kindled," with *'ap*), *'np* (from *'ap*), and *qṣp*. Accumulation of terms may be found, as in Deut. 29:28; Isa. 13:9; or Ps. 78:49. The construct state, which links the nouns to the divine name, usually has → Yahweh (e.g., "the wrath of Yahweh"). Nah. 1:2 describes Yahweh as "full of wrath" (ASV).

Images are used to depict the annihilating power of divine wrath. But things like fire and water are not mere images (contra A. Ritschl). The wrath of God "is quickly kindled" (Ps. 2:12), is "fire" (Ezek. 21:31) or "like fire" (Jer. 4:4), and resembles "a fiery furnace" (Ps. 21:9); it is "poured out" (Jer. 7:20) "like water" (Hos. 5:10), is "like an overflowing stream" (Isa. 30:27-28), and is drunk from a cup (Jer. 25:15).

1.3. Israel is the primary object of this wrath. Yahweh calls them "the people of my wrath" (Isa. 10:6), against whom he will bring Assyria, "the rod of my anger — the club in their hands is my fury!" (v. 5). The → prophets of judgment are the messengers of God's wrath (C. Westermann). From the days of Amos onward, they proclaim inevitable destruction with greater or lesser sharpness and single-mindedness.

Individuals, too, can be the objects of divine wrath. It was "kindled" against Job and "has torn" him (Job 19:11; 16:9). By the wrath of God we are "consumed" and "overwhelmed" (Ps. 90:7).

1.4. According to R. Otto (1869-1937), the wrath

of God in the OT "has no concern whatever with moral qualities" but is "the *tremendum* itself, apprehended and expressed by the aid of a naive analogy from the domain of natural experience." Only later did this wrath begin to be "filled in with elements derived from the moral reason: righteousness in requital, and punishment for moral transgression" (pp. 18-19). There is some truth in this view, for basic experiences such as human perishability and the Babylonian exile led to reflection on the motives for divine wrath as it found expression in OT faith. The prophetic message of judgment contained words of scolding as well as words of warning (→ Prophet, Prophecy 2.4). The → Deuteronomistic writings display a schema of judgment. God directs his wrath against the Israelites because of their disobedience and idolatry, in which "they provoked the LORD to anger" (Judg. 2:12).

1.5. According to the OT, Israel can expect only a limited wrath of God. Yahweh is "slow to anger" (Ps. 103:8). He "does not retain his anger forever" (Mic. 7:18); "his anger is but for a moment; his favor is for a lifetime" (Ps. 30:5). Israel may thus expect to return from exile, and Job can hope for restoration. Eschatological expectation awaits an end to "the period of wrath" (Dan. 8:19). → Grace does not precede wrath. Jerusalem must first drink "the cup of his wrath," and then it will be put into "the hand of your tormentors" (Isa. 51:17, 22-23). Assyria is the instrument of Yahweh's anger, but later it will become the object of that same anger (Isa. 10:5-14).

Some scholars think that the older prophets did not expect Yahweh's anger against Israel to cease (→ Prophets, Prophecy 2.3). Later, however, a prophetic call to repentance accompanies the threat of God's wrath (Jer. 4:4; → Penitence). This motif strengthened the development of legal observance (→ Law 1.3; Sin 1).

Bibliography: W. EICHRODT, *Theology of the OT* (vol. 1; Philadelphia, 1961) 258-69 • J. FICHTNER, "Ὀργή κτλ. B: OT," *TDNT* 5.394-409 • T. E. FRETHEIM, "Theological Reflections on the Wrath of God in the OT," *HBT* 24/2 (2002) 1-26 • H. M. HANEY, *The Wrath of God in the Former Prophets* (New York, 1960) • D. J. McCARTHY, "The Wrath of Yahweh and the Structural Unity of the Deuteronomistic History," *Essays in OT Ethics* (ed. J. L. Crenshaw and J. T. Willis; New York, 1974) 97-110 • R. OTTO, *The Idea of the Holy: An Inquiry into the Non-rational Factor in the Idea of the Divine and Its Relation to the Rational* (2d ed.; London, 1957; orig. pub., 1917) • H. G. L. PEELS, *The Vengeance of God: The Meaning of the Root NQM and the Function of the NQM-Texts in the Context of Divine Revelation in the OT* (Leiden, 1995) • R. V. G. TASKER, *The Biblical Doctrine of the Wrath of God* (London, 1951) • C. WESTERMANN, "Boten des Zorns," *Die Botschaft und die Boten* (ed. J. Jeremias and L. Perlitt; Neukirchen, 1981) 147-56 • E. WÜRTHWEIN, *Tradition und Situation. Studien zur alttestamentlichen Prophetie* (Göttingen, 1963) • E. ZENGER, *A God of Vengeance? Understanding the Psalms of Divine Wrath* (Louisville, Ky., 1996).

RUDOLF SMEND

2. NT

To understand the idea of the wrath of God in the NT, we must refer to the preaching of → John the Baptist, to some aspects of the proclamation of → Jesus, to theological discussions in → Paul, and to many passages in Revelation. The usual Greek word is *orgē*, though *thymos* also occurs. In Revelation the two words appear together as synonyms (14:10; 16:19; 19:15).

2.1. *John the Baptist, Jesus*

The wrath of God is a theological, not a psychological, term. It is not an emotion that exercises control over God. Rather, it denotes the No to → sin that is essential to God's holy nature. This concept of the wrath of God necessarily has a forensic aspect, for divine wrath means divine judgment. In the NT the reference is usually to the approaching → last judgment. The wrath of God is an eschatological term.

We see this sense in the preaching of John the Baptist and its reference to "the wrath to come" (Matt. 3:7; Luke 3:7). Jesus speaks indirectly about the wrath of God in the parable of the wedding feast (Matt. 22:7) and in the apocalyptic address of Luke 21 (v. 23). The wrath of God manifests itself in the wrath of Jesus (Mark 3:5).

2.2. *Paul*

Paul uses the term "wrath of God" somewhat differently. It appears in the authentic Pauline epistles only in 1 Thessalonians and in the theological argument of Romans. In 1 Thess. 1:10 he was perhaps adopting the usage of the missionary literature of Hellenistic Judaism (C. Bussmann). In 1 Thess. 2:16 the wrath of God "has overtaken" the Jews, but in 4:13-18 the imminent approach of the last judgment is very plainly expected. An intensive experience of this imminence may be felt here, a true anticipation of eschatological judgment.

The starting point of Paul's words in Romans about the wrath of God is not anticipation. Rather, his concern is with the theology of → justification. The preaching of the → gospel makes manifest the → righteousness of God (*dikaiosynē theou*, 1:17). According to 1:16-17, justification is a free act of God the Judge. By its nature, however, justification is an event of final judgment. It is already a reality for believers, for in it both → future and present (in that order) coincide. In contrast to 1:16-17, however, 1:18 points to the revelation of the wrath of God that finds its present expression in human perversion (→ Sin 2.1). Future and present coincide in both God's wrath and his righteousness. The future is the essential basis of the present. On the pre-Christian level of legal righteousness (not the works righteousness of 3:27-31), the wrath of God punishes those who do not act according to the law's demands. The → law "brings wrath" (4:15). The justified, however, are saved through Christ from the eschatologically imminent judgment of divine wrath (5:9, with the fut. *sōthēsometha*, "we will be saved"). In 9:22 justification and the eschatological destiny of Israel form the background of what is said about wrath.

The deutero-Pauline authors clearly continue this aspect of God's wrath (e.g., in Col. 3:6; Eph. 2:3; 5:6).

2.3. Revelation

In apocalyptic imagery Revelation speaks Christologically of the wrath of the Lamb (6:16), which is the same as the wrath of God (note "the great day of their [*autōn*] wrath," 6:17; see also 19:15). In speaking of the wrath of God, Revelation often uses *thymos* instead of *orgē* (14:10, 19; 15:1, 7; 16:1; 19:15). Reference is also made to the wrath of the → devil (12:12). And 14:8 reports that the great city of Babylon "has made all nations drink of the wine of the wrath of her fornication."

Bibliography: G. Bornkamm, "The Revelation of God's Wrath (Romans 1-3)," *Early Christian Experience* (New York, 1969) 47-70 • R. Bultmann, *Theology of the NT* (vol. 1; New York, 1970) 288-92 • C. Bussmann, *Themen der paulinischen Missionspredigt auf dem Hintergrund der spätjüdisch-hellenistischen Missionsliteratur* (2d ed.; Bern, 1975) • H. Conzelmann, "Zorn Gottes im Judentum und NT," *RGG* (3d ed.) 6.1931-32 • A. T. Hanson, *The Wrath of the Lamb* (London, 1957) • G. Herold, *Zorn und Gerechtigkeit Gottes bei Paulus* (Bern, 1973) • H. W. Hollander, "Θυμός," *EDNT* 2.159-60 • M. Limbeck, *Zürnt Gott wirklich? Fragen an Paulus* (Stuttgart, 2001) • G. H. C. MacGregor, "The Concept of the Wrath of God in the NT," *NTS* 7 (1961) 101-9 • R. Miggelbrink, *Der zornige Gott. Die Bedeutung einer anstößigen biblischen Tradition* (Darmstadt, 2002) • P. R. Raabe, "Drinking the Cup of God's Wrath: A Biblical Metaphor," *Hear the Word of Yahweh* (ed. D. O. Wenthe, P. L. Schrieber, and L. A. Maxwell; St. Louis, 2002) 45-56 • C. J. Roetzel, *Judgement in the Community* (Leiden, 1972) 79-83 • G. Stählin, "Ὀργή κτλ. E: NT," *TDNT* 5.419-47 • R. V. G. Tasker, *The Biblical Doctrine of the Wrath of God* (London, 1951) • M. Theobald, "Zorn Gottes. Ein nicht zu vernachlässigender Aspekt der Theologie des Römerbriefes," *Studien zum Römerbrief* (Tübingen, 2001) 68-100 • D. E. H. Whiteley, *The Theology of St. Paul* (2d ed.; Oxford, 1974) 61-72.

Hans Hübner

3. Systematics

3.1. Task and Problem

Systematics faces both a task and a problem. The biblical witness uses strongly anthropopathic language when it speaks about the wrath of God. Over the centuries, then, Christian theology has had the task of finding adequate expression for what is meant. It has found two places for the doctrine of the wrath of God. The first is → soteriology — more specifically, the doctrine of → sin (hamartiology and → eschatology) as the terminus a quo of redemption. The wrath of God threatens sinners with temporal penalties and eternal death (→ Last Judgment). But the Christ-event gains the mastery over it by converting sinners and drawing them up into the → love of God. God's working is experienced in a situation of the alienation between God and sinners. This background enables us to speak of the wrath of God.

With this framework in mind, the doctrine of the wrath of God belongs, second, to the actual doctrine of God. Here, however, two problems are involved. First, how does the wrath of God relate to the love of God? Second, how does it fit in with a concept of God that cannot attribute to him either irrational passions or changeability?

3.2. History of Dogma

3.2.1. Early in dogmatic history the comparatively naive witness of the Bible to the wrath of God began to be questioned when Christianity came into contact with the philosophical concept of God in Greek culture (→ God 3). Lactantius (d. ca. 325) wrestled with these problems in his monograph *De ira Dei*. On the one hand, he favored positions that would find only positive predicates for God (love, goodness, grace). On the other hand, he could not attribute emotions of any kind to God (2.9–5.15).

In this encounter with the philosophy of antiquity we also may see the Greek antithesis between philosophical → monotheism and → popular religion. This antithesis found expression in Plato (427-347 B.C.; → Platonism) and Aristotle (384-322; → Aristotelianism) when they criticized the religious ideas that had been mediated by the poets (e.g., Aristotle *Meta.* A.983a1ff.).

3.2.2. Marcion (d. ca. 160; → Marcionites) had argued that the concept of divine wrath was incompatible with a Christian view of God. Negatively, he thought, jealous emotions like wrath characterize the creator of the world (the Demiurge) but not the good God who has manifested himself in Christ. Marcion was offended by the negative passions and the mutability that seemed to be ascribed to the biblical God.

In reaction, the church had two answers to this criticism. It argued first that the wrath of God is both rational and moral; it does not conflict with the divine goodness. It is necessary as God's reaction to human sin and is not an irrational passion incompatible with the divine reason and goodness (Lactantius, *De ira Dei* 16.4-5). Second, an attempt was made to fix limits on the wrath of God by viewing it only as an expression of the divine justice. This was the opinion of → Origen (ca. 185-ca. 254; → Origenism), who, like Philo (15-10 B.C.–A.D. 45-50), found in statements about God's wrath an occasion for allegorizing (→ Allegory; Exegesis, Biblical, 2.1.1). Origen conceded that the literal sense could also be instructive for the many who were not capable of spiritual exposition (*De princ.* 4.2.1 and 8; see also 2.4.4). Only allegorical exposition, however, could meet the challenges of → philosophy, which could find no room for negative passions in God. Both these approaches influenced Western theology.

Academic theology, as a consequence, either omitted the wrath of God altogether or equated it with the divine reaction to human sin, that is, with an unemotional retributive justice (→ Anselm; see also Thomas Aquinas, *Summa theol.* I, q. 3, art. 2, ad 2; also q. 20, art. 1, ad 2). But the wrath of God was still a vital element in the preaching of repentance (→ Penitence 1) and in popular → piety. We see once more the antithesis between the theology of the educated and the piety of the populace.

3.3. *Reformation Theology*

In Reformation theology M. → Luther (1483-1546; → Luther's Theology) gave centrality to the wrath of God. Luther's whole theology focuses on the situation that an assault is made by the wrath of God upon sinners. The doctrine of → justification is the answer to this situation. This theology proposes a doctrine of God that is based on the experience of this God in connection with → law and gospel (see "Against the Antinomians," *LW* 47.107-19; WA 50.660.18). This experience is twofold. The assaults of the law mean, first, a self-distancing from God on the part of sinners who oppose him. → Conscience brings home the reality of this distance to sinners (WA 39/1.352.3-6 and 539.6–541.3; 50.471.22-37).

The preaching of the law clarifies this point (WA 39/1.348.25-30).

Second, however, trust and joy result from the preaching of the → gospel, the good news of the self-giving of God in Christ. God is depicted as the author of the assaults against us, but proclamation of his love portrays him as the one who gives us comfort. Theologians should not try to smooth away God's "negative" attributes. They should not adapt the words of the Bible to meet the demand of a moral or metaphysical concept of God (*De servo arbitrio*, ET *On the Bondage of the Will* = *LW* 33). Rather, they should describe the inner movement in God himself.

Luther's theology of the cross (→ Theologia crucis) depicts God as the God of love breaking into the situation occasioned by his wrath. On the cross he lovingly took upon himself this wrath, replacing it by his love. Emotionally, the experience of this situation transcends the doctrine of the wrath of God (WA 39/1.346.9-10). The result is a description of the wrathful God that ignores the challenges of a metaphysical concept, is not afraid of anthropopathic features, and leaves the demonstration of God's goodness to God himself.

U. → Zwingli (1484-1531; → Zwingli's Theology) and J. → Calvin (1509-64; → Calvin's Theology) put much emphasis on divine impassibility (see Calvin *Inst.* 1.17.13, but see also 3.4.31-35). A return to the principles of Aristotelian → metaphysics may also be seen in Lutheran → orthodoxy (§1), which omitted the anthropopathic features in dealing with God's wrath. It saw "wrath" as another term for the justice that necessarily imposes punishment on sinners (e.g., J. Gerhard, *Loci theologici* 26.1.2.33).

→ Enlightenment theology, with a concept of God derived mainly from rational argument, not from God's revelation in Christ, found no place for divine wrath. A theory of accommodation could be employed in expounding the biblical writings. In revelation God adjusts himself to the terms and concepts of the people of the time. Later ages must purify the contents of revelation according to their more advanced ideas.

3.4. *Nineteenth and Twentieth Centuries*

3.4.1. Beginning in the 19th century, theology found various ways of handling God's wrath, but always in ways to limit its scope. It is no longer seen in equilibrium with God's love. It always comes within the context of a divine will that is wholly determined by → grace. F. D. E. → Schleiermacher (1768-1834; → Schleiermacher's Theology) and A. Ritschl (1822-89) totally rejected a doctrine of divine wrath as being morally unworthy. According to them, it is the consciousness of guilt and the feeling of being alienated from God that establishes a link between sin and evil (i.e., the natural pain experienced in one's life) and that interprets this link by the concept of God's → punishment. But the link is not objective, and once the sense of alienation from God is replaced by trust in God's unlimited love toward sinners, it fades from the scene. Evil, then, is no longer viewed as a punishment. It is a means of education posited by God's love (A. Ritschl, *The Christian Doctrine of Justification and Reconciliation* 3, §§39, 42; see also 2, §§16-21).

An attempt could also be made to see in God's penal activity, summed up in the term "wrath of God," an expression of the same purpose that lies behind God's gracious activity. Thus *F. H. R. Frank* (1827-94) viewed the wrath of God as a means by which God fulfills his goal in creation when faced by rebellious subjects, and *F. Weber* (1836-79) described the wrath of God as a form of his absolute love for sinners.

3.4.2. Among North American theologians *W. → Rauschenbusch* (1861-1918; → Social Gospel) in particular saw correspondence between concepts of God and social forms (→ God 2). The idea of God as an angry despot is a form of religion under a despotic order. In the teaching of Jesus the message of God's love is directly fitting for a liberated society. Opposition to an autocratic society implies opposition to a heavenly autocrat. Social liberation brings with it a democratizing of the concept of God. God is now Father, not Despot, and he gives an experience of redemption (*A Theology of the Social Gospel*, 213ff.).

3.4.3. In his theology *K. → Barth* (1886-1968; → Dialectical Theology) offered a total complex that found a place for the wrath of God in the law that is subjected to the gospel. Barth did not think that the doctrine of divine wrath could claim any independent reality if isolated from the Christ-event and the proclamation of the gospel, nor do we experience it in total antithesis to the gospel of Christ. All that we can say about God's wrath is that it can claim validity only as a mode by which we are both abased and exalted through the Christ-event (*CD* II/1, 407-10). For Barth, sin and → evil *(Nichtige)* are possibilities that are excluded by the decision that God has made to love us and by the corresponding determination that humanity should be the recipient of his love (III/3, §50). For this reason God's opposition to sinners is not a reaction of his anger at sin but a sin-opposing upholding of the determination that humans should be God's covenant partners (IV/1, 735-

39). Those who resist this determination experience God's reaction as wrath, but in reality it is simply an upholding of God's covenant will (see *Evangelium und Gesetz*, esp. 21-22).

Influenced by his concern for the "theology of crisis," *H. R. Niebuhr* (1894-1962; → North American Theology 7.1) engaged in a criticism of → liberal theology in which he demanded reflection on the fact that to understand the gospel we must also proclaim God's wrath.

3.4.4. Roman Catholic theology finds a place for the wrath of God in its discussion of the various attitudes of God that are part of his impenetrable mystery but that may be seen in the context of his saving work and that find full revelation in his turning to us in love (K. → Rahner, *Theological Investigations* [vol. 1; 1961] 117-25). The judgment of God (→ Last Judgment) must be viewed as the reverse side of his love, which we in our guilt reject.

In some tension with the divine revelation of unequivocal love in Christ, Roman Catholic theologians who incline to Luther's opinion (*J. Daniélou* and *H. U. von Balthasar*) point to the cross of Jesus, on which Jesus vicariously bore the penal judgment of God's wrath on human sinners. On the cross Jesus went through the darkness of our sinful state; subjectively, "he can experience it as 'punishment,' although objectively speaking, in his case, it cannot be such" (Balthasar, 4.338).

3.4.5. Most Lutherans resist attempts to unite the wrath of God with his love. They adopt views that rest on a rediscovery of what the wrath of God meant for Luther (T. Harnack). Their starting point is a combination of theological statements and religious experience. They criticize the restriction placed upon theology by preconceived views of God's unity. The ambivalence of religious experience helps us to see that we must claim a "real dialectic" (Elert) of wrath and grace, even in God himself.

W. Elert (1885-1954) pointed out that the existential change that is effected by the preaching of the gospel of grace presupposes an earlier situation of alienation from God under his wrath. We must take this separation into account if we are to understand the gospel (Elert, *Glaube*, §18; see also §5). Analysis of our human situation, of the fact that we have fallen victim to death under God's hiddenness and wrath, serves negatively to prepare us for the gospel. It is itself an experience of God (§§6-16). Through the law God exposes our sinful state (§21; see §24). Only in the gospel does he break into this state. The gospel shows us that his will was to bear the wrath in Christ and in this way to justify sinners

(§24). The unity of God in the antithetical experiences of judgment (wrath) and gospel is something that we can know only through these experiences. It comes to light only when we experience the unequivocal wrath of God, which leaves no place for gospel, and yet also the unequivocal gospel of God, which silences wrath (§23). Faith mediates between wrath and grace. It explains wrath retrospectively as a means of access to the gospel. In this way faith finds wrath an expression of God's love (*Morphologie*, vol. 1, chap. 6).

3.4.6. → Feminist theology has revived Enlightenment criticisms of the doctrine of the wrath of God. It typically discredits all references to God's wrath as depictions of a patriarchal God. The distinction between patriarchal and matriarchal concepts underlies its criticism of Scripture as a whole and acts as a substitute for the distinction (and interrelating) of law and gospel (N. Slenczka).

3.4.7. The doctrine of the wrath of God as a depiction of the human situation before God is indispensable if we are to understand God's loving will as it is made manifest in Christ. We can misunderstand this point only if it is viewed as a problem relating to the unity of the divine will and work, for in this case we rightly favor God's gracious will corresponding to the revelation in Christ. A correct understanding sees God's wrath as a response of opposition to the natural situation of those who are without Christ, who are thus condemned to → death, and whose → freedom of will is damaged by a contingent and anonymous nexus of events (Ps. 90:3-6). Nor is this the only experience of God. The final experience is the reality of death itself (v. 10). The preaching of the law shows that this situation, which always confronts us (v. 11), is our real situation under God's wrath (vv. 7-9).

Only the gospel, the good news of the love of God in Christ, breaks into this situation. We cannot take for granted the unity of God in wrath and love. It finds demonstration only in the event in which the loving will of God prevails against his wrath, showing that his love is triumphant.

Bibliography: H. U. von Balthasar, *Theo-drama: Theological Dramatic Theory* (5 vols.; San Francisco, 1988-98) • K. Barth, "Gospel and Law," *Community, State, and Church* (Garden City, N.Y., 1960) 71-100 • G. Ebeling, "Des Todes Tod," *ZTK* 84 (1987) 162-94 • W. Elert, *Der christliche Glaube* (2d ed.; Berlin, 1941; ET *The Christian Faith* [Columbus, Ohio, 1974]); idem, *Morphologie des Luthertums* (2 vols.; Munich, 1931-32; ET *The Structure of Lutheranism* [St. Louis, Mo., 1962]) • A. von Harnack, *Marcion: The Gospel of the Alien God* (Durham, N.C., 1990; orig. pub., 1921) • Lactantius, *De ira Dei = Vom Zorne Gottes* (Darmstadt, 1957) • B. Lohse, "Gesetz, Tod und Sünde in Luthers Auslegung des 90. Psalms," *Evangelium in der Geschichte* (Göttingen, 1988) 379-94 • E. Mühlenberg, "Marcion's Jealous God," *Disciplina nostra* (Cambridge, Mass., 1979) 93-115 • H. R. Niebuhr, *The Kingdom of God in America* (Middletown, Conn., 1937; repr., 1988) • L. Pinomaa, *Der Zorn Gottes in der Theologie Luthers* (Helsinki, 1938) • W. Rauschenbusch, *A Theology for the Social Gospel* (Louisville, Ky., 1997; orig. pub., 1917) • A. Ritschl, *The Christian Doctrine of Justification and Reconciliation* (vol. 2; Eugene, Oreg., 2004) 119-56 • C. R. Schoonhoven, *The Wrath of Heaven* (Grand Rapids, 1966) • N. Slenczka, "Feministische Theologie," *TRu* 58 (1993) 396-436.

Notger Slenczka

Wycliffe, John

John Wycliffe (also Wyclif[f], ca. 1330-84) was a scholastic philosopher, theologian, and reformer. Born in England near Richmond, Yorkshire, Wycliffe first comes to light in 1356 as a bachelor of arts advancing to higher degrees at Merton College, Oxford. He became master of Balliol in 1359 and in 1361 received Oxford's rich parish of Fillingham. He might have served there briefly, but mainly he used its income to finance his studies. Such absenteeism was common practice, though he would later denounce it (→ Residence, Duty of). He in turn became rector of Ludgershall in 1368, and of Lutterworth in 1374.

Although Wycliffe made small gains in ecclesiastical preferment, his academic prestige was great. Already in 1372, when he took his doctorate in theology, he was, as even his enemies later admitted, Oxford's outstanding philosopher and teacher. Over the years his interest moved away from scholastic disputation to political and religious controversy (→ Polemics). Early in his career Wycliffe converted to → realism, the philosophical position that upheld the substantial reality of universals. He became a passionate defender of this Augustinian tradition against the prevailing → nominalism, which he saw not only as impeding coherent thought but also as undermining Christian virtue and scriptural → authority. Through his realism he developed his radical political ideas.

In 1371 Wycliffe began to advise the Crown. He likely was summoned by the Black Prince, Edward, heir to the throne, but he came to be closest to Edward's brother, John of Gaunt, duke of Lancaster. With the finances of the English crown depleted on account of war with France, Wycliffe defended its case for seizing church property and disavowing papal taxes. He wrote two works on lordship, arguing that dominion over → property belonged strictly to God, who shared it with the righteous alone: those in a state of grace shared in God's lordship over the whole universe; the unrighteous had no proper claim to any ownership. He did not deny the validity of civil power and private property, both needful limits in sinful society, but he concluded that for officers of the church, lordship over wealth was contrary to apostolic poverty and was mired in corruption. He argued for the state to take control of → church finances. So began his call for reform.

Wycliffe's high profile and severe stance made him dangerous to church leaders and a clear target, but his attachment to Gaunt protected him. In 1377 William Courtenay, bishop of London, summoned Wycliffe to convocation at St. Paul's to answer for his teachings. Gaunt, with a retinue of friars and lords, threatened Courtenay, and the meeting ended in disarray. Later in 1377 Pope Gregory XI (1370-78) issued a summons for Wycliffe's arrest on a charge of errors concerning church authority and polity. Wycliffe appeared at Lambeth Palace in 1378 before Archbishop Sudbury but went under the royal protection. This meeting also led to tumult. After Gregory's death and with the election of rival popes, the papal case against Wycliffe was left unpursued.

After 1378 Wycliffe left the political sphere but championed reform and scriptural authority ever more fiercely. His brief hope in Urban VI (1378-89) as a new reforming → pope quickly faded. He went on to develop more extreme conclusions, especially in his predestinarianism (→ Predestination), and published them with harsh invective. He stated that since Christ's true body was the invisible church of the predestined, with Christ alone as its head, the visible church of corrupt leadership lacked genuine authority. He repudiated its civic privileges and "unholy" practices such as → pilgrimage, venerating the → saints, and selling → indulgences. He held that an unworthy priest could not administer the → sacraments, and he promoted the ideal of the primitive, apostolic church, with all members called to sanctity of life in the priesthood of all believers (→ Priest, Priesthood, 4). His realism led him to attack the doctrine of transubstantiation. He viewed it as encouraging idolatry and a false mediating role for the priest. His position was of corporeal remanence,

or residue, with a spiritual Real Presence: "under the form of bread and wine is sacramentally the Body of Christ." He thus ventured into official heresy and lost the support and protection that he had enjoyed at Oxford.

In 1380 Wycliffe defended his writings before a council summoned by Chancellor Berton. Here his allies the friars finally abandoned him; all his support now lay with his disciples among the secular clergy. The Peasants' Revolt in 1381 cast an ill light on Wycliffe, as some held that his teachings on lordship were responsible. In 1382 his longtime foe William Courtney, newly appointed archbishop of Canterbury, had Wycliffe's works condemned at the so-called Blackfriars Synod. Oxford's Chancellor Rigg sympathized with his eminent scholar, but he was forced by Courtney to expel Wycliffe and ban his books. Wycliffe remained free to retire to Lutterworth, where he soon suffered a stroke.

Wycliffe continued, however, to write vigorously and to encourage his disciples, who went forth preaching, restating Wycliffe's scholarly call for reform in terms that came to be relevant to many ordinary, unlettered people. The preaching of these so-called Lollards (from MDut. *lollen*, "mutter"), a term of abuse they soon bore, rested especially on Wycliffe's concern with the supreme authority of Scripture. He had now concluded that Scripture must be set in the vernacular to make its teachings directly available to the people. His urgings led his disciples to undertake the work of translation, which became the first complete Bible in English (→ Bible Versions 3).

Wycliffe died in Lutterworth on December 31, 1384, three days after suffering another stroke while hearing the service of Holy Communion. His call for reform persisted in Lollardy and lent strength to the English Reformation. His scholarship also found a ready audience at the University of Prague and played a part in Jan → Hus's (ca. 1372-1415) attempt at reform in Bohemia (→ Hussites). His works were condemned together with Hus at the Council of Constance in 1415; his bones were soon after exhumed and burned. In the 16th century Wycliffe was heralded as the "morning star" of the Reformation by John Foxe in his *Book of Martyrs*.

Bibliography: Primary sources: De universalibus (ed. I. J. Mueller et al.; Oxford, 1985) • *Latin Works* (36 vols.; Wyclif Society; London, 1883-1922) • *On the Truth of Holy Scripture* (trans. I. C. Levy; Kalamazoo, Mich., 2001) • *On Universals* (trans. A. Kenny; Oxford, 1985) • *Selections from English Wycliffite Writings* (ed. A. Hudson; Toronto, 1997) • *The Wycliffe NT, 1388* (ed. W. R. Cooper; London, 2002).

Secondary works: G. R. EVANS, *John Wyclif: Myth and Reality* (Oxford, 2005) • A. J. P. KENNY, *Wyclif* (Oxford, 1985) • I. LEVY, *John Wyclif: Scriptural Logic, Real Presence, and the Parameters of Orthodoxy* (Milwaukee, Wis., 2003) • K. B. MCFARLANE, *The Origins of Religious Dissent in England* (New York, 1966) • B. SMAL-LEY, "The Bible and Eternity: John Wyclif's Dilemma," *JWCI* 27 (1964) 73-89 • M. TRESCHOW, "The Metaphysics of Scriptural Integrity in John Wyclif's *De Veritate Sacrae Scripturae*," *Dionysius* 13 (1989) 153-96 • H. WORKMAN, *John Wyclif: A Study of the English Medieval Church* (2 vols.; Oxford, 1926).

MICHAEL TRESCHOW

X

Xavier, Francis

Born in 1506 to a family of minor Basque nobility at the castle of Xavier (Javier) in Navarre, Spain, Francis Xavier left his home while still an adolescent to study at the University of Paris. There he lived in the same college with Peter Faber and, later, → Ignatius of Loyola. On August 15, 1534, in the Chapel of the Martyrs at Montmartre, the three of them and four others vowed to travel to the Holy Land and to live in chastity and → poverty (§§4-5). This act constitutes the remote event out of which would evolve the Company of Jesus, known more familiarly as the → Jesuits.

In 1536, having received his master of arts and then completing two years of theological study, Xavier left Paris for Venice to find a ship for the Holy Land. These travel plans were thwarted. Instead, after being ordained to the priesthood, he went to Rome, where Ignatius had already set up his residence. In 1539 the small original group and some others, already working in various apostolic tasks, were formally recognized as a → religious order by Paul III (1534-49), with a formal bull issued in 1540.

At the request of King John III (1521-57) of Portugal, Ignatius sent Francis to do → missionary work in the East Indies. Armed with a papal bull nominating him as an apostolic → nuncio, he sailed from Lisbon, arriving 13 months later in Goa on the western coast of India. His first task was to reform the church in Goa itself. After a valiant effort he managed to halt the atrocious behavior of the colonists toward the Indian people, who were enslaved, raped, and neglected. During the same decade, using Goa as a base, Xavier traveled among the Paravas, low-caste fishermen in southern India, and then on to Ceylon, Malacca, the Moluccas, and the Malay Islands. During these trips, he started small communities of Christians mainly among the poorest classes, with whom he identified through the ascetic manner of his own life and the generosity of his → love for the poor.

During that decade (1541-49) Xavier frequently returned to his base in Goa. In 1549 he decided to move on to Japan. During his missionary efforts in Japan he switched tactics, dressing more regally and offering gifts in order to gain the trust of the mikado (emperor) while identifying himself as a representative of the king of Portugal. His efforts in Japan resulted in a small community of Christians that numbered perhaps 2,000. These Christian communities would suffer a fierce persecution some decades after Francis Xavier's death. In 1552 he was again back in Goa, when he decided to leave for China, where he hoped to ransom some Portuguese prisoners. He never made it to Canton. On an uninhabited island off the coast of China, Xavier died between December 2 and 3, 1552. His body was brought back to Goa in 1554, encased in quicklime, and entombed in the Church of Bom Jesus, where it rests to this day.

Despite his near-constant travel, Francis Xavier

was also an able administrator. He organized the Indian province of the Jesuits, corresponded with both civil and ecclesiastical authorities, and oversaw works of piety and Christian instruction. In Goa itself he formed catechetical schools, ministry to lepers and the poor, as well as services for the needy and the enslaved. During his missionary trips he kept in contact with the community in Goa and the general headquarters in Rome. This huge correspondence was later edited and published between 1899 and 1945 under the title *Monumenta Xaveriana,* in the larger series edited by the Jesuits in Rome, the *Monumenta Historica Societatis Jesu.* That correspondence is important not only for understanding the personality and spirituality of Francis himself but for the information to be gleaned about the religious and social life of the late 16th century.

Francis Xavier was the first great Jesuit missionary, even though his traditional approach to missionary work would be improved upon by later Jesuit missionaries in the East, who would show themselves to be much more sensitive to the cultural conditions of those to whom they preached. Nonetheless, he was universally regarded as a holy person in his own day and a zealous Christian. In 1622 Francis Xavier was canonized by Gregory XV (1621-23), along with three other paradigmatic figures of the Catholic Reformation: Ignatius of Loyola, Philip Neri, and → Teresa of Ávila. The popularity of the saint, especially in the period of the Counterreformation (→ Catholic Reform and Counterreformation), was such that his life was commemorated in all of the major centers of Jesuit activity in Europe. He was the frequent subject of artistic interest, with portraits of him created by such luminaries as Anthony Van Dyck, Peter Paul Rubens, Carlo Dolci, and Luca Giordano. In 1927 Pius XI (1922-39) named him patron of all Catholic foreign missions. He is commemorated in the Roman Catholic liturgy on his feast day, December 3.

Bibliography: J.-L. Monguerre, *St. Francis Xavier* (Garden City, N.Y., 1963) • J. O'Malley, *The First Jesuits* (Cambridge, Mass., 1993).

Lawrence Cunningham

Xenophobia

1. Term
2. Through History
3. Religious Considerations

Of Greek derivation, "xenophobia" is a neologism meaning "fear of strange people or things."

1. Term

"Xenophobia" usually denotes → anxiety at the strange or unknown. This anxiety may promote hostility or hatred. In spite of appearances to the contrary, it was both ancient and widespread, though not universal. Along with it we also find fascination and curiosity about what is strange. Xenophobia often occasions bad individual and social reactions, though analysis in such cases is difficult. The term itself is indispensable.

2. Through History

2.1. The oldest references to xenophobia have the assumption of something that is alien to a group or way of doing things. The basic idea is that what lies outside the macrocosm of early → worldviews developed out of a geocosm that was either chaotic or indwelt by → demons. This negative concept of its background had a great influence upon children. Already at the age of six to eight months they could begin to fear strange people, even if in reality they had nothing to fear. Xenophobia thus developed in societies. Bioethical research has rightly seen here an inborn fact. It has a strong ethical influence, even where education is more humane.

Cultured nations, too, find it hard to grant human names, qualities, or virtues to strangers. Reactions against their alien character vary from social ostracism to physical execution. For example, closed societies among illiterate tribes or elite orders regard the stranger as an enemy (e.g., Lat. *hostis* and Heb. *zār* meant originally "stranger," then also "enemy").

2.2. Early ethics confirmed the elemental nature of xenophobia by establishing new → norms of conduct in relation to strangers. The records portray developing stages in both linguistic and social history.

A lessening of the fear of strangers results in ambivalence. Traditional cultures offered them limited hospitality (often for three days only). Linguistically, the stranger was thus a guest (Heb. *gēr* had both meanings), but similar words might be used for both guest and host (see Old Indian *aryá-,* Gk. *xenos,* Lat. *hospes,* and Eng. "host," from the root *hosp*).

Aliens could achieve permanent status as protected citizens (*gēr,* LXX and Vg *proselytos),* resident aliens (*tôšāb,* LXX *paroikos,* Vg *colonus),* foreigners (*zār,* LXX *allotrios,* Vg *alienus),* or incomers (*nokrî,* LXX *allophylos,* Vg *peregrinus).* Greek law gave recognition to such people, called variously *allogenēs, allodapos, parepidēmos,* and *barbaros;* Roman law, for its part, mentioned *alienigena* and *advena.*

2.3. Neutralizing is today a rival of xenophobia, but it is hard to distinguish between the two.

→ Industrial societies treat resident "guest"

workers as aliens. Traders are often permanent aliens, for example, the Jews (→ Judaism) and → Roma. When those who have sought political asylum threaten the jobs and well-being of native-born workers, xenophobia arises. Atavistic motives are also commonly at work.

A psychological neutralizing of xenophobia takes place when what is strange is relativized merely as the unknown, the untrusted, the odd. A secondary character is thus attributed to strangeness, and it can thus be accepted without prejudice. Sociologically, however, the result might be doubt or uncertainty about the value of one's own culture. When this reaction takes place, it might lead on to a renewing or ensuring of the → identity to which the strangers have contributed. They can then be viewed positively without fear or hatred. Ontologically, the phenomenon of experiencing strangers and their world might assist the discovering of an a priori readiness to accept the strange and to resist xenophobia. Punishments cannot accomplish this end but merely give xenophobia a more solid basis.

3. Religious Considerations

3.1. Xenophobia should not be linked or confused with fear of God. The fear (and love) of God relates to a revealed God, so that what is strange about him is of no concern. Even when God or a divine power is called strange, like the God of Marcion (d. ca. 160; → Marcionites) or the "life" of the → Mandaeans, fear is replaced by a Gnostic trust in an absolutely nonanthropomorphic power to save. → Tertullian (d. ca. 225) speaks of "a new and strange divinity" in Christ (*Adv. Marc.* 1.2.3), and the Mandaean Ginza uses *nukraia* to describe all that is alien to our earthly world. The tendency to ascribe divine transcendence to an external quality that seems to be alien does not have to carry with it a corresponding increase in the fear of God.

3.2. In *The Idea of the Holy* (1923), R. Otto (1869-1937) offered no basis but suggested that there is an emotional analogy between the sense of holy mysteries and the sense of the strange and different when he noted how mysterious and awe-inspiring and astonishing those mysteries are (pp. 27-28).

A transcendental reason was sought for the rise of xenophobia when a difference was found between the macrocosm and the demonic geocosm. "We can regard an object as *fearful* without being afraid *of* it, viz. if we judge of it in such a way that we merely *think* a case in which we would wish to resist it and yet in which all resistance would be altogether vain. Thus the virtuous man fears God without being afraid of Him, because to wish to resist Him and

His commandments he thinks is a case that *he* need not apprehend. But in every such case that he thinks as not impossible, he cognizes Him as fearful" (I. Kant, *Critique of Judgment* [trans. J. H. Bernard; New York, 1951] §28).

3.3. Xenophobia developed along with the → history of religion but was not its basis. The strange and alien, though related to the macrocosm and geocosm, in the final analysis has a nonworldly dimension and cannot be related to these things alone.

What is absolutely alien is a religious object only insofar as it is the transcendental condition of all possible desires that must be explained as foreign to us. On the one side, then, we must posit and resist xenophobia, and yet, on the other, we must seek to maintain or discover our identity with what is alien to us.

→ Prejudice; Racism

Bibliography: A. BEHDAD, *A Forgetful Nation: On Immigration and Cultural Identity in the United States* (Durham, N.C., 2005) • F. CAESTECKER, *Alien Policy in Belgium, 1840-1940: The Creation of Guest Workers, Refugees, and Illegal Aliens* (New York, 2000) • C. COLPE, "Vergleich der biblischen Fremdenterminologien," *Die Restauration der Götter. Antike Religion und Neo-Paganismus* (ed. R. Faber and R. Schlesier; Würzburg, 1986) 87 • B. DIKEN, *Strangers, Ambivalence, and Social Theory* (Aldershot, Vt., 1998) • N. FINZSCH and D. SCHIRMER, eds., *Identity and Intolerance: Nationalism, Racism, and Xenophobia in Germany and the United States* (Washington, D.C., 1998) • D. MACEDO and P. GOUNARI, eds., *The Globalization of Racism* (Boulder, Colo., 2006) • M. MONTEITH and J. WINTERS, "Why We Hate," *PsT* 35/3 (2002) 44-51 • D. S. NORDIN, *A Swedish Dilemma: A Liberal European Nation's Struggle with Racism and Xenophobia, 1990-2000* (Lanham, Md., 2005) • V. REYNOLDS, V. FALGER, and I. VINE, eds., *The Sociobiology of Ethnocentrism: Evolutionary Dimensions of Xenophobia, Discrimination, Racism, and Nationalism* (Athens, Ga., 1987) • O. SCHÄFFTER, ed., *Das Fremde. Erfahrungsmöglichkeiten zwischen Faszination und Bedrohung* (Opladen, 1991) • M. THEUNISSEN, *The Other: Studies in the Social Ontology of Husserl, Heidegger, Sartre, and Buber* (Cambridge, Mass., 1986) • P. THIEME, *Der Fremdling im Rgveda* (Leipzig, 1938; repr., 1966) • J. M. VORSTER, "Racism, Xenophobia, and Human Rights," *ER* 54 (2002) 296-312 • U. WESEL, *Frühformen des Rechts in vorstaatlichen Gesellschaften* (Frankfurt, 1985) • R. S. WISTRICH, ed., *Demonizing the Other: Antisemitism, Racism, and Xenophobia* (Amsterdam, 1999).

CARSTEN COLPE

Y

Yahweh

The divine name "YHWH" occurs over 6,800 times in the OT either alone or in combination (e.g., "house of Yahweh" or "word of Yahweh"). That it was pronounced "Yahweh" is shown by Greek transcriptions. It came to be regarded as unspeakably holy, and so to avoid use of the name it was furnished with the vowels of *'ǎdônāi*, "my Lord, my lords" (cf. LXX *kyrios*), which led to the mixed form "Jehovah." It had already ceased to be used much in the later OT, not occurring at all in Ecclesiastes, Esther, or Song of Solomon (a short form in 8:6?). We also do not find it in Job 3–27 (12:9 being a scribal error), and it is less common in Chronicles than in Samuel. (On its distribution, see E. Jenni, 703-4.) In → Qumran it was written in Old Hebrew script or replaced by four dots.

The OT offers an explanation of the name only in Exod. 3:14 (cf. Hos. 1:9). There the phrase "I will be what I will be" (NRSV marg.) is a reference to the freedom of → God (cf. Exod. 33:19), as well as to the idea that → Israel in the course of its history will and should have future experiences with its God (Mic. 4:5!). Other derivations (from the verbs "to fall," "to fell," or "to blow," or an explanation as "Oh! He!" = *yahuwa*) are grammatically or semantically improbable.

Older extrabiblical examples (esp. the Moabite Stone and ostraca from Arad and Lachish, but not

Ebla) show that the Tetragrammaton YHWH is primary, as compared with the short forms *yāhû* or *yâ* (Exod. 15:2; Hallelujah etc., esp. in proper names, also at Elephantine) or, at the beginning of proper names, Jeho- (*yěhô-*) or Jo- (*yô-*).

Inscriptions from Khirbet el-Qom (west of Hebron, 8th cent.) and Kuntillet 'Ajrud (south of Kadesh) mention "Yahweh of Samaria" (or of Teman; cf. Yahweh of Hebron in 2 Sam. 15:7), which points to a splitting up of Yahweh in popular piety. "Yahweh and his Ashera" is written as well (see U. Winter). This phrase, however, refers not to a goddess next to Yahweh (proper name plus suffix is not customary) but to a cultic column as a reverential symbol of Yahweh. Both are opposed by Deuteronomic/Deuteronomistic theology, with its "YHWH is one" (see Deut. 6:4) and its centralization of worship (chap. 12), which promoted the purity of the cult (→ Deuteronomistic History).

Exod. 3:13-14 and 6:2 show that Yahweh became the God of Israel first with → Moses and through Yahweh's encounter with him in the Midianite territory (Exodus 2–4; 18). In addition, Egyptian texts (Temple of Soleb/Nubia and related documents) mention the "land of the *Š:śu-ywh:*" and link *yhw:* (a region, town, tribe, or mountain?) to the Bedouins between the Negev and the Gulf of Aqaba and in the vicinity of the land of Seir. Since Yahweh is characterized as a deity coming from the south (Judg. 5:4-5; Deut. 33:2; Hab. 3:3), the thesis is plausible that he first became the God of Israel there (cf. Josh. 24:2).

→ Sinai

Bibliography: F. M. Cross, "Yahweh and the God of the Patriarchs," *HTR* 55 (1962) 225-59 • O. Eissfeldt, "El and Yahweh," *JSSt* 1 (1956) 27-37 • D. N. Freedman and M. P. O'Connor, "יהוה YHWH," *TDOT* 5.500-521 • G. Gertoux, *The Name of God Y.eH.oW.aH, Which Is Pronounced as It Is Written I_Eh_oU_Ah* (Lanham, Md., 2002) • E. Jenni, "יהוה Jhwh Jahwe," *THAT* 1.701-7 • B. Lang, "No God but Yahweh! The Origin and Character of Biblical Monotheism," *Monotheism* (ed. C. Geffré and J. P. Jossua; Edinburgh, 1985) 41-49 • L. Lundquist, *The Tetragrammaton and the Christian Greek Scriptures: A Comprehensive Study of the Divine Name (YHWH) in the Original Writings of the Christian Greek Scriptures* (2d ed.; Portland, Oreg., 1998) • E. C. B. Maclaurin, "YHWH: The Origin of the Tetragrammaton," *VT* 12 (1962) 439-63 • G. H. Parke-Taylor, *Yahweh: The Divine Name in the Bible* (Waterloo, Ont., 1975) • M. S. Smith, *The Early History of God: Yahweh and the Other Deities in Ancient Israel* (2d ed.; Grand Rapids, 2002) • U. Winter, *Frau und Göttin. Exegetische und ikonographische Studien zum weiblichen Gottesbild im Alten Israel und in dessen Umwelt* (Freiburg, 1983) 486-90.

HORST DIETRICH PREUSS†

Yemen

	1960	1980	2000
Population (1,000s):	5,247	8,219	18,118
Annual growth rate (%):	2.15	3.31	3.49

Area: 531,869 sq. km. (205,356 sq. mi.)

A.D. 2000

Population density: 34/sq. km. (88/sq. mi.)
Births / deaths: 4.36 / 0.87 per 100 population
Fertility rate: 6.99 per woman
Infant mortality rate: 68 per 1,000 live births
Life expectancy: 60.5 years (m: 59.9, f: 60.9)
Religious affiliation (%): Muslims 98.9, other 1.1.

1. History
2. Present Situation
3. Religious Situation

Located in the southwest part of the Arabian Peninsula, Yemen is unique among its Arab near neighbors in geography, climate, and → poverty. A backbone of mountain ranges in the western highlands runs from north to south, including Jebel an-Nabi Shu'ayb (3,760 m. / 12,336 ft.), the highest peak on the peninsula. The cooler temperatures allow extensive agriculture, which earned Yemen the accolade "Arabia Felix" (happy Arabia) from the ancient Romans. Other landforms include the coastal plains of the Tihama, the eastern highlands of the Hadramaut, and the vast desert of the Rub' al-Khali (empty quarter). Yemen's low oil production (in 2005, est. 387,500 barrels per day), high birthrate (in 2006, an average of 6.8 births per woman), poor infrastructure, and widespread corruption (scoring a low 2.2 out of 10 on Transparency International's latest annual report card) have conspired to keep the country poor. It is ranked at 150 out of the 179 nations in the Human Resources Index of the U.N. Development Programme, well below, for example, Bangladesh at 139.

1. History

Yemen has not always been poor. The queen of Sheba (1 Kgs. 10:1-13; 2 Chr. 9:1-12), a Yemeni ruler according to some Arab legends, brought 4.5 tons of gold as a gift for Solomon. The ancient incense road carrying frankincense and myrrh through Yemen's center attracted much wealth, as did the later coffee monopoly, trading out of the port of Mocha on the Red Sea. The Minaeans, Sabaeans, and Himyarites established kingdoms in its mountain fastnesses. Rome's destruction of the temple in Jerusalem in A.D. 70 brought Jewish emigrants to South Arabia, as well as the Christian message. By the year 350 Christian communities were established.

Dhu Nuwas (515-25), a Himyarite king, changed the state religion to → Judaism and began to massacre Christians. Kaleb, the Christian king of Aksum (Abyssinia), with the encouragement of the Byzantine emperor Justin I (518-27), invaded and annexed a portion of North Yemen. The Aksumite general Abraha, besides repairing the great dam at Ma'rib, constructed an impressive cathedral called al-Qulays at Sana'a to divert → pilgrimage from the Kaaba, which was then a pagan shrine.

The Sassanid Persians invaded in 570 and ruled Yemen until 630, when the country submitted to → Islam, beginning with the conversion of the governor in 628. Descendants of the Prophet established the Zaidi imamate, which survived, with interruptions, up to the 1962 revolution. The Yemen Arab Republic (YAR) was then established in the north.

In 1839 the British occupied Aden, ruling over the south of Yemen until their withdrawal in 1967, in the face of armed revolt. The People's Democratic Republic of Yemen, a socialist state, was established the same year. The decline of Communism caused the two Yemens to unite in 1990. A civil war in 1994 demonstrated that the ideological divide between the conservative tribal north and the more secular south was not completely bridged. Recent years have seen a greater Islamization of the country.

2. Present Situation

The new state, the Republic of Yemen, is a constitutional democracy. It is ruled by Ali Abdullah Saleh, the president of the YAR since 1978, through his party, the General People's Congress (GPC). He was elected president of the reunited Yemen in 1999 and then was reelected in 2006 for another seven-year term. The main opposition comes from the fundamentalist Islah (reform) Party and the declining Yemen Socialist Party. An elected 301-seat House of Representatives, dominated by the GPC, and an appointed 111-member Shura Council share power.

The economy is based on the country's limited oil exports, as well as repatriated incomes from Yemenis who travel out of the country for work. In 1990 an estimated 800,000 Yemenis were expelled from Gulf States when the Yemeni delegation opposed the U.N. Security Council vote condemning the Iraqi invasion of Kuwait. With inflation running at nearly 15 percent, and 35 percent of the workforce unemployed, it is not surprising that over 45 percent of the 23 million population (2007 est.) live below the poverty line. About 70 percent of the population are found in rural areas.

The cultivation of the mildly narcotic khat (Arab. *qāt*) leaves, chewed by millions of Yemenis each day, has provided a reason for Yemeni farmers to stay on the land and has reduced urban drift. Unfortunately, khat's high demand for water is exacerbating the national water crisis. Scarce resources such as arable ground (only 2.9 percent of the total land area) and small family incomes are squandered, and national productivity is lowered as a result of its use.

3. Religious Situation

According to article 2 of the Constitution (1991), Islam is the state religion, and article 3 names Shari'a as the main source of law. Virtually all citizens are Muslims, either of the Zaydi order of Shia Islam or the Shafa'i order of Sunni Islam, representing approximately 30 percent and 70 percent of the total population, respectively. There are also a few thousand Ismailis (mostly of the Bohri sect) in the north. The population is highly armed, with an estimated 60 million guns. The government is acting against international → terrorism. Training camps in the south were closed down following attacks on the USS *Cole* in 2000 and the French oil tanker *Limburgh* in 2002.

There is still a small Jewish community in the north of about 500 people. Most of the Jews left in 1948-50 under Operation Magic Carpet (→ Judaism).

Roman Catholic priests serve as chaplains to the Sisters of Charity, who run orphanages and homes for the handicapped. An Anglican priest is based in Aden as part of the Diocese of Cyprus and the Gulf. In Aden one Anglican and two Roman Catholic churches, seized after the British left, have been returned to their Christian communities. In other places, expatriate Christians have freedom to worship in private homes. In 1998 the country established diplomatic relations with the Vatican and agreed to the construction and operation of a "Christian center" in Sana'a, the capital, since no church buildings exist in the north. This agreement was again mentioned in President Saleh's audience with Pope John Paul II in 2000, but no action has since been undertaken, with "legal reasons" being cited as the reason.

Bibliography: R. L. BIDWELL, *The Two Yemens* (Boulder, Colo., 1983) • S. CARAPICO, *Civil Society in Yemen: The Political Economy of Activism in Modern Arabia* (Cambridge, 1998) • P. DRESCH, *A History of Modern Yemen* (Cambridge, 2000) • J. TOBI, *The Jews of Yemen: Studies in Their History and Culture* (Leiden, 1999).

BERNARD J. POWER

Yezidis

1. History
2. Syncretism
3. Social Organization

1. History

The Yezidis are a religious community in the Syrian district of Sim'ān and across to Ossetia. Though not unlike Iraqi Arabs, their Kurdish dialect (→ Kurds) and distinctive tradition make them a distinct ethnic group. Around 1900 they numbered up to 300,000, but after World War I only 100,000 and by 1983 only around 20,000. In 2005 estimates of the number of Yezidis worldwide ranged up to several times this reduced figure, mainly in Iraq, Syria, Turkey, and Armenia, with a sizable group in Germany as guest workers.

Yezidis call themselves *Dāsin* (pl. *Dawāsin;* Syr. *Dasnīyē*), after an early → Nestorian diocese, and regard the name "Yezidi" as more recent. Sheikh Yezīd, who was thought to be their founder, is more likely an eponymous hero. The often-asserted identification with the Umayyad caliph Yazīd ibn Muʿāwiyah (680-83) makes no sense, since this would presume partisanship for the conqueror of the party of Caliph ʿAlī and his son, Husayn (who was martyred in 680 at the battle of Karbala). The Yezidis, however, were as much enemies of the → Sunnis as were the Shiites (→ Shia, Shiites).

The word "Yezidi" probably comes from a word for God derived from the Old Iranian *yazata* (modern Pers. *īzed* or *yazdān*). The Yezidis worship many *yazatas*, the most important being Malak Ṭāʾūs (Angel Peacock), whose supposedly incorruptible (and inedible) flesh confers → immortality. As the second in a mythological system (→ Myth) that is the basis of a comprehensive but arcane discipline, this *yazata* has oversight of → creation.

The dualistic position (→ Dualism) in which it stands to the unnamed supreme God or Lord is that of a trickster demiurge that permits antitheses in the world. It is antagonistically misunderstood by those who are outside, so that the Malak Ṭāʾūs is given the role of a representative of the principle of → evil. Their neighbors and scholarship have thus wrongly called the Yezidis devil-worshipers. Their reaction was to place the word *Šaiṭān* on their list of → taboos, which already included several foods (the bean, lettuce, the pumpkin), animals (fish, gazelle, hen), and the color blue.

Malak Ṭāʾūs stands on a candelabra in the Yezidis' main → sanctuary in Lalish (northeast of Mosul, Iraq, in the Shaikhan district, near the Sinjār Mountains and west of their central area). There is a pilgrimage there every year in September. It is named after Sheikh ʿAdī (Ibn Musāfir, d. 1162), who is buried there, a Sufi whom Islamic orthodoxy (→ Islam) does not recognize (→ Sufism) but whom the Yezidis revere as a great → saint because Malak Ṭāʾūs or Yezid reappeared in him.

2. Syncretism

The Yezidis continue the → syncretism of antiquity. In addition to their old Iranian or Zoroastrian legacy (→ Iranian Religions 6-7), we see among them a mixture of popular beliefs (burial customs, dream oracles, dances), Jewish features (→ Dietary Laws), Christian (mostly Nestorian) features (a kind of Eucharist, church weddings, the drinking of → wine, infant baptism), Gnostic elements (the transmigration of souls), and Islamic features (the principle of possessing a book, with a "Book of Revelation" and a "Black Book," as well as the veneration of sufi-

sheikhs, → circumcision, → fasting, → sacrifice, → pilgrimages, and burial inscriptions).

3. Social Organization

The social organization of the Yezidis includes endogamous → marriage rules and customs, six clergy grades besides the laity, a brother or sister in the hereafter for each one, elders, and a spiritual and secular head. Armenian Christians and Sunnite Muslims noted these features as early as the 9th and 10th centuries. The Yezidis were also very skilled in agriculture, horticulture, and cattle raising. They were thus subject to retaliation from their Muslim overlords, who were especially oppressive under the Ottoman governors after the 17th century.

A number of enforced requirements were relaxed in post-Ottoman, laicized Turkey, including children having Islamic religious education, young men performing unpaid work, young women being required to marry outside their own religious community, and testators leaving property to nonfamily members. Recently, though, such requirements have again become significant, not only through re-Islamization but, paradoxically, also through redemocratization. Kurdish Sunnis who are large landholders use redemocratization to gain for themselves the authority of village protectors with police powers, which they have then used to expropriate Yezidi villages.

→ Minorities

Bibliography: S. S. Ahmed, *The Yazidis: Their Life and Beliefs* (Coconut Grove, Fla., 1975) • C. Allison, *The Yezidi Oral Tradition in Iraqi Kurdistan* (Richmond, Surrey, 2001) • I. Dulz, *Die Yeziden im Irak. Zwischen "Modelldorf" und Flucht* (Münster, 2001) • N. Fuccaro, *The Other Kurds: Yazidis in Colonial Iraq* (London, 1999) • J. S. Guest, *Survival among the Kurds: A History of the Yezidis* (New York, 1993) • P. G. Kreyenbroek, *Yezidism: Its Background, Observances, and Ritual Traditions* (Lewiston, N.Y., 1995) • J. E. Murad, *The Sacred Poems of the Yazidis: An Anthropological Approach* (Los Angeles, 1993) • E. Spät, *The Yezidis* (London, 2005).

Carsten Colpe

Yoga

Yoga, the Vedic term for "exertion," "strain," or "venture" (related to Gk. *zygon* and Lat. *iugum*, "yoke"), is a technical term used in various senses.

1. In a less technical sense yoga has to do with forms of trance (→ Ecstasy), → asceticism, and → medita-

tion. Two or three such rituals reach back to the end of the second century B.C. in southern Asia. Then in a more crystallized sense we find *jñānayoga, bhaktiyoga,* and *karmayoga* (yoga through the ways of knowledge, surrender/devotion, and action) in the → Bhagavad Gita, and the Yoga Sutras of Patañjali (lived between 2d cent. B.C. and 2d cent. A.D.). Yoga became one of the six classical systems of Indian philosophy. As such, it influenced popular forms in → Hinduism and some of the practices and theories of → Jainism and → Buddhism (the Yogācāra School).

2. Westerners have learned to use Indian terms and categories in developing their own physical, intellectual, and spiritual lives and thus to see a need for redemption relative to their total person. To this extent they have assimilated the methods of yoga. They apply it to breathing therapy and also to redemption through psychological release as they prevent conscious impressions from sinking into the unconscious. One can halt at various stages on this path, for example, practicing love, sympathy, joy, and equanimity. Yoga presupposes a system of spiritual concentration supported by bodily movements that give calm and enable people to discover regions in the cosmos that are homologous to the physical movements.

3. One such exercise is that of → devotion to God. With their concept of God, Christians can view it as part of → creation and not needing apologetic explanation.

Bibliography: M. ELIADE, "Yoga," *EncRel(E)* 15.519-23; idem, *Yoga: Immortality and Freedom* (London, 1958) • G. FEUERSTEIN, "Patañjali," *EncRel(E)* 11.206-7; idem, *The Shambhala Encyclopedia of Yoga* (Boston, 1997); idem, *Yoga: The Technology of Ecstasy* (Los Angeles, 1989); idem, *The Yoga Tradition: Its History, Literature, Philosophy, and Practice* (Prescott, Ariz., 1998) • G. FEUERSTEIN and J. MILLER, *The Essence of Yoga: Essays on the Development of Yogic Philosophy from the Vedas to Modern Times* (Rochester, Vt., 1998) • E. FRAUWALLNER, *History of Indian Philosophy* (2 vols.; New York, 1974) • G. J. LARSON, "Is South Asian *yoga* 'Philosophy,' 'Religion,' Both, or Neither?" *The Notion of "Religion" in Comparative Research* (ed. U. Bianchi; Rome, 1994) 261-70 • PATAÑJALI, *Yoga: Discipline of Freedom; The Yoga Sutra Attributed to Patanjali* (trans. B. S. Miller; Berkeley, Calif., 1996) • I. WHICHER and D. CARPENTER, eds., *Yoga: The Indian Tradition* (London, 2003).

CARSTEN COLPE

Young Men's Christian Association

1. History
2. Basis and Work
3. Impact and Connections
4. Recent Developments

1. History

The Young Men's Christian Association (YMCA) is a product of the 19th-century → revivals, which in North America were greatly influenced by → Methodism. Young male believers gathered for → prayer and Bible reading (→ Bible Study), promoted missionary projects, looked after the socially disadvantaged, and spoke to other young men whose Christianity might be threatened by the developing → industrial society. Out of these gatherings an association arose that, when it spread to Germany, cooperated with and yet also rivaled the → Inner Mission.

Inspired by English merchant and philanthropist George Williams (1821-1905), at the time only 22 years of age, 12 young men met in London in a textile house in 1844 and founded the first group bearing the name "YMCA." They were theological laymen, all engaged in secular jobs, belonging to various → denominations, and all concerned to promote their missionary lifestyle. Branches were soon formed in Montreal (1850), Boston (1851), and Geneva (1852). Henri Dunant (1828-1910) founded it in Geneva and also helped to promote a global expansion. A branch was formed in Paris in 1852, but the Berlin branch came into being only in 1883 and influenced evangelistically and ecumenically the existing groups in Germany.

2. Basis and Work

In 1855 a worldwide alliance was formed on the so-called Paris Basis. The occasion was a meeting in Paris of the Evangelical Alliance (→ World Evangelical Alliance) where 99 delegates from the 338 fellowships in attendance came together. As stated in the basis, "The Young Men's Christian Associations seek to unite those young men who, regarding Jesus Christ as their God and Saviour, according to the Holy Scriptures, desire to be his disciples in their faith and in their life, and to associate their efforts for the extension of his Kingdom amongst young men."

The headquarters of the global YMCA has been in Geneva since 1878. The association has reexamined and reaffirmed this basis, most recently as 1998. Presently there are over 120 national associations, grouped by continents. Over 40 million young men are members. The YMCA coordinates mutual aid, has programs for → refugees, engages in social action (e.g., helping prisoners of war in the two world wars), and since 1875 has held an annual week of prayer together with the → YWCA.

3. Impact and Connections

The Paris Basis was a model also for the founding of the YWCA (1894), the → World Student Christian Federation (1895), and the → World Council of Churches (1948), to which the YMCA was connected as a "related member." Being interdenominational, the YMCA has made a major contribution to the ecumenical movement. Ecumenist John R. → Mott (1865-1955) was president of the global YMCA from 1926 to 1947. In its first beginnings, the YMCA was both evangelical and interdenominational, and today it does not always conform in every respect to the ecumenical ideal. But it has always attempted to bring young men of all churches together in their efforts to win other young men to faith with the → gospel.

The YMCA has won recognition from the → Roman Catholic Church, evident in meetings held in 1984 and 1989 between representatives of the YMCA and the Pontifical Council for Promoting Christian Unity (→ Curia 1.2.4). The World Alliance of YMCAs has consultative status with the Economic and Social Council of the → United Nations, and it is a member of the Conference of NGOs.

4. Recent Developments

Since 1990, YMCAs have been founded in 19 former Communist republics in which they had been banned. In African and Asian countries, notably in India, the societal importance of the YMCA as advocate of youth has increased. In 2001 the International Coalition of YMCA Universities was founded to define common standards of quality, to arrange student-exchange programs, and to define the profile of YMCA professionals.

In 1998, at the 14th World Council of YMCAs, meeting at Frechen, Germany, the World Alliance of YMCAs adopted "Challenge 21." This programmatic statement identifies seven challenges the group faces in the 21st century, in the face of which it made the following declaration: "Affirming the Paris Basis adopted in 1855 as the ongoing foundation statement of the mission of the YMCA, at the threshold of the third millennium, we declare that the YMCA is a world-wide Christian, ecumenical, voluntary movement for women and men with special emphasis on and the genuine involvement of young people and that it seeks to share the Christian

ideal of building a human community of justice with love, peace and reconciliation for the fullness of life for all creation."

→ Ecumenism, Ecumenical Movement

Bibliography: C. Binfield, *This Has Been Tomorrow: The World Alliance of YMCAs since 1955* (Geneva, 1991) • M. D. David, *A Symbol of Asian Solidarity: A History of the Asia Alliance of YMCAs* (Hong Kong, 1998) • C. H. Hopkins, *History of the Y.M.C.A. in North America* (New York, 1951) • C. P. Shedd, *History of the World's Alliance of Young Men's Christian Associations* (London, 1955).

Dieter Roll

Young Women's Christian Association

1. History
2. The Present
3. In Germany and the United States

The Young Women's Christian Association (YWCA) is a global alliance of national associations working on behalf of women. According to its purpose statement, the World YWCA "unites national associations in a worldwide women's volunteer membership movement. Inspired by the Christian faith, the purpose of the World YWCA is to develop the leadership and collective power of women and girls around the world to achieve human → rights, health, security, dignity, → freedom, justice and → peace for all people." Its specific priorities are (1) women's health and the fight against HIV/AIDS, (2) human rights of women and children, (3) world peace with justice, and (4) sustainable → development (including women's economic justice and the → environment).

1. History

The YWCA was founded in the mid-19th century as a product of → revivals. Its aim was to answer the needs and questions posed by the industrial revolution (→ Modern Period 3). It linked prayer and → Bible study to the work of social reform. Two movements in England came together at its founding. With her women friends, Emma Roberts (or Robarts, fl. 1855-77) formed a prayer fellowship in 1855 to protect young women. At the same time Lady Mary Jane Kinnaird (1816-88) set up hostels for young women from rural areas who came to the cities seeking work but also needing protection. The movement quickly spread to other countries in Europe and, in 1858, to the United States, where the first projects were residences for women opened in New York and Boston.

The first world conference was held in 1889, attended by 326 delegates. It adopted a basis very much like the Paris Basis of the → Young Men's Christian Association (§2). It strongly promoted mission, especially in English-speaking countries. In 1894 the YWCA committees of the United States, England, Sweden, and Norway joined together in London to create the World YWCA.

2. The Present

In 2006 the World YWCA was at work in 22,775 local communities in 122 countries around the world, linking 25 million women and girls through 100 affiliated national YWCAs. Its headquarters is in Geneva. The alliance has a consultative role with the → United Nations and its various organizations. It works as a nongovernmental organization with ecumenical and other organizations.

The agenda of the YWCA still includes prayer and Bible study, along with social and political activities. Each year, in the week beginning with the second Sunday of November, it joins forces with the YMCA in the World YWCA/YMCA Week of Prayer and World Fellowship. It distributes a yearly plan of Bible reading with women's experiences in the background. The 2006 booklet, prepared around the theme "Changing Lives: Changing Communities," included Bible studies, a suggested order of worship, and a 12-month Bible reading plan.

The YWCA advocates civil and human rights and strongly opposes violence against women (→ Sexism). It has a concern for migrant workers and → refugees, promotes health and nutrition programs for women, focuses on → ecology and → technology, works for peace and justice, and offers leadership training for young women. By alerts for protest actions in international crisis situations (e.g., in Lebanon, Bosnia, and the Pacific), it reminds the member organizations that they are parts of the largest worldwide society of women.

3. In Germany and the United States

Johannes Burckhardt (1853-1914) founded the German branch of the YWCA in 1893. The Nazi years and the division of Germany after World War II meant that a new beginning had to be made, and the Burckhardt House in Berlin took up the work that had previously been done by the YWCA. With the division of Germany, the West German branch was moved to Gelnhausen, but the East German branch remained in East Berlin. In 1972 the work was incorporated into the Evangelische Frauenarbeit in Deutschland (Protestant Women's Work in Germany). In 2002 this group wished to discontinue the work, which facilitated the establishment of the independent German YWCA.

The U.S. YWCA has long been active in efforts against → racism, holding its first interracial conference in 1915 in Louisville, Kentucky. In 1970 its national convention adopted "One Imperative," namely, "To thrust our collective power toward the elimination of racism, wherever it exists, by any means necessary." To the present, it continues to pursue the goal of full → equality for all. In 2006 the national organization encompassed nearly 300 YWCA associations at close to 1,100 sites, serving 2.6 million members and participants.

Bibliography: N. Boyd, *Emissaries: The Overseas Work of the American YWCA, 1895-1970* (New York, 1986) • H. R. Christensen, "Religion as a Source of Activism: The YWCA in Global Perspective," *Crossing Borders: Re-mapping Women's Movements at the Turn of the Twenty-first Century* (ed. H. Romer; Odense, Den., 2005) 99-118 • *Common Concern* (Geneva) YWCA quarterly, published in English, French, and Spanish • N. Mjagkij and M. Spratt, eds., *Men and Women Adrift: The YMCA and the YWCA in the City* (New York, 1997) • A. A. Rice, *A History of the World's YWCA* (New York, 1947) • W. S. Robins, *Through the Eyes of a Woman: Bible Studies on the Experience of Women* (London, 1986) • C. Seymour-Jones, *Journey of Faith: The History of the World YWCA, 1945-1994* (London, 1994).

HANNE BRAUN and GERHILD FRASCH

Youth

1. As Sociological Construct
2. Problems and Analysis

Youth, as a distinct phase of the life cycle, is not a universal phenomenon. Although the processes of sexual maturation and biological aging are the common experiences of human beings, age is not an equally salient principle of social organization in every → society. Moreover, different societies divide up the spectrum of chronological age at various points for purposes of classifying socially recognized phases of the life cycle. In many preliterate and peasant societies the transition from child to adult is abrupt (→ Childhood) and is ritually marked by → initiation rites or by → marriage (A. van Gennep). In many such cases there is no socially recognized transition stage "youth." A youth stage arises only where fully adult social roles are postponed beyond the point in the life cycle at which puberty typically occurs and where age-homogeneous groupings of young people mark the transition period between childhood and full social maturity.

1. As Sociological Construct

1.1. Youth, in this sociological sense, is a feature of some small-scale and premodern societies. There are even instances where such a stage applies to young males but not to young females, as in some contemporary Arab peasant societies and in some rural parts of the Indian subcontinent where girls are normally married as soon as they are sexually mature, while young males are some years older before they are permitted to marry and take on fully adult responsibilities. It is somewhat paradoxical that in traditional societies the division of labor is importantly structured around age as an organizing principle, but it is uncommon for youth to be a socially important phase of the life cycle, while in modern → industrialized societies the position is the reverse: age declines in importance as a principle of social and economic organization, but youth becomes a recognized and steadily expanding phase in the life cycle for all classes and both sexes.

Over the last century and a half, modern Western societies have created elaborate institutional arrangements through which the young receive education and training beyond the family to prepare them for complex adult social and economic roles. Since the achievement of mass literacy and universal formal education, the number of years typically spent in full-time education has been steadily increased, and the age of full adulthood postponed. Over the same historical period better nutrition has led to an earlier average age of puberty, and an extended period of "adolescence," or youth, has thus emerged. Youth as we know it is therefore a historical creation of modern Western society.

1.2. Because youth is a social and historical construct rather than a simple biological category, there are many potential delineations of the concept. In the social sciences, definitions of youth typically include both biological features (chronological age and sexual maturation) and more variable social markers. Prominent among the latter are features of political, economic, and familial dependency combined with limited measures of personal autonomy, as well as the importance of both formal and informal groupings of young people — from educational institutions, through adult-led youth organizations and youth movements, to autonomous youth subcultures such as dating systems, street gangs, friendship cliques, or fluid stylistic → subcultures organized around fashion, music, sport, and the like.

Important among the formal social markers of youth as a status are legal definitions such as the age of criminal responsibility, the age of consent (to sexual activity), the minimum school-leaving age, and the age at which voting rights or the right to make legally binding contracts are conferred. Typically in modern Western societies adult rights and duties are acquired piecemeal over a prolonged period rather than in one ritual moment. Hence, there is an emphasis on youth as a transition stage between dependency and maturity that is characterized by a contradictory mixture of both.

2. Problems and Analysis

2.1. Certain "problem" features of youth in Western societies have been the focus of both public concern and social research. One of these themes is "adolescence" as a time of emotional turbulence and instability. Comparative studies, notably those of the anthropologist Margaret Mead (1901-78), suggest, however, that adolescent "moodinesss" is a specific consequence of the contradictions of modern Western life rather than an invariable psychological accompaniment of the process of psychological maturation (→ Development 2). A related concern has been with the problem of youthful delinquency, in particular the tendency for young males to display high rates of deviance and petty criminality, especially in urban areas and among disadvantaged groups. Interpretations of this and of related features of youthful "deviance" range from Marxist class theory (→ Marxism), through theories of subcultural variation, to psychosocial theories of inadequate or deviant → socialization.

A closely connected issue is the potential of youth for rebellious or revolutionary → politics (→ Revolution). Although only a minority of young people were involved, it is notable that youth movements were prominent aspects both of 19th-century Romantic nationalism (→ Nation, Nationalism) and of all the successful political revolutions of the 20th century from Russia to Iran. The student protests of the late 1960s, which formed part of the American civil rights movement and the demonstrations against the Viet Nam War, are more limited examples of the political impact of youth movements in times of cultural and political change. Some observers link this propensity for rebellion to the broader attraction of young people to moral, political, and religious idealism.

2.2. The most comprehensive theoretical treatment of these issues is S. N. Eisenstadt's analysis of youth culture as a functionally necessary feature of complex modern societies. The child's world in the private family is in sharp disjunction with the competitive principles of → work and politics (→ Achievement and Competition). Youth culture is a "moratorium," a protected enclave within which the young learn to adjust to the transition, but it remains an unstable world because it is by definition composed of contradictory elements, hence the volatility of youth. Other theorists more influenced by the thinking of K. → Marx (1818-83), notably A. Gramsci (1891-1937), have stressed the class and ethnic subcultures among youth and have interpreted stylistic deviance such as that of hippies or punks as a form of cultural → class struggle.

Since the 1950s affluence has created a flourishing youth market for fashion, rock music, and commercial → leisure pursuits. It has been the spearhead for the spread of an individualistic and hedonistic consumer culture (→ Consumption) of an international scale dominated by Anglo-American images and products. Its libertarian and sexually permissive messages (→ Sexuality) are in tension both with formal educational institutions and the churches, while the secular rituals of rock music offer competition to religion proper.

Conservative churches function as a shelter from the anarchic liberalism of secular youth culture for a growing minority of Western youth (→ Conservatism 2), while liberal churches can often draw upon the idealism and internationalism that remain within popular youth culture (e.g., Bob Geldof's charity project "Band Aid"). Undoubtedly, however, all the churches have accommodated themselves to the style if not wholly to the content of youth culture both in their → evangelism and training of the young and in their provision for Christian youth groups (→ Youth Work).

→ Confirmation; Identity; Pedagogy; Religious Education; Youth Religions

Bibliography: T. Brabazon, *From Revolution to Revelation: Generation X, Popular Memory, and Cultural Studies* (Aldershot, 2005) • M. Brake, *Comparative Youth Culture: The Sociology of Youth Cultures and Youth Subcultures in America, Britain, and Canada* (London, 1985) • K. C. Dean, *Practicing Passion: Youth and the Quest for a Passionate Church* (Grand Rapids, 2004) • S. N. Eisenstadt, *From Generation to Generation* (3d ed.; New Brunswick, N.J., 2003) • A. van Gennep, *The Rites of Passage* (Chicago, 1960; orig. pub., 1908) • S. Hall and T. Jefferson, eds., *Resistance through Rituals: Youth Subcultures in Post-war Britain* (2d ed.; New York, 2006) • B. Hooper, *Youth in China* (New York, 1985) • B. Martin, *A Sociology of Contemporary Cultural Change* (Oxford, 1981) • M. Mead, *From the South Seas: Studies of Adolescence and Sex in Primitive Societies* (3 vols. in 1; New York, 1939) • F. Musgrove, *Youth and the Social Order* (Bloomington, Ind., 1965) • A. Nayak, *Race, Place, and Globalization: Youth Cultures in a Changing World* (New York, 2003) • U. Nembach, ed., *Jugend–2000 Jahre nach Jesus. Jugend und Religion in Europa II* (Frankfurt, 1996); idem, ed., *Jugend und Religion in Europa* (2d ed.; Frankfurt, 1990) • E. C. Roehlkepartain et al., eds., *The Handbook of Spiritual Development in Childhood and Adolescence* (Thousand Oaks, Calif., 2006) • J. Street, *Rebel Rock: The Politics of Popular Music* (Oxford, 1986) • S. Turner, *Hungry for Heaven: Rock 'n' Roll and the Search for Redemption* (rev. ed.; Downers Grove, Ill., 1995) • V. W. Turner, *The Ritual Process: Structure and Anti-structure* (New York, 1995).

BERNICE MARTIN

Youth Religions

1. Term
2. Movements
3. Spread
4. Effect

1. Term

1.1. F. W. Haack used the term "youth religions" in 1974 for the religious and parareligious movements that sprang up since the end of the 1960s that had a particular appeal to young people and young adults between the ages of 18 and 35 (→ Youth) and that, in their teaching and practice, involved a certain infantile regression on the part of their adherents. The → Unification Church (or Moonies), for example, deliberately sets out to win supporters from young people and young adults.

1.2. The attraction of youth religions for their members rests on the unconditional commitment that they demand and the resultant sense of battling for a new world. They offer a visible "saved family" with a "holy master" of absolute, divine → authority who has a remedy by which to solve all individual and global problems and indeed to resolve the all-or-nothing contradiction. Another mark of youth religions is the esoteric gulf between goals and views within the youth religions and the aims propagated to outsiders. Thus some groups claim to be medical or religious reform movements, while they really view themselves internally as the definitive new revelation or even the root of all religions.

Traditional religions are seen as outmoded props of the old era that must be defeated or that at best can simply be used as recruiting grounds for new adherents.

1.3. Members of the youth religions very often evidence a drastic and rapid personality shift that leaves no place for criticism but takes the form of total commitment. These powerful personality changes and the new and strict ethical and moral orientations often lead to conflicts with the law and to social and family problems. The term "destructive cults" has been used because of their negative effects on youthful adherents.

2. Movements

The youth religions might be classified as follows:

First we have Indian-Hindu guru movements like → Ānanda Mārga, the Bhagwan movement (→ Bhagwan Shree Rajneesh), the → Divine Light Mission (DLM), the International Society for → Krishna Consciousness (ISKCON), and → Transcendental Meditation (TM). Some of these groups are linked to the Vishva Hindu Parishad (VHP), a kind of world Hindu missionary council. They are part of a planned Hindu missionary movement and are thus to be seen less in terms of their target and more in terms of their motivations and origins (→ Hinduism).

Then we have new Christian → sects like the → Children of God and The Way International.

Next are new syncretistic and spiritist movements (→ Spiritism; Syncretism) like the Moon movement, or Unification Church.

Finally, we have philosophical-therapeutic groups (psycho-cults) like the → Scientology Church, → EST, and the Action-Analytic Organization (AAO) of the Vienna artist Otto Mühl (b. 1925).

3. Spread

Some youth religions try to organize an elite, while others try to reach as many people as possible, for example, by use of the → mass media and cultural activity. Various membership figures are given, ranging from the hundreds to the thousands in different countries. Many more might take courses, for example, in Scientology or TM, than are actually members. The solid membership of the Moon movement is not especially large.

4. Effect

Youth religions are an especially dubious part of the worldwide movement of → new religions that embraces both church movements and non-Christian religious movements. As distinct from the classic Christian sects, the work of youth religions is not a reaction to Christian proclamation and action. They are active in all highly industrialized countries, including non-Christian Japan and the countries of eastern Europe. They present the churches with the problem of communicating viable Christian practice in modern society, and they also bring to their attention social tasks in relation to young people.

→ Counterculture

Bibliography: J. T. BIERMANS, *The Odyssey of New Religions Today: A Case Study of the Unification Church* (Lewiston, N.Y., 1988) • G. D. CHRYSSIDES and M. Z. WILKINS, eds., *A Reader in New Religious Movements* (New York, 2006) • F. CONWAY and J. SIEGELMAN, *Snapping: America's Epidemic of Sudden Personality Change* (2d ed.; New York, 1995) • J. R. GASCARD, *Neue Jugendreligionen. Zwischen Sehnsucht und Sucht* (Freiburg, 1984) • F.-W. HAACK, *Guruismus und Guru-Bewegungen* (Munich, 1982); idem, *Jugendreligionen. Ursachen, Trends, Reaktionen* (Munich, 1979); idem, *Die neuen Jugendreligionen* (Munich, 1974; 24th ed., 1988) • F.-W. HAACK, with T. GANDOW, *Jugendsekten. Vorbeugen, Hilfe, Auswege* (Weinheim, 1991) • S. J. HUNT, *Alternative Religions: A Sociological Introduction* (Aldershot, 2003) • P. C. LUCAS and T. ROBBINS, eds., *New Religious Movements in the Twenty-first Century: Legal, Political, and Social Challenges in Global Perspective* (New York, 2004) • J. A. MACCOLLAM, *Carnival of Souls: Religious Cults and Young People* (New York, 1979) • S. A. WRIGHT, *Leaving Cults: The Dynamics of Defection* (Washington, D.C., 1987).

THOMAS GANDOW

Youth Work

1. Target

According to the → United Nations *World Youth Report, 2005* (WYR), individuals between the ages of 15 and 24 are referred to as → youth (p. 22). Most international Christian youth organizations, however, target those between 18 and 30. In their youth work, the churches orient themselves to national practice. The range is from the high school period, to which many of the young people in European and North American churches belong, to the age of 35 in some less-developed countries. According to the WYR, there are 1.2 billion young people living in the world today, which represents 18 percent of the world's population (p. 73). (Note that there is currently a trend toward a smaller percentage of youth, from 19.4 percent in 1985 to 14 percent forecast in 2050.) The important fact for international youth work is that more than 80 percent of youth are living in less-developed countries, and it is expected that this number will increase up to 90 percent in 2050 (p. 74).

Young people are under enormous social pressures, including (1) → poverty and malnutrition (→ Hunger) in less-developed countries and stifling affluence in more-developed countries, (2) unequal educational possibilities, and (3) inadequate opportunities in the areas of work and vocation. The 2005 WYR indicates that global youth → unemployment increased from 11.7 percent in 1993 to an all-time high of 14.4 percent (88 million) in 2003. At the regional level, youth unemployment was highest in western Asia and North Africa (25.6 percent) and sub-Saharan Africa (21 percent), and lowest in East Asia (7 percent) and the industrialized economies (13.4 percent; p. 15).

Globalization has brought about substantial changes in the job market, to which young people, as newcomers, may be particularly vulnerable. Trade liberalization has forced companies to become more flexible and competitive. Foreign investment often creates job opportunities in and around cities, inducing rural workers to move to urban areas. Young people have always constituted a significant proportion of migrant workers. In 2003 nearly half (48 percent) of the global population lived in urban areas, and this figure is projected to rise to more than 50 percent by 2007. In 2002 there were 175 million international migrants. Relevant statistics suggest that an estimated 26 million migrants, or around 15 percent of the total, are youth (p. 11).

Young people are regarded as a problem in many lands, for example, in publications that describe them as the lost generation. We should see here, however, a crisis in society as a whole. The task of youth work today is to respond to this crisis.

2. Aims

Youth work takes place within the community of Jesus Christ. Church youth work is part of the fulfillment of the church's commission (Matt. 28:19-20). Youth is both an instrument and an object of the mission of God in the world. Two aspects in particular have come into view in the course of history: the missionary and the emancipatory.

2.1. The *missionary* aspect emphasizes the fact that youth work is primarily pledged to the → gospel. Thus in the 19th century separate youth fellowships were set up alongside the established church, the better to reach and win those who were alienated from the church. But youth also plays an active role in the church's missionary efforts, for example, in Third World churches, in which it offers primary support for the church's evangelistic work (→ Mission). Youth work today reflects changes in the understanding of mission and has three different dimensions:

- sending for *propagation of the gospel,* which includes → proclamation, → Bible study, → spirituality, → youth religions, and → worship;
- sending for *service to the needy,* which includes → diakonia, studying the causes of social injustice, working out a strategy of → development (§1), → solidarity, and cooperation with youth and national movements; and
- sending in a *prophetic ministry,* which includes not only working for → peace, justice, social change (→ Society), liberation, and → peace education but also studying political revolution and seeking social forms that are more just.

2.2. The *emancipatory* aspect stresses the need for an → emancipation of youth in the church and its organizations as a countermeasure to the marginalization (→ Marginalized Groups), oppression, and exploitation of young people in the world. This task covers such matters as rediscovered → identity, generational conflict and the unity of the church, and participation in the process of decision.

Although the two aspects form a single whole, they are easily polarized and viewed as alternatives.

3. Organization

3.1. Youth work takes place primarily in the → congregation, for young people are an integral part of the visible body of Christ. Such ministry is recognized to be a basic task of each congregation. Various forms must be used to reach as many people as possible. Youth work offers young people a chance to engage in living discussion of the faith. The fact that there are separate youth groups, youth organizations, and student unions that almost replace church youth work in many countries (e.g., the Luther League in the U.S. Lutheran Church) is in tension with the claim of the living body of Christ to include every generation.

Young people meet regularly to discuss relevant themes. They look for appropriate activities for their groups (→ Group and Group Dynamics), including Bible study, singing, → play, → sports, and outgoing youth work (see 4). The situation differs in less-developed countries, where young people are more closely integrated into congregational life. An issue in more-developed countries is the so-called crisis in traditional → worship, which does not attract young people. Other issues are youth → spirituality (→ Taizé Community) and distrust of → institutions run by adults.

In the Third World the congregation and confession are a home for young people, and ecumenical contacts with the youth groups of other denominations are sought as an implication of believing. In more-developed countries ecumenical cooperation offers some young people a hope of escaping from the crisis of confidence vis-à-vis their own churches. Serious problems that → ecumenism must wrestle with are the achieving of full ecumenical fellowship and the avoiding of the wrong kind of → proselytism (→ Local Ecumenism). Some ecumenical groups have spontaneously overcome these problems, often in the form of diaconal fellowships with social and political programs.

3.2. Denominational unions give youth work an international dimension that transcends divisions between East and West, North and South. Examples are the International Anglican Youth Network (London), International Movement of Catholic Agricultural and Rural Youth (Brussels), International Youth Catholic Students (Paris), International Youth Christian Workers (Brussels), Syndesmos: The World Fellowship of Orthodox Youth (Holargos, Greece; in 2006 it encompassed 121 member movements worldwide), World Federation of Catholic Youth (Brussels), Youth Committee of the World Methodist Council (Denver), and Youth Department of the Baptist World Alliance (Falls Church, Va.).

Since 1981 the → Lutheran World Federation (→ Lutheran Churches) has had its own youth section, "Youth in Church and Society." Like other such ministries it offers the following programs: conferences, local and global consultations, a youth newsletter, and visits and exchanges with a view to strengthening youth participation in the life of the federation, awakening responsibility for the church's

tasks in the world, and promoting youth work in the member churches.

3.3. International ecumenical youth organizations give added depth to youth work. Thus we have the → YMCA and → YWCA, with regionally structured and globally coordinated work of various kinds in different countries. Then we have the Student Christian Movement (Birmingham, Eng.) and the International Fellowship of Evangelical Students (Oxford) working among students in many different countries, with both evangelistic and social programs. There is also Frontier Internship in Mission, based in Geneva. The → World Council of Churches in Geneva also has the World Youth Program, which focuses on the development and coordination of the ecumenical youth movement.

→ Child Labor; Development 2.3; Socialization; Student Christian Movements; World Student Christian Federation

Bibliography: A. J. van der Bent, *From Generation to Generation: The Story of Youth in the World Council of Churches* (Geneva, 1986) • Evangelical Lutheran Church in America, *Studies on Education: Our Calling in Education; A Lutheran Study* (Minneapolis, 2004) • A. Grimm, *Lass' doch der Jugend ihren Lauf. Probleme und Perspektiven kirchlicher Jugendarbeit* (Rehburg-Loccum, 1994) • B. Grom, *Methoden für Religionsunterricht, Jugendarbeit und Erwachsenenbildung* (Düsseldorf, 1992) • H. Hobelsberger et al., eds., *Experiment Jugendkirche, Event und Spiritualität* (Kevelaer, 2003) • I. Holzapfel, ed., *Jugend und Religion* (Stuttgart, 1992) • R. D. Martinson, *Effective Youth Ministry: A Congregational Approach* (Minneapolis, 1988) • J. Pahl, *Youth Ministry in Modern America: 1930 to the Present* (Peabody, Mass., 2000) • A. L. Reid, *Raising the Bar: Ministry to Youth in the New Millennium* (Grand Rapids, 2004) • H. Spies, *Neue Religiosität als Herausforderung an Theologie und Jugendarbeit* (Bochum, 1995) • M. P. Strommen and R. A. Hardel, *Passing on the Faith: A Radical New Model for Youth and Family Ministry* (Winona, Minn., 2000) • D. F. White, *Practicing Discernment with Youth: A Transformative Youth Ministry Approach* (Cleveland, 2005) • *World Youth Report, 2005: Young People Today and in 2015* (New York, 2005).

JÚLIUS FILO, with ONDREJ PROSTREDNIK

4. Forms and Methods

The forms and methods of youth work are not an arbitrary matter; they are vital. Attention is thus paid to them in the literature. Their selection and use will be determined by the target and goals.

4.1. Forms

The most important and common form is the → group. Groups may be formed according to age, needs, or material goals — for example, groups for children, adolescents, or graduates; groups for fellowship, → play, or discussion; and groups for Bible study, voluntary social service, or cooperative ventures.

Free groups with their own goals are significant, for example, in work for peace or environmental protection or Third World trade. Groups of this kind enable young people to engage freely in both fellowship and service. Honorary presidents and associates are available for → counseling and → pastoral care. Activities might include discussion, films, concerts, seminars, weekend conferences, vacation projects, social programs, youth worship, national conferences, and → evangelism.

4.2. Methods

The forms of youth work, unless they are traditional, might also be regarded as methods to achieve the aims. Methods have been defined as planned modes of action or forms of organization that in a given situation best facilitate the addressing of questions and interests, the tackling of problems, the shaping of learning processes, the mastering of tasks, and the achieving of goals (P. Müller, 281).

Church youth work uses methods from social and group pedagogics, group dynamics, and educational theory (→ Pedagogy). W. Erl distinguished between methods that are oriented to the group, triggering group processes and fostering the group and individuals within it, and those that are governed by the principle of individual activity (p. 7). Criteria of selection are whether the method serves self-discovery, improves mutual acceptance and → communication, and facilitates self-determination and group determination. The same criteria apply also to the selection of forms of leadership.

Means are chosen for the sake of their effectiveness in achieving motivation, understanding, communication, comprehension of complex matters, actualization of experiences, independent activity on the part of participants, and competent training (Müller, 282).

Experience with forms and methods in youth work has increasingly been applied to other spheres of the church's ministry.

→ Catechesis; Christian Education

Bibliography: T. Celek and D. Zander, Inside the Soul of a New Generation: Insights and Strategies for Reaching Busters (Grand Rapids, 1996) • K. C. Dean, Practicing Passion: Youth and the Quest for a Passionate Church (Grand Rapids, 2004) • W. Erl, Methoden moderner Jugendarbeit (7th ed.; Tübingen, 1977) • P. Hendricks, Hungry Souls, Holy Companions: Mentoring a New Generation of Christians (Harrisburg, Pa., 2006) • T. Jones, Postmodern Youth Ministry: Exploring Cultural Shift, Creating Holistic Connections, Cultivating Authentic Community (Grand Rapids, 2001) • P. Müller, "Methoden," Kirchliche Jugendarbeit in Grundbegriffen. Stichworte zu einer ökumenischen Bilanz (ed. M. Affolderbach and H. Steinkamp; Düsseldorf, 1985) 272-92 • P. C. Olsen, Youth at Risk: Ministry to the Least, the Lost, and the Last (Cleveland, 2003) • M. Ungar, ed., Handbook for Working with Children and Youth: Pathways to Resilience across Cultures and Contexts (Thousand Oaks, Calif., 2005) • A. Wheal, Adolescence: Positive Approaches for Working with Young People (2d ed.; Lyme Regis, Dorset, 2004).

GÜNTHER HEGELE

5. United States

5.1. Factors

Christian youth work in the United States has been expressed in three ways: youth activities, youth ministry, and youth movements. In youth activities adults use activities appealing to young people in order to produce moral character. Youth ministry includes the dynamics of youth activity but focuses on achieving results that conform to sectarian values. Christian youth movements, by contrast, are led by older adolescents and express Christian ideals. In these, adults play a secondary and supportive role.

5.2. Context

These expressions of American youth work have arisen in a somewhat cyclic fashion. Every 35 to 50 years for the past two centuries, new strategies have been developed for reaching and holding middle adolescents within the Christian community. Changes in youth work at the college and university level evolve more slowly. Both appear to be the response of Christian leaders to a sense of lost control over the lives of church youth occasioned by economic or social change and spiritual instability within the → culture.

5.3. Youth Activities

Taking a holistic view of life, youth activities employed by concerned adults develop character qualities in participating youth. The activities primarily include intellectual pursuits, social activities, and athletic competition or nature-related activities. The → YMCA in America exemplifies this approach. A similar approach is employed by the Boy Scouts and Girl Scouts, whose early leadership shared a Christian → worldview. Youth athletic programs, while weakened by a small minority of volunteer leadership seeking to win at all costs, teach life skills of discipline, cooperation, and fair play. Challenging this approach is the growing diversity of values vying for inclusion in publicly funded activities.

5.4. Youth Ministry

The most distinctively American contribution to Christian youth work is the youth society. Popularized by Congregationalist minister Francis E. Clark (1851-1927) in 1881, when he established the Christian Endeavor Society in his church in Portland, Maine, the society quickly spawned similar societies in most of the Protestant → denominations. The primary function of youth societies was to maintain the values of the host churches while providing a forum for developing a new generation of church leadership. With the emergence of youth directors and youth pastors in the second half of the 20th century, much of the work with teenagers was professionalized in North America and portions of the United Kingdom.

5.4.1. Global Expressions

As the growth of Christianity exploded in the Majority World (Africa, Latin American, and Asia) in the 20th century, churches attempted to pass on their faith to the rising generation. The predominant approach to youth ministry was a variation on the youth society pioneered by Clark more than a century earlier. In societies where "youth" was understood to mean everyone from childhood through their late 20s or early 30s, youth societies were led by older youth who served as officers and provided spiritual leadership modeled loosely after the forms of worship experienced in their adult church. Camping experiences led by Christian adults consistently have the greatest impact on the spiritual development of, and evangelistic outreach to, the youth of the world.

5.4.2. Parachurch Youth Ministry

With fragmentation of youth ministries along denominational lines during the first quarter of the 20th century, much of youth ministry had lost a sense of the Christian mission. This vacuum was filled by a movement that sought to do youth → evangelism. Best known for evangelist Billy Graham (b. 1918; the first full-time employee of Youth for Christ), the movement included Young Life and Fellowship of Christian Athletes. Using radio broadcasts, weekly evangelistic rallies, club programs, and camps, the movement rapidly changed the focal point of youth ministry from the church to the public high school. By the 1960s many local churches had adopted the creative methodologies of the movement.

5.4.3. Parachurch University Youth Ministries

At the same time, a British export, Inter-Varsity Christian Fellowship, developed → Bible study chapters on university campuses. This ministry was followed by the Navigators and Campus Crusade for Christ, employing much more American models of ministry for late adolescents. Paid staff workers developed spiritually aware student leaders, who created networks of Christian cells on university campuses with the intent of evangelizing peers open to the Christian message and strengthening those already committed to the Christian gospel. The major criticism of these parachurch groups is their tendency to compete with local-church ministries.

5.5. Youth Movements

With influence far out of proportion to their numbers, Christian youth movements have had the most profound effect of any aspect of youth work in the United States. It was from the "haystack prayer meeting" in 1806 that Samuel J. Mills (1783-1818) and his fellow collegians at Williams College (Williamstown, Mass.) gave birth to the modern American missionary movement. Exactly 80 years later, in 1886, students meeting with evangelist D. L. → Moody (1837-99) gained a world vision, and the Student Volunteer Movement was born, with the purpose of "the evangelization of the world in this generation." As a result, over 20,000 students went into foreign mission service. Another 80 years passed before the → Jesus Movement, again led by later adolescents, took the radicalism of the movement against the Viet Nam War (1964-75) and turned it into a means to evangelize the drug culture of American society. At the same time, it modified many churches' forms of worship and methods of evangelization.

With the emergence of postmodern perspectives in the early 21st century, the movement of the locus of Christianity from Europe and North America to the Majority World, the fall of Communism, and the increased influence of → Islam, Christian youth movements can be expected to emerge in the Majority World and have a global impact, as has happened in previous periods of instability and change.

→ Student Christian Movements

Bibliography: K. C. Dean, C. Clark, and D. Rahn, eds., *Starting Right: Thinking Theologically about Youth Ministry* (Grand Rapids, 2001) • R. R. Dunn and M. H. Senter III, eds., *Reaching a Generation for Christ: A Comprehensive Guide to Youth Ministry* (Chicago, 1997) • S. N. Eisenstadt, *From Generation to Generation* (3d ed.; New Brunswick, N.J., 2003) • F. O. Erb, *The Development of the Young People's Movement* (Chicago, 1917) • C. H. HOPKINS, *History of the Y.M.C.A. in North America* (New York, 1951) • D. M. HOWARD, *Student Power in World Evangelism* (Downers Grove, Ill., 1971) • K. HUNT and G. HUNT, *For Christ and the University: The Story of Intervarsity Christian Fellowship–USA, 1940-1990* (Downers Grove, Ill., 1992) • J. F. KETT, *Rites of Passage: Adolescence in America* (New York, 1977) • T. LADD and J. A. MATHISEN, *Muscular Christianity: Evangelical Protestants and the Development of American Sport* (Grand Rapids, 1999) • M. H. SENTER, *The Coming Revolution in Youth Ministry* (Wheaton, Ill., 1992); idem, *The Youth for Christ Movement as an Educational Agency and Its Impact upon Protestant Churches: 1931-1979* (Ann Arbor, Mich., 1990) • M. J. TAYLOR, ed., *An Introduction to Christian Education* (Nashville, 1966).

MARK H. SENTER III

Yugoslavia / Montenegro; Serbia

	1960	1980	2000
Population (1,000s):	8,050	9,522	10,502
Annual growth rate (%):	0.84	0.67	0.02
Area: 102,173 sq. km. (39,449 sq. mi.)			

A.D. 2000

Population density: 103/sq. km. (266/sq. mi.)
Births / deaths: 1.30 / 1.05 per 100 population
Fertility rate: 1.80 per woman
Infant mortality rate: 17 per 1,000 live births
Life expectancy: 73.3 years (m: 70.6, f: 76.1)
Religious affiliation (%): Christians 69.8 (Orthodox 63.7, Roman Catholics 3.6, indigenous 1.4, Protestants 1.0, other Christians 0.1), Muslims 16.3, nonreligious 10.3, atheists 3.5, other 0.1.

1. Background
2. Montenegro
   2.1. General Situation
   2.2. Religious Situation
3. Serbia
   3.1. General Situation
   3.2. Religious Situation

1. Background

"Yugoslavia" (lit. "land of the south Slavs") is the name of a former country of southeast Europe occupying part of the Balkan Peninsula. The first use of the name was in the Kingdom of Yugoslavia (1929-41). This entity was formed in 1918 as the Kingdom of Serbs, Croats, and Slovenes, with the name changed in 1929. During World War II it was invaded and quickly conquered by the Axis powers.

After the war a socialist, federative Yugoslavia replaced the former kingdom. Embracing the six republics of Bosnia and Herzegovina, Croatia, Macedonia, Montenegro, Serbia, and Slovenia, it was successively named the Democratic Federation of Yugoslavia (from its first organization in exile in 1943), the Federal People's Republic of Yugoslavia (1946), and the Socialist Federal Republic of Yugoslavia (1963-91). Its first prime minister was Josip Tito (1892-1980), who was elected president in 1953 and later was named "president for life." Tito and his successors were effective in pursuing policies independent of both the Soviet Union and the West.

In 1989 Slobodan Milošević (1941-2006) became president of the Serbian Republic. His calls for Serbian domination of the federation led to its violent breakup, with Croatia and Slovenia declaring their independence in June 1991, followed by Macedonia (September 1991) and Bosnia and Herzegovina (March 1992). In April 1992 the two remaining republics, Serbia and Montenegro, re-formed themselves as the Federal Republic of Yugoslavia. Under Milošević, Serbia took military steps to unite ethnic Serbs in neighboring republics in a "Greater Serbia," an unsuccessful attempt that ended only with the signing of the Dayton Peace Accords in 1995. Serbian efforts in 1998/99 to expel ethnic Albanians from its province of Kosovo led to NATO bombing of Serbia, the stationing of NATO-led forces in Kosovo, and ultimately the arrest of Milošević and his trial in The Hague on the charge of crimes against humanity (→ International Law).

In February 2003 negotiations between the two republics led to a new, looser federation called simply Serbia and Montenegro. It was agreed that, after three years, either republic could hold a referendum on independence from the union. Montenegro exercised this option on May 21, 2006, with voters choosing independence, thus ending the last remnant of the Yugoslav federation.

2. Montenegro

2.1. *General Situation*

Montenegro (meaning "black mountain" in many Romance languages, as does Crna Gora, its name in Serbo-Croatian) was integrated politically into Serbia at the turn of the 13th century by the Serbian ruling family Nemanja; shortly thereafter it was brought into the Serbian Orthodox Church by Sava Nemanja, or St. Sava (1169-1236). In 1360 it became independent under the name "Zeta"; it was named Montenegro for the first time in 1435. In 1439 the cities on the Adriatic coast were occupied by the Venetians, and the Montenegrin rulers in the rest of the country were forced to recognize the authority of the Turks, though they were able to retain their own internal administration.

In 1878 the Great Powers of Europe, meeting at the Congress of Berlin, recognized Montenegro as an independent state. In 1910 it became a kingdom, with Nicholas I its only ruler. During World War I Montenegro supported the Allies, but from January 1916 to October 1918 it was occupied by Austria-Hungary. In December 1918 Montenegro joined the Kingdom of the Serbs, Croats, and Slovenes, and in 1945 it became one of the Yugoslav socialist republics. Following the fall of the Socialist Federal Republic of Yugoslavia, and together with Serbia, Montenegro in 1992 joined the Federal Republic of Yugoslavia. It was reorganized in 2003 and renamed Serbia and Montenegro. Since June 3, 2006, it has been an independent state.

The Republic of Montenegro, whose capital is Podgorica, has an area of 13,812 sq. km. (5,333 sq. mi.). In 2002 its population was 620,000. The country is rich in bauxite; in recent years it has been ranked as the fastest-growing → tourism destination in the world.

2.2. *Religious Situation*

Roman Catholic church history includes a ninth-century reference to the Diocese of Bar, which in 1034 was elevated to an archdiocese; from this date also, the archbishop of Bar simultaneously held the title "primate of Serbia." Today Catholics are a small minority in Montenegro. In 2004 the Archdiocese of Bar had 11,500 Catholics in 19 parishes, with 5 diocesan priests and 8 religious priests. Since 1969 the Diocese of Kotor (10,000 members in 28 parishes, with 11 diocesan priests and 2 religious priests) has been integrated into the church province of Split-Makarska (Croatia).

Within the → Orthodox Church, the Diocese of Zeta became a metropolitanate in 1389. In 1593 the Montenegrin assembly elected Ruvim II Njeguš, a monk from Cetinje, to combined political and ecclesiastical leadership and proclaimed the Montenegrin Orthodox Church as autocephalous. Subsequently, under the Turkish occupation, the Orthodox metropolitans of Zeta functioned as theocratic leaders of the country. In the mid-19th century the autocephalous status of the Montenegrin Orthodox Church was recognized by the → patriarch of Constantinople. In 1920 the metropolitan of Zeta and the bishops of Nikšič and Peć (joined to Montenegro since 1912) agreed to join the Serbian Patriarchate of Belgrade. In 1993 the church renewed its claim to → autocephaly, which the Serbian Orthodox Church has so far not recognized.

The Islamic congregations in Montenegro have their headquarters in Podgorica (→ Islam). There are 70 mosques in the country, in which 60 imams are active.

3. Serbia
3.1. *General Situation*

Serbia was Christianized in the 9th century by → Byzantium, but in the 11th century it found itself oriented to the West and the → Roman Catholic Church. In the struggle for political independence, Serbian king Stefan I Nemanja (d. 1200), together with his son St. Sava, organized the independent Serbian Orthodox Church. In 1217, however, a legate of Pope Honorius III (1216-27) honored Stefan I's son Stefan II Nemanja (d. 1228) by crowning him king of Raška, a medieval Serbian state. He was thereafter known as Stefan Prvovenčani (lit. "first crowned"). Roman Catholic gains in Serbia ended when St. Sava, Stefan II's brother, secured an archbishopric from the patriarch of Constantinople and, in 1219, crowned Stefan II the Orthodox king of the Serbs.

Constantinople recognized the Serbian Orthodox Church in 1219, and in 1346 a church-state council in Shopje raised it to the rank of a patriarchate, though without the agreement of the patriarch of Constantinople. Its seat was first in Žiće, then in Peć. Reconciliation with the ecumenical patriarch did not take place until 1374. During the Turkish occupation, which began with the Turks' decisive victory in the battle of Kosovo in June 1389, Orthodoxy became for the Serbs an expression of their struggle for political and ecclesiastical independence. In 1830 the Serbs finally won their autonomy under the Turks, and in 1882 they became a kingdom.

The Patriarchate of Peć, which was dissolved from 1463 to 1557 and placed under the archbishop of Ohrid and the patriarch of Constantinople, regained domestic control in 1832. During the Turkish occupation many Serbs left the country, resettling mostly in Hungary and Croatia (→ Refugees). In 1920, following the founding of the Kingdom of Serbs, Croats, and Slovenes, the Serbian Patriarchate was recognized by the ecumenical patriarch. At that time all of the Orthodox in Yugoslavia were placed under the patriarch of Belgrade.

After 1945 Serbia became one of the six socialist republics of Yugoslavia. At that time all religious communities were subjected to severe → persecution, and many Serbs left the country because of the fear of Communist terror. After the fall of Yugoslavia in 1991, Serbia and Montenegro formed the Federal Republic of Yugoslavia, later the loose federation

Serbia and Montenegro. On June 5, 2006, following Montenegro's decision to leave the federation, Serbia declared itself an independent state, the successor to the previous union of Serbia and Montenegro.

The Republic of Serbia has an area of 88,361 sq. km. (34,116 sq. mi.). Its capital is Belgrade. In 2004 its population was 7,489,000. Ethnically, 82 percent of the population were Serbs, with 21 national minorities also present. Since the fall of Milošević, Serbia's economy has experienced solid growth, although many sectors have not recovered from the serious disruptions of the 1990s.

3.2. *Religious Situation*

The Serbian Orthodox Church is the official → state church of Serbia. Today in Serbia it possesses an archbishopric (Archdiocese of Belgrade-Karlovci, with the seat of the ecumenical patriarch) and 13 dioceses (Bačka, Banat, Braničevo, Budimije and Nikšić, Mileševo, Niš, Ras and Prizren, Šabac-Valjevo, Srem, Šumadija, Timok, Vranje, and Žiće). Outside of Serbia there are 4 metropolitanates (Dabro-Bosna, Montenegro and the Coastlands, Midwestern America, and Zagreb and Ljubljana), with a total of 17 dioceses throughout the Balkans and the world. Its highest ecclesial body is a four-person → synod chaired by the patriarch. The Holy Synod comprises all the bishops of the church, who meet once a year. The church, which is estimated to number some nine million faithful worldwide, maintains seminaries for candidates for the priesthood (in the states of Belgrade and Prizren, as well as Krka and Sremski Karlovci) and a theological faculty in Belgrade.

The Roman Catholic Church was organized in Serbia in the 16th century (the Diocese of Smederevo, which in 1729 was united with the Diocese of Belgrade). In 1914 the Kingdom of Serbia concluded a → concordat with the Holy See to regulate the legal status of the Catholic Church in Serbia. As a result, the Archdiocese of Belgrade-Smederevo was founded, with the first archbishop being named in 1924. In 1986 the Metropolitanate of Belgrade was established. In 2004 it encompassed 15

parishes and 23 priests, as well as the Dioceses of Subotica (114 parishes, 102 priests) and Zrenjanin (40 parishes, 26 priests) and the Apostolic Administration of Prizren (23 parishes, 55 priests), with a total of about 500,000 Catholics. In 1997 the Bishops' Conference was established, consisting of the archbishops of Belgrade and Bar, as well as the bishops and apostolic administrator. Following the fall of the federation of Serbia and Montenegro in 2006, and because the archbishop of Bar is in Montenegro, the conference became an international bishops' conference.

Before the fall of Yugoslavia there were well over a half million Catholics (mostly Croats, Slovenians, Hungarians, and Albanians) in Serbia, many of whom subsequently left the country. The number in Belgrade alone fell from 34,800 to 8,500.

The Reformed Christian Church was formed in the middle of the 19th century, becoming independent in 1920. Today it exists in 18 congregations in Bačka and 8 in Banat.

The Moslem community in Serbia is fairly strong, with 529 mosques. The grand mufti's seat is in Belgrade.

Bibliography: S. ALEXANDER, *Church and State in Yugoslavia since 1945* (Cambridge, 1979) • D. B. BARRETT, G. T. KURIAN, and T. M. JOHNSON, *WCE* (2d ed.) 1.812-16 • D. DJOKIC, ed., *Yugoslavism: Histories of a Failed Idea, 1918-1992* (London, 2003) • G. DUIJZINGS, *Religion and the Politics of Identity in Kosovo* (New York, 2000) • V. PERICA, *Balkan Idols: Religion and Nationalism in Yugoslav States* (Oxford, 2002) • S. P. RAMET, *Balkan Babel: The Disintegration of Yugoslavia from the Death of Tito to the Fall of Milosevic* (4th ed.; Boulder, Colo., 2002); eadem, "Religion and Nationality in Yugoslavia," *Religion and Nationalism in Soviet and East European Politics* (ed. P. Ramet; 2d ed.; Durham, N.C., 1989) 299-327; eadem, "The Serbian Orthodox Church," *Christianity under Stress,* vol. 1, *Eastern Christianity and Politics in the Twentieth Century* (ed. P. Ramet; Durham, N.C., 1988) 232-48.

FRANCE M. DOLINAR

Z

Zaire / Congo-Kinshasa

	1960	*1980*	*2000*
Population (1,000s):	15,333	27,009	51,749
Annual growth rate (%):	2.71	3.20	2.98

Area: 2,345,095 sq. km. (905,446 sq. mi.)

A.D. 2000

Population density: 22/sq. km. (57/sq. mi.)
Births / deaths: 4.22 / 1.21 per 100 population
Fertility rate: 5.78 per woman
Infant mortality rate: 82 per 1,000 live births
Life expectancy: 54.7 years (m: 53.1, f: 56.3)
Religious affiliation (%): Christians 95.9 (Roman Catholics 49.9, indigenous 28.4, Protestants 23.0, unaffiliated 4.6, marginal 1.2), tribal religionists 1.9, Muslims 1.1, other 1.1.

1. General Situation
2. Mission Work and Christian Churches
   2.1. Protestants
   2.2. Roman Catholics
   2.3. Kimbanguists
3. Interchurch Relations
4. Church and State
5. Other Religions

Since 1997 Zaire has been named the Democratic Republic of Congo (DRC). Its capital is Kinshasa, a city of 7-8 million people (2006) and a major port on the Congo River. The country, commonly called Congo-Kinshasa, should not be confused with Republic of the Congo, or Congo-Brazzaville.

1. General Situation

1.1. The DRC is one of the largest countries in Africa (third in area, fourth in population). The vast majority of the population are Bantu peoples. Smaller numbers belong to Sudanese, Nilotic, and Hamitic ethnic groups in the north and east. The Pygmies (approximately 0.5 percent) are considered to be the original inhabitants of the Congo Basin. Among the over 200 languages spoken, Kikongo, Lingala, Swahili, and Tshiluba are the four national languages; French is the official language. The cultural heritage is rich regarding language, music, dance, sculpture, and religion. The vast territory is administratively divided into ten provinces plus Kinshasa.

Colonization, urbanization, and political unrest since the late 1980s are the main causes for an ongoing social change in the traditional societies. The economic potential is immense, for the DRC is rich in mineral reserves, hydroelectric power, agriculture, and forestry. After 1975 the effects of an increasing economic crisis surfaced in a serious reduction of productivity, high → unemployment, inflation, and foreign debt. Ruthless exploitation in colonial and postcolonial times (→ Colonialism), along with the ubiquitous corruption and merciless kleptocracy of both the Mobutu and (Laurent) Kabila regimes, made the DRC an impoverished country on the brink of economic collapse.

1.2. The modern history of the DRC starts with the exploration of the Congo Basin between 1874 and 1877 by Henry M. Stanley (1841-1904). It continues with colonial domination by the Congo Free State (1885-1908), under the control of Belgian king Leopold II, and then the Belgian Congo colony (1908-60). Independence was gained in 1960.

Colonel Joseph Désiré Mobutu (as of 1972, Mobutu Sese Seko) seized power in November 1965. He established his rule with the Mouvement Populaire de la Révolution (MPR, Popular Movement of the Revolution), founded in 1967 (which later became the state party), and promoted an ideology of "authenticity," which accounts for the renaming of Congo as Zaïre in 1971, the prohibiting of Christian names in favor of traditional names, and similar decrees. After uprisings in the east and international pressure, Mobutu in early 1990 announced the start of democratic reforms, including establishment of a multiparty system and presidential and parliamentary elections. Elections, however, were never held under Mobutu.

The 1990s were marked by accelerated disintegration of both the national government and territorial unity. Delay in the democratization process gave momentum to the Alliance des Forces Démocratiques pour la Libération du Congo-Zaïre (AFDL, Alliance of Democratic Forces for the Liberation of Congo-Zaire) — a coalition of four rebel movements arising in eastern Zaire and supported by Uganda, Rwanda, Burundi, Angola, and South Africa and led by General Laurent Désiré Kabila — to push for Mobutu's downfall. In May 1997 they were successful in driving Mobutu out of the country. Mobutu died in exile in Morocco in September 1997.

After he replaced Mobutu, Kabila was unfortunately unable to achieve a democratic turnaround. Instead, he had to face accusations that the AFDL, dominated by Tutsis, was responsible for the killing of up to 200,000 Hutu refugees in the east. In 1998 Rwanda and Uganda started to wage war against the Kinshasa government, primarily by supporting a number of rebel and militia groups that were operating in the east and the north, among them the Rassemblement Congolais pour la Démocratie (RCD, Congolese Movement for Democracy), controlling the city and area of Goma, and the Mouvement pour la Libération du Congo (MLC, Congolese Liberation Movement), controlling the north.

These two neighboring countries, along with Burundi, began plundering the treasures of the soil (diamonds, gold, cobalt, copper, and coltran [vital in the manufacture of electronics], plus rare timber), and so too did foreign allies of the central government like Angola, Zimbabwe, and Namibia, which controlled the south and the west. Neither Kabila's troops nor the rebel militias were able to defeat the other, and the civil war continued, with enormous and widespread suffering. The fighting included the recruiting and exploitation of hundreds of child soldiers.

Laurent Kabila was assassinated in January 2001 and was succeeded by his son Joseph Kabila, head of the armed forces, who was sworn in as president the same month. Joseph Kabila's initial declarations indicated a shift in policy toward ending the war by resuming peace talks and allowing U.N. troops to be stationed in the conflict areas. In December 2002 the Pretoria Accord brought about an official but fragile peace between the government of the DRC and the main rebel factions for the purpose of establishing a government of national unity.

In December 2005 a new constitution was accepted by referendum and was promulgated by the president in February 2006. The long-awaited elections for presidency and for the National Assembly, many times postponed, finally took place in July 2006. The presidential results were inconclusive, since no candidate gained a majority of the votes cast. In runoff elections in October, Kabila defeated Vice-President Jean-Pierre Bemba. In late November the Supreme Court dismissed Bemba's appeal, which paved the way for the swearing in of Kabila as president in December 2006.

The human cost of these decades of instability and corruption has been staggering: since 1996 over 3.9 million people have lost their lives in the civil war, with over a half million people forced to flee their homes (→ Refugees). In 2006 a U.N. peacekeeping force of 19,800, then the largest in the world, was stationed in the DRC, but still an average of 1,200 people were dying daily because of the conflict.

2. Mission Work and Christian Churches

In 2006 the number of Christians in the DRC was just under 50 million. Of these, the largest number were Roman Catholics (between 50 and 60 percent of all Christians), followed by those affiliated with mainline Protestant churches (over 20 percent), adherents of independent, Pentecostal, and → charismatic movements (12-14 percent), and Kimbanguists (6-8 percent). In addition, small Greek

Orthodox and Egyptian Coptic communities are found in the urban centers.

Christianity arrived in Congo in two stages. Missionary activity by → Franciscans, → Dominicans, and → Jesuits began in 1491 after Diogo Cão (fl. 1480-86) had made the first contacts with Congolese in 1483 and following the baptism of Congolese king Nzinga Nkumu (d. ca. 1506). This first missionary period ended with little success in 1835.

2.1. *Protestants*

In 1878 the first Protestant mission station was founded in Mpalabala (Lower Congo) by the Livingstone Inland Mission. Shortly afterward, pioneers of the Baptist Missionary Society (→ Baptists) advanced up to the Stanley Pool and founded stations, starting at Kintambo (Kinshasa) and going upstream as far as the Equator region. The → British missions were immediately followed by → Scandinavian and → North American missions. In the course of the decades over 70 mission organizations, mostly from the United States, gained a foothold in Congo, focusing mainly on evangelization (→ Evangelism) and on programs of medical and educational development.

The first translation of the NT was published in 1893. Since then, either the entire Bible or parts of it have been translated into over 60 languages. One of the recent projects of the Bible Society of the DRC, carried out with Roman Catholic participation, is the translation of the Bible into the Lomongo, Kituba, and Lingala languages (→ Bible Versions).

The vision of a united church in Congo, outlined for the first time in a joint venture by → missionaries in 1902, survived from 1924 onward in the Conseil Protestant du Congo (CPC, Protestant Council of Congo) and was given at least a structural shape in 1970 by the creation of the Église du Christ au Zaïre (ECZ, Church of Christ in Zaire). This body meant the end of Protestant missions, for henceforth all *communautés,* or religious communities originating from missions, were placed under Congolese leadership and recognized by the government as member churches of the ECZ. More than 60 *communautés* joined the ECZ, which in 1999 became the Église du Christ au Congo (ECC, Church of Christ in Congo).

The main traditions represented in the ECC are Presbyterian (→ Reformed and Presbyterian Churches), → Baptist, → Methodist, → Mennonite, → Pentecostal, → Disciples of Christ, and → Assemblies of God. Many of the smaller churches trace their origin to → evangelical missions or to separatist movements. Thus the ECC embraces today episcopal, congregationalist, and synodal church models.

Protestant schools obtained recognition by the colonial government and the right to public subsidies only in 1948. The Protestant philosophy of education and their schools were coordinated on a national level by the Office of Protestant Education (BEP) at ECC headquarters in Kinshasa. Landmarks in the history of Congolese Protestantism include the foundation of the Protestant Theological Seminary in 1959, expanded in 1994 to become the Université Protestante au Zaïre (UPZ), now the Université Protestante au Congo (UPC), and formation in 1963 of the Université Libre du Congo (ULC). The majority of the pastors receive their training in regional theological schools (Instituts Supérieurs de Théologie, later upgraded to theological seminaries). In the meantime, women have been admitted to theological training in greater numbers, but thus far relatively few have gained access to the ministry. Also numerous Bible schools offer training to catechists and community leaders.

The ECC is involved in social activities, coordinated by the central office Entr'aide Protestante (Protestant Mutual Aid), with noteworthy performances in health services (e.g., hospitals, dispensaries, pharmacies) and in development and relief work. During the Mobutu regime the National Synod and the leaders of the ECZ had to face the challenges of an increasingly unjust dictatorship failing to meet the needs of the population and committing egregious violations of human → rights. In the ongoing transformation of Congolese society, the ECC, together with the other churches, is called to proclaim and live the liberating power of the gospel in a credible way.

2.2. *Roman Catholics*

The second era of → Catholic missions started in 1880 simultaneously in the west and in the east. French Spiritans founded the mission station Boma in the Lower Congo, while the White Fathers (Missionaries of Africa) founded the mission station Mulweva at the western shore of Lake Tanganyika. Beginning in 1888, the Belgian Missionaries of Scheut (C.I.C.M.) undertook an ongoing mission that has lasted up to the present time. Belgian Sisters followed, working mostly in → education and in health. In the following decades over 150 different religious communities of women and men, as well as contemplative orders, arrived in Congo. In 1954 the first university in Congo was established, which was designated a Catholic university in 1957. Named Lovanium, it was given the status of an African branch of the University of Louvain. The same year a Faculté de Théologie (Department of Theology), the first in all Africa, was incorporated.

In 1959, on the eve of independence, the Catholic → hierarchy was established in the DRC. According to Vatican statistics for 2004, the → Roman Catholic Church, the largest in Africa, was organized in the DRC in 47 ecclesiastical territories (6 metropolitan, 41 episcopal). They were administered by indigenous → bishops, who oversaw a church totaling roughly 30 million baptized persons. The pastoral workforce included 7,577 women religious, 4,612 priests belonging either to the diocesan clergy (2,903) or to → religious orders (1,709), 1,340 laymen religious, 106 lay missionaries, and 63,447 catechists.

In the late 1970s Joseph Cardinal Malula (1917-89) decided to promote the lay ministry in the Archdiocese of Kinshasa by appointing married men as *bakambi* (sing. *mokambi*), or responsible parish leaders. After pastoral training, these lay ministers accomplish their task beside their professional work. The *mokambi* is bound to share his ministry with his wife, who likewise assumes certain responsibilities in the parish. Mostly in urban areas, small → base communities (*communautés ecclésiales de base*) have increasingly emerged. These communities are the very environment where African Christians can express and share their faith with one another in solidarity and celebration.

Established in 1969, the Catholic Office for Development coordinates a large number of projects, mainly in the fields of education, health, agriculture, social justice, and the promotion of women. Guided by the vision of an integral development, the church is involved in the realization of economic, social, and political conditions that embody justice, and also in the field of research and formation. This work is documented by numerous publications of the local bishops or the Bishops' Conference, as well as by the broad educational work of the Centre d'Études pour l'Action Sociale (CEPAS, Study Center for Social Action), directed by the Jesuits.

Since the 1970s the Catholic Church in Congo has played a leading part in the struggle for an authentic Africanization of Christian witness and practice, based on a true recognition by the universal church of the African particular churches (i.e., dioceses) in their respective cultural contexts (→ Culture and Christianity). Thanks to Cardinal Malula, a committed promoter of the emergence of a truly African church with an authentic African liturgy, the Congolese Catholic Church took the lead in this process, supported by theological research and teaching (→ African Theology), as well as by → preaching and → liturgy.

Since 1972 a climate of tension between the Catholic Church and the government arose from the ideology of authenticity imposed by Mobutu's one-party rule, with its corollary of interfering with the efforts of democratic participation, plus its disregard for human rights and the implementation of socioeconomic justice. If there was at times reluctance on the side of the individual bishops to speak up, the episcopal conference (Conférence épiscopale nationale du Congo [CENCO]) regularly addressed itself in different ways to the burning political issues.

2.3. *Kimbanguists*

The → Kimbanguist Church, or Église de Jésus-Christ sur la terre par son envoyé spécial (*before 1987*: par le prophète) Simon Kimbangu (EJCSK, Church of Jesus Christ on earth by his messenger [*formerly*: by his prophet] Simon Kimbangu), claims a membership of roughly 5 million faithful, 3-4 million being in Congo, the rest in neighboring countries like Angola, Congo-Brazzaville, and Zambia, as well as in European countries. The Kimbanguists are spread throughout all of Congo, with the greatest numbers in the Lower Congo and in Kinshasa. Generally, they belong to the modest social strata of the population. Like the other churches, the EJCSK has schools and social and development projects, which are financed to a remarkable extent by its own means. In 1969 the EJCSK was received as a member of the → World Council of Churches (WCC). In 1971 a theological school was established to offer training for the pastors, and in 1977 it developed into a theological faculty at the university level.

The spiritual strength of the Kimbanguist Church is seen in its rich tradition of → prayers and → hymns, reaching back as far as 1921. Annually, thousands of Kimbanguists go on → pilgrimage up to Nkamba Jerusalem, or New Jerusalem, in the Lower Congo — the place of its historical origin. There one finds the mausoleum of the prophet Simon Kimbangu (1889?-1951 or, in Kimbanguist sources, 1887?-1951) and, beside it, a large temple. Visible from far away, it was dedicated in 1981 after many years of building efforts by the faithful.

From its beginning as an officially recognized church in December 1959 until 1992, the spiritual head of the EJCSK was Joseph Diangienda Kuntima (1918-92), the second son of Simon Kimbangu. His death left a vacuum in leadership that was not bridged by his older brother Salomon Dialungana Kiangani (1916-2001), who was followed in 2001 by his son Simon Kimbangu Kiangani (b. 1951).

For many years the EJCSK has struggled to consolidate the church, which is divided into rival factions because of conflicts over leadership and doctrine. In this complex situation, many attempts to overcome the crisis by reconciling the disputing parties with the support of internal or external mediation and ecumenical dialogue initiated by the WCC, the → All Africa Conference of Churches, and other Christian partners have thus far not produced a lasting solution to the problem. More fundamentally, the EJCSK must face the question whether it is, or still wants to be, a Christian church.

3. Interchurch Relations

In the DRC there are no formal interdenominational structures. Ecumenical cooperation happens mostly on a parish or community level (→ Local Ecumenism) and often within the framework of development projects. Occasionally, church leaders have joined together for common interventions regarding important issues (e.g., education). Reciprocal invitations are usually extended at important church events (e.g., the centenaries of both the Protestant and the Roman Catholic Church) or visits (e.g., Philip Potter, general secretary of the WCC, in April 1978; Pope Shenouda III, in October 1979; and Pope John Paul II, in May 1980).

The doctrinal controversies within the EJCSK have created tensions between it and the main churches (the ECC and the Roman Catholic Church), leading the latter to distance itself somewhat from the Kimbanguists. In July 2004 the Bishops' Conference issued a declaration prohibiting Catholics from practicing "spiritual ecumenism" with the Kimbanguists. Having transformed the biblically based Christian doctrine of the Trinity into one based instead on Simon Kimbangu, they are considered to be no longer a Christian church but a non-Christian religion, which would require another type of approach and relationship.

Thus for the time being the ecumenical climate seems not very promising for enhancing cooperation between the various Christian denominations. There is, however, a spirit of mutual interest and support regarding theological teaching and research between the institutions of theological learning.

4. Church and State

According to its new constitution, the Democratic Republic of Congo is a secular state that guarantees freedom of thought, conscience, and → religion (art. 22). Since 1971 the Roman Catholic Church, the ECC, and the EJCSK have been officially recognized. In 1972 this recognition was extended also to Moslems (→ Islam), Jews (→ Judaism), and the Greek → Orthodox Church. Many of the numerous Christian communities of Pentecostal or charis-

matic origin or those who had broken away from mainline churches have been tolerated, whereas others have at times been prohibited for political reasons, such as the → Jehovah's Witnesses, in 1986.

From the outbreak of the civil war in 1998 up to the present, the churches from the various denominations have been victims of aggression, damage, destruction, and theft both by raiding rebels and by soldiers of the army. They not only have destroyed numerous schools, hospitals, churches, and development projects but also have driven away countless people and thus scattered members of families and civil and Christian communities.

5. Other Religions

Because of the extensive Christian mission the traditional African religions in the DRC have sharply declined. They have proved, however, to be a steady undercurrent in the lives of people, and thus there still are → healings of the sick according to traditional methods and different forms of → fetish cult and magical practices (→ Magic). At important transitional stages of life such as birth, puberty, marriage, and death, traditional rituals and customs emerge (→ Initiation Rites). Christian theologians have been challenged by research done in the realm of science of religion and anthropology to appreciate and treasure anew the traditional belief in God and the cult of the → ancestors. New theological approaches and projects take into account the religious traditions of African ancestors.

Islam is increasingly present and influential in the east and northeast. Congolese Muslims are descendants from those converted in the 19th century. They are → Sunnis, but their beliefs and practices betray the ongoing influence of the African religious tradition. Other Muslim groups are represented by immigrants who come mostly from Arab countries, India, and Pakistan. The relationship between Muslims and Christians follows everyday patterns of neighborhood and trade relations. Thus far no significant efforts have been made by either side to open a dialogue with the other (→ Islam and Christianity).

Bibliography: Journals: Cahiers africains (Tervuren, Belg., Royal Museum for Central Africa) • *Congo-Afrique (Zaïre-Afrique). Economie-Culture-Vie sociale* (published since 1961 by the Centre d'Études pour l'Action Sociale, Kinshasa) • *Review of African Political Economy* (Brussels) 29, nos. 93-94 (2002).

Works in English: D. B. BARRETT, G. T. KURIAN, and T. M. JOHNSON, *WCE* (2d ed.) 1.211-16 • F. S. BOBB, ed., *Historical Dictionary of Democratic Republic of the Congo (Zaire)* (Lanham, Md., 1999) • J. DIANGIENDA,

Out of Africa: Kimbanguism (London, 1979) • C. Irvine, comp., *The Church of Christ in Zaïre: A Handbook of Protestant Churches, Missions, and Communities, 1878-1978* (Indianapolis, 1978) • L. N. Kayongo, "Kimbanguism: Its Present Christian Doctrine and the Problems Raised by It," *Exchange* 34/3 (2005) 227-47 • G. Mianda, "Democratic Republic of Congo," *Encyclopedia of Twentieth-Century African History* (ed. P. T. Zeleza; London, 2003) 141-43 • G. Nzongola-Ntalaja, *The Congo: From Leopold to Kabila; A People's History* (London, 2002) • *Statistical Yearbook of the Church, 2004* (Vatican City, 2006) • K. Vlassenroot and T. Raeymaekers, "The Formation of Centres of Profit, Power, and Protection: Conflict and Social Transformation in Eastern DR Congo" (University of Copenhagen, Centre of African Studies, 2005) • M. Wrong, *In the Footsteps of Mr Kurtz: Living on the Brink of Disaster in the Congo* (London, 2000).

Works in French: F. Bontinck, *L'évangélisation du Zaïre* (Kinshasa, 1980) • Diangienda Kuntima, *Histoire du Kimbanguisme* (Kinshasa, 1984) • P. B. Kabongo-Mbaya, *L'Église du Christ au Zaïre. Formation et adaptation d'un protestantisme en situation de dictature* (Paris, 1992) • O. Lanotte, *Guerres sans frontières en République démocratique du Congo* (Brussels, 2003) • O. Lanotte, C. Roosens, and C. Clément, eds., *La Belgique et l'Afrique centrale, de 1960 à nos jours* (Brussels, 2000) • C. Makiobo, *Église catholique et mutations socio-politiques au Congo-Zaïre. La contestation du régime Mobutu* (Paris, 2004) • P. M. Mantuba-Ngoma, ed., *La nouvelle histoire du Congo. Mélanges eurafricains offerts à Frans Bontinck* (Tervuren, Belg., 2004) • I. Ndaywel è Nziem, *Histoire générale du Congo. De l'héritage ancien à la République Démocratique* (Brussels, 1998) • L. Ngomo Okitembo, *L'engagement politique de l'Église catholique au Zaïre, 1960-1992* (Paris, 1998) • J.-L. Vellut, *Simon Kimbangu, 1921. De la prédication à la déportation. Les sources* (Brussels, 2005) • G. de Villers, with J. Tshonda Omasombo, *La transition manquée, 1990-1997* (Tervuren, Belg., 1998) • G. de Villers, with J. Tshonda Omasombo and E. Kennes, *République démocratique du Congo. Guerre et politique; Les trente derniers mois de L. D. Kabila, août 1998–janvier 2001* (Paris, 2001) • G. de Villers and J.-C. Willame, with J. Tshonda Omasombo and E. Kennes, *République démocratique du Congo. Chronique politique d'un entre-deux-guerres, octobre 1996–juillet 1998* (Tervuren, Belg., 1999) • D. Wamu Oyatambwe, *Église catholique et pouvoir politique au Congo-Zaïre. La quête démocratique* (Paris, 1997); idem, *Les mots de la démocratie au Congo-Zaïre, 1990-1997* (Paris, 2006).

Paul Stadler

Zambia

	1960	1980	2000
Population (1,000s):	3,141	5,738	9,133
Annual growth rate (%):	2.80	2.22	2.49
Area: 752,614 sq. km. (290,586 sq. mi.)			

A.D. 2000

Population density: 12/sq. km. (31/sq. mi.)
Births / deaths: 4.07 / 1.59 per 100 population
Fertility rate: 5.01 per woman
Infant mortality rate: 90 per 1,000 live births
Life expectancy: 45.5 years (m: 44.7, f: 46.2)
Religious affiliation (%): Christians 82.9 (Roman Catholics 32.3, Protestants 22.3, indigenous 19.3, marginal 3.8, Anglicans 3.4, unaffiliated 3.2, other Christians 0.1), tribal religionists 13.7, Baha'is 1.8, Muslims 1.1, other 0.5.

1. General Situation
2. History of the Church
3. Religions and Churches Today
4. Interchurch Cooperation
5. Church and State

1. General Situation

The Republic of Zambia, the former British protectorate of Northern Rhodesia, is a country in the interior of southern Africa. Small farming and copper mines are its economic basis. The latter have given it what is for Africa a high urban population (44 percent in 2006).

In 1964, under the leadership of the United National Independence Party (UNIP) and its president, Kenneth D. Kaunda, Zambia achieved independence. A one-party system followed up to 1991, when Frederick Chiluba of the Movement for Multiparty Democracy succeeded Kaunda as president. After independence, the government failed to diversify the economy, and fluctuations in the world price of copper, along with massive indebtedness, produced a steadily worsening economic situation, so that the relatively prosperous country of the 1960s became one of the poorest countries, with an average annual income of only $380 (2003).

2. History of the Church

Although the missionary and geographer David Livingstone (1813-73) explored the area between 1853 and 1860 with a view to missionary work (→ Mission), only toward the end of the 19th century did missionary societies establish themselves in this territory in inland Africa, far from the coasts, along with the British South Africa Company of Cecil Rhodes (1853-1902), which ruled the country until 1924 with a mandate from the British crown. The first important missions were those of the London Missionary Society (LMS; → British Missions 1.2) at the south end of Lake Tanganyika (1883), the Paris Evangelical Missionary Society (→ French Missions) in the kingdom of Barotseland to the west of modern Zambia (1885), the Roman Catholic White Fathers (→ Catholic Missions) in the Bemba area to the north (1895), and the mission of the Dutch Reformed Church from South Africa in the east (1899). Up to World War I Christian Missions in Many Lands, an international group belonging to the Christian Brethren, and the interdenominational South Africa General Mission were also at work in the northwest, while the South African Baptists and the Free Church of Scotland (→ British Missions 1.2.2) evangelized other parts of the country.

Many of these agencies entered into comity agreements with each other, but on the more accessible Tonga plateau to the south, many other groups were at work: two Methodist societies (→ Methodism; Methodist Churches), → Adventists, → Jesuits, the → Salvation Army, the Brethren in Christ (→ Brethren Churches), the U.S. Church of Christ, and the Anglican Universities Mission to Central Africa. Between the world wars the Italian Franciscans and Irish Capuchins (→ Franciscans 3) reinforced Roman Catholic work in the country. Thus most of the main denominational streams flowed into Zambia.

The Watchtower movement has also been important. From its first entry in 1911 it has always had a specifically African character (H.-J. Greschat; → Independent Churches) but is now part of the worldwide organization of → Jehovah's Witnesses. Perhaps because of it, independent African churches are not so numerous as in neighboring lands. The anticolonial Lumpa (lit. "better than all others") Church, founded in 1954 by Alice Lenshina (ca. 1924-78), turned against the independent state and was suppressed after causing disorders in 1964.

3. Religions and Churches Today

Over 80 percent of the people of Zambia view themselves as Christian, and approximately 14 percent belong to traditional African religions (→ Guinea 2; Tribal Religions). Indian immigrants, a small but economically important minority, are → Hindus or Muslims. → Islam tried to make massive inroads from 1991 onward, especially in the eastern province, with Arab financial support.

Great denominational variety exists in Zambia. The comity principle has made many churches into tribal churches. Even the → Roman Catholic Church, the largest and most widespread, is strongest in the Bemba area to the north. Though there is national leadership, at least formally, national priests are few in number, comprising only 20 percent of the total of 560. Latent conflicts between missionaries and nationals flared up in the 1980s around the archbishop of Lusaka, Emmanuel Milingo (1969-83), who, as a result of missionary interventions, was reassigned to a relatively unimportant post in Rome. Milingo espoused a charismatic African Christianity and practiced faith → healing and → exorcism.

The over 40 Protestant churches are small in proportion but have played a large part in public life. The largest is the United Church of Zambia (1 million adherents in 2000), formed in 1965 as a union church, bringing together Congregationalists (LMS), French Reformed, Presbyterians, and Methodists (P. Bolink). Already in 1925, preceding this union, and independently of the whites, African Christians of different regional and denominational origins had joined forces in the Copperbelt (J. V. Taylor and D. Lehmann).

The next largest is the New Apostolic Church, from South Africa (→ Apostolic Churches), which has grown rapidly since around 1980. In 2000 it was the third largest religious Christian community in the country, with 800,000 affiliates.

Next in numbers come the Reformed Church of Zambia, the Seventh-day Adventists, the Jehovah's Witnesses, the Church of God (Cleveland, Tenn.), and the → Anglican Church. Smaller groups include the Pentecostal Assemblies of God of Zambia, the Christian Brethren, the Evangelical Church in Zambia, the Baptist Union, the Baptist Convention, and the African Methodist Episcopal Church, which, with roots in the United States, was established in the cities from 1931 onward.

A significant number of Christians belong to the more than 70 African → Independent Churches. These include not only the Lumpa Church but the Masowe Apostles from Zimbabwe and the Bamulonda (Watchman Healing Mission), a Watchtower split.

The number of Jehovah's Witnesses is large; they constitute one of the largest religious groups in the country and are widespread. Globally, Zambia has a higher proportion of Witnesses than any other country in the world. The monthly *Watchtower* comes out in four languages: Bemba, Nyanje, Lozi, and Luvale. The refusal of Witnesses to take an active part in constructing the new state led in 1967-69 to clashes with the UNIP and to repressive legal measures against them.

4. Interchurch Cooperation

Preceding the Christian Council of Zambia (CCZ; → National Councils of Churches), founded under another name in 1945, was the General Missionary Conference of Northern Rhodesia, which first met in 1914 and became an important forum for interdenominational cooperation in such matters as education (P. D. Snelson). Today 11 churches, mostly liberal ecumenical, belong to the council. In addition, 18 smaller evangelical churches have formed the Evangelical Fellowship of Zambia (EFZ). Some churches belong to both groupings. Ten independent churches belong to the Association of Independent Churches.

In 1970 Protestants and Roman Catholics formed the Churches Medical Association of Zambia to coordinate their medical work, which in 2000 was providing up to 30 percent of the national health care, and up to 50 percent in rural areas (→ Medical Missions). Facilities run by this organization are usually better equipped, given their overseas help.

The Mindolo Ecumenical Foundation, in the Copperbelt, in which Roman Catholics also play a part, is important for interdenominational work (D. M'Passou). Its facilities are often used for development-oriented courses and for conferences (→ Development 1).

5. Church and State

The constitution of Zambia guarantees → religious liberty (→ Church and State). Nevertheless, religious societies must register with the state, which has led to conflict in the case of the Lumpa Church and Jehovah's Witnesses. In 1974 the state took over church primary schools founded by missionaries in the colonial era. The churches, however, still retain control over some high schools.

Former president Kaunda, who took up many Christian ideas in his philosophy of "Zambian humanism" (→ Social Ethics 4), expressly called himself a (Protestant) Christian, as did Chiluba, his successor, who declared Zambia a Christian nation when he assumed power in 1991.

At the change from a one-party to a multiparty system (1989-91), the churches, the most influential institutions in public life, supported the multiparty movement against the UNIP. It was thanks to them that the transition took place peacefully.

The two Protestant groupings and the Roman Catholics join forces on many political matters and questions of social ethics, at times in criticism of the government. One example is the ecumenical → pastoral letter "Christian Liberation, Justice, and Development," issued jointly in 1987 by the CCZ,

the EFZ, and the Roman Catholic Zambia Episcopal Conference.

Bibliography: D. B. BARRETT, G. T. KURIAN, and T. M. JOHNSON, *WCE* (2d ed.) 1.817-20 • P. BOLINK, *Towards Church Union in Zambia* (Franeker, 1967) • P. FRESTON, *Evangelicals and Politics in Asia, Africa, and Latin America* (Cambridge, 2001) • P. GIFFORD, *African Christianity: Its Public Role* (London, 1998) • H.-J. GRESCHAT, *Kitawala. Ursprung, Ausbreitung und Religion der Watch-Tower-Bewegung in Zentralafrika* (Marburg, 1967) • R. HENKEL, *Christian Missions in Africa: A Social Geographical Study of the Impact of Their Activities in Zambia* (Berlin, 1989) • K. D. KAUNDA, *Humanism in Zambia and a Guide to Its Implementation* (2 vols.; Lusaka, 1967-74) • U. LUIG, *Conversion as a Social Process: A History of Missionary Christianity among the Valley Tonga, Zambia* (Münster, 1997) • P. MEYNS, *Zambia in der 3. Republik. Demokratische Transition und politische Kontinuität* (Hamburg 1995) • D. M'PASSOU, *Mindolo: A Story of the Ecumenical Movement in Africa* (Lusaka, 1983) • A. ROBERTS, *A History of Zambia* (London, 1976) • P. D. SNELSON, *Educational Development in Northern Rhodesia, 1883-1945* (Lusaka, 1974) • J. V. TAYLOR and D. LEHMANN, *Christians of the Copperbelt* (London, 1961) • J. WELLER and J. LINDEN, *Mainstream Christianity to 1980 in Malawi, Zambia, and Zimbabwe* (Gweru, 1984).

REINHARD HENKEL

Zealots

"Zealots" (Gk. *zēlōtai*, Heb. *qanna'im*, "enthusiasts") was the name given to the radical rebels who led the Jewish people in the war against Rome (A.D. 66-73). The term is a symbolic honorific (the revered Phinehas ben Eleazar was considered the first "zealot," Num. 25:6-13) that may well have included various Jewish revolutionary groups, including the Sicarii. In order to bring about the onset of the kingdom of God, that is, theocratic rule (→ Kingdom of God; Eschatology; Theocracy), the Zealots demanded recognition of God alone as ruler and thus violent action against Roman governance (→ Messianism).

Josephus (ca. 37-ca. 100) holds the Zealots responsible for the downfall of the Jewish nation. In accordance with contemporary Roman legal usage, he also refers to them as "robbers."

Zealot characteristics are already found in the Maccabean revolt (1 Macc. 2:24-27, 49-50), and later in the "robber captain" Hezekiah, who was executed in 47-46 B.C. by → Herod I (73-4 B.C.). The roots of a "party," however, probably first appear in the group led by Hezekiah's son, Judas the Galilean. Outraged by the (second) census of Quirinius (A.D. 6-7) as an insufferable affront to the rule of God, Judas incited the Jews to revolt. This uprising was quickly subdued, but the movement survived. Because of increasing mismanagement by the Roman procurators, its influence steadily grew among the Jews in the period leading up to the Jewish War.

Some NT texts are best understood against a background of active Zealotism. Simon the Zealot (Luke 6:15; Acts 1:13) may have been a member of the group. → Jesus was executed between two "robbers." Barabbas is described as an insurrectionist, robber, and murderer (Mark 15:6-7, 27 and par.; Acts 3:14). The → early church was occasionally counted among contemporary revolutionary groups such as the movement behind Judas the Galilean (Acts 5:34-39). Certain sayings of Jesus show similarities between his own movement and the Zealots, while rejecting their understanding of both the → kingdom (§1) and the will of God (Matt. 11:12; Mark 12:13-17 and par.; 14:47 and par.). Zealot resistance ultimately came to an end with the defeat of Simeon bar Kokhba in A.D. 135.

→ Apocalypticism 3; Judaism; New Testament Era, History of; Roman Empire

Bibliography: Primary sources: Josephus *J.W.,* with par. in *Ant.* • Hippolytus *Haer.* 9.26 • *m. Sanh.* 9:6 • *b. Git.* 56a • *Qoh. Rab.* 7:12 • *'Abot R. Nat.* 6:8 A/B.

Secondary works: O. CULLMANN, *Jesus and the Revolutionaries* (New York, 1970) • W. R. FARMER, *Maccabees, Zealots, and Josephus: An Inquiry into Jewish Nationalism in the Greco-Roman Period* (New York, 1956; repr., Westport, Conn., 1973) • M. HENGEL, *The Zealots: Investigations into the Jewish Freedom Movement in the Period from Herod I until 70 A.D.* (Edinburgh, 1989) • R. A. HORSLEY and J. S. HANSON, *Bandits, Prophets, and Messiahs: Popular Movements in the Time of Jesus* (Minneapolis, 1985) 190-243 • W. KLASSEN, "Jesus and the Zealot Option," *The Wisdom of the Cross* (ed. S. Hauerwas et al.; Grand Rapids, 1999) 131-49 • E. SCHÜRER, *The History of the Jewish People in the Age of Jesus Christ (175 B.C.–A.D. 135)* (3 vols.; Edinburgh, 1973-87) 2.598-606 • A. STUMPFF, "Ζηλόω, ζηλωτής C: Zelotism," *TDNT* 2.884-86.

PAUL A. CATHEY

Zechariah, Book of

1. Text
2. Theology

1. Text

The 11th and largest book of the → Minor Prophets, Zechariah, divides into two distinct parts. *Chapters 1–8* contain eight night visions concerning the restoration of Judah and → Jerusalem, arranged chronologically beginning with October/November 520 B.C., and a series of oracles of the coming messianic age. Zechariah son of Berechiah son of Iddo was probably of priestly and possibly aristocratic background. He was likely among those who recently returned from captivity in Babylon and ministered until 518 B.C. during the reign of the Persian king Darius I. Concerned about the plight of the returned exiles amid adverse conditions in Judah, Zechariah regarded proper → worship and → sacrifice as essential to Israel's salvation. He called the people to repentance and insisted upon social justice (5:1-4; 7:9-10), blaming their pitiable situation on → sin and unfaithfulness. Like his contemporary Haggai, he advocated the reconstruction of the Jerusalem → temple (§2) and supported the dual leadership of the Zadokite high priest Joshua and the governor Zerubbabel, whom he considered to be heir to the Davidic throne.

Chapters 9–14, often called Second (or Deutero-) Zechariah, contrast sharply with the hopeful expectation of reconstruction in the first part of the book and the instrumental role of the Jerusalem priesthood. The anonymous author (or authors, thought by some to be disciples or a "school" of Zechariah) appears to have been outside the power structure of postexilic Judah. Scholars disagree concerning the unity of these chapters (some identify chaps. 12–14 as Third Zechariah) and suggest that they may have been added as late as the fifth or even the third century B.C.

The two oracles in the second part, which bear similarity to the Book of Malachi, are largely apocalyptic in nature. In the first (chaps. 9–11), → Yahweh is portrayed as the divine warrior, wreaking vengeance on Israel and the nations. The second (12–14) displays an increasingly intense expectation of the terrible day of the Lord. It depicts a city purged of its sin and a tranquil new age, an ideal world in which a faithful remnant of Judah and believers from all nations will worship at the purified temple.

2. Theology

Zechariah's vivid imagery and symbolic language represent a significant development in the formation of Jewish → apocalyptic thought. → Angels appear as mediators and interpreters, and cataclysmic struggles are fought between forces of good and evil.

The Book of Revelation frequently echoes Zechariah (note the symbolism in Rev. 6:1-8).

The book displays a clear understanding of Yahweh as sovereign in creation (10:1) and history (4:6-10; 10:3-12). The prophet exhorts faithfulness to the divine will so that the people might avoid another catastrophe, such as the exile, as renewed punishment for covenant disobedience, even as he provides assurance of God's continued loyalty to Jerusalem and Zion.

Of particular importance is Zechariah's interest in God's anointed, the messianic king. The imagery of the Suffering Servant (12:10) and the Good Shepherd sacrificed for the flock (13:7) are used in the NT portrayal of Jesus as Messiah (John 19:37; Mark 14:27; cf. Rev. 1:7). In their accounts of Jesus' entry into Jerusalem on Palm Sunday, the Gospels draw on Zechariah's prophecy of Zion's king, the Prince of Peace, "humble and riding on a donkey" (9:9, quoted in Matt. 21:5; John 12:15; cf. Mark 11:2-7; Luke 19:30-36). Matthew's account of the fee paid to Judas (Matt. 27:9) reflects Zech. 11:12-13.

Bibliography: Commentaries: C. L. Meyers and E. M. Meyers, *Haggai, Zechariah 1–8* (AB; Garden City, N.Y., 1987); idem, *Zechariah 9–14* (AB; New York, 1993) • D. L. Petersen, *Zechariah 9–14 and Malachi* (OTL; Philadelphia, 1995) • P. L. Redditt, *Haggai, Zechariah, Malachi* (NCBC; Grand Rapids, 1995) • R. L. Smith, *Micah–Malachi* (WBC; Waco, Tex., 1984).

Other works: M. Butterworth, *Structure and the Book of Zechariah* (Sheffield, 1992) • D. L. Petersen, *Late Israelite Prophecy: Studies in Deutero-prophetic Literature and in Chronicles* (Missoula, Mont., 1977).

Allen C. Myers

Zen

Zen Buddhism is an orientation in Japanese → Buddhism that stresses → meditation (Jpn. *zen*). The word *zen* comes from Chin. *ch'an,* from Skt. *dhyāna* (meditation). The *ch'an,* or *zen,* school did not exist in India, the home of Buddhism. Bodhidharma, a Buddhist monk who came from India to → China at the beginning of the sixth century A.D., triggered a Chinese development that reveals an antiformalistic, Taoist influence (→ Taoism). The teaching work of Hui-neng (638-713) was a high point in China. He advocated a principle of sudden illumination. A radical discontinuity ensued between the state of illumination and the ordinary practices of the monks.

The most important sects of Japanese Buddhism were rooted in Chinese models. Eisai (1141-1215) introduced the Rinzai school to Japan. Enigmatic questions *(kōan)* would break through the boundaries of normal → logic in favor of illumination. The Sōtō school introduced by Dōgen (1200-1253) took the position that meditation when sitting *(zazen)* leads to an experience of the true nature of Buddhism. Dōgen's main work, the *Shōbōgenzō,* was regarded as a normative text by the Sōtō school.

The simplicity of nature, which Zen Buddhism emphasized, found expression in Japan in such things as the Japanese garden, the tea ceremony, and Japanese art, calligraphy, and poetry. Western acceptance is due partly to the cultural achievements and partly to the energetic advocacy of apologists such as D. T. Suzuki (1870-1966). In Japan the adherents of Zen Buddhism share in the religious life of Japan (including → ancestor worship), and for this reason the Zen experience has had only a limited success in the West.

Bibliography: H. J. Baroni, *The Illustrated Encyclopedia of Zen Buddhism* (New York, 2002) • H. Dumoulin, *Zen Buddhism: A History* (2 vols.; Bloomington, Ind., 2005) • H. M. Enomiya-Lassalle, *The Practice of Zen Meditation* (ed. R. Ropers and B. Snela; London, 1995); idem, *Zen Meditation for Christians* (La Salle, Ill., 1974) • R. L. F. Habito, *Healing Breath: Zen for Christians and Buddhists in a Wounded World* (rev. ed.; Boston, 2006) • S. Heine and D. S. Wright, eds., *Zen Classics: Formative Texts in the History of Zen Buddhism* (New York, 2006) • K. Sekida, *Zen Training: Methods and Philosophy* (New York, 1975; repr., Boston, 2005) • D. T. Suzuki, *Zen and Japanese Culture* (2d ed.; New York, 1959); idem, *Zen Buddhism: Selected Writings of D. T. Suzuki* (ed. W. Barrett; New York, 1996).

Michael Pye

Zephaniah, Book of

Zephaniah is the ninth book of the → Minor Prophets. Although the precise circumstances of the prophet's life are unknown, his prophecies suggest that he was of Judean origin, a member of a prominent and possibly royal family, and active during the first half of the reign of → Josiah (639-609 B.C.). Zephaniah's preaching falls within the tradition of Amos, Isaiah, and Micah, his eighth-century predecessors. His utterances in turn may have influenced the prophecy of Jeremiah, a contemporary of his.

The book consists of three chapters. Although some scholars find evidence of exilic and postexilic expansion, the book in its final form is a closely woven unity. Its organization reflects the characteristic eschatological pattern of oracles of disaster and judgment, followed by oracles of salvation as found in the major writing prophets. Warning of judgment on the day of the Lord's → wrath (1:2–2:3) is followed by announcement of judgment upon foreign nations (the neighboring Philistines, Moab, and Ammon, as well as Ethiopia and Assyria) and upon Jerusalem itself (2:4–3:8). The book concludes with prophecies of universal salvation (3:9-20).

The central focus of Zephaniah's theology is his proclamation of the coming terrible "day of the LORD" (1:7, 14) as → punishment for Judah's corrupt religious and political leadership, in particular the idolatrous reigns of Manasseh and Amon (see 2 Kings 21), and for the people's dalliance with foreign deities and for their unethical behavior in general. More fully than any other prophet, Zephaniah depicts the Lord's final war against his covenant people and the destruction of all creation.

The prophecy, however, is not only of coming judgment but also of hope and compassion upon the whole world. These cataclysmic events will bring purification for Israel and the nations through punishment, a purging judgment that issues in salvation. In the course of this turbulence the fate of the chosen people will be radically altered through the re-creative work of the Lord. A "remnant" (2:7, 9; 3:13) will not only survive the judgment but receive a new way of life, purified of pride and deceit, and become the firstfruits of the future (cf. 1 Pet. 2:9).

Zephaniah's heralding of the final intervention and imminent great consummation anticipates the coming cosmic judgment later proclaimed in the NT by Jesus and especially in the Book of Revelation (Matt. 13:41; Rev. 6:17; 14:5; 16:1). The day of the Lord came to be associated with the day of the Son of Man (Matt. 24:42-44; Luke 17:24, 30; Acts 17:31; Rom. 2:16). The prophet's oracle of impending disaster (1:14-16) is echoed in the medieval hymn *Dies irae*, "Day of Wrath," and other literary and musical works and liturgies.

In addition to expounding upon the book's eschatological theme, Christian commentators have interpreted Zephaniah as a summons to simple, righteous, and penitent living (Clement *Paed.* 2.13; → Cyprian *Ad Quir.* 3.47, 106 and *De pat.* 21), a call for social reform (J. → Calvin, see comm. on Zephaniah), and proclamation of salvation for the nations (→ Augustine *De civ. Dei* 18.33).

→ Prophet, Prophecy

Bibliography: Commentaries: E. ACHTEMEIER, *Nahum–Malachi* (Interp.; Atlanta, 1986) • A. BERLIN, *Zephaniah* (AB; New York, 1994) • R. MASON, *Zephaniah, Habakkuk, Joel* (OTGu; Sheffield, 1994) • J. J. M. ROBERTS, *Nahum, Habakkuk, and Zephaniah* (OTL; Louisville, Ky., 1991) • O. P. ROBERTSON, *The Books of Nahum, Habakkuk, and Zephaniah* (NICOT; Grand Rapids, 1990) • R. L. SMITH, *Micah–Malachi* (WBC; Waco, Tex., 1984).

Other works: I. J. BALL, *Zephaniah: A Rhetorical Study* (Berkeley, Calif., 1988) • E. BEN ZVI, *A Historical-Critical Study of the Book of Zephaniah* (Berlin, 1991) • A. S. KAPELRUD, *The Message of the Prophet Zephaniah* (Oslo, 1975).

ALLEN C. MYERS

Zimbabwe

	1960	1980	2000
Population (1,000s):	3,812	7,126	12,423
Annual growth rate (%):	3.17	3.27	2.11

Area: 390,757 sq. km. (150,872 sq. mi.)

A.D. 2000

Population density: 32/sq. km. (82/sq. mi.)
Births / deaths: 3.40 / 1.29 per 100 population
Fertility rate: 4.17 per woman
Infant mortality rate: 60 per 1,000 live births
Life expectancy: 50.8 years (m: 50.0, f: 51.6)
Religious affiliation (%): Christians 67.4 (indigenous 36.4, Protestants 12.1, Roman Catholics 9.3, unaffiliated 6.6, Anglicans 2.4, other Christians 0.7), tribal religionists 30.1, nonreligious 1.0, other 1.5.

1. General Situation
2. Religions
3. Christianity
4. Interdenominational Organizations
5. Church and State

1. General Situation

Zimbabwe is the name of the nation-state born when Britain granted its people independence in 1980. The country was part of the British South Africa Company from 1889 until 1923, when it became the crown colony of Southern Rhodesia. Then between 1953 and 1963 it joined with Northern Rhodesia (now Zambia) and Nyasaland (now Malawi) in the Federation of Rhodesia and Nyasaland. After a lengthy war of liberation Zimbabwe became independent in 1980, with Robert Mugabe (b. 1924) as the first prime minister and then, from 1987, its first executive president.

Zimbabwe began as the most industrialized of all countries in black Africa, with mining (coal, copper) as its main resource. Through commercial farming, there was an abundance of food crops for local consumption and export, and tobacco was a major export crop, with Zimbabwe the leading producer in Africa. This positive situation changed in 1999 with Mugabe's introduction of a program to forcibly transfer land ownership from whites to blacks. This redistribution plan has plunged the country into an economic crisis, with millions of its people now suffering from poverty and the AIDS pandemic.

2. Religions

Zimbabwe is a secular state with large numbers of civic groups who are religious. Its constitution identifies no faith or religious tradition as the official state religion. → Religious liberty is guaranteed by the constitution as a fundamental human right. The population is mostly religious. Zimbabwean society is pluralistic in its religious beliefs, though closer examination finds it predominantly Christian. According to a survey by the Bible Society of Zimbabwe, over 60 percent of the people are practicing Christians. Close to one-third are adherents of the traditional religions (→ Guinea 2), mainly in the rural areas. About one-third of this number are members of a Christian church. Quite a few Christians are attached to traditional religions without perceiving any contradiction. Christians often participate in the traditional death and burial rites for their relatives (→ Funeral 4), and some communities have begun to inject Christian ideas into these ceremonies by celebrating Mass and singing hymns from church. In Matonjeni, the old shrine for the high god Mwari continues to receive visitors, even though "Mwari" has become the most popular name for the biblical God, whom Christians try to keep separate from all other gods.

No more than 1 percent of the people are Muslims (→ Islam). The majority of these are either of Asian origin or Malawians who came to work in mines or on farms during the colonial era. Few Zimbabweans are Muslims. Other religious traditions include → Hinduism and → Baha'i, whose adherents mostly came from Asia. The different traditions tolerate one another. Thus far, however, there has been minimal interreligious → dialogue. The Zimbabwe Council of Churches has arranged meetings at which Hindus and even Muslims have expressed a desire for closer cooperation on matters of mutual interest such as human rights and AIDS.

Zimbabwe is one of the few African countries that mandates → religious and → moral education in the schools. Through a multifaith approach, chil-

dren of all religious groups study together (→ Education 3.3). Although the syllabi must draw from every religious tradition, they are heavily biased toward Christianity.

3. Christianity

The Christian community can be divided into three main groups: the Roman Catholic Church, the Protestant churches, and the African Initiated Churches. Also making an impact on these communities, and adding to the spectrum of churches in Zimbabwe today, is the current wave of → Pentecostal churches, with roots in the United States.

Christian mission began in 1560 with the coming of the → Jesuits under the leadership of G. da Silveira (1521/24-61). The mission ended in failure with the execution of Silveira by King Mutapa. Up to 1775 Roman Catholics made other attempts to spread Christianity. They found it difficult to make converts until the 19th century, when the British South Africa Company colonized the country and brought groups of white settlers to take over the land (→ Colonialism and Mission). The defeat of the Shona and Ndebele peoples in the 1896/97 uprisings significantly contributed to the Christianization of the land. European missionaries now came under the protection of a colonial power led by Cecil John Rhodes (1853-1902) with effective military superiority. The colonial regime provided missionaries with land, which they used to establish permanent bases from which to spread Christianity throughout Southern Rhodesia. Christianity and colonialism were closely linked, which explains the conflicting attitudes about the liberation war. Some nationalists brushed aside the teaching of their churches against the ancestors by venerating them during the guerrilla war, while others used the gospel to justify the war against racism. When Zimbabwe achieved independence in 1980, Christianity had become socially and culturally rooted among the people, enough to lead Robert Mugabe to appoint Methodist bishop Canaan Banana (1936-2003) as Zimbabwe's first president. Churches became the major civic groups, to which the majority of Zimbabweans now belong.

3.1. The → Roman Catholic Church dates back to 1879, which makes it the oldest denomination. Today there are two archdioceses, in Harare and Bulawayo, with a total of seven bishops and a little over a million members. Its contribution to the educational and medical welfare of Zimbabwe is enormous, with its 75 primary schools, 42 secondary schools, 1 tertiary college, 35 hospitals, and 12 clinics. It was also very much involved in development projects after independence (e.g., the joint Lutheran and Catholic water project in Matabeleland). Its Justice and Peace Commission effectively championed human → rights and was a voice for the voiceless in the colonial and postcolonial periods. Candidates for the priesthood are trained at the major seminary in Chishawasha, which is affiliated with the University of Zimbabwe. Ecumenically, the Roman Catholic Church belongs to the Heads of Denominations and, since the founding of the Zimbabwe Council of Churches (ZCC) in 1964, has held observer status in the council (→ National Councils of Churches).

3.2. There are several large Protestant churches in Zimbabwe. The Anglican Church (→ Anglican Communion), with its four dioceses (Harare, Lundi, Manicaland, and Matabeleland), is part of the Church of the Province of Central Africa, which covers also Malawi, Botswana, and Zambia. This church dates back to 1889 and was the established church from 1890 to 1980 (→ Church and State 1.2). It has many private and government-aided schools, a large hospital at Bonda, four clinics, and several orphanages.

Methodist churches consist of the Methodist Church in Zimbabwe (founded in 1889), the United Methodist Church (founded 1897, with roots in the United States), the African Methodist Episcopal Church, and the Free Methodist Church. Before 2000, the Methodists supported many schools, 3 hospitals, and 14 clinics, with the United Methodist Church itself covering all the expense of running them. It pioneered the ordination of women (→ Ordination 1.5.2) and established the first private university — Africa University, located outside Mutare. The Free Methodist Church also does educational and medical work.

The Evangelical Lutheran Church in Zimbabwe, initiated by the Svenska Kyrkans Mission (→ Lutheran Churches; Scandinavian Missions 1.2), dates back to 1903. It is strongest in the south (Mberengwa, Gwanda, and Beitbridge), which often suffers from drought and has a high level of poverty. Also before 2000, it supported six secondary schools, four hospitals, two Bible schools, a youth center, and a women's center. Helped by the → Lutheran World Federation, it has contributed to many significant development projects (water, agriculture, drought relief, refugee work, and informal educational programs). Its men and women pastors are trained at the United Theological College in Harare, an ecumenical center jointly owned by most of the Protestant churches. The Ruwadzano movement is made up of women from the Methodist and Lutheran Churches of Zimbabwe. They are distin-

guished by uniforms worn at prayer meetings to give expression to evangelical teaching about Christ as their personal Savior. They also dress in uniforms to make the presence of the Ruwadzano felt in Zimbabwean society, which they do by gathering by the thousands in open-air prayer meetings.

Other denominations in this group are the Reformed Church in Zimbabwe (1891; → Reformed and Presbyterian Churches), the Dutch Reformed Church (1894), the Presbyterian Church of Southern Africa (1896), and the United Church of Christ (1892), originating in the United States. Also at work are the → Adventists, the → Salvation Army, and → Jehovah's Witnesses.

3.3. For the most part, African → Independent Churches (AIC) arose as a result of splits from established churches. Some began as revival movements within these churches that failed to find acceptance and thus became separate bodies. Nationalist ideas and access to the Scriptures inspired others. There are thousands of such churches, and their number keeps growing, for new groups typically form after the death of their leaders. While a few indigenous churches have not yet joined the African Independent Churches Conference, many have joined and are thus provisional members of the ZCC. The indigenous churches tend to be provisional rather than full members because of the norms of faith used by the World Council of Churches, to which the national council of churches is accountable.

Suspicion about indigenous churches arises from the fact that many express the Christian faith in an African manner, using cultural symbols that the missionary-established churches reject. Some practice polygamy and follow other traditional customs. Others have drawn attention to themselves by teaching against the use of biomedicine because of their belief in the healing power of the Holy Spirit. This teaching has resulted in conflicts with the government, which insists that biomedicine be used to protect life. Nevertheless, healing physical and psychological problems through counseling and prayer remains the most attractive feature of AICs.

3.4. The Pentecostal churches are illustrated by the Zimbabwe Assemblies of God Africa (ZAOGA, founded in 1965, with 1.6 million persons affiliated), the majority of African Initiated Churches (such as the popular African Apostles, with origins in the 1930s), newer churches such as the Rhema Bible Churches (which teaches a prosperity gospel), and the Assemblies of God (founded in 1958 from South Africa). Also resulting from the new wave of Pentecostalism in sub-Saharan Africa are hundreds of new churches scattered throughout Zimbabwe where the chosen styles of worship draw attention to beliefs in the Holy Spirit as the sign of the presence of God during worship.

4. Interdenominational Organizations

The most important interdenominational organization is the ZCC, to which 20 member churches belong. The Roman Catholic Church and the ZAOGA have observer status. The ZCC is the successor of the Rhodesian Christian Council (1964), which was founded by the African Methodist Church, African Methodist Episcopal Church, Anglican dioceses of Matabeleland and Mashonaland, Bible Society, Christian Marching Church, Evangelical Lutheran Church, Independent African Church, London Missionary Society, Methodist Church (U.K.), Methodist Church Conference (U.S.A.), Presbyterian Church in Southern Africa, Salisbury Council of Churches, Salvation Army, Society of → Friends, Southern Rhodesia Christian Conference, United Church of Christ (American Board), United Congregational Church of Southern Africa, and → YWCA. The new name, which emphasizes the churches, was adopted after independence. Other Christian organizations are associate members.

The council is meant to be a forum through which the churches can support Zimbabwean aspirations for self-government and reduce problems of violence, oppression, and corruption. Before independence, the council provided relief for the families of political prisoners and detainees, and also scholarships for black students both at home and abroad. Protests were made against death sentences passed on political prisoners. In 1967 the ZCC established Christian Care as the agency responsible for emergency relief work. Since independence the churches and associate members have played a part in the development of the country. More recently, public meetings have been arranged where leaders of member churches can discuss problems of violence during election campaigns, in which political parties opposing Robert Mugabe have clashed with soldiers and other supporters of the government.

Another interdenominational body is the Heads of Denominations (HOD). Most of the churches, including the Roman Catholics, participate. HOD enables church leaders to discuss matters of mutual concern, to decide swiftly on joint action, and to arrange meetings with government authorities. It has organized workshops, for example, on AIDS. In 1974 HOD established the Zimbabwe Association of Church-Related Hospitals (ZACH), which in 2004 oversaw 126 hospitals and clinics, as well as nurses'

training schools. ZACH has worked with the state on all medical matters.

On the whole, ecumenical relations in Zimbabwe are good. Though there is no serious discussion of unity, the churches no longer compete with one another. They also respect one another. Some churches (e.g., the Anglican and Lutheran) have entered into dialogue that aims at better understanding and closer sharing (→ Ecumenical Dialogue).

5. Church and State

In Zimbabwe the → church and the state are separate entities. In the past the government has pledged not to interfere in the work of the churches, but it often has used the press to warn the churches to stay out of politics. There has been close cooperation in the areas of health and education. The government much appreciates the contribution of the churches toward the development of Zimbabwe. Indeed, many state development projects may be entrusted to church bodies (e.g., the Lutheran World Federation) for implementation, the state providing the funding. In other areas church and state simply tolerate one another. According to the secretary of the ZCC, these areas include the need for land distribution (Economic Structural Adjustment Program), in which the church detects violation of human rights.

Since the ruthless murder of Ndebele people during the mid-1980s by President Robert Mugabe's Fifth Brigade, the state has had to face criticisms made by churches concerning abuses of power. In 2000 Robert Mugabe declared the Third Chimurenga (Shona for "war of liberation"). He used the army to seize land from white commercial farmers, which caused the displacement of thousands of migrant farmworkers and the imposition of sanctions against Zimbabwe by European countries and by the United States. The Catholic Justice and Peace Commission, leaders of the ZCC, and the Evangelical Fellowship of Zimbabwe have used the press to complain about violations of human rights by supporters of the government, call for the restoration of peace and justice, and increase awareness about democracy.

As the number of complaints grew, the state reacted by insisting on the separation of church and state. Churches, however, continue to provide services that the state needs. For example, numerous schools are run by churches. The ZCC provides the government with board members for hospitals and appoints representatives to various state commissions (e.g., Development, National Affairs, Employment Creation). Overall, relationships that could be cordial have become quite mixed because of the escalation of problems of oppression.

→ African Theology

Bibliography: C. S. Banana, *Christianity and the Struggle for Socialism in Zimbabwe* (Harare, 1987) • N. Bhebhe, *The ZAPU and ZANU Guerrilla Warfare and the Evangelical Lutheran Church in Zimbabwe* (Gweru, 1999) • M. F. C. Bourdillion, *Where Are the Ancestors? Changing Culture in Zimbabwe* (Harare, 1993) • M. L. Daneel, *African Earthkeepers,* vol. 1, *Interfaith Missions in Earth-Care* (Pretoria, 1998); idem, *Old and New in Shona Independent Churches* (2 vols.; The Hague, 1971-74) • P. Gifford, *The Religious Right in Zimbabwe* (Harare, 1989) • C. F. Hallencreutz and A. M. Moyo, eds., *Church and State in Zimbabwe* (Gweru, 1988) • G. Hansson, *The Rise of Vashandiri: The Ruwadzano Movement in the Lutheran Church in Zimbabwe* (Uppsala, 1991) • M. Hinfelaar, *Respectable and Responsible Women: Methodist and Roman Catholic Women's Organisations in Harare, Zimbabwe (1919-1985)* (Zoetermeer, 2001) • D. Lan, *Guns and Rain: Guerrillas and Spirit Mediums in Zimbabwe* (London, 1985) • M. Lapsley, *Neutrality or Cooption? Anglican Church and State from 1948 until the Independence of Zimbabwe* (Gweru, 1986) • E. C. Mandivenga, *Islam in Zimbabwe* (Gweru, 1983) • I. Mukonyora, "Foundations for Democracy among Evangelical Christians in Zimbabwe," *The Bible and the Ballot Box: Evangelical Faith and Third World Politics* (New York, forthcoming); eadem, *Wandering a Gendered Wilderness: Suffering and Healing in an African Initiated Church* (New York, 2007) • R. H. Randolph, *Dawn in Zimbabwe* (Gweru, 1985) • C. D. Watyoka, *The Zimbabwe Council of Churches: Twenty-five Years of Struggle* (Harare, 1989).

Ambrose M. Moyo and Isabel Mukonyora

Zinzendorf, Nikolaus

Nikolaus Ludwig, Reichsgraf von (count of) Zinzendorf and Pottendorf (1700-1760), was a German Protestant theologian and founder and organizer of the Moravian Brethren (Herrnhut community). Born in Dresden, Zinzendorf was the son of a high Saxon court official, descended from old Austrian nobility. After his father's early death and the remarriage of his mother, Zinzendorf was raised in the Upper Lusatia region of eastern Germany by his grandmother Henriette von Gersdorf, who had a strong influence on him.

From 1710 to 1716 Zinzendorf attended, with ambivalent experiences, A. H. → Francke's Peda-

gogium in Halle. While still there, he began to establish "societies," or religious friendship associations. From 1716 to 1719 Zinzendorf deferred to his family's wishes and studied law at Wittenberg, which was dominated by Lutheran → orthodoxy (§1) and where he continued these societies. The youthful Zinzendorf had a plan for peace talks between the theologians of Halle and those of Wittenberg, but it was hindered by his family, who sent him off instead on the customary Grand Tour of Europe (1719-20). In Holland he learned about confessional variety and came to value it in the name of a "religion of the heart." In Paris he began a lasting friendship with Cardinal-Archbishop L.-A. de Noailles. After he returned to Germany, he began working in 1721 in a minor government post in electoral Saxony at the behest of his grandmother.

Following his marriage in 1722 to Countess Erdmuthe Dorothea of Reuss, Zinzendorf purchased his grandmother's estate of Berthelsdorf in Upper Lusatia. There he allowed the settlement of the first emigrant families from Bohemia and Moravia, under the leadership of Christian David (1690-1751). Out of this humble start grew the community of Herrnhut (lit. "under the Lord's watch," or "on watch for the Lord"). Tensions over voting processes among the local Berthelsdorf congregation, Zinzendorf's own palace congregation, and the (in part, separatistic) Moravians resolved themselves in August 1727 in a unifying experience of a common celebration of the → Eucharist, which became viewed as the birth of the renewed → Moravian Church, the revival of the ancient Unitas Fratrum (Unity of the Brethren). This was a religiously based community of life and service that Zinzendorf strove to keep within the provincial church.

In 1727 Zinzendorf reduced his government work, and in 1732 he gave it up altogether so he could dedicate himself to the building up of the Herrnhut community life. In 1727 he began organization of the community into "choirs," or homogeneous groupings based on age, sex, and marital status. He also established common children's education and new forms of religious assembly, and he wrote → hymns and, from 1728, daily devotional texts (→ Devotional Literature 3). Zinzendorf also worked tirelessly on the outward activities of the developing Brethren Church, including maintenance of contacts with Protestant minorities, especially in eastern Europe, and sponsorship of foreign → missions, beginning with the Danish West Indies (1732) and Greenland (1733).

In an attempt to bolster his ties with the Lutheran Church, Zinzendorf formally entered the Lutheran ministry, passing examinations at the hands of theologians at Stralsund, in northwestern Germany, and at Tübingen. At the same time, he allowed the missionary David Nitschmann (1696-1772) in 1735, and himself in 1737, to be consecrated as → bishop (though without any leadership function) in Berlin by the elderly Daniel Jablonski (1660-1741), one of the two remaining bishops of the → Bohemian Brethren. This action did not improve the tense relations with the Lutherans.

In 1736 Zinzendorf was banished from Electoral Saxony through the efforts of the Pietists of Halle and others; he resettled in Wetterau in Hesse and built up the Pilgergemeine Herrenhaag (Pilgrim Community of Herrenhaag), which brought together various Reformed separatists. His travels took him to the Baltic area of eastern Europe, the West Indies, England (where he made contact with John → Wesley), and North America. He established congregations in New York and Pennsylvania (including at Bethlehem, Pa.) and did pioneer mission work among the Indians. Back in Herrenhaag he labored to give a stronger biblical base to what had become an intensified practice of a → piety focused on Christ's blood and wounds, which, admittedly, he had originally fostered. In the context of these controversies, Zinzendorf refined his Christocentric theology, whose ecumenical breadth is clear in his doctrine of "tropes," according to which the various confessions (→ Denomination), with their differing modes of understanding and communicating religious truth, are all valid expressions of the one true church of Christ.

Although his banishment from Saxony was lifted in 1747, and although the authorities there formally recognized the Unitas Fratrum in 1749, allowing it freedom to preach and organize congregations, Zinzendorf spent the years 1750-55 mostly in England. The English Parliament similarly recognized the Moravians in 1749. In spite of basic differences Zinzendorf was of great significance for emerging → Methodism.

Following the death of Erdmuthe in 1756, Zinzendorf married his coworker Anna Nitschmann in 1757. His last decade was clouded by difficult financial crises of the Moravian Church. The unavoidable increase in institutionalization necessary to overcome these crises was carried out after Zinzendorf's death (1760) in Herrnhut by his successor, August Spangenberg (1704-92).

Zinzendorf is remembered equally for his broad ecumenism, for his call within Protestantism to view cross-cultural mission as an essential activity of the church, and for his cultivation of a sincere and expressive religion of the heart.

Bibliography: Primary sources: Hauptschriften (6 vols.; ed. E. Beyreuther and G. Meyer; Hildesheim, 1962-63) • Ergänzungsbände zu den Hauptschriften (vols. 1-14, ed. E. Beyreuther and G. Meyer; vol. 15, ed. G. Clemens; Hildesheim, 1964-2001).

Secondary works: E. Beyreuther, Der junge Zinzendorf (2d ed.; Marburg, 1974; orig. pub., 1957); idem, Studien zur Theologie Zinzendorfs (2d ed.; Hildesheim, 2000; orig. pub., 1962) • M. Brecht and P. Peucker, eds., Neue Aspekte der Zinzendorf-Forschung (Göttingen, 2006) • A. J. Freeman, An Ecumenical Theology of the Heart: The Theology of Count Nicholas Ludwig von Zinzendorf (Bethlehem, Pa., 1998) • G. S. Kinkel, Our Dear Mother the Spirit: An Investigation of Count Zinzendorf's Theology and Praxis (Lanham, Md., 1990) • J. C. S. Mason, The Moravian Church and the Missionary Awakening in England, 1760-1800 (Woodbridge, Suffolk, 2001) • W. H. Wagner, The Zinzendorf-Muhlenberg Encounter: A Controversy in Search of Understanding (Nazareth, Pa., 2002) • W. R. Ward "Zinzendorf and the Moravians," The Protestant Evangelical Awakening (Cambridge, 1992) 116-59 • J. R. Weinlick, Count Zinzendorf: The Story of His Life and Leadership in the Renewed Moravian Church (Bethlehem, Pa., 1989).

Bernd Oberdorfer

Zion → Jerusalem

Zionism

1. In Antiquity
2. Nineteenth-Century Developments
3. Theodor Herzl
4. Christian Restorationism
5. Twentieth-Century Developments before 1948
6. After the Formation of Modern Israel

1. In Antiquity

Zionism is the national movement to establish Jewish sovereignty in the biblical land of Israel (Eretz Yisrael). "Zion" itself is the name of a Jerusalem hillock, but as early as the biblical period the name was used to signify the Holy City and the entire land of Israel. The word "Zion" appears in Hebrew Scriptures 180 times; following the Babylonian destruction of the First Temple in 586 b.c.e., the term represented the spiritual hope of remembrance, return, reconstruction, and redemption.

Following the → Roman Empire's destruction of the Second Temple in 70 C.E., "Zion" became the overall term for the creation of a future independent Jewish state with → Jerusalem as its capital, as it had been during the reign of King → David (ca. 980 B.C.E.). Typical of this early meaning of Zion is Ps. 137:1: "By the rivers of Babylon — there we sat down and there we wept when we remembered Zion." A traditional prayer asks God to "let our eyes behold Your return in mercy to Zion," and the medieval poet Judah ha-Levi (ca. 1075-1141), who lived in Spain, wrote:

> My heart is in the east, and I am in the farthest west,
> How can I find savor in food? How shall it be sweet to me?
> How shall I render my vows and my bonds, while yet
> Zion lieth beneath the fetter of Edom . . .
> Zion, I am the harp for all thy songs.
>
> (C. Potok, *Wanderings*
> [New York, 1978] 275)

There are numerous other examples of Jewish prayers, prose, and poems that describe a collective longing for the physical restoration of the Jewish people to their ancient homeland. While some Jews always lived in Eretz Yisrael, the Jews of the → diaspora (dispersion) hoped and prayed for Zion to be restored. But that longing was often only spiritual in nature or was reflected in a series of philanthropic programs that assisted Jews who actually resided, frequently in poverty, in the Holy Land.

2. Nineteenth-Century Developments

With the rise of European nationalism in the mid-19th century, several Jewish writers and thinkers posited the idea of a Jewish nationalism that would create a nation-state in Eretz Yisrael (→ Nation, Nationalism). Moses Hess (1812-75), a German Jew from Bonn who was influenced by the rise of Italian nationalism, published *Rom und Jerusalem. Die letzte Nationalitätsfrage* (1862; ET *Rome and Jerusalem: A Study in Jewish Nationalism* [New York, 1918]). Hess declared, "As long as an independent Jewish state does not exist and is not recognized in international law as a member of the family of civilized nations, the Jews who live in exile . . . are by no means abandoning the hope of ultimate restoration of the Jewish state" (A. Hertzberg, 139). Then in 1882 Leo Pinsker (1821-91), a Russian Jewish physician from Odessa, published, initially anonymously, *Autoemanzipation* (ET *Auto-Emancipation* [London, 1932]), a book that asserted that the "proper

and only remedy" for the desperate situation of the Jewish people was "the creation of a Jewish nationality, of a people living on its own soil . . . [gaining] their emancipation . . . by the acquisition of a home of their own. . . . Let 'now or never' be our watchword" (ibid., 198).

While Hess, Pinsker, and others called for Jews to create a national state, there was no effective political action until the 1890s, when the spiritual yearning and acts of charity were converted into a political mass movement. The specific term "Zionism" was first used in 1890 by Nathan Birnbaum (pseud. Mathias Acher, 1864-1937), an Austrian Jewish journalist.

Earlier, however, many young Jews in pogrom-plagued eastern Europe, especially lands under czarist control, had rejected traditional prayers and philanthropy, calling them inadequate responses to the painful daily existence endured by millions of their fellow Jews. Young Jews organized "Lovers of Zion" societies (*Hibbat Tzion*) throughout Jewish communities in eastern Europe, and in 1882 they issued a formal manifesto calling for "a home in our country [*Eretz Yisrael*]." To achieve this goal, they called for political action, not merely personal acts of piety. It was the beginning of Zionism as a political force.

The infusion of young Jews into Zionist activities included the establishment of agricultural colonies in Palestine, then controlled by the Ottoman Empire. Ironically, these early Zionist settlements of farmers, shepherds, and vintners were frequently funded by wealthy philanthropic Jews who lived outside Eretz Yisrael.

3. Theodor Herzl

It took, however, the charismatic leadership of Theodor Herzl (1860-1904) to create the institutions of political Zionism. Herzl, a Viennese journalist posted by his newspaper to Paris in the 1890s, witnessed the infamous Dreyfus Affair, in which a French Jewish artillery officer was falsely convicted of treason. The presence of → anti-Semitism within several significant sectors of French society, especially the military and the → Roman Catholic Church, was a decisive force in Dreyfus's trial and subsequent conviction and imprisonment.

Like Dreyfus, Herzl was a thoroughly acculturated European Jew, but in 1896 he reacted to the virulent anti-Semitism he had witnessed by writing a book, *Der Judenstaat* (ET *The Jewish State* [London, 1896]), that called for the establishment of a Jewish nation-state as a response to the anti-Semitism present throughout the Jewish diaspora. That publication catapulted Herzl and Zionism onto the world stage. Not surprisingly, the highly assimilated Herzl did not know of Hess, Pinsker, or the 1882 "Hibbat Tzion" manifesto, and he had little personal knowledge of the ancient religious tradition that intensely focused on Zion restored.

In 1897 Herzl convened the first Zionist Congress, thereby breaking the centuries-old pattern of merely praying for a return to Zion. The event had to take place in Basel, Switzerland, because the Jewish leadership in Herzl's preferred city, Munich, was opposed to Herzl's "wild scheme" of a Jewish state. The congress adopted a statement of purpose that succinctly summed up the movement's methods and goal: "Zionism seeks to secure for the Jewish people a publicly recognized, legally secured home in Palestine." Herzl was to attend only five other Zionist Congresses before he died, but he was able to set up the basic organization and structure of the Zionist movement, which have remained for over a century.

Despite Herzl's "political" version of Zionism, the movement retained much of its spiritual foundations and messianic fervor. Indeed, Herzl's most enthusiastic followers were Jews from eastern Europe who brought with them the religious and emotional qualities that Herzl and other more assimilated Zionist leaders lacked. As a result of this blending of piety, philanthropy, and politics, modern Zionism from its very inception was a diverse movement. It has always been an amalgam of religionists, mystics, political activists, and revolutionaries. Modern Zionism is a kind of biblical "tent of meeting" that has always attracted varied and distinct supporters. All of them, however, were united in the overall goal of returning and restoring the Jewish people to a Palestinian homeland.

4. Christian Restorationism

During the 19th century, many Christians, particularly in the United States and Great Britain, became part of the "Christian restorationism" movement. Restorationism asserted that the Jewish people must return to their ancient homeland and establish a sovereign Jewish state in order to fulfill biblical prophecy. Two of the best-known Christian restorationists were Lord Anthony Ashley Cooper, Seventh Earl of Shaftesbury (1801-85) of Britain, and the American William Blackstone (1844-1933).

In 1891, at Blackstone's urging and five years before Herzl and the emergence of modern Zionism, 400 prominent Americans signed a declaration calling for a Jewish state. They sensed an "opportunity to further the purposes of God concerning His ancient people" (M. B. Oren, 278). Signatories in-cluded John D. Rockefeller, J. Pierpont Morgan, Congressman William McKinley, and Charles Scribner. Another prominent restorationist was Lew Wallace, author of the immensely popular novel *Ben-Hur* (1880).

Fifty years earlier George Bush (1796-1859), a New York University professor of Hebrew, urged that Jews be "elevated to a rank of honorable repute among the nations of the earth" (Oren, 141) by establishing a Jewish state. This professor was a 19th-century relative of two future U.S. presidents.

5. Twentieth-Century Developments before 1948

In the years before 1917, Zionism attracted only a small number of Jews in western Europe, the United Kingdom, Canada, and the United States. Some → rabbis and other community leaders perceived the concept of a Jewish state in the Middle East as either an impossible goal or a threat to their newly won status as fully participating citizens of Western democratic nations. For such people, being Jewish was solely a religious identity devoid of any national elements. Indeed, many dismissed both Herzl and Zionism as misguided at best and dangerous at worst.

In 1914 in the United States, however, Kentucky-born Supreme Court Justice Louis D. Brandeis (1856-1941) became a leader of the Zionist movement. He linked the pragmatic democratic ideals of America with President Woodrow Wilson's (1856-1924) concept of national self-determinism. Brandeis's endorsement of Zionism gave the movement great credibility. His closest Zionist ally was America's most prominent rabbi, Stephen S. Wise (1874-1949).

In 1903 Herzl, desperate to establish his *Judenstaat*, was willing to accept the British government's offer of Uganda in Africa as a possible "Jewish national home" instead of Eretz Yisrael. Chaim Weizmann (1874-1952), however, a prominent Zionist leader from eastern Europe, bitterly opposed the Uganda plan and insisted that only the historic land of Israel could be the site of a future Jewish state. The Uganda proposal was defeated, and afterward all Zionist efforts were directed solely to rebuilding the biblical Holy Land.

One of Zionism's lasting achievements was the revitalization of the → Hebrew language, which for nearly 2,000 years had been used mainly for prayer and study. Eliezer Ben-Yehuda (1858-1922), who studied at the Sorbonne, devoted his life to compiling the first modern Hebrew dictionary and campaigning for the use of Hebrew as the daily language of Zionism and the Jewish community in Palestine.

Following Herzl's death, the Zionist leadership

passed mainly to eastern European Jews like David Ben-Gurion (1886-1973) and Weizmann. The former later served as Israel's first prime minister, beginning in 1948, while the latter was the Jewish state's first president. Weizmann, a professional chemist by training, moved to England in 1904 and became a faculty member at Manchester University. With his personal charm, he enlisted many prominent English Christians to the Zionist cause, most notably Arthur J. Balfour (1848-1930), a leading British politician.

Primarily as a result of Weizmann's efforts, in November 1917 the British Cabinet, led by Prime Minister David Lloyd George (1863-1945) and Foreign Secretary Balfour, sent the following letter to Lord Walter Rothschild (1868-1937), a prominent English Zionist: "His Majesty's Government views with favour the establishment in Palestine of a national home for the Jewish people, and will use their best endeavours to facilitate the achievement of this objective, it being clearly understood that nothing shall be done which might prejudice the civil and religious rights of existing non-Jewish communities in Palestine, or the rights and political status enjoyed by Jews in any other country" (W. Laqueur, 198). Despite its nuanced language and cautious tone, which left the future of Palestine wide open, this "Balfour Declaration," as the statement came to be called, represented the first official endorsement of Zionist aspirations by a major government. (Exactly 30 years later, in November 1947, Zionism achieved its second and greatest diplomatic success: U.N. General Assembly Resolution 181, calling for Palestine to be partitioned into a Jewish and an Arab state.)

In 1920 the League of Nations granted Great Britain a mandate over Palestine, a situation that lasted until May 14, 1948, when Israel declared its independence and began its War of Independence with neighboring Arab states. During the British Mandate, the Jewish population of Palestine increased, as did Arab hostility toward Zionism. After Nazi leader Adolf Hitler (1889-1945) came to power in Germany in 1933, Zionist leaders pressured Great Britain, the United States, and other nations to increase Jewish immigration, but with limited success.

Facing both the Nazi threat in Europe and Arab enmity in the Middle East, the Zionist movement itself became divided. The militant revisionist wing was led by Vladimir Jabotinsky (1880-1940), who called for mass immigration, combined with a strong Jewish fighting force in Palestine. Jabotinsky greatly influenced many Zionist leaders, including Menachem Begin (1913-92), who was elected Israeli prime minister in 1977. Weizmann, Ben-Gurion, and others opposed the revisionists and remained more conciliatory toward Britain, despite London's restrictions on Jewish immigration to Palestine during the 1930s and 1940s.

One of the most important and influential Zionist leaders was Rabbi Abraham Isaac Kook (1865-1935). Kook was a strong proponent of "religious Zionism," which was a bridge between observant and nonobservant Jews in Mandate Palestine. He wrote, "Deep in the heart of every Jew . . . there blazes the fire of Israel. . . . The real and organic holiness of Jewry can become manifest only by the return of the people to its land" (S. Noveck, 114, 122-23).

6. After the Formation of Modern Israel

Following the catastrophic Nazi "War against the Jews," culminating in World War II's → Holocaust, the Zionist movement sharply increased its activities in all parts of the world. The murder of six million Jews forced many Jews to rally behind the call for a Jewish state as a haven for both the surviving remnant of European Jews and the Jews in Arab nations who suffered persecution and discrimination from the Muslim majority population.

With the creation of Israel in 1948, many felt that the goal of Zionism had been fulfilled. Indeed, the movement was called the scaffolding necessary during the construction of a house. Once the house was completed, however, the scaffolding was no longer required.

Zionism, however, has remained a viable movement since 1948. Its leaders mounted an educational campaign that has reached the global Jewish community, and the Zionist movement continually calls for Jews to "make Aliyah" (i.e., immigrate to Israel). Nevertheless, more Jews continue to live outside Israel than in the Jewish state. At the same time, Israel will soon become the single largest Jewish community in the world, surpassing the Jewish community in the United States, a notable feat that was accomplished in little more than a hundred years.

Modern Israel's adversaries have participated in a constant anti-Zionist campaign that seeks to delegitimize the Jewish state. Anti-Zionism frequently has three targets: the continued existence of modern Israel, the Israeli Jews, and the Jews of the diaspora who support Israel. The Vatican has criticized anti-Zionism, calling it "a screen for anti-Semitism" (Pontifical Council for Justice and Peace, par. 15).

In 1975 the U.N. General Assembly, backed by the world's Muslim nations and the Soviet Union, adopted Resolution 3379, which termed Zionism "a form of racism and racial discrimination." The

United States led most Western democracies in condemning the resolution, as did a large number of Christian leaders, including the general secretaries of the → World Council of Churches and the → National Council of Churches of Christ in the U.S.A., the Greek Orthodox patriarch of North and South America, and the president of the U.S. Conference of Catholic Bishops.

Despite the strong negative reaction to this U.N. declaration, it was not rescinded until 1991 in General Assembly Resolution 46/86, following the collapse of the Soviet Union and the end of the first Persian Gulf War. Many Christian leaders were in the forefront to repeal the "Zionism is racism" resolution. Despite this U.N. action, Israel's foes continue to use "Zionism" as an epithet. At the same time others, including many Christians, see Zionism as the national liberation of the Jewish people.

Bibliography: S. AVINERI, The Making of Modern Zionism (New York, 1981) • A. ELON, Herzl (New York, 1975) • B. HALPERN, The Idea of the Jewish State (Cambridge, Mass., 1969) • A. HERTZBERG, ed., The Zionist Idea: A Historical Analysis and Reader (New York, 1960) • A. J. HESCHEL, Israel: An Echo of Eternity (New York, 1969) • W. LAQUEUR, A History of Zionism: From the French Revolution to the Establishment of the State of Israel (New York, 2003) • S. NOVECK, ed., Contemporary Jewish Thought: A Reader (New York, 1963) • C. C. O'BRIEN, The Siege: The Saga of Israel and Zionism (New York, 1986) • M. B. OREN, Power, Faith, and Fantasy: America in the Middle East, 1776 to the Present (New York, 2007) • J. W. PARKES, Whose Land? A History of the Peoples of Palestine (New York, 1970) • PONTIFICAL COUNCIL FOR JUSTICE AND PEACE, The Church and Racism: Toward a More Fraternal Society (Vatican City, 1988) • J. REINHARZ and A. SHAPIRO, eds., Essential Papers on Zionism (New York, 1996) • A. J. RUDIN, Israel for Christians: Understanding Modern Israel (Philadelphia, 1983) • H. M. SACHER, A History of Israel: From the Rise of Zionism to Our Time (New York, 1996) • C. WEIZMANN, Trial and Error (New York, 1949).

A. JAMES RUDIN

Zoroastrianism → Iranian Religions 7

Zwingli, Ulrich

Ulrich (Huldrych, Huldreich) Zwingli (1484-1531), a Zurich reformer, was perhaps the most important figure in German Switzerland and southwest Germany for the initial phase of the early → Reformation. His theology, distinctively formed above all in the theological argument with Martin → Luther and related particularly to the urban experience, represents a specific interpretation of the Reformation message and forms an essential theological-historical element of the development of the Reformed confession, which had been evolving since the late 1520s.

Zwingli was born on January 1, 1484, in Wildhaus in the Toggenburg valley in eastern Switzerland. He left his home early to stay under the care of his uncle, a priest, in the small city of Wesen, where he began his school education. He attended Latin schools in Basel (from 1494) and Vienna (from 1496). His university education course in the liberal arts was completed in Vienna and Basel (1498-1506). Following several months of theological study, Zwingli was ordained as a → priest in 1506 and took a position as a → pastor in Glarus, which he held until 1516. The extremely broad collection of books in Zwingli's library witnesses to his intellectual interests, showing that he intensively studied not only secular antiquity and scholastic philosophy but also the → church fathers and the theologians and philosophers of the Italian → Renaissance. An educational experience that was essential to Zwingli's spiritual development and determined the entire direction of his Reformation theology consisted of his study of the work of → Erasmus of Rotterdam (1469?-1536), whom he met personally in 1515 in Basel.

Between 1516 and 1518 Zwingli worked in → pastoral care in the pilgrimage center of Einsiedeln. Then at the end of 1518 he was appointed people's (or preaching) priest at the Großmünster (Great minster) of Zurich. Existentially influenced by a bout with the plague, as well as by various writings, especially Luther's Bible expositions, Zwingli after 1519 underwent a process of intensive exegetical work and maturing theological development that centered on his understanding of the Bible as a personal word of → salvation, upon the → justification of the sinner through → faith alone, and upon the crucified Christ as the foundation and guarantor of salvation.

After some of the laity closest to him had flouted the church fasting laws during Lent in 1522, Zwingli published his first reform writing: a tract On Choice and the Liberty of Meals. Conflict erupted with the bishop of Constance, coming to the fore in the First Zurich Disputation (January 29, 1523), which the town council convened as a means of dealing with Zwingli's religious questions. For this disputation

Zwingli had published his Sixty-seven Articles, which he conceived as the basis for discussion. The council agreed that Zwingli's teaching was in conformity with Scripture and directed the ministers in the canton to preach likewise. Zwingli thus became famous as the leader of the first successful city reformation.

With the implementation of reforming changes in the Zurich church in 1524-25, Zwingli assumed an important role among the city clergy. They followed his lead in theology and in liturgical reform (e.g., removing images from the churches and suppressing the use of church organs). Zwingli likewise had an influential role with regard to the reforming process in other cities of Switzerland and southern Germany. He accepted the direct influence of the city council on the church and acquiesced in its decisions against the → Anabaptists.

In wide areas of Switzerland and southern Germany, Zwingli influenced the theological attitudes of clergy in their understanding of Reformation thought through his foundational theological writings (*Interpretation of the Articles* [1523], *Commentary on True and False Religion* [1525]) and his Bible commentaries. The latter were composed in close connection with the "Prophezey," or daily Bible readings and exegesis for both clergy and laymen, which Zwingli began in 1525.

Beginning in 1524/25, Zwingli was in animated debate with the Anabaptists, whom he stubbornly fought with the support of the leading aristocracy of the city. In his literary debate with Martin Luther (1526-27), Zwingli was regarded by his contemporaries as the most effective representative of a symbolic view of the Lord's Supper. Despite his unshakable convictions about the issues, he had a more intensive interest than Luther in a lasting church solidarity of "evangelicals," which the Marburg Colloquy (1529) failed to achieve.

Zwingli's prophetic understanding of church office led him to follow political interests; in connection with Landgrave Philip of Hesse, he supported an all-European anti-Hapsburg coalition. He also supported Zurich's military forces, which on October 11, 1531, responded to an attack by five nonreforming cantons. Zwingli accompanied the troops as a chaplain and was killed, thus depriving German-speaking Protestantism in Switzerland and southern Germany of its charismatic leader.

Bibliography: Primary sources: Sämtliche Werke (12 vols.; Zurich, 1982; repr. of Berlin, 1905-63) • *Selected Works of Huldreich Zwingli* (ed. S. M. Jackson; Philadelphia, 1901) • *Zwingli and Bullinger* (trans. G. W. Bromiley; Philadelphia, 1953) 47-279.

Bibliographies: U. Gäbler, ed., *Huldrych Zwingli im 20. Jahrhundert. Forschungsbericht und annotierte Bibliographie, 1897-1972* (Zurich, 1975) • H. W. Pipkin, comp., *A Zwingli Bibliography* (Pittsburgh, 1972).

Secondary works: E. F. Furcha and H. W. Pipkin, eds., *Prophet, Pastor, Protestant: The Work of Huldrych Zwingli after Five Hundred Years* (Allison Park, Pa., 1984) • U. Gäbler, *Huldrych Zwingli: His Life and Work* (Philadelphia, 1986) • B. Hamm, *Zwinglis Reformation der Freiheit* (Neukirchen, 1988) • G. W. Locher, *Zwingli's Thought: New Perspectives* (Leiden, 1981) • W. P. Stephens, *The Theology of Huldrych Zwingli* (New York, 1986); idem, *Zwingli: An Introduction to His Thought* (New York, 1992) • R. C. Walton, *Zwingli's Theocracy* (Toronto, 1967) • L. P. Wandel, "Zwingli and Reformed Practice," *Educating People of Faith* (ed. J. van Engen; Grand Rapids, 2004) 270-93.

Thomas Kaufmann

Zwingli's Theology

Overview
1. Teaching
  1.1. God
  1.2. Christ
  1.3. The Holy Spirit
  1.4. Human Beings
  1.5. The Bible
  1.6. Salvation
  1.7. Sacraments
  1.8. Church and Society
2. Influence

Overview

Ulrich (Huldrych or Huldreich) Zwingli (1484-1531) expounded his theology most comprehensively in *Auslegen und Gründe der Schlußreden* (1523) and *De vera et falsa religione commentarius* (1525) and most succinctly in *Fidei ratio* (1530) and *Fidei expositio* (1531). His other works include commentaries, treatises, and letters. Zwingli's theology has often been misrepresented when based on a narrow selection of his works, especially the more philosophical ones, or when interpreted primarily in the light of Martin → Luther (1483-1546). The strongest influences, with the Bible, are patristic (esp. → Augustine), humanist (esp. → Erasmus; → Humanism 1), and scholastic (Scotus and *via antiqua;* → Scotism 2).

Humanist and Erasmian influence led Zwingli to the sources (Scripture and the Fathers), to the biblical languages, and to the historical-critical approach to the text. It is evident in a biblical, Christ-centered theology, in the stress on the Spirit and inward → piety, in the Platonist view of body and soul, and in the → sacraments (e.g., in the role of faith and the use of John 6:63). Augustine's pervasive influence is seen especially in the sovereignty of God, but also in many areas of Erasmian influence, such as the interpretation of Scripture and the sacraments. Scotist influence is probable in the emphasis on the will of God and in the contrast between the Creator and the creature.

Zwingli's theology is theocentric, though not as opposed to being Christocentric. This focus is manifest in every doctrine (e.g., Christ, the Spirit, Scripture, salvation, sacraments, church, and state) and in his stress on the glory of God.

1. Teaching

1.1. *God*

Zwingli allows that all people can have knowledge of → God (§7), but with the traditional distinction between knowing *that* he is and knowing *who* he is. This knowledge is not inherent but comes from God (Rom. 1:19). Religion stems from God's initiative, as in his calling to Adam (Gen. 3:9).

In discussing God, Zwingli argues both in the scholastic tradition (e.g., beginning with the being of God or with God as the *summum bonum,* or highest good; → Scholasticism 2.4) and in the biblical tradition (drawing on Exod. 3:14; Gen. 1:31; and Luke 18:19). All goodness and being are from God. Zwingli affirms God's aseity and simplicity. His → righteousness (§1.1) and → grace (§4) are part of his goodness.

The conviction of God's → providence pervades Zwingli's works and life. It is used to reject free will and merit (as, later, → predestination is), to assert that God is the cause of all things, and to deny the role of secondary causes. Human beings are God's instruments, not causes. The doctrine of providence is also used pastorally (in guidance and encouragement), as well as theologically.

1.2. *Christ*

The central significance of Christ (→ Christology 2.4) finds expression in the text "Come to me . . ." (Matt. 11:28), which appears on the title page of all Zwingli's works. Christ is example and teacher, as with Erasmus, but more fundamentally he is the Son of God, who died for us. (Zwingli emphasizes Christ's divinity rather than his humanity, for only God can save us.) Zwingli understands Christ's death primarily as a → sacrifice (§3; → Soteriology) for sins to satisfy God's righteousness (see → Anselm), but as in Scripture, Zwingli mentions other interpretations of his death.

In Zwingli, as in → Irenaeus, Christ recapitulates all that happened in Adam, a comparison in which Zwingli refers, following → Athanasius, to Christ's becoming man (→ Incarnation 3.4) so that we might become gods. In addition, his death was victory over or liberation from sin, death, and the devil. On occasion, Zwingli's writings reveal an almost Abelardian sense of the power of God's love displayed in Christ.

Christ's sinlessness, which is essential for his atoning death, is related to the → virgin birth. Zwingli asserts that Mary is ever-virgin on biblical, not traditional, grounds (appealing to Ezek. 44:2). He held Mary in high regard but maintained that the highest honor we can do her is to honor her Son. Zwingli stressed the distinction between Christ's divine and human natures. With his → ascension, Christ's body is in heaven; like Augustine, Zwingli insisted that a human body can be in only one place at one time.

Christ is present now in his divinity. Zwingli's strong distinction of Christ's natures is used soteriologically to safeguard his humanity, especially in the eucharistic controversy (→ Eucharist 3.3; Reformers 3.2). Some regard his views as → Nestorian, though Zwingli himself always insisted on the unity of Christ's person.

1.3. *The Holy Spirit*

Zwingli's theocentric emphasis is evident in his stress on the → Holy Spirit. It is the Spirit who gives faith rather than the Word (even the words of Jesus or the apostles) or the sacraments. The Spirit acts inwardly on the mind or heart. He may use outward means, but he is not bound to them, having to act through them and not being able to act apart from them. He is free. He moves where he wills (John 3:8). He is, moreover, not limited to Palestine. Having created the whole world, he is also active among pagans (e.g., through → natural law).

The Spirit, as the author of Scripture, is also its interpreter. To understand the Word read or proclaimed, we need the Spirit. Zwingli thus characteristically uses the order "Spirit and Word," rather than Luther's order "Word and Spirit." Zwingli differs from the Anabaptists and Spirituals, who in his view separate the Spirit from the Word. On occasion the Word, as God's Word, is portrayed as powerful and effective.

1.4. *Human Beings*

Human beings are made in the image of God, but through the → sin (§3) of Adam they are born as sinners. Zwingli makes the traditional distinction between original and actual sin, but he relates → guilt only to actual sin. Sin is a disease or fundamental defect (*morbus* or *prästen,* which G. W. Locher translates "incurable breach"). It is self-love and powerlessness. In describing human beings, Zwingli uses the biblical contrast of Spirit and flesh, so that the whole person as sinful is flesh. But he also contrasts spirit/soul with flesh/body. This Platonist opposition has some influence on his understanding of Word and sacrament.

1.5. *The Bible*

The Bible as the → Word of God (§3) is true and authoritative. Human words are not, for human beings are untruthful (Rom. 3:4). The teachings of the Fathers, the → councils, and the → popes are all human words and therefore come under the judgment of Scripture, which is God's Word. At first Zwingli stressed the contrast between the OT and the NT, but later he emphasized their unity. This unity rests on the conviction that there are not two covenants, one in the OT and one in the NT, but only one → covenant (§3; this position leads to covenant theology), for there is only one God and only one people of God. The people in the OT believed in Christ who is to come; Christians believe in the Christ who has come. Zwingli's belief in the unity of Scripture underlies the way he used the OT in controversy with → Anabaptists, who argued from the NT. His emphasis on the whole of Scripture contrasts with Luther's "canon within the canon."

In his exegesis Zwingli insisted on the natural meaning of the text, but he also used → typology, especially interpreting OT figures as pointing to Christ. He was prepared to accept allegorizing but, unlike → Origen (ca. 185-ca. 254), insisted that an allegorical interpretation must be explicit elsewhere in Scripture (→ Allegory). Zwingli could use non-Christian authors such as Plato and Seneca positively, for, like → Jerome and Augustine, he believed that all → truth comes from God. Non-Christian works, however, are to be tested by Christ and Scripture, whose author is the Spirit. A few of Zwingli's works, especially *De providentia Dei anamnema* (1530), are strongly philosophical, though even in them he insists on the sovereign authority of Scripture, which he sees as the foundation of all his teaching.

The Spirit, given to the whole church and not just to the bishops, is the interpreter of Scripture. Zwingli criticized the Anabaptists and the Spirituals for appealing to the inspiration of the Spirit (not testing their spirit by Scripture), for misunderstanding the Scripture through their ignorance of Hebrew and Greek, and for failing, unlike Jesus and the apostles, to take the OT seriously. For Zwingli, unlike the Anabaptists, knowledge of the biblical languages was necessary for interpretation. He started the so-called prophesyings (based on 1 Corinthians 14), where both the Hebrew and the Greek text were studied, before a final preaching of the word to the people. (The Zurich Bible came out of these meetings.) Zwingli used humanist principles of interpretation (→ Humanism), but he also particularly emphasized the role of faith ("If you do not believe, you will not understand") and the comparing of Scripture with Scripture in arriving at a true interpretation. Unlike Luther, Zwingli does not oppose faith and reason. Reason can be the reason of the flesh, but it can also be the reason of the believing person.

1.6. *Salvation*

God's sovereignty is fundamental in our salvation. It is expressed in election, in the death of Christ as a sacrifice for sin, in the role of the Spirit leading people to faith, and in the use of texts such as John 6:44-45. Zwingli contrasts faith in God not with works, as Luther did, but with faith in the creature, in all that is not God, whether works, sacraments, or the saints. Faith in anything other than God is idolatry. This conviction led to Zwingli's removal of → images (→ Saints, Veneration of).

In 1526 Zwingli developed a doctrine of election (→ Predestination 3), though there are earlier references to election or predestination. (It is intimately related to providence, which can be described as the "mother" of predestination.) He used the doctrine not only to deny the role of free will, works, and sacraments in salvation but also to assert God's initiative in salvation. The elect may know their election by their having faith but cannot be certain of the election of others. Faith and love are signs of election, and lack of faith and love could be signs of reprobation. (They will be absent or only apparent in those not elect.) Like Augustine, but unlike John → Calvin (1509-64), Zwingli emphasized election.

The doctrine of election underlies his giving a place in → heaven to people like Theseus and Socrates (in *Fidei expositio*). Zwingli's view of salvation is not that of Pelagius (→ Pelagianism) or the Renaissance. The salvation of pagans is not based on their good works but on God's election, on Christ's redeeming work, which undid the effects of Adam's sin, and on the freedom of the Spirit. It is supported by biblical examples such as Jethro and Cornelius. Support is also found in what Romans 2 says about Gentiles who, though they do not have the law, do by nature what the law demands and who, though they do not have outward circumcision, have circumcision of the heart. Zwingli explicitly rejected universalism, a belief he attributed to the Anabaptists.

→ Justification, meaning both reckoning and making righteous, is not a central theme in Zwingli's exposition of salvation, as it was for Luther. Law, as the expression of God's will, has a positive role for Christians (the so-called third use), as well as the negative one of exposing sin. Hence, unlike Luther, Zwingli speaks of gospel and law rather than → law and gospel. Although, like Luther, he can oppose gospel to law, he also describes the law as gospel (good news) for believers, but not for unbelievers. Believers delight to learn God's will for their lives so that they may live in accordance with it. Divine righteousness, which is inward (e.g., loving), is contrasted with human righteousness, which is outward (e.g., not stealing). The latter, which involves outward words and deeds, is the concern of the → state (§2).

1.7. *Sacraments*

Zwingli did not like the term → "sacrament" (§2.4.2) because it was misused and misunderstood (e.g., as meaning taking away sin). The Spirit uses Word and sacrament but is not bound by them or to them. Sacraments are "signs of a sacred thing" (Augustine). A sign is not the same as what it signifies but is distinguished from it. It is a sign of grace already given rather than a → means of grace. Zwingli opposed Roman Catholic, Lutheran, and Anabaptist reliance on the sacraments. Signs cannot save. They are badges whereby we can recognize Christians. They are also pledges — at first, God's pledge to us and our pledge to God, the former emphasizing God's initiative, the latter our response. Later he refers to them as signs of God's covenant and promise. This position suits infant baptism as well as adult baptism better than the understanding of sacraments as our pledge. Writings in 1530-31 use the appeal of the sacraments to our senses to express Zwingli's more positive understanding of the sacraments.

Zwingli's view of → baptism (§2.2.3) is largely expounded in controversy with Anabaptists and in his defense of infant baptism. Salvation, he holds, depends neither on baptism nor ultimately on faith but on election. Adults are baptized when they respond to the Word with a confession of faith. But lack of faith is no argument against infant baptism. The elect are elect before they are born, and therefore infants may be elect and consequently belong to God's people, though not yet having faith. Zwingli argues for infant baptism on many grounds, but especially from the analogy of baptism with circumcision and the unity of the covenant. There is only one → covenant in both the OT and the NT. Therefore, as the NT is no less comprehensive and no less gracious than the OT, it also includes infants in the cov-

enant. Unbaptized children are not rejected. Zwingli argues on several grounds that the early death of the children of Christian parents is a sign of their election, just as much as faith is in adults, for original sin has been expiated by Christ and they are too young to be under the law, so as to be stained by actual sin.

The → Eucharist, or thanksgiving, is not a sacrifice but the memorial of Christ's sacrifice. Faith in Christ is fundamental to the sacrament. In John 6 eating is believing, as in Augustine, but we believe in Christ as slain, not eaten. Salvation is promised to faith, not to eating the sacramental bread. Controversy with Luther is focused in Christ's presence in the sacrament. In 1524 Zwingli used Cornelius Honius's (d. 1524) exposition of "this is" as "this signifies" to support a symbolic view, which he may have held from the beginning. He argues against Christ's bodily presence (Christ's body is in heaven) and against bodily eating ("the flesh is useless," John 6:63). The one point of disagreement in the Marburg Articles (1529) concerned Christ's bodily presence. For Zwingli Christ is present in his divinity and is eaten spiritually (by faith) as food for the soul, but not physically. Zwingli did not believe in "the real absence." On the contrary, in 1531 he insisted on Christ's true presence, adding that "we do not believe it is the Lord's supper unless Christ is present." In his earliest writings Zwingli held, as did Luther, that the sacraments strengthen faith. He later rejected this view, but in 1530-31 he reaffirmed it, relating it to the way that the sacraments appeal to the senses, which might otherwise lead us astray.

Zwingli's views are shaped by his insistence that salvation depends on God, not on us — hence his stress on the role of God's election, Christ's saving death, and the freedom of the Spirit rather than on the sacraments. Also influential was his Platonist opposition of body and soul, which meant that outward things, like water, bread, and wine, are unable to affect the soul or spirit.

1.8. *Church and Society*

Zwingli's understanding of the Christian life differs from Luther's in being communal rather than individual. Christians are members of the → church (§3.5). The NT describes the church as both local and universal, and it is also visible and invisible. The local church (or → congregation) exercises discipline, including → excommunication for serious offenses. Zwingli rejects the Anabaptist vision of a pure church. The visible church is a mixed body. The invisible church, which is visible to God, is defined sometimes as believers, sometimes as elect. Its Head is Christ, not the pope, who in usurping the place of Christ is described as antichrist. The church's ministers, as prophets or watchmen, are concerned with the whole life of society (social, political, and economic). Zwingli's understanding of church and society is taken from the whole Bible. In the OT rulers were referred to as shepherds of the people, which is one reason for Zwingli's giving them a role in the church and its discipline. Zwingli's view differed here from that of Johannes Oecolampadius (1482-1531) and Calvin, as well as from Anabaptist views. To him, the situation of the church in his day resembled the situation under the prophets in Israel rather than that of the apostles in the Roman Empire.

Zwingli's view was theocratic (→ Theocracy). He had a vision of society under the rule of God, with both minister and magistrate seeking to establish that rule. He did not mean government to be subject to the church or the church to the government. All people, however, including bishops and popes, are to obey the government (Rom. 13:1). Rulers must govern in accordance with God's law, which ministers have a duty to expound to them. The laws they pass must correspond with God's will, a view that does not mean a literal application of biblical laws to the laws of the land. Zwingli's concern for the reformation of society is to be related to his sense that God's → wrath (§3) is against a rebellious society and not just rebellious individuals. His patriotism and his long opposition to mercenary service find expression in this political concern. A sense of patriotism was present from Zwingli's earliest years.

Civil government is necessary on account of → sin (§3). It is appointed by God to punish the evil and protect the righteous (Rom. 13:3-4). It must be obeyed, not because those governing are good, but because God has instituted government and rules through it. If, however, it acts contrary to God's law, it should not be obeyed. If it rejects God's rule, it can (with qualifications) be deposed (→ Resistance, Right of, 2). The Anabaptists are criticized because they separate the church and secular government and do not allow Christians to be magistrates or soldiers. Zwingli defended his position on both NT and OT grounds.

Zwingli draws on classical and Christian discussion in recognizing three main forms of government: monarchy, aristocracy, and → democracy — the rule of one, of the best, or of the people. Each of them has a corrupt form: tyranny, oligarchy, and sedition, in which people act without any restraint. Where Zwingli expresses a preference, it is for aristocracy, which was the form in Zurich, with its elected council. He held that monarchy usually led to tyranny, which was harder to change than a council.

The closing words of *De vera et falsa religione commentarius* show Zwingli's priorities: God, society, and the individual. "All I have said, I have said to the glory of God, for the benefit of the commonwealth of Christ, and the good of conscience."

2. Influence

Zwingli's influence was strongest in Switzerland and southern Germany. Through Heinrich Bullinger (1504-75) and returning exiles, as well as his own works, it also spread to England and other parts of Europe. Areas of influence include his theology of the sacraments, his exposition of the covenant, his stress on the distinction of Christ's natures, his understanding of gospel and law, his view of Spirit and Word, his interrelating of church and society, and his use of prophesy (prophesyings), with its exposition and examination of the Bible in the original languages.

Bibliography: Primary sources: E. EGLI, G. FINSLER, et al., *Huldreich Zwinglis Sämtliche Werke* (Berlin, Leipzig, Zurich, 1905-) • M. SCHULER and J. SCHULTESS, *Huldreich Zwingli's Werke* (Zurich, 1828-42).

English translations: Commentary on True and False Religion (ed. S. M. Jackson and C. N. Heller; Durham, N.C., 1981; orig. pub., 1929) • *Early Writings* (ed. S. M. Jackson; Durham, N.C., 1987; orig. publ., 1912) • *On Providence, and Other Essays* (ed. S. M. Jackson and W. J. Hinke; Durham, N.C., 1983; orig. pub., 1922) • *Selected Works of Huldreich Zwingli* (ed. S. M. Jackson; Philadelphia, 1972; orig. pub., 1901) • *Selected Writings of Huldrych Zwingli*, vol. 1, *The Defense of the Reformed Faith* (trans. E. J. Furcha; Allison Park, Pa., 1984); vol. 2, *In Search of True Religion: Reformation, Pastoral, and Eucharistic Writings* (trans. H. W. Pipkin; Allison Park, Pa., 1984) • *Zwingli and Bullinger* (trans. G. W. Bromiley; London, 1953).

Bibliographies: G. FINSLER, *Zwingli-Bibliographie* (Zurich, 1897) • U. GÄBLER, *Huldrych Zwingli im 20. Jahrhundert* (Zurich, 1975) and since Gäbler in *Zwingliana* (Zurich, 1897-).

Secondary works: D. BAGCHI and D. C. STEINMETZ, eds., *Reformation Theology* (Cambridge, 2004) • A. BARCLAY, *The Protestant Doctrine of the Lord's Supper* (Glasgow, 1927) • J. COURVOISIER, *Zwingli: A Reformed Theologian* (London, 1964) • E. J. FURCHA and H. W. PIPKIN, eds., *Prophet, Pastor, Protestant* (Allison Park, Pa., 1984) • U. GÄBLER, *Huldrych Zwingli: His Life and Work* (Edinburgh, 1987) • T. GEORGE, *Theology of the Reformers* (Nashville, 1988) • S. M. JACKSON, *Huldreich Zwingli, the Reformer of German Switzerland, 1484-1531* (2d ed.; New York, 1972; orig. pub., 1901) •

W. Köhler, *Zwingli und Luther. Ihr Streit über das Abendmahl nach seinen politischen und religiösen Beziehungen* (2 vols.; Leipzig, 1924, and Gütersloh, 1953) • G. W. Locher, *Die Theologie Huldrych Zwinglis im Lichte seiner Christologie,* vol. 1, *Die Gotteslehre* (Zurich, 1952); idem, *Zwingli's Thought* (Leiden, 1981) • R. Pfister, *Das Problem der Erbsünde bei Zwingli* (Leipzig, 1953) • J. V. Pollet, "Zwinglianisme," *DTC* 15.3745-928 • G. R. Potter, *Zwingli* (Cambridge, 1976) • J. Rilliet, *Zwingli, Third Man of the Reformation* (London, 1964) • W. P. Stephens, *The Theology of Huldrych Zwingli* (Oxford, 1986); idem, *Zwingli: An Introduction to His Thought* (Oxford, 1992) • R. C. Walton, *Zwingli's Theocracy* (Toronto, 1967).

W. P. Stephens